COMPUTATIONAL ANALYSIS OF PRESENT-DAY AMERICAN ENGLISH

COMPUTATIONAL ANALYSIS OF

PRESENT-DAY AMERICAN ENGLISH

By Henry Kučera and W. Nelson Francis

WITH A FOREWORD BY W. F. TWADDELL, A STUDY BY MARY LOIS MARCKWORTH AND
LAURA M. BELL, AND AN ANALYTICAL ESSAY BY JOHN B. CARROLL

BROWN UNIVERSITY PRESS · PROVIDENCE, RHODE ISLAND · 1967

This book was designed by David Ford.

It was set in Monotype Modern Number 8
by the Riverside Press.

It was printed on University Text
and bound by Wm. J. Keller Inc.

FOREWORD

Readers can expect to find many parts of this volume tantalizing. The definiteness of the answers to certain questions irresistibly provokes more questions. The happy feature is that the book provides information required to limit the effect to that of tantalizing rather than frustrating. For there is given here a wholly adequate description of the nature of the Corpus of Present-Day Edited American English on which this study is based, the details of its constituents, and the modes of its transfer to tape. A replica of that tape is available at a small cost in money, which is minuscule compared to the cost in time needed to produce a like corpus. Accordingly, any reader who seriously wants answers to further questions can set about getting those answers.

The advantages and disadvantages of basing linguistic statements on a specific corpus are familiar. A corpus protects against gross lapses of recall to which introspection is liable. Statistical statements depending on subjective judgment are unreliable in the extreme. On the other hand, a corpus of manageable size will underrepresent some units and structures that introspection can supply and specify adequately. A corpus of one million words (a "megaword" corpus) is small for many purposes. No reader of this volume, for example, will find in the Corpus lists of all the vocabulary items he recognizes and produces. The low-frequency items have

to be assigned definite relative-frequency-of-occurrence numbers that are not particularly meaningful; the frequencies of thousands of the items occurring once or twice could be exchanged without implausibility. But the studies of type-token ratios make it clear that to attain statistically reliable data on those words that are low-frequency words in the megaword Corpus a tremendous increase in corpus size would be required at an impractical expenditure of time and money in the present state of the art. As of now, prudence dictates asking those questions that can be answered from an available corpus of a given size. Several of the studies in this volume throw light on the limits of valid questionings.

A corpus of this size and kind is material for two quite different kinds of investigation:

1. It is a reservoir of linguistic usage in a form (computer tape) that makes it relatively easy to extract exhaustively all available specimens of a given word or describable grammatical item. Thus the megaword Corpus has already been mined via various concordance and index programs for several investigations of lexicographical and phonological matters which include a study by George K. Monroe on the mechanical phonemic transcription of graphic postbase affixes in English (Ph.D. dissertation, Brown University, 1965); an analysis of *The Meanings*

of the Modals by Madeline E. Ehrman (The Hague, 1966); Mary Lois Marckworth's study of sentence length and structure in different genres of American English (a portion of which is included in this volume); an investigation of front-heavy sentences in English by Patricia L. Damian (Master's thesis, Brown University, in preparation); and other research projects in progress. As such a reservoir, the Corpus corresponds in kind to a card file of examples of the well-established sort that has been the basis of the great grammars. The difference is that it is not a wholly relevant card file filtered through intelligent selection, and it is gathered much more rapidly than a traditional card file and can be searched enormously more rapidly and exhaustively.

2. A corpus is also an entity in itself with structures that can be investigated purely for an expression aspect without regard to any semantic content of its constituent types and tokens. Such an investigation of vocabulary utilization in various types of writing and the correlation between lexical properties of a sample and the notion of "semantic information" has been conducted by Henry Kučera and will be published as a separate monograph. (It is unfortunate that the term "lexicostatistics" has been used as a rough synonym for various glottochronological theorems and theories, for it would be the proper name for such studies and rather more lovable than "computational linguistics".)

The studies of the distribution of occurrence of frequent word-types display some suggestive constants and variables. It is not a priori surprising that every one of the one hundred most frequent words in the entire Corpus occurs in each of the genres (with a relative frequency of .010 per cent or more). But—surprising or not—the table on pages 277–93 attests the fact, which is not a mere hunch. The distribution-of-occurrence table also shows

some of the interesting variations along with the partial uniformities of high-frequency vocabulary items. For example, in all genres the most frequent item is *the*. But the second most frequent word is *of* in ten genres, *and* in five. Already at rank 2 genre difference affects the occupancy of a rank. The effect of genre difference on the relative frequency of a given (frequent) word is also impressive: *if* (rank 50 for the total Corpus) ranges from .116 to .360 per cent relative frequency in the genres; rank 51, *out*, from .093 to .467 per cent; rank 100, *well*, from .048 to .150 per cent; rank 101, *down*, from .010 to .263 per cent.

The frequency distribution tables on pages 300–57 can readily yield many kinds of statements of uniformities and differences at the 2,000-word level. The proportion of the total vocabulary represented by the *hapax legomena* varies within limits, to be sure, but the range is considerable for smaller samples. For the entire Corpus the *hapax* percentage is 44.72. For a sample 100,000-word subset it is 51.64. The representative subset of fifty 2,000-word samples, summarized in Tables B8–B57, shows the following distribution of *hapax* percentages:

Range of *Hapax* Percentages	Number of Samples
56.00–57.99	3
58.00–59.99	3
60.00–61.99	2
62.00–63.99	3
64.00–65.99	9
66.00–67.99	8
68.99–69.99	7
70.00–71.99	5
72.00–73.99	5
74.00–75.99	3
76.00–77.99	1
78.00–79.99	1

Accordingly there is a strong indication from the various samples that the proportion of *hapax legomena* is sensitive to some

quantitative constraints of corpus size and probably also to qualitative genre influences.

The relation between type-token ratio and sample size as it is displayed on page 356 is one of the tantalizing topics. How far dare we extrapolate—for a composite-author corpus? For an individual-author corpus? The calculations of John B. Carroll on pages 406-24 are suggestive of some of the answers.

Two studies of ratios can be considered as fairly definitive, since there is no reason to believe that a much larger corpus would substantially alter the findings. The study of relative frequency of words of grapheme length 1 . . . n appears to be permanently reliable for a corpus of this kind, regardless of size. Significant differences from this distribution should be indicative of a significant difference in the type of corpus. The theoretically parallel study of relative frequency of sentences of word length 1 . . . n is, naturally, more complex and shows interesting associations with genre differences. The double peak in several graphs suggests that, so far as word-number length of sentences is concerned, there may be two populations of sentences in the Corpus or in certain genres of it—and hence, perhaps, in English. The tables and discussion on pages 368–405 clearly point toward two populations of genres as determining the distribution of sentence lengths.

Among the tables and graphs those dealing with the fits to a "Zipf's constant" line for various samples show a suggestively narrow range of variation with hints of dependence upon sample size. It would be equally injudicious to be awed by the display or to dismiss it as unimportant.

There are pedagogical questions that may well be within the proper scope of a megaword corpus. For example, what kinds of clumping of vocabulary items take place and in what proportion? Consider those words with an absolute frequency of 10 in the Corpus. How many of these 10-occurrence words occur once in each of ten 100,000-word subcorpuses? How many occur in nine? How many in each of the various possible distributions? A related question would pursue the "careers" of the *hapax legomena* of a particular subcorpus (say 100,000) when that subcorpus is joined by one or more. For example, how many of the *hapax legomena* of subcorpus A are also *hapax legomena* in subcorpus B, so that in the collection AB they together constitute two-frequency items?

The massive lists (pp. 5–137 and 139–271) constitute two orderings of lexical data, both of which fill needs, some pedagogical, some relevant to stylistic studies. The relevance of frequency lists for the construction of materials for elementary and intermediate language teaching (in this case for teaching English as a foreign language or to children who are native speakers of English) is often overstated, but relevance there is. An interesting stylistic characteristic of a text or a genre would be revealed by comparing the distribution therein of words of various frequency levels in the Corpus as a whole. It will probably happen that a reader who at first considers only one list relevant to his curiosities will find that he can use the other, unexpectedly.

In general, it can be foreseen that of this, and possibly of later volumes of this kind, it will be true that the thoughtful user will begin by saying "Da muß sich manches Rätsel lösen" and quickly recognize "Doch manches Rätsel knüpft sich auch."

W. F. Twaddell

ACKNOWLEDGMENTS

The lexical and statistical information presented in this book could not have been assembled without the collaboration of a number of research assistants and computer programmers who aided us in the compilation of the Standard Corpus of Present-Day Edited American English and in the subsequent analyses of the Corpus.

The Corpus was assembled at Brown University during 1963 and 1964 under the direction of W. Nelson Francis. The several members of the Corpus project staff contributed greatly to the successful and timely completion of the project. Anne Robb Taylor, Hall Peyton, Jr., and Mary Lois Marckworth assumed many of the administrative responsibilities for the selection and procurement of the material, for securing of permissions from copyright holders, and for the various editorial duties in the preparation of the material for keypunching. Loretta Felice competently and cheerfully punched almost all of the approximately one million words of the Corpus. Robert Staudte wrote the ingenious and efficient computer programs for the automatic proofreading of the data, for organization of the Corpus on magnetic tape, and for its updating and correction. Several other undergraduate and graduate students aided us in the visual proofreading of the punched text.

A number of other persons assisted us with the various aspects of the Corpus analysis, performed under the direction of Henry Kučera at the Brown University Computing Laboratory during 1965 and the first part of 1966. Our appreciation goes especially to Carol Easthope who served as research assistant and computer programmer during the last year of the project and who was responsible not only for many of the editorial and administrative chores connected with the final organization of the book but also for much of the computer programming for the statistical calculations included in this volume as well as for the organization of the computer-produced word lists and word-frequency tables.

Among the others who contributed in various ways to the Corpus analysis project, only a few names can be mentioned here. Stanley E. Legum and George K. Monroe developed the algorithms and programs for the generation of the stripped version of the Corpus and related programs that eventually made it possible to perform the word-frequency analyses efficiently. John D. Garberson wrote a number of programs for the correction and updating of the Corpus and was responsible as well for the type-token ratio analysis and the least-squares fit approximations of the word-frequency distributions in the Corpus and in its various subsets. Frank Merewether contributed a

flexible program for the retrieval of any desired subset of data from the Corpus.

There are others to whom we owe our thanks. We would like to mention, at least, the staff of the Computing Laboratory at Brown University and its director, Walter Freiberger, who were often helpful to us much beyond the call of duty, and Christine Murray, who gave her able assistance in the preparation of the final manuscript. We would also like to thank Grant Dugdale, director of the Brown University Press, for his general encouragement and support and Barbara Dickinson for her very helpful and patient editorial assistance.

The assembling of the Corpus itself was supported through the Cooperative Research Program of the Office of Education, U. S. Department of Health, Education, and Welfare. The printing of the computer-produced lists and tables for reproduction in this book was supported by National Science Foundation Grant GP-4825. In performing the computations incorporated in his contribution on the lognormal law of word-frequency distribution, John B. Carroll was helped by Mary Burke Betts of the Graduate School of Education, Harvard University, to whom he wishes to express his appreciation. The computations themselves were performed at the Harvard Computing Center with subsidy funds provided by National Science Foundation Grant GP-2723. Mary Lois Marckworth was aided in her research by an IBM Graduate Fellowship for computer research in the humanities. The analysis project was supported by Brown University, which provided the computer time necessary for its completion. Our thanks go primarily to Merton P. Stoltz, provost of the University, for his encouragement of computer-oriented research in linguistics.

We are also grateful to colleagues at Brown University and at other institutions as well as to students who have used the Corpus in their own research and who offered many valuable comments about the organization of the data.

CONTENTS

THE CORPUS VOCABULARY

ANALYSES OF THE CORPUS

WORD LENGTH

SENTENCE-LENGTH DISTRIBUTION IN THE CORPUS BY MARY LOIS MARCKWORTH AND LAURA M. BELL

INTRODUCTION

This volume presents a collection of lexical and statistical information obtained from analysis of the Standard Corpus of Present-Day Edited American English, a computer-processible corpus of language texts assembled at Brown University during 1963–64. This body of data, referred to subsequently simply as the "Corpus," has been made available at cost to persons and institutions engaged in computer-based research in the English language.

The main objective of this book is the presentation of lexical and statistical data about the Corpus. Our primary aim has not been to test the validity of various mathematical models of language which have been proposed by linguists and statisticians in the past nor to suggest new ones. Not infrequently, mathematical models have been based on insufficiently large and improperly selected samples of language and as a result have not always withstood the test of further empirical observations. It is hoped that the studies presented here, especially the numerous tables that summarize the results of the word-frequency analysis of the Corpus and its various subsets, will offer useful material for the development and improvement of statistical procedures of linguistic analysis and will make possible the construction of more satisfactory mathematical models of language.

The term "standard" in the full title of the Corpus is not intended as a qualitative description of the texts included. Rather, it is an expression of the hope that the Corpus, being a carefully selected and fully described body of natural-language texts, may serve as a standard of comparison for a variety of studies and analyses of present-day English. It was felt that there was a distinct need for such a standard body of data, and this feeling has been justified by the interest that has been evinced since copies of the Corpus have been made available. Most previous studies in those fields of linguistics where the analysis of a body of utterances was essential (statistically oriented studies, stylo-statistics, studies of the manifestation of grammatical elements and of grammatical structure in actual utterances, etc.) have relied on samples selected from a single genre of writing or a single author or have used samples for no better reason than that the data was readily available. The present Corpus, selected by a method that makes it reasonably representative of current printed American English and prepared with care, supplies a more reliable body of data. Because of its subdivision into distinct samples of approximately equal size, easily isolable individually or in homogeneous sets, it is possible for any individual genre of writing represented or any desired combination of genres to be retrieved and analyzed separately.

The compilation of this Corpus and the various frequency counts extracted from it have a rather different aim than the several word counts of English published before and thus cannot be easily compared to such previous results. The results published here, unlike those of many other frequency counts, do not aim at a determination of the basic vocabulary or of the "most common" words of English. Rather, the aim has been to compile a corpus of printed American English and present a basic analysis of the data according to the following criteria:

1. Definite and specific delimitation of the language texts included, so that scholars using the Corpus may have a precise notion of the composition of the material

2. Complete synchronicity; texts published in a single calendar year only are included

3. A predetermined ratio of the various genres represented and a selection of individual samples through a random sampling procedure

4. Accessibility of the Corpus to automatic retrieval of all information contained in it which can be formally identified

5. An accurate and complete description of the basic statistical properties of the Corpus and of several subsets of the Corpus with the possibility of expanding such analysis to other sections or properties of the Corpus as may be required.

The Corpus

The Corpus is a body of 1,014,232 words of natural-language text, coded for processing on IBM and other types of data-processing equipment. It is fully described in the *Manual of Information* (Providence: Department of Linguistics, Brown University, 1964) which is issued with all copies of the Corpus tape or is available separately. In the description that follows only those details are given which are necessary for the understanding and use of the lists, tables, and graphs included in this volume. Readers interested in further details are referred to the *Manual*.

The Corpus is divided into 500 samples of approximately 2,000 words each. It was intended that all samples should contain at least 2,000 words, but owing to errors in counting, 18 fell below that number, all but 3 of which have at least 1,990 words. The shortest sample (E09) contains 1,948 words, the longest (J77) 2,246, and the mean sample length is 2,028.46 words, with a standard deviation of 37.59. All the samples are of continuous discourse. In most cases the material in a single sample is one continuous passage from a single source. In some categories, however, notably newspaper reportage, some of the samples consist of collections of shorter pieces, sometimes from different sources. The *Manual* gives detailed information about the constitution and source of each sample.

The idea that governed the selection and preparation of the text making up the Corpus was that it should be synchronic, representative of a wide range of styles, and accurate. Each of these characteristics required careful decisions about procedures. The major decisions were made in a conference held at Brown University in February, 1963, participated in by John B. Carroll, W. Nelson Francis, Philip B. Gove, Henry Kučera, Patricia O'Connor, and Randolph Quirk. Later procedural decisions were made by the staff of the project, especially W. Nelson Francis, Henry Kučera, Hall Peyton, Jr., and Anne Robb Taylor. Synchronicity was assured by confining the data to texts first printed in the year 1961 (though, of course, many of them may have been written some time before publication). Further restrictions imposed were that the material should be printed in the United States, written so far as could be determined by American

writers, in prose, with no more than 50 per cent of any selection in dialogue (this automatically excluded drama as well as some fiction). To insure representativeness, the 500 samples were distributed among fifteen categories, representing the full range of subject matter and prose styles, from the sports page of the newspaper to the scientific journal and from popular romantic fiction to abstruse philosophical discussion. The number and content of the categories and the proportion of the 500 samples to be assigned to each of them were determined by consensus of those taking part in the conference mentioned above. The conference also determined the proportions to be allotted to various subdivisions of the main categories. In most cases these decisions were closely adhered to, but in one or two of the categories where it became apparent that the proportions decided upon were significantly out of line with the amount of material available, the numbers were changed.

Each category was given a code letter, and the individual samples were numbered serially within each category. The categories and numbers of selections assigned to each are as follows:

A.	Press: Reportage	44
B.	Press: Editorial	27
C.	Press: Reviews	17
D.	Religion	17
E.	Skills and Hobbies	36
F.	Popular Lore	48
G.	Belles Lettres, Biography, etc.	75
H.	Miscellaneous	30
J.	Learned and Scientific Writings	80
K.	Fiction: General	29
L.	Fiction: Mystery and Detective	24
M.	Fiction: Science	6
N.	Fiction: Adventure and Western	29
P.	Fiction: Romance and Love Story	29
R.	Humor	9

Once these categories and the subcategories within them were established, the actual samples were selected by a variety of random procedures. In most categories the holdings of the Brown University Library and the Providence Athenaeum were treated as the universe from which the random selections were made. But for certain categories it was necessary to go beyond these two collections. For the daily press, for example, the list of American newspapers of which the New York Public Library keeps microfilm files was used (with the addition of the easily available *Providence Journal*). Certain categories of ephemeral material necessitated rather arbitrary procedures: thus some periodical materials in the categories Skills and Hobbies and Popular Lore were chosen from the contents of one of the largest secondhand magazine stores in New York City.

In the case of short items the selection began at the beginning; in the case of longer items such as books a page number was chosen at random. In either case the selection ran on continuously, omitting such things as footnotes, tables, and picture captions, and ended at the first sentence break after a rough count of 2,000 words. Later an accurate count was made with the aid of a computer program. Defining criteria for words will be given below.

Various steps were taken to insure accuracy. The text was read and marked before being keypunched and then was proofread three times before being transferred to magnetic tape. The third proofreading was done with the aid of a listing by the computer of all items appearing no more than twice in a given group of samples. This made it easy to detect misspellings and spacing errors in the keypunching. Errors and questionable readings in the original text were allowed to stand, but were recorded in the *Manual*. Even after the material had been transferred to magnetic tape, some errors were detected and rectified by means of a correction program. It is possible that a few errors remain, but in general the reader may be

confident that erroneous or unconventional words and spellings appearing in the lists in this volume go back to the original printed texts from which the samples were derived.

Since the generally available computer coding system has only the twenty-six letters of the alphabet (in capital form); ten numerals (including zero); and the punctuation marks comma, period, plus sign, equal sign, parentheses, asterisk, hyphen-minus sign, apostrophe–single-quotation mark, slash, and dollar sign, it was necessary to use arbitrary coding in order to incorporate as much as possible of the graphic detail of the original into the Corpus. The basic system was that used by the U. S. Patent Office and presented in the pamphlet *A Notation System for Transliterating Technical and Scientific Texts for Use in Data Processing Systems*, by Simon M. Newman, Rowena W. Swanson, and Kenneth Knowlton (Patent Office Research and Development Reports No. 15, U. S. Department of Commerce [Washington, D.C., 1959]). The coding procedure is described in detail in the Corpus *Manual;* those features that appear in the lists in this book will be given on page 4.

Combinations of letters and numbers not constituting genuine words and not followed by a period were considered symbols and in the Corpus were marked by the code **J. Since the stripping procedure that was applied to the Corpus before the listings were made normally removed initial **J from symbols and the abbreviation period from abbreviations, these symbols often fall together with normal words and abbreviations in the lists. But the rare occurrences of **J within a graphic unit are preserved.

Combinations of letters, numbers, and other symbols that also include operator symbols (such as plus sign, minus sign, exponents, subscripts) were defined as formulas and replaced by the code **F with space on either side. Each formula, no matter how long, was thus considered a single word in the over-all word count. There are 1,010 formulas in the total Corpus; their distribution among the individual samples is given in the *Manual*. Because of this treatment of formulas, the lists in this volume do not record accurately the frequencies of various numerical combinations. Numbers that are not part of formulas are, however, included in the lists.

By means of this coding system it was possible to include in the full version of the Corpus (Form A) most of the graphic detail of the original text. But before the frequency lists in this volume were prepared, a version of the Corpus (Form B) from which most of the punctuation marks and other coding symbols had been stripped was produced. If this had not been done, the number of individual words (types) would have been greatly and undesirably increased, since, for example, a word followed by a comma would be treated as different from the otherwise identical word not followed by a comma. The stripping program that produced Form B removed all marks of punctuation— except the hyphen and the apostrophe— that were followed by another mark of punctuation or by space. It also removed all other coding symbols attached to the beginning or ending of genuine words. It removed **J from the beginning of symbols (as defined above) but left all other coding. All punctuation marks and coding symbols within words (i.e., with no space on either side) were left. This occasionally produced rather bizarre graphic combinations. The alternative, however, would be to increase the number of types undesirably.

Definitions

An "individual word" (token), for purposes of the lists and tables in this volume,

can be simply defined as a continuous string of letters, numerals, punctuation marks, and other symbols (i.e., of graphemes), uninterrupted by space, in the stripped (Form B) version of the Corpus. The graphic, rather than the phonemic or lexical, word is thus the unit that is used. Owing to some of the structural peculiarities of the English graphic system, the application of this criterion (the only practical one for computer-produced word counts) sometimes leads one to identify as words graphic combinations that would not normally be recognized as such. Such a combination as LOS ANGELES-*SAN FRANCISCO, for example, will be considered three "words": LOS, ANGELES-*SAN, and FRANCISCO. Note that the internal mark of capitalization on *SAN is preserved, since it is not preceded by space and thus was not removed by the stripping program. Results such as this could, of course, have been avoided by preediting the text: in this case by arbitrarily hyphenating the city names and spacing on both sides of the hyphen linking them, thus producing LOS-*ANGELES - SAN-*FRANCISCO, which the computer would then have recognized as two words. But it was felt that the principle of adhering faithfully to the graphics of the original text was more important. It is expected, after all, that the Corpus will be used for other purposes beside word counts, quite possibly including the study of the English graphic system. Editorial interference with the original texts would have distorted the material to an undesirable extent for studies of that kind.

A "distinct word" (type) can also be simply defined as a set of identical individual words, as defined above. This again is the only feasible criterion for computer-produced classification. To attempt to separate homographs and group alternate spellings would have required extensive editorial time, or intricate programming, or both. The reader thus should

be aware of some of the consequences of this criterion:

1. Homographs (words identical in spelling but different in pronunciation and meaning) and homologs (words identical in spelling and pronunciation but different in meaning) are lumped together as the same type. Thus *sow*, 'plant seed' and *sow*, 'female pig' are not distinguished nor are *bear*, 'carry' and *bear*, 'animal.'

2. Variant spellings of phonologically and lexically identical words are listed and counted separately. Thus *catalogue* and *catalog* are separated as are *non-conformist* and *nonconformist*.

3. Morphologically and syntactically variant graphic forms of lexically identical words are listed separately. Thus *cannot*, *can't*, and *c'n* appear as separate types, while *can not* will simply be counted as one instance each of *can* and *not*. In fact, it will not be possible to derive from these tables an accurate count of the auxiliary *can*, even if the morphological variants are counted, since all tokens of the noun *can* are lumped with verbal *can*.

These consequences of basing the lists uncompromisingly on the graphic word as unit undeniably restrict the usefulness of the counts, especially for stylistic analysis. But it is hard to see how any other procedure short of a completely "semantic" count like that of Lorge is possible. In the present state of the art a semantic count, even if desirable, is beyond the reach of computer technology. We can only advise the user of the word lists in this book to be aware of how homographs, variant spellings, and morphological variation may influence his conclusions.

The Lists, Tables, Graphs, and Analyses

This volume contains two main types of material: word lists, and statistical tables and graphs. The bulk of the book comprises two frequency lists of the words in the

Corpus, the first in descending order of frequency and the second alphabetical. The rest comprises a number of tables and graphs resulting from various counts, calculations, and studies and two essays analyzing some of the results.

Word-Frequency Lists. The first of the word lists contains the complete vocabulary of the Corpus, arranged in order of frequency of occurrence from the most frequent to those of single occurrence. For the lower frequencies the reader who wants to know the total number of words of a given frequency, but not the individual words, may readily derive this information from the statistical tables later in this volume. The second list also contains all the distinct words found in the Corpus and the frequency and range of occurrence of each, arranged in alphabetical order. For the convenience of the reader words that begin with special symbols not letters of the alphabet have been moved to the end of the list, since the usual computer sorting procedures would place them at the beginning.

A word entry in either list is preceded by three figures, separated by dashes. The first figure gives the actual frequency of occurrence of the word in the Corpus. The second figure designates the number of genre subdivisions in which the word occurs, and the third figure gives the number of samples in which the word is found.

In addition to these two main lists an additional list of the first one hundred most frequent words of the Corpus has also been included in which the distribution of occurrence of these most frequent items in the various portions of the Corpus has been specified. The distribution list contains the information as to the relative frequency of occurrence of each of the one hundred words in each subsection of the Corpus designated by the code letters A to R; these letter subdivisions essentially divide the Corpus into subsets according to the various genres represented in it.

For each of the most frequent one hundred words, a chi-square analysis test has been performed from which it is possible to estimate whether the differences in the relative frequency of occurrence of any word in the various subsections of the Corpus might be due simply to chance or whether such differences might be indicative of a statistically significant concentration of the word occurrences in a particular genre of the Corpus. The result of the chi-square analysis for each word is included directly in the distribution list.

While the information specifying the distribution of occurrence has been retrieved for all the words of the Corpus, space limitations permitted us to include in this volume only the data and the chi-square calculations for the most frequent words.

Word-Frequency Tables and Graphs. All the basic information on word frequencies is summarized, whenever possible, in the form of tables and corresponding graphs. These are essentially of two types, depending on the nature of the data they represent. First, there are those that pertain to the entire Corpus and thus are based on the analysis of the entire 1,014,232 words of the text. Secondly, there are those that summarize, for purposes of comparison, the statistical information obtained from various subsets of the Corpus (for example, a subset containing approximately 100,000 words of running text, selected so as to be a representative sample of the Corpus as a whole). The analysis of subsets of various lengths can produce significant conclusions concerning those statistical variables that are affected by the total size of the sample analyzed, such as the ratio of different words (types) to the number of running words (tokens).

In addition to representative (cross-sectional) subsets of various sizes some nonrepresentative subsets were also analyzed. Some of these results are presented also. The nonrepresentative samples were

obtained by dividing the Corpus into ten subsets of equal size (approximately 100,000 tokens), each of which was skewed toward one particular genre represented in the Corpus, such as newspapers, fiction, or scientific writing. A comparative study of the results obtained from these non-representative samples offers information on the degree of stability of various statistical properties of language, such as the type-token ratio or the rank-frequency relationship, in texts of different character.

Word-Length Analysis. The book includes two tables and one graph that offer information on word-length distribution in the Corpus; the length of a word is defined as the number of graphic characters composing it. This data is given, first of all, for the vocabulary of the Corpus, showing how many word-types of which length occur. Secondly, it is given for the running words, showing how many tokens of which length there are in the Corpus.

Sentence-Length Analysis. The entire Corpus was analyzed for information on the length of sentences in terms of the number of graphic words that constitute a graphic sentence. The number of sentences of each specific length is given in a table, and an accompanying graph displays the sentence-length distribution curve. The second section of this study contains an analysis of the sentence-length distribution for each genre represented in the Corpus and a discussion of sentence length as a significant parameter in the quantitative description of writing style in the various literary prose genres of the Corpus. Again, all the relevant information is summarized in tables and graphs.

Analysis of a Lognormal Model of Word-Frequency Distribution. In his analytical essay John B. Carroll of Educational Testing Service gives new results on the application of the lognormal distribution to word frequencies. He shows that a lognormal distribution with given parameters implies a finite rather than an infinite

number of word-types in the theoretical population. Further, he shows that when finite samples are drawn from the population, the statistics of such samples are systematically biased and that there are systematic deviations from the lognormal distribution. This statistical development results in a definite solution for the type-token function. Mr. Carroll applies these developments to the Corpus and shows that the data are in good agreement with the lognormal model.

Because of space limitations, many items of information which already have been retrieved from the Corpus or which are easily retrievable have not been included in this book. This is particularly true of the complete index of the Corpus, which has been compiled and is stored on magnetic tape. This index contains, in addition to each word entry and its frequency (corresponding to the alphabetic list printed in this volume), all the location markers that specify the sample code and the line within a sample in which a given word occurs, so that all words of the Corpus can be easily located in all their contexts. If printed, this index would comprise probably no less than 2,000 pages; it is hoped that it can eventually be published.

An example of the kind of information that may be retrieved with the aid of the index from the Corpus is a complete or partial concordance. A computer program that uses the index tape in conjunction with the full Corpus tape and constructs a complete list of all three-line contexts in which the specified Corpus words can be found is available at Brown University.

Another kind of information the Corpus index can readily supply for any word or any set of words is the complete distribution of occurrence among the genres of the Corpus. As already mentioned, this information is given in this volume for the first one hundred most frequent words only. Similar information for any other

words can be easily obtained from the index. Together with the range that is given here for each word, which simply states the number of genres and samples in which a word occurs, the exact specification of the relative frequency of occurrence of a word in the genres may be useful, for example, for the precise evaluation of the frequency count of a word or for the study of its stylistic function.

Data-Processing Information

The principal format of the Corpus comprises one computer magnetic tape about 1,600 feet long. The termination of the Corpus text on the tape is indicated by a Tape Mark symbol (BCD code 8421). The Corpus is recorded on tape in the standard binary coded decimal seven-bit code (known as BCD code) in which each character is represented by a six-bit code and one check bit. The density of this tape is 556 characters per inch. An alternate Corpus tape is also available in the IBM System/360 Extended Binary Coded Decimal Interchange Code (EBCDIC) on a nine-channel tape with the density of 800 characters per inch.

The organization of the data on tape corresponds to the card format in which the text was originally punched. The data is recorded on tape in card-image form, i.e., all cards (including correction cards and other incompletely filled cards) are reproduced in their entirety. However, for reasons of operating efficiency in processing the Corpus data, the card-image records are grouped on tape by a blocking factor of twenty, so that the tape is composed of a series of fixed-length tape records each containing 1,600 characters (i.e., twenty cards). The tape records are separated from each other by a three-fourths inch interrecord gap on the seven-channel tape, by a six-tenths inch gap on the nine-channel tape.

The Corpus is also available in a format (Form B) from which all punctuation symbols and codes have been removed, except hyphens, apostrophes (coded **A), and symbols for formulas (**F) and ellipses (**H). In all other respects this format is identical with Form A.

The processing of data for obtaining the word-frequency lists and the information needed for the tables and graphs was performed principally on the IBM 7070 Data Processing System at the Brown University Computing Laboratory. The IBM 1401 computer was used in an auxiliary capacity, primarily for smaller problems involving data organization and checking. Some statistical calculations and the printout of the word-frequency lists was performed on the IBM System/360. The necessary computer programs for the IBM 7070 were written by several programmers (the individual contributions are specified in the preface), mainly in the two available 7070 assembly programming languages, Autocoder 74 and Autocoder 76; in Fortran; and for the System/360 in assembly language.

The processing of the Corpus data was done essentially in three stages: (1) segmentation of the texts into words, (2) sorting of the segmented words in an ascending (that is alphabetical) order, and (3) the merging of identical words and a count of their frequencies of occurrence.

The segmentation of the Corpus text into individual words was performed by a computer program that identified all strings with a space on each side that occurred in the stripped-down version (Form B) of the Corpus tape. The words thus segmented were stored in the format of fixed-length records on another magnetic tape. This output tape was then sorted with the aid of the IBM Sort 90 program. The sorted tape was processed by a merge program that included all identical words under a single entry and counted the frequency of occurrence of each word.

The merged output then provided, with some additional modifications and partial reorganization of the data, the source for the computer-produced alphabetical word list included in this volume. This procedure also produced, in addition to the tables printed in this volume, a complete word index of the Corpus, described above but not printed here.

The first word list reproduced here (i.e., the list sorted by descending frequencies) was obtained from the alphabetical list by a sort on the frequency fields. It will be noted that in this list those sets of words that occur with identical frequencies are organized alphabetically.

The statistical information required for the compilation of tables and graphs was obtained mainly with the aid of several FORTRAN programs. The various subsets of the Corpus which were utilized in the statistical analysis were retrieved from the complete word index of the Corpus by a flexible IBM 1401 program.

THE CORPUS VOCABULARY

EXPLANATION

Each of the two lists in this section contains a complete listing of all the 50,406 distinct graphic words (types) that occur in the Corpus.

A word entry in either list is preceded by three figures separated by dashes. The first figure gives the actual frequency of occurrence of the word in the Corpus. The second figure designates the number of genre subdivisions in which the word occurs; there are altogether fifteen genre subdivisions in the Corpus (the Introduction contains a description of the composition of these genre subdivisions). The third figure gives the number of samples in which the word is found; the Corpus is composed of 500 samples of roughly equal length.

For example, the entry 4381-15-490 BUT means that the word *but* occurs 4,381 times in the whole Corpus and can be found in all fifteen genres and in 490 of the 500 samples.

The first list is ordered by descending frequency of occurrence. When there is more than one word of the same frequency, the order of such words within the respective frequency is alphabetical.

The second list is ordered alphabetically; for the reader's convenience all types that begin with a character not a letter of the alphabet have been moved to the end of the list, since the usual computer sorting procedures would place them at the beginning.

Detailed information about the word-frequency distribution of the Corpus can be found in Tables B1 and B3 in the latter part of this book.

To determine the rank of any word in terms of its Corpus frequency (the most frequent word having the rank 1, the second most frequent the rank 2, etc.), it is only necessary to find the Corpus frequency of occurrence for the desired entry in either list and then proceed through Table B1 on page 300 until the same frequency is found in column 2 (labeled X). The figure in the first column of Table B1 corresponding to this frequency is then the rank of the word; in those cases when the frequency in column 2 of Table B1 is applicable to more than one word, column 1 specifies the rank range of those words. For example, the reader interested in the rank of the word *our* can find in the alphabetical list that its frequency is 1,252 and determine from Table B1 that for $X = 1,252$ the corresponding number in column 1 is 79. This is the Corpus rank of the word *our*.

The reader should bear in mind that the "word" **F, which occurs with the frequency of 1,010 and ranks ninety-second in the rank list, stands for *any* formula in the Corpus, not a particular one.

Coding Symbols

Within regular words (as distinct from symbols and numbers), the only punctuation marks that appear are the hyphen and the apostrophe. Other codings that appear occasionally in abbreviated, symbolic, and numerical "words" are the following:

* letter immediately following is a capital

+ plus sign or ampersand

*(beginning bracket

*) closing bracket

*= begin italics or underscoring

*$ end italics or underscoring

*/ begin Roman numeral

*, end Roman numeral

**B character(s) for which no specific code is used

**C colon

**S semicolon

D diaeresis or umlaut (follows letter over which it appears; thus NAIDVE equals naïve)

**H points of ellipsis; there are 721 occurrences of this, each counted as one word

**J begin symbol (combinations of letters and numbers not constituting genuine words and not followed by a period were considered symbols); domain extends to next space or punctuation mark

**K per cent sign

**Q begin quotation (used for quotations set off either by double quotation marks or by blocking in the text)

**U end quotation (used for quotations set off either by double quotation marks or by blocking in the text)

**- dash

*+0 degree symbol

**= begin boldface type

**$ end boldface type

**(begin all capital letters

**) end all capital letters

**. abbreviation period

**.. abbreviation period at end of sentence

Y lower case Greek letter follows (in the case of a few long Greek words the initial **Y was erroneously removed from the first letter, e.g., SYA**YK**YO**YS equals σακος)

**Z capital Greek letter follows

Greek Letters

A	alpha	I	iota	R	rho
B	beta	K	kappa	S	sigma
G	gamma	L	lambda	T	tau
D	delta	M	mu	U	upsilon
E	epsilon	N	nu	F	phi
Z	zeta	X	xi	C	chi
H	eta	O	omicron	Y	psi
J	theta	P	pi	Q	omega

THE RANK LIST

69971-15-500	THE	923-15-203	YOUR	442-14-134	WATER	315-13-122	SERVICE
36411-15-500	OF	909-15-363	WAY	438-15-236	LESS	313-15-188	CERTAIN
28852-15-500	AND	897-15-383	WELL	438-14-180	PUBLIC	313-15-186	KIND
26149-15-500	TO	895-15-297	DOWN	437-15-251	PUT	313-15-154	PROBLEM
23237-15-500	A	888-15-320	SHOULD	433-15-219	THINK	312-15-177	BEGAN
21341-15-500	IN	883-15-344	BECAUSE	432-15-256	ALMOST	312-15-181	DIFFERENT
10595-15-500	THAT	877-15-320	EACH	431-15-220	HAND	312-15-124	DOOR
10099-15-485	IS	872-15-321	JUST	430-15-256	ENOUGH	312-13-180	THUS
9816-15-466	WAS	850-15-367	THOSE	427-15-258	FAR	311-15-184	HELP
9543-15-428	HE	847-15-288	PEOPLE	426-15-227	TOOK	311-15-163	SENSE
9489-15-500	FOR	839-15-148	MR	424-15-190	HEAD	310-14-168	MEANS
8756-15-500	IT	834-15-333	HOW	419-15-241	YET	309-15-192	WHOLE
7289-15-500	WITH	832-15-336	TOO	417-13-135	GOVERNMENT	308-15-196	MATTER
7250-15-500	AS	831-15-324	LITTLE	416-14-133	SYSTEM	307-15-192	PERHAPS
6997-15-435	HIS	808-14-198	STATE	414-15-233	BETTER	304-15-171	ITSELF
6742-15-500	ON	807-15-319	GOOD	414-15-234	SET	302-14-149	IT'S
6377-15-499	BE	796-15-344	VERY	413-15-185	TOLD	301-13-126	YORK
5378-15-500	AT	794-15-365	MAKE	412-15-219	NOTHING	300-15-194	TIMES
5305-15-498	BY	787-15-270	WORLD	411-15-183	NIGHT	299-14-130	HUMAN
5173-15-338	I	782-15-348	STILL	410-15-246	END	299-14-099	LAW
5146-15-495	THIS	772-15-339	OWN	404-15-201	WHY	298-15-150	LINE
5133-15-422	HAD	772-15-336	SEE	401-15-233	CALLED	296-15-173	ABOVE
4609-15-495	NOT	763-14-145	MEN	401-14-145	DIDN'T	294-15-162	NAME
4393-15-453	ARE	760-15-311	WORK	401-15-161	EYES	292-15-166	EXAMPLE
4381-15-490	BUT	755-15-338	LONG	399-15-245	FIND	291-15-142	ACTION
4369-15-500	FROM	750-15-276	GET	399-15-196	GOING	290-15-107	COMPANY
4207-15-492	OR	750-15-315	HERE	399-15-210	LOOK	289-15-149	HANDS
3941-15-498	HAVE	730-15-316	BETWEEN	398-15-200	ASKED	288-15-114	LOCAL
3747-15-498	AN	730-15-337	BOTH	397-15-234	LATER	287-15-190	SHOW
3618-15-482	THEY	721-15-196	**H	395-15-171	KNEW	286-15-165	FIVE
3562-15-474	WHICH	715-15-279	LIFE	395-15-223	POINT	286-13-135	HISTORY
3292-15-496	ONE	712-15-334	BEING	394-15-238	NEXT	286-15-170	WHETHER
3286-15-297	YOU	707-15-334	UNDER	394-13-119	PROGRAM	285-15-176	GAVE
3284-15-453	WERE	698-15-307	NEVER	393-15-156	CITY	284-15-206	EITHER
3037-15-253	HER	686-15-288	DAY	392-15-165	BUSINESS	284-14-161	TODAY
3001-15-491	ALL	686-15-336	SAME	391-15-249	GIVE	283-14-123	ACT
2859-15-228	SHE	683-15-348	ANOTHER	390-15-190	GROUP	283-15-131	FEET
2724-15-467	THERE	683-15-271	KNOW	386-15-216	TOWARD	282-15-176	ACROSS
2714-15-448	WOULD	680-15-329	WHILE	385-15-190	YOUNG	282-12-127	3
2670-15-465	THEIR	676-15-296	LAST	384-15-216	DAYS	281-15-186	PAST
2653-15-364	WE	672-15-310	MIGHT	384-15-206	LET	281-15-173	QUITE
2619-15-350	HIM	672-15-233	US	383-15-159	ROOM	281-15-198	TAKEN
2472-15-477	BEEN	665-15-291	GREAT	382-13-110	PRESIDENT	280-15-166	ANYTHING
2439-15-408	HAS	660-15-256	OLD	380-15-201	SIDE	279-15-190	HAVING
2331-15-468	WHEN	660-15-213	YEAR	380-15-123	SOCIAL	279-15-180	SEEN
2252-15-420	WHO	639-15-267	OFF	377-15-225	GIVEN	277-15-132	DEATH
2244-15-408	WILL	630-15-303	COME	377-15-213	PRESENT	276-15-142	BODY
2216-15-475	MORE	628-15-313	SINCE	377-15-234	SEVERAL	276-15-121	EXPERIENCE
2201-15-469	NO	626-15-268	AGAINST	376-15-202	ORDER	275-15-168	HALF
2199-15-453	IF	626-15-275	GO	375-13-143	NATIONAL	275-15-168	REALLY
2096-15-453	OUT	622-15-261	CAME	373-15-226	POSSIBLE	275-15-136	WEEK
1984-15-467	SO	613-15-265	RIGHT	373-15-232	RATHER	274-13-078	CAR
1961-15-317	SAID	612-15-240	USED	373-15-223	SECOND	274-15-125	FIELD
1908-15-424	WHAT	611-15-297	TAKE	371-15-189	FACE	274-15-153	WORD
1895-15-430	UP	610-15-288	THREE	371-09-096	PER	274-15-154	WORDS
1858-15-427	ITS	605-14-182	STATES	370-15-214	AMONG	273-15-193	ALREADY
1815-15-426	ABOUT	803-15-246	HIMSELF	370-14-171	FORM	270-15-176	THEMSELVES
1791-15-464	INTO	601-15-311	FEW	369-15-211	IMPORTANT	269-14-115	INFORMATION
1789-15-456	THAN	591-14-195	HOUSE	368-15-206	OFTEN	268-13-111	I'M
1789-15-429	THEM	589-15-261	USE	368-15-201	THINGS	268-15-154	TELL
1772-15-401	CAN	585-15-265	DURING	367-15-170	LOOKED	267-13-078	COLLEGE
1747-15-460	ONLY	583-15-312	WITHOUT	366-15-209	EARLY	267-15-107	SHALL
1702-15-462	OTHER	578-15-287	AGAIN	365-14-156	WHITE	267-15-192	TOGETHER
1635-15-388	NEW	571-15-292	PLACE	362-15-202	CASE	265-14-143	MONEY
1617-15-440	SOME	569-14-199	AMERICAN	362-13-119	JOHN	265-14-149	PERIOD
1599-15-396	COULD	561-15-254	AROUND	361-15-211	BECOME	264-15-168	HELD
1599-15-447	TIME	552-15-282	HOWEVER	361-15-214	LARGE	264-14-178	KEEP
1573-15-413	THESE	547-15-243	HOME	360-15-182	BIG	264-15-169	SURE
1412-15-429	TWO	542-15-243	SMALL	360-15-204	NEED	261-15-183	PROBABLY
1400-15-343	MAY	536-15-271	FOUND	359-15-214	FOUR	260-15-148	FREE
1377-15-408	THEN	534-13-101	MRS	359-15-195	WITHIN	260-15-156	REAL
1363-15-396	DO	515-15-237	THOUGHT	357-15-184	FELT	259-15-146	SEEMS
1360-15-430	FIRST	507-15-222	WENT	355-15-222	ALONG	258-15-150	BEHIND
1345-15-433	ANY	504-15-242	SAY	355-15-132	CHILDREN	258-14-150	CANNOT
1319-15-251	MY	500-15-301	PART	352-15-184	SAW	258-14-073	MISS
1314-15-394	NOW	499-15-262	ONCE	351-15-226	BEST	258-13-103	POLITICAL
1303-15-400	SUCH	497-13-208	GENERAL	348-13-081	CHURCH	257-15-128	AIR
1290-15-362	LIKE	497-15-250	HIGH	345-15-208	EVER	257-15-151	QUESTION
1252-15-280	OUR	496-10-160	1	343-15-211	LEAST	255-15-175	MAKING
1236-15-412	OVER	495-15-235	UPON	342-15-156	POWER	255-14-127	OFFICE
1207-15-319	MAN	492-15-139	SCHOOL	334-12-120	DEVELOPMENT	253-15-179	BROUGHT
1181-15-234	ME	491-15-274	EVERY	333-15-168	LIGHT	252-15-171	WHOSE
1171-15-402	EVEN	489-14-176	DON'T	333-15-203	THING	250-14-155	SPECIAL
1160-15-396	MOST	485-15-250	DOES	332-14-186	SEEMED	247-15-147	HEARD
1125-15-416	MADE	482-14-191	GOT	331-15-149	FAMILY	247-14-143	MAJOR
1070-15-378	AFTER	482-13-153	UNITED	330-15-170	INTEREST	247-14-136	PROBLEMS
1069-15-383	ALSO	480-15-250	LEFT	329-15-173	WANT	246-15-163	AGO
1044-15-325	DID	472-15-204	NUMBER	325-14-134	MEMBERS	246-15-151	BECAME
1030-15-365	MANY	465-15-259	COURSE	325-15-182	MIND	246-11-066	FEDERAL
1016-15-383	BEFORE	464-15-165	WAR	324-15-163	COUNTRY	246-14-151	MOMENT
1013-15-349	MUST	461-15-273	UNTIL	323-14-145	AREA	246-14-117	STUDY
1010-07-048	**F	458-15-240	ALWAYS	323-15-212	OTHERS	245-14-118	AVAILABLE
969-15-372	THROUGH	456-15-242	AWAY	320-15-199	DONE	245-15-161	KNOWN
967-15-308	BACK	450-15-222	SOMETHING	320-15-183	TURNED	244-13-147	RESULT
949-15-346	YEARS	450-13-176	2	319-15-194	ALTHOUGH	244-14-111	STREET
938-15-372	WHERE	447-15-233	FACT	319-15-193	OPEN	243-11-086	ECONOMIC
937-15-368	MUCH	442-15-245	THOUGH	318-14-091	GOD	242-13-115	BOY

241-15-146 POSITION
241-15-170 REASON
240-15-138 CHANGE
240-15-095 SOUTH
239-14-083 BOARD
239-11-131 INDIVIDUAL
238-13-135 JOB
237-14-101 SOCIETY
236-10-120 AREAS
235-14-115 WEST
234-15-166 CLOSE
233-15-164 TURN
232-15-103 LOVE
231-12-086 COMMUNITY
231-15-155 TRUE
230-13-064 COURT
230-15-122 FORCE
230-15-166 FULL
229-13-087 COST
229-15-154 SEEM
228-15-121 AM
228-15-115 WIFE
227-15-125 AGE
227-15-134 FUTURE
226-15-130 VOICE
226-14-129 WANTED
225-13-082 DEPARTMENT
224-15-115 CENTER
224-15-107 WOMAN
223-14-132 COMMON
223-14-119 CONTROL
222-14-142 NECESSARY
222-10-070 POLICY
221-15-139 FOLLOWING
221-15-122 FRONT
221-15-131 SOMETIMES
220-15-101 GIRL
220-15-147 SIX
219-15-149 CLEAR
218-15-148 FURTHER
217-15-105 LAND
216-15-167 ABLE
216-15-145 FEEL
216-13-089 MOTHER
216-15-064 MUSIC
216-15-087 PARTY
216-13-123 PROVIDE
214-12-069 EDUCATION
214-13-086 UNIVERSITY
213-14-089 CHILD
213-15-137 EFFECT
213-14-108 LEVEL
213-13-062 STUDENTS
212-12-077 MILITARY
212-15-137 RUN
212-15-158 SHORT
212-15-116 STOOD
212-14-103 TOWN
211-15-121 MORNING
211-12-109 TOTAL
210-15-136 OUTSIDE
209-14-109 FIGURE
209-11-084 RATE
208-14-079 ART
207-15-092 CENTURY
207-14-070 CLASS
206-14-088 NORTH
206-15-137 USUALLY
206-11-089 WASHINGTON
205-15-136 LEAVE
205-15-095 PLAN
205-15-135 THEREFORE
204-14-121 EVIDENCE
204-14-073 MILLION
204-15-127 SOUND
204-15-128 TOP
203-14-100 BLACK
202-15-140 HARD
202-14-133 STRONG
201-15-131 VARIOUS
200-15-130 BELIEVE
200-15-106 PLAY
200-14-112 SAYS
200-13-074 SURFACE
200-13-114 TYPE
200-12-101 VALUE
199-15-130 MEAN
199-15-106 SOON
198-15-110 LINES
198-15-106 MODERN
198-15-140 NEAR
198-13-086 PEACE
198-14-106 TABLE
197-15-101 RED
197-14-084 ROAD
197-10-039 TAX
196-14-100 MINUTES

196-15-109 PERSONAL
196-14-087 PROCESS
196-15-126 SITUATION
196-11-110 4
195-15-145 ALONE
195-15-087 ENGLISH
195-15-139 GONE
195-15-127 IDEA
195-11-095 INCREASE
195-15-138 NOR
195-13-059 SCHOOLS
195-15-097 WOMEN
194-13-095 AMERICA
194-15-138 LIVING
194-15-121 STARTED
193-15-100 BOOK
193-15-141 LONGER
192-15-111 CUT
192-13-068 DR
191-15-144 FINALLY
191-15-125 NATURE
191-14-102 PRIVATE
191-13-066 SECRETARY
190-15-129 THIRD
189-15-118 MONTHS
189-14-082 SECTION
188-15-129 CALL
188-14-119 GREATER
187-14-123 EXPECTED
187-14-103 FIRE
187-14-133 NEEDED
186-15-109 GROUND
186-15-136 KEPT
186-14-101 THAT'S
186-12-064 VALUES
186-14-127 VIEW
185-14-106 DARK
185-15-122 EVERYTHING
185-14-084 PRESSURE
184-14-112 BASIS
184-14-082 SPACE
183-13-083 EAST
183-15-105 FATHER
182-12-107 REQUIRED
182-14-089 SPIRIT
182-13-071 UNION
181-15-118 COMPLETE
181-15-137 EXCEPT
181-12-080 I'LL
181-15-122 MOVED
181-14-081 WROTE
180-12-097 CONDITIONS
180-15-106 RETURN
180-12-108 SUPPORT
179-15-129 ATTENTION
179-15-123 LATE
179-14-112 PARTICULAR
179-13-120 RECENT
178-15-114 HOPE
177-15-122 LIVE
176-13-069 BROWN
176-09-047 COSTS
176-14-125 ELSE
175-15-127 BEYOND
175-11-092 COULDN'T
175-13-078 FORCES
175-15-110 HOURS
175-11-057 NATIONS
175-15-119 PERSON
175-15-142 TAKING
174-15-132 COMING
174-15-102 DEAD
174-15-085 INSIDE
174-14-103 LOW
174-12-094 MATERIAL
174-15-082 REPORT
174-14-085 STAGE
173-10-048 DATA
173-15-098 HEART
173-15-138 INSTEAD
173-15-122 LOOKING
173-14-131 LOST
173-15-083 MILES
173-15-114 READ
172-15-128 ADDED
172-15-099 AMOUNT
172-14-109 FEELING
172-15-126 FOLLOWED
172-15-122 MAKES
172-14-102 PAY
172-13-112 SINGLE
171-10-096 BASIC
171-15-098 COLD
171-14-104 HUNDRED
171-14-128 INCLUDING
171-10-055 INDUSTRY
171-14-121 MOVE

171-11-072 RESEARCH
170-13-107 DEVELOPED
170-15-124 SIMPLY
170-15-123 TRIED
170-09-070 1960
169-14-106 CAN'T
169-15-120 HOLD
169-14-117 REACHED
168-10-063 COMMITTEE
167-11-063 DEFENSE
167-14-078 EQUIPMENT
167-15-057 ISLAND
166-15-128 ACTUALLY
166-13-091 SHOWN
166-14-083 SON
165-12-061 RELIGIOUS
165-13-069 RIVER
165-15-119 TEN
164-14-121 BEGINNING
164-12-084 CENTRAL
164-15-122 GETTING
164-13-120 SORT
163-15-124 DOING
163-15-106 RECEIVED
163-15-119 REST
163-13-061 ST
163-15-120 TERMS
163-15-119 TRYING
162-15-104 CARE
162-15-098 FRIENDS
162-15-119 INDEED
162-13-049 MEDICAL
162-14-098 PICTURE
161-09-065 ADMINISTRATION
161-15-127 DIFFICULT
161-15-111 FINE
161-15-113 SIMPLE
161-15-104 SUBJECT
160-15-105 BUILDING
160-15-126 ESPECIALLY
160-13-088 HIGHER
160-15-089 RANGE
160-14-087 WALL
159-14-080 MEETING
159-13-092 WALKED
158-13-131 BRING
158-11-053 CENT
158-15-093 FLOOR
158-13-083 FOREIGN
157-15-088 PAPER
157-14-101 PASSED
157-14-113 SIMILAR
156-15-106 FINAL
156-14-097 NATURAL
156-13-061 PROPERTY
156-12-055 TRAINING
155-13-062 COUNTY
155-11-061 GROWTH
155-09-075 INTERNATIONAL
155-12-057 MARKET
155-12-052 POLICE
154-15-066 ENGLAND
154-15-107 START
154-15-100 TALK
154-13-083 WASN'T
154-14-097 WRITTEN
153-14-110 HEAR
153-15-080 STORY
153-13-098 SUDDENLY
152-15-115 ANSWER
152-09-053 CONGRESS
152-14-074 HALL
152-11-082 ISSUE
152-15-095 NEEDS
151-14-110 CONSIDERED
151-11-054 COUNTRIES
151-14-101 LIKELY
151-14-115 WORKING
151-13-070 YOU'RE
150-15-061 EARTH
150-14-080 SAT
149-14-114 ENTIRE
149-15-102 HAPPENED
149-10-068 LABOR
149-14-107 PURPOSE
149-11-092 RESULTS
148-14-094 CASES
148-14-093 DIFFERENCE
148-13-083 HAIR
148-14-102 MEET
148-12-072 PRODUCTION
148-15-117 STAND
148-13-077 WILLIAM
147-14-106 FALL
147-15-066 FOOD
147-15-105 INVOLVED
147-14-063 STOCK

146-13-106 EARLIER
146-14-093 INCREASED
146-15-116 PARTICULARLY
146-15-095 WHOM
145-13-089 BELOW
145-14-065 CLUB
145-14-107 EFFORT
145-13-103 KNOWLEDGE
145-15-070 LETTER
145-14-086 PAID
145-15-104 SENT
145-15-100 THINKING
145-11-050 U**.*S
145-15-095 USING
144-12-043 CHRISTIAN
144-15-099 HOUR
144-14-089 YES
143-14-071 BILL
143-14-085 BLUE
143-11-070 BOYS
143-14-107 CERTAINLY
143-12-071 IDEAS
143-11-057 INDUSTRIAL
143-13-078 POINTS
143-14-111 READY
143-15-070 SQUARE
143-13-074 TRADE
143-13-090 10
142-13-099 ADDITION
142-15-089 BAD
142-15-057 DEAL
142-14-092 DUE
142-15-063 GIRLS
142-12-081 METHOD
142-11-091 METHODS
142-15-063 MORAL
141-14-087 COLOR
141-15-107 DECIDED
141-13-102 DIRECTLY
141-15-108 NEARLY
141-15-116 NEITHER
141-15-101 SHOWED
141-15-083 STATEMENT
141-14-106 THROUGHOUT
141-13-096 WEEKS
140-15-105 ANYONE
140-07-038 KENNEDY
140-14-094 QUESTIONS
140-15-074 READING
140-15-105 TRY
139-14-098 ACCORDING
139-12-071 FRENCH
139-15-096 LAY
139-13-073 NATION
139-10-056 PROGRAMS
139-10-070 SERVICES
139-12-039 +
138-13-083 PHYSICAL
138-15-099 REMEMBER
138-15-082 SIZE
137-14-103 COMES
137-14-087 MEMBER
137-15-083 RECORD
137-12-053 SOUTHERN
137-15-105 UNDERSTAND
137-15-075 WESTERN
136-15-072 NORMAL
136-09-053 POPULATION
136-14-079 STRENGTH
135-15-100 APPEARED
135-12-103 CONCERNED
135-10-057 DISTRICT
135-13-100 MERELY
135-11-073 S
135-09-032 TEMPERATURE
135-11-049 VOLUME
134-14-082 DIRECTION
134-15-065 MAYBE
134-14-084 RAN
134-15-079 SUMMER
134-14-039 TRIAL
134-15-097 TROUBLE
134-09-051 1961
134-10-077 5
133-15-096 CONTINUED
133-14-083 EVENING
133-14-083 FRIEND
133-15-067 LIST
133-12-053 LITERATURE
133-09-036 SALES
132-14-067 ARMY
132-13-067 ASSOCIATION
132-14-100 GENERALLY
132-12-075 INFLUENCE
132-14-107 LED
132-14-093 MET
132-12-084 PROVIDED

Code	Word	Code	Word	Code	Word	Code	Word
131-15-099	CHANCE	119-14-082	CHIEF	108-12-077	DESIGNED	100-14-078	TALKING
131-13-078	CHANGES	119-14-062	DECISION	108-14-074	DISTANCE	100-08-048	THOMAS
131-14-090	FORMER	119-14-082	DETERMINED	108-11-087	ESTABLISHED	100-12-066	WALK
131-15-067	HUSBAND	119-13-046	IMAGE	108-14-081	EXPECT	99-11-055	FACILITIES
131-15-093	OPENED	119-14-098	MAIN	108-15-080	GROWING	99-14-080	FILLED
131-13-052	SCIENCE	119-12-069	OH	108-13-079	IMPORTANCE	99-15-062	GLASS
131-14-093	STEP	119-14-044	RELIGION	108-14-082	INDICATED	99-07-057	HADN'T
131-12-053	STUDENT	119-13-079	REPORTED	108-15-095	NONE	99-08-016	JAZZ
130-11-069	AID	119-12-070	STEPS	108-12-044	PRICE	99-14-071	KNOWS
130-13-081	AVERAGE	119-13-071	TEST	108-09-040	PRODUCTS	99-12-038	POET
130-11-076	C	119-14-066	WINDOW	107-14-071	ATTITUDE	99-11-053	TECHNIQUES
130-14-099	CAUSE	118-13-083	APPEAR	107-12-048	CITIES	98-13-031	BRIDGE
130-14-077	HOT	118-13-058	BRITISH	107-13-085	CONTINUE	98-14-073	CAUGHT
130-14-082	MONTH	118-14-083	CHARACTER	107-12-067	DETERMINE	98-11-046	CHICAGO
130-13-076	SERIES	118-13-056	EUROPE	107-09-049	DIVISION	98-10-044	CLAIM
130-15-079	WORKS	118-09-034	GUN	107-10-052	ELEMENTS	98-13-072	CONCERN
129-15-094	DIRECT	118-14-082	MIDDLE	107-12-066	EXISTENCE	98-14-071	ENTERED
129-10-089	EFFECTIVE	118-11-059	RESPONSIBILITY	107-11-064	LEADERS	98-13-074	FIGHT
129-13-068	GEORGE	117-13-086	ACCOUNT	107-14-075	PRETTY	98-11-039	GAS
129-15-089	LEAD	117-09-064	B	107-15-084	SERVE	98-14-065	HAPPY
129-13-077	MYSELF	117-14-045	HORSE	107-09-035	STRESS	98-07-042	HE'D
129-14-074	PIECE	117-15-087	LEARNED	106-12-075	AFTERNOON	98-08-046	INSTITUTIONS
129-11-056	PLANNING	117-12-072	WRITING	106-10-046	AGREEMENT	98-13-073	POPULAR
129-09-036	SOVIET	116-12-061	ACTIVITY	106-13-066	APPLIED	98-13-065	SHARE
129-15-096	STOPPED	116-05-026	FISCAL	106-13-076	CLOSED	98-13-054	STYLE
129-12-053	SYSTEMS	116-13-077	GREEN	106-15-083	EASILY	98-09-066	12
129-11-049	THEORY	116-14-073	LENGTH	106-10-059	FACTORS	98-08-047	1959
129-13-077	WOULDN'T	116-15-090	ONES	106-14-089	HARDLY	97-09-020	CATTLE
129-15-091	WRONG	116-14-088	SERIOUS	106-13-081	LIMITED	97-10-030	CHRIST
128-15-090	ASK	116-10-068	TYPES	106-13-086	REACH	97-09-042	COMMUNIST
128-14-104	CLEARLY	115-13-060	ACTIVITIES	106-14-065	SCENE	97-14-058	DOLLARS
128-13-063	FORMS	115-14-047	AUDIENCE	106-14-074	WRITE	97-15-087	FOLLOW
128-12-074	FREEDOM	115-15-064	CORNER	106-09-063	30	97-13-045	HEAT
128-15-078	MOVEMENT	115-14-080	FORWARD	105-12-059	ATTACK	97-13-076	INCLUDED
128-15-104	WAYS	115-14-064	HIT	105-15-079	DRIVE	97-13-065	ISN'T
128-15-098	WORKED	115-14-055	LETTERS	105-12-066	HEALTH	97-08-044	MATERIALS
127-15-080	BEAUTIFUL	115-14-084	LIVED	105-14-077	INTERESTED	97-06-012	RADIATION
127-13-070	BED	115-10-035	NUCLEAR	105-13-057	MARRIED	97-10-057	STATUS
127-13-091	CONSIDER	115-09-056	OBTAINED	105-15-063	PROFESSIONAL	97-14-072	SUPPOSE
127-13-084	EFFORTS	115-14-092	RETURNED	105-15-087	REMAINED	97-15-065	THOUSAND
127-15-073	FEAR	115-13-078	SLOWLY	105-08-019	RHODE	96-14-074	ACCEPTED
127-14-093	LOT	115-11-076	SPECIFIC	105-12-050	SEASON	96-11-046	BEHAVIOR
127-15-076	MEANING	114-11-046	DESIGN	105-13-049	STATION	96-14-066	BOOKS
127-14-095	NOTE	114-15-092	DOUBT	105-13-086	SUGGESTED	96-12-057	CHARLES
127-11-071	ORGANIZATION	114-12-062	JUSTICE	105-13-074	WON'T	96-10-031	CHURCHES
127-13-061	PRESS	114-13-083	LATTER	104-15-068	COVERED	96-11-061	CONFERENCE
127-15-090	SOMEWHAT	114-14-090	MOVING	104-12-073	CURRENT	96-12-078	CONSIDERABLE
127-14-076	SPRING	114-15-088	OBVIOUSLY	104-13-077	DESPITE	96-13-036	FILM
127-11-052	TREATMENT	114-10-038	PLANE	104-15-073	EIGHT	96-14-083	GIVING
126-12-060	HOTEL	114-13-071	QUALITY	104-09-057	I'D	96-11-066	OPINION
126-14-097	PLACED	114-15-080	STRAIGHT	104-08-033	NEGRO	96-11-061	PRIMARY
126-15-078	TRUTH	113-14-062	BORN	104-14-071	PLAYED	96-13-070	SITTING
125-15-100	APPARENTLY	113-13-075	CHOICE	104-13-064	ROLE	96-15-077	USUAL
125-14-097	CARRIED	113-15-074	FIGURES	104-15-084	SPENT	95-13-078	ATTEMPT
125-14-081	DEGREE	113-11-054	FUNCTION	104-10-068	8	95-15-079	CHANGED
125-15-100	EASY	113-09-082	INCLUDE	103-14-068	BUILT	95-10-049	CONSTRUCTION
125-13-039	FARM	113-13-071	OPERATION	103-09-049	COMMISSION	95-07-046	FUNDS
125-12-073	GROUPS	113-13-074	PARTS	103-10-044	COUNCIL	95-11-053	HELL
125-12-069	HE'S	113-13-065	PATTERN	103-13-065	DATE	95-13-044	MARRIAGE
125-14-069	HERSELF	113-15-079	PLANS	103-15-086	EXACTLY	95-14-071	PROPER
125-12-076	I'VE	113-14-075	POOR	103-11-036	MACHINE	95-15-052	SEA
125-14-077	MAN'S	113-14-089	SAYING	103-13-064	MOUTH	95-12-042	SIR
125-12-072	NUMBERS	113-15-075	SEVEN	103-14-078	ORIGINAL	95-12-073	SUCCESSFUL
125-10-044	PLANT	113-12-062	STAFF	103-12-054	RACE	94-12-061	ARM
125-13-079	RESPECT	113-14-085	STAY	103-11-077	REASONS	94-11-062	DISCUSSION
125-15-094	WIDE	113-12-077	6	103-12-053	STUDIES	94-14-071	EVERYONE
124-12-068	J	112-13-048	CARS	103-11-036	TEETH	94-14-075	HIGHLY
124-15-101	MANNER	112-14-082	GIVES	103-11-052	UNIT	94-12-044	PARK
124-11-048	REACTION	112-13-052	SHOT	102-10-074	BECOMES	94-13-069	PRACTICE
123-15-085	APPROACH	112-14-067	SUN	102-13-058	DEMAND	94-11-071	SHOWS
123-08-024	FEED	112-15-087	WHATEVER	102-15-079	NEWS	94-13-056	SIGN
123-12-051	GAME	111-15-054	FAITH	102-12-075	PREPARED	94-14-068	SOMEONE
123-15-095	IMMEDIATELY	111-13-030	POOL	102-09-040	RATES	94-12-070	SOURCE
123-15-084	LARGER	110-12-081	BALL	102-10-072	RELATED	94-10-053	TRADITION
123-13-079	LOWER	110-12-081	COMPLETELY	102-11-064	RELATIONS	94-12-062	WAIT
123-14-101	RECENTLY	110-10-072	EXTENT	102-13-072	RISE	94-15-074	WORTH
123-15-082	RUNNING	110-13-086	HEAVY	102-14-069	SUPPLY	93-12-054	AMERICANS
122-13-079	CHARGE	110-12-048	HOSPITAL	101-13-073	BIT	93-11-060	ANNUAL
122-15-084	COUPLE	110-14-088	LACK	101-14-055	DIRECTOR	93-12-059	AUTHORITY
122-13-059	DAILY	110-13-065	MASS	101-15-076	DROPPED	93-11-054	JUNE
122-13-062	DE	110-14-078	SPEAK	101-09-063	E	93-12-037	LORD
122-13-075	EYE	110-11-062	STANDARD	101-14-069	EVENTS	93-11-045	OIL
122-12-065	PERFORMANCE	110-15-082	WAITING	101-12-060	JAMES	93-14-067	OLDER
121-15-086	ARMS	110-15-087	WISH	101-12-050	OFFICER	93-13-058	PROJECT
121-14-069	BLOOD	109-15-081	AHEAD	101-15-056	PLAYING	93-15-074	REMAIN
121-14-077	OPPORTUNITY	109-12-041	CORPS	101-15-085	RAISED	93-11-061	SUCCESS
121-13-076	PERSONS	109-15-078	DEEP	101-15-068	SIDES	92-13-073	FELL
121-13-080	UNDERSTANDING	109-08-038	DEMOCRATIC	101-13-074	STANDING	92-11-033	JACK
120-11-085	ADDITIONAL	109-12-063	EFFECTS	101-13-052	SUNDAY	92-12-076	LEADERSHIP
120-12-082	DESCRIBED	109-13-065	FIRM	101-12-057	TREES	92-14-074	OBVIOUS
120-11-068	MARCH	109-12-036	INCOME	101-14-076	UNLESS	92-14-042	PIECES
120-12-078	PROGRESS	109-13-068	LANGUAGE	100-10-061	ACTUAL	92-12-061	PRINCIPAL
120-14-043	RADIO	109-12-061	PRINCIPLE	100-10-022	CLAY	92-14-062	THIN
120-13-082	SERVED	109-13-075	THERE'S	100-11-044	DOCTOR	91-13-052	BASE
120-13-086	STOP	109-15-078	VISIT	100-14-047	ENERGY	91-10-053	CIVIL
120-13-062	TECHNICAL	109-11-060	15	100-14-069	MEANT	91-09-059	COMPLEX
119-12-086	BASED	108-09-053	ANALYSIS	100-15-082	PLACES	91-14-065	CONDITION

Code	Word	Code	Word	Code	Word	Code	Word
91-13-061	DINNER	85-11-040	GERMAN	80-11-043	SESSION	74-10-043	PERSONNEL
91-15-072	ENTIRELY	85-14-061	MARKED	80-11-038	TEACHER	74-13-065	POINTED
91-13-066	FREQUENTLY	85-14-061	MUSICAL	80-15-067	TWENTY	74-12-051	POSITIVE
91-08-032	MANAGEMENT	85-10-067	RELATIVELY	79-14-061	ATMOSPHERE	74-13-060	RICH
91-11-061	MEASURE	85-13-039	RULES	79-14-072	DESIRE	74-10-050	SELECTED
91-07-010	MIKE	85-14-061	SHAPE	79-06-046	DIFFERENCES	74-12-063	SEND
91-10-055	OBJECTIVE	85-09-066	SIGNIFICANT	79-09-049	ECONOMY	74-09-046	STANDARDS
91-13-044	PARENTS	85-12-053	STATED	79-11-050	EXPRESSION	74-12-043	STORE
91-13-056	RECORDS	85-09-019	STATIONS	79-10-042	MAXIMUM	74-13-059	TWICE
91-11-050	SECURITY	85-12-071	VARIETY	79-13-070	MENTIONED	73-12-052	ADVANTAGE
91-12-061	STRUCTURE	84-11-057	AFFAIRS	79-13-044	PROCEDURE	73-14-060	BRIEF
91-08-040	U	84-09-063	APPEARS	79-11-049	REALITY	73-11-044	BROTHER
91-11-053	WEIGHT	84-14-068	AWARE	79-11-062	REDUCED	73-15-049	DIE
91-11-061	7	84-14-070	BEGIN	79-09-026	SAM	73-15-064	DISCOVERED
90-12-052	BALANCE	84-13-069	BROAD	79-14-062	SEPARATE	73-10-054	INDIVIDUALS
90-14-071	CAUSED	84-08-022	CATHOLIC	79-14-071	STUDIED	73-12-036	LOUIS
90-07-028	CORPORATION	84-13-068	CIRCUMSTANCES	79-11-056	TERM	73-07-025	MEMBERSHIP
90-10-062	D	84-14-043	COLLECTION	78-11-055	BESIDE	73-14-063	NEVERTHELESS
90-13-040	DANCE	84-15-073	IMPOSSIBLE	78-10-036	COFFEE	73-12-050	OBSERVED
90-14-069	EQUAL	84-15-069	LEARN	78-13-057	EDGE	73-13-041	POWERS
90-13-054	KITCHEN	84-12-051	M	78-12-064	ENTER	73-12-054	PULLED
90-13-069	NOTED	84-14-065	NAMED	78-13-064	FAST	73-12-050	RULE
90-12-066	PRODUCED	84-09-044	OPERATIONS	78-13-061	FAVOR	73-11-034	VALLEY
90-13-055	PURPOSES	84-11-050	POST	78-12-038	LITERARY	73-11-042	WRITER
89-12-054	CLOTHES	84-11-053	PROPOSED	78-14-062	LOOKS	73-11-032	WRITERS
89-13-065	DEVELOP	84-11-078	REMAINS	78-15-045	MISSION	72-12-048	ACCEPT
89-13-056	FAILURE	84-13-065	REPORTS	78-12-058	PICKED	72-13-060	ALLOW
89-14-062	FAMOUS	84-12-030	SEX	78-15-056	SECRET	72-15-061	ASSUMED
89-14-074	GOES	84-13-068	STRANGE	78-14-064	SMALLER	72-11-025	BOAT
89-12-050	LONDON	84-11-056	W	78-13-039	TONE	72-13-061	BROKE
89-14-055	NAMES	83-10-036	BANK	78-10-058	TRADITIONAL	72-13-040	COMMAND
89-15-063	PASS	83-14-052	CAPACITY	77-13-041	ADDRESS	72-12-024	DAUGHTER
89-12-053	PUBLISHED	83-08-032	GOVERNOR	77-01-002	ANODE	72-13-050	DETAIL
89-14-071	QUICKLY	83-10-052	HENRY	77-14-061	BELIEVED	72-14-055	EVERYBODY
89-13-069	REGARD	83-13-064	HOUSES	77-12-025	EDITOR	72-12-033	EVIL
89-10-055	YOU'LL	83-12-049	INTERESTS	77-09-030	ELECTION	72-13-059	FACES
89-08-044	1958	83-12-056	MARK	77-14-057	FAIR	72-14-062	FAMILIAR
88-12-059	ACTIVE	83-14-069	OFFERED	77-11-061	FOLLOWS	72-13-056	FIELDS
88-12-063	ADD	83-11-052	OFFICERS	77-13-044	JUDGE	72-04-016	FIG
88-15-068	ANNOUNCED	83-14-063	OPENING	77-14-066	LAID	72-14-051	FIGHTING
88-12-050	BOTTOM	83-10-046	P	77-12-032	MODEL	72-08-046	HILL
88-13-077	BREAK	83-12-061	PREVENT	77-13-058	PERMIT	72-08-036	INCREASES
88-13-075	CARRY	83-15-063	REGULAR	77-13-056	RESPONSE	72-11-039	ITEMS
88-12-057	CHECK	83-14-064	REMEMBERED	77-14-047	RIGHTS	72-11-026	JONES
88-14-064	COVER	83-09-051	REQUIREMENTS	77-15-060	SOLID	72-13-040	LEGAL
88-11-035	ENEMY	83-12-056	ROBERT	77-13-044	TITLE	72-13-054	MASTER
88-13-071	GREATEST	83-14-037	SHIP	77-06-011	VOCATIONAL	72-07-009	MORGAN
88-13-060	KEY	83-13-067	SLIGHTLY	76-08-024	BOTTLE	72-11-050	ORDINARY
88-13-038	KING	83-12-052	SPEED	76-12-043	BUILDINGS	72-08-036	PHASE
88-12-042	LAWS	83-13-070	SPREAD	76-14-060	DIFFICULTY	72-08-016	PLATFORM
88-13-073	LEAVING	83-11-035	TEAM	76-12-056	FORMED	72-13-055	PLUS
88-12-040	MANAGER	83-14-053	WINTER	76-12-041	HEARING	72-11-040	RESOURCES
88-13-036	MARY	83-11-038	YESTERDAY	76-10-021	KNIFE	72-11-044	RUSSIA
88-13-063	MOREOVER	82-12-034	BAR	76-14-056	MEMORY	72-15-059	SHARP
88-12-044	PAIN	82-12-035	CRISIS	76-14-060	PRESENCE	72-15-062	SOMEHOW
88-09-025	POETRY	82-11-044	DRINK	76-15-059	QUIET	72-14-051	UPPER
88-14-062	RELATIONSHIP	82-13-061	FRESH	76-13-056	RECEIVE	72-13-045	VILLAGE
88-09-052	SOURCES	82-15-068	INSTANCE	76-11-047	REGION	72-12-024	WINE
88-09-063	20	82-13-070	INTERESTING	76-12-046	TELEPHONE	71-07-042	APPROXIMATELY
87-08-035	ASSISTANCE	82-05-015	POEMS	76-13-061	WATCHING	71-11-041	APRIL
87-13-058	BATTLE	82-13-069	PRESENTED	75-10-034	CAMP	71-13-044	BEAUTY
87-13-060	BRIGHT	82-13-063	PRODUCE	75-12-028	DOG	71-14-060	CARRYING
87-13-069	CAREFULLY	82-14-045	TRAIN	75-11-059	EXPRESSED	71-12-059	CHOSEN
87-10-035	COMPANIES	82-14-044	YOUTH	75-10-057	FIT	71-12-034	COLUMN
87-13-068	DOESN'T	82-10-058	25	75-10-030	JUNIOR	71-12-054	COMPARED
87-15-069	FACTS	81-13-056	AGREED	75-13-050	KILLED	71-12-055	CONSTANT
87-14-070	FINISHED	81-12-039	APARTMENT	75-11-033	MURDER	71-10-052	FACTOR
87-15-057	FIXED	81-12-037	CAMPAIGN	75-13-049	NICE	71-14-061	FORTH
87-09-044	OPERATING	81-06-013	CELLS	75-15-060	OFFICIAL	71-10-048	HISTORICAL
87-13-070	POSSIBILITY	81-13-053	CREATED	75-14-058	PLANNED	71-03-007	MERCER
87-09-044	PRODUCT	81-13-059	ESSENTIAL	75-15-059	REMOVED	71-11-049	PRINCIPLES
87-13-064	SPOKE	81-12-062	EVENT	75-14-042	ROCK	71-13-062	PROVED
87-15-062	TOUCH	81-12-027	FILE	75-13-061	STAYED	71-15-059	RESPONSIBLE
87-10-044	UNITS	81-15-066	FORCED	75-13-049	TREATED	71-09-037	RICHARD
86-12-060	ALLOWED	81-12-033	GERMANY	75-14-062	TURNING	71-09-050	SMILED
86-14-056	BUILD	81-14-071	IMMEDIATE	75-11-031	VIRGINIA	71-10-037	UNITY
86-13-052	CITIZENS	81-08-015	INDEX	75-09-037	VOTE	71-09-025	UNIVERSE
86-15-062	DIED	81-13-062	LIVES	74-12-054	ABILITY	71-15-058	WANTS
86-11-051	FINANCIAL	81-11-054	NECK	74-09-025	BERLIN	70-10-019	AIRCRAFT
86-11-025	INCHES	81-13-056	NINE	74-14-043	CHAPTER	70-15-041	BOX
86-13-062	LOSS	81-11-061	OPPOSITE	74-11-041	CLAIMS	70-12-043	BUY
86-15-069	OTHERWISE	81-10-056	PROVIDES	74-12-052	CONTRAST	70-12-053	CALLS
86-13-028	PATIENT	81-14-055	ROUND	74-10-018	DU	70-12-050	CLEAN
86-11-036	PHILOSOPHY	81-10-033	SUBJECTS	74-09-018	FACULTY	70-09-024	COMMUNISM
86-12-076	PREVIOUS	81-13-058	TRIP	74-14-059	FAILED	70-12-054	DANGER
86-10-066	REQUIRE	81-13-068	WATCH	74-12-058	FOURTH	71-11-026	DOGS
86-13-065	ROSE	81-13-063	WATCHED	74-12-042	FRAME	70-14-065	DRAWN
86-09-047	SCIENTIFIC	80-13-062	EXPLAINED	74-12-039	FRANCE	70-13-038	DUST
86-15-066	SEEING	80-12-054	FEATURES	74-10-036	GAIN	70-09-036	EDUCATIONAL
86-13-066	SIGHT	80-12-069	FULLY	74-08-047	H	70-12-039	EXCHANGE
86-14-077	TAKES	80-13-053	GRAY	74-10-059	INCREASING	70-08-047	F
86-11-036	WORKERS	80-12-065	INDICATE	74-10-020	INTERIOR	70-11-032	FOOT
85-10-040	CAPITAL	80-13-042	LADY	74-08-020	JEWISH	70-08-032	INDEPENDENCE
85-10-024	CAPTAIN	80-13-071	OFFER	74-09-030	JR	70-11-047	INDEPENDENT
85-09-036	CLASSES	80-08-019	PROVIDENCE	74-09-044	LEADER	70-14-063	NATURALLY
85-09-046	CONCEPT	80-13-063	RECOGNIZED	74-12-052	NOBODY	70-11-038	RAIN
85-08-038	DISTRIBUTION	80-11-036	RUSSIAN	74-15-042	NOVEMBER	70-08-036	REVOLUTION

70-10-027	ROME	66-14-050	CAPABLE	63-14-054	POWERFUL	60-14-043	LEARNING
70-14-039	SAN	66-13-048	CHAIR	63-08-043	RELATION	60-08-022	MACHINERY
70-09-023	SECTIONS	66-12-049	CLOSELY	63-09-020	RIFLE	60-12-046	MAINTAIN
70-07-013	SHELTER	66-08-024	CUTTING	63-13-043	SHOP	60-12-026	MOON
70-12-031	SONG	66-11-052	DECLARED	63-12-032	SIGNAL	60-10-042	NOSE
70-12-039	SWEET	66-12-046	ENDS	63-08-050	SUFFICIENT	60-12-047	ONTO
70-09-055	WAITED	66-07-027	EXPERIMENTS	63-09-018	TOM	60-11-024	ORCHESTRA
70-13-046	WALLS	66-12-050	FINGERS	63-11-039	TOMORROW	60-14-048	REFUSED
70-08-044	100	66-09-021	FOREST	63-15-052	UNUSUAL	60-10-037	SCALE
69-15-055	ANCIENT	66-11-022	GROSS	63-14-045	WIND	60-14-052	SETTING
69-12-029	CHINA	66-04-004	HANOVER	63-10-047	9	60-11-046	SLOW
69-13-055	COMPLETED	66-14-054	HELPED	62-11-051	ACHIEVED	60-13-049	SOMEWHERE
69-14-058	CONNECTION	66-12-045	HONOR	62-08-035	AGENCIES	60-09-044	STARED
69-14-052	FASHION	66-12-042	INTELLECTUAL	62-12-037	APPEAL	60-11-047	STREETS
69-09-028	LEAGUE	66-10-041	ISSUES	62-15-054	ARRIVED	60-13-049	TASK
69-09-044	LEVELS	66-10-032	MEASURED	62-08-021	ASSIGNMENT	60-09-041	TECHNIQUE
69-10-036	LIBERAL	66-12-046	OURSELVES	62-12-038	BABY	60-10-020	TEXT
69-10-044	LIPS	66-14-046	PAGE	62-08-016	BILLION	59-11-028	BIBLE
69-14-050	ORDERED	66-13-041	PLAYS	62-14-056	CAREFUL	59-07-026	BUDGET
69-12-038	POLITICS	66-10-031	PROPERTIES	62-11-043	CONCERNING	59-12-048	CONCLUSION
69-14-058	REALIZE	66-11-044	R	62-13-035	COOL	59-13-051	DROP
69-13-057	REALIZED	66-15-052	RELIEF	62-10-044	DECEMBER	59-10-050	EXIST
69-13-057	SEEK	66-11-035	SCORE	62-10-048	DROVE	59-12-049	FINDS
69-12-058	SETTLED	66-13-050	SEARCH	62-14-049	EQUALLY	59-07-027	FORMULA
69-11-028	TEACHERS	66-11-051	SIGNIFICANCE	62-11-050	EXTREME	59-13-042	HEADED
69-09-027	TEXAS	66-09-046	SUBSTANTIAL	62-10-032	FUND	59-08-026	HOUSING
69-11-053	WEATHER	65-07-027	ACHIEVEMENT	62-10-054	GREATLY	59-14-049	LIE
69-14-056	WILLING	65-09-031	ATTORNEY	62-13-036	GUESTS	59-14-043	MINE
68-11-049	ACTIONS	65-15-037	CALIFORNIA	62-10-036	HOMES	59-14-050	NOTICE
68-12-037	ANIMAL	65-06-018	CELL	62-10-036	INTERNAL	59-10-031	NOVEL
68-11-042	APPLICATION	65-10-044	DESK	62-11-022	LIBRARY	59-12-028	PAINTING
68-10-049	APPROPRIATE	65-14-054	DISCUSSED	62-08-048	OFFICIALS	59-12-039	PARTIES
68-10-035	ARTICLE	65-06-026	DOMINANT	62-14-051	PLEASE	59-11-029	PLANTS
68-12-046	BEAT	65-08-024	EMPLOYEES	62-12-049	PLEASURE	59-12-051	PROVIDING
68-08-049	CHARACTERISTIC	65-13-050	ESCAPE	62-12-040	PORTION	59-14-048	REPEATED
68-13-051	DIRECTED	65-12-049	GETS	62-12-047	RECOGNIZE	59-13-033	ROOF
68-10-051	DREW	65-12-040	HEADQUARTERS	62-08-044	REDUCE	59-10-043	SENSITIVE
68-10-042	DRY	65-13-057	HOLDING	62-13-044	RISING	59-07-018	SEXUAL
68-14-039	ELECTRIC	65-11-051	HUNG	62-12-047	SAVE	59-13-029	SNOW
68-08-014	ELECTRONIC	65-14-051	IMAGINATION	62-06-026	SENATE	59-11-047	SOLUTION
68-08-030	EMOTIONAL	65-10-043	JOBS	62-09-035	SETS	59-10-024	SONGS
68-13-055	EXCELLENT	65-13-045	JOIN	62-13-056	SPEAKING	59-12-040	STORIES
68-11-045	FAMILIES	65-11-039	JULY	62-09-019	WILSON	59-14-047	STRUCK
68-14-056	FIFTY	65-13-043	NEWSPAPER	62-09-047	11	59-12-045	TASTE
68-11-054	FRANK	65-12-045	OBJECT	61-12-043	ACTING	59-14-038	TENSION
68-09-033	HORSES	65-09-038	OBJECTS	61-09-045	ASSOCIATED	59-12-047	THIRTY
68-11-050	INITIAL	65-13-041	ONE'S	61-12-035	BEACH	59-11-032	TREE
68-06-017	KHRUSHCHEV	65-15-053	PASSING	61-12-035	BOSTON	59-09-030	TUESDAY
68-11-053	LARGELY	65-04-007	PHIL	61-14-049	CLOSER	59-13-042	ULTIMATE
68-14-046	LEADING	65-14-055	RAPIDLY	61-14-042	COAST	59-07-036	USES
68-12-046	LET'S	65-10-041	SLEEP	61-09-036	COMMERCIAL	58-12-033	ANIMALS
68-08-030	MONDAY	65-14-054	SUPPOSED	61-10-051	CONTINUING	58-14-049	AVOID
68-14-050	OUGHT	65-13-039	THEY'RE	61-09-021	COURSES	58-14-049	BUSY
68-14-046	PICTURES	65-10-052	TYPICAL	61-14-046	DUTY	58-09-041	CAUSES
68-07-036	POLICIES	65-11-047	WORE	61-13-042	EAT	58-06-030	COMMERCE
68-11-052	PRACTICAL	64-10-051	ASPECTS	61-08-030	EUROPEAN	58-10-042	CRITICAL
68-08-028	PROJECTS	64-13-042	BELIEF	61-12-035	FEELINGS	58-10-034	CULTURE
68-11-035	PROTECTION	64-13-047	BODIES	61-14-044	FRIENDLY	58-05-010	DALLAS
68-14-060	QUICK	64-12-037	CREDIT	61-09-032	GOVERNMENTS	58-10-049	EMPHASIS
68-10-037	SIGNS	64-12-033	DREAM	61-09-028	GREEK	58-09-043	ESTABLISH
68-14-055	STANDS	64-13-050	EMPTY	61-11-040	IDEAL	58-09-043	ETC
68-13-054	STARTING	64-15-055	EXPLAIN	61-13-049	IMAGINE	58-12-033	EXERCISE
68-12-037	STATEMENTS	64-15-051	GREW	61-10-027	KID	58-12-051	FAIRLY
68-11-035	TRAFFIC	64-06-018	JESUS	61-11-037	LA	58-14-047	GROUNDS
68-10-046	WON	64-05-013	LAOS	61-13-039	METAL	58-08-039	HENCE
67-14-056	ANSWERED	64-10-048	LOCATED	61-11-029	MINISTER	58-10-031	HOLE
67-15-060	ASIDE	64-11-034	MAINTENANCE	61-10-035	ORGANIZATIONS	58-10-020	INDIA
67-13-056	ASKING	64-14-050	MATTERS	61-14-051	POSSIBLY	58-10-031	LEG
67-12-052	BACKGROUND	64-13-039	MESSAGE	61-07-025	PRICES	58-12-047	LIKED
67-13-046	CAREER	64-10-045	MINIMUM	61-08-034	PROCEDURES	58-13-051	LOSE
67-08-042	CHAIRMAN	64-09-045	PRIMARILY	61-13-027	SHORE	58-13-047	MINOR
67-11-035	COMMUNICATION	64-12-051	REASONABLE	61-12-043	SHOULDER	58-07-017	NEGROES
67-12-045	DRESS	64-08-019	RESOLUTION	61-12-043	SHOWING	58-12-036	NEIGHBORHOOD
67-10-042	ESTIMATED	64-08-024	SITE	61-11-049	SOFT	58-15-048	OCCASION
67-12-046	FLAT	64-10-032	SPIRITUAL	61-14-045	SPEECH	58-14-042	ORDERS
67-11-043	FLOW	64-14-039	TOWARDS	61-10-028	TESTS	58-10-038	PALE
67-12-045	IMPACT	64-10-038	WE'LL	61-13-042	TRAVEL	58-13-045	PERFECT
67-08-022	JURY	64-10-028	YARDS	61-13-054	VAST	58-11-049	PREVIOUSLY
67-12-043	LEGS	64-10-041	50	61-11-034	VICTORY	58-10-027	RAILROAD
67-13-049	OCCURRED	63-11-048	ARGUMENT	61-11-046	WE'RE	58-11-042	REMOVE
67-12-040	PARIS	63-13-050	ASSUME	61-12-035	WEAPONS	58-10-027	ROADS
67-10-046	POTENTIAL	63-14-044	BENEFIT	60-11-044	ADVANCE	58-11-026	ROMAN
67-13-043	REFERENCE	63-12-052	BROKEN	60-10-034	ARMED	58-13-049	SAFE
67-10-039	SATURDAY	63-11-031	COMPETITION	60-08-023	CHEMICAL	58-13-043	SKY
67-05-020	SHE'D	63-13-037	CONTACT	60-10-040	CIRCLE	58-12-045	SMILE
67-14-050	SIT	63-11-039	CONTEMPORARY	60-12-039	CONTAINED	58-14-039	STONE
67-09-034	TEACHING	63-10-036	DOMESTIC	60-11-034	CONTRACT	58-11-044	SURPRISED
67-11-049	THICK	63-12-049	DRAMATIC	60-12-047	ENDED	58-12-046	TALKED
67-14-055	WARM	63-09-034	EXPERIMENT	60-09-042	EXISTING	58-14-055	UNDERSTOOD
67-14-055	WONDER	63-14-055	FELLOW	60-13-037	FAT	58-13-046	UNIQUE
67-12-041	YOU'VE	63-13-050	GROW	60-10-034	FRIDAY	58-11-045	USEFUL
67-12-052	YOURSELF	63-15-049	HAPPEN	60-12-037	GARDEN	58-11-038	WONDERED
66-10-052	ADEQUATE	63-11-049	HIGHEST	60-11-044	GOAL	57-12-043	AFRAID
66-12-038	ARTS	63-13-041	KILL	60-13-055	HEAVILY	57-13-048	ALIVE
66-13-059	BESIDES	63-07-037	LOCATION	60-11-049	JUDGMENT	57-12-051	APART
66-11-032	BIRTH	63-12-049	NARROW	60-14-048	KEEPING	57-13-052	APPARENT
66-14-039	BLOCK	63-06-009	PARKER			57-13-050	APPEARANCE

57-10-034	ARTIST	55-11-039	ROOMS	52-11-045	DETAILED	50-12-039	NOTICED
57-09-015	BASEBALL	55-12-026	RUNS	52-08-012	DETECTIVE	50-13-043	PAIR
57-13-028	BAY	55-12-046	SOUGHT	52-09-037	DEVELOPING	50-11-026	PHILADELPHIA
57-15-046	BEAR	55-11-044	SOUNDS	52-12-047	DOZEN	50-12-045	PROUD
57-13-052	BECOMING	55-10-045	TALL	52-12-032	ELEMENT	50-12-030	STRIKE
57-12-040	BENEATH	55-08-034	THEME	52-12-043	ESTABLISHMENT	50-11-037	TAUGHT
57-11-033	BIRDS	55-07-025	WAGON	52-13-045	EVENTUALLY	50-11-036	TELEVISION
57-11-037	CHARGED	55-11-038	WIN	52-09-034	FLESH	50-11-033	TILL
57-12-043	COMBINATION	55-11-047	WISHED	52-12-038	GOLD	50-13-042	TINY
57-06-020	COMPLETION	55-13-042	WOOD	52-13-031	HERO	50-11-021	TOWNS
57-04-010	CONGO	55-12-044	WORRY	52-14-028	INDIAN	50-13-040	WELCOME
57-12-049	DETAILS	55-12-041	YELLOW	52-11-046	INTRODUCED	50-11-030	WOODEN
57-05-007	DICTIONARY	55-09-042	14	52-11-032	LOS	50-13-045	WORSE
57-12-047	ENJOYED	54-11-039	ATTEND	52-12-039	RAISE	50-08-038	18
57-12-036	ENTRANCE	54-11-046	CREATE	52-10-041	SILENCE	49-11-038	ACCEPTANCE
57-13-034	FLOWERS	54-10-038	DEAR	52-13-045	TELLING	49-10-044	CONSIDERATION
57-10-027	GOODS	54-10-036	DECISIONS	52-09-028	THEATER	49-05-019	CONSTITUTION
57-14-044	INFORMED	54-11-037	DESCRIPTION	52-14-039	TRUST	49-14-041	COUNT
57-07-011	LEWIS	54-14-051	FACED	52-11-042	WIDELY	49-09-028	CREATIVE
57-10-039	MAJORITY	54-14-042	FORGET	51-10-031	ABROAD	49-11-043	DEPENDS
57-14-040	NOTES	54-14-042	HUGE	51-10-032	AGES	49-10-020	DRIVER
57-13-045	PERMITTED	54-11-040	INTERPRETATION	51-12-040	AGREE	49-11-042	EMPLOYED
57-10-030	PROCESSES	54-10-020	ITEM	51-09-029	APPROVAL	49-11-042	FIRMLY
57-11-035	PROFESSOR	54-07-014	JEWS	51-09-029	ARTHUR	49-10-023	HOLY
57-13-037	REPLIED	54-12-024	LAKE	51-13-048	BEGUN	49-11-042	IMPRESSIVE
57-11-051	REQUIRES	54-09-025	MACHINES	51-10-012	BOATS	49-13-037	INCIDENT
57-08-023	SAMPLE	54-05-020	MEASUREMENTS	51-11-032	COLORS	49-13-039	LEAVES
57-08-044	SHOOK	54-10-030	PHONE	51-09-035	CONVENTIONAL	49-11-040	MEASURES
57-11-040	SOMEBODY	54-09-043	POSITIONS	51-09-015	COUSIN	49-08-026	MILK
57-12-047	SPOT	54-09-031	PREPARATION	51-10-028	DAVID	49-12-036	MILLIONS
57-10-025	TRUCK	54-14-044	PUTTING	51-13-040	DEVOTED	49-06-011	OPERATOR
57-13-052	TRULY	54-06-020	REPUBLICAN	51-13-038	EASIER	49-13-040	PARTLY
57-11-027	UNCLE	54-12-036	RISK	51-04-009	ELECTIONS	49-12-041	PASSAGE
56-10-026	ACADEMIC	54-09-027	RURAL	51-11-033	ESTATE	49-08-018	PAYMENTS
56-10-035	AGENCY	54-10-035	SEAT	51-06-012	FOODS	49-11-035	REQUEST
56-08-044	APPLY	54-10-036	SMITH	51-14-046	GRADUALLY	49-09-036	RIDE
56-12-049	BOUGHT	54-11-023	SOIL	51-11-029	GUY	49-11-043	SILENT
56-10-023	CHINESE	54-12-047	SUGGEST	51-11-037	INVESTIGATION	49-08-023	SPEAKER
56-12-045	CONFIDENCE	54-11-048	SUPPORTED	51-08-040	LAUGHED	49-10-030	SPORTS
56-12-040	DOUBLE	54-13-035	SYMBOL	51-13-043	LISTEN	49-10-040	TENDENCY
56-13-045	DRAW	54-12-044	THOUGHTS	51-09-043	NECESSARILY	49-10-023	TRAGEDY
56-10-037	ENTITLED	54-12-042	TRAINED	51-07-035	NODDED	49-10-035	24
56-12-043	EVIDENT	54-13-047	UNABLE	51-11-034	OCTOBER	48-10-030	ANGER
56-13-048	FIFTEEN	54-11-047	WALKING	51-13-029	OPPORTUNITIES	48-10-041	ATTITUDES
56-12-042	GRANTED	53-12-040	ABSENCE	51-12-036	PAPERS	48-09-015	CHARLIE
56-10-044	GUESS	53-07-031	ADMINISTRATIVE	51-08-016	PLAYER	48-08-024	CO
56-11-037	HAT	53-10-032	ASSIGNED	51-07-016	PROTESTANT	48-10-038	COMPARISON
56-11-031	INTENSITY	53-11-042	AUGUST	51-13-042	PULL	48-12-027	CONCRETE
56-13-046	JOINED	53-13-035	BAND	51-09-030	REAR	48-10-034	CRY
56-11-040	LOVED	53-12-048	BITTER	51-13-044	SHOULDERS	48-10-030	DESTROY
56-13-046	MINDS	53-11-032	BREAKFAST	51-12-035	SICK	48-10-029	DRINKING
56-10-033	MOTOR	53-12-036	BREATH	51-11-032	SITUATIONS	48-09-035	FORMAL
56-13-045	ORGANIZED	53-12-033	CHEST	51-09-024	STAGES	48-09-025	FUNCTIONS
56-05-007	PALMER	53-11-040	CONTENT	51-09-033	STREAM	48-12-039	GRAND
56-11-040	PURE	53-13-040	CROWD	51-11-033	SUPREME	48-12-032	GUARD
56-13-047	REGARDED	53-07-032	DEPTH	51-14-046	SURPRISE	48-01-002	HEARST
56-11-042	REPRESENTED	53-10-021	DISEASE	51-11-031	THROAT	48-10-041	HOPED
56-08-035	REVIEW	53-11-042	DRIVING	51-13-032	UNIFORM	48-13-043	HOPES
56-12-038	SEPTEMBER	53-09-040	EXAMPLES	51-09-036	VIEWS	48-09-024	INTEGRATION
56-09-030	SOLDIERS	53-12-046	EXPERIENCED	51-07-020	WARREN	48-10-024	INTELLIGENCE
56-11-049	SPITE	53-11-036	EXPERIENCES	51-08-017	WAVES	48-12-040	LIMIT
56-13-038	VISION	53-14-048	FINDING	51-09-038	16	48-07-018	LIQUID
56-11-043	VITAL	53-12-034	GRASS	50-12-026	ADVERTISING	48-08-035	MAINTAINED
56-07-011	WAGE	53-13-040	HANDLE	50-10-032	ASSEMBLY	48-02-004	MANTLE
56-10-028	WHEEL	53-08-016	HUDSON	50-10-022	AUTOMOBILE	48-12-027	MILE
56-13-044	WILD	53-10-032	JANUARY	50-12-036	BRILLIANT	48-09-015	MISSILE
55-09-026	ARTISTS	53-11-022	JAPANESE	50-12-034	BURNING	48-12-042	OCCASIONALLY
55-11-042	BEGINS	53-11-043	LARGEST	50-10-025	CHAIN	48-10-032	OPERATE
55-09-027	BRITAIN	53-13-046	LOOSE	50-08-022	CHILDHOOD	48-12-029	PERSONALITY
55-06-028	COMPONENTS	53-13-049	MINUTE	50-14-039	CHOOSE	48-13-031	PINK
55-11-038	CONDUCT	53-08-036	NEGATIVE	50-12-037	CONVERSATION	48-13-038	PLAIN
55-09-037	CONDUCTED	53-08-023	PAYMENT	50-12-042	CONVICTION	48-07-019	POEM
55-13-045	CROSS	53-08-021	PERCENT	50-13-044	CONVINCED	48-11-039	PRECISELY
55-09-032	CULTURAL	53-13-047	PRACTICALLY	50-12-024	COURTS	48-12-042	QUIETLY
55-11-043	DEMANDS	53-09-030	PRACTICES	50-10-039	DESIRED	48-10-023	RESISTANCE
55-13-031	DEVICE	53-14-044	PROVE	50-09-028	EFFICIENCY	48-10-029	ROYAL
55-12-049	DIVIDED	53-11-045	PUSHED	50-07-020	EISENHOWER	48-11-031	SCREEN
55-10-040	EXECUTIVE	53-12-040	REMARKS	50-10-021	ENGINE	48-09-034	SHE'S
55-11-048	EXTENDED	53-08-023	SIN	50-10-044	EXPENSE	48-10-018	SHOOTING
55-08-023	FIRMS	53-13-044	SLIGHT	50-15-041	EXTRA	48-11-036	SORRY
55-11-020	FORT	53-15-045	SPEND	50-09-041	EXTREMELY	48-13-039	SUIT
55-12-028	GAMES	53-09-027	TROOPS	50-12-033	FEMALE	48-11-034	SWUNG
55-10-037	GENERATION	53-09-016	VEHICLES	50-14-039	FILL	48-11-040	TIRED
55-10-028	IDENTITY	53-10-030	VERSION	50-09-038	FUNDAMENTAL	48-12-042	TWELVE
55-11-042	IMPROVED	53-08-037	WELFARE	50-08-036	G	48-08-017	VIA
55-12-041	INNER	53-11-040	WET	50-13-038	HILLS	47-11-029	ANGELES
55-10-023	JOE	53-12-039	WHAT'S	50-08-020	INSTITUTE	47-11-038	ASPECT
55-10-035	JOSEPH	53-13-038	WINDOWS	50-11-038	ISSUED	47-11-028	BILLS
55-11-036	L	53-14-044	WONDERFUL	50-14-043	KNOWING	47-13-036	BLIND
55-08-013	MARINE	52-12-040	ADVANCED	50-11-033	LATIN	47-15-026	BOARDS
55-10-023	MARTIN	52-05-013	ALFRED	50-09-029	MASSACHUSETTS	47-07-017	BONDS
55-14-037	MOTION	52-10-034	BEDROOM	50-12-045	MENTION	47-10-029	CONCENTRATION
55-11-028	O	52-10-032	CENTERS	50-13-041	MOMENTS	47-07-012	CONGREGATION
55-14-042	PICK	52-06-032	CHARACTERISTICS	50-08-010	MOTORS	47-12-040	CONSIDERING
55-13-045	PLENTY ——	52-10-042	CONFLICT			47-11-026	COOK
55-14-046	PROPERLY	52-13-044	CONTRARY			47-09-020	CUBA
55-07-029	PUBLICATION	52-13-041	CORRECT			47-10-030	DENIED

47-11-039 DENY	46-05-005 WRIGHT	44-15-043 MOSTLY	42-07-012 ENGINEER
47-09-026 EMPLOYMENT	46-07-024 1954	44-10-036 NEARBY	42-07-025 ENVIRONMENT
47-11-038 ENGAGED	46-09-029 1957	44-12-031 ODD	42-10-032 EXCESS
47-09-039 ESSENTIALLY	46-09-034 23	44-10-024 OPINIONS	42-09-035 EXISTS
47-13-041 EVERYWHERE	45-09-035 ADOPTED	44-10-035 ORIGIN	42-12-032 EXPRESS
47-10-033 EXPANSION	45-10-028 AFRICA	44-13-033 PATH	42-11-030 FED
47-11-029 EXPENSES	45-10-021 ALEXANDER	44-10-019 PILOT	42-11-029 GOLDEN
47-09-020 FEARS	45-10-036 ANGRY	44-09-033 RECOGNITION	42-10-023 GUNS
47-08-035 GRANT	45-12-041 APPROACHED	44-11-032 SALE	42-07-009 HARDY
47-13-041 HONEST	45-10-017 BALLET	44-12-040 SEEKING	42-10-029 HATE
47-12-032 HUMOR	45-12-022 BRAIN	44-10-036 SHOES	42-11-041 HOLDS
47-10-033 INSTRUMENT	45-12-043 CALLING	44-07-014 SLAVES	42-12-036 INCREASINGLY
47-11-027 ITALIAN	45-13-030 CAST	44-08-013 SNAKE	42-09-016 JOURNAL
47-14-036 LIGHTS	45-10-031 CHARGES	44-11-026 SPIRITS	42-02-002 LINDA
47-10-023 LINCOLN	45-12-037 CONTAIN	44-07-022 SUFFERING	42-13-033 LOTS
47-09-034 LUCK	45-08-033 CONTAINING	44-10-026 TABLES	42-08-017 MUSCLE
47-08-021 MAIL	45-10-024 CUP	44-04-012 THICKNESS	42-10-023 NINETEENTH
47-05-021 MANUFACTURERS	45-05-012 CURVE	44-11-023 VOLUMES	42-08-039 OBTAIN
47-12-039 MERE	45-09-036 DEPEND	44-11-030 WARNING	42-06-012 PARTICLES
47-10-025 MODELS	45-05-018 DIAMETER	44-08-015 WASHING	42-09-031 POSSIBILITIES
47-06-019 MOSCOW	45-10-023 DISCOVERY	44-12-035 WISDOM	42-14-037 PRIDE
47-11-028 MOVEMENTS	45-07-024 EDWARD	44-13-035 YOUNGER	42-09-025 PRISON
47-12-034 NORTHERN	45-12-039 ELSEWHERE	44-08-015 60	42-05-005 RACHEL
47-10-041 NUMEROUS	45-07-016 EXPENDITURES	43-11-030 BELIEVES	42-07-021 REACTIONS
47-11-023 OPERA	45-10-029 FEBRUARY	43-10-028 BUREAU	42-07-026 REDUCTION
47-10-028 PATTERNS	45-11-036 FEELS	43-13-036 CATCH	42-11-032 REFLECTED
47-10-037 PERIODS	45-08-028 ICE	43-10-025 CLOTH	42-07-023 REGIONAL
47-10-034 PRIOR	45-12-036 IMPRESSION	43-09-023 COAT	42-11-035 REPLACED
47-10-034 PROVISION	45-09-037 INCLUDES	43-14-036 COMFORT	42-12-031 REPLY
47-09-026 PURCHASE	45-12-040 INTENDED	43-12-027 CONCERNS	42-04-006 SEEDS
47-11-040 REMARKABLE	45-07-015 INTERFERENCE	43-09-033 CONSISTS	42-10-031 SKILL
47-10-042 REPRESENTATIVE	45-10-010 LOAD	43-08-030 DANCING	42-11-028 SMOOTH
47-14-032 RING	45-04-004 LUCY	43-10-031 DARKNESS	42-12-036 SUFFICIENTLY
47-10-032 ROLLED	45-10-017 MEAT	43-10-037 DEALING	42-10-033 THREAT
47-10-027 SAFETY	45-10-027 MEDIUM	43-10-027 DIRT	42-13-037 THROW
47-12-028 SINGING	45-07-009 MOLD	43-11-030 DRAMA	42-10-036 TOUCHED
47-10-033 SKIN	45-12-029 MOUNTED	43-08-026 EMOTIONS	42-12-040 UNLIKE
47-11-031 SOLD	45-10-034 OFFERS	43-12-031 EXPLANATION	42-09-022 URBAN
47-10-033 SOUL	45-10-026 OFFICES	43-09-026 EXTERNAL	42-10-034 VARIED
47-08-027 STAIRS	45-11-032 PENNSYLVANIA	43-12-030 FLYING	42-11-035 VARYING
47-13-036 SUPPLIES	45-09-026 PERCENTAGE	43-14-037 GROWN	42-09-017 WAGES
47-13-040 SURELY	45-10-026 PRIME	43-14-034 HEADS	42-10-031 WATERS
47-08-025 TESTIMONY	45-12-035 PROMISE	43-12-033 HEAVEN	42-12-028 WEAPON
47-12-035 THOUSANDS	45-12-040 PROMISED	43-10-030 I**.E	42-12-029 WIRE
47-14-042 UNKNOWN	45-10-036 QUALITIES	43-09-029 IDENTIFICATION	41-08-013 ARC
47-10-019 VACATION	45-12-034 REFERRED	43-13-040 INSISTED	41-07-030 ASSUMPTION
47-11-040 WEARING	45-09-018 RESIDENTIAL	43-07-021 INVESTMENT	41-04-008 ATOMS
47-09-037 13	45-11-029 RIDING	43-12-034 IRON	41-11-020 BREAD
46-08-022 AIN'T	45-12-027 SHEET	43-13-030 LAWYER	41-13-034 BROTHERS
46-10-039 ANYWAY	45-12-031 STEEL	43-13-036 LIFTED	41-07-014 CARL
46-03-005 ARTERY	45-10-032 SUM	43-13-030 LIQUOR	41-09-026 COMMUNITIES
46-09-025 ATOMIC	45-08-024 TAXES	43-04-009 MARKETING	41-07-037 COMPARABLE
46-09-037 AUTHOR	45-12-038 TERRIBLE	43-14-035 MENTAL	41-11-040 CONSTANTLY
46-11-031 AVENUE	45-05-013 U**.*N	43-10-027 MOUNTAINS	41-08-032 CONTINUES
46-06-016 AWARD	45-08-026 UNIVERSAL	43-11-033 OCCUR	41-04-009 COOLING
46-06-020 BOND	45-04-006 VALUABLE	44-04-012 OXYGEN	41-10-036 DESCRIBE
46-10-031 CENTURIES	45-04-006 WATSON	43-11-034 PACE	41-12-033 DISPLAY
46-09-023 CHAMBER	45-09-036 21	43-09-026 PORCH	41-12-031 DISTINCTION
46-13-039 CONSCIOUS	45-09-034 22	43-07-020 POUNDS	41-09-017 DOWNTOWN
46-10-034 CREATION	44-12-039 ACCOMPLISHED	43-10-037 RAPID	41-12-031 FAVORITE
46-14-037 CURIOUS	44-10-017 ACRES	43-13-028 RAW	41-11-023 FRANCISCO
46-12-041 DANGEROUS	44-05-009 ADAM	43-14-036 REACHING	41-08-024 FUNNY
46-10-026 DECADE	44-11-036 ADMITTED	43-10-027 READER	41-02-002 HENRIETTA
46-10-039 DIFFICULTIES	44-09-026 AGENT	43-09-035 READILY	41-09-029 INSTITUTION
46-05-026 DOCTRINE	44-11-033 AMOUNTS	43-11-033 RECORDED	41-08-030 INVOLVES
46-11-032 DOLLAR	44-12-034 ANSWERS	43-07-015 RECREATION	41-02-004 KATE
46-08-019 ELECTRICAL	44-13-037 ARRANGED	43-11-034 REPUBLIC	41-10-038 LIMITS
46-10-033 ENCOURAGE	44-11-032 ASIA	43-07-034 RESULTING	41-12-032 MATCH
46-08-016 ENGINEERING	44-12-033 BRUSH	43-09-028 ROUTE	41-08-021 MUSICIANS
46-11-031 EQUIVALENT	44-11-040 BURDEN	43-12-025 SALARY	41-11-028 N
46-06-019 FICTION	44-10-036 CHANGING	43-11-034 SAVED	41-08-038 OPPOSED
46-13-033 FLIGHT	44-09-035 CLIMBED	43-11-035 SEPARATED	41-09-028 PARTICIPATION
46-12-035 FOUGHT	44-09-035 COLLECTED	43-11-023 SHIPS	41-04-005 PIKE
46-08-016 GEORGIA	44-12-037 CONFUSED	43-11-039 SUFFERED	41-12-036 PLEASED
46-12-036 IDENTIFIED	44-12-039 CONFUSION	43-09-035 SWITCH	41-12-032 PROPOSAL
46-09-017 INSURANCE	44-12-040 CONSIDERABLY	43-08-027 TECHNOLOGY	41-09-018 QUEEN
46-07-028 LEGISLATION	44-10-032 CONTINUOUS	43-09-034 TEND	41-11-036 RARE
46-11-027 LIBERTY	44-08-037 CONTRIBUTE	43-10-026 TOUR	41-11-034 RARELY
46-09-020 LOAN	44-10-033 DEVELOPMENTS	43-07-026 TRANSPORTATION	41-11-035 REMAINING
46-10-025 LOSSES	44-11-031 DRIVEN	43-07-024 WARFARE	41-08-019 REMOVAL
46-12-028 NATIVE	44-09-021 EM	43-13-038 WHENEVER	41-07-028 REPRESENTATIVES
46-09-032 OPPOSITION	44-13-038 ENJOY	43-11-033 YEAR'S	41-08-021 RESTAURANT
46-08-013 PANELS	44-10-029 ERRORS	42-09-012 ADAMS	41-10-036 ROUGH
46-09-028 POCKET	44-10-035 EXPENSIVE	42-07-014 ANNE	41-12-033 SAKE
46-09-027 PRECISION	44-10-034 EXTENSIVE	42-07-016 ANXIETY	41-09-014 SEED
46-11-033 RECOMMENDED	44-11-028 FIRED	42-13-037 ANYBODY	41-13-032 SELL
46-10-038 RELATIVE	44-12-031 FUN	42-12-034 APPOINTED	41-09-031 SHIFT
46-12-025 SALT	44-05-008 HANS	42-08-029 BAG	41-10-033 SMOKE
46-13-040 SERIOUSLY	44-11-032 HELPING	42-12-039 BOUND	41-08-023 SOCIETIES
46-08-012 SHARES	44-12-032 HUNDREDS	42-09-026 CIVILIZATION	41-11-025 SPENDING
46-10-037 SHUT	44-12-041 LIES	42-14-033 COMMENT	41-12-036 STEADY
46-10-034 SUPERIOR	44-11-032 LISTED	42-10-030 CROSSED	41-11-036 STEPPED
46-13-036 THREW	44-12-032 LOVELY	42-11-036 DEMANDED	41-06-021 STORAGE
46-09-034 TREND	44-04-007 MAMA	42-11-033 DISTINCT	41-11-035 TEACH
46-09-030 VIOLENCE	44-06-010 MANCHESTER	42-13-036 DISTINGUISHED	41-06-012 TISSUE
46-13-024 WAVE	44-10-013 MOBILE	42-11-035 EASE	41-09-028 VICE
46-12-027 WEAKNESS		42-07-019 EDITORIAL	41-10-033 VIRTUALLY

41-13-035 VISITED	39-10-033 DETERMINATION	38-10-031 SIMULTANEOUSLY	36-11-034 AREN'T		
41-09-035 WHEREAS	39-11-029 EMERGENCY	38-09-028 SISTER	36-09-031 ASSISTANT		
41-10-027 WRITES	39-09-027 ESTIMATE	38-11-035 SPECIFICALLY	36-10-031 ATTENDED		
40-12-034 AFFORD	39-12-030 FINISH	38-11-029 SUDDEN	36-12-027 AUTOMATICALLY		
40-08-027 APPROVED	39-14-030 FOREVER	38-05-011 THOMPSON	36-03-012 BAKER		
40-07-020 ATLANTIC	39-10-024 FURNITURE	38-02-003 THYROID	36-09-027 BEINGS		
40-10-023 AUTOMATIC	39-12-035 FURTHERMORE	38-10-029 TONIGHT	36-01-001 BINOMIAL		
40-10-018 BARS	39-11-033 GAINED	38-12-027 TRACK	36-10-022 BOMB		
40-07-018 BOB	39-10-024 GUEST	38-09-016 TRANSFER	36-11-017 CAMERA		
40-10-032 BRINGS	39-11-020 HOLES	38-12-036 TURNS	36-13-022 CARDS		
40-12-033 BURNED	39-05-007 HYDROGEN	38-10-031 VOICES	36-11-026 CASH		
40-10-021 CODE	39-11-034 ILL	38-08-027 17	36-11-031 CHALLENGE		
40-08-035 COMBINED	39-10-033 IMPROVE	38-10-034 200	36-08-022 CHARACTERS		
40-09-033 COMPOSED	39-12-034 INTRODUCTION	38-07-023 31	36-11-027 CLASSIC		
40-09-022 CONSCIENCE	39-10-031 JOINT	38-09-034 40	36-03-004 COATING		
40-07-034 CRITICISM	39-07-023 LAWRENCE	38-01-002 *=*C*$	36-09-019 COLUMNS		
40-11-023 CUSTOMERS	39-05-013 LEGISLATURE	37-13-035 ACCOMPANIED	36-10-028 CONCLUSIONS		
40-07-022 DEAN	39-11-033 LISTENING	37-12-033 ADMIT	36-09-020 CREW		
40-12-037 DECIDE	39-07-020 LONG-RANGE	37-09-033 AIM	36-09-029 DESIRABLE		
40-06-019 DEMOCRATS	39-09-019 MAD	37-10-032 ASSURE	36-09-028 DIRTY		
40-08-033 DEPENDENT	39-08-023 MAGAZINE	37-07-009 ATOM	36-13-030 DOORS		
40-04-005 DESEGREGATION	39-08-023 MANKIND	37-07-016 AUTHORIZED	36-09-029 DRESSED		
40-11-039 DISCOVER	39-06-013 MATURITY	37-09-018 BANKS	36-09-027 EQUIPPED		
40-11-036 DRAWING	39-09-021 MISSISSIPPI	37-13-033 BELONG	36-08-027 ERROR		
40-13-034 ELEVEN	39-07-023 MYSTERY	37-11-016 BLOCKS	36-08-021 EXTENSION		
40-12-033 EXCEPTION	39-07-017 NEUTRAL	37-12-024 CHICKEN	36-07-012 FELLOWSHIP		
40-12-034 EXISTED	39-10-033 O'CLOCK	37-10-029 CHOSE	36-10-024 FILLING		
40-13-033 FINGER	39-06-027 OBJECTIVES	37-08-019 CLEANING	36-10-020 FOOTBALL		
40-13-034 FOCUS	39-09-019 PROVISIONS	37-07-020 COLONEL	36-12-031 FORTY		
40-11-034 GLANCE	39-04-006 RAYBURN	37-12-033 COMFORTABLE	36-11-030 GUIDE		
40-08-022 GOALS	39-12-034 RECALL	37-10-027 CONSTRUCTED	36-10-024 HOST		
40-09-030 GRACE	39-08-029 REPRESENTS	37-08-016 CONSUMER	36-07-030 HURRY		
40-10-030 GUIDANCE	39-10-031 REVEALED	37-09-033 CONTRIBUTION	36-10-023 INDUSTRIES		
40-09-029 HANDSOME	39-08-036 SATISFACTORY	37-11-024 CORE	36-10-035 INTENTION		
40-12-037 HAPPENS	39-08-026 SELECTION	37-12-031 DEEPER	36-09-020 JACKSON		
40-12-023 HIGHWAY	39-12-033 SEVERE	37-14-036 DEFINITE	36-08-017 JIM		
40-08-026 ILLINOIS	39-14-033 SLEEPING	37-12-035 DELIVERED	36-13-032 KINDS		
40-08-026 IMPROVEMENT	39-09-019 SOLDIER	37-09-027 DEVICES	36-10-022 LICENSE		
40-09-023 INCH	39-11-026 STICK	37-11-031 DISTANT	36-11-033 LYING		
40-08-029 INDICATES	39-10-035 STRIKING	37-09-028 DRUNK	36-13-033 MANAGED		
40-10-037 INTENSE	39-06-011 TRIALS	37-10-021 EDGES	36-01-002 MARIS		
40-12-032 JOY	38-12-030 ACCOUNTS	37-09-016 EDITION	36-08-016 MEETS		
40-09-021 LABORATORY	38-07-018 AGRICULTURAL	37-10-034 EFFECTIVELY	36-10-026 MOTHER'S		
40-06-016 LANGUAGES	38-12-034 ARRANGEMENTS	37-12-036 ENORMOUS	36-09-029 MOVES		
40-07-029 LEGISLATIVE	38-11-036 ATTEMPTS	37-11-032 FAIL	36-09-025 MULTIPLE		
40-12-035 MISSED	38-05-009 AXIS	37-12-031 FEATURE	36-08-030 NATION'S		
40-12-036 NECESSITY	38-14-036 BRIEFLY	37-04-004 FOAM	36-10-027 NORMALLY		
40-12-029 NEIGHBORS	38-13-035 BRINGING	37-10-030 FOOL	36-12-030 OCCUPIED		
40-10-027 NOTION	38-08-017 CANDIDATES	37-11-025 FORMATION	36-08-026 OUTLOOK		
40-06-020 OBSERVATIONS	38-13-025 CLOUDS	37-10-021 GATE	36-09-021 PAINTINGS		
40-08-019 ORLEANS	38-07-028 CONTAINS	37-11-022 HARBOR	36-12-020 PATIENTS		
40-12-026 PAINTED	38-11-025 COPY	37-07-007 HOLMES	36-09-023 PEOPLES		
40-04-008 PAPA	38-07-025 CORRESPONDING	37-09-031 HURT	36-07-019 PETER		
40-07-026 PARALLEL	38-08-019 COTTON	37-07-016 ILLUSION	36-10-025 PRINTED		
40-11-034 PERMANENT	38-08-026 DEFINITION	37-11-029 ILLUSTRATED	36-07-014 PROBABILITY		
40-12-032 PERSONALLY	38-11-026 DESTRUCTION	37-06-023 IMAGES	36-04-018 RATIO		
40-07-016 POPE	38-06-014 DISTRICTS	37-11-022 INNOCENT	36-10-034 SATISFIED		
40-09-035 PRESUMABLY	38-06-022 EXPERIMENTAL	37-11-022 MAGIC	36-08-027 SCHEDULE		
40-13-032 PROMINENT	38-09-027 EXPERTS	37-12-029 MALE	36-10-020 SCHOLARSHIP		
40-12-027 PROOF	38-09-032 FATHER'S	37-08-024 MIXED	36-10-026 SCIENTISTS		
40-08-028 PSYCHOLOGICAL	38-11-031 FIFTH	37-09-030 MOOD	36-11-028 SEES		
40-11-033 REGARDING	38-11-035 FORGOTTEN	37-09-025 NAVY	36-12-027 SHADOW		
40-08-024 REGIONS	38-07-024 FOUNDATION	37-13-027 NOISE	36-09-029 SIMILARLY		
40-09-026 RODE	38-13-033 GLAD	37-13-033 OCCASIONAL	36-11-027 SMILING		
40-13-029 SELF	38-11-025 GOD'S	37-07-030 OUTSTANDING	36-12-026 SPANISH		
40-10-026 SENATOR	38-10-030 HANDED	37-07-015 P**.M	36-11-020 STORED		
40-11-036 SHARED	38-08-026 HANDLING	37-10-022 PAINT	36-08-028 SUBSTANTIALLY		
40-02-003 SHEAR	38-08-027 HAVEN'T	37-11-030 PLOT	36-10-031 SUPPLIED		
40-10-030 SHOUTED	38-11-035 INEVITABLY	37-11-029 PROFESSION	36-06-008 SUSAN		
40-09-022 STRANGER	38-10-026 INSTANT	37-11-030 PUSH	36-08-018 SYMBOLS		
40-11-037 STUDYING	38-10-020 JAPAN	37-03-005 QUESTIONNAIRE	36-11-024 SYMPATHY		
40-12-032 TALENT	38-10-032 KNEES	37-11-026 READERS	36-11-031 THANK		
40-13-036 THOROUGHLY	38-10-029 LEANED	37-12-026 RELEASE	36-12-031 TOUGH		
40-12-032 THROWN	38-06-015 MAYOR	37-07-020 RESERVE	36-06-019 VARIABLE		
40-10-028 TODAY'S	38-12-030 NEWSPAPERS	37-07-032 RESULTED	36-13-034 VISITING		
40-09-020 TOOL	38-10-025 OHIO	37-07-007 ROBERTS	36-13-029 VISITORS		
40-08-017 TREASURY	38-02-003 ONSET	37-06-010 ROY	36-14-032 WEAR		
40-08-014 VISUAL	38-05-015 ORGANIC	37-08-033 SERVES	36-12-029 WISE		
40-09-028 WALTER	38-10-019 PALACE	37-11-030 SIGNED	36-12-024 WORSHIP		
40-04-005 WINSTON	38-10-029 PAUL	37-08-021 SKILLS	36-09-027 YOU'D		
39-08-030 ACTS	38-08-020 PIANO	37-07-018 SPECIES	35-10-033 ACCURATE		
39-08-026 AGENTS	38-11-032 PLEASANT	37-14-028 SPOKEN	35-07-020 ADJUSTMENT		
39-02-002 ALLOTMENT	38-06-007 PONT	37-01-001 STAINING	35-10-030 AFFECT		
39-12-033 ANYWHERE	38-11-022 PRESSURES	37-06-015 STATE'S	35-06-010 ATLANTA		
39-13-037 ASSURED	38-11-029 PRIMITIVE	37-10-029 STOMACH	35-09-019 BENCH		
39-13-032 ATTRACTIVE	38-07-017 PROCESSING	37-11-029 STRONGER	35-06-008 BOMBS		
39-09-026 AUTHORITIES	38-09-019 RANDOM	37-13-032 STRONGLY	35-08-023 CALCULATED		
39-09-022 COLLEGES	38-11-028 RECEPTION	37-10-025 SUPPER	35-11-032 CALM		
39-08-018 COMEDY	38-10-032 REGARDLESS	37-11-029 SURVEY	35-10-028 CLAIMED		
39-08-024 COMMUNISTS	38-09-028 RELATIONSHIPS	37-09-020 SWIMMING	35-08-013 CLARK		
39-08-021 CONCERT	38-10-031 REPRESENT	37-08-023 TESTED	35-05-025 CONTEXT		
39-10-036 CONTRIBUTED	38-05-009 ROBINSON	37-12-032 THANKS	35-09-021 COUNTIES		
39-11-038 CONTROLLED	38-09-028 SACRED	37-12-033 TREMENDOUS	35-12-026 DIGNITY		
39-13-036 DEEPLY	38-12-032 SCHEDULED	37-09-019 WASH	35-11-033 DISAPPEARED		
39-06-029 DEFINED	38-10-032 SERVING	36-07-021 ACCURACY	35-10-021 EGGS		
39-10-026 DERIVED	38-14-035 SHARPLY	36-09-031 AFFECTED	35-12-024 FISH		
39-10-033 DESTROYED			35-11-022 FRUIT		

Code	Word	Code	Word	Code	Word	Code	Word
35-07-022	GRADE	34-09-023	MECHANICAL	33-07-017	NAVAL	32-01-001	SKYWAVE
35-07-017	HARRY	34-08-017	METROPOLITAN	33-13-030	NIGHTS	32-10-029	SLIPPED
35-13-028	HEIGHT	34-12-030	MISTAKE	33-10-022	OWNER	32-12-029	SO-CALLED
35-12-024	INSTALLED	34-08-018	NET	33-08-019	PARKED	32-12-026	SPOTS
35-08-023	INSTRUCTIONS	34-12-022	OCEAN	33-02-002	PATHOLOGY	32-10-029	STUFF
35-08-027	ISOLATED	34-11-029	OPENLY	33-09-022	PERFORMANCES	32-09-023	SURVIVAL
35-08-012	JANE	34-09-029	OWNED	33-06-008	POLAND	32-11-018	SWIFT
35-10-032	JUMPED	34-07-014	PENCIL	33-09-028	PRECISE	32-10-030	T
35-10-022	KNEE	34-13-033	PHRASE	33-08-026	PRESENTATION	32-10-028	TEMPORARY
35-12-030	LATEST	34-10-020	PRESIDENTIAL	33-10-026	PRESENTS	32-06-016	TESTING
35-07-010	LUMBER	34-09-030	PROTECT	33-06-014	PRINCE	32-10-018	THEY'LL
35-01-001	MATSUO	34-14-028	QUARTER	33-02-004	PROKOFIEFF	32-10-020	TRANSITION
35-13-035	MEANWHILE	34-12-029	RAISING	33-11-026	QUANTITY	32-08-019	UNIVERSITIES
35-07-018	MYTH	34-08-026	REALISTIC	33-03-003	RECTOR	32-10-022	VAN
35-05-012	NATIONALISM	34-10-032	REASONABLY	33-11-030	REJECTED	32-06-018	VARIATION
35-07-015	OUTPUT	34-12-032	RECEIVING	33-06-012	REV	32-08-018	WE'D
35-10-024	OVER-ALL	34-09-019	REPORTERS	33-11-014	RICE	32-11-023	WEAK
35-11-026	OWNERS	34-07-015	RETURNS	33-12-024	SCHEME	32-09-021	WEDDING
35-06-011	PAT	34-08-025	ROLES	33-04-015	SLAVERY	32-09-016	WILLIAMS
35-04-010	PATENT	34-08-022	SAMUEL	33-09-019	STEMS	32-09-019	*T*V
35-10-029	PERFORMED	34-13-030	SELDOM	33-09-030	STRICTLY	31-06-023	ACCORDINGLY
35-09-027	PHENOMENON	34-11-027	SENDING	33-11-027	SUBSTANCE	31-09-027	ALLOWING
35-12-029	PREPARE	34-09-025	SENIOR	33-15-030	SUCCEEDED	31-09-023	ARTICLES
35-14-031	PRESENTLY	34-11-022	SENTENCE	33-09-027	SUFFER	31-11-028	BARELY
35-14-032	PRESERVE	34-11-029	SHORTLY	33-13-027	SURVIVE	31-08-010	BASEMENT
35-09-030	PRODUCING	34-12-024	SING	33-08-018	SYMPHONY	31-10-025	BIRD
35-12-025	RETIRED	34-09-025	SMELL	33-09-029	THEREBY	31-10-022	CEILING
35-14-033	RETURNING	34-11-030	STRETCHED	33-03-010	THERMAL	31-09-026	CHECKED
35-08-020	REVENUE	34-09-016	SUGAR	33-11-023	THURSDAY	31-06-015	CHRISTIANITY
35-12-029	ROLL	34-09-030	SUGGESTION	33-08-026	TRAGIC	31-10-021	COLORED
35-13-031	ROUTINE	34-09-031	SUITABLE	33-11-031	UNFORTUNATELY	31-04-020	COMPETITIVE
35-10-027	ROW	34-12-028	SWEPT	33-12-029	VIOLENT	31-06-014	COMPOSER
35-12-025	SAD	34-10-027	TEARS	33-08-027	26	31-09-025	CONSEQUENTLY
35-08-015	SCIENCES	34-14-030	TELLS	32-09-026	AWARENESS	31-07-025	CONSERVATIVE
35-07-011	SEPT	34-08-028	TENDS	32-07-012	BEEF	31-07-022	CONSIDERATIONS
35-07-020	SEQUENCE	34-12-028	TIED	32-05-014	CASTRO	31-08-016	COUNTER
35-11-030	SOUNDED	34-10-019	TOOLS	32-07-007	CHANDLER	31-07-011	DANCER
35-07-010	STANLEY	34-08-028	VARY	32-11-022	CIRCLES	31-08-016	DANCERS
35-11-020	STORES	34-11-029	VISIBLE	32-08-010	COAL	31-04-008	DAVE
35-05-013	SYMBOLIC	34-11-027	WE'VE	32-08-020	COLLECTIVE	31-07-021	DECLINE
35-09-024	SYMPATHETIC	34-11-030	WORST	32-07-023	CONCEPTION	31-09-020	DEFEAT
35-09-014	TAPE	34-09-030	19	32-11-027	CONCLUDED	31-08-025	ENDING
35-11-023	TONGUE	34-04-014	1962	32-12-031	CONFRONTED	31-07-024	ENTERPRISE
35-13-031	URGED	33-14-023	ACCIDENT	32-11-025	COOKING	31-04-018	EVALUATION
35-09-019	VEHICLE	33-09-017	ADJUSTED	32-11-028	COURAGE	31-08-025	EXTEND
35-10-017	VIRGIN	33-08-019	ADMISSION	32-12-029	COVERING	31-10-028	EXTRAORDINARY
35-08-021	WASHED	33-11-027	ADVISED	32-12-027	COVERS	31-03-008	FALLOUT
35-09-028	WASTE	33-12-030	AFFAIR	32-12-029	CROWDED	31-08-018	FILMS
35-09-027	WEDNESDAY	33-17-031	ALERT	32-02-002	CURT	31-09-022	FINANCE
35-11-030	WORLD'S	33-03-004	ANDY	32-09-019	DEBATE	31-11-027	FOURTEEN
35-09-028	WORRIED	33-09-019	ARTISTIC	32-08-030	DEPENDING	31-06-007	FREQUENCIES
35-08-024	YARD	33-12-029	ATTEMPTED	32-10-023	DISCUSSIONS	31-09-014	GALLERY
35-09-022	YIELD	33-07-019	BENEFITS	32-11-027	EASTERN	31-10-024	GENTLY
34-08-020	ABSTRACT	33-13-029	BLOW	32-11-025	EATING	31-09-020	HE'LL
34-09-024	ALTERNATIVE	33-11-026	BONE	32-08-025	EFFECTIVENESS	31-10-024	HELPS
34-12-028	ARRANGEMENT	33-10-022	BRANCH	32-13-026	EFFICIENT	31-08-013	HORN
34-13-031	BADLY	33-10-019	BRANCHES	32-11-029	ELABORATE	31-09-022	IDENTICAL
34-11-022	BEER	33-08-014	BRIDE	32-03-006	ELECTRONICS	31-13-031	INVARIABLY
34-11-029	BENT	33-13-032	BURST	32-01-003	EMISSION	31-09-026	INVOLVE
34-12-026	BIGGER	33-07-015	CAMPUS	32-07-015	ENGINEERS	31-02-003	JUNIORS
34-12-031	BLAME	33-06-011	CATHOLICS	32-11-027	EXCITEMENT	31-08-017	KANSAS
34-08-020	BUS	33-08-014	CHARTER	32-09-016	FACTORY	31-08-027	KNOCKED
34-11-026	CANADA	33-09-016	CHILD'S	32-11-028	FALLS	31-13-031	LETTING
34-09-020	CANDIDATE	33-02-002	CHLORINE	32-08-024	FARTHER	31-12-028	LIGHTLY
34-09-017	CLERK	33-10-024	CLASSICAL	32-10-019	FISHING	31-05-007	LOCKING
34-10-027	CONSEQUENCES	33-13-032	CONNECTED	32-09-019	GARDENS	31-10-018	MAID
34-08-029	COOPERATION	33-10-022	DAMAGE	32-12-030	GATHERED	31-11-030	MAINLY
34-09-021	CORN	33-08-026	DEMONSTRATED	32-12-024	GESTURE	31-07-018	MARKETS
34-12-020	CRAZY	33-08-027	DETERMINING	32-01-001	GORTON	31-08-024	MATURE
34-11-023	CRIME	33-04-005	DRILL	32-06-012	HAROLD	31-11-017	MOVIES
34-09-029	CURRENTLY	33-10-025	ELECTED	32-08-015	HEADING	31-10-019	MUSCLES
34-05-025	DAMN	33-05-014	EQUATION	32-10-026	HOUSEHOLD	31-12-023	OUTER
34-08-026	DECADES	33-10-031	EXAMINE	32-06-017	HOWARD	31-09-017	PACIFIC
34-06-015	DISPUTE	33-10-027	FALLING	32-10-029	INADEQUATE	31-11-026	PAGES
34-08-020	DIVINE	33-08-019	FARMERS	32-09-017	INDIANS	31-08-017	PANEL
34-10-026	DUTIES	33-10-026	FATE	32-09-017	INITIATIVE	31-07-014	PARKING
34-11-025	DYING	33-09-027	FAVORABLE	32-09-024	KIDS	31-10-029	PERFECTLY
34-08-024	EMOTION	33-09-028	FEWER	32-07-028	LACKING	31-07-017	PLASTIC
34-13-029	EXPOSED	33-08-022	FILED	32-03-009	LOANS	31-07-018	POETIC
34-13-031	FACING	33-11-025	FLY	32-05-015	LONG-TERM	31-11-027	PROTECTED
34-11-031	FALLEN	33-12-022	FUNERAL	32-08-018	MILLS	31-08-015	RECORDING
34-07-016	FINANCING	33-12-030	GIFT	32-07-011	MISSILES	31-08-022	REDUCING
34-08-021	FINDINGS	33-10-026	GRAVE	32-09-021	MUD	31-09-019	REMARK
34-12-021	FOLK	33-10-021	GUILT	32-07-018	MUSEUM	31-06-021	RESPECTIVELY
34-10-031	FREQUENT	33-09-017	HARMONY	32-09-027	NAKED	31-10-026	RULED
34-11-033	GENUINE	33-09-021	HEALTHY	32-08-011	PA	31-09-022	RUSSIANS
34-08-014	GOLF	33-11-025	INEVITABLE	32-10-022	PARTNER	31-02-004	SALINE
34-08-017	HARVARD	33-08-029	INVOLVING	32-04-006	PLASTICS	31-08-023	SECONDARY
34-09-019	HUNTING	33-09-027	JACKET	32-06-016	POETS	31-10-021	SELLING
34-08-018	INTERVIEW	33-01-001	JESS	32-08-023	PROMOTE	31-11-021	SEVENTH
34-11-023	ITALY	33-11-030	LEADS	32-10-023	REFLECTION	31-11-026	SHOCK
34-09-016	JOHNSON	33-10-028	LUNCH	32-11-025	REMARKED	31-09-024	SOFTLY
34-07-014	KEYS	33-13-029	MASSIVE	32-11-026	REMOTE	31-09-026	SPONSORED
34-07-020	LEE	33-07-018	MATCHING	32-09-024	ROMANTIC	31-09-028	STARTS
34-09-017	LISTS	33-12-029	MISSING	32-04-015	SALVATION	31-10-029	STRAIN
34-11-026	LOGICAL	33-10-021	MOUNTAIN	32-01-001	SCOTTY	31-07-022	STRUCTURES
34-05-017	MEASUREMENT	33-07-026	NAMELY	32-11-022	SHOUTING	31-09-017	STUDIO

31-09-027 SUCCESSFULLY	30-07-017 VOTING	29-06-013 UNIONS	28-11-024 TIGHT
31-09-023 TERRITORY	30-10-026 WIDESPREAD	29-07-019 UTILITY	28-10-019 TONS
31-09-023 TOSSED	30-01-001 WOODRUFF	29-09-028 VIGOROUS	28-09-021 UPSTAIRS
31-11-017 TRAIL	30-08-018 WORKER	29-08-017 VOLUNTEERS	28-06-013 VERSE
31-12-028 TROUBLED	29-08-024 ALBERT	29-01-001 **ZG	28-12-025 WARMTH
31-06-012 TUBE	29-08-016 ALLIED	28-09-021 ABSENT	28-11-025 WITNESS
31-07-018 V	29-06-011 ANN	28-09-020 ADVANTAGES	28-07-022 WORTHY
31-09-024 WINNING	29-11-022 ANXIOUS	28-11-021 AFRICAN	28-12-020 WOUND
31-06-019 1952	29-08-018 APPARATUS	28-09-022 APPOINTMENT	28-04-009 YANKEES
30-09-023 ABSOLUTE	29-09-023 APPLYING	28-09-025 ARISE	28-07-020 1956
30-03-004 ALEX	29-07-021 ARGUE	28-07-012 BROOKLYN	27-13-021 ABSOLUTELY
30-06-019 ALLIES	29-12-026 ARGUED	28-08-019 BULLET	27-09-024 ACQUIRE
30-10-028 ALTOGETHER	29-08-022 ASLEEP	28-06-012 CALENDAR	27-07-009 AIDS
30-09-023 ASSOCIATIONS	29-10-026 BARE	28-09-020 CLARITY	27-13-023 APPROACHING
30-11-019 BLANKET	29-09-017 BARN	28-11-023 CLOSING	27-04-009 BUILDERS
30-10-023 BUYING	29-12-021 BELT	28-10-018 CLOUD	27-06-012 BUTTER
30-03-007 CARBON	29-01-001 BRANNON	28-07-010 COLONY	27-01-001 CADY
30-10-023 CITIZEN	29-01-001 BRONCHIAL	28-09-019 COMMANDER	27-09-018 CAP
30-10-024 COMMENTS	29-04-010 BUILDER	28-10-024 COMMITTED	27-08-018 CHIN
30-10-026 COMPLICATED	29-01-001 CARLETON	28-08-019 COMMUNICATIONS	27-11-019 CHRISTMAS
30-07-023 CONCENTRATED	29-07-021 COMMONLY	28-08-026 COMPARE	27-03-008 CLAYTON
30-09-019 CONSCIOUSNESS	29-06-028 CONSTITUTE	28-07-025 CONSISTENT	27-05-011 CLINICAL
30-09-025 CONSEQUENCE	29-08-025 CONTRIBUTIONS	28-09-018 CONVENTION	27-12-018 COMBAT
30-08-023 CONTROLS	29-09-012 COW	28-07-016 CURE	27-09-017 COMPANY'S
30-10-025 CRIED	29-11-027 CREATING	28-10-023 DAWN	27-10-024 CONCEIVED
30-11-024 CRUCIAL	29-07-026 DELIGHT	28-07-024 DEMONSTRATE	27-07-018 CONCEPTS
30-08-024 CUTS	29-10-016 DIVORCE	28-07-019 DESIGNS	27-08-022 CONSISTING
30-03-005 DARTMOUTH	29-07-012 DRYING	28-10-023 DINING	27-08-016 CUSTOMER
30-09-024 DATES	29-10-025 EAR	28-08-020 DIPLOMATIC	27-03-006 DAN
30-07-015 DEALERS	29-02-002 ECUMENICAL	28-10-026 DISCUSS	27-05-013 DAVIS
30-10-026 DELIBERATELY	29-11-026 ENCOURAGED	28-10-023 DRIED	27-07-016 DEFINE
30-08-016 DENSITY	29-09-018 ENTERTAINMENT	28-04-008 DRUGS	27-07-009 DELAWARE
30-07-020 DIMENSIONS	29-09-021 ETERNAL	28-09-027 ENCOUNTER	27-13-027 DELICATE
30-11-017 DIRECTIONS	29-06-017 ETHICAL	28-12-026 ENTHUSIASM	27-11-025 DISCIPLINE
30-10-021 DOCTORS	29-08-021 EXAMINATION	28-11-025 EXAMINED	27-08-017 DISTRIBUTED
30-12-020 DREAMS	29-11-024 EXCITING	28-12-025 EXCLUSIVE	27-10-026 DULL
30-07-022 E**.G	29-09-027 EXTENDING	28-11-025 EXPANDING	27-09-027 EAGER
30-06-008 EDDIE	29-04-008 FABRICS	28-11-021 FLED	27-12-020 ENEMIES
30-03-009 ELECTRON	29-08-026 FALSE	28-04-004 FOLKLORE	27-11-023 EXACT
30-10-026 ENCOUNTERED	29-07-013 FEES	28-11-024 FORMERLY	27-09-025 EXCUSE
30-11-023 ERA	29-08-021 FURNISH	28-08-013 FREIGHT	27-08-018 FESTIVAL
30-12-022 ET	29-11-022 GLASSES	28-12-027 GATHERING	27-03-004 FIBER
30-10-024 EXCESSIVE	29-12-027 GUILTY	28-12-025 GENTLEMAN	27-11-024 FLEW
30-13-026 EXPERT	29-11-026 HELPFUL	28-04-006 HAL	27-04-010 FRED
30-05-006 FELIX	29-13-028 IGNORED	28-09-024 HANGING	27-08-020 FRIENDSHIP
30-10-019 FENCE	29-08-015 JET	28-10-023 HAPPENING	27-09-018 FROZEN
30-04-008 FLUX	29-05-011 JURISDICTION	28-09-017 HARRIS	27-10-025 GENTLE
30-07-019 FRANKLIN	29-09-023 LESSON	28-09-022 HATED	27-06-016 GERMANS
30-09-021 FRONTIER	29-08-012 LIEUTENANT	28-08-021 HUMANITY	27-10-019 GRAIN
30-12-023 GAY	29-08-020 LIGHTED	28-07-012 INNOCENCE	27-07-009 GREENWICH
30-10-023 GRADUATE	29-06-016 MAGNITUDE	28-09-016 IRISH	27-05-005 HOLDER
30-07-024 GRINNED	29-10-027 MERIT	28-09-021 JOURNEY	27-12-022 HORIZON
30-06-012 HISTORIAN	29-09-027 MIGHTY	28-08-017 JUDGMENTS	27-04-007 HUGHES
30-11-027 HOPING	29-10-026 MODEST	28-10-023 LADIES	27-10-023 IMAGINED
30-11-025 IMPRESSED	29-08-018 MORALITY	28-09-021 LAUGH	27-09-018 INJURY
30-09-027 INSTANCES	29-04-005 MORSE	28-04-006 LIBRARIES	27-11-026 INSIST
30-11-017 ISLANDS	29-10-020 MOVIE	28-09-021 LIMITATIONS	27-07-015 JEFFERSON
30-06-016 JOHNNY	29-12-027 NOWHERE	28-10-028 LOSING	27-04-004 JULIA
30-08-017 LANE	29-07-017 PERCEPTION	28-09-025 MAINTAINING	27-07-022 LAUGHING
30-09-026 LISTENED	29-10-027 PERFORM	28-11-025 MARKS	27-11-025 LITERALLY
30-11-024 LOCKED	29-02-002 PETITIONER	28-05-011 MECHANISM	27-12-026 MAGNIFICENT
30-08-014 LOUISIANA	29-06-013 PLAYERS	28-08-025 MEETINGS	27-09-012 MARRIAGES
30-08-020 MEAL	29-12-028 POURED	28-04-006 MICKEY	27-09-015 MARSHALL
30-04-014 MEASURING	29-13-022 PRECIOUS	28-08-011 MINES	27-04-009 MINIMAL
30-11-019 MEDICINE	29-10-027 PRESSED	28-07-020 MUNICIPAL	27-10-021 MIRROR
30-01-001 MIRIAM	29-09-017 PRESTIGE	28-08-023 NEWLY	27-02-002 MYRA
30-08-022 MIXTURE	29-09-021 PROPORTION	28-12-022 OFFERING	27-06-009 NEWPORT
30-09-016 NETWORK	29-05-016 PROPOSALS	28-01-004 OPTIMAL	27-07-021 OBSERVATION
30-06-012 OCCURRENCE	29-10-028 QUESTIONED	28-08-022 PASSION	27-06-019 OCCURS
30-10-023 PRECEDING	29-08-017 RECOVERY	28-08-024 PAUSED	27-09-023 OPERATED
30-08-021 PROPAGANDA	29-07-020 REGULATIONS	28-01-001 POLYNOMIAL	27-06-007 ORAL
30-08-027 PURELY	29-10-026 REMINDED	28-10-018 POT	27-12-023 OURS
30-09-023 RADICAL	29-06-016 REPUBLICANS	28-09-010 POUND	27-07-015 OUTDOOR
30-10-028 RANGING	29-10-021 RESIDENCE	28-06-013 POWDER	27-10-020 PASSES
30-07-017 REFORM	29-05-012 SAMPLES	28-09-020 PRAYER	27-10-027 PECULIAR
30-07-027 REPLACE	29-08-022 SANG	28-06-015 PRESIDENT'S	27-09-016 PERMISSION
30-07-025 REPRESENTING	29-09-023 SCENES	28-09-020 PRIZE	27-06-022 PERMITS
30-12-026 REVEAL	29-05-007 SEWAGE	28-10-019 PROFIT	27-08-016 PISTOL
30-10-022 ROOT	29-11-021 SHAPES	28-12-025 PROMPTLY	27-11-024 PLACING
30-11-025 SACRIFICE	29-03-008 SHERMAN	28-11-026 QUARTERS	27-09-025 PREFER
30-08-025 SECURE	29-05-005 SHORTS	28-01-001 RAMEY	27-10-023 PREVENTED
30-02-012 SEN	29-08-016 SHOTS	28-09-021 RENDERED	27-06-009 PREVENTION
30-06-011 SHAKESPEARE	29-10-017 SIGNALS	28-08-017 ROOSEVELT	27-11-027 PROFOUND
30-02-002 SHARPE	29-11-026 SILVER	28-10-018 SAND	27-12-023 PUBLICITY
30-11-020 SHEETS	29-06-019 SOLUTIONS	28-07-013 SANTA	27-13-025 PUBLICLY
30-08-018 SKILLED	29-12-021 SONS	28-12-026 SATISFACTION	27-01-002 PULMONARY
30-09-012 SLAVE	29-09-023 STARS	28-08-017 SENSITIVITY	27-01-004 PURSUANT
30-03-008 SOVEREIGN	29-05-010 STEM	28-06-013 SERGEANT	27-06-016 RANCH
30-09-024 SPLIT	29-08-027 SUBSEQUENT	28-10-019 SHADE	27-09-024 REFER
30-06-020 STABLE	29-08-016 SUBURBAN	28-08-022 SOUTHEAST	27-04-004 REORGANIZATION
30-09-021 STRIP	29-06-027 SUGGESTS	28-05-008 SOVEREIGNTY	27-10-025 REPUTATION
30-10-025 SURPRISING	29-08-019 TASKS	28-07-020 SPECIFIED	27-07-022 REQUIREMENT
30-12-026 SUSPECT	29-09-022 TESTAMENT	28-07-013 STAINED	27-09-022 RESERVED
30-10-018 SUSPENDED	29-08-017 THEATRE	28-06-015 SURFACES	27-07-015 RESPONSES
30-07-026 THEY'D	29-10-026 THREATENED	28-09-024 TALENTS	27-10-024 RESTRICTIONS
30-06-017 UNCONSCIOUS	29-11-018 TRANSFERRED	28-09-020 TEA	27-06-017 ROOTS
30-09-021 VIRTUE	29-09-023 TRIPS	28-05-008 TEXTILE	27-12-023 RUSHED

Code	Word	Code	Word	Code	Word	Code	Word
27-10-025	SCATTERED	26-10-020	PEACEFUL	25-13-022	GRATEFUL	24-07-021	CATEGORIES
27-08-013	SCHOLARS	26-08-020	PERSPECTIVE	25-13-024	HARM	24-13-023	CHANCES
27-08-025	SCOPE	26-08-020	PHENOMENA	25-10-018	HIRED	24-10-021	CHARMING
27-12-020	SECONDS	26-08-018	PHILOSOPHICAL	25-09-018	HONEY	24-10-021	CHEAP
27-01-001	SHAYNE	26-11-015	PLANES	25-05-010	HOUSTON	24-09-022	CITED
27-05-020	SHIRT	26-09-024	POINTING	25-09-016	IMPRESSIONS	24-08-017	CIVILIAN
27-09-020	SHOOT	26-11-023	PREFERRED	25-10-022	INSPIRED	24-08-018	CLUBS
27-09-020	SHOPPING	26-03-009	PREMIER	25-09-023	INTERVALS	24-05-009	COACH
27-07-021	SLEPT	26-09-014	PROMOTION	25-07-017	JERSEY	24-10-018	CONSISTED
27-04-006	SUBMARINE	26-10-022	QUOTED	25-09-018	LANDS	24-10-018	CONTRACTS
27-08-015	SUITE	26-12-026	RECALLED	25-08-018	LONELY	24-09-015	CRIMINAL
27-08-015	SUPPORTING	26-13-021	REGISTER	25-11-014	MAGAZINES	24-07-021	CYCLE
27-08-017	SURPLUS	26-11-022	RELEASED	25-05-008	MAGNETIC	24-08-016	DECLARATION
27-11-024	SURROUNDING	26-12-023	REPEAT	25-06-015	MARGINAL	24-05-015	DEMOCRACY
27-10-025	SUSPICION	26-07-014	RETIREMENT	25-09-013	MOTHERS	24-08-020	DEPRESSION
27-05-016	THEOLOGICAL	26-03-006	REVENUES	25-02-003	NICK	24-10-021	DESIRES
27-10-018	UPWARD	26-04-005	SARAH	25-06-010	NIXON	24-03-005	DIFFUSION
27-12-025	UTTERLY	26-09-018	SESSIONS	25-10-023	NOON	24-09-012	DRAFT
27-09-023	VETERAN	26-08-013	SETTLEMENT	25-09-018	NORTHWEST	24-09-013	DRIVERS
27-08-023	VICTIM	26-08-018	SIXTH	25-01-001	O'*BANION	24-06-011	DRUG
27-08-022	VOTED	26-03-003	SNAKES	25-13-022	OBSERVE	24-05-008	EMPLOYEE
27-08-021	WEEKEND	26-09-021	SOPHISTICATED	25-05-013	OPERATIONAL	24-10-023	ENTERING
27-12-026	WHEREVER	26-04-009	SOUTHERNERS	25-06-006	OWEN	24-11-024	ENTHUSIASTIC
27-11-019	WINGS	26-07-023	STARING	25-09-020	PACK	24-07-021	ESTIMATES
27-08-019	WOMEN'S	26-06-007	STOCKHOLDERS	25-12-025	PAINFUL	24-09-021	EXCLUSIVELY
27-08-017	*A	26-11-020	STORM	25-10-017	PARADE	24-07-019	EXPLICIT
26-06-013	A**.M	26-10-017	STRETCH	25-12-023	PARTIALLY	24-10-022	EXPRESSING
26-09-026	ACQUIRED	26-04-004	SWITCHES	25-08-013	PATROL	24-10-018	FACTORIES
26-04-017	AESTHETIC	26-01-002	TANGENT	25-02-006	PENNY	24-10-018	FIRING
26-03-003	ANTI-TRUST	26-06-013	TEMPERATURES	25-10-020	PILE	24-08-016	FORD
26-11-023	APPRECIATE	26-11-024	THREATENING	25-08-011	PITTSBURGH	24-09-012	FORGIVE
26-02-002	ARLENE	26-03-005	TRADERS	25-05-009	POND	24-09-014	FULL-TIME
26-06-021	ASSIST	26-09-021	TREAT	25-11-022	PRESSING	24-06-016	FUNCTIONAL
26-10-018	BATH	26-08-021	TREMBLING	25-11-022	PROCEEDED	24-06-009	HEATING
26-07-015	BEARD	26-09-024	UNHAPPY	25-07-015	PRODUCTIVE	24-09-021	HONORED
26-08-016	BEARS	26-01-001	URETHANE	25-10-019	PROSPECT	24-10-016	ILLUSTRATION
26-06-012	BILLY	26-03-011	VARIABLES	25-08-019	PULLING	24-09-023	INSURE
26-06-012	BRIDGES	26-06-013	VELOCITY	25-09-013	PUPILS	24-08-023	INTERPRETED
26-09-018	CARD	26-10-023	WARS	25-06-013	RACIAL	24-04-016	JAN
26-06-008	CAVALRY	26-10-018	WIDOW	25-04-016	RATIONAL	24-10-020	JUMP
26-07-010	CELLAR	26-03-003	ZEN	25-10-022	RECOMMEND	24-10-021	LEATHER
26-10-023	CHARM	26-07-020	1953	25-08-021	REFLECT	24-06-009	MANAGERS
26-10-024	CLIMATE	25-11-024	ABANDONED	25-06-008	REGIMENT	24-07-013	MANUFACTURING
26-04-012	CONCERTS	25-08-015	ABOARD	25-10-020	RESPONSIBILITIE S	24-08-015	MASTERS
26-09-019	CONTEST	25-08-020	ACCUSED			24-05-009	MATHEMATICAL
26-09-022	CONTROVERSY	25-08-016	ADULT	25-08-012	RITUAL	24-08-020	MEANINGFUL
26-03-003	COOLIDGE	25-01-001	ALEC	25-05-012	SADDLE	24-08-012	MEXICAN
26-08-021	CRITICS	25-05-007	ALLOWANCES	25-07-009	SHELTERS	24-07-010	MOORE
26-08-017	DELIGHTFUL	25-08-015	AMATEUR	25-03-013	STADIUM	24-06-010	MOTEL
26-08-021	DESPERATE	25-06-015	APPLICATIONS	25-09-021	STAR	24-04-013	NARRATIVE
26-08-021	DISASTER	25-08-020	APPROACHES	25-05-017	STRUCTURAL	24-12-018	NEAREST
26-10-025	DISTURBED	25-12-022	ATTACHED	25-08-022	SUBTLE	24-09-020	NEIGHBORING
26-04-004	EILEEN	25-12-022	ATTACKED	25-10-015	SUCCESSION	24-12-020	NERVOUS
26-01-001	EKSTROHM	25-12-022	ATTRACTED	25-08-015	SUITS	24-03-010	NORMS
26-00-016	ELECTRICITY	25-03-011	AUG	25-11-022	TERROR	24-11-020	OCCUPATION
26-06-025	ELIMINATE	29-01-001	BANG-*JENSEN	25-01-001	TILGHMAN	24-04-011	OCT
26-12-024	EMERGED	25-01-001	BARTON	25-02-005	TIM	24-04-007	PEAS
26-11-019	ENTRY	25-12-022	BEARING	25-10-021	TORN	24-09-020	PHASES
26-06-020	ESTABLISHING	25-04-005	BLANCHE	25-07-013	TRADING	24-02-004	PORTLAND
26-07-021	EXCEPTIONS	25-11-023	BREAKING	25-05-010	TRANSFORMED	24-09-020	PRELIMINARY
26-07-014	FEEDING	25-07-011	CANCER	25-06-011	TRUSTEES	24-10-022	PROBABLE
26-08-019	FIST	25-07-015	CAROLINA	25-10-021	TWENTY-FIVE	24-10-021	PROMISING
26-05-008	FRAMES	25-09-015	CENTS	25-11-024	VAGUE	24-10-019	PROSPECTS
26-08-024	FRIGHTENED	25-08-020	CIGARETTE	25-09-014	VEIN	24-05-009	PUERTO
26-06-009	GEAR	25-09-015	COCKTAIL	25-10-023	VIEWED	24-10-021	QUALIFIED
26-02-002	GREG	25-04-018	COMPONENT	25-08-022	VIVID	24-08-019	RANK
26-01-001	GYRO	25-07-019	COMPOSITION	25-03-003	WALLY	24-09-021	REACHES
26-11-023	HANDLED	25-05-012	CONDUCTOR	25-06-010	WARD	24-08-015	REALISM
26-11-024	HANG	25-08-020	CONFERENCES	25-09-024	WILDLY	24-11-022	REALIZATION
26-01-001	HELVA	25-07-018	CONSTITUTIONAL	25-10-018	WOODS	24-09-011	RECOMMENDATION
26-07-022	IDENTIFY	25-08-016	CONTACTS	25-04-014	YEAH	24-09-020	RELIEVED
26-06-022	INHERENT	25-10-024	CONTINUALLY	25-11-020	YOURS	24-09-017	RIGID
26-11-020	INSTRUCTION	25-06-015	CONTINUITY	25-06-018	1955	24-10-022	ROUGHLY
26-11-018	INSTRUMENTS	25-06-010	CORPORATIONS	25-08-021	300	24-06-015	RULING
26-13-022	INTELLIGENT	25-10-019	CORRESPONDENCE	25-08-016	*B	24-10-022	SCARCELY
26-11-023	INVITED	25-06-015	COVERAGE	24-09-017	ABSORBED	24-10-018	SEATED
26-04-011	JEW	25-09-025	CRITIC	24-08-015	ACADEMY	24-10-019	SEIZED
26-02-002	JOHNNIE	25-05-014	DEALER	24-09-017	ACCESS	24-08-019	SEVENTEEN
26-10-022	JUSTIFY	25-09-019	DELAYED	24-08-020	ACCOMPLISH	24-04-004	SITTER
26-05-018	KENNEDY'S	25-09-020	DEMONSTRATION	24-08-019	ACCURATELY	24-08-019	SLID
26-08-015	KINGDOM	25-06-014	DEPARTMENTS	24-06-014	ACTOR	24-05-006	SPECIMEN
26-10-018	LANDING	25-07-017	DESTRUCTIVE	24-07-014	ADVISORY	24-08-020	STUPID
26-07-018	LEGEND	25-03-004	DETERGENT	24-09-021	AIMED	24-10-018	SUBJECTED
26-04-009	LIBERALS	25-08-017	DEVIL	24-08-015	AL	24-11-020	SWING
26-07-020	LIVELY	25-09-018	DILEMMA	24-10-015	ANGELS	24-10-015	TAIL
26-07-012	MARSHAL	25-03-006	DISK	24-08-020	ANNOUNCEMENT	24-10-023	TENDED
26-10-020	MEALS	25-05-009	EUGENE	24-09-021	ARRIVE	24-01-001	THERESA
26-06-010	MITCHELL	25-09-019	EVIDENTLY	24-10-020	ASSEMBLED	24-04-006	TRACTOR
26-11-020	MOUNT	25-09-019	EXHIBIT	24-06-006	ASTRONOMY	24-08-019	TRIBUTE
26-08-020	MUTUAL	25-07-013	EXPLORATION	24-08-011	AUTOMOBILES	24-06-009	TUBES
26-10-024	MYSTERIOUS	25-09-017	EXPOSURE	24-09-018	BACKED	24-11-020	UNDOUBTEDLY
26-08-018	OUTCOME	25-09-024	FAINT	24-08-015	BARREL	24-03-004	UTOPIA
26-10-025	OVERCOME	25-06-017	FLEXIBLE	24-09-019	BEND	24-12-019	WEEKLY
26-01-001	PALFREY	25-09-018	FOG	24-11-023	BIGGEST	24-11-022	WHOLLY
26-07-009	PART-TIME	25-10-017	FORTUNE	24-09-021	BORE	24-02-002	WINES
26-02-002	PATCHEN	25-08-023	GENEROUS	24-10-021	BRAVE	24-08-022	WISHES
26-11-024	PAYING	25-07-021	GLANCED	24-08-018	BROADWAY	24-06-013	WORKSHOP

24-06-014 ZERO	23-07-019 MEMORIAL	22-08-019 DEALT	22-10-016 STRATEGY
24-02-007 1/2	23-08-019 MIDNIGHT	22-01-001 DEEGAN	22-09-021 SUBSTITUTE
24-01-002 *=*Q*$	23-08-019 MONTHLY	22-09-017 DESCRIBES	22-08-012 SUCCESSES
23-09-018 ADULTS	23-06-011 MUSICIAN	22-09-022 DESPERATELY	22-09-018 SUITED
23-07-019 AGRICULTURE	23-11-021 NOBLE	22-07-018 DESTINY	22-09-014 SURRENDER
23-05-015 AMENDMENT	23-10-020 ORANGE	22-05-007 DI	22-07-009 TARGETS
23-02-002 ANTI-*SEMITISM	23-10-023 ORIGINALLY	22-10-021 DOUBTFUL	22-07-013 TEAMS
23-10-021 ANTICIPATED	23-03-004 OXIDATION	22-08-014 DRESSING	22-08-019 THRUST
23-11-023 ARRIVAL	23-04-007 PETE	22-08-015 DRINKS	22-09-017 TIP
23-05-009 ASSESSMENT	23-03-003 PIP	22-09-020 EARLIEST	22-06-008 TIRE
23-05-016 ASSUMPTIONS	23-06-010 PLASTER	22-04-016 ECONOMICAL	22-10-021 TOTALLY
23-10-021 ATTEMPTING	23-10-014 PLATES	22-08-018 EIGHTEENTH	22-10-020 TRAVELED
23-09-022 ATTENDING	23-05-007 PLUG	22-04-004 ELAINE	22-09-020 TRIUMPH
23-04-010 AUTHORS	23-10-021 PROTEST	22-08-022 ELIMINATED	22-10-018 TROUBLES
23-08-018 BASES	23-05-011 PUBLICATIONS	22-06-018 EMPIRE	22-06-013 TRUCKS
23-08-016 BELIEFS	23-01-001 QUINEY	22-10-018 ENGAGEMENT	22-10-021 UNCERTAIN
23-08-012 BELLY	23-09-013 RADAR	22-06-016 EXHIBITION	22-08-020 UNEASY
23-05-006 BOATING	23-07-020 REFLECTS	22-09-021 EXPECTS	22-10-019 UNFORTUNATE
23-04-008 BOBBY	23-07-009 REFRIGERATOR	22-09-018 FAULT	22-06-019 VALID
23-08-015 BOWL	23-07-018 REGIME	22-01-001 FOAMS	22-07-012 VIENNA
23-06-006 BROWN'S	23-12-020 REGISTERED	22-06-010 FORESTS	22-06-016 VOLUNTARY
23-06-009 BURNS	23-06-009 REGISTRATION	22-06-016 FORMULAS	22-08-016 WARNED
-23-10-013 CABIN	23-06-020 RELEVANT	22-08-018 FORTUNATE	22-08-017 WEALTH
23-03-007 CASEY	23-11-021 RESUMED	22-10-020 FREELY	22-08-020 WEREN'T
23-09-015 CAT	23-06-012 RIFLES	22-05-013 FREQUENCY	22-11-021 WOMAN'S
23-08-017 CATEGORY	23-09-016 ROCKS	22-07-013 GANG	22-06-015 YELLED
23-10-020 CHAIRS	23-05-008 RUTH	22-09-018 GROWS	21-07-016 ACCEPTABLE
23-07-013 CHAMPION	23-05-019 SAVINGS	22-09-016 GULF	21-09-020 ACCEPTING
23-07-008 CHANNELS	23-11-021 SEARCHING	22-06-010 HEN	21-07-012 ADDRESSES
23-06-016 CHILDREN'S	23-09-021 SELECT	22-04-009 HERD	21-03-005 ANGLO-*SAXON
23-09-016 CIRCUIT	23-09-020 SENTIMENT	22-08-020 HIDE	21-12-017 ANNIVERSARY
23-10-021 CIVIC	23-11-022 SETTLE	22-07-010 HITS	21-07-018 ARBITRARY
23-10-018 CLEARED	23-10-020 SHARING	22-01-001 HYPOTHALAMIC	21-09-019 ASSOCIATE
23-09-018 COLLEAGUES	-23-08-011 SHEEP	22-08-017 IMPLICATIONS	21-06-015 AVAILABILITY
23-08-021 COMPETE	23-09-019 SINK	22-07-022 INSIGHT	21-01-001 B'DIKKAT
23-08-021 CONTINUOUSLY	23-11-021 SPARE	22-09-020 INTENTIONS	21-08-012 BEAM
23-09-021 CONTROLLING	23-02-002 SPENCER	22-05-013 INVESTIGATIONS	21-06-018 BEHALF
23-10-016 CRAFT	23-03-007 SUBSTANCES	22-10-017 JOKE	21-02-002 BELGIANS
23-06-009 CRYSTAL	23-01-005 SUBSTRATE	22-10-017 LAUGHTER	21-11-015 BEN
23-10-020 CURIOSITY	23-10-020 SUGGESTIONS	22-02-002 LO	21-08-021 BOLD
23-09-014 DANCES	23-06-019 SWEAT	22-10-020 LOADED	21-09-019 BREATHING
23-07-012 DECK	23-09-012 TENNESSEE	22-10-019 LOYALTY	21-01-001 BRIDGET
23-09-022 DEDICATED	23-12-021 THINKS	22-05-008 MEANINGS	21-07-013 BULLETS
23-05-016 DEGREES	23-10-018 TIE	22-09-014 MELTING	21-08-014 CERTAINTY
23-08-013 DISCRIMINATION	23-11-020 TRACE	22-05-011 MERCHANTS	21-06-016 CHARACTERIZED
23-04-010 DISPLACEMENT	23-09-021 ULTIMATELY	22-09-013 MESS	21-03-003 CHOLESTEROL
23-04-008 DIVE	23-08-021 UNEXPECTED	22-04-010 MIAMI	21-06-012 CIRCULAR
23-07-015 DON	23-08-019 VARIATIONS	22-03-005 MIDDLE-CLASS	21-09-014 CITY'S
23-06-015 DOUGLAS	23-06-013 VICTOR	22-08-013 MILLER	21-05-013 CLASSIFICATION
23-10-013 EIGHTH	23-11-019 WAKE	22-09-017 MODERATE	21-03-006 CM
23-04-009 EMPIRICAL	23-05-006 WESTMINSTER	22-05-014 MOTIVE	21-08-015 COLONIAL
23-09-020 ENABLE	23-06-010 WHISKY	22-09-020 NERVES	21-07-018 COLORFUL
23-08-021 ENCOURAGING	23-07-017 WHISPERED	22-08-016 NOVELS	21-06-009 COMMODITIES
23-11-022 EXCITED	23-10-022 WORN	22-07-017 OBLIGATIONS	21-11-019 COMPETENT
23-07-015 EXERCISES	23-05-015 WOUNDED	22-12-020 OCCASIONS	21-05-009 COMPLEMENT
23-07-014 EXPECTATIONS	23-03-006 0	22-08-015 OVERSEAS	21-05-010 COMPUTED
-23-08-012 FARMER	23-09-021 27	22-06-016 OWNERSHIP	21-05-012 CONGRESSMAN
23-05-007 FIBERS	23-01-001 *S*B*A	22-07-013 PALM	21-07-015 CONVERSION
23-09-022 FLOWER	22-10-020 ADDING	22-09-021 PANIC	21-09-020 COPE
23-02-002 FOGG	22-07-013 AH	22-09-016 PARTICIPATE	21-08-019 CRACK
23-07-015 FRACTION	22-05-008 ALASKA	22-11-020 PATIENCE	21-07-013 CRISES
23-08-018 FURNISHED	22-02-004 ALIENATION	22-09-012 PHYSICS	21-05-005 CROMWELL
23-03-012 GEN	22-08-017 ALTERED	22-05-009 PHYSIOLOGICAL	21-11-021 CROSSING
23-07-018 GENERATIONS	22-07-014 AMBASSADOR	22-09-017 PITCH	21-10-019 DARE
23-08-016 GENIUS	22-06-016 AMBIGUOUS	22-06-006 PLANETS	21-09-017 DEDICATION
23-12-020 GIANT	22-08-022 AMERICA'S	22-07-012 PLATE	21-07-021 DEFEND
23-05-006 GIN	22-11-019 APPRECIATION	22-09-019 POSSESSED	21-09-017 DEFINITELY
23-06-017 GOVERNMENTAL	22-07-015 ARCHITECT	22-06-013 POSTS	21-09-019 DELAY
23-07-016 GRADES	22-02-004 ARISTOTLE	22-11-022 PREPARING	21-12-017 DESERT
23-09-020 HABIT	22-07-018 ATTACKS	22-09-015 RACING	21-09-019 DESPAIR
23-06-014 HAPPINESS	22-07-013 AUNT	22-06-016 RALPH	21-07-015 DETROIT
23-10-021 HARDER	22-08-014 AUTO	22-06-017 RECOMMENDATIONS	21-09-013 DIET
23-10-020 HEARTS	22-08-014 AUTUMN	22-02-002 REFUND	21-10-015 DISHES
23-09-016 HEELS	22-11-021 BACKWARD	22-10-021 REGULARLY	21-08-020 DISPLAYED
23-09-014 HEIGHTS	22-10-017 BALANCED	22-04-008 REHABILITATION	21-07-013 DISPLAYS
23-09-016 HISTORIC	22-09-017 BALTIMORE	22-08-017 RELATIVES	21-07-014 DRAWINGS
23-06-012 HOLLYWOOD	22-08-016 BELONGS	22-06-020 RELIABLE	21-05-014 DYNAMIC
23-10-017 HUNGRY	22-07-015 BID	22-08-021 RESIST	21-10-017 EDUCATED
23-08-019 HURRIED	22-04-009 BLUES	22-07-022 RESPECTS	21-07-020 ENJOYMENT
23-04-005 IMITATION	22-01-001 BOBBIE	22-10-020 RETAINED	21-06-013 ENVELOPE
23-11-020 INCREDIBLE	22-06-007 BOMBERS	22-09-016 RHYTHM	21-09-013 FANS
23-07-010 INSECTS	22-09-022 BOTHER	22-03-007 SAMPLING	21-02-003 FAULKNER
23-06-013 INVENTORY	22-05-012 CAPABILITIES	22-02-002 SANDBURG	21-10-017 FLASH
23-06-014 JEAN	22-05-012 CAPITOL	22-10-022 SAVAGE	21-08-012 FLUID
23-06-017 JUSTIFIED	22-09-020 CARRIES	22-09-015 SERVANTS	21-08-019 FORMING
23-07-014 KILLING	22-12-021 CASUAL	22-07-010 SHELL	21-07-018 FRANCIS
23-08-015 LAWYERS	22-07-015 CHART	22-08-019 SHOULDN'T	21-06-011 GARAGE
23-04-013 LENGTHS	22-07-018 CHIEFLY	22-08-020 SIGHED	21-11-018 GENTLEMEN
23-12-018 LIFT	22-07-021 COMPLAINED	22-08-008 SIXTIES	21-03-009 GIANTS
23-09-017 LIGHTING	22-06-017 CONGRESSIONAL	22-06-010 SOAP	21-07-012 GLORY
23-09-014 LOCK	22-06-012 CONSPIRACY	22-07-014 SOULS	21-08-015 GOVERNING
23-07-016 LUNCHEON	22-07-018 CONVENIENT	22-06-018 SPECTACULAR	21-08-018 HABITS
23-07-011 MADISON	22-06-010 D**.*C	22-09-015 SPHERE	21-10-015 HELPLESS
23-02-003 MAGGIE		22-08-014 SPONSOR	21-09-014 HERITAGE
23-07-014 MANUFACTURER		22-09-015 STATISTICS	21-07-017 HEROIC
23-09-013 MARYLAND		22-10-021 STEADILY	21-08-019 HESITATED
23-06-007 MASON		22-10-017 STICKS	21-01-001 HOAG

Code	Word	Code	Word	Code	Word	Code	Word
21-12-017	INCLINED	21-06-013	TAXPAYERS	20-05-013	GRABBED	20-09-018	SOLVE
21-03-007	INDIRECT	21-05-011	TAYLOR	20-05-006	GRAINS	20-08-017	SPLENDID
21-12-020	INSPECTION	21-05-007	TELEGRAPH	20-04-007	GRANTS	20-07-015	STAKE
21-04-013	INTERMEDIATE	21-08-019	THEIRS	20-10-018	GREETED	20-08-017	STRIKES
21-10-018	INTIMATE	21-05-015	THEORETICAL	20-08-017	GRIP	20-08-018	STRONGEST
21-06-013	JAIL	21-08-021	THOROUGH	20-09-017	GUIDED	20-09-018	STRUGGLING
21-07-008	JOHN'S	21-05-016	TRADITIONS	20-08-013	GUYS	20-07-016	STYLES
21-04-005	JOHNSTON	21-09-015	TRENDS	20-10-019	HAPPILY	20-05-010	SUBMARINES
21-04-006	JOYCE	21-01-001	TSUNAMI	20-11-014	HASN'T	20-04-009	SUITCASE
21-03-007	KATANGA	21-08-015	UGLY	20-08-017	HATRED	20-08-017	SUPPLEMENT
21-03-004	KAY	21-12-019	UNLIKELY	20-07-016	HIDDEN	20-08-016	TACTICS
21-11-019	KEEPS	21-10-019	URGE	20-06-017	HISTORIANS	20-07-016	TEMPORARILY
21-02-002	KEITH	21-13-019	URGENT	20-09-012	HOSPITALS	20-04-006	TENT
21-06-015	KILLER	21-02-006	UTOPIAN	20-08-014	HOTELS	20-04-014	THEORIES
21-08-015	LAUNCHED	21-05-017	VERBAL	20-06-011	IDEOLOGICAL	20-08-020	THEREAFTER
21-02-006	LINEAR	21-07-010	VERMONT	20-10-016	ILLNESS	20-08-014	TONES
21-06-011	LOOP	21-05-009	VERNON	20-07-015	IMPROVEMENTS	20-05-005	TOOTH
21-08-015	LOWERED	21-06-009	WAGNER	20-09-018	IMPULSE	20-04-007	TOURNAMENT
21-09-019	LUCKY	21-05-008	WARWICK	20-06-013	INC	20-04-012	TRANSFORMATION
21-10-019	LUXURY	21-09-016	WHEELS	20-08-020	INDICATION	20-09-014	TRAP
21-07-015	MARBLE	21-10-017	WINDS	20-10-019	INJURED	20-06-009	TREATY
21-05-010	MARS	21-08-016	WITNESSES	20-02-005	INPUT	20-08-014	TRIM
21-09-019	MASSES	21-07-011	WIVES	20-07-013	INTERVENTION	20-08-018	TWENTIETH
21-07-012	MATE	21-09-020	WONDERING	20-06-011	INVENTION	20-06-018	UNDERLYING
21-01-001	MAUDE	21-09-018	1950	20-09-018	INVITATION	20-09-011	VACUUM
21-08-015	MELODY	20-03-004	ABEL	20-04-009	JUDGES	20-04-014	VOTERS
21-06-009	MERGER	20-07-017	ACCORDANCE	20-05-008	JUNGLE	20-07-015	VOTES
21-07-013	MICHIGAN	20-07-011	ADJUSTMENTS	20-08-020	K	20-06-019	WARRANT
21-02-002	MILLIGRAMS	20-08-012	ALABAMA	20-09-013	LANDSCAPE	20-08-015	WIT
21-09-015	MISSOURI	20-10-020	ALIKE	20-05-007	LAURA	20-07-012	WORRIES
21-05-011	MODE	20-07-017	ALLEN	20-08-019	LEAN	20-06-015	1946
21-08-015	MONUMENT	20-06-013	ALLIANCE	20-08-016	LEAPED	20-07-014	1948
21-05-012	MORRIS	20-09-020	AMAZING	20-06-012	LEGISLATORS	20-06-015	1949
21-11-021	NEAT	20-06-014	ANTICIPATION	20-08-017	LIKES	20-07-017	1951
21-04-011	NOV	20-09-016	ANYHOW	20-07-012	LISTENERS	20-09-018	28
21-06-008	NUTS	20-05-011	ARNOLD	20-07-013	LOBBY	20-06-008	34
21-07-016	OBLIGED	20-11-019	AROUSED	20-08-017	LOUD	20-06-017	70
21-05-015	OCCURRING	20-08-018	ATTAIN	20-06-012	LUNGS	20-05-007	*N*A*T*O
21-11-014	PAINTER	20-09-015	AUTHENTIC	20-11-020	MANAGE	19-09-016	ACHIEVEMENTS
21-05-009	PARTICLE	20-08-019	AWAKE	20-06-010	MANHATTAN	19-08-017	ADDRESSED
21-06-010	PARTISAN	20-07-017	BASICALLY	20-07-013	MATHEMATICS	19-11-016	AFFECTS
21-10-016	PASSENGERS	20-08-017	BET	20-07-013	MERCHANT	19-08-012	AIRPORT
21-05-007	PATIENT'S	20-07-011	BINDING	20-11-018	MERCY	19-08-016	ALLOWS
21-10-017	PAUSE	20-04-007	BIOLOGICAL	20-03-003	MICHELANGELO	19-09-016	AMBITION
21-10-018	PERSUADED	20-06-015	BLONDE	20-06-015	MINORITY	19-04-005	AMEN
21-07-021	PERTINENT	20-08-015	BONES	20-09-016	MOTIVES	19-06-014	APPEALS
21-07-012	PHILIP	20-06-015	BOOTS	20-02-006	MUSTARD	19-06-017	APPLIES
21-05-011	PITCHER	20-01-001	BORDEN	20-05-011	NEGOTIATIONS	19-09-014	ARREST
21-06-011	PLANET	20-11-018	BORDER	20-08-011	NEST	19-07-014	ARRESTED
21-04-005	PLANETARY	20-10-016	BOSS	20-10-017	NEWER	19-04-014	ASSERT
21-01-001	PODGER	20-09-017	BRUSHED	20-07-013	NINTH	19-02-002	ASSESSORS
21-07-016	PORT	20-06-011	BUCK	20-08-020	NOTABLE	19-11-018	ASSURANCE
21-09-019	POSSESSION	20-08-012	BUNDLE	20-06-011	NUDE	19-10-016	ATTRACT
21-07-009	PRAIRIE	20-10-015	CAFE	20-06-014	OBSERVERS	19-10-019	AVOIDED
21-06-011	PRISONERS	20-10-016	CAPE	20-01-002	OEDIPUS	19-05-007	B**.*C
21-04-009	PROCUREMENT	20-02-002	CATHY	20-06-015	OKAY	19-08-012	BLOWING
21-07-013	PROFITS	20-06-016	CHAPEL	20-09-016	ORDERLY	19-09-015	BRASS
21-08-019	PROSPECTIVE	20-07-016	CHEEK	20-09-019	OVERWHELMING	19-07-014	BROADER
21-05-008	PROTEIN	20-05-007	CHRIST'S	20-09-015	PACKAGE	19-06-011	BUSINESSES
21-07-017	PUNISHMENT	20-09-015	CLOCK	20-09-014	PARKS	19-04-014	CALIF
21-10-018	QUESTIONING	20-10-019	CLOTHING	20-08-018	PASSAGES	19-11-016	CANVAS
21-10-015	RACES	20-06-009	COMPROMISE	20-05-015	PEERED	19-07-014	CAUTION
21-05-011	RANG	20-06-009	CONDITIONED	20-07-018	PHYSICALLY	19-08-016	COMBINATIONS
21-08-012	RENT	20-11-018	CONFIRMED	20-10-015	PIONEER	19-05-012	COMMISSIONER
21-09-019	REPLACEMENT	20-09-015	CONVERTED	20-07-012	PIPE	19-09-018	COMPANION
21-08-016	RESOLVED	20-06-017	CONVICTIONS	20-02-004	PLATO	19-06-013	COMPREHENSIVE
21-10-020	RESPECTABLE	20-06-010	COOPERATIVE	20-08-018	POVERTY	19-07-015	CONDEMNED
21-09-019	RESPOND	20-09-016	CRASH	20-04-004	PROBABILITIES	19-07-018	CONSISTENTLY
21-05-014	REVEALS	20-07-016	CRAWLED	20-11-019	PROMISES	19-07-014	CONTINENTAL
21-06-012	REVEREND	20-09-012	CREAM	20-06-007	PUPIL	19-06-016	CONVENIENCE
21-07-015	REVOLUTIONARY	20-09-016	CREATURES	20-09-017	PURCHASED	19-07-014	CORPORATE
21-03-006	RICO	20-07-014	CROP	20-07-018	PURSUE	19-11-015	COTTAGE
21-02-002	RUSS	20-08-019	DECENT	20-11-019	PUTS	19-09-011	CROWN
21-10-020	SAVING	20-09-018	DISPOSAL	20-08-016	QUARREL	19-03-011	CUBAN
21-07-013	SCARED	20-05-018	DISTINCTIVE	20-09-017	RANKS	19-05-008	CURVES
21-05-007	SCREW	20-04-006	DOC	20-05-007	REACTIONARY	19-04-005	DAIRY
21-10-020	SHAKING	20-02-002	DOLORES	20-07-019	RECEIVES	19-08-015	DAMNED
21-08-018	SHAME	20-08-018	DOMINATED	20-06-014	RELATING	19-05-008	DATED
21-09-019	SHINING	20-06-011	DONALD	20-07-012	RENAISSANCE	19-05-005	DAYTIME
21-01-001	SHU	20-04-008	EL	20-10-018	REPAIR	19-09-017	DEADLY
21-08-016	SIDEWALK	20-09-019	EMPHASIZE	20-08-010	REPORTER	19-06-017	DECISIVE
21-11-021	SIXTY	20-11-017	ENDLESS	20-05-015	RESIDENTS	19-10-017	DELIVERY
21-07-015	SKIRT	20-10-020	ENFORCED	20-12-019	RESPONDED	19-10-017	DEMANDING
21-09-018	SMART	20-08-018	EXPANDED	20-06-012	RETAIL	19-10-016	DEPTHS
21-05-011	SOCIALIST	20-07-019	EXPLAINS	20-08-016	RISES	19-10-016	DEVOTION
21-10-020	SPEECHES	20-09-018	FANTASTIC	20-09-020	RUSH	19-07-016	DIM
21-08-015	SPRINGS	20-09-018	FASCINATING	20-08-014	SAILING	19-08-016	DIRECTORS
21-07-019	STARTLED	20-05-014	FEB	20-02-003	SAUCE	19-08-012	DISCHARGE
21-01-002	STEELE	20-08-017	FIGURED	20-06-008	SECRETS	19-08-009	DISEASES
21-09-017	STIFF	20-08-017	FITTED	20-09-019	SHADOWS	19-06-016	DISTANCES
21-09-019	STUMBLED	20-08-013	FLORIDA	20-05-009	SHERIFF	19-04-014	DISTINGUISH
21-08-018	SUBMITTED	20-09-010	FOIL	20-10-019	SIXTEEN	19-08-015	DOCUMENTS
21-05-016	SUMMARY	20-11-017	FORTUNATELY	20-01-001	SKYROS	19-06-015	DRANK
21-10-021	SURROUNDED	20-09-018	FOUNDED	20-08-013	SLIDE	19-09-017	DREAMED
21-10-018	SUSPECTED	20-02-005	FRACTIONS	20-08-012	SLIM	19-05-012	EARNINGS
21-10-015	TALE	20-01-001	FREDDY	20-06-010	SOCIALISM	19-06-016	ELEMENTARY
21-08-018	TALES	20-12-020	GATHER	20-06-017	SOLELY	19-05-009	EMPEROR

Code	Word	Code	Word	Code	Word	Code	Word
19-05-009	ENFORCEMENT	19-08-018	SLENDER	18-03-006	CONGREGATIONS	18-05-014	PRIORITY
19-04-007	ENTRIES	19-10-013	SLIP	18-08-016	CONSISTENCY	18-08-015	PRIVILEGE
19-05-013	ESSAY	19-10-014	SLOPE	18-06-012	CONSUMPTION	18-06-018	PROCEED
19-06-012	ETHICS	19-06-017	SMELLED	18-06-011	CONTINUATION	18-07-014	PROCEEDINGS
19-07-012	EVE	19-07-017	SNAPPED	18-07-012	COPIES	18-09-017	PRONOUNCED
19-05-011	EXCEED	19-09-015	SOBER	18-10-016	CORNERS	18-08-017	PROPORTIONS
19-06-012	EXCEPTIONAL	19-09-018	SOLVED	18-08-013	COSMIC	18-06-012	RANGED
19-07-015	FATAL	19-08-014	SPAN	18-05-013	COSTUMES	18-04-012	RATIOS
19-07-014	FATHERS	19-10-014	SPECIALISTS	18-07-010	CROPS	18-07-013	REBEL
19-03-004	FATS	19-10-016	SPELL	18-08-012	CUSTOMS	18-06-015	REFERRING
19-08-011	FEVER	19-11-016	STARTLING	18-02-003	CYLINDER	18-06-016	REFERS
19-03-008	FIGS	19-05-015	STRAIGHTENED	18-07-016	DEFENDED	18-07-008	RELIGIONS
19-03-013	FILING	19-08-014	STRESSES	18-09-015	DELIVER	18-07-016	REMARKABLY
19-07-014	FLOOD	19-10-016	STRING	18-09-013	DENIAL	18-10-018	REPEATEDLY
19-09-014	FREDERICK	19-07-014	STROKE	18-04-008	DESIGNER	18-05-011	REPRESENTATION
19-07-012	FURY	19-08-013	SUPERVISION	18-06-011	DICK	18-08-014	RESENTMENT
19-08-013	GAINS	19-07-009	TANGIBLE	18-07-016	DIFFER	18-07-015	RESTS
19-04-008	GLUED	19-06-015	TENSIONS	18-07-017	DISPOSED	18-08-015	REVERSE
19-02-011	GOV	19-01-001	TETRACHLORIDE	18-05-010	DOCTOR'S	18-08-016	RIDGE
19-07-011	GUARDS	19-05-010	THEOLOGY	18-05-007	DRAIN	18-06-014	ROARED
19-06-010	GUITAR	19-02-002	THERAPIST	18-05-008	DRIFT	18-04-005	ROD
19-03-008	HAM	19-07-010	TIMBER	18-07-013	DROPS	18-08-015	RUBBED
19-01-001	HANEY	19-09-013	TOAST	18-08-015	EARNED	18-09-015	SANK
19-05-011	HAY	19-08-011	TOBACCO	18-09-017	EARNEST	18-01-001	SAXON
19-02-002	HELION	19-09-015	TOES	18-05-012	EDITORS	18-07-013	SELECTIVE
19-07-017	HOSTILE	19-09-018	TRAVELING	18-01-001	EFFLUENT	18-01-004	SERUM
19-02-002	HYPOTHALAMUS	19-08-014	TWISTED	18-10-018	EMERGE	18-09-014	SHIFTED
19-09-016	IGNORE	19-10-015	UNDERGROUND	18-03-012	EMPHASIZED	18-06-015	SHRUGGED
19-03-008	IMMORTALITY	19-02-004	VECTOR	18-03-006	EMPLOYES	18-06-011	SIMPLER
19-09-018	IMPOSED	19-10-010	VENTURE	18-06-013	EPIC	18-11-016	SOLE
19-08-018	INDIVIDUALLY	19-01-002	VERTEX	18-02-003	ERECTED	18-08-013	SPEAKS
19-11-016	INFINITE	19-08-016	VICTIMS	18-09-018	ERNIE	18-08-014	SPECIALIZED
19-09-017	INSISTENCE	19-06-011	VINCENT	18-07-016	ESCAPED	18-07-016	SPECTACLE
19-11-019	INSTANTLY	19-07-019	WHEREBY	18-07-018	EXERCISED	18-02-003	SPECTRA
19-01-001	KILLPATH	19-08-011	WHIP	18-10-016	EXPECTING	18-05-014	SQUAD
19-08-014	LABEL	19-04-006	WILDLIFE	18-08-012	FADED	18-09-017	SQUEEZED
19-09-018	LACKED	19-08-018	WIPED	18-07-015	FAME	18-06-008	STALL
19-10-013	LADDER	19-07-011	WISCONSIN	18-10-018	FAN	18-04-007	STEIN
19-08-013	LAP	19-06-015	YOUNGSTERS	18-07-012	FASTER	18-07-012	STEPHEN
19-01-001	LETCH	19-06-011	1927	18-09-013	FAVORED	18-05-007	STEVENS
19-03-004	LID	19-09-019	35	18-07-013	FELLOWS	18-01-001	STEVIE
19-04-008	LIVESTOCK	19-05-015	75	18-09-016	FOLKS	18-10-015	STOLEN
19-07-010	LODGE	18-10-015	ABRUPT	18-07-013	FOLKS	18-03-013	SUBJECTIVE
19-07-017	LOVER	18-05-014	ABRUPTLY	18-09-016	FORGOT	18-08-018	SUBMIT
19-09-018	LOVES	18-09-013	ABUSE	18-06-018	FORMALLY	18-09-013	SUBURBS
19-05-006	MA	18-11-017	ACTED	18-07-009	FOUNTAIN	18-07-009	SUE
19-05-012	MAKERS	18-03-003	ADOLESCENCE	18-02-002	GRAMS	18-08-015	SUNG
19-05-011	MALES	18-08-015	ADVANCES	18-09-016	HALFWAY	18-08-018	SURPRISINGLY
19-09-014	MECHANICS	18-09-018	AFFECTION	18-04-006	HARVEY	18-04-013	SYSTEMATIC
19-09-019	MEN'S	18-08-013	AGED	18-07-016	HUMBLE	18-06-016	TALKS
19-08-013	MEXICO	18-05-012	ALUMINUM	18-07-011	HUNTER	18-07-011	TANKS
19-10-018	MIDST	18-05-009	AMMUNITION	18-04-012	HYPOTHESIS	18-09-012	TAP
19-04-005	MOVABLE	18-01-001	ANDREI	18-09-014	INFORMAL	18-04-014	TECHNOLOGICAL
19-07-012	MURDERER	18-08-011	ANGEL	18-06-015	INITIALLY	18-09-016	TERRIBLY
19-12-016	NEATLY	18-07-017	ANNOUNCE	18-08-015	INTERRUPTED	18-01-002	THEOREM
19-01-001	NONSPECIFIC	18-06-015	APPLICABLE	18-06-010	INTERVAL	18-05-007	TOKYO
19-02-003	NOTTE	18-06-010	ARKANSAS	18-04-009	INTERVIEWS	18-04-004	TOMMY
19-04-012	NUMERICAL	18-09-015	AROSE	18-06-013	INTUITION	18-06-013	TRANSPORT
19-03-008	OPTICAL	18-10-016	ASKS	18-05-012	INVESTIGATED	18-07-010	TRAY
19-06-013	ORTHODOX	18-06-014	ASSIGN	18-01-002	IODINE	18-11-017	TWIST
19-09-019	PACKED	18-07-012	ASSIGNMENTS	18-08-016	IT'LL	18-06-015	UNDERTAKEN
19-03-013	PAMELA	18-06-009	ATHLETIC	18-07-012	JUVENILE	18-01-001	UPTON
19-04-007	PATENTS	18-08-016	ATTRIBUTED	18-09-014	KICKED	18-08-015	WHO'S
19-02-002	PAULA	18-04-011	AUSTIN	18-01-001	KITTI	18-07-015	WING
19-08-015	PEOPLE'S	18-06-008	AUTONOMY	18-07-010	KNIGHT	18-07-013	YANKEE
19-03-006	PLANTATION	18-01-001	BARCO	18-01-002	KOWALSKI	18-06-016	1945
19-06-011	POLICEMAN	18-08-012	BAT	18-07-010	LAMP	18-08-017	29
19-09-015	POLISH	18-07-013	BATHROOM	18-01-001	LANGFORD	18-07-015	400
19-08-015	POLITICIANS	18-07-009	BATTERY	18-08-012	LEMON	18-05-009	50**K
19-07-018	PRESERVED	18-09-017	BELL	18-07-016	LESSER	17-08-015	ABANDON
19-07-017	PRODUCES	18-09-015	BELOVED	18-08-016	LIKEWISE	17-07-017	ABSURD
19-08-017	PUZZLED	18-06-010	BIBLICAL	18-11-016	LIP	17-05-009	ACCELERATION
19-08-016	RAY	18-09-018	BIRTHDAY	18-05-013	LOCATIONS	17-01-001	ACCELEROMETER
19-01-004	REACTIVITY	18-08-012	BISHOP	18-10-017	LOYAL	17-07-015	ACCOMPANYING
19-07-017	REALM	18-08-016	BITTERNESS	18-01-001	MADDEN	17-05-006	ACQUISITION
19-02-002	REALTORS	18-08-014	BRAINS	18-06-010	MANUFACTURE	17-01-002	ADA
19-08-013	RELAX	18-09-016	BRICK	18-06-011	MARRY	17-08-015	ADMIRED
19-10-019	REMAINDER	18-04-008	BRIGHTNESS	18-05-012	MECHANISMS	17-09-014	AGGRESSIVE
19-07-018	RESPECTIVE	18-07-009	BULLETIN	18-07-010	MEDIEVAL	17-04-008	ALLOCATION
19-12-016	RESTING	18-04-006	BUNK	18-04-006	MEREDITH	17-08-014	ALTERNATIVES
19-09-019	RID	18-07-015	BURIED	18-08-010	MILLING	17-05-012	AND/OR
19-08-016	RIDICULOUS	18-01-003	CAMPING	18-10-017	NEGLECTED	17-01-001	ANGIE
19-05-005	ROB	18-07-013	CAMPS	18-10-014	NINETEEN	17-02-002	ANNISTON
19-10-019	ROLLING	18-07-011	CANDLE	18-09-011	OBJECTION	17-06-011	ANONYMOUS
19-01-002	ROURKE	18-06-011	CATS	18-08-016	OFFICIALLY	17-06-009	APARTMENTS
19-02-003	ROUSSEAU	18-09-017	CAUSING	18-10-017	OVERHEAD	17-08-017	ARTIFICIAL
19-07-012	RUGGED	18-08-017	CEREMONY	18-06-017	OVERNIGHT	17-08-015	ASSUMING
19-04-008	SALEM	18-09-013	CHASE	18-05-009	OXFORD	17-06-013	AWARDED
19-06-006	SALESMEN	18-09-013	CHORUS	18-07-016	PARLOR	17-03-007	AWARDS
19-03-005	SEC	18-06-007	CLASSROOM	18-05-009	PARTNERSHIP	17-09-014	AWFUL
19-01-003	SERA	18-02-022	COBB	18-08-013	PEN	17-03-006	BALLISTIC
19-09-014	SERVANT	18-04-007	COLT	18-05-010	PHOTOGRAPH	17-08-014	BALLS
19-05-009	SHIPPING	18-06-012	COLUMBIA	18-07-012	PHRASES	17-08-011	BAPTIST
19-08-018	SHOCKED	18-08-017	COMMENTED	18-08-017	PLAINLY	17-04-009	BARGAINING
19-09-018	SHORTER	18-06-014	COMMITTEES	18-07-012	POLE	17-08-015	BARRIERS
19-07-011	SITUATED	18-08-016	COMPELLED	18-07-014	PREDICTED	17-08-012	BASKET
19-05-009	SKETCHES	18-07-012	COMPETENCE	18-09-014	PRINT	17-09-015	BELONGED
				18-05-010	PRINTING		

16-09-016	LEGITIMATE	16-04-008	SOLAR	15-08-013	CARED	15-04-011	HONORS

Code	Word	Code	Word	Code	Word	Code	Word
16-09-016	LEGITIMATE	16-04-008	SOLAR	15-08-013	CARED	15-04-011	HONORS
16-01-001	LEVELING	16-08-012	SOUP	15-06-015	CEASE	15-06-013	HORRIBLE
16-11-016	LINED	16-08-015	SOUTHWEST	15-09-014	CELEBRATION	15-06-010	IMPORTS
16-11-016	LINK	16-08-014	SPECIALIST	15-06-010	CEMETERY	15-09-015	INDISPENSABLE
16-07-015	LINKED	16-06-013	SPOTTED	15-10-013	CIRCUMSTANCE	15-03-005	INDUSTRY'S
16-07-010	LIVER	16-08-012	SPRAY	15-07-012	CLEARER	15-10-013	INTEND
16-07-012	LOCATE	16-09-016	SPREADING	15-06-009	CLIENT	15-05-010	INTENSIVE
16-05-006	LUNG	16-07-013	SPUN	15-08-015	CLUE	15-05-005	ISRAEL
16-02-002	MAE	16-03-013	STAGED	15-04-008	COALITION	15-04-005	JAY
16-08-011	MAILED	16-09-015	STATING	15-01-001	COLLAGE	15-05-010	JERRY
16-07-013	MAINTAINS	16-06-011	STATISTICAL	15-07-012	COMMANDED	15-08-013	JOINING
16-06-007	MARE	16-07-013	STIRRING	15-04-007	COMMANDS	15-01-001	JUANITA
16-07-011	MATCHED	16-07-012	STRENGTHEN	15-07-015	COMMONPLACE	15-06-011	JUDGED
16-06-009	MESSAGES	16-09-014	STRIDE	15-05-014	COMPARATIVELY	15-08-009	JUDGING
16-06-009	METAPHYSICAL	16-07-011	STRINGS	15-08-014	COMPETING	15-02-003	KATIE
16-05-014	MINIMIZE	16-05-009	STUART	15-09-013	CONNECTIONS	15-06-012	KISSED
16-08-013	MIRACLE	16-09-015	STURDY	15-06-014	CONSIDERS	15-09-013	KNOCK
16-09-012	MISSIONS	16-06-010	SUCCESSOR	15-08-013	CONSTRUCTIVE	15-04-004	LAGOON
16-08-015	MISTAKES	16-07-014	SWINGING	15-08-014	CONTEMPT	15-06-015	LANDED
16-05-007	MONK	16-09-012	SWITCHED	15-07-012	CONTOURS	15-09-012	LAWN
16-05-006	MONTGOMERY	16-03-009	SYNTHESIS	15-08-014	CONTRIBUTING	15-06-014	LEANING
16-07-011	MUSCULAR	16-07-015	TAXI	15-05-009	COP	15-06-011	LECTURES
16-07-009	NELSON	16-08-011	TELEPHONED	15-06-012	COUNTRY'S	15-03-009	LIBERALISM
16-06-007	NETWORKS	16-04-009	THEREOF	15-07-011	CRACKING	15-03-005	LITERAL
16-01-001	NICOLAS	16-06-010	THEY'VE	15-08-013	CREATURE	15-06-015	LOSES
16-06-009	NINETEENTH-CENT	16-06-011	TICKET	15-08-014	CRUDE	15-09-014	LOVING
	URY	16-04-006	TILE	15-07-014	CRUEL	15-02-002	LUBLIN
16-09-011	NORTHEAST	16-07-009	TOLL	15-07-014	CRYING	15-04-007	LYRICS
16-09-014	NOTABLY	16-05-012	TOURIST	15-03-003	CUBIC	15-06-006	MADAME
16-08-016	NOTING	16-04-005	TRAILS	15-04-009	DAD	15-09-015	MANNERS
16-06-013	OBLIGATION	16-08-015	TRAINS	15-08-014	DAY'S	15-06-011	MARCHING
16-07-013	OBSERVER	16-04-007	TRANSIT	15-08-014	DAYLIGHT	15-10-014	MEANINGLESS
16-09-016	OCCUPY	16-11-015	TRANSLATE	15-06-014	DEALS	15-07-014	MEMORIES
16-10-015	OPENS	16-09-014	TRANSLATED	15-06-013	DECREASE	15-08-013	MENTALLY
16-01-001	OPERAND	16-06-012	TRANSLATION	15-07-012	DEEMED	15-05-005	MILEAGE
16-02-002	OPIUM	16-05-011	TRANSMISSION	15-08-013	DEFEATED	15-06-014	MISERY
16-03-011	OPTIMUM	16-05-006	TROOP	15-09-015	DELIBERATE	15-04-006	MM
16-10-011	ORBIT	16-06-014	TYPICALLY	15-03-005	DENOMINATIONS	15-03-004	MOLDING
16-08-013	ORIENTAL	16-05-010	UNEMPLOYMENT	15-06-013	DESERTED	15-03-006	MORTON
16-08-011	ORIENTATION	16-11-016	UNNECESSARY	15-09-012	DEVOTE	15-05-006	NEEDLE
16-08-012	OUTFIT	16-05-009	UNTO	15-09-013	DIMENSION	15-07-014	NEWEST
16-01-001	P,	16-05-007	VEGETABLES	15-06-014	DISAPPOINTED	15-05-015	NORMAN
16-08-012	PAN	16-06-011	VERTICAL	15-09-015	DISAPPOINTMENT	15-02-010	NOVELIST
16-04-009	PARLIAMENT	16-06-010	VESSEL	15-05-011	DISAPPROVAL	15-07-009	NUT
16-09-013	PARTNERS	16-06-007	VETERANS	15-07-013	DISCOURAGED	15-08-014	OAK
16-02-002	PAYNE	16-03-007	VIET	15-05-011	DISSOLVED	15-03-003	OILS
16-04-006	PAYROLL	16-06-010	VIEWPOINT	15-04-011	DISTINCTIONS	15-04-005	ONION
16-05-013	PEAK	16-03-006	VOLTAGE	15-06-011	DISTRESS	15-05-013	OPERATES
16-04-015	PERSISTENT	16-07-011	VS	15-06-010	DIVISIONS	15-06-007	OPPONENT
16-07-012	PHILOSOPHER	16-08-015	WANTING	15-06-010	DOMINATION	15-06-015	OPPOSE
16-07-015	PHOTOGRAPHS	16-08-015	WASTED	15-07-012	DOORWAY	15-10-014	OPTIMISM
16-07-016	PILED	16-09-016	WAVED	15-08-015	DRAG	15-06-013	OPTIMISTIC
16-08-013	PIN	16-06-012	WEIGHED	15-08-014	DRAGGED	15-11-015	ORIGINATED
16-05-010	PITCHING	16-05-007	WHITES	15-06-014	DRAGGING	15-06-013	OWED
16-06-013	POSSESS	16-01-001	WILLIS	15-06-009	DRUMS	15-07-014	PAINS
16-04-005	POTTERY	16-01-001	*B*O*D	15-08-015	DUG	15-07-012	PARENT
16-06-007	PRIEST	15-10-014	ACCUSTOMED	15-06-010	DUTCH	15-06-011	PARTICIPATING
16-07-011	PRIESTS	15-04-007	ACE	15-07-010	ELDER	15-06-008	PENETRATION
16-06-014	PRO	15-07-014	ACHIEVING	15-08-013	ELIMINATING	15-08-013	PERSONALITIES
16-08-016	PROCEEDS	15-07-012	ACTORS	15-09-014	ELIZABETH	15-05-009	PETITION
16-09-014	PRODUCER	15-06-012	ADMINISTRATOR	15-05-010	EMERGING	15-06-008	PICNIC
16-08-013	PROFESSORS	15-05-010	ADVOCATE	15-08-013	EMPLOYER	15-05-005	PILL
16-08-015	PROLONGED	15-02-002	AEGEAN	15-03-004	ENGLISHMAN	15-04-011	PLACEMENT
16-07-013	PROPOSITION	15-07-011	AGREEMENTS	15-07-014	ESSENCE	15-08-015	PLUNGED
16-10-015	PROVES	15-09-014	ALONGSIDE	15-01-001	EUGENIA	15-06-012	POLICEMEN
16-05-010	PURCHASES	15-08-013	ALTER	15-10-014	EVENINGS	15-02-002	PONT'S
16-08-013	PURSUIT	15-06-013	AMBITIONS	15-05-008	EXCELLENCE	15-05-007	POOLS
16-10-013	QUALIFICATIONS	15-04-005	AMY	15-08-013	EXECUTION	15-05-007	POTATO
16-06-011	QUEST	15-07-011	ANCHOR	15-10-014	EXHAUSTED	15-09-011	POTATOES
16-08-014	RAGE	15-06-007	APPRENTICE	15-07-009	EXPEDITION	15-04-006	POWELL
16-10-015	RAIL	15-06-014	APT	15-10-012	EXPLANATIONS	15-09-013	PRACTICING
16-06-009	RAILROADS	15-08-013	ARGUMENTS	15-08-013	EXPLOSION	15-07-014	PRECEDED
16-08-015	RAISES	15-04-006	ARMIES	15-06-012	EXPRESSIONS	15-08-012	PREPARATIONS
16-08-013	READS	15-08-014	ARRIVING	15-06-008	FABRIC	15-06-007	PREVENTIVE
16-09-015	REASONING	15-05-012	ASSAULT	15-06-011	FEASIBLE	15-03-006	PROFILE
16-07-010	REFERENCES	15-09-015	ASSOCIATES	15-06-012	FEDERATION	15-06-011	PROVINCE
16-07-016	REFUSE	15-09-013	ATTRACTION	15-03-004	FLUIDS	15-07-013	QUALIFY
16-06-014	REQUIRING	15-09-013	BACKS	15-06-015	FOLDED	15-08-013	QUIT
16-07-013	RESUME	15-04-008	BANKERS	15-07-015	FORBIDDEN	15-04-006	RANCHER
16-07-012	REVISED	15-06-012	BATHING	15-05-006	FORGIVENESS	15-03-005	RAZOR
16-08-010	RIDER	15-01-002	BATTENS	15-07-009	FOSTER	15-07-013	REACT
16-01-001	ROLEPLAYING	15-05-010	BATTING	15-07-009	FREEZING	15-08-013	READINESS
16-09-012	ROWS	15-08-014	BEATEN	15-02-002	FROMM	15-08-013	REALITIES
16-08-013	RUINED	15-05-005	BEES	15-01-001	FROMM'S	15-09-014	REFUSAL
16-10-014	SAINT	15-02-003	BERGER	15-08-015	GAINING	15-09-014	RELUCTANT
16-09-015	SATISFY	15-01-001	BLACKMAN	15-07-011	GATES	15-08-013	REMIND
16-06-012	SCOTT	15-06-011	BLAST	15-07-011	GOVERNED	15-07-008	RENTAL
16-01-001	SECANTS	15-06-013	BOOST	15-06-007	GRAHAM	15-09-011	RESCUE
16-06-011	SECULAR	15-08-012	BOTTLES	15-07-014	GUESSED	15-11-015	RESTRICTED
16-08-016	SEVERELY	15-09-014	BOW	15-01-001	HARDY'S	15-11-014	REWARD
16-05-010	SHIPMENTS	15-07-013	BURN	15-07-013	HASTILY	15-04-011	ROGER
16-07-011	SHORTAGE	15-02-002	BURTON	15-03-005	HAVANA	15-06-012	ROPE
16-06-009	SIMPLICITY	15-08-012	BUSINESSMEN	15-08-013	HEAVIER	15-10-014	ROUNDED
16-06-013	SINS	15-05-006	CAFETERIA	15-03-003	HELIUM	15-07-013	RUBBER
16-07-010	SITES	15-07-011	CAMBRIDGE	15-07-013	HEY	15-02-002	RYAN
16-06-011	SKETCH	15-09-013	CARDINAL	15-08-012	HIRE	15-06-010	SCHOLAR
16-06-014	SLAMMED			15-01-002	HOMERIC	15-05-009	SCORED

15-04-006 SCORES	14-01-001 BEOWULF	14-08-012 FORK	14-07-014 PREFERABLY
15-08-011 SEATS	14-05-007 BEVERLY	14-05-010 FOUNDATIONS	14-06-013 PRESCRIBED
15-05-009 SEGREGATED	14-07-011 BLANK	14-10-013 FRAMED	14-07-010 PRESIDENTS
15-01-001 SELDEN	14-07-012 BORED	14-09-014 FRIGHTENING	14-05-005 PROCLAMATION
15-06-014 SELECTING	14-08-014 BORROWED	14-05-010 FRUITS	14-08-009 PRODUCERS
15-05-009 SELECTIONS	14-10-013 BOTHERED	14-02-004 FT	14-07-014 PROFITABLE
15-03-003 SELF-HELP	14-07-011 BOUNDARIES	14-01-001 GARRYOWEN	14-07-013 PROJECTED
15-07-013 SENSES	14-06-013 BOXES	14-02-002 GARTH	14-07-012 PRONE
15-07-014 SENTIMENTAL	14-06-008 BRACE	14-04-005 GENERATOR	14-01-006 PROPORTIONAL
15-09-015 SHEER	14-10-012 BREEZE	14-05-013 GLOOM	14-04-010 PROSE
15-07-009 SHOWER	14-08-014 BROODING	14-08-011 GODS	14-08-011 PROSPERITY
15-07-011 SIGHTS	14-06-007 BUBBLES	14-04-008 GOVERNOR'S	14-09-013 PROTECTIVE
15-07-012 SILLY	14-08-011 BULL	14-03-004 GRADIENT	14-02-005 PROTEINS
15-09-014 SINCERE	14-04-006 BUSH	14-01-001 GREVILLE	14-03-006 PROTESTANTS
15-07-014 SIZABLE	14-01-001 CANNERY	14-06-014 GRIM	14-06-013 PSYCHOLOGY
15-03-003 SLOAN	14-04-005 CAPABILITY	14-05-011 GROVE	14-07-011 PUBLISHING
15-08-013 SMASHED	14-06-010 CAPITALISM	14-04-007 GUM	14-09-013 PURSE
15-08-013 SOCIALLY	14-07-011 CAREERS	14-04-004 HABITAT	14-07-014 PURSUED
15-02-002 SOCIOLOGY	14-07-013 CARVED	14-03-006 HAMMARSKJOLD	14-01-001 PYTHON
15-02-002 SOILS	14-09-014 CELEBRATED	14-02-003 HARLEM	14-06-012 REFORMS
15-03-004 STALIN	14-06-011 CENTERED	14-08-013 HATS	14-04-007 REGULATION
15-08-012 STATURE	14-06-011 CEREMONIES	14-04-005 HAWK	14-08-013 RELAXED
15-02-002 STEINBERG	14-05-007 CHANCELLOR	14-07-012 HEAP	14-07-013 REQUESTS
15-05-008 STEVENSON	14-03-005 CHARCOAL	14-07-009 HEATER	14-04-004 RESONANCE
15-05-012 STIMULUS	14-06-013 CHILL	14-05-006 HEMISPHERE	14-07-013 RESTORED
15-09-014 STIRRED	14-05-008 CHUCK	14-05-006 HODGES	14-08-013 RETREAT
15-08-012 STOVE	14-06-010 CLASSIFIED	14-07-012 HOPELESS	14-06-013 REVELATION
15-07-012 STRAW	14-04-013 CLIMAX	14-07-010 HUSBANDS	14-05-008 REVOLVER
15-08-014 SUBSTITUTED	14-07-013 CLUNG	14-01-002 ILIAD	14-05-010 RIPE
15-09-015 SUCCEED	14-07-012 COLUMBUS	14-07-010 ILLUMINATED	14-07-013 RUIN
15-07-014 SUPPORTS	14-01-002 COMEDIE	14-07-013 IMMENSE	14-01-001 RUPEES
15-06-014 SUSTAINED	14-05-013 COMPLAINT	14-07-010 IMPERSONAL	14-05-010 RUSSIA'S
15-10-015 SWEEP	14-08-011 COMPLEXITY	14-06-014 INCIDENTALLY	14-06-013 SCENERY
15-07-013 SWIFTLY	14-07-014 CONCEIVE	14-06-014 INFLUENCES	14-05-006 SCREWED
15-07-010 SWIM	14-05-008 CONDITIONING	14-07-012 INFLUENTIAL	14-06-013 SCRUTINY
15-01-001 TAPPET	14-04-006 CONFEDERATE	14-06-009 INSECT	14-09-014 SEEMING
15-07-008 TENNIS	14-04-005 CONGREGATIONAL	14-05-011 INSTINCT	14-08-013 SENSATION
15-07-011 TENSE	14-01-002 CONJUGATES	14-07-012 INTACT	14-07-013 SENSIBLE
15-06-013 TENTATIVE	14-07-012 CONVICTED	14-08-014 INTENT	14-07-011 SHALLOW
15-09-015 TERMED	14-06-010 CORRUPTION	14-04-009 INTERSTATE	14-08-010 SHELLS
15-05-008 TEXTILES	14-10-014 COUNTLESS	14-07-011 INVITATIONS	14-11-013 SHOE
15-09-013 TEXTURE	14-05-013 COUPLED	14-01-001 IRENAEUS	14-03-007 SHORT-TERM
15-07-009 THREAD	14-06-012 CREATOR	14-07-013 IRRELEVANT	14-06-008 SINGULAR
15-05-009 THRESHOLD	14-06-011 CREEK	14-01-001 JESS'S	14-08-014 SOLITARY
15-09-013 TIES	14-06-011 CRIMES	14-01-002 JESSICA	14-09-012 SPEAKERS
15-09-013 TIGHTLY	14-05-010 CRITICIZED	14-04-010 JOAN	14-05-009 SPECTRUM
15-08-014 TORE	14-07-011 CUPS	14-06-008 KENT	14-05-006 SPEEDS
15-06-014 TOUCHING	14-06-013 CUSTOM	14-08-012 KENTUCKY	14-08-013 STARE
15-06-012 TRICK	14-10-014 CUSTOMARY	14-04-010 KHRUSHCHEV'S	14-11-014 STOPPING
15-04-004 TURNPIKE	14-07-009 DANIEL	14-07-010 KING'S	14-05-009 STRIPS
15-01-001 ULYATE	14-08-011 DARED	14-09-013 LE	14-02-003 STRUCTURED
15-08-010 UNDERWATER	14-07-011 DAUGHTERS	14-08-012 LEAP	14-04-006 SUNSET
15-09-014 UNPLEASANT	14-03-010 DEBUT	14-09-013 LEND	14-05-011 SUPERB
15-07-014 VALIDITY	14-05-009 DECAY	14-03-006 LEVER	14-06-012 SUPERIORITY
15-08-013 VANISHED	14-01-003 DECOMPOSITION	14-05-010 LIGHTNING	14-08-010 SURVIVED
15-07-014 VIRTUES	14-05-009 DESIGNERS	14-06-007 MANPOWER	14-07-011 SURVIVING
15-02-002 WADDELL	14-05-014 DETERMINES	14-02-002 MARTY	14-08-012 SUSTAIN
15-07-012 WIFE'S	14-04-008 DEVIATION	14-07-014 MERITS	14-05-006 SWEATER
15-06-014 WRITINGS	14-01-001 DIAGONALIZABLE	14-09-014 MILD	14-06-007 SWISS
15-04-010 1910	14-02-002 DIANE	14-06-008 MINERALS	14-05-010 SWORE
15-07-011 1940	14-06-007 DICE	14-07-012 MIST	14-07-009 SYMPTOMS
15-07-014 1944	14-05-012 DISCLOSED	14-05-008 MOMENTUM	14-04-009 TERRITORIAL
15-06-012 48	14-04-010 DISCRETION	14-07-011 MONOPOLY	14-06-012 THEODORE
15-01-003 *=*T*$	14-07-013 DISLIKE	14-06-008 NAILS	14-09-013 THIRTY-FIVE
15-02-007 *=N*$	14-10-014 DISMISSED	14-04-005 NASSAU	14-05-007 THOU
15-02-003 *=P*$	14-07-010 DIVIDE	14-08-013 NEARER	14-07-014 THOUGHTFULLY
15-01-003 *=T*$	14-02-005 DOMINICAN	14-06-008 NEIGHBOR	14-10-013 THREATS
14-09-013 ACCOMMODATE	14-09-013 DRAWS	14-04-005 NEON	14-08-010 THUNDER
14-07-010 ADMINISTERED	14-08-012 DRIVEWAY	14-09-014 ODDS	14-06-009 TICKETS
14-06-012 ADVENTURE	14-01-001 EDYTHE	14-06-011 ODOR	14-07-014 TOUCHES
14-10-014 ADVENTURES	14-06-012 EGYPT	14-06-009 OKLAHOMA	14-06-010 TOWN'S
14-03-003 AFFIXED	14-03-003 EICHMANN	14-10-013 OLDEST	14-05-010 TREASURER
14-09-014 AFTERWARDS	14-07-011 ELEGANT	14-07-010 ONE-THIRD	14-08-010 TREATS
14-05-006 ALICE	14-04-010 ELIGIBLE	14-07-010 ORDINARILY	14-07-013 TWENTY-FOUR
14-04-009 AMENDED	14-04-005 EMANCIPATION	14-07-012 ORGANIZE	14-02-003 ULTRAVIOLET
14-06-013 AMID	14-01-001 EMORY	14-06-011 ORGANS	14-09-014 UNIFORMS
14-07-012 AMUSING	14-08-014 ENCOURAGEMENT	14-10-014 PAINFULLY	14-08-012 UPRIGHT
14-02-002 ANACONDA	14-08-013 ENGAGE	14-06-013 PAIRS	14-11-014 UPSET
14-06-014 ANALYZED	14-06-009 ENTERPRISES	14-05-007 PARAGRAPHS	14-04-008 USAGE
14-06-011 ANNUALLY	14-08-011 ENTERTAIN	14-07-012 PASSENGER	14-06-010 VALUED
14-09-014 ANSWERING	14-04-011 EVOLUTION	14-05-008 PASTURE	14-02-004 VERDICT
14-07-013 APPEALING	14-06-009 EXAMINER	14-07-010 PATHS	14-09-013 VIGOR
14-06-014 APPEARANCES	14-07-013 EXCLAIMED	14-09-013 PENALTY	14-07-009 VOCAL
14-07-012 APPLAUSE	14-08-014 EXECUTED	14-08-010 PENDING	14-09-012 VULNERABLE
14-06-012 APPROVE	14-01-001 EXPORT-*IMPORT	14-09-014 PENETRATING	14-06-008 WAX
14-01-001 AQUEOUS	14-07-014 FAILS	14-07-009 PHYSICIAN	14-07-014 WEEP
14-08-013 ARISES	14-03-004 FANTASY	14-05-010 PIANIST	14-01-001 WELCH
14-03-003 ARROW	14-10-014 FAREWELL	14-06-006 PICASSO	14-03-012 WIDTH
14-08-011 ATTACH	14-05-007 FASTENED	14-08-014 PICKING	14-07-013 WOKE
14-07-010 AUDITORIUM	14-05-012 FAVORABLY	14-06-010 PICKUP	14-08-012 WRAPPED
14-02-003 BACTERIAL	14-10-013 FEARED	14-07-007 PIE	14-02-002 YALTA
14-02-002 BARI	14-07-013 FEATHERS	14-07-011 PINE	14-03-003 YARN
14-05-012 BARK	14-07-009 FISTS	14-07-010 PIT	14-07-014 10,000
14-05-005 BASTARDS	14-08-014 FIX	14-07-012 PITY	14-06-006 15TH
14-06-009 BEACHES	14-07-009 FLAMES	14-08-011 PLAINS	14-06-013 1947
14-05-005 BELGIAN	14-08-010 FLIGHTS	14-03-006 PLATO'S	14-06-012 500
14-07-013 BELIEVING	14-04-011 FLUNG	14-11-013 POLISHED	14-06-013 65

Code	Word	Code	Word	Code	Word	Code	Word
14-05-009	$1	13-04-008	DETECTION	13-04-004	LAFAYETTE	13-08-012	RESIDENT
14-01-006	*=*P*$	13-06-011	DIAGNOSIS	13-03-006	LANTERN	13-07-013	RESOLVE
14-07-011	*C	13-05-010	DICTATORSHIP	13-09-013	LASTING	13-08-013	RESTLESS
13-01-001	A**.*L**.*A**.*M	13-07-011	DIFFERED	13-06-008	LESTER	13-04-010	RESTRAINED
13-06-010	ABILITIES	13-08-013	DISPOSITION	13-07-011	LEVELED	13-06-012	REVIEWED
13-08-011	ABSORB	13-05-013	DIVERSE	13-03-004	LIME	13-04-010	ROAR
13-09-011	ABUNDANCE	13-02-006	DIVERSITY	13-03-004	LINGUIST	13-06-008	ROCKETS
13-07-013	ACCELERATED	13-06-011	DOCUMENT	13-03-005	LITIGATION	13-04-006	ROCKING
13-06-009	ACID	13-05-006	DOSES	13-05-008	LOU	13-07-010	ROMANCE
13-08-013	ACUTE	13-06-009	DOT	13-09-013	LOWEST	13-07-008	ROUNDS
13-06-013	ADAPTED	13-08-012	DOUBTLESS	13-02-003	LUCILLE	13-08-011	RUG
13-07-011	ADJOINING	13-06-006	DOUGH	13-01-001	LUDIE	13-09-013	SAFELY
13-06-012	ADOPT	13-07-009	DRAINAGE	13-01-002	MALRAUX	13-04-004	SALLY
13-09-011	AFTERNOONS	13-06-009	DUMB	13-02-003	MANIFOLD	13-09-012	SATISFYING
13-05-007	ALCOHOL	13-06-010	DWELLING	13-07-011	MAP	13-05-009	SCOTLAND
13-06-010	ALOUD	13-07-011	EAGERLY	13-06-009	MAPS	13-05-012	SCREAM
13-05-011	ANALOGY	13-08-012	EARNESTLY	13-06-010	MATCHES	13-05-010	SEALED
13-02-009	ANALYSES	13-07-011	EGO	13-04-006	MAYS	13-07-010	SECTOR
13-04-008	ANDERSON	13-09-013	ELDERLY	13-01-001	MC*FEELEY	13-06-011	SELLS
13-03-003	ANTENNA	13-03-003	ELECTORAL	13-07-010	MEDIA	13-08-010	SENTENCES
13-05-011	APPEALED	13-07-009	ELITE	13-06-010	METHODIST	13-05-012	SEPARATELY
13-04-007	ARCH	13-06-013	EMBRACE	13-05-009	MINISTRY	13-08-010	SHADES
13-01-001	ARGIENTO	13-06-010	EMOTIONALLY	13-07-009	MINNESOTA	13-06-012	SHATTERED
13-01-001	ARLEN	13-05-011	ENABLING	13-07-011	MISERABLE	13-08-013	SHY
13-04-007	ASSETS	13-06-013	ENTERS	13-06-012	MIX	13-06-012	SINCERITY
13-01-001	ATHABASCAN	13-03-008	EQUILIBRIUM	13-04-006	MODERNIZATION	13-04-009	SINGERS
13-01-001	AUTISTIC	13-07-009	ERECT	13-04-012	MODIFIED	13-07-012	SINISTER
13-03-008	AVE	13-06-008	ETHNIC	13-03-003	MONITORING	13-06-010	SISTERS
13-03-005	AVERAGED	13-05-011	EVALUATE	13-06-012	MONSTROUS	13-01-002	SKELETAL
13-03-003	BARBECUE	13-07-013	EXAGGERATED	13-04-009	MOONLIGHT	13-06-012	SLICE
13-05-008	BEAMS	13-05-010	EXERTED	13-06-008	MUTUALLY	13-08-013	SLIGHTEST
13-06-012	BEATING	13-07-011	EXPAND	13-02-005	MYTHOLOGICAL	13-05-009	SMALLEST
13-05-010	BEGGED	13-06-010	EXPERIMENTATION	13-03-006	NAM	13-05-009	SOLIDARITY
13-07-013	BEHAVE	13-09-013	EXPLAINING	13-05-006	NAZI	13-01-002	SOLIDS
13-09-011	BEHAVED	13-08-011	FAMILIARITY	13-06-009	NECESSITIES	13-02-004	SOX
13-08-013	BELONGING	13-08-012	FEARFUL	13-07-012	NIGHT'S	13-05-007	SPECIMENS
13-07-009	BIOGRAPHY	13-05-006	FIAT	13-01-001	NIGHTTIME	13-07-011	SPECTATORS
13-06-008	BIRMINGHAM	13-04-007	FICTIONAL	13-09-012	NONSENSE	13-05-010	SPOKESMAN
13-06-010	BLADE	13-07-010	FILES	13-01-003	NUCLEI	13-06-010	SPOKESMEN
13-08-012	BLESSED	13-09-012	FITS	13-03-003	NULL	13-07-012	SPRANG
13-09-013	BOOT	13-09-013	FOND	13-05-008	NURSERY	13-08-012	SPUR
13-05-010	BREAKDOWN	13-10-012	FORCING	13-06-013	OBJECTED	13-06-007	SQUARES
13-06-011	BRUTALITY	13-06-009	FOREIGNERS	13-09-013	OBJECTIONS	13-06-012	STABILITY
13-05-009	BUDDY	13-02-002	FOUNDATION'S	13-07-013	OBSERVING	13-06-010	STANDPOINT
13-06-013	BURSTING	13-07-008	FOX	13-01-001	OERSTED	13-04-007	STATEWIDE
13-04-004	BUZZ	13-07-013	FRANKLY	13-03-004	OFFICER'S	13-08-013	STATIC
13-08-011	CAKE	13-02-004	FRIEZE	13-06-011	OMITTED	13-03-006	STATUTE
13-06-009	CARPET	13-04-007	FUR	13-07-013	OPPONENTS	13-03-005	STATUTORY
13-01-001	CASEWORK	13-06-007	FUSION	13-07-011	OPPOSING	13-06-010	STEEP
13-07-013	CASUALLY	13-01-002	GARIBALDI	13-04-009	ORDERING	13-06-009	STIMULATION
13-05-006	CHAMPAGNE	13-04-006	GENTILE	13-08-013	OUTSET	13-05-006	STREETCAR
13-04-006	CHARLOTTE	13-09-013	GIFTED	13-07-009	OWNS	13-01-003	SUBSECTION
13-06-012	CHEEKS	13-01-001	GLENDORA	13-02-002	PACKARD	13-06-011	SUBURB
13-06-010	CHEWING	13-09-012	GLOBE	13-06-009	PAINTERS	13-09-013	SUGGESTING
13-04-008	CHICKENS	13-04-006	GOSPEL	13-01-001	PANSIES	13-07-011	SUNNY
13-05-010	CLARIFY	13-06-012	GOSSIP	13-05-008	PAR	13-06-011	SUPPLYING
13-06-011	CLUSTER	13-06-011	GRADUATED	13-02-002	PARAMAGNETIC	13-05-010	SURVIVORS
13-09-012	COLLAPSED	13-04-004	GRANDMA	13-07-011	PARTICIPATED	13-09-012	SUSPICIOUS
13-08-011	COLLECTING	13-04-006	GREENE	13-06-012	PATCH	13-09-013	SWEEPING
13-07-011	COLORADO	13-08-013	GRIN	13-05-008	PENSION	13-01-001	TAPPETS
13-07-011	COMMITMENT	13-06-011	GUARANTEED	13-08-011	PENTAGON	13-04-005	TAXED
13-06-011	COMMUNICATE	13-02-002	HAN	13-03-007	PEPPER	13-07-013	TEMPTED
13-05-009	COMPASS	13-08-013	HANDFUL	13-05-008	PERCEIVE	13-02-002	THAYER
13-09-011	COMPLETING	13-03-005	HANDICAPPED	13-06-010	PERFORMERS	13-04-007	THERAPEUTIC
13-05-009	COMPOSERS	13-08-012	HANDY	13-07-012	PERMANENTLY	13-06-011	TIPS
13-01-001	COMPULSIVITY	13-04-005	HART	13-01-001	PHOSPHOR	13-02-005	TISSUES
13-04-006	COMPUTER	13-04-010	HELEN	13-01-001	PIEPSAM	13-06-007	TOILET
13-03-003	CONDITIONER	13-01-001	HINO	13-04-005	PINT	13-05-006	TON
13-08-012	CONDUCTING	13-02-002	HORMONE	13-01-001	PIP'S	13-01-004	TORY
13-03-004	CONE	13-05-006	HULL	13-07-012	PLANNERS	13-05-010	TOWER
13-06-010	CONSERVATION	13-03-005	HUT	13-02-006	PLASMA	13-06-010	TRANSPARENT
13-05-009	CONSULTING	13-01-001	HYMEN	13-05-009	POET'S	13-08-010	TRIBUNE
13-06-009	CONSUMED	13-07-011	IDEOLOGY	13-06-009	POLITICIAN	13-06-010	TRIES
13-07-010	CONTRADICTION	13-09-011	IDLE	13-06-011	PORTABLE	13-05-010	TRUMAN
13-07-012	CONVEY	13-07-012	IMAGINATIVE	13-09-013	POSTURE	13-05-009	TUB
13-04-008	COORDINATED	13-08-013	IMPERIAL	13-06-012	PRAISED	13-05-012	TUMBLED
13-01-002	COPERNICUS	13-05-011	IMPLICIT	13-07-011	PRIVATELY	13-06-012	UNAWARE
13-07-012	COPPER	13-02-002	INCEST	13-06-007	PROCLAIM	13-08-013	UNCOMFORTABLE
13-04-010	CORP	13-03-009	INCOMPLETE	13-02-003	PROGRAMING	13-09-013	UNDERSTANDABLE
13-07-013	CORRECTLY	13-05-011	INCORPORATED	13-07-012	PROGRESSED	13-07-013	UNDERTAKE
13-08-010	COUPLES	13-05-007	INDIANA	13-06-009	PROHIBITION	13-08-013	UNDUE
13-07-012	CREATES	13-04-008	INDUCED	13-06-011	PROMOTING	13-08-013	UNFAIR
13-08-013	CRUELTY	13-08-012	INHABITANTS	13-08-011	PROPOSE	13-06-010	UNLIMITED
13-06-009	CUMULATIVE	13-01-001	INQUIRER	13-05-012	PROTESTED	13-06-011	UTTER
13-05-010	CURB	13-07-011	INSANE	13-06-009	PURPLE	13-07-012	VIGOROUSLY
13-06-011	CURLED	13-02-007	INSERT	13-02-003	RABBI	13-04-005	VIRUS
13-08-011	CURTAIN	13-06-008	INSPECTOR	13-06-012	RADICALLY	13-08-013	VISITOR
13-06-013	DEBT	13-06-012	INTEGRAL	13-07-011	REBELLION	13-06-010	VOCABULARY
13-07-012	DEEPEST	13-01-002	INVARIANT	13-05-010	RECEIVER	13-06-012	WALKS
13-06-008	DEER	13-08-012	INVENTED	13-03-005	REFRIGERATION	13-06-013	WAVING
13-07-010	DEFECTS	13-04-008	INVENTORIES	13-09-012	RELIEVE	13-07-012	WHOEVER
13-07-013	DEFENDING	13-03-011	INVESTIGATORS	13-09-013	RELY	13-07-013	WIRES
13-04-009	DEMOCRAT	13-07-010	INVOLVEMENT	13-04-010	REMEDY	13-09-013	WITNESSED
13-03-005	DEPOT	13-07-009	IRELAND	13-05-011	REMEMBERS	13-06-010	YALE
13-05-008	DEPUTIES	13-04-011	IRONIC	13-02-004	REP	13-06-012	YOUNGEST
13-05-012	DERIVE	13-08-011	JOURNALISM	13-10-013	REPETITION	13-04-008	1900
		13-01-001	KOHNSTAMM	13-07-012	RESEMBLANCE	13-07-011	32

Code	Word
13-05-012	45
13-03-004	800
13-05-008	$600
13-04-008	*D
13-01-001	*T*S*H
13-01-001	*W*T*V
12-04-009	ABSORPTION
12-07-012	ACCOUNTING
12-07-012	ACKNOWLEDGE
12-08-011	ACKNOWLEDGED
12-08-011	ACQUAINTED
12-06-012	ACTIVELY
12-05-009	ADJACENT
12-03-004	ADOLESCENT
12-04-011	ADVISERS
12-06-008	AFFIRM
12-04-011	ANDREW
12-01-001	ANDRUS
12-02-002	ANTI-SLAVERY
12-01-001	ANTIBODY
12-01-001	ANTIGEN
12-06-007	ANTIQUE
12-07-012	ARDENT
12-05-009	ASPIRATIONS
12-03-005	ATLAS
12-06-009	ATTENDANCE
12-04-009	ATTENDANT
12-04-007	ATTRIBUTES
12-06-009	BABIES
12-04-004	BAKE
12-04-010	BALLOT
12-04-006	BAPTIZED
12-04-008	BASTARD
12-06-010	BEDS
12-02-004	BEETHOVEN
12-06-010	BENJAMIN
12-07-011	BITS
12-08-010	BLADES
12-05-010	BLEW
12-05-010	BLINDNESS
12-07-012	BLOCKED
12-06-008	BLOOM
12-09-010	BOIL
12-07-011	BORDERS
12-01-001	BRASSNOSE
12-07-012	BREAKS
12-05-007	BRYAN
12-08-008	BUBBLE
12-05-010	BUTT
12-05-007	CAB
12-04-010	CALCULATION
12-07-009	CANE
12-04-007	CANYON
12-01-001	CAPPY
12-02-002	CARRYOVER
12-03-004	CAVITY
12-08-012	CEASED
12-09-012	CHALLENGING
12-07-009	CHOICES
12-02-003	CHRIS
12-04-004	CHURCHILL
12-05-011	CIGARETTES
12-04-008	CLERGY
12-08-010	CLIMB
12-06-008	CO-OPERATION
12-02-003	COATINGS
12-05-009	COINCIDE
12-03-008	COLLABORATION
12-03-003	COMBUSTION
12-07-011	COMFORTABLY
12-07-009	COMPACT
12-07-011	COMPOUNDED
12-02-002	CONGOLESE
12-08-012	CONSCIOUSLY
12-04-011	CONSTRUCT
12-03-006	CONSULTANT
12-06-011	CONTENDED
12-03-004	CONTRACTION
12-05-008	CONTROVERSIAL
12-08-012	CONVERT
12-06-007	COOLER
12-04-004	COOPER
12-05-007	COORDINATION
12-07-010	CORRESPONDENT
12-06-009	COUCH
12-05-011	COUNTING
12-07-010	COUNTS
12-07-010	CRASHED
12-06-011	CREDITED
12-04-008	CREST
12-06-009	CROSSROADS
12-08-012	CROWDS
12-06-010	CULTURES
12-06-006	CURRENCY
12-06-010	DARING
12-06-007	DEAF
12-06-009	DEBTS
12-08-011	DECIDES
12-06-009	DECIDING
12-01-001	DEDUCT
12-05-007	DEDUCTION
12-09-010	DEFENSES
12-05-008	DEFICIT
12-06-006	DEL
12-01-001	DELPHINE
12-02-002	DEMOGRAPHIC
12-04-004	DENTAL
12-04-006	DENTIST
12-04-010	DEPENDENCE
12-05-009	DEPRECIATION
12-06-010	DESERVE
12-10-012	DESERVED
12-06-011	DETACHED
12-02-008	DETECTED
12-05-009	DIALOGUE
12-01-001	DIALYSIS
12-07-011	DIES
12-02-002	DILL
12-06-012	DIMLY
12-05-011	DISCOUNT
12-07-012	DISTINCTLY
12-03-004	DOLLS
12-05-012	DOWNSTAIRS
12-07-011	DURABLE
12-07-011	DWIGHT
12-03-008	EARL
12-08-011	EATEN
12-06-010	EFFECTED
12-04-006	EGG
12-07-011	ELEVATOR
12-07-011	EMPLOY
12-10-012	ENABLED
12-04-008	ENACTED
12-05-010	ENTERTAINING
12-09-011	EPISODE
12-06-010	EQUALITY
12-04-005	ESSEX
12-07-009	EVERYDAY
12-05-011	EVIDENCED
12-06-011	EXPENDED
12-08-011	EXPLORE
12-08-011	EXTENDS
12-06-009	FAITHFUL
12-07-010	FASHIONABLE
12-07-011	FAVORITES
12-01-001	FEATHERTOP
12-06-010	FEEDS
12-04-006	FIFTIES
12-06-009	FLIES
12-07-012	FLOATING
12-08-010	FLOORS
12-01-001	FLUORESCENCE
12-08-012	FOCUSED
12-07-008	FOLIAGE
12-07-012	FOREMOST
12-01-001	FORMULAIC
12-08-012	FREED
12-05-010	FROWNING
12-05-009	FULFILLMENT
12-06-010	FUNCTIONING
12-06-010	FURIOUSLY
12-02-003	GABRIEL
12-03-003	GARRY
12-05-009	GASOLINE
12-06-007	GAUGE
12-06-012	GAZE
12-02-002	GM
12-02-007	GOIN
12-09-011	GRANDFATHER
12-06-008	GREY
12-02-003	GRILL
12-06-010	GRIPPED
12-03-003	GUAM
12-05-010	GUERRILLA
12-06-009	HAIRS
12-05-010	HALTED
12-05-008	HARDENED
12-07-012	HARSH
12-07-011	HARVEST
12-07-011	HAZARD
12-07-009	HERBERT
12-01-001	HETMAN
12-05-007	HOLIDAYS
12-06-009	HOLLOW
12-07-010	HONESTLY
12-05-010	HONORABLE
12-09-012	HOPEFUL
12-07-011	HOUSED
12-03-005	HOWE
12-09-010	ICY
12-06-010	IGNORANT
12-06-010	ILLUSTRATIONS
12-06-011	IMPLY
12-05-010	IMPULSES
12-06-009	INCENTIVE
12-05-009	INDEPENDENTLY
12-05-009	INDICTMENT
12-01-004	INDIVIDUALISM
12-03-005	INFRARED
12-06-010	INITIATED
12-03-004	INNING
12-04-007	INSOLUBLE
12-07-009	INSPECT
12-02-007	INSTALLATION
12-07-010	INSTITUTED
12-05-010	INTELLECTUALS
12-06-009	INTERPRETATIONS
12-01-002	INTERSECTIONS
12-06-008	INTERVIEWED
12-06-011	IRONY
12-05-011	JERKED
12-02-002	JOEL
12-06-008	JOINTS
12-05-006	KEN
12-08-010	KICKING
12-04-004	KID'S
12-01-001	KOHNSTAMM-POSITIVE
12-03-006	KOREA
12-04-006	LANDLORD
12-10-012	LASTED
12-05-012	LATELY
12-05-009	LAYER
12-08-012	LAYING
12-05-009	LEAF
12-04-005	LENS
12-05-010	LIGHTER
12-04-012	LIMP
12-05-005	LIQUIDATION
12-07-012	LOGICALLY
12-08-012	LOOSELY
12-05-007	LORD'S
12-06-010	LOUDER
12-05-007	LOUSY
12-06-007	LUMINOUS
12-02-002	LUMUMBA
12-04-007	LYRIC
12-04-005	MAGICAL
12-07-008	MAIDS
12-05-008	MAKER
12-06-006	MANNED
12-09-012	MARIA
12-06-008	MAX
12-04-005	MC*CLELLAN
12-06-011	MEANTIME
12-03-003	MEATS
12-01-001	MELTZER
12-05-006	MERCENARIES
12-02-003	METAPHYSICS
12-01-001	MEXICANS
12-02-003	MICROORGANISMS
12-01-001	MIMESIS
12-06-010	MINERAL
12-07-009	MINING
12-06-010	MINISTERS
12-03-005	MOLDED
12-04-004	MONROE
12-05-006	MONSIEUR
12-04-005	MURDERS
12-03-006	NAI**DVE
12-05-007	NAVY'S
12-05-005	NAZIS
12-06-012	NEARING
12-07-010	NEGLECT
12-09-012	NERVE
12-01-002	NIGGER
12-01-001	NILPOTENT
12-05-008	NINETY
12-06-007	NITROGEN
12-06-012	NOD
12-04-006	NOMINATION
12-06-011	NOWADAYS
12-08-012	OMINOUS
12-07-009	ORGAN
12-08-012	OUTLINE
12-05-010	OVERALL
12-01-001	PALAZZO
12-06-010	PARAGRAPH
12-06-009	PAROCHIAL
12-05-012	PASSIONATE
12-03-005	PASSIONS
12-03-008	PATROLMAN
12-05-006	PEARSON
12-06-009	PEASANTS
12-05-010	PERCEIVED
12-01-001	PERSIANS
12-04-009	PHONY
12-03-005	PIRATES
12-07-010	PLEADING
12-07-008	PLOW
12-08-010	POISED
12-06-009	POLES
12-09-011	POPULATED
12-02-003	POROUS
12-07-009	PRAY
12-08-010	PRAYED
12-06-010	PRAYERS
12-04-010	PREMIUM
12-05-011	PRESUMED
12-06-010	PRETENDING
12-08-010	PRIVACY
12-04-008	PRO-*WESTERN
12-04-008	PROCEEDING
12-03-004	PROCESSED
12-08-011	PROMOTED
12-07-009	PROVINCES
12-01-002	PTOLEMAIC
12-01-001	PURDEW
12-07-012	PURITY
12-08-012	QUAINT
12-06-012	RACED
12-08-010	RAILWAY
12-06-010	REACTED
12-07-012	REALIZING
12-08-012	RECALLS
12-07-011	REQUESTED
12-06-012	RESORT
12-09-012	RESTAURANTS
12-06-011	RESULTANT
12-04-007	RETENTION
12-04-010	RHYTHMS
12-05-009	RIBBON
12-04-005	RICHARDSON
12-09-010	RICHMOND
12-05-009	RIDERS
12-06-011	RIVAL
12-02-002	ROBERTS'
12-05-010	ROCKEFELLER
12-05-009	RUSSELL
12-06-011	SADLY
12-05-007	SAIL
12-07-010	SALESMAN
12-06-010	SALOON
12-01-001	SANSOM
12-05-007	SCRATCHING
12-01-001	SECANT
12-01-001	SELKIRK
12-06-009	SERMON
12-05-006	SETTLERS
12-07-009	SHELF
12-04-006	SHELLEY
12-06-011	SILK
12-06-010	SIXTEENTH
12-05-010	SIZES
12-05-008	SKIES
12-06-012	SMOOTHLY
12-06-010	SNAP
12-02-005	SODIUM
12-08-012	SOLEMN
12-06-012	SOMEDAY
12-07-012	SORTS
12-04-008	SOVIETS
12-06-009	SPARK
12-06-012	STAGGERED
12-01-001	STATE-OWNED
12-05-008	STATESMAN
12-01-001	STEELE'S
12-04-007	STEREO
12-04-006	STEREOTYPE
12-03-004	STOCKADE
12-05-009	STONES
12-08-011	STRAY
12-06-011	STRENGTHENING
12-03-006	STROKES
12-09-012	STUBBORN
12-08-012	SUCCESSIVE
12-04-005	SUMMIT
12-08-011	SUPPOSEDLY
12-04-007	SURVEYS
12-05-009	SUSPENSION
12-08-011	SWALLOWED
12-04-010	SWITZERLAND
12-05-010	SWOLLEN
12-02-007	SYNTHETIC
12-08-010	TANK
12-02-003	TAR
12-05-009	TECHNICIANS
12-04-004	TEEN-AGERS
12-06-010	TEMPER
12-07-010	TEMPTATION
12-05-006	TENURE
12-04-007	TERMINAL
12-06-012	TERMINATE
12-09-012	THEATRICAL
12-02-006	THERAPY
12-03-006	THY
12-08-011	TILTED

Code	Word
12-08-009	TIN
12-06-009	TIRES
12-06-010	TITLED
12-01-001	TORRIO
12-08-012	TOURISTS
12-06-010	TRACED
12-08-011	TRACKS
12-03-004	TRAILERS
12-01-001	TRANSFEROR
12-01-001	TREVELYAN'S
12-02-002	TRI-*STATE
12-04-007	TRIBES
12-04-009	TRIGGER
12-03-004	TROT
12-01-002	TRUJILLO
12-05-006	TURKISH
12-06-012	TURMOIL
12-06-007	TWINS
12-06-011	TWO-THIRDS
12-01-001	UNADJUSTED
12-06-011	UNDERGOING
12-04-009	UNLOCKED
12-01-001	UNSTRUCTURED
12-02-002	UNWED
12-07-011	URGENCY
12-03-004	VAPOR
12-05-009	VESSELS
12-05-009	VILLAGES
12-07-012	VIOLENTLY
12-01-001	WATERCOLOR
12-04-009	WAYNE
12-06-009	WEALTHY
12-07-011	WELCOMED
12-08-011	WHIPPED
12-07-011	WHISPER
12-05-006	WINCHESTER
12-05-009	WORLD-WIDE
12-05-011	WRINKLED
12-03-006	X-RAY
12-01-002	YANG
12-07-012	YEARLY
12-07-011	YIELDED
12-06-010	YOUTHFUL
12-05-006	1912
12-05-009	1913
12-06-011	20TH
12-03-003	7TH
12-08-012	90
12-02-002	.22
12-05-010	$100
12-05-010	$500
12-02-003	*=F*$
12-02-005	*G*O*P
11-06-009	A**.*M
11-06-010	ACCUMULATION
11-04-005	ACQUIRING
11-07-009	ACREAGE
11-01-001	ACRYLIC
11-07-010	AD
11-05-010	ADJUSTING
11-06-010	ADOPTING
11-05-009	ADOPTION
11-06-010	ADVERSE
11-01-001	AERATOR
11-06-011	AFFORDED
11-05-007	AGREEABLE
11-06-009	AGREES
11-08-011	AIDED
11-08-009	AIRPLANE
11-07-009	ALBANY
11-05-007	ALTERNATE
11-06-011	AMAZED
11-04-004	AMBIGUITY
11-03-006	ANGLES
11-02-003	ANGLICAN
11-08-011	ANTICIPATE
11-04-007	APPETITE
11-08-011	APPRECIATED
11-08-010	APPREHENSION
11-04-008	APPROPRIATED
11-03-009	APPROXIMATE
11-03-004	ARCHAEOLOGY
11-05-007	ARCHED
11-07-009	ARCHITECTURE
11-05-009	ARISING
11-05-011	ARRAY
11-05-010	ARTILLERY
11-05-008	ASH
11-04-006	ASSEMBLIES
11-05-009	ASSISTANTS
11-08-009	AUSTRALIA
11-01-001	AUTONOMIC
11-02-002	AVOCADO
11-06-011	AVOIDING
11-05-008	AWKWARD
11-01-004	B)
11-05-010	BANDS
11-06-008	BARBED
11-01-002	BARNETT
11-04-007	BAROQUE
11-04-005	BEE
11-07-010	BEG
11-04-008	BENEFICIAL
11-06-009	BLANKETS
11-05-009	BLOND
11-05-010	BOREDOM
11-04-005	BOULEVARD
11-07-008	BREAST
11-10-010	BRONZE
11-01-001	BRUMIDI
11-05-010	BURIAL
11-08-009	BUSHES
11-06-008	BUYS
11-04-008	CALCIUM
11-02-002	CALENDARS
11-06-008	CALF
11-06-009	CALMLY
11-04-007	CARRIAGE
11-06-008	CARRIERS
11-08-011	CATASTROPHE
11-06-011	CEMENT
11-04-006	CENSUS
11-07-011	CHAMBERS
11-05-008	CHEAPER
11-06-009	CHILDISH
11-07-010	CHOOSING
11-03-009	CHRONIC
11-06-009	CIVILIZED
11-05-006	CLAUDE
11-05-008	CLIFF
11-06-010	CLIMBING
11-04-006	COEXISTENCE
11-03-004	COHESIVE
11-07-010	COINCIDENCE
11-04-010	COMMANDING
11-04-010	COMMERCIALLY
11-06-008	COMMISSIONS
11-05-010	COMMUNION
11-06-008	COMPARTMENT
11-03-005	COMPILATION
11-06-010	COMPLAIN
11-07-008	COMPOUND
11-05-010	COMPRISE
11-03-005	COMPUTING
11-07-010	CONCEDED
11-06-010	CONCEIVABLE
11-06-011	CONCENTRATE
11-03-006	CONCERTO
11-06-008	CONCLUSIVE
11-05-009	CONFESS
11-01-001	CONGRUENCE
11-05-009	CONSTITUTED
11-05-011	CONSTITUTES
11-08-011	CONSULT
11-07-010	CONTRASTING
11-06-009	CONTRASTS
11-06-010	CONVINCING
11-06-010	COOPERATE
11-04-008	COUNTERPARTS
11-06-008	CRAWL
11-06-010	CREPT
11-04-008	CRITERIA
11-07-009	CRITERION
11-06-010	CRITICISMS
11-01-001	CROMBIE
11-01-001	CUBISM
11-05-007	CULT
11-06-011	CURIOUSLY
11-06-010	CURSE
11-06-011	CURSED
11-02-006	CYLINDRICAL
11-06-010	DASH
11-07-009	DECLARES
11-02-002	DEDUCTIONS
11-05-007	DEFICIENCY
11-05-010	DELEGATION
11-05-009	DEPRESSED
11-07-011	DESCENT
11-07-011	DEVELOPS
11-04-005	DILLON
11-02-004	DIMENSIONAL
11-05-011	DISAGREEMENT
11-07-010	DISAPPEAR
11-06-010	DISARMAMENT
11-06-011	DISCIPLINED
11-05-008	DISCREPANCY
11-05-011	DISGUISED
11-05-010	DISLIKED
11-04-011	DISTORTED
11-06-007	DODGE
11-04-008	DOMINANCE
11-07-009	DOSE
11-04-006	DOTS
11-04-011	DOUBLED
11-07-010	DOZENS
11-06-009	DRASTIC
11-06-010	DREAMING
11-06-009	DRIFTING
11-07-011	DRUM
11-03-005	DUKE
11-06-011	DURATION
11-02-003	DYLAN
11-07-010	EASTER
11-04-008	ECCENTRIC
11-07-010	ECONOMICALLY
11-07-011	EDWIN
11-05-009	EIGHTY
11-05-009	EISENHOWER'S
11-06-009	ELEMENTAL
11-07-011	ELEVATED
11-08-011	ELOQUENT
11-08-011	EMBARRASSING
11-07-010	ENCLOSED
11-06-009	ENDURED
11-05-011	ENERGETIC
11-03-007	ENERGIES
11-07-010	ENLISTED
11-02-006	ENSEMBLE
11-07-008	ENTERTAINED
11-04-008	ENTITIES
11-02-004	ENZYMES
11-04-005	EPIDEMIC
11-05-007	EQUITABLE
11-03-005	EVALUATED
11-07-010	EVENTUAL
11-08-011	EXERT
11-08-011	EXPECTATION
11-06-010	EXPENDITURE
11-07-011	EXPLORED
11-04-005	EXPORTS
11-05-009	FACILITY
11-06-011	FATIGUE
11-05-006	FERRY
11-03-006	FINITE
11-08-011	FIXING
11-06-009	FLUSH
11-04-009	FOREGOING
11-05-011	FORMULATED
11-03-007	FORMULATIONS
11-05-010	FORTHCOMING
11-06-010	FRAMEWORK
11-07-011	FRANTIC
11-05-008	FREEMAN
11-04-005	FRIGHTEN
11-05-009	FRUSTRATION
11-04-011	FULFILLED
11-03-005	FURNACE
11-05-010	GENERATED
11-04-004	GHETTO
11-06-010	GHOST
11-06-010	GIFTS
11-02-002	GLAZE
11-05-006	GRADUATION
11-06-009	GRASPED
11-08-011	GREATNESS
11-05-010	GRIMLY
11-01-001	GYMNASTICS
11-06-009	HAMPSHIRE
11-09-011	HAPPIER
11-07-010	HARDEST
11-08-010	HARDWARE
11-05-010	HAVEN
11-07-008	HERALD
11-06-010	HERE'S
11-01-001	HESPERUS
11-06-010	HIDEOUS
11-01-001	HILLSBORO
11-04-004	HIROSHIMA
11-06-009	HISTORIES
11-02-003	HOGAN
11-06-008	HONEYMOON
11-04-007	HONG
11-02-002	HUB
11-03-005	IMPROVES
11-04-011	INCAPABLE
11-07-010	INCIDENTS
11-07-011	INDIFFERENT
11-03-008	INDIVIDUAL'S
11-04-005	INFANCY
11-07-011	INFANT
11-05-010	INJURIES
11-01-004	INORGANIC
11-06-007	INSTRUMENTAL
11-07-011	INTEGRATED
11-05-010	INTELLIGIBLE
11-06-009	INTERIM
11-06-010	INTERPRET
11-10-011	INTRODUCE
11-06-009	INVESTED
11-06-011	INVESTIGATE
11-09-010	INVITE
11-01-001	ISTIQLAL
11-05-006	JACK'S
11-01-001	JASTROW
11-06-010	JIMMY
11-06-008	JUICE
11-08-011	KEEN
11-01-001	KEHL
11-04-005	KONG
11-06-007	KOREAN
11-04-011	KREMLIN
11-07-011	LEISURE
11-07-011	LENGTHY
11-06-011	LIKING
11-07-009	LIMITING
11-03-003	LINGUISTS
11-04-007	LOADING
11-06-010	LOCALLY
11-04-010	LOCATING
11-05-007	LOG
11-02-002	MAGNUM
11-01-001	MAHAYANA
11-01-001	MAHZEER
11-04-005	MAINLAND
11-07-010	MANUFACTURED
11-03-004	MARINES
11-06-009	MARKING
11-07-011	MARVELOUS
11-03-004	MAXWELL
11-01-001	MC*BRIDE
11-04-004	MC*KINLEY
11-06-011	MEMORABLE
11-03-005	METERS
11-05-010	MICHAEL
11-05-005	MIDWEST
11-02-005	MILITIA
11-06-007	MILL
11-05-010	MISUNDERSTANDING
11-01-004	ML
11-07-010	MOIST
11-01-001	MORITZ
11-05-005	MORTAR
11-04-005	MOTIVATION
11-05-008	MOUND
11-07-009	MOUNTING
11-04-009	MUFFLED
11-05-009	N**.*Y
11-08-009	NAILED
11-02-002	NARRATOR
11-07-009	NATIVES
11-05-010	NECESSITATED
11-05-009	NEEDLESS
11-05-009	NOMINAL
11-07-010	NOTICEABLE
11-05-007	NUCLEUS
11-04-007	OBTAINABLE
11-04-005	OCCUPATIONAL
11-02-002	ODYSSEY
11-05-008	OREGON
11-05-008	ORIENTED
11-02-003	ORIOLES
11-02-002	OUTCOMES
11-04-010	OVERT
11-06-007	PACED
11-06-010	PARADOXICALLY
11-04-006	PARISH
11-06-011	PARTIAL
11-03-004	PASO
11-07-009	PASSIVE
11-05-010	PAVEMENT
11-05-010	PERFECTION
11-06-006	PHILLIPS
11-04-006	PHILOSOPHIC
11-05-007	PHOTOGRAPHIC
11-03-003	PITUITARY
11-07-009	PLANTED
11-06-009	PLEA
11-03-006	PLOWING
11-03-004	PLYMOUTH
11-02-002	POHL
11-05-010	POLITICALLY
11-03-003	POLLEN
11-03-003	POPS
11-07-011	PORTIONS
11-07-010	POSE
11-03-003	POSSE
11-07-009	POSSESSIONS
11-06-009	POSTED
11-03-009	POSTWAR
11-04-005	POULTRY
11-04-007	PREACHER
11-05-009	PREJUDICE
11-06-011	PREOCCUPIED
11-06-008	PRESBYTERIAN
11-06-008	PRESERVES
11-05-010	PRESIDENCY

Code	Word	Code	Word	Code	Word	Code	Word
11-07-009	PROMPT	11-06-009	TOMB	10-06-008	ARGUING	10-03-007	DESCRIPTIONS
11-06-007	PROPRIETOR	11-04-007	TONY	10-06-009	ARRANGE	10-05-010	DETECT
11-03-004	PROTESTANTISM	11-04-006	TOWELS	10-05-008	ASIAN	10-06-006	DEVOTING
11-05-010	PROTESTS	11-06-010	TOWERING	10-03-005	ASSESSING	10-04-007	DIAGNOSTIC
11-05-011	PROVEN	11-05-005	TOYS	10-07-010	ASSURING	10-05-007	DIAGRAM
11-04-007	PSYCHOLOGISTS	11-02-004	TRAILER	10-01-001	AUTOCODER	10-05-007	DIALECT
11-06-008	PUBLISHERS	11-07-007	TRANSFERS	10-03-007	AVERAGES	10-04-009	DIFFERS
11-02-002	PULLEY	11-05-009	TREATING	10-05-007	AWFULLY	10-08-009	DIG
11-03-006	PUMP	11-04-008	TREATMENTS	10-06-009	BACON	10-06-008	DIMINISHED
11-06-010	QUANTITIES	11-07-011	TRIVIAL	10-04-006	BAGS	10-03-003	DISABLED
11-01-001	QUINT	11-08-009	TROPICAL	10-07-008	BALLOON	10-05-008	DISCOURSE
11-05-010	QUO	11-06-011	TRUSTED	10-03-007	BARBARA	10-06-009	DISCOVERIES
11-05-007	RABBIT	11-06-011	TWISTING	10-07-009	BATON	10-05-006	DISTILLED
11-04-004	RAKE	11-07-011	TYRANNY	10-06-008	BEARDED	10-03-006	DISTRIBUTIONS
11-06-009	RECONSTRUCTION	11-08-010	UNANIMOUSLY	10-06-009	BEGGING	10-06-008	DISTURB
11-07-010	RECORDINGS	11-04-004	UNDERGRADUATE	10-07-010	BITE	10-04-009	DISTURBANCE
11-06-010	RECOVER	11-06-009	UNDERNEATH	10-06-010	BLEAK	10-04-006	DITCH
11-01-001	REEF	11-09-011	UNEXPECTEDLY	10-05-009	BLESSING	10-05-008	DOLL
11-05-011	REGRETTED	11-04-009	UNIFIED	10-05-008	BLOC	10-05-009	DOOMED
11-05-010	REJECTION	11-04-006	UNIFORMITY	10-03-004	BLOOMING	10-05-008	DRAMATICALLY
11-05-009	REJECTS	11-07-010	UNPRECEDENTED	10-05-008	BOILED	10-07-009	DRASTICALLY
11-06-009	RENDER	11-07-011	UNQUESTIONABLY	10-06-010	BOLT	10-06-010	DREADFUL
11-08-009	RENDERING	11-07-011	UNUSUALLY	10-01-001	BORIS	10-05-009	DRESSES
11-05-008	REPAIRED	11-05-009	USEFULNESS	10-04-005	BOULDER	10-02-003	DREXEL
11-05-011	RESPECTED	11-07-008	VACANT	10-07-008	BOUNDS	10-04-005	DRILLING
11-06-009	RESTORATION	11-04-010	VARIES	10-02-004	BRANDT	10-05-007	DULY
11-06-011	RESTRAINT	11-02-002	VASES	10-02-002	BRENNER	10-02-002	DUMONT
11-05-010	RESTRICT	11-04-005	VENUS	10-01-001	BRODIE	10-06-010	EARTHY
11-07-011	RETAIN	11-04-006	VICE-PRESIDENT	10-06-007	BROTHER'S	10-06-010	ECHO
11-06-009	REUNION	11-01-001	VINCE	10-02-002	BULL'S-EYE	10-05-007	EDITIONS
11-06-011	REVEALING	11-01-001	VIOLA	10-01-001	BUMBLEBEES	10-05-009	EDITORIALS
11-07-009	RHYTHMIC	11-03-008	VIOLIN	10-03-004	BUTTON	10-03-003	EDUCATOR
11-05-009	RIBS	11-01-001	VIVIAN	10-05-006	BUTTONS	10-05-008	ELBOW
11-06-010	ROLLS	11-06-010	WAIST	10-04-007	CALCULATIONS	10-05-008	ELEANOR
11-05-006	ROSS	11-08-010	WAKING	10-03-004	CALHOUN	10-03-004	ELECTRONS
11-02-007	ROTATING	11-03-005	WALNUT	10-06-009	CARING	10-05-009	ELEGANCE
11-05-007	ROTATION	11-07-010	WARN	10-01-001	CARMER	10-06-008	ELEPHANTS
11-05-008	RUBBING	11-02-002	WART	10-01-002	CATHODE	10-05-006	ELLEN
11-06-008	SANCTION	11-03-008	WEIGHTS	10-06-010	CAUTIOUS	10-05-009	EMBODIMENT
11-06-010	SANITATION	11-07-011	WELLS	10-02-004	CELLULOSE	10-04-004	EMMA
11-06-007	SATISFACTORILY	11-05-008	WHOLESOME	10-07-007	CHAINS	10-04-010	EMPLOYING
11-03-003	SCHOOLHOUSE	11-06-010	WILDERNESS	10-03-008	CHAMPIONS	10-05-008	ENDURING
11-02-002	SCOTTY'S	11-03-007	WILLIE	10-06-010	CHEERFUL	10-07-009	ENJOYS
11-08-009	SCRIPT	11-06-009	WILLINGNESS	10-05-009	CHESTER	10-07-010	ENTITY
11-05-007	SCRIPTURES	11-01-001	WINSLOW	10-05-007	CHICAGO'S	10-02-006	EQUATIONS
11-05-007	SCULPTURE	11-07-011	WIRED	10-06-009	CIGAR	10-03-004	ERNEST
11-08-011	SECURED	11-05-011	WONDERFULLY	10-05-008	CITES	10-01-001	EROMONGA
11-08-011	SETTLING	11-05-009	Y	10-05-007	CLERGYMAN	10-03-004	EVANS
11-05-006	SEVENTEENTH	11-07-008	YE	10-05-008	CLIENTS	10-04-009	EXCEEDS
11-05-008	SEXES	11-05-007	YOUTHS	10-07-010	CLUES	10-07-009	EXHIBITED
11-07-008	SHAFT	11-05-008	ZONE	10-07-009	COARSE	10-04-007	EXPORT
11-06-011	SHAKEN	11-05-009	1.5	10-04-006	COATS	10-02-002	EXPRESSWAY
11-04-007	SHAKESPEARE'S	11-06-007	1,000	10-08-010	COIN	10-05-008	EXTENSIVELY
11-07-008	SHED	11-03-007	1000	10-05-009	COMBINING	10-04-005	FAKE
11-06-011	SHIFTING	11-01-001	104	10-03-006	COMMERCIALS	10-07-010	FAVORS
11-05-009	SHIVERING	11-06-009	1920	10-01-001	COMMUTE	10-06-009	FEMININE
11-02-002	SHOWMANSHIP	11-05-011	1930	10-01-001	COMMUTER	10-03-004	FERTILITY
11-08-011	SIGH	11-05-008	1941	10-07-008	COMPETITORS	10-02-002	FINALS
11-05-009	SLEEVE	11-06-009	1942	10-05-008	COMPILED	10-03-007	FLA
11-08-011	SLIDING	11-05-008	1943	10-03-006	COMPOSITIONS	10-06-008	FLEEING
11-07-011	SMILES	11-07-011	250	10-04-004	COMPULSIVE	10-04-008	FLOCK
11-05-010	SNATCHED	11-02-009	41	10-04-005	COMRADES	10-04-008	FOLLY
11-05-009	SOCIOLOGICAL	11-05-010	55	10-06-010	CONCEIVABLY	10-06-009	FORECAST
11-08-011	SOMETIME	11-05-007	$1,000	10-03-003	CONCORD	10-03-003	FORGE
11-05-008	SPACES	11-01-003	*=*R*$	10-06-010	CONFORM	10-06-006	FORUM
11-04-009	SPECIFY	11-02-005	*U*N	10-06-010	CONFRONTING	10-01-001	FOSDICK
11-01-001	SPELMAN	11-04-005	*V	10-06-007	CONGRESSMEN	10-06-010	FOUNDER
11-06-008	SPINNING	10-05-009	ABANDONMENT	10-01-001	CONJUGATE	10-07-009	FRAGILE
11-06-008	SPIT	10-06-008	ABOLITION	10-02-003	CONRAD	10-04-007	FRAGMENTS
11-06-009	SPRAWLED	10-06-008	ACCOMPLISHMENTS	10-06-008	CONSCIENTIOUS	10-06-008	FRAMING
11-08-011	SQUARELY	10-04-010	ACCUMULATED	10-04-008	CONSECUTIVE	10-04-010	FRUSTRATED
11-08-009	SQUEEZE	10-06-008	ACCUSE	10-03-004	CONSERVATISM	10-04-004	GAZETTE
11-05-009	STRAINED	10-07-009	ADAPTATION	10-07-007	CONSTITUENTS	10-05-006	GENERALS
11-06-009	STREAMS	10-05-010	ADDS	10-07-010	CONSULTATION	10-05-009	GENUINELY
11-06-011	STRENUOUS	10-05-007	ADMIRABLE	10-07-009	CONTAINER	10-10-010	GIGANTIC
11-08-011	STRICT	10-05-007	ADMIRATION	10-07-009	CONTRIBUTES	10-07-007	GIRL'S
11-04-005	SUBDIVISION	10-08-010	ADMIRE	10-07-009	CONVERSATIONS	10-06-007	GLOWING
11-06-011	SUBSEQUENTLY	10-07-009	ADS	10-05-006	CONVERTIBLE	10-03-006	GOLDBERG
11-03-007	SURGEON	10-05-009	ADVANCEMENT	10-06-007	COOKED	10-05-009	GORDON
11-05-011	SWELLING	10-06-010	ADVISE	10-02-002	COOPERATIVES	10-05-009	GRACEFUL
11-05-009	SYMBOLIZED	10-07-010	AGGRESSION	10-06-008	COSTUME	10-02-004	GRAM
11-01-001	SZOLD	10-05-006	AIRPLANES	10-06-008	COUNSELING	10-02-002	GREG'S
11-01-001	TALIESIN	10-07-010	AKIN	10-06-010	CREEP	10-07-008	GRIEF
11-04-006	TAXATION	10-08-010	ALAS	10-08-008	CRUSHED	10-08-010	GUARANTEE
11-06-009	TAXPAYER	10-01-002	ALBUMIN	10-06-009	CULTIVATED	10-09-010	GUIDING
11-08-009	TEACHES	10-01-001	ALEX'S	10-05-008	DANCED	10-06-009	HAIL
11-07-011	TEAR	10-06-008	ALLEGED	10-03-006	DEADLOCK	10-01-002	HALFBACK
11-05-010	TENDER	10-01-001	ALLOTMENTS	10-06-008	DECEASED	10-07-010	HALT
11-04-007	TESTIFIED	10-05-007	ALLOTTED	10-07-010	DECENCY	10-02-002	HANSEN
11-04-005	THEATERS	10-08-009	AMAZEMENT	10-06-010	DECLARING	10-01-001	HARD-SURFACE
11-02-005	THERETO	10-05-010	ANALYZE	10-02-004	DEFENDANTS	10-04-007	HARNESS
11-08-010	THIRTEEN	10-05-010	ANCHORED	10-04-007	DEFICIENCIES	10-01-001	HAWKSLEY
11-09-011	THOUGHTFUL	10-01-003	ANIONIC	10-06-010	DEFINING	10-07-008	HAZARDS
11-07-010	THREATEN	10-01-005	AP)**T**-	10-09-010	DENYING	10-05-007	HEBREW
11-08-011	TIDE	10-02-003	APPENDIX	10-07-010	DEPARTING	10-08-010	HELLO
11-05-008	TIMING	10-05-006	APPLICANTS	10-05-007	DEPOSITED	10-07-007	HERMAN
11-02-002	TIMOTHY	10-06-007	ARGUES	10-07-009	DESCENDING	10-03-003	HERR

10-06-010 HESITATE	10-05-005 MULTIPLY	10-05-008 ROMANS	10-04-008 UNDESIRABLE
10-06-008 HINTS	10-04-007 MUSEUMS	10-06-008 ROTARY	10-07-009 UNFAMILIAR
10-06-009 HIP	10-05-007 MUZZLE	10-05-006 RUSHING	10-05-009 UNIQUELY
10-02-007 HOLSTER	10-06-010 NATIONALLY	10-04-006 RUSK	10-06-009 UNITE
10-06-008 HONESTY	10-04-006 NEGLIGIBLE	10-04-006 RUST	10-06-007 UNIVERSITY'S
10-06-009 HOW'S	10-03-005 NEGOTIATE	10-02-003 RUSTLING	10-06-010 URGING
10-04-009 HUDDLED	10-05-008 NEUROTIC	10-03-006 SAILED	10-06-010 UTILIZE
10-01-001 HUFF	10-04-005 NEWMAN	10-08-009 SANDS	10-04-008 UTILIZED
10-08-009 HUNT	10-03-009 NICKNAME	10-06-009 SANDWICH	10-01-001 VAGINA
10-06-009 HYSTERICAL	10-05-009 NON	10-06-009 SCANNED	10-05-010 VAIN
10-05-010 IDEALLY	10-01-001 NON-VIOLENT	10-05-006 SCAR	10-06-010 VASTLY
10-03-006 IDENTITIES	10-05-010 NONETHELESS	10-07-009 SCARS	10-05-009 VEGETABLE
10-03-008 IMAGERY	10-04-010 NORM	10-07-010 SCHEDULES	10-06-009 VENGEANCE
10-05-008 IMMIGRANTS	10-09-010 OBSTACLE	10-04-006 SCOTTISH	10-07-010 VENT
10-04-005 IMMIGRATION	10-04-007 OCCURRENCES	10-06-007 SCREENS	10-04-007 VETO
10-08-010 IMPATIENCE	10-05-009 OILY	10-01-004 SCREWS	10-05-007 VIEWING
10-06-009 IMPATIENT	10-06-010 OUTWARD	10-05-007 SEAS	10-02-003 VISCOSITY
10-06-010 IMPERATIVE	10-07-008 OWE	10-02-002 SECEDE	10-05-006 VITAMINS
10-06-010 IMPLICATION	10-02-003 OXEN	10-06-009 SECTORS	10-06-008 VOID
10-06-009 INDEBTED	10-03-007 PAINTS	10-06-010 SEEKS	10-02-002 VUE
10-07-010 INDIGNANT	10-02-002 PAPA'S	10-05-009 SEGMENT	10-02-004 WAITER
10-06-010 INGENIOUS	10-05-007 PASTE	10-03-006 SEGMENTS	10-06-006 WALES
10-06-009 INSISTS	10-07-010 PATCHES	10-04-005 SEGREGATION	10-06-010 WARMED
10-07-008 INSTINCTIVELY	10-02-004 PATHET	10-03-003 SEMESTER	10-02-003 WARSAW
10-03-004 INSULATION	10-06-007 PATRIOT	10-04-005 SEMINARY	10-07-008 WATERFRONT
10-07-009 INTEGRITY	10-04-009 PATRIOTIC	10-02-005 SENATORS	10-06-007 WEIRD
10-06-010 INTENSELY	10-06-007 PATRONAGE	10-04-007 SENSATIONS	10-07-010 WHEELED
10-07-010 INTRICATE	10-01-001 PEDERSEN	10-07-009 SERENE	10-07-010 WHIRLING
10-01-001 IRRADIATION	10-05-009 PERFUME	10-04-006 SEWER	10-07-010 WIPE
10-05-006 ISAAC	10-05-005 PERSIAN	10-05-005 SEWING	10-05-007 WITTY
10-04-007 JAWS	10-07-010 PERSISTED	10-02-002 SHEA	10-07-010 WOOL
10-03-004 JOHNSON'S	10-04-006 PHILHARMONIC	10-02-002 SIMMONS	10-05-007 WRIST
10-06-009 JOURNALIST	10-01-001 PHONOLOGIC	10-08-010 SIMPLEST	10-04-005 ZINC
10-02-003 JULIE	10-06-008 PIOUS	10-03-007 SINGER	10-04-005 17TH
10-01-001 KEELSON	10-10-010 PLEASANTLY	10-03-006 SINGLED	10-03-003 1859
10-01-001 KENNINGS	10-06-009 PLEASING	10-03-005 SINGS	10-06-006 1917
10-07-009 KNIT	10-04-008 PLOTTED	10-01-001 SKORICH	10-08-008 1935
10-01-002 LARKIN	10-05-008 POISON	10-05-007 SLASHED	10-06-010 1937
10-09-010 LATTER'S	10-04-007 POLARIS	10-04-006 SLATE	10-01-001 2**C36**JH
10-07-010 LAUNCH	10-07-009 POLITELY	10-07-009 SLAUGHTER	10-03-006 71
10-01-002 LAUREN	10-05-008 POLLS	10-06-007 SLUG	10-05-010 72
10-05-006 LAYERS	10-01-001 POLYNOMIALS	10-05-007 SOLIDLY	10-01-001 *A*I*A
10-03-008 LEARNS	10-04-006 PONY	10-06-009 SORE	10-05-009 *A,
10-06-008 LEASE	10-04-006 PORK	10-04-006 SPADE	10-05-008 *E
10-03-004 LEGENDS	10-04-006 PRATT	10-02-003 SPATIAL	10-02-002 *V*A
10-03-008 LEONARD	10-05-009 PREDICTION	10-07-009 SPECIALIZATION	9-06-008 ABUNDANT
10-07-009 LICKED	10-08-010 PRESENTING	10-02-004 SPECIFICITY	9-06-009 ACCENT
10-05-010 LIFETIME	10-06-007 PRESERVING	10-08-010 SPONSORS	9-05-006 ACCIDENTAL
10-09-010 LIKELIHOOD	10-07-007 PRESIDING	10-07-010 SPREADS	9-05-008 ACCORD
10-01-001 LILLY	10-06-007 PREVENTING	10-02-002 STACY	9-05-009 ACQUAINTANCE
10-04-009 LIMITATION	10-07-009 PREVENTS	10-06-008 STAINS	9-05-006 ACRE
10-02-005 LINGUISTIC	10-05-007 PRINCESS	10-05-008 STEAK	9-05-009 ADDITIONS
10-04-005 LISTENER	10-08-010 PRINCIPALLY	10-02-002 STEICHEN	9-05-008 ADDRESSING
10-01-001 LITTLEPAGE	10-05-009 PRINTS	10-04-010 STOLE	9-05-008 ADHERENCE
10-05-010 LLOYD	10-07-009 PRIVILEGED	10-03-009 STREAK	9-02-002 ADMISSIBLE
10-04-007 LOADS	10-05-008 PRIVILEGES	10-05-009 STRODE	9-05-007 ADVERTISED
10-05-009 LONGING	10-09-009 PROFESSIONALS	10-01-001 STURLEY	9-01-001 AERATED
10-06-010 LOOMING	10-03-006 PROJECTIONS	10-05-008 SUBSISTENCE	9-06-009 AGONY
10-08-010 LOVERS	10-04-006 PROSTITUTION	10-01-002 SUBSYSTEMS	9-06-008 AIDE
10-01-001 LUCIEN	10-03-007 PSYCHOLOGIST	10-07-009 SUMMONED	9-04-007 ALLY
10-06-006 LUGGAGE	10-03-007 PURIFIED	10-03-004 SUNRISE	9-03-003 ALUMNI
10-02-003 LUNAR	10-09-009 PUZZLE	10-08-010 SWALLOW	9-01-002 ALVEOLAR
10-04-005 MAGNIFICATION	10-03-003 QUEENS	10-04-009 SWEAR	9-07-009 AMUSED
10-01-001 MAJDANEK	10-05-007 RADIOACTIVE	10-02-004 SWEDEN	9-03-005 ANALYTICAL
10-06-009 MAJESTIC	10-05-007 RAG	10-06-009 SYSTEMATICALLY	9-04-005 ANATOMICAL
10-04-004 MANAGERIAL	10-05-006 RAID	10-06-008 TACKLE	9-07-007 ANATOMY
10-04-008 MARGARET	10-06-010 RALLY	10-08-010 TASTED	9-05-008 ANECDOTE
10-06-009 MARGIN	10-02-003 RAMSEY	10-08-010 TASTES	9-06-009 ANNOYANCE
10-02-002 MARIJUANA	10-06-009 RANGES	10-03-007 TECH	9-04-004 ANTAGONISM
10-03-004 MARINA	10-03-005 RATING	10-02-002 TENTS	9-01-002 ANTIBODIES
10-03-005 MARITAL	10-05-005 RATION	10-01-001 TEXT-FORM	9-06-007 ANXIOUSLY
10-04-005 MARY'S	10-05-007 REARED	10-06-008 THEFT	9-06-009 APPALLING
10-07-009 MASTERY	10-05-010 RECOGNIZES	10-04-004 THERMOMETER	9-04-006 APPLE
10-04-006 MATES	10-08-010 RECOGNIZING	10-05-008 THESIS	9-01-001 APPORTIONMENT
10-02-002 MEEK	10-04-004 RECRUIT	10-05-007 THREE-DIMENSION	9-03-007 APPROPRIATIONS
10-01-001 MEEKER	10-04-008 REFRAIN	AL	9-06-008 ARIZONA
10-01-002 MEGATONS	10-08-009 REFUSING	10-03-006 THRU	9-05-007 ASSEMBLE
10-04-006 MELODIES	10-02-002 REGULUS	10-06-010 THUMB	9-07-008 ASSESSED
10-06-009 MERCURY	10-05-007 REINFORCE	10-01-001 TODMAN	9-05-009 ASSIGNING
10-08-008 MERGE	10-06-009 REJECT	10-06-008 TOKEN	9-05-008 ATHLETE
10-05-010 MESSENGER	10-03-007 RELEVANCE	10-05-010 TOPICS	9-04-005 ATHLETICS
10-05-005 MICE	10-07-009 REPLIES	10-06-007 TOPS	9-03-004 ATMOSPHERIC
10-05-008 MISCELLANEOUS	10-04-006 REPRESENTATIONS	10-05-008 TOUGHER	9-06-009 ATTACKING
10-06-010 MISFORTUNE	10-05-009 RESERVOIR	10-05-008 TOURS	9-06-009 ATTAINMENT
10-05-009 MISLEADING	10-08-009 RESTRAIN	10-08-010 TRADITIONALLY	9-03-008 ATTORNEYS
10-04-004 MISSIONARIES	10-04-004 RETRIEVED	10-02-002 TRANSDUCER	9-05-008 ATTRACTIONS
10-05-007 MISTER	10-05-009 REVIEWING	10-06-010 TREMBLE	9-06-008 AUGMENTED
10-04-007 MIXING	10-07-007 REVULSION	10-06-009 TREMENDOUSLY	9-02-003 AUSTRALIAN
10-06-007 MOB	10-03-005 RICHARDS	10-01-001 TRIG	9-02-003 AV
10-05-008 MOISTURE	10-07-008 RIDES	10-06-010 TUNE	9-04-007 AVERAGING
10-06-007 MONKS	10-06-010 RINGING	10-05-005 TUNNEL	9-05-007 AWAIT
10-01-001 MONTERO	10-08-009 RISEN	10-01-001 TURNPIKES	9-06-008 AWOKE
10-07-010 MORNINGS	10-03-004 RIVERSIDE	10-06-007 TWENTIES	9-02-002 BADNESS
10-06-008 MORTAL	10-04-006 ROAST	10-05-009 TYPEWRITER	9-02-007 BARNES
10-01-001 MOSQUE	10-06-010 ROBBED	10-06-009 UNCONSCIOUSLY	9-06-009 BARRIER
10-04-006 MOUSE	10-02-004 ROBBERY	10-06-010 UNDERDEVELOPED	9-04-008 BASKETBALL
10-06-008 MUDDY	10-07-010 ROCKY	10-07-009 UNDERGONE	9-06-009 BATTERED

9-04-006 BEANS	9-02-003 DA	9-01-002 GENERATORS	9-08-009 LADIES'
9-06-009 BEGINNINGS	9-06-008 DAZZLING	9-04-006 GEOMETRY	9-04-007 LARRY
9-05-005 BERMUDA	9-01-002 DECLARATIVE	9-02-004 GEORGIA'S	9-06-007 LATENT
9-03-009 BERNARD	9-06-009 DECLINING	9-02-003 GERMANIC	9-06-008 LAZY
9-04-006 BERRY	9-06-009 DELIVERING	9-02-003 GLAND	9-06-009 LESSENED
9-01-001 BIENVILLE	9-04-004 DEMON	9-04-006 GLOVE	9-05-006 LOCKER
9-03-004 BIN	9-04-005 DENOMINATIONAL	9-03-004 GODDAMN	9-03-007 LONELINESS
9-01-001 BIWA	9-03-005 DENOTED	9-02-002 GONZALES	9-03-005 LOUNGE
9-01-001 BLATZ	9-07-009 DENSE	9-07-009 GRACIOUS	9-03-004 LUIS
9-06-008 BLEND	9-05-009 DEPARTED	9-01-001 GRAN	9-06-009 MAINE
9-04-008 BLESS	9-05-009 DEPENDED	9-06-006 GRANDMOTHER	9-03-005 MALAISE
9-07-009 BLOWN	9-06-006 DEPOSIT	9-05-006 GRATITUDE	9-04-008 MANIFEST
9-05-008 BLUNT	9-06-009 DERIVES	9-03-006 GRAVEL	9-05-007 MANIFESTATIONS
9-05-008 BOILING	9-06-009 DESIGNING	9-06-008 GRAVES	9-01-002 MANN'S
9-06-009 BORROW	9-07-007 DESTINATION	9-07-008 GREASE	9-03-008 MANUAL
9-04-005 BOUNCING	9-07-009 DESTINED	9-05-009 GRIPS	9-04-008 MARCHED
9-05-007 BOUNDED	9-03-004 DEVELOPMENTAL	9-06-009 GROCERY	9-03-005 MARVIN
9-01-001 BRAQUE	9-05-008 DICTATES	9-01-001 GROSSE	9-05-006 MASK
9-04-006 BREASTS	9-07-009 DINNERS	9-04-008 GROTESQUE	9-04-008 MASTERPIECE
9-08-009 BREATHED	9-05-007 DISADVANTAGES	9-04-005 GROUPINGS	9-03-005 MAYOR'S
9-05-009 BRILLIANTLY	9-07-008 DISCHARGED	9-05-008 GRUNTED	9-05-008 MELANCHOLY
9-03-007 BROADCASTING	9-01-001 DISCHARGES	9-05-008 GUARDIAN	9-07-008 MELTED
9-04-006 BROADENING	9-05-009 DISCLOSE	9-06-009 GUARDING	9-08-009 MENACE
9-01-001 BRONCHIOLES	9-07-009 DISCOURAGE	9-06-009 GUIDES	9-06-007 METALLIC
9-05-005 BRONX	9-06-008 DISSATISFACTION	9-04-007 GUTS	9-03-006 MILWAUKEE
9-04-005 BROOD	9-01-003 DISTAL	9-01-001 HAGUE	9-05-007 MINIATURE
9-07-009 BUD	9-01-001 DOCHERTY	9-01-001 HALF-MAN	9-05-007 MINNEAPOLIS
9-03-004 BUDDHISM	9-01-001 DOGTOWN	9-05-006 HAMMER	9-04-004 MONETARY
9-05-008 BULKY	9-04-009 DOMAIN	9-04-006 HANDKERCHIEF	9-03-004 MONKEY
9-04-008 BUSINESSMAN	9-05-009 DOUBTED	9-05-009 HANDLES	9-01-001 MORPHOPHONEMICS
9-01-001 BUTYRATE	9-01-001 DOUGLASS	9-05-008 HARDSHIP	9-05-006 MORTALITY
9-06-007 BYRD	9-07-009 DRAPED	9-04-005 HARRIET	9-05-008 MOSES
9-04-005 CADILLAC	9-06-008 DREAD	9-06-007 HASTE	9-06-007 MOSS
9-05-006 CAGE	9-06-009 DRIFTED	9-06-008 HASTENED	9-04-009 MOTIVATED
9-07-008 CAMERAS	9-05-009 DUAL	9-06-008 HAULED	9-01-001 MULLER
9-01-001 CAMPERS	9-05-008 DUCK	9-07-009 HEARTILY	9-03-005 MUNICIPALITIES
9-04-007 CAREFREE	9-04-004 DULLES	9-05-006 HEAVENLY	9-05-008 MURDERED
9-07-008 CARES	9-04-008 DUMPED	9-06-007 HEAVENS	9-07-009 NAGGING
9-05-006 CARNIVAL	9-03-007 DUSK	9-07-008 HEEL	9-07-009 NARROWED
9-06-006 CARRIER	9-07-009 EARNING	9-01-001 HENGESBACH	9-03-005 NEPHEW
9-06-009 CATCHING	9-02-002 EARTHQUAKE	9-06-009 HIERARCHY	9-06-009 NICELY
9-04-009 CAUTIOUSLY	9-02-002 EARTHQUAKES	9-04-007 HILLSIDE	9-06-007 NIGHTMARE
9-05-007 CAVE	9-04-008 ECCLESIASTICAL	9-05-009 HINT	9-03-004 NORTON
9-05-006 CENTRALIZED	9-06-006 EDEN	9-01-001 HOHLBEIN	9-07-007 NOTICES
9-04-005 CERAMIC	9-04-005 EFFICACY	9-01-001 HOLDEN	9-08-009 NUMBERED
9-04-006 CHAIRMEN	9-04-006 ELDERS	9-06-006 HOMELY	9-01-001 O'*BANION'S
9-05-008 CHALLENGED	9-01-001 ELEC	9-04-004 HOOT	9-04-007 OBEDIENCE
9-05-009 CHARTS	9-02-002 ELECTROSTATIC	9-04-008 HORIZONTAL	9-02-005 OBTAINING
9-07-008 CHEESE	9-04-008 ELIMINATION	9-04-005 HOSE	9-05-007 OCCUPANTS
9-04-007 CHEF	9-06-009 ELSE'S	9-04-008 HUGH	9-08-009 ODDLY
9-03-003 CHIEN	9-06-009 EMERGES	9-07-008 HUMANS	9-05-007 OFFSET
9-06-007 CHOCOLATE	9-07-009 EMINENT	9-06-006 HUNGARIAN	9-07-008 ONE-HALF
9-05-006 CHOKE	9-06-006 EMPLOYS	9-04-007 HYMN	9-03-004 ORBITS
9-01-001 CHRISTIANA	9-06-009 ENABLES	9-05-009 ILLEGAL	9-04-006 ORDINANCE
9-03-004 CHROMATIC	9-04-005 ENCHANTING	9-05-007 ILLS	9-01-001 ORTHODONTIC
9-01-002 CHROMATOGRAPHY	9-05-006 ENFORCE	9-04-008 ILLUMINATION	9-01-001 ORTHODONTIST
9-02-006 CINCINNATI	9-05-009 ENGENDERED	9-07-009 IMMENSELY	9-08-009 OSCAR
9-05-009 CIRCLED	9-06-008 ENORMOUSLY	9-04-009 IMPATIENTLY	9-09-009 OTHER'S
9-07-007 CLASSICS	9-05-008 ENROLLED	9-05-008 IMPOSE	9-01-001 OTHON
9-03-006 CLAUSE	9-06-008 ESCORT	9-02-006 IMPURITIES	9-05-008 OUTLET
9-05-007 CLEANER	9-02-002 ESTHER	9-05-007 INCURRED	9-06-009 OUTRIGHT
9-05-008 CLERICAL	9-02-002 ETCETERA	9-03-005 INDICATORS	9-04-004 OVERCAST
9-07-009 CLOSEST	9-02-003 EVANGELISM	9-04-008 INDIES	9-01-001 PALATABILITY
9-04-007 CLUB'S	9-05-006 EVILS	9-07-009 INDIGNATION	9-01-001 PALFREY'S
9-01-001 CO-OPTATION	9-07-009 EXECUTIVES	9-03-005 INDONESIA	9-03-006 PAMPHLETS
9-06-007 COINS	9-02-004 EXISTENTIAL	9-04-009 INDUCE	9-04-008 PANTING
9-03-005 COLLABORATED	9-06-009 EXPLOIT	9-05-008 INDULGE	9-06-009 PANTS
9-05-007 COLLEAGUE	9-06-009 EXPLOITED	9-04-006 INDUSTRIALIZED	9-05-008 PARADOX
9-03-004 COLOGNE	9-05-009 EXPRESSES	9-04-006 INGREDIENTS	9-06-009 PARAMOUNT
9-06-008 COMIC	9-05-007 EXTRACTED	9-04-008 INN	9-02-006 PARTY'S
9-05-008 COMPARING	9-07-008 EXTREMES	9-05-007 INSPIRATION	9-01-001 PASTERN
9-05-008 COMPRESSED	9-02-003 EXTRUDED	9-05-008 INSTITUTIONAL	9-02-004 PATHOLOGICAL
9-03-008 CONCENTRATIONS	9-04-007 EYEBROWS	9-01-002 INTERCOURSE	9-07-009 PATIENTLY
9-04-007 CONCEPTIONS	9-05-007 FACETS	9-08-009 INTERFERE	9-06-007 PATRONS
9-03-006 CONDENSED	9-01-001 FAULKNER'S	9-03-005 INTERLOCKING	9-06-009 PEARL
9-03-004 CONFEDERACY	9-01-001 FIEDLER	9-06-008 INTRODUCING	9-05-008 PEERING
9-06-009 CONFLICTS	9-04-008 FIFTEENTH	9-01-002 INVASIONS	9-01-001 PELTS
9-04-006 CONQUEST	9-06-008 FIGHTER	9-01-001 INVOLUTION	9-06-009 PENINSULA
9-03-004 CONSOLIDATION	9-02-002 FILLY	9-07-009 INWARD	9-03-006 PENNANT
9-01-002 CONSONANTAL	9-03-005 FILTER	9-02-004 IONS	9-03-007 PERCEPTIONS
9-03-005 CONSTANTS	9-05-009 FINISHING	9-05-008 IRREGULAR	9-05-009 PERIODIC
9-06-008 CONSUMERS	9-05-007 FLASHES	9-07-009 IRRESPONSIBLE	9-05-009 PERMITTING
9-04-007 CONTENTION	9-05-009 FLOODED	9-03-005 ISLAND'S	9-04-006 PERSISTENCE
9-03-005 CONTROLLER	9-02-002 FOAMED	9-03-005 IVY	9-04-008 PERSUASION
9-03-007 CONVENTIONS	9-02-002 FORBES	9-03-003 JENKINS	9-04-005 PETER'S
9-04-007 CONVERSELY	9-03-005 FORECASTING	9-06-009 JOKES	9-05-007 PHILOSOPHERS
9-06-008 CONVEYED	9-04-005 FORMAT	9-01-001 JUBAL	9-02-004 PHOENIX
9-03-003 COOMBS	9-04-007 FORMULATE	9-04-008 JUMPING	9-06-008 PICKET
9-05-007 COORDINATE	9-03-009 FREUD	9-03-003 JUPITER	9-04-008 PICTURESQUE
9-04-004 CORK	9-04-008 FULFILL	9-01-001 KAYABASHI	9-03-005 PIGMENT
9-06-009 CORRECTED	9-06-009 FUNDAMENTALLY	9-01-001 KEARTON	9-06-008 PILGRIMAGE
9-04-008 COUNTERPART	9-06-008 FURNISHINGS	9-02-002 KIRBY	9-05-005 PINEAPPLE
9-03-004 COUPLING	9-04-005 GARLAND	9-02-004 KIROV	9-05-008 PLUMBING
9-06-007 COUSINS	9-01-002 GARSON	9-01-001 KOHNSTAMM-NEGAT IVE	9-01-003 PLYWOOD
9-03-005 CREATIVITY	9-02-002 GAVIN'S		9-04-007 POLL
9-04-007 CURRENTS	9-04-008 GENE	9-05-009 LABELED	9-07-009 POSITIVELY
9-05-006 CYNICAL	9-02-007 GENERALIZED	9-04-008 LABORATORIES	

Code	Word	Code	Word	Code	Word	Code	Word
9-06-007	POSTPONED	9-05-009	SHE'LL	9-07-009	UNHAPPILY	8-04-006	ARCHITECTS
9-06-008	POTENT	9-05-007	SHORES	9-04-005	UNIFICATION	8-05-005	ARCHITECTURAL
9-07-008	POUR	9-04-009	SHOUT	9-06-008	UNIMPORTANT	8-01-001	ARCS
9-06-009	POURING	9-04-006	SIDNEY	9-04-006	UNPAID	8-04-005	ARITHMETIC
9-04-006	PP	9-05-009	SIMILARITY	9-05-009	UNSUCCESSFUL	8-04-008	ARTICULATE
9-04-007	PRECEDENT	9-03-006	SIMPLIFIED	9-06-009	UNTOUCHED	8-01-001	ARTIE
9-03-007	PRECIPITATED	9-04-008	SIMPLIFY	9-03-006	UTILIZATION	8-04-004	ASSIMILATION
9-02-002	PREDISPOSITIONS	9-05-008	SIMULTANEOUS	9-03-004	VACATIONS	8-04-008	ASSUMES
9-05-009	PREFERENCE	9-04-006	SIXTY-FIVE	9-05-008	VERSES	8-05-008	ASTONISHING
9-06-008	PREOCCUPATION	9-02-002	SKIFF	9-04-008	VERSIONS	8-04-006	ATHENS
9-04-005	PRESSES	9-06-008	SKILLFUL	9-04-006	VERSUS	8-04-007	ATTAINED
9-01-001	PREVOT	9-06-009	SKINNY	9-03-004	VINEGAR	8-03-004	AUTHENTICITY
9-08-009	PROCLAIMED	9-04-005	SLAB	9-07-009	VITALLY	8-07-007	AUTHORITATIVE
9-03-008	PROJECTION	9-08-009	SLACK	9-04-006	VIVIDLY	8-03-004	AUTOMOTIVE
9-05-007	PROPORTIONATE	9-05-008	SLOWER	9-02-002	VOLTAIRE	8-06-008	AVOIDANCE
9-05-007	PROPORTIONATELY	9-05-006	SMELLS	9-05-009	VOLUNTARILY	8-03-005	BABE
9-02-002	PROPRIETORSHIP	9-05-008	SMOKED	9-06-008	VOLUNTEER	8-06-008	BACKING
9-05-007	PROSECUTION	9-05-008	SNAPPING	9-03-005	VON	8-03-006	BACTERIA
9-06-009	PROUDLY	9-04-007	SOAKING	9-01-001	WAGNER-*PEYSER	8-05-006	BAKED
9-05-008	PROVINCIAL	9-06-008	SOLEMNLY	9-01-001	WALTON	8-04-007	BALLAD
9-05-006	PUBLISHER	9-03-007	SOLOIST	9-06-009	WARMING	8-02-005	BALLROOM
9-05-007	PULLS	9-07-008	SON'S	9-05-008	WARNINGS	8-05-006	BANKRUPTCY
9-06-008	PULSE	9-02-004	SONATA	9-04-009	WEIGHING	8-05-008	BANNER
9-08-009	PURSUING	9-06-009	SORROW	9-06-008	WELL-BEING	8-03-005	BARBER
9-01-001	PUSH-*PULL	9-06-008	SPACIOUS	9-06-007	WEPT	8-01-001	BARCO'S
9-04-008	PUZZLING	9-06-009	SPARED	9-03-005	WHEAT	8-02-003	BARKER
9-01-001	QUACK	9-04-009	SPAT	9-04-007	WHO'D	8-02-002	BARNEY
9-01-001	QUACKS	9-05-008	SPECIALLY	9-05-009	WICKED	8-07-008	BARRED
9-04-007	QUANTITATIVE	9-04-007	SPECIFICATIONS	9-02-003	WILLOW	8-05-007	BARRELS
9-04-005	QUARTET	9-07-009	SPECTATOR	9-06-007	WINDING	8-01-001	BEAUCLERK
9-06-008	QUESTIONABLE	9-06-007	SPED	9-05-009	WISHFUL	8-04-004	BELLOWS
9-02-002	QUILL	9-04-007	SPONTANEOUSLY	9-01-001	WISMAN	8-05-006	BELLS
9-05-009	RACK	9-06-006	SPORTING	9-06-009	WITHDREW	8-04-006	BELTS
9-01-001	RADIOPASTEURIZA TION	9-06-007	SPY	9-06-009	WORKABLE	8-06-007	BENCHES
		9-07-009	STACK	9-05-007	WORLDLY	8-04-008	BETRAYED
9-03-005	RADIUS	9-07-008	STACKED	9-05-006	WOVEN	8-03-006	BIAS
9-06-009	RAGGED	9-01-003	STEEPLE	9-04-009	WRATH	8-05-005	BITES
9-05-006	RAILS	9-04-005	STEER	9-02-002	WRIGHT'S	8-07-008	BLINDLY
9-01-001	RANDOLPH	9-06-008	STEERING	9-06-007	WYOMING	8-01-001	BLOAT
9-02-002	RANKIN	9-07-008	STEPPING	9-05-006	YELL	8-06-008	BLOODY
9-03-007	RATED	9-06-008	STERILE	9-06-008	YIELDING	8-06-008	BLUNTLY
9-02-005	RATINGS	9-06-007	STICKY	9-05-007	ZOO	8-05-006	BOAST
9-04-009	RAYS	9-03-007	STIFFLY	9-03-006	0.1	8-06-008	BOLDLY
9-07-008	RECKLESS	9-06-008	STILLNESS	9-02-005	0.5	8-03-003	BOMBER
9-04-004	RECONNAISSANCE	9-06-008	STIMULATING	9-03-006	10-YEAR	8-06-008	BOOM
9-07-008	RECOVERED	9-04-009	STRETCHES	9-05-008	100,000	8-07-008	BORNE
9-02-002	REDCOATS	9-06-007	SUBORDINATES	9-05-009	150	8-05-005	BORROWING
9-06-009	REGRET	9-02-002	SUDS	9-03-005	18TH	8-05-007	BOSOM
9-04-008	REINS	9-02-008	SUGGESTIVE	9-05-006	1924	8-04-005	BOTTOMS
9-06-009	REPEATING	9-05-009	SULLEN	9-04-009	1925	8-05-006	BOUNCE
9-05-009	REPLACING	9-03-009	SUMMARIZED	9-06-008	1933	8-05-006	BOURBON
9-06-009	REPORTEDLY	9-08-009	SUNDAYS	9-04-005	2**K	8-03-003	BOYCOTT
9-05-007	RESEMBLES	9-05-008	SUPERBLY	9-05-009	3,000	8-02-002	BRANDON
9-04-007	RESERVATIONS	9-04-007	SUPPLEMENTARY	9-05-007	40,000	8-04-006	BRAZIL
9-04-008	RESIGNED	9-06-009	SURGE	9-05-008	46	8-04-006	BRETHREN
9-02-003	RESIN	9-04-007	SURVEYED	9-04-009	85	8-07-008	BRIGHTER
9-05-009	RESISTED	9-05-007	SWAYED	9-04-009	$10,000	8-03-006	BROADEN
9-07-008	RESOURCE	9-06-006	SWEETHEART	9-01-002	*=*D*$	8-04-004	BRUISES
9-06-009	RESTORE	9-01-002	SYLLABLES	9-01-002	*=*P*$,	8-04-005	BUDAPEST
9-03-005	RESUMPTION	9-04-008	SYMBOLIZE	9-01-002	*=*T*$.	8-03-004	BUDDHA
9-05-008	RETAINS	9-02-005	SYMPOSIUM	9-01-002	*=*V*$	8-05-007	BUGS
9-07-009	RETIRE	9-07-009	TAILORED	9-04-004	*B-52	8-01-001	BUNS
9-02-005	REVIEWS	9-06-009	TAN	9-01-002	*O	8-06-007	BUSILY
9-06-008	REVISIONS	9-02-003	TAX-FREE	9-04-004	*T	8-02-002	BUTCHER
9-01-002	RITTER	9-04-004	TAXING	8-03-005	A**.*D	8-03-004	CALIBER
9-05-008	ROARING	9-05-009	TEARING	8-05-007	ABOLISH	8-04-005	CANVASES
9-01-001	ROEBUCK	9-07-008	TECHNICALLY	8-02-007	ABORIGINES	8-01-001	CAPILLARY
9-06-007	ROGERS	9-05-007	TENANTS	8-07-009	ABSURDITY	8-03-004	CARAVAN
9-04-006	ROOKIE	9-05-008	TERRACE	8-01-001	ACCELEROMETERS	8-04-006	CARDINALS
9-07-009	ROSY	9-05-008	TERRITORIES	8-06-009	ACCIDENTS	8-06-008	CARELESS
9-06-008	RULERS	9-02-003	TEXANS	8-05-007	ACCOMMODATIONS	8-03-005	CARNEGIE
9-05-006	SALAD	9-05-007	THEOLOGIANS	8-04-007	ACCOMPANY	8-05-006	CATALOGUE
9-02-002	SALTER	9-05-008	THEREIN	8-05-007	ACCUSING	8-06-008	CATHEDRAL
9-03-005	SANCTIONS	9-06-007	THIEVES	8-01-001	ACTIVES	8-03-004	CATHOLICISM
9-06-006	SANCTUARY	9-06-006	THIGH	8-03-007	ACTUALITY	8-03-004	CELESTIAL
9-04-006	SATIRE	9-03-003	THOR	8-05-008	ADMITTING	8-01-001	CENTIMETERS
9-05-005	SAVANNAH	9-06-008	TIMED	8-03-006	AERIAL	8-05-005	CEREBRAL
9-01-002	SAVIOUR	9-04-007	TIMELY	8-03-008	AFFLICTED	8-02-003	CF
9-03-004	SCENIC	9-07-008	TOE	8-03-007	AGGREGATE	8-04-006	CHAMPIONSHIP
9-01-001	SCHAFFNER	9-07-009	TOLERANCE	8-01-002	AGRARIAN	8-04-008	CHARACTERIZATION
9-06-007	SCHOLASTIC	9-05-007	TOLERANT	8-06-008	ALARMED		
9-04-005	SCHWEITZER	9-03-004	TONAL	8-03-004	ALIBI	8-06-008	CHARGING
9-05-009	SCRAMBLED	9-05-008	TOPIC	8-04-006	ALLEY	8-05-005	CHARITY
9-06-009	SCRATCH	9-07-009	TORTURED	8-05-007	ANALOGOUS	8-03-005	CHARLEY
9-07-008	SCRUB	9-05-006	TOSS	8-05-007	ANALYZING	8-05-007	CHEER
9-05-008	SE	9-03-003	TOWNE	8-05-008	ANCESTRY	8-05-006	CHOIR
9-03-003	SEAM	9-03-003	TOYNBEE	8-02-003	ANGELO	8-06-008	CHOOSES
9-04-004	SEAMS	9-06-009	TRACES	8-06-008	ANGUISH	8-04-007	CHUCKLED
9-06-009	SEARCHED	9-05-006	TRADES	8-06-006	ANKLE	8-05-007	CHURCH'S
9-05-008	SECRECY	9-07-009	TRIFLE	8-03-004	ANTI-*COMMUNIST	8-02-002	CHURCHYARD
9-06-009	SECRETARIES	9-04-007	TRIO	8-03-004	APERTURE	8-01-002	CIVILIZATIONAL
9-05-005	SECRETARY'S	9-04-006	TRUSTEE	8-04-004	APPLIANCES	8-03-003	CLAIMANT
9-04-006	SENSORY	9-05-008	TURKEY	8-03-004	APPLICANT	8-05-007	CLAMPED
9-05-008	SETTINGS	9-05-007	TWENTIETH-CENTU RY	8-03-003	APPORTIONED	8-05-007	CLARENCE
9-01-001	SHANN			8-05-008	APPRAISAL	8-05-008	CLARIFIED
9-05-008	SHAVED	9-07-009	UNCHANGED	8-02-002	ARCHAEOLOGICAL		
9-03-004	SHAW	9-04-005	UNDERGRADUATES	8-03-004	ARCHBISHOP		

Code	Word	Code	Word	Code	Word	Code	Word
8-04-004	CLEANERS	8-07-008	DOWNRIGHT	8-06-008	HEED	8-05-006	MATING
8-06-008	CLICKED	8-05-008	DRAWER	8-01-001	HELVA'S	8-01-001	MATSON
8-05-008	CLOCKS	8-03-004	DUNES	8-01-001	HEMPHILL	8-01-001	MEL
8-04-008	CLUTCHING	8-05-006	DUPLICATION	8-03-004	HEREBY	8-05-006	MEMPHIS
8-03-003	COALS	8-05-007	DWELL	8-05-008	HERETOFORE	8-04-007	MENTIONING
8-06-008	COLDLY	8-01-001	DYSTOPIAS	8-01-001	HETMAN'S	8-02-002	MERCER'S
8-05-008	COLLECTIONS	8-05-007	EASED	8-06-008	HIPS	8-03-007	MERCHANDISING
8-04-004	COLLECTOR	8-07-008	ECHOES	8-04-006	HITLER	8-05-007	MERRY
8-04-004	COLTS	8-04-008	EFFICIENTLY	8-05-006	HOLLAND	8-01-002	METEORITES
8-08-008	COMFORTING	8-05-008	EH	8-04-006	HOMOGENEOUS	8-02-002	METROPOLIS
8-07-008	COMMENCING	8-04-007	ELECT	8-03-007	HONORING	8-01-001	MICROMETEORITE
8-04-005	COMMENTARY	8-06-008	EMBARRASSED	8-04-006	HOOVER	8-04-004	MICROSCOPE
8-04-007	COMPANIONS	8-05-008	EMBARRASSMENT	8-05-007	HOPEFULLY	8-03-005	MICROSCOPIC
8-04-008	COMPELLING	8-05-007	EMERSON	8-07-008	HORNS	8-07-007	MIDDLE-AGED
8-06-008	COMPLAINTS	8-05-007	EMPTIED	8-04-007	HOSTESS	8-05-007	MIDWAY
8-02-002	COMPOST	8-05-007	ENCOUNTERS	8-03-003	HUMIDITY	8-04-006	MILITANT
8-02-002	COMPRESSION	8-06-008	ENDURE	8-05-006	HURRICANE	8-07-008	MINGLED
8-04-007	COMPRISED	8-04-004	ENEMY'S	8-03-007	HYPOTHETICAL	8-05-008	MINUS
8-05-007	COMPULSION	8-04-007	ENGAGEMENTS	8-03-007	ILLITERATE	8-06-007	MIRACLES
8-06-008	CONCEALED	8-03-007	ENGAGING	8-03-005	IMMEDIACY	8-04-007	MO
8-06-007	CONCEDE	8-02-003	ENGLISHMEN	8-03-006	IMPARTIAL	8-04-006	MOBILITY
8-05-008	CONCLUDING	8-05-007	ENSURE	8-04-008	IMPASSIONED	8-07-008	MOCK
8-05-008	CONFIDED	8-06-007	ENTAILS	8-05-007	IMPLEMENTATION	8-03-007	MODES
8-04-007	CONFLICTING	8-03-004	EQUALS	8-05-007	IMPORTANTLY	8-05-006	MOLECULES
8-06-008	CONFRONT	8-01-003	EQUATE	8-05-007	IMPORTED	8-06-007	MOMENTOUS
8-01-002	CONNALLY	8-04-005	EQUIVALENTS	8-04-008	INAUGURAL	8-06-008	MONOTONOUS
8-05-008	CONSPICUOUSLY	8-02-004	EROTIC	8-05-007	INAUGURATION	8-05-007	MONUMENTS
8-03-003	CONSTANTINE	8-04-006	ESSAYS	8-05-007	INCLINATION	8-04-007	MOODS
8-06-007	CONTENTED	8-06-007	ESTABLISHMENTS	8-04-004	INDEFINITE	8-05-005	MOTIF
8-06-007	CONTESTS	8-04-006	EVERLASTING	8-04-006	INDICATOR	8-03-007	MOUNTS
8-05-007	CONTRACTED	8-05-008	EVOLVED	8-07-008	INESCAPABLE	8-04-006	MOURNING
8-04-004	COOKS	8-05-007	EXAGGERATE	8-06-008	INFECTION	8-07-008	MOUTHS
8-01-001	COPERNICAN	8-05-007	EXAMINATIONS	8-01-004	INHIBIT	8-02-003	MULTIPLICITY
8-04-006	COPING	8-06-008	EXCEEDINGLY	8-04-008	INSISTENT	8-04-005	MULTIPLYING
8-05-007	CORRUPT	8-05-008	EXCEPTIONALLY	8-07-008	INSPIRING	8-04-007	MURRAY
8-05-008	COUNTERS	8-06-008	EXCLUDED	8-03-006	INSTALL	8-04-007	MUTTERING
8-04-005	COURT'S	8-03-004	EXEMPTION	8-06-007	INSTRUCTOR	8-02-002	MUTTON
8-06-006	COURTYARD	8-03-007	EXPERIMENTALLY	8-04-005	INTENSIFICATION	8-05-007	NEGOTIATING
8-05-006	COWARD	8-04-005	EXPLODED	8-04-007	INTERDEPENDENT	8-03-004	NEUTRALIST
8-03-006	CRAWLING	8-05-007	EXPOSE	8-01-001	INTERLOBULAR	8-03-004	NEWARK
8-03-005	CREDO	8-06-006	EXTENSIONS	8-07-008	INTERPRETER	8-01-001	NEWT
8-05-006	CREED	8-03-007	EXTERIOR	8-05-008	INTERRUPTION	8-04-005	NIECE
8-07-008	CREEPING	8-03-004	FABRICATION	8-02-002	INTONATION	8-01-001	NOGOL
8-07-007	CRIMSON	8-03-004	FARMHOUSE	8-06-007	INVESTIGATING	8-04-005	NOMINATED
8-04-007	CRISP	8-04-006	FAULTY	8-06-008	INVISIBLE	8-05-008	NOSTALGIA
8-05-005	CRUSADE	8-05-007	FEATURED	8-07-008	INVITING	8-04-006	NOTIFY
8-01-001	CRUZ	8-06-008	FEEBLE	8-01-002	IODIDE	8-05-008	NOTORIOUS
8-02-003	CRYSTALS	8-05-006	FESTIVITIES	8-04-008	IONIC	8-01-002	NUTRITION
8-05-008	CURSING	8-04-004	FIDELITY	8-03-007	IRRATIONAL	8-04-006	O**.*K
8-01-001	CURT'S	8-06-008	FIERCE	8-06-008	IRREGULARITIES	8-06-008	OBEY
8-05-008	CURTAINS	8-06-008	FINANCIALLY	8-04-005	IRRESISTIBLE	8-03-008	OBSERVES
8-05-006	CUSHION	8-05-006	FITNESS	8-03-007	ISOLATE	8-05-008	ODORS
8-01-001	CYCLIST	8-05-007	FLAIR	8-03-003	JACQUES	8-03-007	OFFENSE
8-04-004	DANISH	8-04-006	FLASHLIGHT	8-06-008	JAMMED	8-05-008	OFFENSIVE
8-06-007	DASHED	8-01-001	FLATNESS	8-03-003	JED	8-02-003	ONE-SHOT
8-05-007	DEATHS	8-05-008	FLOUR	8-02-002	JENNY	8-01-001	ONTOLOGICAL
8-05-006	DEBRIS	8-05-006	FLU	8-02-002	JIG	8-01-004	OP
8-05-008	DECLARE	8-06-006	FOCAL	8-03-004	JUDY	8-06-007	ORGANIZING
8-06-007	DECORATION	8-04-006	FOE	8-01-001	JUET	8-05-008	OUTGOING
8-05-007	DECORATIONS	8-02-004	FOLLOW-UP	8-06-008	JULIAN	8-06-008	OUTSIDERS
8-04-006	DECORATIVE	8-05-007	FOOTSTEPS	8-05-006	JUNK	8-06-007	OVAL
8-02-006	DECREASED	8-05-007	FORCEFUL	8-02-003	KERN	8-05-007	OVERBOARD
8-02-006	DECREASES	8-06-007	FORESEEN	8-07-007	KILLS	8-06-008	OVERLY
8-07-008	DEED	8-06-007	FRAIL	8-01-001	KILOMETER	8-02-003	OYSTERS
8-07-008	DEEDS	8-02-002	FRANCESCA	8-06-006	KINDLY	8-05-006	P**.*M
8-03-006	DELEGATE	8-01-001	FRANKS	8-01-006	KINETIC	8-02-003	P*H
8-04-005	DENOMINATION	8-05-007	FRANTICALLY	8-05-007	KNELT	8-03-005	PAD
8-05-007	DEPENDABLE	8-04-005	FRAUD	8-05-008	KNIGHTS	8-05-007	PALMS
8-04-005	DEPICTED	8-03-006	FRENCHMAN	8-03-003	KNITTED	8-02-002	PAM
8-04-007	DEPRIVED	8-02-002	FRESCO	8-06-008	KNOT	8-01-001	PAPA-SAN
8-05-007	DES	8-05-007	FRESHMAN	8-05-008	KNUCKLES	8-01-007	PARAMETERS
8-06-008	DESCENDED	8-04-008	FROWNED	8-01-001	KRIM'S	8-01-001	PARASYMPATHETIC
8-03-005	DETECTABLE	8-05-006	FULLER	8-04-005	LAKES	8-07-008	PARDON
8-05-007	DETERRENT	8-04-006	FURIOUS	8-04-006	LEAGUES	8-03-006	PARLIAMENTARY
8-05-007	DEVISE	8-05-006	GAIETY	8-03-006	LIBERATED	8-07-008	PATHETIC
8-06-006	DIAGRAMS	8-03-004	GAIT	8-03-005	LIBERTIES	8-07-007	PEAKS
8-04-006	DIAMOND	8-01-002	GARIBALDI'S	8-06-008	LIFTING	8-06-007	PECULIARLY
8-03-008	DIFFERENTIATION	8-07-007	GAZING	8-04-008	LOGS	8-05-006	PEER
8-05-008	DIMINISHING	8-05-008	GENEROUSLY	8-01-001	LOLOTTE	8-05-007	PEERS
8-06-007	DIRECTIONAL	8-02-003	GEOLOGICAL	8-06-008	LONE	8-06-008	PENETRATED
8-04-008	DISAPPEARANCE	8-04-005	GIBSON	8-02-002	LOTION	8-06-007	PERIL
8-07-008	DISCARDED	8-04-008	GLANCING	8-02-002	LOWER-CLASS	8-05-008	PERILOUS
8-05-007	DISCERNIBLE	8-02-002	GLUE	8-04-005	LT	8-03-006	PERIPHERAL
8-06-007	DISCONTENT	8-04-007	GOVERNORS	8-02-003	LUCIA	8-04-006	PERPETUAL
8-07-008	DISMAL	8-06-007	GRACEFULLY	8-01-001	MACKLIN	8-04-007	PERRY
8-02-007	DISPATCH	8-04-008	GRANTING	8-02-002	MAGNETISM	8-04-008	PET
8-04-006	DISPELLED	8-01-001	GRATT	8-03-004	MAHOGANY	8-03-003	PETERSON
8-04-006	DISPUTES	8-02-002	GREASY	8-03-003	MAILING	8-02-004	PETITIONS
8-06-008	DISTASTE	8-05-005	GRINDING	8-01-001	MALRAUX'S	8-06-007	PETTY
8-04-006	DIVIDENDS	8-06-007	GUESSING	8-02-003	MAMMA	8-01-001	PHONEMIC
8-06-008	DIVORCED	8-01-001	GUIDEPOSTS	8-05-008	MANAGING	8-05-007	PIG
8-01-001	DOATY	8-06-007	HALF-HOUR	8-03-003	MANEUVERS	8-05-007	PILLOW
8-04-005	DOCK	8-01-001	HAMRICK	8-04-004	MANSION	8-05-006	PILLS
8-05-006	DOMES	8-05-008	HAUNTED	8-06-008	MANUSCRIPT	8-04-004	PILOTS
8-07-008	DOMINATE	8-05-007	HAUNTING	8-04-005	MARCHES	8-06-007	PITCHED
8-04-007	DOMINION	8-04-007	HEADLIGHTS	8-02-003	MARTYR	8-02-006	PITCHERS
8-01-001	DORSET	8-04-006	HEARINGS	8-06-007	MARX	8-01-001	PLANKING

8-06-007	PLOTS	8-04-004	SCOUT	8-04-004	THANKSGIVING	8-04-007	47
8-01-002	POETICS	8-07-008	SCRAP	8-03-007	THEMES	8-03-007	53
8-04-004	POLLOCK	8-06-008	SCRAPED	8-06-007	THIEF	8-03-005	58
8-05-008	POP	8-07-007	SEASONAL	8-05-007	THIRTIES	8-05-008	600
8-05-007	POPULATIONS	8-03-005	SECURITIES	8-02-002	THORNBURG	8-04-005	61
8-04-008	POSSESSES	8-06-007	SELFISH	8-07-008	THRUSTING	8-03-003	99
8-03-005	POST-WAR	8-03-006	SENSIBILITY	8-01-001	THYROXINE	8-04-006	$2
8-05-008	POTENTIALITIES	8-05-008	SENSING	8-01-001	TOLL-ROAD	8-05-006	$5
8-02-002	POTTERS	8-05-007	SENTENCED	8-04-005	TRADED	8-01-002	**YF
8-06-008	PRACTICED	8-04-007	SENTIMENTS	8-03-004	TRADER	8-01-001	**ZG.
8-06-008	PREACH	8-06-007	SERIOUSNESS	8-04-008	TRAILED	8-01-002	*=*Q*$.
8-05-008	PREACHED	8-06-008	SETUP	8-05-008	TRANSMITTED	8-01-001	*=F(T)*$
8-06-007	PRECARIOUS	8-04-007	SHAPING	8-04-006	TRAPS	8-01-002	*=R*$
8-06-008	PRECAUTION	8-04-006	SHELDON	8-05-007	TRAVELER	8-01-002	*=S*$
8-03-003	PRECINCT	8-06-008	SHELVES	8-06-008	TRAVELERS	8-01-001	*A**U
8-05-006	PREDICT	8-04-004	SHERRY	8-06-008	TRICKS	8-02-004	*F*B*I
8-07-008	PREDICTABLE	8-05-006	SHIELD	8-07-008	TRIUMPHANTLY	8-03-006	*R
8-06-007	PREGNANT	8-04-005	SHOTGUN	8-02-005	TROPHY	7-06-007	AARON
8-06-007	PREMISES	8-03-007	SHOVED	8-01-003	TRUNK	7-06-007	ABANDONING
8-06-008	PRETEND	8-04-007	SHREWD	8-02-002	TUMORS	7-04-007	ABBEY
8-06-007	PROFOUNDLY	8-03-004	SIOUX	8-03-004	TURTLE	7-05-007	ABIDE
8-07-007	PROHIBITED	8-05-006	SIPPING	8-05-006	TWENTY-ONE	7-01-002	ABORIGINE
8-04-007	PROMINENTLY	8-02-002	SIXTY-ONE	8-06-007	TWENTY-TWO	7-03-007	ABSTRACTIONS
8-03-004	PROPAGATION	8-05-008	SKIPPED	8-05-006	TWO-STORY	7-04-004	ABUSES
8-03-005	PROSECUTOR	8-04-007	SLAPPED	8-01-001	ULTRASONIC	7-06-007	ACCESSORIES
8-04-006	PROSPEROUS	8-06-007	SLEEVES	8-04-006	UMBRELLA	7-04-005	ACCOMPANIMENT
8-01-001	PTOLEMY	8-03-004	SLIPS	8-07-008	UNCOMMON	7-06-007	ACCOMPLISHMENT
8-01-001	PUBLIC-LIMIT	8-04-005	SLUM	8-07-008	UNCONCERNED	7-01-001	ACCREDITATION
8-05-008	PUMPING	8-04-007	SLUMP	8-06-007	UNDERGO	7-02-002	ACCRUING
8-05-008	QUALIFICATION	8-04-007	SLUMPED	8-05-008	UNDERMINE	7-02-003	ACETATE
8-01-002	QUIRT	8-06-006	SLUMS	8-02-003	UNITARIAN	7-03-005	ACIDS
8-05-006	RADIANT	8-05-008	SMOKING	8-03-006	UNNATURAL	7-02-002	ACTIVATION
8-01-001	RADISH	8-04-006	SNARLED	8-05-007	UNSATISFACTORY	7-03-003	ADAPTATIONS
8-05-008	RAGED	8-01-001	SOCIAL-CLASS	8-04-005	UNSTABLE	7-05-006	ADLAI
8-02-003	RAYBURN'S	8-05-006	SOLVING	8-06-007	UPSIDE	7-02-003	ADOLESCENTS
8-05-006	REALISTICALLY	8-04-006	SOPHISTICATION	8-02-002	URBANIZATION	7-02-002	AERATION
8-06-007	REASSURANCE	8-01-001	SORBED	8-06-007	URGES	7-01-001	AEROSOL
8-04-006	RECIPE	8-03-005	SOUTHERNER	8-05-008	USABLE	7-07-007	AFFILIATED
8-04-004	RECIPROCAL	8-06-006	SOUTHWARD	8-04-007	UTILIZING	7-04-005	AFLOAT
8-03-007	RECITAL	8-05-007	SPACED	8-06-007	VARIETIES	7-05-006	AGREEING
8-05-007	RECOMMENDING	8-04-006	SPECULATIVE	8-02-002	VECCHIO	7-03-007	AIDING
8-04-006	RECREATIONAL	8-07-008	SPENDS	8-07-007	VEIL	7-04-007	AIRBORNE
8-06-006	RECRUITS	8-03-007	SPHERICAL	8-02-004	VERANDA	7-05-007	AIRY
8-01-001	REFERRALS	8-02-003	SPINDLE	8-03-007	VICTORIA	7-01-004	ALA
8-04-008	RELATES	8-02-003	SPIRAL	8-05-008	VICTORIAN	7-02-002	ALGAE
8-06-007	RELEASES	8-04-007	SPIRITED	8-05-007	VINES	7-01-002	ALMA
8-04-008	RELIED	8-02-002	SPOILAGE	8-06-008	WANDER	7-04-007	ALTERATION
8-05-008	RELISH	8-03-004	SPRAYING	8-05-008	WANDERED	7-03-005	ALTERATIONS
8-07-008	REMINDER	8-05-008	SPRUNG	8-04-006	WARDROBE	7-07-007	ALTERNATELY
8-04-007	REMINDS	8-04-007	STAFFS	8-04-006	WARMLY	7-03-007	AMBIGUITIES
8-06-008	REMOVING	8-03-005	STAG	8-06-007	WEAKER	7-03-004	AMBUSH
8-04-007	RENEWAL	8-05-007	STAIRCASE	8-03-007	WEEK'S	7-04-007	AMENDMENTS
8-06-007	REPAIRS	8-06-008	STAMP	8-06-007	WEEPING	7-05-006	AMUSEMENT
8-05-007	REPEL	8-06-007	STATESMEN	8-02-003	WENDELL	7-02-003	ANALYST
8-05-007	REQUESTING	8-06-007	STATUTES	8-05-007	WESTON	7-04-005	ANARCHY
8-06-008	RESEMBLE	8-08-008	STICKING	8-02-003	WESTWARD	7-05-007	ANCESTOR
8-07-007	RESEMBLED	8-05-008	STIFFENED	8-01-002	WHEREOF	7-01-001	ANDRENA
8-04-008	RESENT	8-03-005	STOOL	8-05-007	WINKED	7-05-007	ANGRILY
8-07-008	RESENTED	8-06-008	STOPS	8-04-007	WINNER	7-06-007	ANKLES
8-06-006	RESERVATION	8-06-006	STORMY	8-04-005	WINS	7-04-005	ANNA
8-04-006	RESIDUE	8-05-007	STRAIGHTFORWARD	8-05-007	WIRY	7-02-002	ANNAPOLIS
8-01-001	RESPONDENT	8-06-008	STRAINS	8-05-008	WISELY	7-05-007	ANNOUNCING
8-01-001	RESPONDENTS	8-08-008	STRANGELY	8-04-005	WITCHES	7-05-007	ANNOYED
8-01-001	RESTORATIVE	8-02-007	STRANGERS	8-05-007	WITHDRAW	7-02-002	ANTELOPE
8-05-008	RESTRICTION	8-01-001	STRASBOURG	8-05-008	WITHHELD	7-04-007	ANTHROPOLOGY
8-03-007	RETIRING	8-02-002	STRAVINSKY	8-03-005	WITHHOLDING	7-01-001	ANTITHYROID
8-04-007	RETREATED	8-05-008	STRIKINGLY	8-02-005	WOLFE	7-04-006	ANTS
8-03-007	REVERSED	8-06-008	STRUGGLED	8-05-008	WONDERS	7-02-007	APPRECIABLY
8-05-008	REVISION	8-04-008	STUMBLING	8-01-001	WORKBENCH	7-02-006	APPROXIMATION
8-06-007	REVIVAL	8-05-007	STUNNED	8-07-008	WORTHWHILE	7-05-006	APRON
8-05-008	REVIVE	8-06-008	STUPIDITY	8-04-005	WOUNDS	7-04-006	ARCHES
8-05-007	REVOLT	8-06-008	SUBDUED	8-03-004	WREATH	7-01-006	ARENA
8-04-004	RHODES	8-05-008	SUCCEEDS	8-05-008	WRECK	7-01-001	ARGON
8-06-008	RIGIDLY	8-04-007	SUCKING	8-06-007	YEARS'	7-06-007	ARRIVES
8-03-005	RITE	8-03-005	SULLIVAN	8-01-002	YIN	7-02-002	ARTERIAL
8-01-001	ROBARDS	8-06-008	SUNSHINE	8-05-005	YOURSELVES	7-03-005	ARTIST'S
8-06-006	ROCKED	8-05-008	SUPER	8-06-008	ZEAL	7-04-007	ASCERTAIN
8-04-004	ROOTED	8-01-001	SUPER-*SET	8-01-001	ZING	7-05-007	ASSERTION
8-06-006	ROT	8-05-007	SUPERSTITION	8-05-006	100**K	7-07-007	ASSISTED
8-04-007	ROUSING	8-04-007	SUPPLEMENTS	8-01-001	1040	7-04-006	ASSISTING
8-01-001	RUANDA-*URUNDI	8-04-007	SUPPORTERS	8-06-008	180	7-06-006	ATTENDANTS
8-04-007	RUINS	8-06-008	SURROUNDINGS	8-04-004	1861	7-03-005	ATTRIBUTABLE
8-05-006	RUMOR	8-02-003	SURVEYING	8-04-005	1896	7-04-006	AUTHOR'S
8-05-006	RUSTY	8-01-001	SWADESH	8-04-007	19TH	7-05-006	AUXILIARY
8-02-003	RUTH'S	8-04-007	SYMBOLISM	8-05-008	1914	7-05-007	AWAITED
8-01-001	RYUSENJI	8-05-007	SYMPATHIES	8-04-007	1920'S	7-04-006	AWAITING
8-05-007	SACK	8-04-006	TACTICAL	8-04-007	1921	7-04-006	AWAKEN
8-06-006	SAILORS	8-01-001	TACTUAL	8-05-007	1922	7-04-005	AXES
8-06-008	SALARIES	8-07-007	TANGLE	8-07-008	1938	7-06-007	BACKGROUNDS
8-05-005	SALOONS	8-06-007	TAUT	8-03-007	1963	7-03-004	BAIL
8-05-005	SANE	8-02-004	TAXABLE	8-01-001	2-56	7-03-005	BALLADS
8-05-007	SATELLITE	8-03-005	TEAMSTERS	8-04-007	2,000	7-04-007	BAN
8-05-006	SCANDAL	8-02-006	TELEGRAM	8-01-001	24-**JHR	7-05-006	BANG
8-05-007	SCHOLARLY	8-03-004	TERMINATION	8-06-007	350	7-03-005	BANISHED
8-05-006	SCHOLARSHIPS	8-04-007	TERRAIN	8-05-007	36	7-05-006	BAREFOOT
8-01-001	SCIENCE-FICTION	8-05-008	TESTIFY	8-04-006	38	7-06-007	BARGAIN
8-03-004	SCOTS	8-02-006	TEX	8-04-005	4TH	7-06-006	BARGE

7-05-007 BARREN	7-06-006 CHORD	7-05-005 DELIBERATIONS	7-05-005 EXCHANGED
7-06-006 BASIN	7-05-007 CHORE	7-04-005 DELINQUENCY	7-05-007 EXCITEDLY
7-04-007 BATHED	7-04-005 CHRONOLOGICAL	7-02-005 DELTA	7-05-007 EXCLUDE
7-02-002 BATISTA	7-05-006 CIRCUS	7-03-004 DEMONS	7-03-005 EXCLUSION
7-06-007 BATTLES	7-04-006 CITE	7-01-003 DENOTES	7-04-007 EXECUTE
7-04-005 BAZAAR	7-04-007 CLAD	7-04-007 DENOUNCED	7-06-007 EXHAUST
7-07-007 BEAST	7-01-001 CLERFAYT	7-05-007 DEPART	7-04-007 EXIT
7-03-005 BEATNIK	7-04-006 CLERKS	7-06-007 DEPARTURES	7-06-007 EXOTIC
7-03-004 BEATRICE	7-03-003 CLIENT'S	7-04-005 DERBY	7-05-007 EXPEDIENT
7-05-007 BECKONED	7-06-007 CLINGING	7-01-005 DESCRIPTIVE	7-03-006 EXPERIENCING
7-01-001 BEEBREAD	7-05-007 CLUTCHED	7-05-007 DESPERATION	7-03-004 EXPERIMENTING
7-04-006 BENDING	7-03-004 CO-OPERATIVE	7-05-007 DESPISE	7-05-005 EXPLODING
7-01-001 BENINGTON	7-03-004 COCONUT	7-04-005 DESSERT	7-05-006 EXPRESSIVE
7-07-007 BESET	7-05-006 COFFIN	7-02-002 DETERMINISTIC	7-04-007 EXUBERANT
7-05-007 BESTOWED	7-05-005 COL	7-04-005 DIAMONDS	7-03-006 EYED
7-03-003 BIDDING	7-05-007 COLLAPSE	7-02-002 DIANA	7-05-005 EYELIDS
7-04-004 BILLIONS	7-04-006 COLLECTORS	7-02-002 DIAPHRAGM	7-04-006 FACADE
7-05-007 BIOLOGY	7-05-005 COLLISION	7-01-001 DIARRHEA	7-04-005 FACTO
7-04-006 BIZARRE	7-07-007 COLONIES	7-04-005 DICTATOR	7-05-007 FACTUAL
7-06-007 BLAMED	7-04-004 COLORING	7-02-004 DIFFRACTION	7-05-006 FAINTLY
7-04-006 BLAZE	7-06-007 COMBINES	7-01-001 DIGBY	7-04-007 FARE
7-04-004 BLIZZARD	7-05-007 COMMENCED	7-06-007 DIGGING	7-04-006 FARMER'S
7-04-005 BLOSSOM	7-03-006 COMMEND	7-05-005 DIGNIFIED	7-05-007 FASCINATED
7-04-006 BLOSSOMS	7-03-004 COMMODITY	7-01-003 DILUTION	7-05-007 FASHIONED
7-01-001 BOA	7-04-005 COMMONWEALTH	7-05-007 DIRECTING	7-06-006 FASTEST
7-06-007 BODILY	7-05-006 COMMUNICATING	7-04-006 DIRECTORY	7-03-003 FATTY
7-05-007 BOLTED	7-01-001 COMPILER	7-03-004 DISAGREE	7-05-007 FAULTS
7-04-004 BONY	7-02-002 COMPLETIONS	7-06-007 DISAPPOINTING	7-02-002 FE
7-03-005 BOOKED	7-02-003 COMPLICITY	7-04-006 DISCOMFORT	7-04-005 FEARLESS
7-03-006 BOOTH	7-05-007 COMPREHENSION	7-03-004 DISCONTINUED	7-04-004 FERGUSON
7-04-005 BOUT	7-05-006 COMPULSORY	7-07-007 DISCOVERING	7-02-004 FIDEL
7-07-007 BOWED	7-06-006 COMPUTATION	7-03-005 DISCRETE	7-05-007 FIERY
7-02-003 BRAHMS	7-04-005 COMPUTE	7-05-007 DISCRIMINATING	7-05-007 FILTHY
7-03-005 BRAKES	7-04-005 CON	7-05-005 DISCS	7-02-003 FIREARMS
7-05-007 BRANDY	7-04-004 CONANT	7-04-005 DISMISSAL	7-03-004 FISHERMEN
7-01-001 BRANDYWINE	7-05-007 CONCEAL	7-01-001 DISOBEDIENCE	7-01-001 FLANNAGAN
7-04-006 BRAVADO	7-04-005 CONCENTRATES	7-03-004 DISORDER	7-06-006 FLATLY
7-04-007 BREADTH	7-05-007 CONCENTRATING	7-03-005 DISORDERS	7-05-007 FLATTERED
7-05-007 BREATHE	7-02-002 CONCESSIONAIRES	7-03-005 DISPERSED	7-05-005 FLEETING
7-04-004 BREEDING	7-04-007 CONCESSIONS	7-04-005 DISPLEASED	7-03-003 FLETCHER
7-05-005 BRIGADIER	7-03-006 CONCLUSIVELY	7-03-005 DISTORTION	7-04-007 FLOATED
7-06-007 BRISK	7-03-006 CONCURRENT	7-05-007 DISTRESSING	7-03-004 FLOORING
7-04-004 BROADCASTS	7-03-005 CONDEMNATION	7-02-003 DISTRIBUTOR	7-05-007 FOLD
7-06-006 BROADENED	7-02-004 CONDENSATION	7-04-005 DIVERSIFIED	7-04-007 FORE
7-05-007 BROADLY	7-05-007 CONFESSED	7-04-006 DIVERSION	7-02-002 FORENSIC
7-04-005 BROWNING	7-02-005 CONFIGURATION	7-05-007 DIVIDING	7-03-004 FORERUNNER
7-04-007 BRUISED	7-06-007 CONFINEMENT	7-04-004 DIVINITY	7-06-006 FORGETTING
7-06-006 BRUTAL	7-05-007 CONFINES	7-03-005 DOMINATES	7-02-002 FORKS
7-04-006 BUCKET	7-05-007 CONFIRMATION	7-06-007 DONATED	7-02-004 FORMATIONS
7-02-002 BUCKLEY	7-04-007 CONGENIAL	7-01-001 DONOVAN	7-04-006 FORTIES
7-01-001 BUCKSKIN	7-05-006 CONGRATULATIONS	7-05-006 DOUBLING	7-05-007 FORTIFIED
7-03-005 BUDGETING	7-03-006 CONSENSUS	7-04-006 DRAINED	7-06-007 FORTY-FIVE
7-05-006 BUILDS	7-02-006 CONSEQUENT	7-05-006 DRIPPING	7-05-007 FOSTERED
7-04-006 BULB	7-05-007 CONSTRUCTING	7-05-007 DRUNKEN	7-03-006 FRAGMENTARY
7-01-001 BULTMANN'S	7-03-005 CONSULTANTS	7-05-007 DUBIOUS	7-01-001 FRANKFURT
7-04-005 BUM	7-04-007 CONTEMPLATE	7-02-002 DUCLOS	7-01-001 FRANKFURTERS
7-04-005 BUNDLES	7-06-007 CONTINENTS	7-01-001 DUGOUT	7-01-001 FRONTAGE
7-05-007 BURDENS	7-03-006 CONTINUUM	7-04-006 DWELLINGS	7-04-005 FRONTS
7-02-005 BUREAUCRACY	7-02-003 CONTRACTUAL	7-01-001 DYSTOPIAN	7-05-007 FRUITFUL
7-03-005 BURKE	7-05-007 CONVENIENTLY	7-04-006 EASIEST	7-01-001 FUDO
7-03-003 BURNSIDE	7-05-006 COOPERATING	7-06-007 ECHOED	7-05-007 FUTILITY
7-04-004 BURR	7-02-002 CORONARY	7-03-006 ECONOMIES	7-06-007 FUZZY
7-03-003 BUST	7-04-007 CORPSE	7-04-004 EDGED	7-03-005 GADGETS
7-01-002 C)	7-04-004 CORPUS	7-03-004 EDITED	7-03-006 GALA
7-04-005 CABINS	7-04-007 CORRESPOND	7-06-007 EDUCATE	7-01-001 GALAXIES
7-04-006 CABLE	7-01-001 CORSO	7-05-006 ELASTIC	7-01-001 GALL
7-06-007 CALCULATING	7-01-002 CORTEX	7-03-007 ELBOWS	7-01-001 GAPT
7-05-007 CALLOUS	7-05-006 COSMETICS	7-05-005 ELEPHANT	7-06-006 GARBAGE
7-02-002 CALORIES	7-01-001 COSTAGGINI	7-03-003 ELIZABETHAN	7-05-007 GASES
7-06-007 CANADIAN	7-03-006 COUGH	7-04-004 ELLIS	7-05-007 GATHERINGS
7-04-005 CANCEL	7-06-007 COUNTRYSIDE	7-03-003 EMBASSIES	7-05-007 GAUDY
7-03-003 CANNING	7-05-007 COURTESY	7-04-007 EMBODIED	7-05-006 GAZED
7-04-006 CANNON	7-04-005 CRACKS	7-06-006 EMERGENCIES	7-01-001 GEELY
7-04-004 CANOE	7-04-004 CRADLE	7-05-007 EN	7-04-007 GENERALIZATIONS
7-04-005 CAPTAIN'S	7-04-007 CRASHING	7-05-005 ENACT	7-03-005 GENERATE
7-05-005 CAR'S	7-03-006 CREDITS	7-04-006 ENACTMENT	7-03-006 GENERATING
7-05-005 CARCASS	7-03-004 CROUCH	7-06-006 ENCLOSURE	7-06-007 GENEROSITY
7-04-005 CARGO	7-05-006 CROWNED	7-04-007 ENDEAVOR	7-06-007 GESTURES
7-05-005 CARIBBEAN	7-05-006 CRUISING	7-07-007 ENDLESSLY	7-02-002 GIBBS
7-05-005 CARTER	7-05-006 CRUSHING	7-04-007 ENDOWED	7-01-001 GIBBY
7-04-007 CASTLE	7-02-003 CUBIST	7-04-004 ENGAGES	7-02-002 GILES
7-01-001 CATATONIA	7-03-003 CURED	7-05-007 ENLARGE	7-03-007 GLARE
7-02-004 CEASE-FIRE	7-03-005 CURVED	7-06-007 ENLARGED	7-04-007 GLARING
7-01-002 CELTIC	7-06-007 CYCLES	7-06-007 ENLIGHTENED	7-05-007 GLEN
7-01-001 CENTRIFUGED	7-01-001 CYLINDERS	7-04-007 ENTIRETY	7-03-003 GLOUCESTER
7-06-006 CERTIFICATE	7-05-005 CYPRESS	7-02-005 ENVIRONMENTAL	7-05-005 GLOVES
7-03-004 CERTIFIED	7-03-005 DAG	7-04-007 ENVY	7-01-001 GORBODUC
7-04-006 CHARACTERISTICA	7-05-007 DAMAGED	7-02-002 EPITHETS	7-04-004 GORE
LLY	7-03-004 DAME	7-04-004 EQUITY	7-05-007 GORGEOUS
7-04-004 CHARLES'	7-03-006 DAMMIT	7-03-005 ERRAND	7-01-001 GOULDING
7-02-004 CHARTING	7-05-006 DARKENED	7-06-007 ERUPTED	7-04-006 GOVERN
7-05-006 CHATTER	7-05-007 DEALINGS	7-02-002 ESCALATION	7-04-005 GRADUATING
7-03-007 CHIC	7-05-006 DEFECTIVE	7-03-006 EVALUATING	7-05-007 GRAPES
7-04-006 CHILLED	7-04-007 DEFIANCE	7-02-002 EVANSTON	7-05-007 GRAVELY
7-04-005 CHIMNEY	7-05-007 DEFY	7-04-007 EVOKED	7-05-006 GRAVEYARD
7-04-007 CHOKED	7-02-003 DEI	7-04-007 EXALTED	7-04-006 GRAVITY
7-06-007 CHOKING	7-01-001 DEJA	7-04-007 EXAMINING	7-05-005 GREET

7-04-007 GRINNING	7-01-001 KARNS	7-04-007 NARROWER	7-04-006 PREMISE
7-03-006 GROPED	7-01-001 KENNAN	7-02-004 NASHVILLE	7-05-005 PREPARATORY
7-04-006 GRUDGE	7-03-006 KIDDING	7-03-005 NEGOTIATED	7-04-007 PREVAIL
7-06-007 GRUMBLE	7-04-004 KINGS	7-04-006 NEWCOMER	7-06-007 PREVAILED
7-05-007 GUARANTEES	7-02-002 KITTY	7-04-007 NEWCOMERS	7-03-005 PREVAILS
7-02-003 GUBERNATORIAL	7-06-006 KNIVES	7-04-004 NICHOLAS	7-05-007 PREY
7-03-005 GUILD	7-01-001 KODYKE	7-02-002 NICK'S	7-03-005 PRICING
7-04-005 GUNFIRE	7-01-001 KYOTO	7-03-005 NICKEL	7-03-002 PRINCETON
7-05-007 HAILED	7-04-006 LABOR-MANAGEMEN T	7-03-004 NIKITA	7-05-006 PRISONER
7-03-007 HALF-MILE		7-04-006 NOBEL	7-02-006 PROBATION
7-04-007 HALLWAY	7-03-004 LACE	7-04-007 NODDING	7-04-005 PROCEDURAL
7-03-005 HAMLET	7-04-005 LAMB	7-02-002 NOMENCLATURE	7-05-007 PRODUCTIONS
7-02-002 HAMM	7-01-001 LAMBS	7-05-007 NOTEWORTHY	7-05-007 PROMPTED
7-04-005 HANGED	7-04-005 LANDMARKS	7-03-005 NOTHIN	7-05-006 PROP
7-02-003 HANOVERIAN	7-04-007 LARGE-SCALE	7-03-007 NOVELTIES	7-04-007 PROPOSES
7-05-005 HARMONIES	7-02-002 LAUNDERING	7-04-005 NUMBERING	7-05-007 PROPRIETY
7-01-002 HARRINGTON	7-05-005 LEDGER	7-03-005 OATS	7-05-007 PROTESTING
7-04-005 HAZE	7-04-005 LEGION	7-06-007 OBEYED	7-01-001 PROTOZOA
7-05-006 HEADLINES	7-03-003 LEGISLATOR	7-06-007 OBSCURED	7-05-005 PROVISIONAL
7-06-007 HEARS	7-01-001 LEMMA	7-06-007 OBSTACLES	7-05-007 PROVOCATIVE
7-01-001 HEBEPHRENIC	7-03-005 LENDING	7-05-007 OCCUPYING	7-04-007 PROVOKED
7-02-002 HEE	7-03-005 LEO	7-01-001 OERSTED'S	7-02-003 PROXY
7-05-007 HEIR	7-04-004 LESSENING	7-03-005 OFFSPRING	7-05-007 PSYCHE
7-01-001 HEISER	7-04-004 LEVY	7-05-007 OLD-FASHIONED	7-02-005 PSYCHOANALYTIC
7-03-004 HERB	7-05-006 LEXINGTON	7-01-001 OLGIVANNA	7-04-007 PUNISHED
7-01-001 HEREUNTO	7-04-006 LIABILITY	7-04-005 OLIVER	7-01-001 QUADRIC
7-03-006 HESITATION	7-01-001 LILIAN	7-04-006 OLYMPIC	7-01-002 PUTT
7-01-001 HEZ	7-03-003 LINDEN	7-05-006 OPENINGS	7-04-006 QUARRY
7-06-007 HIGH-PITCHED	7-05-007 LINGER	7-02-003 ORGANISMS	7-03-006 QUARTERLY
7-04-007 HINTED	7-05-005 LINKS	7-03-003 ORGASM	7-04-007 QUIVERING
7-05-006 HITLER'S	7-04-006 LISTING	7-04-006 ORIGINS	7-04-006 RADIOS
7-05-006 HOOD	7-03-003 LOCKS	7-01-001 OSO	7-05-007 RAGS
7-02-005 HOOFS	7-02-005 LONGED	7-03-003 OUTBOARD	7-04-007 RAINING
7-05-007 HOOKED	7-01-001 LOOKUP	7-05-007 OUTRAGED	7-02-005 RANCHERS
7-05-005 HOPELESSLY	7-05-007 LORE	7-05-005 OVEN	7-03-006 RATTLING
7-04-005 HOPKINS	7-03-006 LUMP	7-05-006 OVERCOMES	7-05-007 RAUCOUS
7-06-007 HOTTER	7-07-007 LURE	7-07-007 OVERLOOKED	7-02-003 REACTOR
7-05-007 HOUND	7-04-006 LYRICAL	7-04-006 OVERWHELMINGLY	7-04-007 REASSURING
7-05-006 HOUSEKEEPING	7-01-001 MACNEFF	7-06-007 PACES	7-05-007 RECALLING
7-02-007 HUGGING	7-04-007 MAGNIFICENTLY	7-06-007 PACING	7-05-006 RECEIPTS
7-05-006 HUNCH	7-04-004 MAILS	7-04-005 PACKAGING	7-03-006 RECESSION
7-04-005 HUNTED	7-05-007 MANDATE	7-03-003 PAGEANT	7-04-006 RECIPIENT
7-06-007 HYPOCRISY	7-05-006 MANIPULATION	7-04-003 PAKISTAN	7-04-006 RECKON
7-04-006 HYSTERIA	7-02-003 MAO	7-02-003 PALESTINE	7-04-007 RECOGNIZABLE
7-04-007 IDIOM	7-04-006 MAPLE	7-03-004 PAPAL	7-05-005 RECORDER
7-05-007 IDOL	7-03-003 MAPPING	7-01-004 PARAMETER	7-02-002 RECRUITMENT
7-03-007 ILLUSIONS	7-04-005 MAR	7-05-007 PARTICIPANTS	7-03-004 REDHEAD
7-03-007 ILLUSTRATES	7-04-006 MARCUS	7-04-005 PARTICIPATES	7-02-005 REDUCES
7-05-006 IMMATURE	7-02-002 MARINAS	7-02-002 PATCHEN'S	7-04-006 REFLECTIONS
7-04-004 IMMORTAL	7-02-002 MARKSMAN	7-01-002 PATRICIA	7-05-007 REFUGE
7-04-004 IMMUNITY	7-01-001 MARTINELLI	7-04-007 PATTED	7-03-004 REFUGEE
7-03-007 IMPAIRED	7-04-006 MASCULINE	7-02-002 PAULING	7-04-006 REFUGEES
7-04-006 IMPLYING	7-05-006 MASTER'S	7-01-001 PAXTON	7-04-007 REGARDS
7-05-007 IMPOSING	7-03-007 MATERIALISM	7-02-002 PEAKED	7-03-006 REGISTRY
7-03-005 INACTIVE	7-04-006 MAURICE	7-05-007 PEASANT	7-01-003 REGRESSION
7-02-004 INCIDENCE	7-02-003 MAXIMIZATION	7-04-007 PENETRATE	7-06-006 REGULATED
7-06-007 INCREDIBLY	7-04-005 MC*CARTHY	7-05-007 PENSIONS	7-04-004 REHEARSED
7-01-002 INDICES	7-02-004 MC*CORMICK	7-02-006 PERCEPTUAL	7-05-006 REIGN
7-05-006 INEFFICIENT	7-05-005 MEADOWS	7-02-003 PERCUSSIVE	7-05-006 REINFORCED
7-06-006 INEXPERIENCED	7-04-007 MEDAL	7-05-005 PERFORMER	7-03-007 RELATE
7-03-005 INFERENCE	7-07-007 MEDITERRANEAN	7-03-006 PERSECUTION	7-04-006 RELAXATION
7-04-007 INFERIOR	7-01-001 MEEKER'S	7-04-007 PERSISTS	7-03-007 RELIANCE
7-06-007 INFORM	7-01-001 MENSHIKOV	7-06-006 PHONES	7-05-007 RELUCTANTLY
7-01-001 INFRINGEMENT	7-05-007 MENTIONS	7-02-003 PHOSPHATE	7-05-006 RENDEZVOUS
7-05-007 INHUMAN	7-04-006 MERCHANDISE	7-01-001 PHOTOCATHODE	7-03-003 RENO
7-05-007 INITIATION	7-04-007 METALS	7-01-001 PHOTOCHEMICAL	7-05-006 RENTED
7-04-006 INJECTION	7-01-002 METEORITIC	7-04-006 PHOTOGRAPHY	7-06-006 REPAY
7-03-004 INK	7-01-001 MEYNELL	7-03-005 PHOTOS	7-02-003 REPEAL
7-05-007 INNOVATION	7-01-001 MG/**JL	7-04-007 PINCHED	7-06-007 REPRODUCE
7-02-003 INSCRIBED	7-02-002 MIKE'S	7-05-007 PIPES	7-05-007 REPRODUCED
7-04-007 INSOFAR	7-05-007 MILDLY	7-01-001 PISTON	7-04-005 REPUTABLE
7-05-007 INSUFFICIENT	7-06-006 MINT	7-04-007 PLANK	7-04-007 RESIGNATION
7-07-007 INSULT	7-04-004 MISPLACED	7-01-001 PLANTATIONS	7-01-002 RESISTORS
7-04-006 INTAKE	7-02-004 MOLDS	7-02-002 PLATOON	7-03-007 RESPONDS
7-04-006 INTEGRATE	7-01-001 MOLESWORTH	7-02-004 PLAYER'S	7-03-005 RESTRAINING
7-02-002 INTERFAITH	7-02-002 MOLOTOV	7-04-005 PLEADED	7-03-003 RESTRAINTS
7-03-007 INTERVIEWING	7-03-003 MONASTIC	7-05-007 PLENTIFUL	7-03-005 RESTRICTIVE
7-03-006 INTUITIVE	7-06-007 MONOTONY	7-05-007 PLIGHT	7-06-007 RETAINING
7-06-007 INVALID	7-01-001 MONTPELIER	7-04-005 POLAR	7-04-006 RETARDED
7-04-006 INVENT	7-04-006 MORALLY	7-06-007 POLITE	7-05-007 REVENGE
7-06-007 INVENTOR	7-04-006 MORALS	7-01-001 POLYETHER	7-06-006 REVOLUTIONS
7-04-006 INVITES	7-01-001 MORE'S	7-01-002 POLYMERIZATION	7-02-002 RHINE
7-02-002 IODINATED	7-04-007 MORES	7-01-001 PONDS	7-04-007 RIGOROUS
7-04-005 IRONS	7-01-001 MORPHOPHONEMIC	7-05-007 POPULARLY	7-05-006 RIOT
7-04-006 IRRITATION	7-02-003 MOTELS	7-05-005 PORTRAITS	7-05-006 ROCKET
7-04-007 ISSUANCE	7-06-007 MOTIONLESS	7-05-006 PORTRAYAL	7-01-001 ROONEY
7-04-006 ITALIANS	7-01-001 MOUSIE	7-06-007 POSED	7-03-006 ROSES
7-01-001 JELKE	7-05-006 MOUTHPIECE	7-01-001 POSITIVIST	7-04-006 ROUGE
7-02-002 JEN	7-01-001 MULLINS	7-02-006 POSTAL	7-04-004 ROYALTY
7-05-005 JERUSALEM	7-04-006 MULTIPLIED	7-05-005 POSTCARD	7-02-002 RUSSELL'S
7-03-003 JIST	7-03-004 MURPHY	7-06-006 POSTPONE	7-06-007 RUTHLESS
7-05-007 JOINTLY	7-01-001 MUSSORGSKY	7-03-006 POSTULATED	7-01-001 SABELLA
7-05-007 JOYS	7-06-007 MYRIAD	7-04-006 POTENTIALLY	7-04-007 SAGA
7-05-006 JUAN	7-03-007 MYSTERIES	7-03-004 POWDERED	7-03-003 SALAMI
7-06-007 JUNCTION	7-05-007 NAIVE	7-04-007 PRECAUTIONS	7-04-006 SAMPLED
7-01-001 KAHLER	7-04-006 NAPOLEON	7-03-007 PREDOMINANTLY	7-04-004 SATELLITES
7-05-005 KARL	7-02-002 NARCOTICS	7-04-006 PREFERENCES	7-04-005 SATURATED

Code	Word	Code	Word	Code	Word	Code	Word
7-01-001	SAXONS	7-01-002	SUPPORTIVE	7-06-007	WARY	6-06-006	AGITATION
7-03-003	SCANDALS	7-03-004	SUPPRESSION	7-05-007	WASHINGTON'S	6-02-002	AGNESE
7-03-003	SCHUYLKILL	7-01-002	SURFACE-ACTIVE	7-05-006	WASTEFUL	6-02-003	AILMENTS
7-05-006	SCRAPING	7-05-007	SURGED	7-04-007	WATERED	6-02-002	AIRFIELDS
7-04-007	SCRATCHED	7-03-006	SURRENDERED	7-05-007	WEAKEN	6-03-003	AIRWAYS
7-04-006	SCREECHING	7-05-006	SUSPICIONS	7-04-006	WEEKENDS	6-05-005	AISLE
7-04-005	SCULPTURES	7-02-002	SWEDISH	7-05-006	WHIPPING	6-02-004	ALBUM
7-02-003	SEAMAN	7-06-007	SWELL	7-02-003	WHIPPLE	6-04-006	ALIENATED
7-03-006	SEATTLE	7-04-007	SWITCHING	7-03-004	WHITEHEAD	6-02-002	ALIGNED
7-04-007	SECURING	7-06-007	SWORD	7-06-006	WHOLESALE	6-01-001	ALL-*NEGRO
7-01-001	SELF-CERTAINTY	7-01-001	SYMMETRIC	7-01-001	WILLINGS	6-04-005	ALL-OUT
7-03-004	SELF-DETERMINAT ION	7-03-003	SYMMETRY	7-04-006	WINK	6-02-002	ALPHA
7-01-004	SEMANTIC	7-06-007	SYMPATHIZE	7-03-004	WINKING	6-03-005	ALVIN
7-05-007	SEPARATING	7-03-003	SYMPHONIC	7-06-007	WISER	6-04-005	AMBASSADORS
7-03-005	SERIAL	7-04-006	SYMPTOMATIC	7-05-005	WORKMEN	6-05-006	AMBIVALENT
7-04-004	SESAME	7-01-002	TABLESPOONS	7-06-006	WORLDS	6-03-004	AMBULANCE
7-01-001	SHAEFER	7-04-004	TAILS	7-03-006	WRETCHED	6-03-005	AMORPHOUS
7-02-003	SHEARING	7-02-002	TAIWAN	7-06-007	WRINKLES	6-02-002	AMPLIFIED
7-02-003	SHELLEY'S	7-03-007	TALENTED	7-02-005	WRIT	6-02-002	AMPLIFIER
7-02-002	SHERMAN'S	7-03-006	TALLER	7-02-004	YANK	6-02-004	AMPLITUDE
7-04-007	SHORTENED	7-01-001	TALLYHO	7-07-007	YEARNING	6-03-004	ANALYSTS
7-03-004	SHORTSTOP	7-02-002	TAMMANY	7-04-007	YIELDS	6-01-001	ANASTOMOSES
7-04-006	SHRILL	7-04-006	TAPERED	7-01-001	YOKUTS	6-05-005	ANCESTORS
7-05-007	SHRINE	7-07-007	TAPPED	7-07-007	YORK'S	6-05-005	ANEW
7-01-001	SHYLOCK	7-04-007	TART	7-05-005	YORKER	6-05-005	ANNIHILATION
7-01-001	SIDDO	7-03-005	TED	7-05-005	YOUNGSTER	6-05-005	ANNOUNCEMENTS
7-05-007	SIGHTED	7-07-007	TEMPERAMENT	7-01-001	YUGOSLAV	6-04-006	ANNOYING
7-06-007	SIGNING	7-06-007	TENTH	7-01-001	1/8	6-04-005	ANT
7-01-001	SIMPKINS	7-02-002	TERRACES	7-04-006	10**K	6-03-005	ANTISEPTIC
7-02-003	SIMULATED	7-05-007	TERRIFIED	7-05-007	110	6-03-005	ANTONIO
7-03-006	SINCERELY	7-05-007	TERRIFYING	7-01-001	1105	6-04-006	ANYONE'S
7-03-005	SINNER	7-03-007	TERRY	7-03-004	1819	6-05-006	APOLOGETICALLY
7-04-005	SKEPTICAL	7-01-001	TESSIE	7-01-001	1832	6-02-002	APPLES
7-03-004	SKIING	7-03-006	THIGHS	7-05-005	1908	6-05-006	APPOINT
7-05-007	SKINS	7-05-006	THIRTY-FOUR	7-04-007	1923	6-05-006	APPOINTMENTS
7-04-005	SLACKS	7-06-007	THREADS	7-04-007	1929	6-05-005	ARABIC
7-04-007	SLICK	7-03-003	TIBET	7-03-005	1930'S	6-01-002	ARISTOTLE'S
7-04-006	SLIPPERS	7-06-006	TIGER	7-03-006	1931	6-01-001	ARM-ELEVATION
7-05-007	SLIPPING	7-02-004	TITAN	7-03-006	1960'S	6-03-004	ARMSTRONG
7-03-005	SLOGAN	7-05-005	TOPPED	7-01-001	2**C37**JH	6-02-002	ARP
7-05-007	SLOPES	7-04-007	TORSO	7-01-001	203	6-04-004	ARREARS
7-04-007	SLOPING	7-04-007	TOTALED	7-05-007	24TH	6-03-003	ARROWS
7-05-007	SMOOTHED	7-04-004	TOURING	7-04-005	25,000	6-04-005	ARTIFICIALLY
7-05-006	SMUG	7-04-004	TOWNSHIP	7-05-007	33	6-05-006	ARTISTS'
7-01-001	SNELLING	7-05-005	TRACTORS	7-05-006	37	6-05-005	ASHES
7-03-003	SNOWS	7-06-007	TRAGEDIES	7-04-004	40**K	6-03-004	ASHORE
7-04-005	SOAK	7-07-007	TRAILING	7-05-007	5,000	6-04-005	ASSASSIN
7-05-006	SOCKS	7-03-007	TRANSFORM	7-03-005	52	6-04-006	ASSAULTED
7-06-007	SOFTENED	7-06-007	TRAPPED	7-05-006	57	6-05-005	ASSEMBLING
7-01-002	SOILED	7-05-007	TRIGGERED	7-02-003	69	6-05-005	ASSESS
7-05-007	SOLO	7-03-003	TROOPER	7-04-005	7**C30	6-04-006	ASSESSMENTS
7-06-007	SOMEBODY'S	7-05-005	TROTTED	7-01-003	7-1	6-04-006	ASSURES
7-02-002	SOMERS	7-03-007	TROUBLESOME	7-05-006	8,000	6-04-006	ASTONISHED
7-01-001	SONAR	7-03-006	TROUSERS	7-04-007	86	6-06-006	ASTONISHINGLY
7-01-001	SOPHIA	7-05-006	TRUMPET	7-01-002	9TH	6-05-006	ASTRONOMICAL
7-06-006	SPAIN	7-03-005	TRUSTS	7-04-007	$10	6-05-005	ATOP
7-04-004	SPEAR	7-02-003	TSHOMBE	7-05-007	$200	6-04-004	ATTACKER
7-04-006	SPECK	7-04-006	TUNES	7-04-007	$300	6-03-005	ATTAINING
7-03-007	SPECULATE	7-05-006	TWENTY-THREE	7-04-007	$50	6-04-006	ATTENDS
7-03-006	SPIRITUALLY	7-05-005	TWIN	7-01-002	**YC	6-05-005	ATTIRE
7-05-006	SPLENDOR	7-05-005	TYPING	7-01-004	*=*A*$	6-02-002	ATTRIBUTE
7-05-006	SPONGE	7-05-005	UGLINESS	7-01-001	*=*C*$-PLANE	6-01-001	AUGUSTA
7-03-005	SPONTANEITY	7-05-005	UNAVAILABLE	7-01-002	*=*C*$,	6-06-006	AUSPICES
7-03-006	SPORADIC	7-04-005	UNAVOIDABLE	7-02-002	*A.	6-02-003	AUTHORIZATIONS
7-05-005	SPRINKLE	7-05-007	UNBROKEN	7-01-001	*A*D*C	6-05-006	AUTOMATION
7-04-007	SPRINKLING	7-05-007	UNCOVERED	7-01-001	*A*M	6-03-004	AVANT-GARDE
7-01-001	SQUALL	7-07-007	UNDERTOOK	7-01-001	*C*D	6-02-005	AX
7-06-007	SQUAT	7-06-007	UNIFORMED	7-01-001	*C*D*C	6-02-004	AXE
7-04-006	SQUATTING	7-03-003	UNLOAD	7-01-002	*D*E*A*E-CELLUL OSE	6-02-003	BABY'S
7-04-006	STALKED	7-06-007	UNMISTAKABLE			6-04-006	BACHELOR
7-06-007	STAMPED	7-03-005	UNRELATED			6-01-001	BAILIFF
7-04-006	STARK	7-04-007	UNWILLING	7-03-004	*I*B*M	6-01-001	BANG-*JENSEN'S
7-05-007	STARVATION	7-06-007	UPHOLD	7-02-002	*N	6-03-004	BANGS
7-04-006	STATES'	7-04-005	UPTURN	7-01-001	*P*B*S	6-03-004	BANQUET
7-05-006	STATUES	7-04-005	UTILITIES ~	7-02-002	*S*A*C	6-02-003	BARLEY
7-05-005	STERLING	7-06-007	UTMOST	6-05-006	ABDOMEN	6-02-003	BARTENDER
7-04-007	STIMULATED	7-04-005	VA	6-06-006	ABORTION	6-04-004	BATES
7-05-007	STIR	7-02-002	VAGINAL	6-05-005	ABRAHAM	6-03-005	BATS
7-06-006	STRAIGHTEN	7-05-007	VALUATION	6-03-005	ABSENTLY	6-02-002	BAYONET
7-06-007	STRAINING	7-06-007	VANITY	6-05-005	ACCELERATING	6-05-006	BEAMING
7-04-004	STRAND	7-01-004	VECTORS	6-04-006	ACCEPTS	6-05-005	BEARINGS
7-05-006	STRANDED	7-02-003	VENICE	6-06-006	ACCIDENTALLY	6-02-003	BEAVERTON
7-05-006	STREAMING	7-04-005	VERBS	6-05-006	ACHING	6-01-001	BECKETT
7-05-007	STRIDES	7-01-001	VERMEJO	6-01-001	ACROPOLIS	6-02-002	BEECH
7-06-006	STRIVE	7-04-007	VICTORIES	6-04-005	ACTRESS	6-04-006	BELLOWED
7-02-002	STUD	7-02-002	VIENTIANE	6-03-004	ADHESIVE	6-02-002	BERMAN
7-02-002	STYRENE	7-04-007	VIOLATE	6-02-002	ADIOS	6-04-005	BETRAYAL
7-01-002	SUBGROUPS	7-02-003	VIOLET	6-04-004	ADJUNCT	6-03-006	BEWILDERED
7-05-007	SUBMERGED	7-03-007	VISIONS	6-02-005	ADMINISTRATION'S	6-01-001	BEY
7-04-004	SUBSCRIBERS	7-01-001	VOLTAIC			6-02-003	BIDS
7-04-005	SUBSIDIARY	7-02-003	VOWEL	6-04-006	ADMIRABLY	6-03-003	BIRTHPLACE
7-01-001	SUBSPACE	7-05-007	VULGAR	6-01-001	ADONIRAM	6-03-005	BISHOPS
7-04-005	SUBWAY	7-02-002	VULNERABILITY	6-03-005	ADVISER	6-01-001	BISQUE
7-01-001	SUMMED	7-06-007	WAGED	6-05-006	ADVOCATING	6-02-004	BITCH
7-04-007	SUMMED	7-02-004	WALLPAPER	6-05-006	AFFECTIONATE	6-04-005	BITING
7-05-007	SUMMER'S	7-06-007	WANDERING	6-05-006	AFFIRMED	6-02-003	BLACK'S
7-05-007	SUPERFICIAL	7-02-002	WARRIORS	6-01-001	AGGLUTININ	6-03-003	BLAKE

6-03-005	BLAZING	6-05-005	COMMANDERS	6-04-006	DISTRIBUTE	6-04-005	FLOWERING
6-04-006	BLINKED	6-06-006	COMMOTION	6-04-005	DISTRUST	6-04-006	FLUSHED
6-05-005	BLOOMED	6-03-006	COMMUNICATIVE	6-03-003	DIVAN	6-01-001	FOAMING
6-06-006	BLOT	6-03-006	COMPARES	6-05-006	DIVERGENT	6-03-004	FOCUSING
6-06-006	BLURRED	6-03-005	COMPARISONS	6-04-005	DIVIDEND	6-03-005	FOES
6-04-005	BLUSHED	6-02-002	COMPLEXES	6-01-001	DIVIDES	6-05-006	FOREFINGER
6-05-005	BOASTED	6-04-006	COMPLEXION	6-01-001	DOATY'S	6-03-003	FORGIVEN
6-01-001	BODYBUILDER	6-03-006	COMPLIANCE	6-05-005	DOCUMENTED	6-02-002	FORSYTHE
6-01-001	BONG	6-04-005	COMPLIED	6-04-004	DOINGS	6-05-006	FORTE
6-01-001	BONNER	6-05-005	COMPOSE	6-01-001	DOOLIN	6-05-006	FORTHRIGHT
6-01-001	BOOKING	6-05-006	CONFIDENTIAL	6-02-004	DOUBLES	6-03-006	FORTRESS
6-01-001	BOSIS	6-04-004	CONGESTION	6-01-001	DOWEX-2-CHLORID	6-05-005	FORTUNES
6-04-006	BOTHERING	6-03-005	CONNECTING		E	6-03-005	FORTY-FOUR
6-01-001	BOURBONS	6-03-005	CONSOLIDATED	6-05-006	DOWNHILL	6-04-004	FOUNDERS
6-02-002	BOXCAR	6-01-001	CONSTRICTOR	6-03-005	DRAFTING	6-04-006	FRAGMENT
6-06-006	BREACH	6-03-004	CONSTRUED	6-04-006	DRAMAS	6-03-004	FRAGRANCE
6-05-005	BREAKTHROUGH	6-03-004	CONTEMPLATING	6-01-001	DREADNOUGHT	6-03-003	FRAN
6-01-001	BREASTED	6-06-006	CONTEMPLATION	6-05-005	DREARY	6-06-006	FRANCE'S
6-03-003	BRICKS	6-04-006	CONTEMPORARIES	6-05-005	DRIFTS	6-04-005	FRATERNITY
6-05-006	BRIGHTLY	6-05-006	CONTEMPTUOUS	6-03-006	DRIPPED	6-05-005	FREEZE
6-04-006	BRITAIN'S	6-03-006	CONTEND	6-05-005	DRIVES	6-05-006	FRENZY
6-05-006	BROTHERHOOD	6-05-006	CONTINUANCE	6-05-006	DROWNED	6-04-005	FRIED
6-05-006	BROW	6-03-005	CONTOUR	6-02-003	DUCTS	6-04-006	FRIGHTFUL
6-01-001	BRUMIDI'S	6-03-004	CONTRACTOR	6-04-004	DUNN	6-01-001	FRITZIE
6-04-005	BRUSHES	6-05-006	CONTRIBUTORS	6-04-004	DUPLICATE	6-02-002	FRIVOLOUS
6-04-006	BRUSHING	6-05-005	CONVERSIONS	6-04-004	DUSTING	6-04-005	FROST
6-05-006	BRUTE	6-03-005	CONVICT	6-01-001	E)	6-01-001	FUCKEN
6-01-001	BUCHHEISTER	6-03-006	COOKIES	6-02-002	EAGLES	6-05-005	FUTILE
6-04-006	BUCKS	6-03-005	COORDINATES	6-02-003	EARTHLY	6-02-002	GALLON
6-04-006	BUFFET	6-01-001	COPENHAGEN	6-03-003	ECONOMIST	6-04-004	GALLONS
6-04-004	BUGGY	6-01-001	COPERNICUS'	6-04-006	ECSTASY	6-04-004	GANGS
6-01-001	BULL'S-EYES	6-05-006	CORD	6-04-005	EDUCATORS	6-01-001	GANSEVOORT
6-02-002	BURGUNDY	6-06-006	CORDIAL	6-01-001	EICHMANN'S	6-03-004	GARMENT
6-01-001	BURLINGTON	6-02-006	CORRESPONDS	6-05-006	ELABORATELY	6-03-004	GARMENTS
6-03-006	BURNT	6-04-004	COSTING	6-02-002	ELEMENTARY-SCHO	6-04-005	GAUNT
6-05-006	BURY	6-04-006	COTTAGES		OL	6-04-005	GENERAL'S
6-03-003	BUSES	6-02-002	COUGHLIN	6-04-005	ELICITED	6-03-005	GEOGRAPHIC
6-03-005	BUZZING	6-02-005	COUNCIL'S	6-03-003	ELMER	6-02-005	GEOGRAPHICALLY
6-04-005	CAESAR	6-04-005	COUNCILS	6-02-002	EMERALDS	6-02-002	GERMANIUM
6-01-001	CALDERONE	6-04-006	COUNTENANCE	6-04-006	ENDORSE	6-04-006	GHASTLY
6-02-002	CALIBRATION	6-04-006	COUNTRYMEN	6-04-006	ENROLLMENT	6-01-001	GLADDY
6-05-006	CALMED	6-04-005	COURTEOUS	6-01-003	ENTREPRENEUR	6-03-004	GLANDS
6-02-002	CALVES	6-02-003	CREAKED	6-03-004	ENZYME	6-03-005	GLEAMING
6-04-004	CANCELED	6-03-005	CRIES	6-01-001	EPICYCLES	6-03-003	GLENN
6-03-005	CANDIDACY	6-03-005	CRIMINALS	6-04-005	EPISCOPAL	6-03-006	GLISTENING
6-03-003	CANNED	6-05-006	CRIPPLED	6-05-005	EPISODES	6-05-005	GLITTERING
6-04-004	CANONS	6-06-006	CRIPPLING	6-03-005	EPOCH	6-04-005	GLOWED
6-02-002	CAPER	6-05-005	CRUTCHES	6-01-001	ERIKSON	6-04-004	GOAT
6-05-005	CAPITALIST	6-03-003	CUTTERS	6-04-005	EROSION	6-04-005	GOODBYE
6-02-002	CAPONE	6-04-005	DAKOTA	6-02-003	ESPRIT	6-04-005	GRANDCHILDREN
6-05-006	CAPS	6-03-004	DANNY	6-05-005	ETERNITY	6-04-006	GRANDEUR
6-02-003	CARBINE	6-05-005	DAPPER	6-05-006	EVER-PRESENT	6-03-003	GRANNY
6-03-003	CARPENTER	6-04-006	DARTED	6-03-006	EVOKE	6-05-006	GRAPHIC
6-05-006	CARRIAGES	6-04-006	DEADLINE	6-03-006	EXCEEDING	6-02-002	GRASSLANDS
6-04-005	CARTOONS	6-03-005	DEBATES	6-02-003	EXCERPT	6-02-002	GREER
6-03-004	CARTRIDGE	6-01-001	DEBENTURES	6-03-004	EXCLAMATION	6-05-006	GREETINGS
6-04-004	CARVING	6-02-002	DECKS	6-04-006	EXERCISING	6-05-006	GRENADES
6-05-006	CASTS	6-04-005	DECLINES	6-02-004	EXHIBITING	6-04-006	GRIPPING
6-01-001	CAUSAL	6-04-006	DECORATED	6-02-003	EXPANDABLE	6-06-006	GROUNDED
6-05-006	CAUTIONED	6-02-006	DECREASING	6-04-004	EXPEDITIONS	6-01-001	GROUNDWAVE
6-05-005	CAVES	6-03-006	DEDUCED	6-04-005	EXPERIMENTED	6-03-005	GRUDGINGLY
6-05-006	CENTENNIAL	6-01-001	DEERSTALKER	6-03-005	EXPLICITLY	6-03-006	GUISE
6-02-005	CENTRALLY	6-02-003	DEFENDANT	6-05-006	EXPLODE	6-01-001	GUNNY
6-01-002	CENTUM	6-04-006	DEFENDERS	6-05-005	EXPOSITION	6-01-001	GYP
6-05-005	CHANTED	6-03-005	DEFINITIONS	6-04-005	EXTRACT	6-01-001	GYRO-STABILIZED
6-01-004	CHAPMAN	6-04-005	DELINQUENT	6-04-006	FABULOUS	6-04-004	HAMBURGER
6-04-006	CHARACTERIZE	6-04-005	DELIVERS	6-02-004	FACTIONS	6-05-006	HANDICAP
6-04-005	CHARTED	6-02-002	DELLA	6-04-006	FAIRNESS	6-05-006	HANDING
6-05-006	CHATTERING	6-03-005	DEMONSTRATES	6-03-003	FAMILY'S	6-01-001	HANDLER
6-04-005	CHERRY	6-05-005	DEMONSTRATING	6-04-005	FARRELL	6-06-006	HARASSED
6-03-004	CHIEFS	6-01-001	DEMYTHOLOGIZATI	6-05-006	FASCINATION	6-02-002	HARCOURT
6-01-001	CHILI		ON	6-04-006	FEAT	6-05-006	HATCHING
6-04-004	CHIPPING	6-04-006	DENIES	6-03-003	FEATHER	6-03-003	HAWAIIAN
6-03-006	CHORDS	6-04-005	DEPICTING	6-02-005	FELLA	6-04-006	HAWTHORNE
6-03-005	CLAMBERED	6-03-003	DEPLETION	6-04-006	FETCH	6-02-003	HAYS
6-02-002	CLAMPS	6-04-005	DEPOSITS	6-02-003	FEUDAL	6-03-005	HEADACHES
6-04-006	CLAPPING	6-02-002	DESEGREGATED	6-01-001	FIBROSIS	6-04-004	HEALED
6-03-006	CLASSIFY	6-05-006	DESOLATE	6-06-006	FIGHTS	6-04-005	HEALING
6-04-006	CLEAR-CUT	6-05-006	DETECTING	6-05-006	FIGURING	6-01-002	HEARST'S
6-03-004	CLERGYMEN	6-05-006	DEVOID	6-01-001	FILLE	6-01-001	HEIDENSTAM
6-03-005	CLICHE	6-01-005	DIALECTIC	6-04-006	FILTERED	6-05-006	HEIGHTENED
6-06-006	CLING	6-02-004	DICTION	6-03-004	FILTERING	6-02-003	HELLENIC
6-04-006	CLIP	6-02-004	DIETARY	6-05-005	FINALE	6-03-004	HELPER
6-04-004	CLOSES	6-02-004	DIGITAL	6-05-005	FINANCES	6-05-005	HERDS
6-05-005	CLOUDED	6-02-005	DILUTED	6-01-002	FINGERPRINT	6-01-001	HERNANDEZ
6-05-006	CLUMSY	6-06-006	DIP	6-04-006	FIREPLACE	6-01-001	HESIOMETER
6-03-004	COACHING	6-03-004	DIPLOMATS	6-04-005	FIRMER	6-05-006	HI
6-04-005	COASTS	6-01-002	DIPPER	6-05-006	FIRST-CLASS	6-03-003	HICKORY
6-04-006	COCKED	6-05-005	DISBELIEF	6-03-003	FITZGERALD	6-03-004	HID
6-04-005	COD	6-02-004	DISC	6-05-006	FLAMING	6-03-003	HIGHLANDS
6-04-005	COHESION	6-05-006	DISGUSTED	6-03-003	FLARES	6-01-001	HIGHROAD
6-02-003	COIL	6-04-006	DISPLAYING	6-03-006	FLASHING	6-03-004	HIND
6-05-006	COINCIDED	6-04-006	DISREGARD	6-05-006	FLATTENED	6-01-001	HIREY
6-03-006	COLLINS	6-04-005	DISSATISFIED	6-06-006	FLOODS	6-04-006	HIRING
6-01-001	COLMER	6-02-003	DISSEMINATED	6-03-005	FLOPPED	6-02-004	HOMICIDE
6-03-005	COMB	6-04-006	DISSOLVE	6-05-006	FLOURISHED	6-02-002	HON
6-04-004	COMIN	6-03-006	DISTINGUISHING	6-05-006	FLOWED	6-02-002	HONOLULU

6-04-005	RESIDING	6-03-006	SLIT	6-04-006	TERMINOLOGY	6-04-005	WALLACE
6-04-006	RESOLUTIONS	6-04-005	SLOT	6-04-006	TERRESTRIAL	6-05-005	WALLET
6-04-005	RESPONDING	6-04-004	SLOWING	6-04-004	TERRIER	6-04-006	WARTIME
6-04-006	RESTORING	6-06-006	SMALL-TOWN	6-03-003	TEXTURES	6-04-004	WASTES
6-04-006	RETALIATION	6-04-005	SMOTHERED	6-04-005	THANKED	6-02-002	WAVELENGTHS
6-03-005	REVERSIBLE	6-04-005	SNACK	6-03-004	THANKFUL	6-06-006	WEAKENED
6-03-004	REVERSING	6-04-006	SNEAKED	6-05-006	THAW	6-03-005	WEAKENING
6-05-006	REVIVED	6-03-006	SNIFFED	6-01-001	THELMA	6-05-005	WEAKNESSES
6-03-005	REVOLVING	6-02-004	SNORING	6-04-006	THENCE	6-04-005	WEB
6-01-001	REXROTH	6-04-006	SOAKED	6-01-001	THERMOMETERS	6-05-006	WEEK-END
6-04-005	RIBBONS	6-03-003	SOCIALIZATION	6-02-003	THERMOSTAT	6-01-001	WEIDER
6-03-006	RIDDEN	6-03-003	SOFA	6-04-006	THINKER	6-01-001	WELCH'S
6-01-001	RIFLEMEN	6-04-005	SOFTENING	6-04-006	THINKERS	6-04-006	WELL-INFORMED
6-03-004	RIGHT-HAND	6-04-006	SOLACE	6-03-003	THINNER	6-02-003	WERNER
6-04-006	RIGHTEOUSNESS	6-03-004	SOLICITOR	6-02-002	THOMAS'	6-02-002	WESTFIELD
6-04-005	RINGS	6-05-006	SOMEPLACE	6-01-001	THOMAS'S	6-01-001	WEXLER
6-02-002	RINSE	6-02-004	SONATAS	6-02-002	THROAT'S	6-04-005	WHATSOEVER
6-05-006	RIP	6-03-005	SOPRANO	6-04-006	THROATS	6-04-004	WHERE'S
6-04-006	RIPPED	6-02-003	SOUVANNA	6-03-003	THROTTLE	6-04-005	WHEREUPON
6-05-005	RIVALRY	6-02-002	SOYBEANS	6-04-005	THROWS	6-05-006	WHICHEVER
6-04-005	ROAM	6-03-004	SPACING	6-01-001	THURBER	6-01-002	WHIG
6-02-002	ROBBERS	6-02-003	SPECTRAL	6-02-005	TIGHTENED	6-02-004	WHIGS
6-03-004	ROBBINS	6-06-006	SPEEDY	6-04-004	TILES	6-03-003	WHINING
6-05-006	ROBE	6-05-006	SPELLED	6-05-005	TINGLING	6-04-004	WHIRLED
6-01-001	ROBERTA	6-01-001	SPENCER'S	6-06-006	TOLERATED	6-05-006	WHISTLED
6-02-002	ROCOCO	6-05-006	SPINE	6-01-001	TOLLEY	6-02-003	WHITEY
6-01-001	RODGERS	6-05-006	SPOILED	6-02-002	TOOTHBRUSH	6-01-001	WHOLE-WHEAT
6-01-001	ROSSOFF	6-05-006	SPOON	6-03-003	TOPOGRAPHY	6-03-004	WILEY
6-05-006	ROTATED	6-01-003	SPORTSMEN	6-02-002	TORIES	6-05-006	WILLED
6-01-001	ROTOR	6-04-006	SPOTLIGHT	6-04-005	TORONTO	6-02-002	WILLIAM'S
6-04-004	ROTUNDA	6-05-005	SPRAYED	6-04-006	TOTALING	6-03-003	WILMINGTON
6-04-004	ROUTES	6-03-003	SPROUTING	6-06-006	TOTALITARIAN	6-03-004	WINDSHIELD
6-05-005	RUB	6-06-006	SPURRED	6-04-006	TOTALS	6-04-006	WIPING
6-05-006	RUDE	6-05-006	STAGGERING	6-02-002	TOUCHDOWN	6-01-001	WISMAN'S
6-05-005	RUE	6-04-006	STAIN	6-05-005	TOUGHNESS	6-06-006	WITHDRAWAL
6-04-004	RUMORS	6-06-006	STAIRWAY	6-05-005	TOWEL	6-05-006	WITNESSING
6-04-004	RUNAWAY	6-04-006	STANCE	6-05-006	TRAITS	6-03-005	WOLF
6-01-001	RUPEE	6-03-006	STARVING	6-01-001	TRANS-ILLUMINAT	6-05-005	WORKINGS
6-04-006	SACRIFICES	6-04-006	STEALING		ED	6-04-004	WORKMANSHIP
6-06-006	SADNESS	6-01-004	STENGEL	6-02-005	TRANSCENDS	6-03-006	WORKOUT
6-03-006	SAINTS	6-03-003	STEWART	6-04-006	TRAVERSED	6-03-005	WORKSHOPS
6-03-003	SALESMANSHIP	6-04-006	STIMULATE	6-03-006	TREACHEROUS	6-03-003	WRANGLER
6-03-005	SALTS	6-05-006	STINT	6-04-004	TREASON	6-04-005	WRAPPING
6-05-006	SANDY	6-06-006	STORMS	6-06-006	TREASURES	6-04-005	WRECKED
6-03-003	SAVAGES	6-04-005	STRAIGHTENING	6-05-006	TRIBAL	6-06-006	WRISTS
6-03-005	SAVIOR	6-05-005	STRANGLED	6-04-004	TROOPERS	6-04-006	WRITHING
6-02-002	SAX	6-01-002	STRATFORD	6-04-004	TUBERCULOSIS	6-03-004	WRONGS
6-04-005	SCAFFOLD	6-03-003	STRAYS	6-03-003	TUBING	6-02-002	YARNS
6-05-006	SCARCE	6-04-006	STREAKS	6-05-006	TUCKED	6-02-004	YELLING
6-04-006	SCENT	6-06-006	STRENGTHENED	6-02-003	TURBINE	6-06-006	YESTERDAY'S
6-05-006	SCHEMES	6-04-005	STREWN	6-04-006	TURNER	6-03-004	YURI
6-01-001	SCHIZOPHRENIC	6-05-006	STRICKEN	6-03-005	TWISTS	6-02-002	ZENITH
6-01-001	SCHNABEL	6-06-006	STRIFE	6-02-002	UDALL	6-03-003	ZION
6-01-001	SCHNABEL'S	6-03-004	STRONGHOLD	6-03-005	UH	6-04-006	ZONING
6-03-005	SCHWARTZ	6-03-006	STUNNING	6-04-006	UNBEARABLE	6-01-001	1-*JUNE
6-01-001	SCHWARZKOPF	6-03-004	SUBJECTIVELY	6-06-006	UNDERSTANDS	6-03-005	120
6-03-003	SCRATCHES	6-03-005	SUBMITTING	6-05-005	UNDERWORLD	6-02-004	13TH
6-03-003	SCULPTOR	6-05-006	SUBORDINATE	6-05-005	UNDULY	6-03-003	1815
6-06-006	SECRETLY	6-04-006	SUBTLY	6-05-006	UNEASILY	6-04-005	1883
6-04-006	SEIZE	6-01-001	SUBTRACTION	6-04-006	UNEVEN	6-03-004	1888
6-04-005	SEIZURE	6-04-004	SUCCEEDING	6-04-005	UNFRIENDLY	6-03-005	1895
6-04-005	SELLER	6-04-006	SUCCESSORS	6-04-006	UNHAPPINESS	6-03-005	1905
6-05-005	SENSATIONAL	6-03-006	SUCKED	6-04-006	UNIFORMLY	6-03-005	1919
6-05-006	SENSELESS	6-03-006	SUNDAY'S	6-04-006	UNIVERSALLY	6-05-005	1926
6-02-005	SENSIBILITIES	6-04-006	SUNDOWN	6-04-006	UNMARRIED	6-03-005	1934
6-01-001	SENSORS	6-05-006	SUNK	6-05-005	UNORTHODOX	6-04-006	1936
6-05-006	SENSUAL	6-03-006	SUPERIMPOSED	6-03-004	UNPOPULAR	6-04-006	1939
6-04-006	SENTRY	6-04-006	SUPPLEMENTED	6-06-006	UNPREPARED	6-05-006	25**K
6-01-001	SEPTA	6-02-004	SUPPLIER	6-04-004	UNREAL	6-03-004	28TH
6-03-005	SEQUENCES	6-05-006	SUPPRESS	6-05-006	UNWANTED	6-05-006	300,000
6-04-006	SERENITY	6-05-005	SURGERY	6-04-006	UPHELD	6-01-001	353
6-03-006	SETTLEMENTS	6-05-005	SURVEILLANCE	6-04-006	UPKEEP	6-03-006	39
6-05-006	SEVERED	6-06-006	SUSCEPTIBLE	6-05-005	UPWARDS	6-02-003	5**K
6-02-002	SEW	6-05-006	SUSPENSE	6-02-002	URANIUM	6-03-006	56
6-02-002	SEXUALLY	6-02-002	SUTHERLAND	6-03-005	URGENTLY	6-02-004	68
6-05-006	SHADED	6-01-001	SUVOROV	6-03-006	USERS	6-04-005	700
6-01-001	SHAFER	6-03-005	SWAM	6-04-004	UTAH	6-03-006	74
6-01-001	SHAKESPEAREAN	6-04-006	SWEETLY	6-04-005	VACANCY	6-05-006	76
6-03-005	SHATTERING	6-04-006	SYNDICATE	6-02-002	VANDIVER	6-04-006	95
6-05-006	SHAVE	6-03-005	SYNTAX	6-05-006	VANTAGE	6-04-006	$150
6-03-004	SHAVING	6-02-002	TABLESPOON	6-01-001	VAULTS	6-04-006	$2,000
6-01-001	SHERLOCK	6-04-006	TACT	6-03-005	VEILED	6-02-004	$20
6-04-005	SHIPPED	6-06-006	TAGGED	6-05-006	VEINS	6-04-006	$20,000
6-05-005	SHORELINE	6-01-001	TANGENTS	6-02-003	VELOCITIES	6-03-006	$5,000
6-04-006	SHOVING	6-02-004	TANNED	6-02-002	VENDING	6-02-004	$60
6-04-005	SIBERIA	6-05-005	TAPPING	6-03-004	VENETIAN	6-04-005	$800
6-05-006	SICKNESS	6-02-004	TAX-EXEMPT	6-03-005	VENTILATION	6-01-001	*=*C*$.
6-04-006	SIDEWISE	6-04-006	TEACHINGS	6-03-006	VERIFIED	6-02-002	*=*N*$
6-04-006	SIEGE	6-04-005	TEASE	6-03-005	VERSA	6-01-001	*=*N'*$
6-05-006	SIGNATURE	6-05-005	TECHNICIAN	6-04-006	VIBRANT	6-01-002	*=*Q*$,
6-01-001	SIMILITUDE	6-03-006	TEDIOUS	6-05-006	VICINITY	6-01-001	*=*R*$-STAGE
6-01-001	SINGLE-VALUED	6-02-002	TEEN	6-02-004	VIETNAMESE	6-03-003	*A'S
6-05-006	SINKING	6-03-005	TELEPHONES	6-03-005	VILLA	6-01-001	*B*T*U
6-03-004	SINNED	6-02-003	TEMPTATIONS	6-04-005	VIRTUOUS	6-02-002	*C*T*A
6-04-005	SITS	6-04-006	TENOR	6-06-006	VISIBLY	6-01-005	*F
6-06-006	SLAPPING	6-05-006	TENTATIVELY	6-04-006	VOGUE	6-03-004	*N*B*C
6-03-006	SLEEPY	6-03-005	TENUOUS	6-05-005	VOLLEY	6-01-001	*N*S

6-04-005	*R*C*A	
6-01-001	*S*A*A*M*I'S	
5-01-003	A)	
5-02-003	ABERRANT	
5-01-002	ABERRATIONS	
5-05-005	ABIDING	
5-04-005	ABREAST	
5-03-004	ABSTENTION	
5-04-005	ABUSED	
5-02-003	ACADEMICALLY	
5-01-001	ACALA	
5-03-005	ACCELERATE	
5-04-004	ACCELERATOR	
5-04-005	ACCENTS	
5-04-005	ACCESSIBLE	
5-04-004	ACCOUNTED	
5-05-005	ACHIEVES	
5-02-005	ACQUIESCENCE	
5-03-003	ACTIVATED	
5-03-005	ACUTELY	
5-04-005	ADAMANT	
5-04-005	ADAPT	
5-05-005	ADDITIONALLY	
5-01-001	ADELIA	
5-03-005	ADHERED	
5-04-004	ADHERENTS	
5-05-005	ADMINISTRATORS	
5-04-005	ADVANTAGEOUS	
5-03-005	ADVENT	
5-03-004	ADVENTUROUS	
5-04-005	ADVERSARY	
5-01-001	ADVERTISERS	
5-02-003	ADVISORS	
5-04-005	AFFECTING	
5-04-005	AFFILIATIONS	
5-04-005	AFFINITY	
5-03-005	AFFORDS	
5-04-004	AFT	
5-04-004	AGE-OLD	
5-04-005	AGENDA	
5-02-003	AGGRESSIVENESS	
5-02-005	AIMING	
5-05-005	AIMLESS	
5-03-004	AIRFIELD	
5-02-003	AIRLINES	
5-02-003	ALAN	
5-01-001	ALCOVES	
5-01-001	ALEC'S	
5-02-004	ALGERIAN	
5-03-004	ALL-IMPORTANT	
5-03-003	ALL-WHITE	
5-03-004	ALLEGATIONS	
5-03-004	ALLEVIATE	
5-04-005	ALLOCATED	
5-03-003	ALLOWABLE	
5-03-005	ALLUSIONS	
5-03-003	ALMIGHTY	
5-04-005	ALOOF	
5-01-001	ALPERT	
5-04-004	ALTAR	
5-03-005	AMBIVALENCE	
5-04-004	AMERICANA	
5-05-005	AMOUNTED	
5-04-005	ANCESTRAL	
5-01-001	ANEMIA	
5-04-005	ANIMATED	
5-05-005	ANOTHER'S	
5-01-001	ANTA	
5-02-003	ANTERIOR	
5-01-001	ANTI-PARTY	
5-01-001	ANTISUBMARINE	
5-04-004	APOCALYPTIC	
5-04-004	APOLLO	
5-04-005	APOLOGIZED	
5-01-001	APPESTAT	
5-05-005	APPLAUD	
5-02-002	APPLIANCE	
5-03-003	APPOINTEES	
5-03-005	APPRECIABLE	
5-04-004	APPREHENSIONS	
5-05-005	APPROPRIATELY	
5-03-004	APPROPRIATION	
5-04-005	APPROXIMATED	
5-02-004	ARBITER	
5-03-005	ARBITRARILY	
5-01-001	ARBUCKLE	
5-02-003	ARCHAIC	
5-01-001	ARICARAS	
5-01-001	ARIZ	
5-02-004	ARMY'S	
5-01-001	ARNOLPHE	
5-03-005	AROUSE	
5-03-005	ARRESTING	
5-01-001	ARTERY-PULMONAR Y	
5-03-005	ARTISTICALLY	
5-01-001	ARUNDEL	

5-03-005	ASCRIBED	
5-01-001	ASKINGTON	
5-05-005	ASS	
5-03-005	ASSERTS	
5-03-005	ASSET	
5-04-005	ASTONISHMENT	
5-04-005	ASTOUNDING	
5-03-004	ATHLETES	
5-02-005	ATMOSPHERES	
5-04-005	ATTACHMENT	
5-03-005	ATTENTIVE	
5-03-005	ATTRITION	
5-03-003	AUDUBON	
5-01-001	AUREOMYCIN	
5-01-001	AUTOCOLLIMATOR	
5-04-005	AUSTERE	
5-03-005	AUTHORITARIAN	
5-04-005	AUTHORIZE	
5-04-004	AUTHORIZING	
5-03-005	AUTOBIOGRAPHY	
5-04-005	AVENUES	
5-03-004	AVIATION	
5-01-001	AVOCADOS	
5-05-005	AWE	
5-05-005	AWED	
5-05-005	AWKWARDLY	
5-02-002	AXLE	
5-02-003	BACKLOG	
5-02-003	BACKWOODS	
5-04-005	BADGE	
5-01-001	BAER	
5-04-004	BAFFLED	
5-01-001	BALAFREJ	
5-03-004	BALCONY	
5-04-005	BALD	
5-01-002	BALF	
5-02-002	BALLPLAYER	
5-02-003	BANCROFT	
5-02-003	BANDSTAND	
5-04-004	BANISTER	
5-04-004	BANKER	
5-04-004	BANKRUPT	
5-02-002	BANTER	
5-01-001	BARBELL	
5-03-003	BARITONE	
5-03-003	BARNARD	
5-05-005	BARRAGE	
5-01-001	BARRE	
5-01-001	BARTH	
5-04-005	BATCH	
5-04-004	BATHS	
5-04-005	BATTLEFIELD	
5-04-005	BEACON	
5-03-004	BEAN	
5-01-001	BEARDENS	
5-04-005	BEARDS	
5-05-005	BEAUTIES	
5-05-005	BEDSIDE	
5-02-003	BEGOTTEN	
5-04-005	BELIEVERS	
5-04-005	BELLIGERENT	
5-02-002	BEQUEST	
5-02-003	BERGER'S	
5-01-001	BERN	
5-03-003	BERTHA	
5-04-004	BETH	
5-03-004	BETTING	
5-03-004	BEVERAGE	
5-03-004	BICYCLE	
5-04-005	BILL'S	
5-01-002	BIRDIE	
5-04-005	BISCUITS	
5-02-004	BIVOUAC	
5-03-004	BLACKENED	
5-04-005	BLACKNESS	
5-04-005	BLACKOUT	
5-02-004	BLASPHEMOUS	
5-02-003	BLEACHED	
5-04-005	BLEACHERS	
5-01-001	BLENHEIM	
5-02-004	BOARD'S	
5-05-005	BOARDED	
5-05-005	BOARDING	
5-02-002	BOGEY	
5-04-005	BOMBING	
5-03-005	BONN	
5-03-004	BOOKKEEPING	
5-03-005	BORDERING	
5-04-005	BORING	
5-03-003	BOROUGH	
5-01-001	BOSPHORUS	
5-05-005	BOSSES	
5-02-002	BOUN	
5-03-003	BOYD	
5-03-004	BOYHOOD	
5-04-005	BRACED	
5-02-004	BRADFORD	

5-04-005	BRANDISHING	
5-05-005	BREATHLESS	
5-01-001	BREVARD	
5-01-001	BRIAN	
5-02-002	BRIDE'S	
5-04-005	BRISKLY	
5-04-004	BROTHER-IN-LAW	
5-04-005	BROWS	
5-03-005	BUCKLE	
5-02-002	BUDD	
5-03-004	BUDDIES	
5-03-004	BUDGETS	
5-03-004	BUDS	
5-03-004	BUFF	
5-05-005	BULGE	
5-05-005	BULWARK	
5-05-005	BUMP	
5-05-005	BUNCHED	
5-01-001	BURNSIDES	
5-02-002	BUTCHERY	
5-04-005	BUTTS	
5-04-005	BUYERS	
5-03-003	BYZANTINE	
5-04-004	C'MON	
5-04-004	CABINETS	
5-02-002	CAFES	
5-02-003	CAIRO	
5-01-001	CALENDA	
5-03-004	CANDLES	
5-02-003	CANON	
5-03-003	CANS	
5-03-005	CAPACITIES	
5-04-004	CAPSULE	
5-02-004	CAPT	
5-03-005	CAPTIVE	
5-04-005	CARDBOARD	
5-03-003	CARESSES	
5-03-005	CARESSING	
5-01-001	CAREY	
5-02-003	CARRUTHERS	
5-04-004	CART	
5-04-004	CARTRIDGES	
5-03-003	CARTS	
5-01-001	CARVEY	
5-04-004	CASTRO'S	
5-03-004	CATASTROPHES	
5-03-003	CATASTROPHIC	
5-03-004	CATHARSIS	
5-01-001	CATKINS	
5-02-002	CATSKILL	
5-05-005	CELEBRATING	
5-02-004	CENSORSHIP	
5-04-004	CENTERING	
5-02-002	CERTIFY	
5-01-001	CERV	
5-04-004	CEYLON	
5-02-002	CHAMBRE	
5-01-001	CHANGEABLE	
5-01-001	CHANNING	
5-03-005	CHAOTIC	
5-03-003	CHAP	
5-04-004	CHAPLAIN	
5-05-005	CHARITABLE	
5-05-005	CHAT	
5-03-003	CHECKBOOK	
5-03-004	CHECKING	
5-03-005	CHEEKBONES	
5-04-005	CHEERFULLY	
5-04-005	CHEMICALLY	
5-04-004	CHERISH	
5-03-005	CHESTNUT	
5-01-001	CHILDHOOD'S	
5-04-005	CHILLING	
5-04-004	CHILLY	
5-01-001	CHINES	
5-02-002	CHING	
5-03-003	CHLORIDE	
5-03-005	CHOPPING	
5-01-001	CHOREOGRAPHED	
5-02-002	CHOREOGRAPHER	
5-03-005	CHRISTOPHER	
5-03-005	CHRONICLE	
5-04-005	CHRONOLOGY	
5-04-004	CHUCKLE	
5-03-003	CHUNKS	
5-01-001	CICERO	
5-04-004	CIRCULATING	
5-02-005	CITATION	
5-02-002	CLAIMANTS	
5-03-005	CLARIFICATION	
5-05-005	CLASH	
5-04-004	CLASSROOMS	
5-04-005	CLATTERED	
5-04-005	CLENCHED	
5-02-002	CLERK'S	
5-03-004	CLICHES	
5-04-005	CLIFFORD	

5-05-005	CLOTHED	
5-02-004	CLUBHOUSE	
5-04-005	CLUSTERS	
5-04-005	CLUTCH	
5-02-005	COACHES	
5-01-001	COCHANNEL	
5-02-003	COCK	
5-01-001	COE	
5-05-005	COHERENT	
5-02-003	COINCIDES	
5-04-005	COLDER	
5-04-005	COLLECTS	
5-03-005	COLUMNIST	
5-04-005	COMEDIAN	
5-03-003	COMFORTS	
5-04-005	COMMENDABLE	
5-04-005	COMMENTING	
5-05-005	COMMITTING	
5-02-002	COMMUNES	
5-01-001	COMMUNESE	
5-03-004	COMMUTING	
5-05-005	COMPASSION	
5-03-005	COMPETENTLY	
5-04-005	COMPLAINING	
5-03-005	COMPLETES	
5-04-005	COMPLICATIONS	
5-05-005	COMPLY	
5-04-005	COMPREHEND	
5-04-005	COMPUTERS	
5-03-005	CONCERTOS	
5-01-001	CONCHITA	
5-02-002	CONDITIONERS	
5-02-004	CONDUCTIVITY	
5-05-005	CONFERRED	
5-03-005	CONFORMS	
5-03-005	CONFRONTS	
5-04-005	CONFUSE	
5-01-001	CONJUGATED	
5-03-005	CONNOTATION	
5-04-005	CONSPICUOUS	
5-02-002	CONSTABLE	
5-02-003	CONSTANCY	
5-02-004	CONSTITUENT	
5-04-005	CONSUMING	
5-05-005	CONTEMPLATED	
5-04-004	CONTENDS	
5-05-005	CONTESTANTS	
5-04-004	CONTINGENCIES	
5-03-004	CONTINUAL	
5-02-005	CONTRADICTIONS	
5-05-005	CONVERSE	
5-03-004	CONVERTS	
5-01-001	COO**OPERATION	
5-05-005	COOLLY	
5-02-003	COOLNESS	
5-01-003	COORDINATOR	
5-03-003	CORAL	
5-04-004	CORINTHIAN	
5-04-004	CORNELL	
5-03-004	CORONER	
5-02-002	CORPORATION'S	
5-05-005	CORPSES	
5-03-004	CORRAL	
5-05-005	CORRECTION	
5-04-004	CORRESPONDENTS	
5-03-005	CORRUPTIBLE	
5-02-002	COUNCILMAN	
5-03-004	COUNTERPOINT	
5-02-002	COUNTIN	
5-01-001	COUPERIN	
5-01-001	COUPLER	
5-01-003	COURTIER	
5-02-004	COX	
5-04-005	CRAFTSMANSHIP	
5-04-004	CRANE	
5-03-003	CRATERS	
5-04-005	CREAKING	
5-01-001	CREEK-*TURN	
5-02-002	CRIB	
5-01-001	CRITICALITY	
5-04-005	CRITICALLY	
5-04-005	CROPPED	
5-02-002	CROSBY	
5-04-004	CROSS-SECTION	
5-04-005	CROWDING	
5-02-003	CRYSTALLINE	
5-01-001	CRYSTALLOGRAPHI C	
5-02-003	CUBANS	
5-04-005	CULMINATES	
5-03-005	CULTURALLY	
5-01-001	CUNARD	
5-04-005	CUNNING	
5-02-002	CUNNINGHAM	
5-03-005	CURLY	
5-01-003	CURVATURE	
5-02-002	CURZON	

Code	Word	Code	Word	Code	Word	Code	Word
5-01-001	CUSTER	5-03-003	DRS	5-01-002	FAIRWAY	5-04-005	GLITTER
5-03-004	CUTE	5-03-005	DRUGGED	5-04-005	FAITHFULLY	5-02-002	GLYCERINE
5-04-004	CZECHOSLOVAKIA	5-01-001	DRUGSTORE	5-04-005	FAMED	5-01-001	GODOT
5-01-001	DAER	5-04-005	DUCKED	5-04-005	FANNING	5-02-004	GOOD-BY
5-03-003	DALE	5-02-003	DUEL	5-01-001	FAROUK	5-04-005	GOOD-BYE
5-04-004	DAM	5-04-005	DYNAMITE	5-05-005	FASHIONS	5-01-001	GOSSON
5-03-004	DARES	5-01-001	DYNASTY	5-01-001	FAVRE	5-04-004	GOTTA
5-01-001	DE*KALB	5-05-005	EAGLE	5-04-005	FEARING	5-01-001	GRA**DFIN
5-02-003	DEACON	5-01-003	EARTHMEN	5-05-005	FERTILE	5-05-005	GRABBING
5-04-005	DEBATED	5-02-003	EASEL	5-02-005	FERVENT	5-01-001	GRABSKI
5-02-003	DEBUTANTE	5-01-001	EASTWICK	5-02-002	FIBERGLAS	5-02-003	GRADIENTS
5-04-005	DECEIVED	5-04-005	ECONOMISTS	5-02-003	FIBROUS	5-01-003	GRADY
5-02-005	DECISIVELY	5-03-004	EDGING	5-03-004	FIGURATIVE	5-03-003	GRAFTON
5-05-005	DECORATOR	5-02-002	EDIBLE	5-04-005	FILLS	5-01-001	GRAMMATIC
5-03-004	DECREES	5-03-005	EDITING	5-02-002	FINE-LOOKING	5-04-004	GRANDSON
5-03-004	DEDUCTIBLE	5-01-001	EDWARD'S	5-03-004	FIREMEN	5-01-001	GRAPHITE
5-05-005	DEFERENCE	5-04-005	EGYPTIAN	5-04-005	FIREWORKS	5-01-002	GREATCOAT
5-04-005	DEFINES	5-04-004	EIGHTEENTH-CENTURY	5-03-004	FISHER	5-04-004	GREEDY
5-04-005	DEFINITIVE			5-04-004	FISHERMAN	5-04-005	GREEKS
5-01-002	DEFORMATION	5-01-001	EIGHTY-SIXTH	5-01-001	FISKE	5-04-005	GREENS
5-04-005	DELHI	5-03-004	ELAPSED	5-02-002	FISSION	5-03-004	GREETING
5-04-005	DELICACY	5-01-002	ELASTICITY	5-02-004	FLAGS	5-01-001	GRIGORSS
5-03-003	DELL	5-03-004	ELDEST	5-05-005	FLANKED	5-01-001	GROK
5-02-003	DENOTING	5-01-002	ELECTRODE	5-04-005	FLARED	5-04-004	GROOM
5-04-005	DENOUNCE	5-01-002	ELECTROPHORESIS	5-01-002	FLASK	5-04-004	GROPING
5-05-005	DEPRESSING	5-05-005	ELLIOTT	5-02-003	FLEMISH	5-02-004	GROUPED
5-04-005	DEPT	5-02-002	ELMAN	5-01-001	FLEXURAL	5-02-005	GUARDED
5-04-005	DESERTS	5-04-005	ELONGATED	5-02-004	FLICKED	5-03-003	GULLY
5-04-004	DESIGNATE	5-03-005	EMBARK	5-02-003	FLORENCE	5-04-005	GUSHED
5-05-005	DESIRING	5-02-003	EMBROIDERED	5-05-005	FLOURISH	5-01-001	GYROS
5-04-005	DESOLATION	5-01-001	EMILE	5-04-005	FLOWS	5-05-005	HABITUAL
5-04-004	DESPOTISM	5-03-003	EMMETT	5-03-003	FLUENT	5-04-005	HAIRY
5-04-005	DEVASTATING	5-03-003	EMPIRICALLY	5-03-004	FOGGY	5-01-002	HALF-BREED
5-02-002	DEVELOPER	5-04-005	ENCHANTED	5-03-004	FOOLS	5-02-004	HAMMARSKJOLD'S
5-01-001	DEVEY	5-04-005	ENCOURAGES	5-05-005	FORBIDS	5-01-001	HAMMOCK
5-03-005	DEVIL'S	5-04-005	ENCROACHMENT	5-04-005	FORECASTS	5-04-004	HAMPER
5-02-003	DI*MAGGIO	5-04-004	ENDEAVORS	5-05-005	FORESIGHT	5-01-001	HANCH
5-01-001	DI-IODOTYROSINE	5-04-004	ENFORCING	5-02-005	FORESTALL	5-05-005	HANDWRITING
5-03-004	DICTATED	5-03-005	ENGLANDER	5-02-003	FORMOSA	5-04-005	HAPPENINGS
5-02-003	DIEGO	5-04-005	ENGULFED	5-03-004	FORMULAE	5-03-005	HARDSHIPS
5-03-003	DIETRICH	5-04-005	ENHANCE	5-04-004	FRAGMENTATION	5-04-005	HARMLESS
5-02-005	DIFFERENTIATED	5-02-005	ENHANCED	5-04-004	FRANCHISE	5-03-005	HARMONIOUS
5-04-005	DINGY	5-04-004	ENJOINED	5-04-004	FRAUDS	5-02-002	HARPER'S
5-01-001	DIOCESAN	5-04-005	ENLIST	5-03-004	FREER	5-03-005	HARSHLY
5-05-005	DIPLOMAT	5-04-005	ENRICH	5-03-003	FREEWAY	5-02-002	HARTMAN
5-01-002	DIPOLE	5-03-004	ENROLL	5-02-002	FREEWAYS	5-01-001	HARTSFIELD
5-03-005	DIRECTS	5-04-005	ENSUED	5-04-005	FRIGID	5-01-001	HARTWEGER
5-05-005	DISABILITY	5-05-005	ENTAIL	5-04-004	FRINGED	5-05-005	HASTY
5-04-005	DISAPPEARING	5-04-005	ENTERPRISING	5-04-005	FRONTIERS	5-04-004	HATCH
5-04-005	DISCIPLES	5-03-004	ENTHUSIASTICALLY	5-02-002	FROZE	5-04-005	HAUL
5-04-004	DISCOUNTS			5-02-005	FRUITLESS	5-04-005	HAUNCHES
5-03-005	DISCOURAGING	5-03-003	ENTITLE	5-04-005	FULLEST	5-02-004	HAYES
5-04-004	DISCREPANCIES	5-03-005	ENTRENCHED	5-03-005	FUMBLED	5-03-004	HAZARDOUS
5-03-005	DISFIGURED	5-04-005	ENVIED	5-05-005	FUMES	5-03-005	HAZY
5-02-005	DISGUISE	5-01-001	EPHESIANS	5-03-004	FUND-RAISING	5-04-005	HEADACHE
5-04-005	DISINTEGRATION	5-01-001	EPIPHYSIS	5-05-005	FUNDAMENTALS	5-03-003	HELPLESSNESS
5-04-005	DISINTERESTED	5-03-004	EQUATED	5-03-004	FURNISHES	5-03-003	HEMORRHAGE
5-05-005	DISMAY	5-03-004	ERECTION	5-01-001	FURROW	5-01-001	HEMUS
5-03-004	DISMISS	5-01-001	ERNST	5-02-003	FURS	5-02-003	HEREINAFTER
5-03-004	DISMOUNTED	5-04-005	ESCAPING	5-04-005	FUSE	5-01-001	HERFORD
5-04-005	DISORGANIZED	5-04-005	ESCORTED	5-03-004	GA	5-02-003	HEROINE
5-03-004	DISPATCHED	5-03-004	ESPIONAGE	5-02-003	GABRIEL'S	5-01-001	HETTIE
5-04-004	DISPOSE	5-03-004	ESTATES	5-03-004	GAILY	5-04-004	HEYWOOD
5-03-005	DISRUPT	5-03-005	ESTEEM	5-04-004	GAL	5-01-001	HIBACHI
5-05-005	DISRUPTED	5-05-005	EUROPEANS	5-05-005	GALLANT	5-05-005	HIDES
5-04-005	DISSENT	5-04-005	EVACUATION	5-03-003	GAMBLERS	5-05-005	HIGH-PRICED
5-02-004	DISTINGUISHES	5-04-004	EVALUATIONS	5-02-002	GAMMA	5-05-005	HIGH-SCHOOL
5-04-004	DISTRACTED	5-02-003	EVANGELICAL	5-01-001	GANTRY	5-05-005	HIGH-SPEED
5-02-002	DIURNAL	5-04-005	EVASIVE	5-03-004	GARAGES	5-01-001	HILUM
5-03-004	DIVED	5-04-005	EVER-CHANGING	5-02-004	GARRISON	5-01-001	HIPPODROME
5-04-004	DIVING	5-03-005	EVIDENCES	5-01-001	GARTH'S	5-04-005	HITCH
5-05-005	DIVISIVE	5-03-004	EVOKES	5-02-004	GARY	5-02-004	HOARSE
5-04-005	DIZZY	5-03-005	EVOLVE	5-04-005	GASPED	5-03-004	HOLDERS
5-03-004	DO-IT-YOURSELF	5-05-005	EXAGGERATION	5-04-005	GASPING	5-04-005	HOLOCAUST
5-03-004	DOCTRINES	5-04-005	EXASPERATION	5-03-005	GASPS	5-01-004	HOMELAND
5-01-004	DODGERS	5-04-005	EXCEEDED	5-02-003	GEHRIG	5-03-004	HOMOGENEITY
5-01-002	DOLCE	5-04-005	EXCELLENTLY	5-04-005	GENERALIZE	5-01-001	HOMOZYGOUS
5-03-003	DONOR	5-03-004	EXCERPTS	5-04-005	GENERATES	5-02-004	HOOK
5-01-001	DONORS	5-04-004	EXCHANGES	5-02-002	GENETIC	5-05-005	HOPPED
5-04-004	DORIS	5-01-001	EXCHEQUER	5-04-004	GENIAL	5-03-004	HORACE
5-04-004	DORMANT	5-04-005	EXEMPT	5-01-001	GENTILE-*JEWISH	5-04-004	HORSE'S
5-04-005	DOWN-TO-EARTH	5-02-002	EXISTENT	5-04-005	GEOGRAPHY	5-01-002	HORSEPOWER
5-05-005	DOWNED	5-05-005	EXPANSE	5-04-005	GEOLOGY	5-01-001	HOSS
5-05-005	DOWNFALL	5-04-005	EXPELLED	5-02-002	GERTRUDE	5-01-001	HOSSES
5-04-004	DOWNS	5-03-003	EXPERIMENTER	5-02-002	GHETTOS	5-04-005	HOST'S
5-04-004	DOWNSTREAM	5-05-005	EXPIRED	5-04-005	GHOSTS	5-02-002	HOSTILITIES
5-03-005	DOZED	5-04-005	EXPLOITATION	5-01-001	GINNING	5-05-005	HOSTS
5-04-004	DRAB	5-04-005	EXPLORING	5-04-004	GIRLISH	5-01-001	HOTEI
5-04-005	DRAFTED	5-03-003	EXTANT	5-01-001	GIVIN	5-05-005	HOUSEWIVES
5-02-002	DRAINS	5-04-005	EXTRACTION	5-04-005	GLAMOROUS	5-05-005	HUH
5-05-005	DRAWERS	5-05-005	EXTRAVAGANT	5-04-005	GLAMOUR	5-04-004	HUM
5-02-004	DRILLED	5-01-001	FABER	5-04-005	GLANCES	5-03-005	HUMANE
5-04-004	DRIVE-IN	5-04-005	FACILITATE	5-03-005	GLARED	5-02-005	HUMANISM
5-02-003	DRIVER'S	5-04-005	FACTION	5-03-004	GLAZED	5-03-004	HUMILITY
5-02-002	DRIZZLE	5-04-004	FACULTIES	5-04-005	GLIMPSED	5-02-002	HUNTER-KILLER
5-01-001	DROMOZOA	5-04-005	FADING	5-04-005	GLINTING	5-02-002	HUNTLEY
5-03-004	DROUGHT	5-01-001	FAGET			5-05-005	HURLING

Code	Word	Code	Word	Code	Word	Code	Word
5-04-004	HURTLING	5-01-001	KASAVUBU	5-01-001	MANU	5-02-002	NEPHEWS
5-01-001	HYDROLYSIS	5-01-001	KEMBLE	5-03-003	MARKER	5-03-003	NEUTRALISM
5-01-001	HYS	5-03-003	KERR	5-03-003	MARROW	5-03-005	NEUTRALIZED
5-02-002	I**.*Q	5-04-004	KIDNEYS	5-01-001	MARSDEN	5-01-001	NEWBURYPORT
5-05-005	IDENTIFIABLE	5-03-004	KINDA	5-04-005	MARSHES	5-03-004	NOBLEST
5-04-005	IGNITION	5-02-004	KINDNESS	5-03-003	MARTHA	5-04-005	NONDESCRIPT
5-03-005	IGNORES	5-03-003	KINGSTON	5-02-002	MARTIAN	5-02-002	NORTHERNERS
5-04-004	ILLUMINATING	5-04-005	KITCHENS	5-02-004	MASTERED	5-02-002	NORTHWARD
5-04-005	IMITATE	5-04-004	KITTEN	5-02-004	MAT	5-05-005	NOTICING
5-04-005	IMMACULATE	5-02-002	KITTENS	5-05-005	MATERIALLY	5-05-005	NOURISHED
5-04-005	IMMORAL	5-05-005	KITTY'S	5-05-005	MATERNAL	5-03-005	NOVELTY
5-03-005	IMPEDED	5-01-001	KIZZIE	5-04-005	MATHEMATICALLY	5-02-003	NUGENT
5-02-004	IMPINGING	5-04-005	KNEEL	5-03-005	MATTERED	5-03-003	NUISANCE
5-03-003	IMPLEMENTS	5-03-005	KNEELING	5-02-003	MAXIMIZING	5-02-003	NUTRIENTS
5-05-005	IMPOSITION	5-03-003	KNOCKING	5-02-003	MAYER	5-02-002	O**.*E**.*C**.* D
5-05-005	IMPRACTICAL	5-02-004	KNOX	5-04-005	MD		
5-03-003	IMPUTED	5-02-002	KOREANS	5-03-004	MEASURABLE	5-04-004	O'*CONNOR
5-04-005	INACCURATE	5-01-001	KRUGER	5-05-005	MECHANIC	5-01-001	OAKWOOD
5-03-005	INCARNATION	5-03-005	LABORED	5-02-003	MECHANIZED	5-01-001	OBESITY
5-03-005	INCIDENTAL	5-04-005	LADY'S	5-03-005	MEDICINES	5-03-005	OBNOXIOUS
5-04-005	INCOMING	5-03-004	LAISSEZ-FAIRE	5-04-005	MEDIOCRE	5-03-003	OBSCURITY
5-04-005	INCONSISTENT	5-04-004	LANDSCAPES	5-01-001	MEE	5-03-004	OBSESSED
5-04-005	INCORRECT	5-01-002	LARSON	5-04-005	MELODIC	5-04-005	OBSESSION
5-03-005	INCUR	5-03-005	LAS	5-05-005	MENU	5-02-004	OBSOLETE
5-03-005	INDECENT	5-03-004	LATCH	5-04-005	MERGERS	5-03-005	OCCASIONED
5-04-004	INDECISION	5-04-005	LATITUDE	5-03-005	MERGING	5-02-003	OL
5-03-003	INDELIBLE	5-03-003	LAUNDRY	5-04-005	MERITED	5-01-001	OLE
5-01-001	INDIAN'S	5-03-003	LAVENDER	5-03-004	METAPHOR	5-04-004	OLIVE
5-02-005	INDIVIDUALIZED	5-05-005	LAWNS	5-01-001	MICELLES	5-03-003	ONE-
5-03-005	INDOORS	5-02-002	LAY-OFFS	5-01-001	MICROMETEORITES	5-03-004	ONE-MAN
5-03-005	INDULGED	5-01-001	LB**./CU	5-01-003	MICRONS	5-03-004	ONE-STORY
5-02-003	INDULGENCE	5-01-002	LEAKED	5-03-005	MIDDAY	5-05-005	ONE-TENTH
5-03-005	INERT	5-01-002	LEESONA	5-04-004	MIGRATION	5-03-003	ONESELF
5-02-002	INFECTIONS	5-02-004	LEFT-HAND	5-02-002	MILLIE	5-01-001	ONSETS
5-03-005	INFERIORITY	5-02-004	LEGACY	5-01-001	MILLIGRAM	5-03-005	OPERATIC
5-04-004	INFLATION	5-04-005	LEGALLY	5-01-002	MIN	5-05-005	OPPRESSED
5-05-005	INFORMALLY	5-04-005	LEISURELY	5-05-005	MINDFUL	5-01-001	OPTIMALITY
5-03-005	INGENUITY	5-05-005	LENSES	5-02-002	MINERALOGY	5-03-005	OPTION
5-02-004	INHIBITED	5-04-005	LENT	5-02-002	MINERS	5-02-003	ORATOR
5-05-005	INITIATE	5-03-005	LEON	5-04-005	MINIMIZED	5-04-004	ORCHARDS
5-02-004	INJECTING	5-01-001	LEONA	5-04-005	MINK	5-01-001	ORGANIFICATION
5-02-002	INJUNCTIONS	5-04-005	LESSEN	5-05-005	MINORITIES	5-04-005	ORGANIZATIONAL
5-02-002	INQUEST	5-04-005	LETHAL	5-04-004	MINORS	5-02-002	ORIOLE
5-03-005	INQUIRING	5-03-004	LETS	5-01-001	MINUTEMEN	5-01-001	OSLO
5-03-005	INSCRUTABLE	5-01-002	LEWIS'S	5-03-005	MISCHIEF	5-02-002	OTTER
5-04-005	INSECURITY	5-03-004	LIBERATION	5-03-004	MISDEEDS	5-03-003	OUT-OF-DOORS
5-04-005	INSIGNIFICANT	5-02-003	LIBRARIAN	5-05-005	MISGIVINGS	5-01-003	OUTING
5-02-005	INSTALLING	5-03-004	LIDS	5-03-004	MISSES	5-02-003	OUTPUTS
5-02-003	INSTALLMENT	5-04-004	LIEU	5-04-005	MISTRESS	5-01-001	OUTREACH
5-04-004	INSTANTANEOUS	5-05-005	LIGHTWEIGHT	5-04-005	MISUSE	5-02-003	OVERALLS
5-03-003	INTELLECT	5-03-004	LILLIAN	5-01-001	MIIYUKH	5-02-005	OVERCOAT
5-05-005	INTELLECTUALLY	5-05-005	LIMB	5-04-005	MOBILIZATION	5-04-005	OVERRUN
5-03-005	INTENSITIES	5-04-005	LIMBS	5-05-005	MOCKING	5-04-005	OVERTHROW
5-02-004	INTENTIONAL	5-03-004	LINCOLN'S	5-03-003	MODIFIER	5-02-005	OVERTURE
5-03-005	INTER-*AMERICAN	5-05-005	LINGERING	5-01-001	MOLIERE'S	5-03-004	OVERWEIGHT
5 03-004	INTERCONTINENTA L	5-02-002	LINGUISTICS	5-01-001	MOLL	5-05-005	OWES
		5-02-002	LIPTON	5-03-004	MOLLY	5-03-004	OX
5-01-002	INTERFACES	5-03-003	LIQUIDATED	5-05-005	MOMENT'S	5-04-005	PACT
5-05-005	INTERFERED	5-05-005	LIVELIHOOD	5-05-005	MOMENTARILY	5-05-005	PADDED
5-05-005	INTERLUDE	5-02-004	LIVERY	5-01-001	MONACLE	5-02-004	PADS
5-02-003	INTERMEDIATES	5-01-003	LOADINGS	5-01-001	MONEI	5-02-002	PAGEANTS
5-02-002	INTERRELATED	5-03-003	LOBES	5-02-002	MONOPOLIES	5-04-005	PALACES
5-02-002	INTERSTELLAR	5-02-004	LOCALITY	5-03-005	MONTE	5-03-003	PALETTE
5-05-005	INTIMATED	5-03-004	LODGING	5-01-001	MONTERO'S	5-03-003	PANTHEON
5-04-005	INTIMIDATION	5-04-005	LOFTY	5-05-005	MONTHS'	5-01-001	PARKHOUSE
5-02-005	INTRINSIC	5-04-004	LOGGING	5-04-005	MONUMENTAL	5-02-003	PAROLE
5-03-004	INVADE	5-01-003	LONG-RUN	5-04-005	MOODY	5-02-002	PARSONS
5-05-005	INVADERS	5-02-002	LONGHORNS	5-02-002	MORIARTY	5-05-005	PARTICULARS
5-04-005	INVALUABLE	5-02-004	LOUISE	5-02-003	MOROCCO	5-04-005	PATCHED
5-01-001	INVERSE	5-01-001	LOVELESS	5-02-002	MORPHOLOGICAL	5-02-002	PATRICE
5-01-001	INVERSELY	5-05-005	LOWERING	5-01-001	MORSC'S	5-03-003	PATTERSON
5-02-003	IRONING	5-03-003	LTD	5-03-005	MORTGAGES	5-05-005	PAVED
5-01-001	IRRADIATED	5-03-003	LUCIAN	5-03-003	MOTIFS	5-04-005	PEACEFULLY
5-03-005	IRREGULARLY	5-03-003	LUGGED	5-04-005	MOTIVATIONS	5-01-002	PEANUTS
5-03-005	IRRITABLE	5-05-005	LUKEWARM	5-02-003	MOTORISTS	5-03-004	PECK
5-03-005	IRRITATED	5-03-004	LULLABY	5-04-004	MT	5-03-004	PEDDLER
5-04-005	ISLE	5-03-005	LURCHED	5-01-001	MUCOSA	5-03-004	PEDESTAL
5-03-005	ISOLATING	5-05-005	LUSH	5-04-005	MUMBLED	5-05-005	PEELED
5-01-001	ISTANBUL	5-05-005	LUST	5-03-004	MURDERERS	5-01-001	PELHAM
5-04-005	ITCH	5-04-004	LUTHER	5-05-005	MURKY	5-04-005	PENANCE
5-01-001	JACOBY	5-01-001	LYFORD	5-03-005	MUSTACHE	5-02-002	PENDLETON
5-04-005	JAGGED	5-02-004	LYNN	5-03-005	MUSTN'T	5-03-004	PENN
5-02-002	JAGUAR	5-01-001	LYTTLETON	5-04-004	MYSTICAL	5-04-004	PENNIES
5-02-002	JASON	5-04-005	MA'AM	5-02-003	MYSTIQUE	5-02-005	PERFECTED
5-02-002	JEFFERSON'S	5-02-002	MAGNUMS	5-01-001	NAGRIN	5-05-005	PERIODICALS
5-03-005	JEROME	5-01-001	MAGUIRE	5-02-005	NANCY	5-02-005	PERIPHERY
5-04-005	JOCKEY	5-01-001	MAHZEER'S	5-04-005	NASTY	5-04-005	PERMISSIVE
5-04-004	JOE'S	5-05-005	MAKE-UP	5-01-001	NATE	5-03-005	PERPETUATE
5-01-001	JOHN-AND-*LINDA	5-02-003	MAMMALIAN	5-03-005	NATHAN	5-04-005	PERSUADING
5-05-005	JOKING	5-01-001	MANDO	5-04-005	NATIONWIDE	5-04-004	PERTAINING
5-03-003	JONATHAN	5-05-005	MANEUVER	5-04-005	NECESSITATE	5-01-003	PERTAINS
5-04-005	JOURNALS	5-05-005	MANIA	5-01-001	NEEDHAM	5-04-004	PERVERSE
5-02-004	JOYOUS	5-05-005	MANIFESTLY	5-03-005	NEEDING	5-03-003	PETERSBURG
5-04-005	JUSTIFIABLY	5-04-005	MANOR	5-02-004	NEGATION	5-03-003	PHALANX
5-04-005	JUSTLY			5-02-005	NEGLECTING	5-02-002	PHARMACY
5-01-001	KAFKA			5-04-005	NEHRU	5-01-001	PHILIPPI
5-02-004	KAPPA			5-01-001	NEOCORTEX		

5-04-005 PHONED	5-03-003 RANKING	5-04-005 SARGENT	5-01-001 SLOAN'S
5-01-001 PHONOLOGY	5-05-005 RANSOM	5-02-003 SATIN	5-01-001 SLOANAKER
5-02-003 PHOTO	5-04-005 RAPE	5-03-004 SATURATION	5-04-004 SLOGANS
5-04-004 PHOTOGRAPHER	5-03-003 RATIFICATION	5-02-002 SAUCES	5-03-005 SLOTS
5-03-004 PHYSICIST	5-03-004 RATIONALIZE	5-02-002 SAUSAGES	5-05-005 SLY
5-03-003 PICTORIAL	5-04-005 RATTLE	5-04-005 SAVES	5-04-005 SMELLING
5-03-004 PIES	5-03-003 RATTLESNAKES	5-03-003 SAYIN	5-04-004 SMITH'S
5-04-005 PILLARS	5-02-002 RE-ENTER	5-02-003 SCABBARD	5-03-003 SMOKY
5-01-001 PIMEN	5-04-005 READY-MADE	5-03-005 SCALES	5-03-004 SMOOTHNESS
5-05-005 PINPOINT	5-01-001 REALTOR	5-04-004 SCAN	5-04-005 SOARING
5-03-003 PIPING	5-01-001 REAMA	5-03-005 SCANT	5-04-005 SOFTER
5-05-005 PLAGUED	5-03-005 REASSURED	5-02-005 SCENTED	5-03-004 SOFTNESS
5-01-001 PLAINTIFF	5-02-002 REBS	5-01-002 SCEPTICISM	5-02-002 SOJOURN
5-03-004 PLANKS	5-05-005 REBUILD	5-03-005 SCHOOLING	5-02-002 SOLES
5-04-005 PLANTING	5-03-004 RECEDING	5-04-004 SCOOP	5-03-005 SOLOISTS
5-04-005 PLASTERED	5-03-003 RECEIVERS	5-03-005 SCORING	5-01-001 SOLVENT
5-04-005 PLATFORMS	5-02-002 RECEPTIONIST	5-03-004 SCORNFUL	5-04-005 SOMEONE'S
5-04-005 PLEAD	5-03-004 RECIPIENTS	5-03-003 SCOTCH	5-03-003 SOPHOMORE
5-03-004 PLEDGED	5-02-002 RECOIL	5-01-001 SCOURS	5-03-004 SOUNDER
5-03-003 PLOWED	5-03-004 RECOLLECTION	5-03-004 SCRAWLED	5-03-004 SOUTH'S
5-03-004 PLUMB	5-03-004 RECTANGULAR	5-03-004 SCREECHED	5-04-004 SOUTHEASTERN
5-04-004 PLUNGE	5-03-003 REDEVELOPMENT	5-03-005 SCREENING	5-01-001 SOUTHPAW
5-03-005 POISONOUS	5-05-005 REED	5-04-004 SCULPTURED	5-01-001 SOYBEAN
5-04-005 POKING	5-05-005 REFINEMENT	5-04-005 SEASHORE	5-01-001 SPACERS
5-03-003 POLARITY	5-05-005 REFINEMENTS	5-03-004 SEASONED	5-01-002 SPAHN
5-04-005 POLITENESS	5-02-002 REFLECTOR	5-03-003 SEATING	5-03-005 SPANS
5-02-002 POLYESTER	5-01-004 REFORMATION	5-04-004 SECOND-RATE	5-04-005 SPARKLING
5-01-001 POLYPHOSPHATES	5-04-004 REFRESHED	5-03-005 SECONDLY	5-04-005 SPARKS
5-01-001 POMPEII	5-02-002 REFRIGERATED	5-04-005 SECRETARIAT	5-05-005 SPARSE
5-03-005 POPULOUS	5-03-003 REGISTERS	5-04-005 SECURELY	5-04-005 SPECIALTIES
5-01-001 PORTAGO	5-04-004 REGULATORY	5-01-001 SEIGNER	5-05-005 SPIN
5-03-005 PORTRAYS	5-05-005 RELAXING	5-04-005 SELECTS	5-03-003 SPIRE
5-01-003 POTASSIUM	5-05-005 RELENTLESS	5-03-005 SELF-CONSCIOUS	5-04-004 SPITTING
5-04-005 POTS	5-05-005 RELENTLESSLY	5-04-005 SELF-CONSCIOUS	5-03-004 SPONSORSHIP
5-02-003 POWDERS	5-03-003 RELUCTANCE	ESS	5-03-005 SPORTSMAN
5-01-001 POYNTING-*ROBER	5-03-005 RELYING	5-03-005 SELF-CONTAINED	5-03-005 SPRAWLING
TSON	5-04-004 REMINDING	5-02-002 SELF-DISCIPLINE	5-04-004 SPRUCE
5-02-003 PRECINCTS	5-01-001 REMINGTON	5-03-005 SELF-EVIDENT	5-02-003 SQUARED
5-05-005 PREDECESSOR	5-02-004 REMOVES	5-03-003 SELF-EXAMINATIO	5-02-002 SQUIRE
5-04-005 PREFERS	5-03-004 RENTING	N	5-04-005 STACCATO
5-05-005 PRELUDE	5-04-005 REPELLED	5-02-002 SELF-SUSTAINING	5-05-005 STAGNANT
5-03-004 PREMIERE	5-04-005 REPERTORY	5-04-004 SENSUALITY	5-05-005 STAKES
5-04-004 PREPOSTEROUS	5-02-003 REPRODUCIBLE	5-02-002 SERGE	5-03-004 STALIN'S
5-03-003 PRESCRIBE	5-03-005 REPUTED	5-01-001 SERVO	5-05-005 STAMPING
5-04-005 PRESCRIPTION	5-03-004 RESERVES	5-03-003 SEVERITY	5-04-005 STATEN
5-01-002 PRESIDENT-ELECT	5-04-005 RESISTANT	5-01-001 SEWARD	5-03-004 STATIONED
5-04-005 PREVALENT	5-03-004 RESORTED	5-04-004 SHABBY	5-05-005 STAYS
5-04-005 PRICELESS	5-04-005 RESPECTABILITY	5-03-003 SHADOWING	5-03-005 STEAD
5-04-005 PRIMACY	5-04-005 RESPECTING	5-03-004 SHAKES	5-05-005 STEAL
5-04-005 PRIMEVAL	5-01-001 RESPONDENTS'	5-04-005 SHAKY	5-05-005 STEALTH
5-03-004 PRIORITIES	5-02-003 RESULTANTS	5-04-005 SHAPELESS	5-05-005 STEAMED
5-04-005 PRO-*COMMUNIST	5-03-004 RETAILERS	5-04-005 SHARPENED	5-05-005 STEAMING
5-05-005 PROBING	5-02-002 RETAILING	5-04-005 SHERIFF'S	5-03-004 STEEPED
5-04-005 PROCESSION	5-04-005 RETREATING	5-04-004 SHIELDED	5-02-002 STEPHENS
5-02-002 PROCREATION	5-01-001 REUVENI	5-02-002 SHIELDING	5-03-004 STEREOTYPED
5-04-005 PROFESS	5-03-005 REVERED	5-04-004 SHINE	5-01-001 STERILIZATION
5-03-005 PROFESSED	5-04-005 REVERENCE	5-04-004 SHINGLES	5-04-004 STEW
5-05-005 PROFESSIONALLY	5-03-005 REVISE	5-03-003 SHIP'S	5-02-002 STICKNEY
5-03-004 PROFESSIONS	5-02-003 REVIVALS	5-02-003 SHIRLEY	5-03-004 STIMULI
5-04-004 PROFICIENT	5-03-004 REX	5-05-005 SHOCKS	5-04-005 STING
5-02-004 PROGRAMMING	5-02-004 REYNOLDS	5-04-005 SHONE	5-02-005 STOCKINGS
5-04-005 PROLIFERATION	5-02-002 RHETORIC	5-04-005 SHORTCOMINGS	5-03-003 STOICISM
5-01-001 PROLUSION	5-03-003 RICHARD'S	5-03-004 SHORTSIGHTED	5-04-004 STONY
5-05-005 PROMINENCE	5-04-005 RICHER	5-04-005 SHOUTS	5-01-001 STOWEY
5-04-005 PROPHECY	5-01-001 RICHERT	5-03-004 SHOVEL	5-02-002 STRAIT
5-03-005 PROPHET	5-04-005 RICHEST	5-02-004 SHOWERED	5-04-004 STRENGTHENS
5-04-004 PROPRIETORS	5-03-005 RICHLY	5-03-004 SHREDS	5-03-005 STRESSING
5-03-004 PROSECUTED	5-03-004 RICHNESS	5-04-005 SHRIEK	5-03-004 STRIPED
5-04-005 PROVERB	5-04-005 RIDICULE	5-04-005 SHRINK	5-04-005 STRIPES
5-03-005 PROVING	5-04-005 RIG	5-03-004 SHRIVER	5-04-005 STUDDED
5-03-004 PROVOCATION	5-03-004 RIGHTEOUS	5-03-005 SHUDDER	5-05-005 STUFFED
5-03-005 PROXIMITY	5-05-005 RIM	5-04-005 SHUDDERED	5-05-005 STUMPS
5-01-001 PSALMIST	5-01-002 RINSING	5-01-001 SHUNTS	5-02-002 SUB
5-01-001 PSITHYRUS	5-04-004 RIPPLE	5-01-001 SHUTTER	5-03-004 SUBCOMMITTEE
5-02-003 PSYCHIATRIC	5-03-003 RIPPLES	5-02-002 SHUTTERS	5-04-005 SUBSIDED
5-02-004 PSYCHIATRISTS	5-05-005 RISKS	5-03-004 SIDEWALKS	5-03-005 SUBSTITUTES
5-01-003 PSYCHOANALYSIS	5-04-004 ROADWAY	5-04-004 SIDING	5-04-005 SUCCUMBED
5-03-004 PULP	5-03-004 ROASTED	5-02-004 SIGHING	5-03-005 SUCK
5-04-004 PUMPS	5-02-003 ROMANTICS	5-05-005 SIGNALING	5-04-005 SUFFERS
5-04-004 PUNCH	5-02-002 RONALD	5-01-002 SIGNATURES	5-04-005 SUFFICE
5-01-001 PUPPETS	5-02-002 RONNIE	5-04-005 SILENCED	5-03-005 SUFFOCATING
5-03-005 PURITAN	5-05-005 ROOFS	5-02-002 SILHOUETTES	5-04-005 SUFFRAGE
5-05-005 PURPOSELY	5-03-004 ROOSEVELT'S	5-02-003 SIMMER	5-04-005 SUFFUSED
5-02-002 PUSSY	5-05-005 ROUNDING	5-02-004 SIMPSON	5-02-003 SUITCASES
5-01-001 PYREX	5-02-002 RPM	5-01-002 SINGLE-SHOT	5-01-002 SUNBURN
5-01-002 QUANTUM	5-04-004 RUNNERS	5-04-005 SINGLY	5-04-005 SUNDRY
5-05-005 QUARRELING	5-01-001 S**.*K	5-01-001 SITUS	5-03-005 SUPERSEDED
5-01-003 QUARTERBACK	5-01-001 SADIE	5-03-004 SKEPTICISM	5-05-005 SUPERVISE
5-04-005 QUOTATIONS	5-03-005 SAFEGUARD	5-02-002 SKI	5-03-005 SUPERVISOR
5-04-005 QUOTES	5-05-005 SAFER	5-04-005 SKILLFULLY	5-04-005 SUPERVISORS
5-05-005 RABBITS	5-04-004 SAILOR	5-04-005 SKIMMED	5-04-004 SUPREMACY
5-05-005 RACKET	5-02-003 SALISBURY	5-03-004 SKIP	5-04-005 SURPRISES
5-03-004 RADIAL	5-04-005 SALUTARY	5-05-005 SKYLINE	5-05-005 SURROUND
5-03-005 RAIDS	5-04-004 SALVAGE	5-03-005 SLASHING	5-04-004 SURVEYOR
5-05-005 RAINS	5-03-004 SANDALS	5-01-001 SLATER	5-02-002 SUSIE
5-03-004 RAINY	5-01-001 SANDMAN	5-04-005 SLIDES	5-02-002 SWAMP
5-02-002 RALL	5-01-001 SANTE	5-05-005 SLIPPERY	5-04-004 SWAY

Code	Word	Code	Word	Code	Word	Code	Word
5-03-004	SWEATY	5-02-003	U**.*S**.*S**.*R	5-05-005	WESTERLY	4-02-004	ACCLAIM
5-03-005	SWIRLED	5-04-004	UH-HUH	5-04-005	WHEREABOUTS	4-03-004	ACCLAIMED
5-03-004	SWIVEL	5-03-003	ULCER	5-04-004	WHEREIN	4-04-004	ACCORDED
5-04-005	SWOOPED	5-01-001	ULTRACENTRIFUGATION	5-04-004	WHISPERING	4-02-003	ACCOUNTABILITY
5-03-005	SWORN			5-04-005	WHISTLING	4-02-002	ACES
5-03-005	SYDNEY	5-03-004	UM	5-04-005	WIDEN	4-01-002	ACETONE
5-03-005	SYMBOLICALLY	5-03-004	UNANIMITY	5-04-005	WIDENED	4-03-004	ACHE
5-03-005	SYMPATHETICALLY	5-04-005	UNANIMOUS	5-04-005	WIDOWED	4-01-001	ADA'S
5-03-004	SYMPTOM	5-03-005	UNBREAKABLE	5-01-003	WIDTHS	4-02-003	ADDICTS
5-04-004	TAG	5-04-004	UNCANNY	5-04-004	WILLY	4-02-002	ADDITIVES
5-03-004	TAKIN	5-05-005	UNCERTAINTIES	5-04-005	WISHING	4-02-003	ADENAUER
5-04-005	TAME	5-04-004	UNCLE'S	5-03-003	WITCH	4-04-004	ADEPT
5-03-005	TANGLED	5-03-004	UNCOMPROMISING	5-04-005	WITS	4-02-004	ADHERE
5-04-004	TAPESTRY	5-03-005	UNDENIABLE	5-03-005	WOE	4-02-004	ADJECTIVES
5-05-005	TARIFF	5-04-005	UNDERSIDE	5-03-005	WOODED	4-03-003	ADJOURNMENT
5-04-004	TATTERED	5-04-005	UNDERTAKING	5-04-004	WOODWORK	4-02-002	ADJUDICATION
5-01-002	TEE	5-03-004	UNEASINESS	5-04-005	WORMS	4-03-004	ADMINISTERING
5-03-004	TEENAGERS	5-02-004	UNEMPLOYED	5-02-003	WORRYING	4-04-004	ADMIRING
5-04-005	TEENS	5-03-005	UNEQUIVOCALLY	5-05-005	WOULD-BE	4-01-001	ADO
5-01-001	TEKTITES	5-05-005	UNFAVORABLE	5-04-005	WRAP	4-01-002	ADOLF
5-02-002	TELEGRAPHERS	5-02-005	UNFOLDING	5-03-003	WRECKING	4-02-002	ADRIAN
5-01-001	TEMPLATE	5-01-001	UNICONER	5-04-005	WRY	4-04-004	ADVANCING
5-02-002	TEMPORAL	5-01-001	UNIFIL	5-01-001	XYDIS	4-03-003	ADVISABILITY
5-04-005	TENACITY	5-05-005	UNINTERRUPTED	5-03-005	YANKED	4-03-004	ADVOCATED
5-04-005	TENANT	5-05-005	UNIQUENESS	5-01-001	YOW	4-01-001	AEROSPACE
5-03-005	TENDENCIES	5-01-001	UNITIZED	5-04-004	YUGOSLAVIA	4-02-002	AESCHYLUS
5-02-002	TENSILE	5-05-005	UNLOADED	5-04-005	ZEST	4-03-004	AFFECTIONS
5-04-004	TERRIFIC	5-04-004	UNLOADING	5-03-003	111	4-02-004	AFFILIATION
5-04-004	TEXAN	5-04-004	UNMISTAKABLY	5-05-005	130	4-03-004	AFFIRMATION
5-01-001	THANT	5-04-005	UNOFFICIAL	5-02-004	16TH	4-02-003	AFFIRMATIVE
5-05-005	THAT'LL	5-01-001	UNRECONSTRUCTED	5-05-005	160	4-03-004	AFFLUENCE
5-02-004	THEOLOGIAN	5-05-005	UNREST	5-01-001	1625	4-03-003	AFRICANS
5-02-005	THEORETICALLY	5-04-005	UNSCRUPULOUS	5-04-005	1776	4-01-001	AFRO-*ASIAN
5-01-001	THER	5-04-005	UNSEEN	5-03-004	1793	4-03-004	AFTERMATH
5-03-004	THEREFROM	5-04-005	UNSPEAKABLE	5-02-003	1810	4-01-001	AGGLUTINATION
5-05-005	THEREUPON	5-05-005	UNWELCOME	5-04-005	1821	4-04-004	AGING
5-03-004	THICKENED	5-03-005	UNWILLINGNESS	5-02-002	1834	4-02-003	AIDES
5-04-004	THICKER	5-05-005	UNWITTINGLY	5-02-004	1844	4-03-003	AILMENT
5-05-005	THICKLY	5-04-005	UNWORTHY	5-02-003	1845	4-01-001	AIRMAIL
5-04-005	THIRSTY	5-02-002	UPPER-MIDDLE-CLASS	5-02-003	1865	4-02-003	AIRPORTS
5-01-001	THOM			5-03-005	1915	4-01-001	ALASTOR
5-01-002	THOMPSON'S	5-03-003	UPSTREAM	5-03-005	1916	4-03-003	ALCOHOLICS
5-05-005	THREATENS	5-01-003	UPTAKE	5-03-003	1928	4-03-004	ALERTING
5-04-004	THREE-PART	5-04-004	UPTOWN	5-03-003	1965	4-03-003	ALEXANDRIA
5-03-004	THREE-YEAR	5-02-003	UTOPIANS	5-01-001	2**C35	4-01-001	ALICIA
5-01-001	THRIFT	5-03-004	UTTERANCE	5-02-002	2-YEAR-OLD	4-02-004	ALIGNMENT
5-04-005	THRILL	5-05-005	UTTERED	5-03-004	20**K	4-01-002	ALKALI
5-04-005	THRIVED	5-04-004	VALLEYS	5-04-005	20,000	4-03-004	ALLAN
5-04-004	THRONE	5-04-004	VANISH	5-02-003	2000	4-03-003	ALLEGEDLY
5-04-005	THRUSTS	5-05-005	VARIOUSLY	5-02-003	23D	4-03-004	ALLEGIANCE
5-03-005	THUMPING	5-02-002	VAUDEVILLE	5-03-003	260	4-02-002	ALLIGATOR
5-03-004	TILT	5-03-005	VEGAS	5-04-005	29TH	4-01-001	ALLSTATES
5-04-004	TIMBERS	5-05-005	VENERABLE	5-03-003	30**K	4-01-001	ALMAGEST
5-04-005	TIMID	5-05-005	VENTURED	5-05-005	30,000	4-03-003	ALPHABETICAL
5-05-005	TOOLING	5-04-005	VERBALLY	5-03-005	30TH	4-01-001	ALTENBURG
5 01 001	TORQUE	5-04-005	VERIFY	5-02-003	63	4-03-004	ALTERING
5-01-001	TORQUER	5-01-001	VESOLE	5-03-005	49	4-01-001	ALTHO
5-05-005	TOSSING	5-03-004	VIABLE	5-04-004	51	4-03-003	ALTITUDE
5-03-004	TOURNAMENTS	5-03-005	VIBRATION	5-03-005	54	4-04-004	ALTO
5-04-005	TOWERS	5-04-005	VICES	5-03-005	6,000	4-01-003	ALVEOLI
5-05-005	TRACTS	5-04-005	VILE	5-04-004	6TH	4-01-001	AMADEE
5-03-004	TRANSACTION	5-02-003	VINEYARDS	5-05-005	63	4-01-001	AMETHYSTINE
5-03-004	TRANSACTIONS	5-03-005	VIRTUAL	5-01-001	8**C30	4-02-002	AMMO
5-03-003	TRANSITIONAL	5-02-002	VISA	5-03-003	96	4-04-004	AMONGST
5-03-005	TRANSITIONS	5-03-005	VISIBILITY	5-02-002	$135	4-04-004	AMPLY
5-04-004	TRANSPORTED	5-01-002	VITA	5-04-005	$15	4-01-001	ANACONDAS
5-05-005	TRANSPORTS	5-04-004	VITAMIN	5-03-005	$4	4-03-003	ANALOGIES
5-04-005	TRANSPOSED	5-04-005	VOICED	5-02-002	$5000	4-02-004	ANDERSON'S
5-03-005	TRAVELS	5-02-003	VOLATILE	5-01-001	**YA	4-02-002	ANDREA
5-03-003	TRAVERSE	5-05-005	VOLUNTEERED	5-01-001	*=*D'*$	4-01-001	ANDRENAS
5-04-005	TREAD	5-04-005	VOWED	5-01-001	*=*T*$,	4-01-001	ANDY'S
5-03-005	TREMBLED	5-03-003	VOWS	5-01-002	*=*X*$	4-03-003	ANECDOTES
5-04-005	TRIANGULAR	5-01-001	WACO	5-02-002	*=E*$	4-01-001	ANGELINA
5-03-005	TRIBUNAL	5-01-001	WAGE-PRICE	5-01-001	*=K*$	4-02-003	ANNALS
5-03-005	TRINITY	5-05-005	WAILING	5-01-001	*=L*$,	4-03-003	ANNE'S
5-02-005	TRIPLE	5-02-004	WAITERS	5-01-001	*=T*$.	4-04-004	ANTAGONISTIC
5-04-004	TRIUMPHANT	5-02-002	WAKEFUL	5-01-001	*A*B*O	4-01-001	ANTAGONISTS
5-04-005	TROLLEY	5-01-001	WALITZEE	5-01-001	*B*W	4-01-002	ANTHOLOGY
5-04-005	TRUCE	5-03-004	WALNUTS	5-01-001	*C*O*A*H*R	4-01-001	ANTI-**J*A
5-05-005	TRUNKS	5-04-004	WALT	5-01-001	*D*A	4-01-001	ANTI-**J*B
5-05-005	TRUTHFULLY	5-02-003	WANNA	5-01-001	*D*C	4-01-001	ANTI-*SEMITIC
5-02-002	TUBS	5-05-005	WARLIKE	5-01-001	*D*I*O*C*S	4-01-001	ANTI-MONOPOLY
5-03-004	TUCKER	5-03-003	WARRANTS	5-01-001	*D*U*F	4-03-004	ANTICS
5-03-004	TUITION	5-02-003	WARRIOR	5-03-003	*H	4-04-004	ANTIPATHY
5-03-004	TURK	5-04-004	WARTS	5-03-003	*M	4-03-004	ANTIQUATED
5-02-003	TURKS	5-01-001	WASHES	5-01-001	*RH	4-01-001	ANTISERUM
5-01-001	TUXAPOKA	5-04-005	WASTING	5-03-003	*S	4-04-004	ANYMORE
5-03-005	TWEED	5-05-005	WATER'S	5-02-002	*S*E*A*T*O	4-03-004	APEX
5-05-005	TWELFTH	5-02-002	WATSON'S	4-03-003	A**.*M**.*A	4-02-004	APOLOGIES
5-03-005	TWENTY-EIGHT	5-05-005	WEARS	4-03-003	ABDOMINAL	4-02-002	APOSTOLIC
5-04-005	TWENTY-SIX	5-02-003	WEAVING	4-04-004	ABETTED	4-04-004	APPLAUDED
5-03-004	TWIRLING	5-03-005	WEBSTER	4-02-003	ABODE	4-02-002	APPRAISE
5-01-001	TWO-DIGIT	5-03-005	WEE	4-03-003	ABOLITIONISTS	4-03-004	APPREHENSIVELY
5-03-004	TWO-YEAR	5-04-005	WEEDS	4-02-004	ABSTRACTS	4-03-004	APTLY
5-04-004	TYING	5-04-005	WELCOMING	4-04-004	ABYSS	4-04-004	ARCHIVES
5-01-001	U**.*N**.*F**.*P	5-02-002	WELLS'S	4-01-001	ACCACIA	4-01-001	ARCTIC
						4-03-004	ARDUOUS

4-03-003 ARISEN	4-01-002 BELLBOY	4-03-003 CANTERBURY	4-03-004 COMPEL
4-04-004 ARISTOCRACY	4-03-003 BELLOW	4-03-004 CAPES	4-03-004 COMPENSATED
4-02-004 ARISTOCRATIC	4-04-004 BELONGINGS	4-04-004 CAPITALIZE	4-02-003 COMPILING
4-02-002 ARLINGTON	4-04-004 BENEFACTOR	4-02-002 CAPITALS	4-04-004 COMPLACENCY
4-02-003 ARMAMENTS	4-04-004 BENEVOLENCE	4-03-003 CAPTIVITY	4-04-004 COMPLEMENTARY
4-03-004 ARMCHAIR	4-02-002 BENGAL	4-02-003 CARESSED	4-03-003 COMPLETENESS
4-01-003 ARMISTICE	4-02-002 BENNINGTON	4-01-001 CARL'S	4-02-003 COMPLEXITIES
4-02-004 ARMOR	4-03-003 BENNY	4-03-003 CARPENTRY	4-03-004 COMPLICATION
4-02-002 ARTE	4-03-003 BEREAVEMENT	4-03-003 CARPETS	4-03-004 COMPLIMENTS
4-03-004 ARTFULLY	4-02-002 BERLE	4-03-003 CARROTS	4-04-004 COMPOSURE
4-04-004 ASCENDING	4-02-003 BERLIN'S	4-03-004 CASTING	4-04-004 COMPROMISING
4-02-004 ASCERTAINED	4-03-004 BERTH	4-03-004 CASTLES	4-01-001 COMPSON
4-04-004 ASSAILED	4-03-004 BESTOWAL	4-04-004 CATALOGUED	4-02-002 COMPTROLLER
4-03-003 ASSASSINATION	4-04-004 BETRAY	4-03-004 CATER	4-01-001 COMPULSIVES
4-03-004 ASSAULTS	4-02-002 BEVERAGES	4-03-004 CATHERINE	4-03-003 COMRADE
4-04-004 ASSENT	4-04-004 BILLING	4-01-001 CATHODOLUMINESCENT	4-02-003 CONCAVE
4-04-004 ASSERTING	4-04-004 BIND		4-02-003 CONCEPTUAL
4-02-004 ASSIGNS	4-01-004 BIOGRAPHICAL	4-01-001 CATT	4-03-004 CONCLUDES
4-04-004 ASSIMILATED	4-01-001 BIRDIED	4-03-004 CELEBRATE	4-03-004 CONCUR
4-03-003 ASSUREDLY	4-01-001 BIRTH-CONTROL	4-03-004 CELERY	4-04-004 CONCURRENCE
4-01-001 ATHENIANS	4-03-004 BIRTHS	4-01-001 CELL-FREE	4-02-003 CONDEMN
4-01-002 ATLANTA'S	4-01-001 BLACK-BODY	4-03-003 CEMENTED	4-03-004 CONDEMNING
4-01-001 ATROPHY	4-01-001 BLANCHING	4-01-001 CENTRALITY	4-02-002 CONDUCTS
4-03-004 ATTACHMENTS	4-02-003 BLASPHEMY	4-03-003 CENTRALIZATION	4-01-003 CONFEDERATION
4-04-004 ATTESTED	4-03-004 BLASTED	4-01-002 CEREALS	4-04-004 CONFIDENTIALLY
4-04-004 ATTRACTING	4-04-004 BLASTS	4-03-003 CETERA	4-02-004 CONFUSIONS
4-02-004 ATTY	4-04-004 BLENDED	4-02-002 CH	4-04-004 CONGEALED
4-01-002 AUCTION	4-03-004 BLINDED	4-04-004 CHAGRIN	4-02-004 CONGRATULATE
4-04-004 AUDIBLE	4-03-003 BLINK	4-04-004 CHALLENGES	4-04-004 CONN
4-02-003 AUDIO-VISUAL	4-04-004 BLISS	4-03-004 CHARACTERIZES	4-03-003 CONNOISSEUR
4-02-002 AUDIT	4-03-004 BLISSFUL	4-03-004 CHARITIES	4-03-003 CONQUER
4-01-001 AUDITORS	4-03-003 BLOODSTREAM	4-01-001 CHARLAYNE	4-03-004 CONSENTED
4-03-004 AUGUSTINE	4-02-003 BLOTS	4-03-004 CHARTERED	4-02-003 CONSERVATIVES
4-04-004 AUGUSTUS	4-02-002 BLOWER	4-03-004 CHARTERS	4-03-004 CONSIDERATE
4-04-004 AUNTS	4-04-004 BLUFFS	4-03-004 CHAUFFEUR	4-02-002 CONSOLES
4-02-004 AUSTRIA	4-04-004 BLUSHING	4-01-001 CHAVEZ	4-01-002 CONSONANTS
4-02-002 AUSTRIAN	4-01-003 BLVD	4-04-004 CHEATED	4-03-004 CONSPIRATORS
4-01-001 AUTOCRACIES	4-01-001 BO**OO**DK	4-03-004 CHEERS	4-02-003 CONSTELLATIONS
4-04-004 AUTOS	4-01-001 BOMBUS	4-04-004 CHEMICALS	4-01-003 CONSTITUTIONS
4-04-004 AVAIL	4-01-001 BONIFACE	4-01-001 CHEMISCHE	4-03-003 CONSTRUCTIONS
4-03-004 AWAKENED	4-01-001 BONNOR	4-04-004 CHEMISTS	4-03-004 CONSUMMATED
4-04-004 AWAKENING	4-02-003 BOOBY	4-02-003 CHESAPEAKE	4-01-001 CONSUMMATION
4-04-004 AWESOME	4-04-004 BOOZE	4-04-004 CHESTS	4-03-004 CONTACTED
4-03-004 AWHILE	4-03-003 BOUGHS	4-03-003 CHEVROLET	4-03-004 CONTAINERS
4-04-004 BACH	4-02-002 BOUQUET	4-02-003 CHEWED	4-02-003 CONTAMINATION
4-01-001 BACHELORS	4-01-001 BOXELL	4-03-003 CHIANG	4-01-001 CONTRACEPTION
4-04-004 BACKBONE	4-04-004 BOYISH	4-01-001 CHICKASAWS	4-01-001 CONTRACEPTIVES
4-01-002 BACKERS	4-03-003 BRACES	4-04-004 CHIEFTAIN	4-04-004 CONTRADICT
4-01-001 BACKSTITCH	4-02-002 BRADLEY	4-03-003 CHILDISHNESS	4-02-004 CONTRASTED
4-04-004 BAFFLING	4-02-004 BRANDS	4-02-003 CHILDLIKE	4-02-002 CONTROVERSIES
4-03-003 BAGGAGE	4-01-001 BRAQUE'S	4-04-004 CHIPPED	4-02-004 CONVENT
4-03-003 BAGGY	4-04-004 BRAVELY	4-02-004 CHISEL	4-03-004 CONVEYS
4-02-004 BAIRD	4-03-004 BRAVERY	4-02-002 CHOREOGRAPHERS	4-03-003 CONVICTS
4-02-003 BAKING	4-04-004 BRAZILIAN	4-02-002 CHROME	4-03-004 CONVINCE
4-03-004 BALANCING	4-02-002 BRETT	4-01-001 CHROMIUM	4-02-002 COOLANT
4-01-001 BALDRIGE	4-04-004 BREW	4-03-003 CIRCUITS	4-02-004 COOLERS
4-03-003 BALES	4-03-004 BRIGHTEST	4-03-004 CIRCULATED	4-02-002 COOLEST
4-03-003 BALLETS	4-03-004 BRILLIANCE	4-03-003 CIVILIZATIONS	4-02-002 CORNE
4-03-004 BANANA	4-04-004 BRIM	4-02-004 CLAPPED	4-01-003 COROLLARY
4-03-004 BANDAGE	4-02-003 BRISTLES	4-03-003 CLARET	4-01-001 CORONER'S
4-02-003 BANDAGED	4-02-002 BROKERS	4-04-004 CLASPING	4-03-003 CORPORAL
4-03-004 BANGED	4-01-001 BRONCHIOLE	4-03-003 CLASSIFICATIONS	4-03-003 CORRESPONDED
4-04-004 BANGING	4-01-001 BRONCHUS	4-04-004 CLASSMATES	4-03-003 CORROSION
4-02-002 BANISH	4-03-004 BRUCE	4-02-002 CLAUSES	4-04-004 CORROSIVE
4-04-004 BANKED	4-01-001 BRUCKNER	4-04-004 CLEANSING	4-03-003 CORRUGATED
4-02-002 BAPTISM	4-02-003 BUCKETS	4-04-004 CLEARANCE	4-01-001 COSSACKS
4-03-003 BAPTISTS	4-03-003 BUCKING	4-03-004 CLEVERLY	4-01-001 COTTEN
4-01-001 BARBARIANS	4-03-004 BUDDHIST	4-02-003 CLIMACTIC	4-04-004 COUNSELOR
4-01-001 BARCUS	4-01-003 BUFFERED	4-01-003 CLINT	4-02-004 COUNTERACT
4-02-004 BARNS	4-02-002 BUG	4-04-004 CLIPPINGS	4-04-004 COUP
4-01-001 BARNUMVILLE	4-03-004 BUILD-UP	4-03-003 CLODS	4-01-001 COUPLERS
4-03-003 BARRICADES	4-03-004 BULLETINS	4-02-003 CLOSE-UP	4-04-004 COURAGEOUS
4-02-003 BASEBALL'S	4-04-004 BULLY	4-02-003 CLUMP	4-01-001 COURTENAY
4-02-002 BASEMAN	4-01-001 BULTMANN	4-03-004 CLUMPS	4-04-004 COURTIERS
4-04-004 BASING	4-02-004 BURDENED	4-04-004 CLUSTERED	4-04-004 COVETED
4-04-004 BATHE	4-03-004 BURGEONING	4-04-004 CO-OPERATE	4-04-004 COWBOYS
4-04-004 BATHTUB	4-02-003 BURGLARY	4-03-004 COASTAL	4-02-004 COWHAND
4-01-001 BATTENKILL	4-02-002 BURMESE	4-02-003 COATED	4-03-004 COY
4-03-003 BAYREUTH	4-01-001 BURNSIDE'S	4-04-004 COERCION	4-02-003 CRACKERS
4-02-002 BEADLE	4-02-002 BURROW	4-02-002 COGNAC	4-04-004 CRAFTSMEN
4-04-004 BEADS	4-02-002 BUSHELS	4-02-002 COHN	4-03-004 CRAZILY
4-01-001 BEARDEN	4-04-004 BUTLER	4-02-002 COKE	4-01-001 CREAMER
4-04-004 BEARER	4-03-003 BYRON'S	4-02-004 COLDEST	4-04-004 CREDITABLE
4-01-001 BEATIE	4-02-002 CABANA	4-03-004 COLDNESS	4-03-003 CRIMINALITY
4-01-001 BEATNIKS	4-02-003 CABBAGE	4-04-004 COLLABORATORS	4-03-003 CRITICIZE
4-04-004 BEATS	4-01-001 CABRINI	4-03-004 COLLECTIVELY	4-01-001 CROSS-LICENSING
4-01-001 BECKETT'S	4-04-004 CADET	4-03-004 COLLEGIATE	4-02-003 CROSS-SECTIONAL
4-01-001 BECKWORTH	4-03-003 CALAMITY	4-03-003 COLONIALISM	4-02-003 CROSSES
4-03-004 BEDROOMS	4-03-004 CALCULATE	4-04-004 COMBED	4-04-004 CRUELLY
4-04-004 BEDTIME	4-01-001 CALCUTTA	4-03-004 COMBO	4-03-003 CRUISER
4-03-003 BEEBE	4-03-004 CALISTHENICS	4-04-004 COMMENDED	4-03-004 CRUMPLED
4-01-001 BEEP	4-02-002 CALVIN	4-03-004 COMMENSURATE	4-01-001 CRUS
4-03-003 BEHAVING	4-01-001 CAMARET	4-02-002 COMMITTEEMEN	4-03-004 CRUSH
4-02-003 BEHOLD	4-03-004 CAMPAIGNED	4-02-003 COMMONS	4-03-003 CUBES
4-03-003 BEL	4-03-003 CAMPAIGNING	4-03-003 COMMUNAL	4-03-003 CULMINATION
4-02-003 BELCHED	4-03-004 CAMPBELL	4-03-004 COMMUNE	4-03-004 CULTIVATION
4-03-004 BELIEVER	4-01-001 CAMUSFEARNA	4-04-004 COMPANIONSHIP	4-04-004 CULTS

Code	Word
4-02-003	CULTURED
4-03-004	CUPPED
4-02-002	CURE-ALL
4-03-004	CURSORY
4-04-004	CURTAIL
4-04-004	CURVING
4-02-002	CUSHIONING
4-03-004	CUSTOMARILY
4-02-002	CUTTER
4-03-003	CYNICISM
4-03-003	CYRUS
4-01-002	CYTOPLASM
4-01-001	D'*ALBERT
4-03-004	DADDY
4-02-004	DALTON
4-03-003	DANES
4-03-004	DANGLING
4-03-004	DARKENING
4-04-004	DARNED
4-02-003	DASHING
4-01-001	DATELINED
4-04-004	DATING
4-03-003	DAUGHTER'S
4-02-002	DAVENPORT
4-03-003	DAVID'S
4-03-004	DAZED
4-04-004	DEARLY
4-04-004	DEBATING
4-04-004	DECAYED
4-04-004	DECAYING
4-04-004	DECEPTIVE
4-03-004	DECIDEDLY
4-03-004	DECOR
4-03-003	DECORATING
4-02-003	DECORATORS
4-02-003	DEDUCTED
4-03-004	DEFENDS
4-04-004	DEFIED
4-03-004	DELEGATED
4-03-004	DELICIOUS
4-04-004	DELIGHTFULLY
4-04-004	DELUGE
4-04-004	DEMISE
4-04-004	DEMOLISHED
4-02-003	DEMONSTRATIONS
4-04-004	DENIALS
4-03-003	DENMARK
4-02-004	DENOTE
4-03-004	DENOUNCING
4-02-002	DENTISTS
4-01-002	DENTON
4-04-004	DENUNCIATION
4-01-001	DEPEW
4-03-004	DERISION
4-03-004	DERIVATION
4-02-004	DERIVING
4-03-004	DESCEND
4-04-004	DESCENDANTS
4-03-004	DESIGNATION
4-02-003	DESKS
4-02-004	DESPAIRING
4-02-004	DESPAIRINGLY
4-04-004	DETACHMENT
4-02-002	DETERGENTS
4-03-004	DETERIORATED
4-03-003	DETRIMENTAL
4-01-002	DEUX
4-02-004	DEVIATIONS
4-03-003	DEVOUT
4-01-001	DIA
4-03-004	DIABETES
4-01-001	DIAGONAL
4-03-004	DIAGONALLY
4-03-004	DIALECTS
4-01-002	DIALYZED
4-02-003	DIAMETERS
4-02-002	DIANE'S
4-04-004	DIARY
4-03-003	DICTATORS
4-04-004	DICTUM
4-01-001	DIETHYLSTILBESTROL
4-03-004	DIFFUSE
4-03-004	DIME
4-03-003	DIRECTIVES
4-03-004	DIRECTNESS
4-02-002	DIRECTORATE
4-02-002	DISADVANTAGE
4-04-004	DISAPPROVE
4-03-004	DISAPPROVED
4-04-004	DISASTERS
4-03-004	DISCERN
4-02-004	DISCIPLE
4-04-004	DISCIPLINES
4-03-004	DISCLOSURES
4-03-004	DISCONCERTING
4-03-004	DISCONNECTED
4-01-001	DISCONTINUITY
4-02-002	DISCUSSES
4-04-004	DISGUSTING
4-04-004	DISKS
4-04-004	DISLIKES
4-04-004	DISOBEYED
4-03-004	DISPARATE
4-04-004	DISPENSE
4-04-004	DISPLEASURE
4-04-004	DISREGARDED
4-02-003	DISSOCIATION
4-01-002	DISTINGUISHABLE
4-02-004	DISTORT
4-03-003	DISTRESSED
4-04-004	DISTRIBUTING
4-02-004	DISTRIBUTORS
4-03-004	DIVERSIONS
4-02-004	DIVES
4-01-001	DIVESTITURE
4-01-001	DIVISIBLE
4-01-001	DJANGO
4-04-004	DOCILE
4-04-004	DOCTORED
4-03-003	DOCUMENTARY
4-04-004	DOGMA
4-03-004	DOGMATIC
4-03-003	DOGMATISM
4-01-001	DOLLY
4-03-003	DOLPHINS
4-01-001	DONNA
4-01-001	DONNYBROOK
4-03-004	DOORMAN
4-02-002	DORADO
4-02-002	DORIC
4-03-004	DORMITORIES
4-01-001	DOSAGE
4-01-002	DOSAGES
4-01-001	DOUBLE-WALL
4-04-004	DOUBLY
4-02-003	DOVE
4-02-002	DOVER
4-03-003	DOW
4-03-003	DOYLE
4-02-002	DRAPER
4-03-004	DRAPERIES
4-03-004	DREAMY
4-03-003	DREGS
4-03-003	DRILLS
4-02-002	DROSS
4-04-004	DROWNING
4-04-004	DRUMMING
4-04-004	DRUNKENLY
4-03-004	DRUNKENNESS
4-01-001	DRYER
4-03-004	DRYLY
4-01-001	DRYWALL
4-03-004	DUBBED
4-03-004	DUCKS
4-04-004	DUMP
4-02-003	DUMPING
4-02-002	DUNBAR
4-01-001	DUNCAN
4-01-001	DUNNE
4-04-004	DWINDLING
4-03-004	DYED
4-01-001	DYNAFAC
4-02-004	DYNAMICS
4-02-003	EAST-*WEST
4-04-004	EASTWARD
4-03-004	ECCENTRICITY
4-03-003	ECLIPSES
4-04-004	ECSTATIC
4-03-003	EDITH
4-03-004	EDITOR'S
4-03-004	ELEVENTH
4-01-002	ELIGIBILITY
4-04-004	ELIMINATES
4-02-003	ELIOT
4-01-001	ELLIPSOIDS
4-03-004	ELSIE
4-01-001	ELUTION
4-03-003	EMBANKMENT
4-04-004	EMBEDDED
4-03-003	EMBRACED
4-04-004	EMBRACES
4-03-004	EMBRACING
4-01-001	EMBROIDERY
4-04-004	EMINENCE
4-03-004	EMINENTLY
4-02-002	EMPERORS
4-03-004	EMPHASIZING
4-01-002	EMPHYSEMA
4-03-003	EMPIRES
4-04-004	ENACTING
4-03-004	ENCOMPASS
4-04-004	ENDORSED
4-03-003	ENDOWMENTS
4-03-004	ENGRAVED
4-02-004	ENGROSSING
4-04-004	ENIGMA
4-03-004	ENLARGEMENT
4-02-002	ENSIGN
4-04-004	ENSUING
4-03-004	ENTITLES
4-03-004	ENTOURAGE
4-01-001	ENTROPY
4-02-002	ENVER
4-04-004	ENVIABLE
4-02-003	ENVIRONMENTS
4-04-004	ENVIRONS
4-04-004	ENVISIONED
4-01-003	ENZYMATIC
4-03-004	EPHEMERAL
4-02-002	EPITAPH
4-02-004	EQUIVALENCE
4-02-003	ERICH
4-03-004	ERODED
4-04-004	ERRONEOUS
4-02-004	ESCAPES
4-03-003	ESOTERIC
4-03-004	ESTABLISHES
4-01-001	ESTELLA
4-03-003	ESTIMATION
4-01-001	ETA
4-02-002	ETHAN
4-02-004	ETHIC
4-03-004	ETHOS
4-02-002	ETHYL
4-03-004	EVELYN
4-03-004	EVENLY
4-04-004	EVERYBODY'S
4-02-004	EVERYONE'S
4-03-003	EVOLUTIONARY
4-03-004	EXAGGERATING
4-02-002	EXCELSIOR
4-02-003	EXCISE
4-01-001	EXCITABILITY
4-01-001	EXCITATORY
4-03-004	EXCLAIMING
4-03-004	EXCOMMUNICATED
4-04-004	EXILE
4-03-004	EXODUS
4-04-004	EXPECTANCY
4-02-002	EXPERIENTIAL
4-04-004	EXPERIMENTERS
4-03-003	EXPLANATORY
4-01-002	EXPLICABLE
4-04-004	EXPLOITS
4-02-003	EXPLORATORY
4-03-004	EXPLORER
4-03-004	EXPOSING
4-02-004	EXPULSION
4-02-004	EXTRACTING
4-03-004	EXTRACTS
4-02-002	EXTRAPOLATED
4-01-002	EXTRAPOLATION
4-03-003	EXTREMISTS
4-03-004	EXTREMITY
4-04-004	EYEBROW
4-04-004	EYEING
4-01-001	FABIAN
4-04-004	FABLED
4-02-003	FACE-SAVING
4-03-004	FAILURES
4-04-004	FAIRY
4-02-002	FALCON
4-04-004	FAMILIAL
4-03-003	FANATICISM
4-02-003	FANNED
4-03-004	FANTASIES
4-03-004	FAR-REACHING
4-02-002	FARMERS'
4-02-002	FARO
4-03-004	FASTEN
4-04-004	FATALLY
4-01-001	FAUST
4-02-004	FAVORING
4-02-002	FAVORITISM
4-01-001	FAWKES
4-03-003	FAYETTE
4-03-003	FEARFULLY
4-03-003	FEATHERED
4-04-004	FEATURING
4-01-001	FELICE
4-04-004	FELICITY
4-01-001	FENCE-LINE
4-03-003	FENCING
4-03-004	FENDER
4-01-001	FERMENTED
4-04-004	FERTILIZER
4-03-004	FERVOR
4-04-004	FEVERISH
4-04-004	FIASCO
4-01-001	FIBER-COUPLED
4-02-003	FIERCELY
4-02-002	FILMED
4-03-004	FILTERS
4-03-003	FINALITY
4-03-004	FINED
4-03-004	FINELY
4-01-002	FINGERPRINTS
4-01-001	FINITE-DIMENSIONAL
4-02-002	FINK
4-01-001	FIORELLO
4-04-004	FIRMNESS
4-03-003	FIRST-RATE
4-01-001	FISCAL-TAX
4-03-004	FIVE-YEAR
4-04-004	FLAKES
4-03-004	FLANNEL
4-03-003	FLAPPED
4-04-004	FLAPPING
4-01-001	FLAT-BED
4-02-002	FLAT-BOTTOMED
4-02-002	FLINT
4-04-004	FLIP
4-03-004	FLOORBOARDS
4-02-002	FLORENTINE
4-04-004	FLOURISHES
4-04-004	FLOWN
4-03-003	FLUORESCENT
4-04-004	FLURRY
4-03-003	FLUSHING
4-04-004	FLUTTERING
4-01-002	FLUXES
4-03-003	FLYER
4-04-004	FONDLY
4-04-004	FONDNESS
4-01-001	FOOD-PRESERVATION
4-04-004	FORBID
4-04-004	FOREBODING
4-02-003	FOREIGNER
4-03-004	FOREMAN
4-04-004	FORESEEABLE
4-01-003	FORKED
4-03-004	FORMULATING
4-03-003	FORTS
4-02-002	FORTY-NINE
4-02-003	FORTY-SEVEN
4-04-004	FOUL
4-02-002	FOUNTAINS
4-03-003	FRAGMENTED
4-01-001	FRANCIE
4-03-004	FRANKNESS
4-02-004	FREAK
4-01-001	FREDDY'S
4-02-002	FREIGHTER
4-01-001	FRELINGHUYSEN
4-03-003	FRESHNESS
4-03-004	FRIENDLINESS
4-03-004	FRIENDSHIPS
4-03-003	FRUSTRATE
4-03-004	FRUSTRATIONS
4-02-002	FUCHS
4-01-001	FUCK
4-04-004	FULLNESS
4-04-004	FUMBLING
4-03-004	FUNCTIONALLY
4-03-004	FUNDAMENTALIST
4-02-002	FUNK
4-04-004	FURNISHING
4-03-003	FUSS
4-03-003	GABLES
4-03-003	GADGET
4-03-003	GAG
4-03-004	GAGE
4-02-002	GAIETIES
4-03-003	GALLEY
4-02-002	GALLEYS
4-01-001	GALLIUM
4-03-004	GALLOP
4-01-002	GAME'S
4-03-004	GAMUT
4-03-004	GANGSTERS
4-01-001	GANNON
4-03-003	GARDENER
4-03-003	GARDNER
4-01-001	GARDNER'S
4-03-004	GARLIC
4-01-001	GASKET
4-01-001	GASTROCNEMIUS
4-02-002	GAULLE
4-03-003	GEE
4-02-002	GELDING
4-04-004	GEM
4-03-003	GENERALE
4-03-004	GENERALIZATION
4-03-004	GENESIS

4-03-003	GENTEEL
4-01-001	GERAGHTY
4-01-001	GERRY
4-03-004	GHANA
4-03-004	GIGGLES
4-02-004	GISELLE
4-04-004	GIT
4-04-004	GIVEAWAY
4-04-004	GLADLY
4-03-003	GLAMOR
4-04-004	GLEAM
4-03-004	GLEAMED
4-03-004	GLIBLY
4-01-001	GLIMCO
4-03-004	GLIMPSES
4-02-004	GLISTEN
4-03-004	GLISTENED
4-02-003	GLOBAL
4-01-002	GLOBULIN
4-04-004	GLORIES
4-03-004	GLORIFIED
4-03-004	GNAWING
4-03-003	GODDAM
4-01-001	GODKIN
4-03-003	GODWIN
4-01-002	GOLFERS
4-03-004	GOOD-LOOKING
4-01-001	GOODIS
4-03-004	GOOSE
4-01-001	GORHAM
4-03-004	GOSH
4-03-004	GOSPELS
4-02-004	GOTHIC
4-03-004	GRACES
4-03-003	GRAMMAR
4-03-004	GRAMMATICAL
4-04-004	GRAPPLING
4-03-003	GRASSHOPPERS
4-03-003	GRATIFICATION
4-02-004	GRATIFIED
4-03-003	GRAVEST
4-01-002	GRAVITATIONAL
4-04-004	GRAVY
4-02-004	GRAYING
4-01-001	GRAZIE
4-02-004	GRECIAN
4-04-004	GREGARIOUS
4-01-001	GREGORIO
4-03-004	GREGORY
4-01-001	GREVILLE'S
4-03-003	GRIFFIN
4-01-001	GROGGINS
4-02-004	GROIN
4-01-001	GROKKED
4-01-001	GROKKING
4-03-004	GROOMED
4-03-004	GROSSLY
4-03-004	GROTESQUELY
4-01-001	GROTH
4-01-001	GROTH'S
4-02-004	GROUPING
4-01-001	GROVER
4-03-003	GROVES
4-03-004	GROWL
4-03-004	GROWLED
4-03-004	GROWN-UP
4-03-003	GRUFF
4-02-004	GUARD'S
4-03-004	GUARDIANS
4-02-004	GUMS
4-02-002	GUNMEN
4-01-001	GYMNASTIC
4-01-001	GYMNASTS
4-04-004	GYPSY
4-01-001	HABITANTS
4-04-004	HALF-WAY
4-03-004	HALLS
4-02-002	HAMBURGERS
4-03-004	HANGS
4-04-004	HARBORS
4-02-004	HARMFUL
4-02-003	HATCHET
4-02-004	HATES
4-03-004	HAULING
4-03-004	HAUNT
4-03-004	HEADLINE
4-03-003	HEADWATERS
4-03-004	HEAPED
4-02-002	HEARTBEAT
4-04-004	HEARTENING
4-02-003	HEARTH
4-04-004	HEARTY
4-04-004	HEAVED
4-04-004	HEAVING
4-02-004	HELM
4-03-003	HELPFULLY
4-03-004	HEM

4-01-001	HEMOGLOBIN
4-03-004	HENCEFORTH
4-03-003	HENS
4-02-003	HEREAFTER
4-01-001	HEROLD
4-02-003	HETEROGENEOUS
4-02-002	HIGH-ENERGY
4-01-001	HIGH-GAIN
4-04-004	HIGH-LEVEL
4-03-004	HIGHBALL
4-04-004	HIKE
4-03-004	HIKES
4-01-001	HILAR
4-01-001	HILO
4-04-004	HINGES
4-04-004	HISSING
4-02-002	HITTERS
4-02-002	HOARSELY
4-03-004	HOBBY
4-04-004	HOLDINGS
4-03-004	HOLLYWOOD'S
4-01-001	HOMECOMING
4-03-003	HOMEMADE
4-01-001	HONEYBEES
4-01-001	HONOTASSA
4-04-004	HOPPING
4-01-001	HOPPLES
4-03-004	HORRIFIED
4-03-004	HORRORS
4-03-004	HOSPITABLE
4-02-003	HOSPITALIZATION
4-03-004	HOTTEST
4-02-003	HOUGHTON
4-03-004	HOUSEWIFE
4-03-004	HOVER
4-04-004	HOWL
4-03-003	HOYT
4-02-003	HUDDLE
4-02-003	HUMANIST
4-04-004	HUMBLY
4-03-004	HUMILIATING
4-02-003	HUNGARY
4-04-004	HURLED
4-02-002	HUROK
4-04-004	HURRYING
4-04-004	HURTS
4-02-003	HUSH
4-03-004	HUSTLER
4-01-002	HUTCHINS
4-01-001	HWANG
4-01-001	HYDE
4-01-001	HYDROCHLORIDE
4-01-001	HYPOTHALAMIC-CORTICAL
4-02-002	HYPOTHESES
4-01-001	IBRAHIM
4-02-002	ICELAND
4-02-003	IDEALIST
4-02-002	IDEALIZED
4-02-004	IDYLLIC
4-03-004	IGNORING
4-03-004	IKE
4-04-004	ILL-STARRED
4-02-002	ILLEGITIMACY
4-04-004	ILLUSTRATING
4-04-004	IMBEDDED
4-04-004	IMITATED
4-04-004	IMMERSED
4-03-004	IMMIGRANT
4-03-003	IMMOBILITY
4-02-002	IMMORALITY
4-04-004	IMPAIR
4-04-004	IMPART
4-03-004	IMPARTED
4-03-004	IMPENDING
4-04-004	IMPERFECT
4-03-004	IMPLEMENT
4-04-004	IMPOSES
4-03-004	IMPRESS
4-03-004	IMPRISONED
4-03-004	IN-GROUP
4-04-004	INAPPROPRIATE
4-03-004	INAUGURATED
4-02-003	INCENTIVES
4-03-004	INCESSANT
4-03-004	INCIPIENT
4-03-003	INCISIVE
4-02-002	INCLINE
4-04-004	INCLUSIVE
4-04-004	INCOHERENT
4-03-004	INCOMPARABLE
4-03-003	INCOMPETENCE
4-02-003	INCUBATION
4-02-003	INCUMBENT
4-04-004	INDESCRIBABLE
4-04-004	INDETERMINATE
4-02-004	INDIVIDUALISTIC

4-04-004	INDIVIDUALITY
4-02-003	INDOLENT
4-04-004	INDOOR
4-02-003	INDUCING
4-02-004	INFAMOUS
4-02-003	INFATUATION
4-04-004	INFECTED
4-02-004	INFERENCES
4-01-001	INFESTATIONS
4-03-004	INFLECTIONS
4-03-004	INFLICT
4-04-004	INFLICTED
4-04-004	INFLUX
4-04-004	INFORMING
4-04-004	INFREQUENT
4-04-004	INGESTED
4-03-004	INGRATIATING
4-04-004	INHERIT
4-03-003	INHUMANE
4-03-004	INITIATING
4-04-004	INLAND
4-02-003	INLET
4-03-004	INNATE
4-02-003	INNINGS
4-03-004	INNOVATIONS
4-01-001	INPUT/#OUTPUT
4-02-004	INSEPARABLE
4-03-004	INSIDES
4-04-004	INSTABILITY
4-04-004	INSTINCTS
4-02-003	INSTRUMENTATION
4-04-004	INSULATED
4-03-004	INSULTING
4-01-003	INTEGER
4-04-004	INTENSIFIED
4-03-004	INTENSIFY
4-04-004	INTENTIONALLY
4-03-004	INTENTLY
4-01-001	INTERAMA
4-02-002	INTERCOLLEGIATE
4-02-002	INTERFEROMETER
4-02-003	INTERIORS
4-03-004	INTERLACED
4-04-004	INTERMINABLE
4-02-004	INTERNATIONALLY
4-04-004	INTERRELATION
4-02-004	INTERRELATIONS
4-04-004	INTERRUPT
4-04-004	INTERTWINED
4-03-003	INTERVENED
4-03-004	INTERWOVEN
4-02-003	INTONED
4-04-004	INTRIGUE
4-03-004	INTRINSICALLY
4-03-004	INTRODUCES
4-03-003	INVENTIONS
4-01-001	INVENTORS
4-03-004	INVESTIGATOR
4-03-004	INVOKE
4-03-004	INVOKING
4-04-004	IOWA
4-04-004	IRREGULARITY
4-03-004	IRRITATING
4-03-003	IRVING
4-01-001	ISFAHAN
4-03-004	ISLES
4-01-001	ISOTONIC
4-02-002	ISRAELI
4-02-003	ISSUING
4-03-003	ITCHING
4-02-003	IVAN
4-01-002	JACKIE
4-02-002	JACQUELINE
4-04-004	JANITOR
4-03-003	JANSSEN
4-01-001	JAPS
4-03-004	JARGON
4-03-004	JAVA
4-04-004	JEALOUS
4-03-004	JEALOUSY
4-01-001	JENSEN
4-03-004	JEOPARDIZE
4-04-004	JEOPARDY
4-03-004	JERKY
4-04-004	JETS
4-02-002	JIM'S
4-03-003	JOCULAR
4-01-001	JOLLIFFE
4-03-003	JOLLY
4-03-004	JOLT
4-01-001	JONATHAN'S
4-03-003	JORDAN
4-02-002	JORGE
4-03-003	JOSHUA
4-01-001	JOSSY
4-01-001	JOUR
4-01-001	JOUVET

4-03-004	JOWLS
4-02-002	JUDITH
4-02-003	JULIUS
4-03-004	JUMBLE
4-03-004	JUNCTURE
4-02-004	JUNGLES
4-02-003	JURISTS
4-01-001	JUROR
4-01-001	JURORS
4-03-003	JUSTIFIABLE
4-02-002	JUSTINIAN
4-03-003	KARAMAZOV
4-01-001	KARIPO
4-01-001	KATE'S
4-03-004	KATHY
4-01-001	KEDGEREE
4-01-001	KEO
4-03-003	KEYBOARD
4-02-002	KEYNOTE
4-01-001	KILLINGSWORTH
4-01-001	KILOWATT-HOUR
4-01-001	KIMMEL
4-01-001	KIMPTON
4-01-001	KINESTHETIC
4-04-004	KISSES
4-04-004	KNACK
4-04-004	KNOTTED
4-04-004	KNOW-HOW
4-03-004	KNOWINGLY
4-01-001	KRYSTALLOGRAPHIE
4-01-001	KULTURBUND
4-01-001	LABAN
4-04-004	LABELING
4-03-003	LABOUR
4-04-004	LACY
4-01-003	LAIN
4-03-003	LANES
4-03-004	LANGUID
4-02-003	LAOTIAN
4-04-004	LAPSES
4-02-002	LARD
4-01-001	LAJCHLI
4-03-004	LAUGHS
4-02-002	LAVATORY
4-04-004	LAVISHLY
4-03-003	LAWMAKERS
4-01-001	LAY-SISTERS
4-01-003	LEAGUE'S
4-04-004	LEAPS
4-01-001	LEAR
4-01-001	LEDOUX
4-02-004	LEERING
4-04-004	LENDS
4-02-002	LENGTHWISE
4-03-004	LETHARGY
4-04-004	LETTERING
4-02-002	LEVITT
4-02-002	LEW
4-01-003	LEWISOHN
4-01-001	LEXICOSTATISTICS
4-03-004	LIBERALLY
4-04-004	LIBERATE
4-01-001	LIFEBOAT
4-01-001	LIFTERS
4-03-004	LIGHTENED
4-01-001	LIGNITE
4-03-003	LILAC
4-02-002	LIMOUSINE
4-01-001	LINEARLY
4-03-003	LINER
4-03-003	LINT
4-01-001	LISA
4-03-003	LITHE
4-04-004	LITTERED
4-03-003	LOAF
4-01-002	LOANED
4-03-004	LOATHED
4-03-004	LOATHSOME
4-02-002	LOCALES
4-03-004	LOCALITIES
4-04-004	LOGISTICS
4-04-004	LONG-TIME
4-02-002	LONGHORN
4-01-001	LOOMIS
4-02-004	LOOSENED
4-04-004	LOUDEST
4-04-004	LOUNGING
4-02-002	LOVE-MAKING
4-03-003	LOVELINESS
4-02-002	LOWER-MIDDLE
4-03-003	LUCID
4-01-001	LUMPE
4-02-002	LUNGE
4-02-003	LUNGED
4-01-001	LUXEMBURG

Code	Word	Code	Word	Code	Word	Code	Word
4-01-001	LYFORD'S	4-02-003	MODULAR	4-01-001	ORVILLE	4-03-004	PLODDING
4-02-002	M**.*A	4-02-002	MODULATION	4-01-004	OUTFIELDER	4-03-004	PLUCKED
4-03-004	MACON	4-02-002	MOISE	4-03-004	OUTGROW	4-03-003	PLUMBER
4-02-004	MADLY	4-04-004	MOLE	4-03-004	OUTLAWED	4-03-004	PLUMP
4-03-003	MAESTRO	4-03-003	MONOPOLIZE	4-04-004	OUTMODED	4-01-002	PLUMPNESS
4-03-003	MAGICIAN	4-02-002	MONTREAL	4-04-004	OUTRAGE	4-02-003	POE
4-01-001	MAGWITCH'S	4-03-004	MOPPED	4-04-004	OUTRUN	4-01-001	POETRY-AND-JAZZ
4-01-001	MAHLER'S	4-02-002	MORRISON	4-04-004	OUTWEIGHED	4-04-004	POISONED
4-01-002	MAILBOXES	4-04-004	MOSAIC	4-04-004	OVERGROWN	4-03-004	POKED
4-02-002	MAJOR-LEAGUE	4-03-003	MOSCOW'S	4-03-003	OVERLAP	4-03-004	POLITIC
4-03-003	MAKINGS	4-02-003	MOTHERS'	4-04-004	OVERLOOK	4-02-004	POLO
4-02-002	MALFORMED	4-03-004	MOTTO	4-03-003	OVERLOOKS	4-02-003	POLYETHYLENE
4-03-003	MALNUTRITION	4-02-002	MOUNTAINSIDE	4-01-001	OVERPAYMENT	4-01-001	POLYMERS
4-03-004	MAMMOTH	4-02-002	MOVERS	4-03-004	OVERSIMPLIFIED	4-02-003	PONDERED
4-04-004	MANAGES	4-03-004	MULE	4-03-004	OVERTONES	4-01-001	PONS
4-01-001	MANAS	4-01-001	MULLIGAN'S	4-04-004	OVERWHELMED	4-03-003	POPULACE
4-04-004	MANEUVERING	4-04-004	MURDEROUS	4-03-004	OWING	4-02-002	PORTS
4-04-004	MANIAC	4-04-004	MURMURING	4-01-001	OYABUN	4-03-003	PORTSMOUTH
4-03-004	MANKIND'S	4-03-004	MUSE	4-01-001	OZAGEN	4-04-004	PORTUGAL
4-01-001	MANNING'S	4-02-004	MUSED	4-01-001	PA'S	4-01-002	POSITIVISM
4-03-004	MANSIONS	4-01-001	MUSMANNO	4-02-002	PAGAN	4-04-004	POSSESSIVE
4-02-003	MANSLAUGHTER	4-01-001	MYRA'S	4-01-001	PAH	4-02-002	POST-ATTACK
4-03-004	MANUALS	4-03-003	N**.*C	4-03-004	PAIL	4-03-003	POSTER
4-01-003	MANUFACTURER'S	4-02-004	NAME'S	4-04-004	PAILS	4-02-002	POSTERS
4-02-002	MANUSCRIPTS	4-04-004	NAMING	4-03-004	PALL	4-02-004	POSTMASTER
4-01-002	MARIN	4-03-003	NANTUCKET	4-04-004	PANAMA	4-01-001	POTEMKIN
4-01-001	MARINE'S	4-03-003	NAP	4-03-004	PANORAMA	4-02-003	POTENTIALS
4-01-001	MARIS'S	4-03-004	NARROWING	4-03-004	PARALLELED	4-02-003	POTTER
4-02-002	MARITIME	4-02-004	NATIONALIST	4-03-003	PARASITES	4-04-004	POUNDED
4-03-004	MARKEDLY	4-03-003	NATIONALISTIC	4-01-001	PAREDON	4-02-004	POWERFULLY
4-01-001	MARKETABLE	4-02-003	NATIONALS	4-01-002	PARENCHYMA	4-01-001	POZZATTI
4-03-003	MARKSMANSHIP	4-03-004	NATURALISTIC	4-02-002	PARKERSBURG	4-03-004	PRAGMATIC
4-01-002	MARLOWE	4-02-003	NATURES	4-03-003	PARODY	4-04-004	PREAMBLE
4-03-003	MARQUIS	4-01-001	NAVONA	4-02-003	PARTICIPANT	4-04-004	PRECLUDE
4-04-004	MARRED	4-02-002	NEAL	4-03-004	PARTING	4-02-002	PREDISPOSITION
4-02-002	MARSH	4-03-003	NEGLIGENCE	4-03-004	PASSAGEWAY	4-02-003	PREFERENTIAL
4-02-003	MARX'S	4-02-002	NEGRO'S	4-03-004	PASTIME	4-01-001	PREGNANCY
4-01-001	MASARYK	4-01-002	NEIMAN-*MARCUS	4-02-003	PASTRY	4-03-004	PREJUDICED
4-02-003	MASKED	4-01-001	NEITZBOHR	4-04-004	PATRON	4-04-004	PREJUDICES
4-02-002	MATED	4-02-002	NEMESIS	4-02-002	PATTING	4-03-003	PREJUDICIAL
4-03-003	MATH	4-01-004	NESTED	4-01-001	PAVILION	4-03-003	PREMIERES
4-02-003	MATTHEW	4-01-001	NEUROSES	4-01-001	PAWTUXET	4-04-004	PREPARES
4-03-004	MAYFLOWER	4-01-001	NEUTROPHILS	4-03-004	PEACETIME	4-01-001	PREPOLYMER
4-01-002	MC*AULIFFE	4-01-001	NEWBURY	4-02-002	PEACOCKS	4-03-004	PRESUMPTUOUS
4-03-004	MECHANICALLY	4-02-003	NEWSLETTER	4-04-004	PECULIARITIES	4-03-004	PRETENCE
4-04-004	MECHANIZATION	4-01-004	NEWSMEN	4-03-004	PEDAL	4-02-003	PRETTIER
4-01-001	MECHOLYL	4-02-002	NIGHTCLUBS	4-02-002	PEERLESS	4-03-003	PRETTIEST
4-04-004	MEDALS	4-03-004	NIGHTFALL	4-02-002	PEG	4-04-004	PREVALENCE
4-03-003	MEDDLING	4-03-003	NIGHTINGALE	4-01-001	PEMBINA	4-02-003	PRICED
4-03-004	MEDITATIONS	4-02-002	NIKOLAIS	4-02-003	PENALTIES	4-03-004	PRINCIPALS
4-01-001	MEDIUMS	4-01-001	NISCHWITZ	4-01-001	PENCILS	4-02-002	PRIVY
4-01-001	MELIES	4-03-004	NOBILITY	4-03-004	PENNED	4-01-002	PROCESSOR
4-03-004	MELODIOUS	4-04-004	NOBODY'S	4-02-002	PENSACOLA	4-03-003	PROCLAIMING
4-04-004	MELODRAMATIC	4-04-004	NOISILY	4-01-001	PERALTA	4-03-003	PROCLAIMS
4-04-004	MELT	4-02-002	NON-*CATHOLICS	4-04-004	PERCHED	4-03-003	PROCTOR
4-02-004	MELVIN	4-02-003	NONFICTION	4-02-002	PERCUSSION	4-01-002	PROCURE
4-01-001	MELZI	4-01-001	NONMETALLIC	4-02-002	PERFORMS	4-03-004	PROCURED
4-02-004	MEMOIRS	4-01-001	NORDMANN	4-03-004	PERIODICAL	4-04-004	PRODIGIOUS
4-04-004	MENACING	4-03-003	NORMALCY	4-03-004	PERPETUATING	4-03-004	PROF
4-03-004	MERCIFULLY	4-02-002	NORTHERNER	4-01-001	PERSIA	4-04-004	PROFANITY
4-02-004	MERGED	4-02-002	NORTHWESTERN	4-04-004	PERSON'S	4-01-002	PROFITABLY
4-02-002	MERRIMACK	4-04-004	NOTIFIED	4-04-004	PERSUASIVE	4-03-004	PROHIBITING
4-03-004	MESH	4-03-003	NOTWITHSTANDING	4-03-003	PERU	4-01-001	PROLUSIONS
4-01-001	METEORS	4-02-004	NOVELISTS	4-03-003	PERVASIVE	4-03-004	PROMOTERS
4-02-003	METERED	4-03-004	NOZZLE	4-03-003	PEST	4-04-004	PROMOTES
4-04-004	METHODICAL	4-04-004	NUMB	4-03-003	PETALS	4-02-002	PRONOUN
4-01-001	MG/**JL.	4-04-004	NUNS	4-02-002	PETERS	4-03-004	PRONOUNS
4-02-003	MICH	4-02-003	NURSES	4-03-004	PETITIONED	4-01-001	PROPAGANDISTIC
4-01-001	MICKIE	4-04-004	NURTURE	4-01-001	PFAFF	4-01-002	PROPAGANDISTS
4-03-004	MICROPHONE	4-02-002	NUTMEG	4-01-001	PHENOTHIAZINE	4-03-004	PROPEL
4-03-003	MICROPHONES	4-03-003	NYMPHOMANIAC	4-04-004	PHILANTHROPIC	4-03-004	PROPHESIED
4-03-003	MICROSCOPY	4-01-001	O**.-*B	4-03-003	PHILIPPINES	4-03-004	PROPHETS
4-02-002	MICROSECONDS	4-04-004	OBLIGATED	4-01-001	PHILMONT	4-01-001	PROTEASES
4-01-003	MIDDLE-	4-02-002	OBSERVATIONAL	4-04-004	PHOTOGRAPHED	4-02-004	PROTECTS
4-02-002	MIDGE	4-04-004	OBSTRUCT	4-02-003	PHOUMA	4-03-004	PROTRUDED
4-03-004	MILESTONE	4-04-004	OBSTRUCTED	4-02-003	PHRASING	4-04-004	PROVERBIAL
4-02-003	MILIEU	4-01-002	OCCLUDED	4-01-001	PHYFE	4-04-004	PROVOKES
4-03-004	MILLENNIUM	4-03-004	OCCUPANCY	4-02-002	PIANIST'S	4-01-002	PSALM
4-01-001	MILSTEIN	4-04-004	OCCUPANT	4-04-004	PICKS	4-03-004	PSYCHIATRIST
4-01-001	MINARETS	4-03-004	OCCUPIES	4-04-004	PICTURED	4-02-002	PSYCHICAL
4-01-002	MINUMUM	4-01-001	OEDIPAL	4-02-002	PIERCED	4-03-004	PSYCHOLOGICALLY
4-03-004	MIRACULOUS	4-03-004	OFFEND	4-03-004	PIETY	4-04-004	PUBLISHES
4-02-004	MIRRORS	4-01-001	OILSEEDS	4-04-004	PILGRIM	4-03-003	PUFFED
4-03-004	MISCONCEPTION	4-03-004	OLD-TIME	4-03-003	PINNED	4-02-002	PULLEN
4-04-004	MISHAP	4-01-001	OLIVETTI	4-03-003	PIRATE	4-04-004	PULPIT
4-03-003	MISSOURI'S	4-03-004	ONE-FIFTH	4-02-003	PIROUETTE	4-03-004	PUNCTUATED
4-03-003	MISTRUST	4-04-004	ONIONS	4-03-003	PISTOLS	4-04-004	PUNGENT
4-04-004	MISTY	4-04-004	ONRUSH	4-03-004	PITIFUL	4-03-003	PURCHASERS
4-01-003	MIXTURES	4-04-004	ONSLAUGHT	4-03-003	PITS	4-02-004	PURIFICATION
4-03-004	MOBILIZED	4-04-004	OPPRESSIVE	4-03-003	PLAQUES	4-02-004	PURPORTED
4-02-003	MOBS	4-02-004	OPTIONAL	4-02-002	PLASTICITY	4-01-001	PURVIS
4-02-004	MODERATES	4-02-003	ORCHESTRAL	4-03-003	PLATINUM	4-02-002	PUSH-UPS
4-03-003	MODERATOR	4-04-004	ORCHESTRAS	4-02-002	PLATONISM	4-03-003	PUZZLES
4-03-003	MODERNIZING	4-03-004	ORDAINED	4-03-004	PLAUSIBLE	4-03-004	QUAKERS
4-04-004	MODESTY	4-03-004	ORIENT	4-03-004	PLAYGROUND	4-02-004	QUANTITATIVELY
4-03-004	MODIFICATION	4-01-002	ORLEANS'	4-01-002	PLAYHOUSE	4-04-004	QUARRELED
4-01-003	MODIFYING	4-03-003	ORNAMENT	4-02-003	PLENARY	4-03-004	QUARRELS

Code	Word
4-03-004	QUIETER
4-03-004	QUINCY
4-01-001	QUINZAINE
4-03-004	QUITTING
4-01-002	QUIXOTE
4-04-004	QUOTA
4-02-003	QUOTATION
4-01-001	RACE-DRIVERS
4-04-004	RADIATED
4-04-004	RADIATOR
4-01-001	RADIC
4-03-004	RADICALISM
4-03-003	RADICALS
4-02-003	RADII
4-03-003	RAFT
4-03-003	RAINBOW
4-04-004	RAINED
4-03-004	RAKED
4-02-002	RAMEAU'S
4-04-004	RAMPANT
4-02-004	RANKED
4-02-002	RAPHAEL
4-03-004	RAPIDITY
4-03-004	RAPPED
4-02-003	RAPPORT
4-03-004	RATIFIED
4-01-002	RATIONALISM
4-03-003	RATIONS
4-01-001	RAWLINGS
4-02-004	RE-EXAMINE
4-03-004	REACTING
4-03-004	READER'S
4-04-004	REASONED
4-03-004	REBELLED
4-03-004	REBUFF
4-04-004	REBUFFED
4-03-003	REBUILT
4-02-003	RECEIPT
4-02-004	RECONCILE
4-03-004	RECONSIDER
4-03-004	RECONSIDERATION
4-02-002	RECONSIDERED
4-03-004	RECOVERING
4-03-004	RECRUITED
4-04-004	RECRUITING
4-02-003	RECTANGLE
4-02-004	RECURRENT
4-02-004	REDEMPTION
4-02-003	REDS
4-03-004	REDUCTIONS
4-03-004	REDUNDANCY
4-03-003	REDUNDANT
4-01-001	REF
4-03-004	REFLEX
4-02-004	REGAINED
4-04-004	REGISTERING
4-01-001	REGISTRANT
4-01-001	REGISTRIES
4-03-003	REGULATING
4-04-004	REHEARSAL
4-02-002	REHEARSALS
4-03-004	REJECTING
4-04-004	REJOICING
4-03-004	RELIES
4-02-003	RELIGIOUSLY
4-04-004	RELINQUISHED
4-02-004	RELINQUISHING
4-03-004	REMINISCENT
4-04-004	REMOTELY
4-04-004	RENEW
4-03-003	RENTS
4-03-004	REORGANIZED
4-03-004	REPEATS
4-02-003	REPLENISH
4-04-004	REPOSITORY
4-02-002	REPUBLICANISM
4-02-002	REPUDIATION
4-03-003	REPULSIVE
4-03-003	REPUTEDLY
4-04-004	REREAD
4-04-004	RESEARCHERS
4-03-004	RESERVING
4-02-004	RESIDES
4-04-004	RESISTING
4-04-004	RESOLUTE
4-02-002	RESONANT
4-03-004	RESPECTFUL
4-03-004	RESPONSIVE
4-02-002	RESPONSIVENESS
4-02-003	RESTATEMENT
4-03-003	RESTRICTING
4-03-004	RESUMING
4-04-004	RETORT
4-04-004	RETRIBUTION
4-04-004	REVOLVED
4-04-004	REWARDING
4-03-004	REWARDS
4-02-003	REWRITE
4-01-001	RICCO
4-01-001	RICKARDS
4-03-003	RIDGES
4-03-003	RIFLEMAN
4-03-003	RIGHTFUL
4-03-003	RIGHTLY
4-03-003	RIGOROUSLY
4-04-004	RIGORS
4-03-003	RIGS
4-03-004	RIO
4-03-004	RISKED
4-01-001	RITCHIE
4-03-004	RITES
4-02-003	RITUALS
4-02-002	ROAD'S
4-04-004	ROADSIDE
4-04-004	ROBES
4-03-004	ROCKER
4-01-001	RODDING
4-04-004	RODS
4-03-003	ROLAND
4-02-004	RON
4-03-004	ROOKIES
4-02-003	ROPES
4-01-001	ROSA
4-01-001	ROSBURG
4-02-003	ROSEBUDS
4-02-003	ROSENBERG
4-04-004	ROULETTE
4-02-002	ROVER
4-03-004	ROWDY
4-03-004	RUBBISH
4-04-004	RUDIMENTARY
4-02-003	RUDY
4-01-001	RUGER
4-03-004	RUGS
4-02-003	RUNWAY
4-02-002	RUNWAYS
4-03-003	RUSTLE
4-02-002	RUSTLER
4-02-003	RYE
4-01-001	SACREDNESS
4-04-004	SADDLED
4-04-004	SAFEST
4-04-004	SAG
4-02-004	SAGGING
4-03-004	SAITH
4-03-003	SALIENT
4-03-004	SALINGER
4-02-002	SALIVA
4-03-003	SALTED
4-03-004	SALTY
4-02-004	SAM'S
4-02-002	SAMENESS
4-03-004	SANCTIONED
4-02-004	SANDWICHES
4-03-004	SANITARY
4-04-004	SANITY
4-01-001	SARA
4-04-004	SARATOGA
4-03-003	SATIRIC
4-04-004	SATISFACTIONS
4-02-002	SAUERKRAUT
4-03-003	SAVORY
4-02-003	SAVOY
4-01-002	SAVOY
4-01-001	SAXOPHONE
4-02-003	SCALP
4-02-002	SCANNING
4-04-004	SCANTY
4-01-001	SCAPIN
4-02-002	SCARF
4-01-001	SCHAEFER
4-01-001	SCHIELE
4-01-001	SCHILLINGER
4-03-003	SCHUBERT'S
4-02-002	SCIATICA
4-03-004	SCIENTIFICALLY
4-03-004	SCOOTED
4-02-004	SCOREBOARD
4-04-004	SCORN
4-04-004	SCOURING
4-04-004	SCOWLED
4-04-004	SCRAWNY
4-02-002	SCRIBE
4-03-004	SCRIPTURE
4-01-001	SEABOARD
4-04-004	SEALING
4-03-004	SEALS
4-04-004	SECRETARIAL
4-01-001	SECRETION
4-01-001	SEDANS
4-02-002	SEDIMENTS
4-01-001	SEEBOHM
4-01-001	SELENA
4-04-004	SELF-CONFIDENCE
4-03-004	SELF-ESTEEM
4-03-004	SELF-IMPOSED
4-02-003	SELF-INDULGENCE
4-04-004	SELF-RESPECT
4-03-004	SELF-SATISFACTION
4-01-002	SELF-UNLOADING
4-01-001	SELKIRK'S
4-02-003	SELVES
4-03-004	SEMINAR
4-03-004	SENATE'S
4-04-004	SENDS
4-04-004	SENSIBLY
4-04-004	SERVICEABLE
4-04-004	SERVICING
4-04-004	SET-UP
4-03-004	SEVENTY
4-03-004	SEWERS
4-02-003	SEXTET
4-03-004	SEXUALITY
4-03-003	SHADING
4-01-001	SHAYOL
4-02-004	SHEATH
4-03-004	SHEDS
4-01-001	SHEIK
4-04-004	SHELTERED
4-04-004	SHINES
4-03-004	SHIVER
4-03-004	SHIVERED
4-04-004	SHOCKING
4-01-002	SHOOTER
4-04-004	SHORTEN
4-01-002	SHOUP
4-03-004	SHOWDOWN
4-02-003	SHRIEKED
4-03-004	SHRINES
4-03-003	SHRUBS
4-03-004	SHYLY
4-02-003	SIAMESE
4-01-001	SIBYLLA
4-03-003	SIC
4-02-003	SICKENED
4-01-001	SIGMEN
4-03-004	SILHOUETTE
4-03-004	SILL
4-03-004	SIMON
4-02-003	SIMULATE
4-03-003	SINATRA
4-02-004	SINE
4-03-004	SINNERS
4-04-004	SIZED
4-02-003	SKETCHED
4-03-004	SKETCHING
4-01-001	SKIFFS
4-04-004	SKIMMING
4-01-001	SKINLESS
4-01-001	SKIPJACK
4-03-004	SKIPPING
4-04-004	SKIRMISH
4-04-004	SKIRTS
4-01-001	SKOLOVSKY
4-01-001	SKOPAS
4-03-004	SLAMMING
4-03-004	SLANTING
4-04-004	SLICED
4-03-004	SLOB
4-03-004	SLOWNESS
4-01-001	SLUDGE
4-02-004	SLUGGED
4-02-003	SLUGGER
4-04-004	SLUGS
4-03-003	SMACK
4-02-002	SMALLWOOD
4-03-004	SMARTLY
4-04-004	SMASH
4-02-003	SMYTHE
4-04-004	SNATCH
4-03-003	SNOBBERY
4-01-002	SNOPES
4-03-004	SNORTED
4-04-004	SNOWING
4-04-004	SNOWY
4-02-004	SNUGGLED
4-02-003	SO'S
4-02-003	SO-SO
4-02-004	SOARED
4-03-004	SOBERLY
4-02-002	SOCIETAL
4-03-004	SOCK
4-03-004	SOFTEN
4-01-001	SOKOL
4-01-001	SOLDER
4-03-003	SOLIDITY
4-01-002	SON-IN-LAW
4-01-001	SONGAU
4-03-004	SONOFABITCH
4-02-004	SOOTHING
4-04-004	SORTED
4-01-001	SPADES
4-04-004	SPARKLE
4-04-004	SPEAKER'S
4-03-004	SPECIALIZING
4-03-004	SPECIALTY
4-03-004	SPECIFIES
4-03-004	SPECULATING
4-04-004	SPECULATIONS
4-03-004	SPEEDING
4-02-004	SPELLING
4-02-003	SPHERES
4-02-004	SPICE
4-01-001	SPINCO
4-03-004	SPLENDIDLY
4-02-002	SPLINTER
4-01-001	SPORTIN
4-01-001	SPOSATO
4-03-004	SPOUSES
4-03-004	SPREE
4-04-004	SPRINGTIME
4-03-003	SPRINKLED
4-01-001	SQ
4-03-004	SQUATTED
4-03-003	SQUEEZING
4-03-003	SR
4-02-004	STABILIZING
4-01-001	STAFFE
4-01-001	STALAG
4-03-004	STALE
4-03-004	STALLED
4-04-004	STALWART
4-02-003	STAMFORD
4-04-004	STAMMERED
4-02-002	STAMPEDE
4-03-003	STAMPS
4-02-004	STANDARDIZED
4-02-002	STANLEY'S
4-04-004	STANTON
4-01-001	STARBIRD
4-01-001	STARCH
4-04-004	STARTLINGLY
4-01-003	STAT
4-04-004	STATELY
4-03-004	STATION'S
4-02-004	STATISTICALLY
4-03-003	STEAKS
4-03-003	STEEPLES
4-03-003	STEERED
4-01-001	STEIN'S
4-02-002	STETTIN
4-03-004	STIFFENING
4-03-003	STITCHES
4-04-004	STOOP
4-03-003	STOOPING
4-03-003	STORING
4-03-004	STORYTELLER
4-01-001	STRAM
4-02-004	STRATEGISTS
4-04-004	STREAKED
4-03-004	STREAMED
4-03-003	STREAMLINED
4-02-003	STRENGTHS
4-02-002	STRIPE
4-04-004	STRIVING
4-03-004	STROLL
4-04-004	STROLLED
4-03-004	STROLLING
4-04-004	STROVE
4-04-004	STRUNG
4-02-002	STRYCHNINE
4-01-001	STUBBLEFIELD
4-01-001	STUBBLEFIELDS
4-03-003	STUCCO
4-04-004	STUDENTS'
4-03-004	STUPOR
4-03-003	SUBCONSCIOUS
4-03-004	SUBCONSCIOUSLY
4-03-003	SUBMISSION
4-02-002	SUBMISSIVE
4-03-003	SUBORDINATED
4-04-004	SUBSCRIPTION
4-03-003	SUBSIDIZE
4-03-004	SUBSIDIZED
4-04-004	SUBSTITUTING
4-02-004	SUBTLETIES
4-03-003	SUBTRACTED
4-03-004	SUED
4-02-004	SUFFERINGS
4-04-004	SUITES
4-02-003	SUKARNO
4-04-004	SULKY
4-02-002	SULTANS
4-04-004	SUMMERTIME
4-02-002	SUMPTUOUS
4-04-004	SUN'S
4-01-001	SUPER-CONDAMINE
4-03-003	SUPERIMPOSE

Rank	Entry	Rank	Entry	Rank	Entry	Rank	Entry
4-01-001	SUPERIORS	4-03-004	TONGUES	4-02-003	UNSPECIFIED	4-03-004	WINCED
4-02-003	SUPERNATURALISM	4-02-003	TOPICAL	4-01-001	UNSTRESSED	4-02-002	WINNERS
4-02-002	SUPERSONIC	4-03-004	TORMENT	4-03-004	UNTRAMMELED	4-02-002	WINOOSKI
4-04-004	SUPERVISED	4-01-001	TORQUERS	4-04-004	UNWARRANTED	4-04-004	WISTFULLY
4-04-004	SUPPRESSED	4-04-004	TORRENT	4-02-004	UPHOLDING	4-03-004	WITHDRAWING
4-03-004	SUPREMELY	4-03-004	TOY	4-03-004	URBANIZED	4-04-004	WITHDRAWN
4-03-003	SURPLUSES	4-02-002	TRADITIONALIST	4-03-004	USER	4-01-001	WOLLMAN
4-03-003	SURRENDERING	4-03-003	TRAITORS	4-03-004	UTILIZES	4-04-004	WOLVES
4-03-003	SUSPECTS	4-03-003	TRANCE	4-03-004	VACATED	4-03-004	WOODROW
4-03-004	SUSPICIOUSLY	4-03-003	TRANQUILITY	4-01-001	VALE	4-04-004	WOOLEN
4-02-003	SWARTHY	4-03-003	TRANQUILIZERS	4-02-004	VALVES	4-02-002	WOONSOCKET
4-04-004	SWEATERS	4-03-004	TRANSCRIPT	4-03-004	VANISHING	4-03-004	WORDED
4-04-004	SWEATING	4-02-002	TRANSFUSIONS	4-04-004	VARIANT	4-03-004	WORDING
4-01-001	SWEENEY	4-02-002	TRANSMITTER	4-01-001	VARLAAM	4-02-003	WORKER'S
4-03-003	SWELLS	4-04-004	TRANSMUTED	4-03-003	VASE	4-03-004	WORM
4-03-003	SWIRLING	4-01-001	TRANSPIRATION	4-04-004	VATICAN	4-03-003	WRITERS'
4-02-004	SWISHED	4-01-001	TRANSPIRING	4-03-004	VELVET	4-01-001	XYLEM
4-03-004	SWORDS	4-02-002	TRANSVERSE	4-02-002	VENTS	4-02-002	Y'ALL
4-03-004	SYNONYMOUS	4-04-004	TRAVELLED	4-04-004	VENTURES	4-02-003	YA
4-03-003	SYRUP	4-04-004	TRAVELLING	4-03-004	VERB	4-02-002	YACHT
4-01-001	SZOLDS	4-04-004	TREASURE	4-03-004	VERIFICATION	4-02-003	YANKS
4-02-004	TABULATED	4-03-003	TREATIES	4-04-004	VERITABLE	4-01-001	YARROW
4-02-003	TACK	4-02-003	TRENCHANT	4-02-003	VERSATILITY	4-03-004	YEAR-ROUND
4-03-004	TACTIC	4-02-002	TRENTON	4-03-004	VERVE	4-02-002	YIDDISH
4-03-003	TAHOE	4-01-001	TRI-IODOTHYRONINE	4-03-004	VEST	4-01-001	YR
4-03-004	TAKE-OFF	4-01-001	TRIAMCINOLONE	4-03-004	VETERINARY	4-02-003	ZEALOUS
4-01-001	TAKE-UP	4-03-004	TRIANGLE	4-03-003	VIC	4-02-004	ZIGZAGGING
4-03-004	TALKATIVE	4-04-004	TRIBE	4-02-004	VICAR	4-02-004	0.2
4-02-003	TALLY	4-03-003	TRIBUNALS	4-04-004	VICTIM'S	4-02-002	0.4
4-03-003	TALMUD	4-01-003	TRILOGY	4-03-004	VIEWER	4-01-003	0.8
4-02-004	TANG	4-03-004	TRIMMED	4-03-003	VIGILANCE	4-01-001	1**C10
4-04-004	TANTALIZING	4-03-003	TRIMMINGS	4-03-004	VILLAINS	4-01-001	1*,-**J*A
4-01-002	TAO	4-03-004	TRIPLED	4-03-004	VINDICATION	4-02-004	1-1/2
4-02-002	TAOISM	4-02-004	TRISTANO	4-04-004	VINE	4-04-004	10-YEAR-OLD
4-02-003	TAPES	4-02-002	TROUT	4-02-002	VINYL	4-01-001	1040**J*A
4-01-001	TARTUFFE	4-04-004	TRUDGED	4-01-001	VIOLA'S	4-03-003	108
4-01-001	TARZAN	4-04-004	TRUSTING	4-03-004	VIOLATED	4-01-001	11**C20
4-04-004	TAUNT	4-03-004	TRUTHS	4-04-004	VIOLATING	4-03-003	114
4-04-004	TAVERNS	4-03-004	TUBULAR	4-02-003	VIOLINIST	4-02-004	133
4-03-004	TAWNY	4-03-003	TUDOR	4-02-003	VIRGINIAN	4-01-001	14-1/2
4-01-001	TEASPOON	4-03-004	TULIP	4-02-002	VIRGINITY	4-03-003	14TH
4-02-003	TEDDY	4-01-001	TULTUL	4-04-004	VIRILE	4-03-004	15**K
4-04-004	TEEN-AGE	4-01-003	TUNGSTEN	4-01-002	VISCERAL	4-02-002	154
4-04-004	TEENAGE	4-02-002	TURBULENT	4-01-002	VISCOELASTIC	4-01-001	1629
4-04-004	TELESCOPE	4-01-001	TURPENTINE	4-03-004	VISUALLY	4-01-001	1632
4-03-004	TELEVISED	4-01-001	TUSSLE	4-01-002	VITRO	4-02-002	1801
4-02-002	TELLER	4-03-003	TUTOR	4-01-002	VIVO	4-02-003	1812
4-04-004	TEMPLES	4-01-002	TUTTLE	4-01-002	VOLTAGES	4-02-004	1817
4-03-004	TEMPO	4-03-003	TWILIGHT	4-03-004	VOTER	4-01-001	1818
4-04-004	TENABLE	4-04-004	TWINED	4-02-003	VOYAGEURS	4-02-002	1840
4-04-004	TENDERLY	4-02-002	TWISTER	4-03-003	VULTURE	4-02-003	1851
4-04-004	TENDERNESS	4-03-004	TWITCHED	4-02-002	WABASH	4-01-001	1875
4-03-004	TENDING	4-03-004	TWO-DAY	4-01-001	WADE-*EVANS	4-03-003	1876
4-03-004	TENSELY	4-03-004	TWO-HOUR	4-02-002	WARDEN	4-02-003	1887
4-03-004	TERMINALS	4-03-004	TWOFOLD	4-04-004	WAREHOUSE	4-03-004	1891
4-03-004	TERMINATED	4-02-003	U**.*S**.*A	4-02-003	WAREHOUSES	4-04-004	1892
4-02-004	TESTIFIES	4-03-004	U**.S	4-03-003	WARMER	4-03-004	1898
4-03-004	TEXTBOOK	4-01-001	UHHU	4-01-001	WARP	4-03-004	1901
4-04-004	TEXTS	4-03-004	ULTRA-VIOLET	4-01-002	WARPING	4-04-004	1907
4-03-003	THAILAND	4-02-002	UMBER	4-04-004	WATCHES	4-03-004	1909
4-03-004	THERE'D	4-03-004	UN-*AMERICAN	4-04-004	WATERING	4-04-004	1920S
4-03-004	THIEVING	4-03-004	UNAFRAID	4-02-002	WATERSHEDS	4-03-004	1950'S
4-01-001	THIRD-GRADE	4-03-004	UNAIDED	4-02-002	WAVELENGTH	4-02-002	1959-1960
4-03-003	THIRDS	4-03-003	UNARMED	4-04-004	WAXED	4-02-004	1966
4-04-004	THIRST	4-03-004	UNBELIEVABLE	4-02-004	WEAVE	4-02-003	1980
4-04-004	THIRTY-SIX	4-03-004	UNBORN	4-01-003	WEAVER	4-02-003	2.1
4-01-001	THOR'S	4-03-004	UNCHARGED	4-03-004	WEDDED	4-02-003	2.5
4-01-001	THORPE	4-04-004	UNCLEAN	4-03-004	WEDGE	4-02-003	2.6
4-02-004	THREADED	4-03-003	UNCONDITIONAL	4-01-001	WEIGAND	4-02-004	2**C30
4-02-003	THREE-MONTH	4-03-004	UNCONTROLLED	4-04-004	WEIGH	4-01-001	2**C35**JH
4-04-004	THREE-QUARTERS	4-02-004	UNCOVER	4-03-004	WEIGHS	4-02-004	2D
4-03-003	THREEFOLD	4-04-004	UNDEFINED	4-03-004	WEIGHTED	4-03-004	200,000
4-03-004	THRILLING	4-01-001	UNDEPICTED	4-04-004	WEIGHTY	4-03-003	250,000
4-04-004	THRIVING	4-04-004	UNDERESTIMATE	4-02-002	WELD	4-03-003	275
4-01-001	THRONEBERRY	4-03-004	UNDERFOOT	4-02-003	WELL-EDUCATED	4-03-004	280
4-01-001	THROWIN	4-04-004	UNDERSTATEMENT	4-04-004	WELL-KEPT	4-01-001	3.15
4-04-004	THWARTED	4-03-003	UNDERTAKINGS	4-02-002	WELSH	4-02-004	3.5
4-01-001	THYROID-STIMULATING	4-03-004	UNDERWRITERS	4-03-003	WESTCHESTER	4-03-004	3-1/2
4-01-001	TICONDEROGA	4-04-004	UNDEVELOPED	4-02-003	WETTING	4-01-001	348
4-02-003	TIDES	4-03-003	UNDONE	4-02-002	WHARF	4-04-004	360
4-04-004	TIGHTENING	4-04-004	UNEXPLAINED	4-03-004	WHEELER	4-01-001	381
4-04-004	TILED	4-04-004	UNEXPLORED	4-02-003	WHERE'D	4-01-001	381(A
4-01-001	TILGHMAN'S	4-02-004	UNFETTERED	4-02-003	WHINE	4-01-001	4.2
4-02-004	TIMETABLE	4-03-004	UNFOLDED	4-02-004	WHISPERS	4-01-001	4-**J*H
4-04-004	TIPPED	4-02-002	UNFOLDS	4-03-003	WHISTLE	4-02-002	45*+0
4-02-004	TIRELESS	4-02-002	UNHEALTHY	4-02-002	WHITE'S	4-04-004	450
4-04-004	TIRING	4-03-004	UNIFYING	4-01-001	WHITEMAN	4-01-003	50-MEGATON
4-01-002	TITER	4-03-003	UNIMPRESSED	4-03-003	WHITNEY	4-03-004	5000
4-01-001	TITERS	4-02-004	UNINHIBITED	4-03-004	WICK	4-03-004	59
4-01-002	TO-DAY	4-03-004	UNNAMED	4-04-004	WICKER	4-01-001	6-**JHR
4-03-003	TOAD	4-04-004	UNNOTICED	4-03-003	WILDCAT	4-03-004	7.5
4-02-002	TOILETS	4-01-001	UNPAIRED	4-03-004	WILHELM	4-03-003	70,000
4-03-004	TOLERATE	4-03-004	UNRELIABLE	4-02-003	WILLARD	4-01-001	707
4-03-003	TOM'S	4-04-004	UNRELIEVED	4-01-003	WILLIE'S	4-01-001	7070/7074
4-01-001	TOMAS	4-03-004	UNSETTLED	4-04-004	WILLINGLY	4-03-003	73
4-02-004	TOMATO	4-02-002	UNSINKABLE	4-03-003	WILLY-NILLY	4-02-003	75**K
				4-02-003	WILMETTE	4-02-003	750

Code	Word
4-03-004	77
4-04-004	90**K
4-03-003	97
4-02-002	.300
4-01-001	.44
4-01-002	.45
4-02-003	$1,500
4-03-003	$100,000
4-02-004	$25,000
4-02-004	$250
4-01-001	$28
4-03-003	$3,000
4-02-002	$45
4-02-003	$700
4-03-004	$75
4-01-001	**F-STAGE
4-01-002	**YT
4-01-002	*=*P*$.
4-01-002	*=B*$
4-02-002	*=H*$
4-01-001	*=L*$
4-01-001	*=VS*$
4-02-002	*A+**J*M
4-01-001	*A*I*D
4-01-002	*A-**J*Z
4-01-001	*B**U
4-01-001	*B*A*M
4-02-002	*B-70
4-01-001	*C*T*C*A
4-02-003	*C,
4-01-001	*E*Q*U
4-01-003	*F.
4-02-003	*K
4-01-001	*K*C
4-01-001	*P-20
4-01-002	*S*M*U
4-01-002	*S*M*U.
4-01-001	*T*A*S*S
4-01-001	*T*R
4-01-001	*T,
4-02-002	*U*S
4-03-003	*V-SHAPED
3-02-003	A**.*B
3-02-002	ABBE
3-03-003	ABE
3-03-003	ABERRATION
3-02-003	ABEYANCE
3-03-003	ABJECT
3-03-003	ABLAZE
3-03-003	ABNORMAL
3-02-003	ABORTIVE
3-01-001	ABSCESSES
3-03-003	ABSENCES
3-03-003	ABSENT-MINDED
3-02-003	ABSENT-MINDEDLY
3-03-003	ABSOLUTES
3-03-003	ABSORBING
3-02-002	ABSTRACTED
3-01-001	ABSTRACTING
3-01-001	ABSTRACTIONISTS
3-01-001	ACACIA
3-03-003	ACADEMIES
3-01-001	ACCELERATORS
3-03-003	ACCENTED
3-03-003	ACCENTUATED
3-02-003	ACCOMPANIMENTS
3-03-003	ACCOMPLISHING
3-02-002	ACCRETION
3-01-002	ACCRUED
3-03-003	ACCUMULATE
3-02-003	ACCUMULATING
3-03-003	ACCUSATION
3-03-003	ACCUSATIONS
3-01-001	ACETONEMIA
3-01-001	ACEY
3-03-003	ACHED
3-02-003	ACOUSTICAL
3-03-003	ACQUAINT
3-02-003	ACQUIESCE
3-03-003	ACTRESSES
3-03-003	ADAGE
3-01-002	ADAGIO
3-01-001	ADAMS'
3-03-003	ADAPTING
3-03-003	ADDICTED
3-03-003	ADDICTION
3-01-001	ADDITIVE
3-03-003	ADEQUACY
3-01-001	ADJECTIVAL
3-01-001	ADLER
3-02-003	ADMINISTER
3-03-003	ADMIRER
3-03-003	ADMISSIONS
3-03-003	ADMITTEDLY
3-02-003	ADMONITIONS
3-01-001	ADOLESCENT'S
3-02-003	ADORABLE
3-01-001	ADRIATIC
3-01-001	ADSORBED
3-03-003	ADULTERY
3-02-002	ADULTHOOD
3-03-003	ADVERSARIES
3-02-003	ADVERSELY
3-03-003	ADVERTISE
3-02-002	ADVERTISEMENTS
3-03-003	ADVISING
3-02-002	ADVOCACY
3-01-001	AEROSOLIZED
3-01-001	AEROSOLS
3-03-003	AFFECTIONATELY
3-02-002	AFGHAN
3-03-003	AFLAME
3-03-003	AFTERNOON'S
3-03-003	AGGLOMERATION
3-03-003	AGGRAVATED
3-01-002	AGGRESSIONS
3-02-002	AGGRIEVED
3-02-003	AGILITY
3-03-003	AGONIZING
3-01-001	AHMET
3-02-003	AIRS
3-02-003	ALABASTER
3-02-002	ALBANIA
3-01-001	ALBRIGHT
3-03-003	ALCOHOLIC
3-03-003	ALERTED
3-02-002	ALEXANDER'S
3-01-001	ALFRED'S
3-02-002	ALFREDO
3-01-001	ALGEBRAICALLY
3-01-001	ALGOL
3-02-002	ALIENS
3-02-003	ALIGHT
3-03-003	ALL-TIME
3-03-003	ALLEGING
3-02-002	ALLEGORICAL
3-03-003	ALLEGORY
3-01-001	ALLOCABLE
3-02-003	ALLOCATE
3-02-002	ALLOY
3-01-001	ALLOYS
3-03-003	ALLUSION
3-01-001	ALMONDS
3-03-003	ALOFT
3-01-002	ALSATIAN
3-02-002	ALSOP
3-01-001	ALTERNATIVELY
3-02-002	ALVAREZ
3-03-003	AMATEURISH
3-03-003	AMAZE
3-03-003	AMAZINGLY
3-02-002	AMBER
3-02-003	AMENABLE
3-01-001	AMERICANEGRO
3-01-001	AMICI
3-02-003	AMIDST
3-01-002	AMORTIZATION
3-02-002	AMOS
3-02-002	AMSTERDAM
3-02-003	AMUSE
3-03-003	ANACHRONISM
3-03-003	ANALYST'S
3-03-003	ANDOVER
3-02-003	ANDRE
3-01-001	ANDROFSKI
3-02-002	ANGEL'S
3-02-002	ANGELES'
3-02-002	ANGOLA
3-02-003	ANIMAL'S
3-03-003	ANIMOSITY
3-03-003	ANNOUNCES
3-03-003	ANNUM
3-01-002	ANTAGONIST
3-02-003	ANTE
3-02-003	ANTE-BELLUM
3-03-003	ANTENNAE
3-01-001	ANTHEA
3-02-002	ANTI-*FRENCH
3-01-001	ANTI-*SEMITES
3-02-003	ANTI-INTELLECTUAL
3-02-002	ANTI-SUBMARINE
3-03-003	ANTICIPATIONS
3-02-003	ANTIQUES
3-02-003	ANTIQUITY
3-02-003	ANTITHESIS
3-01-001	ANTLER
3-01-001	ANTOINE'S
3-02-002	AORTA
3-02-002	APACHES
3-02-002	APARTHEID
3-02-002	APATHY
3-03-003	APE
3-03-003	APOLOGETIC
3-01-002	APOLOGY
3-01-001	APOTHECARY
3-02-002	APPAREL
3-03-003	APPARITION
3-03-003	APPEASEMENT
3-02-003	APPETITES
3-02-002	APPRENTICES
3-03-003	APPROXIMATIONS
3-02-003	APTITUDE
3-03-003	ARABLE
3-01-002	ARBITRATE
3-01-001	ARBOGAST
3-03-003	ARCADE
3-01-001	ARCHANGEL
3-02-002	ARDEN
3-02-002	ARDOR
3-03-003	ARENAS
3-01-001	ARGER
3-02-002	ARIADNE
3-03-003	ARM'S
3-01-001	ARMHOLE
3-03-003	ARMORED
3-01-001	AROMA
3-03-003	AROUSAL
3-02-003	AROUSING
3-02-002	ARRESTS
3-02-002	ARRIVALS
3-03-003	ARROGANCE
3-01-001	ARROYO
3-03-003	ARSENAL
3-01-001	ARTERIOLAR
3-02-002	ARTHRITIS
3-02-003	ARTISTRY
3-01-001	ARYLESTERASE
3-03-003	ASPHALT
3-02-003	ASPIRATION
3-03-003	ASPIRE
3-03-003	ASPIRIN
3-03-003	ASSAIL
3-03-003	ASSEMBLAGE
3-02-003	ASSENTED
3-03-003	ASSERTIONS
3-02-003	ASSES
3-03-003	ASSURANCES
3-03-003	ASTRAY
3-03-003	ASTRIDE
3-02-002	ASTROPHYSICS
3-03-003	ATHEISTS
3-01-001	ATROPHIC
3-02-003	ATTACHING
3-03-003	ATTACKERS
3-02-002	ATTORNEY'S
3-03-003	ATTRACTS
3-03-003	ATTRIBUTING
3-02-003	ATTUNED
3-03-003	AUDACITY
3-01-002	AUDITION
3-02-002	AUNTIE
3-02-002	AUTHORITY'S
3-03-003	AUTHORSHIP
3-03-003	AUTOBIOGRAPHICAL
3-01-001	AUTOFLUORESCENCE
3-02-002	AUTOGRAPH
3-01-001	AUTOLOADER
3-02-002	AUTOPSY
3-02-002	AUXILIARIES
3-03-003	AVERTED
3-03-003	AVERTING
3-02-002	AVIATOR
3-03-003	AVOIDS
3-02-003	AW
3-02-002	AWAITS
3-02-002	AWARDING
3-03-003	AXIOMATIC
3-02-002	AZALEAS
3-01-002	B**.*S
3-02-002	BABEL
3-02-002	BABES
3-03-003	BACKYARDS
3-02-002	BAILEY
3-01-001	BAILING
3-01-001	BAILLY
3-03-003	BALLOONS
3-01-001	BALLPLAYERS
3-03-003	BALTIC
3-02-003	BALUSTRADE
3-01-001	BANDAGES
3-02-002	BANDIT
3-03-003	BANDITS
3-03-003	BANQUETS
3-01-001	BANTUS
3-01-001	BARBECUES
3-01-001	BARD
3-03-003	BAREST
3-02-002	BARGAINS
3-03-003	BARGES
3-03-003	BARRACKS
3-03-003	BARRICADE
3-02-002	BARRING
3-03-003	BARRY
3-01-001	BARSTOW
3-02-002	BARTLETT
3-01-001	BARTON'S
3-01-001	BAS-RELIEF
3-01-001	BASCOM
3-01-001	BATAVIA
3-02-003	BATHROBE
3-02-003	BATISTA'S
3-02-002	BATTALION
3-01-001	BATTEN
3-01-002	BATTERIES
3-02-003	BATTLING
3-01-001	BAULLARI
3-02-002	BAVARIA
3-03-003	BAWDY
3-02-003	BAYED
3-01-002	BAYONETS
3-01-001	BEAME
3-02-003	BEAUMONT
3-02-003	BEAVER
3-03-003	BECKONS
3-01-001	BECKSTROM
3-02-002	BEDDING
3-01-001	BEDE
3-01-001	BEEPS
3-02-003	BEGUILING
3-02-002	BEHAVIORAL
3-01-001	BEHAVIOUR
3-03-003	BEHELD
3-02-002	BEIN
3-02-003	BELIED
3-02-003	BELLINI
3-01-001	BENEDICK
3-02-003	BENEDICTION
3-02-003	BENEFICIARIES
3-02-003	BENEFITED
3-03-003	BEQUESTS
3-03-003	BERATED
3-01-001	BERTO
3-02-003	BESS
3-02-003	BETRAYS
3-03-003	BETS
3-03-003	BETTERMENT
3-02-002	BETTY
3-01-001	BEVELED
3-02-003	BEVY
3-03-003	BEWARE
3-03-003	BEWILDERMENT
3-01-001	BICEPS
3-02-002	BICKERING
3-03-003	BIDDERS
3-02-002	BILE
3-02-003	BILLED
3-02-002	BILLIE
3-02-003	BIOCHEMICAL
3-01-001	BIREFRINGENCE
3-01-001	BIRKHEAD
3-03-003	BITTEN
3-01-001	BIZERTE
3-02-002	BLACKBERRY
3-03-003	BLACKED
3-01-001	BLACKMER
3-03-003	BLACKS
3-01-001	BLACKWELL
3-02-002	BLAKEY
3-02-003	BLAND
3-02-002	BLANKS
3-01-001	BLASINGAME
3-03-003	BLDG
3-03-003	BLEAKLY
3-02-003	BLED
3-02-002	BLESSINGS
3-03-003	BLEST
3-03-003	BLIGHTED
3-03-003	BLINDS
3-03-003	BLINKING
3-03-003	BLISTER
3-03-003	BLITHELY
3-03-003	BLITZ
3-03-003	BLOATED
3-03-003	BLOCKING
3-02-002	BLONDE'S
3-03-003	BLOODLESS
3-03-003	BLOODSHED
3-02-003	BLOOMS
3-03-003	BLOTTED
3-03-003	BLUDGEON
3-01-003	BLUE-EYED
3-03-003	BLUE-GREEN
3-03-003	BLUEPRINTS
3-02-003	BLUMBERG
3-03-003	BLUR

Code	Word	Code	Word	Code	Word	Code	Word
3-02-003	BLURTED	3-03-003	BUSTED	3-03-003	CHESS	3-03-003	COMPENSATIONS
3-03-003	BOASTING	3-02-002	BUSTER	3-02-002	CHEYENNES	3-03-003	COMPENSATORY
3-01-001	BOATMAN	3-01-001	BUSTS	3-02-002	CHICK	3-03-003	COMPETITOR
3-02-003	BOATSWAIN	3-03-003	BUTLERS	3-02-002	CHIEF'S	3-02-002	COMPLAINS
3-02-003	BOBBING	3-01-001	BUTTED	3-03-003	CHILDBIRTH	3-03-003	COMPLIMENT
3-02-003	BODY'S	3-02-003	BY-PRODUCT	3-03-003	CHIMNEYS	3-03-003	COMPLYING
3-02-002	BOEING	3-02-003	BYPASS	3-02-003	CHINA'S	3-03-003	COMPOSING
3-01-001	BOGUS	3-02-003	BYPRODUCTS	3-03-003	CHIPS	3-02-003	COMPREHENDING
3-02-002	BOLDNESS	3-02-002	BYRD'S	3-01-001	CHISHOLM	3-03-003	COMPRESSES
3-03-003	BOLSTER	3-02-003	CACKLED	3-01-001	CHOCTAWS	3-02-003	COMPRISES
3-01-001	BOLT-ACTION	3-02-003	CADENZA	3-02-003	CHOP	3-02-003	COMPRISING
3-01-001	BOMBPROOF	3-03-003	CADRE	3-02-002	CHOPPED	3-03-003	COMPULSIVELY
3-02-002	BONDAGE	3-02-002	CAKES	3-02-002	CHOPPY	3-01-001	CONANT'S
3-01-001	BONDI	3-02-002	CALDWELL	3-03-003	CHOPS	3-03-003	CONCEDING
3-03-003	BONFIRE	3-01-001	CALIBERS	3-01-003	CHOREOGRAPHIC	3-02-003	CONCERTED
3-01-001	BONN'S	3-03-003	CALIBRATED	3-02-002	CHOREOGRAPHY	3-02-003	CONCESSION
3-02-003	BONNET	3-02-003	CALIFORNIA'S	3-03-003	CHORTLED	3-02-003	CONCURS
3-02-003	BOOK'S	3-02-002	CALLERS	3-03-003	CHRISTENDOM	3-01-002	CONDEMNS
3-03-003	BOOKER	3-01-001	CALORIC	3-01-002	CHROMATOGRAPHIC	3-02-002	CONDITIONAL
3-01-001	BOOKIES	3-01-001	CALVING	3-03-003	CHRYSLER	3-01-002	CONEY
3-02-003	BOOKSHELVES	3-03-003	CAMOUFLAGE	3-03-003	CHURCHGOING	3-01-001	CONFABULATION
3-03-003	BOON	3-01-001	CAMPER	3-02-002	CHURCHMEN	3-03-003	CONFER
3-03-003	BOOSTED	3-01-001	CAMPGROUND	3-03-003	CHURNING	3-02-002	CONFESSES
3-03-003	BOOSTING	3-03-003	CANAL	3-01-001	CILIATED	3-03-003	CONFESSING
3-03-003	BOOTHS	3-03-003	CANDID	3-02-003	CINCH	3-03-003	CONFIDE
3-02-002	BOOTY	3-02-002	CANTO	3-03-003	CINEMA	3-03-003	CONFIGURATIONS
3-02-002	BOP	3-03-003	CANVASS	3-01-001	CINEMATIC	3-03-003	CONFINING
3-03-003	BORDERLINE	3-02-002	CAPITAL'S	3-02-003	CIRCUMFERENCE	3-02-003	CONFIRMS
3-01-001	BORIS'	3-02-002	CAPSULES	3-03-003	CIRCUMSPECT	3-02-002	CONFORMATION
3-02-003	BOSS'S	3-03-003	CARELESSLY	3-02-002	CITING	3-03-003	CONFORMED
3-02-002	BOTANY	3-02-002	CARLOAD	3-02-003	CITIZENRY	3-02-003	CONFORMIST
3-03-003	BOTHERS	3-02-002	CARLSON	3-02-003	CITIZENSHIP	3-02-002	CONFORMISTS
3-03-003	BOTTLED	3-01-001	CARMER'S	3-01-002	CIUDAD	3-01-002	CONFUCIAN
3-02-002	BOULDERS	3-01-001	CARNE	3-03-003	CLAM	3-02-002	CONFUCIANISM
3-02-002	BOUNTY	3-01-001	CAROLI	3-03-003	CLAMPING	3-02-003	CONGRATULATED
3-01-001	BOURCIER	3-02-002	CAROLINIANS	3-03-003	CLARA	3-01-001	CONGREGATIONALISTS
3-02-003	BOURGEOIS	3-02-002	CARPENTER'S	3-02-003	CLARIFYING		
3-03-003	BOUTS	3-03-003	CARPENTERS	3-02-003	CLASPED	3-02-002	CONGRESS'
3-01-002	BOWING	3-02-003	CARPETED	3-02-003	CLASSMATE	3-02-002	CONGRUENT
3-03-003	BOWLS	3-03-003	CARPING	3-03-003	CLAWS	3-03-003	CONJECTURE
3-02-002	BOWMAN	3-01-001	CARRAWAY	3-01-002	CLAYTON'S	3-03-003	CONJOINED
3-02-003	BOWS	3-03-003	CARTOON	3-02-002	CLEMENTE	3-02-002	CONJUGAL
3-02-003	BOYS'	3-01-001	CARTOONIST	3-02-003	CLEMENTS	3-03-003	CONNECT
3-02-002	BRACING	3-02-003	CARVE	3-03-003	CLEVERNESS	3-02-002	CONNECTIVE
3-03-003	BRACKISH	3-01-001	CASBAH	3-01-001	CLIBURN	3-03-003	CONNOTATIONS
3-01-001	BRANDEL	3-01-001	CASCADING	3-03-003	CLIENTELE	3-03-003	CONQUERED
3-01-003	BRAVES	3-03-003	CASTE	3-03-003	CLIFTON	3-02-002	CONQUERING
3-03-003	BREAKDOWNS	3-02-003	CASUALTIES	3-03-003	CLINGS	3-02-003	CONSERVATORY
3-03-003	BREAKUP	3-02-002	CASUALTY	3-02-002	CLINIC	3-03-003	CONSERVE
3-03-003	BREATH-TAKING	3-02-002	CATALOG	3-01-001	CLINICO-PATHOLOGIC	3-03-003	CONSOLATION
3-03-003	BREATHTAKING	3-03-003	CATALOGUES			3-02-002	CONSONANT
3-01-001	BRENNAN	3-02-002	CATALYST	3-01-002	CLINTON	3-02-003	CONSPIRED
3-01-001	BRENNER'S	3-01-003	CATEGORICAL	3-02-003	CLIPPED	3-02-003	CONSTANTINOPLE
3-03-003	BREVITY	3-03-003	CATERING	3-02-002	CLOAK	3-02-002	CONSTITUENCY
3-03-003	BRIBED	3-03-003	CATHEDRALS	3-03-003	CLOCKWISE	3-03-003	CONSTITUTING
3-02-002	BRICKLAYERS	3-02-002	CATHETER	3-03-003	CLOT	3-02-002	CONSTRICTION
3-03-003	BRICKLAYING	3-01-002	CATSUP	3-03-003	CLOUDBURST	3-01-003	CONSUL
3-03-003	BRIDEGROOM	3-02-002	CATTLEMEN	3-03-003	CLOWN	3-01-003	CONSUMMATE
3-02-003	BRIGADE	3-02-003	CEASELESS	3-03-003	CLOYING	3-01-001	CONSUMPTIVE
3-03-003	BRINK	3-03-003	CEASES	3-03-003	CLUCK	3-02-002	CONTAMINATED
3-01-002	BRISBANE	3-02-003	CECILIA	3-03-003	CLUTCHES	3-02-003	CONTESTED
3-03-003	BRISTLE	3-03-003	CEDRIC	3-01-001	CM,	3-03-003	CONTINGENCY
3-02-003	BRISTLED	3-03-003	CELEBRITIES	3-01-001	COACHMAN	3-02-003	CONTINGENT
3-03-003	BRISTLING	3-01-001	CELEBRITY	3-02-002	COASTED	3-02-003	CONTORTED
3-02-003	BRISTOL	3-02-002	CELLULAR	3-03-003	COAXED	3-03-003	CONTRACTING
3-03-003	BRITTLE	3-03-003	CENSURE	3-02-003	COBRA	3-03-003	CONTRIVED
3-03-003	BROAD-BRIMMED	3-01-001	CENSUSES	3-02-003	COCKY	3-03-003	CONTROLLERS
3-03-003	BROADSIDE	3-03-003	CERAMICS	3-01-002	COCONUTS	3-01-002	CONVERGE
3-02-003	BROCADE	3-03-003	CEREMONIAL	3-02-002	COCOON	3-03-003	CONVERSATIONAL
3-01-001	BRONC	3-02-002	CERTIFICATION	3-01-001	CODIFICATION	3-03-003	CONVEYOR
3-01-002	BRONCHI	3-01-001	CESIUM-137	3-01-001	CODING	3-01-001	CONVOCATION
3-02-002	BRONCS	3-03-003	CHALK	3-02-003	COEFFICIENT	3-02-003	CONVOY
3-01-002	BROODS	3-02-002	CHAMBERMAID	3-02-003	COEFFICIENTS	3-02-002	CONVULSIVE
3-02-003	BROOK	3-02-002	CHAMPLAIN	3-02-003	COHEN	3-03-003	CONVULSIVELY
3-03-003	BROTH	3-03-003	CHAMPS	3-02-003	COINED	3-01-001	CONYERS'
3-02-002	BROUN	3-02-002	CHANCED	3-01-001	COLDE	3-01-001	COO**DRDINATION
3-01-001	BRUCKNER'S	3-01-003	CHANDELIER	3-01-001	COLLAGEN	3-01-001	COOKE
3-02-002	BRUISE	3-03-003	CHANNELED	3-03-003	COLLAPSING	3-01-001	COOLIDGES
3-02-002	BRUSSELS	3-03-003	CHANTS	3-02-002	COLLUSION	3-01-001	COONS
3-03-003	BUBBLING	3-02-002	CHAPLIN	3-01-001	COLMAN	3-02-003	COOP
3-03-003	BUDGE	3-01-001	CHARGE-EXCESS	3-01-001	COLONNADE	3-03-003	COOPERS
3-02-003	BUDGETARY	3-03-003	CHARIOT	3-02-003	COLORLESS	3-02-003	COORDINATING
3-01-001	BUGGING	3-01-001	CHARLOTTE'S	3-03-003	COLOSSAL	3-03-003	COPIED
3-02-002	BUICK	3-03-003	CHARLOTTESVILLE	3-01-001	COMMANDER-IN-CHIEF	3-01-001	CORE-*NEGRO
3-03-003	BUILT-IN	3-03-003	CHARMED			3-01-002	CORES
3-02-003	BULBS	3-03-003	CHASING	3-01-003	COMMENCE	3-01-002	CORINTHIANS
3-02-003	BULGED	3-02-002	CHATEAU	3-02-002	COMMENCEMENT	3-03-003	CORKSCREW
3-03-003	BULGING	3-01-002	CHATHAM	3-02-002	COMMENTARIES	3-03-003	CORNERSTONE
3-02-003	BULLSHIT	3-03-003	CHATTANOOGA	3-03-003	COMMENTATOR	3-03-003	CORRECTNESS
3-03-003	BUNDLED	3-03-003	CHATTERED	3-03-003	COMMISSION'S	3-02-003	CORRELATE
3-01-002	BUNKER	3-02-002	CHEAPLY	3-01-001	COMMODORE	3-03-003	CORRELATED
3-02-002	BUNT	3-02-002	CHEAT	3-02-002	COMMONWEAL	3-02-002	CORRUPTING
3-02-002	BUREAUCRACIES	3-03-003	CHECKLIST	3-03-003	COMMUNICATED	3-01-002	CORTICAL
3-02-002	BUREAUCRATIC	3-02-003	CHEERY	3-01-001	COMMUNICATOR	3-01-001	CORTLANDT
3-01-001	BURI	3-01-001	CHEN	3-03-003	COMMUNISM'S	3-02-002	COSMOLOGY
3-03-003	BURLY	3-01-001	CHENOWETH	3-03-003	COMMUNITY'S	3-03-003	COSMOS
3-01-001	BUSHELL	3-01-001	CHERKASOV	3-02-003	COMPENSATE	3-01-002	COSSACK

Code	Word	Code	Word	Code	Word	Code	Word
3-01-001	COST-OF-LIVING	3-03-003	DECREE	3-02-003	DISCREDITED	3-03-003	EATS
3-02-002	COUGHING	3-02-003	DEDUCE	3-03-003	DISCREET	3-01-001	EBONY
3-02-002	COUNSELED	3-03-003	DEDUCTIVE	3-03-003	DISCRIMINATORY	3-03-003	EBULLIENT
3-01-002	COUNSELORS	3-03-003	DEEP-SET	3-03-003	DISDAIN	3-02-003	ECLECTIC
3-02-002	COUNTERATTACK	3-01-001	DEERSKINS	3-03-003	DISGRACE	3-02-002	ECLIPTIC
3-02-003	COURAGEOUSLY	3-03-003	DEFEATING	3-03-003	DISILLUSIONMENT	3-02-003	ECONOMIZE
3-01-001	COURCY	3-03-003	DEFECT	3-03-003	DISINTEREST	3-01-002	EDIFICE
3-02-002	COURTEOUSLY	3-01-003	DEFENDER	3-02-003	DISMAYING	3-02-002	EDISON
3-01-001	COURTHOUSE	3-03-003	DEFENSELESS	3-02-003	DISMISSING	3-03-003	EDNA
3-03-003	COURTING	3-02-003	DEFENSIBLE	3-02-003	DISORDERED	3-03-003	EDUCATING
3-03-003	COVENANT	3-02-003	DEFIANT	3-02-003	DISORDERLY	3-03-003	EDWARDS
3-01-001	COWARD'S	3-03-003	DEFICIENT	3-03-003	DISPASSIONATELY	3-01-003	EFFECTING
3-03-003	COWARDLY	3-01-002	DEFOE	3-02-002	DISPATCHES	3-02-002	EFFICIENCIES
3-01-001	COWBIRDS	3-02-002	DEFORMITY	3-03-003	DISPATCHING	3-01-002	EGOTISM
3-03-003	CRADLED	3-02-002	DEFUNCT	3-03-003	DISPEL	3-01-003	EGYPTIANS
3-02-003	CRAFTS	3-02-002	DELANEY	3-03-003	DISPENSATION	3-02-002	EIGHTY-*FOUR
3-02-003	CRAMMED	3-02-003	DELAYS	3-02-003	DISPERSION	3-02-002	EIGHTY-THREE
3-02-002	CRAP	3-03-003	DELIGHTS	3-03-003	DISPLACE	3-01-001	EILEEN'S
3-02-002	CRAWFORD	3-02-002	DELINEATION	3-02-003	DISPROVE	3-03-003	EINSTEIN
3-03-003	CREATIONS	3-03-003	DELINQUENTS	3-03-003	DISREGARDING	3-02-002	EINSTEIN'S
3-03-003	CREATIVELY	3-02-002	DELIRIUM	3-02-002	DISRUPTION	3-03-003	EJACULATED
3-03-003	CREDULITY	3-02-002	DELUDED	3-02-002	DISSECTION	3-02-003	ELABORATED
3-02-002	CREEPERS	3-01-003	DEMOCRATIZE	3-02-003	DISSENSION	3-03-003	ELATED
3-02-002	CREIGHTON	3-01-001	DEMOGRAPHY	3-03-003	DISSIMILAR	3-02-002	ELECTORS
3-02-002	CRESTS	3-02-003	DEMONSTRABLE	3-03-003	DISSOLUTION	3-01-001	ELENA
3-02-002	CRIBS	3-02-003	DEMORALIZE	3-03-003	DISSOLVING	3-02-002	ELEVATION
3-03-003	CRICKET	3-03-003	DEMURE	3-02-003	DISSUADE	3-02-003	ELICIT
3-02-003	CRINGING	3-03-003	DENNIS	3-02-002	DIST	3-01-002	ELINOR
3-02-002	CRISS-CROSSED	3-01-001	DENTIST'S	3-02-002	DISTILLATION	3-02-002	ELISABETH
3-01-001	CRITTENDEN	3-02-002	DEPENDENCY	3-03-003	DISTRACTION	3-03-003	ELM
3-02-002	CRITTERS	3-02-003	DEPICT	3-01-003	DISTURBANCES	3-01-001	ELONGATION
3-03-003	CROOK	3-02-002	DEPLORES	3-03-003	DISUNITY	3-03-003	EMACIATED
3-03-003	CROOKED	3-02-002	DEPLOYED	3-02-003	DITTIES	3-01-001	EMBLEMATIC
3-03-003	CROUCHING	3-03-003	DEPOSITION	3-03-003	DIVERS	3-03-003	EMBODIES
3-02-003	CROWING	3-01-001	DEPOSITIONS	3-01-002	DIVERSIFICATION	3-03-003	EMBODYING
3-03-003	CROWNING	3-02-002	DEPRAVITY	3-03-003	DIVERTED	3-03-003	EMERALD
3-02-002	CRUCIFIX	3-03-003	DEPREDATIONS	3-03-003	DIVERTING	3-02-003	EMERGENCE
3-01-001	CRUMB	3-02-002	DEPRESSIONS	3-01-001	DIVINATION	3-02-002	EMERITUS
3-03-003	CRUMBLED	3-03-003	DEPRIVE	3-03-003	DIVINELY	3-02-003	EMITTED
3-02-002	CRUMMY	3-03-003	DEPRIVING	3-02-002	DIVINITIES	3-03-003	EMPEROR'S
3-02-003	CRYPTIC	3-01-002	DERRICK	3-02-003	DIXIELAND	3-02-002	EMPHASIZES
3-01-002	CRYSTALLITES	3-03-003	DERVISHES	3-02-002	DIXON	3-03-003	EMPHATICALLY
3-02-002	CRYSTALLIZATION	3-02-002	DESIGNATING	3-02-002	DOCTRINAL	3-03-003	EMPTIES
3-02-002	CUES	3-01-003	DESPISED	3-02-002	DOCUMENTATION	3-03-003	EMULATE
3-03-003	CULTIVATE	3-01-003	DESTINIES	3-02-002	DOIN	3-03-003	ENCAMPMENT
3-03-003	CUMBERLAND	3-02-003	DESTROYERS	3-01-001	DOLLEY	3-03-003	ENCHANTMENT
3-02-003	CUMBERSOME	3-02-002	DETECTIVE'S	3-02-003	DOMAINS	3-02-003	ENCOMPASSED
3-03-003	CUNNINGLY	3-02-002	DETECTOR	3-02-002	DONATE	3-03-003	ENDANGERING
3-01-001	CUPFUL	3-01-001	DETERGENCY	3-01-001	DONNAY	3-02-002	ENDEARED
3-01-001	CUPPLY	3-02-003	DETERIORATION	3-02-003	DONNED	3-03-003	ENDEARING
3-02-002	CURBING	3-02-002	DETESTED	3-02-003	DOOM	3-01-001	ENDINGS
3-02-002	CURBS	3-02-002	DETONATED	3-03-003	DOORKNOB	3-01-001	ENDOGAMY
3-03-003	CURBSIDE	3-02-002	DETONATION	3-02-003	DOORMEN	3-02-002	ENGINEERS'
3-02-003	CURES	3-03-003	DEVASTATED	3-01-002	DOORSTEP	3-01-001	ENGLANDERS
3-01-001	CURIA	3-01-003	DEVIANT	3-03-003	DOORWAYS	3-03-003	ENLARGING
3-01-001	CURIAE	3-03-003	DEVILISH	3-03-003	DOROTHY	3-03-003	ENLIGHTENING
3-01-002	CURRENCIES	3-01-001	DEVOL	3-01-001	DORR	3-02-003	ENRICHMENT
3-03-003	CURRICULA	3-03-003	DEVOTEES	3-01-001	DOUBLE-STAGE	3-01-001	ENRIGHT
3-03-003	CURSES	3-02-002	DEW	3-01-001	DOUBLE-STEP	3-03-003	ENSEMBLES
3-02-002	CURTIS	3-03-003	DEWEY	3-03-003	DOUBTING	3-03-003	ENTERTAINERS
3-02-002	CURY	3-03-003	DEXTER	3-03-003	DOWNGRADED	3-03-003	ENTERTAINMENTS
3-01-001	CURZON'S	3-03-003	DIAGNOSE	3-03-003	DOWNPOUR	3-02-003	ENTHRALLING
3-03-003	CUSTODIAN	3-02-003	DIALED	3-02-002	DOWNWIND	3-03-003	ENTHUSIASTS
3-01-001	CYNEWULF	3-03-003	DIAPERS	3-03-003	DOZING	3-03-003	ENTRANCED
3-03-003	CYNICS	3-01-001	DIARRHOEA	3-02-002	DRAFTS	3-02-003	ENVELOPES
3-02-002	CYSTS	3-01-001	DICKEY	3-03-003	DRAINING	3-02-003	ENVISION
3-01-001	CZARINA'S	3-01-001	DICKSON	3-03-003	DRAMATIZE	3-01-001	EPICENTER
3-02-002	D**.*A	3-02-003	DICTATE	3-02-003	DRAWLED	3-03-003	EPILEPTIC
3-01-001	D'*ARTAGUETTE	3-03-003	DIETS	3-03-003	DRIER	3-02-002	EPIPHANY
3-03-003	DAINTY	3-01-001	DIFFERENTIABLE	3-01-001	DRIERS	3-02-002	EPISTEMOLOGY
3-02-003	DAISIES	3-02-002	DIFFUSING	3-02-002	DRINKER	3-03-003	EPITOMIZED
3-01-001	DALLOWAY	3-03-003	DIGEST	3-03-003	DRONE	3-01-001	EQN
3-02-002	DAMAGES	3-03-003	DIGESTIVE	3-01-002	DROPLETS	3-02-003	EQUATING
3-03-003	DAMAGING	3-03-003	DIGNITARIES	3-02-002	DROPOUTS	3-03-003	EQUATOR
3-02-002	DAMASCUS	3-03-003	DILAPIDATED	3-03-003	DROWN	3-01-001	ERADICATION
3-02-002	DAMNATION	3-02-002	DILATATION	3-03-003	DRUNKARD	3-02-003	ERECTING
3-03-003	DAMPENED	3-03-003	DILIGENCE	3-02-002	DRUNKARDS	3-01-001	ERHART
3-03-003	DAMS	3-01-001	DILL'S	3-02-003	DRUNKS	3-03-003	ERIC
3-01-001	DAN'S	3-03-003	DILUTING	3-02-002	DRURY	3-01-001	ERIKSON'S
3-02-002	DANA	3-01-001	DIMENSIONING	3-02-002	DUCKING	3-02-003	ERRATIC
3-01-001	DANA'S	3-02-003	DIMES	3-01-001	DUFFEL	3-02-003	ERRED
3-03-003	DANGEROUSLY	3-01-003	DIMINISH	3-03-003	DULLED	3-03-003	ERUDITE
3-03-003	DANUBE	3-02-003	DIMINISHES	3-02-003	DULLY	3-02-002	ESKIMO
3-03-003	DARN	3-02-003	DIMINUTIVE	3-02-002	DUMMY	3-01-001	ESPLANADE
3-01-001	DARTMOUTH'S	3-02-003	DINED	3-02-002	DUNKIRK	3-03-003	ESQUIRE
3-01-001	DASHIELL	3-02-002	DINNERTIME	3-01-001	DURIN	3-02-003	EST
3-03-003	DAVIDSON	3-03-003	DIPPED	3-01-002	DURKHEIM	3-02-003	ESTEEMED
3-02-003	DAY-BY-DAY	3-01-001	DIPYLON	3-03-003	DWARF	3-03-003	ESTHETIC
3-02-003	DAY-TO-DAY	3-02-003	DIRKSEN	3-01-001	DWYER	3-02-003	ESTHETICS
3-01-001	DE*PUGH	3-01-002	DISABLING	3-03-003	DYER	3-03-003	ESTRANGED
3-02-002	DEALERS'	3-02-003	DISAGREED	3-02-002	DYNASTIC	3-02-003	ETHEL
3-03-003	DEARTH	3-03-003	DISAPPEARS	3-01-001	DYNASTS	3-03-003	ETHEREAL
3-03-003	DEBACLE	3-01-001	DISARMED	3-03-003	EAGERNESS	3-03-003	ETIQUETTE
3-01-001	DEBONNIE	3-02-003	DISARMING	3-03-003	EARNESTNESS	3-01-001	EURIPIDES
3-01-001	DECANTING	3-03-003	DISCHARGING	3-02-002	EARRINGS	3-02-003	EUROPE'S
3-02-002	DECCA	3-02-002	DISCONTINUOUS	3-02-003	EASING	3-01-001	EUSTIS
3-01-001	DECIMAL	3-03-003	DISCOURAGEMENT	3-01-001	EAST-WEST	3-02-003	EVACUATED

Code	Word	Code	Word	Code	Word	Code	Word
3-01-001	EVADNA	3-03-003	FLARE	3-03-003	GALAXY	3-03-003	GRIEVING
3-03-003	EVER-EXPANDING	3-03-003	FLARING	3-02-003	GALLANTRY	3-01-001	GRIGGS
3-03-003	EVERETT	3-03-003	FLASHY	3-01-001	GALLERY'S	3-01-001	GRIGORI'S
3-03-003	EVERYTHING'S	3-03-003	FLATS	3-01-001	GALLI	3-01-001	GRILLE
3-02-002	EXACERBATION	3-02-003	FLATTERY	3-03-003	GALVANIZING	3-03-003	GRIMACE
3-03-003	EXCAVATION	3-03-003	FLAW	3-01-001	GAMBLE	3-01-001	GRINDERS
3-02-003	EXCESSES	3-01-001	FLAX	3-01-001	GANNETT	3-02-002	GRITS
3-03-003	EXCESSIVELY	3-01-001	FLAXSEED	3-02-002	GAPED	3-02-002	GROANED
3-02-003	EXCHANGING	3-01-001	FLEISCHMANNS	3-03-003	GARB	3-03-003	GROCERS
3-03-003	EXCITE	3-02-003	FLIPPED	3-03-003	GARCIA	3-02-003	GROOVES
3-02-002	EXCLUDES	3-02-003	FLOAT	3-03-003	GARDENING	3-03-003	GROUNDWORK
3-02-002	EXCLUSIVENESS	3-01-001	FLOC	3-01-001	GASCONY	3-02-002	GROWERS
3-03-003	EXCUSED	3-03-003	FLORAL	3-03-003	GASP	3-02-002	GROWNUPS
3-02-002	EXECUTIONS	3-01-001	FLORY	3-03-003	GATEWAY	3-01-001	GRUBB
3-02-002	EXEMPLIFIED	3-03-003	FLOWERED	3-03-003	GEESE	3-03-003	GRUDGES
3-02-002	EXERTS	3-02-002	FOAMY	3-03-003	GENERALITY	3-01-001	GUARDINO
3-03-003	EXHAUSTING	3-02-002	FOCUSSED	3-02-002	GENETICIST	3-03-003	GUATEMALA
3-03-003	EXHIBITIONS	3-01-001	FOGG'S	3-03-003	GENTILITY	3-03-003	GUESSES
3-02-002	EXPANDS	3-02-003	FOIBLES	3-03-003	GENTLER	3-03-003	GUINEA
3-01-002	EXPANSIONS	3-03-003	FOLDING	3-02-002	GEOLOGISTS	3-02-002	GUITARS
3-03-003	EXPANSIVENESS	3-02-002	FOLDS	3-02-002	GEORGE'S	3-03-003	GULPED
3-03-003	EXPECTANT	3-02-003	FOLKSY	3-01-001	GEORGE-*BARDEN	3-03-003	GUNMAN
3-03-003	EXPERTISE	3-03-003	FOLLOWER	3-03-003	GEORGETOWN	3-01-001	GURSEL
3-01-002	EXPIRATION	3-02-003	FOOLED	3-02-002	GEORGIAN	3-02-003	GUS
3-03-003	EXPLORERS	3-03-003	FOOLING	3-01-001	GERAGHTY'S	3-02-002	GUSTS
3-03-003	EXPLOSIVES	3-03-003	FOOLISHLY	3-01-002	GERALD	3-03-003	GUTTURAL
3-03-003	EXPORTED	3-03-003	FOOTING	3-03-003	GERM	3-02-003	GUY'S
3-02-003	EXPRESSIONISM	3-02-003	FOOTNOTE	3-03-003	GESTURED	3-02-002	H**.*M**.*S
3-03-003	EXPRESSLY	3-02-003	FOOTNOTES	3-02-003	GIGGLED	3-02-003	HACK
3-03-003	EXQUISITE	3-03-003	FOOTSTEP	3-03-003	GILBERT	3-02-002	HAFTA
3-03-003	EXQUISITELY	3-01-001	FORAGE	3-01-001	GILBORN'S	3-02-003	HAGGLING
3-03-003	EXTENUATING	3-03-003	FORAGING	3-02-002	GILLESPIE	3-03-003	HALF-CLOSED
3-03-003	EXTINCTION	3-03-003	FORCIBLY	3-01-001	GILMAN	3-03-003	HALF-DOZEN
3-02-002	EXTRA-SENSORY	3-02-002	FORDS	3-02-003	GILT	3-02-003	HALF-HEARTED
3-02-002	EXTRANEOUS	3-02-002	FOREARM	3-01-001	GIORGIO	3-01-001	HALF-INCH
3-03-003	EXTRAORDINARILY	3-03-003	FOREGO	3-02-003	GIOVANNI	3-02-002	HALLECK
3-02-002	EXTRATERRESTRIAL	3-03-003	FORESEE	3-02-003	GIUSEPPE	3-02-002	HALLMARK
3-02-002	FORFEIT	3-01-001	GIVEAWAYS	3-01-001	HAMILTON'S
3-03-003	EXULTATION	3-03-003	FORGED	3-01-001	GLADDEN	3-02-002	HAMMERED
3-03-003	EYEGLASSES	3-03-003	FORGETFULNESS	3-01-001	GLAZES	3-03-003	HAMPERED
3-02-002	F**.*D**.*R	3-03-003	FORLORN	3-02-003	GLEE	3-03-003	HANDBAG
3-03-003	FACE-TO-FACE	3-02-003	FORTITUDE	3-03-003	GLIMMER	3-03-003	HANDCLASP
3-01-001	FACET-PLANES	3-02-003	FORWARDED	3-01-001	GLOBOCNIK	3-01-001	HANDE
3-02-003	FAINTEST	3-01-001	FOSDICK'S	3-03-003	GLOOMILY	3-01-001	HANDGUN
3-01-001	FAIRING	3-01-001	FOSS	3-02-003	GLOOMY	3-01-001	HANDSPIKES
3-01-001	FAIRVIEW	3-02-002	FOSSILIZED	3-01-001	GLORIANA	3-01-001	HANDSTANDS
3-03-003	FAITHS	3-02-002	FOSTERS	3-02-002	GLOSSARY	3-03-003	HAPPIEST
3-01-002	FALSITY	3-02-002	FOULING	3-01-001	GLOTTOCHRONOLOGICAL	3-02-003	HARBORED
3-03-003	FALTERED	3-03-003	FOUR-HOUR	3-01-001	HARDTACK
3-02-003	FAMINE	3-02-002	FOUR-YEAR	3-03-003	GLOWERED	3-02-002	HARDWICK
3-03-003	FANNY	3-02-002	FOURTEENTH	3-02-002	GLOWERING	3-01-002	HARK
3-02-003	FARCE	3-03-003	FOYER	3-02-002	GLUTTONS	3-02-002	HARPERS
3-01-003	FARES	3-01-001	FRACTIONATED	3-03-003	GOADED	3-02-002	HARPING
3-02-003	FARFETCHED	3-01-002	FRACTIONATION	3-02-002	GOD-GIVEN	3-02-003	HARTFORD
3-03-002	FARTHEST	3-03-003	FRAGRANT	3-03-003	GODDESS	3-02-002	HARVESTER
3-01-001	FASCICLES	3-03-002	FRANCAISE	3-01-001	GOETHE	3-02-003	HARVESTING
3-03-002	FASCINATE	3-03-003	FRANCISCO'S	3-03-002	GOITRE	3-01-001	HARVIE
3-02-003	FASCISM	3-02-002	FRANCS	3-02-003	GOLDWATER	3-03-002	MASTEN
3-03-003	FASTIDIOUS	3-03-003	FRAYED	3-01-002	GOLF'S	3-02-003	HATEFUL
3-02-003	FATEFUL	3-01-001	FRAYNE	3-02-002	GOLFER	3-03-003	HATH
3-03-003	FATES	3-02-003	FRECKLES	3-02-003	GOOD-NATURED	3-01-001	HAVISHAM
3-01-002	FATHOM	3-02-002	FREEDMEN	3-01-001	GORDIN	3-03-003	HAVOC
3-03-003	FATIGUED	3-03-003	FREEDOMS	3-01-001	GORTON'S	3-02-003	HEADLESS
3-03-003	FATTER	3-02-003	FREEHAND	3-02-003	GOUGED	3-03-003	HEADMASTER
3-01-003	FEASIBILITY	3-02-002	FREEHOLDERS	3-03-003	GOUGING	3-02-003	HEALTHFUL
3-02-003	FEAST	3-02-002	FREEING	3-03-003	GOVERNESS	3-03-003	HECTIC
3-03-003	FEATS	3-02-003	FRESCOES	3-03-003	GRABS	3-01-001	HEGELIAN
3-01-003	FEEDBACK	3-02-002	FRESHMEN	3-03-003	GRACIOUSLY	3-01-001	HEIDENSTAM'S
3-01-001	FEELY	3-01-001	FRESNEL	3-03-003	GRANDIOSE	3-02-003	HELL'S
3-02-002	FELLOWSHIPS	3-03-003	FREUDIAN	3-01-002	GRANDMA'S	3-03-003	HELPLESSLY
3-02-002	FEMALE'S	3-01-001	FREYA	3-03-003	GRANDMOTHER'S	3-02-003	HEMMED
3-02-002	FENCED	3-02-003	FRICK	3-02-002	GRANDPARENTS	3-02-002	HEMPSTEAD
3-03-003	FERMENTATION	3-02-002	FRIDAYS	3-01-001	GRANDS	3-02-002	HENDERSON
3-01-001	FERRAROS	3-02-003	FRIEZES	3-02-002	GRANITE	3-01-001	HENDL
3-01-001	FERRELL	3-03-003	FRILLS	3-02-002	GRANT-IN-AID	3-02-003	HEPATITIS
3-01-002	FERTILIZED	3-02-002	FRISCO	3-01-001	GRANTS-IN-AID	3-01-001	HERBERET
3-01-001	FERTILIZERS	3-02-003	FRONTAL	3-01-002	GRANULAR	3-02-003	HERBS
3-02-002	FESTIVALS	3-03-003	FRONTING	3-02-003	GRAPE	3-03-003	HERCULES
3-03-003	FETCHING	3-03-003	FROSTBITE	3-01-002	GRAPE-ARBOR	3-01-001	HERDIN
3-02-002	FETE	3-03-003	FRUSTRATING	3-02-003	GRAPEFRUIT	3-03-003	HEREDITY
3-03-003	FEVERISHLY	3-01-001	FUDOMAE	3-03-003	GRAPEVINE	3-03-003	HEREIN
3-02-002	FIELDER	3-01-001	FUELOIL	3-02-002	GRATE	3-03-003	HERO'S
3-02-002	FIELDING	3-03-003	FUGITIVE	3-02-002	GRATEFULLY	3-03-003	HEROISM
3-03-003	FIEND	3-03-003	FULFILLING	3-03-003	GRATIFYING	3-01-001	HERRY
3-03-003	FIFTEEN-MINUTE	3-01-001	FULKE	3-02-003	GRATUITOUS	3-01-001	HERTER
3-01-001	FIGGER	3-03-003	FUNCTIONED	3-02-002	GRAVITATION	3-02-003	HESITANT
3-02-002	FILIBUSTER	3-01-002	FUND'S	3-03-003	GRAY-HAIRED	3-02-003	HESSIANS
3-01-001	FILLINGS	3-02-002	FUROR	3-01-001	GRAZIN	3-01-001	HESTER
3-03-003	FINGERED	3-02-002	FURTHERED	3-03-003	GRAZING	3-01-001	HEVIN
3-01-001	FINNEY	3-03-003	FUSED	3-01-001	GREASES	3-01-002	HEXAMETER
3-03-003	FIRST-HAND	3-02-002	FUSES	3-02-002	GREED	3-03-003	HEYDAY
3-03-003	FIXTURE	3-03-003	FUSSY	3-03-003	GREENLAND	3-02-002	HEYDRICH
3-01-002	FIXTURES	3-02-003	FUZZ	3-01-002	GREENVILLE	3-03-003	HIDEOUSLY
3-03-003	FLAGRANT	3-02-002	G)	3-03-003	GREGG	3-02-002	HIGH-SPIRITED
3-01-001	FLAILING	3-03-003	GABRIELLE	3-02-002	GRENADE	3-02-003	HIGH-VALUE
3-02-003	FLAMBOYANT	3-03-003	GADFLY	3-01-001	GRIEVANCE	3-03-003	HIGHLIGHTS
3-01-001	FLANNAGANS	3-02-002	GAINES	3-03-003	GRIEVANCES	3-02-003	HILLBILLY

3-01-001 HILPRECHT	3-02-003 IMPLEMENTING	3-03-003 INTERMITTENT	3-03-003 KEYHOLE
3-02-003 HILT	3-03-003 IMPLICITLY	3-02-003 INTERPERSONAL	3-01-001 KEYS'S
3-02-002 HILTON	3-02-003 IMPOVERISHED	3-01-001 INTERPLANETARY	3-01-001 KHAJU
3-03-003 HINDERED	3-02-002 IMPRECISELY	3-02-002 INTERPRETS	3-03-003 KICKS
3-01-002 HINDU	3-02-002 IMPRESSIONIST	3-03-003 INTERRUPTIONS	3-03-003 KIDNAPED
3-01-002 HINTON	3-03-003 IMPROMPTU	3-01-001 INTERSTAGE	3-01-001 KIKUYU
3-03-003 HIRAM	3-01-002 IMPROVISED	3-02-002 INTIMA	3-02-003 KILOMETERS
3-01-001 HISTOCHEMISTRY	3-03-003 IMPUDENT	3-03-003 INTIMACY	3-03-003 KINDERGARTEN
3-02-002 HISTORIAN'S	3-03-003 IMPUNITY	3-03-003 INTIMIDATED	3-03-003 KINDRED
3-03-003 HITCHED	3-03-003 INADEQUACY	3-02-003 INTOLERABLE	3-03-003 KINSHIP
3-02-003 HITCHING	3-03-003 INBOARD	3-03-003 INTRIGUES	3-03-003 KIPLING'S
3-02-002 HITHERTO	3-03-003 INCANDESCENT	3-03-003 INTRIGUING	3-01-001 KIRBY'S
3-01-001 HOBBIES	3-03-003 INCENSED	3-03-003 INTRODUCTORY	3-02-002 KITCHENETTE
3-03-003 HOC	3-01-001 INCEPTING	3-01-001 INTROJECT	3-01-001 KIZ
3-01-001 HODGKIN	3-01-002 INCESTUOUS	3-02-003 INTRUSION	3-02-002 KLAN
3-01-001 HOEVE	3-03-003 INCITE	3-02-002 INVADING	3-02-002 KLUX
3-02-003 HOG	3-02-003 INCITED	3-03-003 INVENTIVE	3-01-001 KNIFE'S
3-01-001 HOIJER	3-01-002 INCITEMENT	3-03-003 INVERTED	3-02-003 KNUCKLE
3-01-001 HOIJER'S	3-02-003 INCLUSION	3-03-003 INVEST	3-01-001 KODIAK
3-02-002 HOLLERING	3-02-003 INCOMPARABLY	3-03-003 INVESTIGATIVE	3-01-001 KOEHLER
3-01-002 HOLSTERED	3-03-003 INCONCLUSIVE	3-03-003 INVETERATE	3-01-001 KORNBLUTH'S
3-02-002 HOMEMAKER	3-03-003 INCONSEQUENTIAL	3-03-003 INVIOLATE	3-01-001 KOUSSEVITZKY
3-02-002 HOMEMAKERS	3-03-003 INCONVENIENCE	3-03-003 INVOLUNTARY	3-01-001 KROGERS
3-02-002 HOMEOWNERS	3-03-003 INCONVENIENT	3-01-001 INVOLUTIONS	3-01-002 KRUTCH'S
3-01-002 HOMERS	3-03-003 INCORPORATES	3-01-001 INVOLUTORIAL	3-02-002 KU
3-01-001 HOMESICK	3-03-003 INCORPORATION	3-03-003 INWARDLY	3-01-001 KWHR
3-01-001 HOMESTEADERS	3-02-003 INDEXING	3-01-001 IODINATING	3-01-001 L'*TURU
3-01-001 HOMOSEXUALS	3-02-002 INDIGENOUS	3-02-002 IONIZED	3-01-001 LA**OUTNER
3-03-003 HONEYSUCKLE	3-03-003 INDIGNITIES	3-01-001 IONOSPHERE	3-01-001 LA*GUARDIA
3-02-002 HONORABLY	3-02-003 INDISCRIMINATE	3-03-003 IRAQ	3-02-002 LAB
3-02-002 HOODLUM	3-02-002 INDISPOSED	3-03-003 IRRECONCILABLE	3-02-002 LABELS
3-02-002 HOODLUMS	3-03-003 INDISTINGUISHAB	3-02-003 IRRESPECTIVE	3-03-002 LAG
3-02-002 HOOP	LE	3-03-003 IRRESPONSIBILIT	3-02-003 LAGS
3-02-003 HOOPS	3-01-001 INDIVIDUALIST	Y	3-01-001 LAGUERRE
3-03-003 HOPED-FOR	3-02-002 INDUCES		3-01-001 LAITY
3-02-003 HOPELESSNESS	3-02-002 INDUCTED	3-02-002 IRRIGATION	3-01-002 LAMAR
3-02-003 HORIZONTALLY	3-02-003 INDUSTRIOUS	3-03-003 IRRITABLY	3-01-001 LAMBETH
3-03-003 HOROWITZ	3-03-003 INEFFECTIVE	3-03-003 IRRITATIONS	3-01-001 LAMINATE
3-02-003 HORRIFYING	3-03-003 INELIGIBLE	3-03-003 ISLAM	3-03-003 LAMPLIGHT
3-02-002 HORSEBACK	3-01-001 INERTIAL	3-02-002 ISLAMIC	3-03-003 LANCE
3-03-003 HORSEMANSHIP	3-03-003 INEXHAUSTIBLE	3-01-001 ISOTROPIC	3-01-001 LANDIS
3-03-003 HORSEMEN	3-03-003 INEXORABLE	3-02-002 IT'D	3-03-003 LANDMARK
3-03-003 HORSES'	3-03-003 INEXORABLY	3-01-001 ITALICS	3-03-003 LANDSCAPED
3-01-001 HOSTAGES	3-03-003 INEXPERIENCE	3-01-002 ITEMIZED	3-01-001 LANGER
3-03-003 HOSTESSES	3-02-003 INFALLIBLE	3-03-003 ITINERARY	3-03-003 LAPSED
3-01-003 HOUK	3-02-002 INFANTS	3-01-001 IZAAK	3-02-002 LARAMIE
3-02-003 HOUNDS	3-02-002 INFERRED	3-01-001 IZAAK'S	3-02-002 LARKSPUR
3-01-002 HOW'D	3-03-002 INFINITELY	3-02-002 JACKETED	3-03-003 LASHED
3-03-003 HOWLING	3-02-002 INFINITESIMAL	3-03-003 JAILS	3-03-003 LASTLY
3-02-003 HOWLS	3-03-003 INFLATED	3-02-002 JANITORS	3-02-002 LATHER
3-01-001 HR,	3-02-002 INFLECTED	3-03-003 JANITORS'	3-02-002 LATHERED
3-03-003 HUBERT	3-02-003 INFLECTION	3-01-001 JARS	3-01-001 LATTIMER
3-03-003 HUDDLING	3-03-003 INFLEXIBLE	3-01-001 JAYCEES	3-02-002 LAUDANUM
3-02-003 HUG	3-03-003 INFLICTING	3-01-001 JEFF	3-02-003 LAUNCHES
3-01-001 HUGO	3-02-003 INFLICTION	3-01-001 JEJUNUM	3-03-003 LAUNCHING
3-03-003 HULKS	3-03-003 INFURIATED	3-03-003 JELLY	3-03-003 LAUREL
3-03-003 HUMANITARIAN	3-02-002 INHERENTLY	3-01-001 JENNIE	3-02-002 LAURENCE
3-03-003 HUMMED	3-03-003 INHIBITIONS	3-02-002 JENNINGS	3-03-003 LAVISH
3-03-003 HURDLE	3-01-001 INHOLDINGS	3-01-001 JEREBOHMS	3-02-002 LAWMAKING
3-03-003 HURL	3-03-003 INITIALS	3-03-003 JEREMIAH	3-03-003 LAX
3-02-002 HURRAH	3-01-001 INJUN	3-03-003 JERKING	3-03-003 LAYMAN
3-01-001 HURRAYS	3-01-001 INJUNCTION	3-01-002 JESSE	3-01-001 LE*SOURD
3-02-002 HURTING	3-03-003 INLETS	3-02-002 JESUIT	3-03-003 LEAFLETS
3-02-003 HUSKY	3-02-002 INNA	3-03-003 JEWELRY	3-01-002 LEAGUER
3-01-001 HYDRIDES	3-02-003 INNOCENTLY	3-03-003 JEWELS	3-02-002 LEAKS
3-01-002 HYDROCARBON	3-03-003 INQUISITION	3-01-001 JOINER	3-02-002 LEASES
3-01-001 HYDROGENS	3-03-003 INROADS	3-01-001 JUBAL'S	3-02-002 LEASH
3-02-003 HYGIENE	3-02-002 INSANITY	3-03-003 JUDE	3-02-003 LEASING
3-01-001 HYM	3-02-002 INSECURE	3-02-003 JUDICIARY	3-02-002 LEAVIN
3-01-001 I**.D	3-03-003 INSENSITIVE	3-03-003 JUDSON	3-02-002 LECTURING
3-03-003 ICEBOX	3-03-003 INSINUATIONS	3-01-001 JUET'S	3-01-001 LEE'S
3-02-002 IDAHO	3-01-001 INSOMNIA	3-03-003 JUMBLED	3-02-003 LEERED
3-02-003 IDEALISM	3-03-003 INSPECTIONS	3-01-001 JUNTA	3-01-001 LEESONA'S
3-02-003 IDENTIFYING	3-02-003 INSPIRE	3-01-001 JURE	3-01-003 LEFT-HANDED
3-03-003 IDEOLOGIES	3-03-003 INSTITUTIONALIZ	3-03-003 JURISDICTIONAL	3-01-003 LEGITIMIZED
3-02-002 IDIOMS	ED	3-02-002 JURISPRUDENCE	3-01-001 LEIGH
3-03-003 IDIOSYNCRASIES	3-02-003 INSTRUCT	3-02-003 JURIST	3-03-003 LEMONADE
3-02-003 IDIOTIC	3-02-003 INSTRUCTIONAL	3-02-002 JUSTICES	3-02-002 LEN
3-01-001 IDJE	3-03-003 INSTRUCTIVE	3-02-003 JUSTIFICATIONS	3-02-002 LENA
3-03-003 IDLENESS	3-02-002 INSTRUMENTALIST	3-01-001 JUSTIFYING	3-03-003 LENGTHENING
3-01-001 IERULLI	S	3-02-003 JUXTAPOSITION	3-03-003 LENIENT
3-01-001 IGBO	3-03-003 INSTRUMENTALITI	3-01-001 KAISER'S	3-03-003 LENINGRAD
3-02-003 IGOR	ES	3-02-003 KAN	3-03-003 LEOPOLDVILLE
3-02-003 IL	3-02-002 INSTRUMENTALLY	3-02-003 KAREN	3-03-003 LES
3-02-003 ILL-CONCEIVED	3-03-003 INSUFFICIENTLY	3-01-001 KATYA	3-03-003 LEUKEMIA
3-02-002 ILLEGITIMATE	3-03-003 INSULARITY	3-01-001 KEEGAN	3-01-001 LEVER-ACTION
3-03-003 ILLICIT	3-02-002 INSULIN	3-02-003 KEELER	3-01-001 LEVERKU**DHN
3-02-002 ILLUMINED	3-03-003 INSULTS	3-01-001 KEENE	3-03-003 LEWD
3-03-003 ILLUSTRIOUS	3-03-003 INTANGIBLES	3-03-003 KEENLY	3-02-002 LIAR
3-03-003 IMAGINES	3-02-003 INTEGRALS	3-01-001 KEEPER	3-02-002 LIBERAL-CONSERV
3-01-001 IMITATIONS	3-02-003 INTELLIGENTLY	3-01-001 KEITH'S	ATIVE
3-02-002 IMMANENT	3-02-003 INTERACTIONS	3-02-003 KENNAN'S	3-02-002 LIBERALITY
3-03-003 IMMINENT	3-03-003 INTERCEPTED	3-01-001 KENNEL	3-03-003 LICK
3-01-001 IMPACTS	3-03-003 INTERCHANGEABLE	3-01-001 KERNEL	3-01-001 LIEUTENANT'S
3-03-003 IMPETUOUS	3-03-003 INTERESTINGLY	3-01-001 KERNELS	3-01-001 LIEUTENANTS
3-03-003 IMPINGE	3-01-002 INTERFACE	3-01-001 KERYGMA	3-02-003 LIFELIKE
3-03-003 IMPLACABLE	3-01-002 INTERGROUP	3-03-003 KETTLE	3-02-003 LIGHT-WEIGHT
		3-02-002 KEYED	

3-03-003	LIKENED
3-03-003	LIKENESS
3-01-001	LILACS
3-01-001	LILLY'S
3-03-003	LILTING
3-01-001	LINDA'S
3-01-001	LINDEMANN
3-02-002	LINEUP
3-03-003	LINGO
3-01-001	LINKAGE
3-01-001	LIONESS
3-03-003	LIPPMANN
3-02-003	LIPSTICK
3-01-001	LITERALNESS
3-02-002	LITERATE
3-02-002	LITIGANTS
3-03-003	LITTER
3-02-002	LITTERS
3-01-001	LIVRES
3-02-002	LLOYD'S
3-03-003	LOATH
3-03-003	LOAVES
3-01-003	LOBE
3-03-003	LOCALE
3-03-003	LOCKHEED
3-01-002	LOESSER
3-01-002	LOLA
3-01-001	LOLLY
3-01-002	LONDON'S
3-02-003	LONG-AWAITED
3-03-003	LONGSTANDING
3-01-001	LONGUE
3-01-001	LONSDALE
3-02-002	LOOKIT
3-03-003	LOOMED
3-03-003	LOOSEN
3-03-003	LOOT
3-02-003	LOOTED
3-03-003	LOOTING
3-01-001	LOPER
3-03-003	LORDS
3-02-002	LORDSHIP
3-03-003	LOUNGED
3-03-003	LOUSE
3-01-001	LOVEJOY
3-02-003	LOVELIEST
3-03-003	LOW-DOWN
3-01-001	LOW-WAGE
3-01-002	LOWER-MIDDLE-CL
	ASS
3-03-003	LOYALTIES
3-02-002	LUCIFER
3-03-003	LUCKILY
3-03-003	LUCRATIVE
3-03-003	LUDICROUS
3-02-003	LUDWIG
3-03-003	LUKE
3-03-003	LUMPS
3-02-002	LUMUMBA'S
3-02-003	LURCH
3-03-003	LURED
3-03-003	LURID
3-02-003	LURKED
3-03-003	LURKING
3-03-003	LUSTY
3-02-002	LUTHERAN
3-03-003	LUXURIES
3-03-003	LYNDON
3-02-002	LYON
3 01-001	MAC*PHERSON
3-02-002	MACKEY
3-01-001	MACRO-INSTRUCTI
	ONS
3-01-001	MADDEN'S
3-01-001	MADELEINE
3-03-003	MADMEN
3-03-003	MADONNA
3-01-002	MADRIGALS
3-02-003	MAGDALENE
3-01-001	MAGGIE'S
3-03-003	MAGICALLY
3-01-001	MAGISTRATE
3-02-002	MAGISTRATES
3-03-003	MAGNET
3-03-003	MAGNIFYING
3-01-001	MAHLER
3-01-001	MAILINGS
3-03-003	MAIS
3-03-003	MAJORITIES
3-01-003	MAJORS
3-01-001	MAKU
3-01-001	MALADJUSTED
3-02-003	MALARIA
3-03-003	MALCOLM
3-02-003	MALENESS
3-02-003	MALL
3-03-003	MALTA

3-02-002	MALTESE
3-01-001	MAMMALS
3-02-002	MANA
3-03-003	MANEUVERED
3-01-001	MANHOURS
3-01-001	MANKOWSKI
3-02-003	MANNING
3-02-002	MANSERVANT
3-03-003	MANTEL
3-01-001	MANTHEY
3-01-001	MANUALLY
3-03-003	MANUFACTURERS'
3-03-003	MANY-SIDED
3-02-002	MAPLES
3-02-002	MARBLES
3-02-002	MARION
3-03-003	MARKETED
3-02-002	MARKETINGS
3-02-003	MARKETPLACE
3-01-001	MARLBOROUGH
3-01-001	MARMARA
3-03-003	MAROON
3-02-002	MARRIES
3-02-003	MARRYING
3-02-002	MARSICANO
3-02-002	MARSTON
3-01-001	MARTIANS
3-02-002	MARTINEZ
3-02-002	MARV
3-02-002	MARXIST
3-02-002	MASHED
3-02-002	MASKS
3-01-003	MASONIC
3-02-002	MASONS
3-02-002	MASSACHUSETTS'
3-01-001	MASSEUR
3-03-003	MATERIALIZE
3-01-001	MATRICULATED
3-03-003	MATRIMONY
3-03-003	MATRON
3-02-002	MATT
3-01-001	MATTEI
3-01-001	MATUNUCK
3-03-003	MATURATION
3-02-002	MATURING
3-01-001	MAUREEN
3-03-003	MAVERICK
3-02-003	MAXIMAL
3-01-002	MAXIMIZES
3-01-002	MAZEROSKI
3-01-001	MC*CULLOUGH
3-01-001	MC*IVER
3-02-002	MC*KEE
3-01-001	MC*KENZIE
3-01-001	MC*LISH
3 01-001	MC*NAIR
3-02-002	MC*NAMARA
3-02-003	MEANDERING
3-03-003	MEANNESS
3-01-001	MEDFIELD
3-01-001	MEDICO-MILITARY
3-01-001	MEDIUMISTIC
3-02-002	MEKONG
3-02-002	MELFF
3-01-001	MELISSA
3-02-003	MELODRAMA
3-02-003	MELVILLE
3-02-002	MEMORANDUM
3-02-002	MEMORIALS
3-03-003	MEMORIZE
3-03-003	MEMORIZED
3-01-001	MENARCHE
3-01-002	MENCKEN
3-03-003	MENDING
3-02-003	MENTALITY
3-03-003	MERCILESS
3-03-003	MERCILESSLY
3-03-003	MEREST
3-03-003	MERRIMENT
3-01-001	MESSRS
3-03-003	MESSY
3-01-003	METAPHORS
3-01-001	METAPHYSIC
3-02-002	METEOR
3-02-002	METEOROLOGICAL
3-02-002	METHODOLOGICAL
3-01-001	METRECAL
3-03-003	METRO
3-02-002	METRONOME
3-03-003	MEXICO'S
3-01-001	MEYNER
3-01-001	MG/**JL,
3-03-003	MI
3-02-003	MIAMI'S
3-02-002	MICKEY'S
3-03-003	MICROCOSM
3-02-003	MID-*JUNE

3-03-003	MID-*SEPTEMBER
3-02-003	MID-THIRTIES
3-02-003	MID-TWENTIETH
3-01-002	MIDDLETOWN
3-03-003	MIDSUMMER
3-02-002	MIGRANT
3-02-002	MIGRATORY
3-01-001	MIJ
3-01-001	MIJBIL
3-02-003	MILDER
3-02-003	MILITARILY
3-01-001	MILITARISM
3-02-003	MILLENNIA
3-01-001	MILLIDEGREE
3-01-001	MILLIDEGREES
3-03-003	MILLIMETER
3-01-001	MIMETIC
3-03-003	MINDED
3-03-003	MINDLESS
3-02-002	MINED
3-03-003	MINIMIZING
3-02-003	MINISTERING
3-02-002	MINISTRIES
3-01-001	MINNETT
3-02-003	MINNIE
3-02-003	MINUTEMAN
3-01-003	MIRACULOUSLY
3-03-003	MIRANDA
3-01-001	MISBEHAVIOR
3-03-003	MISCHIEVOUS
3-02-003	MISERABLY
3-03-003	MISLED
3-01-001	MISSAIL
3-02-003	MISSISSIPPI'S
3-02-003	MISTAKENLY
3-01-001	MIZELL
3-02-002	MOBILIZING
3-03-003	MOCKED
3-01-001	MODAL
3-03-003	MODELED
3-02-003	MODERATION
3-03-003	MODERNIZED
3-03-003	MODERNS
3-03-003	MODESTLY
3-02-002	MOLIERE
3-02-002	MOLOCH
3-02-003	MOLTEN
3-01-001	MOLVAR
3-03-003	MOM
3-02-003	MONARCH
3-01-002	MONDAY'S
3-01-001	MONDRIAN
3-01-001	MONEL
3-03-003	MONET
3-01-001	MONIC
3-02-003	MONITOR
3-01-001	MONMOUTH
3-01-001	MONO-IODOTYROSI
	NE
3-02-002	MONOLOGUE
3-02-001	MONOTONE
3-02-002	MONSOON
3-03-003	MONSTERS
3-03-003	MONSTROSITY
3-03-003	MONTICELLO
3-02-002	MOONS
3-01-001	MOOS
3-03-003	MOP
3-03-003	MOPPING
3-01-001	MOROCCAN
3-03-003	MORSEL
3-01-002	MOSK
3-02-002	MOSLEM
3-03-003	MOTION-PICTURE
3-03-003	MOTIVATES
3-02-003	MOTIVATING
3-02-002	MOTLEY
3-01-001	MOTORS'
3-01-001	MOTTLED
3-01-001	MOUTHFUL
3-03-003	MULES
3-01-001	MULLER'S
3-03-003	MULTITUDE
3-02-003	MUNDANE
3-03-003	MUNITIONS
3-02-003	MURDERING
3-02-003	MURMUR
3-01-001	MURTAUGH
3-01-001	MUSCOVY
3-01-001	MUSIAL
3-02-003	MUSICALLY
3-03-003	MUSICALS
3-02-003	MUSICIANSHIP
3-03-003	MUSKETS
3-02-002	MUSLIM
3-02-003	MUSTACHED

3-03-003	MUSTER
3-03-003	MUTE
3-03-003	MUTED
3-03-003	MUTILATED
3-03-003	MUTINY
3-02-002	MYERS
3-01-001	MYNHEER
3-01-001	MYOCARDIAL
3-02-002	MYSTIC
3-03-003	MYSTICS
3-02-002	MYTHOLOGY
3-01-001	N**.C
3-01-001	NADINE'S
3-01-001	NAKAMURA
3-03-003	NAKEDNESS
3-03-003	NAPKIN
3-02-002	NAPLES
3-01-001	NARRATIVES
3-03-003	NARROWS
3-03-003	NATION-WIDE
3-03-003	NATIONALITY
3-01-002	NATIONS'
3-03-003	NATURALIZED
3-03-003	NATURE'S
3-03-003	NAUSEA
3-02-003	NEAR-BY
3-02-003	NEARED
3-01-002	NEARNESS
3-03-003	NEBULOUS
3-02-003	NECESSITATES
3-02-003	NECKLACE
3-02-002	NECKLINE
3-01-001	NECROSIS
3-02-002	NECTAR
3-03-003	NEIGHBOR'S
3-02-003	NEIL
3-03-003	NEPTUNE
3-02-002	NERO
3-01-003	NERVOUSLY
3-03-003	NESTLED
3-02-002	NESTS
3-03-003	NETHERLANDS
3-02-003	NETS
3-01-001	NEURAL
3-03-003	NEUTRALITY
3-01-001	NEVERSINK
3-03-003	NEW-FOUND
3-02-002	NEWFOUNDLAND
3-01-002	NEWTON'S
3-03-003	NICHE
3-02-002	NICODEMUS
3-01-001	NIEMAN
3-01-001	NIGGERS
3-03-003	NIGHTLY
3-02-002	NILE
3-03-003	NINETIES
3-03-003	NINETY-NINE
3-03-003	NIP
3-01-001	NISHIMA
3-01-001	NITRATE
3-02-003	NOCTURNAL
3-02-002	NOCTURNE
3-03-003	NOMINALLY
3-03-003	NOMINATE
3-02-002	NOMINEE
3-01-001	NON-FICTION
3-03-003	NON-MILITARY
3-02-003	NON-PROFIT
3-01-001	NON-SERVICE-CON
	NECTED
3-01-001	NON-SUPERVISORY
3-01-001	NON-TAXABLE
3-02-002	NON-VIOLENCE
3-03-003	NONEXISTENT
3-01-001	NONREACTIVITY
3-01-001	NONRESIDENT
3-01-001	NONSINGULAR
3-01-001	NONSPECIFICALLY
3-01-001	NONVERBAL
3-02-002	NONWHITE
3-02-002	NOOSE
3-02-002	NORTHFIELD
3-02-003	NOSTRILS
3-02-003	NOTATION
3-02-003	NOTHINGNESS
3-02-002	NOUNS
3-02-002	NOVELIST'S
3-02-003	NOVICE
3-02-002	NOZZLES
3-03-003	NUANCES
3-01-001	NUCLIDE
3-01-002	NUTCRACKER
3-03-003	NUTRITIONAL
3-02-002	O*NEILL
3-01-001	OAKES
3-03-003	OATHS
3-03-003	OBEYING

Code	Word	Code	Word	Code	Word	Code	Word
3-01-001	OBJECTIONABLE	3-01-001	OVERLORDS	3-02-003	PERSUASIVELY	3-03-003	POWDERY
3-03-003	OBJECTIVELY	3-01-001	OVERNIGHTERS	3-02-003	PERVERSELY	3-03-003	POWERLESS
3-02-003	OBSERVABLE	3-03-003	OVERREACH	3-01-001	PETRIE	3-01-002	PRAGUE
3-03-003	OBSERVANT	3-03-003	OVERRIDING	3-01-001	PEZZA	3-01-001	PRAISEGOD
3-02-003	OBSERVATORY	3-03-003	OVERSIMPLIFICATION	3-01-001	PFOHL	3-03-003	PRANCING
3-03-003	OCCUPATIONS	3-03-003	OVERTAKE	3-03-003	PHILIPPINE	3-03-003	PRAYING
3-02-003	OCEANOGRAPHY	3-02-003	OVERTHROWN	3-01-002	PHILLIES	3-01-001	PREAMBLES
3-02-002	OCEANS	3-02-002	OVERTIME	3-03-003	PHONOGRAPH	3-03-003	PRECARIOUSLY
3-03-003	OCTAGONAL	3-02-003	OVERTLY	3-03-003	PHOTOGRAPHING	3-03-003	PRECEDE
3-01-001	OCTILLION	3-03-003	OVERTURES	3-02-003	PHRASED	3-02-003	PRECEDENCE
3-01-001	ODER	3-02-002	OWNERSHIPS	3-02-003	PHRASEOLOGY	3-03-003	PRECEDENTS
3-03-003	ODIOUS	3-02-003	OWNING	3-02-002	PI	3-03-003	PRECEPTS
3-03-003	OFF-*BROADWAY	3-01-002	OXIDE	3-03-003	PIANISTS	3-03-003	PRECOCIOUS
3-03-003	OFF-DUTY	3-01-001	OXYGENS	3-01-001	PICASSO'S	3-03-003	PREDETERMINED
3-02-003	OFFENDED	3-01-001	OXYTETRACYCLINE	3-02-002	PICK-UP	3-02-003	PREDICAMENT
3-03-003	OFFERINGS	3-01-001	OZONE	3-01-001	PICKERS	3-03-003	PREDICTIONS
3-01-001	OFFICIATED	3-01-001	P**.*D**.*I	3-01-001	PICKLED	3-02-003	PREDICTIVE
3-02-003	OFFSHORE	3-01-001	PACERS	3-01-001	PICKOFF	3-03-003	PREDICTS
3-01-001	OGDEN	3-02-003	PACIFISM	3-03-003	PICNICS	3-01-001	PREDNISONE
3-02-002	OILCLOTH	3-02-003	PACKET	3-02-003	PICTURING	3-01-003	PREFACE
3-02-003	OILED	3-02-003	PACKS	3-01-001	PIDDINGTON	3-02-002	PREMARITAL
3-03-003	OINTMENT	3-03-003	PADDING	3-03-003	PIER	3-03-003	PREMATURE
3-01-003	OKLA	3-01-001	PAIE	3-03-003	PIERCING	3-02-003	PREMATURELY
3-01-001	OLEOPHILIC	3-03-003	PAINLESS	3-01-002	PIEZOELECTRIC	3-01-001	PREMIX
3-01-001	OLIVER'S	3-02-002	PAINTER'S	3-02-003	PIGEON	3-01-002	PREPARATIVE
3-01-001	OMELET	3-03-003	PAJAMAS	3-03-003	PIGMENTS	3-01-001	PREPOSITIONAL
3-03-003	OMINOUSLY	3-02-002	PALLADIO	3-02-002	PILLAGE	3-01-001	PRESSER
3-03-003	OMISSION	3-03-003	PALLID	3-01-001	PILLOWS	3-01-001	PRESUME
3-03-003	OMISSIONS	3-01-001	PAMPHLET	3-02-002	PIMP	3-03-003	PRESUMES
3-03-003	ON-THE-JOB	3-03-003	PANE	3-02-003	PIONEERED	3-01-001	PRESUMPTION
3-02-003	ONE-ROOM	3-03-003	PANES	3-02-002	PIONEERING	3-03-003	PRETEXT
3-02-003	ONE-TIME	3-02-003	PANS	3-01-001	PIONEERS	3-01-001	PRICE-CONSCIOUSNESS
3-01-001	ONLEH	3-01-001	PANZA	3-01-001	PISTONS	3-02-002	PRICE-EARNINGS
3-03-003	OPEN-MOUTHED	3-02-003	PAOT	3-01-001	PIT-RUN	3-01-001	PRINCE'S
3-03-003	OPUS	3-02-003	PARABLE	3-03-003	PITFALL	3-02-003	PRINCES
3-02-002	ORATION	3-02-003	PARADES	3-03-003	PITIABLE	3-01-002	PRINTER
3-03-003	ORATORY	3-02-003	PARADOXICAL	3-03-003	PIZZA	3-02-002	PRISONERS'
3-03-003	ORBITING	3-02-002	PARALLELISM	3-01-001	PLACE-KICKING	3-02-003	PRISONS
3-02-002	ORCHARD	3-01-001	PARAPSYCHOLOGY	3-01-001	PLACE-NAMES	3-02-003	PROBED
3-02-003	ORCHESTRATION	3-03-003	PARASOL	3-01-001	PLAINFIELD	3-01-001	PROBES
3-03-003	ORCHIDS	3-03-003	PARISHIONERS	3-02-003	PLAINTIFFS	3-02-002	PROBLEMATIC
3-02-003	ORDEAL	3-02-002	PARISIAN	3-01-001	PLANER	3-03-003	PROCLAMATIONS
3-03-003	ORDINANCES	3-01-001	PARRILLO	3-03-003	PLATEAU	3-02-002	PROCURER
3-01-001	ORDO	3-01-001	PARS	3-02-003	PLATONIC	3-03-003	PRODDED
3-03-003	ORE	3-03-003	PARTICULATE	3-03-003	PLATOONS	3-02-003	PRODIGY
3-01-001	ORES	3-01-001	PASHA	3-02-003	PLAY'S	3-03-003	PROFESSEDLY
3-02-003	ORGANDY	3-03-003	PASSIONATELY	3-03-003	PLAYFUL	3-02-003	PROFFERED
3-03-003	ORGANICALLY	3-03-003	PASTEL	3-03-003	PLAYWRIGHT	3-02-003	PROFICIENCY
3-01-002	ORGANIZATION'S	3-02-003	PATENTED	3-03-003	PLEAS	3-02-002	PROFILES
3-03-003	ORGANIZERS	3-01-002	PATHWAYS	3-02-002	PLEDGE	3-01-001	PROFIT-MAXIMIZING
3-02-003	ORIENTING	3-02-002	PATRICK'S	3-03-003	PLEDGES	3-02-003	PROFITED
3-01-001	ORIGEN	3-03-003	PATROLLING	3-03-003	PLOWS	3-03-003	PROFUNDITY
3-01-001	ORIGINALS	3-03-003	PATRONIZED	3-03-003	PLUGGED	3-03-003	PROFUSELY
3-02-002	ORIGINATING	3-01-001	PATRONNE	3-02-003	PLUNGING	3-03-003	PROGRAMMED
3-01-001	ORLICK	3-02-002	PATTER	3-01-001	PLUS-ONE	3-01-001	PROGRAMMER
3-01-001	ORLICK'S	3-03-003	PAW	3-03-003	PLUSH	3-02-002	PROGRESSIONS
3-02-003	ORNAMENTED	3-02-002	PAWNSHOP	3-02-003	PNEUMONIA	3-01-002	PROGRESSIVISM
3-02-003	ORNAMENTS	3-02-002	PAWS	3-01-002	PO	3-02-003	PROLETARIAT
3-01-001	ORTHODONTICS	3-01-001	PAX-ORDO	3-01-001	PO*K	3-01-001	PROMENADE
3-01-001	ORTHODONTISTS	3-02-003	PAYABLE	3-01-001	POCASSET	3-02-003	PRONOUNCEMENT
3-02-003	ORTHODOXY	3-02-003	PAYDAY	3-02-003	POCKETBOOK	3-03-003	PROPAGANDIST
3-01-001	ORTHOGRAPHIC	3-02-002	PAYNE'S	3-01-001	POD	3-03-003	PROPHETICALLY
3-02-002	ORTHOPEDIC	3-03-003	PEACEABLE	3-02-002	POHL'S	3-03-003	PROPPED
3-01-001	ORY	3-03-003	PEACH	3-03-003	POINTEDLY	3-01-001	PROPRIETORSHIPS
3-02-003	OSCILLATION	3-02-002	PEALE	3-03-003	POINTER	3-02-002	PROSCRIPTION
3-01-001	OSMOTIC	3-02-003	PEBBLES	3-03-003	POISONING	3-03-003	PROSECUTING
3-03-003	OSTENSIBLE	3-03-003	PEDIGREE	3-01-001	POITRINE	3-01-002	PROSODIC
3-03-003	OTIS	3-03-003	PEDRO	3-03-003	POKES	3-02-003	PROSPER
3-02-002	OTTOMAN	3-02-003	PEE	3-02-002	POLARIZED	3-03-003	PROSTITUTES
3-03-003	OUNCE	3-03-003	PEEL	3-02-003	POLICING	3-02-003	PROTECTING
3-01-001	OUNCES	3-01-001	PELVIC	3-02-002	POLICY-MAKERS	3-02-003	PROTESTATIONS
3-01-002	OUST	3-03-003	PENALIZED	3-01-001	POLLING	3-03-003	PROTOCOL
3-01-001	OUT-OF-POCKET	3-03-003	PENNILESS	3-01-002	POLYCRYSTALLINE	3-01-001	PROTOGEOMETRIC
3-01-001	OUTBACK	3-01-002	PENNY'S	3-01-001	POLYPROPYLENE	3-02-002	PROTON
3-02-002	OUTBREAKS	3-01-001	PEONY	3-02-002	POMPOUS	3-02-002	PROTONS
3-01-002	OUTCRY	3-02-003	PEPPERY	3-01-001	PONCHO	3-02-003	PROTOTYPE
3-03-003	OUTDATED	3-01-002	PERCEIVES	3-03-003	PONDEROUS	3-03-003	PROTRUDING
3-03-003	OUTDISTANCED	3-03-003	PERCEPTIVE	3-02-003	POORER	3-01-003	PROVINCIALISM
3-03-003	OUTDO	3-01-001	PERDIDO	3-03-003	POOREST	3-03-003	PROVISO
3-02-002	OUTFIELD	3-02-003	PERFECTING	3-02-002	POPE'S	3-03-003	PROVOKE
3-02-003	OUTLIVED	3-02-003	PERFORATED	3-03-003	PORES	3-02-002	PROXIMATE
3-03-003	OUTPOST	3-03-003	PERILOUSLY	3-01-001	PORNSEN	3-02-002	PSYCHIATRY
3-02-003	OUTRAGES	3-02-002	PERJURY	3-02-002	PORTAL	3-03-003	PSYCHIC
3-01-001	OUTRIGGER	3-01-001	PERLMAN	3-03-003	PORTICO	3-02-003	PSYCHOPATHIC
3-03-003	OUTSIDER	3-02-003	PERMEATED	3-01-001	PORTO	3-01-001	PSYLLIUM
3-03-003	OUTSKIRTS	3-03-003	PERPETRATED	3-02-003	PORTUGUESE	3-01-001	PUBESCENT
3-02-003	OUTWARDLY	3-03-003	PERPETUALLY	3-03-003	POSING	3-03-003	PUBLIC-SPIRITED
3-01-001	OVER/UNDER	3-03-003	PERSECUTED	3-01-001	POSITIVISTS	3-01-001	PUBLICK
3-03-003	OVERCAME	3-03-003	PERSISTENTLY	3-03-003	POST-*WORLD	3-03-003	PUBLISH
3-02-003	OVERCROWDED	3-01-002	PERSONAGES	3-02-002	POSTGRADUATE	3-01-001	PUCCINI'S
3-03-003	OVERDEVELOPED	3-03-003	PERSONALIZED	3-03-003	POSTPONING	3-02-002	PULITZER
3-01-001	OVERFALL	3-01-001	PERSONALLY-OWNED	3-03-003	POSTSCRIPT	3-03-003	PULSATING
3-02-002	OVERHAUL	3-03-003	PERSONIFICATION	3-03-003	POSTULATE	3-03-003	PUMPED
3-03-003	OVERHAULING	3-02-003	PERSONIFIES	3-01-001	POTEMKIN'S	3-01-002	PUNCHER
3-03-003	OVERLAPPED	3-02-003	PERSPECTIVES	3-03-003	POTENTIALITY	3-03-003	PUNCTURED
3-03-003	OVERLAPPING			3-03-003	POTTED		
3-03-003	OVERLOAD			3-01-001	POULTICE		

Code	Word
3-02-003	PUNISH
3-03-003	PUREST
3-03-003	PURGES
3-01-002	PURITANS
3-02-003	PURPOSEFUL
3-01-002	PURPOSIVE
3-02-003	PURRING
3-02-003	PURSED
3-02-003	PURSUITS
3-02-002	PUSH-UP
3-01-001	PUSHERS
3-02-002	PUSHES
3-01-001	PYROMETER
3-03-003	QUART
3-01-001	QUASIMODO
3-03-003	QUELL
3-03-003	QUERIED
3-03-003	QUERIES
3-03-003	QUIETED
3-02-002	QUIETNESS
3-02-003	QUINTET
3-01-001	QUINTUS
3-03-003	QUOTING
3-01-001	RACE-DRIVER
3-01-001	RACKETEERS
3-03-003	RACKETS
3-01-001	RADAR-CONTROLLED
3-03-003	RADIANCE
3-02-002	RADIATIONS
3-03-003	RADIO-**J*T*V
3-03-003	RADIOACTIVITY
3-01-001	RADIOCHLORINE
3-03-003	RAILING
3-03-003	RAILROAD'S
3-02-003	RAINFALL
3-02-003	RALLIES
3-03-003	RAMBLE
3-01-001	RAMEY'S
3-03-003	RAMIFICATIONS
3-03-003	RAMMED
3-02-003	RANCOR
3-02-002	RANSACKED
3-01-001	RAPPING
3-03-003	RAPTURE
3-01-001	RATCLIFF
3-03-003	RATIONALIST
3-03-003	RATIONALLY
3-03-003	RATIONED
3-02-002	RATIONING
3-02-002	RATON
3-02-002	RATS
3-02-002	RATTLESNAKE
3-02-003	RAVING
3-01-001	RAWLINS
3-02-003	RAWSON
3-01-003	RD
3-02-003	RE-ELECTED
3-01-001	REACTANTS
3-02-001	REAFFIRMED
3-01-001	REAGENTS
3-03-003	REALIZES
3-03-003	REAP
3-03-003	REAPPEARED
3-03-003	REAPPEARS
3-02-002	REARRANGE
3-03-003	REASSEMBLE
3-03-003	REBELLING
3-03-003	REBELLIOUSLY
3-03-003	REBORN
3-02-003	RECAPTURE
3-03-003	RECEDE
3-03-003	RECITALS
3-03-003	RECITATION
3-02-003	RECKONED
3-02-003	RECKONING
3-03-003	RECLINING
3-03-003	RECOLLECTIONS
3-03-003	RECONCILED
3-01-002	RECONSTRUCTED
3-03-003	RECOUNTING
3-02-003	RECOUNTS
3-03-003	RECRIMINATIONS
3-02-002	RECTIFIER
3-01-001	RECTOR'S
3-02-003	RECURRED
3-01-002	RED-HAIRED
3-01-001	REDBIRDS
3-02-003	REDDER
3-03-003	REDDISH
3-02-003	REDECORATING
3-01-002	REDEPOSITION
3-03-003	REDOUBLED
3-01-001	REDOUTE
3-01-001	REESE
3-01-001	REFILL
3-02-003	REFINE
3-01-001	REFLECTORS
3-01-002	REFORMED
3-03-003	REFORMER
3-02-002	REFUTED
3-03-003	REGAINING
3-02-003	REGION'S
3-02-003	REGRETS
3-02-002	REID
3-03-003	REIGNING
3-03-003	REIN
3-02-002	REINED
3-01-001	REINFORCEMENTS
3-02-003	REINFORCES
3-03-003	RELATIVISTIC
3-03-003	RELATIVITY
3-03-003	RELAXES
3-03-003	RELENTED
3-01-001	REMARQUE
3-02-003	RENAMED
3-02-002	RENDITIONS
3-03-003	RENOIR
3-02-003	RENOVATED
3-01-002	REPAID
3-01-002	REPAYMENT
3-03-003	REPEALED
3-03-003	REPENT
3-01-001	REPETITIONS
3-03-003	REPRESSED
3-03-003	REPRINTS
3-03-003	REPRISAL
3-03-003	REPROACH
3-03-003	REPRODUCES
3-02-003	REPS
3-03-003	REPUDIATED
3-01-001	RESEARCH-STAFF
3-02-003	RESEARCHER
3-02-002	RESENTFUL
3-03-003	RESERVOIRS
3-02-003	RESIDED
3-02-002	RESIDUES
3-02-002	RESISTOR
3-03-003	RESOLVES
3-03-003	RESOLVING
3-01-002	RESONANCES
3-02-003	RESORTING
3-02-002	RESOURCEFUL
3-03-003	RESTFUL
3-01-001	RESTORABILITY
3-02-002	RESURGENCE
3-01-001	RESUSPENDED
3-03-003	RETARD
3-01-002	RETARDATION
3-01-001	RETICULATE
3-01-001	RETINAL
3-03-003	RETORTED
3-03-003	RETRACTED
3-02-002	RETROGRADE
3-03-003	RETROSPECT
3-03-003	REUBEN
3-02-002	REVAMPED
3-03-003	REVEL
3-02-003	REVELATIONS
3-02-003	REVERENT
3-02-003	REVERT
3-01-001	REVOLUTIONIBUS
3-03-003	REVOLUTIONIZED
3-02-003	REWARDED
3-02-002	RHEUMATISM
3-02-002	RHINOCEROS
3-02-003	RHYME
3-01-001	RIEFLING
3-02-002	RIGGED
3-01-001	RIGHTFIELD
3-02-002	RIGHTFULLY
3-01-001	RIM-FIRES
3-01-001	RIMANELLI
3-03-003	RIPENING
3-03-003	RIPPING
3-02-003	RIPPLING
3-02-003	RISKY
3-02-003	RIVALRIES
3-02-002	RIVERBANK
3-03-003	ROADBLOCK
3-03-003	ROAMING
3-03-003	ROBBERIES
3-02-002	ROBBIE
3-01-001	ROBOTS
3-01-001	ROCKFORK
3-02-002	ROCKIES
3-01-001	RODDER
3-02-002	RODENT
3-02-002	RODENTS
3-01-001	RODNEY
3-02-002	ROILING
3-02-003	ROLLER
3-02-002	ROLLS-*ROYCE
3-03-003	ROMEO
3-01-002	ROOMING
3-03-003	ROOSTER
3-02-003	ROSARIES
3-01-001	ROSE'S
3-03-003	ROTS
3-02-003	ROTTING
3-01-001	ROUGHCAST
3-03-003	ROUGHNESS
3-01-001	ROUNDHEAD
3-03-003	ROUNDUP
3-01-001	ROURKE'S
3-01-003	ROUSSEAU'S
3-03-003	ROUTINES
3-02-002	ROYCE
3-03-003	RUDDY
3-01-001	RUDOLPH
3-03-003	RUEFULLY
3-02-003	RUFFLED
3-03-003	RULER
3-03-003	RUM
3-03-003	RUMMAGING
3-02-003	RUNDOWN
3-02-003	RUNG
3-01-001	RUNYON
3-01-001	RUPTURE
3-03-003	RUSHES
3-01-001	RUSK'S
3-02-003	RUSTIC
3-03-003	RUTHLESSNESS
3-02-002	SABOTAGE
3-03-003	SACRAMENTO
3-01-001	SADDLEBAGS
3-03-003	SADISM
3-03-003	SAGGED
3-01-001	SAILBOATS
3-02-002	SALADS
3-01-001	SALEDO
3-01-001	SALESLADY
3-03-003	SALMON
3-02-002	SALONS
3-03-003	SALUTE
3-03-003	SALUTED
3-02-002	SALVADOR
3-02-003	SALVE
3-01-001	SALYER'S
3-01-001	SANCHO
3-02-003	SANCTITY
3-01-001	SANDALPHON
3-03-003	SANDBURG'S
3-01-001	SANT
3-02-002	SANTAYANA
3-02-003	SAPIO
3-02-003	SAPPED
3-01-001	SARAH'S
3-01-001	SARTORIS
3-02-003	SASH
3-03-003	SATAN
3-01-001	SATIRES
3-03-003	SATIRICAL
3-01-001	SATISFIES
3-02-003	SATURDAY'S
3-01-001	SATURN
3-01-002	SAUCEPAN
3-03-003	SAVAGELY
3-03-003	SAVORED
3-03-003	SAVORING
3-03-003	SAWDUST
3-02-002	SAWS
3-01-001	SAWTIMBER
3-02-002	SCAFFOLDING
3-02-003	SCANDALIZED
3-03-003	SCARCITY
3-03-003	SCARE
3-03-003	SCARLET
3-01-001	SCEPTICAL
3-01-001	SCHAACK
3-01-001	SCHEMA
3-01-003	SCHEMATIC
3-01-001	SCHEMATICALLY
3-03-003	SCHEMING
3-01-001	SCHIELE'S
3-02-003	SCHOOL'S
3-03-003	SCHOOLBOY
3-01-001	SCHOOLMASTER
3-01-002	SCHOOLROOM
3-02-002	SCHOONER
3-02-002	SCHUYLER
3-02-003	SCOFFED
3-02-003	SCOOPED
3-03-003	SCOURED
3-03-003	SCOUTING
3-03-003	SCRAPE
3-03-003	SCRAPS
3-01-001	SCREVANE
3-01-002	SCRIVENER
3-03-003	SCRUBBING
3-03-003	SCRUTINIZED
3-03-003	SCRUTINIZING
3-02-003	SCURRIED
3-03-003	SEACOAST
3-02-002	SEAFOOD
3-03-003	SEARCHES
3-02-003	SEASON'S
3-02-002	SEAWEED
3-01-001	SECCO
3-03-003	SECESSIONIST
3-03-003	SECLUSION
3-02-003	SECONDARILY
3-02-002	SECULARIZED
3-01-001	SEDGWICK
3-01-001	SEDIMENT
3-03-003	SEDUCTION
3-03-003	SEEKERS
3-01-001	SEGOVIA
3-03-003	SEGREGATIONIST
3-03-003	SELF-APPOINTED
3-02-003	SELF-CONFIDENT
3-03-003	SELF-CONSCIOUSLY
3-02-003	SELF-CONTROL
3-02-003	SELF-DEFENSE
3-03-003	SELF-DESTRUCTION
3-03-003	SELF-DESTRUCTIVE
3-02-003	SELF-PITY
3-02-002	SELF-RELIANT
3-02-003	SELF-SUFFICIENT
3-03-003	SENATORIAL
3-01-002	SENSOR
3-02-002	SEPARATES
3-01-001	SEPTIC
3-01-001	SERENISSIMUS
3-03-003	SERPENTS
3-01-001	SERVICE-CONNECTED
3-02-003	SETBACK
3-03-003	SETBACKS
3-02-002	SETTLER
3-03-003	SEVER
3-01-001	SEWARD'S
3-02-003	SEXTON
3-02-003	SHADOWED
3-02-003	SHAKERS
3-02-002	SHAMROCK
3-01-001	SHAN
3-03-003	SHANTY
3-02-003	SHAREHOLDERS
3-03-003	SHARKS
3-02-002	SHARON
3-02-002	SHARPE'S
3-03-003	SHARPENING
3-03-003	SHARPER
3-02-002	SHAWL
3-01-001	SHAWOMET
3-03-003	SHEAF
3-03-003	SHEEPSKIN
3-01-001	SHEERAN
3-02-003	SHENANIGANS
3-02-003	SHEPHERD
3-02-003	SHERATON-*BILTMORE
3-03-003	SHERIFFS
3-03-003	SHERWOOD
3-02-002	SHIED
3-03-003	SHIMMERING
3-03-003	SHIN
3-03-003	SHINY
3-03-003	SHIPBUILDING
3-01-001	SHIPPER
3-01-001	SHIRES
3-01-001	SHIRL
3-02-003	SHOALS
3-03-003	SHOCKINGLY
3-03-003	SHORT-LIVED
3-02-003	SHORT-RUN
3-03-003	SHORTAGES
3-03-003	SHORTENING
3-03-003	SHORTEST
3-03-003	SHOULDERED
3-02-002	SHOVELS
3-02-003	SHOWCASE
3-03-003	SHOWERS
3-02-003	SHOWMAN
3-03-003	SHRED
3-01-002	SHREVEPORT
3-03-003	SHRILLY
3-02-002	SHRINKAGE
3-03-003	SHRINKING
3-03-003	SHRIVELED
3-02-003	SHUCKS
3-03-003	SHUDDERING
3-02-003	SHUFFLE
3-02-003	SHUFFLING

3-01-001	SHULD	3-03-003	SOUNDLY
3-01-001	SHUTDOWN	3-01-001	SOUNION
3-02-002	SHUTDOWNS	3-03-003	SOUR
3-03-003	SICILIAN	3-03-003	SOURLY
3-02-003	SICILY	3-02-002	SOVEREIGNS
3-03-003	SIDEWAYS	3-02-003	SOW
3-01-001	SIEBERN	3-03-003	SOWN
3-03-003	SIFTED	3-01-001	SPACECRAFT
3-03-003	SIGHTING	3-03-003	SPACIOUSNESS
3-01-002	SIGNORA	3-03-003	SPARKED
3-03-003	SILENCES	3-01-001	SPARKY
3-03-003	SILHOUETTED	3-03-003	SPARRING
3-02-003	SIMILARITIES	3-03-003	SPASM
3-01-002	SIMS	3-03-003	SPECIALIZE
3-03-003	SINFUL	3-01-001	SPECIFICATION
3-02-002	SINFULNESS	3-02-003	SPECIFYING
3-01-001	SINGLE-STEP	3-03-003	SPECTACLES
3-02-003	SINLESS	3-03-003	SPECTER
3-02-003	SIRED	3-01-001	SPECTROSCOPY
3-02-003	SIS	3-03-003	SPECULATION
3-03-003	SITWELL	3-02-003	SPEECHLESS
3-02-003	SKEPTICS	3-03-003	SPEEDED
3-01-001	SKOLMAN	3-03-003	SPEEDILY
3-03-003	SKULL	3-01-001	SPICE-*NICE
3-02-002	SKULLCAP	3-01-001	SPICED
3-03-003	SLACKENED	3-03-003	SPICES
3-01-001	SLAKED	3-02-002	SPIKES
3-01-001	SLAM	3-02-002	SPILLED
3-01-001	SLANDERER	3-03-003	SPILLING
3-03-003	SLANT	3-02-002	SPIRES
3-03-003	SLANTED	3-02-002	SPIRITO
3-03-003	SLASH	3-03-003	SPLASH
3-03-003	SLATED	3-03-003	SPLASHED
3-03-003	SLAUGHTERED	3-03-003	SPLASHING
3-02-003	SLAYING	3-03-003	SPLITTING
3-02-003	SLEEPILY	3-03-003	SPOIL
3-03-003	SLICKER	3-03-003	SPONSORING
3-03-003	SLIPPER	3-02-002	SPORES
3-01-001	SLOANE	3-02-002	SPORTSWRITER
3-02-003	SLOCUM	3-01-001	SPOTLESS
3-03-003	SLOPPY	3-03-003	SPOUSE
3-01-002	SLOVENLY	3-03-003	SPOUTED
3-03-003	SLUGGING	3-01-001	SPRAGUE
3-03-003	SLUMBER	3-03-003	SPRAWL
3-02-003	SMELT	3-03-003	SPRINGFIELD
3-03-003	SMIRK	3-01-001	SPRINKEL
3-02-002	SMITH-*HUGHES	3-02-002	SPROUTED
3-02-002	SMITHFIELD	3-01-001	SPURDLE
3-01-001	SMITHSONIAN	3-03-003	SPURS
3-02-003	SMOOTHER	3-03-003	SQUABBLES
3-02-003	SMUGGLED	3-03-003	SQUADRON
3-02-003	SNACKS	3-02-003	SQUINTED
3-02-002	SNAG	3-02-003	SQUINTING
3-02-003	SNAKED	3-03-003	STAB
3-03-003	SNARLING	3-02-002	STABILIZATION
3-01-002	SNATCHES	3-03-003	STABLES
3-02-003	SNEAKERS	3-03-003	STAFFED
3-02-002	SNORT	3-01-001	STAGECOACH
3-02-002	SNOW'S	3-03-003	STAGING
3-03-003	SNOWSTORM	3-01-001	STAKE-OUT
3-03-003	SNUBBED	3-01-001	STALLION
3-02-002	SOAPS	3-03-003	STALLS
3-01-003	SOBERED	3-02-002	STAN
3-02-003	SOBERING	3-01-001	STAND-INS
3-03-003	SOBS	3-02-002	STANDBY
3-01-001	SOCCER	3-01-001	STAR'S
3-02-001	SOCIAL-ECONOMIC	3-03-003	STARTER
3-01-003	SOCIALISTIC	3-02-003	STARVED
3-02-003	SOCIALIZED	3-02-002	STASIS
3-02-003	SOCIETY'S	3-03-003	STAUNCH
3-02-002	SOCIO-ECONOMIC	3-02-003	STAUNCHEST
3-01-001	SOCIOECONOMIC	3-01-001	STAVROPOULOS
3-03-003	SOCKET	3-03-003	STEADIER
3-01-003	SOD	3-02-003	STEAMBOAT
3-02-003	SODA	3-03-003	STEAMSHIP
3-02-002	SOFAS	3-01-001	STEARNS
3-02-003	SOGGY	3-01-001	STEELS
3-02-002	SOJOURNER	3-01-001	STEINHA**DGER
3-03-003	SOL	3-03-003	STEMMED
3-03-003	SOLICITUDE	3-02-002	STEPMOTHER
3-03-003	SOLOS	3-02-002	STEPSON
3-02-003	SOLUBLE	3-01-003	STEPWISE
3-01-002	SOLVENTS	3-03-003	STERNLY
3-03-003	SOMBER	3-02-003	STEVE
3-02-002	SOMERSAULTS	3-02-002	STILTS
3-01-001	SOMERSET	3-02-002	STIMULATES
3-01-003	SOMETHIN	3-02-002	STINK
3-01-001	SOMMERS	3-02-002	STIRLING
3-02-002	SONNET	3-02-002	STIRS
3-02-002	SOPHOCLES	3-02-002	STITCH
3-01-003	SORDID	3-02-002	STOIC
3-03-003	SORELY	3-03-003	STOMACHS
3-02-002	SORES	3-01-001	STONEWARE
3-01-001	SORGHUM	3-03-003	STOOPED
3-01-001	SORRENTINO	3-01-001	STOREHOUSE
3-02-003	SOUL'S	3-03-003	STORMED
3-03-003	SOUNDING	3-03-003	STOUT

3-03-003	STRADDLING	3-02-002	TAFT-*HARTLEY
3-03-003	STRAITS	3-01-001	TAILIN
3-03-003	STRANDS	3-03-003	TAILOR-MADE
3-02-003	STRANGER'S	3-01-001	TANGENCY
3-02-002	STRAPPING	3-02-002	TANTAMOUNT
3-02-002	STRATTON	3-01-001	TAOIST
3-01-001	STRATUM	3-03-003	TAPER
3-03-003	STRAUSS	3-02-002	TARAS
3-02-002	STRAWS	3-01-001	TARGO
3-03-003	STRINGY	3-03-003	TARNISHED
3-02-002	STRIVES	3-02-003	TASTING
3-02-002	STRIVINGS	3-03-003	TAXIS
3-02-003	STROKED	3-03-003	TEASING
3-03-003	STRUGGLES	3-01-001	TEASPOONS
3-03-003	STRUT	3-01-001	TELEGRAPHER
3-03-003	STUB	3-02-002	TELEGRAPHIC
3-02-003	STUBBORNLY	3-02-003	TELEPATHY
3-03-003	STUBBY	3-02-003	TELEPHONING
3-02-002	STUCK-UP	3-03-003	TELL-TALE
3-03-003	STUDENT'S	3-02-003	TEN-FOOT
3-01-001	STUDS	3-02-002	TEN-YEAR
3-03-003	STUPENDOUS	3-02-002	TENDERFOOT
3-03-003	STYLED	3-03-003	TENEMENTS
3-03-003	STYLIST	3-02-002	TERMINI
3-01-001	SUB-INTERVAL	3-03-003	TERRORIZED
3-02-003	SUBJUGATION	3-02-003	TETHERED
3-02-002	SUBLIME	3-01-002	TEXAS'
3-02-002	SUBMITS	3-01-001	THAMES
3-03-003	SUBSCRIBED	3-03-003	THANKING
3-01-002	SUBSECTIONS	3-02-003	THAWED
3-03-003	SUBSERVIENT	3-02-002	THERE'LL
3-03-003	SUBSIDIES	3-03-003	THEREWITH
3-03-003	SUBSIDY	3-01-001	THERMOCOUPLE
3-01-001	SUBSPECIES	3-01-001	THERMOCOUPLES
3-03-003	SUBSTANTIVE	3-01-001	THERMOMETRY
3-01-002	SUBSTRATES	3-01-002	THET
3-03-003	SUBTITLED	3-02-002	THICKNESSES
3-02-002	SUBTRACTING	3-02-002	THINKIN
3-01-001	SUBTYPE	3-02-003	THINLY
3-02-003	SUFFERER	3-01-001	THIOURACIL
3-01-001	SUGGESTIBILITY	3-03-003	THIRTY-ONE
3-03-003	SUITABLY	3-03-003	THIRTY-TWO
3-02-003	SUITORS	3-02-002	THORN
3-01-001	SULLAM	3-03-003	THOROUGHFARE
3-03-003	SULPHUR	3-02-003	THOUGHTLESS
3-01-001	SULTAN	3-02-002	THOUSANDTH
3-01-001	SULZBERGER	3-02-002	THRASHED
3-02-003	SUMMARIZE	3-03-003	THREADBARE
3-01-003	SUMMARIZING	3-03-003	THREADING
3-03-003	SUMMATION	3-03-003	THREE-DAY
3-03-003	SUMMON	3-03-003	THREE-HOUR
3-02-003	SUNKEN	3-01-001	THREE-INCH-WIDE
3-01-001	SUNNYVALE	3-03-003	THREE-MAN
3-01-001	SUPER-*SETS	3-02-002	THREES
3-02-003	SUPERFICIALLY	3-03-003	THREESOME
3-03-003	SUPERFLUOUS	3-03-003	THRIFTY
3-03-003	SUPERLATIVE	3-02-003	THRILLED
3-02-002	SUPERMARKETS	3-03-003	THROBBED
3-03-003	SUPERVISING	3-02-003	THROBBING
3-02-003	SUPPLANT	3-03-003	THRONG
3-03-003	SUPPLEMENTAL	3-01-001	THRUST-TO-WEIGHT
3-03-003	SUPPLEMENTING		
3-01-002	SUPPORTER	3-02-003	THUD
3-02-002	SUPPOSITIONS	3-03-003	THUMBS
3-01-001	SUPRA	3-03-003	THUMP
3-03-003	SUR	3-03-003	THWART
3-01-001	SURNAME	3-03-003	TIBETAN
3-03-003	SURREPTITIOUSLY	3-03-003	TICK
3-02-003	SUSPEND	3-01-002	TIDEWATER
3-02-003	SUSTENANCE	3-03-003	TIDINGS
3-02-003	SWAGGERED	3-01-001	TIEPOLO
3-02-003	SWALLOWING	3-03-003	TIERS
3-03-003	SWAN	3-02-003	TIGHTEN
3-03-003	SWARM	3-01-001	TIMBERLANDS
3-03-003	SWARMED	3-02-002	TIME-HONORED
3-03-003	SWARMING	3-03-003	TINIEST
3-02-002	SWATCHES	3-03-003	TIRESOME
3-03-003	SWAYING	3-03-003	TITANIC
3-03-003	SWEARING	3-03-003	TOLERABLE
3-02-002	SWEDEN'S	3-01-001	TOLLEY'S
3-01-001	SWEENEYS	3-02-002	TOLLS
3-01-001	SWEET-SOUR	3-02-003	TOMATOES
3-03-003	SWEETNESS	3-03-003	TOMORROW'S
3-03-003	SWELLED	3-01-001	TONER
3-02-002	SWINE	3-02-002	TOOT
3-03-003	SWINGS	3-02-002	TOP-LEVEL
3-02-003	SWOOPING	3-02-002	TORMENTED
3-02-003	SYMBOLIZES	3-02-002	TORSOS
3-03-003	SYMPHONIES	3-02-002	TORTOISE
3-02-003	SYNAGOGUE	3-03-003	TORTUOUS
3-03-003	SYNONYM	3-02-003	TORTURE
3-02-002	SYNONYMS	3-01-003	TOTALITARIANISM
3-02-002	SYSTEM'S	3-01-001	TOTALLED
3-01-001	SYSTEMIC	3-02-002	TOUGHS
3-01-001	TABLESPOONFUL	3-01-001	TOXIC
3-02-002	TABLET	3-02-003	TRACEABLE
3-02-003	TABOO	3-02-003	TRACKED

3-02-002	TRACKING	3-03-003	UNDERSEA	3-02-002	VIABILITY	3-03-003	WOBBLE
3-03-003	TRADEMARK	3-01-003	UNDERSHIRT	3-02-002	VICE-*PRESIDENT	3-03-003	WOO
3-02-002	TRADITIONALISM	3-03-003	UNDERSTANDABLY	3-02-002	VICKERY	3-02-002	WOODSIDE
3-01-001	TRAFTON	3-03-003	UNDERSTANDINGLY	3-03-003	VICKSBURG	3-03-003	WOODSMOKE
3-02-003	TRAIT	3-03-003	UNDERTAKES	3-01-001	VICKY	3-03-003	WOODWARD
3-03-003	TRAMPLE	3-03-003	UNDERWAY	3-01-001	VIETH	3-03-003	WOOLLY
3-03-003	TRANSACT	3-02-003	UNDERWEAR	3-03-003	VIETNAM	3-01-002	WORCESTERSHIRE
3-02-003	TRANSCENDENTAL	3-03-003	UNDERWRITE	3-02-003	VIEWERS	3-03-003	WORKERS'
3-03-003	TRANSCENDING	3-03-003	UNDIMINISHED	3-02-002	VIEWPOINTS	3-01-001	WORKING-CLASS
3-02-003	TRANSCRIBED	3-02-003	UNDISCIPLINED	3-01-001	VIKINGS	3-01-002	WORKOUTS
3-01-001	TRANSFEROR'S	3-03-003	UNDISTINGUISHED	3-03-003	VILLAIN	3-02-003	WORLD-FAMOUS
3-01-002	TRANSFORMS	3-03-003	UNDISTURBED	3-03-003	VINDICATED	3-03-003	WORLD-RENOWNED
3-02-002	TRANSIENT	3-03-003	UNDO	3-02-002	VINTAGE	3-01-002	WORSHIPING
3-03-003	TRANSLATIONS	3-03-003	UNDRESSING	3-02-003	VIOLATIONS	3-02-003	WORTHLESS
3-02-003	TRANSLUCENT	3-02-003	UNECONOMICAL	3-02-002	VIRGINIA'S	3-02-003	WOVE
3-03-003	TRANSMIT	3-03-003	UNENDING	3-02-003	VIRILITY	3-03-003	WREATHS
3-02-002	TRANSMUTATION	3-01-001	UNFITTING	3-02-003	VIRTUOSO	3-02-002	WRIGLEY
3-01-001	TRANSPIRED	3-03-003	UNFORGETTABLE	3-03-003	VIRULENCE	3-03-003	WROUGHT
3-03-003	TRANSPORTING	3-02-002	UNHEARD	3-01-001	VISCOELASTICITY	3-03-003	WRYLY
3-03-003	TRAPPINGS	3-03-003	UNHESITATINGLY	3-02-002	VISCOUNT	3-03-003	WYATT
3-03-003	TRASTEVERE	3-02-002	UNHURRIED	3-02-003	VISTA	3-03-003	YACHTS
3-02-003	TRAVELLER	3-01-001	UNIFIES	3-02-003	VISTAS	3-02-003	YEA
3-03-003	TRAYS	3-02-003	UNILATERAL	3-03-003	VISUALIZE	3-01-001	YEAR-'ROUND
3-03-003	TRESPASSED	3-03-003	UNISON	3-03-003	VIVACIOUS	3-03-003	YEARNED
3-01-001	TRESPASSES	3-02-003	UNIVERSALITY	3-03-003	VOCATION	3-02-003	YEAST
3-01-001	TRIANDOS	3-02-002	UNJUST	3-02-003	VOCIFEROUS	3-01-001	YELLOW-DWARF
3-02-002	TRILL	3-02-002	UNKIND	3-03-003	VOLUMINOUS	3-02-002	YELLOW-GREEN
3-01-002	TRIMBLE	3-03-003	UNLEASHED	3-02-002	VOLUPTUOUS	3-03-003	YEN
3-01-001	TRIPLETS	3-02-002	UNLINED	3-02-003	VOMITING	3-03-003	YESTERYEAR
3-02-002	TRIPOD	3-03-003	UNLOCK	3-02-002	VOUS	3-03-003	YOKE
3-02-003	TRIUMPHS	3-03-003	UNMOVED	3-02-002	VOWELS	3-01-001	YOSEMITE
3-02-002	TROPIC	3-03-003	UNNECESSARILY	3-03-003	VYING	3-03-003	YOUNG'S
3-02-002	TROUGH	3-03-003	UNOBTAINABLE	3-02-002	WAGER	3-03-003	ZEALAND
3-02-002	TROUP	3-03-003	UNOBTRUSIVE	3-02-003	WAIL	3-03-003	ZEALOUSLY
3-03-003	TROUPE	3-03-003	UNOCCUPIED	3-03-003	WAILED	3-01-001	ZIMMERMAN
3-03-003	TROUSER	3-03-003	UNPUBLISHED	3-01-001	WAKEFULNESS	3-02-002	ZODIACAL
3-03-003	TROY	3-03-003	UNREALISTIC	3-01-001	WALLY'S	3-03-003	ZONES
3-02-003	TRUISM	3-02-003	UNREASONABLE	3-02-003	WANDERINGS	3-02-003	0.3
3-02-003	TRUMAN'S	3-03-003	UNRESTRICTED	3-03-003	WANTON	3-01-001	05
3-03-003	TRUNCATED	3-03-003	UNSIGNED	3-02-003	WAR'S	3-02-002	1.0
3-02-002	TRUSTWORTHY	3-02-002	UNSKILLED	3-02-002	WARDS	3-03-003	1.1
3-02-002	TUCSON	3-02-002	UNSOLD	3-03-003	WARNS	3-02-003	1.8
3-03-003	TUG	3-03-003	UNSOLVED	3-02-003	WARPED	3-01-001	1**C256
3-02-002	TUMBLE	3-03-003	UNSPOKEN	3-02-003	WARRANTED	3-02-002	1**C4
3-03-003	TUMBLING	3-01-002	UNSTAINED	3-01-001	WASHIZU	3-01-001	1/16
3-03-003	TUNED	3-03-003	UNSUITABLE	3-01-001	WASPISH	3-02-003	1,500
3-01-001	TUNING	3-03-003	UNSUNG	3-03-003	WASTELAND	3-01-001	100-109**+0
3-02-003	TUNISIA	3-02-002	UNSYMPATHETIC	3-03-003	WATCHDOG	3-02-002	11TH
3-01-001	TUNISIAN	3-02-003	UNTHINKABLE	3-01-001	WATERCOLORS	3-02-002	113
3-03-003	TUNNELS	3-02-003	UNUSED	3-02-002	WATERSHED	3-02-003	12**K
3-03-003	TURBULENCE	3-02-003	UNVEILED	3-02-003	WATERWAYS	3-01-001	12-GAUGE
3-03-003	TURF	3-02-003	UNWISE	3-03-003	WATERY	3-02-003	12,000
3-02-002	TURNOUT	3-03-003	UP-TO-DATE	3-03-003	WAVER	3-03-003	125
3-02-002	TURQUOISE	3-03-003	UPDATED	3-03-003	WAYWARD	3-03-003	126
3-01-001	TURRET	3-02-003	UPGRADE	3-03-003	WEAKEST	3-01-001	128
3-03-003	TUSKS	3-03-003	UPHEAVAL	3-03-003	WEAKLY	3-02-002	13.5
3-02-002	TWENTY-FIRST	3-02-003	UPHOLSTERY	3-02-003	WEATHERPROOF	3-03-003	14**K
3-01-002	TWENTY-SECOND	3-02-002	UPLANDS	3-02-002	WEEK-LONG	3-03-003	140
3-03-003	TWINGE	3-01-001	UPPER-	3-02-002	WEEKLIES	3-01-001	15-30
3-02-003	TWINKLE	3-03-003	UPPERMOST	3-03-003	WELDED	3-02-003	156
3-02-002	TWIRLER	3-01-001	UPPON	3-02-003	WELL-DEFINED	3-01-002	1582
3-03-003	TWITCH	3-03-003	UPSETS	3-03-003	WELL-ESTABLISHED	3-03-003	16,000
3-02-003	TYPED	3-03-003	UPSURGE			3-03-003	1600
3-01-001	TYPHUS	3-02-003	USAGES	3-03-003	WELL-FED	3-02-002	1602
3-01-001	TYPICALITY	3-02-003	USELESSLY	3-03-003	WELL-MADE	3-02-002	1609
3-01-001	TYPOGRAPHY	3-03-003	UTENSILS	3-03-003	WELL-MEANING	3-01-001	1610
3-01-001	TYROSINE	3-02-003	UTILITARIAN	3-02-002	WELLESLEY	3-02-002	1611
3-01-001	U**.*M**.*C**.*	3-02-003	VACATIONING	3-02-002	WESLEYAN	3-02-002	1643
	I**.*A	3-03-003	VAGUENESS	3-02-003	WEST'S	3-03-003	168
3-03-003	UKRAINIAN	3-01-001	VAIL	3-03-003	WESTINGHOUSE	3-01-003	1700
3-01-001	ULANYS	3-02-002	VALERY	3-01-001	WHAT'S-HIS-NAME	3-03-003	1707
3-03-003	ULTIMATUM	3-03-003	VALVE	3-02-002	WHEELOCK	3-01-002	1783
3-01-002	ULTRACENTRIFUGE	3-03-003	VANGUARD	3-02-002	WHENCE	3-01-001	1788
3-02-003	UMBRELLAS	3-01-001	VAPOR-PRESSURE	3-02-002	WHEREFORE	3-02-003	1789
3-03-003	UNABASHED	3-02-002	VARIABILITY	3-03-003	WHIR	3-02-002	1791
3-02-002	UNACCOMPANIED	3-02-002	VASA	3-03-003	WHIRL	3-02-002	1792
3-03-003	UNAFFECTED	3-01-002	VASCULAR	3-02-002	WHISKERS	3-02-002	1797
3-01-001	UNALLOCABLE	3-02-002	VAUGHAN	3-03-003	WHITE-CLAD	3-01-001	1803
3-02-003	UNAMBIGUOUS	3-03-003	VAULTING	3-01-001	WHITEMARSH	3-02-003	1820
3-01-001	UNANALYZED	3-02-003	VEERED	3-02-002	WHITENED	3-02-003	1835
3-03-003	UNATTRACTIVE	3-03-003	VEGETATION	3-02-002	WHOSOEVER	3-03-003	1848
3-02-003	UNAVOIDABLY	3-03-003	VEHEMENCE	3-03-003	WICKEDNESS	3-03-003	1850
3-03-003	UNAWARENESS	3-03-003	VEILS	3-03-003	WIDE-RANGING	3-03-003	1863
3-02-002	UNBALANCED	3-02-002	VELVETY	3-03-003	WIDEST	3-02-003	1864
3-02-002	UNCHARTED	3-03-003	VENERATION	3-03-003	WIELDED	3-02-002	1868
3-03-003	UNCLES	3-01-001	VENEREAL	3-03-003	WIGGLED	3-03-003	1872
3-02-002	UNCOMFORTABLY	3-02-002	VENEZUELA	3-01-002	WILLAMETTE	3-02-003	1882
3-03-003	UNCOMMITTED	3-02-002	VENTRICLE	3-02-003	WILSON'S	3-02-002	1885
3-03-003	UNCONVENTIONAL	3-03-003	VERACITY	3-03-003	WILT	3-02-002	1890
3-01-002	UNCOUNTED	3-01-001	VERBENAS	3-01-001	WINDER	3-03-003	1890'S
3-02-003	UNCRITICAL	3-02-002	VERDI	3-01-003	WINDOWLESS	3-02-002	1893
3-02-003	UND	3-03-003	VERMILION	3-03-003	WINGED	3-02-003	1897
3-01-001	UNDER-ACHIEVEMENT	3-01-001	VERNAVA	3-02-002	WINNINGS	3-03-003	1899
		3-01-001	VERNON'S	3-02-003	WINTHROP	3-01-003	1902
3-02-002	UNDERCURRENT	3-03-003	VERSATILE	3-03-003	WITHSTAND	3-02-003	1903
3-03-003	UNDERPRIVILEGED	3-01-001	VERTEBRAL	3-03-003	WITHSTOOD	3-03-003	1904
3-03-003	UNDERSCORED	3-03-003	VESTED	3-03-003	WIZARD	3-02-003	1906

```
3-02-002  1911
3-01-001  1912-13
3-02-002  1918
3-02-003  1932
3-02-003  1950S
3-01-001  1955-57
3-03-003  1964
3-03-003  1970
3-01-001  1986
3-01-003  2.4
3-02-002  2**C20
3-01-001  2**C25
3-01-001  2**C30.3-**C36
3-01-001  2-YEAR-OLDS
3-03-003  2-1/2
3-03-003  2ND
3-02-002  21ST
3-02-002  2100
3-02-002  22ND
3-03-003  23RD
3-02-003  230
3-01-001  29-*OCT
3-01-001  3**K
3-02-002  3,500
3-02-002  330
3-02-002  332
3-02-003  375
3-01-001  375*+0**J*C
3-01-001  38-43*+0
3-01-001  4.3
3-02-003  4**C30
3-02-002  4-INCH
3-03-003  4,000
3-02-003  420
3-02-002  44
3-02-002  44-YEAR-OLD
3-01-003  5.5
3-02-002  5.7
3-02-002  5-1
3-01-002  50-FOOT
3-02-002  500,000
3-02-003  6**K
3-01-001  6-3
3-02-003  60,000
3-02-003  64
3-01-001  7-2
3-02-002  70**K
3-01-001  7070
3-03-003  75,000
3-03-003  8TH
3-02-003  800,000
3-02-003  81
3-01-002  90*+0
3-03-003  900
3-03-003  92
3-02-003  93
3-03-003  98
3-01-001  .07
3-03-003  .22-CALIBER
3-02-002  .38
3-03-003  $1.1
3-03-003  $125
3-02-002  $14
3-01-002  $15,000
3-02-002  $17,000
3-01-003  $25
3-03-003  $3
3-02-003  $30,000
3-01-002  $37
3-02-002  $40
3-02-003  $400
3-02-002  $450
3-02-002  $5,000,000
3-01-002  $500,000
3-02-002  $7
3-02-002  $750
3-02-002  $85
3-03-003  $900
3-01-001  **F-FOLD
3-02-003  **YL
3-01-002  **YL,
3-01-002  **ZG,
3-01-001  *==C'*$
3-01-001  *=*F*$
3-01-002  *=*H*$
3-01-001  *=*X*$,
3-01-002  *=A*$
3-01-002  *=G*$
3-01-001  *=G(T)*$
3-02-003  *=N*$,
3-01-001  *=P*$,
3-01-003  *=Q*$
3-01-002  *=T*$,
3-01-001  *=X*$
3-03-003  *A*F*L-**J*C*I*
                         O,
3-01-001  *A*I*M*O

3-01-001  *A*P)**T**-
3-01-001  *A*W*O*C
3-01-001  *B*O*D.
3-03-003  *B,
3-01-001  *C*D*C.
3-01-001  *C*O
3-01-001  *CR
3-03-003  *D.
3-01-001  *D*L*I*N*E
3-01-001  *D*R*D*W
3-01-001  *D*T*F,
3-02-003  *D,
3-03-003  *E**U
3-01-001  *E*S*P
3-01-001  *F*H*A
3-01-001  *F*I*T*C
3-01-001  *G*N*P
3-02-002  *H.
3-02-002  *I
3-02-002  *I*C*B*M
3-01-001  *L*D
3-01-001  *MC/SEC
3-01-001  *MME
3-01-001  *MMES
3-02-002  *N*A*T*O,
3-01-001  *N*B*S
3-01-001  *N*W,
3-01-002  *O*A*S
3-01-001  *O*H
3-01-001  *P*A*B*A.
3-02-002  *P*T*A
3-01-001  *R+*D
3-01-001  *R*A*F
3-01-001  *R*D*W*S
3-01-001  *S*R,
3-03-003  *S*S
3-01-003  *S*W
3-01-001  *T*S*H,
3-03-003  *T*V,
3-01-001  *U*S*P
3-01-001  *V-1
3-01-001  *W-REGION
3-02-003  *X
3-01-001  *Y-CELL
3-01-001  -78**0
3-01-001  A-COMING
2-01-001  A-1
2-02-002  ABACK
2-02-002  ABASEMENT
2-01-001  ABBAS
2-01-001  ABBOT
2-01-001  ABBOTT
2-01-001  ABERNATHY
2-02-002  ABIDES
2-01-001  ABIGAIL
2-01-001  ABILENE
2-01-001  ABLARD
2-01-001  ABLATION
2-01-001  ABLER
2-02-002  ABLY
2-02-002  ABOLISHED
2-02-002  ABOUNDED
2-01-002  ABOUT-FACED
2-02-002  ABOVE-MENTIONED
2-01-001  ABOVEGROUND
2-01-002  ABREACTION
2-01-001  ABSOLUTENESS
2-01-002  ABSOLUTION
2-01-001  ABSORPTIONS
2-02-002  ABSURDITIES
2-02-002  ABUNDANTLY
2-02-002  ABYSMAL
2-01-001  ACADEMICS
2-01-001  ACCELERATIONS
2-01-001  ACCEPTABILITY
2-02-002  ACCESSIBILITY
2-02-002  ACCOLADE
2-01-001  ACCOMMODATES
2-02-002  ACCOMMODATING
2-02-002  ACCOMPLICE
2-01-002  ACCUSED
2-02-002  ACCOUNTANT
2-02-002  ACCREDITED
2-01-002  ACCRETIONS
2-02-002  ACCUMULATES
2-01-002  ACCUSES
2-02-002  ACCUSINGLY
2-01-001  ACHESON
2-01-002  ACKNOWLEDGEMENT
2-02-002  ACKNOWLEDGES
2-02-002  ACKNOWLEDGMENT
2-01-002  ACQUIRES
2-02-002  ACQUISITIONS
2-02-002  ACQUITTAL
2-02-002  ACQUITTED
2-02-002  ACROBATIC
2-02-002  ACTIVATE

2-02-002  ACTIVISM
2-01-002  ACTUALITIES
2-01-002  ACTUATED
2-01-001  ADAIR
2-02-002  ADAM'S
2-02-002  ADAPTABLE
2-01-001  ADAPTERS
2-01-001  ADDABBO
2-02-002  ADELE
2-02-002  ADHERENT
2-02-002  ADHESION
2-01-002  ADHESIVES
2-02-002  ADIRONDACK
2-02-002  ADJECTIVE
2-02-002  ADJOINED
2-02-002  ADJOINS
2-02-002  ADJOURNED
2-02-002  ADJUSTABLE
2-02-002  ADJUSTS
2-01-001  ADMASSY
2-01-001  ADMASSY'S
2-01-001  ADMIRERS
2-01-001  ADMITS
2-02-002  ADMONISHED
2-01-001  ADOBE
2-02-002  ADOPTS
2-01-001  ADORE
2-02-002  ADORED
2-02-002  ADRENAL
2-01-001  ADRIEN
2-01-001  ADULTERERS
2-01-002  ADVERBIAL
2-02-002  ADVERBS
2-02-002  ADVERSITY
2-02-002  ADVERTISEMENT
2-01-001  ADVISEMENT
2-02-002  ADVISES
2-02-002  AERONAUTICS
2-02-002  AFAR
2-02-002  AFFIDAVITS
2-02-002  AFFIRMING
2-02-002  AFFLUENT
2-02-002  AFFORDING
2-01-001  AFFRONT
2-02-002  AFOREMENTIONED
2-01-002  AFORESAID
2-02-002  AFRESH
2-02-002  AFTER-SCHOOL
2-02-002  AGAMEMNON
2-01-001  AGATHA
2-01-001  AGE-AND-SEX
2-02-002  AGELESS
2-01-001  AGGIE
2-01-001  AGGIES
2-01-001  AGGLOMERATE
2-01-001  AGGLUTININS
2-02-002  AGGRESSIVELY
2-02-002  AGGRESSOR
2-02-002  AGILE
2-02-002  AGIN
2-01-001  AGONE
2-02-002  AGONIZES
2-02-002  AHMAD'S
2-01-001  AILEY
2-01-001  AILEY'S
2-02-002  AILING
2-01-001  AIR-CONDITIONIN
                         G
2-02-002  AIRED
2-02-002  AIRILY
2-02-002  AIRLESS
2-02-002  AIRLINE
2-02-002  AIRSTRIP
2-01-002  AJAR
2-02-002  AL'S
2-01-001  ALABAMAS
2-02-002  ALACRITY
2-01-001  ALARMINGLY
2-01-001  ALBANIAN
2-01-001  ALBANIANS
2-01-002  ALBEIT
2-01-001  ALBERTO
2-01-001  ALBRIGHT'S
2-01-001  ALBUMS
2-01-001  ALCOHOLS
2-02-002  ALCORN
2-01-001  ALDEN
2-01-001  ALDERMEN
2-02-002  ALECK
2-02-002  ALERTNESS
2-01-002  ALEXANDRE
2-01-001  ALEXIS
2-01-001  ALF
2-01-002  ALFRESCO
2-01-001  ALGEBRA
2-01-001  ALGERIA
2-02-002  ALIENATE

2-02-002  ALIGN
2-02-002  ALIMONY
2-01-001  ALIX
2-01-002  ALKALINE
2-01-001  ALKALIS
2-01-002  ALL-*AMERICAN
2-01-002  ALL-POWERFUL
2-02-002  ALL-WEATHER
2-02-002  ALLA
2-01-002  ALLAY
2-02-002  ALLEGORIC
2-02-002  ALLEGRO
2-02-002  ALLERGIC
2-01-002  ALLEVIATION
2-01-001  ALLOCATIONS
2-01-001  ALOES
2-02-002  ALONENESS
2-02-002  ALORS
2-01-001  ALPERS
2-01-001  ALPHABET
2-02-002  ALPS
2-02-002  ALTERNATION
2-02-002  ALTON
2-01-001  ALUSIK'S
2-02-002  ALVA
2-01-001  ALVISE
2-02-002  ALWIN
2-02-002  AMASS
2-01-001  AMATEURS
2-01-001  AMAZON
2-02-002  AMBUSHED
2-01-001  AMEAUX
2-01-001  AMELIA'S
2-02-002  AMEND
2-02-002  AMIABLE
2-01-001  AMIGO
2-02-002  AMISS
2-01-001  AMONASRO
2-02-002  AMORAL
2-02-002  AMOROUS
2-01-001  AMORTIZE
2-01-002  AMPLIFICATION
2-01-001  AMUSEMENTS
2-02-002  AMUSINGLY
2-02-002  ANACHRONISMS
2-01-001  ANACONDA'S
2-01-001  ANALEPTIC
2-02-002  ANALOGOUSLY
2-01-001  ANALYSED
2-02-002  ANALYZES
2-01-001  ANARCHICAL
2-01-001  ANATOMICALLY
2-01-001  ANCHORITE
2-01-002  ANCHORS
2-02-002  ANCILLARY
2-01-002  ANDEAN
2-01-002  ANDERS
2-01-001  ANDREI'S
2-02-002  ANDREWS
2-01-001  ANGELIC
2-01-001  ANGELO'S
2-02-002  ANGLICANS
2-01-001  ANGLO-*AMERICA
2-01-001  ANGST
2-02-002  ANGUISHED
2-01-001  ANI
2-01-001  ANIMATION
2-01-001  ANISE
2-01-001  ANISEIKONIC
2-02-002  ANITA
2-02-002  ANKLE-DEEP
2-01-001  ANN'S
2-02-002  ANNOUNCER
2-02-002  ANNOY
2-02-002  ANONYMITY
2-02-002  ANTAGONISMS
2-02-002  ANTECEDENTS
2-02-002  ANTHROPOLOGIS
2-02-002  ANTHROPOLOGIS
2-02-002  ANTI-*AMERICA
2-02-002  ANTI-*NAZI
2-01-001  ANTI-*SEMITE
2-01-001  ANTI-*SOVIET
2-01-001  ANTI-AIRCRAFT
2-01-001  ANTI-HUMAN
2-01-001  ANTI-INFECTIV
2-01-001  ANTI-ORGANIZA
2-01-001  ANTI-SECRECY
2-02-002  ANTICIPATES
2-02-002  ANTICIPATING
2-02-002  ANTIDOTE
2-02-002  ANTIETAM
2-01-001  ANTISERA
2-02-002  ANTISOCIAL
2-01-002  ANTON
2-02-002  ANTONY
```

Code	Word	Code	Word
2-02-002	ANYBODY'S	2-01-002	ATHENIAN
2-02-002	APIECE	2-02-002	ATKINSON
2-02-002	APOCALYPSE	2-02-002	ATLANTIS
2-02-002	APOGEE	2-01-001	ATONEMENT
2-01-001	APOLLINAIRE	2-02-002	ATREUS
2-02-002	APOSTLE	2-02-002	ATROCITIES
2-02-002	APOSTLES	2-01-001	ATT
2-02-002	APP	2-02-002	ATTA
2-02-002	APPALLED	2-02-002	ATTACHES
2-02-002	APPEASE	2-01-001	ATTAKAPAS
2-02-002	APPEASED	2-02-002	ATTEST
2-02-002	APPENDED	2-02-002	AUBURN
2-01-001	APPETIZING	2-02-002	AUDIO
2-02-002	APPLAUDING	2-02-002	AUDITED
2-02-002	APPLICABILITY	2-01-001	AUDITIONS
2-02-002	APPOINTEE	2-01-001	AUF
2-01-001	APPORTIONMENTS	2-02-002	AUGMENTING
2-02-002	APPRAISALS	2-02-002	AURALLY
2-02-002	APPRECIATIVE	2-02-002	AURELIUS
2-02-002	APPRECIATIVELY	2-01-001	AURORA
2-02-002	APPREHENDED	2-02-002	AUSTIN'S
2-02-002	APPRENTICESHIP	2-02-002	AUTHENTICALLY
2-02-002	APPROPRIATENESS	2-01-002	AUTHORITARIANISM
2-02-002	APPROPRIATING	2-01-002	AUTHORIZATION
2-02-002	APPROVINGLY	2-02-002	AUTHORIZES
2-01-001	AQUIDNECK	2-01-001	AUTISM
2-02-002	AQUINAS	2-02-002	AUTOMATED
2-02-002	ARAB	2-01-001	AUTONOMIC-SOMATIC
2-02-002	ARABIAN		
2-01-001	ARAPACIS	2-01-002	AVAILABILITIES
2-02-002	ARBITRATION	2-01-001	AVAILED
2-01-001	ARCADES	2-02-002	AVARICE
2-01-001	ARCHIPELAGO	2-01-002	AVENGE
2-02-002	ARCHITECT'S	2-02-002	AVENGING
2-01-001	AREA'S	2-02-002	AVERELL
2-01-002	AREA-WIDE	2-01-002	AVERSION
2-02-002	ARID	2-02-002	AVOWED
2-02-002	ARIDITY	2-02-002	AWFULNESS
2-01-001	ARIMATHEA	2-02-002	AWNINGS
2-01-001	ARISTIDE	2-02-002	AWRY
2-02-002	ARISTOCRATS	2-02-002	AXIAL
2-01-001	ARISTOTELIAN	2-01-001	AXIOMS
2-01-001	ARM-LEVITATION	2-01-002	AYLESBURY
2-01-001	ARMADILLO	2-01-001	AZALEA
2-01-001	ARMATA	2-02-002	B),
2-02-002	ARMCHAIRS	2-02-002	B**.*A
2-01-001	ARMOUR	2-02-002	BABBITT
2-02-002	ARMPIT	2-02-002	BABBLED
2-02-002	ARNOLD'S	2-01-001	BABIN
2-02-002	AROMAS	2-01-001	BABY-DEAR
2-01-001	AROMATIC	2-02-002	BABYLON
2-02-002	AROUSES	2-02-002	BABYLONIAN
2-02-002	ARRAIGNED	2-02-002	BABYLONIANS
2-01-002	ARRAYED	2-02-002	BACILLUS
2-02-002	ARROGANT	2-01-001	BACKBENDS
2-01-001	ARSON	2-02-002	BACKDROP
2-02-002	ART'S	2-01-001	BACKSTAGE
2-01-001	ARTERIOLES	2-02-002	BACKWARDS
2-01-001	ARTERIOLOSCLEROSIS	2-02-002	BACKYARD
2-02-002	ARTICULATED	2-01-001	BAILEEFE
2-02-002	ARTISAN	2-02-002	BAIT
2-02-002	ARTISANS	2-01-002	BAKERY
2-02-002	ARTLESS	2-01-001	BALAGUER
2-02-002	ARTURO	2-02-002	BALCONIES
2-01-002	ASCENDED	2-02-002	BALDING
2-02-002	ASHEN	2-01-001	BALDNESS
2-01-001	ASHEVILLE	2-01-002	BALDWIN
2-02-002	ASININE	2-02-002	BALI
2-01-001	ASPEN	2-02-002	BALKAN
2-01-001	ASPENCADES	2-02-002	BALKANS
2-01-002	ASPIRANT	2-02-002	BALKED
2-02-002	ASPIRANTS	2-02-002	BALLAST
2-01-001	ASS'N	2-02-002	BALLESTRE
2-02-002	ASSAILANT	2-02-002	BALLOTS
2-01-001	ASSAM	2-02-002	BALMY
2-01-001	ASSAYING	2-01-001	BALTIMORE'S
2-02-002	ASSERTIVE	2-02-002	BALZAC
2-01-001	ASSESSOR	2-01-002	BANAL
2-01-001	ASSIGNEE	2-02-002	BANDED
2-02-002	ASSIMILATE	2-02-002	BANISTERS
2-01-001	ASSINIBOIA	2-02-002	BANJO
2-01-001	ASSINIBOINE	2-02-002	BANKING
2-01-001	ASSN	2-02-002	BANNED
2-01-001	ASSOCIATING	2-02-002	BANNERS
2-02-002	ASSORTED	2-02-002	BANSHEES
2-02-002	ASSUAGED	2-01-001	BARBECUED
2-01-001	ASSYRIAN	2-02-002	BARBS
2-01-001	ASTERIA	2-02-002	BARDS
2-01-001	ASTERISKS	2-01-001	BARKING
2-01-001	ASTOR	2-02-002	BARON
2-02-002	ASTOUNDED	2-01-002	BARRINGTON
2-01-002	ASTRONAUT	2-01-001	BARTLEBY
2-01-001	ASYMMETRIC	2-01-001	BAS-RELIEFS
2-01-001	ASYMMETRICALLY	2-02-002	BASEL
2-01-001	ASYNCHRONY	2-01-001	BASEMENTS
2-01-001	ATHALIE	2-01-001	BASHAW

Code	Word	Code	Word
2-02-002	BASHFUL	2-01-001	BERRA
2-01-001	BASIL'S	2-02-002	BERRIES
2-01-001	BASKETS	2-02-002	BERYL
2-01-001	BASKING	2-02-002	BESIEGED
2-01-001	BASLOT	2-01-001	BESIEGERS
2-02-002	BASOPHILIC	2-02-002	BESPECTACLED
2-02-002	BASSO	2-02-002	BESSARABIA
2-01-001	BASTING	2-02-002	BESTOW
2-02-002	BASTION	2-01-001	BESTSELLER
2-01-001	BATEAU	2-01-002	BETA
2-01-002	BATHYRANS	2-01-002	BETANCOURT
2-01-002	BATTED	2-01-002	BETIDE
2-02-002	BATTER	2-01-001	BETSEY
2-02-002	BATTERING	2-01-001	BEVEL
2-01-001	BATTERY-POWERED	2-01-001	BEVO
2-01-001	BATTLEFIELDS	2-02-002	BEWITCHED
2-02-002	BATTLEGROUND	2-01-001	BEYELER
2-01-001	BAUM	2-01-001	BI
2-01-001	BAWH	2-01-001	BIANCO
2-02-002	BAWLED	2-02-002	BIB
2-01-001	BAYEZIT	2-01-001	BIBLIOGRAPHIES
2-01-001	BAYLOR	2-02-002	BIBLIOGRAPHY
2-01-001	BAYOU	2-02-002	BICYCLES
2-01-002	BAYS	2-02-002	BIDDER
2-02-002	BEA	2-02-002	BIFOCALS
2-02-002	BEACHHEAD	2-02-002	BIGOTRY
2-01-001	BEAKER	2-02-002	BILATERAL
2-02-002	BEALE	2-01-001	BILGE
2-01-001	BEALL	2-02-002	BILKED
2-01-001	BEARISH	2-01-001	BILLBOARDS
2-02-002	BEASTS	2-01-001	BILLIKEN
2-02-002	BEATINGS	2-01-001	BILLIKENS
2-02-002	BEAU	2-01-001	BINDERS
2-01-001	BEAUJOLAIS	2-01-002	BINDS
2-01-001	BECCARIA	2-02-002	BING
2-02-002	BECKET	2-02-002	BINOCULARS
2-02-002	BECKONING	2-02-002	BINS
2-02-002	BEDFORD	2-01-001	BIO-ASSAY
2-02-002	BEDRIDDEN	2-01-001	BIO-MEDICINE
2-01-002	BEDSPREAD	2-02-002	BIOLOGIST
2-01-001	BEECHER	2-01-001	BIOLOGISTS
2-01-001	BEEFED-UP	2-02-002	BIOPHYSICAL
2-01-001	BEETLING	2-01-001	BIOPSY
2-02-002	BEETS	2-02-002	BIPARTISAN
2-01-001	BEFALL	2-01-001	BIPLANE
2-02-002	BEFOREHAND	2-02-002	BIRCH
2-02-002	BEFUDDLED	2-01-001	BIRDIES
2-02-002	BEGGAR	2-01-001	BIRDS'
2-02-002	BEGGARS	2-01-001	BIRTH-PREVENTION
2-01-002	BEGINNER'S		
2-01-001	BEGINNERS'	2-01-001	BISCAYNE
2-01-001	BEGLEY	2-02-002	BISCUIT
2-02-002	BEGRUDGE	2-01-001	BISHOPSGATE
2-02-002	BEGUILED	2-02-002	BITTEREST
2-01-002	BEHAVES	2-01-002	BIZ
2-01-001	BEING?	2-01-001	BLACKBOARD
2-01-001	BELABORING	2-01-001	BLACKFEET
2-01-001	BELASCO	2-01-001	BLACKJACK
2-02-002	BELATED	2-02-002	BLACKMAIL
2-02-002	BELCH	2-01-001	BLACKMAILER
2-02-002	BELCHING	2-02-002	BLACKSMITH
2-01-001	BELGE	2-02-002	BLAINE
2-02-002	BELGIUM	2-02-002	BLAMING
2-01-001	BELIEVETH	2-01-001	BLANCHARD
2-01-001	BELLA	2-02-002	BLANCHARD'S
2-02-002	BELLBOYS	2-02-002	BLANDLY
2-01-001	BELLETCH	2-01-001	BLASPHEMIES
2-02-002	BELLIES	2-02-002	BLASTING
2-02-002	BELLIGERENCE	2-02-002	BLATANT
2-01-001	BELLMAN	2-01-001	BLAUBERMAN
2-02-002	BELLOWING	2-02-002	BLAZED
2-02-002	BELMONT	2-02-002	BLEACHING
2-01-001	BELOWGROUND	2-02-002	BLEARY
2-02-002	BELTED	2-02-002	BLEED
2-01-001	BELTON	2-02-002	BLEMISH
2-02-002	BELVEDERE	2-02-002	BLENDS
2-02-002	BELVIDERE	2-01-001	BLEVINS
2-01-001	BENCHED	2-02-002	BLIGHT
2-01-001	BENCHMARKS	2-01-002	BLINDFOLDED
2-02-002	BENDS	2-01-001	BLINDING
2-02-002	BENEFACTOR'S	2-02-002	BLISSFULLY
2-02-002	BENEFICIARY	2-01-001	BLISTERED
2-01-001	BENELUX	2-02-002	BLISTERS
2-02-002	BENET	2-01-001	BLITHE
2-02-002	BENEVOLENT	2-02-002	BLOB
2-02-002	BENIGHTED	2-02-002	BLOCH
2-01-001	BENTHAM	2-01-002	BLOCKADING
2-01-001	BENTLEY	2-01-002	BLOCKY
2-01-001	BENZENE	2-01-001	BLOMDAHL
2-02-002	BEQUEATHED	2-02-002	BLOODHOUNDS
2-02-002	BEREFT	2-01-001	BLOTTING
2-01-001	BERIBERI	2-02-002	BLUE-BLACK
2-01-001	BERKELY	2-01-002	BLUISH
2-02-002	BERKSHIRES	2-01-001	BLUM
2-02-002	BERNHARDT	2-02-002	BLUNDER
2-01-001	BERNINI'S	2-02-002	BLUNDERED
2-01-001	BERNOULLI	2-01-001	BLUNTNESS

2-02-002 BLUSH	2-02-002 BRIEFING	2-02-002 BYE	2-02-002 CAROUSING
2-01-002 BOASTS	2-02-002 BRIG	2-02-002 BYGONE	2-02-002 CARPETING
2-01-002 BOATYARDS	2-01-001 BRIGHT'S	2-02-002 BYPRODUCT	2-01-002 CARPORT
2-01-001 BOAZ	2-01-002 BRIGHT-EYED	2-01-001 BYRNES	2-02-002 CARR
2-02-002 BOBBED	2-02-002 BRIGHTENED	2-01-001 C**.*C**.*B	2-02-002 CARRE
2-01-001 BOBBIE'S	2-01-001 BRITTANY	2-01-001 C'EST	2-02-002 CARSON
2-01-001 BOBBSEY	2-01-002 BRITTEN	2-02-002 CA	2-02-002 CARTILAGE
2-02-002 BODICE	2-02-002 BROACHED	2-01-001 CAB'S	2-02-002 CARTWHEELS
2-02-002 BODIN	2-01-001 BROADCASTERS	2-01-001 CABANAS	2-02-002 CARUSO
2-01-001 BODYBUILDERS	2-01-001 BROADCASTINGS	2-02-002 CABLES	2-02-002 CARVALHO
2-01-001 BOGEYED	2-01-002 BROADENS	2-02-002 CABOT	2-02-002 CARVINGS
2-02-002 BOGEYS	2-02-002 BROCHURE	2-02-002 CADENCE	2-01-001 CARWOOD
2-01-001 BOGY	2-02-002 BROCHURES	2-02-002 CADILLACS	2-01-001 CASANOVA
2-02-002 BOILER	2-01-001 BROCKLIN	2-02-002 CADMIUM	2-02-002 CASASSA
2-02-002 BOILS	2-01-001 BROGLIO	2-01-001 CAETANI	2-01-002 CASE-HISTORY
2-02-002 BOIS	2-02-002 BROIL	2-02-002 CAFETERIAS	2-01-001 CASEY'S
2-02-002 BOLDER	2-02-002 BROILED	2-01-001 CAGES	2-02-002 CASHMERE
2-01-001 BOLGER	2-02-002 BROILER	2-02-002 CAGEY	2-02-002 CASINO
2-01-001 BOLIOU	2-02-002 BROKERAGE	2-02-002 CAIN	2-01-001 CASTANEDA
2-01-001 BOLKER	2-02-002 BROODY	2-01-001 CAKED	2-01-001 CASTOR
2-02-002 BOLOGNA	2-02-002 BROOKE	2-02-002 CAL	2-01-001 CASTROISM
2-02-002 BOLSHEVIKS	2-01-001 BROOKFIELD	2-01-001 CALABRIA	2-01-001 CASTROS
2-02-002 BOMBINGS	2-02-002 BROOM	2-02-002 CALAMITOUS	2-01-001 CATALOGS
2-01-001 BON	2-02-002 BROTHELS	2-01-001 CALDER	2-01-001 CATALYSTS
2-01-001 BONANZA	2-02-002 BROTHERLY	2-02-002 CALDWELL'S	2-02-002 CATALYTIC
2-01-001 BONAVENTURE	2-01-001 BROTHERS'	2-01-001 CALIBRE	2-02-002 CATAPULTED
2-02-002 BONDED	2-02-002 BROWNING'S	2-02-002 CALICO	2-02-002 CATASTROPHICALLY
2-02-002 BONE-WEARY	2-01-001 BROWNLOW	2-01-001 CALINDA	
2-02-002 BONTEMPO	2-01-001 BROWNY-HAIRED	2-01-001 CALIPER	2-02-002 CATCHES
2-02-002 BONUS	2-01-001 BROXODENT	2-02-002 CALLAS	2-01-001 CATE'S
2-01-001 BONZES	2-02-002 BRUISING	2-02-002 CALLER	2-02-002 CATECHISM
2-02-002 BOOGIE	2-01-001 BRUMBY	2-02-002 CALLOUSED	2-01-001 CATFISH
2-01-001 BOOKCASE	2-02-002 BRUSHFIRE	2-02-002 CALLOUSNESS	2-01-001 CATHERINE'S
2-01-001 BOOKLETS	2-01-001 BRUSHY	2-02-002 CALMER	2-01-001 CATHERWOOD
2-01-001 BOONE	2-02-002 BRUTALLY	2-02-002 CALMING	2-01-001 CATKIN
2-01-001 BOOS	2-02-002 BRYAN'S	2-02-002 CALMNESS	2-02-002 CATSKILLS
2-01-001 BOOTLE	2-02-002 BRYCE	2-01-001 CALORIMETER	2-01-001 CAUCUS
2-01-002 BOOTLEGGERS	2-01-001 BRYN	2-01-001 CALVARY	2-02-002 CAUSE-AND-EFFECT
2-01-001 BORDEAUX	2-02-002 BUBBLED	2-02-002 CAMARADERIE	
2-01-001 BORDEL	2-02-002 BUCHANAN	2-02-002 CAMDEN	2-01-001 CAVANAGH
2-01-001 BORDERED	2-01-001 BUCKBOARD	2-02-002 CAMILLA	2-02-002 CAVORTING
2-02-002 BORES	2-02-002 BUCKLED	2-02-002 CAMOUFLAGED	2-01-001 CAYENNE
2-01-001 BORGLUM	2-02-002 BUCKLES	2-01-001 CAMPAIGNERS	2-01-001 CC
2-02-002 BOROUGHS	2-01-001 BUCKRA	2-01-002 CAMPFIRE	2-02-002 CEASING
2-01-001 BORROMINI'S	2-01-001 BUDDHISTS	2-01-001 CAMPGROUNDS	2-01-001 CEECEE
2-02-002 BORROWER	2-02-002 BUDGETED	2-01-001 CAMPITELLI	2-02-002 CELEBRANTS
2-02-002 BOSCH	2-02-002 BUFFETED	2-01-001 CAMPSITES	2-02-002 CELEBRATES
2-02-002 BOSTON'S	2-02-002 BUGGED	2-02-002 CANADIANS	2-02-002 CELEBRATIONS
2-01-001 BOTANISTS	2-02-002 BUGLE	2-02-002 CANCELLATION	2-02-002 CELLIST
2-02-002 BOTTLENECK	2-02-002 BUILDER'S	2-02-002 CANDIDLY	2-01-001 CEN-*TENNIAL
2-02-002 BOUCHER	2-01-001 BUILDERS'	2-02-002 CANDIES	2-02-002 CENSORED
2-02-002 BOUFFANT	2-01-001 BUILDING'S	2-02-002 CANDOR	2-01-001 CENSORS
2-01-001 BOUGH	2-02-002 BUILDUP	2-01-001 CANISTER	2-01-002 CENSURES
2-02-002 BOULEVARDS	2-01-001 BULBA	2-01-001 CANNIBALS	2-02-002 CENTER'S
2-02-002 BOUNDING	2-01-001 BULL-SESSIONS	2-01-001 CANNY	2-01-001 CENTER-PUNCH
2-02-002 BOUNDLESS	2-02-002 BULLIES	2-02-002 CANOES	2-01-001 CENTIMETER
2-01-001 BOUTON	2-01-001 BULLOCH	2-02-002 CANONIZED	2-01-001 CENTRAL'S
2-01-001 BOVINE	2-02-002 BULLS	2-01-001 CANOPY	2-01-001 CENTRAL-CITY
2-01-001 BOWDEN	2-01-001 BUMBLEBEE	2-01-001 CANTEEN	2-02-002 CENTRALIZING
2-01-001 BOXCARS	2-02-002 BUMPED	2-01-001 CANTOR	2-01-001 CENTRE
2-02-002 BOXED	2-02-002 BUMPER	2-01-001 CANVASSERS	2-01-001 CENTRIFUGE
2-01-001 BOYER	2-02-002 BUMPING	2-02-002 CANYONS	2-01-001 CENTS-PER-HOUR
2-02-002 BRACKETS	2-02-002 BUMS	2-02-002 CAPACITOR	2-02-002 CENTURIES-OLD
2-01-001 BRADBURY'S	2-02-002 BUNDY	2-01-001 CAPET	2-02-002 CERTIORARI
2-02-002 BRAG	2-02-002 BUNYAN	2-01-001 CAPITALISTIC	2-01-001 CESTRE
2-01-001 BRAGG	2-02-002 BUOYANT	2-02-002 CAPITALISTS	2-02-002 CEZANNE
2-02-002 BRAGGED	2-02-002 BURBANK	2-02-002 CAPITALIZING	2-01-001 CH'AN
2-01-001 BRAHMAPUTRA	2-01-001 BURCH	2-01-002 CAPITULATED	2-01-001 CH'IN
2-02-002 BRAHMSIAN	2-02-002 BUREAUS	2-01-001 CAPITULATION	2-01-001 CHABRIER
2-02-002 BRAKE	2-01-001 BUREN	2-01-001 CAPO	2-01-001 CHABRIER'S
2-02-002 BRANCHED	2-01-001 BURGESS	2-02-002 CAPPED	2-01-001 CHADWICK
2-02-002 BRAND-NEW	2-02-002 BURGLARS	2-02-002 CAPTIVATED	2-02-002 CHAFING
2-02-002 BRANDED	2-01-001 BURKES	2-02-002 CAPTIVATING	2-01-001 CHAIKOFF
2-02-002 BRANDENBURG	2-01-001 BURL	2-02-002 CAPTIVES	2-01-001 CHAMFER
2-01-001 BRANDON'S	2-02-002 BURLESQUE	2-01-002 CAPTORS	2-01-001 CHAMPASSAK
2-02-002 BRASSIERE	2-01-001 BURLINGHAM	2-01-002 CAPTURES	2-01-002 CHANCERY
2-02-002 BRASSY	2-01-001 BURMAN	2-02-002 CAPTURING	2-02-002 CHANDLER'S
2-02-002 BRAVER	2-02-002 BURNERS	2-02-002 CARAVAGGIO	2-01-002 CHANGE-OVER
2-02-002 BRAVING	2-01-001 BURNET	2-02-002 CARAVANS	2-01-001 CHANNEL-TYPE
2-01-001 BRAZOS	2-02-002 BURNINGS	2-02-002 CARAWAY	2-01-001 CHANSONS
2-02-002 BREACHING	2-01-001 BURROWS	2-01-001 CARBIDE	2-02-002 CHANT
2-02-002 BREAK-EVEN	2-02-002 BURSTS	2-02-002 CARBINES	2-01-001 CHANTEY
2-02-002 BREAKFASTED	2-01-001 BURTON'S	2-01-001 CARBOLOY	2-02-002 CHANTING
2-02-002 BREAKFASTS	2-01-001 BUSBOY	2-01-001 CARBONDALE	2-02-002 CHAPELS
2-02-002 BREAKWATER	2-01-001 BUSCH	2-01-001 CARBONS	2-02-002 CHARACTERIZATION
2-02-002 BREATHES	2-02-002 BUSIEST	2-02-002 CARELESSNESS	
2-02-002 BREED'S	2-01-002 BUSSES	2-02-002 CARICATURE	2-02-002 CHARLESTON
2-02-002 BREEZES	2-02-002 BUSTLE	2-02-002 CARLO	2-01-001 CHARLIE'S
2-02-002 BREWERY	2-01-001 BUTTERFLY	2-01-001 CARMACK	2-02-002 CHARMS
2-02-002 BRIC-A-BRAC	2-02-002 BUTTON-DOWN	2-01-001 CARMEN	2-01-001 CHARTIST
2-02-002 BRIDAL	2-02-002 BUYER	2-02-002 CARMICHAEL	2-01-002 CHARTRES
2-01-001 BRIDEGROOM'S	2-02-002 BUYER'S	2-02-002 CARMINE	2-01-001 CHARTROOM
2-02-002 BRIDES	2-02-002 BUZZED	2-01-001 CARMODY	2-01-001 CHASES
2-02-002 BRIDESMAIDS	2-02-002 BUZZES	2-02-002 CARNAL	2-02-002 CHASM
2-02-002 BRIDGEHEAD	2-01-001 BY-LAWS	2-01-001 CARNEGEY	2-02-002 CHASTISEMENT
2-02-002 BRIEFED	2-02-002 BY-PASSING	2-01-001 CAROL	2-02-002 CHASTITY
2-02-002 BRIEFER	2-02-002 BY-PRODUCTS	2-02-002 CAROLINE	2-02-002 CHATTED

2-02-002	CHATTING
2-01-001	CHAUFFEUR-DRIVEN
2-02-002	CHAUNCEY
2-01-001	CHAVIS
2-02-002	CHECKUP
2-02-002	CHEERED
2-02-002	CHEKHOV
2-02-002	CHERISHING
2-02-002	CHEROKEE
2-02-002	CHERRIES
2-02-002	CHESTNUTS
2-02-002	CHEW
2-01-001	CHEYENNE
2-02-002	CHICO
2-02-002	CHIDE
2-01-001	CHILBLAINS
2-01-001	CHILDISHLY
2-02-002	CHILLS
2-01-001	CHINLESS
2-01-001	CHINNING
2-02-002	CHINS
2-02-002	CHISELED
2-02-002	CHIVALROUS
2-02-002	CHIVALRY
2-01-001	CHLOROTHIAZIDE
2-02-002	CHOICEST
2-02-002	CHOPIN
2-02-002	CHORAL
2-01-001	CHORINES
2-02-002	CHORUSES
2-01-001	CHOU
2-02-002	CHOW
2-01-001	CHRISTENED
2-01-001	CHRISTI
2-01-001	CHRISTIANS'
2-01-001	CHRISTIANSEN
2-01-002	CHRISTIE
2-01-001	CHRISTINE
2-01-001	CHRISTMASTIME
2-01-002	CHRONICLES
2-02-002	CHRONOLOGICALLY
2-02-002	CHUBBY
2-02-002	CHUGGING
2-02-002	CHUNK
2-02-002	CHURCH-STATE
2-02-002	CHURCHILL'S
2-02-002	CHUTE
2-01-001	CIDER
2-02-002	CIGARS
2-01-001	CINDER
2-02-002	CINDERS
2-01-002	CIPHERS
2-01-002	CIRCLING
2-01-001	CIRCULARITY
2-02-002	CIRCULATE
2-02-002	CIRCULATORY
2-01-002	CIRCUMSCRIBING
2-02-002	CISTERN
2-02-002	CITIZEN'S
2-01-001	CITIZENS'
2-02-002	CITY-WIDE
2-02-002	CITYSCAPES
2-02-002	CIVILIANS
2-01-001	CLAIR
2-02-002	CLAMMY
2-02-002	CLAMOR
2-02-002	CLAMS
2-02-002	CLAN
2-02-002	CLAPS
2-02-002	CLASHES
2-02-002	CLASSED
2-02-002	CLASSICALLY
2-02-002	CLATTER
2-02-002	CLAUS
2-02-002	CLAWED
2-01-001	CLEANLY
2-01-001	CLEAR-CHANNEL
2-01-001	CLEARNESS
2-01-001	CLEAVAGE
2-01-002	CLEFT
2-02-002	CLEMENCEAU
2-01-001	CLEMENCY
2-02-002	CLEMENS
2-01-001	CLEMENS'
2-02-002	CLICK
2-02-002	CLICKS
2-02-002	CLIFFS
2-02-002	CLIMAXED
2-02-002	CLINCH
2-02-002	CLINICS
2-02-002	CLIPS
2-02-002	CLIQUE
2-02-002	CLOG
2-01-002	CLOGGED
2-02-002	CLOGGING
2-01-001	CLOSED-DOOR
2-01-002	CLOSETS
2-02-002	CLOSEUPS
2-01-001	CLOTHESHORSE
2-02-002	CLOUDLESS
2-02-002	CLOUDY
2-01-002	CLOVES
2-02-002	CLOWNS
2-02-002	CLUBBED
2-02-002	CLUCKS
2-01-001	CLURMAN
2-02-002	CLUSTERING
2-02-002	CLUTTERED
2-02-002	CLYDE
2-02-002	CO-CHAIRMEN
2-02-002	CO-OP
2-02-002	CO-ORDINATION
2-02-002	CO-WORKERS
2-01-001	COACHMEN
2-01-001	COATES
2-02-002	COBALT
2-01-002	COCKROACHES
2-01-002	COCKTAILS
2-01-001	COCOA
2-02-002	COCTEAU
2-01-001	CODDINGTON
2-01-002	CODDLED
2-02-002	COERCE
2-01-002	COERCIVE
2-01-002	COFFEEPOT
2-02-002	COGNITIVE
2-02-002	COGNIZANCE
2-02-002	COGNIZANT
2-02-002	COILS
2-02-002	COINCIDENCES
2-01-001	COLCORD'S
2-02-002	COLDS
2-02-002	COLEMAN
2-01-002	COLERIDGE'S
2-02-002	COLLABORATE
2-01-001	COLLAGES
2-02-002	COLLEGE'S
2-02-002	COLLIE
2-01-001	COLLINGWOOD
2-02-002	COLLISIONS
2-01-001	COLLOIDAL
2-02-002	COLLOQUIAL
2-01-001	COLLOQUIUM
2-01-001	COLO
2-02-002	COLOMBIAN
2-01-001	COLON
2-02-002	COLONEL'S
2-02-002	COLONNA
2-01-001	COLOR-**J*T*V
2-01-001	COLORATION
2-02-002	COLORATURA
2-01-001	COLOSSEUM
2-02-002	COLOSSUS
2-01-001	COLQUITT
2-01-002	COLUMNISTS
2-01-002	COMBATANT
2-01-001	COMBELLACK
2-02-002	COMEBACK
2-02-002	COMEDIANS
2-01-001	COMEDIE'S
2-01-001	COMEDIES
2-01-001	COMET
2-02-002	COMETS
2-01-002	COMICALLY
2-02-002	COMMA
2-01-002	COMMANDMENT
2-02-002	COMMANDO
2-02-002	COMMEMORATE
2-02-002	COMMEMORATED
2-02-002	COMMENDING
2-02-002	COMMENTATORS
2-02-002	COMMIES
2-02-002	COMMISSARY
2-02-002	COMMISSIONED
2-02-002	COMMITS
2-01-002	COMMITTEE'S
2-01-001	COMMITTEEWOMAN
2-02-002	COMMON-SENSE
2-02-002	COMMONPLACES
2-01-001	COMMUNICATIONAL
2-02-002	COMMUNIST-LED
2-02-002	COMMUNISTIC
2-02-002	COMMUTED
2-01-001	COMMUTES
2-02-002	COMPASSIONATE
2-02-002	COMPASSIONATELY
2-02-002	COMPELS
2-02-002	COMPENSATING
2-02-002	COMPETED
2-02-002	COMPETITIVELY
2-01-001	COMPEYSON
2-01-002	COMPILATIONS
2-01-001	COMPLEMENTS
2-02-002	COMPLICATE
2-02-002	COMPLIMENTARY
2-02-002	COMPLIMENTED
2-01-001	COMPOSES
2-02-002	COMPREHENDED
2-02-002	COMPREHENSIVELY
2-02-002	COMPRESS
2-01-002	COMPRESSIVE
2-01-001	COMPRESSOR
2-01-001	COMPROMISED
2-01-001	COMPUTES
2-01-001	COMRADESHIP
2-01-001	COMUS
2-01-002	CONAN
2-02-002	CONCEALMENT
2-02-002	CONCEALS
2-02-002	CONCEITS
2-02-002	CONCEIVES
2-02-002	CONCEIVING
2-01-001	CONCENTRIC
2-01-001	CONCEPTUALITY
2-01-001	CONCESSIONAIRE
2-01-001	CONCETTA'S
2-01-001	CONCIERGE
2-02-002	CONCILIATORY
2-02-002	CONCLAVE
2-01-001	CONCORDANT
2-01-001	CONCRETELY
2-01-002	CONCRETISTIC
2-02-002	CONCURRED
2-01-001	CONDESCENDING
2-01-001	CONDESCENSION
2-02-002	CONDIMENTS
2-02-002	CONDUCIVE
2-01-001	CONDUCTION
2-02-002	CONDUCTOR'S
2-01-001	CONE-SPHERE
2-02-002	CONES
2-01-002	CONESTOGA
2-02-002	CONFEDERATES
2-02-002	CONFEREES
2-01-001	CONFESSIONAL
2-02-002	CONFESSIONS
2-02-002	CONFIDENTLY
2-02-002	CONFIDING
2-02-002	CONFINE
2-02-002	CONFIRMING
2-02-002	CONFISCATED
2-02-002	CONFORMANCE
2-01-001	CONFORMATIONAL
2-02-002	CONFOUNDED
2-02-002	CONFUCIUS
2-01-002	CONFUSING
2-02-002	CONGESTED
2-01-002	CONGESTIVE
2-02-002	CONGRATULATORY
2-02-002	CONGREGATE
2-01-001	CONGREGATIONAL- *BAPTIST
2-01-001	CONGREGATIONALIST
2-01-001	CONGRESSWOMAN
2-01-001	CONIC
2-01-001	CONING
2-02-002	CONJECTURES
2-02-002	CONJURED
2-02-002	CONJURES
2-02-002	CONNECTS
2-01-001	CONNEXION
2-02-002	CONNOISSEURS
2-02-002	CONQUERORS
2-02-002	CONQUESTS
2-01-001	CONQUETE
2-01-001	CONRAD'S
2-01-001	CONSANGUINITY
2-02-002	CONSCRIPTED
2-02-002	CONSCRIPTION
2-01-001	CONSEIL
2-02-002	CONSERVING
2-02-002	CONSIDERATELY
2-01-002	CONSIGN
2-02-002	CONSOLED
2-02-002	CONSOLIDATE
2-02-002	CONSOLIDATING
2-02-002	CONSORTING
2-02-002	CONSPIRACIES
2-02-002	CONSTRAINED
2-01-001	CONSTRAINT
2-02-002	CONSTRICTED
2-02-002	CONSTRICTING
2-02-002	CONSTRUCTIVELY
2-02-002	CONSULTATIONS
2-02-002	CONSUME
2-01-001	CONTACTING
2-02-002	CONTADINI
2-02-002	CONTAGION
2-02-002	CONTAGIOUS
2-02-002	CONTAINMENT
2-02-002	CONTEMPTIBLE
2-02-002	CONTEMPTUOUSLY
2-02-002	CONTENDER
2-02-002	CONTENTIONS
2-02-002	CONTEXTS
2-01-001	CONTINGENT-FEE
2-02-002	CONTINUITIES
2-01-001	CONTRACTORS
2-02-002	CONTRADICTED
2-01-002	CONTRADICTORILY
2-02-002	CONTRADICTS
2-02-002	CONTRETEMPS
2-02-002	CONTRIBUTOR
2-02-002	CONTROLLER'S
2-01-001	CONVECTION
2-02-002	CONVENED
2-02-002	CONVENIENCES
2-02-002	CONVENING
2-02-002	CONVERTING
2-02-002	CONVINCINGLY
2-01-001	COOCH
2-02-002	COOK'S
2-01-001	COOKY
2-01-001	COOLIDGE'S
2-01-001	COOLIDGES'
2-01-002	COOLS
2-02-002	COOPED
2-02-002	COOPER'S
2-02-002	COOPERATED
2-01-001	COOPERMAN
2-01-001	COOSA
2-02-002	COPELAND
2-02-002	COPLAND
2-01-001	COPOLYMERS
2-02-002	COPPERY
2-02-002	COPRA
2-01-002	COQUETTE
2-02-002	CORCORAN
2-01-001	CORDER
2-02-002	CORDON
2-02-002	CORDS
2-01-001	CORELLI
2-01-001	CORKED
2-02-002	CORNMEAL
2-01-001	CORNS
2-01-001	CORNWALLIS
2-01-002	CORONADO
2-02-002	CORRECTIONS
2-02-002	CORRELATING
2-01-002	CORRELATIONS
2-02-002	CORRESPONDINGLY
2-02-002	CORRIDORS
2-01-001	CORROBORATE
2-02-002	CORROBORATED
2-01-001	CORROBOREES
2-01-001	CORRUPTED
2-01-001	CORTICO-FUGAL
2-01-001	CORTICO-HYPOTHALAMIC
2-02-002	COSMOLOGICAL
2-01-001	COSMOLOGISTS
2-02-002	COSMOPOLITAN
2-01-001	COSMOPOLITANISM
2-02-002	COSPONSORED
2-01-001	COST-DATA
2-01-001	COST-RAISING
2-01-001	COTILLION
2-02-002	COUCHED
2-02-002	COUGHED
2-01-002	COUNTERACTED
2-02-002	COUNTERACTING
2-02-002	COUNTERBALANCE
2-02-002	COUNTERED
2-02-002	COUNTRYWIDE
2-01-001	COUNTS/MINUTE
2-01-001	COUNTY'S
2-01-001	COUNTY-WIDE
2-02-002	COUPE
2-02-002	COUPS
2-02-002	COURTESAN
2-01-001	COURTLY
2-02-002	COURTROOM
2-02-002	COURTSHIP
2-02-002	COVE
2-01-001	COVENT
2-01-001	COVERALL
2-02-002	COVERINGS
2-02-002	COVERLET
2-02-002	COVERT
2-02-002	COVETOUSNESS
2-02-002	COVINGTON
2-02-002	COWARDICE
2-01-001	COWLEY
2-01-001	COWMAN
2-02-002	COWORKERS

Code	Word
2-02-002	COYNESS
2-01-002	CPS
2-02-002	CRABS
2-02-002	CRACKLE
2-02-002	CRACKPOTS
2-02-002	CRAFTSMAN
2-02-002	CRAGS
2-02-002	CRAIG
2-02-002	CRAMP
2-01-001	CRAMPS
2-02-002	CRANE'S
2-02-002	CRANNIES
2-02-002	CRASS
2-01-001	CRATE
2-01-001	CRATER
2-02-002	CRATES
2-02-002	CRAVE
2-02-002	CRAVED
2-02-002	CRAVEN
2-01-002	CRAVING
2-02-002	CRAWLS
2-01-002	CRAZE
2-02-002	CRAZED
2-02-002	CREASED
2-01-001	CREATORS
2-02-002	CREDENTIALS
2-01-002	CREDIBLE
2-02-002	CREDITORS
2-02-002	CRESCENDO
2-02-002	CRESCENT
2-01-001	CREVICE
2-01-001	CREWEL
2-02-002	CREWS
2-02-002	CRICKETS
2-01-002	CRIMEAN
2-02-002	CRINGED
2-01-001	CRIP
2-01-001	CRISPNESS
2-01-002	CRITICIZING
2-01-001	CRONE
2-02-002	CRONIES
2-02-002	CROOKS
2-01-002	CROONED
2-02-002	CROSBY'S
2-02-002	CROSS-LEGGED
2-01-001	CROSS-STRIATION S
2-01-001	CROSSMAN
2-01-001	CROSSON
2-01-001	CROSSON'S
2-02-002	CROW
2-01-001	CROWDER
2-02-002	CROWED
2-02-002	CROWS
2-02-002	CRUCIFIED
2-02-002	CRUCIFYING
2-02-002	CRUDELY
2-02-002	CRUISE
2-02-002	CRUISERS
2-02-002	CRUMBLE
2-02-002	CRUMBLING
2-02-002	CRUNCH
2-02-002	CRUPPER
2-01-002	CRUSADERS
2-02-002	CRUX
2-02-002	CRYSTALLIZING
2-02-002	CRYSTALLOGRAPHY
2-02-002	CUBA'S
2-02-002	CUBS
2-02-002	CUDGELS
2-02-002	CUFFS
2-02-002	CULMINATE
2-02-002	CULMINATED
2-02-002	CULMINATING
2-02-002	CULPRIT
2-02-002	CULPRITS
2-02-002	CULTIST
2-01-002	CULTIVATING
2-01-001	CULVER
2-02-002	CUNNINGHAM'S
2-02-002	CUPBOARD
2-02-002	CUPBOARDS
2-02-002	CURATOR
2-02-002	CURD
2-02-002	CURIE
2-01-001	CURIO
2-02-002	CURL
2-02-002	CURLING
2-02-002	CURRICULAR
2-02-002	CURRY
2-01-002	CURTAILED
2-02-002	CURTISS
2-02-002	CURTLY
2-02-002	CUSHIONS
2-01-001	CUSP
2-02-002	CUSTODY
2-01-001	CYLINDER'S
2-02-002	CYNTHIA
2-01-001	CZARINA
2-01-002	D'ETAT
2-01-002	DABBING
2-02-002	DABBLING
2-01-001	DACTYLS
2-02-002	DADDY'S
2-02-002	DADE
2-02-002	DAIS
2-02-002	DALEY
2-01-001	DAMED
2-02-002	DAMPEN
2-02-002	DAMPNESS
2-01-001	DANAHER
2-02-002	DANE
2-01-002	DANGLED
2-01-001	DANIELS
2-02-002	DANTE
2-02-002	DARK-HAIRED
2-02-002	DARKER
2-02-002	DARKEST
2-02-002	DARKLING
2-01-002	DARKLY
2-01-002	DARWINISM
2-02-002	DAS
2-02-002	DASHBOARD
2-02-002	DASHES
2-01-002	DATA-PROCESSING
2-02-002	DAUNTLESS
2-01-001	DAVIDSON'S
2-02-002	DAVIS'
2-02-002	DAVY
2-02-002	DAWNING
2-02-002	DAY-AFTER-DAY
2-01-001	DAY-WATCH
2-02-002	DAYS'
2-02-002	DAZZLED
2-02-002	DE*PAUL
2-01-001	DE-IODINATING
2-01-001	DEACTIVATION
2-02-002	DEADLIEST
2-02-002	DEADLINESS
2-01-001	DEALER'S
2-01-001	DEAN'S
2-02-002	DEARBORN
2-02-002	DEAREST
2-01-001	DEATH'S-*HEAD
2-02-002	DEATHBED
2-01-001	DEAUVILLE
2-01-002	DEBAUCHERY
2-02-002	DEBILITATED
2-02-002	DEBILITATING
2-01-001	DEBILITY
2-01-001	DEBORA
2-02-002	DEBS
2-02-002	DEBUNKING
2-01-002	DEBUTING
2-02-002	DECADENCE
2-02-002	DECADENT
2-01-001	DECANTED
2-01-001	DECEDENT
2-02-002	DECEIT
2-01-001	DECELERATION
2-02-002	DECISIVENESS
2-01-001	DECKING
2-01-002	DECLAIMED
2-02-002	DECLARATIONS
2-02-002	DECLIVITY
2-01-001	DECOMPOSES
2-02-002	DECOMPOSING
2-01-002	DECORATE
2-02-002	DECORUM
2-01-001	DECREMENT
2-02-002	DECRIED
2-01-002	DECRY
2-02-002	DEDICATES
2-01-001	DEEGAN'S
2-01-001	DEEP-SEA
2-02-002	DEEP-SEATED
2-02-002	DEFPENED
2-01-002	DEFAULT
2-02-002	DEFEATS
2-02-002	DEFECTION
2-01-002	DEFENSIVENESS
2-01-001	DEFERENT
2-02-002	DEFIANTLY
2-01-001	DEFINITION-SPEC IALIZATION
2-01-001	DEFOCUSING
2-01-001	DEFRAUD
2-02-002	DEFRAY
2-02-002	DEFT
2-02-002	DEFYING
2-02-002	DEGRADATION
2-02-002	DEITIES
2-02-002	DELEGATING
2-02-002	DELEGATIONS
2-01-001	DELIBERATION
2-02-002	DELICACIES
2-01-001	DELICATELY
2-01-001	DELINEATING
2-02-002	DELIVERANCE
2-01-001	DELLER
2-01-001	DELON
2-02-002	DELPHINE'S
2-01-001	DELTOIDS
2-01-002	DELUDE
2-02-002	DELUSION
2-01-001	DELUXE
2-02-002	DELVING
2-01-001	DEMARCATION
2-02-002	DEMEANOR
2-01-001	DEMOCRATIC-ENDO RSED
2-02-002	DEMOCRATIZATION
2-02-002	DEMONIAC
2-02-002	DEMONSTRABLY
2-01-001	DEMORALIZES
2-02-002	DEMURRER
2-01-001	DEMYTHOLOGIZE
2-01-001	DEMYTHOLOGIZED
2-01-002	DEN
2-01-001	DENNY
2-01-001	DENOMINATION'S
2-02-002	DENOUEMENT
2-01-002	DENSITIES
2-02-002	DENT
2-02-002	DENTING
2-02-002	DENUNCIATIONS
2-01-001	DEODORANT
2-02-002	DEPARTS
2-01-002	DEPENDENTS
2-02-002	DEPERSONALIZATI ON
2-02-002	DEPLORABLE
2-02-002	DEPLORED
2-01-001	DEPORTEES
2-01-001	DEPOSED
2-01-001	DEPPY
2-02-002	DEPRAVED
2-02-002	DEPRESSINGLY
2-01-001	DEPUTY'S
2-01-001	DEQUINDRE
2-02-002	DER
2-02-002	DERANGED
2-01-002	DERELICTION
2-01-001	DESCARTES
2-01-002	DESCENDANT
2-02-002	DESCENDS
2-02-002	DESERTION
2-02-002	DESERVING
2-02-002	DESIRABILITY
2-01-001	DESLONDE
2-01-002	DESPATCHED
2-02-002	DESPONDENCY
2-02-002	DESPONDENT
2-02-002	DESPOT
2-02-002	DESSERTS
2-02-002	DESTITUTE
2-02-002	DESTROYER
2-02-002	DETACHABLE
2-02-002	DETECTORS
2-01-001	DETENTE
2-02-002	DETENTION
2-02-002	DETERIORATING
2-01-002	DETERMINANTS
2-01-002	DETERMINATIONS
2-02-002	DETERMINEDLY
2-01-002	DETESTABLE
2-02-002	DETOURED
2-02-002	DETRIMENT
2-02-002	DEVASTATION
2-01-002	DEVELOPERS
2-01-001	DEVERY
2-01-001	DEVIANCE
2-02-002	DEVIANTS
2-01-001	DEVILS
2-02-002	DEVOTIONS
2-02-002	DEVOUR
2-01-002	DEXAMETHASONE
2-02-002	DEXTROUS
2-02-002	DEY
2-01-002	DIABETIC
2-02-002	DIAGNOSED
2-02-002	DIAGNOSING
2-01-002	DIAGNOSTICIANS
2-01-001	DIALECTICS
2-01-002	DIALOGUES
2-01-001	DIAM
2-02-002	DIAMETRICALLY
2-01-002	DIAPHRAGMIC
2-02-002	DIARIES
2-01-002	DIARIO
2-01-001	DIATOMIC
2-02-002	DICK'S
2-01-001	DICKENS'
2-02-002	DICKS
2-02-002	DICTATING
2-01-001	DIDN
2-02-002	DIEM
2-01-002	DIETHYLAMINOETH YL
2-02-002	DIETY
2-01-001	DIFFERENTIABILI TY
2-02-002	DIFFERENTIATE
2-02-002	DIFFIDENCE
2-02-002	DIFFUSED
2-02-002	DIGESTING
2-01-001	DIGGER
2-01-001	DILATE
2-02-002	DILATED
2-02-002	DILATION
2-02-002	DILEMMAS
2-02-002	DILIGENT
2-01-001	DIMETHYLGLYOXIM E
2-02-002	DIMITRI
2-02-002	DINE
2-01-001	DIONYSIAN
2-02-002	DIOXIDE
2-01-001	DIRECT-SUM
2-02-002	DIRECTIVE
2-02-002	DIRGE
2-02-002	DISABILITIES
2-02-002	DISABUSE
2-02-002	DISAGREEMENTS
2-02-002	DISAGREES
2-02-002	DISAPPOINTMENTS
2-02-002	DISARM
2-02-002	DISARRAY
2-02-002	DISBANDED
2-01-001	DISBURSEMENT
2-02-002	DISBURSEMENTS
2-02-002	DISCERNED
2-02-002	DISCERNING
2-01-001	DISCIPLESHIP
2-01-001	DISCLOSURE
2-02-002	DISCONTINUE
2-02-002	DISCORDANTLY
2-01-001	DISCORPORATE
2-02-002	DISCOUNTED
2-02-002	DISCOURSES
2-02-002	DISCOURTEOUS
2-02-002	DISCOVERS
2-02-002	DISCREDIT
2-02-002	DISCREETLY
2-01-001	DISCRETIONARY
2-02-002	DISDAINFUL
2-02-002	DISDAINING
2-01-001	DISENFRANCHISEM ENT
2-01-001	DISENTANGLE
2-02-002	DISHEARTEN
2-01-001	DISHEVELED
2-02-002	DISHONEST
2-02-002	DISHONESTY
2-02-002	DISHONOR
2-02-002	DISILLUSIONED
2-01-001	DISINCLINATION
2-02-002	DISINTEGRATE
2-02-002	DISLOCATIONS
2-02-002	DISLODGE
2-02-002	DISLOYAL
2-02-002	DISLOYALTY
2-01-002	DISMALLY
2-02-002	DISMEMBERED
2-01-002	DISMEMBERMENT
2-01-001	DISMOUNTING
2-01-001	DISOBEDIENT
2-02-002	DISOWNED
2-02-002	DISPARAGEMENT
2-02-002	DISPARITY
2-02-002	DISPENSED
2-02-002	DISPERSE
2-02-002	DISPLACED
2-02-002	DISPOSSESSED
2-02-002	DISPROPORTIONAT E
2-01-002	DISPUTED
2-01-002	DISREPAIR
2-02-002	DISREPUTE
2-01-002	DISRESPECT
2-02-002	DISRUPTING
2-02-002	DISSEMINATION
2-01-002	DISSENTING
2-02-002	DISSENTS
2-02-002	DISSIPATED
2-02-002	DISTASTEFULLY
2-01-001	DISTINCTIVELY
2-02-002	DISTORTIONS

2-02-002 DISTRACT
2-02-002 DISTRIBUTES
2-02-002 DISTRIBUTIVE
2-02-002 DISTRUSTED
2-01-002 DITCHES
2-01-001 DITMARS
2-02-002 DIVERGENCE
2-02-002 DIVERTIMENTO
2-01-001 DIVISION'S
2-01-001 DIVISIONAL
2-02-002 DIVORCEE
2-01-001 DJANGOLOGY
2-01-001 DOCKSIDE
2-01-002 DOCTRINAIRE
2-01-001 DOCUMENTARIES
2-01-002 DODGED
2-02-002 DODGING
2-02-002 DOG'S
2-02-002 DOGGED
2-02-002 DOGGEDLY
2-01-002 DOGMAS
2-02-002 DOGMATICALLY
2-01-001 DOLAN
2-02-002 DOMED
2-01-001 DOMINA
2-02-002 DOMINATING
2-02-002 DOMINEERING
2-01-001 DOMOKOUS
2-01-002 DONALDSON
2-02-002 DONATION
2-01-002 DONATIONS
2-02-002 DOO
2-01-001 DOOKIYOON
2-01-001 DOOLITTLE
2-02-002 DOORBELL
2-02-002 DOPE
2-02-002 DORA
2-01-001 DORAN
2-02-002 DORIA
2-02-002 DORMITORY
2-01-001 DOSED
2-02-002 DOSTOEVSKY
2-02-002 DOTING
2-02-002 DOTTED
2-02-002 DOTTING
2-02-002 DOUBLE-BREASTED
2-01-001 DOUBLE-ENTENDRE
2-01-001 DOUBLE-VALUED
2-02-002 DOUBTFULLY
2-02-002 DOUR
2-01-001 DOUSMAN
2-01-001 DOWEL
2-02-002 DOWNCAST
2-02-002 DOWNTRODDEN
2-02-002 DOWNTURN
2-02-002 DOWRY
2-01-002 DOYLE'S
2-02-002 DRAFTY
2-02-002 DRAGNET
2-02-002 DRAGONS
2-02-002 DRAKE
2-02-002 DRAMATIST
2-02-002 DRAMATIZES
2-01-001 DRAPERS
2-02-002 DRAPERY
2-02-002 DRAUGHTS
2-01-001 DRAW-FILE
2-02-002 DRAWBACK
2-02-002 DRAWING-ROOM
2-02-002 DRAWL
2-02-002 DREADED
2-01-001 DREAM-*MISS
2-02-002 DREAMER
2-01-002 DREAMLIKE
2-01-001 DRESBACH'S
2-01-001 DRESSERS
2-01-001 DRESSY
2-02-002 DRIFTIN
2-02-002 DRINKERS
2-01-001 DRIZZLING
2-01-001 DRONES
2-01-001 DRONK
2-02-002 DROUGHTS
2-01-002 DRUMMED
2-02-002 DRUMMER
2-01-002 DRUNCKE
2-01-001 DRUNKER
2-01-001 DRYFOOS
2-01-001 DRYIN
2-02-002 DRYNESS
2-02-002 DU**DRER
2-01-001 DU**SSELDORF
2-02-002 DUBLIN
2-01-001 DUELING
2-01-001 DUFFERS
2-02-002 DUFFY
2-01-001 DUGAN

2-02-002 DUKE'S
2-02-002 DUKES
2-02-002 DULLER
2-02-002 DULLEST
2-01-001 DUMBBELL
2-02-002 DUNG
2-02-002 DUNGEON
2-01-001 DUNKEL
2-02-002 DUPLICATED
2-02-002 DURABILITY
2-02-002 DURANTE
2-01-001 DUREN
2-01-001 DURKIN
2-02-002 DUSKY
2-02-002 DUTCHESS
2-02-002 DUTIFULLY
2-02-002 DUTTON
2-02-002 DWARFS
2-02-002 DWELLER
2-02-002 DWELLERS
2-02-002 DWINDLE
2-02-002 DWINDLED
2-02-002 DYNAMO
2-01-001 DYSTOPIA
2-02-002 DYSTROPHY
2-01-001 E**.*G**.*T
2-02-002 EARNS
2-02-002 EARSPLITTING
2-01-001 EASEMENT
2-01-001 EASEMENTS
2-01-001 EATON
2-02-002 EBBING
2-02-002 ECCENTRICS
2-01-001 ECHELON
2-02-002 ECHOING
2-01-001 ECKENFELDER
2-02-002 ECLIPSE
2-02-002 ECOLOGICAL
2-02-002 ECONOMIZING
2-01-001 EDDY
2-01-001 EDEMA
2-02-002 EDGAR
2-02-002 EDGEWATER
2-02-002 EDGY
2-01-002 EDIT
2-01-002 EDITORIALLY
2-01-002 EDMUND
2-01-001 EDYTHE'S
2-01-001 EEL
2-02-002 EERIE
2-02-002 EERILY
2-01-001 EFFECTUATE
2-02-002 EFFICACIOUS
2-01-001 EFFICACIOUSLY
2-01-001 EGALITARIANISM
2-02-002 EGOTIST
2-01-001 EIGHT-INCH
2-02-002 EIGHTIES
2-01-001 EIGHTY-FIFTH
2-02-002 EIGHTY-FIVE
2-01-001 EIGHTY-SEVENTH
2-01-002 EIN
2-02-002 EIRE
2-01-001 EJECTED
2-01-001 EJECTION
2-01-001 EKED
2-02-002 ELABORATION
2-02-002 ELATION
2-02-002 ELDON
2-01-001 ELEAZAR
2-01-001 ELECTOR
2-02-002 ELECTRICALLY
2-01-001 ELECTROCARDIOGRAPH
2-01-001 ELECTROSHOCK
2-02-002 ELEGIAC
2-02-002 ELI
2-01-001 ELI'S
2-01-002 ELIZABETHANS
2-02-002 ELLIPSES
2-01-002 ELOQUENCE
2-02-002 ELOQUENTLY
2-01-001 ELSINORE
2-01-001 ELUARD
2-02-002 ELUDED
2-02-002 ELUDING
2-02-002 ELUSIVE
2-01-002 ELVIS
2-02-002 ELYSEES
2-02-002 EMANATING
2-02-002 EMANATION
2-02-002 EMANCIPATE
2-01-002 EMANCIPATED
2-01-001 EMANUELE
2-02-002 EMBARGO
2-02-002 EMBARKED

2-02-002 EMBOLDENED
2-02-002 EMBRYONIC
2-02-002 EMERGENT
2-02-002 EMERSON'S
2-01-001 EMIGRANT
2-01-001 EMILE'S
2-02-002 EMISSARY
2-01-001 EMMA'S
2-01-001 EMMERICH
2-01-001 EMMERT
2-01-001 EMOTIONALISM
2-01-002 EMPEDOCLES
2-01-002 EMPHASES
2-02-002 EMPHATIC
2-01-002 EMPIRICISM
2-02-002 EMPLOYERS'
2-02-002 EMPOWERED
2-02-002 EMPTIER
2-02-002 EMPTINESS
2-02-002 ENAMELING
2-02-002 ENCIRCLED
2-02-002 ENCROACHING
2-02-002 ENCRUSTED
2-02-002 ENCUMBERED
2-01-001 END-PRODUCT
2-01-002 END-USE
2-02-002 ENDEARMENTS
2-01-002 ENDEAVORED
2-02-002 ENDEAVORING
2-02-002 ENDORSEMENT
2-01-001 ENDOTHERMIC
2-02-002 ENDOW
2-02-002 ENDOWMENT
2-02-002 ENDURABLE
2-02-002 ENDURES
2-01-001 ENEMY-*JEW
2-02-002 ENERGETICALLY
2-02-002 ENERVATING
2-01-002 ENFORCEABLE
2-01-002 ENGENDER
2-01-001 ENGINE'S
2-01-001 ENGINEERING-MANAGEMENT
2-02-002 ENGLISH-SPEAKING
2-02-002 ENGRAVING
2-02-002 ENGROSSED
2-01-002 ENIGMATIC
2-01-002 ENJOYABLE
2-01-002 ENLIGHTENMENT
2-02-002 ENLIVENED
2-02-002 ENMESHED
2-01-002 ENRICHED
2-02-002 ENRICO
2-02-002 ENROLLMENTS
2-02-002 ENSCONCED
2-01-001 ENSLAVE
2-02-002 ENSLAVEMENT
2-02-002 ENSUE
2-02-002 ENSUES
2-02-002 ENSURING
2-01-001 ENTERTAINER
2-01-001 ENTHALPY
2-02-002 ENTHUSIAST
2-01-002 ENTRANT
2-01-002 ENTREATED
2-02-002 ENTRUST
2-02-002 ENTRUSTED
2-01-001 ENTRY-LIMITING
2-02-002 ENTWINED
2-01-002 ENUMERATED
2-02-002 ENVELOPING
2-01-002 ENVISIONS
2-02-002 EPHESUS
2-01-002 EPICS
2-02-002 EPICURE
2-01-001 EPIDEMICS
2-02-002 EPIDERMIS
2-02-002 EPIGRAMS
2-01-002 EPIGRAPH
2-01-001 EPIPHYSEAL-DIAPHYSEAL
2-01-001 EPITHET
2-01-002 EPITOME
2-02-002 EPOXY
2-02-002 EPSOM
2-01-002 EQ
2-02-002 EQUANIMITY
2-01-002 EQUILIBRATED
2-01-001 EQUINOX
2-02-002 EQUITABLY
2-01-002 ERA'S
2-02-002 ERADICATE
2-01-002 ERAS
2-02-002 ERASED
2-01-001 ERASER
2-02-002 ERASING

2-01-001 ERDO**DS
2-02-002 ERIE
2-02-002 ERIK
2-01-001 EROS
2-02-002 ERSATZ
2-01-002 ERUPT
2-02-002 ERUPTION
2-01-002 ERVIN
2-02-002 ESCAPADES
2-01-001 ESCHEAT
2-02-002 ESCORTING
2-01-001 ESCRITOIRE
2-02-002 ESCUTCHEON
2-01-001 ESKIMOS
2-01-001 ESMARCH
2-02-002 ESPOUSED
2-02-002 ESSAYED
2-01-001 ESSE
2-02-002 ESSENCES
2-02-002 ESSENTIALS
2-01-001 ESTERASES
2-02-002 ESTIMATING
2-02-002 ETCHED
2-02-002 ETHICALLY
2-02-002 ETHICIST
2-01-001 EUCLID'S
2-01-001 EUGENE'S
2-02-002 EUPHORIA
2-01-001 EURYDICE
2-02-002 EVADED
2-02-002 EVAPORATED
2-02-002 EVAPORATION
2-01-001 EVER-GROWING
2-01-002 EVER-INCREASING
2-02-002 EVEREST
2-02-002 EVICTED
2-01-002 EVOCATIONS
2-01-002 EVOCATIVE
2-02-002 EVOLVING
2-02-002 EX
2-01-001 EX-*MRS
2-02-002 EX-*PRESIDENT
2-01-001 EX-LIBERALS
2-02-002 EXACERBATED
2-01-002 EXACTING
2-02-002 EXACTS
2-02-002 EXASPERATED
2-02-002 EXCELLENCY
2-01-001 EXCLAMATIONS
2-02-002 EXCRUCIATING
2-02-002 EXCURSION
2-02-002 EXCURSIONS
2-02-002 EXCUSES
2-01-001 EXEC
2-02-002 EXECUTIONER
2-01-002 EXECUTOR
2-01-001 EXECUTORS
2-01-002 EXEMPLAR
2-02-002 EXEMPLIFY
2-02-002 EXEMPTIONS
2-02-002 EXERTING
2-02-002 EXHALED
2-01-002 EXHAUSTIVE
2-02-002 EXHILARATING
2-02-002 EXIGENCIES
2-02-002 EXILED
2-02-002 EXISTENTIALIST
2-01-001 EXOGAMY
2-01-002 EXONERATE
2-01-001 EXONERATION
2-01-002 EXPECIALLY
2-02-002 EXPECTANTLY
2-02-002 EXPEDIENCY
2-02-002 EXPEDITING
2-02-002 EXPEDITIOUS
2-02-002 EXPEL
2-02-002 EXPERTLY
2-02-002 EXPIATION
2-01-001 EXPONENTS
2-02-002 EXPOSES
2-02-002 EXPOSURES
2-01-002 EXPOUNDED
2-02-002 EXPRESSIONIST
2-01-001 EXPRESSIONISTS
2-01-001 EXPRESSIONLESS
2-02-002 EXTERMINATE
2-02-002 EXTERNALLY
2-01-001 EXTRACTOR
2-02-002 EXTRICATE
2-02-002 EXUBERANCE
2-01-002 EXUBERANTLY
2-02-002 EXUDED
2-01-001 EYE-UNDECEIVING
2-02-002 EYEBALL
2-02-002 EYEWITNESS
2-02-002 EYING
2-02-002 EZRA

2-02-002 F**.*B**.*I	2-01-001 FIELD-FLATTENIN G	2-01-001 FLYNN	2-02-002 FRUGALITY	
2-01-001 F**.*R		2-01-001 FOAL	2-02-002 FRUITION	
2-01-001 FABER'S	2-02-002 FIELDERS	2-01-001 FOCUSES	2-02-002 FRY	
2-02-002 FABLE	2-01-001 FIELDWORK	2-02-002 FOLK-LORE	2-01-001 FUDO'S	
2-01-001 FABLES	2-01-001 FIFTY-FIFTH	2-02-002 FOLLIES	2-01-001 FUJIMOTO	
2-02-002 FACET	2-02-002 FIFTY-FIVE	2-01-002 FOODSTUFFS	2-02-002 FULBRIGHT	
2-01-002 FACIAL	2-02-002 FIFTY-NINTH	2-01-002 FOOLHARDY	2-02-002 FULFILLS	
2-02-002 FACILITATES	2-01-001 FIFTY-ODD	2-01-001 FOOLISHNESS	2-02-002 FULL-FLEDGED	
2-02-002 FAD	2-02-002 FIFTY-THREE	2-02-002 FOOLPROOF	2-02-002 FULL-GROWN	
2-01-002 FADE	2-02-002 FIFTY-TWO	2-02-002 FOOT-LOOSE	2-02-002 FULL-SCALE	
2-01-001 FAIR'S	2-02-002 FIGMENT	2-02-002 FORBEARS	2-01-001 FULLBACK	
2-02-002 FAIR-SIZED	2-01-001 FIGONE	2-02-002 FORBIDDING	2-02-002 FUMED-OAK	
2-02-002 FAIR-WEATHER	2-01-001 FIKE	2-01-001 FOREGROUND	2-02-002 FUN-LOVING	
2-01-001 FAIRBROTHERS	2-02-002 FIL	2-02-002 FOREHEADS	2-02-002 FUNCTIONALISM	
2-02-002 FAIRCHILD	2-01-001 FILBERTS	2-02-002 FOREIGN-POLICY	2-02-002 FUNCTIONARY	
2-01-001 FAIRFAX	2-02-002 FILIPINO	2-02-002 FORESAW	2-02-002 FUNGUS	
2-02-002 FAIRIES	2-02-002 FILIPPO	2-02-002 FORESEEING	2-02-002 FUNNIEST	
2-01-001 FAIRMONT	2-01-001 FILL-INS	2-02-002 FORGAVE	2-01-001 FUNSTON	
2-01-001 FAIRMOUNT	2-02-002 FILTH	2-01-002 FORGETFUL	2-01-001 FURIOUSER	
2-01-001 FAIRWAYS	2-02-002 FIN	2-01-002 FORGIT	2-02-002 FURLOUGH	
2-02-002 FAKED	2-02-002 FINANCIER	2-02-002 FORGIVING	2-02-002 FURNACES	
2-01-001 FALL-IN	2-01-001 FINBERG	2-02-002 FORMA	2-02-002 FURROWED	
2-02-002 FALSEHOOD	2-02-002 FINDER	2-01-001 FORMALISM	2-01-002 FURTHERING	
2-01-001 FALSEHOODS	2-02-002 FINER	2-02-002 FORMALITIES	2-02-002 FUSSING	
2-02-002 FALSIFY	2-02-002 FINES	2-02-002 FORMALITY	2-02-002 GABLE	
2-02-002 FALTER	2-01-001 FING	2-02-002 FORMALIZE	2-02-002 GAGARIN	
2-02-002 FANATICAL	2-01-001 FINGER-POST	2-01-002 FORMALIZED	2-02-002 GAGES	
2-01-002 FANATICS	2-02-002 FINGERNAILS	2-02-002 FORMATIVE	2-01-001 GAGS	
2-01-002 FANCIED	2-02-002 FINGERTIPS	2-02-002 FORREST	2-01-001 GALATIANS	
2-02-002 FANCIFUL	2-02-002 FINISHES	2-01-002 FORSAKEN	2-02-002 GALE	
2-02-002 FANGS	2-01-002 FINLAND	2-01-001 FORTESCUE	2-02-002 GALENA	
2-02-002 FANTASIA	2-02-002 FINLEY	2-02-002 FORTHRIGHTNESS	2-01-001 GALILEE	
2-02-002 FANTASTICALLY	2-01-001 FINNEGAN	2-02-002 FORTIFICATIONS	2-01-001 GALLIUM/GERMANI UM	
2-02-002 FARGO	2-01-001 FINNEY'S	2-01-002 FORTIFY		
2-01-002 FARING	2-01-001 FIR	2-01-001 FORTMAN	2-02-002 GALLOWS	
2-02-002 FARNESE	2-01-001 FIRE'S	2-01-001 FORTRESSES	2-02-002 GALS	
2-02-002 FASCIST	2-01-001 FIRE-FIGHTING	2-02-002 FORTY-SIX	2-02-002 GALT	
2-01-001 FASCISTS	2-02-002 FIRECRACKERS	2-01-002 FORTY-THREE	2-02-002 GALVANIC	
2-02-002 FASHIONING	2-02-002 FIRELIGHT	2-02-002 FORTY-TWO	2-01-002 GALVESTON	
2-01-001 FAST-CLOSING	2-01-001 FIRM'S	2-02-002 FOSTERING	2-02-002 GALWAY	
2-01-001 FAST-OPENING	2-01-001 FIRST-LEVEL	2-02-002 FOUL-SMELLING	2-02-002 GAMBIT	
2-02-002 FATALITIES	2-01-001 FISHERMAN'S	2-02-002 FOULED	2-01-001 GAMING-CARD	
2-02-002 FATHERED	2-02-002 FISHES	2-01-001 FOUR-ELEMENT	2-02-002 GANGES	
2-01-001 FATIGUES	2-02-002 FISK	2-02-002 FOUR-LANE	2-02-002 GANGSTER	
2-01-001 FATTENING	2-02-002 FITTEST	2-02-002 FOUR-LETTER	2-01-001 GANTLET	
2-02-002 FATUOUS	2-01-001 FIVE-*ELEMENTS	2-02-002 FOUR-O'CLOCK	2-02-002 GAPING	
2-01-001 FAUST'S	2-02-002 FIVE-CENT	2-01-001 FOUR-WOOD	2-02-002 GAPS	
2-01-002 FAUSTUS	2-02-002 FIVE-GALLON	2-02-002 FOURS	2-01-001 GAR-*DENE	
2-01-002 FAVOUR	2-01-002 FIVE-MONTH	2-02-002 FOWLER	2-01-001 GARGERY	
2-02-002 FEARLESSLY	2-01-001 FIVES	2-01-002 FOXHOLES	2-01-001 GARGLE	
2-02-002 FEASTS	2-01-002 FJORDS	2-01-001 FOY	2-02-002 GARRICK	
2-01-001 FEATHERTOP'S	2-02-002 FLAKY	2-01-001 FPS,	2-01-001 GARTER	
2-02-002 FEATURELESS	2-01-001 FLANDERS	2-02-002 FRACTURES	2-01-001 GARVIER	
2-02-002 FEBRUARY'S	2-02-002 FLANGE	2-02-002 FRANCES	2-01-002 GASEOUS	
2-01-001 FEDERAL-STATE	2-02-002 FLANK	2-02-002 FRANCESCO	2-02-002 GASHES	
2-02-002 FEDERALISM	2-01-001 FLATIRON	2-02-002 FRANCISCANS	2-02-002 GASSED	
2-02-002 FEDORA	2-02-002 FLATTENING	2-01-002 FRANCO	2-02-002 GASTON	
2-02-002 FEEBLY	2-01-001 FLATUS	2-02-002 FRANCOIS	2-02-002 GASTROINTESTINA L	
2-01-001 FEED-LOT	2-02-002 FLAUNTED	2-01-001 FRANKFURTER'S		
2-01-001 FEEDER	2-02-002 FLAVORED	2-01-001 FRANS	2-01-001 GATLINBURG	
2-01-001 FEEDING-PAIN	2-01-001 FLAVORING	2-02-002 FRANZ	2-01-001 GATOR	
2-02-002 FEELERS	2-02-002 FLAVORS	2-01-001 FRAUD'S	2-01-001 GAUER	
2-01-001 FEINT	2-02-002 FLAWLESS	2-01-001 FRAYNE'S	2-02-002 GAUGED	
2-02-002 FELICITIES	2-02-002 FLEA	2-01-001 FREAKS	2-02-002 GAUNTLET	
2-02-002 FELINE	2-02-002 FLEAS	2-01-001 FRED'S	2-01-001 GAUSS	
2-01-001 FELIX'S	2-02-002 FLEDGLING	2-02-002 FREDDIE	2-01-002 GAUSSIAN	
2-02-002 FELLED	2-01-001 FLEISCHMAN	2-01-002 FREE-LANCE	2-02-002 GEARED	
2-02-002 FELLING	2-01-001 FLEM	2-01-001 FREEDOM'S	2-02-002 GEARS	
2-01-001 FELLINI	2-02-002 FLEMING	2-02-002 FREES	2-01-002 GEL	
2-02-002 FELONIOUS	2-02-002 FLESHY	2-02-002 FREEST	2-01-002 GEMS	
2-01-002 FELONS	2-02-002 FLEX	2-01-002 FRENCH-*CANADIA N	2-01-001 GENDER	
2-02-002 FEMININITY	2-01-002 FLEXED		2-01-001 GENE-*PRINCESS	
2-01-001 FENNEL	2-02-002 FLICK	2-02-002 FRENCHMEN	2-01-001 GENERALISTS	
2-01-001 FER	2-02-002 FLICKER	2-01-001 FRESCOS	2-02-002 GENRE	
2-02-002 FERDINAND	2-02-002 FLICKERED	2-02-002 FRESHLY	2-02-002 GENTLENESS	
2-01-001 FERGUSON'S	2-02-002 FLIER	2-02-002 FRETTING	2-01-001 GENUS	
2-01-001 FERMENT	2-01-001 FLIMSY	2-02-002 FREUD'S	2-01-001 GEOCENTRIC	
2-02-002 FEROCIOUS	2-02-002 FLING	2-01-001 FRIABLE	2-02-002 GEOCHEMISTRY	
2-02-002 FEROCIOUSLY	2-02-002 FLIPPING	2-01-001 FRICTIONAL	2-02-002 GEOLOGIST	
2-02-002 FEROCITY	2-02-002 FLIRTATION	2-01-002 FRIDAY'S	2-01-002 GEORGES	
2-01-001 FERRARO	2-02-002 FLOCKED	2-01-001 FRIEDENWALD	2-01-001 GEORGIA-*PACIF	
2-02-002 FERRIS	2-02-002 FLOGGED	2-02-002 FRIEND'S		
2-01-001 FERRO	2-02-002 FLOODING	2-01-002 FRIENDLIER	2-02-002 GERALDINE	
2-01-001 FERROMAGNETIC	2-02-002 FLORID	2-02-002 FRIGHT	2-02-002 GERMANE	
2-02-002 FERVENTLY	2-01-001 FLORIDA'S	2-01-001 FRITO	2-02-002 GERMANTOWN	
2-02-002 FESTIVE	2-01-001 FLORIST'S	2-02-002 FRITZ	2-01-001 GERMANY'S	
2-01-001 FESTIVUS	2-02-002 FLOUNDERING	2-02-002 FRIVOLITY	2-01-001 GERMINATE	
2-01-002 FETED	2-01-001 FLOWERPOT	2-02-002 FROCK	2-01-001 GEROSA	
2-02-002 FETID	2-02-002 FLOYD	2-02-002 FROLIC	2-02-002 GEROSA'S	
2-01-002 FETISH	2-02-002 FLOYD'S	2-02-002 FROLICKING	2-01-001 GERUNDIAL	
2-01-001 FEUCHTWANGER	2-02-002 FLUCTUATING	2-02-002 FRONT-LINE	2-01-002 GET-TOGETHER	
2-02-002 FEUDS	2-02-002 FLUIDITY	2-02-002 FRONT-PAGE	2-01-002 GETTYSBURG	
2-01-001 FIBRIN	2-01-002 FLUORIDE	2-02-002 FRONTIERSMEN	2-02-002 GEYSERS	
2-02-002 FICTITIOUS	2-02-002 FLUTTER	2-02-002 FROST-BITTEN	2-01-001 GHOREYEB	
2-01-001 FIDDLE	2-02-002 FLUTTERED	2-02-002 FROTHING	2-02-002 GHOSTLY	
2-01-001 FIELD'S	2-02-002 FLYERS	2-01-001 FROTHINGHAM	2-01-001 GHOULS	
		2-02-002 FROTHY	2-01-001 GIANICOLO	

Code	Word	Code	Word	Code	Word	Code	Word
2-01-001	GIANTS'	2-02-002	GREASED	2-02-002	HANDBOOK	2-01-001	HELPERS
2-01-001	GIBAULT	2-02-002	GREAT-GRANDFATHER	2-02-002	HANDCUFFS	2-01-002	HEMINGWAY
2-02-002	GIBBON			2-01-001	HANDGUNS	2-01-001	HEMORRHAGING
2-02-002	GIDDY	2-02-002	GREEN'S	2-01-001	HANDLERS	2-01-001	HEMOSIDERIN
2-01-001	GIFFEN'S	2-01-001	GREEN-BROWN	2-02-002	HANDMADE	2-01-001	HEMPEL
2-02-002	GILDED	2-01-001	GREENBERG	2-02-002	HANDSOMER	2-02-002	HENCHMEN
2-01-001	GILELS	2-01-002	GREENEST	2-01-001	HANDYMAN	2-01-001	HENDRICKS
2-02-002	GILL	2-01-001	GREENFIELD	2-01-001	HANEY'S	2-01-001	HENLEY'S
2-01-001	GIMBEL	2-02-002	GREENHOUSE	2-01-001	HANGIN	2-01-001	HENRI'S
2-02-002	GINGER	2-02-002	GREENING	2-01-001	HANGOVER	2-01-001	HENRIETTA'S
2-02-002	GINGERLY	2-02-002	GREENISH	2-01-001	HANNAH	2-02-002	HENRY'S
2-02-002	GINGHAM	2-02-002	GREENLEAF	2-02-002	HANSEN'S	2-02-002	HERALDED
2-01-001	GINMILL	2-01-001	GREGORIUS	2-01-001	HAPGOOD	2-02-002	HERDED
2-02-002	GIRDLE	2-01-001	GRENIER	2-02-002	HAPHAZARD	2-02-002	HEREABOUTS
2-02-002	GIRLISHLY	2-02-002	GRIEF-STRICKEN	2-01-001	HAPLESS	2-01-001	HEREDITARY
2-02-002	GIRLS'	2-01-001	GRIGORI	2-02-002	HAPPENSTANCE	2-01-002	HERESY
2-01-001	GIVETH	2-01-001	GRILLED	2-02-002	HARANGUING	2-01-002	HEREWITH
2-01-002	GIZENGA	2-02-002	GRILLWORK	2-02-002	HARASSING	2-02-002	HEROICS
2-01-001	GLADDEN'S	2-02-002	GRIMACED	2-01-001	HARBERT	2-02-002	HEROIN
2-01-001	GLADDY'S	2-02-002	GRIMM	2-01-001	HARBURG	2-01-001	HERONS
2-01-001	GLADIUS	2-02-002	GRIND	2-02-002	HARD-BOILED	2-01-001	HERPETOLOGISTS
2-01-002	GLASGOW	2-02-002	GRINS	2-02-002	HARD-FOUGHT	2-01-001	HERRICK
2-01-001	GLASS-FIBER	2-01-001	GRINSFELDER	2-01-001	HARD-LIQUOR	2-02-002	HERRING
2-01-001	GLASSY	2-02-002	GRISLY	2-01-001	HARDBOILED	2-02-002	HESITANCY
2-02-002	GLAZER	2-02-002	GRIST	2-02-002	HARDING	2-02-002	HESITANTLY
2-01-002	GLAZING	2-02-002	GROCER'S	2-02-002	HARDNESS	2-02-002	HESSIAN
2-01-002	GLEASON	2-02-002	GROCERIES	2-01-001	HARDWICKE-*ETTER	2-01-001	HETEROZYGOUS
2-01-002	GLENDA	2-02-002	GROOMS			2-01-001	HETTY
2-02-002	GLIDE	2-02-002	GROOVE	2-02-002	HAREM	2-01-001	HEUVELMANS
2-02-002	GLINT	2-01-002	GROSVENOR	2-02-002	HARMED	2-02-002	HEX
2-01-002	GLINTED	2-02-002	GROUNDING	2-02-002	HARMONIC	2-01-002	HEXAGONAL
2-01-001	GLISON	2-01-002	GRUB	2-02-002	HARNESSED	2-02-002	HIAWATHA
2-02-002	GLOATED	2-02-002	GRUBBY	2-01-001	HARPER	2-01-001	HIBERNATE
2-01-001	GLOMERULAR	2-02-002	GRUESOME	2-02-002	HARRIMAN	2-01-001	HIDE-OUT
2-01-001	GLORIFY	2-01-002	GRUMBLED	2-02-002	HARRIS'S	2-01-001	HIERONYMUS
2-02-002	GLOVED	2-02-002	GRUNT	2-02-002	HARRISON	2-02-002	HIGH-CEILINGED
2-02-002	GLYCERIN	2-02-002	GRUNTING	2-01-001	HARROW	2-02-002	HIGH-DENSITY
2-01-002	GLYCEROL	2-01-001	GUAR	2-02-002	HARROWING	2-02-002	HIGH-POWERED
2-01-001	GLYCOL	2-01-001	GUERIN	2-01-001	HARTES	2-02-002	HIGH-PROTEIN
2-02-002	GNASHING	2-02-002	GUESTS'	2-02-002	HARVESTS	2-01-001	HIGH-QUALITY
2-01-001	GOAT'S	2-02-002	GUIANA	2-01-001	HASKELL	2-01-001	HIGH-REP
2-02-002	GOBBLED	2-02-002	GUIDEBOOK	2-01-001	HASSELTINE	2-01-001	HIGH-SET
2-01-001	GODDAMMIT	2-01-001	GUILFORD-*MARTIN	2-02-002	HASTENING	2-02-002	HIGH-SOUNDING
2-01-001	GODDAMNED			2-02-002	HATCHED	2-02-002	HIGHLIGHT
2-02-002	GODLESS	2-02-002	GUITARIST	2-01-001	HATCHWAY	2-02-002	HIGHLIGHTING
2-02-002	GODSEND	2-02-002	GULLIBLE	2-01-001	HATFIELD	2-02-002	HIGHPOINT
2-02-002	GOGGLE-EYED	2-02-002	GULP	2-02-002	HATHAWAY	2-02-002	HIGHS
2-02-002	GOGH	2-02-002	GUMMY	2-02-002	HATING	2-01-001	HIJACKED
2-02-002	GOING-OVER	2-01-001	GUNNAR	2-02-002	HAUGHTY	2-02-002	HIJACKERS
2-01-001	GOITROGEN	2-02-002	GUNNERS	2-02-002	HAULS	2-02-002	HIJACKING
2-01-001	GOITROGENS	2-02-002	GUNPOWDER	2-02-002	HAUNTS	2-02-002	HIKING
2-01-002	GOLLY	2-01-001	GURION	2-02-002	HAUTE	2-01-002	HILARIOUS
2-02-002	GOMEZ	2-02-002	GUST	2-01-001	HAVERFIELD	2-01-001	HILLMAN
2-01-001	GONTRAN	2-02-002	GUSTO	2-02-002	HAVERHILL	2-02-002	HILLYER
2-01-001	GONZALEZ	2-02-002	GUSTY	2-02-002	HAWKINS	2-02-002	HIMALAYAS
2-01-001	GOODBODY	2-01-001	GUTE	2-01-001	HAY-SHAKERS	2-02-002	HINDRANCES
2-02-002	GOODMAN	2-02-002	GUTTERS	2-02-002	HAYDN	2-02-002	HINDUISM
2-02-002	GOODNIGHT	2-02-002	GYM	2-02-002	HAZEL	2-01-001	HINO'S
2-01-001	GOODWIN	2-01-001	GYMS	2-02-002	HAZLITT	2-01-001	HIRSCH
2-01-001	GOODY	2-01-001	GYNECOLOGISTS	2-02-002	HEAD-ON	2-02-002	HISS
2-01-001	GORD	2-01-001	GYPSUM	2-02-002	HEAD-TOSSING	2-02-002	HISSED
2-02-002	GORDON'S	2-01-001	GYROCOMPASS	2-01-001	HEADWALLS	2-02-002	HISTORIOGRAPHY
2-01-001	GORTONISTS	2-01-001	H**.*M	2-02-002	HEADY	2-01-001	HIT-RUN
2-02-002	GOSSIPING	2-01-001	HA	2-02-002	HEAL	2-02-002	HITCHCOCK
2-02-002	GOULD	2-02-002	HABITABLE	2-02-002	HEALER	2-02-002	HITHER
2-01-001	GOULDING'S	2-02-002	HABITUALLY	2-01-002	HEALTHIER	2-02-002	HITTER
2-01-001	GOURD	2-02-002	HACKED	2-02-002	HEALTHILY	2-02-002	HIVE
2-01-001	GOURMET	2-02-002	HACKING	2-01-001	HEARE	2-01-001	HOAG'S
2-02-002	GUUT	2-01-002	HACKNEYED	2-02-002	HEARER	2-02-002	HOBBLED
2-02-002	GOVERNS	2-01-001	HADDIX	2-02-002	HEARERS	2-01-001	HODGES'
2-02-002	GOWNS	2-01-001	HAFIZ	2-02-002	HEARSAY	2-02-002	HUFFA
2-01-001	GRACIAS	2-02-002	HAGGARD	2-02-002	HEARTBREAKING	2-02-002	HOFFMAN
2-01-001	GRAD	2-01-001	HAIJAC	2-02-002	HEATHEN	2-02-002	HOGS
2-02-002	GRADATIONS	2-01-002	HAIRCUT	2-02-002	HEATHER	2-02-002	HOISTED
2-02-002	GRADED	2-01-002	HALE	2-02-002	HEAVE	2-01-001	HOLDEN'S
2-02-002	GRADER	2-01-002	HALF-CENTURY	2-01-001	HEAVERS	2-01-001	HOLDUP
2-01-001	GRADS	2-01-002	HALF-CONSCIOUS	2-02-002	HEAVIEST	2-02-002	HOLIER-THAN-THOU
2-02-002	GRAIL	2-01-002	HALF-DRUNK	2-02-002	HEAVINESS		
2-02-002	GRANARY	2-01-002	HALF-FILLED	2-01-001	HEAVY-ELECTRICAL-GOODS	2-02-002	HOLINESS
2-01-001	GRAND-DAUGHTER	2-01-001	HALF-INTENSITY			2-01-002	HOLLERED
2-02-002	GRANDDAUGHTER	2-01-001	HALF-TIME	2-01-001	HEDGE	2-01-001	HOLMES'
2-02-002	GRANDE	2-02-002	HALL'S	2-02-002	HEDGES	2-02-002	HOLYOKE
2-01-001	GRANDE-*BRETAGNE	2-02-002	HALLMARKS	2-01-001	HEDISON	2-02-002	HOMAGE
		2-02-002	HALLOWED	2-01-001	HEDONISTIC	2-02-002	HOME-GROWN
2-02-002	GRANVILLE	2-01-001	HALO	2-02-002	HEEDLESS	2-01-001	HOME-RUN
2-02-002	GRAPHICALLY	2-01-002	HALS	2-01-001	HEEL-*MIRACLE	2-02-002	HOMESTEAD
2-01-001	GRAS	2-02-002	HALTING	2-02-002	HEGEL	2-01-001	HOMOGENATE
2-01-001	GRASPING	2-02-002	HALTINGLY	2-01-001	HEIDEGGER'S	2-01-001	HOMOGENEOUSLY
2-02-002	GRASSY	2-02-002	HALVES	2-02-002	HEIGHTENING	2-02-002	HOMOSEXUAL
2-02-002	GRATED	2-02-002	HAMMETT	2-01-001	HEILMAN	2-01-001	HON'BLE
2-01-001	GRATTAN	2-01-001	HAMMETT'S	2-01-001	HEINKEL	2-02-002	HONAN
2-02-002	GRATUITOUSLY	2-02-002	HAMMOND	2-02-002	HEIRS	2-01-001	HONE
2-02-002	GRAVER	2-02-002	HAMPTON	2-01-001	HELION'S	2-01-001	HONEYBEE
2-02-002	GRAVES'	2-01-001	HAMRICK'S	2-01-001	HELIOPOLIS	2-01-001	HONEYMOONED
2-02-002	GRAVEYARDS	2-02-002	HAND-IN-GLOVE	2-01-001	HELIUM-4	2-01-001	HONORARY
2-01-001	GRAVID	2-02-002	HAND-TO-HAND	2-01-002	HELLFIRE	2-02-002	HONOUR
2-02-002	GRAZED	2-02-002	HAND-WOVEN	2-02-002	HELMETS	2-02-002	HOODS

2-02-002	HOOF
2-02-002	HOOKS
2-02-002	HOOKUP
2-01-001	HOOPER
2-02-002	HOOVES
2-01-002	HOP
2-02-002	HOPEFULS
2-01-001	HOPKINSIAN
2-02-002	HOPPER
2-02-002	HORDE
2-02-002	HORDES
2-02-002	HORMONES
2-02-002	HORNE
2-02-002	HORRIBLY
2-01-001	HORSE-RADISH
2-01-001	HORSELY
2-02-002	HORSEPLAY
2-01-001	HOSAKA
2-02-002	HOSES
2-02-002	HOSTAGE
2-01-001	HOSTLER
2-02-002	HOT-SHOT
2-01-001	HOTHAM
2-02-002	HOTLY
2-01-001	HOUGH'S
2-02-002	HOUR-LONG
2-02-002	HOURLY
2-01-002	HOUSE'S
2-02-002	HOUSEHOLDS
2-02-002	HOUSEKEEPER
2-02-002	HOUSEWORK
2-01-002	HOUSMAN'S
2-01-001	HOUTZ
2-02-002	HOVEL
2-01-001	HOWORTH
2-01-001	HOWSE
2-01-001	HOWSER
2-01-001	HUBBA
2-02-002	HUBS
2-02-002	HUCKSTER
2-01-001	HUES
2-02-002	HUGGED
2-01-001	HUGHES'
2-01-001	HUHMUN
2-01-001	HUL
2-02-002	HULK
2-02-002	HULKING
2-02-002	HUMANISTIC
2-01-002	HUMANITIES
2-02-002	HUMANNESS
2-01-002	HUME
2-01-001	HUME'S
2-02-002	HUMILIATED
2-02-002	HUMMOCKS
2-01-001	HUMORISTS
2-01-001	HUMP
2-01-001	HUN
2-02-002	HUNCHED
2-01-002	HUNDRED-ODD
2-02-002	HUNDREDTH
2-02-002	HUNK
2-01-002	HUNKERED
2-02-002	HUNTS
2-02-002	HURRIEDLY
2-02-002	HUSBANDRY
2-02-002	HUSHED
2-02-002	HUSTLE
2-02-002	HUSTLED
2-01-001	HUTCHINSON
2-02-002	HUTTON
2-01-002	HUXLEY'S
2-01-002	HYANNIS
2-02-002	HYDRIDE
2-01-001	HYDROPHILIC
2-01-001	HYDROPHOBIC
2-01-001	HYDROXYL-RICH
2-01-001	HYPERBOLE
2-02-002	HYPERBOLIC
2-01-001	HYPEREMIA
2-01-001	HYPFREMIC
2-01-001	HYPERTROPHY
2-02-002	HYPHENATED
2-02-002	HYPOCRISIES
2-02-002	HYPOCRITE
2-02-002	HYPOCRITES
2-01-001	HYPOCRITICAL
2-01-002	HYPOTHESIZED
2-01-001	I**.*R**.*S
2-01-001	I-TH
2-01-001	ICE-FILLED
2-01-001	IDA
2-01-001	IDEALISTIC
2-02-002	IDEALIZATION
2-01-001	IDENTIFICATIONS
2-02-002	IDIOSYNCRATIC
2-02-002	IDIOT
2-02-002	IDLING
2-02-002	IDOLS
2-01-001	IDYLL
2-02-002	IGNITE
2-02-002	IGNORAMUS
2-02-002	ILL-EQUIPPED
2-02-002	ILL-FATED
2-02-002	ILLEGALLY
2-02-002	ILLNESSES
2-01-002	ILLUSIVE
2-02-002	ILLUSORY
2-01-002	IMAGING
2-02-002	IMBIBED
2-01-002	IMITATES
2-02-002	IMITATING
2-02-002	IMITATORS
2-02-002	IMMATERIAL
2-02-002	IMMEASURABLE
2-02-002	IMMEMORIAL
2-02-002	IMMENSITY
2-01-002	IMMERSION
2-02-002	IMPACTED
2-02-002	IMPALED
2-01-002	IMPARTIALITY
2-02-002	IMPASSABLE
2-02-002	IMPASSE
2-02-002	IMPECCABLY
2-01-002	IMPERFECTIONS
2-01-002	IMPERFECTLY
2-02-002	IMPERIALISM
2-02-002	IMPERIOUSLY
2-01-002	IMPERSONATION
2-02-002	IMPERVIOUS
2-02-002	IMPIOUS
2-02-002	IMPLICATED
2-02-002	IMPLORED
2-02-002	IMPOLITIC
2-02-002	IMPORTATION
2-02-002	IMPOTENCE
2-02-002	IMPOTENT
2-01-002	IMPRESSING
2-02-002	IMPRIMATUR
2-02-002	IMPROBABLE
2-02-002	IMPROPER
2-02-002	IMPROPERLY
2-02-002	IMPROVISATIONS
2-02-002	IMPROVISE
2-02-002	IMPRUDENTLY
2-01-002	IMPURITY
2-01-002	IMPUTATION
2-02-002	IN-LAWS
2-02-002	INACCURACY
2-01-001	INACTIVATE
2-01-002	INACTIVATION
2-02-002	INADEQUACIES
2-02-002	INADEQUATELY
2-02-002	INADVERTENT
2-02-002	INADVERTENTLY
2-02-002	INALIENABLE
2-02-002	INANIMATE
2-01-001	INAPPLICABLE
2-02-002	INAUDIBLE
2-01-002	INCANTATION
2-02-002	INCAPACITATED
2-02-002	INCARNATE
2-02-002	INCENSE
2-01-002	INCESSANTLY
2-01-001	INCINERATOR
2-01-001	INCIPIENCY
2-02-002	INCLEMENT
2-01-001	INCLUSIONS
2-02-002	INCOMPATIBLE
2-02-002	INCOMPETENT
2-02-002	INCOMPETENTS
2-02-002	INCOMPLETELY
2-02-002	INCOMPREHENSIBLE
2-02-002	INCONGRUITIES
2-02-002	INCORPORATE
2-02-002	INCORRUPTIBLE
2-02-002	INCULCATED
2-02-002	INCULCATION
2-02-002	INCURABLE
2-02-002	INCURABLY
2-02-002	IND
2-02-002	INDECISIVE
2-02-002	INDEFENSIBLE
2-02-002	INDEFINABLE
2-02-002	INDEMNITY
2-02-002	INDENTURE
2-01-002	INDEXES
2-01-001	INDIA'S
2-02-002	INDICTED
2-01-002	INDICTMENTS
2-01-001	INDIGENES
2-02-002	INDIGESTION
2-02-002	INDISCREET
2-01-001	INDIVIDUAL-CONTRIBUTOR
2-01-002	INDIVIDUALISTS
2-02-002	INDOCHINA
2-02-002	INDUCEMENT
2-02-002	INDULGENT
2-02-002	INDUSTRIALIST
2-02-002	INDUSTRIALIZATION
2-02-002	INDUSTRIOUSLY
2-02-002	INDWELLING
2-02-002	INEPT
2-02-002	INEPTNESS
2-02-002	INERTIA
2-02-002	INEVITABILITY
2-02-002	INEXACT
2-02-002	INEXCUSABLE
2-02-002	INFANTILE
2-02-002	INFANTRYMAN
2-01-002	INFERENTIAL
2-02-002	INFERNO
2-02-002	INFESTATION
2-02-002	INFIDELITY
2-01-001	INFILTRATED
2-02-002	INFINITUM
2-02-002	INFINITY
2-02-002	INFLOW
2-02-002	INFLUENCING
2-01-001	INFLUENT
2-01-002	INFLUENZA
2-01-001	INFORMANT
2-01-002	INFORMATIONAL
2-02-002	INFORMATIVE
2-02-002	INFREQUENTLY
2-02-002	INFURIATING
2-01-002	INHIBITING
2-01-001	INHIBITOR
2-02-002	INHIBITORS
2-01-001	INHIBITORY
2-02-002	INHIBITS
2-02-002	INITIATES
2-01-001	INITIATOR
2-02-002	INJECTED
2-02-002	INJURIOUS
2-01-001	INNESFREE
2-01-002	INOCULATION
2-01-002	INORDINATELY
2-01-001	INSECTICIDES
2-02-002	INSHORE
2-02-002	INSIDERS
2-02-002	INSIDIOUS
2-01-002	INSIDIOUSLY
2-02-002	INSINUATION
2-02-002	INSOLENT
2-02-002	INSPECTED
2-02-002	INSPECTING
2-01-002	INSPECTOR'S
2-01-001	INSTALLMENTS
2-02-002	INSTANTANEOUSLY
2-01-001	INSTINCTIVE
2-02-002	INSTINCTUAL
2-02-002	INSTRUCTING
2-01-001	INSTRUCTS
2-01-001	INSUBORDINATE
2-02-002	INSUBORDINATION
2-02-002	INSUBSTANTIAL
2-02-002	INSULATE
2-01-001	INSULATING
2-02-002	INSULTED
2-02-002	INSUPERABLE
2-02-002	INSURMOUNTABLE
2-01-001	INSURRECTION
2-02-002	INTEGRATES
2-01-002	INTEGRATING
2-02-002	INTENSIFYING
2-02-002	INTER
2-01-001	INTER-AMERICAN
2-02-002	INTERACT
7-01-001	INTERCHANGES
2-01-001	INTERDENOMINATIONAL
2-02-002	INTERFERES
2-01-001	INTERLAYER
2-01-001	INTERLIBRARY
2-01-001	INTERLINING
2-02-002	INTERLUDES
2-02-002	INTERMENT
2-01-002	INTERMITTENTLY
2-02-002	INTERN
2-01-002	INTERNALIZED
2-02-002	INTERNATIONALIST
2-02-002	INTERNE
2-01-001	INTERPENETRATES
2-02-002	INTERPOSITION
2-02-002	INTERPRETING
2-02-002	INTERREGNUM
2-01-002	INTERRELATIONSHIPS
2-02-002	INTERROGATION
2-02-002	INTERSECTING
2-01-001	INTERSTITIAL
2-02-002	INTERVENE
2-02-002	INTERVIEWER
2-02-002	INTIMIDATE
2-01-002	INTOLERANCE
2-01-001	INTONACO
2-01-002	INTRACTABLE
2-01-001	INTRAMURAL
2-01-002	INTRANSIGENCE
2-02-002	INTRIGUED
2-02-002	INTRIGUINGLY
2-02-002	INTROSPECTIVE
2-02-002	INTRUSIONS
2-02-002	INTRUSIVE
2-02-002	INURED
2-02-002	INVALIDATE
2-02-002	INVERSION
2-02-002	INVESTOR
2-02-002	INVIGORATION
2-02-002	INVINCIBLE
2-02-002	INVISIBLY
2-02-002	INWARDNESS
2-01-001	IODINATION
2-01-002	IRA
2-02-002	IRAN
2-01-001	IRAQW
2-02-002	IRELAND'S
2-02-002	IRENE
2-02-002	IRINA
2-02-002	IRONED
2-02-002	IRONICAL
2-02-002	IRREDEEMABLE
2-02-002	IRREMEDIABLE
2-02-002	IRREPARABLE
2-01-001	IRREPRODUCIBILT
2-02-002	IRRESOLUTE
2-02-002	IRREVERENCE
2-02-002	IRREVERENT
2-02-002	IRREVERSIBLE
2-02-002	IRREVOCABLE
2-02-002	IRREVOCABLY
2-02-002	ISAACS
2-01-001	ISOCYANATE
2-01-001	ISOPLETHS
2-01-001	ISOTOPIC
2-01-001	ISTIQLAL'S
2-01-001	IT-WIT
2-02-002	ITALY'S
2-02-002	ITEMIZING
2-01-001	IVIES
2-01-001	J**.*D**.*H
2-01-002	JABBED
2-02-002	JABBING
2-01-001	JACKASS
2-02-002	JACKSON'S
2-01-002	JACKSONIAN
2-01-001	JACKSONS
2-02-002	JACKSONVILLE
2-01-001	JACOBS
2-01-001	JACOBY'S
2-01-001	JACOPO
2-02-002	JADED
2-01-002	JAGAN
2-01-001	JAGGERS
2-01-001	JAGGERS'
2-02-002	JAILED
2-01-002	JAMAICA
2-02-002	JAMES'S
2-02-002	JAMS
2-02-002	JANGLING
2-01-001	JANNEQUIN
2-02-002	JARRED
2-02-002	JAUNTY
2-02-002	JEAN-*PAUL
2-01-001	JEFFERSONIANS
2-01-001	JEHOVAH'S
2-01-001	JEREBOHM
2-02-002	JERK
2-02-002	JERSEY'S
2-01-001	JESSIE
2-02-002	JESTING
2-02-002	JESUS'
2-01-001	JEW-BAITER
2-02-002	JEWELED
2-02-002	JEWELER
2-01-001	JEWISHNESS
2-02-002	JIFFY
2-02-002	JILTED
2-02-002	JINGLED
2-02-002	JITTERS
2-02-002	JOAN'S
2-02-002	JOBLESS

Code	Entry
2-01-001	JOEL'S
2-01-002	JOEY
2-01-002	JOINS
2-01-001	JOLLA
2-02-002	JON
2-01-001	JORDA
2-02-002	JOSE
2-02-002	JOSEF
2-02-002	JOSEPH'S
2-02-002	JOSIAH
2-01-001	JOURNALESE
2-02-002	JOURNALISTS
2-02-002	JOURNEY'S
2-02-002	JOURNEYED
2-02-002	JOURNEYS
2-02-002	JOWL
2-01-001	JOYRIDE
2-02-002	JR**.'S
2-01-002	JUBILANT
2-02-002	JUBILANTLY
2-01-001	JUDAISM
2-02-002	JUDAS
2-02-002	JUDICIOUSLY
2-02-002	JUGGLING
2-02-002	JUICES
2-02-002	JUKE
2-02-002	JULEP
2-01-001	JUMPS
2-02-002	JUMPY
2-02-001	JUNCTURES
2-02-002	JUNIOR'S
2-01-001	JUNKERS
2-01-001	JURAS
2-02-002	JUSTICE'S
2-02-002	JUTTING
2-01-001	JUXTAPOSED
2-01-001	KAMIENIEC
2-02-002	KANT
2-01-001	KARSNER
2-01-001	KASAI
2-01-002	KATANGANS
2-02-002	KATIE'S
2-01-001	KAYABASHI'S
2-01-001	KC
2-01-001	KEANE
2-02-002	KEENEST
2-02-002	KEENING
2-02-002	KEG
2-01-001	KEGHAM
2-01-001	KELP
2-01-001	KEMBLE'S
2-02-002	KEMPE
2-02-002	KENNARD
2-01-002	KENNY
2-01-001	KENYON
2-02-002	KEYNOTES
2-02-002	KHAN
2-02-002	KHRUSHCHEVS
2-01-001	KICKOFF
2-01-002	KIDNAPPER
2-01-001	KIEFFER
2-01-001	KILILNGSWORTH
2-01-001	KIMBERLY
2-02-002	KIN
2-02-002	KINGSLEY
2-01-001	KINGSTOWN
2-01-001	KIRKPATRICK
2-01-001	KIRKWOOD
2-01-001	KIT
2-01-001	KITTI'S
2-02-002	KIWANIS
2-01-001	KLAUBER
2-01-001	KLEES
2-01-001	KNAUER
2-01-001	KNEE-LENGTH
2-01-001	KNEE-TYPE
2-01-002	KNEELED
2-01-001	KNIGHT-ERRANT
2-02-002	KNOB
2-02-002	KNOCKS
2-02-002	KNOLL
2-02-002	KNOTTY
2-02-002	KNOWLEDGEABLE
2-01-001	KNOWLTON
2-01-001	KODAMA
2-01-001	KOENIGSBERG
2-01-001	KOINONIA
2-01-001	KOLA
2-01-001	KOLKHOZ
2-02-002	KOLPAKOVA
2-01-001	KONISHI
2-01-001	KONITZ
2-02-002	KOONING
2-01-001	KREMLIN'S
2-01-001	KRETCHMER
2-01-001	KRUGER'S
2-01-001	KRUTCH
2-01-001	KUNKEL
2-01-001	KUNKEL'S
2-01-001	KY
2-01-001	KYNE
2-01-001	L'*UNION
2-02-002	LA*SALLE
2-02-002	LABELLED
2-02-002	LABORIOUSLY
2-02-002	LABORS
2-02-002	LACED
2-02-002	LACERATIONS
2-01-001	LACEY
2-02-002	LACQUER
2-02-002	LACTATE
2-01-001	LACTATING
2-01-001	LADGHAM
2-01-002	LAGGED
2-01-001	LAGOONS
2-02-002	LAGUNA
2-01-001	LALAURIES
2-01-001	LAMBERT
2-02-002	LAME
2-02-002	LAMENTATIONS
2-01-002	LAMENTS
2-01-001	LAMINATED
2-01-002	LAMMERMOOR
2-01-001	LANA
2-01-001	LANCASTER
2-01-001	LANCES
2-02-002	LANDAU
2-01-001	LANDINGS
2-02-002	LANDLORDS
2-02-002	LANDRUM-*GRIFFIN
2-02-002	LANDSLIDE
2-02-002	LANKY
2-02-002	LANTERNS
2-01-001	LANZA
2-02-002	LAODICEAN
2-02-002	LAPELS
2-02-002	LAPPED
2-01-002	LAPPING
2-02-002	LAPS
2-02-002	LARCENY
2-02-002	LAREDO
2-01-001	LARGE-PACKAGE
2-02-002	LARK
2-02-002	LARKS
2-02-002	LASHES
2-01-001	LASHING
2-02-002	LASS
2-01-001	LASSO
2-02-002	LAST-MINUTE
2-02-002	LAST-NAMED
2-01-001	LATEX
2-01-001	LATH
2-01-001	LATS
2-01-002	LATTICE
2-01-002	LAUGHLIN
2-02-002	LAUREATE
2-02-002	LAURELS
2-01-002	LAVALLADE
2-02-002	LAWFUL
2-02-002	LAWLESS
2-01-001	LAWMAN
2-01-001	LAWMEN
2-01-001	LAWRENCE'S
2-01-001	LAWRENCEVILLE
2-02-002	LAWYER'S
2-02-002	LAXNESS
2-01-001	LAYERING
2-01-002	LEADEN
2-01-002	LEAGUERS
2-02-002	LEAK
2-02-002	LEAKY
2-01-002	LEAN-TO
2-01-001	LEAPFROG
2-02-002	LEAPING
2-02-002	LEAPT
2-02-002	LEASED
2-01-001	LEATHERS
2-02-002	LEAVE-TAKING
2-02-002	LEAVENED
2-01-002	LEBANESE
2-02-002	LECTURED
2-01-001	LEEDS'
2-01-001	LEESONA-*HOLT
2-02-002	LEEWAY
2-01-002	LEFTHANDER
2-01-001	LEFTY
2-01-001	LEGALIZED
2-01-001	LEGER
2-01-001	LEGISLATURE'S
2-02-002	LEGISLATURES
2-02-002	LEGITIMACY
2-02-002	LEGITIMATELY
2-02-002	LEGUME
2-02-002	LELAND
2-02-002	LENGTHEN
2-02-002	LENGTHENED
2-02-002	LEROY
2-01-001	LESION
2-02-002	LESLIE
2-01-001	LESSING
2-01-001	LETCH'S
2-01-001	LETITIA
2-01-002	LEVEL-HEADED
2-01-002	LEVELLED
2-01-002	LEVIES
2-01-002	LEVIS
2-02-002	LEX
2-01-001	LEXICAL
2-01-001	LEXICON
2-01-001	LIBEL
2-01-001	LIBERACE
2-02-002	LIBERTARIANS
2-02-002	LIBERTINES
2-01-001	LIBERTY-AND-*UNION
2-01-002	LIBIDO
2-02-002	LIBRETTO
2-01-001	LIBYAN
2-02-002	LICE
2-01-001	LIEDER
2-02-002	LIEN
2-01-002	LIFE-LIKE
2-02-002	LIFE-LONG
2-02-002	LIFELESS
2-02-002	LIFTS
2-01-001	LIGANDS
2-02-002	LIGHT-COLORED
2-02-002	LIGHT-HEADED
2-02-002	LIGHTEST
2-02-002	LIGHTHEARTED
2-01-001	LIKE-MINDED
2-01-001	LILA
2-02-002	LIMBER
2-02-002	LIMBO
2-02-002	LIMPED
2-02-002	LIMPING
2-02-002	LINDSAY
2-02-002	LINEAGE
2-01-001	LINEBACK
2-02-002	LINERS
2-02-002	LINGERED
2-02-002	LINGERIE
2-02-002	LINGERS
2-02-002	LINING
2-02-002	LION'S
2-02-002	LIONEL
2-01-001	LIONESS'
2-02-002	LIONIZED
2-02-002	LIPCHITZ
2-02-002	LIPPMAN
2-01-001	LISSA
2-02-002	LISTENS
2-01-002	LITER
2-01-001	LITERS
2-02-002	LITIGANT
2-01-001	LITURGICAL
2-01-001	LITZ
2-01-002	LIVELIER
2-02-002	LIVELINESS
2-02-002	LIVERPOOL
2-01-001	LIVSHITZ
2-01-001	LIZZY
2-02-002	LOATHING
2-01-001	LOB-SCUSE
2-01-001	LOBULES
2-01-001	LOCALIZATION
2-02-002	LOCKER-ROOM
2-01-001	LOCKIES
2-01-001	LOCKUP
2-02-002	LOCOMOTIVE
2-02-002	LOCUS
2-01-001	LODGES
2-02-002	LODGINGS
2-01-001	LODLEY
2-02-002	LOFT
2-02-002	LOGAN
2-02-002	LOGGED
2-01-002	LOGISTIC
2-02-002	LOINS
2-01-002	LOIS
2-01-001	LONDONDERRY
2-01-001	LONESOME
2-02-002	LONG-DISTANCE
2-02-002	LONG-ESTABLISHED
2-02-002	LONG-LIVED
2-02-002	LONG-SOUGHT
2-02-002	LONGER-LIVED
2-01-001	LONGER-TERM
2-02-002	LONGEVITY
2-02-002	LONGFELLOW'S
2-02-002	LONGHAND
2-02-002	LONGINGS
2-01-001	LONGSTREET
2-01-001	LOOKOUT
2-02-002	LOOMS
2-02-002	LOON
2-02-002	LOOPHOLE
2-02-002	LOOPHOLES
2-02-002	LOOSE-JOINTED
2-02-002	LOOSENESS
2-01-001	LOPE
2-02-002	LOPEZ
2-02-002	LOQUACIOUS
2-02-002	LORDLY
2-02-002	LORENZ
2-02-002	LOTUS
2-02-002	LOUDSPEAKERS
2-02-002	LOUIS'S
2-01-001	LOUVERS
2-01-001	LOUVRE
2-02-002	LOVABLE
2-02-002	LOVE'S
2-01-001	LOVEJOY'S
2-01-001	LOVERING
2-02-002	LOW-CLASS
2-02-002	LOW-GRADE
2-02-002	LOW-KEY
2-02-002	LOW-LEVEL
2-01-001	LOW-MOISTURE
2-01-001	LOW-PASS
2-02-002	LOW-PITCHED
2-01-002	LOW-TEMPERATURE
2-01-001	LOWELL'S
2-02-002	LOWER-STATUS
2-02-002	LOYALIST
2-02-002	LOYALISTS
2-01-001	LUANG
2-01-002	LUBBOCK
2-01-001	LUBELL
2-01-001	LUBLIN'S
2-01-001	LUBRA
2-01-002	LUBRICANT
2-01-001	LUCIUS
2-01-001	LUCRETIA
2-01-001	LUCRETIUS
2-01-001	LUEGER'S
2-02-002	LUG
2-02-002	LUKE'S
2-01-002	LULL
2-01-001	LULLWATER
2-02-002	LUMBERING
2-01-001	LUMIERE
2-02-002	LUMPED
2-02-002	LUMPY
2-01-001	LUNATION
2-02-002	LUNCHEONS
2-02-002	LUNCHTIME
2-02-002	LURCHING
2-02-002	LUSCIOUS
2-02-002	LUSTER
2-02-002	LUSTRE
2-02-002	LUTHER'S
2-01-001	LYKING
2-01-001	LYMPH
2-02-002	LYRICISM
2-02-002	LYRICIST
2-01-001	LYRICISTS
2-02-002	M**.*P
2-01-002	M*EQ
2-01-001	MAC*ARTHUR
2-01-001	MAC*DONALD
2-01-001	MAC*READY
2-01-002	MACABRE
2-01-001	MACAULAY'S
2-02-002	MACHINISTS
2-01-001	MACK'S
2-01-001	MACKEREL
2-02-002	MACKINAC
2-01-001	MACROMOLECULAR
2-01-001	MACROMOLECULES
2-01-001	MACROPATHOLOGICAL
2-02-002	MADAM
2-02-002	MADDENING
2-01-002	MADMAN
2-02-002	MADNESS
2-02-002	MAESTRO'S
2-02-002	MAGENTA
2-01-002	MAGGOTS
2-02-002	MAGICIAN'S
2-01-001	MAGNETIZED
2-02-002	MAGNIFICENCE
2-01-001	MAGOUN
2-02-002	MAGPIES
2-01-001	MAGWITCH

Code	Word	Code	Word	Code	Word	Code	Word
2-01-001	MAH	2-01-002	MC*DANIEL	2-01-001	MINERALOGICAL	2-01-002	MORALIST
2-01-001	MAHMOUD	2-02-002	MC*GEORGE	2-01-001	MINERVA	2-01-001	MORGENTHAU
2-02-002	MAIDEN	2-02-002	MC*NAUGHTON	2-02-002	MINGLE	2-02-002	MORLEY
2-02-002	MAIDENS	2-02-002	MEA	2-02-002	MINISTERED	2-02-002	MORMON
2-02-002	MAILER	2-02-002	MEAD	2-02-002	MINISTERIAL	2-02-002	MORNING'S
2-01-002	MAINSTREAM	2-02-002	MEALTIME	2-02-002	MINISTRATIONS	2-02-002	MOROSE
2-02-002	MALADIES	2-01-001	MEANES	2-01-001	MINN	2-02-002	MOROSELY
2-01-001	MALADJUSTMENTS	2-01-001	MEANIN	2-02-002	MINNESOTA'S	2-01-002	MORPHOLOGY
2-02-002	MALEVOLENCE	2-02-002	MEANINGFULNESS	2-01-001	MINSTREL	2-02-002	MORROW
2-02-002	MALEVOLENT	2-02-002	MEASLES	2-02-002	MINUET	2-02-002	MORT
2-02-002	MALICE	2-01-002	MECUM	2-01-001	MIRIAM'S	2-02-002	MORTALS
2-02-002	MALICIOUS	2-02-002	MEDICALLY	2-02-002	MIRTH	2-01-001	MORTARED
2-02-002	MALIGNED	2-02-002	MEDICATION	2-01-001	MIS-TER	2-01-001	MORTARS
2-02-002	MALINGERING	2-02-002	MEDITATING	2-01-001	MISALIGNMENT	2-02-002	MOSQUES
2-02-002	MAMA'S	2-02-002	MEDITATION	2-02-002	MISCALCULATION	2-02-002	MOTHER-OF-PEARL
2-02-002	MANAGEMENT'S	2-02-002	MEDITATIVE	2-02-002	MISCELLANY	2-02-002	MOTHS
2-01-002	MANAGEMENTS	2-01-001	MEDIUM'S	2-01-001	MISCHA	2-02-002	MOTIONING
2-01-002	MANAGER'S	2-02-002	MEEKLY	2-02-002	MISCONCEPTIONS	2-01-001	MOTORIST
2-01-001	MANASSAS	2-01-001	MEG	2-02-002	MISCONSTRUED	2-01-001	MOUGH
2-01-002	MANES	2-02-002	MEGATON	2-02-002	MISDEMEANOR	2-01-001	MOUNDED
2-01-001	MANIC	2-01-001	MEGAWATT	2-02-002	MISERIES	2-02-002	MOURN
2-02-002	MANILA	2-01-001	MELAMINE	2-02-002	MISGUIDED	2-02-002	MOURNED
2-01-001	MANIN	2-01-001	MELANESIAN	2-02-002	MISINTERPRET	2-01-002	MOURNERS
2-02-002	MANIPULATED	2-02-002	MELLOWED	2-02-002	MISINTERPRETED	2-02-002	MOUTHING
2-01-002	MANIPULATING	2-01-001	MELTZER'S	2-01-001	MISJUDGED	2-01-001	MOZART
2-01-002	MANIPULATIONS	2-02-002	MEMBERS'	2-02-002	MISREPRESENTATI ON	2-02-002	MUCKING
2-01-001	MANLY	2-02-002	MEMBERSHIPS			2-02-002	MUCUS
2-02-002	MANMADE	2-02-002	MEMOIR	2-02-002	MISREPRESENTS	2-02-002	MUDDIED
2-01-001	MANN	2-01-002	MEMORABILIA	2-02-002	MISSHAPEN	2-01-001	MUFFLER
2-02-002	MANNERISM	2-02-002	MEMORIZING	2-02-002	MISSTEP	2-01-001	MUGS
2-01-001	MANNINGHAM	2-01-001	MEMORY-IMAGES	2-01-002	MISSY	2-01-001	MULLEN
2-02-002	MANNY	2-02-002	MENACED	2-02-002	MISTAKING	2-01-001	MULLENAX
2-01-001	MANO	2-02-002	MEND	2-01-002	MISTRIAL	2-02-002	MULTI-MILLION-OLLA
2-01-002	MANUFACTURES	2-01-002	MENDELSSOHN	2-01-001	MISTRUSTED		
2-02-002	MARC	2-01-001	MENDERES	2-02-002	MISTS	2-01-001	MULTI-VALUED
2-02-002	MARCELLUS	2-01-001	MENNONITE	2-01-001	MITCH	2-02-002	MULTI-YEAR
2-01-001	MARDI	2-02-002	MENUS	2-02-002	MITIGATES	2-01-002	MULTIPACTOR
2-02-002	MARE'S	2-01-001	MERC	2-02-002	MITIGATING	2-02-002	MULTIPLIES
2-01-001	MARELLA	2-02-002	MERCIFUL	2-01-001	MITROPOULOS	2-02-002	MULTITUDES
2-01-001	MARGENAU	2-01-001	MEREDITH'S	2-02-002	MITTENS	2-02-002	MULTITUDINOUS
2-01-001	MARGINALITY	2-02-002	MERGES	2-01-001	MIXER	2-01-001	MURKLAND
2-01-001	MARIETTA	2-02-002	MERITORIOUS	2-01-001	MIYAGI	2-02-002	MUSHROOM
2-01-001	MARK'S	2-02-002	MERRILL	2-01-001	MMES	2-02-002	MUSHROOMS
2-02-002	MARKINGS	2-02-002	MERRILY	2-01-001	MMM	2-02-002	MUSIC-LOVING
2-02-002	MARLENE	2-02-002	MERRITT	2-01-001	MOANED	2-01-001	MUSIQUE
2-01-001	MARLIN	2-02-002	MERRY-GO-ROUND	2-01-001	MOBILIZE	2-01-001	MUSLIMS
2-01-001	MARLIN'S	2-01-001	MERZ	2-01-001	MOBUTU	2-02-002	MUSSELS
2-01-001	MARMON	2-02-002	MESSENGERS	2-02-002	MOCCASINS	2-02-002	MUST'VE
2-01-002	MARSHAL'S	2-02-002	MESSIAH	2-02-002	MOCKERY	2-01-002	MUTELY
2-02-002	MART	2-02-002	MESSING	2-02-002	MODERNISM	2-01-001	MYCENAE
2-02-002	MARTINIS	2-02-002	METABOLIC	2-02-002	MODERNISTS	2-01-001	MYLAR
2-02-002	MARVELED	2-02-002	METABOLISM	2-02-002	MODICUM	2-01-001	MYOFIBRILLAE
2-01-001	MARYLAND'S	2-01-001	METALWORKING	2-01-001	MODIFIERS	2-01-001	MYRRH
2-01-001	MARYLANDERS	2-01-001	METAMORPHOSED	2-02-002	MODIFIES	2-02-002	MYSTERIOUSLY
2-02-002	MASQUERADE	2-01-001	METAMORPHOSIS	2-01-001	MOISEYEV	2-02-002	MYSTICISM
2-02-002	MASQUERADES	2-02-002	METAPHORICAL	2-01-001	MOISEYEVA	2-02-002	MYTH-MAKING
2-02-002	MASSAGE	2-02-002	METED	2-02-002	MOISTEN	2-02-002	MYTHIC
2-02-002	MASSED	2-01-001	METERING	2-02-002	MOISTENED	2-02-002	MYTHOLOGIES
2-02-002	MASTERFUL	2-02-002	METHUSELAH	2-01-001	MOLAL	2-01-001	N**.'S
2-02-002	MASTERPIECES	2-01-001	METHYL	2-02-002	MOLINARI	2-01-002	N**.*J
2-02-002	MASTS	2-01-002	METRICAL	2-02-002	MOLLIFY	2-01-001	NACHT
2-02-002	MATCHLESS	2-01-001	METS	2-02-002	MOLLY'S	2-01-001	NADIR
2-01-001	MATCHMAKER	2-01-002	METTLE	2-01-001	MOMMA	2-02-002	NAGASAKI
2-02-002	MATER	2-01-001	MG/**JL/**JHR	2-01-001	MON-*COLUMBIA	2-01-001	NAIRNE
2-02-002	MATERIALISTIC	2-01-001	MIANTONOMI	2-01-001	MON-*FAY	2-01-001	NAKTONG
2-02-002	MATERIEL	2-01-001	MICHAEL'S	2-01-001	MON-*GODDESS	2-02-002	NAMELESS
2-02-002	MATHEMATICIAN	2-01-001	MICHELSON	2-01-001	MON-*KHMER	2-02-002	NAMESAKE
2-02-002	MATHIAS	2-02-002	MICROFILM	2-01-001	MONAGAN	2-02-002	NAN
2-02-002	MATRICULATE	2-01-001	MICROMETEORITIC	2-02-002	MONASTERIES	2-01-001	NAOMI
2-02-002	MATS	2-02-002	MICROMETER	2-02-002	MONASTERY	2-01-002	NAPKINS
2-01-001	MATSUO'S	2-01-001	MICROWAVE	2-02-002	MONDE	2-02-002	NAPOLEON'S
2-02-002	MATTING	2-02-002	MID	2-02-002	MONEY'S	2-02-002	NAPS
2-02-002	MATURED	2-01-001	MID-*OCTOBER	2-01-002	MONEY-SAVING	2-01-001	NARCOTIC
2-01-002	MAUCH	2-01-002	MID-FIFTIES	2-02-002	MONEYS	2-02-002	NARRATION
2-02-002	MAUSOLEUM	2-02-002	MIDAIR	2-01-001	MONICA	2-01-002	NASAL
2-01-001	MAVIS	2-01-001	MIDDLE-*SOUTH	2-01-001	MONITORS	2-01-002	NASSER
2-02-002	MAW	2-02-002	MIDDLE-AGE	2-01-001	MONMOUTH'S	2-02-002	NATAL
2-01-001	MAWR	2-01-001	MIDSHIPMAN	2-01-001	MONO-	2-02-002	NATCHEZ
2-02-002	MAX'S	2-01-001	MIDSHIPMEN	2-01-001	MONO-UNSATURATE D	2-01-001	NATE'S
2-01-002	MAXIMIZE	2-02-002	MIDWEEK			2-01-002	NATHANIEL
2-01-001	MAXIMUMS	2-02-002	MIGRANTS	2-02-002	MONOMER	2-02-002	NATIONALISMS
2-01-001	MAXINE	2-02-002	MIGRATED	2-01-001	MONOPOLISTIC	2-02-002	NATIONALIZED
2-01-001	MAXWELL'S	2-02-002	MIGUEL	2-02-002	MONOSYLLABLES	2-02-002	NATURALNESS
2-01-002	MAYE	2-01-001	MIJBIL'S	2-02-002	MONT	2-02-002	NAUGHT
2-02-002	MAYFAIR	2-01-001	MILCOTE	2-01-002	MONTAIGNE	2-01-002	NAUSEATED
2-02-002	MAYNARD	2-02-002	MILD-MANNERED	2-02-002	MONTANA	2-02-002	NAUTICAL
2-02-002	MAYONNAISE	2-02-002	MILE-LONG	2-02-002	MONTEVERDI	2-01-001	NAUTILUS
2-02-002	MAYORAL	2-02-002	MILITARIST	2-02-002	MONTGOMERY'S	2-02-002	NAVEL
2-02-002	MAYS'	2-02-002	MILKS	2-02-002	MONTH'S	2-02-002	NAVIGATOR
2-01-001	MAZURKA	2-02-002	MILKY	2-01-001	MONTMARTRE	2-02-002	NAY
2-01-001	MC*CAULEY	2-01-001	MILLAY'S	2-01-001	MONTY	2-02-002	NEAPOLITAN
2-01-001	MC*CAY	2-02-002	MILLE	2-02-002	MOON'S	2-02-002	NEAR-AT-HAND
2-02-002	MC*CLELLAN'S	2-01-001	MILLILITER	2-02-002	MOONLIT	2-02-002	NECKLACES
2-01-001	MC*CLOY	2-01-002	MILLIONAIRE	2-02-002	MOORE'S	2-02-002	NECKS
2-01-002	MC*CONNELL	2-01-001	MILLS'S	2-02-002	MOORED	2-02-002	NECKTIE
2-01-001	MC*CRADY	2-01-001	MILORD	2-02-002	MOORISH	2-01-001	NECROPSY
2-01-001	MC*CULLERS	2-01-002	MILT	2-02-002	MOORS	2-02-002	NEGATE

2-02-002	NEGATIVELY
2-02-002	NEGLIGENT
2-01-001	NEGOCIANT
2-01-001	NEISSE
2-01-001	NENNIUS
2-01-001	NEOCORTICAL-HYPOTHALAMIC
2-02-002	NEON-LIT
2-01-001	NERIEN
2-01-001	NERNST
2-02-002	NERVE-SHATTERING
2-01-002	NERVOUSNESS
2-01-002	NESTER
2-01-001	NESTING
2-02-002	NESTLING
2-02-002	NETTLED
2-01-001	NEUROPSYCHIATRIC
2-02-002	NEUTRALISTS
2-01-001	NEUTRALIZATION
2-02-002	NEWBOLD
2-02-002	NEWLYWEDS
2-02-002	NEWSBOY
2-02-002	NEWTONIAN
2-02-002	NIAGARA
2-02-002	NICARAGUA
2-02-002	NICER
2-01-001	NICKEL-IRON
2-02-002	NIEBUHR
2-01-001	NIETZSCHE
2-02-002	NIGER
2-02-002	NIGHTCLUB
2-02-002	NIGHTMARISH
2-01-001	NIHILIST
2-01-001	NIKOLAI
2-02-002	NIMBLY
2-02-002	NINE-THIRTY
2-01-001	NINETEEN-YEAR-OLD
2-01-001	NINETY-SIX
2-01-001	NKRUMAH
2-01-001	NO-HIT
2-02-002	NO-NONSENSE
2-02-002	NOBLEMAN
2-01-001	NOCICEPTIVE
2-01-001	NODES
2-02-002	NOE**DL
2-01-001	NOGARET
2-01-001	NOGAY
2-02-002	NOISEMAKERS
2-01-001	NOMIAS
2-01-001	NON-*CHRISTIANS
2-01-001	NON-*GOD
2-01-001	NON-*JEW
2-02-002	NON-*JEWISH
2-01-001	NON-ACADEMIC
2-01-001	NON-CONTRIBUTORY
2-02-002	NON-EXISTENT
2-02-002	NON-PARTISAN
2-02-002	NON-PARTY
2-02-002	NON-POLITICAL
2-01-001	NON-THERMAL
2-02-002	NON-VERBAL
2-02-002	NONCOMMITTAL
2-01-001	NONCOMPLIANCE
2-02-002	NONCONFORMIST
2-01-001	NONDRYING
2-01-001	NONLINGUISTIC
2-01-001	NONPARTISAN
2-01-001	NONREACTORS
2-01-001	NONRESIDENTIAL
2-01-001	NORELL
2-02-002	NORFOLK
2-01-001	NORMA
2-01-001	NORTH-SOUTH
2-02-002	NORTHAMPTON
2-02-002	NORTHLAND
2-02-002	NORWAY
2-02-002	NORWEGIAN
2-02-002	NOS
2-01-001	NOSEBLEED
2-01-001	NOT-ACE
2-01-001	NOTABLES
2-01-001	NOTCHED
2-02-002	NOTEBOOK
2-02-002	NOTEBOOKS
2-01-002	NOTICEABLY
2-01-001	NOTT
2-02-002	NOVO
2-02-002	NOXIOUS
2-01-001	NUCLEOLI
2-01-002	NUCLEOTIDE
2-02-002	NUDES
2-02-002	NUDGE
2-01-001	NUDGED

2-01-001	NUDITY
2-01-001	NUFF
2-01-001	NUIT
2-01-002	NULLIFIED
2-01-002	NUMBING
2-01-001	NUMBNESS
2-02-002	NUMERICALLY
2-02-002	NUMINOUS
2-02-002	NUN
2-02-002	NURSES'
2-02-002	NUTRIENT
2-02-002	NUTRITIVE
2-02-002	NW
2-01-001	NYBERG
2-02-002	NYMPHOMANIACS
2-01-001	O**.-*C
2-01-001	O'*BRIEN
2-01-001	O'*CLOCK
2-01-001	O'*DONNELL
2-01-001	O'*DWYER
2-01-001	O'*DWYERS
2-01-001	O'*SULLIVAN
2-02-002	OASES
2-01-001	OATNUT
2-02-002	OBEDIENT
2-02-002	OBERLIN
2-02-002	OBITUARIES
2-02-002	OBJECTIFICATION
2-02-002	OBJECTIVITY
2-01-001	OBJECTOR
2-02-002	OBLIGINGLY
2-02-002	OBLITERATE
2-02-002	OBLITERATION
2-02-002	OBLIVION
2-02-002	OBLIVIOUS
2-01-002	OBSCENE
2-02-002	OBSCENITIES
2-01-002	OBSEQUIOUS
2-01-002	OBSESSES
2-02-002	OBSOLESCENT
2-02-002	OBSTRUCTIONIST
2-02-002	OBTRUDES
2-01-001	OCCIDENT
2-02-002	OCCIDENTAL
2-01-001	OCCIPITAL
2-02-002	OCCLUSION
2-01-001	OCEANOGRAPHIC
2-01-001	OCH
2-02-002	OCHRE
2-01-001	OCTAVE
2-02-002	OCTAVES
2-02-002	OCTOROON
2-02-002	OCULAR
2-01-001	OCZAKOV
2-02-002	OFF-BEAT
2-02-002	OFFENDER
2-02-002	OFFENDERS
2-02-002	OFTENTIMES
2-02-002	OGLED
2-01-001	OIL-BEARING
2-01-001	OIL-WATER
2-01-001	OILHEATING
2-01-001	OKAMOTO
2-02-002	OLD-STYLE
2-01-001	OLD-TIMER
2-02-002	OLDSMOBILE
2-02-002	OLDSTERS
2-02-002	OLEANDERS
2-01-001	OLYMPICS
2-01-001	OMAHA
2-02-002	OMEN
2-02-002	OMITS
2-02-002	ON-SITE
2-02-002	ON-THE-SCENE
2-02-002	ONCOMING
2-02-002	ONCT
2-01-001	ONE*$-TWO-THREE
2-02-002	ONE-ARM
2-01-001	ONE-DIGIT
2-01-001	ONE-EIGHTH
2-01-001	ONE-GEE
2-02-002	ONE-NIGHT
2-02-002	ONE-QUARTER
2-02-002	ONE-SIDED
2-02-002	ONE-SIXTH
2-02-002	ONE-STROKE
2-02-002	ONE-THIRTY
2-02-002	ONE-TWENTIETH
2-02-002	ONENESS
2-02-002	ONLOOKER
2-02-002	ONLOOKERS
2-01-001	ONSLAUGHTS
2-02-002	ONUS
2-02-002	OOZE
2-02-002	OOZED
2-02-002	OPELIKA
2-01-002	OPERAS

2-01-002	OPINIONATED
2-01-001	OPPONENT'S
2-01-002	OPPOSES
2-02-002	OPPRESSORS
2-01-001	OPTED
2-01-002	OPTHALMIC
2-01-002	ORACLE
2-02-002	ORALLY
2-02-002	ORATIONS
2-02-002	ORATORICAL
2-02-002	ORATORS
2-01-001	ORBITAL
2-01-001	ORCHESIS
2-01-002	ORCHESTRA'S
2-01-001	ORCHESTRATIONS
2-01-001	ORCUTT
2-01-001	ORDAIN
2-01-002	ORDERINGS
2-01-001	ORESTES
2-01-002	ORGIASTIC
2-02-002	ORGIES
2-01-001	ORIFICES
2-02-002	ORIGINATES
2-02-002	ORLANDO
2-01-001	ORMOC
2-02-002	ORNERY
2-01-001	ORNEY
2-01-001	ORPHANED
2-02-002	ORPHEUS
2-02-002	ORTHICON
2-01-001	ORTHOGRAPHIES
2-01-001	ORVIL
2-02-002	ORWELL
2-01-002	ORWELL'S
2-01-001	OSBORNE
2-01-001	OSO'S
2-01-001	OSSEOUS
2-02-002	OSTENTATIOUS
2-01-001	OTHER-DIRECTED
2-02-002	OTHERS'
2-01-001	OTHERWORLDLY
2-02-002	OUGHTA
2-02-002	OUI
2-02-002	OUM
2-02-002	OUT'N
2-01-001	OUT-MIGRANTS
2-02-002	OUT-OF-THE-WAY
2-01-001	OUTBOARDS
2-02-002	OUTBREAK
2-02-002	OUTBURST
2-01-001	OUTFACE
2-01-002	OUTFLOW
2-01-001	OUTLAW
2-02-002	OUTLAWS
2-01-002	OUTLAY
2-02-002	OUTLINING
2-02-002	OUTLYING
2-02-002	OUTNUMBER
2-02-002	OUTNUMBERED
2-01-002	OUTRAGEOUS
2-02-002	OUTRIGGERS
2-02-002	OUTSMARTED
2-01-001	OUTSPREAD
2-01-001	OUTSTANDINGLY
2-01-001	OUTTA
2-02-002	OUTWEIGH
2-01-001	OVALS
2-02-002	OVATION
2-01-001	OVER-ACHIEVERS
2-02-002	OVER-EMPHASIZED
2-02-002	OVERBEARING
2-01-001	OVERDONE
2-02-002	OVERDUE
2-02-002	OVEREATING
2-02-002	OVERESTIMATION
2-01-002	OVERFLOW
2-01-002	OVERFLOWED
2-01-002	OVERFLOWING
2-02-002	OVERHAND
2-01-001	OVERHANGS
2-02-002	OVERLAY
2-02-002	OVERLOOKING
2-01-002	OVERPOPULATION
2-02-002	OVERPOWERED
2-02-002	OVERREACHED
2-02-002	OVERSHADOW
2-02-002	OVERSHADOWED
2-02-002	OVERSHOES
2-01-001	OVERSIZE
2-02-002	OVERSIZED
2-01-001	OVERSOFT
2-02-002	OVERSUBSCRIBED
2-02-002	OVERTURNED
2-02-002	OVERTURNING
2-02-002	OWL
2-02-002	OWL'S
2-02-002	OWLS

2-02-002	OWNER'S
2-02-002	OWNERS'
2-01-001	OXALATE
2-02-002	OXCART
2-01-001	OXIDISED
2-01-001	OZ
2-02-002	PACIFIST
2-02-002	PACIFY
2-01-001	PACKERS
2-02-002	PADLOCK
2-02-002	PAEAN
2-01-001	PAGNOL'S
2-02-002	PAINSTAKINGLY
2-01-001	PAK
2-01-001	PAKISTANIS
2-02-002	PAL
2-01-001	PALACE'S
2-02-002	PALATE
2-02-002	PALERMO
2-02-002	PALISADES
2-02-002	PALLOR
2-02-002	PALMED
2-02-002	PALPABLE
2-02-002	PALSY
2-01-001	PAMPA
2-01-001	PANDEMIC
2-01-001	PANDORA'S
2-01-001	PANELED
2-02-002	PANGS
2-02-002	PANICKED
2-01-001	PANKOWSKI
2-01-001	PANTAS
2-01-001	PANTHEON'S
2-02-002	PANTOMIME
2-02-002	PANTRY
2-01-001	PANYOTIS
2-02-002	PAPERBACK
2-01-001	PAPERWEIGHT
2-02-002	PAPIER-MACHE
2-01-001	PAPP
2-01-001	PAPRIKA
2-02-002	PARADED
2-02-002	PARADING
2-02-002	PARAGON
2-01-001	PARALANGUAGE
2-01-001	PARALLELS
2-02-002	PARALYZED
2-02-002	PARALYZES
2-01-001	PARAMETRIC
2-01-001	PARANOID
2-01-001	PARAPHRASE
2-01-001	PARASITIC
2-01-001	PARASOLS
2-01-001	PARAXIAL
2-01-001	PARAY
2-02-002	PARCHED
2-01-002	PARDONED
2-02-002	PARE
2-02-002	PAREE
2-01-001	PARENTAGE
2-02-002	PARENTAL
2-01-001	PARICHY
2-01-001	PARINGS
2-01-001	PARKER'S
2-02-002	PARLANCE
2-02-002	PARODIED
2-01-001	PAROLEES
2-01-001	PARRIS
2-02-002	PARSIFAL
2-02-002	PARSON
2-02-002	PARTAKES
2-01-001	PARVENU
2-01-001	PASCHAL
2-01-001	PASLEY
2-02-002	PASTOR'S
2-02-002	PASTURES
2-01-002	PASTY
2-02-002	PAT'S
2-02-002	PATCHWORK
2-02-002	PATE
2-01-001	PATENT-SHARING
2-01-001	PATER
2-01-001	PATERNALISM
2-01-001	PATHOGENIC
2-01-002	PATHOLOGIST
2-01-001	PATIO
2-02-002	PATRIARCH
2-02-002	PATROLLED
2-02-002	PATROLMEN
2-02-002	PATRONIZING
2-01-001	PATTIES
2-01-001	PAULA'S
2-02-002	PAUNCH
2-02-002	PAUNCHY
2-02-002	PAUSES
2-01-001	PAUSON
2-02-002	PAVE

2-02-002 PAVEMENTS	2-01-001 PHONEMICS	2-01-001 POLTAVA	2-02-002 PRETENDS
2-01-001 PAVESE	2-01-001 PHONETIC	2-01-001 POLY-UNSATURATE	2-02-002 PRETEXTS
2-01-001 PAVILIONS	2-02-002 PHONIES	D	2-02-002 PRETTILY
2-02-002 PAVING	2-01-001 PHOTOCATHODES	2-01-001 POLYESTERS	2-01-001 PRETTYMAN
2-01-001 PAWCATUCK	2-01-001 PHOTOELECTRONIC	2-01-001 POLYMERIC	2-01-001 PREVISION
2-02-002 PAWN	2-01-001 PHOTOGENIC	2-01-001 POMHAM	2-01-001 PREVISIONS
2-02-002 PAWTUCKET	2-02-002 PHYLLIS	2-01-001 POMPEY	2-01-001 PRIAM
2-01-002 PAYCHECK	2-02-002 PHYSICISTS	2-02-002 PONDERING	2-02-002 PRICK
2-02-002 PEACE-LOVING	2-01-002 PHYSIOGNOMY	2-02-002 PONTCHARTRAIN	2-02-002 PRICKLY
2-02-002 PEACOCK	2-01-001 PHYSIOLOGIC	2-02-002 POODLE	2-01-001 PRIDE-*STARLETT
2-02-002 PEARLS	2-01-001 PHYSIOLOGIST	2-01-001 POOL-SIDE	E
2-02-002 PEARS	2-02-002 PHYSIOLOGY	2-02-002 POOLING	2-02-002 PRIDES
2-02-002 PECKED	2-01-001 PHYSIQUE	2-01-001 POPISH	2-02-002 PRIMA-FACIE
2-01-001 PECS,	2-02-002 PICCADILLY	2-02-002 POPPY	2-02-002 PRIMARIES
2-01-001 PECTORALIS	2-02-002 PICKETED	2-02-002 PORCELAIN	2-02-002 PRIMED
2-02-002 PEDANTIC	2-01-001 PICKETING	2-01-002 PORCHES	2-01-001 PRIMES
2-01-001 PEDESTRIANS	2-01-001 PICKETS	2-01-001 PORE	2-02-002 PRIMING
2-02-002 PEEKED	2-01-002 PIDGIN	2-01-002 POROSITY	2-02-002 PRIMLY
2-01-001 PEEP	2-02-002 PIECEMEAL	2-02-002 PORTENTOUS	2-01-001 PRINCESSE
2-02-002 PEEPING	2-02-002 PIEDMONT	2-01-001 PORTER'S	2-02-002 PRISTINE
2-01-001 PEGBOARDS	2-02-002 PIERO	2-01-001 PORTFOLIO-MAKER	2-02-002 PRIVATIONS
2-02-002 PEGS	2-01-001 PIERSON	2-01-001 PORTLAND'S	2-02-002 PRIX
2-02-002 PELTING	2-01-001 PIETA	2-02-002 PORTRAYING	2-01-002 PRIZED
2-01-001 PELTRY	2-01-001 PIETRO	2-01-001 PORTWATCHERS	2-02-002 PROBATE
2-01-002 PEMBROKE	2-01-001 PIG-DRUNK	2-01-001 POSSE'S	2-02-002 PROBLEM-SOLVING
2-02-002 PEN-AND-INK	2-01-001 PIKE'S	2-02-002 POSSUM	2-02-002 PROCREATIVE
2-02-002 PENDULUM	2-02-002 PILES	2-01-001 POSSUM-HUNTING	2-02-002 PROD
2-01-001 PENGALLY	2-01-002 PILLAR	2-01-001 POST-BELLUM	2-02-002 PROFESSING
2-02-002 PENNOCK	2-02-002 PILLARED	2-01-002 POSTHUMOUS	2-01-001 PROFESSIONALISM
2-01-002 PENNY-WISE	2-02-002 PILLORIED	2-02-002 POSTMAN	2-02-002 PROFUSE
2-02-002 PENS	2-02-002 PILOT'S	2-02-002 POSTMARK	2-01-002 PROFUSION
2-02-002 PENSIONER	2-02-002 PILOTING	2-02-002 POSTMEN	2-02-002 PROGENY
2-02-002 PEONIES	2-02-002 PILOTS'	2-02-002 POSTPONEMENT	2-02-002 PROGNOSIS
2-01-001 PEOPLE-ORIENTED	2-01-001 PIMEN'S	2-02-002 POSTURES	2-02-002 PROGRAMED
2-01-002 PEPPERED	2-02-002 PIMPS	2-02-002 POTBOILER	2-02-002 PROGRESSING
2-01-001 PEPPERMINTS	2-01-001 PINAR	2-02-002 POTOMAC	2-02-002 PROGRESSION
2-01-002 PEPTIDASES	2-02-002 PINCHING	2-02-002 POUCH	2-02-002 PROHIBIT
2-01-001 PEPTIDES	2-01-001 PINCIAN	2-02-002 POUCHES	2-02-002 PROJECTIVE
2-02-002 PERCY	2-02-002 PINES	2-02-002 POUGHKEEPSIE	2-02-002 PROLIFIC
2-02-002 PERENNIALLY	2-02-002 PINKS	2-01-002 POULTICES	2-01-001 PROLIXITY
2-01-001 PERENNIAN	2-02-002 PIPED	2-02-002 POURS	2-02-002 PROLONGING
2-02-002 PERFORCE	2-02-002 PIQUANT	2-02-002 POUSSIN	2-02-002 PROMPTS
2-02-002 PERFUMED	2-02-002 PIQUE	2-02-002 POVERTY-STRICKE	2-02-002 PROMULGATED
2-01-001 PERIER'S	2-01-001 PITCHFORK	N	2-02-002 PRONOUNCE
2-02-002 PERILS	2-02-002 PITIED	2-01-001 POWELL'S	2-02-002 PRONOUNCEMENTS
2-01-002 PERIPHERALLY	2-01-002 PITIFULLY	2-02-002 POWERED	2-02-002 PROPELLER
2-01-002 PERISH	2-02-002 PITILESS	2-01-001 PRABANG	2-02-002 PROPHETIC
2-01-001 PERKINS	2-01-001 PITT	2-02-002 PRACTICALITY	2-01-002 PROPIONATE
2-02-002 PERKY	2-02-002 PITTSBURGHERS	2-02-002 PRACTISED	2-01-002 PROPITIOUS
2-01-001 PERLUSS	2-02-002 PIUS	2-02-002 PRACTITIONER	2-02-002 PROPONENT
2-02-002 PERMANENCE	2-01-001 PIVOT	2-02-002 PRAGMATISM	2-02-002 PROPOSITIONS
2-02-002 PERMEATES	2-01-002 PL	2-02-002 PRAISES	2-02-002 PROPRIETER
2-01-001 PEROXIDE	2-01-001 PLAIN-CLOTHESME	2-01-001 PRAISING	2-02-002 PROS
2-01-001 PERPENDICULAR	N	2-01-001 PRAYIN	2-02-002 PROSAIC
2-02-002 PERPETUATION	2-02-002 PLAIN-SPOKEN	2-02-002 PRE-*CIVIL	2-02-002 PROSECUTE
2-02-002 PERPLEXED	2-02-002 PLAINTIVE	2-02-002 PRE-HISTORY	2-01-001 PROSECUTORS
2-02-002 PERPLEXING	2-01-001 PLANAR	2-01-001 PRE-PRIMARY	2-02-002 PROSPERED
2-02-002 PERSE	2-02-002 PLANNER	2-02-002 PRE-SEASON	2-02-002 PROSTATE
2-02-002 PERSISTING	2-01-001 PLANT'S	2-01-001 PRE-SELLING	2-02-002 PROSTRATE
2-02-002 PERSONA	2-01-001 PLANTERS	2-01-001 PRE-SHAPED	2-02-002 PROTAGONIST
2-02-002 PERT	2-02-002 PLANTERS'	2-02-002 PREACHERS	2-01-001 PROTEOLYSIS
2-02-002 PERTAIN	2-02-002 PLAQUE	2-02-002 PRECAUTIONARY	2-02-002 PROVOST
2-02-002 PERTINENCE	2-01-002 PLATONIST	2-01-001 PRECEEDING	2-02-002 PROWESS
2-02-002 PERTURBATIONS	2-02-002 PLATTER	2-01-002 PRECIPITATING	2-02-002 PROWL
2-02-002 PERUSAL	2-02-002 PLAYBOY	2-01-002 PRECONCEIVED	2-02-002 PROWLING
2-02-002 PERUVIAN	2-02-002 PLAYED-OUT	2-02-002 PRECONCEPTIONS	2-01-002 PROXIMAL
2-02-002 PERVADES	2-02-002 PLAYMATE	2-01-001 PRECONDITIONED	2-02-002 PRUDENT
2-02-002 PERVADING	2-02-002 PLAYMATES	2-01-001 PREDICATOR	2-01-001 PRUSSIA
2-01-001 PESCE	2-01-001 PLAYOFF	2-02-002 PREDICTABLY	2-01-001 PSEUDO-ANTHROPO
2-01-001 PESTS	2-02-002 PLAZA	2-01-002 PREDOMINANCE	LOGICAL
2-01-001 PETERHOUSE	2-01-002 PLEASES	2-01-002 PREFABRICATED	2-01-001 PSEUDO-CAPITALI
2-01-001 PETIPA-*MINKUS	2-02-002 PLIED	2-01-002 PREFACED	SM
2-01-001 PETITIONER'S	2-02-002 PLODDED	2-01-002 PREFERENTIALLY	2-01-001 PSEUDO-GLAMOROU
2-02-002 PETITS	2-02-002 PLOTTING	2-01-001 PREFLIGHT	S
2-02-002 PETRIFIED	2-02-002 PLUCK	2-02-002 PREHISTORIC	2-01-001 PSEUDO-THINKING
2-02-002 PETTED	2-02-002 PLUGS	2-01-001 PREJUDGED	2-01-001 PSYCHICALLY
2-02-002 PETTING	2-02-002 PLUGUGLY	2-01-001 PRELIMINARIES	2-01-001 PSYCHOACTIVE
2-01-001 PETTIT	2-02-002 PLUME	2-02-002 PREMIUMS	2-02-002 PSYCHOPATH
2-01-002 PHANTASY	2-01-001 PLUMMER	2-02-002 PREMONITION	2-01-001 PUBLIC-OPINION
2-01-002 PHANTOM	2-02-002 PLUMPED	2-02-002 PREP	2-02-002 PUBLIC-SCHOOL
2-02-002 PHARMACEUTICAL	2-02-002 PLUNDER	2-02-002 PREPACKAGED	2-02-002 PUBLICIZING
2-01-002 PHARMACOLOGICAL	2-02-002 PLUNGES	2-02-002 PREPAREDNESS	2-01-001 PUBLIQUE
2-01-001 PHEASANTS	2-02-002 PLUNKING	2-02-002 PREPONDERANCE	2-02-002 PUCKERED
2-02-002 PHENOMENAL	2-02-002 PLURALISTIC	2-01-001 PREPOSITION	2-02-002 PUDDLES
2-01-002 PHI	2-01-001 PODGER'S	2-01-001 PREPREPARED	2-02-002 PUFFING
2-01-001 PHIL'S	2-02-002 POETICALLY	2-01-001 PREREQUISITE	2-02-002 PUFFY
2-01-002 PHILCO	2-01-002 POETIZING	2-02-002 PREROGATIVES	2-01-001 PUGH
2-01-001 PHILIP'S	2-01-001 POGROMS	2-02-002 PRESCRIPTIONS	2-02-002 PUISSANT
2-01-001 PHILIPPOFF	2-01-001 POHLY	2-02-002 PRESENCES	2-01-001 PULLEYS
2-01-001 PHILISTINES	2-02-002 POIGNANCY	2-01-001 PRESENT-TIME	2-01-001 PULLINGS
2-02-002 PHILLIP	2-01-001 POIROT	2-02-002 PRESENTABLE	2-01-001 PULLOVER
2-02-002 PHILOLOGICAL	2-01-002 POISES	2-02-002 PRESIDE	2-01-001 PULOVA
2-02-002 PHILOLOGY	2-02-002 POISONS	2-02-002 PRESTO	2-02-002 PULSATION
2-02-002 PHILOSOPHIES	2-01-001 POITRINE'S	2-02-002 PRESTON	2-02-002 PULSING
2-01-002 PHILOSOPHIZING	2-01-001 POLAND'S	2-02-002 PRESUMING	2-02-002 PULVERIZED
2-01-001 PHIPPS	2-01-001 POLING	2-02-002 PRESUPPOSES	2-01-001 PUMBLECHOOK'S
2-01-001 PHONEMES	2-01-001 POLISHING	2-02-002 PRETENDER	2-01-001 PUMP-ACTION

2-01-001	PUMPED-UP
2-02-002	PUMPKIN
2-02-002	PUNCHING
2-02-002	PUNCTUALLY
2-02-002	PUNCTUATION
2-02-002	PUNISHMENTS
2-02-002	PUNK
2-01-001	PUNNISHED
2-02-002	PUP
2-02-002	PUPPY
2-02-002	PUPS
2-01-002	PURGATION
2-02-002	PURGATORY
2-02-002	PURGE
2-02-002	PURGED
2-02-002	PURGING
2-02-002	PURIFY
2-02-002	PURLED
2-02-002	PURPORT
2-02-002	PURPORTING
2-01-002	PURPORTS
2-02-002	PURSUER
2-02-002	PURSUERS
2-02-002	PURSUES
2-01-001	PUSHIN
2-01-001	PUSHUP
2-02-002	PUTTERING
2-01-001	PYKNOTIC
2-02-002	PYRAMID
2-02-002	Q
2-02-002	QUA
2-01-001	QUADRATIC
2-01-001	QUAKE
2-02-002	QUALIFIES
2-02-002	QUALITATIVELY
2-01-002	QUARRELSOME
2-02-002	QUARTER-CENTURY
2-02-002	QUARTER-MILE
2-01-001	QUASIMODO'S
2-02-002	QUATRAIN
2-02-002	QUAVERING
2-02-002	QUEBEC
2-01-001	QUEENS'
2-02-002	QUEMOY
2-02-002	QUESTIONER
2-01-001	QUETZAL
2-02-002	QUICKENING
2-02-002	QUICKIE
2-02-002	QUICKSILVER
2-02-002	QUICKSTEP
2-02-002	QUIESCENT
2-01-001	QUIETISM
2-01-001	QUIETIST
2-01-001	QUINCE
2-01-001	QUINEY'S
2-01-001	QUINT'S
2-02-002	QUIXOTIC
2-02-002	QUIZ
2-02-002	QUIZZICAL
2-01-001	QUOTAS
2-02-002	R**.'S
2-01-001	R**.*H
2-01-001	R**.P**.M
2-01-001	RABB
2-02-002	RABBLE
2-01-002	RABID
2-01-002	RACETRACK
2-01-001	RACEWAY
2-01-001	RACHEL'S
2-01-002	RACHMANINOFF
2-01-001	RACINE
2-02-002	RACINE'S
2-02-002	RACKETEER
2-02-002	RACKETY
2-02-002	RACKS
2-02-002	RACY
2-01-002	RADIATORS
2-01-001	RADIOED
2-01-001	RADS.
2-02-002	RAE
2-01-001	RAGGING
2-02-002	RAGING
2-02-002	RAIDING
2-02-002	RAILHEAD
2-02-002	RAINCOATS
2-02-002	RAINSTORM
2-01-002	RALLYING
2-02-002	RAM
2-02-002	RAMBLING
2-02-002	RAMEAU
2-01-001	RAMILLIES
2-01-001	RAMIREZ
2-01-001	RAMPART
2-02-002	RANCHES
2-02-002	RANCOROUS
2-02-002	RANDOMLY
2-01-001	RANGELANDS
2-01-001	RANGER
2-02-002	RANGERS
2-01-001	RANGONI'S
2-02-002	RANGY
2-02-002	RANSACK
2-02-002	RAOUL
2-02-002	RAP
2-02-002	RAPED
2-02-002	RAPISTS
2-02-002	RARITY
2-01-002	RASA
2-02-002	RASP
2-02-002	RATA
2-01-001	RATHBONE
2-02-002	RATIONALIZATION
2-02-002	RATTLED
2-02-002	RAVAGES
2-01-002	RAVENOUS
2-02-002	RE
2-01-001	RE-*BIRTH
2-02-002	RE-CREATED
2-01-001	RE-ELECTION
2-02-002	RE-ENACTMENT
2-01-001	RE-SHARPENING
2-02-002	REACTIONARIES
2-01-002	REACTIVATED
2-02-002	READABLE
2-02-002	READJUST
2-02-002	READJUSTMENT
2-02-002	REAFFIRM
2-02-002	REAFFIRMATION
2-01-001	REAL-LIFE
2-02-002	REALIST
2-02-002	REALMS
2-02-002	REALTY
2-02-002	REAMS
2-02-002	REAPPEAR
2-02-002	REAPPEARANCE
2-02-002	REAPPRAISAL
2-02-002	REARING
2-02-002	REASSURINGLY
2-01-001	REAVEY'S
2-01-001	REB
2-02-002	REBELLIOUS
2-02-002	REBOUND
2-02-002	REBUKE
2-01-001	REBUTTAL
2-02-002	REBUTTED
2-01-002	RECALCITRANT
2-02-002	RECAPITULATION
2-02-002	RECEDED
2-02-002	RECEPTIVE
2-02-002	RECESS
2-02-002	RECESSED
2-01-001	RECITATIVE
2-02-002	RECITE
2-02-002	RECITED
2-02-002	RECITING
2-02-002	RECKLESSLY
2-02-002	RECLAIM
2-02-002	RECLAIMED
2-01-001	RECLASSIFIED
2-02-002	RECLUSE
2-01-001	RECOILLESS
2-02-002	RECOMMENDS
2-02-002	RECOUNT
2-02-002	RECOUNTED
2-02-002	RECUR
2-02-002	RED-CLAY
2-01-001	RED-LIGHT
2-01-001	REDACTOR
2-01-001	REDECORATED
2-01-001	REDECORATION
2-02-002	REDEEM
2-02-002	REDISCOVERY
2-02-002	REDISTRIBUTED
2-01-001	REDONDO
2-02-002	REDRESS
2-01-001	REDWOOD
2-01-001	REDWOODS
2-02-002	REEDY
2-02-002	REEK
2-01-001	REEL
2-02-002	REELECTION
2-01-001	REELED
2-02-002	REENACT
2-01-001	REES
2-02-002	REFINING
2-01-001	REFLEXLY
2-02-002	REFORMATORY
2-01-001	REFORMERS
2-02-002	REFRESHINGLY
2-02-002	REFRESHMENT
2-02-002	REFRESHMENTS
2-02-002	REFRIGERATORS
2-02-002	REFUEL
2-02-002	REFUELING
2-01-001	REFUNDS
2-01-001	REFURBISHED
2-02-002	REGAL
2-02-002	REGENTS
2-02-002	REGIMENTS
2-01-001	REGIMES
2-01-001	REGISTRANT'S
2-02-002	REGISTRATIONS
2-02-002	REGIUS
2-01-001	REGRETTABLY
2-02-002	REGULARITY
2-02-002	REGULATE
2-01-001	REGULATIVE
2-02-002	REHASH
2-01-001	REICHENBERG
2-01-001	REIMBURSEABLE
2-01-001	REIMBURSEMENT
2-01-001	REIMBURSEMENTS
2-02-002	REINE
2-02-002	REINFORCEMENT
2-02-002	REINFORCING
2-01-001	REINHARD
2-01-001	REINHARDT
2-01-001	REISSUE
2-02-002	REITERATED
2-02-002	REJOIN
2-01-002	RELATIVISM
2-02-002	RELAY
2-01-001	RELAYED
2-02-002	RELEASING
2-02-002	RELENTLESSNESS
2-02-002	RELEVANCY
2-02-002	RELIABILITY
2-02-002	RELIEVES
2-01-001	RELISHES
2-02-002	RELIVE
2-02-002	RELIVING
2-02-002	RELOADED
2-02-002	REMAKE
2-01-001	REMANDED
2-02-002	REMARKING
2-02-002	REMARRIED
2-02-002	REMBRANDT'S
2-01-002	REMEMBRANCE
2-02-002	REMINDERS
2-02-002	REMINISCENCE
2-02-002	REMNANT
2-02-002	REMNANTS
2-02-002	REMODELING
2-02-002	REMONSTRATED
2-02-002	REMORSELESS
2-02-002	REMOTENESS
2-02-002	REMUNERATION
2-01-002	RENDERS
2-02-002	RENOVATION
2-02-002	RENOWNED
2-02-002	RENSSELAER
2-02-002	RENTALS
2-01-001	REORGANIZATIONS
2-01-001	REORIENTATION
2-02-002	REPAINTING
2-02-002	REPAIRING
2-02-002	REPAIRMEN
2-02-002	REPAYABLE
2-02-002	REPENTANCE
2-02-002	REPERTOIRE
2-02-002	REPETITIOUS
2-02-002	REPLACEMENTS
2-02-002	REPLENISHED
2-01-001	REPNIN
2-02-002	REPOSE
2-02-002	REPREHENSIBLE
2-01-001	REPRESENTATIONAL
2-02-002	REPRESSIVE
2-02-002	REPRIEVE
2-02-002	REPRIMANDED
2-02-002	REPRINTED
2-02-002	REPRISALS
2-02-002	REPRODUCING
2-01-002	REPRODUCTIONS
2-02-002	REPULSIONS
2-02-002	REPUTE
2-02-002	REQUISITIONED
2-01-001	RESALE
2-01-001	RESCIND
2-02-002	RESCUING
2-02-002	RESEMBLING
2-02-002	RESIDE
2-02-002	RESIDENCES
2-02-002	RESIGN
2-01-001	RESIN-SATURATED
2-02-002	RESINS
2-01-001	RESNIK
2-02-002	RESOLUTELY
2-01-001	RESORCINOL
2-02-002	RESOUNDING
2-02-002	RESOURCEFULNESS
2-02-002	RESPECTFULLY
2-01-002	RESPIRATION
2-02-002	RESPITE
2-02-002	RESTLESSLY
2-02-002	RESTLESSNESS
2-02-002	RESTRICTS
2-02-002	RESTUDY
2-02-002	RETALIATORY
2-02-002	RETELLING
2-02-002	RETENTIVE
2-02-002	RETHINK
2-02-002	RETIRES
2-01-002	RETRIEVE
2-02-002	REUNITED
2-01-001	REV'S
2-02-002	REVERBERATED
2-02-002	REVERE
2-02-002	REVERSAL
2-02-002	REVERSES
2-02-002	REVERTED
2-02-002	REVIEWER
2-01-002	REVIEWERS
2-01-001	REVIVALISM
2-02-002	REVIVING
2-02-002	REVOLTING
2-01-001	REVOLTS
2-02-002	REWRITING
2-02-002	REY
2-01-002	RHEUMATIC
2-01-001	RHINOS
2-01-001	RHINOTRACHEITIS
2-02-002	RHYTHMICALLY
2-01-001	RIBES
2-01-002	RICANS
2-02-002	RICHES
2-01-001	RICKENBAUGH
2-02-002	RIDDING
2-02-002	RIDDLED
2-02-002	RIDDLES
2-02-002	RIDDLING
2-02-002	RIDER'S
2-02-002	RIDICULED
2-02-002	RIDICULING
2-02-002	RIDICULOUSLY
2-01-001	RIEGGER
2-02-002	RIGGING
2-01-001	RIGHT-OF-ENTRY
2-02-002	RIGHTNESS
2-01-001	RIGIDITY
2-01-001	RIM-FIRE
2-02-002	RIMMED
2-01-001	RINASCIMENTO
2-02-002	RINGED
2-01-001	RINK
2-01-001	RINKER
2-01-001	RIOTERS
2-02-002	RIOTOUS
2-01-001	RIP-ROARING
2-02-002	RIPENED
2-01-001	RIVALED
2-02-002	RIVERBANKS
2-02-002	RIVIERA
2-01-001	RO**DTTGER
2-02-002	ROACH
2-02-002	ROBBER
2-02-002	ROBBING
2-02-002	ROBERTSON
2-02-002	ROBIN
2-01-001	ROCCO
2-01-001	ROCHDALE
2-02-002	ROCHESTER
2-01-001	ROCHFORD
2-02-002	ROCK-AND-ROLL
2-01-001	ROCKET'S
2-01-001	ROCKLIKE
2-02-002	ROCKPORT
2-02-002	ROGUES
2-02-002	ROMANCES
2-02-002	ROMANTICISM
2-01-001	ROMANTICIZE
2-01-001	ROMANZA
2-01-001	ROME'S
2-02-002	ROOFTOP
2-01-001	ROOMMATES
2-01-001	ROOS
2-02-002	ROOSTERS
2-01-001	ROOTING
2-01-002	ROOTLESS
2-01-001	ROQUEMORE
2-01-001	ROSEN
2-01-001	ROSSI
2-02-002	ROSTER
2-02-002	ROSTRUM
2-02-002	ROTATE
2-02-002	ROTATES
2-01-002	ROTTEN

Code	Word
2-01-001	ROUGH-SANDED
2-02-002	ROUGHENED
2-02-002	ROUNDABOUT
2-02-002	ROUNDHOUSE
2-02-002	ROUNDLY
2-02-002	ROUSE
2-02-002	ROUSED
2-02-002	ROVING
2-02-002	ROWED
2-02-002	ROWLEY
2-01-001	ROYALTIES
2-02-002	RTE
2-02-002	RUDELY
2-02-002	RUFFIAN
2-01-001	RUH
2-01-001	RULINGS
2-02-002	RUMBLE
2-01-001	RUMBLED
2-02-002	RUMBLING
2-01-001	RUMDUM
2-01-001	RUMEN
2-02-002	RUMFORD
2-02-002	RUMORED
2-01-002	RUMP
2-02-002	RUMPLED
2-02-002	RUN-UP
2-02-002	RUNNER-UP
2-01-001	RUNNIN
2-02-002	RUNOFF
2-01-002	RUPTURED
2-02-002	RUSE
2-01-002	RUSTLED
2-02-002	RUTHLESSLY
2-02-002	RUTS
2-02-002	S**.*C
2-02-002	SABBATH
2-01-001	SABINA
2-02-002	SABINE
2-02-002	SABLE
2-02-002	SABRE
2-02-002	SACHEMS
2-02-002	SACRAMENTS
2-01-002	SACRIFICED
2-02-002	SACRIFICIAL
2-02-002	SACRIFICING
2-01-001	SACRIFICIUM
2-02-002	SACRILEGE
2-02-002	SADDLES
2-02-002	SADISTIC
2-02-002	SAFARI
2-02-002	SAGE
2-02-002	SAHARA
2-02-002	SAILS
2-01-001	SAKELLARIADIS
2-02-002	SALACIOUS
2-01-001	SALAMANDER
2-02-002	SALLE
2-01-001	SALLY'S
2-02-002	SALTING
2-02-002	SALUBRIOUS
2-02-002	SALVAGING
2-02-002	SALVO
2-01-001	SAMOVAR
2-01-001	SAMPSON
2-02-002	SANATORIUM
2-02-002	SANCTIMONIOUS
2-02-002	SANDALWOOD
2-02-002	SANDBURGS
2-01-001	SANDERSON
2-01-001	SANDING
2-01-001	SANFORD'S
2-01-001	SANIPRACTOR
2-02-002	SANS
2-01-001	SANTO
2-02-002	SAPLING
2-02-002	SARA'S
2-02-002	SARACENS
2-02-002	SARDINES
2-02-002	SARDONIC
2-01-001	SARKEES
2-01-001	SARPSIS
2-02-002	SARTRE
2-01-002	SASSAFRAS
2-02-002	SATIETY
2-01-001	SATIS
2-02-002	SATURDAYS
2-02-002	SAUCERS
2-01-001	SAUDI
2-02-002	SAUL
2-01-001	SAVANNAKHET
2-01-001	SAVOYARDS
2-01-001	SAXTON
2-01-001	SCALAR
2-02-002	SCALED
2-02-002	SCALLOPED
2-02-002	SCANDINAVIAN
2-02-002	SCANS
2-02-002	SCARRED
2-02-002	SCARSDALE
2-02-002	SCARY
2-01-001	SCATTER
2-01-001	SCATTERBRAINED
2-01-001	SCATTERGUN
2-01-001	SCHAEFFER
2-02-002	SCHEDULING
2-02-002	SCHEHERAZADE
2-02-002	SCHELLING
2-01-001	SCHENK
2-01-001	SCHERER
2-01-001	SCHLEK
2-01-001	SCHLESINGER
2-01-001	SCHMITT
2-01-001	SCHO**DNBERG
2-01-001	SCHOOLMATES
2-01-001	SCHRAMM
2-02-002	SCHUBERT
2-01-001	SCHULTZ
2-01-001	SCHWAB
2-02-002	SCLEROSIS
2-02-002	SCOLDING
2-01-002	SCORCHED
2-01-001	SCORELESS
2-02-002	SCORNED
2-02-002	SCORNFULLY
2-02-002	SCOURGE
2-02-002	SCOUTS
2-02-002	SCOWLING
2-02-002	SCRAGGLY
2-01-001	SCRAMBLE
2-02-002	SCREAMS
2-02-002	SCREENED
2-02-002	SCRIPPS
2-02-002	SCRIPTURAL
2-01-001	SCRUTIN
2-02-002	SCUDDING
2-01-001	SCULPTURAL
2-02-002	SCUTTLED
2-02-002	SEAFARERS
2-02-002	SEAMEN
2-02-002	SEAN
2-02-002	SEAPORTS
2-01-001	SEAQUARIUM
2-01-001	SEAR
2-01-002	SEARCHLIGHT
2-02-002	SEARING
2-01-001	SEARS
2-02-002	SEASIDE
2-02-002	SEASONING
2-01-001	SEATON'S
2-01-002	SECEDED
2-01-002	SECEDING
2-02-002	SECESSION
2-02-002	SECOND
2-01-002	SECOND-DEGREE
2-02-002	SECOND-HALF
2-01-001	SECRETARY-*GENERAL
2-02-002	SECRETARY-TREASURER
2-02-002	SECT
2-02-002	SECTS
2-02-002	SED
2-02-002	SEDAN
2-02-002	SEDATE
2-02-002	SEDATELY
2-01-002	SEDIMENTATION
2-02-002	SEDUCTIVE
2-01-001	SEEDBED
2-01-001	SEEKONK
2-02-002	SEEP
2-02-002	SEEPAGE
2-01-002	SEEPED
2-02-002	SEEPING
2-01-002	SEGMENTAL
2-01-001	SEIDEL
2-01-001	SEIZIN
2-02-002	SELECTIVELY
2-01-001	SELF-ASSERTIVE
2-01-002	SELF-CENTERED
2-02-002	SELF-CRITICISM
2-02-002	SELF-DECEPTION
2-02-002	SELF-DEFEATING
2-02-002	SELF-DELUSION
2-02-002	SELF-DISCOVERY
2-02-002	SELF-EMPLOYED
2-01-001	SELF-GOVERNMENT
2-01-001	SELF-INTEREST
2-02-002	SELF-PRESERVATION
2-02-002	SELF-SACRIFICE
2-02-002	SELF-STYLED
2-02-002	SELF-SUFFICIENCY
2-02-002	SELF-WILL
2-02-002	SELFLESS
2-02-002	SELMA
2-01-001	SEMANTICALLY
2-01-002	SEMBLANCE
2-02-002	SEMESTER'S
2-02-002	SEMI-LITERATE
2-01-001	SEMI-MAJOR
2-01-002	SEMI-RIGID
2-01-002	SEMI-SKILLED
2-02-002	SENILE
2-01-001	SENIORITATIS
2-02-002	SENIORITY
2-01-001	SENOR
2-01-001	SENORA
2-02-002	SENSATIONALISM
2-01-001	SENSITIVES
2-01-001	SENSITIZED
2-01-001	SENSUOUS
2-01-001	SENTIENT
2-02-002	SENTINEL
2-02-002	SENTINELS
2-02-002	SEPARABLE
2-02-002	SEPARATENESS
2-02-002	SEQUOIA
2-02-002	SERENADED
2-01-002	SERGEI
2-02-002	SERMONS
2-01-001	SEROLOGICAL
2-02-002	SERPENT
2-01-001	SERRATUS
2-02-002	SERVILE
2-01-001	SETHNESS
2-01-001	SETTER
2-02-002	SETTLES
2-02-002	SEVENTEENTH-CENTURY
2-01-002	SEVENTIES
2-02-002	SEXY
2-01-001	SEYNES
2-02-002	SHABBILY
2-01-001	SHACKLED
2-01-001	SHACKLES
2-02-002	SHAFTS
2-02-002	SHAGGY
2-01-001	SHAH
2-01-001	SHAKER
2-02-002	SHAKILY
2-02-002	SHAMEFUL
2-01-002	SHAMPOO
2-02-002	SHAPELY
2-02-002	SHATTER
2-02-002	SHAVEN
2-01-001	SHAW'S
2-01-001	SHAWLS
2-02-002	SHAWNEE
2-01-001	SHAYNE'S
2-01-002	SHEATHING
2-02-002	SHEDDING
2-02-002	SHEEN
2-02-002	SHEPARD
2-02-002	SHEPHERDS
2-01-002	SHERATON-*DALLAS
2-02-002	SHERIDAN
2-01-001	SHERRILL
2-02-002	SHIBBOLETH
2-02-002	SHIELDS
2-01-001	SHIFLETT
2-02-002	SHILOH
2-02-002	SHIMMY
2-02-002	SHIPMATE
2-02-002	SHIPMENT
2-02-002	SHIPWRECK
2-02-002	SHIRKING
2-02-002	SHIRTS
2-01-002	SHIT
2-02-002	SHOCKWAVE
2-02-002	SHOD
2-01-001	SHOETTLE
2-01-001	SHOOT-DOWN
2-02-002	SHOOTIN
2-01-001	SHOP'S
2-01-001	SHORT-CONTACT
2-01-001	SHORT-OF-WAR
2-01-001	SHORTCUTS
2-02-002	SHORTHAND
2-02-002	SHOVE
2-02-002	SHOVELED
2-02-002	SHOWINGS
2-01-001	SHRAPNEL
2-02-002	SHREWDLY
2-02-002	SHREWISH
2-01-002	SHRILLED
2-02-002	SHRIMP
2-02-002	SHRINKS
2-02-002	SHRUG
2-01-001	SHRUGS
2-02-002	SHUFFLED
2-02-002	SHUNS
2-02-002	SHUTTERED
2-02-002	SHUTTING
2-01-001	SICILIANS
2-02-002	SICKENING
2-02-002	SICKER
2-02-002	SICKLY
2-02-002	SIDE-STEPPED
2-02-002	SIDLED
2-01-001	SIDNEY'S
2-01-001	SIENNA
2-01-001	SIEPI
2-02-002	SIERRA
2-01-001	SIERRAS
2-01-001	SIESTA
2-01-002	SIGHT-SEEING
2-02-002	SIGNALED
2-01-001	SIGNIFIED
2-02-002	SIGNIFY
2-01-001	SIGNOR
2-02-002	SIGNPOST
2-02-002	SILESIA
2-01-001	SILICA
2-02-002	SILICON
2-02-002	SILOS
2-02-002	SILVERY
2-02-002	SIMPLE-MINDED
2-01-002	SIMPLICITIES
2-02-002	SIMPLIFIES
2-01-001	SIMPLISTIC
2-02-002	SIMPSON'S
2-02-002	SIMULATION
2-02-002	SINEWY
2-02-002	SINGLE-HANDEDL
2-02-002	SINUOUS
2-01-002	SINUSOIDAL
2-01-001	SINUSOIDS
2-02-002	SIP
2-02-002	SIPPED
2-02-002	SIRENS
2-02-002	SIRS
2-01-001	SISK
2-02-002	SISTER'S
2-02-002	SISTER-IN-LAW
2-01-001	SISTERS'
2-01-001	SITTER'S
2-02-002	SITTERS
2-01-001	SITTINGS
2-02-002	SIX-FOOT
2-02-002	SIX-POINT
2-02-002	SIXTY-TWO
2-02-002	SIZZLED
2-02-002	SIZZLING
2-02-002	SKATING
2-02-002	SKEET
2-02-002	SKELETON
2-01-001	SKETCHBOOK
2-01-002	SKID
2-01-002	SKIDDED
2-02-002	SKIDDING
2-02-002	SKIIS
2-01-001	SKILLET
2-01-001	SKIPPERS
2-02-002	SKIRMISHING
2-01-001	SKOLMAN'S
2-01-002	SKULLS
2-01-001	SKY'S
2-01-001	SKYLIGHTS
2-01-001	SKYROS'
2-02-002	SKYSCRAPER
2-02-002	SLACKENING
2-02-002	SLANG
2-02-002	SLAP
2-02-002	SLAPSTICK
2-01-001	SLASH-*B
2-01-001	SLAT
2-01-001	SLAVIC
2-02-002	SLEDDING
2-02-002	SLEEK
2-02-002	SLICES
2-01-001	SLITS
2-01-001	SLOCUM'S
2-01-002	SLOE
2-02-002	SLOP
2-02-002	SLOPPING
2-02-002	SLOWEST
2-01-002	SLUGGERS
2-02-002	SLUGGISH
2-02-002	SLUGGISHLY
2-02-002	SLUICE
2-02-002	SLUICED
2-02-002	SLUICES
2-02-002	SLUNG
2-01-002	SLYLY
2-02-002	SMACKED
2-02-002	SMALL-GAME

2-02-002	SMALLNESS	2-02-002	SPIKE	2-01-001	STEWARDESS	2-02-002	SUMNER
2-02-002	SMALLPOX	2-02-002	SPIKED	2-01-002	STEWARDS	2-02-002	SUMTER
2-02-002	SMARTER	2-02-002	SPILLS	2-02-002	STICKLER	2-02-002	SUNS
2-01-001	SMEAR	2-02-002	SPINACH	2-01-001	STIDGER	2-01-001	SUNSHADES
2-02-002	SMEARED	2-01-001	SPINE-CHILLING	2-02-002	STIFFENS	2-02-002	SUPERHUMAN
2-01-001	SMILIN	2-01-002	SPINELESS	2-02-002	STIFLE	2-02-002	SUPERINTENDENT'S
2-01-002	SMILINGLY	2-02-002	SPITTLE	2-02-002	STIFLED		
2-01-002	SMITHEREENS	2-02-002	SPLASHES	2-02-002	STIFLING	2-01-001	SUPERINTENDENTS
2-01-001	SMOKEHOUSE	2-02-002	SPLEEN	2-02-002	STILLS	2-02-002	SUPERSTITIONS
2-02-002	SMOLDERED	2-02-002	SPLINTERED	2-02-002	STILTED	2-02-002	SUPERVISES
2-02-002	SMOLDERING	2-02-002	SPLITS	2-02-002	STINGING	2-02-002	SUPERVISOR'S
2-02-002	SMOOTHING	2-01-001	SPLOTCHED	2-01-001	STINGS	2-01-001	SUPERVISORY
2-01-001	SNEAD	2-01-001	SPOKANE	2-02-002	STINKING	2-02-002	SUPPLICATING
2-02-002	SNEAK	2-02-002	SPOKES	2-02-002	STIPULATE	2-02-002	SUPPOSING
2-01-001	SNEAKER	2-01-001	SPONGED	2-02-002	STIPULATES	2-01-002	SUPT
2-01-002	SNEAKING	2-02-002	SPONGY	2-02-002	STOCKHOLDER	2-01-001	SURE-SURE
2-02-002	SNEAKY	2-01-001	SPOOKY	2-02-002	STOCKROOM	2-01-001	SURFACTANTS
2-02-002	SNEERS	2-01-002	SPOTTING	2-02-002	STOCKY	2-02-002	SURGING
2-02-002	SNEEZED	2-01-002	SPRAINED	2-02-002	STOLIDLY	2-02-002	SURLY
2-01-001	SNELLVILLE	2-02-002	SPRINGBOARD	2-02-002	STOMPED	2-01-002	SURMISED
2-02-002	SNICKERED	2-02-002	SPRINGING	2-01-002	STONE'S	2-02-002	SURMISES
2-02-002	SNIFF	2-02-002	SPRINTED	2-02-002	STONED	2-01-002	SURMOUNTED
2-02-002	SNIFFING	2-02-002	SPRUE	2-01-001	STOPPER	2-02-002	SURPASSED
2-02-002	SNOBBISH	2-02-002	SPURIOUS	2-01-001	STORYLINE	2-01-001	SURREALISTS
2-02-002	SNODGRASS	2-02-002	SPURT	2-02-002	STOVES	2-01-001	SURVEY-TYPE
2-01-001	SNORKLE	2-02-002	SPUTNIK	2-02-002	STOWED	2-01-001	SURVIVALISTS
2-01-002	SNOWBALL	2-01-001	SPYING	2-02-002	STRADDLED	2-01-001	SUSAN'S
2-01-002	SNOWBALLS	2-02-002	SQUADRONS	2-01-001	STRAFE	2-01-002	SUSCEPTIBILITY
2-01-001	SNOWED	2-02-002	SQUADS	2-02-002	STRAGGLE	2-02-002	SUSHI
2-02-002	SNOWFALL	2-02-002	SQUANDERED	2-01-002	STRAGGLERS	2-02-002	SUSPECTING
2-02-002	SNUG	2-01-001	SQUASH	2-02-002	STRAGGLING	2-02-002	SUSPENSIONS
2-02-002	SNUGLY	2-01-001	SQUEAKED	2-01-001	STRAIGHT-HAIRED	2-01-001	SUSPENSOR
2-02-002	SOAPY	2-02-002	SQUEALED	2-02-002	STRAIGHTAWAY	2-02-002	SUSSEX
2-01-002	SOBBED	2-01-001	SQUIBB	2-02-002	STRANGENESS	2-02-002	SUSTAINING
2-02-002	SOBRIQUET	2-02-002	SQUIRE'S	2-02-002	STRAP	2-01-001	SUVOROV'S
2-01-001	SOCHI	2-02-002	SQUIRMED	2-02-002	STRAPS	2-01-001	SUZERAIN
2-02-002	SOCIABILITY	2-01-001	ST**.-*POL	2-02-002	STRATA	2-01-001	SWADESH'S
2-02-002	SOCIOLOGIST	2-01-001	STA**DDTISCHES	2-02-002	STRATEGICALLY	2-02-002	SWALLOWS
2-02-002	SODDEN	2-02-002	STABBED	2-02-002	STRATIFICATION	2-01-001	SWAMPS
2-01-001	SOFTENER	2-02-002	STABILIZE	2-01-002	STRATIFIED	2-02-002	SWAP
2-01-001	SOKOLOV	2-01-001	STACEY	2-02-002	STRAWBERRIES	2-02-002	SWEARS
2-02-002	SOKOLSKY	2-02-002	STACKING	2-02-002	STREETCARS	2-01-001	SWEATSHIRT
2-01-001	SOLDIERS'	2-02-002	STAGGER	2-02-002	STRENUOUSLY	2-01-001	SWEDES
2-02-002	SOLICITED	2-02-002	STAGGERINGLY	2-01-001	STRESSFUL	2-01-002	SWEEPSTAKES
2-02-002	SOLICITOUS	2-01-001	STAINLESS	2-02-002	STRICTEST	2-01-002	SWEET-SMELLING
2-02-002	SOLITUDE	2-02-002	STAIR	2-02-002	STRIPPERS	2-01-002	SWEETER
2-01-001	SOLLY	2-02-002	STAIRWAYS	2-02-002	STROKING	2-01-002	SWEETEST
2-02-002	SOLOMON	2-02-002	STAKED	2-02-002	STRUCTURALLY	2-02-002	SWEETS
2-02-002	SOLOVIEV	2-02-002	STALEMATE	2-02-002	STRUTTED	2-01-001	SWELLINGS
2-01-002	SOLVES	2-02-002	STALKING	2-01-001	STUBBLE	2-02-002	SWERVE
2-01-002	SOMATIC	2-02-002	STALLING	2-02-002	STUBBORNNESS	2-02-002	SWERVED
2-01-002	SOMBRE	2-01-001	STALLION'S	2-02-002	STUBS	2-02-002	SWERVING
2-01-001	SOMERSAULT	2-02-002	STAMINA	2-02-002	STUDIOS	2-01-002	SWIFT'S
2-01-001	SOMERVILLE	2-01-001	STAMINATE	2-02-002	STUDIOUSLY	2-02-002	SWIG
2-02-002	SOMNOLENT	2-01-001	STANBURY	2-02-002	STUFFING	2-01-001	SWIMMERS
2-02-002	SON-OF-A-BITCH	2-01-001	STANS	2-02-002	STUFFY	2-02-002	SWINBURNE
2-01-001	SONG'S	2-02-002	STARCHED	2-01-001	STUMP	2-02-002	SWINGIN
2-01-002	SONIC	2-01-001	STARCHY	2-01-001	STUNG	2-02-002	SWIPE
2-02-002	SONNETS	2-01-001	STARDEL	2-01-001	STUNTS	2-02-002	SWIRL
2-01-002	SONNY	2-01-001	STARDOM	2-02-002	STUPIDLY	2-01-001	SWITCHGEAR
2-02-002	SOOTHE	2-01-002	STARLET	2-01-001	STURCH	2-02-002	SWOOP
2-02-002	SOOTHED	2-02-002	STARRED	2-02-002	STYLIZATION	2-02-002	SWOOPS
2-02-002	SOOTHSAYERS	2-02-002	STARRING	2-02-002	STYLIZED	2-01-001	SYBIL
2-01-002	SOPHIE	2-01-001	STATE-LOCAL	2-01-001	STYRON	2-01-001	SYLLABICITY
2-02-002	SORREL	2-02-002	STATEROOM	2-02-002	SUAVE	2-01-001	SYLVANIA
2-02-002	SORROWS	2-02-002	STATESMANSHIP	2-01-001	SUB-TESTS	2-01-001	SYMBOLIZING
2-01-002	SORTIE	2-01-002	STATIONARY	2-02-002	SUBDUE	2-01-001	SYMINGTON
2-01-002	SOURDOUGH	2-01-002	STATIONERY	2-01-001	SUBGROSS	2-02-002	SYMMETRICAL
2-01-001	SOUTHAMPTON	2-02-002	STATUARY	2-01-001	SUBIC	2-02-002	SYNAGOGUES
2-01-002	SOUTHWESTERN	2-02-002	STATUS-CONSCIOUS	2-01-001	SUBJECTIVIST	2-02-002	SYNCHRONIZED
2-02-002	SOUVENIR			2-02-002	SUBLIMATE	2-01-001	SYNCHRONIZERS
2-01-001	SOVIET-*CHINESE	2-01-001	STATUS-ROLES	2-02-002	SUBMACHINE	2-02-002	SYNCHRONOUS
2-02-002	SOWBELLY	2-02-002	STATUSES	2-01-001	SUBMUCOSA	2-01-001	SYNCHRONY
2-01-001	SP	2-02-002	STAVE	2-01-001	SUBORDINATOR	2-02-002	SYNDICATED
2-01-001	SPA	2-01-002	STEADIED	2-01-001	SUBPENAS	2-01-001	SYNDROME
2-01-001	SPACER	2-01-001	STEELERS	2-02-002	SUBS	2-01-001	SYNTHESIZED
2-01-001	SPACESHIP	2-01-001	STEEPER	2-02-002	SUBSCRIBING	2-02-002	SYRIA
2-01-001	SPADA	2-02-002	STENDHAL	2-02-002	SUBSIDE	2-02-002	SYRUPY
2-02-002	SPANISH-*AMERICAN	2-02-002	STENGEL'S	2-02-002	SUBSIDIARIES	2-02-002	SYSTEMATIZED
		2-02-002	STEP-BY-STEP	2-02-002	SUBSTANTIATE	2-02-002	SYSTEMATIZING
2-01-001	SPANNED	2-01-001	STEPANOVICH	2-02-002	SUBSTITUTION	2-01-001	SZOLDS'
2-02-002	SPARSELY	2-01-001	STEPHANIE	2-01-002	SUBSYSTEM	2-01-001	T**.*W
2-02-002	SPARTAN	2-01-001	STEPHANOTIS	2-02-002	SUBTILIS	2-01-001	TABULA
2-02-002	SPATE	2-01-001	STEPHENS'S	2-02-002	SUBTRACT	2-01-002	TABULATION
2-01-002	SPATIALLY	2-01-002	STEPHENSON	2-02-002	SUBURBANITE	2-01-002	TABULATIONS
2-02-002	SPATTERED	2-02-002	STEPMOTHERS	2-01-002	SUBVERSIVE	2-01-001	TACIT
2-02-002	SPECIE	2-02-002	STEPPED-UP	2-01-002	SUCCESSIVELY	2-01-002	TACITLY
2-01-002	SPECIOUS	2-01-002	STEPPES	2-02-002	SUCCINCTLY	2-01-001	TACK-SOLDER
2-02-002	SPECKS	2-02-002	STEREOTYPES	2-02-002	SUDDENNESS	2-02-002	TACKED
2-02-002	SPECTACULARLY	2-02-002	STERILITY	2-02-002	SUEZ	2-02-002	TACKING
2-01-001	SPECTROMETER	2-02-002	STERILIZING	2-01-001	SUEZ-*HUNGARY	2-01-001	TACLOBAN
2-02-002	SPECULATED	2-01-001	STEROIDS	2-01-001	SUICIDES	2-01-002	TACTFUL
2-02-002	SPECULATORS	2-01-001	STETHOSCOPE	2-02-002	SULKED	2-01-001	TACTILE
2-02-002	SPEECHLESSNESS	2-02-002	STETSON	2-02-002	SULLENLY	2-01-001	TAFFETA
2-02-002	SPELLS	2-02-002	STEUBEN	2-02-002	SULZBERGER'S	2-02-002	TAHITI
2-02-002	SPIDER	2-02-002	STEVENSON'S	2-01-002	SUMMATE	2-01-002	TAILGATE
2-02-002	SPIES	2-02-002	STEWARD	2-01-002	SUMMERDALE	2-02-002	TAILOR

2-01-001 TAKEOFFS	2-02-002 THENCEFORTH	2-02-002 TONICS	2-02-002 TRIVIALITY
2-02-002 TAKEOVER	2-01-002 THEORISTS	2-01-002 TONIGHT'S	2-01-001 TROPHIES
2-02-002 TAKINGS	2-01-002 THEORIZE	2-01-001 TONSIL	2-02-002 TROUBLE-FREE
2-01-002 TALLIES	2-02-002 THERAPIST'S	2-02-002 TOO-LARGE	2-02-002 TROUBLING
2-02-002 TAMBOURINE	2-01-001 THERAPISTS	2-01-001 TOOBIN	2-02-002 TRUCKING
2-01-001 TAMIRIS'	2-01-001 THERETOFORE	2-01-001 TOODLE	2-02-002 TRUER
2-02-002 TAMPERING	2-01-001 THERMODYNAMIC	2-01-001 TOOKE	2-02-002 TRUEST
2-02-002 TANGO	2-02-002 THERMODYNAMICALLY	2-01-002 TOOL-AND-DIE	2-01-002 TRUJILLO'S
2-02-002 TANKERS	2-01-001 THERMODYNAMICS	2-02-002 TOP-DRAWER	2-01-002 TRUJILLOS
2-01-001 TANNER	2-01-001 THERMOELECTRIC	2-02-002 TOP-GRADE	2-01-001 TRUSSES
2-01-001 TANNHAEUSER	2-01-001 THERMOFORMING	2-01-002 TOP-QUALITY	2-02-002 TRUSTEES'
2-02-002 TANTRUM	2-01-001 THERMONUCLEAR	2-01-001 TOP-TANG	2-01-001 TRUSTETH
2-02-002 TANTRUMS	2-01-001 THICK-WALLED	2-01-001 TOPCOAT	2-02-002 TRUTHFULNESS
2-01-001 TAOISTS	2-02-002 THICKETS	2-01-001 TOPGALLANT	2-01-001 TRYIN
2-02-002 TAPERING	2-02-002 THIN-LIPPED	2-01-001 TOPPING	2-01-001 TSAR'S
2-02-002 TAPESTRIES	2-01-002 THINKE	2-02-002 TOPPLED	2-02-002 TUCK
2-01-001 TAPPAN	2-02-002 THINNING	2-02-002 TOPPLING	2-02-002 TUCKING
2-01-001 TARTARY	2-01-001 THIRD-DIMENSIONAL	2-01-001 TORCH	2-02-002 TUG-OF-WAR
2-02-002 TASMANIA	2-02-002 THIRTEENTH	2-01-001 TORCHES	2-02-002 TUGGED
2-02-002 TASTEFUL	2-02-002 THIRTY-EIGHTH	2-01-001 TORINO	2-01-001 TULAREMIA
2-01-001 TASTY	2-02-002 THIRTY-FOURTH	2-02-002 TORMENTING	2-02-002 TULIPS
2-02-002 TATE	2-01-002 THIRTY-NINE	2-02-002 TORPOR	2-02-002 TUMBLER
2-02-002 TAUNTED	2-02-002 THIRTY-THREE	2-01-002 TORRENCE	2-01-001 TUNG
2-02-002 TAUNTS	2-01-001 THOMSON	2-02-002 TORRENTS	2-01-001 TURBAN
2-01-001 TAUROG	2-02-002 THORNY	2-01-001 TORRID	2-01-001 TURIN
2-01-002 TAUSSIG	2-01-002 THOROUGHGOING	2-01-001 TORRIO-*CAPONE	2-01-001 TURNOUTS
2-02-002 TAVERN	2-01-001 THORP	2-01-002 TORTURES	2-02-002 TURNOVER
2-02-002 TAWDRY	2-01-001 THREE-DIMENSIONALITY	2-02-002 TOSCANINI	2-01-001 TURTLENECK
2-01-001 TAWES	2-01-001 THREE-FIFTHS	2-02-002 TOSSES	2-02-002 TUSCANY
2-01-001 TAX-EXEMPTION	2-02-002 THREE-FOLD	2-01-001 TOTAL-COST	2-02-002 TUTORING
2-02-002 TAXPAYER'S	2-02-002 THREE-FOURTHS	2-02-002 TOTALITY	2-02-002 TWELVE-HOUR
2-01-002 TAXPAYERS'	2-01-001 THREE-ROUND	2-02-002 TOUGHEST	2-02-002 TWENTY-NINE
2-02-002 TAYLOR'S	2-02-002 THREE-WAY	2-02-002 TOURED	2-02-002 TWENTY-YEAR
2-01-002 TCHAIKOVSKY	2-02-002 THRILLS	2-02-002 TOURIST'S	2-02-002 TWINKLING
2-01-001 TEACART	2-01-001 THRO	2-02-002 TOUSLED	2-02-002 TWITCHING
2-02-002 TEACHER'S	2-02-002 THROES	2-01-001 TOWNSMEN	2-01-002 TWO-FOLD
2-02-002 TEAHOUSE	2-01-001 THROWED	2-01-001 TOWSLEY	2-01-001 TWO-RUN
2-01-001 TEAM'S	2-02-002 THROWER	2-02-002 TRACERS	2-02-002 TWO-SEASON
2-02-002 TEAMED	2-02-002 THRUSH	2-02-002 TRACHEA	2-01-001 TWO-SYSTEM
2-01-001 TEAMMATE	2-02-002 THUGS	2-01-002 TRAGEDIANS	2-02-002 TWOS
2-01-002 TEAMMATES	2-02-002 THUNDERED	2-02-002 TRAGER	2-01-002 TYLER
2-02-002 TEARFULLY	2-02-002 THUNDERING	2-01-002 TRAITOR	2-01-001 TYME
2-02-002 TEASED	2-01-002 THUNDEROUS	2-02-002 TRAJECTORY	2-02-002 TYPHOID
2-02-002 TEASPOONFUL	2-01-001 THURBER'S	2-02-002 TRAMPED	2-01-002 TYPIFIED
2-01-001 TEATS	2-01-001 THYNNE	2-02-002 TRANCES	2-02-002 TYRANT
2-02-002 TECHNICALITIES	2-01-001 TIBER	2-02-002 TRANQUIL	2-02-002 U**.*N**.'S
2-02-002 TEDIOUSLY	2-02-002 TICKED	2-02-002 TRANSCENDENCE	2-01-002 U**.*S**.*C
2-01-001 TEE-WAH	2-01-002 TICKLED	2-02-002 TRANSCENDENT	2-02-002 UBIQUITOUS
2-02-002 TEEN-AGER	2-02-002 TICKS	2-02-002 TRANSCENDENTALISM	2-01-001 UGLIER
2-02-002 TEENAGER	2-02-002 TIDBITS	2-01-002 TRANSCRIPTION	2-01-001 ULBRICHT
2-02-002 TEETERING	2-02-002 TIEN	2-02-002 TRANSCRIPTS	2-02-002 UN
2-02-002 TEETOTALER	2-01-001 TIGARD	2-01-001 TRANSDUCERS	2-01-001 UN-*ENGLISH
2-01-001 TEHERAN	2-02-002 TIGHTEST	2-01-001 TRANSFEREE	2-02-002 UNABATED
2-02-002 TELEGRAMS	2-01-001 TILLIE	2-01-001 TRANSFERENCE	2-02-002 UNACCOUNTABLY
2-02-002 TELEGRAPHED	2-01-001 TILLOTSON	2-01-001 TRANSFORMERS	2-02-002 UNACQUAINTED
2-02-002 TELESCOPED	2-02-002 TILTS	2-02-002 TRANSFORMING	2-01-001 UNAMBIGUOUSLY
2-02-002 TELETYPE	2-02-002 TIM'S	2-02-002 TRANSLATING	2-02-002 UNANNOUNCED
2-02-002 TELLERS	2-01-001 TIMBERED	2-01-002 TRANSMITTING	2-02-002 UNASKED
2-02-002 TEMPERATE	2-02-002 TIMBRE	2-02-002 TRANSOMS	2-02-002 UNASSISTED
2-02-002 TEMPERS	2-02-002 TIME'S	2-02-002 TRANSPARENCY	2-02-002 UNATTACHED
2-02-002 TEMPEST	2-01-001 TIME-+-MOTION	2-01-001 TRANSPLANT	2-01-002 UNATTENDED
2-01-001 TEMPLEMAN	2-01-001 TIME-SERVERS	2-01-001 TRANSSHIPMENT	2-02-002 UNAUTHORIZED
2-02-002 TEMPOS	2-02-002 TIME-SPAN	2-01-001 TRANSVERSUS	2-01-001 UNBLINKINGLY
2-02-002 TEMPT	2-01-001 TIME-TEMPERATURE	2-01-001 TRANSYLVANIA	2-01-002 UNBRIDLED
2-01-001 TEMPTING	2-02-002 TIMELESS	2-01-001 TRAPPER	2-02-002 UNCERTAINLY
2-01-001 TEN-GALLON	2-02-002 TIMELINESS	2-02-002 TRAPPING	2-02-002 UNCHALLENGED
2-02-002 TENANCY	2-01-001 TIMEX	2-02-002 TRASH	2-02-002 UNCHANGING
2-02-002 TENDONS	2-01-001 TINES	2-01-001 TRAVELIN	2-02-002 UNCLAIMED
2-02-002 TENEMENT	2-02-002 TINKERING	2-02-002 TRAVELLERS	2-02-002 UNCLEAR
2-02-002 TENETS	2-01-001 TINKLING	2-02-002 TRAVELOGUE	2-02-002 UNCLOUDED
2-01-001 TENITE	2-01-001 TINSEL	2-02-002 TREASURED	2-02-002 UNCONDITIONALLY
2-02-002 TENNYSON	2-01-001 TINTABLE	2-02-002 TREBLE	2-02-002 UNCONNECTED
2-01-001 TENSIONING	2-02-002 TIPSY	2-01-001 TREE-CLUMPS	2-02-002 UNCONSTITUTIONAL
2-02-002 TENTACLES	2-02-002 TIPTOEING	2-02-002 TREK	
2-01-001 TERMINUS	2-02-002 TIREDLY	2-02-002 TREMOR	2-02-002 UNCONTROLLABLE
2-01-001 TERPERS	2-02-002 TIS	2-01-002 TRENCH	2-02-002 UNCONVINCING
2-01-001 TERRACED	2-02-002 TITANIUM	2-01-002 TRENCHARD	2-02-002 UNCOOPERATIVE
2-01-001 TERRIFIES	2-02-002 TITIAN	2-02-002 TRIBESMEN	2-02-002 UNCORKED
2-02-002 TERRY-CLOTH	2-02-002 TITO	2-02-002 TRICKED	2-02-002 UNDEPENDABLE
2-02-002 TERSE	2-02-002 TITRE	2-02-002 TRICKLE	2-01-001 UNDER-DEVELOPED
2-02-002 TERSELY	2-01-001 TITS	2-02-002 TRICKLING	2-01-002 UNDERCUT
2-02-002 TESTAMENTS	2-01-001 TITUS	2-02-002 TRICKSTER	2-01-001 UNDERDOG
2-01-002 TESTICLE	2-02-002 TOASTED	2-02-002 TRIFLING	2-02-002 UNDERESTIMATED
2-02-002 TESTIMONIAL	2-02-002 TOASTING	2-01-002 TRIGGER-HAPPY	2-02-002 UNDERGOES
2-01-001 TEXOMA	2-02-002 TOBIN	2-01-002 TRIGONAL	2-01-001 UNDERLIE
2-01-001 TEXTILE-PRODUCING	2-02-002 TODD	2-01-001 TRIMMER	2-02-002 UNDERLINE
2-02-002 TEXTUAL	2-02-002 TOKENS	2-01-001 TRIMMING	2-02-002 UNDERLINED
2-01-002 TEXTURED	2-02-002 TOLE	2-01-001 TRIPOLYPHOSPHATE	2-01-002 UNDERLINING
2-02-002 THACKERAY	2-01-001 TOMBIGBEE	2-02-002 TRIPPED	2-02-002 UNDERMINED
2-02-002 THANKFULNESS	2-01-001 TOMBLIKE	2-02-002 TRIPPING	2-02-002 UNDERWENT
2-01-001 THAR	2-02-002 TOMBS	2-02-002 TRIPTYCH	2-01-001 UNDERWOOD
2-02-002 THAWING	2-02-002 TOMBSTONE	2-01-001 TRIS	2-02-002 UNDERWRITING
2-01-001 THAXTER	2-02-002 TONGUE-IN-CHEEK	2-01-001 TRISERVICE	2-02-002 UNDETERMINED
2-01-002 THEATRICALLY		2-02-002 TRITE	2-02-002 UNDISPUTED
2-01-001 THEATRICALS		2-02-002 TRIVIA	2-02-002 UNDOING
2-02-002 THEM'S			2-01-002 UNDRESSED
			2-02-002 UNE

Rank	Word	Rank	Word	Rank	Word	Rank	Word
2-02-002	UNEARNED	2-02-002	USHER	2-01-001	VONNEGUT'S	2-02-002	WESLEY
2-02-002	UNEARTHED	2-02-002	USHERED	2-02-002	VOODOO	2-01-001	WESTBROOK
2-02-002	UNEMOTIONAL	2-01-001	UTO-*AZTECAN	2-02-002	VOTIVE	2-02-002	WESTERN-STYLE
2-02-002	UNENTHUSIASTIC	2-02-002	UTTERING	2-02-002	VOW	2-02-002	WESTERNER
2-01-001	UNEQUALLY	2-02-002	VACANCIES	2-02-002	VOWING	2-01-001	WESTMORE
2-02-002	UNERRING	2-02-002	VACCINATION	2-01-001	VP	2-01-001	WESTPHALIA
2-01-002	UNFAILING	2-01-001	VACUOLIZATION	2-02-002	WADDED	2-01-001	WESTPORT
2-02-002	UNFAILINGLY	2-02-002	VACUUM-FORMED	2-02-002	WADE	2-02-002	WHACKED
2-02-002	UNFAIRLY	2-01-001	VACUUMING	2-02-002	WADED	2-02-002	WHADDYA
2-02-002	UNFENCED	2-01-002	VADE	2-02-002	WAGGED	2-02-002	WHARVES
2-02-002	UNFINISHED	2-02-002	VAGABOND	2-02-002	WAGGING	2-01-001	WHEAT-GERM
2-01-001	UNFIRED	2-02-002	VAINLY	2-02-002	WAGNER'S	2-01-002	WHEATON
2-02-002	UNFOLD	2-02-002	VALENTINE	2-01-001	WAILS	2-02-002	WHEELING
2-02-002	UNFORESEEN	2-01-001	VALET	2-02-002	WAITRESS	2-02-002	WHIM
2-02-002	UNFOUNDED	2-02-002	VALIDATE	2-02-002	WAITS	2-01-001	WHINNIED
2-01-001	UNFROZEN	2-02-002	VALUATIONS	2-02-002	WAKED	2-01-001	WHIPSNADE
2-01-002	UNGAINLY	2-01-001	VARANI	2-02-002	WAKES	2-02-002	WHIRLWIND
2-01-001	UNGODLY	2-01-001	VARIAN	2-02-002	WALDO	2-02-002	WHIRRING
2-02-002	UNGRATEFUL	2-01-001	VARLAAM'S	2-01-002	WALDORF-*ASTORIA	2-02-002	WHISKED
2-02-002	UNHEARD-OF	2-01-001	VARMINT	2-02-002	WALL-TO-WALL	2-02-002	WHITE-TOPPED
2-02-002	UNHEATED	2-01-001	VARNISHES	2-01-001	WALLENSTEIN	2-01-001	WHITEFACE
2-01-002	UNHEEDED	2-01-001	VASORUM	2-02-002	WALSH	2-02-002	WHITEHEAD'S
2-02-002	UNHITCHED	2-01-001	VAUGHN	2-02-002	WALTER'S	2-02-002	WHITENESS
2-02-002	UNHURRIEDLY	2-02-002	VAULT	2-02-002	WALTERS	2-01-001	WHITETAIL
2-02-002	UNIFY	2-01-001	VEC*TROL	2-02-002	WAN	2-01-001	WHITING
2-02-002	UNIMAGINABLE	2-01-001	VEC*TROL'S	2-01-001	WANDER-*YEARS	2-02-002	WHITMAN
2-02-002	UNIMPAIRED	2-01-002	VEER	2-02-002	WANDERS	2-01-001	WHITROW
2-02-002	UNIMPEACHABLE	2-02-002	VEERING	2-01-002	WANED	2-01-002	WHIZ
2-02-002	UNIMPRESSIVE	2-02-002	VEHEMENT	2-01-001	WANGENHEIM	2-02-002	WHIZZED
2-02-002	UNIMPROVED	2-02-002	VEINING	2-02-002	WANING	2-01-001	WHOE
2-02-002	UNINITIATED	2-02-002	VENDORS	2-02-002	WAR-RIDDEN	2-01-001	WHOLENESS
2-01-001	UNINJURED	2-02-002	VENERATED	2-01-001	WARDENS	2-01-001	WHOLES
2-02-002	UNINTENDED	2-01-001	VENEZUELAN	2-02-002	WARHEAD	2-02-002	WHOLLY-OWNED
2-02-002	UNINTENTIONALLY	2-01-001	VENN	2-02-002	WARILY	2-02-002	WHOOPING
2-01-002	UNION'S	2-02-002	VENOM	2-01-001	WARSAW'S	2-01-001	WHORE
2-01-002	UNITARIANISM	2-02-002	VENOMOUS	2-02-002	WARSHIPS	2-02-002	WICKEDLY
2-01-002	UNITARIANS	2-02-002	VERA	2-02-002	WASHER	2-02-002	WIGGLING
2-02-002	UNITING	2-01-002	VERBATIM	2-01-002	WASHINGS	2-01-001	WIGMAKER
2-02-002	UNJUSTIFIABLE	2-02-002	VERDI'S	2-01-001	WASP	2-02-002	WIL
2-01-001	UNLEAVENED	2-02-002	VERGE	2-01-001	WASTEBASKET	2-02-002	WILBUR
2-02-002	UNLOCKS	2-01-001	VERLOOP	2-01-001	WASTEWATER	2-01-001	WILCOX
2-01-002	UNLUCKY	2-02-002	VERMONT'S	2-02-002	WATCHERS	2-02-002	WILES
2-02-002	UNMATCHED	2-02-002	VERNACULAR	2-01-002	WATCHFUL	2-01-001	WILFULLY
2-02-002	UNOBTRUSIVELY	2-01-001	VERNIER	2-02-002	WATCHMAKER	2-01-001	WILHELMINA
2-01-001	UNORIGINALS	2-01-001	VERO	2-02-002	WATER-SOLUBLE	2-01-002	WILKES
2-02-002	UNPARALLELED	2-01-001	VERREAU	2-01-001	WATERCOLORIST	2-01-001	WILLCOX
2-01-002	UNPATRIOTIC	2-01-001	VERSAILLES	2-01-001	WATERCOLORISTS	2-02-002	WILLIAMS'S
2-02-002	UNPLOWED	2-01-001	VERSED	2-02-002	WATERFALL	2-01-001	WILLIS'
2-02-002	UNPREDICTABILITY	2-02-002	VERTICALLY	2-02-002	WATERPROOF	2-01-001	WILSHIRE
2-01-001	UNPREDICTABLE	2-01-002	VESTIBULE	2-02-002	WATERWAY	2-01-002	WILY
2-01-001	UNPREDICTABLY	2-02-002	VESTIGE	2-01-001	WATT	2-02-002	WIND-BLOWN
2-02-002	UNPROTECTED	2-02-002	VETERANS'	2-01-001	WATTLES	2-02-002	WIND-SWEPT
2-02-002	UNQUALIFIED	2-02-002	VETERINARIAN	2-01-001	WAVE-LENGTH	2-02-002	WINDED
2-02-002	UNREALITY	2-02-002	VEXED	2-01-001	WAVY	2-02-002	WINDFALL
2-02-002	UNRECOGNIZABLE	2-02-002	VEXING	2-02-002	WAXY	2-01-001	WINDHAM
2-02-002	UNRECOGNIZED	2-01-001	VIA'S	2-02-002	WAYSIDE	2-01-001	WINDOWPANES
2-02-002	UNRESOLVED	2-01-001	VIALL	2-02-002	WEANING	2-02-002	WINDSOR
2-02-002	UNRESPONSIVE	2-02-002	VIBRANCY	2-01-002	WEARINESS	2-02-002	WINDY
2-02-002	UNREWARDING	2-02-002	VICARIOUS	2-02-002	WEARISOME	2-01-001	WINGMAN
2-02-002	UNRULY	2-01-001	VICENZA	2-02-002	WEARYING	2-01-001	WINLESS
2-01-001	UNSALTED	2-02-002	VICIOUSNESS	2-01-001	WEATHER-RESISTANT	2-01-001	WINSLOW'S
2-01-001	UNSATURATED	2-02-002	VICTIMIZED	2-01-001	WEATHERFORD	2-02-002	WINSOR
2-02-002	UNSCATHED	2-02-002	VIDEO	2-01-001	WEATHERING	2-02-002	WINTERED
2-02-002	UNSCIENTIFIC	2-02-002	VIEUX	2-01-001	WEAVES	2-02-002	WINTERS
2-02-002	UNSCREWED	2-01-001	VIEWLESS	2-02-002	WEBER	2-01-002	WINTRY
2-01-002	UNSMILING	2-02-002	VIGILANT	2-01-001	WEBSTERVILLE	2-02-002	WIRING
2-02-002	UNSTEADY	2-02-002	VINDICTIVE	2-01-002	WED	2-02-002	WISECRACKED
2-02-002	UNSTRUNG	2-02-002	VINEYARD	2-02-002	WEDDINGS	2-02-002	WISP
2-02-002	UNTENABLE	2-02-002	VIOLATES	2-02-002	WEDGE-SHAPED	2-02-002	WISPY
2-02-002	UNTIE	2-02-002	VIOLETS	2-02-002	WEDGED	2-02-002	WISTER
2-02-002	UNTOLD	2-01-001	VIRDON	2-01-002	WEDLOCK	2-02-002	WISTFUL
2-02-002	UNTRUE	2-02-002	VIRGIL	2-01-001	WEEK-ENDS	2-02-002	WITHER
2-02-002	UNTRUTH	2-01-001	VIS-A-VIS	2-02-002	WEEKDAY	2-02-002	WITHERED
2-02-002	UNUTTERED	2-02-002	VISAGE	2-02-002	WEEKS'	2-02-002	WITHHOLD
2-01-001	UNWARRANTABLE	2-02-002	VISCERA	2-01-001	WEI	2-02-002	WITT
2-02-002	UNWHOLESOME	2-01-001	VISITATION	2-01-001	WEIGEL'S	2-01-002	WOBBLED
2-02-002	UNWISELY	2-02-002	VISUALIZED	2-02-002	WEIGHTLESSNESS	2-01-002	WOBBLY
2-01-002	UPGRADING	2-02-002	VITALS	2-01-001	WEINSTEIN	2-02-002	WOEFULLY
2-01-002	UPI)**T**-	2-02-002	VITRIOLIC	2-02-002	WEIR	2-01-001	WOHAW
2-01-002	UPLAND	2-01-001	VITTORIO	2-02-002	WELDING	2-01-001	WOLFF
2-02-002	UPPED	2-02-002	VIVACITY	2-01-001	WELDWOOD	2-02-002	WOLFF'S
2-01-001	UPPER-CLASS	2-02-002	VOCABULARIES	2-02-002	WELL'S	2-02-002	WONT
2-01-001	UPPER-MIDDLE-	2-02-002	VOCALIST	2-02-002	WELL-ADJUSTED	2-01-001	WOODBURY
2-02-002	UPRISINGS	2-01-001	VOCALISTS	2-02-002	WELL-DESERVED	2-02-002	WOODLAND
2-02-002	UPROAR	2-01-001	VOCATIONAL-ADVANCEMENT	2-02-002	WELL-DESIGNED	2-01-001	WOODRUFF'S
2-01-001	UPS	2-01-002	VOEGELIN	2-01-002	WELL-DEVELOPED	2-01-001	WOODWARDS
2-02-002	UPSWING	2-01-002	VOL	2-02-002	WELL-TO-DO	2-02-002	WOODWIND
2-01-001	UPWARD-MOBILE	2-01-001	VOLCANIC	2-02-002	WELL-TRAINED	2-02-002	WOODWORKING
2-01-001	URANYL	2-02-002	VOLCANO	2-01-001	WELTER	2-02-002	WORCESTER
2-01-001	URBANISM	2-02-002	VOLITION	2-01-001	WEMMICK	2-02-002	WORDLESSLY
2-01-001	URETHANES	2-01-001	VOLLEY-BALL	2-01-001	WENTWORTH	2-01-001	WORDSWORTH
2-02-002	URGINGS	2-01-001	VOLSTEAD	2-01-002	WERT	2-01-001	WORK-OUT
2-01-002	URINARY	2-01-001	VOLTAIRE'S	2-02-002	WERTHER	2-02-002	WORKMANLIKE
2-02-002	URN	2-02-002	VOLUBLE	2-01-001	WESKER	2-01-001	WORLD-SHAKING
2-02-002	URNS	2-01-002	VOLUMETRIC	2-01-001	WESKER'S	2-01-001	WORRISOME
2-02-002	USELESSNESS	2-01-001	VOLUNTEERING			2-02-002	WORSHIPFUL
						2-02-002	WORSHIPPED

Code	Term
2-02-002	WORSTED
2-02-002	WORTHIEST
2-01-002	WRAITH-LIKE
2-02-002	WRANGLED
2-02-002	WRAPPER
2-02-002	WRAPS
2-01-002	WRECKAGE
2-02-002	WRENCHED
2-02-002	WRENCHES
2-02-002	WRESTLE
2-02-002	WRING
2-02-002	WRINKLE
2-02-002	WRISTWATCH
2-02-002	WRITHE
2-02-002	WRONGDOING
2-01-001	WYLIE
2-01-001	WYNDHAM'S
2-02-002	X-RAYS
2-02-002	XENOPHOBIA
2-01-002	Y'KNOW
2-01-001	Y'RE
2-01-001	YACHTEL
2-02-002	YACHTING
2-01-001	YANKEEFICATION
2-01-002	YANKEES'
2-01-002	YARDAGE
2-02-002	YARDSTICK
2-02-002	YAWN
2-01-002	YAWNING
2-01-001	YE'RE
2-02-002	YEAR-EARLIER
2-01-002	YEAR-TO-YEAR
2-02-002	YEARBOOK
2-02-002	YEARNINGS
2-01-001	YEHHH
2-01-001	YELLER
2-01-002	YELLOWING
2-02-002	YELP
2-01-001	YFF
2-01-001	YIN-*YANG
2-01-001	YODELING
2-01-002	YOGI
2-02-002	YOKEL
2-01-001	YOKNAPATAWPHA
2-01-001	YOKOSUKA
2-01-001	YONEDA
2-02-002	YORE
2-02-002	YORKERS
2-02-002	YORKTOWN
2-02-002	YOUNGISH
2-01-002	YUBA
2-02-002	YUH
2-02-002	YVETTE
2-01-001	ZEISS
2-01-001	ZEMLINSKY
2-01-001	ZENDO
2-01-001	ZERO-MAGNITUDE
2-02-002	ZEROS
2-01-001	ZIEGFELD
2-01-001	ZIFFREN
2-02-002	ZOOLOGIST
2-01-001	ZOUNDS
2-02-002	ZUBKOVSKAYA
2-02-002	ZUR
2-01-001	ZURCHER
2-01-001	ZURICH
2-01-001	ZWORYKIN
2-01-002	0.001
2-01-002	0.16
2-01-002	0.6
2-01-002	0.85**K
2-01-002	06-05
2-01-002	08
2-02-002	1.00
2-01-001	1.07
2-01-002	1.24
2-01-002	1.25-**JCM
2-01-001	1**C12
2-01-002	1**C48
2-01-002	1**C512
2-01-001	1**K
2-01-002	1-1/4
2-01-002	1/**JC
2-02-002	1/3
2-01-002	1/8-INCH
2-01-001	1,083,000
2-02-002	1,600
2-02-002	1,700
2-02-002	10**C30
2-02-002	10,000,000
2-02-002	100-YARD
2-02-002	101
2-02-002	105
2-02-002	106
2-01-001	1065
2-01-001	1066
2-01-002	11**C30
2-01-002	11**K
2-02-002	11-YEAR-OLD
2-01-001	12-1/2-INCH
2-02-002	121
2-02-002	122
2-02-002	124
2-01-001	13/16-INCH
2-02-002	135
2-01-001	14.7
2-01-001	1453
2-02-002	149
2-02-002	15,000
2-01-001	150,000,000
2-02-002	1500
2-01-001	153
2-02-002	1565
2-02-002	1577
2-01-001	1579
2-01-002	1592
2-01-001	1593
2-01-001	1598
2-02-002	160,000
2-01-001	1601
2-02-002	1607
2-01-002	1613
2-01-001	1624
2-02-002	165
2-02-002	169
2-02-002	170
2-02-002	1714
2-02-002	1721
2-02-002	1778
2-02-002	1780
2-02-002	1782
2-01-002	1787
2-01-001	1787-89
2-01-002	18*,E
2-02-002	180**+0
2-01-002	1800
2-01-001	1813
2-02-002	1814
2-01-001	1822
2-02-002	1825
2-01-001	1827
2-02-002	1831
2-02-002	1837
2-02-002	1840'S
2-01-001	1847
2-01-001	1849
2-02-002	1850'S
2-02-002	1855
2-02-002	1857
2-02-002	1858
2-02-002	186
2-01-001	1860-70
2-02-002	1862
2-01-001	1870
2-02-002	1879
2-02-002	188
2-02-002	1880S
2-01-001	1881
2-02-002	1886
2-02-002	189
2-02-002	19TH-CENTURY
2-02-002	1900'S
2-02-002	1909-10
2-02-002	192
2-02-002	1930S
2-01-001	1938-39
2-01-002	195
2-01-001	1959*=A
2-02-002	1959-60
2-02-002	196
2-02-002	1960-61
2-01-001	1961'S
2-01-002	1961-62
2-01-002	1967
2-01-001	2.0
2-01-001	2.512
2-01-001	2.75
2-01-001	2**C01.1**JH
2-01-001	2**C02.3
2-01-001	2**C04.2**JH
2-01-001	2**C1
2-01-001	2**C22
2-01-001	2**C26
2-01-001	2**C30.3-**C35.3
2-01-001	2**C30.3-**C36.1
2-01-001	2**C30-**C34.3
2-01-001	2**C32
2-01-001	2**C32.2**JH
2-01-001	2**C33**JH
2-01-001	2**C34
2-01-001	2**C34**JH
2-01-001	2**C36
2-01-001	2**C40
2-01-001	2-LITER
2-01-001	2-RUN
2-02-002	2-3/4
2-02-002	2-5
2-01-002	2,100
2-01-001	20-TO-1
2-02-002	20-YEAR-OLD
2-01-001	20TH-*CENTURY
2-01-002	21-INCH
2-02-002	210
2-02-002	211
2-02-002	213
2-02-002	214
2-01-002	22-YEAR-OLD
2-02-002	22,000
2-02-002	220
2-01-002	220**+0
2-02-002	229
2-02-002	239
2-01-001	24**K
2-02-002	240
2-01-001	240-GRAIN
2-02-002	25TH
2-01-001	258
2-02-002	26TH
2-01-001	27**C1
2-01-002	27,000
2-01-001	270
2-02-002	29.2
2-01-002	3.03
2-02-002	3.25
2-02-002	3.3
2-01-001	3.46
2-01-001	3**C3
2-01-001	3**C7
2-01-001	3-**JCM
2-01-001	3-3/4
2-01-001	3-94
2-01-001	3/16
2-01-002	3/8-INCH
2-01-001	3,000-FOOT
2-01-002	30-
2-01-002	30-ODD
2-02-002	30S
2-02-002	31ST
2-02-002	3211
2-01-001	337*+0**J*C
2-01-001	346
2-01-002	350,000
2-02-002	354
2-02-002	355
2-02-002	361
2-02-002	362
2-01-001	37*+0
2-01-001	37**0**J*C
2-01-001	381(C
2-01-001	381(C)(6
2-01-002	39,000
2-02-002	392
2-01-002	4.1
2-01-002	4.5
2-02-002	4**C45
2-02-002	4-
2-01-001	4-DAY
2-01-001	4-YEAR
2-01-001	4-0
2-02-002	4,500
2-01-002	40-YEAR-OLD
2-02-002	40,000,000
2-01-002	400,000
2-02-002	407
2-01-001	42-INCH
2-01-001	447
2-02-002	46TH
2-02-002	480
2-01-001	5.6
2-01-001	5**C12
2-02-002	5-DAY
2-02-002	5-FOOT
2-01-001	5-RUN
2-01-002	5-3/4
2-02-002	5-5
2-02-002	5-7
2-01-002	50TH
2-02-002	500-MILE
2-01-001	51ST
2-01-001	54-17
2-02-002	540
2-02-002	565
2-01-001	58TH
2-01-002	6.4
2-01-001	6.9
2-02-002	6**C15
2-01-002	6-FOOT
2-02-002	6-INCH
2-01-001	6-PASSENGER
2-02-002	6-1/2
2-02-002	60-80
2-01-002	6000
2-02-002	605
2-01-001	607
2-02-002	62
2-01-001	65*+0
2-02-002	66
2-02-002	677
2-02-002	7**C00
2-02-002	7**C45
2-02-002	7**K
2-01-001	7-PASSENGER
2-01-001	7-3
2-01-001	7-4
2-02-002	7-6
2-01-001	7/2
2-02-002	7,000
2-01-001	72ND
2-02-002	770
2-02-002	78
2-01-001	78TH
2-01-001	8.6
2-01-001	8.6-**JMM
2-02-002	8**K
2-02-002	8-INCH
2-02-002	8-OZ
2-01-001	8,280
2-02-002	80'S
2-01-001	80**K
2-02-002	80,000
2-02-002	83
2-01-001	85*+0
2-02-002	85**K
2-02-002	87
2-01-001	87TH
2-01-001	9.4
2-01-002	9.8
2-01-001	90-DEGREE
2-01-001	.027
2-01-001	.264
2-01-002	.280
2-01-001	.375
2-01-001	.410
2-01-001	.458
2-02-002	.5
2-01-001	$1.8
2-01-001	$1.9
2-02-002	$1,000,000
2-02-002	$1,200
2-02-002	$1,500,000
2-01-001	$10.50
2-02-002	$11
2-01-001	$110
2-01-001	$12.50
2-01-001	$12,500
2-02-002	$14.00
2-01-001	$15,000,000
2-01-001	$170
2-01-002	$18
2-02-002	$18.9
2-02-002	$2,000,000
2-02-002	$200,000
2-01-001	$23,000,000
2-02-002	$29
2-01-001	$3.00
2-01-002	$3.5
2-01-001	$3,500,000
2-02-002	$30
2-02-002	$32,000
2-01-001	$4,500,000
2-02-002	$40,000
2-02-002	$50,000
2-01-001	$538
2-01-001	$65
2-01-001	$7.00
2-02-002	$8
2-01-001	$8.00
2-01-002	$80,738
2-02-002	$9
2-01-001	$9.50
2-02-002	$90
2-01-001	**K
2-01-001	**YB
2-01-002	**YE
2-01-002	**YF.
2-01-001	**YP,
2-01-001	**ZQ
2-01-001	*(0,*=*T*$*).
2-01-001	*=*H*$.
2-01-001	*=*L*$,
2-01-001	*=*S*$.
2-01-001	*=*V*$.
2-01-001	*=*V*$,
2-01-001	*=*X*$-GYRO
2-01-001	*=*Z*$
2-01-001	*=B(T)*$

2-01-001	*=F*$-PLANE
2-01-001	*=F*$-PLANE.
2-01-001	*=I*$,
2-01-001	*=L*$.
2-02-002	*=N*$.
2-01-002	*=N*$TH
2-01-001	*=U*$,
2-01-001	*A**U.
2-02-002	*A*B
2-02-002	*A*B*C
2-01-001	*A*E*C
2-01-001	*A*I*M*O,
2-01-001	*A*S*W
2-01-001	*AMP
2-01-001	*AMP.
2-01-001	*B+**J*O.
2-01-001	*B**U.
2-01-001	*B*B*B
2-02-002	*B*G
2-01-001	*B*M*E*W*S
2-01-001	*B*O*D/DAY/ACRE
2-02-002	*B-70,
2-01-001	*C**S
2-01-001	*C*D*C'S
2-01-001	*C*O*N*E*L*R*A*D
2-01-001	*CO
2-01-002	*D*E*A*E-CELLULOSE,
2-01-001	*D*I*O*C*S,
2-01-001	*D*S*W
2-01-001	*E*E*G
2-01-001	*E*T*V
2-01-001	*F*E*L*A
2-02-002	*F*M
2-01-001	*F*N
2-01-001	*G*N*P.
2-01-001	*G*N*P,
2-01-001	*I*C*B*M'S
2-01-001	*I*C*B*MS
2-01-001	*I*O*C*S
2-01-001	*I*O*C*S.
2-01-001	*I*O*C*S*I*X*F
2-01-001	*I*O*C*S*I*X*G
2-01-001	*I*R*S*A*C
2-01-001	*K.
2-01-001	*L*I*T*O*R*I*G*I*N
2-01-001	*L*O*C
2-01-001	*L*S*O
2-02-002	*M.
2-01-001	*ME-210
2-01-001	*MRAD
2-01-001	*N*C*T*A
2-01-001	*N*E
2-01-001	*N*E,
2-01-001	*N*L*R*D*A
2-01-001	*N*W.
2-01-001	*N*Y*U
2-02-002	*P**U
2-01-001	*P**U,
2-01-001	*P*H*S
2-01-001	*P*T*C
2-01-001	*P-11
2-01-001	*R*D*W
2-02-002	*R-*N**.*J**.,
2-02-002	*R,
2-01-001	*S+*W
2-02-002	*S**U
2-01-001	*S*A*A*M*I
2-01-001	*S*A*M*O*S
2-01-001	*S*B*A'S
2-01-001	*S*C*R
2-01-001	*S*M*U'S
2-01-001	*S*R*E*L*E*A*S*E
2-01-001	*S*X-21
2-01-001	*S-11
2-01-001	*SP
2-01-001	*T.
2-02-002	*T*N*T
2-01-001	*T*S*E*M
2-01-001	*T-34
2-01-001	*U
2-01-002	*U*P*I)**T**-
2-02-002	*U*S.
2-02-002	*U*S*S*R
2-02-002	*W
2-01-001	*W*B*A*I
2-02-002	*X'S
2-01-001	*X-RAY
2-01-001	*X-REGION
2-01-001	*X-REGION,
2-01-001	-**JISM
2-01-001	/**B/
2-01-001	/L/
1-01-001	A),
1-01-001	A**.*A**.*U
1-01-001	A**.*A**.*U**.'S
1-01-001	A**.*I**.*D
1-01-001	A**.*K**.*C
1-01-001	A**$N
1-01-001	A**$RE
1-01-001	A**YS**YP**YI**YS
1-01-001	A*=NOTH*$ER
1-01-001	A-CROWING
1-01-001	A-DRINKING
1-01-001	A-GRACIOUS
1-01-001	A-RAISING
1-01-001	A-STOOPIN
1-01-001	A-TALL
1-01-001	A-WING
1-01-001	AAA-EE
1-01-001	AAAWWW
1-01-001	AAH
1-01-001	ABARINGE
1-01-001	ABATED
1-01-001	ABATUND
1-01-001	ABBAS'S
1-01-001	ABBE-*DIRECT
1-01-001	ABBE-*SCOTCH
1-01-001	ABBERATIONS
1-01-001	ABBREVIATED
1-01-001	ABBREVIATION
1-01-001	ABBREVIATIONS
1-01-001	ABDALLAH
1-01-001	ABDOMINIS
1-01-001	ABDUCTION
1-01-001	ABED
1-01-001	ABEL'S
1-01-001	ABELL
1-01-001	ABELSON
1-01-001	ABER
1-01-001	ABERNATHYS
1-01-001	ABHORRED
1-01-001	ABHORRENT
1-01-001	ABJECTION
1-01-001	ABJECTLY
1-01-001	ABLATED
1-01-001	ABNER
1-01-001	ABNORMALITIES
1-01-001	ABNORMALLY
1-01-001	ABOLITIONIST
1-01-001	ABORIGINAL
1-01-001	ABORTIONS
1-01-001	ABOUND
1-01-001	ABOUNDING
1-01-001	ABOUNDS
1-01-001	ABOVE-GROUND
1-01-001	ABOVE-NOTED
1-01-001	ABOVE-WATER
1-01-001	ABRA
1-01-001	ABRAMS
1-01-001	ABRASION
1-01-001	ABRIDGED
1-01-001	ABRIDGMENT
1-01-001	ABROADE
1-01-001	ABROGATED
1-01-001	ABRUPTNESS
1-01-001	ABSCISSA
1-01-001	ABSENTED
1-01-001	ABSENTEE
1-01-001	ABSENTEEISM
1-01-001	ABSENTIA
1-01-001	ABSENTMINDEDLY
1-01-001	ABSINTHE
1-01-001	ABSORBENCY
1-01-001	ABSORBER
1-01-001	ABSORBS
1-01-001	ABSORPTIVE
1-01-001	ABSTAIN
1-01-001	ABSTAINING
1-01-001	ABSTINENCE
1-01-001	ABSTRACTEDNESS
1-01-001	ABSTRACTIONISM
1-01-001	ABSTRACTIVE
1-01-001	ABSTRACTLY
1-01-001	ABSTRACTORS
1-01-001	ABSTRUSENESSES
1-01-001	ABSURDLY
1-01-001	ABUSIVE
1-01-001	ABUTMENTS
1-01-001	ABYSSINIANS
1-01-001	ACADEMEH
1-01-001	ACADEMICIANSHIP
1-01-001	ACADIA
1-01-001	ACAPULCO
1-01-001	ACCADEMIA
1-01-001	ACCARDO
1-01-001	ACCEDE
1-01-001	ACCEDED
1-01-001	ACCENTING
1-01-001	ACCENTUAL
1-01-001	ACCENTUATE
1-01-001	ACCENTUATES
1-01-001	ACCESSES
1-01-001	ACCESSIONS
1-01-001	ACCESSORS
1-01-001	ACCESSORY
1-01-001	ACCIDENTAL-WAR
1-01-001	ACCLAIMS
1-01-001	ACCLAMATION
1-01-001	ACCLIMATIZED
1-01-001	ACCOLADES
1-01-001	ACCOMMODATED
1-01-001	ACCOMMODATION
1-01-001	ACCOMODATIONS
1-01-001	ACCOMPANIES
1-01-001	ACCOMPANIMEN
1-01-001	ACCOMPANIST
1-01-001	ACCOMPANISTS
1-01-001	ACCOMPLICES
1-01-001	ACCOMPLISHES
1-01-001	ACCORDION
1-01-001	ACCORDS
1-01-001	ACCOSTING
1-01-001	ACCOUNTABLE
1-01-001	ACCOUNTANTS
1-01-001	ACCOUTERMENTS
1-01-001	ACCRUES
1-01-001	ACCULTURATED
1-01-001	ACCULTURATION
1-01-001	ACHAEANS
1-01-001	ACHAEANS'
1-01-001	ACHES
1-01-001	ACHESON'S
1-01-001	ACHILLES
1-01-001	ACID-FAST
1-01-001	ACIDITY
1-01-001	ACIDULOUS
1-01-001	ACKERLY
1-01-001	ACKNOWLEDGING
1-01-001	ACKNOWLEDGMENTS
1-01-001	ACOLYTE
1-01-001	ACORDING
1-01-001	ACORNS
1-01-001	ACOURSE
1-01-001	ACOUSTIC
1-01-001	ACOUSTICALLY
1-01-001	ACOUSTICS
1-01-001	ACQUIESCED
1-01-001	ACQUIESENCE
1-01-001	ACQUISITIVENESS
1-01-001	ACRE-FEET
1-01-001	ACRID
1-01-001	ACROBACY
1-01-001	ACROBATICS
1-01-001	ACROBATS
1-01-001	ACROSS-THE-BOARD
1-01-001	ACTING-*PRESIDENT
1-01-001	ACTINOMETER
1-01-001	ACTION-ORIENTED
1-01-001	ACTION-PACKED
1-01-001	ACTIVATING
1-01-001	ACTOR'S
1-01-001	ACTOR-*CROONER
1-01-001	ACTUARIAL
1-01-001	ACTUARIALLY
1-01-001	ACTUATE
1-01-001	ACUMEN
1-01-001	AD-LIB
1-01-001	ADAGIOS
1-01-001	ADAIR'S
1-01-001	ADAMANTLY
1-01-001	ADAME
1-01-001	ADAMO
1-01-001	ADAMS'S
1-01-001	ADAMSON
1-01-001	ADAPTAPLEX
1-01-001	ADAPTER
1-01-001	ADCOCK
1-01-001	ADD-ON
1-01-001	ADDICT
1-01-001	ADDISON
1-01-001	ADDLE-BRAINED
1-01-001	ADDRESSEES
1-01-001	ADDUCE
1-01-001	ADE
1-01-001	ADELOS
1-01-001	ADENAUER'S
1-01-001	ADENOMAS
1-01-001	ADERHOLDS
1-01-001	ADHERES
1-01-001	ADIEU
1-01-001	ADIOS-*DIRECT
1-01-001	ADIOS-*ON
1-01-001	ADIOS-*RENA
1-01-001	ADIOS-*TRUSTFUL
1-01-001	ADIPIC
1-01-001	ADIRONDACKS
1-01-001	ADJOURNING
1-01-001	ADJOURNS
1-01-001	ADJUDGED
1-01-001	ADJUDGING
1-01-001	ADJUDICATE
1-01-001	ADJUNCTS
1-01-001	ADMINISTERS
1-01-001	ADMINISTRATIVELY
1-01-001	ADMINSTRATION
1-01-001	ADMIRALS
1-01-001	ADMIRALTY
1-01-001	ADMIRES
1-01-001	ADMIRINGLY
1-01-001	ADMITTANCE
1-01-001	ADMIXED
1-01-001	ADMONISHING
1-01-001	ADMONISHMENTS
1-01-001	ADMONITION
1-01-001	ADNAN
1-01-001	ADOLPHUS
1-01-001	ADONIS
1-01-001	ADORES
1-01-001	ADORN
1-01-001	ADORNED
1-01-001	ADORNS
1-01-001	ADRAR
1-01-001	ADRIANOPLE
1-01-001	ADRIFT
1-01-001	ADROIT
1-01-001	ADROITNESS
1-01-001	ADSORBS
1-01-001	ADULATION
1-01-001	ADULTERATED
1-01-001	ADULTEROUS
1-01-001	ADVANCEMENTS
1-01-001	ADVANTAGEOUSLY
1-01-001	ADVENTISTS
1-01-001	ADVENTISTS'
1-01-001	ADVENTITIOUS
1-01-001	ADVENTURERS
1-01-001	ADVENTURING
1-01-001	ADVERB
1-01-001	ADVERTISER
1-01-001	ADVERTISES
1-01-001	ADVERTISING-CONSCIOUS
1-01-001	ADVISABLE
1-01-001	ADVISEDLY
1-01-001	ADVISOR
1-01-001	ADVOCATES
1-01-001	AEGIS
1-01-001	AEON
1-01-001	AERATE
1-01-001	AERATES
1-01-001	AERIALS
1-01-001	AEROBACTER
1-01-001	AEROBIC
1-01-001	AERODYNAMIC
1-01-001	AEROGENES
1-01-001	AERONAUTICAL
1-01-001	AESCHBACHER
1-01-001	AESCHBACHER'S
1-01-001	AESTHETES
1-01-001	AESTHETICS
1-01-001	AETERNITATIS
1-01-001	AF
1-01-001	AFFABLE
1-01-001	AFFAIRE
1-01-001	AFFAIRES
1-01-001	AFFECTATION
1-01-001	AFFECTINGLY
1-01-001	AFFERENT
1-01-001	AFFIANCED
1-01-001	AFFIED
1-01-001	AFFILIATES
1-01-001	AFFINITIES
1-01-001	AFFIRMATIONS
1-01-001	AFFIRMATIVELY
1-01-001	AFFIRMS
1-01-001	AFFIX
1-01-001	AFFLICTION
1-01-001	AFFLICTIONS
1-01-001	AFFRONTED
1-01-001	AFFRONTING
1-01-001	AFGHANS
1-01-001	AFICIONADO
1-01-001	AFIELD
1-01-001	AFIRE
1-01-001	AFOOT
1-01-001	AFORETHOUGHT
1-01-001	AFRANIO
1-01-001	AFRIKA

1-01-001 AFRIQUE	1-01-001 ALCIBIADES	1-01-001 ALMOND	1-01-001 AMUSEDLY
1-01-001 AFRO-*CUBAN	1-01-001 ALCINOU**DS'	1-01-001 ALOKUT	1-01-001 ANA
1-01-001 AFTER-DUTY	1-01-001 ALCOHOLISM	1-01-001 ALOOFNESS	1-01-001 ANABAPTIST
1-01-001 AFTER-HOURS	1-01-001 ALCOTT'S	1-01-001 ALPERTS	1-01-001 ANABAPTISTS
1-01-001 AFTUH	1-01-001 ALDERMAN	1-01-001 ALPHA-BETA-GAMM	1-01-001 ANABEL
1-01-001 AGAMEMNON'S	1-01-001 ALDO	AS	1-01-001 ANACHRONISTICAL
1-01-001 AGATES	1-01-001 ALDRIDGE	1-01-001 ALPHABETIC	LY
1-01-001 AGAYNE	1-01-001 ALE	1-01-001 ALPHABETIZED	1-01-001 ANAEROBIC
1-01-001 AGED-CARE	1-01-001 ALEMAGNA	1-01-001 ALPHARETTA	1-01-001 ANAESTHESIA
1-01-001 AGEE	1-01-001 ALERTLY	1-01-001 ALPHONSE	1-01-001 ANAGRAM
1-01-001 AGENT'S	1-01-001 ALERTS	1-01-001 ALREADEH	1-01-001 ANALOGUE
1-01-001 AGGLUTINATING	1-01-001 ALESSIO	1-01-001 ALSATIANS	1-01-001 ANALOGUES
1-01-001 AGGRAVATE	1-01-001 ALEXEI	1-01-001 ALSING	1-01-001 ANALYTICALLY
1-01-001 AGGRAVATES	1-01-001 ALEXEYEVA	1-01-001 ALTAIRIANS	1-01-001 ANALYTICITY
1-01-001 AGGREGATION	1-01-001 ALFA	1-01-001 ALTER-EGO	1-01-001 ANALYTROL
1-01-001 AGGREGATIONS	1-01-001 ALFONSO	1-01-001 ALTER-PARENTS	1-01-001 ANALYZABLE
1-01-001 AGHAST	1-01-001 ALGAECIDE	1-01-001 ALTERCATION	1-01-001 ANALYZER
1-01-001 AGILELY	1-01-001 ALGEBRAIC	1-01-001 ALTERMAN	1-01-001 ANANIA
1-01-001 AGITATE	1-01-001 ALGER	1-01-001 ALTERNATED	1-01-001 ANAPLASMOSIS
1-01-001 AGITATED	1-01-001 ALGINATES	1-01-001 ALTERNATING	1-01-001 ANARCHIC
1-01-001 AGITATING	1-01-001 ALGORITHM	1-01-001 ALTERS	1-01-001 ANARCHIST
1-01-001 AGITATOR	1-01-001 ALIA	1-01-001 ALTHAUS	1-01-001 ANARCHIST-ADVEN
1-01-001 AGITATORS	1-01-001 ALIAH	1-01-001 ALTHEA	TURERS
1-01-001 AGLEAM	1-01-001 ALIAS	1-01-001 ALTITUDE-AZIMUT	1-01-001 ANASTOMOSIS
1-01-001 AGNES	1-01-001 ALIBIS	H-MOUNTED	1-01-001 ANASTOMOTIC
1-01-001 AGNOMEN	1-01-001 ALIENATES	1-01-001 ALTRUISM	1-01-001 ANATOLE
1-01-001 AGNOSTICS	1-01-001 ALIENUS	1-01-001 ALTRUISTICALLY	1-01-001 ANATOMIC
1-01-001 AGOENG	1-01-001 ALIGNING	1-01-001 ALUM	1-01-001 ANATOMICALS
1-01-001 AGONALE	1-01-001 ALIGNMENTS	1-01-001 ALUMNAE	1-01-001 ANCEL
1-01-001 AGONIES	1-01-001 ALIQUOTS	1-01-001 ALUNDUM	1-01-001 ANCHORAGE
1-01-001 AGONIZED	1-01-001 ALISON	1-01-001 ALUSIK	1-01-001 ANCHORING
1-01-001 AGREEABLENESS	1-01-001 ALIX'S	1-01-001 ALVEAR	1-01-001 ANCHORITISM
1-01-001 AGREEABLY	1-01-001 ALIZARIN	1-01-001 ALVEOLUS	1-01-001 ANCHOVY
1-01-001 AGREED-ON	1-01-001 ALKALOIDS	1-01-001 ALWAYS-PRESENT	1-01-001 ANCIENTLY
1-01-001 AGREED-UPON	1-01-001 ALKYLARYSULFONA	1-01-001 AMADEE'S	1-01-001 ANCIENTS
1-01-001 AGRICOLAS	TE	1-01-001 AMADO	1-01-001 ANCISTRODON
1-01-001 AGRICULTURALLY	1-01-001 ALKYLBENZENESUL	1-01-001 AMALGAMATED	1-01-001 ANDERLINI
1-01-001 AGRICULTURE'S	FONATES	1-01-001 AMALGAMATION	1-01-001 ANDERSEN
1-01-001 AGRIPPA	1-01-001 ALL-*AMERICAN-B	1-01-001 AMANUENSIS	1-01-001 ANDRES
1-01-001 AGROBACTERIUM	OY	1-01-001 AMARAL	1-01-001 ANDROMACHE
1-01-001 AGUE	1-01-001 ALL-*STAR	1-01-001 AMASSING	1-01-001 ANDRUSES
1-01-001 AH*$-AH	1-01-001 ALL-AUTOMATIC	1-01-001 AMATEURISHNESS	1-01-001 ANECDOTAL
1-01-001 AHAH	1-01-001 ALL-COLLEGE	1-01-001 AMATORY	1-01-001 ANEMATED
1-01-001 AHEM	1-01-001 ALL-CONSUMING	1-01-001 AMAZONS	1-01-001 ANEMIC
1-01-001 AHM	1-01-001 ALL-COUNTY	1-01-001 AMBASSADOR'S	1-01-001 ANESTHETIC
1-01-001 AHMAD	1-01-001 ALL-FEMALE	1-01-001 AMBASSADOR-AT-*	1-01-001 ANESTHETICALLY
1-01-001 AHMIRI	1-01-001 ALL-INCLUSIVE	LARGE	1-01-001 ANESTHETICS
1-01-001 AHRENS	1-01-001 ALL-KNOWING	1-01-001 AMBASSADOR-DESI	1-01-001 ANESTHETIZED
1-01-001 AI	1-01-001 ALL-LESBIAN	GNATE	1-01-001 ANGELES-*PASADE
1-01-001 AID-TO-EDUCATIO	1-01-001 ALL-MARRIED	1-01-001 AMBIANCE	NA
N	1-01-001 ALL-NIGHT	1-01-001 AMBIDEXTROUS	1-01-001 ANGELICA
1-01-001 AIDA	1-01-001 ALL-OVER	1-01-001 AMBITIOUSLY	1-01-001 ANGELICO
1-01-001 AIDE-DE-CAMP	1-01-001 ALL-PERVADING	1-01-001 AMBLED	1-01-001 ANGELL
1-01-001 AIKEN	1-01-001 ALL-PURPOSE	1-01-001 AMBLER	1-01-001 ANGERED
1-01-001 AIKIN	1-01-001 ALL-ROUND	1-01-001 AMBLING	1-01-001 ANGLETERRE
1-01-001 AILERONS	1-01-001 ALL-SOMETHING-O	1-01-001 AMBROSE	1-01-001 ANGLIA
1-01-001 AIMLESSLY	R-THE-OTHER	1-01-001 AMBROSIAL	1-01-001 ANGLICANISM
1-01-001 AINSLEY	1-01-001 ALL-TOO-BRIEF	1-01-001 AMBULANCES	1-01-001 ANGLING
1-01-001 AINSWORTH	1-01-001 ALL-VICTORIOUS	1-01-001 AMBULATORY	1-01-001 ANGLO-*AMERICAN
1-01-001 AINU	1-01-001 ALL-WOMAN	1-01-001 AMBUSCADE	S
1-01-001 AINUS	1-01-001 ALLAH	1-01-001 AMBUSHES	1-01-001 ANGLO-*JEWISH
1-01-001 AIR-CELL	1-01-001 ALLEGE	1-01-001 AMENDING	1-01-001 ANGLO-*PROTESTA
1-01-001 AIR-CONDITIONED	1-01-001 ALLEGHENIES	1-01-001 AMENDMENT'S	NT
1-01-001 AIR-DRIFTS	1-01-001 ALLEGHENY	1-01-001 AMENITSKII	1-01-001 ANGLO-*SAXONS
1-01-001 AIR-FRAME	1-01-001 ALLEGIANCES	1-01-001 AMERICAN'S	1-01-001 ANGLO-SAXON
1-01-001 AIR-TO-SURFACE	1-01-001 ALLEGRETTI	1-01-001 AMERICAN-*JEWIS	1-01-001 ANGLOPHILIA
1-01-001 AIRCRAFT'S	1-01-001 ALLEMANDS	H	1-01-001 ANGLOPHOBIA
1-01-001 AIRDROPS	1-01-001 ALLEN'S	1-01-001 AMERICAN-TRAINE	1-01-001 ANGRIEST
1-01-001 AIREDALE	1-01-001 ALLERGIES	D	1-01-001 ANHALT-*BERNBUR
1-01-001 AIRFLOW	1-01-001 ALLERGY	1-01-001 AMERICAS	G
1-01-001 AIRFRAME	1-01-001 ALLEVIATING	1-01-001 AMICABLE	1-01-001 ANHEMOLYTICUS
1-01-001 AIRLIFT	1-01-001 ALLEYS	1-01-001 AMICABLY	1-01-001 ANHWEI
1-01-001 AIRLINE'S	1-01-001 ALLEYWAYS	1-01-001 AMICAM	1-01-001 ANHYDROUS
1-01-001 AIRLOCK	1-01-001 ALLIANCE'S	1-01-001 AMIDE	1-01-001 ANHYDROUSLY
1-01-001 AIRMAN'S	1-01-001 ALLIANCES	1-01-001 AMINO	1-01-001 ANILINE
1-01-001 AIRMEN	1-01-001 ALLIGATORED	1-01-001 AMIS	1-01-001 ANIMAL-LIKE
1-01-001 AIRPARK	1-01-001 ALLISON	1-01-001 AMITY	1-01-001 ANIMATE
1-01-001 AIRSPEED	1-01-001 ALLISON'S	1-01-001 AMMONIAC	1-01-001 ANIMISM
1-01-001 AIRSTRIPS	1-01-001 ALLITERATION	1-01-001 AMMONIUM	1-01-001 ANIMIZED
1-01-001 AKITA	1-01-001 ALLITERATIVE	1-01-001 AMORALITY	1-01-001 ANION
1-01-001 AKRON	1-01-001 ALLONS	1-01-001 AMORIST	1-01-001 ANIONICS
1-01-001 ALABAMANS	1-01-001 ALLOT	1-01-001 AMORPHOUSLY	1-01-001 ANIONS
1-01-001 ALABAMIAN	1-01-001 ALLOTED	1-01-001 AMORY	1-01-001 ANISOTROPY
1-01-001 ALAI	1-01-001 ALLOTTING	1-01-001 AMOUNTING	1-01-001 ANKARA
1-01-001 ALAIN	1-01-001 ALLSO	1-01-001 AMP/LUMEN	1-01-001 ANNAMORENA
1-01-001 ALAMEIN	1-01-001 ALLSTATES'	1-01-001 AMPHETAMINES	1-01-001 ANNEE
1-01-001 ALAMO	1-01-001 ALLSTATES-*ZENI	1-01-001 AMPHIBIOUS	1-01-001 ANNEX
1-01-001 ALAMOGORDO	TH	1-01-001 AMPHIBOLOGY	1-01-001 ANNIE
1-01-001 ALARMING	1-01-001 ALLUDED	1-01-001 AMPHITHEATER	1-01-001 ANNIHILATE
1-01-001 ALARMIST	1-01-001 ALLUDES	1-01-001 AMPLIFIERS	1-01-001 ANNISBERG
1-01-001 ALARMS	1-01-001 ALLUDING	1-01-001 AMPLIFY	1-01-001 ANNISTON'S
1-01-001 ALBA	1-01-001 ALLURE	1-01-001 AMPLIFYING	1-01-001 ANNIVERSARIES
1-01-001 ALBACORE	1-01-001 ALLUREMENT	1-01-001 AMPUTATED	1-01-001 ANNOUNCER'S
1-01-001 ALBERS	1-01-001 ALLURING	1-01-001 AMRA	1-01-001 ANNOUNCERS
1-01-001 ALBICANS	1-01-001 ALLUSIVENESS	1-01-001 AMT	1-01-001 ANNOYANCES
1-01-001 ALBRIGHTS'	1-01-001 ALMADEN	1-01-001 AMULET	1-01-001 ANNOYS
1-01-001 ALCHEMY	1-01-001 ALMANAC	1-01-001 AMULETS	1-01-001 ANNUNCIATED

1-01-001 ANODES	1-01-001 ANYPLACE	1-01-001 ARCHBISHOPS'	1-01-001 ARTHUR'S
1-01-001 ANOMALIES	1-01-001 ANYTHIN	1-01-001 ARCHDIOCESE	1-01-001 ARTICULATION
1-01-001 ANOMALOUS	1-01-001 ANYWAYS	1-01-001 ARCHENEMY	1-01-001 ARTICULATIONS
1-01-001 ANOMALY	1-01-001 ANZILOTTI	1-01-001 ARCHEOLOGICAL	1-01-001 ARTIFACTS
1-01-001 ANOMIC	1-01-001 AOUELLOUL	1-01-001 ARCHERY	1-01-001 ARTIFICE
1-01-001 ANOMIE	1-01-001 APACHE	1-01-001 ARCHFOOL	1-01-001 ARTIFICER
1-01-001 ANOREXIA	1-01-001 APALACHICOLA	1-01-001 ARCHIMEDES	1-01-001 ARTIFICIALITY
1-01-001 ANORTHIC	1-01-001 APARICIO	1-01-001 ARCHING	1-01-001 ARTILLERIST
1-01-001 ANOUILH	1-01-001 APARTMENT-BUILD ING	1-01-001 ARCHITECTONIC	1-01-001 ARTIST-AUTHOR
1-01-001 ANSELM'S	1-01-001 APATHETIC	1-01-001 ARCHITECTS'	1-01-001 ARTIST-NATURE
1-01-001 ANSELMO	1-01-001 APERGILLUS	1-01-001 ARCHITECTURES	1-01-001 ARTKINO
1-01-001 ANSLEY	1-01-001 APHRODITE	1-01-001 ARCHTYPE	1-01-001 ARTUR
1-01-001 ANSON	1-01-001 APLOMB	1-01-001 ARCHULETA	1-01-001 ARTY
1-01-001 ANSUH	1-01-001 APOCRYPHA	1-01-001 ARCILLA	1-01-001 ARVEY
1-01-001 ANSWERABLE	1-01-001 APOCRYPHAL	1-01-001 ARCLIKE	1-01-001 ARYL
1-01-001 ANTAGONISED	1-01-001 APOLLO'S	1-01-001 ARCO	1-01-001 ARYLESTERASES
1-01-001 ANTAGONIZE	1-01-001 APOLLONIAN	1-01-001 ARCUS	1-01-001 AS-IT-WERE
1-01-001 ANTARCTICA	1-01-001 APOLOGIA	1-01-001 ARDMORE	1-01-001 ASBESTOS
1-01-001 ANTARES	1-01-001 APOLOGIE	1-01-001 AREA(S	1-01-001 ASBESTOS-CEMENT
1-01-001 ANTEATER	1-01-001 APOLOGIST	1-01-001 AREAWAYS	1-01-001 ASCEND
1-01-001 ANTECEDENT	1-01-001 APOLOGIZE	1-01-001 ARENULA	1-01-001 ASCENDANCY
1-01-001 ANTENNAS	1-01-001 APOSTATES	1-01-001 AREOSOL	1-01-001 ASCENT
1-01-001 ANTERIORS	1-01-001 APOTHEOSIS	1-01-001 AREQUIPA	1-01-001 ASCERTAINABLE
1-01-001 ANTHEM	1-01-001 APPALACHIAN	1-01-001 ARES	1-01-001 ASCETIC
1-01-001 ANTHEMS	1-01-001 APPALACHIANS	1-01-001 ARGENTINA	1-01-001 ASCETICISM
1-01-001 ANTHONY'S	1-01-001 APPALLINGLY	1-01-001 ARGIVE	1-01-001 ASCH
1-01-001 ANTHROPOLOGICAL	1-01-001 APPALOOSAS	1-01-001 ARGONAUTS	1-01-001 ASCHENBACH
1-01-001 ANTHROPOLOGICAL -RELIGIOUS	1-01-001 APPANAGE	1-01-001 ARGOS	1-01-001 ASCRIBE
1-01-001 ANTHROPOMORPHIC	1-01-001 APPARELED	1-01-001 ARGOT	1-01-001 ASCRIBES
1-01-001 ANTI	1-01-001 APPARENCY	1-01-001 ARGUMENTATION	1-01-001 ASEPTIC
1-01-001 ANTI-**J*RH	1-01-001 APPEARIN	1-01-001 ARHAT	1-01-001 ASH-*CAN
1-01-001 ANTI-*AMERICANI SM	1-01-001 APPEASING	1-01-001 ARHATS	1-01-001 ASH-BLONDE
1-01-001 ANTI-*CASTRO	1-01-001 APPELLANT	1-01-001 ARIANISM	1-01-001 ASHAM'D
1-01-001 ANTI-*CATHOLIC	1-01-001 APPENDAGES	1-01-001 ARIANIST	1-01-001 ASHER
1-01-001 ANTI-*CATHOLICI SM	1-01-001 APPENDIXES	1-01-001 ARIANISTS	1-01-001 ASHIKAGA
1-01-001 ANTI-*CHRISTIAN	1-01-001 APPIAN	1-01-001 ARIGATO	1-01-001 ASHLEY
1-01-001 ANTI-*COLMER	1-01-001 APPLAUSE-HAPPY	1-01-001 ARISTOCRATICALL Y	1-01-001 ASHMAN
1-01-001 ANTI-*COMMUNISM	1-01-001 APPLE-TREE	1-01-001 ARISTOTELEAN-*T HOMISTIC	1-01-001 ASHMOLEAN
1-01-001 ANTI-*COMMUNIST S	1-01-001 APPLEBY	1-01-001 ARITHMETICAL	1-01-001 ASHTRAYS
1-01-001 ANTI-*KENNEDY	1-01-001 APPLEJACK	1-01-001 ARITHMETIZED	1-01-001 ASIANS
1-01-001 ANTI-*NEGRO	1-01-001 APPLETON	1-01-001 ARKABUTLA	1-01-001 ASIATIC
1-01-001 ANTI-*NEWTONIAN	1-01-001 APPLICATOR	1-01-001 ARKANSAS'	1-01-001 ASILOMAR
1-01-001 ANTI-ASSIGNMENT	1-01-001 APPLIQUES	1-01-001 ARLEIGH	1-01-001 ASIMOV'S
1-01-001 ANTI-AUTHORITAR IAN	1-01-001 APPOINTING	1-01-001 ARLEN'S	1-01-001 ASKANCE
1-01-001 ANTI-CLERICALIS M	1-01-001 APPOINTS	1-01-001 ARLENE'S	1-01-001 ASKEW
1-01-001 ANTI-DEMOCRATIC	1-01-001 APPORTION	1-01-001 ARM-RISE	1-01-001 ASKIN
1-01-001 ANTI-DISCRIMINA TION	1-01-001 APPRAISED	1-01-001 ARMADA'S	1-01-001 ASKINGTON'S
1-01-001 ANTI-DISCRIMINA TORY	1-01-001 APPRAISERS	1-01-001 ARMAGEDDON	1-01-001 ASLEEEP
1-01-001 ANTI-FREEZE	1-01-001 APPRAISING	1-01-001 ARMAMENT	1-01-001 ASOCIAL
1-01-001 ANTI-INTELLECTU ALISM	1-01-001 APPRAISINGLY	1-01-001 ARMBRO	1-01-001 ASPARAGUS
1-01-001 ANTI-LIQUOR	1-01-001 APPRECIATES	1-01-001 ARMENIAN	1-01-001 ASPENCADE
1-01-001 ANTI-MISSILE	1-01-001 APPRECIATING	1-01-001 ARMENTIERES	1-01-001 ASPIRED
1-01-001 ANTI-PERSONALIT Y	1-01-001 APPRECIATIONS	1-01-001 ARMFUL	1-01-001 ASPIRES
1-01-001 ANTI-POLIO	1-01-001 APPREHEND	1-01-001 ARMIDE	1-01-001 ASPIRING
1-01-001 ANTI-RECESSION	1-01-001 APPRENTICED	1-01-001 ARMINES	1-01-001 ASS'NS'
1-01-001 ANTIBIOTIC	1-01-001 APPROACHABLE	1-01-001 ARMISTEADS	1-01-001 ASSAI
1-01-001 ANTIBIOTICS	1-01-001 APPROPRIATES	1-01-001 ARMLOAD	1-01-001 ASSAILANTS
1-01-001 ANTIC	1-01-001 APPROVES	1-01-001 ARMOIRE	1-01-001 ASSAILING
1-01-001 ANTICIPATORY	1-01-001 APPROVING	1-01-001 ARMOND	1-01-001 ASSASSINATED
1-01-001 ANTICOAGULATION	1-01-001 APRICOT	1-01-001 ARMORY	1-01-001 ASSASSINS
1-01-001 ANTICUS	1-01-001 APRIL-*JUNE	1-01-001 ARMORY'S	1-01-001 ASSAULTING
1-01-001 ANTIFUNDAMENTAL IST	1-01-001 APRONS	1-01-001 ARMPITS	1-01-001 ASSAY
1-01-001 ANTIGONE	1-01-001 APROPOS	1-01-001 ARMS-MAKING	1-01-001 ASSAYED
1-01-001 ANTIHISTORICAL	1-01-001 APSES	1-01-001 ARNICA	1-01-001 ASSEMBLAGES
1-01-001 ANTINOMIANS	1-01-001 APTITUDES	1-01-001 ARNOLD-*FOSTER	1-01-001 ASSER
1-01-001 ANTIPHONAL	1-01-001 APTNESS	1-01-001 AROMATICK	1-01-001 ASSERTIVENESS
1-01-001 ANTIPODES	1-01-001 AQUA-LUNG	1-01-001 AROUNY	1-01-001 ASSESMENT
1-01-001 ANTIQUARIAN	1-01-001 AQUACUTIE	1-01-001 ARPEGGIOS	1-01-001 ASSESSOR'S
1-01-001 ANTIQUARIANS	1-01-001 AQUAM	1-01-001 ARRACK	1-01-001 ASSESSORS'
1-01-001 ANTIQUITIES	1-01-001 AQUEDUCTS	1-01-001 ARRAGON	1-01-001 ASSIDUITY
1-01-001 ANTIREDEPOSITIO N	1-01-001 AQUISITION	1-01-001 ARRAIGNING	1-01-001 ASSISTS
1-01-001 ANTISLAVERY	1-01-001 ARABESQUE	1-01-001 ARRANGERS	1-01-001 ASSOCIATION'S
1-01-001 ANTITHETICAL	1-01-001 ARABIA	1-01-001 ARRANGES	1-01-001 ASSOCIATIVELY
1-01-001 ANTITRUST	1-01-001 ARABIAN-*AMERIC AN	1-01-001 ARRINGTON	1-01-001 ASSONANCE
1-01-001 ANTOINE	1-01-001 ARABIANS	1-01-001 ARROGANTLY	1-01-001 ASSORTMENT
1-01-001 ANTOINETTE	1-01-001 ARABS	1-01-001 ARROGATE	1-01-001 ASSYRIOLOGY
1-01-001 ANTONE	1-01-001 ARABS'	1-01-001 ARROWED	1-01-001 ASTAIRES
1-01-001 ANTONINI	1-01-001 ARABY	1-01-001 ARROWHEAD	1-01-001 ASTARTE
1-01-001 ANVIL	1-01-001 ARAK	1-01-001 ARROWHEADS	1-01-001 ASTEROID
1-01-001 ANXIETIES	1-01-001 ARANSAS	1-01-001 ARSENIC	1-01-001 ASTEROIDAL
1-01-001 ANXIETY-RELEASE D	1-01-001 ARATA	1-01-001 ARSHINKOFF	1-01-001 ASTERS
	1-01-001 ARBEITSKOMMANDO	1-01-001 ARSIDE	1-01-001 ASTHMA
1-01-001 ANYBODY'D	1-01-001 ARBITRATED	1-01-001 ARSINES	1-01-001 ASTIN
1-01-001 ANYE	1-01-001 ARBOR	1-01-001 ART-FILLED	1-01-001 ASTOUND
1-01-001 ANYLABEL	1-01-001 ARBOREAL	1-01-001 ART-HISTORIAN	1-01-001 ASTRA
	1-01-001 ARBRITRARY	1-01-001 ART-SHOP	1-01-001 ASTRAL
	1-01-001 ARBUCKLE'S	1-01-001 ARTE'S	1-01-001 ASTRINGENCY
	1-01-001 ARCADED	1-01-001 ARTEMIS	1-01-001 ASTRINGENT
	1-01-001 ARCH-ENEMY	1-01-001 ARTERIOLAR-PULM ONARY	1-01-001 ASTRONOMER
	1-01-001 ARCH-HERETIC	1-01-001 ARTERIOSCLEROSI S	1-01-001 ASTRONOMICALLY
	1-01-001 ARCH-OPPONENT		1-01-001 ASTUTE
	1-01-001 ARCHAEOLOGISTS	1-01-001 ARTERY'S	1-01-001 ASTUTENESS
	1-01-001 ARCHAISM	1-01-001 ARTFUL	1-01-001 ASTWOOD
	1-01-001 ARCHAIZED	1-01-001 ARTFULNESS	1-01-001 ASUNDER
	1-01-001 ARCHANGELS		1-01-001 ASW
			1-01-001 ASYLUM
			1-01-001 ASYMMETRY

Code	Word	Code	Word	Code	Word	Code	Word
1-01-001	ASYMPTOTIC	1-01-001	AVARICIOUS	1-01-001	BAKE-OVEN	1-01-001	BARE-ARMED
1-01-001	ASYMPTOTICALLY	1-01-001	AVEC	1-01-001	BAKERSFIELD	1-01-001	BARE-FOOTED
1-01-001	AT-BATS	1-01-001	AVENTINE	1-01-001	BAKES	1-01-001	BAREFOOTED
1-01-001	ATAVISTIC	1-01-001	AVENTINO	1-01-001	BAKHTIARI	1-01-001	BARFLIES
1-01-001	ATERMAN	1-01-001	AVERT	1-01-001	BAKLAVA	1-01-001	BARGAIN-PRICED
1-01-001	ATH	1-01-001	AVERY	1-01-001	BAKU	1-01-001	BARGEN
1-01-001	ATHEARN	1-01-001	AVIARY	1-01-001	BAL	1-01-001	BARGING
1-01-001	ATHEISTIC	1-01-001	AVIATORS	1-01-001	BALAGUER'S	1-01-001	BARI'S
1-01-001	ATHENA	1-01-001	AVID	1-01-001	BALANCE-OF-PAYM	1-01-001	BARINGER
1-01-001	ATHEROMATOUS	1-01-001	AVIDITY		ENTS	1-01-001	BARIUM
1-01-001	ATHLETE'S	1-01-001	AVIDLY	1-01-001	BALANCE-WISE	1-01-001	BARKEEP
1-01-001	ATHLETES'	1-01-001	AVIS	1-01-001	BALANCES	1-01-001	BARN-BURNER'S
1-01-001	ATHLETICISM	1-01-001	AVIV	1-01-001	BALCOLM	1-01-001	BARNABA
1-01-001	ATLANTES	1-01-001	AVOCATION	1-01-001	BALDY	1-01-001	BARNARD'S
1-01-001	ATLANTICA	1-01-001	AVON	1-01-001	BALEFUL	1-01-001	BARNET
1-01-001	ATLEE	1-01-001	AWAKENS	1-01-001	BALENCIAGA	1-01-001	BARNSFUL
1-01-001	ATM,	1-01-001	AWASH	1-01-001	BALINESE	1-01-001	BARNSTORMER
1-01-001	ATOM-LIKE	1-01-001	AWAYE	1-01-001	BALKANIZE	1-01-001	BARNYARD
1-01-001	ATOMISATION	1-01-001	AWE-INSPIRING	1-01-001	BALKANIZING	1-01-001	BARNYARDS
1-01-001	ATONALLY	1-01-001	AWKWARDNESS	1-01-001	BALKINESS	1-01-001	BAROMETRIC
1-01-001	ATONE	1-01-001	AXIALLY	1-01-001	BALKING	1-01-001	BARONESS
1-01-001	ATROCIOUSLY	1-01-001	AXIOLOGICAL	1-01-001	BALKS	1-01-001	BARONIAL
1-01-001	ATROPHIED	1-01-001	AXIOM	1-01-001	BALL'S	1-01-001	BARONS
1-01-001	ATTACKER'S	1-01-001	AXLES	1-01-001	BALL-CARRIERS	1-01-001	BARONY
1-01-001	ATTACTIVE	1-01-001	AYA	1-01-001	BALL-HAWKING	1-01-001	BARORECEPTOR
1-01-001	ATTAINMENTS	1-01-001	AYE	1-01-001	BALLARD	1-01-001	BARR
1-01-001	ATTAINS	1-01-001	AYE-YAH-AH-AH	1-01-001	BALLARDS	1-01-001	BARRACK
1-01-001	ATTENTIONS	1-01-001	AYES	1-01-001	BALLED	1-01-001	BARRE-*MONTPELI
1-01-001	ATTENTIVELY	1-01-001	AYRES'	1-01-001	BALLERINA		ER
1-01-001	ATTESTING	1-01-001	AYSSHOM	1-01-001	BALLERINAS	1-01-001	BARREL-VAULTED
1-01-001	ATTICA	1-01-001	AYUB	1-01-001	BALLETOMANE	1-01-001	BARREL-WIDE
1-01-001	ATTILIO	1-01-001	AZERBAIJAN	1-01-001	BALLFIELDS	1-01-001	BARRETT
1-01-001	ATTIRED	1-01-001	AZUSA	1-01-001	BALLGOWNS	1-01-001	BARRETTE
1-01-001	ATTIS	1-01-001	B+	1-01-001	BALLING	1-01-001	BARROW
1-01-001	ATTLEE	1-01-001	B**.+*O	1-01-001	BALLISTICS	1-01-001	BARRYMORES
1-01-001	ATTOPEU	1-01-001	B**.*B**.*C	1-01-001	BALLOONING	1-01-001	BARSACS
1-01-001	ATTRACTIVELY	1-01-001	B**.*B**.*C**.'	1-01-001	BALLYHOO	1-01-001	BARTHA
1-01-001	ATTU		S	1-01-001	BALLYHOOEY	1-01-001	BARTHOLF
1-01-001	ATUNE	1-01-001	B**.*D	1-01-001	BALM-OF-*GILEAD	1-01-001	BARTOK
1-01-001	ATWELLS	1-01-001	B**.*S	1-01-001	BALSAMS	1-01-001	BARTOL
1-01-001	ATYPICAL	1-01-001	B**.C	1-01-001	BALTIMOREAN	1-01-001	BARTOLI'S
1-01-001	AUBERGE	1-01-001	B**.T**.U**./SQ	1-01-001	BAMBI	1-01-001	BAS
1-01-001	AUBR	1-01-001	B'DIKKAT'S	1-01-001	BANANAS	1-01-001	BASE-RUNNER
1-01-001	AUBREY'S	1-01-001	BA-A-A	1-01-001	BANBURY	1-01-001	BASE-STEALING
1-01-001	AUCTIONEER	1-01-001	BABATUNDE	1-01-001	BANCROFT'S	1-01-001	BASEBALLIGHT
1-01-001	AUCTIONEER'S	1-01-001	BABBITING	1-01-001	BANDAGING	1-01-001	BASEBALLS
1-01-001	AUDIBLY	1-01-001	BABCOCK	1-01-001	BANDING	1-01-001	BASELESS
1-01-001	AUDITING	1-01-001	BABIN-*FESTIVAL	1-01-001	BANDISH	1-01-001	BASELINE
1-01-001	AUDITIONING	1-01-001	BABY-SITTER	1-01-001	BANDITOS	1-01-001	BASER
1-01-001	AUDITOR	1-01-001	BABYHOOD	1-01-001	BANDOLEERS	1-01-001	BASHIR
1-01-001	AUDITS	1-01-001	BACCARAT	1-01-001	BANDON	1-01-001	BASHO'S
1-01-001	AUDIVI	1-01-001	BACCHUS	1-01-001	BANDWAGON	1-01-001	BASICS
1-01-001	AUDREY	1-01-001	BACHELOR-TYPE	1-01-001	BANDWIDTH	1-01-001	BASIE
1-01-001	AUERBACH'S	1-01-001	BACI	1-01-001	BANEFUL	1-01-001	BASIL
1-01-001	AUGEN	1-01-001	BACK-ISSUE	1-01-001	BANFIELD	1-01-001	BASILEIS
1-01-001	AUGMENT	1-01-001	BACK-LIGHTED	1-01-001	BANG-SASHES	1-01-001	BASKED
1-01-001	AUGURS	1-01-001	BACK-YARD	1-01-001	BANGISH	1-01-001	BASKETBALL-PLAY
1-01-001	AUGUSTA'S	1-01-001	BACKBEND	1-01-001	BANGKOK		ING
1-01-001	AUGUSTAN	1-01-001	BACKLASH	1-01-001	BANGLES	1-01-001	BASLER
1-01-001	AUGUSTIN	1-01-001	BACKPACK	1-01-001	BANI	1-01-001	BASSES
1-01-001	AUGUSTINE'S	1-01-001	BACKSIDE	1-01-001	BANISHES	1-01-001	BASSI
1-01-001	AUJOURD	1-01-001	BACKSTAIRS	1-01-001	BANISHING	1-01-001	BASSINET
1-01-001	AUNT'S	1-01-001	BACKSTITCHING	1-01-001	BANISHMENT	1-01-001	BASSIS
1-01-001	AURA	1-01-001	BACKWATER	1-01-001	BANKER-EDITOR	1-01-001	BAST
1-01-001	AURAL	1-01-001	BACKWOODS-AND-S	1-01-001	BANKHEAD	1-01-001	BASTARD'S
1-01-001	AUSCHWITZ		AND-HILL	1-01-001	BANKS'S	1-01-001	BASTIANINI
1-01-001	AUSPICIOUS	1-01-001	BAD-FITTING	1-01-001	BANNING	1-01-001	BATCHELDER
1-01-001	AUSPICIOUSLY	1-01-001	BADE	1-01-001	BANNNNNNG	1-01-001	BATES'
1-01-001	AUSTERELY	1-01-001	BADEN-*BADEN	1-01-001	BANQUETINGS	1-01-001	BATHAR-ON-*WALL
1-01-001	AUSTERITY	1-01-001	BADGE-TOTER	1-01-001	BANS		
1-01-001	AUSTRALITES	1-01-001	BADGERING	1-01-001	BANSHEE	1-01-001	BATHERS
1-01-001	AUTHENTICATE	1-01-001	BADGES	1-01-001	BANTERED	1-01-001	BATHOS
1-01-001	AUTHENTICATED	1-01-001	BADINAGE	1-01-001	BANTERING	1-01-001	BATHROOMS
1-01-001	AUTHENTICATION	1-01-001	BADLANDS	1-01-001	BANTU	1-01-001	BATHTUBS
1-01-001	AUTHENTICATIONS	1-01-001	BADLY-NEEDED	1-01-001	BAPTISMAL	1-01-001	BATHYRAN
1-01-001	AUTHENTICATOR	1-01-001	BADMEN	1-01-001	BAPTISMS	1-01-001	BATTALIONS
1-01-001	AUTHORITATIVELY	1-01-001	BADMINTON	1-01-001	BAPTIST'S	1-01-001	BATTER'S
1-01-001	AUTHORS'	1-01-001	BADRAWI	1-01-001	BAPTISTE	1-01-001	BATTERIE
1-01-001	AUTO-*EUROPE	1-01-001	BADS	1-01-001	BAPTISTERY	1-01-001	BATTERS
1-01-001	AUTO-LIMITATION	1-01-001	BADURA-*SKODA-*	1-01-001	BAR'L	1-01-001	BATTLE-AX
1-01-001	AUTO-LOADERS		VIENNA	1-01-001	BAR-**J*H,	1-01-001	BATTLE-CRY
1-01-001	AUTOBIOGRAPHIC	1-01-001	BAFFIN	1-01-001	BAR-BUDDY	1-01-001	BATTLE-SHATTER
1-01-001	AUTOCRATIC	1-01-001	BAFFLE	1-01-001	BARACLOUGH		
1-01-001	AUTOCRATS	1-01-001	BAFFLERS	1-01-001	BARAGINING	1-01-001	BATTLEFRONT
1-01-001	AUTOMATE	1-01-001	BAGATELLES	1-01-001	BARATARIA	1-01-001	BATTLEMENTS
1-01-001	AUTOMATON	1-01-001	BAGGED	1-01-001	BARBARIAN	1-01-001	BATWINGS
1-01-001	AUTONAVIGATOR	1-01-001	BAGH	1-01-001	BARBARIC	1-01-001	BAUBLE
1-01-001	AUTOPSIED	1-01-001	BAGLEY	1-01-001	BARBAROUS	1-01-001	BAUBLES
1-01-001	AUTOSUGGESTIBIL	1-01-001	BAGPIPE	1-01-001	BARBED-WIRE	1-01-001	BAUDELAIRE
	ITY	1-01-001	BAH	1-01-001	BARBER'S	1-01-001	BAUER
1-01-001	AUTUMN-TOUCHED	1-01-001	BAHI	1-01-001	BARBITAL	1-01-001	BAUER-*ECSY
1-01-001	AUTUMNAL	1-01-001	BAHIA	1-01-001	BARBITURATE	1-01-001	BAUHAUS
1-01-001	AUX	1-01-001	BAINES	1-01-001	BARBOUR	1-01-001	BAWHS
1-01-001	AVAILING	1-01-001	BAITED	1-01-001	BARBUDOS	1-01-001	BAWLING
1-01-001	AVALANCHE	1-01-001	BAKE-*OFF	1-01-001	BARCUS'	1-01-001	BAY-FRONT
1-01-001	AVALIABLE	1-01-001	BAKE-OFF	1-01-001	BARDALL	1-01-001	BAYADERKA
1-01-001	AVANT	1-01-001	BAKE-OFFS	1-01-001	BARDELL	1-01-001	BAYANIHAN

70

1-01-001 BAYERISCHE	1-01-001 BEGINNERS	1-01-001 BERTHELIER	1-01-001 BIG-GAME
1-01-001 BAYING	1-01-001 BEGS	1-01-001 BERTO'S	1-01-001 BIG-LARGE
1-01-001 BAYLEEFE	1-01-001 BEGUILE	1-01-001 BERTOIA	1-01-001 BIG-LEAGUE
1-01-001 BAYLOR'S	1-01-001 BEHAHN	1-01-001 BERTON	1-01-001 BIG-SHOULDERED
1-01-001 BAYLY	1-01-001 BEHAN	1-01-001 BERTORELLI	1-01-001 BIG-STAGE
1-01-001 BAZAARS	1-01-001 BEHAVIORALLY	1-01-001 BERTRAND	1-01-001 BIG-TICKET
1-01-001 BD	1-01-001 BEHAVIORS	1-01-001 BERYLLIUM	1-01-001 BIG-TOWN
1-01-001 BEACH-DRIFT	1-01-001 BEHEADING	1-01-001 BESEECH	1-01-001 BIGOTED
1-01-001 BEACH-HEAD	1-01-001 BEHOLDS	1-01-001 BESETS	1-01-001 BIGOTS
1-01-001 BEACHING	1-01-001 BEHOOVES	1-01-001 BESETTING	1-01-001 BIJOUTERIE
1-01-001 BEAD	1-01-001 BEIDERBECKE	1-01-001 BESIEGE	1-01-001 BIKINIS
1-01-001 BEADED	1-01-001 BEIGE	1-01-001 BESIEGING	1-01-001 BILHARZIASIS
1-01-001 BEADLES	1-01-001 BEIGE'S	1-01-001 BESMIRCH	1-01-001 BILINEAR
1-01-001 BEADLES'	1-01-001 BEIRUT	1-01-001 BESMIRCHED	1-01-001 BILINGUAL
1-01-001 BEADSMAN	1-01-001 BEISMORTIER	1-01-001 BESMIRCHING	1-01-001 BILLBOARD
1-01-001 BEADY	1-01-001 BEKKAI	1-01-001 BESPEAK	1-01-001 BILLET
1-01-001 BEAKERS	1-01-001 BEL-*AIR	1-01-001 BESPEAKS	1-01-001 BILLETS
1-01-001 BEALLSVILLE	1-01-001 BELA	1-01-001 BESSET	1-01-001 BILLIARD
1-01-001 BEAR'S	1-01-001 BELAFONTE	1-01-001 BESSIE	1-01-001 BILLINGS
1-01-001 BEAR-LIKE	1-01-001 BELANGER	1-01-001 BEST'S	1-01-001 BILLOWED
1-01-001 BEARDLESS	1-01-001 BELATEDLY	1-01-001 BEST-EDUCATED	1-01-001 BILLOWS
1-01-001 BEARDOWN	1-01-001 BELFRY	1-01-001 BEST-GAITED	1-01-001 BIMINI
1-01-001 BEARDSLEE	1-01-001 BELIEVABLE	1-01-001 BEST-HEARTED	1-01-001 BIMOLECULAR
1-01-001 BEARDSLEY'S	1-01-001 BELIEVABLY	1-01-001 BEST-KNOWN	1-01-001 BIMONTHLY
1-01-001 BEASTIES	1-01-001 BELITTLING	1-01-001 BEST-LOOKING	1-01-001 BINDER
1-01-001 BEAT-UP	1-01-001 BELLAMY'S	1-01-001 BEST-PRESERVED	1-01-001 BINDLE
1-01-001 BEATIFIC	1-01-001 BELLE	1-01-001 BEST-SELLER	1-01-001 BINGE
1-01-001 BEATIFICATION	1-01-001 BELLES	1-01-001 BEST-SELLERS	1-01-001 BINGLES
1-01-001 BEATITUDES	1-01-001 BELLEVILLE	1-01-001 BEST-SELLING	1-01-001 BINI
1-01-001 BEAUCHAMPS	1-01-001 BELLHOPS	1-01-001 BEST-TEMPERED	1-01-001 BINUCLEAR
1-01-001 BEAULIEU	1-01-001 BELLICOSITY	1-01-001 BESTED	1-01-001 BIO-
1-01-001 BEAUTEOUS	1-01-001 BELLIGERENTLY	1-01-001 BESTER	1-01-001 BIO-*DYNAMIC
1-01-001 BEAUTIFULLY-BUI	1-01-001 BELLOW'S	1-01-001 BESTES	1-01-001 BIO-MEDICAL
LT	1-01-001 BELLWETHERS	1-01-001 BESTIAL	1-01-001 BIOGRAPHER
1-01-001 BEAUTIFULLY-TAP	1-01-001 BELLWOOD	1-01-001 BESTIMMUNG	1-01-001 BIOGRAPHERS
ERED	1-01-001 BELLYFULL	1-01-001 BESTSELLING	1-01-001 BIOLOGIC
1-01-001 BEAUTIFY	1-01-001 BELSHAZZAR	1-01-001 BESTUBBLED	1-01-001 BIOLOGICALLY
1-01-001 BEAUTIFYING	1-01-001 BELT-DRIVEN	1-01-001 BETE	1-01-001 BIOPHYSICIST
1-01-001 BEAUTY'S	1-01-001 BELTING	1-01-001 BETEL-STAINED	1-01-001 BIOPSIES
1-01-001 BEAUTY-IDIOM	1-01-001 BELZEC	1-01-001 BETHEL	1-01-001 BIOSYNTHESIZED
1-01-001 BEAUX-*ARTS	1-01-001 BEMADDENING	1-01-001 BETHLEHEM	1-01-001 BIRACIAL
1-01-001 BEAVERTAIL	1-01-001 BEMAN	1-01-001 BETHOUGHT	1-01-001 BIRCH-PANELED
1-01-001 BEBOP	1-01-001 BEMOAN	1-01-001 BETRAYER	1-01-001 BIRCHES
1-01-001 BECALMED	1-01-001 BEMOANS	1-01-001 BETRAYING	1-01-001 BIRD'S
1-01-001 BECHHOFER	1-01-001 BEN'S	1-01-001 BETROTHAL	1-01-001 BIRD-BRAIN
1-01-001 BECK	1-01-001 BEN-*GURION	1-01-001 BETROTHED	1-01-001 BIRDBATH
1-01-001 BECKMAN	1-01-001 BEN-HADAD	1-01-001 BETSY	1-01-001 BIRDLIKE
1-01-001 BECKON	1-01-001 BENEDICTINE	1-01-001 BETTER-REMEMBER	1-01-001 BIRDWHISTELL
1-01-001 BECOMETH	1-01-001 BENEFICENCE	ED	1-01-001 BIRDWOOD
1-01-001 BECOMIN	1-01-001 BENEFICIENT	1-01-001 BETTER-THAN-AVE	1-01-001 BIRGIT
1-01-001 BED-HOPPED	1-01-001 BENESI	RAGE	1-01-001 BIRGITTA
1-01-001 BED-TIME	1-01-001 BENET'S	1-01-001 BETTERING	1-01-001 BIRNBAUM
1-01-001 BED-TYPE	1-01-001 BENETS	1-01-001 BETTIES	1-01-001 BIRTHCONTROL
1-01-001 BEDAZZLED	1-01-001 BENGALI	1-01-001 BETTY'S	1-01-001 BIRTHED
1-01-001 BEDAZZLEMENT	1-01-001 BENIGN	1-01-001 BEVELING	1-01-001 BIRTHRIGHT
1-01-001 BEDBUGS	1-01-001 BENITA	1-01-001 BEVELS	1-01-001 BISHOPRY
1-01-001 BEDDED	1-01-001 BENNETT	1-01-001 BEVOR	1-01-001 BISHOPS'
1-01-001 BEDFAST	1-01-001 BENOIT	1-01-001 BEWAIL	1-01-001 BISMARCK
1-01-001 BEDGROUND	1-01-001 BENSON'S	1-01-001 BEWHISKERED	1-01-001 BISMARK
1-01-001 BEDLAM	1-01-001 BENT-*ARM	1-01-001 BEWILDEREDLY	1-01-001 BISON
1-01-001 BEDPOST	1-01-001 BENTLEYS	1-01-001 BEWILDERINGLY	1-01-001 BIT-LIKE
1-01-001 BEDRAGGLED	1-01-001 BENZEDRINE	1-01-001 BEWILDERS	1-01-001 BITER
1-01-001 BEDROOM'S	1-01-001 BENZELL	1-01-001 BEWITCHING	1-01-001 BITTERS
1-01-001 BEDSPRINGS	1-01-001 BEOWULF'S	1-01-001 BEXAR	1-01-001 BITTERSWEET
1-01-001 BEDSTRAW	1-01-001 BERCHE	1-01-001 BEYOND-NORMAL	1-01-001 BIX
1-01-001 BEE'S	1-01-001 BEREA	1-01-001 BHOY	1-01-001 BIZET'S
1-01-001 BEE-*HUNTER	1-01-001 BEREAVEMENTS	1-01-001 BI-MONTHLY	1-01-001 BJERRE'S
1-01-001 BEEBE'S	1-01-001 BERG'S	1-01-001 BIASES	1-01-001 BLABBED
1-01-001 BEEF'S	1-01-001 BERGAMASCHI	1-01-001 BIBB	1-01-001 BLABER
1-01-001 BEEF-FAT	1-01-001 BERGS	1-01-001 BIBLE-EMANCIPAT	1-01-001 BLACK-AND-ORANG
1-01-001 BEEF-FEEDING	1-01-001 BERGSON	ED	E
1-01-001 BEEF-HUNGRY	1-01-001 BERIBBONED	1-01-001 BIBLE-LOVING	1-01-001 BLACK-AND-YELLO
1-01-001 BEEFED	1-01-001 BERINGER	1-01-001 BIBLES	W
1-01-001 BEEFORE	1-01-001 BERKELEY	1-01-001 BIBLICALLY	1-01-001 BLACK-BALLED
1-01-001 BEEFSTEAK	1-01-001 BERKMAN	1-01-001 BIBLIOGRAPHICAL	1-01-001 BLACK-BEARDED
1-01-001 BEEFY	1-01-001 BERLIN-*WEST	1-01-001 BIBLIOPHILES	1-01-001 BLACK-CLAD
1-01-001 BEEHIVE	1-01-001 BERLINERS	1-01-001 BICAMERAL	1-01-001 BLACK-CROWNED
1-01-001 BEER-COOLING	1-01-001 BERLIOZ	1-01-001 BICARBONATE	1-01-001 BLACK-EYED
1-01-001 BEER-RUNNER	1-01-001 BERLITZ	1-01-001 BICEP	1-01-001 BLACK-HAIRED
1-01-001 BEER-RUNNERS	1-01-001 BERMAN'S	1-01-001 BICH	1-01-001 BLACK-MARKET
1-01-001 BEER-RUNNING	1-01-001 BERNADINE'S	1-01-001 BICHES	1-01-001 BLACK-TIPPED
1-01-001 BEERS	1-01-001 BERNARDINE	1-01-001 BICONCAVE	1-01-001 BLACKBIRDS
1-01-001 BEESEMYERS	1-01-001 BERNARDO	1-01-001 BICYCLE-AUTO	1-01-001 BLACKED-IN
1-01-001 BEETHOVEN'S	1-01-001 BERNE	1-01-001 BIDDIES	1-01-001 BLACKENING
1-01-001 BEETLES	1-01-001 BERNET	1-01-001 BIDDLE	1-01-001 BLACKEST
1-01-001 BEFELL	1-01-001 BERNHARD	1-01-001 BIDE	1-01-001 BLACKING
1-01-001 BEFITS	1-01-001 BERNIE	1-01-001 BIEN	1-01-001 BLACKMAILED
1-01-001 BEFITTING	1-01-001 BERNIECE	1-01-001 BIENNIAL	1-01-001 BLACKSTONE
1-01-001 BEFOGGED	1-01-001 BERNINI	1-01-001 BIENNIUM	1-01-001 BLACKWELL'S
1-01-001 BEFOH	1-01-001 BERNSTEIN	1-01-001 BIERCE	1-01-001 BLACKWELLS
1-01-001 BEFOULED	1-01-001 BERNZ-*O-*MATIC	1-01-001 BIETNAR	1-01-001 BLAIR
1-01-001 BEFUDDLES	1-01-001 BERONIO	1-01-001 BIFOCAL	1-01-001 BLANC
1-01-001 BEFUDDLING	1-01-001 BERRA'S	1-01-001 BIFUTEK-SAN	1-01-001 BLANCHE'S
1-01-001 BEGET	1-01-001 BERRELLEZ	1-01-001 BIG-BONED	1-01-001 BLANCHED
1-01-001 BEGGAR'S	1-01-001 BERRY'S	1-01-001 BIG-BUSINESS	1-01-001 BLANDNESS
1-01-001 BEGGARY	1-01-001 BERT	1-01-001 BIG-CHESTED	1-01-001 BLANKETED
1-01-001 BEGINNER	1-01-001 BERTEROS	1-01-001 BIG-DADDY	1-01-001 BLANTON

1-01-001 BLARED	1-01-001 BLYTH	1-01-001 BONGO	1-01-001 BOWDOIN
1-01-001 BLARING	1-01-001 BO	1-01-001 BONHAM	1-01-001 BOWELS
1-01-001 BLASPHEMED	1-01-001 BO'SUN'S	1-01-001 BONHEUR	1-01-001 BOWER
1-01-001 BLASTDOWN	1-01-001 BOADICEA	1-01-001 BONHO**DFFER	1-01-001 BOWERS
1-01-001 BLATANCY	1-01-001 BOAL	1-01-001 BONHOEFFER	1-01-001 BOWES
1-01-001 BLATZ'S	1-01-001 BOAR	1-01-001 BONIFACE'S	1-01-001 BOWIE
1-01-001 BLAUSTEIN	1-01-001 BOARDER	1-01-001 BONITO	1-01-001 BOWSTRING
1-01-001 BLAZER	1-01-001 BOARDING-HOME	1-01-001 BONJOUR	1-01-001 BOX-SIZED
1-01-001 BLAZON	1-01-001 BOARDINGHOUSES	1-01-001 BONNE	1-01-001 BOXED-IN
1-01-001 BLEACHER-TYPE	1-01-001 BOASTFULLY	1-01-001 BONNIE	1-01-001 BOXER
1-01-001 BLEAT	1-01-001 BOASTINGS	1-01-001 BOO	1-01-001 BOXFORD
1-01-001 BLEATING	1-01-001 BOAT'S	1-01-001 BOOBIFY	1-01-001 BOXWOOD
1-01-001 BLEATS	1-01-001 BOAT-YARD	1-01-001 BOOBOO	1-01-001 BOXY
1-01-001 BLEBS	1-01-001 BOATEL	1-01-001 BOOBY-TRAP	1-01-001 BOY-*LADY
1-01-001 BLECKLEY	1-01-001 BOATELS	1-01-001 BOOK-BURNING	1-01-001 BOY-*MARQUITA
1-01-001 BLEEDINGS	1-01-001 BOATERS	1-01-001 BOOK-LINED	1-01-001 BOY-FURIENDO
1-01-001 BLEEKER	1-01-001 BOATHOUSES	1-01-001 BOOK-REVIEW	1-01-001 BOY-MANAGER
1-01-001 BLEEPS	1-01-001 BOATLOAD	1-01-001 BOOK-SELECTION	1-01-001 BOY-MEETS-GIRL
1-01-001 BLEMISHES	1-01-001 BOATLOADS	1-01-001 BOOKCASES	1-01-001 BOY-NAME
1-01-001 BLENDING	1-01-001 BOATMEN	1-01-001 BOOKERS	1-01-001 BOYARS
1-01-001 BLEVINS'	1-01-001 BOATSMEN	1-01-001 BOOKINGS	1-01-001 BOYCE
1-01-001 BLIMP	1-01-001 BOB'S	1-01-001 BOOKISH	1-01-001 BOYCOTTED
1-01-001 BLIND-FOLDED	1-01-001 BOBBINS	1-01-001 BOOKLET	1-01-001 BOYLSTON
1-01-001 BLINKERS	1-01-001 BOBBLES	1-01-001 BOOKLISTS	1-01-001 BRACE'S
1-01-001 BLIPS	1-01-001 BOBBY-SOX	1-01-001 BOOKSELLER	1-01-001 BRACELET
1-01-001 BLISH'S	1-01-001 BOBBY-SOXER	1-01-001 BOOKSHELF	1-01-001 BRACHII
1-01-001 BLITZES	1-01-001 BOBIN-TO-CONE	1-01-001 BOOKWALTER	1-01-001 BRACKEN
1-01-001 BLIZZARDS	1-01-001 BOCK	1-01-001 BOOM-BOOM-BOOM	1-01-001 BRACKET
1-01-001 BLOCK-BUSTER	1-01-001 BOCKWURST	1-01-001 BOOMED	1-01-001 BRAD
1-01-001 BLOCKAGES	1-01-001 BODENHEIM	1-01-001 BOOMERANG	1-01-001 BRADDOCK-AGAINS
1-01-001 BLOCKHOUSE	1-01-001 BODES	1-01-001 BOOMERANGS	T-THE-*INDIANS
1-01-001 BLOIS	1-01-001 BODHISATTVA	1-01-001 BOOMING	1-01-001 BRADEN
1-01-001 BLOKE	1-01-001 BODIED	1-01-001 BOOMTOWN	1-01-001 BRADLEY'S
1-01-001 BLOKES	1-01-001 BODLEIAN	1-01-001 BOONTON	1-01-001 BRADY
1-01-001 BLONDE-HAIRED	1-01-001 BODY-BUILDING	1-01-001 BOORISH	1-01-001 BRADYKININ
1-01-001 BLONDE-HEADED	1-01-001 BODY-TISSUE	1-01-001 BOORS	1-01-001 BRAE
1-01-001 BLONDES	1-01-001 BODYBUILDING	1-01-001 BOOSTER	1-01-001 BRAGGADOCIO
1-01-001 BLOOD-BOUGHT	1-01-001 BODYGUARD	1-01-001 BOOSTS	1-01-001 BRAGGING
1-01-001 BLOOD-CHILLING	1-01-001 BODYWEIGHT	1-01-001 BOOT-WEARER	1-01-001 BRAHM'S
1-01-001 BLOOD-FILLED	1-01-001 BOEHMER	1-01-001 BOOTED	1-01-001 BRAIDED
1-01-001 BLOOD-FLECKED	1-01-001 BOEOTIAN	1-01-001 BOOTHBY	1-01-001 BRAIDING
1-01-001 BLOOD-FLOW	1-01-001 BOG	1-01-001 BOOTLE'S	1-01-001 BRAIDS
1-01-001 BLOOD-KINSHIP	1-01-001 BOGARTIAN	1-01-001 BOOTLEGGER	1-01-001 BRAILLE
1-01-001 BLOOD-LUST	1-01-001 BOGEY-SYMBOL	1-01-001 BOOTLEGGING	1-01-001 BRAILSFORD
1-01-001 BLOOD-SOAKED	1-01-001 BOGEYMEN	1-01-001 BORAK	1-01-001 BRAIN'S
1-01-001 BLOOD-SPECKED	1-01-001 BOGGED	1-01-001 BORATES	1-01-001 BRAIN-WRACKING
1-01-001 BLOOD-STAINED	1-01-001 BOGGLED	1-01-001 BORAX	1-01-001 BRAINARDS
1-01-001 BLOODED	1-01-001 BOGGS	1-01-001 BORDEAU	1-01-001 BRAINWASHING
1-01-001 BLOODIEST	1-01-001 BOGIES	1-01-001 BORDENS	1-01-001 BRAINY
1-01-001 BLOODLUST	1-01-001 BOHART	1-01-001 BORDERLANDS	1-01-001 BRAKKE
1-01-001 BLOODROOT	1-01-001 BOHEME	1-01-001 BORDNER	1-01-001 BRAMANTE'S
1-01-001 BLOODS	1-01-001 BOHEMIAN	1-01-001 BORER	1-01-001 BRAMBLES
1-01-001 BLOODSHOT	1-01-001 BOHLEN	1-01-001 BORLAND	1-01-001 BRAN
1-01-001 BLOODSPOTS	1-01-001 BOHN	1-01-001 BORNEO	1-01-001 BRANCHING
1-01-001 BLOODSTAINED	1-01-001 BOIES	1-01-001 BORNHOLM	1-01-001 BRANCHVILLE
1-01-001 BLOODSTAINS	1-01-001 BOILER-BURNER	1-01-001 BORON	1-01-001 BRANDEIS
1-01-001 BLOOMFIELD	1-01-001 BOILERS	1-01-001 BORRIOBOOLA-*GH	1-01-001 BRANDIN
1-01-001 BLOOPS	1-01-001 BOISBRIANT	A	1-01-001 BRANDT'S
1-01-001 BLOSSOMED	1-01-001 BOISMASSIF	1-01-001 BORROMINI	1-01-001 BRANNON'S
1-01-001 BLOT-APPEARANCE	1-01-001 BOISSONEAULT	1-01-001 BORROWS	1-01-001 BRANUM
1-01-001 BLOT-LIKE	1-01-001 BOISTEROUS	1-01-001 BOSCO	1-01-001 BRAQUES
1-01-001 BLOUSE	1-01-001 BOITE	1-01-001 BOSIS'	1-01-001 BRASH
1-01-001 BLOUSES	1-01-001 BOITES	1-01-001 BOSLER	1-01-001 BRASHNESS
1-01-001 BLOWERS	1-01-001 BOLAND	1-01-001 BOSLEY	1-01-001 BRASS-BOUND
1-01-001 BLOWFISH	1-01-001 BOLDEST	1-01-001 BOSOMS	1-01-001 BRASSBOUND'S
1-01-001 BLOWN-UP	1-01-001 BOLET	1-01-001 BOSSED	1-01-001 BRASSICA
1-01-001 BLOWUP	1-01-001 BOLINGBROKE	1-01-001 BOSSMAN	1-01-001 BRASSTOWN
1-01-001 BLUBBER	1-01-001 BOLINGBROKE'S	1-01-001 BOSTITCH	1-01-001 BRATWURST
1-01-001 BLUE-COLLAR	1-01-001 BOLIVAR	1-01-001 BOSTONIAN	1-01-001 BRAUD
1-01-001 BLUE-DRAPED	1-01-001 BOLIVIA	1-01-001 BOSTONIANS	1-01-001 BRAUN
1-01-001 BLUE-EYES	1-01-001 BOLO	1-01-001 BOTANICAL	1-01-001 BRAVED
1-01-001 BLUE-UNIFORMED	1-01-001 BOLOVENS	1-01-001 BOTHERSOME	1-01-001 BRAVES'
1-01-001 BLUEBERRIES	1-01-001 BOLSHEVISM	1-01-001 BOTTEGA	1-01-001 BRAVEST
1-01-001 BLUEBERRY	1-01-001 BOLSHEVISTIC	1-01-001 BOTTINEAU	1-01-001 BRAVEST-FEATHER
1-01-001 BLUEBIRD	1-01-001 BOLSHOI	1-01-001 BOTTLENECKS	ED
1-01-001 BLUEBONNETS	1-01-001 BOLSTERED	1-01-001 BOTTLING	1-01-001 BRAVO
1-01-001 BLUEBOOK	1-01-001 BOLSTERING	1-01-001 BOTTOM-LIVING	1-01-001 BRAVURA
1-01-001 BLUEBUSH	1-01-001 BOLTING	1-01-001 BOTTOMLESS	1-01-001 BRAWLING
1-01-001 BLUEFISH	1-01-001 BOLTS	1-01-001 BOTULINAL	1-01-001 BRAWL
1-01-001 BLUEPRINT	1-01-001 BOLTZMANN	1-01-001 BOTULINUM	1-01-001 BRAWLE
1-01-001 BLUESTOCKING	1-01-001 BOMB-PROOF	1-01-001 BOUANAHSHA	1-01-001 BRAYING
1-01-001 BLUFFING	1-01-001 BOMBARDING	1-01-001 BOUCLE	1-01-001 BRAZEN
1-01-001 BLUING	1-01-001 BOMBARDMENT	1-01-001 BOUFFE	1-01-001 BRAZENLY
1-01-001 BLUME	1-01-001 BOMBASTIC	1-01-001 BOUGIE	1-01-001 BRAZENNESS
1-01-001 BLUMENTHAL	1-01-001 BOMBAY	1-01-001 BOULEZ	1-01-001 BRAZIER
1-01-001 BLUNDERINGS	1-01-001 BOMBED	1-01-001 BOULLE	1-01-001 BREAK-AWAY
1-01-001 BLUNDERS	1-01-001 BOMBER'S	1-01-001 BOUNCY	1-01-001 BREAK-NECK
1-01-001 BLUNTED	1-01-001 BOMBERS'	1-01-001 BOUQUETS	1-01-001 BREAK-THROUGH
1-01-001 BLUNTER	1-01-001 BONA	1-01-001 BOURGEOISIE	1-01-001 BREAKABLES
1-01-001 BLUNTS	1-01-001 BONAPARTE	1-01-001 BOURGUIBA	1-01-001 BREAKAGE
1-01-001 BLURRY	1-01-001 BONDING	1-01-001 BOURN	1-01-001 BREAKAWAY
1-01-001 BLUSHES	1-01-001 BONDSMAN	1-01-001 BOUT-DE-SOUFFLE	1-01-001 BREAKER
1-01-001 BLUSTER	1-01-001 BONDSMAN'S	1-01-001 BOUTFLOWER	1-01-001 BREAKERS
1-01-001 BLUSTERED	1-01-001 BONE-DEEP	1-01-001 BOUVARDIER	1-01-001 BREAKFAST-TABL
1-01-001 BLUSTERY	1-01-001 BONENFANT	1-01-001 BOUVIER	1-01-001 BREAKIN
1-01-001 BLUTHENZWEIG	1-01-001 BONFIGLIO	1-01-001 BOVINES	1-01-001 BREAKING-OUT
1-01-001 BLUTWURST	1-01-001 BONFIRES	1-01-001 BOWAN	1-01-001 BREAKOFF

1-01-001	BREAKTHROUGHS
1-01-001	BREAKUPS
1-01-001	BREAKWATERS
1-01-001	BREASTWORKS
1-01-001	BREATHER
1-01-001	BREATHLESSLY
1-01-001	BREATHS
1-01-001	BREATHY
1-01-001	BRECKENRIDGE'S
1-01-001	BRED
1-01-001	BREECHES
1-01-001	BREEDS
1-01-001	BREEZY
1-01-001	BREGMAN
1-01-001	BRELIN
1-01-001	BREMERTON
1-01-001	BREMSSTRAHLUNG
1-01-001	BRENDAN
1-01-001	BREST
1-01-001	BREST-*SILEVNIOV
1-01-001	BRESTOWE
1-01-001	BRETON
1-01-001	BREUER
1-01-001	BREVE
1-01-001	BREVET
1-01-001	BREWED
1-01-001	BREWER'S
1-01-001	BREWERS
1-01-001	BREWING
1-01-001	BRIAR
1-01-001	BRIBE
1-01-001	BRIBERS
1-01-001	BRIBES
1-01-001	BRICE
1-01-001	BRICKER
1-01-001	BRICKTOP
1-01-001	BRIDE-GIFT
1-01-001	BRIDEWELL
1-01-001	BRIDGED-*=*T
1-01-001	BRIDGEPORT
1-01-001	BRIDGET'S
1-01-001	BRIDGEWATER
1-01-001	BRIDGEWORK
1-01-001	BRIDLE
1-01-001	BRIEFCASE
1-01-001	BRIEFEST
1-01-001	BRIEFF
1-01-001	BRIEFLY-ILLUMED
1-01-001	BRIEFS
1-01-001	BRIEN
1-01-001	BRIGADES
1-01-001	BRIGADOON
1-01-001	BRIGANTINE
1-01-001	BRIGGS
1-01-001	BRIGHETTI
1-01-001	BRIGHT-GREEN
1-01-001	BRIGHT-LOOKING
1-01-001	BRIGHTENS
1-01-001	BRIMFUL
1-01-001	BRIMMED
1-01-001	BRINDISI
1-01-001	BRINDLE
1-01-001	BRINKLEY
1-01-001	BRINKMANSHIP
1-01-001	BRINSLEY
1-01-001	BRISKER
1-01-001	BRISKNESS
1-01-001	BRITANNIC
1-01-001	BRITANNICA
1-01-001	BRITCHES
1-01-001	BRITISH-*AMERICAN
1-01-001	BRITISH-BORN
1-01-001	BRITISHER
1-01-001	BRITON
1-01-001	BRITONS
1-01-001	BROACH
1-01-001	BROAD-NIBBED
1-01-001	BROAD-SCALE
1-01-001	BROADEST
1-01-001	BROADWAY'S
1-01-001	BROCADED
1-01-001	BROCCOLI
1-01-001	BROCKLE
1-01-001	BROCKLIN'S
1-01-001	BROD
1-01-001	BRODBECK
1-01-001	BROEG
1-01-001	BROGLIE
1-01-001	BROGLIO'S
1-01-001	BROK
1-01-001	BROKEN-BACKED
1-01-001	BROKEN-DOWN
1-01-001	BROKEN-NOSED
1-01-001	BROKENLY
1-01-001	BROKER

1-01-001	BROMFIELD'S
1-01-001	BROMIDES
1-01-001	BROMLEY
1-01-001	BROMPHENOL
1-01-001	BRONCHIOLAR
1-01-001	BRONCHIOLITIS
1-01-001	BRONCOS
1-01-001	BRONISLAW
1-01-001	BRONZED
1-01-001	BRONZY-GREEN-GOLD
1-01-001	BROODINF
1-01-001	BROOK'S
1-01-001	BROOKED
1-01-001	BROOKEN
1-01-001	BROOKLYN'S
1-01-001	BROOKMEYER'S
1-01-001	BROOKMONT
1-01-001	BROOME
1-01-001	BROS
1-01-001	BROTHEL
1-01-001	BROWBEATEN
1-01-001	BROWN-BLACK
1-01-001	BROWN-EDGED
1-01-001	BROWN-PAPER
1-01-001	BROWNAPOPOLUS
1-01-001	BROWNE
1-01-001	BROWNELL
1-01-001	BROWNINGS
1-01-001	BROWNISH
1-01-001	BROWNY
1-01-001	BROWSING
1-01-001	BRUCELLOSIS
1-01-001	BRUCKMANN
1-01-001	BRUEGEL
1-01-001	BRUHN
1-01-001	BRUITED
1-01-001	BRUMIDI-*COSTAGGINI
1-01-001	BRUNCHES
1-01-001	BRUNETTES
1-01-001	BRUNO
1-01-001	BRUNT
1-01-001	BRUSH-OFF
1-01-001	BRUSH-OFF'S
1-01-001	BRUSHCUT
1-01-001	BRUSHLIKE
1-01-001	BRUSHWORK
1-01-001	BRUSQUELY
1-01-001	BRUTALITIES
1-01-001	BRUTALIZED
1-01-001	BRUXELLES
1-01-001	BRYANT
1-01-001	BRYNGE
1-01-001	BRYSON
1-01-001	BUAFORD
1-01-001	BUBBLY
1-01-001	BUBENIK
1-01-001	BUBER
1-01-001	BUBER-THINK
1-01-001	BUCCOLIC
1-01-001	BUCER
1-01-001	BUCHAREST
1-01-001	BUCHENWALD
1-01-001	BUCK'S
1-01-001	BUCKAROOS
1-01-001	BUCKED
1-01-001	BUCKENHAM
1-01-001	BUCKET-SHOP
1-01-001	BUCKHANNON
1-01-001	BUCKHEAD
1-01-001	BUCKHORN'S
1-01-001	BUCKING-UP
1-01-001	BUCKLE-ON
1-01-001	BUCKLING
1-01-001	BUCKMAN
1-01-001	BUCKSHOT
1-01-001	BUCKSKIN'S
1-01-001	BUCKSKINS
1-01-001	BUCKWHEAT
1-01-001	BUCKY
1-01-001	BUCOLIC
1-01-001	BUCS
1-01-001	BUCS'
1-01-001	BUDDED
1-01-001	BUDDING
1-01-001	BUDGET-ALTERING
1-01-001	BUDGET-MAKING
1-01-001	BUDGET-WISE
1-01-001	BUDIESHEIN
1-01-001	BUDLONG
1-01-001	BUDWEISERS
1-01-001	BUDZYN
1-01-001	BUELL
1-01-001	BUELL'S
1-01-001	BUENA
1-01-001	BUENAS

1-01-001	BUENO
1-01-001	BUFFALOES
1-01-001	BUFFETINGS
1-01-001	BUFFETS
1-01-001	BUFFOON
1-01-001	BUFFOONS
1-01-001	BUFFS
1-01-001	BUGATTI
1-01-001	BUGEYED
1-01-001	BUGGERS
1-01-001	BUGGIES
1-01-001	BUGLER
1-01-001	BUILD-BETTER-FOR-LESS
1-01-001	BUILDER-DEALER
1-01-001	BUILDER/ACTIVE
1-01-001	BUILDIN
1-01-001	BUILT-DETERGENT
1-01-001	BUILT-SOAP
1-01-001	BUILTIN
1-01-001	BUL'BA
1-01-001	BULGARIA
1-01-001	BULKED
1-01-001	BULKHEAD
1-01-001	BULKHEADS
1-01-001	BULKS
1-01-001	BULL-LIKE
1-01-001	BULL-NECKED
1-01-001	BULL-ROARING
1-01-001	BULLDOZE
1-01-001	BULLET-RIDDLED
1-01-001	BULLETIN'D
1-01-001	BULLFINCH
1-01-001	BULLHIDE
1-01-001	BULLISH
1-01-001	BULLWHACKERS
1-01-001	BULLYBOYS
1-01-001	BULLYING
1-01-001	BUMBLE-BEE
1-01-001	BUMBRY
1-01-001	BUMMING
1-01-001	BUMPERS
1-01-001	BUMPIN
1-01-001	BUMPS
1-01-001	BUMPTIOUS
1-01-001	BUN
1-01-001	BUNCHA
1-01-001	BUNDESTAG
1-01-001	BUNGALOW
1-01-001	BUNGLED
1-01-001	BUNKERED
1-01-001	BUNKMATE
1-01-001	BUNKMATES
1-01-001	BUNNY
1-01-001	BUNTER
1-01-001	BUNTERS
1-01-001	BUOYANCY
1-01-001	BUOYED
1-01-001	BUOYS
1-01-001	BURCH'S
1-01-001	BURCKHARDT
1-01-001	BURDENSOME
1-01-001	BUREAUCRAT
1-01-001	BUREAUCRATIZATION
1-01-001	BUREAUCRATS
1-01-001	BURFORD
1-01-001	BURGEONED
1-01-001	BURGER
1-01-001	BURGESSES
1-01-001	BURGHARDT
1-01-001	BURGHER
1-01-001	BURGHLEY
1-01-001	BURGLAR
1-01-001	BURGLARPROOF
1-01-001	BURGOMASTER'S
1-01-001	BURGUNDIAN
1-01-001	BURGUNDIES
1-01-001	BURIES
1-01-001	BURKE'S
1-01-001	BURKE-ROSTAGNO
1-01-001	BURKES'
1-01-001	BURKETTE
1-01-001	BURLE
1-01-001	BURLESON
1-01-001	BURLESQUES
1-01-001	BURLEY
1-01-001	BURLINGAME
1-01-001	BURLINGTON'S
1-01-001	BURMAN'S
1-01-001	BURMANS
1-01-001	BURNE
1-01-001	BURNED-OUT
1-01-001	BURNES
1-01-001	BURNHAM
1-01-001	BURNHAM'S
1-01-001	BURNISHED

1-01-001	BURNS'S
1-01-001	BURNSIDES'
1-01-001	BURNT-RED
1-01-001	BURR'S
1-01-001	BURR-HEADED
1-01-001	BURRO
1-01-001	BURROWED
1-01-001	BURROWING
1-01-001	BURRS
1-01-001	BURSITIS
1-01-001	BURT
1-01-001	BUSHEL
1-01-001	BUSHING
1-01-001	BUSHNELL
1-01-001	BUSHWHACKED
1-01-001	BUSHWHACKIN
1-01-001	BUSIED
1-01-001	BUSIER
1-01-001	BUSINESS-LIKE
1-01-001	BUSINESS-MINDED
1-01-001	BUSINESSS
1-01-001	BUSS
1-01-001	BUSTARD
1-01-001	BUSTIN
1-01-001	BUSTLIN
1-01-001	BUSTLING
1-01-001	BUSY-WORK
1-01-001	BUSYNESS
1-01-001	BUTANE
1-01-001	BUTCHERED
1-01-001	BUTTE
1-01-001	BUTTERFAT
1-01-001	BUTTERFLIES
1-01-001	BUTTERNUT
1-01-001	BUTTERWYN
1-01-001	BUTTERY
1-01-001	BUTTING
1-01-001	BUTTOCKS
1-01-001	BUTTON'S
1-01-001	BUTTONED
1-01-001	BUTTONHOLES
1-01-001	BUTTRESSED
1-01-001	BUTTRESSES
1-01-001	BUTTRICK
1-01-001	BUTYL-LITHIUM
1-01-001	BUXOM
1-01-001	BUXTEHUDE
1-01-001	BUXTON
1-01-001	BUYERS'
1-01-001	BUYIN
1-01-001	BUZZ'S
1-01-001	BUZZ-BUZZ-BUZZ
1-01-001	BY-GONE
1-01-001	BY-PASS
1-01-001	BY-PASSED
1-01-001	BY-PASSES
1-01-001	BY-ROADS
1-01-001	BY-THE-*SEA
1-01-001	BY-WAYS
1-01-001	BY-WORD
1-01-001	BYER-*ROLNICK
1-01-001	BYINGE
1-01-001	BYLINE
1-01-001	BYLOT
1-01-001	BYPASSED
1-01-001	BYRONIC
1-01-001	BYRONISM
1-01-001	BYSTANDER
1-01-001	BYSTRZYCA
1-01-001	BYWORD
1-01-001	BYZANTIUM
1-01-001	BYZAS
1-01-001	C)**C
1-01-001	C**.*A**.*I**.*P
1-01-001	C**.*C**.*N**.*Y
1-01-001	C'N
1-01-001	C'UN
1-01-001	C**U
1-01-001	CABARET
1-01-001	CABDRIVER
1-01-001	CABINETMAKERS
1-01-001	CABLED
1-01-001	CABOT'S
1-01-001	CABS
1-01-001	CACAO
1-01-001	CACHE
1-01-001	CACKLY
1-01-001	CACOPHONIST
1-01-001	CACOPHONY
1-01-001	CADAVER
1-01-001	CADAVEROUS
1-01-001	CADDY
1-01-001	CADESI
1-01-001	CAFRITZ
1-01-001	CAGAYAN

1-01-001 CAGED	1-01-001 CANINE	1-01-001 CARNEGIE-*ILLIN OIS	1-01-001 CATERPILLAR
1-01-001 CAHILL	1-01-001 CANISTERS	1-01-001 CARNEIGIE	1-01-001 CATERPILLARS
1-01-001 CAHOOTS	1-01-001 CANKER	1-01-001 CARNEY	1-01-001 CATHODOPHORETIC
1-01-001 CAIN'T	1-01-001 CANNERIES	1-01-001 CARNOCHAN	1-01-001 CATHOLICS'
1-01-001 CAIRNS	1-01-001 CANNIBALISTIC	1-01-001 CAROB	1-01-001 CATHY'S
1-01-001 CAIROLI	1-01-001 CANNONBALL	1-01-001 CAROLINA'S	1-01-001 CATINARI
1-01-001 CAIUS	1-01-001 CANONIST	1-01-001 CAROLINAS	1-01-001 CATLIKE
1-01-001 CAL-*NEVA	1-01-001 CANT	1-01-001 CAROLINGIAN	1-01-001 CATON'S
1-01-001 CALAMITIES	1-01-001 CANTALOUPE	1-01-001 CAROLS	1-01-001 CATTALOE
1-01-001 CALCIFICATION	1-01-001 CANTED	1-01-001 CAROLYN	1-01-001 CATTLE-CAR
1-01-001 CALCIFIED	1-01-001 CANTELOUBE	1-01-001 CARON	1-01-001 CAUCASIAN
1-01-001 CALCULABLE	1-01-001 CANTER	1-01-001 CARPATHIANS	1-01-001 CAUCASUS
1-01-001 CALCULATORS	1-01-001 CANTERED	1-01-001 CARPENTERS'	1-01-001 CAUCUSES
1-01-001 CALCULI	1-01-001 CANTICLE	1-01-001 CARPENTIER	1-01-001 CAUCUSING
1-01-001 CALEB	1-01-001 CANTILEVERS	1-01-001 CARRARA	1-01-001 CAUFFMAN
1-01-001 CALF'S-FOOT	1-01-001 CANTING	1-01-001 CARREER	1-01-001 CAULIFLOWER
1-01-001 CALFSKIN	1-01-001 CANTLES	1-01-001 CARREL	1-01-001 CAUSALLY
1-01-001 CALHOUN'S	1-01-001 CANTONESE	1-01-001 CARREON	1-01-001 CAUSATIVE
1-01-001 CALIBRATING	1-01-001 CANTONMENT	1-01-001 CARREON'S	1-01-001 CAUTERIZE
1-01-001 CALIBRATIONS	1-01-001 CANUTE	1-01-001 CARRIAGE-STEP	1-01-001 CAUTIONS
1-01-001 CALICHE-TOPPED	1-01-001 CANVASSED	1-01-001 CARRIE	1-01-001 CAV
1-01-001 CALIFORNIANS	1-01-001 CANVASSING	1-01-001 CARRIER-BASED	1-01-001 CAV'S
1-01-001 CALIGULA	1-01-001 CANYONSIDE	1-01-001 CARRIER-CURRENT	1-01-001 CAVALCADES
1-01-001 CALIMALA	1-01-001 CAP'N	1-01-001 CARROT	1-01-001 CAVALIERE
1-01-001 CALIPERS	1-01-001 CAP-AND-BALL	1-01-001 CARROZZA	1-01-001 CAVALLINIS
1-01-001 CALIPHS	1-01-001 CAPABLY	1-01-001 CARRYOVERS	1-01-001 CAVALRYMEN
1-01-001 CALL-BACKS	1-01-001 CAPACIOUS	1-01-001 CARSTEN	1-01-001 CAVE-LIKE
1-01-001 CALLABLE	1-01-001 CAPACITANCE	1-01-001 CARTE	1-01-001 CAVE-MEN
1-01-001 CALLAN	1-01-001 CAPACITORS	1-01-001 CARTED	1-01-001 CAVEAT
1-01-001 CALLIGRAPHERS	1-01-001 CAPEK'S	1-01-001 CARTELS	1-01-001 CAVED
1-01-001 CALLIGRAPHY	1-01-001 CAPELLAN	1-01-001 CARTERS	1-01-001 CAVEMEN
1-01-001 CALLIN	1-01-001 CAPELLO	1-01-001 CARTESIAN	1-01-001 CAVERN
1-01-001 CALLOUSLY	1-01-001 CAPERCAILZIE	1-01-001 CARTHAGE	1-01-001 CAVERNOUS
1-01-001 CALLUSES	1-01-001 CAPERING	1-01-001 CARTHAGO	1-01-001 CAVERNS
1-01-001 CALMEST	1-01-001 CAPERS	1-01-001 CARTONS	1-01-001 CAVIAR
1-01-001 CALORIE	1-01-001 CAPETOWN	1-01-001 CARTOONISTS	1-01-001 CAVIN
1-01-001 CALORIE-HEAVY	1-01-001 CAPISTRANO	1-01-001 CARTY	1-01-001 CAVING
1-01-001 CALORIMETRIC	1-01-001 CAPITAL-GAINS	1-01-001 CARVED-OUT-OF-S OLID	1-01-001 CAVITIES
1-01-001 CALTECH	1-01-001 CAPITALIST-DEMO CRATIC		1-01-001 CAVORT
1-01-001 CALTECH'S		1-01-001 CARVEN	1-01-001 CAVORTED
1-01-001 CALUDE	1-01-001 CAPITALISTS'	1-01-001 CARVER	1-01-001 CAWING
1-01-001 CALUMNIATED	1-01-001 CAPITOLINE	1-01-001 CARWOOD'S	1-01-001 CC).
1-01-001 CALUMNY	1-01-001 CAPONE'S	1-01-001 CARYATIDES	1-01-001 CC),
1-01-001 CALVINIST	1-01-001 CAPOTE	1-01-001 CASALS	1-01-001 CEARTAINE
1-01-001 CALYPSO	1-01-001 CAPPY'S	1-01-001 CASCA	1-01-001 CEASELESSLY
1-01-001 CAM	1-01-001 CAPRICIOUS	1-01-001 CASCADE	1-01-001 CECIL
1-01-001 CAMBODIA	1-01-001 CAPRICORN	1-01-001 CASCADED	1-01-001 CEDAR
1-01-001 CAMBODIA'S	1-01-001 CAPSICUM	1-01-001 CASCADES	1-01-001 CEDAR-ROOFED
1-01-001 CAMBRIDGEPORT	1-01-001 CAPSTAN	1-01-001 CASE'S	1-01-001 CEDVET
1-01-001 CAMEL	1-01-001 CAPTAINCY	1-01-001 CASE-BY-CASE	1-01-001 CEIL
1-01-001 CAMELLIAS	1-01-001 CAPTAINS	1-01-001 CASE-HARDENED	1-01-001 CEILINGS
1-01-001 CAMELOT	1-01-001 CAPTIONS	1-01-001 CASE-TO-CASE	1-01-001 CELEBES
1-01-001 CAMELS	1-01-001 CAPTIOUS	1-01-001 CASEBOOK	1-01-001 CELERITY
1-01-001 CAMEO	1-01-001 CARABAO	1-01-001 CASED	1-01-001 CELIA
1-01-001 CAMEO-LIKE	1-01-001 CARACAS	1-01-001 CASEIN	1-01-001 CELIAC
1-01-001 CAMEOS	1-01-001 CARAMEL	1-01-001 CASEWORKERS	1-01-001 CELIE
1-01-001 CAMERA'S	1-01-001 CARAUSIUS	1-01-001 CASHED	1-01-001 CELIE'S
1-01-001 CAMERAMEN	1-01-001 CARAVAN'S	1-01-001 CASHEWS	1-01-001 CELLARS
1-01-001 CAMERON	1-01-001 CARBOHYDRATE	1-01-001 CASINO'S	1-01-001 CELLOPHANE
1-01-001 CAMI	1-01-001 CARBON-HALOGEN	1-01-001 CASK	1-01-001 CELLULOSES
1-01-001 CAMILLE	1-01-001 CARBON-14	1-01-001 CASKETS	1-01-001 CELSO
1-01-001 CAMILO	1-01-001 CARBONATES	1-01-001 CASKS	1-01-001 CEMAL
1-01-001 CAMP'S	1-01-001 CARBONES	1-01-001 CASSIOPEIA	1-01-001 CEMENT-AND-GLAS S
1-01-001 CAMP-MADE	1-01-001 CARBONYL	1-01-001 CASSITE	
1-01-001 CAMPAGNA	1-01-001 CARBORUNDUM	1-01-001 CASSIUS	1-01-001 CENNINI
1-01-001 CAMPAGNOLI	1-01-001 CARBOXY-LABELED	1-01-001 CASSOCKED	1-01-001 CENNINO
1-01-001 CAMPAIGN'S	1-01-001 CARBOXYMETHYL	1-01-001 CAST-IRON	1-01-001 CENSORIAL
1-01-001 CAMPAIGNE	1-01-001 CARCASSES	1-01-001 CASTANETS	1-01-001 CENSURED
1-01-001 CAMPED	1-01-001 CARCINOMA	1-01-001 CASTERS	1-01-001 CENTENARY
1-01-001 CAMPING-OUT	1-01-001 CARDAMOM	1-01-001 CASTIGATED	1-01-001 CENTER-FIRE
1-01-001 CAMPMATE	1-01-001 CARDIAC	1-01-001 CASTIGATES	1-01-001 CENTERLINE
1-01-001 CAMPO	1-01-001 CARDIOMEGALY	1-01-001 CASTIGATION	1-01-001 CENTIGRADE
1-01-001 CAMPOBELLO	1-01-001 CARDIOVASCULAR	1-01-001 CASTILLO	1-01-001 CENTIMETER-
1-01-001 CAMPUSES	1-01-001 CARDIOVASCULATO RY	1-01-001 CASTORBEAN	1-01-001 CENTRAL-*B
1-01-001 CAMS		1-01-001 CASTORBEANS	1-01-001 CENTRALE
1-01-001 CANADA'S	1-01-001 CARE-FREE	1-01-001 CASTRO-HELD	1-01-001 CENTRALIA
1-01-001 CANADIAN'S	1-01-001 CAREENED	1-01-001 CASUALS	1-01-001 CENTREDALE
1-01-001 CANALS	1-01-001 CAREENING	1-01-001 CAT'S	1-01-001 CENTRIC
1-01-001 CANANDAIGUA	1-01-001 CAREER-BOUND	1-01-001 CAT-LIKE	1-01-001 CENTRIFUGAL
1-01-001 CANAVERAL'S	1-01-001 CAREERISM	1-01-001 CATACLYSMIC	1-01-001 CENTRIFUGATION
1-01-001 CANCELING	1-01-001 CAREFULNESS	1-01-001 CATAPULTING	1-01-001 CENTRIFUGING
1-01-001 CANCELLED	1-01-001 CARESS	1-01-001 CATAPULTS	1-01-001 CENTRIST
1-01-001 CANCELLING	1-01-001 CARETAKER	1-01-001 CATCHEE	1-01-001 CENTURY-*FOX
1-01-001 CANCELS	1-01-001 CAREWORN	1-01-001 CATCHER'S	1-01-001 CEPHEUS
1-01-001 CANCER-RIDDEN	1-01-001 CARGILL'S	1-01-001 CATCHERS	1-01-001 CEPT
1-01-001 CANCERS	1-01-001 CARICATURED	1-01-001 CATCHUP	1-01-001 CEPTIN
1-01-001 CANDIDATE-PICKI NG	1-01-001 CARICATURIST	1-01-001 CATCHWORDS	1-01-001 CEREBELLUM
	1-01-001 CARLA'S	1-01-001 CATCHY	1-01-001 CEREBRATED
1-01-001 CANDIDATES'	1-01-001 CARLETON'S	1-01-001 CATECHIZE	1-01-001 CEREMONIALLY
1-01-001 CANDIDE	1-01-001 CARLETONIAN	1-01-001 CATECHOLAMINES	1-01-001 CEREMONIOUSLY
1-01-001 CANDLELIGHT	1-01-001 CARLISLE	1-01-001 CATEGORICALLY	1-01-001 CERISE
1-01-001 CANDLESTICK	1-01-001 CARLOADING	1-01-001 CATEGORIZE	1-01-001 CERTIFICATES
1-01-001 CANDLEWICK	1-01-001 CARLOADS	1-01-001 CATEGORIZED	1-01-001 CERTIFIES
1-01-001 CANDOUR	1-01-001 CARLYLE'S	1-01-001 CATEGORIZING	1-01-001 CERTIFYING
1-01-001 CANE'S	1-01-001 CARNALITY	1-01-001 CATERED	1-01-001 CERTITUDES
1-01-001 CANELI	1-01-001 CARNARVON'S	1-01-001 CATERER'S	1-01-001 CERULEAN
1-01-001 CANESTRANI			1-01-001 CERVANTES

1-01-001 CERVANTES'	1-01-001 CHECKIT	1-01-001 CHOOSY	1-01-001 CITYWIDE
1-01-001 CERVELAT	1-01-001 CHEDDI	1-01-001 CHOPIN'S	1-01-001 CIVIL-RIGHTS
1-01-001 CERVETTO	1-01-001 CHEEKBONE	1-01-001 CHOPPER	1-01-001 CIVILIAN-GROUPS
1-01-001 CESARE	1-01-001 CHEERE	1-01-001 CHORALE	1-01-001 CIVILITY
1-01-001 CESSATION	1-01-001 CHEERFULNESS	1-01-001 CHORING	1-01-001 CIVILIZING
1-01-001 CESSION	1-01-001 CHEERING	1-01-001 CHORTLING	1-01-001 CLADDING
1-01-001 CETERAS	1-01-001 CHEERLEADERS	1-01-001 CHORUSED	1-01-001 CLAIRAUDIENTLY
1-01-001 CEZANNE'S	1-01-001 CHEESECLOTH	1-01-001 CHOUISE	1-01-001 CLAIRVOYANCE
1-01-001 CEZANNES	1-01-001 CHEETAH	1-01-001 CHOWDER	1-01-001 CLAIRVOYANT
1-01-001 CHA-CHAS	1-01-001 CHEETAL	1-01-001 CHOWDERS	1-01-001 CLAMBERING
1-01-001 CHABLIS	1-01-001 CHEHEL	1-01-001 CHRISSAKE	1-01-001 CLAMORED
1-01-001 CHADROE	1-01-001 CHELAS	1-01-001 CHRISTENING	1-01-001 CLAMORING
1-01-001 CHAFE	1-01-001 CHELMNO	1-01-001 CHRISTIANIZING	1-01-001 CLAMOROUS
1-01-001 CHAFFEY	1-01-001 CHEMISE	1-01-001 CHRISTINE'S	1-01-001 CLAMORS
1-01-001 CHAFFING	1-01-001 CHEMIST'S	1-01-001 CHRISTLIKE	1-01-001 CLAMSHELL
1-01-001 CHAHAR	1-01-001 CHEMISTRIES	1-01-001 CHRISTMAS-SEASO	1-01-001 CLANDESTINE
1-01-001 CHAIN-REACTION	1-01-001 CHENG	N	1-01-001 CLANG
1-01-001 CHAINLIKE	1-01-001 CHENNAULT'S		1-01-001 CLANGED
1-01-001 CHAIRING	1-01-001 CHERNISHEV	1-01-001 CHRISTOPHERS'	1-01-001 CLANKING
1-01-001 CHAIRMANSHIP	1-01-001 CHEROKEES	1-01-001 CHRISTSAKE	1-01-001 CLANNISH
1-01-001 CHAIRMANSHIPS	1-01-001 CHERRY-FLAVORED	1-01-001 CHRISTY	1-01-001 CLANNISHNESS
1-01-001 CHAISE	1-01-001 CHERUBIM	1-01-001 CHROMATICS	1-01-001 CLAP
1-01-001 CHALIDALE	1-01-001 CHERWELL	1-01-001 CHROMATOGRAM	1-01-001 CLARE
1-01-001 CHALK-WHITE	1-01-001 CHES	1-01-001 CHROMED	1-01-001 CLARETS
1-01-001 CHALKED	1-01-001 CHESHIRE	1-01-001 CHROMIC	1-01-001 CLARIFIES
1-01-001 CHALKY	1-01-001 CHESLY	1-01-001 CHROMIUM-PLATED	1-01-001 CLARINET
1-01-001 CHALLENGER	1-01-001 CHEST-BACK-**JL	1-01-001 CHROMIUM-SUBSTI	1-01-001 CLARK'S
1-01-001 CHALMERS	AT-SHOULDER	TUTED	1-01-001 CLARKE
1-01-001 CHALON-SUR-*SAO	1-01-001 CHEST-BACK-SHOU	1-01-001 CHROMSPUN	1-01-001 CLARKE'S
NE	LDER	1-01-001 CHRONICALLY	1-01-001 CLASHED
1-01-001 CHAMBERED	1-01-001 CHESTERTON	1-01-001 CHRONICLE'S	1-01-001 CLASS'
1-01-001 CHAMBERLAIN	1-01-001 CHEVALIER	1-01-001 CHRONICLED	1-01-001 CLASS-**J*D
1-01-001 CHAMBERMAIDS	1-01-001 CHEVAUX	1-01-001 CHRONICLERS	1-01-001 CLASS-BIASED
1-01-001 CHAMBRE'S	1-01-001 CHEVY	1-01-001 CHRYSANTHEMUMS	1-01-001 CLASSICIST
1-01-001 CHAMOIS	1-01-001 CHI	1-01-001 CHRYSLER'S	1-01-001 CLASSIEST
1-01-001 CHAMP	1-01-001 CHI-CHI	1-01-001 CHUCK-A-LUCK	1-01-001 CLASSIFICATION-
1-01-001 CHAMPIONSHIPS	1-01-001 CHIAROMONTE	1-01-001 CHUCKLES	ANGLE
1-01-001 CHANCEL	1-01-001 CHIBA	1-01-001 CHUFFING	1-01-001 CLASSIFICATORY
1-01-001 CHANCELLORSVILL	1-01-001 CHICAGO-STYLE	1-01-001 CHUM	1-01-001 CLASSIFIERS
E	1-01-001 CHICAGOANS	1-01-001 CHUMMINESS	1-01-001 CLASSIFYING
1-01-001 CHANCERIES	1-01-001 CHICANERY	1-01-001 CHUMP	1-01-001 CLASSLESS
1-01-001 CHANDELIERS	1-01-001 CHICKS	1-01-001 CHUNG	1-01-001 CLATTERING
1-01-001 CHANDELLE	1-01-001 CHIDED	1-01-001 CHUNKY	1-01-001 CLATTERY
1-01-001 CHANNING'S	1-01-001 CHIDING	1-01-001 CHURCHGOERS	1-01-001 CLAUDE'S
1-01-001 CHANTER	1-01-001 CHIEFDOM	1-01-001 CHURCHILLIAN	1-01-001 CLAUDIA'S
1-01-001 CHANTIER	1-01-001 CHIEFDOMS	1-01-001 CHURCHLY	1-01-001 CLAUDIO
1-01-001 CHANTILLY	1-01-001 CHIEFTAINS	1-01-001 CHURNED	1-01-001 CLAUSTROPHOBIA
1-01-001 CHAPEL-LIKE	1-01-001 CHIETI	1-01-001 CHURNS	1-01-001 CLAW
1-01-001 CHAPELLES	1-01-001 CHIGGERS	1-01-001 CHUTNEY	1-01-001 CLAWING
1-01-001 CHAPERON	1-01-001 CHIGNON	1-01-001 CIAO	1-01-001 CLAY-MINING
1-01-001 CHAPERONE	1-01-001 CHILD-BEARING	1-01-001 CIARDI	1-01-001 CLAYS
1-01-001 CHAPERONED	1-01-001 CHILD-CLOUD	1-01-001 CIBULA'S	1-01-001 CLEAN-SHAVEN
1-01-001 CHAPLAINS	1-01-001 CHILD-FACE	1-01-001 CICADAS	1-01-001 CLEAN-TOP
1-01-001 CHAPPELL	1-01-001 CHILD-REARING	1-01-001 CICERO'S	1-01-001 CLEANS
1-01-001 CHAPS	1-01-001 CHILDE	1-01-001 CICERONIAN	1-01-001 CLEANSED
1-01-001 CHAPTER'S	1-01-001 CHILDLESS	1-01-001 CICIULLA	1-01-001 CLEANTH
1-01-001 CHAR	1-01-001 CHILE	1-01-001 CICOGNANI	1-01-001 CLEANUPS
1-01-001 CHARACTER-EDUCA	1-01-001 CHILLIER	1-01-001 CIECA	1-01-001 CLEAR-HEADED
TION	1-01-001 CHIMERA-CHASING	1-01-001 CIGARET	1-01-001 CLEARS
1-01-001 CHARACTERIZING	1-01-001 CHIMES	1-01-001 CILIA	1-01-001 CLEARWATER
1-01-001 CHARCOAL-BROILE	1-01-001 CHIMIQUES	1-01-001 CILIATES	1-01-001 CLEAT
D	1-01-001 CHIN-UPS	1-01-001 CIMABUE	1-01-001 CLEAVED
1-01-001 CHARCOALED	1-01-001 CHINAMAN	1-01-001 CIMABUE'S	1-01-001 CLEBURNE'S
1-01-001 CHARDON	1-01-001 CHINESE-*SOVIET	1-01-001 CIMOLI	1-01-001 CLEFTS
1-01-001 CHARGE-A-PLATE	1-01-001 CHINESE-INSPIRE	1-01-001 CINCHES	1-01-001 CLEMENCE
1-01-001 CHARGEABLE	D	1-01-001 CINEMACTOR	1-01-001 CLEMENT
1-01-001 CHARGIN	1-01-001 CHINKED	1-01-001 CINERAMA	1-01-001 CLENCH
1-01-001 CHARISMA	1-01-001 CHION	1-01-001 CINQ	1-01-001 CLENCHES
1-01-001 CHARITABLY	1-01-001 CHIP-O'S	1-01-001 CIPHER	1-01-001 CLEOTA'S
1-01-001 CHARLATANS	1-01-001 CHIPPENDALE	1-01-001 CIPOLLA	1-01-001 CLERGYMAN'S
1-01-001 CHARLES'S	1-01-001 CHIPPER	1-01-001 CIPRIANI'S	1-01-001 CLERIC
1-01-001 CHARLEY'S	1-01-001 CHIROPRACTOR	1-01-001 CIR	1-01-001 CLERICAL-LAY
1-01-001 CHARMER	1-01-001 CHIROPRACTOR'S	1-01-001 CIRCA	1-01-001 CLERICIS
1-01-001 CHARMINGLY	1-01-001 CHIRPED	1-01-001 CIRCONSCRIPTION	1-01-001 CLERKING
1-01-001 CHARNOCK	1-01-001 CHIRPING	1-01-001 CIRCONSCRIPTION	1-01-001 CLEVA
1-01-001 CHARRED	1-01-001 CHISELS	S	1-01-001 CLICKING
1-01-001 CHARTACEOS	1-01-001 CHIUCHOW	1-01-001 CIRCUITOUS	1-01-001 CLIENT-SERVICE
1-01-001 CHARTINGS	1-01-001 CHIVE	1-01-001 CIRCUITRY	1-01-001 CLIENTS'
1-01-001 CHARTISTS	1-01-001 CHIVES	1-01-001 CIRCUMCISION	1-01-001 CLIFFHANGING
1-01-001 CHASED	1-01-001 CHIVYING	1-01-001 CIRCUMLOCUTION	1-01-001 CLIMATES
1-01-001 CHASSIS	1-01-001 CHLORIDES	1-01-001 CIRCUMPOLAR	1-01-001 CLIMAXES
1-01-001 CHATTE	1-01-001 CHLORINE-CARBON	1-01-001 CIRCUMSCRIBED	1-01-001 CLIMBS
1-01-001 CHATTELS	1-01-001 CHLORPROMAZINE	1-01-001 CIRCUMSCRIPTION	1-01-001 CLIMES
1-01-001 CHATTY	1-01-001 CHLORTETRACYCLI	S	1-01-001 CLINCHED
1-01-001 CHAUCER	NE	1-01-001 CIRCUMSPECTION	1-01-001 CLINCHER
1-01-001 CHAUFFEUR'S	1-01-001 CHMN	1-01-001 CIRCUMSPECTLY	1-01-001 CLINCHES
1-01-001 CHAUFFEURED	1-01-001 CHOCKFULL	1-01-001 CITATIONS	1-01-001 CLINICALLY
1-01-001 CHAULMOOGRA	1-01-001 CHOCKS	1-01-001 CITO	1-01-001 CLINKED
1-01-001 CHAUTAUQUA	1-01-001 CHOCTAW	1-01-001 CITRATED	1-01-001 CLIPPER
1-01-001 CHAVES	1-01-001 CHOIR'S	1-01-001 CITROE**ON	1-01-001 CLIQUES
1-01-001 CHAW	1-01-001 CHOLE	1-01-001 CITRON	1-01-001 CLIVE
1-01-001 CHE	1-01-001 CHOLELITHIASIS	1-01-001 CITRUS	1-01-001 CLOAKROOMS
1-01-001 CHEAP-MONEY	1-01-001 CHOLERA	1-01-001 CITY-BRED	1-01-001 CLOBBER
1-01-001 CHEATING	1-01-001 CHOLESTEROL-RIC	1-01-001 CITY-DWELLER	1-01-001 CLOBBERED
1-01-001 CHECK-OUT	H	1-01-001 CITY-OWNED	1-01-001 CLOBBERS
1-01-001 CHECKER	1-01-001 CHOLINESTERASE	1-01-001 CITY-TRADING	1-01-001 CLOCKED
1-01-001 CHECKIN	1-01-001 CHOMP	1-01-001 CITYBRED	1-01-001 CLOCKING

52

1-01-001 CLOCKWORK	1-01-001 CODED	1-01-001 COLTSMAN	1-01-001 COMPLAINANT
1-01-001 CLOD	1-01-001 CODETERMINES	1-01-001 COLUMBINES	1-01-001 COMPLAISANCE
1-01-001 CLODDISHNESS	1-01-001 CODFISH	1-01-001 COLUMN-SHAPED	1-01-001 COMPLAISANT
1-01-001 CLODHOPPERS	1-01-001 CODIFIED	1-01-001 COLVIN'S	1-01-001 COMPLEATED
1-01-001 CLOISTERS	1-01-001 CODY	1-01-001 COLZANI	1-01-001 COMPLECTION
1-01-001 CLOMPED	1-01-001 COED	1-01-001 COM	1-01-001 COMPLEMENTING
1-01-001 CLONIC	1-01-001 COEDITORS	1-01-001 COMANCHE	1-01-001 COMPLETELY-RESTORED
1-01-001 CLOSE-IN	1-01-001 COEDS	1-01-001 COMANY'S	1-01-001 COMPLEX-VALUED
1-01-001 CLOSED-CIRCUIT	1-01-001 COERCED	1-01-001 COMAS	1-01-001 COMPLICATING
1-01-001 CLOSELY-PACKED	1-01-001 COEXIST	1-01-001 COMBAT-INFLICTED	1-01-001 COMPLIMENTING
1-01-001 CLOSENESS	1-01-001 COEXISTENT	1-01-001 COMBAT-TESTED	1-01-001 COMPORT
1-01-001 CLOSETED	1-01-001 COFACTORS	1-01-001 COMBATANTS	1-01-001 COMPORTED
1-01-001 CLOSEUP	1-01-001 COFFEE-*HOUSE	1-01-001 COMBATING	1-01-001 COMPORTMENT
1-01-001 CLOSTRIDIUM	1-01-001 COFFEE-HOUSE	1-01-001 COMBATTED	1-01-001 COMPOSER'S
1-01-001 CLOSURE	1-01-001 COFFEECUP	1-01-001 COMBE	1-01-001 COMPOSER-PIANIST-CONDUCTOR
1-01-001 CLOTH-OF-GOLD	1-01-001 COFFERS	1-01-001 COMBINABLE	1-01-001 COMPOSERS'
1-01-001 CLOTHBOUND	1-01-001 COGENTLY	1-01-001 COMBING	1-01-001 COMPOSITES
1-01-001 CLOTHE	1-01-001 COGNATE	1-01-001 COMBS	1-01-001 COMPOSITIONAL
1-01-001 CLOTHESBRUSH	1-01-001 COGS	1-01-001 COMBUSTIBLES	1-01-001 COMPOTE
1-01-001 CLOTHESLINE	1-01-001 COHERE	1-01-001 COME-UPPANCE	1-01-001 COMPOUND-ENGINE
1-01-001 CLOTHESLINES	1-01-001 COHERENCE	1-01-001 COMELY	1-01-001 COMPOUNDING
1-01-001 CLOTHIER	1-01-001 COHESIVELY	1-01-001 COMEND	1-01-001 COMPRESSIBILITY
1-01-001 CLOTTED	1-01-001 COHESIVENESS	1-01-001 COMENICO	1-01-001 COMPRESSING
1-01-001 CLOTURE	1-01-001 COHNFIDUNT	1-01-001 COMER	1-01-001 COMPROMISES
1-01-001 CLOUDCROFT	1-01-001 COHORTS	1-01-001 COMEST	1-01-001 COMPULSIONS
1-01-001 CLOUT	1-01-001 COIFFURE	1-01-001 COMET'S-TAIL	1-01-001 COMPUTATIONAL
1-01-001 CLOV	1-01-001 COILED	1-01-001 COMETARY	1-01-001 COMPUTATIONS
1-01-001 CLOVE	1-01-001 COILING	1-01-001 COMETH	1-01-001 COMROE
1-01-001 CLOWN'S	1-01-001 COINCIDENTAL	1-01-001 COMFORTED	1-01-001 COMSUMER
1-01-001 CLOWNING	1-01-001 COINCIDING	1-01-001 COMICO-ROMANTICO	1-01-001 COMTEMPORARY
1-01-001 CLUBROOMS	1-01-001 COKES	1-01-001 COMICS	1-01-001 CONCEALING
1-01-001 CLUCKED	1-01-001 COLAVITO	1-01-001 COMINFORM	1-01-001 CONCEDEDLY
1-01-001 CLUCKING	1-01-001 COLCHICUM	1-01-001 COMINGS	1-01-001 CONCEDES
1-01-001 CLUMSILY	1-01-001 COLCORD	1-01-001 COMIQUE	1-01-001 CONCENTRATION-CAMP
1-01-001 CLYFFORD	1-01-001 COLD-BLOODED	1-01-001 COMISKEY	1-01-001 CONCEPTUALIZATION
1-01-001 CM.	1-01-001 COLD-BLOODEDLY	1-01-001 COMMAND'S	1-01-001 CONCEPTUALLY
1-01-001 CMDR	1-01-001 COLD-WAR	1-01-001 COMMANDANT	1-01-001 CONCERT-*DISC
1-01-001 CO-AUTHOR	1-01-001 COLE	1-01-001 COMMANDEERED	1-01-001 CONCERTANTE
1-01-001 CO-COLA	1-01-001 COLE'S	1-01-001 COMMANDEERING	1-01-001 CONCERTI
1-01-001 CO-EDUCATIONAL	1-01-001 COLEE	1-01-001 COMMANDER-IN-*CHIEF	1-01-001 CONCERTINA
1-01-001 CO-EXISTENCE	1-01-001 COLEFAX	1-01-001 COMMANDO-TRAINED	1-01-001 CONCERTMASTER
1-01-001 CO-EXTINCTION	1-01-001 COLERIDGE	1-01-001 COMMAWNDED	1-01-001 CONCERTO'S
1-01-001 CO-OCCURRING	1-01-001 COLES	1-01-001 COMMEMORATES	1-01-001 CONCETTA
1-01-001 CO-OPERATED	1-01-001 COLETTA	1-01-001 COMMEMORATING	1-01-001 CONCILIATE
1-01-001 CO-OPERATES	1-01-001 COLFAX	1-01-001 COMMENCEMENTS	1-01-001 CONCILIATOR
1-01-001 CO-OPERATING	1-01-001 COLICKY	1-01-001 COMMENCES	1-01-001 CONCISE
1-01-001 CO-OPS	1-01-001 COLISEUM	1-01-001 COMMENDATION	1-01-001 CONCISENESS
1-01-001 CO-OPTING	1-01-001 COLLABORATOR	1-01-001 COMMENDS	1-01-001 CONCOCTED
1-01-001 CO-ORDINATE	1-01-001 COLLAPSES	1-01-001 COMMERCANTS	1-01-001 CONCORDANCE
1-01-001 CO-ORDINATED	1-01-001 COLLAPSIBLE	1-01-001 COMMERCIALISM	1-01-001 CONCORDE
1-01-001 CO-ORDINATES	1-01-001 COLLAR-TO-COLLAR	1-01-001 COMMERCIALIZATION	1-01-001 CONCRETISTIC-SEEMING
1-01-001 CO-ORDINATING	1-01-001 COLLARBONE	1-01-001 COMMINGE	1-01-001 CONCURRENTLY
1-01-001 CO-ORDINATOR	1-01-001 COLLARED	1-01-001 COMMINGLED	1-01-001 CONCUSSION
1-01-001 CO-SIGNERS	1-01-001 COLLARS	1-01-001 COMMISERATE	1-01-001 CONDEMNATORY
1-01-001 CO-STAR	1-01-001 COLLATED	1-01-001 COMMISSION-CONTROLLED	1-01-001 CONDENSE
1-01-001 COACH'S	1-01-001 COLLATION	1-01-001 COMMISSIONER'S	1-01-001 CONDENSER
1-01-001 COACHWORK	1-01-001 COLLECTIBLE	1-01-001 COMMITTEEMAN	1-01-001 CONDENSING
1-01-001 COAGULATING	1-01-001 COLLECTIVE-BARGAINING	1-01-001 COMMITTMENT	1-01-001 CONDICIONS
1-01-001 COAHSE	1-01-001 COLLECTOR'S	1-01-001 COMMONER	1-01-001 CONDLIFFE
1-01-001 COAL-LIKE	1-01-001 COLLEGE-EDUCATED	1-01-001 COMMONERS	1-01-001 CONDOLENCES
1-01-001 COAL-RAILROAD	1-01-001 COLLEGE-ORIENTED	1-01-001 COMMONEST	1-01-001 CONDONED
1-01-001 COALESCE	1-01-001 COLLEGIANS	1-01-001 COMMONNESS	1-01-001 CONDUCTORS
1-01-001 COALESCED	1-01-001 COLLES	1-01-001 COMMONWEALTHS	1-01-001 CONDUIT
1-01-001 COALESCENCE	1-01-001 COLLETT	1-01-001 COMMUNICATOR'S	1-01-001 CONFABULATED
1-01-001 COALESCES	1-01-001 COLLIDED	1-01-001 COMMUNICATORS	1-01-001 CONFABULATIONS
1-01-001 COARSELY	1-01-001 COLLIMATED	1-01-001 COMMUNIQUES	1-01-001 CONFEDERATIONS
1-01-001 COARSENED	1-01-001 COLLINS'	1-01-001 COMMUNISN	1-01-001 CONFERENCE'S
1-01-001 COARSENESS	1-01-001 COLLINSVILLE	1-01-001 COMMUNIST-INSPIRED	1-01-001 CONFERRING
1-01-001 COAST-TO-COAST	1-01-001 COLLONADED	1-01-001 COMMUNIST-TYPE	1-01-001 CONFERS
1-01-001 COASTLINE	1-01-001 COLLOQUY	1-01-001 COMMUNIZE	1-01-001 CONFESSIONALS
1-01-001 COATTAILS	1-01-001 COLLOSAL	1-01-001 COMMUTATION	1-01-001 CONFESSOR
1-01-001 COAX	1-01-001 COLLYER	1-01-001 COMMUTATOR-LIKE	1-01-001 CONFIDANT
1-01-001 COAXIAL	1-01-001 COLMANS	1-01-001 COMPACTLY	1-01-001 CONFIDANTE
1-01-001 COAXING	1-01-001 COLMER'S	1-01-001 COMPACTS	1-01-001 CONFIDENCES
1-01-001 COBALT-60	1-01-001 COLOMBIA	1-01-001 COMPAGNIE	1-01-001 CONFIDENTIALITY
1-01-001 COBB'S	1-01-001 COLONELS	1-01-001 COMPANIONABLE	1-01-001 CONFINEMENTS
1-01-001 COBBLER'S	1-01-001 COLONIALIST	1-01-001 COMPANIONWAY	1-01-001 CONFISCATING
1-01-001 COBBLESTONE	1-01-001 COLONIALS	1-01-001 COMPANY-PAID	1-01-001 CONFLAGRATION
1-01-001 COBBLESTONES	1-01-001 COLONISTS	1-01-001 COMPANY-WIDE	1-01-001 CONFLICT'S
1-01-001 COBLE	1-01-001 COLONISTS'	1-01-001 COMPARTMENTS	1-01-001 CONFLUENT
1-01-001 COBWEBS	1-01-001 COLONIZED	1-01-001 COMPATABILITY	1-01-001 CONFORMATIONS
1-01-001 COCA-*COLA	1-01-001 COLONNADED	1-01-001 COMPATRIOT	1-01-001 CONFOUNDING
1-01-001 COCAINE	1-01-001 COLONUS	1-01-001 COMPATRIOTS	1-01-001 CONFRERES
1-01-001 COCAO	1-01-001 COLONY'S	1-01-001 COMPELTE	1-01-001 CONFRONTATIONS
1-01-001 COCCIDIOIDOMYCOSIS	1-01-001 COLORADO'S	1-01-001 COMPENDIUM	1-01-001 CONFUSES
1-01-001 COCCIDIOSIS	1-01-001 COLORAMA	1-01-001 COMPENSATES	1-01-001 CONFUSIN
1-01-001 COCHRAN	1-01-001 COLOREDS	1-01-001 COMPETENCY	1-01-001 CONFUTED
1-01-001 COCKATOO	1-01-001 COLORIN	1-01-001 COMPETES	1-01-001 CONG
1-01-001 COCKEYED	1-01-001 COLOSSIANS	1-01-001 COMPILE	1-01-001 CONGDON
1-01-001 COCKIER	1-01-001 COLOUR-PRINTS	1-01-001 COMPLACENT	1-01-001 CONGENIALITY
1-01-001 COCKPITS	1-01-001 COLOURED		1-01-001 CONGENITAL
1-01-001 COCO	1-01-001 COLT'S		1-01-001 CONGO'S
1-01-001 COCONUT-CONTAINING	1-01-001 COLTISH		
1-01-001 COCOPALM			
1-01-001 COCU			

Rank	Word
1-01-001	CONGRATULATION
1-01-001	CONGREGATED
1-01-001	CONGREGATIONALI SM
1-01-001	CONGRESSES
1-01-001	CONGRESSMAN'S
1-01-001	CONJECTURED
1-01-001	CONJUGATING
1-01-001	CONJUGATION
1-01-001	CONJUNCTIONS
1-01-001	CONJURE
1-01-001	CONLOW
1-01-001	CONNALL
1-01-001	CONNEAUT
1-01-001	CONNECTICUT'S
1-01-001	CONNED
1-01-001	CONNELL
1-01-001	CONNELLY
1-01-001	CONNIE
1-01-001	CONNING
1-01-001	CONNIVANCE
1-01-001	CONNIVER
1-01-001	CONNOLLY'S
1-01-001	CONNOR
1-01-001	CONNOTE
1-01-001	CONNOTES
1-01-001	CONPIRED
1-01-001	CONQUEROR
1-01-001	CONS
1-01-001	CONSANGUINEOUS
1-01-001	CONSANGUINEOUSL Y
1-01-001	CONSCIENCES
1-01-001	CONSCIONABLE
1-01-001	CONSCRIPT
1-01-001	CONSDERATIONS
1-01-001	CONSECRATION
1-01-001	CONSENTING
1-01-001	CONSEQUENTIAL
1-01-001	CONSERVATIONIST
1-01-001	CONSERVATIVE-LI BERAL
1-01-001	CONSERVATIVELY- CRAVATED
1-01-001	CONSERVES
1-01-001	CONSIDERIN
1-01-001	CONSIGNED
1-01-001	CONSISENTLY
1-01-001	CONSISTENCE
1-01-001	CONSITUTIONAL
1-01-001	CONSOLING
1-01-001	CONSONANCE
1-01-001	CONSORT
1-01-001	CONSORTED
1-01-001	CONSPICIOUS
1-01-001	CONSPIRATORIAL
1-01-001	CONSPIRE
1-01-001	CONSPIRES
1-01-001	CONSTABLE'S
1-01-001	CONSTABLES
1-01-001	CONSTANCE
1-01-001	CONSTANT-TEMPER ATURE
1-01-001	CONSTANTIN
1-01-001	CONSTANTINO
1-01-001	CONSTANTINOS
1-01-001	CONSTATATION
1-01-001	CONSTELLATION'S
1-01-001	CONSTERNATION
1-01-001	CONSTITUENCIES
1-01-001	CONSTRAINING
1-01-001	CONSTRICTIONS
1-01-001	CONSTRICTORS
1-01-001	CONSTRUCTIONAL
1-01-001	CONSTRUE
1-01-001	CONSTRUING
1-01-001	CONSULAR
1-01-001	CONSULATE
1-01-001	CONSULTATIVE
1-01-001	CONSUMER'S
1-01-001	CONSUMES
1-01-001	CONSUMMATELY
1-01-001	CONTAMINATE
1-01-001	CONTAMINATING
1-01-001	CONTE
1-01-001	CONTEMPLATES
1-01-001	CONTEMPLATIVE
1-01-001	CONTENDERE
1-01-001	CONTENDING
1-01-001	CONTENTEDLY
1-01-001	CONTENTING
1-01-001	CONTENTMENT
1-01-001	CONTIGUOUS
1-01-001	CONTINENCE
1-01-001	CONTINENTALLY
1-01-001	CONTINGENTS
1-01-001	CONTINUO
1-01-001	CONTORTION
1-01-001	CONTOUR-OBLITER ATING
1-01-001	CONTOURING
1-01-001	CONTRABAND
1-01-001	CONTRABASS
1-01-001	CONTRACEPTIVE
1-01-001	CONTRACT-NEGOTI ATION
1-01-001	CONTRACTION-EXT ENSION
1-01-001	CONTRACTOR'S
1-01-001	CONTRACTORS'
1-01-001	CONTRADICTORY
1-01-001	CONTRADISTINCTI ON
1-01-001	CONTRALTO
1-01-001	CONTRAPTIONS
1-01-001	CONTRARIETIES
1-01-001	CONTRARILY
1-01-001	CONTRARY-TO-REA LITY
1-01-001	CONTRIBS
1-01-001	CONTRIBUTORY
1-01-001	CONTRIFUGATION
1-01-001	CONTRITE
1-01-001	CONTRITION
1-01-001	CONTRIVANCES
1-01-001	CONTRIVE
1-01-001	CONTRIVING
1-01-001	CONTROVERSIALIS TS
1-01-001	CONTUSIONS
1-01-001	CONVAIR
1-01-001	CONVALESCENCE
1-01-001	CONVALESCING
1-01-001	CONVENIENT-TYPE
1-01-001	CONVENTIONAL-TY PE
1-01-001	CONVENTIONALITY
1-01-001	CONVENTIONALIZE D
1-01-001	CONVENTIONALLY
1-01-001	CONVERGED
1-01-001	CONVERSANT
1-01-001	CONVERSING
1-01-001	CONVERSION-BY-R ENOVATION
1-01-001	CONVEX
1-01-001	CONVEXITY
1-01-001	CONVEYANCE
1-01-001	CONVEYING
1-01-001	CONVICT'S
1-01-001	CONVICTING
1-01-001	CONVIVIAL
1-01-001	CONVOCATIONS
1-01-001	CONVOLUTED
1-01-001	CONVULSED
1-01-001	CONVULSIONS
1-01-001	CONWAY
1-01-001	COO**ORDINATE
1-01-001	COO**ORDINATED
1-01-001	COO**ORDINATING
1-01-001	COOTING
1-01-001	COOKED-OVER
1-01-001	COOKFIRE
1-01-001	COOKIE
1-01-001	COOLHEADED
1-01-001	COOLING-HEATING
1-01-001	COOLNESSES
1-01-001	COOPERATES
1-01-001	COOPS
1-01-001	COOSIE'S
1-01-001	COPERNICUS-THE- ASTRONOMER
1-01-001	COPES
1-01-001	COPINGS
1-01-001	COPIOUS
1-01-001	COPIOUSLY
1-01-001	COPLEY
1-01-001	COPP
1-01-001	COPYBOOKS
1-01-001	COPYING
1-01-001	COPYRIGHTS
1-01-001	COPYWRITER
1-01-001	CORAL-COLORED
1-01-001	CORAULT
1-01-001	CORBIN
1-01-001	CORDED
1-01-001	CORDIER'S
1-01-001	CORDUROY
1-01-001	CORDUROYS
1-01-001	CORE-CORE
1-01-001	CORE-JACKET
1-01-001	CORE-MARGINAL
1-01-001	CORIANDER
1-01-001	CORINTH
1-01-001	CORIOLANUS
1-01-001	CORKERS
1-01-001	CORKS
1-01-001	CORN-BELT
1-01-001	CORNBREAD
1-01-001	CORNEILUS
1-01-001	CORNELL-*DUBILI ER
1-01-001	CORNER-
1-01-001	CORNER-POSTS
1-01-001	CORNERED
1-01-001	CORNERING
1-01-001	CORNFIELD
1-01-001	CORNIEST
1-01-001	CORNING
1-01-001	CORNSTARCH
1-01-001	CORNUCOPIA
1-01-001	CORNWALL
1-01-001	CORNY
1-01-001	COROLLARIES
1-01-001	CORONA
1-01-001	CORONARIES
1-01-001	CORONATION
1-01-001	CORPOREAL
1-01-001	CORPOREALITY
1-01-001	CORPORIS
1-01-001	CORPSMAN
1-01-001	CORPULENCE
1-01-001	CORPUSCULAR
1-01-001	CORPUSCULAR-RAD IATION
1-01-001	CORRALLING
1-01-001	CORREGGIO
1-01-001	CORRELATIVELY
1-01-001	CORRETTE
1-01-001	CORROBORATING
1-01-001	CORRODE
1-01-001	CORRODING
1-01-001	CORRUGATIONS
1-01-001	CORRUPTER
1-01-001	CORRUPTS
1-01-001	CORSAGE
1-01-001	CORSI
1-01-001	CORSIA
1-01-001	CORTEGE
1-01-001	CORTICALLY
1-01-001	CORTICOSTEROIDS
1-01-001	CORTICOTROPIN
1-01-001	COSEC
1-01-001	COSEQUENCES
1-01-001	COSILY
1-01-001	COSMETIC
1-01-001	COSMICAL
1-01-001	COSMO
1-01-001	COSPONSORS
1-01-001	COST-ACCOUNTING
1-01-001	COST-BILLING
1-01-001	COST-FINDING
1-01-001	COST-PLUS
1-01-001	COSTAGGINI'S
1-01-001	COSTE
1-01-001	COSTIVE
1-01-001	COSTLIER
1-01-001	COSTUMED
1-01-001	COSY
1-01-001	COTMAN
1-01-001	COTT
1-01-001	COTTEN'S
1-01-001	COTTER
1-01-001	COTTER'S
1-01-001	COTTON'S
1-01-001	COTTON-GROWING
1-01-001	COTTONMOUTH
1-01-001	COTTONSEED
1-01-001	COTTY
1-01-001	COUCHES
1-01-001	COUD
1-01-001	COUDN
1-01-001	COUGHLIN'S
1-01-001	COULD'VE
1-01-001	COULDA
1-01-001	COULOMB
1-01-001	COULSON
1-01-001	COUNCILWOMAN
1-01-001	COUNTER-ATTACK
1-01-001	COUNTER-BALANCE D
1-01-001	COUNTER-CLOCKWI SE
1-01-001	COUNTER-DRILL
1-01-001	COUNTER-EFFORTS
1-01-001	COUNTER-ESCALAT ION
1-01-001	COUNTER-MOVES
1-01-001	COUNTER-OFFENSI VE
1-01-001	COUNTER-SUCCESS ES
1-01-001	COUNTERBALANCED
1-01-001	COUNTERBALANCIN G
1-01-001	COUNTERCHALLENG E
1-01-001	COUNTERFEIT
1-01-001	COUNTERFLOW
1-01-001	COUNTERMAN
1-01-001	COUNTERPOINTING
1-01-001	COUNTERPROPOSAL
1-01-001	COUNTERVAILING
1-01-001	COUNTIAN
1-01-001	COUNTREY
1-01-001	COUNTRIMAN
1-01-001	COUNTRY-SQUIREH OOD
1-01-001	COUNTRYMAN
1-01-001	COUP-PROOF
1-01-001	COUPAL
1-01-001	COUPLE'S
1-01-001	COUPON
1-01-001	COUPONS
1-01-001	COURBET
1-01-001	COUREURS
1-01-001	COURIER
1-01-001	COURIER-*JOURNA L
1-01-001	COURSING
1-01-001	COURT-APPOINTED
1-01-001	COURT-LENGTH
1-01-001	COURT-PACKING
1-01-001	COURTED
1-01-001	COURTLINESS
1-01-001	COURTNEY
1-01-001	COURTRAI
1-01-001	COURTYARDS
1-01-001	COUSIN'S
1-01-001	COUSIN-WIFE
1-01-001	COUSINS'
1-01-001	COUTURIER
1-01-001	COUVE
1-01-001	COVENANTS
1-01-001	COVENTRY
1-01-001	COVERTLY
1-01-001	COVES
1-01-001	COVET
1-01-001	COVETING
1-01-001	COW'S
1-01-001	COW-MAN
1-01-001	COW-PEOPLE
1-01-001	COWBIRD
1-01-001	COWBIRDS'
1-01-001	COWBOY'S
1-01-001	COWERING
1-01-001	COWESSETT
1-01-001	COWESSETT-EAST
1-01-001	COWHAND'D
1-01-001	COWHANDS
1-01-001	COWHIDE
1-01-001	COWLING
1-01-001	COWPONY
1-01-001	COWPUNCHER
1-01-001	COWRTIERS
1-01-001	COXCOMBS
1-01-001	COYLY
1-01-001	COYOTE
1-01-001	COYOTES
1-01-001	COZEN
1-01-001	COZIER
1-01-001	COZY
1-01-001	COOLING
1-01-001	CR**-SPE
1-01-001	CRABAPPLE
1-01-001	CRABBED
1-01-001	CRACKER-BOX
1-01-001	CRACKLED
1-01-001	CRACKLES
1-01-001	CRACKLING
1-01-001	CRACKPOT
1-01-001	CRADDOCK
1-01-001	CRADLES
1-01-001	CRAFT-INDUSTRIA L
1-01-001	CRAFTER
1-01-001	CRAFTSMAN'S
1-01-001	CRAFTY
1-01-001	CRAGGY
1-01-001	CRAIG'S
1-01-001	CRAMER
1-01-001	CRANBERRIES
1-01-001	CRANELIKE
1-01-001	CRANES
1-01-001	CRANK
1-01-001	CRANKSHAFT
1-01-001	CRANKY

1-01-001 CRASHER	1-01-001 CROSSBARS	1-01-001 CUSHMAN	1-01-001 DAMON
1-01-001 CRASHES	1-01-001 CROSSINGS	1-01-001 CUSTER'S	1-01-001 DAMPENING
1-01-001 CRASSEST	1-01-001 CROSSOVER	1-01-001 CUSTODIAL	1-01-001 DAMSEL
1-01-001 CRASSNESS	1-01-001 CROSSROADING	1-01-001 CUSTOM-DESIGN	1-01-001 DAN'L
1-01-001 CRATERED	1-01-001 CROSSWALK	1-01-001 CUSTOM-MAKE	1-01-001 DANBURY
1-01-001 CRAWLSPACE	1-01-001 CROSSWAYS	1-01-001 CUSTOMER'S	1-01-001 DANCE-THEATRE
1-01-001 CRAYONS	1-01-001 CROSSWISE	1-01-001 CUSTOMER-COST	1-01-001 DANCELIKE
1-01-001 CRAZING	1-01-001 CROTCHETY	1-01-001 CUSTOMERS'	1-01-001 DANCERS'
1-01-001 CRAZY-WONDERFUL	1-01-001 CROUCH'S	1-01-001 CUSTOMHOUSE	1-01-001 DANCHIN
1-01-001 CREAK	1-01-001 CROUCHIN	1-01-001 CUT-AND-DRIED	1-01-001 DANDELION
1-01-001 CREAKS	1-01-001 CROUPIER	1-01-001 CUT-DOWN	1-01-001 DANDILY
1-01-001 CREAMED	1-01-001 CROWBAIT	1-01-001 CUT-GLASS	1-01-001 DANDY'S
1-01-001 CREAMERY	1-01-001 CROWNS	1-01-001 CUT-OFF	1-01-001 DANEHY
1-01-001 CREAMS	1-01-001 CROYDON	1-01-001 CUT-TO-A-FAMILIAR-PATTERN	1-01-001 DANG
1-01-001 CREAMY	1-01-001 CROZIER	1-01-001 CUTBACK	1-01-001 DANGED
1-01-001 CREASE	1-01-001 CRUCIALLY	1-01-001 CUTEST	1-01-001 DANGLE
1-01-001 CREASES	1-01-001 CRUCIBLE	1-01-001 CUTLASS	1-01-001 DANIEL'S
1-01-001 CREATION'S	1-01-001 CRUCIFIXION	1-01-001 CUTLETS	1-01-001 DANK
1-01-001 CREATIVENESS	1-01-001 CRUDEST	1-01-001 CUTOFF	1-01-001 DANNEHOWER
1-01-001 CREATIVITY-ORIENTED	1-01-001 CRUDITIES	1-01-001 CUTOUTS	1-01-001 DANNY'S
1-01-001 CRECHE	1-01-001 CRUDITY	1-01-001 CUTTERS'	1-01-001 DANS
1-01-001 CREDIBILITY	1-01-001 CRUELEST	1-01-001 CUTTHROAT	1-01-001 DANSEUR
1-01-001 CREDIBLY	1-01-001 CRUISES	1-01-001 CUTTING-EDGE	1-01-001 DANTE'S
1-01-001 CREDULOUS	1-01-001 CRUMBLY	1-01-001 CUTTINGS	1-01-001 DANUBIAN
1-01-001 CREDULOUSNESS	1-01-001 CRUMLEY	1-01-001 CYCLADES	1-01-001 DANVILLE
1-01-001 CREEDAL	1-01-001 CRUMLISH	1-01-001 CYCLED	1-01-001 DANZIG
1-01-001 CREEDS	1-01-001 CRUMP	1-01-001 CYCLICAL	1-01-001 DAPHNE
1-01-001 CREEK-FILLED	1-01-001 CRUNCHED	1-01-001 CYCLOHEXANOL	1-01-001 DAPPERTUTTO
1-01-001 CREEKS	1-01-001 CRUSADER	1-01-001 CYCLORAMA	1-01-001 DAPPLED
1-01-001 CREEPER	1-01-001 CRUSADES	1-01-001 CYCLY	1-01-001 DARBUKA
1-01-001 CREEPS	1-01-001 CRUSADING	1-01-001 CYGNE	1-01-001 DARE-*BASE
1-01-001 CREEPY	1-01-001 CRUSHER	1-01-001 CYNICALLY	1-01-001 DARIN
1-01-001 CREMATE	1-01-001 CRUSHERS	1-01-001 CYPRESS-LIKE	1-01-001 DARIUS
1-01-001 CREMATED	1-01-001 CRUST	1-01-001 CYPRIAN	1-01-001 DARK-BLUE
1-01-001 CREOLE	1-01-001 CRUTCH	1-01-001 CYR	1-01-001 DARK-BROWN
1-01-001 CREON	1-01-001 CRYOSTAT	1-01-001 CYRIL	1-01-001 DARK-GRAY
1-01-001 CREPE	1-01-001 CRYPT	1-01-001 CYTOLYSIS	1-01-001 DARK-GREEN
1-01-001 CRESTED	1-01-001 CRYPTOGRAPHIC	1-01-001 CZAR	1-01-001 DARK-SKINNED
1-01-001 CRESTFALLEN	1-01-001 CRYSTALLITE	1-01-001 CZARSHIP	1-01-001 DARKHAIRED
1-01-001 CRESTON	1-01-001 CRYSTALLIZE	1-01-001 CZERNY	1-01-001 DARLENE
1-01-001 CRESTON'S	1-01-001 CRYSTALLIZED	1-01-001 D)),	1-01-001 DARLIN
1-01-001 CRETACEOUS	1-01-001 CRYSTALLOGRAPHERS	1-01-001 D),	1-01-001 DARLING'S
1-01-001 CREVICES	1-01-001 CT	1-01-001 D**.*J	1-01-001 DARNELL
1-01-001 CREW'S	1-01-001 CU	1-01-001 D**.*D**.*A	1-01-001 DARRELL
1-01-001 CREWCUT	1-01-001 CUB'S	1-01-001 D**.*W	1-01-001 DARROW
1-01-001 CREWMEN	1-01-001 CUBAN-*AMERICAN	1-01-001 D**.W**.GRIFFITH	1-01-001 DARTING
1-01-001 CRIME**H	1-01-001 CUBBYHOLE		1-01-001 DARWEN
1-01-001 CRIMEA	1-01-001 CUBE	1-01-001 D'*=YOU	1-01-001 DARWIN
1-01-001 CRIMSONING	1-01-001 CUBED	1-01-001 D'*AMOURS	1-01-001 DARWIN'S
1-01-001 CRINKLES	1-01-001 CUBISTS	1-01-001 D'*ARGENT	1-01-001 DASHWOOD
1-01-001 CRIPPLE	1-01-001 CUCKOO-BUMBLEBEE	1-01-001 D'*ARLAY	1-01-001 DATA-HANDLING
1-01-001 CRIS	1-01-001 CUD	1-01-001 D'*ART	1-01-001 DATUM
1-01-001 CRISIS-ORIENTED	1-01-001 CUDDLEBACK	1-01-001 D'*AUMONT	1-01-001 DAUBED
1-01-001 CRISIS-TO-CRISIS	1-01-001 CUDKOWICZ	1-01-001 D'*EIFFEL	1-01-001 DAUNT
1-01-001 CRISPIN	1-01-001 CUDMORE	1-01-001 D'*YQUEM	1-01-001 DAUNTED
1-01-001 CRISPLY	1-01-001 CUE-PHRASE	1-01-001 D'ART	1-01-001 DAUPHIN
1-01-001 CRISS-CROSS	1-01-001 CUFF	1-01-001 D'ENTRETENIR	1-01-001 DAUPHINE
1-01-001 CRISS-CROSSING	1-01-001 CUFFLINKS	1-01-001 D'HOTEL	1-01-001 DAVAO
1-01-001 CRISSCROSSED	1-01-001 CUIRASSIERS	1-01-001 D'IDENTITE	1-01-001 DAVE'S
1-01-001 CRISTO	1-01-001 CUISINE	1-01-001 D'UN	1-01-001 DAVITS
1-01-001 CRITIC'S	1-01-001 CULBERTSON	1-01-001 D-C	1-01-001 DAVY'S
1-01-001 CRITICAL-INTELLECTUAL	1-01-001 CULMONE	1-01-001 D-NIGHT	1-01-001 DAWNS
1-01-001 CRITICS'	1-01-001 CULPAS	1-01-001 DA-DA-DA-DUM	1-01-001 DAWSON
1-01-001 CRITIQUE	1-01-001 CULTE	1-01-001 DABBED	1-01-001 DAYBED
1-01-001 CRITTER	1-01-001 CULTIVATES	1-01-001 DABBLED	1-01-001 DAYBREAK
1-01-001 CROAK	1-01-001 CULTURE'S	1-01-001 DABBLER	1-01-001 DAYDREAMED
1-01-001 CROAKED	1-01-001 CULTURE-*PROTESTANTISM	1-01-001 DABBLES	1-01-001 DAYDREAMING
1-01-001 CROAKIN	1-01-001 CULVERS	1-01-001 DABHUMAKSANIGAL-U'AHAI	1-01-001 DAYLIGHT'S
1-01-001 CROAKING	1-01-001 CUMARA	1-01-001 DACHSHUND	1-01-001 DAYLIGHTS
1-01-001 CROAKS	1-01-001 CUMBANCHEROS	1-01-001 DACK-RIHS	1-01-001 DAZZLE
1-01-001 CROCHET	1-01-001 CUMHURIYET	1-01-001 DADAISM	1-01-001 DAZZLER
1-01-001 CROCKED	1-01-001 CUMIN	1-01-001 DADE'S	1-01-001 DAZZLES
1-01-001 CROCKETED	1-01-001 CUMULATE	1-01-001 DAFFODILS	1-01-001 DE*CICCO
1-01-001 CROCKETT	1-01-001 CUMULUS	1-01-001 DAGERS	1-01-001 DE*FOREST
1-01-001 CROCODILE	1-01-001 CUNARD'S	1-01-001 DAGGERMAN	1-01-001 DE*GROOT
1-01-001 CROFTERS	1-01-001 CUR	1-01-001 DAILEY	1-01-001 DE*HAVILAND
1-01-001 CROIX	1-01-001 CURATIVE	1-01-001 DAINTILY	1-01-001 DE*KALB'S
1-01-001 CROMBIE'S	1-01-001 CURDLING	1-01-001 DAINTY-LEGGED	1-01-001 DE*MONTEZ
1-01-001 CROMWELL'S	1-01-001 CURDS	1-01-001 DAIRY-OH	1-01-001 DE*SOTO
1-01-001 CROMWELLIAN	1-01-001 CURETTAGE	1-01-001 DAISES	1-01-001 DE*WITT
1-01-001 CROONING	1-01-001 CURIE-*WEISS	1-01-001 DAK	1-01-001 DE-*KOONING
1-01-001 CROPPING	1-01-001 CURING	1-01-001 DALES	1-01-001 DE-IODINASE
1-01-001 CROSBYS	1-01-001 CURLS	1-01-001 DALI	1-01-001 DE-IODINATE
1-01-001 CROSS-CULTURAL	1-01-001 CURRANT	1-01-001 DALLAS-BASED	1-01-001 DE-IODINATED
1-01-001 CROSS-EXAMINATION	1-01-001 CURRANTS	1-01-001 DALLAS-HEADQUARTERED	1-01-001 DE-IODINATION
1-01-001 CROSS-EYED	1-01-001 CURRICULUMS	1-01-001 DALLES	1-01-001 DEACONS
1-01-001 CROSS-FERTILIZATION	1-01-001 CURRYS	1-01-001 DALTON'S	1-01-001 DEACTIVATED
1-01-001 CROSS-FERTILIZED	1-01-001 CURTAIN-RAISER	1-01-001 DALY	1-01-001 DEAD-END
1-01-001 CROSS-PURPOSES	1-01-001 CURTAINED	1-01-001 DALZELL-*COUSIN	1-01-001 DEAD-WEIGHT
1-01-001 CROSS-TOP	1-01-001 CURTIN	1-01-001 DAMAS	1-01-001 DEADENED
1-01-001 CROSS-WRITING	1-01-001 CURTNESS	1-01-001 DAMMED	1-01-001 DEADHEADS
	1-01-001 CURTSEYED	1-01-001 DAMMED-UP	1-01-001 DEADLINES
	1-01-001 CURVACEOUSLY	1-01-001 DAMNING	1-01-001 DEADNESS
	1-01-001 CUSA	1-01-001 DAMNIT	1-01-001 DEADWEIGHT
			1-01-001 DEADWOOD
			1-01-001 DEAFENED
			1-01-001 DEALERSHIPS

Rank	Word
1-01-001	DEANE
1-01-001	DEANS
1-01-001	DEARER
1-01-001	DEARIE
1-01-001	DEATH-LIKE
1-01-001	DEATH-LOCKED
1-01-001	DEATH-TRAP
1-01-001	DEATH-WISH
1-01-001	DEATHLY
1-01-001	DEATHWARD
1-01-001	DEBATABLE
1-01-001	DEBONAIR
1-01-001	DEBT-FREE
1-01-001	DEBUTS
1-01-001	DECATHLON
1-01-001	DECATUR
1-01-001	DECAYS
1-01-001	DECEIT'S
1-01-001	DECEITFUL
1-01-001	DECEIVE
1-01-001	DECEIVES
1-01-001	DECEIVING
1-01-001	DECELERATE
1-01-001	DECENCIES
1-01-001	DECENTLY
1-01-001	DECENTRALIZATION
1-01-001	DECENTRALIZING
1-01-001	DECEPTION
1-01-001	DECEPTIVELY
1-01-001	DECERTIFY
1-01-001	DECIMALS
1-01-001	DECIMETER-WAVE-LENGTH
1-01-001	DECISION-MAKING
1-01-001	DECISIONAL
1-01-001	DECKED
1-01-001	DECLAMATORY
1-01-001	DECLINATIONS
1-01-001	DECOLLETAGE
1-01-001	DECOMPOSE
1-01-001	DECOMPRESSION
1-01-001	DECORATIVENESS
1-01-001	DECOROUS
1-01-001	DECORTICATED
1-01-001	DECREED
1-01-001	DECREEING
1-01-001	DECRIES
1-01-001	DECRYING
1-01-001	DEDIFFERENTIATED
1-01-001	DEDUCING
1-01-001	DEDUCTABLE
1-01-001	DEDUCTIBILITY
1-01-001	DEDUCTIBLES
1-01-001	DEDUCTING
1-01-001	DCCM
1-01-001	DEEMING
1-01-001	DEEP-EYED
1-01-001	DEEP-SOUNDING
1-01-001	DEEP-TENDON
1-01-001	DEEPEN
1-01-001	DEEPENING
1-01-001	DEEPS
1-01-001	DEF
1-01-001	DEFACING
1-01-001	DEFAULTED
1-01-001	DEFEATISM
1-01-001	DEFEATISTS
1-01-001	DEFECATED
1-01-001	DEFENCE
1-01-001	DEFENDANT'S
1-01-001	DEFER
1-01-001	DEFERENTS
1-01-001	DEFERMENT
1-01-001	DEFERMENTS
1-01-001	DEFERRED
1-01-001	DEFERRING
1-01-001	DEFICITS
1-01-001	DEFINABLE
1-01-001	DEFLATED
1-01-001	DEFORMATIONAL
1-01-001	DEFORMITIES
1-01-001	DEFROST
1-01-001	DEFTNESS
1-01-001	DEGAS
1-01-001	DEGASSED
1-01-001	DEGENERATED
1-01-001	DEGENERATION
1-01-001	DEGLYCEROLIZED
1-01-001	DEGRADE
1-01-001	DEGRADED
1-01-001	DEGRADING
1-01-001	DEHUMANISED
1-01-001	DEHUMANIZE
1-01-001	DEHUMIDIFIED
1-01-001	DEHYDRATED
1-01-001	DEHYDRATION
1-01-001	DEIFICATION
1-01-001	DEIGNED
1-01-001	DEITY
1-01-001	DEJECTEDLY
1-01-001	DEJECTION
1-01-001	DEJEUNER
1-01-001	DEJEUNERS
1-01-001	DEKALB
1-01-001	DELAHANTY
1-01-001	DELANCY
1-01-001	DELANO
1-01-001	DELAWARES
1-01-001	DELECTATION
1-01-001	DELEGATES'
1-01-001	DELENDA
1-01-001	DELIA
1-01-001	DELICATE-BEYOND-DESCRIPTION
1-01-001	DELICATELY-TEXTURED
1-01-001	DELICIOUSLY
1-01-001	DELICTI
1-01-001	DELIGHTING
1-01-001	DELIMIT
1-01-001	DELIMITS
1-01-001	DELINEAMENTS
1-01-001	DELINEATED
1-01-001	DELIVRE
1-01-001	DELLE
1-01-001	DELLS
1-01-001	DELLWOOD
1-01-001	DELMORE
1-01-001	DELORIS
1-01-001	DELOUSED
1-01-001	DELPHI
1-01-001	DELPHIC
1-01-001	DELRAY
1-01-001	DELTAS
1-01-001	DELTOID
1-01-001	DELUDING
1-01-001	DELUGED
1-01-001	DELVIN
1-01-001	DEMAGE
1-01-001	DEMAGNIFICATION
1-01-001	DEMAGOGUES
1-01-001	DEMANDER
1-01-001	DEMANDINGLY
1-01-001	DEMARCATED
1-01-001	DEMEANS
1-01-001	DEMENTED
1-01-001	DEMETRIUS
1-01-001	DEMI-MONDE
1-01-001	DEMINERALIZATION
1-01-001	DEMOCRACIES
1-01-001	DEMOCRATIC-SPONSORED
1-01-001	DEMOCRATIQUE
1-01-001	DEMOCRATS'
1-01-001	DEMODOCUS
1-01-001	DEMOGRAPHIE
1-01-001	DEMOGRAPHIQUES
1-01-001	DEMOLITION
1-01-001	DEMON'S
1-01-001	DEMON-RIDDEN
1-01-001	DEMONSTRATIVES
1-01-001	DEMONSTRATORS
1-01-001	DEMORALIZATION
1-01-001	DEMORALIZED
1-01-001	DEMORALIZING
1-01-001	DEMOTED
1-01-001	DEMURRED
1-01-001	DEMUS-*SCHUBERT
1-01-001	DEMYTHOLOGIZING
1-01-001	DENNY'S
1-01-001	DENOMINATED
1-01-001	DENOMINATIONALLY
1-01-001	DENOMINATORS
1-01-001	DENOUNCES
1-01-001	DENS
1-01-001	DENSEST
1-01-001	DENSITOMETRY
1-01-001	DENSMORE
1-01-001	DENTED
1-01-001	DENTISTRY
1-01-001	DENTURES
1-01-001	DENUDED
1-01-001	DENVER'S
1-01-001	DENVER-AREA
1-01-001	DENVERITE
1-01-001	DENYIN
1-01-001	DEOR
1-01-001	DEPARTMENTAL
1-01-001	DEPECIATION
1-01-001	DEPERSONALIZED
1-01-001	DEPICTION
1-01-001	DEPLORABLY
1-01-001	DEPLORE
1-01-001	DEPLOYING
1-01-001	DEPLOYMENT
1-01-001	DEPORT
1-01-001	DEPOSE
1-01-001	DEPOSITORS
1-01-001	DEPOTS
1-01-001	DEPRAVITIES
1-01-001	DEPRECATORY
1-01-001	DEPRESS
1-01-001	DEPRESSANTS
1-01-001	DEPRESSES
1-01-001	DEPRESSORS
1-01-001	DEPRIVATION
1-01-001	DEPRIVATIONS
1-01-001	DEPUTIZED
1-01-001	DERAILS
1-01-001	DERANGEMENT
1-01-001	DERAS
1-01-001	DERE
1-01-001	DERELICT
1-01-001	DERELICTS
1-01-001	DERISIVELY
1-01-001	DERIVATIONS
1-01-001	DERIVATIVE
1-01-001	DEROGATE
1-01-001	DEROGATORY
1-01-001	DERRIERE
1-01-001	DERVISH
1-01-001	DESCENDENTS
1-01-001	DESECRATED
1-01-001	DESECRATION
1-01-001	DESEGREGATE
1-01-001	DESEGREGATION-FROM-COURT-ORDER
1-01-001	DESENSITIZED
1-01-001	DESIGN-CONSCIOUS
1-01-001	DESIGN-SIDE
1-01-001	DESIGNATES
1-01-001	DESIGNATIONS
1-01-001	DESIGNER'S
1-01-001	DESIROUS
1-01-001	DESMOND
1-01-001	DESOLATIONS
1-01-001	DESPERADOES
1-01-001	DESPINA
1-01-001	DESPISES
1-01-001	DESPISING
1-01-001	DESPOILED
1-01-001	DESPOILERS
1-01-001	DESPOILING
1-01-001	DESPOTS
1-01-001	DESPREZ
1-01-001	DESPUES
1-01-001	DESSIER
1-01-001	DESUETUDE
1-01-001	DESULTORY
1-01-001	DESYNCHRONIZING
1-01-001	DETACH
1-01-001	DETAIN
1-01-001	DETAINED
1-01-001	DETER
1-01-001	DETERIORATE
1-01-001	DETERIORATES
1-01-001	DETERMINABILITY
1-01-001	DETERMINABLE
1-01-001	DETERMINANT
1-01-001	DETERMINATE
1-01-001	DETERMINATIVE
1-01-001	DETERMING
1-01-001	DETERMINISM
1-01-001	DETERRENCE
1-01-001	DETEST
1-01-001	DETESTATION
1-01-001	DETONATING
1-01-001	DETOURS
1-01-001	DETRACT
1-01-001	DETRACTOR
1-01-001	DETRACTORS
1-01-001	DETRIBALIZE
1-01-001	DETROIT'S
1-01-001	DEUS
1-01-001	DEUTERATED
1-01-001	DEUTSCH
1-01-001	DEUTSCHE
1-01-001	DEVASTATE
1-01-001	DEVASTATINGLY
1-01-001	DEVENS
1-01-001	DEVER
1-01-001	DEVEY'S
1-01-001	DEVIATE
1-01-001	DEVIATED
1-01-001	DEVIATING
1-01-001	DEVIL'S-FOOD
1-01-001	DEVIOUS
1-01-001	DEVISEE
1-01-001	DEVISING
1-01-001	DEVONSHIRE
1-01-001	DEVOTEDLY
1-01-001	DEVOTIONAL
1-01-001	DEVOURED
1-01-001	DEVOUTLY
1-01-001	DEWARS
1-01-001	DEWDROPS
1-01-001	DEWY-EYED
1-01-001	DEXEDRINE
1-01-001	DEXTER'S
1-01-001	DEXTERITY
1-01-001	DEXTROUS-FINGERED
1-01-001	DHARMA
1-01-001	DI*GIORGIO
1-01-001	DI*LUZIO
1-01-001	DI*SIMONE
1-01-001	DI*VARCO
1-01-001	DIABOLICAL
1-01-001	DIACHRONIC
1-01-001	DIAGHILEFF
1-01-001	DIAGNOMETER
1-01-001	DIAGNOSABLE
1-01-001	DIAGNOSES
1-01-001	DIAGONALS
1-01-001	DIAGRAMMED
1-01-001	DIAL
1-01-001	DIALECTICAL
1-01-001	DIALECTICALLY
1-01-001	DIALING
1-01-001	DIALS
1-01-001	DIAMETRIC
1-01-001	DIAMOND-
1-01-001	DIAN'S
1-01-001	DIAPHANOUS
1-01-001	DIAPHRAGMS
1-01-001	DIAPIACE
1-01-001	DIATHERMY
1-01-001	DIATHESIS
1-01-001	DIATOMS
1-01-001	DICENDI
1-01-001	DICHONDRA
1-01-001	DICHOTOMY
1-01-001	DICKE
1-01-001	DICKEY'S
1-01-001	DICKINSON
1-01-001	DICTATORIAL
1-01-001	DICTIONARIES
1-01-001	DICTIONARY'S
1-01-001	DIDDLE
1-01-001	DIDDLING
1-01-001	DIDI
1-01-001	DIE-DEAD
1-01-001	DIE-UP
1-01-001	DIEHARD
1-01-001	DIEHARDS
1-01-001	DIENBIENPHU
1-01-001	DIESEL
1-01-001	DIETERS
1-01-001	DIETETIC
1-01-001	DIFU
1-01-001	DIEUX
1-01-001	DIFFERENT-COLOR
1-01-001	DIFFERENTIATING
1-01-001	DIFFERING
1-01-001	DIFFICILE
1-01-001	DIFFRING
1-01-001	DIFFRUNCE
1-01-001	DIFFUSELY
1-01-001	DIFFUSERS
1-01-001	DIFFUSES
1-01-001	DIGBY'S
1-01-001	DIGESTED
1-01-001	DIGESTIBLE
1-01-001	DIGGES
1-01-001	DIGIT
1-01-001	DIGITALIS
1-01-001	DIGITALIZATION
1-01-001	DIGNIFY
1-01-001	DIGRESS
1-01-001	DIGRESSIONS
1-01-001	DIGS
1-01-001	DIISOCYANATE
1-01-001	DIJON
1-01-001	DILATES
1-01-001	DILATING
1-01-001	DILETTANTE
1-01-001	DILIGENTLY
1-01-001	DILLINGER
1-01-001	DILTHEY
1-01-001	DILUENTS
1-01-001	DILUTE
1-01-001	DILWORTH

1-01-001	DILYS
1-01-001	DIMAGGIO
1-01-001	DIMAN
1-01-001	DIMAN'S
1-01-001	DIMENSIONALLY
1-01-001	DIMERS
1-01-001	DIMESIZE
1-01-001	DIMINUTION
1-01-001	DIMLY-OUTLINED
1-01-001	DIN
1-01-001	DINEEN
1-01-001	DINES
1-01-001	DINGHY
1-01-001	DINGO
1-01-001	DINGY-LOOKING
1-01-001	DINH
1-01-001	DINING-ROOM
1-01-001	DINNERWARE
1-01-001	DINOSAUR
1-01-001	DINOSAURS
1-01-001	DINSMORE
1-01-001	DIOCESE
1-01-001	DIOCS**-
1-01-001	DIODATI
1-01-001	DION
1-01-001	DIONIE
1-01-001	DIONIGI
1-01-001	DIONYSUS
1-01-001	DIOR
1-01-001	DIORAH
1-01-001	DIORAMAS
1-01-001	DIOXALATE
1-01-001	DIPHOSPHOPYRIDINE
1-01-001	DIPLOMAT'S
1-01-001	DIPOLES
1-01-001	DIPPING
1-01-001	DIPS
1-01-001	DIRE
1-01-001	DIRECTIONALITY
1-01-001	DIRECTIONALLY
1-01-001	DIRECTIVITY
1-01-001	DIRECTOR'S
1-01-001	DIRECTOR-GENERAL
1-01-001	DIRECTORSHIP
1-01-001	DIRECTRICES
1-01-001	DIRION
1-01-001	DIRON
1-01-001	DIRT-CATCHER
1-01-001	DIS*$HONEST
1-01-001	DISABLE
1-01-001	DISAFFECTED
1-01-001	DISAFFECTION
1-01-001	DISAFFILIATE
1-01-001	DISAFFILIATED
1-01-001	DISAFFILIATION
1-01-001	DISAGREEABLE
1-01-001	DISALLOWED
1-01-001	DISAPPROBATION
1-01-001	DISAPPROVES
1-01-001	DISAPPROVINGLY
1-01-001	DISARRANGED
1-01-001	DISASSEMBLE
1-01-001	DISASSEMBLY
1-01-001	DISBELIEVE
1-01-001	DISBELIEVED
1-01-001	DISBELIEVES
1-01-001	DISBELIEVING
1-01-001	DISBURSED
1-01-001	DISCARD
1-01-001	DISCERNABLE
1-01-001	DISCERNMENT
1-01-001	DISCIPLINARY
1-01-001	DISCIPLINING
1-01-001	DISCLAIMED
1-01-001	DISCLAIMER
1-01-001	DISCLOSES
1-01-001	DISCOID
1-01-001	DISCOLORED
1-01-001	DISCOLORS
1-01-001	DISCONCERT
1-01-001	DISCONCERTINGLY
1-01-001	DISCONTENTED
1-01-001	DISCONTINUANCE
1-01-001	DISCORD
1-01-001	DISCORPORATED
1-01-001	DISCOUNTING
1-01-001	DISCOURS
1-01-001	DISCOVERER
1-01-001	DISCRIMINATE
1-01-001	DISCURSIVENESS
1-01-001	DISCUSSANT
1-01-001	DISDAINS
1-01-001	DISEASED
1-01-001	DISEMBODIED
1-01-001	DISENFRANCHISED

1-01-001	DISENGAGE
1-01-001	DISENGAGEMENT
1-01-001	DISFAVOR
1-01-001	DISGRACED
1-01-001	DISGRACEFUL
1-01-001	DISGRUNTLED
1-01-001	DISGUISES
1-01-001	DISGUST
1-01-001	DISHARMONY
1-01-001	DISHEARTENING
1-01-001	DISHED
1-01-001	DISHONORED
1-01-001	DISHONOURING
1-01-001	DISHWASHERS
1-01-001	DISHWATER
1-01-001	DISILLUSIONING
1-01-001	DISINTEGRATING
1-01-001	DISINTEGRATIVE
1-01-001	DISINTERRED
1-01-001	DISJOINTED
1-01-001	DISKING
1-01-001	DISLIKING
1-01-001	DISLOCATED
1-01-001	DISLOCATION
1-01-001	DISLODGED
1-01-001	DISMAYED
1-01-001	DISMISSES
1-01-001	DISNEYLAND
1-01-001	DISOBEYING
1-01-001	DISORDERLINESS
1-01-001	DISORGANIZATION
1-01-001	DISORIENTED
1-01-001	DISOWN
1-01-001	DISPARITIES
1-01-001	DISPASSIONATE
1-01-001	DISPELL
1-01-001	DISPENSARY
1-01-001	DISPENSER
1-01-001	DISPENSERS
1-01-001	DISPENSING
1-01-001	DISPERSAL
1-01-001	DISPERSEMENT
1-01-001	DISPERSING
1-01-001	DISPLACES
1-01-001	DISPLACING
1-01-001	DISPOSITIONS
1-01-001	DISPOSSESSION
1-01-001	DISPROPORTIONATELY
1-01-001	DISPROVING
1-01-001	DISPUTABLE
1-01-001	DISQUALIFIED
1-01-001	DISQUALIFY
1-01-001	DISQUIET
1-01-001	DISQUIETING
1-01-001	DISQUIETUDE
1-01-001	DISQUISITION
1-01-001	DISREPUTABLE
1-01-001	DISROBE
1-01-001	DISRUPTIONS
1-01-001	DISRUPTS
1-01-001	DISSATISFACTIONS
1-01-001	DISSECT
1-01-001	DISSEMBLING
1-01-001	DISSEMINATING
1-01-001	DISSENSIONS
1-01-001	DISSENTED
1-01-001	DISSENTER
1-01-001	DISSENTERS
1-01-001	DISSERVICE
1-01-001	DISSIDENT
1-01-001	DISSIMULATION
1-01-001	DISSIPATING
1-01-001	DISSOCIATED
1-01-001	DISSOLUTIONS
1-01-001	DISSONANCES
1-01-001	DISTALLY
1-01-001	DISTANTLY
1-01-001	DISTASTEFUL
1-01-001	DISTENSION
1-01-001	DISTIL
1-01-001	DISTILLER
1-01-001	DISTILLERS
1-01-001	DISTILLING
1-01-001	DISTORTABLE
1-01-001	DISTRACTEDLY
1-01-001	DISTRACTING
1-01-001	DISTRACTIONS
1-01-001	DISTRAUGHT
1-01-001	DISTRESSES
1-01-001	DISTRIBUTOR'S
1-01-001	DISTRIBUTORSHIP
1-01-001	DISTURBER
1-01-001	DISTURBINGLY
1-01-001	DISUNION
1-01-001	DISUNITED

1-01-001	DITCHER
1-01-001	DITES
1-01-001	DITMAR
1-01-001	DITTY
1-01-001	DIVA
1-01-001	DIVAN-LIKE
1-01-001	DIVANS
1-01-001	DIVER
1-01-001	DIVERGING
1-01-001	DIVERSIONARY
1-01-001	DIVERSITIES
1-01-001	DIVERT
1-01-001	DIVEST
1-01-001	DIVIDER
1-01-001	DIVINE'S
1-01-001	DIVINING
1-01-001	DIVULGING
1-01-001	DIXIE
1-01-001	DIXIECRATS
1-01-001	DIZZILY
1-01-001	DIZZINESS
1-01-001	DJAKARTA
1-01-001	DJANGO'S
1-01-001	DNIEPER
1-01-001	DO*(C*)TERS
1-01-001	DO-GOOD
1-01-001	DO-GOODER
1-01-001	DO-GOODERS
1-01-001	DOAN
1-01-001	DOBBINS
1-01-001	DOBBS
1-01-001	DOBERMAN
1-01-001	DOBLE
1-01-001	DOCILELY
1-01-001	DOCKED
1-01-001	DOCKETED
1-01-001	DOCKS
1-01-001	DOCTERS
1-01-001	DOCTORATE
1-01-001	DOCTORS'
1-01-001	DOCTRINALLY
1-01-001	DOCUMENTARY-TYPE
1-01-001	DODD
1-01-001	DODGE'S
1-01-001	DODGER
1-01-001	DODINGTON
1-01-001	DOE
1-01-001	DOERNER'S
1-01-001	DOERS
1-01-001	DOESN'S
1-01-001	DOFFING
1-01-001	DOG-EARED
1-01-001	DOG-PIN
1-01-001	DOGBERRY
1-01-001	DOGGONE**H
1-01-001	DOGHOUSE
1-01-001	DOGLEG
1-01-001	DOGTROT
1-01-001	DOGUMENTI
1-01-001	DOGWOOD
1-01-001	DOHNANYI
1-01-001	DOLDRUMS
1-01-001	DOLE
1-01-001	DOLED
1-01-001	DOLEFUL
1-01-001	DOLLAR-*BRITTEN
1-01-001	DOLLAR-*DE
1-01-001	DOLLAR-AND-CENTS
1-01-001	DOLLAR-SIGN
1-01-001	DOLLARETTE
1-01-001	DOLLARS'
1-01-001	DOLLARS-AND-CENTS
1-01-001	DOLLIES
1-01-001	DOLMABAHCE
1-01-001	DOLPHIN
1-01-001	DOLTISH
1-01-001	DOMESDAY
1-01-001	DOMESTICALLY
1-01-001	DOMESTICITY
1-01-001	DOMI
1-01-001	DOMICILE
1-01-001	DOMICILED
1-01-001	DOMICILIUM
1-01-001	DOMINANTLY
1-01-001	DOMINIC
1-01-001	DOMINIQUE
1-01-001	DOMITIAN'S
1-01-001	DON'T-KNOW'S
1-01-001	DONATES
1-01-001	DONATING
1-01-001	DONATO
1-01-001	DONIZETTI'S
1-01-001	DONKEY
1-01-001	DONNELL

1-01-001	DONNELLY
1-01-001	DONNER
1-01-001	DONNING
1-01-001	DOOLEY
1-01-001	DOOLEYS
1-01-001	DOOLIN'S
1-01-001	DOOLITTLE'S
1-01-001	DOOMS
1-01-001	DOOMSDAY
1-01-001	DOOR-FRAME
1-01-001	DOOR-FRONTED
1-01-001	DOOR-TO-DOOR
1-01-001	DOORKEEPER
1-01-001	DOPE-RIDDEN
1-01-001	DOPED
1-01-001	DOPPLER
1-01-001	DORCAS
1-01-001	DORENS
1-01-001	DORENZO
1-01-001	DORIS'
1-01-001	DORSEY
1-01-001	DOS
1-01-001	DOST
1-01-001	DOSTOEVSKY'S
1-01-001	DOUBLE-
1-01-001	DOUBLE-*FIGURE
1-01-001	DOUBLE-BOGEYED
1-01-001	DOUBLE-CROSSED
1-01-001	DOUBLE-CROSSER
1-01-001	DOUBLE-CROSSING
1-01-001	DOUBLE-GLAZE
1-01-001	DOUBLE-HEADER
1-01-001	DOUBLE-MARRIED
1-01-001	DOUBLE-MEANING
1-01-001	DOUBLE-STRENGTH
1-01-001	DOUBLE-TALK
1-01-001	DOUBLEHEADER
1-01-001	DOUBLOON
1-01-001	DOUBTE
1-01-001	DOUBTINGLY
1-01-001	DOUCE
1-01-001	DOUG
1-01-001	DOUGHNUTTERY
1-01-001	DOURLY
1-01-001	DOUSED
1-01-001	DOVES
1-01-001	DOVETAIL
1-01-001	DOW-*JONES
1-01-001	DOWAGER
1-01-001	DOWELING
1-01-001	DOWER
1-01-001	DOWGUARD
1-01-001	DOWLING'S
1-01-001	DOWN-AND-OUT
1-01-001	DOWN-AND-OUTERS
1-01-001	DOWN-PAYMENTS
1-01-001	DOWNBEAT
1-01-001	DOWNERS
1-01-001	DOWNGRADE
1-01-001	DOWNING
1-01-001	DOWNPAYMENT
1-01-001	DOWNTALKING
1-01-001	DOWNTREND
1-01-001	DOXIADIS
1-01-001	DRAB-HAIRED
1-01-001	DRACO
1-01-001	DRAFTEE
1-01-001	DRAFTEES
1-01-001	DRAFTERS
1-01-001	DRAGGER
1-01-001	DRAGON
1-01-001	DRAGONETTI
1-01-001	DRAGOONED
1-01-001	DRAGOSLAV
1-01-001	DRAHVE
1-01-001	DRAM
1-01-001	DRAMA-FILLED
1-01-001	DRAMATICAL
1-01-001	DRAMATICS
1-01-001	DRAMATISTS
1-01-001	DRAMATIZATION
1-01-001	DRAMATIZING
1-01-001	DRAOUGHT
1-01-001	DRAPES
1-01-001	DRAUGHT
1-01-001	DRAUGHTY
1-01-001	DRAWBRIDGE
1-01-001	DRAWIN
1-01-001	DRAWING-ROOMS
1-01-001	DRAWLING
1-01-001	DRAWN-BACK
1-01-001	DRAWN-OUT
1-01-001	DREADFULLY
1-01-001	DREAM-*LUSTY
1-01-001	DREAM-*NEXT
1-01-001	DREAM-*SWEETMITE

A J b

1-01-001 DREAM-*TORKIN	1-01-001 DUMAS	1-01-001 EAVE	1-01-001 EKWANOK
1-01-001 DREAM-*WAY	1-01-001 DUMBBELLS	1-01-001 EBB	1-01-001 ELABORATES
1-01-001 DREAM-RIDDEN	1-01-001 DUMMIES	1-01-001 EBBETTS	1-01-001 ELAINE'S
1-01-001 DREAMBOAT	1-01-001 DUMMKOPF	1-01-001 EBBS	1-01-001 ELAN
1-01-001 DREAMIN	1-01-001 DUMPS	1-01-001 EBEN	1-01-001 ELAPSE
1-01-001 DREAMLESS	1-01-001 DUMPTY	1-01-001 EBER	1-01-001 ELAPSES
1-01-001 DREAMLESSLY	1-01-001 DUN	1-01-001 ECCENTRICITIES	1-01-001 ELBA
1-01-001 DREAMT	1-01-001 DUNDEEN	1-01-001 ECHELONS	1-01-001 ELBOWING
1-01-001 DREARINESS	1-01-001 DUNE	1-01-001 ECKART	1-01-001 ELBURN
1-01-001 DRED	1-01-001 DUNK	1-01-001 ECLAT	1-01-001 ELECTING
1-01-001 DREISER	1-01-001 DUNLOP	1-01-001 ECLECTICALLY	1-01-001 ELECTIVES
1-01-001 DREISER'S	1-01-001 DUNN'S	1-01-001 ECLIPSED	1-01-001 ELECTORATE
1-01-001 DREISERS	1-01-001 DUNN-*ATHERTON	1-01-001 ECLIPSING	1-01-001 ELECTRA
1-01-001 DRENCHED	1-01-001 DUNSTON	1-01-001 ECOLE	1-01-001 ELECTRESS
1-01-001 DRESBACH	1-01-001 DUPED	1-01-001 ECONOMIST'S	1-01-001 ELECTRIC'S
1-01-001 DRESBACHS	1-01-001 DUPLEX	1-01-001 ECUADOR	1-01-001 ELECTRIC-SEWER-
1-01-001 DRESBACHS'	1-01-001 DUPLICABLE	1-01-001 ECUMENICISTS	WATER
1-01-001 DRESSER	1-01-001 DUPONT	1-01-001 ECUMENIST	1-01-001 ELECTRIC-UTILIT
1-01-001 DRESSINGS	1-01-001 DUPONTS	1-01-001 ECUMENISTS	Y
1-01-001 DREWE	1-01-001 DUQUE	1-01-001 EDDIE'S	1-01-001 ELECTRIFICATION
1-01-001 DREXEL'S	1-01-001 DURATIONS	1-01-001 EDDIES	1-01-001 ELECTRIFYING
1-01-001 DRIB-DROOL	1-01-001 DURESS	1-01-001 EDDYMAN	1-01-001 ELECTRIQUES
1-01-001 DRIBBLED	1-01-001 DURLACH	1-01-001 EDEMATOUS	1-01-001 ELECTRO-MAGNETI
1-01-001 DRIED-OUT	1-01-001 DUROCHER	1-01-001 EDENTULOUS	C
1-01-001 DRIED-UP	1-01-001 DURRELL'S	1-01-001 EDGARDO	1-01-001 ELECTROCARDIOGR
1-01-001 DRIES	1-01-001 DURWOOD	1-01-001 EDGERTON'S	AM
1-01-001 DRINKHOUSE	1-01-001 DUSSA	1-01-001 EDGEWISE	1-01-001 ELECTRODYNAMICS
1-01-001 DRIP	1-01-001 DUSSELDORF	1-01-001 EDIFIED	1-01-001 ELECTROLYSIS
1-01-001 DRIP-	1-01-001 DUST-SETTLING	1-01-001 EDIFYING	1-01-001 ELECTROMAGNET
1-01-001 DRIPS	1-01-001 DUST-SWIRLING	1-01-001 EDISON'S	1-01-001 ELECTROMAGNETIS
1-01-001 DRIVE-YOURSELF	1-01-001 DUST-THICK	1-01-001 EDITORIALIST	M
1-01-001 DRIVERS'	1-01-001 DUSTBIN	1-01-001 EDITORSHIP	1-01-001 ELECTROMYOGRAPH
1-01-001 DRIVEWAYS	1-01-001 DUSTED	1-01-001 EDMONIA	Y
1-01-001 DRIZZLY	1-01-001 DUSTIN	1-01-001 EDUARD	1-01-001 ELECTRON-MICROS
1-01-001 DROMOZOOTIC	1-01-001 DUSTS	1-01-001 EDUCATIONS	COPICAL
1-01-001 DRONK'S	1-01-001 DUSTY-GREEN	1-01-001 EDUCATOR'S	1-01-001 ELECTRONICALLY
1-01-001 DROOP	1-01-001 DUSTY-SLIPPERED	1-01-001 EDW	1-01-001 ELECTRONOGRAPHY
1-01-001 DROOPED	1-01-001 DUTCHMAN	1-01-001 EDWARDES	1-01-001 ELECTROPHORUS
1-01-001 DROOPING	1-01-001 DUVERGER	1-01-001 EDWINA	1-01-001 ELECTROSHOCKS
1-01-001 DROP-BLOCK	1-01-001 DUYVIL	1-01-001 EE-FAKET	1-01-001 ELECTROTHERAPIS
1-01-001 DROPPINGS	1-01-001 DVORAK	1-01-001 EFFACES	T
1-01-001 DROUGHT-SEARED	1-01-001 DWARFED	1-01-001 EFFECTE	1-01-001 ELEGANCES
1-01-001 DROUTH	1-01-001 DWARFMISTLETOE	1-01-001 EFFECTINGE	1-01-001 ELEGANTLY
1-01-001 DROVERS	1-01-001 DWELLS	1-01-001 EFFECTUAL	1-01-001 ELEGIES
1-01-001 DROVES	1-01-001 DWELT	1-01-001 EFFEMINATE	1-01-001 ELEGY
1-01-001 DROWNS	1-01-001 DWOR	1-01-001 EFFETE	1-01-001 ELEPHANT'S
1-01-001 DROWSED	1-01-001 DWYER'S	1-01-001 EFFIE	1-01-001 ELEPHANTINE
1-01-001 DROWSILY	1-01-001 DYEING	1-01-001 EFFLORESCE	1-01-001 ELEVATES
1-01-001 DROWSING	1-01-001 DYEREAR	1-01-001 EFFLUENTS	1-01-001 ELEVENTH-FLOOR
1-01-001 DROWSY	1-01-001 DYKE	1-01-001 EFFLUVIUM	1-01-001 ELFIN
1-01-001 DRUDGERY	1-01-001 DYNAMICAL	1-01-001 EFFORTLESS	1-01-001 ELGIN
1-01-001 DRUGGAN-*LAKE	1-01-001 DYNAMICALLY	1-01-001 EFFORTLESSLY	1-01-001 ELICITS
1-01-001 DRUGGING	1-01-001 DYNAMITED	1-01-001 EFFUSIVE	1-01-001 ELIGIO
1-01-001 DRUGLESS	1-01-001 DYNASTIES	1-01-001 EGERTON	1-01-001 ELIJAH
1-01-001 DRUGSTORES	1-01-001 DYNODES	1-01-001 EGG-HATCHING	1-01-001 ELIMINATIONS
1-01-001 DRUID	1-01-001 DYSENTERY	1-01-001 EGG-SIZED	1-01-001 ELIOS
1-01-001 DRUMLIN	1-01-001 DYSPEPTIC	1-01-001 EGGED	1 01-001 ELIOT-OR-*MARTI
1-01-001 DRUMMER'S	1-01-001 DYSPLASIA	1-01-001 EGGHEAD	N
1-01-001 DRUMMERS	1-01-001 E),	1-01-001 EGGSHELL	1-01-001 ELISHA
1-01-001 DRUNK-AND-DISOR	1-01-001 E**.*O	1-01-001 EGILS	1-01-001 ELK
DERLIES	1-01-001 E**.*T	1-01-001 EGNINEERS	1-01-001 ELKS
1-01-001 DRUNKARD'S	1-01-001 E**U	1-01-001 EGO'S	1-01-001 ELL
1-01-001 DRUTHER	1-01-001 E**YU**YM**YM**	1-01-001 EGO-ADAPTIVE	1-01-001 ELLA
1-01-001 DRY-DOCK	YE**YL**YI**YH*	1-01-001 EGOCENTRIC	1-01-001 ELLANAE
1-01-001 DRY-EYED	*YS	1-01-001 EGON	1-01-001 ELLIE
1-01-001 DRY-GULCHIN	1-01-001 EADES	1-01-001 EGOTIST'S	1-01-001 ELLIPSIS
1-01-001 DRYFOOS'	1-01-001 EAGLE'S	1-01-001 EGREGIOUSLY	1-01-001 ELLIPSOID
1-01-001 DU*VOL	1-01-001 EAR-*MUFFS	1-01-001 EGRETS	1-01-001 ELLIPTICAL
1-01-001 DUAL-CHANNEL	1-01-001 EARDRUMS	1-01-001 EHLERS	1-01-001 ELLISON'S
1-01-001 DUAL-LADDER	1-01-001 EARED	1-01-001 EIDETIC	1-01-001 ELLO
1-01-001 DUAL-ROAD-UP	1-01-001 EARLY-MORNING	1-01-001 EIES	1-01-001 ELLSWORTH
1-01-001 DUALISM	1-01-001 EARLY-SEASON	1-01-001 EIGHT-AND-A-HAL	1-01-001 ELLWOOD
1-01-001 DUALITIES	1-01-001 EARMARKED	F-FOOT	1-01-001 ELMIRA
1-01-001 DUANE	1-01-001 EARNED-RUN	1-01-001 EIGHT-BAR	1-01-001 ELMS
1-01-001 DUBIN	1-01-001 EARP	1-01-001 EIGHT-BY-TEN	1-01-001 ELOI
1-01-001 DUBOIS	1-01-001 EARPHONES	1-01-001 EIGHT-FOOT	1-01-001 ELOISE
1-01-001 DUBOVSKOI	1-01-001 EARTH-BOUND	1-01-001 EIGHT-THIRTY	1-01-001 ELOPED
1-01-001 DUCES	1-01-001 EARTH-TOUCHING	1-01-001 EIGHT-WEEK	1-01-001 ELUATE
1-01-001 DUCHESS	1-01-001 EARTH-WEEK	1-01-001 EIGHT-YEAR	1-01-001 ELUATES
1-01-001 DUCT	1-01-001 EARTH-WEEKS	1-01-001 EIGHTEEN-YEAR-O	1-01-001 ELUCIDATED
1-01-001 DUCTWORK	1-01-001 EARTHENWARE	LD	1-01-001 ELUCIDATION
1-01-001 DUD	1-01-001 EARTHMEN'S	1-01-001 EIGHTEENTH-	1-01-001 ELUDES
1-01-001 DUDLEY	1-01-001 EARTHMOVING	1-01-001 EIGHTY-FOUR	1-01-001 ELUSIVENESS
1-01-001 DUDS	1-01-001 EARTHWORM	1-01-001 EIGHTY-NINE	1-01-001 ELUTED
1-01-001 DUDS'D	1-01-001 EASTERNERS	1-01-001 EIGHTY-ONE	1-01-001 EMANATED
1-01-001 DUELS	1-01-001 EASTHAMPTON	1-01-001 EIGHTY-YEAR-OLD	1-01-001 EMANATIONS
1-01-001 DUET	1-01-001 EASTLAND	1-01-001 EINE	1-01-001 EMANUEL
1-01-001 DUETS	1-01-001 EASTMAN	1-01-001 EINSATZKOMMANDO	1-01-001 EMASCULATED
1-01-001 DUFFER	1-01-001 EASY-GOING	S	1-01-001 EMASCULATION
1-01-001 DUFRESNE	1-01-001 EASY-TO-OPERATE	1-01-001 EINSTEINIAN	1-01-001 EMBALMERS'
1-01-001 DUFRESNE'S	1-01-001 EASY-TO-REACH	1-01-001 EISENHHOWER	1-01-001 EMBARCADERO
1-01-001 DUHAGON	1-01-001 EASY-TO-SPOT	1-01-001 EISLER	1-01-001 EMBARRASSINGLY
1-01-001 DULCET	1-01-001 EASYGOING	1-01-001 EITHER-OR	1-01-001 EMBATTLED
1-01-001 DULL-GRAY	1-01-001 EATABLE	1-01-001 EJECT	1-01-001 EMBELLISHED
1-01-001 DULLES'S	1-01-001 EATABLES	1-01-001 EKATERINOSLAV	1-01-001 EMBEZZLE
1-01-001 DULLNESS	1-01-001 EATERS	1-01-001 EKBERG	1-01-001 EMBEZZLEMENT
1-01-001 DULLS	1-01-001 EATINGS	1-01-001 EKSTROHM'S	1-01-001 EMBEZZLING

1-01-001 EMBITTERED	1-01-001 ENGLISH-BORN	1-01-001 EQUALIZERS	1-01-001 EVALUATIVE
1-01-001 EMBODIMENTS	1-01-001 ENGLISH-DIALOGU E	1-01-001 EQUALIZING	1-01-001 EVANGELICALISM
1-01-001 EMBODY		1-01-001 EQUALLED	1-01-001 EVANGELIST
1-01-001 EMBOSSED	1-01-001 ENGLISHY	1-01-001 EQUATORIAL	1-01-001 EVANGELISTS
1-01-001 EMBOUCHURE	1-01-001 ENGRAVER	1-01-001 EQUIDISTANT	1-01-001 EVANSVILLE
1-01-001 EMBROIDERIES	1-01-001 ENGRAVINGS	1-01-001 EQUIDISTANTLY	1-01-001 EVAPORATE
1-01-001 EMBROILED	1-01-001 ENGULFING	1-01-001 EQUILIBRIUMS	1-01-001 EVAPORATIVE
1-01-001 EMBRYO	1-01-001 ENGULFS	1-01-001 EQUINE	1-01-001 EVASION
1-01-001 EMCEE	1-01-001 ENHANCES	1-01-001 EQUINES	1-01-001 EVASIONS
1-01-001 EMIGRATED	1-01-001 ENHANCING	1-01-001 EQUIP	1-01-001 EVEGENI
1-01-001 EMIGRATING	1-01-001 ENJOIN	1-01-001 EQUIPOTENT	1-01-001 EVEN-HANDED
1-01-001 EMIGRATION	1-01-001 ENJOINDER	1-01-001 EQUIPPING	1-01-001 EVENING'S
1-01-001 EMIL	1-01-001 ENLARGD	1-01-001 EQUIVALENT-CHOI CE	1-01-001 EVENSEN
1-01-001 EMILIO	1-01-001 ENLARGEMENTS		1-01-001 EVENSONG
1-01-001 EMINONU	1-01-001 ENLIGHTEN	1-01-001 EQUIVOCAL	1-01-001 EVENTFULLY
1-01-001 EMISSARIES	1-01-001 ENLISTMENT	1-01-001 ERASE	1-01-001 EVENTSHAH-LEH
1-01-001 EMIT	1-01-001 ENLISTS	1-01-001 ERASERS	1-01-001 EVENTSHAHLEH
1-01-001 EMITTING	1-01-001 ENMITIES	1-01-001 ERASMUS'S	1-01-001 EVENTUALITIES
1-01-001 EMMANUEL	1-01-001 ENMITY	1-01-001 ERDE	1-01-001 EVENTUALITY
1-01-001 EMMETT'S	1-01-001 ENNIS	1-01-001 ERDMANN'S	1-01-001 EVENTUATE
1-01-001 EMOTIONALITY	1-01-001 ENNY	1-01-001 ERE	1-01-001 EVENUTALLY
1-01-001 EMPATHY	1-01-001 ENOCH	1-01-001 ERECTS	1-01-001 EVER'BODY
1-01-001 EMPHYSEMATOUS	1-01-001 ENORMITY	1-01-001 ERGOTROPIC	1-01-001 EVER-EXISTENT
1-01-001 EMPLOYE	1-01-001 ENOS	1-01-001 ERICKSON	1-01-001 EVER-LOVIN
1-01-001 EMPLOYEE'S	1-01-001 ENQUETES	1-01-001 ERLENMEYER	1-01-001 EVER-TIGHTENING
1-01-001 EMPLOYEE-CONTRI BUTED	1-01-001 ENQUIRED	1-01-001 ERNIE'S	1-01-001 EVERGLADES
1-01-001 EMPLOYMENTS	1-01-001 ENQUIRER	1-01-001 EROTICA	1-01-001 EVERGREEN
1-01-001 EMPOWER	1-01-001 ENRAGE	1-01-001 EROTICALLY	1-01-001 EVERLASTINGLY
1-01-001 EMPOWERING	1-01-001 ENRAGED	1-01-001 ERR	1-01-001 EVERMOUNTING
1-01-001 EMPTYING	1-01-001 ENRAPTURED	1-01-001 ERRATICALLY	1-01-001 EVERY-DAY
1-01-001 EMSELVES	1-01-001 ENRICHING	1-01-001 ERROL	1-01-001 EVIDENCING
1-01-001 EMULATED	1-01-001 ENRIGHT'S	1-01-001 ERRONEOUSLY	1-01-001 EVIDENTIAL
1-01-001 EMULSIFIED	1-01-001 ENRIQUE	1-01-001 ERRS	1-01-001 EVILDOERS
1-01-001 EMULSION	1-01-001 ENROLLEES	1-01-001 ERSKINE	1-01-001 EVINCED
1-01-001 EN-LAI	1-01-001 ENROLLING	1-01-001 ERUDITION	1-01-001 EVOCATION
1-01-001 EN-LAI'S	1-01-001 ENSLAVED	1-01-001 ERUPTING	1-01-001 EVOKING
1-01-001 ENAMEL	1-01-001 ENSLAVING	1-01-001 ERUPTS	1-01-001 EVOLUTIONISTS
1-01-001 ENAMELLED	1-01-001 ENSOLITE	1-01-001 ERWIN	1-01-001 EVOLVES
1-01-001 ENCAMP	1-01-001 ENSURES	1-01-001 ERYSIPELAS	1-01-001 EVZONE
1-01-001 ENCAMPED	1-01-001 ENTANGLEMENT	1-01-001 ERYTHROID	1-01-001 EWE
1-01-001 ENCASED	1-01-001 ENTER'D	1-01-001 ESCADRILLE	1-01-001 EWEN
1-01-001 ENCEPHALITIS	1-01-001 ENTEROTOXEMIA	1-01-001 ESCAPADE	1-01-001 EX*PE
1-01-001 ENCEPHALOGRAPHI C	1-01-001 ENTERPRISINGLY	1-01-001 ESCAPE'S	1-01-001 EX-*COMMUNIST
	1-01-001 ENTERTEYNED	1-01-001 ESCAPEES	1-01-001 EX-*GOV
1-01-001 ENCHAINED	1-01-001 ENTHRALLED	1-01-001 ESCAPIST	1-01-001 EX-*JUSTICE
1-01-001 ENCHANT	1-01-001 ENTHRONE*(S	1-01-001 ESCHEW	1-01-001 EX-*NATIONAL
1-01-001 ENCHANTINGLY	1-01-001 ENTHUSIASMS	1-01-001 ESCHEWED	1-01-001 EX-*ORIOLE
1-01-001 ENCIPHERED	1-01-001 ENTICEMENTS	1-01-001 ESCHEWING	1-01-001 EX-*PRESIDENTS
1-01-001 ENCIRCLE	1-01-001 ENTICING	1-01-001 ESCHEWS	1-01-001 EX-*TORY
1-01-001 ENCLAVES	1-01-001 ENTOMBED	1-01-001 ESCORTS	1-01-001 EX-*YANKEE
1-01-001 ENCLOSES	1-01-001 ENTOMOLOGIST	1-01-001 ESCUTCHEONS	1-01-001 EX-BANDITS
1-01-001 ENCLOSING	1-01-001 ENTRANCEWAY	1-01-001 ESHLEMAN	1-01-001 EX-CONVICT
1-01-001 ENCOMIUMS	1-01-001 ENTREAT	1-01-001 ESNARDS	1-01-001 EX-CONVICTS
1-01-001 ENCOMPASSES	1-01-001 ENTREPRENEURS	1-01-001 ESPAGNOL	1-01-001 EX-CUSE
1-01-001 ENCORES	1-01-001 ENTROPY-INCREAS ING	1-01-001 ESPANOL	1-01-001 EX-FIGHTER
1-01-001 ENCOURAGINGLY	1-01-001 ENTRUSTING	1-01-001 ESPERANZA	1-01-001 EX-GAMBLER
1-01-001 ENCROACH	1-01-001 ENTRY-LIMIT	1-01-001 ESPOUSAL	1-01-001 EX-JAZZ
1-01-001 ENCROACHED	1-01-001 ENTRY-LIMITED	1-01-001 ESPOUSES	1-01-001 EX-MARINE
1-01-001 ENCUMBRANCES	1-01-001 ENTWHISTLE	1-01-001 ESPOUSING	1-01-001 EX-MAYOR
1-01-001 ENCYCLOPEDIA	1-01-001 ENUMERATION	1-01-001 ESSAYISTS	1-01-001 EX-MUSICIAN
1-01-001 ENCYCLOPEDIAS	1-01-001 ENUNCIATE	1-01-001 ESTELLA'S	1-01-001 EX-PRISON
1-01-001 ENCYCLOPEDIC	1-01-001 ENUNCIATED	1-01-001 ESTEP	1-01-001 EX-PRIZE
1-01-001 ENCYLOPEDIA	1-01-001 ENUNCIATION	1-01-001 ESTERS	1-01-001 EX-SCHOOLTEACHE R
1-01-001 END-TO-END	1-01-001 ENVENOMED	1-01-001 ESTES	
1-01-001 ENDANGER	1-01-001 ENVIABLY	1-01-001 ESTHERSON	1-01-001 EX-SINGER
1-01-001 ENDANGERED	1-01-001 ENVIOUS	1-01-001 ESTRANGEMENT	1-01-001 EX-TRUCK
1-01-001 ENDEARMENT	1-01-001 ENVIOUSLY	1-01-001 ESTRANGING	1-01-001 EXACERBATES
1-01-001 ENDEAVOUR	1-01-001 ENVIRONING	1-01-001 ESTUARIES	1-01-001 EXACERBATIONS
1-01-001 ENDEAVOURS	1-01-001 ENVIRONMENT**H	1-01-001 ET'S	1-01-001 EXACT-SIZE
1-01-001 ENDEVOR	1-01-001 ENVISAGED	1-01-001 ETES	1-01-001 EXACTED
1-01-001 ENDGAME	1-01-001 ENVISAGES	1-01-001 ETHANOL	1-01-001 EXAGGERATIONS
1-01-001 ENDOGAMOUS	1-01-001 ENVOYS	1-01-001 ETHER	1-01-001 EXALT
1-01-001 ENDOGENOUS	1-01-001 ENZO	1-01-001 ETHERS	1-01-001 EXALTATION
1-01-001 ENDORSING	1-01-001 EOSINOPHILIC	1-01-001 ETHICISTS	1-01-001 EXALTATIONS
1-01-001 ENDOSPERM	1-01-001 EPAULETS	1-01-001 ETHIOPIANS	1-01-001 EXALTING
1-01-001 ENDOTHELIAL	1-01-001 EPH	1-01-001 ETRUSCAN	1-01-001 EXAMIANTION
1-01-001 ENDOWS	1-01-001 EPICUREAN	1-01-001 ETTORE	1-01-001 EXAMINERS
1-01-001 ENDPOINTS	1-01-001 EPICURUS	1-01-001 ETUDES	1-01-001 EXAMINES
1-01-001 ENDURINGLY	1-01-001 EPICYCLE	1-01-001 FTYMOLOGICAL	1-01-001 EXAMININ
1-01-001 ENERGIZED	1-01-001 EPICYCLICAL	1-01-001 EUCALYPTUS	1-01-001 EXASPERATE
1-01-001 ENERGIZES	1-01-001 EPICYCLICALLY	1-01-001 EUGENIC	1-01-001 EXASPERATING
1-01-001 ENERVATION	1-01-001 EPIDEMIOLOGICAL	1-01-001 EULOGIZE	1-01-001 EXASPERATINGLY
1-01-001 ENFANT	1-01-001 EPIGENETIC	1-01-001 EULOGIZED	1-01-001 EXBOYFRIEND
1-01-001 ENFIELD	1-01-001 EPIGRAMMATIC	1-01-001 EULOGIZERS	1-01-001 EXCAVATIONS
1-01-001 ENFORCERS	1-01-001 EPILOGUE	1-01-001 EUPHEMISM	1-01-001 EXCEL
1-01-001 ENFORCES	1-01-001 EPISTLES	1-01-001 EUPHORIC	1-01-001 EXCELLENCES
1-01-001 ENG	1-01-001 EPISTOLATORY	1-01-001 EURASIAN	1-01-001 EXCELS
1-01-001 ENGAGINGLY	1-01-001 EPITOMIZE	1-01-001 EURATOM	1-01-001 EXCELSIN
1-01-001 ENGH	1-01-001 EPITOMIZES	1-01-001 EUROPEANISH	1-01-001 EXCEPTING
1-01-001 ENGISCH	1-01-001 EPOCH-MAKING	1-01-001 EUROPEANIZATION	1-01-001 EXCISED
1-01-001 ENGLAND'S	1-01-001 EPPLER	1-01-001 EUROPEANIZED	1-01-001 EXCLAIM
1-01-001 ENGLAND-BORN	1-01-001 EPSILON	1-01-001 EUTECTIC	1-01-001 EXCLAIMS
1-01-001 ENGLE'S	1-01-001 EPSTEIN	1-01-001 EVA	1-01-001 EXCLUSIONS
1-01-001 ENGLISH-*DUTCH	1-01-001 EQNS	1-01-001 EVACUATE	1-01-001 EXCORIATE
1-01-001 ENGLISH-*SCOTTI SH-*FRENCH	1-01-001 EQUALIZATION	1-01-001 EVADE	1-01-001 EXCRETION
	1-01-001 EQUALIZE	1-01-001 EVADES	1-01-001 EXCURSUS
		1-01-001 EVADING	1-01-001 EXCUSABLE

1-01-001 EXECUTING	1-01-001 EXTRAPOLATES	1-01-001 FAMILARITY	1-01-001 FAZIO
1-01-001 EXECUTIONER'S	1-01-001 EXTRAPOLATIONS	1-01-001 FAMILIARLY	1-01-001 FEALTY
1-01-001 EXECUTIVE'S	1-01-001 EXTRAS	1-01-001 FAMILIARNESS	1-01-001 FEAR-FILLED
1-01-001 EXEGETE	1-01-001 EXTRAVAGANZAS	1-01-001 FAMILISM	1-01-001 FEAR-MADDENED
1-01-001 EXEMPLIFIES	1-01-001 EXTREMA	1-01-001 FAMILISTICAL	1-01-001 FEARE
1-01-001 EXERTION	1-01-001 EXTREMIS	1-01-001 FAMILLE	1-01-001 FEARSOME
1-01-001 EXERTIONS	1-01-001 EXTREMITIES	1-01-001 FAMILY-COMMUNITY	1-01-001 FEASTING
1-01-001 EXHALING	1-01-001 EXTROVERT	1-01-001 FAMILY-ORIENTED	1-01-001 FEATHER-LIKE
1-01-001 EXHAUSTIBLE	1-01-001 EXTRUDER	1-01-001 FAMILY-WELFARE	1-01-001 FEATHERBED
1-01-001 EXHAUSTINGLY	1-01-001 EXTRUDING	1-01-001 FAN'S	1-01-001 FEATHERBEDDING
1-01-001 EXHAUSTION	1-01-001 EXULTANTLY	1-01-001 FANCIER	1-01-001 FEATHERWEIGHT
1-01-001 EXHAUSTIVELY	1-01-001 EYD	1-01-001 FANCIES	1-01-001 FEATHERY
1-01-001 EXHAUSTS	1-01-001 EYE-BEAMINGS	1-01-001 FANCY-FREE	1-01-001 FEBRILE
1-01-001 EXHIBITORS	1-01-001 EYE-DECEIVING	1-01-001 FANCYING	1-01-001 FECUND
1-01-001 EXHILARATED	1-01-001 EYE-FILLING	1-01-001 FANEUIL	1-01-001 FECUNDITY
1-01-001 EXHORTATIONS	1-01-001 EYE-GOUGING	1-01-001 FANFARE	1-01-001 FEDERAL-QUESTION
1-01-001 EXHORTING	1-01-001 EYE-MACHINE	1-01-001 FANSHAWE	1-01-001 FEDERAL-RIGHT
1-01-001 EXHUMATIONS	1-01-001 EYE-STRAIN	1-01-001 FANTASIST	1-01-001 FEDERALIST
1-01-001 EXHUSBAND	1-01-001 EYE-TO-EYE	1-01-001 FANTODS	1-01-001 FEDERALIZE
1-01-001 EXILES	1-01-001 EYEBALLS	1-01-001 FAR-AWAY	1-01-001 FEDERALS
1-01-001 EXILING	1-01-001 EYEFUL	1-01-001 FAR-FAMED	1-01-001 FEDERICO
1-01-001 EXISTENTIALISM	1-01-001 EYELASHES	1-01-001 FAR-FLUNG	1-01-001 FEDS
1-01-001 EXISTENTIALISTS	1-01-001 EYELETS	1-01-001 FAR-OFF	1-01-001 FEE-PER-CASE
1-01-001 EXITS	1-01-001 EYELID	1-01-001 FAR-OUT	1-01-001 FEE-PER-DAY
1-01-001 EXOGAMOUS	1-01-001 EYEPIECE	1-01-001 FAR-RANGING	1-01-001 FEEDINGS
1-01-001 EXONERATED	1-01-001 EYESIGHT	1-01-001 FAR-SIGHTED	1-01-001 FEELING-STATE
1-01-001 EXORBITANT	1-01-001 EYETEETH	1-01-001 FARCES	1-01-001 FEENEY
1-01-001 EXORCISE	1-01-001 EYKE	1-01-001 FARDULLI'S	1-01-001 FEIGNED
1-01-001 EXOTHERMIC	1-01-001 F),	1-01-001 FARINA	1-01-001 FEIGNING
1-01-001 EXPANSION-CONTRACTION	1-01-001 F**.*S**.*C	1-01-001 FARLEY	1-01-001 FEIS
1-01-001 EXPANSIONIST	1-01-001 F**.*SUPP**.235	1-01-001 FARMED	1-01-001 FELER
1-01-001 EXPANSIVE	1-01-001 F'OVUH	1-01-001 FARMER-IN-THE-*DELL	1-01-001 FELICE'S
1-01-001 EXPANSIVELY	1-01-001 F'R	1-01-001 FARMER-TYPE	1-01-001 FELICITOUS
1-01-001 EXPECTABLE	1-01-001 F-PLANE	1-01-001 FARMHOUSES	1-01-001 FELLAS
1-01-001 EXPECTEDLY	1-01-001 F-PLANE,	1-01-001 FARMINGTON	1-01-001 FELLER
1-01-001 EXPEDITIOUSLY	1-01-001 FABRICATE	1-01-001 FARMLAND	1-01-001 FELLERS
1-01-001 EXPELLING	1-01-001 FABRICATED	1-01-001 FARMLANDS	1-01-001 FELLOW-COUNTRYMAN
1-01-001 EXPEND	1-01-001 FABRICATING	1-01-001 FARMWIFE'S	1-01-001 FELLOW-CRAFTSMEN
1-01-001 EXPENDABLE	1-01-001 FABRICIUS	1-01-001 FARNESES	1-01-001 FELLOW-CREATURES
1-01-001 EXPERIENTIALLY	1-01-001 FACADED	1-01-001 FARNUM	1-01-001 FELLOW-EMPLOYEES
1-01-001 EXPERIMENTALISM	1-01-001 FACADES	1-01-001 FARNWORTH	1-01-001 FELLOW-MEN
1-01-001 EXPERIMENTATIONS	1-01-001 FACE-LIFTING	1-01-001 FARR	1-01-001 FELLOWFEELING
1-01-001 EXPIATING	1-01-001 FACE-TO-WALL	1-01-001 FARRAR	1-01-001 FELON
1-01-001 EXPIRE	1-01-001 FACELESS	1-01-001 FARRELLS	1-01-001 FELONY
1-01-001 EXPIRES	1-01-001 FACET-PLANE'S	1-01-001 FARVEL-*TOPSY	1-01-001 FELSKE
1-01-001 EXPLICITNESS	1-01-001 FACETIOUS	1-01-001 FASCICULATIONS	1-01-001 FEMINIST
1-01-001 EXPLODES	1-01-001 FACETIOUSLY	1-01-001 FASCINATES	1-01-001 FEMME
1-01-001 EXPLODING-WIRE	1-01-001 FACILE	1-01-001 FASCINATINGLY	1-01-001 FEMMES
1-01-001 EXPLOITERS	1-01-001 FACILITATED	1-01-001 FASCIO-*COMMUNIST	1-01-001 FENDERS
1-01-001 EXPLOITING	1-01-001 FACILITATING	1-01-001 FAST-FIRING	1-01-001 FENS
1-01-001 EXPLORATIONS	1-01-001 FACILITATORY	1-01-001 FAST-FROZEN	1-01-001 FENSTER
1-01-001 EXPLORES	1-01-001 FACIUNT	1-01-001 FAST-GROSSING	1 01-001 FENUGREEK
1-01-001 EXPLOSIVELY	1-01-001 FACSIMILE	1-01-001 FAST-GROWING	1 01-001 FENWAY
1-01-001 EXPONENTIAL	1-01-001 FACSIPORT	1-01-001 FAST-MOVING	1-01-001 FENWICK
1-01-001 EXPORTERS	1-01-001 FACTORY-TO-*YOU	1-01-001 FAST-SPREADING	1-01-001 FERBER
1-01-001 EXPORTING	1-01-001 FADE-IN	1-01-001 FASTENING	1-01-001 FERDINANDO
1-01-001 EXPOSITED	1-01-001 FADEOUT	1-01-001 FASTENINGS	1-01-001 FERGESON
1-01-001 EXPOSITIONS	1-01-001 FADS	1-01-001 FASTENS	1-01-001 FERGUSSON
1-01-001 EXPOSITORY	1-01-001 FAERY	1-01-001 FAT'S	1-01-001 FERINGA
1-01-001 EXPOSURE-TIME	1-01-001 FAGAN	1-01-001 FAT-SOLUBLE	1-01-001 FERLENGHETTI
1-01-001 EXPOUNDING	1-01-001 FAGET'S	1-01-001 FATALISTS	1-01-001 FERMATE
1-01-001 EXPRESSIBLE	1-01-001 FAHEY	1-01-001 FATALITY	1-01-001 FERMENTATIONS
1-01-001 EXPRESSIONISTIC	1-01-001 FAHRENHEIT	1-01-001 FATBOY	1-01-001 FERMENTING
1-01-001 EXPRESSIVENESS	1-01-001 FAIER	1-01-001 FATHER-*GOD	1-01-001 FERN
1-01-001 EXPRESSIVNESS	1-01-001 FAIL-SAFE	1-01-001 FATHER-AND-SON	1-01-001 FERNAND
1-01-001 EXPRESSWAYS	1-01-001 FAIM	1-01-001 FATHER-BROTHER	1-01-001 FERNBERGER
1-01-001 EXPROPRIATED	1-01-001 FAIN	1-01-001 FATHER-CONFESSOR	1-01-001 FERNERY
1-01-001 EXPUNGE	1-01-001 FAINTED	1-01-001 FATHERLY	1-01-001 FERNS
1-01-001 EXPUNGING	1-01-001 FAIR-LOOKING	1-01-001 FATHOMS	1-01-001 FERRET
1-01-001 EXPURGATION	1-01-001 FAIR-PRICED	1-01-001 FATHUH	1-01-001 FERRETED
1-01-001 EXQUISITENESS	1-01-001 FAIRER	1-01-001 FATIMA	1-01-001 FERRIED
1-01-001 EXTEMPORE	1-01-001 FAIRES	1-01-001 FATSO	1-01-001 FERRIES
1-01-001 EXTEMPORIZE	1-01-001 FAIREST	1-01-001 FATTEN	1-01-001 FERVORS
1-01-001 EXTENDIBLES	1-01-001 FAIRGOERS	1-01-001 FAUCET	1-01-001 FESS
1-01-001 EXTENSOR	1-01-001 FAIRLESS	1-01-001 FAULKNERIAN	1-01-001 FESTERING
1-01-001 EXTENUATE	1-01-001 FAIRS	1-01-001 FAULTED	1-01-001 FETES
1-01-001 EXTERIORS	1-01-001 FAIRY-LAND	1-01-001 FAULTLESS	1-01-001 FETISHIZE
1-01-001 EXTERMINATIN	1-01-001 FAIRY-TALE	1-01-001 FAUNA	1-01-001 FEUD
1-01-001 EXTERMINATING	1-01-001 FAKER	1-01-001 FAUNTLEROY	1-01-001 FEUDALISM
1-01-001 EXTERMINATION	1-01-001 FALCONS'	1-01-001 FAUSTIAN	1-01-001 FEUDALISTIC
1-01-001 EXTERN	1-01-001 FALEGNAMI	1-01-001 FAUSTO	1-01-001 FEUERMANN
1-01-001 EXTERNALIZATION	1-01-001 FALL'S	1-01-001 FAUTEUIL	1-01-001 FEVERED
1-01-001 EXTINCT	1-01-001 FALL-OFF	1-01-001 FAVORE	1-01-001 FEVERSHAM
1-01-001 EXTINGUISH	1-01-001 FALL-OUTS	1-01-001 FAVORER	1-01-001 FEYER'S
1-01-001 EXTINGUISHED	1-01-001 FALLA'S	1-01-001 FAVRE'S	1-01-001 FFORTESCUE
1-01-001 EXTIRPATED	1-01-001 FALLACIOUS	1-01-001 FAWCETT	1-01-001 FFREIND
1-01-001 EXTIRPATING	1-01-001 FALLACY	1-01-001 FAWN	1-01-001 FIANCE
1-01-001 EXTRA-CURRICULAR	1-01-001 FALLIBLE	1-01-001 FAWN-COLORED	1-01-001 FIATS
1-01-001 EXTRA-THICK	1-01-001 FALLOFF	1-01-001 FAWNED	1-01-001 FIBER-PHOTOCATHODE
1-01-001 EXTRACTORS	1-01-001 FALLOW	1-01-001 FAWNING	1-01-001 FIBROCALCIFIC
1-01-001 EXTRALEGAL	1-01-001 FALMOUTH	1-01-001 FAY	1-01-001 FICHE
1-01-001 EXTRAMARITAL	1-01-001 FALSE-FRONTED	1-01-001 FAZE	
1-01-001 EXTRANEOUSNESS	1-01-001 FALSIFYING		
1-01-001 EXTRAPOLATE	1-01-001 FALSTAFF		
	1-01-001 FALTERS		
	1-01-001 FAMES		
	1-01-001 FAMILAR		

1-01-001	FICHTE	
1-01-001	FICKLE	
1-01-001	FICTION-WRITER' S	
1-01-001	FICTION-WRITING	
1-01-001	FICTIVE	
1-01-001	FIDDLES	
1-01-001	FIDDLESTICKS	
1-01-001	FIDDLING	
1-01-001	FIDE	
1-01-001	FIEDGLING	
1-01-001	FIEDLER'S	
1-01-001	FIEFDOM	
1-01-001	FIELD-HANDS'	
1-01-001	FIELD-SEQUENTIA L	
1-01-001	FIELDED	
1-01-001	FIELDER'S	
1-01-001	FIELDMICE	
1-01-001	FIELDSTONE	
1-01-001	FIENDISH	
1-01-001	FIERCENESS	
1-01-001	FIERCEST	
1-01-001	FIESTA	
1-01-001	FIFE	
1-01-001	FIFTEEN-MILE	
1-01-001	FIFTEEN-SIXTEEN THS	
1-01-001	FIFTEENTH-CENTU RY	
1-01-001	FIFTH-CENTURY	
1-01-001	FIFTIETH	
1-01-001	FIFTY-CENT	
1-01-001	FIFTY-DOLLAR	
1-01-001	FIFTY-FIFTY	
1-01-001	FIFTY-FOUR	
1-01-001	FIFTY-NINE	
1-01-001	FIFTY-ONE	
1-01-001	FIFTY-PIECE	
1-01-001	FIFTY-POUND	
1-01-001	FIFTY-SEVEN	
1-01-001	FIFTY-THIRD	
1-01-001	FIFTY-YEAR	
1-01-001	FIG**.1	
1-01-001	FIGARO	
1-01-001	FIGGERED	
1-01-001	FIGHTIN	
1-01-001	FIGURAL	
1-01-001	FIGURINES	
1-01-001	FILAGREE	
1-01-001	FILAMENT	
1-01-001	FILAMENTS	
1-01-001	FILBERT	
1-01-001	FILCHED	
1-01-001	FILDE	
1-01-001	FILETS	
1-01-001	FILIAL	
1-01-001	FILIBUSTERS	
1-01-001	FILIGREE	
1-01-001	FILIGREED	
1-01-001	FILIPINOS	
1-01-001	FILL-IN	
1-01-001	FILLER	
1-01-001	FILLIES	
1-01-001	FILLIP	
1-01-001	FILM'S	
1-01-001	FILMDOM	
1-01-001	FILMING	
1-01-001	FILMSTRIPS	
1-01-001	FILMY	
1-01-001	FINALIST	
1-01-001	FINALISTS	
1-01-001	FINAN	
1-01-001	FINDERS	
1-01-001	FINDSOME	
1-01-001	FINE-BONED	
1-01-001	FINE-CHISELED	
1-01-001	FINE-DRAWN	
1-01-001	FINE-FEATHERED	
1-01-001	FINE-FEATURED	
1-01-001	FINE-GRAINED	
1-01-001	FINE-POINT	
1-01-001	FINE-TOOTH	
1-01-001	FINELY-SPUN	
1-01-001	FINENESS	
1-01-001	FINGER-HELD	
1-01-001	FINGER-PAINT	
1-01-001	FINGER-SUCKING	
1-01-001	FINGER-TIPS	
1-01-001	FINGERING	
1-01-001	FINGERINGS	
1-01-001	FINGERPRINTING	
1-01-001	FINIAL	
1-01-001	FINICKY	
1-01-001	FINISHER	
1-01-001	FINK'S	
1-01-001	FINN	
1-01-001	FINNED	
1-01-001	FINNISH	
1-01-001	FINNS	
1-01-001	FINNSBURG	
1-01-001	FINOT	
1-01-001	FIORI	
1-01-001	FIRE-COLORED	
1-01-001	FIRE-CRACKERS	
1-01-001	FIRE-RESISTANT	
1-01-001	FIREBREAKS	
1-01-001	FIREBUG	
1-01-001	FIRECRACKER	
1-01-001	FIREHOUSES	
1-01-001	FIREMAN	
1-01-001	FIREPLACES	
1-01-001	FIREPOWER	
1-01-001	FIRESIDE	
1-01-001	FIRMA	
1-01-001	FIRST-*BORN	
1-01-001	FIRST-AID	
1-01-001	FIRST-DEGREE	
1-01-001	FIRST-FAMILIES	
1-01-001	FIRST-FLOOR	
1-01-001	FIRST-ORDER	
1-01-001	FIRST-PLACE	
1-01-001	FIRST-RUN	
1-01-001	FIRSTHAND	
1-01-001	FIRZITE	
1-01-001	FISHERS	
1-01-001	FISHERY	
1-01-001	FISHING-BOAT	
1-01-001	FISHKILL	
1-01-001	FISHMONGERS	
1-01-001	FISHPOND	
1-01-001	FISSURED	
1-01-001	FIST-FIGHTING	
1-01-001	FISTED	
1-01-001	FISTOULARI'S	
1-01-001	FITCH	
1-01-001	FITFUL	
1-01-001	FITFULLY	
1-01-001	FITTINGS	
1-01-001	FITZHUGH	
1-01-001	FITZROY	
1-01-001	FIVE-A-WEEK	
1-01-001	FIVE-AND-A-HALF	
1-01-001	FIVE-AND-DIME	
1-01-001	FIVE-AND-TWENTY	
1-01-001	FIVE-COLUMN	
1-01-001	FIVE-COORDINATE	
1-01-001	FIVE-DAY	
1-01-001	FIVE-DAYS-A-WEE K	
1-01-001	FIVE-FOLD	
1-01-001	FIVE-FOOT	
1-01-001	FIVE-HOME	
1-01-001	FIVE-HUNDRED	
1-01-001	FIVE-HUNDRED-DO LLAR	
1-01-001	FIVE-HUNDRED-YE AR-OLD	
1-01-001	FIVE-MEMBER	
1-01-001	FIVE-MINUTE	
1-01-001	FIVE-PLY	
1-01-001	FIVE-ROUND	
1-01-001	FIVE-SEVENTEEN	
1-01-001	FIVE-VOLUME	
1-01-001	FIXATIONS	
1-01-001	FIXERS	
1-01-001	FIZZLED	
1-01-001	FLAG-STICK	
1-01-001	FLAG-WAVERS	
1-01-001	FLAGELLATED	
1-01-001	FLAGELLATION	
1-01-001	FLAGEOLET	
1-01-001	FLAGLER'S	
1-01-001	FLAGPOLES	
1-01-001	FLAGRANTLY	
1-01-001	FLAIL	
1-01-001	FLAILED	
1-01-001	FLAKE	
1-01-001	FLAMBOYANTLY	
1-01-001	FLAME-THROWERS	
1-01-001	FLAMED	
1-01-001	FLAMMABLE	
1-01-001	FLANAGAN	
1-01-001	FLANKING	
1-01-001	FLANNAGANS'	
1-01-001	FLANNELS	
1-01-001	FLAPPER	
1-01-001	FLAPPERS	
1-01-001	FLASH-BULBS	
1-01-001	FLASHBACK	
1-01-001	FLASHLIGHT-TYPE	
1-01-001	FLAT-FOOTED	
1-01-001	FLAT-TOPPED	
1-01-001	FLATHEAD	
1-01-001	FLATLAND	
1-01-001	FLATNESSES	
1-01-001	FLATTEN	
1-01-001	FLATTER	
1-01-001	FLATTERING	
1-01-001	FLATTERINGLY	
1-01-001	FLATTEST	
1-01-001	FLATULENCE	
1-01-001	FLAUNTING	
1-01-001	FLAUTIST	
1-01-001	FLAUTIST'S	
1-01-001	FLAVORINGS	
1-01-001	FLAVUS	
1-01-001	FLAWS	
1-01-001	FLAXEN	
1-01-001	FLEAWORT	
1-01-001	FLECK	
1-01-001	FLECKED	
1-01-001	FLEDERMAUS	
1-01-001	FLEDGLINGS	
1-01-001	FLEE	
1-01-001	FLEES	
1-01-001	FLEET'S	
1-01-001	FLEETEST	
1-01-001	FLEETS	
1-01-001	FLEISHER	
1-01-001	FLEISHER'S	
1-01-001	FLEMINGS	
1-01-001	FLICKING	
1-01-001	FLICKS	
1-01-001	FLIMSIES	
1-01-001	FLINCHING	
1-01-001	FLINTLESS	
1-01-001	FLIPPANT	
1-01-001	FLIPPERS	
1-01-001	FLIPS	
1-01-001	FLIRT	
1-01-001	FLIRTATIOUS	
1-01-001	FLIRTED	
1-01-001	FLITE-*KING	
1-01-001	FLITTING	
1-01-001	FLNG	
1-01-001	FLOATER	
1-01-001	FLOATING-LOAD	
1-01-001	FLOATS	
1-01-001	FLOCCULATED	
1-01-001	FLOCCULATION	
1-01-001	FLOCK'S	
1-01-001	FLOCKING	
1-01-001	FLOCKS	
1-01-001	FLOE	
1-01-001	FLOES	
1-01-001	FLOG	
1-01-001	FLOOD'S	
1-01-001	FLOOD-LIGHTED	
1-01-001	FLOOD-RAVAGED	
1-01-001	FLOODHEADS	
1-01-001	FLOODLIGHT	
1-01-001	FLOODLIT	
1-01-001	FLOOR-LENGTH	
1-01-001	FLOOR-TO-CEILIN G	
1-01-001	FLOORSHOW	
1-01-001	FLOP	
1-01-001	FLOPPY	
1-01-001	FLOPS	
1-01-001	FLOR	
1-01-001	FLORA	
1-01-001	FLORESVILLE	
1-01-001	FLORICAN-*INVER NESS	
1-01-001	FLORICAN-*MY	
1-01-001	FLORIDIAN	
1-01-001	FLORIDIANS	
1-01-001	FLORIST	
1-01-001	FLORODORA	
1-01-001	FLOTATION-TYPE	
1-01-001	FLOTILLA	
1-01-001	FLOTILLAS	
1-01-001	FLOTTE	
1-01-001	FLOTTE'S	
1-01-001	FLOUNCED	
1-01-001	FLOUNDER	
1-01-001	FLOUNDERED	
1-01-001	FLOUNDERS	
1-01-001	FLOUR-MILLING	
1-01-001	FLOURED	
1-01-001	FLOURISHING	
1-01-001	FLOUTING	
1-01-001	FLOWER'S	
1-01-001	FLOWER-SCENTED	
1-01-001	FLU**DGEL	
1-01-001	FLUBBED	
1-01-001	FLUCTUATES	
1-01-001	FLUCTUATIONS	
1-01-001	FLUENCY	
1-01-001	FLUENTLY	
1-01-001	FLUFF	
1-01-001	FLUFFY	
1-01-001	FLUID-FILLED	
1-01-001	FLUKE	
1-01-001	FLUMENOPHOBE	
1-01-001	FLUORESCEIN	
1-01-001	FLUORESCEIN-LAB ELED	
1-01-001	FLUORESCES	
1-01-001	FLUORINATED	
1-01-001	FLUORINE	
1-01-001	FLURRIED	
1-01-001	FLUSHING-*MAIN	
1-01-001	FLUSTERED	
1-01-001	FLUTE	
1-01-001	FLUTED	
1-01-001	FLUTING	
1-01-001	FLUTIST	
1-01-001	FLY-BOY	
1-01-001	FLY-DOTTED	
1-01-001	FLYAWAY	
1-01-001	FLYER-*CASTLE	
1-01-001	FLYING-MOUNT	
1-01-001	FLYNN'S	
1-01-001	FLYWAYS	
1-01-001	FOALS	
1-01-001	FOAM'S	
1-01-001	FOAMED-CORE	
1-01-001	FOAMED-IN-PLACE	
1-01-001	FOAMY-NECKED	
1-01-001	FOCALLY	
1-01-001	FOCI	
1-01-001	FODDER	
1-01-001	FOG-ENSHROUDED	
1-01-001	FOGELSON	
1-01-001	FOGGED	
1-01-001	FOGGIA	
1-01-001	FOGY	
1-01-001	FOH	
1-01-001	FOILED	
1-01-001	FOILES	
1-01-001	FOISTED	
1-01-001	FOKINE'S	
1-01-001	FOLDER	
1-01-001	FOLDERS	
1-01-001	FOLEY	
1-01-001	FOLK-DANCE	
1-01-001	FOLK-MUSIC	
1-01-001	FOLK-TALE	
1-01-001	FOLKLIKE	
1-01-001	FOLKS'	
1-01-001	FOLKSONGS	
1-01-001	FOLKSTON	
1-01-001	FOLLICULAR	
1-01-001	FOLLOW-THROUGH	
1-01-001	FOLLOW-UPS	
1-01-001	FOLLOWETH	
1-01-001	FOLLOWIN	
1-01-001	FOLSOM	
1-01-001	FONDER	
1-01-001	FONDS	
1-01-001	FONTA	
1-01-001	FONTAINEBLEAU	
1-01-001	FONTANA	
1-01-001	FONTANEL	
1-01-001	FOOD-PROCESSING	
1-01-001	FOOT-HIGH	
1-01-001	FOOTAGE	
1-01-001	FOOTBALL'S	
1-01-001	FOOTBALLER'S	
1-01-001	FOOTBALLS	
1-01-001	FOOTBRIDGE	
1-01-001	FOOTE	
1-01-001	FOOTFALL	
1-01-001	FOOTFALLS	
1-01-001	FOOTHILL	
1-01-001	FOOTHILLS	
1-01-001	FOOTMAN	
1-01-001	FOOTPATH	
1-01-001	FOOTSTOOL	
1-01-001	FOOTWEAR	
1-01-001	FOOTWORK	
1-01-001	FOPPISH	
1-01-001	FORAGES	
1-01-001	FORAND	
1-01-001	FORAY	
1-01-001	FORAYS	
1-01-001	FORBAD	
1-01-001	FORBADE	
1-01-001	FORBES'S	
1-01-001	FORBORE	
1-01-001	FORBORNE	
1-01-001	FORCE'S	
1-01-001	FORCE-FEAR	
1-01-001	FORCE-RATE	
1-01-001	FORCEFULNESS	

56

1-01-001 FORE-PLAY
1-01-001 FOREARMS
1-01-001 FOREBEARING
1-01-001 FOREBEARS
1-01-001 FORECASTERS
1-01-001 FORECLOSED
1-01-001 FORECLOSING
1-01-001 FOREFATHERS
1-01-001 FOREFEET
1-01-001 FOREFINGERS
1-01-001 FOREGONE
1-01-001 FOREIGN-AID
1-01-001 FOREIGN-ENTRY-LIMIT
1-01-001 FOREIGN-SOUNDING
1-01-001 FOREKNOWLEDGE
1-01-001 FOREKNOWN
1-01-001 FORELEG
1-01-001 FORELLEN
1-01-001 FOREMAN'S
1-01-001 FOREPART
1-01-001 FOREPAWS
1-01-001 FORERUNNERS
1-01-001 FORESHORTENED
1-01-001 FORESHORTENING
1-01-001 FORESTRY
1-01-001 FORETELL
1-01-001 FORETHOUGHT
1-01-001 FOREVER-*CATHY
1-01-001 FORFEITED
1-01-001 FORGERIES
1-01-001 FORGERY
1-01-001 FORGING
1-01-001 FORGITFUL
1-01-001 FORGO
1-01-001 FORISQUE
1-01-001 FORK-LIFT
1-01-001 FORKLIFT
1-01-001 FORM-CREATING
1-01-001 FORM-DICTIONARY
1-01-001 FORMABILITY
1-01-001 FORMATS
1-01-001 FORMBY
1-01-001 FORMBY'S
1-01-001 FORMED-TOOTH
1-01-001 FORMIDABLY
1-01-001 FORMOSAN
1-01-001 FORSAKE
1-01-001 FORSAKES
1-01-001 FORSAN
1-01-001 FORSTER'S
1-01-001 FORSWEARS
1-01-001 FORSYTH
1-01-001 FORTE-PIANOS
1-01-001 FORTHRIGHTLY
1-01-001 FORTIER
1-01-001 FORTIN
1-01-001 FORTIORI
1-01-001 FORTNIGHT
1-01-001 FORTUNE-HAPPY
1-01-001 FORTUNE-TELLERS
1-01-001 FORTY-EIGHT
1-01-001 FORTY-FIFTH
1-01-001 FORTY-NINERS
1-01-001 FORTY-SECOND
1-01-001 FORTY-THIRD
1-01-001 FORTY-YEAR
1-01-001 FORUMS
1-01-001 FORWARD-MOVING
1-01-001 FORWARDING
1-01-001 FOSTER'S
1-01-001 FOSTERITE
1-01-001 FOSTERITES
1-01-001 FOULEST
1-01-001 FOULLY
1-01-001 FOUNDATION-STONE
1-01-001 FOUNDER-CONDUCTOR
1-01-001 FOUNDER-ORIGINATOR
1-01-001 FOUNDERING
1-01-001 FOUNDLING
1-01-001 FOUNDRY
1-01-001 FOUNTAIN-FALLS
1-01-001 FOUNTAIN-HEAD
1-01-001 FOUNTAINHEAD
1-01-001 FOUR-FOLD
1-01-001 FOUR-JET
1-01-001 FOUR-SIDED
1-01-001 FOUR-STORY
1-01-001 FOUR-SYLLABLE
1-01-001 FOUR-THIRTY
1-01-001 FOUR-WHEEL-DRIVE
1-01-001 FOURSOME

1-01-001 FOURTEEN-NATION
1-01-001 FOURTEEN-TEAM
1-01-001 FOURTEEN-YEAR-OLD
1-01-001 FOURTH-CENTURY
1-01-001 FOURTH-CLASS
1-01-001 FOURTH-DOWN
1-01-001 FOURTH-FLIGHT
1-01-001 FOURTH-HAND
1-01-001 FOURTH-OF-*JULY
1-01-001 FOWL
1-01-001 FOX'S
1-01-001 FOX-HOUNDS
1-01-001 FOX-TERRIER
1-01-001 FOXX
1-01-001 FRA
1-01-001 FRACASES
1-01-001 FRACTIONAL
1-01-001 FRACTIOUS
1-01-001 FRACTURE
1-01-001 FRACTURED
1-01-001 FRAGMENTARILY
1-01-001 FRAGONARD
1-01-001 FRAGRANCES
1-01-001 FRAILEST
1-01-001 FRAMBESIA
1-01-001 FRAMER
1-01-001 FRAN'S
1-01-001 FRANC
1-01-001 FRANCE-*GERMANY
1-01-001 FRANCESCA'S
1-01-001 FRANCHISES
1-01-001 FRANCIE'S
1-01-001 FRANCISCAN
1-01-001 FRANCK
1-01-001 FRANCO-*GERMAN
1-01-001 FRANCO-*IRISHMAN
1-01-001 FRANCOISETTE
1-01-001 FRANGIPANI
1-01-001 FRANKER
1-01-001 FRANKEST
1-01-001 FRANKFORD
1-01-001 FRANKFORT
1-01-001 FRANKLIN'S
1-01-001 FRANKS-IN-BUNS
1-01-001 FRANNY
1-01-001 FRATERNISATION
1-01-001 FRATERNITIES
1-01-001 FRATERNIZE
1-01-001 FRATERNIZED
1-01-001 FRAU
1-01-001 FRAY
1-01-001 FRAZZLED
1-01-001 FREAKISH
1-01-001 FRECKLED
1-01-001 FREDERIC
1-01-001 FREDERICKSBURG
1-01-001 FREDERIK
1-01-001 FREDRICO
1-01-001 FREDRIK
1-01-001 FREDRIKSHALL
1-01-001 FREE-*WILL
1-01-001 FREE-BLOWN
1-01-001 FREE-BUYING
1-01-001 FREE-DRINK
1-01-001 FREE-FOR-ALL
1-01-001 FREE-HOLDERS
1-01-001 FREE-WHEELING
1-01-001 FREE-WORLD
1-01-001 FREEBOOTERS
1-01-001 FREEDOM-CONSCIOUS
1-01-001 FREEDOM-LOVING
1-01-001 FREEHOLDER
1-01-001 FREEMAN'S
1-01-001 FREEPORT
1-01-001 FREETHINKERS
1-01-001 FREEWHEELERS
1-01-001 FREEZER
1-01-001 FREEZERS
1-01-001 FREEZES
1-01-001 FREIDA
1-01-001 FREIGHT'S
1-01-001 FREIGHT-BUMS
1-01-001 FREIGHT-CAR
1-01-001 FREIGHT-JUMPER
1-01-001 FREIGHTERS
1-01-001 FREIGHTS
1-01-001 FREINKEL
1-01-001 FRELINGHUYSEN'S
1-01-001 FRENCH-*CANADIANS
1-01-001 FRENCH-BORN
1-01-001 FRENCH-POLISHED
1-01-001 FRENCHMAN'S

1-01-001 FRENETIC
1-01-001 FRENZIED
1-01-001 FRENZIEDLY
1-01-001 FRENZY-FREE
1-01-001 FREQUENCY-INDEPENDENT
1-01-001 FREQUENCY-MODULATION
1-01-001 FREQUENTED
1-01-001 FRESCOED
1-01-001 FRESCOING
1-01-001 FRESH-GROUND
1-01-001 FRESHBORN
1-01-001 FRESHENED
1-01-001 FRESHLY-GROUND
1-01-001 FRESNO
1-01-001 FRET
1-01-001 FRETTED
1-01-001 FRIAR
1-01-001 FRIARS
1-01-001 FRICTION-FREE
1-01-001 FRICTIONS
1-01-001 FRIEDMAN
1-01-001 FRIEDRICH
1-01-001 FRIENDLILY
1-01-001 FRIENDS'
1-01-001 FRIGHTENINGLY
1-01-001 FRIGHTFULLY
1-01-001 FRILLY
1-01-001 FRINGED-WRAPPED
1-01-001 FRISE
1-01-001 FRIST
1-01-001 FRITTERS
1-01-001 FRITZIE'S
1-01-001 FRIZZLED
1-01-001 FRIZZLING
1-01-001 FROG
1-01-001 FROG-EATING
1-01-001 FROG-HAIKU
1-01-001 FROG-MARCHED
1-01-001 FROGS
1-01-001 FROHOCK
1-01-001 FROISSART
1-01-001 FROLICS
1-01-001 FRONDEL
1-01-001 FRONT-BACK
1-01-001 FRONTED
1-01-001 FROST'S
1-01-001 FROST-*DEBBY
1-01-001 FROSTED
1-01-001 FROSTING
1-01-001 FROSTS
1-01-001 FROSTY
1-01-001 FROTH
1-01-001 FROTHIER
1-01-001 FROWN
1-01-001 FROWNINGLY
1-01-001 FROWNS
1-01-001 FROWZY
1-01-001 FRUGALLY
1-01-001 FRUITFULLY
1-01-001 FRUITFULNESS
1-01-001 FRUITLESSLY
1-01-001 FT.
1-01-001 FU**DHRER
1-01-001 FUCHSIA
1-01-001 FUCKS
1-01-001 FUELED
1-01-001 FUELS
1-01-001 FUGITIVES
1-01-001 FUGUAL
1-01-001 FUHRMANN
1-01-001 FUHRMANN'S
1-01-001 FUJI
1-01-001 FULL-BANDED
1-01-001 FULL-BLOWN
1-01-001 FULL-BODIED
1-01-001 FULL-CLAD
1-01-001 FULL-DRESS
1-01-001 FULL-OF-THE-MOON
1-01-001 FULL-SISTERS
1-01-001 FULL-SIZED
1-01-001 FULL-YEAR
1-01-001 FULLBACKING
1-01-001 FULMINATE
1-01-001 FULMINATING
1-01-001 FUMBLE
1-01-001 FUMED
1-01-001 FUMING
1-01-001 FUMIO'S
1-01-001 FUN-FILLED
1-01-001 FUNARI
1-01-001 FUND-RAISER
1-01-001 FUND-RAISERS
1-01-001 FUNDAMENTALISM
1-01-001 FUNDING

1-01-001 FUNERAL-ACCESSORIES
1-01-001 FUNERALS
1-01-001 FUNGAL
1-01-001 FUNGICIDES
1-01-001 FUNNEL
1-01-001 FUNNELED
1-01-001 FUNNELS
1-01-001 FUNNIER
1-01-001 FUR-PIECE
1-01-001 FURBISHING
1-01-001 FURHMANN'S
1-01-001 FURIES
1-01-001 FURLED
1-01-001 FURLONGS
1-01-001 FURLOUGHED
1-01-001 FURNACE'S
1-01-001 FURROWS
1-01-001 FURTIVE
1-01-001 FURTIVELY
1-01-001 FUSELAGE
1-01-001 FUSIFORM
1-01-001 FUSILLADES
1-01-001 FUSING
1-01-001 FUSSILY
1-01-001 FUSTY
1-01-001 FUTHERMORE
1-01-001 FUTOTSU
1-01-001 FUTURE-DAY
1-01-001 FUTURE-TIME
1-01-001 FUZZED
1-01-001 FY
1-01-001 FYODOR
1-01-001 G**.*B**.*S
1-01-001 G**.*D**.*P
1-01-001 G'AHN
1-01-001 G-**JP
1-01-001 GAAFER
1-01-001 GAB
1-01-001 GABARDINE
1-01-001 GABBLE
1-01-001 GABBLING
1-01-001 GABLER
1-01-001 GADGETRY
1-01-001 GAETAN
1-01-001 GAGGED
1-01-001 GAGGING
1-01-001 GAGGLE
1-01-001 GAGING
1-01-001 GAGLINE
1-01-001 GAGWRITERS
1-01-001 GAI
1-01-001 GAINER
1-01-001 GAINERS
1-01-001 GAINESVILLE
1-01-001 GAINFUL
1-01-001 GAITED
1-01-001 GAITERS
1-01-001 GAITHER
1-01-001 GAL.
1-01-001 GALACTIC
1-01-001 GALAHAD
1-01-001 GALANTUOMO
1-01-001 GALAPAGOS
1-01-001 GALATA
1-01-001 GALEN
1-01-001 GALINA
1-01-001 GALINDEZ
1-01-001 GALLANTS
1-01-001 GALLBLADDER
1-01-001 GAILED
1-01-001 GALLERIES
1-01-001 GALLET
1-01-001 GALLING
1-01-001 GALLIVANTIN
1-01-001 GALLON-*LOREN
1-01-001 GALLONAGE
1-01-001 GALLOPED
1-01-001 GALLOPING
1-01-001 GALLS
1-01-001 GALLSTONE
1-01-001 GALLSTONES
1-01-001 GALLUP
1-01-001 GALLUS-SNAPPING
1-01-001 GALOPHONE-*KIMBERLY
1-01-001 GALOPHONE-*PRISSY
1-01-001 GALTIER
1-01-001 GALTIER'S
1-01-001 GALVANISM
1-01-001 GALVESTON-*PORT
1-01-001 GAMBITS
1-01-001 GAMBLER-POLITICIAN
1-01-001 GAMBLES
1-01-001 GAME-MANAGEMENT

1-01-001 GAMEBIRD	1-01-001 GEMEINSCHAFT	1-01-001 GINKGO	1-01-001 GNOMON
1-01-001 GAMECOCK	1-01-001 GEMLIKE	1-01-001 GINNER'S	1-01-001 GO**DTTERDA**DMMERUNG
1-01-001 GAMING	1-01-001 GENDERS	1-01-001 GINNIN	
1-01-001 GANADO	1-01-001 GENEALOGIES	1-01-001 GINO	1-01-001 GO**DTTINGEN
1-01-001 GANDER	1-01-001 GENERA	1-01-001 GINS	1-01-001 GO-GO-GO
1-01-001 GANESSA	1-01-001 GENERAL-APPEAL	1-01-001 GINSBERG'S	1-01-001 GO-IT-ALONE
1-01-001 GANG'S	1-01-001 GENERAL-PURPOSE	1-01-001 GIOCONDA	1-01-001 GO-TO-WAR
1-01-001 GANGLAND	1-01-001 GENERALIST	1-01-001 GIRD	1-01-001 GOA
1-01-001 GANGLING	1-01-001 GENERALITIES	1-01-001 GIRDERS	1-01-001 GOAD
1-01-001 GANGPLANK	1-01-001 GENERATION'S	1-01-001 GIRL-FRIEND	1-01-001 GOAL-LINE
1-01-001 GANGWAY	1-01-001 GENES	1-01-001 GIRL-SAN	1-01-001 GOAL-ORIENTED
1-01-001 GANNETT'S	1-01-001 GENEVIEVE	1-01-001 GIRLIE	1-01-001 GOAL-VALUES
1-01-001 GANNON'S	1-01-001 GENIE	1-01-001 GIRTH	1-01-001 GOB
1-01-001 GARAGED	1-01-001 GENII	1-01-001 GISELE	1-01-001 GOBBLEDYGOOK
1-01-001 GARBED	1-01-001 GENIUSES	1-01-001 GISORS	1-01-001 GOBBLERS
1-01-001 GARBLED	1-01-001 GENNARO	1-01-001 GIST	1-01-001 GOBBLES
1-01-001 GARDE	1-01-001 GENRES	1-01-001 GIUBBONARI	1-01-001 GOD-CURST
1-01-001 GARDENED	1-01-001 GENTIAN	1-01-001 GIULIETTA	1-01-001 GOD-FORSAKEN
1-01-001 GARDENERS	1-01-001 GENTIANS	1-01-001 GIUSTINIANI	1-01-001 GOD-LIKE
1-01-001 GARDENIA	1-01-001 GENTILES	1-01-001 GIVE-AND-TAKE	1-01-001 GODAMIT
1-01-001 GARDENIAS	1-01-001 GENTLEMANLY	1-01-001 GIVE-AWAY	1-01-001 GODDAMIT
1-01-001 GARGANTUAN	1-01-001 GENTRY	1-01-001 GIVENNESS	1-01-001 GODFREY
1-01-001 GARGERY'S	1-01-001 GEO-POLITICAL	1-01-001 GIVER	1-01-001 GODHEAD
1-01-001 GARINE	1-01-001 GEOCENTRICISM	1-01-001 GIVERS	1-01-001 GODLIKE
1-01-001 GARISH	1-01-001 GEODETIC	1-01-001 GLACIER	1-01-001 GODLINESS
1-01-001 GARISHNESS	1-01-001 GEOGRAPHERS	1-01-001 GLACIER-LIKE	1-01-001 GODUNOV
1-01-001 GARLANDED	1-01-001 GEOMETRICAL	1-01-001 GLACIERS	1-01-001 GOERING
1-01-001 GARNER	1-01-001 GEOMETRICALLY	1-01-001 GLADIATOR	1-01-001 GOETHE'S
1-01-001 GARNET	1-01-001 GEOPOLITICAL	1-01-001 GLADNESS	1-01-001 GOG
1-01-001 GARNETT	1-01-001 GEORGETOWN'S	1-01-001 GLAMORIZE	1-01-001 GOGGLES
1-01-001 GARRARD'S	1-01-001 GEORGI	1-01-001 GLANDERS	1-01-001 GOGO
1-01-001 GARRETT	1-01-001 GEORGIANS	1-01-001 GLANDULAR	1-01-001 GOGOL
1-01-001 GARRISONED	1-01-001 GERAGHTYS'	1-01-001 GLARINGLY	1-01-001 GOGOL'S
1-01-001 GARRISONIAN	1-01-001 GERBY	1-01-001 GLASS-BOTTOM	1-01-001 GOINGS
1-01-001 GARRULOUS	1-01-001 GERHARD	1-01-001 GLASS-LIKE	1-01-001 GOLD-FILLED
1-01-001 GARSTUNG	1-01-001 GERIATRIC	1-01-001 GLASSLESS	1-01-001 GOLD-PHONE
1-01-001 GARZA	1-01-001 GERMAN'S	1-01-001 GLAUCOMA	1-01-001 GOLD-WIRE
1-01-001 GAS-FIRED	1-01-001 GERMAN-LANGUAGE	1-01-001 GLAYRE	1-01-001 GOLDA
1-01-001 GAS-GLASS	1-01-001 GERMANIA	1-01-001 GLAZER-*FINE	1-01-001 GOLDEN-CRUSTED
1-01-001 GASH	1-01-001 GERMANIZED	1-01-001 GLEAN	1-01-001 GOLDFISH
1-01-001 GASKET'S	1-01-001 GERMANO-*SLAVIC	1-01-001 GLEANED	1-01-001 GOLDSMITH
1-01-001 GASKETS	1-01-001 GERMINAL	1-01-001 GLEE-CLUB	1-01-001 GOLFING
1-01-001 GASLIGHTS	1-01-001 GERMS	1-01-001 GLEEFUL	1-01-001 GOMPACHI
1-01-001 GASPARD	1-01-001 GEROGE	1-01-001 GLEEFULLY	1-01-001 GONNE
1-01-001 GASPEE	1-01-001 GEROME	1-01-001 GLEES	1-01-001 GOOD-HUMOREDLY
1-01-001 GASPINGLY	1-01-001 GERSHWIN	1-01-001 GLENDALE	1-01-001 GOOD-LIVING
1-01-001 GASSE	1-01-001 GERSHWINS	1-01-001 GLENDORA'S	1-01-001 GOOD-NEWS
1-01-001 GASSER	1-01-001 GERSHWINS'	1-01-001 GLENNON	1-01-001 GOOD-NIGHT
1-01-001 GASSET	1-01-001 GERSTA**DCKER	1-01-001 GLIB	1-01-001 GOOD-SIZE
1-01-001 GASSING	1-01-001 GESAMTKUNSTWERK	1-01-001 GLIDE-BOMBED	1-01-001 GOOD-WILL
1-01-001 GASSINGS	1-01-001 GESANGVEREIN	1-01-001 GLIDED	1-01-001 GOODBY
1-01-001 GASSY	1-01-001 GESTAPO	1-01-001 GLIDERS	1-01-001 GOODIES
1-01-001 GASTRONOMES	1-01-001 GESTICULATED	1-01-001 GLIDES	1-01-001 GOODNESS'
1-01-001 GASTRONOMY	1-01-001 GESTICULATING	1-01-001 GLIMCO'S	1-01-001 GOODWILL
1-01-001 GATE-POST	1-01-001 GESTURING	1-01-001 GLIMMERING	1-01-001 GOOEY
1-01-001 GATEWAYS	1-01-001 GESUALDO	1-01-001 GLISSADE	1-01-001 GOOFED
1-01-001 GATHERING-IN	1-01-001 GETAWAY	1-01-001 GLITTERED	1-01-001 GOOLICK
1-01-001 GATHERS	1-01-001 GETTIN	1-01-001 GLOATS	1-01-001 GOOOOLICK
1-01-001 GATSBY	1-01-001 GETZ	1-01-001 GLOB-FLAKES	1-01-001 GOOSHEY
1-01-001 GAUCHE	1-01-001 GETZ'S	1-01-001 GLOBALLY	1-01-001 GORE'S
1-01-001 GAUCHERIE	1-01-001 GEVURTZ	1-01-001 GLOBE-*DEMOCRAT	1-01-001 GORGE
1-01-001 GAUCHERIES	1-01-001 GEYSERING	1-01-001 GLOBE-GIRDLING	1-01-001 GORGEOUSLY
1-01-001 GAUGUIN	1-01-001 GHADIALI	1-01-001 GLOBES	1-01-001 GORGES
1-01-001 GAUL	1-01-001 GHAZAL	1-01-001 GLOBETROTTER	1-01-001 GORGING
1-01-001 GAULEITER	1-01-001 GHAZALS	1-01-001 GLOBIGII	1-01-001 GORHAM'S
1-01-001 GAUNTLEY	1-01-001 GHENT	1-01-001 GLOBOCNIK'S	1-01-001 GORKY
1-01-001 GAUTIER	1-01-001 GHERKINS	1-01-001 GLOBULINS	1-01-001 GORSHEK
1-01-001 GAUZE	1-01-001 GHIBERTI	1-01-001 GLOCESTER	1-01-001 GORSHIN
1-01-001 GAVESTON	1-01-001 GHORMLEY	1-01-001 GLOMMED	1-01-001 GOSAIMASU
1-01-001 GAVOTTES	1-01-001 GHOSTED	1-01-001 GLORIA	1-01-001 GOSPEL-SINGER
1-01-001 GAWDAMIGHTY	1-01-001 GHOSTLIKE	1-01-001 GLORIFICATION	1-01-001 GOSPELERS
1-01-001 GAWKY	1-01-001 GHOUL	1-01-001 GLORIFIES	1-01-001 GOSSAMER
1-01-001 GAY-ESS	1-01-001 GIACOMETTI	1-01-001 GLORIOUSLY	1-01-001 GOSSIPED
1-01-001 GAYETY	1-01-001 GIACOMO	1-01-001 GLORYING	1-01-001 GOSSON'S
1-01-001 GAYLOR	1-01-001 GIAOUR	1-01-001 GLOSS	1-01-001 GOTHAM
1-01-001 GAYLOR'S	1-01-001 GIBBET	1-01-001 GLOSSED	1-01-001 GOTHICISM
1-01-001 GAYNOR	1-01-001 GIBE	1-01-001 GLOSSY	1-01-001 GOTT
1-01-001 GAZELLE	1-01-001 GIBES	1-01-001 GLOTTAL	1-01-001 GOUGE
1-01-001 GAZER	1-01-001 GIBLET	1-01-001 GLOTTOCHRONOLOGY	1-01-001 GOULDINGS
1-01-001 GAZES	1-01-001 GIDDINESS		1-01-001 GOURMET'S
1-01-001 GAZETTES	1-01-001 GIDDINGS	1-01-001 GLOVER	1-01-001 GOURMETS
1-01-001 GAZINOSU	1-01-001 GIDE	1-01-001 GLOWS	1-01-001 GOUTTE
1-01-001 GEAR-SETS	1-01-001 GIG	1-01-001 GLUM	1-01-001 GOUVERNE
1-01-001 GEARING	1-01-001 GIGENZA	1-01-001 GLUMLY	1-01-001 GOUVERNEMENT
1-01-001 GEARY	1-01-001 GIGGLE	1-01-001 GLUTAMIC	1-01-001 GOVERNMEN
1-01-001 GEATISH	1-01-001 GIGGLING	1-01-001 GLUTINOUS	1-01-001 GOVERNMENT-BLES...SE?
1-01-001 GEDDES	1-01-001 GIL	1-01-001 GLUTTED	
1-01-001 GEE'S	1-01-001 GILD	1-01-001 GLYCERINATED	1-01-001 GOVERNMENT-CON...ROLLE?
1-01-001 GEEING	1-01-001 GILDAS	1-01-001 GLYCEROLIZED	
1-01-001 GEELY'S	1-01-001 GILKSON	1-01-001 GLYCOLS	1-01-001 GOVERNMENT-OWN?
1-01-001 GEERED	1-01-001 GILLIS	1-01-001 GLYCOSIDES	
1-01-001 GEGENSCHEIN	1-01-001 GILMORE	1-01-001 GNARLED	1-01-001 GOVERNMENT-SUP...ORTE?
1-01-001 GEIGER	1-01-001 GILROY	1-01-001 GNAW	
1-01-001 GEISHA	1-01-001 GIMBALED	1-01-001 GNAWED	1-01-001 GOVERNMENT-TO-?...OVERNMEN?
1-01-001 GELATIN-LIKE	1-01-001 GIMME	1-01-001 GNOME	
1-01-001 GELDINGS	1-01-001 GIMPY	1-01-001 GNOMELIKE	1-01-001 GOVERNMENTALLY
1-01-001 GELLY	1-01-001 GINGHAMS	1-01-001 GNOMES	

8⁴1

1-01-001 GOVERNOR-*GENERAL	1-01-001 GREAT-NIECES	1-01-001 GROWTHS	1-01-001 GYNECOLOGIST
1-01-001 GOWNED	1-01-001 GREATCOATED	1-01-001 GRUBS	1-01-001 GYP'LL
1-01-001 GOYETTE	1-01-001 GREATE	1-01-001 GRULLER	1-01-001 GYPSIES
1-01-001 GPD,	1-01-001 GREECE'S	1-01-001 GRUMBLING	1-01-001 GYRATION
1-01-001 GRA**DFIN'S	1-01-001 GREEDILY	1-01-001 GRUNNFEU	1-01-001 GYRATIONS
1-01-001 GRABBIN	1-01-001 GREEK-BORN	1-01-001 GRUONDED	1-01-001 GYRO-PLATFORM-SERVO
1-01-001 GRABSKI'S	1-01-001 GREEK-SPEAKING	1-01-001 GRZESIAK	1-01-001 GYROSCOPES
1-01-001 GRACED	1-01-001 GREEN-BUGS	1-01-001 GUANIDINE	1-01-001 H)
1-01-001 GRACIE	1-01-001 GREEN-SCALED	1-01-001 GUARANTEED-NEUTRAL	1-01-001 H**.*L
1-01-001 GRACIE'S	1-01-001 GREEN-TINTED		1-01-001 H**.*P**.*R
1-01-001 GRADE-*A	1-01-001 GREENHOUSES	1-01-001 GUARANTY	1-01-001 H**.*W
1-01-001 GRADE-CONSTRUCTED	1-01-001 GREENLY	1-01-001 GUARD-ROOM	1-01-001 H'ALL
1-01-001 GRADE-EQUIVALENT	1-01-001 GREENNESS	1-01-001 GUARDEDNESS	1-01-001 HAAEK
1-01-001 GRADE-EQUIVALENTS	1-01-001 GREENOCK	1-01-001 GUARDHOUSE	1-01-001 HAASE
	1-01-001 GREENSWARD	1-01-001 GUARDIA	1-01-001 HABE
1-01-001 GRADING	1-01-001 GREENTREE	1-01-001 GUARDINI	1-01-001 HABERDASHERIES
1-01-001 GRADUALIST	1-01-001 GREENWARE	1-01-001 GUARDINO'S	1-01-001 HABERDASHERY
1-01-001 GRAFF	1-01-001 GREENWICH-*POTOWOMUT	1-01-001 GUATEMALAN	1-01-001 HABIB
1-01-001 GRAFFITI	1-01-001 GREENWOOD	1-01-001 GUERILLA	1-01-001 HABLA
1-01-001 GRAFT	1-01-001 GREGORY'S	1-01-001 GUERRILLA-TH'-WISP	1-01-001 HABLE
1-01-001 GRAHAMSTOWN	1-01-001 GRENOBLE		1-01-001 HABSBURG
1-01-001 GRAIN-STORAGE	1-01-001 GRENVILLE	1-01-001 GUEVARA	1-01-001 HACKERS
1-01-001 GRAINING	1-01-001 GRESHAM	1-01-001 GUFFAWS	1-01-001 HACKETT
1-01-001 GRAM-NEGATIVE	1-01-001 GRET	1-01-001 GUGGENHEIM	1-01-001 HACKETTSTOWN
1-01-001 GRAMMARIANS	1-01-001 GRETCHEN	1-01-001 GUGLIELMO	1-01-001 HACKLES
1-01-001 GRAMMATICALLY	1-01-001 GREV	1-01-001 GUIDE'S	1-01-001 HACKMANN
1-01-001 GRAMMOPHON	1-01-001 GREVILE	1-01-001 GUIDELINES	1-01-001 HACKSAW
1-01-001 GRAN'DAD	1-01-001 GREVOUSELYE	1-01-001 GUIDEPOSTS'	1-01-001 HACKSTAFF
1-01-001 GRAND-LOOKING	1-01-001 GREVYLES	1-01-001 GUIFTES	1-01-001 HACKWORK
1-01-001 GRAND-SLAM	1-01-001 GREY'S	1-01-001 GUIGNOL	1-01-001 HADD
1-01-001 GRANDER	1-01-001 GREY-HAIRED	1-01-001 GUILE	1-01-001 HADDOCK
1-01-001 GRANDFATHER-FATHER-TO	1-01-001 GREY-SKIED	1-01-001 GUILELESS	1-01-001 HADRIAN
1-01-001 GRANDFATHERS	1-01-001 GREYHOUND	1-01-001 GUILFORD	1-01-001 HAEC
1-01-001 GRANDILOQUENT	1-01-001 GREYING	1-01-001 GUILFORD-MARTIN	1-01-001 HAESTIER
1-01-001 GRANDLY	1-01-001 GREYLAG	1-01-001 GUILLAUME	1-01-001 HAFLIS
1-01-001 GRANDMOTHERS	1-01-001 GRIDLEY	1-01-001 GUILTINESS	1-01-001 HAGERTY'S
1-01-001 GRANDMOTHERS'	1-01-001 GRIEVOUS	1-01-001 GUILTLESS	1-01-001 HAGGARDLY
1-01-001 GRANDSONS	1-01-001 GRIFFIN'S	1-01-001 GUIMET	1-01-001 HAGGLE
1-01-001 GRANDSTAND	1-01-001 GRIFFIN-*BYRD	1-01-001 GUISES	1-01-001 HAGNER
1-01-001 GRANITE'S	1-01-001 GRIFFITH'S	1-01-001 GUITAR-STRUMMING	1-01-001 HAILS
1-01-001 GRANNY'S	1-01-001 GRIFFITH-*JONES		1-01-001 HAILSTORM
1-01-001 GRANT'S	1-01-001 GRIGORY	1-01-001 GUIZOT	1-01-001 HAINT
1-01-001 GRANTHER	1-01-001 GRILLE-ROUTE	1-01-001 GULF'S	1-01-001 HAIR-RAISING
1-01-001 GRANULAR-TYPE	1-01-001 GRILLEWORK	1-01-001 GULL	1-01-001 HAIR-TRIGGER
1-01-001 GRANULES	1-01-001 GRIMED	1-01-001 GULLAH	1-01-001 HAIRCUTS
1-01-001 GRANULOCYTIC	1-01-001 GRIMESBY	1-01-001 GULLED	1-01-001 HAIRDOS
1-01-001 GRAPEVINES	1-01-001 GRIMM'S	1-01-001 GULLET	1-01-001 HAIRIER
1-01-001 GRAPHED	1-01-001 GRIMMER	1-01-001 GULLEY	1-01-001 HAIRLESS
1-01-001 GRAPHICAL	1-01-001 GRIMNESS	1-01-001 GULLIBILITY	1-01-001 HAIRPIN
1-01-001 GRAPHS	1-01-001 GRINDINGS	1-01-001 GULLIES	1-01-001 HAIRSHIRT
1-01-001 GRAPPELLY	1-01-001 GRINDLAY	1-01-001 GULLING	1-01-001 HAIRTONIC
1-01-001 GRAPPELY	1-01-001 GRINDS	1-01-001 GULLIVER'S	1-01-001 HAITIAN
1-01-001 GRAPPLE	1-01-001 GRINDSTONE	1-01-001 GULPS	1-01-001 HAJIME
1-01-001 GRAPPLED	1-01-001 GRIPES	1-01-001 GUM-CHEWING	1-01-001 HAL'S
1-01-001 GRASS-FED	1-01-001 GRIS	1-01-001 GUMMING	1-01-001 HALCYON
1-01-001 GRASS-GREEN	1-01-001 GRISTMILL	1-01-001 GUMPTION	1-01-001 HALDA
1-01-001 GRASS-ROOTS	1-01-001 GRISTON	1-01-001 GUN'S	1-01-001 HALE'S
1-01-001 GRASSED	1-01-001 GRIT	1-01-001 GUN-SHOT	1-01-001 HALF-A-DOZEN
1-01-001 GRASSERS	1-01-001 GRIT-IMPREGNATED	1-01-001 GUN-SLINGER	1-01-001 HALF-ACCEPTANCE
1-01-001 GRASSES		1-01-001 GUN-SLINGING	1-01-001 HALF-ACRE
1-01-001 GRASSFIRE	1-01-001 GRITTY	1-01-001 GUNBARREL	1-01-001 HALF-ALOUD
1-01-001 GRASSLAND	1-01-001 GRITTY-EYED	1-01-001 GUNFIGHTER	1-01-001 HALF-BLOOD
1-01-001 GRASSROOTS	1-01-001 GRIZZLED	1-01-001 GUNFIGHTS	1-01-001 HALF-BOTTLES
1-01-001 GRASSROOTS-FUELED	1-01-001 GRIZZLIES'	1-01-001 GUNFLINT	1-01-001 HALF-BROTHER
	1-01-001 GRIZZLY	1-01-001 GUNK	1-01-001 HALF-BROTHERS
1-01-001 GRATA	1-01-001 GROAN	1-01-001 GUNNER	1-01-001 HALF-CITY
1-01-001 GRATIFY	1-01-001 GROANING	1-01-001 GUNNING	1-01-001 HALF-CLAD
1-01-001 GRATIFYINGLY	1-01-001 GROAT	1-01-001 GUNPLAY	1-01-001 HALF-COCKED
1-01-001 GRATING	1-01-001 GROCER	1-01-001 GUNSLINGER	1-01-001 HALF-CRAZY
1-01-001 GRATINGLY	1-01-001 GROGGY	1-01-001 GUNTHER	1-01-001 HALF-CROCKED
1-01-001 GRATINGS	1-01-001 GROOMING	1-01-001 GURGLE	1-01-001 HALF-DARKNESS
1-01-001 GRATIS	1-01-001 GROOMSMEN	1-01-001 GURKHAS	1-01-001 HALF-DIGESTED
1-01-001 GRAUNT	1-01-001 GROOT	1-01-001 GURLA	1-01-001 HALF-DRESSED
1-01-001 GRAVEN	1-01-001 GROOVED	1-01-001 GURU	1-01-001 HALF-EDUCATED
1-01-001 GRAVESEND	1-01-001 GROPE	1-01-001 GUSH	1-01-001 HALF-EXPRESSED
1-01-001 GRAVESTONE	1-01-001 GROSS'S	1-01-001 GUSHER	1-01-001 HALF-FORGOTTEN
1-01-001 GRAY-BACKS	1-01-001 GROSSMAN	1-01-001 GUSSETS	1-01-001 HALF-GAINER
1-01-001 GRAY-LOOKING	1-01-001 GROTESQUES	1-01-001 GUSTAF	1-01-001 HALF-GOURD
1-01-001 GRAY-THATCHED	1-01-001 GROTTOES	1-01-001 GUSTAVE	1-01-001 HALF-GROWN
1-01-001 GRAYBEARD	1-01-001 GROUND-GLASS	1-01-001 GUSTAVUS	1-01-001 HALF-HEARTEDLY
1-01-001 GRAYBEARDS	1-01-001 GROUND-LEVEL	1-01-001 GUT	1-01-001 HALF-LIFE
1-01-001 GRAYED	1-01-001 GROUND-SWELL	1-01-001 GUT-FLATTENING	1-01-001 HALF-LIGHT
1-01-001 GRAYER	1-01-001 GROUND-TRUCK	1-01-001 GUTHMAN	1-01-001 HALF-MELTED
1-01-001 GRAYSON	1-01-001 GROUNDER	1-01-001 GUTHRIE	1-01-001 HALF-MILLION
1-01-001 GRAZE	1-01-001 GROUNDLESS	1-01-001 GUTHRIE'S	1-01-001 HALF-MINCING
1-01-001 GRAZER	1-01-001 GROUP'S	1-01-001 GUTTED	1-01-001 HALF-MOONS
1-01-001 GRE	1-01-001 GROVEL	1-01-001 GUTTER	1-01-001 HALF-MURMURED
1-01-001 GRE'T	1-01-001 GROVELIKE	1-01-001 GUTTERED	1-01-001 HALF-OFF
1-01-001 GREASE-REMOVAL	1-01-001 GROVELING	1-01-001 GUTTMAN-TYPE	1-01-001 HALF-PAST
1-01-001 GREAT'S	1-01-001 GROVERS	1-01-001 GUTZON	1-01-001 HALF-REACHED
1-01-001 GREAT-GRANDMOTHER	1-01-001 GROWER	1-01-001 GUZZLE	1-01-001 HALF-RELUCTANT
	1-01-001 GROWERS'	1-01-001 GUZZLED	1-01-001 HALF-SISTER
1-01-001 GREAT-GRANDSON	1-01-001 GROWING-WAITING	1-01-001 GWEN	1-01-001 HALF-SMILE
	1-01-001 GROWLING	1-01-001 GYMNASIUM	1-01-001 HALF-STANDARD
	1-01-001 GROWNUPS'	1-01-001 GYMNAST	1-01-001 HALF-STARVED
	1-01-001 GROWTH-STUNTING	1-01-001 GYNECOLOGICAL	

1-01-001 HALF-STRAIGHTEN ED
1-01-001 HALF-SWAMPED
1-01-001 HALF-SWIMMING
1-01-001 HALF-TRANSPAREN T
1-01-001 HALF-TURNED
1-01-001 HALF-UNDERSTOOD
1-01-001 HALF-WITTED
1-01-001 HALF-YEAR
1-01-001 HALFBACKS
1-01-001 HALFHEARTED
1-01-001 HALFTIME
1-01-001 HALFWAYS
1-01-001 HALIBURTON
1-01-001 HALIDES
1-01-001 HALKETT
1-01-001 HALL-*MILLS
1-01-001 HALL-MARK
1-01-001 HALLELUJAH
1-01-001 HALLELUJAHS
1-01-001 HALLOWEEN
1-01-001 HALLOWELL'S
1-01-001 HALLUCINATING
1-01-001 HALLUCINATIONS
1-01-001 HALLWAYS
1-01-001 HALMA
1-01-001 HALOGENS
1-01-001 HALOS
1-01-001 HALTER
1-01-001 HALTS
1-01-001 HALVAH
1-01-001 HAM-LIKE
1-01-001 HAM-RADIO
1-01-001 HAMBRIC
1-01-001 HAMEY
1-01-001 HAMILTON-ORIENT ED
1-01-001 HAMILTONIAN
1-01-001 HAMILTONIANS
1-01-001 HAMM'S
1-01-001 HAMMARSKJO**DLD
1-01-001 HAMMERLESS
1-01-001 HAMMERSKJOLD
1-01-001 HAMMING
1-01-001 HAMMONS
1-01-001 HAMPERS
1-01-001 HAMPTON'S
1-01-001 HAMS
1-01-001 HAN'S
1-01-001 HANCOCK
1-01-001 HAND-BLOWER
1-01-001 HAND-COVERED
1-01-001 HAND-CRAFTED
1-01-001 HAND-FILED
1-01-001 HAND-HEWN
1-01-001 HAND-HOLDING
1-01-001 HAND-LEVEL
1-01-001 HAND-MADE
1-01-001 HAND-ME-DOWN
1-01-001 HAND-PAINTED
1-01-001 HAND-SCREENED
1-01-001 HAND-WRITTEN
1-01-001 HANDBOOKS
1-01-001 HANDER
1-01-001 HANDFULS
1-01-001 HANDHOLD
1-01-001 HANDICAPS
1-01-001 HANDICRAFTS
1-01-001 HANDICRAFTSMAN
1-01-001 HANDIER
1-01-001 HANDIEST
1-01-001 HANDIWORK
1-01-001 HANDKERCHIEFS
1-01-001 HANDLEBARS
1-01-001 HANDLERS'
1-01-001 HANDLESS
1-01-001 HANDMAIDEN
1-01-001 HANDS-OFF
1-01-001 HANDS-OFF-ALL-S WEETS
1-01-001 HANDSHAKE
1-01-001 HANDSOMELY
1-01-001 HANDSOMEST
1-01-001 HANDSTAND
1-01-001 HANDYMAN-CARPEN TER
1-01-001 HANDYMEN
1-01-001 HANGAR
1-01-001 HANGARS
1-01-001 HANGERS
1-01-001 HANGERS-ON
1-01-001 HANGMAN
1-01-001 HANGMAN'S
1-01-001 HANGOUTS
1-01-001 HANGOVERS
1-01-001 HANKERED

1-01-001 HANKERIN
1-01-001 HANNIBAL
1-01-001 HANOVER'S
1-01-001 HANOVER-*BERTIE
1-01-001 HANOVER-*CEYWAY
1-01-001 HANOVER-*CHALID ALE
1-01-001 HANOVER-*JUSTIT IA
1-01-001 HANOVER-*LUCY
1-01-001 HANOVER-*MAURI
1-01-001 HANOVER-*MISTY
1-01-001 HANOVER-*PEBBLE
1-01-001 HANOVER-*PRECIO US
1-01-001 HANOVER-*SALLY
1-01-001 HANOVER-*SUPERM ARKET
1-01-001 HANSOM
1-01-001 HANUKKAH
1-01-001 HAP
1-01-001 HAPHAZARDLY
1-01-001 HAQVIN
1-01-001 HARANGUED
1-01-001 HARASS
1-01-001 HARBOR'S
1-01-001 HARBORING
1-01-001 HARBURG'S
1-01-001 HARD'S
1-01-001 HARD-*HEARTED
1-01-001 HARD-BITTEN
1-01-001 HARD-COME-BY
1-01-001 HARD-EARNED
1-01-001 HARD-HIT
1-01-001 HARD-NOSED
1-01-001 HARD-SELL
1-01-001 HARD-TO-GET
1-01-001 HARD-TO-PLEASE
1-01-001 HARD-WON
1-01-001 HARDBAKE
1-01-001 HARDBOARD
1-01-001 HARDEE'S
1-01-001 HARDEN
1-01-001 HARDENER
1-01-001 HARDINGS
1-01-001 HARDSCRABBLE
1-01-001 HARDSHELL
1-01-001 HARDTACK-BOX
1-01-001 HARDWICKE
1-01-001 HARDWOODS
1-01-001 HARDWORKING
1-01-001 HARE
1-01-001 HARELIPS
1-01-001 HARFORD
1-01-001 HARGETT
1-01-001 HARLAN-*HICKORY
1-01-001 HARLAN-*MARCIA
1-01-001 HARLEM'S
1-01-001 HARLEY'S
1-01-001 HARLINGEN
1-01-001 HARMLESSLY
1-01-001 HARMON
1-01-001 HARMONIOUSLY
1-01-001 HARMONIZATION
1-01-001 HARMONY'S
1-01-001 HARNACK
1-01-001 HARNESSING
1-01-001 HARNICK
1-01-001 HARP
1-01-001 HARPSICHORD
1-01-001 HARPSICHORDIST
1-01-001 HARPY
1-01-001 HARRASSMENT
1-01-001 HARRIED
1-01-001 HARRIET'S
1-01-001 HARRINGTON'S
1-01-001 HARRIS'
1-01-001 HARRISON'S
1-01-001 HARRITY
1-01-001 HARRO
1-01-001 HARROWED
1-01-001 HARROWS
1-01-001 HARRUMPHING
1-01-001 HARRY'S
1-01-001 HARSHENED
1-01-001 HARSHER
1-01-001 HARSHNESS
1-01-001 HARTLEY
1-01-001 HARTLIB
1-01-001 HARTSELLE
1-01-001 HARTWELL
1-01-001 HARUO
1-01-001 HARVARD'S
1-01-001 HARVE
1-01-001 HARVESTED
1-01-001 HARVEYS
1-01-001 HASH

1-01-001 HASHER
1-01-001 HASKINS
1-01-001 HASPS
1-01-001 HAST
1-01-001 HASTILY-SUMMONE D
1-01-001 HASTINGS
1-01-001 HATCHET-FACED
1-01-001 HATLESS
1-01-001 HATTED
1-01-001 HATTERAS
1-01-001 HATTERS
1-01-001 HATTES
1-01-001 HATTIE
1-01-001 HATTIESBURG
1-01-001 HAUGHTILY
1-01-001 HAUGHTINESS
1-01-001 HAUGHTON'S
1-01-001 HAULAGE
1-01-001 HAUMD
1-01-001 HAUMD'S
1-01-001 HAUPTS'
1-01-001 HAUSMAN
1-01-001 HAUSMAN'S
1-01-001 HAVENS
1-01-001 HAVILLAND
1-01-001 HAVISHAM'S
1-01-001 HAW
1-01-001 HAWAIIAN-*AMERI CANS
1-01-001 HAWING
1-01-001 HAWK-FACED
1-01-001 HAWKED
1-01-001 HAWKER
1-01-001 HAWKERS
1-01-001 HAWKINS'
1-01-001 HAWKINSES
1-01-001 HAWKS
1-01-001 HAWKSWORTH
1-01-001 HAY-WAGON
1-01-001 HAYDN'S
1-01-001 HAYDON
1-01-001 HAYEK
1-01-001 HAYFIELDS
1-01-001 HAYING
1-01-001 HAYNES
1-01-001 HAYSTACK
1-01-001 HAYSTACKS
1-01-001 HAYTER
1-01-001 HAYWARD
1-01-001 HAYWOOD
1-01-001 HAZELNUTS
1-01-001 HAZES
1-01-001 HEAD-AND-SHOULD ERS
1-01-001 HEAD-COLD
1-01-001 HEAD-IN-THE-CLO UDS
1-01-001 HEADBOARD
1-01-001 HEADDRESS
1-01-001 HEADE
1-01-001 HEADER
1-01-001 HEADINGS
1-01-001 HEADLAND
1-01-001 HEADLANDS
1-01-001 HEADLINESE
1-01-001 HEADLINING
1-01-001 HEADQUARTER
1-01-001 HEADROOM
1-01-001 HEADSMAN
1-01-001 HEADSTAND
1-01-001 HEADSTANDS
1-01-001 HEADSTONES
1-01-001 HEALTHIEST
1-01-001 HEAPS
1-01-001 HEAREST
1-01-001 HEARING-AID
1-01-001 HEARN
1-01-001 HEARSE
1-01-001 HEART'S
1-01-001 HEART-MEASURING
1-01-001 HEART-STOPPING
1-01-001 HEART-WARMING
1-01-001 HEARTBREAK
1-01-001 HEARTFELT
1-01-001 HEARTIEST
1-01-001 HEARTLESS
1-01-001 HEAT'S
1-01-001 HEAT-ABSORBING
1-01-001 HEAT-DENATURED
1-01-001 HEAT-PROCESSING
1-01-001 HEATEDLY
1-01-001 HEATERS
1-01-001 HEATHENISH
1-01-001 HEATWOLE
1-01-001 HEAVEN'S
1-01-001 HEAVENWARD

1-01-001 HEAVES
1-01-001 HEAVILY-UPHOLST ERED
1-01-001 HEAVY-ARMED
1-01-001 HEAVY-COATED
1-01-001 HEAVY-DUTY
1-01-001 HEAVY-FACED
1-01-001 HEAVY-FRAMED
1-01-001 HEAVY-HANDED
1-01-001 HEAVY-WEIGHT
1-01-001 HEBRAIC
1-01-001 HEBREWS
1-01-001 HECATOMB
1-01-001 HECK
1-01-001 HECKMAN
1-01-001 HECTOR
1-01-001 HECTOR'S
1-01-001 HEDDA
1-01-001 HEDGED
1-01-001 HEDONISM
1-01-001 HEEDED
1-01-001 HEEL-
1-01-001 HEEL-*BERYL
1-01-001 HEEL-*BETTY
1-01-001 HEEL-*HOLIDAY
1-01-001 HEEL-*KAOLA
1-01-001 HEEL-*LOTUS
1-01-001 HEEL-*TERKA
1-01-001 HEELERS
1-01-001 HEENAN
1-01-001 HEFFER
1-01-001 HEFFERNAN
1-01-001 HEFTED
1-01-001 HEFTY
1-01-001 HEGEL'S
1-01-001 HEGEMONY
1-01-001 HEIDEGGER
1-01-001 HEIDELBERG
1-01-001 HEIDEMAN
1-01-001 HEIGH-HO
1-01-001 HEIGHT-TO-DIAM TE
1-01-001 HEIGHTEN
1-01-001 HEINE
1-01-001 HEINZE
1-01-001 HEINZES
1-01-001 HEIRESS
1-01-001 HEISTED
1-01-001 HEITSCHMIDT
1-01-001 HEL
1-01-001 HELENA
1-01-001 HELENE
1-01-001 HELICOPTER
1-01-001 HELICOPTER-BOR
1-01-001 HELIOCENTRIC
1-01-001 HELIOTROPE
1-01-001 HELL-BOUND
1-01-001 HELL-FIRE
1-01-001 HELL-FOR-LEATH
1-01-001 HELL-RAISING
1-01-001 HELLS
1-01-001 HELLUVA
1-01-001 HELMET
1-01-001 HELMSMAN
1-01-001 HELMUT
1-01-001 HELPFULNESS
1-01-001 HELPMATE
1-01-001 HELSQ'IYOKOM
1-01-001 HEMENWAY'S
1-01-001 HEMINGWAY'S
1-01-001 HEMISPHERE'S
1-01-001 HEMISPHERICAL
1-01-001 HEMLOCKS
1-01-001 HEMMING
1-01-001 HEMOLYTIC
1-01-001 HEMORRHAGES
1-01-001 HEMORRHOIDS
1-01-001 HEN'S
1-01-001 HENCHMAN
1-01-001 HENDRICKS'
1-01-001 HENDRIK
1-01-001 HENDRY
1-01-001 HENG-*SHAN
1-01-001 HENH
1-01-001 HENPECKED
1-01-001 HENRIK
1-01-001 HENS'
1-01-001 HEOROT
1-01-001 HEPHZIBAH
1-01-001 HEPKER
1-01-001 HEPTACHLOR
1-01-001 HERACLITUS
1-01-001 HERALD-*EXAMI
1-01-001 HERBERET'S

66

1-01-001 HERBLOCK	1-01-001 HIGHER-DENSITY	1-01-001 HOLDUPS	1-01-001 HORN-RIM
1-01-001 HERCULE	1-01-001 HIGHER-PRICED	1-01-001 HOLED	1-01-001 HORN-RIMMED
1-01-001 HERCULEAN	1-01-001 HIGHER-QUALITY	1-01-001 HOLIES	1-01-001 HORNE'S
1-01-001 HERD-OWNER	1-01-001 HIGHEST-PAID	1-01-001 HOLLANDER	1-01-001 HORNED
1-01-001 HERDING	1-01-001 HIGHFIELD	1-01-001 HOLLEY	1-01-001 HORNS'
1-01-001 HEREFORD	1-01-001 HIGHLAND	1-01-001 HOLLINGSHEAD	1-01-001 HOROSCOPE
1-01-001 HERETIC	1-01-001 HIGHNESS	1-01-001 HOLLOWAY	1-01-001 HORRID
1-01-001 HERETICS	1-01-001 HIGHSCHOOL	1-01-001 HOLLOWELL	1-01-001 HORRIFYINGLY
1-01-001 HERETOFORE-ACCE PTED	1-01-001 HIGHWAYMAN	1-01-001 HOLLOWNESS	1-01-001 HORS
1-01-001 HERFORD'S	1-01-001 HIKED	1-01-001 HOLLOWS	1-01-001 HORSE-BLANKET
1-01-001 HERGESHEIMER	1-01-001 HILARIOUSLY	1-01-001 HOLLOWWARE	1-01-001 HORSE-CHESTNUT
1-01-001 HERITAGES	1-01-001 HILARITY	1-01-001 HOLLYHOCK	1-01-001 HORSE-PLAYING
1-01-001 HERMAN'S	1-01-001 HILDY	1-01-001 HOLLYHOCKS	1-01-001 HORSE-TRADING
1-01-001 HERMANOVSKI	1-01-001 HILLARY	1-01-001 HOLMAN	1-01-001 HORSE-TRAIL
1-01-001 HERMENEUTICS	1-01-001 HILLCREST	1-01-001 HOLORED	1-01-001 HORSEDOM
1-01-001 HERMETIC	1-01-001 HILLEL	1-01-001 HOLSTEIN	1-01-001 HORSEFLESH
1-01-001 HERO-WORSHIP	1-01-001 HILLIARD	1-01-001 HOLT'S	1-01-001 HORSEHAIR
1-01-001 HERO-WORSHIPPER S	1-01-001 HILLMAN'S	1-01-001 HOLTY	1-01-001 HORSELIKE
1-01-001 HEROICALLY	1-01-001 HILLSDALE	1-01-001 HOLYSTONES	1-01-001 HORSEMAN
1-01-001 HERON	1-01-001 HILLTOPS	1-01-001 HOLZMAN	1-01-001 HORSEWOMAN
1-01-001 HERPETOLOGIST	1-01-001 HILPRECHT'S	1-01-001 HOME'S	1-01-001 HORSTMAN
1-01-001 HERPETOLOGY	1-01-001 HIMMLER	1-01-001 HOME-AND-HOME	1-01-001 HORTON
1-01-001 HERRIDGE	1-01-001 HIMSELFE	1-01-001 HOME-BLEND	1-01-001 HOSPICE
1-01-001 HERRIN-*MURPHYS BORO-*WEST	1-01-001 HINCKLEY	1-01-001 HOME-BOUND	1-01-001 HOSPITAL-CARE
1-01-001 HERRINGBONE	1-01-001 HINDEMITH'S	1-01-001 HOME-BRED	1-01-001 HOSPITALIZED
1-01-001 HERRINGTON	1-01-001 HINDERING	1-01-001 HOME-BUILDING	1-01-001 HOST-SPECIFIC
1-01-001 HERRMANN	1-01-001 HINDERS	1-01-001 HOME-CITY	1-01-001 HOSTARIA
1-01-001 HERRY'S	1-01-001 HINDMOST	1-01-001 HOME-COMINGS	1-01-001 HOSTE
1-01-001 HERSEY	1-01-001 HINDOO	1-01-001 HOME-FOR-THE-NI GHT	1-01-001 HOSTELRIES
1-01-001 HERSHEL	1-01-001 HINDQUARTERS	1-01-001 HOME-KEEPING	1-01-001 HOT-BLOODED
1-01-001 HERSHEY'S	1-01-001 HINDUS	1-01-001 HOME-MADE	1-01-001 HOT-COLORED
1-01-001 HERTZ	1-01-001 HINGE	1-01-001 HOME-OFFICE	1-01-001 HOT-HONEY
1-01-001 HERZFELD	1-01-001 HINGED	1-01-001 HOME-OWNERS	1-01-001 HOT-SLOUGH
1-01-001 HERZOG	1-01-001 HINKLE	1-01-001 HOMEBOUND	1-01-001 HOT-WATER
1-01-001 HESITANCE	1-01-001 HINSDALE	1-01-001 HOMEBUILDERS	1-01-001 HOTBED
1-01-001 HESITATES	1-01-001 HINTERLANDS	1-01-001 HOMEBUILDING	1-01-001 HOTDOGS
1-01-001 HESITATING	1-01-001 HINTING	1-01-001 HOMECOMINGS	1-01-001 HOTEL'S
1-01-001 HESITATINGLY	1-01-001 HIP-POCKET	1-01-001 HOMEFOLK	1-01-001 HOTEL-MOTEL
1-01-001 HESPERUS'	1-01-001 HIPLINE	1-01-001 HOMEMASTER	1-01-001 HOTELMAN'S
1-01-001 HESS	1-01-001 HIPSTER	1-01-001 HOMER'S	1-01-001 HOTHOUSE
1-01-001 HETEROGAMOUS	1-01-001 HIR	1-01-001 HOMERISTS	1-01-001 HOTROD
1-01-001 HETTY'S	1-01-001 HIRELINGS	1-01-001 HOMERUN	1-01-001 HOUDINI
1-01-001 HEUSEN	1-01-001 HIRES	1-01-001 HOMESICKNESS	1-01-001 HOUGHTON'S
1-01-001 HEUTE	1-01-001 HIREY'S	1-01-001 HOMESTEADS	1-01-001 HOUR'S
1-01-001 HEV	1-01-001 HIRSCH'S	1-01-001 HOMEWARD	1-01-001 HOURS'
1-01-001 HEWED	1-01-001 HIRSCHEY	1-01-001 HOMEWARDS	1-01-001 HOUSE-BUILDING
1-01-001 HEWETT	1-01-001 HISSELF	1-01-001 HOMICIDAL	1-01-001 HOUSE-CLEANING
1-01-001 HEWLETT-*WOODME RE	1-01-001 HISTOCHEMICAL	1-01-001 HOMING	1-01-001 HOUSEBOATS
1-01-001 HEWLITT	1-01-001 HISTOLOGY	1-01-001 HOMO	1-01-001 HOUSEBREAKERS
1-01-001 HEXAGON	1-01-001 HISTORICISM	1-01-001 HOMOGENIZATION	1-01-001 HOUSEBREAKING
1-01-001 HEXAMETAPHOSPHA TE	1-01-001 HISTORICITY	1-01-001 HOMOGENIZE	1-01-001 HOUSEBROKEN
1-01-001 HEXEN	1-01-001 HISTRIONICS	1-01-001 HOMOPOLYMERS	1-01-001 HOUSEHOLD-TYPE
1-01-001 HI-FI	1-01-001 HIT'S	1-01-001 HONDO	1-01-001 HOUSEHOLDER
1-01-001 HI-GRADERS	1-01-001 HIT-AND-MISS	1-01-001 HONEST-TO-*BETS Y	1-01-001 HOUSEHOLDERS
1-01-001 HICCUPS	1-01-001 HIT-AND-RUN	1-01-001 HONEY-IN-THE-SU N	1-01-001 HOUSEPAINT
1-01-001 HICK	1-01-001 HITLERS		1-01-001 HOUSMAN
1-01-001 HICK-SELF	1-01-001 HITLESS	1-01-001 HONEYCOMBED	1-01-001 HOVARTER
1-01-001 HICKOK	1-01-001 HMM	1-01-001 HONEYMOONERS	1-01-001 HOVE
1-01-001 HICKS	1-01-001 HMPF	1-01-001 HONEYMOONING	1-01-001 HOVERED
1-01-001 HIDEAWAY	1-01-001 HO**OLDERLIN	1-01-001 HONKY-TONK	1-01-001 HOVERING
1-01-001 HIDEOUT	1-01-001 HO**DVDINGAR	1-01-001 HONKYTONKS	1-01-001 HOVERS
1-01-001 HIERARCHIES	1-01-001 HOA-WHUP	1-01-001 HONOREE	1-01-001 HOW-2
1-01-001 HIFALUTIN	1-01-001 HOAGY	1-01-001 HONOURED	1-01-001 HOWARD'S
1-01-001 HIGH'S	1-01-001 HOAK	1-01-001 HONSHU	1-01-001 HOWDA
1-01-001 HIGH-	1-01-001 HOAPS	1-01-001 HOO-PIG	1-01-001 HOWDY
1-01-001 HIGH-BACKED	1-01-001 HOARSENESS	1-01-001 HOOCH	1-01-001 HOWE'S
1-01-001 HIGH-CLASS	1-01-001 HOAXES	1-01-001 HOOD'S	1-01-001 HOWELL
1-01-001 HIGH-COST	1-01-001 HOB	1-01-001 HOOF-AND-MOUTH	1-01-001 HOWLED
1-01-001 HIGH-CURRENT	1-01-001 HOBART	1-01-001 HOOFMARKS	1-01-001 HOWRY
1-01-001 HIGH-END	1-01-001 HOBBES	1-01-001 HOOGHLI	1-01-001 HOWSABOUT
1-01-001 HIGH-INTEREST	1-01-001 HOBBES'	1-01-001 HOOKER'S	1-01-001 HOWSAM
1-01-001 HIGH-LEGGED	1-01-001 HOBBING	1-01-001 HOOKING	1-01-001 HOWSAM'S
1-01-001 HIGH-MINDED	1-01-001 HOBBLE	1-01-001 HOOKUPS	1-01-001 HOWSOMEVER
1-01-001 HIGH-POSITIVE	1-01-001 HOBDAY	1-01-001 HOOKWORM	1-01-001 HOXA
1-01-001 HIGH-POWER	1-01-001 HOBO	1-01-001 HOOLIGANISM	1-01-001 HOY
1-01-001 HIGH-RESOLUTION	1-01-001 HOCK'S	1-01-001 HOOPLA	1-01-001 HOYDENISH
1-01-001 HIGH-SALARIED	1-01-001 HOCKADAY	1-01-001 HOORAY	1-01-001 HOYLE'S
1-01-001 HIGH-STEPPED	1-01-001 HOCKETT	1-01-001 HOOSEGOW	1-01-001 HR.
1-01-001 HIGH-SUDSING	1-01-001 HOCKEY	1-01-001 HOOSEGOWS	1-01-001 HROTHGAR
1-01-001 HIGH-TAILED	1-01-001 HOCKING	1-01-001 HOOSIER	1-01-001 HROTHGAR'S
1-01-001 HIGH-TEMPERATUR E	1-01-001 HODGE-PODGE	1-01-001 HOOTED	1-01-001 HUAI
1-01-001 HIGH-TENSION	1-01-001 HODGEPODGE	1-01-001 HOOTING	1-01-001 HUANG-TI
1-01-001 HIGH-TOPPED	1-01-001 HODOSH	1-01-001 HOOTS	1-01-001 HUBAY
1-01-001 HIGH-UP	1-01-001 HOE-*DOWN	1-01-001 HOP-SKIPPED	1-01-001 HUBBELL
1-01-001 HIGH-VELOCITY	1-01-001 HOES	1-01-001 HOPE'S	1-01-001 HUBBUB
1-01-001 HIGH-VOLTAGE	1-01-001 HOFFER	1-01-001 HOPEDALE	1-01-001 HUBBY
1-01-001 HIGH-WAGE	1-01-001 HOGAN'S	1-01-001 HOPEI	1-01-001 HUBERMANN
1-01-001 HIGH-WATER	1-01-001 HOGE'S	1-01-001 HOPKINS'	1-01-001 HUBIE'S
1-01-001 HIGHBOARD	1-01-001 HOGGING	1-01-001 HOPPLED	1-01-001 HUBRIS
1-01-001 HIGHBOY	1-01-001 HOI-POLLOI	1-01-001 HOPS	1-01-001 HUCK
1-01-001 HIGHER-	1-01-001 HOIST	1-01-001 HOPSCOTCH	1-01-001 HUCKSTER'S
	1-01-001 HOKAN	1-01-001 HORACE'S	1-01-001 HUE
	1-01-001 HOLABIRD	1-01-001 HORATIO'S	1-01-001 HUEY
	1-01-001 HOLBROOK	1-01-001 HORD	1-01-001 HUFF'S
	1-01-001 HOLD-BACK		1-01-001 HUFFMAN
	1-01-001 HOLDIN		1-01-001 HUGGINGS
	1-01-001 HOLDOVERS		1-01-001 HUGGINS

2 ? 6

1-01-001 HUGO'S
1-01-001 HUH-UH
1-01-001 HUI
1-01-001 HUITOTOES
1-01-001 HULL-FIRST
1-01-001 HULTBERG
1-01-001 HUMAINE
1-01-001 HUMANELY
1-01-001 HUMANISTS
1-01-001 HUMANIZE
1-01-001 HUMANLY
1-01-001 HUMBLED
1-01-001 HUMID
1-01-001 HUMILATION
1-01-001 HUMILIATINGLY
1-01-001 HUMLY
1-01-001 HUMOUR
1-01-001 HUMPED
1-01-001 HUMPTY
1-01-001 HUNCHED-UP
1-01-001 HUNCHES
1-01-001 HUNDRED-AND-EIG HTY-DEGREE
1-01-001 HUNDRED-AND-FIF TY
1-01-001 HUNDRED-LEAF
1-01-001 HUNDRED-YEN
1-01-001 HUNGARIAN-BORN
1-01-001 HUNGARY-*SUEZ
1-01-001 HUNGRIER
1-01-001 HUNKERISH
1-01-001 HUNTER'S
1-01-001 HUNTINGTON
1-01-001 HUNTINGTONS
1-01-001 HUO-*SHAN
1-01-001 HURDLED
1-01-001 HURDLES
1-01-001 HURLER
1-01-001 HURLERS
1-01-001 HURLEY
1-01-001 HURRAY
1-01-001 HURTLED
1-01-001 HUSBAND-STEALER
1-01-001 HUSBAND-WIFE
1-01-001 HUSBUN
1-01-001 HUSKILY
1-01-001 HUSKINESS
1-01-001 HUSKY-VOICED
1-01-001 HUSTLING
1-01-001 HUSTON
1-01-001 HUTCHINS'
1-01-001 HUTMENT
1-01-001 HUTMENTS
1-01-001 HUZZAHS
1-01-001 HWA-*SHAN
1-01-001 HYACINTHS
1-01-001 HYALINE
1-01-001 HYALINIZATION
1-01-001 HYBRID
1-01-001 HYDE'S
1-01-001 HYDRATED
1-01-001 HYDRAULIC
1-01-001 HYDRAULICALLY
1-01-001 HYDRAULICS
1-01-001 HYDRIDO
1-01-001 HYDRO-*ELECTRIC
1-01-001 HYDROCARBONS
1-01-001 HYDROCHEMISTRY
1-01-001 HYDROLYZED
1-01-001 HYDROPHOBIA
1-01-001 HYDROSTATIC
1-01-001 HYDROUS
1-01-001 HYDROXAZINE
1-01-001 HYDROXIDES
1-01-001 HYDROXYLATION
1-01-001 HYENA
1-01-001 HYMENS
1-01-001 HYNDE
1-01-001 HYNDMAN
1-01-001 HYPED-UP
1-01-001 HYPERBOLICALLY
1-01-001 HYPERCELLULARIT Y
1-01-001 HYPERFINE
1-01-001 HYPERPLASIA
1-01-001 HYPERTROPHIED
1-01-001 HYPERVELOCITY
1-01-001 HYPNOSIS
1-01-001 HYPNOTIC
1-01-001 HYPNOTICALLY
1-01-001 HYPNOTIZED
1-01-001 HYPO-
1-01-001 HYPOACTIVE
1-01-001 HYPOADRENOCORTI CISM
1-01-001 HYPOCELLULARITY
1-01-001 HYPODERMIC

1-01-001 HYPOPHYSEAL
1-01-001 HYPOPHYSECTOMIS ED
1-01-001 HYPOSTATIZATION
1-01-001 HYPOTHALAMICALL Y
1-01-001 HYPOTHESIZE
1-01-001 HYPOTHESIZING
1-01-001 HYPOTHYROIDISM
1-01-001 HYSTERECTOMY
1-01-001 HYSTERON-PROTER ON
1-01-001 HYTT
1-01-001 I**.*B**.*M
1-01-001 I**.*L
1-01-001 I**.*M**.*F
1-01-001 I**$N
1-01-001 I**$T
1-01-001 IBERIA
1-01-001 IBN
1-01-001 IBSEN
1-01-001 ICE-CHEST
1-01-001 ICE-COLD
1-01-001 ICE-CUBES
1-01-001 ICE-FEELING
1-01-001 ICED
1-01-001 ICELANDIC
1-01-001 ICELANDIC-SPEAK ING
1-01-001 ICH
1-01-001 ICICLE
1-01-001 ICING
1-01-001 ICONOCLASM
1-01-001 IDAL
1-01-001 IDEA-EXCHANGE
1-01-001 IDEALOGICAL
1-01-001 IDEATIONAL
1-01-001 IDENTICALLY
1-01-001 IDEOLOGIST
1-01-001 IDIOCIES
1-01-001 IDIOMATIC
1-01-001 IDIOT'S
1-01-001 IDIOT-GRIN
1-01-001 IDIOTICALLY
1-01-001 IDLED
1-01-001 IDLER
1-01-001 IDLERS
1-01-001 IDOL-WORSHIP
1-01-001 IDOLATRY
1-01-001 IDOLIZE
1-01-001 IDOLIZED
1-01-001 IDOLS'
1-01-001 IFNI
1-01-001 IGLEHART
1-01-001 IGNAZIO
1-01-001 IGNEOUS
1-01-001 IGNITED
1-01-001 IHMSEN
1-01-001 IIJIMA
1-01-001 IJ
1-01-001 IKE'S
1-01-001 IKEY-KIKEY
1-01-001 IKLE
1-01-001 ILEUM
1-01-001 ILIAC
1-01-001 ILKA
1-01-001 ILL-PREPARED
1-01-001 ILLE
1-01-001 ILLINOIS'
1-01-001 ILLOGICAL
1-01-001 ILLUMINATE
1-01-001 ILLUMINATIONS
1-01-001 ILLUMINE
1-01-001 ILLUMINES
1-01-001 ILLUSIONARY
1-01-001 ILLUSTRATOR
1-01-001 ILLUSTRATORS
1-01-001 ILONA
1-01-001 ILYUSHIN
1-01-001 IMAGE-PROVOKING
1-01-001 IMAGINATIONS
1-01-001 IMAGINATIVELY
1-01-001 IMAGINING
1-01-001 IMAGININGS
1-01-001 IMAGNATION
1-01-001 IMBALANCE
1-01-001 IMBALANCES
1-01-001 IMBECILE
1-01-001 IMBIBE
1-01-001 IMBODEN
1-01-001 IMBRIUM
1-01-001 IMBROGLIO
1-01-001 IMBRUING
1-01-001 IMBUED
1-01-001 IMCOMPARABLE
1-01-001 IMCOMPATIBLES
1-01-001 IMCOMPLETE

1-01-001 IMITATION-CANIN G
1-01-001 IMITATION-WOODG RAIN
1-01-001 IMITATIVE
1-01-001 IMMATURITY
1-01-001 IMMEASURABLY
1-01-001 IMMEDIACIES
1-01-001 IMMENSITIES
1-01-001 IMMINENCE
1-01-001 IMMODERATE
1-01-001 IMMODEST
1-01-001 IMMODESTY
1-01-001 IMMORALITIES
1-01-001 IMMORTALIZED
1-01-001 IMMOVABLE
1-01-001 IMMUNIZATION
1-01-001 IMMUNOELECTROPH ORESIS
1-01-001 IMMUTABLE
1-01-001 IMPAIRMENT
1-01-001 IMPALING
1-01-001 IMPARTATION
1-01-001 IMPARTS
1-01-001 IMPASSIVE
1-01-001 IMPASSIVELY
1-01-001 IMPEDIMENT
1-01-001 IMPELLING
1-01-001 IMPENETRABLE
1-01-001 IMPERCEPTIBLE
1-01-001 IMPERCEPTIBLY
1-01-001 IMPERFECTABILIT Y
1-01-001 IMPERFECTION
1-01-001 IMPERIALES
1-01-001 IMPERIALIST
1-01-001 IMPERIALISTS
1-01-001 IMPERIL
1-01-001 IMPERILED
1-01-001 IMPERILLED
1-01-001 IMPERIOUS
1-01-001 IMPERISHABLE
1-01-001 IMPERSONALIZED
1-01-001 IMPERSONALLY
1-01-001 IMPERSONATED
1-01-001 IMPERSONATES
1-01-001 IMPERTINENT
1-01-001 IMPERTURBABLE
1-01-001 IMPIETY
1-01-001 IMPLANT
1-01-001 IMPLANTATION
1-01-001 IMPLANTED
1-01-001 IMPLAUSIBLY
1-01-001 IMPLEMENTED
1-01-001 IMPLORE
1-01-001 IMPLORING
1-01-001 IMPONDERABLE
1-01-001 IMPORTANT-LOOKI NG
1-01-001 IMPORTUNATELY
1-01-001 IMPORTUNITIES
1-01-001 IMPOSSIBILITY
1-01-001 IMPOSSIBLY
1-01-001 IMPOTENCY
1-01-001 IMPOUNDMENTS
1-01-001 IMPRACTICABLE
1-01-001 IMPRECATES
1-01-001 IMPRECATIONS
1-01-001 IMPRECISE
1-01-001 IMPRESARIO
1-01-001 IMPRESSER
1-01-001 IMPRESSES
1-01-001 IMPRESSIONISM
1-01-001 IMPRESSIONISTIC
1-01-001 IMPRESSIONISTS
1-01-001 IMPRINT
1-01-001 IMPRINTED
1-01-001 IMPRISONS
1-01-001 IMPROBABLY
1-01-001 IMPROPRIETY
1-01-001 IMPROVISATION
1-01-001 IMPROVISER
1-01-001 IMPROVISES
1-01-001 IMPROVISING
1-01-001 IMPUDENCE
1-01-001 IMPUDENTLY
1-01-001 IMPULSIVE
1-01-001 IMPURITY-DOPED
1-01-001 IMPUTE
1-01-001 IN*$DECENT
1-01-001 IN-FIGHTING
1-01-001 IN-GROUPS
1-01-001 IN-MIGRANTS
1-01-001 IN-PERSON
1-01-001 IN-PLANT
1-01-001 IN-STATE
1-01-001 INACCESSIBLE

1-01-001 INACCURACIES
1-01-001 INACTIVITY
1-01-001 INADVERTENCE
1-01-001 INADVISABLE
1-01-001 INANE
1-01-001 INAPPROPRIATENE SS
1-01-001 INAPT
1-01-001 INARTICULATE
1-01-001 INASMUCH
1-01-001 INATTENTIVE
1-01-001 INAUGURATING
1-01-001 INBOARDS
1-01-001 INBORN
1-01-001 INBREEDING
1-01-001 INCA
1-01-001 INCALCULABLE
1-01-001 INCANTED
1-01-001 INCAPACITY
1-01-001 INCARCERATED
1-01-001 INCAUTIOUS
1-01-001 INCENDIARIES
1-01-001 INCEPTED
1-01-001 INCEPTOR
1-01-001 INCERTAIN
1-01-001 INCHED
1-01-001 INCIDENTALS
1-01-001 INCIPIENCE
1-01-001 INCISE
1-01-001 INCISIVENESS
1-01-001 INCITEMENTS
1-01-001 INCITING
1-01-001 INCLINATIONS
1-01-001 INCLOSED
1-01-001 INCLUSIVENESS
1-01-001 INCOHERENTLY
1-01-001 INCOMES
1-01-001 INCOMPATIBILIT
1-01-001 INCOMPLETENESS
1-01-001 INCOMPREHENSIO
1-01-001 INCONCEIVABLE
1-01-001 INCONGRUITY
1-01-001 INCONGRUOUS
1-01-001 INCONSIDERABLE
1-01-001 INCONSISTENCIE
1-01-001 INCONSISTENCY
1-01-001 INCONSPICUOUS
1-01-001 INCONSPICUOUSL
1-01-001 INCONTESTABLE
1-01-001 INCONTROVERTIB
1-01-001 INCONVENIENTLY
1-01-001 INCORPORATING
1-01-001 INCORRIGIBLE
1-01-001 INCORRUPTIBILI
1-01-001 INCREDULITY
1-01-001 INCREDULOUSLY
1-01-001 INCREMENTAL
1-01-001 INCRIMINATING
1-01-001 INCUBATED
1-01-001 INCUBATING
1-01-001 INCUBI
1-01-001 INCUBUS
1-01-001 INCUMBENTS
1-01-001 INCURRING
1-01-001 INCURS
1-01-001 INCURSION
1-01-001 INDECIPHERABLE
1-01-001 INDECISIVELY
1-01-001 INDECISIVENESS
1-01-001 INDEFATIGABLE
1-01-001 INDEFINITENES
1-01-001 INDEFINITY
1-01-001 INDELIBLY
1-01-001 INDELICATE
1-01-001 INDENTATIONS
1-01-001 INDEPENDENTS
1-01-001 INDESTRUCTIBL
1-01-001 INDIANA'S
1-01-001 INDIANS'
1-01-001 INDIGATION
1-01-001 INDIGENT
1-01-001 INDIGESTIBLE
1-01-001 INDIGNANTLY
1-01-001 INDIGO
1-01-001 INDIRECTION
1-01-001 INDISCRIMINAN
1-01-001 INDISCRIMINAT
1-01-001 INDISPENSIBLE
1-01-001 INDISPOSITION
1-01-001 INDISPUTABLY
1-01-001 INDISTINCT
1-01-001 INDIUM
1-01-001 INDIVIDUALIZI

30

1-01-001 INDIVIDUATION	1-01-001 INHERES	1-01-001 INSURRECTIONS	1-01-001 INTRA-CITY
1-01-001 INDIVISIBILITY	1-01-001 INHERITING	1-01-001 INTACTIBLE	1-01-001 INTRA-COMPANY
1-01-001 INDIVISIBLE	1-01-001 INHERITORS	1-01-001 INTEGERS	1-01-001 INTRA-MURAL
1-01-001 INDO-*CHINA	1-01-001 INHERITS	1-01-001 INTEGRATIVE	1-01-001 INTRA-STELLAR
1-01-001 INDOCTRINATED	1-01-001 INHOMOGENEOUS	1-01-001 INTELLECTUAL-LI	1-01-001 INTRADEPARTMENT
1-01-001 INDOCTRINATING	1-01-001 INHOSPITABLE	TERARY	AL
1-01-001 INDOCTRINATION	1-01-001 INHUMANITIES	1-01-001 INTELLECTUALITY	1-01-001 INTRAEPITHELIAL
1-01-001 INDOLENCE	1-01-001 INIMICAL	1-01-001 INTELLECTUS	1-01-001 INTRAMUSCULARLY
1-01-001 INDOLENTLY	1-01-001 INIMPASSIONED	1-01-001 INTELLIGENTSIA	1-01-001 INTRANASAL
1-01-001 INDOMITABLE	1-01-001 INIQUITIES	1-01-001 INTEMPERANCE	1-01-001 INTRANSIGENTS
1-01-001 INDONESIAN	1-01-001 INIQUITOUS	1-01-001 INTENDANT	1-01-001 INTRAPULMONARY
1-01-001 INDORSED	1-01-001 INITIALED	1-01-001 INTENDANTS	1-01-001 INTRATISSUE
1-01-001 INDUBITABLE	1-01-001 INIURE	1-01-001 INTENDING	1-01-001 INTREPID
1-01-001 INDUCEMENTS	1-01-001 INJECTION-MOLDE	1-01-001 INTENSIVELY	1-01-001 INTRICATELY
1-01-001 INDUCTEES	D	1-01-001 INTENTIONED	1-01-001 INTRODUCTIONS
1-01-001 INDUCTIONS	1-01-001 INJUN'S	1-01-001 INTER-PLANT	1-01-001 INTROJECTED
1-01-001 INDULGENCES	1-01-001 INJUNCTIVE	1-01-001 INTER-RELATION	1-01-001 INTROJECTS
1-01-001 INDULGING	1-01-001 INJUNS	1-01-001 INTER-RELATIONS	1-01-001 INTROSPECTION
1-01-001 INDUSTRALIZATIO	1-01-001 INJURING	HIPS	1-01-001 INTROVERTED
N	1-01-001 INJUSTICES	1-01-001 INTER-SPECIES	1-01-001 INTRUDE
1-01-001 INDUSTRIALISM	1-01-001 INKLING	1-01-001 INTER-TOWN	1-01-001 INTRUDED
1-01-001 INDUSTRIALISTES	1-01-001 INKS	1-01-001 INTER-TRIBAL	1-01-001 INTRUDER
1-01-001 INDUSTRIALISTS	1-01-001 INLAID	1-01-001 INTERACTING	1-01-001 INTRUDERS
1-01-001 INDUSTRIALLY	1-01-001 INMATE	1-01-001 INTERACTS	1-01-001 INTRUDES
1-01-001 INDUSTRY-WIDE	1-01-001 INNERMOST	1-01-001 INTERAXIAL	1-01-001 INTRUDING
1-01-001 INEFFABLE	1-01-001 INNOCENTS	1-01-001 INTERCEDE	1-01-001 INTUITIONS
1-01-001 INEFFECTIVELY	1-01-001 INNOVATE	1-01-001 INTERCEPTOR	1-01-001 INTUITIVELY
1-01-001 INEFFECTIVENESS	1-01-001 INNOVATORS	1-01-001 INTERCEPTS	1-01-001 INUNDATED
1-01-001 INEFFECTUAL	1-01-001 INNS	1-01-001 INTERCLASS	1-01-001 INUNDATING
1-01-001 INEFFICIENCY	1-01-001 INNUENDO	1-01-001 INTERCONNECTED	1-01-001 INUNDATIONS
1-01-001 INELUCTABLE	1-01-001 INNUENDOES	1-01-001 INTERCONNECTEDN	1-01-001 INURE
1-01-001 INEPTLY	1-01-001 INNUENDOS	ESS	1-01-001 INVADER
1-01-001 INEQUALITY	1-01-001 INOCULATIONS	1-01-001 INTERCRISIS	1-01-001 INVADES
1-01-001 INESCAPABLY	1-01-001 INOPERABLE	1-01-001 INTERDEPARTMENT	1-01-001 INVALIDATED
1-01-001 INEVITABILITIES	1-01-001 INOPPORTUNE	AL	1-01-001 INVALIDISM
1-01-001 INEXPERT	1-01-001 INPOST	1-01-001 INTEREFERENCE	1-01-001 INVALIDS
1-01-001 INEXPLICABLY	1-01-001 INPUT/OUTPUT	1-01-001 INTERFERENCE-LI	1-01-001 INVARIABLE
1-01-001 INEXPRESSIBLE	1-01-001 INQUISITIVE	KE	1-01-001 INVASION-THEORY
1-01-001 INEXPRESSIBLY	1-01-001 INQUISITOR	1-01-001 INTERFEROMETERS	1-01-001 INVEIGH
1-01-001 INEXTRICABLE	1-01-001 INQUISITOR-*GEN	1-01-001 INTERGLACIAL	1-01-001 INVENTING
1-01-001 INFAMY	ERAL	1-01-001 INTERGOVERNMENT	1-01-001 INVERCALT
1-01-001 INFANT'S	1-01-001 INSANELY	AL	1-01-001 INVERT
1-01-001 INFANTRYMEN	1-01-001 INSATIABLE	1-01-001 INTERJECTED	1-01-001 INVESTIGATES
1-01-001 INFARCT	1-01-001 INSCRIPTIONS	1-01-001 INTERLACING	1-01-001 INVESTING
1-01-001 INFARCTION	1-01-001 INSCRUTABILITY	1-01-001 INTERLOCUTOR	1-01-001 INVESTS
1-01-001 INFECT	1-01-001 INSECTICIDE	1-01-001 INTERMARRIAGE	1-01-001 INVICTUS
1-01-001 INFER	1-01-001 INSEMINATION	1-01-001 INTERMEDIARY	1-01-001 INVIGORATING
1-01-001 INFERNALLY	1-01-001 INSERTION	1-01-001 INTERMESHED	1-01-001 INVIOLABILITY
1-01-001 INFERTILE	1-01-001 INSERTIONS	1-01-001 INTERMISSION	1-01-001 INVIOLABLE
1-01-001 INFEST	1-01-001 INSERTS	1-01-001 INTERMISSIONS	1-01-001 INVITATIONAL
1-01-001 INFESTED	1-01-001 INSET	1-01-001 INTERMOLECULAR	1-01-001 INVITEES
1-01-001 INFIDEL	1-01-001 INSETS	1-01-001 INTERNAL-EXTERN	1-01-001 INVOCATION
1-01-001 INFIDELS	1-01-001 INSIGNIFICANCE	AL	1-01-001 INVOICES
1-01-001 INFIELDER	1-01-001 INSIGNIFICANCES	1-01-001 INTERNATIONALE	1-01-001 INVOLUNTARILY
1-01-001 INFIGHTING	1-01-001 INSINCERE	1-01-001 INTERNATIONALIS	1-01-001 INVOLUNTARY-CON
1-01-001 INFILTRATING	1-01-001 INSINUATED	TS	TROL
1-01-001 INFINITESIMALLY	1-01-001 INSINUATES	1-01-001 INTERNATIONALIZ	1-01-001 INVOLVEMENTS
1-01-001 INFINITIVE	1-01-001 INSINUATING	ED	1-01-001 INVULNERABILITY
1-01-001 INFIRM	1-01-001 INSIPID	1-01-001 INTERNED	1-01-001 INVULNERABLE
1-01-001 INFIRMARY	1-01-001 INSOLENTLY	1-01-001 INTERNIST'S	1-01-001 IO
1-01-001 INFIRMITY	1-01-001 INSOMMA	1-01-001 INTERNS	1-01-001 IODIDE-CONCENTR
1-01-001 INFLAME	1-01-001 INSOMNIACS	1-01-001 INTERPENETRATE	ATING
1-01-001 INFLAMED	1-01-001 INSOUCIANCE	1-01-001 INTERPEOPLE	1-01-001 IODINATE
1-01-001 INFLAMMATION	1-01-001 INSPIRATIONAL	1-01-001 INTERPOLATED	1-01-001 IODDAMINO
1-01-001 INFLAMMATORY	1-01-001 INSPIRATIONS	1-01-001 INTERPOLATION	1-01-001 IODOCOMPOUNDS
1-01-001 INFLATE	1-01-001 INSPIRES	1-01-001 INTERPOLATIONS	1-01-001 IODOPROTEIN
1-01-001 INFLECTING	1-01-001 INSTALMENTS	1-01-001 INTERPOSED	1-01-001 IODOTHYRONINES
1-01-001 INFLUENZA-PNEUM	1-01-001 INSTANCY	1-01-001 INTERPOSING	1-01-001 IODOTYROSINES
ONIA	1-01-001 INSTANT'S	1-01-001 INTERPRETABLE	1-01-001 IONE
1-01-001 INFORMALITY	1-01-001 INSTIGATE	1-01-001 INTERPRETATIVE	1-01-001 IOSOLA
1-01-001 INFORMANTS	1-01-001 INSTIGATING	1-01-001 INTERPRETOR	1-01-001 IOTA
1-01-001 INFORMATION-CEL	1-01-001 INSTIGATION	1-01-001 INTERRED	1-01-001 IPSO
L	1-01-001 INSTIGATOR	1-01-001 INTERRELATIONSH	1-01-001 IRAJ
1-01-001 INFORMATION-SEE	1-01-001 INSTILLATION	IP	1-01-001 IRATE
KING	1-01-001 INSTITUT	1-01-001 INTERROGATIVES	1-01-001 IRE
1-01-001 INFRA	1-01-001 INSTITUTE'S	1-01-001 INTERROGATOR	1-01-001 IRELANDS'
1-01-001 INFRACTION	1-01-001 INSTITUTES	1-01-001 INTERSCIENCE	1-01-001 IRENAEUS'
1-01-001 INFRINGEMENTS	1-01-001 INSTITUTING	1-01-001 INTERSPECIES	1-01-001 IRIDIUM
1-01-001 INFURIATE	1-01-001 INSTITUTION'S	1-01-001 INTERSPERSED	1-01-001 IRISHMAN
1-01-001 INFURIATION	1-01-001 INSTITUTION-WID	1-01-001 INTERSTICES	1-01-001 IRISHMEN
1-01-001 INFUSION	E	1-01-001 INTERVENES	1-01-001 IRKSOME
1-01-001 ING	1-01-001 INSTITUTIONALIZ	1-01-001 INTERVENING	1-01-001 IRMA
1-01-001 INGBAR	ATION	1-01-001 INTERVIEWEE	1-01-001 IRON-CLAD
1-01-001 INGENIOUSLY	1-01-001 INSTRUCTOR'S	1-01-001 INTERVIEWEES	1-01-001 IRON-POOR
1-01-001 INGESTION	1-01-001 INSTRUCTORS	1-01-001 INTERVIEWERS	1-01-001 IRON-SHOD
1-01-001 INGLESIDE	1-01-001 INSTRUMENT-JAMM	1-01-001 INTERWEAVING	1-01-001 IRONIES
1-01-001 INGLESIDE'S	ED	1-01-001 INTESTINE	1-01-001 IRONPANTS
1-01-001 INGLORIOUS	1-01-001 INSTRUMENTAL-RE	1-01-001 INTESTINES	1-01-001 IRONSIDE
1-01-001 INGO	WARD	1-01-001 INTIAL	1-01-001 IROQUOIS
1-01-001 INGRATITOODE	1-01-001 INSTRUMENTALS	1-01-001 INTIMAL	1-01-001 IRRATIONALITY
1-01-001 INGRATITUDE	1-01-001 INSULATOR	1-01-001 INTIMATING	1-01-001 IRRATIONALLY
1-01-001 INHABIT	1-01-001 INSULATORS	1-01-001 INTIMATIONS	1-01-001 IRRAWADDY
1-01-001 INHABITATION	1-01-001 INSUPERABLY	1-01-001 INTOLERANT	1-01-001 IRREDEEMABLY
1-01-001 INHABITING	1-01-001 INSURES	1-01-001 INTONATIONS	1-01-001 IRREDENTISM
1-01-001 INHALATION	1-01-001 INSURGENCE	1-01-001 INTOXICATED	1-01-001 IRREDUCIBLE
1-01-001 INHALING	1-01-001 INSURGENT	1-01-001 INTOXICATING	1-01-001 IRREGULARS
1-01-001 INHARMONIOUS	1-01-001 INSURGENTS	1-01-001 INTRA	1-01-001 IRREPARABLY

1-01-001 IRRESISTIBLY	1-01-001 JANIS	1-01-001 JOBLOT	1-01-001 K**.*G
1-01-001 IRRESOLUTION	1-01-001 JANISSARIES	1-01-001 JOBS-TEARS	1-01-001 K**.*J**.*P
1-01-001 IRRESOLVABLE	1-01-001 JANITOR'S	1-01-001 JOCK	1-01-001 K'ANG-SI
1-01-001 IRREVERSIBLY	1-01-001 JANITSCH	1-01-001 JOCKEYING	1-01-001 KABALEVSKY
1-01-001 IRRIGATE	1-01-001 JANNEQUIN'S	1-01-001 JOCOSE	1-01-001 KABOOM
1-01-001 IRRIGATING	1-01-001 JANSSEN	1-01-001 JOCULARLY	1-01-001 KADDISH
1-01-001 IRRITABILITY	1-01-001 JANSEN	1-01-001 JOCUND	1-01-001 KADER
1-01-001 IRRITANT	1-01-001 JANSENIST	1-01-001 JODY	1-01-001 KAGANOVICH
1-01-001 IRRITATES	1-01-001 JANUARY'S	1-01-001 JOGS	1-01-001 KAHLER-*CRAFT
1-01-001 IRRUPTIONS	1-01-001 JANUS-FACED	1-01-001 JOHANN	1-01-001 KAHN
1-01-001 IRV	1-01-001 JAP'S	1-01-001 JOHANNESBURG	1-01-001 KAHN'S
1-01-001 IRVIN	1-01-001 JARDIN	1-01-001 JOHANSEN	1-01-001 KAI-SHEK
1-01-001 IRWIN	1-01-001 JAROSS	1-01-001 JOHN'LL	1-01-001 KAI-SHEK'S
1-01-001 ISA	1-01-001 JARVIS	1-01-001 JOHN-*HENRY	1-01-001 KAISER
1-01-001 ISAACSON	1-01-001 JAS	1-01-001 JOHNNIE'S	1-01-001 KAISERS
1-01-001 ISABEL	1-01-001 JASPER	1-01-001 JOHNS-*MANVILLE	1-01-001 KAJAR
1-01-001 ISABELL	1-01-001 JAVERT	1-01-001 JOIE	1-01-001 KAKUTANI
1-01-001 ISAIAH	1-01-001 JAWAHARLAL	1-01-001 JOINERS	1-01-001 KALAMAZOO
1-01-001 ISHAM	1-01-001 JAWBONE	1-01-001 JOKED	1-01-001 KALE
1-01-001 ISHII	1-01-001 JAYCEE	1-01-001 JOKERS	1-01-001 KALEIDESCOPE
1-01-001 ISHTAR	1-01-001 JAZZMEN	1-01-001 JOLLYING	1-01-001 KALEIDOSCOPE
1-01-001 ISIS	1-01-001 JAZZY	1-01-001 JOLTING	1-01-001 KALENTIEV
1-01-001 ISLAM'S	1-01-001 JE	1-01-001 JONES'	1-01-001 KALI
1-01-001 ISLANDIA	1-01-001 JEALOUSIES	1-01-001 JONES'S	1-01-001 KALMUK
1-01-001 ISLANDS'	1-01-001 JEALOUSLY	1-01-001 JONES-*IMBODEN	1-01-001 KALONJI
1-01-001 ISOCYANATE-LABE LED	1-01-001 JEAN-*HONORE	1-01-001 JONESBOROUGH	1-01-001 KAMCHATKA
1-01-001 ISODINE	1-01-001 JEAN-*MARIE	1-01-001 JONESES	1-01-001 KAMENS
1-01-001 ISOLATIONISM	1-01-001 JEAN-*PIERRE	1-01-001 JONQUIERES	1-01-001 KAMIKAZE
1-01-001 ISOLATIONISTIC	1-01-001 JEANNIE	1-01-001 JONQUILS	1-01-001 KAMINSKY
1-01-001 ISOLDE	1-01-001 JEANS	1-01-001 JOPLIN	1-01-001 KANDINSKY
1-01-001 ISOMERS	1-01-001 JEB	1-01-001 JORDA'S	1-01-001 KANIN
1-01-001 ISOTHERMAL	1-01-001 JED'S	1-01-001 JORDON	1-01-001 KANKAKEE
1-01-001 ISOTHERMALLY	1-01-001 JEE	1-01-001 JOSEPHUS	1-01-001 KANS
1-01-001 ISRAEL'S	1-01-001 JEEPERS	1-01-001 JOSHUAL	1-01-001 KANSAS-*NEBRASK A
1-01-001 ISRAELITE	1-01-001 JEERS	1-01-001 JOSS	1-01-001 KANTO
1-01-001 ISRAELITES	1-01-001 JEFFERSONIAN	1-01-001 JOSTLE	1-01-001 KAPLAN
1-01-001 IST	1-01-001 JEHOVAH	1-01-001 JOT	1-01-001 KAPNEK
1-01-001 ISTVAN	1-01-001 JELLIES	1-01-001 JOTTED	1-01-001 KAPOK-FILLED
1-01-001 IT**H	1-01-001 JELLINEK'S	1-01-001 JOTTING	1-01-001 KARE
1-01-001 ITALICIZED	1-01-001 JELLYBY	1-01-001 JOURNAL-*AMERIC AN	1-01-001 KARET
1-01-001 ITALO	1-01-001 JEMELA	1-01-001 JOURNAL-*BULLET IN	1-01-001 KARIPO'S
1-01-001 ITALO-*AMERICAN	1-01-001 JENA	1-01-001 JOURNAL-*BULLET IN'S	1-01-001 KARL-*BIRGER
1-01-001 ITASCA	1-01-001 JENKINS'S		1-01-001 KARLHEINZ
1-01-001 ITCHES	1-01-001 JENNI	1-01-001 JOUST	1-01-001 KARLIS
1-01-001 ITEM-*CATEGORIE S	1-01-001 JENNI'S	1-01-001 JOVIAL	1-01-001 KARNS'
	1-01-001 JENNIE'S	1-01-001 JOVIALITY	1-01-001 KAROL
1-01-001 ITEMIZATION	1-01-001 JENNIFER	1-01-001 JOVIAN	1-01-001 KAROLINERNA
1-01-001 ITHACA	1-01-001 JENNY'S	1-01-001 JOYFUL	1-01-001 KARP'S
1-01-001 ITHACAN	1-01-001 JENS	1-01-001 JOYFULLY	1-01-001 KARSHILAMA
1-01-001 ITINERANT	1-01-001 JEOPARDIZING	1-01-001 JOYOUSLY	1-01-001 KAS.
1-01-001 ITO	1-01-001 JEREZ	1-01-001 JUANITA'S	1-01-001 KASKASKIA
1-01-001 ITOIZ	1-01-001 JERKINGS	1-01-001 JUBILATION	1-01-001 KASSEM
1-01-001 IUVABIT	1-01-001 JERKS	1-01-001 JUDEA	1-01-001 KASTER'S
1-01-001 IVORY-INLAY	1-01-001 JEROBOAM	1-01-001 JUDEO-*CHRISTIA N	1-01-001 KATANGAN
1-01-001 IVY-COVERED	1-01-001 JEROBOAMS		1-01-001 KATHARINE'S
1-01-001 IZVESTIA	1-01-001 JERRY'S	1-01-001 JUDGE'S	1-01-001 KATHERINE'S
1-01-001 J)	1-01-001 JERVIS	1-01-001 JUDGE-MADE	1-01-001 KATHLEEN
1-01-001 J**.*H	1-01-001 JESSICA'S	1-01-001 JUDGEMENT	1-01-001 KATHLEEN-*MASON
1-01-001 J'AI	1-01-001 JESSY	1-01-001 JUDGES'	1-01-001 KATOW
1-01-001 J*P'S	1-01-001 JEST	1-01-001 JUDGESHIP	1-01-001 KAUFFELD
1-01-001 JAB	1-01-001 JESUITS	1-01-001 JUDICIARIES	1-01-001 KAUFFMANN
1-01-001 JABBERINGS	1-01-001 JESUS'S	1-01-001 JUDICIOUS	1-01-001 KAUFNABB
1-01-001 JABS	1-01-001 JET-BLACK	1-01-001 JUDSONS	1-01-001 KAVA
1-01-001 JACCHIA	1-01-001 JETLINERS	1-01-001 JUICIEST	1-01-001 KAWECKI
1-01-001 JACINTO	1-01-001 JETTING	1-01-001 JUJU	1-01-001 KAYABASHI-*=SAN
1-01-001 JACK-AN-*APES	1-01-001 JEUNES	1-01-001 JULEPS	1-01-001 KAYO
1-01-001 JACK-OF-ALL-TRA DES	1-01-001 JEW-AS-ENEMY	1-01-001 JULES	1-01-001 KAZAN
1-01-001 JACKBOOTED	1-01-001 JEW-HATERS	1-01-001 JULIET	1-01-001 KAZOO
1-01-001 JACKBOOTS	1-01-001 JEWEL	1-01-001 JULIO	1-01-001 KEATING'S
1-01-001 JACKDAWS	1-01-001 JEWEL-BRIGHT	1-01-001 JUMPER	1-01-001 KEATS'S
1-01-001 JACKIE'S	1-01-001 JEWELER'S	1-01-001 JUNGIAN	1-01-001 KEBOB
1-01-001 JACKMAN	1-01-001 JEWELLED	1-01-001 JUNIOR-GRADE	1-01-001 KEDDAH
1-01-001 JACKY	1-01-001 JEWETT	1-01-001 JUNIOR-PHILOSOP HICAL	1-01-001 KEDZIE
1-01-001 JACOB	1-01-001 JEWISH-*GENTILE		1-01-001 KEE-REIST
1-01-001 JACOBEAN	1-01-001 JEWS'	1-01-001 JUNIOR-SENIOR	1-01-001 KEEEERIST
1-01-001 JACOBITE	1-01-001 JIBES	1-01-001 JUNIOR-YEAR-ABR OAD	1-01-001 KEERIST
1-01-001 JACQUELYN'S	1-01-001 JIOGE		1-01-001 KEESHOND
1-01-001 JADE	1-01-001 JIFFY-*COUCH-A- *BED	1-01-001 JUNIORS'	1-01-001 KEGFUL
1-01-001 JADE-HANDLED	1-01-001 JIGGER	1-01-001 JUNKERDOM	1-01-001 KEGS
1-01-001 JAG	1-01-001 JIGGLING	1-01-001 JUNKETEERING	1-01-001 KEINE
1-01-001 JAGER	1-01-001 JIMBO'S	1-01-001 JUNKIES	1-01-001 KEIZER
1-01-001 JAGGEDLY	1-01-001 JIMENEZ	1-01-001 JUNKS	1-01-001 KEKISHEVA
1-01-001 JAHR	1-01-001 JIMMIE	1-01-001 JURIDICAL	1-01-001 KEL
1-01-001 JAI	1-01-001 JIMMIED	1-01-001 JURIES	1-01-001 KELLEY'S
1-01-001 JAKARTA	1-01-001 JINGLING	1-01-001 JURISDICTIONS	1-01-001 KELLUM
1-01-001 JAKES	1-01-001 JINNY	1-01-001 JURISPRUDENTIAL LY	1-01-001 KELLY
1-01-001 JALOPY	1-01-001 JINX		1-01-001 KELSEYVILLE
1-01-001 JAMAICAN	1-01-001 JITTERBUG	1-01-001 JURY-TAMPERING	1-01-001 KELTS
1-01-001 JAMES'	1-01-001 JITTERY	1-01-001 JUSSEL	1-01-001 KEMCHENJUNGA
1-01-001 JAMESON	1-01-001 JIU-JITSU	1-01-001 JUSTE	1-01-001 KEMM
1-01-001 JAMESTOWN	1-01-001 JIVING	1-01-001 JUSTINE	1-01-001 KENG
1-01-001 JAMMED-TOGETHER	1-01-001 JOANNE	1-01-001 JUSTITIA	1-01-001 KENILWORTH
1-01-001 JANA	1-01-001 JOAQUIN	1-01-001 JUSTNESS	1-01-001 KENNETT
1-01-001 JANE'S	1-01-001 JOB-	1-01-001 JUTISH	1-01-001 KENNING
1-01-001 JANET	1-01-001 JOB-SEEKERS	1-01-001 K**.*C	1-01-001 KENO
	1-01-001 JOBLESSNESS		1-01-001 KENTFIELD

1-01-001 KENTUCK	1-01-001 KLUCKHOHN	1-01-001 KRIST	1-01-001 LAND-LOCKED
1-01-001 KENZO	1-01-001 KM	1-01-001 KRISTALLSTRUKTU	1-01-001 LANDER
1-01-001 KEPLER	1-01-001 KNACKWURST	REN	1-01-001 LANDES
1-01-001 KERBY	1-01-001 KNAPPERTSBUSCH	1-01-001 KRO**DGER	1-01-001 LANDESCO
1-01-001 KERCHEVAL	1-01-001 KNEAD	1-01-001 KROENING	1-01-001 LANDIS'
1-01-001 KERCHIEF	1-01-001 KNECHT	1-01-001 KROGER	1-01-001 LANDLORD'S
1-01-001 KERR'S	1-01-001 KNEE-DEEP	1-01-001 KROGER'S	1-01-001 LANDON
1-01-001 KERRVILLE	1-01-001 KNEECAP	1-01-001 KROGERS'	1-01-001 LANDOWNERS
1-01-001 KERRY	1-01-001 KNEELS	1-01-001 KROMY	1-01-001 LANDSCAPING
1-01-001 KERSHBAUM	1-01-001 KNICK-KNACKS	1-01-001 KRONENBERGER	1-01-001 LANDSLIDES
1-01-001 KESTNER	1-01-001 KNICKERBOCKER	1-01-001 KRUMPP	1-01-001 LANESMANSHIP
1-01-001 KETCHES	1-01-001 KNIFE-EDGE	1-01-001 KRUPA	1-01-001 LANESVILLE
1-01-001 KETCHUP	1-01-001 KNIFE-GRINDER	1-01-001 KRZYWY-*ROG	1-01-001 LANG
1-01-001 KEY-PUNCHED	1-01-001 KNIFE-MEN	1-01-001 KSU'U'PELI'AFO	1-01-001 LANGE
1-01-001 KEYBOARDING	1-01-001 KNIFE/COATING	1-01-001 KUBEK	1-01-001 LANGELAND
1-01-001 KEYSTONE	1-01-001 KNIFELIKE	1-01-001 KUHN	1-01-001 LANGHORNE
1-01-001 KEZZIAH	1-01-001 KNIGHT-ERRANTRY	1-01-001 KUPCINET	1-01-001 LANGSDORF
1-01-001 KHAKI	1-01-001 KNIGHTES	1-01-001 KURD	1-01-001 LANGUISHED
1-01-001 KHAKI-BOUND	1-01-001 KNIGHTFALL	1-01-001 KURIGALZU	1-01-001 LANGUISHING
1-01-001 KHANEH	1-01-001 KNIGHTLY	1-01-001 KURT	1-01-001 LANIN'S
1-01-001 KHARTOUM	1-01-001 KNILL'S	1-01-001 KWAME	1-01-001 LANTE
1-01-001 KHASI	1-01-001 KNITE	1-01-001 KWANGO	1-01-001 LANTHANUM
1-01-001 KHMER	1-01-001 KNITTING	1-01-001 KWASHIORKOR	1-01-001 LAO-TSE
1-01-001 KHRUSH	1-01-001 KNOBBY-KNUCKLED	1-01-001 KWHR.	1-01-001 LAOTIANS
1-01-001 KI-YI-ING	1-01-001 KNOBS	1-01-001 KYO	1-01-001 LAPEL
1-01-001 KIANG	1-01-001 KNOCK-DOWN	1-01-001 KYO-ZAN	1-01-001 LAPIDARY
1-01-001 KIBBUTZIM	1-01-001 KNOCKDOWN	1-01-001 L**.*S**.*U	1-01-001 LAPLACE
1-01-001 KICK-OFF	1-01-001 KNOE	1-01-001 L*ANGE	1-01-001 LAPPENBURG-*KEM
1-01-001 KICK-OFFS	1-01-001 KNOT-TYING	1-01-001 L*ARCADE	BLE
1-01-001 KICKBACKS	1-01-001 KNOTS	1-01-001 L*ASSISTANCE	1-01-001 LAPPETS
1-01-001 KID-*ISOLETTA	1-01-001 KNOTT	1-01-001 L*ASTREE	1-01-001 LAPSING
1-01-001 KIDDER	1-01-001 KNOW-*NOTHING	1-01-001 L*IMPERIALE	1-01-001 LARDER
1-01-001 KIDNAPER	1-01-001 KNOW-NOTHINGS	1-01-001 L*INDEPENDANCE	1-01-001 LARGE-AREA
1-01-001 KIDNAPPED	1-01-001 KNOWED	1-01-001 L*INSTITUT	1-01-001 LARGE-ENOUGH
1-01-001 KIDNAPPERS	1-01-001 KNOWETH	1-01-001 L*OSSERVATORE	1-01-001 LARGELY-SILENT
1-01-001 KIDNAPPING	1-01-001 KNOWLTON'S	1-01-001 L*UNITA	1-01-001 LARGESSE
1-01-001 KIEFFERM	1-01-001 KNOXVILLE	1-01-001 L*UNIVERSITE	1-01-001 LARIMER
1-01-001 KIKA	1-01-001 KNUCKLE-DUSTER	1-01-001 L'ACTIVITE	1-01-001 LARKIN'S
1-01-001 KIKIYUS	1-01-001 KNUCKLEBALL	1-01-001 L'IDENTITE	1-01-001 LARKINS
1-01-001 KILHOUR	1-01-001 KNUCKLED	1-01-001 L'ORCHESTRE	1-01-001 LARS
1-01-001 KILLABLE	1-01-001 KOAN	1-01-001 L'S	1-01-001 LARSON'S
1-01-001 KILLEBREW	1-01-001 KOB	1-01-001 L-5-VINYL-2-THI	1-01-001 LARVAL
0-01-001 KILLERS	1-01-001 KOBAYASHI	O-OXAZOLIDONE	1-01-001 LASCAR
1-01-001 KILLIN	1-01-001 KOCH	1-01-001 LA**DCHELN	1-01-001 LASCIVIOUS
1-01-001 KILOTON	1-01-001 KOCHANEK	1-01-001 LA**DNDLER	1-01-001 LASHINGS
1-01-001 KILOWATT	1-01-001 KOCHANEKS	1-01-001 LA*GOW	1-01-001 LASSES
1-01-001 KILOWATT-HOURS	1-01-001 KODAKS	1-01-001 LA*GUARDIA'S	1-01-001 LASSUS
1-01-001 KILOWATTS	1-01-001 KOENIG	1-01-001 LABANS	1-01-001 LASSWITZ'S
1-01-001 KILTS	1-01-001 KOFANES	1-01-001 LABILE	1-01-001 LAST-DITCH
1-01-001 KIMBALL	1-01-001 KOH	1-01-001 LABOR'S	1-01-001 LAST-MENTIONED
1-01-001 KIMBELL-*DIAMON	1-01-001 KOHI	1-01-001 LABOR-BASED	1-01-001 LAST-ROUND
D	1-01-001 KOHNSTAMM-POSTI	1-01-001 LABOR-SAVING	1-01-001 LASTS
1-01-001 KIMBOLTON	VE	1-01-001 LABORIOUS	1-01-001 LASWICK
1-01-001 KIMONO	1-01-001 KOK	1-01-001 LABOTHE	1-01-001 LATCHED
1-01-001 KIND'S	1-01-001 KOKOSCHKA	1-01-001 LABOUISSE	1-01-001 LATCHES
1-01-001 KINDER	1-01-001 KOLB	1-01-001 LABRADOR	1-01-001 LATE-COMERS
1-01-001 KINDEST	1-01-001 KOLKHOZES	1-01-001 LABYRINTH	1-01-001 LATE-SUMMER
1-01-001 KINDLED	1-01-001 KOMBO	1-01-001 LACE-DRAWN	1-01-001 LATEINER
1-01-001 KINDLINESS	1-01-001 KOMLEVA	1-01-001 LACERATE	1-01-001 LATFRAL
1-01-001 KINDNESSES	1-01-001 KOMURASAKI	1-01-001 LACERATED	1-01-001 LATERAN
1-01-001 KINESICS	1-01-001 KONGA	1-01-001 LACES	1-01-001 LATHE
1-01-001 KINESTHETICALLY	1-01-001 KONRAD	1-01-001 LACKADAISICAL	1-01-001 LATHES
1-01-001 KINGAN	1-01-001 KONSTANTIN	1-01-001 LACKEYS	1-01-001 LATINOVICH
1-01-001 KINGDOM-WIDE	1-01-001 KONZERTHAUS	1-01-001 LACQUERED	1-01-001 LATITUDES
1-01-001 KINGDOMS	1-01-001 KOOKS	1-01-001 LAD'S	1-01-001 LATS.
1-01-001 KINGPIN	1-01-001 KOOL-*AID	1-01-001 LADLE	1-01-001 LATTER-DAY
1-01-001 KINGWOOD	1-01-001 KOOP	1-01-001 LADS	1-01-001 LATTIMER'S
1-01-001 KINSELL	1-01-001 KOPSTEIN	1-01-001 LADY-BUGS	1-01-001 LAUCHLI'S
1-01-001 KINSEY	1-01-001 KORMAN	1-01-001 LADYLIKE	1-01-001 LAUDABLY
1-01-001 KIOSK	1-01-001 KORNBLUTH	1-01-001 LAFE	1-01-001 LAUDE
1-01-001 KIOWA	1-01-001 KORNEVEY	1-01-001 LAGERLO**DF	1-01-001 LAUDER
1-01-001 KIPLING	1-01-001 KORNEYEV	1-01-001 LAGERS	1-01-001 LAUE
1-01-001 KIRA	1-01-001 KORNEYEVA	1-01-001 LAGRANGE'S	1-01-001 LAUGHINGLY
1-01-001 KIRK	1-01-001 KORNGOLD	1-01-001 LAHK	1-01-001 LAUGHINGSTOCKS
1-01-001 KIRKLAND	1-01-001 KORRA	1-01-001 LAICOS	1-01-001 LAUNCH-CONTROL
1-01-001 KIROV'S	1-01-001 KOSHARE	1-01-001 LAIRS	1-01-001 LAUNCHER
1-01-001 KISSAK	1-01-001 KOSHER	1-01-001 LAK	1-01-001 LAUNCHINGS
1-01-001 KISSIN	1-01-001 KOTOWAZA	1-01-001 LAKEWOOD	1-01-001 LAUNDER-*OMETER
1-01-001 KISSINGS	1-01-001 KOUSSEVITZKY'S	1-01-001 LALAURIE'S	1-01-001 LAUNDERED
1-01-001 KITCHIN	1-01-001 KOWALSKI'S	1-01-001 LALAURIES'	1-01-001 LAUNDERINGS
1-01-001 KITE	1-01-001 KOZINTSEV	1-01-001 LAMBARENE	1-01-001 LAUNDRY-TYPE
1-01-001 KITS	1-01-001 KRAEMER	1-01-001 LAMECHIAN	1-01-001 LAURANCE
1-01-001 KITTENISH	1-01-001 KRAFT	1-01-001 LAMECHIANS	1-01-001 LAURENTIAN
1-01-001 KITTLER	1-01-001 KRAKATOA	1-01-001 LAMENT	1-01-001 LAURENTS'
1-01-001 KITTREDGE	1-01-001 KRAKOW	1-01-001 LAMENTATION	1-01-001 LAURI
1-01-001 KIVU	1-01-001 KRAKOWIAK	1-01-001 LAMINATING	1-01-001 LAURIE
1-01-001 KLAUS	1-01-001 KRAMER'S	1-01-001 LAMMED	1-01-001 LAURITSEN
1-01-001 KLAXON	1-01-001 KRAPP'S	1-01-001 LAMMING	1-01-001 LAURITZ
1-01-001 KLEENEX	1-01-001 KRASNIK	1-01-001 LAMON	1-01-001 LAUSANNE
1-01-001 KLEIBER	1-01-001 KRAUT	1-01-001 LAMPOON	1-01-001 LAVA
1-01-001 KLEIN	1-01-001 KRAUTHEADS	1-01-001 LANCASHIRE	1-01-001 LAVA-ROCKS
1-01-001 KLEIST	1-01-001 KRAUTS	1-01-001 LANCED	1-01-001 LAVATO
1-01-001 KLEMPERER'S	1-01-001 KREISLER	1-01-001 LANCRET	1-01-001 LAVAUGHN
1-01-001 KLIMT	1-01-001 KRIMS	1-01-001 LAND'S	1-01-001 LAVISHED
1-01-001 KLINE	1-01-001 KRISHNA	1-01-001 LAND-	1-01-001 LAVISHING
1-01-001 KLINICO	1-01-001 KRISHNAISTS	1-01-001 LAND-*ROVER	1-01-001 LAVOISIER
1-01-001 KLOMAN	1-01-001 KRISS	1-01-001 LAND-BASED	1-01-001 LAW-ABIDING

1-01-001 LAW-BREAKING	1-01-001 LEHNER	1-01-001 LIBERTINE	1-01-001 LINVILLE
1-01-001 LAW-ENFORCEMENT	1-01-001 LEIBOWITZ	1-01-001 LIBERTY'S	1-01-001 LINZ
1-01-001 LAW-GOVERNED	1-01-001 LEIDEN	1-01-001 LIBRARIAN'S	1-01-001 LIONESSES
1-01-001 LAW-UNTO-ITSELF	1-01-001 LEIGHTON	1-01-001 LIBRARIAN-BOARD	1-01-001 LIONS'
1-01-001 LAWFORD	1-01-001 LEILA	1-01-001 LIBRETTISTS	1-01-001 LIP-SUCKING
1-01-001 LAWMAN'S	1-01-001 LEITMOTIF	1-01-001 LICENSEE	1-01-001 LIPOWA
1-01-001 LAWSUIT	1-01-001 LEITMOTIV	1-01-001 LICHTENSTEIN	1-01-001 LIPPI
1-01-001 LAWSUITS	1-01-001 LEMMAS	1-01-001 LICKING	1-01-001 LIPPINCOTT
1-01-001 LAWYERS'	1-01-001 LEMME	1-01-001 LIDLESS	1-01-001 LIPSON
1-01-001 LAXATIVE	1-01-001 LEMON-MERINGUE	1-01-001 LIEBERMAN	1-01-001 LIQUEUR
1-01-001 LAY-UP	1-01-001 LEMONS	1-01-001 LIEBLER	1-01-001 LIQUID-GLASS
1-01-001 LAYERED	1-01-001 LEMUEL	1-01-001 LIENS	1-01-001 LIQUIDATING
1-01-001 LAYETTE	1-01-001 LENDRUM	1-01-001 LIEUT	1-01-001 LIQUIDATIONS
1-01-001 LAYMAN'S	1-01-001 LENGTHILY	1-01-001 LIEUTENANT-*COL ONEL	1-01-001 LIQUIDITY
1-01-001 LAYMEN'S	1-01-001 LENI	1-01-001 LIEUTENANT-*GOV ERNOR	1-01-001 LIQUOR-CRAZED
1-01-001 LAYOFFS	1-01-001 LENIN'S	1-01-001 LIEUTENANT-GOVE RNOR	1-01-001 LISBON
1-01-001 LAYTON	1-01-001 LENINGRAD'S	1-01-001 LIFE-AND-DEATH	1-01-001 LISE
1-01-001 LAZARUS	1-01-001 LENINGRAD-*KIRO V	1-01-001 LIFE-CONTRACTS	1-01-001 LISLE
1-01-001 LAZE	1-01-001 LENINISM-*MARXI SM	1-01-001 LIFE-DEATH	1-01-001 LISPING
1-01-001 LAZILY	1-01-001 LENNIE	1-01-001 LIFE-PRESERVERS	1-01-001 LISS
1-01-001 LAZZERI	1-01-001 LENNY	1-01-001 LIFE-SIZE	1-01-001 LISTE
1-01-001 LBJ.	1-01-001 LENOBEL'S	1-01-001 LIFE-SUPPORTING	1-01-001 LISTENER'S
1-01-001 LB**S	1-01-001 LENTILS	1-01-001 LIFEBLOOD	1-01-001 LISTENER-SUPPOR TED
1-01-001 LB-PLUS	1-01-001 LENYGON	1-01-001 LIFEBOATS	1-01-001 LISTENIN
1-01-001 LB/DAY	1-01-001 LENYGON'S	1-01-001 LIFEGUARDS	1-01-001 LISTINGS
1-01-001 LE*CLAIR	1-01-001 LEONATO	1-01-001 LIFELONG	1-01-001 LISTLESS
1-01-001 LEACHES	1-01-001 LEONATO'S	1-01-001 LIFER	1-01-001 LISTLESSLY
1-01-001 LEADED	1-01-001 LEONE	1-01-001 LIFSON	1-01-001 LITERALISM
1-01-001 LEADERLESS	1-01-001 LEONORE	1-01-001 LIGAMENT	1-01-001 LITERATURES
1-01-001 LEADINGS	1-01-001 LEOPARD'S	1-01-001 LIGAND	1-01-001 LITHOGRAPH
1-01-001 LEADSMAN	1-01-001 LEOPARDS	1-01-001 LIGGET	1-01-001 LITHOGRAPHS
1-01-001 LEAFED	1-01-001 LEOPOLD	1-01-001 LIGHT-DUTY	1-01-001 LITLE
1-01-001 LEAFHOPPER	1-01-001 LEOPOLD'S	1-01-001 LIGHT-FLARED	1-01-001 LITOWSKI
1-01-001 LEAFIEST	1-01-001 LEPRAE	1-01-001 LIGHT-HEADEDNES S	1-01-001 LITTA
1-01-001 LEAFLET	1-01-001 LEPROSY		1-01-001 LITTAU
1-01-001 LEAFMOLD	1-01-001 LERNER	1-01-001 LIGHT-HEARTED	1-01-001 LITTERBUG
1-01-001 LEAFY	1-01-001 LESBIANS	1-01-001 LIGHT-MINDEDNES S	1-01-001 LITTERING
1-01-001 LEAGUED	1-01-001 LESCAUT		1-01-001 LITTLE-GIRL
1-01-001 LEAKAGE	1-01-001 LESS-DEVELOPED	1-01-001 LIGHT-REFLECTIN G	1-01-001 LITTLE-KNOWN
1-01-001 LEALE	1-01-001 LESS-DRAMATIC		1-01-001 LITTLE-TOWN
1-01-001 LEAMINGTON	1-01-001 LESS-HURRIED	1-01-001 LIGHT-TRANSMITT ING	1-01-001 LITTLEPAGE'S
1-01-001 LEANS	1-01-001 LESS-INDOMITABL E		1-01-001 LITTLEST
1-01-001 LEARNERS		1-01-001 LIGHT-YEAR	1-01-001 LITTLETON'S
1-01-001 LEARY	1-01-001 LESS-THAN-CARLO AD	1-01-001 LIGHTENS	1-01-001 LIVABILITY
1-01-001 LEASHES	1-01-001 LESS-TRAVELED	1-01-001 LIGHTER'N	1-01-001 LIVABLE
1-01-001 LEASURE	1-01-001 LESSENS	1-01-001 LIGHTERS	1-01-001 LIVE-OAK
1-01-001 LEATHER-BOUND	1-01-001 LESSER-KNOWN	1-01-001 LIGHTFOOT	1-01-001 LIVERIED
1-01-001 LEATHER-HARD	1-01-001 LESTER'S	1-01-001 LIGHTHOUSES	1-01-001 LIVERMORE
1-01-001 LEATHERED	1-01-001 LET'S-MAKE-YOUR -HOUSE-OUR-CLUB	1-01-001 LIGHTNESS	1-01-001 LIVERS
1-01-001 LEATHERMAN		1-01-001 LIGHTNING-OCCUR RENCE	1-01-001 LIVID
1-01-001 LEATHERNECK	1-01-001 LET-DOWN		1-01-001 LIVING-ROOM
1-01-001 LEATHERY	1-01-001 LETHALITY	1-01-001 LIGHTYEARS	1-01-001 LIVINGSTON
1-01-001 LEAVENING	1-01-001 LETHARGIES	1-01-001 LIGNE	1-01-001 LIZ
1-01-001 LEAVENWORTH	1-01-001 LETTERED	1-01-001 LIKEE	1-01-001 LIZARD'S
1-01-001 LEAVINGS	1-01-001 LETTERHEAD	1-01-001 LIL	1-01-001 LIZARDS
1-01-001 LEAVITT'S	1-01-001 LETTERMAN	1-01-001 LILI	1-01-001 LIZZIE'S
1-01-001 LEBENSRAUM	1-01-001 LETTERMEN	1-01-001 LILIES	1-01-001 LLEWELLYN
1-01-001 LECHER	1-01-001 LETTIN	1-01-001 LILIPUTIAN	1-01-001 LO**DBL
1-01-001 LECKY	1-01-001 LEV	1-01-001 LILLIAN'S	1-01-001 LOADER
1-01-001 LEDFORD	1-01-001 LEVEE	1-01-001 LILLIPUTIAN	1-01-001 LOADERS
1-01-001 LEDGERS	1-01-001 LEVEL'S	1-01-001 LILT	1-01-001 LOAFED
1-01-001 LEDGES	1-01-001 LEVERAGE	1-01-001 LILY	1-01-001 LOB
1-01-001 LEDYARD	1-01-001 LEVERETT	1-01-001 LIMBIC	1-01-001 LOBAR
1-01-001 LEEDS	1-01-001 LEVI-CLAD	1-01-001 LIMELIGHT	1-01-001 LOBBIED
1-01-001 LEES	1-01-001 LEVIED	1-01-001 LIMERICK	1-01-001 LOBBIES
1-01-001 LEET	1-01-001 LEVIN	1-01-001 LIMITED-TIME	1-01-001 LOBLOLLY
1-01-001 LEFT-CENTERFIEL D	1-01-001 LEVINGER'S	1-01-001 LIMITLESS	1-01-001 LOBO
	1-01-001 LEVITATION	1-01-001 LIMOUSINES	1-01-001 LOBSCOUSE
1-01-001 LEFT-FRONT	1-01-001 LEVITTOWN	1-01-001 LIMP-LOOKING	1-01-001 LOBSTER
1-01-001 LEFT-JUSTIFIED	1-01-001 LEVITY	1-01-001 LIMPID	1-01-001 LOBSTER-BACKED
1-01-001 LEFT-OF-CENTER	1-01-001 LEW'S	1-01-001 LIMPLY	1-01-001 LOBULAR
1-01-001 LEFTFIELD	1-01-001 LEWDLY	1-01-001 LIMPS	1-01-001 LOBULARITY
1-01-001 LEFTHANDERS	1-01-001 LEWELLEYN	1-01-001 LINDBERGH'S	1-01-001 LOBULE
1-01-001 LEFTIST	1-01-001 LEWELLYN	1-01-001 LINDEMANNS	1-01-001 LOCALISMS
1-01-001 LEG'S	1-01-001 LEWIS'	1-01-001 LINDSEY'S	1-01-001 LOCALIZE
1-01-001 LEG-SPLIT	1-01-001 LEXICOSTATISTIC	1-01-001 LINDSKOG	1-01-001 LOCALIZED
1-01-001 LEGACIES	1-01-001 LEYDEN	1-01-001 LINDY	1-01-001 LOCATIN
1-01-001 LEGALITY	1-01-001 LI'L	1-01-001 LINE-DENSITY	1-01-001 LOCATION-MINDE
1-01-001 LEGATEE	1-01-001 LIABILITIES	1-01-001 LINE-DRIVEN	1-01-001 LOCK-OUTS
1-01-001 LEGATION	1-01-001 LIAISONS	1-01-001 LINE-DRYING	1-01-001 LOCKE'S
1-01-001 LEGATION'S	1-01-001 LIAR'S	1-01-001 LINE-FRAGMENTS	1-01-001 LOCKHEED'S
1-01-001 LEGATIONS	1-01-001 LIARS	1-01-001 LINE-PAIRS	1-01-001 LOCKIAN
1-01-001 LEGATO	1-01-001 LIBELLOS	1-01-001 LINEAGES	1-01-001 LOCOMOTIVES
1-01-001 LEGERS	1-01-001 LIBELOUS	1-01-001 LINEAL	1-01-001 LODGED
1-01-001 LEGGED	1-01-001 LIBER	1-01-001 LINEBACKERS	1-01-001 LODGMENT
1-01-001 LEGGETT	1-01-001 LIBERAL'S	1-01-001 LINEMAN	1-01-001 LODOWICK
1-01-001 LEGGINGS	1-01-001 LIBERAL-*RADICA L	1-01-001 LINEN-COVERED	1-01-001 LOEB
1-01-001 LEGGY		1-01-001 LINGUIST-ANTHRO POLOGIST	1-01-001 LOEN
1-01-001 LEGIBILITY	1-01-001 LIBERAL-LED		1-01-001 LOESER
1-01-001 LEGIONS	1-01-001 LIBERALIZING	1-01-001 LINGUISTICALLY	1-01-001 LOESSER'S
1-01-001 LEGISLATE	1-01-001 LIBERATING	1-01-001 LINIMENT	1-01-001 LOEW'S
1-01-001 LEGISLATED	1-01-001 LIBERIA	1-01-001 LINIMENTS	1-01-001 LOEWE
1-01-001 LEGISLATION-DEL AYING	1-01-001 LIBERTARIAN	1-01-001 LINOLEUM	1-01-001 LOG-HOUSE
	1-01-001 LIBERTIE	1-01-001 LINUS	1-01-001 LOG-JAM
1-01-001 LEGUMINOUS			1-01-001 LOGARITHM
1-01-001 LEHMAN			1-01-001 LOGARITHMS
1-01-001 LEHMANN			

Rank	Word
1-01-001	LOGGER
1-01-001	LOGIC-RHETORIC
1-01-001	LOGISTICAL
1-01-001	LOHMANS
1-01-001	LOIN
1-01-001	LOINCLOTH
1-01-001	LOIRE
1-01-001	LOLLING
1-01-001	LOLOTTE'S
1-01-001	LOMBARD
1-01-001	LOND
1-01-001	LONDON-BASED
1-01-001	LONDON-BRED
1-01-001	LONDONER
1-01-001	LONELIER
1-01-001	LONELIEST
1-01-001	LONERS
1-01-001	LONG-
1-01-001	LONG-ACTING
1-01-001	LONG-BODIED
1-01-001	LONG-CHAIN
1-01-001	LONG-CRUISE
1-01-001	LONG-ENDURANCE
1-01-001	LONG-FAMILIAR
1-01-001	LONG-FAR
1-01-001	LONG-FOR
1-01-001	LONG-HAIR
1-01-001	LONG-HAUL
1-01-001	LONG-KEEPING
1-01-001	LONG-KNOWN
1-01-001	LONG-LIFE
1-01-001	LONG-LINE
1-01-001	LONG-OVERDUE
1-01-001	LONG-SETTLED
1-01-001	LONG-SHANKED
1-01-001	LONG-SLEEVED
1-01-001	LONG-STEMMED
1-01-001	LONG-VANISHED
1-01-001	LONG-VIEW
1-01-001	LONGFELLOW
1-01-001	LONGINOTTI
1-01-001	LONGISH
1-01-001	LONGITUDE
1-01-001	LONGITUDES
1-01-001	LONGITUDINAL
1-01-001	LONGRUN
1-01-001	LONGS
1-01-001	LONGSHOREMEN
1-01-001	LONGSHOREMEN'S
1-01-001	LONGSHOT
1-01-001	LONGSUFFERING
1-01-001	LONGTIME
1-01-001	LONGWOOD
1-01-001	LONSDALE'S
1-01-001	LUUK-SEE
1-01-001	LOOKY
1-01-001	LOOPED
1-01-001	LOOPS
1-01-001	LOOSE-JOWLED
1-01-001	LOOSE-KNIT
1-01-001	LOOSE-LEAF
1-01-001	LOOSE-LOADED
1-01-001	LOOSELY-TAPED
1-01-001	LOOSENING
1-01-001	LOOSENS
1-01-001	LOOSEST
1-01-001	LOOSLI
1-01-001	LOP
1-01-001	LOPATNIKOFF'S
1-01-001	LOPED
1-01-001	LOPPED
1-01-001	LOPSIDEDLY
1-01-001	LOQUACITY
1-01-001	LORAIN
1-01-001	LORCA
1-01-001	LORDE
1-01-001	LORELEI
1-01-001	LOREN
1-01-001	LORENA
1-01-001	LORLYN
1-01-001	LORRAIN
1-01-001	LORRAINE
1-01-001	LOSER
1-01-001	LOSERS
1-01-001	LOTHARIO
1-01-001	LOTIONS
1-01-001	LOTTE
1-01-001	LOTTERY
1-01-001	LOTTIE
1-01-001	LOUCHHEIM
1-01-001	LOUD-VOICED
1-01-001	LOUDON'S
1-01-001	LOUDSPEAKER
1-01-001	LOUIS'
1-01-001	LOUISA
1-01-001	LOUISIANAN
1-01-001	LOUISIANE
1-01-001	LOUNGES
1-01-001	LOUSED
1-01-001	LOUSIE
1-01-001	LOUSINESS
1-01-001	LOVE-IN-ACTION
1-01-001	LOVELACE
1-01-001	LOVELIES
1-01-001	LOVELORN
1-01-001	LOVER'S
1-01-001	LOVERS'
1-01-001	LOVETT
1-01-001	LOVEWAYS
1-01-001	LOVIE
1-01-001	LOVIN
1-01-001	LOVINGLY
1-01-001	LOVINGOOD
1-01-001	LOW-BOILING
1-01-001	LOW-BUDGET
1-01-001	LOW-CALORY
1-01-001	LOW-CEILINGED
1-01-001	LOW-DUTY
1-01-001	LOW-FLYING
1-01-001	LOW-FOAM
1-01-001	LOW-FREQUENCY
1-01-001	LOW-HEELED
1-01-001	LOW-LYING
1-01-001	LOW-POWER
1-01-001	LOW-PRICED
1-01-001	LOW-SPEED
1-01-001	LOW-SUDSING
1-01-001	LOW-TENSION
1-01-001	LOW-VOLTAGE
1-01-001	LOW-WATER
1-01-001	LOWDOWN
1-01-001	LOWE
1-01-001	LOWE'S
1-01-001	LOWER-CUT
1-01-001	LOWER-LEVEL
1-01-001	LOWER-PAID
1-01-001	LOWER-PRICED
1-01-001	LOWERS
1-01-001	LOWLANDS
1-01-001	LOWLIEST
1-01-001	LOWN
1-01-001	LOWS
1-01-001	LOY
1-01-001	LP
1-01-001	LUBBERLANDERS
1-01-001	LUBRICATED
1-01-001	LUBRICATION
1-01-001	LUCAS
1-01-001	LUCAS'S
1-01-001	LUCIDITY
1-01-001	LUCIFER'S
1-01-001	LUCILLE'S
1-01-001	LUCKED
1-01-001	LUCKIER
1-01-001	LUCKS
1-01-001	LUCY'S
1-01-001	LUDICROUSNESS
1-01-001	LUDLOW
1-01-001	LUDMILLA
1-01-001	LUDWICK
1-01-001	LUECHTEFELD
1-01-001	LUETTE
1-01-001	LUFTWAFFE
1-01-001	LUGER
1-01-001	LUI
1-01-001	LUIS'S
1-01-001	LUISA
1-01-001	LUISE
1-01-001	LUKUKLU
1-01-001	LULLED
1-01-001	LULLS
1-01-001	LULLY
1-01-001	LULU
1-01-001	LUMBAR
1-01-001	LUMBERED
1-01-001	LUMEN
1-01-001	LUMEN-WATT
1-01-001	LUMIA
1-01-001	LUMINARIES
1-01-001	LUMINESCENCE
1-01-001	LUMINESCENT
1-01-001	LUMINOSITY
1-01-001	LUMMOX
1-01-001	LUMMUS
1-01-001	LUMPISH
1-01-001	LUNATIC
1-01-001	LUNATIC-FRINGE
1-01-001	LUNCHEON-TABLE
1-01-001	LUNCHROOM
1-01-001	LUND
1-01-001	LUNDEEN
1-01-001	LUNDY
1-01-001	LURA
1-01-001	LURAY
1-01-001	LURCAT
1-01-001	LURING
1-01-001	LURK
1-01-001	LURKS
1-01-001	LUSHES
1-01-001	LUSIGNAN
1-01-001	LUSTFUL
1-01-001	LUSTILY
1-01-001	LUSTROUS
1-01-001	LUSTS
1-01-001	LUTE
1-01-001	LUTHULI
1-01-001	LUTIHAW
1-01-001	LUTTE
1-01-001	LUXER
1-01-001	LUXURIANCE
1-01-001	LUXURIOSLY-UPHOLSTERED
1-01-001	LUZON
1-01-001	LYCIDAS
1-01-001	LYDIA
1-01-001	LYIN
1-01-001	LYLE
1-01-001	LYMAN
1-01-001	LYMINGTON
1-01-001	LYMPHOCYTES
1-01-001	LYMPHOMA
1-01-001	LYNCHED
1-01-001	LYOPHILIZED
1-01-001	LYRICIST'S
1-01-001	LYRIIST
1-01-001	M**.'S
1-01-001	M**.*D
1-01-001	M**)C**(CLELLAN
1-01-001	M**YM
1-01-001	M*V
1-01-001	M-M-M
1-01-001	MA*=IES*STIE
1-01-001	MAC
1-01-001	MAC*ARTHUR-*HELEN
1-01-001	MAC*DONALD'S
1-01-001	MAC*GREGORS
1-01-001	MAC*ISAACS
1-01-001	MAC*LEAN
1-01-001	MAC*LEISHES
1-01-001	MAC*PHAIL
1-01-001	MAC*WHORTER
1-01-001	MACASSAR
1-01-001	MACAULAY
1-01-001	MACCABEUS
1-01-001	MACEDON
1-01-001	MACH*T
1-01-001	MACHADO
1-01-001	MACHIAVELLI
1-01-001	MACHINE-FAMILY
1-01-001	MACHINE-GUN
1-01-001	MACHINE-GUNNED
1-01-001	MACHINE-MASTERS
1-01-001	MACHINEGUN
1-01-001	MACHINELIKE
1-01-001	MACHINISTS'
1-01-001	MACINTOSH
1-01-001	MACK
1-01-001	MACKINACK
1-01-001	MACKINAW
1-01-001	MACKINTOSH
1-01-001	MACKLIN'S
1-01-001	MACMILLAN
1-01-001	MACROPATHOLOGY
1-01-001	MACROPHAGES
1-01-001	MACROSCOPICALLY
1-01-001	MACWHYTE
1-01-001	MADAGASCAR
1-01-001	MADAMA
1-01-001	MADARIPUR
1-01-001	MADDALENA
1-01-001	MADDING
1-01-001	MADEIRA
1-01-001	MADEMOISELLE
1-01-001	MADHOUSE
1-01-001	MADISON'S
1-01-001	MADONNA'S
1-01-001	MADRID
1-01-001	MADRIGALING
1-01-001	MADSTONES
1-01-001	MAE'S
1-01-001	MAECKER
1-01-001	MAELSTROM
1-01-001	MAETERLINCK
1-01-001	MAG
1-01-001	MAGARRELL
1-01-001	MAGAZINE'S
1-01-001	MAGEE
1-01-001	MAGET
1-01-001	MAGGOTY
1-01-001	MAGI
1-01-001	MAGIC-PRACTICING
1-01-001	MAGICIANS
1-01-001	MAGNANIMITY
1-01-001	MAGNATE
1-01-001	MAGNATES
1-01-001	MAGNETICALLY
1-01-001	MAGNETISMS
1-01-001	MAGNIFIES
1-01-001	MAGNITUDES
1-01-001	MAGNOLIA
1-01-001	MAGOG
1-01-001	MAGPIE
1-01-001	MAGUIRES
1-01-001	MAH-JONGG
1-01-001	MAHAYANIST
1-01-001	MAHONE
1-01-001	MAHT
1-01-001	MAHUA
1-01-001	MAI
1-01-001	MAI'TEIPA
1-01-001	MAID'S
1-01-001	MAIER
1-01-001	MAILBOX
1-01-001	MAILED-FIST-IN-VELVET-GLOVE
1-01-001	MAILMAN
1-01-001	MAIMED
1-01-001	MAIN-D'*OEUVRE
1-01-001	MAINLINER-*HIGHLAND
1-01-001	MAINS
1-01-001	MAITLAND
1-01-001	MAITLAND'S
1-01-001	MAITRE
1-01-001	MAITRES
1-01-001	MAJ
1-01-001	MAJDAN-*TARTARSKI
1-01-001	MAJESTERIAL
1-01-001	MAJESTICALLY
1-01-001	MAJESTIES
1-01-001	MAJESTY
1-01-001	MAJESTY'S
1-01-001	MAJOR-*LEAGUE
1-01-001	MAJOR-MARKET
1-01-001	MAJORED
1-01-001	MAJUH
1-01-001	MAKE-BELIEVE
1-01-001	MAKE-READY
1-01-001	MAKE-WORK
1-01-001	MAKEPEACE
1-01-001	MAKESHIFTS
1-01-001	MAKEUP
1-01-001	MAL
1-01-001	MALABAR
1-01-001	MALADAPTIVE
1-01-001	MALADROIT
1-01-001	MALADY
1-01-001	MALAMUD
1-01-001	MALAPROPISM
1-01-001	MALAY
1-01-001	MALDEN
1-01-001	MALEDICTION
1-01-001	MALENKOV
1-01-001	MALESHERBES
1-01-001	MALEVOLENCIES
1-01-001	MALFEASANT
1-01-001	MALFORMATIONS
1-01-001	MALFUNCTIONING
1-01-001	MALI
1-01-001	MALIA
1-01-001	MALICIOUSLY
1-01-001	MALIGN
1-01-001	MALIGNANCIES
1-01-001	MALIGNANCY
1-01-001	MALINOVSKY
1-01-001	MALLEABLE
1-01-001	MALLINCKRODT
1-01-001	MALLORY
1-01-001	MALLORY'S
1-01-001	MALMESBURY
1-01-001	MALMROS
1-01-001	MALMUD
1-01-001	MALNOURISHED
1-01-001	MALONE
1-01-001	MALPOSED
1-01-001	MALT
1-01-001	MALTED
1-01-001	MALTREAT
1-01-001	MAMARONECK
1-01-001	MAMBO
1-01-001	MAME
1-01-001	MAMMAL
1-01-001	MAMMAS
1-01-001	MAN-HOURS
1-01-001	MAN-TO-MAN

1-01-001	MANAGEMENT-TRAINED	1-01-001	MARMEE	1-01-001	MATLOWSKY	1-01-001	MEANS'S
1-01-001	MANAGUA	1-01-001	MARMI	1-01-001	MATRIARCH	1-01-001	MEARS
1-01-001	MANCHESTER'S	1-01-001	MAROC	1-01-001	MATRIARCHAL ✓	1-01-001	MEASURABLY
1-01-001	MANDAMUS	1-01-001	MAROCAINE	1-01-001	MATRIMONIAL	1-01-001	MEAT-WAGON
1-01-001	MANDARIN	1-01-001	MAROONED	1-01-001	MATRIX	1-01-001	MEATY
1-01-001	MANDATED	1-01-001	MAROY	1-01-001	MATSU	1-01-001	MECCA
1-01-001	MANDERSCHEID	1-01-001	MARQUEES	1-01-001	MATSYENDRA	1-01-001	MECHANIC'S
1-01-001	MANDHATA	1-01-001	MARQUESS	1-01-001	MATTATHIAS	1-01-001	MECHANIST
1-01-001	MANDREL	1-01-001	MARQUET	1-01-001	MATTER-OF-FACTNESS	1-01-001	MECHANISTIC
1-01-001	MANERET	1-01-001	MARQUETTE			1-01-001	MECHANOCHEMICALLY
1-01-001	MANEUVERABILITY	1-01-001	MARQUIS'	1-01-001	MATTIE		
1-01-001	MANFRED	1-01-001	MARR'S	1-01-001	MATTRESSES	1-01-001	MED-*CHEMICAL
1-01-001	MANGANESE	1-01-001	MARRING	1-01-001	MATURATIONAL	1-01-001	MEDALLIONS
1-01-001	MANGLED	1-01-001	MARROWBONES	1-01-001	MATURITIES	1-01-001	MEDDLE
1-01-001	MANHATTAN'S	1-01-001	MARSEILLES	1-01-001	MAUDE'S	1-01-001	MEDEA
1-01-001	MANIACAL	1-01-001	MARSH'S	1-01-001	MAUDLIN	1-01-001	MEDECINE
1-01-001	MANIACS	1-01-001	MARSHA	1-01-001	MAULDIN	1-01-001	MEDFIELD'S
1-01-001	MANIC-DEPRESSIVE	1-01-001	MARSHALING	1-01-001	MAULER	1-01-001	MEDIAEVALIST
		1-01-001	MARSHALL'S	1-01-001	MAULING	1-01-001	MEDIAN
1-01-001	MANICLIKE	1-01-001	MARSHALLED	1-01-001	MAURIER	1-01-001	MEDIATING
1-01-001	MANIFESTING	1-01-001	MARSHALLING	1-01-001	MAURINE	1-01-001	MEDICALE
1-01-001	MANIKIN	1-01-001	MARSHLANDS	1-01-001	MAUVE	1-01-001	MEDICI
1-01-001	MANIKINS	1-01-001	MARSHMALLOWS	1-01-001	MAUVE-COLORED	1-01-001	MEDICINAL
1-01-001	MANIPULATORS	1-01-001	MARSKMEN	1-01-001	MAVERICKS	1-01-001	MEDICIS
1-01-001	MANITOBA	1-01-001	MARTHA'S	1-01-001	MAWKISH	1-01-001	MEDICO'S
1-01-001	MANJUCRI	1-01-001	MARTIN'S	1-01-001	MAXENTIUS	1-01-001	MEDICS
1-01-001	MANLEY'S	1-01-001	MARTINGALE	1-01-001	MAXIM	1-01-001	MEDIOCRITIES
1-01-001	MANLINESS	1-01-001	MARTINIQUE	1-01-001	MAXIM'S	1-01-001	MEDIOCRITY
1-01-001	MANNEQUIN	1-01-001	MARTS	1-01-001	MAXIMILIAN	1-01-001	MEDITATE
1-01-001	MANNERED	1-01-001	MARTY'S	1-01-001	MAXIMIZED	1-01-001	MEDITATED
1-01-001	MANNERHOUSE	1-01-001	MARTYRDOM	1-01-001	MAXINE'S	1-01-001	MEDIUM-SIZED
1-01-001	MANNERISMS	1-01-001	MARTYRS	1-01-001	MAYANS	1-01-001	MEDIUMSHIP
1-01-001	MANON	1-01-001	MARUM	1-01-001	MAYHEM	1-01-001	MEDLEY
1-01-001	MANORS	1-01-001	MARVELLED	1-01-001	MAYNOR	1-01-001	MEDMENHAM
1-01-001	MANS	1-01-001	MARVELOUSLY	1-01-001	MAYO	1-01-001	MEEHAN
1-01-001	MANSE	1-01-001	MARVELS	1-01-001	MAYOR-ELECT	1-01-001	MEEK-MANNERED
1-01-001	MANSION'S	1-01-001	MARXIST-*LENINIST	1-01-001	MAYOR-NOMINATE	1-01-001	MEEKEST
1-01-001	MANTEGNA			1-01-001	MAYORSHIP	1-01-001	MEETIN
1-01-001	MANTIC	1-01-001	MARYED	1-01-001	MAYST	1-01-001	MEGAKARYOCYTIC
1-01-001	MANTLEPIECE	1-01-001	MARYINSKY	1-01-001	MAZOWSZE	1-01-001	MEGALOMANIA
1-01-001	MANTRAP	1-01-001	MASCARA	1-01-001	MC	1-01-001	MEGALOPOLISES
1-01-001	MANUMISSION	1-01-001	MASCULINITY	1-01-001	MC*ALESTER	1-01-001	MEGARIANS
1-01-001	MANUMITTED	1-01-001	MASER	1-01-001	MC*ALISTER	1-01-001	MEHITABEL
1-01-001	MANURE-SCENTED	1-01-001	MASH	1-01-001	MC*CAFFERTY	1-01-001	MEINCKIAN
1-01-001	MANVILLE	1-01-001	MASHING	1-01-001	MC*CARTHY'S	1-01-001	MEINUNG
1-01-001	MANY-BODIED	1-01-001	MASKERS'	1-01-001	MC*CLOY'S	1-01-001	MEIR
1-01-001	MANY-FACED	1-01-001	MASKING	1-01-001	MC*CLUSKEY	1-01-001	MEISENHEIMER
1-01-001	MANY-MUCH	1-01-001	MASON'S	1-01-001	MC*CONE	1-01-001	MEISTER
1-01-001	MANY-TIMES	1-01-001	MASQUE	1-01-001	MC*CONE'S	1-01-001	MEISTERSINGER
1-01-001	MANYE	1-01-001	MASQUERADING	1-01-001	MC*CONNELL'S	1-01-001	MELANDERI
1-01-001	MANZANITA	1-01-001	MASQUERS	1-01-001	MC*CRACKEN	1-01-001	MELANGE
1-01-001	MANZANOLA	1-01-001	MASS-BUILDING	1-01-001	MC*DERMOTT	1-01-001	MELBOURNE
1-01-001	MAPLECREST	1-01-001	MASS-DISTRIBUTION	1-01-001	MC*DONNELL	1-01-001	MELCHER
1-01-001	MAPPED			1-01-001	MC*EACHERN	1-01-001	MELD
1-01-001	MAQUET	1-01-001	MASS-PRODUCTION	1-01-001	MC*ELVANEY	1-01-001	MELIORATION
1-01-001	MARATHON	1-01-001	MASSACRE	1-01-001	MC*ELYEE	1-01-001	MELISANDE
1-01-001	MARAUDERS	1-01-001	MASSACRED	1-01-001	MC*ENROE'S	1-01-001	MELLAL
1-01-001	MARBLEIZED	1-01-001	MASSACRES	1-01-001	MC*FARLAND	1-01-001	MELLOW
1-01-001	MARBLEIZING	1-01-001	MASSAGING	1-01-001	MC*FEE	1-01-001	MELODICALLY
1-01-001	MARCEL	1-01-001	MASSEY-*FERGUSON	1-01-001	MC*GEHEE	1-01-001	MELON
1-01-001	MARCEL'S			1-01-001	MC*GHIE	1-01-001	MELON-LIKE
1-01-001	MARCELLO	1-01-001	MASSIFS	1-01-001	MC*GLYNN	1-01-001	MEM
1-01-001	MARCHAND	1-01-001	MASSIMO	1-01-001	MC*GOVERN'S	1-01-001	MEME
1-01-001	MARCHIN	1-01-001	MASSING	1-01-001	MC*GRUDER	1-01-001	MEMENTO
1-01-001	MARCILE	1-01-001	MASSON	1-01-001	MC*INTOSH	1-01-001	MEMENTOES
1-01-001	MARCIUS	1-01-001	MASSUH	1-01-001	MC*INTYRE	1-01-001	MEMENTOS
1-01-001	MARCMANN	1-01-001	MASTER-RACE	1-01-001	MC*KELLAR	1-01-001	MEMINISSE
1-01-001	MARCOS	1-01-001	MASTERFULLY	1-01-001	MC*KENNA	1-01-001	MEMO
1-01-001	MARDIS	1-01-001	MASTERING	1-01-001	MC*KINLEY'S	1-01-001	MEMORANDA
1-01-001	MARENZIO	1-01-001	MASTERLY	1-01-001	MC*KINNEY	1-01-001	MEMORIALIZED
1-01-001	MARES	1-01-001	MASTERMINDING	1-01-001	MC*LAUCHLIN	1-01-001	MEMORIZATION
1-01-001	MARGARETVILLE	1-01-001	MASTERPICE	1-01-001	MC*LEMORE	1-01-001	MEMORY-PICTURE
1-01-001	MARGARITO	1-01-001	MASTIC	1-01-001	MC*LENDON	1-01-001	MEMORY-PICTURES
1-01-001	MARGINALLY	1-01-001	MASTIFF	1-01-001	MC*LENDON-*EBONY	1-01-001	MEMOS
1-01-001	MARGO	1-01-001	MASTODONS			1-01-001	MEN-FOLK
1-01-001	MARIANO	1-01-001	MASTOIDEUS	1-01-001	MC*LEOD	1-01-001	MEN-OF-WAR
1-01-001	MARILYN	1-01-001	MASU'S	1-01-001	MC*N	1-01-001	MENAGERIE
1-01-001	MARIMBA	1-01-001	MATAMORAS	1-01-001	MC*NEAR	1-01-001	MENARCHES
1-01-001	MARINADE	1-01-001	MATCH-WIDTH	1-01-001	MC*NEIL	1-01-001	MENAS
1-01-001	MARINATED	1-01-001	MATCHING-FUND	1-01-001	MC*NEILL	1-01-001	MENCIUS
1-01-001	MARINATING	1-01-001	MATCHMAKING	1-01-001	MC*PHERSON	1-01-001	MENDACIOUS
1-01-001	MARINER	1-01-001	MATEO	1-01-001	MC*PHERSON'S	1-01-001	MENDED
1-01-001	MARIO	1-01-001	MATERIAL'S	1-01-001	MC*QUILLAN	1-01-001	MENDELSSOHN'S
1-01-001	MARIONETTES	1-01-001	MATERIAL-FORMAL	1-01-001	MC*ROBERTS	1-01-001	MENDOZA
1-01-001	MARITAIN'S	1-01-001	MATERIAL/HR**./	1-01-001	MC*SORLEY'S	1-01-001	MENELAUS'
1-01-001	MARJORIE		**+0*F**./IN	1-01-001	MC*WHINNEY	1-01-001	MENET
1-01-001	MARK-UP	1-01-001	MATERIALIZED	1-01-001	MCCORMACK	1-01-001	MENFOLK
1-01-001	MARKEL	1-01-001	MATERIALS'	1-01-001	MCCORMICK	1-01-001	MENIAL
1-01-001	MARKERS	1-01-001	MATERIALS-HANDLING	1-01-001	ME'A	1-01-001	MENILMONTANT
1-01-001	MARKET-PLACE			1-01-001	MEAL-TO-MEAL	1-01-001	MENLO
1-01-001	MARKETABILITY	1-01-001	MATHESON	1-01-001	MEALIE-MEAL	1-01-001	MENNEN
1-01-001	MARKETWISE	1-01-001	MATHEWSON	1-01-001	MEALYNOSE	1-01-001	MENNONITES
1-01-001	MARKOVITZ	1-01-001	MATHIAS'	1-01-001	MEALYNOSED	1-01-001	MENSTRUATION
1-01-001	MARKSMAN'S	1-01-001	MATHUES	1-01-001	MEAN-SQUARE	1-01-001	MENTALITIES
1-01-001	MARLOWE'S	1-01-001	MATINALS	1-01-001	MEANDERED	1-01-001	MENTOR
1-01-001	MARMALADE	1-01-001	MATISSE	1-01-001	MEANEST	1-01-001	MENUHIN
		1-01-001	MATISSES	1-01-001	MEANINGFULLY		

64

1-01-001 MENUHIN-*AMADEU S	1-01-001 MICROSCOPICAL	1-01-001 MINACES	1-01-001 MISUNDERSTANDIN GS
1-01-001 MEPHISTOPHELES	1-01-001 MICROSOMAL	1-01-001 MINBER	1-01-001 MISWRITTEN
1-01-001 MERCE	1-01-001 MICROWAVES	1-01-001 MINCE	1-01-001 MITCHELL'S
1-01-001 MERCEDES	1-01-001 MID-*APRIL	1-01-001 MINCING	1-01-001 MITE
1-01-001 MERCENARY	1-01-001 MID-*ATLANTIC	1-01-001 MINDANAO	1-01-001 MITE-BOX
1-01-001 MERCERS	1-01-001 MID-*JULY	1-01-001 MINE-SAFETY	1-01-001 MITER
1-01-001 MERCIER	1-01-001 MID-*VICTORIAN	1-01-001 MINER	1-01-001 MITIGATE
1-01-001 MERCURIAL	1-01-001 MID-AIR	1-01-001 MINERAL-RICH	1-01-001 MITIGATION
1-01-001 MERETRICIOUS	1-01-001 MID-CENTURY	1-01-001 MINERALIZED	1-01-001 MITRAL
1-01-001 MERIWETHER	1-01-001 MID-CONTINENT	1-01-001 MINERALOGIES	1-01-001 MITRE
1-01-001 MERLE	1-01-001 MID-FLIGHT	1-01-001 MINGLES	1-01-001 MIUCHI
1-01-001 MERLEAU-*PONTY	1-01-001 MID-RANGE	1-01-001 MINGLING	1-01-001 MIXERS
1-01-001 MERMAID	1-01-001 MID-SECTION	1-01-001 MINGUS	1-01-001 ML,
1-01-001 MERNER	1-01-001 MID-SHIMMY	1-01-001 MINH	1-01-001 MMMM
1-01-001 MERRICK	1-01-001 MID-TWENTIETH-C ENTURY	1-01-001 MINIATURES	1-01-001 MOAN
1-01-001 MERRIEST	1-01-001 MID-WATCH	1-01-001 MINIFYING	1-01-001 MOANS
1-01-001 MERRIMAC	1-01-001 MID-WEEK	1-01-001 MINIMALLY	1-01-001 MOB'S
1-01-001 MERRYMAKING	1-01-001 MID-1890'S	1-01-001 MINIMIZES	1-01-001 MOBCAPS
1-01-001 MERTON'S	1-01-001 MID-19TH	1-01-001 MINISCULE	1-01-001 MOBSTERS
1-01-001 MERVEILLEUX	1-01-001 MID-1948	1-01-001 MINISTER'S	1-01-001 MOCCASIN
1-01-001 MERVIN	1-01-001 MID-1950'S	1-01-001 MINIVER	1-01-001 MOCKINGLY
1-01-001 MESA	1-01-001 MID-1950S	1-01-001 MINKS	1-01-001 MODALITY
1-01-001 MESENTERIC	1-01-001 MID-1958	1-01-001 MINNS	1-01-001 MODELING
1-01-001 MESMERIZED	1-01-001 MID-1960	1-01-001 MINOAN-*MYCENAE AN	1-01-001 MODERATE-INCOME
1-01-001 MESSED	1-01-001 MID-1960'S	1-01-001 MINOSO	1-01-001 MODERATING
1-01-001 MESSES	1-01-001 MID-1963	1-01-001 MINOT	1-01-001 MODERN-DANCE
1-01-001 MESSHALL	1-01-001 MIDAS	1-01-001 MINSTRELS	1-01-001 MODERNISTIC
1-01-001 MESSIEURS	1-01-001 MIDDLE-*EASTERN	1-01-001 MINTER	1-01-001 MODERNIZE
1-01-001 MESSINA	1-01-001 MIDDLE-*GAELIC	1-01-001 MINUTE'S	1-01-001 MODIGLIANI
1-01-001 MESSINESI	1-01-001 MIDDLE-RANGE	1-01-001 MINUTELY	1-01-001 MODISH
1-01-001 MESTA	1-01-001 MIDDLE-SCHOOL	1-01-001 MINUTIAE	1-01-001 MODULATED
1-01-001 METABOLITES	1-01-001 MIDDLE-SIZED	1-01-001 MIO	1-01-001 MODULATIONS
1-01-001 METABOLIZED	1-01-001 MIDDLE-SOUTH	1-01-001 MIRA	1-01-001 MODULES
1-01-001 METAL-CLEANING	1-01-001 MIDDLES	1-01-001 MIRANDA'S	1-01-001 MODUS
1-01-001 METAL-HYDRIDO	1-01-001 MIDI	1-01-001 MIRIANI'S	1-01-001 MOFFETT
1-01-001 METAL-TASTING	1-01-001 MIDMORNING	1-01-001 MIRO	1-01-001 MOHAMMAD
1-01-001 METAL-WORKING	1-01-001 MIDPOINT	1-01-001 MIRRORED	1-01-001 MOHAMMED
1-01-001 METALSMITHS	1-01-001 MIDSTREAM	1-01-001 MIRSKY'S	1-01-001 MOHAMMEDANISM
1-01-001 METAMORPHIC	1-01-001 MIDSTS	1-01-001 MIRTHLESS	1-01-001 MOI
1-01-001 METAMORPHOSE	1-01-001 MIDWESTERNERS	1-01-001 MIS-READING 40	1-01-001 MOINEAU
1-01-001 METAPHOSPHATE	1-01-001 MIDWIFE	1-01-001 MISANTHROPE	1-01-001 MOIRE
1-01-001 METAPHYSICALS	1-01-001 MIDWOOD	1-01-001 MISBEGOTTEN	1-01-001 MOISTENING
1-01-001 METEORIC	1-01-001 MIEN	1-01-001 MISBRANDED	1-01-001 MOLAR
1-01-001 METEROLOGICAL	1-01-001 MIFFED	1-01-001 MISCALCULATED	1-01-001 MOLARD
1-01-001 METHACRYLATE	1-01-001 MIG	1-01-001 MISCALCULATIONS	1-01-001 MOLARS
1-01-001 METHODE	1-01-001 MIGHTIEST	1-01-001 MISCARRIED	1-01-001 MOLASSES
1-01-001 METHODISM	1-01-001 MIGHTILY	1-01-001 MISCEGENATION	1-01-001 MOLDAVIAN
1-01-001 METHODISTS	1-01-001 MIGLIA	1-01-001 MISCELLANIES	1-01-001 MOLDBOARD
1-01-001 METHODOLOGY	1-01-001 MIGNON	1-01-001 MISCONSTRUCTION	1-01-001 MOLECULES/**F
1-01-001 METHUSELAHS	1-01-001 MIGRATE	1-01-001 MISCONSTRUCTION S	1-01-001 MOLEST
1-01-001 METICULOUS	1-01-001 MIGRATES		1-01-001 MOLESTING
1-01-001 METIER	1-01-001 MIGRATING	1-01-001 MISCOUNT	1-01-001 MOLLER
1-01-001 METIS	1-01-001 MIGS	1-01-001 MISCREANT	1-01-001 MOLLIFIED
1-01-001 METRAZOL	1-01-001 MIKEEN	1-01-001 MISCREANTS	1-01-001 MOLLUSKS
1-01-001 METRE	1-01-001 MIKHAIL	1-01-001 MISDEMEANANTS	1-01-001 MOLLYCODDLE
1-01-001 METRICALLY	1-01-001 MIKOYAN	1-01-001 MISDIRECTORS	1-01-001 MOLUCCAS
1-01-001 METROPOLIAN	1-01-001 MII	1-01-001 MISES	1-01-001 MOM'S
1-01-001 METROPOLITANIZA TION	1-01-001 MILAN	1-01-001 MISFIRED	1-01-001 MOMENTOES
1-01-001 METROPOLITIAN	1-01-001 MILANOFF	1-01-001 MISFORTUNES	1-01-001 MOMMOR
1-01-001 METTLESOME	1-01-001 MILBANKES	1-01-001 MISGAUGED	1-01-001 MOMMY
1-01-001 METTWURST	1-01-001 MILD-VOICED	1-01-001 MISINFORMATION	1-01-001 MOMMY'S
1-01-001 MEURONS	1-01-001 MILD-WINTER	1-01-001 MISINTERPRETATI ON	1-01-001 MON
1-01-001 MEW	1-01-001 MILDEW		1-01-001 MONARQUE
1-01-001 MEWED	1-01-001 MILENOFF	1-01-001 MISINTERPRETERS	1-01-001 MONASTICISM
1-01-001 MEYERBEER'S	1-01-001 MILESTONES	1-01-001 MISLEADS	1-01-001 MONAURAL
1-01-001 MEYERS	1-01-001 MILHAUD	1-01-001 MISMANAGED	1-01-001 MONDAYS
1-01-001 MEYLE	1-01-001 MILHAUD'S	1-01-001 MISNAMED	1-01-001 MONDONVILLE
1-01-001 MEYNELL'S	1-01-001 MILIARIS	1-01-001 MISNOMER	1-01-001 MONEY-FED
1-01-001 MEYNER'S	1-01-001 MILITANTLY	1-01-001 MISO	1-01-001 MONEY-HANDLING
1-01-001 MEZZO	1-01-001 MILITARIST'S	1-01-001 MISOGYNIST	1-01-001 MONEY-HUNGRY
1-01-001 MFG	1-01-001 MILITARY-MEDICA L	1-01-001 MISPERCEIVES	1-01-001 MONEY-MAKER
1-01-001 MG/**JL**J*B*0* D	1-01-001 MILITATED	1-01-001 MISPLACEMENTS	1-01-001 MONEY-MAKING
	1-01-001 MILL-POND	1-01-001 MISPLACING 70	1-01-001 MONEY-MINDED
1-01-001 MG/**JL/**JHR.	1-01-001 MILL-WHEEL	1-01-001 MISPRONUNCIATIO N	1-01-001 MONEY-WINNER
1-01-001 MIASMAL	1-01-001 MILLAY		1-01-001 MONEYED
1-01-001 MICA	1-01-001 MILLEDGEVILLE	1-01-001 MISQUOTED	1-01-001 MONEYMAKING
1-01-001 MICAWBER	1-01-001 MILLENARIANISM	1-01-001 MISRELATED	1-01-001 MONGI
1-01-001 MICHAELS	1-01-001 MILLENIUM	1-01-001 MISREPRESENTATI ONS	1-01-001 MONGOLIA
1-01-001 MICHAELSON	1-01-001 MILLIAMPERES/CE LL		1-01-001 MONGOLIA'S
1-01-001 MICHELANGELO'S		1-01-001 MISREPRESENTING	1-01-001 MONIES
1-01-001 MICHILIMACKINAC	1-01-001 MILLINERY	1-01-001 MISSA	1-01-001 MONILIA
1-01-001 MICK	1-01-001 MILLIONAIRES	1-01-001 MISSILE'S	1-01-001 MONITORED
1-01-001 MICKY	1-01-001 MILLIVOLTMETER	1-01-001 MISSILE-TYPE	1-01-001 MONIUSZKO'S
1-01-001 MICRO-MICROCURI E	1-01-001 MILLSTONE	1-01-001 MISSISSIPPIANS	1-01-001 MONKEY-GLAND
	1-01-001 MILMAN	1-01-001 MISSIVE	1-01-001 MONKEYS
1-01-001 MICROANALYSIS	1-01-001 MILQUETOAST	1-01-001 MISSOULA	1-01-001 MONKISH
1-01-001 MICROBIAL	1-01-001 MILQUETOASTS	1-01-001 MISSOURI-*ILLIN OIS	1-01-001 MONOCHROMES
1-01-001 MICROCHEMISTRY	1-01-001 MILTIES		1-01-001 MONOCITE
1-01-001 MICROCYTOCHEMIS TRY	1-01-001 MILTONIC	1-01-001 MIST-LIKE	1-01-001 MONOCLINIC
	1-01-001 MILWAUKEE'S	1-01-001 MISTED	1-01-001 MONODISPERSE
1-01-001 MICROFOSSILS	1-01-001 MIMETICALLY	1-01-001 MISTOOK	1-01-001 MONOGAMOUS
1-01-001 MICROMETERS	1-01-001 MIMI	1-01-001 MISTY-EYED	1-01-001 MONOGAMY
1-01-001 MICROORGANISM	1-01-001 MIMIEUX	1-01-001 MISUNDERSTAND	1-01-001 MONOGRAPH
1-01-001 MICROPHONING	1-01-001 MIN.	1-01-001 MISUNDERSTANDER S	1-01-001 MONOGRAPHS
1-01-001 MICROSCOPES	1-01-001 MIN,		1-01-001 MONOLITH
			1-01-001 MONOLITHIC

1-01-001	MONOLITHICALLY
1-01-001	MONOLOGIST
1-01-001	MONOMERS
1-01-001	MONONUCLEAR
1-01-001	MONOPHONIC
1-01-001	MONOPOLISTS
1-01-001	MONOPOLIZATION
1-01-001	MONOSYLLABLE
1-01-001	MONSOON-SHROUDED
1-01-001	MONTENEGRIN
1-01-001	MONTEREY
1-01-001	MONTEVIDEO
1-01-001	MONTFAUCON
1-01-001	MONTH-LONG
1-01-001	MONTMORILLONITES
1-01-001	MONTRACHET
1-01-001	MONTREUX
1-01-001	MONUMENTALITY
1-01-001	MONUMENTALLY
1-01-001	MOODILY
1-01-001	MOOED
1-01-001	MOON-DRENCHED
1-01-001	MOON-FACED
1-01-001	MOON-ROUND
1-01-001	MOON-SPLASHED
1-01-001	MOON-WASHED
1-01-001	MOONAN
1-01-001	MOONCURSERS
1-01-001	MOONLIKE
1-01-001	MOONTRACK
1-01-001	MOORING
1-01-001	MOOSILAUKE
1-01-001	MOOT
1-01-001	MOPS
1-01-001	MOR
1-01-001	MOR-EE-AIR-TEEEEE
1-01-001	MORAINE'S
1-01-001	MORALE-ENHANCING
1-01-001	MORALISTIC
1-01-001	MORALITIES
1-01-001	MORASS
1-01-001	MORATORIUM
1-01-001	MORAVIAN
1-01-001	MORBID
1-01-001	MORBID-MINDED
1-01-001	MORE'N
1-01-001	MORE-THAN-AVERAGE
1-01-001	MORE-THAN-ORDINARY
1-01-001	MOREHOUSE
1-01-001	MOREL
1-01-001	MORGART
1-01-001	MORGEN
1-01-001	MORGENTHAU'S
1-01-001	MORGUE
1-01-001	MORIARTY'S
1-01-001	MORIKAWA
1-01-001	MORNING-FRIGHTENED
1-01-001	MORNING-GLORY
1-01-001	MORNINGSTAR
1-01-001	MOROCCO-BOUND
1-01-001	MORPHEMIC
1-01-001	MORPHINE
1-01-001	MORPHOLOGIC
1-01-001	MORRIS'
1-01-001	MORSELS
1-01-001	MORTALLY
1-01-001	MORTARING
1-01-001	MORTICIANS
1-01-001	MORTIFICATION
1-01-001	MORTON'S
1-01-001	MOS
1-01-001	MOSAIC-LIKE
1-01-001	MOSAICS
1-01-001	MOSCONE
1-01-001	MOSCOW-ALLIED
1-01-001	MOSLEMS
1-01-001	MOSQUITO
1-01-001	MOSQUITO-PLAGUED
1-01-001	MOSQUITOES
1-01-001	MOSSBERG
1-01-001	MOSSBERG'S
1-01-001	MOST-VALUABLE
1-01-001	MOST-VALUABLE-PLAYER
1-01-001	MOT
1-01-001	MOTEL-KEEPERS
1-01-001	MOTEL-KEEPING
1-01-001	MOTET
1-01-001	MOTETS

1-01-001	MOTH
1-01-001	MOTH'S
1-01-001	MOTH-EATEN
1-01-001	MOTHER-IN-LAW
1-01-001	MOTHER-INTROJECT
1-01-001	MOTHER-NAKED
1-01-001	MOTHERED
1-01-001	MOTHERHOOD
1-01-001	MOTHERLAND
1-01-001	MOTHERLY
1-01-001	MOTHERS-IN-LAW
1-01-001	MOTHERWELL
1-01-001	MOTION-PATTERN
1-01-001	MOTIONAL
1-01-001	MOTIONAL-MODIFIED
1-01-001	MOTIONED
1-01-001	MOTIVATE
1-01-001	MOTOR-CAR
1-01-001	MOTORING
1-01-001	MOTORISTS'
1-01-001	MOTORSCOOTERS
1-01-001	MOULD
1-01-001	MOULDERING
1-01-001	MOULDING
1-01-001	MOULTON
1-01-001	MOULTONS
1-01-001	MOUNDS
1-01-001	MOUNE
1-01-001	MOUNTAINEERING
1-01-001	MOUNTAINOUSLY
1-01-001	MOUNTAINSIDES
1-01-001	MOUNTINGS
1-01-001	MOURNFUL
1-01-001	MOURNFULLY
1-01-001	MOUSTACHE
1-01-001	MOUSY
1-01-001	MOUTH-WATERING
1-01-001	MOUTHED
1-01-001	MOUTHPIECES
1-01-001	MOUVEMENT
1-01-001	MOVIE-GOER
1-01-001	MOVIE-TO-BE
1-01-001	MOVINGLY
1-01-001	MOWED
1-01-001	MOZART'S
1-01-001	MPH
1-01-001	MPH**-
1-01-001	MSEC
1-01-001	MTS
1-01-001	MU**DLLERIN
1-01-001	MUBARAK
1-01-001	MUCH-COPIED
1-01-001	MUCH-CRAVED
1-01-001	MUCH-DISCUSSED
1-01-001	MUCH-NEEDED
1-01-001	MUCH-THUMBED
1-01-001	MUCILAGE
1-01-001	MUCK
1-01-001	MUCK'S
1-01-001	MUCKER
1-01-001	MUD-BEPLASTERED
1-01-001	MUD-CAKED
1-01-001	MUD-SWEAT-AND-TEARS
1-01-001	MUDDLEHEADED
1-01-001	MUDDLING
1-01-001	MUDDY-TASTING
1-01-001	MUDGUARD
1-01-001	MUDSLINGING
1-01-001	MUDUGNO
1-01-001	MUDWAGON
1-01-001	MUEZZIN
1-01-001	MUFF
1-01-001	MUFFINS
1-01-001	MUFFLING
1-01-001	MUG
1-01-001	MUGGERS
1-01-001	MUGGY
1-01-001	MUHAMMAD
1-01-001	MUIR
1-01-001	MULATTO'S
1-01-001	MULCHING
1-01-001	MULE-DRAWN
1-01-001	MULLAH
1-01-001	MULLENDORE
1-01-001	MULLIGAN
1-01-001	MULLIGATAWNY
1-01-001	MULLING
1-01-001	MULTI-
1-01-001	MULTI-COLORED
1-01-001	MULTI-FAMILY
1-01-001	MULTI-LINGUAL
1-01-001	MULTI-MILLIONAIRE
1-01-001	MULTI-PHASE

1-01-001	MULTI-PRODUCT
1-01-001	MULTI-PURPOSE
1-01-001	MULTI-STATE
1-01-001	MULTICHANNEL
1-01-001	MULTICOLOR
1-01-001	MULTICOLORED
1-01-001	MULTIDIMENSIONAL
1-01-001	MULTIFIGURE
1-01-001	MULTILATERAL
1-01-001	MULTIMEGATON
1-01-001	MULTIMILLIONAIRE
1-01-001	MULTIPHASTIC
1-01-001	MULTIPLE-CHOICE
1-01-001	MULTIPLE-PURPOSE
1-01-001	MULTIPURPOSE
1-01-001	MULTISTAGE
1-01-001	MULTIVALENT
1-01-001	MULTIVERSITY
1-01-001	MUM
1-01-001	MUMBLE
1-01-001	MUMBLING
1-01-001	MUMBO-JUMBO
1-01-001	MUMFORD
1-01-001	MUMMIES
1-01-001	MUMMIFIED
1-01-001	MUNCH
1-01-001	MUNCHED
1-01-001	MUNCHING
1-01-001	MUNCIPAL
1-01-001	MUNDT
1-01-001	MUNDT'S
1-01-001	MUNGER
1-01-001	MUNGUS
1-01-001	MUNICH'S
1-01-001	MUNICIPALITY
1-01-001	MUNICIPALITY'S
1-01-001	MUNICIPALLY
1-01-001	MUNICIPALLY-SPONSORED
1-01-001	MUNOZ
1-01-001	MUNROE
1-01-001	MUONG
1-01-001	MURAL
1-01-001	MURAT
1-01-001	MURDERER'S
1-01-001	MURPHY'S
1-01-001	MURRAY'S
1-01-001	MURRIN
1-01-001	MURROW
1-01-001	MURVILLE
1-01-001	MUSCLE-BOUND
1-01-001	MUSCLE-SHAPING
1-01-001	MUSCLED
1-01-001	MUSCLEMEN
1-01-001	MUSCULATURE
1-01-001	MUSEE
1-01-001	MUSES
1-01-001	MUSHR
1-01-001	MUSHROOMING
1-01-001	MUSIC-HALL
1-01-001	MUSIC-MAKING
1-01-001	MUSICA
1-01-001	MUSICALE
1-01-001	MUSICALITY
1-01-001	MUSICIAN'S
1-01-001	MUSICOLOGISTS
1-01-001	MUSIL'S
1-01-001	MUSING
1-01-001	MUSINGS
1-01-001	MUSKADELL
1-01-001	MUSKEGON
1-01-001	MUSKOKA
1-01-001	MUSMANNO'S
1-01-001	MUSN'T
1-01-001	MUSSETT
1-01-001	MUSSOLINI
1-01-001	MUSSOLINI'S
1-01-001	MUSSOLINIS
1-01-001	MUSSORGSKY'S
1-01-001	MUSTA
1-01-001	MUSTACHES
1-01-001	MUSTACHIOED
1-01-001	MUSTANG
1-01-001	MUSTANGS
1-01-001	MUSTERED
1-01-001	MUSTERING
1-01-001	MUSTINESS
1-01-001	MUSTS
1-01-001	MUTANTS
1-01-001	MUTATIONAL
1-01-001	MUTATIONS
1-01-001	MUTILATION
1-01-001	MUTINEER
1-01-001	MUTINIES

1-01-001	MUTTER
1-01-001	MUTTERERS
1-01-001	MUTTERS
1-01-001	MUTUAL-AID
1-01-001	MUTUALITY
1-01-001	MUZAK
1-01-001	MUZO
1-01-001	MUZYKA
1-01-001	MUZZLES
1-01-001	MYCOBACTERIA
1-01-001	MYCOLOGY
1-01-001	MYELOFIBROSIS
1-01-001	MYELOID
1-01-001	MYN
1-01-001	MYNE
1-01-001	MYOCARDIUM
1-01-001	MYOFIBRILS
1-01-001	MYOPIA
1-01-001	MYOPIC
1-01-001	MYOSIN
1-01-001	MYRON
1-01-001	MYRTLE
1-01-001	MYSTERY-STORY
1-01-001	MYSTICISMS
1-01-001	MYSTIFICATION
1-01-001	MYSTIFIED
1-01-001	MYTTON
1-01-001	NJ,
1-01-001	N*)0
1-01-001	N**.*A
1-01-001	N**.*C**.'S
1-01-001	N**.*D
1-01-001	N**.*L
1-01-001	N**.*M
1-01-001	N**.*Y**.*U
1-01-001	N'TH
1-01-001	N-NO
1-01-001	NAB
1-01-001	NABBED
1-01-001	NABISCO
1-01-001	NAE
1-01-001	NAGAMO
1-01-001	NAGEL
1-01-001	NAGGED
1-01-001	NAGLE
1-01-001	NAGRIN'S
1-01-001	NAHCE
1-01-001	NAI**DVETE
1-01-001	NAILING
1-01-001	NAIROBI
1-01-001	NAIVELY
1-01-001	NAIVETE
1-01-001	NAKAYASU
1-01-001	NAKEDLY
1-01-001	NAKOMA
1-01-001	NAM'S
1-01-001	NAME-DROPPER
1-01-001	NANOOK
1-01-001	NAPHTA
1-01-001	NAPOLEONIC
1-01-001	NAPPED
1-01-001	NAPPING
1-01-001	NAPRAPATH
1-01-001	NARBONNE
1-01-001	NARCOSIS
1-01-001	NARCOTIZES
1-01-001	NARRATED
1-01-001	NARROW-MINDED
1-01-001	NARROWNESS
1-01-001	NARY
1-01-001	NASALED
1-01-001	NASCENT
1-01-001	NASSAU'S
1-01-001	NASSER'S
1-01-001	NASTIER
1-01-001	NASTIEST
1-01-001	NAT
1-01-001	NATALIE
1-01-001	NATCH
1-01-001	NATHANAEL
1-01-001	NATION-BUILDING
1-01-001	NATION-STATES
1-01-001	NATIONALCAR
1-01-001	NATIONALISTS
1-01-001	NATIONALIZE
1-01-001	NATIONALIZING
1-01-001	NATIONHOOD
1-01-001	NATIONS'S
1-01-001	NATIVE-BORN
1-01-001	NATRONA
1-01-001	NATTY
1-01-001	NATURAL-LAW
1-01-001	NATURALISM
1-01-001	NATURALIST
1-01-001	NATURAM
1-01-001	NATURED
1-01-001	NATUROPATH

1-01-001 NAUGHTIER	1-01-001 NEURALGIA	1-01-001 NIGRAS	1-01-001 NON-CODE
1-01-001 NAUGHTY	1-01-001 NEURASTHENIC	1-01-001 NIGS	1-01-001 NON-COLLEGE
1-01-001 NAVELS	1-01-001 NEURENSCHATZ	1-01-001 NIHILISM	1-01-001 NON-COLOR
1-01-001 NAVIGABLE	1-01-001 NEURITIS	1-01-001 NIHILISTIC	1-01-001 NON-COM
1-01-001 NAVIGATE	1-01-001 NEUROLOGICAL	1-01-001 NIJINSKY	1-01-001 NON-COMMISSIONE D
1-01-001 NAVIGATING	1-01-001 NEUROLOGIST	1-01-001 NIKE-ZEUS	1-01-001 NON-COMPARABLE
1-01-001 NAVIGATORS	1-01-001 NEUROMUSCULAR	1-01-001 NIKKO	1-01-001 NON-COMPETITIVE
1-01-001 NAVY-BLUE	1-01-001 NEURON	1-01-001 NIL	1-01-001 NON-CONFORMISTS
1-01-001 NAW	1-01-001 NEURONAL	1-01-001 NILLY	1-01-001 NON-DEALER
1-01-001 NAWT	1-01-001 NEUROPATHOLOGY	1-01-001 NILSEN	1-01-001 NON-DISCRIMINAT ION
1-01-001 NAWTH	1-01-001 NEUSTETER	1-01-001 NILSSON	
1-01-001 NAXOS	1-01-001 NEUSTETERS	1-01-001 NIMBLER	1-01-001 NON-DRAMAS
1-01-001 NAZARENE	1-01-001 NEUTER	1-01-001 NINA	1-01-001 NON-ENZYMATIC
1-01-001 NAZAROVA	1-01-001 NEUTRALIZE	1-01-001 NINE-CHAMBERED	1-01-001 NON-EXEMPT
1-01-001 NAZI-MINDED	1-01-001 NEUTRON	1-01-001 NINE-GAME	1-01-001 NON-FARM
1-01-001 NAZISM	1-01-001 NEUTROPHILIS	1-01-001 NINE-STATE	1-01-001 NON-FIGURATIVE
1-01-001 NDOLA	1-01-001 NEV	1-01-001 NINE-TO-FIVE	1-01-001 NON-FORTHCOMING
1-01-001 NE	1-01-001 NEVAH	1-01-001 NINE-YEAR	1-01-001 NON-FREEZING
1-01-001 NE**)GROES	1-01-001 NEVEH	1-01-001 NINETEEN-SIXTY	1-01-001 NON-HYDROGEN-BO NDED
1-01-001 NEANDERTHAL	1-01-001 NEVER-PREDICTAB LE	1-01-001 NINETIETH	
1-01-001 NEAR-*BALKANIZA TION		1-01-001 NINETY-EIGHT	1-01-001 NON-IDENTITY
	1-01-001 NEVER-TO-BE-FOR GOTTEN	1-01-001 NINETY-FIVE	1-01-001 NON-INSTINCTIVE
1-01-001 NEAR-*COMMUNIST S		1-01-001 NINEVEH	1-01-001 NON-INSTITUTION ALIZED
	1-01-001 NEVSKY	1-01-001 NIOBE	
1-01-001 NEAR-ABSENCE	1-01-001 NEW-*ENGLAND	1-01-001 NIPE'S	1-01-001 NON-INTELLECTUA L
1-01-001 NEAR-BLIND	1-01-001 NEW-*WAVER	1-01-001 NIPPED	
1-01-001 NEAR-EQUIVALENT S	1-01-001 NEW-*YORK	1-01-001 NIPPLES	1-01-001 NON-INTERFERENC E
	1-01-001 NEW-HOUSE	1-01-001 NIPPUR	
1-01-001 NEAR-MISSES	1-01-001 NEW-RICH	1-01-001 NIPS	1-01-001 NON-ITEMIZED
1-01-001 NEAR-MUTINY	1-01-001 NEW-SPILLED	1-01-001 NIRVANA	1-01-001 NON-JOB-CONNECT ED
1-01-001 NEAR-STRANGERS	1-01-001 NEWARKER	1-01-001 NISE	
1-01-001 NEAR-SYNONYMS	1-01-001 NEWBERY	1-01-001 NISF-I-JAHAN	1-01-001 NON-LINEAR
1-01-001 NEARSIGHTED	1-01-001 NEWBIGGIN	1-01-001 NISHIMO	1-01-001 NON-LITERARY
1-01-001 NEARSIGHTEDLY	1-01-001 NEWBIGGIN'S	1-01-001 NITRATES	1-01-001 NON-NEGATIVE
1-01-001 NEATEST	1-01-001 NEWBURGER	1-01-001 NITROGEN-MUSTAR D	1-01-001 NON-NEWTONIAN
1-01-001 NEATNESS	1-01-001 NEWBURGH		1-01-001 NON-NONSENSE
1-01-001 NEBULA	1-01-001 NEWCASTLE	1-01-001 NITROGLYCERINE	1-01-001 NON-OBJECTIVE
1-01-001 NEBULAR	1-01-001 NEWEL	1-01-001 NIVEN	1-01-001 NON-OBJECTS
1-01-001 NEC	1-01-001 NEWELLS	1-01-001 NIXON'S	1-01-001 NON-PATHOGENIC
1-01-001 NECESSARIES	1-01-001 NEWFOUND	1-01-001 NJUST	1-01-001 NON-POETRY
1-01-001 NECESSITATING	1-01-001 NEWLY-APPOINTED	1-01-001 NNUOLAPERTAR-IT -VUH-KARTI-BIRI -PITKNOUMEN	1-01-001 NON-POLICE
1-01-001 NECKING	1-01-001 NEWLY-CREATED		1-01-001 NON-POLYGYNOUS
1-01-001 NECROMANTIC	1-01-001 NEWLY-EMERGING		1-01-001 NON-PRODUCTIVE
1-01-001 NECROTIC	1-01-001 NEWLY-MARRIED	1-01-001 NO*$WHERE	1-01-001 NON-PROFESSIONA L
1-01-001 NECTAREOUS	1-01-001 NEWLY-PLOWED	1-01-001 NO-*CAL	
1-01-001 NECTARIES	1-01-001 NEWLY-SCRUBBED	1-01-001 NO-*NAME	1-01-001 NON-PROPAGANDIS TIC
1-01-001 NEEDHAM'S	1-01-001 NEWLYWED	1-01-001 NO-BACK	
1-01-001 NEEDLE-SHARP	1-01-001 NEWPORT'S	1-01-001 NO-DRIVING	1-01-001 NON-PROPAGATING
1-01-001 NEEDLED	1-01-001 NEWPORT-BASED	1-01-001 NO-GOAL	1-01-001 NON-PUBLIC
1-01-001 NEEDLESSLY	1-01-001 NEWSLETTERS	1-01-001 NO-GOOD	1-01-001 NON-PUBLISHERS
1-01-001 NEESEN	1-01-001 NEWSMAN	1-01-001 NO-MAN'S-LAND	1-01-001 NON-READERS
1-01-001 NEGATIVISM	1-01-001 NEWSOM	1-01-001 NO-O	1-01-001 NON-REPETITIOUS
1-01-001 NEGLECTS	1-01-001 NEWSPAPERMEN	1-01-001 NO-ONE	1-01-001 NON-REPRESENTAT ION
1-01-001 NEGOCIANTS	1-01-001 NEWSPAPERS'	1-01-001 NO-TRADING	
1-01-001 NEGROES'	1-01-001 NEWSREEL	1-01-001 NO-VALUED	1-01-001 NON-RESIDENTS
1-01-001 NEGROID	1-01-001 NEWSSTAND	1-01-001 NOAH	1-01-001 NON-RESISTANTS
1-01-001 NEHF	1-01-001 NEWSWEEK	1-01-001 NOB	1-01-001 NON-ROMANTIC
1-01-001 NEHRU'S	1-01-001 NEWTOWN	1-01-001 NOBLER	1-01-001 NON-SCIENTIFIC
1-01-001 NEIGHBORLINESS	1-01-001 NEWTS	1-01-001 NOBLES	1-01-001 NON-SCIENTIST
1-01-001 NEIGHBORS'	1-01-001 NEXT-DOOR	1-01-001 NOBLESSE	1-01-001 NON-SENTIMENTAL
1-01-001 NEIGHBORHOOD	1-01-001 NEXT-TO-LAST	1-01-001 NOBODY'D	1-01-001 NON-SERVICE
1-01-001 NEIGHBOURS	1-01-001 NGANDLU	1-01-001 NOCES	1-01-001 NON-SKID
1-01-001 NEILSON	1-01-001 NGO	1-01-001 NOCTILUCA	1-01-001 NON-SOCIAL
1-01-001 NEISSE-*ODER	1-01-001 NIBBLE	1-01-001 NODS	1-01-001 NON-STOP
1-01-001 NELL	1-01-001 NIBBLERS	1-01-001 NODULAR	1-01-001 NON-SUCCESS
1-01-001 NEO-	1-01-001 NIBELUNGENLIED	1-01-001 NODULES	1-01-001 NON-SYSTEMATIC
1-01-001 NEO-*CLASSICISM	1-01-001 NIBS'	1-01-001 NOES	1-01-001 NON-TIME
1-01-001 NEO-*CLASSICIST S	1-01-001 NICCOLO	1-01-001 NOIR	1-01-001 NON-VIOLENTLY
	1-01-001 NICE-LOOKING	1-01-001 NOIRE	1-01-001 NON-VOLATILE
1-01-001 NEO-*ECCLESIAST ICISM	1-01-001 NICEST	1-01-001 NOISELESS	1-01-001 NON-WAGE
	1-01-001 NICETIES	1-01-001 NOISIER	1-01-001 NON-WHITE
1-01-001 NEO-*JAZZ	1-01-001 NICHOLS	1-01-001 NOLAN	1-01-001 NON-WRITERS
1-01-001 NEO-*PAGANISM	1-01-001 NICHOLSON	1-01-001 NOLENS	1-01-001 NONACID
1-01-001 NEO-*POPULARISM	1-01-001 NICHTIGE	1-01-001 NOLI	1-01-001 NONAGRICULTURAL
1-01-001 NEO-*ROMANTICIS M	1-01-001 NICKED	1-01-001 NOLL	1-01-001 NONCE
	1-01-001 NICKELS	1-01-001 NOLLE	1-01-001 NONCHALANT
1-01-001 NEO-CLASSICISM	1-01-001 NICKLAUS	1-01-001 NOLO	1-01-001 NONCHURCHGOING
1-01-001 NEO-DADAIST	1-01-001 NICKNAMED	1-01-001 NOMIA	1-01-001 NONCOMBATANT
1-01-001 NEO-STAGNATIONI ST	1-01-001 NICKNAMES	1-01-001 NOMINATING	1-01-001 NONCOMMISSIONED
	1-01-001 NICOLAS'S	1-01-001 NON-*COMMUNIST	1-01-001 NONCOMMITTALLY
1-01-001 NEO-SWING	1-01-001 NICOTINE-CHOKED	1-01-001 NON-*DISSONANT	1-01-001 NONCONFORMISTS
1-01-001 NEOLIBERAL	1-01-001 NIECES	1-01-001 NON-*ENGLISH	1-01-001 NONDEFEATIST
1-01-001 NEON-LIGHTED	1-01-001 NIEPCE	1-01-001 NON-*FEDERAL	1-01-001 NONDESCRIPTLY
1-01-001 NEONATAL	1-01-001 NIGERIA	1-01-001 NON-*GREEK	1-01-001 NONDISCRIMINATO RY
1-01-001 NEPAL	1-01-001 NIGGERTOWN	1-01-001 NON-*INDIAN	
1-01-001 NERVE-ENDS	1-01-001 NIGH	1-01-001 NON-*JEWS	1-01-001 NONDRIVER
1-01-001 NERVELESS	1-01-001 NIGHT-COACH	1-01-001 NON-*SOVIET	1-01-001 NONEQUIVALENCE
1-01-001 NESTOR	1-01-001 NIGHT-SIGHT	1-01-001 NON-*WESTERN	1-01-001 NONEQUIVALENT
1-01-001 NET-LIKE	1-01-001 NIGHT-WATCHMAN	1-01-001 NON-ABSORBENT	1-01-001 NONFOOD
1-01-001 NETHER	1-01-001 NIGHTCLUB'S	1-01-001 NON-ALGEBRAICAL LY	1-01-001 NONFUNCTIONAL
1-01-001 NETTED	1-01-001 NIGHTDRESS		1-01-001 NONIONIC
1-01-001 NETTING	1-01-001 NIGHTED	1-01-001 NON-ARTISTIC	1-01-001 NONISM
1-01-001 NETTLESOME	1-01-001 NIGHTERS	1-01-001 NON-AUTHORITATI VE	1-01-001 NONLITERARY
1-01-001 NETWORK'S	1-01-001 NIGHTINGALES		1-01-001 NONMAGICAL
1-01-001 NETWORKS'	1-01-001 NIGHTMARES	1-01-001 NON-BEARING	1-01-001 NONMUSICAL
1-01-001 NEUBERGER	1-01-001 NIGHTSHIRT	1-01-001 NON-BOOKS	1-01-001 NONMYTHOLOGICAL
1-01-001 NEUMANN		1-01-001 NON-CHURCH	

1-01-001 NONOBSERVANT	1-01-001 NOWACKI	1-01-001 OCCUPATION'S	1-01-001 OLSON
1-01-001 NONOCCURRENCE	1-01-001 NOYES	1-01-001 OCEAN-GOING	1-01-001 OLSON'S
1-01-001 NONOGENARIAN	1-01-001 NOYON-LA-*SAINTE	1-01-001 OCEANA	1-01-001 OLVEY
1-01-001 NONPARTICULATE		1-01-001 OCEANIA	1-01-001 OLYMPIAN
1-01-001 NONPAYMENT	1-01-001 NOZZE	1-01-001 OCEANSIDE	1-01-001 OMAN
1-01-001 NONPOISONOUS	1-01-001 NUANCE	1-01-001 OCELOT	1-01-001 OMEGA
1-01-001 NONPOLITICAL	1-01-001 NUBBINS	1-01-001 OCHER	1-01-001 OMIT
1-01-001 NONPROFIT	1-01-001 NUBILE	1-01-001 OCTAHEDRON	1-01-001 OMMISSION
1-01-001 NONRACIAL	1-01-001 NUCLEATED	1-01-001 OCTAVIA	1-01-001 OMNIPOTENCE
1-01-001 NONSEGREGATED	1-01-001 NUCLEIC	1-01-001 OCTET	1-01-001 OMNISCIENT
1-01-001 NONSENSICAL	1-01-001 NUDGING	1-01-001 OCTOPUS	1-01-001 OMSK
1-01-001 NONSERVICE-CONNECTED	1-01-001 NUDISM	1-01-001 ODDITIES	1-01-001 ON-AGAIN-OFF-AGAIN
1-01-001 NONSHIFTERS	1-01-001 NUDIST	1-01-001 ODDS-ON	
1-01-001 NONSTOP	1-01-001 NUF	1-01-001 ODELL	1-01-001 ON-LEVEL
1-01-001 NONSYSTEMATIC	1-01-001 NUFS	1-01-001 ODESSA	1-01-001 ON-STAGE
1-01-001 NONVIOLENT	1-01-001 NUGENT'S	1-01-001 ODILO	1-01-001 ON-SURE
1-01-001 NOOKS	1-01-001 NUGGET	1-01-001 ODOM	1-01-001 ON-THE-SPOT
1-01-001 NOONTIME	1-01-001 NUISANCES	1-01-001 ODYSSEUS	1-01-001 ON-TO-*SPOKANE
1-01-001 NOPE	1-01-001 NULL-TYPE	1-01-001 OFF-COLOR	1-01-001 ONCE-A-MONTH
1-01-001 NORADRENALIN	1-01-001 NULLIFIERS	1-01-001 OFF-FARM	1-01-001 ONCE-DRY
1-01-001 NORANDA	1-01-001 NULLIFY	1-01-001 OFF-FLAVOR	1-01-001 ONCE-IN-A-LIFETIME
1-01-001 NORBORNE	1-01-001 NULLITY	1-01-001 OFF-FLAVORS	
1-01-001 NORDSTROM	1-01-001 NUMBINGLY	1-01-001 OFF-KEY	1-01-001 ONCE-OVER
1-01-001 NORDYKE	1-01-001 NUMENOUS	1-01-001 OFF-LEVEL	1-01-001 ONCE-OVER-LIGHTLY
1-01-001 NORETHANDROLONE	1-01-001 NUMERAL	1-01-001 OFF-ROAD	
1-01-001 NORI	1-01-001 NUMERALS	1-01-001 OFF-SHORE	1-01-001 ONCE-POPULAR
1-01-001 NORMALIZE	1-01-001 NUMEROLOGICAL	1-01-001 OFF-STAGE	1-01-001 OND
1-01-001 NORMALIZED	1-01-001 NUMEROLOGY	1-01-001 OFF-THE-CUFF	1-01-001 ONE-*LEG
1-01-001 NORMALS	1-01-001 NUNES	1-01-001 OFFAL	1-01-001 ONE-*STEP
1-01-001 NORMANDY	1-01-001 NUOVO	1-01-001 OFFBEAT	1-01-001 ONE-ACT
1-01-001 NORMATIVE	1-01-001 NUPER	1-01-001 OFFENBACH'S	1-01-001 ONE-ACT-PLAY
1-01-001 NORRIS	1-01-001 NURSE'S	1-01-001 OFFENCES	1-01-001 ONE-ARMED
1-01-001 NORRIS-*LA*GUARDIA	1-01-001 NURSERY-	1-01-001 OFFENDING	1-01-001 ONE-COLOR
1-01-001 NORRISTOWN	1-01-001 NUT-HOUSE	1-01-001 OFFENSIVELY	1-01-001 ONE-DAY
1-01-001 NORTH-BOUND	1-01-001 NUT-LIKE	1-01-001 OFFENSIVES	1-01-001 ONE-DUMBBELL
1-01-001 NORTHEASTERN	1-01-001 NUTRITIOUS	1-01-001 OFFERSEY	1-01-001 ONE-HORSE
1-01-001 NORTHENERS	1-01-001 NUTSHELL	1-01-001 OFFHAND	1-01-001 ONE-IRON
1-01-001 NORTHERLY	1-01-001 NUTTALL	1-01-001 OFFICE'S	1-01-001 ONE-KILOTON
1-01-001 NORTHERNMOST	1-01-001 NUX	1-01-001 OFFICEHOLDERS	1-01-001 ONE-MINUTE
1-01-001 NORTHERS	1-01-001 NUZZLED	1-01-001 OFFICERED	1-01-001 ONE-O'CLOCK
1-01-001 NORTHROP	1-01-001 NYLON	1-01-001 OFFICIALDOM	1-01-001 ONE-OVER-PAR
1-01-001 NORTHS	1-01-001 NYMPH	1-01-001 OFFICIATE	1-01-001 ONE-PLANE
1-01-001 NORTHUMBERLAND	1-01-001 NYMPHS	1-01-001 OFFICIATING	1-01-001 ONE-REEL
1-01-001 NOSEBAG	1-01-001 O'*CASEY	1-01-001 OFFICIELLE	1-01-001 ONE-SIXTEENTH
1-01-001 NOSING	1-01-001 O'*CONNOR'S	1-01-001 OFFICIO	1-01-001 ONE-THOUSAND-ZLOTY
1-01-001 NOSKOVA	1-01-001 O'*DONNELL'S	1-01-001 OFFICIOUS	
1-01-001 NOSTALGICALLY	1-01-001 O'*GARA	1-01-001 OFFING	1-01-001 ONE-THOUSANDTH
1-01-001 NOSTRADAMUS	1-01-001 O'*HARE	1-01-001 OFFSADDLED	1-01-001 ONE-WAY
1-01-001 NOSTRIL	1-01-001 O'ER	1-01-001 OFFSETTING	1-01-001 ONE-WEEK-OLD
1-01-001 NOT-**J*=*A	1-01-001 O*K	1-01-001 OFFSTAGE	1-01-001 ONE-YEAR
1-01-001 NOT-KNOWING	1-01-001 OAFS	1-01-001 OFFUTT	1-01-001 ONEASY
1-01-001 NOT-LESS-DEADLY	1-01-001 OAK-LOG	1-01-001 OFT	1-01-001 ONEIDA
1-01-001 NOT-QUITE-PERFECT	1-01-001 OAKEN	1-01-001 OFT-REPEATED	1-01-001 ONELY
1-01-001 NOT-SO-LONELY	1-01-001 OAKLAND	1-01-001 OFTEN-BLOOD	1-01-001 ONETIME
1-01-001 NOT-SO-PALE	1-01-001 OAKMONT	1-01-001 OFTENER	1-01-001 ONEUPMANSHIP
1-01-001 NOT-STRICTLY-PRACTICAL	1-01-001 OAKS	1-01-001 OGLETHORPE	1-01-001 ONRUSHING
1-01-001 NOT-YET-MARRIED	1-01-001 OATH-TAKING	1-01-001 OGRESS	1-01-001 ONTARIO
1-01-001 NOTARIUS	1-01-001 OATHE	1-01-001 OH-THE-PAIN-OF-IT	1-01-001 ONTARIO'S
1-01-001 NOTARIZED	1-01-001 OATMEAL		1-01-001 ONTOLOGICALLY
1-01-001 NOTCHED-STICK	1-01-001 OATS'S	1-01-001 OHMIC	1-01-001 ONWARD
1-01-001 NOTCHING	1-01-001 OBEDIENCE-TRAINED	1-01-001 OIL-BATH	1-01-001 ONWARD-DRIVING
1-01-001 NOTHER		1-01-001 OIL-FIELD	1-01-001 ONWARDS
1-01-001 NOTHING'S	1-01-001 OBEDIENCES	1-01-001 OIL-WELL	1-01-001 OOOO
1-01-001 NOTHING-DOWN	1-01-001 OBEYS	1-01-001 OILERS	1-01-001 OOPS
1-01-001 NOTHINGS	1-01-001 OBJECTING	1-01-001 OILMAN-RANCHER	1-01-001 OOPSIE-*COLA
1-01-001 NOTIFICATION	1-01-001 OBJECTIVENESS	1-01-001 OILSEED	1-01-001 OPALESCENT
1-01-001 NOTIFYING	1-01-001 OBJECTORS	1-01-001 OISTRAKH	1-01-001 OPEN-AIR
1-01-001 NOTITIA	1-01-001 OBJETS	1-01-001 OITICICA	1-01-001 OPEN-COLLARED
1-01-001 NOTORIETY	1-01-001 OBLIGATIONAL	1-01-001 OKADA	1-01-001 OPEN-END
1-01-001 NOTORIOUSLY	1-01-001 OBLIGE	1-01-001 OKINAWA	1-01-001 OPEN-ENDED
1-01-001 NOTRE-*DAME	1-01-001 OBLIQUE	1-01-001 OKS	1-01-001 OPEN-FACE
1-01-001 NOTTE,JR	1-01-001 OBLIQUELY	1-01-001 OLAF	1-01-001 OPEN-FLAME
1-01-001 NOUGH	1-01-001 OBLITERANS	1-01-001 OLATUNJI	1-01-001 OPEN-HANDED
1-01-001 NOUN	1-01-001 OBLITERATED	1-01-001 OLD-AGE	1-01-001 OPEN-MEETING
1-01-001 NOURISHES	1-01-001 OBLONG	1-01-001 OLD-GRAD-TYPE	1-01-001 OPEN-MINDED
1-01-001 NOURISHING	1-01-001 OBOIST	1-01-001 OLD-LINE	1-01-001 OPEN-WORK
1-01-001 NOURISHMENT	1-01-001 OBSCENITY	1-01-001 OLD-SCHOOL	1-01-001 OPENING-DAY
1-01-001 NOUVELLE	1-01-001 OBSCURELY	1-01-001 OLD-TIMERS	1-01-001 OPERA**)'S
1-01-001 NOUVELLE-*HELOI**DSE	1-01-001 OBSCURES	1-01-001 OLDE	1-01-001 OPERABLE
	1-01-001 OBSCURITIES	1-01-001 OLDEN	1-01-001 OPERAGOERS
1-01-001 NOVA	1-01-001 OBSEQUIES	1-01-001 OLDENBURG	1-01-001 OPERANDS
1-01-001 NOVAK	1-01-001 UBSERVANCES	1-01-001 OLDENBURG'S	1-01-001 OPERATIONALLY
1-01-001 NOVAYA	1-01-001 OBSERVER'S	1-01-001 OLDIES	1-01-001 OPIATES
1-01-001 NOVEL'S	1-01-001 OBSESSIONS	1-01-001 OLEG	1-01-001 OPPENHEIM
1-01-001 NOVELIZED	1-01-001 OBSESSIVE	1-01-001 OLEOMARGARINE	1-01-001 OPPORTUNE
1-01-001 NOVEMBER-*DECEMBER	1-01-001 OBSESSIVE-COMPULSIVE	1-01-001 OLEOPHOBIC	1-01-001 OPPORTUNISM
		1-01-001 OLERICHS	1-01-001 OPPORTUNISTIC
1-01-001 NOVITIATE	1-01-001 OBSIDIAN	1-01-001 OLIM	1-01-001 OPPROBRIUM
1-01-001 NOVOSIBIRSK	1-01-001 OBSOLETING	1-01-001 OLIVE-FLUSHED	1-01-001 OPTICALLY
1-01-001 NOVOSTI	1-01-001 OBSTINATE	1-01-001 OLIVE-GREEN	1-01-001 OPTICS
1-01-001 NOW-FAMOUS	1-01-001 OBTAINE	1-01-001 OLIVEFACED	1-01-001 OPTIMIZATION
1-01-001 NOW-HISTORIC	1-01-001 OBTRUSIVENESS	1-01-001 OLIVES	1-01-001 OPTIMIZING
	1-01-001 OBVERSE	1-01-001 OLIVET	1-01-001 OPTIMO
1-01-001 NOW-MISPLACED	1-01-001 OBVIOUSNESS	1-01-001 OLIVIA	1-01-001 OPTIONS
	1-01-001 OCARINA	1-01-001 OLNEY	1-01-001 OPULENT
	1-01-001 OCCLUSIVE	1-01-001 OLOGIES	1-01-001 ORACLES
	1-01-001 OCCUPANCIES	1-01-001 OLSEN	1-01-001 ORATE

Rank	Word	Rank	Word	Rank	Word	Rank	Word
1-01-001	ORATIO	1-01-001	OUTCLASS	1-01-001	OVERLOADED	1-01-001	PAINED
1-01-001	ORATORIO	1-01-001	OUTCLASSED	1-01-001	OVERLOUD	1-01-001	PAINLESSLY
1-01-001	ORB	1-01-001	OUTCROPS	1-01-001	OVERLYING	1-01-001	PAINS-TAKING
1-01-001	ORCHESTER	1-01-001	OUTDISTANCING	1-01-001	OVERPAID	1-01-001	PAINSTAKING
1-01-001	ORCHESTRE	1-01-001	OUTDREW	1-01-001	OVERPLAYED	1-01-001	PAINTBRUSH
1-01-001	ORDERLINESS	1-01-001	OUTFIELDERS	1-01-001	OVERPOPULATED	1-01-001	PAINTED-IN
1-01-001	ORDINARIUS	1-01-001	OUTFITTED	1-01-001	OVERPOWERING	1-01-001	PAINTERESQUE
1-01-001	ORDINARY'S	1-01-001	OUTFOUGHT	1-01-001	OVERPOWERS	1-01-001	PAIX
1-01-001	ORDINATES	1-01-001	OUTFOX	1-01-001	OVERPRESSURE	1-01-001	PAJAMA
1-01-001	ORDNANCE	1-01-001	OUTGENERALED	1-01-001	OVERPRICED	1-01-001	PAKISTANI
1-01-001	OREGONIANS	1-01-001	OUTGRIP	1-01-001	OVERPROTECTION	1-01-001	PAL'S
1-01-001	ORESME	1-01-001	OUTGROWTH	1-01-001	OVERPROTECTIVE	1-01-001	PALACHE
1-01-001	ORESTEIA	1-01-001	OUTHOUSE	1-01-001	OVERRAN	1-01-001	PALASTS
1-01-001	ORGANISED	1-01-001	OUTLANDERS	1-01-001	OVERRATED	1-01-001	PALATABLE
1-01-001	ORGANISMIC	1-01-001	OUTLANDISH	1-01-001	OVERREACHES	1-01-001	PALATES
1-01-001	ORGANIST	1-01-001	OUTLAWRY	1-01-001	OVERRIDDEN	1-01-001	PALAZZI
1-01-001	ORGANIZATION-PO SITION	1-01-001	OUTLAYS	1-01-001	OVERRIDE	1-01-001	PALAZZOS
1-01-001	ORGANIZATIONALL Y	1-01-001	OUTMANEUVERED	1-01-001	OVERRODE	1-01-001	PALE-BLUE
1-01-001	ORGANIZES	1-01-001	OUTMATCHED	1-01-001	OVERSEER	1-01-001	PALED
1-01-001	ORGANTION	1-01-001	OUTPATIENT	1-01-001	OVERSHOOTS	1-01-001	PALELY
1-01-001	ORGASMS	1-01-001	OUTPLAYED	1-01-001	OVERSHOT	1-01-001	PALENESS
1-01-001	ORGONE	1-01-001	OUTPOSTS	1-01-001	OVERSIGHT	1-01-001	PALEO-
1-01-001	ORGY	1-01-001	OUTPOURING	1-01-001	OVERSOFTNESS	1-01-001	PALEOCORTICAL
1-01-001	ORIENTATIONS	1-01-001	OUTPUT-AXIS	1-01-001	OVERSTEPPING	1-01-001	PALEOEXPLOSION
1-01-001	ORIGIN/DESTINAT ION	1-01-001	OUTPUTTING	1-01-001	OVERSTRAINING	1-01-001	PALES
1-01-001	ORIGINATION	1-01-001	OUTS	1-01-001	OVERTAKEN	1-01-001	PALEST
1-01-001	ORIN	1-01-001	OUTSCORING	1-01-001	OVERTAKIN	1-01-001	PALINDROMES
1-01-001	ORINOCO	1-01-001	OUTSIZED	1-01-001	OVERTAXED	1-01-001	PALING
1-01-001	ORIOLES'	1-01-001	OUTSKIRT'S	1-01-001	OVERTOOK	1-01-001	PALLADIAN
1-01-001	ORISSA	1-01-001	OUTSTATE	1-01-001	OVERVAULTING	1-01-001	PALLADIUM
1-01-001	ORKNEY	1-01-001	OUTSTRIPPING	1-01-001	OVERWHELM	1-01-001	PALLAVICINI
1-01-001	ORLY	1-01-001	OUTSVILLE	1-01-001	OVERWORKED	1-01-001	PALLET
1-01-001	ORMSBY	1-01-001	OUTWIT	1-01-001	OVERWRITTEN	1-01-001	PALLETIZED
1-01-001	ORNAMENTATION	1-01-001	OUTWORN	1-01-001	OVIFORM	1-01-001	PALLIATIVE
1-01-001	ORNATE	1-01-001	OUZO	1-01-001	OWENS	1-01-001	PALM-LINED
1-01-001	ORNATELY	1-01-001	OVA	1-01-001	OWLY	1-01-001	PALM-STUDDED
1-01-001	ORNRAIER	1-01-001	OVENS	1-01-001	OWNE	1-01-001	PALO
1-01-001	ORPHAN	1-01-001	OVER-	1-01-001	OWNSELF	1-01-001	PALOMAR
1-01-001	ORPHANAGE	1-01-001	OVER-ACHIEVEMEN T	1-01-001	OXALOACETIC	1-01-001	PALPABLY
1-01-001	ORPHANS	1-01-001	OVER-ARRANGED	1-01-001	OXEN'S	1-01-001	PALS
1-01-001	ORPHIC	1-01-001	OVER-CHILLING	1-01-001	OXFORD'S	1-01-001	PAM'S
1-01-001	ORSO	1-01-001	OVER-CORRECTED	1-01-001	OXIDES	1-01-001	PAMASU
1-01-001	ORTEGA	1-01-001	OVER-EMPHASIZE	1-01-001	OXNARD	1-01-001	PAMELA'S
1-01-001	ORTEGA'S	1-01-001	OVER-HAND	1-01-001	OXYGEN/**JHR/** JHP	1-01-001	PAMPER
1-01-001	ORTHODONTIST'S	1-01-001	OVER-LARGE			1-01-001	PAMPERED
1-01-001	ORTHOPHOSPHATE	1-01-001	OVER-NIGHT	1-01-001	OXYHYDROXIDES	1-01-001	PAMPHILI
1-01-001	ORTHOPHOSPHATES	1-01-001	OVER-OCCUPIED	1-01-001	OYAJIMA	1-01-001	PANACEAS
1-01-001	ORTHORHOMBIC	1-01-001	OVER-PRETENDED	1-01-001	OYSTCHERS	1-01-001	PANCHO
1-01-001	ORWELLIAN	1-01-001	OVER-PRODUCE	1-01-001	OYSTCHERS'LL	1-01-001	PANCRAZIO
1-01-001	ORZAE	1-01-001	OVER-SIMPLE	1-01-001	OZAGENIANS	1-01-001	PANDANUS
1-01-001	OS	1-01-001	OVER-SIMPLIFICA TION	1-01-001	OZARKS	1-01-001	PANDELLI'S
1-01-001	OSBERT	1-01-001	OVER-SPENT	1-01-001	OZON	1-01-001	PANDERS
1-01-001	OSCILLATING	1-01-001	OVER-STITCHED	1-01-001	OZZIE	1-01-001	PANDORA
1-01-001	OSCILLATOR	1-01-001	OVER-SUBSCRIBED	1-01-001	P*$	1-01-001	PANEL'S
1-01-001	OSERVED	1-01-001	OVER-THE-COUNTE R	1-01-001	P**.*G	1-01-001	PANELIZATION
1-01-001	OSHKOSH	1-01-001	OVERACTIVE	1-01-001	P**.*L	1-01-001	PANELIZED
1-01-001	OSIPENKO	1-01-001	OVERAGE	1-01-001	P**.-*T**.*A	1-01-001	PANICKY
1-01-001	OSIS	1-01-001	OVERAGGRESSIVE	1-01-001	P'LITE	1-01-001	PANJANDRUM
1-01-001	OSKAR	1-01-001	OVERBLOWN	1-01-001	P-AMINOBENZOIC	1-01-001	PANORAMAS
1-01-001	OSMIUM	1-01-001	OVERBURDEN	1-01-001	PA'D	1-01-001	PANORAMIC
1-01-001	OSRAM	1-01-001	OVERBURDENED	1-01-001	PABLO	1-01-001	PANT-LEGS
1-01-001	OSRIC	1-01-001	OVERCEREBRAL	1-01-001	PABOR	1-01-001	PANTASAPH
1-01-001	OSSIFY	1-01-001	OVERCOATS	1-01-001	PACE-SETTER	1-01-001	PANTED
1-01-001	OSTENSIBLY	1-01-001	OVERCONFIDENT	1-01-001	PACEM	1-01-001	PANTHEIST
1-01-001	OSTEOPOROSIS	1-01-001	OVERCOOKED	1-01-001	PACEMAKER	1-01-001	PANTHER
1-01-001	OSTINATO	1-01-001	OVERCOOLED	1-01-001	PACER	1-01-001	PANTHERS
1-01-001	OSTRACISM	1-01-001	OVERCROWDING	1-01-001	PACHE	1-01-001	PANTIES
1-01-001	OSTRACIZED	1-01-001	OVERCURIOUS	1-01-001	PACHELBEL	1-01-001	PANTOMIMED
1-01-001	OT	1	OVERDOING	1-01-001	PACHES	1-01-001	PANTOMIMIC
1-01-001	OTHELLO	1-01-001	OVERDRIVING	1-01-001	PACHINKO	1-01-001	PANTS-LEGS
1-01-001	OTHON'S	1-01-001	OVEREAGER	1-01-001	PACIFIER	1-01-001	PAP
1-01-001	OTTAUQUECHEE	1-01-001	OVEREAT	1-01-001	PACIFIES	1-01-001	PAP-PAP-PAP-HEY
1-01-001	OTTAWA	1-01-001	OVEREMPHASIS	1-01-001	PACIFISTIC	1-01-001	PAPANICOLAOU
1-01-001	OTTERMOLE	1-01-001	OVEREMPHASIZED	1-01-001	PACKARDS	1-01-001	PAPER'S
1-01-001	OTTO	1-01-001	OVERESTIMATED	1-01-001	PACKETS	1-01-001	PAPERBACKS
1-01-001	OUD	1-01-001	OVERESTIMATES	1-01-001	PACKWOOD	1-01-001	PAPERWADS
1-01-001	OULD	1-01-001	OVEREXCITED	1-01-001	PACTA	1-01-001	PAPERY
1-01-001	OURAY	1-01-001	OVEREXPLOITATIO N	1-01-001	PADDIES	1-01-001	PAPIERS
1-01-001	OUSE	1-01-001	OVEREXPLOITED	1-01-001	PADDLE	1-01-001	PAPILLARY
1-01-001	OUSTED	1-01-001	OVEREXPOSE	1-01-001	PADDOCK	1-01-001	PAPPAS
1-01-001	OUSTER	1-01-001	OVERFEED	1-01-001	PADLOCKED	1-01-001	PAPPIES
1-01-001	OUSTING	1-01-001	OVERFILL	1-01-001	PAEANS	1-01-001	PAR-3
1-01-001	OUT-DATED	1-01-001	OVERGENEROUS	1-01-001	PAESTUM	1-01-001	PAR-5
1-01-001	OUT-GROUP	1-01-001	OVERGRAZING	1-01-001	PAGANINI	1-01-001	PARABLES
1-01-001	OUT-MODED	1-01-001	OVERHANG	1-01-001	PAGANISM	1-01-001	PARACHUTE
1-01-001	OUT-OF-BOUNDS	1-01-001	OVERHEARING	1-01-001	PAGANS	1-01-001	PARACHUTES
1-01-001	OUT-OF-DOOR	1-01-001	OVERHEAT	1-01-001	PAGEANTRY	1-01-001	PARADIGMATIC
1-01-001	OUT-OF-MIND	1-01-001	OVERHEATED	1-01-001	PAGET	1-01-001	PARADIGMS
1-01-001	OUT-OF-SCHOOL	1-01-001	OVERHEATING	1-01-001	PAGINATED	1-01-001	PARAGRAPHING
1-01-001	OUT-OF-SIGHT	1-01-001	OVERINDULGED	1-01-001	PAGING	1-01-001	PARAKEETS
1-01-001	OUT-OF-STEP	1-01-001	OVERLAID	1-01-001	PAGLIERI'S	1-01-001	PARALINGUISTIC
1-01-001	OUT-REACHING	1-01-001	OVERLAND	1-01-001	PAGNOL	1-01-001	PARALLELING
1-01-001	OUTCAST	1-01-001	OVERLAPS	1-01-001	PAGODA	1-01-001	PARALYZE
1-01-001	OUTCASTS			1-01-001	PAGODAS	1-01-001	PARAMAGNET
				1-01-001	PAID-FOR	1-01-001	PARAMILITARY
				1-01-001	PAIDE	1-01-001	PARANOIAC
				1-01-001	PAINE	1-01-001	PARANORMAL

1-01-001 PARAOXON	1-01-001 PASTRY-LINED	1-01-001 PEDIMENTED	1-01-001 PERMISSIBILITY
1-01-001 PARAPET	1-01-001 PATAGONIANS	1-01-001 PEED	1-01-001 PERMISSIBLE
1-01-001 PARAPETS	1-01-001 PATENTEES	1-01-001 PEEKING	1-01-001 PERNICIOUS
1-01-001 PARAPHERNALIA	1-01-001 PATENTING	1-01-001 PEELS	1-01-001 PERNOD
1-01-001 PARAPHRASES	1-01-001 PATERNALISTIC	1-01-001 PEEPY	1-01-001 PERPENDICULARLY
1-01-001 PARAPHRASING	1-01-001 PATERNALLY	1-01-001 PEER-GROUP	1-01-001 PERPETRATION
1-01-001 PARASITE	1-01-001 PATEROLLERS	1-01-001 PEETER	1-01-001 PERPETRATOR
1-01-001 PARATROOPERS	1-01-001 PATERSON	1-01-001 PEGGED	1-01-001 PERPETUATED
1-01-001 PARATROOPS	1-01-001 PATHLESS	1-01-001 PEGGED-DOWN	1-01-001 PERPLEX
1-01-001 PARBOILED	1-01-001 PATHOGENESIS	1-01-001 PEGGIN	1-01-001 PERPLEXITY
1-01-001 PARCEL	1-01-001 PATHOLOGIC	1-01-001 PEGGING	1-01-001 PERRIN'S
1-01-001 PARCELED	1-01-001 PATHOS	1-01-001 PEGLER	1-01-001 PERSECUTORY
1-01-001 PARCELS	1-01-001 PATI	1-01-001 PEIPING	1-01-001 PERSEVERANCE
1-01-001 PARCHMENT	1-01-001 PATIL	1-01-001 PEKING	1-01-001 PERSEVERE
1-01-001 PARDONABLE	1-01-001 PATINA	1-01-001 PELLAGRA	1-01-001 PERSEVERES
1-01-001 PARDONS	1-01-001 PATINAS	1-01-001 PELLEGRINI	1-01-001 PERSHING
1-01-001 PARELLA	1-01-001 PATISSERIES	1-01-001 PELLETS	1-01-001 PERSIANESQUE
1-01-001 PARENT'S	1-01-001 PATMORE	1-01-001 PELTZ	1-01-001 PERSIFLAGE
1-01-001 PARENT-CHILD	1-01-001 PATRIARCHAL	1-01-001 PELVIS	1-01-001 PERSIMMONS
1-01-001 PARENT-TEACHER	1-01-001 PATRIARCHY	1-01-001 PEMBERTON	1-01-001 PERSON-TO-PERSON
1-01-001 PARENTHESES	1-01-001 PATRICIAN	1-01-001 PEMMICAN	
1-01-001 PARENTHETICALLY	1-01-001 PATRICK	1-01-001 PENA	1-01-001 PERSONAE
1-01-001 PARI-MUTUEL	1-01-001 PATRIMONY	1-01-001 PENAL	1-01-001 PERSONAGE
1-01-001 PARIAH	1-01-001 PATRIOTS	1-01-001 PENCHANT	1-01-001 PERSONIFIED
1-01-001 PARICHY-HAMM	1-01-001 PATRISTIC-CIVILIAN-CANONIST-SCHOLASTIC	1-01-001 PENCIL-AND-SEPIA	1-01-001 PERSONIFYING
1-01-001 PARIMUTUELS			1-01-001 PERSPIRATION
1-01-001 PARIOLI		1-01-001 PENCIL-PUSHER	1-01-001 PERSPIRED
1-01-001 PARIS'	1-01-001 PATROLMAN'S	1-01-001 PENCILED	1-01-001 PERSPIRING
1-01-001 PARISHES	1-01-001 PATROLS	1-01-001 PENDANT	1-01-001 PERSUADERS
1-01-001 PARISINA	1-01-001 PATRONESS	1-01-001 PENDLETON'S	1-01-001 PERSUASIONS
1-01-001 PARISOLOGY	1-01-001 PATRONIZE	1-01-001 PENICILLIN	1-01-001 PERTAINED
1-01-001 PARKINSON'S	1-01-001 PATRONNE'S	1-01-001 PENMAN	1-01-001 PERTURBATION
1-01-001 PARKISH	1-01-001 PATSY	1-01-001 PENNA	1-01-001 PERTURBED
1-01-001 PARKLIKE	1-01-001 PATTERED	1-01-001 PENNANTS	1-01-001 PERUSING
1-01-001 PARLAYED	1-01-001 PATTI	1-01-001 PENNELL	1-01-001 PERVADED
1-01-001 PARLEY	1-01-001 PATTON	1-01-001 PENROSE	1-01-001 PERVAPORATION
1-01-001 PARLIAMENTARIANS	1-01-001 PATTY	1-01-001 PENSIVE	1-01-001 PERVASIVELY
	1-01-001 PAUCITY	1-01-001 PENTAGON'S	1-01-001 PERVERTED
1-01-001 PARLIAMENTS	1-01-001 PAUL'S	1-01-001 PENTECOSTAL	1-01-001 PESSIMISTS
1-01-001 PARLORS	1-01-001 PAUL-MINNEAPOLIS	1-01-001 PENTHOUSE	1-01-001 PESTER
1-01-001 PARMER		1-01-001 PENULTIMATE	1-01-001 PESTERING
1-01-001 PARODIES	1-01-001 PAULAH	1-01-001 PENURIOUS	1-01-001 PESTICIDES
1-01-001 PARQUET	1-01-001 PAULEYS	1-01-001 PENURY	1-01-001 PESTILENT
1-01-001 PARRIED	1-01-001 PAULING'S	1-01-001 PENUTIAN	1-01-001 PESTLE
1-01-001 PARROT	1-01-001 PAULUS	1-01-001 PEOPLED	1-01-001 PETE'S
1-01-001 PARROTING	1-01-001 PAUPER'S	1-01-001 PEOPLES'	1-01-001 PETERED
1-01-001 PARROTLIKE	1-01-001 PAUS'L	1-01-001 PEPINSKY	1-01-001 PETERMANN
1-01-001 PARROTS	1-01-001 PAVLETICH	1-01-001 PEPPERONI	1-01-001 PETEY
1-01-001 PARRY	1-01-001 PAVLOV	1-01-001 PEPPING	1-01-001 PETIPA
1-01-001 PARRY'S	1-01-001 PAVLOVITCH	1-01-001 PEPTIDE	1-01-001 PETIPA-*TSCHAIKOWSKY
1-01-001 PARSIMONIOUS	1-01-001 PAVLOVSKY	1-01-001 PEPTIZING	
1-01-001 PARSIMONY	1-01-001 PAWING	1-01-001 PER-DAY	1-01-001 PETIT
1-01-001 PARSLEY	1-01-001 PAWTUCKET'S	1-01-001 PER-GAME	1-01-001 PETITE
1-01-001 PARSONAGE	1-01-001 PAX	1-01-001 PER-YEAR	1-01-001 PETRARCHAN
1-01-001 PARSYMPATHETIC	1-01-001 PAXAM	1-01-001 PERASSO	1-01-001 PETRINI
1-01-001 PARTAKE	1-01-001 PAYMASTER	1-01-001 PERCEIVING	1-01-001 PETROLEUM
1-01-001 PARTAKER	1-01-001 PAYNES	1-01-001 PERCEPTIBLE	1-01-001 PETRUCHKA
1-01-001 PARTAKING	1-01-001 PAYOFF	1-01-001 PERCH	1-01-001 PETTERSSON
1-01-001 PARTI	1-01-001 PAYSON	1-01-001 PERCHANCE	1-01-001 PETTIBONE
1-01-001 PARTICULARISTIC	1-01-001 PEABODY	1-01-001 PERCOLATOR	1-01-001 PETTIGREW
1-01-001 PARTICULARISTIC-SEEMING	1-01-001 PEABODY'S	1-01-001 PERELMAN	1-01-001 PETTIGREW'S
	1-01-001 PEACE-TREATY	1-01-001 PEREMPTORY	1-01-001 PETTINESS
1-01-001 PARTICULARITY	1-01-001 PEACEMAKING	1-01-001 PEREZ	1-01-001 PETTINESSES
1-01-001 PARTINGS	1-01-001 PEACHES	1-01-001 PERFECTABILITY	1-01-001 PETULANCE
1-01-001 PARTISANS	1-01-001 PEAKY	1-01-001 PERFECTIBILITY	1-01-001 PETULANT
1-01-001 PARTITIONS	1-01-001 PEAL	1-01-001 PERFECTIONISM	1-01-001 PEUGEOT
1-01-001 PARTLOW'S	1-01-001 PEALE'S	1-01-001 PERFECTIONISTS	1-01-001 PEWS
1-01-001 PARTNERED	1-01-001 PEALS	1-01-001 PERFIDIOUS	1-01-001 PFAU
1-01-001 PARTOOK	1-01-001 PEARL-GRAY	1-01-001 PERFORATIONS	1-01-001 PFC
1-01-001 PARTS-SUPPLIERS	1-01-001 PEARLY	1-01-001 PERFORMANCE-CAPACITY	1-01-001 PFENNIG
1-01-001 PARTY-LINE	1-01-001 PEASANTHOOD		1-01-001 PFFFT*$-ED
1-01-001 PASADENA'S	1-01-001 PEBBLE	1-01-001 PERFUMERY	1-01-001 PHAGOCYTES
1-01-001 PASCAGOULA	1-01-001 PEBWORTH	1-01-001 PERFUMES	1-01-001 PHARMACIST
1-01-001 PASCAL	1-01-001 PECAN	1-01-001 PERFUNCTORILY	1-01-001 PHARMACOPOEIA
1-01-001 PASCATAQUA	1-01-001 PECANS	1-01-001 PERFUNCTORY	1-01-001 PHARMICAL
1-01-001 PASCHALL	1-01-001 PECCADILLOES	1-01-001 PERFUSION	1-01-001 PHEASANT
1-01-001 PASSABLE	1-01-001 PECCAVI	1-01-001 PERGAMON	1-01-001 PHELAN
1-01-001 PASSAVANT	1-01-001 PECKS	1-01-001 PERGOLESI'S	1-01-001 PHELPS
1-01-001 PASSER-BY	1-01-001 PECORONE	1-01-001 PERICLEAN	1-01-001 PHENOMENOLOGICAL
1-01-001 PASSERBY	1-01-001 PECOS	1-01-001 PERICLES	
1-01-001 PASSERS-BY	1-01-001 PECS.	1-01-001 PERIDONTAL	1-01-001 PHENONENON
1-01-001 PASSIVELY	1-01-001 PECS.	1-01-001 PERILLA	1-01-001 PHILADELPHIA'S
1-01-001 PASSIVENESS	1-01-001 PECTORAL-FRONT	1-01-001 PERIMETER	1-01-001 PHILANTHROPIES
1-01-001 PASSIVITY	1-01-001 PECTORAL-RIBCAGE	1-01-001 PERINETTI	1-01-001 PHILANTHROPIST
1-01-001 PASSOS		1-01-001 PERIODICITY	1-01-001 PHILANTROPHY
1-01-001 PAST-FANTASY	1-01-001 PECTORALS	1-01-001 PERIPHRASTIC	1-01-001 PHILANTROPISTS
1-01-001 PASTEL-LIKE	1-01-001 PECULIARITY	1-01-001 PERISCOPES	1-01-001 PHILCO-SPONSORED
1-01-001 PASTELS	1-01-001 PEDAGOGICAL	1-01-001 PERISHABLE	
1-01-001 PASTERNAK	1-01-001 PEDAGOGUE	1-01-001 PERISHED	1-01-001 PHILHARMONIQUE
1-01-001 PASTERNS	1-01-001 PEDALS	1-01-001 PERISHES	1-01-001 PHILIBERT
1-01-001 PASTES	1-01-001 PEDDLE	1-01-001 PERISHING	1-01-001 PHILIPPE
1-01-001 PASTEURIZATION	1-01-001 PEDDLED	1-01-001 PERIWINKLES	1-01-001 PHILIPPIANS
1-01-001 PASTILLES	1-01-001 PEDDLERS	1-01-001 PERK	1-01-001 PHILLY
1-01-001 PASTIMES	1-01-001 PEDDLERS'	1-01-001 PERKEN	1-01-001 PHILOLOGISTS
1-01-001 PASTING	1-01-001 PEDEN	1-01-001 PERLE	1-01-001 PHILOSOPHICALLY
1-01-001 PASTNESS	1-01-001 PEDERSEN'S	1-01-001 PERMEATE	1-01-001 PHILOSOPHIZED
1-01-001 PASTORS'	1-01-001 PEDIGREED	1-01-001 PERMIAN	1-01-001 PHINEOPPUS

78

1-01-001	PHIS
1-01-001	PHLOEM
1-01-001	PHOBIC-LIKE
1-01-001	PHONETICS
1-01-001	PHONIC
1-01-001	PHONOGRAPHS
1-01-001	PHOSGENE
1-01-001	PHOSPHATE-BUFFE RED
1-01-001	PHOSPHATES
1-01-001	PHOSPHIDE
1-01-001	PHOSPHINES
1-01-001	PHOSPHOR-SCREEN
1-01-001	PHOSPHORESCENT
1-01-001	PHOSPHORS
1-01-001	PHOSPHORUS
1-01-001	PHOSPHORUS-BRID GED
1-01-001	PHOTEK
1-01-001	PHOTO-MONTAGE
1-01-001	PHOTO-OFFSET
1-01-001	PHOTOELECTRONS
1-01-001	PHOTOFLOODLIGHT S
1-01-001	PHOTOGRAPHICALL Y
1-01-001	PHOTOLUMINESCEN CE
1-01-001	PHOTOMICROGRAPH
1-01-001	PHOTOMICROGRAPH Y
1-01-001	PHOTON-COUNTING
1-01-001	PHOTOREALISM
1-01-001	PHOTOSENSITIVE
1-01-001	PHOUMA'S
1-01-001	PHRASEMAKING
1-01-001	PHRASINGS
1-01-001	PHTHALATE
1-01-001	PHYLA
1-01-001	PHYSICAL-CHEMIC AL
1-01-001	PHYSICALNESS
1-01-001	PHYSICIAN.**RST
1-01-001	PHYSICIAN'S
1-01-001	PHYSICOCHEMICAL
1-01-001	PHYSIOCHEMICAL
1-01-001	PHYSIOLOGICALLY
1-01-001	PHYSIOTHERAPIST
1-01-001	PIANISM
1-01-001	PIANISTIC
1-01-001	PIANOS
1-01-001	PIAZZAS
1-01-001	PIAZZO
1-01-001	PICAYUNE
1-01-001	PICKAXE
1-01-001	PICKER
1-01-001	PICKERING
1-01-001	PICKETT'S
1-01-001	PICKFAIR
1-01-001	PICKFORD
1-01-001	PICKINS
1-01-001	PICKLE
1-01-001	PICKLES
1-01-001	PICKMAN
1-01-001	PICKOFFS
1-01-001	PICNICKED
1-01-001	PICNICKERS
1-01-001	PICON
1-01-001	PICTORIALLY
1-01-001	PICTURE-IMAGES
1-01-001	PICTURE-PALACE
1-01-001	PIDDLING
1-01-001	PIECEWISE
1-01-001	PIEPSAM'S
1-01-001	PIER-TABLE
1-01-001	PIERPONT
1-01-001	PIERSEE
1-01-001	PIETISM
1-01-001	PIETRO'S
1-01-001	PIEZOELECTRICIT Y
1-01-001	PIG-INFESTED
1-01-001	PIGEN
1-01-001	PIGEONHOLE
1-01-001	PIGEONS
1-01-001	PIGMENTED
1-01-001	PIGPENS
1-01-001	PIGSKIN
1-01-001	PILATE
1-01-001	PILATE'S
1-01-001	PILFERING
1-01-001	PILGRIM'S
1-01-001	PILGRIMAGES
1-01-001	PILLAGED
1-01-001	PILLSBURY
1-01-001	PILS
1-01-001	PIMPLED
1-01-001	PIMPLES
1-01-001	PIMPLIKE
1-01-001	PIN-CURL
1-01-001	PIN-POINT
1-01-001	PINAFORES
1-01-001	PINBALL
1-01-001	PINCH-HIT
1-01-001	PINCH-HITTER
1-01-001	PINCH-HITTERS
1-01-001	PINE-KNOT
1-01-001	PING-PONG
1-01-001	PINGING
1-01-001	PINHEAD
1-01-001	PINHOLES
1-01-001	PINIONED
1-01-001	PINK-PETTICOATE D
1-01-001	PINKIE
1-01-001	PINKISH-WHITE
1-01-001	PINKLY
1-01-001	PINNACLE
1-01-001	PINNACLES
1-01-001	PINNING
1-01-001	PINNINGS
1-01-001	PINOCHLE
1-01-001	PINPOINTING
1-01-001	PINPOINTS
1-01-001	PINSCHER
1-01-001	PINSK
1-01-001	PINT-SIZED
1-01-001	PINTO
1-01-001	PIONEER'S
1-01-001	PIOUSLY
1-01-001	PIPERS
1-01-001	PIPGRAS
1-01-001	PIRACY
1-01-001	PIRAEUS
1-01-001	PIRANDELLO
1-01-001	PIRANESI
1-01-001	PIRARO
1-01-001	PIRATES'
1-01-001	PIRIE
1-01-001	PIROGUES
1-01-001	PISCES
1-01-001	PISS
1-01-001	PISTACHIO
1-01-001	PISTOL-PACKING
1-01-001	PISTOL-WHIPPED
1-01-001	PISTOL-WHIPPING
1-01-001	PISTOLEERS
1-01-001	PITEOUS
1-01-001	PITFALLS
1-01-001	PITH
1-01-001	PITHY
1-01-001	PITILESSLY
1-01-001	PITNEY-*BOWES
1-01-001	PITT-*RIVERS
1-01-001	PITTENGER
1-01-001	PITTSBURO
1-01-001	PITYINGLY
1-01-001	PIVOTAL
1-01-001	PIVOTING
1-01-001	PIWEN
1-01-001	PIXIES
1-01-001	PIZARRO
1-01-001	PIZZICATO
1-01-001	PLACATING
1-01-001	PLACE-KICKER
1-01-001	PLACELESS
1-01-001	PLACENTIA
1-01-001	PLAGIARISM
1-01-001	PLAID
1-01-001	PLAIDS
1-01-001	PLAIN-OUT
1-01-001	PLAINCLOTHES
1-01-001	PLAINEST
1-01-001	PLAINTIFF'S
1-01-001	PLAINVIEW
1-01-001	PLAN'S
1-01-001	PLANED
1-01-001	PLANELOAD
1-01-001	PLANET'S
1-01-001	PLANETARIUM
1-01-001	PLANETEN
1-01-001	PLANETOID
1-01-001	PLANETOIDS
1-01-001	PLANOCONCAVE
1-01-001	PLANT-LOCATION
1-01-001	PLANTAIN
1-01-001	PLANTINGS
1-01-001	PLASM
1-01-001	PLASTER-OF-*PAR IS
1-01-001	PLASTERER
1-01-001	PLASTERING
1-01-001	PLASTERS
1-01-001	PLASTI-*BARS
1-01-001	PLASTIC-COVERED
1-01-001	PLASTICALLY
1-01-001	PLASTISOLS
1-01-001	PLATED
1-01-001	PLATFORM-CONTRO LLER
1-01-001	PLATH
1-01-001	PLATITUDINOUS
1-01-001	PLATONICA
1-01-001	PLATTED
1-01-001	PLATTERS
1-01-001	PLAY-ACTING
1-01-001	PLAY-GIRL
1-01-001	PLAY-OFF
1-01-001	PLAYA
1-01-001	PLAYABLE
1-01-001	PLAYBACK
1-01-001	PLAYBACKS
1-01-001	PLAYBOY-*SHOW-* BIZ
1-01-001	PLAYERS'
1-01-001	PLAYES
1-01-001	PLAYHOUSES
1-01-001	PLAYIN
1-01-001	PLAYROOM
1-01-001	PLAYTIME
1-01-001	PLAYWRIGHT-DIRE CTOR
1-01-001	PLAYWRIGHTS
1-01-001	PLAYWRITING
1-01-001	PLAZAS
1-01-001	PLAZEK
1-01-001	PLEADER
1-01-001	PLEADS
1-01-001	PLEASANCE
1-01-001	PLEASANTNESS
1-01-001	PLEASIN
1-01-001	PLEASINGLY
1-01-001	PLEASURE-BOAT
1-01-001	PLEATS
1-01-001	PLEBEIAN
1-01-001	PLEBIAN
1-01-001	PLEE-*ZING
1-01-001	PLENIPOTENTIARY
1-01-001	PLENITUDE
1-01-001	PLEXIGLAS
1-01-001	PLIABLE
1-01-001	PLIANT
1-01-001	PLIERS
1-01-001	PLINKING
1-01-001	PLINY'S
1-01-001	PLOD
1-01-001	PLOPPED
1-01-001	PLOWMAN'S
1-01-001	PLOWSHARES
1-01-001	PLUCKING
1-01-001	PLUGGING
1-01-001	PLUM
1-01-001	PLUMBED
1-01-001	PLUMED
1-01-001	PLUMMETING
1-01-001	PLUNDERERS
1-01-001	PLUNDERING
1-01-001	PLUNKERS
1-01-001	PLURALISM
1-01-001	PLUTARCH
1-01-001	PLYMPTON
1-01-001	POACH
1-01-001	POACHES
1-01-001	POARK
1-01-001	POCKET'S
1-01-001	POCKET-SIZE
1-01-001	POCKETBOOKS
1-01-001	POCKETED
1-01-001	POCKETFUL
1-01-001	POCKMANSTER'S
1-01-001	POCONOS
1-01-001	PODGERS
1-01-001	PODIUM
1-01-001	PODOLIA
1-01-001	PODS
1-01-001	POEMS-IN-DRAWIN G-AND-TYPE
1-01-001	POEPLE'S
1-01-001	POESY
1-01-001	POET-PAINTER
1-01-001	POETRIE
1-01-001	POETRY'S
1-01-001	POGUE
1-01-001	POIGNANTLY
1-01-001	POINDEXTER
1-01-001	POINT-BLANK
1-01-001	POINTERS
1-01-001	POINTLESS
1-01-001	POKE
1-01-001	POKENEU
1-01-001	POKERFACED
1-01-001	POLARITIES
1-01-001	POLARIZE
1-01-001	POLARIZING
1-01-001	POLAROID
1-01-001	POLDOWSKI
1-01-001	POLECAT
1-01-001	POLEMIC
1-01-001	POLEMICAL
1-01-001	POLEMICS
1-01-001	POLICE-DODGING
1-01-001	POLICED
1-01-001	POLICEMAN'S
1-01-001	POLICEMAN-MURDE RER
1-01-001	POLICEMEN'S
1-01-001	POLICY-MAKING
1-01-001	POLICY-ORIENTED
1-01-001	POLIO
1-01-001	POLIS
1-01-001	POLISHES
1-01-001	POLITBURO
1-01-001	POLITICKING
1-01-001	POLITICO
1-01-001	POLITICO-SOCIOL OGICAL
1-01-001	POLITICOS
1-01-001	POLITICS-RIDDEN
1-01-001	POLITIES
1-01-001	POLITY
1-01-001	POLK'S
1-01-001	POLKA
1-01-001	POLKA-DOTTED
1-01-001	POLLED
1-01-001	POLLEN-AND-NECT AR
1-01-001	POLLOCK'S
1-01-001	POLLUTED
1-01-001	POLOLU
1-01-001	POLONAISE
1-01-001	POLTAWA
1-01-001	POLYANKA
1-01-001	POLYBUTENE
1-01-001	POLYBUTENES
1-01-001	POLYCHEMICALS
1-01-001	POLYELECTROLYTE S
1-01-001	POLYETHER-TYPE
1-01-001	POLYETHERS
1-01-001	POLYGYNOUS
1-01-001	POLYISOBUTYLENE
1-01-001	POLYISOCYANATE
1-01-001	POLYISOCYANATES
1-01-001	POLYMER
1-01-001	POLYMERIZATIONS
1-01-001	POLYMYOSITIS
1-01-001	POLYPHOSPHATE
1-01-001	POLYSILOXANES
1-01-001	POLYSTYRENE
1-01-001	POLYTECHNIC
1-01-001	POLYTONAL
1-01-001	POLYUNSATURATED
1-01-001	POMADED
1-01-001	POMERANIA
1-01-001	POMP
1-01-001	POMPADOUR
1-01-001	POMPANO
1-01-001	POMPEII'S
1-01-001	POMPONS
1-01-001	POMPOUSLY
1-01-001	POMPOUSNESS
1-01-001	PONCE
1-01-001	PONCHARIRAIN
1-01-001	PONCHIELLI
1-01-001	PONDER
1-01-001	PONKOB
1-01-001	PONOLUU
1-01-001	PONT-*GENERAL
1-01-001	PONTIAC
1-01-001	PONTIFF
1-01-001	PONTIFICAL
1-01-001	PONTIFICATES
1-01-001	PONTISSARA
1-01-001	PONTIUS
1-01-001	PONY'S
1-01-001	POOCHED
1-01-001	POOH-POOHED
1-01-001	POOL-CARE
1-01-001	POOL-EQUIPMENT
1-01-001	POOL-OWNERS
1-01-001	POOLED
1-01-001	POOR'S
1-01-001	POOR-MOUTH
1-01-001	POOR-WHITE-TRAS H
1-01-001	POP'LAR
1-01-001	POP'S
1-01-001	POPES

1-01-001 POPLAR	1-01-001 PRAM	1-01-001 PREFERMENT	1-01-001 PRINCESS-IN-A-C ARRIAGE
1-01-001 POPLIN	1-01-001 PRAMS	1-01-001 PREFERRING	1-01-001 PRINCIPIA
1-01-001 POPPIES	1-01-001 PRANDTL	1-01-001 PREFIXES	1-01-001 PRINTABLE
1-01-001 POPPYSEED	1-01-001 PRANHA	1-01-001 PREFUH	1-01-001 PRINTEMPS
1-01-001 POPULAIRE	1-01-001 PRANK	1-01-001 PREISOLATED	1-01-001 PRINTER'S
1-01-001 POPULARISM	1-01-001 PRANKS	1-01-001 PRELITERATE	1-01-001 PRINTMAKING
1-01-001 POPULARIZM	1-01-001 PRATAKKU	1-01-001 PRELUDES	1-01-001 PRIOR-YEAR
1-01-001 POPULATE	1-01-001 PRATT'S	1-01-001 PREMONITIONS	1-01-001 PRIORY
1-01-001 PORCUPINES	1-01-001 PRATTVILLE	1-01-001 PREMONITORY	1-01-001 PRIPET
1-01-001 PORED	1-01-001 PRAYER-REQUESTS	1-01-001 PRENCE	1-01-001 PRISCA
1-01-001 PORGY	1-01-001 PRAYER-TIME	1-01-001 PRENTICE'S	1-01-001 PRIVATE-EYE
1-01-001 PORING	1-01-001 PRAYERBOOKS	1-01-001 PRENTICE-*HALL	1-01-001 PRIVATE-SCHOOL
1-01-001 PORK-BARREL	1-01-001 PRAYERFUL	1-01-001 PRENTISS'	1-01-001 PRIVATELY-OWNED
1-01-001 PORNOGRAPHER	1-01-001 PRAYERFULLY	1-01-001 PREOCCUPATIONS	1-01-001 PRIVET
1-01-001 PORNOGRAPHIC	1-01-001 PRAYERS/*SHALL	1-01-001 PREOCCUPIES	1-01-001 PRIVIES
1-01-001 PORPOISES	1-01-001 PRE*$-ATTACK	1-01-001 PREORDAINMENT	1-01-001 PRIZE-FIGHT
1-01-001 PORRIDGE	1-01-001 PRE-*ANGLO-*SAX ON	1-01-001 PREPARATION-*IN QUIRERS'	1-01-001 PRIZE-WINNING
1-01-001 PORTA	1-01-001 PRE-*EASTER	1-01-001 PREPAYMENT	1-01-001 PRO-*CASTRO
1-01-001 PORTAGE	1-01-001 PRE-*FAIR	1-01-001 PREPONDERANTLY	1-01-001 PRO-*EUROPE
1-01-001 PORTANT	1-01-001 PRE-*FRENCH	1-01-001 PREPONDERATING	1-01-001 PRO-*HEARST
1-01-001 PORTENDED	1-01-001 PRE-*HAN	1-01-001 PREPRINTING	1-01-001 PRO-*TRUJILLO
1-01-001 PORTENTS	1-01-001 PRE-*LEGISLATIV E	1-01-001 PREPUBESCENT	1-01-001 PRO-*U**.*N**.* F**.*P
1-01-001 PORTERHOUSE	1-01-001 PRE-*PUNIC	1-01-001 PREPUBLICATION	1-01-001 PRO-*YANKEE
1-01-001 PORTERS	1-01-001 PRE-*REVOLUTION ARY	1-01-001 PREPUPAL	1-01-001 PRO-BALL
1-01-001 PORTFOLIO	1-01-001 PRE-*WORLD-*WAR -*/1	1-01-001 PRERADIATION	1-01-001 PRO-NEUTRALIST
1-01-001 PORTIA	1-01-001 PRE-ACADEMIC	1-01-001 PREROGATIVE	1-01-001 PRO-TEM
1-01-001 PORTLY	1-01-001 PRE-ASSAULT	1-01-001 PRESAGE	1-01-001 PROBABILISTIC
1-01-001 PORTRAITURE	1-01-001 PRE-CAST	1-01-001 PRESAGED	1-01-001 PROBINGS
1-01-001 PORTWATCHERS'	1-01-001 PRE-CONDITIONS	1-01-001 PRESBYTERIAN-*S T	1-01-001 PROBITY
1-01-001 POSEIDON	1-01-001 PRE-CONSCIOUS	1-01-001 PRESBYTERIANISM	1-01-001 PROBL'Y
1-01-001 POSES	1-01-001 PRE-COOLED	1-01-001 PRESCHOOL	1-01-001 PROBLEMATICAL
1-01-001 POSEUR	1-01-001 PRE-DECORATION	1-01-001 PRESCRIBES	1-01-001 PROBLY
1-01-001 POSEURS	1-01-001 PRE-DETERMINED	1-01-001 PRESCRIPTIVE	1-01-001 PROCAINE
1-01-001 POSEY	1-01-001 PRE-DRILLED	1-01-001 PRESENTATIONAL	1-01-001 PROCESS-SERVER
1-01-001 POSHEST	1-01-001 PRE-EMINENT	1-01-001 PRESENTE	1-01-001 PROCESSIONAL
1-01-001 POSITIONED	1-01-001 PRE-EMPLOYMENT	1-01-001 PRESENTER	1-01-001 PROCESSORS
1-01-001 POSSEMAN	1-01-001 PRE-EMPTING	1-01-001 PRESENTLYE	1-01-001 PROCLIVITIES
1-01-001 POSSEMEN	1-01-001 PRE-EMPTION	1-01-001 PRESENTMENTS	1-01-001 PROCRASTINATE
1-01-001 POSSES	1-01-001 PRE-EXISTENCE	1-01-001 PRESENTNESS	1-01-001 PROCRASTINATION
1-01-001 POSSESSOR	1-01-001 PRE-EXISTENT	1-01-001 PRESIDED	1-01-001 PROCREATIVITY
1-01-001 POSSIBLITIES	1-01-001 PRE-HISTORIC	1-01-001 PRESIDES	1-01-001 PROCTORS
1-01-001 POSSIBLE	1-01-001 PRE-INAUGURAL	1-01-001 PRESLEY	1-01-001 PRODDING
1-01-001 POST*$'S	1-01-001 PRE-LEGISLATIVE	1-01-001 PRESSED-PAPER	1-01-001 PRODIGAL
1-01-001 POST*$-ATTACK	1-01-001 PRE-LITERATE	1-01-001 PRESSURE-COOKER	1-01-001 PRODIGALL
1-01-001 POST-*A**.*D	1-01-001 PRE-MARITAL	1-01-001 PRESSURE-FORMED	1-01-001 PRODIGALLY
1-01-001 POST-*CIVIL	1-01-001 PRE-NUPTIAL	1-01-001 PRESSURE-HAPPY	1-01-001 PRODIGIES
1-01-001 POST-*DISPATCH	1-01-001 PRE-PACKED	1-01-001 PRESSURE-MEASUR ING	1-01-001 PRODUCER-HUBBY
1-01-001 POST-*GRADUATE	1-01-001 PRE-PENICILLIN	1-01-001 PRESSURE-SENSIN G	1-01-001 PRODUCERS'
1-01-001 POST-*INAUGURAL	1-01-001 PRE-PLANNING	1-01-001 PRESSURE-VOLUME -TEMPERATURE	1-01-001 PRODUCIN
1-01-001 POST-*SERIALISM	1-01-001 PRE-SCHOOL		1-01-001 PRODUCTIVITY-SH ARE
1-01-001 POST-CENSUS	1-01-001 PRE-SET	1-01-001 PRESTIDIGITATOR	1-01-001 PROFANE
1-01-001 POST-INDEPENDEN CE	1-01-001 PRE-VISION	1-01-001 PRESUMPTIONS	1-01-001 PROFESSES
1-01-001 POST-MORTEM	1-01-001 PRE-1960	1-01-001 PRESUPPOSE	1-01-001 PROFESSEUR
1-01-001 POST-OPERATIVE	1-01-001 PREACHER-SINGER	1-01-001 PRESUPPOSED	1-01-001 PROFESSOR'S
1-01-001 POST-REAPPORTIO NMENT	1-01-001 PREACHES	1-01-001 PRESUPPOSITION	1-01-001 PROFESSORSHIP
1-01-001 POSTAGE-PREPAID	1-01-001 PREARRANGED	1-01-001 PRESUPPOSITIONS	1-01-001 PROFET
1-01-001 POSTCARDS	1-01-001 PRECEDENT-BASED	1-01-001 PRETENSES	1-01-001 PROFILI
1-01-001 POSTMASTER'S	1-01-001 PRECEDES	1-01-001 PRETENSIONS	1-01-001 PROFIT-MOTIVATE D
1-01-001 POSTMASTERS	1-01-001 PRECEEDED	1-01-001 PRETEST	1-01-001 PROFIT-SHARING
1-01-001 POSTULATES	1-01-001 PRECEPT	1-01-001 PRETRIAL	1-01-001 PROFITABILITY
1-01-001 POTBOILERS	1-01-001 PRECHLORINATION	1-01-001 PRETTINESS	1-01-001 PROFOUNDEST
1-01-001 POTENTIOMETER	1-01-001 PRECIPICE	1-01-001 PREVAILE	1-01-001 PROFOUNDITY
1-01-001 POTHOLE	1-01-001 PRECIPICE-WALLE D	1-01-001 PREVAILIN	1-01-001 PROGANDIST
1-01-001 POTIONS	1-01-001 PRECIPITATE	1-01-001 PREVAYLE	1-01-001 PROGNOSES
1-01-001 POTLATCHES	1-01-001 PRECIPITIN	1-01-001 PREVIEW	1-01-001 PROGNOSTICATION
1-01-001 POTOWOMUT	1-01-001 PRECLUDED	1-01-001 PREVOST	1-01-001 PROGNOSTICATOR
1-01-001 POTPOURRI	1-01-001 PRECOCIOUSLY	1-01-001 PREWAR	1-01-001 PROGRAM'S
1-01-001 POTSDAM	1-01-001 PRECOCITY	1-01-001 PREXY	1-01-001 PROGRAMMES
1-01-001 POTTAWATOMIE	1-01-001 PRECONDITION	1-01-001 PREYING	1-01-001 PROHIBITIVE
1-01-001 POTTING	1-01-001 PRECONDITIONS	1-01-001 PRICE-CUTTING	1-01-001 PROHIBITON
1-01-001 POUILLY-*FUISSE	1-01-001 PRECONSCIOUS	1-01-001 PRICE-LEVEL	1-01-001 PROHIBITS
1-01-001 POULTRY-LOVING	1-01-001 PRECOOKED	1-01-001 PRICE-SETTING	1-01-001 PROJECTILE
1-01-001 POUND-FOOLISH	1-01-001 PRECUT	1-01-001 PRICE-WISE	1-01-001 PROJECTILES
1-01-001 POUND-OF-FLESH	1-01-001 PREDESTINED	1-01-001 PRICKED	1-01-001 PROJECTOR
1-01-001 POUNDS'	1-01-001 PREDICTABILITY	1-01-001 PRICKING	1-01-001 PROLIFERATED
1-01-001 POUPIN	1-01-001 PREDICTING-MACH INES	1-01-001 PRICKS	1-01-001 PROLONG
1-01-001 POURED-IN-PLACE	1-01-001 PREDICTORS	1-01-001 PRIDDY	1-01-001 PROLONGATION
1-01-001 POUSSIN'S	1-01-001 PREDIGESTED	1-01-001 PRIDE'S	1-01-001 PROLONGS
1-01-001 POUSSINS	1-01-001 PREDILECTIONS	1-01-001 PRIDE-*VENUS	1-01-001 PROMAZINE
1-01-001 POUT	1-01-001 PREDISPOSED	1-01-001 PRIE-DIEU	1-01-001 PROMENADES
1-01-001 POUTED	1-01-001 PREDOMINANT	1-01-001 PRIEST'S	1-01-001 PROMETHEUS
1-01-001 POWDERPUFF	1-01-001 PREDOMINATED	1-01-001 PRIESTLY	1-01-001 PROMOTER
1-01-001 POWER'S	1-01-001 PREDOMINATELY	1-01-001 PRIM	1-01-001 PROMPTINGS
1-01-001 POWER-*SEEK	1-01-001 PREDOMINATES	1-01-001 PRIMAL	1-01-001 PROMULGATING
1-01-001 POWER-HUNGRY	1-01-001 PREDOMINATING	1-01-001 PRIMATE	1-01-001 PROMULGATORS
1-01-001 POWER-STARVED	1-01-001 PREDOMINATION	1-01-001 PRIMATES	1-01-001 PRONENESS
1-01-001 POWERFULNESS	1-01-001 PREEMPLOYMENT	1-01-001 PRIMERS	1-01-001 PRONOUNCING
1-01-001 POWERPLANTS	1-01-001 PREENING	1-01-001 PRIMITIVE-ECLOG UE	1-01-001 PRONTO
1-01-001 POWERS-THAT-BE	1-01-001 PREFAB	1-01-001 PRIMITIVISM	1-01-001 PROPAGATE
1-01-001 POWICKE	1-01-001 PREFECTURE	1-01-001 PRIMPING	1-01-001 PROPAGATED
1-01-001 POZATTI	1-01-001 PREFECTURES	1-01-001 PRINCES'	1-01-001 PROPELLED
1-01-001 PRACTICABILITY			1-01-001 PROPELLER-DRIV
1-01-001 PRACTISING			
1-01-001 PRADO			
1-01-001 PRAI			

Code	Word
1-01-001	PROPELLING
1-01-001	PROPERTIUS
1-01-001	PROPHECIES
1-01-001	PROPHESIES
1-01-001	PROPITIATE
1-01-001	PROPORTIONALITY
1-01-001	PROPORTIONALLY
1-01-001	PROPOSITIONED
1-01-001	PROPPING
1-01-001	PROPRIETORY
1-01-001	PROPULSIONS
1-01-001	PROPYLAEA
1-01-001	PROPYLTHIOURACIL
1-01-001	PRORATE
1-01-001	PROSCENIUMS
1-01-001	PROSCRIBE
1-01-001	PROSCRIBED
1-01-001	PROSECUTION'S
1-01-001	PROSECUTIONS
1-01-001	PROSELYTIZING
1-01-001	PROSODIES
1-01-001	PROSOPOPOEIA
1-01-001	PROSPERING
1-01-001	PROSPERS
1-01-001	PROSSED
1-01-001	PROSSER
1-01-001	PROTEASE
1-01-001	PROTECTIVELY
1-01-001	PROTECTORATE
1-01-001	PROTEGE
1-01-001	PROTEIN-BOUND
1-01-001	PROTEOLYTIC
1-01-001	PROTESTANT-DOMINATED
1-01-001	PROTITCH
1-01-001	PROTO-*ATHABASCAN
1-01-001	PROTO-*YOKUTS
1-01-001	PROTO-SENILITY
1-01-001	PROTOPLASM
1-01-001	PROTOPLASMIC
1-01-001	PROTOTYPICAL
1-01-001	PROTOZOAN
1-01-001	PROTRACTED
1-01-001	PROTRUDE
1-01-001	PROTRUSION
1-01-001	PROTUBERANCE
1-01-001	PROUDER
1-01-001	PROUDEST
1-01-001	PROUDHON
1-01-001	PROUST
1-01-001	PROVDIED
1-01-001	PROVENANCE
1-01-001	PROVERBS
1-01-001	PROVIDENCE'S
1-01-001	PROVIDENTIAL
1-01-001	PROVINCETOWN
1-01-001	PROVISIONED
1-01-001	PROVISONS
1-01-001	PROVOCATEURS
1-01-001	PROVOCATIVELY
1-01-001	PROW
1-01-001	PROWAZWKI
1-01-001	PROWLED
1-01-001	PROWLERS
1-01-001	PROXMIRE
1-01-001	PRUDENTIAL
1-01-001	PRUDENTIALLY
1-01-001	PRUDENLY
1-01-001	PRUNE
1-01-001	PRUNED
1-01-001	PRUNES
1-01-001	PRURIENT
1-01-001	PRUSSIAN
1-01-001	PRUTA
1-01-001	PRYING
1-01-001	PSEUDO
1-01-001	PSEUDO-EMOTION
1-01-001	PSEUDO-FEELING
1-01-001	PSEUDO-HAPPINESS
1-01-001	PSEUDO-PATRIOTISM
1-01-001	PSEUDO-QUESTIONS
1-01-001	PSEUDO-SCIENTIFIC
1-01-001	PSEUDO-SOPHISTICATION
1-01-001	PSEUDO-SYMMETRIC
1-01-001	PSEUDO-WILLING
1-01-001	PSEUDOMONAS
1-01-001	PSEUDONYM
1-01-001	PSEUDYNOM
1-01-001	PSI
1-01-001	PSI.
1-01-001	PSI,
1-01-001	PSYCHES
1-01-001	PSYCHICALLY-BLIND
1-01-001	PSYCHO-PHYSIOLOGY
1-01-001	PSYCHOANALYST
1-01-001	PSYCHOLOGICAL-INTELLECTUAL
1-01-001	PSYCHOLOGICAL-INTELLECTUAL-VOLITIONAL
1-01-001	PSYCHOPHARMACOLOGICAL
1-01-001	PSYCHOPOMP
1-01-001	PSYCHOSOMATIC
1-01-001	PSYCHOTHERAPEUTIC
1-01-001	PSYCHOTHERAPIST
1-01-001	PSYCHOTIC
1-01-001	PT
1-01-001	PTERYGIA
1-01-001	PTOLEMAISTS
1-01-001	PUALANI
1-01-001	PUB
1-01-001	PUBERTY
1-01-001	PUBLIC-ADDRESS
1-01-001	PUBLICALLY
1-01-001	PUBLICISTS
1-01-001	PUBS
1-01-001	PUCKERING
1-01-001	PUCKISH
1-01-001	PUDDINGS
1-01-001	PUDDINGSTONE
1-01-001	PUDDLE
1-01-001	PUERI
1-01-001	PUERILE
1-01-001	PUFF
1-01-001	PUFFS
1-01-001	PUG-NOSED
1-01-001	PUKE
1-01-001	PULASKI
1-01-001	PULLMAN
1-01-001	PULLMAN'S
1-01-001	PULLMANS
1-01-001	PULPITS
1-01-001	PULSATIONS
1-01-001	PULSE-JET
1-01-001	PULSE-TIMING
1-01-001	PULSED
1-01-001	PULVERIZING
1-01-001	PUMBLECHOOK
1-01-001	PUMMELED
1-01-001	PUMP-PRIMING
1-01-001	PUN
1-01-001	PUNCHBOWL
1-01-001	PUNCHED
1-01-001	PUNCHED-CARD
1-01-001	PUNCHES
1-01-001	PUNCTUALITY
1-01-001	PUNCTURING
1-01-001	PUNDITRY
1-01-001	PUNDITS
1-01-001	PUNGENCY
1-01-001	PUNGENTLY
1-01-001	PUNISHABLE
1-01-001	PUNISHES
1-01-001	PUNISHING
1-01-001	PUNITIVE
1-01-001	PUNKS
1-01-001	PUNSTER
1-01-001	PUNTED
1-01-001	PUPATED
1-01-001	PUPATES
1-01-001	PUPPET'S
1-01-001	PUPPIES
1-01-001	PUPPYISH
1-01-001	PURCELL
1-01-001	PURCHASER'S
1-01-001	PURDUE'S
1-01-001	PURIFYING
1-01-001	PURISM
1-01-001	PURISTS
1-01-001	PURITANICAL
1-01-001	PURLING
1-01-001	PURLOINED
1-01-001	PURPLE-BLACK
1-01-001	PURPLING
1-01-001	PURPORTEDLY
1-01-001	PURPOSED
1-01-001	PURPOSEFULLY
1-01-001	PURPOSELESS
1-01-001	PURPOSIVELY
1-01-001	PURSES
1-01-001	PURSEWARDEN
1-01-001	PURTIEST
1-01-001	PURVEYOR
1-01-001	PURVEYORS
1-01-001	PUSH-*=UP
1-01-001	PUSSYCAT
1-01-001	PUT-UPON
1-01-001	PUTAINS
1-01-001	PUTAS
1-01-001	PUTOUT
1-01-001	PUTTANA
1-01-001	PUTTED
1-01-001	PUTTER
1-01-001	PUTTIN
1-01-001	PUTTY
1-01-001	PUTTY-LIKE
1-01-001	PUZZLEMENT
1-01-001	PUZZLER
1-01-001	PVT
1-01-001	PYE
1-01-001	PYHRRIC
1-01-001	PYNTE
1-01-001	PYOCANEA
1-01-001	PYORRHEA
1-01-001	PYRAMIDAL
1-01-001	PYRAMIDS
1-01-001	PYRE
1-01-001	PYROMETERS
1-01-001	PYROPHOSPHATE
1-01-001	PYSCHIATRIST
1-01-001	PYTHAGOREANS
1-01-001	Q*=T
1-01-001	QUACKED
1-01-001	QUADRENNIAL
1-01-001	QUADRICEPS
1-01-001	QUADRILLE
1-01-001	QUADRILLION
1-01-001	QUADRIPARTITE
1-01-001	QUADRUPLE
1-01-001	QUADRUPLED
1-01-001	QUADRUPLING
1-01-001	QUAGMIRE
1-01-001	QUAKE'S
1-01-001	QUAKERESS
1-01-001	QUAKING
1-01-001	QUALIFYING
1-01-001	QUALMS
1-01-001	QUAM
1-01-001	QUARRYMEN
1-01-001	QUARTER-CENTURY-OLD
1-01-001	QUARTER-INCH
1-01-001	QUARTER-TO-QUARTER
1-01-001	QUARTERBACKS
1-01-001	QUARTERMASTER
1-01-001	QUARTS
1-01-001	QUARTZ
1-01-001	QUASHED
1-01-001	QUASI-FOLK
1-01-001	QUASI-GOVERNMEN
1-01-001	QUASI-MECHANISTIC
1-01-001	QUASI-PERFORMER
1-01-001	QUASI-RECITATIVE
1-01-001	QUAVER
1-01-001	QUAVERED
1-01-001	QUE
1-01-001	QUEASINESS
1-01-001	QUEBEC'S
1-01-001	QUEEN'S
1-01-001	QUEERER
1-01-001	QUEEREST
1-01-001	QUELCH
1-01-001	QUELLING
1-01-001	QUENCH
1-01-001	QUENCHING
1-01-001	QUERULOUS
1-01-001	QUERULOUSLY
1-01-001	QUERY
1-01-001	QUERYING
1-01-001	QUESTION-AND-ANSWER
1-01-001	QUESTIONAIRE
1-01-001	QUESTIONERS
1-01-001	QUESTIONINGLY
1-01-001	QUEUED
1-01-001	QUI
1-01-001	QUIBBLE
1-01-001	QUIBS
1-01-001	QUIBUSDAM
1-01-001	QUICK-*WATE
1-01-001	QUICK-DRYING
1-01-001	QUICK-FROZEN
1-01-001	QUICK-HANDLING
1-01-001	QUICK-KILL
1-01-001	QUICKEN
1-01-001	QUICKENED
1-01-001	QUICKEST
1-01-001	QUICKNESS
1-01-001	QUIET-SPOKEN
1-01-001	QUILTED
1-01-001	QUINTANA
1-01-001	QUINTETS
1-01-001	QUINTILLION
1-01-001	QUIPPING
1-01-001	QUIRINAL
1-01-001	QUIRK
1-01-001	QUIRKING
1-01-001	QUIRKS
1-01-001	QUITELY
1-01-001	QUITS
1-01-001	QUIVERED
1-01-001	QUIVERS
1-01-001	QUOD
1-01-001	QUOK
1-01-001	QUYNE
1-01-001	QUYNEY
1-01-001	R)
1-01-001	R**.*A**.*F
1-01-001	R**.*L
1-01-001	RABAT
1-01-001	RABAUL
1-01-001	RABBETING
1-01-001	RABBI'S
1-01-001	RABIES
1-01-001	RACCOON
1-01-001	RACERS
1-01-001	RACIALLY
1-01-001	RACIE
1-01-001	RACIN
1-01-001	RACISTS
1-01-001	RACKED
1-01-001	RACKING
1-01-001	RACKMIL
1-01-001	RACQUET
1-01-001	RADAR-TYPE
1-01-001	RADETZKY
1-01-001	RADHAKRISHNAN
1-01-001	RADIATE
1-01-001	RADIATES
1-01-001	RADIATING
1-01-001	RADIATION-PRODUCED
1-01-001	RADIO-TRANSMITTER
1-01-001	RADIOCARBON
1-01-001	RADIOCLAST
1-01-001	RADIOGRAPHY
1-01-001	RADIOMEN
1-01-001	RADIONIC
1-01-001	RADIOSTERILIZED
1-01-001	RADS
1-01-001	RAESZ
1-01-001	RAFAEL
1-01-001	RAFER
1-01-001	RAFFISH
1-01-001	RAFTER
1-01-001	RAFTERED
1-01-001	RAFTERS
1-01-001	RAFTS
1-01-001	RAGES
1-01-001	RAGGEDNESS
1-01-001	RAIDED
1-01-001	RAIDERS
1-01-001	RAIDERS'
1-01-001	RAIL-MOBILE
1-01-001	RAILBIRDS
1-01-001	RAILLERY
1-01-001	RAILROADER
1-01-001	RAILROADING
1-01-001	RAILWAY-BASED
1-01-001	RAILWAYS
1-01-001	RAIMU
1-01-001	RAIN'S
1-01-001	RAIN-SLICK
1-01-001	RAINBOW-HUED
1-01-001	RAINDROPS
1-01-001	RAINE
1-01-001	RAINIER
1-01-001	RAINLESS
1-01-001	RAISER
1-01-001	RAISIN
1-01-001	RAJAH
1-01-001	RAK
1-01-001	RAKESTRAW
1-01-001	RAKISH
1-01-001	RAKISHLY
1-01-001	RALLIED
1-01-001	RAMBLES
1-01-001	RAMBLINGS
1-01-001	RAMIFICATION
1-01-001	RAMMIN

Code	Word	Code	Word	Code	Word	Code	Word
1-01-001	RAMMING	1-01-001	RE-ENACTING	1-01-001	RECONDITIONING	1-01-001	REFLECTANCE-MEASURING
1-01-001	RAMPAGE	1-01-001	RE-ENACTMENTS	1-01-001	RECONNAISSANACE	1-01-001	REFOCUSING
1-01-001	RAMPS	1-01-001	RE-ENFORCES	1-01-001	RECONSTRUCTS	1-01-001	REFOLDED
1-01-001	RAMSPERGER	1-01-001	RE-ESTABLISH	1-01-001	RECONTAMINATION	1-01-001	REFORMING
1-01-001	RANAVAN	1-01-001	RE-ESTABLISHING	1-01-001	RECONVENED	1-01-001	REFORMISM
1-01-001	RANCHO	1-01-001	RE-EVALUATE	1-01-001	RECONVENES	1-01-001	REFORMULATED
1-01-001	RANCIDITY	1-01-001	RE-EVALUATION	1-01-001	RECONVENTION	1-01-001	REFRACTED
1-01-001	RAND	1-01-001	RE-EXAMINED	1-01-001	RECONVERTING	1-01-001	REFRACTION
1-01-001	RANDALL	1-01-001	RE-EXAMINES	1-01-001	RECOONED	1-01-001	REFRACTIVE
1-01-001	RANDOM-STORAGE	1-01-001	RE-EXPLORE	1-01-001	RECOPIED	1-01-001	REFRACTORY
1-01-001	RANDOMIZATION	1-01-001	RE-EXPORT	1-01-001	RECORD-HIGH	1-01-001	REFRAINED
1-01-001	RANDY	1-01-001	RE-INCORPORATED	1-01-001	RECORD-TYING	1-01-001	REFRESH
1-01-001	RANK-AND-FILE	1-01-001	RE-INTRODUCTION	1-01-001	RECOUPED	1-01-001	REFRESHER
1-01-001	RANKE	1-01-001	RE-LIVING	1-01-001	RECOVERABLE	1-01-001	REFUNDED
1-01-001	RANKEST	1-01-001	RE-MORALIZING	1-01-001	RECOVERS	1-01-001	REFURBISHING
1-01-001	RANKIN'S	1-01-001	RE-RUN	1-01-001	RECREATE	1-01-001	REFUSE-LITTERED
1-01-001	RANKLES	1-01-001	RE-RUNS	1-01-001	RECREATED	1-01-001	REFUTE
1-01-001	RANSACKING	1-01-001	RE-SCHEDULED	1-01-001	RECREATES	1-01-001	REGAIN
1-01-001	RANSY	1-01-001	RE-SET	1-01-001	RECREATING	1-01-001	REGAINS
1-01-001	RANTED	1-01-001	RE-THINKING	1-01-001	RECRIMINATION	1-01-001	REGALED
1-01-001	RANYARD	1-01-001	RE-USE	1-01-001	RECRUITER	1-01-001	REGALIA
1-01-001	RAPES	1-01-001	RE-USED	1-01-001	RECTILINEAR	1-01-001	REGATTAS
1-01-001	RAPHAEL'S	1-01-001	RE-VISION	1-01-001	RECTITUDE	1-01-001	REGENCY
1-01-001	RAPHAELS	1-01-001	REACQUAINTED	1-01-001	RECTLINEARLY	1-01-001	REGENERATES
1-01-001	RAPID-FIRE	1-01-001	REACTS	1-01-001	RECUMBENT	1-01-001	REGENERATING
1-01-001	RAPID-TRANSIT	1-01-001	READ'S	1-01-001	RECUPERATING	1-01-001	REGENERATION
1-01-001	RAPIDLY-DIMINISHING	1-01-001	READAPTING	1-01-001	RECURRENCE	1-01-001	REGI
1-01-001	RAPIER	1-01-001	READING-ROOMS	1-01-001	RECURRENTLY	1-01-001	REGIMEN
1-01-001	RAPING	1-01-001	READJUSTED	1-01-001	RECURSIVE	1-01-001	REGIMENT'S
1-01-001	RAPOPORT	1-01-001	READYING	1-01-001	RECUSANT	1-01-001	REGIMENTATION
1-01-001	RAPPROCHEMENT	1-01-001	REAFFIRMS	1-01-001	RED'S	1-01-001	REGIMENTED
1-01-001	RAPT	1-01-001	REAGENT	1-01-001	RED-AND-YELLOW	1-01-001	REGINA
1-01-001	RAPTURES	1-01-001	REAL-ANALYTIC	1-01-001	RED-BELLIED	1-01-001	REGINALD
1-01-001	RAPUNZEL	1-01-001	REALER	1-01-001	RED-BLOODED	1-01-001	REGIONALISM
1-01-001	RARER	1-01-001	REALEST	1-01-001	RED-FACED	1-01-001	REGIONALLY
1-01-001	RARIFIED	1-01-001	REALIGNING	1-01-001	RED-NECKED	1-01-001	REGISTRANTS
1-01-001	RASCAL	1-01-001	REALISMO	1-01-001	RED-PRONE	1-01-001	REGISTRANTS'
1-01-001	RASCALS	1-01-001	REALNESS	1-01-001	RED-RIMMED	1-01-001	REGISTRAR
1-01-001	RASH	1-01-001	REALTOR'S	1-01-001	RED-TAILED	1-01-001	REGRETFULLY
1-01-001	RASPBERRY	1-01-001	REAPED	1-01-001	RED-TILE	1-01-001	REGRETTABLE
1-01-001	RASPED	1-01-001	REAPING	1-01-001	RED-TURBANED	1-01-001	REGROUND
1-01-001	RASPING	1-01-001	REAPPEARING	1-01-001	RED-VISORED	1-01-001	REGROUPED
1-01-001	RASPS	1-01-001	REAPPORTIONED	1-01-001	REDACTIONS	1-01-001	REGROUPING
1-01-001	RASTUS	1-01-001	REAPPORTIONMENT	1-01-001	REDBIRDS'	1-01-001	REGULAR-FEATURED
1-01-001	RAT'S	1-01-001	REAPPRAISALS	1-01-001	REDDENED		
1-01-001	RAT-A-TAT-TATTY	1-01-001	REAR-GUARD	1-01-001	REDDING	1-01-001	REGULATOR
1-01-001	RAT-FACE	1-01-001	REAR-LOOKING	1-01-001	REDEDICATE	1-01-001	REGULI
1-01-001	RAT-HOLES	1-01-001	REARGUARD	1-01-001	REDEEMED	1-01-001	REHABILITATING
1-01-001	RATABLE	1-01-001	REARMED	1-01-001	REDEEMIN	1-01-001	REHABILITATIONS
1-01-001	RATCLIFFE	1-01-001	REARRANGED	1-01-001	REDEEMING	1-01-001	REHARMONIZATION
1-01-001	RATEABLE	1-01-001	REARRANGING	1-01-001	REDEFINED	1-01-001	REHEARING
1-01-001	RATHBONES	1-01-001	REASSEMBLED	1-01-001	REDEFINITION	1-01-001	REHEARSE
1-01-001	RATIFY	1-01-001	REASSERT	1-01-001	REDEMPTIVE	1-01-001	REHEARSING
1-01-001	RATIOCINATING	1-01-001	REASSERTING	1-01-001	REDEVELOPERS	1-01-001	REICHSTAG
1-01-001	RATIONALISTIC	1-01-001	REASSIGN	1-01-001	REDHEADED	1-01-001	REIFENRATH
1-01-001	RATIONALITY	1-01-001	REASSURE	1-01-001	REDHEADER	1-01-001	REIGNED
1-01-001	RATIONALIZATIONS	1-01-001	REAVEY	1-01-001	REDHEADS	1-01-001	REIGNS
		1-01-001	REAWAKEN	1-01-001	REDHOOK	1-01-001	REIK
1-01-001	RATIONALIZED	1-01-001	REBECCA	1-01-001	REDIRECT	1-01-001	REILLY
1-01-001	RATOR	1-01-001	REBELLIONS	1-01-001	REDIRECTING	1-01-001	REILY'S
1-01-001	RATTAIL	1-01-001	REBIRTH	1-01-001	REDISCOVER	1-01-001	REIMBURSE
1-01-001	RATTLER	1-01-001	REBUILDS	1-01-001	REDISCOVERING	1-01-001	REIMBURSED
1-01-001	RATTLERS	1-01-001	REBUKED	1-01-001	REDISCOVERS	1-01-001	REIMBURSES
1-01-001	RATTLES	1-01-001	RECALCULATED	1-01-001	REDISTRICTING	1-01-001	REINCARNATED
1-01-001	RATTO	1-01-001	RECALCULATION	1-01-001	REDNECK	1-01-001	REINSTALL
1-01-001	RATTZHENFUUT	1-01-001	RECANTED	1-01-001	REDO	1-01-001	REINSTATED
1-01-001	RAUCOUSLY	1-01-001	RECAPITULATE	1-01-001	REDRESSED	1-01-001	REINSTITUTION
1-01-001	RAUSCHENBERG	1-01-001	RECAPTURED	1-01-001	REDSTONE	1-01-001	REINTERPRET
1-01-001	RAUSCHENBUSCH	1-01-001	RECEAVE	1-01-001	REDUCER	1-01-001	REINTERPRETED
1-01-001	RAVEL-LIKE	1-01-001	RECENTLY-PASSED	1-01-001	REEDBUCK	1-01-001	REINTRODUCES
1-01-001	RAVENCROFT	1-01-001	RECEPTACLE	1-01-001	REEDER	1-01-001	REINVESTIGATION
1-01-001	RAVINE	1-01-001	RECEPTIONIST'S	1-01-001	REEDVILLE	1-01-001	REINVIGORATION
1-01-001	RAVINES	1-01-001	RECEPTIONS	1-01-001	REEFS	1-01-001	REIPUBLICAE
1-01-001	RAWBONED	1-01-001	RECHARTERING	1-01-001	REEKED	1-01-001	REISS
1-01-001	RAWHIDE	1-01-001	RECHECK	1-01-001	REEKING	1-01-001	REITERATE
1-01-001	RAYBURN-*JOHNSON	1-01-001	RECHERCHE	1-01-001	REELECTED	1-01-001	REITERATES
		1-01-001	RECHERCHES	1-01-001	REELING	1-01-001	REITERATING
1-01-001	RAYMONDVILLE	1-01-001	RECIPES	1-01-001	REELS	1-01-001	REJECTIONS
1-01-001	RAYMONT	1-01-001	RECIPROCATE	1-01-001	REEMERGED	1-01-001	REJOICE
1-01-001	RAYNAL	1-01-001	RECIT	1-01-001	REENTERED	1-01-001	REJOICED
1-01-001	RAZING	1-01-001	RECKLESSNESS	1-01-001	REESTABLISH	1-01-001	REJOICES
1-01-001	RAZOR-EDGED	1-01-001	RECKONINGS	1-01-001	REEVALUATION	1-01-001	REJOINDER
1-01-001	RAZOR-SHARP	1-01-001	RECKONS	1-01-001	REEVES-TYPE	1-01-001	REJOINING
1-01-001	RAZORBACK	1-01-001	RECLASSIFICATION	1-01-001	REEXAMINATION	1-01-001	REKINDLING
1-01-001	RE-ACTIVATE			1-01-001	REEXAMINE	1-01-001	RELATEDNESS
1-01-001	RE-ADOPT	1-01-001	RECOGNISED	1-01-001	REFASHION	1-01-001	RELATIONAL
1-01-001	RE-ARGUING	1-01-001	RECOILED	1-01-001	REFECTORIES	1-01-001	RELATIONSHIP-BILDIN
1-01-001	RE-ASSUMED	1-01-001	RECOLLECT	1-01-001	REFEREE		
1-01-001	RE-CREATES	1-01-001	RECOLLECTED	1-01-001	REFERENCE-POINTS	1-01-001	RELATIVIST
1-01-001	RE-CREATION	1-01-001	RECOMMENCE			1-01-001	RELAYING
1-01-001	RE-DECLARED	1-01-001	RECOMPENCE	1-01-001	REFERENDUM	1-01-001	RELEARNS
1-01-001	RE-ECHO	1-01-001	RECOMPENSE	1-01-001	REFERENT	1-01-001	RELIABLY
1-01-001	RE-EMERGED	1-01-001	RECONCILES	1-01-001	REFERRIN	1-01-001	RELICT
1-01-001	RE-EMERGENCE	1-01-001	RECONCILIATION	1-01-001	REFILLED	1-01-001	RELIEVING
1-01-001	RE-EMPHASISE	1-01-001	RECONCILING	1-01-001	REFINANCE	1-01-001	RELIGIONISTS
1-01-001	RE-ENACTED	1-01-001	RECOND	1-01-001	REFLECTANCE	1-01-001	RELIGIOSITY
		1-01-001	RECONDITE				

1-01-001 RELIGIOUSNESS	1-01-001 REPUGNANCE	1-01-001 REUPHOLSTERING	1-01-001 RIFLE-SHOTGUN
1-01-001 RELISHING	1-01-001 REPUGNANT	1-01-001 REUTHER	1-01-001 RIFLED
1-01-001 RELIVES	1-01-001 REPULSED	1-01-001 REV'REND	1-01-001 RIFLEMAN'S
1-01-001 RELOCATION	1-01-001 REPULSION	1-01-001 REVALUATION	1-01-001 RIFLEMEN'S
1-01-001 RELYRICED	1-01-001 REPUTATION'S	1-01-001 REVAMPING	1-01-001 RIFLEMEN-RANGERS
1-01-001 REMAKING	1-01-001 REPUTATIONS	1-01-001 REVELATORY	1-01-001 RIFLING
1-01-001 REMANDING	1-01-001 REQUESTERS	1-01-001 REVELED	1-01-001 RIFT
1-01-001 REMARRY	1-01-001 REQUISITES	1-01-001 REVELING	1-01-001 RIG-*VEDA
1-01-001 REMARRYING	1-01-001 REQUISITION	1-01-001 REVELLERS	1-01-001 RIGGER
1-01-001 REMBRANDT	1-01-001 REREMAINED	1-01-001 REVELLING	1-01-001 RIGGERS
1-01-001 REMEDIAL	1-01-001 RESCINDED	1-01-001 REVELLINGS	1-01-001 RIGGS
1-01-001 REMEMBRANCES	1-01-001 RESEALED	1-01-001 REVELRY	1-01-001 RIGHT-ANGLE
1-01-001 REMINISCED	1-01-001 RESEARCHABLE	1-01-001 REVELS	1-01-001 RIGHT-ANGLED
1-01-001 REMINISCENCES	1-01-001 RESEARCHES	1-01-001 REVENGE-SEEKING	1-01-001 RIGHT-HANDED
1-01-001 REMINISCES	1-01-001 RESEARCHING	1-01-001 REVENUERS	1-01-001 RIGHT-WING
1-01-001 REMINISCING	1-01-001 RESERPINE	1-01-001 REVERBERATION	1-01-001 RIGHTHANDER
1-01-001 REMISSIONS	1-01-001 RESETTLEMENT	1-01-001 REVERBERATIONS	1-01-001 RIGHTHANDLER
1-01-001 REMITTED	1-01-001 RESETTLING	1-01-001 REVERDY	1-01-001 RIGHTIST
1-01-001 REMODELED	1-01-001 RESHAPED	1-01-001 REVERENTLY	1-01-001 RIGHTS-OF-WAY
1-01-001 REMOLDING	1-01-001 RESHAPES	1-01-001 REVERIE	1-01-001 RIGIDS
1-01-001 REMONSTRATE	1-01-001 RESIDENTIALLY	1-01-001 REVERSE-SURFACE	1-01-001 RILKE
1-01-001 REMORSE	1-01-001 RESIDUAL	1-01-001 REVERSIBILITY	1-01-001 RILLY
1-01-001 REMORSEFUL	1-01-001 RESIFTED	1-01-001 REVERY	1-01-001 RIM-*FIRE
1-01-001 REMOTER	1-01-001 RESIGNATIONS	1-01-001 REVETMENTS	1-01-001 RIMBAUD
1-01-001 REMOTEST	1-01-001 RESIGNEDLY	1-01-001 REVILED	1-01-001 RIME
1-01-001 REMOUNTING	1-01-001 RESIGNING	1-01-001 REVISING	1-01-001 RIMINI
1-01-001 REMOVABLE	1-01-001 RESIGNS	1-01-001 REVISIONIST	1-01-001 RIMLESS
1-01-001 REMPHAN	1-01-001 RESILIENCE	1-01-001 REVISITED	1-01-001 RIMS
1-01-001 REMUDA	1-01-001 RESINLIKE	1-01-001 REVITALIZE	1-01-001 RING-AROUND-A
1-01-001 REMUNERATIVE	1-01-001 RESINY	1-01-001 REVIVIFIED	1-01-001 RING-AROUND-THE-ROSIE
1-01-001 REMUS	1-01-001 RESISTANCES	1-01-001 REVOKED	1-01-001 RING-LABELED
1-01-001 REMY	1-01-001 RESISTIVE	1-01-001 REVOLTED	1-01-001 RINGEL
1-01-001 RENAL	1-01-001 RESISTS	1-01-001 REVOLUTION'S	1-01-001 RINGERS
1-01-001 RENATURATION	1-01-001 RESONABLE	1-01-001 REVOLUTIONARIES	1-01-001 RINGINGS
1-01-001 RENAULTS	1-01-001 RESORCINAL	1-01-001 REVOLUTIONISTS	1-01-001 RINGLER'S
1-01-001 REND	1-01-001 RESORTS	1-01-001 REVOLVE	1-01-001 RINGLETS
1-01-001 RENDERINGS	1-01-001 RESOUNDS	1-01-001 REVOLVES	1-01-001 RINGSIDE
1-01-001 RENDITION	1-01-001 RESOURCE-USE	1-01-001 REVVED	1-01-001 RINGSIDERS
1-01-001 RENEWABLE	1-01-001 RESOURCEFULLY	1-01-001 REWRITES	1-01-001 RIOTED
1-01-001 RENEWING	1-01-001 RESPIRATORS	1-01-001 REWRITTEN	1-01-001 RIOTING
1-01-001 RENEWS	1-01-001 RESPLENDENT	1-01-001 REWT	1-01-001 RIOTS
1-01-001 RENFREW	1-01-001 RESPONDENT'S	1-01-001 REXROTH'S	1-01-001 RIPA
1-01-001 RENFRO	1-01-001 RESPONSIBLY	1-01-001 REYES	1-01-001 RIPPLED
1-01-001 RENNELL	1-01-001 RESPONSIVELY	1-01-001 RF	1-01-001 RISKING
1-01-001 RENO-*LAKE	1-01-001 REST-ROOM	1-01-001 RHEA'S	1-01-001 RITIUALITY
1-01-001 RENOUNCING	1-01-001 RESTATES	1-01-001 RHEIMS	1-01-001 RITSCHL
1-01-001 RENOVO	1-01-001 RESTATING	1-01-001 RHEINHOLDT	1-01-001 RITTENHOUSE
1-01-001 RENOWN	1-01-001 RESTAURATEUR	1-01-001 RHEINHOLDT'S	1-01-001 RITTER'S
1-01-001 RENSSELAERWYCK	1-01-001 RESTITUTION	1-01-001 RHENISH	1-01-001 RITUALIZED
1-01-001 RENUNCIATION	1-01-001 RESTIVE	1-01-001 RHENIUM	1-01-001 RITZ
1-01-001 RENUNCIATIONS	1-01-001 RESTIVELY	1-01-001 RHETORICIANS	1-01-001 RIVAL'S
1-01-001 RENVILLE	1-01-001 RESTOCK	1-01-001 RHEUM	1-01-001 RIVALLED
1-01-001 REOPEN	1-01-001 RESTORERS	1-01-001 RHEUMATICS	1-01-001 RIVALS
1-01-001 REOPENED	1-01-001 RESTRAINS	1-01-001 RHINE-*MAIN	1-01-001 RIVEN
1-01-001 REOPENING	1-01-001 RESTRUCTURED	1-01-001 RHINE-*WESTPHALIA	1-01-001 RIVER'S
1-01-001 REORDER	1-01-001 RESUBLIMED	1-01-001 RHINESTONES	1-01-001 RIVERBOAT
1-01-001 REORGANIZE	1-01-001 RESURGENT	1-01-001 RHODESIA	1-01-001 RIVERSIDE'S
1-01-001 REORGANIZING	1-01-001 RESURRECTED	1-01-001 RHODODENDRON	1-01-001 RIVERVIEW
1-01-001 REORIENTED	1-01-001 RESURRECTING	1-01-001 RHU-*=BEB	1-01-001 RIVETS
1-01-001 REP'TATION	1-01-001 RESURRECTION	1-01-001 RHU-BEB-NI-ICE	1-01-001 RIVULETS
1-01-001 REPARATION	1-01-001 RESUSPENSION	1-01-001 RHYMES	1-01-001 RIZZUTO
1-01-001 REPARTEE	1-01-001 RETAILER	1-01-001 RHYMING	1-01-001 ROAD-CIRCUIT
1-01-001 REPEATER	1-01-001 RETAINERS	1-01-001 RHYTHM-*WILY	1-01-001 ROAD-CROSSING
1-01-001 REPELLENT	1-01-001 RETALIATE	1-01-001 RHYTHM-AND-BLUES	1-01-001 ROAD-SHOW
1-01-001 REPELS	1-01-001 RETALIATED	1-01-001 RHYTHMICAL	1-01-001 ROAD-SHY
1-01-001 REPENTANT	1-01-001 RETALIATING	1-01-001 RIB	1-01-001 ROADBED
1-01-001 REPERCUSSIONS	1-01-001 RETARDING	1-01-001 RIBALD	1-01-001 ROADBUILDING
1-01-001 REPETITIVE	1-01-001 RETCH	1-01-001 RIBAS	1-01-001 ROADHOUSE
1-01-001 REPHRASED	1-01-001 RETCHING	1-01-001 RIBBING	1-01-001 ROADSTER
1-01-001 REPLANTED	1-01-001 RETELL	1-01-001 RIBCAGE	1-01-001 ROADWAYS
1-01-001 REPLENISHMENT	1-01-001 RETENTIVENESS	1-01-001 RIBOFLAVIN	1-01-001 ROAMED
1-01-001 REPLETE	1-01-001 RETIED	1-01-001 RIBONUCLEIC	1-01-001 ROARINGEST
1-01-001 REPLICA	1-01-001 RETINA	1-01-001 RICAN	1-01-001 ROARS
1-01-001 REPLICATION	1-01-001 RETINUE	1-01-001 RICCI	1-01-001 ROASTS
1-01-001 REPLYING	1-01-001 RETIREMENTS	1-01-001 RICHARDS'	1-01-001 ROB'S
1-01-001 REPONSES	1-01-001 RETOLD	1-01-001 RICHARDSON'S	1-01-001 ROBARDS'
1-01-001 REPORTAGE	1-01-001 RETOUCHING	1-01-001 RICHEY	1-01-001 ROBBY
1-01-001 REPORTORIAL	1-01-001 RETRACE	1-01-001 RICHMOND-*PETERSBURG	1-01-001 ROBBY'S
1-01-001 REPOSED	1-01-001 RETRACED		1-01-001 ROBED
1-01-001 REPOSITORIES	1-01-001 RETRACING	1-01-001 RICHTER-*HAASER	1-01-001 ROBERTO
1-01-001 REPRESS	1-01-001 RETRACTION	1-01-001 RICKETTSIA	1-01-001 ROBERTSONS
1-01-001 REPRESSIONS	1-01-001 RETRAINING	1-01-001 RICKETY	1-01-001 ROBINSON'S
1-01-001 REPROACHES	1-01-001 RETRANSLATED	1-01-001 RICKEY'S	1-01-001 ROBINSONVILLE
1-01-001 REPROBATE	1-01-001 RETREATS	1-01-001 RICKSHAW	1-01-001 ROBOT
1-01-001 REPROBATING	1-01-001 RETRENCHING	1-01-001 RICOCHETED	1-01-001 ROBOTISM
1-01-001 REPRODUCIBILITIES	1-01-001 RETRIEVAL	1-01-001 RIDDANCE	1-01-001 ROBS
1-01-001 REPRODUCIBILITY	1-01-001 RETRIEVER	1-01-001 RIDDLE	1-01-001 ROBUSTNESS
1-01-001 REPRODUCIBLY	1-01-001 RETROGRADATIONS	1-01-001 RIDER-FASHION	1-01-001 ROCK'N'ROLL
1-01-001 REPRODUCTIVE	1-01-001 RETROGRESSIVE	1-01-001 RIDGEFIELD	1-01-001 ROCK-CARVED
1-01-001 REPROOF	1-01-001 RETROSPECTIVE	1-01-001 RIDGWAY	1-01-001 ROCK-LIKE
1-01-001 REPROVINGLY	1-01-001 RETROVISION	1-01-001 RIDPATH	1-01-001 ROCK-RIBBED
1-01-001 REPUBLICAN-CONTROLLED	1-01-001 REUB	1-01-001 RIEMAN'S	1-01-001 ROCK-STEADY
	1-01-001 REUNION-*HALLOWEEN	1-01-001 RIESMAN	1-01-001 ROCK-STREWN
1-01-001 REPUBLICANS'	1-01-001 REUNIONS	1-01-001 RIFFLE	1-01-001 ROCKABYE
1-01-001 REPUDIATE	1-01-001 REUNITE	1-01-001 RIFLE'S	1-01-001 ROCKAWAYS
1-01-001 REPUDIATING	1-01-001 REUNITING		

1-01-001 ROCKBOUND	1-01-001 ROTONDA	1-01-001 RUNABOUT	1-01-001 SAINTLINESS
1-01-001 ROCKERS	1-01-001 ROTTOSEI	1-01-001 RUNDFUNK	1-01-001 SAINTSBURY
1-01-001 ROCKET-BOMB	1-01-001 ROTUND	1-01-001 RUNDFUNK-*SINFO	1-01-001 SAKELLARIADISES
1-01-001 ROCKET-BOMBS	1-01-001 ROTUNDITY	NIE-*ORCHESTER	1-01-001 SAKO
1-01-001 ROCKETTES	1-01-001 ROUBEN	1-01-001 RUNDFUNKCHOR	1-01-001 SAL*FININISTAS
1-01-001 ROCKHALL	1-01-001 ROUGH-AND-TUMBL	1-01-001 RUNES	1-01-001 SALABLE
1-01-001 ROCKIN	E	1-01-001 RUNING	1-01-001 SALARIED
1-01-001 ROCKSTREWN	1-01-001 ROUGH-HEWN	1-01-001 RUNNER	1-01-001 SALES-BUILDING
1-01-001 ROCKVILLE	1-01-001 ROUGH-HOUSING	1-01-001 RUNT	1-01-001 SALES-CONSCIOUS
1-01-001 ROD'S	1-01-001 ROUGH-TOUGH	1-01-001 RUNYON'S	1-01-001 SALESGIRL
1-01-001 RODEO	1-01-001 ROUGHED	1-01-001 RUPPERT	1-01-001 SALESMAN'S
1-01-001 RODEOS	1-01-001 ROUGHER	1-01-001 RUSHALL	1-01-001 SALFININISTAS
1-01-001 RODEPH	1-01-001 ROUGHEST	1-01-001 RUSHMORE	1-01-001 SALIDA
1-01-001 RODGERS'	1-01-001 ROUGHISH	1-01-001 RUSSE	1-01-001 SALISH
1-01-001 RODNEY-*HONOR	1-01-001 ROUGHNECK	1-01-001 RUSSET-COLORED	1-01-001 SALIVARY
1-01-001 RODNEY-*MISS	1-01-001 ROUGHSHOD	1-01-001 RUSSIAN-DOMINAT	1-01-001 SALIVATE
1-01-001 RODNEY-*THE	1-01-001 ROUGHTLY	ED	1-01-001 SALK
1-01-001 ROE	1-01-001 ROULETTE'S	1-01-001 RUSSIANS'	1-01-001 SALLIES
1-01-001 ROEMER	1-01-001 ROUND'S	1-01-001 RUSSO-*AMERICAN	1-01-001 SALLOW
1-01-001 ROGUE	1-01-001 ROUND-BOTTOM	1-01-001 RUSTED	1-01-001 SALLYING
1-01-001 ROGUES'	1-01-001 ROUND-EYED	1-01-001 RUSTING	1-01-001 SALOMONOVICH
1-01-001 ROI	1-01-001 ROUND-FACED	1-01-001 RUSTLER-HUNTER	1-01-001 SALON
1-01-001 ROLE-EXPERIMENT	1-01-001 ROUND-TABLE	1-01-001 RUSTLERS	1-01-001 SALOONKEEPER
1-01-001 ROLE-EXPERIMENT	1-01-001 ROUND-THE-CLOCK	1-01-001 RUSTLIN	1-01-001 SALPETRIERE
ATION	1-01-001 ROUND-TIPPED	1-01-001 RUSTPROOF	1-01-001 SALSICH
1-01-001 ROLEPLAYED	1-01-001 ROUNDNESS	1-01-001 RUT	1-01-001 SALT-CRUSTED
1-01-001 ROLETTE	1-01-001 ROUNDUPS	1-01-001 RUTABAGA	1-01-001 SALT-EDGED
1-01-001 ROLLED-UP	1-01-001 ROUSSEAUAN	1-01-001 RUTABAGAS	1-01-001 SALT-FRACTIONAT
1-01-001 ROLLICKING	1-01-001 ROUTED	1-01-001 RUTHENIUM	ION
1-01-001 ROLLICKINGLY	1-01-001 ROUTINELY	1-01-001 RUTHERFORD	1-01-001 SALTBUSH
1-01-001 ROLLIE	1-01-001 ROUTINGS	1-01-001 RUTSTEIN	1-01-001 SALTER'S
1-01-001 ROLLINS	1-01-001 ROUTO-*JIG	1-01-001 RUTSTIN	1-01-001 SALTIS-*MC*ERLA
1-01-001 ROLLS-*ROYCES	1-01-001 ROVE	1-01-001 RUTTED	NE
1-01-001 ROLNICK	1-01-001 ROVED	1-01-001 RUYSCH	1-01-001 SALTON
1-01-001 ROLOFF	1-01-001 ROWLANDS'	1-01-001 RY	1-01-001 SALTONSTALL
1-01-001 ROMAGNOSI	1-01-001 ROWSWELL	1-01-001 RYC	1-01-001 SALU
1-01-001 ROMAN-CAMP	1-01-001 ROXY	1-01-001 RYCHARD	1-01-001 SALUTARIS
1-01-001 ROMANCERS	1-01-001 ROY'S	1-01-001 RYDER	1-01-001 SALUTATION
1-01-001 ROMANCING	1-01-001 ROYALE	1-01-001 RYERSON	1-01-001 SALVATORE
1-01-001 ROMANIUK	1-01-001 ROYALTY-FREE	1-01-001 RYLIE	1-01-001 SALVES
1-01-001 ROMANO	1-01-001 ROYAUX	1-01-001 RYNE	1-01-001 SALVOS
1-01-001 ROMANTICALLY	1-01-001 ROYLOTT'S	1-01-001 S*$**(HE'D	1-01-001 SAMAR
1-01-001 ROMANTICIZING	1-01-001 ROZELLA	1-01-001 S**.*P**.*C**.*	1-01-001 SAMBA
1-01-001 ROMANTICK	1-01-001 ROZELLE	A	1-01-001 SAMBUR
1-01-001 ROMEO'S	1-01-001 RPM,	1-01-001 S**.*S	1-01-001 SAMMARTINI
1-01-001 ROMMEL'S	1-01-001 RUARK'S	1-01-001 S**.*S**.*R	1-01-001 SAMMY
1-01-001 ROMP	1-01-001 RUBBER-LIKE	1-01-001 S**$0	1-01-001 SAMOA
1-01-001 ROMPED	1-01-001 RUBBERIZED	1-01-001 S'ACCUSE	1-01-001 SAMOS
1-01-001 ROMPING	1-01-001 RUBBERY	1-01-001 S'EXCUSE	1-01-001 SAMPLERS
1-01-001 ROMULO	1-01-001 RUBBIN	1-01-001 S'POSIN	1-01-001 SAMUELS
1-01-001 RONDO	1-01-001 RUBBLE	1-01-001 S**YA**YK**YO**	1-01-001 SAN*ANTONIO
1-01-001 RONNEL	1-01-001 RUBDOWN	YS	1-01-001 SANA
1-01-001 ROOFED	1-01-001 RUBE	1-01-001 S*S	1-01-001 SANCHEZ
1-01-001 ROOFER	1-01-001 RUBENS	1-01-001 S-S-SAHJUNT	1-01-001 SANCTAM
1-01-001 ROOFER'S	1-01-001 RUBICUND	1-01-001 SAABYE	1-01-001 SANCTIFIED
1-01-001 ROOFING	1-01-001 RUBIES	1-01-001 SAADI	1-01-001 SANCTUARY'S
1-01-001 ROOFTOPS	1-01-001 RUBRIC	1-01-001 SABA	1-01-001 SANDBARS
1-01-001 ROOFTREE	1-01-001 RUCELLAI	1-01-001 SABER	1-01-001 SANDE'S
1-01-001 ROOKIE-OF-THE	1-01-001 RUCKUS	1-01-001 SABINAS	1-01-001 SANDER
1-01-001 ROOKLYN	1-01-001 RUDDER	1-01-001 SABLES	1-01-001 SANDPAPER
1-01-001 ROOM**-FACILITI	1-01-001 RUDDERLESS	1-01-001 SABOL	1-01-001 SANDRA
ES	1-01-001 RUDDINESS	1-01-001 SABRAS	1-01-001 SANDWICH-TYPE
1-01-001 ROOM'S	1-01-001 RUDENESS	1-01-001 SABRE-RATTLING	1-01-001 SANER
1-01-001 ROOMBERG	1-01-001 RUDKOEBING	1-01-001 SACHEMS'	1-01-001 SANEST
1-01-001 ROOMFUL	1-01-001 RUDOLF	1-01-001 SACHEVERELL	1-01-001 SANG-FROID
1-01-001 ROOMMATE	1-01-001 RUDYARD	1-01-001 SACKER	1-01-001 SANGALLO
1-01-001 ROOMY	1-01-001 RUEFULNESS	1-01-001 SACKES	1-01-001 SANGALLO'S
1-01-001 ROOSEVELTIAN	1-01-001 RUFFIANS	1-01-001 SACKING	1-01-001 SANGAREE
1-01-001 ROOST	1-01-001 RUFFLES	1-01-001 SACKS	1-01-001 SANGER-*HARRIS
1-01-001 ROOSTER'S	1-01-001 RUFUS	1-01-001 SACRAL	1-01-001 SANGIOVANNI
1-01-001 ROPED	1-01-001 RUGER'S	1-01-001 SACRAMENT	1-01-001 SANGUINEOUS
1-01-001 ROPERS	1-01-001 RUGGEDLY	1-01-001 SACRE	1-01-001 SANGUINEUM
1-01-001 RORSCHACH	1-01-001 RUGGIERO	1-01-001 SACRESTIA	1-01-001 SANHEDRIN
1-01-001 ROSABELLE	1-01-001 RUIDOSO	1-01-001 SACROSANCT	1-01-001 SANITAIRE
1-01-001 ROSALIE	1-01-001 RUINING	1-01-001 SADDENED	1-01-001 SANITARIUM
1-01-001 ROSE-OF-*SHARON	1-01-001 RUINOUS	1-01-001 SADDER	1-01-001 SANSOME
1-01-001 ROSE-PINK	1-01-001 RUIZ	1-01-001 SADIST	1-01-001 SANTA'S
1-01-001 ROSE-TEA	1-01-001 RUL	1-01-001 SAFAVIDS	1-01-001 SANTAYANA'S
1-01-001 ROSEBUSH	1-01-001 RULERS'	1-01-001 SAFE-CONDUCT	1-01-001 SAP
1-01-001 ROSELLA	1-01-001 RULING'S	1-01-001 SAFE-CRACKING	1-01-001 SAPONINS
1-01-001 ROSEMARY	1-01-001 RULING-CLASS	1-01-001 SAFE-DRIVING	1-01-001 SAPPING
1-01-001 ROSENMUELLER	1-01-001 RUM-TUM-TUM	1-01-001 SAFEGUARDS	1-01-001 SAPPY
1-01-001 ROSETTES	1-01-001 RUMANIA	1-01-001 SAFEKEEPING	1-01-001 SAPS
1-01-001 ROSIE	1-01-001 RUMANIAN	1-01-001 SAFETIES	1-01-001 SARAN
1-01-001 ROSLEV	1-01-001 RUMANIANS	1-01-001 SAFFRON	1-01-001 SARASATE
1-01-001 ROSSILINI'S	1-01-001 RUMBLES	1-01-001 SAGAMI	1-01-001 SARASON
1-01-001 ROSTAGNO	1-01-001 RUMINANTS	1-01-001 SAGEBRUSH	1-01-001 SARASOTA
1-01-001 ROSTAGNOS	1-01-001 RUMMAGED	1-01-001 SAGES	1-01-001 SARCASM
1-01-001 ROSWELL	1-01-001 RUMMEL	1-01-001 SAGO	1-01-001 SARCASMS
1-01-001 ROSY-FINGERED	1-01-001 RUMMY	1-01-001 SAGS	1-01-001 SARCASTIC
1-01-001 ROTARIANS	1-01-001 RUMPUS	1-01-001 SAHJUNT	1-01-001 SARCASTICALLY
1-01-001 ROTATIONALLY	1-01-001 RUMSCHEIDT	1-01-001 SAIGON	1-01-001 SARCOLEMMAL
1-01-001 ROTATIONS	1-01-001 RUN-DOWN	1-01-001 SAILBOAT	1-01-001 SARDANAPALUS
1-01-001 ROTELLI	1-01-001 RUN-OF-THE-MINE	1-01-001 SAILORLY	1-01-001 SARI
1-01-001 ROTENONE	1-01-001 RUN-SCORING	1-01-001 SAINT-*SAENS	1-01-001 SARMI
1-01-001 ROTHKO	1-01-001 RUN-UPS	1-01-001 SAINTED	1-01-001 SARSAPARILLA
1-01-001 ROTOGRAVURES	1-01-001 RUN/CHAMBER	1-01-001 SAINTHOOD	1-01-001 SARTI

1-01-001	SARUM'S	1-01-001	SCHO**DNE	1-01-001	SCRIM	1-01-001	SEGREGATING
1-01-001	SASHAYED	1-01-001	SCHOCKLER	1-01-001	SCRIMMAGE	1-01-001	SEGUR
1-01-001	SASHIMI	1-01-001	SCHOLAR-BUSINES	1-01-001	SCRIMMAGED	1-01-001	SEGURA
1-01-001	SASSING		SMAN	1-01-001	SCRIPT'S	1-01-001	SEISMIC
1-01-001	SATAN'S	1-01-001	SCHOLASTICA	1-01-001	SCROOGE-LIKE	1-01-001	SEISMOGRAPH
1-01-001	SATIATE	1-01-001	SCHOLASTICALLY	1-01-001	SCROUNGING	1-01-001	SEISMOGRAPHS
1-01-001	SATIN-COVERED	1-01-001	SCHOLASTICS	1-01-001	SCRUBBED	1-01-001	SEISMOLOGICAL
1-01-001	SATIRICALLY	1-01-001	SCHOOL-AGE	1-01-001	SCRUMPTIOUS	1-01-001	SEIZING
1-01-001	SATIRIST	1-01-001	SCHOOL-LEAVING	1-01-001	SCRUPULOSITY	1-01-001	SELDES
1-01-001	SATIRIZES	1-01-001	SCHOOLBOOKS	1-01-001	SCRUPULOUS	1-01-001	SELECTION-REJEC
1-01-001	SATTERFIELD	1-01-001	SCHOOLBOYS	1-01-001	SCRUPULOUSLY		TION
1-01-001	SATURDAY-NIGHT	1-01-001	SCHOOLCHILDREN	1-01-001	SCUFF	1-01-001	SELECTIVITY
1-01-001	SAUCY	1-01-001	SCHOOLDAYS	1-01-001	SCUFFLE	1-01-001	SELECTMEN
1-01-001	SAUD	1-01-001	SCHOOLED	1-01-001	SCULPTED	1-01-001	SELECTORS
1-01-001	SAUD'S	1-01-001	SCHOOLERS	1-01-001	SCULPTOR'S	1-01-001	SELF'S
1-01-001	SAUDI-*AMERICAN	1-01-001	SCHOOLGIRL	1-01-001	SCULPTORS	1-01-001	SELF-ACCEPTANCE
1-01-001	SAUNDERS	1-01-001	SCHOOLGIRLISH	1-01-001	SCURRILOUS	1-01-001	SELF-AGGRANDISE
1-01-001	SAUSAGE	1-01-001	SCHOOLGIRLS	1-01-001	SCURVY		MENT
1-01-001	SAUSAGE-MEAT	1-01-001	SCHOOLMARM	1-01-001	SCUSE	1-01-001	SELF-AGGRANDIZE
1-01-001	SAUTE	1-01-001	SCHOOLMASTER'S	1-01-001	SCUTTLING		MENT
1-01-001	SAUTERNE	1-01-001	SCHOOLMATE	1-01-001	SEA'S	1-01-001	SELF-ANALYSIS
1-01-001	SAUTERNES	1-01-001	SCHOOLWORK	1-01-001	SEA-BEACH	1-01-001	SELF-ASSERTION
1-01-001	SAVAGERY	1-01-001	SCHOPENHAUER	1-01-001	SEA-BLESSED	1-01-001	SELF-AWARENESS
1-01-001	SAVER	1-01-001	SCHOPENHAUER'S	1-01-001	SEA-DAMP	1-01-001	SELF-BETRAYAL
1-01-001	SAVONAROLA	1-01-001	SCHOTT	1-01-001	SEA-FOOD	1-01-001	SELF-COMPLETION
1-01-001	SAVOR	1-01-001	SCHRAFFTS	1-01-001	SEA-HORSES	1-01-001	SELF-CONCEITED
1-01-001	SAVVY	1-01-001	SCHRUNK	1-01-001	SEA-ROAD	1-01-001	SELF-CONGRATULA
1-01-001	SAW-HORSE	1-01-001	SCHU**DTZ	1-01-001	SEA-VILLAGE		TION
1-01-001	SAWALISCH	1-01-001	SCHUBERT-*BEETH	1-01-001	SEABORG	1-01-001	SELF-CONSISTENT
1-01-001	SAWALLISCH		OVEN-*MOZART	1-01-001	SEABROOK	1-01-001	SELF-CONSUMING
1-01-001	SAWED-OFF	1-01-001	SCHULZ	1-01-001	SEAFARING	1-01-001	SELF-CONTENT
1-01-001	SAWING	1-01-001	SCHUMAN	1-01-001	SEAGOVILLE	1-01-001	SELF-CORRECTING
1-01-001	SAWMILL	1-01-001	SCHUMAN'S	1-01-001	SEAGULLS	1-01-001	SELF-CRIMINATIO
1-01-001	SAWNDERS	1-01-001	SCHUMANN'S	1-01-001	SEAHORSE		N
1-01-001	SAWYER	1-01-001	SCHUYLER'S	1-01-001	SEAMANSHIP	1-01-001	SELF-CRITICAL
1-01-001	SAXONY	1-01-001	SCHWADA	1-01-001	SEAMLESS	1-01-001	SELF-DECEIVING
1-01-001	SAXOPHONIST	1-01-001	SCHWARZEN	1-01-001	SEAQUAKE	1-01-001	SELF-DECEPTIONS
1-01-001	SAXTON'S	1-01-001	SCHWEITZERS	1-01-001	SEARCHINGLY	1-01-001	SELF-DEFEAT
1-01-001	SAY-SO	1-01-001	SCHWEIZER	1-01-001	SEARCHINGS	1-01-001	SELF-DELUDED
1-01-001	SAY-SPEAK	1-01-001	SCIENCE'S	1-01-001	SEARCHLIGHTS	1-01-001	SELF-DEPRECATIO
1-01-001	SAYED	1-01-001	SCIENTIFICALLY-	1-01-001	SEARLES		N
1-01-001	SAYERS		TRAINED	1-01-001	SEASONALLY	1-01-001	SELF-DICTATE
1-01-001	SAYINGS	1-01-001	SCIENTIFIQUE	1-01-001	SEATON	1-01-001	SELF-DRAMATIZAT
1-01-001	SAYONARA	1-01-001	SCIMITAR	1-01-001	SECESH		ION
1-01-001	SCABBED	1-01-001	SCIMITAR-WIELDI	1-01-001	SECLUDE	1-01-001	SELF-EFFACEMENT
1-01-001	SCABROUS		NG	1-01-001	SECLUDED	1-01-001	SELF-EFFACING
1-01-001	SCAFFOLDINGS	1-01-001	SCIMITARS	1-01-001	SECOND-CLASS	1-01-001	SELF-ENCLOSED
1-01-001	SCAIRT	1-01-001	SCINTILLATING	1-01-001	SECOND-ECHELON	1-01-001	SELF-ENERGIZING
1-01-001	SCALA	1-01-001	SCION	1-01-001	SECOND-FLOOR	1-01-001	SELF-EXILE
1-01-001	SCALD	1-01-001	SCIONS	1-01-001	SECOND-HAND	1-01-001	SELF-EXTINGUISH
1-01-001	SCALDED	1-01-001	SCISSORING	1-01-001	SECOND-LEVEL		ING
1-01-001	SCALDING	1-01-001	SCISSORS	1-01-001	SECOND-LOOK	1-01-001	SELF-FLAGELLATI
1-01-001	SCALLOPS	1-01-001	SCLEROTIC	1-01-001	SECOND-ORDER		ON
1-01-001	SCAMPERING	1-01-001	SCOBEE-*FRAZIER	1-01-001	SECOND-PLACE	1-01-001	SELF-IMAGE
1-01-001	SCAMPINI	1-01-001	SCOFFING	1-01-001	SECOND-STAGE	1-01-001	SELF-IMAGES
1-01-001	SCANDALIZING	1-01-001	SCULATTI	1-01-001	SECOND-STORY	1-01-001	SELF-INSURANCE
1-01-001	SCANDINAVIA	1-01-001	SCOOPING	1-01-001	SECONDHAND	1-01-001	SELF-JUDGING
1-01-001	SCANDINAVIANS	1-01-001	SCOOTING	1-01-001	SECRETARIATE	1-01-001	SELF-LOCKING
1-01-001	SCANNERS	1-01-001	SCOP	1-01-001	SECRETARIES'	1-01-001	SELF-MASTERY
1-01-001	SCAPEGOAT	1-01-001	SCOPED	1-01-001	SECRETARY-DESIG	1-01-001	SELF-OBSERVATIO
1-01-001	SCAPEGOATS	1-01-001	SCOPES		NATE		N
1-01-001	SCAPULARS	1-01-001	SCOPS	1-01-001	SECRETED	1-01-001	SELF-ORDAINED
1-01-001	SCARBOROUGH	1-01-001	SCORCHER	1-01-001	SECRETIONS	1-01-001	SELF-PACIFICATI
1-01-001	SCARCELY-TAPPED	1-01-001	SCOREBOARDS	1-01-001	SECTARIAN		ON
1-01-001	SCARECROWISH	1-01-001	SCORECARD	1-01-001	SECTIONALIZED	1-01-001	SELF-PERCEIVED
1-01-001	SCARFACE	1-01-001	SCOT	1-01-001	SECULARISM	1-01-001	SELF-PITYING
1-01-001	SCARIFY	1-01-001	SCOT-FREE	1-01-001	SECULARIST	1-01-001	SELF-PLAGIARISM
1-01-001	SCARING	1-01-001	SCOTCH-*IRISH-*	1-01-001	SECULARISTS		S
1-01-001	SCATHING		SCANDINAVIAN	1-01-001	SEDATIVE	1-01-001	SELF-PORTRAIT
1-01-001	SCATHINGLY	1-01-001	SCOTCH-AND-SODA	1-01-001	SEDENTARY	1-01-001	SELF-PORTRAITS
1-01-001	SCATTERING	1-01-001	SCOTCHGARD	1-01-001	SEDIMENTARY	1-01-001	SELF-PROCLAIMED
1-01-001	SCATTERS	1-01-001	SCOTCHMAN	1-01-001	SEDITION	1-01-001	SELF-PROTECTION
1-01-001	SCAVENGER	1-01-001	SCOTIAN	1-01-001	SEDITIOUS	1-01-001	SELF-REALIZED
1-01-001	SCAVENGING	1-01-001	SCOTT'S	1-01-001	SEDUCED	1-01-001	SELF-REDEFINITI
1-01-001	SCENARIO	1-01-001	SCOUNDREL	1-01-001	SEDUCER		ON
1-01-001	SCENARIOS	1-01-001	SCOUNDRELS	1-01-001	SEDULOUSLY	1-01-001	SELF-RELIANCE
1-01-001	SCENERIES	1-01-001	SCOUR	1-01-001	SEE-LECTIVE	1-01-001	SELF-RESTRAINT
1-01-001	SCENICS	1-01-001	SCOUT'S	1-01-001	SEE-THROUGH	1-01-001	SELF-RIGHTEOUSN
1-01-001	SCHANG	1-01-001	SCOUTED	1-01-001	SEEBOHM'S		ESS
1-01-001	SCHAPIRO	1-01-001	SCRAMBLING	1-01-001	SEED-BEARING	1-01-001	SELF-RULE
1-01-001	SCHEMATA	1-01-001	SCRAPBOOK	1-01-001	SEED-PODS	1-01-001	SELF-SACRIFICIN
1-01-001	SCHERZO	1-01-001	SCRAPES	1-01-001	SEEDCOAT		G
1-01-001	SCHILLING	1-01-001	SCRAPINGS	1-01-001	SEEDCOATS	1-01-001	SELF-SEEKING
1-01-001	SCHISM	1-01-001	SCRAPIRON	1-01-001	SEEDLESS	1-01-001	SELF-SERVE
1-01-001	SCHLEIERMACHER	1-01-001	SCRAPPED	1-01-001	SEEDLINGS	1-01-001	SELF-VICTIMIZED
1-01-001	SCHLEY	1-01-001	SCRATCHINESS	1-01-001	SEEEMD	1-01-001	SELFE
1-01-001	SCHLIEREN	1-01-001	SCRATCHY	1-01-001	SEEIN	1-01-001	SELFEFFACING
1-01-001	SCHMALMA	1-01-001	SCREECH	1-01-001	SEEKER	1-01-001	SELFISHNESS
1-01-001	SCHMALZRIED	1-01-001	SCREECHES	1-01-001	SEEKIN	1-01-001	SELFLESSNESS
1-01-001	SCHMIDL-*SEEBER	1-01-001	SCREECHY	1-01-001	SEEKINGLY	1-01-001	SELKIRKERS
	G	1-01-001	SCREENINGS	1-01-001	SEELEY	1-01-001	SELLE
1-01-001	SCHMIDT	1-01-001	SCREENLAND	1-01-001	SEEREY	1-01-001	SELLER'S
1-01-001	SCHNABEL-*PRO	1-01-001	SCREENPLAY	1-01-001	SEERS	1-01-001	SELLERS
1-01-001	SCHNABELIAN	1-01-001	SCREW-LOOSE	1-01-001	SEERSUCKER	1-01-001	SELLERS'
1-01-001	SCHNAPPS	1-01-001	SCREWBALL	1-01-001	SEGAL'S	1-01-001	SELLIN
1-01-001	SCHNOOKS	1-01-001	SCRIBBLED	1-01-001	SEGOVIA'S	1-01-001	SELLOUT
1-01-001	SCHO**DNBERG'S	1-01-001	SCRIBING	1-01-001	SEGREGATE	1-01-001	SEMENOV

1-01-001 SEMI-ABSTRACT	1-01-001 SERVICEMEN	1-01-001 SHAREHOLDER	1-01-001 SHOPPER
1-01-001 SEMI-ABSTRACTIO NS	1-01-001 SERVIETTES	1-01-001 SHARERS	1-01-001 SHOPPING-CENTER
1-01-001 SEMI-AMBIGUOUS	1-01-001 SERVINGS	1-01-001 SHARI	1-01-001 SHOPWORN
1-01-001 SEMI-AUTONOMOUS	1-01-001 SERVITORS	1-01-001 SHARK'S	1-01-001 SHORELINES
1-01-001 SEMI-CATATONIC	1-01-001 SESSHU	1-01-001 SHARK-INFESTED	1-01-001 SHORES'
1-01-001 SEMI-CIRCLE	1-01-001 SET'S	1-01-001 SHARKEY	1-01-001 SHORT'S
1-01-001 SEMI-CITY	1-01-001 SETON	1-01-001 SHARP-LIMBED	1-01-001 SHORT-BARREL
1-01-001 SEMI-CONDUCTORS	1-01-001 SEURAT	1-01-001 SHARPEN	1-01-001 SHORT-CHANGING
1-01-001 SEMI-CONSCIOUS	1-01-001 SEVEN-	1-01-001 SHARPEST	1-01-001 SHORT-CUT
1-01-001 SEMI-HEIGHTS	1-01-001 SEVEN-CONCERT	1-01-001 SHARPNESS	1-01-001 SHORT-CUTTING
1-01-001 SEMI-INDEPENDEN T	1-01-001 SEVEN-HIT	1-01-001 SHARPSHOOTERS	1-01-001 SHORT-RANGE
	1-01-001 SEVEN-INCH	1-01-001 SHARTZER'S	1-01-001 SHORT-SKIRTED
1-01-001 SEMI-INFLATED	1-01-001 SEVEN-IRON	1-01-001 SHATILOV	1-01-001 SHORT-STORY
1-01-001 SEMI-ISOLATED	1-01-001 SEVEN-O'CLOCK	1-01-001 SHATTERINGLY	1-01-001 SHORT-TIME
1-01-001 SEMI-MINOR	1-01-001 SEVEN-SHOT	1-01-001 SHATTERPROOF	1-01-001 SHORTCUT
1-01-001 SEMI-NUDE	1-01-001 SEVEN-STORIES	1-01-001 SHATTERS	1-01-001 SHORTNESS
1-01-001 SEMI-PRECIOUS	1-01-001 SEVEN-THIRTY	1-01-001 SHAVINGS	1-01-001 SHORTSIGHTEDNES S
1-01-001 SEMI-PRIVATE	1-01-001 SEVEN-WEEK	1-01-001 SHAWANO	
1-01-001 SEMI-PROCESSED	1-01-001 SEVEN-WORD	1-01-001 SHAY	1-01-001 SHOTGUN-TYPE
1-01-001 SEMI-PROFESSION ALLY	1-01-001 SEVENTEEN-INCH	1-01-001 SHE'ARIM	1-01-001 SHOTGUNS
	1-01-001 SEVENTEEN-YEAR- OLD	1-01-001 SHEA'S	1-01-001 SHOTSHELLS
1-01-001 SEMI-PUBLIC	1-01-001 SEVENTY-EIGHT	1-01-001 SHEARING'S	1-01-001 SHOTWELL
1-01-001 SEMI-SERIOUS	1-01-001 SEVENTY-FIFTH	1-01-001 SHEARN	1-01-001 SHOUDERS
1-01-001 SEMI-SPECIAL	1-01-001 SEVENTY-FIVE	1-01-001 SHECKLEY'S	1-01-001 SHOULDDA
1-01-001 SEMIARID	1-01-001 SEVENTY-FIVE-FO OT	1-01-001 SHEEP-LINED	1-01-001 SHOULDER-HIGH
1-01-001 SEMIAUTOMATIC		1-01-001 SHEEPE	1-01-001 SHOULDER-TO-SHO ULDER
1-01-001 SEMICIRCULAR	1-01-001 SEVENTY-FOOT	1-01-001 SHEERED	
1-01-001 SEMIDRYING	1-01-001 SEVENTY-FOUR	1-01-001 SHEET-METAL	1-01-001 SHOULDERING
1-01-001 SEMIEMPIRICAL	1-01-001 SEVENTY-FOURTH	1-01-001 SHEETED	1-01-001 SHOW-DOWN
1-01-001 SEMINAL	1-01-001 SEVENTY-ODD	1-01-001 SHEETING	1-01-001 SHOW-OFFY
1-01-001 SEMINARIANS	1-01-001 SEVENTY-SIX	1-01-001 SHEILA	1-01-001 SHOWERHEAD
1-01-001 SEMINARIO	1-01-001 SEVENTY-TWO	1-01-001 SHELAGH	1-01-001 SHOWERING
1-01-001 SEMINOLE	1-01-001 SEVERALLY	1-01-001 SHELBY	1-01-001 SHOWIN
1-01-001 SEMIPUBLIC	1-01-001 SEVERALTY	1-01-001 SHELL-PSYCHOLOG Y	1-01-001 SHOWMEN
1-01-001 SEMIQUANTITATIV E	1-01-001 SEVERE-LOOKING		1-01-001 SHOWPIECE
	1-01-001 SEVERING	1-01-001 SHELLED	1-01-001 SHOWROOM
1-01-001 SEMIRAMIS	1-01-001 SEVERLY	1-01-001 SHELVED	1-01-001 SHOWY
1-01-001 SEMISECRET	1-01-001 SEVERNA	1-01-001 SHENANDOAH	1-01-001 SHRANK
1-01-001 SEMITRANCE	1-01-001 SEVERS	1-01-001 SHENSI	1-01-001 SHREDDED
1-01-001 SEMITROPICAL	1-01-001 SEVIGLI	1-01-001 SHEP	1-01-001 SHREDDER
1-01-001 SEMMES	1-01-001 SEWANEE	1-01-001 SHEPHERD'S	1-01-001 SHREDDING
1-01-001 SEMPER	1-01-001 SEWED	1-01-001 SHERBET-COLORED	1-01-001 SHREWDEST
1-01-001 SEMPLE-*LISLE	1-01-001 SEWER'S	1-01-001 SHEVCHENKO	1-01-001 SHRIEKING
1-01-001 SEMRA	1-01-001 SEWICKLEY	1-01-001 SHEWE	1-01-001 SHRILLING
1-01-001 SENATOR'S	1-01-001 SEWN	1-01-001 SHH	1-01-001 SHRILLNESS
1-01-001 SENDERS	1-01-001 SEX-MANUALS	1-01-001 SHIBBOLETHS	1-01-001 SHROUDED
1-01-001 SENESAC	1-01-001 SEXTILLION	1-01-001 SHIES	1-01-001 SHROVE
1-01-001 SENESE	1-01-001 SEXTUOR	1-01-001 SHIETZ	1-01-001 SHRUB
1-01-001 SENILIS	1-01-001 SEXUALIZED	1-01-001 SHIFTE	1-01-001 SHRUB-COVERED
1-01-001 SENIOR-GRADUATE	1-01-001 SEYMOUR	1-01-001 SHIFTERS	1-01-001 SHRUBBERY
1-01-001 SENIORS	1-01-001 SEZ	1-01-001 SHIFTLESS	1-01-001 SHRUBBERY-LINED
1-01-001 SENIUM	1-01-001 SFORZANDO	1-01-001 SHIFTY	1-01-001 SHRUNKEN
1-01-001 SENS	1-01-001 SFORZT	1-01-001 SHIH	1-01-001 SHU-TT
1-01-001 SENSELESSLY	1-01-001 SH-TS	1-01-001 SHILL	1-01-001 SHUDDERY
1-01-001 SENSITIVE-AREA	1-01-001 SHA	1-01-001 SHILLINGS	1-01-001 SHUTSKI
1-01-001 SENSITIVELY	1-01-001 SHABBAT	1-01-001 SHILLONG	1-01-001 SHULDE
1-01-001 SENSITIVITIES	1-01-001 SHACK	1-01-001 SHILLS	1-01-001 SHUN
1-01-001 SENTENCE-STRUCT URE	1-01-001 SHACK-UP	1-01-001 SHIM	1-01-001 SHUNNED
	1-01-001 SHACKED	1-01-001 SHIMMER	1-01-001 SHUNNING
1-01-001 SENTENCING	1-01-001 SHACKS	1-01-001 SHIMMING	1-01-001 SHUNT
1-01-001 SENTIMENTALISTS	1-01-001 SHADE-DARKENED	1-01-001 SHIMS	1-01-001 SHUNTED
1-01-001 SENTIMENTALITY	1-01-001 SHADINGS	1-01-001 SHINBONE	1-01-001 SHUTE
1-01-001 SENTIMENTALIZE	1-01-001 SHADOWY	1-01-001 SHININGLY	1-01-001 SHUTS
1-01-001 SENTRY'S	1-01-001 SHADY	1-01-001 SHINTOISM	1-01-001 SHUTTLED
1-01-001 SEOUL	1-01-001 SHAEFER'S	1-01-001 SHIP-TO-SURFACE	1-01-001 SHUTTLING
1-01-001 SEPARATIONS	1-01-001 SHAFER'S	1-01-001 SHIPBOARD	1-01-001 SHUZ
1-01-001 SEPARATORS	1-01-001 SHAFFNER	1-01-001 SHIPLEY	1-01-001 SHYLOCKIAN
1-01-001 SEPIA	1-01-001 SHAG	1-01-001 SHIPMAN	1-01-001 SI
1-01-001 SEPTATION	1-01-001 SHAHN	1-01-001 SHIPMATES	1-01-001 SIBERIAN
1-01-001 SEPTEMBER-*OCTO BER	1-01-001 SHAK	1-01-001 SHIPPERS	1-01-001 SIBILANT
	1-01-001 SHAKESPEARIAN	1-01-001 SHIPPIN	1-01-001 SIBLEY
1-01-001 SEPTILLION	1-01-001 SHAKYA	1-01-001 SHIPS'	1-01-001 SIBLING
1-01-001 SEPTUAGENARIAN' S	1-01-001 SHALLOWER	1-01-001 SHIPSHAPE	1-01-001 SIBLY
	1-01-001 SHALLOWNESS	1-01-001 SHIPWRECKED	1-01-001 SIBYLLA'S
1-01-001 SEPTUM	1-01-001 SHALOM	1-01-001 SHIPYARDS	1-01-001 SIBYLS
1-01-001 SEPULCHRED	1-01-001 SHAM	1-01-001 SHIRLEY'S	1-01-001 SICILIANA
1-01-001 SEQ	1-01-001 SHAMBLED	1-01-001 SHIRT-SLEEVED	1-01-001 SICKISH
1-01-001 SEQUEL	1-01-001 SHAMBLING	1-01-001 SHIRTFRONT	1-01-001 SICKLY-TOLERANT
1-01-001 SEQUENCED	1-01-001 SHAMED	1-01-001 SHIRTSLEEVE	1-01-001 SICKROOM
1-01-001 SEQUESTRATION	1-01-001 SHAMEFACEDLY	1-01-001 SHISH	1-01-001 SICURELLA
1-01-001 SEQUINS	1-01-001 SHAMES	1-01-001 SHIT-SICK	1-01-001 SID
1-01-001 SERAFIN	1-01-001 SHAMS	1-01-001 SHITTS	1-01-001 SIDE'S
1-01-001 SERAPHIM	1-01-001 SHAN'T	1-01-001 SHIVERY	1-01-001 SIDE-ARM
1-01-001 SERBANTIAN	1-01-001 SHANGRI-*LA	1-01-001 SHO	1-01-001 SIDE-CONCLUSION S
1-01-001 SERENADE	1-01-001 SHANK	1-01-001 SHOCKER	
1-01-001 SERENELY	1-01-001 SHANN'S	1-01-001 SHODDY	1-01-001 SIDE-EFFECTS
1-01-001 SERFS	1-01-001 SHANNON	1-01-001 SHOE-STRING	1-01-001 SIDE-LOOKING
1-01-001 SERGEANTS	1-01-001 SHANSI	1-01-001 SHOELACE	1-01-001 SIDE-RACK
1-01-001 SERIEUSES	1-01-001 SHANTIES	1-01-001 SHOELACES	1-01-001 SIDE-STEP
1-01-001 SERIF	1-01-001 SHANTUNG	1-01-001 SHOESTRING	1-01-001 SIDEARMS
1-01-001 SERIOUS-MINDED	1-01-001 SHANTUNG-LIKE	1-01-001 SHOESTRINGS	1-01-001 SIDEBOARD
1-01-001 SERLOIN	1-01-001 SHANTZ	1-01-001 SHOJI	1-01-001 SIDEBOARDS
1-01-001 SERPENTINE	1-01-001 SHAPE-UP	1-01-001 SHOLOM	1-01-001 SIDECHAIRS
1-01-001 SERRA	1-01-001 SHARDS	1-01-001 SHOOING	1-01-001 SIDED
1-01-001 SERVANDA	1-01-001 SHARE-HOLDERS	1-01-001 SHOOTERS	1-01-001 SIDELIGHT
1-01-001 SERVATIUS	1-01-001 SHARECROP	1-01-001 SHOOTINGS	1-01-001 SIDELINE
		1-01-001 SHOPKEEPERS	1-01-001 SIDELINES

1-01-001 SIDELONG	1-01-001 SINGLING	1-01-001 SKYSCRAPERS	1-01-001 SMASHING
1-01-001 SIDEMEN	1-01-001 SINGSONGED	1-01-001 SKYWAY	1-01-001 SMATTERINGS
1-01-001 SIDESHOW	1-01-001 SINGULARITY	1-01-001 SL	1-01-001 SMELTS
1-01-001 SIDESTEPS	1-01-001 SINGULARLY	1-01-001 SLACKING	1-01-001 SMERDYAKOV
1-01-001 SIDEWINDER	1-01-001 SINKHOLE	1-01-001 SLADANG	1-01-001 SMIRKED
1-01-001 SIDLE	1-01-001 SINKT	1-01-001 SLANDEROUS	1-01-001 SMITH-*COLMER
1-01-001 SIE	1-01-001 SINNING	1-01-001 SLANDERS	1-01-001 SMITHTOWN
1-01-001 SIEBEN	1-01-001 SINO-*SOVIET	1-01-001 SLANT-WISE	1-01-001 SMITHY
1-01-001 SIECLE	1-01-001 SINTERED	1-01-001 SLANTS	1-01-001 SMITTEN
1-01-001 SIECLES	1-01-001 SINTON	1-01-001 SLAPS	1-01-001 SMOG
1-01-001 SIEGFRIED	1-01-001 SINUOUSLY	1-01-001 SLASH-MOUTHED	1-01-001 SMOKE-FILLED
1-01-001 SIENKIEWICZ	1-01-001 SINUOUSNESS	1-01-001 SLASHES	1-01-001 SMOKE-STAINED
1-01-001 SIEUX	1-01-001 SINUS	1-01-001 SLATER'S	1-01-001 SMOKERS
1-01-001 SIEVE	1-01-001 SINUSES	1-01-001 SLATS	1-01-001 SMOKES
1-01-001 SIEVERS	1-01-001 SIPHONED	1-01-001 SLATTED	1-01-001 SMOKESCREEN
1-01-001 SIFTING	1-01-001 SIPPERS	1-01-001 SLAUGHTERING	1-01-001 SMOKIES
1-01-001 SIGEMUND	1-01-001 SIREN	1-01-001 SLAVE'S	1-01-001 SMOLDERINGLY
1-01-001 SIGHS	1-01-001 SIRINJANI	1-01-001 SLAVE-LABORERS	1-01-001 SMOLDERS
1-01-001 SIGHTSEEING	1-01-001 SISTERS-IN-LAW	1-01-001 SLAVE-OWNERS	1-01-001 SMOOCHING
1-01-001 SIGHTSEERS	1-01-001 SISTINE	1-01-001 SLAVERED	1-01-001 SMOOTHBORE
1-01-001 SIGMA	1-01-001 SIT-DOWN	1-01-001 SLAVISH	1-01-001 SMOOTHEST
1-01-001 SIGMUND	1-01-001 SIT-IN	1-01-001 SLAVS	1-01-001 SMOTHERING
1-01-001 SIGNAL-INTENSIT Y	1-01-001 SIT-INS	1-01-001 SLEEK-HEADED	1-01-001 SMUDGED
1-01-001 SIGNAL-TO-NOISE	1-01-001 SITU	1-01-001 SLEEP-WAKEFULNE SS	1-01-001 SMUGGLE
1-01-001 SIGNALIZES	1-01-001 SIVA		1-01-001 SMUGGLERS
1-01-001 SIGNALLY	1-01-001 SIX-DOLLAR	1-01-001 SLEEPER	1-01-001 SMUGGLERS'
1-01-001 SIGNBOARD	1-01-001 SIX-FOUR	1-01-001 SLEEPER'S	1-01-001 SMUGGLING
1-01-001 SIGNERS	1-01-001 SIX-GALLON	1-01-001 SLEEPERS	1-01-001 SNAGS
1-01-001 SIGNIFICANTS	1-01-001 SIX-INCH	1-01-001 SLEEPLESS	1-01-001 SNAIL
1-01-001 SIGNIFIES	1-01-001 SIX-MAN	1-01-001 SLEEPLESSLY	1-01-001 SNAIL'S
1-01-001 SIGNIGICANT	1-01-001 SIX-MONTH	1-01-001 SLEEPS	1-01-001 SNAILS
1-01-001 SIGNORE	1-01-001 SIX-SHOOTER	1-01-001 SLEEPWALKER	1-01-001 SNAKE-LIKE
1-01-001 SIGNPOSTS	1-01-001 SIX-THIRTY	1-01-001 SLEEPY-EYED	1-01-001 SNAKE-RAIL
1-01-001 SIGUE	1-01-001 SIX-TON	1-01-001 SLEET	1-01-001 SNAKESTRIKE
1-01-001 SIHANOUK	1-01-001 SIXTEEN-YEAR-OL D	1-01-001 SLEIGHT	1-01-001 SNAP-IN
1-01-001 SIHANOUK'S		1-01-001 SLENCZYNKA	1-01-001 SNAPBACK
1-01-001 SILAS	1-01-001 SIXTH-GRADE	1-01-001 SLENDER-WAISTED	1-01-001 SNAPDRAGONS
1-01-001 SILENCING	1-01-001 SIXTH-SENSE	1-01-001 SLENDERER	1-01-001 SNAPPER
1-01-001 SILICA-GLASS	1-01-001 SIXTIES'	1-01-001 SLEUTHING	1-01-001 SNAPPY
1-01-001 SILICATE	1-01-001 SIXTY-DAY	1-01-001 SLICK-HEADED	1-01-001 SNAPSHOTS
1-01-001 SILICATES	1-01-001 SIXTY-EIGHT	1-01-001 SLICKERS	1-01-001 SNARE
1-01-001 SILICONE	1-01-001 SIXTY-EIGHTH	1-01-001 SLIDE-LOCK	1-01-001 SNARED
1-01-001 SILKE	1-01-001 SIXTY-FIVE-MILE	1-01-001 SLIGHTER	1-01-001 SNATCHING
1-01-001 SILKEN	1-01-001 SIXTY-NINE	1-01-001 SLIGHTLY-SMOKIN G	1-01-001 SNAZZY
1-01-001 SILKWORMS	1-01-001 SIXTY-SEVEN		1-01-001 SNEAKS
1-01-001 SILKY	1-01-001 SIZEABLE	1-01-001 SLIGHTS	1-01-001 SNEED
1-01-001 SILLIEST	1-01-001 SIZOVA	1-01-001 SLIM-WAISTED	1-01-001 SNEER
1-01-001 SILO	1-01-001 SIZZLE	1-01-001 SLIMED	1-01-001 SNEERED
1-01-001 SILONE	1-01-001 SKATE	1-01-001 SLIMLY	1-01-001 SNEERING
1-01-001 SILVAS	1-01-001 SKATES	1-01-001 SLIMMER	1-01-001 SNEEZING
1-01-001 SILVER-GRAY	1-01-001 SKELETONS	1-01-001 SLING	1-01-001 SNICK
1-01-001 SILVER-PAINTED	1-01-001 SKEPTICALLY	1-01-001 SLINGING	1-01-001 SNIFFLE
1-01-001 SILVERS	1-01-001 SKEWER	1-01-001 SLINGS	1-01-001 SNIGGERED
1-01-001 SILVIO	1-01-001 SKI-JORING	1-01-001 SLINGSHOT	1-01-001 SNIPER
1-01-001 SIMAK'S	1-01-001 SKIDDY	1-01-001 SLIPPAGE	1-01-001 SNIPER'S
1-01-001 SIMBA	1-01-001 SKIDS	1-01-001 SLIPSTREAM	1-01-001 SNIPING
1-01-001 SIMCA	1-01-001 SKIFF'S	1-01-001 SLITTER	1-01-001 SNIPPY
1-01-001 SIMILE	1-01-001 SKILFUL	1-01-001 SLITTERS	1-01-001 SNIPS
1-01-001 SIMMEL	1-01-001 SKILFULLY	1-01-001 SLIVERY	1-01-001 SNIVELINGS
1-01-001 SIMMERED	1-01-001 SKILLFULNESS	1-01-001 SLO-*FLO	1-01-001 SNOB-CLANNISH
1-01-001 SIMMONS'	1-01-001 SKIMPY	1-01-001 SLOGANEERING	1-01-001 SNOBBISHLY
1-01-001 SIMMONSVILLE	1-01-001 SKIN-PERCEPTIVE NESS	1-01-001 SLOOP	1-01-001 SNOBS
1-01-001 SIMON'S		1-01-001 SLOPE'S	1-01-001 SNOOK
1-01-001 SIMONELLI	1-01-001 SKINDIVE	1-01-001 SLOPPED	1-01-001 SNOOP
1-01-001 SIMONSON'S	1-01-001 SKINDIVING	1-01-001 SLOPPILY	1-01-001 SNOOPING
1-01-001 SIMPLE-SEEMING	1-01-001 SKINFOLDS	1-01-001 SLOSHED	1-01-001 SNOUT
1-01-001 SIMPLES	1-01-001 SKINNER	1-01-001 SLOTHFUL	1-01-001 SNOW-COVERED
1-01-001 SIMPLETON	1-01-001 SKINNIN	1-01-001 SLOTTED	1-01-001 SNOW-FENCE
1-01-001 SIMPLEX	1-01-001 SKIPJACK'S	1-01-001 SLOUCH	1-01-001 SNOW-WHITE
1-01-001 SIMPLICITER	1-01-001 SKIPPER	1-01-001 SLOUCHES	1-01-001 SNOWFLAKES
1-01-001 SIMPLICITUDE	1-01-001 SKIPS	1-01-001 SLOUGH	1-01-001 SNUBBING
1-01-001 SIN-NED	1-01-001 SKIRMISHED	1-01-001 SLOVENLINESS	1-01-001 SNUCK
1-01-001 SINAI	1-01-001 SKIRMISHERS	1-01-001 SLOW-ACTING	1-01-001 SNUFFBOXES
1-01-001 SINAN	1-01-001 SKIRMISHES	1-01-001 SLOW-BAKED	1-01-001 SNUFFED
1-01-001 SINCEREST	1-01-001 SKIRTED	1-01-001 SLOW-BOUNCING	1-01-001 SNUFFER
1-01-001 SIND	1-01-001 SKIRTING	1-01-001 SLOW-FIRING	1-01-001 SNUG-*GRIP
1-01-001 SINEWS	1-01-001 SKIS	1-01-001 SLOW-GROWING	1-01-001 SNUG-FITTING
1-01-001 SINFONICA	1-01-001 SKIT	1-01-001 SLOW-MOVING	1-01-001 SNYDER
1-01-001 SING'S	1-01-001 SKITS	1-01-001 SLOW-SCRAMBLING	1-01-001 SNYDER'S
1-01-001 SING-SONG	1-01-001 SKIWAY	1-01-001 SLOWLY-MENDING	1-01-001 SO-FAR
1-01-001 SINGED	1-01-001 SKOLKAU	1-01-001 SLUICEHOUSE	1-01-001 SOAPSUDS
1-01-001 SINGER'S	1-01-001 SKOLOVSKY'S	1-01-001 SLUICING	1-01-001 SOBA
1-01-001 SINGERS'	1-01-001 SKOUTING	1-01-001 SLUMBERED	1-01-001 SOBBING
1-01-001 SINGLE-BARREL	1-01-001 SKULK	1-01-001 SLURPED	1-01-001 SOBBINGLY
1-01-001 SINGLE-COLOR	1-01-001 SKULL-BASHINGS	1-01-001 SLURRIES	1-01-001 SOBIBOR
1-01-001 SINGLE-CRYSTAL	1-01-001 SKUNKS	1-01-001 SLYNESS	1-01-001 SOBRIETY
1-01-001 SINGLE-DOSE	1-01-001 SKY-CARVING	1-01-001 SMACKS	1-01-001 SOCAL
1-01-001 SINGLE-FOOT	1-01-001 SKY-GOD	1-01-001 SMALL-ARMS	1-01-001 SOCIABLE
1-01-001 SINGLE-HANDED	1-01-001 SKY-REACHING	1-01-001 SMALL-BOAT	1-01-001 SOCIAL-CLIMBING
1-01-001 SINGLE-LANE	1-01-001 SKY-TAPPING	1-01-001 SMALL-CAR	1-01-001 SOCIAL-POLITICA L-ECONOMICAL
1-01-001 SINGLE-MINDED	1-01-001 SKYBOLT	1-01-001 SMALL-SCALE	1-01-001 SOCIAL-REGISTER
1-01-001 SINGLE-SEEDED	1-01-001 SKYE	1-01-001 SMALLER-SIZE	1-01-001 SOCIAL-ROLE
1-01-001 SINGLE-SPACED	1-01-001 SKYJACKED	1-01-001 SMALLISH	1-01-001 SOCIAL-WELFARE
1-01-001 SINGLEHANDEDLY	1-01-001 SKYJACKERS	1-01-001 SMALLTIME	1-01-001 SOCIALITY
1-01-001 SINGLENESS	1-01-001 SKYLARK	1-01-001 SMARTED	1-01-001 SOCIALIZE
1-01-001 SINGLES	1-01-001 SKYLARKING	1-01-001 SMASH-'EM-DOWN	1-01-001 SOCIALIZES
	1-01-001 SKYLIGHT	1-01-001 SMASHED-OUT	

Code	Entry
1-01-001	SOCIALLY-ORIENTED
1-01-001	SOCIETE
1-01-001	SOCINIANISM
1-01-001	SOCIO-ARCHAEOLOGICAL
1-01-001	SOCIO-POLITICAL
1-01-001	SOCIO-STRUCTURAL
1-01-001	SOCIOLOGICALLY
1-01-001	SOCIOLOGISTS
1-01-001	SOCKDOLOGIZING
1-01-001	SOCKED
1-01-001	SOCKETS
1-01-001	SOCOLA
1-01-001	SOCONOCO
1-01-001	SODDENLY
1-01-001	SODDIES
1-01-001	SODS
1-01-001	SOE
1-01-001	SOEREN
1-01-001	SOFAR
1-01-001	SOFT-
1-01-001	SOFT-DRINK
1-01-001	SOFT-DRINKS
1-01-001	SOFT-HEADED
1-01-001	SOFT-HEARTEDNESS
1-01-001	SOFT-LOOKING
1-01-001	SOFT-SHELL
1-01-001	SOFT-SHOE
1-01-001	SOFT-SPOKEN
1-01-001	SOFTENS
1-01-001	SOFTEST
1-01-001	SOFTWOOD
1-01-001	SOHN
1-01-001	SOIGNEE
1-01-001	SOIL-BEARING
1-01-001	SOIL-REMOVAL
1-01-001	SOIREE
1-01-001	SOIREES
1-01-001	SOJOURNERS
1-01-001	SOKOLEV
1-01-001	SOLACED
1-01-001	SOLAR-CORPUSCULAR-RADIATION
1-01-001	SOLAR-ELECTROMAGNETIC-
1-01-001	SOLAR-RADIATION
1-01-001	SOLAR-WIND
1-01-001	SOLD-OUT
1-01-001	SOLDERED
1-01-001	SOLDERING
1-01-001	SOLDIER'S
1-01-001	SOLDIER-MASTERS
1-01-001	SOLDIERING
1-01-001	SOLDIERLY
1-01-001	SOLDIERY
1-01-001	SOLEMNIS
1-01-001	SOLEMNITY
1-01-001	SOLENOID
1-01-001	SOLESMES
1-01-001	SOLICIT
1-01-001	SOLICITING
1-01-001	SOLICITOUSNESS
1-01-001	SOLICITS
1-01-001	SOLID-FUELED
1-01-001	SOLID-STATE
1-01-001	SOLIDIFIES
1-01-001	SOLIPSISM
1-01-001	SOLITUDES
1-01-001	SOLITUDINEM
1-01-001	SOLOISTS'
1-01-001	SOLOMON'S
1-01-001	SOLOVIEV-*SEDOI
1-01-001	SOLSTICE
1-01-001	SOLUTION-TYPE
1-01-001	SOLVATING
1-01-001	SOLVENCY
1-01-001	SOMA
1-01-001	SOMAY
1-01-001	SOMEBODY'LL
1-01-001	SOMEONE'LL
1-01-001	SOMERSAULTING
1-01-001	SOMETIMES-NECESSARY
1-01-001	SOMEWHERES
1-01-001	SOMMELIER
1-01-001	SOMNOLENCE
1-01-001	SOMPIN
1-01-001	SONAMBULA
1-01-001	SONATES
1-01-001	SONENBERG
1-01-001	SONG-WRITING
1-01-001	SONGBAG
1-01-001	SONGBOOK
1-01-001	SONGFUL
1-01-001	SONNY-BOY
1-01-001	SONOGRAM
1-01-001	SONOMA
1-01-001	SONORA
1-01-001	SONORITIES
1-01-001	SONORITY
1-01-001	SONOROUS
1-01-001	SONUVABITCH
1-01-001	SOOMED
1-01-001	SOON'S
1-01-001	SOOT
1-01-001	SOOTHINGLY
1-01-001	SOOTHSAYER
1-01-001	SOP
1-01-001	SOPHIA'S
1-01-001	SOPHIAS
1-01-001	SOPHISTICATE
1-01-001	SOPHISTICATES
1-01-001	SOPHOCLEAN
1-01-001	SOPHOMORES
1-01-001	SOPPING
1-01-001	SOPRANOS
1-01-001	SOPS
1-01-001	SOPSAISANA
1-01-001	SOR'L
1-01-001	SORCERY
1-01-001	SORE-RIDDEN
1-01-001	SORENESS
1-01-001	SOREST
1-01-001	SORORITIES
1-01-001	SORORITY
1-01-001	SORPTION
1-01-001	SORPTION-DESORPTION
1-01-001	SORRENTINE
1-01-001	SORRENTINE'S
1-01-001	SORRIEST
1-01-001	SORTING
1-01-001	SOTUN
1-01-001	SOU
1-01-001	SOUBRIQUET
1-01-001	SOUCI
1-01-001	SOUFFLE
1-01-001	SOUKHOUMA
1-01-001	SOUL-SEARCHING
1-01-001	SOULD
1-01-001	SOULE
1-01-001	SOULFUL
1-01-001	SOULFULLY
1-01-001	SOULS'
1-01-001	SOUND-TRUCK
1-01-001	SOUNDNESS
1-01-001	SOUNDPROOF
1-01-001	SOUPHANOUVONG
1-01-001	SOURS
1-01-001	SOUSA
1-01-001	SOUTANE
1-01-001	SOUTH-*ASIAN
1-01-001	SOUTH-*EAST
1-01-001	SOUTH-CENTRAL
1-01-001	SOUTH-EASTERN
1-01-001	SOUTHBOUND
1-01-001	SOUTHERN-*REPUBLICAN
1-01-001	SOUTHERN-CENTRAL
1-01-001	SOUTHERNER'S
1-01-001	SOUTHERNISMS
1-01-001	SOUTHEY
1-01-001	SOUTHFIELD
1-01-001	SOUTHLAND
1-01-001	SOUTHS
1-01-001	SOUVENIRS
1-01-001	SOVIET'S
1-01-001	SOVIET-*WESTERN
1-01-001	SOVIETS'
1-01-001	SOVIETSKAYA
1-01-001	SOVKHOZES
1-01-001	SOWERED
1-01-001	SOWING
1-01-001	SOXHLET
1-01-001	SOY
1-01-001	SOYABURGERS
1-01-001	SPACE-TIME
1-01-001	SPACESUIT
1-01-001	SPACESUITS
1-01-001	SPACINGS
1-01-001	SPAGHETTI
1-01-001	SPAGNA
1-01-001	SPAHN'S
1-01-001	SPAHNIE
1-01-001	SPALDING
1-01-001	SPANDRELS
1-01-001	SPANGLE
1-01-001	SPANGLED
1-01-001	SPANIEL'S
1-01-001	SPANIEL-LIKE
1-01-001	SPANISH-BORN
1-01-001	SPANNING
1-01-001	SPARES
1-01-001	SPARING
1-01-001	SPARKLED
1-01-001	SPARKLES
1-01-001	SPARLING
1-01-001	SPARLING'S
1-01-001	SPARROW'S
1-01-001	SPARROW-SIZE
1-01-001	SPARTA
1-01-001	SPASMS
1-01-001	SPATIALITY
1-01-001	SPATS
1-01-001	SPATTER
1-01-001	SPAVINED
1-01-001	SPEAK-EASY
1-01-001	SPEAKERSHIP
1-01-001	SPEAKIN
1-01-001	SPEAR-THROWING
1-01-001	SPEARED
1-01-001	SPEARHEAD
1-01-001	SPEC
1-01-001	SPECIAL-INTEREST
1-01-001	SPECIALIZES
1-01-001	SPECIES-DEPENDENT
1-01-001	SPECIFICS
1-01-001	SPECIMENTALIA
1-01-001	SPECKLED
1-01-001	SPECKLES
1-01-001	SPECTATOR-TYPE
1-01-001	SPECTERS
1-01-001	SPECTOR
1-01-001	SPECTRALLY
1-01-001	SPECTRE
1-01-001	SPECTROMETRIC
1-01-001	SPECTROPHOTOMETER
1-01-001	SPECTROPHOTOMETRIC
1-01-001	SPECULAR
1-01-001	SPECULATIVELY
1-01-001	SPECULATOR
1-01-001	SPEECH-MAKING
1-01-001	SPEEDBOAT
1-01-001	SPEEDOMETER
1-01-001	SPEEDUP
1-01-001	SPEER
1-01-001	SPEGITITGNININO
1-01-001	SPEIDEL
1-01-001	SPELL-BINDING
1-01-001	SPELLBOUND
1-01-001	SPENCERIAN
1-01-001	SPENDERS
1-01-001	SPENGLERIAN
1-01-001	SPEWING
1-01-001	SPEWINGS
1-01-001	SPHERULES
1-01-001	SPHINX
1-01-001	SPHYNXES
1-01-001	SPIC
1-01-001	SPICE-LADEN
1-01-001	SPICY
1-01-001	SPIDER-LEG
1-01-001	SPIDERY
1-01-001	SPIGOTS
1-01-001	SPIKE-HAIRED
1-01-001	SPILL
1-01-001	SPILLANE'S
1-01-001	SPILLER
1-01-001	SPIN-SPIN
1-01-001	SPINLEY'S
1-01-001	SPINNABILITY
1-01-001	SPINNERET
1-01-001	SPINRAD
1-01-001	SPIRALED
1-01-001	SPIRALING
1-01-001	SPIRALIS
1-01-001	SPIRIT-GUM
1-01-001	SPIRITUALITY
1-01-001	SPIRITUALS
1-01-001	SPIRITUALS'
1-01-001	SPLASHY
1-01-001	SPLATTERED
1-01-001	SPLAYED
1-01-001	SPLEEN-CRUSHING
1-01-001	SPLENDIDE
1-01-001	SPLENETIC
1-01-001	SPLENOMEGALY
1-01-001	SPLICE
1-01-001	SPLICED
1-01-001	SPLICING
1-01-001	SPLINTERS
1-01-001	SPLINTERY
1-01-001	SPLINTING
1-01-001	SPLIT-BAMBOO
1-01-001	SPLIT-LEVEL
1-01-001	SPLOTCHES
1-01-001	SPLURGE
1-01-001	SPOFFORD
1-01-001	SPOILABLES
1-01-001	SPOILING
1-01-001	SPOILS
1-01-001	SPONGES
1-01-001	SPONGING
1-01-001	SPONSOR'S
1-01-001	SPOOF
1-01-001	SPOONED
1-01-001	SPOONFUL
1-01-001	SPORT-*KING
1-01-001	SPORTIEST
1-01-001	SPORTSMANSHIP
1-01-001	SPORTSMEN'S
1-01-001	SPOT-NEWS
1-01-001	SPOT-PROMOTED
1-01-001	SPOTLIGHTS
1-01-001	SPOTTY
1-01-001	SPOUT
1-01-001	SPOUTING
1-01-001	SPRAGUE'S
1-01-001	SPRAINS
1-01-001	SPRAY-DRIED
1-01-001	SPRAYS
1-01-001	SPREAD-EAGLED
1-01-001	SPREAD-OUT
1-01-001	SPREADER
1-01-001	SPRIG
1-01-001	SPRIGHTLY
1-01-001	SPRING-BACK
1-01-001	SPRING-JOINTS
1-01-001	SPRING-TRAINING
1-01-001	SPRINGFIELD'S
1-01-001	SPRITE
1-01-001	SPROUT
1-01-001	SPRUCED
1-01-001	SPUME
1-01-001	SPUMONI'S
1-01-001	SPURNED
1-01-001	SPURNS
1-01-001	SPURRING
1-01-001	SPUTNIKS
1-01-001	SPUTTER
1-01-001	SPUTTERED
1-01-001	SPUYTEN
1-01-001	SPYCKET
1-01-001	SQUABBLING
1-01-001	SQUADROOM
1-01-001	SQUALID
1-01-001	SQUALLS
1-01-001	SQUARE'S
1-01-001	SQUARE-BUILT
1-01-001	SQUARE-MILE
1-01-001	SQUARESVILLE
1-01-001	SQUASHED
1-01-001	SQUASHED-LOOKING
1-01-001	SQUASHING
1-01-001	SQUASHY
1-01-001	SQUAT-STYLE
1-01-001	SQUATS
1-01-001	SQUATTER'S
1-01-001	SQUAW
1-01-001	SQUAWK
1-01-001	SQUEAK
1-01-001	SQUEAKING
1-01-001	SQUEAKY
1-01-001	SQUEAL
1-01-001	SQUEALING
1-01-001	SQUEALS
1-01-001	SQUEAMISH
1-01-001	SQUEAMISHNESS
1-01-001	SQUELCHED
1-01-001	SQUINT
1-01-001	SQUIRES
1-01-001	SQUIRMS
1-01-001	SQUIRREL
1-01-001	SQUIRT
1-01-001	SQUIRTED
1-01-001	SQUIRTING
1-01-001	SSSSHOO
1-01-001	ST-STORY
1-01-001	STABAT
1-01-001	STABILITIES
1-01-001	STABILIZED
1-01-001	STABILIZERS
1-01-001	STABILIZES
1-01-001	STABILIZING-CONSERVING
1-01-001	STABLE-GARAGE
1-01-001	STABLED
1-01-001	STABLEMAN
1-01-001	STABS

Code	Word	Code	Word
1-01-001	STACCATOS	1-01-001	STEAM-GENERATION
1-01-001	STACKS	1-01-001	STEAMER
1-01-001	STAFF'S	1-01-001	STEAMILY
1-01-001	STAFFING	1-01-001	STEED
1-01-001	STAFFORD	1-01-001	STEEL-EDGED
1-01-001	STAFFORDSHIRE	1-01-001	STEELED
1-01-001	STAGE-PLAYS	1-01-001	STEELMAKER
1-01-001	STAGER	1-01-001	STEELMAKERS'
1-01-001	STAGINESS	1-01-001	STEELY
1-01-001	STAGNATION	1-01-001	STEEPEST
1-01-001	STAGS	1-01-001	STEEPLY
1-01-001	STAID	1-01-001	STEERS
1-01-001	STAIGER	1-01-001	STEEVES
1-01-001	STAINED-GLASS	1-01-001	STEFFENS
1-01-001	STAINLESS-STEEL	1-01-001	STEINBECK'S
1-01-001	STAIR-STEP	1-01-001	STEINBECKS
1-01-001	STAIR-WELL	1-01-001	STEINER
1-01-001	STAIRCASES	1-01-001	STEINERS
1-01-001	STAIRWELLS	1-01-001	STEINKERQUE
1-01-001	STALEY	1-01-001	STELLA
1-01-001	STALINGR	1-01-001	STELLAR
1-01-001	STALINIST	1-01-001	STEM/ITEM
1-01-001	STALINIST-CORRUPTED	1-01-001	STENCH
1-01-001	STALINS	1-01-001	STENDLER
1-01-001	STALLARD	1-01-001	STENNIS
1-01-001	STALLINGS	1-01-001	STENOGRAPHY
1-01-001	STAMENS	1-01-001	STENTON
1-01-001	STAMMERING	1-01-001	STEOREOTYPED
1-01-001	STAMPEDED	1-01-001	STEP-CONE
1-01-001	STANCES	1-01-001	STEPCHILD
1-01-001	STANCH	1-01-001	STEPHANE
1-01-001	STANCHEST	1-01-001	STEPHEN'S
1-01-001	STAND-UPS	1-01-001	STEPLADDERS
1-01-001	STANDARD-*TIMES	1-01-001	STEPRELATIONSHIP
1-01-001	STANDARD-WEIGHT	1-01-001	STEREOPHONIC
1-01-001	STANDARDIZING	1-01-001	STERILIZE
1-01-001	STANDETH	1-01-001	STERILIZED
1-01-001	STANDIN	1-01-001	STERIOS
1-01-001	STANDSTILL	1-01-001	STERN-FACED
1-01-001	STANFORD	1-01-001	STERN-TO
1-01-001	STANHOPE	1-01-001	STERNAL
1-01-001	STANISLAS	1-01-001	STERNO-CLEIDO
1-01-001	STANISLAS'	1-01-001	STERNS
1-01-001	STANNARD	1-01-001	STERNUM
1-01-001	STANSBERY	1-01-001	STEROID
1-01-001	STANZA-FORM	1-01-001	STEROID-INDUCED
1-01-001	STAPLE	1-01-001	STETSONS
1-01-001	STAPLES	1-01-001	STEVEDORE
1-01-001	STAPLING	1-01-001	STEVENSES'
1-01-001	STAR-*SPANGLED	1-01-001	STEWARDESSES
1-01-001	STARBOARD	1-01-001	STEWARDSHIP
1-01-001	STARES	1-01-001	STEWART'S
1-01-001	STARKEY	1-01-001	STEWED
1-01-001	STARKLY	1-01-001	STEWS
1-01-001	STARLIGHT	1-01-001	STICKMAN
1-01-001	STARLINGS	1-01-001	STICKPIN
1-01-001	STARR	1-01-001	STICKY-FINGERED
1-01-001	STARRE	1-01-001	STICLE
1-01-001	STARTIN	1-01-001	STIFF-BACKED
1-01-001	STARTLE	1-01-001	STIFFER
1-01-001	STARTLED-HORSE	1-01-001	STIFFNESS
1-01-001	STARTUPS	1-01-001	STIFFS
1-01-001	STARVE	1-01-001	STIGMA
1-01-001	STASHED	1-01-001	STIGMATA
1-01-001	STATE'	1-01-001	STILES
1-01-001	STATE'S-RESPONSIBILITY	1-01-001	STILETTO
1-01-001	STATE-*LOCAL	1-01-001	STILL-BUILDING
1-01-001	STATE-ADMINISTERED	1-01-001	STILL-DARK
1-01-001	STATE-LAW	1-01-001	STILLBIRTHS
1-01-001	STATE-SPONSORED	1-01-001	STILLWELL
1-01-001	STATE-SUPPORTED	1-01-001	STIMSON
1-01-001	STATELESS	1-01-001	STIMULANT
1-01-001	STATES-*YUGOSLAV	1-01-001	STIMULANTS
1-01-001	STATESMANLIKE	1-01-001	STIMULATIONS
1-01-001	STATIONMASTER	1-01-001	STIMULATORY
1-01-001	STATIONS'	1-01-001	STINGY
1-01-001	STATISTICIANS	1-01-001	STINKPOTTERS
1-01-001	STATISTIQUE	1-01-001	STINKY
1-01-001	STATOR	1-01-001	STIPULATION
1-01-001	STATU	1-01-001	STIRRIN
1-01-001	STATUETTE	1-01-001	STIRRINGLY
1-01-001	STATUTO	1-01-001	STIRRINGS
1-01-001	STAUNTON	1-01-001	STIRRUP
1-01-001	STAVED	1-01-001	STIRRUP-GUARD
1-01-001	STAVROPOULOS'	1-01-001	STIRUPS
1-01-001	STEADFASTLY	1-01-001	STITCHED
1-01-001	STEADINESS	1-01-001	STOBER'S
1-01-001	STEADY-STATE	1-01-001	STOCHASTIC
1-01-001	STEALER	1-01-001	STOCK'S
1-01-001	STEALIN	1-01-001	STOCK-MARKET
1-01-001	STEALS	1-01-001	STOCKBROKER
1-01-001	STEALTHILY	1-01-001	STOCKGROWERS'
1-01-001	STEAM-BATHS	1-01-001	STOCKHAUSEN
		1-01-001	STOCKING
		1-01-001	STOCKPILING

Code	Word	Code	Word
1-01-001	STOCKYNGES	1-01-001	STRIDING
1-01-001	STODGY	1-01-001	STRIKEBREAKERS
1-01-001	STOIC-PATRISTIC	1-01-001	STRINDBERG
1-01-001	STOICS	1-01-001	STRINDBERG'S
1-01-001	STOKED	1-01-001	STRINGED
1-01-001	STOKER	1-01-001	STRINGENTLY
1-01-001	STOLID	1-01-001	STRINGING
1-01-001	STOLL	1-01-001	STRIPTEASE
1-01-001	STOLZENBACH	1-01-001	STRITCH
1-01-001	STOMACH-BELLY	1-01-001	STRIVEN
1-01-001	STOMACK	1-01-001	STRONG-MADE
1-01-001	STOMPING	1-01-001	STRONGHEART
1-01-001	STONE-BLIND	1-01-001	STRONGROOMS
1-01-001	STONE-GRAY	1-01-001	STROPHE
1-01-001	STONE-STILL	1-01-001	STROPPED
1-01-001	STONEHENGE	1-01-001	STROPPING
1-01-001	STONESTOWN	1-01-001	STRUCTURING
1-01-001	STONILY	1-01-001	STRUKTURBERICHT
1-01-001	STONY-METEORITE	1-01-001	STRUMMING
1-01-001	STOOGES	1-01-001	STRUTTING
1-01-001	STOOOOOMP	1-01-001	STUART-FAMILY
1-01-001	STOP-OVERS	1-01-001	STUBBED
1-01-001	STOPOVER	1-01-001	STUBBS
1-01-001	STOPOVERS	1-01-001	STUDEBAKER
1-01-001	STOPPAGE	1-01-001	STUDENT-DIRECTED
1-01-001	STOPPAGES	1-01-001	STUDENT-LOAN
1-01-001	STOPPING-POINT	1-01-001	STUDENT-PHYSICISTS
1-01-001	STORE-FRONT	1-01-001	STUDIOUS
1-01-001	STORED-UP	1-01-001	STULTIFYING
1-01-001	STOREFRONT	1-01-001	STUMBLE
1-01-001	STOREHOUSES	1-01-001	STUMBLES
1-01-001	STOREKEEPERS	1-01-001	STUMBLING-BLOCK
1-01-001	STORERIA	1-01-001	STUMPAGE
1-01-001	STOREROOM	1-01-001	STUMPED
1-01-001	STORIED	1-01-001	STUMPING
1-01-001	STORMBOUND	1-01-001	STUMPY
1-01-001	STORMING	1-01-001	STUNK
1-01-001	STORY-BOOK	1-01-001	STUNNINGLY
1-01-001	STORYLINES	1-01-001	STUNT
1-01-001	STORYTELLER'S	1-01-001	STUPEFYING
1-01-001	STOUT'S	1-01-001	STUPIDEST
1-01-001	STOUTLY	1-01-001	STUPIDITIES
1-01-001	STOWE	1-01-001	STURBRIDGE
1-01-001	STOWE'S	1-01-001	STURGEON
1-01-001	STRAFACI	1-01-001	STURLEY'S
1-01-001	STRAFING	1-01-001	STUTTGART
1-01-001	STRAGGLED	1-01-001	STYLEMARK
1-01-001	STRAIGHT-**J*A	1-01-001	STYLING
1-01-001	STRAIGHT-*ARM	1-01-001	STYLISH
1-01-001	STRAIGHT-ARMED	1-01-001	STYLISTIC
1-01-001	STRAIGHT-BACKED	1-01-001	STYMIED
1-01-001	STRAIGHT-LINE	1-01-001	STYRENE'S
1-01-001	STRAIGHT-OUT	1-01-001	STYRENES
1-01-001	STRAIGHTENS	1-01-001	STYRYL-LITHIUM
1-01-001	STRAIGHTWAY	1-01-001	SUABILITY
1-01-001	STRAININ	1-01-001	SUABLE
1-01-001	STRAIT-LACED	1-01-001	SUAVITY
1-01-001	STRAM'S	1-01-001	SUB-*CHRISTIAN
1-01-001	STRAMONIUM	1-01-001	SUB-ASSEMBLY
1-01-001	STRANAHAN	1-01-001	SUB-CHIEFDOM
1-01-001	STRANDING	1-01-001	SUB-CHIEFS
1-01-001	STRANG	1-01-001	SUB-CONSCIOUS-LEVEL
1-01-001	STRANGE-SOUNDING	1-01-001	SUB-FREEZING
1-01-001	STRANGERS'	1-01-001	SUB-GROUP
1-01-001	STRANGEST	1-01-001	SUB-HUMAN
1-01-001	STRANGULATION	1-01-001	SUB-STATION
1-01-001	STRAPPED	1-01-001	SUB-SURFACE
1-01-001	STRASNY	1-01-001	SUB-ZERO
1-01-001	STRATAGEMS	1-01-001	SUBALTERN
1-01-001	STRATEGEM	1-01-001	SUBATOMIC
1-01-001	STRATFORD'S	1-01-001	SUBBING
1-01-001	STRATFORDE	1-01-001	SUBCONTINENT
1-01-001	STRATIFY	1-01-001	SUBCONTRACTING
1-01-001	STRATOSPHERE	1-01-001	SUBDIVISIONS
1-01-001	STRAVINSKY'S	1-01-001	SUBDUES
1-01-001	STRAW-COLORED	1-01-001	SUBDUING
1-01-001	STRAW-HAT	1-01-001	SUBFIGURES
1-01-001	STRAYED	1-01-001	SUBHUMANITY
1-01-001	STREAM'S	1-01-001	SUBJECT'S
1-01-001	STREAM-OF-CONSCIOUSNESS	1-01-001	SUBJECTIVISTS
1-01-001	STREAMER	1-01-001	SUBJECTIVITY
1-01-001	STREAMLINER	1-01-001	SUBJECTS'
1-01-001	STREAMSIDE	1-01-001	SUBJUGATE
1-01-001	STREET'S	1-01-001	SUBLEASE
1-01-001	STREETERS	1-01-001	SUBLIMED
1-01-001	STREETLIGHT	1-01-001	SUBLITERARY
1-01-001	STRENGTHENED	1-01-001	SUBLUNARY
1-01-001	STRENGTH/DENSITY	1-01-001	SUBMARINE-BALL
1-01-001	STREPTOCOCCUS	1-01-001	SUBMARINERS
1-01-001	STRESS-TEMPERATURE	1-01-001	SUBMERGING
1-01-001	STRETCHER	1-01-001	SUBMISSIONS
1-01-001	STRICKLAND	1-01-001	SUBNORMAL
1-01-001	STRICTURES	1-01-001	SUBPARAGRAPH
		1-01-001	SUBPARTS

1-01-001 SUBPENAED	1-01-001 SUMMITRY	1-01-001 SURREALISM	1-01-001 SYMBOLICAL
1-01-001 SUBPOENA	1-01-001 SUMMONS	1-01-001 SURREALIST	1-01-001 SYMBOLISTS
1-01-001 SUBROGATION	1-01-001 SUN'LL	1-01-001 SURREPTITIOUS	1-01-001 SYMES'S
1-01-001 SUBROUTINE	1-01-001 SUN-*TIMES	1-01-001 SURTOUT	1-01-001 SYMMETRICALLY
1-01-001 SUBROUTINES	1-01-001 SUN-BAKED	1-01-001 SURVIVABILITY	1-01-001 SYMONDS
1-01-001 SUBSCRIBE	1-01-001 SUN-BLEACHED	1-01-001 SURVIVALIST	1-01-001 SYMPATHIQUE
1-01-001 SUBSCRIPTS	1-01-001 SUN-BROWNED	1-01-001 SURVIVALS	1-01-001 SYMPATHIZED
1-01-001 SUBSEDIES	1-01-001 SUN-BURNED	1-01-001 SURVIVES	1-01-001 SYMPATHIZING
1-01-001 SUBSERVIENCE	1-01-001 SUN-INFLAMED	1-01-001 SURVIVOR	1-01-001 SYMPHONY'S
1-01-001 SUBSIST	1-01-001 SUN-SUIT	1-01-001 SURVIVORS'	1-01-001 SYNAPSES
1-01-001 SUBSISTENT	1-01-001 SUN-TAN	1-01-001 SUS	1-01-001 SYNCE
1-01-001 SUBSOIL	1-01-001 SUN-TANNED	1-01-001 SUSIE'S	1-01-001 SYNCHRONISM
1-01-001 SUBSPACES	1-01-001 SUN-WARMED	1-01-001 SUSPENDERS	1-01-001 SYNCHRONIZE
1-01-001 SUBSTANTIATES	1-01-001 SUNAY	1-01-001 SUSTAINS	1-01-001 SYNDIC
1-01-001 SUBSTANTIATION	1-01-001 SUNBAKED	1-01-001 SUT	1-01-001 SYNDICATE'S
1-01-001 SUBSTANTIVELY	1-01-001 SUNBONNET	1-01-001 SUTPEN	1-01-001 SYNDICATES
1-01-001 SUBSTANTIVELY	1-01-001 SUNBURNT	1-01-001 SUZANNE	1-01-001 SYNDICATION
1-01-001 SUBSTERILIZATIO N	1-01-001 SUNDAY-SCHOOL	1-01-001 SUZERAINTY	1-01-001 SYNERGISM
1-01-001 SUBSTITUTIONARY	1-01-001 SUNDER	1-01-001 SUZUKI	1-01-001 SYNERGISTIC
1-01-001 SUBSTITUTIONS	1-01-001 SUNDIALS	1-01-001 SVELTE	1-01-001 SYNOD
1-01-001 SUBSTRATUM	1-01-001 SUNG-*SHAN	1-01-001 SVENSKARNA	1-01-001 SYNONYMY
1-01-001 SUBSTRUCTURE	1-01-001 SUNMAN	1-01-001 SVEVO	1-01-001 SYNTACTIC
1-01-001 SUBSUMED	1-01-001 SUNNING	1-01-001 SW**-FT	1-01-001 SYNTACTICAL
1-01-001 SUBSURFACE	1-01-001 SUNSHIELD	1-01-001 SWABBED	1-01-001 SYNTACTICALLY
1-01-001 SUBTENDED	1-01-001 SUNSHINY	1-01-001 SWAGGERING	1-01-001 SYNTHESISED
1-01-001 SUBTENDS	1-01-001 SUNSPOT	1-01-001 SWAHILI	1-01-001 SYNTHESIZE
1-01-001 SUBTERFUGES	1-01-001 SUNT	1-01-001 SWALLOW-*BARN	1-01-001 SYNTHESIZES
1-01-001 SUBTLER	1-01-001 SUNTAN	1-01-001 SWAMI	1-01-001 SYNTHESIZINE
1-01-001 SUBTLETY	1-01-001 SUP	1-01-001 SWAMPED	1-01-001 SYNTHETICS
1-01-001 SUBTYPES	1-01-001 SUPER-*HERCULEA N	1-01-001 SWAMPING	1-01-001 SYRACUSE
1-01-001 SUBURBANITES		1-01-001 SWAMPY	1-01-001 SYRIAN
1-01-001 SUBURBANIZED	1-01-001 SUPER-*PROTEIN	1-01-001 SWANK	1-01-001 SYRIANS
1-01-001 SUBURBIA	1-01-001 SUPER-CHARGED	1-01-001 SWANKY	1-01-001 SYRINGA
1-01-001 SUBVERSION	1-01-001 SUPER-CITY	1-01-001 SWANLIKE	1-01-001 SYRINGE
1-01-001 SUBVERSIVES	1-01-001 SUPER-EMPIRICAL	1-01-001 SWANS	1-01-001 SYSTEMATICALLY- SIMPLE
1-01-001 SUBVERTED	1-01-001 SUPER-EXPERIMEN T	1-01-001 SWARMS	
1-01-001 SUBVERTING		1-01-001 SWART	1-01-001 SYSTEMATIZATION
1-01-001 SUBWAYS	1-01-001 SUPER-HIGH	1-01-001 SWARTZ	1-01-001 SYSTEME
1-01-001 SUCCESS-ORIENTE D	1-01-001 SUPER-IMPOSED	1-01-001 SWASTIKA	1-01-001 SYSTEMIZATION
1-01-001 SUCCESSORS-IN-S PIRIT	1-01-001 SUPER-SECRET	1-01-001 SWATH	1-01-001 SZELENYI
	1-01-001 SUPERCEDED	1-01-001 SWATHED	1-01-001 T**.*B
1-01-001 SUCCESSORSHIP	1-01-001 SUPERCILIOUS	1-01-001 SWATHINGS	1-01-001 T'AI-*SHAN
1-01-001 SUCCINCT	1-01-001 SUPERCRITICAL	1-01-001 SWAY-BACKED	1-01-001 T'GETHUH
1-01-001 SUCCOR	1-01-001 SUPEREGO	1-01-001 SWEARING-IN	1-01-001 T'HI-IM
1-01-001 SUCCUMB	1-01-001 SUPERFICIALITY	1-01-001 SWEARINGE	1-01-001 T'IEN
1-01-001 SUCCUMBING	1-01-001 SUPERHIGHWAYS	1-01-001 SWEAT-SATURATED	1-01-001 T'JAWN
1-01-001 SUCESS	1-01-001 SUPERIEURE	1-01-001 SWEAT-SOAKED	1-01-001 T'LAH
1-01-001 SUCKER-ROLLING	1-01-001 SUPERIMPOSES	1-01-001 SWEAT-SUITS	1-01-001 T'S
1-01-001 SUCKERS	1-01-001 SUPERIMPOSING	1-01-001 SWEATBAND	1-01-001 T**U
1-01-001 SUCTION	1-01-001 SUPERINTEND	1-01-001 SWEATED	1-01-001 TAB
1-01-001 SUDANESE	1-01-001 SUPERLATIVES	1-01-001 SWEATHRUNA	1-01-001 TAB-LIFTER
1-01-001 SUDDEN-END	1-01-001 SUPERLUNARY	1-01-001 SWEAZEY	1-01-001 TABAC
1-01-001 SUDIER	1-01-001 SUPERMACHINE	1-01-001 SWEEPINGLY	1-01-001 TABB
1-01-001 SUDSING	1-01-001 SUPERMARKET	1-01-001 SWEEPINGS	1-01-001 TABELLEN
1-01-001 SUES	1-01-001 SUPERMATIC	1-01-001 SWEET-CLOVER	1-01-001 TABERNACLE
1-01-001 SUEY	1-01-001 SUPERNATANT	1-01-001 SWEET-FACED	1-01-001 TABERNACLES
1-01-001 SUFFERERS	1-01-001 SUPERNORMAL	1-01-001 SWEET-SHRUB	1-01-001 TABIT
1-01-001 SUFFICIENCY	1-01-001 SUPERPOSED	1-01-001 SWEET-SOUNDING	1-01-001 TABLE'S
1-01-001 SUFFIX	1-01-001 SUPERPOSITION	1-01-001 SWEET-THROATED	1-01-001 TABLE-TENNIS
1-01-001 SUFFIXES	1-01-001 SUPERSENSITIVE	1-01-001 SWEET-TONGUED	1-01-001 TABLE-TOP
1-01-001 SUFFOCATED	1-01-001 SUPERSTITIOUS	1-01-001 SWEETHEART-SECR ETARY	1-01-001 TABLEAU
1-01-001 SUFFOCATION	1-01-001 SUPERSTRUCTURE		1-01-001 TABLECLOTHS
1-01-001 SUFFRAGETTES	1-01-001 SUPERVENED	1-01-001 SWEETHEARTS	1-01-001 TABLELAND
1-01-001 SUFFUSE	1-01-001 SUPERVISORS'	1-01-001 SWEETISH	1-01-001 TABLESPOONFULS
1-01-001 SUGARED	1-01-001 SUPINE	1-01-001 SWEETPEAS	1-01-001 TABLETS
1-01-001 SUGGS	1-01-001 SUPINELY	1-01-001 SWELTERING	1-01-001 TABLOIDS
1-01-001 SUHTHUHN	1-01-001 SUPPERS	1-01-001 SWIFT-FOOTED	1-01-001 TABOOS
1-01-001 SUING	1-01-001 SUPPLANTED	1-01-001 SWIFT-STRIDING	1-01-001 TABULATE
1-01-001 SUITABILITY	1-01-001 SUPPLANTING	1-01-001 SWIFTEST	1-01-001 TACITUS
1-01-001 SUITABLY-LOADED	1-01-001 SUPPLENESS	1-01-001 SWIFTNESS	1-01-001 TACKLES
1-01-001 SUITE'S	1-01-001 SUPPLIERS	1-01-001 SWIMMERS'	1-01-001 TACTICALLY
1-01-001 SUITOR	1-01-001 SUPPOSES	1-01-001 SWIMSUIT	1-01-001 TACTLESSNESS
1-01-001 SUKARNO'S	1-01-001 SUPRA-*EXPRESSI ONISM	1-01-001 SWINDLED	1-01-001 TACTUALLY
1-01-001 SUKUMA		1-01-001 SWINDLING	1-01-001 TADPOLES
1-01-001 SULAMITE	1-01-001 SUPRA-PERSONAL	1-01-001 SWINGY	1-01-001 TAFFY
1-01-001 SULAMITH	1-01-001 SUPRANATIONAL	1-01-001 SWIPED	1-01-001 TAFFYCOLORED
1-01-001 SULCER	1-01-001 SUPRANATIONALIS M	1-01-001 SWIPING	1-01-001 TAFT
1-01-001 SULFAQUINOXALIN E		1-01-001 SWISS-BORN	1-01-001 TAGGING
	1-01-001 SURCEASE	1-01-001 SWITCH-HITTER	1-01-001 TAGS
1-01-001 SULFIDE	1-01-001 SURCLIFFE	1-01-001 SWITCHBLADE	1-01-001 TAGUA
1-01-001 SULFUR	1-01-001 SURCLIFFES'	1-01-001 SWITCHBOARD	1-01-001 TAHSE
1-01-001 SULKILY	1-01-001 SURE-ENOUGH	1-01-001 SWITZER	1-01-001 TAHSE'S
1-01-001 SULKING	1-01-001 SURF	1-01-001 SWIVELS	1-01-001 TAI
1-01-001 SULKS	1-01-001 SURFACE-ANALYZE R	1-01-001 SWOLLEN-LOOKING	1-01-001 TAILBACK
1-01-001 SULKY'S		1-01-001 SWORDE	1-01-001 TAILIN'S
1-01-001 SULLYING	1-01-001 SURFACE-DECLARI NG	1-01-001 SWUM	1-01-001 TAILOR-MAKE
1-01-001 SULPHURED		1-01-001 SYBERT	1-01-001 TAIN'T
1-01-001 SULTANE	1-01-001 SURFACED	1-01-001 SYCOPHANTIC	1-01-001 TAINT
1-01-001 SULTRY	1-01-001 SURFACENESS	1-01-001 SYCOPHANTICALLY	1-01-001 TAINTED
1-01-001 SUMAC	1-01-001 SURFACTANT	1-01-001 SYCOPHANTS	1-01-001 TAIPEI
1-01-001 SUMATRA	1-01-001 SURFEIT	1-01-001 SYLLABIFICATION	1-01-001 TAKEING
1-01-001 SUMMARIZATION	1-01-001 SURFEITED	1-01-001 SYLLABLE	1-01-001 TAKEOFF
1-01-001 SUMMARIZES	1-01-001 SURGEONS	1-01-001 SYLPHIDE	1-01-001 TAKSIM
1-01-001 SUMMER-WINTER	1-01-001 SURGICAL	1-01-001 SYLVAN	1-01-001 TALBOTT'S
1-01-001 SUMMERSPACE	1-01-001 SURMISE	1-01-001 SYLVIE	1-01-001 TALISMANIC
1-01-001 SUMMING	1-01-001 SURMOUNT	1-01-001 SYMBOLIC-SOUNDI NG	1-01-001 TALK-ABOUTIVENE SS
	1-01-001 SURPASS		

Rank	Word	Rank	Word	Rank	Word	Rank	Word
1-01-001	TALKER	1-01-001	TEACHER-EMPLOYEE	1-01-001	TENTING	1-01-001	THELMA'S
1-01-001	TALKIN	1-01-001	TEACHERS'	1-01-001	TENUOUSLY	1-01-001	THEMATIC
1-01-001	TALKY	1-01-001	TEAGARDEN	1-01-001	TEPEES	1-01-001	THEOCRACY
1-01-001	TALL-GROWING	1-01-001	TEAHOUSES	1-01-001	TEPID	1-01-001	THEODOR
1-01-001	TALL-MASTED	1-01-001	TEAKETTLE	1-01-001	TER	1-01-001	THEODOSIAN
1-01-001	TALL-TALE	1-01-001	TEAKWOOD	1-01-001	TER-*ARUTUNIAN	1-01-001	THEODOSIUS
1-01-001	TALLAHASSEE	1-01-001	TEAM-MATE	1-01-001	TER-*STEPANOVA	1-01-001	THEOLOGIAN-PHILOSOPHERS
1-01-001	TALLAHOOSA	1-01-001	TEAMING	1-01-001	TERATOLOGIES		
1-01-001	TALLCHIEF	1-01-001	TEAMMATE'S	1-01-001	TERG-*O-*TOMETER	1-01-001	THEOLOGY'S
1-01-001	TALLEYRAND	1-01-001	TEAMMATES'			1-01-001	THEON'S
1-01-001	TALLOW	1-01-001	TEAMS'	1-01-001	TERM-END	1-01-001	THEORETICIANS
1-01-001	TALONS	1-01-001	TEAMSTER	1-01-001	TERMINATES	1-01-001	THEORITICIANS
1-01-001	TAM-O'-SHANTER	1-01-001	TEAMWORK	1-01-001	TERMINATING	1-01-001	THEORIZING
1-01-001	TAMALE	1-01-001	TEAR-FILLED	1-01-001	TERMING	1-01-001	THERAPIES
1-01-001	TAMING	1-01-001	TEAR-SOAKED	1-01-001	TERMINIELLO	1-01-001	THEREABOUTS
1-01-001	TAMIRIS-*DANIEL	1-01-001	TEARDROP	1-01-001	TERRA	1-01-001	THEREBY/*LIKE
1-01-001	TAMP	1-01-001	TEARLE	1-01-001	TERRA-COTTA-COLORED	1-01-001	THEREFOR
1-01-001	TAMPER	1-01-001	TEAS			1-01-001	THEREFORES
1-01-001	TANDEM	1-01-001	TEASPOONFULS	1-01-001	TERRAINS	1-01-001	THEREON
1-01-001	TANEY'S	1-01-001	TEATRO	1-01-001	TERRAL	1-01-001	THEREUNDER
1-01-001	TANGANIKA	1-01-001	TECH'S	1-01-001	TERRAM	1-01-001	THERMALLY
1-01-001	TANGENTIAL	1-01-001	TECHNICAL-LADDER	1-01-001	TERRAMYCIN	1-01-001	THERMISTOR
1-01-001	TANGERE	1-01-001	TECHNOLOGICALLY	1-01-001	TERRESTIAL	1-01-001	THERMOFORMED
1-01-001	TANGIBLY	1-01-001	TECUM	1-01-001	TERRESTRIAL-EXPLOSION	1-01-001	THERMOGRAVIMETRIC
1-01-001	TANGOS	1-01-001	TEDIUM				
1-01-001	TANGY	1-01-001	TEEMING	1-01-001	TERRIERS	1-01-001	THERMOMETRIC
1-01-001	TANIN	1-01-001	TEEMS	1-01-001	TERRITOIRE	1-01-001	THERMOPILE
1-01-001	TANKER	1-01-001	TEEN-AGERS'	1-01-001	TERROR-STRICKEN	1-01-001	THERMOPLASTIC
1-01-001	TANNENBAUM	1-01-001	TEENSY	1-01-001	TERRORISTS	1-01-001	THERMOPYLAE
1-01-001	TANNIN	1-01-001	TEETHING	1-01-001	TERRORIZING	1-01-001	THERMOS
1-01-001	TANNY	1-01-001	TEKTITE	1-01-001	TERROURS	1-01-001	THERMOSTATED
1-01-001	TANSY	1-01-001	TEL	1-01-001	TERTIAN	1-01-001	THERMOSTATICS
1-01-001	TANTALIZINGLY	1-01-001	TELEFUNKEN	1-01-001	TERTIARY	1-01-001	THERMOSTATS
1-01-001	TAOS	1-01-001	TELEGRAPHER'S	1-01-001	TERTRE	1-01-001	THESAURUS
1-01-001	TAPDANCE	1-01-001	TELEGRAPHIE	1-01-001	TESS	1-01-001	THESES
1-01-001	TAPED	1-01-001	TELEGRAPHING	1-01-001	TEST-LIKE	1-01-001	THESPIANS
1-01-001	TAPIS	1-01-001	TELEGRAPHY	1-01-001	TEST-RUN	1-01-001	THESTAGE
1-01-001	TAPLEY	1-01-001	TELEMANN	1-01-001	TESTICULAR	1-01-001	THET'S
1-01-001	TAPS	1-01-001	TELEOLOGICAL	1-01-001	TESTILY	1-01-001	THEVENOW
1-01-001	TAR-SOAKED	1-01-001	TELEOLOGY	1-01-001	TESTIMONIALS	1-01-001	THEWORK
1-01-001	TARA	1-01-001	TELEPATHICALLY	1-01-001	TESTINGS	1-01-001	THIAMIN
1-01-001	TARADAY	1-01-001	TELEPHONE-BOOTH	1-01-001	TETANUS	1-01-001	THICK-SKULLED
1-01-001	TARANTARA	1-01-001	TELEPROMPTER	1-01-001	TETER	1-01-001	THICKEN
1-01-001	TARAS-*TCHAIKOVSKY	1-01-001	TELESCOPES	1-01-001	TETHERS	1-01-001	THICKENERS
1-01-001	TARDILY	1-01-001	TELESCOPIC	1-01-001	TETRAGONAL	1-01-001	THICKENING
1-01-001	TARDINESS	1-01-001	TELESCOPING	1-01-001	TETRAHALIDES	1-01-001	THICKENS
1-01-001	TARDY	1-01-001	TELETYPES	1-01-001	TETRAMERON	1-01-001	THICKEST
1-01-001	TAREYTOWN	1-01-001	TELEVISION-*ELECTRONICS	1-01-001	TETRASODIUM	1-01-001	THICKET
1-01-001	TARGET'S	1-01-001	TELEVISON-RECORD	1-01-001	TEUTONIC	1-01-001	THIEVIN
1-01-001	TARGET-HUNTING			1-01-001	TEWFIK	1-01-001	THIGH-BONE
1-01-001	TARGET-LANGUAGE	1-01-001	TELLI	1-01-001	TEXT-LOOKUP	1-01-001	THIIHNG
1-01-001	TARHEELIA	1-01-001	TELOMERIC	1-01-001	TEXT-ORDERED	1-01-001	THILLS
1-01-001	TARIFF-FREE	1-01-001	TEMERITY	1-01-001	TEXTBOOKS	1-01-001	THIMBLE
1-01-001	TARKINGTON	1-01-001	TEMPEH	1-01-001	TEXTILE'S	1-01-001	THIMBLE-SIZED
1-01-001	TARPAPERED	1-01-001	TEMPERA	1-01-001	TEXTILE-EXPORTING	1-01-001	THIN-SOLED
1-01-001	TARPAULIN	1-01-001	TEMPERANCE	1-01-001	TEXTILE-IMPORTING	1-01-001	THINE
1-01-001	TARPAULINS	1-01-001	TEMPERATELY			1-01-001	THINNED
1-01-001	TARPON	1-01-001	TEMPERED	1-01-001	TEXTRON	1-01-001	THINNESS
1-01-001	TARRANT	1-01-001	TEMPORALLY	1-01-001	TH	1-01-001	THIOCYANATE-PERCHLORATE-FLUOROBORIDE
1-01-001	TARRED	1-01-001	TEMPORE	1-01-001	THADDEUS		
1-01-001	TARRY	1-01-001	TEMPORIZE	1-01-001	THAI	1-01-001	THIOT
1-01-001	TARTAR	1-01-001	TEMPTER	1-01-001	THAKHEK	1-01-001	THIRD-
1-01-001	TARTARUGHE	1-01-001	TEMPTINGLY	1-01-001	THALBERGS	1-01-001	THIRD-DIMENSIONALITY
1-01-001	TARTLY	1-01-001	TEMPTS	1-01-001	THAMNOPHIS		
1-01-001	TARUFFI	1-01-001	TEN-BY-TEN-MILE	1-01-001	THANK-*HEAVEN-*WE'RE-NOT-*INVOLVED	1-01-001	THIRD-INNING
1-01-001	TASKMASTER	1-01-001	TEN-CONCERT			1-01-001	THIRD-RATE
1-01-001	TASSELS	1-01-001	TEN-DAY	1-01-001	THANKLESS	1-01-001	THIRD-SHIFT
1-01-001	TASSO	1-01-001	TEN-FIFTY-FIVE	1-01-001	THAT'D	1-01-001	THIRD-STORY
1-01-001	TASTELESS	1-01-001	TEN-HOUR	1-01-001	THAT-A-WAY	1-01-001	THIRDLY
1-01-001	TASTI-*FREEZE	1-01-001	TEN-MINUTE	1-01-001	THATCHED-ROOF	1-01-001	THIRSTED
1-01-001	TAT	1-01-001	TEN-MONTH	1-01-001	THATCHES	1-01-001	THIRTEENTH-CENTURY
1-01-001	TATIAN	1-01-001	TEN-THOUSAND-DOLLAR	1-01-001	THATT		
1-01-001	TATLER			1-01-001	THAXTERS	1-01-001	THIRTIETH
1-01-001	TATRAS	1-01-001	TEN-TWELVE	1-01-001	THAY	1-01-001	THIRTY-CALIBER
1-01-001	TATTLE-TALE	1-01-001	TEN-YEAR-OLD	1-01-001	THAYER'S	1-01-001	THIRTY-EIGHT
1-01-001	TATTOOED	1-01-001	TENACIOUS	1-01-001	THEA	1-01-001	THIRTY-FOOT
1-01-001	TAU	1-01-001	TENACIOUSLY	1-01-001	THEAF	1-01-001	THIRTY-MILE
1-01-001	TAUI	1-01-001	TENDA	1-01-001	THEARE	1-01-001	THIRTY-NINTH
1-01-001	TAUNTING	1-01-001	TENDERED	1-01-001	THEASE	1-01-001	THIRTY-SEVEN
1-01-001	TAUNTINGLY	1-01-001	TENDERLOIN	1-01-001	THEATER-GOING	1-01-001	THIRTY-SIXTH
1-01-001	TAURIDA	1-01-001	TENEBROUS	1-01-001	THEATERGOER	1-01-001	THIRTY-YEAR
1-01-001	TAUT-NERVED	1-01-001	TENFOLD	1-01-001	THEATERGOERS	1-01-001	THIS'LL
1-01-001	TAWNEY	1-01-001	TENN	1-01-001	THEATERGOING	1-01-001	THITHER
1-01-001	TAX-AIDED	1-01-001	TENNESSEE'S	1-01-001	THEATRE-BY-THE-*SEA	1-01-001	THO
1-01-001	TAX-AVOIDANCE	1-01-001	TENORS			1-01-001	THOM'S
1-01-001	TAX-FREEDOM	1-01-001	TENS	1-01-001	THEATRE-BY-THE-SEA	1-01-001	THONG
1-01-001	TAX-PAYING	1-01-001	TENSED			1-01-001	THOREAU
1-01-001	TAXI-WAYS	1-01-001	TENSES	1-01-001	THEATREGOER	1-01-001	THOREAU'S
1-01-001	TAXICAB	1-01-001	TENSING	1-01-001	THEATRES	1-01-001	THORIATED
1-01-001	TAXIED	1-01-001	TENSIONAL	1-01-001	THEES	1-01-001	THORNS
1-01-001	TAXIING	1-01-001	TENSIONLESS	1-01-001	THEFIN	1-01-001	THORNTON
1-01-001	TAXPAYING	1-01-001	TENSPOT	1-01-001	THEI	1-01-001	THOROUGHBRED
1-01-001	TAYLORS	1-01-001	TENTACLE	1-01-001	THEIR'S	1-01-001	THOROUGHFARES
1-01-001	TCHALO	1-01-001	TENTHS	1-01-001	THEISTIC	1-01-001	THOROUGHNESS
1-01-001	TEA-DRINKING					1-01-001	THORSTEIN
1-01-001	TEA-LEAF					1-01-001	THOUGHTFULNESS

1-01-001 THOUGHTLESSLY	1-01-001 TICKING	1-01-001 TODAY'LL	1-01-001 TORTOISES
1-01-001 THOUSAND-FOLD	1-01-001 TICKLEBRUSH	1-01-001 TODDLERS	1-01-001 TOSCA
1-01-001 THOUSAND-LEGGED	1-01-001 TIDAL	1-01-001 TODE	1-01-001 TOSCANINI'S
1-01-001 THOUSANDTHS	1-01-001 TIDBIT	1-01-001 TODMAN'S	1-01-001 TOTALISTIC
1-01-001 THOUT	1-01-001 TIDELANDS	1-01-001 TOE-TIPS	1-01-001 TOTE
1-01-001 THRASH	1-01-001 TIDIED	1-01-001 TOFFEE	1-01-001 TOTEMIC
1-01-001 THRE	1-01-001 TIDINESS	1-01-001 TOFFENETTI'S	1-01-001 TOTHE
1-01-001 THREATENINGLY	1-01-001 TIDY	1-01-001 TOFU	1-01-001 TOTO
1-01-001 THREE-AXIS	1-01-001 TIDYING	1-01-001 TOGETHERNESS	1-01-001 TOTTED
1-01-001 THREE-BEDROOM	1-01-001 TIE-IN	1-01-001 TOGS	1-01-001 TOTTERING
1-01-001 THREE-BODY	1-01-001 TIECK	1-01-001 TOIL	1-01-001 TOUCHDOWNS
1-01-001 THREE-BUILDING	1-01-001 TIEFES	1-01-001 TOILED	1-01-001 TOUCHSTONE
1-01-001 THREE-DICE	1-01-001 TIEKEN	1-01-001 TOILSOME	1-01-001 TOUCHSTONES
1-01-001 THREE-DIMENTION	1-01-001 TIERED	1-01-001 TOJOS	1-01-001 TOUCHY
AL	1-01-001 TIFT	1-01-001 TOKENISH	1-01-001 TOUGAS
1-01-001 THREE-FAMILY	1-01-001 TIGER'S	1-01-001 TOLAND	1-01-001 TOUGH-LOOKING
1-01-001 THREE-FOOT	1-01-001 TIGERS	1-01-001 TOLEK	1-01-001 TOUJOURS
1-01-001 THREE-FRONT	1-01-001 TIGHT-TURN	1-01-001 TOLERATING	1-01-001 TOULOUSE
1-01-001 THREE-HUNDRED-F	1-01-001 TIGHTER	1-01-001 TOLERATION	1-01-001 TOULOUSE-*LAUTR
OOT	1-01-001 TIGHTEST-FITTIN	1-01-001 TOLL-RATE	EC
1-01-001 THREE-INCH	G	1-01-001 TOLLED	1-01-001 TOURISTS'
1-01-001 THREE-INNING	1-01-001 TIGRESS	1-01-001 TOLLGATE	1-01-001 TOUT
1-01-001 THREE-JUDGE	1-01-001 TIGRIS	1-01-001 TOLLHOUSE	1-01-001 TOW
1-01-001 THREE-MASTED	1-01-001 TIJUANA	1-01-001 TOLSTOY	1-01-001 TOWARDES
1-01-001 THREE-MEN-AND-A	1-01-001 TIKOPIA	1-01-001 TOLSTOY'S	1-01-001 TOWBOATS
-HELPER	1-01-001 TILLED	1-01-001 TOLUBEYEV	1-01-001 TOWED
1-01-001 THREE-NIGHT	1-01-001 TILLER	1-01-001 TOLYLENE	1-01-001 TOWELING
1-01-001 THREE-PANEL	1-01-001 TILLET	1-01-001 TOMATO-RED	1-01-001 TOWER'S
1-01-001 THREE-POWER	1-01-001 TILLICH	1-01-001 TOMBSTONES	1-01-001 TOWNLEY
1-01-001 THREE-ROOM	1-01-001 TILLIE'S	1-01-001 TOMES	1-01-001 TOWNSEND
1-01-001 THREE-SECTIONED	1-01-001 TILLING	1-01-001 TOMKINS	1-01-001 TOWNSHIPS
1-01-001 THREE-STORY	1-01-001 TILT-TOP	1-01-001 TOMMIE	1-01-001 TOWNSMAN
1-01-001 THREE-WEEK	1-01-001 TILTH	1-01-001 TOMMY'S	1-01-001 TOXIN
1-01-001 THREE-WOOD	1-01-001 TILTING	1-01-001 TOMONGGONG	1-01-001 TOYING
1-01-001 THREES-FULFILLE	1-01-001 TIME-*LIFE	1-01-001 TON-MILE	1-01-001 TRABB
D	1-01-001 TIME-*MYNAH	1-01-001 TONALITIES	1-01-001 TRACINGS
1-01-001 THRESHED	1-01-001 TIME-*OLIVETTE	1-01-001 TONALLY	1-01-001 TRACK-SIGNAL
1-01-001 THRESHHOLD	1-01-001 TIME-CAST	1-01-001 TONELESS	1-01-001 TRACKDOWN
1-01-001 THRESHING	1-01-001 TIME-CONSUMING	1-01-001 TONG	1-01-001 TRACKLESS
1-01-001 THRICE	1-01-001 TIME-DELAY	1-01-001 TONGS	1-01-001 TRACTARIANS
1-01-001 THRILLERS	1-01-001 TIME-ON-THE-JOB	1-01-001 TONGUE-THRUSTIN	1-01-001 TRACTOR-TRAILER
1-01-001 THRIVE	1-01-001 TIMEN	G	1-01-001 TRADE-MARK
1-01-001 THRIVES	1-01-001 TIMEPIECE	1-01-001 TONGUE-TIED	1-01-001 TRADE-PREPARATO
1-01-001 THROATY	1-01-001 TIMERS	1-01-001 TONGUE-TWISTER	RY
1-01-001 THROMBI	1-01-001 TIMES-*PICAYUNE	1-01-001 TONGUED	1-01-001 TRADEMARKS
1-01-001 THROMBOSED	1-01-001 TIMETABLES	1-01-001 TONI	1-01-001 TRADERS'
1-01-001 THROMBOSIS	1-01-001 TIMEWORN	1-01-001 TONIC	1-01-001 TRADESMEN
1-01-001 THRONEBERRY'S	1-01-001 TIMIDITY	1-01-001 TONIO	1-01-001 TRADITION-MINDE
1-01-001 THRONES	1-01-001 TIMIDLY	1-01-001 TOO-EXPENSIVE	D
1-01-001 THROTTLED	1-01-001 TIMMY	1-01-001 TOO-HEARTY	1-01-001 TRADITIONALISTI
1-01-001 THROTTLING	1-01-001 TIMON	1-01-001 TOO-NAKED	C
1-01-001 THROUGHPUT	1-01-001 TIMS	1-01-001 TOO-SHINY	1-01-001 TRADITIONALISTS
1-01-001 THROW-RUG	1-01-001 TINCTURE	1-01-001 TOO-SIMPLE-TO-B	1-01-001 TRADITIONALIZED
1-01-001 THRUMMING	1-01-001 TINDAL	E-TRUE	1-01-001 TRADITIONNEL
1-01-001 THRUSTON	1-01-001 TINDER	1-01-001 TOOL-KIT	1-01-001 TRAFFICKED
1-01-001 THRUWAY	1-01-001 TINKERS	1-01-001 TOOLMAKER	1-01-001 TRAFTON'S
1-01-001 THRUWAYS	1-01-001 TINKLED	1-01-001 TOOMEY	1-01-001 TRAGI-COMIC
1-01-001 THUDDING	1-01-001 TINNING	1-01-001 TOONKER	1-01-001 TRAGICALLY
1-01-001 THUDS	1-01-001 TINPLATED	1-01-001 TOOT-TOOT	1-01-001 TRAGICOMIC
1-01-001 THUG	1-01-001 TINT	1-01-001 TOOTH-HURTY	1-01-001 TRAIL-WORN
1-01-001 THUGGEE	1-01-001 TINTED	1-01-001 TOOTH-PASTE	1-01-001 TRAINEESHIPS
1-01-001 THULE	1-01-001 TINTORETTO	1-01-001 TOOTH-STRAIGHTE	1-01-001 TRAINMAN
1-01-001 THUM	1-01-001 TINTS	NING	1-01-001 TRAIPSING
1-01-001 THUMB-	1-01-001 TINTYPE	1-01-001 TOOTHPASTE	1-01-001 TRAITOROUS
1-01-001 THUMB-SUCKING	1-01-001 TIP-TOE	1-01-001 TOOTLEY-TOOT-TO	1-01-001 TRAMMEL
1-01-001 THUMBED	1-01-001 TIPOFF	OTLED	1-01-001 TRAMP
1-01-001 THUMBING	1-01-001 TIPPECANOE	1-01-001 TOOTSIE	1-01-001 TRAMPLED
1-01-001 THUMBNAIL	1-01-001 TIPPERARY	1-01-001 TOP-HEAVY	1-01-001 TRAMPLING
1-01-001 THUMPED	1-01-001 TIPPING	1-01-001 TOP-NOTCH	1-01-001 TRAMWAY
1-01-001 THUNDER-PURPLE	1-01-001 TIPPLE	1-01-001 TOP-PRIORITY	1-01-001 TRANQUILIZER
1-01-001 THUNDERCLAPS	1-01-001 TIRADES	1-01-001 TOP-RANKING	1-01-001 TRANQUILLITY
1-01-001 THUNK	1-01-001 TIREDNESS	1-01-001 TOPCOATS	1-01-001 TRANS-*ATLANTIC
1-01-001 THURMAN	1-01-001 TIRELESSLY	1-01-001 TOPEKA	1-01-001 TRANS-ILLUMINA
1-01-001 THURSDAY'S	1-01-001 TITANS	1-01-001 TOPKAPI	IO
1-01-001 THURSDAY-NIGHT	1-01-001 TITCHE'S	1-01-001 TOPMOST	1-01-001 TRANS-LINGUALL
1-01-001 THUTMOSE	1-01-001 TITHES	1-01-001 TOPNOTCH	1-01-001 TRANS-POLITICA
1-01-001 THWACK	1-01-001 TITIAN-HAIRED	1-01-001 TOPOGRAPHIC	1-01-001 TRANSAMINASE
1-01-001 THWARTING	1-01-001 TITILLATING	1-01-001 TOPPERS	1-01-001 TRANSATLANTIC
1-01-001 THWUMP	1-01-001 TITLE-HOLDER	1-01-001 TOPPINGS	1-01-001 TRANSCEND
1-01-001 THYNKE	1-01-001 TITRATION	1-01-001 TOPPLE	1-01-001 TRANSCENDANT
1-01-001 THYNNES	1-01-001 TITTER	1-01-001 TOPSOIL	1-01-001 TRANSCENDED
1-01-001 THYRATRON	1-01-001 TITTERS	1-01-001 TOPSY-TURVY	1-01-001 TRANSCENDENTAL
1-01-001 THYROIDAL	1-01-001 TITULAR	1-01-001 TORAH	ST
1-01-001 THYROIDS	1-01-001 TIVEDEN	1-01-001 TORMENTERS	1-01-001 TRANSCRIBE
1-01-001 THYRONINE	1-01-001 TIZARD	1-01-001 TORNADO	1-01-001 TRANSCULTURAL
1-01-001 THYROTOXIC	1-01-001 TJOKORDA	1-01-001 TORNADOES	1-01-001 TRANSFER/**JHR
1-01-001 THYROTROPHIC	1-01-001 TO-AND-FRO	1-01-001 TORPEDO	**JH
1-01-001 THYROTROPHIN	1-01-001 TO-DAY'S	1-01-001 TORPEDOES	1-01-001 TRANSFERED
1-01-001 THYROXINE-BINDI	1-01-001 TO-DO	1-01-001 TORPETIUS	1-01-001 TRANSFERORS
NG	1-01-001 TO-MORROW	1-01-001 TORPID	1-01-001 TRANSFERRAL
1-01-001 TI	1-01-001 TO-THE-DEATH	1-01-001 TORQUATO	1-01-001 TRANSFERRING
1-01-001 TIAO	1-01-001 TOADIES	1-01-001 TORQUEMADA	1-01-001 TRANSFORMER
1-01-001 TIBETAN-LIKE	1-01-001 TOADYISM	1-01-001 TORRID-*ADIOS	1-01-001 TRANSGRESSED
1-01-001 TIBIALIS	1-01-001 TOASTED-NUT	1-01-001 TORRID-*BREEZE	1-01-001 TRANSGRESSION
1-01-001 TIBURON	1-01-001 TOBACCO-JUICE	1-01-001 TORRID-*MIGHTY	1-01-001 TRANSIENCE
1-01-001 TIC-*TAC-*TOE	1-01-001 TOCCATA	1-01-001 TORSION	1-01-001 TRANSIENTS
1-01-001 TICKER	1-01-001 TOCH	1-01-001 TORSO-DEFINING	1-01-001 TRANSISTOR

Code	Entry	Code	Entry	Code	Entry	Code	Entry
1-01-001	TRANSISTORS	1-01-001	TRIPHENYLSTIBIN E	1-01-001	TULSA	1-01-001	TWO-LANE
1-01-001	TRANSLATES			1-01-001	TUMBLES	1-01-001	TWO-LINE
1-01-001	TRANSLATOR	1-01-001	TRIPHOSPHOPYRID INE	1-01-001	TUMBRELS	1-01-001	TWO-MILE
1-01-001	TRANSLUCENCE			1-01-001	TUMEFACIENS	1-01-001	TWO-NOSED
1-01-001	TRANSLUCENCY	1-01-001	TRIPLE-CHECKED	1-01-001	TUMOURS	1-01-001	TWO-PART
1-01-001	TRANSLUSCENT	1-01-001	TRIPLE-CROWN	1-01-001	TUMULTUOUS	1-01-001	TWO-RECORD
1-01-001	TRANSMISSIBLE	1-01-001	TRIPLE-TANK	1-01-001	TUNE-BELLY	1-01-001	TWO-ROOM
1-01-001	TRANSMITS	1-01-001	TRIPLET	1-01-001	TUNEFUL	1-01-001	TWO-SEATERS
1-01-001	TRANSMITTABLE	1-01-001	TRIPLICATION	1-01-001	TUNEFULNESS	1-01-001	TWO-STEP
1-01-001	TRANSOCEANIC	1-01-001	TRIPODS	1-01-001	TUNELESSLY	1-01-001	TWO-TAIL
1-01-001	TRANSPIRATING	1-01-001	TRIPOLI	1-01-001	TUNIC	1-01-001	TWO-TERM
1-01-001	TRANSPLANTABLE	1-01-001	TRIPPIN	1-01-001	TUNIS	1-01-001	TWO-TIMED
1-01-001	TRANSPLANTED	1-01-001	TRIS(HYDROXYMET HYL)-AMINOMETHA NE	1-01-001	TUNNARD	1-01-001	TWO-TIMING
1-01-001	TRANSPLANTING			1-01-001	TUNNELED	1-01-001	TWO-TO-THREE
1-01-001	TRANSPOSITION			1-01-001	TUOHY	1-01-001	TWO-VALUED
1-01-001	TRANSVERSALLY	1-01-001	TRISODIUM	1-01-001	TURANDOT	1-01-001	TWO-WAY
1-01-001	TRANSVERSELY	1-01-001	TRISTAN	1-01-001	TURBINATES	1-01-001	TWO-WEEK
1-01-001	TRANSVESTITISM	1-01-001	TROBLES	1-01-001	TURBINES	1-01-001	TWO-WEEKS
1-01-001	TRAPDOOR	1-01-001	TROELTSCH	1-01-001	TURBOFAN	1-01-001	TWO-YEAR-OLD
1-01-001	TRAPDOORS	1-01-001	TROHAN	1-01-001	TURKEYS	1-01-001	TWOSOME
1-01-001	TRAPEZOID	1-01-001	TROIKA	1-01-001	TURN-OUT	1-01-001	TWOTIMING
1-01-001	TRAPP	1-01-001	TROLLOP	1-01-001	TURNAROUND	1-01-001	TYBURN
1-01-001	TRAPPER'S	1-01-001	TROLLS	1-01-001	TURNE	1-01-001	TYCOON
1-01-001	TRAUMA	1-01-001	TROMBONIST	1-01-001	TURNERY	1-01-001	TYGARTIS
1-01-001	TRAUMATIC	1-01-001	TROMPE-L'OEIL	1-01-001	TURNINGS	1-01-001	TYPESCRIPT
1-01-001	TRAVANCORE	1-01-001	TROOPSHIP	1-01-001	TURNIPS	1-01-001	TYPESETTING
1-01-001	TRAVELOGUE-LIKE	1-01-001	TROOPSHIPS	1-01-001	TURNKEY	1-01-001	TYPEWRITERS
1-01-001	TRAVELOGUES	1-01-001	TROPEZ	1-01-001	TURNOFF	1-01-001	TYPEWRITING
1-01-001	TRAVERSING	1-01-001	TROPHO-	1-01-001	TURNTABLE	1-01-001	TYPEWRITTEN
1-01-001	TRAVESTY	1-01-001	TROPICS	1-01-001	TURRETS	1-01-001	TYPHOON
1-01-001	TRAWLER	1-01-001	TROPIDOCLONION	1-01-001	TURTLE-NECK	1-01-001	TYPIFY
1-01-001	TRAXEL	1-01-001	TROPOCOLLAGEN	1-01-001	TURTLEBACKS	1-01-001	TYPIFYING
1-01-001	TREACHERIES	1-01-001	TROTSKY	1-01-001	TURTLES	1-01-001	TYPOGRAPHIC
1-01-001	TREADING	1-01-001	TROTTER	1-01-001	TUSKEGEE	1-01-001	TYPOLOGY
1-01-001	TREADMILL	1-01-001	TROUBIE	1-01-001	TUSSARD'S	1-01-001	TYRANNICAL
1-01-001	TREADWELL	1-01-001	TROUBLE-SHOOTER	1-01-001	TUTORIALS	1-01-001	TYRANNIS
1-01-001	TREASONABLE	1-01-001	TROUBLESHOOTER	1-01-001	TUTORS	1-01-001	TYRANNIZE
1-01-001	TREASONOUS	1-01-001	TROUGHS	1-01-001	TUTTLE'S	1-01-001	TYRANTS
1-01-001	TREASURIES	1-01-001	TROUPES	1-01-001	TUXEDOED	1-01-001	TYSON
1-01-001	TREASURY'S	1-01-001	TROUSERS-POCKET S	1-01-001	TVA	1-01-001	U**.'S
1-01-001	TREATISE			1-01-001	TWAIN	1-01-001	U**.*M**.*T
1-01-001	TREATY-MAKING	1-01-001	TROYES	1-01-001	TWAIN'S	1-01-001	U**.*N**.-CHART ERED
1-01-001	TREDDING	1-01-001	TRUANT	1-01-001	TWEEDY		
1-01-001	TREECE	1-01-001	TRUCK'S	1-01-001	TWEEZED	1-01-001	U**.*S**.'S
1-01-001	TREELIKE	1-01-001	TRUCKDRIVER	1-01-001	TWELVE-YEAR	1-01-001	U**.*S**.*S**.* R**.'S
1-01-001	TREES'	1-01-001	TRUCKED	1-01-001	TWELVE-YEAR-OLD		
1-01-001	TREETOPS	1-01-001	TRUCKEE	1-01-001	TWENTIETH-*CENT URY	1-01-001	U**.*S**.*STEEL 'S
1-01-001	TREGNUMS	1-01-001	TRUCKER				
1-01-001	TREKKED	1-01-001	TRUCKERS	1-01-001	TWENTY-DOLLAR	1-01-001	U**.*S**.-*SOVI ET
1-01-001	TRELLISES	1-01-001	TRUCULENCE	1-01-001	TWENTY-EIGHTH		
1-01-001	TREMBLES	1-01-001	TRUCULENT	1-01-001	TWENTY-FIFTH	1-01-001	U**.N
1-01-001	TREMPLER	1-01-001	TRUE-FALSE	1-01-001	TWENTY-FIRST-CE NTURY	1-01-001	U**DBERMENSCHEN
1-01-001	TREMULOUSLY	1-01-001	TRUMBULL			1-01-001	U*S*N
1-01-001	TRENCHERMEN	1-01-001	TRUMP	1-01-001	TWENTY-FIVE-DOL LAR	1-01-001	UDALL'S
1-01-001	TRENCHES	1-01-001	TRUMPED-UP			1-01-001	UDON
1-01-001	TREND-FOLLOWING	1-01-001	TRUMPETER	1-01-001	TWENTY-FIVE-YEA R-OLD	1-01-001	UGH
1-01-001	TRESTLE	1-01-001	TRUMPS			1-01-001	UH-UH
1-01-001	TRESTLES	1-01-001	TRUNDLE	1-01-001	TWENTY-MILE	1-01-001	UHLES
1-01-001	TRI-MOTOR	1-01-001	TRUNDLING	1-01-001	TWENTY-NINE-FOO T-WIDE	1-01-001	UKRAINIANS
1-01-001	TRIAD	1-01-001	TRUSTEE'S			1-01-001	ULCERATED
1-01-001	TRIAL-BOOK	1-01-001	TRUSTEESHIP	1-01-001	TWENTY-ONE-YEAR -OLD	1-01-001	ULCERATIONS
1-01-001	TRIANGLES	1-01-001	TRUSTFULLY			1-01-001	ULLMAN
1-01-001	TRIANON	1-01-001	TRUSTINGLY	1-01-001	TWENTY-PAGE	1-01-001	ULTRA-EFFICIENT
1-01-001	TRIBE'S	1-01-001	TRUTH-PACKED	1-01-001	TWENTY-SEVEN	1-01-001	ULTRA-FAST
1-01-001	TRIBULATION	1-01-001	TRUTH-REVEALING	1-01-001	TWICE-A-YEAR	1-01-001	ULTRA-HIGH-SPEE D
1-01-001	TRIBUNA	1-01-001	TRUTHFUL	1-01-001	TWICE-AROUND		
1-01-001	TRIBUNE'S	1-01-001	TSAR	1-01-001	TWIGGED	1-01-001	ULTRA-LIBERAL
1-01-001	TRIBUTES	1-01-001	TSAREVICH	1-01-001	TWIGS	1-01-001	ULTRA-MODERN
1-01-001	TRICHIERI	1-01-001	TSARISM	1-01-001	TWINGES	1-01-001	ULTRACENTRIFUGA LLY
1-01-001	TRICHINELLA	1-01-001	TSCHILWYK	1-01-001	TWINS'		
1-01-001	TRICHLOROACETIC	1-01-001	TSH**P	1-01-001	TWIRLED	1-01-001	ULTRAMARINE
1-01-001	TRICHROME	1-01-001	TSHOMBE-*GIZENG A-*GOA-*GHANA	1-01-001	TWIRLINGLY	1-01-001	ULTRAMODERN
1-01-001	TRICKY			1-01-001	TWISE	1-01-001	ULTRASONICALLY
1-01-001	TRICOLOR	1-01-001	TSITOURIS	1-01-001	TWISTER-CONERS	1-01-001	ULTRAVEHEMENT
1-01-001	TRIG'S	1-01-001	TSOU	1-01-001	TWISTY	1-01-001	UMM
1-01-001	TRIGG	1-01-001	TSUNAMI-WARNING	1-01-001	TWITTERED	1-01-001	UMPIRE
1-01-001	TRIKOJUS	1-01-001	TSVETKOV	1-01-001	TWITTERING	1-01-001	UMSCHLAGPLATZ
1-01-001	TRILLED	1-01-001	TT**U.	1-01-001	TWO-*HEAD	1-01-001	UN*$FUNNY
1-01-001	TRILLION	1-01-001	TU	1-01-001	TWO-*STEM	1-01-001	UNABRIDGED
1-01-001	TRIM-YOUR-OWN-F RANKS	1-01-001	TU*HUL*HUL*ZOTE	1-01-001	TWO-AND-A-HALF- MILE	1-01-001	UNACCEPTABLE
		1-01-001	TUALATIN			1-01-001	UNACCOUNTABLE
1-01-001	TRIMESTER	1-01-001	TUBA	1-01-001	TWO-BEDROOM	1-01-001	UNACCUSTOMED
1-01-001	TRIMS	1-01-001	TUBE-NOSED	1-01-001	TWO-BITS'	1-01-001	UNACHIEVABLE
1-01-001	TRINIDAD	1-01-001	TUBERS	1-01-001	TWO-BURNER	1-01-001	UNACHIEVED
1-01-001	TRINITARIAN	1-01-001	TUBORG	1-01-001	TWO-BY-FOUR	1-01-001	UNACKNOWLEDGED
1-01-001	TRINITARIANS	1-01-001	TUBULES	1-01-001	TWO-BY-FOURS	1-01-001	UNADORNED
1-01-001	TRINKET	1-01-001	TUCKER'S	1-01-001	TWO-CLASS	1-01-001	UNADULTERATED
1-01-001	TRINKETS	1-01-001	TUDOR-STYLE	1-01-001	TWO-COLOR	1-01-001	UNAGGRESSIVE
1-01-001	TRIOL	1-01-001	TUFTS	1-01-001	TWO-COLORED	1-01-001	UNAGI
1-01-001	TRIOMPHE	1-01-001	TUG-O'-WAR	1-01-001	TWO-COMPONENT	1-01-001	UNALIENABLE
1-01-001	TRIP-HAMMER	1-01-001	TUGARU	1-01-001	TWO-DIMENSIONAL	1-01-001	UNALLOYED
1-01-001	TRIPARTITE	1-01-001	TUGGING	1-01-001	TWO-DISC	1-01-001	UNALTERABLE
1-01-001	TRIPE	1-01-001	TULANE	1-01-001	TWO-FAMILY	1-01-001	UNAM
1-01-001	TRIPHENYLARSINE	1-01-001	TULIP-SHAPED	1-01-001	TWO-FISTED	1-01-001	UNAMBIGUITY
1-01-001	TRIPHENYLPHOSPH INE	1-01-001	TULLE	1-01-001	TWO-GAME	1-01-001	UNAMUSED
		1-01-001	TULLIO	1-01-001	TWO-INCH	1-01-001	UNANSWERED
		1-01-001	TULLN	1-01-001	TWO-INCHES	1-01-001	UNAPPEASABLE

1-01-001	UNAPPEASABLY	1-01-001	UNDERSTRUCTURE	1-01-001	UNIQUE-INGROWN-	1-01-001	UNQUIET
1-01-001	UNAPPRECIATED	1-01-001	UNDERTAKER		SCREWEDUP	1-01-001	UNRAVEL
1-01-001	UNASHAMEDLY	1-01-001	UNDERTOW	1-01-001	UNITE*(S	1-01-001	UNREADY
1-01-001	UNASTERISKED	1-01-001	UNDERWOOD'S	1-01-001	UNITIES	1-01-001	UNREALISM
1-01-001	UNATTAINABLE	1-01-001	UNDERWRITER	1-01-001	UNIVALENT	1-01-001	UNREALISTICALLY
1-01-001	UNAUTHENTIC	1-01-001	UNDESERVED	1-01-001	UNIVERSAL-*INTE	1-01-001	UNREASON
1-01-001	UNAVAILING	1-01-001	UNDETECTABLE		RNATIONAL	1-01-001	UNREASONABLY
1-01-001	UNBALANCE	1-01-001	UNDETECTED	1-01-001	UNIVERSALISTIC	1-01-001	UNREASONING
1-01-001	UNBEARABLY	1-01-001	UNDID	1-01-001	UNIVERSALIZE	1-01-001	UNREASSURINGLY
1-01-001	UNBEKNOWNST	1-01-001	UNDIFFERENTIATE	1-01-001	UNIVERSALS	1-01-001	UNRECOVERABLE
1-01-001	UNBELIEVABLY		D	1-01-001	UNIVERSITY-EDUC	1-01-001	UNREDEEMED
1-01-001	UNBELIEVING	1-01-001	UNDIGESTED		ATED	1-01-001	UNREELING
1-01-001	UNBENT	1-01-001	UNDILUTED	1-01-001	UNIVERSITY-TRAI	1-01-001	UNREFLECTIVE
1-01-001	UNBIDDEN	1-01-001	UNDIMMED		NED	1-01-001	UNREHEARSED
1-01-001	UNBLEMISHED	1-01-001	UNDISCLOSED	1-01-001	UNIVERSITY-WIDE	1-01-001	UNRELEASED
1-01-001	UNBLUSHING	1-01-001	UNDISGUISED	1-01-001	UNJACKETED	1-01-001	UNRELENTING
1-01-001	UNBOUND	1-01-001	UNDISMAYED	1-01-001	UNJUSTIFIED	1-01-001	UNRELIABILITY
1-01-001	UNBOUNDED	1-01-001	UNDISRUPTED	1-01-001	UNKEMPT	1-01-001	UNREMARKABLE
1-01-001	UNBURDENED	1-01-001	UNDIVIDED	1-01-001	UNKNOWING	1-01-001	UNREMITTING
1-01-001	UNBURNED	1-01-001	UNDREAMED	1-01-001	UNKNOWINGLY	1-01-001	UNREPENTANT
1-01-001	UNCALLED	1-01-001	UNDREAMT	1-01-001	UNKNOWNS	1-01-001	UNREQUITED
1-01-001	UNCAP	1-01-001	UNDRINKABLE	1-01-001	UNLACED	1-01-001	UNRESERVEDLY
1-01-001	UNCAS	1-01-001	UNDULATED	1-01-001	UNLACING	1-01-001	UNRESTRICTEDLY
1-01-001	UNCAUSED	1-01-001	UNDULATING	1-01-001	UNLAMENTED	1-01-001	UNREVEALING
1-01-001	UNCEASING	1-01-001	UNDYING	1-01-001	UNLASHED	1-01-001	UNRIFLED
1-01-001	UNCEASINGLY	1-01-001	UNEARTH	1-01-001	UNLAUNDERED	1-01-001	UNRIPE
1-01-001	UNCERTIFIED	1-01-001	UNEASE	1-01-001	UNLAWFUL	1-01-001	UNROLLED
1-01-001	UNCHANGEABLE	1-01-001	UNECONOMIC	1-01-001	UNLEASH	1-01-001	UNROMANTIC
1-01-001	UNCHECKED	1-01-001	UNEDUCATED	1-01-001	UNLEASHING	1-01-001	UNRUFFLED
1-01-001	UNCHRISTIAN	1-01-001	UNENDURABLE	1-01-001	UNLEVELED	1-01-001	UNSAFE
1-01-001	UNCIRCUMCISION	1-01-001	UNENFORCIBLE	1-01-001	UNLICENSED	1-01-001	UNSAID
1-01-001	UNCIVIL	1-01-001	UNENUNCIATED	1-01-001	UNLINKED	1-01-001	UNSAVORY
1-01-001	UNCKLE	1-01-001	UNENVIABLE	1-01-001	UNLITERARY	1-01-001	UNSCRAMBLE
1-01-001	UNCLASPING	1-01-001	UNENVIED	1-01-001	UNLOADS	1-01-001	UNSCREW
1-01-001	UNCLENCHED	1-01-001	UNEQUAL	1-01-001	UNLOCKING	1-01-001	UNSEALED
1-01-001	UNCLUTTERED	1-01-001	UNEQUALED	1-01-001	UNLOVELY	1-01-001	UNSEASONABLE
1-01-001	UNCO-OPERATIVE	1-01-001	UNEQUALLED	1-01-001	UNLUCKILY	1-01-001	UNSEE
1-01-001	UNCOILING	1-01-001	UNERRINGLY	1-01-001	UNMAGNIFIED	1-01-001	UNSEEMLY
1-01-001	UNCOLORED	1-01-001	UNEXAMINED	1-01-001	UNMALICIOUS	1-01-001	UNSELF-CONSCIOU
1-01-001	UNCOMBABLE	1-01-001	UNEXPENDED	1-01-001	UNMANAGEABLE		S
1-01-001	UNCOMFORATBLE	1-01-001	UNEXPLAINABLE	1-01-001	UNMANAGEABLY	1-01-001	UNSELFCONSCIOUS
1-01-001	UNCOMFORTED	1-01-001	UNFAITHFUL	1-01-001	UNMANAGED		NESS
1-01-001	UNCOMMONLY	1-01-001	UNFALTERINGLY	1-01-001	UNMARKED	1-01-001	UNSELFISH
1-01-001	UNCOMMUNICATIVE	1-01-001	UNFASTENED	1-01-001	UNMASKED	1-01-001	UNSELFISHLY
1-01-001	UNCOMPLAININGLY	1-01-001	UNFATHOMABLE	1-01-001	UNMATED	1-01-001	UNSERVILE
1-01-001	UNCONCERN	1-01-001	UNFELT	1-01-001	UNMERITORIOUS	1-01-001	UNSETTLING
1-01-001	UNCONCERNEDLY	1-01-001	UNFERTILE	1-01-001	UNMESHED	1-01-001	UNSHAKABLE
1-01-001	UNCONDITIONED	1-01-001	UNFERTILIZED	1-01-001	UNMETHODICAL	1-01-001	UNSHAKEABLE
1-01-001	UNCONQUERABLE	1-01-001	UNFIT	1-01-001	UNMINDFUL	1-01-001	UNSHARPENED
1-01-001	UNCONSCIONABLE	1-01-001	UNFIXED	1-01-001	UNMIXED	1-01-001	UNSHAVED
1-01-001	UNCOURAGEOUS	1-01-001	UNFLAGGING	1-01-001	UNMODIFIED	1-01-001	UNSHAVEN
1-01-001	UNCOUSINLY	1-01-001	UNFLATTERING	1-01-001	UNMOLESTED	1-01-001	UNSHEATHE
1-01-001	UNCRITICALLY	1-01-001	UNFOLDMENT	1-01-001	UNMOTIVATED	1-01-001	UNSHEATHING
1-01-001	UNCTION	1-01-001	UNFORGIVABLE	1-01-001	UNMURMURING	1-01-001	UNSHED
1-01-001	UNCURLED	1-01-001	UNFORMED	1-01-001	UNNAMEABLE	1-01-001	UNSHELLED
1-01-001	UNDAMAGED	1-01-001	UNFORSEEN	1-01-001	UNNATURALLY	1-01-001	UNSHELTERED
1-01-001	UNDAUNTED	1-01-001	UNFORTUNATES	1-01-001	UNNATURALNESS	1-01-001	UNSHIELDED
1-01-001	UNDECLARED	1-01-001	UNFROCKING	1-01-001	UNNEEDED	1-01-001	UNSIGHTLY
1-01-001	UNDECORATED	1-01-001	UNFROSTED	1-01-001	UNNERVING	1-01-001	UNSLOPED
1-01-001	UNDEDICATED	1-01-001	UNFULFILLED	1-01-001	UNNNT	1-01-001	UNSMILINGLY
1-01-001	UNDEMOCRATIC	1-01-001	UNFUNNILY	1-01-001	UNNOURISHED	1-01-001	UNSOLDER
1-01-001	UNDENIABLY	1-01-001	UNFURLED	1-01-001	UNNUMBERED	1-01-001	UNSOPHISTICATE
1-01-001	UNDER-ACHIEVERS	1-01-001	UNGALLANT	1-01-001	UNO	1-01-001	UNSPECTACULAR
1-01-001	UNDERACHIEVERS	1-01-001	UNGAVA	1-01-001	UNO'S	1-01-001	UNSPRAYED
1-01-001	UNDERARM	1-01-001	UNGLAMOROUS	1-01-001	UNOFFICIALLY	1-01-001	UNSTAPLED
1-01-001	UNDERBEDDING	1-01-001	UNGLAZED	1-01-001	UNOPENED	1-01-001	UNSTARING
1-01-001	UNDERBELLY	1-01-001	UNGLUED	1-01-001	UNPACK	1-01-001	UNSTEADILY
1-01-001	UNDERBRACING	1-01-001	UNGOVERNED	1-01-001	UNPACKING	1-01-001	UNSTILTED
1-01-001	UNDERBRUSH	1-01-001	UNGRACIOUS	1-01-001	UNPADDED	1-01-001	UNSTUCK
1-01-001	UNDERCLASSMAN	1-01-001	UNGRATIFIED	1-01-001	UNPAINTABLE	1-01-001	UNSTUFFY
1-01-001	UNDERCLOTHES	1-01-001	UNGUIDED	1-01-001	UNPARTISAN	1-01-001	UNSUCCESSFULLY
1-01-001	UNDERCOVER	1-01-001	UNHAPPIEST	1-01-001	UNPATRONIZING	1-01-001	UNSUITABLY
1-01-001	UNDEREDUCATED	1-01-001	UNHARMONIOUS	1-01-001	UNPAVED	1-01-001	UNSUITED
1-01-001	UNDERGIRDING	1-01-001	UNHEEDING	1-01-001	UNPERCEIVED	1-01-001	UNSUPPORTABLE
1-01-001	UNDERGROWTH	1-01-001	UNHESITANT	1-01-001	UNPERFORMED	1-01-001	UNSUPPORTED
1-01-001	UNDERHANDED	1-01-001	UNHINGED	1-01-001	UNPHYSICAL	1-01-001	UNSURE
1-01-001	UNDERHANDEDNESS	1-01-001	UNHOOK	1-01-001	UNPICTURESQUE	1-01-001	UNSURMOUNTABLE
1-01-001	UNDERLAY	1-01-001	UNHURT	1-01-001	UNPLAGUED	1-01-001	UNSURPASSED
1-01-001	UNDERLIES	1-01-001	UNI-DIRECTIONAL	1-01-001	UNPLEASANTLY	1-01-001	UNSUSPECTING
1-01-001	UNDERLING	1-01-001	UNIDENTIFIED	1-01-001	UNPLEASANTNESS	1-01-001	UNTCH
1-01-001	UNDERMINING	1-01-001	UNIDIRECTIONAL	1-01-001	UNPLEASED	1-01-001	UNTEACH
1-01-001	UNDERPAID	1-01-001	UNIFICATIONS	1-01-001	UNPLUMBED	1-01-001	UNTELLABLE
1-01-001	UNDERPINNING	1-01-001	UNILATERALLY	1-01-001	UNPREMEDITATED	1-01-001	UNTENANTED
1-01-001	UNDERPINS	1-01-001	UNIMAGINATIVE	1-01-001	UNPRETENTIOUS	1-01-001	UNTHAW
1-01-001	UNDERPLAYED	1-01-001	UNIMPEACHABLY	1-01-001	UNPROBLEMATIC	1-01-001	UNTHEMATIC
1-01-001	UNDERRATE	1-01-001	UNIMPOSING	1-01-001	UNPROCURABLE	1-01-001	UNTHINKING
1-01-001	UNDERRATED	1-01-001	UNINFLUENCED	1-01-001	UNPRODUCTIVE	1-01-001	UNTIDINESS
1-01-001	UNDERSCORE	1-01-001	UNINITIATE	1-01-001	UNPROFESSIONAL	1-01-001	UNTIDY
1-01-001	UNDERSECRETARY	1-01-001	UNINJECTABLE	1-01-001	UNPROFITABLE	1-01-001	UNTIED
1-01-001	UNDERSECRETARY'	1-01-001	UNINOMINAL	1-01-001	UNPROMISING	1-01-001	UNTIMELY
	S	1-01-001	UNINTELLIGIBLE	1-01-001	UNPROVED	1-01-001	UNTOWARD
1-01-001	UNDERSIZE	1-01-001	UNINTERESTED	1-01-001	UNPROVOCATIVE	1-01-001	UNTRACKED
1-01-001	UNDERSIZED	1-01-001	UNINTERESTING	1-01-001	UNPUNISHED	1-01-001	UNTRADITIONAL
1-01-001	UNDERSTANDED	1-01-001	UNINTERRUPTEDLY	1-01-001	UNQUALIFIEDLY	1-01-001	UNTRAINED
1-01-001	UNDERSTANDINGS	1-01-001	UNINVITED	1-01-001	UNQUENCHED	1-01-001	UNTREATED
1-01-001	UNDERSTATED	1-01-001	UNINVOLVED	1-01-001	UNQUESTIONABLE	1-01-001	UNTRUSTWORTHI
1-01-001	UNDERSTATES	1-01-001	UNION-INDUSTRY	1-01-001	UNQUESTIONINGLY		

1-01-001 UNUTTERABLY	1-01-001 VALIANT	1-01-001 VERLOOP'S	1-01-001 VIRTUOSITY
1-01-001 UNVARYING	1-01-001 VALIANTLY	1-01-001 VERMEERSCH	1-01-001 VIRULENT
1-01-001 UNVENTILATED	1-01-001 VALIDATED	1-01-001 VERMEIL	1-01-001 VISCOMETER
1-01-001 UNWAIVERING	1-01-001 VALIDATING	1-01-001 VERMOUTH	1-01-001 VISCOUS
1-01-001 UNWAVERINGLY	1-01-001 VALIDATION	1-01-001 VERN	1-01-001 VISE
1-01-001 UNWILLINGLY	1-01-001 VALIDLY	1-01-001 VERNAL	1-01-001 VISELIKE
1-01-001 UNWINDING	1-01-001 VALLE	1-01-001 VERNE	1-01-001 VISIGOTHS
1-01-001 UNWIRE	1-01-001 VALLEE	1-01-001 VERNER	1-01-001 VISITATIONS
1-01-001 UNWIRED	1-01-001 VALLEY'S	1-01-001 VERNOR	1-01-001 VISRHANIK
1-01-001 UNWITTING	1-01-001 VALLFART	1-01-001 VERONICA	1-01-001 VISUALIZATION
1-01-001 UNWOMANLY	1-01-001 VALMET	1-01-001 VERPLANCK'S	1-01-001 VISUALIZES
1-01-001 UNWORKABLE	1-01-001 VALOIS	1-01-001 VERRONE	1-01-001 VITAMIN-AND-IRO
1-01-001 UNWORN	1-01-001 VALOR	1-01-001 VERSTANDIG	N
1-01-001 UNWOUNDED	1-01-001 VALUE-JUDGMENTS	1-01-001 VERSTRICHEN	1-01-001 VITIATED
1-01-001 UNWRINKLED	1-01-001 VALUE-ORIENTATI	1-01-001 VERTEBRAE	1-01-001 VITIATES
1-01-001 UNYIELDING	ONS	1-01-001 VERTEBRATE	1-01-001 VITRIOL
1-01-001 UP-AND-COMING	1-01-001 VALUE-PROBLEMS	1-01-001 VERTEBRATES	1-01-001 VITUS
1-01-001 UP-JUTTING	1-01-001 VALUE-SYSTEM	1-01-001 VERTICAL-TAKEOF	1-01-001 VIVA
1-01-001 UP-PP	1-01-001 VALUELESS	F-AND-LANDING	1-01-001 VIVALDI
1-01-001 UPBEAT	1-01-001 VAMP	1-01-001 VERTIGO	1-01-001 VIVE
1-01-001 UPBRINGING	1-01-001 VAMPIRES	1-01-001 VESICULAR	1-01-001 VIVIAN'S
1-01-001 UPCOMING	1-01-001 VANCE'S	1-01-001 VESTMENTS	1-01-001 VIVIDNESS
1-01-001 UPDATE	1-01-001 VANDALISM	1-01-001 VESTS	1-01-001 VIVIER
1-01-001 UPGRADED	1-01-001 VANDALS	1-01-001 VESUVIO'S	1-01-001 VIVIFIED
1-01-001 UPHILL	1-01-001 VANDERVOORT	1-01-001 VET	1-01-001 VIVIFY
1-01-001 UPHOLDERS	1-01-001 VANDRINGSAR	1-01-001 VETERAN'S	1-01-001 VIYELLA
1-01-001 UPHOLDS	1-01-001 VANILLA	1-01-001 VETERINARIANS	1-01-001 VIZ
1-01-001 UPHOLSTERED	1-01-001 VANISHES	1-01-001 VETOED	1-01-001 VLADILEN
1-01-001 UPI).**T**-	1-01-001 VANITIES	1-01-001 VEVAY	1-01-001 VOCABULARIANISM
1-01-001 UPLIFT	1-01-001 VANTAGE-POINTS	1-01-001 VEX	1-01-001 VOCALIC
1-01-001 UPPER-LEVEL	1-01-001 VAPORIZATION	1-01-001 VEXATIOUS	1-01-001 VOCALISM
1-01-001 UPPER-LOWER	1-01-001 VAQUERO	1-01-001 VEXES	1-01-001 VOCALIZATION
1-01-001 UPPER-MIDDLE	1-01-001 VAR	1-01-001 VIALE	1-01-001 VOCALIZE
1-01-001 UPPERCLASSMEN	1-01-001 VARIABLE-SPEED	1-01-001 VIAREGGIO	1-01-001 VOCALLY
1-01-001 UPPERCUT	1-01-001 VARIANCE	1-01-001 VIATOR	1-01-001 VOCALS
1-01-001 UPRAISED	1-01-001 VARICOLORED	1-01-001 VIBES	1-01-001 VOCATIONALLY
1-01-001 UPRISING	1-01-001 VARIEGATED	1-01-001 VIBRATED	1-01-001 VOLE
1-01-001 UPRIVER	1-01-001 VARIGRAD	1-01-001 VIBRATING	1-01-001 VOCIFEROUSLY
1-01-001 UPROARIOUSLY	1-01-001 VARITINTED	1-01-001 VIBRATO	1-01-001 VOCIFEROUSNESS
1-01-001 UPROOTED	1-01-001 VARITYPING	1-01-001 VIBRIONIC	1-01-001 VOICE'S
1-01-001 UPSETTING	1-01-001 VARNER	1-01-001 VIC'S	1-01-001 VOICELESS
1-01-001 UPSHOT	1-01-001 VARNESSA	1-01-001 VICE-CHAIRMAN	1-01-001 VOIDS
1-01-001 UPSHOTS	1-01-001 VARNISH	1-01-001 VICE-CHANCELLOR	1-01-001 VOITURE
1-01-001 UPSON	1-01-001 VARVISO	1-01-001 VICE-PRESIDENTS	1-01-001 VOLARE
1-01-001 UPSTANDING	1-01-001 VASADY	1-01-001 VICE-REGENT	1-01-001 VOLATILIZATION
1-01-001 UPSTATE	1-01-001 VASILIEVITCH	1-01-001 VICELIKE	1-01-001 VOLCANOS
1-01-001 UPTREND	1-01-001 VASKA	1-01-001 VICEROY	1-01-001 VOLENS
1-01-001 UPTURNED	1-01-001 VASSAL	1-01-001 VICHY	1-01-001 VOLKENSTEIN
1-01-001 URBAN-FRINGE	1-01-001 VASTER	1-01-001 VICISSITUDES	1-01-001 VOLKER
1-01-001 URBANA	1-01-001 VAUDOIS	1-01-001 VICKERS	1-01-001 VOLKSGEIST
1-01-001 URBANO	1-01-001 VEAL	1-01-001 VICOLO	1-01-001 VOLKSWAGENS
1-01-001 UREA	1-01-001 VEBLEN	1-01-001 VICTIMIZE	1-01-001 VOLLEYBALL
1-01-001 UREMIA	1-01-001 VEECK'S	1-01-001 VICTOR'S	1-01-001 VOLNEY
1-01-001 URETHRA	1-01-001 VEERS	1-01-001 VICTOR-*BUTLER	1-01-001 VOLTA
1-01-001 URGENCIES	1-01-001 VEGETARIAN	1-01-001 VICTORIA'S	1-01-001 VOLTA'S
1-01-001 URICH	1-01-001 VEHEMENTLY	1-01-001 VICTORIANS	1-01-001 VOLTMETER
1-01-001 URIELITES	1-01-001 VEHICULAR	1-01-001 VICTORIOUS	1-01-001 VOLTS
1-01-001 URINALS	1-01-001 VEILING	1-01-001 VICTORIOUSLY	1-01-001 VOLUMETRICALLY
1-01-001 URINE	1-01-001 VEINED	1-01-001 VICTROLA	1-01-001 VOLUNTARY-CONTR
1-01-001 URSULINE	1-01-001 VELASQUEZ	1-01-001 VICTUALS	OL
1-01-001 URUGUAY	1-01-001 VELDT	1-01-001 VIDA	1-01-001 VOM
1-01-001 USEABLE	1-01-001 VELLUM	1-01-001 VIDAL	1-01-001 VOMICA
1-01-001 USEFULLY	1-01-001 VELOCITER	1-01-001 VIDAL'S	1-01-001 VOORHEES
1-01-001 USURIOUS	1-01-001 VELON	1-01-001 VIED	1-01-001 VOPOS
1-01-001 USURP	1-01-001 VELOUR	1-01-001 VIELLEICHT	1-01-001 VORACIOUSLY
1-01-001 USURPED	1-01-001 VELOURS	1-01-001 VIENNA'S	1-01-001 VOROSHILOV
1-01-001 UTILITY-COST	1-01-001 VENABLE	1-01-001 VIENNE	1-01-001 VORTEX
1-01-001 UTOPIANISM	1-01-001 VENDOME	1-01-001 VIENNESE	1-01-001 VOS
1-01-001 UTOPIAS	1-01-001 VENDOR	1-01-001 VIENOT	1-01-001 VOUCHERS
1-01-001 UTTERANCES	1-01-001 VENEER	1-01-001 VIES	1-01-001 VOUCHING
1-01-001 UTTERMOST	1-01-001 VENETO	1-01-001 VIGIL	1-01-001 VOUCHSAFES
1-01-001 UTTUH	1-01-001 VENISON	1-01-001 VIGILANTISM	1-01-001 VOUILLEMONT
1-01-001 UXBRIDGE	1-01-001 VENTED	1-01-001 VIGNETTE	1-01-001 VOULEZ
1-01-001 VA**DTTERN	1-01-001 VENTI	1-01-001 VIGREUX	1-01-001 VOUME
1-01-001 VACATE	1-01-001 VENTILATED	1-01-001 VIKULOV	1-01-001 VOWEL-*LENGTH
1-01-001 VACATIONERS	1-01-001 VENTILATES	1-01-001 VILAS	1-01-001 VOYAGER
1-01-001 VACATIONLAND	1-01-001 VENTILATING	1-01-001 VILIFYING	1-01-001 VOYAGES
1-01-001 VACCINATING	1-01-001 VENTILATOR	1-01-001 VILLAGER	1-01-001 VRAI
1-01-001 VACCINE	1-01-001 VENTRICLES	1-01-001 VILLAGERS	1-01-001 VRILIUM
1-01-001 VACHELL	1-01-001 VENTURA	1-01-001 VILLAINOUS	1-01-001 VROMAN
1-01-001 VACUOLATED	1-01-001 VENTURESOME	1-01-001 VINDICATE	1-01-001 VUHRANDUH
1-01-001 VACUOUS	1-01-001 VENTURI	1-01-001 VINE-CRISSCROSS	1-01-001 VULCANIZED
1-01-001 VACUUM-	1-01-001 VENUSIANS	ED	1-01-001 VULPINE
1-01-001 VACUUMED	1-01-001 VERACIOUS	1-01-001 VINE-EMBOWERED	1-01-001 VULTURELIKE
1-01-001 VADIM	1-01-001 VERANDAH	1-01-001 VINE-SHADED	1-01-001 VULTURIDAE
1-01-001 VADSTENA	1-01-001 VERANDAS	1-01-001 VINNICUM	1-01-001 W**.'S
1-01-001 VAGABONDS	1-01-001 VERBOORT	1-01-001 VINOGRADOFF	1-01-001 W**.*G
1-01-001 VAGARIES	1-01-001 VERBOTEN	1-01-001 VINSON	1-01-001 W**.*H
1-01-001 VAGRANT	1-01-001 VERDANT	1-01-001 VINTNER	1-01-001 W**.*M
1-01-001 VAGUELY-IMAGINE	1-01-001 VERE	1-01-001 VIOILN	1-01-001 W**.*R
D	1-01-001 VERGES	1-01-001 VIOLINISTS	1-01-001 W**U,
1-01-001 VAGUEST	1-01-001 VERGESSEN	1-01-001 VIOLINS	1-01-001 W-I-D-E
1-01-001 VALEDICTORIAN	1-01-001 VERICT	1-01-001 VIPHAKONE	1-01-001 WAAL'S
1-01-001 VALENTE	1-01-001 VERIDICAL	1-01-001 VIRGILIA	1-01-001 WACKER
1-01-001 VALERIE	1-01-001 VERIE	1-01-001 VIRGINIANS	1-01-001 WACKERS'
1-01-001 VALEUR	1-01-001 VERISIMILITUDE	1-01-001 VIRSALADZE	1-01-001 WACKLIN
1-01-001 VALEWE	1-01-001 VERITY	1-01-001 VIRTUOSI	1-01-001 WACKY

ID	Word	ID	Word	ID	Word	ID	Word
1-01-001	WADS	1-01-001	WARRENTON	1-01-001	WEIRS	1-01-001	WHEREWITH
1-01-001	WAFFLE-PATTERN	1-01-001	WARRING	1-01-001	WEISS	1-01-001	WHETTED
1-01-001	WAFFLES	1-01-001	WART-HOG	1-01-001	WEISSMAN	1-01-001	WHICHEVER-THE-H ELL
1-01-001	WAGE-EARNING	1-01-001	WARTORN	1-01-001	WEISSMULLER		
1-01-001	WAGE-RATE	1-01-001	WARTY	1-01-001	WELBORN	1-01-001	WHIFF
1-01-001	WAGE-RATES	1-01-001	WARWICKSHIRE	1-01-001	WELCOMES	1-01-001	WHIMPER
1-01-001	WAGE-SETTER	1-01-001	WARYS	1-01-001	WELDON	1-01-001	WHIMPERING
1-01-001	WAGGIN	1-01-001	WASH-OUTS	1-01-001	WELL-ADMINISTER ED	1-01-001	WHIMS
1-01-001	WAGGLED	1-01-001	WASH-UP			1-01-001	WHIMSEY
1-01-001	WAGGLING	1-01-001	WASHBASIN	1-01-001	WELL-ARMED	1-01-001	WHIMSICAL
1-01-001	WAGING	1-01-001	WASHBOARD	1-01-001	WELL-BABY	1-01-001	WHINED
1-01-001	WAHTAHM	1-01-001	WASHBOWL	1-01-001	WELL-BALANCED	1-01-001	WHINNY
1-01-001	WAILBRI	1-01-001	WASHED-OUT	1-01-001	WELL-BOUND	1-01-001	WHIP'S
1-01-001	WAINSCOTED	1-01-001	WASHINGTON-*ALE XANDRIA	1-01-001	WELL-BRACED	1-01-001	WHIPLASH
1-01-001	WAIST-*HIGH			1-01-001	WELL-BRED	1-01-001	WHIPLASHES
1-01-001	WAIST-LENGTH	1-01-001	WASHINGTON-*ORE GON	1-01-001	WELL-BRUSHED	1-01-001	WHIPPET
1-01-001	WAISTCOAT			1-01-001	WELL-CEMENTED	1-01-001	WHIPPING-BOYS
1-01-001	WAITE	1-01-001	WASHIZU'S	1-01-001	WELL-DRESSED	1-01-001	WHIPPLE'S
1-01-001	WAITIN	1-01-001	WASHOE	1-01-001	WELL-EQUIPPED	1-01-001	WHIPS
1-01-001	WAITRESSES	1-01-001	WASPISHLY	1-01-001	WELL-FLESHED	1-01-001	WHIPSAWED
1-01-001	WAIVE	1-01-001	WASSON	1-01-001	WELL-GROOVED	1-01-001	WHIRLPOOL
1-01-001	WAIVED	1-01-001	WASTAGE	1-01-001	WELL-HOUSE	1-01-001	WHIRLWIND'S
1-01-001	WAKENED	1-01-001	WASTREL	1-01-001	WELL-MODULATED	1-01-001	WHISKERED
1-01-001	WAKENING	1-01-001	WATCH-SPRING	1-01-001	WELL-MOLDED	1-01-001	WHISKING
1-01-001	WALBRIDGE	1-01-001	WATCHINGS	1-01-001	WELL-NIGH	1-01-001	WHISKY-ON-THE-* OCK
1-01-001	WALCOTT	1-01-001	WATCHMEN	1-01-001	WELL-ORGANIZED		
1-01-001	WALDENSIAN	1-01-001	WATER-BALANCE	1-01-001	WELL-ORIENTED	1-01-001	WHISPERINGS
1-01-001	WALES'	1-01-001	WATER-COOLED	1-01-001	WELL-PLANNED	1-01-001	WHIT
1-01-001	WALFORD	1-01-001	WATER-FILLED	1-01-001	WELL-PLAYED	1-01-001	WHITCOMB
1-01-001	WALK-TO	1-01-001	WATER-HOLDING	1-01-001	WELL-PREPARED	1-01-001	WHITE-COLLAR
1-01-001	WALK-UP	1-01-001	WATER-LINE	1-01-001	WELL-PUBLICIZED	1-01-001	WHITE-COLUMNED
1-01-001	WALK-WAY	1-01-001	WATER-PROOF	1-01-001	WELL-READ	1-01-001	WHITE-DOMINATE*
1-01-001	WALKERS	1-01-001	WATER-SKI	1-01-001	WELL-RECEIVED	1-01-001	WHITE-SHIRTED
1-01-001	WALKIN	1-01-001	WATER-USE	1-01-001	WELL-REGULATED	1-01-001	WHITE-STUCCO
1-01-001	WALKOUT	1-01-001	WATER-WASHED	1-01-001	WELL-ROUNDED	1-01-001	WHITE-SUITED
1-01-001	WALKOVER	1-01-001	WATERBURY	1-01-001	WELL-RULED	1-01-001	WHITEHAIRED
1-01-001	WALKWAYS	1-01-001	WATERFALLS	1-01-001	WELL-SPRINGS	1-01-001	WHITEHALL
1-01-001	WALL-*TEX	1-01-001	WATERFLOWS	1-01-001	WELL-STOCKED	1-01-001	WHITELEAF
1-01-001	WALL-FLOWERS	1-01-001	WATERLINE	1-01-001	WELL-STRETCHED	1-01-001	WHITELEY
1-01-001	WALL-STABILIZED	1-01-001	WATERLOO	1-01-001	WELL-STUFFED	1-01-001	WHITELY
1-01-001	WALL-SWITCH	1-01-001	WATERMELON	1-01-001	WELL-UNDERSTOOD	1-01-001	WHITENING
1-01-001	WALLBOARD	1-01-001	WATERPROOFING	1-01-001	WELL-WEDGED	1-01-001	WHITENS
1-01-001	WALLE	1-01-001	WATERSIDE	1-01-001	WELL-WISHERS	1-01-001	WHITEWASHED
1-01-001	WALLED	1-01-001	WATERSKIING	1-01-001	WELL-WISHING	1-01-001	WHITFIELD
1-01-001	WALLINGFORD	1-01-001	WATLING	1-01-001	WELL-WORN	1-01-001	WHITMAN'S
1-01-001	WALLOP	1-01-001	WATSON-*WATT	1-01-001	WELL-WRITTEN	1-01-001	WHITTAKER
1-01-001	WALLOPED	1-01-001	WATSON-*WATT'S	1-01-001	WELLBEING	1-01-001	WHITTIER
1-01-001	WALLOPING	1-01-001	WATSON-WATT'S	1-01-001	WELLED	1-01-001	WHITTIER'S
1-01-001	WALLOW	1-01-001	WATTENBERG	1-01-001	WELLING	1-01-001	WHIZZING
1-01-001	WALLOWED	1-01-001	WATTERSON	1-01-001	WELLINGTON	1-01-001	WHO'LL
1-01-001	WALLOWING	1-01-001	WAVE-PARTICLE	1-01-001	WELLKNOWN	1-01-001	WHOA
1-01-001	WALLPAPERS	1-01-001	WAVE-SETTING	1-01-001	WELLMAN	1-01-001	WHODUNNIT
1-01-001	WALPOLE	1-01-001	WAVE-TRAVEL	1-01-001	WELLSLEY	1-01-001	WHOLE-HEARTEDL
1-01-001	WALRUS	1-01-001	WAVELAND	1-01-001	WELLSVILLE	1-01-001	WHOLE-HOUSE
1-01-001	WALSH'S	1-01-001	WAVERS	1-01-001	WELMERS	1-01-001	WHOLE-WORD
1-01-001	WALTHAM	1-01-001	WAVY-HAIRED	1-01-001	WELTANSCHAUUNG	1-01-001	WHOLEHEARTEDLY
1-01-001	WALTZ	1-01-001	WAXEN	1-01-001	WELTON	1-01-001	WHOLESALERS
1-01-001	WAND	1-01-001	WAXING	1-01-001	WELTS	1-01-001	WHOLEWHEAT
1-01-001	WANDERER	1-01-001	WAXWORKS	1-01-001	WENDELLS	1-01-001	WHOOP
1-01-001	WANDERERS	1-01-001	WAY'S	1-01-001	WERGELAND	1-01-001	WHOOSH
1-01-001	WANDERJAHR	1-01-001	WAY-OUT	1-01-001	WERT'S	1-01-001	WHOPPERS
1-01-001	WANGEMANS	1-01-001	WAYLAID	1-01-001	WES	1-01-001	WHOPPING
1-01-001	WANGLED	1-01-001	WAYMOUTH	1-01-001	WESLEY'S	1-01-001	WHORES
1-01-001	WANSEE	1-01-001	WE'UNS	1-01-001	WESSON	1-01-001	WHORLS
1-01-001	WANSLEY	1-01-001	WEAKENS	1-01-001	WESTERNERS	1-01-001	WHY'N
1-01-001	WANTA	1-01-001	WEALTHIEST	1-01-001	WESTHAMPTON	1-01-001	WHYFORES
1-01-001	WANTING-TO-BE-A LONE	1-01-001	WEANED	1-01-001	WESTWARDS	1-01-001	WHYN'T
		1-01-001	WEAPONRY	1-01-001	WESTWOOD	1-01-001	WICHITA
1-01-001	WAPPINGER	1-01-001	WEARIED	1-01-001	WETLANDS	1-01-001	WICKET
1-01-001	WAR-DIRTY	1-01-001	WEARIN	1-01-001	WETLY	1-01-001	WICKETS
1-01-001	WAR-TIME	1-01-001	WEASEL	1-01-001	WETNESS	1-01-001	WICKHAM
1-01-001	WARBLING	1-01-001	WEASEL-WORDED	1-01-001	WETTER	1-01-001	WIDE-AWAKE
1-01-001	WARD'S	1-01-001	WEATHER-ROYAL	1-01-001	WEYBOSSET	1-01-001	WIDE-CUT
1-01-001	WARD-HEELERS	1-01-001	WEATHERBEATEN	1-01-001	WHACK	1-01-001	WIDE-DOOR
1-01-001	WARD-PERSONNEL	1-01-001	WEATHERS	1-01-001	WHAH	1-01-001	WIDE-EYED
1-01-001	WARDROOM	1-01-001	WEATHERSTRIP	1-01-001	WHALING	1-01-001	WIDE-GRIP
1-01-001	WARE	1-01-001	WEBB	1-01-001	WHARTON	1-01-001	WIDE-OPEN
1-01-001	WAREHOUSEMAN'S	1-01-001	WEBBER	1-01-001	WHAT'D	1-01-001	WIDE-SHOULDERE
1-01-001	WAREHOUSING	1-01-001	WEBSTER'S	1-01-001	WHAT'RE	1-01-001	WIDE-SWEEPING
1-01-001	WARES	1-01-001	WECHSLER	1-01-001	WHAT-NOTS	1-01-001	WIDE-WINGED
1-01-001	WARFIELD	1-01-001	WEDNESDAY'S	1-01-001	WHAT-WILL-*T	1-01-001	WIDEGRIP
1-01-001	WARFRONT	1-01-001	WEDNESDAYS	1-01-001	WHATMAN	1-01-001	WIDENER
1-01-001	WARLESS	1-01-001	WEED	1-01-001	WHEARE	1-01-001	WIDENS
1-01-001	WARM-BLOODED	1-01-001	WEEDE	1-01-001	WHEE	1-01-001	WIDOWER
1-01-001	WARM-TONED	1-01-001	WEEDED	1-01-001	WHEEDLED	1-01-001	WIDOWHOOD
1-01-001	WARM-UP	1-01-001	WEEK-OLD	1-01-001	WHEELAN'S	1-01-001	WIDOWS
1-01-001	WARMED-OVER	1-01-001	WEEMS'S	1-01-001	WHEELER'S	1-01-001	WIDSITH
1-01-001	WARMHEARTED	1-01-001	WEGENER	1-01-001	WHEELOCK'S	1-01-001	WIDTHWISE
1-01-001	WARMISH	1-01-001	WEIDMAN	1-01-001	WHEEZED	1-01-001	WIEDERUM
1-01-001	WARMONGERING	1-01-001	WEIGHT-HEIGHT	1-01-001	WHEEZES	1-01-001	WIELAND
1-01-001	WARMS	1-01-001	WEIGHTING	1-01-001	WHEEZING	1-01-001	WIELD
1-01-001	WARMUP	1-01-001	WEIGLE	1-01-001	WHELAN	1-01-001	WIELDER
1-01-001	WARNER	1-01-001	WEIL	1-01-001	WHER	1-01-001	WIENERS
1-01-001	WARNINGLY	1-01-001	WEINBERG	1-01-001	WHERE'RE	1-01-001	WIENERS'
1-01-001	WARRANTY	1-01-001	WEINSTEIN'S	1-01-001	WHEREEVER	1-01-001	WIFE-TO-BE
1-01-001	WARRED	1-01-001	WEIRDLY	1-01-001	WHEREFORES	1-01-001	WIFELY
1-01-001	WARREN'S	1-01-001	WEIRDY	1-01-001	WHEREON	1-01-001	WIG

Rank	Entry
1-01-001	WIGGLE
1-01-001	WILCKE
1-01-001	WILD-EYED
1-01-001	WILD-SOUNDING
1-01-001	WILDCATTER
1-01-001	WILDE
1-01-001	WILDENSTEIN
1-01-001	WILDER
1-01-001	WILDER'S
1-01-001	WILDEST
1-01-001	WILDHACK
1-01-001	WILDNESS
1-01-001	WILFRED
1-01-001	WILFRID
1-01-001	WILIGIS
1-01-001	WILKES-*BARRE
1-01-001	WILKEY
1-01-001	WILKINSON
1-01-001	WILL-TO-POWER
1-01-001	WILLA
1-01-001	WILLEM
1-01-001	WILLETT
1-01-001	WILLFUL
1-01-001	WILLFULLY
1-01-001	WILLIAMS'
1-01-001	WILLIAMSBURG
1-01-001	WILLIAMSON'S
1-01-001	WILLINGE
1-01-001	WILLOW-LINED
1-01-001	WILLOWS
1-01-001	WILLOWY
1-01-001	WILLS
1-01-001	WILLYA
1-01-001	WILSONIAN
1-01-001	WILTED
1-01-001	WIMSATT
1-01-001	WINCHELL
1-01-001	WINCHES
1-01-001	WINCING
1-01-001	WIND-AND-WATER
1-01-001	WIND-VELOCITY
1-01-001	WINDBAG
1-01-001	WINDBREAKS
1-01-001	WINDERS
1-01-001	WINDING-CLOTHES
1-01-001	WINDLESS
1-01-001	WINDMILL
1-01-001	WINDOW-WASHING
1-01-001	WINDSTORM
1-01-001	WINDUP
1-01-001	WINE'S
1-01-001	WINE-
1-01-001	WINEHEAD
1-01-001	WINFIELD
1-01-001	WING-SHOOTING
1-01-001	WINGBACK
1-01-001	WINGING
1-01-001	WINNETKA
1-01-001	WINNIPEG
1-01-001	WINNIPESAUKEE
1-01-001	WINNOW
1-01-001	WINOS
1-01-001	WINSETT
1-01-001	WINSOME
1-01-001	WINTERING
1-01-001	WINTERTIME
1-01-001	WIRE-HAIRED
1-01-001	WIS
1-01-001	WISCONSIN'S
1-01-001	WISED
1-01-001	WISENHEIMER
1-01-001	WISEST
1-01-001	WISHART
1-01-001	WISPS
1-01-001	WISSAHICKON
1-01-001	WITH-BUT-AFTER
1-01-001	WITHAL
1-01-001	WITHERING
1-01-001	WITHERSPOON
1-01-001	WITHES
1-01-001	WITHSTANDS
1-01-001	WITOLD
1-01-001	WITTER
1-01-001	WITTINGLY
1-01-001	WIVE'S
1-01-001	WOBBLING
1-01-001	WOBURN
1-01-001	WOD
1-01-001	WOEBEGONE
1-01-001	WOEFUL
1-01-001	WOHAWS
1-01-001	WOHD
1-01-001	WOLCOTT
1-01-001	WOLCYRZ
1-01-001	WOLD
1-01-001	WOLDE
1-01-001	WOLFE'S
1-01-001	WOLFES
1-01-001	WOLFGANG
1-01-001	WOLFISHLY
1-01-001	WOLPE
1-01-001	WOLPE'S
1-01-001	WOLSTENHOLME
1-01-001	WOLVERTON
1-01-001	WOMANHOOD
1-01-001	WOMANLY
1-01-001	WOMB
1-01-001	WOMB-TO-TOMB
1-01-001	WOMEN-TRODDEN
1-01-001	WON-LOST
1-01-001	WONDER-WORKING
1-01-001	WONDERFULNESS
1-01-001	WONDERINGLY
1-01-001	WONDERLAND
1-01-001	WONDROUS
1-01-001	WONDROUSLY
1-01-001	WONDUH
1-01-001	WOOD-GRAINED
1-01-001	WOOD-OIL
1-01-001	WOODBERRY
1-01-001	WOODBURY'S
1-01-001	WOODCARVER
1-01-001	WOODCOCK
1-01-001	WOODCOCK'S
1-01-001	WOODCUTTERS
1-01-001	WOODEN-LEG
1-01-001	WOODGRAINING
1-01-001	WOODIN
1-01-001	WOODMAN'S
1-01-001	WOODPECKER
1-01-001	WOODS'S
1-01-001	WOODSHED
1-01-001	WOODYARD
1-01-001	WOOED
1-01-001	WOOLGATHER
1-01-001	WOOLLCOTT
1-01-001	WOOLLY-HEADED
1-01-001	WOOLLY-MINDED
1-01-001	WOOLWORKERS
1-01-001	WOOLWORTH'S
1-01-001	WOOMERA
1-01-001	WOONASQUATUCKET
1-01-001	WOOOOOSH
1-01-001	WOP
1-01-001	WOPS
1-01-001	WORD-GAMES
1-01-001	WORDY
1-01-001	WORK'S
1-01-001	WORK-OUTS
1-01-001	WORK-PARALYSIS
1-01-001	WORK-SATISFACTION
1-01-001	WORK-STUDY
1-01-001	WORK-SUCCESS
1-01-001	WORK-WEARY
1-01-001	WORK/
1-01-001	WORKDAY
1-01-001	WORKIN
1-01-001	WORKINGMEN
1-01-001	WORKMAN
1-01-001	WORKMAN'S
1-01-001	WORKPIECE
1-01-001	WORKSHEET
1-01-001	WORKTABLE
1-01-001	WORLD-AT-LARGE
1-01-001	WORLD-IGNORING
1-01-001	WORLD-ORIENTED
1-01-001	WORLD-SHATTERING
1-01-001	WORLDERS
1-01-001	WORLDWIDE
1-01-001	WORMY
1-01-001	WORN-FACED
1-01-001	WORN-OUT
1-01-001	WORNOUT
1-01-001	WORRELL
1-01-001	WORRIEDLY
1-01-001	WORRYIN
1-01-001	WORSENED
1-01-001	WORSENS
1-01-001	WORSHIPED
1-01-001	WORSHIPPERS
1-01-001	WORSHIPPING
1-01-001	WORST-MARKED
1-01-001	WORTH-WAITING-FOR
1-01-001	WORTH-WHILE
1-01-001	WORTHLESSNESS
1-01-001	WOULDA
1-01-001	WOULDBE
1-01-001	WOUND-TUMOR
1-01-001	WOUNDING
1-01-001	WOVEN-ROOT
1-01-001	WOW
1-01-001	WOZZEK
1-01-001	WRACK
1-01-001	WRACKED
1-01-001	WRACKING
1-01-001	WRAGGE
1-01-001	WRAPPERS
1-01-001	WRAPPIN
1-01-001	WRATHFUL
1-01-001	WRATTEN
1-01-001	WREAK
1-01-001	WREATHED
1-01-001	WRENCHING
1-01-001	WREST
1-01-001	WRESTLER'S
1-01-001	WRESTLES
1-01-001	WRESTLING
1-01-001	WRESTLINGS
1-01-001	WRETCH
1-01-001	WRETCHEDNESS
1-01-001	WRINGS
1-01-001	WRITER'S
1-01-001	WRITER-TURNED-PAINTER
1-01-001	WRITHED
1-01-001	WRITING-LIKE
1-01-001	WRITS
1-01-001	WRONG-HEADED
1-01-001	WRONG-O
1-01-001	WRONGDOER
1-01-001	WRONGED
1-01-001	WRONGFUL
1-01-001	WRONGLY
1-01-001	WROUGHT-IRON
1-01-001	WRY-FACED
1-01-001	WT
1-01-001	WU
1-01-001	WUH
1-01-001	WUS
1-01-001	WUSTMAN
1-01-001	WYCKOFF
1-01-001	WYCLIFFE
1-01-001	WYCOFF
1-01-001	WYCOFF'S
1-01-001	WYCOMBE
1-01-001	WYMAN
1-01-001	WYN
1-01-001	WYNN
1-01-001	WYNNE
1-01-001	WYNSTON
1-01-001	X
1-01-001	X-*TRU-*COAT
1-01-001	XAVIER
1-01-001	XAVIER'S
1-01-001	XENIA
1-01-001	XENON
1-01-001	XIMENEZ-*VARGAS
1-01-001	YYYY
1-01-001	XYDIS'
1-01-001	XYLOPHONES
1-01-001	Y**.*M**.*C**.*A
1-01-001	Y**.*M**.*H**.*A
1-01-001	Y**.*W**.*C**.*A
1-01-001	Y'R
1-01-001	Y**U
1-01-001	YACHTELS
1-01-001	YACHTERS
1-01-001	YACHTSMAN
1-01-001	YACHTSMEN
1-01-001	YADDO
1-01-001	YAHWE
1-01-001	YAKIMA
1-01-001	YAKOV
1-01-001	YAKS
1-01-001	YALAGALOO
1-01-001	YALE'S
1-01-001	YALE-*ARMY
1-01-001	YALIES
1-01-001	YAMABE
1-01-001	YAMATA
1-01-001	YANCEY-6
1-01-001	YANCY-6
1-01-001	YANKEE-HATRED
1-01-001	YANKING
1-01-001	YANKS'
1-01-001	YANKTON
1-01-001	YAPPING
1-01-001	YAQUI
1-01-001	YARDUMIAN
1-01-001	YASSUHS
1-01-001	YAWL
1-01-001	YAWS
1-01-001	YD
1-01-001	YEAR-END
1-01-001	YEAR-LONG
1-01-001	YEAR-OLD
1-01-001	YEARD
1-01-001	YEARN
1-01-001	YEARNINGLY
1-01-001	YEASTS
1-01-001	YEATS
1-01-001	YEDISAN
1-01-001	YEHUDI
1-01-001	YELLERISH
1-01-001	YELLIN
1-01-001	YELLOW-BELLIED
1-01-001	YELLOW-BROWN
1-01-001	YELLOWED
1-01-001	YELLOWISH
1-01-001	YELPED
1-01-001	YELPING
1-01-001	YELPS
1-01-001	YENI
1-01-001	YESIREE
1-01-001	YIELDING-*MEDITERRANEAN-WOMAN-FLESH-OF-WATER
1-01-001	YINGER
1-01-001	YIP
1-01-001	YODEL
1-01-001	YOGA
1-01-001	YOK
1-01-001	YOKELS
1-01-001	YOKUSUKA
1-01-001	YOLK
1-01-001	YON
1-01-001	YONDER
1-01-001	YONGST
1-01-001	YONKERS
1-01-001	YOOEE
1-01-001	YOORICK
1-01-001	YORI
1-01-001	YORK-*PENNSYLVANIA
1-01-001	YORK-BORN
1-01-001	YORK-MIND
1-01-001	YORK(**JAP
1-01-001	YORKER'S
1-01-001	YOSHIMOTO'S
1-01-001	YOU'S
1-01-001	YOU'UNS
1-01-001	YOU**LL
1-01-001	YOUNGSTER'S
1-01-001	YOUNGUH
1-01-001	YR.
1-01-001	YS
1-01-001	YTIME
1-01-001	YUCATAN
1-01-001	YUCCA
1-01-001	YUJOBO
1-01-001	YUKI
1-01-001	YUM-*YUM
1-01-001	TURBOIIKA
1-01-001	YUSE
1-01-001	YYYY
1-01-001	ZABEL
1-01-001	ZACHRISSON
1-01-001	ZACHRISSON'S
1-01-001	ZADEL
1-01-001	ZAMIATIN'S
1-01-001	ZANZIBAR
1-01-001	ZAPALA
1-01-001	ZAPOROGIAN
1-01-001	ZARA
1-01-001	ZAROUBIN
1-01-001	ZEALOT
1-01-001	ZEBEK
1-01-001	ZEBRA
1-01-001	ZEFFIRELLI
1-01-001	ZEISING
1-01-001	ZEITGEIST
1-01-001	ZEME
1-01-001	ZEMLYA
1-01-001	ZEND-*AVESTA
1-01-001	ZENNIST
1-01-001	ZEROED
1-01-001	ZHITKOV
1-01-001	ZHITZHAKLI
1-01-001	ZHOK
1-01-001	ZIGGY
1-01-001	ZIMINSKA-*SYGIETYNSKA
1-01-001	ZINGGGG-*O
1-01-001	ZINMAN
1-01-001	ZIONISM
1-01-001	ZIONISTS
1-01-001	ZIP
1-01-001	ZIPPED
1-01-001	ZIPPER
1-01-001	ZIRALDO
1-01-001	ZLOTYS
1-01-001	ZOE

ID	Term	ID	Term	ID	Term	ID	Term
1-01-001	ZOMBIE	1-01-001	1,107	1-01-001	110**+0	1-01-001	15-17
1-01-001	ZOMBIES	1-01-001	1,119	1-01-001	110**+0**J*C	1-01-001	15-20
1-01-001	ZONED	1-01-001	1,212	1-01-001	115	1-01-001	15,500-**JLB
1-01-001	ZOOEY	1-01-001	1,212,000	1-01-001	116	1-01-001	150-MILLIAMPERE
1-01-001	ZOOLOGY	1-01-001	1,225	1-01-001	116,000	1-01-001	151
1-01-001	ZOOMING	1-01-001	1,230	1-01-001	1162	1-01-001	1514
1-01-001	ZOOMS	1-01-001	1,253	1-01-001	117	1-01-001	1515
1-01-001	ZOOOOP	1-01-001	1,257,7000	1-01-001	1184	1-01-001	1516
1-01-001	ZORRILLAS	1-01-001	1,286	1-01-001	12.01	1-01-001	1540
1-01-001	ZOTE	1-01-001	1,338,000	1-01-001	12.8	1-01-001	1543
1-01-001	ZU	1-01-001	1,343	1-01-001	12**C01	1-01-001	155
1-01-001	ZWEI	1-01-001	1,400	1-01-001	12**C14	1-01-001	155-YARDER
1-01-001	0.002	1-01-001	1,418,000	1-01-001	12**C50	1-01-001	1550
1-01-001	0.005	1-01-001	1,419,833	1-01-001	12**J0Z	1-01-001	1558
1-01-001	0.025-IN	1-01-001	1,450	1-01-001	12-INCH	1-01-001	157
1-01-001	0.039	1-01-001	1,450,000	1-01-001	12-MONTH	1-01-001	158
1-01-001	0.043	1-01-001	1,488	1-01-001	12-PASSENGER	1-01-001	158-POUNDER
1-01-001	0.075	1-01-001	1,509	1-01-001	12-SHOT	1-01-001	1581
1-01-001	0.080-IN	1-01-001	1,512	1-01-001	12-TO-ONE	1-01-001	1589
1-01-001	0.1-MV**./M	1-01-001	1,524	1-01-001	12-YEAR-OLD	1-01-001	1590
1-01-001	0.10	1-01-001	1,525,000	1-01-001	12-1/2	1-01-001	1594-1674
1-01-001	0.12	1-01-001	1,541,991	1-01-001	12-14	1-01-001	1595
1-01-001	0.15	1-01-001	1,571	1-01-001	12-17	1-01-001	1596
1-01-001	0.154	1-01-001	1,800	1-01-001	12,500	1-01-001	1596/7
1-01-001	0.24	1-01-001	1,800,000	1-01-001	12TH	1-01-001	1597
1-01-001	0.25	1-01-001	1,850	1-01-001	120**+0	1-01-001	1597/8
1-01-001	0.28	1-01-001	1,900	1-01-001	120**+0-160**+0*F	1-01-001	1598/9
1-01-001	0.3**YM	1-01-001	1(**JB	1-01-001	120,000	1-01-001	1599
1-01-001	0.36	1-01-001	1(**JC	1-01-001	1200	1-01-001	16.38
1-01-001	0.5**J**YM	1-01-001	1A	1-01-001	1200-SQUARE-FOOT	1-01-001	16.7
1-01-001	0.5-MV**./M	1-01-001	10			1-01-001	16-HOUR
1-01-001	0.50	1-01-001	10.2	1-01-001	121,000	1-01-001	16-MESH
1-01-001	0.52	1-01-001	10.3	1-01-001	1213	1-01-001	16-PAGE
1-01-001	0.7	1-01-001	10.3-**JCM	1-01-001	1213-15	1-01-001	16-YEAR-OLD
1-01-001	0.70	1-01-001	10.4	1-01-001	1215	1-01-001	16-22
1-01-001	0.78	1-01-001	10.6	1-01-001	122,158	1-01-001	160**+0*F
1-01-001	0.85	1-01-001	10.6**K	1-01-001	1223	1-01-001	160-ML
1-01-001	0.906	1-01-001	10.8**K	1-01-001	123	1-01-001	1600/1
1-01-001	0.95	1-01-001	10**0	1-01-001	1231	1-01-001	1605
1-01-001	035	1-01-001	10**0**J*C	1-01-001	125,000	1-01-001	1608
1-01-001	046	1-01-001	10**B-A-MINUTE	1-01-001	125TH	1-01-001	161
1-01-001	060	1-01-001	10**C00-1**C00	1-01-001	126,000	1-01-001	1615
1-01-001	0600	1-01-001	10**C05	1-01-001	127	1-01-001	162
1-01-001	1.0-**JMG/**JL	1-01-001	10**C10	1-01-001	127-MILE	1-01-001	162-GAME
1-01-001	1.09.3	1-01-001	10**C45	1-01-001	129**K	1-01-001	162,400
1-01-001	1.10.1	1-01-001	10**C50	1-01-001	1290	1-01-001	1622
1-01-001	1.10.4	1-01-001	10-**J**YM-DIAMETER	1-01-001	1298	1-01-001	1626
1-01-001	1.10.8			1-01-001	13.8	1-01-001	1628
1-01-001	1.2	1-01-001	10-DAY	1-01-001	13.9	1-01-001	1628/29
1-01-001	1.23	1-01-001	10-FOOT	1-01-001	13**K	1-01-001	1630
1-01-001	1.25	1-01-001	10-GALLON	1-01-001	13*,-*/15	1-01-001	1631
1-01-001	1.25**K	1-01-001	10-HOUR	1-01-001	13-1/2	1-01-001	1633
1-01-001	1.58	1-01-001	10-MILLIGRAM	1-01-001	13-16	1-01-001	1637
1-01-001	1.8**K	1-01-001	10-O'CLOCK	1-01-001	13-5	1-01-001	1638
1-01-001	1**+0	1-01-001	10-TEAM	1-01-001	13-8	1-01-001	1639
1-01-001	1*+0**J*C	1-01-001	10-YR	1-01-001	13,200	1-01-001	1639-40
1-01-001	1**C00	1-01-001	10-1/2	1-01-001	130-YEAR	1-01-001	164
1-01-001	1**C1	1-01-001	10-15**K	1-01-001	1300	1-01-001	1640
1-01-001	1**C100	1-01-001	10-16	1-01-001	1307	1-01-001	1642
1-01-001	1**C1024	1-01-001	10,500	1-01-001	1310	1-01-001	1644
1-01-001	1**C15	1-01-001	10,517	1-01-001	1311	1-01-001	165-UNIT
1-01-001	1**C16	1-01-001	10TH	1-01-001	132,000	1-01-001	1655
1-01-001	1**C18	1-01-001	100-BRICK	1-01-001	135**+0*C	1-01-001	1657
1-01-001	1**C2	1-01-001	100-MEGATON	1-01-001	138	1-01-001	166
1-01-001	1**C2048	1-01-001	100-MILLION-LB	1-01-001	139	1-01-001	1665
1-01-001	1**C218	1-01-001	100-TON	1-01-001	139-FOOT	1-01-001	1665.32
1-01-001	1**C23	1-01-001	100-105**+0*F	1-01-001	14.2	1-01-001	1667.36
1-01-001	1**C27	1-01-001	100-200	1-01-001	14.5	1-01-001	1671
1-01-001	1**C35	1-01-001	100-230	1-01-001	14-*/1	1-01-001	1678
1-01-001	1**C5	1-01-001	1000-**J**YM-DIAMETER	1-01-001	14-*/2	1-01-001	1680
1-01-001	1**C500			1-01-001	14-POWER	1-01-001	1687
1-01-001	1**C59.3	1-01-001	1001	1-01-001	14-TERM	1-01-001	1688
1-01-001	1**C6	1-01-001	101**J*B	1-01-001	14-1	1-01-001	1690
1-01-001	1**J*=*M	1-01-001	102	1-01-001	140**+0*F	1-01-001	1692
1-01-001	1*,-**J*0	1-01-001	1020	1-01-001	140,000	1-01-001	1693
1-01-001	1-**JHP	1-01-001	103	1-01-001	140,414	1-01-001	17.3
1-01-001	1-**JML	1-01-001	104(**JG	1-01-001	1409	1-01-001	17**C07
1-01-001	1-INCH	1-01-001	1044	1-01-001	141	1-01-001	17*,E
1-01-001	1-TON	1-01-001	105**+0	1-01-001	142	1-01-001	17-1/2-INCH
1-01-001	1-0	1-01-001	105,000	1-01-001	143	1-01-001	17,000
1-01-001	1-1.5	1-01-001	106,500	1-01-001	144	1-01-001	170**+0**J*C
1-01-001	1-1/2-INCH	1-01-001	1068-1159	1-01-001	145	1-01-001	1700'S
1-01-001	1-1/2-STORY	1-01-001	11.2	1-01-001	145-POUND	1-01-001	1702-14
1-01-001	1-3	1-01-001	11.6	1-01-001	1450	1-01-001	1709
1-01-001	1-6	1-01-001	11**C00	1-01-001	147,000	1-01-001	171
1-01-001	1-701	1-01-001	11**C00-12**C00	1-01-001	1479	1-01-001	172
1-01-001	1/2-INCH	1-01-001	11-INCH	1-01-001	1492	1-01-001	172ND
1-01-001	1/20TH	1-01-001	11-MONTH-OLD	1-01-001	15.0-15.5	1-01-001	1720
1-01-001	1/4-INCH	1-01-001	11-SHOT	1-01-001	15.4	1-01-001	1724
1-01-001	1/50TH	1-01-001	11-YEAR	1-01-001	15.8	1-01-001	1727
1-01-001	1/6)(5/6)(1/6	1-01-001	11-12	1-01-001	15**J*A	1-01-001	1728
1-01-001	1,000,000	1-01-001	11-18	1-01-001	15-AND	1-01-001	173
1-01-001	1,018,000	1-01-001	11-3	1-01-001	15-DEGREE	1-01-001	1730
1-01-001	1,040	1-01-001	11-5	1-01-001	15-HIT	1-01-001	1731
1-01-001	1,065	1-01-001	11-7	1-01-001	15-TO-ONE	1-01-001	1732
1-01-001	1,080,062	1-01-001	11,000	1-01-001	15-YEAR-OLD	1-01-001	1733
1-01-001	1,100	1-01-001	11,744	1-01-001	15-1	1-01-001	174

1-01-001	1745	1-01-001	1938-1939	1-01-001	2*,-2	1-01-001	237**K
1-01-001	1746-1748	1-01-001	1940'S	1-01-001	2*,-3	1-01-001	24**+0
1-01-001	1747	1-01-001	1940S	1-01-001	2*,-4	1-01-001	24-*OCT
1-01-001	175	1-01-001	1946-52	1-01-001	2*,-5	1-01-001	24-HOUR
1-01-001	175,000	1-01-001	1947-49	1-01-001	2-*A.	1-01-001	24-HOUR-DAY
1-01-001	1750	1-01-001	1948**C135-75	1-01-001	2-AND-2	1-01-001	24-IN
1-01-001	1751	1-01-001	195-PAGE	1-01-001	2-BASER	1-01-001	24-INCH
1-01-001	1755	1-01-001	1950-1953	1-01-001	2-HOUR-AND-27-MINUTE	1-01-001	24-SHEET
1-01-001	1764	1-01-001	1951-1956			1-01-001	24-YEAR-OLD
1-01-001	1769	1-01-001	1952-1958	1-01-001	2-INCH	1-01-001	24,400
1-01-001	1769-1842	1-01-001	1957**C247-83	1-01-001	2-OVER-PAR	1-01-001	242**K
1-01-001	1770'S	1-01-001	1957-1958	1-01-001	2-SCORE-YEAR	1-01-001	2433
1-01-001	1771	1-01-001	1957B	1-01-001	2-WEEK	1-01-001	2454
1-01-001	1773	1-01-001	1958*=A	1-01-001	2/**JC	1-01-001	247
1-01-001	1774	1-01-001	1958*=B	1-01-001	2/3	1-01-001	25.1**K
1-01-001	1777	1-01-001	1958-60	1-01-001	2/4	1-01-001	25.3
1-01-001	1781	1-01-001	1959**C271-307	1-01-001	2,090	1-01-001	25**JC
1-01-001	1785	1-01-001	1960-1961	1-01-001	2,200,000	1-01-001	25-FOOT
1-01-001	1786	1-01-001	1960-1962	1-01-001	2,300	1-01-001	25-FOOTER
1-01-001	1786-1865	1-01-001	1960S	1-01-001	2,417	1-01-001	25-FT
1-01-001	1788-1873	1-01-001	1963-1972	1-01-001	2,418	1-01-001	25-GALLON
1-01-001	1789-1839	1-01-001	1970S	1-01-001	2,425	1-01-001	25-LITER
1-01-001	1799	1-01-001	1971	1-01-001	2,460	1-01-001	25-MILE-SQUARE
1-01-001	18'.5	1-01-001	1972	1-01-001	2,489,000	1-01-001	25-MINUTE
1-01-001	18**C21-22	1-01-001	1976	1-01-001	2,500	1-01-001	25-YEAR-OLD
1-01-001	18-*MARCH	1-01-001	198	1-01-001	2,700,877	1-01-001	25-30
1-01-001	18-MONTH	1-01-001	1981	1-01-001	2,758	1-01-001	25,000-MAN
1-01-001	18-1/2	1-01-001	1984	1-01-001	2,800	1-01-001	25,000,000
1-01-001	18-1/2-INCH	1-01-001	1991	1-01-001	2,800,000	1-01-001	250-275
1-01-001	18-25	1-01-001	2.1.6	1-01-001	2,887,671	1-01-001	2500
1-01-001	18,792	1-01-001	2.16	1-01-001	2,963	1-01-001	253
1-01-001	18TH-*CENTURY	1-01-001	2.2	1-01-001	2A	1-01-001	254
1-01-001	1800'S	1-01-001	2.21.6	1-01-001	20**+0**J*C	1-01-001	2544
1-01-001	1800-SQUARE-FOOT	1-01-001	2.26	1-01-001	20'S	1-01-001	255
1-01-001	1802	1-01-001	2.295**K	1-01-001	20**JMM	1-01-001	26.8
1-01-001	1803-1895	1-01-001	2.3	1-01-001	20*,TH-CENTURY	1-01-001	26-YEAR-OLD
1-01-001	1804	1-01-001	2.325**K	1-01-001	20-**JCPS	1-01-001	26-2
1-01-001	1805-1879	1-01-001	2.405	1-01-001	20-GAUGE	1-01-001	26-28
1-01-001	1806	1-01-001	2.44	1-01-001	20-INCH-BARREL	1-01-001	26,500
1-01-001	1807-1892	1-260-001	2.5**K	1-01-001	20-MEGATON	1-01-001	260-MEMBER
1-01-001	1808-1895	1-01-001	2.54	1-01-001	20-PIECE	1-01-001	261
1-01-001	1811	1-01-001	2.55	1-01-001	20-22	1-01-001	265
1-01-001	1811-1884	1-01-001	2.58	1-01-001	20-25	1-01-001	268,900
1-01-001	1816	1-01-001	2.7	1-01-001	20-50	1-01-001	2688
1-01-001	182	1-01-001	2.8	1-01-001	20,000,000	1-01-001	269
1-01-001	1823	1-01-001	2**+0**J*C	1-01-001	20S	1-01-001	27**K
1-01-001	1825-1826	1-27-001	2'S	1-01-001	200**+0	1-01-001	27-IN
1-01-001	1830	1-01-001	2**C00.2**JH	1-01-001	200-MAN	1-01-001	27-YEAR-OLD
1-01-001	1833	1-01-001	2**C00.3	1-01-001	200-MEGATON	1-01-001	27-30
1-01-001	1838	1-01-001	2**C01.1	1-01-001	200-ODD	1-01-001	27TH
1-01-001	1841	1-01-001	2**C01.3**JH	1-01-001	202	1-01-001	270,000
1-01-001	1843	1-01-001	2**C02	1-01-001	205-POUND	1-01-001	2705
1-01-001	1846	1-01-001	2**C02.2	1-01-001	2051	1-01-001	271
1-01-001	185	1-01-001	2**C03	1-01-001	206	1-01-001	272
1-01-001	185,000	1-01-001	2**C04	1-01-001	208-POUND	1-01-001	273
1-01-001	185TH	1-01-001	2**C05	1-01-001	21**C121-137	1-01-001	2731
1-01-001	1852	1-01-001	2**C05.1**JH	1-01-001	21**K	1-01-001	275**+0*F
1-01-001	1853	1-01-001	2**C05.2	1-01-001	21-**JCM	1-01-001	275-300
1-01-001	1854	1-01-001	2**C05.3	1-01-001	21-YEAR	1-01-001	278
1-01-001	1859-1929	1-01-001	2**C06.1	1-01-001	21-YEAR-OLD	1-01-001	28-*OCT
1-01-001	1860	1-01-001	2**C06.3**JH	1-01-001	21-2	1-01-001	28-30
1-01-001	1860'S	1-01-001	2**C06**JH	1-01-001	21-75	1-01-001	280-YARD
1-01-001	1865-1868	1-01-001	2**C10	1-01-001	21-9	1-01-001	2809
1-01-001	1866	1-01-001	2**C12	1-01-001	21/64	1-01-001	281
1-01-001	1867	1-01-001	2**C19	1-01-001	2118	1-01-001	2825
1-01-001	1868-70	1-01-001	2**C21	1-01-001	2130	1-01-001	283
1-01-001	1869	1-01-001	2**C24	1-01-001	214,938	1-01-001	285
1-01-001	187.5	1-01-001	2**C26.2	1-01-001	215	1-01-001	29-*JULY
1-01-001	18/-MILE	1-29-001	2**C28**-**C33	1-01-001	216	1-01-001	29-32**+0*C
1-01-001	1870'S	1-01-001	2**C28**-**C36	1-01-001	22**K	1-01-001	29-5
1-01-001	1871	1-01-001	2**C29	1-01-001	22-ACRE	1-01-001	2991
1-01-001	1874	1-01-001	2**C30**-**C33.2	1-01-001	22-DAY	1-01-001	3.0
1-01-001	1878	1-01-001	2**C30**JH	1-01-001	22-1/2	1-01-001	3.1
1-01-001	1880-1900	1-01-001	2**C30-**C36	1-01-001	22-12	1-01-001	3.10
1-01-001	1881-85	1-01-001	2**C31	1-01-001	22-24	1-01-001	3.1416
1-01-001	1884	1-01-001	2**C31.3-**C35.3	1-01-001	22-29	1-01-001	3.190
1-01-001	1889	1-01-001	2**C32.4**JH	1-01-001	22,23	1-01-001	3.28
1-01-001	1890S	1-01-001	2**C33	1-01-001	22,807	1-01-001	3.4
1-01-001	1897-8	1-01-001	2**C33.2**JH	1-01-001	220-YARD	1-01-001	3.5**K
1-01-001	19-FOOT	1-01-001	2**C33.3**JH	1-01-001	221-207	1-01-001	3.7
1-01-001	19-1/2	1-01-001	2**C34.2**JH	1-01-001	22111	1-01-001	3.75
1-01-001	19-12	1-01-001	2**C34**-**C34	1-01-001	2230	1-01-001	3.8
1-01-001	19-23	1-01-001	2**C37.3**-**C36.1**JH	1-01-001	224-170	1-01-001	3.9
1-01-001	19,000			1-01-001	225**J*H*P	1-01-001	3.98
1-01-001	19,000,000	1-01-001	2**C38	1-01-001	225,000	1-01-001	3'S
1-01-001	1908-1910	1-01-001	2**C38**JH	1-01-001	2269	1-01-001	3**C00
1-01-001	1910-14	1-01-001	2**C43.1**-**C38**JH	1-01-001	2274	1-01-001	3*C10-12
1-01-001	1911-1912			1-01-001	228	1-01-001	3**C14
1-01-001	1914-1918	1-01-001	2**C46	1-01-001	228-229	1-01-001	3**C16
1-01-001	1917-18	1-01-001	2**C55	1-01-001	23**C30	1-01-001	3**C17
1-01-001	1918-19	1-01-001	2**C67	1-01-001	23**C34	1-01-001	3**C18
1-01-001	1923-27	1-01-001	2**C8-10	1-01-001	23**J*A	1-01-001	3**C20
1-01-001	1928-29	1-01-001	2**J**YC	1-01-001	23-YEAR-OLD	1-01-001	3**C30
1-01-001	1931-40	1-01-001	2**JLB	1-01-001	23-30	1-01-001	3**C300
1-01-001	1932-33	1-01-001	2*,-*/12	1-01-001	23-36	1-01-001	3**C36
1-01-001	1935-1955			1-01-001	235	1-01-001	3**C5
				1-01-001	236	1-01-001	3**C58

1-01-001 3**C8	1-01-001 372	1-01-001 463*+0**J*C	1-01-001 566
1-01-001 3**C9	1-01-001 376	1-01-001 469	1-01-001 57**K
1-01-001 3*M*M	1-01-001 379,900	1-01-001 47.1**K	1-01-001 570
1-01-001 3-**JHP	1-01-001 38*+0	1-01-001 47.6	1-01-001 573
1-01-001 3-BY-	1-01-001 38-POINT	1-01-001 47**JMG/**K	1-01-001 5777
1-01-001 3-FOOT	1-01-001 38-43*+0*C	1-01-001 470	1-01-001 58.8**K
1-01-001 3-GAME	1-01-001 38-7	1-01-001 470*+0**J*C	1-01-001 5835
1-01-001 3-HITTER	1-01-001 380-FOOT	1-01-001 48,000	1-01-001 5847
1-01-001 3-MONTH	1-01-001 381(C)(14	1-01-001 48,500	1-01-001 589
1-01-001 3-RUN	1-01-001 381(C)(16	1-01-001 49*+0-71*+0*C	1-01-001 59,780
1-01-001 3-TO-0	1-01-001 381(C)(4	1-01-001 49**K	1-01-001 6.2
1-01-001 3-TO-3	1-01-001 381(C)(9	1-01-001 49ERS	1-01-001 6.3
1-01-001 3-YEAR-OLD	1-01-001 385	1-01-001 49TH	1-01-001 6.5
1-01-001 3-0	1-01-001 387	1-01-001 4911	1-01-001 6*+0**J*C
1-01-001 3-10	1-01-001 389	1-01-001 492	1-01-001 6'.7
1-01-001 3-4	1-01-001 39-YEAR-OLD	1-01-001 495	1-01-001 6**C00
1-01-001 3-48	1-01-001 390	1-01-001 5.1	1-01-001 6**C14-15
1-01-001 3-5	1-01-001 390-FOOT	1-01-001 5.3	1-01-001 6**C30
1-01-001 3-6	1-01-001 391	1-01-001 5.4	1-01-001 6**C35
1-01-001 3-7/8	1-01-001 394	1-01-001 5.4**B/**JMBF	1-01-001 6**C50
1-01-001 3/4	1-01-001 395	1-01-001 5.4865771	1-01-001 6**JA
1-01-001 3/64	1-01-001 4.0	1-01-001 5.8	1-01-001 6*,TH
1-01-001 3/8-INCH-THICK	1-01-001 4.00	1-01-001 5*+0**J*C	1-01-001 6-
1-01-001 3,325	1-01-001 4.21	1-01-001 5**C00	1-01-001 6-**J*B
1-01-001 3,399	1-01-001 4.4	1-01-001 5**C1	1-01-001 6-FOOT-10
1-01-001 3,400	1-01-001 4.6	1-01-001 5**C17	1-01-001 6-FOOT-3-INCH
1-01-001 3,450	1-01-001 4.7	1-01-001 5**C18	1-01-001 6-FT
1-01-001 30**B/**JMBF	1-01-001 4.77	1-01-001 5**C24	1-01-001 6-OUNCE
1-01-001 30-INCH	1-01-001 4.8	1-01-001 5**C26	1-01-001 6-YEAR
1-01-001 30-MINUTE	1-01-001 4**C00	1-01-001 5**C30	1-01-001 6-1
1-01-001 30-PIECE	1-01-001 4**C05	1-01-001 5**C4	1-01-001 6-12
1-01-001 30-YEAR	1-01-001 4**C1	1-01-001 5**C45	1-01-001 6-2/3
1-01-001 30-30	1-01-001 4**C18	1-01-001 5-	1-01-001 6-3-3
1-01-001 30-40	1-01-001 4**C3	1-01-001 5-GAME	1-01-001 6-4-2
1-01-001 30,000,000	1-01-001 4**C5	1-01-001 5-MILE	1-01-001 6-5
1-01-001 300-325**0**J*C	1-01-001 4**C7	1-01-001 5-PASSENGER	1-01-001 6-6
1-01-001 300-450	1-01-001 4**K	1-01-001 5-PERCENT	1-01-001 6-7
1-01-001 300TH	1-01-001 4*,-**J*D	1-01-001 5-TO-1	1-01-001 6,768
1-01-001 3000	1-01-001 4*,-1	1-01-001 5-TO-2	1-01-001 600*+0
1-01-001 302	1-01-001 4-CELL	1-01-001 5-TO-3	1-01-001 60*+0*C
1-01-001 312	1-01-001 4-FOR-5	1-01-001 5-1/2	1-01-001 60'S
1-01-001 314	1-01-001 4-HOMER	1-01-001 5-10**J**YM	1-01-001 60**JLB
1-01-001 31730	1-01-001 4-MONTH	1-01-001 5-3	1-01-001 60**JLB**J*B*0*
1-01-001 3181	1-01-001 4-PASSENGER	1-01-001 5-30	D/DAY/ACRE
1-01-001 31978	1-01-001 4-UNDER-PAR	1-01-001 5-4	1-01-001 60**K
1-01-001 32*+0**J*F	1-01-001 4-YEAR-OLD	1-01-001 5-6	1-01-001 60-CITY
1-01-001 32*+0*C	1-01-001 4-1/2**K	1-01-001 5/16	1-01-001 60-DAY
1-01-001 32,000	1-01-001 4-13	1-01-001 5/64	1-01-001 60-INCH
1-01-001 32,589	1-01-001 4-4	1-01-001 5/8-INCH	1-01-001 60-MONTH
1-01-001 320	1-01-001 4-7/8	1-01-001 5,014	1-01-001 60-1
1-01-001 320*T*R	1-01-001 4/4	1-01-001 5,500	1-01-001 60-66
1-01-001 3247	1-01-001 4,000-FOOT	1-01-001 5TH	1-01-001 60S
1-01-001 325	1-01-001 4,122,354	1-01-001 50*+0	1-01-001 600-MILE
1-01-001 327	1-01-001 4,1957	1-01-001 50'S	1-01-001 600-YARD
1-01-001 328	1-01-001 4,369	1-01-001 50-INCH	1-01-001 601
1-01-001 33-MAN	1-01-001 4,427	1-01-001 50-PERCENT	1-01-001 602.2
1-01-001 33-1/2	1-01-001 4,441	1-01-001 50-YEAR	1-01-001 603
1-01-001 33-1/3**K	1-01-001 4,499,608	1-01-001 50-YEAR-OLD	1-01-001 604
1-01-001 33D	1-01-001 4,585	1-01-001 50-100	1-01-001 606
1-01-001 3300	1-01-001 4,622,444	1-01-001 50-50	1-01-001 607-608
1-01-001 334	1-01-001 4,900	1-01-001 50,000	1-01-001 609
1-01-001 34.7	1-01-001 40*+0**J*F	1-01-001 50,000,000	1-01-001 61.2**K
1-01-001 34**C8	1-01-001 40'S	1-01-001 500'S	1-01-001 61ST
1-01-001 34-HOUR	1-01-001 40-GRAIN	1-01-001 5000-WORD	1-01-001 6124
1-01-001 34,000	1-01-001 400-**JLB	1-01-001 5031	1-01-001 613
1-01-001 340*+0**J*C	1-01-001 400-KC	1-01-001 505	1-01-001 619,000
1-01-001 340*T*R	1-01-001 400-POUND	1-01-001 508-YARD	1-01-001 62-YEAR-OLD
1-01-001 340-BLAST	1-01-001 400-401	1-01-001 510	1-01-001 62-63
1-01-001 34220	1-01-001 400,000,000	1-01-001 511	1-01-001 622
1-01-001 343	1-01-001 4000-PLUS	1-01-001 514	1-01-001 63-64
1-01-001 35.3	1-01-001 402	1-01-001 514*C	1-01-001 63,000,000
1-01-001 35**K	1-01-001 41-8	1-01-001 5155	1-01-001 63D
1-01-001 35-FOOT	1-01-001 410	1-01-001 52-YEAR	1-01-001 635
1-01-001 35-MM**.-WIDE	1-01-001 410*+0**J*C	1-01-001 52-YEAR-OLD	1-01-001 637
1-01-001 350TH	1-01-001 412	1-01-001 52ND	1-01-001 63711-R
1-01-001 3500	1-01-001 412-413	1-01-001 520	1-01-001 638,560
1-01-001 35050	1-01-001 415	1-01-001 520-ACRE	1-01-001 64**JC
1-01-001 357	1-01-001 42*+0*F	1-01-001 525	1-01-001 64**K
1-01-001 36-**J*A	1-01-001 42,000	1-01-001 526	1-01-001 64-PAGE
1-01-001 36-IN	1-01-001 42D	1-01-001 53-YEAR-OLD	1-01-001 64-13
1-01-001 36-YEAR-OLD	1-01-001 430,000	1-01-001 532	1-01-001 64-66
1-01-001 36TH	1-01-001 431	1-01-001 54,320	1-01-001 642
1-01-001 360,000	1-01-001 434	1-01-001 54TH	1-01-001 643
1-01-001 3646	1-01-001 44,000	1-01-001 540-**J*K	1-01-001 645-ACRE
1-01-001 365	1-01-001 442	1-01-001 5404	1-01-001 646
1-01-001 367	1-01-001 443	1-01-001 541	1-01-001 65**K
1-01-001 368(A)(1)(*A	1-01-001 45.6	1-01-001 542,250	1-01-001 65-YEAR-OLD
1-01-001 368(A)(1)(*B	1-01-001 45**K	1-01-001 543	1-01-001 65,000
1-01-001 368(A)(1)(*F	1-01-001 45-DEGREE	1-01-001 545-YARD	1-01-001 650
1-01-001 369	1-01-001 45-PASSENGER	1-01-001 55,000	1-01-001 66TH
1-01-001 37-YEAR-OLD	1-01-001 450-MILE-LONG	1-01-001 55,987	1-01-001 67
1-01-001 37-1/2	1-01-001 450,000	1-01-001 553	1-01-001 67-YEAR-OLD
1-01-001 37,000	1-01-001 451	1-01-001 56**J*A	1-01-001 675
1-01-001 37,081	1-01-001 452	1-01-001 56-YARD	1-01-001 676
1-01-001 37,470	1-01-001 46**K	1-01-001 56,000	1-01-001 687.87
1-01-001 37,679	1-01-001 46,000	1-01-001 5612	1-01-001 689-PAGE
1-01-001 37TH	1-01-001 462	1-01-001 562	1-01-001 6934

```
1-01-001  694            1-01-001  87-31          1-01-001  $1.6                 1-01-001  $28.00
1-01-001  695            1-01-001  870,000        1-01-001  $1.60                1-01-001  $28,700,000
1-01-001  7.19           1-01-001  871-892        1-01-001  $1.65                1-01-001  $29,000
1-01-001  7.2            1-01-001  88             1-01-001  $1.7                 1-01-001  $297
1-01-001  7.6**K         1-01-001  88'S           1-01-001  $1.80                1-01-001  $3.11
1-01-001  7**B/**JCWT    1-01-001  883,000        1-01-001  $1,000,000,000       1-01-001  $3.15
1-01-001  7**C10         1-01-001  885            1-01-001  $1,250,000           1-01-001  $3.22
1-01-001  7**C17         1-01-001  8861           1-01-001  $1,276               1-01-001  $3.50
1-01-001  7**C25         1-01-001  899            1-01-001  $1,390               1-01-001  $3,500
1-01-001  7**C50         1-01-001  9.3            1-01-001  $1,450,000,000       1-01-001  $3,675
1-01-001  7**J*A         1-01-001  9**C00         1-01-001  $1,600               1-01-001  $3,825
1-01-001  7-DAY          1-01-001  9**C30         1-01-001  $1,750,000           1-01-001  $30,000,000
1-01-001  7-DAY-WEEK     1-01-001  9**C30-4**C00  1-01-001  $1,800               1-01-001  $300,000
1-01-001  7-ROOM         1-01-001  9**C40         1-01-001  $1,961,000           1-01-001  $300,000,000
1-01-001  7-11           1-01-001  9**C47         1-01-001  $10.00               1-01-001  $306
1-01-001  7-5            1-01-001  9**J*N         1-01-001  $10.1                1-01-001  $31,179,816
1-01-001  7-9            1-01-001  9**JA          1-01-001  $10.3                1-01-001  $310
1-01-001  7/16           1-01-001  9**JB          1-01-001  $10.8                1-01-001  $3100
1-01-001  7,000,000      1-01-001  9**JE          1-01-001  $10,000-PER-YEAR     1-01-001  $325
1-01-001  7,360,187      1-01-001  9-1/2          1-01-001  $10,000,000          1-01-001  $344,000
1-01-001  7,484,268      1-01-001  9-11           1-01-001  $102,285,000         1-01-001  $35
1-01-001  7,500          1-01-001  9-6            1-01-001  $1020                1-01-001  $35,823
1-01-001  7,827          1-01-001  9-7            1-01-001  $109                 1-01-001  $350
1-01-001  70**-NO        1-01-001  9/32           1-01-001  $11.50               1-01-001  $350,000
1-01-001  70'S           1-01-001  9,273          1-01-001  $11,900,000          1-01-001  $36
1-01-001  70-YEAR-OLD    1-01-001  9,748,000      1-01-001  $115,000             1-01-001  $37,500
1-01-001  70-80          1-01-001  9,910,741      1-01-001  $12                  1-01-001  $380
1-01-001  70,000,000     1-01-001  90*+0*F        1-01-001  $12.00               1-01-001  $39.5
1-01-001  70,524         1-01-001  90-DAY         1-01-001  $12.1                1-01-001  $39,000
1-01-001  70TH           1-01-001  90,000         1-01-001  $12.7                1-01-001  $395,000
1-01-001  700-MILE       1-01-001  90S            1-01-001  $12,192,865          1-01-001  $4.9
1-01-001  701            1-01-001  900-CALORIE    1-01-001  $120                 1-01-001  $4.98
1-01-001  701ST          1-01-001  900-STUDENT    1-01-001  $128                 1-01-001  $4/**JMBF
1-01-001  7026           1-01-001  900,000        1-01-001  $133                 1-01-001  $4,000
1-01-001  7034           1-01-001  91             1-01-001  $139.3               1-01-001  $4,000,000
1-01-001  704            1-01-001  92.5           1-01-001  $14,000              1-01-001  $4,177.37
1-01-001  7074           1-01-001  920            1-01-001  $140                 1-01-001  $4,500
1-01-001  710            1-01-001  923,076        1-01-001  $148.50              1-01-001  $4,700
1-01-001  72-HOLE        1-01-001  9230           1-01-001  $15.5                1-01-001  $4,753
1-01-001  725'S          1-01-001  9329           1-01-001  $1500                1-01-001  $4,800
1-01-001  7287           1-01-001  940*Y          1-01-001  $157,460             1-01-001  $40,000,000
1-01-001  734            1-01-001  943            1-01-001  $16                  1-01-001  $4200
1-01-001  74.1           1-01-001  944            1-01-001  $16.00               1-01-001  $43.50
1-01-001  742            1-01-001  949            1-01-001  $16.80               1-01-001  $43,000
1-01-001  742*C          1-01-001  950            1-01-001  $16,000              1-01-001  $44.3-BILLION
1-01-001  75-MINUTE      1-01-001  954            1-01-001  $165                 1-01-001  $450,000
1-01-001  75,000-TON     1-01-001  960-**J*MC     1-01-001  $17                  1-01-001  $451,500
1-01-001  75TH           1-01-001  963            1-01-001  $17.8                1-01-001  $457,000
1-01-001  7599           1-01-001  989            1-01-001  $17,000,000          1-01-001  $46.7
1-01-001  76.7           1-01-001  99.1           1-01-001  $172,000             1-01-001  $47,101,000
1-01-001  76-PER         1-01-001  .0044**K       1-01-001  $172,400             1-01-001  $5.2
1-01-001  760            1-01-001  .01            1-01-001  $18.2                1-01-001  $5.4
1-01-001  762            1-01-001  .020           1-01-001  $184                 1-01-001  $5-8,000
1-01-001  764            1-01-001  .028           1-01-001  $185                 1-01-001  $50,400,000
1-01-001  767            1-01-001  .05            1-01-001  $187                 1-01-001  $52,500
1-01-001  77-234+10IK    1-01-001  .05**K         1-01-001  $19.5                1-01-001  $55,000
1-01-001  78-79          1-01-001  .076           1-01-001  $2.00                1-01-001  $550
1-01-001  79**JC         1-01-001  .09            1-01-001  $2.09                1-01-001  $56
1-01-001  79,400         1-01-001  .1             1-01-001  $2.30/**JMBF         1-01-001  $57,500
1-01-001  790            1-01-001  .130           1-01-001  $2.50                1-01-001  $58,918
1-01-001  795,586        1-01-001  .143           1-01-001  $2.80                1-01-001  $580
1-01-001  798            1-01-001  .179           1-01-001  $2.82                1-01-001  $581
1-01-001  8**C31         1-01-001  .222'S         1-01-001  $2.98                1-01-001  $581,000
1-01-001  8**C36         1-01-001  .243           1-01-001  $2,170               1-01-001  $590,000
1-01-001  8*,.266-366    1-01-001  .255           1-01-001  $2,300               1-01-001  $6
1-01-001  8*,.499-520    1-01-001  .267           1-01-001  $2,300,000           1-01-001  $6,100,000,000
1-01-001  8-**JMM        1-01-001  .270           1-01-001  $2,323,867           1-01-001  $6,666.66
1-01-001  8-*BALLS       1-01-001  .30-30         1-01-001  $2,330,000           1-01-001  $60,000
1-01-001  8-CHANNEL      1-01-001  .306           1-01-001  $2,412,616           1-01-001  $610
1-01-001  8-YEAR-OLD     1-01-001  .308           1-01-001  $2,461,000           1-01-001  $625,561
1-01-001  8-1/2-FOOT     1-01-001  .318           1-01-001  $2,490               1-01-001  $63.8
1-01-001  8-4            1-01-001  .323           1-01-001  $2,500               1-01-001  $634,517,000
1-01-001  8,000,000      1-01-001  .332           1-01-001  $2,557,111           1-01-001  $639
1-01-001  8,100          1-01-001  .338           1-01-001  $2,700               1-01-001  $65,000
1-01-001  8,293          1-01-001  .340           1-01-001  $20,000,000          1-01-001  $650
1-01-001  8,500          1-01-001  .345           1-01-001  $20,000,000,000      1-01-001  $66,000
1-01-001  80**0*C        1-01-001  .365           1-01-001  $20,447,000          1-01-001  $67,000
1-01-001  80-**JHP       1-01-001  .389           1-01-001  $200,000-A-YEAR      1-01-001  $7.20
1-01-001  80TH           1-01-001  .404'S         1-01-001  $200,000,000         1-01-001  $7.50
1-01-001  800'S          1-01-001  .45-CALIBER    1-01-001  $214                 1-01-001  $7,000
1-01-001  81,000         1-01-001  .455           1-01-001  $22                  1-01-001  $7,000,000
1-01-001  817            1-01-001  .50            1-01-001  $22.50               1-01-001  $7,082
1-01-001  82             1-01-001  .500           1-01-001  $222                 1-01-001  $7,500,000
1-01-001  821,220        1-01-001  .7             1-01-001  $227.72              1-01-001  $70
1-01-001  823            1-01-001  .75            1-01-001  $230,000             1-01-001  $70,000
1-01-001  825,000        1-01-001  .7854          1-01-001  $24,926,615          1-01-001  $720
1-01-001  828            1-01-001  +.04           1-01-001  $2400                1-01-001  $73.50
1-01-001  83RD           1-01-001  +.50           1-01-001  $25-A-PLATE          1-01-001  $740
1-01-001  836-901        1-01-001  +.7            1-01-001  $250,000             1-01-001  $740,000
1-01-001  84-FOOT        1-01-001  +C             1-01-001  $2500                1-01-001  $75-BILLION
1-01-001  840,503        1-01-001  $0.9           1-01-001  $251                 1-01-001  $75,000,000
1-01-001  85-PIECE       1-01-001  $1.0           1-01-001  $253,355,000         1-01-001  $750,000
1-01-001  85-STUDENT     1-01-001  $1.00          1-01-001  $26.5-BILLION        1-01-001  $754
1-01-001  85-90**0*F     1-01-001  $1.10          1-01-001  $26,000,000          1-01-001  $77,389,000
1-01-001  86**K          1-01-001  $1.26          1-01-001  $27.50               1-01-001  $79.89
1-01-001  869            1-01-001  $1.4           1-01-001  $278,877,000         1-01-001  $8.5
1-01-001  87-1/2         1-01-001  $1.5                                         1-01-001  $8,250
```

1-01-001 $8,313,514	1-01-001 *=P(*D)*$,	1-01-001 *D*A,	1-01-001 *L-*P
1-01-001 $8,555	1-01-001 *=R*$,	1-01-001 *D*C-7.	1-01-001 *M*E'S
1-01-001 $80	1-01-001 *=R*$TH	1-01-001 *D*C,	1-01-001 *M*F
1-01-001 $800,000	1-01-001 *=RE*$	1-01-001 *D*E*A*E	1-01-001 *M*G*M
1-01-001 $81	1-01-001 *=S*S-VALUES	1-01-001 *D*E*A*E-)	1-01-001 *M*L*S*S
1-01-001 $83,750	1-01-001 *=T-TAU*$	1-01-001 *D*E*A*E-CELLUL OSE.	1-01-001 *M*P'S
1-01-001 $84,000,000	1-01-001 *=U*$.		1-01-001 *M*P*H
1-01-001 $840,000	1-01-001 *=V*$	1-01-001 *D*E*A*E-CELLUL OSE-TREATED	1-01-001 *M*PL,
1-01-001 $842,617	1-01-001 *=W*$		1-01-001 *M*S
1-01-001 $85,000	1-01-001 *=X*$,	1-01-001 *D*E*S	1-01-001 *M*S*)
1-01-001 $88,000	1-01-001 *A)	1-01-001 *D*P*W	1-01-001 *M*V*P
1-01-001 $9.2	1-01-001 *A+**J*I	1-01-001 *D*S*M	1-01-001 *M-*K
1-01-001 $9,841,000	1-01-001 *A+**J*M**-	1-01-001 *D*T*F	1-01-001 *M-1
1-01-001 $94	1-01-001 *A+**J*M,	1-01-001 *D*T*F*S.	1-01-001 *M-4
1-01-001 **=*T*C*U'S**$	1-01-001 *A*$	1-01-001 *D*U	1-01-001 *MESSRS
1-01-001 **=P**$	1-01-001 *A**S	1-01-001 *D-*ORE**..	1-01-001 *MLLE
1-01-001 **=P**$(*=*T*$)	1-01-001 *A*A	1-01-001 *D-496.**T	1-01-001 *MRAD)
1-01-001 **=P**$(*=T*$)	1-01-001 *A*A*A	1-01-001 *D8	1-01-001 *MRADS
1-01-001 **=P**$(*O).	1-01-001 *A*C*S),	1-01-001 *E*D*M*O*V	1-01-001 *MRADS.
1-01-001 **=Q**$.	1-01-001 *A*C*T*H	1-01-001 *E*E*A*E-CELLUL OSE	1-01-001 *MRS
1-01-001 **=Q**$(*=T*$)	1-01-001 *A*D		1-01-001 *N*A*B
1-01-001 **B**U.	1-01-001 *A*D*C**U.	1-01-001 *E*E*G.	1-01-001 *N*A*E*B*M
1-01-001 **F-INCH	1-01-001 *A*E*C'S	1-01-001 *E*Q*U,	1-01-001 *N*A*E*B*M,
1-01-001 **F-VALUES	1-01-001 *A*F+**J*A*M,	1-01-001 *E*S*N,	1-01-001 *N*A*H*B,
1-01-001 **R*O*K'S	1-01-001 *A*F*L-**J*C*I* O	1-01-001 *E*S*P),	1-01-001 *N*A*I*R
1-01-001 **YB,		1-01-001 *E*W*C	1-01-001 *N*A*I*R*O
1-01-001 **YC,	1-01-001 *A*F*L-*C*I*O,	1-01-001 *E*W*C).	1-01-001 *N*A*I*R*O),
1-01-001 **YG	1-01-001 *A*H6	1-01-001 *E,	1-01-001 *N*A*R*E*B
1-01-001 **YG-GLOBULIN	1-01-001 *A*I*CH*E	1-01-001 *ENGRG,	1-01-001 *N*A*R*E*B)
1-01-001 **YJ	1-01-001 *A*I*D'S	1-01-001 *F)	1-01-001 *N*A*R*E*B'S
1-01-001 **YJ.	1-01-001 *A*I*E*E	1-01-001 *F+**J*A	1-01-001 *N*A*T*O.
1-01-001 **YM	1-01-001 *A*L	1-01-001 *F*D*A.	1-01-001 *N*A*T*O)
1-01-001 **YMG	1-01-001 *A*M)	1-01-001 *F*D*A),	1-01-001 *N*A*T*O)**U
1-01-001 **YR	1-01-001 *A*M*A),	1-01-001 *F*D*A'S	1-01-001 *N*A*T*O'S
1-01-001 **Z*G.	1-01-001 *A*R*F)**-	1-01-001 *F*D*A,	1-01-001 *N*B*C-**J*T*V
1-01-001 *(O,*=*T*$*),	1-01-001 *A*S*D*I*C,	1-01-001 *F*D*R.	1-01-001 *N*B*S.
1-01-001 *=*A*$.	1-01-001 *A*S*M*E,	1-01-001 *F*D*R**C	1-01-001 *N*C
1-01-001 *=*A*$**U	1-01-001 *A*S*P*R	1-01-001 *F*D*R,	1-01-001 *N*C*T*A,
1-01-001 *=*A*$,	1-01-001 *A*S*T*M	1-01-001 *F*F*A	1-01-001 *N*E.
1-01-001 *=*B*$	1-01-001 *A*T*P	1-01-001 *F*L*N,	1-01-001 *N*E**S
1-01-001 *=*B*$.	1-01-001 *A*T*P)	1-01-001 *F*O*R*E*A*M*I)	1-01-001 *N*L*R*B
1-01-001 *=*C*$-PLANE,	1-01-001 *A*V*C).	1-01-001 *F-MAJOR	1-01-001 *N*L*R*D*A.
1-01-001 *=*C*$(**=Q**$)	1-01-001 *A*W*O*C)	1-01-001 *F-108	1-01-001 *N*M*R)
1-01-001 *=*C'*$.	1-01-001 *A*W*O*C,	1-01-001 *F-108,	1-01-001 *N*O*P
1-01-001 *=*C'*$,	1-01-001 *A-**J*Z'S	1-01-001 *F,	1-01-001 *N*O*R*A*D
1-01-001 *=*E*$	1-01-001 *A-**J*Z**U,	1-01-001 *G	1-01-001 *N*R
1-01-001 *=*F*$,	1-01-001 *A-BOMBS	1-01-001 *G*A	1-01-001 *N*R*A,
1-01-001 *=*G*$,	1-01-001 *A-26	1-01-001 *G*A*M*I*N**S	1-01-001 *N*R*L
1-01-001 *=*H**$)	1-01-001 *A/3,	1-01-001 *G*E	1-01-001 *N*R*L*D*A'S
1-01-001 *=*H*$	1-01-001 *B)	1-01-001 *G*E**C	1-01-001 *N*S.
1-01-001 *=*M*$	1-01-001 *B+**J*O	1-01-001 *G*N*P),	1-01-001 *N*Y*U,
1-01-001 *=*N*$,	1-01-001 *B+*O	1-01-001 *G*O*P,	1-01-001 *N/G,
1-01-001 *=*N*$.	1-01-001 *B'S	1-01-001 *G,	1-01-001 *N,
1-01-001 *=*P'*$.	1-01-001 *B**U,	1-01-001 *H+*H,	1-01-001 *O*A*G*CO),
1-01-001 *=*P*Q*$	1-01-001 *B*B*B)	1-01-001 *H*B*O	1-01-001 *O*B*E)
1-01-001 *=*R*$.	1-01-001 *B*C*D	1-01-001 *H-BOMBS.	1-01-001 *O*E*P
1-01-001 *=*R*$).	1-01-001 *B*G*S	1-01-001 *H,	1-01-001 *O*K
1-01-001 *=*R*$*$*O*O*H	1-01-001 *B*M*E*W*S.	1-01-001 *I*C*A	1-01-001 *O*K**U**I
1-01-001 *=*R*$,	1-01-001 *B*M*T	1-01-001 *I*C*A'S	1-01-001 *O*K,
1-01-001 *=*R'S*$	1-01-001 *B*O*D'S	1-01-001 *I*C*B*MS.	1-01-001 *O*M*E
1-01-001 *=*S*$	1-01-001 *B*O*D/DAY	1-01-001 *I*C*C	1-01-001 *O*M*E)
1-01-001 *=*S*$,	1-01-001 *B*O*D/DAY/ACRE	1-01-001 *I*J*A*L	1-01-001 *O*W*I**U,
1-01-001 *=*T*$).	1-01-001 *B*O*D/DAY/1,00 0	1-01-001 *I*N*D,	1-01-001 *P
1-01-001 *=*T*$**I		1-01-001 *I*O*C*S*I*X*F,	1-01-001 *P*A*B*A
1-01-001 *=*T*$**S	1-01-001 *B*S*N,	1-01-001 *I*O*C*S*I*X*G,	1-01-001 *P*A*B*A)
1-01-001 *=*U*$	1-01-001 *B*T*U.	1-01-001 *I*Q	1-01-001 *P*B*S.
1-01-001 *=*V*$**S	1-01-001 *B*T*U'S	1-01-001 *I*R*S*A*C)	1-01-001 *P*B*S)
1-01-001 *=*V*$(**=P**$)	1-01-001 *B*T*U'S.	1-01-001 *I*R*S*A*C,	1-01-001 *P*B*S).
1-01-001 *=*Y*$	1-01-001 *B-47	1-01-001 *I-*E	1-01-001 *P*F*C).
1-01-001 *=*Y*$-GYRO	1-01-001 *B-47'S	1-01-001 *I-*E.	1-01-001 *P*M
1-01-001 *=*Z*$-AXIS	1-01-001 *B-52'S,	1-01-001 *J**U	1-01-001 *P*M*R
1-01-001 *=*Z*$-GYRO	1-01-001 *B-52**J*H	1-01-001 *J*A	1-01-001 *P*O*W
1-01-001 *=A*$.	1-01-001 *B-52S	1-01-001 *J*E*D*E*C	1-01-001 *P*T*C,
1-01-001 *=AB*$	1-01-001 *B-58	1-01-001 *J*Y*J	1-01-001 *P*W*A,
1-01-001 *=AL*$	1-01-001 *B70	1-01-001 *J*Y*M	1-01-001 *P-9
1-01-001 *=B*$).	1-01-001 *C.	1-01-001 *J,	1-01-001 *PE
1-01-001 *=B*$-PLANE	1-01-001 *C+**J*O	1-01-001 *J28-6033-1.	1-01-001 *PM
1-01-001 *=B*$-PLANE.	1-01-001 *C+**J*O'S	1-01-001 *J28-6105.	1-01-001 *Q
1-01-001 *=C*$	1-01-001 *C+**J*O-**J*B+ **J*O	1-01-001 *K)	1-01-001 *Q3,
1-01-001 *=F*$.		1-01-001 *K'S	1-01-001 *R)
1-01-001 *=F*$-PLANE**S	1-01-001 *C**-	1-01-001 *K*A*R*L	1-01-001 *R'S**-
1-01-001 *=F*$-PLANE,	1-01-001 *C**U	1-01-001 *K*A*R*L,	1-01-001 *R'S,
1-01-001 *=F(T)*$.	1-01-001 *C*B*S	1-01-001 *K*C-135	1-01-001 *R*A
1-01-001 *=G*$.	1-01-001 *C*B,	1-01-001 *K*CS	1-01-001 *R*A*N*D
1-01-001 *=G(T)*$-AXIS	1-01-001 *C*C*C	1-01-001 *K*K*K	1-01-001 *R*B*IS,
1-01-001 *=H*$.	1-01-001 *C*D,	1-01-001 *K*Q*E*D	1-01-001 *R*C*A-*VICTO
1-01-001 *=I*$.	1-01-001 *C*H	1-01-001 *K*S*A*N,	
1-01-001 *=ITY*$	1-01-001 *C*H**S	1-01-001 *K*V	1-01-001 *R*D*F
1-01-001 *=K*$,	1-01-001 *C*J*S	1-01-001 *K*V.	1-01-001 *R*D*F.
1-01-001 *=K*$TH	1-01-001 *C*O*L*H	1-01-001 *L	1-01-001 *R*D*W*S)
1-01-001 *=L'*$	1-01-001 *C*S*F)	1-01-001 *L**U	1-01-001 *R*O*K
1-01-001 *=L'*$.	1-01-001 *C*T*A.	1-01-001 *L**U,	1-01-001 *R*O*T*C
1-01-001 *=M*$	1-01-001 *C*T*A**P	1-01-001 *L*D056	1-01-001 *R*P*M
1-01-001 *=N*$-DIMENSION AL	1-01-001 *C*T*(*C*A).	1-01-001 *L*D060)	1-01-001 *R*P*M,
	1-01-001 *C*V,	1-01-001 *L*M	1-01-001 *R-*BERGEN,
1-01-001 *=N*$-TRIAL	1-01-001 *CU*K**YA	1-01-001 *L*P	1-01-001 *R-*CAPE
1-01-001 *=P*$.	1-01-001 *D)	1-01-001 *L*S*U,	

```
1-01-001   *R-*WARREN          1-01-001   *Y*M*C*A,
1-01-001   *R-5TH              1-01-001   *Y-*TEEN
1-01-001   *R-6TH              1-01-001   *Y-CELLS
1-01-001   *S*A*C'S            1-01-001   *Y-REGION
1-01-001   *S*A*C,             1-01-001   *Y-REGION,
1-01-001   *S*B*A)             1-01-001   *Y-REGIONS
1-01-001   *S*B*A,             1-01-001   *Z
1-01-001   *S*D                1-01-001   *Z**S
1-01-001   *S*E.               1-01-001   *Z,
1-01-001   *S*E*A*T*O.         1-01-001   -.10
1-01-001   *S*E*T*S*W          1-01-001   -.5
1-01-001   *S*E,               1-01-001   -**J*S*H
1-01-001   *S*H                1-01-001   -CARBONYL
1-01-001   *S*H,               1-01-001   -16**0
1-01-001   *S*M*U,             1-01-001   -20**0
1-01-001   *S*N*P              1-01-001   -20**0**J*C
1-01-001   *S*P-44001).        1-01-001   /R/
1-01-001   *S*P-44002)         1-01-001   (*=A,B*$)
1-01-001   *S*P-44005).
1-01-001   *S*P-44006)
1-01-001   *S*P-44007).
1-01-001   *S*PS.
1-01-001   *S*R
1-01-001   *S*R'S
1-01-001   *S*R*E*S*E*R*V*
             E
1-01-001   *S*R/
1-01-001   *S*S,
1-01-001   *S*T*D*C*R**S
1-01-001   *S*W*A*O
1-01-001   *S*W*C
1-01-001   *S*X-21**U
1-01-001   *S-**J*D
1-01-001   *S-20
1-01-001   *S-20)
1-01-001   *S,
1-01-001   *SB*CS-TYPE
1-01-001   *SC*H.
1-01-001   *SI*H,
1-01-001   *T*C*U,
1-01-001   *T*E*A
1-01-001   *T*H*C
1-01-001   *T*N*T.
1-01-001   *T*N*T)**S
1-01-001   *T*N*T,
1-01-001   *T*S*H.
1-01-001   *T*S*H)
1-01-001   *T*S*H-TREATED
1-01-001   *T*U*C
1-01-001   *T*V**$
1-01-001   *T*V**-
1-01-001   *T*V**P
1-01-001   *T*V**U,
1-01-001   *U.
1-01-001   *U*C*L*A
1-01-001   *U*G*F,
1-01-001   *U*K
1-01-001   *U*S*G*A
1-01-001   *U*S*I*S
1-01-001   *U*S*O
1-01-001   *U*S*O*M,
1-01-001   *U*S*S*R**C
1-01-001   *U*S*S*R,
1-01-001   *U-**J*I
1-01-001   *U-2
1-01-001   *V.
1-01-001   *V*T*O*L
1-01-001   *V*T*O*L)
1-01-001   *V8.
1-01-001   *W*A*C*S
1-01-001   *W*A*C,
1-01-001   *W*A*O
1-01-001   *W*B*A*I,
1-01-001   *W*L*I*B
1-01-001   *W*P*A,
1-01-001   *W*Q*X*R.
1-01-001   *W*W*R*L
1-01-001   *W*W*R*L'S
1-01-001   *W-REGION.
1-01-001   *W-REGION**S
1-01-001   *W-REGION,
1-01-001   *W-2).
1-01-001   *X.
1-01-001   *X**U
1-01-001   *X**U**I
1-01-001   *X*H-834.
1-01-001   *X*R*E*L*E*A*S*
             E
1-01-001   *X*R*E*L*E*A*S*
             E,
1-01-001   *X*R*E*S*E*R*V*
             E
1-01-001   *X-RAY-PROOF
1-01-001   *X-RAYS
1-01-001   *Y
1-01-001   *Y'S
1-01-001   *Y*M*C*A.
```

THE ALPHABETICAL LIST

Freq	Word	Freq	Word	Freq	Word	Freq	Word
23237-15-500	A	4-02-003	ABODE	1-01-001	ABYSSINIANS	2-02-002	ACCOUNTANT
5-01-003	A)	8-05-007	ABOLISH	3-01-001	ACACIA	1-01-001	ACCOUNTANTS
1-01-001	A),	2-02-002	ABOLISHED	1-01-001	ACADEMEH	5-04-004	ACCOUNTED
1-01-001	A**.*A**.*U	10-06-008	ABOLITION	56-10-026	ACADEMIC	12-07-012	ACCOUNTING
1-01-001	A**.*A**.*U**.'	1-01-001	ABOLITIONIST	5-02-003	ACADEMICALLY	38-12-030	ACCOUNTS
	S	4-03-003	ABOLITIONISTS	1-01-001	ACADEMICIANSHIP	1-01-001	ACCOUTERMENTS
3-02-003	A**.*B	1-01-001	ABORIGINAL	2-01-001	ACADEMICS	7-01-001	ACCREDITATION
8-03-005	A**.*D	7-01-002	ABORIGINE	3-03-003	ACADEMIES	2-02-002	ACCREDITED
1-01-001	A**.*I**.*D	8-02-002	ABORIGINES	24-08-015	ACADEMY	3-02-002	ACCRETION
1-01-001	A**.*K**.*C	6-06-006	ABORTION	1-01-001	ACADIA	2-01-001	ACCRETIONS
13-01-001	A**.*L**.*A**.*	1-01-001	ABORTIONS	5-01-001	ACALA	3-01-002	ACCRUED
	M	3-02-003	ABORTIVE	1-01-001	ACAPULCO	1-01-001	ACCRUES
11-06-009	A**.*M	1-01-001	ABOUND	4-01-001	ACCACIA	7-02-002	ACCRUING
4-03-003	A**.*M**.*A	2-02-002	ABOUNDED	1-01-001	ACCADEMIA	1-01-001	ACCULTURATED
26-06-013	A**.M	1-01-001	ABOUNDING	1-01-001	ACCARDO	1-01-001	ACCULTURATION
1-01-001	A**$N	1-01-001	ABOUNDS	1-01-001	ACCEDE	3-03-003	ACCUMULATE
1-01-001	A**$RE	1815-15-426	ABOUT	1-01-001	ACCEDED	10-04-010	ACCUMULATED
1-01-001	A**YS**YP**YI**	2-01-002	ABOUT-FACED	5-03-005	ACCELERATE	2-02-002	ACCUMULATES
	YS	296-15-173	ABOVE	13-07-013	ACCELERATED	3-02-003	ACCUMULATING
1-01-001	A*=NOTH*$ER	1-01-001	ABOVE-GROUND	6-05-005	ACCELERATING	11-06-010	ACCUMULATION
2-01-001	A-COMING	2-02-002	ABOVE-MENTIONED	17-05-009	ACCELERATION	36-07-021	ACCURACY
1-01-001	A-CROWING	1-01-001	ABOVE-NOTED	2-01-001	ACCELERATIONS	35-10-033	ACCURATE
1-01-001	A-DRINKING	1-01-001	ABOVE-WATER	5-04-004	ACCELERATOR	24-08-019	ACCURATELY
1-01-001	A-GRACIOUS	2-01-001	ABOVEGROUND	3-01-001	ACCELERATORS	3-03-003	ACCUSATION
1-01-001	A-RAISING	1-01-001	ABRA	17-01-001	ACCELEROMETER	3-03-003	ACCUSATIONS
1-01-001	A-STOOPIN	6-05-005	ABRAHAM	8-01-001	ACCELEROMETERS	10-06-008	ACCUSE
1-01-001	A-TALL	1-01-001	ABRAMS	9-06-009	ACCENT	25-08-020	ACCUSED
1-01-001	A-WING	3-03-003	ABRASION	3-03-003	ACCENTED	2-01-002	ACCUSES
2-02-002	A-1	2-01-002	ABREACTION	1-01-001	ACCENTING	8-05-007	ACCUSING
1-01-001	AAA-EE	5-04-005	ABREAST	5-04-005	ACCENTS	2-02-002	ACCUSINGLY
1-01-001	AAAWWW	5-04-005	ABRIDGED	1-01-001	ACCENTUAL	15-10-014	ACCUSTOMED
1-01-001	AAH	1-01-001	ABRIDGMENT	1-01-001	ACCENTUATE	15-04-007	ACE
7-06-006	AARON	51-10-031	ABROAD	3-03-003	ACCENTUATED	4-02-003	ACES
2-02-002	ABACK	1-01-001	ABROADE	1-01-001	ACCENTUATES	7-02-003	ACETATE
17-08-015	ABANDON	1-01-001	ABROGATED	72-12-048	ACCEPT	4-01-001	ACETONE
25-11-024	ABANDONED	18-10-015	ABRUPT	2-01-001	ACCEPTABILITY	3-01-001	ACETONEMIA
7-06-007	ABANDONING	18-05-014	ABRUPTLY	21-07-016	ACCEPTABLE	3-01-001	ACEY
10-05-010	ABANDONMENT	1-01-001	ABRUPTNESS	49-11-038	ACCEPTANCE	1-01-001	ACHAEANS
1-01-001	ABARINGE	3-01-001	ABSCESSES	96-14-076	ACCEPTED	1-01-001	ACHAEANS'
2-02-002	ABASEMENT	1-01-001	ABSCISSA	21-09-020	ACCEPTING	4-03-004	ACHE
1-01-001	ABATED	53-12-040	ABSENCE	6-04-006	ACCEPTS	3-03-003	ACHED
1-01-001	ABATUNO	3-03-003	ABSENCES	24-09-017	ACCESS	1-01-001	ACHES
2-01-001	ABBAS	28-09-021	ABSENT	1-01-001	ACCESSES	2-01-001	ACHESON
1-01-001	ABBAS'S	3-03-003	ABSENT-MINDED	2-02-002	ACCESSIBILITY	1-01-001	ACHESON'S
3-02-002	ABBE	3-02-002	ABSENT-MINDEDLY	5-04-005	ACCESSIBLE	51-09-040	ACHIEVE
1-01-001	ABBE-*DIRECT	1-01-001	ABSENTED	1-01-001	ACCESSIONS	62-11-051	ACHIEVED
1-01-001	ABBE-*SCOTCH	1-01-001	ABSENTEE	7-06-007	ACCESSORIES	65-07-027	ACHIEVEMENT
1-01-001	ABBERATIONS	1-01-001	ABSENTEEISM	1-01-001	ACCESSORS	19-09-016	ACHIEVEMENTS
7-04-005	ABBEY	1-01-001	ABSENTIA	1-01-001	ACCESSORY	5-05-005	ACHIEVES
2-01-002	ABBOT	6-03-005	ABSENTLY	33-14-023	ACCIDENT	15-07-014	ACHIEVING
2-01-001	ABBOTT	1-01-001	ABSENTMINDEDLY	9-05-006	ACCIDENTAL	1-01-001	ACHILLES
1-01-001	ABBREVIATED	1-01-001	ABSINTHE	1-01-001	ACCIDENTAL-WAR	6-05-006	ACHING
1-01-001	ABBREVIATION	30-09-023	ABSOLUTE	6-06-006	ACCIDENTALLY	13-06-009	ACID
1-01-001	ABBREVIATIONS	27-13-021	ABSOLUTELY	8-06-007	ACCIDENTS	1-01-001	ACID-FAST
1-01-001	ABDALLAH	2-01-001	ABSOLUTENESS	4-02-004	ACCLAIM	1-01-001	ACIDITY
6-05-006	ABDOMEN	3-03-003	ABSOLUTES	4-03-004	ACCLAIMED	7-03-005	ACIDS
4-03-003	ABDOMINAL	2-01-001	ABSOLUTION	1-01-001	ACCLAIMS	1-01-001	ACIDULOUS
1-01-001	ABDOMINIS	13-08-011	ABSORB	1-01-001	ACCLAMATION	1-01-001	ACKERLY
1-01-001	ABDUCTION	24-09-017	ABSORBED	1-01-001	ACCLIMATIZED	12-07-012	ACKNOWLEDGE
3-03-003	ABE	1-01-001	ABSORBENCY	2-02-002	ACCOLADE	12-08-011	ACKNOWLEDGED
1-01-001	ABED	1-01-001	ABSORBER	1-01-001	ACCOLADES	2-01-002	ACKNOWLEDGEMENT
20-03-004	ABEL	3-03-003	ABSORBING	14-09-013	ACCOMMODATE	2-02-002	ACKNOWLEDGES
1-01-001	ABEL'S	1-01-001	ABSORBS	1-01-001	ACCOMMODATED	1-01-001	ACKNOWLEDGING
1-01-001	ABELL	12-04-009	ABSORPTION	2-01-001	ACCOMMODATES	2-02-002	ACKNOWLEDGMENT
1-01-001	ABELSON	2-01-001	ABSORPTIONS	2-02-002	ACCOMMODATING	1-01-001	ACKNOWLEDGMENTS
1-01-001	ABER	2-02-002	ABSORPTIVE	1-01-001	ACCOMMODATION	1-01-001	ACOLYTE
2-01-001	ABERNATHY	1-01-001	ABSTAIN	8-05-007	ACCOMMODATIONS	1-01-001	ACORDING
1-01-001	ABERNATHYS	1-01-001	ABSTAINING	1-01-001	ACCOMODATIONS	1-01-001	ACORNS
5-02-003	ABERRANT	1-01-001	ABSTENTION	37-13-035	ACCOMPANIED	1-01-001	ACOUSTIC
3-03-003	ABERRATION	34-08-020	ABSTRACT	1-01-001	ACCOMPANIES	3-02-002	ACOUSTICAL
5-01-002	ABERRATIONS	3-02-002	ABSTRACTED	1-01-001	ACCOMPANIMEN	1-01-001	ACOUSTICALLY
4-04-004	ABETTED	1-01-001	ABSTRACTEDNESS	7-04-005	ACCOMPANIMENT	1-01-001	ACOUSTICS
3-02-003	ABEYANCE	3-02-003	ABSTRACTING	3-02-003	ACCOMPANIMENTS	3-03-003	ACQUAINT
1-01-001	ABHORRED	1-01-001	ABSTRACTION	1-01-001	ACCOMPANIST	9-05-009	ACQUAINTANCE
1-01-001	ABHORRENT	1-01-001	ABSTRACTIONISM	1-01-001	ACCOMPANISTS	12-08-011	ACQUAINTED
7-05-007	ABIDE	3-01-001	ABSTRACTIONISTS	8-04-007	ACCOMPANY	3-02-003	ACQUIESCE
2-02-002	ABIDES	7-03-007	ABSTRACTIONS	17-07-015	ACCOMPANYING	1-01-001	ACQUIESCED
5-05-005	ABIDING	2-02-002	ABSTRACTIVE	2-02-002	ACCOMPLICE	5-02-005	ACQUIESCENCE
2-01-001	ABIGAIL	1-01-001	ABSTRACTLY	1-01-001	ACCOMPLICES	1-01-001	ACQUIESENCE
2-01-001	ABILENE	24-08-020	ABSTRACTORS	24-08-020	ACCOMPLISH	27-09-024	ACQUIRE
13-06-010	ABILITIES	1-01-001	ABSTRACTS	44-12-039	ACCOMPLISHED	26-09-026	ACQUIRED
74-12-054	ABILITY	1-01-001	ABSTRUSENESSES	1-01-001	ACCOMPLISHES	2-01-002	ACQUIRES
3-03-003	ABJECT	7-06-007	ABSURD	3-03-003	ACCOMPLISHING	11-04-005	ACQUIRING
1-01-001	ABJECTION	2-02-002	ABSURDITIES	7-06-007	ACCOMPLISHMENT	17-05-006	ACQUISITION
1-01-001	ABJECTLY	8-07-008	ABSURDITY	10-06-008	ACCOMPLISHMENTS	2-02-002	ACQUISITIONS
2-01-001	ABLARD	1-01-001	ABSURDLY	9-05-008	ACCORD	1-01-001	ACQUISITIVENESS
1-01-001	ABLATED	13-09-011	ABUNDANCE	20-07-017	ACCORDANCE	2-01-001	ACQUITTAL
2-01-001	ABLATION	9-06-008	ABUNDANT	4-04-004	ACCORDED	2-02-002	ACQUITTED
3-03-003	ABLAZE	2-02-002	ABUNDANTLY	139-14-098	ACCORDING	9-05-006	ACRE
216-15-167	ABLE	18-09-013	ABUSE	31-06-023	ACCORDINGLY	1-01-001	ACRE-FEET
2-01-002	ABLER	5-04-005	ABUSED	1-01-001	ACCORDION	11-07-009	ACREAGE
2-02-002	ABLY	7-04-004	ABUSES	1-01-001	ACCORDS	44-10-017	ACRES
1-01-001	ABNER	1-01-001	ABUSIVE	2-01-002	ACCOSTED	1-01-001	ACRID
3-03-003	ABNORMAL	1-01-001	ABUTMENTS	1-01-001	ACCOSTING	1-01-001	ACROBACY
1-01-001	ABNORMALITIES	2-02-002	ABYSMAL	117-13-086	ACCOUNT	2-02-002	ACROBATIC
1-01-001	ABNORMALLY	4-04-004	ABYSS	4-02-003	ACCOUNTABILITY	1-01-001	ACROBATICS
25-08-015	ABOARD			1-01-001	ACCOUNTABLE		

1-01-001 ACROBATS	1-01-001 ADE	3-02-003 ADMONITIONS	4-03-004 ADVOCATED
6-01-001 ACROPOLIS	2-02-002 ADELE	1-01-001 ADNAN	1-01-001 ADVOCATES
282-15-176 ACROSS	5-01-001 ADELIA	4-01-001 ADO	6-05-006 ADVOCATING
1-01-001 ACROSS-THE-BOAR D	1-01-001 ADELOS	2-01-001 ADOBE	15-02-002 AEGEAN
	4-02-003 ADENAUER	18-03-003 ADOLESCENCE	1-01-001 AEGIS
11-01-001 ACRYLIC	1-01-001 ADENAUER'S	12-03-004 ADOLESCENT	1-01-001 AEON
283-14-123 ACT	1-01-001 ADENOMAS	3-01-001 ADOLESCENT'S	1-01-001 AERATE
18-11-017 ACTED	4-04-004 ADEPT	7-02-003 ADOLESCENTS	9-01-001 AERATED
61-12-043 ACTING	3-03-003 ADEQUACY	4-01-002 ADOLF	1-01-001 AERATES
1-01-001 ACTING-*PRESIDE NT	66-10-052 ADEQUATE	1-01-001 ADOLPHUS	7-02-002 AERATION
	16-06-015 ADEQUATELY	6-01-001 ADONIRAM	11-01-001 AERATOR
1-01-001 ACTINOMETER	1-01-001 ADERHOLDS	1-01-001 ADONIS	8-03-006 AERIAL
291-15-142 ACTION	4-02-004 ADHERE	13-06-012 ADOPT	1-01-001 AERIALS
1-01-001 ACTION-ORIENTED	5-03-005 ADHERED	45-09-035 ADOPTED	1-01-001 AEROBACTER
1-01-001 ACTION-PACKED	9-05-008 ADHERENCE	11-06-010 ADOPTING	1-01-001 AEROBIC
68-11-049 ACTIONS	2-01-002 ADHERENT	11-05-009 ADOPTION	1-01-001 AERODYNAMIC
2-02-002 ACTIVATE	5-04-004 ADHERENTS	2-02-002 ADOPTS	1-01-001 AEROGENES
5-03-003 ACTIVATED	1-01-001 ADHERES	3-02-003 ADORABLE	1-01-001 AERONAUTICAL
1-01-001 ACTIVATING	2-02-002 ADHESION	2-01-001 ADORE	2-02-002 AERONAUTICS
7-02-002 ACTIVATION	6-03-004 ADHESIVE	2-02-002 ADORED	7-01-001 AEROSOL
88-12-059 ACTIVE	2-01-002 ADHESIVES	1-01-001 ADORES	3-01-001 AEROSOLIZED
12-06-012 ACTIVELY	1-01-001 ADIEU	1-01-001 ADORN	3-01-001 AEROSOLS
8-01-001 ACTIVES	6-02-002 ADIOS	1-01-001 ADORNED	4-01-001 AEROSPACE
2-02-002 ACTIVISM	1-01-001 ADIOS-*DIRECT	1-01-001 ADORNS	1-01-001 AESCHBACHER
115-13-060 ACTIVITIES	1-01-001 ADIOS-*ON	1-01-001 ADRAR	1-01-001 AESCHBACHER'S
116-12-061 ACTIVITY	1-01-001 ADIOS-*RENA	2-02-002 ADRENAL	4-02-002 AESCHYLUS
24-06-014 ACTOR	1-01-001 ADIOS-*TRUSTFUL	4-02-002 ADRIAN	1-01-001 AESTHETES
1-01-001 ACTOR'S	1-01-001 ADIPIC	1-01-001 ADRIANOPLE	26-04-017 AESTHETIC
1-01-001 ACTOR-*CROONER	2-02-002 ADIRONDACK	3-01-001 ADRIATIC	1-01-001 AESTHETICS
15-07-012 ACTORS	1-01-001 ADIRONDACKS	2-01-001 ADRIEN	1-01-001 AETERNITATIS
6-04-005 ACTRESS	12-05-009 ADJACENT	1-01-001 ADRIFT	1-01-001 AF
3-03-003 ACTRESSES	3-01-001 ADJECTIVAL	1-01-001 ADROIT	2-02-002 AFAR
39-08-030 ACTS	2-02-002 ADJECTIVE	1-01-001 ADROITNESS	1-01-001 AFFABLE
100-10-061 ACTUAL	4-02-004 ADJECTIVES	10-07-009 ADS	33-12-030 AFFAIR
2-01-002 ACTUALITIES	2-02-002 ADJOINED	3-01-001 ADSORBED	1-01-001 AFFAIRE
8-03-007 ACTUALITY	13-07-011 ADJOINING	1-01-001 ADSORBS	1-01-001 AFFAIRES
166-15-128 ACTUALLY	2-02-002 ADJOINS	1-01-001 ADULATION	84-11-057 AFFAIRS
1-01-001 ACTUARIAL	2-02-002 ADJOURNED	25-08-016 ADULT	35-10-030 AFFECT
1-01-001 ACTUARIALLY	1-01-001 ADJOURNING	1-01-001 ADULTERATED	1-01-001 AFFECTATION
1-01-001 ACTUATE	4-03-003 ADJOURNMENT	2-01-001 ADULTERERS	36-09-031 AFFECTED
2-01-002 ACTUATED	1-01-001 ADJOURNS	1-01-001 ADULTEROUS	5-04-005 AFFECTING
1-01-001 ACUMEN	1-01-001 ADJUDGED	3-03-003 ADULTERY	1-01-001 AFFECTINGLY
13-08-013 ACUTE	1-01-001 ADJUDGING	3-02-002 ADULTHOOD	18-09-018 AFFECTION
5-03-005 ACUTELY	1-01-001 ADJUDICATE	23-09-018 ADULTS	6-05-006 AFFECTIONATE
11-07-010 AD	4-02-002 ADJUDICATION	60-11-044 ADVANCE	3-03-003 AFFECTIONATELY
1-01-001 AD-LIB	6-04-004 ADJUNCT	52-12-040 ADVANCED	4-03-004 AFFECTIONS
17-01-002 ADA	1-01-001 ADJUNCTS	10-05-009 ADVANCEMENT	19-11-016 AFFECTS
4-01-001 ADA'S	16-09-014 ADJUST	1-01-001 ADVANCEMENTS	1-01-001 AFFERENT
3-03-003 ADAGE	2-02-002 ADJUSTABLE	18-08-015 ADVANCES	1-01-001 AFFIANCED
3-01-002 ADAGIO	33-09-017 ADJUSTED	4-04-004 ADVANCING	2-02-002 AFFIDAVITS
1-01-001 ADAGIOS	11-05-006 ADJUSTING	73-12-052 ADVANTAGE	1-01-001 AFFIED
2-01-001 ADAIR	35-07-020 ADJUSTMENT	5-04-005 ADVANTAGEOUS	7-07-007 AFFILIATED
1-01-001 ADAIR'S	20-07-011 ADJUSTMENTS	1-01-001 ADVANTAGEOUSLY	1-01-001 AFFILIATES
44-05-009 ADAM	2-02-002 ADJUSTS	28-09-020 ADVANTAGES	4-02-004 AFFILIATION
2-02-002 ADAM'S	7-05-006 ADLAI	5-03-005 ADVENT	5-04-005 AFFILIATIONS
5-04-005 ADAMANT	3-01-001 ADLER	1-01-001 ADVENTISTS	1-01-001 AFFINITIES
1-01-001 ADAMANTLY	2-01-001 ADMASSY	1-01-001 ADVENTISTS'	5-04-005 AFFINITY
1-01-001 ADAME	2-01-001 ADMASSY'S	1-01-001 ADVENTITIOUS	12-06-008 AFFIRM
1-01-001 ADAMO	3-02-003 ADMINISTER	14-06-012 ADVENTURE	4-03-004 AFFIRMATION
42-09-012 ADAMS	14-07-010 ADMINISTERED	1-01-001 ADVENTURERS	1-01-001 AFFIRMATIONS
3-01-001 ADAMS'	4-03-004 ADMINISTERING	14-10-014 ADVENTURES	4-02-003 AFFIRMATIVE
1-01-001 ADAMS'S	1-01-001 ADMINISTERS	1-01-001 ADVENTURING	1-01-001 AFFIRMATIVELY
1-01-001 ADAMSON	161-09-065 ADMINISTRATION	5-03-004 ADVENTUROUS	6-05-006 AFFIRMED
5-04-005 ADAPT	6-02-005 ADMINISTRATION'S	1-01-001 ADVERB	2-02-002 AFFIRMING
2-02-002 ADAPTABLE		2-01-002 ADVERBIAL	1-01-001 AFFIRMS
1-01-001 ADAPTAPLEX	53-07-031 ADMINISTRATIVE	2-02-002 ADVERBS	1-01-001 AFFIX
10-07-009 ADAPTATION	1-01-001 ADMINISTRATIVEL Y	3-03-003 ADVERSARIES	14-03-003 AFFIXED
7-03-003 ADAPTATIONS		5-04-005 ADVERSARY	8-03-008 AFFLICTED
13-06-013 ADAPTED	15-06-012 ADMINISTRATOR	11-06-010 ADVERSE	1-01-001 AFFLICTION
1-01-001 ADAPTER	5-05-005 ADMINISTRATORS	3-02-003 ADVERSELY	1-01-001 AFFLICTIONS
2-01-001 ADAPTERS	1-01-001 ADMINSTRATION	2-02-002 ADVERSITY	4-03-004 AFFLUENCE
3-03-003 ADAPTING	10-05-009 ADMIRABLE	3-03-003 ADVERTISE	2-02-002 AFFLUENT
1-01-001 ADCOCK	6-04-006 ADMIRABLY	9-05-007 ADVERTISED	40-12-034 AFFORD
88-12-063 ADD	1-01-001 ADMIRALS	2-02-002 ADVERTISEMENT	11-06-010 AFFORDED
1-01-001 ADD-ON	1-01-001 ADMIRALTY	3-02-002 ADVERTISEMENTS	2-02-002 AFFORDING
2-01-001 ADDABBO	10-05-007 ADMIRATION	1-01-001 ADVERTISER	5-03-005 AFFORDS
172-15-128 ADDED	10-08-010 ADMIRE	5-01-001 ADVERTISERS	2-01-001 AFFRONT
1-01-001 ADDICT	17-08-015 ADMIRED	1-01-001 ADVERTISES	1-01-001 AFFRONTED
3-03-003 ADDICTED	3-03-003 ADMIRER	50-12-026 ADVERTISING	1-01-001 AFFRONTING
3-03-003 ADDICTION	2-02-002 ADMIRERS	1-01-001 ADVERTISING-CON SCIOUS	3-02-002 AFGHAN
4-02-003 ADDICTS	1-01-001 ADMIRES		1-01-001 AFGHANS
22-10-020 ADDING	4-04-004 ADMIRING	51-14-040 ADVICE	1-01-001 AFICIONADO
1-01-001 ADDISON	1-01-001 ADMIRINGLY	4-03-003 ADVISABILITY	1-01-001 AFIELD
142-13-099 ADDITION	9-02-002 ADMISSIBLE	1-01-001 ADVISABLE	1-01-001 AFIRE
120-11-085 ADDITIONAL	33-08-019 ADMISSION	10-06-010 ADVISE	3-03-003 AFLAME
5-05-005 ADDITIONALLY	3-03-003 ADMISSIONS	33-11-027 ADVISED	7-04-005 AFLOAT
9-05-009 ADDITIONS	37-12-033 ADMIT	1-01-001 ADVISEDLY	1-01-001 AFOOT
3-01-001 ADDITIVE	2-01-002 ADMITS	1-01-001 ADVISEMENT	2-02-002 AFOREMENTIONED
4-02-002 ADDITIVES	1-01-001 ADMITTANCE	6-03-005 ADVISER	2-01-001 AFORESAID
1-01-001 ADDLE-BRAINED	44-11-036 ADMITTED	12-04-011 ADVISERS	1-01-001 AFORETHOUGHT
77-13-041 ADDRESS	3-03-003 ADMITTEDLY	2-02-002 ADVISES	57-12-043 AFRAID
19-08-017 ADDRESSED	8-05-008 ADMITTING	3-03-003 ADVISING	1-01-001 AFRANIO
1-01-001 ADDRESSEES	1-01-001 ADMIXED	1-01-001 ADVISOR	2-02-002 AFRESH
21-07-012 ADDRESSES	2-02-002 ADMONISHED	5-02-003 ADVISORS	45-10-028 AFRICA
9-05-008 ADDRESSING	1-01-001 ADMONISHING	24-07-014 ADVISORY	28-11-021 AFRICAN
10-05-010 ADDS	1-01-001 ADMONISHMENTS	3-02-002 ADVOCACY	4-03-003 AFRICANS
1-01-001 ADDUCE	1-01-001 ADMONITION	15-05-010 ADVOCATE	1-01-001 AFRIKA

1-01-001	AFRIQUE	1-01-001	AGRICULTURALLY	1-01-001	ALABAMIAN	16-09-015	ALIEN
4-01-001	AFRO-*ASIAN	23-07-019	AGRICULTURE	3-02-003	ALABASTER	2-02-002	ALIENATE
1-01-001	AFRO-*CUBAN	1-01-001	AGRICULTURE'S	2-01-001	ALACRITY	6-04-006	ALIENATED
5-04-004	AFT	1-01-001	AGRIPPA	1-01-001	ALAI	1-01-001	ALIENATES
1070-15-378	AFTER	1-01-001	AGROBACTERIUM	1-01-001	ALAIN	22-02-004	ALIENATION
1-01-001	AFTER-DUTY	1-01-001	AGUE	1-01-001	ALAMEIN	3-02-002	ALIENS
1-01-001	AFTER-HOURS	22-07-013	AH	1-01-001	ALAMO	1-01-001	ALIENUS
2-02-002	AFTER-SCHOOL	1-01-001	AH*$-AH	1-01-001	ALAMOGORDO	3-02-003	ALIGHT
4-03-004	AFTERMATH	1-01-001	AHAH	5-02-003	ALAN	2-02-002	ALIGN
106-12-075	AFTERNOON	109-15-081	AHEAD	16-08-013	ALARM	6-02-002	ALIGNED
3-03-003	AFTERNOON'S	1-01-001	AHEM	8-06-008	ALARMED	1-01-001	ALIGNING
13-09-011	AFTERNOONS	1-01-001	AHM	1-01-001	ALARMING	4-02-004	ALIGNMENT
16-07-014	AFTERWARD	1-01-001	AHMAD	2-02-002	ALARMINGLY	1-01-001	ALIGNMENTS
14-09-014	AFTERWARDS	2-02-002	AHMAD'S	1-01-001	ALARMIST	20-10-020	ALIKE
1-01-001	AFTUH	3-01-001	AHMET	1-01-001	ALARMS	2-02-002	ALIMONY
578-15-287	AGAIN	1-01-001	AHMIRI	10-08-010	ALAS	1-01-001	ALIQUOTS
626-15-268	AGAINST	1-01-001	AHRENS	22-05-008	ALASKA	1-01-001	ALISON
2-02-002	AGAMEMNON	1-01-001	AI	4-01-001	ALASTOR	57-13-048	ALIVE
1-01-001	AGAMEMNON'S	130-11-069	AID	1-01-001	ALBA	2-01-001	ALIX
1-01-001	AGATES	1-01-001	AID-TO-EDUCATIO	1-01-001	ALBACORE	1-01-001	ALIX'S
2-01-002	AGATHA		N	3-02-002	ALBANIA	1-01-001	ALIZARIN
1-01-001	AGAYNE	1-01-001	AIDA	2-01-001	ALBANIAN	4-01-002	ALKALI
227-15-125	AGE	9-06-008	AIDE	2-01-001	ALBANIANS	2-01-001	ALKALINE
2-01-001	AGE-AND-SEX	1-01-001	AIDE-DE-CAMP	11-07-009	ALBANY	2-01-002	ALKALIS
5-04-004	AGE-OLD	11-08-011	AIDED	2-02-002	ALBEIT	1-01-001	ALKALOIDS
18-08-013	AGED	4-02-003	AIDES	1-01-001	ALBERS	1-01-001	ALKYLARYSULFONA
1-01-001	AGED-CARE	7-03-007	AIDING	29-08-024	ALBERT		TE
1-01-001	AGEE	27-07-009	AIDS	2-01-001	ALBERTO	1-01-001	ALKYLBENZENESUL
2-02-002	AGELESS	1-01-001	AIKEN	1-01-001	ALBICANS		FONATES
62-08-035	AGENCIES	1-01-001	AIKIN	3-01-001	ALBRIGHT	3001-15-491	ALL
56-10-035	AGENCY	1-01-001	AILERONS	2-01-001	ALBRIGHT'S	2-01-002	ALL-*AMERICAN
5-04-005	AGENDA	2-01-001	AILEY	1-01-001	ALBRIGHTS'	1-01-001	ALL-*AMERICAN-B
44-09-026	AGENT	2-01-001	AILEY'S	6-02-004	ALBUM		OY
1-01-001	AGENT'S	2-02-002	AILING	10-01-002	ALBUMIN	6-01-001	ALL-*NEGRO
39-08-026	AGENTS	4-03-003	AILMENT	2-01-001	ALBUMS	1-01-001	ALL-*STAR
51-10-032	AGES	6-02-003	AILMENTS	1-01-001	ALCHEMY	1-01-001	ALL-AUTOMATIC
2-01-001	AGGIE	37-09-033	AIM	1-01-001	ALCIBIADES	1-01-001	ALL-COLLEGE
2-01-001	AGGIES	24-09-021	AIMED	1-01-001	ALCINOU**DS'	1-01-001	ALL-CONSUMING
2-01-001	AGGLOMERATE	5-02-005	AIMING	13-05-007	ALCOHOL	1-01-001	ALL-COUNTY
3-01-002	AGGLOMERATION	5-05-005	AIMLESS	3-03-003	ALCOHOLIC	1-01-001	ALL-FEMALE
1-01-001	AGGLUTINATING	1-01-001	AIMLESSLY	4-03-003	ALCOHOLICS	5-03-004	ALL-IMPORTANT
4-01-001	AGGLUTINATION	16-06-012	AIMS	1-01-001	ALCOHOLISM	1-01-001	ALL-INCLUSIVE
6-01-001	AGGLUTININ	46-08-022	AIN'T	2-01-001	ALCOHOLS	1-01-001	ALL-KNOWING
2-01-001	AGGLUTININS	1-01-001	AINSLEY	2-02-002	ALCORN	1-01-001	ALL-LESBIAN
1-01-001	AGGRAVATE	1-01-001	AINSWORTH	1-01-001	ALCOTT'S	1-01-001	ALL-MARRIED
3-03-003	AGGRAVATED	1-01-001	AINU	5-01-001	ALCOVES	1-01-001	ALL-NIGHT
1-01-001	AGGRAVATES	1-01-001	AINUS	2-01-001	ALDEN	6-04-005	ALL-OUT
8-03-007	AGGREGATE	257-15-128	AIR	1-01-001	ALDERMAN	1-01-001	ALL-OVER
1-01-001	AGGREGATION	1-01-001	AIR-CELL	2-01-001	ALDERMEN	1-01-001	ALL-PERVADING
1-01-001	AGGREGATIONS	1-01-001	AIR-CONDITIONED	1-01-001	ALDO	2-01-002	ALL-POWERFUL
10-07-010	AGGRESSION	2-02-002	AIR-CONDITIONIN	1-01-001	ALDRIDGE	1-01-001	ALL-PURPOSE
3-01-002	AGGRESSIONS		G	1-01-001	ALE	1-01-001	ALL-ROUND
17-09-014	AGGRESSIVE	1-01-001	AIR-DRIFTS	25-01-001	ALEC	1-01-001	ALL-SOMETHING-O
2-02-002	AGGRESSIVELY	1-01-001	AIR-FRAME	5-01-001	ALEC'S		R-THE-OTHER
5-02-003	AGGRESSIVENESS	1-01-001	AIR-TO-SURFACE	2-02-002	ALECK	3-03-003	ALL-TIME
2-02-002	AGGRESSOR	7-04-007	AIRBORNE	1-01-001	ALEMAGNA	1-01-001	ALL-TOO-BRIEF
3-02-002	AGGRIEVED	70-10 019	AIRCRAFT	33-12-031	ALERT	1-01-001	ALL-VICTORIOUS
1-01-001	AGHAST	1-01-001	AIRCRAFT'S	3-03-003	ALERTED	2-02-002	ALL-WEATHER
2-02-002	AGILE	1-01-001	AIRDROPS	4-03-004	ALERTING	5-03-003	ALL-WHITE
1-01-001	AGILELY	2-02-002	AIRED	1-01-001	ALERTLY	1-01-001	ALL-WOMAN
3-02-003	AGILITY	1-01-001	AIREDALE	2-02-002	ALERTNESS	2-02-002	ALLA
2-02-002	AGIN	5-03-004	AIRFIELD	1-01-001	ALERTS	1-01-001	ALLAH
4-04-004	AGING	6-02-002	AIRFIELDS	1-01-001	ALESSIO	4-03-004	ALLAN
1-01-001	AGITATE	1-01-001	AIRFLOW	30-03-004	ALEX	2-01-002	ALLAY
1-01-001	AGITATED	1-01-001	AIRFRAME	10-01-001	ALEX'S	5-03-004	ALLEGATIONS
1-01-001	AGITATING	2-02-002	AIRILY	45-10-021	ALEXANDER	1-01-001	ALLEGE
6-06-006	AGITATION	2-02-002	AIRLESS	3-02-002	ALEXANDER'S	10-06-008	ALLEGED
1-01-001	AGITATOR	1-01-001	AIRLIFT	2-01-001	ALEXANDRE	4-03-003	ALLEGEDLY
1-01-001	AGITATORS	2-02-002	AIRLINE	4-03-003	ALEXANDRIA	1-01-001	ALLEGHENIES
1-01-001	AGLEAM	1-01-001	AIRLINE'S	1-01-001	ALEXEI	1-01-001	ALLEGHENY
1-01-001	AGNES	5-02-003	AIRLINES	1-01-001	ALEXEYEVA	4-03-004	ALLEGIANCE
6-02-002	AGNESE	1-01-001	AIRLOCK	2-01-001	ALEXIS	1-01-001	ALLEGIANCES
1-01-001	AGNOMEN	4-01-001	AIRMAIL	2-01-001	ALF	3-03-003	ALLEGING
1-01-001	AGNOSTICS	1-01-001	AIRMAN'S	1-01-001	ALFA	2-02-002	ALLEGORIC
246-15-163	AGO	1-01-001	AIRMEN	1-01-001	ALFONSO	3-02-002	ALLEGORICAL
1-01-001	AGOENG	1-01-001	AIRPARK	52-05-013	ALFRED	3-03-003	ALLEGORY
1-01-001	AGONALE	11-08-009	AIRPLANE	3-01-001	ALFRED'S	1-01-001	ALLEGRETTI
2-01-001	AGONE	10-05-006	AIRPLANES	3-02-002	ALFREDO	2-02-002	ALLEGRO
1-01-001	AGONIES	19-08-012	AIRPORT	2-02-002	ALFRESCO	1-01-001	ALLEMANDS
1-01-001	AGONIZED	4-02-003	AIRPORTS	7-02-002	ALGAE	20-07-017	ALLEN
2-02-002	AGONIZES	3-02-003	AIRS	1-01-001	ALGAECIDE	1-01-001	ALLEN'S
3-03-003	AGONIZING	1-01-001	AIRSPEED	2-01-001	ALGEBRA	2-02-002	ALLERGIC
9-06-009	AGONY	2-02-002	AIRSTRIP	1-01-001	ALGEBRAIC	1-01-001	ALLERGIES
8-01-002	AGRARIAN	1-01-001	AIRSTRIPS	3-01-001	ALGEBRAICALLY	1-01-001	ALLERGY
51-12-040	AGREE	6-03-003	AIRWAYS	1-01-001	ALGER	5-03-005	ALLEVIATE
11-05-007	AGREEABLE	7-05-007	AIRY	2-01-001	ALGERIA	1-01-001	ALLEVIATING
1-01-001	AGREEABLENESS	6-05-005	AISLE	5-02-004	ALGERIAN	2-01-001	ALLEVIATION
1-01-001	AGREEABLY	2-01-002	AJAR	1-01-001	ALGINATES	8-04-006	ALLEY
81-13-056	AGREED	10-07-010	AKIN	3-01-001	ALGOL	1-01-001	ALLEYS
1-01-001	AGREED-ON	1-01-001	AKITA	1-01-001	ALGORITHM	1-01-001	ALLEYWAYS
1-01-001	AGREED-UPON	1-01-001	AKRON	1-01-001	ALIA	20-06-013	ALLIANCE
7-05-006	AGREEING	24-08-015	AL	1-01-001	ALIAH	1-01-001	ALLIANCE'S
106-10-046	AGREEMENT	2-02-002	AL'S	1-01-001	ALIAS	1-01-001	ALLIANCES
15-07-011	AGREEMENTS	7-01-004	ALA	8-03-004	ALIBI	29-08-016	ALLIED
11-06-009	AGREES	20-08-012	ALABAMA	1-01-001	ALIBIS	30-06-019	ALLIES
1-01-001	AGRICOLAS	1-01-001	ALABAMANS	14-05-006	ALICE	4-02-002	ALLIGATOR
38-07-018	AGRICULTURAL	2-01-001	ALABAMAS	4-01-001	ALICIA	1-01-001	ALLIGATORED

Freq	Word	Freq	Word
1-01-001	ALLISON	3-01-003	ALTERNATIVELY
1-01-001	ALLISON'S	17-08-014	ALTERNATIVES
1-01-001	ALLITERATION	1-01-001	ALTERS
1-01-001	ALLITERATIVE	1-01-001	ALTHAUS
3-01-001	ALLOCABLE	1-01-001	ALTHEA
3-02-002	ALLOCATE	4-01-003	ALTHO
5-04-005	ALLOCATED	319-15-194	ALTHOUGH
17-04-008	ALLOCATION	4-03-003	ALTITUDE
2-01-001	ALLOCATIONS	1-01-001	ALTITUDE-AZIMUTH-MOUNTED
1-01-001	ALLONS	4-04-004	ALTO
1-01-001	ALLOT	30-10-028	ALTOGETHER
1-01-001	ALLOTED	2-02-002	ALTON
39-02-002	ALLOTMENT	1-01-001	ALTRUISM
10-01-001	ALLOTMENTS	1-01-001	ALTRUISTICALLY
10-05-007	ALLOTTED	1-01-001	ALUM
1-01-001	ALLOTTING	18-05-012	ALUMINUM
72-13-060	ALLOW	1-01-001	ALUMNAE
5-03-003	ALLOWABLE	9-03-003	ALUMNI
16-08-012	ALLOWANCE	1-01-001	ALUNDUM
25-05-007	ALLOWANCES	1-01-001	ALUSIK
86-12-060	ALLOWED	3-02-003	ALUSIK'S
31-09-027	ALLOWING	3-02-002	ALVA
19-08-016	ALLOWS	3-02-002	ALVAREZ
3-02-002	ALLOY	1-01-001	ALVEAR
3-01-001	ALLOYS	9-01-002	ALVEOLAR
1-01-001	ALLSO	4-01-003	ALVEOLI
4-01-001	ALLSTATES	1-01-001	ALVEOLUS
1-01-001	ALLSTATES'	6-03-005	ALVIN
1-01-001	ALLSTATES-*ZENITH	2-01-001	ALVISE
1-01-001	ALLUDED	458-15-240	ALWAYS
1-01-001	ALLUDES	1-01-001	ALWAYS-PRESENT
1-01-001	ALLUDING	228-15-121	AM
1-01-001	ALLURE	4-01-001	AMADEE
1-01-001	ALLUREMENT	1-01-001	AMADEE'S
1-01-001	ALLURING	1-01-001	AMADO
3-03-003	ALLUSION	1-01-001	AMALGAMATED
5-03-005	ALLUSIONS	1-01-001	AMALGAMATION
1-01-001	ALLUSIVENESS	1-01-001	AMANUENSIS
9-04-007	ALLY	1-01-001	AMARAL
7-01-002	ALMA	2-02-002	AMASS
1-01-001	ALMADEN	1-01-001	AMASSING
4-01-001	ALMAGEST	25-08-015	AMATEUR
1-01-001	ALMANAC	3-03-003	AMATEURISH
5-03-003	ALMIGHTY	1-01-001	AMATEURISHNESS
1-01-001	ALMOND	2-01-001	AMATEURS
3-01-001	ALMONDS	1-01-001	AMATORY
432-15-256	ALMOST	3-03-003	AMAZE
2-01-001	ALOES	11-06-011	AMAZED
3-03-003	ALOFT	10-08-009	AMAZEMENT
1-01-001	ALOKUT	20-09-020	AMAZING
195-15-145	ALONE	3-03-003	AMAZINGLY
2-02-002	ALONENESS	2-01-001	AMAZON
355-15-222	ALONG	1-01-001	AMAZONS
15-09-014	ALONGSIDE	22-07-014	AMBASSADOR
5-04-005	ALOOF	1-01-001	AMBASSADOR'S
1-01-001	ALOOFNESS	1-01-001	AMBASSADOR-AT-*LARGE
2-02-002	ALORS	1-01-001	AMBASSADOR-DESIGNATE
13-06-010	ALOUD	6-04-005	AMBASSADORS
2-01-001	ALPERS	3-02-002	AMBER
5-01-001	ALPERT	1-01-001	AMBIANCE
1-01-001	ALPERTS	1-01-001	AMBIDEXTROUS
6-02-002	ALPHA	7-03-007	AMBIGUITIES
1-01-001	ALPHA-BETA-GAMMAS	11-04-004	AMBIGUITY
2-01-001	ALPHABET	22-06-016	AMBIGUOUS
1-01-001	ALPHABETIC	19-09-016	AMBITION
4-03-004	ALPHABETICAL	15-06-013	AMBITIONS
1-01-001	ALPHABETIZED	16-08-014	AMBITIOUS
1-01-001	ALPHARETTA	1-01-001	AMBITIOUSLY
1-01-001	ALPHONSE	5-03-005	AMBIVALENCE
2-02-002	ALPS	6-05-006	AMBIVALENT
1-01-001	ALREADEH	1-01-001	AMBLED
273-15-193	ALREADY	1-01-001	AMBLER
3-01-002	ALSATIAN	1-01-001	AMBLING
1-01-001	ALSATIANS	1-01-001	AMBROSE
1-01-001	ALSING	1-01-001	AMBROSIAL
1069-15-383	ALSO	6-03-004	AMBULANCE
3-02-002	ALSOP	1-01-001	AMBULANCES
1-01-001	ALTAIRIANS	1-01-001	AMBULATORY
5-04-004	ALTAR	1-01-001	AMBUSCADE
4-01-001	ALTENBURG	7-03-004	AMBUSH
15-08-013	ALTER	2-02-002	AMBUSHED
1-01-001	ALTER-EGO	1-01-001	AMBUSHES
1-01-001	ALTER-PARENTS	2-01-001	AMEAUX
7-04-005	ALTERATION	1-01-001	AMELIA'S
7-03-005	ALTERATIONS	19-04-005	AMEN
1-01-001	ALTERCATION	3-02-002	AMENABLE
22-08-017	ALTERED	2-02-002	AMEND
4-03-004	ALTERING	14-04-009	AMENDED
1-01-001	ALTERMAN	1-01-001	AMENDING
11-05-007	ALTERNATE	23-05-015	AMENDMENT
1-01-001	ALTERNATED	1-01-001	AMENDMENT'S
7-07-007	ALTERNATELY	7-04-005	AMENDMENTS
1-01-001	ALTERNATING	1-01-001	AMENITSKII
2-02-002	ALTERNATION		
34-09-024	ALTERNATIVE		

Freq	Word	Freq	Word
194-13-095	AMERICA	2-01-001	ANALYSED
22-08-022	AMERICA'S	13-02-009	ANALYSES
569-14-199	AMERICAN	108-09-053	ANALYSIS
1-01-001	AMERICAN'S	7-02-003	ANALYST
1-01-001	AMERICAN-*JEWISH	3-03-003	ANALYST'S
1-01-001	AMERICAN-TRAINED	6-03-004	ANALYSTS
5-04-004	AMERICANA	16-02-004	ANALYTIC
3-01-001	AMERICANEGRO	9-03-005	ANALYTICAL
93-12-054	AMERICANS	1-01-001	ANALYTICALLY
1-01-001	AMERICAS	1-01-001	ANALYTICITY
4-01-001	AMETHYSTINE	1-01-001	ANALYTROL
2-02-002	AMIABLE	1-01-001	ANALYZABLE
1-01-001	AMICABLE	10-05-010	ANALYZE
1-01-001	AMICABLY	14-06-014	ANALYZED
1-01-001	AMICAM	1-01-001	ANALYZER
3-01-001	AMICI	2-02-002	ANALYZES
14-06-013	AMID	8-05-007	ANALYZING
1-01-001	AMIDE	1-01-001	ANANIA
3-02-003	AMIDST	1-01-001	ANAPLASMOSIS
2-01-001	AMIGO	1-01-001	ANARCHIC
1-01-001	AMINO	2-01-001	ANARCHICAL
1-01-001	AMIS	1-01-001	ANARCHIST
2-02-002	AMISS	1-01-001	ANARCHIST-ADVENTURERS
1-01-001	AMITY	7-04-005	ANARCHY
4-02-002	AMMO	6-01-001	ANASTOMOSES
1-01-001	AMMONIAC	1-01-001	ANASTOMOSIS
1-01-001	AMMONIUM	1-01-001	ANASTOMOTIC
18-05-009	AMMUNITION	1-01-001	ANATOLE
2-01-001	AMONASRO	1-01-001	ANATOMIC
370-15-214	AMONG	9-04-005	ANATOMICAL
4-04-004	AMONGST	2-01-001	ANATOMICALLY
2-02-002	AMORAL	1-01-001	ANATOMICALS
1-01-001	AMORALITY	9-07-007	ANATOMY
7-05-007	AMORIST	1-01-001	ANCEL
2-02-002	AMOROUS	7-05-007	ANCESTOR
6-03-005	AMORPHOUS	6-05-005	ANCESTORS
5-04-005	AMORPHOUSLY	5-04-005	ANCESTRAL
1-01-001	AMORTIZATION	8-05-008	ANCESTRY
1-01-001	AMORTIZE	15-07-011	ANCHOR
1-01-001	AMORY	1-01-001	ANCHORAGE
3-02-002	AMOS	10-05-010	ANCHORED
172-15-099	AMOUNT	1-01-001	ANCHORING
5-05-005	AMOUNTED	2-01-001	ANCHORITE
1-01-001	AMOUNTING	1-01-001	ANCHORITISM
44-11-033	AMOUNTS	2-01-002	ANCHORS
1-01-001	AMP/LUMEN	1-01-001	ANCHOVY
1-01-001	AMPHETAMINES	69-15-055	ANCIENT
1-01-001	AMPHIBIOUS	1-01-001	ANCIENTLY
1-01-001	AMPHIBOLOGY	1-01-001	ANCIENTS
1-01-001	AMPHITHEATER	2-02-002	ANCILLARY
16-09-015	AMPLE	1-01-001	ANCISTRODON
2-01-001	AMPLIFICATION	28852-15-500	AND
6-02-002	AMPLIFIED	17-05-012	AND/OR
1-01-001	AMPLIFIER	2-01-001	ANDEAN
1-01-001	AMPLIFIERS	1-01-001	ANDERLINI
1-01-001	AMPLIFY	2-01-001	ANDERS
1-01-001	AMPLIFYING	1-01-001	ANDERSEN
6-02-002	AMPLITUDE	13-04-008	ANDERSON
4-04-004	AMPLY	4-02-004	ANDERSON'S
1-01-001	AMPUTATED	3-03-003	ANDOVER
1-01-001	AMRA	3-02-003	ANDRE
3-02-002	AMSTERDAM	4-02-002	ANDREA
1-01-001	AMT	18-01-001	ANDREI
1-01-001	AMULET	2-01-001	ANDREI'S
1-01-001	AMULETS	7-01-001	ANDRENA
3-02-003	AMUSE	4-01-001	ANDRENAS
9-07-009	AMUSED	1-01-001	ANDRES
1-01-001	AMUSEDLY	12-04-011	ANDREW
7-05-006	AMUSEMENT	2-02-002	ANDREWS
2-02-002	AMUSEMENTS	3-01-001	ANDROFSKI
14-07-012	AMUSING	1-01-001	ANDROMACHE
2-02-002	AMUSINGLY	12-01-001	ANDRUS
15-04-005	AMY	1-01-001	ANDRUSES
3747-15-498	AN	1-01-001	ANDY
1-01-001	ANA	4-01-001	ANDY'S
9-05-008	ANABAPTIST	1-01-001	ANECDOTAL
1-01-001	ANABAPTISTS	9-05-008	ANECDOTE
1-01-001	ANABEL	4-03-003	ANECDOTES
3-03-003	ANACHRONISM	5-01-001	ANEMATED
2-02-002	ANACHRONISMS	5-01-001	ANEMIA
1-01-001	ANACHRONISTICALLY	1-01-001	ANEMIC
14-02-002	ANACONDA	1-01-001	ANESTHETIC
2-01-001	ANACONDA'S	1-01-001	ANESTHETICALLY
4-01-001	ANACONDAS	1-01-001	ANESTHETICS
1-01-001	ANAEROBIC	1-01-001	ANESTHETIZED
1-01-001	ANAESTHESIA	6-05-005	ANEW
1-01-001	ANAGRAM	18-08-011	ANGEL
2-01-001	ANALEPTIC	3-02-002	ANGEL'S
4-03-003	ANALOGIES	47-11-029	ANGELES
8-05-007	ANALOGOUS	3-02-003	ANGELES'
2-02-002	ANALOGOUSLY	1-01-001	ANGELES-*PASADENA
1-01-001	ANALOGUE	2-01-001	ANGELIC
1-01-001	ANALOGUES	1-01-001	ANGELICA
13-05-011	ANALOGY	1-01-001	ANGELICO
		4-01-001	ANGELINA

Code	Word
1-01-001	ANGELL
8-02-003	ANGELO
2-01-001	ANGELO'S
24-10-015	ANGELS
48-10-030	ANGER
1-01-001	ANGERED
17-01-001	ANGIE
51-08-018	ANGLE
11-03-006	ANGLES
1-01-001	ANGLETERRE
1-01-001	ANGLIA
11-02-003	ANGLICAN
1-01-001	ANGLICANISM
2-02-002	ANGLICANS
1-01-001	ANGLING
2-01-001	ANGLO-*AMERICAN
1-01-001	ANGLO-*AMERICANS
1-01-001	ANGLO-*JEWISH
1-01-001	ANGLO-*PROTESTANT
21-03-005	ANGLO-*SAXON
1-01-001	ANGLO-*SAXONS
1-01-001	ANGLO-SAXON
1-01-001	ANGLOPHILIA
1-01-001	ANGLOPHOBIA
3-02-002	ANGOLA
1-01-001	ANGRIEST
7-05-007	ANGRILY
45-10-036	ANGRY
2-01-001	ANGST
8-06-008	ANGUISH
2-02-002	ANGUISHED
16-04-008	ANGULAR
1-01-001	ANHALT-*BERNBURG
1-01-001	ANHEMOLYTICUS
1-01-001	ANHWEI
1-01-001	ANHYDROUS
1-01-001	ANHYDROUSLY
2-01-001	ANI
1-01-001	ANILINE
68-12-037	ANIMAL
3-02-003	ANIMAL'S
1-01-001	ANIMAL-LIKE
58-12-033	ANIMALS
1-01-001	ANIMATE
5-04-005	ANIMATED
2-01-001	ANIMATION
1-01-001	ANIMISM
1-01-001	ANIMIZED
3-03-003	ANIMOSITY
1-01-001	ANION
10-01-003	ANIONIC
1-01-001	ANIONICS
1-01-001	ANIONS
2-01-001	ANISE
2-01-001	ANISEIKONIC
1-01-001	ANISOTROPY
2-02-002	ANITA
1-01-001	ANKARA
8-06-006	ANKLE
2-02-002	ANKLE-DEEP
7-06-007	ANKLES
29-06-011	ANN
2-01-001	ANN'S
7-04-005	ANNA
4-02-003	ANNALS
1-01-001	ANNAMORENA
7-02-002	ANNAPOLIS
42-07-014	ANNE
4-03-003	ANNE'S
1-01-001	ANNEE
1-01-001	ANNEX
1-01-001	ANNIE
1-01-001	ANNIHILATE
6-05-005	ANNIHILATION
1-01-001	ANNISBERG
17-02-002	ANNISTON
1-01-001	ANNISTON'S
1-01-001	ANNIVERSARIES
21-12-017	ANNIVERSARY
18-07-015	ANNOUNCE
88-15-068	ANNOUNCED
24-08-020	ANNOUNCEMENT
6-05-005	ANNOUNCEMENTS
2-02-002	ANNOUNCER
1-01-001	ANNOUNCER'S
1-01-001	ANNOUNCERS
3-03-003	ANNOUNCES
7-05-007	ANNOUNCING
2-02-002	ANNOY
9-06-009	ANNOYANCE
1-01-001	ANNOYANCES
7-05-007	ANNOYED
6-04-006	ANNOYING
1-01-001	ANNOYS
93-11-060	ANNUAL
14-06-011	ANNUALLY
3-03-003	ANNUM
1-01-001	ANNUNCIATED
77-01-002	ANODE
1-01-001	ANODES
1-01-001	ANOMALIES
1-01-001	ANOMALOUS
1-01-001	ANOMALY
1-01-001	ANOMIC
1-01-001	ANOMIE
2-02-002	ANONYMITY
17-06-011	ANONYMOUS
1-01-001	ANOREXIA
1-01-001	ANORTHIC
683-15-348	ANOTHER
5-05-005	ANOTHER'S
1-01-001	ANOUILH
1-01-001	ANSELM'S
1-01-001	ANSELMO
1-01-001	ANSLEY
1-01-001	ANSON
1-01-001	ANSUH
152-15-115	ANSWER
1-01-001	ANSWERABLE
67-14-056	ANSWERED
14-09-014	ANSWERING
44-12-034	ANSWERS
6-04-005	ANT
5-01-001	ANTA
1-01-001	ANTAGONISED
9-04-004	ANTAGONISM
2-02-002	ANTAGONISMS
3-01-002	ANTAGONIST
4-04-004	ANTAGONISTIC
4-01-001	ANTAGONISTS
1-01-001	ANTAGONIZE
1-01-001	ANTARCTICA
1-01-001	ANTARES
3-02-003	ANTE
3-02-003	ANTE-BELLUM
1-01-001	ANTEATER
1-01-001	ANTECEDENT
2-02-002	ANTECEDENTS
7-02-002	ANTELOPE
13-03-003	ANTENNA
3-03-003	ANTENNAE
1-01-001	ANTENNAS
5-02-003	ANTERIOR
1-01-001	ANTERIORS
3-01-001	ANTHEA
1-01-001	ANTHEM
1-01-001	ANTHEMS
4-01-002	ANTHOLOGY
16-07-010	ANTHONY
1-01-001	ANTHONY'S
1-01-001	ANTHROPOLOGICAL
1-01-001	ANTHRUPOLOGICAL-RELIGIOUS
2-02-002	ANTHROPOLOGIST
2-02-002	ANTHROPOLOGISTS
7-04-007	ANTHROPOLOGY
1-01-001	ANTHROPOMORPHIC
1-01-001	ANTI
4-01-001	ANTI-**J*A
4-01-001	ANTI-**J*B
1-01-001	ANTI-**J*RH
2-02-002	ANTI-*AMERICAN
1-01-001	ANTI-*AMERICANISM
1-01-001	ANTI-*CASTRO
1-01-001	ANTI-*CATHOLIC
3-01-001	ANTI-*CATHOLICISM
1-01-001	ANTI-*CHRISTIAN
1-01-001	ANTI-*COLMER
1-01-001	ANTI-*COMMUNISM
1-01-001	ANTI-*COMMUNISTS
3-02-002	ANTI-*FRENCH
1-01-001	ANTI-*KENNEDY
2-02-002	ANTI-*NAZI
42-07-016	ANTI-*NEGRO
1-01-001	ANTI-*NEWTONIAN
2-01-001	ANTI-*SEMITE
3-01-001	ANTI-*SEMITES
4-01-001	ANTI-*SEMITIC
23-02-002	ANTI-*SEMITISM
2-01-001	ANTI-*SOVIET
2-01-001	ANTI-AIRCRAFT
1-01-001	ANTI-ASSIGNMENT
1-01-001	ANTI-AUTHORITARIAN
1-01-001	ANTI-CLERICALISM
1-01-001	ANTI-DEMOCRATIC
1-01-001	ANTI-DISCRIMINATION
1-01-001	ANTI-DISCRIMINATORY
1-01-001	ANTI-FREEZE
2-01-001	ANTI-HUMAN
2-01-001	ANTI-INFECTIVE
3-02-003	ANTI-INTELLECTUAL
1-01-001	ANTI-INTELLECTUALISM
1-01-001	ANTI-LIQUOR
1-01-001	ANTI-MISSILE
4-01-001	ANTI-MONOPOLY
2-01-001	ANTI-ORGANIZATION
5-01-001	ANTI-PARTY
1-01-001	ANTI-PERSONALITY
1-01-001	ANTI-POLIO
1-01-001	ANTI-RECESSION
2-01-001	ANTI-SECRECY
12-02-002	ANTI-SLAVERY
3-02-002	ANTI-SUBMARINE
26-03-003	ANTI-TRUST
8-03-004	ANTIBIOTIC
1-01-001	ANTIBIOTICS
9-01-002	ANTIBODIES
12-01-001	ANTIBODY
1-01-001	ANTIC
11-08-011	ANTICIPATE
23-10-021	ANTICIPATED
2-02-002	ANTICIPATES
2-02-002	ANTICIPATING
20-06-014	ANTICIPATION
3-03-003	ANTICIPATIONS
1-01-001	ANTICIPATORY
1-01-001	ANTICOAGULATION
4-03-004	ANTICS
1-01-001	ANTICUS
2-02-002	ANTIDOTE
2-02-002	ANTIETAM
1-01-001	ANTIFUNDAMENTALIST
12-01-001	ANTIGEN
1-01-001	ANTIGONE
1-01-001	ANTIHISTORICAL
1-01-001	ANTINOMIANS
4-04-004	ANTIPATHY
1-01-001	ANTIPHONAL
1-01-001	ANTIPODES
1-01-001	ANTIQUARIAN
1-01-001	ANTIQUARIANS
4-03-004	ANTIQUATED
12-06-007	ANTIQUE
3-02-003	ANTIQUES
1-01-001	ANTIQUITIES
3-02-003	ANTIQUITY
1-01-001	ANTIREDEPOSITION
6-03-005	ANTISEPTIC
2-01-002	ANTISERA
4-01-001	ANTISERUM
1-01-001	ANTISLAVERY
2-02-002	ANTISOCIAL
5-01-001	ANTISUBMARINE
3-02-003	ANTITHESIS
1-01-001	ANTITHETICAL
7-01-001	ANTITHYROID
1-01-001	ANTITRUST
3-01-001	ANTLER
1-01-001	ANTOINE
3-01-001	ANTOINE'S
1-01-001	ANTOINETTE
2-01-002	ANTON
1-01-001	ANTONE
1-01-001	ANTONINI
6-03-005	ANTONIO
2-02-002	ANTONY
7-04-006	ANTS
1-01-001	ANVIL
1-01-001	ANXIETIES
42-07-016	ANXIETY
1-01-001	ANXIETY-RELEASED
29-11-022	ANXIOUS
9-06-007	ANXIOUSLY
1345-15-433	ANY
42-13-037	ANYBODY
1-01-001	ANYBODY'D
2-02-002	ANYBODY'S
1-01-001	ANYE
20-09-016	ANYHOW
1-01-001	ANYLABEL
4-04-004	ANYMORE
140-15-105	ANYONE
6-04-006	ANYONE'S
1-01-001	ANYPLACE
1-01-001	ANYTHIN
280-15-166	ANYTHING
46-10-039	ANYWAY
1-01-001	ANYWAYS
39-12-033	ANYWHERE
1-01-001	ANZILOTTI
3-02-002	AORTA
1-01-001	AQUELLOUL
10-01-005	AP)**T**-
1-01-001	APACHE
3-02-002	APACHES
1-01-001	APALACHICOLA
1-01-001	APARICIO
57-12-051	APART
3-02-003	APARTHEID
81-12-039	APARTMENT
1-01-001	APARTMENT-BUILDING
17-06-009	APARTMENTS
1-01-001	APATHETIC
3-02-002	APATHY
3-03-003	APE
1-01-001	APERGILLUS
8-03-004	APERTURE
4-03-004	APEX
1-01-001	APHRODITE
2-02-002	APIECE
1-01-001	APLOMB
2-02-002	APOCALYPSE
5-04-004	APOCALYPTIC
1-01-001	APOCRYPHA
1-01-001	APOCRYPHAL
2-02-002	APOGEE
2-01-001	APOLLINAIRE
5-04-004	APOLLO
1-01-001	APOLLO'S
1-01-001	APOLLONIAN
3-03-003	APOLOGETIC
6-05-006	APOLOGETICALLY
1-01-001	APOLOGIA
1-01-001	APOLOGIE
4-02-004	APOLOGIES
1-01-001	APOLOGIST
1-01-001	APOLOGIZE
5-04-005	APOLOGIZED
3-01-002	APOLOGY
1-01-001	APOSTATES
2-02-002	APOSTLE
2-02-002	APOSTLES
4-02-002	APOSTOLIC
3-01-001	APOTHECARY
1-01-001	APOTHEOSIS
2-02-002	APP
1-01-001	APPALACHIAN
1-01-001	APPALACHIANS
2-02-002	APPALLED
9-06-009	APPALLING
1-01-001	APPALLINGLY
1-01-001	APPALOOSAS
1-01-001	APPANAGE
29-08-018	APPARATUS
3-02-002	APPAREL
1-01-001	APPARELED
1-01-001	APPARENCY
57-13-052	APPARENT
125-15-100	APPARENTLY
3-03-003	APPARITION
62-12-037	APPEAL
13-05-011	APPEALED
14-07-013	APPEALING
19-06-014	APPEALS
118-13-083	APPEAR
57-13-050	APPEARANCE
14-06-014	APPEARANCES
135-15-100	APPEARED
1-01-001	APPEARIN
16-09-016	APPEARING
84-09-063	APPEARS
2-02-002	APPEASE
2-02-002	APPEASED
3-03-003	APPEASEMENT
1-01-001	APPEASING
1-01-001	APPELLANT
1-01-001	APPENDAGES
2-02-002	APPENDED
10-02-005	APPENDIX
1-01-001	APPENDIXES
5-01-001	APPESTAT
11-04-007	APPETITE
3-02-003	APPETITES
2-01-001	APPETIZING
1-01-001	APPIAN
5-05-005	APPLAUD
4-04-004	APPLAUDED
2-02-002	APPLAUDING
14-07-012	APPLAUSE

Code	Word	Code	Word	Code	Word	Code	Word
1-01-001	APPLAUSE-HAPPY	1-01-001	AQUAM	1-01-001	AREQUIPA	20-05-011	ARNOLD
9-04-006	APPLE	1-01-001	AQUEDUCTS	1-01-001	ARES	2-02-002	ARNOLD'S
1-01-001	APPLE-TREE	14-01-004	AQUEOUS	1-01-001	ARGENTINA	1-01-001	ARNOLD-*FOSTER
1-01-001	APPLEBY	2-01-001	AQUIDNECK	3-01-001	ARGER	5-01-001	ARNOLPHE
1-01-001	APPLEJACK	2-02-002	AQUINAS	13-01-001	ARGIENTO	3-03-003	AROMA
6-02-002	APPLES	1-01-001	AQUISITION	1-01-001	ARGIVE	2-02-002	AROMAS
1-01-001	APPLETON	2-02-002	ARAB	7-01-001	ARGON	2-01-001	AROMATIC
5-02-002	APPLIANCE	1-01-001	ARABESQUE	1-01-001	ARGONAUTS	1-01-001	AROMATICK
8-04-006	APPLIANCES	1-01-001	ARABIA	1-01-001	ARGOS	18-09-015	AROSE
2-02-002	APPLICABILITY	2-02-002	ARABIAN	1-01-001	ARGOT	561-15-254	AROUND
18-06-015	APPLICABLE	1-01-001	ARABIAN-*AMERICAN	29-07-021	ARGUE	1-01-001	AROUNY
8-03-004	APPLICANT			29-12-026	ARGUED	3-03-003	AROUSAL
10-05-006	APPLICANTS	1-01-001	ARABIANS	10-06-007	ARGUES	5-03-005	AROUSE
68-11-042	APPLICATION	6-05-005	ARABIC	10-06-008	ARGUING	20-11-019	AROUSED
25-06-015	APPLICATIONS	3-03-003	ARABLE	63-11-048	ARGUMENT	2-02-002	AROUSES
1-01-001	APPLICATOR	1-01-001	ARABS	1-01-001	ARGUMENTATION	3-02-003	AROUSING
106-13-066	APPLIED	1-01-001	ARABS'	15-08-013	ARGUMENTS	6-02-002	ARP
19-06-017	APPLIES	1-01-001	ARABY	1-01-001	ARHAT	1-01-001	ARPEGGIOS
1-01-001	APPLIQUES	1-01-001	ARAK	1-01-001	ARHATS	1-01-001	ARRACK
56-08-044	APPLY	1-01-001	ARANSAS	3-02-002	ARIADNE	1-01-001	ARRAGON
29-09-023	APPLYING	2-01-001	ARAPACIS	1-01-001	ARIANISM	2-02-002	ARRAIGNED
6-05-006	APPOINT	1-01-001	ARATA	1-01-001	ARIANIST	1-01-001	ARRAIGNING
42-12-034	APPOINTED	1-01-001	ARBEITSKOMMANDO	1-01-001	ARIANISTS	10-06-009	ARRANGE
2-02-002	APPOINTEE	5-02-004	ARBITER	5-01-001	ARICARAS	44-13-037	ARRANGED
5-03-003	APPOINTEES	5-03-005	ARBITRARILY	2-02-002	ARID	34-12-028	ARRANGEMENT
1-01-001	APPOINTING	21-07-018	ARBITRARY	2-02-002	ARIDITY	38-12-034	ARRANGEMENTS
28-09-022	APPOINTMENT	3-01-002	ARBITRATE	1-01-001	ARIGATO	1-01-001	ARRANGERS
6-05-006	APPOINTMENTS	1-01-001	ARBITRATED	2-01-001	ARIMATHEA	1-01-001	ARRANGES
1-01-001	APPOINTS	2-02-002	ARBITRATION	28-09-025	ARISE	16-10-014	ARRANGING
1-01-001	APPORTION	3-01-001	ARBOGAST	4-03-003	ARISEN	11-05-011	ARRAY
8-03-003	APPORTIONED	1-01-001	ARBOR	11-05-009	ARISES	2-01-002	ARRAYED
9-01-001	APPORTIONMENT	1-01-001	ARBOREAL	2-01-001	ARISING	6-04-004	ARREARS
2-01-001	APPORTIONMENTS	1-01-001	ARBRITRARY	2-01-001	ARISTIDE	19-09-014	ARREST
8-05-008	APPRAISAL	5-01-001	ARBUCKLE	4-04-004	ARISTOCRACY	19-07-014	ARRESTED
2-02-002	APPRAISALS	1-01-001	ARBUCKLE'S	4-02-004	ARISTOCRATIC	5-03-005	ARRESTING
4-02-004	APPRAISE	41-08-013	ARC	1-01-001	ARISTOCRATICALLY	3-02-002	ARRESTS
1-01-001	APPRAISED	3-03-003	ARCADE			1-01-001	ARRINGTON
1-01-001	APPRAISERS	1-01-001	ARCADED	2-02-002	ARISTOCRATS	23-11-023	ARRIVAL
1-01-001	APPRAISING	2-01-001	ARCADES	1-01-001	ARISTOTELEAN-*THOMISTIC	3-02-003	ARRIVALS
1-01-001	APPRAISINGLY	13-04-007	ARCH			24-09-021	ARRIVE
5-03-005	APPRECIABLE	1-01-001	ARCH-ENEMY	2-01-002	ARISTOTELIAN	62-15-054	ARRIVED
7-02-007	APPRECIABLY	1-01-001	ARCH-HERETIC	22-02-004	ARISTOTLE	7-06-007	ARRIVES
26-11-023	APPRECIATE	1-01-001	ARCH-OPPONENT	6-01-002	ARISTOTLE'S	15-08-014	ARRIVING
11-08-011	APPRECIATED	8-02-002	ARCHAEOLOGICAL	8-04-005	ARITHMETIC	3-03-003	ARROGANCE
1-01-001	APPRECIATES	1-01-001	ARCHAEOLOGISTS	1-01-001	ARITHMETICAL	2-02-002	ARROGANT
1-01-001	APPRECIATING	11-03-004	ARCHAEOLOGY	1-01-001	ARITHMETIZED	1-01-001	ARROGANTLY
22-11-019	APPRECIATION	5-02-003	ARCHAIC	5-01-004	ARIZ	1-01-001	ARROGATE
1-01-001	APPRECIATIONS	1-01-001	ARCHAISM	9-06-008	ARIZONA	14-03-003	ARROW
2-02-002	APPRECIATIVE	1-01-001	ARCHAIZED	1-01-001	ARKABUTLA	1-01-001	ARROWED
2-02-002	APPRECIATIVELY	3-01-001	ARCHANGEL	18-06-010	ARKANSAS	1-01-001	ARROWHEAD
1-01-001	APPREHEND	1-01-001	ARCHANGELS	1-01-001	ARKANSAS'	1-01-001	ARROWHEADS
2-02-002	APPREHENDED	8-03-004	ARCHBISHOP	1-01-001	ARLEIGH	6-03-003	ARROWS
11-08-010	APPREHENSION	1-01-001	ARCHBISHOPS'	13-01-001	ARLEN	3-01-001	ARROYO
5-04-004	APPREHENSIONS	1-01-001	ARCHDIOCESE	1-01-001	ARLEN'S	3-03-003	ARSENAL
4-03-004	APPREHENSIVELY	11-05-007	ARCHED	26-02-002	ARLENE	1-01-001	ARSENIC
15-06-007	APPRENTICE	1-01-001	ARCHENEMY	1-01-001	ARLENE'S	1-01-001	ARSHINKOFF
1-01-001	APPRENTICED	1-01-001	ARCHEOLOGICAL	4-02-002	ARLINGTON	1-01-001	ARSIDE
3-02-002	APPRENTICES	1-01-001	ARCHERY	94-12-061	ARM	1-01-001	ARSINES
2-02-002	APPRENTICESHIP	7-04-006	ARCHES	3-03-003	ARM'S	2-01-001	ARSON
123-15-085	APPROACH	1-01-001	ARCHFOOL	6-01-001	ARM-ELEVATION	208-14-079	ART
1-01-001	APPROACHABLE	1-01-001	ARCHIMEDES	2-01-001	ARM-LEVITATION	2-02-002	ART'S
45-12-041	APPROACHED	1-01-001	ARCHING	1-01-001	ARM-RISE	1-01-001	ART-FILLED
25-08-020	APPROACHES	2-01-001	ARCHIPELAGO	1-01-001	ARMADA'S	1-01-001	ART-HISTORIAN
27-13-023	APPROACHING	22-07-015	ARCHITECT	2-01-001	ARMADILLO	1-01-001	ART-SHOP
68-10-049	APPROPRIATE	2-02-002	ARCHITECT'S	1-01-001	ARMAGEDDON	4-02-002	ARTE
11-04-008	APPROPRIATED	1-01-001	ARCHITECTONIC	1-01-001	ARMAMENT	1-01-001	ARTE'S
5-05-005	APPROPRIATELY	8-04-006	ARCHITECTS	4-02-003	ARMAMENTS	1-01-001	ARTEMIS
2-02-002	APPROPRIATENESS	1-01-001	ARCHITECTS'	2-01-001	ARMATA	7-02-002	ARTERIAL
1-01-001	APPROPRIATES	8-05-005	ARCHITECTURAL	1-01-001	ARMBRO	16-04-005	ARTERIES
2-02-002	APPROPRIATING	11-07-009	ARCHITECTURE	4-03-004	ARMCHAIR	3-01-001	ARTERIOLAR
5-03-004	APPROPRIATION	2-02-002	ARCHITECTURES	2-02-002	ARMCHAIRS		ARTERIOLAR-PULMONARY
9-03-007	APPROPRIATIONS	4-04-004	ARCHIVES	60-10-034	ARMED		
51-09-042	APPROVAL	1-01-001	ARCHTYPE	1-01-001	ARMENIAN	2-01-001	ARTERIOLES
14-06-012	APPROVE	1-01-001	ARCHULETA	1-01-001	ARMENTIERES	2-01-001	ARTERIOLOSCLEROSIS
40-08-027	APPROVED	1-01-001	ARCILLA	1-01-001	ARMFUL	1-01-001	ARTERIOSCLEROSIS
1-01-001	APPROVES	1-01-001	ARCLIKE	3-01-001	ARMHOLE		
1-01-001	APPROVING	1-01-001	ARCO	1-01-001	ARMIDE	46-03-005	ARTERY
2-02-002	APPROVINGLY	8-01-001	ARCS	15-04-006	ARMIES	1-01-001	ARTERY'S
11-03-009	APPROXIMATE	4-01-001	ARCTIC	1-01-001	ARMINES	5-01-001	ARTERY-PULMONA
5-04-005	APPROXIMATED	1-01-001	ARCUS	1-01-001	ARMISTEADS		
71-07-042	APPROXIMATELY	3-02-002	ARDEN	4-01-003	ARMISTICE	1-01-001	ARTFUL
7-02-006	APPROXIMATION	12-07-010	ARDENT	1-01-001	ARMLOAD	4-03-004	ARTFULLY
3-03-003	APPROXIMATIONS	1-01-001	ARDMORE	1-01-001	ARMOIRE	1-01-001	ARTFULNESS
1-01-001	APRICOT	3-02-002	ARDOR	1-01-001	ARMOND	3-02-002	ARTHRITIS
71-11-041	APRIL	4-03-004	ARDUOUS	4-02-004	ARMOR	51-09-029	ARTHUR
1-01-001	APRIL-*JUNE	4393-15-453	ARE	3-03-003	ARMORED	1-01-001	ARTHUR'S
7-05-006	APRON	323-14-145	AREA	1-01-001	ARMORY	68-10-035	ARTICLE
1-01-001	APRONS	2-01-001	AREA'S	1-01-001	ARMORY'S	31-09-023	ARTICLES
1-01-001	APROPOS	2-01-002	AREA-WIDE	2-01-001	ARMOUR	8-04-008	ARTICULATE
1-01-001	APSES	1-01-001	AREA(S	2-02-002	ARMPIT	2-02-002	ARTICULATED
15-06-014	APT	236-10-120	AREAS	1-01-001	ARMPITS	2-02-002	ARTICULATION
3-02-003	APTITUDE	1-01-001	AREAWAYS	121-15-086	ARMS	1-01-001	ARTICULATIONS
1-01-001	APTITUDES	36-11-034	AREN'T	1-01-001	ARMS-MAKING	8-01-001	ARTIE
4-03-004	APTLY	7-01-006	ARENA	6-03-004	ARMSTRONG	1-01-001	ARTIFACTS
1-01-001	APTNESS	3-03-003	ARENAS	132-14-067	ARMY	1-01-001	ARTIFICE
1-01-001	AQUA-LUNG	1-01-001	ARENULA	5-02-004	ARMY'S	1-01-001	ARTIFICER
1-01-001	AQUACUTIE	1-01-001	AREOSOL	1-01-001	ARNICA		

```
17-08-017   ARTIFICIAL
1-01-001    ARTIFICIALITY
6-04-005    ARTIFICIALLY
1-01-001    ARTILLERIST
11-05-010   ARTILLERY
2-02-002    ARTISAN
2-02-002    ARTISANS
57-10-034   ARTIST
7-03-005    ARTIST'S
1-01-001    ARTIST-AUTHOR
1-01-001    ARTIST-NATURE
33-09-019   ARTISTIC
5-03-005    ARTISTICALLY
3-02-003    ARTISTRY
55-09-026   ARTISTS
6-05-006    ARTISTS'
1-01-001    ARTKINO
2-02-002    ARTLESS
66-12-038   ARTS
1-01-001    ARTUR
2-02-002    ARTURO
1-01-001    ARTY
5-01-001    ARUNDEL
1-01-001    ARVEY
1-01-001    ARYL
3-01-001    ARYLESTERASE
1-01-001    ARYLESTERASES
7250-15-500 AS
1-01-001    AS-IT-WERE
1-01-001    ASBESTOS
1-01-001    ASBESTOS-CEMENT
1-01-001    ASCEND
1-01-001    ASCENDANCY
2-01-002    ASCENDED
4-04-004    ASCENDING
1-01-001    ASCENT
7-04-007    ASCERTAIN
1-01-001    ASCERTAINABLE
4-02-004    ASCERTAINED
1-01-001    ASCETIC
1-01-001    ASCETICISM
1-01-001    ASCH
1-01-001    ASCHENBACH
1-01-001    ASCRIBE
5-03-005    ASCRIBED
1-01-001    ASCRIBES
1-01-001    ASEPTIC
11-05-008   ASH
1-01-001    ASH-*CAN
1-01-001    ASH-BLONDE
1-01-001    ASHAM'D
16-07-015   ASHAMED
2-02-002    ASHEN
1-01-001    ASHER
6-05-005    ASHES
2-01-001    ASHEVILLE
1-01-001    ASHIKAGA
1-01-001    ASHLEY
1-01-001    ASHMAN
1-01-001    ASHMOLEAN
6-03-004    ASHORE
1-01-001    ASHTRAYS
44-11-032   ASIA
10-05-008   ASIAN
1-01-001    ASIANS
1-01-001    ASIATIC
67-15-060   ASIDE
1-01-001    ASILOMAR
1-01-001    ASIMOV'S
2-02-002    ASININE
128-15-090  ASK
1-01-001    ASKANCE
398-15-200  ASKED
1-01-001    ASKEW
1-01-001    ASKIN
67-13-056   ASKING
5-01-001    ASKINGTON
1-01-001    ASKINGTON'S
18-10-016   ASKS
1-01-001    ASLEEEP
29-08-022   ASLEEP
1-01-001    ASOCIAL
1-01-001    ASPARAGUS
47-11-038   ASPECT
64-10-051   ASPECTS
2-01-001    ASPEN
1-01-001    ASPENCADE
2-01-001    ASPENCADES
3-03-003    ASPHALT
2-01-002    ASPIRANT
2-02-002    ASPIRANTS
3-02-003    ASPIRATION
12-05-009   ASPIRATIONS
3-02-003    ASPIRE
1-01-001    ASPIRED
1-01-001    ASPIRES
3-03-003    ASPIRIN

1-01-001    ASPIRING
5-05-005    ASS
2-01-001    ASS'N
1-01-001    ASS'NS'
1-01-001    ASSAI
3-03-003    ASSAIL
2-02-002    ASSAILANT
1-01-001    ASSAILANTS
4-04-004    ASSAILED
1-01-001    ASSAILING
2-01-001    ASSAM
6-04-005    ASSASSIN
1-01-001    ASSASSINATED
4-03-003    ASSASSINATION
1-01-001    ASSASSINS
15-05-012   ASSAULT
6-04-006    ASSAULTED
1-01-001    ASSAULTING
4-03-004    ASSAULTS
1-01-001    ASSAY
1-01-001    ASSAYED
2-01-002    ASSAYING
3-03-003    ASSEMBLAGE
1-01-001    ASSEMBLAGES
9-05-007    ASSEMBLE
24-10-020   ASSEMBLED
11-04-006   ASSEMBLIES
6-05-006    ASSEMBLING
50-10-032   ASSEMBLY
4-04-004    ASSENT
3-02-003    ASSENTED
1-01-001    ASSER
19-04-014   ASSERT
16-06-014   ASSERTED
4-04-004    ASSERTING
7-05-007    ASSERTION
3-03-003    ASSERTIONS
2-02-002    ASSERTIVE
1-01-001    ASSERTIVENESS
5-03-005    ASSERTS
3-02-003    ASSES
1-01-001    ASSESMENT
6-05-005    ASSESS
9-07-008    ASSESSED
10-03-005   ASSESSING
23-05-009   ASSESSMENT
6-04-006    ASSESSMENTS
2-01-001    ASSESSOR
1-01-001    ASSESSOR'S
19-02-002   ASSESSORS
1-01-001    ASSESSORS'
5-03-005    ASSET
13-04-007   ASSETS
18-06-014   ASSIDUITY
53-10-032   ASSIGN
2-01-001    ASSIGNED
9-05-009    ASSIGNEE
62-08-021   ASSIGNING
18-07-012   ASSIGNMENT
4-02-004    ASSIGNMENTS
2-02-002    ASSIGNS
4-04-004    ASSIMILATE
8-04-004    ASSIMILATED
2-01-001    ASSIMILATION
2-01-001    ASSINIBOIA
26-06-021   ASSINIBOINE
87-08-035   ASSIST
36-09-031   ASSISTANCE
11-05-010   ASSISTANT
7-07-007    ASSISTANTS
7-04-006    ASSISTED
1-01-001    ASSISTING
2-01-001    ASSISTS
21-09-019   ASSN
61-09-045   ASSOCIATE
15-09-015   ASSOCIATED
2-01-002    ASSOCIATES
132-13-067  ASSOCIATING
1-01-001    ASSOCIATION
30-09-023   ASSOCIATION'S
1-01-001    ASSOCIATIONS
1-01-001    ASSOCIATIVELY
1-01-001    ASSONANCE
2-02-002    ASSORTED
1-01-001    ASSORTMENT
2-02-002    ASSUAGED
63-13-050   ASSUME
72-15-061   ASSUMED
8-04-008    ASSUMES
17-08-015   ASSUMING
41-07-030   ASSUMPTION
23-05-016   ASSUMPTIONS
19-11-018   ASSURANCE
3-03-003    ASSURANCES
37-10-032   ASSURE
39-13-037   ASSURED
4-03-003    ASSUREDLY

6-04-006    ASSURES
10-07-010   ASSURING
2-01-001    ASSYRIAN
1-01-001    ASSYRIOLOGY
1-01-001    ASTAIRES
1-01-001    ASTARTE
2-01-001    ASTERIA
2-01-001    ASTERISKS
1-01-001    ASTEROID
1-01-001    ASTEROIDAL
1-01-001    ASTERS
1-01-001    ASTHMA
1-01-001    ASTIN
6-04-006    ASTONISHED
8-05-008    ASTONISHING
6-06-006    ASTONISHINGLY
5-04-005    ASTONISHMENT
2-01-001    ASTOR
1-01-001    ASTOUND
2-02-002    ASTOUNDED
5-04-005    ASTOUNDING
1-01-001    ASTRA
1-01-001    ASTRAL
3-03-003    ASTRAY
3-03-003    ASTRIDE
1-01-001    ASTRINGENCY
1-01-001    ASTRINGENT
2-01-002    ASTRONAUT
1-01-001    ASTRONOMER
6-05-006    ASTRONOMICAL
1-01-001    ASTRONOMICALLY
24-06-006   ASTRONOMY
3-02-002    ASTROPHYSICS
1-01-001    ASTUTE
1-01-001    ASTUTENESS
1-01-001    ASTWOOD
1-01-001    ASUNDER
1-01-001    ASW
1-01-001    ASYLUM
2-01-001    ASYMMETRIC
2-01-001    ASYMMETRICALLY
1-01-001    ASYMMETRY
1-01-001    ASYMPTOTIC
1-01-001    ASYMPTOTICALLY
2-01-001    ASYNCHRONY
5378-15-500 AT
1-01-001    AT-BATS
16-06-013   ATAVISTIC
1-01-001    ATE
1-01-001    ATERMAN
1-01-001    ATH
13-01-001   ATHABASCAN
2-01-001    ATHALIE
1-01-001    ATHEARN
1-01-001    ATHEISTIC
3-03-003    ATHEISTS
1-01-001    ATHENA
2-01-002    ATHENIAN
4-01-001    ATHENIANS
8-04-006    ATHENS
1-01-001    ATHEROMATOUS
9-05-008    ATHLETE
1-01-001    ATHLETE'S
5-03-004    ATHLETES
1-01-001    ATHLETES'
18-06-009   ATHLETIC
1-01-001    ATHLETICISM
9-04-005    ATHLETICS
1-01-001    ATKINSON
35-06-010   ATLANTA
4-01-002    ATLANTA'S
1-01-001    ATLANTES
40-07-020   ATLANTIC
1-01-001    ATLANTICA
2-02-002    ATLANTIS
12-03-005   ATLAS
1-01-001    ATLEE
1-01-001    ATM,
79-14-061   ATMOSPHERE
5-02-003    ATMOSPHERES
9-03-004    ATMOSPHERIC
37-07-009   ATOM
1-01-001    ATOM-LIKE
46-09-025   ATOMIC
1-01-001    ATOMISATION
41-04-008   ATOMS
1-01-001    ATONALLY
1-01-001    ATONE
2-01-001    ATONEMENT
6-05-005    ATOP
2-02-002    ATREUS
1-01-001    ATROCIOUSLY
2-02-002    ATROCITIES
3-01-001    ATROPHIC
1-01-001    ATROPHIED
4-01-001    ATROPHY
2-01-001    ATT

2-02-002    ATTA
14-08-011   ATTACH
25-12-022   ATTACHED
2-02-002    ATTACHES
3-02-003    ATTACHING
5-04-005    ATTACHMENT
4-03-004    ATTACHMENTS
105-12-059  ATTACK
25-12-022   ATTACKED
6-04-004    ATTACKER
1-01-001    ATTACKER'S
3-03-003    ATTACKERS
9-06-009    ATTACKING
22-07-018   ATTACKS
1-01-001    ATTACTIVE
20-08-018   ATTAIN
8-04-007    ATTAINED
6-03-005    ATTAINING
9-06-009    ATTAINMENT
1-01-001    ATTAINMENTS
1-01-001    ATTAINS
2-01-001    ATTAKAPAS
95-13-078   ATTEMPT
33-12-029   ATTEMPTED
23-10-021   ATTEMPTING
38-11-036   ATTEMPTS
54-11-040   ATTEND
12-06-009   ATTENDANCE
12-04-009   ATTENDANT
7-06-006    ATTENDANTS
36-10-031   ATTENDED
23-09-022   ATTENDING
6-04-006    ATTENDS
179-15-129  ATTENTION
1-01-001    ATTENTIONS
5-03-005    ATTENTIVE
1-01-001    ATTENTIVELY
2-02-002    ATTEST
4-04-004    ATTESTED
1-01-001    ATTESTING
16-09-011   ATTIC
1-01-001    ATTICA
1-01-001    ATTILIO
1-01-001    ATTIRE
6-05-005    ATTIRED
1-01-001    ATTIS
107-14-071  ATTITUDE
48-10-041   ATTITUDES
1-01-001    ATTLEE
65-09-031   ATTORNEY
3-02-002    ATTORNEY'S
9-03-008    ATTORNEYS
19-10-016   ATTRACT
25-12-022   ATTRACTED
4-04-004    ATTRACTING
15-09-013   ATTRACTION
9-05-008    ATTRACTIONS
39-13-032   ATTRACTIVE
1-01-001    ATTRACTIVELY
3-03-003    ATTRACTS
7-03-005    ATTRIBUTABLE
6-02-006    ATTRIBUTE
18-08-016   ATTRIBUTED
12-04-007   ATTRIBUTES
3-03-003    ATTRIBUTING
5-03-005    ATTRITION
1-01-001    ATTU
3-02-003    ATTUNED
4-02-004    ATTY
1-01-001    ATUNE
1-01-001    ATWELLS
1-01-001    ATYPICAL
1-01-001    AUBERGE
1-01-001    AUBR
1-01-001    AUBREY'S
2-02-002    AUBURN
4-01-002    AUCTION
1-01-001    AUCTIONEER
1-01-001    AUCTIONEER'S
3-03-003    AUDACITY
4-04-004    AUDIBLE
1-01-001    AUDIBLY
115-14-047  AUDIENCE
16-07-013   AUDIENCES
2-02-002    AUDIO
4-02-003    AUDIO-VISUAL
4-02-002    AUDIT
2-02-002    AUDITED
1-01-001    AUDITING
3-01-001    AUDITION
1-01-001    AUDITIONING
2-01-001    AUDITIONS
1-01-001    AUDITOR
14-07-010   AUDITORIUM
4-01-001    AUDITORS
1-01-001    AUDITS
```

Code	Word
1-01-001	AUDIVI
1-01-001	AUDREY
5-03-003	AUDUBON
1-01-001	AUERBACH'S
2-01-002	AUF
25-03-011	AUG
1-01-001	AUGEN
1-01-001	AUGMENT
9-06-008	AUGMENTED
2-02-002	AUGMENTING
1-01-001	AUGURS
53-11-042	AUGUST
6-01-001	AUGUSTA
1-01-001	AUGUSTA'S
1-01-001	AUGUSTAN
1-01-001	AUGUSTIN
4-03-004	AUGUSTINE
1-01-001	AUGUSTINE'S
4-04-004	AUGUSTUS
1-01-001	AUJOURD
22-07-013	AUNT
1-01-001	AUNT'S
3-02-002	AUNTIE
4-04-004	AUNTS
1-01-001	AURA
1-01-001	AURAL
2-02-002	AURALLY
2-02-002	AURELIUS
5-01-001	AUREOMYCIN
2-01-002	AURORA
1-01-001	AUSCHWITZ
6-06-006	AUSPICES
1-01-001	AUSPICIOUS
1-01-001	AUSPICIOUSLY
5-04-005	AUSTERE
1-01-001	AUSTERELY
1-01-001	AUSTERITY
18-04-011	AUSTIN
2-02-002	AUSTIN'S
11-08-009	AUSTRALIA
9-02-003	AUSTRALIAN
1-01-001	AUSTRALITES
4-02-004	AUSTRIA
4-02-002	AUSTRIAN
20-09-015	AUTHENTIC
2-02-002	AUTHENTICALLY
1-01-001	AUTHENTICATE
1-01-001	AUTHENTICATED
1-01-001	AUTHENTICATION
1-01-001	AUTHENTICATIONS
1-01-001	AUTHENTICATOR
8-03-004	AUTHENTICITY
46-09-037	AUTHOR
7-04-006	AUTHOR'S
5-03-005	AUTHORITARIAN
2-01-002	AUTHORITARIANISM
8-07-007	AUTHORITATIVE
1-01-001	AUTHORITATIVELY
39-09-026	AUTHORITIES
93-12-059	AUTHORITY
3-02-002	AUTHORITY'S
2-01-002	AUTHORIZATION
6-02-003	AUTHORIZATIONS
5-04-005	AUTHORIZE
37-07-016	AUTHORIZED
2-02-002	AUTHORIZES
5-04-004	AUTHORIZING
23-04-010	AUTHORS
1-01-001	AUTHORS'
3-03-003	AUTHORSHIP
2-01-002	AUTISM
13-01-001	AUTISTIC
22-08-014	AUTO
1-01-001	AUTO-*EUROPE
1-01-001	AUTO-LIMITATION
1-01-001	AUTO-LOADERS
1-01-001	AUTOBIOGRAPHIC
3-03-003	AUTOBIOGRAPHICAL
5-03-005	AUTOBIOGRAPHY
10-01-001	AUTOCODER
5-01-001	AUTOCOLLIMATOR
4-01-001	AUTOCRACIES
1-01-001	AUTOCRATIC
1-01-001	AUTOCRATS
3-01-001	AUTOFLUORESCENCE
3-02-002	AUTOGRAPH
3-01-001	AUTOLOADER
1-01-001	AUTOMATE
2-02-002	AUTOMATED
40-10-023	AUTOMATIC
36-12-027	AUTOMATICALLY
6-05-006	AUTOMATION
1-01-001	AUTOMATON
50-10-022	AUTOMOBILE
24-08-011	AUTOMOBILES
8-03-004	AUTOMOTIVE
1-01-001	AUTONAVIGATOR
11-01-001	AUTONOMIC
2-01-001	AUTONOMIC-SOMATIC
18-06-008	AUTONOMY
1-01-001	AUTOPSIED
3-02-003	AUTOPSY
4-04-004	AUTOS
1-01-001	AUTOSUGGESTIBILITY
22-08-014	AUTUMN
1-01-001	AUTUMN-TOUCHED
1-01-001	AUTUMNAL
1-01-001	AUX
3-02-002	AUXILIARIES
7-05-006	AUXILIARY
9-02-003	AV
4-04-004	AVAIL
2-01-002	AVAILABILITIES
21-06-015	AVAILABILITY
245-14-118	AVAILABLE
2-01-001	AVAILED
1-01-001	AVAILING
1-01-001	AVALANCHE
1-01-001	AVALIABLE
1-01-001	AVANT
6-03-004	AVANT-GARDE
2-02-002	AVARICE
1-01-001	AVARICIOUS
13-03-008	AVE
1-01-001	AVEC
2-01-002	AVENGE
2-02-002	AVENGING
1-01-001	AVENTINE
1-01-001	AVENTINO
46-11-031	AVENUE
5-04-005	AVENUES
130-13-081	AVERAGE
13-03-005	AVERAGED
10-03-007	AVERAGES
9-04-007	AVERAGING
2-02-002	AVERELL
2-01-002	AVERSION
1-01-001	AVERT
3-03-003	AVERTED
3-03-003	AVERTING
1-01-001	AVERY
1-01-001	AVIARY
1-01-001	AVIATION
5-03-004	AVIATOR
1-01-001	AVIATORS
1-01-001	AVID
1-01-001	AVIDITY
1-01-001	AVIDLY
1-01-001	AVIS
1-01-001	AVIV
62-12-038	AVOCADO
6-02-003	AVOCADOS
2-01-001	AVOCATION
58-14-049	AVOID
8-06-008	AVOIDANCE
19-10-019	AVOIDED
11-06-011	AVOIDING
3-03-003	AVOIDS
1-01-001	AVON
2-02-002	AVOWED
3-02-003	AW
9-05-007	AWAIT
7-05-007	AWAITED
7-04-006	AWAITING
3-02-003	AWAITS
20-08-019	AWAKE
7-04-006	AWAKEN
4-03-004	AWAKENED
4-04-004	AWAKENING
1-01-001	AWAKENS
46-06-016	AWARD
17-06-013	AWARDED
3-02-002	AWARDING
17-03-007	AWARDS
84-14-068	AWARE
32-09-026	AWARENESS
1-01-001	AWASH
456-15-242	AWAY
1-01-001	AWAYE
5-05-005	AWE
1-01-001	AWE-INSPIRING
5-05-005	AWED
4-04-004	AWESOME
17-09-014	AWFUL
10-05-007	AWFULLY
2-02-002	AWFULNESS
4-03-004	AWHILE
11-05-008	AWKWARD
5-05-005	AWKWARDLY
1-01-001	AWKWARDNESS
2-02-002	AWNINGS
9-06-008	AWOKE
2-02-002	AWRY
6-02-005	AX
6-02-004	AXE
7-04-005	AXES
2-02-002	AXIAL
1-01-001	AXIALLY
1-01-001	AXIOLOGICAL
1-01-001	AXIOM
3-03-003	AXIOMATIC
2-01-001	AXIOMS
38-05-009	AXIS
5-02-002	AXLE
1-01-001	AXLES
1-01-001	AYA
1-01-001	AYE
1-01-001	AYE-YAH-AH-AH
1-01-001	AYES
2-01-002	AYLESBURY
1-01-001	AYRES'
1-01-001	AYSSHOM
1-01-001	AYUB
2-01-001	AZALEA
3-02-002	AZALEAS
1-01-001	AZERBAIJAN
1-01-001	AZUSA
117-09-064	B
11-01-001	B)
2-02-002	B),
1-01-001	B+
1-01-001	B**.+*D
3-01-002	B**.'S
2-02-002	B**.*A
1-01-001	B**.*B**.*C
1-01-001	B**.*B**.*C**.'S
19-05-007	B**.*C
1-01-001	B**.*D
1-01-001	B**.*S
1-01-001	B**.C
1-01-001	B**.T**.U**./SQ
21-01-001	B'DIKKAT
1-01-001	B'DIKKAT'S
1-01-001	BA-A-A
1-01-001	BABATUNDE
1-01-001	BABBITING
1-01-001	BABBITT
2-02-002	BABBLED
1-01-001	BABCOCK
8-03-005	BABE
3-02-002	BABEL
3-03-003	BABES
12-06-009	BABIES
2-01-001	BABIN
1-01-001	BABIN-*FESTIVAL
62-12-038	BABY
6-02-003	BABY'S
2-01-001	BABY-DEAR
1-01-001	BABY-SITTER
1-01-001	BABYHOOD
2-02-002	BABYLON
2-02-002	BABYLONIAN
2-02-002	BABYLONIANS
1-01-001	BACCARAT
1-01-001	BACCHUS
4-04-004	BACH
6-04-006	BACHELOR
1-01-001	BACHELOR-TYPE
4-01-001	BACHELORS
1-01-001	BACI
2-02-002	BACILLUS
967-15-308	BACK
1-01-001	BACK-ISSUE
1-01-001	BACK-LIGHTED
1-01-001	BACK-YARD
1-01-001	BACKBEND
2-01-001	BACKBENDS
4-04-004	BACKBONE
2-02-002	BACKDROP
24-09-018	BACKED
4-01-001	BACKERS
67-12-052	BACKGROUND
7-06-007	BACKGROUNDS
8-06-008	BACKING
1-01-001	BACKLASH
5-02-002	BACKLOG
1-01-001	BACKPACK
15-09-013	BACKS
1-01-001	BACKSIDE
2-01-001	BACKSTAGE
1-01-001	BACKSTAIRS
4-01-001	BACKSTITCH
1-01-001	BACKSTITCHING
22-11-021	BACKWARD
2-02-002	BACKWARDS
1-01-001	BACKWATER
5-02-003	BACKWOODS
1-01-001	BACKWOODS-AND-S AND-HILL
2-02-002	BACKYARD
3-03-003	BACKYARDS
10-06-009	BACON
8-03-006	BACTERIA
14-02-003	BACTERIAL
142-15-089	BAD
1-01-001	BAD-FITTING
1-01-001	BADE
5-04-005	BADEN-*BADEN
5-04-005	BADGE
1-01-001	BADGE-TOTER
1-01-001	BADGERING
1-01-001	BADGES
1-01-001	BADINAGE
1-01-001	BADLANDS
34-13-031	BADLY
1-01-001	BADLY-NEEDED
1-01-001	BADMEN
1-01-001	BADMINTON
9-02-002	BADNESS
1-01-001	BADRAWI
1-01-001	BADS
1-01-001	BADURA-*SKODA-* VIENNA
5-01-001	BAER
1-01-001	BAFFIN
1-01-001	BAFFLE
5-04-004	BAFFLED
1-01-001	BAFFLERS
4-04-004	BAFFLING
42-08-029	BAG
1-01-001	BAGATELLES
4-03-003	BAGGAGE
1-01-001	BAGGED
4-03-003	BAGGY
1-01-001	BAGH
1-01-001	BAGLEY
1-01-001	BAGPIPE
10-04-006	BAGS
1-01-001	BAH
1-01-001	BAHI
1-01-001	BAHIA
7-03-004	BAIL
2-01-001	BAILEEFE
3-02-003	BAILEY
6-01-001	BAILIFF
3-01-001	BAILING
3-01-001	BAILLY
1-01-001	BAINES
4-02-003	BAIRD
2-02-002	BAIT
1-01-001	BAITED
12-04-004	BAKE
1-01-001	BAKE-*OFF
1-01-001	BAKE-OFF
1-01-001	BAKE-OFFS
1-01-001	BAKE-OVEN
8-05-006	BAKED
36-03-012	BAKER
1-01-001	BAKERSFIELD
2-01-002	BAKERY
1-01-001	BAKES
1-01-001	BAKHTIARI
4-02-003	BAKING
1-01-001	BAKLAVA
1-01-001	BAKU
1-01-001	BAL
5-01-001	BALAFREJ
2-01-001	BALAGUER
1-01-001	BALAGUER'S
90-12-052	BALANCE
1-01-001	BALANCE-OF-PAYMENTS
1-01-001	BALANCE-WISE
22-10-017	BALANCED
1-01-001	BALANCES
4-03-004	BALANCING
1-01-001	BALCOLM
2-02-002	BALCONIES
5-03-004	BALCONY
5-04-005	BALD
2-02-002	BALDING
2-01-001	BALDNESS
4-01-001	BALDRIGE
2-01-002	BALDWIN
1-01-001	BALDY
5-01-002	BALE
1-01-001	BALEFUL
1-01-001	BALENCIAGA
4-03-003	BALES
2-02-002	BALI
1-01-001	BALINESE
2-02-002	BALKAN

Code	Word	Code	Word	Code	Word	Code	Word
1-01-001	BALKANIZE	1-01-001	BANKER-EDITOR	9-02-007	BARNES	1-01-001	BASLER
1-01-001	BALKANIZING	15-04-008	BANKERS	1-01-001	BARNET	2-01-001	BASLOT
2-02-002	BALKANS	1-01-001	BANKHEAD	11-01-002	BARNETT	2-01-001	BASOPHILIC
2-02-002	BALKED	2-02-002	BANKING	8-02-002	BARNEY	16-07-011	BASS
1-01-001	BALKINESS	5-04-004	BANKRUPT	4-02-004	BARNS	1-01-001	BASSES
1-01-001	BALKING	8-05-006	BANKRUPTCY	1-01-001	BARNSFUL	1-01-001	BASSI
1-01-001	BALKS	37-09-018	BANKS	1-01-001	BARNSTORMER	1-01-001	BASSINET
110-12-038	BALL	1-01-001	BANKS'S	4-01-001	BARNUMVILLE	1-01-001	BASSIS
1-01-001	BALL'S	2-02-002	BANNED	1-01-001	BARNYARD	2-02-002	BASSO
1-01-001	BALL-CARRIERS	8-05-008	BANNER	1-01-001	BARNYARDS	1-01-001	BAST
1-01-001	BALL-HAWKING	2-02-002	BANNERS	1-01-001	BAROMETRIC	12-04-008	BASTARD
8-04-007	BALLAD	1-01-001	BANNING	2-02-002	BARON	1-01-001	BASTARD'S
7-03-005	BALLADS	1-01-001	BANNNNNNG	1-01-001	BARONESS	14-05-005	BASTARDS
1-01-001	BALLARD	6-03-004	BANQUET	1-01-001	BARONIAL	1-01-001	BASTIANINI
1-01-001	BALLARDS	1-01-001	BANQUETINGS	1-01-001	BARONS	2-01-001	BASTING
2-02-002	BALLAST	3-03-003	BANQUETS	1-01-001	BARONY	2-02-002	BASTION
1-01-001	BALLED	1-01-001	BANS	11-04-007	BAROQUE	18-08-012	BAT
1-01-001	BALLERINA	1-01-001	BANSHEE	1-01-001	BARORECEPTOR	3-01-001	BATAVIA
1-01-001	BALLERINAS	2-02-002	BANSHEES	1-01-001	BARR	5-04-005	BATCH
2-01-001	BALLESTRE	5-02-002	BANTER	1-01-001	BARRACK	1-01-001	BATCHELDER
45-10-017	BALLET	1-01-001	BANTERED	3-03-003	BARRACKS	2-01-001	BATEAU
1-01-001	BALLETOMANE	1-01-001	BANTERING	5-05-005	BARRAGE	6-04-004	BATES
4-03-003	BALLETS	1-01-001	BANTU	5-01-001	BARRE	1-01-001	BATES'
1-01-001	BALLFIELDS	3-01-001	BANTUS	1-01-001	BARRE-*MONTPELI	26-10-018	BATH
1-01-001	BALLGOWNS	4-02-002	BAPTISM		ER	1-01-001	BATHAR-ON-*WALL
1-01-001	BALLING	1-01-001	BAPTISMAL	8-07-008	BARRED				I
17-03-006	BALLISTIC	1-01-001	BAPTISMS	24-08-015	BARREL	4-04-004	BATHE
1-01-001	BALLISTICS	17-08-011	BAPTIST	1-01-001	BARREL-VAULTED	7-04-007	BATHED
10-07-008	BALLOON	1-01-001	BAPTIST'S	1-01-001	BARREL-WIDE	1-01-001	BATHERS
1-01-001	BALLOONING	1-01-001	BAPTISTE	8-05-007	BARRELS	15-06-012	BATHING
3-03-003	BALLOONS	1-01-001	BAPTISTERY	7-05-007	BARREN	1-01-001	BATHOS
12-04-010	BALLOT	4-03-003	BAPTISTS	1-01-001	BARRETT	3-02-003	BATHROBE
2-02-002	BALLOTS	12-04-006	BAPTIZED	1-01-001	BARRETTE	18-07-013	BATHROOM
5-02-002	BALLPLAYER	82-12-034	BAR	3-03-003	BARRICADE	1-01-001	BATHROOMS
3-01-001	BALLPLAYERS	1-01-001	BAR'L	4-03-003	BARRICADES	5-04-004	BATHS
8-02-005	BALLROOM	1-01-001	BAR-**J*H,	9-06-009	BARRIER	4-04-004	BATHTUB
17-08-014	BALLS	1-01-001	BAR-BUDDY	17-08-015	BARRIERS	1-01-001	BATHTUBS
1-01-001	BALLYHOO	1-01-001	BARACLOUGH	3-02-002	BARRING	1-01-001	BATHYRAN
1-01-001	BALLYHUOEY	1-01-001	BARAGINING	2-01-002	BARRINGTON	2-01-001	BATHYRANS
1-01-001	BALM-OF-*GILEAD	1-01-001	BARATARIA	1-01-001	BARROW	7-02-002	BATISTA
2-02-002	BALMY	10-03-007	BARBARA	3-03-003	BARRY	3-02-003	BATISTA'S
1-01-001	BALSAMS	1-01-001	BARBARIAN	1-01-001	BARRYMORES	10-07-009	BATON
3-03-003	BALTIC	4-01-003	BARBARIANS	40-10-018	BARS	6-03-005	BATS
22-09-017	BALTIMORE	1-01-001	BARBARIC	1-01-001	BARSACS	3-02-002	BATTALION
2-01-001	BALTIMORE'S	1-01-001	BARBAROUS	3-01-001	BARSTOW	1-01-001	BATTALIONS
1-01-001	BALTIMOREAN	13-03-003	BARBECUE	6-02-003	BARTENDER	2-01-002	BATTED
3-02-003	BALUSTRADE	2-01-001	BARBECUED	5-01-001	BARTH	3-01-001	BATTEN
2-02-002	BALZAC	3-01-001	BARBECUES	1-01-001	BARTHA	4-01-001	BATTENKILL
1-01-001	BAMBI	11-06-008	BARBED	1-01-001	BARTHOLF	15-01-002	BATTENS
7-04-007	BAN	1-01-001	BARBED-WIRE	2-01-001	BARTLEBY	2-02-002	BATTER
2-01-002	BANAL	5-01-001	BARBELL	3-02-002	BARTLETT	1-01-001	BATTER'S
4-03-004	BANANA	8-03-005	BARBER	1-01-001	BARTOK	9-06-009	BATTERED
1-01-001	BANANAS	1-01-001	BARBER'S	1-01-001	BARTOL	1-01-001	BATTERIE
1-01-001	BANBURY	1-01-001	BARBITAL	1-01-001	BARTOLI'S	3-01-002	BATTERIES
5-02-002	BANCROFT	1-01-001	BARBITURATE	25-01-001	BARTON	2-01-002	BATTERING
1-01-001	BANCROFT'S	1-01-001	BARBOUR	3-01-001	BARTON'S	1-01-001	BATTERS
53-13-035	BAND	2-02-002	BARBS	1-01-001	BAS	18-07-009	BATTERY
4-03-003	BANDAGE	1-01-001	BARBUDOS	3-01-001	BAS-RELIEF	2-01-001	BATTERY-POWERED
4-02-003	BANDAGED	18-01-001	BARCU	2-01-001	BAS-RELIEFS	15-05-010	BATTING
3-01-001	BANDAGES	8-01-001	BARCO'S	3-01-001	BASCOM	87-13-058	BATTLE
1-01-001	BANDAGING	4-01-001	BARCUS	91-13-052	BASE	1-01-001	BATTLE-AX
2-02-002	BANDED	1-01-001	BARCUS'	1-01-001	BASE-RUNNER	1-01-001	BATTLE-CRY
1-01-001	BANDING	3-01-001	BARD	1-01-001	BASE-STEALING	1-01-001	BATTLE-SHATTERE
1-01-001	BANDISH	1-01-001	BARDALL	57-09-015	BASEBALL				D
3-02-002	BANDIT	1-01-001	BARDELL	4-02-003	BASEBALL'S	5-04-005	BATTLEFIELD
1-01-001	BANDITOS	2-02-002	BARDS	1-01-001	BASEBALLIGHT	2-01-001	BATTLEFIELDS
3-03-003	BANDITS	29-10-026	BARE	1-01-001	BASEBALLS	1-01-001	BATTLEFRONT
1-01-001	BANDOLEERS	1-01-001	BARE-ARMED	119-12-086	BASED	2-02-002	BATTLEGROUND
1-01-001	BANDON	1-01-001	BARE-FOOTED	2-02-002	BASEL	1-01-001	BATTLEMENTS
11-05-010	BANDS	7-05-006	BAREFOOT	1-01-001	BASELESS	7-06-007	BATTLES
5-02-003	BANDSTAND	1-01-001	BAREFOOTED	1-01-001	BASELINE	3-02-003	BATTLING
1-01-001	BANDWAGON	31-11-028	BARELY	4-02-002	BASEMAN	2-01-001	BATWINGS
1-01-001	BANDWIDTH	3-03-003	BAREST	31-08-010	BASEMENT	1-01-001	BAUBLE
1-01-001	BANEFUL	1-01-001	BARFLIES	2-01-001	BASEMENTS	1-01-001	BAUBLES
1-01-001	BANFIELD	7-06-007	BARGAIN	1-01-001	BASER	1-01-001	BAUDELAIRE
7-05-006	BANG	1-01-001	BARGAIN-PRICED	23-08-018	BASES	1-01-001	BAUER
25-01-001	BANG-*JENSEN	17-04-009	BARGAINING	2-01-001	BASHAW	1-01-001	BAUER-*ECSY
6-01-001	BANG-*JENSEN'S	3-02-002	BARGAINS	2-02-002	BASHFUL	1-01-001	BAUHAUS
1-01-001	BANG-SASHES	7-06-006	BARGE	1-01-001	BASHIR	3-01-001	BAULLARI
4-03-004	BANGED	1-01-001	BARGEN	1-01-001	BASHO'S	2-01-001	BAUM
4-04-004	BANGING	3-03-003	BARGES	171-10-096	BASIC	3-02-002	BAVARIA
1-01-001	BANGISH	1-01-001	BARGING	20-07-017	BASICALLY	3-03-003	BAWDY
1-01-001	BANGKOK	14-02-002	BARI	1-01-001	BASICS	2-01-001	BAWH
1-01-001	BANGLES	1-01-001	BARI'S	1-01-001	BASIE	1-01-001	BAWHS
6-03-004	BANGS	1-01-001	BARINGER	2-01-001	BASIL	2-02-002	BAWLED
1-01-001	BANI	5-03-004	BARITONE	1-01-001	BASIL'S	1-01-001	BAWLING
4-02-002	BANISH	1-01-001	BARIUM	1-01-001	BASILEIS	57-13-028	BAY
7-03-005	BANISHED	14-05-012	BARK	7-06-006	BASIN	1-01-001	BAY-FRONT
1-01-001	BANISHES	1-01-001	BARKEEP	4-04-004	BASING	1-01-001	BAYADERKA
1-01-001	BANISHING	8-02-003	BARKER	184-14-112	BASIS	1-01-001	BAYANIHAN
1-01-001	BANISHMENT	2-01-001	BARKING	1-01-001	BASKED	3-02-002	BAYED
5-04-004	BANISTER	6-02-003	BARLEY	17-08-012	BASKET	1-01-001	BAYERISCHE
2-02-002	BANISTERS	29-09-017	BARN	9-04-008	BASKETBALL	2-01-001	BAYEZIT
2-02-002	BANJO	1-01-001	BARN-BURNER'S	1-01-001	BASKETBALL-PLAY	1-01-001	BAYING
83-10-036	BANK	1-01-001	BARNABA		ING	1-01-001	BAYLEEFE
4-04-004	BANKED	5-03-003	BARNARD	2-01-001	BASKETS	2-01-001	BAYLOR
5-04-004	BANKER	1-01-001	BARNARD'S	2-02-002	BASKING	1-01-001	BAYLOR'S

1-01-001 BAYLY	2-01-001 BECCARIA	1-01-001 BEGGARY	2-02-002 BELLOWING
6-02-002 BAYONET	1-01-001 BECHHOFER	13-05-010 BEGGED	8-04-004 BELLOWS
3-01-002 BAYONETS	1-01-001 BECK	10-06-009 BEGGING	8-05-006 BELLS
2-01-001 BAYOU	2-02-002 BECKET	84-14-070 BEGIN	1-01-001 BELLWETHERS
4-03-003 BAYREUTH	6-01-001 BECKETT	1-01-001 BEGINNER	1-01-001 BELLWOOD
2-01-002 BAYS	4-01-001 BECKETT'S	2-01-002 BEGINNER'S	23-08-012 BELLY
7-04-005 BAZAAR	1-01-001 BECKMAN	1-01-001 BEGINNERS	1-01-001 BELLYFULL
1-01-001 BAZAARS	1-01-001 BECKON	2-01-001 BEGINNERS'	2-02-002 BELMONT
1-01-001 BD	7-05-007 BECKONED	164-14-121 BEGINNING	37-13-033 BELONG
6377-15-499 BE	2-02-002 BECKONING	9-06-009 BEGINNINGS	17-09-015 BELONGED
2-02-002 BEA	3-03-003 BECKONS	55-11-042 BEGINS	13-08-013 BELONGING
61-12-035 BEACH	3-01-001 BECKSTROM	2-01-001 BEGLEY	4-04-004 BELONGINGS
1-01-001 BEACH-DRIFT	4-01-001 BECKWORTH	5-02-003 BEGOTTEN	22-08-016 BELONGS
1-01-001 BEACH-HEAD	361-15-211 BECOME	2-02-002 BEGRUDGE	18-09-015 BELOVED
14-06-009 BEACHES	102-10-074 BECOMES	1-01-001 BEGS	145-13-089 BELOW
2-02-002 BEACHHEAD	1-01-001 BECOMETH	1-01-001 BEGUILE	2-01-001 BELOWGROUND
1-01-001 BEACHING	1-01-001 BECOMIN	2-02-002 BEGUILED	1-01-001 BELSHAZZAR
5-04-005 BEACON	57-13-052 BECOMING	3-02-003 BEGUILING	29-12-021 BELT
1-01-001 BEAD	127-13-070 BED	51-13-048 BEGUN	1-01-001 BELT-DRIVEN
1-01-001 BEADED	1-01-001 BED-HOPPED	1-01-001 BEHAHN	2-02-002 BELTED
4-02-002 BEADLE	1-01-001 BED-TIME	21-06-018 BEHALF	1-01-001 BELTING
1-01-001 BEADLES	1-01-001 BED-TYPE	1-01-001 BEHAN	2-01-001 BELTON
1-01-001 BEADLES'	1-01-001 BEDAZZLED	13-07-013 BEHAVE	8-04-006 BELTS
4-04-004 BEADS	1-01-001 BEDAZZLEMENT	13-09-011 BEHAVED	2-02-002 BELVEDERE
1-01-001 BEADSMAN	1-01-001 BEDBUGS	2-01-002 BEHAVES	2-01-001 BELVIDERE
1-01-001 BEADY	1-01-001 BEDDED	4-03-003 BEHAVING	1-01-001 BELZEC
2-01-001 BEAKER	3-02-002 BEDDING	96-11-046 BEHAVIOR	1-01-001 BEMADDENING
1-01-001 BEAKERS	3-01-001 BEDE	3-02-002 BEHAVIORAL	1-01-001 BEMAN
2-02-002 BEALE	1-01-001 BEDFAST	1-01-001 BEHAVIORALLY	1-01-001 BEMOAN
2-01-001 BEALL	2-02-002 BEDFORD	1-01-001 BEHAVIORS	1-01-001 BEMOANS
1-01-001 BEALLSVILLE	1-01-001 BEDGROUND	3-01-001 BEHAVIOUR	21-11-015 BEN
21-08-012 BEAM	1-01-001 BEDLAM	1-01-001 BEHEADING	1-01-001 BEN'S
3-01-001 BEAME	1-01-001 BEDPOST	3-03-003 BEHELD	1-01-001 BEN-*GURION
6-05-006 BEAMING	1-01-001 BEDRAGGLED	258-15-150 BEHIND	1-01-001 BEN-HADAD
13-05-008 BEAMS	2-02-002 BEDRIDDEN	4-02-003 BEHOLD	35-09-019 BENCH
5-03-004 BEAN	52-10-034 BEDROOM	1-01-001 BEHOLDS	1-01-001 BENCHED
9-04-006 BEANS	1-01-001 BEDROOM'S	1-01-001 BEHOOVES	8-06-007 BENCHES
57-15-046 BEAR	4-03-004 BEDROOMS	1-01-001 BEIDERBECKE	2-01-001 BENCHMARKS
1-01-001 BEAR'S	12-06-010 BEDS	1-01-001 BEIGE	24-09-019 BEND
1-01-001 BEAR-LIKE	5-05-005 BEDSIDE	1-01-001 BEIGE'S	7-04-006 BENDING
26-07-015 BEARD	2-01-002 BEDSPREAD	3-02-002 BEIN	2-02-002 BENDS
10-06-008 BEARDED	1-01-001 BEDSPRINGS	712-15-334 BEING	57-12-040 BENEATH
4-01-001 BEARDEN	1-01-001 BEDSTRAW	2-01-001 BEINGE	3-01-001 BENEDICK
5-01-001 BEARDENS	4-04-004 BEDTIME	36-09-027 BEINGS	1-01-001 BENEDICTINE
1-01-001 BEARDLESS	11-04-005 BEE	1-01-001 BEIRUT	3-02-003 BENEDICTION
1-01-001 BEARDOWN	1-01-001 BEE'S	1-01-001 BEISMORTIER	4-04-004 BENEFACTOR
5-04-005 BEARDS	1-01-001 BEE-*HUNTER	1-01-001 BEKKAI	2-02-002 BENEFACTOR'S
1-01-001 BEARDSLEE	4-03-003 BEEBE	4-03-003 BEL	1-01-001 BENEFICENCE
1-01-001 BEARDSLEY'S	1-01-001 BEEBE'S	1-01-001 BEL-*AIR	11-04-008 BENEFICIAL
4-04-004 BEARER	7-01-001 BEEBREAD	1-01-001 BELA	3-02-003 BENEFICIARIES
25-12-022 BEARING	6-02-002 BEECH	2-01-001 BELABORING	2-02-002 BENEFICIARY
6-05-005 BEARINGS	2-01-001 BEECHER	1-01-001 BELAFONTE	1-01-001 BENEFICIENT
2-01-001 BEARISH	32-07-012 BEEF	1-01-001 BELANGER	63-13-044 BENEFIT
26-08-016 BEARS	1-01-001 BEEF'S	1-01-001 BELASCO	3-02-003 BENEFITED
7-07-007 BEAST	1-01-001 BEEF-FAT	2-02-002 BELATED	33-07-019 BENEFITS
1-01-001 BEASTIES	1-01-001 BEEF-FEEDING	1-01-001 BELATEDLY	2-01-001 BENELUX
2-02-002 BEASTS	1-01-001 BEEF-HUNGRY	2-02-002 BELCH	1-01-001 BENESI
68-12-046 BEAT	1-01-001 BEEFED	4-02-003 BELCHED	2-02-002 BENET
1-01-001 BEAT-UP	2-02-002 BEEFED-UP	2-02-002 BELCHING	1-01-001 BENET'S
15-08-014 BEATEN	1-01-001 BEEFORE	1-01-001 BELFRY	1-01-001 BENETS
4-01-001 BEATIE	1-01-001 BEEFSTEAK	2-01-001 BELGE	4-04-004 BENEVOLENCE
1-01-001 BEATIFIC	1-01-001 BEEFY	14-05-005 BELGIAN	2-02-002 BENEVOLENT
1-01-001 BEATIFICATION	1-01-001 BEEHIVE	21-02-002 BELGIANS	4-02-002 BENGAL
13-06-012 BEATING	2472-15-477 BEEN	2-02-002 BELGIUM	1-01-001 BENGALI
2-02-002 BEATINGS	4-01-001 BEEP	3-02-003 BELIED	2-02-002 BENIGHTED
1-01-001 BEATITUDES	3-01-001 BEEPS	64-13-042 BELIEF	1-01-001 BENIGN
7-03-003 BEATNIK	34-11-022 BEER	23-08-016 BELIEFS	7-01-001 BENINGTON
4-01-001 BEATNIKS	1-01-001 BEER-COOLING	1-01-001 BELIEVABLE	1-01-001 BENITA
7-03-004 BEATRICE	1-01-001 BEER-RUNNER	1-01-001 BELIEVABLY	12-06-010 BENJAMIN
4-04-004 BEATS	1-01-001 BEER-RUNNERS	200-15-130 BELIEVE	1-01-001 BENNETT
2-02-002 BEAU	1-01-001 BEER-RUNNING	77-14-061 BELIEVED	4-02-002 BENNINGTON
1-01-001 BEAUCHAMPS	1-01-001 BEERS	4-03-004 BELIEVER	4-03-003 BENNY
8-01-001 BEAUCLERK	15-05-005 BEES	5-04-005 BELIEVERS	1-01-001 BENOIT
2-01-001 BEAUJOLAIS	1-01-001 BEESEMYERS	43-11-030 BELIEVES	17-03-003 BENSON
1-01-001 BEAULIEU	12-02-004 BEETHOVEN	2-01-001 BELIEVETH	1-01-001 BENSON'S
3-02-003 BEAUMONT	1-01-001 BEETHOVEN'S	14-07-013 BELIEVING	34-11-029 BENT
1-01-001 BEAUTEOUS	1-01-001 BEETLES	1-01-001 BELITTLING	1-01-001 BENT-*ARM
5-03-005 BEAUTIES	2-01-001 BEETLING	18-09-017 BELL	2-01-002 BENTHAM
127-15-080 BEAUTIFUL	2-02-002 BEETS	2-01-001 BELLA	2-01-001 BENTLEY
16-08-015 BEAUTIFULLY	2-01-002 BEFALL	1-01-001 BELLAMY'S	1-01-001 BENTLEYS
1-01-001 BEAUTIFULLY-BUILT	1-01-001 BEFELL	4-01-001 BELLBOY	1-01-001 BENZEDRINE
	1-01-001 BEFITS	2-02-002 BELLBOYS	1-01-001 BENZELL
1-01-001 BEAUTIFULLY-TAPERED	1-01-001 BEFITTING	1-01-001 BELLE	2-01-001 BENZENE
	1-01-001 BEFOGGED	1-01-001 BELLES	14-01-001 BEOWULF
1-01-001 BEAUTIFY	1-01-001 BEFOH	2-01-001 BELLETCH	1-01-001 BEOWULF'S
1-01-001 BEAUTIFYING	1016-15-383 BEFORE	1-01-001 BELLEVILLE	2-02-002 BEQUEATHED
71-13-044 BEAUTY	2-02-002 BEFOREHAND	1-01-001 BELLHOPS	5-02-003 BEQUEST
1-01-001 BEAUTY'S	1-01-001 BEFOULED	1-01-001 BELLICOSITY	3-03-003 BEQUESTS
1-01-001 BEAUTY-IDIOM	2-02-002 BEFUDDLED	2-02-002 BELLIES	3-03-003 BERATED
1-01-001 BEAUX-*ARTS	1-01-001 BEFUDDLES	2-02-002 BELLIGERENCE	1-01-001 BERCHE
3-02-003 BEAVER	1-01-001 BEFUDDLING	1-01-001 BELLIGERENT	1-01-001 BEREA
1-01-001 BEAVERTAIL	1-01-001 BEG	1-01-001 BELLIGERENTLY	4-03-003 BEREAVEMENT
6-02-003 BEAVERTON	312-15-177 BEGAN	3-02-003 BELLINI	1-01-001 BEREAVEMENTS
1-01-001 BEBOP	1-01-001 BEGET	2-01-001 BELLMAN	2-02-002 BEREFT
1-01-001 BECALMED	2-02-002 BEGGAR	4-03-003 BELLOW	1-01-001 BERG'S
246-15-151 BECAME	1-01-001 BEGGAR'S	1-01-001 BELLOW'S	1-01-001 BERGAMASCHI
883-15-344 BECAUSE	2-02-002 BEGGARS	6-04-006 BELLOWED	15-02-003 BERGER

Code	Word
5-02-003	BERGER'S
1-01-001	BERGS
1-01-001	BERGSON
1-01-001	BERIBBONED
2-02-002	BERIBERI
1-01-001	BERINGER
1-01-001	BERKELEY
2-01-001	BERKELY
1-01-001	BERKMAN
2-02-002	BERKSHIRES
4-02-002	BERLE
74-09-025	BERLIN
4-02-003	BERLIN'S
1-01-001	BERLIN-*WEST
1-01-001	BERLINERS
1-01-001	BERLIOZ
1-01-001	BERLITZ
6-02-002	BERMAN
1-01-001	BERMAN'S
9-05-005	BERMUDA
5-01-001	BERN
1-01-001	BERNADINE'S
9-03-009	BERNARD
1-01-001	BERNARDINE
1-01-001	BERNARDO
1-01-001	BERNE
1-01-001	BERNET
1-01-001	BERNHARD
2-02-002	BERNHARDT
1-01-001	BERNIE
1-01-001	BERNIECE
1-01-001	BERNINI
2-01-001	BERNINI'S
2-01-001	BERNOULLI
1-01-001	BERNSTEIN
1-01-001	BERNZ-*O-*MATIC
1-01-001	BERONIO
2-01-001	BERRA
1-01-001	BERRA'S
1-01-001	BERRELLEZ
2-02-002	BERRIES
9-04-006	BERRY
1-01-001	BERRY'S
1-01-001	BERT
1-01-001	BERTEROS
4-03-004	BERTH
5-03-003	BERTHA
1-01-001	BERTHELIER
3-01-001	BERTO
1-01-001	BERTO'S
1-01-001	BERTOIA
1-01-001	BERTON
1-01-001	BERTORELLI
1-01-001	BERTRAND
2-02-002	BERYL
1-01-001	BERYLLIUM
1-01-001	BESEECH
7-07-007	BESET
1-01-001	BESETS
1-01-001	BESETTING
78-11-055	BESIDE
66-13-059	BESIDES
1-01-001	BESIEGE
2-02-002	BESIEGED
2-01-001	BESIEGERS
1-01-001	BESIEGING
1-01-001	BESMIRCH
1-01-001	BESMIRCHED
1-01-001	BESMIRCHING
1-01-001	BESPEAK
1-01-001	BESPEAKS
2-02-002	BESPECTACLED
3-02-003	BESS
2-02-002	BESSARABIA
1-01-001	BESSET
1-01-001	BESSIE
351-15-226	BEST
1-01-001	BEST'S
1-01-001	BEST-EDUCATED
1-01-001	BEST-GAITED
1-01-001	BEST-HEARTED
1-01-001	BEST-KNOWN
1-01-001	BEST-LOOKING
1-01-001	BEST-PRESERVED
1-01-001	BEST-SELLER
1-01-001	BEST-SELLERS
1-01-001	BEST-SELLING
1-01-001	BEST-TEMPERED
1-01-001	BESTED
1-01-001	BESTER
1-01-001	BESTES
1-01-001	BESTIAL
1-01-001	BESTIMMUNG
2-02-002	BESTOW
4-03-004	BESTOWAL
7-05-007	BESTOWED
2-01-001	BESTSELLER
1-01-001	BESTSELLING
1-01-001	BESTUBBLED
20-08-017	BET
2-01-002	BETA
2-01-002	BETANCOURT
1-01-001	BETE
1-01-001	BETEL-STAINED
5-04-004	BETH
1-01-001	BETHEL
1-01-001	BETHLEHEM
1-01-001	BETHOUGHT
2-01-002	BETIDE
4-04-004	BETRAY
6-04-005	BETRAYAL
8-04-008	BETRAYED
1-01-001	BETRAYER
1-01-001	BETRAYING
3-02-003	BETRAYS
1-01-001	BETROTHAL
1-01-001	BETROTHED
3-03-003	BETS
2-01-001	BETSEY
1-01-001	BETSY
414-15-233	BETTER
1-01-001	BETTER-REMEMBERED
2-02-002	BETTER-THAN-AVERAGE
1-01-001	BETTERING
3-02-003	BETTERMENT
1-01-001	BETTIES
5-03-003	BETTING
3-02-002	BETTY
1-01-001	BETTY'S
730-15-316	BETWEEN
2-01-001	BEVEL
3-01-001	BEVELED
1-01-001	BEVELING
1-01-001	BEVELS
5-03-004	BEVERAGE
4-02-002	BEVERAGES
14-05-007	BEVERLY
2-01-001	BEVO
1-01-001	BEVOR
3-02-003	BEVY
1-01-001	BEWAIL
3-03-003	BEWARE
1-01-001	BEWHISKERED
6-03-006	BEWILDERED
1-01-001	BEWILDEREDLY
1-01-001	BEWILDERINGLY
3-03-003	BEWILDERMENT
1-01-001	BEWILDERS
2-02-002	BEWITCHED
1-01-001	BEWITCHING
1-01-001	BEXAR
6-01-001	BEY
2-01-001	BEYELER
175-15-127	BEYOND
1-01-001	BEYOND-NORMAL
1-01-001	BHOY
2-01-001	BI
1-01-001	BI-MONTHLY
2-02-002	BIANCO
8-03-006	BIAS
1-01-001	BIASES
2-02-002	BIB
1-01-001	BIBB
59-11-028	BIBLE
1-01-001	BIBLE-EMANCIPATED
1-01-001	BIBLE-LOVING
1-01-001	BIBLES
18-06-010	BIBLICAL
1-01-001	BIBLICALLY
1-01-001	BIBLIOGRAPHICAL
2-01-001	BIBLIOGRAPHIES
2-02-002	BIBLIOGRAPHY
1-01-001	BIBLIOPHILES
1-01-001	BICAMERAL
1-01-001	BICARBONATE
4-01-004	BICEP
3-01-001	BICEPS
1-01-001	BICH
1-01-001	BICHES
1-01-001	BICKERING
2-02-002	BICONCAVE
2-01-002	BICYCLE
7-05-007	BICYCLE-AUTO
2-02-002	BICYCLES
22-07-015	BID
2-02-002	BIDDER
3-03-003	BIDDERS
1-01-001	BIDDIES
7-03-003	BIDDING
1-01-001	BIDDLE
1-01-001	BIDE
6-02-003	BIDS
1-01-001	BIEN
1-01-001	BIENNIAL
1-01-001	BIENNIUM
9-01-001	BIENVILLE
1-01-001	BIERCE
1-01-001	BIETNAR
1-01-001	BIFOCAL
2-02-002	BIFOCALS
1-01-001	BIFUTEK-SAN
360-15-182	BIG
1-01-001	BIG-BONED
1-01-001	BIG-BUSINESS
1-01-001	BIG-CHESTED
1-01-001	BIG-DADDY
1-01-001	BIG-GAME
1-01-001	BIG-LARGE
1-01-001	BIG-LEAGUE
1-01-001	BIG-SHOULDERED
1-01-001	BIG-STAGE
1-01-001	BIG-TICKET
1-01-001	BIG-TOWN
34-12-026	BIGGER
24-11-023	BIGGEST
1-01-001	BIGOTED
2-02-002	BIGOTRY
1-01-001	BIGOTS
1-01-001	BIJOUTERIE
1-01-001	BIKINIS
2-02-002	BILATERAL
3-02-002	BILE
2-01-001	BILGE
1-01-001	BILHARZIASIS
1-01-001	BILINEAR
1-01-001	BILINGUAL
2-02-002	BILKED
143-14-071	BILL
5-04-005	BILL'S
1-01-001	BILLBOARD
2-01-001	BILLBOARDS
3-02-003	BILLED
1-01-001	BILLET
1-01-001	BILLETS
1-01-001	BILLIARD
3-02-002	BILLIE
2-01-001	BILLIKEN
2-01-001	BILLIKENS
4-04-004	BILLING
1-01-001	BILLINGS
62-08-016	BILLION
7-04-004	BILLIONS
1-01-001	BILLOWED
1-01-001	BILLOWS
47-11-028	BILLS
26-06-012	BILLY
1-01-001	BIMINI
1-01-001	BIMOLECULAR
1-01-001	BIMONTHLY
9-03-004	BIN
1-01-001	BINDER
2-01-001	BINDERS
20-07-011	BINDING
1-01-001	BINDLE
2-01-002	BINDS
2-02-002	BING
1-01-001	BINGE
1-01-001	BINGLES
1-01-001	BINI
203-14-100	BINOCULARS
36-01-001	BINOMIAL
2-02-002	BINS
2-02-002	BINUCLEAR
1-01-001	BIO-
1-01-001	BIO-*DYNAMIC
2-01-001	BIO-ASSAY
1-01-001	BIO-MEDICAL
2-01-001	BIO-MEDICINE
3-02-003	BIOCHEMICAL
1-01-001	BIOGRAPHER
1-01-001	BIOGRAPHERS
4-01-004	BIOGRAPHICAL
13-07-009	BIOGRAPHY
1-01-001	BIOLOGIC
20-04-007	BIOLOGICAL
1-01-001	BIOLOGICALLY
2-02-002	BIOLOGIST
2-01-002	BIOLOGISTS
7-05-007	BIOLOGY
2-02-002	BIOPHYSICAL
1-01-001	BIOPHYSICIST
1-01-001	BIOPSIES
2-01-001	BIOPSY
1-01-001	BIOSYNTHESIZED
2-02-002	BIPARTISAN
2-01-001	BIPLANE
1-01-001	BIRACIAL
2-02-002	BIRCH
1-01-001	BIRCH-PANELED
1-01-001	BIRCHES
31-10-025	BIRD
1-01-001	BIRD'S
1-01-001	BIRD-BRAIN
1-01-001	BIRDBATH
5-01-002	BIRDIE
4-01-001	BIRDIED
2-01-001	BIRDIES
1-01-001	BIRDLIKE
57-11-033	BIRDS
2-01-001	BIRDS'
1-01-001	BIRDWHISTELL
1-01-001	BIRDWOOD
3-01-001	BIREFRINGENCE
1-01-001	BIRGIT
1-01-001	BIRGITTA
3-01-001	BIRKHEAD
13-06-008	BIRMINGHAM
1-01-001	BIRNBAUM
66-11-032	BIRTH
4-01-001	BIRTH-CONTROL
2-01-001	BIRTH-PREVENTION
1-01-001	BIRTHCONTROL
18-09-018	BIRTHDAY
6-03-004	BIRTHPLACE
1-01-001	BIRTHRIGHT
4-03-004	BIRTHS
2-01-001	BISCAYNE
2-02-002	BISCUIT
5-04-005	BISCUITS
18-08-012	BISHOP
1-01-001	BISHOPRY
6-03-005	BISHOPS
1-01-001	BISHOPS'
2-01-001	BISHOPSGATE
1-01-001	BISMARCK
1-01-001	BISMARK
1-01-001	BISON
6-01-001	BISQUE
101-13-073	BIT
1-01-001	BIT-LIKE
6-02-004	BITCH
10-07-010	BITE
1-01-001	BITER
8-05-005	BITES
6-04-005	BITING
12-07-011	BITS
3-03-003	BITTEN
53-12-048	BITTER
2-02-002	BITTEREST
16-09-014	BITTERLY
18-08-016	BITTERNESS
1-01-001	BITTERS
1-01-001	BITTERSWEET
5-02-004	BIVOUAC
9-01-001	BIWA
1-01-001	BIX
2-01-002	BIZ
1-01-001	BIZARRE
3-01-001	BIZERTE
1-01-001	BIZET'S
1-01-001	BJERRE'S
1-01-001	BLABBED
1-01-001	BLABER
203-14-100	BLACK
6-02-003	BLACK'S
1-01-001	BLACK-AND-ORANGE
1-01-001	BLACK-AND-YELLOW
1-01-001	BLACK-BALLED
1-01-001	BLACK-BEARDED
4-01-001	BLACK-BODY
1-01-001	BLACK-CLAD
1-01-001	BLACK-CROWNED
1-01-001	BLACK-EYED
1-01-001	BLACK-HAIRED
1-01-001	BLACK-MARKET
1-01-001	BLACK-TIPPED
3-02-002	BLACKBERRY
1-01-001	BLACKBIRDS
1-01-001	BLACKBOARD
3-03-003	BLACKED
1-01-001	BLACKED-IN
5-03-004	BLACKENED
1-01-001	BLACKENING
1-01-001	BLACKEST
2-01-001	BLACKFEET
1-01-001	BLACKING
2-01-001	BLACKJACK
2-02-002	BLACKMAIL
1-01-001	BLACKMAILED
2-01-001	BLACKMAILER

15-01-001 BLACKMAN	4-03-004 BLINDED	1-01-001 BLOWN-UP	1-01-001 BOB'S
3-01-001 BLACKMER	2-01-002 BLINDFOLDED	8-08-008 BLOWS	2-02-002 BOBBED
5-04-005 BLACKNESS	2-02-002 BLINDING	1-01-001 BLOWUP	22-01-001 BOBBIE
5-04-004 BLACKOUT	8-07-008 BLINDLY	1-01-001 BLUBBER	2-01-001 BOBBIE'S
3-03-003 BLACKS	12-05-008 BLINDNESS	3-03-003 BLUDGEON	3-02-003 BOBBING
2-02-002 BLACKSMITH	3-03-003 BLINDS	143-14-085 BLUE	1-01-001 BOBBINS
1-01-001 BLACKSTONE	4-03-003 BLINK	2-02-002 BLUE-BLACK	1-01-001 BOBBLES
3-01-001 BLACKWELL	6-04-006 BLINKED	1-01-001 BLUE-COLLAR	2-01-001 BOBBSEY
1-01-001 BLACKWELL'S	1-01-001 BLINKERS	1-01-001 BLUE-DRAPED	23-04-008 BOBBY
1-01-001 BLACKWELLS	3-03-003 BLINKING	3-01-001 BLUE-EYED	1-01-001 BOBBY-SOX
13-06-010 BLADE	1-01-001 BLIPS	1-01-001 BLUE-EYES	1-01-001 BOBBY-SOXER
12-08-010 BLADES	1-01-001 BLISH'S	3-03-003 BLUE-GREEN	1-01-001 BOBIN-TO-CONE
2-02-002 BLAINE	4-04-004 BLISS	1-01-001 BLUE-UNIFORMED	1-01-001 BOCK
1-01-001 BLAIR	4-03-003 BLISSFUL	1-01-001 BLUEBERRIES	1-01-001 BOCKWURST
6-03-003 BLAKE	2-02-002 BLISSFULLY	1-01-001 BLUEBERRY	1-01-001 BODENHEIM
3-02-002 BLAKEY	3-03-003 BLISTER	1-01-001 BLUEBIRD	1-01-001 BODES
34-12-031 BLAME	2-01-001 BLISTERED	1-01-001 BLUEBONNETS	1-01-001 BODHISATTVA
7-06-007 BLAMED	2-02-002 BLISTERS	1-01-001 BLUEBOOK	2-02-002 BODICE
2-02-002 BLAMING	2-01-002 BLITHE	1-01-001 BLUEBUSH	1-01-001 BODIED
1-01-001 BLANC	3-02-003 BLITHELY	1-01-001 BLUEFISH	64-13-047 BODIES
2-01-001 BLANCHARD	3-03-003 BLITZ	1-01-001 BLUEPRINT	7-06-007 BODILY
2-02-002 BLANCHARD'S	1-01-001 BLITZES	3-03-003 BLUEPRINTS	2-02-002 BODIN
25-04-005 BLANCHE	7-04-004 BLIZZARD	22-04-009 BLUES	1-01-001 BODLEIAN
1-01-001 BLANCHE'S	1-01-001 BLIZZARDS	1-01-001 BLUESTOCKING	276-15-142 BODY
1-01-001 BLANCHED	8-01-001 BLOAT	8-06-006 BLUFF	3-02-002 BODY'S
4-01-001 BLANCHING	3-03-003 BLOATED	1-01-001 BLUFFING	1-01-001 BODY-BUILDING
3-02-003 BLAND	2-02-002 BLOB	4-04-004 BLUFFS	1-01-001 BODY-TISSUE
2-02-002 BLANDLY	10-05-008 BLOC	1-01-001 BLUING	6-01-001 BODYBUILDER
1-01-001 BLANDNESS	2-02-002 BLOCH	2-01-002 BLUISH	2-01-001 BODYBUILDERS
14-07-011 BLANK	66-14-039 BLOCK	2-01-001 BLUM	1-01-001 BODYBUILDING
30-11-019 BLANKET	1-01-001 BLOCK-BUSTER	3-02-003 BLUMBERG	1-01-001 BODYGUARD
1-01-001 BLANKETED	16-02-002 BLOCKADE	1-01-001 BLUME	1-01-001 BODYWEIGHT
11-06-009 BLANKETS	2-01-001 BLOCKADING	1-01-001 BLUMENTHAL	3-02-002 BOEING
3-02-002 BLANKS	1-01-001 BLOCKAGES	2-02-002 BLUNDER	1-01-001 BOEOTIAN
1-01-001 BLANTON	12-07-012 BLOCKED	2-02-002 BLUNDERED	1-01-001 BOG
1-01-001 BLARED	1-01-001 BLOCKHOUSE	1-01-001 BLUNDERINGS	1-01-001 BOGARTIAN
1-01-001 BLARING	3-03-003 BLOCKING	1-01-001 BLUNDERS	5-02-002 BOGEY
3-01-001 BLASINGAME	37-11-016 BLOCKS	9-05-008 BLUNT	1-01-001 BOGEY-SYMBOL
1-01-001 BLASPHEMED	1-01-001 BLOCKY	1-01-001 BLUNTED	2-01-001 BOGEYED
2-01-001 BLASPHEMIES	1-01-001 BLOIS	2-01-001 BLUNTER	1-01-001 BOGEYMEN
5-02-004 BLASPHEMOUS	1-01-001 BLOKE	8-06-008 BLUNTLY	2-02-002 BOGEYS
4-02-003 BLASPHEMY	2-01-001 BLOKES	2-01-001 BLUNTNESS	1-01-001 BOGGED
15-06-011 BLAST	1-01-001 BLOMDAHL	1-01-001 BLUNTS	1-01-001 BOGGLED
1-01-001 BLASTDOWN	11-05-009 BLOND	3-03-003 BLUR	1-01-001 BOGGS
4-03-004 BLASTED	20-06-015 BLONDE	6-06-006 BLURRED	1-01-001 BOGIES
2-02-002 BLASTING	3-02-002 BLONDE'S	1-01-001 BLURRY	1-01-001 BOGUS
4-04-004 BLASTS	1-01-001 BLONDE-HAIRED	3-02-003 BLURTED	1-01-001 BOGY
1-01-001 BLATANCY	1-01-001 BLONDE-HEADED	2-02-002 BLUSH	1-01-001 BOHART
2-02-002 BLATANT	1-01-001 BLONDES	6-04-005 BLUSHED	1-01-001 BOHEME
9-01-001 BLATZ	121-14-069 BLOOD	1-01-001 BLUSHES	1-01-001 BOHEMIAN
1-01-001 BLATZ'S	1-01-001 BLOOD-BOUGHT	4-04-004 BLUSHING	1-01-001 BOHLEN
2-01-001 BLAUBERMAN	1-01-001 BLOOD-CHILLING	1-01-001 BLUSTER	1-01-001 BOHN
1-01-001 BLAUSTEIN	1-01-001 BLOOD-FILLED	1-01-001 BLUSTERED	1-01-001 BOIES
7-04-006 BLAZE	1-01-001 BLOOD-FLECKED	1-01-001 BLUSTERY	12-09-012 BOIL
2-02-002 BLAZED	1-01-001 BLOOD-FLOW	1-01-001 BLUTHENZWEIG	10-05-008 BOILED
1-01-001 BLAZER	1-01-001 BLOOD-KINSHIP	1-01-001 BLUTWURST	2-02-002 BOILER
6-03-005 BLAZING	1-01-001 BLOOD-LUST	4-01-003 BLVD	1-01-001 BOILER-BURNER
1-01-001 BLAZON	1-01-001 BLOOD-SOAKED	1-01-001 BLYTH	1-01-001 BOILERS
3-03-003 BLDG	1-01-001 BLOOD-SPECKED	1-01-001 BO	9-05-008 BOILING
5-02-003 BLEACHED	1-01-001 BLOOD-STAINED	1-01-001 BO'SUN'S	2-02-002 BOILS
1-01-001 BLEACHER-TYPE	1-01-001 BLOODED	4-01-001 BO**DO**DK	2-02-002 BOIS
5-04-005 BLEACHERS	2-02-002 BLOODHOUNDS	7-01-001 BOA	1-01-001 BOISBRIANT
2-02-002 BLEACHING	1-01-001 BLOODIEST	1-01-001 BOADICEA	1-01-001 BOISMASSIF
10-06-010 BLEAK	3-02-003 BLOODLESS	1-01-001 BOAL	1-01-001 BOISSONEAULT
3-03-003 BLEAKLY	1-01-001 BLOODLUST	1-01-001 BOAR	1-01-001 BOISTEROUS
2-02-002 BLEARY	1-01-001 BLOODROOT	239-14-083 BOARD	1-01-001 BOITE
1-01-001 BLEAT	1-01-001 BLOODS	5-02-004 BOARD'S	1-01-001 BOITES
1-01-001 BLEATING	3-03-003 BLOODSHED	5-05-005 BOARDED	1-01-001 BOLAND
1-01-001 BLEATS	1-01-001 BLOODSHOT	1-01-001 BOARDER	21-08-021 BOLD
1-01-001 BLEBS	1-01-001 BLOODSPOTS	5-05-005 BOARDING	2-02-002 BOLDER
1-01-001 BLECKLEY	1-01-001 BLOODSTAINED	1-01-001 BOARDING-HOME	1-01-001 BOLDEST
3-02-003 BLED	1-01-001 BLOODSTAINS	1-01-001 BOARDINGHOUSES	8-06-008 BOLDLY
2-02-002 BLEED	4-03-003 BLOODSTREAM	47-15-026 BOARDS	3-02-002 BOLDNESS
16-06-013 BLEEDING	8-06-008 BLOODY	8-05-006 BOAST	1-01-001 BOLET
1-01-001 BLEEDINGS	12-06-008 BLOOM	6-05-005 BOASTED	2-01-001 BOLGER
1-01-001 BLEEKER	6-05-005 BLOOMED	1-01-001 BOASTFULLY	1-01-001 BOLINGBROKE
1-01-001 BLEEPS	1-01-001 BLOOMFIELD	3-03-003 BOASTING	1-01-001 BOLINGBROKE'S
2-02-002 BLEMISH	10-03-004 BLOOMING	1-01-001 BOASTINGS	2-01-001 BOLIOU
1-01-001 BLEMISHES	3-02-003 BLOOMS	2-01-002 BOASTS	1-01-001 BOLIVAR
9-06-008 BLEND	1-01-001 BLOOPS	72-11-025 BOAT	1-01-001 BOLIVIA
4-04-004 BLENDED	7-04-005 BLOSSOM	1-01-001 BOAT'S	2-01-001 BOLKER
1-01-001 BLENDING	1-01-001 BLOSSOMED	1-01-001 BOAT-YARD	1-01-001 BOLO
2-02-002 BLENDS	7-04-006 BLOSSOMS	1-01-001 BOATEL	2-02-002 BOLOGNA
5-01-001 BLENHEIM	6-06-006 BLOT	1-01-001 BOATELS	1-01-001 BOLOVENS
9-04-008 BLESS	1-01-001 BLOT-APPEARANCE	1-01-001 BOATERS	2-02-002 BOLSHEVIKS
13-08-012 BLESSED	1-01-001 BLOT-LIKE	1-01-001 BOATHOUSES	1-01-001 BOLSHEVISM
10-05-009 BLESSING	4-02-003 BLOTS	23-05-006 BOATING	1-01-001 BOLSHEVISTIC
3-02-002 BLESSINGS	3-02-003 BLOTTED	1-01-001 BOATLOAD	1-01-001 BOLSHOI
3-03-003 BLEST	2-01-001 BLOTTING	1-01-001 BOATLOADS	3-03-003 BOLSTER
2-01-001 BLEVINS	1-01-001 BLOUSE	3-01-001 BOATMAN	1-01-001 BOLSTERED
1-01-001 BLEVINS'	1-01-001 BLOUSES	1-01-001 BOATMEN	1-01-001 BOLSTERING
12-05-010 BLEW	33-13-029 BLOW	51-10-012 BOATS	10-06-010 BOLT
2-02-002 BLIGHT	4-02-002 BLOWER	1-01-001 BOATSMEN	3-01-001 BOLT-ACTION
3-03-003 BLIGHTED	1-01-001 BLOWERS	3-02-002 BOATSWAIN	7-05-007 BOLTED
1-01-001 BLIMP	1-01-001 BLOWFISH	2-01-001 BOATYARDS	1-01-001 BOLTING
47-13-036 BLIND	19-08-012 BLOWING	2-01-001 BOAZ	1-01-001 BOLTS
1-01-001 BLIND-FOLDED	9-07-009 BLOWN	40-07-018 BOB	

1-01-001 BOLTZMANN	2-01-001 BOONE	3-03-003 BOTTLED	5-03-004 BOYD
36-10-022 BOMB	1-01-001 BOONTON	2-02-002 BOTTLENECK	2-01-001 BOYER
1-01-001 BOMB-PROOF	1-01-001 BOORISH	1-01-001 BOTTLENECKS	5-03-004 BOYHOOD
1-01-001 BOMBARDING	1-01-001 BOORS	15-08-012 BOTTLES	4-04-004 BOYISH
1-01-001 BOMBARDMENT	2-01-001 BOOS	1-01-001 BOTTLING	1-01-001 BOYLSTON
1-01-001 BOMBASTIC	15-06-013 BOOST	88-12-050 BOTTOM	143-11-070 BOYS
1-01-001 BOMBAY	3-03-003 BOOSTED	1-01-001 BOTTOM-LIVING	3-02-003 BOYS'
1-01-001 BOMBED	1-01-001 BOOSTER	1-01-001 BOTTOMLESS	14-06-008 BRACE
8-03-003 BOMBER	3-03-003 BOOSTING	8-04-005 BOTTOMS	1-01-001 BRACE'S
1-01-001 BOMBER'S	1-01-001 BOOSTS	1-01-001 BOTULINAL	5-04-005 BRACED
22-06-007 BOMBERS	13-09-013 BOOT	1-01-001 BOTULINUM	1-01-001 BRACELET
1-01-001 BOMBERS'	1-01-001 BOOT-WEARER	2-02-002 BOUCHER	4-03-003 BRACES
5-04-005 BOMBING	1-01-001 BOOTED	1-01-001 BOUCLE	1-01-001 BRACHII
2-02-002 BOMBINGS	7-03-006 BOOTH	2-02-002 BOUFFANT	3-02-002 BRACING
3-01-001 BOMBPROOF	1-01-001 BOOTHBY	1-01-001 BOUFFE	1-01-001 BRACKEN
35-06-008 BOMBS	3-03-003 BOOTHS	2-01-001 BOUGH	1-01-001 BRACKET
4-01-001 BOMBUS	2-01-001 BOOTLE	4-03-004 BOUGHS	2-02-002 BRACKETS
2-01-001 BON	1-01-001 BOOTLE'S	56-12-049 BOUGHT	3-03-003 BRACKISH
1-01-001 BONA	1-01-001 BOOTLEGGER	1-01-001 BOUGIE	1-01-001 BRAD
2-01-001 BONANZA	2-01-002 BOOTLEGGERS	10-04-005 BOULDER	2-01-001 BRADBURY'S
1-01-001 BONAPARTE	1-01-001 BOOTLEGGING	3-02-002 BOULDERS	1-01-001 BRADDOCK-AGAINS
2-01-001 BONAVENTURE	20-06-015 BOOTS	11-04-005 BOULEVARD	T-THE-*INDIANS
46-06-020 BOND	3-02-002 BOOTY	2-02-002 BOULEVARDS	1-01-001 BRADEN
3-02-002 BONDAGE	4-04-004 BOOZE	1-01-001 BOULEZ	5-02-004 BRADFORD
2-02-002 BONDED	3-02-002 BOP	1-01-001 BOULLE	4-02-002 BRADLEY
3-01-001 BONDI	1-01-001 BORAK	5-02-002 BOUN	1-01-001 BRADLEY'S
1-01-001 BONDING	1-01-001 BORATES	8-05-006 BOUNCE	1-01-001 BRADY
47-07-017 BONDS	1-01-001 BORAX	16-06-013 BOUNCED	1-01-001 BRADYKININ
1-01-001 BONDSMAN	1-01-001 BORDEAU	9-04-005 BOUNCING	1-01-001 BRAE
1-01-001 BONDSMAN'S	2-01-001 BORDEAUX	1-01-001 BOUNCY	2-02-002 BRAG
33-11-026 BONE	2-01-001 BORDEL	42-12-039 BOUND	2-01-001 BRAGG
1-01-001 BONE-DEEP	20-01-001 BORDEN	14-07-011 BOUNDARIES	1-01-001 BRAGGADOCIO
2-02-002 BONE-WEARY	1-01-001 BORDENS	16-05-007 BOUNDARY	2-02-002 BRAGGED
1-01-001 BONENFANT	20-11-018 BORDER	9-05-007 BOUNDED	1-01-001 BRAGGING
20-08-015 BONES	2-01-001 BORDERED	2-02-002 BOUNDING	1-01-001 BRAHM'S
1-01-001 BONFIGLIO	5-03-005 BORDERING	2-02-002 BOUNDLESS	2-01-001 BRAHMAPUTRA
3-03-003 BONFIRE	1-01-001 BORDERLANDS	10-07-008 BOUNDS	7-02-003 BRAHMS
1-01-001 BONFIRES	3-03-003 BORDERLINE	3-02-002 BOUNTY	2-02-002 BRAHMSIAN
6-01-001 BONG	12-07-011 BORDERS	4-02-002 BOUQUET	1-01-001 BRAIDED
1-01-001 BONGO	1-01-001 BORDNER	1-01-001 BOUQUETS	1-01-001 BRAIDING
1-01-001 BONHAM	24-09-021 BORE	8-05-006 BOURBON	1-01-001 BRAIDS
1-01-001 BONHEUR	14-07-012 BORED	6-01-001 BOURBONS	1-01-001 BRAILLE
1-01-001 BONHO**DFFER	11-05-010 BOREDOM	3-01-001 BOURCIER	1-01-001 BRAILSFORD
1-01-001 BONHOEFFER	1-01-001 BORER	3-02-003 BOURGEOIS	45-12-022 BRAIN
4-01-001 BONIFACE	2-02-002 BORES	1-01-001 BOURGEOISIE	1-01-001 BRAIN'S
1-01-001 BONIFACE'S	2-01-001 BORGLUM	1-01-001 BOURGUIBA	1-01-001 BRAIN-WRACKING
1-01-001 BONITO	1-01-001 BORIS	7-04-005 BOURN	1-01-001 BRAINARDS
1-01-001 BONJOUR	5-04-005 BORIS'	1-01-001 BOUT	18-08-014 BRAINS
5-03-005 BONN	10-01-001 BORLAND	1-01-001 BOUT-DE-SOUFFLE	1-01-001 BRAINWASHING
3-01-001 BONN'S	113-14-062 BORN	1-01-001 BOUTFLOWER	1-01-001 BRAINY
1-01-001 BONNE	8-07-008 BORNE	2-01-001 BOUTON	2-02-002 BRAKE
6-01-001 BONNER	1-01-001 BORNEO	3-03-003 BOUTS	7-03-005 BRAKES
3-02-003 BONNET	1-n1-001 BORNHOLM	1-01-001 BOUVARDIER	1-01-001 BRAKKE
1-01-001 BONNIE	1-01-001 BORON	1-01-001 BOUVIER	1-01-001 BRAMANTE'S
4-01-001 BONNOR	5-03-003 BOROUGH	2-01-002 BOVINE	1-01-001 BRAMBLES
2-02-002 BONTEMPO	2-02-002 BOROUGHS	1-01-001 BOVINES	1-01-001 BRAN
2-02-002 BONUS	1-01-001 BORRIOBOOLA-*GH	15-09-014 BOW	33-10-022 BRANCH
7-04-004 BONY	A	1-01-001 BOWAN	2-02-002 BRANCHED
2-01-001 BONZES		2-01-002 BOWDEN	33-10-019 BRANCHES
1-01-001 BOO	1-01-001 BORROMINI	1-01-001 BOWDOIN	1-01-001 BRANCHING
1-01-001 BOOBIFY	2-01-001 BORROMINI'S	7-07-007 BOWED	1-01-001 BRANCHVILLE
1-01-001 BOOBOO	9-06-009 BORROW	1-01-001 BOWELS	17-07-012 BRAND
4-02-003 BOOBY	14-08-014 BORROWED	1-01-001 BOWER	2-02-002 BRAND-NEW
1-01-001 BOOBY-TRAP	2-02-002 BORROWER	1-01-001 BOWERS	2-02-002 BRANDED
2-02-002 BOOGIE	8-05-005 BORROWING	1-01-001 BOWES	1-01-001 BRANDEIS
193-15-100 BOOK	1-01-001 BORROWS	1-01-001 BOWIE	3-01-001 BRANDEL
3-02-003 BOOK'S	2-02-002 BOSCH	3-01-002 BOWING	2-02-002 BRANDENBURG
1-01-001 BOOK-BURNING	1-01-001 BOSCO	23-08-015 BOWL	1-01-001 BRANDIN
1-01-001 BOOK-LINED	6-01-001 BUSIS	3-03-003 BOWLS	5-04-005 BRANDISHING
1-01-001 BOOK-REVIEW	1-01-001 BOSIS'	3-02-002 BOWMAN	8-02-002 BRANDON
1-01-001 BOOK-SELECTION	1-01-001 BOSLER	3-02-003 BOWS	2-01-001 BRANDON'S
2-01-001 BOOKCASE	1-01-001 BOSLEY	1-01-001 BOWSTRING	4-02-004 BRANDS
1-01-001 BOOKCASES	8-05-007 BOSOM	70-15-041 BOX	10-02-004 BRANDT
7-03-005 BOOKED	1-01-001 BOSOMS	1-01-001 BOX-SIZED	1-01-001 BRANDT'S
3-03-003 BOOKER	5-01-001 BOSPHORUS	6-02-002 BOXCAR	7-05-007 BRANDY
1-01-001 BOOKERS	20-10-016 BOSS	2-01-001 BOXCARS	7-01-001 BRANDYWINE
3-01-001 BOOKIES	3-02-003 BOSS'S	2-02-002 BOXED	29-01-001 BRANNON
6-01-001 BOOKING	1-01-001 BOSSED	1-01-001 BOXED-IN	1-01-001 BRANNON'S
1-01-001 BOOKINGS	5-05-005 BOSSES	4-01-001 BOXELL	1-01-001 BRANUM
1-01-001 BOOKISH	1-01-001 BOSSMAN	1-01-001 BOXER	9-01-001 BRAQUE
5-03-004 BOOKKEEPING	1-01-001 BOSTITCH	14-06-013 BOXES	4-01-001 BRAQUE'S
1-01-001 BOOKLET	61-12-035 BOSTON	1-01-001 BOXFORD	1-01-001 BRAQUES
2-01-002 BOOKLETS	2-02-002 BOSTON'S	1-01-001 BOXWOOD	1-01-001 BRASH
1-01-001 BOOKLISTS	1-01-001 BOSTONIAN	242-13-115 BOY	1-01-001 BRASHNESS
96-14-066 BOOKS	1-01-001 BOSTONIANS	16-08-013 BOY'S	19-09-015 BRASS
1-01-001 BOOKSELLER	1-01-001 BOTANICAL	1-01-001 BOY-*LADY	1-01-001 BRASS-BOUND
1-01-001 BOOKSHELF	2-01-001 BOTANISTS	1-01-001 BOY-*MARQUITA	1-01-001 BRASSBOUND'S
3-02-003 BOOKSHELVES	3-02-002 BOTANY	1-01-001 BOY-FURIENDO	1-01-001 BRASSICA
1-01-001 BOOKWALTER	730-15-337 BOTH	1-01-001 BOY-MANAGER	2-02-002 BRASSIERE
8-06-008 BOOM	22-09-022 BOTHER	1-01-001 BOY-MEETS-GIRL	12-01-001 BRASSNOSE
1-01-001 BOOM-BOOM-BOOM	14-10-013 BOTHERED	1-01-001 BOY-NAME	1-01-001 BRASSTOWN
1-01-001 BOOMED	6-04-006 BOTHERING	1-01-001 BOYARS	2-02-002 BRASSY
1-01-001 BOOMERANG	3-03-003 BOTHERS	1-01-001 BOYCE	1-01-001 BRATWURST
1-01-001 BOOMERANGS	1-01-001 BOTHERSOME	8-03-003 BOYCOTT	1-01-001 BRAUD
1-01-001 BOOMING	1-01-001 BOTTEGA	1-01-001 BOYCOTTED	1-01-001 BRAUN
1-01-001 BOOMTOWN	1-01-001 BOTTINEAU		7-04-006 BRAVADO
3-03-003 BOON	76-08-024 BOTTLE		24-10-021 BRAVE

1-01-001	BRAVED	1-01-001	BREVE	55-09-027	BRITAIN	1-01-001	BROOKMEYER'S
4-04-004	BRAVELY	1-01-001	BREVET	6-04-006	BRITAIN'S	1-01-001	BROOKMONT
2-02-002	BRAVER	3-03-003	BREVITY	1-01-001	BRITANNIC	16-05-007	BROOKS
4-03-004	BRAVERY	4-04-004	BREW	1-01-001	BRITANNICA	2-02-002	BROOM
3-01-003	BRAVES	1-01-001	BREWED	1-01-001	BRITCHES	1-01-001	BROOME
1-01-001	BRAVES'	1-01-001	BREWER'S	118-13-058	BRITISH	1-01-001	BROS
1-01-001	BRAVEST	1-01-001	BREWERS	1-01-001	BRITISH-*AMERIC	3-03-003	BROTH
1-01-001	BRAVEST-FEATHER	2-02-002	BREWERY		AN	1-01-001	BROTHEL
	ED	1-01-001	BREWING	1-01-001	BRITISH-BORN	2-02-002	BROTHELS
2-02-002	BRAVING	5-01-001	BRIAN	1-01-001	BRITISHER	73-11-044	BROTHER
1-01-001	BRAVO	1-01-001	BRIAR	1-01-001	BRITON	10-06-007	BROTHER'S
1-01-001	BRAVURA	1-01-001	BRIBE	1-01-001	BRITONS	5-04-004	BROTHER-IN-LAW
1-01-001	BRAWELING	3-03-003	BRIBED	2-01-001	BRITTANY	6-05-006	BROTHERHOOD
1-01-001	BRAWL	1-01-001	BRIBERS	2-01-002	BRITTEN	2-02-002	BROTHERLY
1-01-001	BRAWLE	1-01-001	BRIBES	3-03-003	BRITTLE	41-13-034	BROTHERS
1-01-001	BRAYING	2-02-002	BRIC-A-BRAC	1-01-001	BROACH	2-01-001	BROTHERS'
1-01-001	BRAZEN	1-01-001	BRICE	2-02-002	BROACHED	253-15-179	BROUGHT
1-01-001	BRAZENLY	18-09-016	BRICK	84-13-069	BROAD	3-02-002	BROUN
1-01-001	BRAZENNESS	1-01-001	BRICKER	3-03-003	BROAD-BRIMMED	6-05-006	BROW
1-01-001	BRAZIER	3-02-002	BRICKLAYERS	1-01-001	BROAD-NIBBED	1-01-001	BROWBEATEN
8-04-006	BRAZIL	3-03-003	BRICKLAYING	1-01-001	BROAD-SCALE	176-13-069	BROWN
4-04-004	BRAZILIAN	6-03-003	BRICKS	16-07-010	BROADCAST	23-06-006	BROWN'S
2-01-001	BRAZOS	1-01-001	BRICKTOP	2-01-001	BROADCASTERS	1-01-001	BROWN-BLACK
6-06-006	BREACH	2-02-002	BRIDAL	9-03-007	BROADCASTING	1-01-001	BROWN-EDGED
2-02-002	BREACHING	33-08-014	BRIDE	2-01-001	BROADCASTINGS	1-01-001	BROWN-PAPER
41-11-020	BREAD	5-02-002	BRIDE'S	7-04-004	BROADCASTS	1-01-001	BROWNAPOPOLUS
7-04-007	BREADTH	1-01-001	BRIDE-GIFT	8-03-006	BROADEN	1-01-001	BROWNE
88-13-077	BREAK	3-03-003	BRIDEGROOM	7-06-006	BROADENED	1-01-001	BROWNELL
1-01-001	BREAK-AWAY	2-01-001	BRIDEGROOM'S	9-04-006	BROADENING	7-04-005	BROWNING
2-02-002	BREAK-EVEN	2-02-002	BRIDES	2-01-002	BROADENS	2-02-002	BROWNING'S
1-01-001	BREAK-NECK	2-02-002	BRIDESMAIDS	19-07-014	BROADER	1-01-001	BROWNINGS
1-01-001	BREAK-THROUGH	1-01-001	BRIDEWELL	1-01-001	BROADEST	1-01-001	BROWNISH
1-01-001	BREAKABLES	98-13-031	BRIDGE	7-05-007	BROADLY	2-01-001	BROWNLOW
1-01-001	BREAKAGE	1-01-001	BRIDGED-*=*T	3-03-003	BROADSIDE	1-01-001	BROWNY
1-01-001	BREAKAWAY	2-02-002	BRIDGEHEAD	24-08-018	BROADWAY	2-01-001	BROWNY-HAIRED
13-05-010	BREAKDOWN	1-01-001	BRIDGEPORT	1-01-001	BROADWAY'S	5-04-005	BROWS
3-03-003	BREAKDOWNS	26-06-012	BRIDGES	3-02-003	BROCADE	1-01-001	BROWSING
1-01-001	BREAKER	21-01-001	BRIDGET	1-01-001	BROCADED	2-01-001	BROXODENT
1-01-001	BREAKERS	1-01-001	BRIDGET'S	1-01-001	BROCCOLI	4-03-004	BRUCE
53-11-032	BREAKFAST	1-01-001	BRIDGEWATER	2-02-002	BROCHURE	1-01-001	BRUCELLOSIS
1-01-001	BREAKFAST-TABLE	1-01-001	BRIDGEWORK	2-02-002	BROCHURES	1-01-001	BRUCKMANN
2-02-002	BREAKFASTED	1-01-001	BRIDLE	1-01-001	BROCKLE	4-01-001	BRUCKNER
2-02-002	BREAKFASTS	73-14-060	BRIEF	2-01-001	BROCKLIN	3-01-001	BRUCKNER'S
1-01-001	BREAKIN	1-01-001	BRIEFCASE	1-01-001	BROCKLIN'S	1-01-001	BRUEGEL
25-11-023	BREAKING	2-02-002	BRIEFED	1-01-001	BROD	1-01-001	BRUHN
1-01-001	BREAKING-OUT	2-02-002	BRIEFER	1-01-001	BRODBECK	3-02-002	BRUISE
1-01-001	BREAKOFF	1-01-001	BRIEFEST	10-01-001	BRODIE	7-04-007	BRUISED
12-07-012	BREAKS	1-01-001	BRIEFF	1-01-001	BROEG	8-04-004	BRUISES
6-05-005	BREAKTHROUGH	2-02-002	BRIEFING	1-01-001	BROGLIE	2-02-002	BRUISING
1-01-001	BREAKTHROUGHS	38-14-036	BRIEFLY	2-01-001	BROGLIO	1-01-001	BRUITED
3-03-003	BREAKUP	1-01-001	BRIEFLY-ILLUMED	1-01-001	BROGLIO'S	2-01-001	BRUMBY
1-01-001	BREAKUPS	1-01-001	BRIEFS	2-02-002	BROIL	11-01-001	BRUMIDI
2-02-002	BREAKWATER	1-01-001	BRIEN	2-02-002	BROILED	6-01-001	BRUMIDI'S
1-01-001	BREAKWATERS	2-02-002	BRIG	2-02-002	BROILER	1-01-001	BRUMIDI-*COSTAG
11-07-008	BREAST	3-02-002	BRIGADE	1-01-001	BROK		GINI
6-01-001	BREASTED	1-01-001	BRIGADES	72-13-061	BROKE	1-01-001	BRUNCHES
9-04-006	BREASTS	7-05-005	BRIGADIER	63-12-052	BROKEN	1-01-001	BRUNETTES
1-01-001	BREASTWORKS	1-01-001	BRIGADOON	1-01-001	BROKEN-BACKED	1-01-001	BRUNO
53-12-036	BREATH	1-01-001	BRIGANTINE	1-01-001	BROKEN-DOWN	1-01-001	BRUNT
3-03-003	BREATH-TAKING	1-01-001	BRIGGS	1-01-001	BROKEN-NOSED	44-12-033	BRUSH
7-05-007	BREATHE	1-01-001	BRIGHETTI	1-01-001	BROKENLY	1-01-001	BRUSH-OFF
9-08-009	BREATHED	87-13-060	BRIGHT	1-01-001	BROKER	1-01-001	BRUSH-OFF'S
1-01-001	BREATHER	2-01-001	BRIGHT'S	2-02-002	BROKERAGE	1-01-001	BRUSHCUT
2-02-002	BREATHES	2-01-002	BRIGHT-EYED	4-02-002	BROKERS	20-09-017	BRUSHED
21-09-019	BREATHING	1-01-001	BRIGHT-GREEN	1-01-001	BROMFIELD'S	6-04-005	BRUSHES
5-05-005	BREATHLESS	1-01-001	BRIGHT-LOOKING	1-01-001	BROMIDES	2-02-002	BRUSHFIRE
1-01-001	BREATHLESSLY	2-02-002	BRIGHTENED	1-01-001	BROMLEY	6-04-006	BRUSHING
1-01-001	BREATHS	1-01-001	BRIGHTENS	1-01-001	BROMPHENOL	1-01-001	BRUSHLIKE
3-03-003	BREATHTAKING	8-07-008	BRIGHTER	3-01-001	BRONC	1-01-001	BRUSHWORK
1-01-001	BREATHY	4-03-004	BRIGHTEST	3-01-002	BRONCHI	2-01-001	BRUSHY
1-01-001	BRECKENRIDGE'S	6-05-006	BRIGHTLY	29-01-001	BRONCHIAL	1-01-001	BRUSQUELY
1-01-001	BRED	18-04-008	BRIGHTNESS	1-01-001	BRONCHIOLAR	3-02-002	BRUSSELS
1-01-001	BREECHES	4-03-004	BRILLIANCE	4-01-001	BRONCHIOLE	7-06-006	BRUTAL
17-05-014	BREED	50-12-036	BRILLIANT	9-01-001	BRONCHIOLES	1-01-001	BRUTALITIES
2-02-002	BREED'S	9-05-009	BRILLIANTLY	1-01-001	BRONCHIOLITIS	13-06-011	BRUTALITY
7-04-004	BREEDING	4-04-004	BRIM	4-01-001	BRONCHUS	1-01-001	BRUTALIZED
1-01-001	BREEDS	1-01-001	BRIMFUL	1-01-001	BRONCOS	2-02-002	BRUTALLY
14-10-012	BREEZE	1-01-001	BRIMMED	3-02-002	BRONCS	6-05-006	BRUTE
2-02-002	BREEZES	1-01-001	BRINDISI	2-02-002	BROODY	1-01-001	BRUXELLES
1-01-001	BREEZY	1-01-001	BRINDLE	9-05-005	BRONX	12-05-007	BRYAN
1-01-001	BREGMAN	158-13-131	BRING	11-10-010	BRONZE	2-02-002	BRYAN'S
1-01-001	BRELIN	38-13-035	BRINGING	1-01-001	BRONZED	1-01-001	BRYANT
1-01-001	BREMERTON	40-10-032	BRINGS	1-01-001	BRONZY-GREEN-GO	2-02-002	BRYCE
1-01-001	BREMSSTRAHLUNG	3-03-003	BRINK		LD	2-01-001	BRYN
1-01-001	BRENDAN	1-01-001	BRINKLEY	9-04-005	BROOD	1-01-001	BRYNGE
3-01-001	BRENNAN	1-01-001	BRINKMANSHIP	1-01-001	BROODINF	1-01-001	BRYSON
10-02-002	BRENNER	1-01-001	BRINSLEY	14-08-014	BROODING	1-01-001	BUAFORD
3-01-001	BRENNER'S	3-01-002	BRISBANE	3-01-002	BROODS	12-08-008	BUBBLE
1-01-001	BREST	7-06-007	BRISK	2-02-002	BROODY	2-02-002	BUBBLED
1-01-001	BREST-*SILEVNIO	1-01-001	BRISKER	3-02-003	BROOK	14-06-007	BUBBLES
	V	5-04-005	BRISKLY	1-01-001	BROOK'S	3-03-003	BUBBLING
1-01-001	BRESTOWE	1-01-001	BRISKNESS	2-02-002	BROOKE	1-01-001	BUBBLY
8-04-006	BRETHREN	3-03-003	BRISTLE	1-01-001	BROOKED	1-01-001	BUBENIK
1-01-001	BRETON	3-02-003	BRISTLED	1-01-001	BROOKEN	1-01-001	BUBER
4-02-002	BRETT	4-02-002	BRISTLES	2-01-001	BROOKFIELD	1-01-001	BUBER-THINK
1-01-001	BREUER	3-03-003	BRISTLING	28-07-012	BROOKLYN	1-01-001	BUCCOLIC
5-01-001	BREVARD	3-02-003	BRISTOL	1-01-001	BROOKLYN'S	1-01-001	BUCER

2-02-002 BUCHANAN	1-01-001 BUILDER/ACTIVE	1-01-001 BUOYS	2-01-001 BURTON'S
1-01-001 BUCHAREST	27-04-009 BUILDERS	2-02-002 BURBANK	6-05-006 BURY
1-01-001 BUCHENWALD	2-01-001 BUILDERS'	2-01-001 BURCH	34-08-020 BUS
6-01-001 BUCHHEISTER	1-01-001 BUILDIN	1-01-001 BURCH'S	2-01-001 BUSBOY
20-06-011 BUCK	160-15-105 BUILDING'S	1-01-001 BURCKHARDT	2-01-001 BUSCH
1-01-001 BUCK'S	2-01-001 BUILDING'S	44-11-040 BURDEN	6-03-003 BUSES
1-01-001 BUCKAROOS	76-12-043 BUILDINGS	4-02-004 BURDENED	14-04-006 BUSH
2-01-001 BUCKBOARD	7-05-006 BUILDS	7-05-007 BURDENS	1-01-001 BUSHEL
1-01-001 BUCKED	2-02-002 BUILDUP	1-01-001 BURDENSOME	3-01-001 BUSHELL
1-01-001 BUCKENHAM	103-14-068 BUILT	43-10-028 BUREAU	4-02-002 BUSHELS
7-04-006 BUCKET	1-01-001 BUILT-DETERGENT	3-02-002 BUREAUCRACIES	11-08-009 BUSHES
1-01-001 BUCKET-SHOP	3-03-003 BUILT-IN	7-02-005 BUREAUCRACY	1-01-001 BUSHING
4-02-003 BUCKETS	1-01-001 BUILT-SOAP	1-01-001 BUREAUCRAT	1-01-001 BUSHNELL
1-01-001 BUCKHANNON	1-01-001 BUILTIN	3-02-002 BUREAUCRATIC	1-01-001 BUSHWHACKED
1-01-001 BUCKHEAD	1-01-001 BUL'BA	1-01-001 BUREAUCRATIZATI	1-01-001 BUSHWHACKIN
1-01-001 BUCKHORN'S	7-04-006 BULB	ON	1-01-001 BUSIED
4-03-003 BUCKING	2-01-001 BULBA	1-01-001 BUREAUCRATS	1-01-001 BUSIER
1-01-001 BUCKING-UP	3-02-003 BULBS	2-02-002 BUREAUS	2-02-002 BUSIEST
5-03-005 BUCKLE	1-01-001 BULGARIA	2-01-001 BUREN	8-06-007 BUSILY
1-01-001 BUCKLE-ON	5-05-005 BULGE	1-01-001 BURFORD	392-15-165 BUSINESS
2-02-002 BUCKLED	3-02-003 BULGED	1-01-001 BURGEONED	1-01-001 BUSINESS-LIKE
2-02-002 BUCKLES	3-03-003 BULGING	4-03-004 BURGEONING	1-01-001 BUSINESS-MINDED
7-02-002 BUCKLEY	16-09-014 BULK	1-01-001 BURGER	19-06-011 BUSINESSES
1-01-001 BUCKLING	1-01-001 BULKED	2-01-002 BURGESS	9-04-008 BUSINESSMAN
1-01-001 BUCKMAN	1-01-001 BULKHEAD	1-01-001 BURGESSES	15-08-012 BUSINESSMEN
2-01-001 BUCKRA	1-01-001 BULKHEADS	1-01-001 BURGHARDT	1-01-001 BUSINESSS
6-04-006 BUCKS	1-01-001 BULKS	1-01-001 BURGHER	1-01-001 BUSS
1-01-001 BUCKSHOT	9-05-008 BULKY	1-01-001 BURGHLEY	2-01-002 BUSSES
7-01-001 BUCKSKIN	14-08-011 BULL	1-01-001 BURGLAR	7-03-003 BUST
1-01-001 BUCKSKIN'S	10-02-002 BULL'S-EYE	1-01-001 BURGLARPROOF	1-01-001 BUSTARD
1-01-001 BUCKSKINS	6-01-001 BULL'S-EYES	2-02-002 BURGLARS	3-03-003 BUSTED
1-01-001 BUCKWHEAT	1-01-001 BULL-LIKE	4-02-003 BURGLARY	3-02-002 BUSTER
1-01-001 BUCKY	1-01-001 BULL-NECKED	1-01-001 BURGOMASTER'S	1-01-001 BUSTIN
1-01-001 BUCOLIC	1-01-001 BULL-ROARING	1-01-001 BURGUNDIAN	2-02-002 BUSTLE
1-01-001 BUCS	2-01-001 BULL-SESSIONS	1-01-001 BURGUNDIES	1-01-001 BUSTLIN
1-01-001 BUCS'	1-01-001 BULLDOZE	6-02-002 BURGUNDY	1-01-001 BUSTLING
9-07-009 BUD	28-08-019 BULLET	3-01-001 BURI	3-01-001 BUSTS
8-04-005 BUDAPEST	1-01-001 BULLET-RIDDLED	11-05-010 BURIAL	58-14-049 BUSY
5-02-002 BUDD	18-07-009 BULLETIN	18-07-015 BURIED	1-01-001 BUSY-WORK
1-01-001 BUDDED	1-01-001 BULLETIN'D	1-01-001 BURIES	1-01-001 BUSYNESS
8-03-004 BUDDHA	4-03-004 BULLETINS	7-03-005 BURKE	4381-15-490 BUT
9-03-004 BUDDHISM	21-07-013 BULLETS	1-01-001 BURKE'S	1-01-001 BUTANE
4-03-004 BUDDHIST	1-01-001 BULLFINCH	1-01-001 BURKE-ROSTAGNO	8-02-002 BUTCHER
2-01-001 BUDDHISTS	1-01-001 BULLHIDE	2-01-001 BURKES	1-01-001 BUTCHERED
5-03-004 BUDDIES	2-02-002 BULLIES	1-01-001 BURKES'	5-02-002 BUTCHERY
1-01-001 BUDDING	1-01-001 BULLISH	1-01-001 BURKETTE	4-04-004 BUTLER
13-05-009 BUDDY	2-01-001 BULLOCH	2-01-001 BURL	3-03-003 BUTLERS
3-03-003 BUDGE	2-02-002 BULLS	1-01-001 BURLE	12-05-010 BUTT
59-07-026 BUDGET	3-02-003 BULLSHIT	1-01-001 BURLESON	1-01-001 BUTTE
1-01-001 BUDGET-ALTERING	1-01-001 BULLWHACKERS	2-02-002 BURLESQUE	3-01-001 BUTTED
1-01-001 BUDGET-MAKING	4-04-004 BULLY	1-01-001 BURLESQUES	27-06-012 BUTTER
3-02-003 BUDGETARY	1-01-001 BULLYBOYS	1-01-001 BURLEY	1-01-001 BUTTERFAT
2-02-002 BUDGETED	4-01-001 BULLYING	2-01-001 BURLINGAME	1-01-001 BUTTERFLIES
7-03-005 BUDGETING	7-01-001 BULTMANN	2-01-001 BURLINGHAM	2-01-002 BUTTERFLY
5-03-004 BUDGETS	5-05-005 BULTMANN'S	6-01-001 BURLINGTON	1-01-001 BUTTERNUT
1-01-001 BUDIESHEIN	7-04-005 BULWARK	1-01-001 BURLINGTON'S	1-01-001 BUTTERWYN
1-01-001 BUDLONG	1-01-001 BUM	3-03-003 BURLY	1-01-001 BUTTERY
5-04-004 BUDS	2-01-001 BUMBLE-BEE	17-06-006 BURMA	1-01-001 BUTTING
1-01-001 BUDWEISERS	10-01-001 BUMBLEBEE	2-01-001 BURMAN	1-01-001 BUTTOCKS
1-01-001 BUDZYN	1-01-001 BUMBLEBEES	1-01-001 BURMAN'S	10-03-004 BUTTON
1-01-001 BUELL	1-01-001 BUMMING	1-01-001 BURMANS	1-01-001 BUTTON'S
1-01-001 BUELL'S	5-05-005 BUMP	4-02-002 BURMESE	2-02-002 BUTTON-DOWN
1-01-001 BUENA	2-02-002 BUMPED	15-07-013 BURN	1-01-001 BUTTONED
1-01-001 BUENAS	2-02-002 BUMPER	1-01-001 BURNE	1-01-001 BUTTONHOLES
1-01-001 BUENO	1-01-001 BUMPERS	40-12-033 BURNED	10-05-006 BUTTONS
5-03-004 BUFF	1-01-001 BUMPIN	1-01-001 BURNED-OUT	1-01-001 BUTTRESSED
16-06-012 BUFFALO	2-02-002 BUMPING	2-02-002 BURNERS	1-01-001 BUTTRESSES
1-01-001 BUFFALOES	1-01-001 BUMPS	1-01-001 BURNES	1-01-001 BUTTRICK
16-02-004 BUFFER	1-01-001 BUMPTIOUS	2-01-001 BURNET	5-04-005 BUTTS
4-01-001 BUFFERED	2-02-002 BUMS	1-01-001 BURNHAM	1-01-001 BUTYL-LITHIUM
6-04-006 BUFFET	1-01-001 BUN	1-01-001 BURNHAM'S	9-01-001 BUTYRATE
2-02-002 BUFFETED	17-09-014 BUNCH	50-12-034 BURNING	1-01-001 BUXOM
1-01-001 BUFFETINGS	1-01-001 BUNCHA	2-02-002 BURNINGS	1-01-001 BUXTEHUDE
1-01-001 BUFFETS	5-05-005 BUNCHED	1-01-001 BURNISHED	1-01-001 BUXTON
1-01-001 BUFFOON	1-01-001 BUNDESTAG	23-06-009 BURNS	70-12-043 BUY
1-01-001 BUFFOONS	20-08-012 BUNDLE	1-01-001 BURNS'S	2-02-002 BUYER
1-01-001 BUFFS	3-03-003 BUNDLED	7-03-003 BURNSIDE	2-02-002 BUYER'S
4-02-002 BUG	7-04-005 BUNDLES	4-01-001 BURNSIDE'S	5-04-005 BUYERS
1-01-001 BUGATTI	2-02-002 BUNDY	5-01-001 BURNSIDES	1-01-001 BUYERS'
1-01-001 BUGEYED	1-01-001 BUNGALOW	1-01-001 BURNSIDES'	1-01-001 BUYIN
2-02-002 BUGGED	1-01-001 BUNGLED	6-03-006 BURNT	30-10-023 BUYING
1-01-001 BUGGERS	18-04-006 BUNK	1-01-001 BURNT-RED	11-06-008 BUYS
1-01-001 BUGGIES	3-01-002 BUNKER	7-04-004 BURR	13-04-004 BUZZ
3-01-001 BUGGING	1-01-001 BUNKERED	1-01-001 BURR'S	1-01-001 BUZZ'S
6-04-004 BUGGY	1-01-001 BUNKMATE	1-01-001 BURR-HEADED	1-01-001 BUZZ-BUZZ-BUZZ
2-02-002 BUGLE	1-01-001 BUNKMATES	1-01-001 BURRO	2-02-002 BUZZED
1-01-001 BUGLER	17-05-007 BUNKS	4-02-002 BURROW	2-02-002 BUZZES
8-05-007 BUGS	1-01-001 BUNNY	1-01-001 BURROWED	6-03-005 BUZZING
3-02-002 BUICK	8-01-001 BUNS	1-01-001 BURROWING	5305-15-498 BY
86-14-056 BUILD	3-02-003 BUNT	2-01-001 BURROWS	1-01-001 BY-GONE
1-01-001 BUILD-BETTER-FO	1-01-001 BUNTER	1-01-001 BURRS	2-01-001 BY-LAWS
R-LESS	1-01-001 BUNTERS	33-13-032 BURST	1-01-001 BY-PASS
4-03-004 BUILD-UP	2-02-002 BUNYAN	13-06-013 BURSTING	1-01-001 BY-PASSED
29-04-010 BUILDER	1-01-001 BUOYANCY	2-02-002 BURSTS	1-01-001 BY-PASSES
2-02-002 BUILDER'S	2-02-002 BUOYANT	1-01-001 BURT	2-02-002 BY-PASSING
1-01-001 BUILDER-DEALER	1-01-001 BUOYED	15-02-002 BURTON	3-02-003 BY-PRODUCT
			2-02-002 BY-PRODUCTS

1-01-001	BY-ROADS	1-01-001	CAIUS
1-01-001	BY-THE-*SEA	13-08-011	CAKE
1-01-001	BY-WAYS	2-01-002	CAKED
1-01-001	BY-WORD	3-02-002	CAKES
2-02-002	BYE	2-02-002	CAL
1-01-001	BYER-*ROLNICK	1-01-001	CAL-*NEVA
2-02-002	BYGONE	2-01-001	CALABRIA
1-01-001	BYINGE	1-01-001	CALAMITIES
1-01-001	BYLINE	2-02-002	CALAMITOUS
1-01-001	BYLOT	4-03-003	CALAMITY
3-02-003	BYPASS	1-01-001	CALCIFICATION
1-01-001	BYPASSED	1-01-001	CALCIFIED
2-02-002	BYPRODUCT	11-04-008	CALCIUM
3-02-002	BYPRODUCTS	1-01-001	CALCULABLE
9-06-007	BYRD	4-03-004	CALCULATE
3-02-002	BYRD'S	35-08-023	CALCULATED
2-01-001	BYRNES	7-06-007	CALCULATING
16-04-006	BYRON	12-04-010	CALCULATION
4-03-003	BYRON'S	10-04-007	CALCULATIONS
1-01-001	BYRONIC	1-01-001	CALCULATORS
1-01-001	BYRONISM	1-01-001	CALCULI
1-01-001	BYSTANDER	4-01-001	CALCUTTA
1-01-001	BYSTRZYCA	2-01-001	CALDER
1-01-001	BYWORD	6-01-001	CALDERONE
5-03-003	BYZANTINE	3-02-002	CALDWELL
1-01-001	BYZANTIUM	2-02-002	CALDWELL'S
1-01-001	BYZAS	1-01-001	CALEB
130-11-076	C	5-01-001	CALENDA
7-01-002	C)	28-06-012	CALENDAR
1-01-001	C)**C	11-02-002	CALENDARS
1-01-001	C**.*A**.*I**.*	11-06-008	CALF
	P	1-01-001	CALF'S-FOOT
2-01-001	C**.*C**.*B	1-01-001	CALFSKIN
1-01-001	C**.*C**.*N**.*	10-03-004	CALHOUN
	Y	1-01-001	CALHOUN'S
2-01-001	C'EST	8-03-004	CALIBER
5-04-004	C'MON	3-01-001	CALIBERS
1-01-001	C'N	3-03-003	CALIBRATED
1-01-001	C'UN	1-01-001	CALIBRATING
1-01-001	C**U	6-02-002	CALIBRATION
2-02-002	CA	1-01-001	CALIBRATIONS
12-05-007	CAB	2-01-002	CALIBRE
2-01-001	CAB'S	1-01-001	CALICHE-TOPPED
4-02-002	CABANA	2-02-002	CALICO
2-01-001	CABANAS	19-04-008	CALIF
1-01-001	CABARET	65-15-037	CALIFORNIA
4-02-003	CABBAGE	3-02-003	CALIFORNIA'S
1-01-001	CABDRIVER	1-01-001	CALIFORNIANS
23-10-013	CABIN	1-01-001	CALIGULA
17-06-013	CABINET	1-01-001	CALIMALA
1-01-001	CABINETMAKERS	2-01-001	CALINDA
5-04-004	CABINETS	2-01-001	CALIPER
7-04-005	CABINS	1-01-001	CALIPERS
7-04-006	CABLE	1-01-001	CALIPHS
1-01-001	CABLED	4-03-004	CALISTHENICS
2-02-002	CABLES	188-15-129	CALL
2-02-002	CABOT	1-01-001	CALL-BACKS
1-01-001	CABOT'S	1-01-001	CALLABLE
4-01-001	CABRINI	1-01-001	CALLAN
1-01-001	CABS	2-02-002	CALLAS
1-01-001	CACAO	401-15-233	CALLED
1-01-001	CACHE	2-02-002	CALLER
3-02-003	CACKLED	3-02-002	CALLERS
1-01-001	CACKLY	1-01-001	CALLIGRAPHERS
1-01-001	CACOPHONIST	1-01-001	CALLIGRAPHY
1-01-001	CACOPHONY	1-01-001	CALLIN
1-01-001	CADAVER	45-12-043	CALLING
1-01-001	CADAVEROUS	7-05-007	CALLOUS
1-01-001	CADDY	2-02-002	CALLOUSED
2-02-002	CADENCE	1-01-001	CALLOUSLY
3-02-003	CADENZA	2-02-002	CALLOUSNESS
1-01-001	CADESI	70-12-053	CALLS
4-04-004	CADET	1-01-001	CALLUSES
9-04-005	CADILLAC	35-11-032	CALM
2-02-002	CADILLACS	6-05-004	CALMED
2-02-002	CADMIUM	2-02-002	CALMER
3-03-003	CADRE	1-01-001	CALMEST
27-01-001	CADY	2-02-002	CALMING
6-04-005	CAESAR	11-06-009	CALMLY
2-01-001	CAETANI	2-02-002	CALMNESS
20-10-015	CAFE	3-01-001	CALORIC
5-02-002	CAFES	1-01-001	CALORIE
15-05-006	CAFETERIA	1-01-001	CALORIE-HEAVY
2-02-002	CAFETERIAS	7-02-002	CALORIES
1-01-001	CAFRITZ	2-01-001	CALORIMETER
1-01-001	CAGAYAN	1-01-001	CALORIMETRIC
9-05-006	CAGE	1-01-001	CALTECH
1-01-001	CAGED	1-01-001	CALTECH'S
2-01-001	CAGES	1-01-001	CALUDE
2-02-002	CAGEY	1-01-001	CALUMNIATED
1-01-001	CAHILL	1-01-001	CALUMNY
1-01-001	CAHOOTS	2-01-001	CALVARY
2-02-002	CAIN	6-02-002	CALVES
1-01-001	CAIN'T	4-02-002	CALVIN
1-01-001	CAIRNS	3-01-001	CALVING
5-02-003	CAIRO	1-01-001	CALVINIST
1-01-001	CAIROLI	1-01-001	CALYPSO

1-01-001	CAM	12-07-009	CANE
2-02-002	CAMARADERIE	1-01-001	CANE'S
4-01-001	CAMARET	1-01-001	CANELI
1-01-001	CAMBODIA	1-01-001	CANESTRANI
1-01-001	CAMBODIA'S	1-01-001	CANINE
15-07-011	CAMBRIDGE	2-01-001	CANISTER
1-01-001	CAMBRIDGEPORT	1-01-001	CANISTERS
2-02-002	CAMDEN	1-01-001	CANKER
622-15-261	CAME	6-03-003	CANNED
1-01-001	CAMEL	1-01-001	CANNERIES
1-01-001	CAMELLIAS	14-01-001	CANNERY
1-01-001	CAMELOT	1-01-001	CANNIBALISTIC
1-01-001	CAMELS	2-01-001	CANNIBALS
1-01-001	CAMEO	7-03-003	CANNING
1-01-001	CAMEO-LIKE	7-04-006	CANNON
1-01-001	CAMEOS	1-01-001	CANNONBALL
36-11-017	CAMERA	258-14-150	CANNOT
1-01-001	CAMERA'S	2-01-001	CANNY
1-01-001	CAMERAMEN	7-04-004	CANOE
9-07-008	CAMERAS	2-02-002	CANOES
1-01-001	CAMERON	5-02-003	CANON
1-01-001	CAMI	1-01-001	CANONIST
2-02-002	CAMILLA	2-02-002	CANONIZED
1-01-001	CAMILLE	6-04-004	CANONS
1-01-001	CAMILO	2-01-001	CANOPY
3-03-003	CAMOUFLAGE	5-03-003	CANS
2-02-002	CAMOUFLAGED	1-01-001	CANT
75-10-034	CAMP	1-01-001	CANTALOUPE
1-01-001	CAMP'S	1-01-001	CANTED
1-01-001	CAMP-MADE	2-01-001	CANTEEN
1-01-001	CAMPAGNA	1-01-001	CANTELOUBE
1-01-001	CAMPAGNOLI	1-01-001	CANTER
81-12-037	CAMPAIGN	4-03-003	CANTERBURY
1-01-001	CAMPAIGN'S	1-01-001	CANTERED
1-01-001	CAMPAIGNE	1-01-001	CANTICLE
4-03-004	CAMPAIGNED	1-01-001	CANTILEVERS
2-01-001	CAMPAIGNERS	1-01-001	CANTING
4-03-003	CAMPAIGNING	1-01-001	CANTLES
17-07-013	CAMPAIGNS	3-02-002	CANTO
4-03-004	CAMPBELL	1-01-001	CANTONESE
1-01-001	CAMPED	1-01-001	CANTONMENT
3-01-001	CAMPER	1-01-001	CANTOR
9-01-001	CAMPERS	1-01-001	CANUTE
2-01-002	CAMPFIRE	19-11-016	CANVAS
3-01-001	CAMPGROUND	8-04-005	CANVASES
2-01-001	CAMPGROUNDS	3-03-003	CANVASS
18-01-003	CAMPING	2-01-001	CANVASSED
2-01-001	CAMPING-OUT	2-01-001	CANVASSERS
1-01-001	CAMPITELLI	1-01-001	CANVASSING
1-01-001	CAMPMATE	12-04-007	CANYON
1-01-001	CAMPO	2-02-002	CANYONS
1-01-001	CAMPOBELLO	1-01-001	CANYONSIDE
18-07-013	CAMPS	27-09-018	CAP
2-01-001	CAMPSITES	1-01-001	CAP'N
33-07-015	CAMPUS	1-01-001	CAP-AND-BALL
1-01-001	CAMPUSES	22-05-012	CAPABILITIES
1-01-001	CAMS	14-04-005	CAPABILITY
4-01-001	CAMUSFEARNA	66-14-050	CAPABLE
1772-15-401	CAN	1-01-001	CAPABLY
169-14-106	CAN'T	1-01-001	CAPACIOUS
34-11-026	CANADA	1-01-001	CAPACITANCE
1-01-001	CANADA'S	5-03-005	CAPACITIES
7-06-007	CANADIAN	2-02-002	CAPACITOR
1-01-001	CANADIAN'S	1-01-001	CAPACITORS
2-02-002	CANADIANS	83-14-052	CAPACITY
3-03-003	CANAL	20-10-016	CAPE
1-01-001	CANALS	1-01-001	CAPEK'S
1-01-001	CANANDAIGUA	1-01-001	CAPELLAN
1-01-001	CANAVERAL'S	1-01-001	CAPELLO
7-04-005	CANCEL	6-02-002	CAPER
6-04-004	CANCELED	1-01-001	CAPERCAILZIE
1-01-001	CANCELING	1-01-001	CAPERING
2-02-002	CANCELLATION	1-01-001	CAPERS
1-01-001	CANCELLED	4-03-004	CAPES
1-01-001	CANCELLING	2-01-001	CAPET
1-01-001	CANCELS	1-01-001	CAPETOWN
25-07-011	CANCER	8-01-004	CAPILLARY
1-01-001	CANCER-RIDDEN	1-01-001	CAPISTRANO
1-01-001	CANCERS	16-03-003	CAPITA
3-03-003	CANDID	85-10-040	CAPITAL
6-03-005	CANDIDACY	3-02-002	CAPITAL'S
34-09-020	CANDIDATE	1-01-001	CAPITAL-GAINS
1-01-001	CANDIDATE-PICKI	14-06-010	CAPITALISM
	NG	6-05-005	CAPITALIST
38-08-017	CANDIDATES	1-01-001	CAPITALIST-DEMO
1-01-001	CANDIDATES'		CRATI
1-01-001	CANDIDE	2-01-002	CAPITALISTIC
2-01-001	CANDIDLY	2-02-002	CAPITALISTS
2-02-002	CANDIES	1-01-001	CAPITALISTS'
18-07-011	CANDLE	4-04-004	CAPITALIZE
1-01-001	CANDLELIGHT	2-02-002	CAPITALIZING
5-03-004	CANDLES	4-02-002	CAPITALS
1-01-001	CANDLESTICK	22-05-012	CAPITOL
1-01-001	CANDLEWICK	1-01-001	CAPITOLINE
2-02-002	CANDOR	2-01-002	CAPITULATED
1-01-001	CANDOUR	2-01-001	CAPITULATION
16-06-011	CANDY	2-01-001	CAPO

Code	Word	Code	Word	Code	Word	Code	Word
6-02-002	CAPONE	7-05-005	CARIBBEAN	1-01-001	CARTELS	1-01-001	CATACLYSMIC
1-01-001	CAPONE'S	2-02-002	CARICATURE	7-05-005	CARTER	3-02-002	CATALOG
1-01-001	CAPOTE	1-01-001	CARICATURED	1-01-001	CARTERS	2-01-001	CATALOGS
2-02-002	CAPPED	1-01-001	CARICATURIST	1-01-001	CARTESIAN	8-05-006	CATALOGUE
12-01-001	CAPPY	10-06-009	CARING	1-01-001	CARTHAGE	4-04-004	CATALOGUED
1-01-001	CAPPY'S	41-07-014	CARL	1-01-001	CARTHAGO	3-03-003	CATALOGUES
1-01-001	CAPRICIOUS	4-01-001	CARL'S	2-02-002	CARTILAGE	3-02-002	CATALYST
1-01-001	CAPRICORN	16-03-003	CARLA	1-01-001	CARTONS	2-01-001	CATALYSTS
6-05-006	CAPS	1-01-001	CARLA'S	3-03-003	CARTOON	2-02-002	CATALYTIC
1-01-001	CAPSICUM	29-01-001	CARLETON	3-01-001	CARTOONIST	2-02-002	CATAPULTED
1-01-001	CAPSTAN	1-01-001	CARLETON'S	1-01-001	CARTOONISTS	1-01-001	CATAPULTING
5-04-006	CAPSULE	1-01-001	CARLETONIAN	6-04-005	CARTOONS	1-01-001	CATAPULTS
3-02-002	CAPSULES	1-01-001	CARLISLE	6-03-004	CARTRIDGE	11-08-011	CATASTROPHE
5-02-004	CAPT	2-02-002	CARLO	5-04-004	CARTRIDGES	5-03-004	CATASTROPHES
85-10-024	CAPTAIN	3-02-002	CARLOAD	5-03-003	CARTS	5-03-003	CATASTROPHIC
7-04-005	CAPTAIN'S	1-01-001	CARLOADING	2-02-002	CARTWHEELS	2-02-002	CATASTROPHICALLY
1-01-001	CAPTAINCY	1-01-001	CARLOADS	1-01-001	CARTY		
1-01-001	CAPTAINS	3-02-002	CARLSON	2-02-002	CARUSO	7-01-001	CATATONIA
1-01-001	CAPTIONS	1-01-001	CARLYLE'S	2-02-002	CARVALHO	43-13-036	CATCH
1-01-001	CAPTIOUS	2-01-002	CARMACK	3-02-003	CARVE	1-01-001	CATCHEE
2-02-002	CAPTIVATED	2-01-002	CARMEN	14-07-013	CARVED	17-04-005	CATCHER
2-02-002	CAPTIVATING	10-01-001	CARMER	1-01-001	CARVED-OUT-OF-SOLID	1-01-001	CATCHER'S
5-03-005	CAPTIVE	3-01-001	CARMER'S			1-01-001	CATCHERS
2-02-002	CAPTIVES	1-01-001	CARMICHAEL	1-01-001	CARVEN	2-02-002	CATCHES
4-03-003	CAPTIVITY	2-02-002	CARMINE	1-01-001	CARVER	9-06-009	CATCHING
2-01-002	CAPTORS	2-01-001	CARMODY	5-01-001	CARVEY	1-01-001	CATCHUP
17-07-017	CAPTURE	2-01-001	CARNAL	6-04-004	CARVING	1-01-001	CATCHWORDS
17-09-013	CAPTURED	2-02-002	CARNALITY	2-02-002	CARVINGS	1-01-001	CATCHY
2-01-002	CAPTURES	1-01-001	CARNARVON'S	2-01-001	CARWOOD	2-01-001	CATE'S
2-02-002	CAPTURING	3-01-001	CARNE	1-01-001	CARWOOD'S	2-02-002	CATECHISM
274-13-078	CAR	2-01-001	CARNEGEY	1-01-001	CARYATIDES	1-01-001	CATECHIZE
7-05-005	CAR'S	8-03-005	CARNEGIE	1-01-001	CASALS	1-01-001	CATECHOLAMINES
1-01-001	CARABAO	1-01-001	CARNEGIE-*ILLINOIS	1-01-001	CASANOVA	3-01-003	CATEGORICAL
1-01-001	CARACAS			2-02-002	CASASSA	1-01-001	CATEGORICALLY
1-01-001	CARAMEL	1-01-001	CARNEIGIE	3-01-001	CASBAH	24-07-021	CATEGORIES
1-01-001	CARAUSIUS	1-01-001	CARNEY	1-01-001	CASCA	1-01-001	CATEGORIZE
2-02-002	CARAVAGGIO	9-05-006	CARNIVAL	1-01-001	CASCADE	1-01-001	CATEGORIZED
8-03-004	CARAVAN	1-01-001	CARNOCHAN	1-01-001	CASCADED	1-01-001	CATEGORIZING
1-01-001	CARAVAN'S	1-01-001	CAROB	1-01-001	CASCADES	23-08-017	CATEGORY
2-02-002	CARAVANS	2-01-001	CAROL	3-01-001	CASCADING	4-03-004	CATER
2-02-002	CARAWAY	3-01-001	CAROLI	362-15-202	CASE	1-01-001	CATERED
2-01-001	CARBIDE	25-07-015	CAROLINA	1-01-001	CASE'S	1-01-001	CATERER'S
6-02-003	CARBINE	1-01-001	CAROLINA'S	1-01-001	CASE-BY-CASE	3-03-003	CATERING
2-02-002	CARBINES	1-01-001	CAROLINAS	1-01-001	CASE-HARDENED	1-01-001	CATERPILLAR
1-01-001	CARBOHYDRATE	2-02-002	CAROLINE	2-01-002	CASE-HISTORY	1-01-001	CATERPILLARS
2-01-001	CARBOLOY	1-01-001	CAROLINGIAN	1-01-001	CASE-TO-CASE	2-01-001	CATFISH
30-03-007	CARBON	3-02-002	CAROLINIANS	1-01-001	CASEBOOK	5-03-004	CATHARSIS
1-01-001	CARBON-HALOGEN	1-01-001	CAROLS	1-01-001	CASED	8-06-008	CATHEDRAL
1-01-001	CARBON-14	1-01-001	CAROLYN	1-01-001	CASEIN	3-03-003	CATHEDRALS
1-01-001	CARBONATES	1-01-001	CARON	148-14-094	CASES	4-03-004	CATHERINE
2-01-001	CARBONDALE	2-02-002	CAROUSING	13-01-001	CASEWORK	2-01-001	CATHERINE'S
1-01-001	CARBONES	1-01-001	CARPATHIANS	1-01-001	CASEWORKERS	2-01-001	CATHERWOOD
2-01-001	CARBONS	6-03-003	CARPENTER	23-03-007	CASEY	3-02-002	CATHETER
1-01-001	CARBONYL	3-02-002	CARPENTER'S	2-01-001	CASEY'S	10-01-002	CATHODE
1-01-001	CARBORUNDUM	3-03-003	CARPENTERS	36-11-026	CASH	4-01-001	CATHODOLUMINESCENT
1-01-001	CARBOXY-LABELED	1-01-001	CARPENTERS'	1-01-001	CASHED		
1-01-001	CARBOXYMETHYL	1-01-001	CARPENTIER	1-01-001	CASHEWS	1-01-001	CATHODOPHORETIC
7-05-005	CARCASS	4-03-003	CARPENTRY	2-02-002	CASHMERE	84-08-022	CATHOLIC
1-01-001	CARCASSES	13-06-009	CARPET	2-02-002	CASINO	8-03-004	CATHOLICISM
1-01-001	CARCINOMA	3-02-003	CARPETED	1-01-001	CASINO'S	33-06-011	CATHOLICS
26-09-018	CARD	2-02-002	CARPETING	1-01-001	CASK	1-01-001	CATHOLICS'
1-01-001	CARDAMOM	4-03-003	CARPETS	1-01-001	CASKETS	20-02-002	CATHY'S
5-04-005	CARDBOARD	3-03-003	CARPING	1-01-001	CASKS	1-01-001	CATINARI
1-01-001	CARDIAC	2-01-002	CARPORT	1-01-001	CASSIOPEIA	2-01-001	CATKIN
15-09-013	CARDINAL	2-02-002	CARR	1-01-001	CASSITE	5-01-001	CATKINS
8-04-006	CARDINALS	1-01-001	CARRARA	1-01-001	CASSIUS	1-01-001	CATLIKE
1-01-001	CARDIOMEGALY	3-01-001	CARRAWAY	1-01-001	CASSOCKED	1-01-001	CATON'S
1-01-001	CARDIOVASCULAR	2-02-002	CARRE	45-13-030	CAST	18-06-011	CATS
1-01-001	CARDIOVASCULATORY	1-01-001	CARREER	1-01-001	CAST-IRON	5-02-002	CATSKILL
		1-01-001	CARREL	2-01-001	CASTANEDA	2-02-002	CATSKILLS
36-13-022	CARDS	1-01-001	CARREON	1-01-001	CASTANETS	3-01-002	CATSUP
162-15-104	CARE	1-01-001	CARREON'S	3-03-003	CASTE	4-01-001	CATT
1-01-001	CARE-FREE	11-04-007	CARRIAGE	1-01-001	CASTERS	1-01-001	CATTALOE
15-08-013	CARED	1-01-001	CARRIAGE-STEP	1-01-001	CASTIGATED	97-09-020	CATTLE
1-01-001	CAREENED	6-05-006	CARRIAGES	1-01-001	CASTIGATES	1-01-001	CATTLE-CAR
1-01-001	CAREENING	1-01-001	CARRIE	1-01-001	CASTIGATION	3-02-002	CATTLEMEN
67-13-046	CAREER	125-14-097	CARRIED	1-01-001	CASTILLO	1-01-001	CAUCASIAN
1-01-001	CAREER-BOUND	9-06-006	CARRIER	4-03-004	CASTING	1-01-001	CAUCASUS
1-01-001	CAREERISM	1-01-001	CARRIER-BASED	7-04-007	CASTLE	2-01-001	CAUCUS
14-07-011	CAREERS	1-01-001	CARRIER-CURRENT	4-03-004	CASTLES	1-01-001	CAUCUSES
9-04-007	CAREFREE	11-06-008	CARRIERS	2-01-001	CASTOR	1-01-001	CAUCUSING
62-14-056	CAREFUL	22-09-020	CARRIES	1-01-001	CASTORBEAN	1-01-001	CAUFFMAN
87-13-069	CAREFULLY	17-04-008	CARROLL	1-01-001	CASTORBEANS	98-14-073	CAUGHT
1-01-001	CAREFULNESS	1-01-001	CARROT	32-05-014	CASTRO	1-01-001	CAULIFLOWER
8-06-008	CARELESS	4-03-003	CARROTS	5-04-004	CASTRO'S	6-01-001	CAUSAL
3-03-003	CARELESSLY	1-01-001	CARROZZA	1-01-001	CASTRO-HELD	1-01-001	CAUSALLY
2-02-002	CARELESSNESS	5-02-003	CARRUTHERS	2-01-001	CASTROISM	1-01-001	CAUSATIVE
9-07-008	CARES	88-13-075	CARRY	2-01-002	CASTROS	1-01-001	CAUSE
1-01-001	CARESS	71-14-060	CARRYING	6-05-006	CASTS	130-14-099	CAUSE
4-02-003	CARESSED	12-02-002	CARRYOVER	22-12-021	CASUAL	2-02-002	CAUSE-AND-EFFECT
5-03-003	CARESSES	1-01-001	CARRYOVERS	13-07-013	CASUALLY		
5-03-005	CARESSING	112-13-048	CARS	1-01-001	CASUALS	90-14-071	CAUSED
1-01-001	CARETAKER	2-02-002	CARSON	3-02-003	CASUALTIES	58-09-041	CAUSES
1-01-001	CAREWORN	1-01-001	CARSTEN	3-02-002	CASUALTY	18-09-017	CAUSING
5-01-003	CAREY	5-04-004	CART	23-09-015	CAT	1-01-001	CAUTERIZE
1-01-001	CARGILL'S	1-01-001	CARTE	1-01-001	CAT'S	19-07-014	CAUTION
7-04-005	CARGO	1-01-001	CARTED	1-01-001	CAT-LIKE	6-05-005	CAUTIONED

1-01-001	CAUTIONS	11-04-006	CENSUS	1-01-001	CHADROE	1-01-001	CHAPERONED
10-06-010	CAUTIOUS	3-01-001	CENSUSES	2-01-001	CHADWICK	5-04-004	CHAPLAIN
9-04-009	CAUTIOUSLY	158-11-053	CENT	1-01-001	CHAFE	1-01-001	CHAPLAINS
1-01-001	CAV	1-01-001	CENTENARY	1-01-001	CHAFFEY	3-02-002	CHAPLIN
1-01-001	CAV'S	6-05-006	CENTENNIAL	1-01-001	CHAFFING	6-01-004	CHAPMAN
1-01-001	CAVALCADES	224-15-115	CENTER	2-02-002	CHAFING	1-01-001	CHAPPELL
1-01-001	CAVALIERE	2-02-002	CENTER'S	4-04-004	CHAGRIN	1-01-001	CHAPS
1-01-001	CAVALLINIS	1-01-001	CENTER-FIRE	1-01-001	CHAHAR	74-14-043	CHAPTER
26-06-008	CAVALRY	2-01-001	CENTER-PUNCH	2-01-001	CHAIKOFF	1-01-001	CHAPTER'S
1-01-001	CAVALRYMEN	14-06-011	CENTERED	50-10-025	CHAIN	16-06-012	CHAPTERS
2-01-001	CAVANAGH	5-04-004	CENTERING	1-01-001	CHAIN-REACTION	1-01-001	CHAR
9-05-007	CAVE	1-01-001	CENTERLINE	1-01-001	CHAINLIKE	118-14-083	CHARACTER
1-01-001	CAVE-LIKE	52-10-032	CENTERS	10-07-007	CHAINS	1-01-001	CHARACTER-EDUCA
1-01-001	CAVE-MEN	1-01-001	CENTIGRADE	66-13-048	CHAIR		TION
1-01-001	CAVEAT	2-01-001	CENTIMETER	1-01-001	CHAIRING	68-08-049	CHARACTERISTIC
1-01-001	CAVED	1-01-001	CENTIMETER-	67-08-042	CHAIRMAN	7-04-006	CHARACTERISTICA
1-01-001	CAVEMEN	8-01-001	CENTIMETERS	1-01-001	CHAIRMANSHIP		LLY
1-01-001	CAVERN	164-12-084	CENTRAL	1-01-001	CHAIRMANSHIPS	52-06-032	CHARACTERISTICS
1-01-001	CAVERNOUS	2-01-001	CENTRAL'S	9-04-006	CHAIRMEN	8-04-008	CHARACTERIZATIO
1-01-001	CAVERNS	2-01-001	CENTRAL-*B	23-10-020	CHAIRS		N
6-05-005	CAVES	2-01-001	CENTRAL-CITY	1-01-001	CHAISE	2-02-002	CHARACTERIZATIO
1-01-001	CAVIAR	1-01-001	CENTRALE	1-01-001	CHALIDALE		NS
1-01-001	CAVIN	1-01-001	CENTRALIA	3-03-003	CHALK	6-04-006	CHARACTERIZE
1-01-001	CAVING	4-01-001	CENTRALITY	1-01-001	CHALK-WHITE	21-06-016	CHARACTERIZED
1-01-001	CAVITIES	4-03-003	CENTRALIZATION	1-01-001	CHALKED	4-03-004	CHARACTERIZES
12-03-004	CAVITY	9-05-006	CENTRALIZED	1-01-001	CHALKY	1-01-001	CHARACTERIZING
1-01-001	CAVORT	2-02-002	CENTRALIZING	36-11-031	CHALLENGE	36-08-022	CHARACTERS
1-01-001	CAVORTED	6-02-005	CENTRALLY	9-05-008	CHALLENGED	14-03-005	CHARCOAL
2-02-002	CAVORTING	2-01-001	CENTRE	1-01-001	CHALLENGER	1-01-001	CHARCOAL-BROILE
1-01-001	CAWING	1-01-001	CENTREDALE	4-04-004	CHALLENGES		D
2-01-001	CAYENNE	1-01-001	CENTRIC	12-09-012	CHALLENGING	1-01-001	CHARCOALED
2-01-001	CC	1-01-001	CENTRIFUGAL	1-01-001	CHALMERS	1-01-001	CHARDON
1-01-001	CC).	1-01-001	CENTRIFUGATION	1-01-001	CHALON-SUR-*SAO	122-13-079	CHARGE
1-01-001	CC),	2-01-001	CENTRIFUGE		NE	1-01-001	CHARGE-A-PLATE
1-01-001	CEARTAINE	7-01-001	CENTRIFUGED	46-09-023	CHAMBER	3-01-001	CHARGE-EXCESS
15-06-015	CEASE	1-01-001	CENTRIFUGING	1-01-001	CHAMBERED	1-01-001	CHARGEABLE
7-02-004	CEASE-FIRE	1-01-001	CENTRIST	1-01-001	CHAMBERLAIN	57-11-037	CHARGED
12-08-012	CEASED	25-09-015	CENTS	3-02-002	CHAMBERMAID	45-10-031	CHARGES
3-02-003	CEASELESS	2-01-001	CENTS-PER-HOUR	1-01-001	CHAMBERMAIDS	1-01-001	CHARGIN
1-01-001	CEASELESSLY	6-01-002	CENTUM	11-07-011	CHAMBERS	8-06-008	CHARGING
3-03-003	CEASES	46-10-031	CENTURIES	5-02-002	CHAMBRE	3-03-003	CHARIOT
2-02-002	CEASING	2-02-002	CENTURIES-OLD	1-01-001	CHAMBRE'S	1-01-001	CHARISMA
1-01-001	CECIL	207-15-092	CENTURY	2-01-001	CHAMFER	5-05-005	CHARITABLE
3-02-003	CECILIA	1-01-001	CENTURY-*FOX	1-01-001	CHAMOIS	1-01-001	CHARITABLY
1-01-001	CEDAR	1-01-001	CEPHEUS	1-01-001	CHAMP	4-03-004	CHARITIES
1-01-001	CEDAR-ROOFED	1-01-001	CEPT	13-05-006	CHAMPAGNE	8-05-005	CHARITY
3-03-003	CEDRIC	1-01-001	CEPTIN	2-01-001	CHAMPASSAK	1-01-001	CHARLATANS
1-01-001	CEDVET	9-04-005	CERAMIC	23-07-013	CHAMPION	4-01-001	CHARLAYNE
2-01-001	CEECEE	3-03-003	CERAMICS	10-03-008	CHAMPIONS	96-12-057	CHARLES
1-01-001	CEIL	17-02-003	CEREAL	8-04-004	CHAMPIONSHIP	7-04-004	CHARLES'
31-10-022	CEILING	4-01-002	CEREALS	1-01-001	CHAMPIONSHIPS	1-01-001	CHARLES'S
1-01-001	CEILINGS	1-01-001	CEREBELLUM	3-02-002	CHAMPLAIN	2-02-002	CHARLESTON
1-01-001	CELEBES	8-05-005	CEREBRAL	3-03-003	CHAMPS	8-03-005	CHARLEY
2-02-002	CELEBRANTS	1-01-001	CEREBRATED	131-15-099	CHANCE	1-01-001	CHARLEY'S
4-03-004	CELEBRATE	3-03-003	CEREMONIAL	3-02-002	CHANCED	48-09-015	CHARLIE
14-09-014	CELEBRATED	1-01-001	CEREMONIALLY	1-01-001	CHANCEL	2-01-001	CHARLIE'S
2-02-002	CELEBRATES	14-06-011	CEREMONIES	14-05-007	CHANCELLOR	13-04-006	CHARLOTTE
5-05-005	CELEBRATING	1-01-001	CEREMONIOUSLY	1-01-001	CHANCELLORSVILL	3-01-001	CHARLOTTE'S
15-09-014	CELEBRATION	18-08-017	CEREMONY		E	3-03-003	CHARLOTTESVILL
2-02-002	CELEBRATIONS	1-01-001	CERISE	1-01-001	CHANCERIES	26-10-023	CHARM
3-03-003	CELEBRITIES	313-15-188	CERTAIN	2-01-001	CHANCERY	3-03-003	CHARMED
3-01-001	CELEBRITY	143-14-107	CERTAINLY	24-13-023	CHANCES	1-01-001	CHARMER
1-01-001	CELERITY	21-08-014	CERTAINTY	3-01-003	CHANDELIER	24-10-021	CHARMING
4-03-004	CELERY	7-06-006	CERTIFICATE	1-01-001	CHANDELIERS	1-01-001	CHARMINGLY
8-03-004	CELESTIAL	1-01-001	CERTIFICATES	1-01-001	CHANDELLE	2-02-002	CHARMS
1-01-001	CELIA	3-02-002	CERTIFICATION	32-07-007	CHANDLER	1-01-001	CHARNOCK
1-01-001	CELIAC	7-03-004	CERTIFIED	2-02-002	CHANDLER'S	1-01-001	CHARRED
1-01-001	CELIE	1-01-001	CERTIFIES	240-15-138	CHANGE	22-07-015	CHART
1-01-001	CELIE'S	5-02-002	CERTIFY	2-01-002	CHANGE-OVER	1-01-001	CHARTACEOS
65-06-018	CELL	1-01-001	CERTIFYING	5-01-001	CHANGEABLE	6-04-005	CHARTED
4-01-001	CELL-FREE	2-02-002	CERTIORARI	95-15-079	CHANGED	33-08-014	CHARTER
26-07-010	CELLAR	1-01-001	CERTITUDES	131-13-078	CHANGES	4-03-003	CHARTERED
1-01-001	CELLARS	1-01-001	CERULEAN	44-10-036	CHANGING	4-03-004	CHARTERS
2-02-002	CELLIST	5-01-001	CERV	16-07-012	CHANNEL	7-02-002	CHARTING
1-01-001	CELLOPHANE	1-01-001	CERVANTES	2-01-001	CHANNEL-TYPE	1-01-001	CHARTINGS
81-06-013	CELLS	1-01-001	CERVANTES'	3-03-003	CHANNELED	2-01-001	CHARTIST
3-02-002	CELLULAR	1-01-001	CERVELAT	23-07-008	CHANNELS	1-01-001	CHARTISTS
10-02-004	CELLULOSE	1-01-001	CERVETTO	5-01-001	CHANNING	2-01-002	CHARTRES
1-01-001	CELLULOSES	1-01-001	CESARE	1-01-001	CHANNING'S	2-01-001	CHARTROOM
1-01-001	CELSO	3-01-001	CESIUM-137	2-01-001	CHANSONS	9-05-009	CHARTS
7-01-002	CELTIC	1-01-001	CESSATION	2-02-002	CHANT	18-09-013	CHASE
1-01-001	CEMAL	2-01-001	CESSION	6-05-005	CHANTED	1-01-001	CHASED
11-06-011	CEMENT	2-01-001	CESTRE	1-01-001	CHANTER	2-01-001	CHASES
1-01-001	CEMENT-AND-GLAS	4-03-003	CETERA	2-01-001	CHANTEY	3-03-003	CHASING
	S	1-01-001	CETERAS	1-01-001	CHANTIER	2-02-002	CHASM
4-03-003	CEMENTED	5-04-004	CEYLON	1-01-001	CHANTILLY	1-01-001	CHASSIS
15-06-010	CEMETERY	2-02-002	CEZANNE	2-02-002	CHANTING	2-02-002	CHASTISEMENT
2-01-001	CEN-*TENNIAL	1-01-001	CEZANNE'S	3-03-003	CHANTS	2-02-002	CHASTITY
1-01-001	CENNINI	1-01-001	CEZANNES	17-07-011	CHAOS	5-05-005	CHAT
1-01-001	CENNINO	8-02-003	CF	5-03-005	CHAOTIC	3-02-002	CHATEAU
2-02-002	CENSORED	4-02-002	CH	5-03-005	CHAP	3-01-002	CHATHAM
1-01-001	CENSORIAL	2-01-001	CH'AN	20-06-016	CHAPEL	3-03-003	CHATTANOOGA
2-01-001	CENSORS	2-01-001	CH'IN	1-01-001	CHAPEL-LIKE	1-01-001	CHATTE
5-02-004	CENSORSHIP	1-01-001	CHA-CHAS	1-01-001	CHAPELLES	2-02-002	CHATTED
3-03-003	CENSURE	1-01-001	CHABLIS	2-02-002	CHAPELS	1-01-001	CHATTELS
1-01-001	CENSURED	2-01-001	CHABRIER	1-01-001	CHAPERON	7-05-006	CHATTER
2-01-002	CENSURES	2-01-001	CHABRIER'S	1-01-001	CHAPERONE	3-03-003	CHATTERED

Freq	Word	Freq	Word
6-05-006	CHATTERING	2-02-002	CHESTNUTS
2-02-002	CHATTING	4-04-004	CHESTS
1-01-001	CHATTY	1-01-001	CHEVALIER
1-01-001	CHAUCER	1-01-001	CHEVAUX
4-03-004	CHAUFFEUR	4-03-003	CHEVROLET
1-01-001	CHAUFFEUR'S	1-01-001	CHEVY
2-01-001	CHAUFFEUR-DRIVEN	2-02-002	CHEW
1-01-001	CHAUFFEURED	1-01-001	CHEWED
1-01-001	CHAULMOOGRA	13-06-010	CHEWING
2-02-002	CHAUNCEY	2-01-001	CHEYENNE
1-01-001	CHAUTAUQUA	3-02-002	CHEYENNES
1-01-001	CHAVES	1-01-001	CHI
4-01-001	CHAVEZ	1-01-001	CHI-CHI
2-01-001	CHAVIS	4-03-003	CHIANG
1-01-001	CHAW	1-01-001	CHIAROMONTE
1-01-001	CHE	1-01-001	CHIBA
24-10-021	CHEAP	7-03-007	CHIC
1-01-001	CHEAP-MONEY	98-11-046	CHICAGO
11-05-008	CHEAPER	10-05-007	CHICAGO'S
3-02-002	CHEAPLY	1-01-001	CHICAGO-STYLE
3-02-003	CHEAT	1-01-001	CHICAGOANS
4-04-004	CHEATED	1-01-001	CHICANERY
1-01-001	CHEATING	3-02-002	CHICK
88-12-057	CHECK	37-12-024	CHICKEN
1-01-001	CHECK-OUT	13-04-008	CHICKENS
5-03-003	CHECKBOOK	1-01-001	CHICKS
31-09-026	CHECKED	2-02-002	CHICO
1-01-001	CHECKER	2-02-002	CHIDE
1-01-001	CHECKIN	1-01-001	CHIDED
5-03-004	CHECKING	1-01-001	CHIDING
1-01-001	CHECKIT	119-14-082	CHIEF
3-03-003	CHECKLIST	3-02-003	CHIEF'S
17-09-014	CHECKS	1-01-001	CHIEFDOM
2-02-002	CHECKUP	1-01-001	CHIEFDOMS
1-01-001	CHEDDI	22-07-018	CHIEFLY
20-07-016	CHEEK	6-03-004	CHIEFS
1-01-001	CHEEKBONE	4-04-004	CHIEFTAIN
5-03-005	CHEEKBONES	1-01-001	CHIEFTAINS
13-06-012	CHEEKS	9-03-003	CHIEN
8-05-007	CHEER	1-01-001	CHIETI
1-01-001	CHEERE	1-01-001	CHIGGERS
2-02-002	CHEERED	1-01-001	CHIGNON
10-06-010	CHEERFUL	2-01-001	CHILBLAINS
5-04-005	CHEERFULLY	213-14-089	CHILD
1-01-001	CHEERFULNESS	33-09-016	CHILD'S
1-01-001	CHEERING	1-01-001	CHILD-BEARING
1-01-001	CHEERLEADERS	1-01-001	CHILD-CLOUD
4-03-004	CHEERS	1-01-001	CHILD-FACE
3-02-003	CHEERY	2-02-002	CHILD-REARING
9-07-008	CHEESE	3-03-003	CHILDBIRTH
1-01-001	CHEESECLOTH	1-01-001	CHILDE
1-01-001	CHEETAH	50-08-022	CHILDHOOD
1-01-001	CHEETAL	5-01-001	CHILDHOOD'S
9-04-007	CHEF	11-06-009	CHILDISH
1-01-001	CHEHEL	2-01-001	CHILDISHLY
2-02-002	CHEKHOV	4-03-003	CHILDISHNESS
1-01-001	CHELAS	4-02-004	CHILDLIKE
1-01-001	CHELMNO	355-15-132	CHILDREN
60-08-023	CHEMICAL	23-06-016	CHILDREN'S
5-04-005	CHEMICALLY	1-01-001	CHILE
4-04-004	CHEMICALS	6-01-001	CHILI
4-01-001	CHEMISCHE	14-06-013	CHILL
1-01-001	CHEMISE	7-04-006	CHILLED
1-01-001	CHEMIST'S	1-01-001	CHILLIER
1-01-001	CHEMISTRIES	5-04-005	CHILLING
16-08-013	CHEMISTRY	2-02-002	CHILLS
4-04-004	CHEMISTS	5-04-004	CHILLY
3-01-001	CHEN	1-01-001	CHIMERA-CHASING
1-01-001	CHENG	1-01-001	CHIMES
1-01-001	CHENNAULT'S	1-01-001	CHIMIQUES
3-01-001	CHENOWETH	7-04-005	CHIMNEY
5-04-004	CHERISH	3-03-003	CHIMNEYS
16-10-015	CHERISHED	27-08-018	CHIN
2-02-002	CHERISHING	1-01-001	CHIN-UPS
3-01-001	CHERKASOV	69-12-029	CHINA
1-01-001	CHERNISHEV	3-02-002	CHINA'S
2-02-002	CHEROKEE	1-01-001	CHINAMAN
1-01-001	CHEROKEES	5-01-001	CHINES
2-02-002	CHERRIES	56-10-023	CHINESE
6-04-005	CHERRY	1-01-001	CHINESE-*SOVIET
1-01-001	CHERRY-FLAVORED	1-01-001	CHINESE-INSPIRED
1-01-001	CHERUBIN	5-02-002	CHING
1-01-001	CHERWELL	1-01-001	CHINKED
1-01-001	CHES	3-03-003	CHINLESS
4-02-003	CHESAPEAKE	2-01-002	CHINNING
1-01-001	CHESHIRE	1-01-001	CHINS
1-01-001	CHESLY	2-01-001	CHION
3-03-003	CHESS	17-04-005	CHIP
53-12-033	CHEST	144-12-043	CHIP-O'S
1-01-001	CHEST-BACK-**JL AT-SHOULDER	9-01-001	CHIPPED
1-01-001	CHEST-BACK-SHOULDER	31-06-015	CHIPPENDALE
10-05-009	CHESTER	17-07-010	CHIPPER
1-01-001	CHESTERTON	2-01-001	CHIPPING
5-03-005	CHESTNUT	3-03-003	CHIPS

Freq	Word	Freq	Word
1-01-001	CHIROPRACTOR	2-01-002	CHRISTIE
1-01-001	CHIROPRACTOR'S	2-01-001	CHRISTINE
1-01-001	CHIRPED	1-01-001	CHRISTINE'S
1-01-001	CHIRPING	1-01-001	CHRISTLIKE
4-02-004	CHISEL	27-11-019	CHRISTMAS
1-01-001	CHISELED	1-01-001	CHRISTMAS-SEASON
1-01-001	CHISELS	2-01-001	CHRISTMASTIME
3-01-002	CHISHOLM	5-03-005	CHRISTOPHER
1-01-001	CHIUCHOW	1-01-001	CHRISTOPHERS'
2-02-002	CHIVALROUS	1-01-001	CHRISTSAKE
2-02-002	CHIVALRY	1-01-001	CHRISTY
1-01-001	CHIVE	9-03-004	CHROMATIC
1-01-001	CHIVES	1-01-001	CHROMATICS
1-01-001	CHIVYING	1-01-001	CHROMATOGRAM
5-03-003	CHLORIDE	3-01-002	CHROMATOGRAPHIC
1-01-001	CHLORIDES	9-01-002	CHROMATOGRAPHY
33-02-002	CHLORINE	4-02-002	CHROME
1-01-001	CHLORINE-CARBON	1-01-001	CHROMED
2-01-001	CHLOROTHIAZIDE	1-01-001	CHROMIC
1-01-001	CHLORPROMAZINE	4-01-001	CHROMIUM
1-01-001	CHLORTETRACYCLINE	1-01-001	CHROMIUM-PLATED
1-01-001	CHMN	1-01-001	CHROMIUM-SUBSTITUTED
1-01-001	CHOCKFULL	1-01-001	CHROMSPUN
9-06-007	CHOCOLATE	11-03-009	CHRONIC
1-01-001	CHOCTAW	1-01-001	CHRONICALLY
3-01-001	CHOCTAWS	5-03-005	CHRONICLE
113-13-075	CHOICE	1-01-001	CHRONICLE'S
12-07-009	CHOICES	1-01-001	CHRONICLED
2-02-002	CHOICEST	1-01-001	CHRONICLERS
8-05-006	CHOIR	2-01-002	CHRONICLES
1-01-001	CHOIR'S	7-04-005	CHRONOLOGICAL
9-05-006	CHOKE	2-02-002	CHRONOLOGICALLY
7-04-007	CHOKED	5-04-005	CHRONOLOGY
7-06-007	CHOKING	1-01-001	CHRYSANTHEMUMS
1-01-001	CHOLE	3-03-003	CHRYSLER
1-01-001	CHOLELITHIASIS	1-01-001	CHRYSLER'S
1-01-001	CHOLERA	2-02-002	CHUBBY
21-03-003	CHOLESTEROL	14-05-008	CHUCK
1-01-001	CHOLESTEROL-RICH	1-01-001	CHUCK-A-LUCK
1-01-001	CHOLINESTERASE	5-04-004	CHUCKLE
1-01-001	CHOMP	8-04-007	CHUCKLED
50-14-039	CHOOSE	1-01-001	CHUCKLES
8-06-008	CHOOSES	1-01-001	CHUFFING
11-07-010	CHOOSING	2-02-002	CHUGGING
1-01-001	CHOOSY	1-01-001	CHUM
3-02-003	CHOP	1-01-001	CHUMMINESS
2-02-002	CHOPIN	1-01-001	CHUMP
1-01-001	CHOPIN'S	1-01-001	CHUNG
3-02-002	CHOPPED	2-02-002	CHUNK
1-01-001	CHOPPER	5-03-003	CHUNKS
5-03-005	CHOPPING	1-01-001	CHUNKY
3-02-002	CHOPPY	348-13-081	CHURCH
3-03-003	CHOPS	8-05-007	CHURCH'S
2-02-002	CHORAL	2-02-002	CHURCH-STATE
1-01-001	CHORALE	96-10-031	CHURCHES
7-06-006	CHORD	1-01-001	CHURCHGOERS
6-03-006	CHORDS	3-03-003	CHURCHGOING
7-05-007	CHORE	12-04-004	CHURCHILL
5-01-001	CHOREOGRAPHED	2-02-002	CHURCHILL'S
5-02-002	CHOREOGRAPHER	1-01-001	CHURCHILLIAN
4-02-002	CHOREOGRAPHERS	1-01-001	CHURCHLY
3-01-001	CHOREOGRAPHIC	3-02-002	CHURCHMEN
3-02-002	CHOREOGRAPHY	8-02-002	CHURCHYARD
16-10-015	CHORES	1-01-001	CHURNED
2-01-001	CHORINES	3-03-003	CHURNING
1-01-001	CHORING	1-01-001	CHURNS
3-03-003	CHORTLED	2-02-002	CHUTE
1-01-001	CHORTLING	1-01-001	CHUTNEY
18-09-013	CHORUS	1-01-001	CIAO
1-01-001	CHORUSED	1-01-001	CIARDI
2-02-002	CHORUSES	1-01-001	CIBULA'S
37-10-029	CHOSE	1-01-001	CICADAS
71-12-059	CHOSEN	5-01-001	CICERO
2-01-001	CHOU	1-01-001	CICERO'S
1-01-001	CHOUISE	1-01-001	CICERONIAN
1-01-001	CHOUSIN	1-01-001	CICIULLA
2-02-002	CHOW	1-01-001	CICOGNANI
1-01-001	CHOWDER	2-01-001	CIDER
1-01-001	CHOWDERS	1-01-001	CIECA
12-02-003	CHRIS	10-06-009	CIGAR
1-01-001	CHRISSAKE	1-01-001	CIGARET
97-10-030	CHRIST	25-08-020	CIGARETTE
20-05-007	CHRIST'S	12-05-011	CIGARETTES
3-03-003	CHRISTENDOM	2-02-002	CIGARS
2-01-002	CHRISTENED	1-01-001	CILIA
1-01-002	CHRISTENING	3-01-001	CILIATED
2-01-001	CHRISTI	1-01-001	CILIATES
144-12-043	CHRISTIAN	1-01-001	CIMABUE
9-01-001	CHRISTIANA	1-01-001	CIMABUE'S
31-06-015	CHRISTIANITY	1-01-001	CIMOLI
1-01-001	CHRISTIANIZING	3-02-003	CINCH
17-07-010	CHRISTIANS	1-01-001	CINCHES
2-01-001	CHRISTIANS'	9-02-006	CINCINNATI
2-01-001	CHRISTIANSEN	2-01-001	CINDER
		2-02-002	CINDERS

Code	Word	Code	Word	Code	Word	Code	Word
3-03-003	CINEMA	1-01-001	CLAIRVOYANT	16-08-016	CLEANED	3-01-001	CLINICO-PATHOLO GIC
1-01-001	CINEMACTOR	3-03-003	CLAM	9-05-007	CLEANER	2-02-002	CLINICS
3-01-001	CINEMATIC	6-03-005	CLAMBERED	8-04-004	CLEANERS	1-01-001	CLINKED
1-01-001	CINERAMA	1-01-001	CLAMBERING	37-08-019	CLEANING	4-01-003	CLINT
1-01-001	CINQ	2-02-002	CLAMMY	2-01-001	CLEANLY	3-01-002	CLINTON
1-01-001	CIPHER	2-02-002	CLAMOR	1-01-001	CLEANS	6-04-006	CLIP
2-01-002	CIPHERS	1-01-001	CLAMORED	1-01-001	CLEANSED	3-02-003	CLIPPED
1-01-001	CIPOLLA	1-01-001	CLAMORING	4-04-004	CLEANSING	1-01-001	CLIPPER
1-01-001	CIPRIANI'S	1-01-001	CLAMOROUS	1-01-001	CLEANTH	4-04-004	CLIPPINGS
1-01-001	CIR	1-01-001	CLAMORS	1-01-001	CLEANUPS	2-02-002	CLIPS
1-01-001	CIRCA	8-05-007	CLAMPED	219-15-149	CLEAR	2-02-002	CLIQUE
60-10-040	CIRCLE	3-03-003	CLAMPING	2-01-001	CLEAR-CHANNEL	1-01-001	CLIQUES
9-05-009	CIRCLED	6-02-002	CLAMPS	6-04-006	CLEAR-CUT	1-01-001	CLIVE
32-11-027	CIRCLES	2-02-002	CLAMS	1-01-001	CLEAR-HEADED	3-02-003	CLOAK
2-01-002	CIRCLING	1-01-001	CLAMSHELL	4-04-004	CLEARANCE	1-01-001	CLOAKROOMS
1-01-001	CIRCONSCRIPTION	2-02-002	CLAN	23-10-018	CLEARED	1-01-001	CLOBBER
1-01-001	CIRCONSCRIPTION S	1-01-001	CLANDESTINE	15-07-012	CLEARER	1-01-001	CLOBBERED
		1-01-001	CLANG	16-10-015	CLEARING	1-01-001	CLOBBERS
23-09-016	CIRCUIT	1-01-001	CLANGED	128-14-104	CLEARLY	20-09-015	CLOCK
1-01-001	CIRCUITOUS	1-01-001	CLANKING	2-02-002	CLEARNESS	1-01-001	CLOCKED
1-01-001	CIRCUITRY	1-01-001	CLANNISH	1-01-001	CLEARS	1-01-001	CLOCKING
4-03-003	CIRCUITS	1-01-001	CLANNISHNESS	1-01-001	CLEARWATER	8-05-006	CLOCKS
21-06-012	CIRCULAR	1-01-001	CLAP	1-01-001	CLEAT	3-03-003	CLOCKWISE
2-01-001	CIRCULARITY	4-02-004	CLAPPED	2-01-001	CLEAVAGE	1-01-001	CLOCKWORK
2-02-002	CIRCULATE	6-04-006	CLAPPING	1-01-001	CLEAVED	1-01-001	CLOD
4-03-004	CIRCULATED	2-02-002	CLAPS	1-01-001	CLEBURNE'S	1-01-001	CLODDISHNESS
5-04-004	CIRCULATING	3-03-003	CLARA	2-01-002	CLEFT	1-01-001	CLODHOPPERS
16-10-015	CIRCULATION	1-01-001	CLARE	1-01-001	CLEFTS	4-03-003	CLODS
2-02-002	CIRCULATORY	1-01-001	CLARENCE	1-01-001	CLEMENCE	2-02-002	CLOG
1-01-001	CIRCUMCISION	4-03-003	CLARET	2-02-002	CLEMENCEAU	2-01-002	CLOGGED
3-02-003	CIRCUMFERENCE	1-01-001	CLARETS	2-01-001	CLEMENCY	2-02-002	CLOGGING
1-01-001	CIRCUMLOCUTION	5-03-005	CLARIFICATION	2-02-002	CLEMENS	1-01-001	CLOISTERS
1-01-001	CIRCUMPOLAR	8-05-008	CLARIFIED	2-01-001	CLEMENS'	1-01-001	CLOMPED
1-01-001	CIRCUMSCRIBED	1-01-001	CLARIFIES	1-01-001	CLEMENT	1-01-001	CLONIC
2-01-002	CIRCUMSCRIBING	13-05-010	CLARIFY	3-02-002	CLEMENTE	234-15-166	CLOSE
1-01-001	CIRCUMSCRIPTION S	3-02-003	CLARIFYING	3-02-003	CLEMENTS	1-01-001	CLOSE-IN
		1-01-001	CLARINET	1-01-001	CLENCH	4-02-003	CLOSE-UP
3-03-003	CIRCUMSPECT	28-09-020	CLARITY	5-04-005	CLENCHED	106-13-076	CLOSED
1-01-001	CIRCUMSPECTION	35-08-013	CLARK	1-01-001	CLENCHES	1-01-001	CLOSED-CIRCUIT
1-01-001	CIRCUMSPECTLY	1-01-001	CLARK'S	1-01-001	CLEOTA'S	2-01-001	CLOSED-DOOR
15-10-013	CIRCUMSTANCE	1-01-001	CLARKE	7-01-001	CLERFAYT	66-12-049	CLOSELY
84-13-068	CIRCUMSTANCES	1-01-001	CLARKE'S	12-04-008	CLERGY	1-01-001	CLOSELY-PACKED
7-05-006	CIRCUS	5-05-005	CLASH	10-05-007	CLERGYMAN	1-01-001	CLOSENESS
2-02-002	CISTERN	1-01-001	CLASHED	1-01-001	CLERGYMAN'S	61-14-049	CLOSER
5-02-005	CITATION	2-02-002	CLASHES	6-03-004	CLERGYMEN	6-04-004	CLOSES
1-01-001	CITATIONS	3-02-003	CLASPED	1-01-001	CLERIC	9-07-009	CLOSEST
7-04-006	CITE	4-04-004	CLASPING	9-05-008	CLERICAL	16-05-013	CLOSET
24-09-022	CITED	207-14-070	CLASS	1-01-001	CLERICAL-LAY	1-01-001	CLOSETED
10-05-008	CITES	1-01-001	CLASS'	1-01-001	CLERICIS	2-01-002	CLOSETS
107-12-048	CITIES	1-01-001	CLASS-**J*D	34-09-017	CLERK	1-01-001	CLOSEUP
3-02-002	CITING	1-01-001	CLASS-BIASED	5-02-002	CLERK'S	2-02-002	CLOSEUPS
30-10-023	CITIZEN	2-02-002	CLASSED	1-01-001	CLERKING	28-11-023	CLOSING
2-02-002	CITIZEN'S	85-09-036	CLASSES	7-04-006	CLERKS	1-01-001	CLOSTRIDIUM
3-02-003	CITIZENRY	36-11-027	CLASSIC	1-01-001	CLEVA	1-01-001	CLOSURE
86-13-052	CITIZENS	33-10-024	CLASSICAL	17-06-010	CLEVELAND	3-03-003	CLOT
2-01-001	CITIZENS'	2-02-002	CLASSICALLY	17-08-016	CLEVER	43-10-025	CLOTH
3-02-003	CITIZENSHIP	1-01-001	CLASSICIST	4-03-004	CLEVERLY	1-01-001	CLOTH-OF-GOLD
1-01-001	CITO	9-07-007	CLASSICS	3-03-003	CLEVERNESS	1-01-001	CLOTHBOUND
1-01-001	CITRATED	1-01-001	CLASSIEST	3-01-001	CLIBURN	1-01-001	CLOTHE
1-01-001	CITROE**DN	21-05-013	CLASSIFICATION	6-03-005	CLICHE	5-05-005	CLOTHED
1-01-001	CITRON	1-01-001	CLASSIFICATION- ANGLE	5-03-004	CLICHES	89-12-054	CLOTHES
1-01-001	CITRUS			2-02-002	CLICK	1-01-001	CLOTHESBRUSH
393-15-156	CITY	4-03-003	CLASSIFICATIONS	8-06-008	CLICKED	2-01-001	CLOTHESHORSE
21-09-014	CITY'S	1-01-001	CLASSIFICATORY	1-01-001	CLICKING	1-01-001	CLOTHESLINE
1-01-001	CITY-BRED	14-06-010	CLASSIFIED	2-02-002	CLICKS	1-01-001	CLOTHESLINES
1-01-001	CITY-DWELLER	1-01-001	CLASSIFIERS	15-06-009	CLIENT	1-01-001	CLOTHIER
1-01-001	CITY-OWNED	6-03-006	CLASSIFY	7-03-003	CLIENT'S	20-10-019	CLOTHING
1-01-001	CITY-TRADING	1-01-001	CLASSIFYING	1-01-001	CLIENT-SERVICE	1-01-001	CLOTTED
2-02-002	CITY-WIDE	1-01-001	CLASSLESS	3-03-003	CLIENTELE	1-01-001	CLOTURE
1-01-001	CITYBRED	3-02-003	CLASSMATE	10-05-008	CLIENTS	28-10-018	CLOUD
2-02-002	CITYSCAPES	4-04-004	CLASSMATES	1-01-001	CLIENTS'	3-03-003	CLOUDBURST
1-01-001	CITYWIDE	18-06-007	CLASSROOM	11-05-008	CLIFF	1-01-001	CLOUDCROFT
3-01-002	CIUDAD	5-04-004	CLASSROOMS	1-01-001	CLIFFHANGING	6-05-005	CLOUDED
23-10-021	CIVIC	2-02-002	CLATTER	5-04-005	CLIFFORD	2-02-002	CLOUDLESS
91-10-053	CIVIL	5-04-005	CLATTERED	2-02-002	CLIFFS	38-13-025	CLOUDS
1-01-001	CIVIL-RIGHTS	1-01-001	CLATTERING	3-03-003	CLIFTON	2-02-002	CLOUDY
24-08-017	CIVILIAN	1-01-001	CLATTERY	4-02-003	CLIMACTIC	1-01-001	CLOUT
1-01-001	CIVILIAN-GROUPS	11-05-006	CLAUDE	26-10-024	CLIMATE	1-01-001	CLOV
2-02-002	CIVILIANS	1-01-001	CLAUDE'S	1-01-001	CLIMATES	1-01-001	CLOVE
1-01-001	CIVILITY	1-01-001	CLAUDIA'S	14-04-013	CLIMAX	16-01-001	CLOVER
42-09-026	CIVILIZATION	1-01-001	CLAUDIO	2-02-002	CLIMAXED	2-01-002	CLOVES
8-01-002	CIVILIZATIONAL	2-02-002	CLAUS	1-01-001	CLIMAXES	3-03-003	CLOWN
4-03-003	CIVILIZATIONS	9-03-006	CLAUSE	12-08-010	CLIMB	1-01-001	CLOWN'S
11-06-009	CIVILIZED	4-02-002	CLAUSES	44-09-035	CLIMBED	1-01-001	CLOWNING
1-01-001	CIVILIZING	1-01-001	CLAUSTROPHOBIA	11-06-010	CLIMBING	2-02-002	CLOWNS
7-04-007	CLAD	1-01-001	CLAW	1-01-001	CLIMBS	3-03-003	CLOYING
1-01-001	CLADDING	2-02-002	CLAWED	1-01-001	CLIMES	145-14-065	CLUB
98-10-044	CLAIM	1-01-001	CLAWING	2-02-002	CLINCH	9-04-007	CLUB'S
8-03-003	CLAIMANT	3-03-003	CLAWS	1-01-001	CLINCHED	2-02-002	CLUBBED
5-02-002	CLAIMANTS	100-10-022	CLAY	1-01-001	CLINCHER	5-02-004	CLUBHOUSE
35-10-028	CLAIMED	1-01-001	CLAY-MINING	1-01-001	CLINCHES	1-01-001	CLUBROOMS
16-10-016	CLAIMING	1-01-001	CLAYS	6-06-006	CLING	24-08-018	CLUBS
74-11-041	CLAIMS	27-03-008	CLAYTON	7-06-007	CLINGING	3-03-003	CLUCK
2-01-001	CLAIR	3-01-002	CLAYTON'S	3-03-003	CLINGS	1-01-001	CLUCKED
1-01-001	CLAIRAUDIENTLY	70-12-050	CLEAN	3-02-002	CLINIC	1-01-001	CLUCKING
16-03-003	CLAIRE	1-01-001	CLEAN-SHAVEN	27-05-011	CLINICAL	2-02-002	CLUCKS
1-01-001	CLAIRVOYANCE	1-01-001	CLEAN-TOP	1-01-001	CLINICALLY		

Freq	Word	Freq	Word	Freq	Word	Freq	Word
15-08-015	CLUE	1-01-001	COBLE	9-06-007	COINS	6-01-001	COLMER
10-07-010	CLUES	3-02-003	COBRA	4-02-002	COKE	1-01-001	COLMER'S
4-02-003	CLUMP	1-01-001	COBWEBS	1-01-001	COKES	2-01-001	COLO
4-03-004	CLUMPS	1-01-001	COCA-*COLA	7-05-005	COL	9-03-004	COLOGNE
1-01-001	CLUMSILY	1-01-001	COCAINE	1-01-001	COLAVITO	1-01-001	COLOMBIA
6-05-006	CLUMSY	1-01-001	COCAO	1-01-001	COLCHICUM	2-02-002	COLOMBIAN
14-07-013	CLUNG	1-01-001	COCCIDIOIDOMYCO SIS	1-01-001	COLCORD	2-01-001	COLON
2-01-001	CLURMAN			2-01-001	COLCORD'S	37-07-020	COLONEL
13-06-011	CLUSTER	1-01-001	COCCIDIOSIS	171-15-098	COLD	2-02-002	COLONEL'S
4-04-004	CLUSTERED	5-01-001	COCHANNEL	1-01-001	COLD-BLOODED	1-01-001	COLONELS
2-02-002	CLUSTERING	1-01-001	COCHRAN	1-01-001	COLD-BLOODEDLY	21-08-015	COLONIAL
5-04-005	CLUSTERS	5-02-003	COCK	4-03-003	COLD-WAR	4-03-003	COLONIALISM
5-04-005	CLUTCH	1-01-001	COCKATOO	3-01-001	COLDE	1-01-001	COLONIALIST
7-05-007	CLUTCHED	6-04-006	COCKED	5-04-005	COLDER	1-01-001	COLONIALS
3-03-003	CLUTCHES	1-01-001	COCKEYED	4-02-004	COLDEST	7-07-007	COLONIES
8-04-008	CLUTCHING	1-01-001	COCKIER	8-06-008	COLDLY	1-01-001	COLONISTS
2-02-002	CLUTTERED	1-01-001	COCKPIT	4-03-004	COLDNESS	1-01-001	COLONISTS'
2-02-002	CLYDE	16-06-007	COCKPITS	2-02-002	COLDS	1-01-001	COLONIZED
1-01-001	CLYFFORD	1-01-001	COCKROACHES	1-01-001	COLE	2-02-002	COLONNA
21-03-006	CM	1-01-001	COCKTAIL	1-01-001	COLE'S	3-01-001	COLONNADE
1-01-001	CM.	1-01-001	COCKTAILS	1-01-001	COLEE	1-01-001	COLONNADED
3-01-001	CM,	1-01-001	COCKY	1-01-001	COLEFAX	1-01-001	COLONUS
1-01-001	CMDR	2-02-002	COCO	2-02-002	COLEMAN	28-07-010	COLONY
48-08-024	CO	2-01-001	COCOA	1-01-001	COLERIDGE	1-01-001	COLONY'S
1-01-001	CO-AUTHOR	7-03-004	COCONUT	2-01-002	COLERIDGE'S	141-14-087	COLOR
2-02-002	CO-CHAIRMEN	1-01-001	COCONUT-CONTAIN ING	1-01-001	COLES	2-01-001	COLOR-**J*T*V
1-01-001	CO-COLA			1-01-001	COLETTA	13-07-011	COLORADO
1-01-001	CO-EDUCATIONAL	3-01-002	COCONUTS	1-01-001	COLFAX	1-01-001	COLORADO'S
1-01-001	CO-EXISTENCE	3-02-002	COCOON	1-01-001	COLICKY	1-01-001	COLORAMA
1-01-001	CO-EXTINCTION	1-01-001	COCOPALM	2-01-001	COLISEUM	1-01-001	COLORATION
1-01-001	CO-OCCURRING	2-02-002	COCTEAU	2-02-002	COLLABORATE	2-02-002	COLORATURA
2-02-002	CO-OP	1-01-001	COCU	9-03-005	COLLABORATED	31-10-021	COLORED
4-04-004	CO-OPERATE	6-04-005	COD	12-03-008	COLLABORATION	1-01-001	COLOREDS
1-01-001	CO-OPERATED	2-01-001	CODDINGTON	1-01-001	COLLABORATOR	21-07-018	COLORFUL
1-01-001	CO-OPERATES	2-01-002	CODDLED	4-04-004	COLLABORATORS	1-01-001	COLORIN
1-01-001	CO-OPERATING	40-10-021	CODE	15-01-001	COLLAGE	7-04-004	COLORING
12-06-008	CO-OPERATION	1-01-001	CODED	3-01-001	COLLAGEN	3-02-003	COLORLESS
7-03-004	CO-OPERATIVE	2-01-001	CODES	2-01-001	COLLAGES	51-11-032	COLORS
1-01-001	CO-OPS	7-05-007	CODETERMINES	7-05-007	COLLAPSE	3-03-003	COLOSSAL
9-01-001	CO-OPTATION	1-01-001	CODFISH	13-09-012	COLLAPSED	2-01-001	COLOSSEUM
1-01-001	CO-OPTING	3-01-001	CODIFICATION	1-01-001	COLLAPSES	1-01-001	COLOSSIANS
1-01-001	CO-ORDINATE	1-01-001	CODIFIED	2-02-002	COLLAPSIBLE	2-02-002	COLOSSUS
1-01-001	CO-ORDINATED	3-03-003	CODING	1-01-001	COLLAPSING	1-01-001	COLOUR-PRINTS
1-01-001	CO-ORDINATES	17-09-016	CODY	1-01-001	COLLAR	1-01-001	COLOURED
1-01-001	CO-ORDINATING	1-01-001	COE	1-01-001	COLLAR-TO-COLLA R	2-01-001	COLQUITT
2-02-002	CO-ORDINATION	1-01-001	COED			18-04-007	COLT
1-01-001	CO-ORDINATOR	1-01-001	COEDITORS	1-01-001	COLLARBONE	1-01-001	COLT'S
1-01-001	CO-SIGNERS	1-01-001	COEDS	1-01-001	COLLARED	1-01-001	COLTISH
1-01-001	CO-STAR	3-02-003	COEFFICIENT	1-01-001	COLLARS	8-04-004	COLTS
2-02-002	CO-WORKERS	3-02-003	COEFFICIENTS	1-01-001	COLLATED	1-01-001	COLTSMAN
24-05-009	COACH	2-02-002	COERCE	1-01-001	COLLATION	18-06-012	COLUMBIA
1-01-001	COACH'S	1-01-001	COERCED	9-05-007	COLLEAGUE	1-01-001	COLUMBINES
5-02-005	COACHES	4-04-004	COERCION	23-09-018	COLLEAGUES	14-07-012	COLUMBUS
6-03-004	COACHING	2-01-002	COERCIVE	16-11-016	COLLECT	71-12-034	COLUMN
3-01-001	COACHMAN	1-01-001	COEXIST	44-09-035	COLLECTED	1-01-001	COLUMN-SHAPED
2-01-001	COACHMEN	11-04-006	COEXISTENCE	1-01-001	COLLECTIBLE	5-03-005	COLUMNIST
1-01-001	COACHWORK	1-01-001	COEXISTENT	13-08-011	COLLECTING	2-01-002	COLUMNISTS
1-01-001	COAGULATING	1-01-001	COFACTORS	84-14-043	COLLECTION	36-09-019	COLUMNS
1-01-001	COAHSE	78-10-036	COFFEE	8-05-008	COLLECTIONS	1-01-001	COLVIN'S
32-08-010	COAL	1-01-001	COFFEE-*HOUSE	32-08-020	COLLECTIVE	1-01-001	COLZANI
2-02-002	COAL-BLACK	1-01-001	COFFEE-HOUSE	1-01-001	COLLECTIVE-BARG AINING	1-01-001	COM
1-01-001	COAL-LIKE	1-01-001	COFFEECUP			1-01-001	COMANCHE
1-01-001	COAL-RAILROAD	2-02-002	COFFEEPOT	4-03-004	COLLECTIVELY	1-01-001	COMANY'S
1-01-001	COALESCE	1-01-001	COFFERS	8-04-004	COLLECTOR	6-03-005	COMAS
1-01-001	COALESCED	7-05-006	COFFIN	1-01-001	COLLECTOR'S	27-12-018	COMBAT
1-01-001	COALESCENCE	1-01-001	COGENTLY	7-04-006	COLLECTORS	1-01-001	COMBAT-INFLICTE D
1-01-001	COALESCES	4-02-002	COGNAC	5-04-005	COLLECTS		
15-04-008	COALITION	1-01-001	COGNATE	267-13-078	COLLEGE	2-01-001	COMBAT-TESTED
8-03-003	COALS	2-02-002	COGNITIVE	2-02-002	COLLEGE'S	1-01-002	COMBATANT
10-07-009	COARSE	2-02-002	COGNIZANCE	1-01-001	COLLEGE-EDUCATE D	1-01-001	COMBATANTS
1-01-001	COARSELY	2-02-002	COGNIZANT			1-01-001	COMBATING
1-01-001	COARSENED	1-01-001	COGS	1-01-001	COLLEGE-ORIENTE D	1-01-001	COMBATTED
1-01-001	COARSENESS	3-02-003	COHEN			1-01-001	COMBE
61-14-042	COAST	1-01-001	COHERE	39-09-022	COLLEGES	4-04-004	COMBED
1-01-001	COAST-TO-COAST	1-01-001	COHERENCE	1-01-001	COLLEGIANS	2-01-001	COMBELLACK
4-03-004	COASTAL	5-05-005	COHERENT	4-03-004	COLLEGIATE	1-01-001	COMBINABLE
3-02-002	COASTED	6-04-005	COHESION	1-01-001	COLLES	57-12-043	COMBINATION
1-01-001	COASTLINE	11-03-004	COHESIVE	1-01-001	COLLETT	1-01-001	COMBINATIONS
6-04-005	COASTS	1-01-001	COHESIVELY	19-08-016	COLLIDED	17-08-014	COMBINE
43-09-023	COAT	1-01-001	COHESIVENESS	2-02-002	COLLIE	40-08-035	COMBINED
4-02-003	COATED	4-02-002	COHN	1-01-001	COLLIMATED	7-06-007	COMBINES
2-01-001	COATES	1-01-001	COHNFIDUNT	2-01-001	COLLINGWOOD	1-01-001	COMBING
36-03-004	COATING	1-01-001	COHORTS	6-03-006	COLLINS	10-05-009	COMBINING
12-02-003	COATINGS	1-01-001	COIFFURE	1-01-001	COLLINS'	4-03-004	COMBO
10-04-006	COATS	6-02-003	COIL	1-01-001	COLLINSVILLE	1-01-001	COMBS
1-01-001	COATTAILS	1-01-001	COILED	7-05-005	COLLISION	1-01-001	COMBUSTIBLES
1-01-001	COAX	1-01-001	COILING	2-02-002	COLLISIONS	12-03-003	COMBUSTION
3-03-003	COAXED	1-01-001	COILS	2-01-001	COLLOIDAL	1-01-001	COME
1-01-001	COAXIAL	10-08-010	COIN	1-01-001	COLLONADED	1-01-001	COME-UPPANCE
1-01-001	COAXING	12-05-009	COINCIDE	2-02-002	COLLOQUIAL	2-02-002	COMEBACK
2-02-002	COBALT	6-05-006	COINCIDED	2-01-001	COLLOQUIUM	5-04-005	COMEDIAN
1-01-001	COBALT-60	11-07-010	COINCIDENCE	1-01-001	COLLOQUY	2-02-002	COMEDIANS
18-02-002	COBB	2-02-002	COINCIDENCES	3-02-002	COLLOSAL	14-01-001	COMEDIE
1-01-001	COBB'S	1-01-001	COINCIDENTAL	1-01-001	COLLUSION	2-01-001	COMEDIE'S
1-01-001	COBBLER'S	1-01-001	COINCIDES	1-01-001	COLLYER	2-01-001	COMEDIES
1-01-001	COBBLESTONE	3-01-001	COINCIDING	2-01-001	COLMAN	39-08-018	COMEDY
1-01-001	COBBLESTONES	3-02-003	COINED	1-01-001	COLMANS		

1-01-001	COMELY	16-07-012	COMMITMENTS	1-01-001	COMPATRIOTS	16-04-008	COMPOSITE
1-01-001	COMEND	2-02-002	COMMITS	4-03-004	COMPEL	1-01-001	COMPOSITES
1-01-001	COMENICO	28-10-024	COMMITTED	18-08-016	COMPELLED	25-07-019	COMPOSITION
1-01-001	COMER	168-10-063	COMMITTEE	8-04-008	COMPELLING	1-01-001	COMPOSITIONAL
137-14-103	COMES	2-01-002	COMMITTEE'S	2-02-002	COMPELS	10-03-006	COMPOSITIONS
1-01-001	COMEST	1-01-001	COMMITTEEMAN	1-01-001	COMPELTE	8-02-002	COMPOST
2-02-002	COMET	4-02-002	COMMITTEEMEN	1-01-001	COMPENDIUM	4-04-004	COMPOSURE
1-01-001	COMET'S-TAIL	18-06-014	COMMITTEES	3-02-003	COMPENSATE	1-01-001	COMPOTE
1-01-001	COMETARY	2-01-001	COMMITTEEWOMAN	4-03-004	COMPENSATED	11-07-008	COMPOUND
1-01-001	COMETH	5-05-005	COMMITTING	1-01-001	COMPENSATES	1-01-001	COMPOUND-ENGINE
2-02-002	COMETS	1-01-001	COMMITMENT	2-02-002	COMPENSATING	12-07-011	COMPOUNDED
43-14-036	COMFORT	21-06-009	COMMODITIES	17-07-014	COMPENSATION	1-01-001	COMPOUNDING
37-12-033	COMFORTABLE	7-03-004	COMMODITY	3-03-003	COMPENSATIONS	16-03-005	COMPOUNDS
12-07-011	COMFORTABLY	3-01-001	COMMODORE	3-03-003	COMPENSATORY	5-04-005	COMPREHEND
1-01-001	COMFORTED	223-14-132	COMMON	23-08-021	COMPETE	2-02-002	COMPREHENDED
8-08-008	COMFORTING	2-02-002	COMMON-SENSE	2-02-002	COMPETED	3-02-003	COMPREHENDING
5-03-003	COMFORTS	1-01-001	COMMONER	18-07-012	COMPETENCE	7-05-007	COMPREHENSION
9-06-008	COMIC	1-01-001	COMMONERS	1-01-001	COMPETENCY	19-06-013	COMPREHENSIVE
2-01-001	COMICALLY	1-01-001	COMMONEST	21-11-019	COMPETENT	2-02-002	COMPREHENSIVELY
1-01-001	COMICO-ROMANTIC	29-07-021	COMMONLY	5-03-005	COMPETENTLY	2-02-002	COMPRESS
	O	1-01-001	COMMONNESS	1-01-001	COMPETES	9-05-008	COMPRESSED
1-01-001	COMICS	15-07-015	COMMONPLACE	15-08-014	COMPETING	3-03-003	COMPRESSES
6-04-004	COMIN	2-02-002	COMMONPLACES	63-11-031	COMPETITION	1-01-001	COMPRESSIBILITY
1-01-001	COMINFORM	4-02-003	COMMONS	31-04-020	COMPETIITIVE	1-01-001	COMPRESSING
174-15-132	COMING	3-02-002	COMMONWEAL	2-02-002	COMPETITIVELY	8-02-002	COMPRESSION
1-01-001	COMINGS	7-04-005	COMMONWEALTH	3-03-003	COMPETITOR	2-01-002	COMPRESSIVE
1-01-001	COMIQUE	1-01-001	COMMONWEALTHS	10-07-008	COMPETITORS	2-01-001	COMPRESSOR
1-01-001	COMISKEY	6-06-006	COMMOTION	2-01-001	COMPEYSON	11-05-010	COMPRISE
2-02-002	COMMA	4-03-003	COMMUNAL	11-03-005	COMPILATION	8-04-007	COMPRISED
72-13-040	COMMAND	4-03-004	COMMUNE	2-01-002	COMPILATIONS	3-02-003	COMPRISES
1-01-001	COMMAND'S	5-02-002	COMMUNES	1-01-001	COMPILE	3-02-003	COMPRISING
1-01-001	COMMANDANT	5-01-001	COMMUNESE	10-05-008	COMPILED	20-07-015	COMPROMISE
15-07-012	COMMANDED	13-06-011	COMMUNICATE	7-01-001	COMPILER	2-01-002	COMPROMISED
1-01-001	COMMANDEERED	3-03-003	COMMUNICATED	4-02-003	COMPILING	1-01-001	COMPROMISES
1-01-001	COMMANDEERING	7-05-006	COMMUNICATING	4-04-004	COMPLACENCY	4-04-004	COMPROMISING
28-09-019	COMMANDER	67-11-035	COMMUNICATION	1-01-001	COMPLACENT	4-01-001	COMPSON
1-01-001	COMMANDER-IN-*C	2-01-001	COMMUNICATIONAL	11-06-010	COMPLAIN	4-02-002	COMPTROLLER
	HIEF	28-08-019	COMMUNICATIONS	1-01-001	COMPLAINANT	8-05-007	COMPULSION
3-01-001	COMMANDER-IN-CH	6-03-005	COMMUNICATIVE	22-07-021	COMPLAINED	1-01-001	COMPULSIONS
	IEF	3-01-001	COMMUNICATOR	5-04-005	COMPLAINING	10-04-004	COMPULSIVE
6-05-005	COMMANDERS	1-01-001	COMMUNICATOR'S	3-02-002	COMPLAINS	3-03-003	COMPULSIVELY
11-04-010	COMMANDING	1-01-001	COMMUNICATORS	14-05-013	COMPLAINT	4-01-001	COMPULSIVES
2-01-002	COMMANDMENT	11-05-010	COMMUNION	8-06-008	COMPLAINTS	13-01-001	COMPULSIVITY
2-02-002	COMMANDO	1-01-001	COMMUNIQUES	1-01-001	COMPLAISANCE	7-05-006	COMPULSORY
1-01-001	COMMANDO-TRAINE	70-09-024	COMMUNISM	1-01-001	COMPLAISANT	7-06-006	COMPUTATION
	D	3-03-003	COMMUNISM'S	1-01-001	COMPLEATED	1-01-001	COMPUTATIONAL
15-04-007	COMMANDS	1-01-001	COMMUNISN	1-01-001	COMPLECTION	1-01-001	COMPUTATIONS
1-01-001	COMMAWNDED	97-09-042	COMMUNIST	21-05-009	COMPLEMENT	7-04-005	COMPUTE
2-02-002	COMMEMORATE	1-01-001	COMMUNIST-INSPI	4-04-004	COMPLEMENTARY	21-05-010	COMPUTED
2-02-002	COMMEMORATED		RED	1-01-001	COMPLEMENTING	13-04-006	COMPUTER
1-01-001	COMMEMORATES	2-02-002	COMMUNIST-LED	2-01-001	COMPLEMENTS	5-04-005	COMPUTERS
1-01-001	COMMEMORATING	1-01-001	COMMUNIST-TYPE	181-15-118	COMPLETE	2-01-001	COMPUTES
3-01-003	COMMENCE	2-02-002	COMMUNISTIC	69-13-055	COMPLETED	11-03-005	COMPUTING
7-05-007	COMMENCED	39-08-024	COMMUNISTS	110-12-081	COMPLETELY	4-03-003	COMRADE
3-02-002	COMMENCEMENT	41-09-026	COMMUNITIES	1-01-001	COMPLETELY-REST	10-04-005	COMRADES
1-01-001	COMMENCEMENTS	231-12-086	COMMUNITY		ORED	2-01-001	COMRADESHIP
1-01-001	COMMENCES	3-03-003	COMMUNITY'S	4-03-003	COMPLETENESS	1-01-001	COMROE
8-07-008	COMMENCING	1-01-001	COMMUNIZE	5-03-005	COMPLETES	1-01-001	COMSUMER
7-03-006	COMMEND	1-01-001	COMMUTATION	13-09-011	COMPLETING	1-01-001	COMTEMPORARY
5-04-005	COMMENDABLE	1-01-001	COMMUTATOR-LIKE	57-06-020	COMPLETION	2-01-001	COMUS
1-01-001	COMMENDATION	10-01-001	COMMUTE	7-02-002	COMPLETIONS	7-04-005	CON
4-04-004	COMMENDED	2-02-002	COMMUTED	91-09-059	COMPLEX	2-01-002	CONAN
2-02-002	COMMENDING	10-01-001	COMMUTER	1-01-001	COMPLEX-VALUED	7-04-004	CONANT
1-01-001	COMMENDS	2-01-001	COMMUTES	6-02-002	COMPLEXES	3-01-001	CONANT'S
4-03-003	COMMENSURATE	5-03-004	COMMUTING	6-04-006	COMPLEXION	4-02-003	CONCAVE
42-14-033	COMMENT	12-07-009	COMPACT	4-02-003	COMPLEXITIES	7-05-007	CONCEAL
3-02-003	COMMENTARIES	1-01-001	COMPACTLY	14-08-011	COMPLEXITY	8-06-008	CONCEALED
8-04-005	COMMENTARY	1-01-001	COMPACTS	6-03-005	COMPLIANCE	1-01-001	CONCEALING
3-03-003	COMMENTATOR	2-02-002	COMPAGNIE	2-02-002	COMPLICATE	2-02-002	CONCEALMENT
2-02-002	COMMENTATORS	87-10-035	COMPANIES	30-10-026	COMPLICATED	2-02-002	CONCEALS
18-08-017	COMMENTED	19-09-018	COMPANION	1-01-001	COMPLICATING	8-06-007	CONCEDE
5-04-005	COMMENTING	1-01-001	COMPANIONABLE	4-03-004	COMPLICATION	11-07-010	CONCEDED
30-10-024	COMMENTS	8-04-007	COMPANIONS	5-04-005	COMPLICATIONS	1-01-001	CONCEDEDLY
1-01-001	COMMERCANTS	4-04-004	COMPANIONSHIP	7-02-002	COMPLICITY	1-01-001	CONCEDES
58-06-030	COMMERCE	1-01-001	COMPANIONWAY	6-04-005	COMPLIED	3-03-003	CONCEDING
61-09-036	COMMERCIAL	290-15-107	COMPANY	3-03-003	COMPLIMENT	2-02-002	CONCEITS
1-01-001	COMMERCIALISM	27-09-017	COMPANY'S	2-02-002	COMPLIMENTARY	11-06-010	CONCEIVABLE
1-01-001	COMMERCIALIZATI	1-01-001	COMPANY-PAID	2-02-002	COMPLIMENTED	10-06-010	CONCEIVABLY
	ON	1-01-001	COMPANY-WIDE	1-01-001	COMPLIMENTING	14-07-014	CONCEIVE
11-04-010	COMMERCIALLY	41-07-037	COMPARABLE	4-03-004	COMPLIMENTS	27-10-024	CONCEIVED
10-03-006	COMMERCIALS	17-04-014	COMPARATIVE	5-05-005	COMPLY	2-02-002	CONCEIVES
2-02-002	COMMIES	15-05-014	COMPARATIVELY	3-03-003	COMPLYING	2-02-002	CONCEIVING
1-01-001	COMMINGE	28-08-026	COMPARE	25-04-018	COMPONENT	11-06-011	CONCENTRATE
1-01-001	COMMINGLED	71-12-054	COMPARED	55-06-028	COMPONENTS	30-07-023	CONCENTRATED
1-01-001	COMMISERATE	6-03-006	COMPARES	1-01-001	COMPORT	7-04-005	CONCENTRATES
2-02-002	COMMISSARY	9-05-008	COMPARING	1-01-001	COMPORTED	7-05-007	CONCENTRATING
103-09-049	COMMISSION	48-10-038	COMPARISON	1-01-001	COMPORTMENT	47-10-029	CONCENTRATION
3-03-003	COMMISSION'S	6-03-005	COMPARISONS	6-05-005	COMPOSE	1-01-001	CONCENTRATION-
1-01-001	COMMISSION-CONT	11-06-008	COMPARTMENT	40-09-033	COMPOSED		AM
	ROLLED	1-01-001	COMPARTMENTS	31-06-014	COMPOSER	9-03-008	CONCENTRATIONS
2-02-002	COMMISSIONED	13-05-009	COMPASS	1-01-001	COMPOSER'S	2-01-001	CONCENTRIC
19-05-012	COMMISSIONER	5-05-005	COMPASSION	1-01-001	COMPOSER-PIANIS	85-09-046	CONCEPT
1-01-001	COMMISSIONER'S	2-02-002	COMPASSIONATE		T-CONDUCTOR	32-07-023	CONCEPTION
16-06-012	COMMISSIONERS	2-02-002	COMPASSIONATELY	13-05-009	COMPOSERS	9-04-007	CONCEPTIONS
11-06-008	COMMISSIONS	1-01-001	COMPATABILITY	1-01-001	COMPOSERS'	27-07-018	CONCEPTS
16-09-014	COMMIT	16-05-014	COMPATIBLE	2-01-001	COMPOSES	4-02-003	CONCEPTUAL
13-07-011	COMMITMENT	1-01-001	COMPATRIOT	3-03-003	COMPOSING	2-01-001	CONCEPTUALITY

1-01-001	CONCEPTUALIZATI ON
1-01-001	CONCEPTUALLY
98-13-072	CONCERN
135-12-103	CONCERNED
62-11-043	CONCERNING
43-12-027	CONCERNS
39-08-021	CONCERT
1-01-001	CONCERT-*DISC
1-01-001	CONCERTANTE
3-02-003	CONCERTED
1-01-001	CONCERTI
1-01-001	CONCERTINA
1-01-001	CONCERTMASTER
11-03-006	CONCERTO
1-01-001	CONCERTO'S
5-03-005	CONCERTOS
26-04-012	CONCERTS
3-02-003	CONCESSION
2-01-001	CONCESSIONAIRE
7-02-002	CONCESSIONAIRES
7-04-007	CONCESSIONS
1-01-001	CONCETTA
2-01-001	CONCETTA'S
5-01-001	CONCHITA
2-01-001	CONCIERGE
1-01-001	CONCILIATE
1-01-001	CONCILIATOR
2-02-002	CONCILIATORY
1-01-001	CONCISE
1-01-001	CONCISENESS
2-02-002	CONCLAVE
16-08-015	CONCLUDE
32-11-027	CONCLUDED
4-03-004	CONCLUDES
8-05-008	CONCLUDING
59-12-048	CONCLUSION
36-10-028	CONCLUSIONS
11-06-008	CONCLUSIVE
7-03-006	CONCLUSIVELY
1-01-001	CONCOCTED
10-03-003	CONCORD
1-01-001	CONCORDANCE
2-01-001	CONCORDANT
1-01-001	CONCORDE
48-12-027	CONCRETE
2-01-002	CONCRETELY
2-01-002	CONCRETISTIC
1-01-001	CONCRETISTIC-SE EMING
4-03-004	CONCUR
2-02-002	CONCURRED
4-04-004	CONCURRENCE
7-03-006	CONCURRENT
1-01-001	CONCURRENTLY
3-02-003	CONCURS
1-01-001	CONCUSSION
4-02-003	CONDEMN
7-03-005	CONDEMNATION
1-01-001	CONDEMNATORY
19-07-015	CONDEMNED
4-03-004	CONDEMNING
3-01-002	CONDEMNS
7-02-004	CONDENSATION
1-01-001	CONDENSE
9-03-006	CONDENSED
1-01-001	CONDENSER
1-01-001	CONDENSING
2-01-001	CONDESCENDING
2-01-001	CONDESCENSION
1-01-001	CONDICIONS
2-02-002	CONDIMENTS
91-14-065	CONDITION
3-02-002	CONDITIONAL
20-06-009	CONDITIONED
13-03-003	CONDITIONER
5-02-002	CONDITIONERS
14-05-008	CONDITIONING
180-12-097	CONDITIONS
1-01-001	CONDLIFFE
1-01-001	CONDOLENCES
1-01-001	CONDONED
2-02-002	CONDUCIVE
55-11-038	CONDUCT
55-09-037	CONDUCTED
13-08-012	CONDUCTING
2-01-001	CONDUCTION
5-02-004	CONDUCTIVITY
25-05-012	CONDUCTOR
2-02-002	CONDUCTOR'S
1-01-001	CONDUCTORS
4-02-002	CONDUCTS
1-01-001	CONDUIT
13-03-004	CONE
2-01-001	CONE-SPHERE
2-02-002	CONES
2-01-002	CONESTOGA

3-01-002	CONEY
1-01-001	CONFABULATED
3-01-001	CONFABULATION
1-01-001	CONFABULATIONS
9-03-004	CONFEDERACY
14-04-006	CONFEDERATE
2-02-002	CONFEDERATES
4-01-003	CONFEDERATION
1-01-001	CONFEDERATIONS
3-03-003	CONFER
2-02-002	CONFEREES
96-11-045	CONFERENCE
1-01-001	CONFERENCE'S
25-08-020	CONFERENCES
5-05-005	CONFERRED
1-01-001	CONFERRING
1-01-001	CONFERS
11-05-009	CONFESS
7-05-007	CONFESSED
3-02-002	CONFESSES
3-03-003	CONFESSING
17-07-013	CONFESSION
2-01-001	CONFESSIONAL
1-01-001	CONFESSIONALS
2-02-002	CONFESSIONS
1-01-001	CONFESSOR
1-01-001	CONFIDANT
1-01-001	CONFIDANTE
10-06-007	CONFIDE
8-05-008	CONFIDED
56-12-045	CONFIDENCE
16-07-016	CONFIDENCES
16-07-016	CONFIDENT
6-05-006	CONFIDENTIAL
1-01-001	CONFIDENTIALITY
4-04-004	CONFIDENTIALLY
2-02-002	CONFIDENTLY
2-02-002	CONFIDING
7-02-005	CONFIGURATION
3-03-003	CONFIGURATIONS
2-02-002	CONFINE
16-06-014	CONFINED
7-06-007	CONFINEMENT
1-01-001	CONFINEMENTS
7-05-007	CONFINES
3-03-003	CONFINING
16-07-015	CONFIRM
7-05-007	CONFIRMATION
20-11-018	CONFIRMED
2-02-002	CONFIRMING
3-02-003	CONFIRMS
2-02-002	CONFISCATED
1-01-001	CONFISCATING
8-01-002	CONFLAGRATION
52-10-042	CONFLICT
1-01-001	CONFLICT'S
8-04-007	CONFLICTING
9-06-009	CONFLICTS
1-01-001	CONFLUENT
10-06-010	CONFORM
2-02-002	CONFORMANCE
3-02-002	CONFORMATION
2-01-001	CONFORMATIONAL
1-01-001	CONFORMATIONS
3-03-003	CONFORMED
3-02-003	CONFORMIST
3-02-002	CONFORMISTS
16-04-007	CONFORMITY
5-03-005	CONFORMS
2-02-002	CONFOUNDED
1-01-001	CONFOUNDING
1-01-001	CONFRERES
8-06-008	CONFRONT
16-06-007	CONFRONTATION
1-01-001	CONFRONTATIONS
32-12-031	CONFRONTED
10-06-010	CONFRONTING
5-03-005	CONFRONTS
3-01-002	CONFUCIAN
3-02-002	CONFUCIANISM
2-02-002	CONFUCIUS
5-04-005	CONFUSE
44-12-037	CONFUSED
1-01-001	CONFUSES
1-01-001	CONFUSIN
2-01-002	CONFUSING
44-12-039	CONFUSION
4-02-004	CONFUSIONS
1-01-001	CONFUTED
1-01-001	CONG
1-01-001	CONGDON
4-04-004	CONGEALED
7-04-007	CONGENIAL
1-01-001	CONGENIALITY
1-01-001	CONGENITAL
2-02-002	CONGESTED
6-04-004	CONGESTION

2-01-002	CONGESTIVE
57-04-010	CONGO
1-01-001	CONGO'S
12-02-002	CONGOLESE
4-02-004	CONGRATULATE
3-02-003	CONGRATULATED
1-01-001	CONGRATULATION
7-05-006	CONGRATULATIONS
2-02-002	CONGRATULATORY
2-02-002	CONGREGATE
1-01-001	CONGREGATED
47-07-012	CONGREGATION
14-04-005	CONGREGATIONAL
2-01-001	CONGREGATIONAL- *BAPTIST
1-01-001	CONGREGATIONALI SM
2-01-001	CONGREGATIONALI ST
3-01-001	CONGREGATIONALI STS
18-03-006	CONGREGATIONS
152-09-058	CONGRESS
3-02-002	CONGRESS'
1-01-001	CONGRESSES
22-06-017	CONGRESSIONAL
21-05-012	CONGRESSMAN
1-01-001	CONGRESSMAN'S
10-06-007	CONGRESSMEN
2-01-001	CONGRESSWOMAN
11-01-001	CONGRUENCE
3-02-003	CONGRUENT
2-01-001	CONIC
2-01-001	CONING
3-03-003	CONJECTURE
1-01-001	CONJECTURED
2-02-002	CONJECTURES
3-02-003	CONJOINED
3-02-002	CONJUGAL
10-01-001	CONJUGATE
5-01-001	CONJUGATED
14-01-002	CONJUGATES
1-01-001	CONJUGATING
1-01-001	CONJUGATION
16-06-014	CONJUNCTION
1-01-001	CONJUNCTIONS
1-01-001	CONJURE
2-02-002	CONJURED
2-02-002	CONJURES
1-01-001	CONLOW
4-04-004	CONN
1-01-001	CONNALL
8-01-002	CONNALLY
1-01-001	CONNEAUT
3-03-003	CONNECT
33-13-032	CONNECTED
17-08-016	CONNECTICUT
1-01-001	CONNECTICUT'S
6-03-005	CONNECTING
69-14-058	CONNECTION
15-09-013	CONNECTIONS
3-02-002	CONNECTIVE
2-02-002	CONNECTS
1-01-001	CONNED
1-01-001	CONNELL
1-01-001	CONNELLY
2-01-001	CONNEXION
1-01-001	CONNIE
1-01-001	CONNING
1-01-001	CONNIVANCE
1-01-001	CONNIVER
4-03-003	CONNOISSEUR
2-02-002	CONNOISSEURS
1-01-001	CONNOLLY'S
1-01-001	CONNOR
5-03-005	CONNOTATION
3-03-003	CONNOTATIONS
1-01-001	CONNOTE
1-01-001	CONNOTES
1-01-001	CONPIRED
4-03-003	CONQUER
3-03-003	CONQUERED
3-02-002	CONQUERING
1-01-001	CONQUEROR
2-02-002	CONQUERORS
9-04-006	CONQUEST
2-02-002	CONQUESTS
2-01-001	CONQUETE
10-02-003	CONRAD
2-01-001	CONRAD'S
1-01-001	CONS
1-01-001	CONSANGUINEOUS
1-01-001	CONSANGUINEOUSL Y
2-01-001	CONSANGUINITY
40-09-022	CONSCIENCE
1-01-001	CONSCIENCES

10-06-008	CONSCIENTIOUS
1-01-001	CONSCIONABLE
46-13-039	CONSCIOUS
12-08-012	CONSCIOUSLY
30-09-019	CONSCIOUSNESS
1-01-001	CONSCRIPT
2-02-002	CONSCRIPTED
2-02-002	CONSCRIPTION
1-01-001	CONSDERATIONS
1-01-001	CONSECRATION
10-04-008	CONSECUTIVE
2-01-001	CONSEIL
7-03-006	CONSENSUS
17-06-012	CONSENT
4-03-004	CONSENTED
1-01-001	CONSENTING
30-09-025	CONSEQUENCE
34-10-027	CONSEQUENCES
7-02-006	CONSEQUENT
1-01-001	CONSEQUENTIAL
31-09-025	CONSEQUENTLY
13-06-010	CONSERVATION
1-01-001	CONSERVATIONIST
10-03-004	CONSERVATISM
31-07-025	CONSERVATIVE
1-01-001	CONSERVATIVE-LI BERAL
1-01-001	CONSERVATIVELY- CRAVATED
4-02-003	CONSERVATIVES
3-02-003	CONSERVATORY
3-03-003	CONSERVE
1-01-001	CONSERVES
2-02-002	CONSERVING
127-13-091	CONSIDER
96-12-078	CONSIDERABLE
44-12-040	CONSIDERABLY
4-03-004	CONSIDERATE
2-02-002	CONSIDERATELY
49-10-044	CONSIDERATION
31-07-022	CONSIDERATIONS
151-14-110	CONSIDERED
1-01-001	CONSIDERIN
47-12-040	CONSIDERING
15-06-014	CONSIDERS
2-01-002	CONSIGN
1-01-001	CONSIGNED
1-01-001	CONSISENTLY
17-07-015	CONSIST
24-10-018	CONSISTED
1-01-001	CONSISTENCE
18-08-016	CONSISTENCY
28-07-025	CONSISTENT
19-07-018	CONSISTENTLY
27-08-022	CONSISTING
43-09-033	CONSISTS
1-01-001	CONSITUTIONAL
3-03-003	CONSOLATION
2-02-002	CONSOLED
4-02-002	CONSOLES
2-02-002	CONSOLIDATE
6-03-005	CONSOLIDATED
2-02-002	CONSOLIDATING
9-03-004	CONSOLIDATION
1-01-001	CONSOLING
1-01-001	CONSONANCE
3-02-002	CONSONANT
9-01-002	CONSONANTAL
4-01-002	CONSONANTS
1-01-001	CONSORT
1-01-001	CONSORTED
2-02-002	CONSORTING
1-01-001	CONSPICIOUS
5-04-005	CONSPICUOUS
8-05-008	CONSPICUOUSLY
2-02-002	CONSPIRACIES
22-06-012	CONSPIRACY
1-01-001	CONSPIRATORIAL
4-03-004	CONSPIRATORS
1-01-001	CONSPIRE
3-02-003	CONSPIRED
1-01-001	CONSPIRES
5-02-002	CONSTABLE
1-01-001	CONSTABLE'S
1-01-001	CONSTABLES
1-01-001	CONSTANCE
5-02-003	CONSTANCY
71-12-055	CONSTANT
1-01-001	CONSTANT-TEMPER ATURE
1-01-001	CONSTANTIN
8-03-003	CONSTANTINE
1-01-001	CONSTANTINO
3-02-003	CONSTANTINOPLE
1-01-001	CONSTANTINOS
41-11-040	CONSTANTLY
9-03-005	CONSTANTS

1-01-001 CONSTATATION	8-06-007 CONTENTED	1-01-001 CONTRITION	10-06-007 COOKED	
1-01-001 CONSTELLATION'S	1-01-001 CONTENTEDLY	1-01-001 CONTRIVANCES	1-01-001 COOKED-OVER	
4-02-003 CONSTELLATIONS	1-01-001 CONTENTING	1-01-001 CONTRIVE	1-01-001 COOKFIRE	
1-01-001 CONSTERNATION	9-04-007 CONTENTION	3-03-003 CONTRIVED	1-01-001 COOKIE	
1-01-001 CONSTITUENCIES	2-02-002 CONTENTIONS	1-01-001 CONTRIVING	6-03-006 COOKIES	
3-02-002 CONSTITUENCY	1-01-001 CONTENTMENT	223-14-119 CONTROL	32-11-025 COOKING	
5-02-004 CONSTITUENT	16-07-014 CONTENTS	39-11-038 CONTROLLED	8-04-004 COOKS	
10-07-007 CONSTITUENTS	26-09-019 CONTEST	9-03-005 CONTROLLER	2-01-001 COOKY	
29-06-028 CONSTITUTE	5-05-005 CONTESTANTS	2-02-002 CONTROLLER'S	62-13-035 COOL	
11-05-009 CONSTITUTED	3-02-003 CONTESTED	3-03-003 CONTROLLERS	4-02-002 COOLANT	
11-05-011 CONSTITUTES	8-06-007 CONTESTS	23-09-021 CONTROLLING	17-07-011 COOLED	
3-03-003 CONSTITUTING	35-05-021 CONTEXT	30-08-023 CONTROLS	12-06-007 COOLER	
49-05-019 CONSTITUTION	2-02-002 CONTEXTS	12-05-008 CONTROVERSIAL	4-02-004 COOLERS	
25-07-018 CONSTITUTIONAL	1-01-001 CONTIGUOUS	1-01-001 CONTROVERSIALIS	4-02-002 COOLEST	
4-01-003 CONSTITUTIONS	1-01-001 CONTINENCE	TS	1-01-001 COOLHEADED	
2-02-002 CONSTRAINED	17-09-016 CONTINENT	4-02-002 CONTROVERSIES	26-03-003 COOLIDGE	
1-01-001 CONSTRAINING	19-07-014 CONTINENTAL	26-09-022 CONTROVERSY	2-01-001 COOLIDGE'S	
2-01-001 CONSTRAINT	1-01-001 CONTINENTALLY	1-01-001 CONTUSIONS	3-01-001 COOLIDGES	
2-02-002 CONSTRICTED	7-06-007 CONTINENTS	1-01-001 CONVAIR	2-01-001 COOLIDGES'	
2-02-002 CONSTRICTING	5-04-004 CONTINGENCIES	1-01-001 CONVALESCENCE	41-04-009 COOLING	
3-02-002 CONSTRICTION	3-03-003 CONTINGENCY	1-01-001 CONVALESCING	1-01-001 COOLING-HEATING	
1-01-001 CONSTRICTIONS	3-02-003 CONTINGENT	2-01-001 CONVECTION	5-05-005 COOLLY	
6-01-001 CONSTRICTOR	2-01-001 CONTINGENT-FEE	2-02-002 CONVENED	5-02-003 COOLNESS	
1-01-001 CONSTRICTORS	1-01-001 CONTINGENTS	19-06-016 CONVENIENCE	1-01-001 COOLNESSES	
12-04-011 CONSTRUCT	5-03-004 CONTINUAL	2-02-002 CONVENIENCES	2-01-002 COOLS	
37-10-027 CONSTRUCTED	25-10-024 CONTINUALLY	22-07-018 CONVENIENT	9-03-003 COOMBS	
7-05-007 CONSTRUCTING	6-05-006 CONTINUANCE	1-01-001 CONVENIENT-TYPE	3-01-001 COONS	
95-10-049 CONSTRUCTION	18-06-011 CONTINUATION	7-05-007 CONVENIENTLY	3-02-003 COOP	
1-01-001 CONSTRUCTIONAL	107-13-085 CONTINUE	2-02-002 CONVENING	2-02-002 COOPED	
4-03-003 CONSTRUCTIONS	133-15-096 CONTINUED	4-02-003 CONVENT	12-04-004 COOPER	
15-08-013 CONSTRUCTIVE	41-08-032 CONTINUES	28-09-018 CONVENTION	2-02-002 COOPER'S	
2-02-002 CONSTRUCTIVELY	61-10-051 CONTINUING	51-09-035 CONVENTIONAL	11-06-010 COOPERATE	
1-01-001 CONSTRUE	2-02-002 CONTINUITIES	1-01-001 CONVENTIONAL-TY	2-02-002 COOPERATED	
6-03-004 CONSTRUED	1-01-001 CONTINUITY	PE	1-01-001 COOPERATES	
1-01-001 CONSTRUING	1-01-001 CONTINUO	1-01-001 CONVENTIONALITY	7-05-006 COOPERATING	
3-01-003 CONSUL	44-10-032 CONTINUOUS	1-01-001 CONVENTIONALIZE	34-08-029 COOPERATION	
1-01-001 CONSULAR	23-08-021 CONTINUOUSLY	D	20-06-010 COOPERATIVE	
1-01-001 CONSULATE	7-03-006 CONTINUUM	1-01-001 CONVENTIONALLY	10-02-002 COOPERATIVES	
11-08-011 CONSULT	3-02-003 CONTORTED	9-03-007 CONVENTIONS	2-01-001 COOPERMAN	
12-03-006 CONSULTANT	1-01-001 CONTORTION	3-01-002 CONVERGE	3-03-003 COOPERS	
7-03-005 CONSULTANTS	6-03-005 CONTOUR	1-01-001 CONVERGED	1-01-001 COOPS	
10-07-010 CONSULTATION	1-01-001 CONTOUR-OBLITER	1-01-001 CONVERGENT	9-05-007 COORDINATE	
2-02-002 CONSULTATIONS	ATING	50-12-037 CONVERSATION	13-04-008 COORDINATED	
1-01-001 CONSULTATIVE	1-01-001 CONTOURING	3-03-003 CONVERSATIONAL	6-03-005 COORDINATES	
17-08-015 CONSULTED	15-07-012 CONTOURS	10-06-009 CONVERSATIONS	3-02-003 COORDINATING	
13-05-009 CONSULTING	1-01-001 CONTRABAND	5-05-005 CONVERSE	12-05-007 COORDINATION	
2-02-002 CONSUME	1-01-001 CONTRABASS	9-04-007 CONVERSELY	5-01-003 COORDINATOR	
13-06-009 CONSUMED	4-01-001 CONTRACEPTION	1-01-001 CONVERSING	2-01-001 COOSA	
37-08-016 CONSUMER	1-01-001 CONTRACEPTIVE	21-07-015 CONVERSION	1-01-001 COOSIE'S	
1-01-001 CONSUMER'S	4-01-001 CONTRACEPTIVES	1-01-001 CONVERSION-BY-R	15-05-009 COP	
9-06-008 CONSUMERS	60-11-034 CONTRACT	ENOVATION	21-09-020 COPE	
1-01-001 CONSUMES	1-01-001 CONTRACT-NEGOTI	6-05-005 CONVERSIONS	2-02-002 COPELAND	
5-04-005 CONSUMING	ATION	12-08-012 CONVERT	6-01-001 COPENHAGEN	
3-01-004 CONSUMMATE	8-05-007 CONTRACTED	20-09-015 CONVERTED	8-01-001 COPERNICAN	
4-03-004 CONSUMMATED	3-03-003 CONTRACTING	10-05-006 CONVERTIBLE	13-01-002 COPERNICUS	
1-01-001 CONSUMMATELY	12-03-004 CONTRACTION	2-02-002 CONVERTING	6-01-001 COPERNICUS'	
4-01-001 CONSUMMATION	1-01-001 CONTRACTION-EXT	5-03-004 CONVERTS	1-01-001 COPERNICUS-THE	
18-06-012 CONSUMPTION	ENSION	1-01-001 CONVEX	ASTRONOME	
3-01-001 CONSUMPTIVE	6-03-004 CONTRACTOR	1-01-001 CONVEXITY	1-01-001 COPES	
63-13-037 CONTACT	1-01-001 CONTRACTOR'S	13-07-012 CONVEY	3-03-003 COPIED	
4-03-004 CONTACTED	2-01-001 CONTRACTORS	1-01-001 CONVEYANCE	18-07-012 COPIES	
2-01-002 CONTACTING	1-01-001 CONTRACTORS'	9-06-008 CONVEYED	8-04-006 COPING	
25-08-016 CONTACTS	24-10-018 CONTRACTS	1-01-001 CONVEYING	1-01-001 COPINGS	
2-02-002 CONTADINI	7-02-003 CONTRACTUAL	3-03-003 CONVEYOR	1-01-001 COPIOUS	
2-02-002 CONTAGION	4-04-004 CONTRADICT	4-03-004 CONVEYS	1-01-001 COPIOUSLY	
2-02-002 CONTAGIOUS	2-02-002 CONTRADICTED	6-03-005 CONVICT	2-02-002 COPLAND	
45-12-037 CONTAIN	13-07-010 CONTRADICTION	1-01-001 CONVICT'S	1-01-001 COPLEY	
60-12-039 CONTAINED	5-02-005 CONTRADICTIONS	14-07-012 CONVICTED	2-01-001 COPOLYMERS	
10-07-008 CONTAINER	2-01-001 CONTRADICTORILY	1-01-001 CONVICTING	1-01-001 COPP	
4-03-004 CONTAINERS	1-01-001 CONTRADICTORY	50-12-042 CONVICTION	13-07-012 COPPER	
45-08-033 CONTAINING	2-02-002 CONTRADICTS	20-06-017 CONVICTIONS	2-02-002 COPPERY	
2-02-002 CONTAINMENT	1-01-001 CONTRADISTINCTI	4-03-003 CONVICTS	2-02-002 COPRA	
38-07-028 CONTAINS	ON	4-03-003 CONVINCE	17-03-011 COPS	
1-01-001 CONTAMINATE	1-01-001 CONTRALTO	50-13-044 CONVINCED	38-11-025 COPY	
3-02-002 CONTAMINATED	1-01-001 CONTRAPTIONS	11-06-010 CONVINCING	1-01-001 COPYBOOKS	
1-01-001 CONTAMINATING	1-01-001 CONTRARIETIES	2-02-002 CONVINCINGLY	1-01-001 COPYING	
4-02-003 CONTAMINATION	1-01-001 CONTRARILY	1-01-001 CONVIVIAL	1-01-001 COPYRIGHTS	
1-01-001 CONTE	52-13-044 CONTRARY	3-01-001 CONVOCATION	1-01-001 COPYWRITER	
7-04-007 CONTEMPLATE	1-01-001 CONTRARY-TO-REA	1-01-001 CONVOCATIONS	2-01-002 COQUETTE	
5-05-005 CONTEMPLATED	LITY	1-01-001 CONVOLUTED	5-03-003 CORAL	
1-01-001 CONTEMPLATES	74-12-052 CONTRAST	3-02-003 CONVOY	1-01-001 CORAL-COLORED	
6-03-004 CONTEMPLATING	4-02-004 CONTRASTED	1-01-001 CONVULSED	1-01-001 CORAULT	
6-06-006 CONTEMPLATION	11-07-010 CONTRASTING	1-01-001 CONVULSIONS	1-01-001 CORBIN	
1-01-001 CONTEMPLATIVE	11-06-009 CONTRASTS	3-02-002 CONVULSIVE	2-02-002 CORCORAN	
6-04-006 CONTEMPORARIES	2-02-002 CONTRETEMPS	3-03-003 CONVULSIVELY	6-05-006 CORD	
63-11-039 CONTEMPORARY	1-01-001 CONTRIBS	1-01-001 CONWAY	1-01-001 CORDED	
15-08-014 CONTEMPT	44-08-037 CONTRIBUTE	3-01-001 CONYERS'	2-01-001 CORDER	
2-02-002 CONTEMPTIBLE	39-10-036 CONTRIBUTED	5-01-001 COO**OPERATION	6-06-006 CORDIAL	
6-05-006 CONTEMPTUOUS	10-07-009 CONTRIBUTES	1-01-001 COO**ORDINATE	1-01-001 CORDIER'S	
2-02-002 CONTEMPTUOUSLY	15-08-014 CONTRIBUTING	1-01-001 COO**ORDINATED	2-02-002 CORDON	
6-03-006 CONTEND	37-09-033 CONTRIBUTION	1-01-001 COO**ORDINATING	2-02-002 CORDS	
12-06-011 CONTENDED	29-08-025 CONTRIBUTIONS	3-01-001 COO**ORDINATION	1-01-001 CORDUROY	
2-02-002 CONTENDER	2-02-002 CONTRIBUTOR	2-01-001 COOCH	1-01-001 CORDUROYS	
1-01-001 CONTENDERE	6-05-006 CONTRIBUTORS	1-01-001 COOING	37-11-024 CORE	
1-01-001 CONTENDING	1-01-001 CONTRIBUTORY	47-11-026 COOK	3-01-001 CORE-*NEGRO	
5-04-004 CONTENDS	1-01-001 CONTRIFUGATION	2-02-002 COOK'S	1-01-001 CORE-CORE	
53-11-040 CONTENT	1-01-001 CONTRITE	3-01-001 COOKE	1-01-001 CORE-JACKET	

1-01-001	CORE-MARGINAL
2-01-002	CORELLI
3-01-002	CORES
1-01-001	CORIANDER
1-01-001	CORINTH
5-04-004	CORINTHIAN
3-01-002	CORINTHIANS
1-01-001	CORIOLANUS
9-04-004	CORK
2-01-001	CORKED
1-01-001	CORKERS
1-01-001	CORKS
3-03-003	CORKSCREW
34-09-021	CORN
1-01-001	CORN-BELT
1-01-001	CORNBREAD
4-02-002	CORNE
1-01-001	CORNEILUS
5-04-004	CORNELL
1-01-001	CORNELL-*DUBILI
	ER
115-15-064	CORNER
1-01-001	CORNER-
1-01-001	CORNER-POSTS
1-01-001	CORNERED
1-01-001	CORNERING
18-10-016	CORNERS
3-03-003	CORNERSTONE
1-01-001	CORNFIELD
1-01-001	CORNIEST
1-01-001	CORNING
2-02-002	CORNMEAL
2-01-001	CORNS
1-01-001	CORNSTARCH
1-01-001	CORNUCOPIA
1-01-001	CORNWALL
2-01-001	CORNWALLIS
1-01-001	CORNY
1-01-001	COROLLARIES
4-01-003	COROLLARY
1-01-001	CORONA
2-01-002	CORONADO
1-01-001	CORONARIES
7-02-002	CORONARY
1-01-001	CORONATION
5-03-004	CORONER
4-01-002	CORONER'S
13-04-010	CORP
4-03-003	CORPORAL
19-07-014	CORPORATE
90-07-028	CORPORATION
5-02-002	CORPORATION'S
25-06-010	CORPORATIONS
1-01-001	CORPOREAL
1-01-001	CORPOREALITY
1-01-001	CORPORIS
109-12-041	CORPS
7-04-007	CORPSE
5-05-005	CORPSES
1-01-001	CORPSMAN
1-01-001	CORPULENCE
7-04-004	CORPUS
1-01-001	CORPUSCULAR
1-01-001	CORPUSCULAR-RAD
	IATION
5-03-004	CORRAL
1-01-001	CORRALLING
52-13-041	CORRECT
9-06-009	CORRECTED
5-05-005	CORRECTION
2-02-002	CORRECTIONS
13-07-013	CORRECTLY
3-03-003	CORRECTNESS
1-01-001	CORREGGIO
3-02-002	CORRELATE
3-03-003	CORRELATED
2-02-002	CORRELATING
16-04-011	CORRELATION
2-01-002	CORRELATIONS
1-01-001	CORRELATIVELY
7-04-007	CORRESPOND
4-03-004	CORRESPONDED
25-10-019	CORRESPONDENCE
12-07-010	CORRESPONDENT
5-04-004	CORRESPONDENTS
38-07-015	CORRESPONDING
2-02-002	CORRESPONDINGLY
6-02-006	CORRESPONDS
1-01-001	CORRETTE
17-05-011	CORRIDOR
2-02-002	CORRIDORS
2-01-002	CORROBORATE
2-02-002	CORROBORATED
1-01-001	CORROBORATING
2-01-001	CORROBOREES
1-01-001	CORRODE
1-01-001	CORRODING

4-03-003	CORROSION
4-04-004	CORROSIVE
4-03-003	CORRUGATED
1-01-001	CORRUGATIONS
8-05-007	CORRUPT
2-01-001	CORRUPTED
1-01-001	CORRUPTER
5-03-005	CORRUPTIBLE
3-02-002	CORRUPTING
14-06-010	CORRUPTION
1-01-001	CORRUPTS
1-01-001	CORSAGE
1-01-001	CORSI
1-01-001	CORSIA
1-01-001	CORSO
7-01-001	CORTEGE
7-01-002	CORTEX
3-01-002	CORTICAL
1-01-001	CORTICALLY
2-01-001	CORTICO-FUGAL
2-01-001	CORTICO-HYPOTHA
	LAMIC
1-01-001	CORTICOSTEROIDS
1-01-001	CORTICOTROPIN
3-01-001	CORTLANDT
1-01-001	COSEC
4-02-004	COSEQUENCES
2-01-002	COSILY
3-02-002	COSMETIC
7-05-006	COSMETICS
18-08-013	COSMIC
1-01-001	COSMICAL
1-01-001	COSMO
2-02-002	COSMOLOGICAL
2-01-001	COSMOLOGISTS
3-02-002	COSMOLOGY
2-02-002	COSMOPOLITAN
1-01-001	COSMOPOLITANISM
3-03-003	COSMOS
2-02-002	COSPONSORED
1-01-001	COSPONSORS
3-01-002	COSSACK
4-01-003	COSSACKS
229-13-087	COST
1-01-001	COST-ACCOUNTING
1-01-001	COST-BILLING
2-01-001	COST-DATA
1-01-001	COST-FINDING
3-01-001	COST-OF-LIVING
1-01-001	COST-PLUS
2-01-001	COST-RAISING
7-01-001	COSTAGGINI
1-01-001	COSTAGGINI'S
1-01-001	COSTE
6-04-004	COSTING
1-01-001	COSTIVE
1-01-001	COSTLIER
16-09-015	COSTLY
176-09-047	COSTS
10-06-008	COSTUME
1-01-001	COSTUMED
18-05-013	COSTUMES
1-01-001	COSY
2-01-001	COTILLION
1-01-001	COTMAN
1-01-001	COTT
19-11-015	COTTAGE
6-04-006	COTTAGES
4-01-001	COTTEN
1-01-001	COTTEN'S
1-01-001	COTTER
1-01-001	COTTER'S
38-08-019	COTTON
1-01-001	COTTON'S
1-01-001	COTTON-GROWING
1-01-001	COTTONMOUTH
1-01-001	COTTONSEED
1-01-001	COTTY
1-01-001	COUCH
1-01-001	COUCHED
1-01-001	COUCHES
1-01-001	COUD
1-01-001	COUDN
32-11-028	COUGH
4-04-004	COUGHED
3-02-002	COUGHING
3-02-002	COUGHLIN
1-01-001	COUGHLIN'S
1-01-001	COULD
1-01-001	COULD'VE
1-01-001	COULDA
175-11-092	COULDN'T
61-09-021	COULOMB
1-01-001	COULSON
103-10-044	COUNCIL
6-02-005	COUNCIL'S
5-02-002	COUNCILMAN

6-04-005	COUNCILS
1-01-001	COUNCILWOMAN
17-07-012	COUNSEL
3-02-002	COUNSELED
10-06-008	COUNSELING
4-04-004	COUNSELOR
3-01-002	COUNSELORS
49-14-041	COUNT
17-10-016	COUNTED
6-04-006	COUNTENANCE
31-08-016	COUNTER
1-01-001	COUNTER-ATTACK
1-01-001	COUNTER-BALANCE
1-01-001	COUNTER-CLOCKWI
	SE
1-01-001	COUNTER-DRILL
1-01-001	COUNTER-EFFORTS
1-01-001	COUNTER-ESCALAT
	ION
1-01-001	COUNTER-MOVES
1-01-001	COUNTER-OFFENSI
	VE
1-01-001	COUNTER-SUCCESS
	ES
4-02-004	COUNTERACT
2-01-002	COUNTERACTED
2-02-002	COUNTERACTING
3-02-002	COUNTERATTACK
2-02-002	COUNTERBALANCE
1-01-001	COUNTERBALANCED
1-01-001	COUNTERBALANCIN
	G
1-01-001	COUNTERCHALLENG
	E
2-02-002	COUNTERED
1-01-001	COUNTERFEIT
1-01-001	COUNTERFLOW
1-01-001	COUNTERMAN
9-04-008	COUNTERPART
11-04-008	COUNTERPARTS
5-03-004	COUNTERPOINT
1-01-001	COUNTERPOINTING
1-01-001	COUNTERPROPOSAL
8-05-008	COUNTERS
1-01-001	COUNTERVAILING
1-01-001	COUNTIAN
35-09-021	COUNTIES
5-02-002	COUNTIN
12-05-011	COUNTING
14-10-014	COUNTLESS
1-01-001	COUNTREY
151-11-054	COUNTRIES
1-01-001	COUNTRIMAN
324-15-163	COUNTRY
15-06-012	COUNTRY'S
1-01-001	COUNTRY-SQUIREH
	OOD
1-01-001	COUNTRYMAN
6-04-006	COUNTRYMEN
7-06-007	COUNTRYSIDE
2-02-002	COUNTRYWIDE
12-07-010	COUNTS
2-01-001	COUNTS/MINUTE
155-13-062	COUNTY
2-01-001	COUNTY'S
2-01-002	COUNTY-WIDE
4-04-004	COUP
1-01-001	COUP-PROOF
1-01-001	COUPAL
2-02-002	COUPE
5-01-001	COUPERIN
122-15-084	COUPLE
1-01-001	COUPLE'S
14-05-013	COUPLED
5-01-001	COUPLER
4-01-001	COUPLERS
13-08-010	COUPLES
9-03-004	COUPLING
1-01-001	COUPON
1-01-001	COUPONS
2-02-002	COUPS
32-11-028	COURAGE
4-04-004	COURAGEOUS
3-02-002	COURAGEOUSLY
1-01-001	COURBET
3-01-001	COURCY
1-01-001	COUREURS
1-01-001	COURIER
1-01-001	COURIER-*JOURNA
	L
465-15-259	COURSE
61-09-021	COURSES
1-01-001	COURSING
230-13-064	COURT
8-04-005	COURT'S
1-01-001	COURT-APPOINTED

1-01-001	COURT-LENGTH
1-01-001	COURT-PACKING
1-01-001	COURTED
4-01-001	COURTENAY
6-04-005	COURTEOUS
3-02-002	COURTEOUSLY
2-02-002	COURTESAN
7-05-007	COURTESY
3-01-001	COURTHOUSE
5-01-003	COURTIER
4-04-004	COURTIERS
3-03-003	COURTING
1-01-001	COURTLINESS
2-01-002	COURTLY
1-01-001	COURTNEY
1-01-001	COURTRAI
2-01-002	COURTROOM
50-12-024	COURTS
2-02-002	COURTSHIP
8-06-006	COURTYARD
1-01-001	COURTYARDS
51-09-015	COUSIN
1-01-001	COUSIN'S
1-01-001	COUSIN-WIFE
9-06-007	COUSINS
1-01-001	COUSINS'
1-01-001	COUTURIER
1-01-001	COUVE
2-02-002	COVE
2-02-002	COVENANT
1-01-001	COVENANTS
2-01-002	COVENT
1-01-001	COVENTRY
88-14-064	COVER
25-06-015	COVERAGE
2-01-001	COVERALL
104-15-068	COVERED
32-12-029	COVERING
2-02-002	COVERINGS
2-02-002	COVERLET
32-12-027	COVERS
2-02-002	COVERT
1-01-001	COVERTLY
1-01-001	COVES
1-01-001	COVET
4-04-004	COVETED
1-01-001	COVETING
2-02-002	COVETOUSNESS
2-02-002	COVINGTON
29-09-012	COW
1-01-001	COW'S
1-01-001	COW-MAN
2-02-002	COW-PEOPLE
8-05-006	COWARD
3-01-001	COWARD'S
2-02-002	COWARDICE
3-03-003	COWARDLY
1-01-001	COWBIRD
3-01-001	COWBIRDS
1-01-001	COWBIRDS'
16-06-007	COWBOY
1-01-001	COWBOY'S
4-04-004	COWBOYS
1-01-001	COWERING
1-01-001	COWESSETT
1-01-001	COWESSETT-*EAST
4-02-002	COWHAND
1-01-001	COWHAND'D
1-01-001	COWHANDS
1-01-001	COWHIDE
2-01-001	COWLEY
1-01-001	COWLING
2-01-001	COWMAN
2-02-002	COWORKERS
1-01-001	COWPONY
1-01-001	COWPUNCHER
1-01-001	COWRTIERS
16-05-008	COWS
5-02-004	COX
1-01-001	COXCOMBS
4-03-004	COY
1-01-001	COYLY
2-02-002	COYNESS
1-01-001	COYOTE
1-01-001	COYOTES
1-01-001	COZEN
1-01-001	COZIER
1-01-001	COZY
1-01-001	COOLING
2-01-002	CPS
1-01-001	CR**-SPE
1-01-001	CRABAPPLE
1-01-001	CRABBED
2-02-002	CRABS
21-08-019	CRACK
17-07-016	CRACKED
1-01-001	CRACKER-BOX

4-02-003 CRACKERS
15-07-011 CRACKING
2-02-002 CRACKLE
1-01-001 CRACKLED
1-01-001 CRACKLES
1-01-001 CRACKLING
1-01-001 CRACKPOT
2-02-002 CRACKPOTS
7-04-005 CRACKS
1-01-001 CRADDOCK
7-04-004 CRADLE
3-03-003 CRADLED
1-01-001 CRADLES
23-10-016 CRAFT
1-01-001 CRAFT-INDUSTRIA L
1-01-001 CRAFTER
3-02-003 CRAFTS
2-02-002 CRAFTSMAN
1-01-001 CRAFTSMAN'S
5-04-005 CRAFTSMANSHIP
4-04-004 CRAFTSMEN
1-01-001 CRAFTY
1-01-001 CRAGGY
2-02-002 CRAGS
2-02-002 CRAIG
1-01-001 CRAIG'S
1-01-001 CRAMER
3-02-003 CRAMMED
2-02-002 CRAMP
2-01-001 CRAMPS
1-01-001 CRANBERRIES
5-04-004 CRANE
2-02-002 CRANE'S
1-01-001 CRANELIKE
1-01-001 CRANES
1-01-001 CRANK
1-01-001 CRANKSHAFT
1-01-001 CRANKY
2-02-002 CRANNIES
16-03-004 CRANSTON
3-02-002 CRAP
20-09-016 CRASH
12-07-010 CRASHED
1-01-001 CRASHER
1-01-001 CRASHES
7-04-007 CRASHING
2-02-002 CRASS
1-01-001 CRASSEST
1-01-001 CRASSNESS
2-01-001 CRATE
2-01-001 CRATER
1-01-001 CRATERED
5-03-003 CRATERS
2-02-002 CRATES
2-02-002 CRAVE
2-02-002 CRAVED
2-02-002 CRAVEN
2-01-001 CRAVING
3-02-002 CRAWFORD
11-06-008 CRAWL
20-07-016 CRAWLED
8-03-006 CRAWLING
2-02-002 CRAWLS
1-01-001 CRAWLSPACE
1-01-001 CRAYONS
2-01-001 CRAZE
2-02-002 CRAZED
4-03-004 CRAZILY
1-01-001 CRAZING
34-12-028 CRAZY
1-01-001 CRAZY-WONDERFUL
1-01-001 CREAK
6-02-003 CREAKED
5-04-005 CREAKING
1-01-001 CREAKS
20-09-012 CREAM
1-01-001 CREAMED
4-01-001 CREAMER
1-01-001 CREAMERY
1-01-001 CREAMS
1-01-001 CREAMY
1-01-001 CREASE
2-02-002 CREASED
1-01-001 CREASES
54-11-046 CREATE
81-13-053 CREATED
13-07-012 CREATES
29-11-027 CREATING
46-10-034 CREATION
1-01-001 CREATION'S
3-03-003 CREATIONS
49-09-028 CREATIVE
3-03-003 CREATIVELY
1-01-001 CREATIVENESS
9-03-005 CREATIVITY

1-01-001 CREATIVITY-ORIE NTED
14-06-012 CREATOR
2-01-001 CREATORS
15-08-013 CREATURE
20-09-016 CREATURES
1-01-001 CRECHE
2-02-002 CREDENTIALS
1-01-001 CREDIBILITY
2-01-002 CREDIBLE
1-01-001 CREDIBLY
64-12-037 CREDIT
4-04-004 CREDITABLE
12-06-011 CREDITED
2-02-002 CREDITORS
7-03-006 CREDITS
8-03-005 CREDO
3-03-003 CREDULITY
1-01-001 CREDULOUS
1-01-001 CREDULOUSNESS
8-05-006 CREED
1-01-001 CREEDAL
1-01-001 CREEDS
14-06-011 CREEK
5-01-001 CREEK-*TURN
1-01-001 CREEK-FILLED
1-01-001 CREEKS
10-06-010 CREEP
1-01-001 CREEPER
3-02-002 CREEPERS
8-07-008 CREEPING
1-01-001 CREEPS
3-02-002 CREEPY
3-02-002 CREIGHTON
1-01-001 CREMATE
1-01-001 CREMATED
1-01-001 CREOLE
1-01-001 CREON
1-01-001 CREPE
11-06-010 CREPT
2-02-002 CRESCENDO
2-02-002 CRESCENT
12-04-008 CREST
1-01-001 CRESTED
1-01-001 CRESTFALLEN
1-01-001 CRESTON
1-01-001 CRESTON'S
3-02-002 CRESTS
1-01-001 CRETACEOUS
2-01-001 CREVICE
1-01-001 CREVICES
36-09-020 CREW
1-01-001 CREW'S
1-01-001 CREWCUT
2-01-001 CREWEL
1-01-001 CREWMEN
5-02-002 CREWS
5-02-002 CRIB
3-02-002 CRIBS
3-03-003 CRICKET
2-02-002 CRICKETS
30-10-025 CRIED
6-03-005 CRIES
34-11-023 CRIME
1-01-001 CRIME**H
1-01-001 CRIMEA
2-01-002 CRIMEAN
14-06-011 CRIMES
24-09-015 CRIMINAL
4-03-003 CRIMINALITY
6-03-005 CRIMINALS
8-07-007 CRIMSON
1-01-001 CRIMSONING
2-02-002 CRINGED
3-02-003 CRINGING
1-01-001 CRINKLES
2-01-001 CRIP
1-01-001 CRIPPLE
6-05-006 CRIPPLED
6-06-006 CRIPPLING
1-01-001 CRIS
21-07-013 CRISES
82-12-035 CRISIS
1-01-001 CRISIS-ORIENTED
1-01-001 CRISIS-TO-CRISI S
8-04-007 CRISP
1-01-001 CRISPIN
1-01-001 CRISPLY
2-01-001 CRISPNESS
1-01-001 CRISS-CROSS
3-02-002 CRISS-CROSSED
1-01-001 CRISS-CROSSING
1-01-001 CRISSCROSSED
1-01-001 CRISTO
11-04-008 CRITERIA
11-07-009 CRITERION

25-09-025 CRITIC
1-01-001 CRITIC'S
58-10-042 CRITICAL
1-01-001 CRITICAL-INTELL ECTUAL
5-01-001 CRITICALITY
5-04-005 CRITICALLY
40-07-034 CRITICISM
11-06-010 CRITICISMS
4-03-004 CRITICIZE
14-05-010 CRITICIZED
2-01-002 CRITICIZING
26-08-021 CRITICS
1-01-001 CRITICS'
1-01-001 CRITIQUE
3-01-001 CRITTENDEN
1-01-001 CRITTER
3-02-002 CRITTERS
1-01-001 CROAK
1-01-001 CROAKED
1-01-001 CROAKIN
1-01-001 CROAKING
1-01-001 CROAKS
1-01-001 CROCHET
1-01-001 CROCKED
1-01-001 CROCKETED
1-01-001 CROCKETT
1-01-001 CROCODILE
1-01-001 CROFTERS
1-01-001 CROIX
11-01-001 CROMBIE
1-01-001 CROMBIE'S
21-05-005 CROMWELL
1-01-001 CROMWELL'S
1-01-001 CROMWELLIAN
2-01-001 CRONE
2-02-002 CRONIES
3-03-003 CROOK
2-02-002 CROOKED
2-02-002 CROOKS
2-01-002 CROONED
1-01-001 CROONING
20-07-014 CROP
5-04-005 CROPPED
1-01-001 CROPPING
18-07-010 CROPS
5-02-002 CROSBY
2-02-002 CROSBY'S
1-01-001 CROSBYS
55-13-045 CROSS
1-01-001 CROSS-CULTURAL
1-01-001 CROSS-EXAMINATI ON
1-01-001 CROSS-EYED
1-01-001 CROSS-FERTILIZA TION
1-01-001 CROSS-FERTILIZE D
2-02-002 CROSS-LEGGED
4-01-001 CROSS-LICENSING
1-01-001 CROSS-PURPOSES
5-04-004 CROSS-SECTION
4-02-003 CROSS-SECTIONAL
2-01-001 CROSS-STRIATION S
1-01-001 CROSS-TOP
1-01-001 CROSS-WRITING
1-01-001 CROSSBARS
42-10-030 CROSSED
4-02-003 CROSSES
21-11-021 CROSSING
1-01-001 CROSSINGS
2-01-001 CROSSMAN
2-01-001 CROSSON
2-01-001 CROSSON'S
1-01-001 CROSSOVER
1-01-001 CROSSROADING
12-06-009 CROSSROADS
1-01-001 CROSSWALK
1-01-001 CROSSWAYS
1-01-001 CROSSWISE
1-01-001 CROTCHETY
7-03-004 CROUCH
1-01-001 CROUCH'S
16-05-010 CROUCHED
1-01-001 CROUCHIN
3-03-003 CROUCHING
1-01-001 CROUPIER
2-02-002 CROW
1-01-001 CROWBAIT
53-13-040 CROWD
32-12-029 CROWDED
2-01-001 CROWDER
5-04-005 CROWDING
12-08-012 CROWDS
2-02-002 CROWED
3-02-003 CROWING

19-09-011 CROWN
7-05-006 CROWNED
3-03-003 CROWNING
1-01-001 CROWNS
2-02-002 CROWS
1-01-001 CROYDON
1-01-001 CROZIER
30-11-024 CRUCIAL
1-01-001 CRUCIALLY
1-01-001 CRUCIBLE
2-02-002 CRUCIFIED
3-02-002 CRUCIFIX
1-01-001 CRUCIFIXION
2-02-002 CRUCIFYING
15-08-014 CRUDE
2-02-002 CRUDELY
1-01-001 CRUDEST
1-01-001 CRUDITIES
1-01-001 CRUDITY
15-07-014 CRUEL
1-01-001 CRUELEST
4-04-004 CRUELLY
13-08-013 CRUELTY
2-02-002 CRUISE
4-03-003 CRUISER
2-02-002 CRUISERS
1-01-001 CRUISES
7-05-006 CRUISING
3-01-001 CRUMB
2-02-002 CRUMBLE
3-03-003 CRUMBLED
2-02-002 CRUMBLING
1-01-001 CRUMBLY
1-01-001 CRUMLEY
1-01-001 CRUMLISH
3-02-002 CRUMMY
1-01-001 CRUMP
4-03-004 CRUMPLED
2-02-002 CRUNCH
1-01-001 CRUNCHED
2-02-002 CRUPPER
4-01-001 CRUS
8-05-005 CRUSADE
1-01-001 CRUSADER
2-01-002 CRUSADERS
1-01-001 CRUSADES
1-01-001 CRUSADING
4-03-004 CRUSH
10-08-008 CRUSHED
1-01-001 CRUSHER
1-01-001 CRUSHERS
7-05-006 CRUSHING
1-01-001 CRUST
1-01-001 CRUTCH
6-05-005 CRUTCHES
2-02-002 CRUX
8-01-001 CRUZ
48-10-034 CRY
15-07-014 CRYING
1-01-001 CRYOSTAT
1-01-001 CRYPT
3-02-003 CRYPTIC
1-01-001 CRYPTOGRAPHIC
23-06-009 CRYSTAL
5-02-002 CRYSTALLINE
1-01-001 CRYSTALLITE
3-01-002 CRYSTALLITES
3-02-002 CRYSTALLIZATI
1-01-001 CRYSTALLIZE
1-01-001 CRYSTALLIZED
2-02-002 CRYSTALLIZING
1-01-001 CRYSTALLOGRAP
5-01-001 CRYSTALLOGRAP
2-02-002 CRYSTALLOGRAP
8-02-003 CRYSTALS
1-01-001 CT
1-01-001 CU
1-01-001 CUB'S
47-09-020 CUBA
2-02-002 CUBA'S
19-03-011 CUBAN
1-01-001 CUBAN-*AMERIC
5-02-003 CUBANS
1-01-001 CUBBYHOLE
1-01-001 CUBE
1-01-001 CUBED
4-03-004 CUBES
15-03-003 CUBIC
11-01-001 CUBISM
7-02-003 CUBIST
1-01-001 CUBISTS
2-02-002 CUBS
1-01-001 CUCKOO-BUMBLE
1-01-001 CUD

```
1-01-001   CUDDLEBACK
2-02-002   CUDGELS
1-01-001   CUDKOWICZ
1-01-001   CUDMORE
1-01-001   CUE-PHRASE
3-02-001   CUES
1-01-001   CUFF
1-01-001   CUFFLINKS
2-02-002   CUFFS
1-01-001   CUIRASSIERS
1-01-001   CUISINE
1-01-001   CULBERTSON
2-02-002   CULMINATE
2-02-002   CULMINATED
5-04-005   CULMINATES
2-02-002   CULMINATING
4-03-003   CULMINATION
1-01-001   CULMONE
1-01-001   CULPAS
2-02-002   CULPRIT
2-02-002   CULPRITS
11-05-007  CULT
1-01-001   CULTE
2-02-002   CULTIST
3-03-003   CULTIVATE
10-06-009  CULTIVATED
1-01-001   CULTIVATES
2-01-001   CULTIVATING
4-03-004   CULTIVATION
4-04-004   CULTS
55-09-032  CULTURAL
5-03-005   CULTURALLY
58-10-034  CULTURE
1-01-001   CULTURE'S
1-01-001   CULTURE-*PROTES
             TANTISM
4-02-003   CULTURED
12-06-010  CULTURES
2-01-001   CULVER
1-01-001   CULVERS
1-01-001   CUMARA
1-01-001   CUMBANCHEROS
3-03-003   CUMBERLAND
3-02-003   CUMBERSOME
1-01-001   CUMHURIYET
1-01-001   CUMIN
1-01-001   CUMULATE
13-06-009  CUMULATIVE
1-01-001   CUMULUS
5-01-001   CUNARD
1-01-001   CUNARD'S
5-04-005   CUNNING
5-02-002   CUNNINGHAM
2-02-002   CUNNINGHAM'S
3-03-003   CUNNINGLY
45-10-024  CUP
2-02-002   CUPBOARD
2-02-002   CUPBOARDS
3-01-001   CUPFUL
4-03-004   CUPPED
3-01-001   CUPPLY
14-07-011  CUPS
1-01-001   CUR
1-01-001   CURATIVE
2-02-002   CURATOR
13-05-010  CURB
3-02-002   CURBING
3-02-002   CURBS
3-03-003   CURBSIDE
2-02-002   CURD
1-01-001   CURDLING
1-01-001   CURDS
28-07-016  CURE
4-02-002   CURE-ALL
7-03-003   CURED
3-02-003   CURES
1-01-001   CURETTAGE
3-01-001   CURIA
3-01-001   CURIAE
2-02-002   CURIE
1-01-001   CURIE-*WEISS
1-01-001   CURING
2-01-001   CURIO
23-10-020  CURIOSITY
46-14-037  CURIOUS
11-05-011  CURIOUSLY
2-02-002   CURL
13-06-011  CURLED
2-02-002   CURLING
1-01-001   CURLS
5-03-005   CURLY
1-01-001   CURRANT
1-01-001   CURRANTS
3-01-002   CURRENCIES
12-06-006  CURRENCY
104-12-073 CURRENT
34-09-029  CURRENTLY

9-04-007   CURRENTS
3-03-003   CURRICULA
2-02-002   CURRICULAR
16-05-010  CURRICULUM
1-01-001   CURRICULUMS
2-02-002   CURRY
1-01-001   CURRYS
1-01-001   CURSE
11-06-010  CURSED
11-06-011  CURSES
3-03-003   CURSING
8-05-008   CURSORY
4-03-004   CURT
32-02-002  CURT'S
8-01-001   CURTAIL
4-04-004   CURTAILED
2-01-002   CURTAILS
13-08-011  CURTAIN
1-01-001   CURTAIN-RAISER
1-01-001   CURTAINED
1-01-001   CURTAINS
8-05-008   CURTIN
3-02-002   CURTIS
2-02-002   CURTISS
2-02-002   CURTLY
1-01-001   CURTNESS
1-01-001   CURTSEYED
1-01-001   CURVACEOUSLY
5-01-003   CURVATURE
45-05-012  CURVE
7-03-005   CURVED
19-05-008  CURVES
4-04-004   CURVING
3-02-002   CURY
5-02-002   CURZON
3-01-001   CURZON'S
1-01-001   CUSA
8-05-006   CUSHION
4-02-002   CUSHIONING
2-02-002   CUSHIONS
1-01-001   CUSHMAN
2-01-001   CUSP
5-01-001   CUSTER
1-01-001   CUSTER'S
1-01-001   CUSTODIAL
3-03-003   CUSTODIAN
2-02-002   CUSTODY
14-06-013  CUSTOM
1-01-001   CUSTOM-DESIGN
1-01-001   CUSTOM-MAKE
4-03-004   CUSTOMARILY
14-10-014  CUSTOMARY
27-08-016  CUSTOMER
1-01-001   CUSTOMER'S
1-01-001   CUSTOMER-COST
40-11-023  CUSTOMERS
1-01-001   CUSTOMERS'
1-01-001   CUSTOMHOUSE
18-08-012  CUSTOMS
192-15-111 CUT
1-01-001   CUT-AND-DRIED
1-01-001   CUT-DOWN
1-01-001   CUT-GLASS
1-01-001   CUT-OFF
1-01-001   CUT-TO-A-FAMILI
             AR-PATTERN
1-01-001   CUTBACK
5-03-004   CUTE
1-01-001   CUTEST
1-01-001   CUTLASS
1-01-001   CUTLETS
1-01-001   CUTOFF
1-01-001   CUTOUTS
30-08-024  CUTS
4-02-002   CUTTER
6-03-003   CUTTERS
1-01-001   CUTTERS'
1-01-001   CUTTHROAT
66-08-024  CUTTING
1-01-001   CUTTING-EDGE
1-01-001   CUTTINGS
1-01-001   CYCLADES
24-07-021  CYCLE
1-01-001   CYCLED
7-06-007   CYCLES
1-01-001   CYCLICAL
8-01-001   CYCLIST
1-01-001   CYCLOHEXANOL
1-01-001   CYCLORAMA
1-01-001   CYCLY
18-02-003  CYLINDER
2-01-001   CYLINDER'S
7-01-001   CYLINDERS
11-02-006  CYLINDRICAL
3-01-001   CYNEWULF
9-05-006   CYNICAL
1-01-001   CYNICALLY

4-03-003   CYNICISM
3-03-003   CYNICS
2-02-002   CYNTHIA
7-05-005   CYPRESS
1-01-001   CYPRESS-LIKE
1-01-001   CYPRIAN
1-01-001   CYR
1-01-001   CYRIL
4-03-003   CYRUS
3-02-002   CYSTS
1-01-001   CYTOLYSIS
4-01-002   CYTOPLASM
1-01-001   CZAR
2-01-001   CZARINA
3-01-001   CZARINA'S
1-01-001   CZARSHIP
5-04-004   CZECHOSLOVAKIA
1-01-001   CZERNY
90-10-062  D
1-01-001   D)),
1-01-001   D),
3-02-002   D**.*A
22-06-010  D**.*C
1-01-001   D**.*J
1-01-001   D**.*O**.*A
1-01-001   D**.*W
1-01-001   D'*=YOU
4-01-001   D'*ALBERT
1-01-001   D'*AMOURS
1-01-001   D'*ARGENT
1-01-001   D'*ARLAY
1-01-001   D'*ART
3-01-001   D'*ARTAGUETTE
1-01-001   D'*AUMONT
1-01-001   D'*EIFFEL
1-01-001   D'*YQUEM
1-01-001   D'ART
1-01-001   D'ENTRETENIR
2-02-002   D'ETAT
1-01-001   D'HOTEL
1-01-001   D'IDENTITE
1-01-001   D'UN
1-01-001   D-C
1-01-001   D-NIGHT
9-02-003   DA
1-01-001   DA-DA-DA-DUM
1-01-001   DABBED
2-01-002   DABBING
1-01-001   DABBLED
1-01-001   DABBLER
1-01-001   DABBLES
2-02-002   DABBLING
1-01-001   DABHUMAKSANIGAL
             U'AHAI
1-01-001   DACHSHUND
1-01-001   DACK-RIHS
2-01-001   DACTYLS
15-04-009  DAD
1-01-001   DADAISM
2-02-002   DADDY
2-02-002   DADDY'S
1-01-001   DADE
1-01-001   DADE'S
5-01-001   DAER
1-01-001   DAFFODILS
7-03-005   DAG
1-01-001   DAGERS
1-01-001   DAGGERMAN
1-01-001   DAILEY
122-13-059 DAILY
1-01-001   DAINTILY
3-03-003   DAINTY
1-01-001   DAINTY-LEGGED
19-04-005  DAIRY
1-01-001   DAIRY-OH
2-02-002   DAIS
1-01-001   DAISES
3-02-002   DAISIES
1-01-001   DAK
6-04-005   DAKOTA
5-03-002   DALE
1-01-001   DALES
2-02-002   DALEY
1-01-001   DALI
58-05-010  DALLAS
1-01-001   DALLAS-BASED
1-01-001   DALLAS-HEADQUAR
             TERED
1-01-001   DALLES
3-01-001   DALLOWAY
4-02-004   DALTON
1-01-001   DALTON'S
1-01-001   DALY
1-01-001   DALZELL-*COUSIN
5-04-004   DAM

33-10-022  DAMAGE
7-05-007   DAMAGED
3-02-002   DAMAGES
3-03-003   DAMAGING
1-01-001   DAMAS
3-02-002   DAMASCUS
7-03-004   DAME
2-01-001   DAMED
1-01-001   DAMMED
1-01-001   DAMMED-UP
7-03-006   DAMMIT
34-05-025  DAMN
3-02-002   DAMNATION
19-08-021  DAMNED
1-01-001   DAMNING
1-01-001   DAMNIT
1-01-001   DAMON
16-08-012  DAMP
2-02-002   DAMPEN
3-03-003   DAMPENED
1-01-001   DAMPENING
2-02-002   DAMPNESS
3-03-003   DAMS
1-01-001   DAMSEL
27-03-006  DAN
1-01-001   DAN'L
3-01-001   DAN'S
3-02-002   DANA
3-01-001   DANA'S
2-01-001   DANAHER
1-01-001   DANBURY
90-13-040  DANCE
1-01-001   DANCE-THEATRE
10-05-008  DANCED
1-01-001   DANCELIKE
31-07-011  DANCER
31-08-016  DANCERS
1-01-001   DANCERS'
23-09-014  DANCES
1-01-001   DANCHIN
43-08-030  DANCING
1-01-001   DANDELION
1-01-001   DANDILY
17-03-003  DANDY
1-01-001   DANDY'S
2-02-002   DANE
1-01-001   DANEHY
4-03-003   DANES
1-01-001   DANG
1-01-001   DANGED
70-12-054  DANGER
46-12-041  DANGEROUS
3-03-003   DANGEROUSLY
16-07-015  DANGERS
1-01-001   DANGLE
2-01-002   DANGLED
4-04-004   DANGLING
14-07-009  DANIEL
1-01-001   DANIEL'S
2-01-001   DANIELS
8-04-004   DANISH
1-01-001   DANK
1-01-001   DANNEHOWER
6-03-004   DANNY
1-01-001   DANNY'S
1-01-001   DANS
1-01-001   DANSEUR
2-02-002   DANTE
1-01-001   DANTE'S
3-03-003   DANUBE
1-01-001   DANUBIAN
1-01-001   DANVILLE
1-01-001   DANZIG
1-01-001   DAPHNE
6-05-005   DAPPER
1-01-001   DAPPERTUTTO
1-01-001   DAPPLED
1-01-001   DARBUKA
21-10-019  DARE
1-01-001   DARE-*BASE
14-08-011  DARED
5-03-004   DARES
1-01-001   DARIN
12-06-010  DARING
1-01-001   DARIUS
185-14-106 DARK
1-01-001   DARK-BLUE
1-01-001   DARK-BROWN
1-01-001   DARK-GRAY
1-01-001   DARK-GREEN
2-02-002   DARK-HAIRED
1-01-001   DARK-SKINNED
7-05-006   DARKENED
4-03-004   DARKENING
2-02-002   DARKER
2-02-002   DARKEST
1-01-001   DARKHAIRED
```

2-02-002	DARKLING	1-01-001	DE-*KOONING	2-01-001	DECEDENT	12-01-001	DEDUCT
2-01-002	DARKLY	1-01-001	DE-IODINASE	2-02-002	DECEIT	1-01-001	DEDUCTABLE
43-10-031	DARKNESS	1-01-001	DE-IODINATE	1-01-001	DECEIT'S	4-02-003	DEDUCTED
1-01-001	DARLENE	1-01-001	DE-IODINATED	1-01-001	DECEITFUL	1-01-001	DEDUCTIBILITY
17-09-013	DARLING	2-01-001	DE-IODINATING	1-01-001	DECEIVE	5-03-004	DEDUCTIBLE
1-01-001	DARLING'S	1-01-001	DE-IODINATION	5-04-005	DECEIVED	1-01-001	DEDUCTIBLES
3-03-003	DARN	5-02-003	DEACON	1-01-001	DECEIVES	1-01-001	DEDUCTING
4-04-004	DARNED	1-01-001	DEACONS	1-01-001	DECEIVING	12-05-007	DEDUCTION
1-01-001	DARNELL	1-01-001	DEACTIVATED	1-01-001	DECELERATE	11-02-002	DEDUCTIONS
1-01-001	DARRELL	2-01-002	DEACTIVATION	2-01-001	DECELERATION	3-03-003	DEDUCTIVE
1-01-001	DARROW	174-15-102	DEAD	62-10-044	DECEMBER	8-07-008	DEED
6-04-006	DARTED	1-01-001	DEAD-END	1-01-001	DECENCIES	8-07-008	DEEDS
1-01-001	DARTING	1-01-001	DEAD-WEIGHT	10-07-010	DECENCY	22-01-001	DEEGAN
30-03-005	DARTMOUTH	1-01-001	DEADENED	20-08-019	DECENT	2-01-001	DEEGAN'S
3-01-001	DARTMOUTH'S	1-01-001	DEADHEADS	1-01-001	DECENTLY	1-01-001	DEEM
1-01-001	DARWEN	2-02-002	DEADLIEST	1-01-001	DECENTRALIZATIO	15-07-012	DEEMED
1-01-001	DARWIN	6-04-006	DEADLINE		N	1-01-001	DEEMING
1-01-001	DARWIN'S	1-01-001	DEADLINES	1-01-001	DECENTRALIZING	109-15-078	DEEP
2-01-002	DARWINISM	2-02-002	DEADLINESS	1-01-001	DECEPTION	1-01-001	DEEP-EYED
2-02-002	DAS	10-03-006	DEADLOCK	4-04-004	DECEPTIVE	2-01-001	DEEP-SEA
11-06-010	DASH	19-09-017	DEADLY	1-01-001	DECEPTIVELY	2-02-002	DEEP-SEATED
2-02-002	DASHBOARD	1-01-001	DEADNESS	1-01-001	DECERTIFY	3-03-003	DEEP-SET
8-06-007	DASHED	1-01-001	DEADWEIGHT	40-12-037	DECIDE	1-01-001	DEEP-SOUNDING
2-02-002	DASHES	1-01-001	DEADWOOD	141-15-107	DECIDED	1-01-001	DEEP-TENDON
3-01-001	DASHIELL	12-06-007	DEAF	4-03-004	DECIDEDLY	1-01-001	DEEPEN
4-02-003	DASHING	1-01-001	DEAFENED	12-08-011	DECIDES	2-02-002	DEEPENED
1-01-001	DASHWOOD	142-15-107	DEAL	12-06-009	DECIDING	1-01-001	DEEPENING
173-10-048	DATA	25-05-014	DEALER	3-01-001	DECIMAL	37-12-031	DEEPER
1-01-001	DATA-HANDLING	2-01-001	DEALER'S	1-01-001	DECIMALS	13-07-012	DEEPEST
2-01-002	DATA-PROCESSING	30-07-015	DEALERS	1-01-001	DECIMETER-WAVE-	39-13-036	DEEPLY
103-13-065	DATE	3-02-002	DEALERS'		LENGTH	1-01-001	DEEPS
19-05-008	DATED	1-01-001	DEALERSHIPS	119-14-062	DECISION	13-06-008	DEER
4-01-001	DATELINED	43-10-037	DEALING	1-01-001	DECISION-MAKING	3-01-001	DEERSKINS
30-09-024	DATES	7-05-007	DEALINGS	1-01-001	DECISIONAL	6-01-001	DEERSTALKER
4-04-004	DATING	15-06-014	DEALS	54-10-036	DECISIONS	1-01-001	DEF
1-01-001	DATUM	22-08-019	DEALT	19-06-017	DECISIVE	1-01-001	DEFACING
1-01-001	DAUBED	40-07-022	DEAN	5-02-005	DECISIVELY	2-02-002	DEFAULT
72-12-043	DAUGHTER	2-01-001	DEAN'S	2-02-002	DECISIVENESS	1-01-001	DEFAULTED
4-03-003	DAUGHTER'S	1-01-001	DEANE	23-07-012	DECK	31-09-020	DEFEAT
14-07-011	DAUGHTERS	1-01-001	DEANS	1-01-001	DECKED	15-08-013	DEFEATED
1-01-001	DAUNT	54-10-038	DEAR	2-01-001	DECKING	3-03-003	DEFEATING
1-01-001	DAUNTED	2-02-002	DEARBORN	6-02-002	DECKS	1-01-001	DEFEATISM
2-02-002	DAUNTLESS	1-01-001	DEARER	2-01-001	DECLAIMED	1-01-001	DEFEATISTS
1-01-001	DAUPHIN	2-02-002	DEAREST	1-01-001	DECLAMATORY	2-02-002	DEFEATS
1-01-001	DAUPHINE	1-01-001	DEARIE	24-08-016	DECLARATION	1-01-001	DEFECATED
1-01-001	DAVAO	4-04-004	DEARLY	2-02-002	DECLARATIONS	3-03-003	DEFECT
31-04-008	DAVE	3-03-003	DEARTH	9-01-002	DECLARATIVE	2-02-002	DEFECTION
1-01-001	DAVE'S	277-15-132	DEATH	8-05-008	DECLARE	7-05-006	DEFECTIVE
4-02-002	DAVENPORT	2-01-001	DEATH'S-*HEAD	66-11-052	DECLARED	13-07-010	DEFECTS
51-10-028	DAVID	1-01-001	DEATH-LIKE	11-07-009	DECLARES	1-01-001	DEFENCE
4-03-003	DAVID'S	1-01-001	DEATH-LOCKED	10-06-010	DECLARING	21-07-021	DEFEND
3-03-003	DAVIDSON	1-01-001	DEATH-TRAP	1-01-001	DECLINATIONS	6-02-003	DEFENDANT
2-01-001	DAVIDSON'S	1-01-001	DEATH-WISH	31-07-021	DECLINE	1-01-001	DEFENDANT'S
27-05-013	DAVIS	2-02-002	DEATHBED	17-09-016	DECLINED	10-02-004	DEFENDANTS
2-02-002	DAVIS'	1-01-001	DEATHLY	6-04-005	DECLINES	18-07-016	DEFENDED
1-01-001	DAVITS	8-05-007	DEATHS	9-06-009	DECLINING	3-01-003	DEFENDER
2-02-002	DAVY	1-01-001	DEATHWARD	2-02-002	DECLIVITY	6-04-006	DEFENDERS
1-01-001	DAVY'S	2-01-001	DEAUVILLE	1-01-001	DECOLLETAGE	13-07-013	DEFENDING
28-10-023	DAWN	3-03-003	DEBACLE	1-01-001	DECOMPOSE	4-03-004	DEFENDS
2-02-002	DAWNING	1-01-001	DEBATABLE	2-01-001	DECOMPOSES	167-11-063	DEFENSE
1-01-001	DAWNS	32-09-019	DEBATE	2-02-002	DECOMPOSING	3-03-003	DEFENSELESS
1-01-001	DAWSON	5-04-005	DEBATED	14-01-003	DECOMPOSITION	12-09-010	DEFENSES
686-15-288	DAY	6-03-005	DEBATES	1-01-001	DECOMPRESSION	3-02-003	DEFENSIBLE
15-08-014	DAY'S	4-04-004	DEBATING	4-03-004	DECOR	17-06-013	DEFENSIVE
2-02-002	DAY-AFTER-DAY	2-02-002	DEBAUCHERY	2-01-001	DECORATE	2-01-001	DEFENSIVENESS
3-02-003	DAY-BY-DAY	6-01-001	DEBENTURES	6-04-006	DECORATED	1-01-001	DEFER
3-02-003	DAY-TO-DAY	2-02-002	DEBILITATED	4-03-003	DECORATING	5-05-005	DEFERENCE
2-01-001	DAY-WATCH	2-02-002	DEBILITATING	8-06-007	DECORATION	2-01-001	DEFERENT
1-01-001	DAYBED	2-01-001	DEBILITY	8-05-007	DECORATIONS	1-01-001	DEFERENTS
1-01-001	DAYBREAK	1-01-001	DEBONAIR	8-04-004	DECORATIVE	1-01-001	DEFERMENT
1-01-001	DAYDREAMED	3-01-001	DEBONNIE	1-01-001	DECORATIVENESS	1-01-001	DEFERMENTS
1-01-001	DAYDREAMING	2-01-001	DEBORA	5-05-005	DECORATOR	1-01-001	DEFERRED
15-08-014	DAYLIGHT	8-05-006	DEBRIS	4-02-003	DECORATORS	1-01-001	DEFERRING
1-01-001	DAYLIGHT'S	2-02-002	DEBS	1-01-001	DECOROUS	7-04-007	DEFIANCE
1-01-001	DAYLIGHTS	13-06-013	DEBT	1-01-001	DECORTICATED	3-02-003	DEFIANT
384-15-216	DAYS	1-01-001	DEBT-FREE	2-02-002	DECORUM	2-02-002	DEFIANTLY
2-02-002	DAYS'	12-06-009	DEBTS	15-06-013	DECREASE	10-04-007	DEFICIENCIES
19-05-005	DAYTIME	2-02-002	DEBUNKING	8-02-006	DECREASED	11-05-007	DEFICIENCY
4-03-004	DAZED	14-03-010	DEBUT	8-02-006	DECREASES	3-03-003	DEFICIENT
1-01-001	DAZZLE	5-02-003	DEBUTANTE	6-02-006	DECREASING	12-05-008	DEFICIT
2-02-002	DAZZLED	2-01-001	DEBUTING	3-03-003	DECREE	1-01-001	DEFICITS
1-01-001	DAZZLER	1-01-001	DEBUTS	1-01-001	DECREED	4-04-004	DEFIED
1-01-001	DAZZLES	17-04-008	DEC	1-01-001	DECREEING	1-01-001	DEFINABLE
9-06-008	DAZZLING	46-10-026	DECADE	5-03-004	DECREES	27-07-016	DEFINE
122-13-062	DE	2-02-002	DECADENCE	2-01-001	DECREMENT	39-06-029	DEFINED
1-01-001	DE*CICCO	2-02-002	DECADENT	2-02-002	DECRIED	5-04-005	DEFINES
1-01-001	DE*FOREST	34-08-026	DECADES	1-01-001	DECRIES	10-06-010	DEFINING
1-01-001	DE*GROOT	2-01-001	DECANTED	2-01-002	DECRY	37-14-036	DEFINITE
1-01-001	DE*HAVILAND	3-01-001	DECANTING	1-01-001	DECRYING	21-09-019	DEFINITELY
5-01-001	DE*KALB	1-01-001	DECATHLON	23-09-022	DEDICATED	38-08-026	DEFINITION
1-01-001	DE*KALB'S	1-01-001	DECATUR	2-02-002	DEDICATES	2-01-001	DEFINITION-SPE
2-02-002	DE*MONTEZ	14-05-009	DECAY	21-09-017	DEDICATION		IALIZATION
2-02-002	DE*PAUL	4-04-004	DECAYED	1-01-001	DEDIFFERENTIATE	6-03-005	DEFINITIONS
3-01-001	DE*PUGH	4-04-004	DECAYING		D	5-04-005	DEFINITIVE
1-01-001	DE*SOTO	3-02-002	DECAYS	3-02-003	DEDUCE	1-01-001	DEFLATED
1-01-001	DE*WITT	3-02-002	DECCA	6-03-006	DEDUCED	2-01-001	DEFOCUSING
		10-06-008	DECEASED	1-01-001	DEDUCING	3-01-002	DEFOE

5-01-002 DEFORMATION	1-01-001 DELIVRE	2-01-001 DEMYTHOLOGIZED	2-01-001 DEPOSED
1-01-001 DEFORMATIONAL	5-03-003 DELL	1-01-001 DEMYTHOLOGIZING	9-06-006 DEPOSIT
1-01-001 DEFORMITIES	1-01-001 DELL'*ARCA	2-01-002 DEN	10-05-007 DEPOSITED
3-02-002 DEFORMITY	6-02-002 DELLA	18-09-013 DENIAL	3-03-003 DEPOSITION
2-01-001 DEFRAUD	1-01-001 DELLE	4-04-004 DENIALS	3-01-001 DEPOSITIONS
2-02-002 DEFRAY	2-01-001 DELLER	47-10-030 DENIED	1-01-001 DEPOSITORS
1-01-001 DEFROST	1-01-001 DELLS	6-04-006 DENIES	6-04-005 DEPOSITS
2-02-002 DEFT	1-01-001 DELLWOOD	4-03-003 DENMARK	13-03-005 DEPOT
1-01-001 DEFTNESS	1-01-001 DELMORE	3-03-003 DENNIS	1-01-001 DEPOTS
3-02-002 DEFUNCT	2-01-001 DELON	2-01-001 DENNY	2-01-001 DEPPY
7-05-007 DEFY	1-01-001 DELORIS	1-01-001 DENNY'S	2-02-002 DEPRAVED
2-02-002 DEFYING	1-01-001 DELOUSED	1-01-001 DENOMINATED	1-01-001 DEPRAVITIES
1-01-001 DEGAS	1-01-001 DELPHI	8-04-005 DENOMINATION	3-02-003 DEPRAVITY
1-01-001 DEGASSED	1-01-001 DELPHIC	2-01-001 DENOMINATION'S	1-01-001 DEPRECATORY
1-01-001 DEGENERATED	12-01-001 DELPHINE	9-04-005 DENOMINATIONAL	12-05-009 DEPRECIATION
1-01-001 DEGENERATION	2-01-001 DELPHINE'S	1-01-001 DENOMINATIONALL Y	3-03-003 DEPREDATIONS
1-01-001 DEGLYCEROLIZED	1-01-001 DELRAY		1-01-001 DEPRESS
2-02-002 DEGRADATION	7-02-005 DELTA	15-03-005 DENOMINATIONS	1-01-001 DEPRESSANTS
1-01-001 DEGRADE	1-01-001 DELTAS	1-01-001 DENOMINATORS	11-05-009 DEPRESSED
1-01-001 DEGRADED	1-01-001 DELTOID	4-02-004 DENOTE	1-01-001 DEPRESSES
1-01-001 DEGRADING	2-01-001 DELTOIDS	9-03-005 DENOTED	5-05-005 DEPRESSING
125-14-081 DEGREE	2-01-001 DELUDE	7-01-003 DENOTES	2-02-002 DEPRESSINGLY
23-05-016 DEGREES	3-02-002 DELUDED	5-02-003 DENOTING	24-08-020 DEPRESSION
1-01-001 DEHUMANISED	1-01-001 DELUDING	2-02-002 DENOUEMENT	3-02-002 DEPRESSIONS
1-01-001 DEHUMANIZE	2-02-002 DELUGE	5-04-005 DENOUNCE	1-01-001 DEPRESSORS
1-01-001 DEHUMIDIFIED	1-01-001 DELUGED	7-04-007 DENOUNCED	1-01-001 DEPRIVATION
1-01-001 DEHYDRATED	1-01-001 DELUSION	1-01-001 DENOUNCES	1-01-001 DEPRIVATIONS
1-01-001 DEHYDRATION	4-03-004 DELUXE	4-03-004 DENOUNCING	3-03-003 DEPRIVE
7-02-003 DEI	1-01-001 DELVIN	1-01-001 DENS	8-04-007 DEPRIVED
1-01-001 DEIFICATION	2-02-002 DELVING	9-07-009 DENSE	3-03-003 DEPRIVING
1-01-001 DEIGNED	1-01-001 DEMAGE	1-01-001 DENSEST	5-04-005 DEPT
2-02-002 DEITIES	1-01-001 DEMAGNIFICATION	2-01-002 DENSITIES	53-07-032 DEPTH
1-01-001 DEITY	1-01-001 DEMAGOGUES	1-01-001 DENSITOMETRY	19-10-016 DEPTHS
7-01-001 DEJA	102-13-058 DEMAND	30-08-016 DENSITY	13-05-008 DEPUTIES
1-01-001 DEJECTEDLY	47-11-036 DEMANDED	1-01-001 DENSMORE	1-01-001 DEPUTIZED
1-01-001 DEJECTION	1-01-001 DEMANDER	2-02-002 DENT	17-06-012 DEPUTY
1-01-001 DEJEUNER	19-10-017 DEMANDING	12-04-004 DENTAL	2-01-001 DEPUTY'S
1-01-001 DEJEUNERS	1-01-001 DEMANDINGLY	1-01-001 DENTED	2-01-001 DEQUINDRE
1-01-001 DEKALB	55-11-043 DEMANDS	2-02-002 DENTING	2-02-002 DER
12-06-006 DEL	1-01-001 DEMARCATED	12-04-004 DENTIST	1-01-001 DERAILS
1-01-001 DELAHANTY	2-01-001 DEMARCATION	3-01-001 DENTIST'S	2-02-002 DERANGED
1-01-001 DELANCY	2-02-002 DEMEANOR	1-01-001 DENTISTRY	1-01-001 DERANGEMENT
3-02-002 DELANEY	1-01-001 DEMEANS	4-02-002 DENTISTS	7-04-005 DERAS
1-01-001 DELANO	1-01-001 DEMENTED	4-01-002 DENTON	7-04-005 DERBY
27-07-009 DELAWARE	1-01-001 DEMETRIUS	1-01-001 DENTURES	1-01-001 DERE
1-01-001 DELAWARES	1-01-001 DEMI-MONDE	1-01-001 DENUDED	1-01-001 DERELICT
21-09-019 DELAY	1-01-001 DEMINERALIZATIO N	4-04-004 DENUNCIATION	2-01-002 DERELICTION
25-09-019 DELAYED		2-02-002 DENUNCIATIONS	1-01-001 DERELICTS
3-02-002 DELAYS	4-04-004 DEMISE	16-05-010 DENVER	4-03-004 DERISION
1-01-001 DELECTATION	1-01-001 DEMOCRACIES	1-01-001 DENVER'S	1-01-001 DERISIVELY
8-03-006 DELEGATE	24-05-015 DEMOCRACY	1-01-001 DENVER-AREA	4-03-004 DERIVATION
4-03-004 DELEGATED	13-04-009 DEMOCRAT	47-11-039 DENVERITE	1-01-001 DERIVATIONS
16-03-008 DELEGATES	109-08-038 DEMOCRATIC	1-01-001 DENY	1-01-001 DERIVATIVE
1-01-001 DELEGATES'	2-01-001 DEMOCRATIC-ENDO RSED	13-05-012 DENYIN	1-01-001 DERIVE
2-02-002 DELEGATING		10-09-010 DENYING	39-10-026 DERIVED
11-05-010 DELEGATION	1-01-001 DEMOCRATIC-SPON SORED	2-01-001 DEODORANT	9-06-009 DERIVES
2-02-002 DELEGATIONS		1-01-001 DEOR	4-02-004 DERIVING
1-01-001 DELENDA	1-01-001 DEMOCRATIQUE	7-05-007 DEPART	1-01-001 DEROGATE
5-04-005 DELHI	2-02-002 DEMOCRATIZATION	9-05-009 DEPARTED	1-01-001 DEROGATORY
1-01-001 DELIA	3-01-003 DEMOCRATIZE	10-07-010 DEPARTING	3-01-002 DERRICK
15-09-015 DELIBERATE	40-06-019 DEMOCRATS	225-13-082 DEPARTMENT	1-01-001 DERRIERE
30-10-026 DELIBERATELY	1-01-001 DEMOCRATS'	17-05-009 DEPARTMENT'S	1-01-001 DERVISH
2-01-001 DELIBERATION	1-01-001 DEMODOCUS	1-01-001 DEPARTMENTAL	3-03-003 DERVISHES
7-05-005 DELIBERATIONS	12-02-002 DEMOGRAPHIC	25-06-014 DEPARTMENTS	8-05-007 DES
2-02-002 DELICACIES	1-01-001 DEMOGRAPHIE	2-02-002 DEPARTS	2-01-001 DESCARTES
5-04-005 DELICACY	1-01-001 DEMOGRAPHIQUES	17-08-015 DEPARTURE	4-03-004 DESCEND
27-13-027 DELICATE	3-01-001 DEMOGRAPHY	7-06-007 DEPARTURES	2-01-002 DESCENDANT
1-01-001 DELICATE-BEYOND -DESCRIPTION	4-04-004 DEMOLISHED	1-01-001 DEPECIATION	4-04-004 DESCENDANTS
	1-01-001 DEMOLITION	45-09-036 DEPEND	8-06-008 DESCENDED
2-01-001 DELICATELY	9-04-004 DEMON	8-05-007 DEPENDABLE	1-01-001 DESCENDENTS
1-01-001 DELICATELY-TEXT URED	1-01-001 DEMON'S	9-05-009 DEPENDED	10-07-009 DESCENDING
	12-04-001 DEMON-RIDDEN	12-04-010 DEPENDENCE	2-02-002 DESCENDS
4-03-004 DELICIOUS	2-02-002 DEMONIAC	3-02-002 DEPENDENCY	11-07-011 DESCENT
1-01-001 DELICIOUSLY	7-03-004 DEMONS	2-01-001 DEPENDENT	41-10-036 DESCRIBE
1-01-001 DELICTI	3-02-003 DEMONSTRABLE	1-01-001 DEPENDENTS	120-12-082 DESCRIBED
29-07-026 DELIGHT	2-02-002 DEMONSTRABLY	32-08-030 DEPENDING	22-09-017 DESCRIBES
16-10-016 DELIGHTED	28-07-024 DEMONSTRATE	2-02-002 DEPENDS	17-08-015 DESCRIBING
26-08-017 DELIGHTFUL	33-08-026 DEMONSTRATED	1-01-001 DEPERSONALIZATI ON	54-11-037 DESCRIPTION
4-04-004 DELIGHTFULLY	6-03-005 DEMONSTRATES		10-03-007 DESCRIPTIONS
1-01-001 DELIGHTING	6-05-005 DEMONSTRATING	1-01-001 DEPERSONALIZED	7-01-005 DESCRIPTIVE
3-03-003 DELIGHTS	25-09-020 DEMONSTRATION	4-01-001 DEPEW	1-01-001 DESECRATED
1-01-001 DELIMIT	4-02-003 DEMONSTRATIONS	3-02-003 DEPICT	1-01-001 DESECRATION
1-01-001 DELIMITS	1-01-001 DEMONSTRATIVES	8-04-005 DEPICTED	1-01-001 DESEGREGATE
1-01-001 DELINEAMENTS	8-04-005 DEMONSTRATORS	6-04-005 DEPICTING	6-02-002 DESEGREGATED
1-01-001 DELINEATED	1-01-001 DEMORALIZATION	1-01-001 DEPICTION	40-04-005 DESEGREGATION
2-01-001 DELINEATING	3-02-003 DEMORALIZE	6-03-003 DEPLETION	1-01-001 DESEGREGATION-F ROM-COURT-ORDER
3-03-003 DELINEATION	1-01-001 DEMORALIZED	2-02-002 DEPLORABLE	
7-04-005 DELINQUENCY	2-01-001 DEMORALIZES	1-01-001 DEPLORABLY	1-01-001 DESENSITIZED
6-04-005 DELINQUENT	1-01-001 DEMORALIZING	2-02-002 DEPLORE	21-12-017 DESERT
3-03-003 DELINQUENTS	1-01-001 DEMOTED	2-02-002 DEPLORED	15-06-013 DESERTED
3-02-002 DELIRIUM	3-03-003 DEMURE	3-02-002 DEPLORES	2-02-002 DESERTION
18-09-015 DELIVER	1-01-001 DEMURRED	5-04-005 DEPLOYED	5-04-005 DESERTS
2-02-002 DELIVERANCE	2-02-002 DEMURRER	12-06-010 DEPLOYING	12-06-010 DESERVE
37-12-035 DELIVERED	1-01-001 DEMUS-*SCHUBERT	12-10-012 DEPLOYMENT	12-10-012 DESERVED
9-06-009 DELIVERING	6-01-001 DEMYTHOLOGIZATI ON	16-07-016 DEPORT	16-07-016 DESERVES
6-04-005 DELIVERS		2-01-001 DEPORTEES	2-02-002 DESERVING
19-10-013 DELIVERY	2-01-001 DEMYTHOLOGIZE	1-01-001 DEPOSE	114-11-046 DESIGN

Freq	Word	Freq	Word	Freq	Word	Freq	Word
1-01-001	DESIGN-CONSCIOUS	4-03-004	DETERIORATED	1-01-001	DEVOUTLY	1-01-001	DICKINSON
1-01-001	DESIGN-SIDE	1-01-001	DETERIORATES	3-02-002	DEW	2-02-002	DICKS
5-04-004	DESIGNATE	2-02-002	DETERIORATING	1-01-001	DEWARS	3-01-001	DICKSON
17-08-017	DESIGNATED	3-02-003	DETERIORATION	1-01-001	DEWDROPS	3-02-003	DICTATE
1-01-001	DESIGNATES	1-01-001	DETERMINABILITY	3-03-003	DEWEY	5-03-004	DICTATED
3-02-003	DESIGNATING	1-01-001	DETERMINABLE	1-01-001	DEWY-EYED	9-05-008	DICTATES
4-03-004	DESIGNATION	1-01-001	DETERMINANT	2-01-001	DEXAMETHASONE	2-02-002	DICTATING
1-01-001	DESIGNATIONS	2-01-002	DETERMINANTS	1-01-001	DEXEDRINE	7-04-005	DICTATOR
108-12-077	DESIGNED	1-01-001	DETERMINATE	3-03-003	DEXTER	1-01-001	DICTATORIAL
18-04-008	DESIGNER	39-10-033	DETERMINATION	1-01-001	DEXTER'S	4-03-003	DICTATORS
1-01-001	DESIGNER'S	2-01-002	DETERMINATIONS	1-01-001	DEXTERITY	13-05-010	DICTATORSHIP
14-05-009	DESIGNERS	1-01-001	DETERMINATIVE	2-02-002	DEXTROUS	6-02-004	DICTION
9-06-009	DESIGNING	107-12-067	DETERMINE	1-01-001	DEXTROUS-FINGERED	1-01-001	DICTIONARIES
28-07-019	DESIGNS	119-14-082	DETERMINED	2-02-002	DEY	57-05-007	DICTIONARY
2-02-002	DESIRABILITY	14-05-014	DETERMINEDLY	1-01-001	DHARMA	1-01-001	DICTIONARY'S
36-09-029	DESIRABLE	1-01-001	DETERMINES	22-05-007	DI	4-04-004	DICTUM
79-14-072	DESIRE	1-01-001	DETERMING	1-01-001	DI*GIORGIO	1044-15-325	DID
50-10-039	DESIRED	33-08-027	DETERMINING	1-01-001	DI*LUZIO	1-01-001	DIDDLE
24-10-021	DESIRES	1-01-001	DETERMINISM	1-01-001	DI*MAGGIO	1-01-001	DIDDLING
5-05-005	DESIRING	7-02-002	DETERMINISTIC	1-01-001	DI*SIMONE	1-01-001	DIDI
1-01-001	DESIROUS	1-01-001	DETERRENCE	1-01-001	DI*VARCO	2-01-001	DIDN
65-10-044	DESK	8-05-007	DETERRENT	5-01-001	DI-IODOTYROSINE	401-14-145	DIDN'T
4-02-003	DESKS	1-01-001	DETEST	4-01-001	DIA	73-15-049	DIE
2-01-001	DESLONDE	2-01-002	DETESTABLE	4-03-003	DIABETES	1-01-001	DIE-DEAD
1-01-001	DESMOND	1-01-001	DETESTATION	2-01-001	DIABETIC	1-01-001	DIE-UP
6-05-006	DESOLATE	3-02-002	DETESTED	1-01-001	DIABOLICAL	86-15-062	DIED
5-04-005	DESOLATION	3-02-002	DETONATED	1-01-001	DIACHRONIC	5-02-003	DIEGO
1-01-001	DESOLATIONS	1-01-001	DETONATING	1-01-001	DIAGHILEFF	1-01-001	DIEHARD
21-09-019	DESPAIR	3-02-002	DETONATION	1-01-001	DIAGNOMETER	1-01-001	DIEHARDS
4-02-004	DESPAIRING	1-01-001	DETOURED	1-01-001	DIAGNOSABLE	2-02-002	DIEM
4-02-004	DESPAIRINGLY	2-02-002	DETOURS	3-03-003	DIAGNOSE	1-01-001	DIENBIENPHU
2-01-002	DESPATCHED	1-01-001	DETRACT	2-02-002	DIAGNOSED	12-07-011	DIES
1-01-001	DESPERADOES	1-01-001	DETRACTOR	1-01-001	DIAGNOSES	1-01-001	DIESEL
26-08-021	DESPERATE	1-01-001	DETRACTORS	2-02-002	DIAGNOSING	21-09-013	DIET
22-09-022	DESPERATELY	1-01-001	DETRIBALIZE	13-06-011	DIAGNOSIS	6-02-004	DIETARY
7-05-007	DESPERATION	1-01-001	DETRIMENT	10-04-007	DIAGNOSTIC	1-01-001	DIETERS
1-01-001	DESPINA	4-03-003	DETRIMENTAL	2-01-002	DIAGNOSTICIANS	1-01-001	DIETETIC
7-05-007	DESPISE	21-07-015	DETROIT	4-01-001	DIAGONAL	2-01-002	DIETHYLAMINOETHYL
3-01-003	DESPISED	1-01-001	DETROIT'S	14-01-001	DIAGONALIZABLE	4-01-001	DIETHYLSTILBESTRO
1-01-001	DESPISES	1-01-001	DEUS	4-03-003	DIAGONALLY	5-03-003	DIETRICH
1-01-001	DESPISING	4-03-003	DEUTERATED	1-01-001	DIAGONALS	3-03-003	DIETS
104-13-077	DESPITE	1-01-001	DEUTSCH	10-05-007	DIAGRAM	2-02-002	DIETY
1-01-001	DESPOILED	1-01-001	DEUTSCHE	1-01-001	DIAGRAMMED	1-01-001	DIEU
1-01-001	DESPOILERS	4-01-002	DEUX	8-06-006	DIAGRAMS	1-01-001	DIEUX
1-01-001	DESPOILING	1-01-001	DEVASTATE	1-01-001	DIAL	18-07-016	DIFFER
2-02-002	DESPONDENCY	3-03-003	DEVASTATED	10-05-007	DIALECT	13-07-011	DIFFERED
2-02-002	DESPONDENT	1-01-001	DEVASTATING	6-01-005	DIALECTIC	148-14-093	DIFFERENCE
2-02-002	DESPOT	5-04-005	DEVASTATINGLY	1-01-001	DIALECTICAL	79-06-046	DIFFERENCES
5-04-004	DESPOTISM	1-01-001	DEVASTATION	1-01-001	DIALECTICALLY	312-15-181	DIFFERENT
1-01-001	DESPOTS	2-02-002	DEVELOP	2-01-001	DIALECTICS	1-01-001	DIFFERENT-COLO
170-13-107	DESPOTS	89-13-065	DEVELOPED	4-03-004	DIALECTS	2-01-001	DIFFERENTIABILIT
1-01-001	DESPREZ	5-02-002	DEVELOPER	3-02-003	DIALED	3-01-001	DIFFERENTIABLE
1-01-001	DESPUES	2-01-002	DEVELOPERS	1-01-001	DIALING	16-03-009	DIFFERENTIAL
7-04-005	DESSERT	52-09-037	DEVELOPING	12-05-009	DIALOGUE	2-02-002	DIFFERENTIATE
2-02-002	DESSERTS	334-12-120	DEVELOPMENT	2-01-002	DIALOGUES	5-02-004	DIFFERENTIATED
1-01-001	DESSIER	9-03-004	DEVELOPMENTAL	1-01-001	DIALS	1-01-001	DIFFERENTIATIN
9-07-007	DESTINATION	44-10-033	DEVELOPMENTS	12-01-001	DIALYSIS	8-03-008	DIFFERENTIATIO
9-07-009	DESTINED	11-07-011	DEVELOPS	4-01-002	DIALYZED	16-10-014	DIFFERENTLY
3-01-003	DESTINIES	1-01-001	DEVENS	2-01-001	DIAM	1-01-001	DIFFERING
22-07-018	DESTINY	1-01-001	DEVER	45-05-018	DIAMETER	10-04-009	DIFFERS
2-02-002	DESTITUTE	1-01-001	DEVERY	4-02-003	DIAMETERS	1-01-001	DIFFICILE
48-10-030	DESTROY	5-01-001	DEVEY	1-01-001	DIAMETRIC	161-15-127	DIFFICULT
39-10-033	DESTROYED	1-01-001	DEVEY'S	2-02-002	DIAMETRICALLY	46-10-039	DIFFICULTIES
2-02-002	DESTROYER	2-01-001	DEVIANCE	8-04-006	DIAMOND	76-14-060	DIFFICULTY
3-02-003	DESTROYERS	3-01-003	DEVIANT	1-01-001	DIAMOND-	2-02-002	DIFFIDENCE
17-07-015	DESTROYING	2-02-002	DEVIANTS	7-04-005	DIAMONDS	7-02-004	DIFFRACTION
38-11-026	DESTRUCTION	1-01-001	DEVIATE	1-01-001	DIAN'S	1-01-001	DIFFRING
25-07-017	DESTRUCTIVE	1-01-001	DEVIATED	7-02-002	DIANA	1-01-001	DIFFRUNCE
1-01-001	DESUETUDE	1-01-001	DEVIATING	14-02-002	DIANE	4-03-004	DIFFUSE
1-01-001	DESULTORY	14-04-008	DEVIATION	4-02-002	DIANE'S	2-02-002	DIFFUSED
1-01-001	DESYNCHRONIZING	4-02-004	DEVIATIONS	3-03-003	DIAPERS	1-01-001	DIFFUSELY
1-01-001	DETACH	55-13-031	DEVICE	1-01-001	DIAPHANOUS	1-01-001	DIFFUSERS
2-02-002	DETACHABLE	37-09-027	DEVICES	7-02-002	DIAPHRAGM	1-01-001	DIFFUSES
12-06-011	DETACHED	25-08-017	DEVIL	2-01-001	DIAPHRAGMIC	3-02-002	DIFFUSING
4-04-004	DETACHMENT	5-03-005	DEVIL'S	1-01-001	DIAPHRAGMS	24-03-005	DIFFUSION
72-13-050	DETAIL	1-01-001	DEVIL'S-FOOD	2-02-002	DIAPIACE	10-08-009	DIG
52-11-045	DETAILED	3-03-003	DEVILISH	2-01-001	DIARIES	7-01-001	DIGBY
57-12-049	DETAILS	2-01-001	DEVILS	2-01-001	DIARIO	1-01-001	DIGBY'S
1-01-001	DETAIN	1-01-001	DEVIOUS	7-01-001	DIARRHEA	3-03-003	DIGEST
1-01-001	DETAINED	8-05-008	DEVISE	3-01-001	DIARRHOEA	1-01-001	DIGESTED
10-05-010	DETECT	16-08-016	DEVISED	4-04-004	DIARY	1-01-001	DIGESTIBLE
8-03-005	DETECTABLE	1-01-001	DEVISEE	1-01-001	DIATHERMY	2-02-002	DIGESTING
12-02-008	DETECTED	1-01-001	DEVISING	1-01-001	DIATHESIS	3-03-003	DIGESTIVE
6-05-006	DETECTING	6-05-006	DEVOID	2-01-001	DIATOMIC	2-01-001	DIGGER
13-04-008	DETECTION	3-01-001	DEVOL	1-01-001	DIATOMS	1-01-001	DIGGES
52-08-012	DETECTIVE	1-01-001	DEVONSHIRE	14-06-007	DICE	7-06-007	DIGGING
3-02-002	DETECTIVE'S	15-09-012	DEVOTE	1-01-001	DICENDI	1-01-001	DIGIT
17-07-010	DETECTIVES	51-13-040	DEVOTED	1-01-001	DICHONDRA	6-02-004	DIGITAL
3-02-002	DETECTOR	1-01-001	DEVOTEDLY	1-01-001	DICHOTOMY	1-01-001	DIGITALIS
2-02-002	DETECTORS	3-03-003	DEVOTEES	18-06-011	DICK	1-01-001	DIGITALIZATIO
2-01-001	DETENTE	10-06-006	DEVOTING	2-02-002	DICK'S	7-05-006	DIGNIFIED
2-02-002	DETENTION	19-10-016	DEVOTION	1-01-001	DICKE	1-01-001	DIGNIFY
1-01-001	DETER	1-01-001	DEVOTIONAL	16-06-008	DICKENS	3-03-003	DIGNITARIES
3-01-001	DETERGENCY	2-02-002	DEVOTIONS	2-01-001	DICKENS'	35-12-026	DIGNITY
25-03-004	DETERGENT	2-02-002	DEVOUR	3-01-001	DICKEY		
4-02-002	DETERGENTS	1-01-001	DEVOURED	1-01-001	DICKEY'S		
1-01-001	DETERIORATE	4-03-003	DEVOUT				

Code	Word	Code	Word	Code	Word	Code	Word
1-01-001	DIGRESS	3-03-003	DIPPED	1-01-001	DISCERNABLE	2-01-001	DISENTANGLE
1-01-001	DIGRESSIONS	6-01-002	DIPPER	2-02-002	DISCERNED	1-01-001	DISFAVOR
1-01-001	DIGS	1-01-001	DIPPING	8-05-007	DISCERNIBLE	5-03-005	DISFIGURED
1-01-001	DIISOCYANATE	1-01-001	DIPS	2-02-002	DISCERNING	3-03-003	DISGRACE
1-01-001	DIJON	3-01-001	DIPYLON	1-01-001	DISCERNMENT	1-01-001	DISGRACED
3-03-003	DILAPIDATED	1-01-001	DIRE	19-08-012	DISCHARGE	1-01-001	DISGRACEFUL
3-02-002	DILATATION	129-15-094	DIRECT	9-07-008	DISCHARGED	1-01-001	DISGRUNTLED
2-01-001	DILATE	2-01-001	DIRECT-SUM	9-01-001	DISCHARGES	5-02-005	DISGUISE
2-02-002	DILATED	68-13-051	DIRECTED	3-03-003	DISCHARGING	11-05-011	DISGUISED
1-01-001	DILATES	7-05-007	DIRECTING	4-02-004	DISCIPLE	1-01-001	DISGUISES
1-01-001	DILATING	134-14-082	DIRECTION	5-04-005	DISCIPLES	1-01-001	DISGUST
2-02-002	DILATION	8-06-007	DIRECTIONAL	2-01-001	DISCIPLESHIP	6-05-006	DISGUSTED
25-09-018	DILEMMA	1-01-001	DIRECTIONALITY	1-01-001	DISCIPLINARY	4-04-004	DISGUSTING
2-02-002	DILEMMAS	27-11-025	DIRECTIONALLY	16-08-012	DISCIPLINE	16-08-012	DISH
1-01-001	DILETTANTE	11-06-011	DIRECTIONS	11-06-011	DISCIPLINED	1-01-001	DISHARMONY
3-03-003	DILIGENCE	4-04-004	DIRECTIVE	4-04-004	DISCIPLINES	2-02-002	DISHEARTEN
2-02-002	DILIGENT	1-01-001	DIRECTIVES	1-01-001	DISCIPLINING	1-01-001	DISHEARTENING
1-01-001	DILIGENTLY	1-01-001	DIRECTIVITY	1-01-001	DISCLAIMED	1-01-001	DISHED
12-02-002	DILL	141-13-102	DIRECTLY	1-01-001	DISCLAIMER	21-10-015	DISHES
3-01-001	DILL'S	4-03-004	DIRECTNESS	9-05-009	DISCLOSE	2-01-002	DISHEVELED
1-01-001	DILLINGER	101-14-055	DIRECTOR	14-05-012	DISCLOSED	2-02-002	DISHONEST
11-04-005	DILLON	1-01-001	DIRECTOR'S	1-01-001	DISCLOSES	2-02-002	DISHONESTY
1-01-001	DILTHEY	1-01-001	DIRECTOR-GENERA L	2-01-001	DISCLOSURE	2-02-002	DISHONOR
1-01-001	DILUENTS			4-03-004	DISCLOSURES	1-01-001	DISHONORED
1-01-001	DILUTE	4-02-002	DIRECTORATE	1-01-001	DISCOID	1-01-001	DISHONOURING
6-02-005	DILUTED	19-08-016	DIRECTORS	1-01-001	DISCOLORED	1-01-001	DISHWASHERS
3-03-003	DILUTING	1-01-001	DIRECTORSHIP	1-01-001	DISCOLORS	1-01-001	DISHWATER
7-01-003	DILUTION	7-04-006	DIRECTORY	7-04-006	DISCOMFORT	2-02-002	DISILLUSIONED
1-01-001	DILWORTH	1-01-001	DIRECTRICES	1-01-001	DISCONCERT	1-01-001	DISILLUSIONING
1-01-001	DILYS	5-03-005	DIRECTS	4-03-004	DISCONCERTING	3-03-003	DISILLUSIONMENT
19-07-016	DIM	2-02-002	DIRGE	1-01-001	DISCONCERTINGLY	2-01-002	DISINCLINATION
1-01-001	DIMAGGIO	1-01-001	DIRION	4-03-004	DISCONNECTED	2-02-002	DISINTEGRATE
1-01-001	DIMAN	3-02-003	DIRKSEN	8-06-007	DISCONTENT	1-01-001	DISINTEGRATING
1-01-001	DIMAN'S	1-01-001	DIRON	1-01-001	DISCONTENTED	5-04-005	DISINTEGRATION
4-03-004	DIME	43-10-027	DIRT	1-01-001	DISCONTINUANCE	1-01-001	DISINTEGRATIVE
15-09-013	DIMENSION	1-01-001	DIRT-CATCHER	2-02-002	DISCONTINUE	3-03-003	DISINTEREST
11-02-004	DIMENSIONAL	36-09-028	DIRTY	7-03-007	DISCONTINUED	5-04-005	DISINTERESTED
1-01-001	DIMENSIONALLY	1-01-001	DIS*$HONEST	4-01-001	DISCONTINUITY	1-01-001	DISINTERRED
3-01-001	DIMENSIONING	2-02-002	DISABILITIES	3-02-002	DISCONTINUOUS	1-01-001	DISJOINTED
30-07-020	DIMENSIONS	5-05-005	DISABILITY	1-01-001	DISCORD	25-03-006	DISK
1-01-001	DIMERS	1-01-001	DISABLE	2-02-002	DISCORDANTLY	1-01-001	DISKING
3-02-003	DIMES	10-03-003	DISABLED	2-01-001	DISCORPORATE	4-04-004	DISKS
1-01-001	DIMESIZE	3-01-002	DISABLING	1-01-001	DISCORPORATED	14-07-013	DISLIKE
2-01-001	DIMETHYLGLYOXIM E	2-02-002	DISABUSE	12-05-011	DISCOUNT	11-05-010	DISLIKED
		4-02-004	DISADVANTAGE	2-02-002	DISCOUNTED	4-04-004	DISLIKES
3-01-003	DIMINISH	9-05-007	DISADVANTAGES	1-01-001	DISCOUNTING	1-01-001	DISLIKING
10-06-008	DIMINISHED	1-01-001	DISAFFECTED	5-04-004	DISCOUNTS	1-01-001	DISLOCATED
3-02-003	DIMINISHES	1-01-001	DISAFFECTION	9-07-009	DISCOURAGE	1-01-001	DISLOCATION
8-05-008	DIMINISHING	1-01-001	DISAFFILIATE	15-07-013	DISCOURAGED	2-02-002	DISLOCATIONS
1-01-001	DIMINUTION	1-01-001	DISAFFILIATED	3-03-003	DISCOURAGEMENT	2-02-002	DISLODGE
3-02-003	DIMINUTIVE	1-01-001	DISAFFILIATION	5-03-005	DISCOURAGING	1-01-001	DISLODGED
2-02-002	DIMITRI	7-02-005	DISAGREE	1-01-001	DISCOURS	2-02-002	DISLOYAL
12-06-012	DIMLY	1-01-001	DISAGREEABLE	10-05-008	DISCOURSE	2-02-002	DISLOYALTY
1-01-001	DIMLY-OUTLINED	3-02-003	DISAGREED	2-02-002	DISCOURSES	8-07-008	DISMAL
1-01-001	DIN	11-05-011	DISAGREEMENT	2-02-002	DISCOURTEOUS	2-01-002	DISMALLY
2-02-002	DINE	2-02-002	DISAGREEMENTS	40-11-039	DISCOVER	5-05-005	DISMAY
3-02-003	DINED	2-02-002	DISAGREES	73-15-064	DISCOVERED	1-01-001	DISMAYED
1-01-001	DINEEN	1-01-001	DISALLOWED	1-01-001	DISCOVERER	3-02-003	DISMAYING
1-01-001	DINES	11-07-010	DISAPPEAR	10-06-009	DISCOVERIES	2-02-002	DISMEMBERED
1-01-001	DINGHY	8-04-008	DISAPPEARANCE	7-07-007	DISCOVERING	2-01-002	DISMEMBERMENT
1-01-001	DINGO	35-11-033	DISAPPEARED	2-02-002	DISCOVERS	5-03-004	DISMISS
5-04-005	DINGY	5-04-005	DISAPPEARING	45-10-023	DISCOVERY	7-04-005	DISMISSAL
1-01-001	DINGY-LOOKING	3-03-003	DISAPPEARS	2-02-002	DISCREDIT	14-10-014	DISMISSED
1-01-001	DINH	15-06-014	DISAPPOINTED	3-02-003	DISCREDITED	1-01-001	DISMISSES
28-10-023	DINING	7-06-007	DISAPPOINTING	3-03-003	DISCREET	3-02-003	DISMISSING
1-01-001	DINING-ROOM	15-09-015	DISAPPOINTMENT	2-02-002	DISCREETLY	5-03-004	DISMOUNTED
91-13-061	DINNER	2-02-002	DISAPPOINTMENTS	5-04-004	DISCREPANCIES	2-01-002	DISMOUNTING
9-07-009	DINNERS	1-01-001	DISAPPROBATION	11-05-008	DISCREPANCY	1-01-001	DISNEYLAND
3-02-002	DINNERTIME	15-05-011	DISAPPROVAL	7-03-005	DISCRETE	7-01-001	DISOBEDIENCE
1-01-001	DINNERWARE	4-04-004	DISAPPROVE	14-04-010	DISCRETION	2-01-001	DISOBEDIENT
1-01-001	DINOSAUR	4-03-004	DISAPPROVED	2-01-001	DISCRETIONARY	4-04-004	DISOBEYED
1-01-001	DINOSAURS	1-01-001	DISAPPROVES	1-01-001	DISCRIMINATE	1-01-001	DISOBEYING
1-01-001	DINSMORE	1-01-001	DISAPPROVINGLY	7-05-007	DISCRIMINATING	7-03-004	DISORDER
5-01-001	DIOCESAN	2-02-002	DISARM	23-08-013	DISCRIMINATION	3-02-003	DISORDERED
1-01-001	DIOCESE	11-06-010	DISARMAMENT	3-03-003	DISCRIMINATORY	1-01-001	DISORDERLINESS
1-01-001	DIOCS**-	3-01-001	DISARMED	7-05-006	DISCS	3-02-003	DISORDERLY
1-01-001	DIODATI	3-02-003	DISARMING	1-01-001	DISCURSIVENESS	7-03-005	DISORDERS
1-01-001	DION	1-01-001	DISARRANGED	28-10-026	DISCUSS	1-01-001	DISORGANIZATION
1-01-001	DIONIE	2-01-002	DISARRAY	1-01-001	DISCUSSANT	5-04-005	DISORGANIZED
1-01-001	DIONIGI	1-01-001	DISASSEMBLE	65-14-054	DISCUSSED	1-01-001	DISORIENTED
2-01-001	DIONYSIAN	1-01-001	DISASSEMBLY	4-02-002	DISCUSSES	2-02-002	DISOWN
1-01-001	DIONYSUS	26-08-021	DISASTER	16-08-016	DISCUSSING	2-02-002	DISOWNED
1-01-001	DIOR	4-04-004	DISASTERS	94-11-062	DISCUSSION	2-02-002	DISPARAGEMENT
1-01-001	DIORAH	16-08-015	DISASTROUS	32-10-023	DISCUSSIONS	4-03-004	DISPARATE
1-01-001	DIORAMAS	2-02-002	DISBANDED	3-03-003	DISDAIN	1-01-001	DISPARITIES
1-01-001	DIOXALATE	6-05-005	DISBELIEF	2-02-002	DISDAINFUL	2-02-002	DISPARITY
2-02-002	DIOXIDE	1-01-001	DISBELIEVE	2-02-002	DISDAINING	2-02-002	DISPASSIONATE
6-06-006	DIP	1-01-001	DISBELIEVED	1-01-001	DISDAINS	3-03-003	DISPASSIONATELY
1-01-001	DIPHOSPHOPYRIDI NE	1-01-001	DISBELIEVES	53-10-021	DISEASE	8-02-007	DISPATCH
		1-01-001	DISBELIEVING	1-01-001	DISEASED	5-03-004	DISPATCHED
17-07-013	DIPLOMACY	1-01-001	DISBURSED	19-08-009	DISEASES	3-02-002	DISPATCHES
5-05-005	DIPLOMAT	2-01-001	DISBURSEMENT	1-01-001	DISEMBODIED	3-03-003	DISPATCHING
1-01-001	DIPLOMAT'S	2-02-002	DISBURSEMENTS	1-01-001	DISENFRANCHISED	3-03-003	DISPEL
28-08-020	DIPLOMATIC	6-02-004	DISC	2-01-001	DISENFRANCHISEM ENT	1-01-001	DISPELL
6-03-004	DIPLOMATS	1-01-001	DISCARD			8-04-006	DISPELLED
5-01-002	DIPOLE	8-07-008	DISCARDED	1-01-001	DISENGAGE	1-01-001	DISPENSARY
1-01-001	DIPOLES	4-03-004	DISCERN	1-01-001	DISENGAGEMENT	3-02-003	DISPENSATION

4-04-004 DISPENSE	19-06-010 DISTANCES	4-02-004 DIVES	75-12-028 DOG
2-02-002 DISPENSED	37-11-031 DISTANT	1-01-001 DIVEST	2-02-002 DOG'S
1-01-001 DISPENSER	1-01-001 DISTANTLY	4-01-001 DIVESTITURE	1-01-001 DOG-EARED
1-01-001 DISPENSERS	8-06-008 DISTASTE	14-07-010 DIVIDE	1-01-001 DOG-PIN
1-01-001 DISPENSING	1-01-001 DISTASTEFUL	55-12-049 DIVIDED	1-01-001 DOGBERRY
1-01-001 DISPERSAL	2-02-002 DISTASTEFULLY	6-04-005 DIVIDEND	2-02-002 DOGGED
2-02-002 DISPERSE	1-01-001 DISTENSION	8-04-006 DIVIDENDS	2-02-002 DOGGEDLY
7-03-005 DISPERSED	1-01-001 DISTIL	1-01-001 DIVIDER	1-01-001 DOGGONE**H
1-01-001 DISPERSEMENT	3-02-002 DISTILLATION	6-01-002 DIVIDES	1-01-001 DOGHOUSE
1-01-001 DISPERSING	10-05-006 DISTILLED	7-05-007 DIVIDING	1-01-001 DOGLEG
3-02-003 DISPERSION	1-01-001 DISTILLER	3-01-001 DIVINATION	4-04-004 DOGMA
3-03-003 DISPLACE	1-01-001 DISTILLERS	34-08-020 DIVINE	2-01-002 DOGMAS
2-02-002 DISPLACED	1-01-001 DISTILLING	1-01-001 DIVINE'S	4-03-004 DOGMATIC
23-04-010 DISPLACEMENT	42-11-033 DISTINCT	3-03-003 DIVINELY	2-02-002 DOGMATICALLY
1-01-001 DISPLACES	41-12-031 DISTINCTION	3-02-002 DIVING	4-03-003 DOGMATISM
1-01-001 DISPLACING	15-04-011 DISTINCTIONS	1-01-001 DIVINING	70-11-026 DOGS
41-12-033 DISPLAY	20-05-018 DISTINCTIVE	3-02-002 DIVINITIES	9-01-001 DOGTOWN
21-08-020 DISPLAYED	2-01-001 DISTINCTIVELY	7-04-004 DIVINITY	1-01-001 DOGTROT
6-04-006 DISPLAYING	12-07-012 DISTINCTLY	4-01-001 DIVISIBLE	1-01-001 DOGUMENTI
21-07-013 DISPLAYS	19-04-014 DISTINGUISH	107-09-049 DIVISION	1-01-001 DOGWOOD
7-04-005 DISPLEASED	4-01-002 DISTINGUISHABLE	2-01-001 DIVISION'S	1-01-001 DOHNANYI
4-04-004 DISPLEASURE	42-13-036 DISTINGUISHED	2-01-001 DIVISIONAL	3-02-002 DOIN
20-09-018 DISPOSAL	5-02-004 DISTINGUISHES	15-06-010 DIVISIONS	163-15-124 DOING
5-04-004 DISPOSE	6-03-006 DISTINGUISHING	5-05-005 DIVISIVE	6-04-004 DOINGS
18-07-017 DISPOSED	4-02-003 DISTORT	29-10-016 DIVORCE	2-01-001 DOLAN
13-08-013 DISPOSITION	1-01-001 DISTORTABLE	8-06-008 DIVORCED	5-01-002 DOLCE
1-01-001 DISPOSITIONS	11-04-011 DISTORTED	2-02-002 DIVORCEE	1-01-001 DOLDRUMS
2-02-002 DISPOSSESSED	7-03-005 DISTORTION	1-01-001 DIVULGING	1-01-001 DOLE
1-01-001 DISPOSSESSION	2-02-002 DISTORTIONS	1-01-001 DIXIE	1-01-001 DOLED
2-02-002 DISPROPORTIONAT E	2-02-002 DISTRACT	1-01-001 DIXIECRATS	1-01-001 DOLEFUL
1-01-001 DISPROPORTIONAT ELY	5-04-004 DISTRACTED	3-02-003 DIXIELAND	10-05-008 DOLL
3-02-003 DISPROVE	1-01-001 DISTRACTEDLY	3-02-002 DIXON	46-11-032 DOLLAR
1-01-001 DISPROVING	1-01-001 DISTRACTING	1-01-001 DIZZILY	1-01-001 DOLLAR-*BRITTEN
1-01-001 DISPUTABLE	3-03-003 DISTRACTION	1-01-001 DIZZINESS	1-01-001 DOLLAR-*DE
34-06-015 DISPUTE	1-01-001 DISTRACTIONS	5-04-005 DIZZY	1-01-001 DOLLAR-AND-CENT S
2-02-002 DISPUTED	1-01-001 DISTRAUGHT	1-01-001 DJAKARTA	1-01-001 DOLLAR-SIGN
8-04-006 DISPUTES	15-06-011 DISTRESS	4-01-001 DJANGO	1-01-001 DOLLARETTE
1-01-001 DISQUALIFIED	4-03-003 DISTRESSED	1-01-001 DJANGO'S	97-14-058 DOLLARS
1-01-001 DISQUALIFY	1-01-001 DISTRESSES	2-01-001 DJANGOLOGY	1-01-001 DOLLARS'
1-01-001 DISQUIET	7-05-007 DISTRESSING	1-01-001 DNIEPER	1-01-001 DOLLARS-AND-CEN TS
1-01-001 DISQUIETING	6-04-006 DISTRIBUTE	1363-15-396 DO	
1-01-001 DISQUIETUDE	27-08-017 DISTRIBUTED	1-01-001 DO*(C*)TERS	3-01-001 DOLLEY
1-01-001 DISQUISITION	2-02-002 DISTRIBUTES	1-01-001 DO-GOOD	1-01-001 DOLLIES
6-04-006 DISREGARD	4-04-004 DISTRIBUTING	1-01-001 DO-GOODER	12-03-004 DOLLS
4-04-004 DISREGARDED	85-08-038 DISTRIBUTION	1-01-001 DO-GOODERS	4-01-001 DOLLY
3-03-003 DISREGARDING	10-03-006 DISTRIBUTIONS	5-03-004 DO-IT-YOURSELF	1-01-001 DOLMABAHCE
2-01-002 DISREPAIR	2-02-002 DISTRIBUTIVE	1-01-001 DOAN	20-02-002 DOLORES
1-01-001 DISREPUTABLE	7-02-003 DISTRIBUTOR	8-01-001 DOATY	1-01-001 DOLPHIN
2-02-002 DISREPUTE	1-01-001 DISTRIBUTOR'S	6-01-001 DOATY'S	4-03-003 DOLPHINS
2-01-002 DISRESPECT	4-02-004 DISTRIBUTORS	1-01-001 DOBBINS	1-01-001 DOLTISH
1-01-001 DISROBE	1-01-001 DISTRIBUTORSHIP	1-01-001 DOBBS	9-04-009 DOMAIN
5-03-005 DISRUPT	135-10-057 DISTRICT	1-01-001 DOBERMAN	3-02-002 DOMAINS
5-05-005 DISRUPTED	38-06-014 DISTRICTS	1-01-001 DOBLE	17-07-008 DOME
2-02-002 DISRUPTING	6-04-005 DISTRUST	20-04-006 DOC	2-02-002 DOMED
3-02-002 DISRUPTION	2-02-002 DISTRUSTED	9-01-001 DOCHERTY	8-05-006 DOMES
1-01-001 DISRUPTIONS	10-06-008 DISTURB	1-01-001 DOCILE	1-01-001 DOMESDAY
4-02-002 DISRUPTIVE	10-04-009 DISTURBANCE	1-01-001 DOCILELY	63-10-036 DOMESTIC
1-01-001 DISRUPTS	3-01-003 DISTURBANCES	4-04-004 DOCK	1-01-001 DOMESTICALLY
9-06-008 DISSATISFACTION	26-10-025 DISTURBED	1-01-001 DOCKED	1-01-001 DOMESTICITY
1-01-001 DISSATISFACTION S	1-01-001 DISTURBER	1-01-001 DOCKETED	1-01-001 DOMI
6-04-005 DISSATISFIED	16-07-013 DISTURBING	1-01-001 DOCKS	1-01-001 DOMICILE
1-01-001 DISSECT	1-01-001 DISTURBINGLY	2-01-001 DOCKSIDE	1-01-001 DOMICILED
3-02-002 DISSECTION	1-01-001 DISUNION	1-01-001 DOCTERS	1-01-001 DOMICILIUM
1-01-001 DISSEMBLING	3-03-003 DISUNITED	100-11-044 DOCTOR	2-01-001 DOMINA
6-02-003 DISSEMINATED	1-01-001 DISUNITY	18-05-010 DOCTOR'S	11-04-008 DOMINANCE
1-01-001 DISSEMINATING	10-04-006 DITCH	1-01-001 DOCTORATE	65-06-026 DOMINANT
2-02-002 DISSEMINATION	1-01-001 DITCHER	4-04-004 DOCTORED	1-01-001 DOMINANTLY
3-02-003 DISSENSION	2-01-002 DITCHES	30-10-021 DOCTORS	8-07-008 DOMINATE
1-01-001 DISSENSIONS	1-01-001 DITES	1-01-001 DOCTORS'	20-08-018 DOMINATED
5-04-005 DISSENT	1-01-001 DITMAR	2-01-002 DOCTRINAIRE	7-03-005 DOMINATES
1-01-001 DISSENTED	2-01-001 DITMARS	3-02-002 DOCTRINAL	2-02-002 DOMINATING
1-01-001 DISSENTER	3-02-002 DITTIES	1-01-001 DOCTRINALLY	15-06-010 DOMINATION
1-01-001 DISSENTERS	1-01-001 DITTY	46-05-026 DOCTRINE	2-02-002 DOMINEERING
2-01-002 DISSENTING	5-02-002 DIURNAL	5-03-004 DOCTRINES	1-01-001 DOMINIC
2-02-002 DISSENTS	13-06-011 DIVA	13-06-011 DOCUMENT	14-02-005 DOMINICAN
1-01-001 DISSERVICE	2-01-001 DIVAN	2-01-001 DOCUMENTARIES	8-04-007 DOMINION
1-01-001 DISSIDENT	4-03-003 DIVAN-LIKE	4-03-003 DOCUMENTARY	1-01-001 DOMINIQUE
3-03-003 DISSIMILAR	1-01-001 DIVANS	1-01-001 DOCUMENTARY-TYP E	1-01-001 DOMITIAN'S
1-01-001 DISSIMULATION	23-04-008 DIVE	3-02-003 DOCUMENTATION	2-01-001 DOMOKOUS
2-02-002 DISSIPATED	5-03-005 DIVED	6-05-006 DOCUMENTED	23-07-015 DON
1-01-001 DISSIPATING	1-01-001 DIVER	19-08-015 DOCUMENTS	489-14-176 DON'T
1-01-001 DISSOCIATED	2-02-002 DIVERGENCE	1-01-001 DODD	1-01-001 DON'T-KNOW'S
4-02-003 DISSOCIATION	6-05-006 DIVERGENT	11-06-007 DODGE	20-06-011 DONALD
3-03-003 DISSOLUTION	1-01-001 DIVERGING	1-01-001 DODGE'S	2-01-002 DONALDSON
1-01-001 DISSOLUTIONS	3-03-003 DIVERS	2-01-002 DODGED	3-02-002 DONATE
6-04-006 DISSOLVE	13-05-013 DIVERSE	1-01-001 DODGER	7-06-007 DONATED
15-05-011 DISSOLVED	3-01-002 DIVERSIFICATION	5-01-004 DODGERS	1-01-001 DONATES
3-03-003 DISSOLVING	5-01-004 DIVERSIFIED	1-01-001 DODGING	1-01-001 DONATING
1-01-001 DISSONANCES	7-04-006 DIVERSION	1-01-001 DODINGTON	2-02-002 DONATION
3-02-003 DISSUADE	1-01-001 DIVERSIONARY	2-01-002 DOE	2-01-002 DONATIONS
3-02-002 DIST	4-03-004 DIVERSIONS	1-01-001 DOERNER'S	1-01-001 DONATO
9-01-003 DISTAL	1-01-001 DIVERSITIES	1-01-001 DOERS	320-15-199 DONE
1-01-001 DISTALLY	13-02-006 DIVERSITY	485-15-250 DOES	1-01-001 DONIZETTI'S
108-14-074 DISTANCE	1-01-001 DIVERT	1-01-001 DOESN'S	1-01-001 DONKEY
	1-01-001 DIVERTED	87-13-068 DOESN'T	4-01-001 DONNA
	2-02-002 DIVERTIMENTO	1-01-001 DOFFING	3-01-001 DONNAY
	3-03-003 DIVERTING		

3-02-003	DONNED	22-10-021	DOUBTFUL	6-04-006	DRAMAS	3-01-001	DRIERS
1-01-001	DONNELL	2-02-002	DOUBTFULLY	63-12-049	DRAMATIC	1-01-001	DRIES
1-01-001	DONNELLY	3-03-003	DOUBTING	1-01-001	DRAMATICAL	18-05-008	DRIFT
1-01-001	DONNER	1-01-001	DOUBTINGLY	10-05-008	DRAMATICALLY	9-06-009	DRIFTED
1-01-001	DONNING	13-08-012	DOUBTLESS	1-01-001	DRAMATICS	2-02-002	DRIFTIN
4-01-001	DONNYBROOK	16-09-015	DOUBTS	2-02-002	DRAMATIST	11-06-009	DRIFTING
5-03-003	DONOR	1-01-001	DOUCE	1-01-001	DRAMATISTS	6-05-005	DRIFTS
5-01-001	DONORS	1-01-001	DOUG	1-01-001	DRAMATIZATION	33-04-005	DRILL
7-01-001	DONOVAN	13-06-006	DOUGH	3-03-003	DRAMATIZE	5-02-004	DRILLED
2-02-002	DOO	1-01-001	DOUGHNUTTERY	2-02-002	DRAMATIZES	10-04-005	DRILLING
2-01-001	DOOKIYOON	23-06-015	DOUGLAS	1-01-001	DRAMATIZING	4-03-003	DRILLS
1-01-001	DOOLEY	9-01-001	DOUGLASS	19-06-015	DRANK	82-11-044	DRINK
1-01-001	DOOLEYS	2-02-002	DOUR	1-01-001	DRAOUGHT	3-02-002	DRINKER
6-01-001	DOOLIN	1-01-001	DOURLY	9-07-009	DRAPED	2-02-002	DRINKERS
1-01-001	DOOLIN'S	1-01-001	DOUSED	4-02-002	DRAPER	1-01-001	DRINKHOUSE
2-01-001	DOOLITTLE	2-01-001	DOUSMAN	4-03-004	DRAPERIES	48-10-029	DRINKING
1-01-001	DOOLITTLE'S	4-02-003	DOVE	2-01-001	DRAPERS	22-08-015	DRINKS
3-02-003	DOOM	4-02-002	DOVER	2-02-002	DRAPERY	1-01-001	DRIP
10-05-009	DOOMED	1-01-001	DOVES	1-01-001	DRAPES	1-01-001	DRIP-
1-01-001	DOOMS	1-01-001	DOVETAIL	11-06-009	DRASTIC	6-03-005	DRIPPED
1-01-001	DOOMSDAY	4-03-003	DOW	10-07-009	DRASTICALLY	7-05-006	DRIPPING
312-13-124	DOOR	1-01-001	DOW-*JONES	1-01-001	DRAUGHT	1-01-001	DRIPS
1-01-001	DOOR-FRAME	1-01-001	DOWAGER	2-02-002	DRAUGHTS	105-15-079	DRIVE
1-01-001	DOOR-FRONTED	2-01-001	DOWEL	1-01-001	DRAUGHTY	5-04-004	DRIVE-IN
1-01-001	DOOR-TO-DOOR	1-01-001	DOWELING	56-13-045	DRAW	1-01-001	DRIVE-YOURSELF
2-02-002	DOORBELL	1-01-001	DOWER	2-01-001	DRAW-FILE	44-11-031	DRIVEN
1-01-001	DOORKEEPER	6-01-001	DOWEX-2-CHLORID	2-02-002	DRAWBACK	49-10-020	DRIVER
3-03-003	DOORKNOB		E	1-01-001	DRAWBRIDGE	5-02-003	DRIVER'S
4-03-004	DOORMAN	1-01-001	DOWGUARD	8-05-008	DRAWER	24-09-013	DRIVERS
3-02-003	DOORMEN	1-01-001	DOWLING'S	5-05-005	DRAWERS	1-01-001	DRIVERS'
36-13-030	DOORS	895-15-297	DOWN	1-01-001	DRAWIN	6-05-005	DRIVES
3-01-002	DOORSTEP	1-01-001	DOWN-AND-OUT	40-11-036	DRAWING	14-08-012	DRIVEWAY
15-07-012	DOORWAY	1-01-001	DOWN-AND-OUTERS	2-02-002	DRAWING-ROOM	1-01-001	DRIVEWAYS
3-03-003	DOORWAYS	1-01-001	DOWN-PAYMENTS	1-01-001	DRAWING-ROOMS	53-11-042	DRIVING
2-02-002	DOPE	5-04-005	DOWN-TO-EARTH	21-07-014	DRAWINGS	5-02-002	DRIZZLE
1-01-001	DOPE-RIDDEN	1-01-001	DOWNBEAT	2-02-002	DRAWL	2-01-001	DRIZZLING
1-01-001	DOPED	2-02-002	DOWNCAST	3-02-003	DRAWLED	1-01-001	DRIZZLY
1-01-001	DOPPLER	5-05-005	DOWNED	1-01-001	DRAWLING	5-01-001	DROMOZOA
2-02-002	DORA	1-01-001	DOWNERS	70-14-065	DRAWN	1-01-001	DROMOZOOTIC
4-02-002	DORADO	5-05-005	DOWNFALL	1-01-001	DRAWN-BACK	3-03-003	DRONE
2-01-001	DORAN	1-01-001	DOWNGRADE	1-01-001	DRAWN-OUT	2-01-001	DRONES
1-01-001	DORCAS	3-03-003	DOWNGRADED	14-09-013	DRAWS	2-01-001	DRONK
1-01-001	DORENS	6-05-006	DOWNHILL	9-06-008	DREAD	1-01-001	DRONK'S
1-01-001	DORENZO	1-01-001	DOWNING	2-02-002	DREADED	1-01-001	DROOP
2-02-002	DORIA	1-01-001	DOWNPAYMENT	10-06-010	DREADFUL	1-01-001	DROOPED
4-02-002	DORIC	3-03-003	DOWNPOUR	1-01-001	DREADFULLY	1-01-001	DROOPING
5-04-004	DORIS	8-07-008	DOWNRIGHT	6-01-001	DREADNOUGHT	59-13-051	DROP
1-01-001	DORIS'	5-04-004	DOWNS	64-12-033	DREAM	1-01-001	DROP-BLOCK
5-04-004	DORMANT	12-05-012	DOWNSTAIRS	1-01-001	DREAM-*LUSTY	3-01-002	DROPLETS
4-03-004	DORMITORIES	5-04-004	DOWNSTREAM	2-01-001	DREAM-*MISS	3-02-002	DROPOUTS
2-02-002	DORMITORY	1-01-001	DOWNTALKING	1-01-001	DREAM-*NEXT	101-15-076	DROPPED
3-03-003	DOROTHY	41-09-017	DOWNTOWN	1-01-001	DREAM-*SWEETMIT	16-09-015	DROPPING
3-01-001	DORR	1-01-001	DOWNTREND		E	1-01-001	DROPPINGS
8-01-001	DORSET	2-02-002	DOWNTRODDEN	1-01-001	DREAM-*TORKIN	18-07-013	DROPS
1-01-001	DORSEY	2-02-002	DOWNTURN	1-01-001	DREAM-*WAY	4-02-004	DROSS
1-01-001	DOS	16-08-014	DOWNWARD	1-01-001	DREAM-RIDDEN	5-03-004	DROUGHT
4-01-001	DOSAGE	3-02-002	DOWNWIND	1-01-001	DREAMBOAT	1-01-001	DROUGHT-SEARED
4-01-002	DOSAGES	2-02-002	DOWRY	19-09-017	DREAMED	2-02-002	DROUGHTS
11-07-009	DOSE	1-01-001	DOXIADIS	2-02-002	DREAMER	1-01-001	DROUTH
2-01-001	DOSED	4-03-003	DOYLE	1-01-001	DREAMIN	62-10-048	DROVE
13-05-006	DOSES	2-01-002	DOYLE'S	11-06-010	DREAMING	1-01-001	DROVERS
1-01-001	DOST	5-03-005	DOZED	1-01-001	DREAMLESS	1-01-001	DROVES
2-02-002	DOSTOEVSKY	52-12-047	DOZEN	1-01-001	DREAMLESSLY	3-03-003	DROWN
1-01-001	DOSTOEVSKY'S	11-07-010	DOZENS	2-01-002	DREAMLIKE	6-05-006	DROWNED
13-06-009	DOT	3-02-003	DOZING	30-12-020	DREAMS	4-04-004	DROWNING
2-02-002	DOTING	192-13-068	DR	1-01-001	DREAMT	1-01-001	DROWNS
11-04-006	DOTS	5-04-004	DRAB	4-03-004	DREAMY	1-01-001	DROWSED
2-02-002	DOTTED	1-01-001	DRAB-HAIRED	1-01-001	DREARINESS	1-01-001	DROWSILY
2-02-002	DOTTING	1-01-001	DRACO	6-05-006	DREARY	1-01-001	DROWSING
56-12-040	DOUBLE	24-09-012	DRAFT	1 01-001	DRED	1-01-001	DROWSY
1-01-001	DOUBLE-*FIGURE	5-04-005	DRAFTED	4-03-003	DREGS	5-03-003	DRS
1-01-001	DOUBLE-BOGEYED	1-01-001	DRAFTEE	1-01-001	DREISER	1-01-001	DRUDGERY
2-02-002	DOUBLE-BREASTED	1-01-001	DRAFTEES	1-01-001	DREISER'S	24-06-011	DRUG
1-01-001	DOUBLE-CROSSED	1-01-001	DRAFTERS	1-01-001	DREISERS	17-01-001	DRUG'S
1-01-001	DOUBLE-CROSSER	6-03-005	DRAFTING	1-01-001	DRENCHED	1-01-001	DRUGGAN-*LAKE
1-01-001	DOUBLE-CROSSING	3-02-002	DRAFTS	1-01-001	DRESBACH	5-03-005	DRUGGED
2-01-001	DOUBLE-ENTENDRE	2-02-002	DRAFTY	2-01-001	DRESBACH'S	1-01-001	DRUGGING
1-01-001	DOUBLE-GLAZE	15-08-015	DRAG	1-01-001	DRESBACHS	28-04-008	DRUGS
1-01-001	DOUBLE-HEADER	15-08-014	DRAGGED	1-01-001	DRESBACHS'	5-01-001	DRUGSTORE
1-01-001	DOUBLE-MARRIED	1-01-001	DRAGGER	67-12-045	DRESS	1-01-001	DRUGSTORES
1-01-001	DOUBLE-MEANING	15-06-014	DRAGGING	36-09-029	DRESSED	1-01-001	DRUID
3-01-001	DOUBLE-STAGE	2-02-002	DRAGNET	1-01-001	DRESSER	11-07-011	DRUM
3-01-001	DOUBLE-STEP	1-01-001	DRAGON	2-01-001	DRESSERS	1-01-001	DRUMLIN
1-01-001	DOUBLE-STRENGTH	1-01-001	DRAGONETTI	10-05-009	DRESSES	2-01-002	DRUMMED
1-01-001	DOUBLE-TALK	2-02-002	DRAGONS	22-08-014	DRESSING	2-02-002	DRUMMER
2-01-001	DOUBLE-VALUED	1-01-001	DRAGOONED	2-02-002	DRESSINGS	1-01-001	DRUMMER'S
4-01-001	DOUBLE-WALL	1-01-001	DRAGOSLAV	68-10-051	DREW	1-01-001	DRUMMERS
11-04-011	DOUBLED	18-05-001	DRAIN	1-01-001	DREWE	4-04-004	DRUMMING
1-01-001	DOUBLEHEADER	13-07-009	DRAINAGE	10-02-003	DREXEL	15-06-009	DRUMS
6-02-004	DOUBLES	7-04-006	DRAINED	1-01-001	DREXEL'S	2-01-001	DRUNCKE
7-05-006	DOUBLING	3-03-003	DRAINING	1-01-001	DRIB-DROOL	37-09-028	DRUNK
1-01-001	DOUBLOON	5-02-002	DRAINS	1-01-001	DRIBBLED	1-01-001	DRUNK-AND-DISOR
4-04-004	DOUBLY	2-02-002	DRAKE	28-10-023	DRIED		DERLIES
14-15-092	DOUBT	1-01-001	DRAM	1-01-001	DRIED-OUT	3-03-003	DRUNKARD
1-01-001	DOUBTE	43-11-030	DRAMA	1-01-001	DRIED-UP	1-01-001	DRUNKARD'S
9-05-009	DOUBTED	1-01-001	DRAMA-FILLED	3-03-003	DRIER	3-02-002	DRUNKARDS

Code	Word	Code	Word	Code	Word	Code	Word
7-05-007	DRUNKEN	1-01-001	DUNDEEN	3-02-002	DYNASTIC	61-13-042	EAT
4-04-004	DRUNKENLY	1-01-001	DUNE	1-01-001	DYNASTIES	1-01-001	EATABLE
4-03-004	DRUNKENNESS	8-03-004	DUNES	3-01-001	DYNASTS	1-01-001	EATABLES
2-02-002	DRUNKER	2-02-002	DUNG	5-01-001	DYNASTY	12-08-011	EATEN
3-02-003	DRUNKS	2-02-002	DUNGEON	1-01-001	DYNODES	1-01-001	EATERS
3-02-002	DRURY	1-01-001	DUNK	1-01-001	DYSENTERY	32-11-025	EATING
1-01-001	DRUTHER	2-01-001	DUNKEL	1-01-001	DYSPEPTIC	1-01-001	EATINGS
68-10-042	DRY	3-02-002	DUNKIRK	1-01-001	DYSPLASIA	2-01-001	EATON
1-01-001	DRY-DOCK	1-01-001	DUNLOP	2-01-001	DYSTOPIA	3-03-003	EATS
1-01-001	DRY-EYED	6-04-004	DUNN	7-01-001	DYSTOPIAN	1-01-001	EAVE
1-01-001	DRY-GULCHIN	1-01-001	DUNN'S	8-01-001	DYSTOPIAS	1-01-001	EBB
4-01-001	DRYER	1-01-001	DUNN-*ATHERTON	2-02-002	DYSTROPHY	1-01-001	EBBETTS
2-01-001	DRYFOOS	4-01-001	DUNNE	101-09-063	E	2-02-002	EBBING
1-01-001	DRYFOOS'	1-01-001	DUNSTON	6-01-001	E)	1-01-001	EBBS
2-01-001	DRYIN	1-01-001	DUPED	1-01-001	E),	1-01-001	EBEN
29-07-012	DRYING	1-01-001	DUPLEX	2-01-001	E**.*G**.*T	1-01-001	EBER
4-03-004	DRYLY	1-01-001	DUPLICABLE	1-01-001	E**.*O	3-01-001	EBONY
2-02-002	DRYNESS	6-04-004	DUPLICATE	1-01-001	E**.*T	3-03-003	EBULLIENT
4-01-001	DRYWALL	2-02-002	DUPLICATED	30-07-022	E**.G	11-04-008	ECCENTRIC
74-10-018	DU	8-05-006	DUPLICATION	1-01-001	E**U	1-01-001	ECCENTRICITIES
2-02-002	DU**DRER	1-01-001	DUPONT	1-01-001	E**YU**YM**YM**	4-03-004	ECCENTRICITY
2-01-001	DU**DSSELDORF	1-01-001	DUPONTS		YE**YL**YI**YH**	2-02-002	ECCENTRICS
1-01-001	DU*VOL	2-02-002	DURABILITY		*YS	9-04-008	ECCLESIASTICAL
9-05-009	DUAL	12-07-011	DURABLE	877-15-320	EACH	2-01-001	ECHELON
1-01-001	DUAL-CHANNEL	2-02-002	DURANTE	1-01-001	EADES	1-01-001	ECHELONS
1-01-001	DUAL-LADDER	11-06-011	DURATION	27-09-027	EAGER	10-06-010	ECHO
1-01-001	DUAL-ROAD-UP	1-01-001	DURATIONS	13-07-011	EAGERLY	7-06-007	ECHOED
1-01-001	DUALISM	2-01-001	DUREN	3-03-003	EAGERNESS	8-07-008	ECHOES
1-01-001	DUALITIES	1-01-001	DURESS	5-05-005	EAGLE	2-02-002	ECHOING
1-01-001	DUANE	3-01-001	DURIN	1-01-001	EAGLE'S	1-01-001	ECKART
4-03-004	DUBBED	585-15-265	DURING	6-02-002	EAGLES	2-01-001	ECKENFELDER
1-01-001	DUBIN	3-01-002	DURKHEIM	29-10-025	EAR	1-01-001	ECLAT
7-05-007	DUBIOUS	2-01-001	DURKIN	1-01-001	EAR-*MUFFS	3-02-003	ECLECTIC
2-02-002	DUBLIN	1-01-001	DURLACH	1-01-001	EARDRUMS	1-01-001	ECLECTICALLY
1-01-001	DUBOIS	1-01-001	DUROCHER	1-01-001	EARED	2-02-002	ECLIPSE
1-01-001	DUBOVSKOI	1-01-001	DURRELL'S	12-03-008	EARL	1-01-001	ECLIPSED
1-01-001	DUCES	1-01-001	DURWOOD	146-13-106	EARLIER	4-03-003	ECLIPSES
1-01-001	DUCHESS	9-03-007	DUSK	22-09-020	EARLIEST	1-01-001	ECLIPSING
9-05-008	DUCK	2-02-002	DUSKY	366-15-209	EARLY	3-02-002	ECLIPTIC
5-04-005	DUCKED	1-01-001	DUSSA	1-01-001	EARLY-MORNING	1-01-001	ECOLE
3-02-003	DUCKING	1-01-001	DUSSELDORF	1-01-001	EARLY-SEASON	2-02-002	ECOLOGICAL
4-03-004	DUCKS	70-13-038	DUST	1-01-001	EARMARKED	243-11-086	ECONOMIC
7-02-002	DUCLOS	1-01-001	DUST-SETTLING	16-06-013	EARN	22-04-016	ECONOMICAL
1-01-001	DUCT	1-01-001	DUST-SWIRLING	18-08-015	EARNED	11-07-010	ECONOMICALLY
6-02-003	DUCTS	1-01-001	DUST-THICK	1-01-001	EARNED-RUN	17-07-016	ECONOMICS
1-01-001	DUCTWORK	1-01-001	DUSTBIN	18-09-017	EARNEST	7-03-006	ECONOMIES
1-01-001	DUD	1-01-001	DUSTED	13-08-012	EARNESTLY	6-03-005	ECONOMIST
1-01-001	DUDLEY	1-01-001	DUSTIN	3-03-003	EARNESTNESS	1-01-001	ECONOMIST'S
1-01-001	DUDS	6-04-004	DUSTING	9-07-009	EARNING	5-04-005	ECONOMISTS
1-01-001	DUDS'D	1-01-001	DUSTS	19-05-012	EARNINGS	3-02-003	ECONOMIZE
142-14-092	DUE	1-01-001	DUSTY	2-02-002	EARNS	2-02-002	ECONOMIZING
5-02-003	DUEL	1-01-001	DUSTY-GREEN	1-01-001	EARP	79-09-049	ECONOMY
2-01-001	DUELING	1-01-001	DUSTY-SLIPPERED	1-01-001	EARPHONES	6-04-006	ECSTASY
1-01-001	DUELS	15-06-010	DUTCH	3-02-002	EARRINGS	4-04-004	ECSTATIC
1-01-001	DUET	2-02-002	DUTCHESS	38-11-033	EARS	1-01-001	ECUADOR
1-01-001	DUETS	1-01-001	DUTCHMAN	2-02-002	EARSPLITTING	29-02-002	ECUMENICAL
3-01-001	DUFFEL	34-10-026	DUTIES	150-15-061	EARTH	1-01-001	ECUMENICISTS
1-01-001	DUFFER	2-02-002	DUTIFULLY	17-07-011	EARTH'S	1-01-001	ECUMENIST
2-01-001	DUFFERS	2-02-002	DUTTON	1-01-001	EARTH-BOUND	1-01-001	ECUMENISTS
2-02-002	DUFFY	61-14-046	DUTY	1-01-001	EARTH-TOUCHING	16-07-011	ED
1-01-001	DUFRESNE	1-01-001	DUVERGER	1-01-001	EARTH-WEEK	30-06-008	EDDIE
1-01-001	DUFRESNE'S	1-01-001	DUYVIL	1-01-001	EARTH-WEEKS	1-01-001	EDDIE'S
15-08-015	DUG	1-01-001	DVORAK	1-01-001	EARTHENWARE	1-01-001	EDDIES
2-01-001	DUGAN	1-01-001	DWARF	6-02-003	EARTHLY	2-01-001	EDDY
7-01-001	DUGOUT	1-01-001	DWARFED	5-01-001	EARTHMEN	1-01-001	EDDYMAN
1-01-001	DUHAGON	1-01-001	DWARFMISTLETOE	1-01-001	EARTHMEN'S	2-01-001	EDEMA
11-03-005	DUKE	2-02-002	DWARFS	1-01-001	EARTHMOVING	1-01-001	EDEMATOUS
2-02-002	DUKE'S	8-05-007	DWELL	9-02-002	EARTHQUAKE	9-06-006	EDEN
2-02-002	DUKES	2-02-002	DWELLER	9-02-002	EARTHQUAKES	1-01-001	EDENTULOUS
1-01-001	DULCET	2-02-002	DWELLERS	1-01-001	EARTHWORM	2-02-002	EDGAR
27-10-026	DULL	13-06-010	DWELLING	10-06-010	EARTHY	1-01-001	EDGARDO
1-01-001	DULL-GRAY	7-04-006	DWELLINGS	42-11-035	EASE	78-13-057	EDGE
3-03-003	DULLED	1-01-001	DWELLS	8-05-007	EASED	7-04-004	EDGED
2-02-002	DULLER	1-01-001	DWELT	5-02-003	EASEL	1-01-001	EDGERTON'S
9-04-004	DULLES	12-07-011	DWIGHT	2-01-001	EASEMENT	37-10-021	EDGES
1-01-001	DULLES'S	2-02-002	DWINDLE	2-01-001	EASEMENTS	2-02-002	EDGEWATER
2-02-002	DULLEST	2-02-002	DWINDLED	51-13-038	EASIER	1-01-001	EDGEWISE
1-01-001	DULLNESS	4-04-004	DWINDLING	7-04-006	EASIEST	5-03-004	EDGING
1-01-001	DULLS	1-01-001	DWOR	106-15-083	EASILY	2-02-002	EDGY
3-02-003	DULLY	3-01-001	DWYER	3-02-003	EASING	5-02-002	EDIBLE
10-05-007	DULY	1-01-001	DWYER'S	183-13-083	EAST	3-01-002	EDIFICE
1-01-001	DUMAS	4-03-004	DYED	4-02-003	EAST-*WEST	1-01-001	EDIFIED
13-06-009	DUMB	1-01-001	DYEING	3-01-001	EAST-WEST	1-01-001	EDIFYING
2-01-001	DUMBBELL	3-02-003	DYER	11-07-010	EASTER	3-02-002	EDISON
1-01-001	DUMBBELLS	1-01-001	DYEREAR	32-11-027	EASTERN	1-01-001	EDISON'S
1-01-001	DUMMIES	34-11-025	DYING	1-01-001	EASTERNERS	2-01-002	EDIT
1-01-001	DUMMKOPF	1-01-001	DYKE	1-01-001	EASTHAMPTON	7-03-004	EDITED
3-02-002	DUMMY	11-02-003	DYLAN	1-01-001	EASTLAND	4-03-004	EDITH
10-02-002	DUMONT	4-01-001	DYNAFAC	1-01-001	EASTMAN	5-03-005	EDITING
4-04-004	DUMP	21-05-014	DYNAMIC	4-04-004	EASTWARD	37-09-016	EDITION
9-04-008	DUMPED	1-01-001	DYNAMICAL	5-01-001	EASTWICK	10-05-007	EDITIONS
4-02-003	DUMPING	1-01-001	DYNAMICALLY	125-15-100	EASY	77-12-025	EDITOR
1-01-001	DUMPS	4-02-004	DYNAMICS	1-01-001	EASY-GOING	4-03-003	EDITOR'S
1-01-001	DUMPTY	5-04-004	DYNAMITE	1-01-001	EASY-TO-OPERATE	42-07-019	EDITORIAL
1-01-001	DUN	1-01-001	DYNAMITED	1-01-001	EASY-TO-REACH	1-01-001	EDITORIALIST
4-02-002	DUNBAR	2-02-002	DYNAMO	1-01-001	EASY-TO-SPOT	2-01-002	EDITORIALLY
4-01-001	DUNCAN			1-01-001	EASYGOING	10-05-009	EDITORIALS

18-05-012	EDITORS	1-01-001	EIGHT-WEEK	2-02-002	ELECTRICALLY	1-01-001	ELLIPSOID
1-01-001	EDITORSHIP	1-01-001	EIGHT-YEAR	26-08-016	ELECTRICITY	4-01-001	ELLIPSOIDS
1-01-001	EDMONIA	17-07-016	EIGHTEEN	1-01-001	ELECTRIFICATION	1-01-001	ELLIPTICAL
2-02-002	EDMUND	1-01-001	EIGHTEEN-YEAR-O	1-01-001	ELECTRIFYING	7-04-004	ELLIS
3-03-003	EDNA		LD	1-01-001	ELECTRIQUES	1-01-001	ELLISON'S
1-01-001	EDUARD	22-08-018	EIGHTEENTH	1-01-001	ELECTRO-MAGNETI	1-01-001	ELLO
7-06-007	EDUCATE	1-01-001	EIGHTEENTH-		C	1-01-001	ELLSWORTH
21-10-017	EDUCATED	5-04-004	EIGHTEENTH-CENT	1-01-001	ELECTROCARDIOGR	1-01-001	ELLWOOD
3-03-003	EDUCATING		URY		AM	3-03-003	ELM
214-12-069	EDUCATION	23-10-013	EIGHTH	2-01-001	ELECTROCARDIOGR	5-02-002	ELMAN
70-09-036	EDUCATIONAL	2-02-002	EIGHTIES		APH	6-03-003	ELMER
1-01-001	EDUCATIONS	11-05-009	EIGHTY	5-01-002	ELECTRODE	1-01-001	ELMIRA
10-03-003	EDUCATOR	3-02-002	EIGHTY-*FOUR	1-01-001	ELECTRODYNAMICS	1-01-001	ELMS
1-01-001	EDUCATOR'S	2-01-001	EIGHTY-FIFTH	1-01-001	ELECTROLYSIS	1-01-001	ELOI
6-04-005	EDUCATORS	2-02-002	EIGHTY-FIVE	1-01-001	ELECTROMAGNET	1-01-001	ELOISE
1-01-001	EDW	1-01-001	EIGHTY-FOUR	1-01-001	ELECTROMAGNETIS	5-04-005	ELONGATED
45-07-024	EDWARD	1-01-001	EIGHTY-NINE		M	3-01-001	ELONGATION
5-01-001	EDWARD'S	1-01-001	EIGHTY-ONE	1-01-001	ELECTROMYOGRAPH	1-01-001	ELOPED
1-01-001	EDWARDES	2-01-001	EIGHTY-SEVENTH		Y	2-01-002	ELOQUENCE
3-03-003	EDWARDS	5-01-001	EIGHTY-SIXTH	30-03-009	ELECTRON	11-08-011	ELOQUENT
11-07-011	EDWIN	3-02-002	EIGHTY-THREE	1-01-001	ELECTRON-MICROS	2-02-002	ELOQUENTLY
1-01-001	EDWINA	1-01-001	EIGHTY-YEAR-OLD		COPICAL	176-14-125	ELSE
14-01-001	EDYTHE	26-04-004	EILEEN	68-08-014	ELECTRONIC	9-06-009	ELSE'S
2-01-001	EDYTHE'S	3-01-001	EILEEN'S	1-01-001	ELECTRONICALLY	45-12-039	ELSEWHERE
1-01-001	EE-FAKET	2-01-002	EIN	32-03-006	ELECTRONICS	4-03-004	ELSIE
2-01-001	EEL	1-01-001	EINE	1-01-001	ELECTRONOGRAPHY	2-01-001	ELSINORE
2-02-002	EERIE	1-01-001	EINSATZKOMMANDO	10-03-004	ELECTRONS	2-01-001	ELUARD
2-02-002	EERILY		S	5-01-002	ELECTROPHORESIS	1-01-001	ELUATE
1-01-001	EFFACES	3-03-003	EINSTEIN	1-01-001	ELECTROPHORUS	1-01-001	ELUATES
213-15-137	EFFECT	3-02-002	EINSTEIN'S	2-01-001	ELECTROSHOCK	1-01-001	ELUCIDATED
1-01-001	EFFECTE	1-01-001	EINSTEINIAN	1-01-001	ELECTROSHOCKS	1-01-001	ELUCIDATION
12-06-010	EFFECTED	2-02-002	EIRE	9-02-002	ELECTROSTATIC	2-02-002	ELUDED
3-01-003	EFFECTING	1-01-001	EISENHHOWER	1-01-001	ELECTROTHERAPIS	1-01-001	ELUDES
1-01-001	EFFECTINGE	50-07-020	EISENHOWER		T	2-02-002	ELUDING
129-10-089	EFFECTIVE	11-05-009	EISENHOWER'S	10-05-009	ELEGANCE	2-07-002	ELUSIVE
37-10-034	EFFECTIVELY	1-01-001	EISLER	1-01-001	ELEGANCES	1-01-001	ELUSIVENESS
32-08-025	EFFECTIVENESS	284-15-206	EITHER	14-07-011	ELEGANT	1-01-001	ELUTED
109-12-063	EFFECTS	1-01-001	EITHER-OR	1-01-001	ELEGANTLY	4-01-001	ELUTION
1-01-001	EFFECTUAL	3-03-003	EJACULATED	2-02-002	ELEGIAC	2-02-002	ELVIS
2-01-001	EFFECTUATE	1-01-001	EJECT	1-01-001	ELEGIES	2-02-002	ELYSEES
1-01-001	EFFEMINATE	2-01-002	EJECTED	1-01-001	ELEGY	44-09-021	EM
1-01-001	EFFETE	2-01-001	EJECTION	52-12-032	ELEMENT	3-03-003	EMACIATED
2-02-002	EFFICACIOUS	1-01-001	EKATERINOSLAV	11-06-009	ELEMENTAL	1-01-001	EMANATED
2-01-001	EFFICACIOUSLY	1-01-001	EKBERG	19-06-016	ELEMENTARY	2-02-002	EMANATING
9-04-005	EFFICACY	2-01-001	EKED	6-02-002	ELEMENTARY-SCHO	2-02-002	EMANATION
3-02-002	EFFICIENCIES	26-01-001	EKSTROHM		OL	1-01-001	EMANATIONS
50-09-028	EFFICIENCY	1-01-001	EKSTROHM'S	107-10-052	ELEMENTS	2-02-002	EMANCIPATE
32-13-026	EFFICIENT	1-01-001	EKWANOK	3-01-001	ELENA	2-01-001	EMANCIPATED
8-04-008	EFFICIENTLY	20-04-008	EL	7-05-005	ELEPHANT	14-04-005	EMANCIPATION
1-01-001	EFFIE	32-11-029	ELABORATE	1-01-001	ELEPHANT'S	1-01-001	EMANUEL
1-01-001	EFFLORESCE	3-02-003	ELABORATED	1-01-001	ELEPHANTINE	2-01-001	EMANUELE
18-01-001	EFFLUENT	6-05-006	ELABORATELY	10-06-008	ELEPHANTS	1-01-001	EMASCULATED
1-01-001	EFFLUENTS	1-01-001	ELABORATES	11-07-011	ELEVATED	1-01-001	EMASCULATION
1-01-001	EFFLUVIUM	2-02-002	ELABORATION	1-01-001	ELEVATES	1-01-001	EMBALMERS'
145-14-107	EFFORT	22-04-004	ELAINE	3-02-002	ELEVATION	4-03-003	EMBANKMENT
1-01-001	EFFORTLESS	1-01-001	ELAINE'S	12-07-011	ELEVATOR	1-01-001	EMBARCADERO
1-01-001	EFFORTLESSLY	1-01-001	ELAN	40-13-034	ELEVEN	2-02-002	EMBARGO
127-13-084	EFFORTS	1-01-001	ELAPSE	4-03-004	ELEVENTH	5-03-005	EMBARK
1-01-001	EFFUSIVE	5-03-004	ELAPSED	1-01-001	ELEVENTH-FLOOR	2-02-002	EMBARKED
2-01-002	EGALITARIANISM	1-01-001	ELAPSES	8-06-008	ELFIN	8-06-008	EMBARRASSED
1-01-001	EGERTON	7-05-006	ELASTIC	1-01-001	ELGIN	11-08-011	EMBARRASSING
12-04-006	EGG	5-01-002	ELASTICITY	2-02-002	ELI	1-01-001	EMBARRASSINGLY
1-01-001	EGG-HATCHING	3-03-003	ELATED	2-01-001	ELI'S	8-05-008	EMBARRASSMENT
1-01-001	EGG-SIZED	2-02-002	ELATION	3-02-003	ELICIT	7-03-003	EMBASSIES
1-01-001	EGGED	1-01-001	ELBA	6-04-005	ELICITED	17-05-010	EMBASSY
1-01-001	EGGHEAD	10-05-008	ELBOW	1-01-001	ELICITS	1-01-001	EMBATTLED
35-10-021	EGGS	1-01-001	ELBOWING	4-01-002	ELIGIBILITY	4-04-004	EMBEDDED
1-01-001	EGGSHELL	7-03-007	ELBOWS	14-04-010	ELIGIBLE	1-01-001	EMBELLISHED
1-01-001	EGILS	1-01-001	ELBURN	1-01-001	ELIGIO	1-01-001	EMBEZZLE
1-01-001	EGNINEERS	15-07-010	ELDER	1-01-001	ELIJAH	1-01-001	EMBEZZLEMENT
13-07-011	EGO	13-09-013	ELDERLY	26-06-025	ELIMINATE	1-01-001	EMBEZZLING
1-01-001	EGO'S	9-04-006	ELDERS	22-08-022	ELIMINATED	1-01-001	EMBITTERED
1-01-001	EGO-ADAPTIVE	5-03-004	ELDEST	4-04-004	ELIMINATES	3-01-001	EMBLEMATIC
1-01-001	EGOCENTRIC	2-02-002	ELDON	15-08-013	ELIMINATING	7-04-007	EMBODIED
1-01-001	EGON	10-05-008	ELEANOR	9-04-008	ELIMINATION	3-03-003	EMBODIES
3-01-002	EGOTISM	2-01-001	ELEAZAR	1-01-001	ELIMINATIONS	10-05-009	EMBODIMENT
2-02-002	EGOTIST	9-01-001	ELEC	3-01-002	ELINOR	1-01-001	EMBODIMENTS
1-01-001	EGOTIST'S	2-01-001	ELEC'S	1-01-001	ELIOS	1-01-001	EMBODY
1-01-001	EGREGIOUSLY	8-04-007	ELECT	4-02-003	ELIOT	3-03-003	EMBODYING
1-01-001	EGRETS	33-10-025	ELECTED	1-01-001	ELIOT-OR-*MARTI	2-02-002	EMBOLDENED
14-06-012	EGYPT	1-01-001	ELECTING		N	1-01-001	EMBOSSED
5-02-003	EGYPTIAN	77-09-030	ELECTION	3-02-002	ELISABETH	1-01-001	EMBOUCHURE
3-01-003	EGYPTIANS	51-04-009	ELECTIONS	1-01-001	ELISHA	13-06-013	EMBRACE
8-05-008	EH	1-01-001	ELECTIVES	13-07-009	ELITE	4-03-003	EMBRACED
1-01-001	EHLERS	2-02-002	ELECTOR	15-09-014	ELIZABETH	4-04-004	EMBRACES
14-03-003	EICHMANN	13-03-003	ELECTORAL	7-03-003	ELIZABETHAN	4-03-004	EMBRACING
6-01-001	EICHMANN'S	1-01-001	ELECTORATE	2-01-002	ELIZABETHANS	5-02-003	EMBROIDERED
1-01-001	EIDETIC	3-02-002	ELECTORS	1-01-001	ELK	1-01-001	EMBROIDERIES
1-01-001	EIES	1-01-001	ELECTRA	1-01-001	ELKS	1-01-001	EMBROIDERY
104-15-073	EIGHT	1-01-001	ELECTRESS	1-01-001	ELL	1-01-001	EMBROILED
1-01-001	EIGHT-AND-A-HAL	68-14-039	ELECTRIC	1-01-001	ELLA	1-01-001	EMBRYO
	F-FOOT	1-01-001	ELECTRIC'S	1-01-001	ELLAMAE	2-02-002	EMBRYONIC
1-01-001	EIGHT-BAR	1-01-001	ELECTRIC-SEWER-	10-05-006	ELLEN	1-01-001	EMCEE
1-01-001	EIGHT-BY-TEN		WATER	1-01-001	ELLIE	3-03-003	EMERALD
1-01-001	EIGHT-FOOT	1-01-001	ELECTRIC-UTILIT	5-05-005	ELLIOTT	6-02-002	EMERALDS
2-01-001	EIGHT-INCH		Y	2-02-002	ELLIPSES	18-08-016	EMERGE
1-01-001	EIGHT-THIRTY	46-08-019	ELECTRICAL	1-01-001	ELLIPSIS	26-12-024	EMERGED

```
3-02-003    EMERGENCE
7-06-006    EMERGENCIES
39-11-029   EMERGENCY
2-02-002    EMERGENT
9-06-009    EMERGES
15-05-010   EMERGING
3-02-002    EMERITUS
8-05-007    EMERSON
2-02-002    EMERSON'S
2-01-001    EMIGRANT
1-01-001    EMIGRATED
1-01-001    EMIGRATING
1-01-001    EMIGRATION
1-01-001    EMIL
5-01-001    EMILE
2-01-001    EMILE'S
1-01-001    EMILIO
4-04-004    EMINENCE
9-07-009    EMINENT
4-03-004    EMINENTLY
1-01-001    EMINONU
1-01-001    EMISSARIES
2-02-002    EMISSARY
32-01-003   EMISSION
1-01-001    EMIT
3-02-003    EMITTED
1-01-001    EMITTING
10-04-004   EMMA
2-01-001    EMMA'S
1-01-001    EMMANUEL
2-01-002    EMMERICH
2-01-001    EMMERT
5-03-003    EMMETT
1-01-001    EMMETT'S
14-01-001   EMORY
34-08-024   EMOTION
68-08-030   EMOTIONAL
2-01-002    EMOTIONALISM
1-01-001    EMOTIONALITY
13-06-010   EMOTIONALLY
43-08-026   EMOTIONS
1-01-001    EMPATHY
2-01-002    EMPEDOCLES
19-05-009   EMPEROR
3-03-003    EMPEROR'S
4-02-002    EMPERORS
2-01-002    EMPHASES
58-10-049   EMPHASIS
20-09-019   EMPHASIZE
18-10-018   EMPHASIZED
3-02-002    EMPHASIZES
4-03-004    EMPHASIZING
2-02-002    EMPHATIC
3-03-003    EMPHATICALLY
4-01-002    EMPHYSEMA
1-01-001    EMPHYSEMATOUS
22-06-018   EMPIRE
4-03-003    EMPIRES
23-04-009   EMPIRICAL
5-03-003    EMPIRICALLY
2-01-002    EMPIRICISM
12-07-011   EMPLOY
1-01-001    EMPLOYE
49-11-042   EMPLOYED
24-05-008   EMPLOYEE
1-01-001    EMPLOYEE'S
1-01-001    EMPLOYEE-CONTRIBUTED
65-08-024   EMPLOYEES
15-08-013   EMPLOYER
17-05-010   EMPLOYERS
2-02-002    EMPLOYERS'
18-03-012   EMPLOYES
10-04-010   EMPLOYING
47-09-026   EMPLOYMENT
1-01-001    EMPLOYMENTS
9-06-006    EMPLOYS
1-01-001    EMPOWER
2-02-002    EMPOWERED
1-01-001    EMPOWERING
8-05-007    EMPTIED
2-02-002    EMPTIER
3-03-003    EMPTIES
2-02-002    EMPTINESS
64-13-050   EMPTY
1-01-001    EMPTYING
1-01-001    EMSELVES
3-03-003    EMULATE
1-01-001    EMULATED
1-01-001    EMULSIFIED
1-01-001    EMULSION
7-05-007    EN
1-01-001    EN-LAI
1-01-001    EN-LAI'S
23-09-020   ENABLE
12-10-012   ENABLED
9-06-009    ENABLES

13-05-011   ENABLING
7-05-006    ENACT
12-04-008   ENACTED
4-04-004    ENACTING
7-04-006    ENACTMENT
1-01-001    ENAMEL
2-02-002    ENAMELING
1-01-001    ENAMELLED
1-01-001    ENCAMP
1-01-001    ENCAMPED
3-03-003    ENCAMPMENT
1-01-001    ENCASED
11-07-010   ENCEPHALITIS
1-01-001    ENCEPHALOGRAPHIC
1-01-001    ENCHAINED
1-01-001    ENCHANT
5-04-005    ENCHANTED
9-04-005    ENCHANTING
1-01-001    ENCHANTINGLY
3-03-003    ENCHANTMENT
1-01-001    ENCIPHERED
1-01-001    ENCIRCLE
2-02-002    ENCIRCLED
1-01-001    ENCLAVES
11-07-010   ENCLOSED
1-01-001    ENCLOSES
1-01-001    ENCLOSING
7-06-006    ENCLOSURE
1-01-001    ENCOMIUMS
4-03-004    ENCOMPASS
3-02-003    ENCOMPASSED
1-01-001    ENCOMPASSES
1-01-001    ENCORES
28-09-027   ENCOUNTER
30-10-026   ENCOUNTERED
8-05-007    ENCOUNTERS
46-10-033   ENCOURAGE
29-11-026   ENCOURAGED
14-08-014   ENCOURAGEMENT
5-04-005    ENCOURAGES
23-08-021   ENCOURAGING
1-01-001    ENCOURAGINGLY
1-01-001    ENCROACH
1-01-001    ENCROACHED
2-02-002    ENCROACHING
5-04-005    ENCROACHMENT
2-02-002    ENCRUSTED
2-02-002    ENCUMBERED
1-01-001    ENCUMBRANCES
1-01-001    ENCYCLOPEDIA
5-03-005    ENCYCLOPEDIAS
3-01-001    ENCYCLOPEDIC
1-01-001    ENCYCLOPEDIA
410-15-246  END
2-01-001    END-PRODUCT
1-01-001    END-TO-END
2-01-002    END-USE
1-01-001    ENDANGER
1-01-001    ENDANGERED
3-03-003    ENDANGERING
3-02-002    ENDEARED
3-03-003    ENDEARING
1-01-001    ENDEARMENT
2-02-002    ENDEARMENTS
7-04-007    ENDEAVOR
2-01-002    ENDEAVORED
2-02-002    ENDEAVORING
5-04-004    ENDEAVORS
1-01-001    ENDEAVOUR
1-01-001    ENDEAVOURS
60-12-047   ENDED
1-01-001    ENDEVOR
1-01-001    ENDGAME
31-08-025   ENDING
3-01-001    ENDINGS
20-11-017   ENDLESS
7-07-007    ENDLESSLY
1-01-001    ENDOGAMOUS
3-01-001    ENDOGAMY
1-01-001    ENDOGENOUS
6-04-006    ENDORSE
4-04-004    ENDORSED
2-02-002    ENDORSEMENT
1-01-001    ENDORSING
1-01-001    ENDOSPERM
17-09-016   ENDOTHELIAL
21-07-020   ENDOTHERMIC
10-07-009   ENDOW
7-04-007    ENDOWED
2-02-002    ENDOWMENT
4-03-003    ENDOWMENTS
1-01-001    ENDOWS
1-01-001    ENDPOINTS
66-12-046   ENDS
2-02-002    ENDURABLE
16-07-012   ENDURANCE

8-06-008    ENDURE
11-06-009   ENDURED
2-02-002    ENDURES
10-05-008   ENDURING
1-01-001    ENDURINGLY
27-12-020   ENEMIES
88-11-035   ENEMY
8-04-004    ENEMY'S
2-01-001    ENEMY-*JEW
11-05-011   ENERGETIC
2-02-002    ENERGETICALLY
11-03-007   ENERGIES
1-01-001    ENERGIZED
1-01-001    ENERGIZES
100-14-047  ENERGY
2-02-002    ENERVATING
1-01-001    ENERVATION
1-01-001    ENFANT
1-01-001    ENFIELD
9-05-006    ENFORCE
2-01-002    ENFORCEABLE
20-10-020   ENFORCED
19-05-009   ENFORCEMENT
1-01-001    ENFORCERS
1-01-001    ENFORCES
5-04-004    ENFORCING
1-01-001    ENG
14-08-013   ENGAGE
47-11-038   ENGAGED
22-10-018   ENGAGEMENT
8-04-007    ENGAGEMENTS
7-04-004    ENGAGES
8-03-007    ENGAGING
1-01-001    ENGAGINGLY
2-01-002    ENGENDER
9-05-009    ENGENDERED
1-01-001    ENGH
50-10-021   ENGINE
2-02-002    ENGINE'S
42-07-012   ENGINEER
46-08-016   ENGINEERING
2-01-001    ENGINEERING-MANAGEMENT
32-07-015   ENGINEERS
3-02-002    ENGINEERS'
17-06-009   ENGINES
1-01-001    ENGISCH
154-15-066  ENGLAND
1-01-001    ENGLAND'S
1-01-001    ENGLAND-BORN
5-03-005    ENGLANDER
3-01-001    ENGLANDERS
1-01-001    ENGLE'S
195-15-087  ENGLISH
1-01-001    ENGLISH-*DUTCH
1-01-001    ENGLISH-*SCOTTISH-*FRENCH
1-01-001    ENGLISH-BORN
1-01-001    ENGLISH-DIALOGUE
2-02-002    ENGLISH-SPEAKING
15-03-004   ENGLISHMAN
8-02-003    ENGLISHMEN
1-01-001    ENGLISHY
4-03-004    ENGRAVED
1-01-001    ENGRAVER
2-02-002    ENGRAVING
1-01-001    ENGRAVINGS
2-02-002    ENGROSSED
1-01-001    ENGROSSING
5-04-005    ENGULFED
1-01-001    ENGULFING
1-01-001    ENGULFS
5-04-005    ENHANCE
5-02-005    ENHANCED
1-01-001    ENHANCES
1-01-001    ENHANCING
4-04-004    ENIGMA
2-01-002    ENIGMATIC
1-01-001    ENJOIN
1-01-001    ENJOINDER
5-04-004    ENJOINED
44-13-038   ENJOY
2-02-002    ENJOYABLE
57-12-047   ENJOYED
17-09-016   ENJOYING
21-07-020   ENJOYMENT
10-07-009   ENJOYS
1-01-001    ENLARGD
91-15-072   ENLARGE
7-04-007    ENLARGED
11-04-008   ENLARGEMENT
4-03-004    ENLARGEMENTS
3-03-003    ENLARGING
1-01-001    ENLIGHTEN
7-06-007    ENLIGHTENED

3-03-003    ENLIGHTENING
2-01-002    ENLIGHTENMENT
5-04-005    ENLIST
11-07-010   ENLISTED
1-01-001    ENLISTMENT
1-01-001    ENLISTS
2-02-002    ENLIVENED
2-02-002    ENMESHED
1-01-001    ENMITIES
1-01-001    ENMITY
1-01-001    ENNIS
1-01-001    ENNY
1-01-001    ENOCH
1-01-001    ENORMITY
37-12-036   ENORMOUS
9-06-008    ENORMOUSLY
1-01-001    ENOS
430-15-256  ENOUGH
1-01-001    ENQUETES
1-01-001    ENQUIRED
1-01-001    ENQUIRER
1-01-001    ENRAGE
1-01-001    ENRAGED
1-01-001    ENRAPTURED
5-04-005    ENRICH
2-01-002    ENRICHED
1-01-001    ENRICHING
3-02-003    ENRICHMENT
2-02-002    ENRICO
3-01-001    ENRIGHT
1-01-001    ENRIGHT'S
1-01-001    ENRIQUE
5-03-004    ENROLL
9-05-008    ENROLLED
1-01-001    ENROLLEES
1-01-001    ENROLLING
6-04-006    ENROLLMENT
2-02-002    ENROLLMENTS
2-02-002    ENSCONCED
11-02-006   ENSEMBLE
3-03-003    ENSEMBLES
4-02-002    ENSIGN
2-01-001    ENSLAVE
1-01-001    ENSLAVED
2-02-002    ENSLAVEMENT
1-01-001    ENSLAVING
1-01-001    ENSOLITE
2-02-002    ENSUE
5-04-005    ENSUED
2-02-002    ENSUES
4-04-004    ENSUING
8-05-007    ENSURE
1-01-001    ENSURES
2-02-002    ENSURING
5-05-005    ENTAIL
8-06-007    ENTAILS
1-01-001    ENTANGLEMENT
78-12-064   ENTER
1-01-001    ENTER'D
98-14-071   ENTERED
24-10-023   ENTERING
1-01-001    ENTEROTOXEMIA
31-07-024   ENTERPRISE
14-06-009   ENTERPRISES
5-04-005    ENTERPRISING
1-01-001    ENTERPRISINGLY
13-06-013   ENTERS
14-08-011   ENTERTAIN
11-07-008   ENTERTAINED
2-01-002    ENTERTAINER
3-03-003    ENTERTAINERS
12-05-010   ENTERTAINING
29-09-018   ENTERTAINMENT
3-03-003    ENTERTAINMENTS
1-01-001    ENTERTEYNED
2-01-001    ENTHALPY
1-01-001    ENTHRALLED
3-02-003    ENTHRALLING
1-01-001    ENTHRONE*(S
28-12-026   ENTHUSIASM
1-01-001    ENTHUSIASMS
2-02-002    ENTHUSIAST
24-11-024   ENTHUSIASTIC
5-03-003    ENTHUSIASTICAL
3-03-003    ENTHUSIASTS
1-01-001    ENTICEMENTS
1-01-001    ENTICING
149-14-114  ENTIRE
91-15-072   ENTIRELY
7-04-007    ENTIRETY
11-04-008   ENTITIES
5-03-003    ENTITLE
56-10-037   ENTITLED
4-03-004    ENTITLES
10-07-010   ENTITY
1-01-001    ENTOMBED
```

Freq.	Word
1-01-001	ENTOMOLOGIST
4-03-004	ENTOURAGE
57-12-036	ENTRANCE
3-03-003	ENTRANCED
1-01-001	ENTRANCEWAY
2-02-002	ENTRANT
1-01-001	ENTREAT
2-01-001	ENTREATED
5-03-005	ENTRENCHED
6-01-003	ENTREPRENEUR
1-01-001	ENTREPRENEURS
19-04-007	ENTRIES
4-01-001	ENTROPY
1-01-001	ENTROPY-INCREASING
2-02-002	ENTRUST
2-02-002	ENTRUSTED
1-01-001	ENTRUSTING
26-11-019	ENTRY
1-01-001	ENTRY-LIMIT
1-01-001	ENTRY-LIMITED
2-01-001	ENTRY-LIMITING
1-01-001	ENTWHISTLE
2-02-002	ENTWINED
2-01-001	ENUMERATED
1-01-001	ENUMERATION
1-01-001	ENUNCIATE
1-01-001	ENUNCIATED
1-01-001	ENUNCIATION
21-06-013	ENVELOPE
3-02-003	ENVELOPES
2-02-002	ENVELOPING
1-01-001	ENVENOMED
4-02-002	ENVER
4-04-004	ENVIABLE
1-01-001	ENVIABLY
5-04-005	ENVIED
1-01-001	ENVIOUS
1-01-001	ENVIOUSLY
1-01-001	ENVIRONING
42-07-025	ENVIRONMENT
1-01-001	ENVIRONMENT**H
7-02-005	ENVIRONMENTAL
42-03-003	ENVIRONMENTS
4-04-004	ENVIRONS
1-01-001	ENVISAGED
1-01-001	ENVISAGES
3-02-003	ENVISION
4-04-004	ENVISIONED
2-01-002	ENVISIONS
1-01-001	ENVOYS
7-04-007	ENVY
1-01-001	ENZO
4-01-003	ENZYMATIC
6-03-004	ENZYME
11-02-004	ENZYMES
1-01-001	EOSINOPHILIC
1-01-001	EPAULETS
1-01-001	EPH
4-03-004	EPHEMERAL
5-01-001	EPHESIANS
2-02-002	EPHESUS
18-03-006	EPIC
3-01-001	EPICENTER
2-01-002	EPICS
2-02-002	EPICURE
1-01-001	EPICUREAN
1-01-001	EPICURUS
1-01-001	EPICYCLE
6-01-001	EPICYCLES
1-01-001	EPICYCLICAL
1-01-001	EPICYCLICALLY
11-04-005	EPIDEMIC
2-01-001	EPIDEMICS
1-01-001	EPIDEMIOLOGICAL
2-02-002	EPIDERMIS
1-01-001	EPIGENETIC
1-01-001	EPIGRAMMATIC
2-02-002	EPIGRAMS
2-01-002	EPIGRAPH
3-03-003	EPILEPTIC
1-01-001	EPILOGUE
3-02-002	EPIPHANY
2-01-001	EPIPHYSEAL-DIAPHYSEAL
5-01-001	EPIPHYSIS
6-04-005	EPISCOPAL
12-09-011	EPISODE
6-05-005	EPISODES
3-02-002	EPISTEMOLOGY
1-01-001	EPISTLES
1-01-001	EPISTOLATORY
4-02-002	EPITAPH
2-01-001	EPITHET
7-02-002	EPITHETS
2-01-002	EPITOME
1-01-001	EPITOMIZE
3-03-003	EPITOMIZED
1-01-001	EPITOMIZES
6-03-005	EPOCH
1-01-001	EPOCH-MAKING
2-02-002	EPOXY
1-01-001	EPPLER
1-01-001	EPSILON
1-01-001	EPSOM
3-03-003	EPSTEIN
1-01-001	EQ
2-01-001	EQN
90-14-069	EQUAL
12-06-010	EQUALITY
1-01-001	EQUALIZATION
1-01-001	EQUALIZE
1-01-001	EQUALIZERS
1-01-001	EQUALIZING
1-01-001	EQUALLED
62-14-049	EQUALLY
8-03-004	EQUALS
2-02-002	EQUANIMITY
8-01-003	EQUATE
5-03-004	EQUATED
3-02-003	EQUATING
33-05-014	EQUATION
10-02-006	EQUATIONS
3-03-003	EQUATOR
1-01-001	EQUATORIAL
1-01-001	EQUIDISTANT
1-01-001	EQUIDISTANTLY
13-03-008	EQUILIBRATED
1-01-001	EQUILIBRIUM
1-01-001	EQUILIBRIUMS
1-01-001	EQUINE
1-01-001	EQUINES
2-01-001	EQUINOX
2-02-002	EQUIP
167-14-078	EQUIPMENT
1-01-001	EQUIPOTENT
36-09-027	EQUIPPED
1-01-001	EQUIPPING
11-05-007	EQUITABLE
2-02-002	EQUITABLY
7-04-004	EQUITY
4-02-003	EQUIVALENCE
46-11-031	EQUIVALENT
1-01-001	EQUIVALENT-CHOICE
8-04-005	EQUIVALENTS
1-01-001	EQUIVOCAL
30-11-023	ERA
2-01-002	ERA'S
2-02-002	ERADICATE
3-01-001	ERADICATION
2-01-002	ERAS
1-01-001	ERASE
2-02-002	ERASED
2-01-001	ERASER
1-01-001	ERASERS
1-01-001	ERASING
1-01-001	ERASMUS'S
1-01-001	ERDE
1-01-001	ERDMANN'S
2-01-001	ERDU**DS
1-01-001	ERE
2-02-002	ERECT
81-13-059	ERECTED
47-09-039	ERECTING
2-02-002	ERECTION
17-04-005	ERECTS
3-02-003	ERGOTROPIC
58-09-043	ERHART
108-11-087	ERIC
4-03-004	ERICH
26-06-020	ERICKSON
52-12-043	ERIE
8-06-007	ERIK
51-11-033	ERIKSON
5-03-004	ERIKSON'S
5-03-005	ERLENMEYER
3-02-003	ERNEST
4-01-001	ERNIE
1-01-001	ERNIE'S
1-01-001	ERNST
2-01-001	ERODED
10-01-001	EROMONGA
2-01-001	EROS
6-04-005	EROSION
8-02-004	EROTIC
3-03-003	EROTICA
3-02-003	EROTICALLY
7-03-005	ERR
2-02-002	ERRAND
7-02-002	ERRATIC
2-02-002	ERRATICALLY
3-02-003	ERRED
1-01-001	ERROL
4-04-004	ERRONEOUS
1-01-001	ERRONEOUSLY
36-08-027	ERROR
44-10-029	ERRORS
1-01-001	ERRS
2-02-002	ERSATZ
1-01-001	ERSKINE
3-03-003	ERUDITE
1-01-001	ERUDITION
2-01-002	ERUPT
7-06-007	ERUPTED
1-01-001	ERUPTING
2-02-002	ERUPTION
1-01-001	ERUPTS
2-01-002	ERVIN
1-01-001	ERWIN
1-01-001	ERYSIPELAS
1-01-001	ERYTHROID
1-01-001	ESCADRILLE
7-02-002	ESCALATION
1-01-001	ESCAPADE
2-02-002	ESCAPADES
65-13-050	ESCAPE
1-01-001	ESCAPE'S
18-09-018	ESCAPED
1-01-001	ESCAPEES
4-02-004	ESCAPES
5-04-005	ESCAPING
1-01-001	ESCAPIST
2-01-001	ESCHEAT
1-01-001	ESCHEW
1-01-001	ESCHEWED
1-01-001	ESCHEWING
1-01-001	ESCHEWS
9-06-008	ESCORT
5-04-005	ESCORTED
2-02-002	ESCORTING
1-01-001	ESCORTS
2-01-001	ESCRITOIRE
2-02-002	ESCUTCHEON
1-01-001	ESCUTCHEONS
1-01-001	ESHLEMAN
3-02-002	ESKIMO
2-01-001	ESKIMOS
2-01-001	ESMARCH
1-01-001	ESNARDS
4-03-003	ESOTERIC
1-01-001	ESPAGNOL
1-01-001	ESPANOL
160-15-126	ESPECIALLY
1-01-001	ESPERANZA
5-03-005	ESPIONAGE
3-01-001	ESPLANADE
1-01-001	ESPOUSAL
2-02-002	ESPOUSE
1-01-001	ESPOUSES
1-01-001	ESPOUSING
6-02-003	ESPRIT
3-03-003	ESQUIRE
19-05-013	ESSAY
2-02-002	ESSAYED
5-04-005	ESSAYISTS
1-01-001	ESSAYS
2-01-001	ESSE
15-07-014	ESSENCE
2-02-002	ESSENCES
81-13-059	ESSENTIAL
47-09-039	ESSENTIALLY
2-02-002	ESSENTIALS
17-04-005	ESSEX
3-02-003	EST
58-09-043	ESTABLISH
108-11-087	ESTABLISHED
4-03-004	ESTABLISHES
26-06-020	ESTABLISHING
52-12-043	ESTABLISHMENT
8-06-007	ESTABLISHMENTS
51-11-033	ESTATE
5-03-004	ESTATES
5-03-005	ESTEEM
3-02-003	ESTEEMED
4-01-001	ESTELLA
1-01-001	ESTELLA'S
1-01-001	ESTEP
2-01-001	ESTERASES
1-01-001	ESTERS
1-01-001	ESTES
9-02-002	ESTHER
1-01-001	ESTHERSON
3-03-003	ESTHETIC
3-02-003	ESTHETICS
39-09-027	ESTIMATE
67-10-042	ESTIMATED
24-07-021	ESTIMATES
2-02-002	ESTIMATING
4-03-003	ESTIMATION
3-03-003	ESTRANGED
1-01-001	ESTRANGEMENT
1-01-001	ESTRANGING
1-01-001	ESTUARIES
30-12-022	ET
1-01-001	ET'S
4-01-001	ETA
58-09-043	ETC
9-02-002	ETCETERA
2-02-002	ETCHED
29-09-021	ETERNAL
6-05-005	ETERNITY
1-01-001	ETES
4-02-002	ETHAN
1-01-001	ETHANOL
3-02-003	ETHEL
1-01-001	ETHER
3-03-003	ETHEREAL
1-01-001	ETHERS
4-02-004	ETHIC
29-06-017	ETHICAL
2-02-002	ETHICALLY
2-02-002	ETHICIST
1-01-001	ETHICISTS
19-06-012	ETHICS
1-01-001	ETHIOPIANS
13-06-008	ETHNIC
4-03-004	ETHOS
4-02-002	ETHYL
3-03-003	ETIQUETTE
1-01-001	ETRUSCAN
1-01-001	ETTORE
1-01-001	ETUDES
1-01-001	ETYMOLOGICAL
1-01-001	EUCALYPTUS
2-01-001	EUCLID'S
25-05-009	EUGENE
2-01-001	EUGENE'S
15-01-001	EUGENIA
1-01-001	EUGENIC
1-01-001	EULOGIZE
1-01-001	EULOGIZED
1-01-001	EULOGIZERS
1-01-001	EUPHEMISM
2-02-002	EUPHORIA
1-01-001	EUPHORIC
1-01-001	EURASIAN
1-01-001	EURATOM
3-01-001	EURIPIDES
118-13-056	EUROPE
3-02-003	EUROPE'S
61-08-030	EUROPEAN
1-01-001	EUROPEANISH
1-01-001	EUROPEANIZATION
1-01-001	EUROPEANIZED
5-05-005	EUROPEANS
2-01-001	EURYDICE
3-01-001	EUSTIS
1-01-001	EUTECTIC
1-01-001	EVA
1-01-001	EVACUATE
3-02-003	EVACUATED
5-04-005	EVACUATION
1-01-001	EVADE
2-02-002	EVADED
1-01-001	EVADES
1-01-001	EVADING
3-01-001	EVADNA
13-05-011	EVALUATE
11-03-010	EVALUATED
7-03-006	EVALUATING
31-04-018	EVALUATION
5-04-004	EVALUATIONS
1-01-001	EVALUATIVE
5-02-003	EVANGELICAL
1-01-001	EVANGELICALISM
9-02-003	EVANGELISM
1-01-001	EVANGELIST
1-01-001	EVANGELISTS
10-03-004	EVANS
7-02-002	EVANSTON
1-01-001	EVANSVILLE
1-01-001	EVAPORATE
2-02-002	EVAPORATED
2-02-002	EVAPORATION
1-01-001	EVAPORATIVE
1-01-001	EVASION
1-01-001	EVASIONS
5-04-005	EVASIVE
19-07-012	EVE
1-01-001	EVEGENI
4-03-004	EVELYN
1171-15-402	EVEN
1-01-001	EVEN-HANDED
133-14-083	EVENING
1-01-001	EVENING'S
15-10-014	EVENINGS

4-03-004	EVENLY	1-01-001	EX-SINGER	4-03-004	EXCOMMUNICATED	3-02-002	EXPANDS
1-01-001	EVENSEN	1-01-001	EX-TRUCK	1-01-001	EXCORIATE	5-05-005	EXPANSE
1-01-001	EVENSONG	2-02-002	EXACERBATED	1-01-001	EXCRETION	47-10-033	EXPANSION
81-12-062	EVENT	1-01-001	EXACERBATES	2-02-002	EXCRUCIATING	1-01-001	EXPANSION-CONTR
1-01-001	EVENTFULLY	3-02-002	EXACERBATION	2-02-002	EXCURSION		ACTION
101-14-069	EVENTS	1-01-001	EXACERBATIONS	2-02-002	EXCURSIONS	1-01-001	EXPANSIONIST
1-01-001	EVENTSHAH-LEH	27-11-023	EXACT	1-01-001	EXCURSUS	3-01-002	EXPANSIONS
1-01-001	EVENTSHAHLEH	1-01-001	EXACT-SIZE	1-01-001	EXCUSABLE	1-01-001	EXPANSIVE
11-07-010	EVENTUAL	1-01-001	EXACTED	27-09-025	EXCUSE	1-01-001	EXPANSIVELY
1-01-001	EVENTUALITIES	2-01-002	EXACTING	3-03-003	EXCUSED	3-03-003	EXPANSIVENESS
1-01-001	EVENTUALITY	103-15-086	EXACTLY	2-02-002	EXCUSES	2-01-002	EXPECIALLY
52-13-045	EVENTUALLY	2-02-002	EXACTS	2-01-001	EXEC	108-14-081	EXPECT
1-01-001	EVENTUATE	8-05-007	EXAGGERATE	7-04-007	EXECUTE	1-01-001	EXPECTABLE
1-01-001	EVENUTALLY	13-07-013	EXAGGERATED	14-08-014	EXECUTED	4-04-004	EXPECTANCY
345-15-208	EVER	4-03-004	EXAGGERATING	1-01-001	EXECUTING	3-03-003	EXPECTANT
1-01-001	EVER'BODY	5-05-005	EXAGGERATION	15-08-013	EXECUTION	2-02-002	EXPECTANTLY
5-04-005	EVER-CHANGING	1-01-001	EXAGGERATIONS	2-02-002	EXECUTIONER	11-08-011	EXPECTATION
1-01-001	EVER-EXISTENT	1-01-001	EXALT	1-01-001	EXECUTIONER'S	23-07-014	EXPECTATIONS
3-03-003	EVER-EXPANDING	3-02-002	EXALTATION	55-10-040	EXECUTIONS	187-14-123	EXPECTED
2-01-001	EVER-GROWING	1-01-001	EXALTATIONS	55-10-040	EXECUTIVE	1-01-001	EXPECTEDLY
2-01-002	EVER-INCREASING	7-04-007	EXALTED	1-01-001	EXECUTIVE'S	18-07-018	EXPECTING
1-01-001	EVER-LOVIN	1-01-001	EXALTING	9-07-008	EXECUTIVES	22-09-021	EXPECTS
6-05-006	EVER-PRESENT	1-01-001	EXAMIANTION	2-01-002	EXECUTOR	2-02-002	EXPEDIENCY
1-01-001	EVER-TIGHTENING	29-08-021	EXAMINATION	2-01-001	EXECUTORS	7-05-007	EXPEDIENT
2-02-002	EVEREST	8-05-007	EXAMINATIONS	1-01-001	EXEGETE	2-02-002	EXPEDITING
3-03-003	EVERETT	33-10-031	EXAMINE	2-01-002	EXEMPLAR	15-07-009	EXPEDITION
1-01-001	EVERGLADES	28-11-025	EXAMINED	3-02-002	EXEMPLIFIED	6-04-005	EXPEDITIONS
1-01-001	EVERGREEN	14-06-009	EXAMINER	1-01-001	EXEMPLIFIES	2-02-002	EXPEDITIOUS
8-04-006	EVERLASTING	1-01-001	EXAMINERS	2-02-002	EXEMPLIFY	1-01-001	EXPEDITIOUSLY
1-01-001	EVERLASTINGLY	1-01-001	EXAMINES	5-04-005	EXEMPT	2-02-002	EXPEL
1-01-001	EVERMOUNTING	1-01-001	EXAMININ	8-03-004	EXEMPTION	5-04-005	EXPELLED
491-15-274	EVERY	7-04-007	EXAMINING	2-02-002	EXEMPTIONS	1-01-001	EXPELLING
1-01-001	EVERY-DAY	292-15-166	EXAMPLE	58-12-033	EXERCISE	1-01-001	EXPEND
72-14-055	EVERYBODY	53-09-040	EXAMPLES	18-07-016	EXERCISED	1-01-001	EXPENDABLE
4-04-004	EVERYBODY'S	1-01-001	EXASPERATE	23-07-015	EXERCISES	12-06-011	EXPENDED
12-07-009	EVERYDAY	2-02-002	EXASPERATED	6-04-006	EXERCISING	11-06-010	EXPENDITURE
94-14-071	EVERYONE	1-01-001	EXASPERATING	11-08-011	EXERT	45-07-016	EXPENDITURES
4-02-004	EVERYONE'S	1-01-001	EXASPERATINGLY	13-05-010	EXERTED	50-10-044	EXPENSE
185-15-122	EVERYTHING	5-04-005	EXASPERATION	2-02-002	EXERTING	47-11-029	EXPENSES
3-03-003	EVERYTHING'S	1-01-001	EXBOYFRIEND	1-01-001	EXERTION	44-10-035	EXPENSIVE
47-13-041	EVERYWHERE	3-03-003	EXCAVATION	1-01-001	EXERTIONS	276-15-121	EXPERIENCE
2-02-002	EVICTED	1-01-001	EXCAVATIONS	3-02-002	EXERTS	53-12-046	EXPERIENCED
204-14-121	EVIDENCE	19-05-011	EXCEED	2-02-002	EXHALED	53-11-036	EXPERIENCES
12-05-011	EVIDENCED	5-04-005	EXCEEDED	1-01-001	EXHALING	7-03-006	EXPERIENCING
5-03-005	EVIDENCES	6-03-006	EXCEEDING	7-06-007	EXHAUST	4-02-002	EXPERIENTIAL
1-01-001	EVIDENCING	8-06-008	EXCEEDINGLY	15-10-014	EXHAUSTED	1-01-001	EXPERIENTIALLY
56-12-043	EVIDENT	10-04-009	EXCEEDS	1-01-001	EXHAUSTIBLE	63-09-034	EXPERIMENT
1-01-001	EVIDENTIAL	1-01-001	EXCEL	3-03-003	EXHAUSTING	38-06-022	EXPERIMENTAL
25-09-019	EVIDENTLY	15-05-008	EXCELLENCE	1-01-001	EXHAUSTINGLY	1-01-001	EXPERIMENTALIS
72-12-033	EVIL	1-01-001	EXCELLENCES	1-01-001	EXHAUSTION	8-03-007	EXPERIMENTALLY
1-01-001	EVILDOERS	2-02-002	EXCELLENCY	2-01-002	EXHAUSTIVE	13-06-010	EXPERIMENTATIO
9-05-006	EVILS	68-13-055	EXCELLENT	1-01-001	EXHAUSTIVELY	1-01-001	EXPERIMENTATIO
1-01-001	EVINCED	5-04-005	EXCELLENTLY	1-01-001	EXHAUSTS		
1-01-001	EVOCATION	1-01-001	EXCELS	25-09-019	EXHIBIT	6-04-005	EXPERIMENTED
2-01-002	EVOCATIONS	1-01-001	EXCELSIN	10-07-009	EXHIBITED	5-03-003	EXPERIMENTER
2-02-002	EVOCATIVE	4-02-002	EXCELSIOR	6-02-004	EXHIBITING	4-04-004	EXPERIMENTERS
6-03-006	EVOKE	181-15-137	EXCEPT	22-06-016	EXHIBITION	7-03-004	EXPERIMENTING
7-04-007	EVOKED	1-01-001	EXCEPTING	3-03-003	EXHIBITIONS	66-07-027	EXPERIMENTS
5-03-004	EVOKES	40-12-033	EXCEPTION	1-01-001	EXHIBITORS	30-13-026	EXPERT
1-01-001	EVOKING	19-06-012	EXCEPTIONAL	16-06-008	EXHIBITS	3-03-003	EXPERTISE
14-04-011	EVOLUTION	8-05-008	EXCEPTIONALLY	1-01-001	EXHILARATED	2-02-002	EXPERTLY
4-03-003	EVOLUTIONARY	26-07-021	EXCEPTIONS	2-02-002	EXHILARATING	38-09-027	EXPERTS
1-01-001	EVOLUTIONISTS	6-02-003	EXCERPT	1-01-001	EXHORTATIONS	1-01-001	EXPIATING
5-03-005	EVOLVE	5-03-004	EXCERPTS	1-01-001	EXHORTING	2-02-002	EXPIATION
8-05-008	EVOLVED	42-10-032	EXCESS	1-01-001	EXHUMATIONS	3-01-002	EXPIRATION
1-01-001	EVOLVES	3-02-003	EXCESSES	1-01-001	EXHUSBAND	1-01-001	EXPIRE
2-02-002	EVOLVING	30-10-024	EXCESSIVE	2-02-002	EXIGENCIES	5-05-005	EXPIRED
1-01-001	EVZONE	3-03-003	EXCESSIVELY	4-04-004	EXILE	1-01-001	EXPIRES
1-01-001	EWE	70-12-039	EXCHANGE	2-02-002	EXILED	64-15-055	EXPLAIN
1-01-001	EWEN	7-05-005	EXCHANGED	1-01-001	EXILES	80-13-062	EXPLAINED
2-02-002	EX	5-04-004	EXCHANGES	1-01-001	EXILING	13-09-013	EXPLAINING
1-01-001	EX*PE	3-02-003	EXCHANGING	59-10-050	EXIST	20-07-019	EXPLAINS
1-01-001	EX-*COMMUNIST	5-01-001	EXCHEQUER	40-12-034	EXISTED	43-12-031	EXPLANATION
1-01-001	EX-*GOV	4-02-003	EXCISE	107-12-066	EXISTENCE	15-10-012	EXPLANATIONS
1-01-001	EX-*JUSTICE	1-01-001	EXCISED	5-02-002	EXISTENT	4-03-004	EXPLANATORY
2-01-001	EX-*MRS	4-01-001	EXCITABILITY	9-02-004	EXISTENTIAL	4-01-002	EXPLICABLE
1-01-001	EX-*NATIONAL	4-01-001	EXCITATORY	1-01-001	EXISTENTIALISM	24-07-019	EXPLICIT
1-01-001	EX-*ORIOLE	3-03-003	EXCITE	1-01-001	EXISTENTIALIST	6-03-005	EXPLICITLY
2-02-002	EX-*PRESIDENT	23-11-022	EXCITED	1-01-001	EXISTENTIALISTS	1-01-001	EXPLICITNESS
1-01-001	EX-*PRESIDENTS	7-05-007	EXCITEDLY	60-09-042	EXISTING	6-05-006	EXPLODE
1-01-001	EX-*TORY	32-11-027	EXCITEMENT	42-09-035	EXISTS	8-04-005	EXPLODED
1-01-001	EX-*YANKEE	29-11-024	EXCITING	7-04-007	EXIT	1-01-001	EXPLODES
1-01-001	EX-BANDITS	1-01-001	EXCLAIM	1-01-001	EXITS	7-05-005	EXPLODING
1-01-001	EX-CONVICT	14-07-013	EXCLAIMED	4-03-004	EXODUS	1-01-001	EXPLODING-WIR
1-01-001	EX-CONVICTS	4-03-004	EXCLAIMING	1-01-001	EXOGAMOUS	9-06-009	EXPLOIT
1-01-001	EX-CUSE	1-01-001	EXCLAIMS	2-01-001	EXOGAMY	5-04-005	EXPLOITATION
1-01-001	EX-FIGHTER	6-03-004	EXCLAMATION	2-01-002	EXONERATE	9-06-009	EXPLOITED
1-01-001	EX-GAMBLER	2-01-001	EXCLAMATIONS	1-01-001	EXONERATED	1-01-001	EXPLOITERS
1-01-001	EX-JAZZ	7-05-007	EXCLUDE	2-01-001	EXONERATION	1-01-001	EXPLOITING
2-01-001	EX-LIBERALS	8-06-008	EXCLUDED	1-01-001	EXORBITANT	4-04-004	EXPLOITS
1-01-001	EX-MARINE	3-02-002	EXCLUDES	1-01-001	EXORCISE	25-07-013	EXPLORATION
1-01-001	EX-MAYOR	16-04-010	EXCLUDING	1-01-001	EXOTHERMIC	1-01-001	EXPLORATIONS
1-01-001	EX-MUSICIAN	7-03-005	EXCLUSION	7-06-007	EXOTIC	4-02-003	EXPLORATORY
1-01-001	EX-PRISON	1-01-001	EXCLUSIONS	13-07-011	EXPAND	12-08-011	EXPLORE
1-01-001	EX-PRIZE	28-12-025	EXCLUSIVE	6-02-003	EXPANDABLE	11-07-011	EXPLORED
1-01-001	EX-SCHOOLTEACHE	24-09-021	EXCLUSIVELY	20-08-018	EXPANDED	4-03-004	EXPLORER
	R	3-02-002	EXCLUSIVENESS	28-11-025	EXPANDING	3-03-003	EXPLORERS

1-01-001 EXPLORES
5-04-005 EXPLORING
15-08-013 EXPLOSION
17-08-016 EXPLOSIVE
1-01-001 EXPLOSIVELY
3-03-003 EXPLOSIVES
1-01-001 EXPONENTIAL
2-01-001 EXPONENTS
10-04-007 EXPORT
14-01-001 EXPORT-*IMPORT
3-02-003 EXPORTED
1-01-001 EXPORTERS
1-01-001 EXPORTING
11-04-005 EXPORTS
8-05-007 EXPOSE
34-13-029 EXPOSED
2-02-002 EXPOSES
4-03-004 EXPOSING
1-01-001 EXPOSITED
6-05-005 EXPOSITION
1-01-001 EXPOSITIONS
1-01-001 EXPOSITORY
25-09-017 EXPOSURE
1-01-001 EXPOSURE-TIME
2-02-002 EXPOSURES
2-01-002 EXPOUNDED
1-01-001 EXPOUNDING
42-12-032 EXPRESS
75-11-059 EXPRESSED
9-05-009 EXPRESSES
1-01-001 EXPRESSIBLE
24-10-022 EXPRESSING
79-11-056 EXPRESSION
3-03-003 EXPRESSIONISM
2-02-002 EXPRESSIONIST
1-01-001 EXPRESSIONISTIC
2-01-001 EXPRESSIONISTS
2-01-002 EXPRESSIONLESS
15-06-012 EXPRESSIONS
7-05-006 EXPRESSIVE
1-01-001 EXPRESSIVENESS
1-01-001 EXPRESSIVNESS
3-03-003 EXPRESSLY
10-02-002 EXPRESSWAY
1-01-001 EXPRESSWAYS
1-01-001 EXPROPRIATED
4-02-003 EXPULSION
1-01-001 EXPUNGE
1-01-001 EXPUNGING
1-01-001 EXPURGATION
3-03-003 EXQUISITE
3-03-003 EXQUISITELY
1-01-001 EXQUISITENESS
5-03-003 EXTANT
1-01-001 EXTEMPORE
1-01-001 EXTEMPORIZE
31-08-025 EXTEND
55-11-048 EXTENDED
1-01-001 EXTENDIBLES
29-09-027 EXTENDING
12-08-011 EXTENDS
36-08-021 EXTENSION
8-06-006 EXTENSIONS
44-10-034 EXTENSIVE
10-05-008 EXTENSIVELY
1-01-001 EXTENSOR
110-10-072 EXTENT
1-01-001 EXTENUATE
3-03-003 EXTENUATING
8-03-007 EXTERIOR
1-01-001 EXTERIORS
2-02-002 EXTERMINATE
1-01-001 EXTERMINATIN
1-01-001 EXTERMINATING
1-01-001 EXTERMINATION
1-01-001 EXTERN
43-09-026 EXTERNAL
1-01-001 EXTERNALIZATION
2-01-001 EXTERNALLY
1-01-001 EXTINCT
3-03-003 EXTINCTION
1-01-001 EXTINGUISH
1-01-001 EXTINGUISHED
1-01-001 EXTIRPATED
1-01-001 EXTIRPATING
50-15-041 EXTRA
1-01-001 EXTRA-CURRICULA R
3-02-002 EXTRA-SENSORY
1-01-001 EXTRA-THICK
6-04-005 EXTRACT
9-05-007 EXTRACTED
4-02-004 EXTRACTING
5-04-005 EXTRACTION
2-01-001 EXTRACTOR
1-01-001 EXTRACTORS
4-03-004 EXTRACTS

1-01-001 EXTRALEGAL
1-01-001 EXTRAMARITAL
3-02-003 EXTRANEOUS
1-01-001 EXTRANEOUSNESS
3-03-003 EXTRAORDINARILY
31-10-028 EXTRAORDINARY
1-01-001 EXTRAPOLATE
4-02-002 EXTRAPOLATED
1-01-001 EXTRAPOLATES
4-01-002 EXTRAPOLATION
1-01-001 EXTRAPOLATIONS
3-02-002 EXTRATERRESTRIA L
5-05-005 EXTRAVAGANT
1-01-001 EXTRAVAGANZAS
1-01-001 EXTREMA
62-11-050 EXTREME
50-09-041 EXTREMELY
9-07-008 EXTREMES
1-01-001 EXTREMIS
4-03-003 EXTREMISTS
1-01-001 EXTREMITIES
4-03-004 EXTREMITY
2-02-002 EXTRICATE
1-01-001 EXTROVERT
9-02-003 EXTRUDED
1-01-001 EXTRUDER
1-01-001 EXTRUDING
2-02-002 EXUBERANCE
7-04-007 EXUBERANT
2-01-002 EXUBERANTLY
2-02-002 EXUDED
1-01-001 EXULTANTLY
3-03-003 EXULTATION
1-01-001 EYD
122-13-075 EYE
1-01-001 EYE-BEAMINGS
1-01-001 EYE-DECEIVING
1-01-001 EYE-FILLING
1-01-001 EYE-GOUGING
1-01-001 EYE-MACHINE
1-01-001 EYE-STRAIN
1-01-001 EYE-TO-EYE
2-01-001 EYE-UNDECEIVING
2-02-002 EYEBALL
1-01-001 EYEBALLS
4-04-004 EYEBROW
9-04-007 EYEBROWS
7-03-006 EYED
1-01-001 EYEFUL
3-03-003 EYEGLASSES
4-04-004 EYEING
1-01-001 EYELASHES
1-01-001 EYELETS
1-01-001 EYELID
7-05-005 EYELIDS
1-01-001 EYEPIECE
401-15-161 EYES
1-01-001 EYESIGHT
1-01-001 EYETEETH
2-02-002 EYEWITNESS
2-02-002 EYING
1-01-001 EYKE
2-02-002 EZRA
70-08-047 F
1-01-001 F),
2-02-002 F**.*B**.*I
3-02-002 F**.*D**.*R
2-01-001 F**.*R
1-01-001 F**.*S**.*C
1-01-001 F**.*SUPP**.235
1-01-001 F'OVUH
1-01-001 F'R
1-01-001 F-PLANE
1-01-001 F-PLANE,
2-02-002 FABER
4-01-001 FABER'S
4-01-001 FABIAN
2-02-002 FABLE
4-04-004 FABLED
2-01-001 FABLES
15-06-008 FABRIC
1-01-001 FABRICATE
1-01-001 FABRICATED
1-01-001 FABRICATING
8-03-004 FABRICATION
1-01-001 FABRICIUS
29-04-008 FABRICS
6-04-006 FABULOUS
7-04-006 FACADE
1-01-001 FACADED
1-01-001 FACADES
371-15-189 FACE
1-01-001 FACE-LIFTING
4-02-003 FACE-SAVING
3-03-003 FACE-TO-FACE

1-01-001 FACE-TO-WALL
54-14-051 FACED
1-01-001 FACELESS
72-13-059 FACES
2-02-002 FACET
1-01-001 FACET-PLANE'S
3-01-001 FACET-PLANES
1-01-001 FACETIOUS
1-01-001 FACETIOUSLY
9-05-007 FACETS
2-01-002 FACIAL
1-01-001 FACILE
5-04-005 FACILITATE
1-01-001 FACILITATED
2-02-002 FACILITATES
1-01-001 FACILITATING
1-01-001 FACILITATORY
99-11-055 FACILITIES
11-05-009 FACILITY
34-13-031 FACING
1-01-001 FACIUNT
1-01-001 FACSIMILE
1-01-001 FACSIPORT
447-15-233 FACT
5-04-005 FACTION
6-02-004 FACTIONS
7-04-005 FACTO
71-10-052 FACTOR
24-10-018 FACTORIES
106-10-059 FACTORS
32-09-016 FACTORY
1-01-001 FACTORY-TO-*YOU
87-15-069 FACTS
7-05-007 FACTUAL
5-04-004 FACULTIES
74-09-018 FACULTY
2-02-002 FAD
2-01-002 FADE
1-01-001 FADE-IN
18-10-016 FADED
1-01-001 FADEOUT
5-04-005 FADING
1-01-001 FADS
2-01-001 FAERY
1-01-001 FAGAN
5-01-001 FAGET
1-01-001 FAGET'S
1-01-001 FAHEY
1-01-001 FAHRENHEIT
1-01-001 FAIER
37-11-032 FAIL
1-01-001 FAIL-SAFE
74-14-059 FAILED
17-06-014 FAILING
14-07-014 FAILS
89-13-056 FAILURE
4-03-004 FAILURES
1-01-001 FAIM
1-01-001 FAIN
25-09-024 FAINT
1-01-001 FAINTED
3-02-003 FAINTEST
7-05-006 FAINTLY
77-14-057 FAIR
2-01-001 FAIR'S
1-01-001 FAIR-LOOKING
1-01-001 FAIR-PRICED
2-02-002 FAIR-SIZED
2-02-002 FAIR-WEATHER
2-01-001 FAIRBROTHERS
2-02-002 FAIRCHILD
1-01-001 FAIRER
1-01-001 FAIRES
1-01-001 FAIREST
2-01-001 FAIRFAX
1-01-001 FAIRGOERS
2-02-002 FAIRIES
3-01-001 FAIRING
1-01-001 FAIRLESS
58-12-051 FAIRLY
2-01-001 FAIRMONT
2-01-001 FAIRMOUNT
6-04-006 FAIRNESS
1-01-001 FAIRS
3-01-001 FAIRVIEW
5-01-002 FAIRWAY
2-01-001 FAIRWAYS
4-04-004 FAIRY
1-01-001 FAIRY-LAND
1-01-001 FAIRY-TALE
111-15-054 FAITH
12-06-009 FAITHFUL
5-04-005 FAITHFULLY
3-03-003 FAITHS
10-04-005 FAKE
2-02-002 FAKED
1-01-001 FAKER

4-02-002 FALCON
1-01-001 FALCONS'
1-01-001 FALEGNAMI
147-14-106 FALL
1-01-001 FALL'S
2-01-001 FALL-IN
1-01-001 FALL-OFF
1-01-001 FALL-OUTS
1-01-001 FALLA'S
1-01-001 FALLACIOUS
1-01-001 FALLACY
34-11-031 FALLEN
1-01-001 FALLIBLE
33-10-027 FALLING
1-01-001 FALLOFF
31-03-008 FALLOUT
1-01-001 FALLOW
32-11-028 FALLS
1-01-001 FALMOUTH
29-08-026 FALSE
1-01-001 FALSE-FRONTED
2-02-002 FALSEHOOD
2-01-001 FALSEHOODS
2-02-002 FALSIFY
1-01-001 FALSIFYING
3-01-002 FALSITY
1-01-001 FALSTAFF
2-02-002 FALTER
3-03-003 FALTERED
1-01-001 FALTERS
18-08-012 FAME
5-04-005 FAMED
1-01-001 FAMES
1-01-001 FAMILAR
1-01-001 FAMILARITY
4-04-004 FAMILIAL
72-14-062 FAMILIAR
13-08-011 FAMILIARITY
1-01-001 FAMILIARLY
1-01-001 FAMILIARNESS
68-11-045 FAMILIES
1-01-001 FAMILISM
1-01-001 FAMILISTICAL
1-01-001 FAMILLE
331-15-149 FAMILY
6-03-003 FAMILY'S
1-01-001 FAMILY-COMMUNIT Y
1-01-001 FAMILY-ORIENTED
1-01-001 FAMILY-WELFARE
3-02-003 FAMINE
89-14-062 FAMOUS
18-07-015 FAN
1-01-001 FAN'S
2-02-002 FANATICAL
4-03-003 FANATICISM
2-01-002 FANATICS
2-01-002 FANCIED
1-01-001 FANCIER
1-01-001 FANCIES
2-02-002 FANCIFUL
16-10-015 FANCY
1-01-001 FANCY-FREE
1-01-001 FANCYING
1-01-001 FANEUIL
1-01-001 FANFARE
2-02-002 FANGS
4-02-003 FANNED
5-04-005 FANNING
3-03-003 FANNY
21-09-013 FANS
1-01-001 FANSHAWE
2-02-002 FANTASIA
4-03-003 FANTASIES
1-01-001 FANTASIST
20-09-018 FANTASTIC
2-02-002 FANTASTICALLY
14-03-004 FANTASY
1-01-001 FANTODS
427-15-258 FAR
1-01-001 FAR-AWAY
1-01-001 FAR-FAMED
1-01-001 FAR-FLUNG
1-01-001 FAR-OFF
1-01-001 FAR-OUT
1-01-001 FAR-RANGING
4-03-004 FAR-REACHING
1-01-001 FAR-SIGHTED
3-02-003 FARCE
1-01-001 FARCES
1-01-001 FARDULLI'S
7-04-007 FARE
3-01-003 FARES
14-10-014 FAREWELL
3-02-003 FARFETCHED
2-02-002 FARGO
1-01-001 FARINA

2-01-002 FARING	19-03-004 FATS	1-01-001 FEDERALIST	7-04-004 FERGUSON
1-01-001 FARLEY	1-01-001 FATSO	1-01-001 FEDERALIZE	2-01-001 FERGUSON'S
125-13-039 FARM	1-01-001 FATTEN	1-01-001 FEDERALS	1-01-001 FERGUSSON
1-01-001 FARMED	2-01-001 FATTENING	15-06-012 FEDERATION	1-01-001 FERINGA
23-08-012 FARMER	3-03-003 FATTER	1-01-001 FEDERICO	1-01-001 FERLENGHETTI
7-04-006 FARMER'S	7-03-003 FATTY	2-02-002 FEDORA	1-01-001 FERMATE
1-01-001 FARMER-IN-THE-* DELL	2-02-002 FATUOUS	1-01-001 FEDS	2-01-001 FERMENT
1-01-001 FARMER-TYPE	2-02-002 FAUCET	16-06-011 FEE	3-03-003 FERMENTATION
33-08-019 FARMERS	1-01-001 FAUCET	1-01-001 FEE-PER-CASE	1-01-001 FERMENTATIONS
4-02-002 FARMERS'	21-02-002 FAULKNER	1-01-001 FEE-PER-DAY	4-01-001 FERMENTED
8-03-004 FARMHOUSE	9-01-001 FAULKNER'S	8-06-008 FEEBLE	1-01-001 FERMENTING
1-01-001 FARMHOUSES	1-01-001 FAULKNERIAN	2-02-002 FEEBLY	1-01-001 FERN
16-03-005 FARMING	22-09-018 FAULT	123-08-024 FEED	1-01-001 FERNAND
1-01-001 FARMINGTON	1-01-001 FAULTED	2-01-001 FEED-LOT	1-01-001 FERNBERGER
1-01-001 FARMLAND	1-01-001 FAULTLESS	3-01-003 FEEDBACK	1-01-001 FERNERY
1-01-001 FARMLANDS	7-05-007 FAULTS	2-01-001 FEEDER	1-01-001 FERNS
16-08-012 FARMS	8-04-006 FAULTY	26-07-014 FEEDING	2-02-002 FEROCIOUS
1-01-001 FARMWIFE'S	1-01-001 FAUNA	2-01-001 FEEDING-PAIN	2-02-002 FEROCIOUSLY
2-02-002 FARNESE	1-01-001 FAUNTLEROY	1-01-001 FEEDINGS	2-02-002 FEROCITY
1-01-001 FARNESES	4-01-001 FAUST	12-06-010 FEEDS	2-01-001 FERRARO
1-01-001 FARNUM	2-01-001 FAUST'S	216-15-145 FEEL	3-01-001 FERRAROS
1-01-001 FARNWORTH	1-01-001 FAUSTIAN	2-02-002 FEELERS	3-01-001 FERRELL
4-02-002 FARO	1-01-001 FAUSTO	3-01-001 FEELEY	1-01-001 FERRET
5-01-001 FAROUK	2-01-002 FAUSTUS	172-14-109 FEELING	1-01-001 FERRETED
1-01-001 FARR	1-01-001 FAUTEUIL	1-01-001 FEELING-STATE	1-01-001 FERRIED
1-01-001 FARRAR	78-13-061 FAVOR	61-12-035 FEELINGS	1-01-001 FERRIES
6-04-005 FARRELL	33-09-027 FAVORABLE	45-11-036 FEELS	2-02-002 FERRIS
1-01-001 FARRELLS	14-05-012 FAVORABLY	1-01-001 FEENEY	2-01-001 FERRO
32-08-024 FARTHER	1-01-001 FAVORE	29-07-013 FEES	2-01-001 FERROMAGNETIC
3-03-003 FARTHEST	18-07-012 FAVORED	283-15-131 FEET	11-05-006 FERRY
1-01-001 FARVEL-*TOPSY	1-01-001 FAVORER	1-01-001 FEIGNED	5-05-005 FERTILE
3-01-001 FASCICLES	4-02-004 FAVORING	1-01-001 FEIGNING	10-03-004 FERTILITY
1-01-001 FASCICULATIONS	41-12-031 FAVORITE	2-01-001 FEINT	3-01-002 FERTILIZED
3-03-003 FASCINATE	12-07-011 FAVORITES	1-01-001 FEIS	4-04-004 FERTILIZER
7-05-007 FASCINATED	4-02-003 FAVORITISM	1-01-001 FELER	3-01-001 FERTILIZERS
1-01-001 FASCINATES	10-07-010 FAVORS	4-01-001 FELICE	5-02-005 FERVENT
20-09-018 FASCINATING	2-01-002 FAVOUR	1-01-001 FELICE'S	2-02-002 FERVENTLY
1-01-001 FASCINATINGLY	5-01-001 FAVRE	2-02-002 FELICITIES	4-03-004 FERVOR
6-05-006 FASCINATION	1-01-001 FAVRE'S	1-01-001 FELICITOUS	1-01-001 FERVORS
1-01-001 FASCIO-*COMMUNIST	1-01-001 FAWCETT	1-01-001 FELICITY	1-01-001 FESS
3-02-003 FASCISM	4-01-001 FAWKES	2-02-002 FELINE	1-01-001 FESTERING
2-02-002 FASCIST	1-01-001 FAWN	30-05-006 FELIX	27-08-018 FESTIVAL
2-01-001 FASCISTS	1-01-001 FAWN-COLORED	2-01-001 FELIX'S	3-02-001 FESTIVALS
69-14-052 FASHION	1-01-001 FAWNED	92-13-073 FELL	2-02-002 FESTIVE
12-07-010 FASHIONABLE	1-01-001 FAWNING	6-02-005 FELLA	8-05-006 FESTIVITIES
7-05-007 FASHIONED	6-02-005 FAY	1-01-001 FELLAS	2-01-001 FESTIVUS
2-02-002 FASHIONING	4-03-003 FAYETTE	2-02-002 FELLED	6-04-005 FETCH
5-05-005 FASHIONS	1-01-001 FAZE	1-01-001 FELLER	3-03-003 FETCHING
78-13-064 FAST	1-01-001 FAZIO	1-01-001 FELLERS	3-02-002 FETE
2-01-001 FAST-CLOSING	7-02-002 FE	2-02-002 FELLING	2-01-002 FETED
1-01-001 FAST-FIRING	1-01-001 FEALTY	2-01-001 FELLINI	1-01-001 FETES
1-01-001 FAST-FROZEN	127-15-073 FEAR	63-14-055 FELLOW	2-02-002 FETID
1-01-001 FAST-GROSSING	1-01-001 FEAR-FILLED	1-01-001 FELLOW-COUNTRYMAN	2-01-002 FETISH
1-01-001 FAST-GROWING	1-01-001 FEAR-MADDENED	1-01-001 FELLOW-CRAFTSMEN	1-01-001 FETISHIZE
1-01-001 FAST-MOVING	1-01-001 FEARE	1-01-001 FELLOW-CREATURES	2-01-001 FEUCHTWANGER
2-01-001 FAST-OPENING	14-10-013 FEARED		1-01-001 FEUD
1-01-001 FAST-SPREADING	13-08-012 FEARFUL	1-01-001 FELLOW-EMPLOYEES	6-02-003 FEUDAL
4-03-004 FASTEN	4-03-004 FEARFULLY		1-01-001 FEUDALISM
14-05-007 FASTENED	5-04-005 FEARING	1-01-001 FELLOW-MEN	1-01-001 FEUDALISTIC
1-01-001 FASTENING	7-04-005 FEARLESS	1-01-001 FELLOWFEELING	2-02-002 FEUDS
1-01-001 FASTENINGS	2-02-002 FEARLESSLY	18-09-013 FELLOWS	1-01-001 FEUERMANN
1-01-001 FASTENS	47-09-020 FEARS	36-07-012 FELLOWSHIP	19-08-011 FEVER
18-10-018 FASTER	1-01-001 FEARSOME	3-02-003 FELLOWSHIPS	1-01-001 FEVERED
7-06-006 FASTEST	3-01-003 FEASIBILITY	1-01-001 FELON	4-04-004 FEVERISH
3-03-003 FASTIDIOUS	15-06-011 FEASIBLE	2-02-002 FELONIOUS	3-03-003 FEVERISHLY
60-13-037 FAT	3-02-003 FEAST	2-01-001 FELONS	1-01-001 FEVERSHAM
1-01-001 FAT'S	1-01-001 FEASTING	1-01-001 FELONY	601-15-311 FEW
1-01-001 FAT-SOLUBLE	2-02-002 FEASTS	1-01-001 FELSKE	33-09-028 FEWER
19-07-015 FATAL	6-04-006 FEAT	357-15-184 FELT	1-01-001 FEYER'S
1-01-001 FATALISTS	6-03-003 FEATHER	50-12-033 FEMALE	1-01-001 FFORTESCUE
2-02-002 FATALITIES	1-01-001 FEATHER-LIKE	3-02-002 FEMALE'S	1-01-001 FFREIND
1-01-001 FATALITY	1-01-001 FEATHERBED	17-04-009 FEMALES	1-01-001 FIANCE
4-04-004 FATALLY	1-01-001 FEATHERBEDDING	10-06-009 FEMININE	4-04-004 FIASCO
1-01-001 FATBOY	4-03-003 FEATHERED	2-02-002 FEMININITY	13-05-006 FIAT
33-10-026 FATE	14-07-013 FEATHERS	1-01-001 FEMINIST	1-01-001 FIATS
3-02-003 FATEFUL	12-01-001 FEATHERTOP	1-01-001 FEMME	27-03-004 FIBER
3-03-003 FATES	2-01-001 FEATHERTOP'S	1-01-001 FEMMES	4-01-001 FIBER-COUPLED
183-15-105 FATHER	1-01-001 FEATHERWEIGHT	30-10-019 FENCE	1-01-001 FIBER-PHOTOCATHODE
38-09-032 FATHER'S	1-01-001 FEATHERY	4-01-001 FENCE-LINE	
1-01-001 FATHER-*GOD	3-03-003 FEATS	3-02-002 FENCED	5-02-002 FIBERGLAS
1-01-001 FATHER-AND-SON	37-12-031 FEATURE	16-06-008 FENCES	23-05-007 FIBERS
1-01-001 FATHER-BROTHER	8-05-007 FEATURED	4-03-003 FENCING	2-01-001 FIBRIN
1-01-001 FATHER-CONFESSOR	2-02-002 FEATURELESS	4-03-003 FENDER	1-01-001 FIBROCALCIFIC
	80-12-054 FEATURES	1-01-001 FENDERS	6-01-001 FIBROSIS
1-01-001 FATHER-MURDER	4-04-004 FEATURING	1-01-001 FENNEL	5-02-003 FIBROUS
2-02-002 FATHERED	20-05-014 FEB	2-01-001 FENS	1-01-001 FICHE
1-01-001 FATHERLY	1-01-001 FEBRILE	1-01-001 FENSTER	1-01-001 FICHTE
19-07-014 FATHERS	45-10-029 FEBRUARY	1-01-001 FENUGREEK	1-01-001 FICKLE
3-01-002 FATHOM	2-02-002 FEBRUARY'S	1-01-001 FENWAY	46-06-019 FICTION
1-01-001 FATHOMS	1-01-001 FECUND	1-01-001 FENWICK	1-01-001 FICTION-WRITER
1-01-001 FATHUH	1-01-001 FECUNDITY	2-01-001 FER	
11-06-017 FATIGUE	42-11-030 FED	1-01-001 FERBER	1-01-001 FICTION-WRITING
3-03-003 FATIGUED	246-11-066 FEDERAL	2-02-002 FERDINAND	13-04-007 FICTIONAL
2-01-001 FATIGUES	1-01-001 FEDERAL-QUESTION	1-01-001 FERDINANDO	2-02-002 FICTITIOUS
1-01-001 FATIMA		1-01-001 FERGESON	1-01-001 FICTIVE
	1-01-001 FEDERAL-RIGHT		2-01-001 FIDDLE
	2-01-001 FEDERAL-STATE		1-01-001 FIDDLES
	2-02-002 FEDERALISM		

Code	Word	Code	Word	Code	Word	Code	Word
1-01-001	FIDDLESTICKS	1-01-001	FILETS	87-14-070	FINISHED	8-05-006	FITNESS
1-01-001	FIDDLING	1-01-001	FILIAL	1-01-001	FINISHER	13-09-012	FITS
1-01-001	FIDE	3-02-002	FILIBUSTER	2-02-002	FINISHES	20-08-018	FITTED
7-02-004	FIDEL	1-01-001	FILIBUSTERS	9-05-009	FINISHING	2-02-002	FITTEST
8-04-004	FIDELITY	1-01-001	FILIGREE	11-03-006	FINITE	17-06-009	FITTING
1-01-001	FIEDGLING	1-01-001	FILIGREED	4-01-001	FINITE-DIMENSIO NAL	1-01-001	FITTINGS
9-01-001	FIEDLER	19-03-007	FILING	4-02-002	FINK	6-03-003	FITZGERALD
1-01-001	FIEDLER'S	2-02-002	FILIPINO	1-01-001	FINK'S	1-01-001	FITZHUGH
1-01-001	FIEFDOM	1-01-001	FILIPINOS	2-01-002	FINLAND	1-01-001	FITZROY
274-15-125	FIELD	2-02-002	FILIPPO	2-02-002	FINLEY	286-15-165	FIVE
2-01-001	FIELD'S	50-14-041	FILL	1-01-001	FINN	2-01-001	FIVE-*ELEMENTS
2-01-001	FIELD-FLATTENIN G	1-01-001	FILL-IN	1-01-001	FINNED	1-01-001	FIVE-A-WEEK
1-01-001	FIELD-HANDS'	1-01-001	FILL-INS	2-01-001	FINNEGAN	1-01-001	FIVE-AND-A-HALF
1-01-001	FIELD-SEQUENTIA L	6-01-001	FILLE	1-01-001	FINNEY	1-01-001	FIVE-AND-DIME
1-01-001	FIELDED	99-14-080	FILLED	2-01-001	FINNEY'S	1-01-001	FIVE-AND-TWENTY
3-02-002	FIELDER	1-01-001	FILLER	1-01-001	FINNISH	2-02-002	FIVE-CENT
1-01-001	FIELDER'S	2-02-002	FILLES	1-01-001	FINNS	1-01-001	FIVE-COLUMN
2-02-002	FIELDERS	1-01-001	FILLIES	1-01-001	FINNSBURG	1-01-001	FIVE-COORDINATE
3-02-002	FIELDING	36-10-024	FILLING	1-01-001	FINOT	1-01-001	FIVE-DAY
1-01-001	FIELDMICE	3-01-001	FILLINGS	5-04-005	FINS	1-01-001	FIVE-DAYS-A-WEE K
72-13-056	FIELDS	1-01-001	FILLIP	4-01-001	FIORELLO	1-01-001	FIVE-FOLD
1-01-001	FIELDSTONE	5-04-005	FILLS	1-01-001	FIORI	1-01-001	FIVE-FOOT
2-01-001	FIELDWORK	9-02-002	FILLY	2-01-002	FIR	2-02-002	FIVE-GALLON
3-03-003	FIEND	96-13-036	FILM	187-14-103	FIRE	1-01-001	FIVE-HOME
1-01-001	FIENDISH	1-01-001	FILM'S	2-01-001	FIRE'S	1-01-001	FIVE-HUNDRED
8-06-008	FIERCE	1-01-001	FILMDOM	1-01-001	FIRE-COLORED	1-01-001	FIVE-HUNDRED-DO LLAR
4-02-003	FIERCELY	4-02-002	FILMED	1-01-001	FIRE-CRACKERS	1-01-001	FIVE-HUNDRED-YE AR-OLD
1-01-001	FIERCENESS	1-01-001	FILMING	2-02-002	FIRE-FIGHTING	1-01-001	FIVE-MEMBER
1-01-001	FIERCEST	31-08-018	FILMS	1-01-001	FIRE-RESISTANT	1-01-001	FIVE-MINUTE
7-05-007	FIERY	1-01-001	FILMSTRIPS	7-02-003	FIREARMS	2-01-002	FIVE-MONTH
1-01-001	FIESTA	1-01-001	FILMY	1-01-001	FIREBREAKS	1-01-001	FIVE-PLY
1-01-001	FIFE	9-03-005	FILTER	1-01-001	FIREBUG	1-01-001	FIVE-ROUND
56-13-048	FIFTEEN	6-04-006	FILTERED	1-01-001	FIRECRACKER	1-01-001	FIVE-SEVENTEEN
1-01-001	FIFTEEN-MILE	6-03-004	FILTERING	2-02-002	FIRECRACKERS	1-01-001	FIVE-VOLUME
3-03-003	FIFTEEN-MINUTE	4-03-004	FILTERS	44-11-028	FIRED	4-03-004	FIVE-YEAR
1-01-001	FIFTEEN-SIXTEEN THS	2-02-002	FILTH	1-01-001	FIREHOUSES	2-01-001	FIVES
9-04-008	FIFTEENTH	7-05-007	FILTHY	2-02-002	FIRELIGHT	14-08-014	FIX
1-01-001	FIFTEENTH-CENTU RY	2-02-002	FIN	1-01-001	FIREMAN	1-01-001	FIXATIONS
38-11-032	FIFTH	156-15-106	FINAL	5-03-004	FIREMEN	87-15-057	FIXED
1-01-001	FIFTH-CENTURY	6-05-005	FINALE	6-04-006	FIREPLACE	1-01-001	FIXERS
12-04-006	FIFTIES	1-01-001	FINALIST	1-01-001	FIREPLACES	11-08-011	FIXING
1-01-001	FIFTIETH	1-01-001	FINALISTS	1-01-001	FIREPOWER	3-03-003	FIXTURE
68-14-056	FIFTY	4-03-003	FINALITY	17-07-012	FIRES	3-01-002	FIXTURES
1-01-001	FIFTY-CENT	191-15-144	FINALLY	1-01-001	FIRESIDE	1-01-001	FIZZLED
1-01-001	FIFTY-DOLLAR	10-02-002	FINALS	5-04-005	FIREWORKS	2-01-002	FJORDS
2-01-001	FIFTY-FIFTH	1-01-001	FINAN	24-10-018	FIRING	10-03-007	FLA
1-01-001	FIFTY-FIFTY	31-09-022	FINANCE	109-13-065	FIRM	16-07-012	FLAG
2-02-002	FIFTY-FIVE	16-07-013	FINANCED	2-01-001	FIRM'S	1-01-001	FLAG-STICK
1-01-001	FIFTY-FOUR	6-05-005	FINANCES	1-01-001	FIRMA	1-01-001	FLAG-WAVERS
1-01-001	FIFTY-NINE	86-11-051	FINANCIAL	6-04-005	FIRMER	1-01-001	FLAGELLATED
2-02-002	FIFTY-NINTH	8-06-008	FINANCIALLY	49-11-042	FIRMLY	1-01-001	FLAGELLATION
2-01-001	FIFTY-ODD	2-01-001	FINANCIER	4-04-004	FIRMNESS	1-01-001	FLAGEOLET
2-01-001	FIFTY-ONE	34-07-016	FINANCING	55-08-023	FIRMS	1-01-001	FLAGLER'S
1-01-001	FIFTY-PIECE	55-08-023	FINBERG	1360-15-430	FIRST	1-01-001	FLAGPOLES
1-01-001	FIFTY-POUND	399-15-245	FIND	1-01-001	FIRST-*BORN	3-03-003	FLAGRANT
1-01-001	FIFTY-SEVEN	2-02-002	FINDER	1-01-001	FIRST-AID	1-01-001	FLAGRANTLY
1-01-001	FIFTY-THIRD	1-01-001	FINDERS	6-05-006	FIRST-CLASS	5-02-004	FLAGS
2-02-002	FIFTY-THREE	53-14-048	FINDING	1-01-001	FIRST-DEGREE	1-01-001	FLAIL
2-02-002	FIFTY-TWO	34-08-021	FINDINGS	1-01-001	FIRST-FAMILIES	1-01-001	FLAILED
1-01-001	FIFTY-YEAR	59-12-049	FINDS	1-01-001	FIRST-FLOOR	3-01-003	FLAILING
72-04-016	FIG	1-01-001	FINDSOME	3-03-003	FIRST-HAND	8-05-007	FLAIR
1-01-001	FIG**.1	161-15-111	FINE	2-01-001	FIRST-LEVEL	1-01-001	FLAKE
1-01-001	FIGARO	1-01-001	FINE-BONED	1-01-001	FIRST-ORDER	4-04-004	FLAKES
3-01-001	FIGGER	1-01-001	FINE-CHISELED	1-01-001	FIRST-PLACE	2-02-002	FLAKY
1-01-001	FIGGERED	1-01-001	FINE-DRAWN	4-03-003	FIRST-RATE	3-02-003	FLAMBOYANT
98-13-074	FIGHT	1-01-001	FINE-FEATHERED	1-01-001	FIRST-RUN	1-01-001	FLAMBOYANTLY
9-06-008	FIGHTER	1-01-001	FINE-FEATURED	1-01-001	FIRSTHAND	17-09-015	FLAME
16-08-012	FIGHTERS	1-01-001	FINE-GRAINED	1-01-001	FIRZITE	1-01-001	FLAME-THROWERS
1-01-001	FIGHTIN	5-02-002	FINE-LOOKING	116-05-026	FISCAL	1-01-001	FLAMED
72-14-051	FIGHTING	1-01-001	FINE-POINT	4-01-001	FISCAL-TAX	14-07-009	FLAMES
6-06-006	FIGHTS	1-01-001	FINE-TOOTH	35-12-024	FISH	6-05-006	FLAMING
2-02-002	FIGMENT	4-03-004	FINED	5-03-004	FISHER	1-01-001	FLAMMABLE
2-01-001	FIGONE	4-03-004	FINELY	5-04-004	FISHERMAN	1-01-001	FLANAGAN
19-03-008	FIGS	1-01-001	FINELY-SPUN	2-01-002	FISHERMAN'S	2-01-001	FLANDERS
1-01-001	FIGURAL	1-01-001	FINENESS	7-03-004	FISHERMEN	2-02-002	FLANGE
5-03-004	FIGURATIVE	2-02-002	FINER	1-01-001	FISHERS	2-02-002	FLANK
209-14-109	FIGURE	2-02-002	FINES	1-01-001	FISHERY	5-05-003	FLANKED
20-08-017	FIGURED	16-06-014	FINEST	2-02-002	FISHES	1-01-001	FLANKING
113-15-074	FIGURES	2-01-001	FING	32-10-019	FISHING	7-01-001	FLANNAGAN
1-01-001	FIGURINES	40-13-033	FINGER	1-01-001	FISHING-BOAT	3-01-001	FLANNAGANS
6-05-006	FIGURING	1-01-001	FINGER-HELD	1-01-001	FISHKILL	1-01-001	FLANNAGANS'
2-01-001	FIKE	1-01-001	FINGER-PAINT	1-01-001	FISHMONGERS	4-03-004	FLANNEL
2-02-002	FIL	2-01-001	FINGER-POST	1-01-001	FISHPOND	1-01-001	FLANNELS
1-01-001	FILAGREE	1-01-001	FINGER-SUCKING	2-02-002	FISK	4-03-003	FLAPPED
1-01-001	FILAMENT	1-01-001	FINGER-TIPS	5-01-001	FISKE	1-01-001	FLAPPER
1-01-001	FILAMENTS	3-03-003	FINGERED	5-02-002	FISSION	1-01-001	FLAPPERS
1-01-001	FILBERT	1-01-001	FINGERING	1-01-001	FISSURED	4-04-004	FLAPPING
2-01-001	FILBERTS	1-01-001	FINGERINGS	26-08-019	FIST	3-03-003	FLARE
1-01-001	FILCHED	2-02-002	FINGERNAILS	1-01-001	FIST-FIGHTING	5-04-003	FLARED
1-01-001	FILDE	6-01-002	FINGERPRINT	1-01-001	FISTED	6-03-003	FLARES
81-12-027	FILE	1-01-001	FINGERPRINTING	1-01-001	FISTOULARI'S	3-03-003	FLARING
33-08-022	FILED	4-01-002	FINGERPRINTS	14-07-009	FISTS	21-10-017	FLASH
13-07-010	FILES	66-12-050	FINGERS	75-15-057	FIT	1-01-001	FLASH-BULBS
		2-02-002	FINGERTIPS	1-01-001	FITCH	1-01-001	FLASHBACK
		1-01-001	FINIAL	1-01-001	FITFUL		
		1-01-001	FINICKY	1-01-001	FITFULLY		
		39-12-030	FINISH				

16-07-014	FLASHED	1-01-001	FLIPPANT	57-13-034	FLOWERS	1-01-001	FOISTED
9-05-007	FLASHES	3-02-003	FLIPPED	17-08-014	FLOWING	1-01-001	FOKINE'S
6-03-004	FLASHING	1-01-001	FLIPPERS	4-04-004	FLOWN	7-05-007	FOLD
8-04-006	FLASHLIGHT	2-02-002	FLIPPING	5-04-005	FLOWS	15-06-015	FOLDED
1-01-001	FLASHLIGHT-TYPE	1-01-001	FLIPS	2-02-002	FLOYD	1-01-001	FOLDER
3-03-003	FLASHY	1-01-001	FLIRT	2-02-002	FLOYD'S	1-01-001	FOLDERS
5-01-002	FLASK	2-02-002	FLIRTATION	8-05-006	FLU	3-03-003	FOLDING
67-12-046	FLAT	1-01-001	FLIRTATIOUS	1-01-001	FLU**DGEL	3-02-002	FOLDS
4-01-001	FLAT-BED	1-01-001	FLIRTED	1-01-001	FLUBBED	1-01-001	FOLEY
4-02-002	FLAT-BOTTOMED	1-01-001	FLITE-*KING	1-01-001	FLUCTUATES	12-07-008	FOLIAGE
1-01-001	FLAT-FOOTED	1-01-001	FLITTING	12-07-008	FLUCTUATING	34-12-021	FOLK
1-01-001	FLAT-TOPPED	1-01-001	FLNG	2-02-002	FLUCTUATING	1-01-001	FOLK-DANCE
1-01-001	FLATHEAD	3-02-003	FLOAT	1-01-001	FLUCTUATIONS	2-01-001	FOLK-LORE
2-01-001	FLATIRON	7-04-007	FLOATED	1-01-001	FLUENCY	1-01-001	FOLK-MUSIC
1-01-001	FLATLAND	1-01-001	FLOATER	5-03-003	FLUENT	1-01-001	FOLK-TALE
7-06-006	FLATLY	12-07-012	FLOATING	1-01-001	FLUENTLY	1-01-001	FOLKLIKE
8-01-001	FLATNESS	1-01-001	FLOATING-LOAD	1-01-001	FLUFF	28-04-004	FOLKLORE
1-01-001	FLATNESSES	1-01-001	FLOATS	1-01-001	FLUFFY	18-07-013	FOLKS
3-03-003	FLATS	3-01-001	FLOC	21-08-012	FLUID	1-01-001	FOLKS'
1-01-001	FLATTEN	1-01-001	FLOCCULATED	1-01-001	FLUID-FILLED	1-01-001	FOLKSONGS
6-05-006	FLATTENED	1-01-001	FLOCCULATION	2-02-002	FLUIDITY	1-01-001	FOLKSTON
2-02-002	FLATTENING	10-04-008	FLOCK	15-03-004	FLUIDS	3-02-002	FOLKSY
1-01-001	FLATTER	1-01-001	FLOCK'S	1-01-001	FLUKE	1-01-001	FOLLICULAR
7-05-007	FLATTERED	2-02-002	FLOCKED	1-01-001	FLUMENOPHOBE	2-02-002	FOLLIES
1-01-001	FLATTERING	1-01-001	FLOCKING	14-04-011	FLUNG	97-15-087	FOLLOW
1-01-001	FLATTERINGLY	1-01-001	FLOCKS	1-01-001	FLUORESCEIN	1-01-001	FOLLOW-THROUGH
3-02-003	FLATTERY	1-01-001	FLOE	1-01-001	FLUORESCEIN-LABELED	8-02-004	FOLLOW-UP
1-01-001	FLATTEST	1-01-001	FLOES	12-01-001	FLUORESCENCE	1-01-001	FOLLOW-UPS
1-01-001	FLATULENCE	1-01-001	FLOG	4-03-003	FLUORESCENT	172-15-126	FOLLOWED
2-01-001	FLATUS	19-07-014	FLOOD	1-01-001	FLUORESCES	3-02-003	FOLLOWER
2-02-002	FLAUNTED	1-01-001	FLOOD'S	2-01-001	FLUORIDE	17-08-015	FOLLOWERS
1-01-001	FLAUNTING	1-01-001	FLOOD-LIGHTED	1-01-001	FLUORINATED	1-01-001	FOLLOWETH
1-01-001	FLAUTIST	1-01-001	FLOOD-RAVAGED	1-01-001	FLUORINE	1-01-001	FOLLOWIN
1-01-001	FLAUTIST'S	9-05-009	FLOODED	1-01-001	FLURRIED	221-15-139	FOLLOWING
16-06-012	FLAVOR	1-01-001	FLOODHEADS	4-04-004	FLURRY	77-11-057	FOLLOWS
2-02-002	FLAVORED	1-01-001	FLOODING	11-06-009	FLUSH	10-04-008	FOLLY
2-01-001	FLAVORING	2-02-002	FLOODING	6-04-006	FLUSHED	1-01-001	FOLSOM
1-01-001	FLAVORINGS	1-01-001	FLOODLIGHT	4-03-003	FLUSHING	13-09-013	FOND
2-02-002	FLAVORS	1-01-001	FLOODLIT	1-01-001	FLUSHING-*MAIN	1-01-001	FONDER
1-01-001	FLAVUS	6-06-006	FLOODS	1-01-001	FLUSTERED	4-04-004	FONDLY
3-03-003	FLAW	158-15-093	FLOOR	1-01-001	FLUTE	4-04-004	FONDNESS
2-02-002	FLAWLESS	1-01-001	FLOOR-LENGTH	1-01-001	FLUTED	1-01-001	FONDS
1-01-001	FLAWS	1-01-001	FLOOR-TO-CEILING	1-01-001	FLUTING	1-01-001	FONTA
3-01-001	FLAX	4-03-004	FLOORBOARDS	1-01-001	FLUTIST	1-01-001	FONTAINEBLEAU
1-01-001	FLAXEN	7-03-004	FLOORING	2-02-002	FLUTTER	1-01-001	FONTANA
3-01-002	FLAXSEED	12-08-010	FLOORS	2-02-002	FLUTTERED	1-01-001	FONTANEL
2-02-002	FLEA	1-01-001	FLOORSHOW	4-04-004	FLUTTERING	147-15-066	FOOD
2-02-002	FLEAS	1-01-001	FLOP	30-04-008	FLUX	4-01-001	FOOD-PRESERVATION
1-01-001	FLEAWORT	6-03-005	FLOPPED	4-01-002	FLUXES	1-01-001	FOOD-PROCESSING
1-01-001	FLECK	1-01-001	FLOPPY	33-11-025	FLY	51-06-012	FOODS
1-01-001	FLECKED	1-01-001	FLOPS	1-01-001	FLY-BOY	2-02-002	FOODSTUFFS
28-11-021	FLED	1-01-001	FLOR	1-01-001	FLY-DOTTED	37-10-030	FOOL
1-01-001	FLEDERMAUS	1-01-001	FLORA	1-01-001	FLYAWAY	3-03-003	FOOLED
2-02-002	FLEDGLING	3-03-003	FLORAL	4-03-003	FLYER	2-01-002	FOOLHARDY
1-01-001	FLEDGLINGS	5-02-003	FLORENCE	1-01-001	FLYER-*CASTLE	3-03-003	FOOLING
1-01-001	FLEE	4-02-002	FLORENTINE	2-02-002	FLYERS	16-08-015	FOOLISH
10-06-008	FLEEING	1-01-001	FLORESVILLE	43-12-030	FLYING	3-03-003	FOOLISHLY
1-01-001	FLEES	1-01-001	FLORICAN-*INVERNESS	1-01-001	FLYING-MOUNT	2-01-001	FOOLISHNESS
17-07-012	FLEET	1-01-001	FLORICAN-*MY	2-01-001	FLYNN	2-02-002	FOOLPROOF
1-01-001	FLEET'S	1-01-001	FLORID	1-01-001	FLYNN'S	5-03-005	FOOLS
1-01-001	FLEETEST	20-08-013	FLORIDA	1-01-001	FLYWAYS	70-11-052	FOOT
7-05-005	FLEETING	2-01-001	FLORIDA'S	2-01-001	FOAL	1-01-001	FOOT-HIGH
1-01-001	FLEETS	1-01-001	FLORIDIAN	1-01-001	FOALS	2-02-002	FOOT-LOOSE
2-01-001	FLEISCHMAN	1-01-001	FLORIDIANS	37-04-004	FOAM	1-01-001	FOOTAGE
3-01-001	FLEISCHMANNS	1-01-001	FLORIST	1-01-001	FOAM'S	36-10-020	FOOTBALL
1-01-001	FLEISHER	2-01-002	FLORIST'S	1-01-001	FOAMED	1-01-001	FOOTBALL'S
1-01-001	FLEISHER'S	1-01-001	FLORODORA	1-01-001	FOAMED-CORE	1-01-001	FOOTBALLER'S
2-01-001	FLEM	3-01-001	FLORY	1-01-001	FOAMED-IN-PLACE	1-01-001	FOOTBALLS
2-02-002	FLEMING	1-01-001	FLOTATION-TYPE	1-01-001	FOAMING	1-01-001	FOOTBRIDGE
1-01-001	FLEMINGS	1-01-001	FLOTILLA	1-01-001	FOAMS	1-01-001	FOOTE
5-02-003	FLEMISH	1-01-001	FLOTILLAS	3-02-002	FOAMY	1-01-001	FOOTFALL
52-09-034	FLESH	1-01-001	FLOTTE	1-01-001	FOAMY-NECKED	1-01-001	FOOTFALLS
2-02-002	FLESHY	1-01-001	FLOTTE'S	8-06-006	FOCAL	1-01-001	FOOTHILL
7-03-003	FLETCHER	1-01-001	FLOUNCED	1-01-001	FOCALLY	1-01-001	FOOTHILLS
27-11-024	FLEW	1-01-001	FLOUNDER	1-01-001	FOCI	3-03-003	FOOTING
2-02-002	FLEX	1-01-001	FLOUNDERED	40-13-034	FOCUS	1-01-001	FOOTMAN
2-01-002	FLEXED	1-01-001	FLOUNDERING	12-08-012	FOCUSED	3-02-003	FOOTNOTE
16-04-010	FLEXIBILITY	1-01-001	FLOUNDERS	2-01-001	FOCUSES	3-02-003	FOOTNOTES
25-06-017	FLEXIBLE	8-05-008	FLOUR	6-03-004	FOCUSING	1-01-001	FOOTPATH
5-01-001	FLEXURAL	1-01-001	FLOUR-MILLING	3-02-003	FOCUSSED	3-03-003	FOOTSTEP
2-02-002	FLICK	1-01-001	FLOURED	1-01-001	FODDER	8-05-007	FOOTSTEPS
5-02-004	FLICKED	1-01-001	FLOURISH	8-04-006	FOE	1-01-001	FOOTSTOOL
2-02-002	FLICKER	5-05-005	FLOURISHED	6-03-005	FOES	1-01-001	FOOTWEAR
2-02-002	FLICKERED	6-05-006	FLOURISHES	25-09-018	FOG	1-01-001	FOOTWORK
1-01-001	FLICKING	4-04-004	FLOURISHING	1-01-001	FOG-ENSHROUDED	1-01-001	FOPPISH
1-01-001	FLICKS	1-01-001	FLOUTED	1-01-001	FOGELSON	9489-15-500	FOR
2-02-002	FLIER	1-01-001	FLOUTING	23-02-002	FOGG	3-01-001	FORAGE
12-06-009	FLIES	67-11-043	FLOW	3-01-001	FOGG'S	1-01-001	FORAGES
46-13-033	FLIGHT	6-05-006	FLOWED	1-01-001	FOGGED	3-03-003	FORAGING
14-08-010	FLIGHTS	23-09-022	FLOWER	1-01-001	FOGGIA	1-01-001	FORAND
1-01-001	FLIMSIES	1-01-001	FLOWER'S	5-03-004	FOGGY	1-01-001	FORAY
2-01-002	FLIMSY	1-01-001	FLOWER-SCENTED	1-01-001	FOGY	1-01-001	FORAYS
1-01-001	FLINCHING	3-03-003	FLOWERED	1-01-001	FOH	1-01-001	FORBAD
2-02-002	FLING	6-04-005	FLOWERING	1-01-001	FOIBLES	1-01-001	FORBADE
4-02-002	FLINT	2-01-001	FLOWERPOT	20-09-010	FOIL	2-02-002	FORBEARS
1-01-001	FLINTLESS			1-01-001	FOILED	9-02-002	FORBES
4-04-004	FLIP			1-01-001	FOILES		

1-01-001	FORBES'S	1-01-001	FORGO	2-02-002	FORTY-TWO	1-01-001	FRACTIOUS
4-04-004	FORBID	18-09-016	FORGOT	1-01-001	FORTY-YEAR	1-01-001	FRACTURE
15-07-015	FORBIDDEN	38-11-035	FORGOTTEN	10-06-006	FORUM	1-01-001	FRACTURED
2-02-002	FORBIDDING	1-01-001	FORISQUE	1-01-001	FORUMS	2-02-002	FRACTURES
5-05-005	FORBIDS	14-08-012	FORK	115-14-080	FORWARD	10-07-009	FRAGILE
1-01-001	FORBORE	1-01-001	FORK-LIFT	1-01-001	FORWARD-MOVING	6-04-006	FRAGMENT
1-01-001	FORBORNE	4-01-003	FORKED	3-02-003	FORWARDED	1-01-001	FRAGMENTARILY
230-15-122	FORCE	1-01-001	FORKLIFT	1-01-001	FORWARDING	7-03-006	FRAGMENTARY
1-01-001	FORCE'S	7-02-002	FORKS	10-01-001	FOSDICK	5-04-005	FRAGMENTATION
1-01-001	FORCE-FEAR	3-03-003	FORLORN	3-01-001	FOSDICK'S	4-03-003	FRAGMENTED
1-01-001	FORCE-RATE	370-14-171	FORM	3-01-001	FOSS	10-04-007	FRAGMENTS
81-15-066	FORCED	1-01-001	FORM-CREATING	3-02-002	FOSSILIZED	1-01-001	FRAGONARD
8-05-007	FORCEFUL	1-01-001	FORM-DICTIONARY	15-07-009	FOSTER	6-03-004	FRAGRANCE
1-01-001	FORCEFULNESS	2-02-002	FORMA	7-05-007	FOSTERED	1-01-001	FRAGRANCES
175-13-078	FORCES	1-01-001	FORMABILITY	2-02-002	FOSTERING	3-03-003	FRAGRANT
3-03-003	FORCIBLY	48-09-035	FORMAL	1-01-001	FOSTERITE	8-06-007	FRAIL
13-10-012	FORCING	2-01-001	FORMALISM	1-01-001	FOSTERITES	1-01-001	FRAILEST
24-08-016	FORD	2-02-002	FORMALITIES	3-02-003	FOSTERS	1-01-001	FRAMBESIA
3-02-002	FORDS	2-02-002	FORMALITY	46-12-035	FOUGHT	74-12-042	FRAME
7-04-007	FORE	2-02-002	FORMALIZE	4-04-004	FOUL	14-10-013	FRAMED
1-01-001	FORE-PLAY	2-01-002	FORMALIZED	2-02-002	FOUL-SMELLING	1-01-001	FRAMER
3-02-003	FOREARM	18-06-018	FORMALLY	2-02-002	FOULED	26-05-008	FRAMES
1-01-001	FOREARMS	9-04-005	FORMAT	1-01-001	FOULEST	11-06-010	FRAMEWORK
1-01-001	FOREBEARING	37-11-025	FORMATION	3-02-002	FOULING	10-06-008	FRAMING
1-01-001	FOREBEARS	7-02-004	FORMATIONS	1-01-001	FOULLY	6-03-003	FRAN
4-04-004	FOREBODING	2-02-002	FORMATIVE	536-15-271	FOUND	1-01-001	FRAN'S
10-06-009	FORECAST	1-01-001	FORMATS	38-07-024	FOUNDATION	1-01-001	FRANC
1-01-001	FORECASTERS	1-01-001	FORMBY	13-02-002	FOUNDATION'S	3-01-002	FRANCAISE
9-03-005	FORECASTING	1-01-001	FORMBY'S	1-01-001	FOUNDATION-STON	74-12-039	FRANCE
5-04-005	FORECASTS	76-12-056	FORMED		E	6-06-006	FRANCE'S
1-01-001	FORECLOSED	1-01-001	FORMED-TOOTH	14-05-010	FOUNDATIONS	1-01-001	FRANCE-*GERMANY
1-01-001	FORECLOSING	131-14-090	FORMER	20-09-018	FOUNDED	2-02-002	FRANCES
1-01-001	FOREFATHERS	28-11-024	FORMERLY	10-06-010	FOUNDER	8-02-007	FRANCESCA
1-01-001	FOREFEET	17-07-016	FORMIDABLE	1-01-001	FOUNDER-CONDUCT	1-01-001	FRANCESCA'S
6-05-006	FOREFINGER	1-01-001	FORMIDABLY		OR	2-02-002	FRANCESCO
1-01-001	FOREFINGERS	21-08-019	FORMING	1-01-001	FOUNDER-ORIGINA	5-04-005	FRANCHISE
3-03-003	FOREGO	5-02-003	FORMOSA		TOR	1-01-001	FRANCHISES
11-04-009	FOREGOING	1-01-001	FORMOSAN	1-01-001	FOUNDERING	4-01-001	FRANCIE
1-01-001	FOREGONE	128-13-063	FORMS	6-04-004	FOUNDERS	1-01-001	FRANCIE'S
2-01-001	FOREGROUND	59-07-027	FORMULA	16-06-012	FOUNDING	21-07-018	FRANCIS
16-07-015	FOREHEAD	5-03-004	FORMULAE	1-01-001	FOUNDLING	1-01-001	FRANCISCAN
2-02-002	FOREHEADS	12-01-001	FORMULAIC	1-01-001	FOUNDRY	2-02-002	FRANCISCANS
158-13-083	FOREIGN	22-06-008	FORMULAS	18-07-009	FOUNTAIN	41-11-023	FRANCISCO
1-01-001	FOREIGN-AID	9-04-007	FORMULATE	1-01-001	FOUNTAIN-FALLS	3-03-003	FRANCISCO'S
1-01-001	FOREIGN-ENTRY-L	11-05-011	FORMULATED	1-01-001	FOUNTAIN-HEAD	1-01-001	FRANCK
	IMIT	4-03-004	FORMULATING	1-01-001	FOUNTAINHEAD	2-01-001	FRANCO
2-02-002	FOREIGN-POLICY	17-04-007	FORMULATION	4-02-002	FOUNTAINS	1-01-001	FRANCO-*GERMAN
1-01-001	FOREIGN-SOUNDIN	11-03-007	FORMULATIONS	359-15-214	FOUR	1-01-001	FRANCO-*IRISHMA
	G	2-02-002	FORREST	2-01-001	FOUR-ELEMENT		N
4-02-003	FOREIGNER	1-01-001	FORSAKE	1-01-001	FOUR-FOLD	2-02-002	FRANCOIS
13-06-009	FOREIGNERS	2-01-002	FORSAKEN	3-03-003	FOUR-HOUR	1-01-001	FRANCOISETTE
1-01-001	FOREKNOWLEDGE	1-01-001	FORSAKES	1-01-001	FOUR-JET	3-02-002	FRANCS
1-01-001	FOREKNOWN	1-01-001	FORSAN	2-02-002	FOUR-LANE	1-01-001	FRANGIPANI
1-01-001	FORELEG	1-01-001	FORSTER'S	2-02-002	FOUR-LETTER	68-11-054	FRANK
1-01-001	FORELLEN	1-01-001	FORSWEARS	2-02-002	FOUR-O'CLOCK	1-01-001	FRANKER
4-03-004	FOREMAN	1-01-001	FORSYTH	1-01-001	FOUR-SIDED	1-01-001	FRANKEST
1-01-001	FOREMAN'S	6-02-002	FORSYTHE	1-01-001	FOUR-STORY	1-01-001	FRANKFORD
12-07-012	FOREMOST	55-11-020	FORT	1-01-001	FOUR-SYLLABLE	7-01-001	FRANKFORT
7-02-002	FORENSIC	6-05-006	FORTE	1-01-001	FOUR-THIRTY	17-02-002	FRANKFURTER
1-01-001	FOREPART	1-01-001	FORTE-PIANOS	1-01-001	FOUR-WHEEL-DRIV	2-01-001	FRANKFURTER'S
1-01-001	FOREPAWS	2-01-001	FORTESCUE		E	7-01-001	FRANKFURTERS
7-03-004	FORERUNNER	71-14-061	FORTH	2-01-001	FOUR-WOOD	17-02-002	FRANKIE
1-01-001	FORERUNNERS	11-05-010	FORTHCOMING	3-02-002	FOUR-YEAR	30-07-019	FRANKLIN
2-02-002	FORESAW	6-05-006	FORTHRIGHT	2-02-002	FOURS	1-01-001	FRANKLIN'S
3-03-003	FORESEE	1-01-001	FORTHRIGHTLY	1-01-001	FOURSOME	13-07-013	FRANKLY
4-04-004	FORESEEABLE	2-02-002	FORTHRIGHTNESS	31-11-027	FOURTEEN	4-03-004	FRANKNESS
2-02-002	FORESEEING	1-01-001	FORTIER	1-01-001	FOURTEEN-NATION	8-01-001	FRANKS
8-06-007	FORESEEN	7-04-006	FORTIES	1-01-001	FOURTEEN-TEAM	1-01-001	FRANKS-IN-BUNS
1-01-001	FORESHORTENED	2-02-002	FORTIFICATIONS	1-01-001	FOURTEEN-YEAR-O	1-01-001	FRANNY
1-01-001	FORESHORTENING	7-05-007	FORTIFIED		LD	2-01-001	FRANS
5-05-005	FORESIGHT	2-01-002	FORTIFY	3-02-003	FOURTEENTH	11-07-011	FRANTIC
66-09-021	FOREST	1-01-001	FORTIN	74-12-058	FOURTH	8-05-007	FRANTICALLY
5-02-005	FORESTALL	1-01-001	FORTIORI	1-01-001	FOURTH-CENTURY	2-02-002	FRANZ
1-01-001	FORESTRY	3-02-003	FORTITUDE	1-01-001	FOURTH-CLASS	1-01-001	FRATERNISATION
22-06-010	FORESTS	2-01-001	FORTMAN	1-01-001	FOURTH-DOWN	1-01-001	FRATERNITIES
1-01-001	FORETELL	1-01-001	FORTNIGHT	1-01-001	FOURTH-FLIGHT	6-04-005	FRATERNITY
1-01-001	FORETHOUGHT	1-01-001	FORTRESS	1-01-001	FOURTH-HAND	1-01-001	FRATERNIZE
39-14-030	FOREVER	6-03-006	FORTRESSES	1-01-001	FOURTH-OF-*JULY	1-01-001	FRATERNIZED
1-01-001	FOREVER-*CATHY	2-01-001	FORTS	2-02-002	FOWL	1-01-001	FRAU
3-02-002	FORFEIT	4-03-003	FORTUNATE	13-07-008	FOWLER	8-04-005	FRAUD
1-01-001	FORFEITED	22-08-018	FORTUNATELY	1-01-001	FOX	2-01-001	FRAUD'S
2-02-002	FORGAVE	20-11-017	FORTUNE	1-01-001	FOX'S	5-04-004	FRAUDS
10-03-003	FORGE	25-10-017	FORTUNE-HAPPY	1-01-001	FOX-HOUNDS	1-01-001	FRAY
3-03-003	FORGED	1-01-001	FORTUNE-TELLERS	1-01-001	FOX-TERRIER	3-03-003	FRAYED
1-01-001	FORGERIES	6-05-005	FORTUNES	2-01-002	FOXHOLES	3-01-001	FRAYNE
1-01-001	FORGERY	36-12-031	FORTY	1-01-001	FOXX	2-01-001	FRAYNE'S
54-14-042	FORGET	1-01-001	FORTY-EIGHT	2-01-001	FOY	1-01-001	FRAZZLED
2-01-001	FORGETFUL	1-01-001	FORTY-FIFTH	3-03-003	FOYER	4-02-004	FREAK
3-03-003	FORGETFULNESS	7-06-007	FORTY-FIVE	2-01-001	FPS,	1-01-001	FREAKISH
7-06-006	FORGETTING	6-03-005	FORTY-FOUR	1-01-001	FRA	2-01-001	FREAKS
1-01-001	FORGING	4-02-002	FORTY-NINE	1-01-001	FRACASES	1-01-001	FRECKLED
2-01-001	FORGIT	1-01-001	FORTY-NINERS	23-07-015	FRACTION	3-02-003	FRECKLES
1-01-001	FORGITFUL	1-01-001	FORTY-SECOND	1-01-001	FRACTIONAL	27-04-010	FRED
24-09-012	FORGIVE	4-02-003	FORTY-SEVEN	3-01-001	FRACTIONATED	2-01-001	FRED'S
6-03-003	FORGIVEN	2-02-002	FORTY-SIX	3-01-002	FRACTIONATION	2-02-002	FREDDIE
15-05-006	FORGIVENESS	1-01-001	FORTY-THIRD	20-02-005	FRACTIONS	20-01-001	FREDDY
2-02-002	FORGIVING	2-01-002	FORTY-THREE				

4-01-001 FREDDY'S	4-03-003 FRESHNESS	1-01-001 FROSTY	2-02-002 FUNCTIONALISM
1-01-001 FREDERIC	3-01-001 FRESNEL	1-01-001 FROTH	4-03-004 FUNCTIONALLY
19-09-014 FREDERICK	1-01-001 FRESNO	1-01-001 FROTHIER	2-02-002 FUNCTIONARY
1-01-001 FREDERICKSBURG	1-01-001 FRET	2-02-002 FROTHING	3-03-003 FUNCTIONED
1-01-001 FREDERIK	1-01-001 FRETTED	2-01-001 FROTHINGHAM	12-06-010 FUNCTIONING
1-01-001 FREDRICO	2-02-002 FRETTING	2-02-002 FROTHY	48-09-025 FUNCTIONS
1-01-001 FREDRIK	9-03-009 FREUD	1-01-001 FROWN	62-10-032 FUND
1-01-001 FREDRIKSHALL	2-02-002 FREUD'S	8-04-008 FROWNED	3-01-002 FUND'S
260-15-148 FREE	3-03-003 FREUDIAN	12-05-010 FROWNING	1-01-001 FUND-RAISER
1-01-001 FREE-*WILL	3-01-001 FREYA	1-01-001 FROWNINGLY	1-01-001 FUND-RAISERS
1-01-001 FREE-BLOWN	2-01-001 FRIABLE	1-01-001 FROWNS	5-03-004 FUND-RAISING
1-01-001 FREE-BUYING	1-01-001 FRIAR	1-01-001 FROWZY	50-09-038 FUNDAMENTAL
1-01-001 FREE-DRINK	1-01-001 FRIARS	5-02-002 FROZE	1-01-001 FUNDAMENTALISM
1-01-001 FREE-FOR-ALL	3-02-003 FRICK	27-09-018 FROZEN	4-03-004 FUNDAMENTALIST
1-01-001 FREE-HOLDERS	17-05-010 FRICTION	2-02-002 FRUGALITY	9-06-009 FUNDAMENTALLY
2-01-002 FREE-LANCE	1-01-001 FRICTION-FREE	1-01-001 FRUGALLY	5-05-005 FUNDAMENTALS
1-01-001 FREE-WHEELING	2-01-001 FRICTIONAL	35-11-022 FRUIT	1-01-001 FUNDING
1-01-001 FREE-WORLD	1-01-001 FRICTIONS	7-05-007 FRUITFUL	95-07-046 FUNDS
1-01-001 FREEBOOTERS	60-10-034 FRIDAY	1-01-001 FRUITFULLY	33-12-022 FUNERAL
12-08-012 FREED	2-01-002 FRIDAY'S	1-01-001 FRUITFULNESS	1-01-001 FUNERAL-ACCESSO
3-02-002 FREEDMEN	3-02-002 FRIDAYS	2-02-002 FRUITION	RIES
128-12-074 FREEDOM	6-04-005 FRIED	5-02-005 FRUITLESS	1-01-001 FUNERALS
2-01-002 FREEDOM'S	2-01-001 FRIEDENWALD	1-01-001 FRUITLESSLY	1-01-001 FUNGAL
1-01-001 FREEDOM-CONSCIO	1-01-001 FRIEDMAN	14-05-010 FRUITS	1-01-001 FUNGICIDES
US	1-01-001 FRIEDRICH	4-03-003 FRUSTRATE	2-02-002 FUNGUS
1-01-001 FREEDOM-LOVING	133-14-083 FRIEND	10-04-010 FRUSTRATED	4-02-002 FUNK
3-03-003 FREEDOMS	2-02-002 FRIEND'S	3-03-003 FRUSTRATING	1-01-001 FUNNEL
3-02-002 FREEHAND	2-01-002 FRIENDLIER	11-05-009 FRUSTRATION	1-01-001 FUNNELED
1-01-001 FREEHOLDER	1-01-001 FRIENDLILY	4-03-004 FRUSTRATIONS	1-01-001 FUNNELS
3-02-002 FREEHOLDERS	4-03-004 FRIENDLINESS	2-02-002 FRY	1-01-001 FUNNIER
3-02-003 FREEING	61-14-044 FRIENDLY	14-02-004 FT	2-02-002 FUNNIEST
22-10-020 FREELY	162-15-098 FRIENDS	1-01-001 FT.	41-08-024 FUNNY
11-05-008 FREEMAN	1-01-001 FRIENDS'	1-01-001 FU**DHRER	2-01-001 FUNSTON
1-01-001 FREEMAN'S	27-08-020 FRIENDSHIP	4-02-002 FUCHS	13-04-007 FUR
1-01-001 FREEPORT	4-03-004 FRIENDSHIPS	1-01-001 FUCHSIA	1-01-001 FUR-PIECE
5-03-004 FREER	13-02-004 FRIEZE	4-01-001 FUCK	1-01-001 FURBISHING
2-02-002 FREES	3-03-003 FRIEZES	6-01-001 FUCKEN	1-01-001 FURHMANN'S
2-02-002 FREEST	2-02-002 FRIGHT	1-01-001 FUCKS	1-01-001 FURIES
1-01-001 FREETHINKERS	7-01-001 FRIGHTEN	7-01-001 FUDO	8-04-006 FURIOUS
5-03-003 FREEWAY	11-04-005 FRIGHTENED	2-01-001 FUDO'S	2-01-001 FURIOUSER
5-02-002 FREEWAYS	26-08-024 FRIGHTENING	3-01-001 FUDOMAE	12-06-010 FURIOUSLY
1-01-001 FREEWHEELERS	14-09-014 FRIGHTENINGLY	17-06-011 FUEL	1-01-001 FURLED
6-05-005 FREEZE	1-01-001 FRIGHTFUL	1-01-001 FUELED	1-01-001 FURLONGS
1-01-001 FREEZE-OUT	6-04-006 FRIGHTFULLY	3-01-001 FUELOIL	2-02-002 FURLOUGH
1-01-001 FREEZER	5-04-005 FRIGID	1-01-001 FUELS	1-01-001 FURLOUGHED
1-01-001 FREEZERS	3-03-003 FRILLS	3-03-003 FUGITIVE	11-03-005 FURNACE
1-01-001 FREEZES	1-01-001 FRILLY	1-01-001 FUGITIVES	1-01-001 FURNACE'S
15-07-009 FREEZING	16-06-009 FRINGE	1-01-001 FUGUAL	2-02-002 FURNACES
1-01-001 FREIDA	5-04-004 FRINGED	1-01-001 FUHRMANN	29-08-021 FURNISH
28-08-013 FREIGHT	1-01-001 FRINGED-WRAPPED	1-01-001 FUHRMANN'S	23-08-018 FURNISHED
1-01-001 FREIGHT'S	3-02-002 FRISCO	1-01-001 FUJI	5-03-004 FURNISHES
1-01-001 FREIGHT-BUMS	1-01-001 FRISE	2-01-001 FUJIMOTO	4-04-004 FURNISHING
1-01-001 FREIGHT-CAR	1-01-001 FRIST	2-02-002 FULBRIGHT	9-06-008 FURNISHINGS
1-01-001 FREIGHT-JUMPER	2-01-001 FRITO	9-04-008 FULFILL	39-10-022 FURNITURE
4-02-003 FREIGHTER	1-01-001 FRITTERS	11-04-011 FULFILLED	3-02-002 FUROR
1-01-001 FREIGHTERS	2-02-002 FRITZ	3-03-003 FULFILLING	5-01-001 FURROW
1-01-001 FREIGHTS	6-01-001 FRITZIE	12-05-009 FULFILLMENT	2-02-002 FURROWED
1-01-001 FREINKEL	1-01-001 FRITZIE'S	2-02-002 FULFILLS	1-01-001 FURROWS
4-01-001 FRELINGHUYSEN	2-02-002 FRIVOLITY	3-01-001 FULKE	5-02-003 FURS
1-01-001 FRELINGHUYSEN'S	6-02-004 FRIVOLOUS	230-15-166 FULL	218-15-148 FURTHER
139-12-071 FRENCH	1-01-001 FRIZZLED	1-01-001 FULL-BANDED	3-02-003 FURTHERED
2-01-002 FRENCH-*CANADIA	1-01-001 FRIZZLING	2-01-001 FULL-BLOWN	2-01-001 FURTHERING
N	2-02-002 FROCK	1-01-001 FULL-BODIED	39-12-035 FURTHERMORE
1-01-001 FRENCH-*CANADIA	1-01-001 FROG	1-01-001 FULL-CLAD	1-01-001 FURTIVE
NS	1-01-001 FROG-EATING	1-01-001 FULL-DRESS	1-01-001 FURTIVELY
1-01-001 FRENCH-BORN	1-01-001 FROG-HAIKU	2-02-002 FULL-FLEDGED	19-07-012 FURY
1-01-001 FRENCH-POLISHED	1-01-001 FROG-MARCHED	2-02-002 FULL-GROWN	5-04-005 FUSE
8-03-006 FRENCHMAN	1-01-001 FROGS	1-01-001 FULL-OF-THE-MOO	3-03-003 FUSED
1-01-001 FRENCHMAN'S	1-01-001 FROHOCK	N	1-01-001 FUSELAGE
2-02-002 FRENCHMEN	1-01-001 FROISSART	2-02-002 FULL-SCALE	3-02-002 FUSES
1-01-001 FRENETIC	2-02-002 FROLIC	1-01-001 FULL-SISTERS	1-01-001 FUSIFORM
1-01-001 FRENZIED	2-02-002 FROLICKING	1-01-001 FULL-SIZED	1-01-001 FUSILLADES
1-01-001 FRENZIEDLY	1-01-001 FROLICS	24-09-014 FULL-TIME	1-01-001 FUSING
6-05-006 FRENZY	4369-15-500 FROM	1-01-001 FULL-YEAR	13-06-007 FUSION
1-01-001 FRENZY-FREE	15-02-002 FROMM	2-01-001 FULLBACK	4-03-003 FUSS
31-06-007 FREQUENCIES	15-01-001 FROMM'S	1-01-001 FULLBACKING	1-01-001 FUSSILY
22-05-013 FREQUENCY	1-01-001 FRONDEL	8-05-006 FULLER	2-02-002 FUSSING
1-01-001 FREQUENCY-INDEP	221-15-122 FRONT	5-04-005 FULLEST	3-03-003 FUSSY
ENDENT	1-01-001 FRONT-BACK	4-04-004 FULLNESS	1-01-001 FUSTY
1-01-001 FREQUENCY-MODUL	2-02-002 FRONT-LINE	80-12-069 FULLY	1-01-001 FUTHERMORE
ATION	2-02-002 FRONT-PAGE	1-01-001 FULMINATE	6-05-005 FUTILE
34-10-031 FREQUENT	7-01-001 FRONTAGE	1-01-001 FULMINATING	7-05-007 FUTILITY
1-01-001 FREQUENTED	3-02-003 FRONTAL	17-03-003 FULTON	1-01-001 FUTOTSU
91-13-066 FREQUENTLY	1-01-001 FRONTED	5-03-005 FUMBLE	227-15-134 FUTURE
8-02-002 FRESCO	30-09-021 FRONTIER	4-04-004 FUMBLED	1-01-001 FUTURE-DAY
1-01-001 FRESCOED	5-04-005 FRONTIERS	1-01-001 FUMBLING	1-01-001 FUTURE-TIME
3-02-002 FRESCOES	2-02-002 FRONTIERSMEN	2-02-002 FUMED	3-02-003 FUZZ
1-01-001 FRESCOING	3-03-003 FRONTING	1-01-001 FUMED-OAK	1-01-001 FUZZED
2-01-001 FRESCOS	7-04-005 FRONTS	5-05-005 FUMES	7-06-007 FUZZY
82-13-061 FRESH	6-04-005 FROST	1-01-001 FUMING	1-01-001 FY
1-01-001 FRESH-GROUND	1-01-001 FROST'S	1-01-001 FUMIO'S	1-01-001 FYODOR
1-01-001 FRESHBORN	1-01-001 FROST-*DEBBY	44-12-031 FUN	50-08-036 G
1-01-001 FRESHENED	2-02-002 FROST-BITTEN	1-01-001 FUN-FILLED	3-02-002 G)
2-02-002 FRESHLY	3-03-003 FROSTBITE	2-02-002 FUN-LOVING	1-01-001 G**.*B**.*S
1-01-001 FRESHLY-GROUND	1-01-001 FROSTED	1-01-001 FUNARI	1-01-001 G**.*O**.*P
8-05-007 FRESHMAN	1-01-001 FROSTING	113-11-054 FUNCTION	1-01-001 G'AHN
3-02-002 FRESHMEN	1-01-001 FROSTS	24-06-016 FUNCTIONAL	1-01-001 G-**JP

5-03-004	GA	2-02-002	GALS	12-03-003	GARRY	26-06-009	GEAR
1-01-001	GAAFER	2-02-002	GALT	14-01-001	GARRYOWEN	1-01-001	GEAR-SETS
1-01-001	GAB	1-01-001	GALTIER	9-01-002	GARSON	2-02-002	GEARED
1-01-001	GABARDINE	1-01-001	GALTIER'S	1-01-001	GARSTUNG	1-01-001	GEARING
1-01-001	GABBLE	2-02-002	GALVANIC	2-01-001	GARTER	2-02-002	GEARS
1-01-001	GABBLING	1-01-001	GALVANISM	14-02-002	GARTH	1-01-001	GEARY
2-02-002	GABLE	3-03-003	GALVANIZING	5-01-001	GARTH'S	1-01-001	GEATISH
1-01-001	GABLER	2-01-002	GALVESTON	2-01-001	GARVIER	1-01-001	GEDDES
4-03-003	GABLES	1-01-001	GALVESTON-*PORT	5-02-004	GARY	4-03-003	GEE
12-02-003	GABRIEL	2-02-002	GALWAY	1-01-001	GARZA	1-01-001	GEE'S
5-02-003	GABRIEL'S	2-02-002	GAMBIT	98-11-039	GAS	1-01-001	GEEING
3-03-003	GABRIELLE	1-01-001	GAMBITS	1-01-001	GAS-FIRED	7-01-001	GEELY
3-03-003	GADFLY	1-01-001	GAMBLE	1-01-001	GAS-GLASS	1-01-001	GEELY'S
4-03-003	GADGET	1-01-001	GAMBLER-POLITICIAN	3-01-001	GASCONY	1-01-001	GEERED
1-01-001	GADGETRY			2-01-002	GASEOUS	3-03-003	GEESE
7-03-005	GADGETS	5-03-003	GAMBLERS	7-05-001	GASES	1-01-001	GEGENSCHEIN
1-01-001	GAETAN	1-01-001	GAMBLES	1-01-001	GASH	5-02-003	GEHRIG
4-03-003	GAG	17-08-013	GAMBLING	2-02-002	GASHES	1-01-001	GEIGER
2-02-002	GAGARIN	123-12-051	GAME	4-01-001	GASKET	1-01-001	GEISHA
4-03-004	GAGE	4-01-002	GAME'S	1-01-001	GASKET'S	2-01-002	GEL
2-02-002	GAGES	1-01-001	GAME-MANAGEMENT	1-01-001	GASKETS	1-01-001	GELATIN-LIKE
1-01-001	GAGGED	1-01-001	GAMEBIRD	1-01-001	GASLIGHTS	4-02-002	GELDING
1-01-001	GAGGING	1-01-001	GAMECOCK	12-05-009	GASOLINE	1-01-001	GELDINGS
1-01-001	GAGGLE	55-12-028	GAMES	3-03-003	GASP	1-01-001	GELLY
1-01-001	GAGING	1-01-001	GAMING	1-01-001	GASPARD	4-04-004	GEM
1-01-001	GAGLINE	2-01-001	GAMING-CARD	5-04-005	GASPED	1-01-001	GEMEINSCHAFT
2-01-001	GAGS	5-02-002	GAMMA	1-01-001	GASPEE	1-01-001	GEMLIKE
1-01-001	GAGWRITERS	4-03-004	GAMUT	5-04-005	GASPING	2-01-002	GEMS
1-01-001	GAI	1-01-001	GANADO	1-01-001	GASPINGLY	23-03-012	GEN
4-02-002	GAIETIES	1-01-001	GANDER	5-03-005	GASPS	2-01-001	GENDER
8-05-006	GAIETY	1-01-001	GANESSA	1-01-001	GASSE	1-01-001	GENDERS
5-05-005	GAILY	22-07-013	GANG	2-02-002	GASSED	9-04-008	GENE
74-10-036	GAIN	1-01-001	GANG'S	1-01-001	GASSER	2-01-001	GENE-*PRINCESS
39-11-033	GAINED	2-02-002	GANGES	1-01-001	GASSET	1-01-001	GENEALOGIES
1-01-001	GAINER	1-01-001	GANGLAND	1-01-001	GASSING	1-01-001	GENERA
1-01-001	GAINERS	1-01-001	GANGLING	1-01-001	GASSINGS	497-13-208	GENERAL
3-02-002	GAINES	1-01-001	GANGPLANK	1-01-001	GASSY	6-04-005	GENERAL'S
1-01-001	GAINESVILLE	6-04-004	GANGS	2-02-002	GASTON	1-01-001	GENERAL-APPEAL
1-01-001	GAINFUL	2-02-002	GANGSTER	4-01-001	GASTROCNEMIUS	1-01-001	GENERAL-PURPOSE
15-08-015	GAINING	4-03-004	GANGSTERS	2-02-002	GASTROINTESTINAL	4-03-003	GENERALE
19-08-013	GAINS	1-01-001	GANGWAY			1-01-001	GENERALIST
8-03-004	GAIT	3-01-001	GANNETT	1-01-001	GASTRONOMES	2-01-001	GENERALISTS
1-01-001	GAITED	1-01-001	GANNETT'S	1-01-001	GASTRONOMY	1-01-001	GENERALITIES
1-01-001	GAITERS	4-01-001	GANNON	37-10-021	GATE	3-03-003	GENERALITY
1-01-001	GAITHER	1-01-001	GANNON'S	1-01-001	GATE-POST	4-03-004	GENERALIZATION
5-04-004	GAL	6-01-001	GANSEVOORT	15-07-011	GATES	7-04-007	GENERALIZATIONS
1-01-001	GAL.	2-01-001	GANTLET	3-03-003	GATEWAY	5-04-005	GENERALIZE
7-03-006	GALA	5-01-001	GANTRY	1-01-001	GATEWAYS	9-02-007	GENERALIZED
1-01-001	GALACTIC	17-08-014	GAP	20-12-020	GATHER	132-14-100	GENERALLY
1-01-001	GALAHAD	3-02-002	GAPED	32-12-030	GATHERED	10-05-006	GENERALS
1-01-001	GALANTUOMO	2-02-002	GAPING	28-12-027	GATHERING	7-03-005	GENERATE
1-01-001	GALAPAGOS	2-02-002	GAPS	1-01-001	GATHERING-IN	11-05-010	GENERATED
1-01-001	GALATA	7-01-001	GAPT	7-05-007	GATHERINGS	5-04-005	GENERATES
2-01-001	GALATIANS	2-01-001	GAR-*DENE	1-01-001	GATHERS	7-03-006	GENERATING
7-01-001	GALAXIES	21-06-011	GARAGE	2-01-001	GATLINBURG	55-10-037	GENERATION
3-03-003	GALAXY	1-01-001	GARAGED	2-01-001	GATOR	1-01-001	GENERATION'S
2-02-002	GALE	5-03-003	GARAGES	1-01-001	GATSBY	23-07-018	GENERATIONS
1-01-001	GALEN	3-03-003	GARB	1-01-001	GAUCHE	14-04-005	GENERATOR
2-02-002	GALENA	7-06-006	GARBAGE	1-01-001	GAUCHERIE	9-01-002	GENERATORS
2-01-001	GALILEE	1-01-001	GARBED	1-01-001	GAUCHERIES	7-06-007	GENEROSITY
1-01-001	GALINA	1-01-001	GARBLED	7-05-007	GAUDY	25-08-023	GENEROUS
1-01-001	GALINDEZ	3-03-003	GARCIA	2-01-001	GAUER	8-05-008	GENEROUSLY
7-01-001	GALL	1-01-001	GARDE	12-06-007	GAUGE	1-01-001	GENES
5-05-005	GALLANT	60-12-037	GARDEN	2-02-002	GAUGED	4-03-004	GENESIS
3-02-003	GALLANTRY	1-01-001	GARDENED	1-01-001	GAUGUIN	5-02-002	GENETIC
1-01-001	GALLANTS	1-01-001	GARDENER	1-01-001	GAUL	3-02-002	GENETICIST
1-01-001	GALLBLADDER	4-03-003	GARDENERS	1-01-001	GAULEITER	17-04-008	GENEVA
1-01-001	GALLED	1-01-001	GARDENIA	4-02-002	GAULLE	1-01-001	GENEVIEVE
1-01-001	GALLERIES	1-01-001	GARDENIAS	6-04-005	GAUNT	5-04-004	GENIAL
31-09-014	GALLERY	3-03-003	GARDENING	2-02-002	GAUNTLET	1-01-001	GENIE
3-01-001	GALLERY'S	32-09-019	GARDENS	1-01-001	GAUNTLEY	1-01-001	GENII
1-01-001	GALLET	1-01-001	GARDNER	2-01-001	GAUSS	23-08-016	GENIUS
4-03-003	GALLEY	4-01-001	GARDNER'S	2-01-002	GAUSSIAN	1-01-001	GENIUSES
4-02-002	GALLEYS	1-01-001	GARGANTUAN	1-01-001	GAUTIER	1-01-001	GENNARO
3-01-001	GALLI	2-01-001	GARGERY	1-01-001	GAUZE	2-02-002	GENRE
1-01-001	GALLING	1-01-001	GARGERY'S	285-15-176	GAVE	1-01-001	GENRES
4-01-001	GALLIUM	1-01-001	GARGLE	1-01-001	GAVESTON	4-03-003	GENTEEL
2-01-001	GALLIUM/GERMANIUM	13-01-002	GARIBALDI	16-02-002	GAVIN	1-01-001	GENTIAN
		8-01-002	GARIBALDI'S	9-02-002	GAVIN'S	1-01-001	GENTIANS
1-01-001	GALLIVANTIN	1-01-001	GARINE	1-01-001	GAVOTTES	13-04-006	GENTILE
6-02-004	GALLON	1-01-001	GARISH	1-01-001	GAWDAMIGHTY	5-01-001	GENTILE-*JEWISH
1-01-001	GALLON-*LOREN	1-01-001	GARISHNESS	1-01-001	GAWKY	1-01-001	GENTILES
1-01-001	GALLONAGE	9-04-005	GARLAND	30-12-023	GAY	3-03-003	GENTILITY
6-04-004	GALLONS	1-01-001	GARLANDED	1-01-001	GAY-ESS	27-10-025	GENTLE
4-03-004	GALLOP	4-03-004	GARLIC	1-01-001	GAYETY	28-12-025	GENTLEMAN
1-01-001	GALLOPED	6-03-004	GARMENT	1-01-001	GAYLOR	1-01-001	GENTLEMANLY
1-01-001	GALLOPING	6-03-004	GARMENTS	1-01-001	GAYLOR'S	21-11-018	GENTLEMEN
2-02-002	GALLOWS	1-01-001	GARNER	1-01-001	GAYNOR	2-02-002	GENTLENESS
1-01-001	GALLS	1-01-001	GARNET	12-06-012	GAZE	3-03-003	GENTLER
1-01-001	GALLSTONE	1-01-001	GARNETT	7-05-006	GAZED	31-10-024	GENTLY
1-01-001	GALLSTONES	1-01-001	GARRARD'S	1-01-001	GAZELLE	1-01-001	GENTRY
1-01-001	GALLUP	1-01-001	GARRETT	1-01-001	GAZER	34-11-033	GENUINE
1-01-001	GALLUS-SNAPPING	2-02-002	GARRICK	1-01-001	GAZES	10-05-009	GENUINELY
1-01-001	GALOPHONE-*KIMBERLY	5-02-004	GARRISON	10-04-004	GAZETTE	2-01-001	GENUS
		1-01-001	GARRISONED	1-01-001	GAZETTES	1-01-001	GEO-POLITICAL
1-01-001	GALOPHONE-*PRISSY	1-01-001	GARRISONIAN	8-07-007	GAZING	2-01-001	GEOCENTRIC
		1-01-001	GARRULOUS	1-01-001	GAZINOSU	1-01-001	GEOCENTRICISM

2-02-002 GEOCHEMISTRY	2-01-001 GHOREYEB	1-01-001 GIULIETTA	1-01-001 GLISSADE	
1-01-001 GEODETIC	1-01-001 GHORMLEY	3-02-003 GIUSEPPE	4-02-004 GLISTEN	
1-01-001 GEOGRAPHERS	11-06-009 GHOST	1-01-001 GIUSTINIANI	4-03-004 GLISTENED	
6-03-005 GEOGRAPHIC	1-01-001 GHOSTED	391-15-249 GIVE	6-03-006 GLISTENING	
16-06-011 GEOGRAPHICAL	1-01-001 GHOSTLIKE	1-01-001 GIVE-AND-TAKE	5-04-005 GLITTER	
6-02-005 GEOGRAPHICALLY	2-02-002 GHOSTLY	1-01-001 GIVE-AWAY	1-01-001 GLITTERED	
5-04-005 GEOGRAPHY	5-04-004 GHOSTS	4-04-004 GIVEAWAY	6-05-005 GLITTERING	
8-02-003 GEOLOGICAL	1-01-001 GHOUL	3-01-001 GIVEAWAYS	2-02-002 GLOATED	
2-02-002 GEOLOGIST	2-01-001 GHOULS	377-15-225 GIVEN	1-01-001 GLOATS	
3-02-002 GEOLOGISTS	1-01-001 GIACOMETTI	1-01-001 GIVENNESS	1-01-001 GLOB-FLAKES	
5-04-004 GEOLOGY	1-01-001 GIACOMO	1-01-001 GIVER	4-02-003 GLOBAL	
17-01-003 GEOMETRIC	2-01-001 GIANICOLO	1-01-001 GIVERS	1-01-001 GLOBALLY	
1-01-001 GEOMETRICAL	23-12-020 GIANT	112-14-082 GIVES	13-09-012 GLOBE	
1-01-001 GEOMETRICALLY	21-03-009 GIANTS	2-01-001 GIVETH	1-01-001 GLOBE-*DEMOCRAT	
9-04-006 GEOMETRY	2-01-001 GIANTS'	5-01-001 GIVIN	1-01-001 GLOBE-GIRDLING	
1-01-001 GEOPOLITICAL	1-01-001 GIAOUR	96-14-083 GIVING	1-01-001 GLOBES	
129-13-068 GEORGE	2-01-001 GIBAULT	2-01-002 GIZENGA	1-01-001 GLOBETROTTER	
3-02-002 GEORGE'S	1-01-001 GIBBET	1-01-001 GLACIER	1-01-001 GLOBIGII	
3-01-001 GEORGE-*BARDEN	2-02-002 GIBBON	1-01-001 GLACIER-LIKE	3-01-001 GLOBOCNIK	
2-01-002 GEORGES	7-02-002 GIBBS	1-01-001 GLACIERS	1-01-001 GLOBOCNIK'S	
3-03-003 GEORGETOWN	7-01-001 GIBBY	38-13-035 GLAD	4-01-002 GLOBULIN	
1-01-001 GEORGETOWN'S	1-01-001 GIBE	3-01-001 GLADDEN	1-01-001 GLOBULINS	
1-01-001 GEORGI	1-01-001 GIBES	2-01-001 GLADDEN'S	2-01-001 GLOCESTER	
46-08-016 GEORGIA	1-01-001 GIBLET	6-01-001 GLADDY	1-01-001 GLOMERULAR	
9-02-004 GEORGIA'S	8-04-005 GIBSON	2-01-001 GLADDY'S	1-01-001 GLOMMED	
2-01-001 GEORGIA-*PACIFIC	1-01-001 GIDDINESS	1-01-001 GLADIATOR	14-05-013 GLOOM	
3-02-003 GEORGIAN	1-01-001 GIDDINGS	2-01-001 GLADIUS	3-03-003 GLOOMILY	
1-01-001 GEORGIANS	2-02-002 GIDDY	4-04-004 GLADLY	3-02-003 GLOOMY	
4-01-001 GERAGHTY	1-01-001 GIDE	1-01-001 GLADNESS	1-01-001 GLORIA	
3-01-001 GERAGHTY'S	17-01-001 GIFFEN	4-03-003 GLAMOR	3-01-001 GLORIANA	
1-01-001 GERAGHTYS'	2-01-001 GIFFEN'S	1-01-001 GLAMORIZE	4-04-004 GLORIES	
3-01-002 GERALD	33-12-030 GIFT	5-04-005 GLAMOROUS	1-01-001 GLORIFICATION	
2-02-002 GERALDINE	13-09-013 GIFTED	5-04-005 GLAMOUR	4-03-004 GLORIFIED	
1-01-001 GERBY	11-06-010 GIFTS	40-11-034 GLANCE	1-01-001 GLORIFIES	
1-01-001 GERHARD	1-01-001 GIG	25-07-021 GLANCED	2-01-001 GLORIFY	
1-01-001 GERIATRIC	10-10-010 GIGANTIC	5-04-005 GLANCES	16-06-014 GLORIOUS	
3-03-003 GERM	1-01-001 GIGENZA	8-04-008 GLANCING	1-01-001 GLORIOUSLY	
85-11-040 GERMAN	1-01-001 GIGGLE	9-02-003 GLAND	21-07-012 GLORY	
1-01-001 GERMAN'S	3-02-003 GIGGLED	1-01-001 GLANDERS	1-01-001 GLORYING	
1-01-001 GERMAN-LANGUAGE	4-03-004 GIGGLES	6-03-004 GLANDS	1-01-001 GLOSS	
2-02-002 GERMANE	1-01-001 GIGGLING	1-01-001 GLANDULAR	3-02-002 GLOSSARY	
1-01-001 GERMANIA	1-01-001 GIL	7-03-007 GLARE	1-01-001 GLOSSED	
9-02-003 GERMANIC	3-03-003 GILBERT	5-03-005 GLARED	1-01-001 GLOSSY	
6-02-002 GERMANIUM	16-01-001 GILBORN	7-04-007 GLARING	1-01-001 GLOTTAL	
1-01-001 GERMANIZED	3-01-001 GILBORN'S	1-01-001 GLARINGLY	3-01-001 GLOTTOCHRONOLOGICAL	
1-01-001 GERMANO-*SLAVIC	1-01-001 GILD	2-01-002 GLASGOW	1-01-001 GLOTTOCHRONOLOGY	
27-06-016 GERMANS	1-01-001 GILDAS	99-15-062 GLASS		
2-02-002 GERMANTOWN	2-02-002 GILDED	1-01-001 GLASS-BOTTOM	7-03-003 GLOUCESTER	
81-12-033 GERMANY	2-01-001 GILELS	2-01-001 GLASS-FIBER	9-04-006 GLOVE	
2-01-001 GERMANY'S	7-02-002 GILES	1-01-001 GLASS-LIKE	2-02-002 GLOVED	
1-01-001 GERMINAL	1-01-001 GILKSON	29-11-022 GLASSES	1-01-001 GLOVER	
2-01-001 GERMINATE	2-02-002 GILL	1-01-001 GLASSLESS	7-05-005 GLOVES	
1-01-001 GERMS	3-02-002 GILLESPIE	2-01-001 GLASSY	16-08-015 GLOW	
1-01-001 GEROGE	1-01-001 GILLIS	1-01-001 GLAUCOMA	6-04-005 GLOWED	
1-01-001 GEROME	3-01-001 GILMAN	1-01-001 GLAYRE	3-03-003 GLOWERED	
2-01-001 GEROSA	1-01-001 GILMORE	11-02-002 GLAZE	3-02-002 GLOWERING	
2-02-002 GEROSA'S	1-01-001 GILROY	5-03-004 GLAZED	10-06-007 GLOWING	
4-01-001 GERRY	3-02-003 GILT	2-02-002 GLAZER	1-01-001 GLOWS	
1-01-001 GERSHWIN	1-01-001 GIMBALED	1-01-001 GLAZER-*FINE	8-02-002 GLUE	
1-01-001 GERSHWINS	2-01-002 GIMBEL	3-01-001 GLAZES	19-04-008 GLUED	
1-01-001 GERSHWINS'	1-01-001 GIMME	2-01-002 GLAZING	1-01-001 GLUM	
1-01-001 GERSTA**DCKER	1-01-001 GIMPY	4-04-004 GLEAM	1-01-001 GLUMLY	
5-02-002 GERTRUDE	23-05-006 GIN	4-03-004 GLEAMED	1-01-001 GLUTAMIC	
2-01-001 GERUNDIAL	2-02-002 GINGER	6-03-005 GLEAMING	1-01-001 GLUTINOUS	
1-01-001 GESAMTKUNSTWERK	2-02-002 GINGERLY	1-01-001 GLEAN	1-01-001 GLUTTED	
1-01-001 GESANGVEREIN	2-02-002 GINGHAM	1-01-001 GLEANED	3-02-002 GLUTTONS	
1-01-001 GESTAPO	1-01-001 GINGHAMS	2-01-002 GLEASON	2-02-002 GLYCERIN	
1-01-001 GESTICULATED	1-01-001 GINKGO	3-02-002 GLEE	1-01-001 GLYCERINATED	
1-01-001 GESTICULATING	2-01-001 GINMILL	1-01-001 GLEE-CLUB	5-02-002 GLYCERINE	
32-12-024 GESTURE	1-01-001 GINNER'S	1-01-001 GLEEFUL	2-01-002 GLYCEROL	
3-03-003 GESTURED	1-01-001 GINNIN	1-01-001 GLEEFULLY	1-01-001 GLYCEROLIZED	
7-06-007 GESTURES	5-01-001 GINNING	1-01-001 GLEES	2-01-001 GLYCOL	
1-01-001 GESTURING	1-01-001 GINO	7-05-007 GLEN	1-01-001 GLYCOLS	
1-01-001 GESUALDO	1-01-001 GINS	2-01-002 GLENDA	1-01-001 GLYCOSIDES	
750-15-276 GET	1-01-001 GINSBERG'S	1-01-001 GLENDALE	12-02-002 GM	
2-01-002 GET-TOGETHER	1-01-001 GIOCONDA	13-01-001 GLENDORA	1-01-001 GNARLED	
1-01-001 GETAWAY	3-01-001 GIORGIO	1-01-001 GLENDORA'S	2-02-002 GNASHING	
65-12-049 GETS	3-02-003 GIOVANNI	6-03-003 GLENN	1-01-001 GNAW	
1-01-001 GETTIN	1-01-001 GIRD	1-01-001 GLENNON	1-01-001 GNAWED	
164-15-122 GETTING	1-01-001 GIRDERS	1-01-001 GLIB	4-03-004 GNAWING	
2-02-002 GETTYSBURG	2-02-002 GIRDLE	4-03-004 GLIBLY	1-01-001 GNOME	
1-01-001 GETZ	220-15-101 GIRL	2-02-002 GLIDE	1-01-001 GNOMELIKE	
1-01-001 GETZ'S	10-07-007 GIRL'S	1-01-001 GLIDE-BOMBED	1-01-001 GNOMES	
1-01-001 GEVURTZ	1-01-001 GIRL-FRIEND	1-01-001 GLIDED	1-01-001 GNOMON	
1-01-001 GEYSERING	1-01-001 GIRL-SAN	1-01-001 GLIDERS	626-15-275 GO	
2-02-002 GEYSERS	1-01-001 GIRLIE	1-01-001 GLIDES	1-01-001 GO**DTTERDA**DMMERUNG	
1-01-001 GHADIALI	5-04-004 GIRLISH	4-01-001 GLIMCO		
4-03-004 GHANA	2-02-002 GIRLISHLY	1-01-001 GLIMCO'S	1-01-001 GO**DTTINGEN	
6-04-006 GHASTLY	142-15-063 GIRLS	3-03-003 GLIMMER	1-01-001 GO-GO-GO	
1-01-001 GHAZAL	2-02-002 GIRLS'	1-01-001 GLIMMERING	1-01-001 GO-IT-ALONE	
1-01-001 GHAZALS	1-01-001 GIRTH	16-06-014 GLIMPSE	1-01-001 GO-TO-WAR	
1-01-001 GHENT	16-06-014 GISELE	5-04-005 GLIMPSED	1-01-001 GOA	
1-01-001 GHERKINS	5-04-005 GISELLE	4-03-004 GLIMPSES	1-01-001 GOAD	
11-04-004 GHETTO	4-03-004 GISORS	2-02-002 GLINT	3-03-003 GOADED	
5-02-002 GHETTOS	2-02-002 GIST	2-01-002 GLINTED	60-11-044 GOAL	
1-01-001 GHIBERTI	4-04-004 GIT	5-04-005 GLINTING	1-01-001 GOAL-LINE	
	1-01-001 GIUBBONARI	2-01-001 GLISON		

Code	Word
1-01-001	GOAL-ORIENTED
1-01-001	GOAL-VALUES
40-08-022	GOALS
6-04-004	GOAT
2-01-001	GOAT'S
1-01-001	GOB
2-02-002	GOBBLED
1-01-001	GOBBLEDYGOOK
1-01-001	GOBBLERS
1-01-001	GOBBLES
318-14-091	GOD
38-11-025	GOD'S
1-01-001	GOD-CURST
1-01-001	GOD-FORSAKEN
3-02-002	GOD-GIVEN
1-01-001	GOD-LIKE
1-01-001	GODAMIT
4-03-003	GODDAM
1-01-001	GODDAMIT
2-01-001	GODDAMMIT
9-03-004	GODDAMN
2-01-001	GODDAMNED
3-03-003	GODDESS
1-01-001	GODFREY
1-01-001	GODHEAD
4-01-001	GODKIN
2-02-002	GODLESS
1-01-001	GODLIKE
1-01-001	GODLINESS
5-01-001	GODOT
14-08-011	GODS
2-02-002	GODSEND
1-01-001	GODUNOV
4-03-003	GODWIN
1-01-001	GOERING
89-14-074	GOES
3-01-001	GOETHE
1-01-001	GOETHE'S
1-01-001	GOG
2-02-002	GOGGLE-EYED
1-01-001	GOGGLES
2-02-002	GOGH
1-01-001	GOGO
1-01-001	GOGOL
1-01-001	GOGOL'S
12-02-007	GOIN
399-15-196	GOING
2-02-002	GOING-OVER
1-01-001	GOINGS
3-01-001	GOITRE
2-01-001	GOITROGEN
2-01-001	GOITROGENS
52-12-038	GOLD
1-01-001	GOLD-FILLED
1-01-001	GOLD-PHONE
1-01-001	GOLD-WIRE
1-01-001	GOLDA
10-03-006	GOLDBERG
42-11-029	GOLDEN
1-01-001	GOLDEN-CRUSTED
1-01-001	GOLDFISH
1-01-001	GOLDSMITH
3-02-003	GOLDWATER
34-08-014	GOLF
3-01-002	GOLF'S
3-02-002	GOLFER
4-01-002	GOLFERS
1-01-001	GOLFING
2-01-001	GOLLY
2-02-002	GOMEZ
1-01-001	GOMPACHI
195-15-139	GONE
16-05-006	GONNA
1-01-001	GONNE
2-01-001	GONTRAN
9-02-002	GONZALES
2-01-001	GONZALEZ
807-15-319	GOOD
5-02-004	GOOD-BY
5-04-005	GOOD-BYE
1-01-001	GOOD-HUMOREDLY
1-01-001	GOOD-LIVING
4-03-004	GOOD-LOOKING
3-02-003	GOOD-NATURED
1-01-001	GOOD-NEWS
1-01-001	GOOD-NIGHT
1-01-001	GOOD-SIZE
1-01-001	GOOD-WILL
2-01-001	GOODBODY
1-01-001	GOODBY
6-04-005	GOODBYE
1-01-001	GOODIES
4-01-001	GOODIS
2-02-002	GOODMAN
16-08-010	GOODNESS
1-01-001	GOODNESS'
2-02-002	GOODNIGHT
57-10-027	GOODS
1-01-001	GOODWILL
2-01-001	GOODWIN
2-01-001	GOODY
1-01-001	GOOEY
1-01-001	GOOFED
1-01-001	GOOLICK
1-01-001	GOOOOLICK
4-03-004	GOOSE
1-01-001	GOOSHEY
7-01-001	GORBODUC
2-01-001	GORD
3-01-001	GORDIN
10-05-009	GORDON
2-02-002	GORDON'S
7-04-004	GORE
1-01-001	GORE'S
1-01-001	GORGE
7-05-007	GORGEOUS
1-01-001	GORGEOUSLY
1-01-001	GORGES
1-01-001	GORGING
4-01-001	GORHAM
1-01-001	GORHAM'S
1-01-001	GORKY
1-01-001	GORSHEK
1-01-001	GORSHIN
32-01-001	GORTON
3-01-001	GORTON'S
2-01-001	GORTONISTS
1-01-001	GOSAIMASU
4-03-004	GOSH
13-04-006	GOSPEL
1-01-001	GOSPEL-SINGER
1-01-001	GOSPELERS
4-03-004	GOSPELS
1-01-001	GOSSAMER
13-06-012	GOSSIP
1-01-001	GOSSIPED
2-02-002	GOSSIPING
5-01-001	GOSSON
1-01-001	GOSSON'S
482-14-191	GOT
1-01-001	GOTHAM
4-02-004	GOTHIC
1-01-001	GOTHICISM
1-01-001	GOTT
5-04-004	GOTTA
16-08-013	GOTTEN
1-01-001	GOUGE
3-02-003	GOUGED
3-03-003	GOUGING
2-02-002	GOULD
1-01-001	GOULDING
7-01-001	GOULDING'S
2-01-001	GOULDINGS
2-01-001	GOURD
2-01-001	GOURMET
1-01-001	GOURMET'S
1-01-001	GOURMETS
2-02-002	GOUT
1-01-001	GOUTTE
1-01-001	GOUVERNE
1-01-001	GOUVERNEMENT
19-02-011	GOV
7-04-006	GOVERN
15-07-011	GOVERNED
3-03-003	GOVERNESS
21-08-015	GOVERNING
1-01-001	GOVERNMEN
417-13-135	GOVERNMENT
16-05-012	GOVERNMENT'S
1-01-001	GOVERNMENT-BLESSED
1-01-001	GOVERNMENT-CONTROLLED
1-01-001	GOVERNMENT-OWNED
1-01-001	GOVERNMENT-SUPPORTED
1-01-001	GOVERNMENT-TO-GOVERNMENT
23-06-017	GOVERNMENTAL
1-01-001	GOVERNMENTALLY
61-09-032	GOVERNMENTS
83-08-032	GOVERNOR
14-04-008	GOVERNOR'S
1-01-001	GOVERNOR-*GENERAL
8-04-007	GOVERNORS
2-02-002	GOVERNS
16-05-012	GOWN
1-01-001	GOWNED
2-02-002	GOWNS
1-01-001	GOYETTE
1-01-001	GPD,
5-01-001	GRA**DFIN
1-01-001	GRA**DFIN'S
16-08-015	GRAB
20-05-013	GRABBED
1-01-001	GRABBIN
5-05-005	GRABBING
3-03-003	GRABS
5-01-001	GRABSKI
1-01-001	GRABSKI'S
40-09-030	GRACE
1-01-001	GRACED
10-05-009	GRACEFUL
8-06-007	GRACEFULLY
4-03-004	GRACES
2-01-001	GRACIAS
1-01-001	GRACIE
1-01-001	GRACIE'S
9-07-009	GRACIOUS
3-03-003	GRACIOUSLY
2-01-001	GRAD
2-02-002	GRADATIONS
35-07-022	GRADE
1-01-001	GRADE-*A
1-01-001	GRADE-CONSTRUCTED
1-01-001	GRADE-EQUIVALENT
1-01-001	GRADE-EQUIVALENTS
2-02-002	GRADED
2-02-002	GRADER
23-07-016	GRADES
14-03-004	GRADIENT
5-02-003	GRADIENTS
1-01-001	GRADING
2-01-001	GRADS
16-07-012	GRADUAL
1-01-001	GRADUALIST
51-14-046	GRADUALLY
30-10-023	GRADUATE
13-06-011	GRADUATED
17-05-013	GRADUATES
7-04-005	GRADUATING
11-05-006	GRADUATION
5-01-003	GRADY
1-01-001	GRAFF
1-01-001	GRAFFITI
1-01-001	GRAFT
5-03-003	GRAFTON
15-06-007	GRAHAM
1-01-001	GRAHAMSTOWN
2-02-002	GRAIL
27-10-019	GRAIN
1-01-001	GRAIN-STORAGE
1-01-001	GRAINING
20-05-006	GRAINS
10-02-004	GRAM
1-01-001	GRAM-NEGATIVE
4-03-003	GRAMMAR
1-01-001	GRAMMARIANS
5-01-001	GRAMMATIC
4-03-004	GRAMMATICAL
1-01-001	GRAMMATICALLY
1-01-001	GRAMMOPHON
18-02-002	GRAMS
9-01-001	GRAN
1-01-001	GRAN'DAD
2-02-002	GRANARY
48-12-039	GRAND
2-01-001	GRAND-DAUGHTER
1-01-001	GRAND-LOOKING
1-01-001	GRAND-SLAM
6-04-005	GRANDCHILDREN
2-02-002	GRANDDAUGHTER
2-02-002	GRANDE
2-01-001	GRANDE-*BRETAGNE
1-01-001	GRANDER
6-04-006	GRANDEUR
12-09-011	GRANDFATHER
1-01-001	GRANDFATHER-FATHER-TO
1-01-001	GRANDFATHERS
1-01-001	GRANDILOQUENT
3-03-003	GRANDIOSE
1-01-001	GRANDLY
13-04-004	GRANDMA
3-01-002	GRANDMA'S
9-06-006	GRANDMOTHER
3-03-003	GRANDMOTHER'S
1-01-001	GRANDMOTHERS
1-01-001	GRANDMOTHERS'
3-02-002	GRANDPARENTS
3-01-001	GRANDS
5-04-004	GRANDSON
1-01-001	GRANDSONS
1-01-001	GRANDSTAND
3-02-002	GRANITE
1-01-001	GRANITE'S
6-03-003	GRANNY
1-01-001	GRANNY'S
47-08-035	GRANT
1-01-001	GRANT'S
3-02-002	GRANT-IN-AID
56-12-042	GRANTED
1-01-001	GRANTHER
8-04-008	GRANTING
20-04-007	GRANTS
3-01-003	GRANTS-IN-AID
3-01-002	GRANULAR
1-01-001	GRANULAR-TYPE
1-01-001	GRANULES
1-01-001	GRANULOCYTIC
2-02-002	GRANVILLE
2-02-003	GRAPE
3-01-002	GRAPE-ARBOR
3-02-003	GRAPEFRUIT
7-05-007	GRAPES
3-03-003	GRAPEVINE
1-01-001	GRAPEVINES
17-01-005	GRAPH
1-01-001	GRAPHED
6-05-006	GRAPHIC
1-01-001	GRAPHICAL
2-02-002	GRAPHICALLY
5-01-001	GRAPHITE
1-01-001	GRAPHS
1-01-001	GRAPPELLY
1-01-001	GRAPPELY
1-01-001	GRAPPLE
1-01-001	GRAPPLED
4-04-004	GRAPPLING
2-01-001	GRAS
17-11-017	GRASP
11-06-009	GRASPED
2-02-002	GRASPING
53-12-034	GRASS
1-01-001	GRASS-FED
1-01-001	GRASS-GREEN
1-01-001	GRASS-ROOTS
1-01-001	GRASSED
1-01-001	GRASSERS
1-01-001	GRASSES
1-01-001	GRASSFIRE
4-03-003	GRASSHOPPERS
1-01-001	GRASSLAND
6-02-002	GRASSLANDS
1-01-001	GRASSROOTS
1-01-001	GRASSROOTS-FUELED
2-02-002	GRASSY
1-01-001	GRATA
3-02-002	GRATE
2-02-002	GRATED
25-13-022	GRATEFUL
3-02-002	GRATEFULLY
4-03-003	GRATIFICATION
4-02-004	GRATIFIED
1-01-001	GRATIFY
3-03-003	GRATIFYING
1-01-001	GRATIFYINGLY
1-01-001	GRATING
1-01-001	GRATINGLY
1-01-001	GRATINGS
1-01-001	GRATIS
9-05-006	GRATITUDE
8-01-001	GRATT
2-01-001	GRATTAN
3-02-003	GRATUITOUS
2-02-002	GRATUITOUSLY
1-01-001	GRAUNT
33-10-026	GRAVE
9-03-006	GRAVEL
7-05-007	GRAVELY
1-01-001	GRAVEN
2-02-002	GRAVER
9-06-008	GRAVES
2-02-002	GRAVES'
1-01-001	GRAVESEND
4-03-003	GRAVEST
1-01-001	GRAVESTONE
7-05-006	GRAVEYARD
2-02-002	GRAVEYARDS
2-01-001	GRAVID
3-02-002	GRAVITATION
4-01-002	GRAVITATIONAL
7-04-006	GRAVITY
4-04-004	GRAVY
80-13-053	GRAY
1-01-001	GRAY-BACKS
3-03-003	GRAY-HAIRED
1-01-001	GRAY-LOOKING
1-01-001	GRAY-THATCHED
1-01-001	GRAYBEARD
1-01-001	GRAYBEARDS

Freq	Word	Freq	Word	Freq	Word	Freq	Word
1-01-001	GRAYED	64-15-051	GREW	1-01-001	GROPE	1-01-001	GUARDINO'S
1-01-001	GRAYER	12-06-008	GREY	7-03-006	GROPED	19-07-011	GUARDS
4-02-004	GRAYING	1-01-001	GREY'S	5-04-004	GROPING	3-03-003	GUATEMALA
1-01-001	GRAYSON	1-01-001	GREY-HAIRED	66-11-022	GROSS	1-01-001	GUATEMALAN
1-01-001	GRAZE	1-01-001	GREY-SKIED	1-01-001	GROSS'S	7-02-003	GUBERNATORIAL
2-02-002	GRAZED	1-01-001	GREYHOUND	1-01-001	GROSSE	1-01-001	GUERILLA
1-01-001	GRAZER	1-01-001	GREYING	9-01-001	GROSSLY	2-01-001	GUERIN
4-01-001	GRAZIE	1-01-001	GREYLAG	4-03-004	GROSSMAN	12-05-010	GUERRILLA
3-01-001	GRAZIN	1-01-001	GRIDLEY	2-01-001	GROSVENOR	1-01-001	GUERRILLA-TH'-W ISP
3-03-003	GRAZING	10-07-008	GRIEF	9-04-008	GROTESQUE	17-03-005	GUERRILLAS
1-01-001	GRE	2-02-002	GRIEF-STRICKEN	4-03-004	GROTESQUELY	56-10-044	GUESS
1-01-001	GRE'T	3-01-001	GRIEVANCE	1-01-001	GROTESQUES	15-07-014	GUESSED
9-07-008	GREASE	3-03-003	GRIEVANCES	4-01-001	GROTH	3-03-003	GUESSES
1-01-001	GREASE-REMOVAL	3-03-003	GRIEVING	4-01-001	GROTH'S	8-06-007	GUESSING
2-02-002	GREASED	1-01-001	GRIEVOUS	1-01-001	GROTTOES	39-10-024	GUEST
3-01-001	GREASES	4-03-003	GRIFFIN	186-15-109	GROUND	62-13-036	GUESTS
8-02-002	GREASY	1-01-001	GRIFFIN'S	1-01-001	GROUND-GLASS	2-02-002	GUESTS'
665-15-291	GREAT	1-01-001	GRIFFIN-*BYRD	1-01-001	GROUND-LEVEL	1-01-001	GUEVARA
1-01-001	GREAT'S	17-03-004	GRIFFITH	1-01-001	GROUND-SWELL	1-01-001	GUFFAWS
2-02-002	GREAT-GRANDFATH ER	1-01-001	GRIFFITH'S	1-01-001	GROUND-TRUCK	1-01-001	GUGGENHEIM
1-01-001	GREAT-GRANDMOTH ER	1-01-001	GRIFFITH-*JONES	6-06-006	GROUNDED	1-01-001	GUGLIELMO
1-01-001	GREAT-GRANDSON	3-01-001	GRIGGS	1-01-001	GROUNDER	2-02-002	GUIANA
1-01-001	GREAT-NIECES	2-01-001	GRIGORI	2-02-002	GROUNDING	40-10-030	GUIDANCE
5-01-002	GREATCOAT	3-01-001	GRIGORI'S	1-01-001	GROUNDLESS	36-11-030	GUIDE
1-01-001	GREATCOATED	5-01-001	GRIGORSS	58-14-047	GROUNDS	1-01-001	GUIDE'S
1-01-001	GREATE	1-01-001	GRIGORY	6-01-001	GROUNDWAVE	2-02-002	GUIDEBOOK
188-14-119	GREATER	12-02-003	GRILL	3-03-003	GROUNDWORK	20-09-017	GUIDED
88-13-071	GREATEST	3-01-001	GRILLE	390-15-190	GROUP	1-01-001	GUIDELINES
62-10-054	GREATLY	1-01-001	GRILLE-ROUTE	1-01-001	GROUP'S	8-01-001	GUIDEPOSTS
11-08-011	GREATNESS	2-01-001	GRILLED	5-02-004	GROUPED	1-01-001	GUIDEPOSTS'
4-02-004	GRECIAN	1-01-001	GRILLEWORK	4-02-004	GROUPING	9-06-009	GUIDES
16-04-010	GREECE	2-02-002	GRILLWORK	9-04-005	GROUPINGS	10-09-010	GUIDING
1-01-001	GREECE'S	14-06-014	GRIM	125-12-073	GROUPS	1-01-001	GUIFTES
3-02-002	GREED	3-03-003	GRIMACE	14-05-011	GROVE	1-01-001	GUIGNOL
1-01-001	GREEDILY	2-02-002	GRIMACED	1-01-001	GROVEL	7-03-005	GUILD
5-04-004	GREEDY	1-01-001	GRIMED	1-01-001	GROVELIKE	1-01-001	GUILE
61-09-028	GREEK	1-01-001	GRIMESBY	1-01-001	GROVELING	1-01-001	GUILELESS
1-01-001	GREEK-BORN	11-05-010	GRIMLY	4-01-001	GROVER	1-01-001	GUILFORD
1-01-001	GREEK-SPEAKING	2-02-002	GRIMM	1-01-001	GROVERS	2-01-001	GUILFORD-*MARTIN
5-04-005	GREEKS	1-01-001	GRIMM'S	4-03-003	GROVES	1-01-001	GUILFORD-MARTIN
116-13-077	GREEN	1-01-001	GRIMMER	63-13-050	GROW	1-01-001	GUILLAUME
2-02-002	GREEN'S	1-01-001	GRIMNESS	3-02-002	GROWER	33-10-021	GUILT
2-01-001	GREEN-BROWN	13-08-013	GRIN	1-01-001	GROWERS'	1-01-001	GUILTINESS
1-01-001	GREEN-BUGS	2-02-002	GRIND	108-15-080	GROWING	1-01-001	GUILTLESS
1-01-001	GREEN-SCALED	3-01-001	GRINDERS	1-01-001	GROWING-WAITING	29-12-027	GUILTY
1-01-001	GREEN-TINTED	8-05-005	GRINDING	4-03-004	GROWL	1-01-001	GUIMET
2-01-001	GREENBERG	1-01-001	GRINDINGS	4-02-004	GROWLED	3-03-003	GUINEA
13-04-006	GREENE	1-01-001	GRINDLAY	1-01-001	GROWLING	6-03-006	GUISE
2-01-002	GREENEST	1-01-001	GRINDS	43-14-037	GROWN	1-01-001	GUISES
2-01-001	GREENFIELD	1-01-001	GRINDSTONE	4-03-004	GROWN-UP	19-06-010	GUITAR
2-02-002	GREENHOUSE	30-07-024	GRINNED	3-02-002	GROWNUPS	1-01-001	GUITAR-STRUMMIN G
1-01-001	GREENHOUSES	7-04-007	GRINNING	1-01-001	GROWNUPS'	2-02-002	GUITARIST
2-02-002	GREENING	2-02-002	GRINS	22-09-018	GROWS	3-02-002	GUITARS
2-02-002	GREENISH	2-01-001	GRINSFELDER	155-11-061	GROWTH	1-01-001	GUIZOT
3-03-003	GREENLAND	20-08-017	GRIP	1-01-001	GROWTH-STUNTING	22-09-016	GULF
2-02-002	GREENLEAF	1-01-001	GRIPES	1-01-001	GROWTHS	1-01-001	GULF'S
1-01-001	GREENLY	12-06-010	GRIPPED	2-01-002	GRUB	1-01-001	GULL
1-01-001	GREENNESS	6-04-006	GRIPPING	3-01-001	GRUBB	1-01-001	GULLAH
1-01-001	GREENOCK	9-05-009	GRIPS	2-02-002	GRUBBY	1-01-001	GULLED
5-04-005	GREENS	2-01-001	GRIS	1-01-001	GRUBS	1-01-001	GULLET
1-01-001	GREENSWARD	2-02-002	GRISLY	7-04-006	GRUDGE	1-01-001	GULLEY
1-01-001	GREENTREE	2-02-002	GRIST	3-02-003	GRUDGES	1-01-001	GULLIBILITY
3-01-002	GREENVILLE	1-01-001	GRISTMILL	6-03-005	GRUDGINGLY	2-02-002	GULLIBLE
1-01-001	GREENWARE	1-01-001	GRISTON	2-02-002	GRUESOME	1-01-001	GULLIES
27-07-009	GREENWICH	1-01-001	GRIT	4-03-003	GRUFF	1-01-001	GULLING
1-01-001	GREENWICH-*POTO WOMUT	1-01-001	GRIT-IMPREGNATE D	1-01-001	GRULLER	1-01-001	GULLIVER'S
1-01-001	GREENWOOD	3-02-002	GRITS	7-06-007	GRUMBLE	5-03-003	GULLY
6-02-002	GREER	1-01-001	GRITTY	2-01-002	GRUMBLED	2-02-002	GULP
7-05-005	GREET	1-01-001	GRITTY-EYED	1-01-001	GRUMBLING	3-03-003	GULPED
20-10-018	GREETED	1-01-001	GRIZZLED	1-01-001	GRUNNFEU	1-01-001	GULPS
5-03-004	GREETING	1-01-001	GRIZZLIES'	2-02-002	GRUNT	14-04-007	GUM
6-05-006	GREETINGS	1-01-001	GRIZZLY	9-05-008	GRUNTED	1-01-001	GUM-CHEWING
26-02-002	GREG	1-01-001	GROAN	2-02-002	GRUNTING	1-01-001	GUMMING
10-02-002	GREG'S	3-02-003	GROANED	1-01-001	GRUONDED	2-02-002	GUMMY
4-04-004	GREGARIOUS	1-01-001	GROANING	1-01-001	GRZESIAK	1-01-001	GUMPTION
3-03-003	GREGG	1-01-001	GROAT	12-03-003	GUAM	4-02-003	GUMS
4-01-001	GREGORIO	1-01-001	GROCER	1-01-001	GUANIDINE	118-09-034	GUN
2-01-001	GREGORIUS	2-02-002	GROCER'S	2-01-001	GUAR	1-01-001	GUN'S
4-03-004	GREGORY	2-02-002	GROCERIES	10-08-010	GUARANTEE	1-01-001	GUN-SHOT
1-01-001	GREGORY'S	3-03-003	GROCERS	13-06-011	GUARANTEED	1-01-001	GUN-SLINGER
3-02-002	GRENADE	9-06-009	GROCERY	1-01-001	GUARANTEED-NEUT RAL	1-01-001	GUN-SLINGING
6-05-006	GRENADES	4-01-001	GROGGINS	7-05-007	GUARANTEES	1-01-001	GUNBARREL
2-01-001	GRENIER	1-01-001	GROGGY	1-01-001	GUARANTY	1-01-001	GUNFIGHTER
1-01-001	GRENOBLE	4-02-002	GROIN	48-12-032	GUARD	1-01-001	GUNFIGHTS
1-01-001	GRENVILLE	5-01-001	GROK	4-02-003	GUARD'S	7-04-005	GUNFIRE
1-01-001	GRESHAM	4-01-001	GROKKED	1-01-001	GUARD-ROOM	1-01-001	GUNFLINT
1-01-001	GRET	4-01-001	GROKKING	5-02-005	GUARDED	1-01-001	GUNK
1-01-001	GRETCHEN	5-04-004	GROOM	1-01-001	GUARDEDNESS	3-03-003	GUNMAN
1-01-001	GREV	4-03-004	GROOMED	1-01-001	GUARDHOUSE	4-02-002	GUNMEN
1-01-001	GREVILE	1-01-001	GROOMING	1-01-001	GUARDIA	2-01-001	GUNNAR
14-01-001	GREVILLE	2-02-002	GROOMS	9-05-008	GUARDIAN	1-01-001	GUNNER
4-01-001	GREVILLE'S	1-01-001	GROOMSMEN	4-03-004	GUARDIANS	2-02-002	GUNNERS
1-01-001	GREVOUSELYE	1-01-001	GROOT	9-06-009	GUARDING	1-01-001	GUNNING
1-01-001	GREVYLES	2-02-002	GROOVE	1-01-001	GUARDINI	6-01-001	GUNNY
		1-01-001	GROOVED	3-01-001	GUARDINO		
		3-02-003	GROOVES				

1-01-001	GUNPLAY	1-01-001	HACKETTSTOWN	1-01-001	HALF-OFF	13-02-002	HAN
2-02-002	GUNPOWDER	2-02-002	HACKING	1-01-001	HALF-PAST	1-01-001	HAN'S
42-10-023	GUNS	1-01-001	HACKLES	1-01-001	HALF-REACHED	5-01-001	HANCH
1-01-001	GUNSLINGER	1-01-001	HACKMANN	1-01-001	HALF-RELUCTANT	1-01-001	HANCOCK
1-01-001	GUNTHER	2-01-002	HACKNEYED	1-01-001	HALF-SISTER	431-15-220	HAND
1-01-001	GURGLE	1-01-001	HACKSAW	1-01-001	HALF-SMILE	1-01-001	HAND-BLOWER
2-01-001	GURION	1-01-001	HACKSTAFF	1-01-001	HALF-STANDARD	1-01-001	HAND-COVERED
1-01-001	GURKHAS	1-01-001	HACKWORK	1-01-001	HALF-STARVED	1-01-001	HAND-CRAFTED
1-01-001	GURLA	5133-15-422	HAD	1-01-001	HALF-STRAIGHTENED	1-01-001	HAND-FILED
3-01-001	GURSEL	1-01-001	HADD			1-01-001	HAND-HEWN
1-01-001	GURU	2-01-001	HADDIX	1-01-001	HALF-SWAMPED	1-01-001	HAND-HOLDING
3-02-003	GUS	1-01-001	HADDOCK	1-01-001	HALF-SWIMMING	2-02-002	HAND-IN-GLOVE
1-01-001	GUSH	99-07-057	HADN'T	2-01-001	HALF-TIME	1-01-001	HAND-LEVEL
5-04-005	GUSHED	1-01-001	HADRIAN	1-01-001	HALF-TRANSPARENT	1-01-001	HAND-MADE
1-01-001	GUSHER	1-01-001	HAEC			1-01-001	HAND-ME-DOWN
1-01-001	GUSSETS	1-01-001	HAESTIER	1-01-001	HALF-TURNED	1-01-001	HAND-PAINTED
2-02-002	GUST	2-01-001	HAFIZ	1-01-001	HALF-UNDERSTOOD	1-01-001	HAND-SCREENED
1-01-001	GUSTAF	1-01-001	HAFLIS	4-04-004	HALF-WAY	2-02-002	HAND-TO-HAND
1-01-001	GUSTAV	3-02-002	HAFTA	1-01-001	HALF-WITTED	2-02-002	HAND-WOVEN
1-01-001	GUSTAVE	1-01-001	HAGERTY'S	1-01-001	HALF-YEAR	1-01-001	HAND-WRITTEN
1-01-001	GUSTAVUS	2-02-002	HAGGARD	10-01-002	HALFBACK	3-03-003	HANDBAG
2-02-002	GUSTO	1-01-001	HAGGARDLY	1-01-001	HALFBACKS	2-02-002	HANDBOOK
3-02-003	GUSTS	1-01-001	HAGGLE	1-01-001	HALFHEARTED	2-02-002	HANDBOOKS
2-02-002	GUSTY	1-01-001	HAGGLING	1-01-001	HALFTIME	3-03-003	HANDCLASP
1-01-001	GUT	1-01-001	HAGNER	18-09-016	HALFWAY	2-02-002	HANDCUFFS
1-01-001	GUT-FLATTENING	9-01-001	HAGUE	1-01-001	HALFWAYS	3-01-001	HANDE
2-01-001	GUTE	2-01-001	HAIJAC	1-01-001	HALIBURTON	38-10-030	HANDED
1-01-001	GUTHMAN	10-06-009	HAIL	1-01-001	HALIDES	1-01-001	HANDER
1-01-001	GUTHRIE	7-05-007	HAILED	1-01-001	HALKETT	13-08-013	HANDFUL
1-01-001	GUTHRIE'S	1-01-001	HAILS	152-14-074	HALL	1-01-001	HANDFULS
9-04-007	GUTS	1-01-001	HAILSTORM	2-02-002	HALL'S	3-01-001	HANDGUN
1-01-001	GUTTED	1-01-001	HAINT	1-01-001	HALL-*MILLS	2-01-001	HANDGUNS
1-01-001	GUTTER	148-13-083	HAIR	1-01-001	HALL-MARK	1-01-001	HANDHOLD
1-01-001	GUTTERED	1-01-001	HAIR-RAISING	3-02-002	HALLECK	6-05-006	HANDICAP
2-02-002	GUTTERS	1-01-001	HAIR-TRIGGER	1-01-001	HALLELUJAH	13-03-005	HANDICAPPED
1-01-001	GUTTMAN-TYPE	2-01-002	HAIRCUT	1-01-001	HALLELUJAHS	1-01-001	HANDICAPS
3-03-003	GUTTURAL	1-01-001	HAIRCUTS	3-02-003	HALLMARK	1-01-001	HANDICRAFTS
1-01-001	GUTZON	1-01-001	HAIRDOS	2-02-002	HALLMARKS	1-01-001	HANDICRAFTSMAN
51-11-029	GUY	1-01-001	HAIRIER	2-02-002	HALLOWED	1-01-001	HANDIER
3-02-003	GUY'S	1-01-001	HAIRLESS	1-01-001	HALLOWEEN	1-01-001	HANDIEST
20-08-013	GUYS	1-01-001	HAIRPIN	1-01-001	HALLOWELL'S	6-05-006	HANDING
1-01-001	GUZZLE	12-06-009	HAIRS	4-03-004	HALLS	1-01-001	HANDIWORK
1-01-001	GUZZLED	1-01-001	HAIRSHIRT	1-01-001	HALLUCINATING	9-04-006	HANDKERCHIEF
1-01-001	GWEN	1-01-001	HAIRTONIC	1-01-001	HALLUCINATIONS	1-01-001	HANDKERCHIEFS
2-02-002	GYM	5-04-005	HAIRY	7-04-007	HALLWAY	53-13-040	HANDLE
1-01-001	GYMNASIUM	1-01-001	HAITIAN	1-01-001	HALLWAYS	1-01-001	HANDLEBARS
1-01-001	GYMNAST	1-01-001	HAJIME	1-01-001	HALMA	26-11-023	HANDLED
4-01-001	GYMNASTIC	28-04-006	HAL	2-01-001	HALO	6-01-001	HANDLER
11-01-001	GYMNASTICS	1-01-001	HAL'S	1-01-001	HALOGENS	2-01-001	HANDLERS
4-01-001	GYMNASTS	1-01-001	HALCYON	1-01-001	HALOS	1-01-001	HANDLERS'
2-01-001	GYMS	1-01-001	HALDA	2-02-002	HALS	9-05-009	HANDLES
1-01-001	GYNECOLOGICAL	2-02-002	HALE	10-07-010	HALT	1-01-001	HANDLESS
1-01-001	GYNECOLOGIST	1-01-001	HALE'S	12-05-010	HALTED	16-01-001	HANDLEY
2-01-001	GYNECOLOGISTS	275-15-168	HALF	1-01-001	HALTER	38-08-026	HANDLING
6-01-001	GYP	1-01-001	HALF-A-DOZEN	2-02-002	HALTING	2-02-002	HANDMADE
1-01-001	GYP'LL	1-01-001	HALF-ACCEPTANCE	2-02-002	HALTINGLY	1-01-001	HANDMAIDEN
1-01-001	GYPSIES	1-01-001	HALF-ACRE	1-01-001	HALTS	289-15-149	HANDS
2-01-001	GYPSUM	1-01-001	HALF-ALOUD	1-01-001	HALVAH	1-01-001	HANDS-OFF
4-04-004	GYPSY	1-01-001	HALF-BLOOD	2-02-002	HALVES	1-01-001	HANDS-OFF-ALL-SWEETS
1-01-001	GYRATION	1-01-001	HALF-BOTTLES	19-03-008	HAM		
1-01-001	GYRATIONS	5-01-002	HALF-BREED	1-01-001	HAM-LIKE	1-01-001	HANDSHAKE
26-01-001	GYRO	1-01-001	HALF-BROTHER	1-01-001	HAM-RADIO	40-09-029	HANDSOME
1-01-001	GYRO-PLATFORM-SERVO	1-01-001	HALF-BROTHERS	1-01-001	HAMBRIC	1-01-001	HANDSOMELY
6-01-001	GYRO-STABILIZED	2-01-002	HALF-CENTURY	6-04-004	HAMBURGER	2-02-002	HANDSOMER
2-01-001	GYROCOMPASS	1-01-001	HALF-CITY	4-02-002	HAMBURGERS	1-01-001	HANDSOMEST
5-01-001	GYROS	1-01-001	HALF-CLAD	1-01-001	HAMEY	3-01-001	HANDSPIKES
1-01-001	GYROSCOPES	3-03-003	HALF-CLOSED	17-04-008	HAMILTON	1-01-001	HANDSTAND
74-08-047	H	1-01-001	HALF-COCKED	3-01-001	HAMILTON'S	3-01-001	HANDSTANDS
1-01-001	H)	2-01-002	HALF-CONSCIOUS	1-01-001	HAMILTON-ORIENTED	5-05-005	HANDWRITING
1-01-001	H**.*L	2-01-002	HALF-CRAZY			13-08-012	HANDY
2-01-001	H**.*M	1-01-001	HALF-CROCKED	1-01-001	HAMILTONIAN	2-01-001	HANDYMAN
3-02-002	H**.*M**.*S	1-01-001	HALF-DARKNESS	1-01-001	HAMILTONIANS	1-01-001	HANDYMAN-CARPENTER
1-01-001	H**.*P**.*R	1-01-001	HALF-DIGESTED	7-03-005	HAMLET		
1-01-001	H**.*W	3-03-003	HALF-DOZEN	7-02-002	HAMM	1-01-001	HANDYMEN
1-01-001	H'ALL	1-01-001	HALF-DRESSED	1-01-001	HAMM'S	19-01-001	HANEY
2-01-001	HA	2-02-002	HALF-DRUNK	1-01-001	HAMMARSKJO**DLD	2-01-001	HANEY'S
1-01-001	HAAEK	1-01-001	HALF-EDUCATED	14-03-006	HAMMARSKJOLD'S	16-01-001	HANFORD
1-01-001	HAASE	1-01-001	HALF-EXPRESSED	5-02-004	HAMMARSKJOLD	26-11-024	HANG
1-01-001	HABE	2-01-002	HALF-FILLED	9-05-006	HAMMER	1-01-001	HANGAR
1-01-001	HABERDASHERIES	9-05-006	HALF-FORGOTTEN	3-02-002	HAMMERED	1-01-001	HANGARS
1-01-001	HABERDASHERY	3-02-002	HALF-GAINER	1-01-001	HAMMERLESS	7-04-005	HANGED
1-01-001	HABIB	1-01-001	HALF-GOURD	1-01-001	HAMMERSKJOLD	1-01-001	HANGERS
23-09-020	HABIT	2-02-002	HALF-GROWN	2-02-002	HAMMETT	1-01-001	HANGERS-ON
2-02-002	HABITABLE	2-01-001	HALF-HEARTED	2-01-001	HAMMETT'S	2-02-002	HANGIN
4-01-001	HABITANTS	1-01-001	HALF-HEARTEDLY	1-01-001	HAMMING	28-09-024	HANGING
14-04-004	HABITAT	8-06-007	HALF-HOUR	5-01-001	HAMMOCK	1-01-001	HANGMAN
21-08-018	HABITS	3-01-001	HALF-INCH	2-01-002	HAMMOND	1-01-001	HANGMAN'S
5-05-005	HABITUAL	2-01-002	HALF-INTENSITY	1-01-001	HAMMONS	1-01-001	HANGOUTS
2-02-002	HABITUALLY	5-04-004	HALF-LIFE	5-04-004	HAMPER	2-01-001	HANGOVER
1-01-001	HABLA	1-01-001	HALF-LIGHT	3-03-003	HAMPERED	1-01-001	HANGOVERS
1-01-001	HABLE	9-01-001	HALF-MAN	1-01-001	HAMPERS	4-03-004	HANGS
1-01-001	HABSBURG	1-01-001	HALF-MELTED	11-06-009	HAMPSHIRE	17-05-007	HANK
3-02-003	HACK	7-03-005	HALF-MILE	2-02-002	HAMPTON	1-01-001	HANKERED
2-02-002	HACKED	1-01-001	HALF-MILLION	1-01-001	HAMPTON'S	1-01-001	HANKERIN
1-01-001	HACKERS	1-01-001	HALF-MINCING	8-01-001	HAMRICK	2-01-001	HANNAH
1-01-001	HACKETT	1-01-001	HALF-MOONS	2-01-001	HAMRICK'S	1-01-001	HANNIBAL
		1-01-001	HALF-MURMURED	1-01-001	HAMS	66-04-004	HANOVER

Code	Word	Code	Word	Code	Word	Code	Word
1-01-001	HANOVER'S	1-01-001	HARE	3-03-003	HASTEN	1-01-001	HAYWARD
1-01-001	HANOVER-*BERTIE	1-01-001	HARELIPS	9-06-008	HASTENED	1-01-001	HAYWOOD
1-01-001	HANOVER-*CEYWAY	2-02-002	HAREM	2-02-002	HASTENING	12-07-011	HAZARD
1-01-001	HANOVER-*CHALID ALE	1-01-001	HARFORD	15-07-013	HASTILY	5-03-004	HAZARDOUS
1-01-001	HANOVER-*JUSTIT IA	1-01-001	HARGETT	1-01-001	HASTILY-SUMMONE D	10-07-008	HAZARDS
		3-01-002	HARK			7-04-005	HAZE
1-01-001	HANOVER-*MAURI	1-01-001	HARLAN-*HICKORY	1-01-001	HASTINGS	2-02-002	HAZEL
1-01-001	HANOVER-*LUCY	1-01-001	HARLAN-*MARCIA	5-05-005	HASTY	1-01-001	HAZELNUTS
1-01-001	HANOVER-*MAURI	14-02-003	HARLEM	56-11-037	HAT	1-01-001	HAZES
1-01-001	HANOVER-*MISTY	1-01-001	HARLEM'S	5-04-004	HATCH	2-02-002	HAZLITT
1-01-001	HANOVER-*PEBBLE	1-01-001	HARLEY'S	2-02-002	HATCHED	5-03-005	HAZY
1-01-001	HANOVER-*PRECIO US	1-01-001	HARLINGEN	4-02-003	HATCHET	9543-15-428	HE
		25-13-024	HARM	1-01-001	HATCHET-FACED	98-07-042	HE'D
1-01-001	HANOVER-*SALLY	2-02-002	HARMED	6-05-006	HATCHING	31-09-020	HE'LL
1-01-001	HANOVER-*SUPERM ARKET	4-02-004	HARMFUL	2-01-001	HATCHWAY	125-12-069	HE'S
		5-04-005	HARMLESS	42-10-029	HATE	424-15-190	HEAD
7-02-003	HANOVERIAN	1-01-001	HARMLESSLY	28-09-022	HATED	1-01-001	HEAD-AND-SHOULD ERS
44-05-008	HANS	1-01-001	HARMON	3-02-003	HATEFUL		
10-02-002	HANSEN	2-02-002	HARMONIC	4-02-004	HATES	1-01-001	HEAD-COLD
2-02-002	HANSEN'S	7-05-005	HARMONIES	2-01-001	HATFIELD	1-01-001	HEAD-IN-THE-CLO UDS
1-01-001	HANSOM	5-03-005	HARMONIOUS	3-03-003	HATH		
1-01-001	HANUKKAH	1-01-001	HARMONIOUSLY	2-02-002	HATHAWAY	2-02-002	HEAD-ON
1-01-001	HAP	1-01-001	HARMONIZATION	2-02-002	HATING	2-02-002	HEAD-TOSSING
2-01-001	HAPGOOD	33-09-017	HARMONY	1-01-001	HATLESS	5-04-005	HEADACHE
2-02-002	HAPHAZARD	1-01-001	HARMONY'S	20-08-017	HATRED	6-03-005	HEADACHES
1-01-001	HAPHAZARDLY	1-01-001	HARNACK	14-08-013	HATS	1-01-001	HEADBOARD
2-01-002	HAPLESS	10-04-007	HARNESS	1-01-001	HATTED	1-01-001	HEADDRESS
63-15-049	HAPPEN	2-02-002	HARNESSED	1-01-001	HATTERAS	1-01-001	HEADE
149-15-102	HAPPENED	1-01-001	HARNESSING	59-13-042	HATTERS	59-13-042	HEADED
28-10-023	HAPPENING	1-01-001	HARNICK	1-01-001	HATTES	1-01-001	HEADER
5-04-005	HAPPENINGS	32-06-012	HAROLD	1-01-001	HATTIE	32-08-015	HEADING
40-12-037	HAPPENS	1-01-001	HARP	1-01-001	HATTIESBURG	1-01-001	HEADINGS
2-02-002	HAPPENSTANCE	2-01-001	HARPER	1-01-001	HAUGHTILY	1-01-001	HEADLAND
11-09-011	HAPPIER	5-02-002	HARPER'S	1-01-001	HAUGHTINESS	1-01-001	HEADLANDS
3-03-003	HAPPIEST	3-02-002	HARPERS	1-01-001	HAUGHTON'S	3-02-003	HEADLESS
20-10-019	HAPPILY	3-02-002	HARPING	2-02-002	HAUGHTY	8-04-007	HEADLIGHTS
23-06-014	HAPPINESS	1-01-001	HARPSICHORD	5-04-005	HAUL	4-03-004	HEADLINE
98-14-065	HAPPY	1-01-001	HARPSICHORDIST	1-01-001	HAULAGE	7-05-006	HEADLINES
1-01-001	HAQVIN	1-01-001	HARPY	9-06-008	HAULED	1-01-001	HEADLINESE
1-01-001	HARANGUED	1-01-001	HARRASSMENT	4-03-004	HAULING	1-01-001	HEADLINING
2-02-002	HARANGUING	1-01-001	HARRIED	2-02-002	HAULS	3-03-003	HEADMASTER
1-01-001	HARASS	9-04-005	HARRIET	1-01-001	HAUMD	1-01-001	HEADQUARTER
6-06-006	HARASSED	1-01-001	HARRIET'S	1-01-001	HAUMD'S	65-12-040	HEADQUARTERS
2-02-002	HARASSING	2-02-002	HARRIMAN	5-04-005	HAUNCHES	1-01-001	HEADROOM
2-01-001	HARBERT	7-01-001	HARRINGTON	4-03-004	HAUNT	43-14-034	HEADS
37-11-022	HARBOR	1-01-001	HARRINGTON'S	8-05-008	HAUNTED	1-01-001	HEADSMAN
1-01-001	HARBOR'S	28-09-017	HARRIS	8-05-007	HAUNTING	1-01-001	HEADSTAND
3-02-003	HARBORED	1-01-001	HARRIS'	2-02-002	HAUNTS	1-01-001	HEADSTANDS
1-01-001	HARBORING	2-02-002	HARRIS'S	1-01-001	HAUPTS'	1-01-001	HEADSTONES
4-04-004	HARBORS	2-02-002	HARRISON	1-01-001	HAUSMAN	2-01-001	HEADWALLS
2-01-001	HARBURG	1-01-001	HARRISON'S	1-01-001	HAUSMAN'S	4-03-003	HEADWATERS
1-01-001	HARBURG'S	1-01-001	HARRITY	2-02-002	HAUTE	2-02-002	HEADY
6-02-002	HARCOURT	1-01-001	HARRO	15-03-005	HAVANA	2-02-002	HEAL
202-15-140	HARD	2-01-001	HARROW	3941-15-498	HAVE	6-04-004	HEALED
1-01-001	HARD'S	1-01-001	HARROWED	11-05-010	HAVEN	2-02-002	HEALER
1-01-001	HARD-*HEARTED	2-02-002	HARROWING	38-08-027	HAVEN'T	6-04-005	HEALING
1-01-001	HARD-BITTEN	1-01-001	HARROWS	1-01-001	HAVENS	105-12-066	HEALTH
2-02-002	HARD-BOILED	1-01-001	HARRUMPHING	2-01-001	HAVERFIELD	3-02-003	HEALTHFUL
1-01-001	HARD-COME-BY	35-07-017	HARRY	2-02-002	HAVERHILL	2-01-002	HEALTHIER
1-01-001	HARD-EARNED	1-01-001	HARRY'S	1-01-001	HAVILLAND	1-01-001	HEALTHIEST
2-02-002	HARD-FOUGHT	12-07-012	HARSH	279-15-190	HAVING	2-02-002	HEALTHILY
1-01-001	HARD-HIT	1-01-001	HARSHENED	3-01-001	HAVISHAM	33-09-021	HEALTHY
2-01-001	HARD-LIQUOR	1-01-001	HARSHER	1-01-001	HAVISHAM'S	14-07-012	HEAP
1-01-001	HARD-NOSED	5-03-005	HARSHLY	3-03-003	HAVOC	4-03-004	HEAPED
1-01-001	HARD-SELL	1-01-001	HARSHNESS	1-01-001	HAW	1-01-001	HEAPS
10-01-001	HARD-SURFACE	13-04-005	HART	16-03-005	HAWAII	153-14-110	HEAR
1-01-001	HARD-TO-GET	2-01-001	HARTES	6-03-003	HAWAIIAN	247-15-147	HEARD
1-01-001	HARD-TO-PLEASE	3-02-003	HARTFORD	1-01-001	HAWAIIAN-*AMERI CANS	2-01-001	HEARE
1-01-001	HARD-WON	1-01-001	HARTLEY			2-02-002	HEARER
1-01-001	HARDBAKE	1-01-001	HARTLIB	1-01-001	HAWING	2-02-002	HEARERS
1-01-001	HARDBOARD	5-02-002	HARTMAN	14-04-005	HAWK	1-01-001	HEAREST
2-01-001	HARDBOILED	1-01-001	HARTSELLE	1-01-001	HAWK-FACED	76-12-041	HEARING
1-01-001	HARDEE'S	5-01-001	HARTSFIELD	1-01-001	HAWKED	1-01-001	HEARING-AID
1-01-001	HARDEN	5-01-001	HARTWEGER	1-01-001	HAWKER	8-04-006	HEARINGS
12-05-008	HARDENED	1-01-001	HARTWELL	1-01-001	HAWKERS	1-01-001	HEARN
1-01-001	HARDENER	1-01-001	HARUO	2-02-002	HAWKINS	7-06-007	HEARS
23-10-021	HARDER	34-08-017	HARVARD	1-01-001	HAWKINS'	2-02-002	HEARSAY
11-07-010	HARDEST	1-01-001	HARVARD'S	1-01-001	HAWKINSES	1-01-001	HEARSE
2-02-002	HARDING	1-01-001	HARVE	1-01-001	HAWKS	48-01-002	HEARST
1-01-001	HARDINGS	12-07-011	HARVEST	10-01-001	HAWKSLEY	6-01-002	HEARST'S
106-14-089	HARDLY	1-01-001	HARVESTED	1-01-001	HAWKSWORTH	173-15-098	HEART
2-02-002	HARDNESS	3-02-002	HARVESTER	6-04-006	HAWTHORNE	1-01-001	HEART'S
1-01-001	HARDSCRABBLE	3-02-003	HARVESTING	19-05-011	HAY	1-01-001	HEART-MEASURING
1-01-001	HARDSHELL	2-02-002	HARVESTS	2-01-001	HAY-SHAKERS	1-01-001	HEART-STOPPING
9-05-008	HARDSHIP	18-04-006	HARVEY	1-01-001	HAY-WAGON	1-01-001	HEART-WARMING
5-03-005	HARDSHIPS	1-01-001	HARVEYS	2-02-002	HAYDN	4-02-002	HEARTBEAT
3-01-001	HARDTACK	3-01-001	HARVIE	1-01-001	HAYDN'S	1-01-001	HEARTBREAK
1-01-001	HARDTACK-BOX	2439-15-408	HAS	1-01-001	HAYDON	2-02-002	HEARTBREAKING
11-08-010	HARDWARE	1-01-001	HASH	1-01-001	HAYEK	4-04-004	HEARTENING
3-02-002	HARDWICK	1-01-001	HASHER	5-02-004	HAYES	1-01-001	HEARTFELT
1-01-001	HARDWICKE	2-01-001	HASKELL	1-01-001	HAYFIELDS	4-02-003	HEARTH
2-01-001	HARDWICKE-*ETTE R	1-01-001	HASKINS	1-01-001	HAYING	1-01-001	HEARTIEST
		20-11-014	HASN'T	1-01-001	HAYNES	9-07-009	HEARTILY
1-01-001	HARDWOODS	1-01-001	HASPS	6-02-003	HAYS	1-01-001	HEARTLESS
1-01-001	HARDWORKING	2-01-001	HASSELTINE	1-01-001	HAYSTACK	23-10-020	HEARTS
42-07-009	HARDY	1-01-001	HAST	1-01-001	HAYSTACKS	4-04-004	HEARTY
15-01-001	HARDY'S	9-06-007	HASTE	1-01-001	HAYTER	97-13-045	HEAT

1-01-001 HEAT'S	1-01-001 HEINZE	2-01-001 HENRIETTA'S	1-01-001 HERZFELD		
1-01-001 HEAT-ABSORBING	1-01-001 HEINZES	1-01-001 HENRIK	1-01-001 HERZOG		
1-01-001 HEAT-DENATURED	7-05-007 HEIR	83-10-052 HENRY	6-01-001 HESIOMETER		
1-01-001 HEAT-PROCESSING	1-01-001 HEIRESS	2-02-002 HENRY'S	1-01-001 HESITANCE		
16-08-015 HEATED	2-02-002 HEIRS	4-03-003 HENS	2-02-002 HESITANCY		
1-01-001 HEATEDLY	7-01-001 HEISER	1-01-001 HENS'	3-02-003 HESITANT		
14-07-009 HEATER	1-01-001 HEISTED	1-01-001 HEOROT	2-02-002 HESITANTLY		
1-01-001 HEATERS	1-01-001 HEITSCHMIDT	3-01-001 HEPATITIS	10-06-010 HESITATE		
2-02-002 HEATHEN	1-01-001 HEL	1-01-001 HEPHZIBAH	21-08-019 HESITATED		
1-01-001 HEATHENISH	264-15-168 HELD	1-01-001 HEPKER	1-01-001 HESITATES		
2-02-002 HEATHER	13-04-010 HELEN	1-01-001 HEPTACHLOR	1-01-001 HESITATING		
24-06-009 HEATING	1-01-001 HELENA	3037-15-253 HER	1-01-001 HESITATINGLY		
1-01-001 HEATWOLE	1-01-001 HELENE	1-01-001 HERACLITUS	7-03-006 HESITATION		
2-02-002 HEAVE	1-01-001 HELICOPTER	11-07-008 HERALD	11-01-001 HESPERUS		
4-04-004 HEAVED	1-01-001 HELICOPTER-BORN E	1-01-001 HERALD-*EXAMINE R	1-01-001 HESPERUS'		
43-12-033 HEAVEN	1-01-001 HELIOCENTRIC	2-02-002 HERALDED	1-01-001 HESS		
1-01-001 HEAVEN'S	19-02-002 HELION	7-03-004 HERB	2-01-001 HESSIAN		
9-05-006 HEAVENLY	2-01-001 HELION'S	3-01-001 HERBERET	3-02-003 HESSIANS		
9-06-007 HEAVENS	2-01-001 HELIOPOLIS	1-01-001 HERBERET'S	3-01-001 HESTER		
1-01-001 HEAVENWARD	1-01-001 HELIOTROPE	12-07-009 HERBERT	1-01-001 HETEROGAMOUS		
2-01-001 HEAVERS	15-03-003 HELIUM	1-01-001 HERBLOCK	4-02-003 HETEROGENEOUS		
1-01-001 HEAVES	2-01-001 HELIUM-4	1-01-001 HERBS	2-01-001 HETEROZYGOUS		
15-08-013 HEAVIER	95-11-053 HELL	1-01-001 HERCULE	12-01-001 HETMAN		
2-02-002 HEAVIEST	3-02-003 HELL'S	1-01-001 HERCULEAN	8-01-001 HETMAN'S		
60-13-055 HEAVILY	1-01-001 HELL-BOUND	3-03-003 HERCULES	5-01-001 HETTIE		
1-01-001 HEAVILY-UPHOLST ERED	1-01-001 HELL-FIRE	22-04-009 HERD	2-01-001 HETTY		
2-02-002 HEAVINESS	1-01-001 HELL-FOR-LEATHE R	1-01-001 HERD-OWNER	1-01-001 HETTY'S		
4-04-004 HEAVING	1-01-001 HELL-RAISING	2-02-002 HERDED	1-01-001 HEUSEN		
110-13-086 HEAVY	6-02-003 HELLENIC	3-01-001 HERDIN	1-01-001 HEUTE		
1-01-001 HEAVY-ARMED	2-01-002 HELLFIRE	1-01-001 HERDING	2-01-001 HEUVELMANS		
1-01-001 HEAVY-COATED	10-08-010 HELLO	6-05-005 HERDS	1-01-001 HEV		
1-01-001 HEAVY-DUTY	1-01-001 HELLS	750-15-315 HERE	3-01-001 HEVIN		
2-01-001 HEAVY-ELECTRICA L-GOODS	1-01-001 HELLUVA	11-06-010 HERE'S	1-01-001 HEWED		
1-01-001 HEAVY-FACED	4-02-004 HELM	2-02-002 HEREABOUTS	1-01-001 HEWETT		
1-01-001 HEAVY-FRAMED	1-01-001 HELMET	4-02-003 HEREAFTER	1-01-001 HEWLETT-*WOODME RE		
1-01-001 HEAVY-HANDED	2-02-002 HELMETS	8-03-004 HEREBY	1-01-001 HEWLITT		
1-01-001 HEAVY-WEIGHT	1-01-001 HELMSMAN	2-01-001 HEREDITARY	2-02-002 HEX		
7-01-001 HEBEPHRENIC	1-01-001 HELMUT	3-03-003 HEREDITY	1-01-001 HEXAGON		
1-01-001 HEBRAIC	311-15-184 HELP	1-01-001 HEREFORD	2-01-002 HEXAGONAL		
10-05-007 HEBREW	66-14-054 HELPED	3-03-003 HEREIN	1-01-001 HEXAMETAPHOSPHA TE		
1-01-001 HEBREWS	6-03-004 HELPER	5-02-003 HEREINAFTER	3-01-002 HEXAMETER		
1-01-001 HECATOMB	2-01-001 HELPERS	2-01-002 HERESY	1-01-001 HEXEN		
1-01-001 HECK	29-11-026 HELPFUL	1-01-001 HERETIC	15-07-013 HEY		
1-01-001 HECKMAN	8-05-008 HELPFULLY	1-01-001 HERETICS	3-03-003 HEYDAY		
3-03-003 HECTIC	1-01-001 HELPFULNESS	8-05-008 HERETOFORE	3-02-002 HEYDRICH		
1-01-001 HECTOR	44-11-032 HELPING	1-01-001 HERETOFORE-ACCE PTED	5-04-004 HEYWOOD		
1-01-001 HECTOR'S	21-10-015 HELPLESS	7-01-001 HEREUNTO	7-01-001 HEZ		
1-01-001 HEDDA	3-03-003 HELPLESSLY	2-01-002 HEREWITH	6-05-006 HI		
2-01-001 HEDGE	5-03-003 HELPLESSNESS	5-01-001 HERFORD	1-01-001 HI-FI		
1-01-001 HEDGED	1-01-001 HELPMATE	1-01-001 HERFORD'S	1-01-001 HI-GRADERS		
2-02-002 HEDGES	31-10-024 HELPS	1-01-001 HERGESHEIMER	2-02-002 HIAWATHA		
2-01-001 HEDISON	1-01-001 HELSQ'IYOKOM	21-09-014 HERITAGE	5-01-001 HIBACHI		
1-01-001 HEDONISM	8-01-001 HELVA	1-01-001 HERITAGES	2-01-001 HIBERNATE		
2-01-001 HEDONISTIC	10-07-007 HELVA'S	10-07-007 HERMAN	1-01-001 HICCUPS		
7-02-002 HEE	4-03-004 HEM	1-01-001 HERMAN'S	1-01-001 HICK		
8-06-008 HEED	1-01-001 HEMENWAY'S	1-01-001 HERMANOVSKI	1-01-001 HICK-SELF		
1-01-001 HEEDED	2-01-002 HEMINGWAY	1-01-001 HERMENEUTICS	1-01-001 HICKOK		
2-02-002 HEEDLESS	1-01-001 HEMINGWAY'S	1-01-001 HERMETIC	6-03-003 HICKORY		
9-07-008 HEEL	14-05-008 HEMISPHERE	6-01-001 HERNANDEZ	1-01-001 HICKS		
1-01-001 HEEL-	1-01-001 HEMISPHERE'S	52-13-031 HERO	6-03-004 HID		
1-01-001 HEEL-*BERYL	1-01-001 HEMISPHERICAL	3-03-003 HERO'S	20-07-016 HIDDEN		
1-01-001 HEEL-*BETTY	1-01-001 HEMLOCKS	1-01-001 HERO-WORSHIP	22-08-020 HIDE		
1-01-001 HEEL-*HOLIDAY	3-02-003 HEMMED	1-01-001 HERO-WORSHIPPER S	2-01-001 HIDE-OUT		
1-01-001 HEEL-*KAOLA	1-01-001 HEMMING	17-07-016 HEROES	1-01-001 HIDEAWAY		
1-01-001 HEEL-*LOTUS	4-01-001 HEMOGLOBIN	21-07-017 HEROIC	11-06-010 HIDEOUS		
2-01-001 HEEL-*MIRACLE	1-01-001 HEMOLYTIC	1-01-001 HEROICALLY	3-03-003 HIDEOUSLY		
1-01-001 HEEL-*TERKA	5-03-003 HEMORRHAGE	2-02-002 HEROICS	1-01-001 HIDEOUT		
1-01-001 HEELERS	1-01-001 HEMORRHAGES	2-02-002 HEROIN	5-05-005 HIDES		
23-09-016 HEELS	2-01-001 HEMORRHAGING	5-02-003 HEROINE	17-07-011 HIDING		
1-01-001 HEENAN	2-02-002 HEMORRHOIDS	3-03-003 HEROISM	1-01-001 HIERARCHIES		
1-01-001 HEFFER	3-03-003 HEMOSIDERIN	4-01-001 HEROLD	9-06-009 HIERARCHY		
1-01-001 HEFFERNAN	4-01-001 HEMPEL	2-01-001 HERON	2-01-001 HIERONYMUS		
1-01-001 HEFTED	1-01-001 HEMPHILL	1-01-001 HERONS	1-01-001 HIFALUTIN		
1-01-001 HEFTY	2-01-001 HEMPSTEAD	2-01-001 HERPETOLOGIST	497-15-250 HIGH		
2-02-002 HEGEL	5-01-001 HEMUS	2-01-001 HERPETOLOGISTS	1-01-001 HIGH'S		
1-01-001 HEGEL'S	22-06-008 HEN	1-01-001 HERPETOLOGY	1-01-001 HIGH-		
1-01-001 HEGELIAN	1-01-001 HEN'S	10-03-003 HERR	1-01-001 HIGH-BACKED		
3-01-001 HEGEMONY	58-08-039 HENCE	2-01-002 HERRICK	2-02-002 HIGH-CEILINGED		
1-01-001 HEIDEGGER	4-03-004 HENCEFORTH	1-01-001 HERRIDGE	1-01-001 HIGH-CLASS		
2-01-001 HEIDEGGER'S	1-01-001 HENCHMAN	1-01-001 HERRIN-*MURPHYS BORO-*WEST	1-01-001 HIGH-COST		
1-01-001 HEIDELBERG	1-01-001 HENCHMEN	2-02-002 HERRING	1-01-001 HIGH-CURRENT		
1-01-001 HEIDEMAN	3-01-001 HENDERSON	1-01-001 HERRINGBONE	2-02-002 HIGH-DENSITY		
6-01-001 HEIDENSTAM	3-01-001 HENDL	1-01-001 HERRINGTON	1-01-001 HIGH-END		
3-01-001 HEIDENSTAM'S	2-01-001 HENDRICKS	1-01-001 HERRMANN	4-02-002 HIGH-ENERGY		
1-01-001 HEIGH-HO	1-01-001 HENDRICKS'	1-01-001 HERRY	4-01-001 HIGH-GAIN		
35-13-028 HEIGHT	1-01-001 HENDRIK	1-01-001 HERRY'S	1-01-001 HIGH-INTEREST		
1-01-001 HEIGHT-TO-DIAME TER	3-01-001 HENDRY	16-07-012 HERS	1-01-001 HIGH-LEGGED		
1-01-001 HEIGHTEN	1-01-001 HENG-*SHAN	125-14-069 HERSELF	4-04-004 HIGH-LEVEL		
6-05-006 HEIGHTENED	9-01-001 HENGESBACH	1-01-001 HERSEY	1-01-001 HIGH-MINDED		
2-02-002 HEIGHTENING	1-01-001 HENH	1-01-001 HERSHEL	7-06-007 HIGH-PITCHED		
23-09-014 HEIGHTS	2-01-001 HENLEY'S	1-01-001 HERSHEY'S	1-01-001 HIGH-POSITIVE		
2-01-001 HEILMAN	1-01-001 HENPECKED	3-01-001 HERTER	1-01-001 HIGH-POWER		
1-01-001 HEINE	16-05-005 HENRI	1-01-001 HERTZ	2-02-002 HIGH-POWERED		
2-01-001 HEINKEL	2-01-001 HENRI'S		5-05-005 HIGH-PRICED		
	41-02-002 HENRIETTA		2-02-002 HIGH-PROTEIN		

E

R

Freq	Term
2-01-001	HIGH-QUALITY
2-01-001	HIGH-REP
1-01-001	HIGH-RESOLUTION
1-01-001	HIGH-SALARIED
5-05-005	HIGH-SCHOOL
2-01-001	HIGH-SET
2-02-002	HIGH-SOUNDING
5-05-005	HIGH-SPEED
3-02-002	HIGH-SPIRITED
1-01-001	HIGH-STEPPED
1-01-001	HIGH-SUDSING
1-01-001	HIGH-TAILED
1-01-001	HIGH-TEMPERATURE
1-01-001	HIGH-TENSION
1-01-001	HIGH-TOPPED
1-01-001	HIGH-UP
3-02-002	HIGH-VALUE
1-01-001	HIGH-VELOCITY
1-01-001	HIGH-VOLTAGE
1-01-001	HIGH-WAGE
1-01-001	HIGH-WATER
4-03-003	HIGHBALL
1-01-001	HIGHBOARD
1-01-001	HIGHBOY
160-13-088	HIGHER
1-01-001	HIGHER-
1-01-001	HIGHER-DENSITY
1-01-001	HIGHER-PRICED
1-01-001	HIGHER-QUALITY
63-11-049	HIGHEST
1-01-001	HIGHEST-PAID
1-01-001	HIGHFIELD
1-01-001	HIGHLAND
6-03-003	HIGHLANDS
2-02-002	HIGHLIGHT
2-02-002	HIGHLIGHTING
3-03-003	HIGHLIGHTS
94-14-075	HIGHLY
1-01-001	HIGHNESS
2-02-002	HIGHPOINT
6-01-001	HIGHROAD
2-02-002	HIGHS
1-01-001	HIGHSCHOOL
40-12-023	HIGHWAY
1-01-001	HIGHWAYMAN
16-05-011	HIGHWAYS
2-01-001	HIJACKED
2-02-002	HIJACKERS
2-02-002	HIJACKING
4-04-004	HIKE
1-01-001	HIKED
4-03-004	HIKES
2-02-002	HIKING
4-01-001	HILAR
2-01-001	HILARIOUS
1-01-001	HILARIOUSLY
1-01-001	HILARITY
1-01-001	HILDY
72-08-046	HILL
1-01-001	HILLARY
3-02-003	HILLBILLY
1-01-001	HILLCREST
1-01-001	HILLEL
1-01-001	HILLIARD
2-01-001	HILLMAN
1-01-001	HILLMAN'S
50-13-038	HILLS
11-01-001	HILLSBORO
1-01-001	HILLSDALE
9-04-007	HILLSIDE
1-01-001	HILLTOPS
2-02-002	HILLYER
4-01-001	HILO
3-01-001	HILPRECHT
1-01-001	HILPRECHT'S
3-02-003	HILT
3-02-002	HILTON
5-01-001	HILUM
2619-15-350	HIM
2-02-002	HIMALAYAS
1-01-001	HIMMLER
603-15-246	HIMSELF
1-01-001	HIMSELFE
1-01-001	HINCKLEY
6-03-004	HIND
1-01-001	HINDEMITH'S
3-03-003	HINDERED
1-01-001	HINDERING
1-01-001	HINDERS
1-01-001	HINDMOST
1-01-001	HINDOO
1-01-001	HINDQUARTERS
2-02-002	HINDRANCES
3-03-003	HINDU
2-02-002	HINDUISM
1-01-001	HINDUS
1-01-001	HINGE
1-01-001	HINGED
4-04-004	HINGES
1-01-001	HINKLE
13-01-001	HINO
2-01-001	HINO'S
1-01-001	HINSDALE
9-05-009	HINT
7-04-007	HINTED
1-01-001	HINTERLANDS
1-01-001	HINTING
3-01-002	HINTON
10-06-008	HINTS
10-06-009	HIP
1-01-001	HIP-POCKET
1-01-001	HIPLINE
5-01-001	HIPPODROME
8-06-008	HIPS
1-01-001	HIPSTER
1-01-001	HIR
6-01-001	HIREY
1-01-001	HIREY'S
6-04-006	HIRING
11-04-004	HIROSHIMA
2-01-001	HIRSCH
1-01-001	HIRSCH'S
1-01-001	HIRSCHEY
6997-15-435	HIS
2-02-002	HISS
2-02-002	HISSED
1-01-001	HISSELF
4-04-004	HISSING
1-01-001	HISTOCHEMICAL
3-01-001	HISTOCHEMISTRY
1-01-001	HISTOLOGY
30-06-012	HISTORIAN
3-02-002	HISTORIAN'S
20-06-017	HISTORIANS
23-09-016	HISTORIC
71-10-048	HISTORICAL
16-06-013	HISTORICALLY
1-01-001	HISTORICISM
1-01-001	HISTORICITY
11-06-009	HISTORIES
2-01-001	HISTORIOGRAPHY
286-13-135	HISTORY
1-01-001	HISTRIONICS
115-14-064	HIT
1-01-001	HIT'S
1-01-001	HIT-AND-MISS
1-01-001	HIT-AND-RUN
2-01-001	HIT-RUN
5-04-005	HITCH
2-02-002	HITCHCOCK
3-03-003	HITCHED
3-02-002	HITCHING
2-02-002	HITHER
3-02-002	HITHERTO
8-04-006	HITLER
7-05-006	HITLER'S
1-01-001	HITLERS
1-01-001	HITLESS
22-07-010	HITS
2-02-002	HITTER
4-02-002	HITTERS
17-07-014	HITTING
2-02-002	HIVE
1-01-001	HMM
1-01-001	HMPF
1-01-001	HO**OLDERLIN
1-01-001	HO**DVDINGAR
1-01-001	HOA-WHUP
21-01-001	HOAG
2-01-001	HOAG'S
1-01-001	HOAGY
1-01-001	HOAK
1-01-001	HOAPS
5-02-004	HOARSE
4-02-004	HOARSELY
1-01-001	HOARSENESS
1-01-001	HOAXES
1-01-001	HOB
1-01-001	HOBART
1-01-001	HOBBES
1-01-001	HOBBES'
3-01-001	HOBBIES
1-01-001	HOBBING
1-01-001	HOBBLE
2-02-002	HOBBLED
4-03-004	HOBBY
1-01-001	HOBDAY
1-01-001	HOBO
3-03-003	HOC
1-01-001	HOCK'S
1-01-001	HOCKADAY
1-01-001	HOCKETT
1-01-001	HOCKEY
1-01-001	HOCKING
1-01-001	HODGE-PODGE
1-01-001	HODGEPODGE
14-05-006	HODGES
2-01-001	HODGES'
3-01-001	HODGKIN
1-01-001	HODOSH
1-01-001	HOE-*DOWN
1-01-001	HOES
3-01-001	HOEVE
2-02-002	HOFFA
1-01-001	HOFFER
2-02-002	HOFFMAN
3-02-003	HOG
11-02-003	HOGAN
1-01-001	HOGAN'S
1-01-001	HOGE'S
1-01-001	HOGGING
2-02-002	HOGS
9-01-001	HOHLBEIN
1-01-001	HOI-POLLOI
3-01-001	HOIJER
3-01-001	HOIJER'S
1-01-001	HOIST
2-02-002	HOISTED
2-01-001	HOKAN
1-01-001	HOLABIRD
1-01-001	HOLBROOK
169-15-120	HOLD
1-01-001	HOLD-BACK
9-01-001	HOLDEN
2-01-001	HOLDEN'S
27-05-005	HOLDER
5-03-004	HOLDERS
1-01-001	HOLDIN
65-13-057	HOLDING
4-04-004	HOLDINGS
1-01-001	HOLDOVERS
42-11-041	HOLDS
2-01-001	HOLDUP
1-01-001	HOLDUPS
58-10-031	HOLE
1-01-001	HOLED
39-11-020	HOLES
17-08-012	HOLIDAY
12-05-007	HOLIDAYS
2-02-002	HOLIER-THAN-THOU
1-01-001	HOLIES
2-02-002	HOLINESS
8-05-006	HOLLAND
1-01-001	HOLLANDER
2-01-001	HOLLERED
3-02-002	HOLLERING
1-01-001	HOLLEY
1-01-001	HOLLINGSHEAD
12-06-009	HOLLOW
1-01-001	HOLLOWAY
1-01-001	HOLLOWELL
1-01-001	HOLLOWNESS
1-01-001	HOLLOWS
1-01-001	HOLLOWWARE
1-01-001	HOLLYHOCK
1-01-001	HOLLYHOCKS
23-06-012	HOLLYWOOD
4-03-004	HOLLYWOOD'S
1-01-001	HOLMAN
37-07-007	HOLMES
2-01-001	HOLMES'
5-04-005	HOLOCAUST
1-01-001	HOLORED
1-01-001	HOLSTEIN
10-02-007	HOLSTER
3-01-002	HOLSTERED
1-01-001	HOLT'S
1-01-001	HOLTY
49-10-023	HOLY
2-02-002	HOLYOKE
1-01-001	HOLYSTONES
1-01-001	HOLZMAN
2-02-002	HOMAGE
547-15-243	HOME
1-01-001	HOME'S
1-01-001	HOME-AND-HOME
1-01-001	HOME-BLEND
1-01-001	HOME-BOUND
1-01-001	HOME-BRED
1-01-001	HOME-BUILDING
1-01-001	HOME-CITY
1-01-001	HOME-COMINGS
1-01-001	HOME-FOR-THE-NIGHT
2-02-002	HOME-GROWN
1-01-001	HOME-KEEPING
1-01-001	HOME-MADE
1-01-001	HOME-OFFICE
1-01-001	HOME-OWNERS
2-01-001	HOME-RUN
1-01-001	HOMEBOUND
1-01-001	HOMEBUILDERS
1-01-001	HOMEBUILDING
4-01-001	HOMECOMING
1-01-001	HOMECOMINGS
1-01-001	HOMEFOLK
5-01-004	HOMELAND
9-06-006	HOMELY
4-03-003	HOMEMADE
3-02-002	HOMEMAKER
3-02-002	HOMEMAKERS
1-01-001	HOMEMASTER
3-02-002	HOMEOWNERS
16-04-008	HOMER
1-01-001	HOMER'S
15-01-001	HOMERIC
1-01-001	HOMERISTS
3-01-002	HOMERS
1-01-001	HOMERUN
62-10-049	HOMES
3-01-001	HOMESICK
1-01-001	HOMESICKNESS
2-02-002	HOMESTEAD
3-01-001	HOMESTEADERS
1-01-001	HOMESTEADS
1-01-001	HOMEWARD
1-01-001	HOMEWARDS
1-01-001	HOMICIDAL
6-02-004	HOMICIDE
1-01-001	HOMING
1-01-001	HOMO
2-01-001	HOMOGENATE
5-03-004	HOMOGENEITY
8-03-005	HOMOGENEOUS
2-02-002	HOMOGENEOUSLY
1-01-001	HOMOGENIZATION
1-01-001	HOMOGENIZE
1-01-001	HOMOPOLYMERS
2-02-002	HOMOSEXUAL
3-01-001	HOMOSEXUALS
5-01-001	HOMOZYGOUS
6-02-002	HON
2-01-001	HON'BLE
2-02-002	HONAN
2-01-001	HONDO
2-01-001	HONE
47-13-041	HONEST
1-01-001	HONEST-TO-*BETSY
12-07-010	HONESTLY
10-06-008	HONESTY
25-09-018	HONEY
1-01-001	HONEY-IN-THE-SUN
2-01-001	HONEYBEE
4-01-001	HONEYBEES
1-01-001	HONEYCOMBED
11-06-008	HONEYMOON
2-01-001	HONEYMOONED
1-01-001	HONEYMOONERS
1-01-001	HONEYMOONING
3-03-003	HONEYSUCKLE
11-04-007	HONG
1-01-001	HONKY-TONK
1-01-001	HONKYTONKS
6-02-002	HONOLULU
66-12-045	HONOR
12-05-010	HONORABLE
3-02-002	HONORABLY
2-01-001	HONORARY
24-09-021	HONORED
1-01-001	HONOREE
8-03-007	HONORING
15-04-011	HONORS
4-01-001	HONOTASSA
2-02-002	HONOUR
1-01-001	HONOURED
1-01-001	HONSHU
1-01-001	HOO-PIG
1-01-001	HOOCH
7-05-006	HOOD
1-01-001	HOOD'S
3-02-002	HOODLUM
3-02-003	HOODLUMS
2-02-002	HOODS
2-02-002	HOOF
1-01-001	HOOF-AND-MOUTH
1-01-001	HOOFMARKS
7-02-005	HOOFS
1-01-001	HOOGHLI
1-01-001	HOOGLI

Code	Word	Code	Word	Code	Word	Code	Word
5-02-004	HOOK	2-02-002	HORSEPLAY	1-01-001	HOVE	2-02-002	HUMANISTIC
7-05-007	HOOKED	5-01-002	HORSEPOWER	2-02-002	HOVEL	1-01-001	HUMANISTS
1-01-001	HOOKER'S	68-09-033	HORSES	4-03-004	HOVER	3-03-003	HUMANITARIAN
1-01-001	HOOKING	3-03-003	HORSES'	1-01-001	HOVERED	2-01-002	HUMANITIES
2-02-002	HOOKS	1-01-001	HORSEWOMAN	1-01-001	HOVERING	28-08-021	HUMANITY
2-02-002	HOOKUP	1-01-001	HORSTMAN	1-01-001	HOVERS	1-01-001	HUMANIZE
1-01-001	HOOKUPS	1-01-001	HORTON	834-15-333	HOW	1-01-001	HUMANLY
1-01-001	HOOKWORM	2-01-001	HOSAKA	3-01-002	HOW'D	2-02-002	HUMANNESS
1-01-001	HOOLIGANISM	9-04-005	HOSE	10-06-009	HOW'S	9-07-008	HUMANS
3-02-002	HOOP	2-02-002	HOSES	1-01-001	HOW-2	18-07-016	HUMBLE
2-01-001	HOOPER	1-01-001	HOSPICE	32-06-017	HOWARD	1-01-001	HUMBLED
1-01-001	HOOPLA	4-03-004	HOSPITABLE	1-01-001	HOWARD'S	4-04-004	HUMBLY
3-02-002	HOOPS	110-12-048	HOSPITAL	1-01-001	HOWDA	2-01-002	HUME
1-01-001	HOORAY	1-01-001	HOSPITAL-CARE	1-01-001	HOWDY	2-01-001	HUME'S
1-01-001	HOOSEGOW	6-04-006	HOSPITALITY	12-03-005	HOWE	1-01-001	HUMID
1-01-001	HOOSEGOWS	4-02-003	HOSPITALIZATION	1-01-001	HOWE'S	8-03-003	HUMIDITY
1-01-001	HOOSIER	1-01-001	HOSPITALIZED	1-01-001	HOWELL	1-01-001	HUMILATION
9-04-004	HOOT	20-09-012	HOSPITALS	1-01-001	HOWELLS	2-02-002	HUMILIATED
1-01-001	HOOTED	5-01-001	HOSS	552-15-282	HOWEVER	4-03-004	HUMILIATING
1-01-001	HOOTING	5-01-001	HOSSES	4-04-004	HOWL	1-01-001	HUMILIATINGLY
1-01-001	HOOTS	36-10-024	HOST	1-01-001	HOWLED	6-04-006	HUMILIATION
8-04-006	HOOVER	5-04-005	HOST'S	3-03-003	HOWLING	5-03-004	HUMILITY
2-02-002	HOOVES	1-01-001	HOST-SPECIFIC	3-02-003	HOWLS	1-01-001	HUMLY
2-01-002	HOP	2-02-002	HOSTAGE	2-01-001	HOWORTH	3-03-003	HUMMED
1-01-001	HOP-SKIPPED	3-01-001	HOSTAGES	1-01-001	HOWRY	6-04-006	HUMMING
178-15-114	HOPE	1-01-001	HOSTARIA	1-01-001	HOWSABOUT	2-02-002	HUMMOCKS
1-01-001	HOPE'S	1-01-001	HOSTE	1-01-001	HOWSAM	47-12-032	HUMOR
48-10-041	HOPED	1-01-001	HOSTELRIES	1-01-001	HOWSAM'S	2-01-001	HUMORISTS
3-03-003	HOPED-FOR	8-04-007	HOSTESS	2-01-001	HOWSE	16-08-012	HUMOROUS
1-01-001	HOPEDALE	3-03-003	HOSTESSES	2-01-001	HOWSER	1-01-001	HUMOUR
12-09-012	HOPEFUL	19-07-017	HOSTILE	1-01-001	HOWSOMEVER	2-01-001	HUMP
8-05-007	HOPEFULLY	5-02-002	HOSTILITIES	1-01-001	HOXA	1-01-001	HUMPED
2-02-002	HOPEFULS	6-04-006	HOSTILITY	1-01-001	HOY	6-03-003	HUMPHREY
1-01-001	HOPEI	2-01-001	HOSTLER	1-01-001	HOYDENISH	1-01-001	HUMPTY
14-07-012	HOPELESS	5-05-005	HOSTS	1-01-001	HOYLE'S	2-01-001	HUN
7-05-005	HOPELESSLY	130-14-077	HOT	4-03-003	HOYT	7-05-006	HUNCH
3-02-003	HOPELESSNESS	1-01-001	HOT-BLOODED	6-01-003	HR	2-02-002	HUNCHED
48-13-043	HOPES	1-01-001	HOT-COLORED	1-01-001	HR.	1-01-001	HUNCHED-UP
30-11-027	HOPING	1-01-001	HOT-HONEY	3-01-001	HR,	1-01-001	HUNCHES
7-04-005	HOPKINS	2-02-002	HOT-SHOT	1-01-001	HROTHGAR	171-14-104	HUNDRED
1-01-001	HOPKINS'	1-01-001	HOT-SLOUGH	1-01-001	HROTHGAR'S	1-01-001	HUNDRED-AND-EIGHTY-DEGREE
2-01-001	HOPKINSIAN	1-01-001	HOT-WATER	1-01-001	HUAI		
5-05-005	HOPPED	1-01-001	HOTBED	1-01-001	HUANG-TI	1-01-001	HUNDRED-AND-FIFTY
2-02-002	HOPPER	1-01-001	HOTDOGS	11-02-002	HUB		
4-04-004	HOPPING	5-01-001	HOTEI	1-01-001	HUBAY	1-01-001	HUNDRED-LEAF
1-01-001	HOPPLED	126-12-060	HOTEL	2-01-001	HUBBA	2-01-002	HUNDRED-ODD
4-01-001	HOPPLES	1-01-001	HOTEL'S	1-01-001	HUBBELL	1-01-001	HUNDRED-YEN
1-01-001	HOPS	1-01-001	HOTEL-MOTEL	1-01-001	HUBBUB	44-12-032	HUNDREDS
1-01-001	HOPSCOTCH	1-01-001	HOTELMAN'S	1-01-001	HUBBY	2-02-002	HUNDREDTH
5-03-004	HORACE	20-08-014	HOTELS	1-01-001	HUBERMANN	65-11-051	HUNG
1-01-001	HORACE'S	2-01-001	HOTHAM	3-03-003	HUBERT	9-06-006	HUNGARIAN
1-01-001	HORATIO'S	1-01-001	HOTHOUSE	1-01-001	HUBIE'S	1-01-001	HUNGARIAN-BORN
1-01-001	HORD	2-02-002	HOTLY	1-01-001	HUBRIS	4-02-003	HUNGARY
2-02-002	HORDE	1-01-001	HOTROD	2-02-002	HUBS	1-01-001	HUNGARY-*SUEZ
2-02-002	HORDES	7-06-007	HOTTER	1-01-001	HUCK	17-09-012	HUNGER
27-12-022	HORIZON	4-03-004	HOTTEST	2-02-002	HUCKSTER	1-01-001	HUNGRIER
6-04-006	HORIZONS	1-01-001	HOUDINI	1-01-001	HUCKSTER'S	23-10-017	HUNGRY
9-04-008	HORIZONTAL	6-02-002	HOUGH	4-02-004	HUDDLE	2-02-002	HUNK
3-02-003	HORIZONTALLY	2-01-001	HOUGH'S	10-04-009	HUDDLED	2-01-002	HUNKERED
13-02-002	HORMONE	4-02-003	HOUGHTON	3-03-003	HUDDLING	2-01-001	HUNKERISH
2-02-002	HORMONES	1-01-001	HOUGHTON'S	53-08-016	HUDSON	10-08-009	HUNT
31-08-013	HORN	3-01-003	HOUK	16-02-003	HUDSON'S	7-04-005	HUNTED
1-01-001	HORN-RIM	7-05-007	HOUND	1-01-001	HUE	18-07-011	HUNTER
1-01-001	HORN-RIMMED	3-02-003	HOUNDS	2-01-001	HUES	1-01-001	HUNTER'S
2-02-002	HORNE	144-15-099	HOUR	1-01-001	HUEY	5-02-002	HUNTER-KILLER
1-01-001	HORNE'S	1-01-001	HOUR'S	10-01-001	HUFF	6-03-006	HUNTERS
1-01-001	HORNED	2-02-002	HOUR-LONG	1-01-001	HUFF'S	34-09-019	HUNTING
8-07-008	HORNS	2-02-002	HOURLY	1-01-001	HUFFMAN	1-01-001	HUNTINGTON
1-01-001	HORNS'	175-15-110	HOURS	3-02-003	HUG	1-01-001	HUNTINGTONS
1-01-001	HOROSCOPE	1-01-001	HOURS'	54-14-042	HUGE	5-02-002	HUNTLEY
3-03-003	HOROWITZ	591-14-195	HOUSE	2-02-002	HUGGED	2-02-002	HUNTS
15-06-013	HORRIBLE	2-01-002	HOUSE'S	7-02-007	HUGGING	1-01-001	HUO-*SHAN
2-02-002	HORRIBLY	1-01-001	HOUSE-BUILDING	1-01-001	HUGGINGS	3-03-003	HURDLE
1-01-001	HORRID	1-01-001	HOUSE-CLEANING	1-01-001	HUGGINS	1-01-001	HURDLED
4-03-004	HORRIFIED	1-01-001	HOUSEBOATS	9-04-008	HUGH	1-01-001	HURDLES
3-02-003	HORRIFYING	1-01-001	HOUSEBREAKERS	27-04-007	HUGHES	3-03-003	HURL
1-01-001	HORRIFYINGLY	1-01-001	HOUSEBREAKING	2-01-001	HUGHES'	4-04-004	HURLED
17-09-015	HORROR	1-01-001	HOUSEBROKEN	3-01-001	HUGO	1-01-001	HURLER
4-03-004	HORRORS	12-07-011	HOUSED	1-01-001	HUGO'S	1-01-001	HURLERS
1-01-001	HORS	32-10-026	HOUSEHOLD	5-05-005	HUH	1-01-001	HURLEY
117-14-045	HORSE	1-01-001	HOUSEHOLD-TYPE	1-01-001	HUH-UH	5-05-005	HURLING
5-04-004	HORSE'S	1-01-001	HOUSEHOLDER	2-01-001	HUHMUN	4-02-002	HUROK
1-01-001	HORSE-BLANKET	1-01-001	HOUSEHOLDERS	1-01-001	HUI	3-02-002	HURRAH
1-01-001	HORSE-CHESTNUT	1-01-001	HOUSEHOLDS	1-01-001	HUITOTOES	1-01-001	HURRAY
1-01-001	HORSE-PLAYING	2-02-002	HOUSEKEEPER	2-01-001	HUL	3-01-001	HURRAYS
2-01-001	HORSE-RADISH	7-05-006	HOUSEKEEPING	2-02-002	HULK	8-05-006	HURRICANE
1-01-001	HORSE-TRADING	1-01-001	HOUSEPAINT	2-02-002	HULKING	23-08-019	HURRIED
1-01-001	HORSE-TRAIL	83-13-064	HOUSES	3-03-003	HULKS	2-02-002	HURRIEDLY
3-02-002	HORSEBACK	4-03-004	HOUSEWIFE	13-05-006	HULL	36-07-030	HURRY
1-01-001	HORSEDOM	5-05-005	HOUSEWIVES	1-01-001	HULL-FIRST	4-04-004	HURRYING
1-01-001	HORSEFLESH	2-02-002	HOUSEWORK	1-01-001	HULTBERG	37-09-031	HURT
1-01-001	HORSEHAIR	59-08-026	HOUSING	5-04-004	HUM	3-02-002	HURTING
1-01-001	HORSELIKE	1-01-001	HOUSMAN	1-01-001	HUMAINE	1-01-001	HURTLED
2-01-001	HORSELY	2-01-002	HOUSMAN'S	299-14-130	HUMAN	5-04-004	HURTLING
1-01-001	HORSEMAN	25-05-010	HOUSTON	5-03-005	HUMANE	4-04-004	HURTS
3-03-003	HORSEMANSHIP	2-01-001	HOUTZ	1-01-001	HUMANELY	131-15-067	HUSBAND
3-03-003	HORSEMEN	1-01-001	HOVARTER	5-02-005	HUMANISM	17-08-015	HUSBAND'S
				4-02-003	HUMANIST		

Code	Word
1-01-001	HUSBAND-STEALER
1-01-001	HUSBAND-WIFE
2-02-002	HUSBANDRY
14-07-010	HUSBANDS
1-01-001	HUSBUN
4-02-003	HUSH
2-02-002	HUSHED
1-01-001	HUSKILY
1-01-001	HUSKINESS
3-02-003	HUSKY
1-01-001	HUSKY-VOICED
2-02-002	HUSTLE
2-02-002	HUSTLED
4-03-004	HUSTLER
1-01-001	HUSTLING
1-01-001	HUSTON
13-03-005	HUT
4-01-003	HUTCHINS
1-01-001	HUTCHINS'
2-01-001	HUTCHINSON
1-01-001	HUTMENT
1-01-001	HUTMENTS
6-02-003	HUTS
2-02-002	HUTTON
6-03-004	HUXLEY
2-01-002	HUXLEY'S
1-01-001	HUZZAHS
1-01-001	HWA-*SHAN
4-01-001	HWANG
1-01-001	HYACINTHS
1-01-001	HYALINE
1-01-001	HYALINIZATION
2-01-002	HYANNIS
1-01-001	HYBRID
4-01-001	HYDE
1-01-001	HYDE'S
1-01-001	HYDRATED
1-01-001	HYDRAULIC
1-01-001	HYDRAULICALLY
1-01-001	HYDRAULICS
2-02-002	HYDRIDE
3-01-001	HYDRIDES
1-01-001	HYDRIDO
1-01-001	HYDRO-*ELECTRIC
3-01-002	HYDROCARBON
1-01-001	HYDROCARBONS
1-01-001	HYDROCHEMISTRY
4-01-001	HYDROCHLORIDE
39-05-007	HYDROGEN
3-01-001	HYDROGENS
5-01-001	HYDROLYSIS
1-01-001	HYDROLYZED
2-01-001	HYDROPHILIC
1-01-001	HYDROPHOBIA
2-01-001	HYDROPHOBIC
1-01-001	HYDROSTATIC
1-01-001	HYDROUS
1-01-001	HYDROXAZINE
1-01-001	HYDROXIDES
2-01-001	HYDROXYL-RICH
1-01-001	HYDROXYLATION
1-01-001	HYENA
3-02-003	HYGIENE
3-01-001	HYM
13-01-001	HYMEN
1-01-001	HYMENS
9-04-007	HYMN
6-04-006	HYMNS
1-01-001	HYNDE
1-01-001	HYNDMAN
1-01-001	HYPED-UP
2-01-001	HYPERBOLE
2-02-002	HYPERBOLIC
1-01-001	HYPERBOLICALLY
1-01-001	HYPERCELLULARITY
2-01-001	HYPEREMIA
2-01-001	HYPEREMIC
1-01-001	HYPERFINE
1-01-001	HYPERPLASIA
1-01-001	HYPERTROPHIED
2-01-001	HYPERTROPHY
1-01-001	HYPERVELOCITY
2-02-002	HYPHENATED
1-01-001	HYPNOSIS
1-01-001	HYPNOTIC
1-01-001	HYPNOTICALLY
1-01-001	HYPNOTIZED
1-01-001	HYPO-
1-01-001	HYPOACTIVE
1-01-001	HYPOADRENOCORTICISM
1-01-001	HYPOCELLULARITY
2-02-002	HYPOCRISIES
7-06-007	HYPOCRISY
2-02-002	HYPOCRITE
2-02-002	HYPOCRITES
2-01-001	HYPOCRITICAL
1-01-001	HYPODERMIC
1-01-001	HYPOPHYSEAL
1-01-001	HYPOPHYSECTOMISED
1-01-001	HYPOSTATIZATION
22-01-001	HYPOTHALAMIC
4-01-001	HYPOTHALAMIC-CORTICAL
1-01-001	HYPOTHALAMICALLY
19-02-002	HYPOTHALAMUS
4-02-002	HYPOTHESES
18-04-012	HYPOTHESIS
6-05-006	HYPOTHESIZE
7-05-007	HYPOTHESIZED
1-01-001	HYPOTHESIZING
8-03-007	HYPOTHETICAL
1-01-001	HYPOTHYROIDISM
5-01-001	HYS
1-01-001	HYSTERECTOMY
7-04-006	HYSTERIA
10-06-009	HYSTERICAL
1-01-001	HYSTERON-PROTERON
1-01-001	HYTT
5173-15-338	I
1-01-001	I**.*B**.*M
1-01-001	I**.*L
1-01-001	I**.*M**.*F
5-02-002	I**.*Q
2-01-001	I**.*R**.*S
3-01-001	I**.D
43-10-030	I**.E
1-01-001	I**$N
1-01-001	I**$T
104-09-057	I'D
181-12-080	I'LL
268-13-111	I'M
125-12-076	I'VE
2-01-001	I-TH
1-01-001	IBERIA
1-01-001	IBN
1-01-001	IBRAHIM
1-01-001	IBSEN
45-08-028	ICE
1-01-001	ICE-CHEST
1-01-001	ICE-COLD
1-01-001	ICE-CUBES
1-01-001	ICE-FEELING
2-01-001	ICE-FILLED
3-03-003	ICEBOX
1-01-001	ICED
4-02-002	ICELAND
1-01-001	ICELANDIC
1-01-001	ICELANDIC-SPEAKING
1-01-001	ICH
1-01-001	ICICLE
1-01-001	ICING
1-01-001	ICONOCLASM
12-09-010	ICY
2-01-001	IDA
3-02-002	IDAHO
1-01-001	IDAL
195-15-127	IDEA
1-01-001	IDEA-EXCHANGE
61-11-040	IDEAL
3-03-003	IDEALISM
4-02-003	IDEALIST
2-01-002	IDEALISTIC
2-02-002	IDEALIZATION
4-02-002	IDEALIZED
10-05-010	IDEALLY
1-01-001	IDEALOGICAL
16-08-013	IDEALS
143-12-071	IDEAS
1-01-001	IDEATIONAL
1-01-001	IDENTICAL
1-01-001	IDENTICALLY
1-01-001	IDENTIFIABLE
5-05-005	IDENTIFICATION
2-01-001	IDENTIFICATIONS
46-12-036	IDENTIFIED
6-05-006	IDENTIFIES
26-07-022	IDENTIFY
3-02-003	IDENTIFYING
10-03-006	IDENTITIES
20-06-011	IDENTITY
3-03-003	IDEOLOGICAL
24-10-016	IDEOLOGIES
12-06-010	IDEOLOGIST
6-03-006	IDEOLOGY
1-01-001	IDIOCIES
1-01-001	IDIOM
1-01-001	IDIOMATIC
3-02-002	IDIOMS
3-03-003	IDIOSYNCRASIES
2-02-002	IDIOSYNCRATIC
2-02-002	IDIOT
1-01-001	IDIOT'S
1-01-001	IDIOT-GRIN
3-02-003	IDIOTIC
1-01-001	IDIOTICALLY
3-01-001	IDJE
13-09-011	IDLE
1-01-001	IDLED
3-03-003	IDLENESS
1-01-001	IDLER
1-01-001	IDLERS
2-02-002	IDLING
6-05-006	IDLY
7-05-007	IDOL
1-01-001	IDOL-WORSHIP
1-01-001	IDOLATRY
1-01-001	IDOLIZE
1-01-001	IDOLIZED
2-02-002	IDOLS
1-01-001	IDOLS'
2-01-001	IDYLL
4-02-004	IDYLLIC
3-01-001	IERULLI
2199-15-453	IF
1-01-001	IFNI
3-01-001	IGBO
1-01-001	IGLEHART
1-01-001	IGNAZIO
1-01-001	IGNEOUS
2-02-002	IGNITE
1-01-001	IGNITED
5-04-004	IGNITION
2-02-002	IGNORAMUS
16-09-015	IGNORANCE
12-06-010	IGNORANT
19-09-016	IGNORE
29-13-028	IGNORED
5-03-005	IGNORES
4-03-004	IGNORING
3-02-003	IGOR
1-01-001	IHMSEN
1-01-001	IIJIMA
1-01-001	IJ
4-03-004	IKE
1-01-001	IKE'S
1-01-001	IKEY-KIKEY
1-01-001	IKLE
3-02-003	IL
1-01-001	ILEUM
1-01-001	ILIAC
14-01-002	ILIAD
1-01-001	ILKA
39-11-034	ILL
3-02-003	ILL-CONCEIVED
2-02-002	ILL-EQUIPPED
2-02-002	ILL-FATED
1-01-001	ILL-PREPARED
4-04-004	ILL-STARRED
1-01-001	ILLE
9-05-009	ILLEGAL
2-02-002	ILLEGALLY
4-02-002	ILLEGITIMACY
3-02-002	ILLEGITIMATE
3-03-003	ILLICIT
40-08-026	ILLINOIS
1-01-001	ILLINOIS'
8-03-007	ILLITERATE
20-10-016	ILLNESS
2-02-002	ILLNESSES
1-01-001	ILLOGICAL
9-05-007	ILLS
1-01-001	ILLUMINATE
1-01-001	ILLUMINATED
14-07-010	ILLUMINATING
5-04-004	ILLUMINATION
9-04-008	ILLUMINATIONS
1-01-001	ILLUMINE
3-02-002	ILLUMINED
1-01-001	ILLUMINES
37-07-016	ILLUSION
1-01-001	ILLUSIONARY
7-03-007	ILLUSIONS
2-01-001	ILLUSIVE
2-02-002	ILLUSORY
17-07-016	ILLUSTRATE
37-11-029	ILLUSTRATED
7-03-007	ILLUSTRATES
4-04-004	ILLUSTRATING
24-10-016	ILLUSTRATION
12-06-010	ILLUSTRATIONS
6-03-006	ILLUSTRATIVE
1-01-001	ILLUSTRATOR
1-01-001	ILLUSTRATORS
3-03-003	ILLUSTRIOUS
1-01-001	ILONA
1-01-001	ILYUSHIN
6-01-001	IM
119-13-046	IMAGE
1-01-001	IMAGE-PROVOKING
10-03-008	IMAGERY
37-06-023	IMAGES
17-08-014	IMAGINARY
65-14-051	IMAGINATION
1-01-001	IMAGINATIONS
13-07-012	IMAGINATIVE
1-01-001	IMAGINATIVELY
61-13-049	IMAGINE
27-10-023	IMAGINED
3-03-003	IMAGINES
2-01-002	IMAGING
1-01-001	IMAGINING
1-01-001	IMAGININGS
1-01-001	IMAGNATION
1-01-001	IMBALANCE
1-01-001	IMBALANCES
1-01-001	IMBECILE
4-04-004	IMBEDDED
1-01-001	IMBIBE
2-02-002	IMBIBED
1-01-001	IMBODEN
1-01-001	IMBRIUM
1-01-001	IMBROGLIO
1-01-001	IMBRUING
1-01-001	IMBUED
1-01-001	IMCOMPARABLE
1-01-001	IMCOMPATIBLES
1-01-001	IMCOMPLETE
5-04-005	IMITATE
4-04-004	IMITATED
2-01-002	IMITATES
2-02-002	IMITATING
23-04-005	IMITATION
1-01-001	IMITATION-CANING
1-01-001	IMITATION-WOODGRAIN
3-01-001	IMITATIONS
1-01-001	IMITATIVE
2-02-002	IMITATORS
5-04-005	IMMACULATE
3-02-002	IMMANENT
2-02-002	IMMATERIAL
7-05-006	IMMATURE
1-01-001	IMMATURITY
2-02-002	IMMEASURABLE
1-01-001	IMMEASURABLY
1-01-001	IMMEDIACIES
8-03-005	IMMEDIACY
81-14-071	IMMEDIATE
123-15-095	IMMEDIATELY
2-02-002	IMMEMORIAL
14-07-013	IMMENSE
9-07-009	IMMENSELY
1-01-001	IMMENSITIES
1-01-001	IMMENSITY
4-04-004	IMMERSED
2-01-002	IMMERSION
4-03-004	IMMIGRANT
10-05-008	IMMIGRANTS
10-04-005	IMMIGRATION
1-01-001	IMMINENCE
3-03-003	IMMINENT
4-03-003	IMMOBILITY
1-01-001	IMMODERATE
1-01-001	IMMODEST
5-04-005	IMMORAL
1-01-001	IMMORALITIES
4-02-002	IMMORALITY
7-04-004	IMMORTAL
19-03-008	IMMORTALITY
1-01-001	IMMORTALIZED
1-01-001	IMMOVABLE
7-04-004	IMMUNITY
1-01-001	IMMUNIZATION
1-01-001	IMMUNOELECTROPORESI
1-01-001	IMMUTABLE
67-12-045	IMPACT
2-02-002	IMPACTED
3-01-001	IMPACTS
4-04-004	IMPAIR
7-03-007	IMPAIRED
1-01-001	IMPAIRMENT
2-02-002	IMPALED
1-01-001	IMPALING
4-04-004	IMPART
1-01-001	IMPARTATION
4-03-004	IMPARTED
8-03-006	IMPARTIAL
2-01-002	IMPARTIALITY
1-01-001	IMPARTS

2-02-002	IMPASSABLE	1-01-001	IMPOUNDMENTS	1-01-001	INASMUCH	1-01-001	INCONSIDERABLE
2-02-002	IMPASSE	3-02-003	IMPOVERISHED	1-01-001	INATTENTIVE	1-01-001	INCONSISTENCIES
8-04-008	IMPASSIONED	1-01-001	IMPRACTICABLE	2-02-002	INAUDIBLE	1-01-001	INCONSISTENCY
1-01-001	IMPASSIVE	5-05-005	IMPRACTICAL	8-04-008	INAUGURAL	5-04-005	INCONSISTENT
1-01-001	IMPASSIVELY	1-01-001	IMPRECATES	4-03-004	INAUGURATED	1-01-001	INCONSPICUOUS
10-08-010	IMPATIENCE	1-01-001	IMPRECATIONS	1-01-001	INAUGURATING	1-01-001	INCONSPICUOUSLY
10-06-009	IMPATIENT	3-02-002	IMPRECISE	8-05-007	INAUGURATION	1-01-001	INCONTESTABLE
9-04-009	IMPATIENTLY	3-03-003	IMPRECISELY	1-01-001	INBOARD	1-01-001	INCONTROVERTIBLE
6-06-006	IMPECCABLE	1-01-001	IMPRESARIO	1-01-001	INBOARDS		
2-02-002	IMPECCABLY	1-01-001	IMPRESS	1-01-001	INBORN	3-03-003	INCONVENIENCE
5-03-005	IMPEDED	30-11-025	IMPRESSED	1-01-001	INBREEDING	3-03-003	INCONVENIENT
1-01-001	IMPEDIMENT	1-01-001	IMPRESSER	20-06-013	INC	1-01-001	INCONVENIENTLY
6-03-005	IMPELLED	1-01-001	IMPRESSES	1-01-001	INCA	2-02-002	INCORPORATE
1-01-001	IMPELLING	2-01-002	IMPRESSING	1-01-001	INCALCULABLE	13-05-010	INCORPORATED
4-03-004	IMPENDING	3-03-003	IMPRESSION	3-03-003	INCANDESCENT	3-03-003	INCORPORATES
1-01-001	IMPENETRABLE	2-01-002	IMPRESSIONISM	1-01-001	INCANTATION	1-01-001	INCORPORATING
10-06-010	IMPERATIVE	3-02-002	IMPRESSIONIST	1-01-001	INCANTED	3-03-003	INCORPORATION
1-01-001	IMPERCEPTIBLE	1-01-001	IMPRESSIONISTIC	11-04-011	INCAPABLE	5-04-005	INCORRECT
1-01-001	IMPERCEPTIBLY	2-02-002	IMPRESSIONISTS	2-02-002	INCAPACITATED	1-01-001	INCORRIGIBLE
4-04-004	IMPERFECT	1-01-001	IMPRESSIONS	1-01-001	INCAPACITY	1-01-001	INCORRUPTIBILITY
1-01-001	IMPERFECTABILITY	1-01-001	IMPRESSIVE	1-01-001	INCARCERATED		
		2-02-002	IMPRIMATUR	2-02-002	INCARNATE	2-02-002	INCORRUPTIBLE
1-01-001	IMPERFECTION	5-03-005	IMPRINT	5-03-005	INCARNATION	195-11-095	INCREASE
2-01-002	IMPERFECTIONS	1-01-001	IMPRINTED	1-01-001	INCAUTIOUS	146-14-093	INCREASED
2-01-002	IMPERFECTLY	1-01-001	IMPRISONED	1-01-001	INCENDIARIES	72-08-036	INCREASES
13-08-013	IMPERIAL	6-04-005	IMPRISONMENT	2-02-002	INCENSE	74-10-059	INCREASING
1-01-001	IMPERIALES	3-03-003	IMPRISONS	3-03-003	INCENSED	42-12-036	INCREASINGLY
2-02-002	IMPERIALISM	12-06-009	IMPROBABLE	12-06-009	INCENTIVE	23-11-020	INCREDIBLE
1-01-001	IMPERIALIST	4-02-003	IMPROBABLY	4-02-003	INCENTIVES	7-06-007	INCREDIBLY
3-03-003	IMPERIALISTS	1-01-001	IMPROMPTU	2-03-004	INCEPTED	1-01-001	INCREDULITY
1-01-001	IMPERIL	3-01-001	IMPROPER	3-01-001	INCEPTING	1-01-001	INCREDULOUSLY
1-01-001	IMPERILED	6-05-006	IMPROPERLY	6-05-006	INCEPTION	1-01-001	INCREMENTAL
1-01-001	IMPERILLED	1-01-001	IMPROPRIETY	1-01-001	INCEPTOR	1-01-001	INCRIMINATING
1-01-001	IMPERIOUS	1-01-001	IMPROVE	1-01-001	INCERTAIN	1-01-001	INCUBATED
2-02-002	IMPERIOUSLY	4-03-004	IMPROVED	1-01-001	INCESSANT	1-01-001	INCUBATING
1-01-001	IMPERISHABLE	2-01-002	IMPROVEMENT	2-01-002	INCESSANTLY	4-02-003	INCUBATION
14-07-010	IMPERSONAL	20-07-015	IMPROVEMENTS	13-02-002	INCEST	1-01-001	INCUBI
1-01-001	IMPERSONALIZED	11-03-005	IMPROVES	3-01-002	INCESTUOUS	1-01-001	INCUBUS
1-01-001	IMPERSONALLY	16-07-015	IMPROVING	40-09-023	INCH	2-02-002	INCULCATED
1-01-001	IMPERSONATED	1-01-001	IMPROVISATION	1-01-001	INCHED	2-02-002	INCULCATION
1-01-001	IMPERSONATES	2-02-002	IMPROVISATIONS	86-11-025	INCHES	4-02-003	INCUMBENT
2-01-002	IMPERSONATION	2-02-002	IMPROVISE	7-02-004	INCIDENCE	1-01-001	INCUMBENTS
1-01-001	IMPERTINENT	3-01-002	IMPROVISED	49-13-037	INCIDENT	5-03-005	INCUR
1-01-001	IMPERTURBABLE	5-03-005	IMPROVISER	5-03-005	INCIDENTAL	2-02-002	INCURABLE
2-02-002	IMPERVIOUS	14-06-014	IMPROVISES	2-02-002	INCIDENTALLY	2-02-002	INCURABLY
3-03-003	IMPETUOUS	1-01-001	IMPROVISING	9-05-007	INCIDENTALS	9-05-007	INCURRED
6-04-006	IMPETUS	11-07-010	IMPRUDENTLY	1-01-001	INCIDENTS	1-01-001	INCURRING
1-01-001	IMPIETY	1-01-001	IMPUDENCE	2-01-001	INCINERATOR	1-01-001	INCURS
3-03-003	IMPINGE	3-03-003	IMPUDENT	1-01-001	INCIPIENCE	1-01-001	INCURSION
5-02-004	IMPINGING	1-01-001	IMPUDENTLY	2-01-001	INCIPIENCY	2-02-002	IND
2-02-002	IMPIOUS	20-09-018	IMPULSE	4-03-004	INCIPIENT	10-06-009	INDEBTED
3-03-003	IMPLACABLE	1-01-001	IMPULSES	1-01-001	INCISE	5-03-005	INDECENT
1-01-001	IMPLANT	4-03-003	IMPULSIVE	5-03-005	INCISIVE	1-01-001	INDECIPHERABLE
1-01-001	IMPLANTATION	1-01-001	IMPUNITY	1-01-001	INCISIVENESS	5-04-004	INDECISION
1-01-001	IMPLANTED	3-03-003	IMPURITIES	2-02-002	INCITE	2-02-002	INDECISIVE
1-01-001	IMPLAUSIBLY	2-01-002	IMPURITY	3-01-002	INCITED	1-01-001	INDECISIVELY
4-03-004	IMPLEMENT	3-01-002	IMPURITY-DOPED	3-01-002	INCITEMENT	1-01-001	INDECISIVENESS
8-05-007	IMPLEMENTATION	1-01-001	IMPUTATION	1-01-001	INCITEMENTS	162-15-119	INDEED
1-01-001	IMPLEMENTED	1-01-001	IMPUTE	1-01-001	INCITING	1-01-001	INDEFATIGABLE
3-02-003	IMPLEMENTING	1-01-001	IMPUTED	1-01-001	INCLEMENT	2-02-002	INDEFENSIBLE
5-03-003	IMPLEMENTS	21341-15-500	IN	8-05-007	INCLINATION	2-02-002	INDEFINABLE
2-02-002	IMPLICATED	1-01-001	IN*$DECENT	1-01-001	INCLINATIONS	8-04-004	INDEFINITE
10-06-010	IMPLICATION	1-01-001	IN-FIGHTING	4-02-002	INCLINE	6-05-006	INDEFINITELY
22-08-017	IMPLICATIONS	4-03-004	IN-GROUP	21-12-017	INCLINED	1-01-001	INDEFINITENESS
13-05-011	IMPLICIT	1-01-001	IN-GROUPS	1-01-001	INCLOSED	1-01-001	INDEFINITY
3-03-003	IMPLICITLY	2-02-002	IN-LAWS	113-09-082	INCLUDE	5-03-003	INDELIBLE
17-05-015	IMPLIED	1-01-001	IN-MIGRANTS	97-13-076	INCLUDED	1-01-001	INDELIBLY
17-05-016	IMPLIES	1-01-001	IN-PERSON	45-09-037	INCLUDES	1-01-001	INDELICATE
1-01-001	IMPLORE	1-01-001	IN-PLANT	171-14-128	INCLUDING	2-02-002	INDEMNITY
2-02-002	IMPLORED	1-01-001	IN-STATE	3-02-002	INCLUSION	1-01-001	INDENTATIONS
1-01-001	IMPLORING	17-08-014	INABILITY	2-01-001	INCLUSIONS	2-02-002	INDENTURE
12-06-011	IMPLY	1-01-001	INACCESSIBLE	4-04-004	INCLUSIVE	70-08-032	INDEPENDENCE
7-04-006	IMPLYING	1-01-001	INACCURACIES	1-01-001	INCLUSIVENESS	70-11-047	INDEPENDENT
2-02-002	IMPOLITIC	2-02-002	INACCURACY	4-04-004	INCOHERENT	12-05-009	INDEPENDENTLY
1-01-001	IMPONDERABLE	5-04-005	INACCURATE	1-01-001	INCOHERENTLY	1-01-001	INDEPENDENTS
17-09-014	IMPORT	6-04-005	INACTION	109-12-036	INCOME	4-04-004	INDESCRIBABLE
108-13-079	IMPORTANCE	2-01-001	INACTIVATE	1-01-001	INCOMES	1-01-001	INDESTRUCTIBLE
369-15-211	IMPORTANT	2-01-002	INACTIVATION	5-04-005	INCOMING	4-04-004	INDETERMINATE
1-01-001	IMPORTANT-LOOKING	7-03-005	INACTIVE	4-03-004	INCOMPARABLE	81-08-015	INDEX
		1-01-001	INACTIVITY	3-02-003	INCOMPARABLY	2-01-001	INDEXES
8-05-007	IMPORTANTLY	2-02-002	INADEQUACIES	1-01-001	INCOMPATIBILITY	3-02-003	INDEXING
2-02-002	IMPORTATION	3-03-003	INADEQUACY	2-02-002	INCOMPATIBLE	58-10-020	INDIA
8-05-007	IMPORTED	32-10-029	INADEQUATE	4-03-003	INCOMPETENCE	52-14-028	INDIAN
15-06-010	IMPORTS	2-02-002	INADEQUATELY	2-02-002	INCOMPETENT	5-01-004	INDIAN'S
1-01-001	IMPORTUNATELY	1-01-001	INADVERTENCE	13-03-009	INCOMPETENTS	13-05-007	INDIANA
1-01-001	IMPORTUNITIES	1-01-001	INADVERTENT	2-02-002	INCOMPLETE	1-01-001	INDIANA'S
9-05-008	IMPOSE	2-02-002	INADVERTENTLY	1-01-001	INCOMPLETELY	6-04-005	INDIANAPOLIS
19-09-018	IMPOSED	1-01-001	INADVISABLE	1-01-001	INCOMPLETENESS	32-09-017	INDIANS
4-04-004	IMPOSES	2-02-002	INALIENABLE	2-02-002	INCOMPREHENSIBLE	1-01-001	INDIANS'
7-05-007	IMPOSING	2-02-002	INANE			80-12-065	INDICATE
5-05-005	IMPOSITION	2-02-002	INANIMATE	1-01-001	INCOMPREHENSION	108-14-082	INDICATED
1-01-001	IMPOSSIBILITY	2-01-001	INAPPLICABLE	1-01-001	INCONCEIVABLE	40-08-029	INDICATES
84-15-073	IMPOSSIBLE	4-04-004	INAPPROPRIATE	3-03-003	INCONCLUSIVE	16-09-015	INDICATING
1-01-001	IMPOSSIBLY	1-01-001	INAPPROPRIATENESS	2-02-002	INCONGRUITIES	20-08-020	INDICATION
2-02-002	IMPOTENCE			1-01-001	INCONGRUITY	16-07-015	INDICATIONS
1-01-001	IMPOTENCY	1-01-001	INAPT	1-01-001	INCONGRUOUS	6-04-006	INDICATIVE
2-02-002	IMPOTENT	1-01-001	INARTICULATE	3-03-003	INCONSEQUENTIAL		

8-04-006 INDICATOR	3-02-003 INDUSTRIOUS	1-01-001 INFLAMMATORY	7-05-007 INHUMAN
9-03-005 INDICATORS	2-02-002 INDUSTRIOUSLY	1-01-001 INFLATE	4-03-003 INHUMANE
7-01-002 INDICES	171-10-055 INDUSTRY	3-03-003 INFLATED	1-01-001 INHUMANITIES
2-02-002 INDICTED	15-03-005 INDUSTRY'S	5-04-004 INFLATION	1-01-001 INIMICAL
12-05-009 INDICTMENT	1-01-001 INDUSTRY-WIDE	3-02-002 INFLECTED	1-01-001 INIMPASSIONED
2-01-002 INDICTMENTS	2-02-002 INDWELLING	1-01-001 INFLECTING	1-01-001 INIQUITIES
9-04-008 INDIES	1-01-001 INEFFABLE	3-02-003 INFLECTION	1-01-001 INIQUITOUS
17-09-016 INDIFFERENCE	3-02-003 INEFFECTIVE	4-03-004 INFLECTIONS	68-11-050 INITIAL
11-07-011 INDIFFERENT	3-03-003 INEFFECTIVELY	3-03-003 INFLEXIBLE	1-01-001 INITIALED
1-01-001 INDIGATION	4-03-004 INEFFECTIVENESS	18-06-015 INFLICT	18-06-015 INITIALLY
2-01-001 INDIGENES	1-01-001 INEFFECTUAL	3-03-003 INFLICTED	3-03-003 INITIALS
3-02-002 INDIGENOUS	1-01-001 INEFFICIENCY	3-03-003 INFLICTING	5-05-005 INITIATE
1-01-001 INDIGENT	7-05-006 INEFFICIENT	3-02-003 INFLICTION	12-06-010 INITIATED
1-01-001 INDIGESTIBLE	3-03-003 INELIGIBLE	2-02-002 INFLOW	2-02-002 INITIATES
2-02-002 INDIGESTION	1-01-001 INELUCTABLE	132-12-075 INFLUENCE	4-03-004 INITIATING
10-07-010 INDIGNANT	2-02-002 INEPT	16-07-015 INFLUENCED	7-05-007 INITIATION
1-01-001 INDIGNANTLY	16-07-015 INEPTLY	14-06-014 INFLUENCES	32-09-017 INITIATIVE
9-07-009 INDIGNATION	14-06-014 INEPTNESS	2-01-001 INFLUENCING	2-01-001 INITIATOR
3-03-003 INDIGNITIES	2-02-002 INEQUALITY	14-07-012 INFLUENT	1-01-001 INIURE
1-01-001 INDIGO	2-01-001 INERT	2-01-002 INFLUENTIAL	6-03-003 INJECT
21-03-007 INDIRECT	5-03-005 INERTIA	1-01-001 INFLUENZA	2-02-002 INJECTED
1-01-001 INDIRECTION	2-02-002 INERTIAL	INFLUENZA-PNEUM ONIA	5-02-004 INJECTING
17-05-015 INDIRECTLY	8-07-008 INESCAPABLE	1-01-001 INFLUX	7-04-006 INJECTION
2-02-002 INDISCREET	1-01-001 INESCAPABLY	4-04-004 INFLUX	1-01-001 INJECTION-MOLDE D
1-01-001 INDISCRIMINANTL Y	1-01-001 INEVITABILITIES	7-06-007 INFORM	3-01-001 INJUN
3-02-003 INDISCRIMINATE	2-02-002 INEVITABILITY	18-09-014 INFORMAL	1-01-001 INJUN'S
1-01-001 INDISCRIMINATIN G	33-11-025 INEVITABLE	1-01-001 INFORMALITY	3-01-001 INJUNCTION
15-09-015 INDISPENSABLE	38-11-035 INEVITABLY	5-05-005 INFORMALLY	5-02-002 INJUNCTIONS
1-01-001 INDISPENSIBLE	2-02-002 INEXACT	2-01-001 INFORMANT	1-01-001 INJUNCTIVE
3-02-002 INDISPOSED	2-02-002 INEXCUSABLE	1-01-001 INFORMANTS	1-01-001 INJUNS
1-01-001 INDISPOSITION	3-03-003 INEXHAUSTIBLE	269-14-115 INFORMATION	20-10-019 INJURED
1-01-001 INDISPUTABLY	3-03-003 INEXORABLE	1-01-001 INFORMATION-CEL L	11-05-010 INJURIES
1-01-001 INDISTINCT	3-03-003 INEXORABLY	1-01-001 INFORMATION-SEE KING	1-01-001 INJURING
3-03-003 INDISTINGUISHAB LE	6-03-006 INEXPENSIVE	2-01-002 INFORMATIONAL	2-02-002 INJURIOUS
1-01-001 INDIUM	1-01-001 INEXPERIENCE	2-02-002 INFORMATIVE	27-09-018 INJURY
239-11-131 INDIVIDUAL	7-06-007 INEXPERIENCED	57-14-044 INFORMED	16-05-008 INJUSTICE
11-03-008 INDIVIDUAL'S	1-01-001 INEXPERT	4-04-004 INFORMING	1-01-001 INJUSTICES
2-01-001 INDIVIDUAL-CONT RIBUTOR	6-04-005 INEXPLICABLE	6-03-005 INFORMS	7-03-004 INK
12-01-004 INDIVIDUALISM	1-01-001 INEXPLICABLY	1-01-001 INFRA	1-01-001 INKLING
3-01-001 INDIVIDUALIST	1-01-001 INEXPRESSIBLE	1-01-001 INFRACTION	1-01-001 INKS
4-02-004 INDIVIDUALISTIC	1-01-001 INEXPRESSIBLY	12-03-005 INFRARED	1-01-001 INLAID
2-01-002 INDIVIDUALISTS	1-01-001 INEXTRICABLE	4-04-004 INFREQUENT	4-04-004 INLAND
4-04-004 INDIVIDUALITY	3-02-003 INFALLIBLE	2-02-002 INFREQUENTLY	4-02-003 INLET
5-02-005 INDIVIDUALIZED	4-02-004 INFAMOUS	7-01-001 INFRINGEMENT	3-03-003 INLETS
1-01-001 INDIVIDUALIZING	1-01-001 INFAMY	1-01-001 INFRINGEMENTS	1-01-001 INMATE
19-08-018 INDIVIDUALLY	11-04-005 INFANCY	1-01-001 INFURIATE	6-03-003 INMATES
73-10-054 INDIVIDUALS	11-07-011 INFANT	3-03-003 INFURIATED	9-04-008 INN
1-01-001 INDIVIDUATION	1-01-001 INFANT'S	2-02-002 INFURIATING	3-02-002 INNA
1-01-001 INDIVISIBILITY	3-03-003 INFANTILE	1-01-001 INFURIATION	4-03-004 INNATE
1-01-001 INDIVISIBLE	16-04-009 INFANTRY	1-01-001 INFUSION	55-12-041 INNER
1-01-001 INDO-*CHINA	2-02-002 INFANTRYMAN	1-01-001 ING	1-01-001 INNERMOST
2-02-002 INDOCHINA	1-01-001 INFANTRYMEN	10-06-010 INGBAR	2-01-001 INNESFREE
1-01-001 INDOCTRINATED	3-02-002 INFANTS	1-01-001 INGENIOUS	12-03-004 INNING
1-01-001 INDOCTRINATING	1-01-001 INFARCT	1-01-001 INGENIOUSLY	4-02-003 INNINGS
1-01-001 INDOCTRINATION	1-01-001 INFARCTION	5-03-005 INGENUITY	28-07-012 INNOCENCE
1-01-001 INDOLENCE	4-02-003 INFATUATION	4-04-004 INGESTED	37-11-022 INNOCENT
4-02-003 INDOLENT	1-01-001 INFECT	1-01-001 INGESTION	3-02-003 INNOCENTLY
1-01-001 INDOLENTLY	5-03-005 INFECTED	1-01-001 INGLESIDE	1-01-001 INNOCENTS
1-01-001 INDOMITABLE	4-04-004 INFECTION	1-01-001 INGLESIDE'S	7-05-007 INNOVATION
9-03-005 INDONESIA	1-01-001 INFECTIONS	1-01-001 INGLORIOUS	4-03-004 INNOVATIONS
1-01-001 INDONESIAN	1-01-001 INFECTIOUS	1-01-001 INGO	1-01-001 INNOVATORS
4-04-004 INDOOR	1-01-001 INFER	4-03-004 INGRATIATING	1-01-001 INNS
5-03-005 INDOORS	7-03-005 INFERENCE	1-01-001 INGRATITOODE	1-01-001 INNUENDO
1-01-001 INDORSED	4-02-004 INFERENCES	1-01-001 INGRATITUDE	1-01-001 INNUENDOES
1-01-001 INDUBITABLE	2-01-002 INFERENTIAL	6-06-006 INGREDIENT	1-01-001 INNUENDOS
9-04-009 INDUCE	7-04-007 INFERIOR	9-04-006 INGREDIENTS	6-05-006 INNUMERABLE
13-04-008 INDUCED	5-03-005 INFERIORITY	2-01-002 INHABIT	2-01-002 INOCULATION
2-02-002 INDUCEMENT	1-01-001 INFERNALLY	13-08-012 INHABITANTS	1-01-001 INOCULATIONS
1-01-001 INDUCEMENTS	2-02-002 INFERNO	1-01-001 INHABITATION	1-01-001 INOPERABLE
3-02-002 INDUCES	3-02-003 INFERRED	6-05-005 INHABITED	1-01-001 INOPPORTUNE
4-02-003 INDUCING	1-01-001 INFERTILE	1-01-001 INHABITING	2-01-002 INORDINATELY
3-02-002 INDUCTED	1-01-001 INFEST	1-01-001 INHALATION	11-01-004 INORGANIC
1-01-001 INDUCTEES	2-02-002 INFESTATION	1-01-001 INHALING	1-01-001 INPOST
6-03-004 INDUCTION	4-01-001 INFESTATIONS	1-01-001 INHARMONIOUS	20-02-005 INPUT
1-01-001 INDUCTIONS	1-01-001 INFESTED	26-06-022 INHERENT	4-01-001 INPUT/*OUTPUT
9-05-008 INDULGE	1-01-001 INFIDEL	3-02-003 INHERENTLY	1-01-001 INPUT/OUTPUT
5-03-005 INDULGED	2-02-002 INFIDELITY	1-01-001 INHERES	5-02-003 INQUEST
5-02-003 INDULGENCE	1-01-001 INFIDELS	1-01-001 INHERIT	6-06-006 INQUIRE
1-01-001 INDULGENCES	6-03-003 INFIELD	6-03-005 INHERITANCE	16-08-013 INQUIRED
2-02-002 INDULGENT	1-01-001 INFIELDER	16-09-016 INHERITED	13-01-001 INQUIRER
1-01-001 INDULGING	1-01-001 INFIGHTING	1-01-001 INHERITING	17-05-009 INQUIRIES
1-01-001 INDUSTRALIZATIO N	2-01-001 INFILTRATED	1-01-001 INHERITORS	5-03-005 INQUIRING
143-11-057 INDUSTRIAL	1-01-001 INFILTRATING	8-01-004 INHERITS	17-06-013 INQUIRY
1-01-001 INDUSTRIALISM	1-01-001 INFILTRATION	5-02-004 INHIBIT	3-03-003 INQUISITION
2-02-002 INDUSTRIALIST	19-11-016 INFINITE	2-01-002 INHIBITED	1-01-001 INQUISITIVE
1-01-001 INDUSTRIALISTES	3-03-003 INFINITELY	6-02-005 INHIBITING	1-01-001 INQUISITOR
1-01-001 INDUSTRIALISTS	3-02-002 INFINITESIMAL	3-03-003 INHIBITION	1-01-001 INQUISITOR-*GEN ERAL
2-02-002 INDUSTRIALIZATI ON	1-01-001 INFINITESIMALLY	2-01-001 INHIBITIONS	3-03-003 INROADS
9-04-006 INDUSTRIALIZED	6-02-005 INFINITIVE	2-02-002 INHIBITOR	13-07-011 INSANE
1-01-001 INDUSTRIALLY	3-03-003 INFINITUM	2-01-001 INHIBITORS	1-01-001 INSANELY
36-10-023 INDUSTRIES	2-01-001 INFINITY	1-01-001 INHIBITORY	3-02-002 INSANITY
	2-02-002 INFIRM	1-01-001 INHIBITS	1-01-001 INSATIABLE
	2-01-001 INFIRMARY	3-01-001 INHOLDINGS	7-02-003 INSCRIBED
	1-01-001 INFIRMITY	1-01-001 INHOMOGENEOUS	6-05-005 INSCRIPTION
	3-01-001 INFLAME	1-01-001 INHOSPITABLE	
	1-01-001 INFLAMED		
	1-01-001 INFLAMMATION		

Code	Word	Code	Word
1-01-001	INSCRIPTIONS	12-07-010	INSTITUTED
1-01-001	INSCRUTABILITY	1-01-001	INSTITUTES
5-03-004	INSCRUTABLE	1-01-001	INSTITUTING
14-06-009	INSECT	41-09-029	INSTITUTION
1-01-001	INSECTICIDE	1-01-001	INSTITUTION'S
2-01-001	INSECTICIDES	1-01-001	INSTITUTION-WID E
23-07-010	INSECTS	9-05-008	INSTITUTIONAL
3-02-002	INSECURE	1-01-001	INSTITUTIONALIZ ATION
5-04-005	INSECURITY	3-03-003	INSTITUTIONALIZ ED
1-01-001	INSEMINATION	98-08-046	INSTITUTIONS
3-03-003	INSENSITIVE	3-02-003	INSTRUCT
4-02-004	INSEPARABLE	16-10-015	INSTRUCTED
13-02-007	INSERT	2-02-002	INSTRUCTING
16-09-012	INSERTED	26-11-020	INSTRUCTION
1-01-001	INSERTION	3-02-003	INSTRUCTIONAL
1-01-001	INSERTIONS	35-08-023	INSTRUCTIONS
1-01-001	INSERTS	3-03-003	INSTRUCTIVE
1-01-001	INSET	8-06-007	INSTRUCTOR
1-01-001	INSETS	1-01-001	INSTRUCTOR'S
2-02-002	INSHORE	1-01-001	INSTRUCTORS
174-15-085	INSIDE	2-01-001	INSTRUCTS
2-02-002	INSIDERS	47-10-033	INSTRUMENT
4-03-004	INSIDES	1-01-001	INSTRUMENT-JAMM ED
2-02-002	INSIDIOUS	11-06-007	INSTRUMENTAL
2-01-002	INSIDIOUSLY	1-01-001	INSTRUMENTAL-RE WARD
22-07-022	INSIGHT	3-02-002	INSTRUMENTALIST S
16-06-013	INSIGHTS	3-03-003	INSTRUMENTALITI ES
1-01-001	INSIGNIFICANCE	3-02-002	INSTRUMENTALLY
1-01-001	INSIGNIFICANCES	1-01-001	INSTRUMENTALS
5-04-005	INSIGNIFICANT	4-02-003	INSTRUMENTATION
1-01-001	INSINCERE	26-11-018	INSTRUMENTS
1-01-001	INSINUATED	2-01-001	INSUBORDINATE
1-01-001	INSINUATES	2-02-002	INSUBORDINATION
1-01-001	INSINUATING	2-02-002	INSUBSTANTIAL
2-02-002	INSINUATION	7-05-007	INSUFFICIENT
3-03-003	INSINUATIONS	3-03-003	INSUFFICIENTLY
1-01-001	INSIPID	3-03-003	INSULARITY
27-11-026	INSIST	2-02-002	INSULATE
43-13-040	INSISTED	4-04-004	INSULATED
19-09-017	INSISTENCE	2-01-001	INSULATING
8-04-008	INSISTENT	10-03-004	INSULATION
6-05-006	INSISTING	1-01-001	INSULATOR
10-06-009	INSISTS	1-01-001	INSULATORS
7-04-007	INSOFAR	3-02-002	INSULIN
6-05-005	INSOLENCE	7-07-007	INSULT
2-02-002	INSOLENT	2-02-002	INSULTED
1-01-001	INSOLENTLY	4-03-004	INSULTING
12-04-007	INSOLUBLE	3-03-003	INSULTS
1-01-001	INSOMMA	2-02-002	INSUPERABLE
3-01-001	INSOMNIA	1-01-001	INSUPERABLY
1-01-001	INSOMNIACS	46-09-017	INSURANCE
1-01-001	INSOUCIANCE	24-09-023	INSURE
12-07-009	INSPECT	6-04-006	INSURED
2-02-002	INSPECTED	1-01-001	INSURES
2-02-002	INSPECTING	1-01-001	INSURGENCE
21-12-020	INSPECTION	1-01-001	INSURGENT
3-03-003	INSPECTIONS	1-01-001	INSURGENTS
13-06-008	INSPECTOR	6-05-006	INSURING
2-01-002	INSPECTOR'S	2-02-002	INSURMOUNTABLE
9-05-007	INSPIRATION	2-01-001	INSURRECTION
1-01-001	INSPIRATIONAL	1-01-001	INSURRECTIONS
1-01-001	INSPIRATIONS	14-07-012	INTACT
3-02-003	INSPIRE	1-01-001	INTACTIBLE
25-10-022	INSPIRED	7-04-005	INTAKE
1-01-001	INSPIRES	6-03-004	INTANGIBLE
8-07-008	INSPIRING	3-03-003	INTANGIBLES
4-04-004	INSTABILITY	4-01-003	INTEGER
8-03-006	INSTALL	1-01-001	INTEGERS
12-02-007	INSTALLATION	13-06-012	INTEGRAL
16-04-008	INSTALLATIONS	3-02-002	INTEGRALS
35-12-024	INSTALLED	7-04-006	INTEGRATE
5-02-005	INSTALLING	11-07-011	INTEGRATED
5-02-003	INSTALLMENT	2-02-002	INTEGRATES
2-01-002	INSTALLMENTS	2-01-002	INTEGRATING
1-01-001	INSTALMENTS	48-09-024	INTEGRATION
82-15-068	INSTANCE	1-01-001	INTEGRATIVE
30-09-027	INSTANCES	10-07-009	INTEGRITY
1-01-001	INSTANCY	5-03-003	INTELLECT
38-10-026	INSTANT	66-12-042	INTELLECTUAL
1-01-001	INSTANT'S	1-01-001	INTELLECTUAL-LI TERARY
5-04-004	INSTANTANEOUS	1-01-001	INTELLECTUALITY
2-02-002	INSTANTANEOUSLY	5-04-005	INTELLECTUALLY
19-11-019	INSTANTLY	12-05-010	INTELLECTUALS
173-15-138	INSTEAD	1-01-001	INTELLECTUS
1-01-001	INSTIGATE	48-10-024	INTELLIGENCE
1-01-001	INSTIGATING	26-13-022	INTELLIGENT
1-01-001	INSTIGATION	3-02-003	INTELLIGENTLY
1-01-001	INSTIGATOR	1-01-001	INTELLIGENTSIA
1-01-001	INSTILLATION	11-05-010	INTELLIGIBLE
14-05-011	INSTINCT		
2-02-002	INSTINCTIVE		
10-07-008	INSTINCTIVELY		
4-04-004	INSTINCTS		
2-02-002	INSTINCTUAL		
1-01-001	INSTITUT		
50-08-027	INSTITUTE		
1-01-001	INSTITUTE'S		

Code	Word	Code	Word
1-01-001	INTEMPERANCE	2-01-001	INTERLINING
15-10-013	INTEND	8-01-001	INTERLOBULAR
1-01-001	INTENDANT	9-03-005	INTERLOCKING
1-01-001	INTENDANTS	1-01-001	INTERLOCUTOR
45-12-040	INTENDED	5-05-005	INTERLUDE
1-01-001	INTENDING	2-02-002	INTERLUDES
6-05-006	INTENDS	1-01-001	INTERMARRIAGE
40-10-037	INTENSE	1-01-001	INTERMEDIARY
10-06-010	INTENSELY	21-04-013	INTERMEDIATE
8-04-005	INTENSIFICATION	5-02-003	INTERMEDIATES
4-04-004	INTENSIFIED	2-02-002	INTERMENT
6-01-001	INTENSIFIER	1-01-001	INTERMESHED
6-01-001	INTENSIFIERS	4-04-004	INTERMINABLE
4-03-004	INTENSIFY	1-01-001	INTERMISSION
2-02-002	INTENSIFYING	1-01-001	INTERMISSIONS
5-03-005	INTENSITIES	3-03-003	INTERMITTENT
56-11-031	INTENSITY	2-01-002	INTERMITTENTLY
15-05-010	INTENSIVE	1-01-001	INTERMOLECULAR
1-01-001	INTENSIVELY	2-02-002	INTERN
14-08-014	INTENT	62-10-036	INTERNAL
36-10-035	INTENTION	1-01-001	INTERNAL-EXTERN AL
5-02-004	INTENTIONAL	2-01-002	INTERNALIZED
4-04-004	INTENTIONALLY	6-01-004	INTERNALLY
1-01-001	INTENTIONED	155-09-075	INTERNATIONAL
22-09-020	INTENTIONS	1-01-001	INTERNATIONALE
4-03-004	INTENTLY	2-02-002	INTERNATIONALIS T
2-02-002	INTER	1-01-001	INTERNATIONALIS TS
5-03-005	INTER-*AMERICAN	1-01-001	INTERNATIONALIZ ED
2-01-001	INTER-AMERICAN	4-02-004	INTERNATIONALLY
1-01-001	INTER-PLANT	2-02-002	INTERNE
1-01-001	INTER-RELATION	1-01-001	INTERNED
1-01-001	INTER-RELATIONS HIPS	1-01-001	INTERNIST'S
1-01-001	INTER-SPECIES	1-01-001	INTERNS
1-01-001	INTER-TOWN	1-01-001	INTERPENETRATE
1-01-001	INTER-TRIBAL	2-01-001	INTERPENETRATES
2-02-002	INTERACT	1-01-001	INTERPEOPLE
1-01-001	INTERACTING	3-02-003	INTERPERSONAL
17-03-008	INTERACTION	3-01-001	INTERPLANETARY
3-02-003	INTERACTIONS	6-03-006	INTERPLAY
1-01-001	INTERACTS	1-01-001	INTERPOLATED
4-01-001	INTERAMA	1-01-001	INTERPOLATION
1-01-001	INTERAXIAL	1-01-001	INTERPOLATIONS
1-01-001	INTERCEDE	1-01-001	INTERPOSED
6-04-005	INTERCEPT	1-01-001	INTERPOSING
3-03-003	INTERCEPTED	2-02-002	INTERPOSITION
1-01-001	INTERCEPTOR	11-06-010	INTERPRET
1-01-001	INTERCEPTS	1-01-001	INTERPRETABLE
6-03-003	INTERCHANGE	54-11-040	INTERPRETATION
3-03-003	INTERCHANGEABLE	12-06-009	INTERPRETATIONS
2-01-001	INTERCHANGES	1-01-001	INTERPRETATIVE
1-01-001	INTERCLASS	24-08-023	INTERPRETED
4-02-002	INTERCOLLEGIATE	8-07-008	INTERPRETER
1-01-001	INTERCONNECTED	2-07-002	INTERPRETING
1-01-001	INTERCONNECTEDN ESS	1-01-001	INTERPRETOR
5-03-004	INTERCONTINENTA L	3-02-002	INTERPRETS
9-01-002	INTERCOURSE	1-01-001	INTERRED
1-01-001	INTERCRISIS	2-02-002	INTERREGNUM
2-01-001	INTERDENOMINATI ONAL	5-02-005	INTERRELATED
1-01-001	INTERDEPARTMENT AL	4-04-004	INTERRELATION
6-02-002	INTERDEPENDENCE	4-02-004	INTERRELATIONS
8-04-007	INTERDEPENDENT	1-01-001	INTERRELATIONSH IP
1-01-001	INTEREFERENCE	2-01-002	INTERRELATIONSH IPS
330-15-170	INTEREST	2-02-002	INTERROGATION
105-14-077	INTERESTED	1-01-001	INTERROGATIVES
82-13-070	INTERESTING	1-01-001	INTERROGATOR
3-03-003	INTERESTINGLY	4-04-004	INTERRUPT
83-12-049	INTERESTS	18-08-015	INTERRUPTED
3-01-002	INTERFACE	8-05-008	INTERRUPTION
5-01-002	INTERFACES	3-03-003	INTERRUPTIONS
6-01-004	INTERFACIAL	1-01-001	INTERSCIENCE
7-02-002	INTERFAITH	6-01-003	INTERSECT
9-08-009	INTERFERE	2-02-002	INTERSECTING
5-05-005	INTERFERED	17-05-007	INTERSECTION
45-07-015	INTERFERENCE	12-01-002	INTERSECTIONS
1-01-001	INTERFERENCE-LI KE	1-01-001	INTERSPECIES
2-02-002	INTERFERES	1-01-001	INTERSPERSED
6-05-006	INTERFERING	3-01-001	INTERSTAGE
4-02-002	INTERFEROMETER	14-04-009	INTERSTATE
1-01-001	INTERFEROMETERS	5-02-002	INTERSTELLAR
1-01-001	INTERGLACIAL	1-01-001	INTERSTICES
1-01-001	INTERGOVERNMENT AL	2-01-001	INTERSTITIAL
3-01-002	INTERGROUP	4-04-004	INTERTWINED
11-06-009	INTERIM	18-06-010	INTERVAL
74-10-020	INTERIOR	25-09-023	INTERVALS
4-02-003	INTERIORS	2-02-002	INTERVENE
1-01-001	INTERJECTED	4-03-003	INTERVENED
4-03-004	INTERLACED	1-01-001	INTERVENES
1-01-001	INTERLACING	1-01-001	INTERVENING
2-01-001	INTERLAYER	20-07-013	INTERVENTION
2-01-001	INTERLIBRARY	34-08-018	INTERVIEW
		12-06-008	INTERVIEWED

Code	Word
1-01-001	INTERVIEWEE
1-01-001	INTERVIEWEES
2-02-002	INTERVIEWER
1-01-001	INTERVIEWERS
7-03-005	INTERVIEWING
18-04-009	INTERVIEWS
1-01-001	INTERWEAVING
4-03-004	INTERWOVEN
1-01-001	INTESTINE
1-01-001	INTESTINES
1-01-001	INTIAL
3-02-002	INTIMA
3-03-003	INTIMACY
1-01-001	INTIMAL
21-10-018	INTIMATE
5-05-005	INTIMATED
6-04-006	INTIMATELY
1-01-001	INTIMATING
1-01-001	INTIMATIONS
2-02-002	INTIMIDATE
3-03-003	INTIMIDATED
5-04-005	INTIMIDATION
1791-15-464	INTO
3-02-003	INTOLERABLE
2-01-002	INTOLERANCE
1-01-001	INTOLERANT
2-01-001	INTONACO
8-02-002	INTONATION
1-01-001	INTONATIONS
4-02-003	INTONED
1-01-001	INTOXICATED
1-01-001	INTOXICATING
1-01-001	INTRA
1-01-001	INTRA-CITY
1-01-001	INTRA-COMPANY
1-01-001	INTRA-MURAL
1-01-001	INTRA-STELLAR
2-01-002	INTRACTABLE
1-01-001	INTRADEPARTMENTAL
1-01-001	INTRAEPITHELIAL
2-01-001	INTRAMURAL
1-01-001	INTRAMUSCULARLY
1-01-001	INTRANASAL
2-01-002	INTRANSIGENCE
1-01-001	INTRANSIGENTS
1-01-001	INTRAPULMONARY
1-01-001	INTRATISSUE
1-01-001	INTREPID
10-07-010	INTRICATE
1-01-001	INTRICATELY
4-04-004	INTRIGUE
2-02-002	INTRIGUED
3-03-003	INTRIGUES
3-03-003	INTRIGUING
2-02-002	INTRIGUINGLY
5-02-005	INTRINSIC
4-03-004	INTRINSICALLY
11-10-011	INTRODUCE
52-11-046	INTRODUCED
4-03-004	INTRODUCES
9-06-008	INTRODUCING
39-12-034	INTRODUCTION
1-01-001	INTRODUCTIONS
3-01-003	INTRODUCTORY
3-01-001	INTROJECT
1-01-001	INTROJECTED
1-01-001	INTROJECTS
1-01-001	INTROSPECTION
2-02-002	INTROSPECTIVE
1-01-001	INTROVERTED
1-01-001	INTRUDE
1-01-001	INTRUDED
1-01-001	INTRUDER
1-01-001	INTRUDERS
1-01-001	INTRUDES
1-01-001	INTRUDING
3-02-003	INTRUSION
2-02-002	INTRUSIONS
2-02-002	INTRUSIVE
18-06-013	INTUITION
1-01-001	INTUITIONS
7-03-006	INTUITIVE
1-01-001	INTUITIVELY
1-01-001	INUNDATED
1-01-001	INUNDATING
1-01-001	INUNDATIONS
1-01-001	INURE
2-02-002	INURED
5-03-004	INVADE
6-06-006	INVADED
1-01-001	INVADER
5-05-005	INVADERS
1-01-001	INVADES
3-02-002	INVADING
7-06-007	INVALID
2-02-002	INVALIDATE
1-01-001	INVALIDATED
1-01-001	INVALIDISM
1-01-001	INVALIDS
5-04-005	INVALUABLE
1-01-001	INVARIABLE
31-13-031	INVARIABLY
13-01-002	INVARIANT
16-06-015	INVASION
1-01-001	INVASION-THEORY
9-01-002	INVASIONS
1-01-001	INVEIGH
7-04-006	INVENT
13-08-012	INVENTED
1-01-001	INVENTING
20-06-011	INVENTION
4-03-003	INVENTIONS
3-03-003	INVENTIVE
7-06-007	INVENTOR
13-04-008	INVENTORIES
4-01-001	INVENTORS
23-06-013	INVENTORY
1-01-001	INVERCALT
5-01-004	INVERSE
5-01-004	INVERSELY
2-02-002	INVERSION
1-01-001	INVERT
3-03-003	INVERTED
3-03-003	INVEST
11-06-009	INVESTED
11-06-011	INVESTIGATE
18-05-012	INVESTIGATED
1-01-001	INVESTIGATES
8-06-007	INVESTIGATING
51-11-037	INVESTIGATION
22-05-013	INVESTIGATIONS
3-03-003	INVESTIGATIVE
4-03-004	INVESTIGATOR
13-03-011	INVESTIGATORS
1-01-001	INVESTING
43-07-021	INVESTMENT
6-05-006	INVESTMENTS
2-02-002	INVESTOR
1-01-001	INVESTORS
1-01-001	INVESTS
3-03-003	INVETERATE
8-06-008	INVIGORATING
1-01-001	INVIGORATION
2-02-002	INVINCIBLE
1-01-001	INVIOLABILITY
1-01-001	INVIOLABLE
3-03-003	INVIOLATE
8-06-008	INVISIBLE
2-02-002	INVISIBLY
20-09-018	INVITATION
1-01-001	INVITATIONAL
14-07-011	INVITATIONS
26-11-023	INVITE
1-01-001	INVITED
7-04-006	INVITEES
8-07-008	INVITES
4-04-004	INVITING
5-03-005	INVOCATION
1-01-001	INVOICES
4-03-004	INVOKE
6-04-006	INVOKED
4-03-004	INVOKING
1-01-001	INVOLUNTARILY
3-03-003	INVOLUNTARY
1-01-001	INVOLUNTARY-CONTROL
9-01-001	INVOLUTION
3-01-001	INVOLUTIONS
3-01-001	INVOLUTORIAL
31-09-026	INVOLVE
147-15-105	INVOLVED
13-07-010	INVOLVEMENT
1-01-001	INVOLVEMENTS
41-08-030	INVOLVES
33-08-029	INVOLVING
1-01-001	INVULNERABILITY
1-01-001	INVULNERABLE
9-07-009	INWARD
3-03-003	INWARDLY
2-02-002	INWARDNESS
1-01-001	IO
8-01-002	IODIDE
1-01-001	IODIDE-CONCENTRATING
1-01-001	IODINATE
7-02-002	IODINATED
3-01-001	IODINATING
1-01-001	IODINATION
18-01-002	IODINE
1-01-001	IODOAMINO
1-01-001	IODOCOMPOUNDS
1-01-001	IODOPROTEIN
1-01-001	IODOTHYRONINES
1-01-001	IODOTYROSINES
6-02-005	ION
1-01-001	IONE
8-04-006	IONIC
3-02-002	IONIZED
6-01-001	IONIZING
3-01-001	IONOSPHERE
9-02-004	IONS
1-01-001	IOSOLA
1-01-001	IOTA
4-04-004	IOWA
1-01-001	IPSO
2-01-002	IRA
1-01-001	IRAJ
2-02-002	IRAN
3-03-003	IRAQ
2-01-001	IRAQW
1-01-001	IRATE
1-01-001	IRE
13-07-009	IRELAND
2-02-002	IRELAND'S
1-01-001	IRELANDS'
14-01-001	IRENAEUS
1-01-001	IRENAEUS'
2-02-002	IRENE
1-01-001	IRIDIUM
2-02-002	IRINA
28-09-016	IRISH
1-01-001	IRISHMAN
1-01-001	IRISHMEN
1-01-001	IRKSOME
1-01-001	IRMA
43-12-034	IRON
1-01-001	IRON-CLAD
1-01-001	IRON-POOR
1-01-001	IRON-SHOD
2-02-002	IRONED
16-03-009	IRONIC
2-02-002	IRONICAL
6-04-005	IRONICALLY
1-01-001	IRONIES
5-02-003	IRONING
1-01-001	IRONPANTS
7-04-005	IRONS
1-01-001	IRONSIDE
12-06-011	IRONY
1-01-001	IROQUOIS
5-01-001	IRRADIATED
10-01-001	IRRADIATION
8-03-007	IRRATIONAL
1-01-001	IRRATIONALITY
1-01-001	IRRATIONALLY
1-01-001	IRRAWADDY
3-03-003	IRRECONCILABLE
2-02-002	IRREDEEMABLE
1-01-001	IRREDEEMABLY
1-01-001	IRREDENTISM
1-01-001	IRREDUCIBLE
9-05-008	IRREGULAR
8-06-006	IRREGULARITIES
4-04-004	IRREGULARITY
5-03-005	IRREGULARLY
1-01-001	IRREGULARS
14-07-013	IRRELEVANT
2-02-002	IRREMEDIABLE
2-02-002	IRREPARABLE
1-01-001	IRREPARABLY
2-01-001	IRREPRODUCIBILITY
8-04-005	IRRESISTIBLE
1-01-001	IRRESISTIBLY
2-02-002	IRRESOLUTE
1-01-001	IRRESOLUTION
1-01-001	IRRESOLVABLE
3-02-003	IRRESPECTIVE
3-03-003	IRRESPONSIBILITY
9-07-009	IRRESPONSIBLE
2-02-002	IRREVERENCE
2-02-002	IRREVERENT
2-02-002	IRREVERSIBLE
1-01-001	IRREVERSIBLY
2-02-002	IRREVOCABLE
2-02-002	IRREVOCABLY
1-01-001	IRRIGATE
1-01-001	IRRIGATING
3-02-002	IRRIGATION
1-01-001	IRRITABILITY
5-03-004	IRRITABLE
3-03-003	IRRITABLY
1-01-001	IRRITANT
5-03-005	IRRITATED
1-01-001	IRRITATES
4-03-004	IRRITATING
7-04-006	IRRITATION
3-03-003	IRRITATIONS
1-01-001	IRRUPTIONS
1-01-001	IRV
1-01-001	IRVIN
4-03-003	IRVING
1-01-001	IRWIN
10099-15-485	IS
1-01-001	ISA
10-05-006	ISAAC
2-02-002	ISAACS
1-01-001	ISAACSON
1-01-001	ISABEL
1-01-001	ISABELL
1-01-001	ISAIAH
4-01-001	ISFAHAN
1-01-001	ISHAM
1-01-001	ISHII
1-01-001	ISHTAR
1-01-001	ISIS
3-03-003	ISLAM
1-01-001	ISLAM'S
3-02-002	ISLAMIC
167-15-057	ISLAND
9-03-005	ISLAND'S
6-03-003	ISLANDERS
1-01-001	ISLANDIA
30-11-017	ISLANDS
1-01-001	ISLANDS'
5-04-005	ISLE
4-03-004	ISLES
97-13-065	ISN'T
1-01-001	ISOCYANATE
1-01-001	ISOCYANATE-LABELED
1-01-001	ISODINE
8-03-007	ISOLATE
35-08-027	ISOLATED
5-03-005	ISOLATING
16-03-009	ISOLATION
1-01-001	ISOLATIONISM
1-01-001	ISOLATIONISTIC
1-01-001	ISOLDE
1-01-001	ISOMERS
2-01-001	ISOPLETHS
1-01-001	ISOTHERMAL
1-01-001	ISOTHERMALLY
4-01-001	ISOTONIC
2-01-002	ISOTOPIC
3-01-001	ISOTROPIC
15-05-006	ISRAEL
1-01-001	ISRAEL'S
4-02-002	ISRAELI
1-01-001	ISRAELITE
1-01-001	ISRAELITES
7-04-007	ISSUANCE
152-11-082	ISSUE
50-11-038	ISSUED
66-10-041	ISSUES
4-02-003	ISSUING
1-01-001	IST
5-01-001	ISTANBUL
11-01-001	ISTIQLAL
2-01-001	ISTIQLAL'S
1-01-001	ISTVAN
8756-15-500	IT
3-02-002	IT'D
18-08-016	IT'LL
302-14-149	IT'S
1-01-001	IT**H
2-01-001	IT-WIT
47-11-027	ITALIAN
7-04-006	ITALIANS
1-01-001	ITALICIZED
3-01-002	ITALICS
1-01-001	ITALO
1-01-001	ITALO-*AMERICA
34-11-023	ITALY
2-02-002	ITALY'S
1-01-001	ITASCA
5-04-004	ITCH
1-01-001	ITCHES
4-03-003	ITCHING
54-10-020	ITEM
1-01-001	ITEM-*CATEGOR
1-01-001	ITEMIZATION
3-01-002	ITEMIZED
2-02-002	ITEMIZING
72-11-039	ITEMS
1-01-001	ITHACA
1-01-001	ITHACAN
1-01-001	ITINERANT
3-03-003	ITINERARY
1-01-001	ITO
1-01-001	ITOIZ
1858-15-427	ITS
304-15-171	ITSELF
1-01-001	IUVABIT

```
4-03-004    JOWLS
40-12-032   JOY
21-04-006   JOYCE
1-01-001    JOYFUL
1-01-001    JOYFULLY
5-02-004    JOYOUS
1-01-001    JOYOUSLY
2-01-001    JOYRIDE
7-05-007    JOYS
74-09-030   JR
2-02-002    JR**.'S
7-05-006    JUAN
15-06-001   JUANITA
1-01-001    JUANITA'S
9-01-001    JUBAL
3-01-001    JUBAL'S
2-01-002    JUBILANT
2-02-002    JUBILANTLY
1-01-001    JUBILATION
2-01-001    JUDAISM
2-02-002    JUDAS
3-03-003    JUDE
1-01-001    JUDEA
1-01-001    JUDEO-*CHRISTIA
                N
77-13-044   JUDGE
1-01-001    JUDGE'S
1-01-001    JUDGE-MADE
15-06-011   JUDGED
1-01-001    JUDGEMENT
20-04-009   JUDGES
1-01-001    JUDGES'
1-01-001    JUDGESHIP
15-08-009   JUDGING
60-11-049   JUDGMENT
28-08-017   JUDGMENTS
16-04-009   JUDICIAL
1-01-001    JUDICIARIES
3-02-003    JUDICIARY
1-01-001    JUDICIOUS
2-02-002    JUDICIOUSLY
4-02-002    JUDITH
3-03-003    JUDSON
1-01-001    JUDSONS
8-03-004    JUDY
8-01-001    JUET
3-01-001    JUET'S
6-05-005    JUG
2-02-002    JUGGLING
11-06-008   JUICE
2-02-002    JUICES
1-01-001    JUICIEST
6-03-004    JUICY
1-01-001    JUJU
2-02-002    JUKE
2-02-002    JULEP
1-01-001    JULEPS
1-01-001    JULES
27-04-004   JULIA
8-06-008    JULIAN
10-02-003   JULIE
1-01-001    JULIET
1-01-001    JULIO
4-02-003    JULIUS
65-11-039   JULY
4-03-004    JUMBLE
3-03-003    JUMBLED
24-10-020   JUMP
35-10-032   JUMPED
1-01-001    JUMPER
9-04-008    JUMPING
2-01-001    JUMPS
2-02-002    JUMPY
7-06-007    JUNCTION
4-03-004    JUNCTURE
2-01-001    JUNCTURES
93-11-054   JUNE
1-01-001    JUNGIAN
20-05-008   JUNGLE
4-02-002    JUNGLES
75-10-030   JUNIOR
2-02-002    JUNIOR'S
1-01-001    JUNIOR-GRADE
1-01-001    JUNIOR-PHILOSOP
                HICAL
1-01-001    JUNIOR-SENIOR
1-01-001    JUNIOR-YEAR-ABR
                OAD
31-02-003   JUNIORS
1-01-001    JUNIORS'
8-05-006    JUNK
1-01-001    JUNKERDOM
2-01-001    JUNKERS
1-01-001    JUNKETEERING
1-01-001    JUNKIES
1-01-001    JUNKS
3-01-001    JUNTA

9-03-003    JUPITER
2-01-001    JURAS
3-01-001    JURE
1-01-001    JURIDICAL
1-01-001    JURIES
29-05-011   JURISDICTION
3-03-003    JURISDICTIONAL
1-01-001    JURISDICTIONS
3-02-002    JURISPRUDENCE
1-01-001    JURISPRUDENTIAL
                LY
3-02-003    JURIST
4-02-003    JURISTS
4-01-001    JUROR
4-01-003    JURORS
67-08-022   JURY
1-01-001    JURY-TAMPERING
1-01-001    JUSSEL
872-15-321  JUST
1-01-001    JUSTE
114-12-062  JUSTICE
2-02-002    JUSTICE'S
3-02-003    JUSTICES
4-03-003    JUSTIFIABLE
5-04-005    JUSTIFIABLY
16-04-013   JUSTIFICATION
3-02-003    JUSTIFICATIONS
23-06-017   JUSTIFIED
26-10-022   JUSTIFY
3-01-002    JUSTIFYING
1-01-001    JUSTINE
4-02-002    JUSTINIAN
1-01-001    JUSTITIA
5-04-005    JUSTLY
1-01-001    JUSTNESS
1-01-001    JUTISH
2-02-002    JUTTING
21-03-004   JUVENILE
18-07-012   JUXTAPOSED
2-01-001    JUXTAPOSED
3-02-003    JUXTAPOSITION
20-08-020   K
1-01-001    K**.*C
1-01-001    K**.*G
1-01-001    K**.*J**.*P
2-01-001    KC
2-01-001    K'ANG-SI
1-01-001    KABALEVSKY
1-01-001    KABOOM
1-01-001    KADDISH
1-01-001    KADER
5-01-001    KAFKA
1-01-001    KAGANOVICH
7-01-001    KAHLER
1-01-001    KAHLER-*CRAFT
1-01-001    KAHN
2-02-002    KAHN'S
1-01-001    KAI-SHEK
1-01-001    KAI-SHEK'S
1-01-001    KAISER
3-01-001    KAISER'S
1-01-001    KAISERS
1-01-001    KAJAR
1-01-001    KAKUTANI
1-01-001    KALAMAZOO
264-14-178  KALE
1-01-001    KALEIDESCOPE
1-01-001    KALEIDOSCOPE
1-01-001    KALENTIEV
1-01-001    KALI
1-01-001    KALMUK
1-01-001    KALONJI
1-01-001    KAMCHATKA
2-01-001    KAMENS
2-01-001    KAMIENIEC
1-01-001    KAMIKAZE
1-01-001    KAMINSKY
3-02-002    KAN
2-02-002    KANDINSKY
1-01-001    KANIN
1-01-001    KANKAKEE
1-01-001    KANS
31-08-017   KANSAS
1-01-001    KANSAS-*NEBRASK
                A
2-02-002    KANT
1-01-001    KANTO
1-01-001    KAPLAN
1-01-001    KAPNEK
1-01-001    KAPOK-FILLED
5-02-004    KAPPA
4-03-003    KARAMAZOV
1-01-001    KARE
3-02-003    KAREN
1-01-001    KARET
4-01-001    KARIPO
1-01-001    KARIPO'S
7-05-005    KARL
1-01-001    KARL-*BIRGER

1-01-001    KARLHEINZ
1-01-001    KARLIS
7-01-001    KARNS
1-01-001    KARNS'
1-01-001    KAROL
1-01-001    KAROLINERNA
1-01-001    KARP'S
1-01-001    KARSHILAMA
2-01-001    KARSNER
1-01-001    KAS
2-01-001    KASAI
5-01-001    KASAVUBU
1-01-001    KASKASKIA
1-01-001    KASSEM
2-01-001    KASTER'S
21-03-007   KATANGA
1-01-001    KATANGAN
2-01-002    KATANGANS
41-02-004   KATE
4-01-002    KATE'S
6-01-001    KATHARINE
1-01-001    KATHARINE'S
6-04-005    KATHERINE
1-01-001    KATHERINE'S
1-01-001    KATHLEEN
1-01-001    KATHLEEN-*MASON
4-03-004    KATHY
15-02-003   KATIE
2-02-002    KATIE'S
1-01-001    KATOW
3-01-001    KATYA
1-01-001    KAUFFELD
1-01-001    KAUFFMANN
1-01-001    KAUFNABB
1-01-001    KAVA
1-01-001    KAWECKI
3-03-003    KAY
9-01-001    KAYABASHI
2-01-001    KAYABASHI'S
1-01-001    KAYABASHI-*=SAN
1-01-001    KAYO
1-01-001    KAZAN
1-01-001    KAZOO
2-01-001    KC
2-01-001    KEANE
9-01-001    KEARTON
1-01-001    KEATING'S
1-01-001    KEATS'S
1-01-001    KEBOB
1-01-001    KEDDAH
4-01-001    KEDGEREE
1-01-001    KEDZIE
1-01-001    KEE-REIST
1-01-001    KEEEERIST
3-01-001    KEEGAN
6-03-003    KEEL
3-02-002    KEELER
10-01-001   KEELSON
11-08-011   KEEN
3-01-001    KEENE
2-02-002    KEENEST
2-02-002    KEENING
1-01-001    KEENLY
264-14-178  KEEP
3-01-001    KEEPER
60-14-048   KEEPING
21-11-019   KEEPS
1-01-001    KEERIST
1-01-001    KEESHOND
2-02-002    KEG
1-01-001    KEGFUL
2-01-001    KEGHAM
1-01-001    KEGS
11-01-001   KEHL
1-01-001    KEINE
21-02-002   KEITH
3-01-001    KEITH'S
1-01-001    KEIZER
1-01-001    KEKISHEVA
1-01-001    KEL
1-01-001    KELLEY'S
1-01-001    KELLUM
1-01-001    KELLY
2-01-001    KELP
6-01-002    KELSEY
1-01-001    KELSEYVILLE
2-01-001    KELTS
5-01-001    KEMBLE
2-01-001    KEMBLE'S
1-01-001    KEMCHENJUNGA
1-01-001    KEMM
2-02-002    KEMPE
12-05-006   KEN
1-01-001    KENG
1-01-001    KENILWORTH
1-01-001    KENNAN
3-02-002    KENNAN'S

2-02-002    KENNARD
140-07-038  KENNEDY
26-05-018   KENNEDY'S
3-01-001    KENNEL
6-03-003    KENNETH
1-01-001    KENNETT
1-01-001    KENNING
10-01-001   KENNINGS
2-01-002    KENNY
1-01-001    KENO
14-06-008   KENT
1-01-001    KENTFIELD
1-01-001    KENTUCK
14-08-012   KENTUCKY
2-01-001    KENYON
1-01-001    KENZO
4-01-001    KEO
1-01-001    KEPLER
186-15-136  KEPT
1-01-001    KERBY
1-01-001    KERCHEVAL
1-01-001    KERCHIEF
8-02-003    KERN
3-01-001    KERNEL
3-01-001    KERNELS
6-03-003    KEROSENE
5-03-003    KERR
1-01-001    KERR'S
1-01-001    KERRVILLE
1-01-001    KERRY
1-01-001    KERSHBAUM
3-01-001    KERYGMA
1-01-001    KESTNER
1-01-001    KETCHES
1-01-001    KETCHUP
6-01-001    KETOSIS
3-03-003    KETTLE
88-13-060   KEY
1-01-001    KEY-PUNCHED
4-03-003    KEYBOARD
1-01-001    KEYBOARDING
3-02-002    KEYED
3-03-003    KEYHOLE
4-02-002    KEYNOTE
2-02-002    KEYNOTES
34-07-014   KEYS
3-01-001    KEYS'S
1-01-001    KEYSTONE
1-01-001    KEZZIAH
3-01-001    KHAJU
1-01-001    KHAKI
1-01-001    KHAKI-BOUND
2-02-002    KHAN
1-01-001    KHANEH
1-01-001    KHARTOUM
1-01-001    KHASI
1-01-001    KHMER
1-01-001    KHRUSH
68-06-017   KHRUSHCHEV
14-04-010   KHRUSHCHEV'S
2-02-002    KHRUSHCHEVS
1-01-001    KI-YI-ING
1-01-001    KIANG
1-01-001    KIBBUTZIM
16-06-008   KICK
1-01-001    KICK-OFF
1-01-001    KICK-OFFS
1-01-001    KICKBACKS
18-09-014   KICKED
12-08-010   KICKING
2-01-001    KICKOFF
3-03-003    KICKS
61-10-027   KID
12-04-004   KID'S
1-01-001    KID-*ISOLETTA
1-01-001    KIDDER
7-03-006    KIDDING
3-03-003    KIDNAPED
1-01-001    KIDNAPER
1-01-001    KIDNAPPED
2-01-001    KIDNAPPER
1-01-001    KIDNAPPERS
1-01-001    KIDNAPPING
6-03-003    KIDNEY
5-04-004    KIDNEYS
32-09-024   KIDS
2-01-001    KIEFFER
1-01-001    KIEFFERM
1-01-001    KIKA
1-01-001    KIKIYUS
3-01-001    KIKUYU
1-01-001    KILHOUR
2-01-001    KILILNGSWORTH
63-13-041   KILL
1-01-001    KILLABLE
1-01-001    KILLEBREW
75-13-050   KILLED
```

21-06-015	KILLER
1-01-001	KILLERS
1-01-001	KILLIN
23-07-014	KILLING
4-01-001	KILLINGSWORTH
19-01-001	KILLPATH
6-01-001	KILLPATH'S
8-07-007	KILLS
8-01-001	KILOMETER
3-02-003	KILOMETERS
1-01-001	KILOTON
1-01-001	KILOWATT
4-01-001	KILOWATT-HOUR
1-01-001	KILOWATT-HOURS
1-01-001	KILOWATTS
1-01-001	KILTS
1-01-001	KIMBALL
1-01-001	KIMBELL-*DIAMOND
2-01-001	KIMBERLY
1-01-001	KIMBOLTON
4-01-001	KIMMELL
1-01-001	KIMONO
4-01-001	KIMPTON
2-02-002	KIN
313-15-186	KIND
1-01-001	KIND'S
5-03-004	KINDA
1-01-001	KINDER
3-03-003	KINDERGARTEN
1-01-001	KINDEST
1-01-001	KINDLED
1-01-001	KINDLINESS
8-06-008	KINDLY
5-02-004	KINDNESS
1-01-001	KINDNESSES
3-03-003	KINDRED
36-13-032	KINDS
1-01-001	KINESICS
4-01-001	KINESTHETIC
1-01-001	KINESTHETICALLY
8-01-006	KINETIC
88-13-038	KING
14-07-010	KING'S
1-01-001	KINGAN
26-08-015	KINGDOM
1-01-001	KINGDOM-WIDE
1-01-001	KINGDOMS
1-01-001	KINGPIN
7-04-004	KINGS
2-02-002	KINGSLEY
5-03-003	KINGSTON
2-01-001	KINGSTOWN
1-01-001	KINGWOOD
1-01-001	KINSELL
1-01-001	KINSEY
3-03-003	KINSHIP
1-01-001	KIOSK
1-01-001	KIOWA
1-01-001	KIPLING
3-03-003	KIPLING'S
1-01-001	KIRA
9-02-002	KIRBY
3-01-001	KIRBY'S
1-01-001	KIRK
1-01-001	KIRKLAND
2-01-001	KIRKPATRICK
2-01-001	KIRKWOOD
9-02-004	KIROV
1-01-001	KIROV'S
17-06-014	KISS
1-01-001	KISSAK
15-06-012	KISSED
4-04-004	KISSES
1-01-001	KISSIN
6-05-006	KISSING
1-01-001	KISSINGS
2-01-001	KIT
90-13-054	KITCHEN
3-02-002	KITCHENETTE
5-04-005	KITCHENS
1-01-001	KITCHIN
1-01-001	KITE
1-01-001	KITS
5-04-004	KITTEN
1-01-001	KITTENISH
5-02-002	KITTENS
18-01-001	KITTI
2-01-001	KITTI'S
1-01-001	KITTLER
1-01-001	KITTREDGE
7-02-002	KITTY
5-01-001	KITTY'S
1-01-001	KIVU
2-02-002	KIWANIS
3-01-001	KIZ
5-01-001	KIZZIE

3-02-002	KLAN
2-01-001	KLAUBER
1-01-001	KLAUS
1-01-001	KLAXON
1-01-001	KLEENEX
2-01-001	KLEES
3-01-001	KLEIBER
7-01-001	KLEIN
1-01-001	KLEIST
1-01-001	KLEMPERER'S
1-01-001	KLIMT
1-01-001	KLINE
1-01-001	KLINICO
1-01-001	KLOMAN
35-10-022	KLUCKHOHN
1-01-001	KLUX
1-01-001	KM
4-04-004	KNACK
1-01-001	KNACKWURST
1-01-001	KNAPPERTSBUSCH
2-01-001	KNAUER
1-01-001	KNEAD
1-01-001	KNECHT
1-01-001	KNEE
1-01-001	KNEE-DEEP
2-01-001	KNEE-LENGTH
2-01-001	KNEE-TYPE
1-01-001	KNEECAP
5-04-005	KNEEL
2-01-002	KNEELED
5-03-005	KNEELING
1-01-001	KNEELS
38-10-032	KNEES
8-05-007	KNELT
395-15-171	KNEW
1-01-001	KNICK-KNACKS
1-01-001	KNICKERBOCKER
76-10-021	KNIFE
3-01-001	KNIFE'S
1-01-001	KNIFE-EDGE
1-01-001	KNIFE-GRINDER
2-02-002	KNIFE-MEN
1-01-001	KNIFE/COATING
1-01-001	KNIFELIKE
18-07-010	KNIGHT
2-01-001	KNIGHT-ERRANT
1-01-001	KNIGHT-ERRANTRY
1-01-001	KNIGHTES
1-01-001	KNIGHTFALL
3-01-001	KNIGHTLY
8-05-008	KNIGHTS
1-01-001	KNILL'S
10-07-009	KNIT
1-01-001	KNITE
8-03-003	KNITTED
1-01-001	KNITTING
7-06-006	KNIVES
2-02-002	KNOB
1-01-001	KNOBBY-KNUCKLED
1-01-001	KNOBS
15-09-013	KNOCK
1-01-001	KNOCK-DOWN
1-01-001	KNOCKDOWN
31-08-027	KNOCKED
5-03-003	KNOCKING
2-02-002	KNOCKS
1-01-001	KNOE
2-02-002	KNOLL
8-06-008	KNOT
1-01-001	KNOT-TYING
1-01-001	KNOTS
1-01-001	KNOTT
4-04-004	KNOTTED
2-02-002	KNOTTY
683-15-271	KNOW
1-01-001	KNOW-*NOTHING
4-04-004	KNOW-HOW
1-01-001	KNOW-NOTHINGS
17-01-001	KNOWED
8-01-001	KNOWETH
50-14-043	KNOWING
4-03-004	KNOWINGLY
145-13-103	KNOWLEDGE
2-02-002	KNOWLEDGEABLE
2-01-001	KNOWLTON
1-01-001	KNOWLTON'S
245-15-161	KNOWN
99-14-071	KNOWS
5-02-004	KNOX
1-01-001	KNOXVILLE
3-02-003	KNUCKLE
1-01-001	KNUCKLE-DUSTER
1-01-001	KNUCKLEBALL
1-01-001	KNUCKLED
8-05-008	KNUCKLES
1-01-001	KOAN
1-01-001	KOB

1-01-001	KOBAYASHI
1-01-001	KOCH
1-01-001	KOCHANEK
1-01-001	KOCHANEKS
1-01-001	KODAKS
2-01-001	KODAMA
3-01-001	KODIAK
7-01-001	KODYKE
3-01-001	KOEHLER
1-01-001	KOENIG
2-01-001	KOENIGSBERG
1-01-001	KOFANES
1-01-001	KOH
1-01-001	KOHI
13-01-001	KOHNSTAMM
9-01-001	KOHNSTAMM-NEGAT IVE
12-01-001	KOHNSTAMM-POSIT IVE
1-01-001	KOHNSTAMM-POSTI VE
2-01-001	KOINONIA
1-01-001	KOK
1-01-001	KOKOSCHKA
2-01-001	KOLA
1-01-001	KOLB
2-01-001	KOLKHOZ
1-01-001	KOLKHOZES
2-02-002	KOLPAKOVA
1-01-001	KOMBO
1-01-001	KOMLEVA
1-01-001	KOMURASAKI
11-04-007	KONG
1-01-001	KONGA
2-01-001	KONISHI
2-01-001	KONITZ
1-01-001	KONRAD
1-01-001	KONSTANTIN
1-01-001	KONZERTHAUS
1-01-001	KOOKS
1-01-001	KOOL-*AID
2-02-002	KOONING
1-01-001	KOOP
1-01-001	KOPSTEIN
12-03-006	KOREA
11-06-007	KOREAN
5-02-002	KOREANS
1-01-001	KORMAN
1-01-001	KORNBLUTH
3-01-001	KORNBLUTH'S
1-01-001	KORNEVEY
1-01-001	KORNEYEV
1-01-001	KORNEYEVA
1-01-001	KORNGOLD
1-01-001	KORRA
1-01-001	KOSHARE
1-01-001	KOSHER
1-01-001	KOIOWALA
3-01-001	KOUSSEVITZKY
1-01-001	KOUSSEVITZKY'S
18-01-002	KOWALSKI
1-01-001	KOWALSKI'S
1-01-001	KOZINTSEV
1-01-001	KRAEMER
1-01-001	KRAFT
149-10-068	KRAKATOA
1-01-001	KRAKOW
1-01-001	KRAKOWIAK
1-01-001	KRAMER'S
1-01-001	KRAPP'S
1-01-001	KRASNIK
1-01-001	KRAUT
1-01-001	KRAUTHEADS
1-01-001	KRAUTS
1-01-001	KREISLER
11-04-011	KREMLIN
2-01-001	KREMLIN'S
2-01-001	KRETCHMER
17-01-001	KRIM
8-01-001	KRIM'S
1-01-001	KRIMS
1-01-001	KRISHNA
1-01-001	KRISHNAISTS
1-01-001	KRISS
1-01-001	KRIST
1-01-001	KRISTALLSTRUKTU REN
1-01-001	KRO**DGER
1-01-001	KROENING
1-01-001	KROGER
3-01-001	KROGER'S
1-01-001	KROGERS
1-01-001	KROGERS'
1-01-001	KROMY
19-09-018	KRONENBERGER
5-01-001	KRUGER
2-01-001	KRUGER'S

1-01-001	KRUMPP
1-01-001	KRUPA
2-01-001	KRUTCH
3-01-002	KRUTCH'S
4-01-001	KRYSTALLOGRAPHI E
1-01-001	KRZYWY-*ROG
1-01-001	KSU'U'PELI'AFO
3-02-002	KU
1-01-001	KUBEK
1-01-001	KUHN
4-01-001	KULTURBUND
2-01-001	KUNKEL
2-01-001	KUNKEL'S
1-01-001	KUPCINET
1-01-001	KURD
1-01-001	KURIGALZU
1-01-001	KURT
1-01-001	KWAME
1-01-001	KWANGO
1-01-001	KWASHIORKOR
3-01-001	KWHR
1-01-001	KWHR.
2-01-001	KY
2-01-001	KYNE
1-01-001	KYO
1-01-001	KYO-ZAN
7-01-001	KYOTO
55-11-036	L
1-01-001	L**.*S**.*U
1-01-001	L'*ANGE
1-01-001	L'*ARCADE
1-01-001	L'*ASSISTANCE
1-01-001	L'*ASTREE
1-01-001	L'*IMPERIALE
1-01-001	L'*INDEPENDANCE
1-01-001	L'*INSTITUT
1-01-001	L'*OSSERVATORE
3-01-001	L'*TURU
2-01-001	L'*UNION
1-01-001	L'*UNITA
1-01-001	L'*UNIVERSITE
1-01-001	L'ACTIVITE
1-01-001	L'IDENTITE
1-01-001	L'ORCHESTRE
1-01-001	L'S
1-01-001	L-5-VINYL-2-THI O-OXAZOLIDONE
61-11-037	LA
1-01-001	LA**DCHELN
1-01-001	LA**DNDLER
3-01-001	LA**DUTNER
1-01-001	LA*GOW
3-01-001	LA*GUARDIA
1-01-001	LA*GUARDIA'S
2-02-002	LA*SALLE
3-02-002	LAB
4-01-001	LABAN
1-01-001	LABANS
19-08-014	LABEL
9-05-009	LABELED
4-04-004	LABELING
2-02-002	LABELLED
3-02-002	LABELS
1-01-001	LABILE
1-01-001	LABOR
1-01-001	LABOR'S
1-01-001	LABOR-BASED
7-04-006	LABOR-MANAGEMEN T
1-01-001	LABOR-SAVING
9-04-008	LABORATORIES
40-09-021	LABORATORY
5-03-005	LABORED
6-04-005	LABORER
6-03-005	LABORERS
1-01-001	LABORIOUS
2-02-002	LABORIOUSLY
2-02-002	LABORS
1-01-001	LABOTHE
1-01-001	LABOUISSE
4-03-003	LABOUR
1-01-001	LABRADOR
1-01-001	LABYRINTH
7-03-004	LACE
1-01-001	LACE-DRAWN
2-02-002	LACED
1-01-001	LACERATE
1-01-001	LACERATED
2-02-002	LACERATIONS
1-01-001	LACES
2-01-001	LACEY
110-14-088	LACK
1-01-001	LACKADAISICAL
19-09-018	LACKED
1-01-001	LACKEYS
32-07-028	LACKING

6-04-005	LACKS	1-01-001	LANDON	676-15-296	LAST	1-01-001	LAVOISIER
2-02-002	LACQUER	1-01-001	LANDOWNERS	1-01-001	LAST-DITCH	299-14-099	LAW
1-01-001	LACQUERED	2-02-002	LANDRUM-*GRIFFIN	1-01-001	LAST-MENTIONED	1-01-001	LAW-ABIDING
2-02-002	LACTATE			2-02-002	LAST-MINUTE	1-01-001	LAW-BREAKING
2-01-001	LACTATING	25-09-018	LANDS	2-01-001	LAST-NAMED	1-01-001	LAW-ENFORCEMENT
4-04-004	LACY	20-09-013	LANDSCAPE	1-01-001	LAST-ROUND	1-01-001	LAW-GOVERNED
6-06-006	LAD	3-03-003	LANDSCAPED	12-10-012	LASTED	1-01-001	LAW-UNTO-ITSELF
1-01-001	LAD'S	5-04-004	LANDSCAPES	13-09-013	LASTING	1-01-001	LAWFORD
19-10-013	LADDER	1-01-001	LANDSCAPING	3-03-003	LASTLY	2-02-002	LAWFUL
6-06-006	LADEN	2-02-002	LANDSLIDE	1-01-001	LASTS	2-02-002	LAWLESS
2-01-001	LADGHAM	1-01-001	LANDSLIDES	1-01-001	LASWICK	4-03-003	LAWMAKERS
28-10-023	LADIES	30-08-017	LANE	5-03-004	LATCH	3-02-002	LAWMAKING
9-08-009	LADIES'	4-03-003	LANES	1-01-001	LATCHED	2-01-001	LAWMAN
1-01-001	LADLE	1-01-001	LANESMANSHIP	1-01-001	LATCHES	1-01-001	LAWMAN'S
1-01-001	LADS	1-01-001	LANESVILLE	179-15-123	LATE	2-01-002	LAWMEN
80-13-042	LADY	1-01-001	LANG	1-01-001	LATE-COMERS	15-09-012	LAWN
5-04-005	LADY'S	1-01-001	LANGE	1-01-001	LATE-SUMMER	5-05-005	LAWNS
1-01-001	LADY-BUGS	1-01-001	LANGELAND	1-01-001	LATEINER	39-07-023	LAWRENCE
1-01-001	LADYLIKE	3-01-001	LANGER	12-05-012	LATELY	2-01-001	LAWRENCE'S
13-04-004	LAFAYETTE	18-01-001	LANGFORD	9-06-007	LATENT	2-01-001	LAWRENCEVILLE
1-01-001	LAFE	1-01-001	LANGHORNE	397-15-234	LATER	88-12-042	LAWS
3-03-003	LAG	1-01-001	LANGSDORF	1-01-001	LATERAL	1-01-001	LAWSUIT
1-01-001	LAGERLO**DF	109-13-068	LANGUAGE	1-01-001	LATERAN	1-01-001	LAWSUITS
1-01-001	LAGERS	40-06-016	LANGUAGES	35-12-030	LATEST	43-13-030	LAWYER
2-01-002	LAGGED	4-03-004	LANGUID	2-01-001	LATEX	2-02-002	LAWYER'S
15-04-004	LAGOON	1-01-001	LANGUISHED	2-01-001	LATH	23-08-015	LAWYERS
2-01-001	LAGOONS	1-01-001	LANGUISHING	1-01-001	LATHE	1-01-001	LAWYERS'
1-01-001	LAGRANGE'S	1-01-001	LANIN'S	3-02-002	LATHER	3-03-003	LAX
3-02-003	LAGS	2-02-002	LANKY	3-02-002	LATHERED	1-01-001	LAXATIVE
3-01-001	LAGUERRE	1-01-001	LANTE	1-01-001	LATHES	2-02-002	LAXNESS
2-02-002	LAGUNA	13-03-006	LANTERN	50-11-033	LATIN	139-15-096	LAY
1-01-001	LAHK	2-02-002	LANTERNS	1-01-001	LATINOVICH	5-02-002	LAY-OFFS
1-01-001	LAICOS	1-01-001	LANTHANUM	5-04-005	LATITUDE	4-01-001	LAY-SISTERS
77-14-066	LAID	2-01-001	LANZA	1-01-001	LATITUDES	1-01-001	LAY-UP
4-01-003	LAIN	17-02-004	LAO	2-01-001	LATS	12-05-009	LAYER
1-01-001	LAIRS	1-01-001	LAO-TSE	1-01-001	LATS.	1-01-001	LAYERED
5-03-004	LAISSEZ-FAIRE	2-02-002	LAODICEAN	114-13-083	LATTER	2-01-001	LAYERING
3-01-001	LAITY	64-05-013	LAOS	10-09-010	LATTER'S	10-05-006	LAYERS
1-01-001	LAK	4-02-003	LAOTIAN	1-01-001	LATTER-DAY	1-01-001	LAYETTE
54-12-024	LAKE	1-01-001	LAOTIANS	2-01-002	LATTICE	12-08-012	LAYING
8-04-005	LAKES	19-08-013	LAP	3-01-001	LATTIMER	3-03-003	LAYMAN
1-01-001	LAKEWOOD	1-01-001	LAPEL	1-01-001	LATTIMER'S	1-01-001	LAYMAN'S
17-01-001	LALAURIE	2-02-002	LAPELS	4-01-001	LAUCHLI	6-05-006	LAYMEN
1-01-001	LALAURIE'S	1-01-001	LAPIDARY	1-01-001	LAUCHLI'S	1-01-001	LAYMEN'S
2-01-001	LALAURIES	1-01-001	LAPLACE	1-01-001	LAUDABLY	1-01-001	LAYOFFS
1-01-001	LALAURIES'	2-02-002	LAPPED	3-02-002	LAUDANUM	6-04-005	LAYOUT
3-01-002	LAMAR	5-01-001	LAPPENBERG	1-01-001	LAUDE	6-04-005	LAYS
7-04-005	LAMB	1-01-001	LAPPENBURG-*KEMBLE	1-01-001	LAUDER	1-01-001	LAYTON
1-01-001	LAMBARENE			6-03-003	LAUDERDALE	1-01-001	LAZARUS
2-01-002	LAMBERT	1-01-001	LAPPETS	1-01-001	LAUE	1-01-001	LAZE
3-01-001	LAMBETH	2-01-002	LAPPING	28-09-021	LAUGH	1-01-001	LAZILY
7-01-001	LAMBS	2-02-002	LAPS	51-08-040	LAUGHED	9-06-008	LAZY
2-02-002	LAME	6-04-005	LAPSE	27-07-022	LAUGHING	2-01-001	LAZYBONES
1-01-001	LAMECHIAN	3-03-003	LAPSED	1-01-001	LAUGHINGLY	1-01-001	LAZZERI
1-01-001	LAMECHIANS	4-04-004	LAPSES	1-01-001	LAUGHINGSTOCKS	17-02-006	LB
1-01-001	LAMENT	1-01-001	LAPSING	2-01-002	LAUGHLIN	1-01-001	LB).
1-01-001	LAMENTATION	3-02-002	LARAMIE	4-03-004	LAUGHS	5-01-001	LB**./CU
2-02-002	LAMENTATIONS	2-02-002	LARCENY	22-10-017	LAUGHTER	1-01-001	LB**S
2-01-002	LAMENTS	4-02-002	LARD	10-07-010	LAUNCH	1-01-001	LB-PLUS
3-01-001	LAMINATE	1-01-001	LARDER	1-01-001	LAUNCH-CONTROL	1-01-001	LB/DAY
2-01-001	LAMINATED	2-02-002	LAREDO	21-08-015	LAUNCHED	6-02-002	LBS
1-01-001	LAMINATING	361-15-214	LARGE	1-01-001	LAUNCHER	14-09-013	LE
1-01-001	LAMMED	1-01-001	LARGE-AREA	3-02-003	LAUNCHES	1-01-001	LE*CLAIR
2-01-002	LAMMERMOOR	1-01-001	LARGE-ENOUGH	3-03-003	LAUNCHING	3-01-001	LE*SOURD
1-01-001	LAMMING	2-01-001	LARGE-PACKAGE	1-01-001	LAUNCHINGS	1-01-001	LEACHES
1-01-001	LAMON	7-04-007	LARGE-SCALE	1-01-001	LAUNDER-*OMETER	129-15-089	LEAD
18-07-010	LAMP	68-11-053	LARGELY	1-01-001	LAUNDERED	1-01-001	LEADED
3-03-003	LAMPLIGHT	1-01-001	LARGELY-SILENT	7-02-002	LAUNDERING	2-01-002	LEADEN
1-01-001	LAMPOON	123-15-084	LARGER	1-01-001	LAUNDERINGS	74-09-044	LEADER
6-04-006	LAMPS	1-01-001	LARGESSE	5-03-003	LAUNDRY	6-03-004	LEADER'S
2-01-001	LANA	53-11-043	LARGEST	1-01-001	LAUNDRY-TYPE	1-01-001	LEADERLESS
1-01-001	LANCASHIRE	1-01-001	LARIMER	20-05-007	LAURA	107-11-064	LEADERS
2-02-002	LANCASTER	1-01-001	LARK	1-01-001	LAURANCE	92-12-046	LEADERSHIP
3-03-003	LANCE	10-01-002	LARKIN	2-02-002	LAUREATE	68-14-060	LEADING
1-01-001	LANCED	1-01-001	LARKIN'S	3-03-003	LAUREL	1-01-001	LEADINGS
2-01-001	LANCES	1-01-001	LARKINS	2-02-002	LAURELS	33-11-030	LEADS
1-01-001	LANCRET	2-02-002	LARKS	10-01-002	LAUREN	1-01-001	LEADSMAN
217-15-105	LAND	3-02-002	LARKSPUR	3-02-003	LAURENCE	12-05-009	LEAF
1-01-001	LAND'S	9-04-007	LARRY	1-01-001	LAURENTIAN	1-01-001	LEAFED
1-01-001	LAND-	1-01-001	LARS	1-01-001	LAURENTS'	1-01-001	LEAFHOPPER
1-01-001	LAND-*ROVER	5-01-002	LARSON	1-01-001	LAURI	1-01-001	LEAFIEST
1-01-001	LAND-BASED	1-01-001	LARSON'S	1-01-001	LAURIE	1-01-001	LEAFLET
1-01-001	LAND-LOCKED	6-01-001	LARVAE	1-01-001	LAURITSEN	3-03-003	LEAFLETS
2-02-002	LANDAU	1-01-001	LARVAL	1-01-001	LAURITZ	1-01-001	LEAFMOLD
15-06-015	LANDED	5-03-005	LAS	6-01-001	LAURO	1-01-001	LEAFY
1-01-001	LANDER	1-01-001	LASCAR	1-01-001	LAUSANNE	69-09-028	LEAGUE
1-01-001	LANDES	1-01-001	LASCIVIOUS	1-01-001	LAVA	4-01-003	LEAGUE'S
1-01-001	LANDESCO	6-05-005	LASH	1-01-001	LAVA-ROCKS	1-01-001	LEAGUED
26-10-018	LANDING	3-03-003	LASHED	2-01-001	LAVALLADE	3-01-002	LEAGUER
2-01-001	LANDINGS	2-02-002	LASHES	1-01-001	LAVATO	2-01-002	LEAGUERS
3-01-001	LANDIS	2-01-001	LASHING	4-02-002	LAVATORY	8-04-006	LEAGUES
1-01-001	LANDIS'	1-01-001	LASHINGS	1-01-001	LAVAUGHN	2-02-002	LEAK
12-04-006	LANDLORD	2-02-002	LASS	5-03-003	LAVENDER	1-01-001	LEAKAGE
1-01-001	LANDLORD'S	1-01-001	LASSES	3-03-003	LAVISH	5-03-005	LEAKED
2-02-002	LANDLORDS	2-01-001	LASSO	1-01-001	LAVISHED	3-02-002	LEAKS
3-03-003	LANDMARK	1-01-001	LASSUS	1-01-001	LAVISHING	2-02-002	LEAKY
7-04-005	LANDMARKS	1-01-001	LASSWITZ'S	4-04-004	LAVISHLY	1-01-001	LEALE

1-01-001	LIFE-SIZE	1-01-001	LIMITED-TIME	1-01-001	LIQUIDATING	2-01-001	LIZZY
1-01-001	LIFE-SUPPORTING	11-07-009	LIMITING	12-05-005	LIQUIDATION	1-01-001	LLEWELLYN
1-01-001	LIFEBLOOD	1-01-001	LIMITLESS	1-01-001	LIQUIDATIONS	10-05-010	LLOYD
4-01-001	LIFEBOAT	41-10-038	LIMITS	1-01-001	LIQUIDITY	3-02-002	LLOYD'S
1-01-001	LIFEBOATS	4-02-002	LIMOUSINE	6-03-003	LIQUIDS	22-02-002	LO
1-01-001	LIFEGUARDS	1-01-001	LIMOUSINES	43-13-030	LIQUOR	1-01-001	LO**DBL
2-02-002	LIFELESS	12-04-012	LIMP	1-01-001	LIQUOR-CRAZED	45-10-033	LOAD
3-02-003	LIFELIKE	1-01-001	LIMP-LOOKING	4-01-001	LISA	22-10-020	LOADED
1-01-001	LIFELONG	2-02-002	LIMPED	1-01-001	LISBON	1-01-001	LOADER
1-01-001	LIFER	1-01-001	LIMPID	1-01-001	LISE	1-01-001	LOADERS
10-05-010	LIFETIME	2-02-002	LIMPING	1-01-001	LISLE	11-04-007	LOADING
1-01-001	LIFSON	1-01-001	LIMPLY	1-01-001	LISPING	5-01-003	LOADINGS
23-12-018	LIFT	1-01-001	LIMPS	1-01-001	LISS	10-04-007	LOADS
43-13-036	LIFTED	47-10-023	LINCOLN	2-01-001	LISSA	4-03-003	LOAF
4-01-001	LIFTERS	5-03-004	LINCOLN'S	133-15-067	LIST	1-01-001	LOAFED
8-06-008	LIFTING	42-02-002	LINDA	1-01-001	LISTE	46-09-020	LOAN
2-02-002	LIFTS	3-01-001	LINDA'S	44-11-032	LISTED	4-01-002	LOANED
1-01-001	LIGAMENT	1-01-001	LINDBERGH'S	51-13-043	LISTEN	32-03-009	LOANS
1-01-001	LIGAND	3-01-001	LINDEMANN	30-09-026	LISTENED	3-03-003	LOATH
2-01-001	LIGANDS	1-01-001	LINDEMANNS	10-04-005	LISTENER	4-03-004	LOATHED
1-01-001	LIGGET	7-03-003	LINDEN	1-01-001	LISTENER'S	2-02-002	LOATHING
333-15-168	LIGHT	2-02-002	LINDSAY	1-01-001	LISTENER-SUPPOR	4-03-004	LOATHSOME
2-02-002	LIGHT-COLORED	1-01-001	LINDSEY'S		TED	3-03-003	LOAVES
1-01-001	LIGHT-DUTY	1-01-001	LINDSKOG	20-07-012	LISTENERS	1-01-001	LOB
1-01-001	LIGHT-FLARED	1-01-001	LINDY	1-01-001	LISTENIN	2-01-001	LOB-SCUSE
2-02-002	LIGHT-HEADED	298-15-150	LINE	39-11-033	LISTENING	1-01-001	LOBAR
1-01-001	LIGHT-HEADEDNES	1-01-001	LINE-DENSITY	2-02-002	LISTENS	1-01-001	LOBBIED
	S	1-01-001	LINE-DRIVEN	7-04-006	LISTING	1-01-001	LOBBIES
1-01-001	LIGHT-HEARTED	1-01-001	LINE-DRYING	1-01-001	LISTINGS	20-07-013	LOBBY
1-01-001	LIGHT-MINDEDNES	1-01-001	LINE-FRAGMENTS	1-01-001	LISTLESS	3-01-003	LOBE
	S	1-01-001	LINE-PAIRS	1-01-001	LISTLESSLY	5-03-003	LOBES
1-01-001	LIGHT-REFLECTIN	2-02-002	LINEAGE	6-01-001	LISTON	1-01-001	LOBLOLLY
	G	1-01-001	LINEAGES	34-09-017	LISTS	1-01-001	LOBO
1-01-001	LIGHT-TRANSMITT	1-01-001	LINEAL	17-08-017	LIT	1-01-001	LOBSCOUSE
	ING	21-02-006	LINEAR	2-01-002	LITER	1-01-001	LOBSTER
3-02-003	LIGHT-WEIGHT	4-01-003	LINEARLY	15-03-005	LITERAL	1-01-001	LOBSTER-BACKED
1-01-001	LIGHT-YEAR	2-01-001	LINEBACK	1-01-001	LITERALISM	1-01-001	LOBULAR
29-08-020	LIGHTED	1-01-001	LINEBACKERS	27-11-025	LITERALLY	1-01-001	LOBULARITY
4-03-004	LIGHTENED	16-11-016	LINED	3-01-001	LITERALNESS	1-01-001	LOBULE
1-01-001	LIGHTENS	1-01-001	LINEMAN	78-12-038	LITERARY	2-01-001	LOBULES
12-05-010	LIGHTER	6-04-005	LINEN	3-02-002	LITERATE	288-15-114	LOCAL
1-01-001	LIGHTER'N	1-01-001	LINEN-COVERED	133-12-053	LITERATURE	3-03-003	LOCALE
1-01-001	LIGHTERS	4-03-003	LINER	1-01-001	LITERATURES	4-02-002	LOCALES
2-02-002	LIGHTEST	2-02-002	LINERS	2-01-001	LITERS	1-01-001	LOCALISMS
1-01-001	LIGHTFOOT	198-15-110	LINES	4-03-004	LITHE	4-03-004	LOCALITIES
2-02-002	LIGHTHEARTED	3-02-002	LINEUP	1-01-001	LITHOGRAPH	5-02-004	LOCALITY
1-01-001	LIGHTHOUSES	7-05-007	LINGER	1-01-001	LITHOGRAPHS	2-01-001	LOCALIZATION
23-09-017	LIGHTING	2-02-002	LINGERED	2-02-002	LITIGANT	1-01-001	LOCALIZE
31-12-028	LIGHTLY	2-02-002	LINGERIE	3-02-003	LITIGANTS	1-01-001	LOCALIZED
1-01-001	LIGHTNESS	5-05-005	LINGERING	13-03-005	LITIGATION	11-06-010	LOCALLY
14-05-010	LIGHTNING	2-02-002	LINGERS	1-01-001	LITLE	16-07-012	LOCATE
1-01-001	LIGHTNING-OCCUR	3-03-003	LINGO	1-01-001	LITOWSKI	64-10-048	LOCATED
	RENCE	13-03-004	LINGUIST	1-01-001	LITTA	1-01-001	LOCATIN
47-14-036	LIGHTS	1-01-001	LINGUIST-ANTHRO	1-01-001	LITTAU	11-04-010	LOCATING
5-05-005	LIGHTWEIGHT		POLOGIST	3-03-003	LITTER	63-07-037	LOCATION
1-01-001	LIGHTYEARS	10-02-005	LINGUISTIC	1-01-001	LITTERBUG	1-01-001	LOCATION-MINDED
1-01-001	LIGNE	1-01-001	LINGUISTICALLY	4-04-004	LITTERED	18-05-013	LOCATIONS
4-01-001	LIGNITE	5-02-002	LINGUISTICS	1-01-001	LITTERING	23-09-014	LOCK
1290-15-362	LIKE	11-03-003	LINGUISTS	3-02-002	LITTERS	1-01-001	LOCK-OUTS
2-01-001	LIKE-MINDED	1-01-001	LINIMENT	831-15-324	LITTLE	1-01-001	LOCKE'S
58-12-047	LIKED	1-01-001	LINIMENTS	1-01-001	LITTLE-GIRL	30-11-024	LOCKED
1-01-001	LIKEE	2-02-002	LINING	1-01-001	LITTLE-KNOWN	9-05-006	LOCKER
10-09-010	LIKELIHOOD	16-11-016	LINK	1-01-001	LITTLE-TOWN	2-02-002	LOCKER-ROOM
151-14-101	LIKELY	3-01-001	LINKAGE	10-01-001	LITTLEPAGE	3-03-003	LOCKHEED
3-03-003	LIKENED	16-07-015	LINKED	1-01-001	LITTLEPAGE'S	1-01-001	LOCKHEED'S
3-03-003	LIKENESS	6-06-006	LINKING	1-01-001	LITTLEST	1-01-001	LOCKIAN
20-08-017	LIKES	7-05-005	LINKS	2-01-001	LITTLETON'S	2-01-001	LOCKIES
18-08-016	LIKEWISE	1-01-001	LINOLEUM	2-01-001	LITURGICAL	31-05-007	LOCKING
11-06-011	LIKING	4-03-003	LINT	2-01-001	LITZ	7-03-003	LOCKS
1-01-001	LIL	1-01-001	LINUS	1-01-001	LIVABILITY	2-01-001	LOCKUP
2-01-001	LILA	1-01-001	LINVILLE	1-01-001	LIVABLE	2-02-002	LOCOMOTIVE
4-03-003	LILAC	1-01-001	LINZ	177-15-122	LIVE	1-01-001	LOCOMOTIVES
3-01-001	LILACS	17-04-006	LION	1-01-001	LIVE-OAK	2-02-002	LOCUS
1-01-001	LILI	2-02-002	LION'S	115-14-084	LIVED	6-02-002	LOCUST
7-01-001	LILIAN	2-02-002	LIONEL	2-01-002	LIVELIER	19-07-010	LODGE
1-01-001	LILIES	3-01-001	LIONESS	5-05-005	LIVELIHOOD	1-01-001	LODGED
1-01-001	LILIPUTIAN	2-01-001	LIONESS'	2-02-002	LIVELINESS	2-01-001	LODGES
5-03-004	LILLIAN	1-01-001	LIONESSES	26-07-020	LIVELY	5-03-004	LODGING
1-01-001	LILLIAN'S	2-02-002	LIONIZED	16-07-010	LIVER	2-02-002	LODGINGS
1-01-001	LILLIPUTIAN	6-04-005	LIONS	1-01-001	LIVERIED	1-01-001	LODGMENT
10-01-001	LILLY	1-01-001	LIONS'	1-01-001	LIVERMORE	2-01-001	LODLEY
3-01-001	LILLY'S	18-11-016	LIP	2-02-002	LIVERPOOL	1-01-001	LODOWICK
1-01-001	LILT	1-01-001	LIP-SUCKING	1-01-001	LIVERS	1-01-001	LOEB
3-03-003	LILTING	2-02-002	LIPCHITZ	5-02-004	LIVERY	1-01-001	LOEN
1-01-001	LILY	1-01-001	LIPOWA	81-13-062	LIVES	1-01-001	LOESER
5-05-005	LIMB	1-01-001	LIPPI	19-04-008	LIVESTOCK	3-01-002	LOESSER
2-02-002	LIMBER	1-01-001	LIPPINCOTT	1-01-001	LIVID	1-01-001	LOESSER'S
1-01-001	LIMBIC	2-02-002	LIPPMAN	194-15-138	LIVING	1-01-001	LOEW'S
2-02-002	LIMBO	3-03-003	LIPPMANN	1-01-001	LIVING-ROOM	1-01-001	LOEWE
5-04-005	LIMBS	69-10-044	LIPS	1-01-001	LIVINGSTON	2-02-002	LOFT
13-03-004	LIME	1-01-001	LIPSON	3-01-001	LIVRES	5-04-005	LOFTY
1-01-001	LIMELIGHT	3-02-003	LIPSTICK	2-01-001	LIVSHITZ	11-05-007	LOG
1-01-001	LIMERICK	5-02-002	LIPTON	1-01-001	LIZ	1-01-001	LOG-HOUSE
48-12-040	LIMIT	1-01-001	LIQUEUR	1-01-001	LIZARD'S	1-01-001	LOG-JAM
10-04-009	LIMITATION	48-07-018	LIQUID	1-01-001	LIZARDS	2-02-002	LOGAN
28-09-021	LIMITATIONS	1-01-001	LIQUID-GLASS	17-01-001	LIZZIE	1-01-001	LOGARITHM
106-13-081	LIMITED	5-03-003	LIQUIDATED	1-01-001	LIZZIE'S	1-01-001	LOGARITHMS

2-02-002	LOGGED	3-01-001	LONGUE
1-01-001	LOGGER	1-01-001	LONGWOOD
5-04-004	LOGGING	3-01-001	LONSDALE
17-11-016	LOGIC	1-01-001	LONSDALE'S
1-01-001	LOGIC-RHETORIC	399-15-210	LOOK
34-11-026	LOGICAL	1-01-001	LOOK-SEE
12-07-012	LOGICALLY	367-15-170	LOOKED
2-01-002	LOGISTIC	173-15-122	LOOKING
1-01-001	LOGISTICAL	3-02-002	LOOKIT
4-04-004	LOGISTICS	2-01-002	LOOKOUT
8-04-008	LOGS	78-14-062	LOOKS
1-01-001	LOHMANS	7-01-001	LOOKUP
1-01-001	LOIN	1-01-001	LOOKY
1-01-001	LOINCLOTH	6-03-003	LOOM
2-02-002	LOINS	3-03-003	LOOMED
1-01-001	LOIRE	10-06-010	LOOMING
2-01-002	LOIS	4-01-001	LOOMIS
3-01-002	LOLA	2-02-002	LOOMS
1-01-001	LOLLING	2-02-002	LOON
3-01-001	LOLLY	21-06-011	LOOP
8-01-001	LOLOTTE	1-01-001	LOOPED
1-01-001	LOLOTTE'S	2-02-002	LOOPHOLE
1-01-001	LOMBARD	2-02-002	LOOPHOLES
1-01-001	LOND	1-01-001	LOOPS
89-12-050	LONDON	53-13-046	LOOSE
3-01-002	LONDON'S	2-02-002	LOOSE-JOINTED
1-01-001	LONDON-BASED	1-01-001	LOOSE-JOWLED
1-01-001	LONDON-BRED	1-01-001	LOOSE-KNIT
2-01-001	LONDONDERRY	1-01-001	LOOSE-LEAF
1-01-001	LONDONER	1-01-001	LOOSE-LOADED
8-06-008	LONE	12-08-012	LOOSELY
1-01-001	LONELIER	1-01-001	LOOSELY-TAPED
1-01-001	LONELIEST	3-03-003	LOOSEN
9-03-007	LONELINESS	4-02-004	LOOSENED
25-08-018	LONELY	2-02-002	LOOSENESS
1-01-001	LONERS	1-01-001	LOOSENING
2-01-002	LONESOME	1-01-001	LOOSENS
755-15-338	LONG	1-01-001	LOOSEST
1-01-001	LONG-	1-01-001	LOOSLI
1-01-001	LONG-ACTING	3-03-003	LOOT
3-02-003	LONG-AWAITED	3-02-003	LOOTED
1-01-001	LONG-BODIED	3-03-003	LOOTING
1-01-001	LONG-CHAIN	1-01-001	LOP
1-01-001	LONG-CRUISE	1-01-001	LOPATNIKOFF'S
2-02-002	LONG-DISTANCE	2-01-001	LOPE
1-01-001	LONG-ENDURANCE	1-01-001	LOPED
2-02-002	LONG-ESTABLISHE	3-01-001	LOPER
	D	2-02-002	LOPEZ
1-01-001	LONG-FAMILIAR	1-01-001	LOPPED
1-01-001	LONG-FAR	1-01-001	LOPSIDEDLY
1-01-001	LONG-FOR	2-02-002	LOQUACIOUS
1-01-001	LONG-HAIR	1-01-001	LOQUACITY
1-01-001	LONG-HAUL	1-01-001	LORAIN
1-01-001	LONG-KEEPING	1-01-001	LORCA
1-01-001	LONG-KNOWN	93-12-037	LORD
1-01-001	LONG-LIFE	12-05-007	LORD'S
1-01-001	LONG-LINE	1-01-001	LORDE
2-02-002	LONG-LIVED	2-02-002	LORDLY
1-01-001	LONG-OVERDUE	3-03-003	LORDS
39-07-020	LONG-RANGE	3-02-002	LORDSHIP
5-01-003	LONG-RUN	7-05-007	LORE
1-01-001	LONG-SETTLED	1-01-001	LORELEI
1-01-001	LONG-SHANKED	1-01-001	LOREN
1-01-001	LONG-SLEEVED	1-01-001	LORENA
2-02-002	LONG-SOUGHT	2-02-002	LORENZ
1-01-001	LONG-STEMMED	1-01-001	LORLYN
32-05-015	LONG-TERM	1-01-001	LORRAIN
4-04-004	LONG-TIME	1-01-001	LORRAINE
1-01-001	LONG-VANISHED	52-11-032	LOS
1-01-001	LONG-VIEW	58-13-051	LOSE
7-02-005	LONGED	1-01-001	LOSER
193-15-141	LONGER	1-01-001	LOSERS
2-02-002	LONGER-LIVED	15-06-015	LOSES
2-01-001	LONGER-TERM	28-10-028	LOSING
6-06-006	LONGEST	86-13-062	LOSS
2-02-002	LONGEVITY	46-10-025	LOSSES
1-01-001	LONGFELLOW	173-14-131	LOST
2-02-002	LONGFELLOW'S	127-14-093	LOT
2-02-002	LONGHAND	1-01-001	LOTHARIO
4-02-002	LONGHORN	8-02-002	LOTION
5-02-002	LONGHORNS	1-01-001	LOTIONS
10-05-009	LONGING	42-13-033	LOTS
2-02-002	LONGINGS	1-01-001	LOTTE
1-01-001	LONGINOTTI	1-01-001	LOTTERY
1-01-001	LONGISH	1-01-001	LOTTIE
1-01-001	LONGITUDE	2-02-002	LOTUS
1-01-001	LONGITUDES	13-05-008	LOU
1-01-001	LONGITUDINAL	1-01-001	LOUCHHEIM
1-01-001	LONGRUN	20-08-017	LOUD
1-01-001	LONGS	1-01-001	LOUD-VOICED
1-01-001	LONGSHOREMEN	12-06-010	LOUDER
1-01-001	LONGSHOREMEN'S	4-04-004	LOUDEST
1-01-001	LONGSHOT	17-08-014	LOUDLY
3-03-003	LONGSTANDING	1-01-001	LOUDON'S
2-01-001	LONGSTREET	1-01-001	LOUDSPEAKER
1-01-001	LONGSUFFERING	2-02-002	LOUDSPEAKERS
1-01-001	LONGTIME	73-12-036	LOUIS

1-01-001	LOUIS'	1-01-001	LOWN
2-02-002	LOUIS'S	1-01-001	LOWS
1-01-001	LOUISA	1-01-001	LOY
5-02-004	LOUISE	18-10-017	LOYAL
30-08-014	LOUISIANA	2-02-002	LOYALIST
1-01-001	LOUISIANAN	2-02-002	LOYALISTS
1-01-001	LOUISIANE	3-03-003	LOYALTIES
6-05-006	LOUISVILLE	22-10-019	LOYALTY
9-03-005	LOUNGE	1-01-001	LP
3-03-003	LOUNGED	8-04-005	LT
1-01-001	LOUNGES	5-03-003	LTD
4-04-004	LOUNGING	2-01-001	LUANG
3-03-003	LOUSE	1-01-001	LUBBERLANDERS
1-01-001	LOUSED	2-01-001	LUBBOCK
1-01-001	LOUSIE	2-01-001	LUBELL
1-01-001	LOUSINESS	15-02-002	LUBLIN
12-05-007	LOUSY	2-01-001	LUBLIN'S
2-01-001	LOUVERS	2-01-001	LUBRA
2-01-001	LOUVRE	2-01-002	LUBRICANT
2-02-002	LOVABLE	1-01-001	LUBRICATED
232-15-103	LOVE	1-01-001	LUBRICATION
2-02-002	LOVE'S	1-01-001	LUCAS
1-01-001	LOVE-IN-ACTION	1-01-001	LUCAS'S
4-02-002	LOVE-MAKING	8-02-003	LUCIA
56-11-040	LOVED	5-03-003	LUCIAN
3-01-001	LOVEJOY	4-03-003	LUCID
2-01-001	LOVEJOY'S	1-01-001	LUCIDITY
1-01-001	LOVELACE	10-01-001	LUCIEN
5-01-001	LOVELESS	3-02-002	LUCIFER
1-01-001	LOVELIES	1-01-001	LUCIFER'S
3-02-003	LOVELIEST	13-02-003	LUCILLE
4-03-003	LOVELINESS	1-01-001	LUCILLE'S
1-01-001	LOVELORN	2-01-001	LUCIUS
44-12-032	LOVELY	47-09-034	LUCK
19-07-017	LOVER	1-01-001	LUCKED
1-01-001	LOVER'S	1-01-001	LUCKIER
2-01-002	LOVERING	3-03-003	LUCKILY
10-08-010	LOVERS	1-01-001	LUCKS
1-01-001	LOVERS'	21-09-019	LUCKY
19-09-018	LOVES	3-03-003	LUCRATIVE
1-01-001	LOVETT	2-01-001	LUCRETIA
1-01-001	LOVEWAYS	2-01-002	LUCRETIUS
1-01-001	LOVIE	45-04-004	LUCY
15-09-014	LOVIN	1-01-001	LUCY'S
1-01-001	LOVING	3-03-003	LUDICROUS
1-01-001	LOVINGLY	1-01-001	LUDICROUSNESS
1-01-001	LOVINGOOD	13-01-001	LUDIE
174-14-103	LOW	1-01-001	LUDLOW
1-01-001	LOW-BOILING	1-01-001	LUDMILLA
1-01-001	LOW-BUDGET	1-01-001	LUDWICK
1-01-001	LOW-CALORY	3-02-003	LUDWIG
1-01-001	LOW-CEILINGED	1-01-001	LUECHTEFELD
2-02-002	LOW-CLASS	2-01-001	LUEGER'S
6-03-005	LOW-COST	1-01-001	LUETTE
3-03-003	LOW-DOWN	1-01-001	LUFTWAFFE
1-01-001	LOW-DUTY	2-02-002	LUG
1-01-001	LOW-FLYING	1-01-001	LUGER
1-01-001	LOW-FOAM	10-06-006	LUGGAGE
1-01-001	LOW-FREQUENCY	5-03-003	LUGGED
2-02-002	LOW-GRADE	1-01-001	LUI
1-01-001	LOW-HEELED	9-03-004	LUIS
2-02-002	LOW-KEY	1-01-001	LUIS'S
2-02-002	LOW-LEVEL	1-01-001	LUISA
1-01-001	LOW-LYING	1-01-001	LUISE
2-01-001	LOW-MOISTURE	3-03-003	LUKE
2-01-001	LOW-PASS	2-02-002	LUKE'S
2-02-002	LOW-PITCHED	5-05-005	LUKEWARM
1-01-001	LOW-POWER	1-01-001	LUKUKLU
1-01-001	LOW-PRICED	2-01-002	LULL
1-01-001	LOW-SPEED	5-03-004	LULLABY
1-01-001	LOW-SUDSING	1-01-001	LULLED
2-01-002	LOW-TEMPERATURE	1-01-001	LULLS
1-01-001	LOW-TENSION	2-01-001	LULLWATER
1-01-001	LOW-VOLTAGE	1-01-001	LULLY
3-01-001	LOW-WAGE	1-01-001	LULU
1-01-001	LOW-WATER	1-01-001	LUMBAR
1-01-001	LOWDOWN	35-07-010	LUMBER
1-01-001	LOWE	1-01-001	LUMBERED
1-01-001	LOWE'S	2-02-002	LUMBERING
6-03-005	LOWELL	1-01-001	LUMEN
2-01-001	LOWELL'S	1-01-001	LUMEN-WATT
123-13-079	LOWER	1-01-001	LUMIA
8-02-003	LOWER-CLASS	2-01-001	LUMIERE
1-01-001	LOWER-CUT	1-01-001	LUMINARIES
1-01-001	LOWER-LEVEL	1-01-001	LUMINESCENCE
4-02-002	LOWER-MIDDLE	1-01-001	LUMINESCENT
3-01-002	LOWER-MIDDLE-CL	1-01-001	LUMINOSITY
	ASS	12-06-007	LUMINOUS
1-01-001	LOWER-PAID	1-01-001	LUMMOX
1-01-001	LOWER-PRICED	1-01-001	LUMMUS
2-02-002	LOWER-STATUS	7-03-006	LUMP
21-08-020	LOWERED	4-01-001	LUMPE
5-05-005	LOWERING	2-02-002	LUMPED
1-01-001	LOWERS	1-01-001	LUMPISH
13-09-013	LOWEST	3-03-003	LUMPS
1-01-001	LOWLANDS	2-02-002	LUMPY
1-01-001	LOWLIEST	12-02-002	LUMUMBA

Code	Word
3-02-002	LUMUMBA'S
10-02-003	LUNAR
1-01-001	LUNATIC
1-01-001	LUNATIC-FRINGE
2-01-001	LUNATION
33-10-028	LUNCH
23-07-016	LUNCHEON
1-01-001	LUNCHEON-TABLE
2-02-002	LUNCHEONS
1-01-001	LUNCHROOM
2-02-002	LUNCHTIME
1-01-001	LUND
1-01-001	LUNDEEN
1-01-001	LUNDY
16-05-006	LUNG
4-02-002	LUNGE
4-02-003	LUNGED
20-06-012	LUNGS
1-01-001	LURA
1-01-001	LURAY
1-01-001	LURCAT
3-02-003	LURCH
5-03-005	LURCHED
2-02-002	LURCHING
7-07-007	LURE
3-03-003	LURED
3-03-003	LURID
1-01-001	LURING
1-01-001	LURK
3-02-003	LURKED
3-03-003	LURKING
1-01-001	LURKS
2-02-002	LUSCIOUS
5-05-005	LUSH
1-01-001	LUSHES
1-01-001	LUSIGNAN
5-05-005	LUST
2-02-002	LUSTER
1-01-001	LUSTFUL
1-01-001	LUSTILY
2-02-002	LUSTRE
1-01-001	LUSTROUS
1-01-001	LUSTS
3-03-003	LUSTY
1-01-001	LUTE
5-04-004	LUTHER
2-02-002	LUTHER'S
3-02-002	LUTHERAN
1-01-001	LUTHULI
1-01-001	LUTIHAW
1-01-001	LUTTE
4-01-001	LUXEMBURG
1-01-001	LUXER
1-01-001	LUXURIANCE
3-03-003	LUXURIES
1-01-001	LUXURIOSLY-UPHO LSTERED
6-04-004	LUXURIOUS
21-10-019	LUXURY
1-01-001	LUZON
1-01-001	LYCIDAS
1-01-001	LYDIA
5-01-001	LYFORD
4-01-001	LYFORD'S
1-01-001	LYIN
36-11-033	LYING
2-01-001	LYKING
1-01-001	LYLE
1-01-001	LYMAN
1-01-001	LYMINGTON
2-01-001	LYMPH
1-01-001	LYMPHOCYTES
1-01-001	LYMPHOMA
1-01-001	LYNCHED
3-03-003	LYNDON
5-02-004	LYNN
3-02-002	LYON
1-01-001	LYOPHILIZED
12-04-007	LYRIC
7-04-006	LYRICAL
2-02-002	LYRICISM
2-02-002	LYRICIST
1-01-001	LYRICIST'S
2-01-001	LYRICISTS
15-04-007	LYRICS
1-01-001	LYRIIST
5-01-001	LYTTLETON
84-12-051	M
1-01-001	M**.'S
4-02-002	M**.*A
1-01-001	M**.*D
2-02-002	M**.*P
6-03-003	M**.P**.H
1-01-001	M**)C**(CLELLAN
1-01-001	M**YM
2-01-002	M*EQ
1-01-001	M*V
1-01-001	M-M-M
19-05-006	MA
5-04-005	MA'AM
1-01-001	MA*=IES*$TIE
1-01-001	MAC
2-01-001	MAC*ARTHUR
1-01-001	MAC*ARTHUR-*HEL EN
2-01-002	MAC*DONALD
1-01-001	MAC*DONALD'S
1-01-001	MAC*GREGORS
1-01-001	MAC*ISAACS
1-01-001	MAC*LEAN
1-01-001	MAC*LEISHES
1-01-001	MAC*PHAIL
3-01-001	MAC*PHERSON
2-01-001	MAC*READY
1-01-001	MAC*WHORTER
2-01-002	MACABRE
1-01-001	MACASSAR
1-01-001	MACAULAY
2-01-001	MACAULAY'S
6-02-002	MACBETH
1-01-001	MACCABEUS
1-01-001	MACEDON
1-01-001	MACH'T
1-01-001	MACHADO
1-01-001	MACHIAVELLI
103-11-036	MACHINE
1-01-001	MACHINE-FAMILY
1-01-001	MACHINE-GUN
1-01-001	MACHINE-GUNNED
1-01-001	MACHINE-MASTERS
1-01-001	MACHINEGUN
1-01-001	MACHINELIKE
60-08-022	MACHINERY
54-09-025	MACHINES
5-03-005	MACHINIST
2-02-002	MACHINISTS
1-01-001	MACHINISTS'
1-01-001	MACINTOSH
1-01-001	MACK
2-01-001	MACK'S
2-01-001	MACKEREL
3-02-002	MACKEY
2-02-002	MACKINAC
1-01-001	MACKINACK
1-01-001	MACKINAW
1-01-001	MACKINTOSH
8-01-001	MACKLIN
1-01-001	MACKLIN'S
1-01-001	MACMILLAN
1-01-001	MACNEFF
4-03-004	MACON
2-01-002	MACROMOLECULAR
2-01-001	MACROMOLECULES
2-01-001	MACROPATHOLOGIC AL
1-01-001	MACROPATHOLOGY
1-01-001	MACROPHAGES
1-01-001	MACROSCOPICALLY
1-01-001	MACWHYTE
39-09-028	MAD
1-01-001	MADAGASCAR
2-02-002	MADAM
1-01-001	MADAMA
15-06-006	MADAME
1-01-001	MADARIPUR
1-01-001	MADDALENA
18-01-001	MADDEN
3-01-001	MADDEN'S
2-02-002	MADDENING
2-02-002	MADDING
1125-15-416	MADE
1-01-001	MADEIRA
3-01-001	MADELEINE
1-01-001	MADEMOISELLE
1-01-001	MADHOUSE
23-07-011	MADISON
1-01-001	MADISON'S
4-02-004	MADLY
2-01-001	MADMAN
3-03-003	MADMEN
2-02-002	MADNESS
1-01-001	MADONNA
1-01-001	MADONNA'S
1-01-001	MADRID
5-01-001	MADRIGAL
1-01-001	MADRIGALING
3-01-002	MADRIGALS
1-01-001	MADSTONES
16-02-002	MAE
1-01-001	MAE'S
1-01-001	MAECKER
1-01-001	MAELSTROM
4-03-003	MAESTRO
2-02-002	MAESTRO'S
1-01-001	MAETERLINCK
1-01-001	MAG
1-01-001	MAGARRELL
39-14-028	MAGAZINE
1-01-001	MAGAZINE'S
25-11-014	MAGAZINES
3-02-003	MAGDALENE
1-01-001	MAGEE
2-02-002	MAGENTA
1-01-001	MAGET
23-02-003	MAGGIE
3-01-001	MAGGIE'S
2-01-002	MAGGOTS
1-01-001	MAGGOTY
1-01-001	MAGI
37-11-022	MAGIC
1-01-001	MAGIC-PRACTICIN G
12-04-005	MAGICAL
3-03-003	MAGICALLY
4-03-003	MAGICIAN
2-02-002	MAGICIAN'S
1-01-001	MAGICIANS
3-01-001	MAGISTRATE
3-02-002	MAGISTRATES
1-01-001	MAGNANIMITY
1-01-001	MAGNATE
1-01-001	MAGNATES
3-03-003	MAGNET
25-05-008	MAGNETIC
1-01-001	MAGNETICALLY
8-02-002	MAGNETISM
1-01-001	MAGNETISMS
2-01-001	MAGNETIZED
10-04-005	MAGNIFICATION
2-02-002	MAGNIFICENCE
27-12-026	MAGNIFICENT
7-04-007	MAGNIFICENTLY
6-06-006	MAGNIFIED
1-01-001	MAGNIFIES
3-03-003	MAGNIFYING
29-06-016	MAGNITUDE
1-01-001	MAGNITUDES
1-01-001	MAGNOLIA
11-02-002	MAGNUM
5-02-002	MAGNUMS
1-01-001	MAGOG
2-01-001	MAGOUN
1-01-001	MAGPIE
2-02-002	MAGPIES
5-01-001	MAGUIRE
1-01-001	MAGUIRES
2-01-001	MAGWITCH
4-01-001	MAGWITCH'S
2-01-001	MAH
1-01-001	MAH-JONGG
11-01-001	MAHAYANA
1-01-001	MAHAYANIST
3-01-001	MAHLER
1-01-001	MAHLER'S
2-01-001	MAHMOUD
8-03-004	MAHOGANY
1-01-001	MAHONE
1-01-001	MAHT
1-01-001	MAHUA
11-01-001	MAHZEER
5-01-001	MAHZEER'S
1-01-001	MAI
1-01-001	MAI'TEIPA
31-01-018	MAID
1-01-001	MAID'S
2-02-002	MAIDEN
2-02-002	MAIDENS
12-07-008	MAIDS
1-01-001	MAIER
47-08-021	MAIL
1-01-001	MAILBOX
4-01-002	MAILBOXES
16-08-011	MAILED
1-01-001	MAILED-FIST-IN- VELVET-GLOVE
2-02-002	MAILER
8-03-003	MAILING
3-01-001	MAILINGS
1-01-001	MAILMAN
7-04-004	MAILS
1-01-001	MAIMED
119-14-098	MAIN
1-01-001	MAIN-D'*OEUVRE
9-06-009	MAINLAND
11-04-005	MAINLINER-*HIGH LAND
31-11-030	MAINLY
1-01-001	MAINS
2-01-002	MAINSTREAM
60-12-046	MAINTAIN
48-08-035	MAINTAINED
28-09-025	MAINTAINING
16-07-013	MAINTAINS
64-11-034	MAINTENANCE
3-03-003	MAIS
1-01-001	MAITLAND
1-01-001	MAITLAND'S
1-01-001	MAITRE
1-01-001	MAITRES
1-01-001	MAJ
1-01-001	MAJDAN-*TARTARS KI
10-01-001	MAJDANEK
1-01-001	MAJESTERIAL
10-06-009	MAJESTIC
1-01-001	MAJESTICALLY
1-01-001	MAJESTIES
1-01-001	MAJESTY
1-01-001	MAJESTY'S
247-14-143	MAJOR
1-01-001	MAJOR-*LEAGUE
4-02-002	MAJOR-LEAGUE
1-01-001	MAJOR-MARKET
1-01-001	MAJORED
3-03-003	MAJORITIES
57-10-039	MAJORITY
3-01-003	MAJORS
1-01-001	MAJUH
794-15-365	MAKE
1-01-001	MAKE-BELIEVE
1-01-001	MAKE-READY
5-05-005	MAKE-UP
1-01-001	MAKE-WORK
1-01-001	MAKEPEACE
12-05-008	MAKER
19-05-012	MAKERS
172-15-122	MAKES
6-05-006	MAKESHIFT
1-01-001	MAKESHIFTS
1-01-001	MAKEUP
255-15-175	MAKING
4-03-003	MAKINGS
3-01-001	MAKU
1-01-001	MAL
1-01-001	MALABAR
1-01-001	MALADAPTIVE
2-02-002	MALADIES
3-01-001	MALADJUSTED
6-01-001	MALADJUSTMENT
2-01-001	MALADJUSTMENTS
1-01-001	MALADROIT
1-01-001	MALADY
9-03-005	MALAISE
1-01-001	MALAMUD
1-01-001	MALAPROPISM
3-02-003	MALARIA
1-01-001	MALAY
3-03-003	MALCOLM
1-01-001	MALDEN
37-12-029	MALE
1-01-001	MALEDICTION
3-02-003	MALENESS
1-01-001	MALENKOV
19-05-010	MALES
1-01-001	MALESHERBES
2-02-002	MALEVOLENCE
1-01-001	MALEVOLENCIES
2-02-002	MALEVOLENT
1-01-001	MALFEASANT
1-01-001	MALFORMATIONS
4-02-002	MALFORMED
1-01-001	MALFUNCTIONING
1-01-001	MALI
1-01-001	MALIA
2-02-002	MALICE
2-02-002	MALICIOUS
1-01-001	MALICIOUSLY
1-01-001	MALIGN
1-01-001	MALIGNANCIES
1-01-001	MALIGNANCY
2-02-002	MALIGNED
2-02-002	MALINGERING
1-01-001	MALINOVSKY
3-02-003	MALL
1-01-001	MALLEABLE
1-01-001	MALLINCKRODT
1-01-001	MALLORY
1-01-001	MALLORY'S
1-01-001	MALMESBURY
1-01-001	MALMROS
1-01-001	MALMUD
1-01-001	MALNOURISHED
4-03-003	MALNUTRITION
6-01-001	MALOCCLUSION
1-01-001	MALONE

1-01-001 MALPOSED	1-01-001 MANLEY'S	1-01-001 MARCMANN	27-09-012 MARRIAGES
13-01-002 MALRAUX	1-01-001 MANLINESS	1-01-001 MARCOS	105-13-057 MARRIED
8-01-001 MALRAUX'S	2-01-001 MANLY	7-04-006 MARCUS	3-02-003 MARRIES
1-01-001 MALT	2-02-002 MANMADE	2-01-001 MARDI	1-01-001 MARRING
3-03-003 MALTA	2-01-001 MANN	1-01-001 MARDIS	5-03-003 MARROW
1-01-001 MALTED	9-01-002 MANN'S	16-06-007 MARE	1-01-001 MARROWBONES
3-02-002 MALTESE	12-06-006 MANNED	2-02-002 MARE'S	18-06-011 MARRY
1-01-001 MALTREAT	1-01-001 MANNEQUIN	2-01-001 MARELLA	3-02-003 MARRYING
44-04-007 MAMA	124-15-101 MANNER	1-01-001 MARENZIO	21-05-010 MARS
2-02-002 MAMA'S	1-01-001 MANNERED	1-01-001 MARES	5-01-001 MARSDEN
1-01-001 MAMARONECK	1-01-001 MANNERHOUSE	10-04-008 MARGARET	1-01-001 MARSEILLES
1-01-001 MAMBO	2-02-002 MANNERISM	1-01-001 MARGARETVILLE	4-02-002 MARSH
1-01-001 MAME	1-01-001 MANNERISMS	1-01-001 MARGARITO	1-01-001 MARSH'S
8-02-002 MAMMA	15-09-015 MANNERS	2-01-001 MARGENAU	1-01-001 MARSHA
1-01-001 MAMMAL	3-02-003 MANNING	10-06-009 MARGIN	26-07-012 MARSHAL
5-02-002 MAMMALIAN	4-01-001 MANNING'S	25-06-015 MARGINAL	2-01-001 MARSHAL'S
3-01-001 MAMMALS	2-01-001 MANNINGHAM	2-01-001 MARGINALITY	1-01-001 MARSHALING
1-01-001 MAMMAS	2-02-002 MANNY	1-01-001 MARGINALLY	27-09-015 MARSHALL
4-03-004 MAMMOTH	2-01-001 MANO	6-03-004 MARGINS	1-01-001 MARSHALL'S
1207-15-319 MAN	6-01-001 MANOMETER	1-01-001 MARGO	1-01-001 MARSHALLED
125-14-077 MAN'S	1-01-001 MANON	12-09-012 MARIA	1-01-001 MARSHALLING
1-01-001 MAN-HOURS	5-04-005 MANOR	1-01-001 MARIANO	5-04-005 MARSHES
6-06-006 MAN-MADE	1-01-001 MANORS	6-04-006 MARIE	1-01-001 MARSHLANDS
1-01-001 MAN-TO-MAN	14-06-007 MANPOWER	2-01-001 MARIETTA	1-01-001 MARSHMALLOWS
3-02-002 MANA	1-01-001 MANS	10-02-002 MARIJUANA	3-02-002 MARSICANO
20-11-020 MANAGE	1-01-001 MANSE	1-01-001 MARILYN	1-01-001 MARSKMEN
36-13-033 MANAGED	3-02-002 MANSERVANT	1-01-001 MARIMBA	3-02-002 MARSTON
91-08-032 MANAGEMENT	8-04-004 MANSION	4-01-002 MARIN	2-02-002 MART
2-02-002 MANAGEMENT'S	1-01-001 MANSION'S	10-03-004 MARINA	5-03-003 MARTHA
1-01-001 MANAGEMENT-TRAINED	4-03-004 MANSIONS	1-01-001 MARINADE	1-01-001 MARTHA'S
2-01-002 MANAGEMENTS	4-02-003 MANSLAUGHTER	7-02-002 MARINAS	5-02-002 MARTIAN
88-12-040 MANAGER	1-01-001 MANTEGNA	170-01-001 MARINATED	3-01-001 MARTIANS
2-01-002 MANAGER'S	3-03-003 MANTEL	1-01-001 MARINATING	55-10-023 MARTIN
10-04-009 MANAGERIAL	3-01-001 MANTHEY	55-08-013 MARINE	1-01-001 MARTIN'S
24-06-009 MANAGERS	1-01-001 MANTIC	4-01-001 MARINE'S	7-01-001 MARTINELLI
4-04-004 MANAGES	48-02-004 MANTLE	1-01-001 MARINER	3-02-002 MARTINEZ
8-05-008 MANAGING	6-01-002 MANTLE'S	11-03-004 MARINES	1-01-001 MARTINGALE
1-01-001 MANAGUA	1-01-001 MANTLEPIECE	1-01-001 MARIO	6-04-006 MARTINI
4-01-001 MANAS	1-01-001 MANTRAP	3-02-003 MARION	1-01-001 MARTINIQUE
2-01-001 MANASSAS	5-01-001 MANU	1-01-001 MARIONETTES	2-02-002 MARTINIS
44-06-010 MANCHESTER	9-03-008 MANUAL	36-01-002 MARIS	1-01-001 MARTS
1-01-001 MANCHESTER'S	3-01-001 MANUALLY	4-01-001 MARIS'S	14-02-002 MARTY
1-01-001 MANDAMUS	4-03-004 MANUALS	1-01-001 MARITAIN'S	1-01-001 MARTY'S
1-01-001 MANDARIN	6-02-002 MANUEL	10-03-005 MARITAL	8-02-003 MARTYR
7-05-007 MANDATE	18-06-010 MANUFACTURE	4-02-002 MARITIME	1-01-001 MARTYRDOM
1-01-001 MANDATED	11-07-010 MANUFACTURED	1-01-001 MARJORIE	1-01-001 MARTYRS
6-05-006 MANDATORY	23-07-015 MANUFACTURER	83-12-056 MARK	1-01-001 MARUM
1-01-001 MANDERSCHEID	4-01-003 MANUFACTURER'S	2-01-001 MARK'S	3-02-002 MARV
1-01-001 MANDHATA	47-05-021 MANUFACTURERS	1-01-001 MARK-UP	6-03-005 MARVEL
5-01-001 MANDO	3-03-003 MANUFACTURERS'	85-14-061 MARKED	2-02-002 MARVELED
1-01-001 MANDREL	2-01-002 MANUFACTURES	4-03-004 MARKEDLY	1-01-001 MARVELLED
1-01-001 MANERET	24-07-013 MANUFACTURING	1-01-001 MARKEL	11-07-011 MARVELOUS
?-01-002 MANES	1-01-001 MANUMISSION	5-03-003 MARKER	1-01-001 MARVELOUSLY
5-05-005 MANEUVER	1-01-001 MANUMITTED	1-01-001 MARKERS	1-01-001 MARVELS
1-01-001 MANEUVERABILITY	6-03-004 MANURE	155-12-057 MARKET	9-03-005 MARVIN
3-03-003 MANEUVERED	1-01-001 MANURE-SCENTED	1-01-001 MARKET-PLACE	8-06-007 MARX
4-04-004 MANEUVERING	1-01-001 MANUSCRIPT	1-01-001 MARKETABILITY	4-02-003 MARX'S
8-03-003 MANEUVERS	8-06-006 MANUSCRIPTS	4-01-001 MARKETABLE	3-02-002 MARXIST
1-01-001 MANFRED	4-02-002 MANUSCRIPTS	3-03-003 MARKETED	1-01-001 MARXIST-*LENINIST
1-01-001 MANGANESE	1-01-001 MANVILLE	43-04-009 MARKETING	
1-01-001 MANGLED	1030-15-365 MANY	3-02-002 MARKETINGS	88-13-036 MARY
20-06-010 MANHATTAN	1-01-001 MANY-BODIED	3-02-003 MARKETPLACE	10-04-006 MARY'S
1-01-001 MANHATTAN'S	1-01-001 MANY-FACED	31-07-018 MARKETS	1-01-001 MARYED
6-03-004 MANHOOD	1-01-001 MANY-MUCH	1-01-001 MARKETWISE	1-01-001 MARYINSKY
3-01-001 MANHOURS	3-03-003 MANY-SIDED	11-06-009 MARKING	23-09-013 MARYLAND
5-05-005 MANIA	1-01-001 MANY-TIMES	2-02-002 MARKINGS	2-01-001 MARYLAND'S
4-04-004 MANIAC	1-01-001 MANYE	1-01-001 MARKOVITZ	2-01-001 MARYLANDERS
1-01-001 MANIACAL	1-01-001 MANZANITA	28-11-025 MARKS	4-01-001 MASARYK
1-01-001 MANIACS	1-01-001 MANZANOLA	7-02-002 MARKSMAN	1-01-001 MASCARA
2-01-001 MANIC	7-02-003 MAO	1-01-001 MARKSMAN'S	7-04-006 MASCULINE
1-01-001 MANIC-DEPRESSIVE	13-07-011 MAP	4-03-003 MARKSMANSHIP	1-01-001 MASCULINITY
	7-04-006 MAPLE	3-01-002 MARLBOROUGH	1-01-001 MASER
1-01-001 MANICLIKE	1-01-001 MAPLECREST	2-02-002 MARLENE	1-01-001 MASH
9-04-008 MANIFEST	3-02-002 MAPLES	2-01-001 MARLIN	3-02-002 MASHED
6-05-006 MANIFESTATION	1-01-001 MAPPED	2-01-001 MARLIN'S	1-01-001 MASHING
9-05-007 MANIFESTATIONS	7-03-003 MAPPING	4-01-002 MARLOWE	9-05-006 MASK
6-04-005 MANIFESTED	13-06-009 MAPS	1-01-001 MARLOWE'S	4-02-003 MASKED
1-01-001 MANIFESTING	1-01-001 MAQUET	1-01-001 MARMALADE	1-01-001 MASKERS'
5-05-005 MANIFESTLY	7-04-005 MAR	3-01-001 MARMARA	1-01-001 MASKING
13-02-003 MANIFOLD	1-01-001 MARATHON	1-01-001 MARMEE	3-02-002 MASKS
1-01-001 MANIKIN	1-01-001 MARAUDERS	1-01-001 MARMI	23-06-007 MASON
1-01-001 MANIKINS	21-07-015 MARBLE	2-01-001 MARMON	1-01-001 MASON'S
2-02-002 MANILA	1-01-001 MARBLEIZED	1-01-001 MAROC	3-01-003 MASONIC
2-01-001 MANIN	1-01-001 MARBLEIZING	1-01-001 MAROCAINE	6-05-005 MASONRY
6-05-006 MANIPULATE	3-02-002 MARBLES	3-03-003 MAROON	3-02-002 MASONS
2-02-002 MANIPULATED	2-02-002 MARC	1-01-001 MAROONED	1-01-001 MASQUE
2-01-001 MANIPULATING	1-01-001 MARCEL	1-01-001 MAROY	2-02-002 MASQUERADE
7-05-006 MANIPULATION	1-01-001 MARCEL'S	1-01-001 MARQUEES	2-02-002 MASQUERADES
2-01-002 MANIPULATIONS	1-01-001 MARCELLO	1-01-001 MARQUESS	1-01-001 MASQUERADING
1-01-001 MANIPULATORS	2-02-002 MARCELLUS	1-01-001 MARQUET	1-01-001 MASQUERS
1-01-001 MANITOBA	120-11-068 MARCH	1-01-001 MARQUETTE	110-13-065 MASS
1-01-001 MANJUCRI	1-01-001 MARCHAND	4-03-003 MARQUIS	1-01-001 MASS-BUILDING
39-08-023 MANKIND	9-04-008 MARCHED	1-01-001 MARQUIS'	1-01-001 MASS-DISTRIBUTION
4-03-004 MANKIND'S	8-04-005 MARCHES	6-01-001 MARR	
3-01-001 MANKOWSKI	1-01-001 MARCHIN	1-01-001 MARR'S	1-01-001 MASS-PRODUCTION
6-02-003 MANLEY	15-06-011 MARCHING	4-04-004 MARRED	50-09-029 MASSACHUSETTS
	1-01-001 MARCILE	95-13-044 MARRIAGE	3-02-002 MASSACHUSETTS'
	1-01-001 MARCIUS		

Code	Word	Code	Word	Code	Word	Code	Word
1-01-001	MASSACRE	35-01-001	MATSUO	2-02-002	MC*CLELLAN'S	5-03-004	MEASURABLE
1-01-001	MASSACRED	2-01-001	MATSUO'S	2-01-001	MC*CLOY	1-01-001	MEASURABLY
1-01-001	MASSACRES	1-01-001	MATSYENDRA	1-01-001	MC*CLOY'S	91-11-061	MEASURE
2-02-002	MASSAGE	3-02-002	MATT	1-01-001	MC*CLUSKEY	66-10-032	MEASURED
1-01-001	MASSAGING	1-01-001	MATTATHIAS	1-01-001	MC*CONE	34-05-017	MEASUREMENT
2-02-002	MASSED	3-01-001	MATTEI	1-01-001	MC*CONE'S	54-05-020	MEASUREMENTS
21-09-018	MASSES	308-15-196	MATTER	2-01-002	MC*CONNELL	49-11-040	MEASURES
3-01-001	MASSEUR	1-01-001	MATTER-OF-FACTN ESS	1-01-001	MC*CONNELL'S	30-04-014	MEASURING
1-01-001	MASSEY-*FERGUSON			7-02-004	MC*CORMICK	45-10-017	MEAT
		5-03-005	MATTERED	1-01-001	MC*CRACKEN	1-01-001	MEAT-WAGON
1-01-001	MASSIFS	64-14-050	MATTERS	2-01-001	MC*CRADY	12-03-003	MEATS
1-01-001	MASSIMO	4-02-003	MATTHEW	2-01-001	MC*CULLERS	1-01-001	MEATY
1-01-001	MASSING	1-01-001	MATTIE	3-01-001	MC*CULLOUGH	5-05-005	MECCA
33-13-029	MASSIVE	2-02-002	MATTING	2-01-002	MC*DANIEL	5-05-005	MECHANIC
1-01-001	MASSON	1-01-001	MATTRESSES	1-01-001	MC*DERMOTT	1-01-001	MECHANIC'S
1-01-001	MASSUH	3-01-001	MATUNUCK	1-01-001	MC*DONNELL	34-09-023	MECHANICAL
6-02-003	MAST	3-03-003	MATURATION	1-01-001	MC*EACHERN	4-03-004	MECHANICALLY
72-13-054	MASTER	1-01-001	MATURATIONAL	1-01-001	MC*ELVANEY	19-09-014	MECHANICS
7-05-006	MASTER'S	31-08-024	MATURE	1-01-001	MC*ELYEE	28-05-011	MECHANISM
1-01-001	MASTER-RACE	1-01-001	MATURED	1-01-001	MC*ENROE'S	18-05-012	MECHANISMS
5-04-005	MASTERED	3-02-002	MATURING	1-01-001	MC*FARLAND	1-01-001	MECHANIST
2-02-002	MASTERFUL	1-01-001	MATURITIES	13-01-001	MC*FEE	1-01-001	MECHANISTIC
1-01-001	MASTERFULLY	39-06-013	MATURITY	1-01-001	MC*FEELEY	4-04-004	MECHANIZATION
1-01-001	MASTERING	1-01-001	MAUCH	1-01-001	MC*GEHEE	5-02-003	MECHANIZED
1-01-001	MASTERLY	21-01-001	MAUDE	2-02-002	MC*GEORGE	1-01-001	MECHANOCHEMICAL LY
1-01-001	MASTERMINDING	1-01-001	MAUDE'S	1-01-001	MC*GHIE		
1-01-001	MASTERPICE	1-01-001	MAUDLIN	1-01-001	MC*GLYNN	4-01-001	MECHOLYL
9-04-008	MASTERPIECE	1-01-001	MAULDIN	1-01-001	MC*GOVERN'S	2-01-002	MECUM
2-02-002	MASTERPIECES	1-01-001	MAULER	1-01-001	MC*GRUDER	1-01-001	MED-*CHEMICAL
24-08-015	MASTERS	1-01-001	MAULING	1-01-001	MC*INTOSH	7-04-007	MEDAL
10-07-009	MASTERY	3-01-001	MAUREEN	1-01-001	MC*INTYRE	1-01-001	MEDALLIONS
1-01-001	MASTIC	7-04-006	MAURICE	3-01-001	MC*IVER	4-04-004	MEDALS
1-01-001	MASTIFF	1-01-001	MAURIER	3-02-002	MC*KEE	1-01-001	MEDDLE
1-01-001	MASTODONS	1-01-001	MAURINE	1-01-001	MC*KELLAR	4-03-003	MEDDLING
1-01-001	MASTOIDEUS	2-02-002	MAUSOLEUM	1-01-001	MC*KENNA	1-01-001	MEDEA
2-02-002	MASTS	1-01-001	MAUVE	3-01-001	MC*KENZIE	1-01-001	MEDECINE
6-01-001	MASU	1-01-001	MAUVE-COLORED	11-04-004	MC*KINLEY	3-01-001	MEDFIELD
1-01-001	MASU'S	3-03-003	MAVERICK	1-01-001	MC*KINLEY'S	1-01-001	MEDFIELD'S
5-02-004	MAT	1-01-001	MAVERICKS	1-01-001	MC*KINNEY	13-07-010	MEDIA
1-01-001	MATAMORAS	2-01-001	MAVIS	1-01-001	MC*LAUCHLIN	1-01-001	MEDIAEVALIST
41-12-032	MATCH	2-02-002	MAW	1-01-001	MC*LEMORE	1-01-001	MEDIAN
1-01-001	MATCH-WIDTH	1-01-001	MAWKISH	1-01-001	MC*LENDON	1-01-001	MEDIATING
16-07-011	MATCHED	2-01-001	MAWR	1-01-001	MC*LENDON-*EBONY	162-13-049	MEDICAL
13-06-010	MATCHES	12-06-008	MAX			1-01-001	MEDICALE
33-07-018	MATCHING	2-02-002	MAX'S	1-01-001	MC*LEOD	2-02-002	MEDICALLY
1-01-001	MATCHING-FUND	1-01-001	MAXENTIUS	3-01-001	MC*LISH	2-02-002	MEDICATION
2-02-002	MATCHLESS	1-01-001	MAXIM	1-01-001	MC*N	1-01-001	MEDICI
2-01-001	MATCHMAKER	1-01-001	MAXIM'S	3-01-001	MC*NAIR	1-01-001	MEDICINAL
1-01-001	MATCHMAKING	1-01-001	MAXIMAL	3-02-002	MC*NAMARA	30-11-019	MEDICINE
21-07-012	MATE	1-01-001	MAXIMILIAN	2-02-002	MC*NAUGHTON	5-03-005	MEDICINES
4-02-002	MATED	7-02-003	MAXIMIZATION	1-01-001	MC*NEAR	1-01-001	MEDICIS
1-01-001	MATEO	2-01-002	MAXIMIZE	1-01-001	MC*NEIL	1-01-001	MEDICO'S
2-02-002	MATER	1-01-001	MAXIMIZED	1-01-001	MC*NEILL	3-01-001	MEDICO-MILITAR
174-12-094	MATERIAL	1-01-001	MAXIMIZES	1-01-001	MC*PHERSON	1-01-001	MEDICS
1-01-001	MATERIAL'S	5-02-003	MAXIMIZING	1-01-001	MC*PHERSON'S	18-07-010	MEDIEVAL
1-01-001	MATERIAL-FORMAL	79-10-042	MAXIMUM	1-01-001	MC*QUILLAN	5-04-005	MEDIOCRE
1-01-001	MATERIAL/HR**./ **O*F**./IN	2-01-001	MAXIMUMS	1-01-001	MC*ROBERTS	1-01-001	MEDIOCRITIES
		2-01-001	MAXINE	1-01-001	MC*SORLEY'S	1-01-001	MEDIOCRITY
7-03-007	MATERIALISM	1-01-001	MAXINE'S	1-01-001	MC*WHINNEY	1-01-001	MEDITATE
2-02-002	MATERIALISTIC	11-03-004	MAXWELL	1-01-001	MCCORMACK	1-01-001	MEDITATED
3-03-003	MATERIALIZE	1-01-001	MAXWELL'S	1-01-001	MCCORMICK	2-02-002	MEDITATING
1-01-001	MATERIALIZED	1400-15-343	MAY	5-04-005	MD	2-02-002	MEDITATION
5-05-005	MATERIALLY	1-01-001	MAYANS	1181-15-234	ME	4-03-004	MEDITATIONS
97-08-044	MATERIALS	134-15-075	MAYBE	1-01-001	ME'A	2-02-002	MEDITATIVE
1-01-001	MATERIALS'	2-01-001	MAYE	2-02-002	MEA	7-07-007	MEDITERRANEAN
1-01-001	MATERIALS-HANDL ING	5-02-003	MAYER	2-02-002	MEAD	45-10-027	MEDIUM
		2-02-002	MAYFAIR	17-07-010	MEADOW	2-01-001	MEDIUM'S
2-02-002	MATERIEL	4-03-004	MAYFLOWER	7-05-005	MEADOWS	1-01-001	MEDIUM-SIZED
5-05-005	MATERNAL	1-01-001	MAYHEM	6-05-006	MEAGER	3-01-001	MEDIUMISTIC
10-04-006	MATES	2-02-002	MAYNARD	30-08-020	MEAL	4-01-001	MEDIUMS
4-03-003	MATH	1-01-001	MAYNOR	1-01-001	MEAL-TO-MEAL	1-01-001	MEDIUMSHIP
24-05-009	MATHEMATICAL	1-01-001	MAYO	1-01-001	MEALIE-MEAL	1-01-001	MEDLEY
5-04-005	MATHEMATICALLY	2-02-002	MAYONNAISE	26-10-020	MEALS	1-01-001	MEDMENHAM
2-02-002	MATHEMATICIAN	38-06-015	MAYOR	2-02-002	MEALTIME	5-01-001	MEE
20-07-013	MATHEMATICS	9-03-005	MAYOR'S	1-01-001	MEALYNOSE	1-01-001	MEEHAN
1-01-001	MATHESON	1-01-001	MAYOR-ELECT	1-01-001	MEALYNOSED	10-02-002	MEEK
1-01-001	MATHEWSON	1-01-001	MAYOR-NOMINATE	199-15-130	MEAN	1-01-001	MEEK-MANNERED
2-02-002	MATHIAS	2-02-002	MAYORAL	1-01-001	MEAN-SQUARE	10-01-001	MEEKER
1-01-001	MATHIAS'	1-01-001	MAYORSHIP	1-01-001	MEANDERED	7-01-001	MEEKER'S
1-01-001	MATHUES	13-04-006	MAYS	3-02-003	MEANDERING	1-01-001	MEEKEST
6-01-001	MATILDA	2-01-002	MAYS'	2-01-001	MEANES	2-02-002	MEEKLY
1-01-001	MATINALS	1-01-001	MAYST	1-01-001	MEANEST	148-14-102	MEET
8-05-006	MATING	6-06-006	MAZE	2-01-001	MEANIN	1-01-001	MEETIN
1-01-001	MATISSE	3-01-002	MAZEROSKI	127-15-076	MEANING	159-14-080	MEETING
1-01-001	MATISSES	1-01-001	MAZOWSZE	24-08-020	MEANINGFUL	28-08-025	MEETINGS
1-01-001	MATLOWSKY	2-01-001	MAZURKA	1-01-001	MEANINGFULLY	36-08-016	MEETS
1-01-001	MATRIARCH	1-01-001	MC	2-02-002	MEANINGFULNESS	2-01-001	MEG
1-01-001	MATRIARCHAL	1-01-001	MC*ALESTER	15-10-014	MEANINGLESS	1-01-001	MEGAKARYOCYTE
2-02-002	MATRICULATE	1-01-001	MC*ALISTER	22-05-008	MEANINGS	1-01-001	MEGALOMANIA
3-01-001	MATRICULATED	4-01-002	MC*AULIFFE	3-03-003	MEANNESS	1-01-001	MEGALOPOLISES
1-01-001	MATRIMONIAL	11-01-001	MC*BRIDE	310-14-168	MEANS	1-01-001	MEGARIANS
3-03-003	MATRIMONY	1-01-001	MC*CAFFERTY	1-01-001	MEANS'S	2-02-002	MEGATON
1-01-001	MATRIX	7-04-005	MC*CARTHY	100-14-069	MEANT	10-01-002	MEGATONS
3-03-003	MATRON	1-01-001	MC*CARTHY'S	12-06-011	MEANTIME	2-01-001	MEGAWATT
2-02-002	MATS	2-01-001	MC*CAULEY	35-13-035	MEANWHILE	1-01-001	MEHITABEL
8-01-001	MATSON	2-01-001	MC*CAY	1-01-001	MEARS	1-01-001	MEINCKIAN
1-01-001	MATSU	12-04-005	MC*CLELLAN	2-02-002	MEASLES	1-01-001	MEINUNG

Code	Term
1-01-001	MEIR
1-01-001	MEISENHEIMER
1-01-001	MEISTER
1-01-001	MEISTERSINGER
3-02-002	MEKONG
8-01-001	MEL
2-01-001	MELAMINE
9-05-008	MELANCHOLY
1-01-001	MELANDERI
2-01-001	MELANESIAN
1-01-001	MELANGE
1-01-001	MELBOURNE
1-01-001	MELCHER
1-01-001	MELD
3-02-002	MELEE
4-01-001	MELIES
1-01-001	MELIORATION
1-01-001	MELISANDE
3-01-001	MELISSA
1-01-001	MELLAL
1-01-001	MELLOW
2-02-002	MELLOWED
5-04-005	MELODIC
1-01-001	MELODICALLY
10-04-006	MELODIES
4-03-004	MELODIOUS
3-02-003	MELODRAMA
4-04-004	MELODRAMATIC
21-08-016	MELODY
1-01-001	MELON
1-01-001	MELON-LIKE
4-04-004	MELT
9-07-008	MELTED
22-09-014	MELTING
12-01-001	MELTZER
2-01-001	MELTZER'S
3-02-003	MELVILLE
4-02-004	MELVIN
4-01-001	MELZI
1-01-001	MEM
137-14-087	MEMBER
325-14-134	MEMBERS
2-02-002	MEMBERS'
73-07-025	MEMBERSHIP
2-02-002	MEMBERSHIPS
6-02-004	MEMBRANE
1-01-001	MEME
1-01-001	MEMENTO
1-01-001	MEMENTOES
1-01-001	MEMENTOS
1-01-001	MEMINISSE
1-01-001	MEMO
2-02-002	MEMOIR
4-02-004	MEMOIRS
2-01-002	MEMORABILIA
11-06-011	MEMORABLE
1-01-001	MEMORANDA
3-02-002	MEMORANDUM
23-07-019	MEMORIAL
1-01-001	MEMORIALIZED
3-02-002	MEMORIALS
15-07-014	MEMORIES
1-01-001	MEMORIZATION
3-03-003	MEMORIZE
3-03-003	MEMORIZED
2-02-002	MEMORIZING
76-14-056	MEMORY
2-01-001	MEMORY-IMAGES
1-01-001	MEMORY-PICTURE
1-01-001	MEMORY-PICTURES
1-01-001	MEMOS
8-05-006	MEMPHIS
763-15-248	MEN
19-09-019	MEN'S
1-01-001	MEN-FOLK
1-01-001	MEN-OF-WAR
9-08-009	MENACE
2-02-002	MENACED
4-04-004	MENACING
1-01-001	MENAGERIE
3-01-001	MENARCHE
1-01-001	MENARCHES
1-01-001	MENAS
1-01-001	MENCIUS
3-01-002	MENCKEN
2-02-002	MEND
1-01-001	MENDACIOUS
1-01-001	MENDED
2-01-002	MENDELSSOHN
1-01-001	MENDELSSOHN'S
2-01-001	MENDERES
3-03-003	MENDING
1-01-001	MENDOZA
1-01-001	MENELAUS'
1-01-001	MENET
1-01-001	MENFOLK
1-01-001	MENIAL
1-01-001	MENILMONTANT
1-01-001	MENLO
2-02-002	MENNEN
2-02-002	MENNONITE
1-01-001	MENNONITES
7-01-001	MENSHIKOV
1-01-001	MENSTRUATION
43-14-035	MENTAL
1-01-001	MENTALITIES
3-02-003	MENTALITY
15-08-013	MENTALLY
50-12-045	MENTION
79-13-070	MENTIONED
8-04-007	MENTIONING
7-05-007	MENTIONS
1-01-001	MENTOR
5-05-005	MENU
1-01-001	MENUHIN
1-01-001	MENUHIN-*AMADEUS
2-02-002	MENUS
1-01-001	MEPHISTOPHELES
2-01-001	MERC
1-01-001	MERCE
3-01-001	MERCEDES
16-06-009	MERCENARIES
1-01-001	MERCENARY
12-02-005	MERCER
2-02-002	MERCER'S
3-02-002	MERCERS
1-01-001	MERCHANDISE
6-01-001	MERCHANDISING
8-01-002	MERCHANT
7-01-002	MERCHANTS
3-02-002	MERCIER
4-01-001	MERCIFUL
6-03-004	MERCIFULLY
4-02-003	MERCILESS
2-01-001	MERCILESSLY
1-01-001	MERCURIAL
11-03-005	MERCURY
1-01-001	MERCY
142-12-081	MERE
1-01-001	MEREDITH
4-04-004	MEREDITH'S
6-06-006	MERELY
1-01-001	MEREST
13-06-010	MERETRICIOUS
1-01-001	MERGE
3-02-002	MERGED
1-01-001	MERGER
142-11-091	MERGERS
2-02-002	MERGES
1-01-001	MERGING
2-01-002	MERIT
1-01-001	MERITED
6-04-006	MERITORIOUS
1-01-001	MERITS
1-01-001	MERIWETHER
1-01-001	MERLE
1-01-001	MERLEAU-*PONTY
3-01-001	MERMAID
2-01-002	MERNER
1-01-001	MERRICK
3-03-003	MERRIEST
3-02-002	MERRILL
1-01-001	MERRILY
8-02-002	MERRIMAC
34-08-017	MERRIMACK
1-01-001	MERRIMENT
1-01-001	MERRITT
2-01-001	MERRY-GO-ROUND
2-01-002	MERRYMAKING
1-01-001	MERTON'S
1-01-001	MERVEILLEUX
1-01-001	MERVIN
1-01-001	MERZ
1-01-001	MESA
24-08-012	MESENTERIC
12-01-001	MESH
19-08-013	MESMERIZED
3-03-003	MESS
6-03-005	MESSAGE
1-01-001	MESSAGES
1-01-001	MESSED
7-01-001	MESSENGER
1-01-001	MESSENGERS
3-01-001	MESSES
1-01-001	MESSHALL
1-01-001	MESSIAH
1-01-001	MESSIEURS
1-01-001	MESSINA
17-01-003	MESSINESI
7-01-001	MESSING
4-01-001	MESSRS
	MESSY
1-01-001	MESTA
132-14-093	MET
2-02-002	METABOLIC
2-02-002	METABOLISM
6-01-001	METABOLITE
1-01-001	METABOLITES
1-01-001	METABOLIZED
61-13-039	METAL
1-01-001	METAL-CLEANING
1-01-001	METAL-HYDRIDO
1-01-001	METAL-TASTING
1-01-001	METAL-WORKING
9-06-007	METALLIC
7-04-007	METALS
1-01-001	METALSMITHS
2-01-001	METALWORKING
1-01-001	METAMORPHIC
1-01-001	METAMORPHOSE
2-01-001	METAMORPHOSED
2-01-002	METAMORPHOSIS
5-03-004	METAPHOR
2-02-002	METAPHORICAL
3-01-003	METAPHORS
1-01-001	METAPHOSPHATE
3-01-001	METAPHYSIC
16-06-009	METAPHYSICAL
12-02-005	METAPHYSICALS
2-02-002	METAPHYSICS
3-02-002	METED
4-01-001	METEOR
1-01-001	METEORIC
6-01-001	METEORITE
8-01-002	METEORITES
7-01-002	METEORITIC
3-02-002	METEOROLOGICAL
4-01-001	METEORS
6-03-004	METER
4-02-003	METERED
2-01-001	METERING
1-01-001	METEROLOGICAL
11-03-005	METERS
5-01-001	METHACRYLATE
2-01-001	METHOD
2-02-002	METHODE
1-01-001	METHODICAL
5-01-003	METHODICALLY
1-01-001	METHODISM
12-02-003	METHODIST
4-03-004	METHODISTS
4-03-003	METHODOLOGICAL
1-01-001	METHODOLOGY
8-04-004	METHODS
1-01-001	METHUSELAH
8-03-005	METHUSELAHS
1-01-001	METHYL
6-01-001	METICULOUS
4-03-003	METICULOUSLY
4-02-002	METIER
1-01-001	METIS
2-01-001	METRAZOL
1-01-001	METRE
2-02-002	METRECAL
1-01-001	METRICAL
1-01-001	METRICALLY
1-01-001	METRO
3-02-003	METRONOME
2-01-001	METROPOLIAN
3-03-003	METROPOLIS
1-01-001	METROPOLITAN
1-01-001	METROPOLITANIZATION
1-01-001	METROPOLITIAN
2-01-002	METS
1-01-001	METTLE
1-01-001	METTLESOME
1-01-001	METTWURST
1-01-001	MEURONS
1-01-001	MEW
3-02-003	MEWED
1-01-001	MEXICAN
1-01-001	MEXICANS
1-01-001	MEXICO
1-01-001	MEXICO'S
1-01-001	MEYER
1-01-001	MEYERBEER'S
1-01-001	MEYERS
1-01-001	MEYLE
1-01-001	MEYNELL
1-01-001	MEYNELL'S
1-01-001	MEYNER
1-01-001	MEYNER'S
1-01-001	MEZZO
2-02-002	MFG
1-01-001	MG
5-03-005	MG/**JL
118-14-082	MG/**JL.
1-01-001	MG/**JL**J*B*O*D
2-01-001	MG/**JL/**JHR
1-01-001	MG/**JL/**JHR.
3-01-001	MG/**JL,
3-03-003	MI
22-04-010	MIAMI
3-02-002	MIAMI'S
2-01-001	MIANTONOMI
1-01-001	MIASMAL
1-01-001	MICA
1-01-001	MICAWBER
10-05-005	MICE
6-01-001	MICELLE
5-01-001	MICELLES
4-02-003	MICH
11-05-010	MICHAEL
2-01-001	MICHAEL'S
1-01-001	MICHAELS
1-01-001	MICHAELSON
20-03-003	MICHELANGELO
1-01-001	MICHELANGELO'S
2-01-001	MICHELSON
21-07-013	MICHIGAN
1-01-001	MICHILIMACKINAC
1-01-001	MICK
28-04-013	MICKEY
3-02-002	MICKEY'S
4-01-001	MICKIE
1-01-001	MICKY
1-01-001	MICRO-MICROCURIE
1-01-001	MICROANALYSIS
1-01-001	MICROBIAL
1-01-001	MICROCHEMISTRY
3-03-003	MICROCOSM
1-01-001	MICROCYTOCHEMISTRY
2-02-002	MICROFILM
1-01-001	MICROFOSSILS
8-01-001	MICROMETEORITE
5-01-001	MICROMETEORITES
2-01-001	MICROMETEORITIC
2-02-002	MICROMETER
1-01-001	MICROMETERS
5-01-003	MICRONS
1-01-001	MICROORGANISM
12-02-003	MICROORGANISMS
4-03-004	MICROPHONE
4-03-003	MICROPHONES
1-01-001	MICROPHONING
8-04-004	MICROSCOPE
1-01-001	MICROSCOPES
8-03-005	MICROSCOPIC
1-01-001	MICROSCOPICAL
6-01-001	MICROSCOPICALLY
4-03-003	MICROSCOPY
4-02-002	MICROSECONDS
1-01-001	MICROSOMAL
2-01-001	MICROWAVE
2-02-002	MICROWAVES
1-01-001	MID
1-01-001	MID-*APRIL
1-01-001	MID-*ATLANTIC
1-01-001	MID-*JULY
3-02-003	MID-*JUNE
2-01-001	MID-*OCTOBER
3-03-003	MID-*SEPTEMBER
1-01-001	MID-*VICTORIAN
1-01-001	MID-AIR
1-01-001	MID-CENTURY
1-01-001	MID-CONTINENT
2-01-002	MID-FIFTIES
1-01-001	MID-FLIGHT
1-01-001	MID-RANGE
1-01-001	MID-SECTION
1-01-001	MID-SHIMMY
3-02-003	MID-THIRTIES
3-02-003	MID-TWENTIETH
1-01-001	MID-TWENTIETH-CENTURY
1-01-001	MID-WATCH
1-01-001	MID-WEEK
1-01-001	MID-1890'S
1-01-001	MID-19TH
1-01-001	MID-1948
1-01-001	MID-1950'S
1-01-001	MID-1950S
1-01-001	MID-1958
1-01-001	MID-1960
1-01-001	MID-1960'S
1-01-001	MID-1963
2-02-002	MIDAIR
1-01-001	MIDAS
5-03-005	MIDDAY
118-14-082	MIDDLE
4-01-003	MIDDLE-

Code	Word
1-01-001	MIDDLE-*EASTERN
1-01-001	MIDDLE-*GAELIC
2-01-001	MIDDLE-*SOUTH
2-02-002	MIDDLE-AGE
8-07-007	MIDDLE-AGED
22-03-005	MIDDLE-CLASS
1-01-001	MIDDLE-RANGE
1-01-001	MIDDLE-SCHOOL
1-01-001	MIDDLE-SIZED
1-01-001	MIDDLE-SOUTH
1-01-001	MIDDLES
3-01-002	MIDDLETOWN
4-02-002	MIDGE
1-01-001	MIDI
1-01-001	MIDMORNING
23-08-019	MIDNIGHT
1-01-001	MIDPOINT
2-01-001	MIDSHIPMAN
2-01-001	MIDSHIPMEN
19-10-018	MIDST
1-01-001	MIDSTREAM
1-01-001	MIDSTS
3-03-003	MIDSUMMER
8-05-007	MIDWAY
2-02-002	MIDWEEK
11-05-005	MIDWEST
6-04-005	MIDWESTERN
1-01-001	MIDWESTERNERS
1-01-001	MIDWIFE
1-01-001	MIDWOOD
1-01-001	MIEN
1-01-001	MIFFED
1-01-001	MIG
672-15-310	MIGHT
1-01-001	MIGHTIEST
1-01-001	MIGHTILY
29-09-027	MIGHTY
1-01-001	MIGLIA
1-01-001	MIGNON
3-02-002	MIGRANT
2-02-002	MIGRANTS
1-01-001	MIGRATE
2-02-002	MIGRATED
1-01-001	MIGRATES
1-01-001	MIGRATING
5-04-004	MIGRATION
3-02-002	MIGRATORY
1-01-001	MIGS
2-02-002	MIGUEL
3-01-001	MIJ
3-01-001	MIJBIL
2-01-001	MIJBIL'S
91-07-010	MIKE
7-02-002	MIKE'S
1-01-001	MIKEEN
1-01-001	MIKHAIL
1-01-001	MIKOYAN
1-01-001	MIL
1-01-001	MILAN
1-01-001	MILANOFF
1-01-001	MILBANKES
2-01-001	MILCOTE
14-09-014	MILD
2-02-002	MILD-MANNERED
1-01-001	MILD-VOICED
1-01-001	MILD-WINTER
3-02-003	MILDER
1-01-001	MILDEW
7-05-007	MILDLY
48-12-027	MILE
2-02-002	MILE-LONG
15-05-005	MILEAGE
1-01-001	MILENOFF
173-15-083	MILES
4-03-004	MILESTONE
1-01-001	MILESTONES
1-01-001	MILHAUD
1-01-001	MILHAUD'S
1-01-001	MILIARIS
4-02-003	MILIEU
8-04-006	MILITANT
1-01-001	MILITANTLY
3-02-003	MILITARILY
3-01-001	MILITARISM
2-02-002	MILITARIST
1-01-001	MILITARIST'S
212-12-077	MILITARY
1-01-001	MILITARY-MEDICAL
1-01-001	MILITATED
11-02-005	MILITIA
49-08-026	MILK
2-02-002	MILKS
2-02-002	MILKY
11-06-007	MILL
1-01-001	MILL-POND
1-01-001	MILL-WHEEL
1-01-001	MILLAY
2-01-001	MILLAY'S
2-02-002	MILLE
1-01-001	MILLEDGEVILLE
1-01-001	MILLENARIANISM
1-01-001	MILLENIUM
3-02-003	MILLENNIA
4-03-004	MILLENNIUM
22-08-013	MILLER
1-01-001	MILLER'S
6-04-001	MILLIAMPERES/CELL
3-01-001	MILLIDEGREE
3-01-001	MILLIDEGREES
5-02-002	MILLIE
5-01-001	MILLIGRAM
21-02-001	MILLIGRAMS
2-01-001	MILLILITER
3-03-003	MILLIMETER
1-01-001	MILLINERY
18-08-010	MILLING
204-14-073	MILLION
2-02-002	MILLIONAIRE
1-01-001	MILLIONAIRES
49-12-036	MILLIONS
1-01-001	MILLIVOLTMETER
32-08-018	MILLS
2-01-001	MILLS'S
1-01-001	MILLSTONE
1-01-001	MILMAN
2-01-001	MILORD
1-01-001	MILQUETOAST
1-01-001	MILQUETOASTS
4-01-001	MILSTEIN
2-01-002	MILT
1-01-001	MILTIES
17-02-005	MILTON
6-01-002	MILTON'S
1-01-001	MILTONIC
9-03-006	MILWAUKEE
1-01-001	MILWAUKEE'S
12-01-001	MIMESIS
3-01-001	MIMETIC
1-01-001	MIMETICALLY
1-01-001	MIMI
1-01-001	MIMIEUX
5-01-002	MIN
1-01-001	MIN.
1-01-001	MIN,
1-01-001	MINACES
4-01-001	MINARETS
1-01-001	MINBER
1-01-001	MINCE
6-01-002	MINCED
1-01-001	MINCING
325-15-182	MIND
6-06-006	MIND'S
1-01-001	MINDANAO
2-01-001	MINDED
5-05-005	MINDFUL
3-03-003	MINDLESS
56-13-046	MINDS
59-14-043	MINE
1-01-001	MINE-SAFETY
3-02-002	MINED
1-01-001	MINER
12-06-010	MINERAL
1-01-001	MINERAL-RICH
1-01-001	MINERALIZED
2-01-001	MINERALOGICAL
1-01-001	MINERALOGIES
5-02-002	MINERALOGY
14-06-008	MINERALS
5-02-002	MINERS
2-01-001	MINERVA
28-08-011	MINES
2-02-002	MINGLE
8-07-008	MINGLED
1-01-001	MINGLES
1-01-001	MINGLING
1-01-001	MINGUS
1-01-001	MINH
9-05-007	MINIATURE
1-01-001	MINIATURES
1-01-001	MINIFYING
27-04-009	MINIMAL
1-01-001	MINIMALLY
16-05-014	MINIMIZE
5-04-005	MINIMIZED
1-01-001	MINIMIZES
3-03-003	MINIMIZING
64-10-045	MINIMUM
12-07-009	MINING
1-01-001	MINISCULE
61-11-029	MINISTER
1-01-001	MINISTER'S
2-02-002	MINISTERED
2-02-002	MINISTERIAL
3-02-002	MINISTERING
12-06-010	MINISTERS
2-02-002	MINISTRATIONS
3-02-002	MINISTRIES
13-05-009	MINISTRY
1-01-001	MINIVER
5-04-005	MINK
1-01-001	MINKS
2-01-001	MINN
9-05-007	MINNEAPOLIS
13-07-009	MINNESOTA
2-02-002	MINNESOTA'S
3-01-001	MINNETT
3-02-003	MINNIE
1-01-001	MINNS
1-01-001	MINOAN-*MYCENAEAN
58-13-047	MINOR
5-05-005	MINORITIES
20-06-015	MINORITY
5-04-004	MINORS
1-01-001	MINOSO
1-01-001	MINOT
2-01-001	MINSTREL
1-01-001	MINSTRELS
7-06-006	MINT
1-01-001	MINTER
2-02-002	MINUET
4-01-002	MINUMUM
8-05-008	MINUS
53-13-049	MINUTE
1-01-001	MINUTE'S
1-01-001	MINUTELY
3-02-003	MINUTEMAN
5-01-001	MINUTEMEN
196-14-100	MINUTES
1-01-001	MINUTIAE
48-09-015	MIO
1-01-001	MIRA
16-08-013	MIRACLE
8-06-007	MIRACLES
4-03-004	MIRACULOUS
3-01-003	MIRACULOUSLY
3-03-003	MIRANDA
1-01-001	MIRANDA'S
30-01-001	MIRIAM
2-01-001	MIRIAM'S
1-01-001	MIRIANI'S
1-01-001	MIRO
27-10-021	MIRROR
1-01-001	MIRRORED
4-02-004	MIRRORS
1-01-001	MIRSKY'S
2-02-002	MIRTH
1-01-001	MIRTHLESS
1-01-001	MIS-READING
2-01-001	MIS-TER
2-01-001	MISALIGNMENT
1-01-001	MISANTHROPE
1-01-001	MISBEGOTTEN
3-01-001	MISBEHAVIOR
1-01-001	MISBRANDED
1-01-001	MISCALCULATED
2-02-002	MISCALCULATION
1-01-001	MISCALCULATIONS
1-01-001	MISCARRIED
1-01-001	MISCEGENATION
10-05-008	MISCELLANEOUS
1-01-001	MISCELLANIES
2-02-002	MISCELLANY
2-01-001	MISCHA
5-03-005	MISCHIEF
3-03-003	MISCHIEVOUS
4-03-004	MISCONCEPTION
2-02-002	MISCONCEPTIONS
1-01-001	MISCONSTRUCTION
1-01-001	MISCONSTRUCTIONS
2-02-002	MISCONSTRUED
1-01-001	MISCOUNT
1-01-001	MISCREANT
1-01-001	MISCREANTS
1-01-001	MISDEEDS
1-01-001	MISDEMEANANTS
2-02-002	MISDEMEANOR
1-01-001	MISDIRECTORS
13-07-011	MISERABLE
3-02-003	MISERABLY
2-02-002	MISERIES
15-06-014	MISERY
1-01-001	MISES
1-01-001	MISFIRED
10-06-010	MISFORTUNE
1-01-001	MISFORTUNES
1-01-001	MISGAUGED
5-05-005	MISGIVINGS
2-02-002	MISGUIDED
4-04-004	MISHAP
1-01-001	MISINFORMATION
2-02-002	MISINTERPRET
1-01-001	MISINTERPRETATION
2-02-002	MISINTERPRETED
1-01-001	MISINTERPRETERS
2-02-002	MISJUDGED
10-05-009	MISLEADING
1-01-001	MISLEADS
3-03-003	MISLED
1-01-001	MISMANAGED
1-01-001	MISNAMED
1-01-001	MISNOMER
1-01-001	MISO
1-01-001	MISOGYNIST
1-01-001	MISPERCEIVES
7-04-004	MISPLACED
1-01-001	MISPLACEMENTS
1-01-001	MISPLACING
1-01-001	MISPRONUNCIATION
1-01-001	MISQUOTED
1-01-001	MISRELATED
2-02-002	MISREPRESENTATION
1-01-001	MISREPRESENTATIONS
1-01-001	MISREPRESENTING
2-02-002	MISREPRESENTS
258-14-073	MISS
1-01-001	MISSA
3-01-001	MISSAIL
40-12-035	MISSED
5-03-004	MISSES
2-02-002	MISSHAPEN
48-09-015	MISSILE
1-01-001	MISSILE'S
1-01-001	MISSILE-TYPE
32-07-011	MISSILES
33-12-028	MISSING
78-15-045	MISSION
10-04-004	MISSIONARIES
17-06-009	MISSIONARY
16-09-012	MISSIONS
39-09-021	MISSISSIPPI
3-02-003	MISSISSIPPI'S
1-01-001	MISSISSIPPIANS
1-01-001	MISSIVE
1-01-001	MISSOULA
21-09-015	MISSOURI
4-03-003	MISSOURI'S
1-01-001	MISSOURI-*ILLINOIS
2-02-002	MISSTEP
2-01-002	MISSY
14-07-012	MIST
1-01-001	MIST-LIKE
34-12-030	MISTAKE
17-11-016	MISTAKEN
3-02-003	MISTAKENLY
16-08-015	MISTAKES
2-02-002	MISTAKING
1-01-001	MISTED
10-05-007	MISTER
1-01-001	MISTOOK
5-04-005	MISTRESS
2-01-002	MISTRIAL
4-03-003	MISTRUST
2-01-001	MISTRUSTED
2-02-002	MISTS
4-04-004	MISTY
1-01-001	MISTY-EYED
1-01-001	MISUNDERSTAND
1-01-001	MISUNDERSTANDED
11-05-010	MISUNDERSTANDING
1-01-001	MISUNDERSTANDINGS
6-05-006	MISUNDERSTOOD
5-04-005	MISUSE
1-01-001	MISWRITTEN
2-01-001	MITCH
26-06-010	MITCHELL
1-01-001	MITCHELL'S
1-01-001	MITE
1-01-001	MITE-BOX
1-01-001	MITER
1-01-001	MITIGATE
2-02-002	MITIGATES
2-02-002	MITIGATING
1-01-001	MITIGATION
1-01-001	MITRAL
1-01-001	MITRE
2-01-001	MITROPOULOS

2-02-002	MITTENS	11-07-010	MOIST	2-02-002	MONICA	2-02-002	MOON'S
5-01-001	MITYUKH	2-02-002	MOISTEN	1-01-001	MONIES	1-01-001	MOON-DRENCHED
1-01-001	MIUCHI	2-02-002	MOISTENED	1-01-001	MONILIA	1-01-001	MOON-FACED
13-06-012	MIX	1-01-001	MOISTENING	3-02-003	MONITOR	1-01-001	MOON-ROUND
37-08-024	MIXED	10-05-008	MOISTURE	1-01-001	MONITORED	1-01-001	MOON-SPLASHED
2-01-001	MIXER	2-01-001	MOLAL	13-03-003	MONITORING	1-01-001	MOON-WASHED
1-01-001	MIXERS	1-01-001	MOLAR	2-01-001	MONITORS	1-01-001	MOONAN
10-04-007	MIXING	1-01-001	MOLARD	1-01-001	MONIUSZKO'S	1-01-001	MOONCURSERS
30-08-022	MIXTURE	1-01-001	MOLARS	16-05-007	MONK	13-04-009	MOONLIGHT
4-01-003	MIXTURES	1-01-001	MOLASSES	9-03-004	MONKEY	1-01-001	MOONLIKE
2-01-001	MIYAGI	45-07-009	MOLD	1-01-001	MONKEY-GLAND	2-02-002	MOONLIT
3-01-001	MIZELL	1-01-001	MOLDAVIAN	1-01-001	MONKEYS	3-02-002	MOONS
11-01-004	ML	1-01-001	MOLDBOARD	1-01-001	MONKISH	1-01-001	MOONTRACK
1-01-001	ML,	12-03-005	MOLDED	10-06-007	MONKS	24-07-010	MOORE
15-04-006	MM	15-03-004	MOLDING	3-01-001	MONMOUTH	2-02-002	MOORE'S
2-01-001	MMES	7-02-004	MOLDS	2-01-001	MONMOUTH'S	2-02-002	MOORED
2-01-001	MMM	4-04-004	MOLE	2-01-001	MONO-	1-01-001	MOORING
1-01-001	MMMM	17-03-010	MOLECULAR	3-01-001	MONO-IODOTYROSI	2-02-002	MOORISH
8-04-007	MO	6-02-004	MOLECULE		NE	2-02-002	MOORS
1-01-001	MOAN	8-05-006	MOLECULES	2-01-001	MONO-UNSATURATE	3-01-001	MOOS
2-01-002	MOANED	1-01-001	MOLECULES/**F		D	1-01-001	MOOSILAUKE
1-01-001	MOANS	1-01-001	MOLEST	1-01-001	MONOCHROMES	1-01-001	MOOT
10-06-007	MOB	1-01-001	MOLESTING	1-01-001	MONOCITE	3-03-003	MOP
1-01-001	MOB'S	7-01-001	MOLESWORTH	1-01-001	MONOCLINIC	4-03-004	MOPPED
1-01-001	MOBCAPS	3-02-002	MOLIERE	1-01-001	MONODISPERSE	3-03-003	MOPPING
44-10-013	MOBILE	5-01-001	MOLIERE'S	1-01-001	MONOGAMOUS	1-01-001	MOPS
8-04-006	MOBILITY	2-02-002	MOLINARI	1-01-001	MONOGRAM	1-01-001	MOR
5-04-005	MOBILIZATION	5-01-001	MOLL	1-01-001	MONOGRAPH	1-01-001	MOR-EE-AIR-TEEE
2-01-002	MOBILIZE	1-01-001	MOLLER	1-01-001	MONOGRAPHS		EE
4-03-004	MOBILIZED	6-01-001	MOLLIE	1-01-001	MONOLITH	1-01-001	MORAINE'S
3-02-002	MOBILIZING	1-01-001	MOLLIFIED	1-01-001	MONOLITHIC	142-15-063	MORAL
4-02-003	MOBS	2-02-002	MOLLIFY	1-01-001	MONOLITHICALLY	17-05-010	MORALE
1-01-001	MOBSTERS	1-01-001	MOLLUSKS	1-01-001	MONOLOGIST	1-01-001	MORALE-ENHANCIN
2-01-001	MOBUTU	5-04-004	MOLLY	3-02-002	MONOLOGUE		G
1-01-001	MOCCASIN	2-02-002	MOLLY'S	2-02-002	MONOMER	2-01-002	MORALIST
2-02-002	MOCCASINS	1-01-001	MOLLYCODDLE	1-01-001	MONOMERS	1-01-001	MORALISTIC
8-07-008	MOCK	3-02-002	MOLOCH	1-01-001	MONONUCLEAR	1-01-001	MORALITIES
3-03-003	MOCKED	7-02-002	MOLOTOV	1-01-001	MONOPHONIC	29-08-018	MORALITY
2-02-002	MOCKERY	3-02-003	MOLTEN	5-02-002	MONOPOLIES	7-04-006	MORALLY
5-05-005	MOCKING	1-01-001	MOLUCCAS	2-01-001	MONOPOLISTIC	7-04-006	MORALS
1-01-001	MOCKINGLY	3-01-001	MOLVAR	1-01-001	MONOPOLISTS	1-01-001	MORASS
3-01-003	MODAL	3-03-003	MOM	1-01-001	MONOPOLIZATION	1-01-001	MORATORIUM
1-01-001	MODALITY	1-01-001	MOM'S	4-03-003	MONOPOLIZE	1-01-001	MORAVIAN
21-05-011	MODE	246-14-151	MOMENT	14-07-011	MONOPOLY	1-01-001	MORBID
77-12-032	MODEL	5-05-005	MOMENT'S	1-01-001	MONOSYLLABLE	1-01-001	MORBID-MINDED
3-03-003	MODELED	5-05-005	MOMENTARILY	2-02-002	MONOSYLLABLES	2216-15-475	MORE
1-01-001	MODELING	6-05-006	MOMENTARY	3-01-001	MONOTONE	1-01-001	MORE'N
47-10-025	MODELS	1-01-001	MOMENTOES	8-06-008	MONOTONOUS	7-01-001	MORE'S
22-09-017	MODERATE	8-06-007	MOMENTOUS	7-06-007	MONOTONY	1-01-001	MORE-THAN-AVERA
1-01-001	MODERATE-INCOME	50-13-041	MOMENTS	12-04-004	MONROE		GE
6-04-005	MODERATELY	14-05-008	MOMENTUM	12-05-006	MONSIEUR	1-01-001	MORE-THAN-ORDIN
4-02-004	MODERATES	2-01-001	MOMMA	3-02-002	MONSOON		ARY
1-01-001	MODERATING	1-01-001	MOMMOR	1-01-001	MONSOON-SHROUDE	1-01-001	MOREHOUSE
3-02-002	MODERATION	1-01-001	MOMMY		D	1-01-001	MOREL
4-03-003	MODERATOR	1-01-001	MOMMY'S	6-04-006	MONSTER	17-01-001	MORELAND
198-15-116	MODERN	3-01-001	MOMOYAMA	3-03-003	MONSTERS	88-13-063	MOREOVER
1-01-001	MODERN-DANCE	1-01-001	MON	3-03-003	MONSTROSITY	7-04-007	MORES
2-02-002	MODERNISM	2-01-001	MON-*COLUMBIA	13-06-012	MONSTROUS	72-07-009	MORGAN
1-01-001	MODERNISTIC	2-01-001	MON-*FAY	2-02-002	MONT	6-02-002	MORGAN'S
2-02-002	MODERNISTS	2-01-001	MON-*GODDESS	2-01-001	MONTAIGNE	1-01-001	MORGART
6-03-003	MODERNITY	2-01-001	MON-*KHMER	2-02-002	MONTANA	1-01-001	MORGEN
13-04-006	MODERNIZATION	5-01-001	MONACLE	5-03-005	MONTE	2-01-001	MORGENTHAU
1-01-001	MODERNIZE	2-01-001	MONAGAN	1-01-001	MONTENEGRIN	1-01-001	MORGENTHAU'S
3-03-003	MODERNIZED	3-02-003	MONARCH	1-01-001	MONTEREY	1-01-001	MORGUE
4-03-003	MODERNIZING	1-01-001	MONARQUE	10-01-001	MONTERO	5-02-002	MORIARTY
3-03-003	MODERNS	2-02-002	MONASTERIES	5-01-001	MONTERO'S	1-01-001	MORIARTY'S
8-03-007	MODES	2-02-002	MONASTERY	2-02-002	MONTEVERDI	1-01-001	MORIKAWA
29-10-026	MODEST	7-03-003	MONASTIC	1-01-001	MONTEVIDEO	11-01-001	MORITZ
3-03-003	MODESTLY	1-01-001	MONASTICISM	1-01-001	MONTFAUCON	2-02-002	MORLEY
4-04-004	MODESTY	1-01-001	MONAURAL	16-05-006	MONTGOMERY	2-02-002	MORMON
2-02-002	MODICUM	68-08-030	MONDAY	2-02-002	MONTGOMERY'S	211-15-121	MORNING
4-03-004	MODIFICATION	3-01-002	MONDAY'S	130-14-082	MONTH	2-02-002	MORNING'S
6-04-006	MODIFICATIONS	1-01-001	MONDAYS	2-02-002	MONTH'S	1-01-001	MORNING-FRIGHTE
13-04-012	MODIFIED	2-02-002	MONDE	1-01-001	MONTH-LONG		NED
5-03-003	MODIFIER	1-01-001	MONDONVILLE	23-08-019	MONTHLY	1-01-001	MORNING-GLORY
2-01-001	MODIFIERS	3-01-001	MONDRIAN	189-15-118	MONTHS	10-07-010	MORNINGS
2-02-002	MODIFIES	5-01-001	MONEI	5-05-005	MONTHS'	1-01-001	MORNINGSTAR
6-04-005	MODIFY	3-01-001	MONEL	3-03-003	MONTICELLO	3-01-001	MOROCCAN
4-01-003	MODIFYING	3-03-003	MONET	2-01-001	MONTMARTRE	5-02-003	MOROCCO
1-01-001	MODIGLIANI	9-04-004	MONETARY	1-01-001	MONTMORILLONITE	1-01-001	MOROCCO-BOUND
1-01-001	MODISH	265-14-143	MONEY		S	2-02-002	MOROSE
4-02-003	MODULAR	2-02-002	MONEY'S	7-01-001	MONTPELIER	2-02-002	MOROSELY
1-01-001	MODULATED	1-01-001	MONEY-FED	1-01-001	MONTRACHET	1-01-001	MORPHEMIC
4-02-002	MODULATION	1-01-001	MONEY-HANDLING	4-02-002	MONTREAL	1-01-001	MORPHINE
1-01-001	MODULATIONS	1-01-001	MONEY-HUNGRY	1-01-001	MONTREUX	1-01-001	MORPHOLOGIC
1-01-001	MODULES	1-01-001	MONEY-MAKER	2-01-001	MONTY	5-02-002	MORPHOLOGICAL
1-01-001	MODUS	1-01-001	MONEY-MAKING	21-08-015	MONUMENT	2-01-002	MORPHOLOGY
1-01-001	MOFFETT	1-01-001	MONEY-MINDED	5-04-005	MONUMENTAL	7-01-001	MORPHOPHONEMIC
1-01-001	MOHAMMAD	2-01-002	MONEY-SAVING	1-01-001	MONUMENTALITY	9-01-001	MORPHOPHONEMICS
1-01-001	MOHAMMED	1-01-001	MONEY-WINNER	1-01-001	MONUMENTALLY	21-05-012	MORRIS
1-01-001	MOHAMMEDANISM	1-01-001	MONEYED	8-05-007	MONUMENTS	1-01-001	MORRIS'
1-01-001	MOI	1-01-001	MONEYMAKING	37-09-030	MOOD	4-02-002	MORRISON
1-01-001	MOINEAU	2-02-002	MONEYS	1-01-001	MOODILY	2-02-002	MORROW
1-01-001	MOIRE	1-01-001	MONGI	8-04-007	MOODS	29-04-005	MORSE
4-02-002	MOISE	1-01-001	MONGOLIA	5-04-005	MOODY	5-01-001	MORSE'S
2-01-001	MOISEYEV	1-01-001	MONGOLIA'S	1-01-001	MOOED	3-03-003	MORSEL
2-01-001	MOISEYEVA	3-01-001	MONIC	60-12-026	MOON	1-01-001	MORSELS

2-02-002 MORT	1-01-001 MOTORSCOOTERS	1-01-001 MUFF	1-01-001 MUNICIPALLY-SPO NSORED
10-06-008 MORTAL	3-01-001 MOTTLED	1-01-001 MUFFINS	3-03-003 MUNITIONS
9-05-006 MORTALITY	4-03-004 MOTTO	11-04-009 MUFFLED	1-01-001 MUNOZ
1-01-001 MORTALLY	2-01-001 MOUGH	2-01-001 MUFFLER	1-01-001 MUNROE
2-02-002 MORTALS	1-01-001 MOULD	1-01-001 MUFFLING	1-01-001 MUONG
11-05-005 MORTAR	1-01-001 MOULDERING	1-01-001 MUG	1-01-001 MURAL
2-01-001 MORTARED	1-01-001 MOULDING	1-01-001 MUGGERS	1-01-001 MURAT
1-01-001 MORTARING	1-01-001 MOULTON	1-01-001 MUGGY	75-11-033 MURDER
2-01-001 MORTARS	1-01-001 MOULTONS	2-01-001 MUGS	9-05-008 MURDERED
17-08-010 MORTGAGE	11-05-008 MOUND	1-01-001 MUHAMMAD	19-07-012 MURDERER
5-03-005 MORTGAGES	2-01-001 MOUNDED	1-01-001 MUIR	1-01-001 MURDERER'S
1-01-001 MORTICIANS	1-01-001 MOUNDS	1-01-001 MULATTO'S	5-03-004 MURDERERS
1-01-001 MORTIFICATION	1-01-001 MOUNE	6-02-002 MULCH	3-02-003 MURDERING
15-03-006 MORTON	26-11-020 MOUNT	1-01-001 MULCHING	4-04-004 MURDEROUS
1-01-001 MORTON'S	33-10-021 MOUNTAIN	4-03-004 MULE	12-04-005 MURDERS
1-01-001 MOS	1-01-001 MOUNTAINEERING	1-01-001 MULE-DRAWN	2-01-001 MURKLAND
4-04-004 MOSAIC	6-05-006 MOUNTAINOUS	3-03-003 MULES	5-05-005 MURKY
1-01-001 MOSAIC-LIKE	1-01-001 MOUNTAINOUSLY	1-01-001 MULLAH	3-02-003 MURMUR
1-01-001 MOSAICS	43-10-027 MOUNTAINS	2-01-001 MULLEN	17-05-013 MURMURED
1-01-001 MOSCONE	4-02-004 MOUNTAINSIDE	2-01-001 MULLENAX	4-03-004 MURMURING
47-06-019 MOSCOW	1-01-001 MOUNTAINSIDES	1-01-001 MULLENDORE	7-03-004 MURPHY
4-03-003 MOSCOW'S	45-12-029 MOUNTED	9-01-001 MULLER	1-01-001 MURPHY'S
1-01-001 MOSCOW-ALLIED	11-07-009 MOUNTING	3-01-001 MULLER'S	8-04-007 MURRAY
6-01-001 MOSE	1-01-001 MOUNTINGS	1-01-001 MULLIGAN	1-01-001 MURRAY'S
9-05-008 MOSES	8-03-007 MOUNTS	4-01-001 MULLIGAN'S	1-01-001 MURRIN
3-01-002 MOSK	2-02-002 MOURN	1-01-001 MULLIGATAWNY	1-01-001 MURROW
3-02-002 MOSLEM	2-02-002 MOURNED	1-01-001 MULLING	3-01-001 MURTAUGH
1-01-001 MOSLEMS	2-01-001 MOURNERS	7-01-001 MULLINS	1-01-001 MURVILLE
10-01-001 MOSQUE	1-01-001 MOURNFUL	1-01-001 MULTI-	42-08-017 MUSCLE
2-02-002 MOSQUES	1-01-001 MOURNFULLY	1-01-001 MULTI-COLORED	1-01-001 MUSCLE-BOUND
1-01-001 MOSQUITO	8-04-006 MOURNING	1-01-001 MULTI-FAMILY	1-01-001 MUSCLE-SHAPING
1-01-001 MOSQUITO-PLAGUE D	10-04-006 MOUSE	1-01-001 MULTI-LINGUAL	1-01-001 MUSCLED
1-01-001 MOSQUITOES	7-01-001 MOUSIE	2-02-002 MULTI-MILLION-D OLLAR	1-01-001 MUSCLEMEN
9-06-007 MOSS	1-01-001 MOUSTACHE	1-01-001 MULTI-MILLIONAI RE	31-10-019 MUSCLES
1-01-001 MOSSBERG	1-01-001 MOUSY	1-01-001 MULTI-PHASE	3-01-001 MUSCOVY
1-01-001 MOSSBERG'S	103-13-064 MOUTH	1-01-001 MULTI-PRODUCT	16-07-011 MUSCULAR
1160-15-396 MOST	1-01-001 MOUTH-WATERING	1-01-001 MULTI-PURPOSE	1-01-001 MUSCULATURE
1-01-001 MOST-VALUABLE	1-01-001 MOUTHED	2-01-001 MULTI-STATE	4-03-004 MUSE
1-01-001 MOST-VALUABLE-P LAYER	3-01-003 MOUTHFUL	1-01-001 MULTI-VALUED	4-02-004 MUSED
44-15-043 MOSTLY	2-02-002 MOUTHING	2-02-002 MULTI-YEAR	1-01-001 MUSEE
1-01-001 MOT	7-05-006 MOUTHPIECE	1-01-001 MULTICHANNEL	1-01-001 MUSES
24-06-010 MOTEL	1-01-001 MOUTHPIECES	1-01-001 MULTICOLOR	32-07-018 MUSEUM
1-01-001 MOTEL-KEEPERS	8-07-008 MOUTHS	1-01-001 MULTICOLORED	10-04-007 MUSEUMS
1-01-001 MOTEL-KEEPING	1-01-001 MOUVEMENT	1-01-001 MULTIDIMENSIONA L	1-01-001 MUSHR
7-02-003 MOTELS	19-04-005 MOVABLE	1-01-001 MULTIFIGURE	2-02-002 MUSHROOM
1-01-001 MOTET	171-14-121 MOVE	1-01-001 MULTILATERAL	1-01-001 MUSHROOMING
1-01-001 MOTETS	181-15-122 MOVED	1-01-001 MULTIMEGATON	2-02-002 MUSHROOMS
1-01-001 MOTH	128-15-078 MOVEMENT	1-01-001 MULTIMILLIONAIR E	3-01-001 MUSIAL
1-01-001 MOTH'S	47-11-028 MOVEMENTS	2-01-001 MULTIPACTOR	216-15-064 MUSIC
1-01-001 MOTH-EATEN	4-02-002 MOVERS	1-01-001 MULTIPHASTIC	1-01-001 MUSIC-HALL
216-13-089 MOTHER	36-09-029 MOVES	36-09-025 MULTIPLE	2-02-002 MUSIC-LOVING
36-10-026 MOTHER'S	29-10-020 MOVIE	1-01-001 MULTIPLE-CHOICE	1-01-001 MUSIC-MAKING
1-01-001 MOTHER-IN-LAW	1-01-001 MOVIE-GOER	1-01-001 MULTIPLE-PURPOS E	1-01-001 MUSICA
1-01-001 MOTHER-INTROJEC T	1-01-001 MOVIE-TO-BE	6-02-003 MULTIPLICATION	85-13-032 MUSICAL
1-01-001 MOTHER-NAKED	31-11-017 MOVIES	8-02-003 MULTIPLICITY	1-01-001 MUSICALE
2-02-002 MOTHER-OF-PEARL	114-14-090 MOVING	7-04-006 MULTIPLIED	1-01-001 MUSICALITY
1-01-001 MOTHERED	1-01-001 MOVINGLY	2-02-002 MULTIPLIES	3-02-003 MUSICALLY
1-01-001 MOTHERHOOD	1-01-001 MOWED	10-05-005 MULTIPLY	3-03-003 MUSICALS
1-01-001 MOTHERLAND	2-01-001 MOZART	8-04-005 MULTIPLYING	23-06-011 MUSICIAN
1-01-001 MOTHERLY	1-01-001 MOZART'S	1-01-001 MULTIPURPOSE	1-01-001 MUSICIAN'S
25-09-013 MOTHERS	1-01-001 MPH	1-01-001 MULTISTAGE	41-08-021 MUSICIANS
4-02-004 MOTHERS'	1-01-001 MPH**-	1-01-001 MULTITUDE	3-02-003 MUSICIANSHIP
1-01-001 MOTHERS-IN-LAW	839-15-148 MR	2-01-001 MULTITUDES	1-01-001 MUSICOLOGISTS
1-01-001 MOTHERWELL	534-13-101 MRS	2-02-002 MULTITUDINOUS	1-01-001 MUSIL'S
2-02-002 MOTHS	1-01-001 MSEC	1-01-001 MULTIVALENT	1-01-001 MUSING
8-05-005 MOTIF	5-04-004 MT	1-01-001 MULTIVERSITY	1-01-001 MUSINGS
5-03-003 MOTIFS	1-01-001 MTS	6-01-002 MULTNOMAH	2-01-001 MUSIQUE
55-14-037 MOTION	1-01-001 MU**DLLERIN	1-01-001 MUM	1-01-001 MUSKADELL
1-01-001 MOTION-PATTERN	1-01-001 MUBARAK	1-01-001 MUMBLE	1-01-001 MUSKEGON
3-03-003 MOTION-PICTURE	937-15-368 MUCH	5-04-005 MUMBLED	6-01-002 MUSKET
1-01-001 MOTIONAL	1-01-001 MUCH-COPIED	1-01-001 MUMBLING	3-03-003 MUSKETS
1-01-001 MOTIONAL-MODIFI ED	1-01-001 MUCH-CRAVED	1-01-001 MUMBO-JUMBO	1-01-001 MUSKOKA
1-01-001 MOTIONED	1-01-001 MUCH-DISCUSSED	1-01-001 MUMFORD	3-02-002 MUSLIM
2-01-001 MOTIONING	1-01-001 MUCH-NEEDED	1-01-001 MUMMIES	2-01-001 MUSLIMS
7-06-007 MOTIONLESS	1-01-001 MUCH-THUMBED	1-01-001 MUMMIFIED	4-01-001 MUSMANNO
17-07-012 MOTIONS	1-01-001 MUCILAGE	1-01-001 MUNCH	1-01-001 MUSMANNO'S
1-01-001 MOTIVATE	1-01-001 MUCK	1-01-001 MUNCHED	1-01-001 MUSN'T
9-04-009 MOTIVATED	1-01-001 MUCK'S	1-01-001 MUNCHING	2-02-002 MUSSELS
3-03-003 MOTIVATES	1-01-001 MUCKER	1-01-001 MUNCIPAL	1-01-001 MUSSETT
3-02-003 MOTIVATING	2-02-002 MUCKING	3-02-003 MUNDANE	1-01-001 MUSSOLINI
11-04-005 MOTIVATION	5-01-001 MUCOSA	1-01-001 MUNDT	1-01-001 MUSSOLINI'S
5-04-005 MOTIVATIONS	2-02-002 MUCUS	1-01-001 MUNDT'S	1-01-001 MUSSOLINIS
22-05-014 MOTIVE	32-09-021 MUD	1-01-001 MUNGER	7-01-001 MUSSORGSKY
20-09-016 MOTIVES	1-01-001 MUD-BEPLASTERED	1-01-001 MUNGUS	1-01-001 MUSSORGSKY'S
3-02-002 MOTLEY	1-01-001 MUD-CAKED	6-03-005 MUNICH	1013-15-349 MUST
56-10-033 MOTOR	1-01-001 MUD-SWEAT-AND-T EARS	1-01-001 MUNICH'S	2-02-002 MUST'VE
1-01-001 MOTOR-CAR	2-02-002 MUDDIED	28-07-020 MUNICIPAL	1-01-001 MUSTA
1-01-001 MOTORING	1-01-001 MUDDLEHEADED	9-03-005 MUNICIPALITIES	5-03-005 MUSTACHE
2-01-001 MOTORIST	1-01-001 MUDDLING	1-01-001 MUNICIPALITY	3-02-003 MUSTACHED
5-02-003 MOTORISTS	10-06-008 MUDDY	1-01-001 MUNICIPALITY'S	1-01-001 MUSTACHES
1-01-001 MOTORISTS'	1-01-001 MUDDY-TASTING	1-01-001 MUNICIPALLY	1-01-001 MUSTACHIOED
50-08-010 MOTORS	1-01-001 MUDGUARD		1-01-001 MUSTANG
3-01-001 MOTORS'	1-01-001 MUDSLINGING		1-01-001 MUSTANGS
	1-01-001 MUDUGNO		20-02-006 MUSTARD
	1-01-001 MUDWAGON		3-03-003 MUSTER
	1-01-001 MUEZZIN		1-01-001 MUSTERED

Code	Word	Code	Word
1-01-001	MUSTERING	3-01-001	NADINE'S
1-01-001	MUSTINESS	2-01-001	NADIR
5-03-004	MUSTN'T	1-01-001	NAE
1-01-001	MUSTS	1-01-001	NAGAMO
1-01-001	MUTANTS	2-02-002	NAGASAKI
1-01-001	MUTATIONAL	1-01-001	NAGEL
1-01-001	MUTATIONS	1-01-001	NAGGED
3-03-003	MUTE	9-07-009	NAGGING
3-03-003	MUTED	1-01-001	NAGLE
2-01-002	MUTELY	5-01-001	NAGRIN
3-03-003	MUTILATED	1-01-001	NAGRIN'S
1-01-001	MUTILATION	1-01-001	NAHCE
1-01-001	MUTINEER	12-03-006	NAI**DVE
1-01-001	MUTINIES	1-01-001	NAI**DVETE
3-03-003	MUTINY	6-05-006	NAIL
1-01-001	MUTTER	11-08-009	NAILED
17-06-014	MUTTERED	1-01-001	NAILING
1-01-001	MUTTERERS	14-06-008	NAILS
8-04-007	MUTTERING	2-01-001	NAIRNE
1-01-001	MUTTERS	1-01-001	NAIROBI
8-02-002	MUTTON	7-05-007	NAIVE
26-08-020	MUTUAL	1-01-001	NAIVELY
1-01-001	MUTUAL-AID	1-01-001	NAIVETE
1-01-001	MUTUALITY	3-01-001	NAKAMURA
13-06-008	MUTUALLY	1-01-001	NAKAYASU
1-01-001	MUZAK	32-09-027	NAKED
1-01-001	MUZO	1-01-001	NAKEDLY
1-01-001	MUZYKA	3-03-003	NAKEDNESS
10-05-007	MUZZLE	1-01-001	NAKOMA
1-01-001	MUZZLES	2-01-001	NAKTONG
1319-15-251	MY	13-03-006	NAM
2-01-001	MYCENAE	1-01-001	NAM'S
1-01-001	MYCOBACTERIA	294-15-162	NAME
1-01-001	MYCOLOGY	4-02-004	NAME'S
1-01-001	MYELOFIBROSIS	1-01-001	NAME-DROPPER
1-01-001	MYELOID	84-14-065	NAMED
3-02-002	MYERS	2-02-002	NAMELESS
2-01-001	MYLAR	33-07-026	NAMELY
1-01-001	MYN	89-14-055	NAMES
1-01-001	MYNE	2-02-002	NAMESAKE
3-01-001	MYNHEER	4-04-004	NAMING
3-01-001	MYOCARDIAL	2-02-002	NAN
1-01-001	MYOCARDIUM	5-02-005	NANCY
2-01-001	MYOFIBRILLAE	1-01-001	NANOOK
1-01-001	MYOFIBRILS	4-03-003	NANTUCKET
1-01-001	MYOPIA	2-01-001	NAOMI
1-01-001	MYOPIC	4-03-003	NAP
1-01-001	MYOSIN	1-01-001	NAPHTA
27-02-002	MYRA	3-03-003	NAPKIN
4-01-001	MYRA'S	2-01-001	NAPKINS
7-06-007	MYRIAD	3-02-002	NAPLES
1-01-001	MYRON	7-04-006	NAPOLEON
2-01-001	MYRRH	2-02-002	NAPOLEON'S
1-01-001	MYRTLE	1-01-001	NAPOLEONIC
129-13-077	MYSELF	1-01-001	NAPPED
1-03-007	MYSTERIES	1-01-001	NAPPING
26-10-024	MYSTERIOUS	1-01-001	NAPRAPATH
2-02-002	MYSTERIOUSLY	2-02-002	NAPS
39-07-023	MYSTERY	6-01-001	NARA
1-01-001	MYSTERY-STORY	1-01-001	NARBONNE
3-02-002	MYSTIC	1-01-001	NARCOSIS
5-04-004	MYSTICAL	2-01-001	NARCOTIC
2-02-002	MYSTICISM	7-02-002	NARCOTICS
1-01-001	MYSTICISMS	1-01-001	NARCOTIZES
3-03-003	MYSTICS	6-03-005	NARRAGANSETT
1-01-001	MYSTIFICATION	1-01-001	NARRATED
1-01-001	MYSTIFIED	2-02-002	NARRATION
5-02-003	MYSTIQUE	24-04-013	NARRATIVE
35-07-018	MYTH	3-01-003	NARRATIVES
2-02-002	MYTH-MAKING	11-02-002	NARRATOR
2-02-002	MYTHIC	63-12-049	NARROW
13-02-005	MYTHOLOGICAL	1-01-001	NARROW-MINDED
2-02-002	MYTHOLOGIES	9-07-009	NARROWED
3-02-002	MYTHOLOGY	7-04-007	NARROWER
6-03-005	MYTHS	4-03-004	NARROWING
1-01-001	MYTTON	6-03-005	NARROWLY
41-11-028	N	1-01-001	NARROWNESS
1-01-001	N),	3-03-003	NARROWS
1-01-001	N*)O	1-01-001	NARY
2-01-001	N**.'S	2-01-002	NASAL
1-01-001	N**.*A	1-01-001	NASALED
4-03-003	N**.*C	1-01-001	NASCENT
1-01-001	N**.*C**.'S	7-02-004	NASHVILLE
1-01-001	N**.*D	14-04-005	NASSAU
2-01-002	N**.*J	1-01-001	NASSAU'S
1-01-001	N**.*L	2-01-002	NASSER
1-01-001	N**.*M	1-01-001	NASSER'S
11-05-009	N**.*Y	1-01-001	NASTIER
1-01-001	N**.*Y**.*U	5-04-005	NASTIEST
3-01-001	N**.*C	1-01-001	NASTY
1-01-001	N'TH	2-02-002	NATAL
1-01-001	N-NO	-1-01-001	NATALIE
1-01-001	NAB	1-01-001	NATCH
1-01-001	NABBED	2-02-002	NATCHEZ
1-01-001	NABISCO	5-01-001	NATE
2-01-001	NACHT	2-01-001	NATE'S
17-01-001	NADINE		

Code	Word	Code	Word
5-03-005	NATHAN	1-01-001	NEAR-SYNONYMS
1-01-001	NATHANAEL	44-10-036	NEARBY
2-01-002	NATHANIEL	3-02-003	NEARED
139-13-073	NATION	14-08-013	NEARER
36-08-030	NATION'S	24-12-018	NEAREST
1-01-001	NATION-BUILDING	12-06-012	NEARING
6-01-001	NATION-STATE	141-15-108	NEARLY
1-01-001	NATION-STATES	3-01-002	NEARNESS
3-03-003	NATION-WIDE	1-01-001	NEARSIGHTED
375-13-143	NATIONAL	1-01-001	NEARSIGHTEDLY
1-01-001	NATIONALCAR	21-11-021	NEAT
35-05-012	NATIONALISM	1-01-001	NEATEST
2-02-002	NATIONALISMS	19-12-017	NEATLY
4-02-004	NATIONALIST	1-01-001	NEATNESS
4-03-003	NATIONALISTIC	6-05-006	NEBRASKA
1-01-001	NATIONALISTS	1-01-001	NEBULA
3-03-003	NATIONALITY	1-01-001	NEBULAR
1-01-001	NATIONALIZE	3-03-003	NEBULOUS
2-02-002	NATIONALIZED	1-01-001	NEC
1-01-001	NATIONALIZING	51-09-043	NECESSARILY
10-06-010	NATIONALLY	222-14-142	NECESSARY
4-02-003	NATIONALS	5-04-005	NECESSITATE
1-01-001	NATIONHOOD	11-05-010	NECESSITATED
175-11-057	NATIONS	3-02-003	NECESSITATES
3-01-002	NATIONS'	1-01-001	NECESSITATING
1-01-001	NATIONS'S	13-06-009	NECESSITIES
5-04-005	NATIONWIDE	40-12-036	NECESSITY
46-12-038	NATIVE	81-11-054	NECK
1-01-001	NATIVE-BORN	1-01-001	NECKING
11-07-009	NATIVES	3-02-003	NECKLACE
1-01-001	NATRONA	2-02-002	NECKLACES
1-01-001	NATTY	3-02-002	NECKLINE
156-14-097	NATURAL	2-02-002	NECKS
1-01-001	NATURAL-LAW	2-02-002	NECKTIE
1-01-001	NATURALISM	1-01-001	NECROMANTIC
1-01-001	NATURALIST	2-01-001	NECROPSY
4-03-004	NATURALISTIC	3-01-001	NECROSIS
3-03-003	NATURALIZED	1-01-001	NECROTIC
70-14-059	NATURALLY	3-02-002	NECTAR
2-02-002	NATURALNESS	1-01-001	NECTAREOUS
1-01-001	NATURAM	1-01-001	NECTARIES
191-15-125	NATURE	360-15-204	NEED
3-03-003	NATURE'S	187-14-133	NEEDED
1-01-001	NATURED	5-01-001	NEEDHAM
4-02-003	NATURES	1-01-001	NEEDHAM'S
1-01-001	NATUROPATH	5-03-005	NEEDING
2-02-002	NAUGHT	15-05-006	NEEDLE
1-01-001	NAUGHTIER	1-01-001	NEEDLE-SHARP
1-01-001	NAUGHTY	1-01-001	NEEDLED
3-03-003	NAUSEA	6-05-005	NEEDLES
2-02-002	NAUSEATED	11-05-009	NEEDLESS
2-02-002	NAUTICAL	1-01-001	NEEDLESSLY
2-01-001	NAUTILUS	152-15-095	NEEDS
33-07-017	NAVAL	6-03-005	NEEDY
2-02-002	NAVEL	1-01-001	NEESEN
1-01-001	NAVELS	2-02-002	NEGATE
1-01-001	NAVIGABLE	3 0£ 004	NEGATION
1-01-001	NAVIGATE	53-08-036	NEGATIVE
1-01-001	NAVIGATING	2-02-002	NEGATIVELY
6-05-006	NAVIGATION	1-01-001	NEGATIVISM
2-02-002	NAVIGATOR	12-07-010	NEGLECT
1-01-001	NAVIGATORS	18-10-017	NEGLECTED
4-01-001	NAVONA	5-02-005	NEGLECTING
37-09-025	NAVY	1-01-001	NEGLECTS
12-05-007	NAVY'S	4-03-003	NEGLIGENCE
1-01-001	NAVY-BLUE	2-02-002	NEGLIGENT
1-01-001	NAW	10-04-006	NEGLIGIBLE
1-01-001	NAWT	2-01-001	NEGOCIANT
1-01-001	NAWTH	1-01-001	NEGOCIANTS
1-01-001	NAXOS	10-03-005	NEGOTIATE
2-02 002	NAY	7-03-005	NEGOTIATED
1-01-001	NAZARENE	8-05-007	NEGOTIATING
1-01-001	NAZAROVA	6-04-005	NEGOTIATION
13-05-006	NAZI	20-05-011	NEGOTIATIONS
1-01-001	NAZI-MINDED	104-08-033	NEGRO
12-05-005	NAZIS	4-02-002	NEGRO'S
1-01-001	NAZISM	6-01-001	NEGRO-APPEAL
1-01-001	NDOLA	58-07-017	NEGROES
1-01-001	NE	1-01-001	NEGROES'
1-01-001	NE**)GROES	1-01-001	NEGROID
4-02-002	NEAL	1-01-001	NEHF
1-01-001	NEANDERTHAL	5-04-005	NEHRU
2-02-002	NEAPOLITAN	1-01-001	NEHRU'S
198-15-140	NEAR	14-06-008	NEIGHBOR
1-01-001	NEAR-*BALKANIZATION	3-03-003	NEIGHBOR'S
1-01-001	NEAR-*COMMUNISTS	58-12-036	NEIGHBORHOOD
1-01-001	NEAR-ABSENCE	17-07-008	NEIGHBORHOODS
2-02-002	NEAR-AT-HAND	24-09-020	NEIGHBORING
1-01-001	NEAR-BLIND	1-01-001	NEIGHBORLINESS
3-02-003	NEAR-BY	40-12-029	NEIGHBORS
1-01-001	NEAR-EQUIVALENTS	1-01-001	NEIGHBORS'
1-01-001	NEAR-MISSES	1-01-001	NEIGHBOURHOOD
1-01-001	NEAR-MUTINY	1-01-001	NEIGHBOURS
1-01-001	NEAR-STRANGERS	3-02-003	NEIL
		1-01-001	NEILSON
		4-01-002	NEIMAN-*MARCUS

Count	Word
2-01-001	NEISSE
1-01-001	NEISSE-*ODER
141-15-116	NEITHER
4-01-001	NEITZBOHR
1-01-001	NELL
6-02-002	NELLIE
16-07-009	NELSON
4-02-002	NEMESIS
2-01-001	NENNIUS
1-01-001	NEO-
1-01-001	NEO-*CLASSICISM
1-01-001	NEO-*CLASSICISTS
1-01-001	NEO-*ECCLESIASTICISM
1-01-001	NEO-*JAZZ
1-01-001	NEO-*PAGANISM
1-01-001	NEO-*POPULARISM
1-01-001	NEO-*ROMANTICISM
1-01-001	NEO-CLASSICISM
1-01-001	NEO-DADAIST
1-01-001	NEO-STAGNATIONIST
1-01-001	NEO-SWING
5-01-001	NEOCORTEX
2-01-001	NEOCORTICAL-HYPOTHALAMIC
1-01-001	NEOLIBERAL
14-04-005	NEON
1-01-001	NEON-LIGHTED
2-02-002	NEON-LIT
1-01-001	NEONATAL
1-01-001	NEPAL
9-03-005	NEPHEW
5-02-002	NEPHEWS
3-03-003	NEPTUNE
\2-01-001	NERIEN
2-01-001	NERNST
3-02-002	NERO
12-09-012	NERVE
1-01-001	NERVE-ENDS
2-02-002	NERVE-SHATTERING
1-01-001	NERVELESS
22-09-020	NERVES
24-12-020	NERVOUS
3-01-003	NERVOUSLY
2-01-001	NERVOUSNESS
20-08-011	NEST
4-01-004	NESTED
2-01-001	NESTER
2-01-001	NESTING
3-03-003	NESTLED
2-02-002	NESTLING
1-01-001	NESTOR
3-02-002	NESTS
34-08-018	NET
1-01-001	NET-LIKE
1-01-001	NETHER
3-03-003	NETHERLANDS
3-02-003	NETS
1-01-001	NETTED
1-01-001	NETTING
2-02-002	NETTLED
1-01-001	NETTLESOME
30-09-016	NETWORK
1-01-001	NETWORK'S
16-06-007	NETWORKS
1-01-001	NETWORKS'
1-01-001	NEUBERGER
1-01-001	NEUMANN
3-01-001	NEURAL
1-01-001	NEURALGIA
1-01-001	NEURASTHENIC
1-01-001	NEURENSCHATZ
1-01-001	NEURITIS
1-01-001	NEUROLOGICAL
1-01-001	NEUROLOGIST
1-01-001	NEUROMUSCULAR
1-01-001	NEURON
1-01-001	NEURONAL
1-01-001	NEUROPATHOLOGY
2-01-001	NEUROPSYCHIATRIC
4-01-001	NEUROSES
6-02-003	NEUROSIS
10-05-008	NEUROTIC
1-01-001	NEUSTETER
1-01-001	NEUSTETERS
1-01-001	NEUTER
39-07-017	NEUTRAL
5-03-003	NEUTRALISM
8-03-004	NEUTRALIST
2-02-002	NEUTRALISTS
3-03-003	NEUTRALITY
2-01-001	NEUTRALIZATION
1-01-001	NEUTRALIZE
5-03-005	NEUTRALIZED
1-01-001	NEUTRON
1-01-001	NEUTROPHILIS
4-01-001	NEUTROPHILS
1-01-001	NEV
6-04-005	NEVADA
1-01-001	NEVAH
1-01-001	NEVEH
698-15-307	NEVER
1-01-001	NEVER-PREDICTABLE
1-01-001	NEVER-TO-BE-FORGOTTEN
3-01-001	NEVERSINK
73-14-063	NEVERTHELESS
1-01-001	NEVSKY
1635-15-388	NEW
1-01-001	NEW-*ENGLAND
1-01-001	NEW-*WAVER
1-01-001	NEW-*YORK
3-03-003	NEW-FOUND
1-01-001	NEW-HOUSE
1-01-001	NEW-RICH
1-01-001	NEW-SPILLED
1-01-001	NEWARK
1-01-001	NEWARKER
1-01-001	NEWBERY
1-01-001	NEWBIGGIN
1-01-001	NEWBIGGIN'S
2-02-002	NEWBOLD
6-05-006	NEWBORN
1-01-001	NEWBURGER
1-01-001	NEWBURGH
4-01-001	NEWBURY
5-01-001	NEWBURYPORT
1-01-001	NEWCASTLE
7-04-006	NEWCOMER
7-04-007	NEWCOMERS
1-01-001	NEWEL
1-01-001	NEWELLS
20-10-017	NEWER
15-07-014	NEWEST
1-01-001	NEWFOUND
3-02-002	NEWFOUNDLAND
28-08-023	NEWLY
1-01-001	NEWLY-APPOINTED
1-01-001	NEWLY-CREATED
1-01-001	NEWLY-EMERGING
1-01-001	NEWLY-MARRIED
1-01-001	NEWLY-PLOWED
1-01-001	NEWLY-SCRUBBED
1-01-001	NEWLY-WEDS
1-01-001	NEWLYWED
2-02-002	NEWLYWEDS
10-04-005	NEWMAN
27-06-009	NEWPORT
1-01-001	NEWPORT'S
1-01-001	NEWPORT-BASED
102-15-079	NEWS
2-02-002	NEWSBOY
4-02-003	NEWSLETTER
1-01-001	NEWSLETTERS
4-01-004	NEWSMEN
1-01-001	NEWSOM
65-13-043	NEWSPAPER
6-03-005	NEWSPAPERMAN
1-01-001	NEWSPAPERMEN
38-12-030	NEWSPAPERS
1-01-001	NEWSPAPERS'
1-01-001	NEWSREEL
1-01-001	NEWSSTAND
1-01-001	NEWSWEEK
8-01-001	NEWT
6-03-005	NEWTON
3-01-002	NEWTON'S
2-02-002	NEWTONIAN
1-01-001	NEWTOWN
1-01-001	NEWTS
394-15-238	NEXT
1-01-001	NEXT-DOOR
1-01-001	NEXT-TO-LAST
1-01-001	NGANDLU
1-01-001	NGO
2-02-002	NIAGARA
1-01-001	NIBBLE
1-01-001	NIBBLERS
1-01-001	NIBELUNGENLIED
1-01-001	NIBS'
2-02-002	NICARAGUA
1-01-001	NICCOLO
75-13-049	NICE
1-01-001	NICE-LOOKING
9-06-009	NICELY
2-02-002	NICER
1-01-001	NICEST
1-01-001	NICETIES
3-03-003	NICHE
7-04-004	NICHOLAS
1-01-001	NICHOLS
1-01-001	NICHOLSON
1-01-001	NICHTIGE
25-02-003	NICK
7-02-002	NICK'S
1-01-001	NICKED
7-03-005	NICKEL
2-01-001	NICKEL-IRON
1-01-001	NICKELS
1-01-001	NICKLAUS
10-03-009	NICKNAME
1-01-001	NICKNAMED
1-01-001	NICKNAMES
3-02-002	NICODEMUS
16-01-001	NICOLAS
1-01-001	NICOLAS'S
1-01-001	NICOTINE-CHOKED
2-02-002	NIEBUHR
8-04-005	NIECE
1-01-001	NIECES
3-01-001	NIEMAN
1-01-001	NIEPCE
2-01-001	NIETZSCHE
2-02-002	NIGER
1-01-001	NIGERIA
12-01-002	NIGGER
3-01-001	NIGGERS
1-01-001	NIGGERTOWN
1-01-001	NIGH
411-15-183	NIGHT
13-07-012	NIGHT'S
1-01-001	NIGHT-COACH
1-01-001	NIGHT-SIGHT
1-01-001	NIGHT-WATCHMAN
2-02-002	NIGHTCLUB
1-01-001	NIGHTCLUB'S
4-02-002	NIGHTCLUBS
1-01-001	NIGHTDRESS
1-01-001	NIGHTED
1-01-001	NIGHTERS
4-03-004	NIGHTFALL
4-03-003	NIGHTINGALE
23-11-021	NIGHTINGALES
2-02-002	NIGHTLY
1-01-001	NIGHTMARE
9-06-007	NIGHTMARES
1-01-001	NIGHTMARISH
2-02-002	NIGHTS
33-13-030	NIGHTSHIRT
1-01-001	NIGHTTIME
13-01-001	NIGRAS
1-01-001	NIGS
1-01-001	NIHILISM
2-01-001	NIHILIST
1-01-001	NIHILISTIC
3-02-003	NIJINSKY
12-06-012	NIKE-ZEUS
51-07-035	NIKITA
7-04-007	NIKKO
2-01-001	NIKOLAI
4-02-002	NIKOLAIS
1-01-001	NIL
1-01-001	NILE
2-02-002	NILLY
6-02-002	NILPOTENT
1-01-001	NILSEN
2-01-001	NILSSON
2-01-001	NIMBLER
8-01-001	NIMBLY
1-01-001	NINA
1-01-001	NINE
37-13-027	NINE-CHAMBERED
1-01-001	NINE-GAME
2-02-002	NINE-STATE
6-05-006	NINE-THIRTY
1-01-001	NINE-TO-FIVE
4-04-004	NINE-YEAR
6-04-006	NINETEEN
1-01-001	NINETEEN-SIXTY
1-01-001	NINETEEN-YEAR-OLD
1-01-001	NINETEENTH
1-01-001	NINETEENTH-CENTURY
7-02-002	NINETIES
1-01-001	NINETIETH
2-01-001	NINETY
11-05-009	NINETY-EIGHT
3-03-003	NINETY-FIVE
3-03-003	NINETY-NINE
8-04-005	NINETY-SIX
1-01-001	NINEVEH
12-04-006	NINTH
3-02-002	NIOBE
3-03-003	NIP
1-01-001	NIPE'S
1-01-001	NIPPED
1-01-001	NIPPLES
1-01-001	NIPPUR
1-01-001	NIPS
1-01-001	NIRVANA
4-01-001	NISCHWITZ
1-01-001	NISE
1-01-001	NISF-I-JAHAN
3-01-001	NISHIMA
1-01-001	NISHIMO
3-01-001	NITRATE
1-01-001	NITRATES
12-06-007	NITROGEN
1-01-001	NITROGEN-MUSTARD
1-01-001	NITROGLYCERINE
1-01-001	NIVEN
25-06-010	NIXON
1-01-001	NIXON'S
1-01-001	NJUST
2-01-001	NKRUMAH
1-01-001	NNUOLAPERTAR-IT-VUH-KARTI-BIRI-PITKNOUMEN
2201-15-469	NO
1-01-001	NO*$WHERE
1-01-001	NO-*CAL
1-01-001	NO-*NAME
1-01-001	NO-BACK
1-01-001	NO-DRIVING
1-01-001	NO-GOAL
1-01-001	NO-GOOD
2-01-002	NO-HIT
1-01-001	NO-MAN'S-LAND
2-02-002	NO-NONSENSE
1-01-001	NO-O
1-01-001	NO-ONE
1-01-001	NO-TRADING
1-01-001	NO-VALUED
1-01-001	NOAH
1-01-001	NOB
7-04-006	NOBEL
4-03-004	NOBILITY
23-11-021	NOBLE
2-02-002	NOBLEMAN
1-01-001	NOBLER
1-01-001	NOBLES
1-01-001	NOBLESSE
5-03-004	NOBLEST
74-12-052	NOBODY
1-01-001	NOBODY'D
4-04-004	NOBODY'S
1-01-001	NOCES
2-01-001	NOCICEPTIVE
1-01-001	NOCTILUCA
3-02-003	NOCTURNAL
3-02-002	NOCTURNE
12-06-012	NOD
51-07-035	NODDED
7-04-007	NODDING
2-01-001	NODES
1-01-001	NODS
1-01-001	NODULAR
1-01-001	NODULES
2-02-002	NOE**DL
6-02-002	NOEL
1-01-001	NOES
2-01-001	NOGARET
2-01-001	NOGAY
8-01-001	NOGOL
1-01-001	NOIR
1-01-001	NOIRE
37-13-027	NOISE
1-01-001	NOISELESS
2-02-002	NOISEMAKERS
6-05-006	NOISES
1-01-001	NOISIER
4-04-004	NOISILY
6-04-006	NOISY
1-01-001	NOLAN
1-01-001	NOLENS
1-01-001	NOLI
1-01-001	NOLL
1-01-001	NOLLE
1-01-001	NOLO
7-02-002	NOMENCLATURE
1-01-001	NOMIA
2-01-001	NOMIAS
11-05-009	NOMINAL
3-03-003	NOMINALLY
3-03-003	NOMINATE
8-04-005	NOMINATED
1-01-001	NOMINATING
12-04-006	NOMINATION
3-02-002	NOMINEE

Freq	Word
10-05-009	NON
6-02-002	NON-*CATHOLIC
4-02-002	NON-*CATHOLICS
2-01-001	NON-*CHRISTIANS
1-01-001	NON-*COMMUNIST
1-01-001	NON-*DISSONANT
1-01-001	NON-*ENGLISH
1-01-001	NON-*FEDERAL
2-01-001	NON-*GOD
1-01-001	NON-*GREEK
1-01-001	NON-*INDIAN
2-01-002	NON-*JEW
2-02-002	NON-*JEWISH
1-01-001	NON-*JEWS
1-01-001	NON-*SOVIET
1-01-001	NON-*WESTERN
1-01-001	NON-ABSORBENT
2-01-001	NON-ACADEMIC
1-01-001	NON-ALGEBRAICALLY
1-01-001	NON-ARTISTIC
1-01-001	NON-AUTHORITATIVE
1-01-001	NON-BEARING
1-01-001	NON-BOOKS
1-01-001	NON-CHURCH
1-01-001	NON-CODE
1-01-001	NON-COLLEGE
1-01-001	NON-COLOR
1-01-001	NON-COM
1-01-001	NON-COMMISSIONED
1-01-001	NON-COMPARABLE
1-01-001	NON-COMPETITIVE
1-01-001	NON-CONFORMISTS
2-01-001	NON-CONTRIBUTORY
1-01-001	NON-DEALER
1-01-001	NON-DISCRIMINATION
1-01-001	NON-DRAMAS
1-01-001	NON-ENZYMATIC
1-01-001	NON-EXEMPT
2-02-002	NON-EXISTENT
1-01-001	NON-FARM
3-01-001	NON-FICTION
1-01-001	NON-FIGURATIVE
1-01-001	NON-FORTHCOMING
1-01-001	NON-FREEZING
1-01-001	NON-HYDROGEN-BONDED
1-01-001	NON-IDENTITY
1-01-001	NON-INSTINCTIVE
1-01-001	NON-INSTITUTIONALIZED
1-01-001	NON-INTELLECTUAL
1-01-001	NON-INTERFERENCE
1-01-001	NON-ITEMIZED
1-01-001	NON-JOB-CONNECTED
1-01-001	NON-LINEAR
1-01-001	NON-LITERARY
3-03-003	NON-MILITARY
1-01-001	NON-NEGATIVE
1-01-001	NON-NEWTONIAN
1-01-001	NON-NONSENSE
1-01-001	NON-OBJECTIVE
1-01-001	NON-OBJECTS
2-02-002	NON-PARTISAN
2-02-002	NON-PARTY
1-01-001	NON-PATHOGENIC
1-01-001	NON-POETRY
1-01-001	NON-POLICE
2-02-002	NON-POLITICAL
1-01-001	NON-POLYGYNOUS
1-01-001	NON-PRODUCTIVE
1-01-001	NON-PROFESSIONAL
3-02-003	NON-PROFIT
1-01-001	NON-PROPAGANDISTIC
1-01-001	NON-PROPAGATING
1-01-001	NON-PUBLIC
1-01-001	NON-PUBLISHERS
1-01-001	NON-READERS
1-01-001	NON-REPETITIOUS
1-01-001	NON-REPRESENTATION
1-01-001	NON-RESIDENTS
1-01-001	NON-RESISTANTS
1-01-001	NON-ROMANTIC
1-01-001	NON-SCIENTIFIC
1-01-001	NON-SCIENTIST
1-01-001	NON-SENTIMENTAL
1-01-001	NON-SERVICE
3-01-001	NON-SERVICE-CONNECTED
1-01-001	NON-SKID
1-01-001	NON-SOCIAL
1-01-001	NON-STOP
1-01-001	NON-SUCCESS
1-01-001	NON-SUPERVISORY
1-01-001	NON-SYSTEMATIC
1-01-001	NON-TAXABLE
1-01-001	NON-THERMAL
1-01-001	NON-TIME
2-02-002	NON-VERBAL
1-01-001	NON-VIOLENCE
1-01-001	NON-VIOLENT
1-01-001	NON-VIOLENTLY
1-01-001	NON-VOLATILE
1-01-001	NON-WAGE
1-01-001	NON-WHITE
206-14-088	NON-WRITERS
1-01-001	NONACID
1-01-001	NONAGRICULTURAL
2-02-002	NONCE
16-09-011	NONCHALANT
1-01-001	NONCHURCHGOING
1-01-001	NONCOMBATANT
1-01-001	NONCOMMISSIONED
47-12-034	NONCOMMITTAL
4-02-002	NONCOMMITTALLY
5-02-002	NONCOMPLIANCE
1-01-001	NONCONFORMIST
1-01-001	NONCONFORMISTS
3-02-002	NONDEFEATIST
2-02-002	NONDESCRIPT
1-01-001	NONDESCRIPTLY
1-01-001	NONDISCRIMINATORY
1-01-001	NONDRIVER
2-01-001	NONDRYING
108-15-095	NONE
1-01-001	NONEQUIVALENCE
1-01-001	NONEQUIVALENT
2-02-002	NONETHELESS
3-03-003	NONEXISTENT
4-02-003	NON-EXISTENT
1-01-001	NONFOOD
1-01-001	NONFUNCTIONAL
1-01-001	NONIONIC
1-01-001	NONISM
1-01-001	NONLINGUISTIC
8-05-008	NONLITERARY
6-05-006	NONMAGICAL
1-01-001	NONMETALLIC
1-01-001	NONMUSICAL
1-01-001	NONMYTHOLOGICAL
3-02-003	NONOBSERVANT
4609-15-495	NONOCCURRENCE
1-01-001	NONOGENARIAN
1-01-001	NONPARTICULATE
2-01-001	NONPARTISAN
1-01-001	NONPAYMENT
1-01-001	NONPOISONOUS
1-01-001	NONPOLITICAL
1-01-001	NONPROFIT
1-01-001	NONRACIAL
1-01-001	NONREACTIVITY
2-01-001	NONREACTORS
1-01-001	NONRESIDENT
20-08-020	NONRESIDENTIAL
2-01-002	NONSEGREGATED
16-09-014	NONSENSE
1-01-001	NONSENSICAL
1-01-001	NONSERVICE-CONNECTED
6-03-004	NONSHIFTERS
2-01-001	NONSINGULAR
1-01-001	NONSPECIFIC
6-01-001	NONSPECIFICALLY
1-01-001	NONSTOP
127-14-095	NONSYSTEMATIC
2-02-002	NONVERBAL
2-02-002	NONVIOLENT
90-13-069	NONWHITE
57-14-040	NOOKS
7-05-007	NOON
1-01-001	NOONTIME
7-03-005	NOOSE
412-15-219	NOPE
195-15-138	NOR
1-01-001	NORADRENALIN
3-02-003	NORANDA
1-01-001	NORBERG
59-14-050	NORBORNE
11-07-010	NORDMANN
2-01-002	NORDSTROM
50-12-039	NORDYKE
9-07-007	NORELL
5-05-005	NORETHANDROLONE
2-02-002	NORFOLK
1-01-001	NORI
10-04-010	NORM
2-01-001	NORMA
136-15-072	NORMAL
4-03-003	NORMALCY
1-01-001	NORMALIZE
1-01-001	NORMALIZED
36-10-027	NORMALLY
1-01-001	NORMALS
15-05-015	NORMAN
1-01-001	NORMANDY
1-01-001	NORMATIVE
1-01-001	NORMS
24-03-010	NORRIS
1-01-001	NORRIS-*LA*GUARDIA
1-01-001	NORRISTOWN
1-01-001	NORTH
3-02-002	NORTH-BOUND
2-01-001	NORTH-SOUTH
2-02-002	NORTHAMPTON
16-09-011	NORTHEAST
1-01-001	NORTHEASTERN
1-01-001	NORTHENERS
1-01-001	NORTHERLY
47-12-034	NORTHERN
21-04-011	NORTHERNER
1-01-001	NORTHERNERS
1-01-001	NORTHERNMOST
1-01-001	NORTHERS
59-10-031	NORTHFIELD
1-01-001	NORTHLAND
15-02-010	NORTHROP
3-02-002	NORTHS
1-01-001	NORTHUMBERLAND
5-02-004	NORTHWARD
25-09-018	NORTHWEST
7-03-007	NORTHWESTERN
5-03-005	NORTON
74-15-042	NORWAY
1-01-001	NORWEGIAN
2-02-002	NOS
3-02-003	NOSE
1-01-001	NOSEBAG
2-02-002	NOSEBLEED
1-01-001	NOSES
1-01-001	NOSING
8-05-008	NOSKOVA
1-01-001	NOSTALGIA
1-01-001	NOSTALGIC
1-01-001	NOSTALGICALLY
1-01-001	NOSTRADAMUS
1-01-001	NOSTRIL
12-06-011	NOSTRILS
29-12-027	NOT
1-01-001	NOT-**J*=*A
1-01-001	NOT-ACE
1-01-001	NOT-KNOWING
1-01-001	NOT-LESS-DEADLY
1-01-001	NOT-QUITE-PERFECT
1-01-001	NOT-SO-LONELY
3-03-003	NOT-SO-PALE
1-01-001	NOT-STRICTLY-PRACTICAL
1-01-001	NOT-YET-MARRIED
1-01-001	NOTABLE
13-01-003	NOTABLES
1-01-001	NOTABLY
2-01-001	NOTARIUS
2-02-002	NOTARIZED
11-05-007	NOTATION
3-01-001	NOTCH
20-06-011	NOTCHED
2-02-002	NOTCHED-STICK
2-02-002	NOTCHES
2-01-001	NOTCHING
1-01-001	NOTE
1-01-001	NOTEBOOK
1-01-001	NOTEBOOKS
2-01-001	NOTED
1-01-001	NOTES
2-01-001	NOTEWORTHY
1-01-001	NOTHER
5-02-003	NOTHIN
1-01-001	NOTHING
1-01-001	NOTHING'S
5-03-004	NOTHING-DOWN
1-01-001	NOTHINGNESS
2-01-001	NOTHINGS
13-03-003	NOTICE
1-01-001	NOTICEABLE
2-01-002	NOTICEABLY
1-01-001	NOTICED
1-01-001	NOTICES
1-01-001	NOTICING
1-01-001	NOTIFICATION
4-04-004	NOTIFIED
8-04-006	NOTIFY
1-01-001	NOTIFYING
16-08-016	NOTING
40-10-027	NOTION
17-05-014	NOTIONS
1-01-001	NOTITIA
1-01-001	NOTORIETY
8-05-008	NOTORIOUS
1-01-001	NOTORIOUSLY
6-02-003	NOTRE
1-01-001	NOTRE-*DAME
2-01-001	NOTT
19-02-003	NOTTE
1-01-001	NOTTE,JR
4-03-003	NOTWITHSTANDING
1-01-001	NOUGH
1-01-001	NOUN
3-02-002	NOUNS
5-05-005	NOURISHED
1-01-001	NOURISHES
1-01-001	NOURISHING
1-01-001	NOURISHMENT
1-01-001	NOUVELLE
1-01-001	NOUVELLE-*HELOI**DSE
1-01-001	NOV
1-01-001	NOVA
1-01-001	NOVAK
1-01-001	NOVAYA
1-01-001	NOVEL
1-01-001	NOVEL'S
15-02-010	NOVELIST
3-02-002	NOVELIST'S
4-02-004	NOVELISTS
1-01-001	NOVELIZED
22-08-016	NOVELS
7-03-007	NOVELTIES
5-03-005	NOVELTY
74-15-042	NOVEMBER
1-01-001	NOVEMBER-*DECEMBER
3-02-003	NOVICE
1-01-001	NOVITIATE
2-02-002	NOVO
1-01-001	NOVOSIBIRSK
1-01-001	NOVOSTI
1314-15-394	NOW
1-01-001	NOW-FAMOUS
1-01-001	NOW-HISTORIC
1-01-001	NOW-MISPLACED
1-01-001	NOWACKI
1-01-001	NOWADAYS
29-12-027	NOWHERE
2-02-002	NOXIOUS
1-01-001	NOYES
1-01-001	NOYON LA-*SAINTE
1-01-001	NOZZE
4-03-004	NOZZLE
3-02-002	NOZZLES
1-01-001	NUANCE
3-03-003	NUANCES
1-01-001	NUBBINS
1-01-001	NUBILE
115-10-035	NUCLEAR
1-01-001	NUCLEATED
13-01-003	NUCLEI
1-01-001	NUCLEIC
2-01-001	NUCLEOLI
2-02-002	NUCLEOTIDE
11-05-007	NUCLEUS
3-01-001	NUCLIDE
20-06-011	NUDE
2-02-002	NUDES
2-02-002	NUDGE
2-01-001	NUDGED
1-01-001	NUDGING
1-01-001	NUDISM
1-01-001	NUDIST
2-01-001	NUDITY
1-01-001	NUF
2-01-001	NUFF
1-01-001	NUFS
5-02-003	NUGENT
1-01-001	NUGENT'S
1-01-001	NUGGET
5-03-004	NUISANCE
1-01-001	NUISANCES
2-01-001	NUIT
13-03-003	NULL
1-01-001	NULL-TYPE
2-01-002	NULLIFIED
1-01-001	NULLIFIERS
1-01-001	NULLIFY
1-01-001	NULLITY

Code	Word
4-04-004	NUMB
472-15-204	NUMBER
9-08-009	NUMBERED
7-04-005	NUMBERING
125-12-072	NUMBERS
2-01-002	NUMBING
1-01-001	NUMBINGLY
2-01-001	NUMBNESS
1-01-001	NUMENOUS
1-01-001	NUMERAL
1-01-001	NUMERALS
19-04-012	NUMERICAL
2-02-002	NUMERICALLY
1-01-001	NUMEROLOGICAL
1-01-001	NUMEROLOGY
47-10-041	NUMEROUS
2-02-002	NUMINOUS
2-02-002	NUN
1-01-001	NUNES
4-04-004	NUNS
1-01-001	NUOVO
1-01-001	NUPER
17-08-014	NURSE
1-01-001	NURSE'S
13-05-008	NURSERY
1-01-001	NURSERY-
4-02-003	NURSES
2-02-002	NURSES'
17-08-012	NURSING
4-04-004	NURTURE
15-07-009	NUT
1-01-001	NUT-HOUSE
1-01-001	NUT-LIKE
3-01-002	NUTCRACKER
4-02-002	NUTMEG
2-02-002	NUTRIENT
5-02-003	NUTRIENTS
8-01-002	NUTRITION
3-03-003	NUTRITIONAL
1-01-001	NUTRITIOUS
2-01-002	NUTRITIVE
21-06-008	NUTS
1-01-001	NUTSHELL
1-01-001	NUTTALL
1-01-001	NUX
1-01-001	NUZZLED
2-02-002	NW
2-01-001	NYBERG
1-01-001	NYLON
1-01-001	NYMPH
4-03-003	NYMPHOMANIAC
2-02-002	NYMPHOMANIACS
1-01-001	NYMPHS
55-11-028	O
5-02-002	O**.*E**.*C**.*D
8-04-006	O**.*K
4-01-001	O**.-*B
2-01-001	O**.-*C
25-01-001	O**BANION
9-01-001	O**BANION'S
2-02-002	O**BRIEN
1-01-001	O**CASEY
2-02-002	O**CLOCK
5-04-004	O**CONNOR
1-01-001	O**CONNOR'S
2-01-001	O**DONNELL
1-01-001	O**DONNELL'S
2-01-001	O**DWYER
2-01-001	O**DWYERS
1-01-001	O**GARA
1-01-001	O**HARE
3-02-002	O**NEILL
2-01-001	O**SULLIVAN
39-10-033	O'CLOCK
1-01-001	O'ER
1-01-001	O*K
1-01-001	OAFS
15-08-014	OAK
1-01-001	OAK-LOG
1-01-001	OAKEN
3-01-001	OAKES
1-01-001	OAKLAND
1-01-001	OAKMONT
1-01-001	OAKS
5-01-001	OAKWOOD
2-02-002	OASES
6-04-005	OATH
1-01-001	OATH-TAKING
1-01-001	OATHE
3-03-003	OATHS
1-01-001	OATMEAL
2-01-001	OATNUT
7-03-005	OATS
1-01-001	OATS'S
9-04-007	OBEDIENCE
1-01-001	OBEDIENCE-TRAINED
1-01-001	OBEDIENCES
2-02-002	OBEDIENT
6-03-003	OBELISK
2-02-002	OBERLIN
5-01-001	OBESITY
8-06-008	OBEY
7-06-007	OBEYED
3-03-003	OBEYING
1-01-001	OBEYS
2-02-002	OBITUARIES
65-12-045	OBJECT
13-06-013	OBJECTED
2-02-002	OBJECTIFICATION
1-01-001	OBJECTING
18-09-011	OBJECTION
3-01-001	OBJECTIONABLE
13-09-013	OBJECTIONS
91-10-055	OBJECTIVE
3-03-003	OBJECTIVELY
1-01-001	OBJECTIVENESS
39-06-027	OBJECTIVES
2-02-002	OBJECTIVITY
2-01-001	OBJECTOR
1-01-001	OBJECTORS
65-09-038	OBJECTS
1-01-001	OBJETS
4-04-004	OBLIGATED
16-06-013	OBLIGATION
1-01-001	OBLIGATIONAL
22-07-017	OBLIGATIONS
1-01-001	OBLIGE
21-07-016	OBLIGED
2-02-002	OBLIGINGLY
1-01-001	OBLIQUE
1-01-001	OBLIQUELY
1-01-001	OBLITERANS
2-02-002	OBLITERATE
1-01-001	OBLITERATED
2-02-002	OBLITERATION
2-02-002	OBLIVION
2-02-002	OBLIVIOUS
1-01-001	OBLONG
5-03-005	OBNOXIOUS
1-01-001	OBOIST
2-01-002	OBSCENE
2-02-002	OBSCENITIES
1-01-001	OBSCENITY
17-10-017	OBSCURE
7-06-007	OBSCURED
1-01-001	OBSCURELY
1-01-001	OBSCURES
1-01-001	OBSCURITIES
5-03-004	OBSCURITY
1-01-001	OBSEQUIES
2-01-002	OBSEQUIOUS
3-02-003	OBSERVABLE
6-03-003	OBSERVANCE
1-01-001	OBSERVANCES
3-03-003	OBSERVANT
27-07-021	OBSERVATION
4-02-002	OBSERVATIONAL
40-06-020	OBSERVATIONS
3-02-002	OBSERVATORY
25-13-022	OBSERVE
73-12-050	OBSERVED
16-07-013	OBSERVER
1-01-001	OBSERVER'S
20-06-014	OBSERVERS
8-03-008	OBSERVES
13-07-013	OBSERVING
5-03-004	OBSESSED
2-01-002	OBSESSES
5-04-005	OBSESSION
1-01-001	OBSESSIONS
1-01-001	OBSESSIVE
1-01-001	OBSESSIVE-COMPULSIVE
1-01-001	OBSIDIAN
2-02-002	OBSOLESCENT
5-02-004	OBSOLETE
1-01-001	OBSOLETING
10-09-010	OBSTACLE
7-06-007	OBSTACLES
1-01-001	OBSTINATE
4-04-004	OBSTRUCT
4-04-004	OBSTRUCTED
2-02-002	OBSTRUCTIONIST
42-08-039	OBTAIN
11-04-007	OBTAINABLE
1-01-001	OBTAINE
115-09-056	OBTAINED
9-02-005	OBTAINING
2-02-002	OBTRUDES
1-01-001	OBTRUSIVENESS
1-01-001	OBVERSE
92-14-074	OBVIOUS
114-15-088	OBVIOUSLY
1-01-001	OBVIOUSNESS
1-01-001	OCARINA
58-15-048	OCCASION
37-13-033	OCCASIONAL
48-12-042	OCCASIONALLY
5-03-005	OCCASIONED
22-12-020	OCCASIONS
2-01-001	OCCIDENT
2-02-002	OCCIDENTAL
2-01-001	OCCIPITAL
4-01-002	OCCLUDED
2-02-002	OCCLUSION
1-01-001	OCCLUSIVE
1-01-001	OCCUPANCIES
4-03-004	OCCUPANCY
4-04-004	OCCUPANT
9-05-007	OCCUPANTS
24-11-020	OCCUPATION
1-01-001	OCCUPATION'S
11-04-005	OCCUPATIONAL
3-03-003	OCCUPATIONS
36-12-030	OCCUPIED
4-03-004	OCCUPIES
16-09-016	OCCUPY
7-05-007	OCCUPYING
43-11-035	OCCUR
67-13-049	OCCURRED
30-06-012	OCCURRENCE
10-04-007	OCCURRENCES
21-05-015	OCCURRING
27-06-019	OCCURS
34-12-022	OCEAN
1-01-001	OCEAN-GOING
1-01-001	OCEANA
1-01-001	OCEANIA
2-01-001	OCEANOGRAPHIC
3-02-002	OCEANOGRAPHY
3-03-003	OCEANS
1-01-001	OCEANSIDE
1-01-001	OCELOT
2-01-001	OCH
1-01-001	OCHER
2-02-002	OCHRE
24-04-011	OCT
3-03-003	OCTAGONAL
1-01-001	OCTAHEDRON
2-01-001	OCTAVE
2-02-002	OCTAVES
1-01-001	OCTAVIA
2-02-002	OCTET
3-01-001	OCTILLION
51-11-034	OCTOBER
1-01-001	OCTOPUS
2-02-002	OCTOROON
2-02-002	OCULAR
2-01-001	OCZAKOV
44-12-031	ODD
17-01-001	ODD-LOT
1-01-001	ODDITIES
9-08-009	ODDLY
14-09-014	ODDS
1-01-001	ODDS-ON
1-01-001	ODELL
3-01-001	ODER
1-01-001	ODESSA
1-01-001	ODILO
3-03-003	ODIOUS
1-01-001	ODOM
14-06-011	ODOR
8-05-008	ODORS
1-01-001	ODYSSEUS
11-02-002	ODYSSEY
4-01-001	OEDIPAL
20-01-002	OEDIPUS
13-01-001	OERSTED
7-01-001	OERSTED'S
36411-15-500	OF
639-15-267	OFF
3-03-003	OFF-*BROADWAY
2-02-002	OFF-BEAT
1-01-001	OFF-COLOR
3-03-003	OFF-DUTY
1-01-001	OFF-FARM
1-01-001	OFF-FLAVOR
1-01-001	OFF-FLAVORS
1-01-001	OFF-KEY
1-01-001	OFF-LEVEL
1-01-001	OFF-ROAD
1-01-001	OFF-SHORE
1-01-001	OFF-STAGE
1-01-001	OFF-THE-CUFF
1-01-001	OFFAL
1-01-001	OFFBEAT
1-01-001	OFFENBACH'S
1-01-001	OFFENCES
4-03-004	OFFEND
3-02-003	OFFENDED
2-02-002	OFFENDER
2-02-002	OFFENDERS
1-01-001	OFFENDING
8-03-007	OFFENSE
6-02-004	OFFENSES
8-05-008	OFFENSIVE
1-01-001	OFFENSIVELY
1-01-001	OFFENSIVES
80-13-071	OFFER
83-14-069	OFFERED
28-12-022	OFFERING
3-03-003	OFFERINGS
45-10-034	OFFERS
1-01-001	OFFERSEY
1-01-001	OFFHAND
255-14-127	OFFICE
1-01-001	OFFICE'S
1-01-001	OFFICEHOLDERS
101-12-050	OFFICER
13-03-004	OFFICER'S
1-01-001	OFFICERED
83-11-052	OFFICERS
6-04-005	OFFICERS'
45-10-026	OFFICES
75-15-060	OFFICIAL
1-01-001	OFFICIALDOM
18-08-016	OFFICIALLY
62-08-048	OFFICIALS
1-01-001	OFFICIATE
3-01-001	OFFICIATED
1-01-001	OFFICIATING
1-01-001	OFFICIELLE
1-01-001	OFFICIO
1-01-001	OFFICIOUS
1-01-001	OFFING
1-01-001	OFFSADDLED
9-05-007	OFFSET
1-01-001	OFFSETTING
3-02-003	OFFSHORE
7-03-005	OFFSPRING
1-01-001	OFFSTAGE
1-01-001	OFFUTT
1-01-001	OFT
1-01-001	OFT-REPEATED
368-15-206	OFTEN
1-01-001	OFTEN-BLOOD
1-01-001	OFTENER
2-02-002	OFTENTIMES
3-01-001	OGDEN
2-02-002	OGLED
1-01-001	OGLETHORPE
1-01-001	OGRESS
119-12-069	OH
1-01-001	OH-THE-PAIN-OF-I
38-10-025	OHIO
1-01-001	OHMIC
93-11-045	OIL
1-01-001	OIL-BATH
2-01-001	OIL-BEARING
1-01-001	OIL-FIELD
2-01-001	OIL-WATER
1-01-001	OIL-WELL
3-02-002	OILCLOTH
3-02-003	OILED
1-01-001	OILERS
2-01-001	OILHEATING
1-01-001	OILMAN-RANCHER
15-03-003	OILS
1-01-001	OILSEED
4-01-001	OILSEEDS
10-05-009	OILY
3-03-003	OINTMENT
1-01-001	OISTRAKH
1-01-001	OITICICA
1-01-001	OKADA
2-01-001	OKAMOTO
20-06-015	OKAY
1-01-001	OKINAWA
3-01-003	OKLA
14-06-009	OKLAHOMA
1-01-001	OKS
5-02-003	OL
1-01-001	OLAF
1-01-001	OLATUNJI
660-15-256	OLD
1-01-001	OLD-AGE
7-05-007	OLD-FASHIONED
1-01-001	OLD-GRAD-TYPE
1-01-001	OLD-LINE
1-01-001	OLD-SCHOOL
2-02-002	OLD-STYLE
4-03-004	OLD-TIME
2-01-001	OLD-TIMER
1-01-001	OLD-TIMERS

Ref	Word
1-01-001	OLDE
1-01-001	OLDEN
1-01-001	OLDENBURG
1-01-001	OLDENBURG'S
93-14-067	OLDER
14-10-013	OLDEST
1-01-001	OLDIES
2-02-002	OLDSMOBILE
2-02-002	OLDSTERS
5-01-001	OLE
2-02-002	OLEANDERS
1-01-001	OLEG
1-01-001	OLEOMARGARINE
3-01-001	OLEOPHILIC
1-01-001	OLEOPHOBIC
1-01-001	OLERICHS
6-03-004	OLGA
7-01-001	OLGIVANNA
1-01-001	OLIM
5-04-004	OLIVE
1-01-001	OLIVE-FLUSHED
1-01-001	OLIVE-GREEN
1-01-001	OLIVEFACED
7-04-005	OLIVER
3-01-001	OLIVER'S
1-01-001	OLIVES
1-01-001	OLIVET
4-01-001	OLIVETTI
1-01-001	OLIVIA
1-01-001	OLNEY
1-01-001	OLOGIES
1-01-001	OLSEN
1-01-001	OLSON
1-01-001	OLSON'S
1-01-001	OLVEY
1-01-001	OLYMPIAN
7-04-006	OLYMPIC
2-01-001	OLYMPICS
2-01-001	OMAHA
1-01-001	OMAN
1-01-001	OMEGA
3-01-001	OMELET
2-02-002	OMEN
12-08-012	OMINOUS
3-03-003	OMINOUSLY
3-03-003	OMISSION
3-03-003	OMISSIONS
1-01-001	OMIT
2-02-002	OMITS
13-06-011	OMITTED
6-04-005	OMITTING
1-01-001	OMMISSION
1-01-001	OMNIPOTENCE
1-01-001	OMNISCIENT
1-01-001	OMSK
6742-15-500	ON
1-01-001	ON-AGAIN-OFF-AGAIN
1-01-001	ON-LEVEL
2-02-002	ON-SITE
1-01-001	ON-STAGE
1-01-001	ON-SURE
3-03-003	ON-THE-JOB
2-02-002	ON-THE-SCENE
1-01-001	ON-THE-SPOT
1-01-001	ON-TO-*SPOKANE
499-15-262	ONCE
1-01-001	ONCE-A-MONTH
1-01-001	ONCE-DRY
1-01-001	ONCE-IN-A-LIFETIME
1-01-001	ONCE-OVER
1-01-001	ONCE-OVER-LIGHTLY
1-01-001	ONCE-POPULAR
2-02-002	ONCOMING
2-01-002	ONCT
1-01-001	OND
3292-15-496	ONE
2-01-001	ONE*$-TWO-THREE
65-13-041	ONE'S
5-03-003	ONE-
1-01-001	ONE-*LEG
1-01-001	ONE-*STEP
1-01-001	ONE-ACT
1-01-001	ONE-ACT-PLAY
2-02-002	ONE-ARM
1-01-001	ONE-ARMED
1-01-001	ONE-COLOR
1-01-001	ONE-DAY
2-01-001	ONE-DIGIT
1-01-001	ONE-DUMBBELL
2-01-002	ONE-EIGHTH
4-03-004	ONE-FIFTH
6-06-006	ONE-FOURTH
2-01-001	ONE-GEE
9-07-008	ONE-HALF
1-01-001	ONE-HORSE
6-01-001	ONE-INCH
1-01-001	ONE-IRON
1-01-001	ONE-KILOTON
5-03-004	ONE-MAN
1-01-001	ONE-MINUTE
2-02-002	ONE-NIGHT
1-01-001	ONE-O'CLOCK
1-01-001	ONE-OVER-PAR
1-01-001	ONE-PLANE
1-01-001	ONE-QUARTER
1-01-001	ONE-REEL
3-02-003	ONE-ROOM
8-02-003	ONE-SHOT
2-02-002	ONE-SIDED
1-01-001	ONE-SIXTEENTH
2-02-002	ONE-SIXTH
5-03-004	ONE-STORY
2-01-001	ONE-STROKE
1-01-001	ONE-TENTH
14-07-010	ONE-THIRD
2-01-001	ONE-THIRTY
1-01-001	ONE-THOUSAND-ZLOTY
1-01-001	ONE-THOUSANDTH
3-02-003	ONE-TIME
2-02-002	ONE-TWENTIETH
1-01-001	ONE-WAY
1-01-001	ONE-WEEK-OLD
1-01-001	ONE-YEAR
1-01-001	ONEASY
1-01-001	ONEIDA
1-01-001	ONELY
1-01-001	ONENESS
116-15-090	ONES
5-03-003	ONESELF
1-01-001	ONETIME
1-01-001	ONEUPMANSHIP
15-04-005	ONION
4-04-004	ONIONS
3-01-001	ONLEH
2-02-002	ONLOOKER
2-02-002	ONLOOKERS
1747-15-460	ONLY
4-04-004	ONRUSH
1-01-001	ONRUSHING
38-02-003	ONSET
5-01-001	ONSETS
4-04-004	ONSLAUGHT
2-01-001	ONSLAUGHTS
1-01-001	ONTARIO
1-01-001	ONTARIO'S
60-12-047	ONTO
8-01-001	ONTOLOGICAL
1-01-001	ONTOLOGICALLY
2-02-002	ONUS
1-01-001	ONWARD
1-01-001	ONWARD-DRIVING
1-01-001	ONWARDS
1-01-001	OOOO
6-04-004	OOPS
1-01-001	OOPSIE-*COLA
2-02-002	OOZE
2-02-002	OOZED
8-01-004	OP
1-01-001	OPALESCENT
6-03-006	OPAQUE
2-02-002	OPELIKA
319-15-193	OPEN
1-01-001	OPEN-AIR
1-01-001	OPEN-COLLARED
1-01-001	OPEN-END
1-01-001	OPEN-ENDED
1-01-001	OPEN-FACE
1-01-001	OPEN-FLAME
1-01-001	OPEN-HANDED
1-01-001	OPEN-MEETING
1-01-001	OPEN-MINDED
3-03-003	OPEN-MOUTHED
1-01-001	OPEN-WORK
131-15-093	OPENED
6-04-006	OPENER
83-14-063	OPENING
1-01-001	OPENING-DAY
7-05-006	OPENINGS
34-11-029	OPENLY
16-10-015	OPENS
47-11-023	OPERA
1-01-001	OPERA**)'S
1-01-001	OPERABLE
2-01-001	OPERAGOERS
16-01-001	OPERAND
1-01-001	OPERANDS
2-01-002	OPERAS
1-01-001	OPERATE
15-05-013	OPERATES
5-03-005	OPERATIC
87-09-044	OPERATING
113-13-071	OPERATION
25-05-013	OPERATIONAL
1-01-001	OPERATIONALLY
84-09-044	OPERATIONS
6-03-004	OPERATIVE
49-06-011	OPERATOR
17-05-013	OPERATORS
6-02-002	OPERETTA
1-01-001	OPIATES
96-11-066	OPINION
2-01-002	OPINIONATED
44-10-024	OPINIONS
16-02-002	OPIUM
1-01-001	OPPENHEIM
15-06-007	OPPONENT
2-01-001	OPPONENT'S
13-07-013	OPPONENTS
1-01-001	OPPORTUNE
1-01-001	OPPORTUNISM
1-01-001	OPPORTUNISTIC
51-13-029	OPPORTUNITIES
121-14-077	OPPORTUNITY
15-06-015	OPPOSE
41-08-038	OPPOSED
2-01-002	OPPOSES
13-07-011	OPPOSING
81-11-061	OPPOSITE
46-09-032	OPPOSITION
5-05-005	OPPRESSED
6-05-006	OPPRESSION
4-04-004	OPPRESSIVE
2-02-002	OPPRESSORS
1-01-001	OPPROBRIUM
2-01-001	OPTED
2-01-001	OPTHALMIC
19-03-008	OPTICAL
1-01-001	OPTICALLY
1-01-001	OPTICS
28-01-004	OPTIMAL
5-01-001	OPTIMALITY
15-10-014	OPTIMISM
15-06-013	OPTIMISTIC
1-01-001	OPTIMIZATION
1-01-001	OPTIMIZING
1-01-001	OPTIMO
16-03-011	OPTIMUM
5-03-005	OPTION
4-02-004	OPTIONAL
1-01-001	OPTIONS
1-01-001	OPULENT
3-03-003	OPUS
2-01-002	OR
1-01-001	ORACLE
1-01-001	ORACLES
27-06-007	ORAL
2-02-002	ORALLY
23-10-020	ORANGE
6-04-004	ORANGES
1-01-001	ORATE
3-02-002	ORATIO
2-02-002	ORATION
2-02-002	ORATIONS
5-02-003	ORATOR
2-02-002	ORATORICAL
1-01-001	ORATORIO
2-02-002	ORATORS
3-03-003	ORATORY
3-03-003	ORB
1-01-001	ORBIT
2-01-001	ORBITAL
3-03-003	ORBITING
9-03-004	ORBITS
3-02-002	ORCHARD
5-04-004	ORCHARDS
2-01-001	ORCHESIS
1-01-001	ORCHESTER
60-11-024	ORCHESTRA
2-01-002	ORCHESTRA'S
4-02-003	ORCHESTRAL
4-04-004	ORCHESTRAS
3-02-003	ORCHESTRATION
2-01-001	ORCHESTRATIONS
1-01-001	ORCHESTRE
3-03-003	ORCHIDS
2-01-001	ORCUTT
2-01-001	ORDAIN
4-03-004	ORDAINED
3-02-003	ORDEAL
376-15-202	ORDER
69-14-050	ORDERED
13-04-009	ORDERING
2-01-002	ORDERINGS
1-01-001	ORDERLINESS
20-09-016	ORDERLY
58-14-042	ORDERS
9-04-006	ORDINANCE
3-03-003	ORDINANCES
14-07-010	ORDINARILY
1-01-001	ORDINARIUS
72-11-050	ORDINARY
1-01-001	ORDINARY'S
1-01-001	ORDINATES
3-01-001	ORDO
3-03-003	ORE
11-05-008	OREGON
1-01-001	OREGONIANS
1-01-001	ORES
1-01-001	ORESME
2-01-001	ORESTEIA
2-01-001	ORESTES
12-07-009	ORGAN
3-02-003	ORGANDY
38-05-015	ORGANIC
3-03-003	ORGANICALLY
5-01-001	ORGANIFICATION
1-01-001	ORGANISED
6-03-004	ORGANISM
1-01-001	ORGANISMIC
7-02-003	ORGANISMS
1-01-001	ORGANIST
127-11-071	ORGANIZATION
3-01-002	ORGANIZATION'S
1-01-001	ORGANIZATION-POSITION
5-04-005	ORGANIZATIONAL
1-01-001	ORGANIZATIONALLY
61-10-035	ORGANIZATIONS
14-07-012	ORGANIZE
56-13-045	ORGANIZED
3-03-003	ORGANIZERS
1-01-001	ORGANIZES
8-06-007	ORGANIZING
14-06-011	ORGANS
1-01-001	ORGANTION
7-03-003	ORGASM
1-01-001	ORGASMS
2-01-001	ORGIASTIC
2-02-002	ORGIES
1-01-001	ORGONE
1-01-001	ORGY
4-03-004	ORIENT
16-08-013	ORIENTAL
16-08-011	ORIENTATION
1-01-001	ORIENTATIONS
11-05-008	ORIENTED
3-02-003	ORIENTING
2-01-001	ORIFICES
3-01-001	ORIGEN
44-10-035	ORIGIN
1-01-001	ORIGIN/DESTINATION
103-14-078	ORIGINAL
6-04-006	ORIGINALITY
23-10-023	ORIGINALLY
3-01-001	ORIGINALS
6-04-005	ORIGINATE
15-11-015	ORIGINATED
2-02-002	ORIGINATES
3-02-002	ORIGINATING
2-01-001	ORIGINATION
7-04-006	ORIGINS
1-01-001	ORIN
1-01-001	ORINOCO
5-02-002	ORIOLE
11-02-003	ORIOLES
1-01-001	ORIOLES'
1-01-001	ORISSA
1-01-001	ORKNEY
2-02-002	ORLANDO
40-08-019	ORLEANS
4-01-002	ORLEANS'
3-01-001	ORLICK
3-01-001	ORLICK'S
1-01-001	ORLY
2-01-001	ORMOC
1-01-001	ORMSBY
4-03-003	ORNAMENT
1-01-001	ORNAMENTATION
3-02-003	ORNAMENTED
3-02-003	ORNAMENTS
1-01-001	ORNATE
1-01-001	ORNATELY
2-02-002	ORNERY
2-01-001	ORNEY
1-01-001	ORNRAIER
1-01-001	ORPHAN
1-01-001	ORPHANAGE
2-01-001	ORPHANED
1-01-001	ORPHANS
2-02-002	ORPHEUS

Count	Word
1-01-001	ORPHIC
1-01-001	ORSO
1-01-001	ORTEGA
1-01-001	ORTEGA'S
2-01-001	ORTHICON
9-01-001	ORTHODONTIC
3-01-001	ORTHODONTICS
9-01-001	ORTHODONTIST
1-01-001	ORTHODONTIST'S
3-01-001	ORTHODONTISTS
19-06-013	ORTHODOX
3-02-003	ORTHODOXY
3-01-001	ORTHOGRAPHIC
2-01-001	ORTHOGRAPHIES
6-01-001	ORTHOGRAPHY
3-02-002	ORTHOPEDIC
1-01-001	ORTHOPHOSPHATE
1-01-001	ORTHOPHOSPHATES
1-01-001	ORTHORHOMBIC
2-01-001	ORVIL
4-01-001	ORVILLE
6-01-001	ORVIS
2-02-002	ORWELL
2-01-002	ORWELL'S
1-01-001	ORWELLIAN
3-01-001	ORY
1-01-001	ORZAE
1-01-001	OS
6-01-002	OSAKA
1-01-001	OSBERT
2-01-001	OSBORNE
9-08-009	OSCAR
1-01-001	OSCILLATING
3-02-003	OSCILLATION
1-01-001	OSCILLATOR
1-01-001	OSERVED
1-01-001	OSHKOSH
1-01-001	OSIPENKO
1-01-001	OSIS
1-01-001	OSKAR
5-01-001	OSLO
1-01-001	OSMIUM
3-01-001	OSMOTIC
7-01-001	OSO
2-01-001	OSO'S
1-01-001	OSRAM
1-01-001	OSRIC
2-01-001	OSSEOUS
6-01-001	OSSIFICATION
1-01-001	OSSIFY
3-03-003	OSTENSIBLE
1-01-001	OSTENSIBLY
2-02-002	OSTENTATIOUS
1-01-001	OSTEOPOROSIS
1-01-001	OSTINATO
1-01-001	OSTRACISM
1-01-001	OSTRACIZED
1-01-001	OT
1-01-001	OTHELLO
1702-15-462	OTHER
9-09-009	OTHER'S
2-01-001	OTHER-DIRECTED
323-15-212	OTHERS
2-02-002	OTHERS'
86-15-069	OTHERWISE
2-01-001	OTHERWORLDLY
9-01-001	OTHON
1-01-001	OTHON'S
3-03-003	OTIS
1-01-001	OTTAUQUECHEE
1-01-001	OTTAWA
5-02-002	OTTER
1-01-001	OTTERMOLE
1-01-001	OTTO
3-02-002	OTTOMAN
1-01-001	OUD
68-14-050	OUGHT
2-02-002	OUGHTA
2-02-002	OUI
1-01-001	OULD
2-02-002	OUM
3-03-003	OUNCE
3-01-001	OUNCES
1252-15-280	OUR
1-01-001	OURAY
27-12-023	OURS
66-12-046	OURSELVES
1-01-001	OUSE
3-01-002	OUST
1-01-001	OUSTED
1-01-001	OUSTER
1-01-001	OUSTING
2096-15-453	OUT
2-02-002	OUT'N
1-01-001	OUT-DATED
1-01-001	OUT-GROUP
2-01-001	OUT-MIGRANTS
1-01-001	OUT-MODED
1-01-001	OUT-OF-BOUNDS
1-01-001	OUT-OF-DOOR
5-03-003	OUT-OF-DOORS
1-01-001	OUT-OF-MIND
3-01-001	OUT-OF-POCKET
1-01-001	OUT-OF-SCHOOL
1-01-001	OUT-OF-SIGHT
6-01-001	OUT-OF-STATE
1-01-001	OUT-OF-STEP
2-02-002	OUT-OF-THE-WAY
6-03-004	OUT-OF-TOWN
1-01-001	OUT-REACHING
3-01-001	OUTBACK
7-03-003	OUTBOARD
2-01-001	OUTBOARDS
2-02-002	OUTBREAK
3-02-002	OUTBREAKS
2-02-002	OUTBURST
6-03-004	OUTBURSTS
1-01-001	OUTCAST
1-01-001	OUTCASTS
2-01-001	OUTCLASS
1-01-001	OUTCLASSED
26-08-018	OUTCOME
11-02-002	OUTCOMES
1-01-001	OUTCROPS
3-01-002	OUTCRY
3-03-003	OUTDATED
3-03-003	OUTDISTANCED
1-01-001	OUTDISTANCING
3-02-002	OUTDO
27-07-015	OUTDOOR
6-05-006	OUTDOORS
1-01-001	OUTDREW
31-12-023	OUTER
2-01-001	OUTFACE
3-02-002	OUTFIELD
4-01-004	OUTFIELDER
1-01-001	OUTFIELDERS
16-08-012	OUTFIT
1-01-001	OUTFITTED
2-01-002	OUTFLOW
1-01-001	OUTFOUGHT
1-01-001	OUTFOX
1-01-001	OUTGENERALED
1-01-001	OUTGOING
1-01-001	OUTGRIP
4-03-004	OUTGROW
1-01-001	OUTGROWTH
1-01-001	OUTHOUSE
5-01-003	OUTING
1-01-001	OUTLANDERS
1-01-001	OUTLANDISH
2-01-001	OUTLAW
4-03-004	OUTLAWED
1-01-001	OUTLAWRY
2-02-002	OUTLAWS
2-01-002	OUTLAY
1-01-001	OUTLAYS
9-05-008	OUTLET
6-05-005	OUTLETS
12-08-012	OUTLINE
6-05-006	OUTLINED
6-06-006	OUTLINES
2-02-002	OUTLINING
3-02-003	OUTLIVED
36-08-026	OUTLOOK
2-02-002	OUTLYING
1-01-001	OUTMANEUVERED
1-01-001	OUTMATCHED
4-04-004	OUTMODED
2-02-002	OUTNUMBER
2-02-002	OUTNUMBERED
1-01-001	OUTPATIENT
1-01-001	OUTPLAYED
3-03-003	OUTPOST
1-01-001	OUTPOSTS
1-01-001	OUTPOURING
35-07-015	OUTPUT
1-01-001	OUTPUT-AXIS
5-02-003	OUTPUTS
1-01-001	OUTPUTTING
4-04-004	OUTRAGE
7-05-007	OUTRAGED
2-01-002	OUTRAGEOUS
3-02-003	OUTRAGES
5-01-001	OUTREACH
3-01-001	OUTRIGGER
2-02-002	OUTRIGGERS
9-06-009	OUTRIGHT
4-04-004	OUTRUN
1-01-001	OUTS
1-01-001	OUTSCORING
13-08-013	OUTSET
210-15-136	OUTSIDE
3-03-003	OUTSIDER
8-06-008	OUTSIDERS
1-01-001	OUTSIZED
2-01-001	OUTSKIRT'S
3-03-003	OUTSKIRTS
2-02-002	OUTSMARTED
6-04-006	OUTSPOKEN
2-01-001	OUTSPREAD
37-07-030	OUTSTANDING
2-01-001	OUTSTANDINGLY
1-01-001	OUTSTATE
1-01-001	OUTSTRIPPING
1-01-001	OUTSVILLE
2-01-001	OUTTA
10-06-010	OUTWARD
3-02-003	OUTWARDLY
2-02-002	OUTWEIGH
4-04-004	OUTWEIGHED
1-01-001	OUTWIT
1-01-001	OUTWORN
1-01-001	OUZO
1-01-001	OVA
8-06-007	OVAL
2-01-001	OVALS
2-02-002	OVATION
7-05-005	OVEN
2-01-001	OVENS
1236-15-412	OVER
1-01-001	OVER-
1-01-001	OVER-ACHIEVEMENT
2-01-001	OVER-ACHIEVERS
35-10-024	OVER-ALL
1-01-001	OVER-ARRANGED
1-01-001	OVER-CHILLING
1-01-001	OVER-CORRECTED
1-01-001	OVER-EMPHASIZE
2-02-002	OVER-EMPHASIZED
1-01-001	OVER-HAND
1-01-001	OVER-LARGE
1-01-001	OVER-NIGHT
1-01-001	OVER-OCCUPIED
1-01-001	OVER-PRETENDED
1-01-001	OVER-PRODUCE
1-01-001	OVER-SIMPLE
1-01-001	OVER-SIMPLIFICATION
1-01-001	OVER-SPENT
1-01-001	OVER-STITCHED
1-01-001	OVER-SUBSCRIBED
1-01-001	OVER-THE-COUNTER
3-01-001	OVER/UNDER
1-01-001	OVERACTIVE
1-01-001	OVERAGE
1-01-001	OVERAGGRESSIVE
12-05-010	OVERALL
5-02-002	OVERALLS
2-02-002	OVERBEARING
1-01-001	OVERBLOWN
8-05-007	OVERBOARD
1-01-001	OVERBURDEN
1-01-001	OVERBURDENED
3-03-003	OVERCAME
9-04-004	OVERCAST
1-01-001	OVERCEREBRAL
5-02-005	OVERCOAT
1-01-001	OVERCOATS
26-10-025	OVERCOME
7-05-006	OVERCOMES
6-05-006	OVERCOMING
1-01-001	OVERCONFIDENT
1-01-001	OVERCOOKED
1-01-001	OVERCOOLED
3-02-003	OVERCROWDED
1-01-001	OVERCROWDING
1-01-001	OVERCURIOUS
3-03-003	OVERDEVELOPED
1-01-001	OVERDOING
2-01-001	OVERDONE
1-01-001	OVERDRIVING
2-02-002	OVERDUE
1-01-001	OVEREAGER
1-01-001	OVEREAT
2-02-002	OVEREATING
1-01-001	OVEREMPHASIS
1-01-001	OVEREMPHASIZED
1-01-001	OVERESTIMATED
1-01-001	OVERESTIMATES
2-02-002	OVERESTIMATION
1-01-001	OVEREXCITED
1-01-001	OVEREXPLOITATION
1-01-001	OVEREXPLOITED
1-01-001	OVEREXPOSE
3-01-001	OVERFALL
1-01-001	OVERFEED
1-01-001	OVERFILL
2-01-002	OVERFLOW
2-02-002	OVERFLOWED
2-01-002	OVERFLOWING
1-01-001	OVERGENEROUS
1-01-001	OVERGRAZING
4-04-004	OVERGROWN
2-02-002	OVERHAND
2-01-001	OVERHANG
2-01-001	OVERHANGS
3-02-002	OVERHAUL
3-03-003	OVERHAULING
18-10-017	OVERHEAD
6-06-006	OVERHEARD
1-01-001	OVERHEARING
1-01-001	OVERHEAT
1-01-001	OVERHEATED
1-01-001	OVERHEATING
1-01-001	OVERINDULGED
1-01-001	OVERLAID
1-01-001	OVERLAND
4-03-003	OVERLAP
3-03-003	OVERLAPPED
3-03-003	OVERLAPPING
1-01-001	OVERLAPS
2-02-002	OVERLAY
3-03-003	OVERLOAD
1-01-001	OVERLOADED
4-04-004	OVERLOOK
7-07-007	OVERLOOKED
2-02-002	OVERLOOKING
4-03-003	OVERLOOKS
3-01-001	OVERLORDS
1-01-001	OVERLOUD
8-06-008	OVERLY
1-01-001	OVERLYING
18-06-017	OVERNIGHT
3-01-001	OVERNIGHTERS
1-01-001	OVERPAID
4-01-001	OVERPAYMENT
1-01-001	OVERPLAYED
1-01-001	OVERPOPULATED
2-01-002	OVERPOPULATION
2-02-002	OVERPOWERED
1-01-001	OVERPOWERING
1-01-001	OVERPOWERS
1-01-001	OVERPRESSURE
1-01-001	OVERPRICED
1-01-001	OVERPROTECTION
1-01-001	OVERPROTECTIVE
1-01-001	OVERRAN
3-01-001	OVERRATED
3-03-003	OVERREACH
2-02-002	OVERREACHED
1-01-001	OVERREACHES
1-01-001	OVERRIDDEN
1-01-001	OVERRIDE
3-03-003	OVERRIDING
1-01-001	OVERRODE
5-04-005	OVERRUN
22-08-015	OVERSEAS
1-01-001	OVERSEER
2-02-002	OVERSHADOW
2-02-002	OVERSHADOWED
2-02-002	OVERSHOES
1-01-001	OVERSHOOTS
1-01-001	OVERSHOT
1-01-001	OVERSIGHT
3-03-003	OVERSIMPLIFICATION
4-03-004	OVERSIMPLIFIED
2-01-001	OVERSIZE
2-02-002	OVERSIZED
2-01-001	OVERSOFT
1-01-001	OVERSOFTNESS
1-01-001	OVERSTEPPING
1-01-001	OVERSTRAINING
2-02-002	OVERSUBSCRIBED
11-04-010	OVERT
3-03-003	OVERTAKE
1-01-001	OVERTAKEN
1-01-001	OVERTAKIN
1-01-001	OVERTAXED
5-04-005	OVERTHROW
3-02-003	OVERTHROWN
3-02-002	OVERTIME
3-02-002	OVERTLY
4-03-004	OVERTONES
1-01-001	OVERTOOK
5-02-002	OVERTURE
3-03-003	OVERTURES
2-02-002	OVERTURNED
2-02-002	OVERTURNING
1-01-001	OVERVAULTING
5-03-004	OVERWEIGHT
1-01-001	OVERWHELM
4-04-004	OVERWHELMED
20-09-019	OVERWHELMING

7-04-006	OVERWHELMINGLY	6-05-006	PACKAGED	1-01-001	PALE-BLUE	2-02-002	PANTRY
1-01-001	OVERWORKED	6-03-003	PACKAGES	1-01-001	PALED	9-06-009	PANTS
1-01-001	OVERWRITTEN	7-04-005	PACKAGING	1-01-001	PALELY	1-01-001	PANTS-LEGS
1-01-001	OVIFORM	13-02-002	PACKARD	1-01-001	PALENESS	2-01-001	PANYOTIS
10-07-008	OWE	1-01-001	PACKARDS	1-01-001	PALEO-	3-01-001	PANZA
15-06-013	OWED	19-09-019	PACKED	1-01-001	PALEOCORTICAL	3-01-001	PAOT
25-06-006	OWEN	2-01-002	PACKERS	1-01-001	PALEOEXPLOSION	1-01-001	PAP
1-01-001	OWENS	3-02-003	PACKET	2-02-002	PALERMO	1-01-001	PAP-PAP-PAP-HEY
5-05-005	OWES	1-01-001	PACKETS	1-01-001	PALES	40-04-008	PAPA
4-03-004	OWING	17-06-011	PACKING	1-01-001	PALEST	10-02-002	PAPA'S
2-02-002	OWL	3-02-003	PACKS	7-02-003	PALESTINE	8-01-001	PAPA-SAN
2-02-002	OWL'S	1-01-001	PACKWOOD	5-03-003	PALETTE	7-03-004	PAPAL
2-02-002	OWLS	5-04-005	PACT	26-01-001	PALFREY	1-01-001	PAPANICOLAOU
1-01-001	OWLY	9-01-001	PACTA	9-01-001	PALFREY'S	157-15-088	PAPER
772-15-339	OWN	8-03-005	PAD	1-01-001	PALINDROMES	1-01-001	PAPER'S
1-01-001	OWNE	5-05-005	PADDED	1-01-001	PALING	2-02-002	PAPERBACK
34-09-029	OWNED	1-01-001	PADDIES	2-02-002	PALISADES	1-01-001	PAPERBACKS
33-10-022	OWNER	3-03-003	PADDING	4-03-004	PALL	51-12-036	PAPERS
2-02-002	OWNER'S	1-01-001	PADDLE	1-01-001	PALLADIAN	1-01-001	PAPERWADS
35-11-026	OWNERS	1-01-001	PADDOCK	3-02-002	PALLADIO	2-01-001	PAPERWEIGHT
2-02-002	OWNERS'	2-02-002	PADLOCK	1-01-001	PALLADIUM	1-01-001	PAPERY
22-06-016	OWNERSHIP	1-01-001	PADLOCKED	1-01-001	PALLAVICINI	2-02-002	PAPIER-MACHE
3-02-002	OWNERSHIPS	5-02-004	PADS	1-01-001	PALLET	1-01-001	PAPIERS
3-02-003	OWNING	2-02-002	PAEAN	1-01-001	PALLETIZED	1-01-001	PAPILLARY
13-07-009	OWNS	1-01-001	PAEANS	1-01-001	PALLIATIVE	2-01-001	PAPP
1-01-001	OWNSELF	1-01-001	PAESTUM	3-03-003	PALLID	1-01-001	PAPPAS
5-02-004	OX	4-02-002	PAGAN	2-02-002	PALLOR	1-01-001	PAPPIES
2-01-001	OXALATE	1-01-001	PAGANINI	22-07-013	PALM	2-01-001	PAPRIKA
1-01-001	OXALOACETIC	1-01-001	PAGANISM	1-01-001	PALM-LINED	13-05-008	PAR
2-02-002	OXCART	1-01-001	PAGANS	1-01-001	PALM-STUDDED	1-01-001	PAR-3
10-02-003	OXEN	66-14-046	PAGE	2-02-002	PALMED	1-01-001	PAR-5
1-01-001	OXEN'S	7-03-003	PAGEANT	56-05-007	PALMER	3-02-003	PARABLE
18-05-009	OXFORD	1-01-001	PAGEANTRY	6-01-002	PALMER'S	1-01-001	PARABLES
1-01-001	OXFORD'S	5-02-002	PAGEANTS	8-05-007	PALMS	1-01-001	PARACHUTE
23-03-004	OXIDATION	31-11-026	PAGES	1-01-001	PALO	1-01-001	PARACHUTES
3-01-002	OXIDE	1-01-001	PAGET	1-01-001	PALOMAR	25-10-017	PARADE
1-01-001	OXIDES	1-01-001	PAGINATED	2-02-002	PALPABLE	2-02-002	PARADED
2-01-001	OXIDISED	1-01-001	PAGING	1-01-001	PALPABLY	3-03-003	PARADES
1-01-001	OXNARD	1-01-001	PAGLIERI'S	1-01-001	PALS	6-03-004	PARADIGM
43-04-012	OXYGEN	1-01-001	PAGNOL	2-02-002	PALSY	1-01-001	PARADIGMATIC
1-01-001	OXYGEN/**JHR/**	2-01-001	PAGNOL'S	8-02-002	PAM	1-01-001	PARADIGMS
	JHP	1-01-001	PAGODA	1-01-001	PAM'S	2-02-002	PARADING
3-01-001	OXYGENS	1-01-001	PAGODAS	1-01-001	PAMASU	12-08-011	PARADISE
1-01-001	OXYHYDROXIDES	4-01-001	PAH	19-03-003	PAMELA	9-05-008	PARADOX
3-01-001	OXYTETRACYCLINE	145-14-086	PAID	1-01-001	PAMELA'S	3-02-003	PARADOXICAL
4-01-001	OYABUN	1-01-001	PAID-FOR	2-01-001	PAMPA	11-06-010	PARADOXICALLY
1-01-001	OYAJIMA	1-01-001	PAIDE	1-01-001	PAMPER	2-02-002	PARAGON
1-01-001	OYSTCHERS	3-01-001	PAIE	1-01-001	PAMPERED	12-06-010	PARAGRAPH
1-01-001	OYSTCHERS'LL	4-03-004	PAIL	1-01-001	PAMPHILI	1-01-001	PARAGRAPHING
6-03-003	OYSTER	4-04-004	PAILS	3-01-001	PAMPHLET	14-05-007	PARAGRAPHS
8-02-003	OYSTERS	88-12-044	PAIN	9-03-006	PAMPHLETS	1-01-001	PARAKEETS
2-01-001	OZ	1-01-001	PAINE	16-08-012	PAN	2-01-001	PARALANGUAGE
4-01-001	OZAGEN	1-01-001	PAINED	1-01-001	PANACEAS	1-01-001	PARALINGUISTIC
1-01-001	OZAGENIANS	25-12-025	PAINFUL	4-04-004	PANAMA	40-07-026	PARALLEL
1-01-001	OZARKS	14-10-014	PAINFULLY	1-01-001	PANCHO	4-03-004	PARALLELED
1-01-001	OZON	3-03-003	PAINLESS	1-01-001	PANCRAZIO	1-01-001	PARALLELING
3-01-001	OZONE	1-01-001	PAINLESSLY	1-01-001	PANDANUS	3-02-002	PARALLELISM
1-01-001	OZZIE	15-07-014	PAINS	1-01-001	PANDELL'S	2-01-001	PARALLELS
83-10-046	P	1-01-001	PAINS-TAKING	2-01-001	PANDEMIC	6-03-003	PARALYSIS
1-01-001	P*$	1-01-001	PAINSTAKING	1-01-001	PANDERS	1-01-001	PARALYZE
3-01-001	P**.*D**.*I	2-02-002	PAINSTAKINGLY	1-01-001	PANDORA	2-02-002	PARALYZED
1-01-001	P**.*G	37-10-022	PAINT	2-01-001	PANDORA'S	2-02-002	PARALYZES
1-01-001	P**.*L	1-01-001	PAINTBRUSH	3-03-003	PANE	1-01-001	PARAMAGNET
8-05-006	P**.*M	40-12-026	PAINTED	31-08-017	PANEL	13-02-002	PARAMAGNETIC
1-01-001	P**.-*T**.*A	1-01-001	PAINTED-IN	1-01-001	PANEL'S	7-01-004	PARAMETER
37-07-015	P**.M	21-11-014	PAINTER	2-01-001	PANELED	8-01-007	PARAMETERS
1-01-001	P'LITE	3-02-002	PAINTER'S	6-04-004	PANELING	2-01-001	PARAMETRIC
8-02-003	P*H	1-01-001	PAINTFRESQUE	1-01-001	PANELIZATION	1-01-001	PARAMILITARY
1-01-001	P-AMINOBENZOIC	13-06-009	PAINTERS	1-01-001	PANELIZED	9-06-009	PARAMOUNT
16-01-001	P,	59-12-028	PAINTING	46-08-013	PANELS	1-01-001	PARANOIAC
32-08-011	PA	36-09-021	PAINTINGS	3-03-003	PANES	2-01-001	PARANOID
1-01-001	PA'D	10-03-007	PAINTS	2-02-002	PANGS	1-01-001	PARANORMAL
4-01-001	PA'S	50-13-043	PAIR	22-09-021	PANIC	1-01-001	PARAOXON
1-01-001	PABLO	6-04-006	PAIRED	2-02-002	PANICKED	1-01-001	PARAPET
1-01-001	PABOR	14-06-013	PAIRS	1-01-001	PANICKY	1-01-001	PARAPETS
43-11-034	PACE	1-01-001	PAIX	1-01-001	PANJANDRUM	1-01-001	PARAPHERNALIA
1-01-001	PACE-SETTER	1-01-001	PAJAMA	2-01-001	PANKOWSKI	2-01-001	PARAPHRASE
11-06-007	PACED	3-03-003	PAJAMAS	4-03-004	PANORAMA	1-01-001	PARAPHRASES
1-01-001	PACEM	2-01-001	PAK	1-01-001	PANORAMAS	1-01-001	PARAPHRASING
1-01-001	PACEMAKER	7-04-005	PAKISTAN	1-01-001	PANORAMIC	3-01-001	PARAPSYCHOLOGY
1-01-001	PACER	1-01-001	PAKISTANI	3-02-003	PANS	1-01-001	PARASITE
3-01-001	PACERS	2-02-002	PAKISTANIS	13-01-001	PANSIES	4-03-003	PARASITES
7-06-007	PACES	2-02-002	PAL	6-01-001	PANSY	2-01-001	PARASITIC
1-01-001	PACHE	1-01-001	PAL'S	1-01-001	PANT-LEGS	3-03-003	PARASOL
1-01-001	PACHELBEL	38-10-019	PALACE	2-01-001	PANTAS	2-01-001	PARASOLS
1-01-001	PACHES	2-01-001	PALACE'S	1-01-001	PANTASAPH	8-01-001	PARASYMPATHETIC
1-01-001	PACHINKO	5-04-005	PALACES	1-01-001	PANTED	1-01-001	PARATROOPERS
31-09-017	PACIFIC	1-01-001	PALACHE	1-01-001	PANTHEIST	1-01-001	PARATROOPS
1-01-001	PACIFIER	1-01-001	PALASTS	5-03-003	PANTHEON	2-01-001	PARAXIAL
1-01-001	PACIFIES	9-01-001	PALATABILITY	2-01-001	PANTHEON'S	2-01-001	PARAY
3-02-002	PACIFISM	1-01-001	PALATABLE	2-01-001	PANTHER	1-01-001	PARBOILED
2-02-002	PACIFIST	2-02-002	PALATE	1-01-001	PANTHERS	1-01-001	PARCEL
1-01-001	PACIFISTIC	1-01-001	PALATES	1-01-001	PANTIES	1-01-001	PARCELED
2-02-002	PACIFY	1-01-001	PALAZZI	9-04-008	PANTING	1-01-001	PARCELS
7-06-007	PACING	12-01-001	PALAZZO	2-02-002	PANTOMIME	2-02-002	PARCHED
25-09-020	PACK	1-01-001	PALAZZOS	1-01-001	PANTOMIMED	1-01-001	PARCHMENT
20-09-015	PACKAGE	58-10-038	PALE	1-01-001	PANTOMIMIC	8-07-008	PARDON

1-01-001	PARDONABLE	7-04-005	PARTICIPATES	2-02-002	PAT'S	2-01-001	PAULA'S
2-01-002	PARDONED	15-06-011	PARTICIPATING	1-01-001	PATAGONIANS	1-01-001	PAULAH
1-01-001	PARDONS	41-09-028	PARTICIPATION	13-06-012	PATCH	1-01-001	PAULEYS
2-01-002	PARE	21-05-009	PARTICLE	5-04-005	PATCHED	7-02-002	PAULING
4-01-001	PAREDON	42-06-012	PARTICLES	26-02-002	PATCHEN	1-01-001	PAULING'S
2-02-002	PAREE	179-14-112	PARTICULAR	7-02-002	PATCHEN'S	1-01-001	PAULUS
1-01-001	PARELLA	1-01-001	PARTICULARISTIC	10-07-010	PATCHES	2-02-002	PAUNCH
4-01-002	PARENCHYMA	1-01-001	PARTICULARISTIC	2-02-002	PATCHWORK	2-01-002	PAUNCHY
15-07-012	PARENT		-SEEMING	2-02-002	PATE	1-01-001	PAUPER'S
1-01-001	PARENT'S	1-01-001	PARTICULARITY	35-04-010	PATENT	1-01-001	PAUS'L
1-01-001	PARENT-CHILD	146-15-116	PARTICULARLY	2-01-001	PATENT-SHARING	21-10-017	PAUSE
1-01-001	PARENT-TEACHER	5-05-005	PARTICULARS	3-02-003	PATENTED	28-08-024	PAUSED
2-01-001	PARENTAGE	3-01-003	PARTICULATE	1-01-001	PATENTEES	2-02-002	PAUSES
2-02-002	PARENTAL	59-12-039	PARTIES	1-01-001	PATENTING	6-05-006	PAUSING
1-01-001	PARENTHESES	4-03-004	PARTING	19-04-007	PATENTS	2-01-001	PAUSON
1-01-001	PARENTHETICALLY	1-01-001	PARTINGS	2-01-001	PATER	2-02-002	PAVE
6-02-003	PARENTHOOD	21-06-010	PARTISAN	2-01-001	PATERNALISM	5-05-005	PAVED
91-13-044	PARENTS	1-01-001	PARTISANS	1-01-001	PATERNALISTIC	11-05-006	PAVEMENT
6-05-006	PARENTS'	6-04-005	PARTITION	1-01-001	PATERNALLY	2-02-002	PAVEMENTS
1-01-001	PARI-MUTUEL	1-01-001	PARTITIONS	1-01-001	PATEROLLERS	2-01-001	PAVESE
1-01-001	PARIAH	9-01-001	PARTLOW	1-01-001	PATERSON	4-01-001	PAVILION
2-01-001	PARICHY	1-01-001	PARTLOW'S	44-13-033	PATH	2-01-001	PAVILIONS
1-01-001	PARICHY-HAMM	49-13-040	PARTLY	10-02-004	PATHET	2-02-002	PAVING
1-01-001	PARIMUTUELS	32-10-022	PARTNER	8-07-008	PATHETIC	1-01-001	PAVLETICH
2-01-001	PARINGS	1-01-001	PARTNERED	1-01-001	PATHLESS	1-01-001	PAVLOV
1-01-001	PARIOLI	16-09-013	PARTNERS	1-01-001	PATHOGENESIS	1-01-001	PAVLOVITCH
67-12-040	PARIS	18-05-009	PARTNERSHIP	2-01-002	PATHOGENIC	1-01-001	PAVLOVSKY
1-01-001	PARIS'	1-01-001	PARTOOK	1-01-001	PATHOLOGIC	3-03-003	PAW
11-04-006	PARISH	113-13-074	PARTS	9-02-004	PATHOLOGICAL	2-01-001	PAWCATUCK
1-01-001	PARISHES	1-01-001	PARTS-SUPPLIERS	2-01-001	PATHOLOGIST	1-01-001	PAWING
3-03-003	PARISHIONERS	216-15-087	PARTY	33-02-002	PATHOLOGY	2-02-002	PAWN
3-02-002	PARISIAN	9-02-006	PARTY'S	1-01-001	PATHOS	3-02-002	PAWNSHOP
1-01-001	PARISINA	1-01-001	PARTY-LINE	14-07-010	PATHS	3-02-003	PAWS
1-01-001	PARISOLOGY	2-01-001	PARVENU	3-01-002	PATHWAYS	2-02-002	PAWTUCKET
94-12-044	PARK	6-02-003	PAS	1-01-001	PATI	1-01-001	PAWTUCKET'S
33-08-019	PARKED	6-03-003	PASADENA	22-11-020	PATIENCE	4-01-001	PAWTUXET
63-06-009	PARKER	1-01-001	PASADENA'S	86-13-028	PATIENT	1-01-001	PAX
2-01-001	PARKER'S	1-01-001	PASCAGOULA	21-05-007	PATIENT'S	3-01-001	PAX-ORDO
4-02-002	PARKERSBURG	1-01-001	PASCAL	9-07-009	PATIENTLY	1-01-001	PAXAM
5-01-001	PARKHOUSE	1-01-001	PASCATAQUA	36-12-020	PATIENTS	7-01-001	PAXTON
31-07-014	PARKING	2-01-001	PASCHAL	1-01-001	PATIL	172-14-102	PAY
1-01-001	PARKINSON'S	1-01-001	PASCHALL	3-02-003	PATINA	3-02-003	PAYABLE
1-01-001	PARKISH	3-01-001	PASHA	1-01-001	PATINAS	2-01-002	PAYCHECK
1-01-001	PARKLIKE	2-01-001	PASLEY	2-01-002	PATIO	3-02-003	PAYDAY
20-09-014	PARKS	11-03-004	PASO	1-01-001	PATISSERIES	26-11-024	PAYING
6-02-003	PARKWAY	89-15-063	PASS	1-01-001	PATMORE	1-01-001	PAYMASTER
2-02-002	PARLANCE	1-01-001	PASSABLE	2-02-002	PATRIARCH	53-08-023	PAYMENT
1-01-001	PARLAYED	49-12-041	PASSAGE	1-01-001	PATRIARCHAL	49-08-018	PAYMENTS
1-01-001	PARLEY	20-08-018	PASSAGES	1-01-001	PATRIARCHY	16-02-002	PAYNE
16-04-009	PARLIAMENT	4-03-004	PASSAGEWAY	5-02-002	PATRICE	3-02-002	PAYNE'S
1-01-001	PARLIAMENTARIAN	1-01-001	PASSAVANT	7-01-006	PATRICIA	1-01-001	PAYNES
	S	157-14-101	PASSED	1-01-001	PATRICIAN	1-01-001	PAYOFF
8-03-006	PARLIAMENTARY	14-07-012	PASSENGER	1-01-001	PATRICK	16-04-006	PAYROLL
1-01-001	PARLIAMENTS	21-10-016	PASSENGERS	3-02-002	PATRICK'S	17-09-016	PAYS
18-07-016	PARLOR	1-01-001	PASSER-BY	1-01-001	PATRIMONY	1-01-001	PAYSON
1-01-001	PARLORS	1-01-001	PASSERBY	10-06-007	PATRIOT	1-01-001	PEABODY
1-01-001	PARMER	1-01-001	PASSERS-BY	10-04-007	PATRIOTIC	1-01-001	PEABODY'S
12-06-009	PAROCHIAL	27-10-020	PASSES	6-03-005	PATRIOTISM	198-13-086	PEACE
2-02-002	PARODIED	65-15-053	PASSING	1-01-001	PATRIOTS	2-02-002	PEACE-LOVING
1-01-001	PARODIES	28-08-022	PASSION	1-01-001	PATRISTIC-CIVIL	1-01-001	PEACE-TREATY
4-03-003	PARODY	12-05-012	PASSIONATE		IAN-CANONIST-SC	3-03-003	PEACEABLE
5-02-003	PAROLE	3-03-003	PASSIONATELY		HOLASTIC	26-10-020	PEACEFUL
2-01-001	PAROLEES	12-03-005	PASSIONS	25-08-013	PATROL	5-04-005	PEACEFULLY
1-01-001	PARQUET	11-07-009	PASSIVE	2-02-002	PATROLLED	1-01-001	PEACEMAKING
1-01-001	PARRIED	1-01-001	PASSIVELY	3-03-003	PATROLLING	4-03-004	PEACETIME
3-01-001	PARRILLO	1-01-001	PASSIVENESS	12-03-008	PATROLMAN	3-03-003	PEACH
2-01-001	PARRIS	1-01-001	PASSIVITY	1-01-001	PATROLMAN'S	1-01-001	PEACHES
1-01-001	PARROT	1-01-001	PASSOS	2-02-002	PATROLMEN	2-02-002	PEACOCK
1-01-001	PARROTING	6-03-003	PASSPORT	1-01-001	PATROLS	4-02-002	PEACOCKS
1-01-001	PARROTLIKE	281-15-186	PAST	4-04-004	PATRON	16-05-013	PEAK
1-01-001	PARROTS	1-01-001	PAST-FANTASY	10-06-007	PATRONAGE	7-02-002	PEAKED
1-01-001	PARRY	10-05-007	PASTE	1-01-001	PATRONESS	8-07-007	PEAKS
1-01-001	PARRY'S	6-02-002	PASTED	1-01-001	PATRONIZE	1-01-001	PEAKY
3-01-001	PARS	3-03-003	PASTEL	3-03-003	PATRONIZED	1-01-001	PEAL
2-02-002	PARSIFAL	1-01-001	PASTEL-LIKE	2-02-002	PATRONIZING	3-02-002	PEALE
1-01-001	PARSIMONIOUS	1-01-001	PASTELS	3-01-001	PATRONNE	1-01-001	PEALE'S
1-01-001	PARSIMONY	9-01-001	PASTERN	1-01-001	PATRONNE'S	1-01-001	PEALS
1-01-001	PARSLEY	1-01-001	PASTERNAK	9-06-007	PATRONS	6-03-003	PEANUT
2-02-002	PARSON	1-01-001	PASTERNS	1-01-001	PATSY	5-01-002	PEANUTS
1-01-001	PARSONAGE	1-01-001	PASTES	7-04-007	PATTED	6-04-004	PEAR
5-02-002	PARSONS	1-01-001	PASTEURIZATION	3-02-002	PATTER	9-06-009	PEARL
1-01-001	PARSYMPATHETIC	1-01-001	PASTILLES	1-01-001	PATTERED	1-01-001	PEARL-GRAY
500-15-301	PART	4-03-004	PASTIME	113-13-068	PATTERN	2-02-002	PEARLS
26-07-009	PART-TIME	1-01-001	PASTIMES	6-04-006	PATTERNED	1-01-001	PEARLY
1-01-001	PARTAKE	1-01-001	PASTING	47-10-028	PATTERNS	2-02-002	PEARS
1-01-001	PARTAKER	1-01-001	PASTNESS	5-03-003	PATTERSON	12-05-006	PEARSON
2-02-002	PARTAKES	17-06-008	PASTOR	1-01-001	PATTI	24-04-007	PEAS
1-01-001	PARTAKING	2-02-002	PASTOR'S	2-01-001	PATTIES	7-05-007	PEASANT
5-02-005	PARTED	6-03-003	PASTORAL	4-02-004	PATTING	1-01-001	PEASANTHOOD
6-01-002	PARTHENON	6-03-003	PASTORS	1-01-001	PATTON	12-06-009	PEASANTS
1-01-001	PARTI	1-01-001	PASTORS'	1-01-001	PATTY	1-01-001	PEBBLE
11-06-011	PARTIAL	4-02-004	PASTRY	1-01-001	PAUCITY	3-02-002	PEBBLES
25-12-023	PARTIALLY	1-01-001	PASTRY-LINED	38-10-029	PAUL	1-01-001	PEBWORTH
4-02-003	PARTICIPANT	14-05-008	PASTURE	1-01-001	PAUL'S	1-01-001	PECAN
7-05-007	PARTICIPANTS	2-02-002	PASTURES	1-01-001	PAUL-MINNEAPOLI	1-01-001	PECANS
22-09-016	PARTICIPATE	2-01-002	PASTY		S	1-01-001	PECCADILLOES
13-07-011	PARTICIPATED	35-06-011	PAT	19-02-002	PAULA	1-01-001	PECCAVI

5-03-004 PECK
2-02-002 PECKED
1-01-001 PECKS
1-01-001 PECORONE
1-01-001 PECOS
1-01-001 PECS
1-01-001 PECS.
2-01-001 PECS,
1-01-001 PECTORAL-FRONT
1-01-001 PECTORAL-RIBCAG E
2-01-001 PECTORALIS
1-01-001 PECTORALS
27-10-027 PECULIAR
4-04-004 PECULIARITIES
1-01-001 PECULIARITY
8-06-007 PECULIARLY
1-01-001 PEDAGOGICAL
1-01-001 PEDAGOGUE
4-03-004 PEDAL
1-01-001 PEDALS
2-02-002 PEDANTIC
1-01-001 PEDDLE
1-01-001 PEDDLED
5-03-004 PEDDLER
1-01-001 PEDDLERS
1-01-001 PEDDLERS'
1-01-001 PEDEN
10-01-001 PEDERSEN
1-01-001 PEDERSEN'S
5-03-004 PEDESTAL
6-02-004 PEDESTRIAN
2-01-001 PEDESTRIANS
3-03-003 PEDIGREE
1-01-001 PEDIGREED
1-01-001 PEDIMENTED
3-03-003 PEDRO
3-02-003 PEE
1-01-001 PEED
2-02-002 PEEKED
1-01-001 PEEKING
3-03-003 PEEL
5-05-005 PEELED
6-03-003 PEELING
1-01-001 PEELS
2-01-001 PEEP
2-02-002 PEEPING
1-01-001 PEEPY
8-05-006 PEER
1-01-001 PEER-GROUP
20-05-015 PEERED
9-05-008 PEERING
4-02-002 PEERLESS
8-05-007 PEERS
1-01-001 PEETER
4-02-002 PEG
6-01-001 PEGBOARD
2-01-001 PEGBOARDS
1-01-001 PEGGED
1-01-001 PEGGED-DOWN
1-01-001 PEGGIN
1-01-001 PEGGING
1-01-001 PEGLER
2-02-002 PEGS
1-01-001 PEIPING
1-01-001 PEKING
5-01-001 PELHAM
1-01-001 PELLAGRA
1-01-001 PELLEGRINI
1-01-001 PELLETS
6-01-001 PELS
2-02-002 PELTING
2-01-001 PELTRY
9-01-001 PELTS
1-01-001 PELTZ
3-01-001 PELVIC
1-01-001 PELVIS
1-01-001 PEMBERTON
4-01-001 PEMBINA
2-01-002 PEMBROKE
1-01-001 PEMMICAN
18-08-013 PEN
2-02-002 PEN-AND-INK
1-01-001 PENA
1-01-001 PENAL
3-03-003 PENALIZED
4-02-003 PENALTIES
14-09-013 PENALTY
5-04-005 PENANCE
1-01-001 PENCHANT
34-07-014 PENCIL
1-01-001 PENCIL-AND-SEPI A
1-01-001 PENCIL-PUSHER
1-01-001 PENCILED
4-01-001 PENCILS
1-01-001 PENDANT

14-08-010 PENDING
5-02-002 PENDLETON
1-01-001 PENDLETON'S
2-02-002 PENDULUM
7-04-007 PENETRATE
8-06-008 PENETRATED
14-09-014 PENETRATING
15-06-008 PENETRATION
2-01-001 PENGALLY
1-01-001 PENICILLIN
9-06-009 PENINSULA
1-01-001 PENMAN
5-03-004 PENN
1-01-001 PENNA
9-03-006 PENNANT
1-01-001 PENNANTS
4-03-004 PENNED
1-01-001 PENNELL
5-04-004 PENNIES
3-03-003 PENNILESS
2-02-002 PENNOCK
45-11-032 PENNSYLVANIA
25-02-006 PENNY
3-01-002 PENNY'S
2-02-002 PENNY-WISE
1-01-001 PENROSE
2-02-002 PENS
4-02-002 PENSACOLA
13-05-008 PENSION
2-02-002 PENSIONER
7-05-007 PENSIONS
1-01-001 PENSIVE
13-08-011 PENTAGON
1-01-001 PENTAGON'S
1-01-001 PENTECOSTAL
1-01-001 PENTHOUSE
1-01-001 PENULTIMATE
1-01-001 PENURIOUS
1-01-001 PENURY
1-01-001 PENUTIAN
2-02-002 PEONIES
3-01-001 PEONY
847-15-288 PEOPLE
19-08-015 PEOPLE'S
2-01-001 PEOPLE-ORIENTED
1-01-001 PEOPLED
36-09-023 PEOPLES
1-01-001 PEOPLES'
1-01-001 PEPINSKY
13-03-007 PEPPER
2-01-002 PEPPERED
2-01-001 PEPPERMINTS
1-01-001 PEPPERONI
3-02-003 PEPPERY
1-01-001 PEPPING
2-01-002 PEPTIDASES
1-01-001 PEPTIDE
2-01-001 PEPTIDES
1-01-001 PEPTIZING
371-09-096 PER
1-01-001 PER-DAY
1-01-001 PER-GAME
1-01-001 PER-YEAR
4-01-001 PERALTA
1-01-001 PERASSO
13-05-008 PERCEIVE
12-05-010 PERCEIVED
3-01-002 PERCEIVES
1-01-001 PERCEIVING
53-08-021 PERCENT
45-09-026 PERCENTAGE
6-04-004 PERCENTAGES
1-01-001 PERCEPTIBLE
29-07-017 PERCEPTION
9-03-007 PERCEPTIONS
3-03-003 PERCEPTIVE
7-02-006 PERCEPTUAL
1-01-001 PERCH
1-01-001 PERCHANCE
4-04-004 PERCHED
1-01-001 PERCOLATOR
4-02-002 PERCUSSION
7-02-003 PERCUSSIVE
2-02-002 PERCY
3-01-001 PERDIDO
1-01-001 PERELMAN
1-01-001 PEREMPTORY
6-05-006 PERENNIAL
2-02-002 PERENNIALLY
2-01-001 PERENNIAN
5-03-004 PEREZ
1-01-001 PERFECT
1-01-001 PERFECTABILITY
5-02-005 PERFECTED
1-01-001 PERFECTIBILITY
3-02-003 PERFECTING
11-05-010 PERFECTION

1-01-001 PERFECTIONISM
1-01-001 PERFECTIONISTS
31-10-029 PERFECTLY
1-01-001 PERFIDIOUS
3-02-002 PERFORATED
1-01-001 PERFORATIONS
2-02-002 PERFORCE
29-10-027 PERFORM
122-12-065 PERFORMANCE
1-01-001 PERFORMANCE-CAP ACITY
33-09-022 PERFORMANCES
35-10-029 PERFORMED
7-05-005 PERFORMER
13-06-010 PERFORMERS
17-06-016 PERFORMING
4-02-004 PERFORMS
10-05-009 PERFUME
2-02-002 PERFUMED
1-01-001 PERFUMERY
1-01-001 PERFUMES
1-01-001 PERFUNCTORILY
1-01-001 PERFUNCTORY
1-01-001 PERFUSION
1-01-001 PERGAMON
1-01-001 PERGOLESI'S
307-15-192 PERHAPS
1-01-001 PERICLEAN
1-01-001 PERICLES
1-01-001 PERIDONTAL
6-01-001 PERIER
2-01-001 PERIER'S
8-06-007 PERIL
1-01-001 PERILLA
8-05-008 PERILOUS
3-03-003 PERILOUSLY
2-02-002 PERILS
1-01-001 PERIMETER
1-01-001 PERINETTI
265-14-149 PERIOD
9-05-009 PERIODIC
4-03-004 PERIODICAL
6-04-005 PERIODICALLY
5-05-005 PERIODICALS
1-01-001 PERIODICITY
47-10-037 PERIODS
8-03-006 PERIPHERAL
2-01-002 PERIPHERALLY
5-02-005 PERIPHERY
1-01-001 PERIPHRASTIC
1-01-001 PERISCOPES
2-01-001 PERISH
1-01-001 PERISHABLE
1-01-001 PERISHED
1-01-001 PERISHES
1-01-001 PERISHING
1-01-001 PERIWINKLES
3-02-002 PERJURY
1-01-001 PERK
1-01-001 PERKEN
2-01-002 PERKINS
2-02-002 PERKY
1-01-001 PERLE
3-01-001 PERLMAN
2-01-001 PERLUSS
2-02-002 PERMANENCE
40-11-034 PERMANENT
13-07-012 PERMANENTLY
1-01-001 PERMEATE
3-01-003 PERMEATED
2-02-002 PERMEATES
1-01-001 PERMIAN
1-01-001 PERMISSIBILITY
1-01-001 PERMISSIBLE
27-09-016 PERMISSION
5-04-005 PERMISSIVE
77-13-058 PERMIT
27-06-022 PERMITS
57-13-045 PERMITTED
9-05-009 PERMITTING
1-01-001 PERNICIOUS
1-01-001 PERNOD
2-01-001 PEROXIDE
1-01-001 PERPENDICULAR
1-01-001 PERPENDICULARLY
3-03-003 PERPETRATED
1-01-001 PERPETRATION
1-01-001 PERPETRATOR
8-04-006 PERPETUAL
3-03-003 PERPETUALLY
5-03-004 PERPETUATE
1-01-001 PERPETUATED
4-03-004 PERPETUATING
2-02-002 PERPETUATION
1-01-001 PERPLEX
4-03-003 PERPLEXED
2-02-002 PERPLEXING

1-01-001 PERPLEXITY
6-01-001 PERRIN
1-01-001 PERRIN'S
8-04-007 PERRY
2-02-002 PERSE
3-03-003 PERSECUTED
7-03-006 PERSECUTION
1-01-001 PERSECUTORY
1-01-001 PERSEVERANCE
1-01-001 PERSEVERE
1-01-001 PERSEVERES
1-01-001 PERSHING
4-01-001 PERSIA
10-05-005 PERSIAN
1-01-001 PERSIANESQUE
12-01-001 PERSIANS
1-01-001 PERSIFLAGE
1-01-001 PERSIMMONS
6-04-005 PERSIST
10-07-010 PERSISTED
9-04-006 PERSISTENCE
16-04-015 PERSISTENT
3-03-003 PERSISTENTLY
2-02-002 PERSISTING
7-04-007 PERSISTS
175-15-119 PERSON
4-04-004 PERSON'S
1-01-001 PERSON-TO-PERSON
2-02-002 PERSONA
1-01-001 PERSONAE
1-01-001 PERSONAGE
3-01-002 PERSONAGES
196-15-109 PERSONAL
15-08-013 PERSONALITIES
48-12-029 PERSONALITY
3-03-003 PERSONALIZED
40-12-032 PERSONALLY
3-01-001 PERSONALLY-OWNE D
3-03-003 PERSONIFICATION
1-01-001 PERSONIFIED
3-02-003 PERSONIFIES
1-01-001 PERSONIFYING
74-10-043 PERSONNEL
121-13-076 PERSONS
26-08-020 PERSPECTIVE
3-02-003 PERSPECTIVES
1-01-001 PERSPIRATION
1-01-001 PERSPIRED
1-01-001 PERSPIRING
17-08-017 PERSUADE
21-10-018 PERSUADED
1-01-001 PERSUADERS
5-04-005 PERSUADING
9-04-008 PERSUASION
1-01-001 PERSUASIONS
4-04-004 PERSUASIVE
3-02-003 PERSUASIVELY
2-02-002 PERT
2-02-002 PERTAIN
1-01-001 PERTAINED
5-04-004 PERTAINING
5-01-003 PERTAINS
2-02-002 PERTINENCE
21-07-021 PERTINENT
1-01-001 PERTURBATION
2-02-002 PERTURBATIONS
1-01-001 PERTURBED
4-03-003 PERU
2-02-002 PERUSAL
1-01-001 PERUSING
2-02-002 PERUVIAN
1-01-001 PERVADED
2-02-002 PERVADES
2-02-002 PERVADING
1-01-001 PERVAPORATION
4-03-004 PERVASIVE
1-01-001 PERVASIVELY
5-04-004 PERVERSE
3-02-003 PERVERSELY
1-01-001 PERVERTED
2-01-001 PESCE
6-03-005 PESSIMISM
6-04-006 PESSIMISTIC
1-01-001 PESSIMISTS
4-03-003 PEST
1-01-001 PESTER
1-01-001 PESTERING
1-01-001 PESTICIDES
1-01-001 PESTILENT
1-01-001 PESTLE
2-01-001 PESTS
8-04-008 PET
4-03-003 PETALS
23-04-007 PETE
1-01-001 PETE'S

36-07-019	PETER	
9-04-005	PETER'S	
1-01-001	PETERED	
2-01-001	PETERHOUSE	
1-01-001	PETERMANN	
4-02-002	PETERS	
5-03-003	PETERSBURG	
8-03-003	PETERSON	
1-01-001	PETEY	
1-01-001	PETIPA	
2-01-002	PETIPA-*MINKUS	
1-01-001	PETIPA-*TSCHAIK	OWSKY
1-01-001	PETIT	
1-01-001	PETITE	
15-05-009	PETITION	
4-03-004	PETITIONED	
29-02-002	PETITIONER	
2-01-001	PETITIONER'S	
8-02-004	PETITIONS	
2-02-002	PETITS	
1-01-001	PETRARCHAN	
3-01-001	PETRIE	
2-02-002	PETRIFIED	
1-01-001	PETRINI	
1-01-001	PETROLEUM	
1-01-001	PETRUCHKA	
6-04-005	PETS	
2-02-002	PETTED	
1-01-001	PETTERSSON	
1-01-001	PETTIBONE	
1-01-001	PETTIGREW	
1-01-001	PETTIGREW'S	
1-01-001	PETTINESS	
1-01-001	PETTINESSES	
2-02-002	PETTING	
2-01-001	PETTIT	
8-06-007	PETTY	
1-01-001	PETULANCE	
1-01-001	PETULANT	
1-01-001	PEUGEOT	
1-01-001	PEWS	
3-01-001	PEZZA	
4-01-001	PFAFF	
1-01-001	PFAU	
1-01-001	PFC	
1-01-001	PFENNIG	
1-01-001	PFFFT*$-ED	
3-01-001	PFOHL	
1-01-001	PHAGOCYTES	
5-03-003	PHALANX	
2-01-001	PHANTASY	
2-02-002	PHANTOM	
2-02-002	PHARMACEUTICAL	
1-01-001	PHARMACIST	
2-01-002	PHARMACOLOGICAL	
1-01-001	PHARMACOPOEIA	
5-02-002	PHARMACY	
1-01-001	PHARMICAL	
72-08-036	PHASE	
24-09-020	PHASES	
1-01-001	PHEASANT	
2-01-001	PHEASANTS	
6-02-003	PHEDRE	
1-01-001	PHELAN	
1-01-001	PHELPS	
26-08-020	PHENOMENA	
2-02-002	PHENOMENAL	
1-01-001	PHENOMENOLOGICA	L
35-09-027	PHENOMENON	
1-01-001	PHENONENON	
4-01-001	PHENOTHIAZINE	
2-01-002	PHI	
65-04-007	PHIL	
2-01-001	PHIL'S	
50-11-026	PHILADELPHIA	
1-01-001	PHILADELPHIA'S	
4-04-004	PHILANTHROPIC	
1-01-001	PHILANTHROPIES	
1-01-001	PHILANTHROPIST	
1-01-001	PHILANTROPHY	
1-01-001	PHILANTROPISTS	
2-02-002	PHILCO	
1-01-001	PHILCO-SPONSORE	D
10-04-006	PHILHARMONIC	
1-01-001	PHILHARMONIQUE	
1-01-001	PHILIBERT	
21-07-012	PHILIP	
2-01-001	PHILIP'S	
1-01-001	PHILIPPE	
5-01-001	PHILIPPI	
1-01-001	PHILIPPIANS	
3-03-003	PHILIPPINE	
4-03-003	PHILIPPINES	
2-01-001	PHILIPPOFF	
2-01-001	PHILISTINES	
3-01-002	PHILLIES	
2-02-002	PHILLIP	
11-06-006	PHILLIPS	
1-01-001	PHILLY	
4-01-001	PHILMONT	
2-02-002	PHILOLOGICAL	
2-02-002	PHILOLOGISTS	
2-02-002	PHILOLOGY	
16-07-012	PHILOSOPHER	
9-05-007	PHILOSOPHERS	
11-04-006	PHILOSOPHIC	
26-08-018	PHILOSOPHICAL	
1-01-001	PHILOSOPHICALLY	
2-02-002	PHILOSOPHIES	
1-01-001	PHILOSOPHIZED	
2-01-002	PHILOSOPHIZING	
86-11-036	PHILOSOPHY	
1-01-001	PHINEOPPUS	
2-02-002	PHIPPS	
1-01-001	PHIS	
1-01-001	PHLOEM	
2-01-001	PHOBIC-LIKE	
1-01-001	PHOENIX	
54-10-030	PHONE	
5-04-005	PHONED	
2-01-001	PHONEMES	
8-01-001	PHONEMIC	
2-01-001	PHONEMICS	
7-06-006	PHONES	
2-01-001	PHONETIC	
1-01-001	PHONETICS	
1-01-001	PHONIC	
2-02-002	PHONIES	
3-03-003	PHONOGRAPH	
1-01-001	PHONOGRAPHS	
10-01-001	PHONOLOGIC	
5-01-001	PHONOLOGY	
12-04-009	PHONY	
1-01-001	PHOSGENE	
7-02-003	PHOSPHATE	
1-01-001	PHOSPHATE-BUFFE	RED
1-01-001	PHOSPHATES	
1-01-001	PHOSPHIDE	
1-01-001	PHOSPHINES	
13-01-001	PHOSPHOR	
1-01-001	PHOSPHOR-SCREEN	
1-01-001	PHOSPHORESCENT	
1-01-001	PHOSPHORS	
1-01-001	PHOSPHORUS	
14-08-014	PHOSPHORUS-BRID	GED
1-01-001	PHOTEK	
5-02-003	PHOTO	
1-01-001	PHOTO-MONTAGE	
1-01-001	PHOTO-OFFSET	
7-01-001	PHOTOCATHODE	
2-01-001	PHOTOCATHODES	
7-01-001	PHOTOCHEMICAL	
2-01-001	PHOTOELECTRONIC	
14-06-010	PHOTOELECTRONS	
15-06-008	PHOTOFLOODLIGHT	S
2-01-001	PHOTOGENIC	
18-05-010	PHOTOGRAPH	
4-04-004	PHOTOGRAPHED	
5-04-004	PHOTOGRAPHER	
6-03-005	PHOTOGRAPHERS	
11-05-007	PHOTOGRAPHIC	
1-01-001	PHOTOGRAPHICALL	Y
3-03-003	PHOTOGRAPHING	
16-07-015	PHOTOGRAPHS	
7-04-006	PHOTOGRAPHY	
1-01-001	PHOTOLUMINESCEN	CE
1-01-001	PHOTOMICROGRAPH	
1-01-001	PHOTOMICROGRAPH	Y
1-01-001	PHOTON-COUNTING	
1-01-001	PHOTOREALISM	
7-03-005	PHOTOS	
1-01-001	PHOTOSENSITIVE	
4-02-003	PHOUMA	
13-01-001	PHOUMA'S	
34-13-033	PHRASE	
3-02-003	PHRASED	
6-03-004	PHRASEMAKING	
3-02-003	PHRASEOLOGY	
18-07-012	PHRASES	
4-02-003	PHRASING	
1-01-001	PHRASINGS	
17-08-012	PHTHALATE	
4-01-001	PHYFE	
1-01-001	PHYLA	
2-02-002	PHYLLIS	
138-13-083	PHYSICAL	
1-01-001	PHYSICAL-CHEMIC	AL
20-07-018	PHYSICALLY	
1-01-001	PHYSICALNESS	
14-07-009	PHYSICIAN	
1-01-001	PHYSICIAN.**RST	
1-01-001	PHYSICIAN'S	
6-05-006	PHYSICIANS	
5-03-004	PHYSICIST	
2-02-002	PHYSICISTS	
1-01-001	PHYSICOCHEMICAL	
22-09-012	PHYSICS	
1-01-001	PHYSIOCHEMICAL	
1-01-001	PHYSIOGNOMY	
2-01-001	PHYSIOLOGIC	
22-05-009	PHYSIOLOGICAL	
1-01-001	PHYSIOLOGICALLY	
2-01-001	PHYSIOLOGIST	
3-03-003	PHYSIOLOGISTS	
1-01-001	PHYSIOLOGY	
1-01-001	PHYSIOTHERAPIST	
2-01-001	PHYSIQUE	
3-02-002	PI	
1-01-001	PIANISM	
14-05-008	PIANIST	
4-02-002	PIANIST'S	
1-01-001	PIANISTIC	
3-03-003	PIANISTS	
38-08-020	PIANO	
1-01-001	PIANOS	
17-02-003	PIAZZA	
1-01-001	PIAZZAS	
1-01-001	PIAZZO	
14-06-006	PICASSO	
3-01-001	PICASSO'S	
1-01-001	PICAYUNE	
2-02-002	PICCADILLY	
55-14-042	PICK	
3-02-002	PICK-UP	
1-01-001	PICKAXE	
78-12-058	PICKED	
1-01-001	PICKER	
1-01-001	PICKERING	
3-01-001	PICKERS	
9-06-008	PICKET	
2-02-002	PICKETED	
2-01-001	PICKETING	
1-01-001	PICKETS	
1-01-001	PICKETT'S	
1-01-001	PICKFAIR	
1-01-001	PICKFORD	
14-08-014	PICKING	
1-01-001	PICKINS	
1-01-001	PICKLE	
3-01-001	PICKLED	
1-01-001	PICKLES	
1-01-001	PICKMAN	
3-01-001	PICKOFF	
1-01-001	PICKOFFS	
4-04-004	PICKS	
14-06-010	PICKUP	
15-06-008	PICNIC	
1-01-001	PICNICKED	
1-01-001	PICNICKERS	
3-03-003	PICNICS	
1-01-001	PICON	
5-03-003	PICTORIAL	
1-01-001	PICTORIALLY	
162-14-098	PICTURE	
1-01-001	PICTURE-IMAGES	
1-01-001	PICTURE-PALACE	
4-04-004	PICTURED	
68-14-046	PICTURES	
9-04-008	PICTURESQUE	
3-02-002	PICTURING	
3-01-001	PIDDINGTON	
1-01-001	PIDDLING	
2-02-002	PIDGIN	
14-07-007	PIE	
129-14-074	PIECE	
2-02-002	PIECEMEAL	
92-14-042	PIECES	
1-01-001	PIECEWISE	
2-02-002	PIEDMONT	
13-01-001	PIEPSAM	
1-01-001	PIEPSAM'S	
3-03-003	PIER	
1-01-001	PIER-TABLE	
6-03-004	PIERCE	
4-02-003	PIERCED	
3-03-003	PIERCING	
2-02-002	PIERO	
1-01-001	PIERPONT	
1-01-001	PIERRE	
6-04-005	PIERS	
1-01-001	PIERSEE	
2-01-001	PIERSON	
5-03-004	PIES	
2-01-001	PIETA	
1-01-001	PIETISM	
2-01-001	PIETRO	
1-01-001	PIETRO'S	
4-03-004	PIETY	
3-01-002	PIEZOELECTRIC	
1-01-001	PIEZOELECTRICIT	Y
8-05-007	PIG	
2-01-001	PIG-DRUNK	
1-01-001	PIG-INFESTED	
1-01-001	PIGEN	
3-02-003	PIGEON	
1-01-001	PIGEONHOLE	
1-01-001	PIGEONS	
9-03-005	PIGMENT	
1-01-001	PIGMENTED	
3-03-003	PIGMENTS	
1-01-001	PIGPENS	
6-04-005	PIGS	
1-01-001	PIGSKIN	
41-04-005	PIKE	
2-01-001	PIKE'S	
1-01-001	PILATE	
1-01-001	PILATE'S	
25-10-020	PILE	
16-07-016	PILED	
2-02-002	PILES	
1-01-001	PILFERING	
4-04-004	PILGRIM	
1-01-001	PILGRIM'S	
9-06-008	PILGRIMAGE	
1-01-001	PILGRIMAGES	
6-02-002	PILGRIMS	
6-05-006	PILING	
15-05-005	PILL	
3-02-002	PILLAGE	
1-01-001	PILLAGED	
2-01-002	PILLAR	
2-02-002	PILLARED	
5-04-005	PILLARS	
2-02-002	PILLORIED	
8-05-007	PILLOW	
3-01-003	PILLOWS	
8-05-006	PILLS	
1-01-001	PILLSBURY	
44-10-019	PILOT	
2-02-002	PILOT'S	
2-02-002	PILOTING	
8-04-004	PILOTS	
2-02-002	PILOTS'	
1-01-001	PILS	
5-01-001	PIMEN	
2-01-001	PIMEN'S	
3-02-002	PIMP	
1-01-001	PIMPLED	
1-01-001	PIMPLES	
1-01-001	PIMPLIKE	
2-02-002	PIMPS	
16-08-013	PIN	
1-01-001	PIN-CURL	
1-01-001	PIN-POINT	
1-01-001	PINAFORES	
2-01-001	PINAR	
1-01-001	PINBALL	
6-03-004	PINCH	
1-01-001	PINCH-HIT	
1-01-001	PINCH-HITTER	
1-01-001	PINCH-HITTERS	
7-04-007	PINCHED	
2-02-002	PINCHING	
2-01-001	PINCIAN	
14-07-011	PINE	
1-01-001	PINE-KNOT	
9-05-005	PINEAPPLE	
2-02-002	PINES	
1-01-001	PING-PONG	
1-01-001	PINGING	
1-01-001	PINHEAD	
1-01-001	PINHOLES	
1-01-001	PINIONED	
48-13-031	PINK	
1-01-001	PINK-PETTICOAT	
1-01-001	PINKIE	
1-01-001	PINKISH-WHITE	
1-01-001	PINKLY	
2-02-002	PINKS	
1-01-001	PINNACLE	
1-01-001	PINNACLES	
4-03-003	PINNED	
1-01-001	PINNING	
1-01-001	PINNINGS	
1-01-001	PINOCHLE	
5-05-005	PINPOINT	
1-01-001	PINPOINTING	

```
1-01-001   PINPOINTS
6-04-005   PINS
1-01-001   PINSCHER
1-01-001   PINSK
13-04-005  PINT
1-01-001   PINT-SIZED
1-01-001   PINTO
20-10-015  PIONEER
1-01-001   PIONEER'S
3-02-003   PIONEERED
3-02-002   PIONEERING
3-01-001   PIONEERS
10-06-008  PIOUS
1-01-001   PIOUSLY
23-03-003  PIP
13-01-001  PIP'S
20-07-012  PIPE
2-02-002   PIPED
6-03-003   PIPELINE
1-01-001   PIPERS
7-05-007   PIPES
1-01-001   PIPGRAS
5-03-003   PIPING
2-02-002   PIQUANT
2-02-002   PIQUE
1-01-001   PIRACY
1-01-001   PIRAEUS
1-01-001   PIRANDELLO
1-01-001   PIRANESI
1-01-001   PIRARO
4-03-003   PIRATE
12-03-006  PIRATES
1-01-001   PIRATES'
1-01-001   PIRIE
1-01-001   PIROGUES
4-02-003   PIROUETTE
1-01-001   PISCES
1-01-001   PISS
1-01-001   PISTACHIO
27-08-016  PISTOL
1-01-001   PISTOL-PACKING
1-01-001   PISTOL-WHIPPED
1-01-001   PISTOL-WHIPPING
1-01-001   PISTOLEERS
4-03-003   PISTOLS
7-01-001   PISTON
3-01-002   PISTONS
14-07-010  PIT
3-01-001   PIT-RUN
22-09-017  PITCH
8-06-007   PITCHED
21-05-011  PITCHER
8-02-006   PITCHERS
6-03-004   PITCHES
2-01-001   PITCHFORK
16-05-010  PITCHING
1-01-001   PITEOUS
3-03-003   PITFALL
1-01-001   PITFALLS
1-01-001   PITH
1-01-001   PITHY
3-03-003   PITIABLE
2-02-002   PITIED
4-03-004   PITIFUL
2-01-001   PITIFULLY
2-02-002   PITILESS
1-01-001   PITILESSLY
1-01-001   PITNEY-*BOWES
4-03-003   PITS
2-01-001   PITT
1-01-001   PITT-*RIVERS
1-01-001   PITTENGER
1-01-001   PITTSBORO
25-08-011  PITTSBURGH
2-02-002   PITTSBURGHERS
11-03-003  PITUITARY
14-07-012  PITY
1-01-001   PITYINGLY
2-02-002   PIUS
2-01-001   PIVOT
1-01-001   PIVOTAL
1-01-001   PIVOTING
1-01-001   PIWEN
1-01-001   PIXIES
1-01-001   PIZARRO
3-03-003   PIZZA
1-01-001   PIZZICATO
2-01-002   PL
1-01-001   PLACATING
571-15-292 PLACE
1-01-001   PLACE-KICKER
3-01-001   PLACE-KICKING
6-01-001   PLACE-NAME
3-01-001   PLACE-NAMES
126-14-097 PLACED
1-01-001   PLACELESS
15-04-011  PLACEMENT

1-01-001   PLACENTIA
100-15-082 PLACES
6-05-006   PLACID
27-11-024  PLACING
1-01-001   PLAGIARISM
6-06-006   PLAGUE
5-05-005   PLAGUED
1-01-001   PLAID
1-01-001   PLAIDS
48-13-038  PLAIN
2-01-001   PLAIN-CLOTHESMEN
1-01-001   PLAIN-OUT
2-02-002   PLAIN-SPOKEN
1-01-001   PLAINCLOTHES
1-01-001   PLAINEST
3-01-002   PLAINFIELD
18-08-017  PLAINLY
14-08-011  PLAINS
5-01-001   PLAINTIFF
1-01-001   PLAINTIFF'S
3-02-003   PLAINTIFFS
2-02-002   PLAINTIVE
1-01-001   PLAINVIEW
205-15-095 PLAN
1-01-001   PLAN'S
1-01-001   PLANAR
114-10-038 PLANE
1-01-001   PLANED
1-01-001   PLANELOAD
3-01-001   PLANER
26-11-015  PLANES
21-06-011  PLANET
1-01-001   PLANET'S
1-01-001   PLANETARIUM
21-04-005  PLANETARY
1-01-001   PLANETEN
1-01-001   PLANETOID
1-01-001   PLANETOIDS
22-06-006  PLANETS
7-04-007   PLANK
8-01-001   PLANKING
5-03-004   PLANKS
75-14-058  PLANNED
2-02-002   PLANNER
13-07-012  PLANNERS
129-11-056 PLANNING
1-01-001   PLANOCONCAVE
113-15-079 PLANS
125-10-044 PLANT
2-01-002   PLANT'S
1-01-001   PLANT-LOCATION
1-01-001   PLANTAIN
19-03-006  PLANTATION
7-01-001   PLANTATIONS
11-07-009  PLANTED
6-02-002   PLANTER
2-01-001   PLANTERS
2-02-002   PLANTERS'
5-04-005   PLANTING
1-01-001   PLANTINGS
59-11-029  PLANTS
2-02-002   PLAQUE
4-03-003   PLAQUES
1-01-001   PLASM
13-02-006  PLASMA
23-06-010  PLASTER
1-01-001   PLASTER-OF-*PARIS
5-04-005   PLASTERED
1-01-001   PLASTERER
1-01-001   PLASTERING
1-01-001   PLASTERS
1-01-001   PLASTI-*BARS
31-07-017  PLASTIC
1-01-001   PLASTIC-COVERED
1-01-001   PLASTICALLY
4-02-002   PLASTICITY
32-04-006  PLASTICS
1-01-001   PLASTISOLS
22-07-012  PLATE
3-03-003   PLATEAU
1-01-001   PLATED
23-10-014  PLATES
72-08-016  PLATFORM
1-01-001   PLATFORM-CONTROLLER
5-04-005   PLATFORMS
1-01-001   PLATH
4-03-003   PLATINUM
1-01-001   PLATITUDINOUS
20-02-004  PLATO
14-03-006  PLATO'S
3-02-003   PLATONIC
1-01-001   PLATONICA
4-02-002   PLATONISM
2-01-002   PLATONIST

7-02-002   PLATOON
3-03-003   PLATOONS
1-01-001   PLATTED
2-02-002   PLATTER
1-01-001   PLATTERS
4-03-004   PLAUSIBLE
200-15-106 PLAY
3-02-003   PLAY'S
1-01-001   PLAY-ACTING
1-01-001   PLAY-GIRL
1-01-001   PLAY-OFF
1-01-001   PLAYA
1-01-001   PLAYABLE
1-01-001   PLAYBACK
1-01-001   PLAYBACKS
2-02-002   PLAYBOY
1-01-001   PLAYBOY-*SHOW-*BIZ
104-14-071 PLAYED
2-02-002   PLAYED-OUT
51-08-016  PLAYER
7-02-004   PLAYER'S
29-06-013  PLAYERS
1-01-001   PLAYERS'
1-01-001   PLAYES
3-03-003   PLAYFUL
4-03-004   PLAYGROUND
4-01-002   PLAYHOUSE
1-01-001   PLAYHOUSES
101-15-056 PLAYING
2-02-002   PLAYMATE
2-02-002   PLAYMATES
2-01-001   PLAYOFF
1-01-001   PLAYROOM
66-13-041  PLAYS
1-01-001   PLAYTIME
3-03-003   PLAYWRIGHT
1-01-001   PLAYWRIGHT-DIRECTOR
1-01-001   PLAYWRIGHTS
1-01-001   PLAYWRITING
2-02-002   PLAZA
1-01-001   PLAZAS
1-01-001   PLAZEK
11-06-009  PLEA
5-04-005   PLEAD
7-04-005   PLEADED
1-01-001   PLEADER
12-07-010  PLEADING
1-01-001   PLEADS
3-03-003   PLEAS
1-01-001   PLEASANCE
38-11-032  PLEASANT
10-10-010  PLEASANTLY
1-01-001   PLEASANTNESS
62-14-051  PLEASE
41-12-036  PLEASED
2-01-002   PLEASES
1-01-001   PLEASIN
10-06-009  PLEASING
1-01-001   PLEASINGLY
62-12-049  PLEASURE
1-01-001   PLEASURE-BOAT
6-06-006   PLEASURES
1-01-001   PLEATS
1-01-001   PLEBEIAN
1-01-001   PLEBIAN
3-02-002   PLEDGE
5-03-004   PLEDGED
3-03-003   PLEDGES
1-01-001   PLEE-*ZING
4-02-003   PLENARY
1-01-001   PLENIPOTENTIARY
1-01-001   PLENITUDE
7-05-007   PLENTIFUL
55-13-045  PLENTY
6-01-001   PLEURA
6-01-001   PLEURAL
1-01-001   PLEXIGLAS
1-01-001   PLIABLE
1-01-001   PLIANT
2-02-002   PLIED
1-01-001   PLIERS
7-05-007   PLIGHT
1-01-001   PLINKING
1-01-001   PLINY'S
1-01-001   PLOD
2-02-002   PLODDED
4-03-004   PLODDING
1-01-001   PLOPPED
37-11-030  PLOT
8-06-007   PLOTS
10-04-008  PLOTTED
2-02-002   PLOTTING
12-07-008  PLOW
5-03-003   PLOWED

11-03-006  PLOWING
1-01-001   PLOWMAN'S
3-03-003   PLOWS
1-01-001   PLOWSHARES
2-02-002   PLUCK
4-03-004   PLUCKED
1-01-001   PLUCKING
23-05-007  PLUG
3-03-003   PLUGGED
1-01-001   PLUGGING
2-02-002   PLUGS
2-02-002   PLUGUGLY
1-01-001   PLUM
5-03-004   PLUMB
1-01-001   PLUMBED
4-03-003   PLUMBER
9-05-008   PLUMBING
2-02-002   PLUME
1-01-001   PLUMED
2-01-001   PLUMMER
1-01-001   PLUMMETING
4-03-004   PLUMP
2-02-002   PLUMPED
4-01-002   PLUMPNESS
2-02-002   PLUNDER
1-01-001   PLUNDERERS
1-01-001   PLUNDERING
5-04-004   PLUNGE
15-08-015  PLUNGED
2-02-002   PLUNGES
3-02-003   PLUNGING
1-01-001   PLUNKERS
2-02-002   PLUNKING
1-01-001   PLURALISM
2-02-002   PLURALISTIC
72-13-055  PLUS
3-01-001   PLUS-ONE
3-03-003   PLUSH
1-01-001   PLUTARCH
11-03-004  PLYMOUTH
1-01-001   PLYMPTON
9-01-003   PLYWOOD
3-02-003   PNEUMONIA
3-01-002   PO
3-01-002   PO'K
1-01-001   POACH
1-01-001   POACHES
1-01-001   POARK
3-01-001   POCASSET
46-09-028  POCKET
1-01-001   POCKET'S
1-01-001   POCKET-SIZE
3-02-003   POCKETBOOK
1-01-001   POCKETBOOKS
1-01-001   POCKETED
1-01-001   POCKETFUL
17-09-016  POCKETS
1-01-001   POCKMANSTER'S
1-01-001   POCONOS
3-01-001   POD
21-01-001  PODGER
2-01-001   PODGER'S
1-01-001   PODGERS
1-01-001   PODIUM
1-01-001   PODOLIA
1-01-001   PODS
4-02-003   POE
48-07-019  POEM
82-05-015  POEMS
1-01-001   POEMS-IN-DRAWING-AND-TYPE
1-01-001   POEPLE'S
1-01-001   POESY
99-12-038  POET
13-05-009  POET'S
1-01-001   POET-PAINTER
31-07-018  POETIC
2-02-002   POETICALLY
8-01-002   POETICS
2-01-001   POETIZING
1-01-001   POETRIE
88-09-025  POETRY
1-01-001   POETRY'S
4-01-001   POETRY-AND-JAZZ
32-06-016  POETS
2-01-001   POGROMS
1-01-001   POGUE
11-02-002  POHL
3-02-002   POHL'S
2-01-001   POHLY
2-02-002   POIGNANCY
6-04-006   POIGNANT
1-01-001   POIGNANTLY
1-01-001   POINDEXTER
395-15-223 POINT
1-01-001   POINT-BLANK
74-13-065  POINTED
```

Freq	Word
3-03-003	POINTEDLY
3-03-003	POINTER
1-01-001	POINTERS
26-09-024	POINTING
1-01-001	POINTLESS
143-13-078	POINTS
2-01-001	POIROT
6-06-006	POISE
12-08-010	POISED
2-01-001	POISES
10-05-008	POISON
4-04-004	POISONED
3-03-003	POISONING
5-03-005	POISONOUS
2-02-002	POISONS
3-01-001	POITRINE
2-01-001	POITRINE'S
1-01-001	POKE
4-03-004	POKED
1-01-001	POKENEU
6-06-006	POKER
1-01-001	POKERFACED
3-03-003	POKES
5-04-005	POKING
33-06-008	POLAND
2-01-001	POLAND'S
7-04-005	POLAR
10-04-007	POLARIS
1-01-001	POLARITIES
5-03-003	POLARITY
6-02-003	POLARIZATION
1-01-001	POLARIZE
3-02-002	POLARIZED
1-01-001	POLARIZING
1-01-001	POLAROID
1-01-001	POLDOWSKI
18-07-012	POLE
1-01-001	POLECAT
1-01-001	POLEMIC
1-01-001	POLEMICAL
1-01-001	POLEMICS
12-06-009	POLES
155-12-056	POLICE
1-01-001	POLICE-DODGING
1-01-001	POLICED
19-06-011	POLICEMAN
1-01-001	POLICEMAN'S
1-01-001	POLICEMAN-MURDERER
15-06-012	POLICEMEN
1-01-001	POLICEMEN'S
68-07-036	POLICIES
3-02-003	POLICING
222-10-070	POLICY
3-02-002	POLICY-MAKERS
1-01-001	POLICY-MAKING
1-01-001	POLICY-ORIENTED
2-01-001	POLING
1-01-001	POLIO
1-01-001	POLIS
19-09-015	POLISH
14-11-013	POLISHED
1-01-001	POLISHES
2-01-001	POLISHING
1-01-001	POLITBURO
7-06-007	POLITE
10-07-009	POLITELY
5-04-005	POLITENESS
4-03-004	POLITIC
258-13-103	POLITICAL
11-05-010	POLITICALLY
13-06-009	POLITICIAN
19-08-015	POLITICIANS
1-01-001	POLITICKING
1-01-001	POLITICO
1-01-001	POLITICO-SOCIOLOGICAL
1-01-001	POLITICOS
69-12-038	POLITICS
1-01-001	POLITICS-RIDDEN
1-01-001	POLITIES
1-01-001	POLITY
1-01-001	POLK'S
1-01-001	POLKA
1-01-001	POLKA-DOTTED
9-04-007	POLL
1-01-001	POLLED
11-03-003	POLLEN
1-01-001	POLLEN-AND-NECTAR
3-01-001	POLLING
8-04-004	POLLOCK
1-01-001	POLLOCK'S
10-05-008	POLLS
1-01-001	POLLUTED
6-04-005	POLLUTION
4-02-004	POLO
1-01-001	POLOLU
1-01-001	POLONAISE
2-01-001	POLTAVA
1-01-001	POLTAWA
2-01-001	POLY-UNSATURATED
1-01-001	POLYANKA
1-01-001	POLYBUTENE
1-01-001	POLYBUTENES
1-01-001	POLYCHEMICALS
3-01-002	POLYCRYSTALLINE
1-01-001	POLYELECTROLYTES
5-02-002	POLYESTER
2-01-001	POLYESTERS
7-01-001	POLYETHER
1-01-001	POLYETHER-TYPE
1-01-001	POLYETHERS
4-02-003	POLYETHYLENE
1-01-001	POLYGYNOUS
1-01-001	POLYISOBUTYLENE
1-01-001	POLYISOCYANATE
1-01-001	POLYISOCYANATES
1-01-001	POLYMER
2-01-001	POLYMERIC
7-01-002	POLYMERIZATION
1-01-001	POLYMERIZATIONS
4-01-001	POLYMERS
1-01-001	POLYMYOSITIS
28-01-001	POLYNOMIAL
10-01-001	POLYNOMIALS
1-01-001	POLYPHOSPHATE
5-01-001	POLYPHOSPHATES
3-01-001	POLYPROPYLENE
1-01-001	POLYSILOXANES
1-01-001	POLYSTYRENE
1-01-001	POLYTECHNIC
1-01-001	POLYTONAL
10-04-006	POLYUNSATURATED
1-01-001	POMADED
1-01-001	POMERANIA
2-01-001	POMHAM
1-01-001	POMP
1-01-001	POMPADOUR
1-01-001	POMPANO
5-01-001	POMPEII
1-01-001	POMPEII'S
2-01-001	POMPEY
1-01-001	POMPONS
3-02-002	POMPOUS
1-01-001	POMPOUSLY
1-01-001	POMPOUSNESS
1-01-001	PONCE
1-01-001	PONCHARTRAIN
1-01-001	PONCHIELLI
3-01-001	PONCHO
25-05-009	POND
1-01-001	PONDER
4-02-003	PONDERED
2-02-002	PONDERING
3-03-003	PONDEROUS
7-01-001	PONDS
6-02-002	PONIES
1-01-001	PONKOB
1-01-001	PONOLUU
38-06-007	PONT
15-02-002	PONT'S
1-01-001	PONT-*GENERAL
2-02-002	PONTCHARTRAIN
1-01-001	PONTIAC
1-01-001	PONTIFF
1-01-001	PONTIFICAL
1-01-001	PONTIFICATES
1-01-001	PONTISSARA
1-01-001	PONTIUS
10-04-006	PONY
1-01-001	PONY'S
1-01-001	POOCHED
2-02-002	POODLE
1-01-001	POOH-POOHED
6-03-003	POOL
1-01-001	POOL'S
1-01-001	POOL-CARE
1-01-001	POOL-EQUIPMENT
1-01-001	POOL-OWNERS
2-01-001	POOL-SIDE
1-01-001	POOLED
2-02-002	POOLING
15-05-007	POOLS
113-14-075	POOR
1-01-001	POOR'S
1-01-001	POOR-MOUTH
1-01-001	POOR-WHITE-TRASH
3-02-003	POORER
3-03-003	POOREST
11-07-010	POORLY
8-05-008	POP
1-01-001	POP'LAR
1-01-001	POP'S
40-07-016	POPE
3-02-002	POPE'S
1-01-001	POPES
2-01-001	POPISH
1-01-001	POPLAR
1-01-001	POPLIN
6-04-006	POPPED
1-01-001	POPPIES
6-04-005	POPPING
2-02-002	POPPY
1-01-001	POPPYSEED
11-03-003	POPS
4-03-003	POPULACE
1-01-001	POPULAIRE
1-01-001	POPULAIRES
98-13-073	POPULAR
1-01-001	POPULARISM
17-08-013	POPULARITY
7-05-007	POPULARLY
1-01-001	POPULATE
12-09-011	POPULATED
136-09-053	POPULATION
8-05-007	POPULATIONS
5-03-005	POPULOUS
2-02-002	PORCELAIN
43-09-026	PORCH
2-01-002	PORCHES
1-01-001	PORCUPINES
2-01-001	PORE
1-01-001	PORED
3-03-003	PORES
1-01-001	PORGY
1-01-001	PORING
10-04-006	PORK
1-01-001	PORK-BARREL
1-01-001	PORNOGRAPHER
1-01-001	PORNOGRAPHIC
3-01-001	PORNSEN
2-01-002	POROSITY
12-02-003	POROUS
1-01-001	PORPOISES
1-01-001	PORRIDGE
21-07-016	PORT
1-01-001	PORTA
13-06-011	PORTABLE
1-01-001	PORTAGE
4-03-003	PORTAGO
1-01-001	PORTAL
1-01-001	PORTANT
1-01-001	PORTENDED
2-02-002	PORTENTOUS
2-01-002	PORTENTS
17-06-009	PORTER
2-01-001	PORTER'S
1-01-001	PORTERHOUSE
1-01-001	PORTERS
1-01-001	PORTFOLIO
1-01-001	PORTFOLIO-MAKER
1-01-001	PORTIA
3-03-003	PORTICO
62-12-040	PORTION
11-07-011	PORTIONS
24-02-004	PORTLAND
2-01-001	PORTLAND'S
1-01-001	PORTLY
3-01-001	PORTO
17-08-015	PORTRAIT
7-05-007	PORTRAITS
1-01-001	PORTRAITURE
6-03-005	PORTRAY
7-05-006	PORTRAYAL
6-04-005	PORTRAYED
2-02-002	PORTRAYING
5-03-005	PORTRAYS
4-02-002	PORTS
4-03-003	PORTSMOUTH
4-04-004	PORTUGAL
3-02-003	PORTUGUESE
2-01-001	PORTWATCHERS
1-01-001	PORTWATCHERS'
11-07-010	POSE
7-06-007	POSED
1-01-001	POSEIDON
1-01-001	POSES
1-01-001	POSEUR
1-01-001	POSEURS
1-01-001	POSEY
1-01-001	POSHEST
3-03-003	POSING
241-15-146	POSITION
1-01-001	POSITIONED
54-09-043	POSITIONS
74-12-051	POSITIVE
9-07-009	POSITIVELY
4-01-002	POSITIVISM
7-01-001	POSITIVIST
3-01-001	POSITIVISTS
11-03-003	POSSE
2-01-001	POSSE'S
1-01-001	POSSEMAN
1-01-001	POSSEMEN
1-01-001	POSSES
16-06-013	POSSESS
22-09-019	POSSESSED
8-04-008	POSSESSES
6-04-006	POSSESSING
21-09-019	POSSESSION
11-07-009	POSSESSIONS
4-04-004	POSSESSIVE
1-01-001	POSSESSOR
42-09-031	POSSIBILITIES
87-13-070	POSSIBILITY
373-15-226	POSSIBLE
1-01-001	POSSIBLITIES
61-14-051	POSSIBLY
2-02-002	POSSUM
2-01-001	POSSUM-HUNTING
1-01-001	POSSIBLE
84-11-050	POST
1-01-001	POST*$'S
1-01-001	POST*$-ATTACK
1-01-001	POST-*A**.*D
1-01-001	POST-*CIVIL
1-01-001	POST-*DISPATCH
1-01-001	POST-*GRADUATE
1-01-001	POST-*INAUGURAL
1-01-001	POST-*SERIALISM
3-03-003	POST-*WORLD
4-02-002	POST-ATTACK
2-01-001	POST-BELLUM
1-01-001	POST-CENSUS
1-01-001	POST-INDEPENDENCE
1-01-001	POST-MORTEM
1-01-001	POST-OPERATIVE
1-01-001	POST-REAPPORTIONMENT
8-03-005	POST-WAR
1-01-001	POSTAGE-PREPAID
7-02-006	POSTAL
7-05-005	POSTCARD
1-01-001	POSTCARDS
11-06-009	POSTED
4-03-003	POSTER
6-02-003	POSTERIOR
6-03-005	POSTERITY
4-02-004	POSTERS
3-02-002	POSTGRADUATE
2-01-002	POSTHUMOUS
2-02-002	POSTMAN
2-02-002	POSTMARK
4-02-004	POSTMASTER
1-01-001	POSTMASTER'S
1-01-001	POSTMASTERS
2-02-002	POSTMEN
7-06-006	POSTPONE
9-06-007	POSTPONED
2-02-002	POSTPONEMENT
3-03-003	POSTPONING
22-06-013	POSTS
3-03-003	POSTSCRIPT
3-03-003	POSTULATE
7-03-006	POSTULATED
1-01-001	POSTULATES
13-09-013	POSTURE
2-02-002	POSTURES
11-03-009	POSTWAR
28-10-018	POT
5-01-001	POTASSIUM
15-05-007	POTATO
15-09-011	POTATOES
2-02-002	POTBOILER
1-01-001	POTBOILERS
4-01-001	POTEMKIN
3-01-001	POTEMKIN'S
6-04-005	POTENCY
9-06-008	POTENT
67-10-046	POTENTIAL
8-05-008	POTENTIALITIES
3-03-003	POTENTIALITY
7-04-006	POTENTIALLY
4-02-003	POTENTIALS
1-01-001	POTENTIOMETER
1-01-001	POTHOLE
1-01-001	POTIONS
1-01-001	POTLATCHES
2-02-002	POTOMAC
1-01-001	POTOWOMUT
1-01-001	POTPOURRI
5-04-005	POTS

```
1-01-001    POTSDAM
1-01-001    POTTAWATOMIE
3-03-003    POTTED
4-02-003    POTTER
8-02-002    POTTERS
16-04-005   POTTERY
1-01-001    POTTING
2-02-002    POUCH
2-02-002    POUCHES
2-02-002    POUGHKEEPSIE
1-01-001    POUILLY-*FUISSE
3-01-001    POULTICE
2-01-002    POULTICES
11-04-005   POULTRY
1-01-001    POULTRY-LOVING
28-09-010   POUND
1-01-001    POUND-FOOLISH
1-01-001    POUND-OF-FLESH
4-04-004    POUNDED
6-06-006    POUNDING
43-07-020   POUNDS
1-01-001    POUNDS'
1-01-001    POUPIN
9-07-008    POUR
29-12-028   POURED
1-01-001    POURED-IN-PLACE
9-06-009    POURING
2-02-002    POURS
2-02-002    POUSSIN
1-01-001    POUSSIN'S
1-01-001    POUSSINS
1-01-001    POUT
1-01-001    POUTED
20-08-018   POVERTY
2-02-002    POVERTY-STRICKEN
28-06-013   POWDER
7-03-004    POWDERED
1-01-001    POWDERPUFF
5-02-003    POWDERS
3-03-003    POWDERY
15-04-006   POWELL
2-01-001    POWELL'S
342-15-156  POWER
1-01-001    POWER'S
1-01-001    POWER-*SEEK
1-01-001    POWER-HUNGRY
1-01-001    POWER-STARVED
2-02-002    POWERED
63-14-054   POWERFUL
4-02-004    POWERFULLY
1-01-001    POWERFULNESS
3-03-003    POWERLESS
1-01-001    POWERPLANTS
73-13-041   POWERS
1-01-001    POWERS-THAT-BE
1-01-001    POWICKE
5-01-001    POYNTING-*ROBERTSON
1-01-001    POZATTI
4-01-001    POZZATTI
9-04-006    PP
2-01-001    PRABANG
1-01-001    PRACTICABILITY
6-02-004    PRACTICABLE
68-11-052   PRACTICAL
2-02-002    PRACTICALITY
53-13-047   PRACTICALLY
94-13-069   PRACTICE
8-06-008    PRACTICED
53-09-030   PRACTICES
15-09-013   PRACTICING
2-02-002    PRACTISED
1-01-001    PRACTISING
2-01-002    PRACTITIONER
6-04-006    PRACTITIONERS
1-01-001    PRADO
4-03-004    PRAGMATIC
2-02-002    PRAGMATISM
3-01-002    PRAGUE
1-01-001    PRAI
21-07-009   PRAIRIE
17-11-017   PRAISE
13-06-012   PRAISED
3-01-001    PRAISEGOD
2-02-002    PRAISES
2-01-001    PRAISING
1-01-001    PRAM
1-01-001    PRAMS
3-03-003    PRANCING
1-01-001    PRANDTL
1-01-001    PRANHA
1-01-001    PRANK
1-01-001    PRANKS
1-01-001    PRATAKKU
10-04-006   PRATT
1-01-001    PRATT'S

1-01-001    PRATTVILLE
12-07-009   PRAY
12-08-010   PRAYED
28-09-020   PRAYER
1-01-001    PRAYER-REQUESTS
1-01-001    PRAYER-TIME
1-01-001    PRAYERBOOKS
1-01-001    PRAYERFUL
1-01-001    PRAYERFULLY
12-06-010   PRAYERS
1-01-001    PRAYERS/*SHALL
2-01-001    PRAYIN
3-03-003    PRAYING
1-01-001    PRE*$-ATTACK
1-01-001    PRE-*ANGLO-*SAXON
2-02-002    PRE-*CIVIL
1-01-001    PRE-*EASTER
1-01-001    PRE-*FAIR
1-01-001    PRE-*FRENCH
1-01-001    PRE-*HAN
1-01-001    PRE-*LEGISLATIVE
1-01-001    PRE-*PUNIC
1-01-001    PRE-*REVOLUTIONARY
1-01-001    PRE-*WORLD-*WAR-*/1
1-01-001    PRE-ACADEMIC
1-01-001    PRE-ASSAULT
1-01-001    PRE-CAST
1-01-001    PRE-CONDITIONS
1-01-001    PRE-CONSCIOUS
1-01-001    PRE-COOLED
1-01-001    PRE-DECORATION
1-01-001    PRE-DETERMINED
1-01-001    PRE-DRILLED
1-01-001    PRE-EMINENT
1-01-001    PRE-EMPLOYMENT
1-01-001    PRE-EMPTING
1-01-001    PRE-EMPTION
1-01-001    PRE-EXISTENCE
1-01-001    PRE-EXISTENT
1-01-001    PRE-HISTORIC
2-02-002    PRE-HISTORY
1-01-001    PRE-INAUGURAL
1-01-001    PRE-LEGISLATIVE
1-01-001    PRE-LITERATE
1-01-001    PRE-MARITAL
1-01-001    PRE-NUPTIAL
1-01-001    PRE-PACKED
1-01-001    PRE-PENICILLIN
1-01-001    PRE-PLANNING
1-01-001    PRE-PRIMARY
2-01-001    PRE-SCHOOL
2-02-002    PRE-SEASON
2-01-001    PRE-SELLING
1-01-001    PRE-SET
2-01-001    PRE-SHAPED
1-01-001    PRE-VISION
6-05-005    PRE-WAR
1-01-001    PRE-1960
8-06-008    PREACH
8-05-008    PREACHED
11-04-007   PREACHER
1-01-001    PREACHER-SINGER
2-02-002    PREACHERS
1-01-001    PREACHES
17-07-010   PREACHING
4-04-004    PREAMBLE
3-01-001    PREAMBLES
1-01-001    PREARRANGED
8-06-007    PRECARIOUS
3-03-003    PRECARIOUSLY
1-01-001    PRECAUTION
8-06-008    PRECAUTIONARY
2-02-002    PRECAUTIONS
7-04-007    PRECEDE
3-03-003    PRECEDED
15-07-014   PRECEDENCE
3-02-003    PRECEDENT
1-01-001    PRECEDENT-BASED
3-03-003    PRECEDENTS
1-01-001    PRECEDES
30-10-023   PRECEDING
1-01-001    PRECEEDED
1-01-001    PRECEEDING
1-01-001    PRECEPT
3-03-003    PRECEPTS
1-01-001    PRECHLORINATION
8-03-003    PRECINCT
5-02-003    PRECINCTS
29-13-022   PRECIOUS
1-01-001    PRECIPICE
1-01-001    PRECIPICE-WALLED
1-01-001    PRECIPITATE

9-03-007    PRECIPITATED
2-01-002    PRECIPITATING
1-01-001    PRECIPITIN
33-09-028   PRECISE
48-11-039   PRECISELY
46-09-027   PRECISION
4-04-004    PRECLUDE
1-01-001    PRECLUDED
3-03-003    PRECOCIOUS
1-01-001    PRECOCIOUSLY
1-01-001    PRECOCITY
2-01-001    PRECONCEIVED
2-02-002    PRECONCEPTIONS
1-01-001    PRECONDITION
2-01-001    PRECONDITIONED
1-01-001    PRECONDITIONS
1-01-001    PRECONSCIOUS
1-01-001    PRECOOKED
5-05-005    PREDECESSOR
6-04-006    PREDECESSORS
1-01-001    PREDESTINED
3-03-003    PREDETERMINED
3-02-003    PREDICAMENT
2-01-001    PREDICATOR
8-05-006    PREDICT
1-01-001    PREDICTABILITY
8-07-008    PREDICTABLE
2-02-002    PREDICTABLY
18-07-014   PREDICTED
6-05-006    PREDICTING
1-01-001    PREDICTING-MACHINES
10-05-009   PREDICTION
3-03-003    PREDICTIONS
3-02-003    PREDICTIVE
1-01-001    PREDICTORS
3-03-003    PREDICTS
1-01-001    PREDIGESTED
1-01-001    PREDILECTIONS
1-01-001    PREDISPOSED
4-02-002    PREDISPOSITION
9-02-002    PREDISPOSITIONS
3-01-001    PREDNISONE
2-01-002    PREDOMINANCE
1-01-001    PREDOMINANT
7-03-007    PREDOMINANTLY
1-01-001    PREDOMINATED
1-01-001    PREDOMINATELY
1-01-001    PREDOMINATES
1-01-001    PREDOMINATING
1-01-001    PREDOMINATION
1-01-001    PREEMPLOYMENT
1-01-001    PREENING
5-04-005    PREFAB
2-01-001    PREFABRICATED
3-01-003    PREFACE
2-01-002    PREFACED
1-01-001    PREFECTURE
1-01-001    PREFECTURES
27-09-025   PREFER
6-06-006    PREFERABLE
14-07-014   PREFERABLY
9-05-009    PREFERENCE
7-04-006    PREFERENCES
4-02-003    PREFERENTIAL
2-01-002    PREFERENTIALLY
1-01-001    PREFERMENT
26-11-023   PREFERRED
1-01-001    PREFERRING
1-01-001    PREFERS
1-01-001    PREFIXES
2-01-001    PREFLIGHT
1-01-001    PREFUH
4-01-001    PREGNANCY
8-06-007    PREGNANT
2-02-002    PREHISTORIC
1-01-001    PREISOLATED
2-01-001    PREJUDGED
11-05-009   PREJUDICE
4-03-004    PREJUDICED
4-04-004    PREJUDICES
4-03-003    PREJUDICIAL
2-01-002    PRELIMINARIES
24-09-020   PRELIMINARY
1-01-001    PRELITERATE
5-05-005    PRELUDE
1-01-001    PRELUDES
3-02-002    PREMARITAL
3-03-003    PREMATURE
3-02-003    PREMATURELY
26-03-009   PREMIER
5-03-004    PREMIERE
4-03-003    PREMIERES
7-04-006    PREMISE
8-06-007    PREMISES
12-04-010   PREMIUM

2-02-002    PREMIUMS
3-01-001    PREMIX
2-02-002    PREMONITION
1-01-001    PREMONITIONS
1-01-001    PREMONITORY
1-01-001    PRENCE
1-01-001    PRENTICE'S
1-01-001    PRENTICE-*HALL
1-01-001    PRENTISS'
9-06-008    PREOCCUPATION
1-01-001    PREOCCUPATIONS
11-06-011   PREOCCUPIED
1-01-001    PREOCCUPIES
1-01-001    PREORDAINMENT
2-02-002    PREP
2-02-002    PREPACKAGED
54-09-031   PREPARATION
1-01-001    PREPARATION-*INQUIRERS'
15-08-012   PREPARATIONS
3-01-002    PREPARATIVE
7-05-005    PREPARATORY
35-12-029   PREPARE
102-12-075  PREPARED
2-02-002    PREPAREDNESS
4-04-004    PREPARES
22-11-022   PREPARING
1-01-001    PREPAYMENT
4-01-001    PREPOLYMER
2-02-002    PREPONDERANCE
1-01-001    PREPONDERANTLY
1-01-001    PREPONDERATING
2-01-001    PREPOSITION
3-01-001    PREPOSITIONAL
5-04-004    PREPOSTEROUS
2-01-001    PREPREPARED
1-01-001    PREPRINTING
1-01-001    PREPUBESCENT
1-01-001    PREPUBLICATION
1-01-001    PREPUPAL
1-01-001    PRERADIATION
2-01-002    PREREQUISITE
1-01-001    PREROGATIVE
2-02-002    PREROGATIVES
1-01-001    PRESAGE
1-01-001    PRESAGED
11-06-008   PRESBYTERIAN
1-01-001    PRESBYTERIAN-*ST
1-01-001    PRESBYTERIANISM
1-01-001    PRESCHOOL
5-03-003    PRESCRIBE
14-06-013   PRESCRIBED
1-01-001    PRESCRIBES
5-04-005    PRESCRIPTION
2-02-002    PRESCRIPTIONS
1-01-001    PRESCRIPTIVE
76-14-060   PRESENCE
2-02-002    PRESENCES
377-15-213  PRESENT
17-06-013   PRESENT-DAY
2-01-001    PRESENT-TIME
2-02-002    PRESENTABLE
33-08-026   PRESENTATION
1-01-001    PRESENTATIONAL
6-04-005    PRESENTATIONS
1-01-001    PRESENTE
82-13-069   PRESENTED
1-01-001    PRESENTER
10-08-010   PRESENTING
35-14-031   PRESENTLY
1-01-001    PRESENTLYE
1-01-001    PRESENTMENTS
1-01-001    PRESENTNESS
33-10-026   PRESENTS
17-06-008   PRESERVATION
35-14-032   PRESERVE
19-07-018   PRESERVED
11-06-008   PRESERVES
10-06-007   PRESERVING
2-02-002    PRESIDE
1-01-001    PRESIDED
11-05-010   PRESIDENCY
382-13-110  PRESIDENT
28-06-015   PRESIDENT'S
5-01-002    PRESIDENT-ELECT
34-10-020   PRESIDENTIAL
14-07-010   PRESIDENTS
10-07-007   PRESIDES
1-01-001    PRESIDING
127-13-061  PRESLEY
29-10-027   PRESS
1-01-001    PRESSED
3-01-001    PRESSED-PAPER
9-04-005    PRESSER
25-11-022   PRESSES
            PRESSING
```

Code	Word	Code	Word	Code	Word	Code	Word
185-14-084	PRESSURE	1-01-001	PRIDE-*VENUS	1-01-001	PRO-TEM	5-03-004	PROFESSIONS
1-01-001	PRESSURE-COOKER	2-02-002	PRIDES	1-01-001	PROBABILISTIC	57-11-035	PROFESSOR
1-01-001	PRESSURE-FORMED	1-01-001	PRIE-DIEU	20-04-004	PROBABILITIES	1-01-001	PROFESSOR'S
1-01-001	PRESSURE-HAPPY	16-06-008	PRIEST	36-07-014	PROBABILITY	16-08-013	PROFESSORS
1-01-001	PRESSURE-MEASURING	1-01-001	PRIEST'S	24-10-022	PROBABLE	1-01-001	PROFESSORSHIP
1-01-001	PRESSURE-SENSING	1-01-001	PRIESTLY	261-15-183	PROBABLY	1-01-001	PROFET
		16-07-011	PRIESTS	2-02-002	PROBATE	3-02-003	PROFFERED
1-01-001	PRESSURE-VOLUME-TEMPERATURE	6-01-001	PRIEUR	7-02-004	PROBATION	3-02-003	PROFICIENCY
		1-01-001	PRIM	6-04-006	PROBE	5-04-005	PROFICIENT
38-11-022	PRESSURES	2-02-003	PRIMA-FACIE	3-02-003	PROBED	15-03-006	PROFILE
1-01-001	PRESTIDIGITATOR	5-04-005	PRIMACY	3-01-001	PROBES	3-02-002	PROFILES
29-09-017	PRESTIGE	3-01-001	PRIMAL	5-05-005	PROBING	1-01-001	PROFILI
2-02-002	PRESTO	2-02-002	PRIMARIES	1-01-001	PROBINGS	28-10-019	PROFIT
2-02-002	PRESTON	64-09-045	PRIMARILY	1-01-001	PROBITY	3-01-001	PROFIT-MAXIMIZING
40-09-035	PRESUMABLY	96-11-061	PRIMARY	1-01-001	PROBL'Y		
3-01-001	PRESUME	1-01-001	PRIMATE	313-15-154	PROBLEM	1-01-001	PROFIT-MOTIVATED
12-05-011	PRESUMED	1-01-001	PRIMATES	2-02-002	PROBLEM-SOLVING		
3-03-003	PRESUMES	45-10-026	PRIME	3-02-002	PROBLEMATIC	1-01-001	PROFIT-SHARING
2-02-002	PRESUMING	2-02-002	PRIMED	1-01-001	PROBLEMATICAL	1-01-001	PROFITABILITY
3-01-001	PRESUMPTION	1-01-001	PRIMERS	247-14-136	PROBLEMS	14-07-014	PROFITABLE
1-01-001	PRESUMPTIONS	2-01-001	PRIMES	1-01-001	PROBLY	4-01-002	PROFITABLY
4-03-004	PRESUMPTUOUS	1-01-001	PRIMEVAL	1-01-001	PROCAINE	3-02-003	PROFITED
1-01-001	PRESUPPOSE	7-04-005	PRIMING	7-04-005	PROCEDURAL	21-07-013	PROFITS
1-01-001	PRESUPPOSED	38-11-029	PRIMITIVE	79-13-044	PROCEDURE	27-11-027	PROFOUND
2-02-002	PRESUPPOSES	1-01-001	PRIMITIVE-ECLOGUE	61-08-034	PROCEDURES	1-01-001	PROFOUNDEST
1-01-001	PRESUPPOSITION			18-06-018	PROCEED	1-01-001	PROFOUNDITY
1-01-001	PRESUPPOSITIONS	1-01-001	PRIMITIVISM	25-11-022	PROCEEDED	8-06-007	PROFOUNDLY
4-03-004	PRETENCE	2-02-002	PRIMLY	12-04-008	PROCEEDING	3-03-003	PROFUNDITY
8-06-008	PRETEND	1-01-001	PRIMPING	18-07-014	PROCEEDINGS	2-02-002	PROFUSE
6-03-006	PRETENDED	33-06-014	PRINCE	16-08-016	PROCEEDS	3-03-003	PROFUSELY
2-02-002	PRETENDER	3-01-001	PRINCE'S	196-14-087	PROCESS	2-01-002	PROFUSION
12-06-010	PRETENDING	3-02-003	PRINCES	1-01-001	PROCESS-SERVER	1-01-001	PROGANDIST
2-02-002	PRETENDS	1-01-001	PRINCES'	12-03-006	PROCESSED	2-02-002	PROGENY
6-02-006	PRETENSE	10-05-007	PRINCESS	57-10-030	PROCESSES	1-01-001	PROGNOSES
1-01-001	PRETENSES	1-01-001	PRINCESS-IN-A-CARRIAGE	38-07-017	PROCESSING	2-02-002	PROGNOSIS
1-01-001	PRETENSIONS			5-04-005	PROCESSION	1-01-001	PROGNOSTICATION
6-03-005	PRETENTIOUS	2-01-001	PRINCESSE	1-01-001	PROCESSIONAL	1-01-001	PROGNOSTICATOR
1-01-001	PRETEST	7-03-004	PRINCETON	4-01-002	PROCESSOR	394-13-119	PROGRAM
3-03-003	PRETEXT	92-12-061	PRINCIPAL	1-01-001	PROCESSORS	1-01-001	PROGRAM'S
2-02-002	PRETEXTS	10-08-010	PRINCIPALLY	13-06-007	PROCLAIM	2-02-002	PROGRAMED
1-01-001	PRETRIAL	4-03-004	PRINCIPALS	9-08-009	PROCLAIMED	13-02-003	PROGRAMING
4-02-003	PRETTIER	109-12-061	PRINCIPIA	4-03-003	PROCLAIMING	3-03-003	PROGRAMMED
4-03-004	PRETTIEST	71-11-049	PRINCIPLE	4-03-004	PROCLAIMS	3-01-001	PROGRAMMER
2-02-002	PRETTILY	18-09-014	PRINCIPLES	14-05-005	PROCLAMATION	1-01-001	PROGRAMMES
1-01-001	PRETTINESS	1-01-001	PRINT	3-03-003	PROCLAMATIONS	5-02-004	PROGRAMMING
107-14-075	PRETTY	36-10-025	PRINTABLE	1-01-001	PROCLIVITIES	139-10-056	PROGRAMS
2-01-001	PRETTYMAN	1-01-001	PRINTED	1-01-001	PROCRASTINATE	120-12-078	PROGRESS
7-04-007	PREVAIL	3-01-002	PRINTEMPS	1-01-001	PROCRASTINATION	13-07-012	PROGRESSED
1-01-001	PREVAILE	1-01-001	PRINTER	1-01-001	PROCREATION	6-04-005	PROGRESSES
7-06-007	PREVAILED	18-05-010	PRINTER'S	1-01-001	PROCREATIVE	2-02-002	PROGRESSING
1-01-001	PREVAILIN	1-01-001	PRINTING	1-01-001	PROCREATIVITY	2-02-002	PROGRESSION
17-06-015	PREVAILING	10-05-009	PRINTMAKING	1-01-001	PROCTOR	3-02-002	PROGRESSIONS
7-03=005	PREVAILS	47-10-034	PRINTS	1-01-001	PROCTORS	17-07-010	PROGRESSIVE
4-04-004	PREVALENCE	1-01-001	PRIOR	4-01-002	PROCURE	6-03-006	PROGRESSIVELY
5-04-005	PREVALENT	5-03-004	PRIOR-YEAR	4-03-004	PROCURED	3-01-001	PROGRESSIVISM
1-01-001	PREVAYLE	18-05-014	PRIORITIES	21-04-009	PROCUREMENT	2-02-002	PROHIBIT
83-12-061	PREVENT	1-01-001	PRIORITY	3-02-002	PROCURER	8-07-007	PROHIBITED
27-10-023	PREVENTED	2-02-002	PRIORY	2-02-002	PROD	4-03-004	PROHIBITING
10-06-007	PREVENTING	3-03-003	PRIPET	3-03-003	PRODDED	13-06-009	PROHIBITION
27-06-009	PREVENTION	1-01-001	PRISCA	1-01-001	PRODDING	1-01-001	PROHIBITIVE
15-06-007	PREVENTIVE	42-09-025	PRISON	1-01-001	PRODIGAL	1-01-001	PROHIBITON
10-07-009	PREVENTS	7-05-006	PRISONER	1-01-001	PRODIGALL	1-01-001	PROHIBITS
1-01-001	PREVIEW	21-06-011	PRISONERS	1-01-001	PRODIGALLY	93-13-058	PROJECT
86-12-076	PREVIOUS	3-02-002	PRISONERS'	1-01-001	PRODIGIES	14-07-013	PROJECTED
58-11-049	PREVIOUSLY	3-02-002	PRISONS	4-04-004	PRODIGIOUS	1-01-001	PROJECTILE
2-01-001	PREVISION	2-02-002	PRISTINE	3-02-003	PRODIGY	1-01-001	PROJECTILES
2-01-001	PREVISIONS	12-08-010	PRIVACY	82-13-063	PRODUCE	6-05-005	PROJECTING
1-01-001	PREVOST	191-14-102	PRIVATE	90-12-066	PRODUCED	9-03-008	PROJECTION
9-01-001	PREVOT	1-01-001	PRIVATE-EYE	16-09-014	PRODUCER	10-03-006	PROJECTIONS
1-01-001	PREWAR	1-01-001	PRIVATE-SCHOOL	1-01-001	PRODUCER-HUBBY	2-02-002	PROJECTIVE
1-01-001	PREXY	13-07-011	PRIVATELY	1-01-001	PRODUCERS	1-01-001	PROJECTOR
7-05-007	PREY	14-08-009	PRIVATELY-OWNED	1-01-001	PRODUCERS'	68-08-028	PROJECTS
1-01-001	PREYING	2-02-002	PRIVATIONS	19-07-017	PRODUCES	33-02-004	PROKOFIEFF
2-01-001	PRIAM	1-01-001	PRIVET	6-01-001	PRODUCIN	6-01-001	PROKOFIEFF'S
108-12-044	PRICE	1-01-001	PRIVIES	35-09-030	PRODUCING	3-02-003	PROLETARIAT
3-01-001	PRICE-CONSCIOUSNESS	18-08-015	PRIVILEGE	87-09-044	PRODUCT	1-01-001	PROLIFERATED
		10-07-009	PRIVILEGED	148-12-072	PRODUCTION	5-04-005	PROLIFERATION
1-01-001	PRICE-CUTTING	10-05-008	PRIVILEGES	7-05-007	PRODUCTIONS	2-02-002	PROLIFIC
3-02-002	PRICE-EARNINGS	1-01-001	PRIVY	25-07-015	PRODUCTIVE	2-01-001	PROLIXITY
1-01-001	PRICE-LEVEL	4-02-002	PRIX	17-06-011	PRODUCTIVITY	1-01-001	PROLONG
1-01-001	PRICE-SETTING	2-02-002	PRIZE	1-01-001	PRODUCTIVITY-SHARE	1-01-001	PROLONGATION
1-01-001	PRICE-WISE	28-09-020	PRIZE-FIGHT			16-08-015	PROLONGED
4-02-003	PRICED	1-01-001	PRIZE-WINNING	108-09-040	PRODUCTS	2-02-002	PROLONGING
5-04-005	PRICELESS	1-01-001	PRIZED	4-03-004	PROF	1-01-001	PROLONGS
61-07-025	PRICES	2-01-002	PRIZES	4-04-004	PROFANE	5-01-001	PROLUSION
7-03-005	PRICING	6-04-005	PRO	5-04-005	PROFANITY	4-01-001	PROLUSIONS
2-02-002	PRICK	16-06-014	PRO-*CASTRO	5-03-005	PROFESS	1-01-001	PROMAZINE
1-01-001	PRICKED	5-04-005	PRO-*COMMUNIST	3-03-003	PROFESSED	3-01-001	PROMENADE
1-01-001	PRICKING	1-01-001	PRO-*EUROPE	1-01-001	PROFESSEDLY	1-01-001	PROMENADES
2-02-002	PRICKLY	1-01-001	PRO-*HEARST	1-01-001	PROFESSES	1-01-001	PROMETHEUS
1-01-001	PRICKS	1-01-001	PRO-*TRUJILLO	1-01-001	PROFESSEUR	5-05-005	PROMINENCE
1-01-001	PRIDDY	1-01-001	PRO-*U**.*N**.*F**.*P	2-02-002	PROFESSING	40-13-032	PROMINENT
42-14-037	PRIDE	12-04-008	PRO-*WESTERN	37-11-029	PROFESSION	8-04-007	PROMINENTLY
1-01-001	PRIDE'S	1-01-001	PRO-*YANKEE	105-15-063	PROFESSIONAL	45-12-035	PROMISE
2-01-001	PRIDE-*STARLETTE	1-01-001	PRO-BALL	2-01-001	PROFESSIONALISM	45-12-040	PROMISED
		1-01-001	PRO-NEUTRALIST	5-05-005	PROFESSIONALLY	20-11-019	PROMISES
				10-09-009	PROFESSIONALS	24-10-021	PROMISING

32-08-023	PROMOTE
12-08-011	PROMOTED
1-01-001	PROMOTER
4-03-004	PROMOTERS
4-04-004	PROMOTES
13-06-011	PROMOTING
26-09-014	PROMOTION
6-03-004	PROMOTIONAL
11-07-009	PROMPT
7-05-007	PROMPTED
1-01-001	PROMPTINGS
28-12-025	PROMPTLY
2-02-002	PROMPTS
2-02-002	PROMULGATED
1-01-001	PROMULGATING
1-01-001	PROMULGATORS
14-07-012	PRONE
1-01-001	PRONENESS
4-02-002	PRONOUN
2-02-002	PRONOUNCE
18-09-017	PRONOUNCED
3-02-003	PRONOUNCEMENT
2-02-002	PRONOUNCEMENTS
1-01-001	PRONOUNCING
4-03-004	PRONOUNS
1-01-001	PRONTO
40-12-027	PROOF
7-05-006	PROP
30-08-021	PROPAGANDA
3-03-003	PROPAGANDIST
4-01-001	PROPAGANDISTIC
4-01-002	PROPAGANDISTS
1-01-001	PROPAGATE
1-01-001	PROPAGATED
8-03-004	PROPAGATION
4-03-004	PROPEL
1-01-001	PROPELLED
2-02-002	PROPELLER
1-01-001	PROPELLER-DRIVEN
1-01-001	PROPELLING
95-14-071	PROPER
55-14-046	PROPERLY
66-10-031	PROPERTIES
1-01-001	PROPERTIUS
156-13-061	PROPERTY
1-01-001	PROPHECIES
5-04-005	PROPHECY
4-03-004	PROPHESIED
1-01-001	PROPHESIES
5-03-005	PROPHET
2-02-002	PROPHETIC
3-03-003	PROPHETICALLY
4-03-004	PROPHETS
2-01-002	PROPIONATE
1-01-001	PROPITIATE
2-01-002	PROPITIOUS
2-02-002	PROPONENT
6-03-003	PROPONENTS
29-09-021	PROPORTION
14-01-006	PROPORTIONAL
1-01-001	PROPORTIONALITY
1-01-001	PROPORTIONALLY
9-05-007	PROPORTIONATE
9-05-007	PROPORTIONATELY
18-08-017	PROPORTIONS
41-12-032	PROPOSAL
29-05-016	PROPOSALS
13-08-011	PROPOSE
84-11-053	PROPOSED
7-04-007	PROPOSES
6-05-006	PROPOSING
16-07-013	PROPOSITION
1-01-001	PROPOSITIONED
2-02-002	PROPOSITIONS
3-03-003	PROPPED
1-01-001	PROPPING
2-02-002	PROPRIETER
11-06-007	PROPRIETOR
5-04-004	PROPRIETORS
9-02-002	PROPRIETORSHIP
3-01-001	PROPRIETORSHIPS
1-01-001	PROPRIETORY
7-05-006	PROPRIETY
6-06-006	PROPS
6-03-004	PROPULSION
1-01-001	PROPULSIONS
1-01-001	PROPYLAEA
1-01-001	PROPYLTHIOURACIL
1-01-001	PRORATE
2-02-002	PROS
2-02-002	PROSAIC
1-01-001	PROSCENIUMS
1-01-001	PROSCRIBE
1-01-001	PROSCRIBED
3-02-002	PROSCRIPTION

14-04-010	PROSE
2-02-002	PROSECUTE
5-03-004	PROSECUTED
3-03-003	PROSECUTING
9-05-007	PROSECUTION
1-01-001	PROSECUTION'S
1-01-001	PROSECUTIONS
8-03-005	PROSECUTOR
2-01-001	PROSECUTORS
1-01-001	PROSELYTIZING
3-01-002	PROSODIC
1-01-001	PROSODIES
1-01-001	PROSOPOPOEIA
25-10-019	PROSPECT
21-08-019	PROSPECTIVE
24-10-019	PROSPECTS
3-02-003	PROSPER
2-02-002	PROSPERED
1-01-001	PROSPERING
14-08-011	PROSPERITY
8-04-006	PROSPEROUS
1-01-001	PROSPERS
1-01-001	PROSSED
1-01-001	PROSSER
2-02-002	PROSTATE
6-02-002	PROSTITUTE
3-03-003	PROSTITUTES
10-04-006	PROSTITUTION
2-02-002	PROSTRATE
2-02-002	PROTAGONIST
2-01-002	PROTEASE
3-02-002	PROTEASES
5-03-005	PROTECT
1-01-001	PROTECTED
7-02-003	PROTECTING
68-11-035	PROTECTION
14-09-013	PROTECTIVE
1-01-001	PROTECTIVELY
1-01-001	PROTECTORATE
4-02-004	PROTECTS
1-01-001	PROTEGE
21-05-008	PROTEIN
1-01-001	PROTEIN-BOUND
14-02-005	PROTEINS
2-01-001	PROTEOLYSIS
1-01-001	PROTEOLYTIC
23-10-021	PROTEST
51-07-016	PROTESTANT
1-01-001	PROTESTANT-DOMINATED
11-03-004	PROTESTANTISM
14-03-006	PROTESTANTS
3-02-003	PROTESTATIONS
13-05-012	PROTESTED
7-05-007	PROTESTING
11-05-010	PROTESTS
1-01-001	PROTITCH
1-01-001	PROTO-*ATHABASCAN
1-01-001	PROTO-*YOKUTS
1-01-001	PROTO-SENILITY
3-03-003	PROTOCOL
3-01-001	PROTOGEOMETRIC
3-02-002	PROTON
3-02-003	PROTONS
1-01-001	PROTOPLASM
1-01-001	PROTOPLASMIC
3-02-003	PROTOTYPE
1-01-001	PROTOTYPICAL
7-01-001	PROTOZOA
1-01-001	PROTOZOAN
1-01-001	PROTRACTED
1-01-001	PROTRUDE
4-03-004	PROTRUDED
3-03-003	PROTRUDING
1-01-001	PROTRUSION
1-01-001	PROTUBERANCE
50-12-045	PROUD
1-01-001	PROUDER
1-01-001	PROUDEST
1-01-001	PROUDHON
9-06-009	PROUDLY
1-01-001	PROUST
1-01-001	PROVDIED
53-14-044	PROVE
71-13-062	PROVED
11-05-011	PROVEN
1-01-001	PROVENANCE
5-04-005	PROVERB
4-04-004	PROVERBIAL
1-01-001	PROVERBS
16-10-015	PROVES
216-13-123	PROVIDE
132-12-084	PROVIDED
80-08-019	PROVIDENCE
1-01-001	PROVIDENCE'S
1-01-001	PROVIDENTIAL

81-10-056	PROVIDES
59-12-051	PROVIDING
15-06-011	PROVINCE
12-07-009	PROVINCES
1-01-001	PROVINCETOWN
9-05-008	PROVINCIAL
3-01-003	PROVINCIALISM
5-03-005	PROVING
47-10-034	PROVISION
7-05-005	PROVISIONAL
1-01-001	PROVISIONED
39-09-019	PROVISIONS
3-03-003	PROVISO
1-01-001	PROVISONS
1-01-001	PROVOCATEURS
5-03-004	PROVOCATION
7-05-007	PROVOCATIVE
1-01-001	PROVOCATIVELY
3-03-003	PROVOKE
7-04-007	PROVOKED
4-04-004	PROVOKES
2-02-002	PROVOST
1-01-001	PROW
1-01-001	PROWAZWKI
2-02-002	PROWESS
2-02-002	PROWL
1-01-001	PROWLED
1-01-001	PROWLERS
2-02-002	PROWLING
2-01-002	PROXIMAL
3-02-002	PROXIMATE
5-03-005	PROXIMITY
1-01-001	PROXMIRE
7-02-003	PROXY
6-03-005	PRUDENCE
2-02-002	PRUDENT
1-01-001	PRUDENTIAL
1-01-001	PRUDENTIALLY
1-01-001	PRUDENTLY
1-01-001	PRUNE
1-01-001	PRUNED
1-01-001	PRUNES
1-01-001	PRURIENT
2-01-001	PRUSSIA
1-01-001	PRUSSIAN
1-01-001	PRUTA
6-05-006	PRY
1-01-001	PRYING
4-01-002	PSALM
5-01-001	PSALMIST
1-01-001	PSEUDO
2-01-001	PSEUDO-ANTHROPOLOGICAL
2-01-001	PSEUDO-CAPITALISM
1-01-001	PSEUDO-EMOTION
1-01-001	PSEUDO-FEELING
2-01-001	PSEUDO-GLAMOROUS
1-01-001	PSEUDO-HAPPINESS
1-01-001	PSEUDO-PATRIOTISM
1-01-001	PSEUDO-QUESTIONS
1-01-001	PSEUDO-SCIENTIFIC
1-01-001	PSEUDO-SOPHISTICATION
1-01-001	PSEUDO-SYMMETRIC
2-01-001	PSEUDO-THINKING
1-01-001	PSEUDO-WILLING
1-01-001	PSEUDOMONAS
1-01-001	PSEUDONYM
6-01-001	PSEUDOPHLOEM
1-01-001	PSEUDYNOM
1-01-001	PSI
1-01-001	PSI.
1-01-001	PSI,
5-01-001	PSITHYRUS
7-05-007	PSYCHE
1-01-001	PSYCHES
5-02-003	PSYCHIATRIC
4-03-004	PSYCHIATRIST
5-02-004	PSYCHIATRISTS
3-02-002	PSYCHIATRY
3-03-003	PSYCHIC
4-02-002	PSYCHICAL
2-01-001	PSYCHICALLY
1-01-001	PSYCHICALLY-BLIND
1-01-001	PSYCHO-PHYSIOLOGY
2-01-001	PSYCHOACTIVE
5-01-003	PSYCHOANALYSIS
1-01-001	PSYCHOANALYST

7-02-005	PSYCHOANALYTIC
40-08-028	PSYCHOLOGICAL
1-01-001	PSYCHOLOGICAL-INTELLECTUAL
1-01-001	PSYCHOLOGICAL-INTELLECTUAL-VOLITIONAL
4-03-004	PSYCHOLOGICALLY
10-03-007	PSYCHOLOGIST
11-04-007	PSYCHOLOGISTS
14-06-013	PSYCHOLOGY
2-02-002	PSYCHOPATH
3-02-003	PSYCHOPATHIC
1-01-001	PSYCHOPHARMACOLOGICAL
1-01-001	PSYCHOPOMP
1-01-001	PSYCHOSOMATIC
1-01-001	PSYCHOTHERAPEUTIC
1-01-001	PSYCHOTHERAPISTS
6-03-005	PSYCHOTHERAPY
1-01-001	PSYCHOTIC
3-01-001	PSYLLIUM
1-01-001	PT
1-01-001	PTERYGIA
12-01-002	PTOLEMAIC
1-01-001	PTOLEMAISTS
8-01-001	PTOLEMY
6-01-001	PTOLEMY'S
1-01-001	PUALANI
1-01-001	PUB
1-01-001	PUBERTY
3-01-001	PUBESCENT
438-14-180	PUBLIC
6-03-006	PUBLIC'S
1-01-001	PUBLIC-ADDRESS
1-01-001	PUBLIC-LIMIT
8-01-001	PUBLIC-OPINION
2-01-001	PUBLIC-SCHOOL
2-02-002	PUBLIC-SPIRITED
3-03-003	PUBLICALLY
55-07-029	PUBLICATION
23-05-011	PUBLICATIONS
1-01-001	PUBLICISTS
27-12-023	PUBLICITY
6-05-006	PUBLICIZED
2-02-002	PUBLICIZING
3-01-001	PUBLICK
27-13-025	PUBLICLY
2-01-001	PUBLIQUE
3-03-003	PUBLISH
89-12-053	PUBLISHED
9-05-006	PUBLISHER
11-06-008	PUBLISHERS
4-04-004	PUBLISHES
14-07-011	PUBLISHING
1-01-001	PUBS
3-01-001	PUCCINI'S
2-02-002	PUCKERED
1-01-001	PUCKERING
1-01-001	PUCKISH
1-01-001	PUDDINGS
1-01-001	PUDDINGSTONE
1-01-001	PUDDLE
2-02-002	PUDDLES
1-01-001	PUERI
1-01-001	PUERILE
24-05-009	PUERTO
1-01-001	PUFF
4-03-003	PUFFED
2-02-002	PUFFING
1-01-001	PUFFS
2-02-002	PUFFY
1-01-001	PUG-NOSED
2-01-001	PUGH
2-02-002	PUISSANT
1-01-001	PUKE
1-01-001	PULASKI
3-02-002	PULITZER
51-13-042	PULL
73-12-054	PULLED
4-02-002	PULLEN
11-02-002	PULLEY
2-01-001	PULLEYS
25-08-019	PULLING
2-01-001	PULLINGS
1-01-001	PULLMAN
1-01-001	PULLMAN'S
1-01-001	PULLMANS
1-01-001	PULLOVER
9-05-007	PULLS
27-01-002	PULMONARY
2-01-001	PULOVA
5-03-004	PULP
4-04-004	PULPIT
1-01-001	PULPITS

3-03-003	PULSATING	13-06-009	PURPLE	1-01-001	QUADRICEPS	1-01-001	QUESTION-AND-AN
2-02-002	PULSATION	1-01-001	PURPLE-BLACK	1-01-001	QUADRILLE		SWER
1-01-001	PULSATIONS	1-01-001	PURPLING	1-01-001	QUADRILLION	9-06-008	QUESTIONABLE
9-06-008	PULSE	2-02-002	PURPORT	1-01-001	QUADRIPARTITE	1-01-001	QUESTIONAIRE
1-01-001	PULSE-JET	4-02-004	PURPORTED	1-01-001	QUADRUPLE	29-10-028	QUESTIONED
1-01-001	PULSE-TIMING	1-01-001	PURPORTEDLY	1-01-001	QUADRUPLED	2-02-002	QUESTIONER
1-01-001	PULSED	2-02-002	PURPORTING	1-01-001	QUADRUPLING	1-01-001	QUESTIONERS
2-02-002	PULSING	2-01-002	PURPORTS	1-01-001	QUAGMIRE	21-10-018	QUESTIONING
2-02-002	PULVERIZED	149-14-107	PURPOSE	12-08-012	QUAINT	1-01-001	QUESTIONINGLY
1-01-001	PULVERIZING	1-01-001	PURPOSED	2-01-001	QUAKE	37-03-005	QUESTIONNAIRE
1-01-001	PUMBLECHOOK	3-02-003	PURPOSEFUL	1-01-001	QUAKE'S	6-01-002	QUESTIONNAIRES
2-01-001	PUMBLECHOOK'S	1-01-001	PURPOSEFULLY	6-05-005	QUAKER	140-14-094	QUESTIONS
1-01-001	PUMMELED	1-01-001	PURPOSELESS	1-01-001	QUAKERESS	2-01-001	QUETZAL
11-03-006	PUMP	5-05-005	PURPOSELY	4-03-004	QUAKERS	2-01-001	QUEUED
2-01-001	PUMP-ACTION	90-13-055	PURPOSES	1-01-001	QUAKING	1-01-001	QUI
1-01-001	PUMP-PRIMING	3-01-002	PURPOSIVE	8-05-008	QUALIFICATION	1-01-001	QUIBBLE
3-03-003	PUMPED	1-01-001	PURPOSIVELY	16-10-013	QUALIFICATIONS	1-01-001	QUIBS
2-01-001	PUMPED-UP	3-02-003	PURRING	24-10-021	QUALIFIED	1-01-001	QUIBUSDAM
8-05-008	PUMPING	14-09-013	PURSE	2-02-002	QUALIFIES	68-14-060	QUICK
2-02-002	PUMPKIN	3-02-003	PURSED	15-07-013	QUALIFY	1-01-001	QUICK-*WATE
5-04-004	PUMPS	1-01-001	PURSES	1-01-001	QUALIFYING	1-01-001	QUICK-DRYING
1-01-001	PUN	1-01-001	PURSEWARDEN	6-03-005	QUALITATIVE	1-01-001	QUICK-FROZEN
5-04-004	PUNCH	27-01-004	PURSUANT	2-02-002	QUALITATIVELY	1-01-001	QUICK-HANDLING
1-01-001	PUNCHBOWL	20-07-018	PURSUE	45-10-036	QUALITIES	1-01-001	QUICK-KILL
1-01-001	PUNCHED	14-07-014	PURSUED	114-13-071	QUALITY	1-01-001	QUICKEN
1-01-001	PUNCHED-CARD	2-02-002	PURSUER	1-01-001	QUALMS	1-01-001	QUICKENED
3-01-002	PUNCHER	2-02-002	PURSUERS	1-01-001	QUAM	2-02-002	QUICKENING
1-01-001	PUNCHES	2-02-002	PURSUES	9-04-007	QUANTITATIVE	6-05-005	QUICKER
2-02-002	PUNCHING	9-08-009	PURSUING	4-02-004	QUANTITATIVELY	1-01-001	QUICKEST
1-01-001	PUNCTUALITY	16-08-013	PURSUIT	11-06-010	QUANTITIES	2-02-002	QUICKIE
2-02-002	PUNCTUALLY	3-02-003	PURSUITS	33-11-026	QUANTITY	89-14-071	QUICKLY
4-03-004	PUNCTUATED	1-01-001	PURTIEST	5-01-002	QUANTUM	1-01-001	QUICKNESS
2-02-002	PUNCTUATION	1-01-001	PURVEYOR	20-08-016	QUARREL	2-02-002	QUICKSILVER
3-03-003	PUNCTURED	1-01-001	PURVEYORS	4-04-004	QUARRELED	2-02-002	QUICKSTEP
1-01-001	PUNCTURING	4-01-001	PURVIS	5-05-005	QUARRELING	2-02-002	QUIESCENT
1-01-001	PUNDITRY	37-11-030	PUSH	4-03-004	QUARRELS	76-15-059	QUIET
1-01-001	PUNDITS	1-01-001	PUSH-*=UP	2-01-002	QUARRELSOME	1-01-001	QUIET-SPOKEN
1-01-001	PUNGENCY	9-01-001	PUSH-*PULL	7-04-007	QUARRY	3-03-003	QUIETED
4-04-004	PUNGENT	3-02-002	PUSH-UP	1-01-001	QUARRYMEN	4-03-004	QUIETER
1-01-001	PUNGENTLY	4-02-002	PUSH-UPS	3-03-003	QUART	2-01-001	QUIETISM
3-02-003	PUNISH	53-11-045	PUSHED	34-14-028	QUARTER	2-01-001	QUIETIST
1-01-001	PUNISHABLE	3-01-001	PUSHERS	2-02-002	QUARTER-CENTURY	48-12-042	QUIETLY
7-04-007	PUNISHED	3-02-002	PUSHES	1-01-001	QUARTER-CENTURY	3-02-002	QUIETNESS
1-01-001	PUNISHES	2-01-001	PUSHIN		-OLD	9-02-002	QUILL
1-01-001	PUNISHING	17-10-017	PUSHING	1-01-001	QUARTER-INCH	1-01-001	QUILTED
21-07-017	PUNISHMENT	2-01-001	PUSHUP	2-02-002	QUARTER-MILE	2-01-001	QUINCE
2-02-002	PUNISHMENTS	5-02-002	PUSSY	1-01-001	QUARTER-TO-QUAR	4-03-004	QUINCY
1-01-001	PUNITIVE	1-01-001	PUSSYCAT		TER	23-01-001	QUINEY
2-02-002	PUNK	437-15-251	PUT	5-01-003	QUARTERBACK	2-01-001	QUINEY'S
1-01-001	PUNKS	1-01-001	PUT-UPON	1-01-001	QUARTERBACKS	11-01-001	QUINT
2-01-001	PUNNISHED	1-01-001	PUTAINS	7-03-006	QUARTERLY	2-01-001	QUINT'S
1-01-001	PUNSTER	1-01-001	PUTAS	1-01-001	QUARTERMASTER	1-01-001	QUINTANA
1-01-001	PUNTED	1-01-001	PUTOUT	28-11-026	QUARTERS	3-02-003	QUINTET
6-03-003	PUNY	20-11-019	PUTS	9-04-005	QUARTET	1-01-001	QUINTETS
2-02-002	PUP	7-01-002	PUTT	1-01-001	QUARTS	1-01-001	QUINTILLION
1-01-001	PUPATED	1-01-001	PUTTANA	1-01-001	QUARTZ	3-01-001	QUINTUS
1-01-001	PUPATES	1-01-001	PUTTED	1-01-001	QUASHED	4-01-001	QUINZAINE
20-06-007	PUPIL	1-01-001	PUTTER	1-01-001	QUASI-FOLK	1-01-001	QUIPPING
25-09-013	PUPILS	2-02-002	PUTTERING	1-01-001	QUASI-GOVERNMEN	1-01-001	QUIRINAL
6-03-003	PUPPET	1-01-001	PUTTIN		TAL	1-01-001	QUIRK
1-01-001	PUPPET'S	54-14-050	PUTTING	1-01-001	QUASI-MECHANIST	1-01-001	QUIRKING
5-01-001	PUPPETS	1-01-001	PUTTY		IC	1-01-001	QUIRKS
1-01-001	PUPPIES	1-01-001	PUTTY-LIKE	1-01-001	QUASI-PERFORMER	8-01-002	QUIRT
2-02-002	PUPPY	10-09-009	PUZZLE	1-01-001	QUASI-RECITATIV	15-08-013	QUIT
1-01-001	PUPPYISH	19-08-017	PUZZLED		E	281-15-173	QUITE
2-02-002	PUPS	1-01-001	PUZZLEMENT	3-01-001	QUASIMODO	1-01-001	QUITELY
1-01-001	PURCELL	1-01-001	PUZZLER	2-01-001	QUASIMODO'S	1-01-001	QUITS
47-09-026	PURCHASE	4-03-003	PUZZLES	2-02-002	QUATRAIN	4-03-004	QUITTING
20-09-017	PURCHASED	9-04-008	PUZZLING	1-01-001	QUAVER	1-01-001	QUIVERED
1-01-001	PURCHASER'S	1-01-001	PVT	1-01-001	QUAVERED	7-04-007	QUIVERING
4-03-003	PURCHASERS	1-01-001	PYE	2-02-002	QUAVERING	1-01-001	QUIVERS
16-05-010	PURCHASES	1-01-001	PYHRRIC	1-01-001	QUE	4-01-002	QUIXOTE
17-05-010	PURCHASING	2-01-001	PYKNOTIC	1-01-001	QUEASINESS	2-02-002	QUIXOTIC
12-01-001	PURDEW	1-01-001	PYNTE	2-02-002	QUEBEC	2-02-002	QUIZ
1-01-001	PURDUE'S	1-01-001	PYOCANEA	1-01-001	QUEBEC'S	2-02-002	QUIZZICAL
56-11-040	PURE	1-01-001	PYORRHEA	41-09-018	QUEEN	11-05-010	QUO
30-08-027	PURELY	1-01-001	PYRAMID	1-01-001	QUEEN'S	1-01-001	QUOD
3-03-003	PUREST	10-03-003	PYRAMIDAL	10-03-003	QUEENS	1-01-001	QUOK
2-01-002	PURGATION	1-01-001	PYRAMIDS	2-01-001	QUEENS'	4-04-004	QUOTA
2-02-002	PURGATORY	1-01-001	PYRE	6-03-006	QUEER	2-01-001	QUOTAS
2-07-002	PURGE	5-01-001	PYREX	1-01-001	QUEERER	4-02-003	QUOTATION
2-02-002	PURGED	3-01-001	PYROMETER	1-01-001	QUEEREST	5-04-005	QUOTATIONS
3-03-003	PURGES	1-01-001	PYROMETERS	1-01-001	QUELCH	17-06-015	QUOTE
2-02-002	PURGING	1-01-001	PYROPHOSPHATE	3-03-003	QUELL	26-10-022	QUOTED
4-02-004	PURIFICATION	1-01-001	PYSCHIATRIST	1-01-001	QUELLING	5-04-005	QUOTES
10-03-007	PURIFIED	1-01-001	PYTHAGOREANS	2-02-002	QUEMOY	3-03-003	QUOTING
2-02-002	PURIFY	14-01-001	PYTHON	1-01-001	QUENCH	1-01-001	QUYNE
1-01-001	PURIFYING	2-02-002	Q	1-01-001	QUENCHING	1-01-001	QUYNEY
1-01-001	PURISM	1-01-001	Q*=T	3-03-003	QUERIED	66-11-044	R
1-01-001	PURISTS	2-02-002	QUA	3-03-003	QUERIES	1-01-001	R)
5-03-005	PURITAN	9-01-001	QUACK	1-01-001	QUERULOUS	2-02-002	R**.'S
1-01-001	PURITANICAL	1-01-001	QUACKED	1-01-001	QUERULOUSLY	1-01-001	R**.*A**.*F
3-01-002	PURITANS	6-01-002	QUACKERY	2-01-001	QUERY	2-01-001	R**.*H
12-07-012	PURITY	9-01-001	QUACKS	1-01-001	QUERYING	1-01-001	R**.*L
2-02-002	PURLED	2-01-001	QUADRATIC	16-06-011	QUEST	2-01-001	R**.P**.M
1-01-001	PURLING	1-01-001	QUADRENNIAL	257-15-151	QUESTION	1-01-001	RABAT
1-01-001	PURLOINED	7-01-001	QUADRIC			1-01-001	RABAUL

2-01-001	RABB	1-01-001	RAFTERS	1-01-001	RANCHO	373-15-232	RATHER
1-01-001	RABBETING	1-01-001	RAFTS	1-01-001	RANCIDITY	5-03-003	RATIFICATION
13-02-003	RABBI	10-05-007	RAG	3-02-003	RANCOR	4-03-004	RATIFIED
1-01-001	RABBI'S	16-08-014	RAGE	2-02-002	RANCOROUS	1-01-001	RATIFY
11-05-007	RABBIT	8-05-008	RAGED	1-01-001	RAND	10-03-005	RATING
5-05-005	RABBITS	1-01-001	RAGES	1-01-001	RANDALL	9-02-005	RATINGS
2-02-002	RABBLE	9-06-009	RAGGED	9-01-001	RANDOLPH	36-04-018	RATIO
2-01-002	RABID	1-01-001	RAGGEDNESS	38-09-019	RANDOM	1-01-001	RATIOCINATING
1-01-001	RABIES	2-01-001	RAGGING	1-01-001	RANDOM-STORAGE	10-05-005	RATION
1-01-001	RACCOON	2-02-002	RAGING	1-01-001	RANDOMIZATION	25-04-016	RATIONAL
103-12-054	RACE	7-05-007	RAGS	2-01-002	RANDOMLY	6-05-005	RATIONALE
3-01-001	RACE-DRIVER	10-05-006	RAID	1-01-001	RANDY	4-01-002	RATIONALISM
4-01-001	RACE-DRIVERS	1-01-001	RAIDED	21-05-017	RANG	3-03-003	RATIONALIST
12-06-012	RACED	1-01-001	RAIDERS	160-15-089	RANGE	1-01-001	RATIONALISTIC
1-01-001	RACERS	1-01-001	RAIDERS'	18-06-012	RANGED	1-01-001	RATIONALITY
21-10-015	RACES	2-02-002	RAIDING	2-01-001	RANGELANDS	2-02-002	RATIONALIZATION
2-01-002	RACETRACK	5-03-005	RAIDS	2-01-001	RANGER	1-01-001	RATIONALIZATIONS
2-01-001	RACEWAY	16-10-015	RAIL	2-02-002	RANGERS		
42-05-005	RACHEL	1-01-001	RAIL-MOBILE	10-06-009	RANGES	5-03-004	RATIONALIZE
2-01-001	RACHEL'S	1-01-001	RAILBIRDS	30-10-028	RANGING	1-01-001	RATIONALIZED
2-01-002	RACHMANINOFF	2-02-002	RAILHEAD	6-01-001	RANGONI	3-03-003	RATIONALLY
25-06-013	RACIAL	3-03-003	RAILING	2-01-001	RANGONI'S	3-03-003	RATIONED
1-01-001	RACIALLY	1-01-001	RAILLERY	2-02-002	RANGY	3-02-002	RATIONING
1-01-001	RACIE	58-10-027	RAILROAD	24-08-019	RANK	4-03-003	RATIONS
1-01-001	RACIN	3-03-003	RAILROAD'S	1-01-001	RANK-AND-FILE	18-04-007	RATIOS
2-01-001	RACINE	1-01-001	RAILROADER	1-01-001	RANKE	3-02-002	RATON
2-02-002	RACINE'S	1-01-001	RAILROADING	4-02-004	RANKED	1-01-001	RATOR
22-09-015	RACING	16-06-009	RAILROADS	1-01-001	RANKEST	3-02-002	RATS
1-01-001	RACISTS	9-05-006	RAILS	9-02-002	RANKIN	1-01-001	RATTAIL
9-05-009	RACK	12-08-010	RAILWAY	1-01-001	RANKIN'S	5-04-005	RATTLE
1-01-001	RACKED	1-01-001	RAILWAY-BASED	5-03-003	RANKING	2-02-002	RATTLED
5-05-005	RACKET	1-01-001	RAILWAYS	1-01-001	RANKLES	1-01-001	RATTLER
2-02-002	RACKFTEER	1-01-001	RAIMU	20-09-017	RANKS	1-01-001	RATTLERS
3-01-003	RACKETEERS	70-11-038	RAIN	2-02-002	RANSACK	1-01-001	RATTLES
3-03-003	RACKETS	1-01-001	RAIN'S	3-02-002	RANSACKED	3-02-002	RATTLESNAKE
2-02-002	RACKETY	1-01-001	RAIN-SLICK	1-01-001	RANSACKING	5-03-003	RATTLESNAKES
1-01-001	RACKING	4-03-003	RAINBOW	5-05-005	RANSOM	7-03-006	RATTLING
1-01-002	RACKMIL	1-01-001	RAINBOW-HUED	1-01-001	RANSY	1-01-001	RATTO
2-02-002	RACKS	1-01-001	RAINCOATS	1-01-001	RANTED	1-01-001	RATTZHENFUUT
1-01-001	RACQUET	1-01-001	RAINDROPS	1-01-001	RANYARD	7-05-007	RAUCOUS
2-02-002	RACY	1-01-001	RAINE	2-02-002	RAOUL	1-01-001	RAUCOUSLY
23-09-013	RADAR	4-04-004	RAINED	2-02-002	RAP	1-01-001	RAUSCHENBERG
3-01-001	RADAR-CONTROLLED	3-02-003	RAINFALL	5-04-005	RAPE	1-01-001	RAUSCHENBUSCH
		1-01-001	RAINIER	2-02-002	RAPED	2-02-002	RAVAGES
1-01-001	RADAR-TYPE	7-04-007	RAINING	1-01-001	RAPES	1-01-001	RAVEL-LIKE
1-01-001	RADETZKY	1-01-001	RAINLESS	4-02-002	RAPHAEL	1-01-001	RAVENCROFT
1-01-001	RADHAKRISHNAN	5-05-005	RAINS	1-01-001	RAPHAEL'S	2-01-002	RAVENOUS
5-03-005	RADIAL	2-02-002	RAINSTORM	1-01-001	RAPHAELS	1-01-001	RAVINE
3-03-003	RADIANCE	5-03-004	RAINY	43-10-037	RAPID	1-01-001	RAVINES
8-05-006	RADIANT	52-12-039	RAISE	1-01-001	RAPID-FIRE	3-02-003	RAVING
1-01-001	RADIATE	101-15-085	RAISED	1-01-001	RAPID-TRANSIT	43-13-028	RAW
4-04-004	RADIATED	1-01-001	RAISER	4-03-004	RAPIDITY	1-01-001	RAWBONED
1-01-001	RADIATES	16-08-015	RAISES	65-14-055	RAPIDLY	1-01-001	RAWHIDE
1-01-001	RADIATING	1-01-001	RAISIN	1-01-001	RAPIDLY-DIMINISHING	4-01-001	RAWLINGS
97-06-012	RADIATION	34-12-029	RAISING			3-01-001	RAWLINS
1-01-001	RADIATION-PRODUCED	1-01-001	RAJAH	1-01-001	RAPIER	3-02-003	RAWSON
		1-01-001	RAK	1-01-001	RAPING	19-08-016	RAY
3-02-002	RADIATIONS	11-04-004	RAKE	2-02-002	RAPISTS	39-04-006	RAYBURN
4-04-004	RADIATOR	4-03-004	RAKED	1-01-001	RAPOPORT	8-02-003	RAYBURN'S
2-01-002	RADIATORS	1-01-001	RAKESTRAW	4-03-004	RAPPED	1-01-001	RAYBURN-*JOHNSON
4-01-001	RADIC	1-01-001	RAKISH	3-01-001	RAPPING		
30-09-023	RADICAL	1-01-001	RAKISHLY	4-02-001	RAPPORT	17-06-014	RAYMOND
4-03-004	RADICALISM	5-02-002	RALL	1-01-001	RAPPROCHEMENT	1-01-001	RAYMONDVILLE
13-06-012	RADICALLY	1-01-001	RALLIED	1-01-001	RAPT	1-01-001	RAYMONT
4-03-003	RADICALS	3-02-003	RALLIES	3-03-003	RAPTURE	1-01-001	RAYNAL
4-02-003	RADII	10-06-010	RALLY	1-01-001	RAPTURES	9-04-009	RAYS
120-14-043	RADIO	2-01-002	RALLYING	1-01-001	RAPUNZEL	1-01-001	RAZING
3-03-003	RADIO-**J*T*V	22-06-016	RALPH	41-11-036	RARE	15-03-005	RAZOR
1-01-001	RADIO-TRANSMITTER	2-02-002	RAM	41-11-034	RARELY	1-01-001	RAZOR-EDGED
		3-03 003	RAMBLE	1-01-001	RARER	1-01-001	RAZOR-SHARP
10-05-007	RADIOACTIVE	1-01-001	RAMBLES	1-01-001	RARIFIED	1-01-001	RAZORBACK
3-03-003	RADIOACTIVITY	2-02-002	RAMBLING	2-02-002	RARITY	3-01-003	RD
1-01-001	RADIOCARBON	1-01-001	RAMBLINGS	2-01-001	RASA	2-02-002	RE
3-01-001	RADIOCHLORINE	2-02-002	RAMEAU	1-01-001	RASCAL	2-01-001	RE-*BIRTH
1-01-001	RADIOCLAST	4-02-002	RAMEAU'S	1-01-001	RASCALS	1-01-001	RE-ACTIVATE
2-01-001	RADIOED	28-01-001	RAMEY	1-01-001	RASH	1-01-001	RE-ADOPT
1-01-001	RADIOGRAPHY	3-01-001	RAMEY'S	2-02-002	RASP	1-01-001	RE-ARGUING
1-01-001	RADIOMEN	1-01-001	RAMIFICATION	1-01-001	RASPBERRY	1-01-001	RE-ASSUMED
1-01-001	RADIONIC	3-03-003	RAMIFICATIONS	1-01-001	RASPED	2-02-002	RE-CREATED
9-01-001	RADIOPASTEURIZATION	2-01-001	RAMILLIES	1-01-001	RASPING	1-01-001	RE-CREATES
		2-01-001	RAMIREZ	1-01-001	RASPS	1-01-001	RE-CREATION
7-04-006	RADIOS	3-03-003	RAMMED	1-01-001	RASTUS	1-01-001	RE-DECLARED
6-01-001	RADIOSTERILIZATION	1-01-001	RAMMIN	6-05-006	RAT	1-01-001	RE-ECHO
		1-01-001	RAMMING	1-01-001	RAT'S	3-02-003	RE-ELECTED
1-01-001	RADIOSTERILIZED	6-04-005	RAMP	1-01-001	RAT-A-TAT-TATTY	2-01-001	RE-ELECTION
8-01-001	RADISH	1-01-001	RAMPAGE	1-01-001	RAT-FACE	1-01-001	RE-EMERGED
9-03-005	RADIUS	4-04-004	RAMPANT	1-01-001	RAT-HOLES	1-01-001	RE-EMERGENCE
1-01-001	RADS	2-01-001	RAMPART	2-02-002	RATA	1-01-001	RE-EMPHASISE
2-01-001	RADS.	1-01-001	RAMPS	1-01-001	RATABLE	1-01-001	RE-ENACTED
2-02-002	RAE	10-02-003	RAMSEY	3-01-001	RATCLIFF	1-01-001	RE-ENACTING
1-01-001	RAESZ	1-01-001	RAMSPERGER	1-01-001	RATCLIFFE	2-02-002	RE-ENACTMENT
1-01-001	RAFAEL	134-14-084	RAN	209-11-084	RATE	1-01-001	RE-ENACTMENTS
1-01-001	RAFER	1-01-001	RANAVAN	1-01-001	RATEABLE	1-01-001	RE-ENFORCES
1-01-001	RAFFISH	27-06-016	RANCH	9-03-007	RATED	1-01-001	RE-ENTER
4-03-004	RAFT	15-04-006	RANCHER	102-09-040	RATES	5-02-002	RE-ESTABLISH
1-01-001	RAFTER	7-02-005	RANCHERS	2-01-001	RATHBONE	1-01-001	RE-ESTABLISHING
1-01-001	RAFTERED	2-02-002	RANCHES	1-01-001	RATHBONES	1-01-001	RE-EVALUATE

1-01-001	RE-EVALUATION	3-03-003	REAPPEARS	1-01-001	RECHERCHE	29-08-017	RECOVERY
4-02-004	RE-EXAMINE	1-01-001	REAPPORTIONED	1-01-001	RECHERCHES	1-01-001	RECREATE
1-01-001	RE-EXAMINED	1-01-001	REAPPORTIONMENT	8-04-006	RECIPE	1-01-001	RECREATED
1-01-001	RE-EXAMINES	2-02-002	REAPPRAISAL	1-01-001	RECIPES	1-01-001	RECREATES
1-01-001	RE-EXPLORE	1-01-001	REAPPRAISALS	7-04-006	RECIPIENT	1-01-001	RECREATING
1-01-001	RE-EXPORT	51-09-030	REAR	5-03-004	RECIPIENTS	43-07-015	RECREATION
1-01-001	RE-INCORPORATED	1-01-001	REAR-GUARD	8-04-004	RECIPROCAL	8-04-006	RECREATIONAL
1-01-001	RE-INTRODUCTION	1-01-001	REAR-LOOKING	1-01-001	RECIPROCATE	1-01-001	RECRIMINATION
1-01-001	RE-LIVING	10-05-007	REARED	1-01-001	RECIT	3-03-003	RECRIMINATIONS
1-01-001	RE-MORALIZING	1-01-001	REARGUARD	8-03-007	RECITAL	10-04-004	RECRUIT
1-01-001	RE-RUN	2-02-002	REARING	3-03-003	RECITALS	4-03-004	RECRUITED
2-02-002	RE-RUNS	1-01-001	REARMED	3-03-003	RECITATION	1-01-001	RECRUITER
1-01-001	RE-SCHEDULED	3-02-002	REARRANGE	2-01-001	RECITATIVE	4-04-004	RECRUITING
1-01-001	RE-SET	2-01-001	REARRANGED	2-02-002	RECITE	7-02-002	RECRUITMENT
2-01-001	RE-SHARPENING	2-02-002	REARRANGING	2-02-002	RECITED	8-06-006	RECRUITS
1-01-001	RE-THINKING	241-15-170	REASON	2-02-002	RECITING	4-02-003	RECTANGLE
1-01-001	RE-USE	64-12-051	REASONABLE	9-07-008	RECKLESS	5-03-004	RECTANGULAR
1-01-001	RE-USED	34-10-032	REASONABLY	2-02-002	RECKLESSLY	3-02-002	RECTIFIER
1-01-001	RE-VISION	4-04-004	REASONED	1-01-001	RECKLESSNESS	1-01-001	RECTILINEAR
106-13-086	REACH	16-09-015	REASONING	7-04-006	RECKON	1-01-001	RECTITUDE
169-14-117	REACHED	103-11-077	REASONS	3-02-003	RECKONED	1-01-001	RECTLINEARLY
24-09-021	REACHES	3-03-003	REASSEMBLE	3-02-003	RECKONING	33-03-003	RECTOR
43-14-036	REACHING	1-01-001	REASSEMBLED	1-01-001	RECKONINGS	3-01-001	RECTOR'S
1-01-001	REACQUAINTED	1-01-001	REASSERT	1-01-001	RECKONS	1-01-001	RECUMBENT
15-07-013	REACT	1-01-001	REASSERTING	2-02-002	RECLAIM	1-01-001	RECUPERATING
3-01-001	REACTANTS	1-01-001	REASSIGN	2-02-002	RECLAIMED	2-02-002	RECUR
12-06-010	REACTED	8-06-007	REASSURANCE	1-01-001	RECLASSIFICATIO N	3-02-003	RECURRED
4-03-004	REACTING	1-01-001	REASSURE			1-01-001	RECURRENCE
124-11-048	REACTION	5-03-005	REASSURED	2-01-001	RECLASSIFIED	4-02-004	RECURRENT
2-02-002	REACTIONARIES	7-04-007	REASSURING	3-03-003	RECLINING	1-01-001	RECURRENTLY
20-05-007	REACTIONARY	2-02-002	REASSURINGLY	2-02-002	RECLUSE	6-02-006	RECURRING
42-07-021	REACTIONS	2-01-001	REAVEY	1-01-001	RECOGNISED	1-01-001	RECURSIVE
2-01-002	REACTIVATED	2-01-001	REAVEY'S	44-09-033	RECOGNITION	1-01-001	RECUSANT
19-01-004	REACTIVITY	1-01-001	REAWAKEN	7-04-007	RECOGNIZABLE	197-15-101	RED
7-02-003	REACTOR	2-01-001	REB	62-12-047	RECOGNIZE	1-01-001	RED'S
6-03-004	REACTORS	18-07-013	REBECCA	80-13-063	RECOGNIZED	1-01-001	RED-AND-YELLOW
1-01-001	REACTS	4-03-004	REBELLED	10-05-010	RECOGNIZES	1-01-001	RED-BELLIED
173-15-114	READ	3-03-003	REBELLING	10-08-010	RECOGNIZING	1-01-001	RED-BLOODED
1-01-001	READ'S	13-07-011	REBELLION	5-02-002	RECOIL	2-01-001	RED-CLAY
2-02-002	READABLE	1-01-001	REBELLIONS	1-01-001	RECOILED	1-01-001	RED-FACED
1-01-001	READAPTING	2-02-002	REBELLIOUS	2-01-001	RECOILLESS	3-01-002	RED-HAIRED
43-10-027	READER	3-03-003	REBELLIOUSLY	1-01-001	RECOLLECT	2-01-001	RED-LIGHT
4-03-004	READER'S	17-07-013	REBELS	1-01-001	RECOLLECTED	1-01-001	RED-NECKED
37-11-026	READERS	1-01-001	REBIRTH	5-03-004	RECOLLECTION	1-01-001	RED-PRONE
43-09-035	READILY	3-03-003	REBORN	3-03-003	RECOLLECTIONS	1-01-001	RED-RIMMED
15-08-014	READINESS	2-02-002	REBOUND	1-01-001	RECOMMENCE	1-01-001	RED-TAILED
140-15-074	READING	5-02-002	REBS	25-10-022	RECOMMEND	1-01-001	RED-TILE
1-01-001	READING-ROOMS	4-03-004	REBUFF	24-09-011	RECOMMENDATION	1-01-001	RED-TURBANED
17-08-011	READINGS	4-04-004	REBUFFED	22-06-017	RECOMMENDATIONS	1-01-001	RED-VISORED
2-02-002	READJUST	5-05-005	REBUILD	46-11-033	RECOMMENDED	1-01-001	REDACTIONS
1-01-001	READJUSTED	6-05-006	REBUILDING	8-05-007	RECOMMENDING	2-01-001	REDACTOR
2-02-002	READJUSTMENT	1-01-001	REBUILDS	2-02-002	RECOMMENDS	3-01-001	REDBIRDS
16-08-013	READS	4-03-003	REBUILT	1-01-001	RECOMPENCE	1-01-001	REDBIRDS'
143-14-111	READY	2-02-002	REBUKE	1-01-001	RECOMPENSE	6-01-001	REDCOAT
5-04-005	READY-MADE	1-01-001	REBUKED	4-02-004	RECONCILE	9-02-002	REDCOATS
1-01-001	READYING	6-02-002	REBUT	3-03-003	RECONCILED	1-01-001	REDDENED
2-02-002	REAFFIRM	2-01-001	REBUTTAL	1-01-001	RECONCILES	3-02-003	REDDER
2-02-002	REAFFIRMATION	2-02-002	REBUTTED	1-01-001	RECONCILIATION	1-01-001	REDDING
3-02-002	REAFFIRMED	2-01-002	RECALCITRANT	1-01-001	RECONCILING	3-03-003	REDDISH
1-01-001	REAFFIRMS	1-01-001	RECALCULATED	1-01-001	RECOND	2-01-001	REDECORATED
1-01-001	REAGENT	1-01-001	RECALCULATION	1-01-001	RECONDITE	3-02-003	REDECORATING
3-01-001	REAGENTS	39-12-034	RECALL	1-01-001	RECONDITIONING	2-01-001	REDECORATION
260-15-156	REAL	26-12-026	RECALLED	1-01-001	RECONNAISSANACE	1-01-001	REDEDICATE
1-01-001	REAL-ANALYTIC	7-05-007	RECALLING	9-04-004	RECONNAISSANCE	2-02-002	REDEEM
2-01-001	REAL-LIFE	12-08-012	RECALLS	4-03-004	RECONSIDER	1-01-001	REDEEMED
1-01-001	REALER	1-01-001	RECANTED	4-03-004	RECONSIDERATION	1-01-001	REDEEMIN
1-01-001	REALEST	1-01-001	RECAPITULATE	4-02-002	RECONSIDERED	1-01-001	REDEEMING
1-01-001	REALIGNING	2-02-002	RECAPITULATION	6-03-006	RECONSTRUCT	1-01-001	REDEFINED
24-08-015	REALISM	3-03-003	RECAPTURE	3-01-002	RECONSTRUCTED	1-01-001	REDEFINITION
1-01-001	REALISMO	1-01-001	RECAPTURED	11-06-009	RECONSTRUCTION	4-02-004	REDEMPTION
2-01-002	REALIST	1-01-001	RECEAVE	1-01-001	RECONSTRUCTS	1-01-001	REDEMPTIVE
34-08-026	REALISTIC	3-03-003	RECEDE	1-01-001	RECONTAMINATION	3-01-002	REDEPOSITION
8-05-006	REALISTICALLY	2-02-002	RECEDED	1-01-001	RECONVENED	1-01-001	REDEVELOPERS
15-08-013	REALITIES	5-03-004	RECEDING	1-01-001	RECONVENES	5-03-003	REDEVELOPMENT
79-11-049	REALITY	4-02-003	RECEIPT	1-01-001	RECONVENTION	7-03-004	REDHEAD
24-11-022	REALIZATION	7-05-006	RECEIPTS	1-01-001	RECONVERTING	1-01-001	REDHEADED
69-14-058	REALIZE	76-13-056	RECEIVE	1-01-001	RECOONED	1-01-001	REDHEADER
69-13-057	REALIZED	163-15-106	RECEIVED	1-01-001	RECOPIED	1-01-001	REDHEADS
3-03-003	REALIZES	13-05-010	RECEIVER	137-15-083	RECORD	1-01-001	REDHOOK
12-07-012	REALIZING	5-03-003	RECEIVERS	1-01-001	RECORD-HIGH	1-01-001	REDIRECT
275-15-168	REALLY	20-07-019	RECEIVES	1-01-001	RECORD-TYING	1-01-001	REDIRECTING
19-07-017	REALM	34-12-032	RECEIVING	43-11-033	RECORDED	1-01-001	REDISCOVER
2-02-002	REALMS	179-13-120	RECENT	7-05-005	RECORDER	1-01-001	REDISCOVERING
1-01-001	REALNESS	123-14-101	RECENTLY	31-08-015	RECORDING	1-01-001	REDISCOVERS
5-01-001	REALTOR	1-01-001	RECENTLY-PASSED	11-07-010	RECORDINGS	2-02-002	REDISCOVERY
1-01-001	REALTOR'S	1-01-001	RECEPTACLE	91-13-056	RECORDS	2-02-002	REDISTRIBUTED
19-02-002	REALTORS	38-11-028	RECEPTION	2-02-002	RECOUNT	1-01-001	REDISTRICTING
2-02-002	REALTY	5-02-002	RECEPTIONIST	2-02-002	RECOUNTED	1-01-001	REDNECK
5-01-001	REAMA	1-01-001	RECEPTIONIST'S	3-03-003	RECOUNTING	2-01-001	REDO
2-02-002	REAMS	1-01-001	RECEPTIONS	3-02-003	RECOUNTS	3-03-003	REDONDO
3-03-003	REAP	2-02-002	RECEPTIVE	1-01-001	RECOUPED	3-01-001	REDOUBLED
1-01-001	REAPED	2-02-002	RECESS	6-04-006	RECOURSE	3-01-001	REDOUTE
1-01-001	REAPING	2-02-002	RECESSED	11-06-010	RECOVER	2-02-002	REDRESS
2-02-002	REAPPEAR	7-03-006	RECESSION	1-01-001	RECOVERABLE	1-01-001	REDRESSED
2-02-002	REAPPEARANCE	1-01-001	RECHARTERING	9-07-008	RECOVERED	4-02-003	REDS
3-03-003	REAPPEARED	1-01-001	RECHECK	4-03-004	RECOVERING	1-01-001	REDSTONE
1-01-001	REAPPEARING			1-01-001	RECOVERS	62-08-044	REDUCE

79-11-062	REDUCED	6-04-006	REFRESHING	1-01-001	REGULATOR	3-03-003	RELAXES

79-11-062	REDUCED	6-04-006	REFRESHING
1-01-001	REDUCER	2-02-002	REFRESHINGLY
7-02-005	REDUCES	2-02-002	REFRESHMENT
31-08-022	REDUCING	2-02-002	REFRESHMENTS
42-07-026	REDUCTION	5-02-002	REFRIGERATED
4-03-004	REDUCTIONS	13-03-005	REFRIGERATION
4-03-004	REDUNDANCY	23-07-009	REFRIGERATOR
4-03-003	REDUNDANT	2-02-002	REFRIGERATORS
2-01-001	REDWOOD	2-02-002	REFUEL
2-01-001	REDWOODS	2-02-002	REFUELING
5-05-005	REED	7-05-007	REFUGE
1-01-001	REEDBUCK	7-03-004	REFUGEE
1-01-001	REEDER	7-04-006	REFUGEES
1-01-001	REEDVILLE	22-07-002	REFUND
2-02-002	REEDY	1-01-001	REFUNDED
11-01-001	REEF	2-01-001	REFUNDS
1-01-001	REEFS	2-01-001	REFURBISHED
2-02-002	REEK	1-01-001	REFURBISHING
1-01-001	REEKED	15-09-014	REFUSAL
1-01-001	REEKING	16-07-016	REFUSE
2-01-001	REEL	1-01-001	REFUSE-LITTERED
1-01-001	REELECTED	60-14-048	REFUSED
2-02-002	REELECTION	6-05-006	REFUSES
2-01-001	REELED	10-08-009	REFUSING
1-01-001	REELING	1-01-001	REFUTE
1-01-001	REELS	3-02-002	REFUTED
1-01-001	REEMERGED	1-01-001	REGAIN
2-02-002	REENACT	4-02-004	REGAINED
1-01-001	REENTERED	3-03-003	REGAINING
2-01-001	REES	1-01-001	REGAINS
3-01-001	REESE	2-02-002	REGAL
1-01-001	REESTABLISH	1-01-001	REGALED
1-01-001	REEVALUATION	1-01-001	REGALIA
1-01-001	REEVES-TYPE	89-13-069	REGARD
1-01-001	REEXAMINATION	56-13-047	REGARDED
1-01-001	REEXAMINE	40-11-033	REGARDING
4-01-001	REF	38-10-032	REGARDLESS
1-01-001	REFASHION	7-04-007	REGARDS
1-01-001	REFECTORIES	1-01-001	REGATTAS
27-09-024	REFER	1-01-001	REGATTAS
1-01-001	REFEREE	1-01-001	REGENCY
67-13-043	REFERENCE	1-01-001	REGENERATES
1-01-001	REFERENCE-POINT	1-01-001	REGENERATING
		2-02-002	REGENERATION
16-07-010	REFERENCES	1-01-001	REGENTS
1-01-001	REFERENDUM	23-07-018	REGI
1-01-001	REFERENT	1-01-001	REGIME
6-01-002	REFERRAL	25-06-008	REGIMEN
8-01-001	REFERRALS	1-01-001	REGIMENT
45-12-034	REFERRED	1-01-001	REGIMENT'S
1-01-001	REFERRIN	1-01-001	REGIMENTATION
18-06-015	REFERRING	1-01-001	REGIMENTED
18-06-016	REFERS	2-02-002	REGIMENTS
3-01-001	REFILL	2-01-001	REGIMES
1-01-001	REFILLED	1-01-001	REGINA
1-01-001	REFINANCE	1-01-001	REGINALD
1-01-001	REFINANCE	76-11-047	REGION
3-02-003	REFINE	3-02-003	REGION'S
6-04-006	REFINED	42-07-023	REGIONAL
5-05-005	REFINEMENT	1-01-001	REGIONALISM
5-05-005	REFINEMENTS	1-01-001	REGIONALLY
2-01-002	REFINING	40-08-024	REGIONS
25-08-021	REFLECT	26-13-021	REGISTER
1-01-001	REFLECTANCE	23-12-020	REGISTERED
1-01-001	REFLECTANCE-MEA	4-04-004	REGISTERING
	SURING	5-03-003	REGISTERS
42-11-032	REFLECTED	4-01-001	REGISTRANT
17-10-015	REFLECTING	2-01-001	REGISTRANT'S
32-10-023	REFLECTION	1-01-001	REGISTRANTS
7-04-006	REFLECTIONS	1-01-001	REGISTRANTS'
6-04-006	REFLECTIVE	1-01-001	REGISTRAR
5-02-002	REFLECTOR	23-06-009	REGISTRATION
3-01-001	REFLECTORS	2-02-002	REGISTRATIONS
23-07-020	REFLECTS	4-01-001	REGISTRIES
4-03-004	REFLEX	7-03-004	REGISTRY
6-03-004	REFLEXES	2-02-002	REGIUS
2-01-001	REFLEXLY	7-01-003	REGRESSION
1-01-001	REFOCUSING	9-06-009	REGRET
1-01-001	REFOLDED	1-01-001	REGRETFULLY
30-07-017	REFORM	3-02-003	REGRETS
5-01-004	REFORMATION	1-01-001	REGRETTABLE
2-02-002	REFORMATORY	2-01-001	REGRETTABLY
3-01-002	REFORMED	11-05-011	REGRETTED
3-03-003	REFORMER	1-01-001	REGROUND
2-01-001	REFORMERS	1-01-001	REGROUPED
1-01-001	REFORMING	1-01-001	REGROUPING
1-01-001	REFORMISM	83-15-063	REGULAR
14-06-012	REFORMS	1-01-001	REGULAR-FEATURE
1-01-001	REFORMULATED		D
1-01-001	REFRACTED	2-02-002	REGULARITY
1-01-001	REFRACTION	22-12-020	REGULARLY
1-01-001	REFRACTIVE	6-04-005	REGULARS
1-01-001	REFRACTORY	2-02-002	REGULATE
10-04-008	REFRAIN	7-06-006	REGULATED
1-01-001	REFRAINED	4-03-003	REGULATING
1-01-001	REFRESH	14-04-007	REGULATION
5-04-004	REFRESHED	29-07-020	REGULATIONS
1-01-001	REFRESHER	2-01-001	REGULATIVE

1-01-001	REGULATOR	3-03-003	RELAXES
5-04-004	REGULATORY	5-05-005	RELAXING
1-01-001	REGULI	2-02-002	RELAY
10-02-002	REGULUS	2-01-001	RELAYED
1-01-001	REHABILITATING	1-01-001	RELAYING
22-04-008	REHABILITATION	1-01-001	RELEARNS
1-01-001	REHABILITATIONS	37-12-026	RELEASE
1-01-001	REHARMONIZATION	26-11-022	RELEASED
2-02-002	REHASH	8-06-007	RELEASES
1-01-001	REHEARING	2-02-002	RELEASING
4-04-004	REHEARSAL	6-06-006	RELEGATED
4-02-002	REHEARSALS	3-03-003	RELENTED
1-01-001	REHEARSE	5-05-005	RELENTLESS
7-04-004	REHEARSED	5-05-005	RELENTLESSLY
1-01-001	REHEARSING	2-02-002	RELENTLESSNESS
6-02-003	REICH	10-03-007	RELEVANCE
2-01-001	REICHENBERG	2-02-002	RELEVANCY
1-01-001	REICHSTAG	23-06-020	RELEVANT
3-02-002	REID	2-02-002	RELIABILITY
1-01-001	REIFENRATH	22-06-020	RELIABLE
7-05-006	REIGN	1-01-001	RELIABLY
1-01-001	REIGNED	7-03-007	RELIANCE
3-03-003	REIGNING	6-05-005	RELIC
1-01-001	REIGNS	1-01-001	RELICT
1-01-001	REIK	8-04-008	RELIED
1-01-001	REILLY	66-15-052	RELIEF
1-01-001	REILY'S	4-03-004	RELIES
1-01-001	REIMBURSE	13-09-012	RELIEVE
2-01-001	REIMBURSEABLE	24-09-020	RELIEVED
1-01-001	REIMBURSED	2-02-002	RELIEVES
2-01-002	REIMBURSEMENT	1-01-001	RELIEVING
2-01-001	REIMBURSEMENTS	119-14-044	RELIGION
1-01-001	REIMBURSES	1-01-001	RELIGIONISTS
3-03-003	REIN	18-07-008	RELIGIONS
1-01-001	REINCARNATED	1-01-001	RELIGIOSITY
2-02-002	REINE	165-12-061	RELIGIOUS
3-02-002	REINED	4-02-003	RELIGIOUSLY
10-05-007	REINFORCE	1-01-001	RELIGIOUSNESS
7-05-006	REINFORCED	6-04-005	RELINQUISH
2-02-002	REINFORCEMENT	4-04-004	RELINQUISHED
3-01-001	REINFORCEMENTS	4-02-004	RELINQUISHING
3-02-003	REINFORCES	8-05-008	RELISH
2-02-002	REINFORCING	2-01-001	RELISHES
2-01-001	REINHARD	1-01-001	RELISHING
2-01-001	REINHARDT	2-02-002	RELIVE
9-04-008	REINS	1-01-001	RELIVES
1-01-001	REINSTALL	2-02-002	RELIVING
1-01-001	REINSTATED	2-02-002	RELOADED
1-01-001	REINSTITUTION	1-01-001	RELOCATION
1-01-001	REINTERPRET	5-03-005	RELUCTANCE
1-01-001	REINTERPRETED	15-09-014	RELUCTANT
1-01-001	REINTRODUCES	7-05-007	RELUCTANTLY
1-01-001	REINVESTIGATION	13-09-013	RELY
1-01-001	REINVIGORATION	5-03-005	RELYING
1-01-001	REIPUBLICAE	1-01-001	RELYRICED
1-01-001	REISS	93-15-074	REMAIN
2-01-001	REISSUE	19-10-019	REMAINDER
1-01-001	REITERATE	105-15-087	REMAINED
2-02-002	REITERATED	41-11-035	REMAINING
1-01-001	REITERATES	84-11-078	REMAINS
1-01-001	REITERATING	2-02-002	REMAKE
10-06-009	REJECT	1-01-001	REMAKING
33-11-030	REJECTED	2-01-001	REMANDED
4-03-004	REJECTING	1-01-001	REMANDING
11-05-010	REJECTION	31-09-019	REMARK
1-01-001	REJECTIONS	47-11-040	REMARKABLE
11-05-009	REJECTS	18-07-016	REMARKABLY
1-01-001	REJOICE	32-11-025	REMARKED
1-01-001	REJOICED	2-02-002	REMARKING
1-01-001	REJOICES	53-12-040	REMARKS
4-04-004	REJOICING	3-01-001	REMARQUE
2-02-002	REJOIN	6-01-001	REMARQUE'S
1-01-001	REJOINDER	2-02-002	REMARRIED
1-01-001	REJOINING	1-01-001	REMARRY
1-01-001	REKINDLING	2-02-002	REMARRYING
7-03-007	RELATE	1-01-001	REMBRANDT
102-10-072	RELATED	2-02-002	REMBRANDT'S
1-01-001	RELATEDNESS	1-01-001	REMEDIAL
8-04-008	RELATES	6-04-006	REMEDIES
20-06-014	RELATING	13-04-010	REMEDY
63-08-043	RELATION	138-15-099	REMEMBER
1-01-001	RELATIONAL	83-14-064	REMEMBERED
102-11-064	RELATIONS	17-09-015	REMEMBERING
88-14-062	RELATIONSHIP	13-05-011	REMEMBERS
1-01-001	RELATIONSHIP-BU	2-01-002	REMEMBRANCE
	ILDING	1-01-001	REMEMBRANCES
15-08-013	RELATIONSHIPS	29-10-026	REMIND
46-10-038	RELATIVE	1-01-001	REMINDED
85-10-067	RELATIVELY	8-07-008	REMINDER
22-08-017	RELATIVES	2-02-002	REMINDERS
2-01-002	RELATIVISM	5-04-004	REMINDING
1-01-001	RELATIVIST	8-04-007	REMINDS
3-03-003	RELATIVISTIC	5-01-001	REMINGTON
3-03-003	RELATIVITY	1-01-001	REMINISCED
19-08-013	RELAX	2-02-002	REMINISCENCE
7-04-006	RELAXATION	1-01-001	REMINISCENCES
14-08-013	RELAXED	4-03-004	REMINISCENT

1-01-001 REMINISCES	7-06-006 REPAY	1-01-001 REPROVINGLY
1-01-001 REMINISCING	2-02-002 REPAYABLE	3-02-003 REPS
1-01-001 REMISSIONS	3-01-002 REPAYMENT	43-11-028 REPUBLIC
1-01-001 REMITTED	7-02-003 REPEAL	54-06-020 REPUBLICAN
2-02-002 REMNANT	3-03-003 REPEALED	1-01-001 REPUBLICAN-CONT ROLLED
2-02-002 REMNANTS	26-12-023 REPEAT	
1-01-001 REMODELED	59-14-048 REPEATED	4-02-002 REPUBLICANISM
2-02-002 REMODELING	18-10-018 REPEATEDLY	29-06-016 REPUBLICANS
1-01-001 REMOLDING	1-01-001 REPEATER	1-01-001 REPUBLICANS'
1-01-001 REMONSTRATE	9-06-009 REPEATING	6-03-005 REPUBLICS
2-02-002 REMONSTRATED	4-03-004 REPEATS	1-01-001 REPUDIATE
1-01-001 REMORSE	8-05-007 REPEL	3-03-003 REPUDIATED
1-01-001 REMORSEFUL	5-04-005 REPELLED	1-01-001 REPUDIATING
2-02-002 REMORSELESS	1-01-001 REPELLENT	4-02-002 REPUDIATION
32-11-026 REMOTE	1-01-001 REPELS	1-01-001 REPUGNANCE
4-04-004 REMOTELY	3-03-003 REPENT	1-01-001 REPUGNANT
2-02-002 REMOTENESS	2-02-002 REPENTANCE	1-01-001 REPULSED
1-01-001 REMOTER	1-01-001 REPENTANT	1-01-001 REPULSION
1-01-001 REMOTEST	1-01-001 REPERCUSSIONS	2-02-002 REPULSIONS
1-01-001 REMOUNTING	2-02-002 REPERTOIRE	4-03-003 REPULSIVE
1-01-001 REMOVABLE	4-03-003 REPERTORY	7-04-005 REPUTABLE
41-08-019 REMOVAL	13-10-013 REPETITION	27-10-025 REPUTATION
58-11-042 REMOVE	2-02-002 REPETITIONS	1-01-001 REPUTATION'S
75-15-059 REMOVED	2-02-002 REPETITIOUS	1-01-001 REPUTATIONS
5-02-004 REMOVES	1-01-001 REPETITIVE	2-02-002 REPUTE
8-06-008 REMOVING	5-03-005 REPHRASED	5-03-005 REPUTED
1-01-001 REMPHAN	1-01-001 REPLACE	4-03-003 REPUTEDLY
1-01-001 REMUDA	42-11-035 REPLACED	49-11-035 REQUEST
2-02-002 REMUNERATION	21-09-016 REPLACEMENT	12-07-011 REQUESTED
1-01-001 REMUNERATIVE	2-02-002 REPLACEMENTS	1-01-001 REQUESTERS
1-01-001 REMUS	6-02-005 REPLACES	8-05-007 REQUESTING
1-01-001 REMY	9-05-009 REPLACING	14-07-013 REQUESTS
20-07-012 RENAISSANCE	1-01-001 REPLANTED	86-10-066 REQUIRE
1-01-001 RENAL	4-02-003 REPLENISH	182-12-107 REQUIRED
3-02-003 RENAMED	2-02-002 REPLENISHED	27-07-022 REQUIREMENT
1-01-001 RENATURATION	1-01-001 REPLENISHMENT	83-09-051 REQUIREMENTS
1-01-001 RENAULTS	1-01-001 REPLETE	57-11-051 REQUIRES
1-01-001 REND	1-01-001 REPLICA	16-06-014 REQUIRING
11-06-009 RENDER	1-01-001 REPLICATION	1-01-001 REQUISITES
28-09-021 RENDERED	57-13-037 REPLIED	1-01-001 REQUISITION
11-08-009 RENDERING	10-07-009 REPLIES	9-07-008 REQUISITIONED
1-01-001 RENDERINGS	42-12-031 REPLY	1-01-001 REREAD
2-01-002 RENDERS	1-01-001 REPLYING	1-01-001 REREMAINED
7-05-006 RENDEZVOUS	2-01-001 REPNIN	2-01-001 RESALE
1-01-001 RENDITION	1-01-001 REPONSES	2-01-001 RESCIND
3-02-002 RENDITIONS	174-15-082 REPORT	1-01-001 RESCINDED
4-04-004 RENEW	1-01-001 REPORTAGE	15-09-011 RESCUE
1-01-001 RENEWABLE	119-13-079 REPORTED	6-06-006 RESCUED
8-04-007 RENEWAL	9-06-009 REPORTEDLY	2-02-002 RESCUING
17-10-015 RENEWED	20-08-010 REPORTER	1-01-001 RESEALED
1-01-001 RENEWING	34-09-019 REPORTERS	171-11-072 RESEARCH
1-01-001 RENEWS	17-07-015 REPORTING	3-01-001 RESEARCH-STAFF
1-01-001 RENFREW	1-01-001 REPORTORIAL	1-01-001 RESEARCHABLE
1-01-001 RENFRO	84-13-065 REPORTS	3-02-003 RESEARCHER
1-01-001 RENNELL	2-02-002 REPOSE	4-04-004 RESEARCHERS
7-03-003 RENO	1-01-001 REPOSED	1-01-001 RESEARCHES
1-01-001 RENO-*LAKE	1-01-001 REPOSITORIES	1-01-001 RESEARCHING
3-03-003 RENOIR	4-04-004 REPOSITORY	13-07-012 RESEMBLANCE
1-01-001 RENOUNCING	2-02-002 REPREHENSIBLE	8-06-008 RESEMBLE
3-02-003 RENOVATED	38-10-031 REPRESENT	8-07-007 RESEMBLED
2-02-002 RENOVATION	18-05-011 REPRESENTATION	9-05-007 RESEMBLES
1-01-001 RENOVO	2-01-001 REPRESENTATIONA L	2-02-002 RESEMBLING
1-01-001 RENOWN		8-04-008 RESENT
2-02-002 RENOWNED	10-04-006 REPRESENTATIONS	8-07-008 RESENTED
2-02-002 RENSSELAER	47-10-042 REPRESENTATIVE	3-02-002 RESENTFUL
1-01-001 RENSSELAERWYCK	41-07-028 REPRESENTATIVES	18-08-014 RESENTMENT
21-08-012 RENT	56-11-042 REPRESENTED	1-01-001 RESERPINE
15-07-008 RENTAL	30-07-025 REPRESENTING	8-06-006 RESERVATION
2-02-002 RENTALS	39-08-029 REPRESENTS	9-04-007 RESERVATIONS
7-05-006 RENTED	1-01-001 REPRESS	37-07-020 RESERVE
5-03-004 RENTING	3-03-003 REPRESSED	27-09-022 RESERVED
4-03-003 RENTS	6-03-006 REPRESSION	5-03-004 RESERVES
1-01-001 RENUNCIATION	1-01-001 REPRESSIONS	4-03-004 RESERVING
1-01-001 RENUNCIATIONS	2-02-002 REPRESSIVE	10-05-009 RESERVOIR
1-01-001 RENVILLE	2-02-002 REPRIEVE	3-03-003 RESERVOIRS
1-01-001 REOPEN	2-02-002 REPRIMANDED	1-01-001 RESETTLEMENT
1-01-001 REOPENED	2-02-002 REPRINTED	1-01-001 RESETTLING
1-01-001 REOPENING	3-03-003 REPRINTS	1-01-001 RESHAPED
1-01-001 REORDER	3-03-003 REPRISAL	1-01-001 RESHAPES
27-04-006 REORGANIZATION	2-02-002 REPRISALS	2-02-002 RESIDE
2-01-002 REORGANIZATIONS	3-03-003 REPROACH	3-02-003 RESIDED
1-01-001 REORGANIZE	1-01-001 REPROACHES	29-10-021 RESIDENCE
4-03-004 REORGANIZED	1-01-001 REPROBATE	2-02-002 RESIDENCES
1-01-001 REORGANIZING	13-08-012 REPROBATING	13-08-012 RESIDENT
2-01-002 REORIENTATION	7-06-007 REPRODUCE	45-09-018 RESIDENTIAL
1-01-001 REORIENTED	7-05-007 REPRODUCED	1-01-001 RESIDENTIALLY
13-02-004 REP	3-03-003 REPRODUCES	20-05-015 RESIDENTS
1-01-001 REP'TATION	1-01-001 REPRODUCIBILITI ES	4-02-004 RESIDES
3-02-002 REPAID		6-04-005 RESIDING
2-02-002 REPAINTING	1-01-001 REPRODUCIBILITY	1-01-001 RESIDUAL
20-10-018 REPAIR	5-02-003 REPRODUCIBLE	8-04-006 RESIDUE
11-05-008 REPAIRED	1-01-001 REPRODUCIBLY	3-02-002 RESIDUES
2-02-002 REPAIRING	2-02-002 REPRODUCING	1-01-001 RESIFTED
2-02-002 REPAIRMEN	6-03-004 REPRODUCTION	2-02-002 RESIGN
8-06-007 REPAIRS	2-01-002 REPRODUCTIONS	7-04-007 RESIGNATION
1-01-001 REPARATION	1-01-001 REPRODUCTIVE	1-01-001 RESIGNATIONS
1-01-001 REPARTEE	1-01-001 REPROOF	9-04-008 RESIGNED

1-01-001 RESIGNEDLY
1-01-001 RESIGNING
1-01-001 RESIGNS
1-01-001 RESILIENCE
9-02-003 RESIN
2-01-001 RESIN-SATURATED
1-01-001 RESINLIKE
2-02-002 RESINS
1-01-001 RESINY
22-08-021 RESIST
48-10-023 RESISTANCE
1-01-001 RESISTANCES
5-04-005 RESISTANT
9-05-009 RESISTED
4-04-004 RESISTING
1-01-001 RESISTIVE
3-02-002 RESISTOR
7-01-002 RESISTORS
1-01-001 RESISTS
2-01-001 RESNIK
4-04-004 RESOLUTE
2-02-002 RESOLUTELY
64-08-019 RESOLUTION
6-04-006 RESOLUTIONS
13-07-013 RESOLVE
21-08-016 RESOLVED
3-03-003 RESOLVES
3-03-003 RESOLVING
1-01-001 RESONABLE
14-04-004 RESONANCE
3-01-002 RESONANCES
4-02-002 RESONANT
1-01-001 RESORCINAL
2-01-001 RESORCINOL
12-06-012 RESORT
5-03-004 RESORTED
3-02-003 RESORTING
1-01-001 RESORTS
2-02-002 RESOUNDING
1-01-001 RESOUNDS
9-07-008 RESOURCE
1-01-001 RESOURCE-USE
3-02-002 RESOURCEFUL
1-01-001 RESOURCEFULLY
2-02-002 RESOURCEFULNESS
72-11-040 RESOURCES
125-13-079 RESPECT
5-04-005 RESPECTABILITY
21-10-020 RESPECTABLE
11-05-011 RESPECTED
4-03-004 RESPECTFUL
2-02-002 RESPECTFULLY
5-04-005 RESPECTING
19-07-018 RESPECTIVE
31-06-021 RESPECTIVELY
22-07-022 RESPECTS
2-01-002 RESPIRATION
1-01-001 RESPIRATORS
17-03-005 RESPIRATORY
2-02-002 RESPITE
21-09-018 RESPLENDENT
20-12-019 RESPOND
8-01-001 RESPONDED
8-01-001 RESPONDENT
1-01-001 RESPONDENT'S
8-01-001 RESPONDENTS
5-01-001 RESPONDENTS'
6-04-005 RESPONDING
7-03-007 RESPONDS
77-13-056 RESPONSE
27-07-015 RESPONSES
25-10-020 RESPONSIBILITI
118-11-059 RESPONSIBILITY
71-15-059 RESPONSIBLE
1-01-001 RESPONSIBLY
4-03-004 RESPONSIVE
1-01-001 RESPONSIVELY
4-02-002 RESPONSIVENESS
163-15-119 REST
1-01-001 REST-ROOM
4-02-003 RESTATEMENT
1-01-001 RESTATES
1-01-001 RESTATING
41-08-021 RESTAURANT
12-09-012 RESTAURANTS
1-01-001 RESTAURATEUR
17-12-016 RESTED
3-03-003 RESTFUL
19-12-016 RESTING
1-01-001 RESTITUTION
1-01-001 RESTIVE
1-01-001 RESTIVELY
13-08-013 RESTLESS
2-02-002 RESTLESSLY
2-02-002 RESTLESSNESS
1-01-001 RESTOCK

```
3-01-001    RESTORABILITY
11-06-009   RESTORATION
8-01-001    RESTORATIVE
9-06-009    RESTORE
14-07-013   RESTORED
1-01-001    RESTORERS
6-04-005    RESTORING
10-08-009   RESTRAIN
13-04-010   RESTRAINED
7-03-005    RESTRAINING
1-01-001    RESTRAINS
11-06-011   RESTRAINT
7-03-003    RESTRAINTS
11-05-010   RESTRICT
15-11-015   RESTRICTED
4-03-003    RESTRICTING
8-05-008    RESTRICTION
27-10-024   RESTRICTIONS
7-03-005    RESTRICTIVE
2-02-002    RESTRICTS
1-01-001    RESTRUCTURED
18-07-015   RESTS
2-02-002    RESTUDY
1-01-001    RESUBLIMED
244-13-147  RESULT
12-06-011   RESULTANT
5-02-003    RESULTANTS
37-07-032   RESULTED
43-07-034   RESULTING
149-11-092  RESULTS
16-07-013   RESUME
23-11-021   RESUMED
4-03-004    RESUMING
9-03-005    RESUMPTION
3-02-002    RESURGENCE
1-01-001    RESURGENT
1-01-001    RESURRECTED
1-01-001    RESURRECTING
1-01-001    RESURRECTION
3-01-001    RESUSPENDED
1-01-001    RESUSPENSION
20-06-012   RETAIL
1-01-001    RETAILER
5-03-004    RETAILERS
5-02-002    RETAILING
11-07-011   RETAIN
22-10-020   RETAINED
1-01-001    RETAINERS
7-06-007    RETAINING
9-05-008    RETAINS
1-01-001    RETALIATE
1-01-001    RETALIATED
1-01-001    RETALIATING
6-04-006    RETALIATION
2-02-002    RETALIATORY
3-03-003    RETARD
3-01-002    RETARDATION
7-04-006    RETARDED
1-01-001    RETARDING
1-01-001    RETCH
1-01-001    RETCHING
1-01-001    RETELL
2-02-002    RETELLING
12-04-007   RETENTION
2-02-002    RETENTIVE
1-01-001    RETENTIVENESS
2-02-002    RETHINK
3-01-001    RETICULATE
1-01-001    RETIED
1-01-001    RETINA
3-01-001    RETINAL
1-01-001    RETINUE
9-07-009    RETIRE
35-12-025   RETIRED
26-07-014   RETIREMENT
1-01-001    RETIREMENTS
2-02-002    RETIRES
8-03-007    RETIRING
1-01-001    RETOLD
4-04-004    RETORT
3-03-003    RETORTED
1-01-001    RETOUCHING
1-01-001    RETRACE
1-01-001    RETRACED
1-01-001    RETRACING
3-03-003    RETRACTED
1-01-001    RETRACTION
1-01-001    RETRAINING
1-01-001    RETRANSLATED
14-08-013   RETREAT
8-04-007    RETREATED
5-04-005    RETREATING
1-01-001    RETREATS
1-01-001    RETRENCHING
4-04-004    RETRIBUTION
1-01-001    RETRIEVAL
2-01-002    RETRIEVE

10-04-004   RETRIEVED
1-01-001    RETRIEVER
1-01-001    RETROGRADATIONS
3-02-002    RETROGRADE
1-01-001    RETROGRESSIVE
3-03-003    RETROSPECT
1-01-001    RETROSPECTIVE
1-01-001    RETROVISION
180-15-106  RETURN
115-14-092  RETURNED
35-14-033   RETURNING
34-07-015   RETURNS
1-01-001    REUB
3-03-003    REUBEN
11-06-009   REUNION
1-01-001    REUNION-*HALLOWEEN
1-01-001    REUNIONS
1-01-001    REUNITE
2-02-002    REUNITED
1-01-001    REUNITING
1-01-001    REUPHOLSTERING
1-01-001    REUTHER
1-01-001    REUVENI
33-06-012   REV
1-01-001    REV'REND
2-01-001    REV'S
1-01-001    REVALUATION
3-02-002    REVAMPED
1-01-001    REVAMPING
30-12-026   REVEAL
39-10-031   REVEALED
11-06-011   REVEALING
21-05-014   REVEALS
3-03-003    REVEL
14-06-013   REVELATION
3-02-003    REVELATIONS
1-01-001    REVELATORY
1-01-001    REVELED
1-01-001    REVELING
1-01-001    REVELLERS
1-01-001    REVELLING
1-01-001    REVELLINGS
1-01-001    REVELRY
1-01-001    REVELS
7-05-007    REVENGE
1-01-001    REVENGE-SEEKING
35-08-020   REVENUE
1-01-001    REVENUERS
26-03-006   REVENUES
2-02-002    REVERBERATED
1-01-001    REVERBERATION
1-01-001    REVERBERATIONS
1-01-001    REVERDY
1-01-001    REVERE
5-03-005    REVERED
5-04-005    REVERENCE
21-06-012   REVEREND
3-02-003    REVERENT
1-01-001    REVERENTLY
1-01-001    REVERIE
2-02-002    REVERSAL
18-08-015   REVERSE
1-01-001    REVERSE-SURFACE
8-03-007    REVERSED
2-02-002    REVERSES
1-01-001    REVERSIBILITY
6-03-005    REVERSIBLE
6-03-004    REVERSING
3-02-003    REVERT
2-02-002    REVERTED
1-01-001    REVERY
1-01-001    REVETMENTS
13-06-012   REVIEW
56-08-035   REVIEWED
13-06-012   REVIEWER
2-01-001    REVIEWERS
6-04-005    REVIEWING
9-02-005    REVIEWS
1-01-001    REVILED
1-01-001    REVISE
8-05-008    REVISED
1-01-001    REVISING
8-05-008    REVISION
1-01-001    REVISIONIST
9-06-008    REVISIONS
1-01-001    REVISITED
1-01-001    REVITALIZE
1-01-001    REVIVAL
8-06-007    REVIVALISM
2-01-001    REVIVALS
5-02-003    REVIVE
8-05-008    REVIVED
6-05-006    REVIVIFIED
1-01-001    REVIVING
2-02-002    REVOKED
8-05-007    REVOLT

1-01-001    REVOLTED
2-02-002    REVOLTING
2-01-001    REVOLTS
70-08-036   REVOLUTION
1-01-001    REVOLUTION'S
1-01-001    REVOLUTIONARIES
21-07-015   REVOLUTIONARY
3-01-001    REVOLUTIONIBUS
1-01-001    REVOLUTIONISTS
3-03-003    REVOLUTIONIZED
7-06-006    REVOLUTIONS
1-01-001    REVOLVE
4-04-004    REVOLVED
14-05-008   REVOLVER
1-01-001    REVOLVES
6-03-005    REVOLVING
10-07-007   REVULSION
1-01-001    REVVED
15-11-014   REWARD
3-02-003    REWARDED
4-04-004    REWARDING
4-03-004    REWARDS
4-02-003    REWRITE
1-01-001    REWRITES
2-02-002    REWRITING
1-01-001    REWRITTEN
1-01-001    REWT
5-03-004    REX
6-01-001    REXROTH
1-01-001    REXROTH'S
2-02-002    REY
1-01-001    REYES
5-02-004    REYNOLDS
1-01-001    RF
1-01-001    RHEA'S
1-01-001    RHEIMS
1-01-001    RHEINHOLDT
1-01-001    RHEINHOLDT'S
1-01-001    RHENISH
1-01-001    RHENIUM
5-02-005    RHETORIC
1-01-001    RHETORICIANS
1-01-001    RHEUM
2-01-001    RHEUMATIC
1-01-001    RHEUMATICS
3-02-002    RHEUMATISM
7-02-002    RHINE
1-01-001    RHINE-*MAIN
1-01-001    RHINE-*WESTPHALIA
1-01-001    RHINESTONES
3-02-002    RHINOCEROS
2-01-001    RHINOS
2-01-001    RHINOTRACHEITIS
105-08-019  RHODE
8-04-004    RHODES
1-01-001    RHODESIA
1-01-001    RHODODENDRON
1-01-001    RHU-*=BEB
1-01-001    RHU-BEB-NI-ICE
3-02-003    RHYME
1-01-001    RHYMES
1-01-001    RHYMING
22-09-016   RHYTHM
1-01-001    RHYTHM-*WILY
1-01-001    RHYTHM-AND-BLUES
11-07-009   RHYTHMIC
1-01-001    RHYTHMICAL
2-02-002    RHYTHMICALLY
12-04-010   RHYTHMS
1-01-001    RIB
1-01-001    RIBALD
1-01-001    RIBAS
1-01-001    RIBBING
12-05-009   RIBBON
6-04-005    RIBBONS
1-01-001    RIBCAGE
2-01-001    RIBES
1-01-001    RIBOFLAVIN
1-01-001    RIBONUCLEIC
11-05-009   RIBS
1-01-001    RICAN
2-01-002    RICANS
1-01-001    RICCI
4-01-001    RICCO
33-11-014   RICE
74-13-060   RICH
71-09-037   RICHARD
5-03-003    RICHARD'S
10-03-005   RICHARDS
12-04-005   RICHARDSON
1-01-001    RICHARDSON'S
5-04-005    RICHER
5-01-001    RICHERT
2-02-002    RICHES

5-04-005    RICHEST
1-01-001    RICHEY
5-03-005    RICHLY
12-09-010   RICHMOND
1-01-001    RICHMOND-*PETERSBURG
5-03-004    RICHNESS
1-01-001    RICHTER-*HAASER
4-01-001    RICKARDS
2-01-001    RICKENBAUGH
1-01-001    RICKETTSIA
1-01-001    RICKETY
1-01-001    RICKEY'S
1-01-001    RICKSHAW
21-03-006   RICO
1-01-001    RICOCHETED
19-09-019   RID
1-01-001    RIDDANCE
6-03-006    RIDDEN
2-02-002    RIDDING
1-01-001    RIDDLE
2-02-002    RIDDLED
2-02-002    RIDDLES
2-02-002    RIDDLING
49-09-036   RIDE
16-08-010   RIDER
2-02-002    RIDER'S
1-01-001    RIDER-FASHION
12-05-009   RIDERS
10-07-008   RIDES
18-08-016   RIDGE
1-01-001    RIDGEFIELD
4-03-003    RIDGES
1-01-001    RIDGWAY
5-04-005    RIDICULE
2-02-002    RIDICULED
2-02-002    RIDICULING
19-08-016   RIDICULOUS
2-02-002    RIDICULOUSLY
45-11-029   RIDING
1-01-001    RIDPATH
3-01-001    RIEFLING
2-01-001    RIEGGER
1-01-001    RIEMANN'S
1-01-001    RIESMAN
1-01-001    RIFFLE
63-09-020   RIFLE
1-01-001    RIFLE'S
1-01-001    RIFLE-SHOTGUN
1-01-001    RIFLED
4-03-003    RIFLEMAN
1-01-001    RIFLEMAN'S
6-01-001    RIFLEMEN
1-01-001    RIFLEMEN'S
1-01-001    RIFLEMEN-RANGERS
23-06-012   RIFLES
1-01-001    RIFLING
1-01-001    RIFT
5-04-005    RIG
1-01-001    RIG-*VEDA
3-02-002    RIGGED
1-01-001    RIGGER
1-01-001    RIGGERS
2-02-002    RIGGING
1-01-001    RIGGS
613-15-265  RIGHT
1-01-001    RIGHT-ANGLE
1-01-001    RIGHT-ANGLED
6-03-004    RIGHT-HAND
1-01-001    RIGHT-HANDED
2-01-001    RIGHT-OF-ENTRY
1-01-001    RIGHT-WING
5-03-004    RIGHTEOUS
6-04-006    RIGHTEOUSNESS
3-01-001    RIGHTFIELD
4-03-004    RIGHTFUL
3-02-003    RIGHTFULLY
1-01-001    RIGHTHANDER
1-01-001    RIGHTHANDLER
1-01-001    RIGHTIST
4-03-003    RIGHTLY
2-02-002    RIGHTNESS
77-14-047   RIGHTS
1-01-001    RIGHTS-OF-WAY
24-09-017   RIGID
2-01-001    RIGIDITY
8-06-008    RIGIDLY
1-01-001    RIGIDS
7-04-007    RIGOROUS
4-03-004    RIGOROUSLY
4-04-004    RIGORS
4-03-003    RIGS
1-01-001    RILKE
1-01-001    RILLY
5-05-005    RIM
1-01-001    RIM-*FIRE
```

2-01-001	RIM-FIRE	1-01-001	ROAD-SHY	3-02-002	RODENTS	2-01-001	ROOMMATES
3-01-001	RIM-FIRES	1-01-001	ROADBED	1-01-001	RODEO	55-11-039	ROOMS
3-01-001	RIMANELLI	3-03-003	ROADBLOCK	1-01-001	RODEOS	1-01-001	ROOMY
1-01-001	RIMBAUD	1-01-001	ROADBUILDING	1-01-001	RODEPH	7-01-001	ROONEY
1-01-001	RIME	1-01-001	ROADHOUSE	6-01-001	RODGERS	2-01-001	ROOS
1-01-001	RIMINI	58-10-027	ROADS	1-01-001	RODGERS'	28-08-017	ROOSEVELT
1-01-001	RIMLESS	4-04-004	ROADSIDE	3-01-001	RODNEY	5-03-004	ROOSEVELT'S
2-02-002	RIMMED	1-01-001	ROADSTER	1-01-001	RODNEY-*HONOR	1-01-001	ROOSEVELTIAN
1-01-001	RIMS	5-04-004	ROADWAY	1-01-001	RODNEY-*MISS	1-01-001	ROOST
2-01-001	RINASCIMENTO	1-01-001	ROADWAYS	1-01-001	RODNEY-*THE	3-03-003	ROOSTER
47-14-032	RING	6-04-005	ROAM	4-04-004	RODS	1-01-001	ROOSTER'S
1-01-001	RING-AROUND-A	1-01-001	ROAMED	1-01-001	ROE	2-02-002	ROOSTERS
1-01-001	RING-AROUND-THE	3-03-003	ROAMING	9-01-001	ROEBUCK	30-10-022	ROOT
	-ROSIE	13-04-010	ROAR	1-01-001	ROEMER	8-04-004	ROOTED
1-01-001	RING-LABELED	18-06-014	ROARED	15-04-011	ROGER	2-01-001	ROOTING
2-02-002	RINGED	9-05-008	ROARING	9-06-007	ROGERS	2-01-002	ROOTLESS
1-01-001	RINGEL	1-01-001	ROARINGEST	1-01-001	ROGUE	27-06-017	ROOTS
1-01-001	RINGERS	1-01-001	ROARS	2-02-002	ROGUES	15-06-012	ROPE
10-06-010	RINGING	10-04-006	ROAST	1-01-001	ROGUES'	1-01-001	ROPED
1-01-001	RINGINGS	5-03-004	ROASTED	1-01-001	ROI	1-01-001	ROPERS
1-01-001	RINGLER'S	1-01-001	ROASTS	3-02-002	ROILING	4-02-003	ROPES
1-01-001	RINGLETS	19-05-005	ROB	4-03-003	ROLAND	2-01-001	ROQUEMORE
6-04-005	RINGS	1-01-001	ROB'S	104-13-064	ROLE	1-01-001	RORSCHACH
1-01-001	RINGSIDE	8-01-001	ROBARDS	1-01-001	ROLE-EXPERIMENT	4-01-001	ROSA
1-01-001	RINGSIDERS	1-01-001	ROBARDS'	1-01-001	ROLE-EXPERIMENT	1-01-001	ROSABELLE
2-01-001	RINK	10-06-010	ROBBED		ATION	1-01-001	ROSALIE
2-01-001	RINKER	2-02-002	ROBBER	1-01-001	ROLEPLAYED	3-02-003	ROSARIES
6-02-002	RINSE	3-03-003	ROBBERIES	16-01-001	ROLEPLAYING	4-01-001	ROSBURG
5-01-002	RINSING	6-02-002	ROBBERS	34-08-025	ROLES	86-13-065	ROSE
4-03-003	RIO	10-02-004	ROBBERY	1-01-001	ROLETTE	3-01-001	ROSE'S
7-05-006	RIOT	3-02-002	ROBBIE	35-12-029	ROLL	1-01-001	ROSE-OF-*SHARO
1-01-001	RIOTED	2-02-002	ROBBING	47-10-032	ROLLED	1-01-001	ROSE-PINK
2-01-001	RIOTERS	6-03-004	ROBBINS	1-01-001	ROLLED-UP	1-01-001	ROSE-TEA
1-01-001	RIOTING	1-01-001	ROBBY	3-03-003	ROLLER	4-02-002	ROSEBUDS
2-02-002	RIOTOUS	1-01-001	ROBBY'S	1-01-001	ROLLICKING	1-01-001	ROSEBUSH
1-01-001	RIOTS	6-05-006	ROBE	1-01-001	ROLLICKINGLY	1-01-001	ROSELLA
6-05-006	RIP	1-01-001	ROBED	1-01-001	ROLLIE	1-01-001	ROSEMARY
2-01-001	RIP-ROARING	83-12-056	ROBERT	19-10-019	ROLLING	2-01-001	ROSEN
1-01-001	RIPA	6-01-001	ROBERTA	1-01-001	ROLLINS	4-02-003	ROSENBERG
14-05-010	RIPE	1-01-001	ROBERTO	11-06-010	ROLLS	1-01-001	ROSENMUELLER
2-02-002	RIPENED	37-07-007	ROBERTS	3-02-002	ROLLS-*ROYCE	7-03-006	ROSES
3-03-003	RIPENING	12-02-002	ROBERTS'	1-01-001	ROLLS-*ROYCES	1-01-001	ROSETTES
6-04-006	RIPPED	2-02-002	ROBERTSON	1-01-001	ROLNICK	1-01-001	ROSIE
3-03-003	RIPPING	1-01-001	ROBERTSONS	1-01-001	ROLOFF	1-01-001	ROSLEV
5-04-004	RIPPLE	4-04-004	ROBES	1-01-001	ROMAGNOSI	11-05-006	ROSS
1-01-001	RIPPLED	2-02-002	ROBIN	58-11-026	ROMAN	2-02-002	ROSSI
5-03-003	RIPPLES	38-05-009	ROBINSON	1-01-001	ROMAN-CAMP	1-01-001	ROSSILINI'S
3-02-002	RIPPLING	1-01-001	ROBINSON'S	13-07-010	ROMANCE	6-01-001	ROSSOFF
102-13-072	RISE	1-01-001	ROBINSONVILLE	1-01-001	ROMANCERS	1-01-001	ROSTAGNO
10-08-009	RISEN	1-01-001	ROBOT	2-02-002	ROMANCES	1-01-001	ROSTAGNOS
20-08-016	RISES	1-01-001	ROBOTISM	1-01-001	ROMANCING	2-02-002	ROSTER
62-13-044	RISING	3-01-001	ROBOTS	1-01-001	ROMANIUK	2-02-002	ROSTRUM
54-12-036	RISK	1-01-001	ROBS	1-01-001	ROMANO	1-01-001	ROSWELL
4-03-004	RISKED	1-01-001	ROBUSTNESS	10-05-008	ROMANS	9-07-009	ROSY
1-01-001	RISKING	2-01-001	ROCCO	32-09-024	ROMANTIC	1-01-001	ROSY-FINGERED
5-05-005	RISKS	2-01-001	ROCHDALE	1-01-001	ROMANTICALLY	8-06-006	ROT
3-02-002	RISKY	2-02-002	ROCHESTER	2-02-002	ROMANTICISM	1-01-001	ROTARIANS
4-01-002	RITCHIE	2-01-001	ROCHFORD	2-01-002	ROMANTICIZE	10-06-008	ROTARY
8-03-005	RITE	75-14-042	ROCK	1-01-001	ROMANTICIZING	2-02-002	ROTATE
4-03-004	RITES	1-01-001	ROCK'N'ROLL	1-01-001	ROMANTICK	6-05-005	ROTATED
1-01-001	RITIUALITY	2-02-002	ROCK-AND-ROLL	5-02-003	ROMANTICS	2-01-002	ROTATING
1-01-001	RITSCHL	1-01-001	ROCK-CARVED	2-01-001	ROMANZA	11-02-007	ROTATING
1-01-001	RITTENHOUSE	1-01-001	ROCK-LIKE	70-10-027	ROME	11-05-007	ROTATION
9-01-002	RITTER	1-01-001	ROCK-RIBBED	2-01-001	ROME'S	1-01-001	ROTATIONALLY
1-01-001	RITTER'S	1-01-001	ROCK-STEADY	3-03-003	ROMEO	1-01-001	ROTATIONS
25-08-012	RITUAL	1-01-001	ROCK-STREWN	1-01-001	ROMEO'S	1-01-001	ROTELLI
1-01-001	RITUALIZED	1-01-001	ROCKABYE	1-01-001	ROMMEL'S	1-01-001	ROTENONE
4-02-002	RITUALS	1-01-001	ROCKAWAYS	1-01-001	ROMP	1-01-001	ROTHKO
1-01-001	RITZ	1-01-001	ROCKBOUND	1-01-001	ROMPED	1-01-001	ROTOGRAVURES
12-06-011	RIVAL	8-06-006	ROCKED	1-01-001	ROMPING	1-01-001	ROTONDA
1-01-001	RIVAL'S	12-05-010	ROCKEFELLER	1-01-001	ROMULO	6-01-001	ROTOR
2-01-001	RIVALED	4-03-004	ROCKER	4-02-004	RON	3-03-003	ROTS
1-01-001	RIVALLED	1-01-001	ROCKERS	5-02-003	RONALD	2-01-002	ROTTEN
3-02-003	RIVALRIES	7-05-006	ROCKET	1-01-001	RONDO	3-02-003	ROTTING
6-05-005	RIVALRY	2-01-001	ROCKET'S	5-02-002	RONNEL	1-01-001	ROTTOSEI
1-01-001	RIVALS	1-01-001	ROCKET-BOMB	1-01-001	RONNIE	1-01-001	ROTUND
1-01-001	RIVEN	1-01-001	ROCKET-BOMBS	59-13-033	ROOF	6-04-004	ROTUNDA
165-13-069	RIVER	13-06-008	ROCKETS	1-01-001	ROOFED	1-01-001	ROTUNDITY
1-01-001	RIVER'S	1-01-001	ROCKETTES	1-01-001	ROOFER	1-01-001	ROUBEN
3-02-002	RIVERBANK	3-01-001	ROCKFORK	1-01-001	ROOFER'S	7-04-006	ROUGE
2-02-002	RIVERBANKS	1-01-001	ROCKHALL	1-01-001	ROOFING	41-10-036	ROUGH
1-01-001	RIVERBOAT	3-02-002	ROCKIES	5-05-005	ROOFS	1-01-001	ROUGH-AND-TUM
17-07-010	RIVERS	1-01-001	ROCKIN	2-02-002	ROOFTOP		
10-03-004	RIVERSIDE	13-04-006	ROCKING	1-01-001	ROOFTOPS	1-01-001	ROUGH-HEWN
1-01-001	RIVERSIDE'S	2-01-001	ROCKLIKE	1-01-001	ROOFTREE	1-01-001	ROUGH-HOUSING
1-01-001	RIVERVIEW	2-02-002	ROCKPORT	9-04-006	ROOKIE	2-01-001	ROUGH-SANDED
1-01-001	RIVETS	23-09-016	ROCKS	1-01-001	ROOKIE-OF-THE	1-01-001	ROUGH-TOUGH
2-02-002	RIVIERA	1-01-001	ROCKSTREWN	4-03-004	ROOKIES	3-01-001	ROUGHCAST
1-01-001	RIVULETS	1-01-001	ROCKVILLE	1-01-001	ROOKLYN	1-01-001	ROUGHED
1-01-001	RIZZUTO	10-07-010	ROCKY	383-15-159	ROOM	2-02-002	ROUGHENED
2-01-001	RO**DTTGER	6-02-002	ROCOCO	1-01-001	ROOM**-FACILITI	1-01-001	ROUGHER
2-02-002	ROACH	18-04-005	ROD		ES	1-01-001	ROUGHEST
197-14-084	ROAD	1-01-001	ROD'S	1-01-001	ROOM'S	1-01-001	ROUGHISH
4-02-002	ROAD'S	3-01-001	RODDER	1-01-001	ROOMBERG	24-10-022	ROUGHLY
1-01-001	ROAD-CIRCUIT	4-01-001	RODDING	1-01-001	ROOMFUL	1-01-001	ROUGHNECK
1-01-001	ROAD-CROSSING	40-09-026	RODE	3-01-002	ROOMING	3-03-003	ROUGHNESS
1-01-001	ROAD-SHOW	3-02-002	RODENT	1-01-001	ROOMMATE	1-01-001	ROUGHSHOD

Freq	Word	Freq	Word	Freq	Word	Freq	Word
1-01-001	ROUGHTLY	6-05-005	RUE	3-03-003	RUSHES	1-01-001	SACRAMENT
4-04-004	ROULETTE	3-03-003	RUEFULLY	10-05-006	RUSHING	3-03-003	SACRAMENTO
1-01-001	ROULETTE'S	1-01-001	RUEFULNESS	1-01-001	RUSHMORE	2-02-002	SACRAMENTS
81-14-055	ROUND	2-02-002	RUFFIAN	10-04-006	RUSK	1-01-001	SACRE
1-01-001	ROUND'S	1-01-001	RUFFIANS	3-01-001	RUSK'S	38-09-028	SACRED
1-01-001	ROUND-BOTTOM	3-02-003	RUFFLED	21-02-002	RUSS	4-01-002	SACREDNESS
1-01-001	ROUND-EYED	1-01-001	RUFFLES	1-01-001	RUSSE	1-01-001	SACRESTIA
1-01-001	ROUND-FACED	1-01-001	RUFUS	12-05-009	RUSSELL	30-11-025	SACRIFICE
1-01-001	ROUND-TABLE	13-08-011	RUG	7-02-002	RUSSELL'S	2-01-002	SACRIFICED
1-01-001	ROUND-THE-CLOCK	4-01-001	RUGER	1-01-001	RUSSET	6-04-006	SACRIFICES
1-01-001	ROUND-TIPPED	1-01-001	RUGER'S	1-01-001	RUSSET-COLORED	2-02-002	SACRIFICIAL
2-02-002	ROUNDABOUT	19-07-015	RUGGED	72-11-044	RUSSIA	2-02-002	SACRIFICING
15-10-014	ROUNDED	1-01-001	RUGGEDLY	14-05-010	RUSSIA'S	2-01-001	SACRIFICIUM
3-01-001	ROUNDHEAD	1-01-001	RUGGIERO	80-11-036	RUSSIAN	2-02-002	SACRILEGE
2-02-002	ROUNDHOUSE	4-03-004	RUGS	1-01-001	RUSSIAN-DOMINAT ED	1-01-001	SACROSANCT
5-05-005	ROUNDING	2-01-001	RUH			35-12-025	SAD
2-02-002	ROUNDLY	1-01-001	RUIDOSO	31-09-022	RUSSIANS	1-01-001	SADDENED
1-01-001	ROUNDNESS	14-07-013	RUIN	1-01-001	RUSSIANS'	1-01-001	SADDER
13-07-008	ROUNDS	16-08-013	RUINED	1-01-001	RUSSO-*AMERICAN	25-05-012	SADDLE
3-03-003	ROUNDUP	1-01-001	RUINING	10-04-006	RUST	3-01-001	SADDLEBAGS
1-01-001	ROUNDUPS	1-01-001	RUINOUS	1-01-001	RUSTED	4-04-004	SADDLED
19-01-002	ROURKE	8-04-007	RUINS	3-02-003	RUSTIC	2-02-002	SADDLES
3-01-001	ROURKE'S	1-01-001	RUIZ	1-01-001	RUSTING	5-01-001	SADIE
2-02-002	ROUSE	1-01-001	RUL	4-03-003	RUSTLE	3-03-003	SADISM
2-02-002	ROUSED	73-12-050	RULE	2-01-002	RUSTLED	1-01-001	SADIST
8-04-007	ROUSING	31-10-026	RULED	4-02-002	RUSTLER	2-02-002	SADISTIC
19-02-003	ROUSSEAU	3-03-003	RULER	1-01-001	RUSTLER-HUNTER	12-06-011	SADLY
3-01-003	ROUSSEAU'S	9-06-008	RULERS	1-01-001	RUSTLERS	6-06-006	SADNESS
1-01-001	ROUSSEAUAN	1-01-001	RULERS'	1-01-001	RUSTLIN	2-02-002	SAFARI
43-09-028	ROUTE	85-13-039	RULES	10-02-003	RUSTLING	1-01-001	SAFAVIDS
1-01-001	ROUTED	24-06-015	RULING	1-01-001	RUSTPROOF	58-13-049	SAFE
6-04-004	ROUTES	1-01-001	RULING'S	8-05-006	RUSTY	1-01-001	SAFE-CONDUCT
35-13-031	ROUTINE	1-01-001	RULING-CLASS	1-01-001	RUT	1-01-001	SAFE-CRACKING
1-01-001	ROUTINELY	2-01-002	RULINGS	1-01-001	RUTABAGA	1-01-001	SAFE-DRIVING
3-03-003	ROUTINES	3-03-003	RUM	1-01-001	RUTABAGAS	5-03-005	SAFEGUARD
1-01-001	ROUTINGS	1-01-001	RUM-TUM-TUM	23-05-008	RUTH	1-01-001	SAFEGUARDS
1-01-001	ROUTO-*JIG	1-01-001	RUMANIA	8-02-003	RUTH'S	1-01-001	SAFEKEEPING
1-01-001	ROVE	1-01-001	RUMANIAN	1-01-001	RUTHENIUM	13-09-013	SAFELY
1-01-001	ROVED	1-01-001	RUMANIANS	1-01-001	RUTHERFORD	5-05-005	SAFER
4-02-002	ROVER	2-02-002	RUMBLE	7-06-007	RUTHLESS	4-04-004	SAFEST
2-02-002	ROVING	2-01-001	RUMBLED	2-02-002	RUTHLESSLY	1-01-001	SAFETIES
35-10-027	ROW	1-01-001	RUMBLES	3-03-003	RUTHLESSNESS	47-10-027	SAFETY
4-03-004	ROWDY	2-02-002	RUMBLING	2-02-002	RUTS	1-01-001	SAFFRON
2-02-002	ROWED	2-01-001	RUMDUM	1-01-001	RUTSTEIN	4-04-004	SAG
1-01-001	ROWLANDS'	2-01-001	RUMEN	1-01-001	RUTTED	7-04-007	SAGA
2-02-002	ROWLEY	2-02-002	RUMFORD	1-01-001	RUYSCH	1-01-001	SAGAMI
16-09-012	ROWS	1-01-001	RUMINANTS	1-01-001	RY	2-02-002	SAGE
1-01-001	ROWSWELL	1-01-001	RUMMAGED	15-02-002	RYAN	1-01-001	SAGEBRUSH
1-01-001	ROXY	3-03-003	RUMMAGING	1-01-001	RYC	1-01-001	SAGES
37-06-010	ROY	1-01-001	RUMMEL	1-01-001	RYCHARD	3-03-003	SAGGED
1-01-001	ROY'S	1-01-001	RUMMY	1-01-001	RYDER	4-02-004	SAGGING
48-10-029	ROYAL	4-02-003	RUMOR	4-02-003	RYE	1-01-001	SAGO
1-01-001	ROYALE	2-02-002	RUMORED	1-01-001	RYERSON	1-01-001	SAGS
2-01-001	ROYALTIES	6-04-004	RUMORS	1-01-001	RYLIE	2-02-002	SAHARA
7-04-004	ROYALTY	2-01-002	RUMP	1-01-001	RYNE	1-01-001	SAHJUNT
1-01-001	ROYALTY-FREE	2-02-002	RUMPLED	8-01-001	RYUSENJI	1961-15-317	SAID
1-01-001	ROYAUX	1-01-001	RUMPUS	135-11-073	S	1-01-001	SAIGON
3-02-002	ROYCE	1-01-001	RUMSCHEIDT	1-01-001	S*$**(HE'D	12-05-007	SAIL
1-01-001	ROYLOTT'S	212-15-137	RUN	2-02-002	S**.*C	1-01-001	SAILBOAT
1-01-001	ROZELLA	1-01-001	RUN-DOWN	5-01-001	S**.*K	3-01-001	SAILBOATS
1-01-001	ROZELLE	1-01-001	RUN-OF-THE-MINE	1-01-001	S**.*P**.*C**.* A	10-03-006	SAILED
5-02-002	RPM	1-01-001	RUN-SCORING			20-08-014	SAILING
1-01-001	RPM,	2-02-002	RUN-UP	1-01-001	S**.*S	5-04-004	SAILOR
2-02-002	RTE	1-01-001	RUN-UPS	1-01-001	S**.*S**.*R	1-01-001	SAILORLY
8-01-001	RUANDA-*URUNDI	1-01-001	RUN/CHAMBER	1-01-001	S**$0	8-06-006	SAILORS
1-01-001	RUARK'S	1-01-001	RUNABOUT	1-01-001	S'ACCUSE	2-02-002	SAILS
6-05-005	RUB	6-04-004	RUNAWAY	1-01-001	S'EXCUSE	16-10-014	SAINT
18-08-015	RUBBED	1-01-001	RUNDFUNK	1-01-001	S'POSIN	1-01-001	SAINT-*SAENS
15-07-013	RUBBER	1-01-001	RUNDFUNK-*SINFO NIE-*ORCHESTER	1-01-001	S**YA**YK**YO** YS	1-01-001	SAINTED
1-01-001	RUBBER-LIKE					1-01-001	SAINTHOOD
1-01-001	RUBBERIZED	1-01-001	RUNDFUNKCHOR	1-01-001	S*S	1-01-001	SAINTLINESS
1-01-001	RUBBERY	3-02-003	RUNDOWN	1-01-001	S-S-SAHJUNT	6-03-006	SAINTS
1-01-001	RUBBIN	1-01-001	RUNES	1-01-001	SAABYE	1-01-001	SAINTSBURY
11-05-008	RUBBING	3-02-003	RUNG	1-01-001	SAADI	4-03-004	SAITH
4-03-004	RUBBISH	1-01-001	RUNING	1-01-001	SABA	41-12-033	SAKE
1-01-001	RUBBLE	1-01-001	RUNNER	2-02-002	SABBATH	2-01-001	SAKELLARIADIS
1-01-001	RUBDOWN	2-02-002	RUNNER-UP	7-01-001	SABELLA	1-01-001	SAKELLARIADISES
1-01-001	RUBE	7-01-001	RUNNERS	1-01-001	SABER	1-01-001	SAKO
1-01-001	RUBENS	2-01-001	RUNNIN	2-01-001	SABINA	1-01-001	SAL*FININISTAS
1-01-001	RUBICUND	123-15-082	RUNNING	1-01-001	SABINAS	1-01-001	SALABLE
1-01-001	RUBIES	2-02-002	RUNOFF	2-02-002	SABINE	2-02-002	SALACIOUS
1-01-001	RUBRIC	55-12-026	RUNS	2-02-002	SABLE	9-05-006	SALAD
1-01-001	RUCELLAI	1-01-001	RUNT	1-01-001	SABLES	3-02-002	SALADS
1-01-001	RUCKUS	4-02-004	RUNWAY	1-01-001	SABOL	2-01-001	SALAMANDER
1-01-001	RUDDER	4-02-002	RUNWAYS	3-02-002	SABOTAGE	7-03-003	SALAMI
1-01-001	RUDDERLESS	3-01-001	RUNYON	1-01-001	SABRAS	1-01-001	SALARIED
1-01-001	RUDDINESS	1-01-001	RUNYON'S	2-02-002	SABRE	8-06-008	SALARIES
3-03-003	RUDDY	6-01-001	RUPEE	1-01-001	SABRE-RATTLING	43-12-025	SALARY
6-05-006	RUDE	14-01-001	RUPEES	2-02-002	SACHEMS	44-11-032	SALE
2-02-002	RUDELY	1-01-001	RUPPERT	1-01-001	SACHEMS'	3-01-001	SALEDO
1-01-001	RUDENESS	3-01-001	RUPTURE	1-01-001	SACHEVERELL	19-04-008	SALEM
4-04-004	RUDIMENTARY	2-01-002	RUPTURED	8-05-007	SACK	133-09-036	SALES
1-01-001	RUDKOEBING	54-09-027	RURAL	1-01-001	SACKER	1-01-001	SALES-BUILDING
1-01-001	RUDOLF	2-02-002	RUSE	1-01-001	SACKES	1-01-001	SALES-CONSCIOUS
3-01-001	RUDOLPH	20-09-020	RUSH	1-01-001	SACKING	1-01-001	SALESGIRL
4-02-003	RUDY	1-01-001	RUSHALL	1-01-001	SACKS	3-01-001	SALESLADY
1-01-001	RUDYARD	27-12-023	RUSHED	1-01-001	SACRAL	12-07-010	SALESMAN

1-01-001	SALESMAN'S	28-10-018	SAND	1-01-001	SATIATE	200-14-112	SAYS
6-03-003	SALESMANSHIP	3-01-001	SANDALPHON	2-02-002	SATIETY	5-02-003	SCABBARD
19-06-006	SALESMEN	5-03-004	SANDALS	5-02-003	SATIN	1-01-001	SCABBED
1-01-001	SALFININISTAS	2-02-002	SANDALWOOD	1-01-001	SATIN-COVERED	1-01-001	SCABROUS
1-01-001	SALIDA	1-01-001	SANDBARS	9-04-006	SATIRE	6-04-005	SCAFFOLD
4-03-003	SALIENT	22-02-002	SANDBURG	3-01-001	SATIRES	3-02-002	SCAFFOLDING
31-02-004	SALINE	3-03-003	SANDBURG'S	4-03-003	SATIRIC	1-01-001	SCAFFOLDINGS
4-03-003	SALINGER	2-02-002	SANDBURGS	3-03-003	SATIRICAL	1-01-001	SCAIRT
5-02-002	SALISBURY	1-01-001	SANDE'S	1-01-001	SATIRICALLY	1-01-001	SCALA
1-01-001	SALISH	1-01-001	SANDER	1-01-001	SATIRIST	2-01-001	SCALAR
4-02-002	SALIVA	2-01-001	SANDERSON	1-01-001	SATIRIZES	1-01-001	SCALD
1-01-001	SALIVARY	2-01-002	SANDING	2-01-001	SATIS	1-01-001	SCALDED
1-01-001	SALIVATE	5-01-001	SANDMAN	28-12-026	SATISFACTION	1-01-001	SCALDING
1-01-001	SALK	1-01-001	SANDPAPER	4-04-004	SATISFACTIONS	60-10-037	SCALE
2-02-002	SALLE	1-01-001	SANDRA	11-06-007	SATISFACTORILY	2-02-002	SCALED
1-01-001	SALLIES	10-08-009	SANDS	39-08-036	SATISFACTORY	5-03-005	SCALES
1-01-001	SALLOW	10-06-009	SANDWICH	36-10-034	SATISFIED	2-02-002	SCALLOPED
13-04-004	SALLY	1-01-001	SANDWICH-TYPE	3-01-001	SATISFIES	1-01-001	SCALLOPS
2-01-001	SALLY'S	4-02-004	SANDWICHES	16-09-015	SATISFY	4-02-003	SCALP
1-01-001	SALLYING	6-05-006	SANDY	13-09-012	SATISFYING	1-01-001	SCAMPERING
3-03-003	SALMON	8-05-005	SANE	1-01-001	SATTERFIELD	1-01-001	SCAMPINI
1-01-001	SALOMONOVICH	1-01-001	SANER	7-04-005	SATURATED	5-04-004	SCAN
1-01-001	SALON	1-01-001	SANEST	5-03-004	SATURATION	8-05-006	SCANDAL
3-02-002	SALONS	2-01-001	SANFORD'S	67-10-039	SATURDAY	3-02-003	SCANDALIZED
12-06-010	SALOON	29-08-022	SANG	3-02-003	SATURDAY'S	1-01-001	SCANDALIZING
1-01-001	SALOONKEEPER	1-01-001	SANG-FROID	1-01-001	SATURDAY-NIGHT	7-03-003	SCANDALS
8-05-005	SALOONS	1-01-001	SANGALLO	2-02-002	SATURDAYS	1-01-001	SCANDINAVIA
1-01-001	SALPETRIERE	1-01-001	SANGALLO'S	3-01-001	SATURN	2-02-002	SCANDINAVIAN
1-01-001	SALSICH	1-01-001	SANGAREE	20-02-003	SAUCE	1-01-001	SCANDINAVIANS
46-12-025	SALT	1-01-001	SANGER-*HARRIS	3-01-002	SAUCEPAN	10-06-009	SCANNED
1-01-001	SALT-CRUSTED	1-01-001	SANGIOVANNI	2-02-002	SAUCERS	1-01-001	SCANNERS
1-01-001	SALT-EDGED	1-01-001	SANGUINEOUS	5-02-002	SAUCES	4-02-002	SCANNING
1-01-001	SALT-FRACTIONAT	1-01-001	SANGUINEUM	1-01-001	SAUCY	2-02-002	SCANS
	ION	1-01-001	SANHEDRIN	1-01-001	SAUD	5-03-005	SCANT
1-01-001	SALTBUSH	2-01-001	SANIPRACTOR	1-01-001	SAUD'S	4-04-004	SCANTY
4-03-003	SALTED	1-01-001	SANITAIRE	2-01-001	SAUDI	1-01-001	SCAPEGOAT
9-02-002	SALTER	1-01-001	SANITARIUM	1-01-001	SAUDI-*AMERICAN	1-01-001	SCAPEGOATS
1-01-001	SALTER'S	4-03-004	SANITARY	4-02-002	SAUERKRAUT	4-01-001	SCAPIN
2-02-002	SALTING	11-06-010	SANITATION	2-02-002	SAUL	1-01-001	SCAPULARS
1-01-001	SALTIS-*MC*ERLA	4-04-004	SANITY	1-01-001	SAUNDERS	10-05-006	SCAR
	NE	18-09-015	SANK	1-01-001	SAUSAGE	1-01-001	SCARBOROUGH
1-01-001	SALTON	2-02-002	SANS	1-01-001	SAUSAGE-MEAT	6-05-006	SCARCE
1-01-001	SALTONSTALL	12-01-001	SANSOM	5-02-002	SAUSAGES	24-10-022	SCARCELY
6-03-005	SALTS	1-01-001	SANSOME	1-01-001	SAUTE	1-01-001	SCARCELY-TAPPED
4-03-004	SALTY	3-01-001	SANT	1-01-001	SAUTERNE	3-03-003	SCARCITY
1-01-001	SALU	28-07-013	SANTA	1-01-001	SAUTERNES	3-03-003	SCARE
2-02-002	SALUBRIOUS	1-01-001	SANTA'S	22-10-022	SAVAGE	1-01-001	SCARECROWISH
1-01-001	SALUTARIS	3-02-002	SANTAYANA	3-03-003	SAVAGELY	21-07-013	SCARED
5-04-005	SALUTARY	1-01-001	SANTAYANA'S	1-01-001	SAVAGERY	4-02-004	SCARF
1-01-001	SALUTATION	5-01-001	SANTE	6-03-003	SAVAGES	1-01-001	SCARFACE
3-03-003	SALUTE	2-01-001	SANTO	9-05-005	SAVANNAH	1-01-001	SCARIFY
3-03-003	SALUTED	1-01-001	SAP	2-01-001	SAVANNAKHET	1-01-001	SCARING
3-02-002	SALVADOR	3-02-002	SAPIO	62-12-047	SAVE	3-03-003	SCARLET
5-04-004	SALVAGE	2-02-002	SAPLING	43-11-034	SAVED	2-02-002	SCARRED
2-02-002	SALVAGING	1-01-001	SAPONINS	1-01-001	SAVER	10-07-009	SCARS
32-04-015	SALVATION	3-02-003	SAPPED	5-04-005	SAVES	2-02-002	SCARSDALE
1-01-001	SALVATORE	1-01-001	SAPPING	21-10-020	SAVING	2-02-002	SCARY
3-02-003	SALVE	1-01-001	SAPPY	23-05-019	SAVINGS	1-01-001	SCATHING
1-01-001	SALVES	1-01-001	SAPS	6-03-005	SAVIOR	1-01-001	SCATHINGLY
2-02-002	SALVO	4-01-001	SARA	9-01-002	SAVIOUR	2-01-001	SCATTER
1-01-001	SALVOS	2-02-002	SARA'S	1-01-001	SAVONAROLA	2-01-001	SCATTERBRAINED
3-01-001	SALYER'S	2-02-002	SARACENS	1-01-001	SAVOR	27-10-025	SCATTERED
79-09-026	SAM	26-04-005	SARAH	3-03-003	SAVORED	2-01-001	SCATTERGUN
4-02-004	SAM'S	3-01-001	SARAH'S	3-03-003	SAVORING	2-01-001	SCATTERING
1-01-001	SAMAR	1-01-001	SARAN	4-03-003	SAVORY	1-01-001	SCATTERS
1-01-001	SAMBA	1-01-001	SARASATE	4-01-002	SAVOY	1-01-001	SCAVENGER
1-01-001	SAMBUR	1-01-001	SARASON	2-01-001	SAVOYARDS	1-01-001	SCAVENGING
686-15-336	SAME	1-01-001	SARASOTA	1-01-001	SAVVY	1-01-001	SCENARIO
4-02-002	SAMENESS	4-04-004	SARATOGA	352-15-184	SAW	1-01-001	SCENARIOS
1-01-001	SAMMARTINI	1-01-001	SARCASM	1-01-001	SAW-HORSE	106-14-065	SCENE
1-01-001	SAMMY	1-01-001	SARCASMS	1-01-001	SAWALISCH	1-01-001	SCENERIES
1-01-001	SAMOA	1-01-001	SARCASTIC	1-01-001	SAWALLISCH	14-06-013	SCENERY
1-01-001	SAMOS	1-01-001	SARCASTICALLY	3-03-003	SAWDUST	29-09-023	SCENES
2-01-001	SAMOVAR	1-01-001	SARCOLEMMAL	1-01-001	SAWED-OFF	9-03-004	SCENIC
57-08-023	SAMPLE	1-01-001	SARDANAPALUS	1-01-001	SAWING	1-01-001	SCENICS
7-04-006	SAMPLED	2-02-002	SARDINES	1-01-001	SAWMILL	6-04-006	SCENT
1-01-001	SAMPLERS	2-02-002	SARDONIC	1-01-001	SAWNDERS	5-02-005	SCENTED
29-05-012	SAMPLES	5-04-005	SARGENT	3-02-002	SAWS	3-01-001	SCEPTICAL
22-03-007	SAMPLING	1-01-001	SARI	3-01-001	SAWTIMBER	5-01-002	SCEPTICISM
2-01-001	SAMPSON	2-01-001	SARKEES	1-01-001	SAWYER	3-01-001	SCHAACK
34-08-022	SAMUEL	1-01-001	SARMI	6-02-002	SAX	4-01-001	SCHAEFER
1-01-001	SAMUELS	2-01-001	SARPSIS	18-01-001	SAXON	2-01-001	SCHAEFFER
70-14-039	SAN	1-01-001	SARSAPARILLA	7-01-001	SAXONS	9-01-001	SCHAFFNER
1-01-001	SAN*ANTONIO	1-01-001	SARTI	1-01-001	SAXONY	1-01-001	SCHANG
1-01-001	SANA	3-01-002	SARTORIS	4-01-001	SAXOPHONE	1-01-001	SCHAPIRO
2-02-002	SANATORIUM	2-02-002	SARTRE	1-01-001	SAXOPHONIST	36-08-027	SCHEDULE
1-01-001	SANCHEZ	1-01-001	SARUM'S	2-01-001	SAXTON	38-12-032	SCHEDULED
3-01-001	SANCHO	3-02-003	SASH	1-01-001	SAXTON'S	10-07-010	SCHEDULES
1-01-001	SANCTAM	1-01-001	SASHAYED	504-15-242	SAY	2-02-002	SCHEDULING
1-01-001	SANCTIFIED	1-01-001	SASHIMI	1-01-001	SAY-SO	2-02-002	SCHEHERAZADE
2-02-002	SANCTIMONIOUS	2-01-002	SASSAFRAS	1-01-001	SAY-SPEAK	2-02-002	SCHELLING
11-06-008	SANCTION	1-01-001	SASSING	1-01-001	SAYED	3-01-001	SCHEMA
4-03-004	SANCTIONED	150-14-080	SAT	1-01-001	SAYERS	1-01-001	SCHEMATA
9-03-005	SANCTIONS	3-03-003	SATAN	5-03-003	SAYIN	3-01-003	SCHEMATIC
3-02-003	SANCTITY	1-01-001	SATAN'S	113-14-089	SAYING	3-01-001	SCHEMATICALLY
9-06-006	SANCTUARY	8-05-007	SATELLITE	1-01-001	SAYINGS	33-12-024	SCHEME
1-01-001	SANCTUARY'S	7-04-004	SATELLITES	1-01-001	SAYONARA	6-05-006	SCHEMES

3-03-003 SCHEMING	8-01-001 SCIENCE-FICTION	12-05-007 SCRATCHING	1-01-001 SEAMLESS
2-01-001 SCHENK	35-08-015 SCIENCES	1-01-001 SCRATCHY	9-04-004 SEAMS
2-01-001 SCHERER	86-09-047 SCIENTIFIC	5-03-004 SCRAWLED	2-02-002 SEAN
1-01-001 SCHERZO	4-03-004 SCIENTIFICALLY	4-04-004 SCRAWNY	2-01-002 SEAPORTS
4-01-001 SCHIELE	1-01-001 SCIENTIFICALLY-TRAINED	13-05-012 SCREAM	1-01-001 SEAQUAKE
3-01-001 SCHIELE'S	1-01-001 SCIENTIFIQUE	17-07-014 SCREAMED	2-01-001 SEAQUARIUM
1-01-001 SCHILLING	17-08-011 SCIENTIST	17-08-016 SCREAMING	2-01-001 SEAR
4-01-001 SCHILLINGER	36-10-026 SCIENTISTS	2-02-002 SCREAMS	66-13-050 SEARCH
1-01-001 SCHISM	1-01-001 SCIMITAR	1-01-001 SCREECH	9-06-009 SEARCHED
6-01-001 SCHIZOPHRENIC	5-03-004 SCIMITAR-WIELDING	5-03-004 SCREECHED	3-03-003 SEARCHES
1-01-001 SCHLEIERMACHER	1-01-001 SCIMITARS	1-01-001 SCREECHES	23-11-021 SEARCHING
2-01-001 SCHLEK	1-01-001 SCINTILLATING	7-04-006 SCREECHING	1-01-001 SEARCHINGLY
2-01-001 SCHLESINGER	1-01-001 SCION	1-01-001 SCREECHY	1-01-001 SEARCHINGS
1-01-001 SCHLEY	1-01-001 SCIONS	48-11-031 SCREEN	2-01-001 SEARCHLIGHT
1-01-001 SCHLIEREN	1-01-001 SCISSORING	2-02-002 SCREENED	1-01-001 SEARCHLIGHTS
1-01-001 SCHMALMA	1-01-001 SCISSORS	5-03-005 SCREENING	2-01-002 SEARING
1-01-001 SCHMALZRIED	2-02-002 SCLEROSIS	1-01-001 SCREENINGS	1-01-001 SEARLES
1-01-001 SCHMIDL-*SEEBERG	1-01-001 SCLEROTIC	1-01-001 SCREENLAND	2-01-001 SEARS
1-01-001 SCHMIDT	1-01-001 SCOBEE-*FRAZIER	1-01-001 SCREENPLAY	10-05-007 SEAS
2-01-001 SCHMITT	3-02-003 SCOFFED	10-06-007 SCREENS	5-04-005 SEASHORE
6-01-001 SCHNABEL	1-01-001 SCOFFING	3-01-001 SCREVANE	2-02-002 SEASIDE
6-01-001 SCHNABEL'S	1-01-001 SCOLATTI	21-05-007 SCREW	105-12-050 SEASON
1-01-001 SCHNABEL-*PRO	2-02-002 SCOLDING	105-12-050 SCREW-LOOSE	3-03-003 SEASON'S
2-02-002 SCHNABELIAN	5-04-004 SCOOP	1-01-001 SCREWBALL	8-07-007 SEASONAL
1-01-001 SCHNAPPS	3-03-003 SCOOPED	14-05-006 SCREWED	1-01-001 SEASONALLY
1-01-001 SCHNOOKS	1-01-001 SCOOPING	10-01-004 SCREWS	5-03-004 SEASONED
2-01-001 SCHO**DNBERG	4-03-004 SCOOTED	1-01-001 SCRIBBLED	2-01-002 SEASONING
1-01-001 SCHO**DNBERG'S	1-01-001 SCOOTING	4-02-002 SCRIBE	17-09-015 SEASONS
1-01-001 SCHO**DNE	1-01-001 SCOP	1-01-001 SCRIBING	54-10-035 SEAT
1-01-001 SCHOCKLER	27-08-025 SCOPE	1-01-001 SCRIM	24-10-018 SEATED
15-06-010 SCHOLAR	1-01-001 SCOPED	1-01-001 SCRIMMAGE	5-03-003 SEATING
1-01-001 SCHOLAR-BUSINESSMAN	1-01-001 SCOPES	1-01-001 SCRIMMAGED	1-01-001 SEATON
8-05-007 SCHOLARLY	1-01-001 SCOPS	2-02-002 SCRIPPS	2-01-001 SEATON'S
27-08-013 SCHOLARS	2-01-002 SCORCHED	11-08-009 SCRIPT	15-08-011 SEATS
36-10-020 SCHOLARSHIP	1-01-001 SCORCHER	1-01-001 SCRIPT'S	7-03-006 SEATTLE
8-05-006 SCHOLARSHIPS	66-11-035 SCORE	2-02-002 SCRIPTURAL	3-02-002 SEAWEED
9-06-007 SCHOLASTIC	4-02-004 SCOREBOARD	4-03-004 SCRIPTURE	19-03-005 SEC
1-01-001 SCHOLASTICA	1-01-001 SCOREBOARDS	11-05-007 SCRIPTURES	12-01-001 SECANT
1-01-001 SCHOLASTICALLY	1-01-001 SCORECARD	3-01-002 SCRIVENER	16-01-001 SECANTS
1-01-001 SCHOLASTICS	15-05-009 SCORED	1-01-001 SCROOGE-LIKE	3-01-001 SECCO
492-15-139 SCHOOL	2-01-001 SCORELESS	1-01-001 SCROUNGING	10-02-002 SECEDE
3-02-003 SCHOOL'S	15-04-006 SCORES	9-07-008 SCRUB	2-01-001 SECEDED
1-01-001 SCHOOL-AGE	5-03-005 SCORING	1-01-001 SCRUBBED	2-01-002 SECEDING
1-01-001 SCHOOL-LEAVING	4-04-004 SCORN	3-03-003 SCRUBBING	1-01-001 SECESH
1-01-001 SCHOOLBOOKS	2-02-002 SCORNED	1-01-001 SCRUMPTIOUS	2-02-002 SECESSION
3-03-003 SCHOOLBOY	5-03-004 SCORNFUL	1-01-001 SCRUPULOSITY	3-03-003 SECESSIONIST
1-01-001 SCHOOLBOYS	2-02-002 SCORNFULLY	1-01-001 SCRUPULOUS	1-01-001 SECLUDE
1-01-001 SCHOOLCHILDREN	2-01-001 SCOT	1-01-001 SCRUPULOUSLY	1-01-001 SECLUDED
1-01-001 SCHOOLDAYS	1-01-001 SCOT-FREE	2-01-001 SCRUTIN	3-03-003 SECLUSION
1-01-001 SCHOOLED	14-06-013 SCOTCH	3-03-003 SCRUTINIZED	373-15-223 SECOND
1-01-001 SCHOOLERS	2-02-002 SCOTCH-*IRISH-*SCANDINAVIAN	3-03-003 SCRUTINIZING	2-02-002 SECOND-
1-01-001 SCHOOLGIRL	1-01-001 SCOTCH-AND-SODA	14-06-013 SCRUTINY	2-01-002 SECOND-CLASS
1-01-001 SCHOOLGIRLISH	1-01-001 SCOTCHGARD	2-01-001 SCUDDING	2-01-001 SECOND-DEGREE
1-01-001 SCHOOLGIRLS	1-01-001 SCOTCHMAN	1-01-001 SCUFF	1-01-001 SECOND-ECHELON
11-03-003 SCHOOLHOUSE	6-03-003 SCOTIAN	1-01-001 SCUFFLE	1-01-001 SECOND-FLOOR
5-03-005 SCHOOLING	1-01-001 SCOTLAND	2-02-002 SCULPTED	2-02-002 SECOND-HALF
1-01-001 SCHOOLMARM	13-05-009 SCOTS	1-01-001 SCULPTOR	1-01-001 SECOND-HAND
3-01-002 SCHOOLMASTER	8-03-004 SCOTT	1-01-001 SCULPTOR'S	1-01-001 SECOND-LEVEL
1-01-001 SCHOOLMASTER'S	16-06-012 SCOTT'S	1-01-001 SCULPTORS	1-01-001 SECOND-LOOK
1-01-001 SCHOOLMATE	1-01-001 SCOTTISH	2-01-001 SCULPTURAL	1-01-001 SECOND-ORDER
2-01-001 SCHOOLMATES	10-04-006 SCOTTY	11-05-007 SCULPTURE	1-01-001 SECOND-PLACE
3-01-002 SCHOOLROOM	32-01-001 SCOTTY'S	5-04-004 SCULPTURED	5-04-004 SECOND-RATE
195-13-059 SCHOOLS	11-02-002 SCOUNDREL	7-04-005 SCULPTURES	1-01-001 SECOND-STAGE
1-01-001 SCHOOLWORK	1-01-001 SCOUNDRELS	1-01-001 SCURRIED	1-01-001 SECOND-STORY
3-02-002 SCHOONER	1-01-001 SCOUR	3-02-003 SCURRILOUS	3-02-003 SECONDARILY
1-01-001 SCHOPENHAUER	2-02-002 SCOURED	1-01-001 SCURVY	31-08-023 SECONDARY
1-01-001 SCHOPENHAUER'S	3-03-003 SCOURED	1-01-001 SCUSE	1-01-001 SECONDHAND
1-01-001 SCHOTT	2-02-002 SCOURGE	2-02-002 SCUTTLED	5-03-005 SECONDLY
1-01-001 SCHRAFFTS	4-04-004 SCOURING	1-01-001 SCUTTLING	27-12-020 SECONDS
2-01-001 SCHRAMM	5-01-001 SCOURS	9-05-008 SE	9-05-008 SECRECY
1-01-001 SCHRUNK	8-04-004 SCOUT	95-15-052 SEA	78-15-056 SECRET
1-01-001 SCHU**DTZ	1-01-001 SCOUT'S	1-01-001 SEA'S	4-04-004 SECRETARIAL
2-02-002 SCHUBERT	1-01-001 SCOUTED	4-04-004 SEA-BEACH	5-04-005 SECRETARIAT
4-03-003 SCHUBERT'S	3-03-003 SCOUTING	1-01-001 SEA-BLESSED	1-01-001 SECRETARIATE
1-01-001 SCHUBERT-*BEETHOVEN-*MOZART	2-02-002 SCOUTS	9-06-009 SEA-DAMP	9-06-009 SECRETARIES
2-01-001 SCHULTZ	4-04-004 SCOWLED	1-01-001 SEA-HORSES	1-01-001 SECRETARIES'
1-01-001 SCHULZ	2-02-002 SCOWLING	9-05-005 SEA-ROAD	191-13-066 SECRETARY
1-01-001 SCHUMAN	2-01-001 SCRAGGLY	2-01-001 SEA-VILLAGE	9-05-005 SECRETARY'S
1-01-001 SCHUMAN'S	1-01-001 SCRAMBLE	4-01-001 SEABOARD	2-01-001 SECRETARY-*GENERAL
9-05-009 SCHUMANN'S	1-01-001 SCRAMBLED	1-01-001 SEABORG	
1-01-001 SCHUMANN'S	1-01-001 SCRAMBLING	1-01-001 SEABROOK	1-01-001 SECRETARY-DESIGNATE
3-02-002 SCHUYLER	8-07-008 SCRAP	3-03-003 SEACOAST	2-02-002 SECRETARY-TREASURER
1-01-001 SCHUYLER'S	1-01-001 SCRAPBOOK	2-02-002 SEAFARERS	
7-03-003 SCHUYLKILL	3-03-003 SCRAPE	1-01-001 SEAFARING	1-01-001 SECRETED
2-01-001 SCHWAB	8-06-008 SCRAPED	3-02-002 SEAFOOD	4-01-002 SECRETION
1-01-001 SCHWADA	1-01-001 SCRAPES	1-01-001 SEAGOVILLE	1-01-001 SECRETIONS
6-03-005 SCHWARTZ	7-05-006 SCRAPING	1-01-001 SEAGULLS	6-06-006 SECRETLY
1-01-001 SCHWARZEN	1-01-001 SCRAPINGS	17-06-008 SEAHORSE	20-06-008 SECRETS
6-01-001 SCHWARZKOPF	1-01-001 SCRAPIRON	13-05-010 SEAL	2-02-002 SECT
9-04-005 SCHWEITZER	1-01-001 SCRAPPED	4-04-004 SEALED	1-01-001 SECTARIAN
1-01-001 SCHWEITZERS	4-03-004 SCRAPS	189-14-082 SEALING	189-14-082 SECTION
1-01-001 SCHWEIZER	9-03-003 SCRATCH	1-01-001 SEALS	1-01-001 SECTIONALIZED
4-02-002 SCIATICA	7-04-007 SCRATCHED	70-09-023 SEAM	70-09-023 SECTIONS
131-13-052 SCIENCE	6-03-003 SCRATCHES	13-07-010 SEAMAN	13-07-010 SECTOR
1-01-001 SCIENCE'S	1-01-001 SCRATCHINESS	10-06-009 SEAMANSHIP	10-06-009 SECTORS
		2-02-002 SEAMEN	2-02-002 SECTS

16-06-011	SECULAR	23-09-021	SELECT	1-01-001	SELF-OBSERVATIO N	1-01-001	SEMIARID
1-01-001	SECULARISM	74-10-050	SELECTED			1-01-001	SEMIAUTOMATIC
1-01-001	SECULARIST	15-06-014	SELECTING	1-01-001	SELF-ORDAINED	1-01-001	SEMICIRCULAR
1-01-001	SECULARISTS	39-08-026	SELECTION	1-01-001	SELF-PACIFICATI ON	1-01-001	SEMIDRYING
3-02-002	SECULARIZED	1-01-001	SELECTION-REJEC TION	1-01-001	SELF-PERCEIVED	1-01-001	SEMIEMPIRICAL
30-08-025	SECURE			3-02-003	SELF-PITY	1-01-001	SEMINAL
11-08-011	SECURED	15-05-009	SELECTIONS	1-01-001	SELF-PITYING	4-03-004	SEMINAR
5-04-005	SECURELY	18-07-013	SELECTIVE	1-01-001	SELF-PLAGIARISM S	1-01-001	SEMINARIANS
7-04-007	SECURING	2-02-002	SELECTIVELY			1-01-001	SEMINARIO
8-03-005	SECURITIES	1-01-001	SELECTIVITY	1-01-001	SELF-PORTRAIT	10-04-005	SEMINARY
91-11-050	SECURITY	1-01-001	SELECTMEN	1-01-001	SELF-PORTRAITS	1-01-001	SEMINOLE
2-02-002	SED	1-01-001	SELECTORS	2-02-002	SELF-PRESERVATI ON	1-01-001	SEMIPUBLIC
2-02-002	SEDAN	5-04-005	SELECTS			1-01-001	SEMIQUANTITATIV E
4-01-001	SEDANS	4-01-001	SELENA	1-01-001	SELF-PROCLAIMED		
2-02-002	SEDATE	40-13-029	SELF	1-01-001	SELF-PROTECTION	1-01-001	SEMIRAMIS
2-02-002	SEDATELY	1-01-001	SELF'S	1-01-001	SELF-REALIZED	1-01-001	SEMISECRET
1-01-001	SEDATIVE	1-01-001	SELF-ACCEPTANCE	1-01-001	SELF-REDEFINITI ON	1-01-001	SEMITRANCE
1-01-001	SEDENTARY	1-01-001	SELF-AGGRANDISE MENT			1-01-001	SEMITROPICAL
3-01-001	SEDGWICK			1-01-001	SELF-RELIANCE	1-01-001	SEMMES
3-01-001	SEDIMENT	1-01-001	SELF-AGGRANDIZE MENT	3-02-002	SELF-RELIANT	1-01-001	SEMPER
1-01-001	SEDIMENTARY			4-04-004	SELF-RESPECT	1-01-001	SEMPLE-*LISLE
2-01-002	SEDIMENTATION	1-01-001	SELF-ANALYSIS	1-01-001	SELF-RESTRAINT	1-01-001	SEMRA
4-02-002	SEDIMENTS	3-03-003	SELF-APPOINTED	1-01-001	SELF-RIGHTEOUSN ESS	30-02-012	SEN
1-01-001	SEDITION	1-01-001	SELF-ASSERTION			62-06-026	SENATE
1-01-001	SEDITIOUS	2-01-001	SELF-ASSERTIVE	1-01-001	SELF-RULE	4-03-004	SENATE'S
1-01-001	SEDUCED	1-01-001	SELF-AWARENESS	2-02-002	SELF-SACRIFICE	40-10-026	SENATOR
1-01-001	SEDUCER	1-01-001	SELF-BETRAYAL	1-01-001	SELF-SACRIFICIN G	1-01-001	SENATOR'S
3-03-003	SEDUCTION	2-01-002	SELF-CENTERED			3-03-003	SENATORIAL
2-02-002	SEDUCTIVE	7-01-001	SELF-CERTAINTY	4-03-004	SELF-SATISFACTI ON	10-02-005	SENATORS
1-01-001	SEDULOUSLY	1-01-001	SELF-COMPLETION			74-12-063	SEND
772-15-336	SEE	1-01-001	SELF-CONCEITED	1-01-001	SELF-SEEKING	1-01-001	SENDERS
1-01-001	SEE-LECTIVE	4-04-004	SELF-CONFIDENCE	1-01-001	SELF-SERVE	34-11-027	SENDING
1-01-001	SEE-THROUGH	3-02-003	SELF-CONFIDENT	2-02-002	SELF-STYLED	4-04-004	SENDS
4-01-001	SEEBOHM	1-01-001	SELF-CONGRATULA TION	2-02-002	SELF-SUFFICIENC Y	1-01-001	SENESAC
1-01-001	SEEBOHM'S					1-01-001	SENESE
41-09-014	SEED	5-03-005	SELF-CONSCIOUS	3-02-003	SELF-SUFFICIENT	2-02-002	SENILE
1-01-001	SEED-BEARING	3-03-003	SELF-CONSCIOUSL Y	5-02-002	SELF-SUSTAINING	1-01-001	SENILIS
1-01-001	SEED-PODS			4-01-002	SELF-UNLOADING	34-09-025	SENIOR
2-01-001	SEEDBED	5-04-005	SELF-CONSCIOUSN ESS	1-01-001	SELF-VICTIMIZED	1-01-001	SENIOR-GRADUATE
1-01-001	SEEDCOAT			2-02-002	SELF-WILL	2-01-001	SENIORITATIS
1-01-001	SEEDCOATS	1-01-001	SELF-CONSISTENT	1-01-001	SELFE	2-02-002	SENIORITY
1-01-001	SEEDLESS	1-01-001	SELF-CONSUMING	1-01-001	SELFEFFACING	1-01-001	SENIORS
1-01-001	SEEDLINGS	5-03-005	SELF-CONTAINED	8-06-007	SELFISH	1-01-001	SENIUM
42-04-006	SEEDS	1-01-001	SELF-CONTENT	1-01-001	SELFISHNESS	2-01-001	SENOR
1-01-001	SEEEMD	3-02-003	SELF-CONTROL	2-02-002	SELFLESS	2-01-001	SENORA
1-01-001	SEEIN	1-01-001	SELF-CORRECTING	1-01-001	SELFLESSNESS	1-01-001	SENS
86-15-066	SEEING	1-01-001	SELF-CRIMINATIO N	12-01-001	SELKIRK	14-08-012	SENSATION
69-13-057	SEEK			4-01-001	SELKIRK'S	6-05-005	SENSATIONAL
1-01-001	SEEKER	1-01-001	SELF-CRITICAL	1-01-001	SELKIRKERS	2-02-002	SENSATIONALISM
3-03-003	SEEKERS	2-02-002	SELF-CRITICISM	41-13-032	SELL	10-04-007	SENSATIONS
1-01-001	SEEKIN	1-01-001	SELF-DECEIVING	1-01-001	SELLE	311-15-163	SENSE
44-12-040	SEEKING	2-02-002	SELF-DECEPTION	6-04-005	SELLER	17-07-014	SENSED
1-01-001	SEEKINGLY	1-01-001	SELF-DECEPTIONS	1-01-001	SELLER'S	6-05-006	SENSELESS
2-01-001	SEEKONK	1-01-001	SELF-DEFEAT	1-01-001	SELLERS	1-01-001	SENSELESSLY
10-06-010	SEEKS	2-02-002	SELF-DEFEATING	1-01-001	SELLERS'	15-07-013	SENSES
1-01-001	SEELEY	3-02-003	SELF-DEFENSE	1-01-001	SELLIN	6-02-005	SENSIBILITIES
229-15-154	SEEM	1-01-001	SELF-DELUDED	31-10-021	SELLING	8-03-006	SENSIBILITY
332-14-186	SEEMED	2-02-002	SELF-DELUSION	1-01-001	SELLOUT	14-07-013	SENSIBLE
14-09-014	SEEMING	1-01-001	SELF-DEPRECATIO N	13-06-011	SELLS	4-04-004	SENSIBLY
17-09-017	SEEMINGLY			2-02-002	SELMA	8-05-008	SENSING
259-15-146	SEEMS	3-03-003	SELF-DESTRUCTIO N	4-02-003	SELVES	59-10-043	SENSITIVE
279-15-180	SEEN			7-01-004	SEMANTIC	1-01-001	SENSITIVE-AREA
2-02-002	SEEP	3-03-003	SELF-DESTRUCTIV E	2-01-001	SEMANTICALLY	1-01-001	SENSITIVELY
2-02-002	SEEPAGE			2-01-002	SEMBLANCE	2-01-001	SENSITIVES
2-01-002	SEEPED	7-03-004	SELF-DETERMINAT ION	1-01-001	SEMENOV	1-01-001	SENSITIVITIES
2-02-002	SEEPING			10-03-003	SEMESTER	28-08-017	SENSITIVITY
1-01-001	SEEREY	1-01-001	SELF-DICTATE	2-02-002	SEMESTER'S	2-01-001	SENSITIZED
1-01-001	SEERS	5-02-002	SELF-DISCIPLINE	1-01-001	SEMI-ABSTRACT	3-01-002	SENSOR
1-01-001	SEERSUCKER	2-02-002	SELF-DISCOVERY	1-01-001	SEMI-ABSTRACTIO NS	6-01-001	SENSORS
36-11-028	SEES	1-01-001	SELF-DRAMATIZAT ION			9-04-006	SENSORY
1-01-001	SEGAL'S			1-01-001	SEMI-AMBIGUOUS	6-05-006	SENSUAL
10-05-009	SEGMENT	1-01-001	SELF-EFFACEMENT	1-01-001	SEMI-AUTONOMOUS	5-04-004	SENSUALITY
2-01-002	SEGMENTAL	1-01-001	SELF-EFFACING	1-01-001	SEMI-CATATONIC	2-01-002	SENSUOUS
10-03-006	SEGMENTS	2-02-002	SELF-EMPLOYED	1-01-001	SEMI-CIRCLE	145-15-104	SENT
3-01-001	SEGOVIA	1-01-001	SELF-ENCLOSED	1-01-001	SEMI-CITY	34-11-022	SENTENCE
1-01-001	SEGOVIA'S	1-01-001	SELF-ENERGIZING	1-01-001	SEMI-CONDUCTORS	1-01-001	SENTENCE-STRUC URE
1-01-001	SEGREGATE	4-03-004	SELF-ESTEEM	1-01-001	SEMI-CONSCIOUS		
15-05-009	SEGREGATED	5-03-005	SELF-EVIDENT	1-01-001	SEMI-HEIGHTS	8-05-007	SENTENCED
1-01-001	SEGREGATING	5-03-003	SELF-EXAMINATIO N	1-01-001	SEMI-INDEPENDEN T	13-08-010	SENTENCES
10-04-005	SEGREGATION					1-01-001	SENTENCING
3-03-003	SEGREGATIONIST	1-01-001	SELF-EXILE	1-01-001	SEMI-INFLATED	2-01-001	SENTIENT
1-01-001	SEGUR	1-01-001	SELF-EXTINGUISH ING	1-01-001	SEMI-ISOLATED	23-09-020	SENTIMENT
1-01-001	SEGURA			2-02-002	SEMI-LITERATE	15-07-014	SENTIMENTAL
2-01-002	SEIDEL	1-01-001	SELF-FLAGELLATI ON	2-01-001	SEMI-MAJOR	1-01-001	SENTIMENTALIST
5-01-001	SEIGNER			1-01-001	SEMI-MINOR	1-01-001	SENTIMENTALITY
1-01-001	SEISMIC	2-01-001	SELF-GOVERNMENT	1-01-001	SEMI-NUDE	1-01-001	SENTIMENTALIZE
1-01-001	SEISMOGRAPH	15-03-003	SELF-HELP	1-01-001	SEMI-PRECIOUS	8-04-007	SENTIMENTS
1-01-001	SEISMOGRAPHS	1-01-001	SELF-IMAGE	1-01-001	SEMI-PRIVATE	2-02-002	SENTINEL
1-01-001	SEISMOLOGICAL	1-01-001	SELF-IMAGES	1-01-001	SEMI-PROCESSED	2-02-002	SENTINELS
6-04-006	SEIZE	4-03-004	SELF-IMPOSED	1-01-001	SEMI-PROFESSION ALLY	6-04-006	SENTRY
24-10-019	SEIZED	4-02-003	SELF-INDULGENCE			1-01-001	SENTRY'S
2-01-001	SEIZIN	1-01-001	SELF-INSURANCE	1-01-001	SEMI-PUBLIC	1-01-001	SEOUL
1-01-001	SEIZING	2-01-002	SELF-INTEREST	2-01-001	SEMI-RIGID	2-02-002	SEPARABLE
6-04-005	SEIZURE	1-01-001	SELF-JUDGING	1-01-001	SEMI-SERIOUS	79-14-062	SEPARATE
15-01-001	SELDEN	1-01-001	SELF-LOCKING	2-01-002	SEMI-SKILLED	43-11-035	SEPARATED
1-01-001	SELDES	1-01-001	SELF-MASTERY	1-01-001	SEMI-SPECIAL	13-05-012	SEPARATELY
34-13-030	SELDOM					2-02-002	SEPARATENESS

3-02-002	SEPARATES	6-03-006	SETTLEMENTS	13-08-010	SHADES	1-01-001	SHARPSHOOTERS
7-05-007	SEPARATING	3-02-002	SETTLER	4-03-004	SHADING	1-01-001	SHARTZER'S
17-07-012	SEPARATION	12-05-006	SETTLERS	1-01-001	SHADINGS	1-01-001	SHATILOV
1-01-001	SEPARATIONS	2-02-002	SETTLES	36-12-027	SHADOW	2-02-002	SHATTER
1-01-001	SEPARATORS	11-08-011	SETTLING	3-02-003	SHADOWED	13-06-012	SHATTERED
1-01-001	SEPIA	8-06-008	SETUP	5-03-003	SHADOWING	6-03-005	SHATTERING
35-07-011	SEPT	1-01-001	SEURAT	20-09-019	SHADOWS	1-01-001	SHATTERINGLY
6-01-001	SEPTA	113-15-075	SEVEN	1-01-001	SHADOWY	1-01-001	SHATTERPROOF
1-01-001	SEPTATION	1-01-001	SEVEN-	1-01-001	SHADY	1-01-001	SHATTERS
56-12-038	SEPTEMBER	1-01-001	SEVEN-CONCERT	7-01-001	SHAEFER	6-05-006	SHAVE
1-01-001	SEPTEMBER-*OCTO BER	1-01-001	SEVEN-HIT	1-01-001	SHAEFER'S	9-05-008	SHAVED
3-01-001	SEPTIC	1-01-001	SEVEN-INCH	6-01-001	SHAFER	2-02-002	SHAVEN
1-01-001	SEPTILLION	1-01-001	SEVEN-IRON	1-01-001	SHAFER'S	6-03-004	SHAVING
1-01-001	SEPTUAGENARIAN'S	1-01-001	SEVEN-O'CLOCK	1-01-001	SHAFFNER	1-01-001	SHAVINGS
1-01-001	SEPTUM	1-01-001	SEVEN-SHOT	11-07-008	SHAFT	9-03-004	SHAW
1-01-001	SEPULCHRED	1-01-001	SEVEN-STORIES	2-02-002	SHAFTS	2-01-001	SHAW'S
1-01-001	SEQ	1-01-001	SEVEN-THIRTY	1-01-001	SHAG	1-01-001	SHAWANO
1-01-001	SEQUEL	1-01-001	SEVEN-WEEK	2-02-002	SHAGGY	3-02-002	SHAWL
35-07-020	SEQUENCE	1-01-001	SEVEN-WORD	2-01-001	SHAH	2-01-001	SHAWLS
1-01-001	SEQUENCED	24-08-019	SEVENTEEN	1-01-001	SHAHN	2-02-002	SHAWNEE
6-03-005	SEQUENCES	1-01-001	SEVENTEEN-INCH	1-01-001	SHAK	3-01-001	SHAWOMET
1-01-001	SEQUESTRATION	1-01-001	SEVENTEEN-YEAR- OLD	17-10-015	SHAKE	1-01-001	SHAY
1-01-001	SEQUINS	11-05-006	SEVENTEENTH	11-06-011	SHAKEN	27-01-001	SHAYNE
2-02-002	SEQUOIA	2-02-002	SEVENTEENTH-CEN TURY	2-01-001	SHAKER	2-01-001	SHAYNE'S
19-01-003	SERA	31-11-021	SEVENTH	3-02-003	SHAKERS	4-01-001	SHAYOL
1-01-001	SERAFIN	2-01-002	SEVENTIES	5-03-004	SHAKES	2859-15-228	SHE
1-01-001	SERAPHIM	4-03-004	SEVENTY	30-06-011	SHAKESPEARE	1-01-001	SHE'ARIM
1-01-001	SERBANTIAN	1-01-001	SEVENTY-EIGHT	11-04-007	SHAKESPEARE'S	67-05-020	SHE'D
1-01-001	SERENADE	1-01-001	SEVENTY-FIFTH	6-01-001	SHAKESPEAREAN	9-05-009	SHE'LL
2-02-002	SERENADED	1-01-001	SEVENTY-FIVE	1-01-001	SHAKESPEARIAN	48-09-034	SHE'S
10-07-009	SERENE	1-01-001	SEVENTY-FIVE-FO OT	2-02-002	SHAKILY	10-02-002	SHEA
1-01-001	SERENELY	1-01-001	SEVENTY-FOOT	21-10-020	SHAKING	1-01-001	SHEA'S
3-01-001	SERENISSIMUS	1-01-001	SEVENTY-FOUR	5-04-005	SHAKY	3-03-003	SHEAF
6-04-006	SERENITY	1-01-001	SEVENTY-FOURTH	1-01-001	SHAKYA	40-02-003	SHEAR
1-01-001	SERFS	1-01-001	SEVENTY-ODD	267-15-107	SHALL	7-02-003	SHEARING
5-02-002	SERGE	1-01-001	SEVENTY-SIX	14-07-011	SHALLOW	1-01-001	SHEARING'S
28-06-013	SERGEANT	1-01-001	SEVENTY-TWO	1-01-001	SHALLOWER	1-01-001	SHEARN
1-01-001	SERGEANTS	3-03-003	SEVER	1-01-001	SHALLOWNESS	4-02-004	SHEATH
2-01-002	SERGEI	377-15-234	SEVERAL	1-01-001	SHALOM	2-01-001	SHEATHING
7-03-005	SERIAL	1-01-001	SEVERALLY	1-01-001	SHAM	1-01-001	SHECKLEY'S
130-13-076	SERIES	1-01-001	SEVERALTY	1-01-001	SHAMBLED	11-07-008	SHED
1-01-001	SERIEUSES	39-12-033	SEVERE	1-01-001	SHAMBLING	2-02-002	SHEDDING
1-01-001	SERIF	1-01-001	SEVERE-LOOKING	21-08-018	SHAME	4-03-004	SHEDS
116-14-088	SERIOUS	6-05-006	SEVERED	1-01-001	SHAMED	23-08-011	SHEEP
1-01-001	SERIOUS-MINDED	16-08-016	SEVERELY	1-01-001	SHAMEFACEDLY	1-01-001	SHEEP-LINED
46-13-040	SERIOUSLY	1-01-001	SEVERING	2-02-002	SHAMEFUL	1-01-001	SHEEPE
8-06-007	SERIOUSNESS	5-03-003	SEVERITY	1-01-001	SHAMES	3-03-003	SHEEPSKIN
1-01-001	SERLOIN	1-01-001	SEVERLY	2-01-001	SHAMPOO	15-09-015	SHEER
12-06-009	SERMON	1-01-001	SEVERNA	3-02-002	SHAMROCK	3-01-001	SHEERAN
2-02-002	SERMONS	1-01-001	SEVERS	1-01-001	SHAMS	1-01-001	SHEERED
2-01-001	SEROLOGICAL	1-01-001	SEVIGLI	3-01-001	SHAN	45-12-027	SHEET
2-02-002	SERPENT	6-02-002	SEW	1-01-001	SHAN'T	1-01-001	SHEET-METAL
1-01-001	SERPENTINE	29-05-007	SEWAGE	1-01-001	SHANGRI-*LA	1-01-001	SHEETED
3-03-003	SERPENTS	1-01-001	SEWANEE	9-01-001	SHANK	1-01-001	SHEETING
1-01-001	SERRA	5-01-001	SEWARD	1-01-001	SHANN	30-11-020	SHEETS
2-01-001	SERRATUS	3-01-001	SEWARD'S	1-01-001	SHANN'S	4-01-001	SHEIK
18-01-004	SERUM	1-01-001	SEWED	1-01-001	SHANNON	1-01-001	SHEILA
1-01-001	SERVANDA	10-04-006	SEWER	1-01-001	SHANSI	1-01-001	SHELAGH
19-09-013	SERVANT	1-01-001	SEWER'S	1-01-001	SHANTIES	1-01-001	SHELBY
22-09-015	SERVANTS	4-03-004	SEWERS	1-01-001	SHANTUNG	8-04-006	SHELDON
1-01-001	SERVATIUS	1-01-001	SEWICKLEY	1-01-001	SHANTUNG-LIKE	12-07-009	SHELF
107-15-084	SERVE	10-05-005	SEWING	3-03-003	SHANTY	22-07-010	SHELL
120-13-082	SERVED	1-01-001	SEWN	1-01-001	SHANTZ	1-01-001	SHELL-PSYCHOLOG Y
37-08-033	SERVES	84-12-030	SEX	85-14-061	SHAPE	1-01-001	SHELLED
315-13-122	SERVICE	1-01-001	SEX-MANUALS	1-01-001	SHAPE-UP	12-04-006	SHELLEY
3-01-001	SERVICE-CONNECT ED	11-05-008	SEXES	17-08-016	SHAPED	7-02-003	SHELLEY'S
4-04-004	SERVICEABLE	4-02-003	SEXTET	5-04-005	SHAPELESS	14-08-010	SHELLS
1-01-001	SERVICEMEN	1-01-001	SEXTILLION	2-02-002	SHAPELY	70-07-013	SHELTER
139-10-070	SERVICES	3-02-003	SEXTON	29-11-021	SHAPES	4-04-004	SHELTERED
4-04-004	SERVICING	1-01-001	SEXTUOR	8-04-007	SHAPING	25-07-009	SHELTERS
1-01-001	SERVIETTES	59-07-018	SEXUAL	1-01-001	SHARDS	1-01-001	SHELVED
2-02-002	SERVILE	4-03-003	SEXUALITY	98-13-065	SHARE	8-06-008	SHELVES
38-10-032	SERVING	1-01-001	SEXUALIZED	1-01-001	SHARE-HOLDERS	1-01-001	SHENANDOAH
1-01-001	SERVINGS	6-02-002	SEXUALLY	1-01-001	SHARECROP	3-02-002	SHENANIGANS
1-01-001	SERVITORS	2-02-002	SEXY	40-11-036	SHARED	1-01-001	SHENSI
5-01-001	SERVO	1-01-001	SEYMOUR	1-01-001	SHAREHOLDER	1-01-001	SHEP
7-04-004	SESAME	2-01-001	SEYNES	3-02-002	SHAREHOLDERS	2-02-002	SHEPARD
1-01-001	SESSHU	1-01-001	SEZ	1-01-001	SHARERS	3-03-003	SHEPHERD
80-11-043	SESSION	1-01-001	SFORZANDO	46-08-012	SHARES	1-01-001	SHEPHERD'S
26-09-018	SESSIONS	1-01-001	SFORZT	1-01-001	SHARI	2-02-002	SHEPHERDS
414-15-234	SET	1-01-001	SH-TS	23-10-020	SHARING	3-02-002	SHERATON-*BILTM ORE
1-01-001	SET'S	1-01-001	SHA	1-01-001	SHARK'S	2-01-002	SHERATON-*DALLA S
4-04-004	SET-UP	1-01-001	SHABBAT	1-01-001	SHARK-INFESTED		
3-02-003	SETBACK	2-02-002	SHABBILY	1-01-001	SHARKEY	1-01-001	SHERBET-COLORED
3-03-003	SETBACKS	5-04-005	SHABBY	3-03-003	SHARKS	2-02-002	SHERIDAN
2-01-001	SETHNESS	1-01-001	SHACK	3-02-002	SHARON	20-05-009	SHERIFF
1-01-001	SETON	1-01-001	SHACK-UP	72-15-059	SHARP	5-04-005	SHERIFF'S
62-09-035	SETS	1-01-001	SHACKED	1-01-001	SHARP-LIMBED	3-03-003	SHERIFFS
2-01-001	SETTER	2-01-001	SHACKLED	30-02-002	SHARPE	6-01-001	SHERLOCK
60-14-052	SETTING	2-01-001	SHACKLES	3-02-002	SHARPE'S	29-03-008	SHERMAN
9-05-008	SETTINGS	1-01-001	SHACKS	1-01-001	SHARPEN	7-02-002	SHERMAN'S
23-11-022	SETTLE	28-10-019	SHADE	5-04-005	SHARPENED	2-01-001	SHERRILL
69-12-058	SETTLED	1-01-001	SHADE-DARKENED	3-03-003	SHARPENING	8-04-004	SHERRY
26-08-013	SETTLEMENT	6-05-006	SHADED	3-03-003	SHARPER	3-03-003	SHERWOOD
				1-01-001	SHARPEST		
				38-14-035	SHARPLY		
				1-01-001	SHARPNESS		

1-01-001	SHEVCHENKO	44-10-036	SHOES	15-07-009	SHOWER	1-01-001	SIBLEY
1-01-001	SHEWE	1-01-001	SHOESTRING	5-02-004	SHOWERED	1-01-001	SIBLING
1-01-001	SHH	1-01-001	SHOESTRINGS	1-01-001	SHOWERHEAD	1-01-001	SIBLY
2-02-002	SHIBBOLETH	2-01-001	SHOETTLE	1-01-001	SHOWERING	4-01-001	SIBYLLA
1-01-001	SHIBBOLETHS	1-01-001	SHOJI	3-03-003	SHOWERS	1-01-001	SIBYLLA'S
3-02-003	SHIED	1-01-001	SHOLOM	1-01-001	SHOWIN	4-03-003	SIC
8-05-006	SHIELD	5-04-005	SHONE	61-12-043	SHOWING	3-03-003	SICILIAN
5-04-004	SHIELDED	1-01-001	SHOOING	2-02-002	SHOWINGS	3-03-003	SICILIANA
5-02-002	SHIELDING	57-08-044	SHOOK	3-02-003	SHOWMAN	1-01-001	SICILIANS
2-02-002	SHIELDS	27-09-020	SHOOT	11-02-002	SHOWMANSHIP	2-01-001	SICILY
1-01-001	SHIES	2-01-001	SHOOT-DOWN	1-01-001	SHOWMEN	3-02-003	SICK
1-01-001	SHIETZ	4-01-002	SHOOTER	166-13-091	SHOWN	51-12-035	SICKENED
2-01-001	SHIFLETT	1-01-001	SHOOTERS	1-01-001	SHOWPIECE	4-02-003	SICKENING
41-09-031	SHIFT	2-02-002	SHOOTIN	1-01-001	SHOWROOM	2-02-002	SICKER
1-01-001	SHIFTE	48-10-018	SHOOTING	94-11-071	SHOWS	2-02-002	SICKISH
18-09-014	SHIFTED	1-01-001	SHOOTINGS	1-01-001	SHOWY	1-01-001	SICKLY
1-01-001	SHIFTERS	63-13-043	SHOP	1-01-001	SHRANK	2-02-002	SICKLY-TOLERANT
11-06-011	SHIFTING	2-01-001	SHOP'S	2-01-002	SHRAPNEL	1-01-001	SICKNESS
1-01-001	SHIFTLESS	1-01-001	SHOPKEEPERS	3-03-003	SHRED	6-05-006	SICKROOM
17-08-013	SHIFTS	1-01-001	SHOPPER	1-01-001	SHREDDED	1-01-001	SICURELLA
1-01-001	SHIFTY	27-09-020	SHOPPING	1-01-001	SHREDDER	1-01-001	SID
1-01-001	SHIH	1-01-001	SHOPPING-CENTER	1-01-001	SHREDDING	1-01-001	SIDDO
1-01-001	SHILL	17-10-016	SHOPS	5-03-004	SHREDS	7-01-001	SIDE
1-01-001	SHILLINGS	1-01-001	SHOPWORN	3-01-002	SHREVEPORT	380-15-201	SIDE'S
1-01-001	SHILLONG	61-13-027	SHORE	8-04-007	SHREWD	1-01-001	SIDE-ARM
1-01-001	SHILLS	6-05-005	SHORELINE	1-01-001	SHREWDEST	1-01-001	SIDE-CONCLUSION S
2-02-002	SHILOH	1-01-001	SHORELINES	2-02-002	SHREWDLY	1-01-001	
1-01-001	SHIM	9-05-007	SHORES	2-02-002	SHREWISH	1-01-001	SIDE-EFFECTS
1-01-001	SHIMMER	1-01-001	SHORES'	5-04-005	SHRIEK	1-01-001	SIDE-LOOKING
3-03-003	SHIMMERING	212-15-158	SHORT	4-02-003	SHRIEKED	1-01-001	SIDE-RACK
1-01-001	SHIMMING	1-01-001	SHORT'S	1-01-001	SHRIEKING	1-01-001	SIDE-STEP
2-02-002	SHIMMY	1-01-001	SHORT-BARREL	7-04-006	SHRILL	2-02-002	SIDE-STEPPED
1-01-001	SHIMS	1-01-001	SHORT-CHANGING	2-01-002	SHRILLED	1-01-001	SIDEARMS
3-03-003	SHIN	2-01-001	SHORT-CONTACT	1-01-001	SHRILLING	1-01-001	SIDEBOARD
1-01-001	SHINBONE	1-01-001	SHORT-CUT	1-01-001	SHRILLNESS	1-01-001	SIDEBOARDS
5-04-004	SHINE	1-01-001	SHORT-CUTTING	3-03-003	SHRILLY	1-01-001	SIDECHAIRS
4-04-004	SHINES	3-03-003	SHORT-LIVED	2-02-002	SHRIMP	1-01-001	SIDED
5-04-004	SHINGLES	2-01-001	SHORT-OF-WAR	7-05-007	SHRINE	1-01-001	SIDELIGHT
21-09-019	SHINING	1-01-001	SHORT-RANGE	4-03-004	SHRINES	1-01-001	SIDELINE
1-01-001	SHININGLY	3-02-003	SHORT-RUN	5-04-005	SHRINK	1-01-001	SIDELINES
1-01-001	SHINTOISM	1-01-001	SHORT-SKIRTED	3-02-002	SHRINKAGE	1-01-001	SIDELONG
3-03-003	SHINY	1-01-001	SHORT-STORY	3-03-003	SHRINKING	1-01-001	SIDEMEN
83-14-037	SHIP	14-03-007	SHORT-TERM	2-02-002	SHRINKS	101-13-068	SIDES
5-03-003	SHIP'S	1-01-001	SHORT-TIME	3-03-003	SHRIVELED	1-01-001	SIDESHOW
1-01-001	SHIP-TO-SURFACE	16-07-011	SHORTAGE	5-03-004	SHRIVER	1-01-001	SIDESTEPS
1-01-001	SHIPBOARD	3-03-003	SHORTAGES	1-01-001	SHROUDED	21-08-016	SIDEWALK
3-03-003	SHIPBUILDING	5-04-005	SHORTCOMINGS	1-01-001	SHROVE	5-03-004	SIDEWALKS
1-01-001	SHIPLEY	1-01-001	SHORTCUT	1-01-001	SHRUB	3-03-003	SIDEWAYS
1-01-001	SHIPMAN	2-01-001	SHORTCUTS	1-01-001	SHRUB-COVERED	1-01-001	SIDEWINDER
2-02-002	SHIPMATE	4-04-004	SHORTEN	1-01-001	SHRUBBERY	6-04-006	SIDEWISE
1-01-001	SHIPMATES	7-04-007	SHORTENED	1-01-001	SHRUBBERY-LINED	5-04-004	SIDING
2-02-002	SHIPMENT	3-03-003	SHORTENING	4-03-003	SHRUBS	1-01-001	SIDLE
16-05-010	SHIPMENTS	19-09-018	SHORTER	2-02-002	SHRUG	2-02-002	SIDLED
6-04-005	SHIPPED	3-03-003	SHORTEST	18-06-015	SHRUGGED	9-04-006	SIDNEY
3-01-001	SHIPPER	2-02-002	SHORTHAND	2-01-001	SHRUGS	2-01-001	SIDNEY'S
1-01-001	SHIPPERS	34-11-029	SHORTLY	1-01-001	SHRUNKEN	1-01-001	SIE
1-01-001	SHIPPIN	1-01-001	SHORTNESS	21-01-001	SHU	1-01-001	SIEBEN
19-05-009	SHIPPING	29-05-005	SHORTS	1-01-001	SHU-TT	3-01-001	SIEBERN
43-11-023	SHIPS	5-03-004	SHORTSIGHTED	3-02-003	SHUCKS	1-01-001	SIECLE
1-01-001	SHIPS'	1-01-001	SHORTSIGHTEDNES S	5-03-004	SHUDDER	1-01-001	SIECLES
1-01-001	SHIPSHAPE			5-04-005	SHUDDERED	6-04-006	SIEGE
2-02-002	SHIPWRECK	7-03-004	SHORTSTOP	3-03-003	SHUDDERING	1-01-001	SIEGFRIED
1-01-001	SHIPWRECKED	112-13-052	SHOT	1-01-001	SHUDDERY	1-01-001	SIENKIEWICZ
1-01-001	SHIPYARDS	8-04-005	SHOTGUN	3-02-003	SHUFFLE	2-01-001	SIENNA
3-01-001	SHIRES	1-01-001	SHOTGUN-TYPE	2-02-002	SHUFFLED	2-01-001	SIEPI
2-02-002	SHIRKING	1-01-001	SHOTGUNS	3-02-003	SHUFFLING	2-02-002	SIERRA
3-01-001	SHIRL	29-08-016	SHOTS	1-01-001	SHUISKI	2-01-001	SIERRAS
5-02-003	SHIRLEY	1-01-001	SHOTSHELLS	3-01-001	SHULD	2-01-001	SIESTA
1-01-001	SHIRLEY'S	1-01-001	SHOTWELL	1-01-001	SHULDE	1-01-001	SIEUX
27-05-020	SHIRT	1-01-001	SHOUDERS	1-01-001	SHUN	1-01-001	SIEVE
1-01-001	SHIRT-SLEEVED	888-15-320	SHOULD	1-01-001	SHUNNED	1-01-001	SIEVERS
1-01-001	SHIRTFRONT	1-01-001	SHOULDDA	1-01-001	SHUNNING	3-03-003	SIFTED
2-02-002	SHIRTS	61-12-043	SHOULDER	2-02-002	SHUNS	1-01-001	SIFTING
1-01-001	SHIRTSLEEVE	1-01-001	SHOULDER-HIGH	1-01-001	SHUNT	1-01-001	SIGEMUND
1-01-001	SHISH	1-01-001	SHOULDER-TO-SHOULDER	1-01-001	SHUNTED	11-08-011	SIGH
2-01-002	SHIT			5-01-001	SHUNTS	22-08-020	SIGHED
1-01-001	SHIT-SICK	3-03-003	SHOULDERED	46-10-037	SHUT	5-02-004	SIGHING
1-01-001	SHITTS	1-01-001	SHOULDERING	3-01-001	SHUTDOWN	1-01-001	SIGHS
4-03-004	SHIVER	51-13-044	SHOULDERS	3-02-002	SHUTDOWNS	86-13-066	SIGHT
4-03-004	SHIVERED	22-08-019	SHOULDN'T	1-01-001	SHUTE	2-01-002	SIGHT-SEEING
11-05-009	SHIVERING	4-01-002	SHOUP	1-01-001	SHUTS	7-05-007	SIGHTED
1-01-001	SHIVERY	9-04-009	SHOUT	5-01-001	SHUTTER	3-03-003	SIGHTING
1-01-001	SHO	40-10-030	SHOUTED	2-02-002	SHUTTERED	15-07-011	SIGHTS
3-02-003	SHOALS	32-11-022	SHOUTING	5-02-004	SHUTTERS	1-01-001	SIGHTSEEING
31-11-026	SHOCK	5-04-005	SHOUTS	2-02-002	SHUTTING	1-01-001	SIGHTSEERS
19-08-018	SHOCKED	2-02-002	SHOVED	1-01-001	SHUTTLED	1-01-001	SIGMA
1-01-001	SHOCKER	8-03-007	SHOVEL	1-01-001	SHUTTLING	4-01-001	SIGMEN
4-04-004	SHOCKING	5-03-004	SHOVELED	1-01-001	SHUZ	1-01-001	SIGMUND
3-03-003	SHOCKINGLY	2-02-002	SHOVELS	13-08-013	SHY	94-13-056	SIGN
5-05-005	SHOCKS	3-02-002	SHOVING	7-01-001	SHYLOCK	63-12-032	SIGNAL
2-02-002	SHOCKWAVE	6-04-006	SHOW	1-01-001	SHYLOCKIAN	1-01-001	SIGNAL-INTENS
2-02-002	SHOD	287-15-190	SHOW-DOWN	4-03-004	SHYLY		
1-01-001	SHODDY	1-01-001	SHOW-OFFY	1-01-001	SI	1-01-001	SIGNAL-TO-NOIS
14-11-013	SHOE	1-01-001	SHOWCASE	4-02-003	SIAMESE	2-02-002	SIGNALED
1-01-001	SHOE-STRING	3-02-003	SHOWDOWN	6-04-005	SIBERIA	5-05-005	SIGNALING
1-01-001	SHOELACE	4-03-004	SHOWED	1-01-001	SIBERIAN	1-01-001	SIGNALIZES
1-01-001	SHOELACES	141-15-101		1-01-001	SIBILANT		

Freq	Word	Freq	Word	Freq	Word	Freq	Word
1-01-001	SIGNALLY	170-15-124	SIMPLY	2-02-002	SISTER'S	42-10-031	SKILL
29-10-017	SIGNALS	5-02-004	SIMPSON	2-02-002	SISTER-IN-LAW	30-08-018	SKILLED
6-05-006	SIGNATURE	2-02-002	SIMPSON'S	13-06-010	SISTERS	2-01-001	SKILLET
5-01-002	SIGNATURES	3-01-002	SIMS	2-01-001	SISTERS'	9-06-008	SKILLFUL
1-01-001	SIGNBOARD	4-02-003	SIMULATE	1-01-001	SISTERS-IN-LAW	5-04-005	SKILLFULLY
37-11-030	SIGNED	7-02-003	SIMULATED	1-01-001	SISTINE	1-01-001	SKILLFULNESS
1-01-001	SIGNERS	2-02-002	SIMULATION	67-14-050	SIT	37-08-021	SKILLS
66-11-051	SIGNIFICANCE	9-05-008	SIMULTANEOUS	1-01-001	SIT-DOWN	5-04-005	SKIMMED
85-09-066	SIGNIFICANT	38-10-031	SIMULTANEOUSLY	1-01-001	SIT-IN	4-04-004	SKIMMING
17-06-011	SIGNIFICANTLY	53-08-023	SIN	1-01-001	SIT-INS	1-01-001	SKIMPY
1-01-001	SIGNIFICANTS	1-01-001	SIN-NED	64-08-024	SITE	47-10-033	SKIN
2-01-001	SIGNIFIED	1-01-001	SINAI	16-07-010	SITES	1-01-001	SKIN-PERCEPTIVE NESS
1-01-001	SIGNIFIES	1-01-001	SINAN	6-04-005	SITS	1-01-001	SKINDIVE
2-02-002	SIGNIFY	4-03-003	SINATRA	24-04-004	SITTER	1-01-001	SKINDIVING
1-01-001	SIGNIGICANT	628-15-313	SINCE	2-01-001	SITTER'S	1-01-001	SKINFOLDS
7-06-007	SIGNING	15-09-014	SINCERE	2-02-002	SITTERS	4-01-001	SKINLESS
2-01-001	SIGNOR	7-03-006	SINCERELY	96-13-070	SITTING	1-01-001	SKINNER
3-01-002	SIGNORA	1-01-001	SINCEREST	2-01-001	SITTINGS	1-01-001	SKINNIN
1-01-001	SIGNORE	13-06-012	SINCERITY	1-01-001	SITU	9-06-009	SKINNY
2-02-002	SIGNPOST	1-01-001	SIND	19-07-011	SITUATED	7-05-007	SKINS
1-01-001	SIGNPOSTS	4-02-004	SINE	196-15-126	SITUATION	5-03-004	SKIP
68-10-037	SIGNS	1-01-001	SINEWS	51-11-032	SITUATIONS	4-01-001	SKIPJACK
1-01-001	SIGUE	2-02-002	SINEWY	5-01-001	SITUS	1-01-001	SKIPJACK'S
1-01-001	SIHANOUK	1-01-001	SINFONICA	3-03-003	SITWELL	8-05-008	SKIPPED
1-01-001	SIHANOUK'S	3-03-003	SINFUL	1-01-001	SIVA	1-01-001	SKIPPER
1-01-001	SILAS	3-02-002	SINFULNESS	220-15-147	SIX	2-01-001	SKIPPERS
52-10-041	SILENCE	34-12-024	SING	1-01-001	SIX-DOLLAR	4-03-004	SKIPPING
5-04-005	SILENCED	1-01-001	SING'S	2-02-002	SIX-FOOT	1-01-001	SKIPS
3-03-003	SILENCES	1-01-001	SING-SONG	1-01-001	SIX-FOUR	4-04-004	SKIRMISH
1-01-001	SILENCING	1-01-001	SINGED	1-01-001	SIX-GALLON	1-01-001	SKIRMISHED
49-11-043	SILENT	10-03-007	SINGER	1-01-001	SIX-INCH	1-01-001	SKIRMISHERS
17-07-016	SILENTLY	1-01-001	SINGER'S	1-01-001	SIX-MAN	1-01-001	SKIRMISHES
2-02-002	SILESIA	13-04-009	SINGERS	1-01-001	SIX-MONTH	2-02-002	SKIRMISHING
4-03-003	SILHOUETTE	1-01-001	SINGERS'	2-02-002	SIX-POINT	21-07-015	SKIRT
3-03-003	SILHOUETTED	47-12-028	SINGING	1-01-001	SIX-SHOOTER	1-01-001	SKIRTED
5-02-002	SILHOUETTES	172-13-112	SINGLE	1-01-001	SIX-THIRTY	1-01-001	SKIRTING
2-01-001	SILICA	1-01-001	SINGLE-BARREL	1-01-001	SIX-TON	4-04-004	SKIRTS
1-01-001	SILICA-GLASS	1-01-001	SINGLE-COLOR	20-10-019	SIXTEEN	1-01-001	SKIS
1-01-001	SILICATE	1-01-001	SINGLE-CRYSTAL	1-01-001	SIXTEEN-YEAR-OLD	1-01-001	SKIT
1-01-001	SILICATES	1-01-001	SINGLE-DOSE			1-01-001	SKITS
2-02-002	SILICON	1-01-001	SINGLE-FOOT	12-06-010	SIXTEENTH	1-01-001	SKIWAY
1-01-001	SILICONE	2-02-002	SINGLE-HANDED	26-08-018	SIXTH	1-01-001	SKOLKAU
12-06-011	SILK	1-01-001	SINGLE-HANDEDLY	1-01-001	SIXTH-GRADE	3-01-001	SKOLMAN
1-01-001	SILKE	1-01-001	SINGLE-LANE	1-01-001	SIXTH-SENSE	2-01-001	SKOLMAN'S
1-01-001	SILKEN	1-01-001	SINGLE-MINDED	22-08-008	SIXTIES	4-01-001	SKOLOVSKY
1-01-001	SILKWORMS	1-01-001	SINGLE-SEEDED	1-01-001	SIXTIES'	1-01-001	SKOLOVSKY'S
1-01-001	SILKY	5-01-002	SINGLE-SHOT	21-11-021	SIXTY	4-01-001	SKOPAS
4-03-004	SILL	1-01-001	SINGLE-SPACED	1-01-001	SIXTY-DAY	10-01-001	SKORICH
1-01-001	SILLIEST	3-01-001	SINGLE-STEP	1-01-001	SIXTY-EIGHT	1-01-001	SKOUTING
15-07-012	SILLY	6-01-001	SINGLE-VALUED	1-01-001	SIXTY-EIGHTH	1-01-001	SKULK
1-01-001	SILO	10-03-006	SINGLED	9-04-006	SIXTY-FIVE	3-03-003	SKULL
1-01-001	SILONE	1-01-001	SINGLEHANDEDLY	1-01-001	SIXTY-FIVE-MILE	1-01-001	SKULL-BASHINGS
2-02-002	SILOS	1-01-001	SINGLENESS	1-01-001	SIXTY-NINE	3-02-002	SKULLCAP
1-01-001	SILVAS	1-01-001	SINGLES	8-02-002	SIXTY-ONE	2-01-002	SKULLS
29-11-026	SILVER	1-01-001	SINGLING	1-01-001	SIXTY-SEVEN	1-01-001	SKUNKS
1-01-001	SILVER-GRAY	5-04-005	SINGLY	2-02-002	SIXTY-TWO	58-13-043	SKY
1-01-001	SILVER-PAINTED	10-03-005	SINGS	15-07-014	SIZABLE	2-01-001	SKY'S
1-01-001	SILVERS	1-01-001	SINGSONGED	138-15-082	SIZE	1-01-001	SKY-CARVING
2-02-002	SILVERY	14-06-008	SINGULAR	1-01-001	SIZEABLE	1-01-001	SKY-GOD
1-01-001	SILVIO	1-01-001	SINGULARITY	4-04-004	SIZED	1-01-001	SKY-REACHING
1-01-001	SIMAK'S	1-01-001	SINGULARLY	12-05-010	SIZES	1-01-001	SKY-TAPPING
1-01-001	SIMBA	13-07-012	SINISTER	1-01-001	SIZOVA	1-01-001	SKYBOLT
1-01-001	SIMCA	23-09-019	SINK	1-01-001	SIZZLE	1-01-001	SKYE
157-14-113	SIMILAR	1-01-001	SINKHOLE	2-02-002	SIZZLED	1-01-001	SKYJACKED
3-02-003	SIMILARITIES	6-05-006	SINKING	2-02-002	SIZZLING	1-01-001	SKYJACKERS
9-05-009	SIMILARITY	1-01-001	SINKT	1-01-001	SKATE	1-01-001	SKYLARK
36-09-029	SIMILARLY	3-02-003	SINLESS	1-01-001	SKATES	1-01-001	SKYLARKING
1-01-001	SIMILE	6-03-004	SINNED	2-02-002	SKATING	1-01-001	SKYLIGHT
6-01-001	SIMILITUDE	7-03-005	SINNER	2-02-002	SKEET	2-01-001	SKYLIGHTS
1-01-001	SIMMEL	4-03-003	SINNERS	13-01-002	SKELETAL	5-05-005	SKYLINE
5-02-003	SIMMER	1-01-001	SINNING	2-02-002	SKELETON	20-01-001	SKYROS
1-01-001	SIMMERED	1-01-001	SINO-*SOVIET	1-01-001	SKELETONS	2-01-001	SKYROS'
10-02-002	SIMMONS	16-06-013	SINS	7-04-005	SKEPTICAL	2-02-002	SKYSCRAPER
1-01-001	SIMMONS'	1-01-001	SINTERED	1-01-001	SKEPTICALLY	1-01-001	SKYSCRAPERS
1-01-001	SIMMONSVILLE	1-01-001	SINTON	5-03-004	SKEPTICISM	32-01-001	SKYWAVE
17-03-003	SIMMS	2-02-002	SINUOUS	3-02-003	SKEPTICS	1-01-001	SKYWAY
4-03-004	SIMON	1-01-001	SINUOUSLY	16-06-011	SKETCH	1-01-001	SL
1-01-001	SIMON'S	1-01-001	SINUOUSNESS	2-01-001	SKETCHBOOK	9-04-005	SLAB
1-01-001	SIMONELLI	1-01-001	SINUS	4-02-003	SKETCHED	9-08-009	SLACK
1-01-001	SIMONSON'S	1-01-001	SINUSES	19-05-009	SKETCHES	3-03-003	SLACKENED
7-01-001	SIMPKINS	2-01-002	SINUSOIDAL	4-03-004	SKETCHING	2-02-002	SLACKENING
161-15-113	SIMPLE	2-01-001	SINUSOIDS	1-01-001	SKEWER	1-01-001	SLACKING
2-02-002	SIMPLE-MINDED	8-03-004	SIOUX	5-02-002	SKI	7-04-005	SLACKS
1-01-001	SIMPLE-SEEMING	2-02-002	SIP	1-01-001	SKI-JORING	1-01-001	SLADANG
18-06-011	SIMPLER	1-01-001	SIPHONED	2-01-002	SKID	3-01-001	SLAKED
1-01-001	SIMPLES	2-02-002	SIPPED	2-01-002	SKIDDED	3-01-002	SLAM
10-08-010	SIMPLEST	1-01-001	SIPPERS	2-02-002	SKIDDING	16-06-014	SLAMMED
1-01-001	SIMPLETON	8-05-006	SIPPING	1-01-001	SKIDDY	4-03-004	SLAMMING
1-01-001	SIMPLEX	95-12-042	SIR	1-01-001	SKIDS	3-01-001	SLANDERER
1-01-001	SIMPLICITER	3-02-003	SIRED	12-05-008	SKIES	1-01-001	SLANDEROUS
2-01-002	SIMPLICITIES	1-01-001	SIREN	9-02-002	SKIFF	1-01-001	SLANDERS
1-01-001	SIMPLICITUDE	2-02-002	SIRENS	1-01-001	SKIFF'S	2-02-002	SLANG
16-06-009	SIMPLICITY	1-01-001	SIRINJANI	4-01-001	SKIFFS	3-03-003	SLANT
9-03-006	SIMPLIFIED	2-02-002	SIRS	7-03-004	SKIING	1-01-001	SLANT-WISE
2-02-002	SIMPLIFIES	3-02-002	SIS	2-02-002	SKIIS	3-03-003	SLANTED
9-04-008	SIMPLIFY	2-01-001	SISK	1-01-001	SKILFUL	4-03-004	SLANTING
2-01-001	SIMPLISTIC	38-09-028	SISTER	1-01-001	SKILFULLY		

Freq	Word	Freq	Word	Freq	Word	Freq	Word
1-01-001	SLANTS	6-03-006	SLIT	1-01-001	SMARTED	4-04-004	SNATCH
2-02-002	SLAP	2-01-001	SLITS	2-02-002	SMARTER	11-05-010	SNATCHED
8-04-007	SLAPPED	1-01-001	SLITTER	4-03-004	SMARTLY	3-01-002	SNATCHES
6-06-006	SLAPPING	1-01-001	SLITTERS	4-04-004	SMASH	1-01-001	SNATCHING
1-01-001	SLAPS	1-01-001	SLIVERY	1-01-001	SMASH-'EM-DOWN	1-01-001	SNAZZY
2-02-002	SLAPSTICK	1-01-001	SLO-*FLO	15-08-013	SMASHED	2-01-001	SNEAD
3-03-003	SLASH	15-03-003	SLOAN	1-01-001	SMASHED-OUT	2-02-002	SNEAK
2-01-001	SLASH-*B	5-01-001	SLOAN'S	1-01-001	SMASHING	6-04-006	SNEAKED
1-01-001	SLASH-MOUTHED	5-01-001	SLOANAKER	1-01-001	SMATTERINGS	2-01-001	SNEAKER
10-05-007	SLASHED	3-01-001	SLOANE	2-01-001	SMEAR	3-02-003	SNEAKERS
1-01-001	SLASHES	4-03-004	SLOB	2-02-002	SMEARED	2-01-001	SNEAKING
5-03-005	SLASHING	3-02-002	SLOCUM	34-09-025	SMELL	1-01-001	SNEAKS
2-01-001	SLAT	2-01-001	SLOCUM'S	19-06-017	SMELLED	2-02-002	SNEAKY
10-04-006	SLATE	2-01-001	SLOE	5-04-005	SMELLING	1-01-001	SNEED
3-03-003	SLATED	7-03-005	SLOGAN	9-05-008	SMELLS	1-01-001	SNEER
5-01-001	SLATER	1-01-001	SLOGANEERING	3-02-002	SMELT	1-01-001	SNEERED
1-01-001	SLATER'S	5-04-004	SLOGANS	1-01-001	SMELTS	1-01-001	SNEERING
1-01-001	SLATS	1-01-001	SLOOP	1-01-001	SMERDYAKOV	2-02-002	SNEERS
1-01-001	SLATTED	2-02-002	SLOP	58-12-045	SMILE	2-02-002	SNEEZED
10-07-009	SLAUGHTER	19-10-014	SLOPE	71-09-050	SMILED	1-01-001	SNEEZING
3-03-003	SLAUGHTERED	1-01-001	SLOPE'S	11-07-011	SMILES	7-01-001	SNELLING
1-01-001	SLAUGHTERING	7-05-007	SLOPES	2-01-001	SMILIN	2-01-001	SNELLVILLE
30-09-012	SLAVE	7-04-007	SLOPING	36-11-027	SMILING	1-01-001	SNICK
1-01-001	SLAVE'S	1-01-001	SLOPPED	2-01-002	SMILINGLY	2-02-002	SNICKERED
1-01-001	SLAVE-LABORERS	1-01-001	SLOPPILY	3-03-003	SMIRK	2-02-002	SNIFF
1-01-001	SLAVE-OWNERS	2-02-002	SLOPPING	1-01-001	SMIRKED	6-03-006	SNIFFED
1-01-001	SLAVERED	3-03-003	SLOPPY	54-10-036	SMITH	2-02-002	SNIFFING
33-04-015	SLAVERY	1-01-001	SLOSHED	5-04-004	SMITH'S	1-01-001	SNIFFLE
44-07-014	SLAVES	1-01-001	SLOT	1-01-001	SMITH-*COLMER	1-01-001	SNIGGERED
2-01-001	SLAVIC	1-01-001	SLOTHFUL	3-02-002	SMITH-*HUGHES	1-01-001	SNIPER
1-01-001	SLAVISH	5-03-005	SLOTS	2-01-002	SMITHEREENS	1-01-001	SNIPER'S
1-01-001	SLAVS	1-01-001	SLOTTED	3-02-002	SMITHFIELD	1-01-001	SNIPING
3-02-003	SLAYING	1-01-001	SLOUCH	3-01-001	SMITHSONIAN	1-01-001	SNIPPY
2-02-002	SLEDDING	1-01-001	SLOUCHES	1-01-001	SMITHTOWN	1-01-001	SNIPS
2-02-002	SLEEK	1-01-001	SLOUGH	1-01-001	SMITHY	1-01-001	SNIVELINGS
1-01-001	SLEEK-HEADED	1-01-001	SLOVENLINESS	1-01-001	SMITTEN	1-01-001	SNOB-CLANNISH
65-10-041	SLEEP	3-01-002	SLOVENLY	1-01-001	SMOG	4-03-003	SNOBBERY
1-01-001	SLEEP-WAKEFULNESS	60-11-046	SLOW	41-10-033	SMOKE	2-02-002	SNOBBISH
1-01-001	SLEEPER	1-01-001	SLOW-ACTING	1-01-001	SMOKE-FILLED	1-01-001	SNOBBISHLY
1-01-001	SLEEPER'S	1-01-001	SLOW-BAKED	1-01-001	SMOKE-STAINED	1-01-001	SNOBS
1-01-001	SLEEPERS	1-01-001	SLOW-BOUNCING	9-05-008	SMOKED	2-02-002	SNODGRASS
3-02-003	SLEEPILY	1-01-001	SLOW-FIRING	2-01-001	SMOKEHOUSE	1-01-001	SNOOK
39-14-033	SLEEPING	1-01-001	SLOW-GROWING	1-01-001	SMOKERS	1-01-001	SNOOP
1-01-001	SLEEPLESS	1-01-001	SLOW-MOVING	1-01-001	SMOKES	1-01-001	SNOOPING
1-01-001	SLEEPLESSLY	1-01-001	SLOW-SCRAMBLING	1-01-001	SMOKESCREEN	4-01-002	SNOPES
1-01-001	SLEEPS	17-08-015	SLOWED	1-01-001	SMOKIES	6-02-004	SNORING
1-01-001	SLEEPWALKER	9-05-008	SLOWER	8-05-008	SMOKING	2-01-001	SNORKLE
6-03-006	SLEEPY	2-02-002	SLOWEST	5-03-003	SMOKY	3-02-002	SNORT
1-01-001	SLEEPY-EYED	6-04-004	SLOWING	2-02-002	SMOLDERED	4-03-004	SNORTED
1-01-001	SLEET	115-13-078	SLOWLY	2-02-002	SMOLDERING	1-01-001	SNOUT
11-05-009	SLEEVE	1-01-001	SLOWLY-MENDING	1-01-001	SMOLDERINGLY	59-13-029	SNOW
8-06-007	SLEEVES	4-03-004	SLOWNESS	1-01-001	SMOLDERS	3-02-002	SNOW'S
1-01-001	SLEIGHT	4-01-001	SLUDGE	1-01-001	SMOOCHING	1-01-001	SNOW-COVERED
1-01-001	SLENCZYNKA	10-06-007	SLUG	42-11-028	SMOOTH	1-01-001	SNOW-FENCE
19-08-018	SLENDER	4-02-004	SLUGGED	1-01-001	SMOOTHBORE	1-01-001	SNOW-WHITE
1-01-001	SLENDER-WAISTED	4-02-003	SLUGGER	7-05-007	SMOOTHED	2-01-002	SNOWBALL
1-01-001	SLENDERER	2-01-002	SLUGGERS	3-02-003	SMOOTHER	2-01-002	SNOWBALLS
27-07-021	SLEPT	3-03-003	SLUGGING	1-01-001	SMOOTHEST	2-01-001	SNOWED
1-01-001	SLEUTHING	2-02-002	SLUGGISH	2-02-002	SMOOTHING	2-02-002	SNOWFALL
13-06-012	SLICE	2-02-002	SLUGGISHLY	12-06-012	SMOOTHLY	1-01-001	SNOWFLAKES
4-04-004	SLICED	4-04-004	SLUGS	5-03-004	SMOOTHNESS	4-04-004	SNOWING
2-02-002	SLICES	2-02-002	SLUICE	6-04-004	SMOTHERED	7-03-003	SNOWS
7-04-007	SLICK	2-02-002	SLUICED	1-01-001	SMOTHERING	3-03-003	SNOWSTORM
1-01-001	SLICK-HEADED	1-01-001	SLUICEHOUSE	7-05-006	SMUDGED	4-04-004	SNOWY
3-03-003	SLICKER	2-02-002	SLUICES	1-01-001	SMUG	3-03-003	SNUBBED
1-01-001	SLICKERS	1-01-001	SLUICING	3-02-002	SMUGGLE	1-01-001	SNUBBING
24-08-019	SLID	8-04-005	SLUM	1-01-001	SMUGGLED	1-01-001	SNUCK
20-08-013	SLIDE	3-03-003	SLUMBER	1-01-001	SMUGGLERS	1-01-001	SNUFFBOXES
1-01-001	SLIDE-LOCK	1-01-001	SLUMBERED	1-01-001	SMUGGLERS'	1-01-001	SNUFFED
5-04-005	SLIDES	8-04-007	SLUMP	1-01-001	SMUGGLING	1-01-001	SNUFFER
11-08-011	SLIDING	8-04-007	SLUMPED	4-02-003	SMYTHE	2-02-002	SNUG
53-13-044	SLIGHT	8-06-006	SLUMS	6-04-004	SNACK	1-01-001	SNUG-*GRIP
1-01-001	SLIGHTER	2-02-002	SLUNG	3-02-003	SNACKS	1-01-001	SNUG-FITTING
13-08-013	SLIGHTEST	1-01-001	SLURPED	3-02-002	SNAG	4-02-004	SNUGGLED
83-13-067	SLIGHTLY	1-01-001	SLURRIES	1-01-001	SNAGS	2-02-002	SNUGLY
1-01-001	SLIGHTLY-SMOKING	5-05-005	SLURRY	1-01-001	SNAIL	1-01-001	SNYDER
1-01-001	SLIGHTS	1-01-001	SLYLY	1-01-001	SNAIL'S	1-01-001	SNYDER'S
20-08-012	SLIM	1-01-001	SLYNESS	1-01-001	SNAILS	1984-15-467	SO
1-01-001	SLIM-WAISTED	4-03-003	SMACK	44-08-013	SNAKE	4-02-003	SO'S
1-01-001	SLIMED	2-02-002	SMACKED	1-01-001	SNAKE-LIKE	32-12-029	SO-CALLED
1-01-001	SLIMLY	1-01-001	SMACKS	1-01-001	SNAKE-RAIL	1-01-001	SO-FAR
1-01-001	SLIMMER	542-15-243	SMALL	3-02-003	SNAKED	4-02-003	SO-SO
1-01-001	SLING	1-01-001	SMALL-ARMS	26-03-003	SNAKES	7-04-005	SOAK
1-01-001	SLINGING	1-01-001	SMALL-BOAT	1-01-001	SNAKESTRIKE	6-04-006	SOAKED
1-01-001	SLINGS	1-01-001	SMALL-CAR	12-06-010	SNAP	9-04-007	SOAKING
1-01-001	SLINGSHOT	2-02-002	SMALL-GAME	1-01-001	SNAP-IN	22-06-010	SOAP
19-10-013	SLIP	1-01-001	SMALL-SCALE	1-01-001	SNAPBACK	3-02-002	SOAPS
1-01-001	SLIPPAGE	6-06-006	SMALL-TOWN	1-01-001	SNAPDRAGONS	1-01-001	SOAPSUDS
32-10-029	SLIPPED	78-14-064	SMALLER	19-07-017	SNAPPED	2-02-002	SOAPY
3-03-003	SLIPPER	1-01-001	SMALLER-SIZE	1-01-001	SNAPPER	4-02-004	SOARED
7-04-006	SLIPPERS	13-05-009	SMALLEST	9-05-008	SNAPPING	5-04-005	SOARING
5-05-005	SLIPPERY	1-01-001	SMALLISH	1-01-001	SNAPPY	1-01-001	SOBA
7-05-007	SLIPPING	2-02-002	SMALLNESS	1-01-001	SNAPSHOTS	2-01-002	SOBBED
8-03-004	SLIPS	2-02-002	SMALLPOX	1-01-001	SNARE	1-01-001	SOBBING
1-01-001	SLIPSTREAM	1-01-001	SMALLTIME	1-01-001	SNARED	1-01-001	SOBBINGLY
		4-02-002	SMALLWOOD	8-04-006	SNARLED	19-09-015	SOBER
		21-09-018	SMART	3-03-003	SNARLING	3-01-003	SOBERED

Code	Word	Code	Word	Code	Word	Code	Word
3-02-003	SOBERING	15-02-003	SOILS	94-14-068	SOMEONE	1-01-001	SORORITY
4-03-004	SOBERLY	1-01-001	SOIREE	1-01-001	SOMEONE'LL	1-01-001	SORPTION
1-01-001	SOBIBOR	1-01-001	SOIREES	5-04-005	SOMEONE'S	1-01-001	SORPTION-DESORP TION
1-01-001	SOBRIETY	5-02-005	SOJOURN	6-05-006	SOMEPLACE		
2-02-002	SOBRIQUET	3-02-002	SOJOURNER	7-02-002	SOMERS	2-02-002	SORREL
3-03-003	SOBS	1-01-001	SOJOURNERS	2-01-001	SOMERSAULT	1-01-001	SORRENTINE
1-01-001	SOCAL	4-01-001	SOKOL	1-01-001	SOMERSAULTING	1-01-001	SORRENTINE'S
3-01-001	SOCCER	1-01-001	SOKOLEV	3-02-002	SOMERSAULTS	3-01-001	SORRENTINO
2-01-001	SOCHI	2-01-001	SOKOLOV	3-01-001	SOMERSET	1-01-001	SORRIEST
2-02-002	SOCIABILITY	2-02-002	SOKOLSKY	2-01-001	SOMERVILLE	9-06-009	SORROW
1-01-001	SOCIABLE	3-03-003	SOL	3-01-003	SOMETHIN	2-02-002	SORROWS
380-15-123	SOCIAL	6-04-006	SOLACE	450-15-222	SOMETHING	48-11-036	SORRY
8-01-001	SOCIAL-CLASS	1-01-001	SOLACED	11-08-011	SOMETIME	164-13-120	SORT
1-01-001	SOCIAL-CLIMBING	16-04-008	SOLAR	221-15-131	SOMETIMES	4-04-004	SORTED
3-02-002	SOCIAL-ECONOMIC	1-01-001	SOLAR-CORPUSCUL AR-RADIATION	1-01-001	SOMETIMES-NECES SARY	2-01-002	SORTIE
1-01-001	SOCIAL-POLITICA L-ECONOMICAL	1-01-001	SOLAR-ELECTROMA GNETIC-	127-15-090	SOMEWHAT	1-01-001	SORTING
1-01-001	SOCIAL-REGISTER	1-01-001	SOLAR-RADIATION	60-13-049	SOMEWHERE	12-07-012	SORTS
1-01-001	SOCIAL-ROLE	1-01-001	SOLAR-WIND	1-01-001	SOMEWHERES	1-01-001	SOTUN
1-01-001	SOCIAL-WELFARE	47-11-031	SOLD	3-01-001	SOMMELIER	1-01-001	SOU
20-06-010	SOCIALISM	1-01-001	SOLD-OUT	1-01-001	SOMMERS	1-01-001	SOUBRIQUET
21-05-011	SOCIALIST	4-01-001	SOLDER	1-01-001	SOMNOLENCE	1-01-001	SOUCI
3-01-003	SOCIALISTIC	1-01-001	SOLDERED	2-02-002	SOMNOLENT	1-01-001	SOUFFLE
1-01-001	SOCIALITY	1-01-001	SOLDERING	1-01-001	SOMPIN	55-12-046	SOUGHT
6-03-003	SOCIALIZATION	39-09-019	SOLDIER	166-14-083	SON	1-01-001	SOUKHOUMA
1-01-001	SOCIALIZE	1-01-001	SOLDIER'S	9-07-008	SON'S	47-10-033	SOUL
3-02-003	SOCIALIZED	1-01-001	SOLDIER-MASTERS	4-01-002	SON-IN-LAW	3-02-003	SOUL'S
1-01-001	SOCIALIZES	1-01-001	SOLDIERING	2-02-002	SON-OF-A-BITCH	1-01-001	SOUL-SEARCHING
15-08-013	SOCIALLY	1-01-001	SOLDIERLY	1-01-001	SONAMBULA	1-01-001	SOULD
1-01-001	SOCIALLY-ORIENT ED	56-09-030	SOLDIERS	7-01-001	SONAR	1-01-001	SOULE
4-02-002	SOCIETAL	2-01-001	SOLDIERS'	9-02-004	SONATA	1-01-001	SOULFUL
1-01-001	SOCIETE	1-01-001	SOLDIERY	6-02-004	SONATAS	1-01-001	SOULFULLY
41-08-023	SOCIETIES	18-11-018	SOLE	1-01-001	SONATES	22-07-014	SOULS
237-14-101	SOCIETY	20-06-017	SOLELY	1-01-001	SONENBERG	1-01-001	SOULS'
3-02-003	SOCIETY'S	12-08-012	SOLEMN	70-12-031	SONG	204-15-127	SOUND
1-01-001	SOCINIANISM	1-01-001	SOLEMNIS	2-01-001	SONG'S	1-01-001	SOUND-TRUCK
1-01-001	SOCIO-ARCHAEOLO GICAL	1-01-001	SOLEMNITY	1-01-001	SONG-WRITING	35-11-030	SOUNDED
3-02-002	SOCIO-ECONOMIC	9-06-008	SOLEMNLY	4-01-001	SONGAU	5-03-004	SOUNDER
1-01-001	SOCIO-POLITICAL	1-01-001	SOLENOID	1-01-001	SONGBAG	3-03-003	SOUNDING
1-01-001	SOCIO-STRUCTURA L	1-01-001	SOLES	1-01-001	SONGBOOK	3-03-003	SOUNDLY
3-01-001	SOCIOECONOMIC	59-10-024	SOLESMES	1-01-001	SONGFUL	1-01-001	SOUNDNESS
11-05-009	SOCIOLOGICAL	1-01-001	SOLICIT	59-10-024	SONGS	1-01-001	SOUNDPROOF
1-01-001	SOCIOLOGICALLY	2-02-002	SOLICITED	2-01-001	SONIC	55-11-044	SOUNDS
2-02-002	SOCIOLOGIST	1-01-001	SOLICITING	3-02-002	SONNET	3-01-001	SOUNION
1-01-001	SOCIOLOGISTS	6-03-004	SOLICITOR	2-02-002	SONNETS	16-08-012	SOUP
15-02-002	SOCIOLOGY	2-02-002	SOLICITOUS	2-01-002	SONNY	1-01-001	SOUPHANOUVONG
4-03-004	SOCK	1-01-001	SOLICITOUSNESS	1-01-001	SONNY-BOY	3-03-003	SOUR
1-01-001	SOCKDOLOGIZING	4-03-004	SOLICITS	4-03-004	SONOFABITCH	94-12-070	SOURCE
1-01-001	SOCKED	1-01-001	SOLICITUDE	1-01-001	SONOGRAM	88-09-052	SOURCES
3-03-003	SOCKET	77-15-060	SOLID	1-01-001	SONOMA	2-01-002	SOURDOUGH
1-01-001	SOCKETS	1-01-001	SOLID-FUELED	1-01-001	SONORA	3-03-003	SOURLY
7-05-006	SOCKS	1-01-001	SOLID-STATE	1-01-001	SONORITIES	1-01-001	SOURS
1-01-001	SOCOLA	13-05-009	SOLIDARITY	1-01-001	SONORITY	1-01-001	SOUSA
1-01-001	SOCONOCO	4-03-003	SOLIDITY	1-01-001	SONOROUS	1-01-001	SOUTANE
3-01-003	SOD	10-05-007	SOLIDLY	29-12-021	SONS	240-15-095	SOUTH
3-02-002	SODA	13-01-002	SOLIDS	1-01-001	SONUVABITCH	5-03-004	SOUTH'S
2-02-002	SODDEN	1-01-001	SOLIPSISM	1-01-001	SOOMED	1-01-001	SOUTH-*ASIAN
1-01-001	SODDENLY	14-08-014	SOLITARY	199-15-146	SOON	1-01-001	SOUTH-*EAST
1-01-001	SODDIES	2-02-002	SOLITUDE	1-01-001	SOON'S	1-01-001	SOUTH-CENTRAL
12-02-005	SODIUM	1-01-001	SOLITUDES	17-09-016	SOONER	1-01-001	SOUTH-EASTERN
1-01-001	SODS	1-01-001	SOLITUDINEM	1-01-001	SOOT	2-01-001	SOUTHAMPTON
1-01-001	SOE	4-02-004	SOLLY	2-02-002	SOOTHE	1-01-001	SOUTHBOUND
1-01-001	SOEREN	1-01-001	SOLO	2-02-002	SOOTHED	28-08-022	SOUTHEAST
6-03-003	SOFA	1-01-001	SOLOIST	4-02-004	SOOTHING	5-04-004	SOUTHEASTERN
1-01-001	SOFAR	5-03-005	SOLOISTS	1-01-001	SOOTHINGLY	137-12-053	SOUTHERN
3-02-002	SOFAS	1-01-001	SOLOISTS'	1-01-001	SOOTHSAYER	1-01-001	SOUTHERN-*REPUB LICAN
61-11-049	SOFT	2-02-002	SOLOMON	2-02-002	SOOTHSAYERS	1-01-001	SOUTHERN-CENTRA L
1-01-001	SOFT-	1-01-001	SOLOMON'S	1-01-001	SOP		
1-01-001	SOFT-DRINK	3-03-003	SOLOS	7-01-001	SOPHIA	8-03-005	SOUTHERNER
1-01-001	SOFT-DRINKS	2-02-002	SOLOVIEV	1-01-001	SOPHIA'S	1-01-001	SOUTHERNER'S
1-01-001	SOFT-HEADED	1-01-001	SOLOVIEV-*SEDOI	1-01-001	SOPHIAS	26-04-009	SOUTHERNERS
1-01-001	SOFT-HEARTEDNES S	1-01-001	SOLSTICE	2-01-002	SOPHIE	1-01-001	SOUTHERNISMS
1-01-001	SOFT-LOOKING	1-01-001	SOLUBLE	1-01-001	SOPHISTICATE	1-01-001	SOUTHEY
1-01-001	SOFT-SHELL	59-11-047	SOLUTION	26-09-021	SOPHISTICATED	1-01-001	SOUTHFIELD
1-01-001	SOFT-SHOE	1-01-001	SOLUTION-TYPE	1-01-001	SOPHISTICATES	1-01-001	SOUTHLAND
1-01-001	SOFT-SPOKEN	29-06-019	SOLUTIONS	8-04-006	SOPHISTICATION	5-01-003	SOUTHPAW
4-03-004	SOFTEN	1-01-001	SOLVATING	1-01-001	SOPHOCLEAN	1-01-001	SOUTHS
7-06-007	SOFTENED	20-09-018	SOLVE	3-02-002	SOPHOCLES	8-06-006	SOUTHWARD
2-01-001	SOFTENER	19-09-018	SOLVED	5-03-003	SOPHOMORE	16-08-015	SOUTHWEST
6-04-005	SOFTENING	1-01-001	SOLVENCY	1-01-001	SOPHOMORES	2-01-001	SOUTHWESTERN
1-01-001	SOFTENS	5-01-001	SOLVENT	1-01-001	SOPPING	6-02-003	SOUVANNA
5-04-005	SOFTER	3-01-002	SOLVENTS	6-03-005	SOPRANO	2-02-002	SOUVENIR
1-01-001	SOFTEST	2-01-001	SOLVES	1-01-001	SOPRANOS	1-01-001	SOUVENIRS
31-09-024	SOFTLY	8-05-006	SOLVING	1-01-001	SOPS	30-03-008	SOVEREIGN
5-03-004	SOFTNESS	1-01-001	SOMA	30-03-008	SOPSAISANA	1-01-001	SOVEREIGNS
1-01-001	SOFTWOOD	2-01-001	SOMATIC	1-01-001	SOR'L	28-05-008	SOVEREIGNTY
3-02-003	SOGGY	3-01-003	SOMAY	8-01-001	SORBED	129-09-036	SOVIET
1-01-001	SOHN	1-01-001	SOMBER	1-01-001	SORCERY	1-01-001	SOVIET'S
1-01-001	SOIGNEE	1-01-001	SOMBRE	2-01-001	SORDID	2-01-001	SOVIET-*CHINESE
54-11-023	SOIL	1617-15-440	SOME	10-06-009	SORE	1-01-001	SOVIET-*WESTERN
1-01-001	SOIL-BEARING	57-11-040	SOMEBODY	1-01-001	SORE-RIDDEN	12-04-008	SOVIETS
1-01-001	SOIL-REMOVAL	1-01-001	SOMEBODY'LL	3-03-003	SORELY	1-01-001	SOVIETS'
7-01-002	SOILED	7-06-007	SOMEBODY'S	1-01-001	SORENESS	1-01-001	SOVIETSKAYA
		12-06-012	SOMEDAY	3-02-002	SORES	1-01-001	SOVKHOZES
		72-15-062	SOMEHOW	1-01-001	SOREST	3-02-002	SOW
				3-01-001	SORGHUM	2-02-002	SOWBELLY
				1-01-001	SORORITIES	1-01-001	SOWERED

1-01-001 SOWING	19-10-014 SPECIALISTS	1-01-001 SPEWING	8-02-002 SPOILAGE
3-03-003 SOWN	10-07-009 SPECIALIZATION	1-01-001 SPEWINGS	6-05-006 SPOILED
13-02-004 SOX	3-03-003 SPECIALIZE	22-09-015 SPHERE	1-01-001 SPOILING
1-01-001 SOXHLET	18-08-014 SPECIALIZED	4-02-003 SPHERES	1-01-001 SPOILS
1-01-001 SOY	1-01-001 SPECIALIZES	8-03-007 SPHERICAL	2-01-001 SPOKANE
1-01-001 SOYABURGERS	4-03-004 SPECIALIZING	1-01-001 SPHERULES	87-13-064 SPOKE
5-01-001 SOYBEAN	9-05-008 SPECIALLY	1-01-001 SPHINX	37-14-028 SPOKEN
6-02-002 SOYBEANS	5-04-005 SPECIALTIES	1-01-001 SPHYNXES	2-02-002 SPOKES
2-01-001 SP	4-03-004 SPECIALTY	1-01-001 SPIC	13-05-010 SPOKESMAN
2-01-001 SPA	2-02-002 SPECIE	4-02-004 SPICE	13-06-010 SPOKESMEN
184-14-082 SPACE	37-07-018 SPECIES	3-01-001 SPICE-*NICE	7-05-006 SPONGE
1-01-001 SPACE-TIME	1-01-001 SPECIES-DEPENDE	1-01-001 SPICE-LADEN	2-01-001 SPONGED
3-01-001 SPACECRAFT	NT	3-01-001 SPICED	1-01-001 SPONGES
8-05-007 SPACED	115-11-076 SPECIFIC	3-03-003 SPICES	1-01-001 SPONGING
2-01-001 SPACER	38-11-035 SPECIFICALLY	1-01-001 SPICY	2-02-002 SPONGY
5-01-001 SPACERS	3-01-001 SPECIFICATION	2-02-002 SPIDER	22-08-014 SPONSOR
11-05-008 SPACES	9-04-007 SPECIFICATIONS	1-01-001 SPIDER-LEG	1-01-001 SPONSOR'S
2-01-001 SPACESHIP	10-02-004 SPECIFICITY	1-01-001 SPIDERY	31-09-026 SPONSORED
1-01-001 SPACESUIT	1-01-001 SPECIFICS	2-02-002 SPIES	3-03-003 SPONSORING
1-01-001 SPACESUITS	28-07-020 SPECIFIED	1-01-001 SPIGOTS	10-08-008 SPONSORS
6-03-004 SPACING	4-03-004 SPECIFIES	2-02-002 SPIKE	5-03-004 SPONSORSHIP
1-01-001 SPACINGS	11-04-009 SPECIFY	1-01-001 SPIKE-HAIRED	7-03-005 SPONTANEITY
9-06-008 SPACIOUS	3-02-003 SPECIFYING	2-02-002 SPIKED	17-06-017 SPONTANEOUS
3-03-003 SPACIOUSNESS	24-05-006 SPECIMEN	3-02-002 SPIKES	9-04-007 SPONTANEOUSLY
2-01-001 SPADA	13-05-007 SPECIMENS	1-01-001 SPILL	1-01-001 SPOOF
10-04-006 SPADE	1-01-001 SPECIMENTALIA	1-01-001 SPILLANE'S	2-01-001 SPOOKY
4-01-001 SPADES	2-01-001 SPECIOUS	3-02-002 SPILLED	6-05-006 SPOON
1-01-001 SPAGHETTI	7-04-006 SPECK	1-01-001 SPILLER	1-01-001 SPOONED
1-01-001 SPAGNA	1-01-001 SPECKLED	3-03-003 SPILLING	1-01-001 SPOONFUL
5-01-002 SPAHN	1-01-001 SPECKLES	2-02-002 SPILLS	7-03-006 SPORADIC
1-01-001 SPAHN'S	2-02-002 SPECKS	5-05-005 SPIN	3-02-002 SPORES
1-01-001 SPAHNIE	18-07-016 SPECTACLE	1-01-001 SPIN-SPIN	17-08-013 SPORT
7-06-006 SPAIN	3-03-003 SPECTACLES	2-02-002 SPINACH	1-01-001 SPORT-*KING
1-01-001 SPALDING	22-06-018 SPECTACULAR	4-01-001 SPINCO	1-01-001 SPORTIEST
19-08-014 SPAN	2-02-002 SPECTACULARLY	8-02-003 SPINDLE	4-01-001 SPORTIN
1-01-001 SPANDRELS	9-07-009 SPECTATOR	6-05-006 SPINE	9-06-006 SPORTING
1-01-001 SPANGLE	1-01-001 SPECTATOR-TYPE	2-01-001 SPINE-CHILLING	49-10-030 SPORTS
1-01-001 SPANGLED	13-07-011 SPECTATORS	2-01-002 SPINELESS	5-03-005 SPORTSMAN
1-01-001 SPANIEL'S	3-03-003 SPECTER	1-01-001 SPINLEY'S	1-01-001 SPORTSMANSHIP
1-01-001 SPANIEL-LIKE	1-01-001 SPECTERS	1-01-001 SPINNABILITY	6-01-003 SPORTSMEN
36-12-026 SPANISH	1-01-001 SPECTOR	1-01-001 SPINNERET	1-01-001 SPORTSMEN'S
2-02-002 SPANISH-*AMERIC	18-02-003 SPECTRA	11-06-008 SPINNING	3-02-002 SPORTSWRITER
AN	6-02-003 SPECTRAL	1-01-001 SPINRAD	4-01-001 SPOSATO
1-01-001 SPANISH-BORN	1-01-001 SPECTRALLY	8-02-003 SPIRAL	57-12-047 SPOT
2-01-001 SPANNED	1-01-001 SPECTRE	1-01-001 SPIRALED	1-01-001 SPOT-NEWS
1-01-001 SPANNING	2-01-001 SPECTROMETER	1-01-001 SPIRALING	1-01-001 SPOT-PROMOTED
5-03-005 SPANS	1-01-001 SPECTROMETRIC	1-01-001 SPIRALIS	3-01-003 SPOTLESS
23-11-021 SPARE	1-01-001 SPECTROPHOTOMET	5-03-003 SPIRE	6-04-006 SPOTLIGHT
9-06-009 SPARED	ER	3-02-002 SPIRES	1-01-001 SPOTLIGHTS
1-01-001 SPARES	1-01-001 SPECTROPHOTOMET	182-14-089 SPIRIT	32-12-026 SPOTS
1-01-001 SPARING	RIC	1-01-001 SPIRIT-GUM	16-06-013 SPOTTED
12-06-009 SPARK	3-01-001 SPECTROSCOPY	8-04-007 SPIRITED	2-02-002 SPOTTING
3-03-003 SPARKED	14-05-009 SPECTRUM	3-02-002 SPIRITO	1-01-001 SPOTTY
4-04-004 SPARKLE	1-01-001 SPECULAR	44-11-026 SPIRITS	3-03-003 SPOUSE
1-01-001 SPARKLED	7-03-007 SPECULATE	64-10-032 SPIRITUAL	4-03-004 SPOUSES
1-01-001 SPARKLES	2-02-002 SPECULATED	1-01-001 SPIRITUALITY	1-01-001 SPOUT
5-04-005 SPARKLING	4-03-004 SPECULATING	7-03-006 SPIRITUALLY	3-03-003 SPOUTED
5-04-005 SPARKS	3-03-003 SPECULATION	1-01-001 SPIRITUALS	1-01-001 SPOUTING
3-01-001 SPARKY	4-04-004 SPECULATIONS	1-01-001 SPIRITUALS'	3-01-001 SPRAGUE
1-01-001 SPARLING	8-04-006 SPECULATIVE	11-06-008 SPIT	1-01-001 SPRAGUE'S
1-01-001 SPARLING'S	1-01-001 SPECULATIVELY	56-11-049 SPITE	2-01-002 SPRAINED
3-03-003 SPARRING	1-01-001 SPECULATOR	5-04-004 SPITTING	1-01-001 SPRAINS
1-01-001 SPARROW'S	2-02-002 SPECULATORS	2-02-002 SPITTLE	13-07-012 SPRANG
1-01-001 SPARROW-SIZE	9-06-009 SPED	3-03-003 SPLASH	3-03-003 SPRAWL
5-05-005 SPARSE	61-14-045 SPEECH	3-03-003 SPLASHED	11-06-009 SPRAWLED
2-02-002 SPARSELY	1-01-001 SPEECH-MAKING	2-02-002 SPLASHES	5-03-005 SPRAWLING
1-01-001 SPARTA	21-10-020 SPEECHES	3-03-003 SPLASHING	16-08-012 SPRAY
2-02-002 SPARTAN	3-02-003 SPEECHLESS	1-01-001 SPLASHY	1-01-001 SPRAY-DRIED
3-03-003 SPASM	2-02-002 SPEECHLESSNESS	1-01-001 SPLATTERED	6-05-005 SPRAYED
1-01-001 SPASMS	83-12-052 SPEED	1-01-001 SPLAYED	8-03-004 SPRAYING
9-04-009 SPAT	1-01-001 SPEEDBOAT	2-02-002 SPLEEN	1-01-001 SPRAYS
2-02-002 SPATE	3-03-003 SPEEDED	1-01-001 SPLEEN-CRUSHING	83-13-070 SPREAD
10-02-003 SPATIAL	3-03-003 SPEEDILY	20-08-017 SPLENDID	1-01-001 SPREAD-EAGLED
1-01-001 SPATIALITY	4-03-004 SPEEDING	1-01-001 SPLENDIDE	1-01-001 SPREAD-OUT
2-01-002 SPATIALLY	1-01-001 SPEEDOMETER	4-03-004 SPLENDIDLY	1-01-001 SPREADER
1-01-001 SPATS	14-05-006 SPEEDS	7-05-006 SPLENDOR	16-09-016 SPREADING
1-01-001 SPATTER	1-01-001 SPEEDUP	1-01-001 SPLENETIC	10-07-010 SPREADS
2-02-002 SPATTERED	6-06-006 SPEEDY	1-01-001 SPLENOMEGALY	4-03-004 SPREE
1-01-001 SPAVINED	1-01-001 SPEER	1-01-001 SPLICE	1-01-001 SPRIG
110-14-078 SPEAK	1-01-001 SPEGITITGNININO	1-01-001 SPLICED	1-01-001 SPRIGHTLY
1-01-001 SPEAK-EASY	1-01-001 SPEIDEL	1-01-001 SPLICING	127-14-076 SPRING
49-08-023 SPEAKER	19-10-016 SPELL	4-02-002 SPLINTER	1-01-001 SPRING-BACK
4-04-004 SPEAKER'S	1-01-001 SPELL-BINDING	2-02-002 SPLINTERED	1-01-001 SPRING-JOINTS
14-09-012 SPEAKERS	1-01-001 SPELLBOUND	1-01-001 SPLINTERS	1-01-001 SPRING-TRAINING
1-01-001 SPEAKERSHIP	6-05-006 SPELLED	1-01-001 SPLINTERY	2-02-002 SPRINGBOARD
1-01-001 SPEAKIN	4-02-004 SPELLING	1-01-001 SPLINTING	3-03-003 SPRINGFIELD
62-13-056 SPEAKING	2-02-002 SPELLS	30-09-024 SPLIT	1-01-001 SPRINGFIELD'S
18-08-013 SPEAKS	11-01-001 SPELMAN	1-01-001 SPLIT-BAMBOO	2-02-002 SPRINGING
7-04-004 SPEAR	23-02-002 SPENCER	1-01-001 SPLIT-LEVEL	21-08-015 SPRINGS
1-01-001 SPEAR-THROWING	6-01-001 SPENCER'S	2-02-002 SPLITS	4-04-004 SPRINGTIME
1-01-001 SPEARED	1-01-001 SPENCERIAN	3-03-003 SPLITTING	3-01-001 SPRINKEL
1-01-001 SPEARHEAD	53-15-045 SPEND	2-01-001 SPLOTCHED	7-05-005 SPRINKLE
1-01-001 SPEC	1-01-001 SPENDERS	1-01-001 SPLOTCHES	4-03-003 SPRINKLED
250-14-155 SPECIAL	41-11-025 SPENDING	1-01-001 SPLURGE	7-04-007 SPRINKLING
1-01-001 SPECIAL-INTERES	8-07-008 SPENDS	1-01-001 SPOFFORD	2-02-002 SPRINTED
T	1-01-001 SPENGLERIAN	3-03-003 SPOIL	1-01-001 SPRITE
16-08-014 SPECIALIST	104-15-084 SPENT	1-01-001 SPOILABLES	1-01-001 SPROUT

3-02-002	SPROUTED	13-06-012	STABILITY	1-01-001	STAMMERING	12-01-001	STATE-OWNED
6-03-003	SPROUTING	3-02-002	STABILIZATION	8-06-008	STAMP	1-01-001	STATE-SPONSORED
5-04-004	SPRUCE	2-02-002	STABILIZE	7-06-007	STAMPED	1-01-001	STATE-SUPPORTED
1-01-001	SPRUCED	1-01-001	STABILIZED	4-02-002	STAMPEDE	85-12-053	STATED
2-02-002	SPRUE	1-01-001	STABILIZERS	1-01-001	STAMPEDED	1-01-001	STATELESS
8-05-008	SPRUNG	1-01-001	STABILIZES	5-05-005	STAMPING	4-04-004	STATELY
1-01-001	SPUME	4-02-004	STABILIZING	4-03-004	STAMPS	141-15-083	STATEMENT
1-01-001	SPUMONI'S	1-01-001	STABILIZING-CON SERVING	3-02-002	STAN	68-12-037	STATEMENTS
16-07-013	SPUN	30-06-020	STABLE	2-01-001	STANBURY	5-04-005	STATEN
13-08-012	SPUR	1-01-001	STABLE-GARAGE	6-04-006	STANCE	2-02-002	STATEROOM
3-01-001	SPURDLE	1-01-001	STABLED	1-01-001	STANCES	605-14-182	STATES
2-02-002	SPURIOUS	1-01-001	STABLEMAN	1-01-001	STANCH	7-04-006	STATES'
1-01-001	SPURNED	3-03-003	STABLES	1-01-001	STANCHEST	1-01-001	STATES-*YUGOSLA V
1-01-001	SPURNS	1-01-001	STABS	148-15-117	STAND		
6-06-006	SPURRED	5-04-005	STACCATO	3-01-001	STAND-INS	12-05-008	STATESMAN
1-01-001	SPURRING	1-01-001	STACCATOS	1-01-001	STAND-UPS	1-01-001	STATESMANLIKE
3-03-003	SPURS	2-01-001	STACEY	110-11-062	STANDARD	2-02-002	STATESMANSHIP
2-02-002	SPURT	9-07-009	STACK	1-01-001	STANDARD-*TIMES	8-04-008	STATESMEN
2-02-002	SPUTNIK	9-07-008	STACKED	1-01-001	STANDARD-WEIGHT	13-04-007	STATEWIDE
1-01-001	SPUTNIKS	2-02-002	STACKING	4-02-004	STANDARDIZED	13-08-013	STATIC
1-01-001	SPUTTER	1-01-001	STACKS	1-01-001	STANDARDIZING	16-09-015	STATING
1-01-001	SPUTTERED	10-02-002	STACY	74-09-046	STANDARDS	105-13-049	STATION
1-01-001	SPUYTEN	25-03-013	STADIUM	3-02-003	STANDBY	4-03-004	STATION'S
9-06-007	SPY	113-12-062	STAFF	1-01-001	STANDETH	2-01-002	STATIONARY
1-01-001	SPYCKET	1-01-001	STAFF'S	1-01-001	STANDIN	5-03-004	STATIONED
2-01-001	SPYING	4-01-001	STAFFE	101-13-074	STANDING	2-01-002	STATIONERY
4-01-001	SQ	3-03-003	STAFFED	13-06-010	STANDPOINT	1-01-001	STATIONMASTER
3-03-003	SQUABBLES	1-01-001	STAFFING	68-14-055	STANDS	85-09-019	STATIONS
1-01-001	SQUABBLING	1-01-001	STAFFORD	1-01-001	STANDSTILL	1-01-001	STATIONS'
18-05-008	SQUAD	1-01-001	STAFFORDSHIRE	1-01-001	STANFORD	16-06-011	STATISTICAL
3-03-003	SQUADRON	8-04-007	STAFFS	1-01-001	STANHOPE	4-02-004	STATISTICALLY
2-02-002	SQUADRONS	8-03-005	STAG	1-01-001	STANISLAS	1-01-001	STATISTICIANS
1-01-001	SQUADROOM	174-14-085	STAGE	1-01-001	STANISLAS'	22-09-015	STATISTICS
2-02-002	SQUADS	1-01-001	STAGE-PLAYS	35-07-010	STANLEY	1-01-001	STATISTIQUE
1-01-001	SQUALID	3-01-001	STAGECOACH	4-02-002	STANLEY'S	1-01-001	STATOR
7-01-001	SQUALL	16-03-013	STAGED	1-01-001	STANNARD	1-01-001	STATU
1-01-001	SQUALLS	1-01-001	STAGER	2-01-001	STANS	2-02-002	STATUARY
2-02-002	SQUANDERED	51-09-024	STAGES	1-01-001	STANSBERY	17-05-009	STATUE
143-15-070	SQUARE	2-02-002	STAGGER	4-04-004	STANTON	7-05-006	STATUES
1-01-001	SQUARE'S	12-06-012	STAGGERED	1-01-001	STANZA-FORM	1-01-001	STATUETTE
1-01-001	SQUARE-BUILT	6-05-006	STAGGERING	1-01-001	STAPLE	15-08-012	STATURE
1-01-001	SQUARE-MILE	2-02-002	STAGGERINGLY	1-01-001	STAPLES	97-10-057	STATUS
5-02-003	SQUARED	1-01-001	STAGINESS	1-01-001	STAPLING	2-02-002	STATUS-CONSCIOU S
11-08-011	SQUARELY	3-03-003	STAGING	25-09-021	STAR		
13-06-007	SQUARES	5-05-005	STAGNANT	3-01-001	STAR'S	2-01-001	STATUS-ROLES
1-01-001	SQUARESVILLE	1-01-001	STAGNATION	1-01-001	STAR-*SPANGLED	2-02-002	STATUSES
2-01-001	SQUASH	1-01-001	STAGS	4-01-001	STARBIRD	13-03-006	STATUTE
1-01-001	SQUASHED	4-01-001	STAID	1-01-001	STARBOARD	8-06-007	STATUTES
1-01-001	SQUASHED-LOOKIN G	2-02-002	STAIGER	4-01-001	STARCH	1-01-001	STATUTO
1-01-001	SQUASHING	6-04-006	STAIN	2-01-001	STARCHED	13-03-005	STATUTORY
1-01-001	SQUASHY	28-07-013	STAINED	2-01-001	STARCHY	3-03-003	STAUNCH
7-06-007	SQUAT	1-01-001	STAINED-GLASS	2-01-002	STARDEL	3-02-003	STAUNCHEST
1-01-001	SQUAT-STYLE	37-01-001	STAINING	1-01-001	STARDOM	1-01-001	STAUNTON
1-01-001	SQUATS	2-01-001	STAINLESS	14-08-013	STARE	2-02-002	STAVE
4-03-004	SQUATTED	1-01-001	STAINLESS-STEEL	60-09-044	STARED	1-01-001	STAVED
1-01-001	SQUATTER'S	10-06-008	STAINS	1-01-001	STARES	3-01-001	STAVROPOULOS
7-04-006	SQUATTING	2-02-002	STAIR	26-07-023	STARING	1-01-001	STAVROPOULOS'
1-01-001	SQUAW	1-01-001	STAIR-STEP	7-04-006	STARK	113-14-085	STAY
1-01-001	SQUAWK	1-01-001	STAIR-WELL	1-01-001	STARKEY	75-13-061	STAYED
1-01-001	SQUEAK	8-05-007	STAIRCASE	1-01-001	STARKLY	17-07-014	STAYING
2-01-001	SQUEAKED	1-01-001	STAIRCASES	2-01-002	STARLET	5-05-005	STAYS
1-01-001	SQUEAKING	47-08-027	STAIRS	1-01-001	STARLIGHT	5-03-005	STEAD
1-01-001	SQUEAKY	6-06-006	STAIRWAY	1-01-001	STARLINGS	1-01-001	STEADFASTLY
1-01-001	SQUEAL	2-02-002	STAIRWAYS	1-01-001	STARR	2-01-002	STEADIED
2-02-002	SQUEALED	1-01-001	STAIRWELLS	2-01-002	STARRE	3-03-003	STEADIER
1-01-001	SQUEALING	20-07-015	STAKE	3-03-003	STARRED	22-10-021	STEADILY
1-01-001	SQUEALS	3-01-001	STAKE-OUT	2-02-002	STARRING	1-01-001	STEADINESS
1-01-001	SQUEAMISH	2-02-002	STAKED	29-09-023	STARS	41-12-036	STEADY
1-01-001	SQUEAMISHNESS	5-05-005	STAKES	154-15-107	START	1-01-001	STEADY-STATE
11-08-009	SQUEEZE	4-01-001	STALAG	194-15-121	STARTED	10-05-008	STEAK
18-09-017	SQUEEZED	4-03-004	STALE	3-03-003	STARTER	4-03-003	STEAKS
4-03-003	SQUEEZING	2-02-002	STALEMATE	1-01-001	STARTIN	5-05-005	STEAL
1-01-001	SQUELCHED	1-01-001	STALEY	68-13-054	STARTING	1-01-001	STEALER
2-01-001	SQUIBB	15-03-004	STALIN	1-01-001	STARTLE	1-01-001	STEALIN
1-01-001	SQUINT	5-03-004	STALIN'S	21-07-019	STARTLED	6-04-006	STEALING
3-02-003	SQUINTED	1-01-001	STALINGR	1-01-001	STARTLED-HORSE	1-01-001	STEALS
3-02-003	SQUINTING	1-01-001	STALINIST	19-11-016	STARTLING	5-05-005	STEALTH
5-02-002	SQUIRE	1-01-001	STALINIST-CORRU PTED	4-04-004	STARTLINGLY	1-01-001	STEALTHILY
2-02-002	SQUIRE'S			31-09-028	STARTS	17-08-011	STEAM
1-01-001	SQUIRES	1-01-001	STALINS	1-01-001	STARTUPS	1-01-001	STEAM-BATHS
2-02-002	SQUIRMED	7-04-006	STALKED	7-05-007	STARVATION	1-01-001	STEAM-GENERATIO N
1-01-001	SQUIRMS	2-02-002	STALKING	1-01-001	STARVE		
1-01-001	SQUIRREL	18-06-008	STALL	3-02-003	STARVED	3-02-002	STEAMBOAT
1-01-001	SQUIRT	1-01-001	STALLARD	6-03-006	STARVING	5-05-005	STEAMED
1-01-001	SQUIRTED	1-01-001	STALLED	1-01-001	STASHED	1-01-001	STEAMER
1-01-001	SQUIRTING	2-02-002	STALLING	3-02-002	STASIS	1-01-001	STEAMILY
4-03-003	SR	1-01-001	STALLINGS	5-05-005	STAT	5-05-005	STEAMING
1-01-001	SSSSHOO	1-01-001	STALLION	808-14-198	STATE	3-03-003	STEAMSHIP
163-13-061	ST	2-01-001	STALLION'S	1-01-001	STATE'	3-01-001	STEARNS
2-01-001	ST**.-*POL	3-03-003	STALLS	37-06-015	STATE'S	1-01-001	STEED
1-01-001	ST-STORY	4-04-004	STALWART	1-01-001	STATE'S-RESPONS IBILITY	45-12-031	STEEL
2-01-001	STA**DDTISCHES	1-01-001	STAMENS	1-01-001	STATE-*LOCAL	1-01-001	STEEL-EDGED
3-03-003	STAB	4-02-003	STAMFORD	1-01-001	STATE-ADMINISTE RED	21-01-002	STEELE
1-01-001	STABAT	2-02-002	STAMINA			12-01-001	STEELE'S
2-02-002	STABBED	2-01-001	STAMINATE	1-01-001	STATE-LAW	1-01-001	STEELED
1-01-001	STABILITIES	4-04-004	STAMMERED	2-01-001	STATE-LOCAL	2-01-001	STEELERS
						1-01-001	STEELMAKER

Code	Word	Code	Word	Code	Word	Code	Word
1-01-001	STEELMAKERS'	18-05-007	STEVENS	1-01-001	STOCKHAUSEN	3-03-003	STRADDLING
3-01-001	STEELS	1-01-001	STEVENSES'	2-02-002	STOCKHOLDER	1-01-001	STRAFACI
1-01-001	STEELY	15-05-008	STEVENSON	26-06-007	STOCKHOLDERS	2-01-001	STRAFE
13-06-010	STEEP	2-02-002	STEVENSON'S	1-01-001	STOCKING	1-01-001	STRAFING
5-03-004	STEEPED	18-01-001	STEVIE	5-02-005	STOCKINGS	2-02-002	STRAGGLE
2-01-001	STEEPER	5-04-004	STEW	1-01-001	STOCKPILING	1-01-001	STRAGGLED
1-01-001	STEEPEST	2-01-001	STEWARD	2-02-002	STOCKROOM	2-01-002	STRAGGLERS
9-01-003	STEEPLE	2-01-001	STEWARDESS	17-03-010	STOCKS	2-02-002	STRAGGLING
4-03-003	STEEPLES	1-01-001	STEWARDESSES	2-02-002	STOCKY	114-15-080	STRAIGHT
1-01-001	STEEPLY	2-01-001	STEWARDS	1-01-001	STOCKYNGES	1-01-001	STRAIGHT-**J*A
9-04-005	STEER	1-01-001	STEWARDSHIP	1-01-001	STODGY	1-01-001	STRAIGHT-*ARM
4-03-003	STEERED	6-03-003	STEWART	3-02-002	STOIC	1-01-001	STRAIGHT-ARMED
9-06-008	STEERING	1-01-001	STEWART'S	1-01-001	STOIC-PATRISTIC	1-01-001	STRAIGHT-BACKED
1-01-001	STEERS	1-01-001	STEWED	5-03-003	STOICISM	2-01-001	STRAIGHT-HAIRED
1-01-001	STEEVES	1-01-001	STEWS	1-01-001	STOICS	1-01-001	STRAIGHT-LINE
1-01-001	STEFFENS	39-11-026	STICK	1-01-001	STOKED	1-01-001	STRAIGHT-OUT
10-02-002	STEICHEN	8-08-008	STICKING	1-01-001	STOKER	2-02-002	STRAIGHTAWAY
18-04-007	STEIN	2-02-002	STICKLER	10-04-010	STOLE	7-06-006	STRAIGHTEN
4-01-001	STEIN'S	1-01-001	STICKMAN	18-10-015	STOLEN	19-05-015	STRAIGHTENED
1-01-001	STEINBECK'S	5-02-002	STICKNEY	1-01-001	STOLID	6-04-005	STRAIGHTENING
1-01-001	STEINBECKS	1-01-001	STICKPIN	2-02-002	STOLIDLY	1-01-001	STRAIGHTENS
15-02-002	STEINBERG	22-10-017	STICKS	1-01-001	STOLL	8-05-007	STRAIGHTFORWARD
1-01-001	STEINER	9-06-007	STICKY	1-01-001	STOLZENBACH	1-01-001	STRAIGHTWAY
1-01-001	STEINERS	1-01-001	STICKY-FINGERED	37-10-029	STOMACH	31-10-029	STRAIN
3-01-001	STEINHA**DGER	1-01-001	STICLE	1-01-001	STOMACH-BELLY	11-05-009	STRAINED
1-01-001	STEINKERQUE	2-01-001	STIDGER	3-03-003	STOMACHS	1-01-001	STRAININ
1-01-001	STELLA	21-09-017	STIFF	1-01-001	STOMACK	7-06-007	STRAINING
1-01-001	STELLAR	1-01-001	STIFF-BACKED	2-02-002	STOMPED	8-06-008	STRAINS
29-05-010	STEM	8-05-008	STIFFENED	1-01-001	STOMPING	5-02-002	STRAIT
1-01-001	STEM/ITEM	4-03-004	STIFFENING	58-14-039	STONE	1-01-001	STRAIT-LACED
3-03-003	STEMMED	2-02-002	STIFFENS	2-01-001	STONE'S	3-03-003	STRAITS
33-09-019	STEMS	1-01-001	STIFFER	1-01-001	STONE-BLIND	4-01-001	STRAM
1-01-001	STENCH	9-03-007	STIFFLY	1-01-001	STONE-GRAY	1-01-001	STRAM'S
2-02-002	STENDHAL	1-01-001	STIFFNESS	1-01-001	STONE-STILL	1-01-001	STRAMONIUM
1-01-001	STENDLER	1-01-001	STIFFS	2-02-002	STONED	1-01-001	STRANAHAN
6-01-004	STENGEL	2-02-002	STIFLE	1-01-001	STONEHENGE	7-04-004	STRAND
2-02-002	STENGEL'S	2-02-002	STIFLED	12-05-009	STONES	7-05-006	STRANDED
1-01-001	STENNIS	2-02-002	STIFLING	1-01-001	STONESTOWN	1-01-001	STRANDING
1-01-001	STENOGRAPHY	1-01-001	STIGMA	3-01-001	STONEWARE	3-03-003	STRANDS
1-01-001	STENTON	1-01-001	STIGMATA	1-01-001	STONILY	1-01-001	STRANG
1-01-001	STEOREOTYPED	1-01-001	STILES	5-04-004	STONY	84-13-068	STRANGE
131-14-093	STEP	1-01-001	STILETTO	1-01-001	STONY-METEORITE	1-01-001	STRANGE-SOUNDING
2-02-002	STEP-BY-STEP	782-15-348	STILL	212-15-116	STOOD		
2-02-002	STEP-CONE	1-01-001	STILL-BUILDING	1-01-001	STOOGES	8-08-008	STRANGELY
2-01-001	STEPANOVICH	1-01-001	STILL-DARK	8-03-005	STOOL	2-02-002	STRANGENESS
1-01-001	STEPCHILD	1-01-001	STILLBIRTHS	1-01-001	STOOOOOMP	40-09-022	STRANGER
1-01-001	STEPHANE	9-06-008	STILLNESS	4-04-004	STOOP	3-02-003	STRANGER'S
2-01-001	STEPHANIE	2-02-002	STILLS	3-03-003	STOOPED	8-02-007	STRANGERS
2-01-001	STEPHANOTIS	1-01-001	STILLWELL	4-03-003	STOOPING	1-01-001	STRANGERS'
18-07-012	STEPHEN	2-02-002	STILTED	120-13-086	STOP	1-01-001	STRANGEST
1-01-001	STEPHEN'S	3-02-002	STILTS	1-01-001	STOP-OVERS	6-05-005	STRANGLED
5-02-002	STEPHENS	1-01-001	STIMSON	1-01-001	STOPOVER	1-01-001	STRANGULATION
2-01-001	STEPHENS'S	1-01-001	STIMULANT	1-01-001	STOPOVERS	2-02-002	STRAP
2-01-002	STEPHENSON	1-01-001	STIMULANTS	1-01-001	STOPPAGE	1-01-001	STRAPPED
1-01-001	STEPLADDERS	6-04-006	STIMULATE	1-01-001	STOPPAGES	3-02-002	STRAPPING
3-02-002	STEPMOTHER	7-04-007	STIMULATED	129-15-096	STOPPED	2-02-002	STRAPS
2-01-001	STEPMOTHERS	3-02-002	STIMULATES	2-01-001	STOPPER	8-01-001	STRASBOURG
41-11-036	STEPPED	9-06-008	STIMULATING	14-11-014	STOPPING	1-01-001	STRASNY
2-02-002	STEPPED-UP	13-06-009	STIMULATION	1-01-001	STOPPING-POINT	2-02-002	STRATA
2-01-002	STEPPES	1-01-001	STIMULATIONS	8-06-008	STOPS	1-01-001	STRATAGEMS
9-07-008	STEPPING	1-01-001	STIMULATORY	41-06-021	STORAGE	1-01-001	STRATEGEM
1-01-001	STEPRELATIONSHIP	5-03-004	STIMULI	74-12-043	STORE	23-06-012	STRATEGIC
		15-05-012	STIMULUS	1-01-001	STORE-FRONT	2-02-002	STRATEGICALLY
119-12-070	STEPS	5-04-005	STING	36-11-020	STORED	4-02-004	STRATEGISTS
3-02-002	STEPSON	2-02-002	STINGING	1-01-001	STORED-UP	22-10-016	STRATEGY
3-01-003	STEPWISE	2-01-001	STINGS	1-01-001	STOREFRONT	6-01-002	STRATFORD
12-04-007	STEREO	1-01-001	STINGY	3-01-001	STOREHOUSE	1-01-001	STRATFORD'S
1-01-001	STEREOPHONIC	1-01-001	STINK	1-01-001	STOREHOUSES	1-01-001	STRATFORDE
12-04-006	STEREOTYPE	3-02-002	STINKING	1-01-001	STOREKEEPERS	2-02-002	STRATIFICATION
5-03-004	STEREOTYPED	2-02-002	STINKING	1-01-001	STORERIA	2-01-001	STRATIFIED
2-01-002	STEREOTYPES	1-01-001	STINKPOTTERS	1-01-001	STOREROOM	1-01-001	STRATIFY
9-06-008	STERILE	1-01-001	STINKY	35-11-020	STORES	1-01-001	STRATOSPHERE
2-02-002	STERILITY	6-05-006	STINT	1-01-001	STORIED	3-02-002	STRATTON
5-01-001	STERILIZATION	2-02-002	STIPULATE	59-12-040	STORIES	3-01-001	STRATUM
1-01-001	STERILIZE	2-02-002	STIPULATES	4-03-003	STORING	3-03-003	STRAUSS
1-01-001	STERILIZED	1-01-001	STIPULATION	26-11-020	STORM	8-02-002	STRAVINSKY
2-02-002	STERILIZING	7-05-007	STIR	1-01-001	STORMBOUND	1-01-001	STRAVINSKY'S
1-01-001	STERIOS	3-02-002	STIRLING	3-03-003	STORMED	15-07-012	STRAW
7-05-005	STERLING	15-09-014	STIRRED	1-01-001	STORMING	1-01-001	STRAW-COLORED
23-11-019	STERN	1-01-001	STIRRIN	6-06-006	STORMS	1-01-001	STRAW-HAT
1-01-001	STERN-FACED	16-07-014	STIRRING	8-06-006	STORMY	2-02-002	STRAWBERRIES
1-01-001	STERN-TO	1-01-001	STIRRINGLY	153-15-080	STORY	3-02-002	STRAWS
1-01-001	STERNAL	1-01-001	STIRRINGS	1-01-001	STORY-BOOK	12-08-011	STRAY
3-03-003	STERNLY	1-01-001	STIRRUP	2-01-001	STORYLINE	1-01-001	STRAYED
1-01-001	STERNO-CLEIDO	1-01-001	STIRRUP-GUARD	1-01-001	STORYLINES	6-03-003	STRAYS
1-01-001	STERNS	3-02-003	STIRS	4-03-004	STORYTELLER	10-03-009	STREAK
1-01-001	STERNUM	1-01-001	STIRUPS	1-01-001	STORYTELLER'S	4-04-004	STREAKED
1-01-001	STEROID	3-02-002	STITCH	3-03-003	STOUT	6-04-006	STREAKS
1-01-001	STEROID-INDUCED	1-01-001	STITCHED	1-01-001	STOUT'S	51-09-033	STREAM
2-01-001	STEROIDS	4-03-003	STITCHES	1-01-001	STOUTLY	1-01-001	STREAM'S
2-01-001	STETHOSCOPE	1-01-001	STOBER'S	15-08-012	STOVE	1-01-001	STREAM-OF-CONSCIOUSNESS
2-02-002	STETSON	1-01-001	STOCHASTIC	2-02-002	STOVES	4-03-004	STREAMED
1-01-001	STETSONS	147-14-063	STOCK	1-01-001	STOWE	1-01-001	STREAMER
4-02-002	STETTIN	1-01-001	STOCK'S	1-01-001	STOWE'S	7-05-006	STREAMING
2-02-002	STEUBEN	1-01-001	STOCK-MARKET	2-02-002	STOWED	4-03-003	STREAMLINED
3-02-003	STEVE	12-03-004	STOCKADE	5-01-001	STOWEY	1-01-001	STREAMLINER
1-01-001	STEVEDORE	1-01-001	STOCKBROKER	2-02-002	STRADDLED		
		1-01-001	STOCKGROWERS'				

Code	Entry
11-06-009	STREAMS
1-01-001	STREAMSIDE
244-14-111	STREET
1-01-001	STREET'S
13-05-006	STREETCAR
2-02-002	STREETCARS
1-01-001	STREETERS
1-01-001	STREETLIGHT
60-11-047	STREETS
1-01-001	STRENGTENED
136-14-079	STRENGTH
1-01-001	STRENGTH/DENSITY
16-07-012	STRENGTHEN
6-06-006	STRENGTHENED
12-06-011	STRENGTHENING
5-04-004	STRENGTHENS
4-02-003	STRENGTHS
11-06-011	STRENUOUS
2-02-002	STRENUOUSLY
1-01-001	STREPTOCOCCUS
107-09-035	STRESS
1-01-001	STRESS-TEMPERATURE
23-11-019	STRESSED
19-08-014	STRESSES
2-01-001	STRESSFUL
5-03-005	STRESSING
26-10-017	STRETCH
34-11-030	STRETCHED
1-01-001	STRETCHER
9-04-009	STRETCHES
17-09-015	STRETCHING
6-04-005	STREWN
6-05-006	STRICKEN
1-01-001	STRICKLAND
11-08-011	STRICT
2-02-002	STRICTEST
33-09-030	STRICTLY
1-01-001	STRICTURES
16-09-014	STRIDE
7-05-007	STRIDES
1-01-001	STRIDING
6-06-006	STRIFE
50-12-030	STRIKE
1-01-001	STRIKEBREAKERS
20-08-017	STRIKES
39-10-035	STRIKING
8-05-008	STRIKINGLY
1-01-001	STRINDBERG
1-01-001	STRINDBERG'S
19-10-016	STRING
1-01-001	STRINGED
1-01-001	STRINGENTLY
1-01-001	STRINGING
16-07-011	STRINGS
3-03-003	STRINGY
30-09-021	STRIP
4-02-002	STRIPE
5-03-004	STRIPED
5-04-005	STRIPES
17-07-015	STRIPPED
2-02-002	STRIPPERS
14-05-009	STRIPS
1-01-001	STRIPTEASE
1-01-001	STRITCH
7-06-006	STRIVE
1-01-001	STRIVEN
3-02-003	STRIVES
4-04-004	STRIVING
3-02-002	STRIVINGS
10-05-009	STRODE
19-07-014	STROKE
3-02-003	STROKED
12-03-006	STROKES
2-02-002	STROKING
4-03-004	STROLL
4-04-004	STROLLED
4-03-004	STROLLING
202-14-133	STRONG
1-01-001	STRONG-MADE
37-11-029	STRONGER
20-08-018	STRONGEST
1-01-001	STRONGHEART
6-03-004	STRONGHOLD
37-13-032	STRONGLY
1-01-001	STRONGROOMS
1-01-001	STROPHE
1-01-001	STROPPED
1-01-001	STROPPING
4-04-004	STROVE
59-14-047	STRUCK
25-05-017	STRUCTURAL
2-02-002	STRUCTURALLY
91-12-061	STRUCTURE
14-02-003	STRUCTURED
31-07-022	STRUCTURES
1-01-001	STRUCTURING
62-12-051	STRUGGLE
8-06-008	STRUGGLED
20-09-018	STRUGGLES
1-01-001	STRUGGLING
1-01-001	STRUKTURBERICHT
1-01-001	STRUMMING
1-01-001	STRUNG
3-03-003	STRUT
2-02-002	STRUTTED
1-01-001	STRUTTING
16-05-009	STUART
1-01-001	STUART-FAMILY
3-03-003	STUB
1-01-001	STUBBED
1-01-001	STUBBLE
4-01-001	STUBBLEFIELD
4-01-001	STUBBLEFIELDS
12-09-012	STUBBORN
3-02-003	STUBBORNLY
2-02-002	STUBBORNNESS
1-01-001	STUBBS
3-03-003	STUBBY
2-02-002	STUCCO
23-09-022	STUCK
3-02-002	STUCK-UP
7-02-002	STUD
5-04-005	STUDDED
1-01-001	STUDEBAKER
131-12-053	STUDENT
31-09-017	STUDENT'S
1-01-001	STUDENT-DIRECTED
1-01-001	STUDENT-LOAN
1-01-001	STUDENT-PHYSICISTS
213-13-062	STUDENTS
4-04-004	STUDENTS'
79-14-071	STUDIED
103-12-053	STUDIES
7-01-002	STUDIO
1-01-001	STUDIOS
2-01-001	STUDIOUS
1-01-001	STUDIOUSLY
3-01-001	STUDS
246-14-117	STUDY
40-11-037	STUDYING
32-10-029	STUFF
5-05-005	STUFFED
2-02-002	STUFFING
2-02-002	STUFFY
1-01-001	STULTIFYING
1-01-001	STUMBLE
1-01-001	STUMBLED
3-02-003	STUMBLES
1-01-001	STUMBLING
2-02-002	STUMBLING-BLOCK
3-02-002	STUMP
1-01-001	STUMPAGE
1-01-001	STUMPED
1-01-001	STUMPING
2-02-002	STUMPS
1-01-001	STUMPY
1-01-001	STUNG
1-01-001	STUNK
20-05-010	STUNNED
7-05-007	STUNNING
1-01-001	STUNNINGLY
4-03-003	STUNT
1-01-001	STUNTS
4-02-002	STUPEFYING
3-02-002	STUPID
21-08-016	STUPIDEST
6-03-005	STUPIDITIES
2-01-001	STUPIDITY
1-01-001	STUPIDLY
6-05-006	STUPOR
4-03-003	STURBRIDGE
9-06-007	STURCH
2-01-001	STURDY
1-01-001	STURGEON
1-01-001	STURLEY
1-01-001	STURLEY'S
2-01-001	STUTTGART
1-01-001	STYKA
1-01-001	STYLE
98-13-054	STYLED
3-02-003	STYLEMARK
1-01-001	STYLES
20-07-016	STYLING
1-01-001	STYLISH
3-03-003	STYLIST
1-01-001	STYLISTIC
2-02-002	STYLIZATION
2-02-002	STYLIZED
1-01-001	STYMIED
7-02-002	STYRENE
1-01-001	STYRENE'S
1-01-001	STYRENES
2-01-001	STYRON
1-01-001	STYRYL-LITHIUM
1-01-001	SUABILITY
1-01-001	SUABLE
1-01-001	SUAVE
5-02-002	SUAVITY
7-04-005	SUB
1-01-001	SUB-*CHRISTIAN
1-01-001	SUB-ASSEMBLY
1-01-001	SUB-CHIEFDOM
1-01-001	SUB-CHIEFS
1-01-001	SUB-CONSCIOUS-LEVEL
1-01-001	SUB-FREEZING
1-01-001	SUB-GROUP
1-01-001	SUB-HUMAN
3-01-001	SUB-INTERVAL
1-01-001	SUB-STATION
2-01-001	SUB-SURFACE
2-01-001	SUB-TESTS
1-01-001	SUB-ZERO
1-01-001	SUBALTERN
2-02-002	SUBATOMIC
1-01-001	SUBBING
5-03-004	SUBCOMMITTEE
4-03-003	SUBCONSCIOUS
4-03-004	SUBCONSCIOUSLY
1-01-001	SUBCONTINENT
1-01-001	SUBCONTRACTING
11-04-005	SUBDIVISION
1-01-001	SUBDIVISIONS
2-02-002	SUBDUE
8-06-008	SUBDUED
1-01-001	SUBDUES
1-01-001	SUBDUING
1-01-001	SUBFIGURES
1-01-001	SUBGROSS
7-01-002	SUBGROUPS
1-01-001	SUBHUMANITY
2-01-001	SUBIC
161-15-104	SUBJECT
1-01-001	SUBJECT'S
24-10-018	SUBJECTED
18-03-013	SUBJECTIVE
6-03-004	SUBJECTIVELY
2-01-001	SUBJECTIVIST
1-01-001	SUBJECTIVISTS
1-01-001	SUBJECTIVITY
81-10-033	SUBJECTS
1-01-001	SUBJECTS'
1-01-001	SUBJUGATE
3-02-003	SUBJUGATION
1-01-001	SUBLEASE
1-01-001	SUBLIMATE
3-02-002	SUBLIME
1-01-001	SUBLIMED
1-01-001	SUBLITERARY
1-01-001	SUBLUNARY
2-02-002	SUBMACHINE
27-04-006	SUBMARINE
1-01-001	SUBMARINE-BALL
1-01-001	SUBMARINERS
20-05-010	SUBMARINES
7-05-007	SUBMERGED
1-01-001	SUBMERGING
4-03-003	SUBMISSION
1-01-001	SUBMISSIONS
4-02-002	SUBMISSIVE
18-08-018	SUBMIT
3-02-002	SUBMITS
21-08-016	SUBMITTED
6-03-005	SUBMITTING
2-01-001	SUBMUCOSA
1-01-001	SUBNORMAL
6-05-006	SUBORDINATE
4-03-003	SUBORDINATED
9-06-007	SUBORDINATES
2-01-001	SUBORDINATOR
1-01-001	SUBPARAGRAPH
1-01-001	SUBPARTS
1-01-001	SUBPENAED
2-01-001	SUBPENAS
1-01-001	SUBPOENA
1-01-001	SUBROGATION
1-01-001	SUBROUTINE
1-01-001	SUBROUTINES
2-02-002	SUBS
1-01-001	SUBSCRIBE
3-03-003	SUBSCRIBED
7-04-005	SUBSCRIBERS
2-02-002	SUBSCRIBING
4-04-004	SUBSCRIPTION
1-01-001	SUBSCRIPTS
13-01-003	SUBSECTION
3-01-002	SUBSECTIONS
1-01-001	SUBSEDIES
29-08-027	SUBSEQUENT
11-06-011	SUBSEQUENTLY
1-01-001	SUBSERVIENCE
3-03-003	SUBSERVIENT
2-02-002	SUBSIDE
5-04-005	SUBSIDED
2-02-002	SUBSIDIARIES
7-04-005	SUBSIDIARY
3-03-003	SUBSIDIES
4-03-003	SUBSIDIZE
4-03-004	SUBSIDIZED
3-03-003	SUBSIDY
1-01-001	SUBSIST
10-05-008	SUBSISTENCE
1-01-001	SUBSISTENT
1-01-001	SUBSOIL
7-01-001	SUBSPACE
1-01-001	SUBSPACES
3-01-001	SUBSPECIES
33-11-027	SUBSTANCE
23-03-007	SUBSTANCES
66-09-046	SUBSTANTIAL
36-08-028	SUBSTANTIALLY
2-02-002	SUBSTANTIATE
1-01-001	SUBSTANTIATES
1-01-001	SUBSTANTIATION
3-03-003	SUBSTANTIVE
1-01-001	SUBSTANTIVELY
1-01-001	SUBSTERILIZATION
22-09-021	SUBSTITUTE
15-08-014	SUBSTITUTED
5-03-004	SUBSTITUTES
4-04-004	SUBSTITUTING
2-02-002	SUBSTITUTION
1-01-001	SUBSTITUTIONARY
1-01-001	SUBSTITUTIONS
23-01-005	SUBSTRATE
3-01-002	SUBSTRATES
1-01-001	SUBSTRATUM
1-01-001	SUBSTRUCTURE
1-01-001	SUBSUMED
1-01-001	SUBSURFACE
2-01-002	SUBSYSTEM
10-01-002	SUBSYSTEMS
1-01-001	SUBTENDED
1-01-001	SUBTENDS
1-01-001	SUBTERFUGES
2-02-002	SUBTILIS
3-03-003	SUBTITLED
25-08-022	SUBTLE
1-01-001	SUBTLER
4-02-004	SUBTLETIES
1-01-001	SUBTLETY
6-04-006	SUBTLY
2-02-002	SUBTRACT
4-03-003	SUBTRACTED
3-02-002	SUBTRACTING
6-01-001	SUBTRACTION
3-01-001	SUBTYPE
1-01-001	SUBTYPES
13-06-011	SUBURB
29-08-016	SUBURBAN
2-02-002	SUBURBANITE
1-01-001	SUBURBANITES
1-01-001	SUBURBANIZED
1-01-001	SUBURBIA
18-09-013	SUBURBS
1-01-001	SUBVERSION
2-01-002	SUBVERSIVE
1-01-001	SUBVERSIVES
1-01-001	SUBVERTED
1-01-001	SUBVERTING
7-04-005	SUBWAY
1-01-001	SUBWAYS
15-09-015	SUCCEED
33-15-030	SUCCEEDED
6-04-004	SUCCEEDING
8-05-008	SUCCEEDS
93-11-061	SUCCESS
1-01-001	SUCCESS-ORIENTED
22-08-012	SUCCESSES
95-12-073	SUCCESSFUL
31-09-027	SUCCESSFULLY
25-10-015	SUCCESSION
12-08-012	SUCCESSIVE
2-01-002	SUCCESSIVELY
16-06-010	SUCCESSOR
6-04-006	SUCCESSORS
1-01-001	SUCCESSORS-IN-SPIRIT
1-01-001	SUCCESSORSHIP

Code	Word	Code	Word	Code	Word	Code	Word
1-01-001	SUCCINCT	1-01-001	SULLYING	1-01-001	SUPER-IMPOSED	1-01-001	SUPRA-*EXPRESSIONISM
2-02-002	SUCCINCTLY	3-03-003	SULPHUR	1-01-001	SUPER-SECRET	1-01-001	SUPRA-PERSONAL
1-01-001	SUCCOR	1-01-001	SULPHURED	14-05-011	SUPERB	1-01-001	SUPRANATIONAL
1-01-001	SUCCUMB	3-01-001	SULTAN	9-05-008	SUPERBLY	1-01-001	SUPRANATIONALISM
5-04-005	SUCCUMBED	1-01-001	SULTANE	1-01-001	SUPERCEDED	5-04-004	SUPREMACY
1-01-001	SUCCUMBING	4-02-002	SULTANS	1-01-001	SUPERCILIOUS	51-11-033	SUPREME
1-01-001	SUCESS	1-01-001	SULTRY	1-01-001	SUPERCRITICAL	4-03-004	SUPREMELY
1303-15-400	SUCH	3-01-001	SULZBERGER	1-01-001	SUPEREGO	2-01-002	SUPT
5-03-005	SUCK	2-02-002	SULZBERGER'S	7-05-007	SUPERFICIAL	3-03-003	SUR
6-03-006	SUCKED	45-10-032	SUM	1-01-001	SUPERFICIALITY	1-01-001	SURCEASE
1-01-001	SUCKER-ROLLING	1-01-001	SUMAC	3-02-003	SUPERFICIALLY	1-01-001	SURCLIFFE
1-01-001	SUCKERS	1-01-001	SUMATRA	3-03-003	SUPERFLUOUS	1-01-001	SURCLIFFES'
8-04-007	SUCKING	1-01-001	SUMMARIZATION	1-01-001	SUPERHIGHWAYS	264-15-169	SURE
1-01-001	SUCTION	3-02-003	SUMMARIZE	2-02-002	SUPERHUMAN	1-01-001	SURE-ENOUGH
1-01-001	SUDANESE	9-03-009	SUMMARIZED	1-01-001	SUPERIEURE	2-01-001	SURE-SURE
38-11-029	SUDDEN	1-01-001	SUMMARIZES	4-03-003	SUPERIMPOSE	47-13-040	SURELY
1-01-001	SUDDEN-END	3-01-003	SUMMARIZING	6-03-006	SUPERIMPOSED	1-01-001	SURF
153-13-098	SUDDENLY	21-05-016	SUMMARY	1-01-001	SUPERIMPOSES	200-13-074	SURFACE
2-02-002	SUDDENNESS	2-01-002	SUMMATE	1-01-001	SUPERIMPOSING	7-01-001	SURFACE-ACTIVE
1-01-001	SUDIER	3-03-003	SUMMATION	1-01-001	SUPERINTEND	1-01-001	SURFACE-ANALYZER
9-02-002	SUDS	7-04-007	SUMMED	17-05-009	SUPERINTENDENT	1-01-001	SURFACE-DECLARING
1-01-001	SUDSING	134-15-079	SUMMER	2-02-002	SUPERINTENDENT'S	1-01-001	SURFACED
18-07-009	SUE	7-05-007	SUMMER'S	2-01-001	SUPERINTENDENTS	1-01-001	SURFACENESS
4-03-004	SUED	1-01-001	SUMMER-WINTER	46-10-034	SUPERIOR	28-06-015	SURFACES
1-01-001	SUES	2-01-002	SUMMERDALE	14-06-012	SUPERIORITY	1-01-001	SURFACTANT
1-01-001	SUEY	17-08-009	SUMMERS	4-01-001	SUPERIORS	1-01-001	SURFACTANTS
2-02-002	SUEZ	1-01-001	SUMMERSPACE	3-03-003	SUPERLATIVE	1-01-001	SURFEIT
2-01-001	SUEZ-*HUNGARY	4-04-004	SUMMERTIME	1-01-001	SUPERLATIVES	1-01-001	SURFEITED
33-09-027	SUFFER	1-01-001	SUMMING	1-01-001	SUPERLUNARY	9-06-009	SURGE
43-11-039	SUFFERED	12-04-005	SUMMIT	1-01-001	SUPERMACHINE	7-05-007	SURGED
3-02-003	SUFFERER	1-01-001	SUMMITRY	1-01-001	SUPERMARKET	11-03-007	SURGEON
1-01-001	SUFFERERS	3-03-003	SUMMON	3-02-002	SUPERMARKETS	1-01-001	SURGEONS
44-07-022	SUFFERING	10-07-009	SUMMONED	1-01-001	SUPERMATIC	6-05-005	SURGERY
4-02-004	SUFFERINGS	1-01-001	SUMMONS	1-01-001	SUPERNATANT	1-01-001	SURGICAL
5-04-005	SUFFERS	2-02-002	SUMPTUOUS	17-04-006	SUPERNATURAL	2-02-002	SURGING
5-04-005	SUFFICE	4-02-002	SUMTER	4-02-003	SUPERNATURALISM	2-02-002	SURLY
1-01-001	SUFFICIENCY	17-07-016	SUMS	1-01-001	SUPERNORMAL	1-01-001	SURMISE
63-08-050	SUFFICIENT	2-02-002	SUMTER	1-01-001	SUPERPOSED	2-01-002	SURMISED
42-12-036	SUFFICIENTLY	112-14-067	SUN	1-01-001	SUPERPOSITION	2-02-002	SURMISES
1-01-001	SUFFIX	1-01-001	SUN'LL	5-03-005	SUPERSEDED	1-01-001	SURMOUNT
1-01-001	SUFFIXES	4-04-004	SUN'S	1-01-001	SUPERSENSITIVE	2-01-002	SURMOUNTED
1-01-001	SUFFOCATED	1-01-001	SUN-*TIMES	4-02-002	SUPERSONIC	3-01-001	SURNAME
5-03-005	SUFFOCATING	1-01-001	SUN-BAKED	8-05-007	SUPERSTITION	1-01-001	SURPASS
1-01-001	SUFFOCATION	1-01-001	SUN-BLEACHED	2-02-002	SUPERSTITIONS	2-02-002	SURPASSED
5-04-005	SUFFRAGE	1-01-001	SUN-BROWNED	1-01-001	SUPERSTITIOUS	27-08-017	SURPLUS
1-01-001	SUFFRAGETTES	1-01-001	SUN-BURNED	1-01-001	SUPERSTRUCTURE	4-03-003	SURPLUSES
1-01-001	SUFFUSE	1-01-001	SUN-INFLAMED	1-01-001	SUPERVENED	51-14-046	SURPRISE
5-04-005	SUFFUSED	1-01-001	SUN-SUIT	5-05-005	SUPERVISE	58-11-044	SURPRISED
34-09-016	SUGAR	5-05-005	SUN-TAN	4-04-004	SUPERVISED	5-04-005	SURPRISES
1-01-001	SUGARED	1-01-001	SUN-TANNED	2-02-002	SUPERVISES	30-10-025	SURPRISING
54-12-047	SUGGEST	1-01-001	SUN-WARMED	3-03-003	SUPERVISING	18-08-018	SURPRISINGLY
105-13-086	SUGGESTED	3-03-003	SUNAY	5-03-005	SUPERVISION	1-01-001	SURREALISM
3-01-001	SUGGESTIBILITY	19-08-013	SUNBAKED	2-02-002	SUPERVISOR	1-01-001	SURREALIST
13-09-013	SUGGESTING	5-03-005	SUNBONNET	5-04-005	SUPERVISOR'S	2-01-001	SURREALISTS
34-09-030	SUGGESTION	5-01-002	SUNBURN	1-01-001	SUPERVISORS	22-09-014	SURRENDER
23-10-020	SUGGESTIONS	5-04-005	SUNBURNT	2-01-001	SUPERVISORS'	7-03-006	SURRENDERED
9-02-008	SUGGESTIVE	101-13-052	SUNDAY	1-01-001	SUPERVISORY	4-03-004	SURRENDERING
29-06-027	SUGGESTS	6-03-006	SUNDAY'S	1-01-001	SUPINE	1-01-001	SURREPTITIOUS
1-01-001	SUGGS	1-01-001	SUNDAY-SCHOOL	1-01-001	SUPINELY	3-03-003	SURREPTITIOUSLY
1-01-001	SUHTHUHN	9-08-009	SUNDAYS	37-10-025	SUPPER	5-05-005	SURROUND
17-10-015	SUICIDE	1-01-001	SUNDER	1-01-001	SUPPERS	21-10-021	SURROUNDED
2-01-002	SUICIDES	37-10-025	SUNDIALS	3-02-003	SUPPLANT	27-11-024	SURROUNDING
1-01-001	SUING	1-01-001	SUNDOWN	1-01-001	SUPPLANTED	8-06-008	SURROUNDINGS
48-13-039	SUIT	6-04-006	SUNDRY	1-01-001	SUPPLANTING	1-01-001	SURTOUT
1-01-001	SUITABILITY	5-04-005	SUNG	1-01-001	SUPPLEMENT	6-05-006	SURVEILLANCE
34-09-031	SUITABLE	18-08-015	SUNG	1-01-001	SUPPLEMENTAL	37-11-029	SURVEY
3-03-003	SUITABLY	6-05-006	SUNG-*SHAN	9-03-006	SUPPLEMENTARY	2-01-001	SURVEY-TYPE
1-01-001	SUITABLY-LOADED	3-02-003	SUNK	6-04-004	SUPPLEMENTED	9-04-007	SURVEYED
20-04-009	SUITCASE	17-07-011	SUNKEN	3-03-003	SUPPLEMENTING	8-02-003	SURVEYING
5-02-003	SUITCASES	1-01-001	SUNLIGHT	8-04-007	SUPPLEMENTS	5-04-004	SURVEYOR
27-08-015	SUITE	1-01-001	SUNMAN	1-01-001	SUPPLENESS	12-04-007	SURVEYS
1-01-001	SUITE'S	13-07-011	SUNNING	2-02-002	SUPPLICATING	1-01-001	SURVIVABILITY
22-09-018	SUITED	3-01-001	SUNNY	36-10-031	SUPPLIED	32-09-023	SURVIVAL
4-04-004	SUITES	10-03-004	SUNNYVALE	6-02-004	SUPPLIER	1-01-001	SURVIVALIST
1-01-001	SUITOR	2-02-002	SUNRISE	1-01-001	SUPPLIERS	2-01-001	SURVIVALISTS
3-02-003	SUITORS	14-04-006	SUNS	47-13-036	SUPPLIES	1-01-001	SURVIVALS
25-08-015	SUITS	2-01-001	SUNSET	102-14-069	SUPPLY	33-13-027	SURVIVE
4-02-003	SUKARNO	1-01-001	SUNSHADES	13-06-011	SUPPLYING	14-08-014	SURVIVED
1-01-001	SUKARNO'S	8-06-008	SUNSHIELD	180-12-108	SUPPORT	1-01-001	SURVIVES
1-01-001	SUKUMA	1-01-001	SUNSHINE	54-11-048	SUPPORTED	14-07-011	SURVIVING
1-01-001	SULAMITE	1-01-001	SUNSHINY	3-01-002	SUPPORTER	1-01-001	SURVIVOR
1-01-001	SULAMITH	1-01-001	SUNSPOT	8-04-007	SUPPORTERS	13-05-010	SURVIVORS
1-01-001	SULCER	1-01-001	SUNT	27-08-021	SUPPORTING	1-01-001	SURVIVORS'
1-01-001	SULFAQUINOXALINE	8-04-007	SUNTAN	7-01-002	SUPPORTIVE	1-01-001	SUS
1-01-001	SULFIDE	8-05-008	SUP	15-07-014	SUPPORTS	36-06-008	SUSAN
1-01-001	SULFUR	27-08-021	SUPER	97-14-072	SUPPOSE	2-01-001	SUSAN'S
2-02-002	SULKED	1-01-001	SUPER-*HERCULEAN	65-14-054	SUPPOSED	2-01-002	SUSCEPTIBILITY
1-01-001	SULKILY	1-01-001	SUPER-*PROTEIN	12-08-011	SUPPOSEDLY	6-06-006	SUSCEPTIBLE
1-01-001	SULKING	8-01-002	SUPER-*SET	1-01-001	SUPPOSES	2-02-002	SUSHI
1-01-001	SULKS	3-01-001	SUPER-*SETS	2-02-002	SUPPOSING	5-02-002	SUSIE
4-04-004	SULKY	1-01-001	SUPER-CHARGED	3-02-002	SUPPOSITIONS	1-01-001	SUSIE'S
1-01-001	SULKY'S	1-01-001	SUPER-CITY	6-05-006	SUPPRESS	30-12-026	SUSPECT
3-01-001	SULLAM	4-01-001	SUPER-CONDAMINE	4-04-004	SUPPRESSED	21-10-018	SUSPECTED
9-05-009	SULLEN	1-01-001	SUPER-EMPIRICAL	7-03-004	SUPPRESSION		
2-02-002	SULLENLY	1-01-001	SUPER-EXPERIMENT	3-01-001	SUPRA		
8-03-005	SULLIVAN	1-01-001	SUPER-HIGH				

Code	Word
2-02-002	SUSPECTING
4-03-004	SUSPECTS
3-02-003	SUSPEND
30-10-018	SUSPENDED
1-01-001	SUSPENDERS
6-05-006	SUSPENSE
12-05-009	SUSPENSION
2-02-002	SUSPENSIONS
2-01-001	SUSPENSOR
27-10-025	SUSPICION
7-05-006	SUSPICIONS
13-09-013	SUSPICIOUS
4-03-004	SUSPICIOUSLY
2-02-002	SUSSEX
14-08-012	SUSTAIN
15-06-014	SUSTAINED
2-02-002	SUSTAINING
1-01-001	SUSTAINS
3-02-003	SUSTENANCE
1-01-001	SUT
6-02-002	SUTHERLAND
1-01-001	SUTPEN
6-01-001	SUVOROV
2-01-001	SUVOROV'S
1-01-001	SUZANNE
2-01-001	SUZERAIN
1-01-001	SUZERAINTY
1-01-001	SUZUKI
1-01-001	SVELTE
1-01-001	SVENSKARNA
1-01-001	SVEVO
1-01-001	SW**-FT
1-01-001	SWABBED
8-01-001	SWADESH
2-01-001	SWADESH'S
3-02-003	SWAGGERED
1-01-001	SWAGGERING
1-01-001	SWAHILI
10-08-010	SWALLOW
1-01-001	SWALLOW-*BARN
12-08-011	SWALLOWED
3-02-003	SWALLOWING
2-02-002	SWALLOWS
6-03-005	SWAM
1-01-001	SWAMI
5-02-002	SWAMP
1-01-001	SWAMPED
1-01-001	SWAMPING
2-01-001	SWAMPS
1-01-001	SWAMPY
3-03-003	SWAN
1-01-001	SWANK
1-01-001	SWANKY
1-01-001	SWANLIKE
1-01-001	SWANS
2-02-002	SWAP
3-03-003	SWARM
3-03-003	SWARMED
3-03-003	SWARMING
1-01-001	SWARMS
1-01-001	SWART
4-02-003	SWARTHY
1-01-001	SWARTZ
1-01-001	SWASTIKA
3-02-002	SWATCHES
1-01-001	SWATH
1-01-001	SWATHED
1-01-001	SWATHINGS
5-04-004	SWAY
1-01-001	SWAY-BACKED
9-05-007	SWAYED
3-03-003	SWAYING
10-04-009	SWEAR
3-03-003	SWEARING
1-01-001	SWEARING-IN
1-01-001	SWEARINGE
2-02-002	SWEARS
23-06-019	SWEAT
1-01-001	SWEAT-SATURATED
1-01-001	SWEAT-SOAKED
1-01-001	SWEAT-SUITS
1-01-001	SWEATBAND
1-01-001	SWEATED
14-05-006	SWEATER
4-04-004	SWEATERS
1-01-001	SWEATHRUNA
4-04-004	SWEATING
2-01-001	SWEATSHIRT
5-03-004	SWEATY
1-01-001	SWEAZEY
10-02-004	SWEDEN
3-02-002	SWEDEN'S
2-01-001	SWEDES
7-02-002	SWEDISH
4-01-001	SWEENEY
3-01-001	SWEENEYS
15-10-015	SWEEP
13-09-013	SWEEPING
1-01-001	SWEEPINGLY
1-01-001	SWEEPINGS
2-01-002	SWEEPSTAKES
70-12-039	SWEET
1-01-001	SWEET-CLOVER
1-01-001	SWEET-FACED
1-01-001	SWEET-SHRUB
54-13-035	SWEET-SMELLING
35-05-013	SWEET-SOUNDING
1-01-001	SWEET-SOUR
1-01-001	SWEET-THROATED
5-03-005	SWEET-TONGUED
8-04-007	SWEETER
1-01-001	SWEETEST
9-04-008	SWEETHEART
11-05-009	SWEETHEART-SECRETARY
3-02-003	SWEETHEARTS
2-01-001	SWEETISH
36-08-018	SWEETLY
1-01-001	SWEETNESS
2-02-002	SWEETPEAS
7-01-001	SWEETS
2-02-002	SWELL
1-01-001	SWELLED
7-03-003	SWELLING
1-01-001	SWELLINGS
35-09-024	SWELLS
5-03-005	SWELTERING
8-05-007	SWEPT
1-01-001	SWERVE
7-06-007	SWERVED
1-01-001	SWERVING
36-11-024	SWIFT
7-03-003	SWIFT'S
3-03-003	SWIFT-FOOTED
33-08-018	SWIFT-STRIDING
1-01-001	SWIFTEST
9-02-005	SWIFTLY
5-03-004	SWIFTNESS
7-04-006	SWIG
14-07-009	SWIM
3-02-003	SWIMMERS
2-02-002	SWIMMERS'
1-01-001	SWIMMING
1-01-001	SWIMSUIT
1-01-001	SWINBURNE
1-01-001	SWINDLED
2-02-002	SWINDLING
2-01-001	SWINE
2-02-002	SWING
2-01-001	SWINGIN
1-01-001	SWINGING
6-04-006	SWINGS
1-01-001	SWINGY
2-02-002	SWIPE
1-01-001	SWIPED
1-01-001	SWIPING
2-01-002	SWIRL
1-01-001	SWIRLED
1-01-001	SWIRLING
1-01-001	SWISHED
3-03-003	SWISS
4-03-004	SWISS-BORN
3-02-002	SWITCH
1-01-001	SWITCH-HITTER
1-01-001	SWITCHBLADE
1-01-001	SWITCHBOARD
1-01-001	SWITCHED
6-03-005	SWITCHES
16-03-009	SWITCHGEAR
1-01-001	SWITCHING
1-01-001	SWITZER
2-01-002	SWITZERLAND
1-01-001	SWIVEL
1-01-001	SWIVELS
12-02-007	SWOLLEN
1-01-001	SWOLLEN-LOOKING
1-01-001	SWOOP
2-02-002	SWOOPED
1-01-001	SWOOPING
1-01-001	SWOOPS
1-01-001	SWORD
1-01-001	SWORDE
4-03-003	SWORDS
2-02-002	SWORE
416-14-133	SWORN
3-02-002	SWUM
18-04-013	SWUNG
1-01-001	SYBERT
10-06-009	SYBIL
1-01-001	SYCOPHANTIC
1-01-001	SYCOPHANTICALLY
1-01-001	SYCOPHANTS
2-02-002	SYDNEY
2-02-002	SYLLABICITY
1-01-001	SYLLABIFICATION
1-01-001	SYLLABLE
9-01-002	SYLLABLES
1-01-001	SYLPHIDE
1-01-001	SYLVAN
2-01-001	SYLVANIA
1-01-001	SYLVIE
54-13-035	SYMBOL
35-05-013	SYMBOLIC
1-01-001	SYMBOLIC-SOUNDING
1-01-001	SYMBOLICAL
5-03-005	SYMBOLICALLY
8-04-007	SYMBOLISM
1-01-001	SYMBOLISTS
9-04-008	SYMBOLIZE
11-05-009	SYMBOLIZED
3-02-003	SYMBOLIZES
2-01-001	SYMBOLIZING
36-08-018	SYMBOLS
1-01-001	SYMES'S
2-02-002	SYMINGTON
7-01-001	SYMMETRIC
2-02-002	SYMMETRICAL
1-01-001	SYMMETRICALLY
7-03-003	SYMMETRY
1-01-001	SYMONDS
35-09-024	SYMPATHETIC
1-01-001	SYMPATHETICALLY
8-05-007	SYMPATHIES
1-01-001	SYMPATHIQUE
7-06-007	SYMPATHIZE
1-01-001	SYMPATHIZED
1-01-001	SYMPATHIZING
44-10-026	SYMPATHY
6-02-002	SYMPHONIC
3-01-001	SYMPHONIES
1-01-001	SYMPHONY
7-01-002	SYMPHONY'S
3-02-002	SYMPOSIUM
1-01-001	SYMPTOM
3-02-003	SYMPTOMATIC
1-01-001	SYMPTOMS
2-01-001	SYNAGOGUE
1-01-001	SYNAGOGUES
4-02-004	SYNAPSES
2-01-002	SYNCE
2-01-002	SYNCHRONISM
2-02-002	SYNCHRONIZE
2-02-002	SYNCHRONIZED
1-01-001	SYNCHRONIZERS
4-02-003	SYNCHRONOUS
2-01-001	SYNCHRONY
2-02-002	SYNDIC
10-06-008	SYNDICATE
1-01-001	SYNDICATE'S
2-01-001	SYNDICATED
6-04-006	SYNDICATES
2-01-002	SYNDICATION
4-03-004	SYNDROME
8-04-006	SYNERGISM
1-01-001	SYNERGISTIC
20-08-016	SYNOD
2-01-001	SYNONYM
1-01-001	SYNONYMOUS
8-01-001	SYNONYMS
1-01-001	SYNONYMY
2-01-001	SYNTACTIC
1-01-001	SYNTACTICAL
3-02-002	SYNTACTICALLY
5-04-004	SYNTAX
6-06-006	SYNTHESIS
1-01-001	SYNTHESISED
1-01-001	SYNTHESIZE
2-02-002	SYNTHESIZED
4-03-003	SYNTHESIZES
1-01-001	SYNTHESIZINE
2-02-002	SYNTHETIC
2-02-002	SYNTHETICS
3-01-001	SYRACUSE
1-01-001	SYRIA
2-02-002	SYRIAN
3-03-003	SYRIANS
1-01-001	SYRINGA
24-10-015	SYRINGE
1-01-001	SYRUP
2-01-002	SYRUPY
3-01-001	SYSTEM
1-01-001	SYSTEM'S
2-02-002	SYSTEMATIC
3-03-003	SYSTEMATICALLY
1-01-001	SYSTEMATICALLY-SIMPLE
9-07-009	SYSTEMATIZATION
7-04-004	SYSTEMATIZED
1-01-001	SYSTEMATIZING
1-01-001	SYSTEME
3-01-001	SYSTEMIC
1-01-001	SYSTEMIZATION
129-12-053	SYSTEMS
1-01-001	SZELENYI
11-01-001	SZOLD
4-01-001	SZOLDS
2-01-001	SZOLDS'
32-10-030	T
1-01-001	T**.*B
2-01-001	T**.*W
1-01-001	T'AI-*SHAN
1-01-001	T'GETHUH
1-01-001	T'HI-IM
1-01-001	T'IEN
1-01-001	T'JAWN
1-01-001	T'LAH
1-01-001	T'S
1-01-001	T**U
1-01-001	TAB
1-01-001	TAB-LIFTER
1-01-001	TABAC
1-01-001	TABB
1-01-001	TABELLEN
1-01-001	TABERNACLE
1-01-001	TABERNACLES
1-01-001	TABIT
198-14-106	TABLE
1-01-001	TABLE'S
1-01-001	TABLE-TENNIS
1-01-001	TABLE-TOP
1-01-001	TABLEAU
1-01-001	TABLECLOTHS
1-01-001	TABLELAND
44-10-026	TABLES
6-02-002	TABLESPOON
3-01-001	TABLESPOONFUL
1-01-001	TABLESPOONFULS
7-01-002	TABLESPOONS
3-02-002	TABLET
1-01-001	TABLETS
1-01-001	TABLOIDS
3-02-003	TABOO
1-01-001	TABOOS
2-01-001	TABULA
1-01-001	TABULATE
4-02-004	TABULATED
2-01-002	TABULATION
2-01-002	TABULATIONS
2-02-002	TACIT
2-02-002	TACITLY
1-01-001	TACITUS
4-02-003	TACK
2-01-001	TACK-SOLDER
2-02-002	TACKED
2-02-002	TACKING
10-06-008	TACKLE
1-01-001	TACKLES
2-01-001	TACLOBAN
6-04-006	TACT
2-01-002	TACTFUL
4-03-004	TACTIC
8-04-006	TACTICAL
1-01-001	TACTICALLY
20-08-016	TACTICS
2-01-001	TACTILE
1-01-001	TACTLESSNESS
8-01-001	TACTUAL
1-01-001	TACTUALLY
2-01-001	TADPOLES
2-01-001	TAFFETA
1-01-001	TAFFY
1-01-001	TAFFYCOLORED
1-01-001	TAFT
3-02-002	TAFT-*HARTLEY
5-04-004	TAG
6-06-006	TAGGED
1-01-001	TAGGING
1-01-001	TAGS
1-01-001	TAGUA
2-02-002	TAHITI
4-03-003	TAHOE
1-01-001	TAHSE
1-01-001	TAHSE'S
1-01-001	TAI
24-10-015	TAIL
1-01-001	TAILBACK
2-01-002	TAILGATE
3-01-001	TAILIN
1-01-001	TAILIN'S
2-02-002	TAILOR
3-03-003	TAILOR-MADE
1-01-001	TAILOR-MAKE
9-07-009	TAILORED
7-04-004	TAILS
1-01-001	TAIN'T
1-01-001	TAINT
1-01-001	TAINTED

Freq	Word	Freq	Word	Freq	Word	Freq	Word
1-01-001	TAIPEI	1-01-001	TAOS	4-03-004	TAWNY	4-02-003	TEDDY
7-02-002	TAIWAN	18-09-012	TAP	197-10-039	TAX	6-03-006	TEDIOUS
611-15-297	TAKE	35-09-014	TAPDANCE	1-01-001	TAX-AIDED	2-02-002	TEDIOUSLY
4-03-004	TAKE-OFF	1-01-001	TAPE	1-01-001	TAX-AVOIDANCE	1-01-001	TEDIUM
4-01-001	TAKE-UP	3-03-003	TAPED	6-02-004	TAX-EXEMPT	5-01-002	TEE
1-01-001	TAKEING	7-04-006	TAPER	2-01-001	TAX-EXEMPTION	2-01-001	TEE-WAH
281-15-198	TAKEN	2-02-002	TAPERED	9-02-003	TAX-FREE	1-01-001	TEEMING
1-01-001	TAKEOFF	4-02-003	TAPERING	1-01-001	TAX-FREEDOM	1-01-001	TEEMS
2-01-001	TAKEOFFS	2-02-002	TAPES	1-01-001	TAX-PAYING	6-02-002	TEEN
2-02-002	TAKEOVER	5-04-004	TAPESTRIES	8-02-004	TAXABLE	4-04-004	TEEN-AGE
86-14-077	TAKES	1-01-001	TAPESTRY	11-04-006	TAXATION	2-02-002	TEEN-AGER
5-03-004	TAKIN	1-01-001	TAPIS	13-04-005	TAXED	12-04-004	TEEN-AGERS
175-15-142	TAKING	1-01-001	TAPLEY	45-08-024	TAXES	1-01-001	TEEN-AGERS'
2-02-002	TAKINGS	2-01-001	TAPPAN	16-07-015	TAXI	4-04-004	TEENAGE
1-01-001	TAKSIM	7-07-007	TAPPED	1-01-001	TAXI-WAYS	2-02-002	TEENAGER
1-01-001	TALBOTT'S	15-01-001	TAPPET	1-01-001	TAXICAB	5-03-004	TEENAGERS
21-10-015	TALE	13-01-001	TAPPETS	1-01-001	TAXIED	5-04-005	TEENS
40-12-032	TALENT	6-05-005	TAPPING	1-01-001	TAXIING	1-01-001	TEENSY
7-03-007	TALENTED	1-01-001	TAPS	9-04-004	TAXING	2-02-002	TEETERING
28-09-024	TALENTS	12-02-003	TAR	3-03-003	TAXIS	103-11-036	TEETH
21-08-018	TALES	1-01-001	TAR-SOAKED	11-06-009	TAXPAYER	1-01-001	TEETHING
11-01-001	TALIESIN	1-01-001	TARA	2-02-002	TAXPAYER'S	2-02-002	TEETOTALER
1-01-001	TALISMANIC	1-01-001	TARADAY	21-06-013	TAXPAYERS	1-01-001	TEHERAN
154-15-100	TALK	3-02-002	TARAS	2-01-001	TAXPAYERS'	1-01-001	TEKTITE
1-01-001	TALK-ABOUTIVENESS	1-01-001	TARAS-*TCHAIKOVSKY	1-01-001	TAXPAYING	5-01-001	TEKTITES
4-03-004	TALKATIVE	1-01-001	TARDILY	21-05-011	TAYLOR	1-01-001	TEL
58-12-046	TALKED	1-01-001	TARDINESS	2-02-002	TAYLOR'S	1-01-001	TELEFUNKEN
1-01-001	TALKER	1-01-001	TARDY	1-01-001	TAYLORS	8-02-006	TELEGRAM
1-01-001	TALKIN	1-01-001	TAREYTOWN	2-01-002	TCHAIKOVSKY	2-02-002	TELEGRAMS
100-14-078	TALKING	45-11-025	TARGET	1-01-001	TCHALO	21-05-007	TELEGRAPH
18-06-016	TALKS	1-01-001	TARGET'S	28-09-020	TEA	2-02-002	TELEGRAPHED
1-01-001	TALKY	1-01-001	TARGET-HUNTING	1-01-001	TEA-DRINKING	3-01-001	TELEGRAPHER
55-10-045	TALL	1-01-001	TARGET-LANGUAGE	1-01-001	TEA-LEAF	1-01-001	TELEGRAPHER'S
1-01-001	TALL-GROWING	22-07-009	TARGETS	2-01-001	TEACART	5-02-002	TELEGRAPHERS
1-01-001	TALL-MASTED	3-01-001	TARGO	41-11-035	TEACH	3-02-002	TELEGRAPHIC
1-01-001	TALL-TALE	1-01-001	TARHEELIA	80-11-038	TEACHER	1-01-001	TELEGRAPHIE
1-01-001	TALLAHASSEE	5-05-005	TARIFF	2-02-002	TEACHER'S	1-01-001	TELEGRAPHING
1-01-001	TALLAHOOSA	1-01-001	TARIFF-FREE	1-01-001	TEACHER-EMPLOYEE	1-01-001	TELEGRAPHY
1-01-001	TALLCHIEF	1-01-001	TARKINGTON	69-11-028	TEACHERS	1-01-001	TELEMANN
7-03-006	TALLER	1-01-001	TARNISHED	1-01-001	TEACHERS'	1-01-001	TELEOLOGICAL
1-01-001	TALLEYRAND	1-01-001	TARPAPERED	11-08-009	TEACHES	1-01-001	TELEOLOGY
2-01-002	TALLIES	1-01-001	TARPAULIN	67-09-034	TEACHING	1-01-001	TELEPATHICALLY
1-01-001	TALLOW	1-01-001	TARPAULINS	6-04-006	TEACHINGS	3-02-003	TELEPATHY
4-02-003	TALLY	1-01-001	TARPON	1-01-001	TEAGARDEN	76-12-046	TELEPHONE
7-01-001	TALLYHO	1-01-001	TARRANT	2-02-002	TEAHOUSE	1-01-001	TELEPHONE-BOOTH
4-03-003	TALMUD	1-01-001	TARRED	1-01-001	TEAHOUSES	16-08-011	TELEPHONED
1-01-001	TALONS	1-01-001	TARRY	1-01-001	TEAKETTLE	6-03-005	TELEPHONES
1-01-001	TAM-O'-SHANTER	7-04-007	TART	1-01-001	TEAKWOOD	3-02-003	TELEPHONING
1-01-001	TAMALE	1-01-001	TARTAR	83-11-035	TEAM	1-01-001	TELEPROMPTER
2-02-002	TAMBOURINE	1-01-001	TARTARUGHE	2-01-001	TEAM'S	4-04-004	TELESCOPE
5-04-005	TAME	2-01-001	TARTARY	1-01-001	TEAM-MATE	2-02-002	TELESCOPED
1-01-001	TAMING	1-01-001	TARTLY	2-02-002	TEAMED	1-01-001	TELESCOPES
2-01-001	TAMIRIS'	4-01-001	TARTUFFE	1-01-001	TEAMING	1-01-001	TELESCOPIC
1-01-001	TAMIRIS-*DANIEL	1-01-001	TARUFFI	2-01-001	TEAMMATE	1-01-001	TELESCOPING
7-02-002	TAMMANY	4-01-001	TARZAN	1-01-001	TEAMMATE'S	2-02-002	TELETYPE
1-01-001	TAMP	60-13-049	TASK	2-01-002	TEAMMATES	1-01-001	TELETYPES
1-01-001	TAMPER	1-01-001	TASKMASTER	1-01-001	TEAMMATES'	4-03-004	TELEVISED
2-02-002	TAMPERING	29-08-019	TASKS	22-07-013	TEAMS	50-11-036	TELEVISION
9-06-009	TAN	2-02-002	TASMANIA	1-01-001	TEAMS'	1-01-001	TELEVISION-*ELECTRONICS
1-01-001	TANDEM	1-01-001	TASSELS	1-01-001	TEAMSTER	1-01-001	TELEVISON-RECORD
1-01-001	TANEY'S	1-01-001	TASSO	8-03-005	TEAMSTERS	268-15-154	TELL
4-02-004	TANG	59-12-045	TASTE	1-01-001	TEAMWORK	3-03-003	TELL-TALE
1-01-001	TANGANIKA	10-08-010	TASTED	11-07-011	TEAR	4-02-002	TELLER
3-01-001	TANGENCY	2-02-002	TASTEFUL	1-01-001	TEAR-FILLED	2-02-002	TELLERS
26-01-002	TANGENT	1-01-001	TASTELESS	1-01-001	TEAR-SOAKED	1-01-001	TELLI
1-01-001	TANGENTIAL	10-08-010	TASTES	1-01-001	TEARDROP	52-13-045	TELLING
6-01-001	TANGENTS	3-02-003	TASTING	2-02-002	TEARFULLY	34-14-030	TELLS
1-01-001	TANGERE	2-01-001	TASTY	9-05-009	TEARING	1-01-001	TELOMERIC
19-07-009	TANGIBLE	1-01-001	TAT	1-01-001	TEARLE	1-01-001	TEMERITY
1-01-001	TANGIBLY	2-02-002	TATE	34-10-027	TEARS	1-01-001	TEMPEH
8-07-007	TANGLE	1-01-001	TATIAN	1-01-001	TEAS	12-06-010	TEMPER
5-03-005	TANGLED	1-01-001	TATLER	6-04-005	TEASE	1-01-001	TEMPERA
2-02-002	TANGO	1-01-001	TATRAS	2-02-002	TEASED	7-07-007	TEMPERAMENT
1-01-001	TANGOS	5-04-004	TATTERED	3-03-003	TEASING	1-01-001	TEMPERANCE
1-01-001	TANGY	1-01-001	TATTLE-TALE	4-01-001	TEASPOON	2-02-002	TEMPERATE
1-01-001	TANIN	1-01-001	TATTOOED	2-02-002	TEASPOONFUL	1-01-001	TEMPERATELY
12-08-010	TANK	1-01-001	TAU	1-01-001	TEASPOONFULS	135-09-032	TEMPERATURE
1-01-001	TANKER	50-11-037	TAUGHT	3-01-001	TEASPOONS	26-06-013	TEMPERATURES
2-02-002	TANKERS	1-01-001	TAUI	1-01-001	TEATRO	1-01-001	TEMPERED
18-07-011	TANKS	4-04-004	TAUNT	2-01-001	TEATS	2-02-002	TEMPERS
6-02-004	TANNED	2-02-002	TAUNTED	10-03-007	TECH	2-02-002	TEMPEST
1-01-001	TANNENBAUM	1-01-001	TAUNTING	1-01-001	TECH'S	5-01-001	TEMPLATE
2-01-001	TANNER	1-01-001	TAUNTINGLY	120-13-062	TECHNICAL	38-09-019	TEMPLE
2-01-001	TANNHAEUSER	2-02-002	TAUNTS	1-01-001	TECHNICAL-LADDER	2-01-001	TEMPLEMAN
1-01-001	TANNIN	1-01-001	TAURIDA	2-02-002	TECHNICALITIES	4-04-004	TEMPLES
1-01-001	TANNY	2-01-001	TAUROG	9-07-008	TECHNICALLY	4-03-004	TEMPO
1-01-001	TANSY	2-01-002	TAUSSIG	6-05-005	TECHNICIAN	5-02-002	TEMPORAL
4-04-004	TANTALIZING	8-06-007	TAUT	12-05-009	TECHNICIANS	1-01-001	TEMPORALLY
1-01-001	TANTALIZINGLY	1-01-001	TAUT-NERVED	60-09-041	TECHNIQUE	20-07-016	TEMPORARILY
3-02-002	TANTAMOUNT	2-02-002	TAVERN	99-11-053	TECHNIQUES	32-10-028	TEMPORARY
2-02-002	TANTRUM	4-04-004	TAVERNS	18-04-014	TECHNOLOGICAL	1-01-001	TEMPORE
2-02-002	TANTRUMS	2-02-002	TAWDRY	1-01-001	TECHNOLOGICALLY	1-01-001	TEMPORIZE
4-01-002	TAO	2-01-001	TAWES	43-08-027	TECHNOLOGY	2-02-002	TEMPOS
4-02-002	TAOISM	1-01-001	TAWNEY	1-01-001	TECUM	2-02-002	TEMPT
3-01-001	TAOIST			7-03-005	TED	12-07-010	TEMPTATION
2-01-001	TAOISTS						

Code	Entry
6-02-003	TEMPTATIONS
13-07-013	TEMPTED
1-01-001	TEMPTER
2-01-002	TEMPTING
1-01-001	TEMPTINGLY
1-01-001	TEMPTS
165-15-119	TEN
1-01-001	TEN-BY-TEN-MILE
1-01-001	TEN-CONCERT
1-01-001	TEN-DAY
1-01-001	TEN-FIFTY-FIVE
3-02-003	TEN-FOOT
2-01-001	TEN-GALLON
1-01-001	TEN-HOUR
1-01-001	TEN-MINUTE
1-01-001	TEN-MONTH
1-01-001	TEN-THOUSAND-DOLLAR
1-01-001	TEN-TWELVE
3-02-002	TEN-YEAR
1-01-001	TEN-YEAR-OLD
4-04-004	TENABLE
1-01-001	TENACIOUS
1-01-001	TENACIOUSLY
5-04-005	TENACITY
2-02-002	TENANCY
5-04-005	TENANT
9-05-007	TENANTS
43-09-034	TEND
1-01-001	TENDA
24-10-023	TENDED
5-03-005	TENDENCIES
49-10-040	TENDENCY
11-05-010	TENDER
1-01-001	TENDERED
3-02-002	TENDERFOOT
1-01-001	TENDERLOIN
4-04-004	TENDERLY
4-04-004	TENDERNESS
4-03-004	TENDING
2-02-002	TENDONS
34-08-028	TENDS
1-01-001	TENEBROUS
2-02-002	TENEMENT
3-03-003	TENEMENTS
2-02-002	TENETS
1-01-001	TENFOLD
2-01-001	TENITE
1-01-001	TENN
23-09-012	TENNESSEE
1-01-001	TENNESSEE'S
15-07-008	TENNIS
2-02-002	TENNYSON
6-04-006	TENOR
1-01-001	TENORS
1-01-001	TENS
15-07-011	TENSE
1-01-001	TENSED
4-03-004	TENSELY
1-01-001	TENSES
5-02-002	TENSILE
1-01-001	TENSING
59-14-038	TENSION
1-01-001	TENSIONAL
2-01-001	TENSIONING
1-01-001	TENSIONLESS
19-06-015	TENSIONS
1-01-001	TENSPOT
20-04-006	TENT
1-01-001	TENTACLE
2-02-002	TENTACLES
15-06-013	TENTATIVE
6-05-006	TENTATIVELY
7-06-007	TENTH
1-01-001	TENTHS
1-01-001	TENTING
10-02-002	TENTS
6-03-005	TENUOUS
1-01-001	TENUOUSLY
12-05-006	TENURE
1-01-001	TEPEES
1-01-001	TEPID
1-01-001	TER
1-01-001	TER-*ARUTUNIAN
1-01-001	TER-*STEPANOVA
1-01-001	TERATOLOGIES
1-01-001	TERESA
1-01-001	TERG-*O-*TOMETER
79-11-056	TERM
1-01-001	TERM-END
15-09-015	TERMED
12-04-007	TERMINAL
4-03-004	TERMINALS
12-06-012	TERMINATE
4-03-004	TERMINATED
1-01-001	TERMINATES

Code	Entry
1-01-001	TERMINATING
8-03-004	TERMINATION
1-01-001	TERMING
3-02-002	TERMINI
1-01-001	TERMINIELLO
6-04-006	TERMINOLOGY
2-01-001	TERMINUS
163-15-120	TERMS
1-01-001	TERPERS
2-01-001	TERRA
1-01-001	TERRA-COTTA-COLORED
9-05-008	TERRACE
1-01-001	TERRACED
1-01-001	TERRACES
4-03-003	TERRAIN
1-01-001	TERRAINS
1-01-001	TERRAL
3-01-001	TERRAM
1-01-001	TERRAMYCIN
1-01-001	TERRESTIAL
36-11-031	TERRESTRIAL
1-01-001	TERRESTRIAL-EXPLOSION
45-12-038	TERRIBLE
6-04-006	TERRIBLY
6-03-004	TERRIER
2-02-002	TERRIERS
3-03-003	TERRIFIC
1-01-001	TERRIFIED
37-12-032	TERRIFIES
8-04-004	TERRIFYING
5-01-001	TERRITOIRE
14-04-009	TERRITORIAL
9-05-008	TERRITORIES
31-09-023	TERRITORY
25-11-022	TERROR
1-01-001	TERROR-STRICKEN
1-01-001	TERRORISTS
3-03-003	TERRORIZED
1-01-001	TERRORIZING
1-01-001	TERROURS
6-05-006	TERRY
3-02-003	TERRY-CLOTH
2-02-002	TERSE
2-01-001	TERSELY
1-01-001	TERTIAN
1-01-001	TERTIARY
13-02-002	TERTRE
1-01-001	TESS
1-01-001	TESSIE
119-13-071	TEST
1-01-001	TEST-LIKE
1-01-001	TEST-RUN
29-09-022	TESTAMENT
2-02-002	TESTAMENTS
37-08-023	TESTED
2-01-002	TESTICLE
1-01-001	TESTICULAR
11-04-007	TESTIFIED
11-04-005	TESTIFIES
29-08-017	TESTIFY
1-01-001	TESTILY
2-02-002	TESTIMONIAL
1-01-001	TESTIMONIALS
47-08-025	TESTIMONY
1-01-001	TESTING
1-01-001	TESTINGS
12-09-012	TESTS
2-01-002	TETANUS
2-01-001	TETER
17-07-010	TETHERED
1-01-001	TETHERS
1-01-001	TETRACHLORIDE
10-06-008	TETRAGONAL
1-01-001	TETRAHALIDES
1-01-001	TETRAMERON
1-01-001	TETRASODIUM
21-08-019	TEUTONIC
1-01-001	TEWFIK
6-01-001	TEX
1-01-001	TEXAN
1-01-001	TEXANS
2-02-002	TEXAS
1-01-001	TEXAS'
55-08-034	TEXOMA
8-03-007	TEXT
1-01-001	TEXT-FORM
1-01-001	TEXT-LOOKUP
1-01-001	TEXT-ORDERED
4-03-004	TEXTBOOK
1-01-001	TEXTBOOKS
1-01-001	TEXTILE
14-06-012	TEXTILE'S
1-01-001	TEXTILE-EXPORTING

Code	Entry
1-01-001	TEXTILE-IMPORTING
2-01-001	TEXTILE-PRODUCING
15-05-008	TEXTILES
19-05-010	TEXTRON
1-01-001	TEXTS
4-04-004	TEXTUAL
2-02-002	TEXTURE
1-01-001	TEXTURED
6-03-003	TEXTURES
1-01-001	TH
2-02-002	THACKERAY
1-01-001	THADDEUS
2-01-001	THAI
4-03-003	THAILAND
1-01-001	THAKHEK
5-01-001	THALBERGS
13-04-007	THAMES
1-01-001	THAMNOPHIS
1789-15-456	THAN
19-02-002	THANK
2-02-002	THANK-*HEAVEN-*WE'RE-NOT-*INVOLVED
4-03-004	THANKED
3-02-002	THANKFUL
109-13-075	THANKFULNESS
1-01-001	THANKING
20-08-020	THANKLESS
33-09-029	THANKS
1-01-001	THANKSGIVING
1-01-001	THANT
205-15-135	THAR
10595-15-500	THAT
5-03-004	THAT'D
9-05-008	THAT'LL
16-04-009	THAT'S
1-01-001	THAT-A-WAY
24-01-001	THATCHED-ROOF
11-02-005	THATCHES
2-01-002	THATT
1-01-001	THAW
5-05-005	THAWED
3-03-003	THAWING
33-03-010	THAXTER
1-01-001	THAXTERS
3-01-001	THAY
3-01-001	THAYER
3-01-001	THAYER'S
69971-15-500	THE
2-02-002	THEA
1-01-001	THEAF
2-01-001	THEARE
2-01-001	THEASE
1-01-001	THEATER
2-01-001	THEATER-GOING
1-01-001	THEATERGOER
1-01-001	THEATERGOERS
10-04-004	THEATERGOING
6-01-001	THEATERS
1-01-001	THEATRE
3-01-001	THEATRE-BY-THE-*SEA
2-01-001	THEATRE-BY-THE-SEA
1-01-001	THEATREGOER
1-01-001	THEATRES
1-01-001	THEATRICAL
1-01-001	THEATRICALLY
1-01-001	THEATRICALS
1-01-001	THEE
1-01-001	THEES
1-01-001	THEFT
10-05-008	THEI
2670-15-465	THEIR
1-01-001	THEIR'S
3-01-002	THEIRS
1-01-001	THEISTIC
1-01-001	THELMA
1-01-001	THELMA'S
1788-15-482	THEM
30-07-026	THEM'S
32-10-018	THEMATIC
65-13-039	THEME
16-06-010	THEMES
270-15-176	THEMSELVES
1377-15-408	THEN
1-01-001	THENCE
2-01-001	THENCEFORTH
1-01-001	THEOCRACY
1-01-001	THEODOR
5-03-004	THEODORE
1-01-001	THEODOSIAN
1-01-001	THEODOSIUS
5-02-004	THEOLOGIAN

Code	Entry
1-01-001	THEOLOGIAN-PHILOSOPHERS
9-05-007	THEOLOGIANS
27-05-016	THEOLOGICAL
19-05-010	THEOLOGY
1-01-001	THEOLOGY'S
1-01-001	THEON'S
18-01-002	THEOREM
21-05-015	THEORETICAL
5-02-005	THEORETICALLY
1-01-001	THEORETICIANS
20-04-014	THEORIES
2-01-002	THEORISTS
1-01-001	THEORITICIANS
2-01-002	THEORIZE
1-01-001	THEORIZING
129-11-049	THEORY
5-01-001	THER
13-04-007	THERAPEUTIC
1-01-001	THERAPIES
19-02-002	THERAPIST
2-01-001	THERAPIST'S
2-01-001	THERAPISTS
12-02-006	THERAPY
2724-15-467	THERE
4-03-004	THERE'D
3-02-002	THERE'LL
109-13-075	THERE'S
1-01-001	THEREABOUTS
20-08-020	THEREAFTER
1-01-001	THEREBY/*LIKE
1-01-001	THEREFOR
205-15-135	THEREFORE
1-01-001	THEREFORES
5-03-004	THEREFROM
9-05-008	THEREIN
16-04-009	THEREOF
1-01-001	THEREON
1-01-001	THERESA
11-02-005	THERETO
2-01-002	THERETOFORE
1-01-001	THEREUNDER
5-05-005	THEREUPON
3-03-003	THEREWITH
33-03-010	THERMAL
1-01-001	THERMALLY
1-01-001	THERMISTOR
3-01-001	THERMOCOUPLE
3-01-001	THERMOCOUPLES
2-01-001	THERMODYNAMIC
2-02-002	THERMODYNAMICALLY
2-01-001	THERMODYNAMICS
2-01-001	THERMOELECTRIC
1-01-001	THERMOFORMED
2-01-001	THERMOFORMING
1-01-001	THERMOGRAVIMETRIC
10-04-004	THERMOMETER
6-01-001	THERMOMETERS
1-01-001	THERMOMETRIC
3-01-001	THERMOMETRY
2-01-001	THERMONUCLEAR
1-01-001	THERMOPILE
1-01-001	THERMOPLASTIC
1-01-001	THERMOPYLAE
1-01-001	THERMOS
6-02-003	THERMOSTAT
1-01-001	THERMOSTATED
1-01-001	THERMOSTATICS
1-01-001	THERMOSTATS
1-01-001	THESAURUS
1573-15-413	THESE
1-01-001	THESES
10-05-008	THESIS
1-01-001	THESPIANS
3-01-002	THESTAGE
1-01-001	THET
1-01-001	THET'S
1-01-001	THEVENOW
1-01-001	THEWORK
3618-15-482	THEY
30-07-026	THEY'D
32-10-018	THEY'LL
65-13-039	THEY'RE
16-06-010	THEY'VE
1-01-001	THIAMIN
67-11-049	THICK
1-01-001	THICK-SKULLED
2-01-001	THICK-WALLED
1-01-001	THICKEN
5-03-004	THICKENED
1-01-001	THICKENERS
1-01-001	THICKENING
1-01-001	THICKENS
5-04-004	THICKER

Code	Word	Code	Word
1-01-001	THICKEST	1-01-001	THORIATED
1-01-001	THICKET	3-02-002	THORN
2-02-002	THICKETS	8-02-002	THORNBURG
5-05-005	THICKLY	1-01-001	THORNS
44-04-012	THICKNESS	1-01-001	THORNTON
3-02-002	THICKNESSES	2-02-002	THORNY
8-06-007	THIEF	21-08-021	THOROUGH
9-06-007	THIEVES	1-01-001	THOROUGHBRED
1-01-001	THIEVIN	3-03-003	THOROUGHFARE
4-03-004	THIEVING	1-01-001	THOROUGHFARES
9-06-006	THIGH	2-01-002	THOROUGHGOING
1-01-001	THIGH-BONE	40-13-036	THOROUGHLY
7-03-006	THIGHS	1-01-001	THOROUGHNESS
1-01-001	THIIHNG	2-01-001	THORP
1-01-001	THILLS	4-01-001	THORPE
1-01-001	THIMBLE	1-01-001	THORSTEIN
1-01-001	THIMBLE-SIZED	850-15-367	THOSE
92-14-062	THIN	14-05-007	THOU
2-02-002	THIN-LIPPED	442-15-245	THOUGH
1-01-001	THIN-SOLED	515-15-237	THOUGHT
1-01-001	THINE	11-09-011	THOUGHTFUL
333-15-203	THING	14-07-014	THOUGHTFULLY
368-15-201	THINGS	1-01-001	THOUGHTFULNESS
433-15-219	THINK	3-02-003	THOUGHTLESS
2-01-002	THINKE	1-01-001	THOUGHTLESSLY
6-04-006	THINKER	54-12-044	THOUGHTS
6-04-006	THINKERS	97-15-065	THOUSAND
3-02-002	THINKIN	1-01-001	THOUSAND-FOLD
145-15-100	THINKING	1-01-001	THOUSAND-LEGGED
23-12-021	THINKS	47-12-035	THOUSANDS
3-03-003	THINLY	3-02-002	THOUSANDTH
1-01-001	THINNED	1-01-001	THOUSANDTHS
6-03-003	THINNER	1-01-001	THOUT
1-01-001	THINNESS	1-01-001	THRASH
2-02-002	THINNING	3-02-003	THRASHED
1-01-001	THIOCYANATE-PERCHLORATE-FLUOROBORIDE	1-01-001	THRE
1-01-001	THIOT	15-07-009	THREAD
3-01-001	THIOURACIL	3-03-003	THREADBARE
190-15-129	THIRD	4-02-004	THREADED
1-01-001	THIRD-	3-03-003	THREADING
2-01-001	THIRD-DIMENSIONAL	7-06-007	THREADS
1-01-001	THIRD-DIMENSIONALITY	42-10-033	THREAT
4-01-001	THIRD-GRADE	11-07-010	THREATEN
1-01-001	THIRD-INNING	29-10-026	THREATENED
1-01-001	THIRD-RATE	26-11-024	THREATENING
1-01-001	THIRD-SHIFT	1-01-001	THREATENINGLY
1-01-001	THIRD-STORY	5-05-005	THREATENS
1-01-001	THIRDLY	14-10-013	THREATS
4-03-003	THIRDS	610-15-288	THREE
4-04-004	THIRST	1-01-001	THREE-AXIS
1-01-001	THIRSTED	1-01-001	THREE-BEDROOM
5-04-005	THIRSTY	1-01-001	THREE-BODY
11-08-010	THIRTEEN	1-01-001	THREE-BUILDING
2-02-002	THIRTEENTH	3-03-003	THREE-DAY
1-01-001	THIRTEENTH-CENTURY	1-01-001	THREE-DICE
8-05-007	THIRTIES	10-05-007	THREE-DIMENSIONAL
1-01-001	THIRTIETH	1-01-001	THREE-DIMENSIONALITY
59-12-047	THIRTY	1-01-001	THREE-DIMENTIONAL
1-01-001	THIRTY-CALIBER	1-01-001	THREE-FAMILY
1-01-001	THIRTY-EIGHT	2-01-001	THREE-FIFTHS
2-02-002	THIRTY-EIGHTH	2-02-002	THREE-FOLD
14-09-013	THIRTY-FIVE	1-01-001	THREE-FOOT
1-01-001	THIRTY-FOOT	2-02-002	THREE-FOURTHS
7-05-006	THIRTY-FOUR	1-01-001	THREE-FRONT
2-02-002	THIRTY-FOURTH	1-01-001	THREE-HOUR
1-01-001	THIRTY-MILE	1-01-001	THREE-HUNDRED-FOOT
2-01-002	THIRTY-NINE	1-01-001	THREE-INCH
1-01-001	THIRTY-NINTH	3-01-001	THREE-INCH-WIDE
3-03-003	THIRTY-ONE	1-01-001	THREE-INNING
1-01-001	THIRTY-SEVEN	1-01-001	THREE-JUDGE
4-04-004	THIRTY-SIX	3-03-003	THREE-MAN
1-01-001	THIRTY-SIXTH	1-01-001	THREE-MASTED
2-01-002	THIRTY-THREE	1-01-001	THREE-MEN-AND-A-HELPER
3-03-003	THIRTY-TWO	4-02-003	THREE-MONTH
1-01-001	THIRTY-YEAR	1-01-001	THREE-NIGHT
5146-15-495	THIS	1-01-001	THREE-PANEL
1-01-001	THIS'LL	5-04-004	THREE-PART
1-01-001	THITHER	1-01-001	THREE-POWER
1-01-001	THO	4-04-004	THREE-QUARTERS
5-01-001	THOM	1-01-001	THREE-ROOM
1-01-001	THOM'S	2-01-001	THREE-ROUND
100-08-048	THOMAS	1-01-001	THREE-SECTIONED
6-02-002	THOMAS'	1-01-001	THREE-STORY
6-01-001	THOMAS'S	2-02-002	THREE-WAY
38-05-011	THOMPSON	1-01-001	THREE-WEEK
5-01-002	THOMPSON'S	1-01-001	THREE-WOOD
2-01-001	THOMSON	5-03-004	THREE-YEAR
1-01-001	THONG	4-03-003	THREEFOLD
9-03-003	THOR	3-02-002	THREES
4-01-001	THOR'S	1-01-001	THREES-FULFILLED
1-01-001	THOREAU	3-03-003	THREESOME
1-01-001	THOREAU'S		

Code	Word	Code	Word
1-01-001	THRESHED	1-01-001	THYNKE
1-01-001	THRESHHOLD	2-01-001	THYNNE
1-01-001	THRESHING	1-01-001	THYNNES
15-05-009	THRESHOLD	1-01-001	THYRATRON
46-13-036	THREW	17-01-001	THYROGLOBULIN
1-01-001	THRICE	38-02-003	THYROID
5-01-001	THRIFT	4-01-001	THYROID-STIMULATING
3-03-003	THRIFTY	1-01-001	THYROIDAL
5-04-005	THRILL	1-01-001	THYROIDS
3-02-003	THRILLED	1-01-001	THYRONINE
1-01-001	THRILLERS	1-01-001	THYROTOXIC
4-03-004	THRILLING	1-01-001	THYROTROPHIC
2-02-002	THRILLS	1-01-001	THYROTROPHIN
1-01-001	THRIVE	8-01-001	THYROXINE
5-04-005	THRIVED	1-01-001	THYROXINE-BINDING
1-01-001	THRIVES	1-01-001	TI
4-04-004	THRIVING	1-01-001	TIAO
2-01-001	THRO	2-01-001	TIBER
51-11-031	THROAT	7-03-003	TIBET
6-02-002	THROAT'S	3-03-003	TIBETAN
6-04-006	THROATS	1-01-001	TIBETAN-LIKE
1-01-001	THROATY	1-01-001	TIBIALIS
3-03-003	THROBBED	1-01-001	TIBURON
3-02-003	THROBBING	1-01-001	TIC-*TAC-*TOE
2-02-002	THROES	3-03-003	TICK
1-01-001	THROMBI	2-02-002	TICKED
1-01-001	THROMBOSED	1-01-001	TICKER
3-03-003	THROMBOSIS	16-06-011	TICKET
1-01-001	THRONE	14-06-009	TICKETS
4-01-001	THRONEBERRY	1-01-001	TICKING
1-01-001	THRONEBERRY'S	1-01-001	TICKLEBRUSH
1-01-001	THRONES	2-01-002	TICKLED
3-03-003	THRONG	2-02-002	TICKS
6-03-003	THROTTLE	4-01-001	TICONDEROGA
1-01-001	THROTTLED	1-01-001	TIDAL
1-01-001	THROTTLING	1-01-001	TIDBIT
969-15-372	THROUGH	2-02-002	TIDBITS
141-14-106	THROUGHOUT	11-08-011	TIDE
1-01-001	THROUGHPUT	1-01-001	TIDELANDS
42-13-037	THROW	4-02-003	TIDES
1-01-001	THROW-RUG	3-01-002	TIDEWATER
2-01-001	THROWED	1-01-001	TIDIED
2-02-002	THROWER	1-01-001	TIDINESS
4-01-001	THROWIN	3-03-003	TIDINGS
17-10-016	THROWING	1-01-001	TIDY
40-12-032	THROWN	1-01-001	TIDYING
6-04-005	THROWS	23-10-018	TIE
10-03-006	THRU	1-01-001	TIE-IN
1-01-001	THRUMMING	1-01-001	TIECK
2-02-002	THRUSH	34-12-028	TIED
22-08-019	THRUST	1-01-001	TIEFES
3-01-001	THRUST-TO-WEIGHT	1-01-001	TIEKEN
8-07-008	THRUSTING	2-02-002	TIEN
1-01-001	THRUSTON	3-01-001	TIEPOLO
5-04-005	THRUSTS	1-01-001	TIERED
1-01-001	THRUWAY	3-03-003	TIERS
1-01-001	THRUWAYS	15-09-013	TIES
3-02-003	THUD	1-01-001	TIFT
1-01-001	THUDDING	2-01-001	TIGARD
1-01-001	THUDS	7-06-006	TIGER
1-01-001	THUG	1-01-001	TIGER'S
1-01-001	THUGGEE	1-01-001	TIGERS
1-01-001	THUGS	28-11-024	TIGHT
1-01-001	THULE	1-01-001	TIGHT-TURN
1-01-001	THUM	3-02-003	TIGHTEN
10-06-010	THUMB	6-02-005	TIGHTENED
1-01-001	THUMB-	4-04-004	TIGHTENING
1-01-001	THUMB-SUCKING	1-01-001	TIGHTER
1-01-001	THUMBED	2-02-002	TIGHTEST
1-01-001	THUMBING	1-01-001	TIGHTEST-FITTING
1-01-001	THUMBNAIL	15-09-013	TIGHTLY
3-03-003	THUMBS	1-01-001	TIGRESS
3-03-003	THUMP	1-01-001	TIGRIS
1-01-001	THUMPED	1-01-001	TIJUANA
1-01-001	THUMPING	1-01-001	TIKOPIA
5-03-005	THUMPING	16-04-006	TILE
14-08-010	THUNDER	4-04-004	TILED
1-01-001	THUNDER-PURPLE	6-04-004	TILES
1-01-001	THUNDERCLAPS	25-01-001	TILGHMAN
2-02-002	THUNDERED	4-01-001	TILGHMAN'S
2-02-002	THUNDERING	50-11-033	TILL
2-01-002	THUNDEROUS	1-01-001	TILLED
1-01-001	THUNK	1-01-001	TILLER
6-01-001	THURBER	1-01-001	TILLET
2-01-001	THURBER'S	1-01-001	TILLICH
1-01-001	THURMAN	2-01-001	TILLIE
33-11-023	THURSDAY	1-01-001	TILLIE'S
1-01-001	THURSDAY'S	1-01-001	TILLING
1-01-001	THURSDAY-NIGHT	2-01-001	TILLOTSON
312-13-180	THUS	5-03-004	TILT
1-01-001	THUTMOSE	1-01-001	TILT-TOP
1-01-001	THWACK	12-08-011	TILTED
1-01-001	THWART	1-01-001	TILTH
3-03-003	THWARTED	1-01-001	TILTING
1-01-001	THWARTING		
1-01-001	THWUMP		
12-03-006	THY		

2-02-002	TILTS	2-02-002	TITIAN
25-02-003	TIM	1-01-001	TITIAN-HAIRED
2-01-001	TIM'S	1-01-001	TITILLATING
19-07-010	TIMBER	77-13-044	TITLE
2-01-001	TIMBERED	1-01-001	TITLE-HOLDER
3-01-001	TIMBERLANDS	12-06-010	TITLED
5-04-004	TIMBERS	17-07-012	TITLES
2-02-002	TIMBRE	2-02-002	TITO
1599-15-447	TIME	1-01-001	TITRATION
2-02-002	TIME'S	2-02-002	TITRE
2-01-001	TIME-+-MOTION	2-01-001	TITS
1-01-001	TIME-*LIFE	1-01-001	TITTER
1-01-001	TIME-*MYNAH	1-01-001	TITTERS
1-01-001	TIME-*OLIVETTE	1-01-001	TITULAR
1-01-001	TIME-CAST	2-01-001	TITUS
1-01-001	TIME-CONSUMING	1-01-001	TIVEDEN
1-01-001	TIME-DELAY	1-01-001	TIZARD
3-02-002	TIME-HONORED	1-01-001	TJOKORDA
1-01-001	TIME-ON-THE-JOB	26149-15-500	TO
2-01-001	TIME-SERVERS	1-01-001	TO-AND-FRO
2-02-002	TIME-SPAN	4-01-002	TO-DAY
2-01-001	TIME-TEMPERATUR	1-01-001	TO-DAY'S
	E	1-01-001	TO-DO
9-05-008	TIMED	1-01-001	TO-MORROW
2-02-002	TIMELESS	1-01-001	TO-THE-DEATH
2-02-002	TIMELINESS	4-03-003	TOAD
9-04-007	TIMELY	1-01-001	TOADIES
1-01-001	TIMEN	1-01-001	TOADYISM
1-01-001	TIMEPIECE	19-09-013	TOAST
1-01-001	TIMERS	2-02-002	TOASTED
300-15-194	TIMES	1-01-001	TOASTED-NUT
1-01-001	TIMES-*PICAYUNE	2-02-002	TOASTING
4-02-004	TIMETABLE	19-08-011	TOBACCO
1-01-001	TIMETABLES	1-01-001	TOBACCO-JUICE
1-01-001	TIMEWORN	2-02-002	TOBIN
2-01-001	TIMEX	1-01-001	TOCCATA
5-04-005	TIMID	1-01-001	TOCH
1-01-001	TIMIDITY	284-14-161	TODAY
1-01-001	TIMIDLY	1-01-001	TODAY'LL
11-05-008	TIMING	40-10-028	TODAY'S
1-01-001	TIMMY	2-02-002	TODD
1-01-001	TIMON	1-01-001	TODDLERS
11-02-002	TIMOTHY	1-01-001	TODE
1-01-001	TIMS	10-01-001	TODMAN
12-08-009	TIN	1-01-001	TODMAN'S
1-01-001	TINCTURE	9-07-008	TOE
1-01-001	TINDAL	1-01-001	TOE-TIPS
1-01-001	TINDER	19-09-015	TOES
2-01-001	TINES	1-01-001	TOFFEE
6-05-005	TINGLING	1-01-001	TOFFENETTI'S
3-03-003	TINIEST	1-01-001	TOFU
2-02-002	TINKERING	267-15-192	TOGETHER
1-01-001	TINKERS	1-01-001	TOGETHERNESS
1-01-001	TINKLED	1-01-001	TOGS
2-01-001	TINKLING	1-01-001	TOIL
1-01-001	TINNING	1-01-001	TOILED
13-06-007	TINPLATED	13-06-007	TOILET
2-01-001	TINSEL	4-02-002	TOILETS
1-01-001	TINT	1-01-001	TOILSOME
2-01-001	TINTABLE	1-01-001	TOJOS
1-01-001	TINTED	10-06-008	TOKEN
1-01-001	TINTORETTO	1-01-001	TOKENISH
1-01-001	TINTS	2-02-002	TOKENS
1-01-001	TINTYPE	18-05-007	TOKYO
50-13-042	TINY	1-01-001	TOLAND
22-09-017	TIP	413-15-185	TOLD
1-01-001	TIP-TOE	2-02-002	TOLE
1-01-001	TIPOFF	1-01-001	TOLEK
1-01-001	TIPPECANOE	3-03-003	TOLERABLE
4-04-004	TIPPED	9-07-009	TOLERANCE
1-01-001	TIPPERARY	9-05-007	TOLERANT
1-01-001	TIPPING	4-03-004	TOLERATE
1-01-001	TIPPLE	6-06-006	TOLERATED
13-06-011	TIPS	1-01-001	TOLERATING
2-02-002	TIPSY	1-01-001	TOLERATION
2-02-002	TIPTOEING	16-07-009	TOLL
1-01-001	TIRADES	1-01-001	TOLL-RATE
22-06-008	TIRE	8-01-001	TOLL-ROAD
48-11-040	TIRED	1-01-001	TOLLED
2-02-002	TIREDLY	6-01-001	TOLLEY
1-01-001	TIREDNESS	3-01-001	TOLLEY'S
4-02-004	TIRELESS	1-01-001	TOLLGATE
1-01-001	TIRELESSLY	1-01-001	TOLLHOUSE
12-06-009	TIRES	3-02-002	TOLLS
3-03-003	TIRESOME	1-01-001	TOLSTOY
4-04-004	TIRING	1-01-001	TOLSTOY'S
2-02-002	TIS	1-01-001	TOLUBEYEV
41-06-012	TISSUE	1-01-001	TOLYLENE
13-02-005	TISSUES	63-09-018	TOM
7-02-004	TITAN	4-03-003	TOM'S
3-03-003	TITANIC	4-01-001	TOMAS
2-02-002	TITANIUM	4-02-004	TOMATO
1-01-001	TITANS	1-01-001	TOMATO-RED
1-01-001	TITCHE'S	3-02-003	TOMATOES
4-01-002	TITER	11-06-009	TOMB
4-01-001	TITERS	2-01-001	TOMBIGBEE
1-01-001	TITHES	2-01-002	TOMBLIKE

2-02-002	TOMBS	1-01-001	TOPPLE
2-02-002	TOMBSTONE	2-02-002	TOPPLED
1-01-001	TOMBSTONES	2-02-002	TOPPLING
1-01-001	TOMES	10-06-007	TOPS
1-01-001	TOMKINS	1-01-001	TOPSOIL
1-01-001	TOMMIE	1-01-001	TOPSY-TURVY
18-04-004	TOMMY	1-01-001	TORAH
1-01-001	TOMMY'S	2-02-002	TORCH
1-01-001	TOMONGGONG	2-01-001	TORCHES
63-11-039	TOMORROW	15-08-014	TORE
3-03-003	TOMORROW'S	6-02-002	TORIES
13-05-006	TON	2-01-001	TORINO
1-01-001	TON-MILE	4-03-004	TORMENT
9-03-004	TONAL	3-02-002	TORMENTED
1-01-001	TONALITIES	1-01-001	TORMENTERS
1-01-001	TONALLY	2-02-002	TORMENTING
78-13-039	TONE	25-10-021	TORN
1-01-001	TONELESS	1-01-001	TORNADO
3-01-001	TONER	1-01-001	TORNADOES
20-08-014	TONES	6-04-005	TORONTO
1-01-001	TONG	1-01-001	TORPEDO
1-01-001	TONGS	1-01-001	TORPEDOES
35-11-023	TONGUE	1-01-001	TORPETIUS
2-02-002	TONGUE-IN-CHEEK	1-01-001	TORPID
1-01-001	TONGUE-THRUSTIN	2-02-002	TORPOR
	G	1-01-001	TORQUATO
1-01-001	TONGUE-TIED	5-01-001	TORQUE
1-01-001	TONGUE-TWISTER	1-01-001	TORQUEMADA
1-01-001	TONGUED	5-01-001	TORQUER
4-03-004	TONGUES	4-01-001	TORQUERS
1-01-001	TONI	2-01-001	TORRENCE
1-01-001	TONIC	4-04-004	TORRENT
2-02-002	TONICS	2-02-002	TORRENTS
38-10-029	TONIGHT	2-01-001	TORRID
2-01-002	TONIGHT'S	1-01-001	TORRID-*ADIOS
1-01-001	TONIO	1-01-001	TORRID-*BREEZE
28-10-019	TONS	1-01-001	TORRID-*MIGHTY
2-01-001	TONSIL	12-01-001	TORRID
11-04-007	TONY	2-01-001	TORRID-*CAPONE
832-15-336	TOO	1-01-001	TORSION
1-01-001	TOO-EXPENSIVE	7-05-005	TORSO
1-01-001	TOO-HEARTY	1-01-001	TORSO-DEFINING
2-02-002	TOO-LARGE	3-02-002	TORSOS
1-01-001	TOO-NAKED	3-02-002	TORTOISE
1-01-001	TOO-SHINY	1-01-001	TORTOISES
1-01-001	TOO-SIMPLE-TO-B	3-03-003	TORTUOUS
	E-TRUE	3-03-003	TORTURE
2-01-001	TOOBIN	9-07-004	TORTURED
2-01-001	TOODLE	2-01-001	TORTURES
426-15-227	TOOK	13-01-004	TORY
2-01-001	TOOKE	1-01-001	TOSCA
40-09-020	TOOL	2-02-002	TOSCANINI
2-01-001	TOOL-AND-DIE	1-01-001	TOSCANINI'S
1-01-001	TOOL-KIT	9-05-006	TOSS
5-05-005	TOOLING	31-09-023	TOSSED
1-01-001	TOOLMAKER	2-02-002	TOSSES
34-10-019	TOOLS	5-05-005	TOSSING
1-01-001	TOOMEY	211-12-109	TOTAL
1-01-001	TOONKER	2-01-001	TOTAL-COST
3-02-002	TOOT	7-04-007	TOTALED
1-01-001	TOOT-TOOT	6-04-006	TOTALING
20-05-005	TOOTH	1-01-001	TOTALISTIC
1-01-001	TOOTH-HURTY	6-06-006	TOTALITARIAN
1-01-001	TOOTH-PASTE	3-01-003	TOTALITARIANISM
1-01-001	TOOTH-STRAIGHTE	2-02-002	TOTALITY
	NING	3-01-001	TOTALLED
6-02-002	TOOTHBRUSH	22-10-021	TOTALLY
1-01-001	TOOTHPASTE	6-04-006	TOTALS
1-01-001	TOOTLEY-TOOT-TO	1-01-001	TOTE
	OTLED	1-01-001	TOTEMIC
1-01-001	TOOTSIE	1-01-001	TOTHE
204-15-128	TOP	1-01-001	TOTO
2-02-002	TOP-DRAWER	1-01-001	TOTTED
2-02-002	TOP-GRADE	1-01-001	TOTTERING
1-01-001	TOP-HEAVY	87-15-062	TOUCH
3-02-002	TOP-LEVEL	6-02-003	TOUCHDOWN
1-01-001	TOP-NOTCH	1-01-001	TOUCHDOWNS
1-01-001	TOP-PRIORITY	42-10-036	TOUCHED
2-01-002	TOP-QUALITY	14-07-014	TOUCHES
1-01-001	TOP-RANKING	15-06-014	TOUCHING
2-01-001	TOP-TANG	1-01-001	TOUCHSTONE
2-01-001	TOPCOAT	1-01-001	TOUCHSTONES
1-01-001	TOPCOATS	1-01-001	TOUCHY
1-01-001	TOPEKA	1-01-001	TOUGAS
2-01-001	TOPGALLANT	36-12-031	TOUGH
9-05-008	TOPIC	1-01-001	TOUGH-LOOKING
4-02-003	TOPICAL	10-05-008	TOUGHER
10-05-010	TOPICS	2-02-002	TOUGHEST
1-01-001	TOPKAPI	6-05-005	TOUGHNESS
1-01-001	TOPMOST	3-02-002	TOUGHS
1-01-001	TOPNOTCH	1-01-001	TOUJOURS
1-01-001	TOPOGRAPHIC	1-01-001	TOULOUSE
6-03-003	TOPOGRAPHY	1-01-001	TOULOUSE-*LAUTR
7-05-006	TOPPED		EC
1-01-001	TOPPERS	43-10-026	TOUR
2-01-002	TOPPING	2-02-002	TOURED
1-01-001	TOPPINGS	7-04-005	TOURING

Code	Word	Code	Word	Code	Word	Code	Word
16-05-012	TOURIST	1-01-001	TRAGICALLY	32-10-020	TRANSITION	1-01-001	TREASONOUS
2-02-002	TOURIST'S	1-01-001	TRAGICOMIC	5-03-003	TRANSITIONAL	4-04-004	TREASURE
12-08-012	TOURISTS	31-11-017	TRAIL	5-03-005	TRANSITIONS	2-02-002	TREASURED
1-01-001	TOURISTS'	1-01-001	TRAIL-WORN	16-11-015	TRANSLATE	14-05-010	TREASURER
20-04-007	TOURNAMENT	8-04-008	TRAILED	16-09-014	TRANSLATED	6-06-006	TREASURES
5-03-004	TOURNAMENTS	11-02-004	TRAILER	1-01-001	TRANSLATES	1-01-001	TREASURIES
10-05-008	TOURS	12-03-004	TRAILERS	2-02-002	TRANSLATING	40-08-017	TREASURY
2-02-002	TOUSLED	7-07-007	TRAILING	16-06-012	TRANSLATION	1-01-001	TREASURY'S
1-01-001	TOUT	16-04-005	TRAILS	3-03-003	TRANSLATIONS	26-09-021	TREAT
1-01-001	TOW	82-14-045	TRAIN	1-01-001	TRANSLATOR	75-13-049	TREATED
386-15-216	TOWARD	54-12-042	TRAINED	1-01-001	TRANSLUCENCE	4-03-003	TREATIES
1-01-001	TOWARDES	1-01-001	TRAINEESHIPS	1-01-001	TRANSLUCENCY	11-05-009	TREATING
64-14-039	TOWARDS	156-12-055	TRAINING	3-02-002	TRANSLUCENT	1-01-001	TREATISE
1-01-001	TOWBOATS	1-01-001	TRAINMAN	1-01-001	TRANSLUSCENT	127-11-052	TREATMENT
1-01-001	TOWED	16-08-015	TRAINS	1-01-001	TRANSMISSIBLE	11-04-006	TREATMENTS
6-05-005	TOWEL	1-01-001	TRAIPSING	16-05-011	TRANSMISSION	14-08-010	TREATS
1-01-001	TOWELING	3-02-003	TRAIT	3-03-003	TRANSMIT	20-06-009	TREATY
11-04-006	TOWELS	2-01-001	TRAITOR	1-01-001	TRANSMITS	1-01-001	TREATY-MAKING
13-05-010	TOWER	1-01-001	TRAITOROUS	1-01-001	TRANSMITTABLE	2-02-002	TREBLE
1-01-001	TOWER'S	4-03-003	TRAITORS	8-05-008	TRANSMITTED	1-01-001	TREDDING
11-06-010	TOWERING	6-05-006	TRAITS	4-02-002	TRANSMITTER	59-11-032	TREE
5-04-005	TOWERS	2-02-002	TRAJECTORY	2-01-002	TRANSMITTING	2-01-001	TREE-CLUMPS
212-14-103	TOWN	1-01-001	TRAMMEL	3-02-002	TRANSMUTATION	1-01-001	TREECE
14-06-010	TOWN'S	1-01-001	TRAMP	4-04-004	TRANSMUTED	1-01-001	TREELIKE
9-03-003	TOWNE	2-02-002	TRAMPED	1-01-001	TRANSOCEANIC	101-12-057	TREES
1-01-001	TOWNLEY	3-03-003	TRAMPLE	17-02-002	TRANSOM	1-01-001	TREES'
50-11-021	TOWNS	1-01-001	TRAMPLED	2-02-002	TRANSOMS	1-01-001	TREETOPS
1-01-001	TOWNSEND	2-02-002	TRAMPLING	2-02-002	TRANSPARENCY	1-01-001	TREGNUMS
7-04-004	TOWNSHIP	1-01-001	TRAMWAY	13-06-010	TRANSPARENT	2-02-002	TREK
1-01-001	TOWNSHIPS	4-03-003	TRANCE	1-01-001	TRANSPIRATING	1-01-001	TREKKED
1-01-001	TOWNSMAN	2-02-002	TRANCES	4-01-001	TRANSPIRATION	1-01-001	TRELLISES
2-01-001	TOWNSMEN	2-02-002	TRANQUIL	3-01-003	TRANSPIRED	10-06-010	TREMBLE
2-01-001	TOWSLEY	4-03-003	TRANQUILITY	4-01-001	TRANSPIRING	5-03-005	TREMBLED
3-01-001	TOXIC	1-01-001	TRANQUILIZER	2-01-001	TRANSPLANT	1-01-001	TREMBLES
1-01-001	TOXIN	4-03-003	TRANQUILIZERS	1-01-001	TRANSPLANTABLE	26-08-021	TREMBLING
4-03-004	TOY	1-01-001	TRANQUILLITY	1-01-001	TRANSPLANTED	37-12-033	TREMENDOUS
1-01-001	TOYING	1-01-001	TRANS-*ATLANTIC	1-01-001	TRANSPLANTING	10-06-009	TREMENDOUSLY
9-03-003	TOYNBEE	6-01-001	TRANS-ILLUMINATED	18-06-013	TRANSPORT	2-02-002	TREMOR
11-05-005	TOYS	1-01-001	TRANS-ILLUMINATION	43-07-026	TRANSPORTATION	1-01-001	TREMPLER
1-01-001	TRABB	1-01-001	TRANS-LINGUALLY	5-04-004	TRANSPORTED	1-01-001	TREMULOUSLY
23-11-020	TRACE	1-01-001	TRANS-POLITICAL	3-03-003	TRANSPORTING	2-01-002	TRENCH
3-02-003	TRACEABLE	3-03-003	TRANSACT	5-05-005	TRANSPORTS	2-01-002	TRENCHANT
12-06-010	TRACED	5-03-004	TRANSACTION	5-04-005	TRANSPOSED	4-02-003	TRENCHARD
2-02-002	TRACERS	5-03-004	TRANSACTIONS	1-01-001	TRANSPOSITION	2-01-002	TRENCHERMEN
9-06-009	TRACES	1-01-001	TRANSAMINASE	2-01-001	TRANSSHIPMENT	1-01-001	TRENCHES
2-02-002	TRACHEA	1-01-001	TRANSATLANTIC	1-01-001	TRANSVERSALLY	46-09-034	TREND
17-06-008	TRACING	1-01-001	TRANSCEND	4-02-002	TRANSVERSE	1-01-001	TREND-FOLLOWING
1-01-001	TRACINGS	1-01-001	TRANSCENDANT	1-01-001	TRANSVERSELY	21-09-015	TRENDS
38-12-027	TRACK	1-01-001	TRANSCENDED	2-01-001	TRANSVERSUS	4-02-002	TRENTON
1-01-001	TRACK-SIGNAL	2-02-002	TRANSCENDENCE	1-01-001	TRANSVESTITISM	3-03-003	TRESPASSED
1-01-001	TRACKDOWN	2-02-002	TRANSCENDENT	2-01-001	TRANSYLVANIA	3-01-001	TRESPASSES
3-02-003	TRACKED	3-02-003	TRANSCENDENTAL	20-09-014	TRAP	1-01-001	TRESTLE
3-02-002	TRACKING	2-02-002	TRANSCENDENTALISM	1-01-001	TRAPDOOR	1-01-001	TRESTLES
1-01-001	TRACKLESS	1-01-001	TRANSCENDENTALISTS	1-01-001	TRAPDOORS	17-01-001	TREVELYAN
12-08-011	TRACKS	3-03-003	TRANSCENDING	1-01-001	TRAPEZOID	12-01-001	TREVELYAN'S
17-08-013	TRACT	6-02-005	TRANSCENDS	1-01-001	TRAPP	12-02-002	TRI-*STATE
1-01-001	TRACTARIANS	1-01-001	TRANSCRIBE	7-06-007	TRAPPED	4-01-001	TRI-IODOTHYRONINE
24-04-006	TRACTOR	3-02-003	TRANSCRIBED	2-01-001	TRAPPER	1-01-001	TRI-MOTOR
1-01-001	TRACTOR-TRAILER	4-03-003	TRANSCRIPT	1-01-001	TRAPPER'S	1-01-001	TRIAD
7-05-005	TRACTORS	2-01-002	TRANSCRIPTION	2-02-002	TRAPPING	134-14-039	TRIAL
5-05-005	TRACTS	2-02-002	TRANSCRIPTS	3-03-003	TRAPPINGS	1-01-001	TRIAL-BOOK
143-13-074	TRADE	1-01-001	TRANSCULTURAL	8-04-006	TRAPS	39-06-011	TRIALS
1-01-001	TRADE-MARK	10-02-002	TRANSDUCER	2-02-002	TRASH	4-01-001	TRIAMCINOLONE
1-01-001	TRADE-PREPARATORY	2-01-001	TRANSDUCERS	3-03-003	TRASTEVERE	3-01-001	TRIANDOS
8-04-005	TRADED	38-09-016	TRANSFER	1-01-001	TRAUMA	4-03-004	TRIANGLE
3-03-003	TRADEMARK	1-01-001	TRANSFER/**JHR/**JHP	1-01-001	TRAUMATIC	1-01-001	TRIANGLES
1-01-001	TRADEMARKS	1-01-001	TRANSFERED	1-01-001	TRAVANCORE	5-04-005	TRIANGULAR
8-03-004	TRADER	1-01-001	TRANSFEREE	61-13-042	TRAVEL	1-01-001	TRIANON
26-03-005	TRADERS	2-01-001	TRANSFERENCE	22-10-020	TRAVELED	6-05-006	TRIBAL
1-01-001	TRADERS'	2-01-001	TRANSFEROR	8-05-007	TRAVELER	4-04-004	TRIBE
9-05-006	TRADES	12-01-001	TRANSFEROR'S	8-06-008	TRAVELERS	1-01-001	TRIBE'S
1-01-001	TRADESMEN	3-01-001	TRANSFERORS	2-01-001	TRAVELIN	12-04-007	TRIBES
25-07-013	TRADING	1-01-001	TRANSFERRAL	19-09-018	TRAVELING	2-02-002	TRIBESMEN
94-10-053	TRADITION	29-11-018	TRANSFERRED	4-04-004	TRAVELLED	1-01-001	TRIBULATION
1-01-001	TRADITION-MINDED	1-01-001	TRANSFERRING	3-02-002	TRAVELLER	1-01-001	TRIBUNA
78-10-058	TRADITIONAL	11-07-007	TRANSFERS	2-02-002	TRAVELLERS	5-03-005	TRIBUNAL
3-02-002	TRADITIONALISM	7-03-007	TRANSFORM	4-04-004	TRAVELLING	4-03-003	TRIBUNALS
4-02-002	TRADITIONALIST	20-04-012	TRANSFORMATION	2-02-002	TRAVELOGUE	13-08-010	TRIBUNE
1-01-001	TRADITIONALISTIC	25-05-010	TRANSFORMED	1-01-001	TRAVELOGUE-LIKE	1-01-001	TRIBUNE'S
1-01-001	TRADITIONALISTS	1-01-001	TRANSFORMER	1-01-001	TRAVELOGUES	24-08-019	TRIBUTE
1-01-001	TRADITIONALIZED	2-01-002	TRANSFORMERS	5-03-005	TRAVELS	1-01-001	TRIBUTES
10-08-010	TRADITIONALLY	2-02-002	TRANSFORMING	5-03-003	TRAVERSE	1-01-001	TRICHIERI
1-01-001	TRADITIONNEL	3-01-002	TRANSFORMS	6-04-006	TRAVERSED	1-01-001	TRICHINELLA
21-05-016	TRADITIONS	4-02-002	TRANSFUSIONS	1-01-001	TRAVERSING	1-01-001	TRICHLOROACETIC
68-11-035	TRAFFIC	1-01-001	TRANSGRESSED	1-01-001	TRAVESTY	1-01-001	TRICHROME
1-01-001	TRAFFICKED	1-01-001	TRANSGRESSION	1-01-001	TRAWLER	15-06-012	TRICK
3-01-001	TRAFTON	1-01-001	TRANSIENCE	15-06-012	TRAXEL	2-02-002	TRICKED
1-01-001	TRAFTON'S	3-02-002	TRANSIENT	18-07-010	TRAY	2-02-002	TRICKLE
2-01-001	TRAGEDIANS	1-01-001	TRANSIENTS	3-03-003	TRAYS	2-02-002	TRICKLING
7-06-007	TRAGEDIES	1-01-001	TRANSISTOR	1-01-001	TREACHERIES	8-06-008	TRICKS
49-10-023	TRAGEDY	1-01-001	TRANSISTORS	6-03-006	TREACHEROUS	2-02-002	TRICKSTER
2-02-002	TRAGER	16-04-007	TRANSIT	5-04-005	TREAD	1-01-001	TRICKY
1-01-001	TRAGI-COMIC			1-01-001	TREADING	1-01-001	TRICOLOR
33-08-026	TRAGIC			1-01-001	TREADMILL	170-15-123	TRIED
				1-01-001	TREADWELL	13-06-010	TRIES
				6-04-004	TREASON	9-07-009	TRIFLE
				1-01-001	TREASONABLE		

2-02-002	TRIFLING	11-08-009	TROPICAL	1-01-001	TSHOMBE-*GIZENG	1-01-001	TURN-OUT
10-01-001	TRIG	1-01-001	TROPICS		A-*GOA-*GHANA	1-01-001	TURNAROUND
1-01-001	TRIG'S	1-01-001	TROPIDOCLONION	1-01-001	TSITOURIS	1-01-001	TURNE
1-01-001	TRIGG	1-01-001	TROPOCOLLAGEN	1-01-001	TSOU	320-15-183	TURNED
12-04-009	TRIGGER	12-03-004	TROT	21-01-001	TSUNAMI	6-04-006	TURNER
2-01-002	TRIGGER-HAPPY	1-01-001	TROTSKY	1-01-001	TSUNAMI-WARNING	1-01-001	TURNERY
7-05-007	TRIGGERED	7-05-005	TROTTED	1-01-001	TSVETKOV	75-14-062	TURNING
2-01-002	TRIGONAL	1-01-001	TROTTER	1-01-001	TT**U.	1-01-001	TURNINGS
1-01-001	TRIKOJUS	1-01-001	TROUBIE	1-01-001	TU	1-01-001	TURNIPS
3-02-002	TRILL	134-15-097	TROUBLE	1-01-001	TU*HUL*HUL*ZOTE	1-01-001	TURNKEY
1-01-001	TRILLED	2-02-002	TROUBLE-FREE	1-01-001	TUALATIN	1-01-001	TURNOFF
1-01-001	TRILLION	1-01-001	TROUBLE-SHOOTER	13-05-009	TUB	3-02-002	TURNOUT
4-01-003	TRILOGY	31-12-028	TROUBLED	1-01-001	TUBA	2-01-001	TURNOUTS
20-08-014	TRIM	22-10-018	TROUBLES	31-06-012	TUBE	2-02-002	TURNOVER
1-01-001	TRIM-YOUR-OWN-F	1-01-001	TROUBLESHOOTER	1-01-001	TUBE-NOSED	15-04-004	TURNPIKE
	RANKS	7-03-007	TROUBLESOME	6-04-004	TUBERCULOSIS	10-01-001	TURNPIKES
3-01-002	TRIMBLE	2-02-002	TROUBLING	1-01-001	TUBERS	38-12-036	TURNS
1-01-001	TRIMESTER	3-02-002	TROUGH	24-06-009	TUBES	1-01-001	TURNTABLE
4-03-004	TRIMMED	1-01-001	TROUGHS	6-03-003	TUBING	4-01-001	TURPENTINE
2-01-001	TRIMMER	3-02-002	TROUP	1-01-001	TUBORG	3-02-002	TURQUOISE
2-01-001	TRIMMING	3-03-003	TROUPE	5-02-002	TUBS	3-01-002	TURRET
4-03-003	TRIMMINGS	1-01-001	TROUPES	4-03-004	TUBULAR	1-01-001	TURRETS
1-01-001	TRIMS	3-03-003	TROUSER	1-01-001	TUBULES	8-03-004	TURTLE
1-01-001	TRINIDAD	7-03-006	TROUSERS	2-02-002	TUCK	1-01-001	TURTLE-NECK
1-01-001	TRINITARIAN	1-01-001	TROUSERS-POCKET	6-05-006	TUCKED	2-01-001	TURTLEBACKS
1-01-001	TRINITARIANS		S	5-03-004	TUCKER	2-01-001	TURTLENECK
5-03-005	TRINITY	4-02-002	TROUT	1-01-001	TUCKER'S	1-01-001	TURTLES
1-01-001	TRINKET	3-03-003	TROY	2-02-002	TUCKING	2-02-002	TUSCANY
1-01-001	TRINKETS	1-01-001	TROYES	3-02-002	TUCSON	1-01-001	TUSKEGEE
9-04-007	TRIO	1-01-001	TRUANT	4-03-003	TUDOR	3-03-003	TUSKS
1-01-001	TRIOL	5-04-005	TRUCE	1-01-001	TUDOR-STYLE	1-01-001	TUSSARD'S
1-01-001	TRIOMPHE	57-10-025	TRUCK	59-09-030	TUESDAY	4-01-001	TUSSLE
81-13-058	TRIP	1-01-001	TRUCK'S	1-01-001	TUFTS	4-03-003	TUTOR
1-01-001	TRIP-HAMMER	1-01-001	TRUCKDRIVER	3-03-003	TUG	1-01-001	TUTORIALS
1-01-001	TRIPARTITE	1-01-001	TRUCKED	1-01-001	TUG-O'-WAR	2-02-002	TUTORING
1-01-001	TRIPE	2-02-002	TRUCKEE	2-02-002	TUG-OF-WAR	1-01-001	TUTORS
1-01-001	TRIPHENYLARSINE	1-01-001	TRUCKER	1-01-001	TUGARU	4-01-002	TUTTLE
1-01-001	TRIPHENYLPHOSPH	1-01-001	TRUCKERS	2-02-002	TUGGED	1-01-001	TUTTLE'S
	INE	2-02-002	TRUCKING	1-01-001	TUGGING	5-01-001	TUXAPOKA
1-01-001	TRIPHENYLSTIBIN	22-06-013	TRUCKS	5-03-004	TUITION	1-01-001	TUXEDOED
	E	1-01-001	TRUCULENCE	1-01-001	TULANE	1-01-001	TVA
1-01-001	TRIPHOSPHOPYRID	1-01-001	TRUCULENT	2-01-001	TULAREMIA	1-01-001	TWAIN
	INE	4-04-004	TRUDGED	4-03-004	TULIP	1-01-001	TWAIN'S
5-02-005	TRIPLE	231-15-155	TRUE	1-01-001	TULIP-SHAPED	5-03-005	TWEED
1-01-001	TRIPLE-CHECKED	1-01-001	TRUE-FALSE	2-02-002	TULIPS	1-01-001	TWEEDY
1-01-001	TRIPLE-CROWN	2-02-002	TRUER	1-01-001	TULLE	1-01-001	TWEEZED
1-01-001	TRIPLE-TANK	2-02-002	TRUEST	1-01-001	TULLIO	5-05-005	TWELFTH
4-03-004	TRIPLED	3-02-003	TRUISM	1-01-001	TULLN	48-12-042	TWELVE
1-01-001	TRIPLET	12-01-002	TRUJILLO	1-01-001	TULSA	2-02-002	TWELVE-HOUR
3-01-001	TRIPLETS	2-01-002	TRUJILLO'S	4-01-001	TULTUL	1-01-001	TWELVE-YEAR
1-01-001	TRIPLICATION	2-01-002	TRUJILLOS	3-02-002	TUMBLE	1-01-001	TWELVE-YEAR-OLD
3-02-002	TRIPOD	57-13-052	TRULY	13-05-012	TUMBLED	10-06-007	TWENTIES
1-01-001	TRIPODS	13-05-010	TRUMAN	2-02-002	TUMBLER	20-08-018	TWENTIETH
1-01-001	TRIPOLI	3-02-003	TRUMAN'S	1-01-001	TUMBLES	1-01-001	TWENTIETH-*CENT
2-01-001	TRIPOLYPHOSPHAT	1-01-001	TRUMBULL	3-03-003	TUMBLING		URY
	E	1-01-001	TRUMP	1-01-001	TUMBRELS	9-05-007	TWENTIETH-CENTU
2-02-002	TRIPPED	1-01-001	TRUMPED-UP	1-01-001	TUMEFACIENS		RY
1-01-001	TRIPPIN	7-05-006	TRUMPET	17-05-005	TUMOR	80-15-067	TWENTY
2-02-002	TRIPPING	1-01-001	TRUMPETER	8-02-002	TUMORS	1-01-001	TWENTY-DOLLAR
29-09-023	TRIPS	1-01-001	TRUMPS	1-01-001	TUMOURS	5-03-005	TWENTY-EIGHT
2-02-002	TRIPTYCH	3-03-003	TRUNCATED	1-01-001	TUMULTUOUS	1-01-001	TWENTY-EIGHTH
2-01-001	TRIS	1-01-001	TRUNDLE	10-06-010	TUNE	1-01-001	TWENTY-FIFTH
1-01-001	TRIS(HYDROXYMET	1-01-001	TRUNDLING	1-01-001	TUNE-BELLY	3-02-003	TWENTY-FIRST
	HYL)-AMINOMETHA	8-01-003	TRUNK	1-01-001	TUNED	1-01-001	TWENTY-FIRST-CE
	NE	5-05-005	TRUNKS	1-01-001	TUNEFUL		NTURY
2-01-001	TRISERVICE	2-01-001	TRUSSES	1-01-001	TUNEFULNESS	25-10-021	TWENTY-FIVE
1-01-001	TRISODIUM	52-14-039	TRUST	1-01-001	TUNELESSLY	1-01-001	TWENTY-FIVE-DOL
1-01-001	TRISTAN	11-06-011	TRUSTED	7-04-006	TUNES		LAR
4-02-002	TRISTANO	9-04-006	TRUSTEE	2-01-001	TUNG	1-01-001	TWENTY-FIVE-YEA
2-02-002	TRITE	1-01-001	TRUSTEE'S	4-01-003	TUNGSTEN		R-OLD
22-09-020	TRIUMPH	25-06-011	TRUSTEES	1-01-001	TUNIC	14-07-013	TWENTY-FOUR
5-04-004	TRIUMPHANT	2-02-002	TRUSTEES'	3-01-001	TUNING	1-01-001	TWENTY-MILE
8-07-008	TRIUMPHANTLY	1-01-001	TRUSTEESHIP	1-01-001	TUNIS	2-02-002	TWENTY-NINE
3-02-003	TRIUMPHS	2-01-001	TRUSTETH	3-02-003	TUNISIA	1-01-001	TWENTY-NINE-FOO
2-02-002	TRIVIA	1-01-001	TRUSTFULLY	3-01-001	TUNISIAN		T-WIDE
11-07-011	TRIVIAL	4-04-004	TRUSTING	1-01-001	TUNNARD	8-05-006	TWENTY-ONE
2-02-002	TRIVIALITY	1-01-001	TRUSTINGLY	10-05-005	TUNNEL	1-01-001	TWENTY-ONE-YEAR
1-01-001	TROBLES	7-03-005	TRUSTS	1-01-001	TUNNELED		-OLD
1-01-001	TROELTSCH	3-02-002	TRUSTWORTHY	3-03-003	TUNNELS	1-01-001	TWENTY-PAGE
1-01-001	TROHAN	126-15-078	TRUTH	1-01-001	TUOHY	3-01-002	TWENTY-SECOND
1-01-001	TROIKA	1-01-001	TRUTH-PACKED	1-01-001	TURANDOT	1-01-001	TWENTY-SEVEN
5-04-005	TROLLEY	1-01-001	TRUTH-REVEALING	2-01-001	TURBAN	5-04-005	TWENTY-SIX
1-01-001	TROLLOP	1-01-001	TRUTHFUL	1-01-001	TURBINATES	7-05-006	TWENTY-THREE
1-01-001	TROLLS	5-05-005	TRUTHFULLY	6-02-003	TURBINE	8-06-007	TWENTY-TWO
1-01-001	TROMBONIST	2-02-002	TRUTHFULNESS	1-01-001	TURBINES	2-02-002	TWENTY-YEAR
1-01-001	TROMPE-L'OEIL	4-03-004	TRUTHS	1-01-001	TURBOFAN	74-13-059	TWICE
16-05-006	TROOP	140-15-105	TRY	3-03-003	TURBULENCE	1-01-001	TWICE-A-YEAR
7-03-003	TROOPER	2-01-001	TRYIN	4-02-003	TURBULENT	1-01-001	TWICE-AROUND
6-04-004	TROOPERS	163-15-119	TRYING	3-03-003	TURF	1-01-001	TWIGGED
53-09-027	TROOPS	1-01-001	TSAR	2-01-001	TURIN	1-01-001	TWIGS
1-01-001	TROOPSHIP	2-01-001	TSAR'S	5-03-004	TURK	4-03-003	TWILIGHT
1-01-001	TROOPSHIPS	1-01-001	TSAREVICH	9-05-008	TURKEY	7-05-006	TWIN
1-01-001	TROPEZ	1-01-001	TSARISM	1-01-001	TURKEYS	4-04-004	TWINED
2-01-001	TROPHIES	1-01-001	TSCHILWYK	12-05-006	TURKISH	3-03-003	TWINGE
1-01-001	TROPHO-	1-01-001	TSH**P	5-02-003	TURKS	1-01-001	TWINGES
8-02-005	TROPHY	7-02-003	TSHOMBE	12-06-012	TURMOIL	3-02-002	TWINKLE
3-02-002	TROPIC			233-15-164	TURN	2-02-002	TWINKLING

Freq	Word
12-06-007	TWINS
1-01-001	TWINS'
1-01-001	TWIRLED
3-02-002	TWIRLER
5-03-004	TWIRLING
1-01-001	TWIRLINGLY
1-01-001	TWISE
18-11-016	TWIST
19-08-014	TWISTED
4-02-002	TWISTER
1-01-001	TWISTER-CONERS
11-06-011	TWISTING
6-03-005	TWISTS
1-01-001	TWISTY
3-03-003	TWITCH
4-03-004	TWITCHED
2-02-002	TWITCHING
1-01-001	TWITTERED
1-01-001	TWITTERING
1412-15-429	TWO
1-01-001	TWO-*HEAD
1-01-001	TWO-*STEM
1-01-001	TWO-AND-A-HALF-MILE
1-01-001	TWO-BEDROOM
1-01-001	TWO-BITS'
1-01-001	TWO-BURNER
1-01-001	TWO-BY-FOUR
1-01-001	TWO-BY-FOURS
1-01-001	TWO-CLASS
1-01-001	TWO-COLOR
1-01-001	TWO-COLORED
1-01-001	TWO-COMPONENT
4-03-004	TWO-DAY
5-01-001	TWO-DIGIT
1-01-001	TWO-DIMENSIONAL
1-01-001	TWO-DISC
1-01-001	TWO-FAMILY
1-01-001	TWO-FISTED
2-01-002	TWO-FOLD
1-01-001	TWO-GAME
4-03-004	TWO-HOUR
1-01-001	TWO-INCH
1-01-001	TWO-INCHES
1-01-001	TWO-LANE
1-01-001	TWO-LINE
1-01-001	TWO-MILE
1-01-001	TWO-NOSED
1-01-001	TWO-PART
1-01-001	TWO-RECORD
1-01-001	TWO-ROOM
2-01-001	TWO-RUN
2-02-002	TWO-SEASON
1-01-001	TWO-SEATERS
1-01-001	TWO-STEP
8-05-006	TWO-STORY
2-01-001	TWO-SYSTEM
1-01-001	TWO-TAIL
1-01-001	TWO-TERM
12-06-011	TWO-THIRDS
1-01-001	TWO-TIMED
1-01-001	TWO-TIMING
1-01-001	TWO-TO-THREE
1-01-001	TWO-VALUED
1-01-001	TWO-WAY
1-01-001	TWO-WEEK
1-01-001	TWO-WEEKS
5-03-004	TWO-YEAR
1-01-001	TWO-YEAR-OLD
4-03-004	TWOFOLD
2-02-002	TWOS
1-01-001	TWOSOME
1-01-001	TWOTIMING
1-01-001	TYBURN
1-01-001	TYCOON
1-01-001	TYGARTIS
5-04-004	TYING
2-01-002	TYLER
2-01-001	TYME
200-13-114	TYPE
3-02-003	TYPED
116-10-068	TYPES
1-01-001	TYPESCRIPT
1-01-001	TYPESETTING
10-05-009	TYPEWRITER
1-01-001	TYPEWRITERS
1-01-001	TYPEWRITING
1-01-001	TYPEWRITTEN
2-02-002	TYPHOID
1-01-001	TYPHOON
3-01-001	TYPHUS
65-10-052	TYPICAL
3-01-001	TYPICALITY
16-06-014	TYPICALLY
2-01-002	TYPIFIED
1-01-001	TYPIFY
1-01-001	TYPIFYING
7-05-005	TYPING
1-01-001	TYPOGRAPHIC
3-01-001	TYPOGRAPHY
1-01-001	TYPOLOGY
1-01-001	TYRANNICAL
1-01-001	TYRANNIS
1-01-001	TYRANNIZE
11-07-011	TYRANNY
2-02-002	TYRANT
1-01-001	TYRANTS
3-01-001	TYROSINE
1-01-001	TYSON
91-08-040	U
1-01-001	U**.'S
3-01-001	U**.*M**.*C**.* I**.*A
1-01-001	U**.*M**.*T
45-05-013	U**.*N
2-02-002	U**.*N**.'S
5-01-001	U**.*N**.*F**.* P
1-01-001	U**.*N**.-CHARTERED
145-11-050	U**.*S
3-02-002	U**.*S**.'S
4-02-003	U**.*S**.*A
2-01-002	U**.*S**.*C
5-02-003	U**.*S**.*S**.* R
1-01-001	U**.*S**.*S**.* R**.'S
2-02-002	U**.*S**.*STEEL 'S
1-01-001	U**.*S**.-*SOVIET
1-01-001	U**.N
4-03-004	U**.S
1-01-001	U**DBERMENSCHEN
1-01-001	U*S*N
2-02-002	UBIQUITOUS
6-02-002	UDALL
1-01-001	UDALL'S
1-01-001	UDON
1-01-001	UGH
1-01-001	UGLIER
2-01-001	UGLINESS
7-05-007	UGLY
21-08-015	UH
6-03-005	UH-HUH
5-04-004	UH-UH
1-01-001	UHHU
1-01-001	UHLES
3-03-003	UKRAINIAN
1-01-001	UKRAINIANS
1-01-001	ULANYS
2-01-001	ULBRICHT
7-05-007	ULCER
1-01-001	ULCERATED
1-01-001	ULCERATIONS
1-01-001	ULLMAN
59-13-042	ULTIMATE
23-09-021	ULTIMATELY
3-03-003	ULTIMATUM
1-01-001	ULTRA-EFFICIENT
1-01-001	ULTRA-FAST
1-01-001	ULTRA-HIGH-SPEED
1-01-001	ULTRA-LIBERAL
1-01-001	ULTRA-MODERN
4-03-004	ULTRA-VIOLET
1-01-001	ULTRACENTRIFUGALLY
5-01-001	ULTRACENTRIFUGATION
3-01-002	ULTRACENTRIFUGE
1-01-001	ULTRAMARINE
1-01-001	ULTRAMODERN
8-01-001	ULTRASONIC
1-01-001	ULTRASONICALLY
1-01-001	ULTRAVEHEMENT
14-02-003	ULTRAVIOLET
15-01-001	ULYATE
5-03-004	UM
4-02-002	UMBER
8-04-006	UMBRELLA
3-02-003	UMBRELLAS
1-01-001	UMM
9-07-009	UMPIRE
1-01-001	UMSCHLAGPLATZ
2-02-002	UN
4-01-001	UN*$FUNNY
3-02-002	UN-*AMERICAN
1-01-001	UN-*ENGLISH
3-03-003	UNABASHED
2-02-002	UNABATED
54-13-047	UNABLE
1-01-001	UNABRIDGED
1-01-001	UNACCEPTABLE
3-02-002	UNACCOMPANIED
1-01-001	UNACCOUNTABLE
2-02-002	UNACCOUNTABLY
1-01-001	UNACCUSTOMED
1-01-001	UNACHIEVABLE
1-01-001	UNACHIEVED
1-01-001	UNACKNOWLEDGED
2-02-002	UNACQUAINTED
12-01-001	UNADJUSTED
1-01-001	UNADORNED
1-01-001	UNADULTERATED
3-03-003	UNAFFECTED
4-03-004	UNAFRAID
1-01-001	UNAGGRESSIVE
1-01-001	UNAGI
4-03-004	UNAIDED
1-01-001	UNALIENABLE
3-01-001	UNALLOCABLE
1-01-001	UNALLOYED
1-01-001	UNALTERABLE
1-01-001	UNAM
1-01-001	UNAMBIGUITY
3-02-003	UNAMBIGUOUS
2-01-002	UNAMBIGUOUSLY
1-01-001	UNAMUSED
3-01-001	UNANALYZED
5-03-004	UNANIMITY
5-04-005	UNANIMOUS
11-08-010	UNANIMOUSLY
2-02-002	UNANNOUNCED
1-01-001	UNANSWERED
1-01-001	UNAPPEASABLE
1-01-001	UNAPPEASABLY
1-01-001	UNAPPRECIATED
4-03-003	UNARMED
1-01-001	UNASHAMEDLY
2-02-002	UNASKED
2-02-002	UNASSISTED
1-01-001	UNASTERISKED
2-02-002	UNATTACHED
1-01-001	UNATTAINABLE
2-01-002	UNATTENDED
3-03-003	UNATTRACTIVE
1-01-001	UNAUTHENTIC
2-02-002	UNAUTHORIZED
7-05-005	UNAVAILABLE
1-01-001	UNAVAILING
7-04-005	UNAVOIDABLE
3-02-003	UNAVOIDABLY
13-06-012	UNAWARE
3-03-003	UNAWARENESS
1-01-001	UNBALANCE
3-02-002	UNBALANCED
6-04-006	UNBEARABLE
1-01-001	UNBEARABLY
1-01-001	UNBEKNOWNST
4-03-004	UNBELIEVABLE
1-01-001	UNBELIEVABLY
2-02-002	UNBELIEVING
1-01-001	UNBENT
1-01-001	UNBIDDEN
1-01-001	UNBLEMISHED
2-01-002	UNBLINKINGLY
1-01-001	UNBLUSHING
4-03-004	UNBORN
1-01-001	UNBOUND
1-01-001	UNBOUNDED
5-03-005	UNBREAKABLE
2-01-002	UNBRIDLED
7-05-007	UNBROKEN
1-01-001	UNBURDENED
1-01-001	UNBURNED
1-01-001	UNCALLED
5-04-004	UNCANNY
1-01-001	UNCAP
1-01-001	UNCAS
1-01-001	UNCAUSED
1-01-001	UNCEASING
1-01-001	UNCEASINGLY
1-01-001	UNCERTAIN
2-02-002	UNCERTAINLY
5-05-005	UNCERTAINTIES
17-08-014	UNCERTAINTY
1-01-001	UNCERTIFIED
2-02-002	UNCHALLENGED
1-01-001	UNCHANGEABLE
9-07-009	UNCHANGED
2-02-002	UNCHANGING
4-01-001	UNCHARGED
3-02-002	UNCHARTED
1-01-001	UNCHECKED
1-01-001	UNCHRISTIAN
1-01-001	UNCIRCUMCISION
1-01-001	UNCIVIL
1-01-001	UNCKLE
2-02-002	UNCLAIMED
1-01-001	UNCLASPING
57-11-027	UNCLE
5-04-004	UNCLE'S
4-04-004	UNCLEAN
2-02-002	UNCLEAR
1-01-001	UNCLENCHED
3-03-003	UNCLES
2-02-002	UNCLOUDED
1-01-001	UNCLUTTERED
1-01-001	UNCO-OPERATIVE
1-01-001	UNCOILING
1-01-001	UNCOLORED
1-01-001	UNCOMBABLE
1-01-001	UNCOMFORATBLE
13-08-013	UNCOMFORTABLE
3-02-003	UNCOMFORTABLY
1-01-001	UNCOMFORTED
3-03-003	UNCOMMITTED
8-07-008	UNCOMMON
1-01-001	UNCOMMONLY
1-01-001	UNCOMMUNICATIVE
1-01-001	UNCOMPLAININGLY
5-03-004	UNCOMPROMISING
1-01-001	UNCONCERN
8-07-008	UNCONCERNED
1-01-001	UNCONCERNEDLY
4-03-003	UNCONDITIONAL
2-02-002	UNCONDITIONALLY
1-01-001	UNCONDITIONED
2-02-002	UNCONNECTED
1-01-001	UNCONQUERABLE
1-01-001	UNCONSCIONABLE
30-06-017	UNCONSCIOUS
10-06-009	UNCONSCIOUSLY
2-02-002	UNCONSTITUTIONAL
2-02-002	UNCONTROLLABLE
4-03-004	UNCONTROLLED
3-03-003	UNCONVENTIONAL
2-02-002	UNCONVINCING
2-02-002	UNCOOPERATIVE
2-02-002	UNCORKED
3-01-002	UNCOUNTED
1-01-001	UNCOURAGEOUS
1-01-001	UNCOUSINLY
4-02-004	UNCOVER
7-05-007	UNCOVERED
3-02-003	UNCRITICAL
1-01-001	UNCRITICALLY
1-01-001	UNCTION
1-01-001	UNCURLED
3-02-003	UND
1-01-001	UNDAMAGED
1-01-001	UNDAUNTED
1-01-001	UNDECLARED
1-01-001	UNDECORATED
1-01-001	UNDEDICATED
4-04-004	UNDEFINED
1-01-001	UNDEMOCRATIC
5-03-005	UNDENIABLE
1-01-001	UNDENIABLY
2-02-002	UNDEPENDABLE
4-01-001	UNDEPICTED
707-15-334	UNDER
3-01-001	UNDER-ACHIEVEMENT
1-01-001	UNDER-ACHIEVERS
2-01-001	UNDER-DEVELOPED
1-01-001	UNDERACHIEVERS
1-01-001	UNDERARM
1-01-001	UNDERBEDDING
1-01-001	UNDERBELLY
1-01-001	UNDERBRACING
1-01-001	UNDERBRUSH
1-01-001	UNDERCLASSMAN
1-01-001	UNDERCLOTHES
1-01-001	UNDERCOVER
3-02-002	UNDERCURRENT
2-01-002	UNDERCUT
10-06-010	UNDERDEVELOPED
2-01-001	UNDERDOG
1-01-001	UNDEREDUCATED
4-04-004	UNDERESTIMATE
2-02-002	UNDERESTIMATED
4-03-004	UNDERFOOT
1-01-001	UNDERGIRDING
8-06-007	UNDERGO
2-02-002	UNDERGOES
12-06-011	UNDERGOING
10-07-009	UNDERGONE
11-04-004	UNDERGRADUATE
9-04-005	UNDERGRADUATES
19-10-015	UNDERGROUND
1-01-001	UNDERGROWTH
1-01-001	UNDERHANDED
1-01-001	UNDERHANDEDNESS
1-01-001	UNDERLAY

Code	Word	Code	Word	Code	Word	Code	Word
2-01-001	UNDERLIE	2-02-002	UNEARNED	2-02-002	UNHEARD-OF	3-02-002	UNJUST
1-01-001	UNDERLIES	1-01-001	UNEARTH	2-02-002	UNHEATED	2-02-002	UNJUSTIFIABLE
2-02-002	UNDERLINE	2-02-002	UNEARTHED	2-01-002	UNHEEDED	1-01-001	UNJUSTIFIED
2-02-002	UNDERLINED	1-01-001	UNEASE	1-01-001	UNHEEDING	1-01-001	UNKEMPT
1-01-001	UNDERLING	6-05-006	UNEASILY	1-01-001	UNHESITANT	3-02-003	UNKIND
2-01-002	UNDERLINING	5-03-004	UNEASINESS	3-02-003	UNHESITATINGLY	1-01-001	UNKNOWING
20-06-018	UNDERLYING	22-08-020	UNEASY	1-01-001	UNHINGED	1-01-001	UNKNOWINGLY
8-05-008	UNDERMINE	1-01-001	UNECONOMIC	2-02-002	UNHITCHED	47-14-042	UNKNOWN
2-02-002	UNDERMINED	3-02-003	UNECONOMICAL	1-01-001	UNHOOK	1-01-001	UNKNOWNS
1-01-001	UNDERMINING	1-01-001	UNEDUCATED	3-02-002	UNHURRIED	1-01-001	UNLACED
11-06-009	UNDERNEATH	2-02-002	UNEMOTIONAL	2-02-002	UNHURRIEDLY	1-01-001	UNLACING
1-01-001	UNDERPAID	5-02-004	UNEMPLOYED	1-01-001	UNHURT	1-01-001	UNLAMENTED
1-01-001	UNDERPINNING	16-05-010	UNEMPLOYMENT	1-01-001	UNI-DIRECTIONAL	1-01-001	UNLASHED
1-01-001	UNDERPINS	3-03-003	UNENDING	1-01-001	UNICONER	1-01-001	UNLAUNDERED
1-01-001	UNDERPLAYED	1-01-001	UNENDURABLE	5-01-001	UNIDENTIFIED	1-01-001	UNLAWFUL
3-03-003	UNDERPRIVILEGED	1-01-001	UNENFORCIBLE	1-01-001	UNIDIRECTIONAL	1-01-001	UNLEASH
1-01-001	UNDERRATE	2-02-002	UNENTHUSIASTIC	9-04-005	UNIFICATION	3-03-003	UNLEASHED
1-01-001	UNDERRATED	1-01-001	UNENUNCIATED	1-01-001	UNIFICATIONS	1-01-001	UNLEASHING
1-01-001	UNDERSCORE	1-01-001	UNENVIABLE	11-04-009	UNIFIED	2-01-001	UNLEAVENED
3-03-003	UNDERSCORED	1-01-001	UNENVIED	3-01-001	UNIFIES	101-14-076	UNLESS
3-03-003	UNDERSEA	1-01-001	UNEQUAL	5-01-001	UNIFIL	1-01-001	UNLEVELED
1-01-001	UNDERSECRETARY	1-01-001	UNEQUALED	51-13-032	UNIFORM	1-01-001	UNLICENSED
1-01-001	UNDERSECRETARY'S	1-01-001	UNEQUALLED	7-06-007	UNIFORMED	42-12-040	UNLIKE
3-01-003	UNDERSHIRT	2-01-001	UNEQUALLY	11-04-006	UNIFORMITY	21-12-019	UNLIKELY
5-04-005	UNDERSIDE	5-03-005	UNEQUIVOCALLY	6-04-006	UNIFORMLY	13-06-010	UNLIMITED
1-01-001	UNDERSIZE	2-02-002	UNERRING	14-09-014	UNIFORMS	3-02-002	UNLINED
1-01-001	UNDERSIZED	1-01-001	UNERRINGLY	2-02-002	UNIFY	1-01-001	UNLINKED
137-15-105	UNDERSTAND	6-04-006	UNEVEN	4-03-004	UNIFYING	1-01-001	UNLITERARY
13-09-013	UNDERSTANDABLE	1-01-001	UNEXAMINED	3-02-003	UNILATERAL	7-03-003	UNLOAD
3-03-003	UNDERSTANDABLY	23-08-021	UNEXPECTED	1-01-001	UNILATERALLY	5-05-005	UNLOADED
1-01-001	UNDERSTANDED	11-09-011	UNEXPECTEDLY	2-02-002	UNIMAGINABLE	5-04-004	UNLOADING
121-13-080	UNDERSTANDING	1-01-001	UNEXPENDED	1-01-001	UNIMAGINATIVE	1-01-001	UNLOADS
3-03-003	UNDERSTANDINGLY	1-01-001	UNEXPLAINABLE	2-02-002	UNIMPAIRED	3-03-003	UNLOCK
1-01-001	UNDERSTANDINGS	4-04-004	UNEXPLAINED	2-02-002	UNIMPEACHABLE	12-04-009	UNLOCKED
6-06-006	UNDERSTANDS	4-04-004	UNEXPLORED	1-01-001	UNIMPEACHABLY	1-01-001	UNLOCKING
1-01-001	UNDERSTATED	2-01-002	UNFAILING	9-06-008	UNIMPORTANT	2-02-002	UNLOCKS
4-04-004	UNDERSTATEMENT	2-02-002	UNFAILINGLY	1-01-001	UNIMPOSING	1-01-001	UNLOVELY
1-01-001	UNDERSTATES	13-08-013	UNFAIR	4-03-003	UNIMPRESSED	1-01-001	UNLUCKILY
58-14-055	UNDERSTOOD	2-02-002	UNFAIRLY	2-02-002	UNIMPRESSIVE	2-01-002	UNLUCKY
1-01-001	UNDERSTRUCTURE	1-01-001	UNFAITHFUL	2-02-002	UNIMPROVED	1-01-001	UNMAGNIFIED
13-07-013	UNDERTAKE	1-01-001	UNFALTERINGLY	1-01-001	UNINFLUENCED	1-01-001	UNMALICIOUS
18-06-015	UNDERTAKEN	10-07-009	UNFAMILIAR	4-02-004	UNINHIBITED	1-01-001	UNMANAGEABLE
1-01-001	UNDERTAKER	1-01-001	UNFASTENED	1-01-001	UNINITIATE	1-01-001	UNMANAGEABLY
3-03-003	UNDERTAKES	5-05-005	UNFATHOMABLE	2-02-002	UNINITIATED	1-01-001	UNMANAGED
5-04-005	UNDERTAKING	1-01-001	UNFAVORABLE	1-01-001	UNINJECTABLE	6-04-006	UNMARKED
4-03-003	UNDERTAKINGS	1-01-001	UNFELT	2-01-001	UNINJURED	1-01-001	UNMARRIED
7-07-007	UNDERTOOK	2-02-002	UNFENCED	1-01-001	UNINOMINAL	1-01-001	UNMASKED
1-01-001	UNDERTOW	1-01-001	UNFERTILE	1-01-001	UNINTELLIGIBLE	2-02-002	UNMATCHED
15-08-010	UNDERWATER	1-01-001	UNFERTILIZED	2-02-002	UNINTENDED	1-01-001	UNMATED
3-03-003	UNDERWAY	4-02-004	UNFETTERED	2-02-002	UNINTENTIONALLY	1-01-001	UNMERITORIOUS
3-02-003	UNDERWEAR	2-02-002	UNFINISHED	1-01-001	UNINTERESTED	1-01-001	UNMESHED
2-02-002	UNDERWENT	2-01-001	UNFIRED	1-01-001	UNINTERESTING	1-01-001	UNMETHODICAL
2-01-001	UNDERWOOD	1-01-001	UNFIT	5-05-005	UNINTERRUPTED	1-01-001	UNMINDFUL
1-01-001	UNDERWOOD'S	3-01-001	UNFITTING	1-01-001	UNINTERRUPTEDLY	7-06-007	UNMISTAKABLE
6-05-005	UNDERWORLD	1-01-001	UNFIXED	1-01-001	UNINVITED	5-04-005	UNMISTAKABLY
3-03-003	UNDERWRITE	1-01-001	UNFLAGGING	1-01-001	UNINVOLVED	1-01-001	UNMIXED
1-01-001	UNDERWRITER	1-01-001	UNFLATTERING	182-13-071	UNION	1-01-001	UNMODIFIED
4-03-004	UNDERWRITERS	2-02-002	UNFOLD	2-01-002	UNION'S	1-01-001	UNMOLESTED
2-02-002	UNDERWRITING	4-03-004	UNFOLDED	1-01-001	UNION-INDUSTRY	1-01-001	UNMOTIVATED
1-01-001	UNDESERVED	5-02-005	UNFOLDING	29-06-013	UNIONS	3-03-003	UNMOVED
10-04-008	UNDESIRABLE	1-01-001	UNFOLDMENT	58-13-046	UNIQUE	1-01-001	UNMURMURING
1-01-001	UNDETECTABLE	4-02-002	UNFOLDS	1-01-001	UNIQUE-INGROWN-SCREWEDUP	1-01-001	UNNAMEABLE
1-01-001	UNDETECTED	2-02-002	UNFORESEEN			4-03-004	UNNAMED
2-02-002	UNDETERMINED	3-03-003	UNFORGETTABLE	10-05-009	UNIQUELY	8-03-006	UNNATURAL
4-04-004	UNDEVELOPED	1-01-001	UNFORGIVABLE	5-05-005	UNIQUENESS	1-01-001	UNNATURALLY
1-01-001	UNDID	1-01-001	UNFORMED	3-03-003	UNISON	1-01-001	UNNATURALNESS
1-01-001	UNDIFFERENTIATED	1-01-001	UNFORSEEN	103-11-052	UNIT	3-03-003	UNNECESSARILY
1-01-001	UNDIGESTED	22-10-019	UNFORTUNATE	8-02-003	UNITARIAN	16-11-016	UNNECESSARY
1-01-001	UNDILUTED	33-11-031	UNFORTUNATELY	2-01-002	UNITARIANISM	1-01-001	UNNEEDED
3-03-003	UNDIMINISHED	1-01-001	UNFORTUNATES	2-01-002	UNITARIANS	1-01-001	UNNERVING
1-01-001	UNDIMMED	2-02-002	UNFOUNDED	10-06-009	UNITE	1-01-001	UNNNT
3-02-003	UNDISCIPLINED	6-04-005	UNFRIENDLY	1-01-001	UNITE*(S	4-04-004	UNNOTICED
1-01-001	UNDISCLOSED	1-01-001	UNFROCKING	482-13-153	UNITED	1-01-001	UNNOURISHED
1-01-001	UNDISGUISED	1-01-001	UNFROSTED	1-01-001	UNITIES	1-01-001	UNNUMBERED
1-01-001	UNDISMAYED	2-01-001	UNFROZEN	2-02-002	UNITING	1-01-001	UNO
2-02-002	UNDISPUTED	1-01-001	UNFULFILLED	5-01-001	UNITIZED	1-01-001	UNO'S
1-01-001	UNDISRUPTED	1-01-001	UNFUNNILY	87-10-044	UNITS	3-03-003	UNOBTAINABLE
3-03-003	UNDISTINGUISHED	1-01-001	UNFURLED	71-10-037	UNITY	3-03-003	UNOBTRUSIVE
3-03-003	UNDISTURBED	2-01-002	UNGAINLY	1-01-001	UNIVALENT	2-02-002	UNOBTRUSIVELY
1-01-001	UNDIVIDED	1-01-001	UNGALLANT	45-08-026	UNIVERSAL	3-03-003	UNOCCUPIED
3-03-003	UNDO	1-01-001	UNGAVA	1-01-001	UNIVERSAL-*INTERNATIONAL	5-04-005	UNOFFICIAL
2-02-002	UNDOING	1-01-001	UNGLAMOROUS	1-01-001	UNIVERSALISTIC	1-01-001	UNOFFICIALLY
4-03-003	UNDONE	1-01-001	UNGLAZED	3-02-003	UNIVERSALITY	1-01-001	UNOPENED
24-11-020	UNDOUBTEDLY	1-01-001	UNGLUED	1-01-001	UNIVERSALIZE	2-01-001	UNORIGINALS
1-01-001	UNDREAMED	2-01-001	UNGODLY	6-04-006	UNIVERSALLY	6-05-005	UNORTHODOX
1-01-001	UNDREAMT	1-01-001	UNGOVERNED	1-01-001	UNIVERSALS	1-01-001	UNPACK
2-01-002	UNDRESSED	1-01-001	UNGRACIOUS	71-09-025	UNIVERSE	1-01-001	UNPACKING
3-03-003	UNDRESSING	2-02-002	UNGRATEFUL	32-08-019	UNIVERSITIES	1-01-001	UNPADDED
1-01-001	UNDRINKABLE	1-01-001	UNGRATIFIED	214-13-086	UNIVERSITY	9-04-006	UNPAID
13-08-013	UNDUE	1-01-001	UNGUIDED	10-06-007	UNIVERSITY'S	1-01-001	UNPAINTABLE
1-01-001	UNDULATED	1-01-001	UNHAPPIEST	1-01-001	UNIVERSITY-EDUCATED	4-01-001	UNPAIRED
1-01-001	UNDULATING	9-07-009	UNHAPPILY			2-02-002	UNPARALLELED
6-05-006	UNDULY	6-04-006	UNHAPPINESS	1-01-001	UNIVERSITY-TRAINED	1-01-001	UNPARTISAN
1-01-001	UNDYING	26-09-024	UNHAPPY			2-01-002	UNPATRIOTIC
		1-01-001	UNHARMONIOUS	1-01-001	UNIVERSITY-WIDE	1-01-001	UNPATRONIZING
2-02-002	UNE	4-02-002	UNHEALTHY			1-01-001	UNPAVED
		3-02-002	UNHEARD	1-01-001	UNJACKETED	1-01-001	UNPERCEIVED

1-01-001	UNPERFORMED	5-04-005	UNSEEN	1-01-001	UNVENTILATED	27-10-018	UPWARD
1-01-001	UNPHYSICAL	1-01-001	UNSELF-CONSCIOU	1-01-001	UNWAIVERING	2-01-001	UPWARD-MOBILE
1-01-001	UNPICTURESQUE		S	6-05-006	UNWANTED	6-05-005	UPWARDS
1-01-001	UNPLAGUED	1-01-001	UNSELFCONSCIOUS	2-01-001	UNWARRANTABLE	6-02-002	URANIUM
15-09-014	UNPLEASANT		NESS	4-04-004	UNWARRANTED	2-01-001	URANYL
1-01-001	UNPLEASANTLY	1-01-001	UNSELFISH	1-01-001	UNWAVERINGLY	42-09-022	URBAN
1-01-001	UNPLEASANTNESS	1-01-001	UNSELFISHLY	12-02-002	UNWED	1-01-001	URBAN-FRINGE
1-01-001	UNPLEASED	1-01-001	UNSERVILE	5-05-005	UNWELCOME	1-01-001	URBANA
2-02-002	UNPLOWED	4-03-004	UNSETTLED	2-02-002	UNWHOLESOME	2-01-001	URBANISM
1-01-001	UNPLUMBED	1-01-001	UNSETTLING	7-04-007	UNWILLING	8-02-002	URBANIZATION
6-03-004	UNPOPULAR	1-01-001	UNSHAKABLE	1-01-001	UNWILLINGLY	4-03-004	URBANIZED
11-07-010	UNPRECEDENTED	5-03-005	UNSHAKEABLE	5-03-005	UNWILLINGNESS	1-01-001	URBANO
2-02-002	UNPREDICTABILIT	1-01-001	UNSHARPENED	1-01-001	UNWINDING	1-01-001	UREA
	Y	1-01-001	UNSHAVED	1-01-001	UNWIRE	1-01-001	UREMIA
2-01-001	UNPREDICTABLE	1-01-001	UNSHAVEN	1-01-001	UNWIRED	26-01-001	URETHANE
2-01-002	UNPREDICTABLY	3-02-003	UNSHEATHE	2-01-001	UNWISE	1-01-001	URETHANES
1-01-001	UNPREMEDITATED	1-01-001	UNSHEATHING	2-02-002	UNWISELY	1-01-001	URETHRA
6-06-006	UNPREPARED	1-01-001	UNSHED	1-01-001	UNWITTING	21-10-019	URGE
1-01-001	UNPRETENTIOUS	5-05-005	UNSHELLED	5-05-005	UNWITTINGLY	35-13-031	URGED
1-01-001	UNPROBLEMATIC	1-01-001	UNSHELTERED	1-01-001	UNWOMANLY	1-01-001	URGENCIES
1-01-001	UNPROCURABLE	1-01-001	UNSHIELDED	1-01-001	UNWORKABLE	12-07-011	URGENCY
1-01-001	UNPRODUCTIVE	1-01-001	UNSIGHTLY	21-13-019	UNWORN	1-01-001	URGENT
1-01-001	UNPROFESSIONAL	3-03-003	UNSIGNED	5-04-005	UNWORTHY	6-03-005	URGENTLY
1-01-001	UNPROFITABLE	4-02-002	UNSINKABLE	1-01-001	UNWOUNDED	8-06-007	URGES
1-01-001	UNPROMISING	3-02-002	UNSKILLED	1-01-001	UNWRINKLED	10-06-010	URGING
2-02-002	UNPROTECTED	1-01-001	UNSLOPED	1-01-001	UNYIELDING	2-02-002	URGINGS
1-01-001	UNPROVED	2-01-002	UNSMILING	1895-15-430	UP	1-01-001	URICH
1-01-001	UNPROVOCATIVE	1-01-001	UNSMILINGLY	1-01-001	UP-AND-COMING	1-01-001	URIELITES
3-03-003	UNPUBLISHED	3-02-002	UNSOLD	1-01-001	UP-JUTTING	1-01-001	URINALS
1-01-001	UNPUNISHED	1-01-001	UNSOLDER	1-01-001	UP-PP	2-01-002	URINARY
2-02-002	UNQUALIFIED	3-03-003	UNSOLVED	3-03-003	UP-TO-DATE	1-01-001	URINE
1-01-001	UNQUALIFIEDLY	1-01-001	UNSOPHISTICATED	1-01-001	UPBEAT	2-02-002	URN
1-01-001	UNQUENCHED	5-04-005	UNSPEAKABLE	1-01-001	UPBRINGING	2-02-002	URNS
1-01-001	UNQUESTIONABLE	4-02-003	UNSPECIFIED	1-01-001	UPCOMING	1-01-001	URSULINE
11-07-011	UNQUESTIONABLY	1-01-001	UNSPECTACULAR	1-01-001	UPDATE	1-01-001	URUGUAY
1-01-001	UNQUESTIONINGLY	3-03-003	UNSPOKEN	3-03-003	UPDATED	672-15-233	US
1-01-001	UNQUIET	1-01-001	UNSPRAYED	3-02-003	UPGRADE	8-05-008	USABLE
1-01-001	UNRAVEL	8-04-005	UNSTABLE	1-01-001	UPGRADED	14-04-008	USAGE
1-01-001	UNREADY	3-01-001	UNSTAINED	2-01-002	UPGRADING	3-02-003	USAGES
6-04-004	UNREAL	1-01-001	UNSTAPLED	3-03-003	UPHEAVAL	589-15-261	USE
1-01-001	UNREALISM	1-01-001	UNSTARING	6-04-006	UPHELD	1-01-001	USEABLE
3-03-003	UNREALISTIC	1-01-001	UNSTEADILY	1-01-001	UPHILL	612-15-240	USED
1-01-001	UNREALISTICALLY	2-02-002	UNSTEADY	7-06-007	UPHOLD	58-11-045	USEFUL
2-02-002	UNREALITY	1-01-001	UNSTILTED	1-01-001	UPHOLDERS	1-01-001	USEFULLY
1-01-001	UNREASON	4-01-001	UNSTRESSED	4-02-004	UPHOLDING	11-05-009	USEFULNESS
3-02-003	UNREASONABLE	12-01-001	UNSTRUCTURED	1-01-001	UPHOLDS	17-07-015	USELESS
1-01-001	UNREASONABLY	2-02-002	UNSTRUNG	1-01-001	UPHOLSTERED	3-02-003	USELESSLY
1-01-001	UNREASONING	3-02-003	UNSTUCK	3-02-003	UPHOLSTERY	2-02-002	USELESSNESS
1-01-001	UNREASSURINGLY	1-01-001	UNSTUFFY	1-01-001	UPI).**T**-	4-03-004	USER
2-02-002	UNRECOGNIZABLE	9-05-009	UNSUCCESSFUL	2-01-002	UPI)**T**-	6-03-036	USERS
2-02-002	UNRECOGNIZED	1-01-001	UNSUCCESSFULLY	6-04-006	UPKEEP	59-07-036	USES
5-01-001	UNRECONSTRUCTED	3-03-003	UNSUITABLE	2-01-002	UPLAND	2-02-002	USHER
1-01-001	UNRECOVERABLE	1-01-001	UNSUITABLY	3-02-002	UPLANDS	2-02-002	USHERED
1-01-001	UNREDEEMED	1-01-001	UNSUITED	1-01-001	UPLIFT	145-15-095	USING
1-01-001	UNREELING	3-03-003	UNSUNG	495-15-235	UPON	96-15-077	USUAL
1-01-001	UNREFLECTIVE	1-01-001	UNSUPPORTABLE	2-02-002	UPPED	206-15-137	USUALLY
1-01-001	UNREHEARSED	1-01-001	UNSUPPORTED	72-14-051	UPPER	1-01-001	USURIOUS
7-03-005	UNRELATED	1-01-001	UNSURE	3-01-001	UPPER-	1-01-001	USURP
1-01-001	UNRELEASED	1-01-001	UNSURMOUNTABLE	2-01-001	UPPER-CLASS	1-01-001	USURPED
1-01-001	UNRELENTING	1-01-001	UNSURPASSED	1-01-001	UPPER-LEVEL	6-04-004	UTAH
1-01-001	UNRELIABILITY	1-01-001	UNSUSPECTING	1-01-001	UPPER-LOWER	3-03-003	UTENSILS
4-03-003	UNRELIABLE	3-02-002	UNSYMPATHETIC	1-01-001	UPPER-MIDDLE	3-02-003	UTILITARIAN
4-04-004	UNRELIEVED	1-01-001	UNTCH	2-01-001	UPPER-MIDDLE-	7-04-005	UTILITIES
1-01-001	UNREMARKABLE	1-01-001	UNTEACH	5-02-002	UPPER-MIDDLE-CL	29-07-019	UTILITY
1-01-001	UNREMITTING	1-01-001	UNTELLABLE		ASS	1-01-001	UTILITY-COST
1-01-001	UNREPENTANT	2-02-002	UNTENABLE	1-01-001	UPPERCLASSMEN	9-03-006	UTILIZATION
1-01-001	UNREQUITED	1-01-001	UNTENANTED	1-01-001	UPPERCUT	10-06-010	UTILIZE
1-01-001	UNRESERVEDLY	1-01-001	UNTHAW	3-03-003	UPPERMOST	10-04-008	UTILIZED
2-02-002	UNRESOLVED	3-02-003	UNTHEMATIC	3-01-001	UPPON	4-03-004	UTILIZES
2-02-002	UNRESPONSIVE	1-01-001	UNTHINKABLE	1-01-001	UPRAISED	8-04-007	UTILIZING
5-05-005	UNREST	1-01-001	UNTHINKING	14-08-012	UPRIGHT	7-06-007	UTMOST
3-03-003	UNRESTRICTED	1-01-001	UNTIDINESS	1-01-001	UPRISING	2-01-001	UTO-*AZTECAN
1-01-001	UNRESTRICTEDLY	1-01-001	UNTIDY	2-02-002	UPRISINGS	24-03-004	UTOPIA
1-01-001	UNREVEALING	2-02-002	UNTIE	1-01-001	UPRIVER	21-02-006	UTOPIAN
2-02-002	UNREWARDING	1-01-001	UNTIED	2-02-002	UPROAR	1-01-001	UTOPIANISM
1-01-001	UNRIFLED	461-15-273	UNTIL	1-01-001	UPROARIOUSLY	5-02-003	UTOPIANS
1-01-001	UNRIPE	1-01-001	UNTIMELY	1-01-001	UPROOTED	1-01-001	UTOPIAS
1-01-001	UNROLLED	16-05-009	UNTO	2-01-001	UPS	13-06-011	UTTER
1-01-001	UNROMANTIC	2-02-002	UNTOLD	14-11-014	UPSET	5-03-004	UTTERANCE
1-01-001	UNRUFFLED	9-06-009	UNTOUCHED	3-03-003	UPSETS	1-01-001	UTTERANCES
2-02-002	UNRULY	1-01-001	UNTOWARD	1-01-001	UPSETTING	5-05-005	UTTERED
1-01-001	UNSAFE	1-01-001	UNTRACKED	1-01-001	UPSHOT	2-02-002	UTTERING
1-01-001	UNSAID	1-01-001	UNTRADITIONAL	1-01-001	UPSHOTS	27-12-025	UTTERLY
2-01-001	UNSALTED	8-06-007	UNTRAINED	1-01-001	UPSIDE	1-01-001	UTTERMOST
8-05-007	UNSATISFACTORY	4-03-004	UNTRAMMELED	1-01-001	UPSON	1-01-001	UTTUH
2-01-001	UNSATURATED	1-01-001	UNTREATED	28-09-021	UPSTAIRS	1-01-001	UXBRIDGE
1-01-001	UNSAVORY	2-02-002	UNTRUE	1-01-001	UPSTANDING	31-07-018	V
2-02-002	UNSCATHED	1-01-001	UNTRUSTWORTHINE	1-01-001	UPSTATE	7-04-005	VA
2-02-002	UNSCIENTIFIC		SS	5-03-003	UPSTREAM	1-01-001	VA**DTTERN
1-01-001	UNSCRAMBLE	2-02-002	UNTRUTH	3-03-003	UPSURGE	2-02-002	VACANCIES
1-01-001	UNSCREW	3-02-003	UNUSED	2-02-002	UPSWING	6-04-005	VACANCY
2-02-002	UNSCREWED	63-15-052	UNUSUAL	5-01-003	UPTAKE	11-07-008	VACANT
5-04-005	UNSCRUPULOUS	11-07-011	UNUSUALLY	18-01-001	UPTON	1-01-001	VACATE
1-01-001	UNSEALED	1-01-001	UNUTTERABLY	5-04-004	UPTOWN	4-03-004	VACATED
1-01-001	UNSEASONABLE	2-02-002	UNUTTERED	1-01-001	UPTREND	47-10-019	VACATION
1-01-001	UNSEE	1-01-001	UNVARYING	7-04-005	UPTURN	1-01-001	VACATIONERS
1-01-001	UNSEEMLY	3-02-003	UNVEILED	1-01-001	UPTURNED	3-02-003	VACATIONING

Code	Word	Code	Word	Code	Word	Code	Word
1-01-001	VACATIONLAND	2-01-001	VARANI	2-02-002	VENDORS	53-10-030	VERSION
9-03-004	VACATIONS	3-02-002	VARIABILITY	1-01-001	VENEER	9-04-008	VERSIONS
1-01-001	VACCINATING	36-06-019	VARIABLE	5-05-005	VENERABLE	1-01-001	VERSTANDIG
2-02-002	VACCINATION	1-01-001	VARIABLE-SPEED	2-02-002	VENERATED	1-01-001	VERSTRICHEN
1-01-001	VACCINE	26-03-011	VARIABLES	3-03-003	VENERATION	9-04-006	VERSUS
1-01-001	VACHELL	2-01-001	VARIAN	3-01-001	VENEREAL	1-01-001	VERTEBRAE
1-01-001	VACUOLATED	1-01-001	VARIANCE	6-03-004	VENETIAN	3-01-001	VERTEBRAL
2-01-001	VACUOLIZATION	4-04-004	VARIANT	1-01-001	VENETO	1-01-001	VERTEBRATE
1-01-001	VACUOUS	32-06-018	VARIATION	3-02-003	VENEZUELA	1-01-001	VERTEBRATES
20-09-011	VACUUM	23-08-019	VARIATIONS	2-01-001	VENEZUELAN	19-01-002	VERTEX
1-01-001	VACUUM-	1-01-001	VARICOLORED	10-06-009	VENGEANCE	16-06-011	VERTICAL
2-01-001	VACUUM-FORMED	42-10-034	VARIED	7-02-005	VENICE	1-01-001	VERTICAL-TAKEOFF-AND-LANDING
1-01-001	VACUUMED	1-01-001	VARIEGATED	1-01-001	VENISON	2-02-002	VERTICALLY
2-01-001	VACUUMING	11-04-010	VARIES	2-01-001	VENN	1-01-001	VERTIGO
2-01-002	VADE	8-06-007	VARIETIES	2-02-002	VENOM	4-03-004	VERVE
1-01-001	VADIM	85-12-071	VARIETY	2-02-002	VENOMOUS	796-15-344	VERY
1-01-001	VADSTENA	1-01-001	VARIGRAD	10-07-010	VENT	1-01-001	VESICULAR
2-02-002	VAGABOND	201-15-131	VARIOUS	1-01-001	VENTED	5-01-001	VESOLE
1-01-001	VAGABONDS	5-05-005	VARIOUSLY	1-01-001	VENTI	16-06-010	VESSEL
1-01-001	VAGARIES	1-01-001	VARITINTED	1-01-001	VENTILATED	12-05-009	VESSELS
10-01-001	VAGINA	1-01-001	VARITYPING	1-01-001	VENTILATES	4-03-004	VEST
7-02-002	VAGINAL	4-01-001	VARLAAM	1-01-001	VENTILATING	3-03-003	VESTED
1-01-001	VAGRANT	2-91-001	VARLAAM'S	6-03-005	VENTILATION	2-01-001	VESTIBULE
25-11-024	VAGUE	2-01-001	VARMINT	1-01-001	VENTILATOR	2-02-002	VESTIGE
17-07-016	VAGUELY	1-01-001	VARNER	3-02-002	VENTRICLE	1-01-001	VESTMENTS
1-01-001	VAGUELY-IMAGINED	1-01-001	VARNESSA	1-01-001	VENTRICLES	1-01-001	VESTS
3-03-003	VAGUENESS	1-01-001	VARNISH	4-02-002	VENTS	1-01-001	VESUVIO'S
1-01-001	VAGUEST	2-01-001	VARNISHES	1-01-001	VENTURA	1-01-001	VET
3-01-001	VAIL	1-01-001	VARVISO	19-10-016	VENTURE	27-09-023	VETERAN
10-05-010	VAIN	34-08-028	VARY	5-05-005	VENTURED	1-01-001	VETERAN'S
2-02-002	VAINLY	42-11-035	VARYING	4-04-004	VENTURES	16-06-007	VETERANS
4-01-001	VALE	3-02-002	VASA	1-01-001	VENTURESOME	2-02-002	VETERANS'
1-01-001	VALEDICTORIAN	1-01-001	VASADY	1-01-001	VENTURI	2-01-002	VETERINARIAN
1-01-001	VALENTE	3-01-002	VASCULAR	11-04-005	VENUS	1-01-001	VETERINARIANS
2-02-002	VALENTINE	4-03-003	VASE	1-01-001	VENUSIANS	4-03-003	VETERINARY
1-01-001	VALERIE	11-02-002	VASES	2-02-002	VERA	10-04-007	VETO
3-02-002	VALERY	1-01-001	VASILIEVITCH	1-01-001	VERACIOUS	1-01-001	VETOED
2-01-002	VALET	1-01-001	VASKA	3-03-003	VERACITY	1-01-001	VEVAY
1-01-001	VALEUR	2-01-001	VASORUM	8-02-004	VERANDA	1-01-001	VEX
1-01-001	VALEWE	1-01-001	VASSAL	1-01-001	VERANDAH	2-02-002	VEXED
1-01-001	VALIANT	61-13-054	VAST	1-01-001	VERANDAS	1-01-001	VEXES
1-01-001	VALIANTLY	1-01-001	VASTER	4-03-004	VERB	2-02-002	VEXING
22-06-019	VALID	10-06-010	VASTLY	21-05-017	VERBAL	48-08-017	VIA
2-02-002	VALIDATE	4-04-004	VATICAN	5-04-005	VERBALLY	2-01-001	VIA'S
1-01-001	VALIDATED	5-02-002	VAUDEVILLE	2-01-001	VERBATIM	3-02-002	VIABILITY
1-01-001	VALIDATING	1-01-001	VAUDOIS	3-01-001	VERBENAS	5-03-004	VIABLE
1-01-001	VALIDATION	3-02-002	VAUGHAN	1-01-001	VERBOORT	1-01-001	VIALE
15-07-014	VALIDITY	2-01-001	VAUGHN	1-01-001	VERBOTEN	2-01-001	VIALL
1-01-001	VALIDLY	2-02-002	VAULT	7-04-005	VERBS	1-01-001	VIAREGGIO
1-01-001	VALLE	3-03-003	VAULTING	1-01-001	VERDANT	1-01-001	VIATOR
1-01-001	VALLEE	6-01-001	VAULTS	3-02-002	VERDI	1-01-001	VIBES
73-11-034	VALLEY	1-01-001	VEAL	2-02-002	VERDI'S	2-02-002	VIBRANCY
1-01-001	VALLEY'S	1-01-001	VEBLEN	14-02-004	VERDICT	6-04-006	VIBRANT
5-04-004	VALLEYS	2-01-001	VEC*TROL	1-01-001	VERE	1-01-001	VIBRATED
1-01-001	VALLFART	2-01-001	VEC*TROL'S	2-02-002	VERGE	1-01-001	VIBRATING
1-01-001	VALMET	8-02-002	VECCHIO	1-01-001	VERGES	5-03-005	VIBRATION
1-01-001	VALOIS	19-02-004	VECTOR	1-01-001	VERGESSEN	1-01-001	VIBRATO
1-01-001	VALOR	7-01-004	VECTORS	1-01-001	VERICT	1-01-001	VIBRIONIC
45-13-039	VALUABLE	1-01-001	VEECK'S	1-01-001	VERIDICAL	4-03-003	VIC
7-05-005	VALUATION	2-01-002	VEER	1-01-001	VERIE	1-01-001	VIC'S
2-02-002	VALUATIONS	3-02-003	VEERED	4-03-004	VERIFICATION	4-02-004	VICAR
200-12-101	VALUE	2-02-002	VEERING	6-03-003	VERIFIED	2-02-002	VICARIOUS
1-01-001	VALUE-JUDGMENTS	1-01-001	VEERS	5-04-005	VERIFY	41-09-028	VICE
1-01-001	VALUE-ORIENTATIONS	5-03-005	VEGAS	1-01-001	VERISIMILITUDE	3-02-003	VICE-*PRESIDENT
1-01-001	VALUE-PROBLEMS	10-05-009	VEGETABLE	4-04-004	VERITABLE	1-01-001	VICE-CHAIRMAN
1-01-001	VALUE-SYSTEM	16-05-007	VEGETABLES	1-01-001	VERITY	1-01-001	VICE-CHANCELLOR
14-06-010	VALUED	1-01-001	VEGETARIAN	2-01-001	VERLOOP	11-04-006	VICE-PRESIDENT
1-01-001	VALUELESS	3-03-003	VEGETATION	1-01-001	VERLOOP'S	1-01-001	VICE-PRESIDENTS
186-12-064	VALUES	3-03-003	VEHEMENCE	1-01-001	VERMEERSCH	1-01-001	VICE-REGENT
3-03-003	VALVE	2-02-002	VEHEMENT	1-01-001	VERMEIL	1-01-001	VICELIKE
4-02-004	VALVES	1-01-001	VEHEMENTLY	7-01-001	VERMEJO	2-01-001	VICENZA
1-01-001	VAMP	35-09-019	VEHICLE	3-03-003	VERMILION	1-01-001	VICEROY
1-01-001	VAMPIRES	53-09-016	VEHICLES	21-07-010	VERMONT	5-04-005	VICES
32-10-022	VAN	1-01-001	VEHICULAR	2-02-002	VERMONT'S	1-01-001	VICHY
1-01-001	VANCE'S	8-07-007	VEIL	1-01-001	VERMOUTH	6-05-006	VICINITY
1-01-001	VANDALISM	6-03-005	VEILED	1-01-001	VERN	17-06-016	VICIOUS
1-01-001	VANDALS	1-01-001	VEILING	2-02-002	VERNACULAR	2-02-002	VICIOUSNESS
1-01-001	VANDERVOORT	2-02-002	VEILS	1-01-001	VERNAL	1-01-001	VICISSITUDES
6-02-002	VANDIVER	3-01-001	VEIN	3-01-001	VERNAVA	1-01-001	VICKERS
1-01-001	VANDRINGSAR	1-01-001	VEINED	1-01-001	VERNE	3-02-002	VICKERY
3-03-003	VANGUARD	2-02-002	VEINING	1-01-001	VERNER	3-03-003	VICKSBURG
1-01-001	VANILLA	6-05-006	VEINS	2-01-001	VERNIER	3-01-001	VICKY
5-04-005	VANISH	1-01-001	VELASQUEZ	21-05-009	VERNON	1-01-001	VICOLO
15-08-013	VANISHED	1-01-001	VELDT	3-01-001	VERNON'S	27-08-023	VICTIM
1-01-001	VANISHES	1-01-001	VELLUM	1-01-001	VERNOR	4-04-004	VICTIM'S
4-03-004	VANISHING	1-01-001	VELOCITER	2-01-001	VERO	1-01-001	VICTIMIZE
1-01-001	VANITIES	6-02-003	VELOCITIES	1-01-001	VERONICA	2-02-002	VICTIMIZED
7-06-007	VANITY	26-06-013	VELOCITY	1-01-001	VERPLANCK'S	19-08-016	VICTIMS
6-05-006	VANTAGE	1-01-001	VELON	2-01-001	VERREAU	23-06-013	VICTOR
1-01-001	VANTAGE-POINTS	1-01-001	VELOUR	1-01-001	VERRONE	1-01-001	VICTOR'S
12-03-004	VAPOR	1-01-001	VELOURS	6-03-005	VERSA	1-01-001	VICTOR-*BUTLER
3-01-001	VAPOR-PRESSURE	4-03-004	VELVET	2-01-001	VERSAILLES	8-03-003	VICTORIA
1-01-001	VAPORIZATION	3-02-002	VELVETY	3-03-003	VERSATILE	1-01-001	VICTORIA'S
1-01-001	VAQUERO	1-01-001	VENABLE	4-02-003	VERSATILITY	8-05-008	VICTORIAN
1-01-001	VAR	6-02-002	VENDING	28-06-013	VERSE	1-01-001	VICTORIANS
		1-01-001	VENDOME	2-02-002	VERSED		
		1-01-001	VENDOR	9-05-008	VERSES		

Code	Word
7-04-006	VICTORIES
1-01-001	VICTORIOUS
1-01-001	VICTORIOUSLY
61-11-034	VICTORY
1-01-001	VICTROLA
1-01-001	VICTUALS
1-01-001	VIDA
1-01-001	VIDAL
1-01-001	VIDAL'S
2-02-002	VIDEO
1-01-001	VIED
1-01-001	VIELLEICHT
22-07-012	VIENNA
1-01-001	VIENNA'S
1-01-001	VIENNE
1-01-001	VIENNESE
1-01-001	VIENOT
7-02-002	VIENTIANE
1-01-001	VIES
16-03-007	VIET
3-01-001	VIETH
3-03-003	VIETNAM
6-02-004	VIETNAMESE
2-02-002	VIEUX
186-14-127	VIEW
25-10-023	VIEWED
4-03-004	VIEWER
3-02-003	VIEWERS
10-05-007	VIEWING
2-01-001	VIEWLESS
16-06-010	VIEWPOINT
3-02-002	VIEWPOINTS
51-09-036	VIEWS
1-01-001	VIGIL
4-03-003	VIGILANCE
2-02-002	VIGILANT
1-01-001	VIGILANTISM
1-01-001	VIGNETTE
14-09-013	VIGOR
29-09-028	VIGOROUS
13-07-012	VIGOROUSLY
1-01-001	VIGREUX
3-01-001	VIKINGS
1-01-001	VIKULOV
1-01-001	VILAS
5-04-005	VILE
1-01-001	VILIFYING
6-03-005	VILLA
72-13-045	VILLAGE
1-01-001	VILLAGER
1-01-001	VILLAGERS
12-05-009	VILLAGES
3-03-003	VILLAIN
1-01-001	VILLAINOUS
4-03-004	VILLAINS
11-01-001	VINCE
19-06-011	VINCENT
1-01-001	VINDICATE
3-03-003	VINDICATED
4-03-004	VINDICATION
2-02-002	VINDICTIVE
4-04-004	VINE
1-01-001	VINE-CRISSCROSS ED
1-01-001	VINE-EMBOWERED
1-01-001	VINE-SHADED
9-03-004	VINEGAR
8-05-007	VINES
2-02-002	VINEYARD
5-02-003	VINEYARDS
1-01-001	VINNICUM
1-01-001	VINOGRADOFF
1-01-001	VINSON
3-02-003	VINTAGE
1-01-001	VINTNER
4-02-002	VINYL
1-01-001	VIOLN
11-01-001	VIOLA
4-01-001	VIOLA'S
7-04-007	VIOLATE
4-03-004	VIOLATED
2-02-002	VIOLATES
4-04-004	VIOLATING
17-07-014	VIOLATION
3-02-003	VIOLATIONS
46-09-030	VIOLENCE
33-12-029	VIOLENT
12-07-012	VIOLENTLY
7-02-003	VIOLET
2-02-002	VIOLETS
11-03-008	VIOLIN
4-02-003	VIOLINIST
1-01-001	VIOLINISTS
1-01-001	VIOLINS
1-01-001	VIPHAKONE
2-01-001	VIRDON
2-02-002	VIRGIL
1-01-001	VIRGILIA
35-10-017	VIRGIN
75-11-031	VIRGINIA
3-02-002	VIRGINIA'S
4-02-003	VIRGINIAN
1-01-001	VIRGINIANS
4-02-002	VIRGINITY
4-04-004	VIRILE
3-02-003	VIRILITY
1-01-001	VIRSALADZE
5-03-005	VIRTUAL
41-10-033	VIRTUALLY
30-09-021	VIRTUE
15-07-014	VIRTUES
1-01-001	VIRTUOSI
1-01-001	VIRTUOSITY
3-02-003	VIRTUOSO
6-04-005	VIRTUOUS
3-03-003	VIRULENCE
1-01-001	VIRULENT
13-04-005	VIRUS
2-01-002	VIS-A-VIS
5-02-002	VISA
2-02-002	VISAGE
2-02-002	VISCERA
4-01-002	VISCERAL
4-01-002	VISCOELASTIC
3-01-001	VISCOELASTICITY
1-01-001	VISCOMETER
10-02-003	VISCOSITY
3-02-002	VISCOUNT
1-01-001	VISCOUS
1-01-001	VISE
1-01-001	VISELIKE
5-03-005	VISIBILITY
34-11-029	VISIBLE
6-06-006	VISIBLY
1-01-001	VISIGOTHS
56-13-038	VISION
7-03-007	VISIONS
109-15-078	VISIT
2-01-001	VISITATION
1-01-001	VISITATIONS
41-13-035	VISITED
36-13-034	VISITING
13-08-013	VISITOR
36-13-029	VISITORS
17-06-011	VISITS
1-01-001	VISRHANIK
3-02-003	VISTA
3-02-003	VISTAS
40-08-014	VISUAL
1-01-001	VISUALIZATION
3-03-003	VISUALIZE
2-02-002	VISUALIZED
1-01-001	VISUALIZES
4-03-004	VISUALLY
5-01-002	VITA
56-11-043	VITAL
17-09-017	VITALITY
9-07-009	VITALLY
2-02-002	VITALS
5-04-004	VITAMIN
1-01-001	VITAMIN-AND-IRO N
10-05-006	VITAMINS
1-01-001	VITIATED
1-01-001	VITIATES
1-01-001	VITRIOL
2-02-002	VITRIOLIC
4-01-002	VITRO
2-01-001	VITTORIO
1-01-001	VITUS
1-01-001	VIVA
3-03-003	VIVACIOUS
2-02-002	VIVACITY
1-01-001	VIVALDI
1-01-001	VIVE
11-01-001	VIVIAN
1-01-001	VIVIAN'S
25-08-022	VIVID
9-04-006	VIVIDLY
1-01-001	VIVIDNESS
1-01-001	VIVIER
2-02-002	VIVIFIED
1-01-001	VIVIFY
4-01-002	VIVO
1-01-001	VIYELLA
1-01-001	VIZ
1-01-001	VLADILEN
1-01-001	VOCABULARIANISM
2-02-002	VOCABULARIES
13-06-010	VOCABULARY
14-07-009	VOCAL
1-01-001	VOCALIC
1-01-001	VOCALISM
2-02-002	VOCALIST
2-01-002	VOCALISTS
1-01-001	VOCALIZATION
1-01-001	VOCALIZE
1-01-001	VOCALLY
1-01-001	VOCALS
3-03-003	VOCATION
77-06-011	VOCATIONAL
2-01-001	VOCATIONAL-ADVA NCEMENT
1-01-001	VOCATIONALLY
1-01-001	VOCE
3-02-003	VOCIFEROUS
1-01-001	VOCIFEROUSLY
1-01-001	VOCIFEROUSNESS
2-01-002	VOEGELIN
6-04-006	VOGUE
226-15-130	VOICE
1-01-001	VOICE'S
5-04-005	VOICED
1-01-001	VOICELESS
38-10-031	VOICES
10-06-008	VOID
1-01-001	VOIDS
1-01-001	VOITURE
2-01-002	VOL
1-01-001	VOLARE
5-02-003	VOLATILE
1-01-001	VOLATILIZATION
2-01-002	VOLCANIC
2-02-002	VOLCANO
1-01-001	VOLCANOS
1-01-001	VOLENS
2-02-002	VOLITION
1-01-001	VOLKENSTEIN
1-01-001	VOLKER
1-01-001	VOLKSGEIST
1-01-001	VOLKSWAGENS
6-05-005	VOLLEY
2-01-001	VOLLEY-BALL
1-01-001	VOLLEYBALL
1-01-001	VOLNEY
2-01-001	VOLSTEAD
1-01-001	VOLTA
1-01-001	VOLTA'S
16-03-006	VOLTAGE
4-01-002	VOLTAGES
7-01-001	VOLTAIC
9-02-002	VOLTAIRE
2-01-001	VOLTAIRE'S
1-01-001	VOLTMETER
1-01-001	VOLTS
2-02-002	VOLUBLE
135-11-049	VOLUME
44-11-023	VOLUMES
2-01-001	VOLUMETRIC
1-01-001	VOLUMETRICALLY
3-03-003	VOLUMINOUS
9-05-009	VOLUNTARILY
22-06-016	VOLUNTARY
1-01-001	VOLUNTARY-CONTR OL
9-06-008	VOLUNTEER
5-05-005	VOLUNTEERED
2-01-001	VOLUNTEERING
29-08-017	VOLUNTEERS
3-02-002	VOLUPTUOUS
1-01-001	VOM
1-01-001	VOMICA
3-03-003	VOMITING
9-03-005	VON
2-01-001	VONNEGUT'S
2-02-002	VOODOO
1-01-001	VOORHEES
1-01-001	VOPOS
1-01-001	VORACIOUSLY
1-01-001	VOROSHILOV
1-01-001	VORTEX
1-01-001	VOS
75-09-037	VOTE
27-08-022	VOTED
4-03-004	VOTER
20-04-014	VOTERS
20-07-015	VOTES
30-07-017	VOTING
2-02-002	VOTIVE
1-01-001	VOUCHERS
1-01-001	VOUCHING
1-01-001	VOUCHSAFES
1-01-001	VOUILLEMONT
1-01-001	VOULEZ
1-01-001	VOUME
2-02-002	VOUS
2-02-002	VOW
5-04-005	VOWED
7-02-002	VOWEL
1-01-001	VOWEL-*LENGTH
3-02-002	VOWELS
2-02-002	VOWING
5-03-003	VOWS
17-04-007	VOYAGE
1-01-001	VOYAGER
1-01-001	VOYAGES
4-02-003	VOYAGEURS
2-01-001	VP
1-01-001	VRAI
1-01-001	VRILIUM
1-01-001	VROMAN
16-07-011	VS
10-02-002	VUE
1-01-001	VUHRANDUH
1-01-001	VULCANIZED
7-05-007	VULGAR
7-02-002	VULNERABILITY
14-09-012	VULNERABLE
1-01-001	VULPINE
4-03-003	VULTURE
1-01-001	VULTURELIKE
1-01-001	VULTURIDAE
3-03-003	VYING
84-11-056	W
1-01-001	W**.'S
1-01-001	W**.*G
1-01-001	W**.*H
1-01-001	W**.*M
1-01-001	W**.*R
1-01-001	W**U,
1-01-001	W-I-D-E
1-01-001	WAAL'S
4-02-002	WABASH
1-01-001	WACKER
1-01-001	WACKERS'
1-01-001	WACKLIN
1-01-001	WACKY
5-01-001	WACO
2-02-002	WADDED
15-02-002	WADDELL
2-02-002	WADE
4-01-001	WADE-*EVANS
2-01-002	WADED
1-01-001	WADS
1-01-001	WAFFLE-PATTERN
1-01-001	WAFFLES
56-07-011	WAGE
1-01-001	WAGE-EARNING
5-01-001	WAGE-PRICE
1-01-001	WAGE-RATE
1-01-001	WAGE-RATES
1-01-001	WAGE-SETTER
7-06-007	WAGED
3-02-002	WAGER
42-09-017	WAGES
2-02-002	WAGGED
1-01-001	WAGGIN
2-02-002	WAGGING
1-01-001	WAGGLED
1-01-001	WAGGLING
21-06-009	WAGNER
2-02-002	WAGNER'S
9-01-001	WAGNER-*PEYSER
55-07-025	WAGON
17-07-010	WAGONS
1-01-001	WAHTAHM
3-02-003	WAIL
1-01-001	WAILBRI
3-03-003	WAILED
5-05-005	WAILING
2-01-001	WAILS
1-01-001	WAINSCOTED
11-06-010	WAIST
1-01-001	WAIST-*HIGH
1-01-001	WAIST-LENGTH
1-01-001	WAISTCOAT
94-12-062	WAIT
1-01-001	WAITE
70-09-055	WAITED
10-02-004	WAITER
5-02-004	WAITERS
1-01-001	WAITIN
110-15-082	WAITING
2-02-002	WAITRESS
1-01-001	WAITRESSES
2-02-002	WAITS
2-02-002	WAIVE
1-01-001	WAIVED
23-11-019	WAKE
2-02-002	WAKED
5-02-002	WAKEFUL
3-01-001	WAKEFULNESS
1-01-001	WAKENED
1-01-001	WAKENING
2-02-002	WAKES
11-08-010	WAKING
1-01-001	WALBRIDGE

Code	Word
1-01-001	WALCOTT
1-01-001	WALDENSIAN
2-02-002	WALDO
2-01-002	WALDORF-*ASTORIA
10-06-006	WALES
1-01-001	WALES'
1-01-001	WALFORD
5-01-001	WALITZEE
100-12-066	WALK
1-01-001	WALK-TO
1-01-001	WALK-UP
1-01-001	WALK-WAY
159-13-092	WALKED
17-05-010	WALKER
1-01-001	WALKERS
1-01-001	WALKIN
54-11-047	WALKING
1-01-001	WALKOUT
1-01-001	WALKOVER
13-06-012	WALKS
1-01-001	WALKWAYS
160-14-087	WALL
1-01-001	WALL-*TEX
1-01-001	WALL-FLOWERS
1-01-001	WALL-STABILIZED
1-01-001	WALL-SWITCH
2-02-002	WALL-TO-WALL
6-04-005	WALLACE
1-01-001	WALLBOARD
1-01-001	WALLE
1-01-001	WALLED
2-01-001	WALLENSTEIN
6-05-005	WALLET
1-01-001	WALLINGFORD
1-01-001	WALLOP
1-01-001	WALLOPED
1-01-001	WALLOPING
1-01-001	WALLOW
1-01-001	WALLOWED
1-01-001	WALLOWING
7-02-004	WALLPAPER
1-01-001	WALLPAPERS
70-13-046	WALLS
25-03-003	WALLY
3-01-001	WALLY'S
11-03-005	WALNUT
5-03-004	WALNUTS
1-01-001	WALPOLE
1-01-001	WALRUS
2-02-002	WALSH
1-01-001	WALSH'S
5-04-004	WALT
40-09-028	WALTER
2-02-002	WALTER'S
2-02-003	WALTERS
1-01-001	WALTHAM
9-01-001	WALTON
1-01-001	WALTZ
2-02-002	WAN
1-01-001	WAND
8-06-008	WANDER
2-01-001	WANDER-*YEARS
8-05-008	WANDERED
1-01-001	WANDERER
1-01-001	WANDERERS
7-06-007	WANDERING
3-02-003	WANDERINGS
1-01-001	WANDERJAHR
2-02-002	WANDERS
2-01-002	WANED
1-01-001	WANGEMANS
2-01-001	WANGENHEIM
1-01-001	WANGLED
2-02-002	WANING
5-02-003	WANNA
1-01-001	WANSEE
1-01-001	WANSLEY
329-15-173	WANT
1-01-001	WANTA
226-14-129	WANTED
16-08-015	WANTING
1-01-001	WANTING-TO-BE-ALONE
3-03-003	WANTON
71-15-058	WANTS
1-01-001	WAPPINGER
64-15-165	WAR
3-03-003	WAR'S
1-01-001	WAR-DIRTY
2-02-002	WAR-RIDDEN
1-01-001	WAR-TIME
1-01-001	WARBLING
25-06-010	WARD
1-01-001	WARD'S
1-01-001	WARD-HEELERS
1-01-001	WARD-PERSONNEL
4-02-002	WARDEN
2-01-001	WARDENS
8-04-006	WARDROBE
1-01-001	WARDROOM
3-02-002	WARDS
1-01-001	WARE
4-04-004	WAREHOUSE
1-01-001	WAREHOUSEMAN'S
4-02-003	WAREHOUSES
1-01-001	WAREHOUSING
1-01-001	WARES
43-07-024	WARFARE
1-01-001	WARFIELD
1-01-001	WARFRONT
2-02-002	WARHEAD
2-02-002	WARILY
1-01-001	WARLESS
5-05-005	WARLIKE
67-14-055	WARM
1-01-001	WARM-BLOODED
1-01-001	WARM-TONED
10-06-010	WARM-UP
1-01-001	WARMED
4-03-003	WARMED-OVER
1-01-001	WARMER
9-06-008	WARMHEARTED
1-01-001	WARMISH
8-04-008	WARMLY
1-01-001	WARMONGERING
1-01-001	WARMS
28-12-025	WARMTH
1-01-001	WARMUP
11-07-010	WARN
22-08-016	WARNED
1-01-001	WARNER
44-11-030	WARNING
1-01-001	WARNINGLY
9-05-008	WARNINGS
3-03-003	WARNS
4-01-001	WARP
3-02-003	WARPED
4-01-002	WARPING
20-06-019	WARRANT
3-02-003	WARRANTED
5-03-003	WARRANTS
1-01-001	WARRANTY
51-07-020	WARREN
1-01-001	WARREN'S
1-01-001	WARRENTON
1-01-001	WARRING
5-02-003	WARRIOR
7-02-002	WARRIORS
26-10-023	WARS
10-02-003	WARSAW
37-09-019	WARSAW'S
2-02-002	WARSHIPS
11-02-002	WART
1-01-001	WART-HOG
6-04-006	WARTIME
1-01-001	WARTORN
5-04-004	WARTS
1-01-001	WARTY
21-05-008	WARWICK
1-01-001	WARWICKSHIRE
7-06-007	WARY
1-01-001	WARYS
9816-15-466	WAS
37-09-019	WASH
1-01-001	WASH-OUTS
1-01-001	WASH-UP
1-01-001	WASHBASIN
1-01-001	WASHBOARD
1-01-001	WASHBOWL
35-08-021	WASHED
1-01-001	WASHED-OUT
5-01-001	WASHER
2-02-002	WASHES
44-08-015	WASHING
2-01-001	WASHINGS
206-11-089	WASHINGTON
7-05-007	WASHINGTON'S
1-01-001	WASHINGTON-*ALEXANDRIA
1-01-001	WASHINGTON-*OREGON
1-01-001	WASHIZU
1-01-001	WASHIZU'S
1-01-001	WASHOE
154-13-083	WASN'T
2-01-001	WASP
3-01-001	WASPISH
1-01-001	WASPISHLY
1-01-001	WASSON
1-01-001	WASTAGE
35-09-028	WASTE
2-01-001	WASTEBASKET
16-08-015	WASTED
7-05-006	WASTEFUL
3-03-003	WASTELAND
6-04-004	WASTES
2-01-001	WASTEWATER
5-04-005	WASTING
1-01-001	WASTREL
81-13-068	WATCH
1-01-001	WATCH-SPRING
3-03-003	WATCHDOG
81-13-063	WATCHED
2-02-002	WATCHERS
4-04-004	WATCHES
2-01-002	WATCHFUL
76-13-061	WATCHING
1-01-001	WATCHINGS
1-01-001	WATCHMAKER
2-02-002	WATCHMEN
442-14-134	WATER
5-05-005	WATER'S
1-01-001	WATER-BALANCE
1-01-001	WATER-COOLED
1-01-001	WATER-FILLED
1-01-001	WATER-HOLDING
1-01-001	WATER-LINE
1-01-001	WATER-PROOF
1-01-001	WATER-SKI
2-02-002	WATER-SOLUBLE
1-01-001	WATER-USE
1-01-001	WATER-WASHED
1-01-001	WATERBURY
12-01-001	WATERCOLOR
2-01-001	WATERCOLORIST
2-01-001	WATERCOLORISTS
3-01-001	WATERCOLORS
7-04-007	WATERED
2-02-002	WATERFALL
1-01-001	WATERFALLS
1-01-001	WATERFLOWS
10-07-008	WATERFRONT
4-03-004	WATERING
1-01-001	WATERLINE
1-01-001	WATERLOO
1-01-001	WATERMELON
2-02-002	WATERPROOF
1-01-001	WATERPROOFING
42-10-031	WATERS
3-02-002	WATERSHED
4-02-002	WATERSHEDS
1-01-001	WATERSIDE
1-01-001	WATERSKIING
2-02-002	WATERWAY
3-02-003	WATERWAYS
3-03-003	WATERY
1-01-001	WATLING
45-04-006	WATSON
5-02-002	WATSON'S
1-01-001	WATSON-*WATT
1-01-001	WATSON-*WATT'S
1-01-001	WATSON-WATT'S
2-01-001	WATT
1-01-001	WATTENBERG
1-01-001	WATTERSON
2-01-001	WATTLES
1-01-001	WAVE
2-01-001	WAVE-LENGTH
1-01-001	WAVE-PARTICLE
1-01-001	WAVE-SETTING
1-01-001	WAVE-TRAVEL
16-09-016	WAVED
1-01-001	WAVELAND
4-02-002	WAVELENGTH
6-02-002	WAVELENGTHS
3-03-003	WAVER
1-01-001	WAVERS
51-08-017	WAVES
13-06-013	WAVING
2-01-002	WAVY
1-01-001	WAVY-HAIRED
14-06-008	WAX
4-04-004	WAXED
1-01-001	WAXEN
1-01-001	WAXING
1-01-001	WAXWORKS
2-02-002	WAXY
909-15-363	WAY
1-01-001	WAY'S
1-01-001	WAY-OUT
1-01-001	WAYLAID
1-01-001	WAYMOUTH
12-04-009	WAYNE
128-15-104	WAYS
2-02-002	WAYSIDE
3-03-003	WAYWARD
2653-15-364	WE
32-08-018	WE'D
64-10-038	WE'LL
61-11-046	WE'RE
1-01-001	WE'UNS
34-11-027	WE'VE
32-11-023	WEAK
7-05-007	WEAKEN
6-06-006	WEAKENED
6-03-005	WEAKENING
1-01-001	WEAKENS
8-06-007	WEAKER
3-03-003	WEAKEST
46-12-027	WEAKNESS
6-05-005	WEAKNESSES
22-08-017	WEALTH
1-01-001	WEALTHIEST
12-06-009	WEALTHY
1-01-001	WEANED
2-02-002	WEANING
42-12-028	WEAPON
1-01-001	WEAPONRY
61-12-035	WEAPONS
36-14-032	WEAR
1-01-001	WEARIED
7-05-007	WEARILY
1-01-001	WEARIN
2-01-002	WEARINESS
47-11-040	WEARING
2-02-002	WEARISOME
5-05-005	WEARS
17-09-016	WEARY
2-02-002	WEARYING
1-01-001	WEASEL
1-01-001	WEASEL-WORDED
69-11-053	WEATHER
2-01-001	WEATHER-RESISTANT
1-01-001	WEATHER-ROYAL
1-01-001	WEATHERBEATEN
2-01-001	WEATHERFORD
2-01-001	WEATHERING
3-02-003	WEATHERPROOF
1-01-001	WEATHERS
1-01-001	WEATHERSTRIP
4-02-004	WEAVE
1-01-001	WEAVER
4-01-003	WEAVES
2-01-001	WEAVING
5-02-003	WEB
6-04-005	WEBB
1-01-001	WEBBER
2-02-002	WEBER
5-03-005	WEBSTER
1-01-001	WEBSTER'S
2-01-001	WEBSTERVILLE
1-01-001	WECHSLER
2-01-002	WED
4-03-004	WEDDED
32-09-021	WEDDING
2-02-002	WEDDINGS
4-03-004	WEDGE
2-02-002	WEDGE-SHAPED
2-02-002	WEDGED
2-01-002	WEDLOCK
35-09-027	WEDNESDAY
1-01-001	WEDNESDAY'S
1-01-001	WEDNESDAYS
5-03-005	WEE
1-01-001	WEED
1-01-001	WEEDE
1-01-001	WEEDED
5-04-005	WEEDS
275-15-136	WEEK
8-03-007	WEEK'S
6-05-006	WEEK-END
2-01-001	WEEK-ENDS
3-02-002	WEEK-LONG
1-01-001	WEEK-OLD
2-02-002	WEEKDAY
27-08-021	WEEKEND
7-04-006	WEEKENDS
3-02-002	WEEKLIES
24-12-019	WEEKLY
141-13-096	WEEKS
2-02-002	WEEKS'
1-01-001	WEEMS'S
14-07-014	WEEP
8-06-007	WEEPING
1-01-001	WEGENER
2-01-001	WEI
6-01-001	WEIDER
1-01-001	WEIDMAN
4-01-001	WEIGAND
2-01-001	WEIGEL'S
4-04-004	WEIGH
16-06-012	WEIGHED
9-04-008	WEIGHING

Freq	Word
4-03-003	WEIGHS
91-11-053	WEIGHT
1-01-001	WEIGHT-HEIGHT
4-03-004	WEIGHTED
1-01-001	WEIGHTING
2-02-002	WEIGHTLESSNESS
11-03-008	WEIGHTS
4-04-004	WEIGHTY
1-01-001	WEIGLE
1-01-001	WEIL
1-01-001	WEINBERG
2-01-001	WEINSTEIN
1-01-001	WEINSTEIN'S
2-02-002	WEIR
10-06-007	WEIRD
1-01-001	WEIRDLY
1-01-001	WEIRDY
1-01-001	WEIRS
1-01-001	WEISS
1-01-001	WEISSMAN
1-01-001	WEISSMULLER
1-01-001	WELBORN
14-01-001	WELCH
6-01-001	WELCH'S
50-13-040	WELCOME
12-07-011	WELCOMED
1-01-001	WELCOMES
5-04-005	WELCOMING
4-02-002	WELD
3-03-003	WELDED
2-02-002	WELDING
1-01-001	WELDON
2-01-001	WELDWOOD
53-08-037	WELFARE
897-15-383	WELL
2-02-002	WELL'S
2-02-002	WELL-ADJUSTED
1-01-001	WELL-ADMINISTERED
1-01-001	WELL-ARMED
1-01-001	WELL-BABY
1-01-001	WELL-BALANCED
9-06-008	WELL-BEING
1-01-001	WELL-BOUND
1-01-001	WELL-BRACED
1-01-001	WELL-BRED
1-01-001	WELL-BRUSHED
1-01-001	WELL-CEMENTED
3-02-003	WELL-DEFINED
2-02-002	WELL-DESERVED
2-02-002	WELL-DESIGNED
2-01-002	WELL-DEVELOPED
1-01-001	WELL-DRESSED
4-02-003	WELL-EDUCATED
1-01-001	WELL-EQUIPPED
3-03-003	WELL-ESTABLISHED
3-03-003	WELL-FED
1-01-001	WELL-FLESHED
1-01-001	WELL-GROOVED
1-01-001	WELL-HOUSE
6-04-006	WELL-INFORMED
4-04-004	WELL-KEPT
17-08-016	WELL-KNOWN
3-03-003	WELL-MADE
3-03-003	WELL-MEANING
1-01-001	WELL-MODULATED
1-01-001	WELL-MOLDED
1-01-001	WELL-NIGH
1-01-001	WELL-ORGANIZED
1-01-001	WELL-ORIENTED
1-01-001	WELL-PLANNED
1-01-001	WELL-PLAYED
1-01-001	WELL-PREPARED
1-01-001	WELL-PUBLICIZED
1-01-001	WELL-READ
1-01-001	WELL-RECEIVED
1-01-001	WELL-REGULATED
1-01-001	WELL-ROUNDED
1-01-001	WELL-RULED
1-01-001	WELL-SPRINGS
1-01-001	WELL-STOCKED
1-01-001	WELL-STRETCHED
1-01-001	WELL-STUFFED
2-02-002	WELL-TO-DO
2-02-002	WELL-TRAINED
1-01-001	WELL-UNDERSTOOD
1-01-001	WELL-WEDGED
1-01-001	WELL-WISHERS
1-01-001	WELL-WISHING
1-01-001	WELL-WORN
1-01-001	WELL-WRITTEN
1-01-001	WELLBEING
1-01-001	WELLED
3-02-002	WELLESLEY
1-01-001	WELLING
1-01-001	WELLINGTON
1-01-001	WELLKNOWN
1-01-001	WELLMAN
11-07-011	WELLS
5-02-002	WELLS'S
1-01-001	WELLSLEY
1-01-001	WELLSVILLE
1-01-001	WELMERS
1-01-001	WELTANSCHAUUNG
2-01-001	WELTER
1-01-001	WELTON
2-01-001	WELTS
8-03-003	WEMMICK
1-01-001	WENDELL
1-01-001	WENDELLS
507-15-222	WENT
2-01-001	WENTWORTH
9-06-007	WEPT
3284-15-453	WERE
22-08-020	WEREN'T
1-01-001	WERGELAND
6-02-003	WERNER
2-01-001	WERT
1-01-001	WERT'S
1-01-001	WERTHER
1-01-001	WES
1-01-001	WESKER
6-01-002	WESKER'S
6-02-004	WESLEY
1-01-001	WESLEY'S
3-02-002	WESLEYAN
1-01-001	WESSON
1-01-001	WEST
1-01-001	WEST'S
1-01-001	WESTBROOK
4-03-003	WESTCHESTER
5-05-005	WESTERLY
137-15-075	WESTERN
2-02-002	WESTERN-STYLE
2-02-002	WESTERNER
1-01-001	WESTERNERS
6-02-002	WESTFIELD
1-01-001	WESTHAMPTON
3-02-003	WESTINGHOUSE
23-05-006	WESTMINSTER
2-01-001	WESTMORE
8-02-003	WESTON
2-01-001	WESTPHALIA
2-01-001	WESTPORT
8-05-007	WESTWARD
1-01-001	WESTWARDS
1-01-001	WESTWOOD
53-11-040	WET
1-01-001	WETLANDS
2-01-001	WETLY
3-03-003	WETNESS
6-04-004	WETTER
4-02-003	WETTING
6-01-001	WEXLER
1-01-001	WEYBOSSET
1-01-001	WHACK
2-02-002	WHACKED
2-02-002	WHADDYA
1-01-001	WHAH
3-02-002	WHALING
17-07-013	WHARF
1-01-001	WHARTON
2-02-002	WHARVES
1908-15-424	WHAT
1-01-001	WHAT'D
1-01-001	WHAT'RE
53-12-039	WHAT'S
3-01-001	WHAT'S-HIS-NAME
1-01-001	WHAT-NOTS
4-02-004	WHAT-WILL-*T
4-03-003	WHATEVER
6-05-006	WHATMAN
5-05-005	WHATSOEVER
1-01-001	WHEARE
1-01-001	WHEAT
365-14-156	WHEAT-GERM
4-02-002	WHEATON
3-03-003	WHEE
1-01-001	WHEEDLED
1-01-001	WHEEL
1-01-001	WHEELAN'S
1-01-001	WHEELED
4-03-004	WHEELER
1-01-001	WHEELER'S
2-02-002	WHEELING
2-01-001	WHEELOCK
1-01-001	WHEELOCK'S
1-01-001	WHEELS
7-03-004	WHEEZED
2-02-002	WHEEZES
1-01-001	WHEEZING
1-01-001	WHELAN
2331-15-468	WHEN
3-02-002	WHENCE
43-13-038	WHENEVER
1-01-001	WHER
938-15-372	WHERE
4-02-003	WHERE'D
1-01-001	WHERE'RE
6-04-004	WHERE'S
5-04-005	WHEREABOUTS
41-09-035	WHEREAS
19-07-019	WHEREBY
1-01-001	WHEREEVER
3-02-002	WHEREFORE
1-01-001	WHEREFORES
5-04-004	WHEREIN
8-01-002	WHEREOF
1-01-001	WHEREON
6-04-005	WHEREUPON
27-12-026	WHEREVER
1-01-001	WHEREWITH
286-15-170	WHETHER
1-01-001	WHETTED
3562-15-474	WHICH
6-05-006	WHICHEVER
1-01-001	WHICHEVER-THE-HELL
1-01-001	WHIFF
6-01-002	WHIG
6-02-004	WHIGS
680-15-329	WHILE
2-02-002	WHIM
1-01-001	WHIMPER
1-01-001	WHIMPERING
1-01-001	WHIMS
1-01-001	WHIMSEY
1-01-001	WHIMSICAL
4-02-003	WHINE
6-03-003	WHINING
2-01-001	WHINNIED
1-01-001	WHINNY
19-08-011	WHIP
1-01-001	WHIP'S
1-01-001	WHIPLASH
1-01-001	WHIPLASHES
12-08-011	WHIPPED
1-01-001	WHIPPET
7-05-006	WHIPPING
1-01-001	WHIPPING-BOYS
7-02-003	WHIPPLE
1-01-001	WHIPPLE'S
1-01-001	WHIPS
1-01-001	WHIPSAWED
2-01-001	WHIPSNADE
3-03-003	WHIR
3-03-003	WHIRL
6-04-004	WHIRLED
10-07-010	WHIRLING
1-01-001	WHIRLPOOL
2-02-002	WHIRLWIND
1-01-001	WHIRLWIND'S
2-02-002	WHIRRING
2-02-002	WHISKED
1-01-001	WHISKERED
3-02-002	WHISKERS
17-07-013	WHISKEY
1-01-001	WHISKING
23-06-010	WHISKY
1-01-001	WHISKY-ON-THE-ROCKS
1-01-001	WHISPER
12-07-011	WHISPERED
23-07-017	WHISPERING
5-04-004	WHISPERINGS
1-01-001	WHISPERS
4-02-004	WHISTLE
4-03-003	WHISTLED
6-05-006	WHISTLING
5-05-005	WHIT
1-01-001	WHITCOMB
365-14-156	WHITE
4-02-002	WHITE'S
3-03-003	WHITE-CLAD
1-01-001	WHITE-COLLAR
1-01-001	WHITE-COLUMNED
1-01-001	WHITE-DOMINATED
1-01-001	WHITE-SHIRTED
1-01-001	WHITE-STUCCO
1-01-001	WHITE-SUITED
2-02-002	WHITE-TOPPED
2-01-001	WHITEFACE
1-01-001	WHITEHAIRED
1-01-001	WHITEHALL
7-03-004	WHITEHEAD
2-02-002	WHITEHEAD'S
1-01-001	WHITELEAF
1-01-001	WHITELEY
1-01-001	WHITELY
4-01-001	WHITEMAN
3-01-001	WHITEMARSH
3-02-002	WHITENED
2-02-002	WHITENESS
1-01-001	WHITENING
1-01-001	WHITENS
16-05-007	WHITES
2-01-001	WHITETAIL
1-01-001	WHITEWASHED
6-02-003	WHITEY
1-01-001	WHITFIELD
2-01-001	WHITING
2-02-002	WHITMAN
1-01-001	WHITMAN'S
4-03-003	WHITNEY
2-01-001	WHITROW
1-01-001	WHITTAKER
1-01-001	WHITTIER
1-01-001	WHITTIER'S
2-01-002	WHIZ
2-02-002	WHIZZED
1-01-001	WHIZZING
2252-15-420	WHO
9-04-007	WHO'D
1-01-001	WHO'LL
18-08-015	WHO'S
1-01-001	WHOA
1-01-001	WHODUNNIT
2-01-001	WHOE
13-07-012	WHOEVER
309-15-192	WHOLE
1-01-001	WHOLE-HEARTEDLY
1-01-001	WHOLE-HOUSE
6-01-001	WHOLE-WHEAT
1-01-001	WHOLE-WORD
1-01-001	WHOLEHEARTEDLY
2-01-001	WHOLENESS
2-01-001	WHOLES
7-06-006	WHOLESALE
1-01-001	WHOLESALERS
11-05-008	WHOLESOME
1-01-001	WHOLEWHEAT
24-11-022	WHOLLY
2-02-002	WHOLLY-OWNED
146-15-095	WHOM
1-01-001	WHOOP
2-02-002	WHOOPING
1-01-001	WHOOSH
1-01-001	WHOPPERS
1-01-001	WHOPPING
2-01-001	WHORE
1-01-001	WHORES
1-01-001	WHORLS
252-15-171	WHOSE
3-02-002	WHOSOEVER
404-15-201	WHY
1-01-001	WHY'N
1-01-001	WHYFORES
1-01-001	WHYN'T
1-01-001	WICHITA
4-03-004	WICK
9-05-009	WICKED
2-02-002	WICKEDLY
3-03-003	WICKEDNESS
4-04-004	WICKER
1-01-001	WICKET
1-01-001	WICKETS
1-01-001	WICKHAM
125-15-094	WIDE
1-01-001	WIDE-AWAKE
1-01-001	WIDE-CUT
1-01-001	WIDE-DOOR
1-01-001	WIDE-EYED
1-01-001	WIDE-GRIP
1-01-001	WIDE-OPEN
3-03-003	WIDE-RANGING
1-01-001	WIDE-SHOULDER
1-01-001	WIDE-SWEEPING
1-01-001	WIDE-WINGED
1-01-001	WIDEGRIP
52-11-042	WIDELY
5-04-004	WIDEN
5-04-005	WIDENED
1-01-001	WIDENER
1-01-001	WIDENS
17-07-015	WIDER
30-10-026	WIDESPREAD
3-03-003	WIDEST
26-10-018	WIDOW
5-04-005	WIDOWED
1-01-001	WIDOWER
1-01-001	WIDOWHOOD
1-01-001	WIDOWS
1-01-001	WIDSITH
14-03-012	WIDTH
5-01-003	WIDTHS

1-01-001	WIDTHWISE	12-05-006	WINCHESTER	6-01-001	WISMAN'S	1-01-001	WONDERLAND
1-01-001	WIEDERUM	1-01-001	WINCING	2-02-002	WISP	8-05-008	WONDERS
1-01-001	WIELAND	63-14-045	WIND	1-01-001	WISPS	1-01-001	WONDROUS
1-01-001	WIELD	1-01-001	WIND-AND-WATER	2-02-002	WISPY	1-01-001	WONDROUSLY
3-03-003	WIELDED	2-02-002	WIND-BLOWN	1-01-001	WISSAHICKON	1-01-001	WONDUH
1-01-001	WIELDER	2-02-002	WIND-SWEPT	2-02-002	WISTER	2-02-002	WONT
1-01-001	WIENERS	1-01-001	WIND-VELOCITY	2-02-002	WISTFUL	3-03-003	WOO
1-01-001	WIENERS'	1-01-001	WINDBAG	4-04-004	WISTFULLY	55-13-042	WOOD
228-15-115	WIFE	1-01-001	WINDBREAKS	20-08-015	WIT	1-01-001	WOOD-GRAINED
15-07-012	WIFE'S	2-02-002	WINDED	5-03-003	WITCH	1-01-001	WOOD-OIL
1-01-001	WIFE-TO-BE	3-01-001	WINDER	8-04-005	WITCHES	1-01-001	WOODBERRY
1-01-001	WIFELY	1-01-001	WINDERS	7289-15-500	WITH	2-01-001	WOODBURY
1-01-001	WIG	2-02-002	WINDFALL	1-01-001	WITH-BUT-AFTER	1-01-001	WOODBURY'S
1-01-001	WIGGLE	2-01-001	WINDHAM	1-01-001	WITHAL	1-01-001	WOODCARVER
3-03-003	WIGGLED	9-06-007	WINDING	8-05-007	WITHDRAW	1-01-001	WOODCOCK
2-02-002	WIGGLING	1-01-001	WINDING-CLOTHES	6-06-006	WITHDRAWAL	1-01-001	WOODCOCK'S
2-01-001	WIGMAKER	1-01-001	WINDLESS	4-03-004	WITHDRAWING	1-01-001	WOODCUTTERS
2-02-002	WIL	1-01-001	WINDMILL	4-04-004	WITHDRAWN	5-03-005	WOODED
2-02-002	WILBUR	119-14-066	WINDOW	9-06-009	WITHDREW	50-11-030	WOODEN
1-01-001	WILCKE	1-01-001	WINDOW-WASHING	2-02-002	WITHER	1-01-001	WOODEN-LEG
2-01-001	WILCOX	3-03-003	WINDOWLESS	2-02-002	WITHERED	1-01-001	WOODGRAINING
56-13-044	WILD	2-01-001	WINDOWPANES	1-01-001	WITHERING	1-01-001	WOODIN
1-01-001	WILD-EYED	53-13-038	WINDOWS	1-01-001	WITHERSPOON	2-02-002	WOODLAND
1-01-001	WILD-SOUNDING	21-10-017	WINDS	1-01-001	WITHES	1-01-001	WOODMAN'S
4-03-003	WILDCAT	6-03-004	WINDSHIELD	8-05-008	WITHHELD	1-01-001	WOODPECKER
1-01-001	WILDCATTER	2-02-002	WINDSOR	2-02-002	WITHHOLD	4-03-004	WOODROW
1-01-001	WILDE	1-01-001	WINDSTORM	8-03-005	WITHHOLDING	30-01-001	WOODRUFF
1-01-001	WILDENSTEIN	2-02-002	WINDUP	359-15-195	WITHIN	2-01-001	WOODRUFF'S
1-01-001	WILDER	72-12-024	WINDY	583-15-312	WITHOUT	25-10-018	WOODS
1-01-001	WILDER'S	1-01-001	WINE	3-03-003	WITHSTAND	1-01-001	WOODS'S
11-06-010	WILDERNESS	1-01-001	WINE'S	1-01-001	WITHSTANDS	1-01-001	WOODSHED
1-01-001	WILDEST	1-01-001	WINE-	3-02-003	WITHSTOOD	3-02-002	WOODSIDE
1-01-001	WILDHACK	1-01-001	WINEHEAD	28-11-025	WITNESS	3-03-003	WOODSMOKE
19-04-006	WILDLIFE	24-02-002	WINES	13-09-013	WITNESSED	3-03-003	WOODWARD
25-09-024	WILDLY	1-01-001	WINFIELD	21-08-016	WITNESSES	2-01-001	WOODWARDS
1-01-001	WILDNESS	18-07-015	WING	6-05-006	WITNESSING	2-02-002	WOODWIND
2-02-002	WILES	1-01-001	WING-SHOOTING	1-01-001	WITOLD	5-04-004	WOODWORK
6-03-004	WILEY	1-01-001	WINGBACK	5-04-005	WITS	2-02-002	WOODWORKING
1-01-001	WILFRED	3-03-003	WINGED	2-02-002	WITT	1-01-001	WOODYARD
1-01-001	WILFRID	1-01-001	WINGING	1-01-001	WITTER	1-01-001	WOOED
2-02-002	WILFULLY	2-01-001	WINGMAN	1-01-001	WITTINGLY	1-01-001	WOOER
4-03-004	WILHELM	27-11-019	WINGS	10-05-007	WITTY	10-07-010	WOOL
2-01-001	WILHELMINA	7-04-006	WINK	1-01-001	WIVE'S	4-04-004	WOOLEN
1-01-001	WILIGIS	8-05-007	WINKED	21-07-011	WIVES	1-01-001	WOOLGATHER
2-01-002	WILKES	7-03-004	WINKING	3-03-003	WIZARD	1-01-001	WOOLLCOTT
1-01-001	WILKES-*BARRE	2-01-001	WINLESS	3-03-003	WOBBLE	3-03-003	WOOLLY
1-01-001	WILKEY	8-04-007	WINNER	2-01-002	WOBBLED	1-01-001	WOOLLY-HEADED
1-01-001	WILKINSON	4-02-002	WINNERS	1-01-001	WOBBLING	1-01-001	WOOLLY-MINDED
2244-15-408	WILL	1-01-001	WINNETKA	2-01-002	WOBBLY	1-01-001	WOOLWORKERS
1-01-001	WILLA	31-09-024	WINNING	1-01-001	WOBURN	1-01-001	WOOLWORTH'S
3-01-001	WILLAMETTE	3-02-002	WINNINGS	1-01-001	WOD	1-01-001	WOOMERA
4-02-003	WILLARD	1-01-001	WINNIPEG	5-03-005	WOE	1-01-001	WOONASQUATUCKET
2-01-001	WILLCOX	1-01-001	WINNIPESAUKEE	1-01-001	WOEBEGONE	4-02-002	WOONSOCKET
6-05-006	WILLED	1-01-001	WINNOW	1-01-001	WOEFUL	1-01-001	WOOODOSH
1-01-001	WILLEM	4-02-002	WINOOSKI	2-02-002	WOEFULLY	1-01-001	WOP
1-01-001	WILLETT	1-01-001	WINOS	2-01-001	WOHAW	1-01-001	WOPS
1-01-001	WILLFUL	8-04-005	WINS	1-01-001	WOHAWS	2-02-002	WORCESTER
1-01-001	WILLFULLY	1-01-001	WINSETT	1-01-001	WOHD	3-01-002	WORCESTERSHIRE
148-13-077	WILLIAM	11-01-001	WINSLOW	14-07-013	WOKE	274-15-153	WORD
6-02-002	WILLIAM'S	2-01-001	WINSLOW'S	1-01-001	WOLCOTT	1-01-001	WORD-GAMES
32-09-016	WILLIAMS	1-01-001	WINSOME	1-01-001	WOLCYRZ	4-03-003	WORDED
1-01-001	WILLIAMS'	2-02-002	WINSOR	1-01-001	WOLD	4-03-004	WORDING
2-02-002	WILLIAMS'S	40-04-005	WINSTON	1-01-001	WOLDE	2-02-002	WORDLESSLY
1-01-001	WILLIAMSBURG	83-14-053	WINTER	6-03-005	WOLF	274-15-154	WORDS
1-01-001	WILLIAMSON'S	2-02-002	WINTERED	8-02-005	WOLFE	1-01-001	WORDSWORTH
11-03-007	WILLIE	1-01-001	WINTERING	1-01-001	WOLFE'S	2-01-001	WORDY
4-01-003	WILLIE'S	2-02-002	WINTERS	1-01-001	WOLFES	65-11-047	WORE
69-14-056	WILLING	1-01-001	WINTERTIME	2-01-001	WOLFF	760-15-311	WORK
1-01-001	WILLINGF	3-02-002	WINTHROP	2-02-002	WOLFF'S	1-01-001	WORK'S
4-04-004	WILLINGLY	2-02-002	WINTRY	1-01-001	WOLFGANG	2-01-001	WORK-OUT
11-06-009	WILLINGNESS	10-07-010	WIPE	1-01-001	WOLFISHLY	1-01-001	WORK-OUTS
7-01-001	WILLINGS	19-08-018	WIPED	4-01-001	WOLLMAN	1-01-001	WORK-PARALYSIS
16-01-001	WILLIS	6-04-006	WIPING	1-01-001	WOLPE	1-01-001	WORK-SATISFACTI ON
2-01-001	WILLIS'	42-12-029	WIRE	1-01-001	WOLPE'S	1-01-001	WORK-STUDY
9-02-003	WILLOW	1-01-001	WIRE-HAIRED	1-01-001	WOLSTENHOLME	1-01-001	WORK-SUCCESS
1-01-001	WILLOW-LINED	11-07-011	WIRED	1-01-001	WOLVERTON	1-01-001	WORK-WEARY
1-01-001	WILLOWS	13-07-013	WIRES	4-04-004	WOLVES	1-01-001	WORK/
1-01-001	WILLOWY	2-02-002	WIRING	224-15-107	WOMAN	9-06-009	WORKABLE
1-01-001	WILLS	8-05-007	WIRY	22-11-021	WOMAN'S	8-01-001	WORKBENCH
5-04-004	WILLY	1-01-001	WIS	1-01-001	WOMANHOOD	1-01-001	WORKDAY
4-03-003	WILLY-NILLY	19-07-011	WISCONSIN	1-01-001	WOMANLY	128-15-098	WORKED
1-01-001	WILLYA	1-01-001	WISCONSIN'S	1-01-001	WOMB	30-08-018	WORKER
4-02-003	WILMETTE	44-12-035	WISDOM	1-01-001	WOMB-TO-TOMB	4-03-003	WORKER'S
6-03-004	WILMINGTON	36-12-029	WISE	195-15-097	WOMEN	86-11-036	WORKERS
2-01-001	WILSHIRE	2-02-002	WISECRACKED	27-08-019	WOMEN'S	3-03-003	WORKERS'
62-09-019	WILSON	1-01-001	WISED	1-01-001	WOMEN-TRODDEN	1-01-001	WORKIN
3-02-003	WILSON'S	8-05-008	WISELY	68-10-046	WON	151-14-115	WORKING
1-01-001	WILSONIAN	1-01-001	WISENHEIMER	105-13-074	WON'T	3-01-001	WORKING-CLASS
3-03-003	WILT	7-06-007	WISER	1-01-001	WON-LOST	1-01-001	WORKINGMEN
1-01-001	WILTED	1-01-001	WISEST	67-14-055	WONDER	6-05-005	WORKINGS
2-01-002	WILY	110-15-087	WISH	1-01-001	WONDER-WORKING	1-01-001	WORKMAN
1-01-001	WIMSATT	1-01-001	WISHART	58-11-038	WONDERED	1-01-001	WORKMAN'S
55-11-038	WIN	55-11-047	WISHED	53-14-044	WONDERFUL	2-02-002	WORKMANLIKE
4-03-004	WINCED	24-08-022	WISHES	11-05-011	WONDERFULLY	6-04-004	WORKMANSHIP
1-01-001	WINCHELL	9-05-009	WISHFUL	1-01-001	WONDERFULNESS	7-05-005	WORKMEN
1-01-001	WINCHES	5-04-005	WISHING	21-09-020	WONDERING	6-03-006	WORKOUT
		9-01-001	WISMAN	1-01-001	WONDERINGLY	3-01-002	WORKOUTS

Count	Word
1-01-001	WORKPIECE
130-15-079	WORKS
1-01-001	WORKSHEET
24-06-013	WORKSHOP
6-03-005	WORKSHOPS
1-01-001	WORKTABLE
787-15-270	WORLD
35-11-030	WORLD'S
1-01-001	WORLD-AT-LARGE
3-02-003	WORLD-FAMOUS
1-01-001	WORLD-IGNORING
1-01-001	WORLD-ORIENTED
3-03-003	WORLD-RENOWNED
2-02-002	WORLD-SHAKING
1-01-001	WORLD-SHATTERING
12-05-009	WORLD-WIDE
1-01-001	WORLDERS
9-05-007	WORLDLY
7-06-006	WORLDS
1-01-001	WORLDWIDE
4-03-004	WORM
5-04-005	WORMS
1-01-001	WORMY
23-10-022	WORN
1-01-001	WORN-FACED
1-01-001	WORN-OUT
1-01-001	WORNOUT
1-01-001	WORRELL
35-09-028	WORRIED
1-01-001	WORRIEDLY
20-07-012	WORRIES
2-01-002	WORRISOME
55-12-044	WORRY
2-02-002	WORRYIN
5-02-005	WORRYING
50-13-045	WORSE
1-01-001	WORSENED
1-01-001	WORSENS
36-12-024	WORSHIP
1-01-001	WORSHIPED
2-02-002	WORSHIPFUL
3-01-002	WORSHIPING
2-02-002	WORSHIPPED
1-01-001	WORSHIPPERS
1-01-001	WORSHIPPING
34-11-030	WORST
1-01-001	WORST-MARKED
2-02-002	WORSTED
94-15-074	WORTH
1-01-001	WORTH-WAITING-FOR
1-01-001	WORTH-WHILE
2-02-002	WORTHIEST
3-02-003	WORTHLESS
1-01-001	WORTHLESSNESS
8-07-008	WORTHWHILE
28-07-022	WORTHY
2714-15-448	WOULD
5-05-005	WOULD-BE
1-01-001	WOULDA
1-01-001	WOULDBE
129-13-077	WOULDN'T
28-12-020	WOUND
1-01-001	WOUND-TUMOR
23-05-015	WOUNDED
1-01-001	WOUNDING
8-04-005	WOUNDS
3-02-003	WOVE
9-05-006	WOVEN
1-01-001	WOVEN-ROOT
1-01-001	WOW
1-01-001	WOZZEK
1-01-001	WRACK
1-01-001	WRACKED
1-01-001	WRACKING
1-01-001	WRAGGE
2-01-002	WRAITH-LIKE
2-02-002	WRANGLED
6-03-003	WRANGLER
5-04-005	WRAP
14-08-012	WRAPPED
2-02-002	WRAPPER
1-01-001	WRAPPERS
1-01-001	WRAPPIN
6-04-005	WRAPPING
2-02-002	WRAPS
9-04-009	WRATH
1-01-001	WRATHFUL
1-01-001	WRATTEN
1-01-001	WREAK
8-03-004	WREATH
1-01-001	WREATHED
3-02-003	WREATHS
8-05-008	WRECK
2-01-002	WRECKAGE
6-04-005	WRECKED
5-03-003	WRECKING
2-02-002	WRENCHED
2-02-002	WRENCHES
1-01-001	WRENCHING
1-01-001	WREST
1-01-001	WRESTLE
1-01-001	WRESTLER'S
1-01-001	WRESTLES
1-01-001	WRESTLING
1-01-001	WRESTLINGS
1-01-001	WRETCH
7-03-006	WRETCHED
1-01-001	WRETCHEDNESS
9-02-008	WRIGHT'S
3-02-002	WRIGLEY
2-02-002	WRING
1-01-001	WRINGS
2-02-002	WRINKLE
12-05-011	WRINKLED
7-06-007	WRINKLES
10-05-007	WRIST
6-06-006	WRISTS
2-02-002	WRISTWATCH
7-02-005	WRIT
106-14-074	WRITE
73-11-042	WRITER
1-01-001	WRITER'S
1-01-001	WRITER-TURNED-PAINTER
73-11-032	WRITERS
4-03-003	WRITERS'
41-10-027	WRITES
2-02-002	WRITHE
1-01-001	WRITHED
6-04-006	WRITHING
117-12-072	WRITING
1-01-001	WRITING-LIKE
15-06-014	WRITINGS
1-01-001	WRITS
154-14-097	WRITTEN
129-15-091	WRONG
1-01-001	WRONG-HEADED
1-01-001	WRONG-O
1-01-001	WRONGDOER
2-02-002	WRONGDOING
1-01-001	WRONGED
1-01-001	WRONGFUL
1-01-001	WRONGLY
6-03-004	WRONGS
181-14-081	WROTE
3-03-003	WROUGHT
1-01-001	WROUGHT-IRON
5-04-005	WRY
1-01-001	WRY-FACED
3-03-003	WRYLY
1-01-001	WT
1-01-001	WU
1-01-001	WUH
1-01-001	WUS
1-01-001	WUSTMAN
3-03-003	WYATT
1-01-001	WYCKOFF
1-01-001	WYCLIFFE
1-01-001	WYCOFF
1-01-001	WYCOFF'S
1-01-001	WYCOMBE
2-01-001	WYLIE
1-01-001	WYMAN
1-01-001	WYN
2-01-001	WYNDHAM'S
1-01-001	WYNN
1-01-001	WYNNE
1-01-001	WYNSTON
9-06-007	WYOMING
1-01-001	X
1-01-001	X-*TRU-*COAT
12-03-006	X-RAY
2-02-002	X-RAYS
1-01-001	XAVIER
1-01-001	XAVIER'S
1-01-001	XENIA
1-01-001	XENON
2-02-002	XENOPHOBIA
1-01-001	XIMENEZ-*VARGAS
1-01-001	XXXX
5-01-001	XYDIS
1-01-001	XYDIS'
1-01-001	XYLEM
1-01-001	XYLOPHONES
11-05-009	Y
1-01-001	Y**.*M**.*C**.*A
1-01-001	Y**.*M**.*H**.*A
1-01-001	Y**.*W**.*C**.*A
4-02-002	Y'ALL
2-01-002	Y'KNOW
1-01-001	Y'R
2-01-001	Y'RE
1-01-001	Y**U
4-03-003	YA
4-02-002	YACHT
2-01-001	YACHTEL
1-01-001	YACHTELS
1-01-001	YACHTERS
2-02-002	YACHTING
3-03-003	YACHTS
1-01-001	YACHTSMAN
1-01-001	YACHTSMEN
9-02-008	YADDO
1-01-001	YAHWE
1-01-001	YAKIMA
1-01-001	YAKOV
1-01-001	YAKS
1-01-001	YALAGALOO
13-06-010	YALE
1-01-001	YALE'S
1-01-001	YALE-*ARMY
1-01-001	YALIES
14-02-002	YALTA
1-01-001	YAMABE
1-01-001	YAMATA
1-01-001	YANCEY-6
1-01-001	YANCY-6
12-01-002	YANG
7-02-004	YANK
5-03-005	YANKED
18-07-013	YANKEE
1-01-001	YANKEE-HATRED
2-01-001	YANKEEFICATION
28-04-009	YANKEES
2-01-002	YANKEES'
1-01-001	YANKING
4-02-003	YANKS
1-01-001	YANKS'
1-01-001	YANKTON
1-01-001	YAPPING
1-01-001	YAQUI
35-08-024	YARD
2-01-001	YARDAGE
64-10-028	YARDS
2-02-002	YARDSTICK
1-01-001	YARDUMIAN
14-03-003	YARN
6-02-002	YARNS
4-01-001	YARROW
1-01-001	YASSUHS
1-01-001	YAWL
2-02-002	YAWN
2-01-002	YAWNING
1-01-001	YAWS
1-01-001	YD
11-07-008	YE
2-01-001	YE'RE
3-02-003	YEA
25-04-014	YEAH
660-15-213	YEAR
43-11-033	YEAR'S
3-01-001	YEAR-'ROUND
2-02-002	YEAR-EARLIER
1-01-001	YEAR-END
1-01-001	YEAR-LONG
1-01-001	YEAR-OLD
4-03-004	YEAR-ROUND
2-01-001	YEAR-TO-YEAR
2-02-002	YEARBOOK
1-01-001	YEARD
12-07-012	YEARLY
1-01-001	YEARN
3-03-003	YEARNED
7-07-007	YEARNING
1-01-001	YEARNINGLY
2-02-002	YEARNINGS
949-15-346	YEARS
8-06-007	YEARS'
3-02-003	YEAST
1-01-001	YEASTS
1-01-001	YEATS
1-01-001	YEDISAN
2-01-001	YEHHH
1-01-001	YEHUDI
9-05-006	YELL
22-06-015	YELLED
2-01-001	YELLER
1-01-001	YELLERISH
1-01-001	YELLIN
6-02-004	YELLING
55-12-041	YELLOW
1-01-001	YELLOW-BELLIED
1-01-001	YELLOW-BROWN
3-01-001	YELLOW-DWARF
3-02-002	YELLOW-GREEN
1-01-001	YELLOWED
2-01-002	YELLOWING
1-01-001	YELLOWISH
2-02-002	YELP
1-01-001	YELPED
1-01-001	YELPING
1-01-001	YELPS
3-03-003	YEN
1-01-001	YENI
144-14-089	YES
1-01-001	YESIREE
83-11-038	YESTERDAY
6-06-006	YESTERDAY'S
3-03-003	YESTERYEAR
419-15-241	YET
2-01-001	YFF
4-02-002	YIDDISH
35-09-022	YIELD
12-07-011	YIELDED
9-06-008	YIELDING
1-01-001	YIELDING-*MEDITERRANEAN-WOMAN-FLESH-OF-WATER
7-04-007	YIELDS
8-01-002	YIN
2-01-001	YIN-*YANG
1-01-001	YINGER
1-01-001	YIP
1-01-001	YODEL
2-01-001	YODELING
1-01-001	YOGA
2-01-002	YOGI
1-01-001	YOK
3-03-003	YOKE
2-02-002	YOKEL
1-01-001	YOKELS
2-01-001	YOKNAPATAWPHA
2-01-001	YOKOSUKA
1-01-001	YOKUSUKA
7-01-001	YOKUTS
1-01-001	YOLK
1-01-001	YON
1-01-001	YONDER
2-01-001	YONEDA
1-01-001	YONGST
1-01-001	YONKERS
1-01-001	YOODEE
1-01-001	YOORICK
2-02-002	YORE
1-01-001	YORI
301-13-126	YORK
7-07-007	YORK'S
1-01-001	YORK-*PENNSYLVANIA
1-01-001	YORK-BORN
1-01-001	YORK-MIND
1-01-001	YORKI(**JAP
7-05-005	YORKER
1-01-001	YORKER'S
2-02-002	YORKERS
2-02-002	YORKTOWN
3-01-002	YOSEMITE
1-01-001	YOSHIMOTO'S
3286-15-297	YOU
36-09-027	YOU'D
89-10-055	YOU'LL
151-13-076	YOU'RE
1-01-001	YOU'S
1-01-001	YOU'UNS
67-12-041	YOU'VE
1-01-001	YOU**LL
385-15-190	YOUNG
3-03-003	YOUNG'S
44-13-035	YOUNGER
13-06-012	YOUNGEST
2-02-002	YOUNGISH
7-05-005	YOUNGSTER
1-01-001	YOUNGSTER'S
19-06-015	YOUNGSTERS
1-01-001	YOUNGUH
923-15-203	YOUR
25-11-020	YOURS
67-12-052	YOURSELF
8-05-005	YOURSELVES
82-14-044	YOUTH
12-06-010	YOUTHFUL
11-05-007	YOUTHS
5-01-001	YOW
4-01-001	YR
1-01-001	YR.
1-01-001	YS
1-01-001	YTIME
2-01-001	YUBA
1-01-001	YUCATAN
1-01-001	YUCCA
7-01-001	YUGOSLAV
5-04-004	YUGOSLAVIA

Code	Term
2-02-002	YUH
1-01-001	YUJOBO
1-01-001	YUKI
1-01-001	YUM-*YUM
6-03-004	YURI
1-01-001	YUROCHKA
1-01-001	YUSE
2-02-002	YVETTE
1-01-001	YYYY
1-01-001	ZABEL
1-01-001	ZACHRISSON
1-01-001	ZACHRISSON'S
1-01-001	ZADEL
1-01-001	ZAMIATIN'S
1-01-001	ZANZIBAR
1-01-001	ZAPALA
1-01-001	ZAPOROGIAN
1-01-001	ZARA
1-01-001	ZAROUBIN
8-06-008	ZEAL
3-03-003	ZEALAND
1-01-001	ZEALOT
4-02-003	ZEALOUS
3-03-003	ZEALOUSLY
1-01-001	ZEBEK
1-01-001	ZEBRA
1-01-001	ZEFFIRELLI
1-01-001	ZEISING
2-01-001	ZEISS
1-01-001	ZEITGEIST
1-01-001	ZEME
2-01-001	ZEMLINSKY
1-01-001	ZEMLYA
26-03-003	ZEN
1-01-001	7END-*AVESTA
2-01-001	ZENDO
6-02-002	ZENITH
1-01-001	ZENNIST
24-06-014	ZERO
2-01-001	ZERO-MAGNITUDE
1-01-001	ZEROED
2-02-002	ZEROS
5-04-005	ZEST
1-01-001	ZHITKOV
1-01-001	ZHITZHAKLI
1-01-001	ZHOK
2-01-001	ZIEGFELD
2-01-001	ZIFFREN
1-01-001	ZIGGY
4-02-004	ZIGZAGGING
1-01-001	ZIMINSKA-*SYGIETYNSKA
3-01-001	ZIMMERMAN
10-04-005	ZINC
8-01-001	ZING
1-01-001	ZINGGGG-*0
1-01-001	ZINMAN
6-03-003	ZION
1-01-001	ZIONISM
1-01-001	ZIONISTS
1-01-001	ZIP
1-01-001	ZIPPED
1-01-001	ZIPPER
1-01-001	ZIRALDO
1-01-001	ZLOTYS
3-02-002	ZODIACAL
1-01-001	ZOE
1-01-001	ZOMBIE
1-01-001	ZOMBIES
11-05-008	ZONE
1-01-001	ZONED
3-03-003	ZONES
6-04-006	ZONING
9-05-007	ZOO
1-01-001	ZOOEY
2-02-002	ZOOLOGIST
1-01-001	ZOOLOGY
1-01-001	ZOOMING
1-01-001	ZOOMS
1-01-001	ZOOOOP
1-01-001	ZORRILLAS
1-01-001	ZOTE
2-01-001	ZOUNDS
1-01-001	ZU
2-02-002	ZUBKOVSKAYA
2-02-002	ZUR
2-01-001	ZURCHER
2-01-001	ZURICH
1-01-001	ZWEI
2-01-001	ZWORYKIN
23-03-006	0
2-01-001	0.001
1-01-001	0.002
1-01-001	0.005
1-01-001	0.025-IN
1-01-001	0.039
1-01-001	0.043
1-01-001	0.075
1-01-001	0.080-IN
9-03-006	0.1
1-01-001	0.1-MV**./M
1-01-001	0.10
1-01-001	0.12
1-01-001	0.15
1-01-001	0.154
2-01-002	0.16
4-02-004	0.2
1-01-001	0.24
1-01-001	0.25
1-01-001	0.28
3-02-003	0.3
1-01-001	0.3**YM
1-01-001	0.36
4-02-002	0.4
9-02-005	0.5
1-01-001	0.5**J**YM
1-01-001	0.5-MV**./M
1-01-001	0.50
1-01-001	0.52
2-01-001	0.6
1-01-001	0.7
1-01-001	0.70
1-01-001	0.78
4-01-003	0.8
1-01-001	0.85
2-01-001	0.85**K
1-01-001	0.906
1-01-001	0.95
1-01-001	035
1-01-001	046
3-01-001	05
2-01-001	06-05
1-01-001	060
1-01-001	0600
2-01-001	08
496-10-160	1
3-02-002	1.0
1-01-001	1.0-**JMG/**JL
2-02-002	1.00
2-01-001	1.07
1-01-001	1.09.3
3-03-003	1.1
1-01-001	1.10.1
1-01-001	1.10.4
1-01-001	1.10.8
1-01-001	1.2
1-01-001	1.23
2-01-002	1.24
1-01-001	1.25
1-01-001	1.25**K
2-01-001	1.25-**JCM
11-05-009	1.5
1-01-001	1.58
3-02-003	1.8
1-01-001	1.8**K
1-01-001	1**+0
1-01-001	1**+0**J*C
1-01-001	1**C00
1-01-001	1**C1
4-01-001	1**C10
1-01-001	1**C100
1-01-001	1**C1024
2-01-001	1**C12
1-01-001	1**C15
1-01-001	1**C16
1-01-001	1**C18
1-01-001	1**C2
1-01-001	1**C2048
1-01-001	1**C218
1-01-001	1**C23
3-01-001	1**C256
1-01-001	1**C27
1-01-001	1**C35
3-02-002	1**C4
2-01-002	1**C48
1-01-001	1**C5
1-01-001	1**C500
2-01-001	1**C512
1-01-001	1**C59.3
1-01-001	1**C6
1-01-001	1**J*=*M
2-01-001	1**K
4-01-001	1*,-**J*A
1-01-001	1*,-**J*0
1-01-001	1-**JHP
1-01-001	1-**JML
6-01-001	1-*JUNE
1-01-001	1-INCH
1-01-001	1-0
1-01-001	1-1.5
1-01-001	1-1/2
1-01-001	1-1/2-INCH
1-01-001	1-1/2-STORY
2-01-002	1-1/4
1-01-001	1-3
1-01-001	1-6
1-01-001	1-701
2-01-001	1/**JC
3-01-003	1/16
24-02-007	1/2
1-01-001	1/2-INCH
1-01-001	1/20TH
2-02-002	1/3
17-02-006	1/4
1-01-001	1/4-INCH
1-01-001	1/50TH
1-01-001	1/6)(5/6)(1/6
7-01-001	1/8
2-01-001	1/8-INCH
11-06-007	1,000
1-01-001	1,000,000
1-01-001	1,018,000
1-01-001	1,040
1-01-001	1,065
1-01-001	1,080,062
2-01-001	1,083,000
1-01-001	1,100
1-01-001	1,107
1-01-001	1,119
1-01-001	1,212
1-01-001	1,212,000
1-01-001	1,225
1-01-001	1,230
1-01-001	1,253
1-01-001	1,257,7000
1-01-001	1,286
1-01-001	1,338,000
1-01-001	1,343
1-01-001	1,400
1-01-001	1,418,000
1-01-001	1,419,833
1-01-001	1,450
1-01-001	1,450,000
1-01-001	1,488
3-02-003	1,500
1-01-001	1,509
1-01-001	1,512
1-01-001	1,524
1-01-001	1,525,000
1-01-001	1,541,991
1-01-001	1,571
2-02-002	1,600
2-02-002	1,700
1-01-001	1,800
1-01-001	1,800,000
1-01-001	1,850
1-01-001	1,900
1-01-001	1(**JB
1-01-001	1(**JC
1-01-001	1A
1-01-001	10
143-13-090	10
1-01-001	10.2
1-01-001	10.3
1-01-001	10.3-**JCM
1-01-001	10.4
1-01-001	10.6
1-01-001	10.6**K
1-01-001	10.8**K
1-01-001	10*+0
1-01-001	10*+0**J*C
1-01-001	10**B-A-MINUTE
1-01-001	10**C00-1**C00
1-01-001	10**C05
1-01-001	10**C10
2-02-002	10**C30
1-01-001	10**C45
1-01-001	10**C50
7-04-006	10**K
1-01-001	10-**J**YM-DIAMETER
1-01-001	10-DAY
1-01-001	10-FOOT
1-01-001	10-GALLON
1-01-001	10-HOUR
1-01-001	10-MILLIGRAM
1-01-001	10-O'CLOCK
1-01-001	10-TEAM
9-03-006	10-YEAR
4-04-006	10-YEAR-OLD
1-01-001	10-YR
1-01-001	10-1/2
1-01-001	10-15**K
1-01-001	10-16
14-07-014	10,000
2-02-002	10,000,000
1-01-001	10,500
1-01-001	10,517
1-01-001	10TH
70-08-044	100
8-05-006	100**K
1-01-001	100-BRICK
1-01-001	100-MEGATON
1-01-001	100-MILLION-LB
1-01-001	100-TON
2-02-002	100-YARD
1-01-001	100-105*+0*F
3-01-001	100-109*+0
1-01-001	100-200
1-01-001	100-230
9-05-008	100,000
11-03-007	1000
1-01-001	1000-**J**YM-DIAMETER
1-01-001	1001
2-02-002	101
1-01-001	101**J*B
1-01-001	102
1-01-001	1020
1-01-001	103
11-01-001	104
1-01-001	104(**JG
8-01-001	1040
4-01-001	1040**J*A
1-01-001	1044
2-02-002	105
1-01-001	105*+0
1-01-001	105,000
2-02-002	106
1-01-001	106,500
2-01-001	1065
2-01-001	1066
1-01-001	1068-1159
4-03-003	108
62-09-047	11
1-01-001	11.2
1-01-001	11.6
1-01-001	11**C00
1-01-001	11**C00-12**C00
1-01-001	11**C20
2-01-002	11**C30
2-01-002	11**K
1-01-001	11-INCH
1-01-001	11-MONTH-OLD
1-01-001	11-SHOT
1-01-001	11-YEAR
2-02-002	11-YEAR-OLD
1-01-001	11-12
1-01-001	11-18
1-01-001	11-3
1-01-001	11-5
1-01-001	11-7
1-01-001	11,000
1-01-001	11,744
3-02-002	11TH
7-05-007	110
1-01-001	110*+0
1-01-001	110*+0**J*C
7-01-001	1105
5-03-003	111
3-02-002	113
4-03-003	114
1-01-001	115
1-01-001	116
1-01-001	116,000
1-01-001	1162
1-01-001	117
1-01-001	1184
98-09-066	12
1-01-001	12.01
1-01-001	12.8
1-01-001	12**C01
1-01-001	12**C14
1-01-001	12**C50
1-01-001	12**JOZ
3-02-003	12**K
3-01-001	12-GAUGE
1-01-001	12-INCH
1-01-001	12-MONTH
1-01-001	12-PASSENGER
1-01-001	12-SHOT
1-01-001	12-TO-ONE
1-01-001	12-YEAR-OLD
1-01-001	12-1/2
2-01-001	12-1/2-INCH
1-01-001	12-14
1-01-001	12-17
3-02-003	12,000
1-01-001	12,500
1-01-001	12TH
6-03-005	120
1-01-001	120*+0
1-01-001	120*+0-160*+0*F
1-01-001	120,000
1-01-001	1200
1-01-001	1200-SQUARE-FOOT

Code	Word	Code	Word	Code	Word	Code	Word
2-02-002	121	2-01-001	150,000,000	1-01-001	1680	1-01-001	1807-1892
1-01-001	121,000	2-02-002	1500	1-01-001	1687	1-01-001	1808-1895
1-01-001	1213	1-01-001	151	1-01-001	1688	5-02-003	1810
1-01-001	1213-15	1-01-001	1514	2-02-002	169	1-01-001	1811
1-01-001	1215	1-01-001	1515	1-01-001	1690	1-01-001	1811-1884
2-02-002	122	1-01-001	1516	1-01-001	1692	4-02-003	1812
1-01-001	122,158	2-01-001	153	1-01-001	1693	2-01-001	1813
1-01-001	1223	4-02-002	154	38-08-027	17	2-02-002	1814
1-01-001	123	1-01-001	1540	1-01-001	17.3	6-03-003	1815
1-01-001	1231	1-01-001	1543	1-01-001	17**C07	1-01-001	1816
2-02-002	124	1-01-001	155	1-01-001	17*,E	4-02-004	1817
3-03-003	125	1-01-001	155-YARDER	1-01-001	17-1/2-INCH	4-01-001	1818
1-01-001	125,000	1-01-001	1550	1-01-001	17,000	7-03-004	1819
1-01-001	125TH	1-01-001	1558	10-04-005	17TH	1-01-001	182
3-03-003	126	3-02-003	156	2-02-002	170	3-02-002	1820
1-01-001	126,000	2-02-002	1565	1-01-001	170*+0**J*C	5-04-005	1821
1-01-001	127	1-01-001	157	3-01-003	1700	2-01-001	1822
1-01-001	127-MILE	2-01-002	1577	1-01-001	1700'S	1-01-001	1823
3-01-001	128	2-01-001	1579	1-01-001	1702-14	2-02-002	1825
1-01-001	129**K	1-01-001	158	3-03-003	1707	1-01-001	1825-1826
1-01-001	1290	1-01-001	158-POUNDER	1-01-001	1709	2-01-001	1827
1-01-001	1298	1-01-001	1581	1-01-001	171	1-01-001	1830
47-09-037	13	3-01-002	1582	2-02-002	1714	2-02-002	1831
3-02-002	13.5	1-01-001	1589	1-01-001	172	7-01-003	1832
1-01-001	13.8	1-01-001	1590	1-01-001	172ND	1-01-001	1833
1-01-001	13.9	2-01-002	1592	1-01-001	1720	5-02-002	1834
1-01-001	13**K	2-01-001	1593	2-02-002	1721	2-02-003	1835
1-01-001	13*,-*/15	1-01-001	1594-1674	1-01-001	1724	2-02-002	1837
1-01-001	13-1/2	1-01-001	1595	1-01-001	1727	1-01-001	1838
1-01-001	13-16	1-01-001	1596	1-01-001	1728	4-02-002	1840
1-01-001	13-5	1-01-001	1596/7	1-01-001	173	2-02-002	1840'S
1-01-001	13-8	1-01-001	1597	1-01-001	1730	1-01-001	1841
2-01-001	13/16-INCH	1-01-001	1597/8	1-01-001	1731	1-01-001	1843
1-01-001	13,200	1-01-001	1598	1-01-001	1732	5-02-004	1844
6-02-004	13TH	1-01-001	1598/9	1-01-001	1733	5-02-003	1845
5-05-005	130	1-01-001	1599	1-01-001	174	1-01-001	1846
1-01-001	130-YEAR	51-09-038	16	1-01-001	1745	2-01-001	1847
1-01-001	1300	1-01-001	16.38	1-01-001	1746-1748	3-03-003	1848
1-01-001	1307	1-01-001	16.7	1-01-001	1747	2-01-001	1849
1-01-001	1310	1-01-001	16-HOUR	1-01-001	175	1-01-001	185
1-01-001	1311	1-01-001	16-MESH	1-01-001	175,000	1-01-001	185,000
1-01-001	132,000	1-01-001	16-PAGE	1-01-001	1750	1-01-001	185TH
4-02-004	133	1-01-001	16-YEAR-OLD	1-01-001	1751	3-03-003	1850
2-02-002	135	1-01-001	16-22	1-01-001	1755	2-02-002	1850'S
1-01-001	135*+0*C	3-03-003	16,000	1-01-001	1764	4-02-003	1851
1-01-001	138	5-02-004	16TH	1-01-001	1769	1-01-001	1852
1-01-001	139	5-05-005	160	1-01-001	1769-1842	1-01-001	1853
1-01-001	139-FOOT	1-01-001	160*+0*F	1-01-001	1770'S	1-01-001	1854
55-09-042	14	1-01-001	160-ML	1-01-001	1771	2-02-002	1855
1-01-001	14.2	2-02-002	160,000	1-01-001	1773	2-02-002	1857
1-01-001	14.5	3-03-003	1600	1-01-001	1774	2-02-002	1858
2-01-001	14.7	1-01-001	1600/1	5-04-005	1776	10-03-003	1859
3-03-003	14**K	2-01-001	1601	1-01-001	1777	1-01-001	1859-1929
1-01-001	14-*/1	3-02-002	1602	2-02-002	1778	2-02-002	186
1-01-001	14-*/2	1-01-001	1605	2-02-002	1780	1-01-001	1860
1-01-001	14-POWER	2-02-002	1607	1-01-001	1781	1-01-001	1860'S
1-01-001	14-TERM	1-01-001	1608	2-02-002	1782	2-01-001	1860-70
1-01-001	14-1	3-02-002	1609	3-01-002	1783	8-04-004	1861
4-01-001	14-1/2	1-01-001	161	1-01-001	1785	2-02-002	1862
4-03-003	14TH	3-01-001	1610	1-01-001	1786	3-03-003	1863
3-03-003	140	3-02-002	1611	1-01-001	1786-1865	3-02-002	1864
1-01-001	140*+0*F	2-01-002	1613	2-01-002	1787	5-04-005	1865
1-01-001	140,000	1-01-001	1615	2-01-001	1787-89	1-01-001	1865-1868
1-01-001	140,414	1-01-001	162	3-01-001	1788	1-01-001	1866
1-01-001	1409	1-01-001	162-GAME	1-01-001	1788-1873	1-01-001	1867
1-01-001	141	1-01-001	162,400	3-02-003	1789	3-02-002	1868
1-01-001	142	1-01-001	1622	1-01-001	1789-1839	1-01-001	1868-70
1-01-001	143	2-01-001	1624	3-02-002	1791	1-01-001	1869
1-01-001	144	5-01-001	1625	3-02-002	1792	1-01-001	187.5
1-01-001	145	1-01-001	1626	5-03-004	1793	1-01-001	187-MILE
1-01-001	145-POUND	1-01-001	1628	3-02-002	1797	2-01-001	1870
1-01-001	1450	1-01-001	1628/29	1-01-001	1799	1-01-001	1870'S
2-01-001	1453	4-01-001	1629	50-08-038	18	1-01-001	1871
1-01-001	147,000	1-01-001	1630	1-01-001	18'.5	3-03-003	1872
1-01-001	1479	1-01-001	1631	1-01-001	18**C21-22	1-01-001	1874
2-02-002	149	4-01-001	1632	2-01-001	18*,E	4-01-001	1875
1-01-001	1492	1-01-001	1633	1-01-001	18-*MARCH	4-03-003	1876
109-11-060	15	1-01-001	1637	1-01-001	18-MONTH	1-01-001	1878
1-01-001	15.0-15.5	1-01-001	1638	1-01-001	18-1/2	1-01-001	1879
1-01-001	15.4	1-01-001	1639	1-01-001	18-1/2-INCH	2-02-002	188
1-01-001	15.8	1-01-001	1639-40	1-01-001	18-25	1-01-001	1880-1900
1-01-001	15**J*A	1-01-001	164	1-01-001	18,792	2-02-002	1880S
4-03-004	15**K	1-01-001	1640	9-03-005	18TH	2-01-001	1881
1-01-001	15-AND	1-01-001	1642	1-01-001	18TH-*CENTURY	1-01-001	1881-85
1-01-001	15-DEGREE	3-02-002	1643	8-06-008	180	3-02-002	1882
1-01-001	15-HIT	1-01-001	1644	2-02-002	180*+0	6-04-005	1883
1-01-001	15-TO-ONE	2-02-002	165	2-01-002	1800	1-01-001	1884
1-01-001	15-YEAR-OLD	1-01-001	165-UNIT	1-01-001	1800'S	3-02-002	1885
1-01-001	15-1	1-01-001	1655	1-01-001	1800-SQUARE-FOO T	2-02-002	1886
1-01-001	15-17	1-01-001	1657			4-02-003	1887
1-01-001	15-20	1-01-001	166	4-02-002	1801	6-03-004	1888
3-01-001	15-30	1-01-001	1665	1-01-001	1802	1-01-001	1889
2-02-002	15,000	1-01-001	1665.32	3-01-001	1803	2-02-002	189
1-01-001	15,500-**JLB	1-01-001	1667.36	1-01-001	1803-1895	3-02-002	1890
14-06-006	15TH	1-01-001	1671	1-01-001	1804	3-03-003	1890'S
9-05-009	150	1-01-001	1678	1-01-001	1805-1879	1-01-001	1890S
1-01-001	150-MILLIAMPERE	3-03-003	168	1-01-001	1806	4-03-004	1891

Ref	Word	Ref	Word	Ref	Word	Ref	Word
4-04-004	1892	1-01-001	1950-1953	1-01-001	2**C10	1-01-001	2,887,671
3-02-002	1893	3-02-003	1950S	1-01-001	2**C12	1-01-001	2,963
6-03-005	1895	20-07-017	1951	1-01-001	2**C19	1-01-001	2A
8-04-005	1896	1-01-001	1951-1956	3-02-002	2**C20	4-02-004	2D
3-02-003	1897	31-06-019	1952	1-01-001	2**C21	3-03-003	2ND
1-01-001	1897-8	1-01-001	1952-1958	2-01-001	2**C22	88-09-063	20
4-03-004	1898	26-07-020	1953	1-01-001	2**C24	1-01-001	20**+0**J*C
3-03-003	1899	46-07-024	1954	3-01-001	2**C25	1-01-001	20'S
34-09-030	19	25-06-018	1955	2-01-001	2**C26	1-01-001	20**JMM
1-01-001	19-FOOT	3-01-001	1955-57	1-01-001	2**C26.2	5-03-004	20**K
1-01-001	19-1/2	28-07-020	1956	1-01-001	2**C28**-**C33	1-01-001	20*,TH-CENTURY
1-01-001	19-12	46-09-029	1957	1-01-001	2**C28**-**C36	1-01-001	20-**JCPS
1-01-001	19-23	1-01-001	1957**C247-83	1-01-001	2**C29	1-01-001	20-GAUGE
1-01-001	19,000	1-01-001	1957-1958	4-02-004	2**C30	1-01-001	20-INCH-BARREL
1-01-001	19,000,000	1-01-001	1957B	2-01-001	2**C30.3-**C35.3	1-01-001	20-MEGATON
8-04-007	19TH	89-08-044	1958	3-01-001	2**C30.3-**C36	1-01-001	20-PIECE
2-02-002	19TH-CENTURY	1-01-001	1958*=A	2-01-001	2**C30.3-**C36.1	2-01-001	20-TO-1
13-04-008	1900	1-01-001	1958*=B	1-01-001	2**C30**-**C33.2	2-02-002	20-YEAR-OLD
2-02-002	1900'S	1-01-001	1958-60	1-01-001	2**C30**JH	1-01-001	20-22
4-03-004	1901	98-08-047	1959	2-01-001	2**C30-**C34.3	1-01-001	20-25
3-01-003	1902	1-01-001	1959**C271-307	1-01-001	2**C30-**C36	1-01-001	20-50
3-02-003	1903	2-01-001	1959*=A	1-01-001	2**C31	5-04-005	20,000
3-03-003	1904	4-02-002	1959-1960	1-01-001	2**C31.3-**C35.3	1-01-001	20,000,000
6-03-004	1905	2-02-002	1959-60	2-01-001	2**C32	1-01-001	20S
3-02-003	1906	2-02-002	196	2-01-001	2**C32.2**JH	12-06-011	20TH
4-04-004	1907	170-09-070	1960	2-01-001	2**C32.4**JH	2-01-001	20TH-*CENTURY
7-05-005	1908	7-03-006	1960'S	1-01-001	2**C33	38-10-034	200
1-01-001	1908-1910	1-01-001	1960-1961	1-01-001	2**C33.2**JH	1-01-001	200*+0
4-03-004	1909	1-01-001	1960-1962	1-01-001	2**C33.3**JH	1-01-001	200-MAN
2-02-002	1909-10	2-02-002	1960-61	2-01-002	2**C33**JH	1-01-001	200-MEGATON
15-04-010	1910	1-01-001	1960S	2-01-001	2**C34	1-01-001	200-ODD
1-01-001	1910-14	134-09-051	1961	1-01-001	2**C34.2**JH	4-03-004	200,000
3-02-002	1911	2-01-001	1961'S	1-01-001	2**C34**-**C34	5-02-003	2000
1-01-001	1911-1912	2-01-002	1961-62	2-01-001	2**C34**JH	1-01-001	202
12-05-006	1912	34-04-014	1962	5-01-001	2**C35	7-01-001	203
3-01-001	1912-13	8-03-007	1963	4-01-001	2**C35**JH	1-01-001	205-POUND
12-05-009	1913	1-01-001	1963-1972	2-01-001	2**C36	1-01-001	2051
8-05-008	1914	3-03-003	1964	10-01-001	2**C36**JH	1-01-001	206
1-01-001	1914-1918	5-03-004	1965	1-01-001	2**C37.3**-**C36.1**JH	1-01-001	208-POUND
5-03-005	1915	4-02-004	1966	7-01-001	2**C37**JH	45-09-036	21
5-03-005	1916	2-01-002	1967	1-01-001	2**C38	1-01-001	21**C121-137
10-06-006	1917	3-03-003	1970	1-01-001	2**C38**JH	1-01-001	21**K
1-01-001	1917-18	1-01-001	1970S	2-01-001	2**C40	1-01-001	21-**JCM
3-02-002	1918	1-01-001	1971	1-01-001	2**C43.1**-**C38**JH	2-01-002	21-INCH
1-01-001	1918-19	1-01-001	1972	1-01-001	2**C46	1-01-001	21-YEAR
6-03-005	1919	1-01-001	1976	1-01-001	2**C55	1-01-001	21-YEAR-OLD
2-02-002	192	4-02-003	1980	1-01-001	2**C67	1-01-001	21-2
11-06-009	1920	1-01-001	1981	1-01-001	2**C8-10	1-01-001	21-75
8-04-007	1920'S	1-01-001	1984	1-01-001	2**J**YC	1-01-001	21-9
4-04-004	1920S	3-01-001	1986	1-01-001	2**JLB	1-01-001	21/64
8-04-007	1921	1-01-001	1991	9-04-005	2**K	3-02-002	21ST
8-05-007	1922	450-13-176	2	1-01-001	2*,-*/12	2-02-002	210
7-04-007	1923	2-01-001	2.0	1-01-001	2*,-2	3-02-002	2100
1-01-001	1923-27	4-02-003	2.1	1-01-001	2*,-3	2-02-002	211
9-05-006	1924	1-01-001	2.1.6	1-01-001	2*,-4	1-01-001	2118
9-04-009	1925	1-01-001	2.16	1-01-001	2*,-5	2-02-002	213
6-05-005	1926	1-01-001	2.2	1-01-001	2-*A.	1-01-001	2130
19-06-011	1927	1-01-001	2.21.6	1-01-001	2-AND-2	2-02-002	214
5-03-005	1928	1-01-001	2.26	1-01-001	2-BASER	1-01-001	214,938
1-01-001	1928-29	1-01-001	2.295**K	1-01-001	2-HOUR-AND-27-MINUTE	1-01-001	215
7-04-007	1929	1-01-001	2.3	1-01-001	2-INCH	1-01-001	216
11-05-011	1930	1-01-001	2.325**K	2-01-001	2-LITER	45-09-034	22
7-03-005	1930'S	3-01-003	2.4	1-01-001	2-OVER-PAR	1-01-001	22**K
2-02-002	1930S	1-01-001	2.405	2-01-001	2-RUN	1-01-001	22-ACRE
7-03-006	1931	1-01-001	2.44	1-01-001	2-SCORE-YEAR	1-01-001	22-DAY
1-01-001	1931-40	4-01-004	2.5	1-01-001	2-WEEK	2-01-001	22-YEAR-OLD
3-02-003	1932	1-01-001	2.5**K	5-02-002	2-YEAR-OLD	1-01-001	22-1/2
1-01-001	1932-33	2-01-001	2.512	3-01-001	2-YEAR-OLDS	1-01-001	22-12
9-06-008	1933	1-01-001	2.54	3-03-003	2-1/2	1-01-001	22-24
6-03-005	1934	1-01-001	2.55	2-02-002	2-3/4	1-01-001	22-29
10-08-008	1935	1-01-001	2.58	2-02-002	2-5	2-02-002	22,000
1-01-001	1935-1955	4-02-003	2.6	8-01-001	2-56	1-01-001	22,23
6-04-006	1936	1-01-001	2.7	1-01-001	2/**JC	1-01-001	22,807
10-06-010	1937	2-01-001	2.75	1-01-001	2/3	3-02-002	22ND
8-07-008	1938	1-01-001	2.8	1-01-001	2/4	2-02-002	220
1-01-001	1938-1939	1-01-001	2**+0**J*C	8-04-007	2,000	2-01-001	220*+0
2-01-001	1938-39	1-01-001	2'S	1-01-001	2,090	1-01-001	220-YARD
6-04-006	1939	1-01-001	2**C00.2**JH	2-01-002	2,100	1-01-001	221-207
15-07-011	1940	1-01-001	2**C00.3	1-01-001	2,200,000	1-01-001	22111
1-01-001	1940'S	1-01-001	2**C01.1	1-01-001	2,300	1-01-001	2230
1-01-001	1940S	2-01-001	2**C01.1**JH	1-01-001	2,417	1-01-001	224-170
11-05-008	1941	1-01-001	2**C01.3**JH	1-01-001	2,418	1-01-001	225**J*H*P
11-06-009	1942	1-01-001	2**C02	1-01-001	2,425	1-01-001	225,000
11-05-008	1943	1-01-001	2**C02.2	1-01-001	2,460	1-01-001	2269
15-07-011	1944	2-01-001	2**C02.3	1-01-001	2,489,000	1-01-001	2274
18-06-016	1945	1-01-001	2**C03	1-01-001	2,500	1-01-001	228
20-06-015	1946	1-01-001	2**C04	1-01-001	2,700,877	1-01-001	228-229
1-01-001	1946-52	2-01-001	2**C04.2**JH	1-01-001	2,758	2-02-002	229
14-06-013	1947	1-01-001	2**C05	1-01-001	2,800	46-09-034	23
1-01-001	1947-49	1-01-001	2**C05.1**JH	1-01-001	2,800,000	1-01-001	23**C30
20-07-014	1948	1-01-001	2**C05.2			1-01-001	23**C34
1-01-001	1948**C135-75	1-01-001	2**C05.3			1-01-001	23**J*A
20-06-015	1949	1-01-001	2**C06.1			1-01-001	23-YEAR-OLD
2-01-002	195	1-01-001	2**C06.3**JH			1-01-001	23-30
1-01-001	195-PAGE	1-01-001	2**C06**JH			1-01-001	23-36
21-09-018	1950	2-01-001	2**C1			5-02-002	23D
4-03-004	1950'S					3-03-003	23RD

Code	Term	Code	Term	Code	Term	Code	Term
3-02-003	230	1-01-001	29-*JULY	6-05-006	300,000	4-01-001	381
1-01-001	235	3-01-001	29-*OCT	1-01-001	300TH	4-01-001	381(A
1-01-001	236	1-01-001	29-32*+0*C	1-01-001	3000	2-01-001	381(C
1-01-001	237**K	1-01-001	29-5	1-01-001	302	1-01-001	381(C)(14
2-02-002	239	5-04-005	29TH	38-07-023	31	1-01-001	381(C)(16
49-10-035	24	1-01-001	2991	2-02-002	31ST	1-01-001	381(C)(4
1-01-001	24**+0	282-12-127	3	1-01-001	312	2-01-001	381(C)(6
2-01-001	24**K	1-01-001	3.0	1-01-001	314	1-01-001	381(C)(9
8-01-001	24-**JHR	2-01-002	3.03	1-01-001	31730	1-01-001	385
1-01-001	24-*OCT	1-01-001	3.1	1-01-001	3181	1-01-001	387
1-01-001	24-HOUR	1-01-001	3.10	1-01-001	31978	1-01-001	389
1-01-001	24-HOUR-DAY	1-01-001	3.1416	13-07-011	32	6-03-006	39
1-01-001	24-IN	4-01-001	3.15	1-01-001	32*+0**J*F	1-01-001	39-YEAR-OLD
1-01-001	24-INCH	1-01-001	3.190	1-01-001	32*+0*C	2-01-002	39,000
1-01-001	24-SHEET	2-02-002	3.25	1-01-001	32,000	1-01-001	390
1-01-001	24-YEAR-OLD	1-01-001	3.28	1-01-001	32,589	1-01-001	390-FOOT
1-01-001	24,400	2-02-002	3.3	1-01-001	320	1-01-001	391
7-05-007	24TH	1-01-001	3.4	1-01-001	320*T*R	2-02-002	392
2-02-002	240	2-01-001	3.46	2-02-002	3211	1-01-001	394
2-01-001	240-GRAIN	4-02-004	3.5	1-01-001	3247	1-01-001	395
1-01-001	242**K	1-01-001	3.5**K	1-01-001	325	196-11-110	4
1-01-001	2433	1-01-001	3.7	1-01-001	327	1-01-001	4.0
1-01-001	2454	1-01-001	3.75	1-01-001	328	1-01-001	4.00
1-01-001	247	1-01-001	3.8	7-05-007	33	2-01-002	4.1
82-10-058	25	1-01-001	3.9	1-01-001	33-MAN	4-01-001	4.2
1-01-001	25.1**K	1-01-001	3.98	1-01-001	33-1/2	1-01-001	4.21
1-01-001	25.3	1-01-001	3'S	1-01-001	33-1/3**K	3-01-001	4.3
1-01-001	25**JC	1-01-001	3**C00	1-01-001	33D	1-01-001	4.4
6-05-006	25**K	1-01-001	3**C10-12	3-02-002	330	2-01-002	4.5
1-01-001	25-FOOT	1-01-001	3**C14	1-01-001	3300	1-01-001	4.6
1-01-001	25-FOOTER	1-01-001	3**C16	3-02-002	332	1-01-001	4.7
1-01-001	25-FT	1-01-001	3**C17	1-01-001	334	1-01-001	4.77
1-01-001	25-GALLON	1-01-001	3**C18	2-01-001	337*+0**J*C	1-01-001	4.8
1-01-001	25-LITER	1-01-001	3**C20	20-06-008	34	1-01-001	4**C00
1-01-001	25-MILE-SQUARE	2-01-001	3**C3	1-01-001	34.7	1-01-001	4**C05
1-01-001	25-MINUTE	1-01-001	3**C30	1-01-001	34**C8	1-01-001	4**C1
1-01-001	25-YEAR-OLD	1-01-001	3**C300	1-01-001	34-HOUR	1-01-001	4**C18
1-01-001	25-30	1-01-001	3**C36	1-01-001	34,000	1-01-001	4**C3
7-04-005	25,000	1-01-001	3**C5	1-01-001	340*+0**J*C	3-02-003	4**C30
1-01-001	25,000-MAN	1-01-001	3**C58	1-01-001	340*T*R	2-02-002	4**C45
1-01-001	25,000,000	2-01-001	3**C7	1-01-001	340-BLAST	1-01-001	4**C5
2-02-002	25TH	1-01-001	3**C8	1-01-001	34220	1-01-001	4**C7
11-07-011	250	1-01-001	3**C9	1-01-001	343	1-01-001	4**K
1-01-001	250-275	1-01-001	3**K	2-01-001	346	1-01-001	4*,-**J*D
4-03-003	250,000	3-01-001	3*M*M	4-01-001	348	1-01-001	4*,-1
1-01-001	2500	2-01-001	3-**JCM	19-09-019	35	2-02-002	4-
1-01-001	253	1-01-001	3-**JHP	1-01-001	35.3	4-01-001	4-**J*H
1-01-001	254	1-01-001	3-BY-	1-01-001	35**K	1-01-001	4-CELL
1-01-001	2544	1-01-001	3-FOOT	1-01-001	35-FOOT	2-01-001	4-DAY
1-01-001	255	1-01-001	3-GAME	1-01-001	35-MM**.-WIDE	1-01-001	4-FOR-5
2-01-001	258	1-01-001	3-HITTER	8-06-007	350	1-01-001	4-HOMER
33-08-027	26	1-01-001	3-MONTH	2-01-002	350,000	3-02-002	4-INCH
1-01-001	26.8	1-01-001	3-RUN	1-01-001	350TH	1-01-001	4-MONTH
1-01-001	26-YEAR-OLD	1-01-001	3-TO-0	1-01-001	3500	1-01-001	4-PASSENGER
1-01-001	26-2	1-01-001	3-TO-3	1-01-001	35050	1-01-001	4-UNDER-PAR
1-01-001	26-28	1-01-001	3-YEAR-OLD	6-01-001	353	2-01-002	4-YEAR
1-01-001	26,500	1-01-001	3-0	2-02-002	354	1-01-001	4-YEAR-OLD
2-01-002	26TH	4-03-004	3-1/2	2-02-002	355	2-01-001	4-0
5-03-003	260	1-01-001	3-10	1-01-001	357	1-01-001	4-1/2**K
1-01-001	260-MEMBER	2-01-001	3-3/4	8-05-007	36	1-01-001	4-13
1-01-001	261	1-01-001	3-4	1-01-001	36-**J*A	1-01-001	4-4
1-01-001	265	1-01-001	3-48	1-01-001	36-IN	1-01-001	4-7/8
1-01-001	268,900	1-01-001	3-5	1-01-001	36-YEAR-OLD	1-01-001	4/4
1-01-001	2688	1-01-001	3-6	1-01-001	36TH	3-03-003	4,000
1-01-001	269	1-01-001	3-7/8	4-04-004	360	1-01-001	4,000-FOOT
23-09-021	27	2-01-001	3-94	1-01-001	360,000	1-01-001	4,122,354
2-01-001	27**C1	1-01-001	3/16	2-02-002	361	1-01-001	4,1957
1-01-001	27**K	1-01-001	3/4	2-02-002	362	1-01-001	4,369
1-01-001	27-IN	1-01-001	3/64	1-01-001	3646	1-01-001	4,427
1-01-001	27-YEAR-OLD	2-01-002	3/8-INCH	1-01-001	365	1-01-001	4,441
1-01-001	27-30	1-01-001	3/8-INCH-THICK	1-01-001	367	1-01-001	4,499,608
2-01-002	27,000	9-05-009	3,000	1-01-001	368(A)(1)(*A	2-02-002	4,500
1-01-001	27TH	2-01-001	3,000-FOOT	1-01-001	368(A)(1)(*B	1-01-001	4,585
2-01-001	270	1-01-001	3,325	1-01-001	368(A)(1)(*F	1-01-001	4,622,444
1-01-001	270,000	1-01-001	3,399	1-01-001	369	1-01-001	4,900
1-01-001	2705	1-01-001	3,400	7-05-006	37	8-04-005	4TH
1-01-001	271	1-01-001	3,450	2-01-001	37*+0	38-09-034	40
1-01-001	272	3-02-002	3,500	2-01-001	37*+0**J*C	1-01-001	40*+0**J*F
1-01-001	273	5-02-003	3RD	1-01-001	37-YEAR-OLD	1-01-001	40'S
1-01-001	2731	106-09-063	30	1-01-001	37-1/2	7-04-004	40**K
4-03-003	275	1-01-001	30**B/**JMBF	1-01-001	37,000	1-01-001	40-GRAIN
1-01-001	275*+0*F	5-03-005	30**K	1-01-001	37,081	2-01-002	40-YEAR-OLD
1-01-001	275-300	2-01-002	30-	1-01-001	37,470	9-05-007	40,000
1-01-001	278	1-01-001	30-INCH	1-01-001	37,679	2-02-002	40,000,000
20-09-018	28	1-01-001	30-MINUTE	1-01-001	37TH	18-07-015	400
1-01-001	28-*OCT	2-01-002	30-ODD	1-01-001	372	1-01-001	400-**JLB
1-01-001	28-30	1-01-001	30-PIECE	3-02-003	375	1-01-001	400-KC
6-03-004	28TH	1-01-001	30-YEAR	3-01-001	375*+0**J*C	1-01-001	400-POUND
4-03-004	280	1-01-001	30-30	1-01-001	376	1-01-001	400-401
1-01-001	280-YARD	1-01-001	30-40	1-01-001	379,900	2-01-002	400,000
1-01-001	2809	5-05-005	30,000	8-04-006	38	1-01-001	400,000,000
1-01-001	281	1-01-001	30,000,000	1-01-001	38*+0	1-01-001	4000-PLUS
1-01-001	2825	2-02-002	30S	1-01-001	38-POINT	1-01-001	402
1-01-001	283	5-03-005	30TH	3-01-001	38-43**0	2-02-002	407
1-01-001	285	25-08-021	300	1-01-001	38-43*+0*C	11-02-009	41
18-08-017	29	1-01-001	300-325*+0**J*C	1-01-001	38-7	1-01-001	41-8
2-02-002	29.2	1-01-001	300-450	1-01-001	380-FOOT	1-01-001	410

Ref	Term
1-01-001	410*+0**J*C
1-01-001	412
1-01-001	412-413
1-01-001	415
17-08-015	42
1-01-001	42*+0*F
2-01-001	42-INCH
1-01-001	42,000
1-01-001	42D
3-02-003	420
5-03-003	43
1-01-001	430,000
1-01-001	431
1-01-001	434
3-02-003	44
3-02-002	44-YEAR-OLD
1-01-001	44,000
1-01-001	442
1-01-001	443
2-01-001	447
13-05-012	45
1-01-001	45.6
4-02-002	45*+0
1-01-001	45**K
1-01-001	45-DEGREE
1-01-001	45-PASSENGER
4-04-004	450
1-01-001	450-MILE-LONG
1-01-001	450,000
1-01-001	451
1-01-001	452
9-05-008	46
1-01-001	46**K
1-01-001	46,000
2-02-002	46TH
1-01-001	462
1-01-001	463*+0**J*C
1-01-001	469
8-04-007	47
1-01-001	47.1**K
1-01-001	47.6
1-01-001	47**JMG/**JL
1-01-001	470
1-01-001	470*+0**J*C
15-06-012	48
1-01-001	48,000
1-01-001	48,500
2-02-002	480
5-03-005	49
1-01-001	49*+0-71**0*C
1-01-001	49**K
1-01-001	49ERS
1-01-001	49TH
1-01-001	4911
1-01-001	492
1-01-001	495
134-10-077	5
1-01-001	5.1
1-01-001	5.3
1-01-001	5.4
1-01-001	5.4**B/**JMBF
1-01-001	5.4865771
3-01-003	5.5
2-01-001	5.6
3-02-002	5.7
1-01-001	5.8
1-01-001	5*+0**J*C
1-01-001	5**C00
1-01-001	5**C1
2-01-001	5**C12
1-01-001	5**C17
1-01-001	5**C18
1-01-001	5**C24
1-01-001	5**C26
1-01-001	5**C30
1-01-001	5**C4
1-01-001	5**C45
6-02-003	5**K
1-01-001	5-
2-02-002	5-DAY
2-02-002	5-FOOT
1-01-001	5-GAME
1-01-001	5-MILE
1-01-001	5-PASSENGER
1-01-001	5-PERCENT
2-01-001	5-RUN
1-01-001	5-TO-1
1-01-001	5-TO-2
1-01-001	5-TO-3
3-02-002	5-1
1-01-001	5-1/2
1-01-001	5-10**J**YM
1-01-001	5-3
2-01-001	5-3/4
1-01-001	5-30
1-01-001	5-4
2-02-002	5-5
1-01-001	5-6
2-02-002	5-7
1-01-001	5/16
1-01-001	5/64
1-01-001	5/8-INCH
7-05-007	5,000
1-01-001	5,014
1-01-001	5,500
1-01-001	5TH
64-10-041	50
1-01-001	50*+0
1-01-001	50'S
18-05-009	50**K
3-01-002	50-FOOT
1-01-001	50-INCH
4-01-003	50-MEGATON
1-01-001	50-PERCENT
1-01-001	50-YEAR
1-01-001	50-YEAR-OLD
1-01-001	50-100
1-01-001	50-50
1-01-001	50,000
1-01-001	50,000,000
2-01-002	50TH
14-06-012	500
1-01-001	500'S
2-02-002	500-MILE
3-02-002	500,000
4-03-004	5000
1-01-001	5000-WORD
1-01-001	5031
1-01-001	505
1-01-001	508-YARD
5-04-004	51
2-01-001	51ST
1-01-001	510
1-01-001	511
1-01-001	514
1-01-001	514*C
1-01-001	5155
7-03-005	52
1-01-001	52-YEAR
1-01-001	52-YEAR-OLD
1-01-001	52ND
1-01-001	520
1-01-001	520-ACRE
1-01-001	525
1-01-001	526
8-03-007	53
1-01-001	53-YEAR-OLD
1-01-001	532
5-03-005	54
2-01-001	54-17
1-01-001	54,320
1-01-001	54TH
2-02-002	540
1-01-001	540-**J*K
1-01-001	5404
1-01-001	541
1-01-001	542,250
1-01-001	543
1-01-001	545-YARD
11-05-010	55
1-01-001	55,000
1-01-001	55,987
1-01-001	553
6-03-006	56
1-01-001	56**J*A
1-01-001	56-YARD
1-01-001	56,000
1-01-001	5612
1-01-001	562
2-02-002	565
1-01-001	566
7-05-006	57
1-01-001	57**K
1-01-001	570
1-01-001	573
1-01-001	5777
8-03-005	58
1-01-001	58.8**K
2-01-001	58TH
1-01-001	5835
1-01-001	5847
1-01-001	589
4-03-004	59
1-01-001	59,780
113-12-077	6
1-01-001	6.2
1-01-001	6.3
2-01-002	6.4
1-01-001	6.5
2-01-001	6.9
1-01-001	6*+0**J*C
1-01-001	6'.7
1-01-001	6**C00
1-01-001	6**C14-15
2-02-002	6**C15
1-01-001	6**C30
1-01-001	6**C35
1-01-001	6**C50
1-01-001	6**JA
3-02-003	6**K
1-01-001	6*,TH
1-01-001	6-
4-01-001	6-**J*B
2-01-002	6-**JHR
2-01-002	6-FOOT
1-01-001	6-FOOT-10
1-01-001	6-FOOT-3-INCH
1-01-001	6-FT
2-02-002	6-INCH
1-01-001	6-OUNCE
2-01-001	6-PASSENGER
1-01-001	6-YEAR
1-01-001	6-1
2-02-002	6-1/2
1-01-001	6-12
1-01-001	6-2/3
3-01-002	6-3
1-01-001	6-3-3
1-01-001	6-4-2
1-01-001	6-5
1-01-001	6-6
1-01-001	6-7
5-03-005	6,000
1-01-001	6,768
1-01-001	600*+0
5-04-004	6TH
44-08-036	60
1-01-001	60*+0*C
1-01-001	60'S
1-01-001	60**JLB
1-01-001	60**JLB**J*B*0* D/DAY/ACRE
1-01-001	60**K
1-01-001	60-CITY
1-01-001	60-DAY
1-01-001	60-INCH
1-01-001	60-MONTH
1-01-001	60-1
1-01-001	60-66
2-02-002	60-80
3-02-003	60,000
1-01-001	60S
8-05-008	600
1-01-001	600-MILE
1-01-001	600-YARD
2-01-002	6000
1-01-001	601
1-01-001	602.2
1-01-001	603
1-01-001	604
2-02-002	605
1-01-001	606
2-01-001	607
1-01-001	607-608
1-01-001	609
8-04-005	61
1-01-001	61.2**K
1-01-001	61ST
1-01-001	6124
1-01-001	613
1-01-001	619,000
2-02-002	62
1-01-001	62-YEAR-OLD
1-01-001	62-63
1-01-001	622
5-05-005	63
1-01-001	63-64
1-01-001	63,000,000
1-01-001	63D
1-01-001	635
1-01-001	637
1-01-001	63711-R
1-01-001	638,560
3-02-003	64
1-01-001	64**JC
1-01-001	64**K
1-01-001	64-PAGE
1-01-001	64-13
1-01-001	64-66
1-01-001	642
1-01-001	643
1-01-001	645-ACRE
1-01-001	646
14-06-013	65
2-01-001	65*+0
1-01-001	65**K
1-01-001	65-YEAR-OLD
1-01-001	65,000
1-01-001	650
2-02-002	66
1-01-001	66TH
1-01-001	67
1-01-001	67-YEAR-OLD
1-01-001	675
1-01-001	676
2-02-002	677
6-02-004	68
1-01-001	687.87
1-01-001	689-PAGE
7-02-003	69
1-01-001	6934
1-01-001	694
1-01-001	695
91-11-061	7
1-01-001	7.19
1-01-001	7.2
4-03-004	7.5
1-01-001	7.6**K
1-01-001	7**B/**JCWT
2-02-002	7**C00
1-01-001	7**C10
1-01-001	7**C17
1-01-001	7**C25
7-04-005	7**C30
2-02-002	7**C45
1-01-001	7**C50
1-01-001	7**J*A
2-02-002	7**K
1-01-001	7-DAY
1-01-001	7-DAY-WEEK
2-01-001	7-PASSENGER
1-01-001	7-ROOM
7-01-003	7-1
1-01-001	7-11
3-01-001	7-2
2-01-001	7-3
2-01-001	7-4
1-01-001	7-5
2-02-002	7-6
1-01-001	7-9
1-01-001	7/16
2-01-001	7/2
2-02-002	7,000
1-01-001	7,000,000
1-01-001	7,360,187
1-01-001	7,484,268
1-01-001	7,500
1-01-001	7,827
12-03-003	7TH
20-06-017	70
1-01-001	70**-NO
1-01-001	70'S
3-02-002	70**K
1-01-001	70-YEAR-OLD
1-01-001	70-80
4-03-003	70,000
1-01-001	70,000,000
1-01-001	70,524
1-01-001	70TH
6-04-005	700
1-01-001	700-MILE
1-01-001	701
1-01-001	701ST
1-01-001	7026
1-01-001	7034
1-01-001	704
4-01-001	707
3-01-001	7070
4-01-001	7070/7074
1-01-001	7074
10-03-006	71
1-01-001	710
10-05-010	72
1-01-001	72-HOLE
2-01-001	72ND
1-01-001	725'S
1-01-001	7287
4-03-003	73
1-01-001	734
6-03-006	74
1-01-001	74.1
1-01-001	742
1-01-001	742*C
19-05-015	75
4-02-003	75**K
1-01-001	75-MINUTE
3-03-003	75,000
1-01-001	75,000-TON
1-01-001	75TH
4-02-003	750
1-01-001	7599
6-05-006	76
1-01-001	76.7
1-01-001	76-PER
1-01-001	760
1-01-001	762
1-01-001	764
1-01-001	767

4-03-004	77	1-01-001	9,273	1-01-001	$1.00	1-01-001	$2.82
1-01-001	77-294**+0*K	1-01-001	9,748,000	3-03-003	$1.1	1-01-001	$2.98
2-02-002	770	1-01-001	9,910,741	1-01-001	$1.10	6-04-006	$2,000
2-02-002	78	7-01-002	9TH	1-01-001	$1.26	2-02-002	$2,000,000
1-01-001	78-79	12-08-012	90	1-01-001	$1.4	1-01-001	$2,170
2-01-001	78TH	3-01-002	90**+0	1-01-001	$1.5	1-01-001	$2,300
1-01-001	79**JC	1-01-001	90**+0*F	1-01-001	$1.6	1-01-001	$2,300,000
1-01-001	79,400	4-04-004	90**K	1-01-001	$1.60	1-01-001	$2,323,867
1-01-001	790	1-01-001	90-DAY	1-01-001	$1.65	1-01-001	$2,330,000
1-01-001	795,586	2-01-001	90-DEGREE	1-01-001	$1.7	1-01-001	$2,412,616
1-01-001	798	1-01-001	90,000	2-01-001	$1.8	1-01-001	$2,461,000
104-10-068	8	1-01-001	90S	1-01-001	$1.80	1-01-001	$2,490
2-01-001	8.6	3-03-003	900	2-01-001	$1.9	1-01-001	$2,500
2-01-001	8.6-**JMM	1-01-001	900-CALORIE	11-05-007	$1,000	1-01-001	$2,557,111
5-01-004	8**C30	1-01-001	900-STUDENT	2-02-002	$1,000,000	1-01-001	$2,700
1-01-001	8**C31	1-01-001	900,000	1-01-001	$1,000,000,000	6-02-004	$20
1-01-001	8**C36	1-01-001	91	2-02-002	$1,200	6-04-006	$20,000
2-02-002	8**K	3-03-003	92	1-01-001	$1,250,000	1-01-001	$20,000,000
1-01-001	8*,.266-366	1-01-001	92.5	1-01-001	$1,276	1-01-001	$20,000,000,000
1-01-001	8*,.499-520	1-01-001	920	1-01-001	$1,390	1-01-001	$20,447,000
1-01-001	8-**JMM	1-01-001	923,076	1-01-001	$1,450,000,000	7-05-007	$200
1-01-001	8-*BALLS	3-02-003	93	4-02-003	$1,500	2-02-002	$200,000
1-01-001	8-CHANNEL	1-01-001	9329	2-02-002	$1,500,000	1-01-001	$200,000-A-YEAR
2-02-002	8-INCH	1-01-001	940*Y	1-01-001	$1,600	1-01-001	$200,000,000
2-02-002	8-OZ	1-01-001	943	1-01-001	$1,750,000	1-01-001	$214
1-01-001	8-YEAR-OLD	1-01-001	944	1-01-001	$1,800	1-01-001	$22
1-01-001	8-1/2-FOOT	1-01-001	949	1-01-001	$1,961,000	1-01-001	$22.50
1-01-001	8-4	6-04-006	95	7-04-007	$10	1-01-001	$222
7-05-006	8,000	1-01-001	950	1-01-001	$10.00	1-01-001	$227.72
1-01-001	8,000,000	1-01-001	954	1-01-001	$10.1	2-01-001	$23,000,000
1-01-001	8,100	5-03-003	96	1-01-001	$10.3	1-01-001	$230,000
2-01-001	8,280	1-01-001	960-**J*MC	2-01-001	$10.50	1-01-001	$24,926,615
1-01-001	8,293	1-01-001	963	1-01-001	$10.8	1-01-001	$2400
1-01-001	8,500	4-03-003	97	9-04-009	$10,000	3-01-003	$25
3-03-003	8TH	3-03-003	98	1-01-001	$10,000-PER-YEAR	1-01-001	$25-A-PLATE
17-07-016	80	1-01-001	989			4-02-004	$25,000
1-01-001	80**+0*C	8-03-003	99	1-01-001	$10,000,000	4-02-004	$250
2-02-002	80'S	1-01-001	99.1	12-05-010	$100	1-01-001	$250,000
2-01-001	80**K	1-01-001	.0044**K	4-03-003	$100,000	1-01-001	$2500
1-01-001	80-**JHP	1-01-001	.01	1-01-001	$102,285,000	1-01-001	$251
2-02-002	80,000	1-01-001	.020	1-01-001	$1020	1-01-001	$253,355,000
1-01-001	80TH	2-01-001	.027	1-01-001	$109	1-01-001	$26.5-BILLION
13-03-004	800	1-01-001	.028	2-02-002	$11	1-01-001	$26,000,000
1-01-001	800'S	1-01-001	.05	1-01-001	$11.50	1-01-001	$27.50
3-02-003	800,000	1-01-001	.05**K	1-01-001	$11,900,000	1-01-001	$278,877,000
3-02-003	81	3-01-001	.07	2-01-001	$110	4-01-001	$28
1-01-001	81,000	1-01-001	.076	1-01-001	$115,000	1-01-001	$28.00
1-01-001	817	1-01-001	.09	1-01-001	$12	1-01-001	$28,700,000
1-01-001	82	1-01-001	.1	1-01-001	$12.00	2-02-002	$29
1-01-001	821,220	1-01-001	.130	1-01-001	$12.1	1-01-001	$29,000
1-01-001	823	1-01-001	.143	2-01-001	$12.50	1-01-001	$297
1-01-001	825,000	1-01-001	.179	1-01-001	$12.7	3-03-003	$3
1-01-001	828	12-02-002	.22	1-01-001	$12,192,865	2-01-001	$3.00
2-02-002	83	3-03-003	.22-CALIBER	2-01-001	$12,500	1-01-001	$3.11
1-01-001	83RD	1-01-001	.222'S	1-01-001	$120	1-01-001	$3.15
1-01-001	836-901	1-01-001	.243	3-03-003	$125	1-01-001	$3.22
1-01-001	84-FOOT	1-01-001	.255	1-01-001	$128	2-01-002	$3.5
1-01-001	840,503	2-01-001	.264	5-02-002	$135	1-01-001	$3.50
9-04-009	85	1-01-001	.267	1-01-001	$139.3	4-03-003	$3,000
2-01-001	85**0	1-01-001	.270	3-02-002	$14	1-01-001	$3,500
2-02-002	85**K	2-01-002	.280	2-02-002	$14.00	2-01-002	$3,500,000
1-01-001	85-PIECE	1-01-001	.30-30	1-01-001	$14,000	1-01-001	$3,675
1-01-001	85-STUDENT	4-02-002	.300	1-01-001	$140	1-01-001	$3,825
1-01-001	85-90*+0*F	1-01-001	.306	1-01-001	$148.50	2-02-002	$30
7-04-007	86	1-01-001	.308	5-04-005	$15	3-02-003	$30,000
1-01-001	86**K	1-01-001	.318	1-01-001	$15.5	1-01-001	$30,000,000
1-01-001	869	1-01-001	.323	3-01-002	$15,000	7-04-007	$300
2-02-002	87	1-01-001	.332	2-01-002	$15,000,000	1-01-001	$300,000
1-01-001	87-1/2	1-01-001	.338	6-04-006	$150	1-01-001	$300,000,000
1-01-001	87-31	1-01-001	.340	1-01-001	$1500	1-01-001	$306
2-01-001	87TH	1-01-001	.345	1-01-001	$157,460	1-01-001	$31,179,816
1-01-001	870,000	1-01-001	.365	1-01-001	$16	1-01-001	$310
1-01-001	871-892	2-01-001	.375	1-01-001	$16.00	2-02-002	$32,000
1-01-001	88	3-02-002	.38	1-01-001	$16.80	1-01-001	$325
1-01-001	88'S	1-01-001	.389	1-01-001	$16,000	1-01-001	$344,000
1-01-001	883,000	1-01-001	.404'S	1-01-001	$165	1-01-001	$35
1-01-001	885	2-01-001	.410	1-01-001	$17	1-01-001	$35,823
1-01-001	8861	4-01-001	.44	1-01-001	$17.8	1-01-001	$350
1-01-001	899	4-01-002	.45	3-02-003	$17,000	1-01-001	$350,000
63-10-047	9	1-01-001	.45-CALIBER	1-01-001	$17,000,000	1-01-001	$36
1-01-001	9.3	1-01-001	.455	2-01-001	$170	3-01-002	$37
2-02-002	9.4	2-01-001	.458	1-01-001	$172,000	1-01-001	$37,500
2-01-002	9.8	2-02-002	.5	1-01-001	$172,400	1-01-001	$380
1-01-001	9**C00	1-01-001	.50	2-01-002	$18	1-01-001	$39.5
1-01-001	9**C30	1-01-001	.500	1-01-001	$18.2	1-01-001	$39,000
1-01-001	9**C30-4**C00	1-01-001	.7	2-02-002	$18.9	1-01-001	$395,000
1-01-001	9**C40	1-01-001	.75	1-01-001	$184	5-03-005	$4
1-01-001	9**C47	1-01-001	.7854	1-01-001	$185	1-01-001	$4.9
1-01-001	9**J*N	139-12-039	+	1-01-001	$187	1-01-001	$4.98
1-01-001	9**JA	1-01-001	+.04	1-01-001	$19.3	1-01-001	$4/**JMBF
1-01-001	9**JB	1-01-001	+.50	8-04-006	$2	1-01-001	$4,000
1-01-001	9**JE	1-01-001	+.7	1-01-001	$2.00	1-01-001	$4,000,000
1-01-001	9-1/2	1-01-001	+C	1-01-001	$2.09	1-01-001	$4,177.37
1-01-001	9-11	14-05-009	$1	1-01-001	$2.30/**JMBF	1-01-001	$4,500
1-01-001	9-6	1-01-001	$1.0	1-01-001	$2.50	2-01-001	$4,500,000
1-01-001	9-7			1-01-001	$2.80	1-01-001	$4,700
1-01-001	9/32						

Code	Term
1-01-001	$4,753
1-01-001	$4,800
3-02-002	$40
2-02-002	$40,000
1-01-001	$40,000,000
3-02-003	$400
1-01-001	$4200
1-01-001	$43.50
1-01-001	$43,000
1-01-001	$44.3-BILLION
4-02-002	$45
3-02-002	$450
1-01-001	$450,000
1-01-001	$451,500
1-01-001	$457,000
1-01-001	$46.7
1-01-001	$47,101,000
8-05-006	$5
1-01-001	$5.2
1-01-001	$5.4
1-01-001	$5-8,000
6-03-006	$5,000
3-02-002	$5,000,000
7-04-007	$50
2-02-002	$50,000
1-01-001	$50,400,000
12-05-010	$500
3-01-003	$500,000
5-02-002	$5000
1-01-001	$52,500
2-01-001	$538
1-01-001	$55,000
1-01-001	$550
1-01-001	$56
1-01-001	$57,500
1-01-001	$58,918
1-01-001	$580
1-01-001	$581
1-01-001	$581,000
1-01-001	$590,000
1-01-001	$6
1-01-001	$6,100,000,000
1-01-001	$6,666.66
6-02-004	$60
1-01-001	$60,000
13-05-008	$600
1-01-001	$610
1-01-001	$625,561
1-01-001	$63.8
1-01-001	$634,517,000
2-01-002	$65
1-01-001	$65,000
1-01-001	$650
1-01-001	$66,000
1-01-001	$67,000
3-02-002	$7
2-01-001	$7.00
1-01-001	$7.20
1-01-001	$7.50
1-01-001	$7,000
1-01-001	$7,000,000
1-01-001	$7,082
1-01-001	$7,500,000
1-01-001	$70
1-01-001	$70,000
4-02-003	$700
1-01-001	$720
1-01-001	$73.50
1-01-001	$740
1-01-001	$740,000
4-03-004	$75
1-01-001	$75-BILLION
1-01-001	$75,000,000
3-01-002	$750
1-01-001	$750,000
1-01-001	$754
1-01-001	$77,389,000
1-01-001	$79.89
2-02-002	$8
2-01-001	$8.00
1-01-001	$8.5
1-01-001	$8,250
1-01-001	$8,313,514
1-01-001	$8,555
1-01-001	$80
2-01-002	$80,738
6-04-005	$800
1-01-001	$800,000
1-01-001	$81
1-01-001	$83,750
1-01-001	$84,000,000
1-01-001	$840,000
1-01-001	$842,617
3-02-003	$85
1-01-001	$85,000
1-01-001	$88,000
2-02-002	$9
1-01-001	$9.2
2-01-001	$9.50
1-01-001	$9,841,000
2-02-002	$90
3-03-003	$900
1-01-001	$94
1-01-001	**=*T*C*U'S**$
1-01-001	**=P**$
1-01-001	**=P**$(*=*T*$)
1-01-001	**=P**$(*=T*$)
1-01-001	**=P**$(*0).
1-01-001	**=Q**$.
1-01-001	**=Q**$(*=T*$)
1-01-001	**B**U.
1010-07-048	**F
3-01-001	**F-FOLD
1-01-001	**F-INCH
4-01-001	**F-STAGE
1-01-001	**F-VALUES
721-15-196	**H
2-01-002	**K
1-01-001	**R*0*K'S
5-01-002	**YA
2-01-001	**YB
1-01-001	**YB,
7-01-002	**YC
1-01-001	**YC,
2-01-001	**YE
8-01-002	**YF
2-01-002	**YF.
1-01-001	**YG
1-01-001	**YG-GLOBULIN
1-01-001	**YJ
1-01-001	**YJ.
3-02-003	**YL
3-01-002	**YL,
1-01-001	**YM
1-01-001	**YMG
2-01-001	**YP,
1-01-001	**YR
4-01-002	**YT
1-01-001	**Z*G.
29-01-001	**ZG
8-01-001	**ZG.
3-01-001	**ZG,
2-01-002	**ZQ
2-01-001	*(0,*=*T*$*).
1-01-001	*(0,*=*T*$*),
7-01-004	*=*A*$
1-01-001	*=*A*$.
1-01-001	*=*A*$**U
1-01-001	*=*A*$,
1-01-001	*=*B*$
1-01-001	*=*B*$.
38-01-001	*=*C*$
6-01-001	*=*C*$.
7-01-001	*=*C*$-PLANE
1-01-001	*=*C*$-PLANE,
7-01-002	*=*C*$,
1-01-001	*=*C*$(**=Q**$)
3-01-001	*=*C'*$
1-01-001	*=*C'*$.
1-01-001	*=*C'*$,
9-01-002	*=*D*$
5-01-001	*=*D'*$
1-01-001	*=*E*$
3-01-001	*=*F*$
1-01-001	*=*F*$,
1-01-001	*=*G*$,
3-01-002	*=*H*$
1-01-001	*=*H*$)
1-01-001	*=*H*$,
2-01-001	*=*L*$,
1-01-001	*=*M*$,
6-02-002	*=*N*$,
1-01-001	*=*N'*$
6-01-001	*=*N'*$
14-01-006	*=*P*$.
4-01-002	*=*P*$,
9-01-002	*=*P*$,
1-01-001	*=*P'*$,
1-01-001	*=*P*Q*$
24-01-002	*=*Q*$
8-01-002	*=*Q*$.
6-01-002	*=*Q*$,
11-01-003	*=*R*$
1-01-001	*=*R*$,
1-01-001	*=*R*$).
1-01-001	*=*R*$*0*0*H
6-01-001	*=*R*$-STAGE
1-01-001	*=*R*$,
1-01-001	*=*R'S*$
1-01-001	*=*S*$
2-01-001	*=*S*$.
1-01-001	*=*S*$,
15-01-003	*=*T*$
9-01-003	*=*T*$.
1-01-001	*=*T*$).
1-01-001	*=*T*$**I
1-01-001	*=*T*$**S
5-01-004	*=*T*$,
1-01-001	*=*U*$
9-01-002	*=*V*$
2-01-001	*=*V*$.
1-01-001	*=*V*$**S
2-01-001	*=*V*$,
1-01-001	*=*V*$(**=P**$)
5-01-002	*=*X*$
2-01-001	*=*X*$-GYRO
3-01-001	*=*X*$,
1-01-001	*=*Y*$
1-01-001	*=*Y*$-GYRO
2-01-001	*=*Z*$
1-01-001	*=*Z*$-AXIS
1-01-001	*=*Z*$-GYRO
3-01-002	*=A*$
1-01-001	*=A*$.
1-01-001	*=AB*$
1-01-001	*=AL*$
4-01-002	*=B*$
1-01-001	*=B*$).
1-01-001	*=B*$-PLANE
1-01-001	*=B*$-PLANE.
2-01-001	*=B(T)*$
1-01-001	*=C*$
5-02-002	*=E*$
12-02-003	*=F*$
1-01-001	*=F*$.
2-01-001	*=F*$-PLANE
2-01-001	*=F*$-PLANE.
1-01-001	*=F*$-PLANE**S
1-01-001	*=F*$-PLANE,
8-01-001	*=F(T)*$
1-01-001	*=F(T)*$.
3-01-002	*=G*$
1-01-001	*=G*$.
3-01-001	*=G(T)*$
1-01-001	*=G(T)*$-AXIS
4-02-002	*=H*$
1-01-001	*=H*$.
2-01-001	*=I*$.
2-01-001	*=I*$,
1-01-001	*=ITY*$
5-01-001	*=K*$
1-01-001	*=K*$,
4-01-001	*=K*$TH
2-01-001	*=L*$
5-01-001	*=L*$,
1-01-001	*=L'*$
1-01-001	*=L'*$.
1-01-001	*=M*$
15-02-007	*=N*$
2-02-002	*=N*$.
1-01-001	*=N*$-DIMENSION AL
1-01-001	*=N*$-TRIAL
3-02-003	*=N*$,
2-01-002	*=N*$TH
15-02-003	*=P*$
1-01-001	*=P*$.
3-01-002	*=P*$,
1-01-001	*=P(*D)*$,
3-01-003	*=Q*$
8-01-002	*=R*$
1-01-001	*=R*$,
1-01-001	*=R*$TH
1-01-001	*=RE*$
8-01-002	*=S*$
1-01-001	*=S*$-VALUES
15-01-001	*=T*$
5-01-001	*=T*$,
3-01-002	*=T*$,
1-01-001	*=T-TAU*$
1-01-001	*=U*$.
2-01-001	*=U*$,
1-01-001	*=V*$
4-01-001	*=VS*$
3-01-001	*=W*$
1-01-001	*=X*$
1-01-001	*=X*$,
27-08-017	*A
7-07-002	*A.
1-01-001	*A)
4-02-002	*A+**J*I
1-01-001	*A+**J*M
1-01-001	*A+**J*M**-
1-01-001	*A+**J*M,
1-01-001	*A*$
6-03-003	*A'S
1-01-001	*A**S
8-01-001	*A**U
2-01-001	*A**U.
1-01-001	*A*A
1-01-001	*A*A*A
2-02-002	*A*B
2-02-002	*A*B*C
5-01-001	*A*B*D
1-01-001	*A*C*S),
1-01-001	*A*C*T*H
1-01-001	*A*D
7-01-001	*A*D*C
1-01-001	*A*D*C**U.
2-01-001	*A*E*C
1-01-001	*A*E*C'S
1-01-001	*A*F+**J*A*M,
1-01-001	*A*F*L-**J*C*I* O
3-03-003	*A*F*L-**J*C*I* O,
1-01-001	*A*F*L-*C*I*0,
1-01-001	*A*H6
10-01-001	*A*I*A
1-01-001	*A*I*CH*E
4-01-001	*A*I*D
1-01-001	*A*I*D'S
1-01-001	*A*I*E*E
3-01-001	*A*I*M*0
2-01-001	*A*I*M*0,
1-01-001	*A*L
7-01-001	*A*M
1-01-001	*A*M)
1-01-001	*A*M*A),
3-01-001	*A*P)**T**-
1-01-001	*A*R*F)**-
1-01-001	*A*S*D*I*C,
1-01-001	*A*S*M*E,
1-01-001	*A*S*P*R
1-01-001	*A*S*T*M
2-01-001	*A*S*W
1-01-001	*A*T*P
1-01-001	*A*T*P)
3-01-001	*A*V*C).
1-01-001	*A*W*0*C
1-01-001	*A*W*0*C,
4-01-001	*A-**J*Z
1-01-001	*A-**J*Z'S
1-01-001	*A-**J*Z**U,
1-01-001	*A-BOMBS
1-01-001	*A-26
1-01-001	*A/3,
10-05-009	*A,
2-01-001	*AMP
2-01-001	*AMP.
25-08-016	*B
1-01-001	*B)
1-01-001	*B***J*0
2-01-001	*B***J*0.
1-01-001	*B**0
1-01-001	*B'S
4-01-001	*B**U
2-01-001	*B**U.
1-01-001	*B**U,
4-01-001	*B*A*M
2-01-001	*B*B*R
1-01-001	*B*B*B)
1-01-001	*B*C*D
2-02-002	*B*G
1-01-001	*B*G*S
2-01-001	*B*M*E*W*S
1-01-001	*B*M*E*W*S.
1-01-001	*B*M*T
16-01-001	*B*0*D
3-01-001	*B*0*D.
1-01-001	*B*0*D'S
1-01-001	*B*0*D/DAY
1-01-001	*B*0*D/DAY/ACRE
2-01-001	*B*0*D/DAY/ACRE
1-01-001	*B*0*D/DAY/1,00 0
1-01-001	*B*S*N,
6-01-001	*B*T*U
1-01-001	*B*T*U.
1-01-001	*B*T*U'S
1-01-001	*B*T*U'S.
5-01-001	*B*W
1-01-001	*B-47
1-01-001	*B-47'S
9-04-004	*B-52
1-01-001	*B-52'S,
1-01-001	*B-52**J*H
1-01-001	*B-52S
1-01-001	*B-58
4-02-002	*B-70
2-02-002	*B-70,
3-03-003	*B,

1-01-001	*B70	1-01-001	*F*D*A,	1-01-001	*M*G*M	1-01-001	*P*T*C,
14-07-011	*C	1-01-001	*F*D*R.	1-01-001	*M*L*S*S	1-01-001	*P*W*A,
1-01-001	*C.	1-01-001	*F*D*R**C	1-01-001	*M*P'S	2-01-001	*P-11
1-01-001	*C+**J*0	1-01-001	*F*D*R,	1-01-001	*M*P*H	4-01-001	*P-20
1-01-001	*C+**J*0'S	2-01-001	*F*E*L*A	1-01-001	*M*PL,	1-01-001	*P-9
1-01-001	*C+**J*0-**J*B+	1-01-001	*F*F*A	1-01-001	*M*S	1-01-001	*PE
	**J*0	3-01-001	*F*H*A	1-01-001	*M*S*)	1-01-001	*PM
1-01-001	*C**-	3-01-001	*F*I*T*C	1-01-001	*M*V*P	1-01-001	*Q
2-01-001	*C**S	1-01-001	*F*L*N,	1-01-001	*M-*K	1-01-001	*Q3,
1-01-001	*C**U	2-02-002	*F*M	1-01-001	*M-1	8-03-006	*R
1-01-001	*C*B*S	2-01-001	*F*N	1-01-001	*M-4	1-01-001	*R)
1-01-001	*C*B,	1-01-001	*F*0*R*E*A*M*I)	3-01-001	*MC/SEC	3-01-001	*R+*D
1-01-001	*C*C*C	1-01-001	*F-MAJOR	2-01-001	*ME-210	1-01-001	*R'S
7-01-001	*C*D	1-01-001	*F-108	1-01-001	*MESSRS	1-01-001	*R'S**-
7-01-001	*C*D*C.	1-01-001	*F-108,	1-01-001	*MLLE	1-01-001	*R'S,
3-01-001	*C*D*C.	1-01-001	*F,	3-01-001	*MME	1-01-001	*R*A
2-01-001	*C*D*C'S	1-01-001	*G	3-01-001	*MMES	3-01-001	*R*A*F
1-01-001	*C*D,	1-01-001	*G*A	2-01-001	*MRAD	1-01-001	*R*A*N*D
1-01-001	*C*H	1-01-001	*G*A*M*I*N**S	1-01-001	*MRAD)	1-01-001	*R*B*IS,
1-01-001	*C*H**S	1-01-001	*G*E	1-01-001	*MRADS	6-04-005	*R*C*A
1-01-001	*C*J*S	1-01-001	*G*E**C	1-01-001	*MRADS.	1-01-001	*R*C*A-*VICTOR'
3-01-001	*C*0	3-01-001	*G*N*P	1-01-001	*MRS		S
5-01-001	*C*0*A*H*R	2-01-001	*G*N*P.	7-02-002	*N	1-01-001	*R*D*F
1-01-001	*C*0*L*H	1-01-001	*G*N*P),	1-01-001	*N*A*B	1-01-001	*R*D*F.
2-01-001	*C*0*N*E*L*R*A*	2-01-001	*G*N*P,	1-01-001	*N*A*E*B*M	2-01-001	*R*D*W
	D	12-02-005	*G*0*P	1-01-001	*N*A*E*B*M,	3-01-001	*R*D*W*S
1-01-001	*C*S*F)	1-01-001	*G*0*P,	1-01-001	*N*A*H*B,	1-01-001	*R*D*W*S)
6-02-002	*C*T*A	1-01-001	*G,	1-01-001	*N*A*I*R	1-01-001	*R*0*K
1-01-001	*C*T*A.	5-03-003	*H	1-01-001	*N*A*I*R*0	1-01-001	*R*0*T*C
1-01-001	*C*T*A**P	3-02-002	*H.	1-01-001	*N*A*I*R*0),	1-01-001	*R*P*M
4-01-001	*C*T*C*A	1-01-001	*H+*H,	1-01-001	*N*A*R*E*B	1-01-001	*R*P*M,
1-01-001	*C*T*C*A).	1-01-001	*H*B*0	1-01-001	*N*A*R*E*B)	1-01-001	*R-*BERGEN,
1-01-001	*C*V,	1-01-001	*H-BOMBS.	1-01-001	*N*A*R*E*B'S	1-01-001	*R-*CAPE
4-02-003	*C,	1-01-001	*H,	20-05-007	*N*A*T*0	2-02-002	*R-*N**.*J**.,
2-01-001	*CD	3-02-002	*I	1-01-001	*N*A*T*0.	1-01-001	*R-*WARREN
3-01-001	*CR	7-03-004	*I*B*M	1-01-001	*N*A*T*0)	1-01-001	*R-5TH
1-01-001	*CU*K**YA	1-01-001	*I*C*A	1-01-001	*N*A*T*0)**U	1-01-001	*R-6TH
13-04-008	*D	1-01-001	*I*C*A'S	1-01-001	*N*A*T*0'S	2-02-002	*R,
3-03-003	*D.	3-02-002	*I*C*B*M	3-02-002	*N*A*T*0,	5-01-001	*RH
1-01-001	*D)	2-01-001	*I*C*B*M'S	6-03-004	*N*B*C	5-03-003	*S
5-01-001	*D*A	2-01-001	*I*C*B*MS	1-01-001	*N*B*C-**J*T*V	2-01-001	*S+*W
1-01-001	*D*A,	1-01-001	*I*C*B*MS.	3-01-001	*N*B*S	2-02-002	*S**U
5-01-001	*D*C	1-01-001	*I*C*C	1-01-001	*N*B*S.	2-01-001	*S*A*A*M*I
1-01-001	*D*C-7.	1-01-001	*I*J*A*L	1-01-001	*N*C	6-01-001	*S*A*A*M*I'S
1-01-001	*D*C,	1-01-001	*I*N*D,	2-01-001	*N*C*T*A	7-02-002	*S*A*C
1-01-001	*D*E*A*E	1-01-001	*I*0*C*S	1-01-001	*N*C*T*A,	1-01-001	*S*A*C'S
1-01-001	*D*E*A*E-)	2-01-001	*I*0*C*S.	2-01-001	*N*E	1-01-001	*S*A*C,
7-01-002	*D*E*A*E-CELLUL	2-01-001	*I*0*C*S*I*X*F	1-01-001	*N*E.	2-01-001	*S*A*M*0*S
	OSE	1-01-001	*I*0*C*S*I*X**F,	1-01-001	*N*E**S	23-01-001	*S*B*A
1-01-001	*D*E*A*E-CELLUL	2-01-001	*I*0*C*S*I*X*G	2-01-001	*N*E,	1-01-001	*S*B*A)
	OSE.	1-01-001	*I*0*C*S*I*X*G,	1-01-001	*N*L*R*B	2-01-001	*S*B*A'S
1-01-001	*D*E*A*E-CELLUL	1-01-001	*I*Q	2-01-001	*N*L*R*D*A	1-01-001	*S*B*A,
	OSE-TREATED	2-01-001	*I*R*S*A*C	1-01-001	*N*L*R*D*A.	2-01-001	*S*C*R
2-01-002	*D*E*A*E-CELLUL	1-01-001	*I*R*S*A*C)	1-01-001	*N*M*M*R)	1-01-001	*S*D
	OSE,	1-01-001	*I*R*S*A*C,	1-01-001	*N*0*P	1-01-001	*S*E.
1-01-001	*D*E*S	1-01-001	*I-*E	1-01-001	*N*0*R*A*D	5-02-002	*S*E*A*T*0
5-01-001	*D*I*0*C*S	1-01-001	*I-*E.	1-01-001	*N*R	1-01-001	*S*E*A*T*0.
2-01-001	*D*I*0*C*S,	1-01-001	*J**U	1-01-001	*N*R*A,	1-01-001	*S*E*T*S*W
3-01-001	*D*L*I*N*E	1-01-001	*J*A	1-01-001	*N*R*L	1-01-001	*S*E,
1-01-001	*D*P*W	1-01-001	*J*E*D*E*C,	1-01-001	*N*R*L*D*A'S	1-01-001	*S*H
3-01-001	*D*R*D*W	1-01-001	*J*Y*J	6-01-001	*N*S	1-01-001	*S*H,
1-01-001	*D*S*M	1-01-001	*J*Y*M	1-01-001	*N*S.	4-01-002	*S*M*U
2-01-001	*D*S*W	1-01-001	*J,	2-01-001	*N*W,	4-01-002	*S*M*U.
1-01-001	*D*T*F	1-01-001	*J28-6033-1.	3-01-001	*N*Y*U	2-01-001	*S*M*U'S
1-01-001	*D*T*F*S.	1-01-001	*J28-6105.	2-01-001	*N*Y*U,	1-01-001	*S*M*U,
3-01-001	*D*T*F,	4-02-003	*K	1-01-001	*N/G,	1-01-001	*S*N*P
1-01-001	*D*U	2-01-001	*K.	1-01-001	*N,	1-01-001	*S*P-44001).
5-01-001	*D*U*F	1-01-001	*K)	9-01-002	*O	1-01-001	*S*P-44002)
1-01-001	*D-*ORE**..	1-01-001	*K'S	1-01-001	*O*A*G*CO),	1-01-001	*S*P-44005).
1-01-001	*D-496.**T	1-01-001	*K*A*R*L	3-01-002	*O*A*S	1-01-001	*S*P-44006)
3-02-003	*D,	1-01-001	*K*A*R*L,	1-01-001	*O*B*E)	1-01-001	*S*P-44007).
1-01-001	*D8	4-01-001	*K*C	1-01-001	*O*E*P	1-01-001	*S*PS.
10-05-008	*E	1-01-001	*K*C-135	3-01-001	*O*H	1-01-001	*S*R
3-03-003	*E**U	1-01-001	*K*CS	1-01-001	*O*K	1-01-001	*S*R'S
1-01-001	*E*0*M*0*V	1-01-001	*K*K*K	1-01-001	*O*K**U**I	2-01-001	*S*R*E*L*E*A*S
1-01-001	*E*E*A*E-CELLUL	1-01-001	*K*Q*E*D	1-01-001	*O*K,	1-01-001	*S*R*E*S*E*R*V
	OSE	1-01-001	*K*S*A*N,	1-01-001	*O*M*E	1-01-001	*S*R/
2-01-001	*E*E*G	1-01-001	*K*V	1-01-001	*O*M*E)	3-01-001	*S*R,
1-01-001	*E*E*G.	1-01-001	*K*V.	1-01-001	*O*W*I**U,	3-03-003	*S*S
4-01-001	*E*Q*U	1-01-001	*L	1-01-001	*P	1-01-001	*S*S,
1-01-001	*E*Q*U,	1-01-001	*L**U	2-02-002	*P**U	1-01-001	*S*T*D*C*R**S
1-01-001	*E*S*N,	1-01-001	*L**U,	2-01-001	*P**U,	3-01-003	*S*W
3-01-001	*E*S*P	1-01-001	*L*D	1-01-001	*P*A*B*A	1-01-001	*S*W*A*0
1-01-001	*E*S*P),	1-01-001	*L*D056	3-01-001	*P*A*B*A.	1-01-001	*S*W*C
2-01-001	*E*T*V	1-01-001	*L*D060)	1-01-001	*P*A*B*A)	2-01-001	*S*X-21
1-01-001	*E*W*C	2-01-001	*L*I*T*0*R*I*G*	7-01-001	*P*B*S	1-01-001	*S*X-21**U
1-01-001	*E*W*C).		I*N	1-01-001	*P*B*S.	1-01-001	*S-**J*D
1-01-001	*E,	1-01-001	*L*M	1-01-001	*P*B*S)	2-01-001	*S-11
1-01-001	*ENGRG,	2-01-001	*L*0*C	1-01-001	*P*B*S).	1-01-001	*S-20
6-01-005	*F	1-01-001	*L*P	1-01-001	*P*F*C).	1-01-001	*S-20)
4-01-003	*F.	2-01-001	*L*S*0	2-01-001	*P*H*S	1-01-001	*S,
1-01-001	*F)	1-01-001	*L*S*U,	1-01-001	*P*M	1-01-001	*SB*CS-TYPE
1-01-001	*F+**J*A	1-01-001	*L-*P	1-01-001	*P*M*R	1-01-001	*SC*H.
8-02-004	*F*B*I	5-03-003	*M	1-01-001	*P*O*W	1-01-001	*SI*H,
1-01-001	*F*D*A.	2-02-002	*M.	3-02-002	*P*T*A	2-01-001	*SP
1-01-001	*F*D*A),	1-01-001	*M*E'*S	2-01-001	*P*T*C		
1-01-001	*F*D*A'S	1-01-001	*M*F				

9-04-004	*T	1-01-001	*Z
2-01-001	*T.	1-01-001	*Z**S
4-01-001	*T*A*S*S	1-01-001	*Z,
1-01-001	*T*C*U,	1-01-001	-.10
1-01-001	*T*E*A	1-01-001	-.5
1-01-001	*T*H*C	1-01-001	-**J*S*H
2-02-002	*T*N*T	2-01-001	-**JISM
1-01-001	*T*N*T.	1-01-001	-CARBONYL
1-01-001	*T*N*T)**S	1-01-001	-16**0
1-01-001	*T*N*T,	1-01-001	-20**0
4-01-001	*T*R	1-01-001	-20**0**J*C
2-01-001	*T*S*E*M	3-01-001	-78**0
13-01-001	*T*S*H	2-01-001	/**B/
1-01-001	*T*S*H.	2-01-001	/L/
1-01-001	*T*S*H)	1-01-001	/R/
1-01-001	*T*S*H-TREATED	1-01-001	(*=A,B*$)
3-01-001	*T*S*H,		
1-01-001	*T*U*C		
32-09-019	*T*V		
1-01-001	*T*V**$		
1-01-001	*T*V**-		
1-01-001	*T*V**P		
1-01-001	*T*V**U,		
3-03-003	*T*V,		
2-01-001	*T-34		
4-01-001	*T,		
2-01-001	*U		
1-01-001	*U.		
1-01-001	*U*C*L*A		
1-01-001	*U*G*F,		
1-01-001	*U*K		
11-02-005	*U*N		
2-01-002	*U*P*I)**T**-		
4-02-002	*U*S		
2-02-002	*U*S.		
1-01-001	*U*S*G*A		
1-01-001	*U*S*I*S		
1-01-001	*U*S*0		
1-01-001	*U*S*0*M,		
3-01-001	*U*S*P		
2-02-002	*U*S*S*R		
1-01-001	*U*S*S*R**C		
1-01-001	*U*S*S*R,		
1-01-001	*U-**J*I		
1-01-001	*U-2		
11-04-005	*V		
1-01-001	*V.		
10-02-002	*V*A		
1-01-001	*V*T*0*L		
1-01-001	*V*T*0*L)		
4-03-003	*V-SHAPED		
3-01-001	*V-1		
1-01-001	*V8.		
2-02-002	*W		
1-01-001	*W*A*C*S		
1-01-001	*W*A*C,		
1-01-001	*W*A*0		
2-01-001	*W*B*A*I		
1-01-001	*W*B*A*I,		
1-01-001	*W*L*I*B		
1-01-001	*W*P*A,		
1-01-001	*W*Q*X*R.		
13-01-001	*W*T*V		
1-01-001	*W*W*R*L		
1-01-001	*W*W*R*L'S		
3-01-001	*W-REGION		
1-01-001	*W-REGION.		
1-01-001	*W-REGION**S		
1-01-001	*W-REGION,		
1-01-001	*W-2).		
3-02-003	*X		
1-01-001	*X.		
2-02-002	*X'S		
1-01-001	*X**U		
1-01-001	*X**U**I		
1-01-001	*X*H-834.		
1-01-001	*X*R*E*L*E*A*S*E		
1-01-001	*X*R*E*L*E*A*S*E,		
1-01-001	*X*R*E*S*E*R*V*E		
2-01-001	*X-RAY		
1-01-001	*X-RAY-PROOF		
1-01-001	*X-RAYS		
2-01-001	*X-REGION		
2-01-001	*X-REGION,		
1-01-001	*Y		
1-01-001	*Y'S		
1-01-001	*Y*M*C*A.		
1-01-001	*Y*M*C*A,		
1-01-001	*Y-*TEEN		
3-01-001	*Y-CELL		
1-01-001	*Y-CELLS		
1-01-001	*Y-REGION		
1-01-001	*Y-REGION,		
1-01-001	*Y-REGIONS		

ANALYSES OF THE CORPUS

DISTRIBUTION OF OCCURRENCE
OF FREQUENT WORDS

Explanation of Table A1

The range figures in the two word lists in the preceding section of this book specify in how many genres and in how many samples of the Corpus each word-type actually occurs. These range indications are of importance in evaluating the significance of the frequency of occurrence, particularly in the case of middle- and low-frequency words.

High-frequency words, however, generally occur in all the genres and all or most of the samples of the Corpus. Thus, the simple range figures offer little information about the relative distribution of high-frequency words in the individual genres of the Corpus. In order to judge how evenly such high-frequency words are distributed throughout the genres, the relative frequencies of occurrence of each word in the individual genre subdivisions must be compared.

Table A1 represents such a tabulation of the distribution of occurrence of the one hundred most frequent word-types in the Corpus.

For each type there are three lines of data. The first line gives the frequency rank of the type, the word-type entry, and the actual number of times the type occurs

in each of the fifteen genre subdivisions of the Corpus (designated by the letters A through R; see the Introduction, p. xix, for a description of the contents of each subdivision). The last entry on this line is the total frequency of the type in the Corpus.

The second line gives the expected frequency of the word-type in each subdivision, assuming an even distribution of each type throughout the fifteen genres of the Corpus. (The expected value equals the ratio of the total number of tokens in a genre subdivision to the total number of tokens in the Corpus, multiplied by the total number of Corpus occurrences of the respective type.) The entry in the extreme right-hand column is the chi-square value, computed on the basis of the observed frequency o and expected frequency e in each genre subdivision, according to the usual formula:

$$\chi^2 = \sum \frac{(o - e)^2}{e}.$$

On the third line the ratio of the number of occurrences of the type in the respective subdivision to the total number of tokens in that subdivision is given. The ratio is expressed as a percentage.

All of the chi-square values for the one hundred most frequent words of the Corpus

are significant, even at the 1 per cent level of significance. (At $P = 0.01$ for fourteen degrees of freedom the critical value of $\chi^2 = 29.1$.) Thus the hypothesis that the uneven frequency distribution of the common words (most of which are function words) among the subdivisions of the Corpus is due solely to chance has to be rejected. Rather, it is reasonable to assume that style and content characteristics of the genres represented in the various subdivisions affect significantly the frequency of occurrence of even the most common words in English.

It should be noted that there is no word of rank 92 in Table A1. This omission is due to the fact that rank 92 in the Corpus is occupied by the "word" **F, which has a frequency of 1,010. The code **F stands for any formula, i.e., any combination of letters, numbers, and other symbols that also include operator symbols (such as plus sign, equal sign, exponents, etc.). It should be emphasized that **F designates any formula, not a specific one. Since the determination of the distribution of formulas in the various genres would be of little linguistic interest, the code **F was omitted from the calculations in Table A1, and the list of frequent words was extended to include one hundred actual linguistic words, having the ranks 1 to 101.

For the sake of completeness, however, the code **F is included in both word lists in the preceding section of this book as well as in all the frequency distribution tables in the subsequent section.

Table A1   Distribution of Occurrence of the 100 Most Frequent Word-Types in the Corpus

RANK	WORD		GENRES															TOTAL	X^2
			A	B	C	D	E	F	G	H	J	K	L	M	N	P	R		
		Frequency																		
		Expected frequency																		
		Ratio, as % of freq. to total no. words in genre																		
1	the		6385	3961	2370	2480	4757	6976	10758	4621	12536	3792	2817	723	3780	2988	1027	69971	
			6122.5	3764.8	2441.6	2385.1	5009.1	6711.0	10500.6	4311.5	11183.3	4030.3	3331.3	831.9	4033.7	4050.9	1261.5		
			7.19	7.26	6.70	7.17	6.55	7.17	7.07	7.39	7.73	6.49	5.83	5.99	6.46	5.09	5.62		688.7
2	of		2858	1994	1340	1505	2411	3696	6382	3059	7454	1423	913	329	1327	1202	518	36411	
			3185.9	1959.1	1270.5	1241.6	2606.5	3492.2	5464.2	2243.6	5819.4	2097.3	1733.5	432.9	2098.9	2107.9	656.4		
			3.22	3.65	3.79	4.35	3.32	3.80	4.19	4.89	4.60	2.44	1.89	2.73	2.27	2.05	2.83		2362.6
3	and		2185	1357	1162	962	2178	2833	4460	1947	4282	1770	1282	294	1706	1905	529	28852	
			2524.5	1552.4	1006.7	983.9	2065.4	2767.2	4329.8	1777.8	4611.3	1661.8	1373.6	343.0	1663.2	1670.3	520.2		
			2.46	2.49	3.28	2.78	2.99	2.91	2.93	3.12	2.64	3.03	2.65	2.44	2.92	3.24	2.89		200.2
4	to		2143	1583	726	904	1836	2579	4164	1853	3948	1508	1295	306	1322	1517	465	26149	
			2288.1	1406.9	912.5	891.7	1871.9	2508.0	3924.3	1611.3	4179.4	1506.2	1244.9	310.9	1507.4	1513.9	471.4		
			2.41	2.90	2.05	2.61	2.53	2.65	2.74	2.96	2.44	2.58	2.68	2.54	2.26	2.58	2.54		160.9
5	a		2160	1171	932	696	1844	2436	3458	977	3452	1339	1198	235	1433	1383	523	23237	
			2033.3	1250.3	810.9	792.4	1663.5	2228.7	3487.2	1431.9	3713.9	1338.5	1106.3	276.3	1339.6	1345.3	418.9		
			2.43	2.15	2.63	2.01	2.54	2.50	2.27	1.56	2.13	2.29	2.48	1.95	2.45	2.36	2.86		292.0
6	in		2020	1091	728	774	1543	2195	3409	1471	4097	971	695	164	893	930	360	21341	
			1867.4	1148.3	744.7	727.8	1527.8	2046.9	3202.7	1315.0	3410.9	1229.3	1016.0	253.7	1230.3	1235.5	384.8		
			2.28	1.99	2.06	2.24	2.12	2.26	2.24	2.35	2.53	1.66	1.44	1.36	1.53	1.58	1.97		556.3

Table A1 (cont.)   Distribution of Occurrence of the 100 Most Frequent Word-Types in the Corpus

RANK	WORD		GENRES															TOTAL	X²
		A	B	C	D	E	F	G	H	J	K	L	M	N	P	R		
		Frequency																
		Expected frequency																
		Ratio, as %; of freq. to total no. of words in genre																
7	that	829	596	348	492	526	1005	1960	503	1711	572	526	131	532	612	252	10595	
		927.1	570.1	369.7	361.3	758.5	1016.2	1590.0	652.9	1693.4	610.3	504.4	125.9	610.8	613.4	191.0		
		0.93	1.09	0.98	1.42	0.72	1.03	1.29	0.80	1.06	0.98	1.09	1.09	0.91	1.04	1.38		285.3
8	is	733	751	513	537	969	1016	1815	656	2409	151	120	50	100	158	121	10099	
		883.7	543.4	352.4	344.4	722.9	968.6	1515.6	622.3	1614.1	581.7	480.8	120.1	582.2	584.7	182.1		
		0.83	1.38	1.45	1.55	1.33	1.04	1.19	1.05	1.49	0.26	0.25	0.41	0.17	0.27	0.66		2186.2
9	was	717	311	227	214	265	961	1470	223	1115	1091	828	200	919	999	276	9816	
		858.9	528.2	342.5	334.7	702.7	941.5	1473.1	604.9	1568.9	565.4	467.3	116.7	565.9	568.3	176.9		
		0.81	0.57	0.64	0.62	0.36	0.99	0.97	0.36	0.69	1.87	1.71	1.66	1.57	1.70	1.51		2269.3
10	he	642	364	239	206	196	683	1536	169	388	1308	1076	191	1283	1068	194	9543	
		835.0	513.5	333.0	325.4	683.2	915.3	1432.1	588.0	1525.3	549.7	454.3	113.5	550.1	552.5	172.1		
		0.72	0.67	0.68	0.60	0.27	0.70	1.01	0.27	0.24	2.24	2.23	1.58	2.19	1.82	1.06		5128.8
11	for	969	541	300	315	857	941	1291	858	1568	414	378	100	358	441	158	9489	
		830.3	510.6	331.1	323.6	679.3	910.1	1424.0	584.7	1516.6	546.6	451.8	112.8	547.0	549.4	171.1		
		1.09	0.99	0.85	0.91	1.18	0.97	0.85	1.37	0.97	0.71	0.78	0.83	0.61	0.75	0.86		350.9
12	it	478	498	269	337	606	746	1372	322	1146	606	653	158	638	717	210	8756	
		766.2	471.1	305.5	298.6	626.8	839.8	1314.0	539.5	1399.5	504.4	416.9	104.1	504.8	506.9	157.9		
		0.54	0.91	0.76	0.97	0.83	0.77	0.90	0.52	0.71	1.04	1.35	1.31	1.09	1.22	1.15		588.2

Table A1 (cont.)   Distribution of Occurrence of the 100 Most Frequent Word-Types in the Corpus

Frequency
Expected frequency
Ratio, as % of freq. to total no. words in genre

RANK	WORD		A	B	C	D	E	F	G	H	J	K	L	M	N	P	R	TOTAL	X²
											GENRES							TOTAL	X²
13	with	Freq	567	329	284	222	624	716	1095	376	1158	483	336	73	420	473	133	7289	74.9
		Exp	637.8	392.2	254.3	248.6	521.8	699.1	1093.9	449.1	1165.0	419.9	347.0	86.7	420.2	421.9	131.4		
		Ratio	.639	.603	.802	.642	.859	.736	.719	.602	.714	.827	.696	.605	.718	.805	.727		
14	as	Freq	516	391	276	314	494	759	1261	480	1291	322	301	72	338	302	133	7250	172.5
		Exp	634.4	390.1	252.9	247.2	519.0	695.4	1088.0	446.7	1158.8	417.6	345.2	86.2	417.9	419.7	130.7		
		Ratio	.581	.716	.780	.908	.680	.780	.828	.768	.796	.551	.623	.597	.578	.514	.727		
15	his	Freq	428	269	231	177	258	526	1447	149	454	797	565	102	846	603	145	6997	2117.2
		Exp	612.2	376.5	244.2	238.6	500.9	671.1	1050.1	431.2	1118.3	403.0	333.1	83.2	403.4	405.1	126.1		
		Ratio	0.48	0.49	0.65	0.51	0.36	0.54	0.95	0.24	0.28	1.36	1.17	0.85	1.45	1.03	0.79		
16	on	Freq	691	347	197	170	537	636	831	424	954	450	441	90	469	375	130	6742	166.4
		Exp	589.9	362.8	235.3	229.9	482.7	646.6	1011.8	415.4	1077.6	388.3	320.9	80.2	388.7	390.3	121.6		
		Ratio	.779	.636	.557	.491	.740	.654	.546	.678	.588	.770	.913	.746	.802	.639	.711		
17	be	Freq	526	422	154	243	524	570	844	604	1361	256	234	80	188	292	79	6377	463.3
		Exp	557.9	343.1	222.5	217.5	456.5	611.6	957.0	392.9	1019.0	367.3	303.6	75.8	367.6	369.2	114.9		
		Ratio	.593	.773	.435	.703	.722	.586	.554	.966	.840	.438	.485	.663	.322	.497	.432		
18	at	Freq	637	217	196	121	355	488	707	254	739	397	332	55	342	431	107	5378	248.4
		Exp	470.6	289.4	187.7	183.4	385.0	515.8	807.1	331.4	859.6	309.8	256.1	63.9	310.0	311.4	96.9		
		Ratio	.718	.398	.554	.350	.489	.502	.464	.406	.456	.680	.687	.456	.585	.734	.585		

Table A1 (cont.)   Distribution of Occurrence of the 100 Most Frequent Word-Types in the Corpus

Frequency
Expected frequency
Ratio, as %, of freq. to total no. of words in genre

RANK WORD	GENRES															TOTAL	X²
	A	B	C	D	E	F	G	H	J	K	L	M	N	P	R		
19 by	504	308	207	192	346	591	833	438	1216	173	117	37	156	114	73	5305	
	464.1	285.4	185.1	180.9	379.7	508.7	795.9	326.8	847.7	305.5	252.5	63.1	305.8	307.1	95.6		562.4
	.568	.564	.585	.555	.476	.607	.547	.701	.749	.296	.242	.307	.267	.194	.399		
20 I	185	204	49	155	155	264	845	100	182	511	583	98	652	950	240	5173	
	452.6	278.3	180.5	176.4	370.3	496.2	776.3	318.8	826.8	297.9	246.3	61.5	298.2	299.5	93.3		3867.3
	0.21	0.37	0.14	0.45	0.21	0.27	0.56	0.16	0.11	0.87	1.21	0.81	1.12	1.62	1.31		
21 this	320	327	184	257	441	482	791	440	993	176	172	61	239	187	76	5146	
	450.3	276.9	179.6	175.5	368.4	493.6	772.3	317.1	822.5	296.4	245.0	61.2	296.7	297.9	92.8		308.9
	.361	.599	.520	.743	.607	.495	.520	.704	.613	.301	.356	.506	.409	.318	.416		
22 had	281	132	71	84	86	463	809	49	331	728	520	143	592	695	149	5133	
	449.1	276.2	179.1	175.0	367.5	492.3	770.3	316.3	820.4	295.7	244.4	61.0	295.9	297.2	92.5		2904.4
	0.32	0.24	0.20	0.24	0.12	0.48	0.53	0.08	0.20	1.25	1.08	1.19	1.01	1.18	0.81		
23 not	257	307	155	236	223	420	832	208	783	314	219	95	203	273	84	4609	
	403.3	247.9	160.8	157.2	329.9	442.1	691.7	284.0	736.7	265.5	219.4	54.8	265.7	266.8	83.1		247.7
	.290	.563	.438	.682	.307	.432	.547	.333	.483	.537	.454	.788	.347	.465	.459		
24 are	330	298	195	194	532	481	649	416	993	52	52	26	53	78	44	4393	
	384.4	236.4	153.3	149.8	314.5	421.3	659.3	270.7	702.1	253.0	209.2	52.2	253.2	254.3	79.2		992.9
	.372	.546	.551	.561	.733	.494	.426	.666	.613	.089	.108	.216	.091	.133	.241		

Table A1 (cont.)   Distribution of Occurrence of the 100 Most Frequent Word-Types in the Corpus

Frequency
Expected frequency
Ratio, as %, of freq. to total no. words in genre

RANK	WORD	A	B	C	D	E	F	G	GENRES H	J	K	L	M	N	P	R	TOTAL	X²
25	but	283	293	170	175	221	391	772	119	501	297	266	89	316	387	101	4381	378.9
		383.3	235.7	152.9	149.4	313.6	420.2	657.5	269.9	700.2	252.3	208.6	52.1	252.6	253.6	78.9		
		.319	.537	.480	.506	.304	.402	.507	.190	.309	.508	.551	.738	.540	.659	.552		
26	from	353	219	143	143	295	489	684	249	792	235	181	46	270	209	61	4369	50.4
		382.3	235.1	152.5	148.9	312.8	419.0	655.7	269.2	698.3	251.7	208.0	51.9	251.9	252.9	78.8		
		.398	.401	.404	.413	.406	.503	.449	.398	.489	.402	.375	.381	.462	.356	.334		
27	or	176	198	100	168	461	506	597	400	905	173	139	31	119	165	69	4207	527.1
		368.2	226.4	146.8	143.5	301.2	403.6	631.5	259.3	672.6	242.4	200.3	50.0	242.6	243.6	75.9		
		.198	.363	.283	.486	.635	.520	.392	.640	.558	.296	.288	.257	.204	.281	.377		
28	have	265	275	124	194	375	396	633	223	551	169	222	6I	133	264	56	3941	184.0
		344.8	212.1	137.5	134.4	282.1	377.9	591.4	242.8	629.9	227.0	187.6	46.9	227.2	228.2	71.1		
		.299	.504	.350	.561	.516	.407	.416	.357	.340	.289	.460	.506	.227	.450	.306		
29	an	311	194	172	126	243	395	603	227	739	160	133	33	169	161	81	3747	112.3
		327.8	201.6	130.7	127.7	268.2	359.3	562.2	230.8	598.7	215.8	178.3	44.5	215.9	216.9	67.5		
		.350	.355	.486	.364	.335	.406	.396	.363	.455	.274	.275	.274	.289	.274	.443		
30	they	268	184	98	133	217	400	609	119	405	313	165	67	305	237	98	3618	269.3
		316.6	194.7	126.2	123.4	259.0	347.0	542.9	222.9	578.3	208.4	172.3	43.0	208.6	209.5	65.2		
		.302	.337	.277	.385	.299	.411	.400	.190	.250	.536	.342	.556	.522	.404	.536		

Table A1 (cont.) Distribution of Occurrence of the 100 Most Frequent Word-Types in the Corpus

RANK WORD		A	B	C	D	E	F	G	H	J	K	L	M	N	P	R	TOTAL	X²
									GENRES									
	Frequency																	
	Expected frequency																	
	Ratio, as %, of freq. to total no. of words in genre																	
31 which	Frequency	245	191	124	202	253	277	682	265	835	124	61	33	102	106	62	3562	458.5
	Expected	311.7	191.7	124.3	121.5	254.9	341.6	534.6	219.5	569.3	205.2	169.6	42.3	205.3	206.2	64.2		
	Ratio	.276	.350	.350	.584	.348	.285	.448	.424	.515	.212	.126	.274	.174	.181	.339		
32 one	Frequency	213	173	125	104	286	361	550	125	518	184	172	39	183	182	77	3292	82.3
	Expected	288.1	177.1	114.9	112.3	235.7	315.7	494.0	202.9	526.2	189.6	156.7	39.1	189.8	190.6	59.4		
	Ratio	.240	.317	.353	.301	.394	.371	.361	.200	.320	.315	.356	.323	.313	.310	.421		
33 you	Frequency	66	90	37	123	434	242	220	86	42	282	416	96	446	558	148	3286	2865.1
	Expected	287.5	176.8	114.7	112.1	235.2	315.2	493.1	202.5	525.2	189.3	156.4	39.1	189.4	190.2	59.2		
	Ratio	.074	.165	.105	.356	.598	.249	.145	.138	.026	.483	.861	.796	.763	.950	.809		
34 were	Frequency	252	109	87	92	106	349	525	126	633	240	157	59	251	214	84	3284	225.6
	Expected	287.4	176.7	114.6	111.9	235.1	314.9	492.8	202.4	524.9	189.2	156.4	39.0	189.3	190.1	59.2		
	Ratio	.284	.200	.246	.266	.146	.359	.345	.202	.390	.411	.325	.489	.429	.364	.459		
35 her	Frequency	121	39	90	8	17	315	289	3	132	413	311	82	469	680	68	3037	3466.5
	Expected	265.7	163.4	105.9	103.6	217.4	291.3	455.8	187.1	485.4	174.9	144.6	36.1	175.1	175.8	54.8		
	Ratio	.136	.071	.254	.023	.023	.324	.190	.005	.081	.707	.644	.680	.802	1.16	.372		
36 all	Frequency	181	155	143	123	214	242	477	169	362	209	165	66	191	242	62	3001	149.5
	Expected	262.6	161.5	104.7	102.3	214.8	287.8	450.4	184.9	479.7	172.9	142.9	35.7	173.0	173.7	54.1		
	Ratio	.204	.284	.404	.356	.295	.249	.313	.270	.223	.358	.342	.547	.327	.412	.339		

Table A1 (cont.) Distribution of Occurrence of the 100 Most Frequent Word-Types in the Corpus

RANK WORD		A	B	C	D	E	F	G	H	J	K	L	M	N	P	R	TOTAL	X²
									GENRES									
	Frequency / Expected frequency / Ratio, as % of freq. to total no. words in genre																	
37 she	Freq.	77	61	52	12	29	310	230	1	67	425	350	59	377	728	81	2859	3995.9
	Exp.	250.2	153.8	99.8	97.5	204.7	274.2	429.1	176.2	456.9	164.7	136.1	33.9	164.8	165.5	51.5		
	Ratio	.087	.112	.147	.035	.040	.319	.151	.002	.041	.727	.725	.489	.645	1.24	.443		
38 there	Freq.	188	120	94	102	147	225	374	98	412	219	232	44	192	235	42	2724	222.6
	Exp.	238.4	146.6	95.1	92.9	195.0	261.3	408.8	167.9	435.4	156.9	129.7	32.4	157.0	157.7	49.1		
	Ratio	.212	.220	.266	.295	.202	.231	.246	.157	.254	.375	.480	.365	.328	.400	.230		
39 would	Freq.	246	185	48	69	83	188	397	120	321	291	189	80	194	247	56	2714	442.2
	Exp.	237.5	146.0	94.7	92.6	194.3	260.3	407.3	167.2	433.8	156.3	129.2	32.3	156.5	157.1	48.9		
	Ratio	.277	.339	.136	.199	.114	.193	.261	.192	.198	.498	.391	.663	.332	.421	.306		
40 their	Freq.	231	131	68	115	157	310	520	178	369	166	50	41	162	119	53	2670	442.2
	Exp.	233.6	143.7	93.2	91.1	191.1	256.1	400.7	164.5	426.7	153.8	127.1	31.7	153.9	154.6	48.1		
	Ratio	.260	.240	.192	.332	.216	.319	.342	.285	.228	.284	.104	.340	.277	.203	.290		
41 we	Freq.	107	227	45	218	159	177	513	145	526	118	94	45	119	109	51	2653	135.7
	Exp.	232.1	142.7	92.6	90.5	189.9	254.5	398.1	163.5	424.0	152.8	126.3	31.5	152.9	153.6	47.8		
	Ratio	.121	.416	.127	.630	.219	.182	.337	.232	.324	.202	.195	.373	.204	.186	.279		
42 him	Freq.	93	106	40	94	49	167	373	26	98	382	330	58	415	340	48	2619	452.4
	Exp.	229.2	140.9	91.4	89.3	187.5	251.2	393.0	161.4	418.6	150.9	124.7	31.1	150.9	151.6	47.2		
	Ratio	.105	.194	.113	.272	.067	.172	.245	.042	.060	.654	.683	.481	.710	.579	.262		2020.5

Table A1 (cont.) Distribution of Occurrence of the 100 Most Frequent Word-Types in the Corpus

Frequency
Expected frequency
Ratio, as %, of freq. to total no. of words in genre

RANK WORD		A	B	C	D	E	F	G	H	J	K	L	M	N	P	R	TOTAL	X²
									GENRES									
43 been	Freq.	212	151	70	76	115	235	376	130	409	157	152	40	131	179	39	2472	
	Exp.	216.3	133.0	86.3	84.3	176.9	237.1	370.9	152.3	395.1	142.4	117.7	29.4	142.5	143.1	44.6		57.9
	Ratio	.239	.277	.198	.220	.158	.242	.247	.208	.252	.269	.315	.332	.224	.305	.213		
44 has	Freq.	301	261	195	111	236	226	405	153	431	27	17	9	15	26	26	2439	
	Exp.	213.4	131.2	85.1	83.2	174.6	233.9	366.0	150.3	389.8	140.5	116.1	28.9	140.6	141.2	43.9		749.5
	Ratio	.339	.478	.551	.321	.325	.232	.266	.245	.266	.046	.035	.075	.026	.044	.142		
45 when	Freq.	169	123	60	68	164	250	345	68	312	192	154	28	173	163	62	2331	
	Exp.	203.9	125.4	81.3	79.5	166.9	223.6	349.8	143.6	372.6	134.3	110.9	27.7	134.4	134.9	42.0		134.1
	Ratio	.190	.225	.170	.197	.226	.257	.227	.109	.192	.329	.319	.232	.296	.278	.339		
46 who	Freq.	268	177	130	102	104	261	461	77	214	112	94	13	95	95	49	2252	
	Exp.	197.1	121.2	78.6	76.8	161.2	215.9	337.9	138.8	359.9	129.7	107.2	26.8	129.8	130.4	40.6		286.1
	Ratio	.302	.324	.367	.295	.143	.268	.303	.123	.132	.192	.195	.108	.162	.162	.268		
47 will	Freq.	389	235	61	72	269	178	246	244	339	56	25	17	51	49	13	2244	
	Exp.	196.4	120.7	78.3	76.5	160.6	215.2	336.8	138.3	358.7	129.3	106.8	26.7	129.4	129.9	40.5		711.3
	Ratio	.438	.431	.172	.208	.370	.183	.162	.390	.209	.096	.052	.141	.087	.083	.071		
48 more	Freq.	184	144	107	65	194	231	376	126	395	84	79	21	84	89	37	2216	
	Exp.	193.9	119.2	77.3	75.6	158.6	212.5	332.6	136.5	354.2	127.6	105.5	26.3	127.7	128.3	39.9		89.1
	Ratio	.207	.264	.302	.188	.267	.237	.247	.202	.244	.144	.164	.174	.144	.152	.202		

Table A1 (cont.)   Distribution of Occurrence of the 100 Most Frequent Word-Types in the Corpus

Frequency
Expected frequency
Ratio, as %, of freq. to total no. words in genre

RANK WORD		A	B	C	D	E	F	G	H	J	K	L	M	N	P	R	TOTAL	X²
									GENRES									
49 no		126	122	68	88	134	191	329	74	285	162	188	61	174	163	36	2201	222.5
		192.6	118.4	76.8	75.1	157.6	211.1	330.3	135.6	351.8	126.8	104.8	26.2	126.9	127.4	39.7		
		.142	.224	.192	.254	.185	.196	.216	.118	.176	.277	.389	.506	.298	.278	.197		
50 if		103	134	48	96	181	208	301	113	332	128	174	29	140	170	42	2199	133.3
		192.4	118.3	76.7	74.9	157.4	210.9	330.0	135.5	351.5	126.7	104.7	26.1	126.8	127.3	39.6		
		.116	.246	.136	.278	.249	.214	.198	.181	.205	.219	.360	.240	.239	.289	.230		
51 out		162	87	56	54	87	171	247	58	160	224	214	36	273	223	44	2096	694.6
		183.4	112.8	73.1	71.5	150.1	201.0	314.6	129.2	335.0	120.7	99.8	24.9	120.8	121.3	37.8		
		.183	.159	.158	.156	.120	.176	.162	.093	.099	.383	.443	.299	.467	.380	.241		
52 so		81	111	76	99	121	182	334	83	226	135	126	26	136	192	56	1984	193.3
		173.6	106.8	69.2	67.7	142.0	190.3	297.7	122.3	317.1	114.3	94.5	23.6	114.4	114.9	35.8		
		.091	.203	.215	.286	.167	.187	.219	.133	.139	.231	.261	.216	.233	.327	.306		
53 said		406	52	12	27	11	89	161	18	35	194	204	45	288	331	88	1961	1959.5
		171.6	105.5	68.4	66.9	140.4	188.1	294.3	120.8	313.4	112.9	93.4	23.3	113.0	113.5	35.4		
		.457	.095	.034	.078	.015	.091	.106	.029	.022	.332	.422	.373	.493	.564	.481		
54 what		95	113	56	86	108	162	314	58	177	186	146	41	149	171	46	1908	287.3
		166.9	102.7	66.6	65.1	136.6	183.0	286.3	117.6	304.9	109.9	90.8	22.7	109.9	110.5	34.4		
		.107	.207	.158	.249	.149	.167	.206	.093	.109	.318	.302	.340	.255	.291	.252		

Table A1 (cont.) Distribution of Occurrence of the 100 Most Frequent Word-Types in the Corpus

Frequency
Expected frequency
Ratio, as %, of freq. to total no. of words in genre

RANK WORD	GENRES															TOTAL	X²
	A	B	C	D	E	F	G	H	J	K	L	M	N	P	R		
55 up	168	76	57	37	107	169	180	36	134	191	217	33	227	212	51	1895	689.9
	165.8	101.9	66.1	64.6	135.7	181.8	284.4	116.8	302.9	109.2	90.2	22.5	109.2	109.7	34.2		
	.189	.139	.161	.107	.147	.174	.118	.058	.083	.327	.449	.274	.388	.361	.279		
56 its	178	131	96	87	160	198	310	151	300	54	23	14	70	70	16	1858	170.5
	162.6	99.9	64.8	63.4	133.0	178.2	278.8	114.5	296.9	107.0	88.5	22.1	107.1	107.6	33.5		
	.201	.240	.271	.252	.220	.204	.204	.242	.185	.092	.048	.116	.120	.119	.087		
57 about	147	63	75	64	102	166	257	77	217	171	133	18	124	165	36	1815	157.9
	158.8	97.7	63.3	61.9	129.9	174.1	272.4	111.8	290.1	104.5	86.4	21.6	104.6	105.1	32.7		
	.166	.115	.212	.185	.140	.171	.169	.123	.134	.293	.275	.149	.212	.281	.197		
58 into	115	78	45	82	108	163	247	65	223	148	143	22	180	137	35	1791	191.3
	156.7	96.4	62.5	61.1	128.2	171.8	268.8	110.4	286.3	103.2	85.3	21.3	103.2	103.7	32.3		
	.130	.143	.127	.237	.149	.168	.162	.104	.138	.253	.296	.182	.308	.233	.191		
59 than	138	109	80	69	159	189	322	117	334	47	62	13	60	65	25	1789	112.3
	156.5	96.3	62.4	61.0	128.1	171.6	268.5	110.2	285.9	103.1	85.2	21.3	103.1	103.6	32.3		
	.155	.200	.226	.199	.219	.194	.212	.187	.206	.080	.128	.108	.103	.111	.137		
60 them	96	67	45	74	128	183	298	63	149	172	120	47	156	142	49	1789	271.3
	156.5	96.3	62.4	61.0	128.1	171.6	268.5	110.2	285.9	103.1	85.2	21.3	103.1	103.6	32.3		
	.108	.123	.127	.214	.176	.188	.196	.101	.092	.294	.248	.390	.267	.242	.268		

Table A1 (cont.) Distribution of Occurrence of the 100 Most Frequent Word-Types in the Corpus

RANK WORD		GENRES															TOTAL	X²
		A	B	C	D	E	F	G	H	J	K	L	M	N	P	R		
	Frequency																	
	Expected frequency																	
	Ratio, as %, of freq. to total no. words in genre																	
61 can		94	124	45	84	276	170	249	119	367	39	45	16	48	79	17	1772	348.2
		155.1	95.3	61.8	60.4	126.9	169.9	265.9	109.2	283.2	102.1	84.4	21.1	102.2	102.6	31.9		
		.106	.227	.127	.243	.380	.175	.164	.190	.226	.067	.093	.133	.082	.135	.093		
62 only		111	80	69	95	126	148	301	73	336	80	56	20	105	114	33	1747	81.4
		152.9	93.9	60.9	59.6	125.1	167.6	262.2	107.6	279.2	100.6	83.2	20.8	100.7	101.1	31.5		
		.125	.147	.195	.275	.174	.152	.198	.117	.207	.137	.116	.166	.180	.194	.180		
63 other		164	92	58	60	141	145	267	200	293	48	51	22	61	71	29	1702	153.7
		148.9	91.6	59.4	58.0	121.8	163.2	255.4	104.9	272.0	98.0	81.0	20.2	98.1	98.5	30.7		
		.185	.169	.164	.173	.194	.149	.175	.320	.181	.082	.106	.182	.104	.121	.159		
64 new		241	134	90	99	149	162	278	150	147	49	29	9	32	46	20	1635	358.1
		143.1	87.9	57.1	55.8	117.0	156.8	245.4	100.7	261.3	94.2	77.8	19.4	94.3	94.7	29.5		
		.272	.246	.254	.286	.205	.167	.183	.240	.091	.084	.060	.075	.055	.078	.109		
65 some		113	105	59	69	107	183	260	68	311	90	82	20	57	73	20	1617	62.7
		141.5	87.0	56.4	55.1	115.8	155.1	242.7	99.6	258.5	93.1	76.9	19.2	93.2	93.6	29.2		
		.127	.192	.167	.199	.147	.188	.171	.109	.192	.154	.170	.166	.097	.124	.109		
66 time		103	74	44	35	133	178	231	104	210	103	83	34	129	94	44	1599	73.1
		139.9	86.0	55.8	54.5	114.5	153.4	239.9	98.5	255.6	92.1	76.1	19.0	92.2	92.6	28.8		
		.116	.136	.124	.101	.183	.183	.152	.166	.130	.176	.172	.282	.221	.160	.241		

Table A1 (cont.)   Distribution of Occurrence of the 100 Most Frequent Word-Types in the Corpus

Frequency
Expected frequency
Ratio, as % of freq. to total no. of words in genre

RANK	WORD		A	B	C	D	E	F	G	H	J	K	L	M	N	P	R	TOTAL	X²
67	could	Freq.	87	57	40	59	59	142	215	38	159	168	145	49	153	195	33	1599	
		Exp.	139.9	86.0	55.8	54.5	114.5	153.4	239.9	98.5	255.6	92.1	76.1	19.0	92.2	92.6	28.8		
		Ratio	.098	.104	.113	.171	.081	.146	.141.	.061	.098	.288	.300	.406	.262	.332	.180		464.9
68	these	Freq.	70	82	35	75	141	157	271	156	421	47	20	15	34	31	18	1573	
		Exp.	137.6	84.6	54.9	53.6	112.6	150.9	236.1	96.9	251.4	90.6	74.9	18.7	90.7	91.1	28.4		
		Ratio	.079	.150	.099	.217	.194	.161	.178	.250	.260	.080	.041	.124	.058	.053	.098		352.8
69	two	Freq.	174	68	40	27	118	132	191	71	250	76	89	10	88	52	26	1412	
		Exp.	123.6	75.9	49.3	48.2	101.1	135.4	211.9	87.0	225.7	81.3	67.2	16.8	81.4	81.7	25.5		
		Ratio	.196	.125	.113	.078	.163	.136	.125	.114	.154	.130	.184	.083	.150	.089	.142		64.5
70	may	Freq.	93	79	47	79	143	170	221	179	334	10	15	4	7	11	8	1400	
		Exp.	122.5	75.3	48.9	47.7	100.2	134.3	210.1	86.3	223.8	80.6	66.7	16.6	80.7	81.1	25.2		
		Ratio	.105	.145	.133	.228	.197	.175	.145	.286	.206	.017	.031	.033	.012	.019	.044		461.3
71	then	Freq.	73	63	32	59	87	125	161	17	172	119	134	18	137	143	37	1377	
		Exp.	120.5	74.1	48.1	46.9	98.6	132.1	206.7	84.9	220.1	79.3	65.6	16.4	79.4	79.7	24.8		
		Ratio	.082	.115	.090	.171	.120	.128	.106	.027	.106	.204	.277	.149	.234	.244	.202		294.9
72	do	Freq.	64	112	40	54	125	115	186	51	137	95	102	26	99	121	36	1363	
		Exp.	119.3	73.3	47.6	46.5	97.6	130.7	204.5	83.9	217.8	78.5	64.9	16.2	78.6	78.9	24.6		
		Ratio	.072	.205	.113	.156	.172	.118	.122	.082	.085	.163	.211	.216	.169	.206	.197		166.3

GENRES

Table A1 (cont.)   Distribution of Occurrence of the 100 Most Frequent Word-Types in the Corpus

RANK WORD	GENRES															TOTAL	X^2
	A	B	C	D	E	F	G	H	J	K	L	M	N	P	R		
	Frequency / Expected frequency / Ratio, as %, of freq. to total no. words in genre																
73 first	158 119.0 .178	72 73.2 .132	69 47.5 .195	29 46.4 .084	126 97.4 .174	161 130.4 .165	201 204.1 .132	62 83.8 .099	243 217.4 .150	55 78.3 .094	40 64.7 .083	17 16.2 .141	59 78.4 .101	53 78.7 .090	15 24.5 .082	1360	86.8
74 any	95 117.7 .107	82 72.4 .150	30 46.9 .085	60 45.9 .173	92 96.3 .127	120 129.0 .123	215 201.8 .141	149 82.9 .238	214 214.9 .132	55 77.5 .094	69 64.0 .143	19 15.9 .158	58 77.5 .099	68 77.9 .116	19 24.2 .104	1345	85.3
75 my	43 115.4 .048	53 70.9 .097	11 46.0 .031	75 44.9 .217	44 94.4 .061	58 126.5 .060	240 197.9 .158	29 81.3 .046	39 210.8 .024	131 75.9 .224	117 62.8 .242	32 15.7 .265	189 76.0 .323	177 76.4 .301	81 23.8 .443	1319	885.0
76 now	87 114.9 .098	89 70.7 .163	27 45.9 .076	45 44.8 .130	75 94.1 .103	102 126.0 .105	173 197.2 .114	54 80.9 .086	124 210.0 .076	130 75.7 .223	114 62.6 .236	27 15.6 .224	127 75.7 .217	112 76.1 .191	28 23.7 .153	1314	216.9
77 such	74 114.0 .083	65 70.1 .119	36 45.5 .102	73 44.4 .211	94 93.3 .129	116 124.9 .119	189 195.5 .124	195 80.3 .312	316 208.3 .195	28 75.1 .048	23 62.0 .048	12 15.5 .100	23 75.1 .039	24 75.4 .041	35 23.5 .191	1303	386.9
78 like	48 112.9 .054	50 69.4 .092	40 45.0 .113	19 43.9 .055	70 92.3 .096	89 123.7 .091	184 193.6 .121	21 79.5 .034	88 206.2 .054	151 74.3 .258	139 61.4 .288	25 15.3 .207	141 74.4 .241	189 74.7 .322	36 23.3 .197	1290	608.0

Table A1 (cont.)   Distribution of Occurrence of the 100 Most Frequent Word-Types in the Corpus

RANK	WORD		GENRES																TOTAL	X²
			A	B	C	D	E	F	G	H	J	K	L	M	N	P	R		
		Frequency Expected frequency Ratio, as %, of freq. to total no. of words in genre																		
79	our		60 109.6 .068	130 67.4 .238	12 43.7 .034	84 42.7 .243	87 89.6 .120	96 120.1 .099	306 187.9 .201	164 77.1 .262	142 200.1 .088	44 72.1 .075	17 59.6 .035	6 14.9 .050	44 72.2 .075	28 72.5 .048	32 22.6 .175	1252	426.4
80	over		119 108.2 .134	61 66.5 .112	23 43.1 .065	33 42.1 .095	80 88.5 .110	119 118.5 .122	150 185.5 .099	55 76.2 .088	132 197.6 .081	102 71.2 .175	108 58.8 .224	16 14.7 .133	123 71.3 .210	88 71.6 .150	27 22.3 .148	1236	145.0
81	man		74 105.6 .083	56 64.9 .103	58 42.1 .164	68 41.2 .197	19 86.4 .026	90 115.8 .093	231 181.1 .152	12 74.4 .019	73 192.9 .045	112 69.5 .192	107 57.5 .222	18 14.3 .149	166 69.6 .284	100 69.9 .170	23 21.8 .126	1207	145.0
82	me		31 103.3 .035	35 63.5 .064	11 41.2 .031	33 40.3 .095	16 84.5 .022	58 113.3 .060	207 177.2 .136	12 72.8 .019	44 188.8 .027	137 68.0 .234	116 56.2 .240	21 14.0 .174	210 68.1 .359	194 68.4 .330	56 21.3 .306	1181	449.3
83	even		61 102.5 .069	67 63.0 .123	34 40.9 .096	49 39.9 .142	74 83.8 .102	123 112.3 .126	223 175.7 .146	31 72.2 .050	157 187.2 .097	64 67.5 .110	67 55.8 .139	12 13.9 .099	84 67.5 .144	86 67.8 .146	39 21.1 .213	1171	1056.4
84	most		81 101.5 .091	76 62.4 .139	57 40.5 .161	52 39.6 .150	124 83.0 .171	161 111.3 .165	214 174.1 .141	55 71.5 .088	198 185.4 .122	36 66.8 .062	18 55.2 .037	12 13.8 .010	28 66.9 .048	31 67.2 .053	17 20.9 .093	1160	90.2

Table A1 (cont.)   Distribution of Occurrence of the 100 Most Frequent Word-Types in the Corpus

RANK WORD		GENRES															TOTAL	X²
		A	B	C	D	E	F	G	H	J	K	L	M	N	P	R		
		Frequency																
		Expected frequency																
		Ratio, as % of freq. to total no. words in genre																
85 made		107	45	35	28	72	112	147	118	164	60	60	15	77	62	23	1125	
		98.4	60.5	39.3	38.4	80.5	107.9	168.8	69.3	179.8	64.8	53.6	13.4	64.9	65.1	20.3		51.6
		.121	.082	.099	.081	.099	.115	.097	.189	.101	.103	.124	.124	.132	.106	.126		
86 after		151	38	36	22	74	121	158	43	127	66	56	13	67	69	29	1070	
		93.6	57.6	37.3	36.5	76.6	102.6	160.6	65.9	171.0	61.6	50.9	12.7	61.7	61.9	19.3		77.3
		.170	.069	.102	.064	.102	.124	.104	.069	.078	.113	.116	.108	.115	.116	.159		
87 also		129	47	35	57	110	99	185	89	227	8	30	2	22	16	13	1069	
		93.5	57.5	37.3	36.5	76.5	102.5	160.4	65.9	170.9	61.6	50.9	12.7	61.6	61.9	19.3		197.9
		.145	.086	.099	.165	.151	.102	.122	.142	.140	.014	.062	.017	.038	.027	.071		
88 did		64	36	23	34	25	91	179	18	111	123	55	38	90	127	30	1044	
		91.4	56.2	36.4	35.6	74.7	100.1	156.7	64.3	166.9	60.1	49.7	12.4	60.2	60.4	18.8		323.4
		.072	.066	.065	.098	.034	.094	.118	.029	.068	.211	.114	.315	.154	.216	.164		
89 many		72	72	42	52	125	137	158	86	161	29	16	11	24	28	17	1030	
		90.1	55.4	35.9	35.1	73.7	98.8	154.6	63.5	164.6	59.3	49.0	12.2	59.4	59.6	18.6		152.2
		.081	.132	.119	.150	.172	.141	.104	.138	.099	.050	.033	.091	.041	.048	.093		
90 before		93	34	26	27	68	104	148	42	112	85	72	13	90	91	11	1016	
		88.7	54.6	35.4	34.6	72.6	97.3	152.2	62.5	162.1	58.4	48.3	12.1	58.5	58.7	18.3		96.6
		.105	.062	.073	.078	.094	.107	.097	.067	.068	.145	.149	.108	.154	.155	.060		

Table A1 (cont.)   Distribution of Occurrence of the 100 Most Frequent Word-Types in the Corpus

RANK	WORD		GENRES A	B	C	D	E	F	G	H	J	K	L	M	N	P	R	TOTAL	X²
		Frequency / Expected frequency / Ratio, as % of freq. to total no. of words in genre																	
91	must	Freq	53	55	19	54	84	96	171	102	203	55	31	8	27	46	9	1013	104.6
		Exp	88.6	54.5	35.3	34.5	72.5	97.2	152.0	62.4	161.9	58.3	48.2	12.0	58.4	58.6	18.3		
		Ratio	.060	.101	.054	.156	.116	.099	.112	.163	.125	.094	.064	.066	.046	.078	.049		
93	through	Freq	56	23	29	49	78	97	139	60	145	63	58	16	80	58	18	969	52.9
		Exp	84.7	52.1	33.8	33.0	69.3	92.8	145.3	59.6	154.7	55.8	46.1	11.5	55.8	56.0	17.5		
		Ratio	.063	.042	.082	.142	.106	.100	.091	.096	.089	.108	.120	.133	.137	.099	.098		
94	back	Freq	73	36	19	15	42	60	82	10	39	104	158	19	166	128	16	967	830.0
		Exp	84.6	52.0	33.7	32.9	69.2	92.7	145.1	59.6	154.6	55.7	46.0	11.5	55.7	55.9	17.4		
		Ratio	.082	.066	.054	.043	.058	.062	.054	.016	.024	.178	.327	.158	.284	.218	.087		
95	years	Freq	102	63	33	37	80	110	157	106	88	44	25	16	32	35	21	949	111.3
		Exp	83.0	51.1	33.1	32.4	67.9	91.0	142.4	58.5	151.7	54.7	45.2	11.3	54.7	54.9	17.1		
		Ratio	.115	.115	.093	.107	.110	.113	.103	.170	.054	.075	.052	.133	.055	.060	.115		
96	where	Freq	59	45	29	21	77	111	114	48	127	89	71	15	58	58	16	938	67.9
		Exp	82.1	50.5	32.7	31.9	67.2	89.9	140.8	57.8	149.9	54.0	44.7	11.2	54.1	54.3	16.9		
		Ratio	.066	.082	.082	.061	.106	.114	.075	.077	.078	.152	.147	.124	.099	.099	.087		
97	much	Freq	51	56	37	29	82	76	160	29	150	50	59	14	55	70	19	937	46.1
		Exp	81.9	50.4	32.7	31.9	67.1	89.9	140.6	57.7	149.8	53.9	44.6	11.1	54.0	54.2	16.9		
		Ratio	.057	.103	.105	.084	.113	.078	.105	.046	.093	.086	.122	.116	.094	.119	.104		

Table A1 (cont.) Distribution of Occurrence of the 100 Most Frequent Word-Types in the Corpus

RANK WORD	GENRES															TOTAL	X²
	A	B	C	D	E	F	G	H	J	K	L	M	N	P	R		
	Frequency																
	Expected frequency																
	Ratio, as % of freq. to total no. words in genre																
98 your	13	36	12	41	279	59	54	55	21	42	70	18	69	116	38	923	1059.9
	80.8	49.7	32.2	31.5	66.1	88.5	138.5	56.9	147.5	53.2	43.9	10.9	53.2	53.4	16.6		
	.015	.066	.034	.119	.384	.061	.035	.088	.013	.072	.145	.149	.118	.198	.208		
99 way	47	45	35	33	77	86	157	23	90	63	62	14	65	84	28	909	101.1
	79.5	48.9	31.7	30.9	65.1	87.2	136.4	56.0	145.3	52.4	43.3	10.8	52.4	52.6	16.4		
	.053	.082	.099	.095	.106	.088	.103	.037	.056	.108	.128	.116	.111	.143	.153		
100 well	43	35	53	24	78	79	161	41	124	54	54	15	49	72	15	897	63.9
	78.5	48.3	31.3	30.6	64.2	86.0	134.6	55.3	143.4	51.7	42.7	10.7	51.7	51.9	16.2		
	.048	.064	.150	.069	.107	.081	.106	.066	.076	.092	.112	.124	.084	.123	.082		
101 down	51	34	14	15	46	70	98	6	34	129	83	11	154	127	23	895	645.8
	78.3	48.2	31.2	30.5	64.1	85.8	134.3	55.1	143.0	51.6	42.6	10.6	51.6	51.8	16.1		
	.057	.062	.040	.043	.063	.072	.064	.010	.021	.221	.172	.091	.263	.216	.126		

WORD-FREQUENCY DISTRIBUTION

Explanation of Tables B1 to B59 and Graphs Bɪ to Bᴠ

In the explanations that accompany the tables and graphs in this section the following terms are consistently used:

The term "Corpus" refers to the entire Standard Corpus of Present-Day Edited American English, described in detail on pp. xviii–xx of the Introduction.

A "sample" is any of the five hundred natural-language texts, each consisting of approximately two thousand running words (tokens), which compose the Corpus.

A "representative subset" of the Corpus refers to a set of samples selected in such a way that the set is reasonably representative of the genres of writing included in the Corpus. This selection was performed by retrieving from the Corpus every nth sample needed to compose a subset of desired length. For example, the selection of a representative subset of fifty samples (approximately one hundred thousand tokens) was achieved by extracting every tenth sample.

A "nonrepresentative subset" of the Corpus, on the other hand, is a set of samples selected in such a way that this subset does *not* contain the same proportion of various genres of writing as does the Corpus as a whole.

A "word" is any string of graphemes bounded by spaces in the stripped version (Form B) of the Corpus (see pp. xx–xxi of the Introduction for details).

A "token" is any individual word identified in any specified selection from the Corpus or in the Corpus as a whole. The number of tokens is thus synonymous with the number of running words.

A "type" is any distinct word that is defined as a set of identical individual words identifiable in any specified subset of the Corpus or in the entire Corpus. The number of types is thus synonymous with the number of distinct words. A detailed explanation of a type is given with examples on p. xxi of the Introduction.

Frequency Tables. Tables B1, B2, and B3 give the word-frequency figures in *descending* order, i.e., the highest frequency first and the *hapax legomena* (words occurring only once) in the last row. Table B1 represents the word-frequency distribution in the whole Corpus, Table B2 gives the data for a representative subset of the

Corpus consisting of 125 samples (253,538 tokens), and Table B3 gives the data for a representative subset of the Corpus consisting of 50 samples (101,566 tokens).

Tables B4 to B57 give the word-frequency figures in *ascending* order, i.e., the *hapax legomena* first and the word of the highest frequency of occurrence in the last row. Table B4 displays the distribution for the whole Corpus; Table B5, for a representative Corpus subset of 125 samples (253,538 tokens); Table B6, for a representative subset of 50 samples (101,566 tokens); and Table B7, for a subset consisting of 5 samples (10,051 tokens). Tables B8 to B57 give the word-frequency distribution for 50 individual samples selected from the Corpus (by taking every tenth sample); each of these samples consists of approximately 2,000 tokens, the exact number of tokens in each case being indicated in each table.

The organization of the tables and the labeling of columns is identical in all the tables with the minor exception of Table B1, which includes one more column than the other tables. The first column in Table B1, which has no parallel in the other tables, represents the designation of the Corpus rank of the word or the words whose frequency is given in column two (labeled X) of Table B1. Since Table B1 summarizes the word frequencies in descending order, the rank number in the first column of B1 makes it possible to read off the Corpus rank of any word or words of frequency X. It is only necessary to look up the Corpus frequency of a word in either word list in the preceding section of this book and then proceed through Table B1 until the same frequency X is located in the second column; the figure in the first column corresponding to this X is the Corpus rank of the word. In those cases when the frequency in Table B1 applies to more than one type, column one gives the rank range of these words.

For example, the reader interested in the Corpus rank of the word *it* will find in the alphabetical word list that *it* has a frequency of 8,756. In Table B1 for $X = 8,756$ the first column gives the value 12. This is the Corpus rank of the word *it*.

With the exception of the additional rank column of Table B1, all tables in this section have identical configurations. Reading from left to right, the column labeled X gives the frequency of occurrence. The following column labeled FX, i.e., f_x, gives the number of distinct words (types) of the frequency X. Thus we find, for example, in Table B4 that for $X = 2$, $FX = 7,233$, which indicates that there are 7,233 different words in the Corpus which occur exactly twice.

The column labeled SUM FX, i.e., $\sum_x f_x$, contains the sum of types, counting from the top of the table, and the next column, CUM % FX, i.e., $\% \sum_x f_x$, expresses this figure as a cumulative percentage of the total number of types found in the analyzed text. The SUM FX column thus gives the total number of types, and the CUM % FX column, the percentage of types that are due to frequency X and to preceding values of X. For example, Table B1, summarizing the frequency distribution for the whole Corpus in descending order, shows that the first one hundred most frequent words of the Corpus account for only 0.198 per cent of the types in the Corpus. On the other hand, Table B4, which gives the data for the Corpus in ascending order of frequency, shows that low-frequency words occurring no more than ten times include 42,487 types and constitute 84.290 per cent of the total number of different words in the Corpus.

The fifth column (sixth in Table B1) gives the product FX*X, i.e., $f_x X$, or the number of types of the respective frequency multiplied by the frequency. In other words, this column shows the number of running words (tokens) accounted for by the types of frequency X. The next

column SUM FX*X, i.e., $\sum_{x} f_x X$, lists the cumulative number of tokens due to frequency X and preceding values of X, and the following column, labeled CUM % FX*X, i.e., $\% \sum_{x} f_x X$, expresses this figure as a percentage of the total number of running words (tokens) in the analyzed text. The cumulative count and percentage of tokens thus makes it possible to determine quickly, among other things, the proportion of the text accounted for by words of high frequency (in the descending tables B1–B3) or by low-frequency words (in the ascending tables B4–B57).

For example, the following information can be read off from Table B1: the first one hundred most frequent words of the Corpus (which constitute only 0.198 per cent of all types) account for 481,055 tokens, i.e., 47.430 per cent of all the running words of the Corpus. From Table B4 the information may be read off that the words occurring no more than ten times (which constitute 84.290 per cent of all the types of the Corpus) account for only 101,776 tokens, i.e., only 10.035 per cent of the running words of the Corpus.

The basic statistical values were calculated for each word-frequency distribution and are given at the end of each table. S_0 is the sum of *SUM FX* taken over all values of X and represents thus the total number of types in the analyzed set of data. The first moment of the distribution S_1 equals the sum of *SUM FX*X* taken over all values of X and represents the total number of tokens in the set. S_2 is the second moment of the distribution $\sum_{x} f_x X^2$.

Also included for each distribution is the mean M, the standard deviation SD, i.e., σ, the coefficient of variation V and Yule's characteristic K.

The characteristic K is a statistical parameter of a frequency distribution, devised by the English statistician G. Udny Yule (*The Statistical Study of Literary Vocabulary* [Cambridge, Eng., 1944]). The characteristic is based on the Poisson probability law and was developed by Yule as the result of his work on accidents and "repeated events."

K can be said to measure the repeat rate of words and thus indicate the concentration of vocabulary in the text. A large value of K implies a proportionately greater use of the commoner words (i.e., words of high frequency of occurrence) than a smaller value of K. Conversely, a small value of K implies that the text depends to a relatively larger extent on rare words (i.e., words of low frequency) than a sample with a larger value of K.

The characteristic K is calculated from the formula

$$K = 10,000 \frac{S_2 - S_1}{S_1{}^2}$$

where

$$S_1 = \sum_{x} f_x X$$

is the first moment of the distribution about zero as origin, and

$$S_2 = \sum_{x} f_x X^2$$

the second moment. The quantity 10,000 is introduced to avoid dealing with small decimals.

Because K is based on the second and first moments of the distribution, it is theoretically independent of size of sample. In taking random samples of various sizes from a population, the frequency distribution of these samples will exhibit the same constant "characteristic," which will also be the same as the "characteristic" of the distribution of the whole population.

It is important that the samples be a random, sufficiently spread, selection from the population. It is this condition that conversely implies that K, in practice, may not be always independent of the size of the sample. For a large population taking only a small sample from one section will "localize" the distribution, and therefore

the resulting distribution and its characteristic will be valid only for the local sample space.

The values of K given at the end of each frequency distribution table in this section illustrate well the relative independence of Yule's characteristic of sample size.

Individual Samples. Tables B8 to B57 give the frequency distribution (in ascending order) for 50 samples selected from the Corpus by taking every tenth sample of the 500 samples composing the entire Corpus. The 50 samples whose frequency distribution is displayed in these tables are of approximately equal length, about 2,000 words each, with the exact number of tokens specified at the end of each table. This makes it possible to compare the statistical properties of 50 samples of almost equal size and evaluate the significant differences of the word-frequency distributions of these samples.

The sources from which the 50 samples have been taken are briefly identified at the head of each table. Further details about the sources can be found in the *Manual of Information.*

Type-Token Ratios. Table B58 gives a summary of the information on the number of distinct words (types) and the number of running words (tokens) in the Corpus as a whole and in several subsets of the Corpus, including representative subsets (marked by R) and nonrepresentative subsets of the Corpus (designated by N). The representative subsets were selected from the Corpus in such a manner as to contain—as much as possible—the same proportion of individual genres as the Corpus as a whole: subsets consisting of 5, 25, 50, and 125 samples (i.e., approximately of 10,000, 50,000, 100,000, and 250,000 tokens) were chosen in this manner. The nonrepresentative subsets, each consisting of 50 samples (i.e., approximately 100,000 tokens) were selected so that they would contain samples from as few of the fifteen genres as possible (one, two, or three

genres, with four genres being represented only in a single subset). Because of the organization of the Corpus, this could be done simply by dividing the Corpus into ten consecutive sections, each section consisting of exactly 50 samples. The subset designated N1 thus represents the first 50 samples of the Corpus, N2 the second 50 samples, and so on.

For each subset, as well as the Corpus as a whole, Table B58 also gives the type-token ratio and the logarithmic type-token ratio.

Least-Squares Fits to the Rank vs. Frequency and Frequency vs. Number of Types Distributions. Table B59a gives the results of least-squares fits of a straight line to the log rank versus log frequency curve for the Corpus (as represented in Graph B$_I$) and the various Corpus subsets described in the preceding table. Table B59b gives the results of least-squares fits of a straight line to the log frequency versus log number of types of that frequency for the whole Corpus (as represented in Graph B$_{II}$).

Since the rank of certain words (where more than one type has the same frequency) was arbitrarily determined on the basis of their alphabetical order within the respective frequency set, a modified average-rank least-squares fit was also made for the Corpus to ascertain whether this procedure would result in significantly different values (designated by A in the table).

In Table B59, a is the slope of the straight line, b its y-intercept, and σ the standard deviation of the straight line from the actual distribution curve.

Graphs. The data from the frequency distribution tables of the Corpus and its subsets have been plotted in several different graphs to show the relation of the elements of the distribution to the frequency. In the description of the following graphs the logarithm is always to the base 10.

Graph B$_I$—Log Rank vs. Log Frequency

for the Entire Corpus: full logarithmic paper was used for this graph. Each individual word was assigned a rank, the most frequent word having the rank of 1, the next most frequent word the rank of 2, etc. The logarithm of the rank was then plotted on the x-axis (horizontal), the logarithm of the frequency of the word of that rank on the y-axis (vertical). The curve is "stepped" at the extremities, but consists of an almost straight line at the middle. The graph was made using an average rank for words of rank 1,000 through 50,406.

A least-squares fit of a straight line for this curve as well as for the log rank vs. log frequency distribution for various subsets of the Corpus can be found in Table B59 on p. 357.

Graph Bii—Log Frequency vs. Log Number of Types of That Frequency for (a) the entire Corpus and (b) the representative subset of 50 samples (101,566 words): full logarithmic paper was used for this graph. The x-axis represents the logarithm of the frequency X, the y-axis the logarithm of the number of types. For a given frequency the number of types of that frequency is plotted. The resulting complex curve was fitted to a straight line by the method of least squares. The slope, y-intercept, and standard deviation for this line are given in Table B59.

Since the number of types of higher frequencies would be extremely difficult to plot individually, Graph Bii shows, in the higher frequency range, points that represent sums of types falling into a given frequency range. This is the case with all types of frequency higher than 20.

However, in order to show better the properties of distribution by individual frequencies, the graph also contains an extended partial curve that gives the number of types plotted by individual frequencies. This is shown for all frequencies up to 110.

Graph Biii—Log Frequency vs. Cumulative Percentage of Types for (a) the entire Corpus and (b) the representative subset of 50 samples (101,566 words): probability vs. logarithmic paper was used for this graph. The logarithm of a particular frequency X is plotted along the x-axis, and the cumulative percentage of types due to that frequency or less is plotted along the y-axis. The mean of the resulting curve can be obtained by dropping a perpendicular from the point where the curve crosses the 50 per cent line to the x-axis; the standard deviation, by dropping a perpendicular from the point where the curve crosses the 16 per cent line or 84 per cent line to the x-axis. The curve approximates a straight line.

Graph Biv—Log Frequency vs. Cumulative Percentage of Tokens for (a) the entire Corpus and (b) the representative subset of 50 samples (101,566 words): this graph is plotted in the same way as the previous graph, except that the y-axis represents the cumulative percentage of tokens. Probability vs. logarithmic paper was used.

Graph Bv—Log Frequency vs. Cumulative Percentage of Types and Tokens for (a) the entire Corpus and (b) the representative subset of 50 samples (101,566 words): to better show the relationship of the type and the token curves to each other, Graphs Biii and Biv were superimposed in Graph Bv.

Symbols Used in Tables B1 to B59

X   Frequency of occurrence

$FX = f_x$ Number of types of frequency X

$SUM\ FX = \sum_x f_x$ Sum of types due to frequency X and preceding values of X

$CUM\ \%\ FX = \%\sum_x f_x$ Per cent of types due to frequency X and preceding values of X

$FX^*X = f_x X$ Number of tokens accounted for by types of frequency X

$SUM\ FX^*X = \sum_x f_x X$ Sum of tokens due to frequency X and preceding values of X

$CUM\ \%\ FX^*X = \%\sum_x f_x X$ Per cent of tokens due to frequency X and preceding values of X

$S0 = S_0 = SUM\ FX$ $\sum_x f_x$ taken over all values of X; the total number of types

$S1 = S_1 = SUM\ FX^*X$ $\sum_x f_x X$ taken over all values of X; the total number of tokens; the first moment of the distribution

$S2 = S_2 = SUM\ FX^*X^2$ $\sum_x f_x X^2$; the second moment of the distribution

M   The mean of the distribution

SD   The standard deviation

V   The coefficient of variation

K Yule's characteristic, $K = 10{,}000\,\dfrac{S_2 - S_1}{S_1{}^2}$

a The slope of the straight line in Table B59 and in Graphs B$_I$ and B$_{II}$

b The y-intercept of the straight line in Table B59 and in Graphs B$_I$ and B$_{II}$

σ The standard deviation of the straight line from the actual distribution curve in Table B59 and Graphs B$_I$ and B$_{II}$

TABLE B1   THE CORPUS WITH RANK IN DESCENDING ORDER

RANK	X	FX	SUM FX	FX*X	SUM FX*X	CUM% FX	CUM% FX*X
1	69971	1	1	69971	69971	0.002	6.899
2	36411	1	2	36411	106382	0.004	10.489
3	28852	1	3	28852	135234	0.006	13.334
4	26149	1	4	26149	161383	0.008	15.912
5	23237	1	5	23237	184620	0.010	18.203
6	21341	1	6	21341	205961	0.012	20.307
7	10595	1	7	10595	216556	0.014	21.352
8	10099	1	8	10099	226655	0.016	22.347
9	9816	1	9	9816	236471	0.018	23.315
10	9543	1	10	9543	246014	0.020	24.256
11	9489	1	11	9489	255503	0.022	25.192
12	8756	1	12	8756	264259	0.024	26.055
13	7289	1	13	7289	271548	0.026	26.774
14	7250	1	14	7250	278798	0.028	27.489
15	6997	1	15	6997	285795	0.030	28.178
16	6742	1	16	6742	292537	0.032	28.843
17	6377	1	17	6377	298914	0.034	29.472
18	5378	1	18	5378	304292	0.036	30.002
19	5305	1	19	5305	309597	0.038	30.525
20	5173	1	20	5173	314770	0.040	31.035
21	5146	1	21	5146	319916	0.042	31.543
22	5133	1	22	5133	325049	0.044	32.049
23	4609	1	23	4609	329658	0.046	32.503
24	4393	1	24	4393	334051	0.048	32.936
25	4381	1	25	4381	338432	0.050	33.368
26	4369	1	26	4369	342801	0.052	33.799
27	4207	1	27	4207	347008	0.054	34.214
28	3941	1	28	3941	350949	0.056	34.602
29	3747	1	29	3747	354696	0.058	34.972
30	3618	1	30	3618	358314	0.060	35.329
31	3562	1	31	3562	361876	0.062	35.680
32	3292	1	32	3292	365168	0.063	36.004
33	3286	1	33	3286	368454	0.065	36.328
34	3284	1	34	3284	371738	0.067	36.652
35	3037	1	35	3037	374775	0.069	36.952
36	3001	1	36	3001	377776	0.071	37.247

TABLE B1 (CONT.)   THE CORPUS WITH RANK IN DESCENDING ORDER

RANK	X	FX	SUM FX	CUM% FX	FX*X	SUM FX*X	CUM% FX*X
37	2859	1	37	0.073	2859	380635	37.529
38	2724	1	38	0.075	2724	383359	37.798
39	2714	1	39	0.077	2714	386073	38.066
40	2670	1	40	0.079	2670	388743	38.329
41	2653	1	41	0.081	2653	391396	38.590
42	2619	1	42	0.083	2619	394015	38.849
43	2472	1	43	0.085	2472	396487	39.092
44	2439	1	44	0.087	2439	398926	39.333
45	2331	1	45	0.089	2331	401257	39.563
46	2252	1	46	0.091	2252	403509	39.785
47	2244	1	47	0.093	2244	405753	40.006
48	2216	1	48	0.095	2216	407969	40.224
49	2201	1	49	0.097	2201	410170	40.441
50	2199	1	50	0.099	2199	412369	40.658
51	2096	1	51	0.101	2096	414465	40.865
52	1984	1	52	0.103	1984	416449	41.061
53	1961	1	53	0.105	1961	418410	41.254
54	1908	1	54	0.107	1908	420318	41.442
55	1895	1	55	0.109	1895	422213	41.629
56	1858	1	56	0.111	1858	424071	41.812
57	1815	1	57	0.113	1815	425886	41.991
58	1791	1	58	0.115	1791	427677	42.168
59 THRU 60	1789	2	60	0.119	3578	431255	42.520
61	1772	1	61	0.121	1772	433027	42.695
62	1747	1	62	0.123	1747	434774	42.867
63	1702	1	63	0.125	1702	436476	43.035
64	1635	1	64	0.127	1635	438111	43.196
65	1617	1	65	0.129	1617	439728	43.356
66 THRU 67	1599	2	67	0.133	3198	442926	43.671
68	1573	1	68	0.135	1573	444499	43.826
69	1412	1	69	0.137	1412	445911	43.965
70	1400	1	70	0.139	1400	447311	44.103
71	1377	1	71	0.141	1377	448688	44.239
72	1363	1	72	0.143	1363	450051	44.374
73	1360	1	73	0.145	1360	451411	44.508
74	1345	1	74	0.147	1345	452756	44.640

TABLE B1 (CONT.) THE CORPUS WITH RANK IN DESCENDING ORDER

RANK	X	FX	SUM FX	CUM% FX	FX*X	SUM FX*X	CUM% FX*X
75	1319	1	75	0.149	1319	454075	44.770
76	1314	1	76	0.151	1314	455389	44.900
77	1303	1	77	0.153	1303	456692	45.028
78	129C	1	78	0.155	1290	457982	45.156
79	1252	1	79	0.157	1252	459234	45.279
80	1236	1	80	0.159	1236	460470	45.401
81	1207	1	81	0.161	1207	461677	45.520
82	1181	1	82	C.163	1181	462858	45.636
83	1171	1	83	0.165	1171	464029	45.752
84	1160	1	84	0.167	1160	465189	45.866
85	1125	1	85	0.169	1125	466314	45.977
86	107C	1	86	0.171	1070	467384	46.083
87	1069	1	87	0.173	1069	468453	46.188
88	1044	1	88	0.175	1044	469497	46.291
89	1030	1	89	0.177	1030	470527	46.392
90	1016	1	90	0.179	1016	471543	46.493
91	1013	1	91	0.181	1013	472556	46.592
92	1010	1	92	0.183	1010	473566	46.692
93	969	1	93	0.185	969	474535	46.788
94	967	1	94	0.186	967	475502	46.883
95	949	1	95	0.188	949	476451	46.977
96	938	1	96	0.190	938	477389	47.069
97	937	1	97	0.192	937	478326	47.161
98	923	1	98	0.194	923	479249	47.252
99	909	1	99	0.196	909	480158	47.342
100	897	1	100	0.198	897	481055	47.430
101	895	1	101	0.200	895	481950	47.519
102	888	1	102	0.202	888	482838	47.606
103	883	1	103	0.204	883	483721	47.693
104	877	1	104	0.206	877	484598	47.780
105	872	1	105	0.208	872	485470	47.866
106	85C	1	106	0.210	850	486320	47.950
107	847	1	107	0.212	847	487167	48.033
108	839	1	108	0.214	839	488006	48.116
109	834	1	109	0.216	834	488840	48.198
110	832	1	110	0.218	832	489672	48.280

TABLE B1 (CONT.) THE CORPUS WITH RANK IN DESCENDING ORDER

RANK	X	FX	SUM FX	CUM% FX	FX*X	SUM FX*X	CUM% FX*X
111	831	1	111	0.220	831	490503	48.362
112	808	1	112	0.222	808	491311	48.442
113	807	1	113	0.224	807	492118	48.521
114	796	1	114	0.226	796	492914	48.600
115	794	1	115	0.228	794	493708	48.678
116	787	1	116	0.230	787	494495	48.756
117	782	1	117	0.232	782	495277	48.833
118 THRU 119	772	2	119	0.236	1544	496821	48.985
120	763	1	120	0.238	763	497584	49.060
121	760	1	121	0.240	760	498344	49.135
122	755	1	122	0.242	755	499099	49.210
123 THRU 124	750	2	124	0.246	1500	500599	49.357
125 THRU 126	730	2	126	0.250	1460	502059	49.501
127	721	1	127	0.252	721	502780	49.572
128	715	1	128	0.254	715	503495	49.643
129	712	1	129	0.256	712	504207	49.713
130	707	1	130	0.258	707	504914	49.783
131	698	1	131	0.260	698	505612	49.852
132 THRU 133	686	2	133	0.264	1372	506984	49.987
134 THRU 135	683	2	135	0.268	1366	508350	50.122
136	680	1	136	0.270	680	509030	50.189
137	676	1	137	0.272	676	509706	50.255
138 THRU 139	672	2	139	0.276	1344	511050	50.388
140	665	1	140	0.278	665	511715	50.453
141 THRU 142	660	2	142	0.282	1320	513035	50.584
143	639	1	143	0.284	639	513674	50.647
144	630	1	144	0.286	630	514304	50.709
145	628	1	145	0.288	628	514932	50.771
146 THRU 147	626	2	147	0.292	1252	516184	50.894
148	622	1	148	0.294	622	516806	50.955
149	613	1	149	0.296	613	517419	51.016
150	612	1	150	0.298	612	518031	51.076
151	611	1	151	0.300	611	518642	51.136
152	610	1	152	0.302	610	519252	51.197
153	605	1	153	0.304	605	519857	51.256
154	603	1	154	0.306	603	520460	51.316

TABLE 81 (CONT.) THE CORPUS WITH RANK IN DESCENDING ORDER

RANK	X	FX	SUM FX	CUM% FX	FX*X	SUM FX*X	CUM% FX*X
155	601	1	155	0.308	601	521061	51.375
156	591	1	156	0.309	591	521652	51.433
157	585	1	157	0.311	589	522241	51.491
158	585	1	158	0.313	585	522826	51.549
159	583	1	159	0.315	583	523409	51.606
160	578	1	160	0.317	578	523987	51.663
161	571	1	161	0.319	571	524558	51.720
162	565	1	162	0.321	569	525127	51.776
163	561	1	163	0.323	561	525688	51.831
164	552	1	164	0.325	552	526240	51.886
165	547	1	165	0.327	547	526787	51.939
166	542	1	166	0.329	542	527329	51.993
167	536	1	167	0.331	536	527865	52.046
168	534	1	168	0.333	534	528399	52.098
169	515	1	169	0.335	515	528914	52.149
170	507	1	170	0.337	507	529421	52.199
171	504	1	171	0.339	504	529925	52.249
172	500	1	172	0.341	500	530425	52.298
173	495	1	173	0.343	499	530924	52.347
174 THRU 175	497	2	175	0.347	994	531918	52.445
176	496	1	176	0.349	496	532414	52.494
177	495	1	177	0.351	495	532909	52.543
178	492	1	178	0.353	492	533401	52.592
179	491	1	179	0.355	491	533892	52.640
180	489	1	180	0.357	489	534381	52.688
181	485	1	181	0.359	485	534866	52.736
182 THRU 183	482	2	183	0.363	964	535830	52.831
184	480	1	184	0.365	480	536310	52.878
185	472	1	185	0.367	472	536782	52.925
186	465	1	186	0.369	465	537247	52.971
187	464	1	187	0.371	464	537711	53.017
188	461	1	188	0.373	461	538172	53.062
189	458	1	189	0.375	458	538630	53.107
190	456	1	190	0.377	456	539086	53.152
191 THRU 192	450	2	192	0.381	900	539986	53.241
193	447	1	193	0.383	447	540433	53.285

TABLE 81 (CONT.) THE CORPUS WITH RANK IN DESCENDING ORDER

RANK	X	FX	SUM FX	CUM% FX	FX*X	SUM FX*X	CUM% FX*X
194 THRU 195	442	2	195	0.387	884	541317	53.372
196 THRU 197	438	2	197	0.391	876	542193	53.458
198	437	1	198	0.393	437	542630	53.502
199	433	1	199	0.395	433	543063	53.544
200	432	1	200	0.397	432	543495	53.587
201	431	1	201	0.399	431	543926	53.629
202	430	1	202	0.401	430	544356	53.672
203	427	1	203	0.403	427	544783	53.714
204	426	1	204	0.405	426	545209	53.756
205	424	1	205	0.407	424	545633	53.798
206	419	1	206	0.409	419	546052	53.839
207	417	1	207	0.411	417	546469	53.880
208	416	1	208	0.413	416	546885	53.921
209 THRU 210	414	2	210	0.417	828	547713	54.003
211	413	1	211	0.419	413	548126	54.043
212	412	1	212	0.421	412	548538	54.084
213	411	1	213	0.423	411	548949	54.125
214	410	1	214	0.425	410	549359	54.165
215	404	1	215	0.427	404	549763	54.205
216 THRU 218	401	3	218	0.432	1203	550966	54.323
219 THRU 221	399	3	221	0.438	1197	552163	54.441
222	398	1	222	0.440	398	552561	54.481
223	397	1	223	0.442	397	552958	54.520
224 THRU 225	395	2	225	0.446	790	553748	54.598
226 THRU 227	394	2	227	0.450	788	554536	54.675
228	393	1	228	0.452	393	554929	54.714
229	392	1	229	0.454	392	555321	54.753
230	391	1	230	0.456	391	555712	54.791
231	390	1	231	0.458	390	556102	54.830
232	386	1	232	0.460	386	556488	54.868
233	385	1	233	0.462	385	556873	54.906
234 THRU 235	384	2	235	0.466	768	557641	54.982
236	383	1	236	0.468	383	558024	55.019
237	382	1	237	0.470	382	558406	55.057
238 THRU 239	380	2	239	0.474	760	559166	55.132
240 THRU 242	377	3	242	0.480	1131	560297	55.243

TABLE B1 (CONT.) THE CORPUS WITH RANK IN DESCENDING ORDER

RANK	X	FX	SUM FX	CUM% FX	FX*X	SUM FX*X	CUM% FX*X
243	376	1	243	0.482	376	560673	55.281
244	375	1	244	0.484	375	561048	55.318
245 THRU 247	373	3	247	0.490	1119	562167	55.428
248 THRU 249	371	2	249	0.494	742	562909	55.501
250 THRU 251	370	2	251	0.498	740	563649	55.574
252	369	1	252	0.500	369	564018	55.610
253 THRU 254	368	2	254	0.504	736	564754	55.683
255	367	1	255	0.506	367	565121	55.719
256	366	1	256	0.508	366	565487	55.755
257	365	1	257	0.510	365	565852	55.791
258 THRU 259	362	2	259	0.514	724	566576	55.863
260 THRU 261	361	2	261	0.518	722	567298	55.934
262 THRU 263	360	2	263	0.522	720	568018	56.005
264 THRU 265	359	2	265	0.526	718	568736	56.076
266	357	1	266	0.528	357	569093	56.111
267 THRU 268	355	2	268	0.532	710	569803	56.181
269	352	1	269	0.534	352	570155	56.215
270	351	1	270	0.536	351	570506	56.250
271	348	1	271	0.538	348	570854	56.284
272	345	1	272	0.540	345	571199	56.318
273	343	1	273	0.542	343	571542	56.352
274	342	1	274	0.544	342	571884	56.386
275	334	1	275	0.546	334	572218	56.419
276 THRU 277	333	2	277	0.550	666	572884	56.484
278	332	1	278	0.552	332	573216	56.517
279	331	1	279	0.554	331	573547	56.550
280	330	1	280	0.555	330	573877	56.582
281	329	1	281	0.557	329	574206	56.615
282 THRU 283	325	2	283	0.561	650	574856	56.679
284	324	1	284	0.563	324	575180	56.711
285 THRU 286	323	2	286	0.567	646	575826	56.775
287 THRU 288	320	2	288	0.571	640	576466	56.838
289 THRU 290	319	2	290	0.575	638	577104	56.901
291	318	1	291	0.577	318	577422	56.932
292	315	1	292	0.579	315	577737	56.963
293 THRU 295	313	3	295	0.585	939	578676	57.056

TABLE B1 (CONT.) THE CORPUS WITH RANK IN DESCENDING ORDER

RANK	X	FX	SUM FX	CUM% FX	FX*X	SUM FX*X	CUM% FX*X
296 THRU 299	312	4	299	0.593	1248	579924	57.179
300 THRU 301	311	2	301	0.597	622	580546	57.240
302	310	1	302	0.599	310	580856	57.271
303	309	1	303	0.601	309	581165	57.301
304	308	1	304	0.603	308	581473	57.331
305	307	1	305	0.605	307	581780	57.362
306	304	1	306	0.607	304	582084	57.392
307	302	1	307	0.609	302	582386	57.421
308	301	1	308	0.611	301	582687	57.451
309	300	1	309	0.613	300	582987	57.481
310 THRU 311	295	2	311	0.617	598	583585	57.540
312	298	1	312	0.619	298	583883	57.569
313	296	1	313	0.621	296	584179	57.598
314	294	1	314	0.623	294	584473	57.627
315	292	1	315	0.625	292	584765	57.656
316	291	1	316	0.627	291	585056	57.685
317	290	1	317	0.629	290	585346	57.713
318	289	1	318	0.631	289	585635	57.742
319	288	1	319	0.633	288	585923	57.770
320	287	1	320	0.635	287	586210	57.798
321 THRU 323	286	3	323	0.641	858	587068	57.883
324	285	1	324	0.643	285	587353	57.911
325 THRU 326	284	2	326	0.647	568	587921	57.967
327 THRU 328	283	2	328	0.651	566	588487	58.023
329 THRU 330	282	2	330	0.655	564	589051	58.079
331 THRU 333	281	3	333	0.661	843	589894	58.162
334	280	1	334	0.663	280	590174	58.189
335 THRU 336	279	2	336	0.667	558	590732	58.244
337	277	1	337	0.669	277	591009	58.272
338 THRU 339	276	2	339	0.673	552	591561	58.326
340 THRU 342	275	3	342	0.678	825	592386	58.407
343 THRU 346	274	4	346	0.686	1096	593482	58.515
347	273	1	347	0.688	273	593755	58.542
348	270	1	348	0.690	270	594025	58.569
349	269	1	349	0.692	269	594294	58.595
350 THRU 351	268	2	351	0.696	536	594830	58.648

TABLE B1 (CONT.) THE CORPUS WITH RANK IN DESCENDING ORDER

RANK		X	FX	SUM FX	CUM% FX	FX*X	SUM FX*X	CUM% FX*X
352 THRU	354	267	3	354	0.702	801	595631	58.727
355 THRU	356	265	2	356	0.706	530	596161	58.780
357 THRU	359	264	3	359	0.712	792	596953	58.858
360		261	1	360	0.714	261	597214	58.883
361 THRU	362	260	2	362	0.718	520	597734	58.935
363		259	1	363	0.720	259	597993	58.960
364 THRU	367	258	4	367	0.728	1032	599025	59.062
368 THRU	369	257	2	369	0.732	514	599539	59.113
370 THRU	371	255	2	371	0.736	510	600049	59.163
372		253	1	372	0.738	253	600302	59.188
373		252	1	373	0.740	252	600554	59.213
374		250	1	374	0.742	250	600804	59.237
375 THRU	377	247	3	377	0.748	741	601545	59.310
378 THRU	382	246	5	382	0.758	1230	602775	59.432
383 THRU	384	245	2	384	0.762	490	603265	59.480
385 THRU	386	244	2	386	0.766	488	603753	59.528
387		243	1	387	0.768	243	603996	59.552
388		242	1	388	0.770	242	604238	59.576
389 ↑THRU	390	241	2	390	0.774	482	604720	59.623
391 THRU	392	240	2	392	0.778	480	605200	59.671
393 THRU	394	239	2	394	0.782	478	605678	59.718
395		238	1	395	0.784	238	605916	59.741
396		237	1	396	0.786	237	606153	59.765
397		236	1	397	0.788	236	606389	59.788
398		235	1	398	0.790	235	606624	59.811
399		234	1	399	0.792	234	606858	59.834
400		233	1	400	0.794	233	607091	59.857
401		232	1	401	0.796	232	607323	59.880
402 THRU	403	231	2	403	0.800	462	607785	59.926
404 THRU	406	230	3	406	0.805	690	608475	59.994
407 THRU	408	229	2	408	0.809	458	608933	60.039
409 THRU	410	228	2	410	0.813	456	609389	60.084
411 THRU	412	227	2	412	0.817	454	609843	60.129
413 THRU	414	226	2	414	0.821	452	610295	60.173
415		225	1	415	0.823	225	610520	60.195
416 THRU	417	224	2	417	0.827	448	610968	60.239

TABLE B1 (CONT.) THE CORPUS WITH RANK IN DESCENDING ORDER

RANK		X	FX	SUM FX	CUM% FX	FX*X	SUM FX*X	CUM% FX*X
418 THRU	419	223	2	419	0.831	446	611414	60.283
420 THRU	421	222	2	421	0.835	444	611858	60.327
422 THRU	424	221	3	424	0.841	663	612521	60.393
425 THRU	426	220	2	426	0.845	440	612961	60.436
427		219	1	427	0.847	219	613180	60.458
428		218	1	428	0.849	218	613398	60.479
429		217	1	429	0.851	217	613615	60.500
430 THRU	435	216	6	435	0.863	1296	614911	60.628
436 THRU	437	214	2	437	0.867	428	615339	60.670
438 THRU	441	213	4	441	0.875	852	616191	60.754
442 THRU	446	212	5	446	0.885	1060	617251	60.859
447 THRU	448	211	2	448	0.889	422	617673	60.901
449		210	1	449	0.891	210	617883	60.921
450 THRU	451	209	2	451	0.895	418	618301	60.962
452		208	1	452	0.897	208	618509	60.983
453 THRU	454	207	2	454	0.901	414	618923	61.024
455 THRU	457	206	3	457	0.907	618	619541	61.085
458 THRU	460	205	3	460	0.913	615	620156	61.145
461 THRU	464	204	4	464	0.921	816	620972	61.226
465		203	1	465	0.923	203	621175	61.246
466 THRU	467	202	2	467	0.926	404	621579	61.286
468		201	1	468	0.928	201	621780	61.305
465 THRU	474	200	6	474	0.940	1200	622980	61.424
475 THRU	476	199	2	476	0.944	398	623378	61.463
477 THRU	481	198	5	481	0.954	990	624368	61.561
482 THRU	484	197	3	484	0.960	591	624959	61.619
485 THRU	489	196	5	489	0.970	980	625939	61.716
490 THRU	497	195	8	497	0.986	1560	627499	61.869
498 THRU	500	194	3	500	0.992	582	628081	61.927
501 THRU	502	193	2	502	0.996	386	628467	61.965
503 THRU	504	192	2	504	1.000	384	628851	62.003
505 THRU	508	191	4	508	1.008	764	629615	62.078
509		190	1	509	1.010	190	629805	62.097
510 THRU	511	189	2	511	1.014	378	630183	62.134
512 THRU	513	188	2	513	1.018	376	630559	62.171
514 THRU	516	187	3	516	1.024	561	631120	62.226

TABLE 81 (CONT.) THE CORPUS WITH RANK IN DESCENDING ORDER

RANK	x	FX	SUM FX	CUM% FX	FX*X	SUM FX*X	CUM% FX*X
517 THRU 521	186	5	521	1.034	930	632050	62.318
522 THRU 524	185	3	524	1.040	555	632605	62.373
525 THRU 526	184	2	526	1.044	368	632973	62.409
527 THRU 528	183	2	528	1.047	366	633339	62.445
529 THRU 531	182	3	531	1.053	546	633885	62.499
532 THRU 536	181	5	536	1.063	905	634790	62.588
537 THRU 539	180	3	539	1.069	540	635330	62.641
540 THRU 543	179	4	543	1.077	716	636046	62.712
544	178	1	544	1.079	178	636224	62.730
545	177	1	545	1.081	177	636401	62.747
546 THRU 548	176	3	548	1.087	528	636929	62.799
549 THRU 555	175	7	555	1.101	1225	638154	62.920
556 THRU 562	174	7	562	1.115	1218	639372	63.040
563 THRU 569	173	7	569	1.129	1211	640583	63.159
570 THRU 576	172	7	576	1.143	1204	641787	63.278
577 THRU 583	171	7	583	1.157	1197	642984	63.396
584 THRU 587	170	4	587	1.165	680	643664	63.463
588 THRU 590	169	3	590	1.170	507	644171	63.513
591	168	1	591	1.172	168	644339	63.530
592 THRU 594	167	3	594	1.178	501	644840	63.579
595 THRU 597	166	3	597	1.184	498	645338	63.628
598 THRU 600	165	3	600	1.190	495	645833	63.677
601 THRU 604	164	4	604	1.198	656	646489	63.742
605 THRU 610	163	6	610	1.210	978	647467	63.838
611 THRU 615	162	5	615	1.220	810	648277	63.918
616 THRU 620	161	5	620	1.230	805	649082	63.997
621 THRU 625	160	5	625	1.240	800	649882	64.076
626 THRU 627	159	2	627	1.244	318	650200	64.108
628 THRU 631	158	4	631	1.252	632	650832	64.170
632 THRU 634	157	3	634	1.258	471	651303	64.216
635 THRU 638	156	4	638	1.266	624	651927	64.278
639 THRU 643	155	5	643	1.276	775	652702	64.354
644 THRU 648	154	5	648	1.286	770	653472	64.430
649 THRU 651	153	3	651	1.292	459	653931	64.475
652 THRU 656	152	5	656	1.301	760	654691	64.550
657 THRU 661	151	5	661	1.311	755	655446	64.625

TABLE 81 (CONT.) THE CORPUS WITH RANK IN DESCENDING ORDER

RANK	x	FX	SUM FX	CUM% FX	FX*X	SUM FX*X	CUM% FX*X
662 THRU 663	150	2	663	1.315	300	655746	64.654
664 THRU 668	149	5	668	1.325	745	656491	64.728
669 THRU 675	148	7	675	1.339	1036	657527	64.830
676 THRU 679	147	4	679	1.347	588	658115	64.888
680 THRU 683	146	4	683	1.355	584	658699	64.946
684 THRU 693	145	10	693	1.375	1450	660149	65.089
694 THRU 696	144	3	696	1.381	432	660581	65.131
697 THRU 707	143	11	707	1.403	1573	662154	65.286
708 THRU 715	142	8	715	1.418	1136	663290	65.398
716 THRU 724	141	9	724	1.436	1269	664559	65.523
725 THRU 729	140	5	729	1.446	700	665259	65.592
730 THRU 736	139	7	736	1.460	973	666232	65.688
737 THRU 739	138	3	739	1.466	414	666646	65.729
740 THRU 745	137	6	745	1.478	822	667468	65.810
746 THRU 748	136	3	748	1.484	408	667876	65.850
749 THRU 755	135	7	755	1.498	945	668821	65.944
756 THRU 763	134	8	763	1.514	1072	669893	66.049
764 THRU 769	133	6	769	1.526	798	670691	66.128
770 THRU 776	132	7	776	1.539	924	671615	66.219
777 THRU 784	131	8	784	1.555	1048	672663	66.322
785 THRU 792	130	8	792	1.571	1040	673703	66.425
793 THRU 805	129	13	805	1.597	1677	675380	66.590
806 THRU 812	128	7	812	1.611	896	676276	66.679
813 THRU 825	127	13	825	1.637	1651	677927	66.841
826 THRU 828	126	3	828	1.643	378	678305	66.879
829 THRU 842	125	14	842	1.670	1750	680055	67.051
843 THRU 845	124	3	845	1.676	372	680427	67.088
846 THRU 853	123	8	853	1.692	984	681411	67.185
854 THRU 859	122	6	859	1.704	732	682143	67.257
860 THRU 864	121	5	864	1.714	605	682748	67.317
865 THRU 872	120	8	872	1.730	960	683708	67.411
873 THRU 884	119	12	884	1.754	1428	685136	67.552
885 THRU 891	118	7	891	1.768	826	685962	67.634
892 THRU 896	117	5	896	1.778	585	686547	67.691
897 THRU 903	116	7	903	1.791	812	687359	67.771
904 THRU 915	115	12	915	1.815	1380	688739	67.907

TABLE B1 (CONT.) THE CORPUS WITH RANK IN DESCENDING ORDER

RANK	THRU	X	FX	SUM FX	CUM% FX	FX*X	SUM FX*X	CUM% FX*X
916 THRU	924	114	9	924	1.833	1026	689765	68.009
925 THRU	939	113	15	939	1.863	1695	691460	68.176
940 THRU	944	112	5	944	1.873	560	692020	68.231
945 THRU	946	111	2	946	1.877	222	692242	68.253
947 THRU	957	110	11	957	1.899	1210	693452	68.372
958 THRU	969	109	12	969	1.922	1308	694760	68.501
970 THRU	980	108	11	980	1.944	1188	695948	68.618
981 THRU	991	107	11	991	1.966	1177	697125	68.734
992 THRU	1003	106	12	1003	1.990	1272	698397	68.860
1004 THRU	1015	105	12	1015	2.014	1260	699657	68.984
1016 THRU	1025	104	10	1025	2.033	1040	700697	69.086
1026 THRU	1038	103	13	1038	2.059	1339	702036	69.218
1039 THRU	1047	102	9	1047	2.077	918	702954	69.309
1048 THRU	1061	101	14	1061	2.105	1414	704368	69.448
1062 THRU	1070	100	9	1070	2.123	900	705268	69.537
1071 THRU	1078	99	8	1078	2.139	792	706060	69.615
1079 THRU	1094	98	16	1094	2.170	1568	707628	69.770
1095 THRU	1107	97	13	1107	2.196	1261	708889	69.894
1108 THRU	1120	96	13	1120	2.222	1248	710137	70.017
1121 THRU	1130	95	10	1130	2.242	950	711087	70.111
1131 THRU	1143	94	13	1143	2.268	1222	712309	70.231
1144 THRU	1153	93	10	1153	2.287	930	713239	70.323
1154 THRU	1160	92	7	1160	2.301	644	713883	70.387
1161 THRU	1178	91	18	1178	2.337	1638	715521	70.548
1179 THRU	1188	90	10	1188	2.357	900	716421	70.637
1189 THRU	1201	89	13	1201	2.383	1157	717578	70.751
1202 THRU	1223	88	22	1223	2.426	1936	719514	70.942
1224 THRU	1238	87	15	1238	2.456	1305	720819	71.070
1239 THRU	1256	86	18	1256	2.492	1548	722367	71.223
1257 THRU	1271	85	15	1271	2.522	1275	723642	71.349
1272 THRU	1291	84	20	1291	2.561	1680	725322	71.514
1292 THRU	1314	83	23	1314	2.607	1909	727231	71.703
1315 THRU	1326	82	12	1326	2.631	984	728215	71.800
1327 THRU	1348	81	22	1348	2.674	1782	729997	71.975
1349 THRU	1361	80	13	1361	2.700	1040	731037	72.078
1362 THRU	1375	79	14	1375	2.728	1106	732143	72.187

TABLE B1 (CONT.) THE CORPUS WITH RANK IN DESCENDING ORDER

RANK	THRU	X	FX	SUM FX	CUM% FX	FX*X	SUM FX*X	CUM% FX*X
1376 THRU	1389	78	14	1389	2.756	1092	733235	72.295
1390 THRU	1405	77	16	1405	2.787	1232	734467	72.416
1406 THRU	1418	76	13	1418	2.813	988	735455	72.513
1419 THRU	1435	75	17	1435	2.847	1275	736730	72.639
1436 THRU	1464	74	29	1464	2.904	2146	738876	72.851
1465 THRU	1480	73	16	1480	2.936	1168	740044	72.966
1481 THRU	1513	72	33	1513	3.002	2376	742420	73.200
1514 THRU	1533	71	20	1533	3.041	1420	743840	73.340
1534 THRU	1561	70	28	1561	3.097	1960	745800	73.533
1562 THRU	1580	69	19	1580	3.135	1311	747111	73.663
1581 THRU	1617	68	37	1617	3.208	2516	749627	73.911
1618 THRU	1644	67	27	1644	3.262	1809	751436	74.089
1645 THRU	1675	66	31	1675	3.323	2046	753482	74.291
1676 THRU	1704	65	29	1704	3.381	1885	755367	74.477
1705 THRU	1728	64	24	1728	3.428	1536	756903	74.628
1729 THRU	1757	63	29	1757	3.486	1827	758730	74.808
1758 THRU	1791	62	34	1791	3.553	2108	760838	75.016
1792 THRU	1828	61	37	1828	3.627	2257	763095	75.239
1829 THRU	1860	60	32	1860	3.690	1920	765015	75.428
1861 THRU	1893	59	33	1893	3.756	1947	766962	75.620
1894 THRU	1935	58	42	1935	3.839	2436	769398	75.860
1936 THRU	1973	57	38	1973	3.914	2166	771564	76.074
1974 THRU	2006	56	33	2006	3.980	1848	773412	76.256
2007 THRU	2050	55	44	2050	4.067	2420	775832	76.495
2051 THRU	2081	54	31	2081	4.128	1674	777506	76.660
2082 THRU	2126	53	45	2126	4.218	2385	779891	76.895
2127 THRU	2153	52	27	2153	4.271	1404	781295	77.033
2154 THRU	2199	51	46	2199	4.363	2346	783641	77.264
2200 THRU	2245	50	46	2245	4.454	2300	785941	77.491
2246 THRU	2273	49	28	2273	4.509	1372	787313	77.627
2274 THRU	2316	48	43	2316	4.595	2064	789377	77.830
2317 THRU	2376	47	60	2376	4.714	2820	792197	78.108
2377 THRU	2429	46	53	2429	4.819	2438	794635	78.348
2430 THRU	2485	45	56	2485	4.930	2520	797155	78.597
2486 THRU	2545	44	60	2545	5.049	2640	799795	78.857
2546 THRU	2604	43	59	2604	5.166	2537	802332	79.107

TABLE B1 (CCNT.) THE CORPUS WITH RANK IN DESCENDING ORDER

RANK	x	FX	SUM FX	CUM% FX	FX*X	SUM FX*X	CUM% FX*X
11120 THRU 12398	6	1279	12398	24.596	7674	946422	93.314
12399 THRU 14218	5	1820	14218	28.207	9100	955522	94.211
14219 THRU 16683	4	2465	16683	33.097	9860	965382	95.184
16684 THRU 20630	3	3947	20630	40.928	11841	977223	96.351
20631 THRU 27863	2	7233	27863	55.277	14466	991689	97.777
27864 THRU 50406	1	22543	50406	100.000	22543	1014232	100.000

$$\text{TYPES} = S0 = 50406 \qquad S2 = 10154742794$$
$$\text{TOKENS} = S1 = 1014232 \qquad K = 98.7077$$
$$\text{MEAN} = 20.1213 \qquad SD = 448.3906 \qquad V = 22.2844$$

TABLE B1 (CCNT.) THE CORPUS WITH RANK IN DESCENDING ORDER

RANK	x	FX	SUM FX	CUM% FX	FX*X	SUM FX*X	CUM% FX*X
2605 THRU 2663	42	59	2663	5.283	2478	804810	79.352
2664 THRU 2719	41	56	2719	5.394	2296	807106	79.578
2720 THRU 2796	40	77	2796	5.547	3080	810186	79.882
2797 THRU 2854	39	58	2854	5.662	2262	812448	80.105
2855 THRU 2927	38	73	2927	5.807	2774	815222	80.378
2928 THRU 3005	37	78	3005	5.962	2886	818108	80.663
3006 THRU 3087	36	82	3087	6.124	2952	821060	80.954
3088 THRU 3157	35	70	3157	6.263	2450	823510	81.195
3158 THRU 3244	34	87	3244	6.436	2958	826468	81.487
3245 THRU 3331	33	87	3331	6.608	2871	829339	81.770
3332 THRU 3415	32	84	3415	6.775	2688	832027	82.035
3416 THRU 3501	31	86	3501	6.946	2666	834693	82.298
3502 THRU 3593	30	92	3593	7.128	2760	837453	82.570
3594 THRU 3691	29	98	3691	7.323	2842	840295	82.850
3692 THRU 3793	28	102	3793	7.525	2856	843151	83.132
3794 THRU 3906	27	113	3906	7.749	3051	846202	83.433
3907 THRU 4019	26	113	4019	7.973	2938	849140	83.722
4020 THRU 4148	25	129	4148	8.229	3225	852365	84.040
4149 THRU 4270	24	122	4270	8.471	2928	855293	84.329
4271 THRU 4426	23	156	4426	8.781	3588	858881	84.683
4427 THRU 4584	22	158	4584	9.094	3476	862357	85.026
4585 THRU 4777	21	193	4777	9.477	4053	866410	85.425
4778 THRU 4984	20	207	4984	9.888	4140	870550	85.833
4985 THRU 5182	19	198	5182	10.281	3762	874312	86.204
5183 THRU 5403	18	221	5403	10.719	3978	878290	86.597
5404 THRU 5658	17	255	5658	11.225	4335	882625	87.024
5659 THRU 5972	16	314	5972	11.848	5024	887649	87.519
5973 THRU 6273	15	301	6273	12.445	4515	892164	87.964
6274 THRU 6597	14	324	6597	13.088	4536	896700	88.412
6598 THRU 6987	13	390	6987	13.861	5070	901770	88.912
6988 THRU 7421	12	434	7421	14.722	5208	906978	89.425
7422 THRU 7919	11	498	7919	15.710	5478	912456	89.965
7920 THRU 8478	10	559	8478	16.819	5590	918046	90.516
8479 THRU 9173	9	695	9173	18.198	6255	924301	91.133
9174 THRU 9998	8	825	9998	19.835	6600	930901	91.784
9999 THRU 11119	7	1121	11119	22.059	7847	938748	92.558

TABLE B2   A REPRESENTATIVE CORPUS SUBSET OF 125 SAMPLES IN DESCENDING ORDER

X	FX	SUM FX	CUM% FX	FX*X	SUM FX*X	CUM% FX*X
17359	1	1	0.004	17359	17359	6.847
8998	1	2	0.008	8998	26357	10.396
7268	1	3	0.013	7268	33625	13.262
6434	1	4	0.017	6434	40059	15.800
5737	1	5	0.021	5737	45796	18.063
5512	1	6	0.025	5512	51308	20.237
2571	1	7	0.030	2571	53879	21.251
2536	1	8	0.034	2536	56415	22.251
2528	1	9	0.038	2528	58943	23.248
2434	1	10	0.042	2434	61377	24.208
2322	1	11	0.047	2322	63699	25.124
2193	1	12	0.051	2193	65892	25.989
1886	1	13	0.055	1886	67778	26.733
1822	1	14	0.059	1822	69600	27.451
1744	1	15	0.063	1744	71344	28.139
1691	1	16	0.068	1691	73035	28.806
1557	1	17	0.072	1557	74592	29.420
1427	1	18	0.076	1427	76019	29.983
1373	1	19	0.080	1373	77392	30.525
1311	1	20	0.085	1311	78703	31.042
1300	1	21	0.089	1300	80003	31.555
1275	1	22	0.093	1275	81278	32.058
1191	1	23	0.097	1191	82469	32.527
1127	1	24	0.101	1127	83596	32.972
1111	1	25	0.106	1111	84707	33.410
1099	1	26	0.110	1099	85806	33.843
1075	1	27	0.114	1075	86881	34.267
958	1	28	0.118	958	87839	34.645
955	1	29	0.123	955	88794	35.022
909	1	30	0.127	909	89703	35.380
885	1	31	0.131	885	90588	35.730
883	1	32	0.135	883	91471	36.078
866	1	33	0.140	866	92337	36.419
853	1	34	0.144	853	93190	36.756
740	1	35	0.148	740	93930	37.048
714	1	36	0.152	714	94644	37.329

TABLE B2 (CONT.)   A REPRESENTATIVE CORPUS SUBSET OF 125 SAMPLES IN DESC. ORDER

X	FX	SUM FX	CUM% FX	FX*X	SUM FX*X	CUM% FX*X
696	1	37	0.156	696	95340	37.604
690	1	38	0.161	690	96030	37.876
685	1	39	0.165	685	96715	38.146
616	1	40	0.169	616	97331	38.389
615	1	41	0.173	615	97946	38.632
613	1	42	0.178	613	98559	38.873
568	1	43	0.182	568	99127	39.097
567	1	44	0.186	567	99694	39.321
560	1	45	0.190	560	100254	39.542
555	1	46	0.194	555	100809	39.761
538	1	47	0.199	538	101347	39.973
533	1	48	0.203	533	101880	40.183
520	1	49	0.207	520	102400	40.388
518	1	50	0.211	518	102918	40.593
497	1	51	0.216	497	103415	40.789
485	1	52	0.220	485	103900	40.980
484	1	53	0.224	484	104384	41.171
482	1	54	0.228	482	104866	41.361
476	1	55	0.233	476	105342	41.549
462	1	56	0.237	462	105804	41.731
459	1	57	0.241	459	106263	41.912
453	2	59	0.249	906	107169	42.269
449	1	60	0.254	449	107618	42.446
434	1	61	0.258	434	108052	42.618
414	2	63	0.266	828	108880	42.944
401	1	64	0.271	401	109281	43.102
399	1	65	0.275	399	109680	43.260
396	1	66	0.279	396	110076	43.416
383	2	68	0.287	766	110842	43.718
374	1	69	0.292	374	111216	43.866
371	1	70	0.296	371	111587	44.012
366	1	71	0.300	366	111953	44.156
352	1	72	0.304	352	112305	44.295
342	1	73	0.309	342	112647	44.430
334	1	74	0.313	334	112981	44.562
331	1	75	0.317	331	113312	44.692

TABLE B2 (CONT.) A REPRESENTATIVE CORPUS SUBSET OF 125 SAMPLES IN DESC. ORDER

X	FX	SUM FX	CUM% FX	FX*X	SUM FX*X	CUM% FX*X
330	1	76	0.321	330	113642	44.822
328	3	79	0.334	984	114626	45.211
326	1	80	0.338	326	114952	45.339
319	1	81	0.342	319	115271	45.465
297	1	82	0.347	297	115568	45.582
296	1	83	0.351	296	115864	45.699
285	1	84	0.355	285	116149	45.811
275	1	85	0.359	275	116424	45.920
271	1	86	0.364	271	116695	46.027
261	1	87	0.368	261	116956	46.130
259	2	89	0.376	518	117474	46.334
256	1	90	0.380	256	117730	46.435
255	1	91	0.385	255	117985	46.535
253	1	92	0.389	253	118238	46.635
250	1	93	0.393	250	118488	46.734
249	1	94	0.397	249	118737	46.832
241	1	95	0.402	241	118978	46.927
239	1	96	0.406	239	119217	47.021
238	1	97	0.410	238	119455	47.115
228	1	98	0.414	228	119683	47.205
227	1	99	0.419	227	119910	47.295
226	2	101	0.427	452	120362	47.473
218	2	103	0.435	436	120798	47.645
215	1	104	0.440	215	121013	47.730
212	3	107	0.452	636	121649	47.981
211	1	108	0.457	211	121860	48.064
207	1	109	0.461	207	122067	48.145
206	1	110	0.465	206	122273	48.227
205	1	111	0.469	205	122478	48.308
203	1	112	0.473	203	122681	48.388
202	1	113	0.478	202	122883	48.467
201	1	114	0.482	201	123084	48.547
200	1	115	0.486	200	123284	48.625
198	2	117	0.495	396	123680	48.782
192	1	118	0.499	192	123872	48.857
190	2	120	0.507	380	124252	49.007

TABLE B2 (CONT.) A REPRESENTATIVE CORPUS SUBSET OF 125 SAMPLES IN DESC. ORDER

X	FX	SUM FX	CUM% FX	FX*X	SUM FX*X	CUM% FX*X
187	1	121	0.512	187	124439	49.081
185	1	122	0.516	185	124624	49.154
182	1	123	0.520	182	124806	49.226
181	2	125	0.528	362	125168	49.369
179	1	126	0.533	179	125347	49.439
177	1	127	0.537	177	125524	49.509
175	3	130	0.550	525	126049	49.716
174	1	131	0.554	174	126223	49.785
173	2	133	0.562	346	126569	49.921
170	1	134	0.566	170	126739	49.988
168	1	135	0.571	168	126907	50.054
167	1	136	0.575	167	127074	50.120
166	2	138	0.583	332	127406	50.251
163	1	139	0.588	163	127569	50.316
162	3	142	0.600	486	128055	50.507
161	1	143	0.605	161	128216	50.571
160	1	144	0.609	160	128376	50.634
159	3	147	0.621	477	128853	50.822
156	3	150	0.634	468	129321	51.007
155	2	152	0.643	310	129631	51.129
153	2	154	0.651	306	129937	51.250
151	3	157	0.664	453	130390	51.428
149	1	158	0.668	149	130539	51.487
146	1	159	0.672	146	130685	51.545
144	2	161	0.681	288	130973	51.658
143	1	162	0.685	143	131116	51.715
141	2	164	0.693	282	131398	51.826
139	1	165	0.698	139	131537	51.881
138	1	166	0.702	138	131675	51.935
136	1	167	0.706	136	131811	51.989
132	2	169	0.714	264	132075	52.093
131	2	171	0.723	262	132337	52.196
128	3	174	0.736	384	132721	52.348
126	2	176	0.744	252	132973	52.447
122	1	177	0.748	122	133095	52.495
121	2	179	0.757	242	133337	52.591

TABLE B2 (CONT.) A REPRESENTATIVE CORPUS SUBSET OF 125 SAMPLES IN DESC. ORDER

X	FX	SUM FX	CUM% FX	FX*X	SUM FX*X	CUM% FX*X
120	1	180	0.761	120	133457	52.638
119	2	182	0.769	238	133695	52.732
118	2	184	0.778	236	133931	52.825
117	2	186	0.786	234	134165	52.917
116	3	189	0.799	348	134513	53.054
115	1	190	0.803	115	134628	53.100
114	4	194	0.820	456	135084	53.280
113	4	198	0.837	452	135536	53.458
112	3	201	0.850	336	135872	53.590
111	4	205	0.867	444	136316	53.766
110	3	208	0.879	330	136646	53.896
109	1	209	0.884	109	136755	53.939
107	2	211	0.892	214	136969	54.023
106	2	213	0.900	212	137181	54.107
105	1	214	0.905	105	137286	54.148
104	2	216	0.913	208	137494	54.230
103	4	220	0.930	412	137906	54.393
102	2	222	0.938	204	138110	54.473
101	4	226	0.955	404	138514	54.632
100	2	228	0.964	200	138714	54.711
99	1	229	0.968	99	138813	54.750
98	7	236	0.998	686	139499	55.021
97	3	239	1.010	291	139790	55.136
95	3	242	1.023	285	140075	55.248
94	5	247	1.044	470	140545	55.433
93	3	250	1.057	279	140824	55.544
92	5	255	1.078	460	141284	55.725
91	3	258	1.091	273	141557	55.833
89	3	261	1.103	267	141824	55.938
88	2	263	1.112	176	142000	56.007
87	4	267	1.129	348	142348	56.145
86	2	269	1.137	172	142520	56.212
85	1	270	1.141	85	142605	56.246
84	5	275	1.163	420	143025	56.412
83	5	280	1.184	415	143440	56.575
82	6	286	1.209	492	143932	56.769

TABLE B2 (CCNT.) A REPRESENTATIVE CORPUS SUBSET OF 125 SAMPLES IN DESC. ORDER

X	FX	SUM FX	CUM% FX	FX*X	SUM FX*X	CUM% FX*X
81	5	291	1.230	405	144337	56.929
80	3	294	1.243	240	144577	57.024
79	4	298	1.260	316	144893	57.148
78	6	304	1.285	468	145361	57.333
77	5	309	1.306	385	145746	57.485
76	6	315	1.332	456	146202	57.665
75	4	319	1.349	300	146502	57.783
74	7	326	1.378	518	147020	57.987
73	4	330	1.395	292	147312	58.103
72	1	331	1.399	72	147384	58.131
71	2	333	1.408	142	147526	58.187
70	4	337	1.425	280	147806	58.297
69	5	342	1.446	345	148151	58.433
68	3	345	1.458	204	148355	58.514
67	8	353	1.492	536	148891	58.725
66	6	359	1.518	396	149287	58.882
65	6	365	1.543	390	149677	59.035
64	4	369	1.560	256	149933	59.136
63	7	376	1.590	441	150374	59.310
62	9	385	1.628	558	150932	59.530
61	11	396	1.674	671	151603	59.795
60	5	401	1.695	300	151903	59.913
59	15	416	1.759	885	152788	60.262
58	9	425	1.797	522	153310	60.468
57	7	432	1.826	399	153709	60.626
56	7	439	1.856	392	154101	60.780
55	12	451	1.907	660	154761	61.041
54	6	457	1.932	324	155085	61.168
53	13	470	1.987	689	155774	61.440
52	9	479	2.025	468	156242	61.625
51	11	490	2.071	561	156803	61.846
50	15	505	2.135	750	157553	62.142
49	13	518	2.190	637	158190	62.393
48	8	526	2.224	384	158574	62.544
47	12	538	2.274	564	159138	62.767
46	16	554	2.342	736	159874	63.057

TABLE B2 (CONT.) A REPRESENTATIVE CORPUS SUBSET OF 125 SAMPLES IN DESC. ORDER

X	FX	SUM FX	CUM% FX	FX*X	SUM FX*X	CUM% FX*X
45	17	571	2.414	765	160639	63.359
44	21	592	2.503	924	161563	63.723
43	19	611	2.583	817	162380	64.044
42	13	624	2.638	546	162926	64.261
41	20	644	2.722	820	163746	64.584
40	22	666	2.815	880	164626	64.931
39	29	695	2.938	1131	165757	65.378
38	21	716	3.027	798	166555	65.692
37	25	741	3.133	925	167480	66.057
36	28	769	3.251	1008	168488	66.455
35	27	796	3.365	945	169433	66.827
34	21	817	3.454	714	170147	67.109
33	44	861	3.640	1452	171599	67.582
32	24	885	3.741	768	172367	67.985
31	23	908	3.839	713	173080	68.266
30	28	936	3.957	840	173920	68.597
29	42	978	4.134	1218	175138	69.078
28	38	1016	4.295	1064	176202	69.497
27	40	1056	4.464	1080	177282	69.923
26	42	1098	4.642	1092	178374	70.354
25	32	1130	4.777	800	179174	70.669
24	56	1186	5.014	1344	180518	71.200
23	62	1248	5.276	1426	181944	71.762
22	77	1325	5.601	1694	183638	72.430
21	79	1404	5.935	1659	185297	73.085
20	84	1488	6.290	1680	186977	73.747
19	91	1579	6.675	1729	188706	74.429
18	99	1678	7.094	1782	190488	75.132
17	92	1770	7.483	1564	192052	75.749
16	124	1894	8.007	1984	194036	76.531
15	132	2026	8.565	1980	196016	77.312
14	152	2178	9.207	2128	198144	78.152
13	190	2368	10.011	2470	200614	79.126
12	203	2571	10.869	2436	203050	80.087
11	205	2776	11.735	2255	205305	80.976
10	288	3064	12.953	2880	208185	82.112

TABLE B2 (CONT.) A REPRESENTATIVE CORPUS SUBSET OF 125 SAMPLES IN DESC. ORDER

X	FX	SUM FX	CUM% FX	FX*X	SUM FX*X	CUM% FX*X
9	286	3350	14.162	2574	210759	83.127
8	374	3724	15.743	2992	213751	84.307
7	473	4197	17.743	3311	217062	85.613
6	515	4712	19.920	3090	220152	86.832
5	828	5540	23.420	4140	224292	88.465
4	1213	6753	28.548	4852	229144	90.379
3	1943	8696	36.762	5829	234973	92.678
2	3606	12302	52.006	7212	242185	95.522
1	11353	23655	100.000	11353	253538	100.000

TYPES = S0 = 23655   TOKENS = S1 = 253538   S2 = 629404334

MEAN = 10.7182   SD = 162.7660   V = 15.1860   K = 97.8743

TABLE B3 A REPRESENTATIVE CORPUS SUBSET OF 50 SAMPLES IN DESCENDING ORDER

X	FX	SUM FX	CUM%	FX*X	SUM FX*X	CUM% FX*X
7042	1	1	0.007	7042	7042	6.933
3574	1	2	0.015	3574	10616	10.452
2952	1	3	0.022	2952	13568	13.359
2617	1	4	0.029	2617	16185	15.935
2430	1	5	0.036	2430	18615	18.328
2268	1	6	0.044	2268	20883	20.561
1110	1	7	0.051	1110	21993	21.654
1019	1	8	0.058	1019	23012	22.657
985	1	9	0.066	985	23997	23.627
926	1	10	0.073	926	24923	24.539
918	1	11	0.080	918	25841	25.443
866	1	12	0.088	866	26707	26.295
737	1	13	0.095	737	27444	27.021
683	1	14	0.102	683	28127	27.693
680	1	15	0.109	680	28807	28.363
633	1	16	0.117	633	29440	28.986
622	1	17	0.124	622	30062	29.598
557	1	18	0.131	557	30619	30.147
548	1	19	0.139	548	31167	30.686
540	1	20	0.146	540	31707	31.218
515	1	21	0.153	515	32222	31.725
491	1	22	0.161	491	32713	32.209
454	1	23	0.168	454	33167	32.656
440	1	24	0.175	440	33607	33.089
437	1	25	0.182	437	34044	33.519
423	1	26	0.190	423	34467	33.936
417	1	27	0.197	417	34884	34.346
409	1	28	0.204	409	35293	34.749
380	1	29	0.212	380	35673	35.123
377	1	30	0.219	377	36050	35.494
356	1	31	0.226	356	36406	35.845
351	1	32	0.233	351	36757	36.190
330	1	33	0.241	330	37087	36.515
320	1	34	0.248	320	37407	36.830
305	1	35	0.255	305	37712	37.131
291	1	36	0.263	291	38003	37.417

TABLE B3 (CONT.) A REPRESENTATIVE CORPUS SUBSET OF 50 SAMPLES IN DESC. ORDER

X	FX	SUM FX	CUM% FX	FX*X	SUM FX*X	CUM% FX*X
290	1	37	0.270	290	38293	37.703
284	1	38	0.277	284	38577	37.982
268	1	39	0.285	268	38845	38.246
254	1	40	0.292	254	39099	38.496
253	1	41	0.299	253	39352	38.745
251	1	42	0.306	251	39603	38.992
249	1	43	0.314	249	39852	39.238
241	1	44	0.321	241	40093	39.475
232	1	45	0.328	232	40325	39.703
228	2	47	0.343	456	40781	40.152
215	2	49	0.358	430	41211	40.576
208	1	50	0.365	208	41419	40.780
203	1	51	0.372	203	41622	40.980
198	1	52	0.379	198	41820	41.175
192	1	53	0.387	192	42012	41.364
190	1	54	0.394	190	42202	41.551
189	1	55	0.401	189	42391	41.737
184	1	56	0.409	184	42575	41.919
181	3	59	0.430	543	43118	42.453
179	1	60	0.438	179	43297	42.629
174	1	61	0.445	174	43471	42.801
169	1	62	0.452	169	43640	42.967
167	1	63	0.460	167	43807	43.132
166	1	64	0.467	166	43973	43.295
161	1	65	0.474	161	44134	43.454
159	2	67	0.489	318	44452	43.767
157	1	68	0.496	157	44609	43.921
156	1	69	0.503	156	44765	44.075
155	1	70	0.511	155	44920	44.227
147	1	71	0.518	147	45067	44.372
142	1	72	0.525	142	45209	44.512
137	1	73	0.533	137	45346	44.647
136	2	75	0.547	272	45618	44.915
135	1	76	0.555	135	45753	45.048
129	1	77	0.562	129	45882	45.175
126	2	79	0.576	252	46134	45.423

TABLE B3 (CONT.) A REPRESENTATIVE CORPUS SUBSET OF 50 SAMPLES IN DESC. ORDER

X	FX	SUM FX	CUM% FX	FX*X	SUM FX*X	CUM% FX*X
125	1	80	0.584	125	46259	45.546
122	1	81	0.591	122	46381	45.666
120	2	83	0.606	240	46621	45.902
119	1	84	0.613	119	46740	46.019
115	1	85	0.620	115	46855	46.133
113	1	86	0.627	113	46968	46.244
110	2	88	0.642	220	47188	46.460
108	1	89	0.649	108	47296	46.567
102	2	91	0.664	204	47500	46.768
99	1	92	0.671	99	47599	46.865
98	1	93	0.679	98	47697	46.962
96	1	94	0.686	96	47793	47.056
95	2	96	0.700	190	47983	47.243
94	1	97	0.708	94	48077	47.336
93	1	98	0.715	93	48170	47.427
92	1	99	0.722	92	48262	47.518
91	1	100	0.730	91	48353	47.607
89	1	101	0.737	89	48442	47.695
88	1	102	0.744	88	48530	47.782
87	2	104	0.759	174	48704	47.953
86	1	105	0.766	86	48790	48.038
84	1	106	0.773	84	48874	48.120
83	5	111	0.810	415	49289	48.529
82	1	112	0.817	82	49371	48.610
81	1	113	0.824	81	49452	48.690
80	1	114	0.832	80	49532	48.768
79	3	117	0.854	237	49769	49.002
77	1	118	0.861	77	49846	49.077
76	2	120	0.876	152	49998	49.227
75	2	122	0.890	150	50148	49.375
73	3	125	0.912	219	50367	49.590
72	3	128	0.934	216	50583	49.803
71	1	129	0.941	71	50654	49.873
70	1	130	0.948	70	50724	49.942
69	2	132	0.963	138	50862	50.078
68	2	134	0.978	136	50998	50.212

TABLE B3 (CONT.) A REPRESENTATIVE CORPUS SUBSET OF 50 SAMPLES IN DESC. ORDER

X	FX	SUM FX	CUM% FX	FX*X	SUM FX*X	CUM% FX*X
67	4	138	1.007	268	51266	50.476
66	3	141	1.029	198	51464	50.670
65	2	143	1.043	130	51594	50.798
64	2	145	1.058	128	51722	50.925
63	1	146	1.065	63	51785	50.987
62	3	149	1.087	186	51971	51.170
61	3	152	1.109	183	52154	51.350
60	1	153	1.116	60	52214	51.409
59	3	156	1.138	177	52391	51.583
58	3	159	1.160	174	52565	51.755
57	5	164	1.197	285	52850	52.035
56	5	169	1.233	280	53130	52.311
55	1	170	1.240	55	53185	52.365
54	3	173	1.262	162	53347	52.524
53	1	174	1.270	53	53400	52.577
52	4	178	1.299	208	53608	52.781
51	2	180	1.313	102	53710	52.882
50	8	188	1.372	400	54110	53.276
49	1	189	1.379	49	54159	53.324
48	2	191	1.394	96	54255	53.418
47	4	195	1.423	188	54443	53.604
46	5	200	1.459	230	54673	53.830
45	1	201	1.467	45	54718	53.874
44	6	207	1.510	264	54982	54.134
43	3	210	1.532	129	55111	54.261
42	9	219	1.598	378	55489	54.633
41	10	229	1.671	410	55899	55.037
40	7	236	1.722	280	56179	55.313
39	4	240	1.751	156	56335	55.466
38	11	251	1.831	418	56753	55.878
37	8	259	1.890	296	57049	56.169
36	8	267	1.948	288	57337	56.453
35	9	276	2.014	315	57652	56.763
34	3	279	2.036	102	57754	56.864
33	14	293	2.138	462	58216	57.318
32	9	302	2.203	288	58504	57.602

TABLE 83 (CCNT.) A REPRESENTATIVE CORPUS SUBSET OF 50 SAMPLES IN DESC. ORDER

X	FX	SUM FX	CUM% FX	FX*X	SUM FX*X	CUM% FX*X
31	11	313	2.284	341	58845	57.938
30	17	330	2.408	510	59355	58.440
29	23	353	2.576	667	60022	59.097
28	13	366	2.670	364	60386	59.455
27	16	382	2.787	432	60818	59.880
26	19	401	2.926	494	61312	60.367
25	30	431	3.145	750	62062	61.105
24	25	456	3.327	600	62662	61.696
23	28	484	3.531	644	63306	62.330
22	25	509	3.714	550	63856	62.871
21	24	533	3.889	504	64360	63.368
20	38	571	4.166	760	65120	64.116
19	33	604	4.407	627	65747	64.733
18	45	649	4.735	810	66557	65.531
17	50	699	5.100	850	67407	66.368
16	54	753	5.494	864	68271	67.218
15	59	812	5.924	885	69156	68.090
14	60	872	6.362	840	69996	68.917
13	82	954	6.960	1066	71062	69.966
12	89	1043	7.610	1068	72130	71.018
11	126	1169	8.529	1386	73516	72.382
10	136	1305	9.521	1360	74876	73.722
9	159	1464	10.681	1431	76307	75.130
8	228	1692	12.345	1824	78131	76.926
7	245	1937	14.132	1715	79846	78.615
6	332	2269	16.555	1992	81838	80.576
5	476	2745	20.028	2380	84218	82.919
4	705	3450	25.171	2820	87038	85.696
3	1094	4544	33.153	3282	90320	88.927
2	2084	6628	48.358	4168	94488	93.031
1	7078	13706	100.000	7078	101566	100.000

TYPES = SO = 13706   TOKENS = S1 = 101566   S2 = 103190852

MEAN = 7.4103   SD = 86.4521   V = 11.6664   K = 99.9348

TABLE 84 (CONT.) THE CORPUS IN ASCENDING ORDER

X	FX	SUM FX	CUM% FX	FX*X	SUM FX*X	CUM% FX*X
1	22543	22543	44.723	22543	22543	2.223
2	7233	29776	59.072	14466	37009	3.649
3	3947	33723	66.903	11841	48850	4.816
4	2465	36188	71.793	9860	58710	5.789
5	1820	38008	75.404	9100	67810	6.686
6	1279	39287	77.941	7674	75484	7.442
7	1121	40408	80.165	7847	83331	8.216
8	825	41233	81.802	6600	89931	8.867
9	695	41928	83.181	6255	96186	9.484
10	559	42487	84.290	5590	101776	10.035
11	498	42985	85.278	5478	107254	10.575
12	434	43419	86.135	5208	112462	11.088
13	390	43809	86.912	5070	117532	11.588
14	324	44133	87.555	4536	122068	12.036
15	301	44434	88.152	4515	126583	12.481
16	314	44748	88.775	5024	131607	12.976
17	255	45003	89.281	4335	135942	13.403
18	221	45224	89.719	3978	139920	13.796
19	198	45422	90.112	3762	143682	14.167
20	207	45629	90.523	4140	147822	14.575
21	193	45822	90.906	4053	151875	14.974
22	158	45980	91.219	3476	155351	15.317
23	156	46136	91.529	3588	158939	15.671
24	122	46258	91.771	2928	161867	15.960
25	129	46387	92.027	3225	165092	16.278
26	113	46500	92.251	2938	168030	16.567
27	113	46613	92.475	3051	171081	16.868
28	102	46715	92.677	2856	173937	17.150
29	98	46813	92.872	2842	176779	17.430
30	92	46905	93.054	2760	179539	17.702
31	86	46991	93.225	2666	182205	17.965
32	84	47075	93.392	2688	184893	18.230
33	87	47162	93.564	2871	187764	18.513
34	87	47249	93.737	2958	190722	18.805
35	70	47319	93.876	2450	193172	19.046
36	82	47401	94.038	2952	196124	19.337
37	78	47479	94.193	2886	199010	19.622
38	73	47552	94.338	2774	201784	19.895
39	58	47610	94.453	2262	204046	20.118
40	77	47687	94.606	3080	207126	20.422
41	56	47743	94.717	2296	209422	20.648
42	59	47802	94.834	2478	211900	20.893
43	59	47861	94.951	2537	214437	21.143
44	60	47921	95.070	2640	217077	21.403
45	56	47977	95.181	2520	219597	21.652
46	53	48030	95.286	2438	222035	21.892
47	60	48090	95.405	2820	224855	22.170
48	43	48133	95.491	2064	226919	22.373
49	28	48161	95.546	1372	228291	22.509
50	46	48207	95.637	2300	230591	22.736
51	46	48253	95.729	2346	232937	22.967
52	27	48280	95.782	1404	234341	23.105
53	45	48325	95.872	2385	236726	23.340
54	31	48356	95.933	1674	238400	23.505
55	44	48400	96.020	2420	240820	23.744
56	33	48433	96.086	1848	242668	23.926
57	38	48471	96.161	2166	244834	24.140
58	42	48513	96.244	2436	247270	24.380
59	33	48546	96.310	1947	249217	24.572
60	32	48578	96.373	1920	251137	24.761
61	37	48615	96.447	2257	253394	24.984
62	34	48649	96.514	2108	255502	25.192
63	29	48678	96.572	1827	257329	25.372
64	24	48702	96.619	1536	258865	25.523
65	29	48731	96.677	1885	260750	25.709
66	31	48762	96.738	2046	262796	25.911
67	27	48789	96.792	1809	264605	26.089
68	37	48826	96.865	2516	267121	26.337
69	19	48845	96.903	1311	268432	26.467
70	28	48873	96.959	1960	270392	26.660
71	20	48893	96.998	1420	271812	26.800
72	33	48926	97.064	2376	274188	27.034

TABLE B4 (CONT.) THE CORPUS IN ASCENDING ORDER

X	FX	SUM FX	CUM% FX	FX*X	SUM FX*X	CUM% FX*X
73	16	48942	97.096	1168	275356	27.149
74	29	48971	97.153	2146	277502	27.361
75	17	48988	97.187	1275	278777	27.486
76	13	49001	97.213	988	279765	27.584
77	16	49017	97.244	1232	280997	27.705
78	14	49031	97.272	1092	282089	27.813
79	14	49045	97.300	1106	283195	27.922
80	13	49058	97.326	1040	284235	28.025
81	22	49080	97.365	1782	286017	28.200
82	12	49092	97.393	984	287001	28.297
83	23	49115	97.435	1909	288910	28.486
84	20	49135	97.478	1680	290590	28.651
85	15	49150	97.508	1275	291865	28.777
86	18	49168	97.544	1548	293413	28.930
87	15	49183	97.574	1305	294718	29.058
88	22	49205	97.617	1936	296654	29.249
89	13	49218	97.643	1157	297811	29.363
90	10	49228	97.663	900	298711	29.452
91	18	49246	97.699	1638	300349	29.613
92	7	49253	97.713	644	300993	29.677
93	10	49263	97.732	930	301923	29.769
94	13	49276	97.758	1222	303145	29.889
95	10	49286	97.778	950	304095	29.983
96	13	49299	97.804	1248	305343	30.106
97	13	49312	97.830	1261	306604	30.230
98	16	49328	97.861	1568	308172	30.385
99	8	49336	97.877	792	308964	30.463
100	9	49345	97.895	900	309864	30.552
101	14	49359	97.923	1414	311278	30.691
102	9	49368	97.941	918	312196	30.782
103	13	49381	97.967	1339	313535	30.914
104	10	49391	97.986	1040	314575	31.016
105	12	49403	98.010	1260	315835	31.140
106	12	49415	98.034	1272	317107	31.266
107	11	49426	98.056	1177	318284	31.382
108	11	49437	98.078	1188	319472	31.499

TABLE B4 (CONT.) THE CORPUS IN ASCENDING ORDER

X	FX	SUM FX	CUM% FX	FX*X	SUM FX*X	CUM% FX*X
109	12	49449	98.101	1308	320780	31.628
110	11	49460	98.123	1210	321990	31.747
111	2	49462	98.127	222	322212	31.769
112	5	49467	98.137	560	322772	31.824
113	15	49482	98.167	1695	324467	31.991
114	9	49491	98.185	1026	325493	32.093
115	12	49503	98.209	1380	326873	32.229
116	7	49510	98.222	812	327685	32.309
117	5	49515	98.232	585	328270	32.366
118	7	49522	98.246	826	329096	32.448
119	12	49534	98.270	1428	330524	32.589
120	8	49542	98.286	960	331484	32.683
121	5	49547	98.296	605	332089	32.743
122	6	49553	98.308	732	332821	32.815
123	8	49561	98.324	984	333805	32.912
124	3	49564	98.330	372	334177	32.949
125	14	49578	98.357	1750	335927	33.121
126	3	49581	98.363	378	336305	33.159
127	13	49594	98.389	1651	337956	33.321
128	7	49601	98.403	896	338852	33.410
129	13	49614	98.429	1677	340529	33.575
130	8	49622	98.445	1040	341569	33.678
131	8	49630	98.460	1048	342617	33.781
132	7	49637	98.474	924	343541	33.872
133	6	49643	98.486	798	344339	33.951
134	8	49651	98.502	1072	345411	34.056
135	7	49658	98.516	945	346356	34.150
136	3	49661	98.522	408	346764	34.190
137	6	49667	98.534	822	347586	34.271
138	3	49670	98.540	414	348000	34.312
139	7	49677	98.554	973	348973	34.408
140	5	49682	98.564	700	349673	34.477
141	9	49691	98.582	1269	350942	34.602
142	8	49699	98.597	1136	352078	34.714
143	11	49710	98.619	1573	353651	34.869
144	3	49713	98.625	432	354083	34.911

TABLE 84 (CCNT.) THE CORPUS IN ASCENDING ORDER

X	FX	SUM FX	CUM% FX	FX*X	SUM FX*X	CUM% FX*X
145	10	49723	98.645	1450	355533	35.054
146	4	49727	98.653	584	356117	35.112
147	4	49731	98.661	588	356705	35.170
148	7	49738	98.675	1036	357741	35.272
149	5	49743	98.685	745	358486	35.346
150	2	49745	98.689	300	358786	35.375
151	5	49750	98.699	755	359541	35.450
152	5	49755	98.708	760	360301	35.525
153	3	49758	98.714	459	360760	35.570
154	5	49763	98.724	770	361530	35.646
155	5	49768	98.734	775	362305	35.722
156	4	49772	98.742	624	362929	35.784
157	3	49775	98.748	471	363400	35.830
158	4	49779	98.756	632	364032	35.892
159	2	49781	98.760	318	364350	35.924
160	5	49786	98.770	800	365150	36.003
161	5	49791	98.780	805	365955	36.082
162	5	49796	98.790	810	366765	36.162
163	6	49802	98.802	978	367743	36.258
164	4	49806	98.810	656	368399	36.323
165	3	49809	98.816	495	368894	36.372
166	3	49812	98.822	498	369392	36.421
167	3	49815	98.828	501	369893	36.470
168	1	49816	98.829	168	370061	36.487
169	3	49819	98.835	507	370568	36.537
170	4	49823	98.843	680	371248	36.604
171	7	49830	98.857	1197	372445	36.722
172	7	49837	98.871	1204	373649	36.841
173	7	49844	98.885	1211	374860	36.960
174	7	49851	98.899	1218	376078	37.080
175	7	49858	98.913	1225	377303	37.201
176	3	49861	98.919	528	377831	37.253
177	1	49862	98.921	177	378008	37.270
178	1	49863	98.923	178	378186	37.288
179	4	49867	98.931	716	378902	37.359
180	3	49870	98.937	540	379442	37.412

TABLE 84 (CCNT.) THE CORPUS IN ASCENDING ORDER

X	FX	SUM FX	CUM% FX	FX*X	SUM FX*X	CUM% FX*X
181	5	49875	98.947	905	380347	37.501
182	3	49878	98.952	546	380893	37.555
183	2	49880	98.956	366	381259	37.591
184	2	49882	98.960	368	381627	37.627
185	3	49885	98.966	555	382182	37.682
186	5	49890	98.976	930	383112	37.774
187	3	49893	98.982	561	383673	37.829
188	2	49895	98.986	376	384049	37.866
189	2	49897	98.990	378	384427	37.903
190	1	49898	98.992	190	384617	37.922
191	4	49902	99.000	764	385381	37.997
192	2	49904	99.004	384	385765	38.035
193	2	49906	99.008	386	386151	38.073
194	3	49909	99.014	582	386733	38.131
195	8	49917	99.030	1560	388293	38.284
196	5	49922	99.040	980	389273	38.381
197	3	49925	99.046	591	389864	38.439
198	5	49930	99.056	990	390854	38.537
199	2	49932	99.060	398	391252	38.576
200	6	49938	99.072	1200	392452	38.694
201	1	49939	99.074	201	392653	38.714
202	2	49941	99.077	404	393057	38.754
203	1	49942	99.079	203	393260	38.774
204	4	49946	99.087	816	394076	38.855
205	3	49949	99.093	615	394691	38.915
206	3	49952	99.099	618	395309	38.976
207	2	49954	99.103	414	395723	39.017
208	1	49955	99.105	208	395931	39.038
209	2	49957	99.109	418	396349	39.079
210	1	49958	99.111	210	396559	39.099
211	2	49960	99.115	422	396981	39.141
212	5	49965	99.125	1060	398041	39.246
213	4	49969	99.133	852	398893	39.330
214	2	49971	99.137	428	399321	39.372
216	6	49977	99.149	1296	400617	39.500
217	1	49978	99.151	217	400834	39.521

TABLE B4 (CONT.) THE CORPUS IN ASCENDING ORDER

X	FX	SUM FX	CUM% FX	FX*X	SUM FX*X	CUM% FX*X
218	1	49979	99.153	218	401052	39.542
219	1	49980	99.155	219	401271	39.564
220	2	49982	99.159	440	401711	39.607
221	3	49985	99.165	663	402374	39.673
222	2	49987	99.169	444	402818	39.717
223	2	49989	99.173	446	403264	39.761
224	2	49991	99.177	448	403712	39.805
225	1	49992	99.179	225	403937	39.827
226	2	49994	99.183	452	404389	39.871
227	2	49996	99.187	454	404843	39.916
228	2	49998	99.191	456	405299	39.961
229	2	50000	99.195	458	405757	40.006
230	3	50003	99.200	690	406447	40.074
231	2	50005	99.204	462	406909	40.120
232	1	50006	99.206	232	407141	40.143
233	1	50007	99.208	233	407374	40.166
234	1	50008	99.210	234	407608	40.189
235	1	50009	99.212	235	407843	40.212
236	1	50010	99.214	236	408079	40.235
237	1	50011	99.216	237	408316	40.259
238	1	50012	99.218	238	408554	40.282
239	2	50014	99.222	478	409032	40.329
240	2	50016	99.226	480	409512	40.377
241	2	50018	99.230	482	409994	40.424
242	1	50019	99.232	242	410236	40.448
243	1	50020	99.234	243	410479	40.472
244	2	50022	99.238	488	410967	40.520
245	2	50024	99.242	490	411457	40.568
246	5	50029	99.252	1230	412687	40.690
247	3	50032	99.258	741	413428	40.763
250	1	50033	99.260	250	413678	40.787
252	1	50034	99.262	252	413930	40.812
253	1	50035	99.264	253	414183	40.837
255	2	50037	99.268	510	414693	40.887
257	2	50039	99.272	514	415207	40.938
258	4	50043	99.280	1032	416239	41.040

TABLE B4 (CONT.) THE CORPUS IN ASCENDING ORDER

X	FX	SUM FX	CUM% FX	FX*X	SUM FX*X	CUM% FX*X
259	1	50044	99.282	259	416498	41.065
260	2	50046	99.286	520	417018	41.117
261	1	50047	99.288	261	417279	41.142
264	3	50050	99.294	792	418071	41.220
265	2	50052	99.298	530	418601	41.273
267	3	50055	99.304	801	419402	41.352
268	2	50057	99.308	536	419938	41.405
269	1	50058	99.310	269	420207	41.431
270	1	50059	99.312	270	420477	41.458
273	1	50060	99.314	273	420750	41.485
274	4	50064	99.322	1096	421846	41.593
275	3	50067	99.327	825	422671	41.674
276	2	50069	99.331	552	423223	41.728
277	1	50070	99.333	277	423500	41.756
279	2	50072	99.337	558	424058	41.811
280	1	50073	99.339	280	424338	41.838
281	3	50076	99.345	843	425181	41.921
282	2	50078	99.349	564	425745	41.977
283	2	50080	99.353	566	426311	42.033
284	2	50082	99.357	568	426879	42.089
285	1	50083	99.359	285	427164	42.117
286	3	50086	99.365	858	428022	42.202
287	1	50087	99.367	287	428309	42.230
288	1	50088	99.369	288	428597	42.258
289	1	50089	99.371	289	428886	42.287
290	1	50090	99.373	290	429176	42.315
291	1	50091	99.375	291	429467	42.344
292	1	50092	99.377	292	429759	42.373
294	1	50093	99.379	294	430053	42.402
296	1	50094	99.381	296	430349	42.431
298	1	50095	99.383	298	430647	42.460
299	2	50097	99.387	598	431245	42.519
300	1	50098	99.389	300	431545	42.549
301	1	50099	99.391	301	431846	42.579
302	1	50100	99.393	302	432148	42.608
304	1	50101	99.395	304	432452	42.638

TABLE B4 (CONT.) THE CORPUS IN ASCENDING ORDER

X	FX	SUM FX	CUM% FX	FX*X	SUM FX*X	CUM% FX*X
307	1	50102	99.397	307	432759	42.669
308	1	50103	99.399	308	433067	42.699
309	1	50104	99.401	309	433376	42.729
310	1	50105	99.403	310	433686	42.760
311	2	50107	99.407	622	434308	42.821
312	4	50111	99.415	1248	435556	42.944
313	3	50114	99.421	939	436495	43.037
315	1	50115	99.423	315	436810	43.068
318	1	50116	99.425	318	437128	43.099
319	2	50118	99.429	638	437766	43.162
320	2	50120	99.433	640	438406	43.225
323	2	50122	99.437	646	439052	43.289
324	1	50123	99.439	324	439376	43.321
325	2	50125	99.443	650	440026	43.385
329	1	50126	99.445	329	440355	43.418
330	1	50127	99.446	330	440685	43.450
331	1	50128	99.448	331	441016	43.483
332	1	50129	99.450	332	441348	43.515
333	2	50131	99.454	666	442014	43.581
334	1	50132	99.456	334	442348	43.614
342	1	50133	99.458	342	442690	43.648
343	1	50134	99.460	343	443033	43.682
345	1	50135	99.462	345	443378	43.716
348	1	50136	99.464	348	443726	43.750
351	1	50137	99.466	351	444077	43.785
352	1	50138	99.468	352	444429	43.819
355	2	50140	99.472	710	445139	43.889
357	1	50141	99.474	357	445496	43.924
359	2	50143	99.478	718	446214	43.995
360	2	50145	99.482	720	446934	44.066
361	2	50147	99.486	722	447656	44.137
362	2	50149	99.490	724	448380	44.209
365	1	50150	99.492	365	448745	44.245
366	1	50151	99.494	366	449111	44.281
367	1	50152	99.496	367	449478	44.317
368	2	50154	99.500	736	450214	44.390

TABLE B4 (CONT.) THE CORPUS IN ASCENDING ORDER

X	FX	SUM FX	CUM% FX	FX*X	SUM FX*X	CUM% FX*X
369	1	50155	99.502	369	450583	44.426
370	2	50157	99.506	740	451323	44.499
371	2	50159	99.510	742	452065	44.572
373	3	50162	99.516	1119	453184	44.682
375	1	50163	99.518	375	453559	44.719
376	1	50164	99.520	376	453935	44.757
377	3	50167	99.526	1131	455066	44.868
380	2	50169	99.530	760	455826	44.943
382	1	50170	99.532	382	456208	44.981
383	1	50171	99.534	383	456591	45.018
384	2	50173	99.538	768	457359	45.094
385	1	50174	99.540	385	457744	45.132
386	1	50175	99.542	386	458130	45.170
390	1	50176	99.544	390	458520	45.209
391	1	50177	99.546	391	458911	45.247
392	1	50178	99.548	392	459303	45.286
393	1	50179	99.550	393	459696	45.325
394	2	50181	99.554	788	460484	45.402
395	2	50183	99.558	790	461274	45.480
397	1	50184	99.560	397	461671	45.519
398	1	50185	99.562	398	462069	45.559
399	3	50188	99.568	1197	463266	45.677
401	3	50191	99.573	1203	464469	45.795
404	1	50192	99.575	404	464873	45.835
410	1	50193	99.577	410	465283	45.875
411	1	50194	99.579	411	465694	45.916
412	1	50195	99.581	412	466106	45.957
413	1	50196	99.583	413	466519	45.997
414	2	50198	99.587	828	467347	46.079
416	1	50199	99.589	416	467763	46.120
417	1	50200	99.591	417	468180	46.161
419	1	50201	99.593	419	468599	46.202
424	1	50202	99.595	424	469023	46.244
426	1	50203	99.597	426	469449	46.286
427	1	50204	99.599	427	469876	46.328
430	1	50205	99.601	430	470306	46.371

TABLE B4 (CONT.)   THE CORPUS IN ASCENDING ORDER

X	FX	SUM FX	CUM% FX	FX*X	SUM FX*X	CUM% FX*X
431	1	50206	99.603	431	470737	46.413
432	1	50207	99.605	432	471169	46.456
433	1	50208	99.607	433	471602	46.498
437	1	50209	99.609	437	472039	46.542
438	2	50211	99.613	876	472915	46.628
442	2	50213	99.617	884	473799	46.715
447	1	50214	99.619	447	474246	46.759
450	2	50216	99.623	900	475146	46.848
456	1	50217	99.625	456	475602	46.893
458	1	50218	99.627	458	476060	46.938
461	1	50219	99.629	461	476521	46.983
464	1	50220	99.631	464	476985	47.029
465	1	50221	99.633	465	477450	47.075
472	1	50222	99.635	472	477922	47.122
480	1	50223	99.637	480	478402	47.169
482	2	50225	99.641	964	479366	47.264
485	1	50226	99.643	485	479851	47.312
489	1	50227	99.645	489	480340	47.360
491	1	50228	99.647	491	480831	47.408
492	1	50229	99.649	492	481323	47.457
495	1	50230	99.651	495	481818	47.506
496	1	50231	99.653	496	482314	47.555
497	2	50233	99.657	994	483308	47.653
499	1	50234	99.659	499	483807	47.702
500	1	50235	99.661	500	484307	47.751
504	1	50236	99.663	504	484811	47.801
507	1	50237	99.665	507	485318	47.851
515	1	50238	99.667	515	485833	47.902
534	1	50239	99.669	534	486367	47.954
536	1	50240	99.671	536	486903	48.007
542	1	50241	99.673	542	487445	48.060
547	1	50242	99.675	547	487992	48.114
552	1	50243	99.677	552	488544	48.169
561	1	50244	99.679	561	489105	48.224
565	1	50245	99.681	569	489674	48.280
571	1	50246	99.683	571	490245	48.337

TABLE B4 (CONT.)   THE CORPUS IN ASCENDING ORDER

X	FX	SUM FX	CUM% FX	FX*X	SUM FX*X	CUM% FX*X
578	1	50247	99.685	578	490823	48.394
583	1	50248	99.687	583	491406	48.451
585	1	50249	99.689	585	491991	48.509
589	1	50250	99.691	589	492580	48.567
591	1	50251	99.692	591	493171	48.625
601	1	50252	99.694	601	493772	48.684
603	1	50253	99.696	603	494375	48.744
605	1	50254	99.698	605	494980	48.803
610	1	50255	99.700	610	495590	48.864
611	1	50256	99.702	611	496201	48.924
612	1	50257	99.704	612	496813	48.984
613	1	50258	99.706	613	497426	49.045
622	1	50259	99.708	622	498048	49.106
626	2	50261	99.712	1252	499300	49.229
628	1	50262	99.714	628	499928	49.291
630	1	50263	99.716	630	500558	49.353
639	1	50264	99.718	639	501197	49.416
66C	2	50266	99.722	1320	502517	49.547
665	1	50267	99.724	665	503182	49.612
672	2	50269	99.728	1344	504526	49.745
676	1	50270	99.730	676	505202	49.811
680	1	50271	99.732	680	505882	49.878
683	2	50273	99.736	1366	507248	50.013
686	2	50275	99.740	1372	508620	50.148
698	1	50276	99.742	698	509318	50.217
7C7	1	50277	99.744	707	510025	50.287
712	1	50278	99.746	712	510737	50.357
715	1	50279	99.748	715	511452	50.428
721	1	50280	99.750	721	512173	50.499
730	2	50282	99.754	1460	513633	50.643
750	2	50284	99.758	1500	515133	50.790
755	1	50285	99.760	755	515888	50.865
760	1	50286	99.762	760	516648	50.940
763	1	50287	99.764	763	517411	51.015
772	2	50289	99.768	1544	518955	51.167
782	1	50290	99.770	782	519737	51.244

TABLE B4 (CONT.) THE CORPUS IN ASCENDING ORDER

X	FX	SUM FX	CUM% FX	FX*X	SUM FX*X	CUM% FX*X
787	1	50291	99.772	787	520524	51.322
794	1	50292	99.774	794	521318	51.400
796	1	50293	99.776	796	522114	51.479
807	1	50294	99.778	807	522921	51.558
808	1	50295	99.780	808	523729	51.638
831	1	50296	99.782	831	524560	51.720
832	1	50297	99.784	832	525392	51.802
834	1	50298	99.786	834	526226	51.884
839	1	50299	99.788	839	527065	51.967
847	1	50300	99.790	847	527912	52.050
850	1	50301	99.792	850	528762	52.134
872	1	50302	99.794	872	529634	52.220
877	1	50303	99.796	877	530511	52.307
883	1	50304	99.798	883	531394	52.394
888	1	50305	99.800	888	532282	52.481
895	1	50306	99.802	895	533177	52.570
897	1	50307	99.804	897	534074	52.658
909	1	50308	99.806	909	534983	52.748
923	1	50309	99.808	923	535906	52.839
937	1	50310	99.810	937	536843	52.931
938	1	50311	99.812	938	537781	53.023
949	1	50312	99.814	949	538730	53.117
967	1	50313	99.815	967	539697	53.212
969	1	50314	99.817	969	540666	53.308
1010	1	50315	99.819	1010	541676	53.408
1013	1	50316	99.821	1013	542689	53.507
1016	1	50317	99.823	1016	543705	53.608
1030	1	50318	99.825	1030	544735	53.709
1044	1	50319	99.827	1044	545779	53.812
1069	1	50320	99.829	1069	546848	53.917
1070	1	50321	99.831	1070	547918	54.023
1125	1	50322	99.833	1125	549043	54.134
1160	1	50323	99.835	1160	550203	54.248
1171	1	50324	99.837	1171	551374	54.364
1181	1	50325	99.839	1181	552555	54.480
1207	1	50326	99.841	1207	553762	54.599
1236	1	50327	99.843	1236	554998	54.721
1252	1	50328	99.845	1252	556250	54.844
1290	1	50329	99.847	1290	557540	54.972
1303	1	50330	99.849	1303	558843	55.100
1314	1	50331	99.851	1314	560157	55.230
1319	1	50332	99.853	1319	561476	55.360
1345	1	50333	99.855	1345	562821	55.492
1360	1	50334	99.857	1360	564181	55.626
1363	1	50335	99.859	1363	565544	55.761
1377	1	50336	99.861	1377	566921	55.897
1400	1	50337	99.863	1400	568321	56.035
1412	1	50338	99.865	1412	569733	56.174
1573	1	50339	99.867	1573	571306	56.329
1599	2	50341	99.871	3198	574504	56.644
1617	1	50342	99.873	1617	576121	56.804
1635	1	50343	99.875	1635	577756	56.965
1702	1	50344	99.877	1702	579458	57.133
1747	1	50345	99.879	1747	581205	57.305
1772	1	50346	99.881	1772	582977	57.480
1789	2	50348	99.885	3578	586555	57.832
1791	1	50349	99.887	1791	588346	58.009
1815	1	50350	99.889	1815	590161	58.188
1858	1	50351	99.891	1858	592019	58.371
1895	1	50352	99.893	1895	593914	58.558
1908	1	50353	99.895	1908	595822	58.746
1961	1	50354	99.897	1961	597783	58.939
1984	1	50355	99.899	1984	599767	59.135
2096	1	50356	99.901	2096	601863	59.342
2199	1	50357	99.903	2199	604062	59.559
2201	1	50358	99.905	2201	606263	59.776
2216	1	50359	99.907	2216	608479	59.994
2244	1	50360	99.909	2244	610723	60.215
2252	1	50361	99.911	2252	612975	60.437
2331	1	50362	99.913	2331	615306	60.667
2439	1	50363	99.915	2439	617745	60.908
2472	1	50364	99.917	2472	620217	61.151

TABLE B4 (CONT.) THE CORPUS IN ASCENDING ORDER

X	FX	SUM FX	CUM% FX	FX*X	SUM FX*X	CUM% FX*X
2619	1	50365	99.919	2619	622836	61.410
2653	1	50366	99.921	2653	625489	61.671
2670	1	50367	99.923	2670	628159	61.934
2714	1	50368	99.925	2714	630873	62.202
2724	1	50369	99.927	2724	633597	62.471
2859	1	50370	99.929	2859	636456	62.753
3001	1	50371	99.931	3001	639457	63.048
3037	1	50372	99.933	3037	642494	63.348
3284	1	50373	99.935	3284	645778	63.672
3286	1	50374	99.937	3286	649064	63.996
3292	1	50375	99.938	3292	652356	64.320
3562	1	50376	99.940	3562	655918	64.671
3618	1	50377	99.942	3618	659536	65.028
3747	1	50378	99.944	3747	663283	65.398
3941	1	50379	99.946	3941	667224	65.786
4207	1	50380	99.948	4207	671431	66.201
4369	1	50381	99.950	4369	675800	66.632
4381	1	50382	99.952	4381	680181	67.064
4393	1	50383	99.954	4393	684574	67.497
4609	1	50384	99.956	4609	689183	67.951
5133	1	50385	99.958	5133	694316	68.457
5146	1	50386	99.960	5146	699462	68.965
5173	1	50387	99.962	5173	704635	69.475
5305	1	50388	99.964	5305	709940	69.998
5378	1	50389	99.966	5378	715318	70.528
6377	1	50390	99.968	6377	721695	71.157
6742	1	50391	99.970	6742	728437	71.822
6997	1	50392	99.972	6997	735434	72.511
7250	1	50393	99.974	7250	742684	73.226
7289	1	50394	99.976	7289	749973	73.945
8756	1	50395	99.978	8756	758729	74.808
9489	1	50396	99.980	9489	768218	75.744
9543	1	50397	99.982	9543	777761	76.685
9816	1	50398	99.984	9816	787577	77.653
10099	1	50399	99.986	10099	797676	78.648
10595	1	50400	99.988	10595	808271	79.693

TABLE B4 (CONT.) THE CORPUS IN ASCENDING ORDER

X	FX	SUM FX	CUM% FX	FX*X	SUM FX*X	CUM% FX*X
21341	1	50401	99.990	21341	829612	81.797
23237	1	50402	99.592	23237	852849	84.088
26149	1	50403	99.994	26149	878998	86.666
28852	1	50404	99.996	28852	907850	89.511
36411	1	50405	99.998	36411	944261	93.101
65971	1	50406	100.000	69971	1014232	100.000

TYPES = S0 = 50406   TOKENS = S1 = 1014232   S2 = 10154742794

MEAN = 20.1213   SD = 448.3906   V = 22.2844   K = 98.7077

TABLE 85 A REPRESENTATIVE CORPUS SUBSET OF 125 SAMPLES IN ASCENDING ORDER

X	FX	SUM FX	CUM% FX	FX*X	SUM FX*X	CUM% FX*X
1	11353	11353	47.994	11353	11353	4.478
2	3606	14959	63.238	7212	18565	7.322
3	1943	16902	71.452	5829	24394	9.621
4	1213	18115	76.580	4852	29246	11.535
5	828	18943	80.080	4140	33386	13.168
6	515	19458	82.257	3090	36476	14.387
7	473	19931	84.257	3311	39787	15.693
8	374	20305	85.838	2992	42779	16.873
9	286	20591	87.047	2574	45353	17.888
10	288	20879	88.265	2880	48233	19.024
11	205	21084	89.131	2255	50488	19.913
12	203	21287	89.989	2436	52924	20.874
13	190	21477	90.793	2470	55394	21.848
14	152	21629	91.435	2128	57522	22.688
15	132	21761	91.993	1980	59502	23.469
16	124	21885	92.517	1984	61486	24.251
17	92	21977	92.906	1564	63050	24.868
18	99	22076	93.325	1782	64832	25.571
19	91	22167	93.710	1729	66561	26.253
20	84	22251	94.065	1680	68241	26.915
21	79	22330	94.399	1659	69900	27.570
22	77	22407	94.724	1694	71594	28.238
23	62	22469	94.986	1426	73020	28.800
24	56	22525	95.223	1344	74364	29.331
25	32	22557	95.358	800	75164	29.646
26	42	22599	95.536	1092	76256	30.077
27	40	22639	95.705	1080	77336	30.503
28	38	22677	95.866	1064	78400	30.922
29	42	22719	96.043	1218	79618	31.403
30	28	22747	96.161	840	80458	31.734
31	23	22770	96.255	713	81171	32.015
32	24	22794	96.360	768	81939	32.318
33	44	22838	96.546	1452	83391	32.891
34	21	22859	96.635	714	84105	33.173
35	27	22886	96.745	945	85050	33.545
36	28	22914	96.867	1008	86058	33.943

TABLE 85 (CONT.) A REPRESENTATIVE CORPUS SUBSET OF 125 SAMPLES IN ASC. ORDER

X	FX	SUM FX	CUM% FX	FX*X	SUM FX*X	CUM% FX*X
37	25	22939	96.973	925	86983	34.308
38	21	22960	97.062	798	87781	34.622
39	29	22989	97.185	1131	88912	35.068
40	22	23011	97.278	880	89792	35.416
41	20	23031	97.362	820	90612	35.739
42	13	23044	97.417	546	91158	35.954
43	19	23063	97.497	817	91975	36.277
44	21	23084	97.586	924	92899	36.641
45	17	23101	97.658	765	93664	36.943
46	16	23117	97.726	736	94400	37.233
47	12	23129	97.776	564	94964	37.456
48	8	23137	97.810	384	95348	37.607
49	13	23150	97.865	637	95985	37.858
50	15	23165	97.929	750	96735	38.154
51	11	23176	97.975	561	97296	38.375
52	9	23185	98.013	468	97764	38.560
53	13	23198	98.068	689	98453	38.832
54	6	23204	98.093	324	98777	38.959
55	12	23216	98.144	660	99437	39.220
56	7	23223	98.174	392	99829	39.374
57	7	23230	98.203	399	100228	39.532
58	9	23239	98.241	522	100750	39.738
59	15	23254	98.305	885	101635	40.087
60	5	23259	98.326	300	101935	40.205
61	11	23270	98.372	671	102606	40.470
62	9	23279	98.410	558	103164	40.690
63	7	23286	98.440	441	103605	40.864
64	4	23290	98.457	256	103861	40.965
65	6	23296	98.482	390	104251	41.118
66	6	23302	98.508	396	104647	41.275
67	8	23310	98.542	536	105183	41.486
68	3	23313	98.554	204	105387	41.567
69	5	23318	98.575	345	105732	41.703
70	4	23322	98.592	280	106012	41.813
71	2	23324	98.601	142	106154	41.869
72	1	23325	98.605	72	106226	41.897

TABLE 85 (CCNT.) A REPRESENTATIVE CORPUS SUBSET OF 125 SAMPLES IN ASC. ORDER

X	FX	SUM FX	CUM% FX	FX*X	SUM FX*X	CUM% FX*X
73	4	23329	98.622	292	106518	42.013
74	7	23336	98.651	518	107036	42.217
75	4	23340	98.668	300	107336	42.335
76	6	23346	98.694	456	107792	42.515
77	5	23351	98.715	385	108177	42.667
78	6	23357	98.740	468	108645	42.852
79	4	23361	98.757	316	108961	42.976
80	3	23364	98.770	240	109201	43.071
81	5	23369	98.791	405	109606	43.231
82	6	23375	98.816	492	110098	43.425
83	5	23380	98.837	415	110513	43.588
84	5	23385	98.859	420	110933	43.754
85	1	23386	98.863	85	111018	43.788
86	2	23388	98.871	172	111190	43.855
87	4	23392	98.888	348	111538	43.993
88	2	23394	98.897	176	111714	44.062
89	3	23397	98.909	267	111981	44.167
91	3	23400	98.922	273	112254	44.275
92	5	23405	98.943	460	112714	44.456
93	3	23408	98.956	279	112993	44.566
94	5	23413	98.977	470	113463	44.752
95	3	23416	98.990	285	113748	44.864
97	3	23419	99.002	291	114039	44.979
98	7	23426	99.032	686	114725	45.250
99	1	23427	99.036	99	114824	45.289
100	2	23429	99.045	200	115024	45.368
101	4	23433	99.061	404	115428	45.527
102	2	23435	99.070	204	115632	45.607
103	4	23439	99.087	412	116044	45.770
104	2	23441	99.095	208	116252	45.852
105	1	23442	99.100	105	116357	45.893
106	2	23444	99.108	212	116569	45.977
107	2	23446	99.116	214	116783	46.061
109	1	23447	99.121	109	116892	46.104
110	3	23450	99.133	330	117222	46.234
111	4	23454	99.150	444	117666	46.410

TABLE 85 (CCNT.) A REPRESENTATIVE CORPUS SUBSET OF 125 SAMPLES IN ASC. ORDER

X	FX	SUM FX	CUM% FX	FX*X	SUM FX*X	CUM% FX*X
112	3	23457	99.163	336	118002	46.542
113	4	23461	99.180	452	118454	46.720
114	4	23465	99.197	456	118910	46.900
115	1	23466	99.201	115	119025	46.946
116	3	23469	99.214	348	119373	47.083
117	2	23471	99.222	234	119607	47.175
118	2	23473	99.231	236	119843	47.268
119	2	23475	99.239	238	120081	47.362
120	1	23476	99.243	120	120201	47.409
121	2	23478	99.252	242	120443	47.505
122	1	23479	99.256	122	120565	47.553
126	2	23481	99.264	252	120817	47.652
128	3	23484	99.277	384	121201	47.804
131	2	23486	99.286	262	121463	47.907
132	2	23488	99.294	264	121727	48.011
136	1	23489	99.298	136	121863	48.065
138	1	23490	99.302	138	122001	48.119
139	1	23491	99.307	139	122140	48.174
141	2	23493	99.315	282	122422	48.285
143	1	23494	99.319	143	122565	48.342
144	2	23496	99.328	288	122853	48.455
146	1	23497	99.332	146	122999	48.513
149	1	23498	99.336	149	123148	48.572
151	3	23501	99.349	453	123601	48.750
153	2	23503	99.357	306	123907	48.871
155	2	23505	99.366	310	124217	48.993
156	3	23508	99.379	468	124685	49.178
159	3	23511	99.391	477	125162	49.366
160	1	23512	99.395	160	125322	49.429
161	1	23513	99.400	161	125483	49.453
162	3	23516	99.412	486	125969	49.684
163	1	23517	99.417	163	126132	49.749
166	2	23519	99.425	332	126464	49.880
167	1	23520	99.429	167	126631	49.946
168	1	23521	99.434	168	126799	50.012
170	1	23522	99.438	170	126969	50.079

TABLE B5 (CCNT.) A REPRESENTATIVE CORPUS SUBSET OF 125 SAMPLES IN ASC. ORDER

X	FX	SUM FX	CUM% FX	FX*X	SUM FX*X	CUM% FX*X
173	2	23524	99.446	346	127315	50.215
174	1	23525	99.450	174	127489	50.284
175	3	23528	99.463	525	128014	50.491
177	1	23529	99.467	177	128191	50.561
179	1	23530	99.472	179	128370	50.631
181	2	23532	99.480	362	128732	50.774
182	1	23533	99.484	182	128914	50.846
185	1	23534	99.488	185	129099	50.919
187	1	23535	99.493	187	129286	50.993
190	2	23537	99.501	380	129666	51.143
192	1	23538	99.505	192	129858	51.218
198	2	23540	99.514	396	130254	51.375
200	1	23541	99.518	200	130454	51.453
201	1	23542	99.522	201	130655	51.533
202	1	23543	99.527	202	130857	51.612
203	1	23544	99.531	203	131060	51.692
205	1	23545	99.535	205	131265	51.773
206	1	23546	99.539	206	131471	51.855
207	1	23547	99.543	207	131678	51.936
211	1	23548	99.548	211	131889	52.019
212	3	23551	99.560	636	132525	52.270
215	1	23552	99.565	215	132740	52.355
218	2	23554	99.573	436	133176	52.527
226	2	23556	99.581	452	133628	52.705
227	1	23557	99.586	227	133855	52.795
228	1	23558	99.590	228	134083	52.885
238	1	23559	99.594	238	134321	52.979
239	1	23560	99.598	239	134560	53.073
241	1	23561	99.603	241	134801	53.168
249	1	23562	99.607	249	135050	53.266
250	1	23563	99.611	250	135300	53.365
253	1	23564	99.615	253	135553	53.465
255	1	23565	99.620	255	135808	53.565
256	1	23566	99.624	256	136064	53.666
259	2	23568	99.632	518	136582	53.870
261	1	23569	99.636	261	136843	53.973

TABLE B5 (CCNT.) A REPRESENTATIVE CORPUS SUBSET OF 125 SAMPLES IN ASC. ORDER

X	FX	SUM FX	CUM% FX	FX*X	SUM FX*X	CUM% FX*X
271	1	23570	99.641	271	137114	54.080
275	1	23571	99.645	275	137389	54.189
285	1	23572	99.649	285	137674	54.301
296	1	23573	99.653	296	137970	54.418
297	1	23574	99.658	297	138267	54.535
319	1	23575	99.662	319	138586	54.661
326	1	23576	99.666	326	138912	54.789
328	3	23579	99.679	984	139896	55.178
330	1	23580	99.683	330	140226	55.308
331	1	23581	99.687	331	140557	55.438
334	1	23582	99.691	334	140891	55.570
342	1	23583	99.696	342	141233	55.705
352	1	23584	99.700	352	141585	55.844
366	1	23585	99.704	366	141951	55.988
371	1	23586	99.708	371	142322	56.134
374	1	23587	99.713	374	142696	56.282
383	2	23589	99.721	766	143462	56.584
396	1	23590	99.725	396	143858	56.740
399	1	23591	99.729	399	144257	56.898
401	1	23592	99.734	401	144658	57.056
414	2	23594	99.742	828	145486	57.382
434	1	23595	99.746	434	145920	57.553
445	1	23596	99.751	449	146369	57.731
453	2	23598	99.755	906	147275	58.088
455	1	23599	99.763	459	147734	58.269
462	1	23600	99.767	462	148196	58.451
476	1	23601	99.772	476	148672	58.639
482	1	23602	99.776	482	149154	58.829
484	1	23603	99.780	484	149638	59.020
485	1	23604	99.784	485	150123	59.211
497	1	23605	99.789	497	150620	59.407
518	1	23606	99.793	518	151138	59.612
520	1	23607	99.797	520	151658	59.817
533	1	23608	99.801	533	152191	60.027
538	1	23609	99.806	538	152729	60.239
555	1	23610	99.810	555	153284	60.458

TABLE 85 (CCNT.) A REPRESENTATIVE CORPUS SUBSET OF 125 SAMPLES IN ASC. ORDER

X	FX	SUM FX	CUM% FX	FX*X	SUM FX*X	CUM% FX*X
560	1	23611	99.814	560	153844	60.679
567	1	23612	99.818	567	154411	60.902
568	1	23613	99.822	568	154979	61.127
613	1	23614	99.827	613	155592	61.368
615	1	23615	99.831	615	156207	61.611
616	1	23616	99.835	616	156823	61.854
685	1	23617	99.839	685	157508	62.124
690	1	23618	99.844	690	158198	62.396
696	1	23619	99.848	696	158894	62.671
714	1	23620	99.852	714	159608	62.952
740	1	23621	99.856	740	160348	63.244
853	1	23622	99.860	853	161201	63.581
866	1	23623	99.865	866	162067	63.922
883	1	23624	99.869	883	162950	64.270
885	1	23625	99.873	885	163835	64.619
909	1	23626	99.877	909	164744	64.978
955	1	23627	99.882	955	165699	65.355
958	1	23628	99.886	958	166657	65.733
1075	1	23629	99.890	1075	167732	66.157
1099	1	23630	99.894	1099	168831	66.590
1111	1	23631	99.899	1111	169942	67.028
1127	1	23632	99.903	1127	171069	67.473
1191	1	23633	99.907	1191	172260	67.942
1275	1	23634	99.911	1275	173535	68.445
1300	1	23635	99.915	1300	174835	68.958
1311	1	23636	99.920	1311	176146	69.475
1373	1	23637	99.924	1373	177519	70.017
1427	1	23638	99.928	1427	178946	70.580
1557	1	23639	99.932	1557	180503	71.194
1651	1	23640	99.937	1651	182194	71.861
1744	1	23641	99.941	1744	183938	72.548
1822	1	23642	99.945	1822	185760	73.267
1886	1	23643	99.949	1886	187646	74.011
2193	1	23644	99.953	2193	189839	74.876
2322	1	23645	99.958	2322	192161	75.792
2434	1	23646	99.962	2434	194595	76.752

TABLE 85 (CCNT.) A REPRESENTATIVE CORPUS SUBSET OF 125 SAMPLES IN ASC. ORDER

X	FX	SUM FX	CUM% FX	FX*X	SUM FX*X	CUM% FX*X
2528	1	23647	99.966	2528	197123	77.749
2536	1	23648	99.970	2536	199659	78.749
2571	1	23649	99.975	2571	202230	79.763
5512	1	23650	99.979	5512	207742	81.937
5737	1	23651	99.983	5737	213479	84.200
6434	1	23652	99.987	6434	219913	86.738
7268	1	23653	99.992	7268	227181	89.604
8998	1	23654	99.996	8998	236179	93.153
17359	1	23655	100.000	17359	253538	100.000

TYPES = SO = 23655   TOKENS = S1 = 253538   S2 = 629404334

MEAN = 10.7182   SD = 162.7660   V = 15.1860   K = 97.8743

TABLE OF FOUR? A REPRESENTATIVE CORPUS SUBSET OF 50 SAMPLES IN ASC. ORDER

X	FX	SUM FX	CUM% FX	FX*X	SUM FX*X	CUM% FX*X
1	7078	7078	51.642	7078	7078	6.969
2	2084	9162	66.347	4168	11246	11.073
3	1094	10256	74.829	3282	14528	14.304
4	705	10961	79.972	2820	17348	17.081
5	476	11437	83.445	2380	19728	19.424
6	332	11769	85.867	1992	21720	21.385
7	245	12014	87.655	1715	23435	23.074
8	228	12242	89.319	1824	25259	24.870
9	159	12401	90.475	1431	26690	26.278
10	136	12537	91.471	1360	28050	27.618
11	126	12663	92.390	1386	29436	28.982
12	89	12752	93.040	1068	30504	30.034
13	82	12834	93.638	1066	31570	31.083
14	60	12894	94.076	840	32410	31.910
15	59	12953	94.506	885	33295	32.782
16	54	13007	94.900	864	34159	33.632
17	50	13057	95.265	850	35009	34.469
18	45	13102	95.593	810	35819	35.267
19	33	13135	95.834	627	36446	35.884
20	38	13173	96.111	760	37206	36.632
21	24	13197	96.286	504	37710	37.129
22	25	13222	96.465	550	38260	37.670
23	28	13250	96.673	644	38904	38.304
24	25	13275	96.855	600	39504	38.895
25	30	13305	97.074	750	40254	39.633
26	19	13324	97.213	494	40748	40.120
27	16	13340	97.330	432	41180	40.545
28	13	13353	97.424	364	41544	40.903
29	23	13376	97.592	667	42211	41.560
30	17	13393	97.716	510	42721	42.062
31	11	13404	97.797	341	43062	42.398
32	9	13413	97.862	288	43350	42.682
33	14	13427	97.964	462	43812	43.136
34	3	13430	97.986	102	43914	43.237
35	9	13439	98.052	315	44229	43.547
36	8	13447	98.110	288	44517	43.831
37	8	13455	98.169	296	44813	44.122
38	11	13466	98.249	418	45231	44.534
39	4	13470	98.278	156	45387	44.687
40	7	13477	98.329	280	45667	44.963
41	10	13487	98.402	410	46077	45.367
42	9	13496	98.468	378	46455	45.739
43	3	13499	98.490	129	46584	45.866
44	6	13505	98.533	264	46848	46.126
45	1	13506	98.541	45	46893	46.170
46	5	13511	98.577	230	47123	46.396
47	4	13515	98.606	188	47311	46.582
48	2	13517	98.621	96	47407	46.676
49	1	13518	98.628	49	47456	46.724
50	8	13526	98.687	400	47856	47.118
51	2	13528	98.701	102	47958	47.219
52	4	13532	98.730	208	48166	47.423
53	1	13533	98.738	53	48219	47.476
54	3	13536	98.760	162	48381	47.635
55	1	13537	98.767	55	48436	47.689
56	5	13542	98.803	280	48716	47.965
57	5	13547	98.840	285	49001	48.245
58	3	13550	98.862	174	49175	48.417
59	3	13553	98.884	177	49352	48.591
60	1	13554	98.891	60	49412	48.650
61	3	13557	98.913	183	49595	48.830
62	3	13560	98.935	186	49781	49.013
63	1	13561	98.942	63	49844	49.075
64	2	13563	98.957	128	49972	49.201
65	2	13565	98.971	130	50102	49.329
66	3	13568	98.993	198	50300	49.524
67	4	13572	99.022	268	50568	49.788
68	2	13574	99.037	136	50704	49.922
69	2	13576	99.051	138	50842	50.058
70	1	13577	99.059	70	50912	50.127
71	1	13578	99.066	71	50983	50.197
72	3	13581	99.088	216	51199	50.410

TABLE 86 (CONT.) A REPRESENTATIVE CORPUS SUBSET OF 50 SAMPLES IN ASC. ORDER

X	FX	SUM FX	CUM% FX	FX*X	SUM FX*X	CUM% FX*X
73	3	13584	99.110	219	51418	50.625
75	2	13586	99.124	150	51568	50.773
76	2	13588	99.139	152	51720	50.923
77	1	13589	99.146	77	51797	50.998
79	3	13592	99.168	237	52034	51.232
80	1	13593	99.176	80	52114	51.310
81	1	13594	99.183	81	52195	51.390
82	1	13595	99.190	82	52277	51.471
83	5	13600	99.227	415	52692	51.880
84	1	13601	99.234	84	52776	51.962
86	1	13602	99.241	86	52862	52.047
87	2	13604	99.256	174	53036	52.218
88	1	13605	99.263	88	53124	52.305
89	1	13606	99.270	89	53213	52.393
91	1	13607	99.278	91	53304	52.482
92	1	13608	99.285	92	53396	52.573
93	1	13609	99.292	93	53489	52.664
94	1	13610	99.300	94	53583	52.757
95	2	13612	99.314	190	53773	52.944
96	1	13613	99.321	96	53869	53.038
98	1	13614	99.329	98	53967	53.135
99	1	13615	99.336	99	54066	53.232
102	2	13617	99.351	204	54270	53.433
108	1	13618	99.358	108	54378	53.540
110	2	13620	99.373	220	54598	53.756
113	1	13621	99.380	113	54711	53.867
115	1	13622	99.387	115	54826	53.981
119	1	13623	99.394	119	54945	54.098
120	2	13625	99.409	240	55185	54.334
122	1	13626	99.416	122	55307	54.454
125	1	13627	99.424	125	55432	54.577
126	2	13629	99.438	252	55684	54.825
129	1	13630	99.445	129	55813	54.952
135	1	13631	99.453	135	55948	55.085
136	2	13633	99.467	272	56220	55.353
137	1	13634	99.475	137	56357	55.488

TABLE 86 (CONT.) A REPRESENTATIVE CORPUS SUBSET OF 50 SAMPLES IN ASC. ORDER

X	FX	SUM FX	CUM% FX	FX*X	SUM FX*X	CUM% FX*X
142	1	13635	99.482	142	56499	55.628
147	1	13636	99.489	147	56646	55.773
155	1	13637	99.497	155	56801	55.925
156	1	13638	99.504	156	56957	56.079
157	1	13639	99.511	157	57114	56.233
159	2	13641	99.526	318	57432	56.546
161	1	13642	99.533	161	57593	56.705
166	1	13643	99.540	166	57759	56.868
167	1	13644	99.548	167	57926	57.033
169	1	13645	99.555	169	58095	57.199
174	1	13646	99.562	174	58269	57.371
179	1	13647	99.570	179	58448	57.547
181	3	13650	99.591	543	58991	58.081
184	1	13651	99.599	184	59175	58.263
189	1	13652	99.606	189	59364	58.449
190	1	13653	99.613	190	59554	58.636
192	1	13654	99.621	192	59746	58.825
198	1	13655	99.628	198	59944	59.020
203	1	13656	99.635	203	60147	59.220
208	1	13657	99.642	208	60355	59.424
215	2	13659	99.657	430	60785	59.848
228	2	13661	99.672	456	61241	60.297
232	1	13662	99.679	232	61473	60.525
241	1	13663	99.686	241	61714	60.762
249	1	13664	99.694	249	61963	61.008
251	1	13665	99.701	251	62214	61.255
253	1	13666	99.708	253	62467	61.504
254	1	13667	99.715	254	62721	61.754
268	1	13668	99.723	268	62989	62.018
284	1	13669	99.730	284	63273	62.297
290	1	13670	99.737	290	63563	62.583
291	1	13671	99.745	291	63854	62.869
305	1	13672	99.752	305	64159	63.170
320	1	13673	99.759	320	64479	63.485
330	1	13674	99.767	330	64809	63.810
351	1	13675	99.774	351	65160	64.155

TABLE 86 (CCNT..) A REPRESENTATIVE CORPUS SUBSET OF 50 SAMPLES IN ASC. ORDER

X	FX	SUM FX	CUM% FX	FX*X	SUM FX*X	CUM% FX*X
356	1	13676	99.781	356	65516	64.506
377	1	13677	99.788	377	65893	64.877
380	1	13678	99.796	380	66273	65.251
409	1	13679	99.803	409	66682	65.654
417	1	13680	99.810	417	67099	66.064
423	1	13681	99.818	423	67522	66.481
437	1	13682	99.825	437	67959	66.911
440	1	13683	99.832	440	68399	67.344
454	1	13684	99.839	454	68853	67.791
491	1	13685	99.847	491	69344	68.275
515	1	13686	99.854	515	69859	68.782
540	1	13687	99.861	540	70399	69.314
548	1	13688	99.869	548	70947	69.853
557	1	13689	99.876	557	71504	70.402
622	1	13690	99.883	622	72126	71.014
633	1	13691	99.891	633	72759	71.637
680	1	13692	99.898	680	73439	72.307
683	1	13693	99.905	683	74122	72.979
737	1	13694	99.912	737	74859	73.705
866	1	13695	99.920	866	75725	74.557
918	1	13696	99.927	918	76643	75.461
926	1	13697	99.934	926	77569	76.373
985	1	13698	99.942	985	78554	77.343
1019	1	13699	99.949	1019	79573	78.346
1110	1	13700	99.956	1110	80683	79.439
2268	1	13701	99.964	2268	82951	81.672
2430	1	13702	99.971	2430	85381	84.065
2617	1	13703	99.978	2617	87998	86.641
2952	1	13704	99.985	2952	90950	89.548
3574	1	13705	99.993	3574	94524	93.067
7042	1	13706	100.000	7042	101566	100.000

TYPES = S0 = 13706   TOKENS = S1 = 101566   S2 = 103190852

MEAN = 7.4103   SD = 86.4521   V = 11.6664   K = 99.9348

TABLE B7 A CORPUS SUBSET OF 5 SAMPLES IN ASCENDING ORDER

X	FX	SUM FX	CUM% FX	FX*X	SUM FX*X	CUM% FX*X
1	1933	1933	64.241	1933	1933	19.232
2	472	2405	79.927	944	2877	28.624
3	207	2612	86.806	621	3498	34.802
4	120	2732	90.794	480	3978	39.578
5	43	2775	92.223	215	4193	41.717
6	50	2825	93.885	300	4493	44.702
7	32	2857	94.948	224	4717	46.931
8	23	2880	95.713	184	4901	48.761
9	16	2896	96.245	144	5045	50.194
10	11	2907	96.610	110	5155	51.288
11	9	2916	96.909	99	5254	52.273
12	11	2927	97.275	132	5386	53.587
13	3	2930	97.375	39	5425	53.975
14	6	2936	97.574	84	5509	54.810
15	5	2941	97.740	75	5584	55.557
16	3	2944	97.840	48	5632	56.034
17	4	2948	97.973	68	5700	56.711
18	5	2953	98.139	90	5790	57.606
19	5	2958	98.305	95	5885	58.551
20	1	2959	98.338	20	5905	58.750
21	2	2961	98.405	42	5947	59.168
22	2	2963	98.471	44	5991	59.606
23	1	2964	98.504	23	6014	59.835
24	3	2967	98.604	72	6086	60.551
25	1	2968	98.637	25	6111	60.800
26	2	2970	98.704	52	6163	61.317
27	2	2972	98.770	54	6217	61.855
28	2	2974	98.837	56	6273	62.412
29	1	2975	98.870	29	6302	62.700
31	2	2977	98.937	62	6364	63.317
35	1	2978	98.970	35	6399	63.665
36	1	2979	99.003	36	6435	64.023
37	1	2980	99.036	37	6472	64.392
39	1	2981	99.069	39	6511	64.780
41	1	2982	99.103	41	6552	65.188
42	1	2983	99.136	42	6594	65.605

TABLE B7 (CONT.) A CORPUS SUBSET OF 5 SAMPLES IN ASCENDING ORDER

X	FX	SUM FX	CUM% FX	FX*X	SUM FX*X	CUM% FX*X
44	1	2984	99.169	44	6638	66.043
45	1	2985	99.202	45	6683	66.491
46	1	2986	99.236	46	6729	66.949
47	1	2987	99.269	47	6776	67.416
49	1	2988	99.302	49	6825	67.904
50	1	2989	99.335	50	6875	68.401
53	1	2990	99.369	53	6928	68.928
56	1	2991	99.402	56	6984	69.486
60	1	2992	99.435	60	7044	70.083
61	1	2993	99.468	61	7105	70.689
62	1	2994	99.501	62	7167	71.306
64	1	2995	99.535	64	7231	71.943
67	1	2996	99.568	67	7298	72.610
76	1	2997	99.601	76	7374	73.366
86	1	2998	99.634	86	7460	74.221
91	1	2999	99.668	91	7551	75.127
95	1	3000	99.701	95	7646	76.072
101	1	3001	99.734	101	7747	77.077
126	1	3002	99.767	126	7873	78.331
131	1	3003	99.801	131	8004	79.634
212	1	3004	99.834	212	8216	81.743
226	1	3005	99.867	226	8442	83.992
228	1	3006	99.900	228	8670	86.260
237	1	3007	99.934	237	8907	88.618
442	1	3008	99.967	442	9349	93.016
702	1	3009	100.000	702	10051	100.000

TYPES = S0 = 3009   TOKENS = S1 = 10051   S2 = 1052813

MEAN = 3.3403   SD = 18.4046   V = 5.5099   K = 103.2207

TABLE BY SAMPLE A11, PRESS, REPORTAGE, SPORTS ('THE SUN,' BALTIMORE)

X	FX	SUM FX	CUM% FX	FX*X	SUM FX*X	CUM% FX*X
1	592	592	67.273	592	592	29.423
2	134	726	82.500	268	860	42.744
3	64	790	89.773	192	1052	52.286
4	27	817	92.841	108	1160	57.654
5	18	835	94.886	90	1250	62.127
6	13	848	96.364	78	1328	66.004
7	9	857	97.386	63	1391	69.135
8	4	861	97.841	32	1423	70.726
9	3	864	98.182	27	1450	72.068
10	1	865	98.295	10	1460	72.565
11	3	868	98.636	33	1493	74.205
12	1	869	98.750	12	1505	74.801
14	1	870	98.864	14	1519	75.497
15	2	872	99.091	30	1549	76.988
17	1	873	99.205	17	1566	77.833
22	1	874	99.318	22	1588	78.926
40	1	875	99.432	40	1628	80.915
49	1	876	99.545	49	1677	83.350
55	1	877	99.659	55	1732	86.083
58	1	878	99.773	58	1790	88.966
71	1	879	99.886	71	1861	92.495
151	1	880	100.000	151	2012	100.000

TYPES = S0 = 880   TOKENS = S1 = 2012   S2 = 44252   K = 104.3441
MEAN = 2.2864   SD = 6.7126   V = 2.9359

TABLE BY SAMPLE A10 PRESS, REPORTAGE POLITICAL ('THE ATLANTA CONSTITUTION')

X	FX	SUM FX	CUM% FX	FX*X	SUM FX*X	CUM% FX*X
1	518	518	65.404	518	518	26.056
2	138	656	82.828	275	794	39.940
3	44	700	88.384	132	926	46.579
4	30	730	92.172	120	1046	52.616
5	16	746	94.192	80	1126	56.640
6	10	756	95.455	60	1186	59.658
7	3	759	95.833	21	1207	60.714
8	1	760	95.960	8	1215	61.117
9	6	766	96.717	54	1269	63.833
10	3	769	97.096	30	1299	65.342
11	1	770	97.222	11	1310	65.895
12	3	773	97.601	36	1346	67.706
13	2	775	97.854	26	1372	69.014
14	3	778	98.232	42	1414	71.127
15	1	779	98.359	15	1429	71.881
18	2	781	98.611	36	1465	73.692
19	1	782	98.737	19	1484	74.648
21	1	783	98.864	21	1505	75.704
22	1	784	98.990	22	1527	76.811
24	1	785	99.116	24	1551	78.018
28	1	786	99.242	28	1579	79.427
40	2	788	99.495	80	1659	83.451
54	1	789	99.621	54	1713	86.167
55	1	790	99.747	55	1768	88.934
65	1	791	99.874	65	1833	92.203
155	1	792	100.000	155	1988	100.000

TYPES = S0 = 792   TOKENS = S1 = 1988   S2 = 46092   K = 111.5951
MEAN = 2.5101   SD = 7.2039   V = 2.8700

TABLE B10 SAMPLE A21, PRESS, REPORTAGE, SPOT NEWS ('THE DETROIT NEWS')

X	FX	SUM FX	CUM% FX	FX*X	SUM FX*X	CUM% FX*X
1	592	592	67.044	592	592	29.570
2	157	749	84.824	314	906	45.255
3	54	803	90.940	162	1068	53.347
4	19	822	93.092	76	1144	57.143
5	14	836	94.677	70	1214	60.639
6	10	846	95.810	60	1274	63.636
7	8	854	96.716	56	1330	66.434
8	5	859	97.282	40	1370	68.432
9	4	863	97.735	36	1406	70.230
10	1	864	97.848	10	1416	70.729
12	1	865	97.961	12	1428	71.329
13	1	866	98.075	13	1441	71.978
14	2	868	98.301	28	1469	73.377
16	2	870	98.528	32	1501	74.975
17	3	873	98.867	51	1552	77.522
18	1	874	98.981	18	1570	78.422
21	1	875	99.094	21	1591	79.471
26	1	876	99.207	26	1617	80.769
28	1	877	99.320	28	1645	82.168
40	1	878	99.434	40	1685	84.166
44	1	879	99.547	44	1729	86.364
51	1	880	99.660	51	1780	88.911
52	1	881	99.773	52	1832	91.508
54	1	882	99.887	54	1886	94.206
116	1	883	100.000	116	2002	100.000

TYPES = SO = 883   TOKENS = S1 = 2002   S2 = 33378   K = 78.2833

MEAN = 2.2673   SD = 5.7149   V = 2.5206

TABLE B11 SAMPLE A31, PRESS, REPORTAGE, CULTURAL ('THE MIAMI HERALD')

X	FX	SUM FX	CUM% FX	FX*X	SUM FX*X	CUM% FX*X
1	665	665	71.892	665	665	32.791
2	126	791	85.514	252	917	45.217
3	46	837	90.486	138	1055	52.022
4	31	868	93.838	124	1179	58.136
5	12	880	95.135	60	1239	61.095
6	6	886	95.784	36	1275	62.870
7	5	891	96.324	35	1310	64.596
8	9	900	97.297	72	1382	68.146
9	4	904	97.730	36	1418	69.921
10	2	906	97.946	20	1438	70.907
11	3	909	98.270	33	1471	72.535
12	4	913	98.703	48	1519	74.901
15	1	914	98.811	15	1534	75.641
19	1	915	98.919	19	1553	76.578
20	1	916	99.027	20	1573	77.564
21	1	917	99.135	21	1594	78.600
24	1	918	99.243	24	1618	79.783
39	1	919	99.351	39	1657	81.706
41	1	920	99.459	41	1698	83.728
43	2	922	99.676	86	1784	87.968
48	1	923	99.784	48	1832	90.335
67	1	924	99.892	67	1899	93.639
129	1	925	100.000	129	2028	100.000

TYPES = SO = 925   TOKENS = S1 = 2028   S2 = 37216   K = 85.5576

MEAN = 2.1924   SD = 5.9520   V = 2.7148

TABLE B12 SAMPLE A41, PRESS, REPORTAGE (ROBERT WALLACE, 'THIS IS THE WAY IT CAME ABOUT', IN 'LIFE' MAGAZINE)

X	FX	SUM FX	CUM% FX	FX*X	SUM FX*X	CUM% FX*X
1	589	589	72.626	589	589	29.391
2	98	687	84.710	196	785	39.172
3	39	726	89.519	117	902	45.010
4	24	750	92.478	96	998	49.800
5	9	759	93.588	45	1043	52.046
6	7	766	94.451	42	1085	54.142
7	7	773	95.314	49	1134	56.587
8	4	777	95.808	32	1166	58.184
9	2	779	96.054	18	1184	59.082
10	3	782	96.424	30	1214	60.579
11	4	786	96.917	44	1258	62.774
12	1	787	97.041	12	1270	63.373
13	4	791	97.534	52	1322	65.968
14	3	794	97.904	42	1364	68.064
15	4	798	98.397	60	1424	71.058
16	1	799	98.520	16	1440	71.856
17	1	800	98.644	17	1457	72.705
18	1	801	98.767	18	1475	73.603
20	2	803	99.014	40	1515	75.599
25	1	804	99.137	25	1540	76.846
28	1	805	99.260	28	1568	78.243
34	1	806	99.383	34	1602	79.940
44	1	807	99.507	44	1646	82.136
45	1	808	99.630	45	1691	84.381
56	1	809	99.753	56	1747	87.176
74	1	810	99.877	74	1821	90.868
183	1	811	100.000	183	2004	100.000

TYPES = S0 = 811   TOKENS = S1 = 2004   S2 = 56342   K = 135.3032

MEAN = 2.4710   SD = 7.9603   V = 3.2215

TABLE B13 SAMPLE B07, PRESS, EDITORIAL ('THE NEW YORK TIMES')

X	FX	SUM FX	CUM% FX	FX*X	SUM FX*X	CUM% FX*X
1	602	602	71.074	602	602	29.728
2	116	718	84.770	232	834	41.185
3	44	762	89.965	132	966	47.704
4	21	783	92.444	84	1050	51.852
5	14	797	94.097	70	1120	55.309
6	12	809	95.514	72	1192	58.864
7	9	818	96.576	63	1255	61.975
8	2	820	96.812	16	1271	62.765
9	2	822	97.048	18	1289	63.654
11	4	826	97.521	44	1333	65.827
12	2	828	97.757	24	1357	67.012
13	2	830	97.993	26	1383	68.296
15	1	831	98.111	15	1398	69.037
16	3	834	98.465	48	1446	71.407
17	1	835	98.583	17	1463	72.247
19	2	837	98.819	38	1501	74.123
20	2	839	99.055	40	1541	76.099
22	1	840	99.174	22	1563	77.185
28	1	841	99.292	28	1591	78.568
38	1	842	99.410	38	1629	80.444
44	1	843	99.528	44	1673	82.617
56	1	844	99.646	56	1729	85.383
62	1	845	99.764	62	1791	88.444
78	1	846	99.882	78	1869	92.296
156	1	847	100.000	156	2025	100.000

TYPES = S0 = 847   TOKENS = S1 = 2025   S2 = 49273   K = 115.2214

MEAN = 2.3908   SD = 7.2428   V = 3.0294

TABLE B14 SAMPLE B17, PRESS, EDITORIAL, LETTERS ('WHAT READERS HAVE TO SAY,' IN 'NEWARK EVENING NEWS' AND 'LETTERS TO THE EDITOR,' IN 'WASHINGTON POST')

X	FX	SUM FX	CUM% FX	FX*X	SUM FX*X	CUM% FX*X
1	552	552	69.260	552	552	27.313
2	112	664	83.312	224	776	38.397
3	48	712	89.335	144	920	45.522
4	21	733	91.970	84	1004	49.678
5	18	751	94.228	90	1094	54.132
6	9	760	95.358	54	1148	56.804
7	4	764	95.859	28	1176	58.189
8	5	769	96.487	40	1216	60.168
9	3	772	96.863	27	1243	61.504
10	4	776	97.365	40	1283	63.483
13	3	779	97.742	39	1322	65.413
15	1	780	97.867	15	1337	66.155
17	4	784	98.369	68	1405	69.520
18	1	785	98.494	18	1423	70.411
19	1	786	98.620	19	1442	71.351
21	1	787	98.745	21	1463	72.390
22	2	789	98.996	44	1507	74.567
24	1	790	99.122	24	1531	75.755
30	1	791	99.247	30	1561	77.239
42	1	792	99.373	42	1603	79.317
46	1	793	99.498	46	1649	81.593
48	1	794	99.624	48	1697	83.968
82	1	795	99.749	82	1779	88.026
93	1	796	99.875	93	1872	92.627
149	1	797	100.000	149	2021	100.000

TYPES = S0 = 797 TOKENS = S1 = 2021 S2 = 52917

MEAN = 2.5358 SD = 7.7437 V = 3.0538 K = 124.6094

TABLE B15 SAMPLE B27, PRESS, EDITORIAL, LETTERS ('LETTERS TO THE EDITOR,' IN 'SATURDAY REVIEW')

X	FX	SUM FX	CUM% FX	FX*X	SUM FX*X	CUM% FX*X
1	514	514	65.146	514	514	25.420
2	136	650	82.383	272	786	38.872
3	56	706	89.480	168	954	47.181
4	16	722	91.508	64	1018	50.346
5	13	735	93.156	65	1083	53.561
6	12	747	94.677	72	1155	57.122
7	7	754	95.564	49	1204	59.545
8	4	758	96.071	32	1236	61.128
9	6	764	96.831	54	1290	63.798
10	2	766	97.085	20	1310	64.787
11	4	770	97.592	44	1354	66.963
12	2	772	97.845	24	1378	68.150
13	3	775	98.226	39	1417	70.079
14	2	777	98.479	28	1445	71.464
19	1	778	98.606	19	1464	72.404
22	1	779	98.733	22	1486	73.492
23	1	780	98.859	23	1509	74.629
24	1	781	98.986	24	1533	75.816
25	1	782	99.113	25	1558	77.052
27	1	783	99.240	27	1585	78.388
40	1	784	99.366	40	1625	80.366
46	1	785	99.493	46	1671	82.641
57	2	787	99.747	114	1785	88.279
82	1	788	99.873	82	1867	92.334
155	1	789	100.000	155	2022	100.000

TYPES = S0 = 789 TOKENS = S1 = 2022 S2 = 49798 K = 116.8550

MEAN = 2.5627 SD = 7.5198 V = 2.9343

TABLE B16 SAMPLE C1C, PRESS, REVIEWS ('THE PROVIDENCE JOURNAL')

x	FX	SUM FX	CUM% FX	FX*X	SUM FX*X	CUM% FX*X
1	672	672	73.684	672	672	32.432
2	115	787	86.294	230	902	43.533
3	41	828	90.789	123	1025	49.469
4	31	859	94.189	124	1149	55.454
5	16	875	95.943	80	1229	59.315
6	3	878	96.272	18	1247	60.183
7	3	881	96.601	21	1268	61.197
8	3	884	96.930	24	1292	62.355
9	4	888	97.368	36	1328	64.093
10	2	890	97.588	20	1348	65.058
11	3	893	97.917	33	1381	66.651
12	1	894	98.026	12	1393	67.230
13	4	898	98.465	52	1445	69.739
15	2	900	98.684	30	1475	71.187
17	1	901	98.794	17	1492	72.008
19	1	902	98.904	19	1511	72.925
20	1	903	99.013	20	1531	73.890
30	1	904	99.123	30	1561	75.338
34	1	905	99.232	34	1595	76.979
37	1	906	99.342	37	1632	78.764
48	1	907	99.452	48	1680	81.081
51	1	908	99.561	51	1731	83.542
62	2	910	99.781	124	1855	89.527
81	1	911	99.890	81	1936	93.436
136	1	912	100.000	136	2072	100.000

TYPES = SO = 912   TOKENS = S1 = 2072   S2 = 47126

MEAN = 2.2719   SD = 6.8199   V = 3.0018   K = 104.9431

TABLE B17 SAMPLE D03, RELIGION (EDWARD E. KELLY, S.J., 'CHRISTIAN UNITY IN ENGLAND,' IN 'AMERICA' MAGAZINE)

x	FX	SUM FX	CUM% FX	FX*X	SUM FX*X	CUM% FX*X
1	523	523	67.571	523	523	25.253
2	115	638	82.429	230	753	36.359
3	45	683	88.243	135	888	42.878
4	18	701	90.568	72	960	46.354
5	12	713	92.119	60	1020	49.252
6	12	725	93.669	72	1092	52.728
7	5	730	94.315	35	1127	54.418
8	6	736	95.090	48	1175	56.736
9	7	743	95.995	63	1238	59.778
10	2	745	96.253	20	1258	60.744
11	3	748	96.641	33	1291	62.337
12	2	750	96.899	24	1315	63.496
13	1	751	97.028	13	1328	64.124
14	3	754	97.416	42	1370	66.152
15	4	758	97.933	60	1430	69.049
16	1	759	98.062	16	1446	69.821
17	3	762	98.450	51	1497	72.284
18	1	763	98.579	18	1515	73.153
20	1	764	98.708	20	1535	74.119
24	1	765	98.837	24	1559	75.278
25	2	767	99.096	50	1609	77.692
33	1	768	99.225	33	1642	79.285
39	1	769	99.354	39	1681	81.169
49	1	770	99.483	49	1730	83.535
55	1	771	99.612	55	1785	86.190
63	1	772	99.742	63	1848	89.232
94	1	773	99.871	94	1942	93.771
129	1	774	100.000	129	2071	100.000

TYPES = SO = 774   TOKENS = S1 = 2071   S2 = 47267

MEAN = 2.6757   SD = 7.3423   V = 2.7440   K = 105.3755

TABLE B18 SAMPLE D13, RELIGION (DONALD H. ANDREWS, 'THE NEW SCIENCE AND THE NEW FAITH' AND GEORGE B. LONGSTEET, 'THE SEEING IMPOSSIBLE,' BOTH IN 'SCIENCE OF MIND' MAGAZINE)

X	FX	SUM FX	CUM% FX	FX*X	SUM FX*X	CUM% FX*X
1	408	408	64.353	408	408	20.248
2	83	491	77.445	166	574	28.486
3	48	539	85.016	144	718	35.633
4	25	564	88.959	100	818	40.596
5	14	578	91.167	70	888	44.069
6	4	582	91.798	24	912	45.261
7	7	589	92.902	49	961	47.692
8	4	593	93.533	32	993	49.280
9	9	602	94.953	81	1074	53.300
10	1	603	95.110	10	1084	53.797
11	3	606	95.584	33	1117	55.434
12	2	608	95.899	24	1141	56.625
13	1	609	96.057	13	1154	57.270
14	4	613	96.688	56	1210	60.050
15	3	616	97.161	45	1255	62.283
17	4	620	97.792	68	1323	65.658
19	1	621	97.950	19	1342	66.600
20	1	622	98.107	20	1362	67.593
22	1	623	98.265	22	1384	68.685
26	1	624	98.423	26	1410	69.975
28	1	625	98.580	28	1438	71.365
30	1	626	98.738	30	1468	72.854
33	1	627	98.896	33	1501	74.491
42	1	628	99.054	42	1543	76.576
44	1	629	99.211	44	1587	78.759
45	1	630	99.369	45	1632	80.993
64	1	631	99.527	64	1696	84.169
68	1	632	99.685	68	1764	87.543
94	1	633	99.842	94	1858	92.208
157	1	634	100.000	157	2015	100.000

TYPES = S0 = 634   TOKENS = S1 = 2015   S2 = 59553

MEAN = 3.1782   SD = 5.1559   V = 2.8808   K = 141.7113

TABLE B19 SAMPLE E06, SKILLS AND HOBBIES (JOSEPH E. CHOATE, 'THE AMERICAN BOATING SCENE,' IN 'RUDDER' MAGAZINE)

X	FX	SUM FX	CUM% FX	FX*X	SUM FX*X	CUM% FX*X
1	565	565	69.926	565	565	28.264
2	110	675	83.540	220	785	39.270
3	44	719	88.985	132	917	45.873
4	23	742	91.832	92	1009	50.475
5	18	760	94.059	90	1099	54.977
6	8	768	95.049	48	1147	57.379
7	5	773	95.668	35	1182	59.130
8	6	779	96.411	48	1230	61.531
9	4	783	96.906	36	1266	63.332
10	3	786	97.277	30	1296	64.832
11	1	787	97.401	11	1307	65.383
12	2	789	97.648	24	1331	66.583
14	2	791	97.896	28	1359	67.984
16	1	792	98.020	16	1375	68.784
17	4	796	98.515	68	1443	72.186
18	2	798	98.762	36	1479	73.987
19	1	799	98.886	19	1498	74.937
26	1	800	99.010	26	1524	76.238
29	1	801	99.134	29	1553	77.689
34	1	802	99.257	34	1587	79.390
47	1	803	99.381	47	1634	81.741
49	1	804	99.505	49	1683	84.192
54	1	805	99.629	54	1737	86.893
64	1	806	99.752	64	1801	90.095
70	1	807	99.876	70	1871	93.597
128	1	808	100.000	128	1999	100.000

TYPES = S0 = 808   TOKENS = S1 = 1999   S2 = 42561

MEAN = 2.4740   SD = 6.8230   V = 2.7579   K = 101.5064

TABLE B20 SAMPLE E16, SKILLS AND HOBBIES (HAL KELLY, "BUILD HOTEL," IN "MECHANIX ILLUSTRATED" MAGAZINE)

X	FX	SUM FX	CUM% FX	FX*X	SUM FX*X	CUM% FX*X
1	386	386	59.385	386	386	19.261
2	115	501	77.077	230	616	30.739
3	45	546	84.000	135	751	37.475
4	30	576	88.615	120	871	43.463
5	17	593	91.231	85	956	47.705
6	7	600	92.308	42	998	49.800
7	10	610	93.846	70	1068	53.293
8	9	619	95.231	72	1140	56.886
9	4	623	95.846	36	1176	58.683
10	4	627	96.462	40	1216	60.679
11	4	631	97.077	44	1260	62.874
12	2	633	97.385	24	1284	64.072
13	2	635	97.692	26	1310	65.369
14	2	637	98.000	28	1338	66.766
15	1	638	98.154	15	1353	67.515
19	1	639	98.308	19	1372	68.463
25	3	642	98.769	75	1447	72.206
32	1	643	98.923	32	1479	73.802
44	1	644	99.077	44	1523	75.998
45	2	646	99.385	90	1613	80.489
51	1	647	99.538	51	1664	83.034
62	1	648	99.692	62	1726	86.128
84	1	649	99.846	84	1810	90.319
194	1	650	100.000	194	2004	100.000

TYPES = S0 = 650   TOKENS = S1 = 2004   S2 = 66308

MEAN = 3.0831   SD = 9.6181   V = 3.1196   K = 160.1189

TABLE B21 SAMPLE E26, SKILLS AND HOBBIES (BERN DIBNER, "OERSTED AND THE DISCOVERY OF ELECTROMAGNETISM," IN "ELECTRICAL ENGINEERING" MAGAZINE)

X	FX	SUM FX	CUM% FX	FX*X	SUM FX*X	CUM% FX*X
1	565	565	70.099	565	565	28.081
2	115	680	84.367	230	795	39.513
3	45	725	89.950	135	930	46.223
4	23	748	92.804	92	1022	50.795
5	11	759	94.165	55	1077	53.529
6	8	767	95.161	48	1125	55.915
7	8	775	96.154	56	1181	58.698
8	4	779	96.650	32	1213	60.288
10	2	781	96.898	20	1233	61.282
11	2	783	97.146	22	1255	62.376
12	4	787	97.643	48	1303	64.761
13	4	791	98.139	52	1355	67.346
14	3	794	98.511	42	1397	69.433
17	1	795	98.635	17	1414	70.278
22	1	796	98.759	22	1436	71.372
24	1	797	98.883	24	1460	72.565
31	2	799	99.132	62	1522	75.646
35	1	800	99.256	35	1557	77.386
48	1	801	99.380	48	1605	79.771
51	1	802	99.504	51	1656	82.306
74	1	803	99.628	74	1730	85.984
78	1	804	99.752	78	1808	89.861
82	1	805	99.876	82	1890	93.936
122	1	806	100.000	122	2012	100.000

TYPES = S0 = 806   TOKENS = S1 = 2012   S2 = 47860

MEAN = 2.4963   SD = 7.2903   V = 2.9205   K = 113.2568

TABLE B22 SAMPLE E36, SKILLS AND HOBBIES (ETHEL NORLING, 'RENTING A CAR IN EUROPE,' IN 'PLAYBILL' MAGAZINE)

X	FX	SUM FX	CUM% FX	FX*X	SUM FX*X	CUM% FX*X
1	446	446	65.588	446	446	22.068
2	94	540	79.412	188	634	31.371
3	43	583	85.735	129	763	37.754
4	24	607	89.265	96	859	42.504
5	14	621	91.324	70	929	45.967
6	9	630	92.647	54	983	48.639
7	5	635	93.382	35	1018	50.371
8	7	642	94.412	56	1074	53.142
9	6	648	95.294	54	1128	55.814
10	1	649	95.441	10	1138	56.309
11	5	654	96.176	55	1193	59.030
12	2	656	96.471	24	1217	60.218
13	3	659	96.912	39	1256	62.147
15	3	662	97.353	45	1301	64.374
16	1	663	97.500	16	1317	65.166
17	1	664	97.647	17	1334	66.007
22	1	665	97.794	22	1356	67.095
23	4	669	98.382	92	1448	71.648
27	1	670	98.529	27	1475	72.984
28	1	671	98.676	28	1503	74.369
32	1	672	98.824	32	1535	75.952
39	1	673	98.971	39	1574	77.882
41	1	674	99.118	41	1615	79.911
44	1	675	99.265	44	1659	82.088
47	1	676	99.412	47	1706	84.414
54	1	677	99.559	54	1760	87.086
68	1	678	99.706	68	1828	90.450
69	1	679	99.853	69	1897	93.864
124	1	680	100.000	124	2021	100.000

TYPES = S0 = 680 TOKENS = S1 = 2021 S2 = 46327

MEAN = 2.9721 SD = 7.7003 V = 2.5909 K = 108.4750

TABLE B23 SAMPLE F10, POPULAR LORE (JACK KAPLAN, 'THE HEALTH MACHINE MENACE: THERAPY BY WITCHCRAFT,' IN 'TODAY'S HEALTH' MAGAZINE)

X	FX	SUM FX	CUM% FX	FX*X	SUM FX*X	CUM% FX*X
1	530	530	66.250	530	530	26.421
2	134	664	83.000	268	798	39.781
3	49	713	89.125	147	945	47.109
4	22	735	91.875	88	1033	51.495
5	13	748	93.500	65	1098	54.736
6	5	753	94.125	30	1128	56.231
7	9	762	95.250	63	1191	59.372
8	5	767	95.875	40	1231	61.366
9	6	773	96.625	54	1285	64.058
10	4	777	97.125	40	1325	66.052
11	1	778	97.250	11	1336	66.600
12	1	779	97.375	12	1348	67.198
13	1	780	97.500	13	1361	67.846
14	2	782	97.750	28	1389	69.242
15	2	784	98.000	30	1419	70.738
16	1	785	98.125	16	1435	71.535
17	1	786	98.250	17	1452	72.383
19	1	787	98.375	19	1471	73.330
20	3	790	98.750	60	1531	76.321
25	1	791	98.875	25	1556	77.567
26	1	792	99.000	26	1582	78.863
28	1	793	99.125	28	1610	80.259
32	1	794	99.250	32	1642	81.854
34	1	795	99.375	34	1676	83.549
44	1	796	99.500	44	1720	85.743
49	1	797	99.625	49	1769	88.185
71	1	798	99.750	71	1840	91.725
72	1	799	99.875	72	1912	95.314
94	1	800	100.000	94	2006	100.000

TYPES = S0 = 800 TOKENS = S1 = 2006 S2 = 35056

MEAN = 2.5075 SD = 6.1264 V = 2.4432 K = 82.1314

TABLE B24 SAMPLE F20, POPULAR LORE (KENNETH ALLSOP, 'THE BOOTLEGGERS AND THEIR ERA')

X	FX	SUM FX	CUM% FX	FX*X	SUM FX*X	CUM% FX*X
1	726	726	79.171	726	726	36.155
2	99	825	89.967	198	924	46.016
3	32	857	93.457	96	1020	50.797
4	19	876	95.529	76	1096	54.582
5	6	882	96.183	30	1126	56.076
6	5	887	96.728	30	1156	57.570
7	4	891	97.165	28	1184	58.964
8	1	892	97.274	8	1192	59.363
9	5	897	97.819	45	1237	61.604
11	1	898	97.928	11	1248	62.151
12	1	899	98.037	12	1260	62.749
13	1	900	98.146	13	1273	63.396
15	1	901	98.255	15	1288	64.143
18	1	902	98.364	18	1306	65.040
20	2	904	98.582	40	1346	67.032
22	1	905	98.691	22	1368	68.127
24	1	906	98.800	24	1392	69.323
25	1	907	98.909	25	1417	70.568
31	1	908	99.019	31	1448	72.112
34	1	909	99.128	34	1482	73.805
38	1	910	99.237	38	1520	75.697
46	1	911	99.346	46	1566	77.988
50	1	912	99.455	50	1616	80.478
55	1	913	99.564	55	1671	83.217
68	1	914	99.673	68	1739	86.604
70	1	915	99.782	70	1809	90.090
81	1	916	99.891	81	1890	94.123
118	1	917	100.000	118	2008	100.000

TYPES = S0 = 917   TOKENS = S1 = 2008   S2 = 47388

MEAN = 2.1897   SD = 6.8471   V = 3.1269   K = 112.5478

TABLE B25 SAMPLE F30, POPULAR LORE (FREDERIC A. BIRMINGHAM, 'THE IVY LEAGUE TODAY')

X	FX	SUM FX	CUM% FX	FX*X	SUM FX*X	CUM% FX*X
1	631	631	72.696	631	631	31.534
2	116	747	86.060	232	863	43.128
3	46	793	91.359	138	1001	50.025
4	21	814	93.779	84	1085	54.223
5	7	821	94.585	35	1120	55.972
6	11	832	95.853	66	1186	59.270
7	8	840	96.774	56	1242	62.069
8	1	841	96.889	8	1250	62.469
9	4	845	97.350	36	1286	64.268
10	1	846	97.465	10	1296	64.768
11	3	849	97.811	33	1329	66.417
12	2	851	98.041	24	1353	67.616
13	2	853	98.272	26	1379	68.916
14	1	854	98.387	14	1393	69.615
15	3	857	98.733	45	1438	71.864
16	1	858	98.848	16	1454	72.664
21	1	859	98.963	21	1475	73.713
23	1	860	99.078	23	1498	74.863
25	1	861	99.194	25	1523	76.112
26	1	862	99.309	26	1549	77.411
34	1	863	99.424	34	1583	79.110
60	1	864	99.539	60	1643	82.109
62	1	865	99.654	62	1705	85.207
68	1	866	99.770	68	1773	88.606
78	1	867	99.885	78	1851	92.504
150	1	868	100.000	150	2001	100.000

TYPES = S0 = 868   TOKENS = S1 = 2001   S2 = 49491

MEAN = 2.3053   SD = 7.1905   V = 3.1191   K = 118.6063

TABLE B26 SAMPLE F40, POPULAR LORE (WILLIAM GREENLEAF, 'MONOPOLY ON WHEELS')

X	FX	SUM FX	CUM% FX	FX*X	SUM FX*X	CUM% FX*X
1	590	590	72.215	590	590	29.426
2	104	694	84.945	208	798	39.800
3	42	736	90.086	126	924	46.085
4	16	752	92.044	64	988	49.277
5	14	766	93.758	70	1058	52.768
6	3	769	94.125	18	1076	53.666
7	12	781	95.594	84	1160	57.855
8	8	789	96.573	64	1224	61.047
9	3	792	96.940	27	1251	62.394
10	2	794	97.185	20	1271	63.392
11	2	796	97.430	22	1293	64.489
12	5	801	98.042	60	1353	67.481
13	2	803	98.286	26	1379	68.778
15	1	804	98.409	15	1394	69.526
16	1	805	98.531	16	1410	70.324
17	1	806	98.654	17	1427	71.172
19	2	808	98.898	38	1465	73.067
23	1	809	99.021	23	1488	74.214
25	1	810	99.143	25	1513	75.461
26	1	811	99.266	26	1539	76.758
33	1	812	99.388	33	1572	78.404
42	1	813	99.510	42	1614	80.499
43	1	814	99.633	43	1657	82.643
58	1	815	99.755	58	1715	85.536
115	1	816	99.878	115	1830	91.272
175	1	817	100.000	175	2005	100.000

TYPES = S0 = 817   TOKENS = S1 = 2005   S2 = 60179

MEAN = 2.4541   SD = 8.2241   V = 3.3512   K = 144.7105

TABLE B27 SAMPLE G02, BELLES LETTRES (ARTHUR S. MILLER, 'TOWARD A CONCEPT OF NATIONAL RESPONSIBILITY,' IN 'THE YALE REVIEW')

X	FX	SUM FX	CUM% FX	FX*X	SUM FX*X	CUM% FX*X
1	537	537	69.922	537	537	26.440
2	107	644	83.854	214	751	36.977
3	36	680	88.542	108	859	42.294
4	19	699	91.016	76	935	46.036
5	15	714	92.969	75	1010	49.729
6	13	727	94.661	78	1088	53.570
7	7	734	95.573	49	1137	55.982
8	1	735	95.703	8	1145	56.376
9	5	740	96.354	45	1190	58.592
10	4	744	96.875	40	1230	60.561
11	3	747	97.266	33	1263	62.186
12	4	751	97.786	48	1311	64.549
13	3	754	98.177	39	1350	66.470
16	1	755	98.307	16	1366	67.257
17	1	756	98.438	17	1383	68.095
18	1	757	98.568	18	1401	68.981
20	1	758	98.698	20	1421	69.966
21	1	759	98.828	21	1442	70.999
26	1	760	98.958	26	1468	72.280
30	1	761	99.089	30	1498	73.757
40	1	762	99.219	40	1538	75.726
42	1	763	99.349	42	1580	77.794
46	1	764	99.479	46	1626	80.059
51	1	765	99.609	51	1677	82.570
55	1	766	99.740	55	1732	85.278
115	1	767	99.870	115	1847	90.940
184	1	768	100.000	184	2031	100.000

TYPES = S0 = 768   TOKENS = S1 = 2031   S2 = 66567

MEAN = 2.6445   SD = 8.9265   V = 3.3755   K = 156.4523

TABLE B28 SAMPLE G12; BELLES LETTRES (TOM F. DRIVER, 'BECKETT BY THE MADELEINE,' IN 'COLUMBIA UNIVERSITY FORUM')

X	FX	SUM FX	CUM% FX	FX*X	SUM FX*X	CUM% FX*X
1	451	451	64.892	451	451	22.250
2	107	558	80.288	214	665	32.807
3	42	600	86.331	126	791	39.023
4	21	621	89.353	84	875	43.167
5	14	635	91.367	70	945	46.621
6	10	645	92.806	60	1005	49.581
7	8	653	93.957	56	1061	52.343
8	5	658	94.676	40	1101	54.317
9	4	662	95.252	36	1137	56.093
10	4	666	95.827	40	1177	58.066
11	2	668	96.115	22	1199	59.151
12	2	670	96.403	24	1223	60.335
13	2	672	96.691	26	1249	61.618
14	2	674	96.978	28	1277	62.999
15	1	675	97.122	15	1292	63.740
16	1	676	97.266	16	1308	64.529
17	2	678	97.554	34	1342	66.206
18	2	680	97.842	36	1378	67.982
19	2	682	98.129	38	1416	69.857
21	1	683	98.273	21	1437	70.893
23	1	684	98.417	23	1460	72.028
28	1	685	98.561	28	1488	73.409
29	1	686	98.705	29	1517	74.840
31	1	687	98.849	31	1548	76.369
39	1	688	98.993	39	1587	78.293
42	1	689	99.137	42	1629	80.365
43	1	690	99.281	43	1672	82.486
52	1	691	99.424	52	1724	85.052
54	1	692	99.568	54	1778	87.716
57	1	693	99.712	57	1835	90.528
62	1	694	99.856	62	1897	93.587
130	1	695	100.000	130	2027	100.000

TYPES = S0 = 695   TOKENS = S1 = 2027   S2 = 45731

MEAN = 2.9165   SD = 7.5693   V = 2.5953   K = 106.3686

TABLE B29 SAMPLE G22; BELLES LETTRES (KENNETH REINER, 'COPING WITH RUNAWAY TECHNOLOGY,' IN 'THE ETHICAL OUTLOOK')

X	FX	SUM FX	CUM% FX	FX*X	SUM FX*X	CUM% FX*X
1	585	585	70.567	585	585	28.889
2	106	691	83.353	212	797	39.358
3	47	738	89.023	141	938	46.321
4	25	763	92.039	100	1038	51.259
5	7	770	92.883	35	1073	52.988
6	10	780	94.089	60	1133	55.951
7	7	787	94.934	49	1182	58.370
8	8	795	95.899	64	1246	61.531
9	7	802	96.743	63	1309	64.642
10	1	803	96.864	10	1319	65.136
11	2	805	97.105	22	1341	66.222
12	3	808	97.467	36	1377	68.000
13	2	810	97.708	26	1403	69.284
14	3	813	98.070	42	1445	71.358
15	2	815	98.311	30	1475	72.839
16	2	817	98.552	32	1507	74.420
17	1	818	98.673	17	1524	75.259
18	1	819	98.794	18	1542	76.148
19	1	820	98.914	19	1561	77.086
22	2	822	99.156	44	1605	79.259
27	1	823	99.276	27	1632	80.593
45	1	824	99.397	45	1677	82.815
53	1	825	99.517	53	1730	85.432
54	1	826	99.638	54	1784	88.099
67	1	827	99.759	67	1851	91.407
75	1	828	99.879	75	1926	95.111
99	1	829	100.000	99	2025	100.000

TYPES = S0 = 829   TOKENS = S1 = 2025   S2 = 36787

MEAN = 2.4427   SD = 6.1974   V = 2.5371   K = 84.7724

TABLE B30   SAMPLE G32, BELLES LETTRES (FINIS FARR, 'FRANK LLOYD WRIGHT')

X	FX	SUM FX	CUM% FX	FX*X	SUM FX*X	CUM% FX*X
1	556	556	69.937	556	556	27.620
2	119	675	84.906	238	794	39.444
3	36	711	89.434	108	902	44.809
4	19	730	91.824	76	978	48.584
5	15	745	93.711	75	1053	52.310
6	11	756	95.094	66	1119	55.589
7	3	759	95.472	21	1140	56.632
8	2	761	95.723	16	1156	57.427
9	2	763	95.975	18	1174	58.321
10	4	767	96.478	40	1214	60.308
11	3	770	96.855	33	1247	61.947
12	2	772	97.107	24	1271	63.140
13	3	775	97.484	39	1310	65.077
14	1	776	97.610	14	1324	65.772
15	2	778	97.862	30	1354	67.263
17	1	779	97.987	17	1371	68.107
18	2	781	98.239	36	1407	69.896
19	2	783	98.491	38	1445	71.783
20	1	784	98.616	20	1465	72.777
24	1	785	98.742	24	1489	73.969
29	1	786	98.868	29	1518	75.410
30	1	787	98.994	30	1548	76.900
34	1	788	99.119	34	1582	78.589
38	1	789	99.245	38	1620	80.477
44	1	790	99.371	44	1664	82.663
58	1	791	99.497	58	1722	85.544
61	2	793	99.748	122	1844	91.605
66	1	794	99.874	66	1910	94.883
103	1	795	100.000	103	2013	100.000

TYPES = SO = 795   TOKENS = S1 = 2013   S2 = 39755

MEAN = 2.5321   SD = 6.6026   V = 2.6076   K = 93.1402

TABLE B31   SAMPLE G42, BELLES LETTRES (HAROLD D. LASSWELL, 'EPILOGUE,' TO 'THE JEW IN A GENTILE WORLD, AN ANTHOLOGY OF WRITINGS ABOUT JEWS BY NON-JEWS')

X	FX	SUM FX	CUM% FX	FX*X	SUM FX*X	CUM% FX*X
1	551	551	68.447	551	551	27.129
2	122	673	83.602	244	795	39.143
3	56	729	90.559	168	963	47.415
4	22	751	93.292	88	1051	51.748
5	9	760	94.410	45	1096	53.964
6	6	766	95.155	36	1132	55.736
7	8	774	96.149	56	1188	58.493
8	3	777	96.522	24	1212	59.675
9	2	779	96.770	18	1230	60.561
10	3	782	97.143	30	1260	62.038
11	3	785	97.516	33	1293	63.663
12	2	787	97.764	24	1317	64.845
14	2	789	98.012	28	1345	66.224
15	2	791	98.261	30	1375	67.701
17	2	793	98.509	34	1409	69.375
19	2	795	98.758	38	1447	71.246
21	2	797	99.006	42	1489	73.314
27	1	798	99.130	27	1516	74.643
34	1	799	99.255	34	1550	76.317
41	1	800	99.379	41	1591	78.336
53	1	801	99.503	53	1644	80.945
56	1	802	99.627	56	1700	83.703
57	1	803	99.752	57	1757	86.509
121	1	804	99.876	121	1878	92.467
153	1	805	100.000	153	2031	100.000

TYPES = SO = 805   TOKENS = S1 = 2031   S2 = 57867

MEAN = 2.5230   SD = 8.0944   V = 3.2083   K = 135.3613

TABLE B32 SAMPLE G52, BELLES LETTRES (ROBERT L. DUNCAN, 'THE RELUCTANT GENERAL')

X	FX	SUM FX	CUM% FX	FX*X	SUM FX*X	CUM% FX*X
1	541	541	70.443	541	541	26.624
2	105	646	84.115	210	751	36.959
3	51	697	90.755	153	904	44.488
4	15	712	92.708	60	964	47.441
5	10	722	94.010	50	1014	49.902
6	8	730	95.052	48	1062	52.264
7	4	734	95.573	28	1090	53.642
8	5	739	96.224	40	1130	55.610
9	3	742	96.615	27	1157	56.939
10	3	745	97.005	30	1187	58.415
12	1	746	97.135	12	1199	59.006
14	2	748	97.396	28	1227	60.384
15	1	749	97.526	15	1242	61.122
17	1	750	97.656	17	1259	61.959
18	1	751	97.786	18	1277	62.844
19	3	754	98.177	57	1334	65.650
22	1	755	98.307	22	1356	66.732
25	1	756	98.438	25	1381	67.963
30	2	758	98.698	60	1441	70.915
32	1	759	98.828	32	1473	72.490
34	1	760	98.958	34	1507	74.163
41	1	761	99.089	41	1548	76.181
43	1	762	99.219	43	1591	78.297
45	1	763	99.349	45	1636	80.512
58	1	764	99.479	58	1694	83.366
59	2	766	99.740	118	1812	89.173
75	1	767	99.870	75	1887	92.864
145	1	768	100.000	145	2032	100.000

TYPES = S0 = 768   TOKENS = S1 = 2032   S2 = 53334

MEAN = 2.6458   SD = 7.9022   V = 2.9867   K = 124.2473

TABLE B33 SAMPLE G62, BELLES LETTRES (C. H. CRAMER, 'NEWTON D. BAKER')

X	FX	SUM FX	CUM% FX	FX*X	SUM FX*X	CUM% FX*X
1	655	655	74.686	655	655	32.250
2	102	757	86.317	204	859	42.294
3	54	811	92.474	162	1021	50.271
4	14	825	94.071	56	1077	53.028
5	13	838	95.553	65	1142	56.228
6	6	844	96.237	36	1178	58.001
7	4	848	96.693	28	1206	59.380
8	3	851	97.035	24	1230	60.561
9	4	855	97.491	36	1266	62.334
10	3	858	97.834	30	1296	63.811
11	1	859	97.948	11	1307	64.353
12	2	861	98.176	24	1331	65.534
13	1	862	98.290	13	1344	66.174
14	2	864	98.518	28	1372	67.553
17	3	867	98.860	51	1423	70.064
19	1	868	98.974	19	1442	70.999
20	1	869	99.088	20	1462	71.984
29	1	870	99.202	29	1491	73.412
43	1	871	99.316	43	1534	75.529
48	1	872	99.430	48	1582	77.893
53	1	873	99.544	53	1635	80.502
58	1	874	99.658	58	1693	83.358
62	1	875	99.772	62	1755	86.411
91	1	876	99.886	91	1846	90.891
185	1	877	100.000	185	2031	100.000

TYPES = S0 = 877   TOKENS = S1 = 2031   S2 = 63441

MEAN = 2.3158   SD = 8.1839   V = 3.5338   K = 148.8741

TABLE B34 SAMPLE G72, BELLES LETTRES (J. W. FULBRIGHT, 'FOR A CONCERT OF FREE NATIONS,' IN 'FOREIGN AFFAIRS' MAGAZINE)

X	FX	SUM FX	CUM% FX	FX*X	SUM FX*X	CUM% FX*X
1	471	471	65.782	471	471	23.340
2	112	583	81.425	224	695	34.440
3	39	622	86.871	117	812	40.238
4	19	641	89.525	76	888	44.004
5	23	664	92.737	115	1003	49.703
6	11	675	94.274	66	1069	52.973
7	8	683	95.391	56	1125	55.748
8	7	690	96.369	56	1181	58.523
9	1	691	96.508	9	1190	58.969
10	1	692	96.648	10	1200	59.465
11	5	697	97.346	55	1255	62.190
12	1	698	97.486	12	1267	62.785
13	2	700	97.765	26	1293	64.073
14	2	702	98.045	28	1321	65.461
16	1	703	98.184	16	1337	66.254
17	2	705	98.464	34	1371	67.939
20	1	706	98.603	20	1391	68.930
24	1	707	98.743	24	1415	70.119
25	1	708	98.883	25	1440	71.358
34	1	709	99.022	34	1474	73.043
39	1	710	99.162	39	1513	74.975
41	1	711	99.302	41	1554	77.007
44	1	712	99.441	44	1598	79.187
54	1	713	99.581	54	1652	81.863
64	1	714	99.721	64	1716	85.035
138	1	715	99.860	138	1854	91.873
164	1	716	100.000	164	2018	100.000

TYPES = S0 = 716   TOKENS = S1 = 2018   S2 = 66726
MEAN = 2.8184   SD = 9.2330   V = 3.2759   K = 158.8970

TABLE B35 SAMPLE H07, MISCELLANEOUS, GOVERNMENT DOCUMENTS (RHODE ISLAND LEGISLATIVE COUNCIL, 'UNIFORM FISCAL YEAR FOR MUNICIPALITIES')

X	FX	SUM FX	CUM% FX	FX*X	SUM FX*X	CUM% FX*X
1	403	403	60.968	403	403	19.063
2	108	511	77.307	216	619	29.281
3	38	549	83.056	114	733	34.674
4	24	573	86.687	96	829	39.215
5	17	590	89.259	85	914	43.236
6	15	605	91.528	90	1004	47.493
7	11	616	93.192	77	1081	51.135
8	4	620	93.797	32	1113	52.649
9	8	628	95.008	72	1185	56.055
10	2	630	95.310	20	1205	57.001
11	5	635	96.067	55	1260	59.603
12	1	636	96.218	12	1272	60.170
13	3	639	96.672	39	1311	62.015
14	1	640	96.823	14	1325	62.677
15	1	641	96.974	15	1340	63.387
16	3	644	97.428	48	1388	65.658
18	1	645	97.579	18	1406	66.509
19	2	647	97.882	38	1444	68.307
20	2	649	98.185	40	1484	70.199
24	1	650	98.336	24	1508	71.334
25	1	651	98.487	25	1533	72.517
26	1	652	98.638	26	1559	73.746
32	2	654	98.941	64	1623	76.774
43	1	655	99.092	43	1666	78.808
49	1	656	99.244	49	1715	81.126
50	1	657	99.395	50	1765	83.491
63	1	658	99.546	63	1828	86.471
76	1	659	99.697	76	1904	90.066
85	1	660	99.849	85	1989	94.087
125	1	661	100.000	125	2114	100.000

TYPES = S0 = 661   TOKENS = S1 = 2114   S2 = 51730
MEAN = 3.1982   SD = 8.2481   V = 2.5790   K = 111.0227

TABLE B36 SAMPLE H17, MISCELLANEOUS, GOVERNMENT DOCUMENTS (U.S. REPORTS, 'CASES ADJUDGED IN THE SUPREME COURT, OCTOBER TERM 1959, AUGUST SPECIAL TERM 1960')

x	FX	SUM FX	CUM% FX	FX*X	SUM FX*X	CUM% FX*X
1	404	404	62.250	404	404	18.012
2	98	502	77.350	196	600	26.750
3	41	543	83.667	123	723	32.234
4	19	562	86.595	76	799	35.622
5	20	582	89.676	100	899	40.080
6	12	594	91.525	72	971	43.290
7	7	601	92.604	49	1020	45.475
8	4	605	93.220	32	1052	46.901
9	8	613	94.453	72	1124	50.111
10	3	616	94.915	30	1154	51.449
11	3	619	95.377	33	1187	52.920
12	2	621	95.686	24	1211	53.990
13	1	622	95.840	13	1224	54.570
14	2	624	96.148	28	1252	55.818
16	3	627	96.610	48	1300	57.958
17	2	629	96.918	34	1334	59.474
18	1	630	97.072	18	1352	60.276
19	1	631	97.226	19	1371	61.123
20	2	633	97.535	40	1411	62.907
21	1	634	97.689	21	1432	63.843
22	1	635	97.843	22	1454	64.824
24	1	636	97.997	24	1478	65.894
26	1	637	98.151	26	1504	67.053
28	1	638	98.305	28	1532	68.301
30	1	639	98.459	30	1562	69.639
32	1	640	98.613	32	1594	71.066
40	1	641	98.767	40	1634	72.849
42	1	642	98.921	42	1676	74.721
48	2	644	99.230	96	1772	79.001
49	1	645	99.384	49	1821	81.186
51	1	646	99.538	51	1872	83.460
88	2	648	99.846	176	2048	91.306
195	1	649	100.000	195	2243	100.000

TYPES = S0 = 649   TOKENS = S1 = 2243   S2 = 79363

MEAN = 3.4561   SD = 10.5043   V = 3.0394   K = 153.2881

TABLE B37 SAMPLE H27, MISCELLANEOUS, INDUSTRY REPORTS (LEESONA CORPORATION, 'ANNUAL REPORT FOR THE YEAR 1960')

x	FX	SUM FX	CUM% FX	FX*X	SUM FX*X	CUM% FX*X
1	493	493	64.783	493	493	24.037
2	122	615	80.815	244	737	35.934
3	44	659	86.597	132	869	42.370
4	28	687	90.276	112	981	47.830
5	21	708	93.035	105	1086	52.950
6	8	716	94.087	48	1134	55.290
7	3	719	94.481	21	1155	56.314
8	5	724	95.138	40	1195	58.264
9	6	730	95.926	54	1249	60.897
10	6	736	96.715	60	1309	63.823
11	3	739	97.109	33	1342	65.431
12	3	742	97.503	36	1378	67.187
13	1	743	97.635	13	1391	67.821
14	1	744	97.766	14	1405	68.503
15	2	746	98.029	30	1435	69.966
17	1	747	98.160	17	1452	70.795
19	1	748	98.292	19	1471	71.721
20	2	750	98.555	40	1511	73.671
21	1	751	98.686	21	1532	74.695
23	2	753	98.949	46	1578	76.930
24	1	754	99.080	24	1602	78.108
30	1	755	99.212	30	1632	79.571
41	1	756	99.363	41	1673	81.570
49	1	757	99.474	49	1722	83.959
69	1	758	99.606	69	1791	87.323
71	1	759	99.737	71	1862	90.785
76	1	760	99.869	76	1938	94.490
113	1	761	100.000	113	2051	100.000

TYPES = S0 = 761   TOKENS = S1 = 2051   S2 = 42655

MEAN = 2.6951   SD = 6.9848   V = 2.5916   K = 96.5245

TABLE B38   SAMPLE J07, LEARNED AND SCIENTIFIC WRITINGS (J. F. VEDDER, "MICROMETEORITES," IN "SATELLITE ENVIRONMENT HANDBOOK")

x	FX	SUM FX	CUM% FX	FX*X	SUM FX*X	CUM% FX*X
1	362	362	56.386	362	362	16.963
2	124	486	75.701	248	610	28.585
3	49	535	83.333	147	757	35.473
4	23	558	86.916	92	849	39.784
5	22	580	90.343	110	959	44.939
6	15	595	92.679	90	1049	49.157
7	9	604	94.081	63	1112	52.109
8	7	611	95.171	56	1168	54.733
9	2	613	95.483	18	1186	55.576
10	3	616	95.950	30	1216	56.982
11	2	618	96.262	22	1238	58.013
12	1	619	96.417	12	1250	58.575
13	1	620	96.573	13	1263	59.185
14	1	621	96.729	14	1277	59.841
15	3	624	97.196	45	1322	61.949
16	3	627	97.664	48	1370	64.199
17	1	628	97.819	17	1387	64.995
18	1	629	97.975	18	1405	65.839
19	2	631	98.287	38	1443	67.619
23	1	632	98.442	23	1466	68.697
25	2	634	98.754	50	1516	71.040
31	1	635	98.910	31	1547	72.493
40	1	636	99.065	40	1587	74.367
43	1	637	99.221	43	1630	76.382
46	1	638	99.377	46	1676	78.538
50	1	639	99.533	50	1726	80.881
51	1	640	99.688	51	1777	83.271
111	1	641	99.844	111	1888	88.472
246	1	642	100.000	246	2134	100.000

TYPES = S0 = 642   TOKENS = S1 = 2134   S2 = 93880

MEAN = 3.3240   SD = 11.6268   V = 3.4978   K = 201.4644

TABLE B39   SAMPLE J17, LEARNED AND SCIENTIFIC WRITINGS (E. GELLHORN, "PROLEGOMENA TO A THEORY OF THE EMOTIONS," IN "PERSPECTIVES IN BIOLOGY AND MEDICINE")

x	FX	SUM FX	CUM% FX	FX*X	SUM FX*X	CUM% FX*X
1	376	376	56.712	376	376	18.094
2	128	504	76.018	256	632	30.414
3	59	563	84.917	177	809	38.932
4	33	596	89.894	132	941	45.284
5	15	611	92.157	75	1016	48.893
6	8	619	93.363	48	1064	51.203
7	5	624	94.118	35	1099	52.887
8	3	627	94.570	24	1123	54.042
9	5	632	95.324	45	1168	56.208
10	2	634	95.626	20	1188	57.170
11	5	639	96.380	55	1243	59.817
12	5	644	97.134	60	1303	62.705
14	1	645	97.285	14	1317	63.378
15	2	647	97.587	30	1347	64.822
16	1	648	97.738	16	1363	65.592
17	1	649	97.888	17	1380	66.410
18	1	650	98.039	18	1398	67.276
19	3	653	98.492	57	1455	70.019
20	1	654	98.643	20	1475	70.982
22	2	656	98.944	44	1519	73.099
26	1	657	99.095	26	1545	74.350
38	1	658	99.246	38	1583	76.179
51	1	659	99.397	51	1634	78.633
76	1	660	99.548	76	1710	82.291
79	1	661	99.698	79	1789	86.092
97	1	662	99.849	97	1886	90.760
192	1	663	100.000	192	2078	100.000

TYPES = S0 = 663   TOKENS = S1 = 2078   S2 = 71954

MEAN = 3.1342   SD = 9.9350   V = 3.1698   K = 161.8218

TABLE B40 SAMPLE J27, LEARNED AND SCIENTIFIC WRITINGS (DALE L. WOMBLE, "FUNCTIONAL MARRIAGE COURSE FOR THE ALREADY MARRIED," IN 'MARRIAGE AND FAMILY LIVING' MAGAZINE)

X	FX	SUM FX	CUM% FX	FX*X	SUM FX*X	CUM% FX*X
1	444	444	65.007	444	444	22.035
2	90	534	78.184	180	624	30.968
3	44	578	84.627	132	756	37.519
4	29	607	88.873	116	872	43.275
5	11	618	90.483	55	927	46.005
6	11	629	92.094	66	993	49.280
7	6	635	92.972	42	1035	51.365
8	8	643	94.143	64	1099	54.541
9	3	646	94.583	27	1126	55.881
10	5	651	95.315	50	1176	58.362
11	3	654	95.754	33	1209	60.000
12	4	658	96.340	48	1257	62.382
13	2	660	96.632	26	1283	63.672
14	2	662	96.925	28	1311	65.062
15	2	664	97.218	30	1341	66.551
16	1	665	97.365	16	1357	67.365
17	2	667	97.657	34	1391	69.032
18	1	668	97.804	18	1409	69.926
19	1	669	97.950	19	1428	70.868
20	1	670	98.097	20	1448	71.861
21	2	672	98.389	42	1490	73.945
27	1	673	98.536	27	1517	75.285
28	2	675	98.829	56	1573	78.064
29	1	676	98.975	29	1602	79.504
33	1	677	99.122	33	1635	81.141
35	1	678	99.268	35	1670	82.878
48	1	679	99.414	48	1718	85.261
58	1	680	99.561	58	1776	88.139
60	1	681	99.707	60	1836	91.117
66	1	682	99.854	66	1902	94.392
113	1	683	100.000	113	2015	100.000

TYPES = S0 = 683   TOKENS = S1 = 2015   S2 = 40645

MEAN = 2.9502   SD = 7.1282   V = 2.4162   K = 95.1523

TABLE B41 SAMPLE J37, LEARNED AND SCIENTIFIC WRITINGS (DOUGLAS ASHFORD, "ELECTIONS IN MOROCCO: PROGRESS OR CONFUSION?" IN 'MIDDLE EAST JOURNAL')

X	FX	SUM FX	CUM% FX	FX*X	SUM FX*X	CUM% FX*X
1	491	491	66.712	491	491	24.489
2	115	606	82.337	230	721	35.960
3	44	650	88.315	132	853	42.544
4	23	673	91.440	92	945	47.132
5	9	682	92.663	45	990	49.377
6	14	696	94.565	84	1074	53.566
7	8	704	95.652	56	1130	56.359
8	5	709	96.332	40	1170	58.354
9	3	712	96.739	27	1197	59.701
10	2	714	97.011	20	1217	60.698
11	4	718	97.554	44	1261	62.893
12	3	721	97.962	36	1297	64.688
13	2	723	98.234	26	1323	65.985
16	1	724	98.370	16	1339	66.783
17	1	725	98.505	17	1356	67.631
19	2	727	98.777	38	1394	69.526
25	1	728	98.913	25	1419	70.773
32	1	729	99.049	32	1451	72.369
34	1	730	99.185	34	1485	74.065
37	1	731	99.321	37	1522	75.910
41	1	732	99.457	41	1563	77.955
55	1	733	99.592	55	1618	80.698
58	1	734	99.728	58	1676	83.591
114	1	735	99.864	114	1790	89.277
215	1	736	100.000	215	2005	100.000

TYPES = S0 = 736   TOKENS = S1 = 2005   S2 = 77585

MEAN = 2.7242   SD = 5.8992   V = 3.6338   K = 188.0088

TABLE B42 SAMPLE J47, LEARNED AND SCIENTIFIC WRITINGS (WILLIAM B. RAGAN, "TEACHING AMERICA'S CHILDREN")

X	FX	SUM FX	CUM% FX	FX*X	SUM FX*X	CUM% FX*X
1	470	470	64.828	470	470	23.371
2	117	587	80.965	234	704	35.007
3	39	626	86.345	117	821	40.825
4	25	651	89.793	100	921	45.798
5	21	672	92.690	105	1026	51.019
6	7	679	93.655	42	1068	53.108
7	6	685	94.483	42	1110	55.196
8	4	689	95.034	32	1142	56.788
9	6	695	95.862	54	1196	59.473
10	3	698	96.276	30	1226	60.965
11	2	700	96.552	22	1248	62.059
12	3	703	96.966	36	1284	63.849
13	2	705	97.241	26	1310	65.142
14	1	706	97.379	14	1324	65.838
15	1	707	97.517	15	1339	66.584
16	2	709	97.793	32	1371	68.175
17	3	712	98.207	51	1422	70.711
18	2	714	98.483	36	1458	72.501
21	2	716	98.759	42	1500	74.590
23	1	717	98.897	23	1523	75.733
25	1	718	99.034	25	1548	76.977
26	1	719	99.172	26	1574	78.270
33	1	720	99.310	33	1607	79.910
65	1	721	99.448	65	1672	83.143
66	1	722	99.586	66	1738	86.425
72	1	723	99.724	72	1810	90.005
76	1	724	99.862	76	1886	93.784
125	1	725	100.000	125	2011	100.000

TYPES = S0 = 725   TOKENS = S1 = 2011   S2 = 46229

MEAN = 2.7738   SD = 7.4880   V = 2.6996   K = 109.3389

TABLE B43 SAMPLE J57, LEARNED AND SCIENTIFIC WRITINGS (J. H. HEXTER, "THOMAS MORE: ON THE MARGINS OF MODERNITY," IN "JOURNAL OF BRITISH STUDIES")

X	FX	SUM FX	CUM% FX	FX*X	SUM FX*X	CUM% FX*X
1	482	482	67.038	482	482	23.897
2	114	596	82.893	228	710	35.201
3	42	638	88.734	126	836	41.448
4	18	656	91.238	72	908	45.017
5	14	670	93.185	70	978	48.488
6	5	675	93.880	30	1008	49.975
7	7	682	94.854	49	1057	52.405
8	3	685	95.271	24	1081	53.594
9	3	688	95.688	27	1108	54.933
10	3	691	96.106	30	1138	56.420
11	5	696	96.801	55	1193	59.147
12	5	701	97.497	60	1253	62.122
15	3	704	97.914	45	1298	64.353
19	1	705	98.053	19	1317	65.295
20	2	707	98.331	40	1357	67.278
22	1	708	98.470	22	1379	68.369
24	1	709	98.609	24	1403	69.559
25	1	710	98.748	25	1428	70.798
36	1	711	98.887	36	1464	72.583
46	1	712	99.026	46	1510	74.864
47	1	713	99.165	47	1557	77.194
50	1	714	99.305	50	1607	79.673
54	1	715	99.444	54	1661	82.350
56	1	716	99.583	56	1717	85.126
58	1	717	99.722	58	1775	88.002
107	1	718	99.861	107	1882	93.307
135	1	719	100.000	135	2017	100.000

TYPES = S0 = 719   TOKENS = S1 = 2017   S2 = 55269

MEAN = 2.8053   SD = 8.3066   V = 2.9611   K = 130.8953

TABLE B44 SAMPLE J67, LEARNED AND SCIENTIFIC WRITINGS (WILLIAM WHALLON, 'THE DICTION OF BEOWULF,' IN 'PMLA')

X	FX	SUM FX	CUM% FX	FX*X	SUM FX*X	CUM% FX*X
1	500	500	67.476	500	500	24.826
2	107	607	81.916	214	714	35.452
3	50	657	88.664	150	864	42.900
4	19	676	91.228	76	940	46.673
5	12	688	92.847	60	1000	49.652
6	3	691	93.252	18	1018	50.546
7	6	697	94.062	42	1060	52.632
8	7	704	95.007	56	1116	55.412
9	4	708	95.547	36	1152	57.200
10	5	713	96.221	50	1202	59.682
11	4	717	96.761	44	1246	61.867
12	3	720	97.166	36	1282	63.654
13	1	721	97.301	13	1295	64.300
14	3	724	97.706	42	1337	66.385
15	3	727	98.111	45	1382	68.620
16	1	728	98.246	16	1398	69.414
17	2	730	98.516	34	1432	71.102
21	1	731	98.650	21	1453	72.145
23	1	732	98.785	23	1476	73.287
25	1	733	98.920	25	1501	74.528
28	1	734	99.055	28	1529	75.919
34	1	735	99.190	34	1563	77.607
49	1	736	99.325	49	1612	80.040
52	2	738	99.595	104	1716	85.204
65	1	739	99.730	65	1781	88.431
85	1	740	99.865	85	1866	92.651
148	1	741	100.000	148	2014	100.000

TYPES = SO = 741   S1 = 2014   S2 = 51536
TOKENS = S1 = 2014   K = 122.0898
MEAN = 2.7179   SD = 7.3843   V = 2.9008

TABLE B45 SAMPLE J77, LEARNED AND SCIENTIFIC WRITINGS (WILLIAM D. APPEL, ED., '1961 TECHNICAL MANUAL OF THE AMERICAN ASSOCIATION OF TEXTILE CHEMISTS AND COLORISTS')

X	FX	SUM FX	CUM% FX	FX*X	SUM FX*X	CUM% FX*X
1	379	379	57.078	379	379	16.874
2	112	491	73.946	224	603	26.848
3	53	544	81.928	159	762	33.927
4	32	576	86.747	128	890	39.626
5	17	593	89.307	85	975	43.410
6	15	608	91.566	90	1065	47.418
7	6	614	92.470	42	1107	49.288
8	12	626	94.277	96	1203	53.562
10	7	633	95.331	70	1273	56.679
11	5	638	96.084	55	1328	59.127
12	1	639	96.235	12	1340	59.662
13	3	642	96.687	39	1379	61.398
14	2	644	96.988	28	1407	62.645
16	1	645	97.139	16	1423	63.357
17	2	647	97.440	34	1457	64.871
18	1	648	97.590	18	1475	65.672
19	1	649	97.741	19	1494	66.518
20	1	650	97.892	20	1514	67.409
21	1	651	98.042	21	1535	68.344
22	1	652	98.193	22	1557	69.323
24	2	654	98.494	48	1605	71.460
26	1	655	98.645	26	1631	72.618
28	1	656	98.795	28	1659	73.865
34	1	657	98.946	34	1693	75.378
42	1	658	99.096	42	1735	77.248
48	1	659	99.247	48	1783	79.386
50	1	660	99.398	50	1833	81.612
59	1	661	99.548	59	1892	84.239
67	1	662	99.699	67	1959	87.222
94	1	663	99.849	94	2053	91.407
193	1	664	100.000	193	2246	100.000

TYPES = SO = 664   S1 = 2246   S2 = 73426
TOKENS = S1 = 2246   K = 141.1037
MEAN = 3.3825   SD = 9.9569   V = 2.9436

TABLE B46   SAMPLE K07, FICTION, GENERAL (FRANCIS POLLINI, 'NIGHT')

X	FX	SUM FX	CUM% FX	FX*X	SUM FX*X	CUM% FX*X
1	425	425	61.773	425	425	21.197
2	108	533	77.471	216	641	31.970
3	38	571	82.994	114	755	37.656
4	29	600	87.209	116	871	43.441
5	21	621	90.262	105	976	48.678
6	13	634	92.151	78	1054	52.569
7	13	647	94.041	91	1145	57.107
8	6	653	94.913	48	1193	59.501
9	5	658	95.640	45	1238	61.746
10	5	663	96.366	50	1288	64.239
11	2	665	96.657	22	1310	65.337
12	1	666	96.802	12	1322	65.935
13	2	668	97.093	26	1348	67.232
14	4	672	97.674	56	1404	70.025
17	2	674	97.965	34	1438	71.721
19	3	677	98.401	57	1495	74.564
24	1	678	98.547	24	1519	75.761
26	1	679	98.692	26	1545	77.057
28	1	680	98.837	28	1573	78.454
31	1	681	98.983	31	1604	80.000
32	1	682	99.128	32	1636	81.596
37	1	683	99.273	37	1673	83.441
43	1	684	99.419	43	1716	85.586
52	2	686	99.709	104	1820	90.773
75	1	687	99.855	75	1895	94.514
110	1	688	100.000	110	2005	100.000

TYPES = SO = 688   TOKENS = S1 = 2005   S2 = 38123

MEAN = 2.9142   SD = 6.8497   V = 2.3504   K = 89.8452

TABLE B47   SAMPLE K17, FICTION, GENERAL (LEON URIS, 'MILA 18')

X	FX	SUM FX	CUM% FX	FX*X	SUM FX*X	CUM% FX*X
1	539	539	68.575	539	539	26.843
2	106	645	82.061	212	751	37.400
3	44	689	87.659	132	883	43.974
4	25	714	90.840	100	983	48.954
5	18	732	93.130	90	1073	53.436
6	11	743	94.525	66	1139	56.723
7	3	746	94.911	21	1160	57.769
8	6	752	95.674	48	1208	60.159
9	6	758	96.438	54	1262	62.849
10	2	760	96.692	20	1282	63.845
11	3	763	97.074	33	1315	65.488
12	3	766	97.455	36	1351	67.281
13	5	771	98.092	65	1416	70.518
14	1	772	98.219	14	1430	71.215
15	1	773	98.346	15	1445	71.962
16	1	774	98.473	16	1461	72.759
18	1	775	98.600	18	1479	73.655
21	1	776	98.728	21	1500	74.701
22	1	777	98.855	22	1522	75.797
28	1	778	98.982	28	1550	77.191
30	1	779	99.109	30	1580	78.685
39	1	780	99.237	39	1619	80.627
40	1	781	99.364	40	1659	82.620
46	2	783	99.618	92	1751	87.201
58	1	784	99.746	58	1809	90.090
75	1	785	99.873	75	1884	93.825
124	1	786	100.000	124	2008	100.000

TYPES = SO = 786   TOKENS = S1 = 2008   S2 = 40790

MEAN = 2.5547   SD = 6.7357   V = 2.6366   K = 96.1840

TABLE B48   SAMPLE A27, FICTION, GENERAL (E. LUCAS MYERS, 'THE VINDICATION OF DR. NESTOR,' IN 'SEWANEE REVIEW')

X	FX	SUM FX	CUM% FX	FX*X	SUM FX*X	CUM% FX*X
1	577	577	72.215	577	577	28.354
2	102	679	84.981	204	781	38.378
3	36	715	89.487	108	889	43.686
4	20	735	91.990	80	969	47.617
5	11	746	93.367	55	1024	50.319
6	9	755	94.493	54	1078	52.973
7	9	764	95.620	63	1141	56.069
8	5	769	96.245	40	1181	58.034
9	3	772	96.621	27	1208	59.361
10	1	773	96.746	10	1218	59.853
11	1	774	96.871	11	1229	60.393
12	5	779	97.497	60	1289	63.342
13	1	780	97.622	13	1302	63.980
14	1	781	97.747	14	1316	64.668
15	3	784	98.123	45	1361	66.880
16	2	786	98.373	32	1393	68.452
19	1	787	98.498	19	1412	69.386
22	2	789	98.748	44	1456	71.548
23	1	790	98.874	23	1479	72.678
25	2	792	99.124	50	1529	75.135
38	1	793	99.249	38	1567	77.002
40	1	794	99.374	40	1607	78.968
47	1	795	99.499	47	1654	81.278
57	1	796	99.625	57	1711	84.079
62	1	797	99.750	62	1773	87.125
71	1	798	99.875	71	1844	90.614
191	1	799	100.000	191	2035	100.000

TYPES = S0 = 799   TOKENS = S1 = 2035   S2 = 62701

MEAN = 2.5469   SD = 8.4845   V = 3.3313   K = 146.4929

TABLE B49   SAMPLE L08, FICTION, MYSTERY AND DETECTIVE (DELL SHANNON, 'THE ACE OF SPADES')

X	FX	SUM FX	CUM% FX	FX*X	SUM FX*X	CUM% FX*X
1	392	392	59.847	392	392	19.272
2	97	489	74.656	194	586	28.810
3	42	531	81.069	126	712	35.005
4	31	562	85.802	124	836	41.101
5	14	576	87.939	70	906	44.543
6	13	589	89.924	78	984	48.378
7	10	599	91.450	70	1054	51.819
8	4	603	92.061	32	1086	53.392
9	12	615	93.893	108	1194	58.702
10	6	621	94.809	60	1254	61.652
11	5	626	95.573	55	1309	64.356
12	4	630	96.183	48	1357	66.716
13	1	631	96.336	13	1370	67.355
14	4	635	96.947	56	1426	70.108
16	2	637	97.252	32	1458	71.681
17	1	638	97.405	17	1475	72.517
18	2	640	97.710	36	1511	74.287
19	1	641	97.863	19	1530	75.221
20	1	642	98.015	20	1550	76.205
22	3	645	98.473	66	1616	79.449
25	1	646	98.626	25	1641	80.678
26	1	647	98.779	26	1667	81.957
32	1	648	98.931	32	1699	83.530
34	1	649	99.084	34	1733	85.202
36	1	650	99.237	36	1769	86.971
39	1	651	99.389	39	1808	88.889
52	1	652	99.542	52	1860	91.445
55	1	653	99.695	55	1915	94.149
57	1	654	99.847	57	1972	96.952
62	1	655	100.000	62	2034	100.000

TYPES = S0 = 655   TOKENS = S1 = 2034   S2 = 29706

MEAN = 3.1053   SD = 5.9757   V = 1.9243   K = 66.8865

TABLE B50 SAMPLE L18, FICTION, MYSTERY AND DETECTIVE (GEORGE HARMON COXE, 'ERROR OF JUDGMENT')

X	FX	SUM FX	CUM% FX	FX*X	SUM FX*X	CUM% FX*X
1	411	411	62.273	411	411	20.519
2	103	514	77.879	206	617	30.804
3	45	559	84.697	135	752	37.544
4	27	586	88.788	108	860	42.936
5	19	605	91.667	95	955	47.678
6	7	612	92.727	42	997	49.775
7	4	616	93.333	28	1025	51.173
8	8	624	94.545	64	1089	54.368
9	6	630	95.455	54	1143	57.064
10	5	635	96.212	50	1193	59.561
11	2	637	96.515	22	1215	60.659
13	1	638	96.667	13	1228	61.308
14	3	641	97.121	42	1270	63.405
15	1	642	97.273	15	1285	64.154
16	2	644	97.576	32	1317	65.751
17	1	645	97.727	17	1334	66.600
18	1	646	97.879	18	1352	67.499
19	1	647	98.030	19	1371	68.447
20	1	648	98.182	20	1391	69.446
22	1	649	98.333	22	1413	70.544
26	1	650	98.485	26	1439	71.842
28	1	651	98.636	28	1467	73.240
37	2	653	98.939	74	1541	76.935
40	2	655	99.242	80	1621	80.929
41	1	656	99.394	41	1662	82.976
58	1	657	99.545	58	1720	85.871
73	1	658	99.697	73	1793	89.516
98	1	659	99.848	98	1891	94.408
112	1	660	100.000	112	2003	100.000

TYPES = SO = 66C TOKENS = S1 = 2003 S2 = 47595

MEAN = 3.0348 SD = 7.9312 V = 2.6134 K = 113.6388

TABLE B51 SAMPLE N04, FICTION, SCIENCE (JIM HARMON, 'THE PLANET WITH NO NIGHTMARE,' IN 'IF' MAGAZINE)

X	FX	SUM FX	CUM% FX	FX*X	SUM FX*X	CUM% FX*X
1	515	515	68.032	515	515	25.724
2	100	615	81.242	200	715	35.714
3	50	665	87.847	150	865	43.207
4	24	689	91.017	96	961	48.002
5	8	697	92.074	40	1001	50.000
6	10	707	93.395	60	1061	52.997
7	7	714	94.320	49	1110	55.445
8	6	720	95.112	48	1158	57.842
9	2	722	95.376	18	1176	58.741
10	4	726	95.905	40	1216	60.739
11	2	728	96.169	22	1238	61.838
12	1	729	96.301	12	1250	62.438
13	3	732	96.697	39	1289	64.386
14	4	736	97.226	56	1345	67.183
15	1	737	97.358	15	1360	67.932
16	2	739	97.622	32	1392	69.530
17	1	740	97.754	17	1409	70.380
18	1	741	97.886	18	1427	71.279
19	1	742	98.018	19	1446	72.228
20	1	743	98.151	20	1466	73.227
21	1	744	98.283	21	1487	74.276
22	1	745	98.415	22	1509	75.375
23	1	746	98.547	23	1532	76.523
25	1	747	98.679	25	1557	77.772
26	2	749	98.943	52	1609	80.370
28	1	750	99.075	28	1637	81.768
30	1	751	99.207	30	1667	83.267
35	1	752	99.339	35	1702	85.015
38	1	753	99.472	38	1740	86.913
43	1	754	99.604	43	1783	89.061
48	1	755	99.736	48	1831	91.459
49	1	756	99.868	49	1880	93.906
122	1	757	100.000	122	2002	100.000

TYPES = SO = 757 TOKENS = S1 = 2002 S2 = 36608

MEAN = 2.6446 SD = 6.4316 V = 2.4319 K = 86.3422

TABLE B52 SAMPLE N08, FICTION, ADVENTURE AND WESTERN (MARY SAVAGE, 'JUST FOR TONIGHT')

X	FX	SUM FX	CUM% FX	FX*X	SUM FX*X	CUM% FX*X
1	607	607	74.115	607	607	30.064
2	98	705	86.081	196	803	39.772
3	39	744	90.842	117	920	45.567
4	18	762	93.040	72	992	49.133
5	12	774	94.505	60	1052	52.105
6	4	778	94.994	24	1076	53.294
7	8	786	95.971	56	1132	56.067
8	5	791	96.581	40	1172	58.049
9	3	794	96.947	27	1199	59.386
10	6	800	97.680	60	1259	62.358
11	1	801	97.802	11	1270	62.902
13	1	802	97.924	13	1283	63.546
14	2	804	98.168	28	1311	64.933
17	1	805	98.291	17	1328	65.775
18	1	806	98.413	18	1346	66.667
20	2	808	98.657	40	1386	68.648
29	1	809	98.779	29	1415	70.084
31	1	810	98.901	31	1446	71.620
34	1	811	99.023	34	1480	73.304
36	1	812	99.145	36	1516	75.087
41	1	813	99.267	41	1557	77.117
55	1	814	95.389	55	1612	79.841
56	1	815	99.512	56	1668	82.615
62	1	816	99.634	62	1730	85.686
76	1	817	99.756	76	1806	89.450
89	1	818	99.878	89	1895	93.858
124	1	819	100.000	124	2019	100.000

TYPES = S0 = 819   TOKENS = S1 = 2019   S2 = 50745

MEAN = 2.4652   SD = 7.4755   V = 3.0324   K = 119.5331

TABLE B53 SAMPLE N18, FICTION, ADVENTURE AND WESTERN (PETER BAINS, 'WITH WOMEN ... EDUCATION PAYS OFF,' IN 'MONSIEUR' MAGAZINE)

X	FX	SUM FX	CUM% FX	FX*X	SUM FX*X	CUM% FX*X
1	427	427	63.636	427	427	21.371
2	112	539	80.328	224	651	32.583
3	32	571	85.097	96	747	37.387
4	26	597	88.972	104	851	42.593
5	12	609	90.760	60	911	45.596
6	8	617	91.952	48	959	47.998
7	10	627	93.443	70	1029	51.501
8	4	631	94.035	32	1061	53.103
9	5	636	94.784	45	1106	55.355
10	4	640	95.380	40	1146	57.357
11	1	641	95.529	11	1157	57.908
12	5	646	96.274	60	1217	60.911
13	1	647	96.423	13	1230	61.562
14	2	649	96.721	28	1258	62.963
15	4	653	97.317	60	1318	65.966
16	1	654	97.466	16	1334	66.767
17	1	655	97.615	17	1351	67.618
18	1	656	97.765	18	1369	68.519
23	1	657	97.914	23	1392	69.670
24	1	658	98.063	24	1416	70.871
26	1	659	98.212	26	1442	72.172
27	1	660	98.361	27	1469	73.524
29	2	662	98.659	58	1527	76.426
31	1	663	98.808	31	1558	77.978
33	1	664	98.957	33	1591	79.630
35	1	665	99.106	35	1626	81.381
39	1	666	99.255	39	1665	83.333
46	1	667	99.404	46	1711	85.636
57	1	668	99.553	57	1768	88.488
64	1	669	99.702	64	1832	91.692
81	1	670	99.851	81	1913	95.746
85	1	671	100.000	85	1998	100.000

TYPES = S0 = 671   TOKENS = S1 = 1998   S2 = 39124

MEAN = 2.9776   SD = 7.0314   V = 2.3614   K = 93.0009

TABLE B54 SAMPLE N28, FICTION, ADVENTURE AND WESTERN (RALPH GRIMSHAW, 'MRS. HACKSAW: NEW ORLEANS' SOCIETY KILLER,' IN 'SIR' MAGAZINE)

X	FX	SUM FX	CUM% FX	FX*X	SUM FX*X	CUM% FX*X
1	677	677	76.067	677	677	33.565
2	96	773	86.854	192	869	43.084
3	42	815	91.573	126	995	49.331
4	17	832	93.483	68	1063	52.702
5	13	845	94.944	65	1128	55.925
6	9	854	95.955	54	1182	58.602
7	7	861	96.742	49	1231	61.031
8	1	862	96.854	8	1239	61.428
9	4	866	97.303	36	1275	63.213
10	2	868	97.528	20	1295	64.204
11	3	871	97.865	33	1328	65.840
12	1	872	97.978	12	1340	66.435
14	1	873	98.090	14	1354	67.129
15	1	874	98.202	15	1369	67.873
16	1	875	98.315	16	1385	68.666
17	3	878	98.652	51	1436	71.195
23	2	880	98.876	46	1482	73.475
24	1	881	98.989	24	1506	74.665
26	1	882	99.101	26	1532	75.954
30	1	883	99.213	30	1562	77.442
34	1	884	99.326	34	1596	79.127
39	1	885	99.438	39	1635	81.061
42	1	886	99.551	42	1677	83.143
50	1	887	99.663	50	1727	85.622
54	1	888	99.775	54	1781	88.299
87	1	889	99.888	87	1868	92.613
149	1	890	100.000	149	2017	100.000

TYPES = S0 = 890 TOKENS = S1 = 2017 S2 = 48179

MEAN = 2.2663 SD = 6.9998 V = 3.0887 K = 113.4678

TABLE B55 SAMPLE P09, FICTION, ROMANCE AND LOVE STORY (JESSE HILL FORD, 'MOUNTAINS OF GILEAD')

X	FX	SUM FX	CUM% FX	FX*X	SUM FX*X	CUM% FX*X
1	441	441	66.920	441	441	22.150
2	83	524	79.514	166	607	30.487
3	39	563	85.432	117	724	36.364
4	27	590	89.530	108	832	41.788
5	12	602	91.351	60	892	44.802
6	11	613	93.020	66	958	48.117
7	9	622	94.385	63	1021	51.281
8	2	624	94.685	16	1037	52.084
9	1	625	94.841	9	1046	52.536
10	4	629	95.448	40	1086	54.545
11	2	631	95.751	22	1108	55.650
12	2	633	96.055	24	1132	56.856
14	6	639	96.965	84	1216	61.075
15	1	640	97.117	15	1231	61.828
16	1	641	97.265	16	1247	62.632
17	1	642	97.420	17	1264	63.486
18	1	643	97.572	18	1282	64.390
19	1	644	97.724	19	1301	65.344
20	3	647	98.179	60	1361	68.358
23	1	648	98.331	23	1384	69.513
25	1	649	98.483	25	1409	70.768
27	1	650	98.634	27	1436	72.125
28	1	651	98.786	28	1464	73.531
31	1	652	98.938	31	1495	75.088
40	1	653	99.090	40	1535	77.097
44	1	654	99.241	44	1579	79.307
45	1	655	99.393	45	1624	81.567
47	1	656	99.545	47	1671	83.928
89	1	657	99.697	89	1760	86.398
98	1	658	99.848	98	1858	93.320
133	1	659	100.000	133	1991	100.000

TYPES = S0 = 659 TOKENS = S1 = 1991 S2 = 54275

MEAN = 3.0212 SD = 6.5576 V = 2.8325 K = 131.8943

TABLE B56 SAMPLE P29, FICTION, ROMANCE AND LOVE STORY ("THIS CANCER VICTIM MAY RUIN MY LIFE," IN "MEDICAL STORY" MAGAZINE)

X	FX	SUM FX	CUM% FX	FX*X	SUM FX*X	CUM% FX*X
1	371	371	58.242	371	371	18.531
2	115	486	76.295	230	601	30.020
3	36	522	81.947	108	709	35.415
4	28	550	86.342	112	821	41.009
5	21	571	89.639	105	926	46.254
6	15	586	91.994	90	1016	50.749
7	7	593	93.093	49	1065	53.197
8	4	597	93.721	32	1097	54.795
9	7	604	94.815	63	1160	57.942
10	5	609	95.604	50	1210	60.440
11	2	611	95.918	22	1232	61.538
12	2	613	96.232	24	1256	62.737
13	2	615	96.546	26	1282	64.036
14	1	616	96.703	14	1296	64.735
15	2	618	97.017	30	1326	66.234
17	3	621	97.488	51	1377	68.781
20	1	622	97.645	20	1397	69.780
23	1	623	97.802	23	1420	70.929
24	1	624	97.959	24	1444	72.128
25	2	626	98.273	50	1494	74.625
27	1	627	98.430	27	1521	75.974
31	1	628	98.587	31	1552	77.522
32	1	629	98.744	32	1584	79.121
33	1	630	98.901	33	1617	80.769
35	1	631	99.058	35	1652	82.517
42	2	633	99.372	84	1736	86.713
45	1	634	99.529	45	1781	88.961
61	1	635	99.686	61	1842	92.008
77	1	636	99.843	77	1919	95.854
83	1	637	100.000	83	2002	100.000

TYPES = S0 = 637 TOKENS = S1 = 2002 S2 = 36590

MEAN = 3.1429 SD = 6.8966 V = 2.1944 K = 86.2973

TABLE B57 SAMPLE P29, FICTION, ROMANCE AND LOVE STORY (ROBERT CARSON, "MY HERO")

X	FX	SUM FX	CUM% FX	FX*X	SUM FX*X	CUM% FX*X
1	675	675	74.751	675	675	33.733
2	100	775	85.825	200	875	43.728
3	42	817	90.476	126	1001	50.025
4	31	848	93.909	124	1125	56.222
5	12	860	95.238	60	1185	59.220
6	5	865	95.792	30	1215	60.720
7	2	867	96.013	14	1229	61.419
8	5	872	96.567	40	1269	63.418
10	4	876	97.010	40	1309	65.417
11	4	880	97.453	44	1353	67.616
12	3	883	97.785	36	1389	69.415
13	1	884	97.896	13	1402	70.065
14	1	885	98.007	14	1416	70.765
15	2	887	98.228	30	1446	72.264
16	1	888	98.339	16	1462	73.063
17	1	889	98.450	17	1479	73.913
18	1	890	98.560	18	1497	74.813
19	2	892	98.782	38	1535	76.712
20	1	893	98.893	20	1555	77.711
21	1	894	99.003	21	1576	78.761
24	1	895	99.114	24	1600	79.960
25	1	896	99.225	25	1625	81.209
29	1	897	99.336	29	1654	82.659
32	1	898	99.446	32	1686	84.258
46	1	899	99.557	46	1732	86.557
48	1	900	99.668	48	1780	88.956
54	1	901	99.779	54	1834	91.654
80	1	902	99.889	80	1914	95.652
87	1	903	100.000	87	2001	100.000

TYPES = S0 = 903 TOKENS = S1 = 2001 S2 = 31781

MEAN = 2.2159 SD = 5.5031 V = 2.4834 K = 74.3756

Table B58   Type-Token Ratios in the Corpus and Various Subsets

No. of Samples	Types	Tokens	Ratio	Log Ratio
5R	3009	10051	.299	.869
25R	8749	50721	.172	.838
50R	13706	101566	.135	.826
125R	23655	253538	.093	.809
Corpus	50406	1014232	.050	.783
25N1	14110	100847	.140	.829
25N2	14244	102262	.139	.829
25N3	13616	100891	.135	.826
25N4	13733	101627	.135	.826
25N5	13201	101259	.130	.823
25N6	11821	103193	.115	.812
25N7	11076	100909	.110	.808
25N8	13474	101392	.133	.825
25N9	11092	100596	.110	.809
25N10	12328	101256	.122	.817

where R = representative
      N = nonrepresentative

Table B59a   Least-Squares Fits of $ax + b$ to Log Rank vs. Log Frequency

Number of Samples	a	b	σ
5R	−0.8380	2.734	0.0838
25R	−0.9345	3.567	0.0752
50R	−1.022	4.113	0.0792
125R	−1.135	4.848	0.0834
Corpus	−1.170	5.445	0.1091
Corpus *	−1.172	5.451	0.1087
Corpus A	−1.316	6.076	0.0604
25N1	−1.022	4.125	0.0796
25N2	−1.004	4.046	0.0779
25N3	−1.026	4.132	0.0794
25N4	−1.012	4.071	0.0784
25N5	−1.017	4.070	0.0769
25N6	−1.092	4.343	0.0864
25N7	−1.101	4.364	0.0864
25N8	−1.020	4.097	0.0790
25N9	−1.084	4.255	0.0782
25N10	−1.039	4.107	0.0805

Table B59b   Least-Squares Fits of $ax + b$ to Log Frequency vs. Log (No. of Types of That Frequency)

	a	b	σ
Corpus	−0.9478	2.859	0.4167
Corpus A	−1.0135	2.515	0.4426

A signifies that an average rank was used
* signifies words of rank 1–10 removed from sample

Graph B1   Log Rank vs. Log Frequency for the Entire Corpus

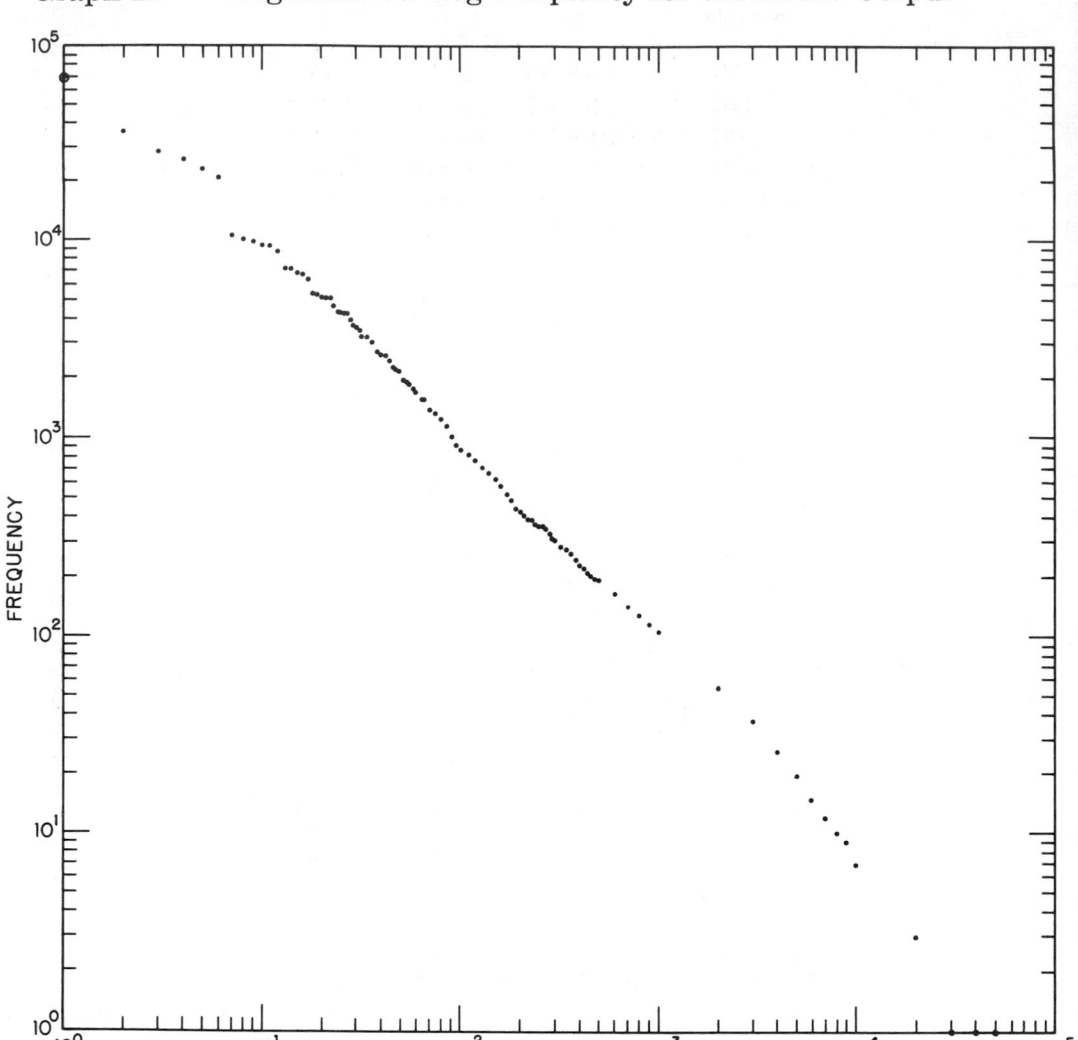

Graph B₁₁   Log Frequency vs. Log Number of Types of That Frequency

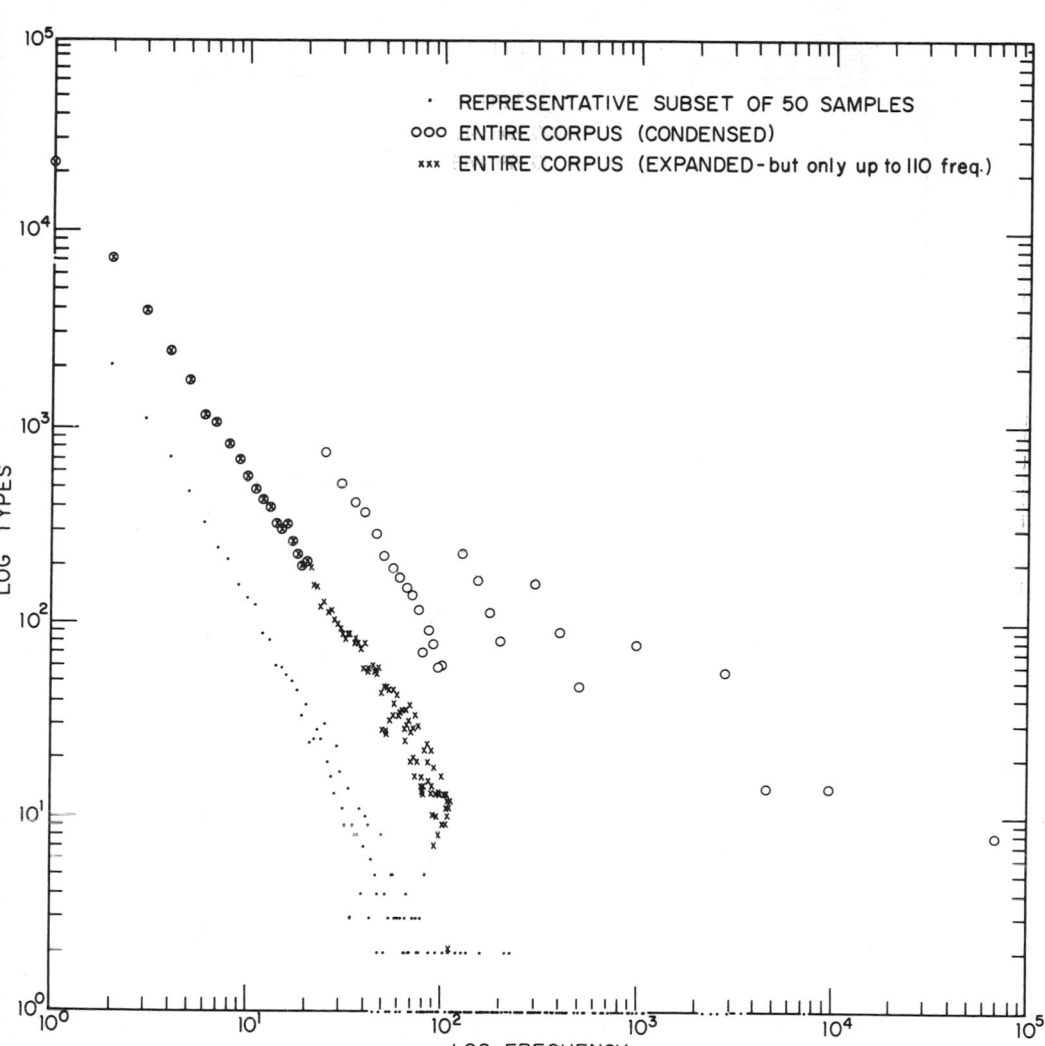

Graph B<small>III</small>   Log Frequency vs. Cumulative Percentage of Types

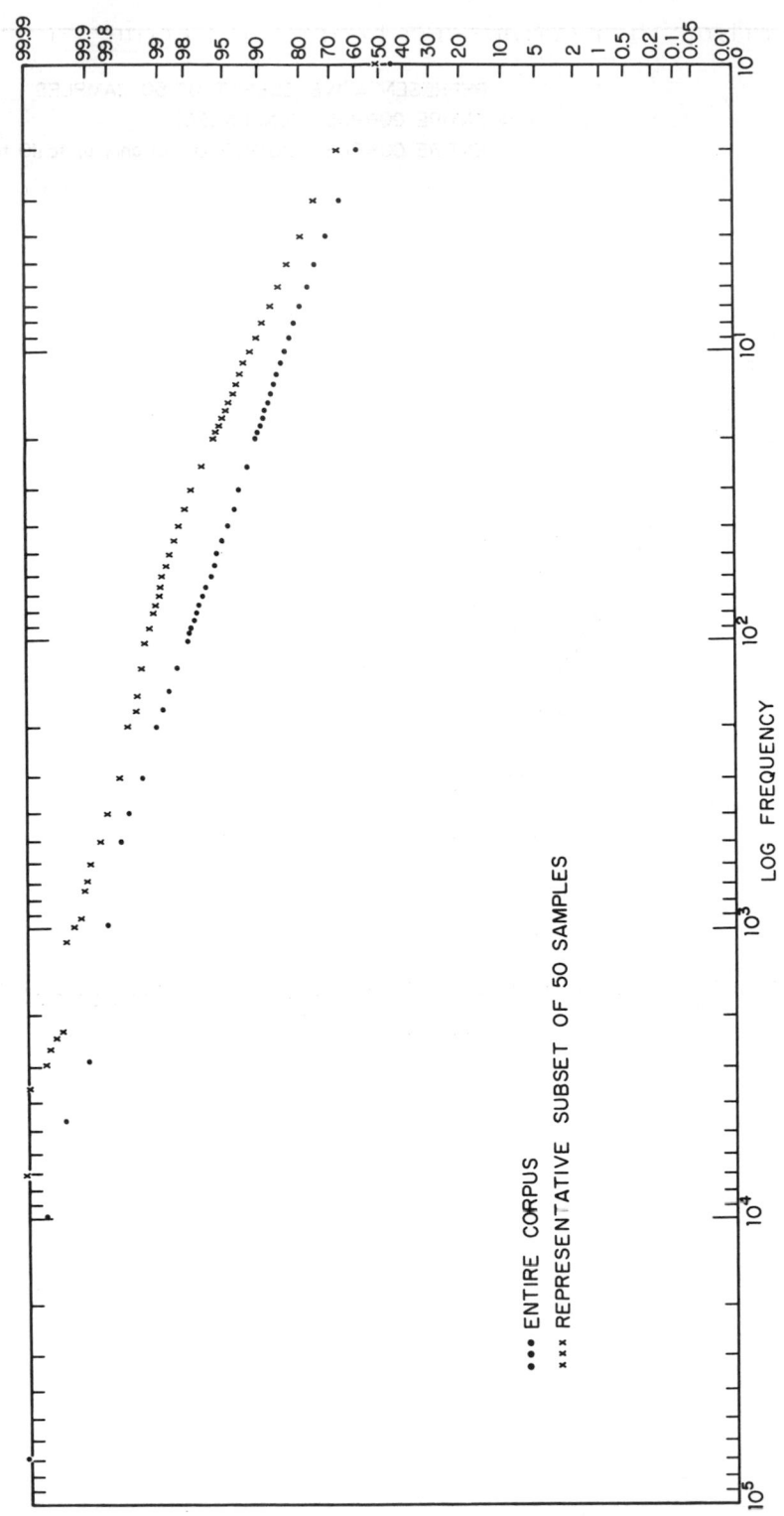

Graph B iv   Log Frequency vs. Cumulative Percentage of Tokens

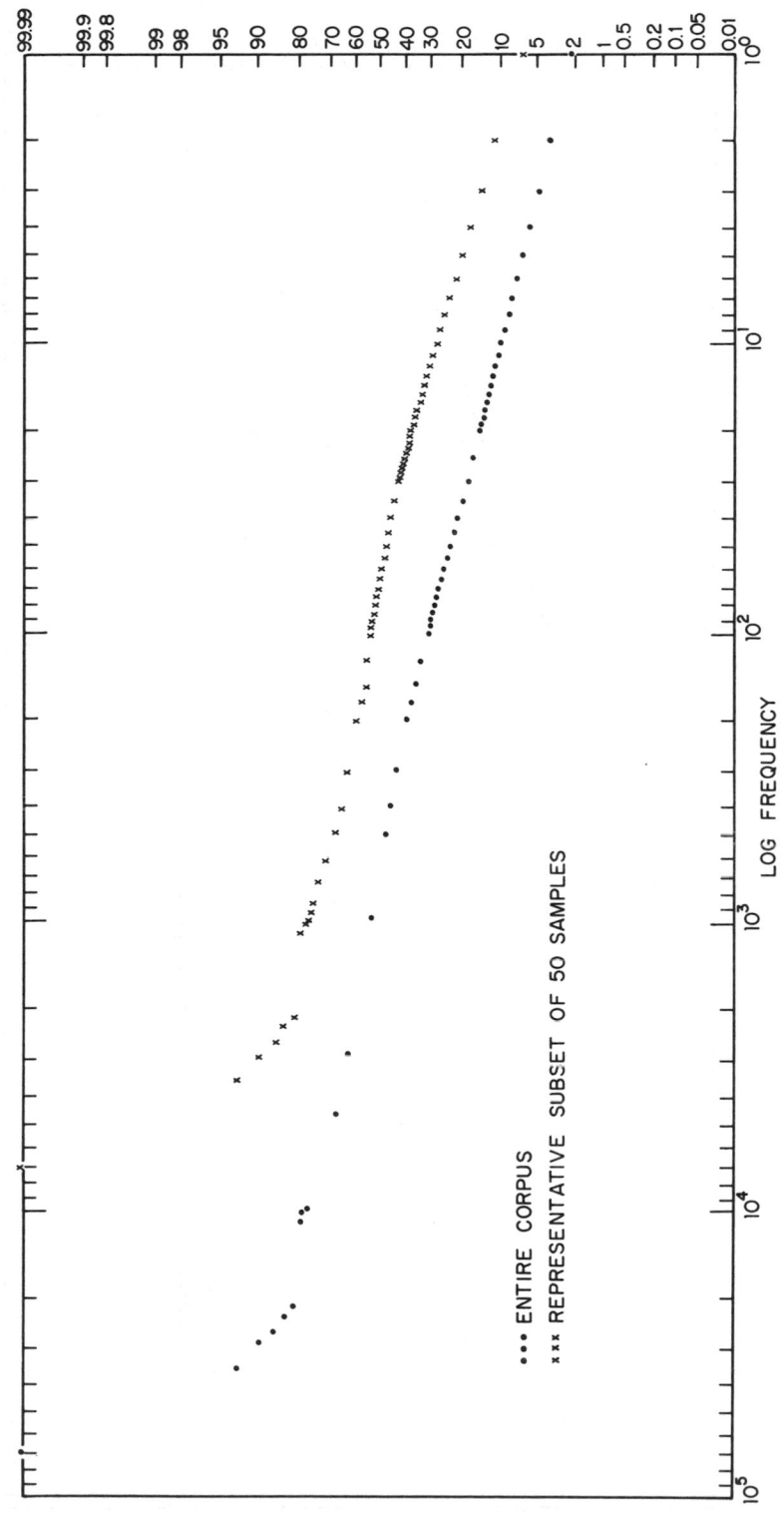

Graph Bv   Log Frequency vs. Cumulative Percentage of Types and Tokens

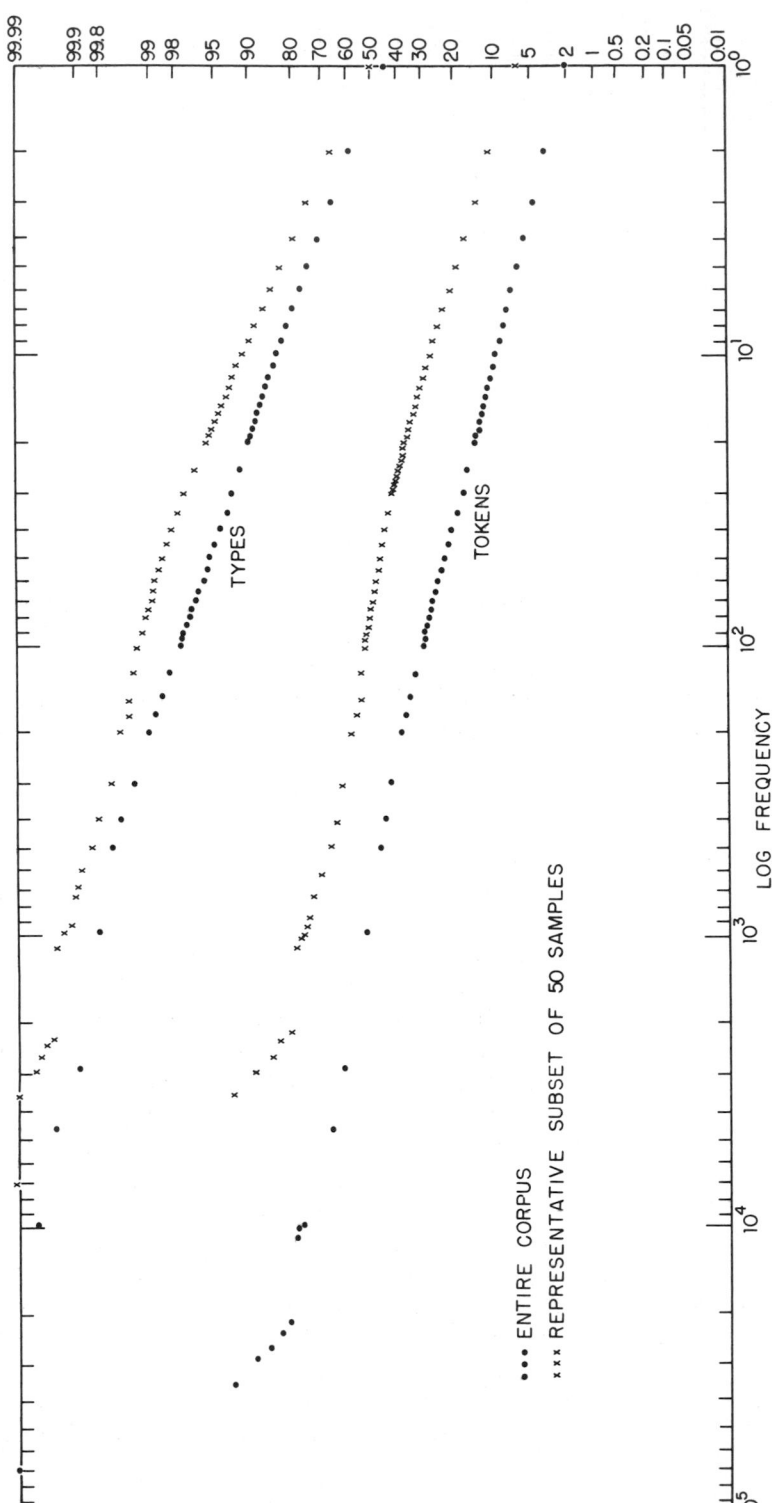

WORD LENGTH

Explanation of Tables C1 and C2 and Graph C1

Tables C1 and C2 summarize the analysis of the length of all the words in the Corpus, the length of a word being defined as the number of graphic characters composing it.

Table C1 represents the data for the types of the Corpus; it thus gives the basic information about the graphic composition of the dictionary of the Corpus.

The first column X specifies the number of graphic characters, and the second column FX, the number of types (i.e., different words) of length X. The third column SUM FX gives the total number of types of length X and shorter, and the following column CUM % FX expresses this figure as a percentage of the total number of types in the entire Corpus.

The fifth column, the product FX*X, is the number of graphic characters in the dictionary of the Corpus accounted for by types of length X. The next column SUM FX*X gives the total number of graphic characters composing the types of length X or shorter, and the last column CUM % FX*X expresses this figure as a percentage of the total number of graphic characters in the dictionary of the Corpus.

From the statistical parameters at the end of Table C1 it can be seen that there

are altogether 50,406 different words in the Corpus (S_0) and that these types consist of a total of 409,826 characters (S_1).

Table C2 summarizes the graphic-length data for the tokens of the Corpus and gives thus the basic information about the graphic composition of all the running words in the stripped version (Form B) of the Corpus.

The first column X specifies the number of graphic characters, and the second column FX, the number of tokens (i.e., running words) of length X. The third column SUM FX gives the total number of tokens of length X and shorter, and the following column CUM % FX expresses this figure as a percentage of the total number of tokens in the entire Corpus.

The fifth column, the product FX*X, is the number of graphic characters in the Corpus accounted for by tokens of length X. The next column SUM FX*X gives the total number of graphic characters composing the tokens of length X or shorter, and the last column CUM % FX*X expresses this figure as a percentage of the total number of graphic characters in the Corpus.

The statistical parameters at the end of Table C2 indicate that there are 1,014,232

tokens in the Corpus (S_0) and 4,807,066 graphic characters (S_1) in the stripped version of the Corpus.

The frequency distributions in Tables C1 and C2 are displayed in Graph C1. Semilogarithmic paper was used for this graph, with the number of graphic characters plotted on a uniform scale and the number of word-types and word-tokens of a given length plotted on the logarithmic scale.

TABLE C1   GRAPHIC CHARACTERS BY TYPES

X	FX	SUM FX	CUM% FX	FX*X	SUM FX*X	CUM% FX*X
1	36	36	0.071	36	36	0.009
2	277	313	0.621	554	590	0.144
3	1193	1506	2.988	3579	4169	1.017
4	3025	4531	8.989	12100	16269	3.970
5	4619	9150	18.153	23095	39364	9.605
6	6470	15620	30.988	38820	78184	19.077
7	7356	22976	45.582	51492	129676	31.642
8	6999	29975	59.467	55992	185668	45.304
9	6073	36048	71.515	54657	240325	58.641
10	4823	40871	81.084	48230	288555	70.409
11	3436	44307	87.900	37796	326351	79.632
12	2335	46642	92.533	28020	354371	86.469
13	1443	48085	95.395	18759	373130	91.046
14	881	48966	97.143	12334	385464	94.056
15	534	49500	98.203	8010	393474	96.010
16	331	49831	98.859	5296	398770	97.302
17	194	50025	99.244	3298	402068	98.107
18	120	50145	99.482	2160	404228	98.634
19	87	50232	99.655	1653	405881	99.037
20	56	50288	99.766	1120	407001	99.311
21	46	50334	99.857	966	407967	99.546
22	19	50353	99.895	418	408385	99.648
23	10	50363	99.915	230	408615	99.704
24	6	50369	99.927	144	408759	99.740
25	9	50378	99.944	225	408984	99.795
26	6	50384	99.956	156	409140	99.833
27	7	50391	99.970	189	409329	99.879
28	3	50394	99.976	84	409413	99.899
29	2	50396	99.980	58	409471	99.913
30	2	50398	99.984	60	409531	99.928
32	1	50399	99.986	32	409563	99.936
33	1	50400	99.988	33	409596	99.944
34	1	50401	99.990	34	409630	99.952
36	1	50402	99.992	36	409666	99.961
37	1	50403	99.994	37	409703	99.970
38	1	50404	99.996	38	409741	99.979
41	1	50405	99.998	41	409782	99.989
44	1	50406	100.000	44	409826	100.000

TYPES = S0 = 50406   GRAPHEMES = S1 = 409826   S2 =   3783288
MEAN = 8.1305   SD =   2.9919   V = 0.3680

TABLE C2   GRAPHIC CHARACTERS BY TOKENS

X	FX	SUM FX	CUM% FX	FX*X	SUM FX*X	CUM% FX*X
1	32048	32048	3.1598	32048	32048	0.6667
2	172161	204209	20.1343	344322	376370	7.8295
3	214935	419144	41.3262	644805	1021175	21.2432
4	159015	578159	57.0046	636060	1657235	34.4750
5	110066	688225	67.8568	550330	2207565	45.9233
6	86458	774683	76.3812	518748	2726313	56.7147
7	78336	853019	84.1049	548352	3274665	68.1219
8	57033	910052	89.7282	456264	3730929	77.6134
9	40897	950949	93.7605	368073	4099002	85.2703
10	28055	979004	96.5266	280550	4379552	91.1065
11	16047	995051	98.1088	176517	4556069	94.7786
12	9300	1004351	99.0258	111600	4667669	97.1002
13	4901	1009252	99.5090	63713	4731382	98.4256
14	2661	1011913	99.7713	37254	4768636	99.2005
15	1007	1012920	99.8706	15105	4783741	99.5148
16	508	1013428	99.9207	8128	4791869	99.6839
17	275	1013703	99.9478	4675	4796544	99.7811
18	219	1013922	99.9694	3942	4800486	99.8631
19	115	1014037	99.9808	2185	4802671	99.9086
20	61	1014098	99.9868	1220	4803891	99.9339
21	54	1014152	99.9921	1134	4805025	99.9575
22	24	1014176	99.9945	528	4805553	99.9685
23	11	1014187	99.9955	253	4805806	99.9738
24	7	1014194	99.9962	168	4805974	99.9773
25	10	1014204	99.9972	250	4806224	99.9825
26	6	1014210	99.9978	156	4806380	99.9857
27	7	1014217	99.9985	189	4806569	99.9897
28	3	1014220	99.9988	84	4806653	99.9914
29	2	1014222	99.9990	58	4806711	99.9926
30	2	1014224	99.9992	60	4806771	99.9939
32	1	1014225	99.9993	32	4806803	99.9945
33	1	1014226	99.9994	33	4806836	99.9952
34	1	1014227	99.9995	34	4806870	99.9959
36	1	1014228	99.9996	36	4806906	99.9967
37	1	1014229	99.9997	37	4806943	99.9974
38	1	1014230	99.9998	38	4806981	99.9982
41	1	1014231	99.9999	41	4807022	99.9991
44	1	1014232	100.0000	44	4807066	100.0000

TOKENS = S0 = 1014232   GRAPHEMES = S1 = 4807066   S2 = 29951248

MEAN = 4.7396   SD = 2.6584   V = 0.5609

Graph Cɪ   Length in Graphic Characters vs. Number of
Types and Tokens

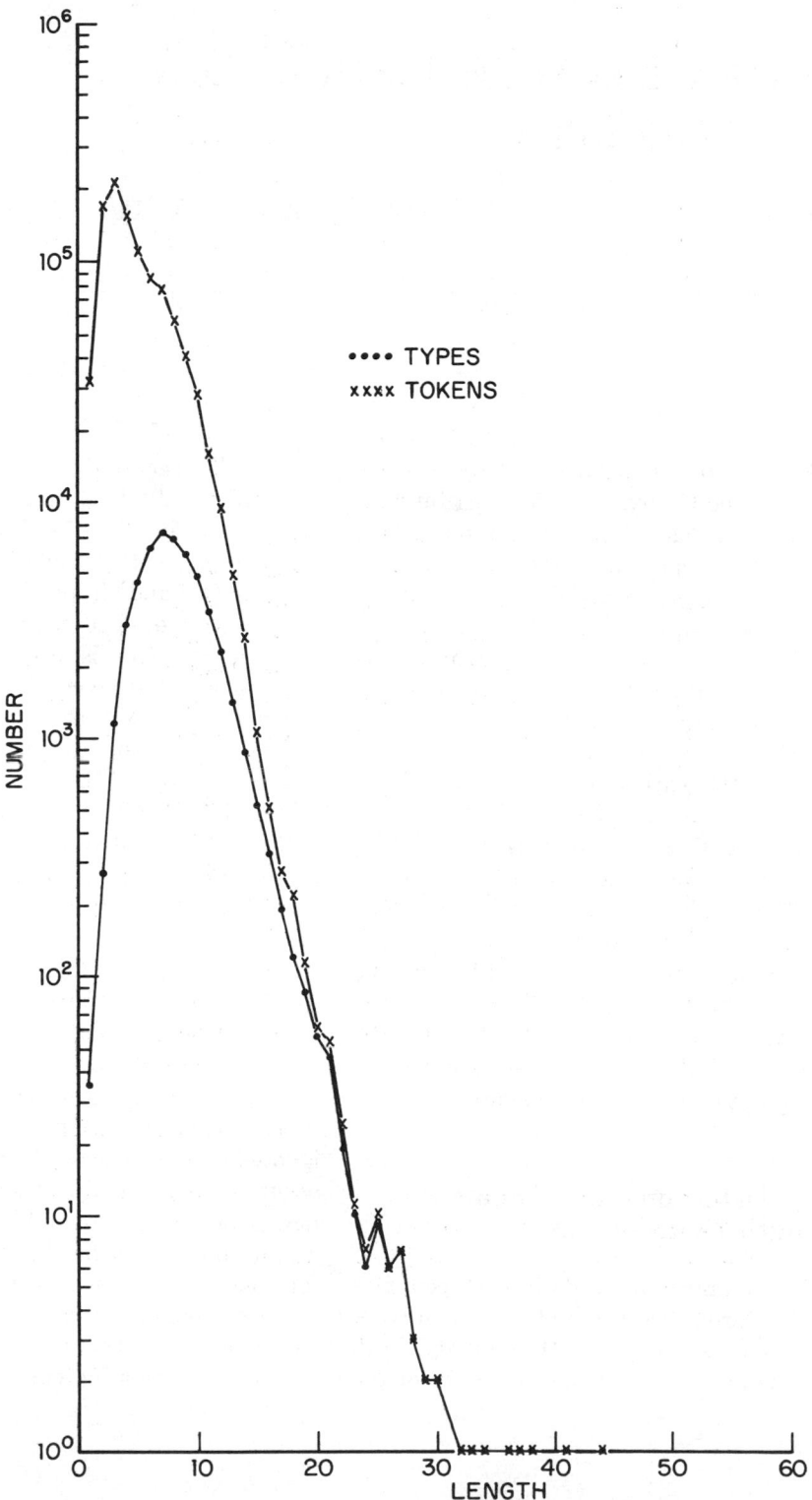

SENTENCE-LENGTH DISTRIBUTION IN THE CORPUS

BY MARY LOIS MARCKWORTH AND LAURA M. BELL

Because of its size and variety of composition the Corpus provides a useful data set for a range of stylistic studies. This study is the report of an effort (a) to establish the sentence-length distribution of the whole population of the English Corpus and of each of the genres of which it is composed and (b) to determine whether sentence length is a significant parameter in the quantitative description of writing style in the various literary prose genres of the Corpus; i.e., does the genre impose some sort of constraint in this matter on the individual practitioner? Assuming such constraints to be present, no attempt will be made here to say whether they are determined for an author by context, precept, or previous example, but some nonquantitative similarities between genres will be pointed out in cases where there are quantitative correspondences.

The Determination of Sentence-Length Distributions

The number of words in each sentence in the Corpus was counted and the number of sentences of each length tabulated, both for the entire Corpus and for each of the genres. The genre distributions are given in Tables D12–D26 and are displayed graphically in Graphs D$_{II}$–D$_{XVI}$. The distribution for the whole Corpus is given in Table D11 and Graph D$_I$. In Table D11 the number of sentences (FX) of each given length (X) is displayed, together with the cumulative count of all sentences of length X or less ($SUM\ FX$); the percentage of all the Corpus sentences accounted for by $SUM\ FX$ is given in the column labeled CUM % FX.

It should be noted here that genre word totals found in this study are not identical with those used in the sections of this book dealing with the statistics of word distribution. For example, the word count used in this study for Genre A is 87,812, while for the calculation of word-level statistics it is 88,751. The reason for this discrepancy is that the computer program used to extract the figures for this study ignored nonsentence heading materials that occurred in the body of such samples as newspaper headlines and datelines, paragraph and section headings, free-standing formulas, etc. The word-level statistics, on the other hand, are based on all words in the Corpus, without reference to the sentence or nonsentence structures in

which they occur. The total Corpus discrepancy is 6,983 words: 1,007,249 words actually involved in sentence structures and 1,014,232 words in the complete Corpus.

In making the sentence-length tabulations, "word" and "sentence" were defined as follows: a word was generally regarded as any sequence of characters set off by spaces, although there were some exceptions to this rule. The slash counted as a space. Thus the word sequence "and/or" was counted as two words. The points of ellipsis, although set off by spaces in the code, were not counted as a word. For example, the sequence "I think . . ." counted as two words rather than three. Formulas (signaled by **F) and special items, such as typographical ornaments, for which no specific coding was available (signaled by **B) were counted as individual words when combined with other material within a sentence. When such a device appeared by itself, it was not counted.

The most reliable delimiter of the graphic sentence boundary is the end punctuation mark. The simple period followed by a space was found to be the only completely unambiguous signal for the end of a sentence. (An abbreviation period or point has a distinctive machine code.) Without exception all punctuation marks other than the period followed by a space were found to occur both within sentences and at sentence ends.

Most sentences in the Corpus ended with a simple period followed by a space. In those that did not, the end punctuation marks that created the greatest difficulty were the points of ellipsis, the long dash, the question mark, and the exclamation point. All of these marks may occur regularly within a sentence as well as at its end. The points of ellipsis and the long dash are used, in addition, to begin sentences. Such difficulties of punctuation analysis occurred most often when the writer of a sample used unconventional or complex punctuation and capitalization for stylistic reasons, such as for dialogue or for stream-of-consciousness writing. The ambiguities had to be resolved through an examination of context. For example, if points of ellipsis, a long dash, a question mark, or an exclamation point were followed by a capital letter, points of ellipsis, a long dash, a mathematical formula, or all capital letters, a sentence ending was assumed. Finally, the end of a sample or the end of a paragraph was automatically considered the end of a sentence, no matter what punctuation marks appeared, even when such marks (commas, colons, semicolons) would have normally been found in the middle of a sentence.

The following example illustrates some of the complexities and ambiguities of punctuation: " ' "Help! help! HELP!" But help never came.' is an example of unusual punctuation." The computer program would have counted the word sequence within the single quotation marks as three sentences of two, one, and four words. The program also would have counted "is an example of unusual punctuation" as a fourth sentence of six words. The criteria established to resolve ambiguities determining the end of a sentence are as follows:

1. The end of a sample and/or the end of a paragraph, without regard for what follows

2. A period followed by a space before the occurrence of the next word

3. The punctuation marks in the left-hand column below, if followed by any one of the conditions in the right-hand column before the occurrence of the next word—

End States	*Beginning States*
Points of ellipsis	Points of ellipsis
Long dash	Long dash
Question mark	Capital letter
Exclamation point	Mathematical formula
	All capitals

Comparison of Genre Distributions

When the sentences of the Corpus had been counted and tabulated, the chi-square test was made on the genre sentence-length distributions to determine the significance of their deviation from the normal population expressed by the sentence-length distribution of the Corpus. Because of the large size of the Corpus and the unusual skewness of its distribution curve, two tests were run. In the first test the chi-square matrix was set up with the fifteen genres as populations and six ranges that compared short sentences, a group of sentences on either side of the Corpus mean sentence length, and three groups of longer sentences. In the second test the fifteen genres were again used as populations, and the ranges were established arbitrarily at every tenth sentence length with the exception of the last, which included all sentences above fifty words in length.

In the first test with ranges set at sentence length 11, 18, 26, 40, 55, and 240, chi-square = 7,878. In the second test with arbitrary ranges at 10, 20, 30, 40, 50, and 240, chi-square = 8,020. At 70 degrees of freedom both of these numbers may be accepted as highly significant, since at that level chi-square = 104.22 is significant at the .005 percentile. This significance showed the genre distributions to be highly deviant from the expected distribution and gave support to the hypothesis that sentence length is a meaningful variable of genre style. As a consequence, further statistical tests were made on the individual genre distributions to determine the extent of their difference from each other and from the Corpus as a whole.

Mean sentence length was computed for each genre, together with the standard deviation and the coefficient of variation, the median, the mode, and the average number of sentences in each 2,000-word sample of the Corpus. These data are given in Table D1 and show immediately that the major division of the Corpus in terms of the sentence-length parameter is into the two large categories of informative and imaginative prose (hereafter Category I and Category II). When the mean sentence lengths are ranked in descending order (see Table D2), this major division is so marked that, excluding the means for Genre H and Genre R (the highest ranked in each category), it is possible to say that any mean in Category I or Category II is closer in value to every other mean of its own category than to any mean of the opposite category. The unusual cases of Genre H and Genre R will be discussed later.

The range of standard deviations for the genres (Table D1) is quite narrow, extending only from 9.3350 to 16.2514, and indicates that in all genres there is a fairly similar degree of clustering of sentences about the mean length. This tendency toward clustering can also be seen graphically in the leptokurtic nature of the curves shown in the graphs. The coefficients of variation (calculated by dividing the standard deviation by the mean) range from .5231 to .7897.

When the genres were ranked by mean sentence length it was evident that, in broad terms, there might be a relationship between a high percentage of quoted material in a genre (data given in Table D3) and a low mean sentence length. For the imaginative prose genres it may be assumed that a large proportion of the material within quotation marks is fictional dialogue. For the informative prose genres this material may be either the representation of spoken material or a quotation from another written source. Table D3 shows that, while all Category I genres have higher mean sentence lengths than all Category II genres, thus indicating the basic influence of quoted content on the sentence-length distribution, there is not an exact correlation. (It would be well to

remember that in the fiction sections of the Corpus dialogue represents artistic rather than actual rendering of spoken language. It is quite possible that many actual spoken utterances are not nearly so terse as might be supposed.)

Several examples of a lack of correlation between low mean sentence length and high percentage of dialogue were found. Genre E has the lowest mean sentence length of Category I (19.8694), but it has a dialogue percentage of only 5.7 per cent, as compared with a high for Category I of 11.9 per cent. Genre R has the highest mean sentence length in Category II—only .715 word below the mean for the whole Corpus and a large step (4.161 words) above its nearest neighbor in Category II—but its average dialogue percentage falls halfway down the ranking of those values for Category II.

A possible explanation lies in the fact that sentence structures in Genre E, which has a content of skills and hobbies literature, may be expected to be quite heavily weighted with short declarative or imperative sentences in the "how-to-do-it" style. Genre R (Humorous Literature) while it is in the imaginative prose category (II), contains at least six samples (out of a total of nine) of nonfiction, chiefly informal essays. The other genres of Category II contain only fiction samples. Stylistically, the light essay of Genre R may have more in common with the belles lettres genre (G) than it has with narrative fiction, especially in terms of the use of complexly embedded or lengthily modified structures. On this basis it would seem fair to conclude that, while a high average dialogue content is, in general, correlated with a low mean sentence length, there are a variety of stylistic factors that may override this correlation.

The data presented above show that, in addition to a major division between the Category I and Category II genres, there are significant variations in the sentence-length distributions within Category I. The genres of this category cover a much wider field of stylistic types than those of Category II. The range of mean sentence lengths in Category II is only from 12.7639 to 14.3898, excluding Genre R, which, as has been pointed out, is much more closely akin to some members of Category I than to its more immediate neighbors in Category II. The means of the Category I genres range from 18.5510 (if R is included) to 25.4863.

Examination of the content of the five genres with the highest mean sentence lengths—H (Miscellaneous: Government Documents and House Organs), 25.4863; J (Learned and Scientific Writings), 23.8045; D (Religion), 23.1870; G (Belles Lettres), 22.7004; and C (Press: Reviews), 22.3744—shows three possible factors associated with their ranking in this group. These three stylistic elements may occur alone or in combination in a genre. They are as follows:

1. The genre is one in which author and projected audience share an awareness of, and a critical interest in, stylish expository prose; how elegantly things are said is of great importance. This factor operates in the genres of Belles Lettres (G) and, probably to a lesser extent, in Press: Reviews (C).

2. The genre is one in which it is necessary for the author to make highly precise statements that exclude a set of further possibilities; i.e., the statements are likely to be extensively modified for the purposes of exactness. The most outstanding example of this factor is in Genre H, half of which is made up of samples from technical governmental legal statements, in which every possible loophole on one subject must be stopped before another subject is introduced. Genre J (Learned and Scientific Writings) also exhibits this factor by virtue of the highly specialized sorts of information exchanged by cognoscenti in a subject field. The title of Genre D (Reli-

gion) is ambiguous in regard to its stylistic level, but examination of the constituent samples shows that many of them belong to a type similar to Genre J. Three of the seventeen samples could be classed as popular literature, three as semipopular, and the remaining eleven as learned theology.

3. The genre is one in which a specialized set of concepts is assumed to be available to the audience. This is most evidently a factor in Genre J and in Genre D wherever it is similar to J. It is also a factor in Genre C (Press Reviews) insofar as a general critical apparatus is recognized. It is, in addition, probably a factor in much of Genre E (Skills and Hobbies), which has a relatively low mean sentence length, so that in this case the factor is overridden by the didactic requirement of the "cookbook" language.

With the exception of Genre E just noted, none of the remaining genres of Category I exhibit any of these three factors to a marked degree. This would seem to indicate that such paralinguistic elements do have a significant effect on authors, at least in terms of the specific quantitative measure under discussion here.

As another method of determining variation between genres, a rough measure of the skewness of each distribution curve was taken, using Pearson's formula (F. C. Mills, *Statistical Methods* [New York, 1924]): mean minus mode divided by standard deviation equals skew. This formula will give a result of zero for a normal distribution, where mean and mode coincide. The result for a non-normal distribution may be positive or negative: positive if the mode falls to the left of the mean and negative if it falls to the right. The theoretical limits of the measure are determined only by the left- and right-hand points of the curve. The results for the individual genre distributions are in Table D4. All values found here are positive. The larger the positive value, the greater the deviation of the distribution from a normal bell-shaped curve.

The skew factors for the genres range from a low of .185 to a high of .908. It should be noted that for Genre D and Genre P it was necessary to use artificial modes in the calculation. In the case of P this value is probably reliable, as the two peaks of the curve were at sentence lengths 6 and 7, and a value of 6.5 was used in the formula. However, due to the peculiar shape of the D curve, there were peaks at sentence-lengths 12 and 20, and an artificial figure of 16 had to be used—a somewhat greater exercise of latitude in curve-smoothing.

All of the genre curves are skewed because of their long right-hand tails (produced by the stringing-out of a few hyperlong sentences in each genre subdivision). In the Category II genres, however, this factor has combined with a heavy concentration of short sentences to produce particularly skewed curves. Here the genres K through R vary only between .736 and .908. Among the Category I genres, J (Learned and Scientific Writings), B (Press: Editorial), and C (Press: Reviews) have the least skewed curves. Genre C, in particular, with a measure of .185, approaches most closely a normal curve. The chief interest of this measure is that it, like the more sophisticated measures used, shows a fairly clear line of demarcation between the two major categories.

Sentence-Length Variety

A rather different measure of the role of sentence length in genre style description was found when determinations were made of the variety of different sentence lengths occurring in the various genres. In other words, did an author in a particular genre typically use a limited number of sentence lengths or a great variety of them, and did this factor differ between genres? It was

suspected from inspection of the genre sentence-length distributions that genre size and the number of different sentence lengths were relatively independent of each other. Table D5 presents data that support this hypothesis. The figures show that, while the largest data set (the whole Corpus) is 58.118 times larger than the smallest (Genre M), the Corpus has only 2.372 times as many different sentence lengths in it as M. In addition, the ranking of genres by size between these two extremes in no way corresponds to a ranking by the number of different sentence lengths present; Genre E with 3,615 sentences has 74 different sentence lengths, and Genre D with 1,476 sentences has the same number of different sentence lengths, but Genre N with 4,461 sentences has only 63 different sentence lengths.

A somewhat more sophisticated measure of the amount of variation in sentence length was made for each genre using Yule's K factor (G. Udny Yule, *The Statistical Study of Literary Vocabulary* [Cambridge, Eng., 1944]). A list of K factors will be found in Table D6. Although this factor was designed to measure the rate of vocabulary repetition in a text, it proved useful in this case for measuring the variety of sentence types used in a particular genre, where a type is a distinctive sentence length. Yule's formula for the K factor is

$$K = \frac{S_2 - S_1}{S_1{}^2} * 10{,}000$$

where

$$S_1 = \sum_x f_x X \quad \text{and} \quad S_2 = \sum_x f_x X^2.$$

For the calculation made here X equals the number of times a sentence length has occurred, and f_x equals the number of cases of X. For example, where $X = 1$ and $f_x = 7$, the statement is that there were seven cases in which a sentence length had only one occurrence. The limits of this measure are reached (a) when X equals

the total number of sentences in the data set and $f_x = 1$; for example, for Genre A, $X = 4{,}110$ and $f_x = 1$ would indicate that all of the sentences in A were of the same length; or (b) when $X = 1$ and f_x equals the total number of sentences in the data set, in which case no two sentences would be of the same length.

The Yule calculation has the advantage of being free of using the actual length in words of the sentences involved. It measures instead the degree of sentence-length variety only in regard to the frequency of occurrence of distinctive lengths and thus maintains its independence of sample size. A low K-factor value indicates a low rate of repetition of a sentence length and thus a greater diversity of sentence lengths present.

The most immediately evident result of the K-factor analysis is that it divides the genres into very nearly the same blocs as does the ranking by mean sentence length. The K factors, from the lowest to highest, arrange the genres in the following order: D, H, G, J, C, Corpus, F, R, B, A, E, K, M, P, N, L. The five lowest K factors (and thus the five genres with the greatest sentence-length diversity) are found for D, H, G, J, and C, and they correspond to the five longest mean sentence lengths, although they are not in the same order. The imaginative prose genres, with the exception of R, are again set off from the informative—this time by a consistently high K factor. Genre R, on the other hand, has moved even deeper into Category I, being eighth highest in the group of sixteen. The K factor for the whole Corpus, instead of dividing Category I and Category II, falls high in Category I, just below the first group of five. The remaining four genres of Category I—F, B, A, and E—maintain their central position, although in a different order from that of the mean sentence-length ranking.

The ranking of genres by the K factor may indicate roughly the variety of struc-

tural variants an author uses without feeling that he is violating the level of style imposed by the genre within which he is working. Most evidently this variety is greatest in those genres that are most concerned with elegance of style, with precise modification, and with a shared store of knowledge. The variety is least where the amount of dialogue representation is greatest: elegance of style is not commonly the concern of the casual spoken utterance.

Teachers of rhetoric have long preached that deliberate variation of sentence length makes an interesting composition, and critics have recognized sentence length as an aspect of individual style (G. Udny Yule, "On Sentence Length as a Statistical Characteristic of Style in Prose: With Application to Two Cases of Disputed Authorship," *Biometrika*, XXX [1939], 363–90). However, the *K* factor, when applied to a set of data large enough to transcend the individual author's attempts to apply this rule, gives a possible measure of a much deeper level of style. It may be the indicator of the range of grammatical stylistic devices allowed within the confines of a genre pattern.

Sentence-Length Homogeny

An attempt was made to discover what sort of internal consistency the genres had, in terms of sentence-length distributions. How similar were the distribution patterns of the samples composing a genre? Was there variation in this matter between genres, indicating that some types of writing have a more or less powerful pattern than others, or was there only a random occurrence of various distributions? This parameter was first investigated by Lubomir Doležel ("The Prague School and the Statistical Theory of Poetic Language," talk given at Brown University under the auspices of the Department of Slavic Languages, March 28, 1966) of Charles

University, Prague, in his sentence-length determinations of the homogeny of a genre. As he has so far dealt with small samples, he makes his comparisons in terms of mean sentence lengths.

For a text of the size of the Corpus a homogeny determination was begun by first running a chi-square test on each of the genres, using ranges that compared one group of short sentences, two groups roughly on either side of the mean and two groups of long sentences. These ranges vary between genres and are given in Table D8. All of the chi-squares are highly significant —below the .005 percentile—as was the figure for the whole Corpus. Table D7 gives the genre chi-squares, the number of degrees of freedom, and for purposes of comparison, the chi-square for the appropriate degree of freedom at the .005 percentile. By comparing the actual chi-square with this figure, an estimate of the significance can be made.

The data in Table D7 indicate that in no genre do the samples follow a strongly homogenous pattern. However, within the framework of this restriction, there are observable variations. The comparison of Genre C and Genre D is a case in point. Genres C (Press: Reviews) and D (Religion) were both in the top group of five in the mean sentence-length comparison, and both are the same size, having 64 degrees of freedom in the chi-square matrix. But the chi-square value for C is 112.8320, and that for D is 393.3181. Because we are dealing with values below the .005 percentile level, it is difficult to say just how significant such a variation really is.

Another, more revealing, test was made to rank the genres by amount of homogeny present. The mean sentence length for each of the 500 samples in the Corpus was determined. Frequency distributions were made of these sample means for each of the fifteen genres, and a mean of the means, a standard deviation, and a coefficient of variation computed for each distribution.

These data are given in Table D9. The coefficient of variation is derived from the formula standard deviation divided by the mean. As such, it indicates the rate at which items in the distribution move away from the mean. Thus, in terms of the measurement of the sentence-length homogeny of the samples whose mean sentence lengths make up the frequency distribution, the lower the coefficient of variation, the greater the degree of homogeny in the samples. Table D10 gives the genres in the order of this coefficient of variation (derived from the mean and the standard deviation of a frequency distribution whose members are the mean sentence lengths of the genre's constituent samples). The list is in order of decreasing homogeny. Thus in terms of sentence-length distribution patterns, the individual samples of Genre K are less alike than those of Genre A. These data may be further interpreted in regard to style by saying that more different combinatorial sentence-length patterns are characteristic of the genres with the least homogeny, while those with the greatest homogeny adhere most closely to a similar sentence-length distribution.

Press: Reportage (Genre A) shows the greatest degree of homogeny in the Corpus, perhaps understandably in the light of the stringent restrictions of the short news story and the oft-repeated behest to the journalist to "tell who, what, when, where, and how, and don't speculate." Imaginative prose genres are scattered through the list (Table D10 shows sentence length in such genres), with R (Humor), P (Romance), and K (General Fiction) at the bottom of the rank, showing the least homogeny of the whole Corpus; and L (Mystery), M (Fiction: Science), and N (Adventure) in the top, or most homogenous, half of the list. This measure is especially interesting in that it shows the diversity of the creative fiction genres. In other measures applied in this paper to determine the parameters of sentence length in genre style, the fiction genres have tended to operate as a bloc, but this measure sets off, as showing the most homogeny, those genres (L, M, and N) which—although they have many excellent practitioners—are most often associated with potboilers and pulp magazines.

The following conclusions may be drawn from this study. Within this sampling of written American English, sentence length is a measurably significant variable of genre style. Sentence-length distribution is highly dependent upon the classification of the genre as informative or imaginative prose, and, more speculatively, is subtly dependent upon the expected relationship between author and audience, the nature and/or purpose of the information being conveyed, and the expected patterns set by previous examples of the genre.

The variety of different sentence lengths occurring in a genre (determined by Yule's K factor) is another significant parameter of style. This factor may provide an index to the number of other stylistic variables, chiefly grammatical, that are used by an author within the confines of a genre. Genres can be ranked by degree of internal homogeny of sentence-length distribution patterns. This parameter is particularly useful in distinguishing differences in stylistic patterns between members of the imaginative prose category.

The chief value of this experiment, over and above the determination of the factual results above, has been to demonstrate again that, using a text of sufficient size to minimize the idiosyncrasies of individual authors, strictly quantitative measurements can be made of what has heretofore been the preserve of the aesthetic elements of language style.

Table D1 Mean Sentence Length, Standard Deviation, Coefficient of Variation, Median, Mode, and Average Number of Sentences per 2,000-Word Sample

Genre	Mean	Standard Deviation	Variation	Median*	Mode	Number of Sentences per Sample
A	21.36545000	11.17565000	0.52307112	19.34	16	93.41
B	20.36163700	11.48993400	0.56429323	18.00	16	97.70
C	22.37444300	12.82045000	0.57299526	19.93	20	92.53
D	23.18699100	15.09900500	0.65118432	20.00	16	86.82
E	19.86943200	11.08184600	0.55773340	17.67	14	100.43
F	21.30654300	12.28865400	0.57675494	18.47	13	94.88
G	22.70037300	13.59918600	0.59907323	19.67	17	89.27
H	25.48629500	16.25144500	0.63765427	21.79	16	80.27
J	23.80537000	12.60137400	0.52935005	21.15	19	84.26
K	14.38979600	11.29509300	0.78493767	10.92	5	139.24
L	12.76386300	9.44916820	0.74030630	9.98	5	157.04
M	13.38598400	10.03004700	0.74929471	10.63	6	149.83
N	13.09302800	9.33498740	0.71297391	10.61	6	153.83
P	13.72067400	10.83493700	0.78967964	10.19	6.5	147.28
R	18.55100000	12.71579300	0.68545054	15.94	7	111.11
Corpus	19.26561600	12.73860600	0.66120937	16.41	12	104.50

* The medians do not represent actual sentence lengths, but are hypothetical values determined by the point on the sentence-length axis when half of the total sentences in a genre have been summed.

Table D2   Genres Ranked by Mean Sentence Length

Genre	Mean	Content
H	25.4863	Miscellaneous: Government Documents, etc.
J	23.8054	Learned and Scientific Writings
D	23.1870	Religion
G	22.7004	Belles Lettres
C	22.3744	Press: Reviews
A	21.3655	Press: Reportage
F	21.3065	Popular Lore
B	20.3616	Press: Editorial
E	19.8694	Skills and Hobbies
Corpus	19.2656	
R	18.5510	Humor
K	14.3898	Fiction: General
P	13.7207	Fiction: Romance and Love Story
M	13.3860	Fiction: Science
N	13.0930	Fiction: Adventure and Western
L	12.7639	Fiction: Mystery and Detective

Table D3   Correlation of Mean Sentence Length in Descending Order with Average Percentage of Quoted Material per Genre

Genre	Mean	Per Cent of Quoted Material
H	25.4863	4.5
J	23.8054	2.8
D	23.1870	10.5
G	22.7004	11.9
C	22.3744	7.5
A	21.3655	10.6
F	21.3065	7.4
B	20.3616	8.6
E	19.8694	5.7
Corpus	19.2656	10.8
R	18.5510	20.2
K	14.3898	14.9
P	13.7207	22.3
M	13.3860	26.8
N	13.0930	20.9
L	12.7639	22.9

Table D4   Pearson's Skew Factor by Genre

Genre	Skew
A	.470
B	.380
C	.185
D	.476
E	.530
F	.676
G	.419
H	.584
J	.381
K	.830
L	.817
M	.736
N	.760
P	.666
R	.908
Corpus	.570

Table D5 Number of Sentences and Number of Different Sentence Lengths for Each Genre

Genre	No. of Sentences per Genre	No. of Sentence Lengths per Genre
A	4,110	72
B	2,638	69
C	1,573	74
D	1,476	74
E	3,615	74
F	4,554	80
G	6,695	97
H	2,408	93
J	6,741	94
K	4,038	76
L	3,769	60
M	899	51
N	4,461	63
P	4,271	73
R	1,000	65
Corpus	52,248	121

Table D6 K Factors for Each Genre

Genre	K Factor
A	276.80039
B	273.89969
C	261.95384
D	217.73855
E	302.38842
F	269.54349
G	247.36929
H	233.41008
J	259.35562
K	355.71923
L	402.32838
M	368.07675
N	393.81783
P	382.01806
R	272.42000
Corpus	266.24033

Table D7 Chi-Squares, Degrees of Freedom, and Comparative Chi-Square Values at the .005 Percentile Level

Genre	Chi-Square	Degree of Freedom	Chi-Square Values at .005 Percentile
A	422.7734	172	c. 223.00
B	344.4497	104	144.89
C	112.8320	64	96.88
D	393.3181	64	96.88
E	558.9766	140	186.85
F	996.5313	188	c. 223.00
G	1301.8359	296	c. 366.00
H	422.2070	116	158.97
J	1136.2500	316	c. 366.00
K	731.4675	112	154.29
L	260.0007	92	130.49
M	91.7031	20	39.99
N	472.9258	112	154.29
P	623.8085	112	154.29
R	174.8928	32	56.33

Table D8   Ranges for the Chi-Square Computation to Determine Genre Homogeny

Genre	Range for Chi-Square Computation				
A	10	20	27	34	107
B	10	20	27	34	88
C	10	20	27	34	121
D	15	20	24	29	123
E	10	17	20	24	143
F	10	20	25	29	124
G	15	20	25	29	160
H	15	23	26	29	240
J	10	21	25	29	116
K	9	12	15	19	100
L	9	12	17	24	163
M	9	12	17	24	83
N	9	12	15	19	133
P	9	12	15	19	111
R	10	17	22	29	111

Table D9   Mean, Standard Deviation, and Coefficient of Variation for Frequency Distributions of the 2,000-Word-Sample Means of Each Genre

Genre	Mean	Standard Deviation	Coefficient of Variation
A	21.6386	2.4253	0.1121
B	20.8891	3.4951	0.1673
C	22.6492	2.7881	0.1231
D	25.0600	7.1900	0.2869
E	20.5706	3.8289	0.1861
F	22.4925	5.6461	0.2510
G	24.0029	6.0054	0.2502
H	26.8586	6.4785	0.2412
J	24.6724	4.9937	0.2024
K	15.9085	5.7905	0.3640
L	12.9874	1.6951	0.1305
M	13.7462	2.3885	0.1738
N	13.6375	2.8221	0.2069
P	14.9360	4.7751	0.3197
R	19.6883	5.2183	0.2650

Table D10   Genres Ranked by Coefficient of Variation from Table D9

Genre	Variation
A	0.1121
C	0.1231
L	0.1305
B	0.1673
M	0.1738
E	0.1861
J	0.2024
N	0.2069
H	0.2412
G	0.2502
F	0.2510
R	0.2650
D	0.2869
P	0.3197
K	0.3640

Table D11   Sentence-Length Distribution Statistics for the Whole Corpus

X	FX	SUM FX	CUM % FX	X	FX	SUM FX	CUM % FX
1	421	421	0.805	44	212	50053	95.798
2	716	1137	2.176	45	204	50257	96.189
3	973	2110	4.038	46	183	50440	96.539
4	1331	3441	6.585	47	166	50606	96.857
5	1590	5031	9.629	48	126	50732	97.098
6	1666	6697	12.817	49	117	50849	97.322
7	1837	8534	16.333	50	115	50964	97.542
8	1852	10386	19.878	51	137	51101	97.804
9	1717	12103	23.164	52	108	51209	98.011
10	1846	13949	26.697	53	91	51300	98.185
11	1861	15810	30.259	54	91	51391	98.359
12	1979	17789	34.047	55	67	51458	98.487
13	1917	19706	37.716	56	63	51521	98.608
14	1960	21666	41.467	57	54	51575	98.711
15	1838	23504	44.985	58	61	51636	98.828
16	1850	25354	48.526	59	65	51701	98.953
17	1794	27148	51.959	60	43	51744	99.035
18	1727	28875	55.265	61	46	51790	99.123
19	1687	30562	58.494	62	32	51822	99.184
20	1621	32183	61.596	63	32	51854	99.245
21	1498	33681	64.463	64	39	51893	99.320
22	1423	35104	67.187	65	33	51926	99.383
23	1383	36487	69.834	66	29	51955	99.439
24	1320	37807	72.360	67	27	51982	99.490
25	1090	38897	74.446	68	30	52012	99.548
26	1138	40035	76.624	69	16	52028	99.578
27	1112	41147	78.753	70	15	52043	99.607
28	941	42088	80.554	71	11	52054	99.628
29	883	42971	82.244	72	9	52063	99.645
30	813	43784	83.800	73	11	52074	99.666
31	790	44574	85.312	74	18	52092	99.701
32	693	45267	86.638	75	16	52108	99.732
33	667	45934	87.915	76	6	52114	99.743
34	555	46489	88.977	77	6	52120	99.755
35	549	47038	90.028	78	4	52124	99.762
36	471	47509	90.929	79	3	52127	99.768
37	438	47947	91.768	80	9	52136	99.785
38	399	48346	92.531	81	5	52141	99.795
39	357	48703	93.215	82	6	52147	99.806
40	308	49011	93.804	83	7	52154	99.820
41	326	49337	94.428	84	4	52158	99.827
42	255	49592	94.916	85	7	52165	99.841
43	249	49841	95.393	86	9	52174	99.858

Table D11 (cont.)   Sentence-Length Distribution Statistics
for the Whole Corpus

X	FX	SUM FX	CUM % FX	X	FX	SUM FX	CUM % FX
87	1	52175	99.860	111	4	52227	99.959
88	8	52183	99.875	112	1	52228	99.961
89	8	52191	99.890	115	2	52230	99.965
90	4	52195	99.898	116	2	52232	99.969
92	3	52198	99.904	117	1	52233	99.971
93	2	52200	99.908	121	2	52235	99.975
94	3	52203	99.913	122	1	52236	99.977
95	1	52204	99.915	123	1	52237	99.978
96	1	52205	99.917	124	2	52239	99.982
99	1	52206	99.919	126	2	52241	99.986
100	5	52211	99.929	129	1	52242	99.988
101	2	52213	99.933	133	1	52243	99.990
102	2	52215	99.936	143	1	52244	99.992
104	2	52217	99.940	154	1	52245	99.994
106	2	52219	99.944	160	1	52246	99.996
107	2	52221	99.948	163	1	52247	99.998
108	1	52222	99.950	240	1	52248	100.000
110	1	52223	99.952				

Table D12   Sentence-Length Distribution of Genre A,
Press, Reportage

Words per Sentence	Number of Sentences	Words per Sentence	Number of Sentences	Words per Sentence	Number of Sentences
1	3	36	42	71	0
2	12	37	52	72	0
3	17	38	38	73	1
4	44	39	32	74	0
5	66	40	18	75	0
6	76	41	34	76	0
7	98	42	21	77	0
8	96	43	21	78	0
9	110	44	13	79	0
10	118	45	17	80	2
11	126	46	15	81	0
12	143	47	13	82	1
13	153	48	9	83	0
14	146	49	9	84	0
15	159	50	12	85	1
16	168	51	7	86	0
17	163	52	9	87	0
18	166	53	2	88	0
19	139	54	7	89	0
20	153	55	2	90	2
21	150	56	5	—	—
22	150	57	3	107	1
23	134	58	1	—	
24	123	59	3		4,110
25	118	60	4		
26	138	61	4		
27	109	62	1		
28	84	63	0		
29	89	64	0		
30	84	65	1		
31	96	66	5		
32	78	67	2		
33	71	68	2		
34	58	69	1		
35	59	70	0		

Table D13   Sentence-Length Distribution of Genre B,
Press, Editorial

Words per Sentence	Number of Sentences	Words per Sentence	Number of Sentences	Words per Sentence	Number of Sentences
1	23	36	21	71	0
2	21	37	24	72	0
3	25	38	26	73	1
4	27	39	25	74	1
5	54	40	12	75	0
6	45	41	24	76	0
7	68	42	15	77	0
8	75	43	12	78	0
9	88	44	10	79	0
10	90	45	9	80	0
11	87	46	6	81	2
12	98	47	5	82	0
13	88	48	7	83	0
14	112	49	8	84	0
15	96	50	2	85	0
16	124	51	10	86	0
17	103	52	3	87	0
18	94	53	3	88	1
19	91	54	3	89	0
20	101	55	2		
21	89	56	6		2,638
22	78	57	2		
23	67	58	4		
24	85	59	6		
25	71	60	4		
26	75	61	2		
27	70	62	2		
28	52	63	0		
29	53	64	1		
30	44	65	0		
31	53	66	0		
32	39	67	1		
33	33	68	0		
34	24	69	1		
35	34	70	0		

Table D14 Sentence-Length Distribution of Genre C, Press, Reviews

Words per Sentence	Number of Sentences	Words per Sentence	Number of Sentences	Words per Sentence	Number of Sentences
1	3	36	15	71	0
2	5	37	22	72	0
3	18	38	21	73	0
4	17	39	13	74	0
5	22	40	8	75	0
6	19	41	10	76	0
7	31	42	8	77	0
8	46	43	8	78	0
9	40	44	13	79	1
10	39	45	10	80	0
11	40	46	4	81	0
12	60	47	4	82	0
13	62	48	3	83	1
14	53	49	3	84	0
15	45	50	7	85	0
16	46	51	3	86	0
17	64	52	3	87	0
18	56	53	3	88	0
19	53	54	4	89	1
20	73	55	0	—	—
21	46	56	1	100	1
22	54	57	2	101	1
23	65	58	3	102	1
24	53	59	3	104	1
25	37	60	3	121	1
26	49	61	2		
27	36	62	3		1,573
28	48	63	1		
29	37	64	4		
30	31	65	1		
31	27	66	0		
32	23	67	0		
33	34	68	0		
34	24	69	1		
35	22	70	1		

Table D15   Sentence-Length Distribution of Genre D, Religion

Words per Sentence	Number of Sentences	Words per Sentence	Number of Sentences	Words per Sentence	Number of Sentences
1	9	36	15	71	1
2	17	37	20	72	3
3	23	38	12	73	2
4	38	39	24	74	1
5	22	40	11	75	0
6	28	41	17	76	0
7	34	42	17	77	1
8	43	43	12	78	0
9	44	44	6	79	0
10	41	45	13	80	0
11	47	46	10	81	0
12	49	47	3	82	0
13	38	48	5	83	0
14	45	49	12	84	0
15	47	50	6	85	0
16	43	51	11	86	0
17	47	52	4	87	0
18	36	53	7	88	0
19	39	54	4	89	2
20	49	55	2	—	—
21	41	56	3	104	1
22	48	57	0	106	1
23	35	58	4	123	1
24	35	59	3		—
25	34	60	0		1,476
26	35	61	7		
27	48	62	0		
28	30	63	5		
29	24	64	5		
30	23	65	5		
31	28	66	3		
32	21	67	4		
33	25	68	2		
34	24	69	0		
35	21	70	0		

Table D16   Sentence-Length Distribution of Genre E,
   Skills and Hobbies

Words per Sentence	Number of Sentences	Words per Sentence	Number of Sentences	Words per Sentence	Number of Sentences
1	9	36	34	71	0
2	25	37	24	72	0
3	32	38	15	73	1
4	37	39	16	74	0
5	44	40	15	75	1
6	72	41	21	76	0
7	86	42	21	77	0
8	99	43	18	78	0
9	122	44	11	79	0
10	141	45	15	80	0
11	126	46	10	81	0
12	150	47	11	82	1
13	144	48	8	83	1
14	182	49	3	84	0
15	134	50	9	85	1
16	139	51	4	86	0
17	158	52	7	87	0
18	161	53	1	88	1
19	133	54	4	89	0
20	171	55	3	—	—
21	133	56	6	115	1
22	112	57	3	124	1
23	111	58	4	143	1
24	118	59	3		
25	97	60	0		—
26	85	61	1		3,615
27	72	62	0		
28	82	63	2		
29	68	64	0		
30	73	65	1		
31	49	66	1		
32	58	67	1		
33	39	68	2		
34	38	69	0		
35	32	70	0		

Table D17   Sentence-Length Distribution of Genre F, Popular Lore

Words per Sentence	Number of Sentences	Words per Sentence	Number of Sentences	Words per Sentence	Number of Sentences
1	11	36	48	71	1
2	20	37	37	72	1
3	40	38	38	73	0
4	54	39	20	74	0
5	76	40	42	75	1
6	75	41	35	76	0
7	110	42	25	77	0
8	122	43	20	78	0
9	127	44	23	79	1
10	158	45	14	80	1
11	163	46	11	81	1
12	165	47	26	82	0
13	191	48	16	83	0
14	186	49	12	84	0
15	178	50	11	85	0
16	180	51	21	86	0
17	160	52	8	87	0
18	173	53	15	88	1
19	189	54	11	89	2
20	137	55	7	90	1
21	158	56	4	—	—
22	147	57	6	100	1
23	124	58	5	124	1
24	137	59	5	—	
25	93	60	8		4,554
26	104	61	6		
27	105	62	3		
28	104	63	5		
29	104	64	7		
30	86	65	4		
31	98	66	2		
32	71	67	3		
33	71	68	0		
34	59	69	4		
35	62	70	2		

Table D18   Sentence-Length Distribution of Genre G, Belles Lettres

Words per Sentence	Number of Sentences	Words per Sentence	Number of Sentences	Words per Sentence	Number of Sentences
1	14	36	90	71	4
2	32	37	65	72	2
3	42	38	80	73	2
4	65	39	69	74	6
5	111	40	60	75	5
6	139	41	59	76	1
7	154	42	39	77	2
8	202	43	56	78	2
9	177	44	38	79	0
10	174	45	38	80	2
11	224	46	38	81	0
12	235	47	36	82	0
13	211	48	19	83	1
14	242	49	17	84	1
15	225	50	17	85	1
16	225	51	23	86	2
17	246	52	23	87	0
18	236	53	19	88	1
19	245	54	18	89	1
20	223	55	22	——	——
21	212	56	16	92	2
22	201	57	18	94	1
23	209	58	18	99	1
24	199	59	12	100	1
25	153	60	4	101	1
26	168	61	6	102	1
27	183	62	8	106	1
28	138	63	6	112	1
29	146	64	9	115	1
30	134	65	8	117	1
31	127	66	7	121	1
32	117	67	3	160	1
33	114	68	8		——
34	84	69	3		6,695
35	85	70	5		

Table D19 Sentence-Length Distribution of Genre H, Miscellaneous

Words per Sentence	Number of Sentences	Words per Sentence	Number of Sentences	Words per Sentence	Number of Sentences
1	9	36	30	71	2
2	7	37	32	72	1
3	17	38	29	73	4
4	21	39	25	74	3
5	34	40	29	75	3
6	18	41	22	76	3
7	42	42	19	77	1
8	30	43	14	78	0
9	31	44	26	79	0
10	51	45	16	80	3
11	66	46	18	81	1
12	68	47	16	82	2
13	86	48	12	83	2
14	87	49	9	84	1
15	90	50	11	85	1
16	91	51	14	86	4
17	88	52	13	87	0
18	75	53	8	88	0
19	73	54	11	89	0
20	74	55	10	—	—
21	76	56	6	94	1
22	89	57	5	101	1
23	77	58	2	111	2
24	72	59	7	122	1
25	66	60	3	123	1
26	78	61	6	126	2
27	70	62	5	129	1
28	54	63	2	154	1
29	58	64	4	240	1
30	60	65	5		—
31	40	66	4		2,408
32	36	67	4		
33	34	68	6		
34	31	69	2		
35	38	70	4		

Table D20   Sentence-Length Distribution of Genre J,
Learned and Scientific Writings

Words per Sentence	Number of Sentences	Words per Sentence	Number of Sentences	Words per Sentence	Number of Sentences
1	20	36	89	71	1
2	18	37	86	72	1
3	23	38	80	73	1
4	18	39	83	74	5
5	48	40	66	75	3
6	76	41	69	76	2
7	108	42	48	77	0
8	114	43	55	78	1
9	125	44	48	79	1
10	177	45	42	80	0
11	179	46	48	81	1
12	232	47	30	82	0
13	222	48	29	83	1
14	233	49	25	84	2
15	248	50	25	85	2
16	263	51	25	86	2
17	228	52	25	87	0
18	262	53	16	88	1
19	279	54	17	89	2
20	237	55	9	—	—
21	225	56	11	92	1
22	240	57	12	93	1
23	237	58	16	94	1
24	222	59	11	95	1
25	206	60	9	96	1
26	193	61	9	100	1
27	204	62	4	107	1
28	160	63	6	108	1
29	150	64	5	116	1
30	131	65	6		—
31	137	66	5		6,741
32	135	67	5		
33	116	68	8		
34	102	69	2		
35	113	70	1		

Table D21   Sentence-Length Distribution of Genre K, Fiction, General

Words per Sentence	Number of Sentences	Words per Sentence	Number of Sentences	Words per Sentence	Number of Sentences
1	71	36	21	71	0
2	122	37	20	72	1
3	171	38	22	73	0
4	215	39	16	74	2
5	239	40	9	75	0
6	227	41	10	76	0
7	218	42	10	77	1
8	226	43	10	78	0
9	177	44	5	79	0
10	196	45	6	80	0
11	171	46	7	81	0
12	165	47	8	82	0
13	162	48	5	83	0
14	142	49	6	84	0
15	122	50	4	85	0
16	121	51	6	86	1
17	129	52	3	87	1
18	99	53	5	88	1
19	96	54	5	89	0
20	83	55	4	90	1
21	79	56	3	—	—
22	61	57	1	93	1
23	71	58	0	100	1
24	55	59	3		
25	44	60	3		4,038
26	51	61	2		
27	40	62	0		
28	52	63	4		
29	29	64	2		
30	48	65	1		
31	31	66	0		
32	29	67	1		
33	41	68	1		
34	24	69	1		
35	16	70	1		

Table D22   Sentence-Length Distribution of Genre L, Fiction, Mystery and Detective

Words per Sentence	Number of Sentences	Words per Sentence	Number of Sentences	Words per Sentence	Number of Sentences
1	78	36	9	71	0
2	113	37	5	72	0
3	161	38	11	73	0
4	202	39	5	74	0
5	259	40	9	75	2
6	234	41	7	76	0
7	243	42	4	77	0
8	210	43	5	78	0
9	200	44	2	79	0
10	189	45	4	80	0
11	173	46	5	81	0
12	162	47	2	82	0
13	145	48	2	83	0
14	140	49	0	84	0
15	132	50	0	85	1
16	132	51	2	86	0
17	78	52	2	87	0
18	92	53	2	88	1
19	90	54	1	89	0
20	81	55	1	—	—
21	86	56	0	163	1
22	60	57	0		—
23	62	58	2		3,769
24	54	59	0		
25	44	60	0		
26	43	61	0		
27	41	62	1		
28	37	63	0		
29	30	64	0		
30	23	65	0		
31	19	66	0		
32	19	67	1		
33	23	68	0		
34	16	69	0		
35	11	70	0		

Table D23   Sentence-Length Distribution of Genre M,
Fiction, Science

Words per Sentence	Number of Sentences	Words per Sentence	Number of Sentences	Words per Sentence	Number of Sentences
1	29	36	4	71	0
2	25	37	1	72	0
3	43	38	2	73	0
4	45	39	1	74	0
5	57	40	3	75	0
6	60	41	2	76	0
7	50	42	1	77	1
8	50	43	0	78	0
9	42	44	1	79	0
10	32	45	0	80	0
11	27	46	2	81	0
12	30	47	1	82	0
13	41	48	3	83	1
14	36	49	0	84	0
15	29	50	0	85	0
16	30	51	0	86	0
17	19	52	0	87	0
18	28	53	1	88	0
19	22	54	0	89	0
20	28	55	1		—
21	22	56	0		899
22	12	57	0		
23	17	58	0		
24	13	59	0		
25	11	60	0		
26	10	61	0		
27	10	62	1		
28	10	63	0		
29	12	64	0		
30	7	65	0		
31	2	66	0		
32	4	67	0		
33	7	68	0		
34	6	69	0		
35	7	70	0		

Table D24   Sentence-Length Distribution of Genre N, Fiction, Adventure and Western

Words per Sentence	Number of Sentences	Words per Sentence	Number of Sentences	Words per Sentence	Number of Sentences
1	72	36	20	71	0
2	124	37	24	72	0
3	185	38	6	73	0
4	251	39	12	74	0
5	264	40	7	75	0
6	284	41	4	76	0
7	273	42	11	77	0
8	260	43	4	78	0
9	174	44	6	79	0
10	221	45	4	80	0
11	203	46	2	81	0
12	219	47	2	82	1
13	187	48	1	83	0
14	177	49	4	84	0
15	158	50	2	85	0
16	126	51	1	86	0
17	153	52	3	87	0
18	127	53	1	88	0
19	108	54	2	89	0
20	112	55	2	—	—
21	82	56	0	116	1
22	84	57	1	133	1
23	69	58	0	—	—
24	63	59	0		4,461
25	52	60	1		
26	60	61	0		
27	62	62	0		
28	30	63	0		
29	29	64	1		
30	30	65	0		
31	28	66	0		
32	20	67	0		
33	18	68	0		
34	18	69	1		
35	12	70	1		

Table D25   Sentence-Length Distribution of Genre P, Fiction,
Romance and Love Story

Words per Sentence	Number of Sentences	Words per Sentence	Number of Sentences	Words per Sentence	Number of Sentences
1	65	36	24	71	1
2	160	37	18	72	0
3	156	38	14	73	0
4	261	39	11	74	0
5	253	40	11	75	1
6	275	41	5	76	0
7	275	42	12	77	0
8	237	43	11	78	1
9	218	44	5	79	0
10	181	45	10	80	0
11	198	46	5	81	0
12	178	47	5	82	0
13	154	48	6	83	0
14	147	49	8	84	0
15	149	50	4	85	0
16	131	51	9	86	0
17	113	52	3	87	0
18	90	53	5	88	1
19	99	54	3	89	0
20	75	55	1	—	—
21	70	56	1	110	1
22	66	57	1	111	1
23	77	58	1		
24	65	59	6		4,271
25	42	60	4		
26	36	61	1		
27	49	62	4		
28	42	63	1		
29	35	64	1		
30	31	65	1		
31	38	66	1		
32	30	67	1		
33	20	68	0		
34	29	69	0		
35	27	70	0		

Table D26   Sentence-Length Distribution of Genre R, Humor

Words per Sentence	Number of Sentences	Words per Sentence	Number of Sentences	Words per Sentence	Number of Sentences
1	5	36	9	71	1
2	15	37	6	72	0
3	20	38	5	73	0
4	36	39	5	74	0
5	41	40	7	75	0
6	38	41	7	76	0
7	47	42	4	77	0
8	42	43	3	78	0
9	42	44	5	79	0
10	38	45	6	80	1
11	31	46	2	81	0
12	25	47	4	82	1
13	33	48	1	83	0
14	32	49	1	84	0
15	26	50	5	85	0
16	31	51	1	86	0
17	45	52	2	87	0
18	32	53	3	88	0
19	31	54	1	89	0
20	24	55	1	—	—
21	29	56	1	111	1
22	21	57	0		—
23	28	58	1		1,000
24	26	59	3		
25	22	60	0		
26	13	61	0		
27	13	62	0		
28	18	63	0		
29	19	64	0		
30	8	65	0		
31	17	66	1		
32	13	67	1		
33	21	68	1		
34	18	69	0		
35	10	70	0		

Graph Dɪ   Sentence-Length Distribution of the Whole Corpus

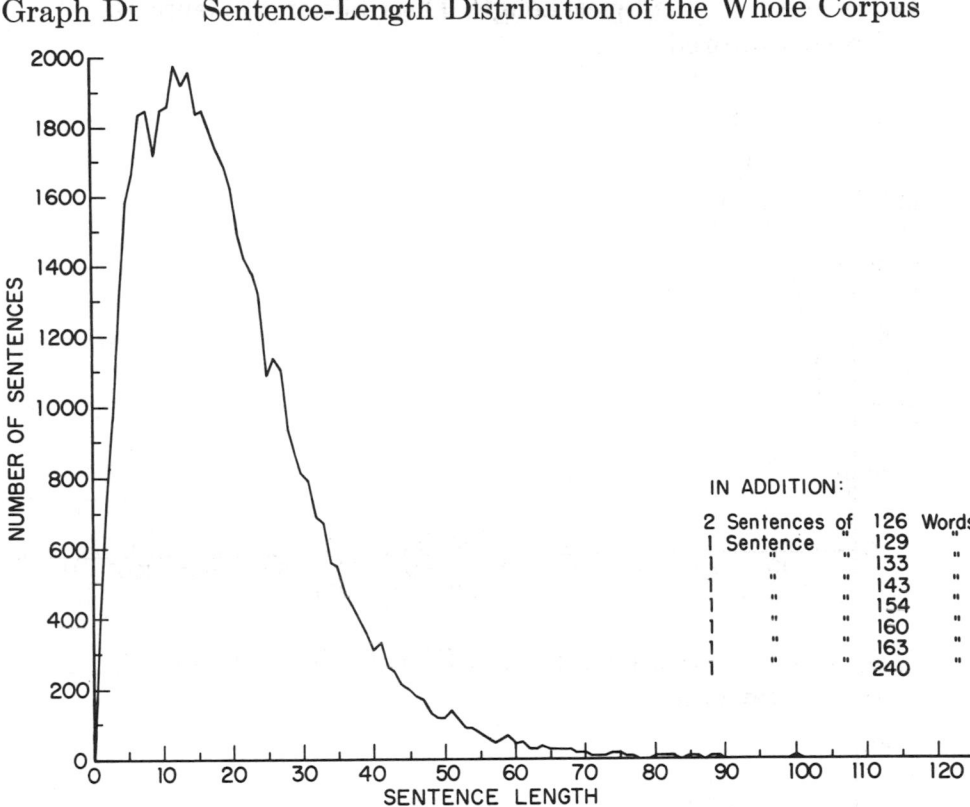

IN ADDITION:

2 Sentences of 126 Words
1 Sentence   "   129   "
1   "   "   133   "
1   "   "   143   "
1   "   "   154   "
1   "   "   160   "
1   "   "   163   "
1   "   "   240   "

Graph Dɪɪ   Sentence-Length Distribution of Genre A,
Press, Reportage

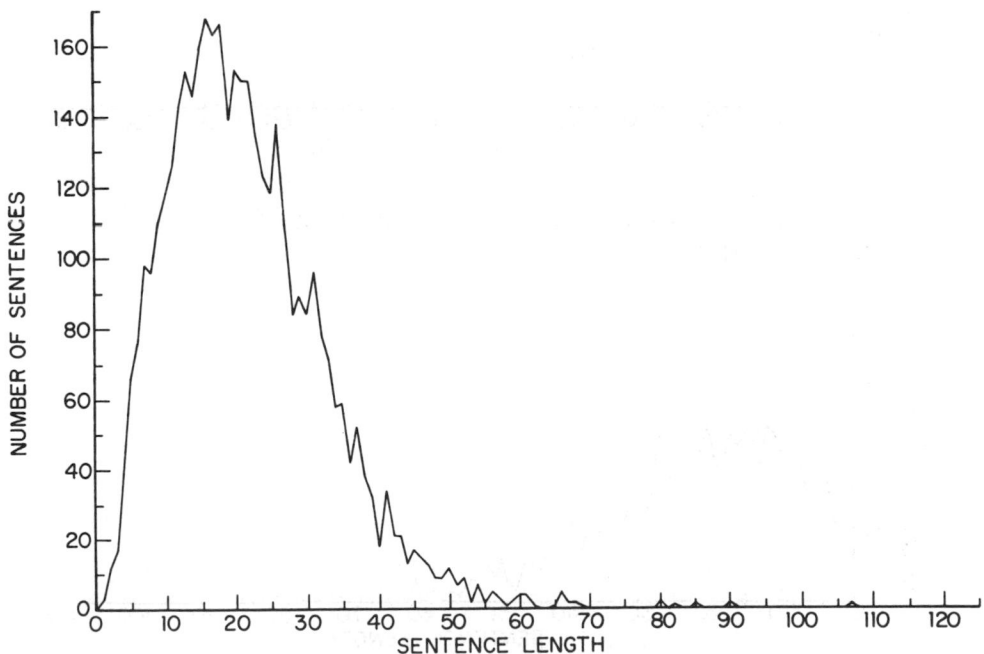

Graph Dɪɪɪ   Sentence-Length Distribution of Genre B, Press, Editorial

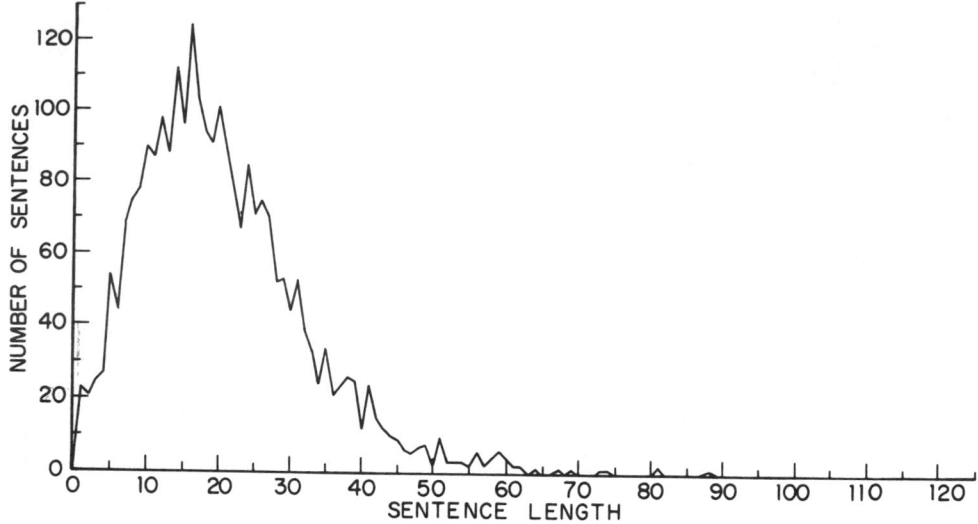

Graph Dɪᴠ   Sentence-Length Distribution of Genre C, Press, Reviews

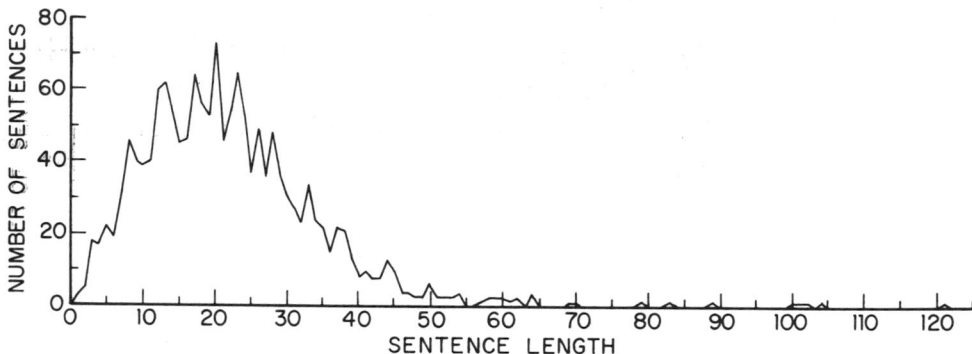

Graph Dᴠ   Sentence-Length Distribution of Genre D, Religion

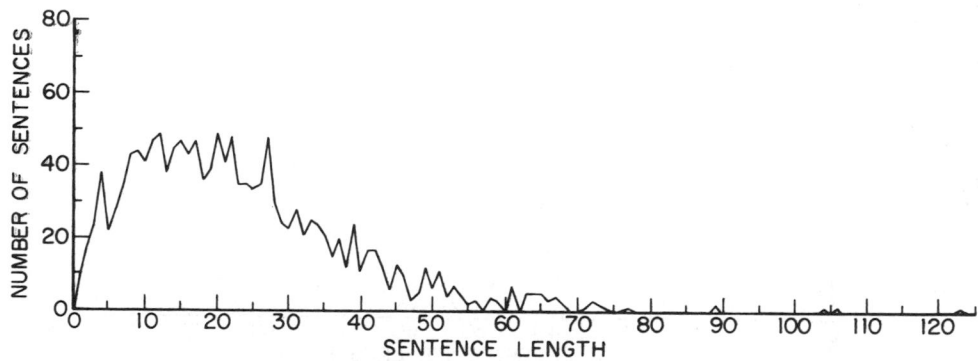

Graph Dvɪ   Sentence-Length Distribution of Genre E, Skills and Hobbies

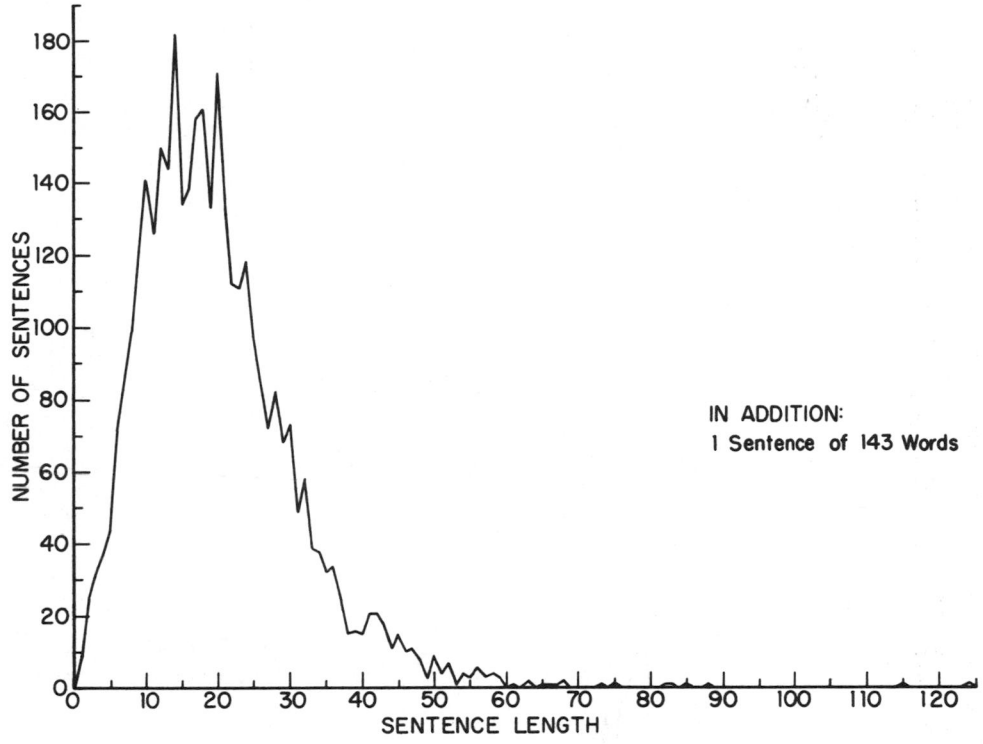

IN ADDITION:
1 Sentence of 143 Words

Graph Dvɪɪ   Sentence-Length Distribution of Genre F, Popular Lore

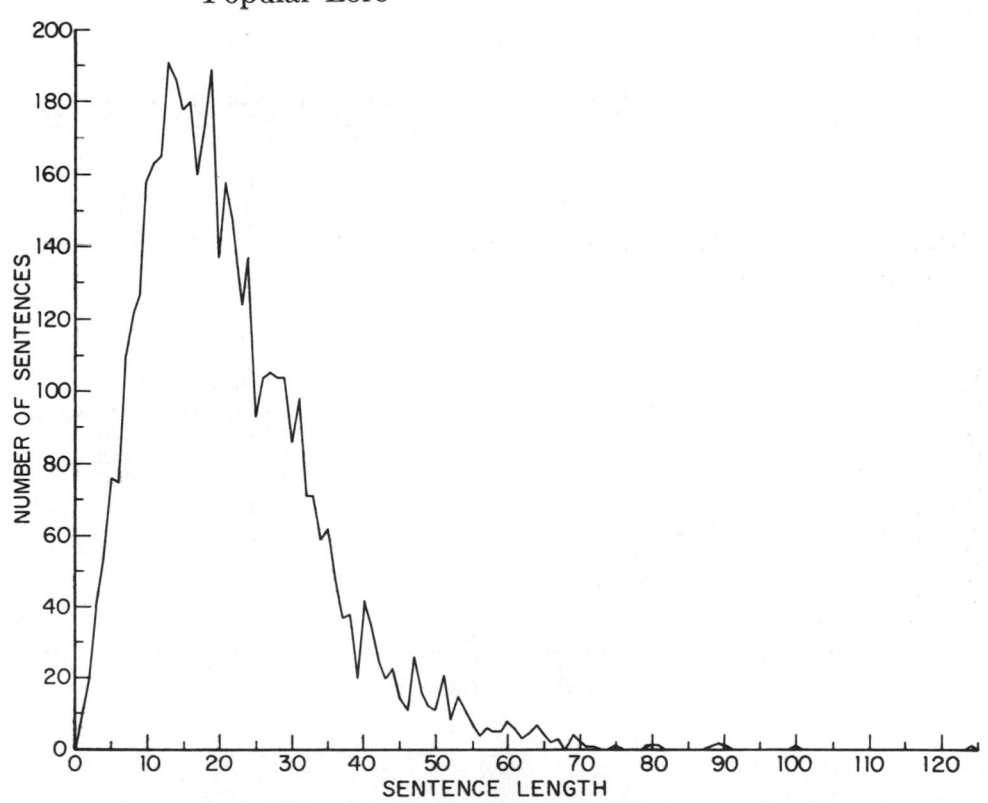

Graph Dᴠɪɪɪ   Sentence-Length Distribution of Genre G,
   Belles Lettres

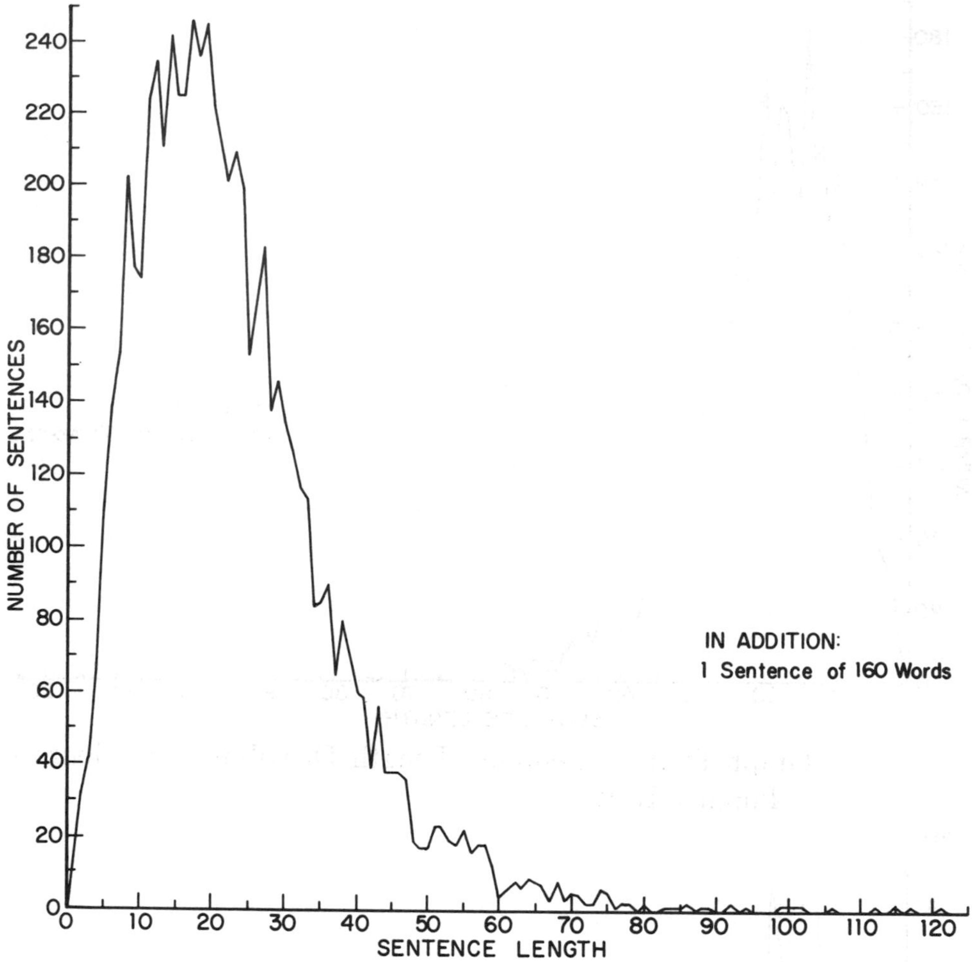

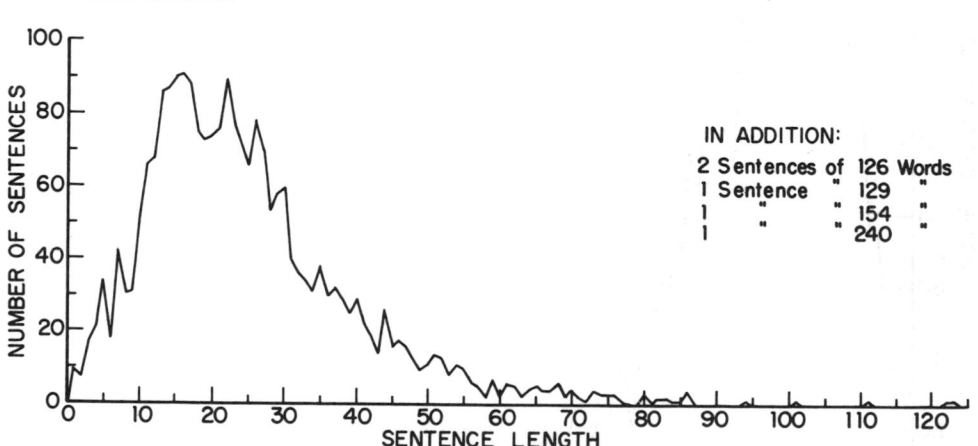

IN ADDITION:
1 Sentence of 160 Words

Graph Dɪx   Sentence-Length Distribution of Genre H,
   Miscellaneous

IN ADDITION:

2 Sentences of 126 Words
1 Sentence   "   129   "
1   "   "   154   "
1   "   "   240   "

Graph Dx   Sentence-Length Distribution of Genre J,
Learned and Scientific Writings

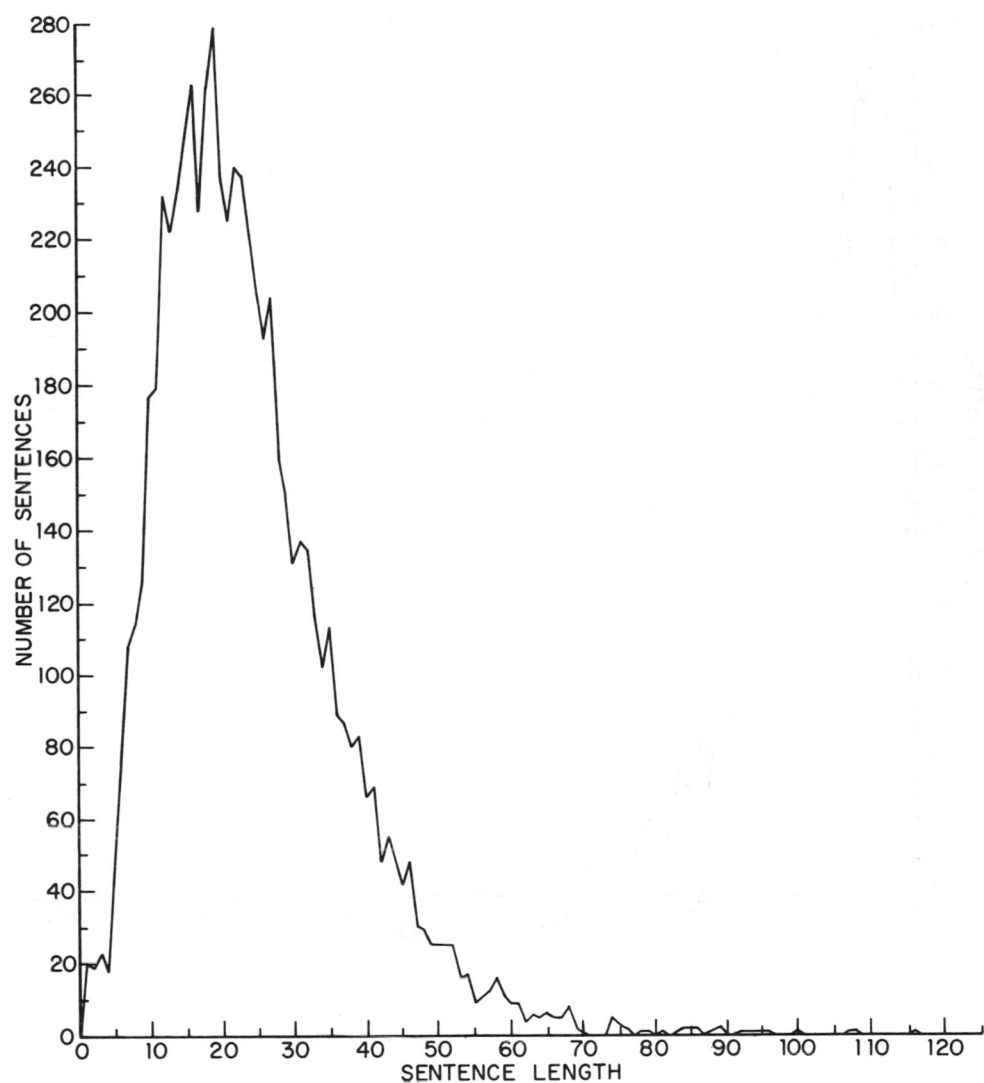

Graph Dxɪ   Sentence-Length Distribution of Genre K,
  Fiction, General

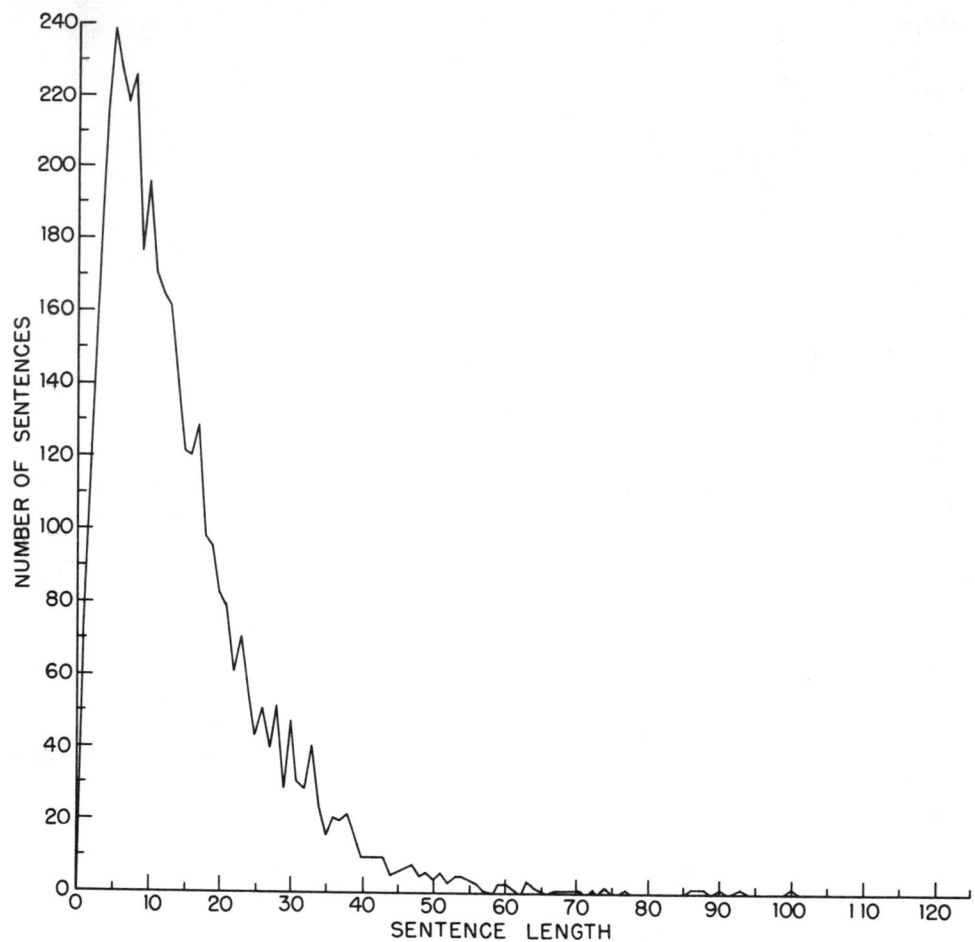

Graph Dxɪɪ   Sentence-Length Distribution of Genre L, Fiction, Mystery and Detective

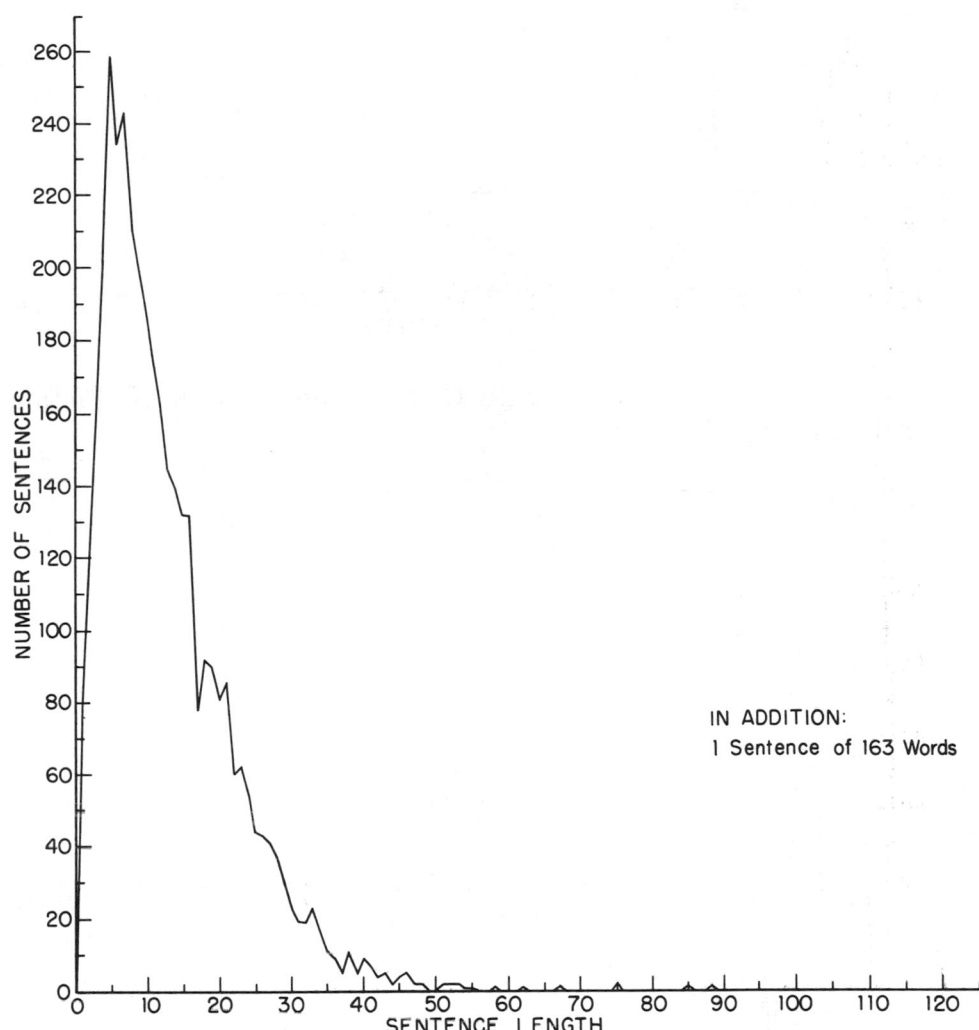

IN ADDITION:
1 Sentence of 163 Words

Graph DXIII   Sentence-Length Distribution of Genre M,
Fiction, Science

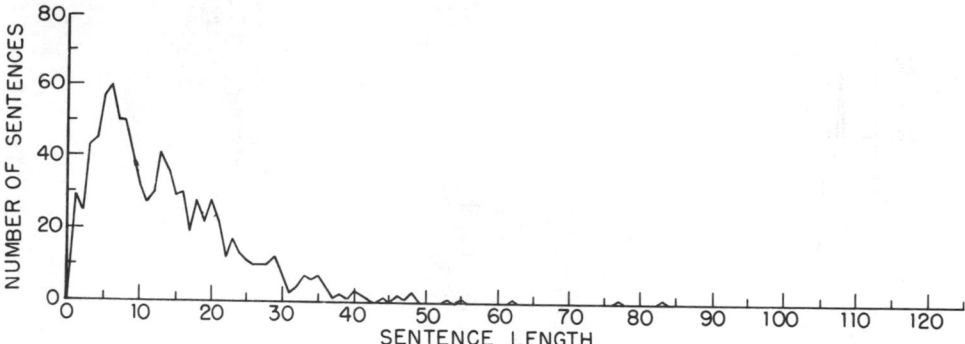

Graph DXIV   Sentence-Length Distribution of Genre N, Fiction,
Adventure and Western

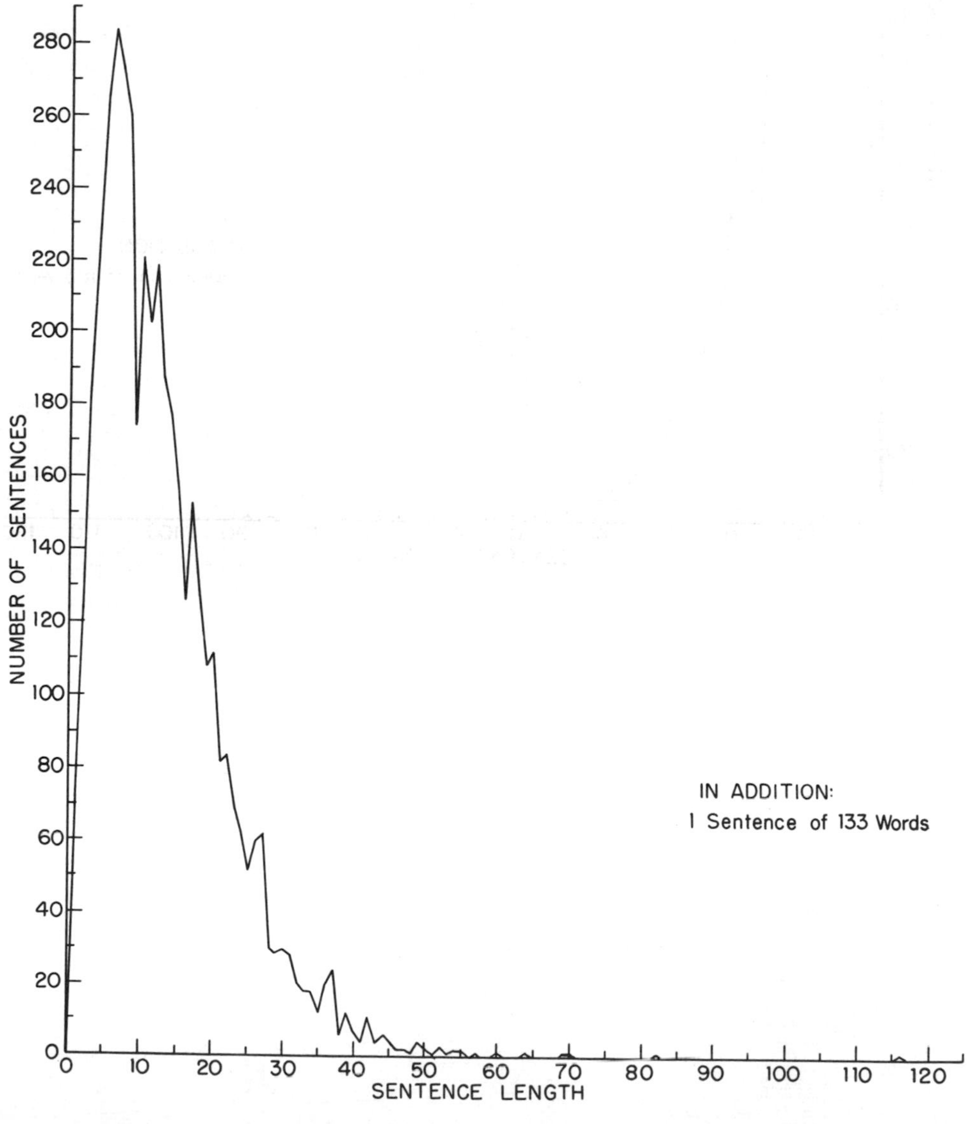

IN ADDITION:
1 Sentence of 133 Words

Graph Dxv   Sentence-Length Distribution of Genre P, Fiction, Romance and Love Story

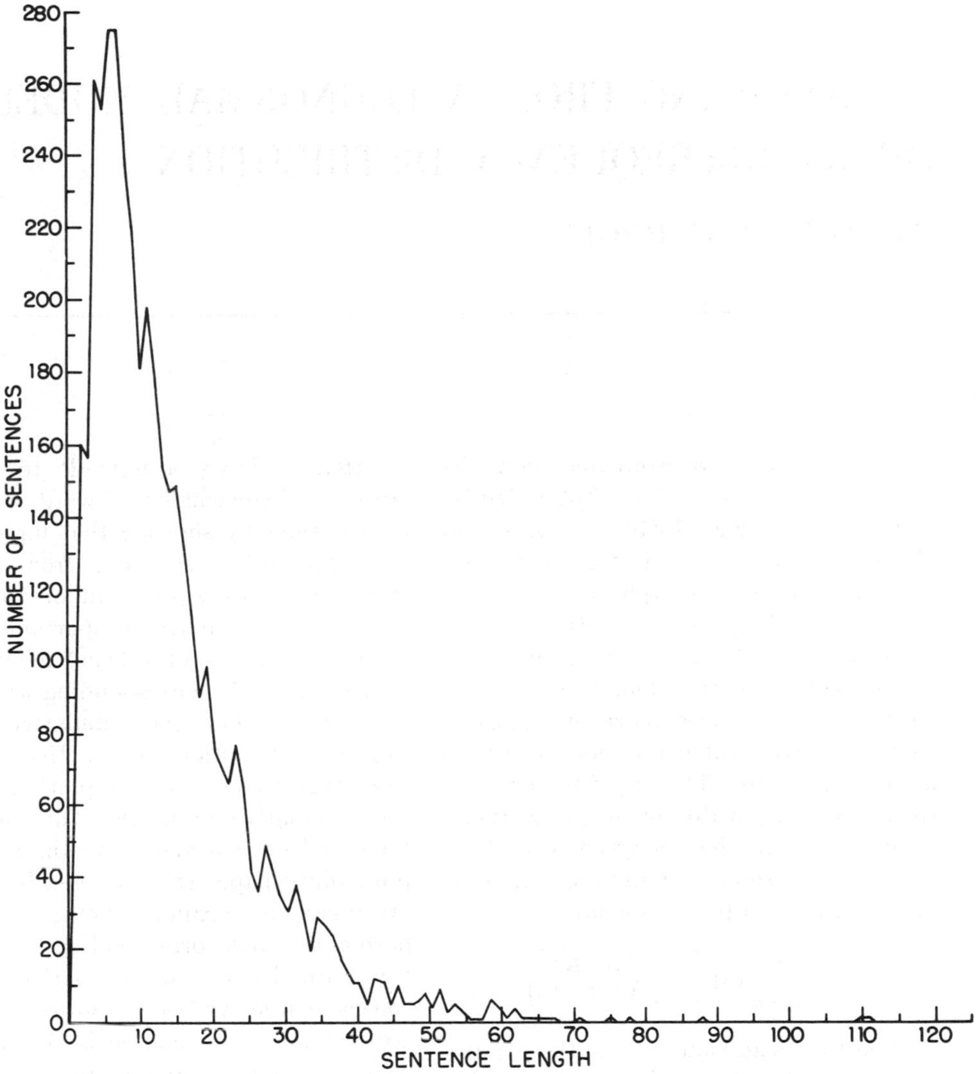

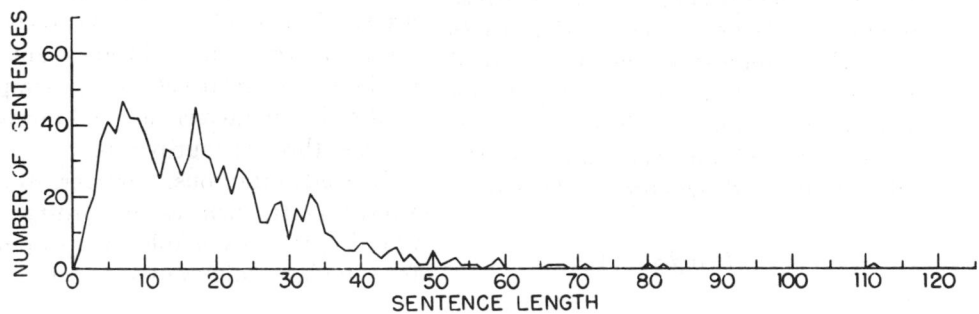

Graph Dxvi   Sentence-Length Distribution of Genre R, Humor

ON SAMPLING FROM A LOGNORMAL MODEL
OF WORD-FREQUENCY DISTRIBUTION

BY JOHN B. CARROLL

In the literature of word-frequency distribution (G. Herdan, *Type-Token Mathematics* [The Hague, 1960], 42–55; David Howes, "Application of the Word-Frequency Concept to Aphasia," in *Ciba Foundation Symposium on Disorders of Language*, ed. A. V. S. de Reuck and Maeve O'Connor [London, 1964], 47–75) there is considerable support for supposing that the theoretical population is distributed lognormally. That is, if we let ϕ be the common logarithm of the proportional frequency with which a given word type appears in a sample of infinite size, ϕ is distributed according to the law

$$z = \frac{1}{\sqrt{2\pi}} \exp\left[-\frac{1}{2}\left(\frac{\phi-\mu}{\sigma}\right)^2 \right],$$

μ being the mean value of ϕ in the population and σ its standard deviation and z being the proportional frequency of types in the population having a given value of ϕ. A segment of the density curve of width $d\phi$ and height z represents the proportional frequency of tokens in the population having a given value of ϕ. The parameters of the law are scaled in such a way that the total area of the distribution is 1; that is,

$$\int_{-\infty}^{+\infty} f(\phi)\, d\phi = 1 .$$

Attempts have been made to demonstrate the lognormality of word-frequency distributions by showing that for samples of appreciable size, say, from several thousand up to several million tokens, a plot of the cumulative proportions of the sample (in terms of tokens) against the logarithms of the corresponding word-type frequencies follows the cumulative normal (ogive) distribution curve. Usually, the word-type frequencies are plotted against the cumulative proportions of tokens in the samples on so-called logarithmic normal probability paper (the abscissa being logarithmic, the ordinate being scaled in normal deviates corresponding to cumulative normal curve areas) so that the resulting curve will be approximately a straight line. An example is Graph EI in which the data for one of the constituent samples in the present Corpus (sample E06, with 1,999 tokens), given in Table E1, are so plotted. The deviations of points in Graph EI from strict linearity are typical of data from relatively small samples, as is also the characteristic bend upwards for the last three or four points.

It is advantageous, however, to convert word-type frequencies to word-type probabilities, for this enables one to plot data for samples of different sizes on a common

scale. Further, it is desirable to convert the probabilities to common logarithms. Graph EII shows such plots for five samples from the present Corpus, one of the samples being the entire Corpus and another being the small sample plotted in Graph EI. The plot is on so-called arithmetic normal probability paper, since the word-type probabilities are already scaled logarithmically. The cumulative proportional areas are plotted against the presumed upper boundaries of the logarithmic word-probability intervals; that is, for a word-type frequency f against log

$$\left(\frac{f + \frac{1}{2}}{N}\right),$$

when N is the number of tokens in the sample. Some investigators appear to have customarily plotted the cumulative proportional areas directly against the frequency values rather than their upper boundaries. The method of plotting used here is preferable, however, because it may be assumed that a given observed word-type frequency represents theoretical word probabilities varying continuously through an interval from $(f - .5)/N$ to $(f + .5)/N$.

From such a plot it is customary to estimate the median, $Mdn_{\phi'}$, and standard deviation, $s_{\phi'}$, of the word-frequency distribution for the sample. (ϕ' denotes a value of ϕ estimated from sample data.) The median is the word-type probability corresponding to a cumulative proportional area of .5; that is, half the tokens in the sample have word probabilities greater than this value. The standard deviation can be estimated from the slope of a straight line fitted to the curve. Because the first three or four points are usually somewhat irregular, it seems advisable to fit the curve by minimizing the squares of deviations in a vertical direction, i.e., using the regression of $\xi_{\phi'}$ on ϕ', where $\xi_{\phi'}$ is the normal deviate corresponding to the cumulative area for a given value of ϕ'.

Further, for reasons that will not be discussed here, in the least-square fitting of the curve it seems advisable to weight the points by the respective numbers of types represented; in this way the points at the lower left of the plot will receive more weight than those towards the upper right. If b is the slope of such a regression line, $s_{\phi'} = 1/b$. (In practice, the line is often fitted by eye, but this does not adequately reflect the suggested weighting of the points.) Table E2 gives the $Mdn_{\phi'}$ and $s_{\phi'}$, determined by regression line, for each of the samples plotted in Graph EII.

It will be noticed that $Mdn_{\phi'}$ and $s_{\phi'}$ vary systematically as a function of sample size; that is, they appear to be biased estimates of the population value. (In statistical sampling theory a statistic whose mean value over samples differs systematically from the population value is said to be a biased statistic.) Furthermore, the curves tend to bend downward at the lower end; this tendency is most marked for the smaller samples. The question naturally arises, are the samples really samples from a theoretical lognormally distributed population? (For the purposes of the present discussion it is assumed that the five samples studied are random samples from a single population with mean μ and variance σ^2, although there are good reasons for thinking that they are not, since the smaller samples, at least, are "clustered" samples—continuous texts rather than being composed of words sampled purely at random from a pool of indefinite size.) In ordinary sampling theory no bias is expected in the usual measures of central tendency applied to samples of different sizes, and the bias in estimates of the population variance is negligible for large samples and is easily adjusted for by using the number of degrees of freedom as the denominator in the calculation of the variance.

These observations lead us to note an interesting property of the lognormal dis-

tribution of word probabilities: the variable whose distribution we are considering, namely ϕ, is a determinant of the probable composition of any sample drawn from the population. If we draw one word (token) at random from the population, that word is more likely to be a high-frequency word than a low-frequency word; in fact, the word most likely to be drawn is the most frequent. Only as we increase the sample size indefinitely will the expected or mean value of the logarithmic word probabilities in a sample approach μ, the value for the population. Similarly, the dispersion of logarithmic word probabilities in a sample will be attenuated because the rare words are less likely to appear in the sample.

Furthermore, if we consider the lognormal plot of a finite sample of words, we see that it is inevitably truncated. Word probabilities computed from a sample are biased estimates of the true word probabilities; this is clear from the fact that the minimum value of a word probability computed from a sample is $1/N$, where N is the size of the sample. There will be a large number of word types in the population that will not appear even once in the sample. The probability that a word type of a given probability will appear once or more times in a sample is a function of that word probability; only the more frequent words will have very high probabilities of appearing at least once in a sample of moderate size. This fact is the explanation for the tendency of the lognormal plots of moderately sized samples to bend downward at their lower end (as may be seen in Graph EII). In effect, such a plot is a representation of the function

$$A_{\phi'} = \int^{\phi'} f(\phi')\, d\phi',$$

where ϕ' is a (biased) estimate of the true word probability and $A_{\phi'}$ is the cumulative area to a given value of ϕ'.

Specification of the Characteristics of the Theoretical Lognormal Word-Frequency Distribution

To examine whether finite-sized samples can be considered as samples from theoretical lognormal distributions, our best course is to study the characteristics of such distributions and of the samples we might expect to draw from them by random sampling. A computer program has been written for doing this for given pairs of parameters μ and σ and for one or more sample sizes (the sample size itself being limited to approximately 10^9). In this section we discuss the computation of the theoretical lognormal distribution. For convenience and clarity the discussion refers to Table E3, which is taken from the computer printouts for a population with $\mu = -3.2370$ and $\sigma = 1.4116$. (The selection of these values will be explained later.)

The goal of the computations is to specify certain quantities associated with arbitrarily chosen intervals of the continuously varying quantity ϕ. Essentially, two types of intervals are used: (a) the tail portions of the curve, one to the left of $\phi = \phi_L$ and the one to the right of

$$\phi = \phi_U \ (\phi_U > \phi_L);$$

and (b) equally spaced intervals, each $\Delta\phi$ in width, between ϕ_L and ϕ_U. The argument of the computation is ξ, the normal-curve deviate corresponding to ϕ by the equation $\xi = (\phi - \mu)/\sigma$, so that the intervals are chosen in terms of ξ_L, ξ_U, and increments of ξ between ξ_L and ξ_U.

In choosing ξ_U, it may be noted that when $\phi > 0$, the probability of a word is greater than one. But it is also the case that the number of word-types that could have such probabilities, at least for the parameters likely to be chosen for the distribution, is virtually zero. Therefore, ξ_U may safely be chosen as somewhat less

than $-\mu/\sigma$, the value of ξ corresponding to $\phi = 0$. For Table E3

$$-\mu/\sigma = -(-3.2370/1.4116) = 2.2931,$$

and ξ_U was chosen as $+2.00$.

The value of ξ_L should be chosen so that the lower tail interval is likely to contribute less than one word (token) to the largest size of sample that one is likely to investigate. The exact determination of this value is complex since it depends partly on the parameters μ and σ and the resulting distribution of types. For the range of parameters likely to be used with word-frequency data the value -5.00, used in Table E3, will suffice for the investigation of samples as large as about five million. (In the more precise computations used for other data reported here, ξ_L was chosen as -6.00, which proved satisfactory for a sample size of one hundred million.)

The size of the intervals of ξ between ξ_U and ξ_L is to be chosen as reasonably small to give good approximations to what might be computed with infinitesimal increments. For Table E3 the increment chosen was .1, in order to make the table of reasonable length, but the more accurate results used in the remainder of this text were computed with an increment of .02.

The quantities computed are as follows (see columns of Table E3):

(A) Interval number. The computations for interval 1 concern the tail of the normal curve to the right of ξ_U. The computations for the last interval (number 72 in the table) concern the tail to the left of ξ_L. The remaining intervals (numbers 2 to 71 in the table) are for the intervals between ξ_U and ξ_L.

(B) Lower boundary of interval in terms of ξ.

(C) Lower boundary of interval in terms of ϕ.

(D) Word probability for the interval $p_i = $ antilog ϕ at the midpoint of the interval, considered as representative for all words in the interval. For the tail intervals these are computed from ϕ corresponding to the mean ξ for the truncated tail of a normal curve ($\bar{\xi}_L = -z/A_L$; $\bar{\xi}_U = z/A_U$, where z is the ordinate at ξ_L or ξ_U and A_L and A_U are the respective tail areas). (Because of special problems in computing values of p for extremely low values of ξ, p for the lower tail interval was arbitrarily made equal to one-tenth of the value of p for the immediately preceding interval.) For the interior intervals these are computed from the mean of ϕ at the upper boundary and at the lower boundary of the interval. For example, for interval 2,

$$p = \text{antilog } \tfrac{1}{2}(-0.4138 - 0.5550)$$
$$= .327807.$$

(E) Proportional area below the interval. This is the proportion of the normal curve area up to ξ at the lower boundary of the interval. It can be regarded as the proportion of tokens in the theoretical population that have logarithmic word probabilities equal to or less than ϕ at the lower boundary of the interval. (For values of ξ less than -3.0 the algorithm used for approximating the proportional area below the interval is increasingly inaccurate, but for reasons that will not be entered into here, the inaccuracy does not significantly affect the final results.)

(F) Proportional area in the interval, A_i. This is obtained from the successive differences of column E; for example, for interval 2, $.977250 - .971283 = .005967$. It can be regarded as the proportional frequency of tokens in the theoretical population that have logarithmic word probabilities between ϕ at the upper boundary of the interval and ϕ at the lower boundary of the interval; the estimated mean word probability for these words is p (column D).

(G) Number of word-types in the in-

terval, computed as A_i/p_i. It is a remarkable property of the lognormal word frequency distribution that this quantity has an absolute rather than a relative magnitude. That this is so can be seen from the following example: Suppose that there are two word-types in an interval, each having a word-probability of .1. Together, then, they would constitute $2 \times (.1)$, or .2 of the population. Therefore, if we have a representative value for the word probability of the types in a given interval, as well as an estimate of the proportion of the total population constituted by the corresponding tokens, we can estimate the absolute number of word-types in that interval by dividing the proportional area by the word probability. The values of ϕ in terms of types are normally distributed with a mean of $(\mu - 2.3026\sigma^2)$ or -7.8252 for the data of Table E3. (Because of special problems in computing data for intervals having extremely low values of ξ, the numbers of types in the intervals below the interval corresponding to the mean of the lognormal distribution of types were computed by producing a mirror image of the distribution down to that interval with an appropriate adjustment for the interpolated midpoint of the distribution.)

(H) The cumulative number of word types, starting at $\xi = +\infty$ and running downwards to the lower boundary of the interval, cumulated from the values in column G. It will be noted that the last value in this column is the theoretical absolute size of the vocabulary implied by the given values of μ and σ. It can be shown that the common logarithm of this value is $(1.1513\sigma^2 - \mu)$.

(I) Cumulative number of types (integral). These quantities are rounded off from values in column H.

(J) Number of types in the interval (integral). These quantities are obtained from the successive differences of values in column I rather than being rounded off directly from values in column G, in order to take advantage of the cumulative values computed in column H.

While the computations outlined above are efficient and reasonably accurate for the middle portion of the type distribution, they do not yield correct values for the first few (say, one hundred) types at the top of the distribution. Therefore, a special computing procedure was developed to yield estimates of the word probabilities of the first X word-types. This was done by successively interpolating in column H of Table E3 until exactly one word-type was accumulated. The probability assigned to each such word-type was the proportional area it occupied in the theoretical curve. (These computations are not shown in Table E3.)

The information developed in this way gives us a notion of the theoretical distribution of the probabilities of word-types, if we assume that they are lognormally distributed. As we have already remarked, the numbers of types to be found in particular intervals of the distribution are absolute magnitudes, and their sum, found as the last value in column H in Table E3, is also a finite, absolute magnitude. Any given values of μ and σ imply a definite upper limit to the size of vocabulary (i.e., number of word-types) in samples drawn from a theoretical population specified in this way.

Cumulative Word-Types in Samples

Because the numbers of word-types with given word probabilities are absolute magnitudes, we should expect that theoretically expected values would correspond closely to the cumulative numbers of word-types found with given word probabilities in samples, the closeness of the fit increasing with the size of the sample. This reasoning has been tested by plotting in Graph EIII the theoretical curve of cumulative num-

bers of word-types (for the parameters used in Table E3) against decreasing word probability and also the curves derived from four variously sized samples from the present Corpus. It can be seen that the fit of observed data to the theoretical is quite close, particularly for the larger samples and for smaller values of word probabilities. On the whole, the data of Graph EIII give strong support to the lognormal theory of word-frequency distribution.

Computation of the Characteristics of Samples

An even stronger confirmation of the theory of lognormally distributed word probabilities results if we obtain a close fit between observed data from samples of given size and the characteristics of a sample of that size predicted from a theoretical population.

Given information on a theoretical population such as that contained in Table E3, one can apply Yule's compound Poisson distribution procedure (G. Udny Yule, *The Statistical Study of Literary Vocabulary* [Cambridge, Eng., 1944] pp. 48–52) to predict the characteristics of a sample of given size. (Yule did not have available the theory of lognormally distributed word probabilities. Instead, he applied the compound Poisson distribution to a very crude model of the distribution, using relatively small numbers of strata.) The basic Poisson distribution specifies that if there are m elements, each with a population probability p, the number of these elements that will occur $n = 0, 1, 2, \ldots$ times in a sample of size N is given by the series

$$\frac{m}{e^{Np}}\left[1, \frac{(Np)}{1!}, \frac{(Np)^2}{2!}, \frac{(Np)^3}{3!}, \ldots, \frac{(Np)^n}{n!}\right].$$

(Np) is the mean number of occurrences and also the variance of the number of occurrences. The Poisson distribution is appropriate for small probabilities, say $p \ll .1$, and is therefore appropriate for our problem. To produce the compound Poisson distribution, the basic Poisson distribution is applied to each stratum (i.e., each interval) of the theoretical lognormal distribution, the results being summed over strata to yield the total number of word-types that will occur $0, 1, 2, \ldots$ times in the sample. Word-types occurring zero times in the sample are eliminated, of course, from further computations, but it is of use to note the number of word-types from each stratum which do not occur in a sample of given size.

For large values of Np, say $Np > 10$, it is satisfactory to consider the Poisson distribution as approximated by a normal distribution with mean and variance Np. If $m = 1$, it may be assumed that that one element will occur exactly Np times in a sample of size N; if $m = 2$, it may be assumed that one of the elements will occur a number of times corresponding to the mean of the left half of the normal curve approximation to the binomial, and the other element will occur a number of times corresponding to the mean of the right half of the normal curve. This reasoning may be extended to a procedure for distributing a small number of elements to portions of the normal curve, so that the frequencies of words occurring a given number of times will be integral and yet approximate the frequencies expected in the Poisson distribution.

Except for the first X word-types, whose probabilities are computed by a special procedure, the integral values in column J of Table E3 are the elements distributed by the Poisson distribution or the approximation thereto. For each of the first X word-types the frequency is taken as equal to Np.

Computations have been performed to predict the word-frequency distributions for the five variously sized samples from the present Corpus. Table E4 shows the observed and expected data. Values of μ

and σ for the theoretical distributions were determined by iteration until the fit was satisfactorily close for the largest size sample ($N = 1,014,232$). That is, values of μ and σ were adjusted until the parameters of the lognormal regression line for the predicted sample, with points weighted by the number of types, were sufficiently close to those for the observed data for the sample with $N = 1,014,232$. Graphs Eiv and Ev show lognormal plots for the largest and smallest of the samples, affording a comparison between observed and expected data. The closeness of the fit for the larger sample is a strong confirmation of the theory of lognormally distributed word probabilities. The expected lognormal plot for this sample even displays a considerable downward displacement at the lower end, in comparison with the theoretical straight line for the population, and a slight upward displacement at the upper end. The expected lognormal plot for the smaller sample (Graph Ev) also shows similar displacements, but the fit of the observed data to the theoretical is not as good as it is for the larger sample. This lack of fit is probably to be accounted for partly by reason of the fact that this was a sample of continuous text rather than a sample of words chosen from the total Corpus by a purely random process, as is assumed by the sampling theory used here.

Table E4 also shows certain expected data for samples of several other sizes (1, 100, 10,000,000, and 100,000,000). It is to be noted that the expected value of $Mdn_{\phi'}$ shows a nonmonotonic relation with the size of sample, descending to a value of -3.4553 for the sample of 10,000,000 and then rising again to the population value of -3.2370. On the other hand, $s_{\phi'}$ has a monotonic relation to sample size, reaching the value 1.4116 with a sample of infinite size.

Table E4 further shows observed and expected data for the number of types as a function of sample size. For a sample of infinite size, i.e., for the theoretical population with the given values of μ and σ, there would be 340,193 word-types. The number of word-types expected for the sample of 1,014,232 is 50,963, a value that is quite close to the number of word-types observed, viz., 50,406.

The several values of expected and observed numbers of word-types as a function of sample size have been plotted in Graph Evi together with the theoretical asymptote. The values for numbers of word-types approach the asymptote quite slowly. A sample of 1,014,232 tokens yields only about 15 per cent of the total number of types in the theoretical population and can therefore be regarded as a relatively small sample. Even a sample of 100,000,000 is expected to yield only about 61 per cent of the total number of types.

Although for the sake of convenience Graph Evi is plotted with logarithmic coordinates, the fact that the theoretical curve is nonlinear is a definite indication that the logarithmic type-token ratio is not a constant.

The Distribution of Word Probabilities of Types

In the preceding discussion we have been dealing essentially with the distribution of the word probabilities of tokens; the claim is that if we assign its word probability to each token in a population, these will be distributed lognormally. It should be noted, however, that all tokens that are the same word-type are assigned the same word probability values. In our previous computations we derived the number of types occurring within a given interval of ϕ, the logarithmic word probability, by dividing the area by the word probability, as explained previously.

Herdan has pointed out that the distribution of word-type probabilities when each word-type is regarded as occurring

only once is the first-moment distribution with respect to the distribution of token probabilities. He refers to J. Aitchison and J. A. C. Brown (*The Lognormal Distribution* [Cambridge, Eng., 1957]), who have shown that the jth moment of a lognormal distribution with mean μ and variance σ^2 (measured in common logarithms) will have a mean

$$= \mu + (\log_e 10)j\sigma^2 = \mu + 2.3026j\sigma^2.$$

The variance of the jth moment distribution remains the same as that of the original distribution.

Accordingly, we should expect the theoretical distribution of word-type probabilities to have a mean

$$- [3.2370 + 2.3026(1.4116)^2] = -7.8252.$$

This is also the value at which one-half the types in the population would be expected to have word probabilities equal to or greater than this value. From these considerations we can compute the expected proportion of word-types for each interval and make a lognormal plot for the theoretical population as shown in Graph Evii. Again, word probability has been used as the abscissa. Also, the actual and predicted values for four samples of different sizes have been plotted. For the Corpus as a whole the fit between observed and expected points is very good. It should be noted that all of the expected lognormal plots for samples are markedly nonlinear and displaced from the theoretical population curve. The nonlinearity and downward displacement are due to the fact that the lower the probability of a type and the smaller the sample, the less likely it is to appear in the sample. Also, it should be remembered that the smaller samples studied here are not random samples but cluster samples.

In our investigations thus far we have not yet arrived at an efficient method for estimating the parameters of the theoretical population from the characteristics of a sample. The procedure used to determine these parameters for the present data was one of trial and error and iteration, using several values of μ and σ until the predicted sample characteristics were satisfactorily close to the observed. The direct mathematical estimation of the parameters of a population from sample statistics is a matter for further investigation. This, as well as the problem of the exact form of the type-token function, is beyond the scope of the present paper.

Table E1   Word-Frequency Distribution for Sample E06

Occurrence Frequency	No. of Types with This Frequency	No. of Tokens with This Frequency	Cumulative Tokens	Cumulative Proportion of Tokens
1	565	565	565	.2826
2	110	220	785	.3927
3	44	132	917	.4587
4	23	92	1009	.5048
5	18	90	1099	.5498
6	8	48	1147	.5738
7	5	35	1182	.5913
8	6	48	1230	.6153
9	4	36	1266	.6333
10	3	30	1296	.6483
11	1	11	1307	.6538
12	2	24	1331	.6658
14	2	28	1359	.6798
16	1	16	1375	.6878
17	4	68	1443	.7219
18	2	36	1479	.7399
19	1	19	1498	.7494
26	1	26	1524	.7624
29	1	29	1553	.7769
34	1	34	1587	.7939
47	1	47	1634	.8174
49	1	49	1683	.8419
54	1	54	1737	.8689
64	1	64	1801	.9010
70	1	70	1871	.9360
128	1	128	1999	1.0000

Table E2   Values of $Mdn_{\phi'}$ and $s_{\phi'}$ Computed from Regression Lines Fitted to Data for Five Samples, the Points Being Weighted by the Number of Types with a Given Value of ϕ'

Sample Size (N)	$Mdn_{\phi'}$	$s_{\phi'}$
1,014,232	−3.3928	1.2260
253,538	−3.3923	1.0953
101,566	−3.3627	1.0045
10,051	−3.0075	0.9689
1,999	−2.6329	0.8699

Table E3　　Specification of the Theoretical Lognormal Token and Type Distributions for Given Parameters Mu and Sigma

MU= -3.2370, SIGMA= 1.4116, IN INCREMENTS OF 0.10 FROM XI= -5.00 TO 2.00
THEORETICAL MEAN FOR TYPES= -7.8252

A	B	C	D*	E*	F*	G*	H*	I	J
INT. NO.	DOWN TO XI=	PHI AT LOWER BOUNDARY	P AT MIDPOINT OF INTERVAL	PROPORTIONAL AREA BELOW INTERVAL	PROPORTION OF AREA IN INTERVAL	NUMBER OF TYPES IN INTERVAL	CUM. TYPES TO BOTTOM OF INTERVAL	INTEGRAL TYPES (CUM.)	INTEGRAL TYPES IN INTERVAL
1	2.00	-0.4138	0.129712E 01	0.977250E 00	0.227504E-01	0.175391E-01	0.175391E-01	0.	0.
2	1.90	-0.5550	0.327807E 00	0.971283E 00	0.596642E-02	0.182010E-01	0.357401E-01	0.	0.
3	1.80	-0.6961	0.236842E 00	0.964069E 00	0.721365E-02	0.304577E-01	0.661978E-01	0.	0.
4	1.70	-0.8373	0.171119E 00	0.955434E 00	0.863528E-02	0.504637E-01	0.116661E 00	0.	0.
5	1.60	-0.9784	0.123634E 00	0.945200E 00	0.102339E-01	0.827757E-01	0.199437E 00	0.	0.
6	1.50	-1.1196	0.893258E-01	0.933192E 00	0.120080E-01	0.134429E 00	0.333867E 00	0.	0.
7	1.40	-1.2608	0.645382E-01	0.919243E 00	0.139495E-01	0.216143E 00	0.550009E 00	1.	1.
8	1.30	-1.4019	0.466290E-01	0.903199E 00	0.160439E-01	0.344076E 00	0.894085E 00	1.	0.
9	1.20	-1.5431	0.336896E-01	0.884930E 00	0.182694E-01	0.542285E 00	0.143637E 01	1.	0.
10	1.10	-1.6842	0.243408E-01	0.864333E 00	0.205966E-01	0.846174E 00	0.228254E 01	2.	1.
11	1.00	-1.8254	0.175863E-01	0.841344E 00	0.229892E-01	0.130722E 01	0.358976E 01	4.	2.
12	0.90	-1.9666	0.127062E-01	0.815939E 00	0.254049E-01	0.199942E 01	0.558918E 01	6.	2.
13	0.80	-2.1077	0.918028E-02	0.788144E 00	0.277954E-01	0.302773E 01	0.861691E 01	9.	3.
14	0.70	-2.2489	0.663278E-02	0.758035E 00	0.301083E-01	0.453931E 01	0.131562E 02	13.	4.
15	0.60	-2.3900	0.479222E-02	0.725746E 00	0.322895E-01	0.673790E 01	0.198941E 02	20.	7.
16	0.50	-2.5312	0.346240E-02	0.691461E 00	0.342845E-01	0.990195E 01	0.297961E 02	30.	10.
17	0.40	-2.6724	0.250160E-02	0.655421E 00	0.360407E-01	0.144071E 02	0.442031E 02	44.	14.
18	0.30	-2.8135	0.180741E-02	0.617910E 00	0.375103E-01	0.207536E 02	0.649568E 02	65.	21.
19	0.20	-2.9547	0.130586E-02	0.579258E 00	0.386518E-01	0.295987E 02	0.945554E 02	95.	30.
20	0.10	-3.0958	0.943491E-03	0.539827E 00	0.394319E-01	0.417935E 02	0.136349E 03	136.	41.
21	-0.00	-3.2370	0.681676E-03	0.499999E 00	0.398278E-01	0.584263E 02	0.194775E 03	195.	59.
22	-0.10	-3.3782	0.492513E-03	0.460171E 00	0.398278E-01	0.808665E 02	0.275642E 03	276.	81.
23	-0.20	-3.5193	0.355843E-03	0.420739E 00	0.394318E-01	0.110812E 03	0.386454E 03	386.	110.
24	-0.30	-3.6605	0.257097E-03	0.382087E 00	0.386517E-01	0.150339E 03	0.536792E 03	537.	151.
25	-0.40	-3.8016	0.185754E-03	0.344577E 00	0.375102E-01	0.201935E 03	0.738727E 03	739.	202.
26	-0.50	-3.9428	0.134208E-03	0.308537E 00	0.360407E-01	0.268543E 03	0.100727E 04	1007.	268.
27	-0.60	-4.0840	0.969659E-04	0.274252E 00	0.342844E-01	0.353571E 03	0.136084E 04	1361.	354.
28	-0.70	-4.2251	0.700582E-04	0.241963E 00	0.322894E-01	0.460894E 03	0.182173E 04	1822.	461.
29	-0.80	-4.3663	0.506173E-04	0.211855E 00	0.301082E-01	0.594819E 03	0.241655E 04	2417.	595.
30	-0.90	-4.5074	0.365712E-04	0.184059E 00	0.277952E-01	0.760030E 03	0.317658E 04	3177.	760.
31	-1.00	-4.6486	0.264229E-04	0.158655E 00	0.254046E-01	0.961464E 03	0.413805E 04	4138.	961.
32	-1.10	-4.7898	0.190907E-04	0.135666E 00	0.229890E-01	0.120420E 04	0.534225E 04	5342.	1204.
33	-1.20	-4.9309	0.137931E-04	0.115070E 00	0.205962E-01	0.149322E 04	0.683547E 04	6835.	1493.
34	-1.30	-5.0721	0.996559E-05	0.968005E-01	0.182691E-01	0.183322E 04	0.866869E 04	8669.	1834.
35	-1.40	-5.2132	0.720019E-05	0.807567E-01	0.160438E-01	0.222824E 04	0.108969E 05	10897.	2228.
36	-1.50	-5.3544	0.520216E-05	0.668074E-01	0.139493E-01	0.268144E 04	0.135784E 05	13578.	2681.
37	-1.60	-5.4956	0.375859E-05	0.547996E-01	0.120078E-01	0.319476E 04	0.167731E 05	16773.	3195.
38	-1.70	-5.6367	0.271560E-05	0.445658E-01	0.102338E-01	0.376854E 04	0.205417E 05	20542.	3769.

Table E3 (cont.) Specification of the Theoretical Lognormal Token and Type Distributions for Given Parameters Mu and Sigma

MU= -3.2370, SIGMA= 1.4116, IN INCREMENTS OF 0.10 FROM XI= -5.00 TO 2.00
THEORETICAL MEAN FOR TYPES= -7.8252

A	B	C	D*	E*	F*	G*	H*	I	J
INT. NO.	DOWN TO XI=	PHI AT LOWER BOUNDARY	P AT MIDPOINT OF INTERVAL	PROPORTIONAL AREA BELOW INTERVAL	PROPORTION OF AREA IN INTERVAL	NUMBER OF TYPES IN INTERVAL	CUM. TYPES TO BOTTOM OF INTERVAL	INTEGRAL TYPES (CUM.)	INTEGRAL TYPES IN INTERVAL
39	-1.80	-5.7779	0.196204E-05	0.359307E-01	0.863510E-02	0.440109E 04	0.249428E 05	24943.	4401.
40	-1.90	-5.9190	0.141758E-05	0.287171E-01	0.721362E-02	0.508868E 04	0.300314E 05	30031.	5088.
41	-2.00	-6.0602	0.102421E-05	0.227506E-C1	0.596649E-02	0.582546E 04	0.358569E 05	35857.	5826.
42	-2.10	-6.2014	0.739997E-06	0.178647E-01	0.488583E-02	0.660250E 04	0.424594E 05	42459.	6602.
43	-2.20	-6.3425	0.534652E-06	0.139039E-01	0.396086E-02	0.740830E 04	0.498677E 05	49868.	7409.
44	-2.30	-6.4837	0.386288E-06	0.107244E-01	0.317951E-02	0.823091E 04	0.580986E 05	58099.	8231.
45	-2.40	-6.6248	0.279095E-06	0.819797E-02	0.252641E-02	0.905215E 04	0.671507E 05	67151.	9052.
46	-2.50	-6.7660	0.201648E-06	0.620966E-02	0.198831E-02	0.986031E 04	0.770111E 05	77011.	9860.
47	-2.60	-6.9071	0.145692E-06	0.466197E-02	0.154769E-02	0.106231E 05	0.876341E 05	87634.	10623.
48	-2.70	-7.0483	0.105263E-06	0.346742E-02	0.119454E-02	0.113482E 05	0.989822E 05	98982.	11348.
49	-2.80	-7.1895	0.760534E-07	0.255635E-02	0.911070E-03	0.119794E 05	0.110961E 06	110962.	11980.
50	-2.90	-7.3306	0.549491E-07	0.186664E-02	0.689710E-03	0.125518E 05	0.123513E 06	123513.	12551.
51	-3.00	-7.4718	0.397012E-07	0.135053E-02	0.516110E-03	0.129999E 05	0.136513E 06	136513.	13000.
52	-3.10	-7.6129	0.286844E-07	0.967844E-C3	0.382690E-03	0.133414E 05	0.149854E 06	149854.	13341.
53	-3.20	-7.7541	0.207244E-07	0.688218E-03	0.279626E-C3	0.134926E 05	0.163347E 06	163347.	13493.
54	-3.30	-7.8953	0.149735E-07	0.487445E-03	0.200773E-03	0.134085E 05	0.176755E 06	176756.	13409.
55	-3.40	-8.0364	0.108185E-07	0.341478E-03	0.145967E-03	0.134924E 05	0.190248E 06	190248.	13492.
56	-3.50	-8.1776	0.781643E-08	0.237191E-C3	0.104287E-03	0.133420E 05	0.203590E 06	203590.	13342.
57	-3.60	-8.3187	0.564743E-08	0.163762E-03	0.734295E-04	0.130023E 05	0.216592E 06	216592.	13002.
58	-3.70	-8.4599	0.408031E-08	0.112537E-03	0.512242E-04	0.125540E 05	0.229146E 06	229146.	12554.
59	-3.80	-8.6011	0.294805E-08	0.772083E-04	0.353290E-04	0.119838E 05	0.241130E 06	241130.	11984.
60	-3.90	-8.7422	0.212996E-08	0.530285E-04	0.241798E-04	0.113522E 05	0.252482E 06	252482.	11352.
61	-4.00	-8.8834	0.153891E-08	0.366732E-C4	0.163553E-04	0.106279E 05	0.263110E 06	263110.	10628.
62	-4.10	-9.0245	0.111188E-08	0.257044E-04	0.109688E-04	0.986513E 04	0.272975E 06	272975.	9865.
63	-4.20	-9.1657	0.803338E-09	0.184282E-04	0.727618E-05	0.905743E 04	0.282032E 06	282032.	9057.
64	-4.30	-9.3069	0.580418E-09	0.136475E-04	0.478062E-05	0.823652E 04	0.290269E 06	290269.	8237.
65	-4.40	-9.4480	0.419350E-09	0.105383E-04	0.310928E-05	0.741453E 04	0.297684E 06	297684.	7415.
66	-4.50	-9.5892	0.302983E-09	0.853633E-05	0.200194E-05	0.660743E 04	0.304291E 06	304291.	6607.
67	-4.60	-9.7303	0.218908E-09	0.725983E-05	0.127650E-05	0.583122E 04	0.310122E 06	310122.	5831.
68	-4.70	-9.8715	0.158163E-09	0.645431E-05	0.805515E-06	0.509296E 04	0.315215E 06	315215.	5093.
69	-4.80	-10.0126	0.114274E-09	0.595086E-05	0.503446E-06	0.440562E 04	0.319621E 06	319621.	4406.
70	-4.90	-10.1538	0.825623E-10	0.563934E-C5	0.311528E-06	0.377325E 04	0.323394E 06	323394.	3773.
71	-5.00	-10.2950	0.596519E-10	0.544852E-05	0.190818E-06	0.319886E 04	0.326593E 06	326593.	3199.
72	-INF.	-INF.	0.596518E-11	0.0	0.0	0.136000E 05	0.340193E 06	340193.	13600.

*VALUES IN THIS COLUMN ARE IN E-NOTATION. TO OBTAIN THE VALUE IN CONVENTIONAL NOTATION, MOVE THE DECIMAL POINT TO THE RIGHT (+) OR LEFT (-) THE NUMBER OF PLACES INDICATED BY THE NUMBER FOLLOWING E.

Table E4   Observed and Theoretically Expected Values for Several Sample Sizes Drawn from a Population with $\mu = -3.2370$ and $\sigma = 1.4116$

Sample Size	Median ϕ' Obs.	Median ϕ' Exp.	$s_{\phi'}$ Obs.	$s_{\phi'}$ Exp.	No. of Types Obs.	No. of Types Exp.
1	—	—	—	—	(1)	1
100	—	−2.4368	—	.7460	—	87
1,999	−2.6329	−2.9427	.8699	.9005	808	1,063
10,051	−3.0075	−3.1457	.9689	1.0392	3,009	3,576
101,566	−3.3627	−3.3312	1.0045	1.1344	13,706	15,865
253,538	−3.3923	−3.3751	1.0953	1.1670	23,655	26,218
1,014,232*	−3.3928	−3.4030	1.2260	1.2230	50,406	50,963
10,000,000	—	−3.4553	—	1.2593	—	118,624
100,000,000	—	−3.2607	—	1.3925	—	206,309
∞	—	−3.2370	—	1.4116	—	340,193

* The theoretical values of μ and σ were estimated by iterating the calculations until the observed and expected values of $Mdn_{\phi'}$ and $s_{\phi'}$, respectively, were approximately equal for the sample of size $N = 1,014,232$. Further iterations could have been carried out to make these equalities more precise but were not deemed worthwhile. The next iteration would have input $\mu = -3.2273$ and $\sigma = 1.4151$ as the estimated theoretical parameters.

Graph E1   Plot of Word-Frequency Data for
   Sample E06

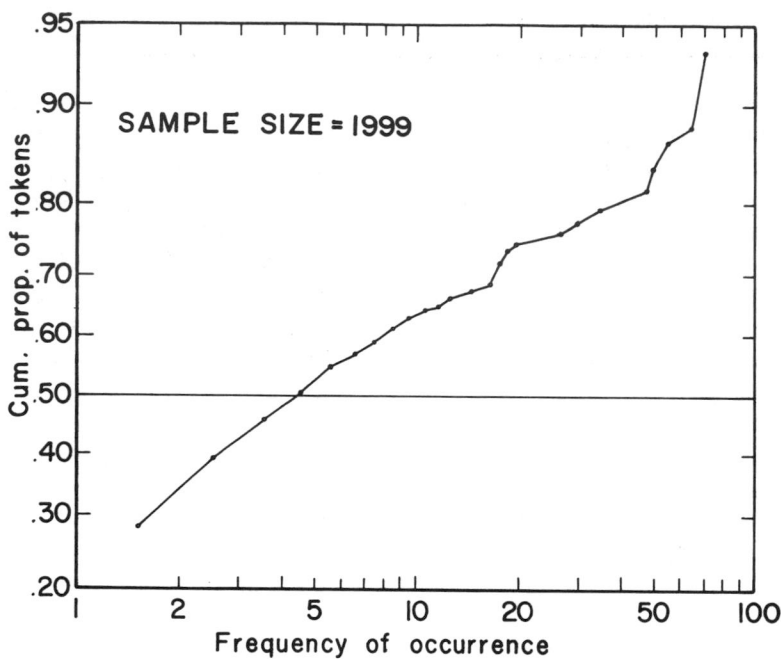

This graph was drawn on logarithmic normal probability paper.

Graph E11   Plots of Word-Frequency Data for Five Samples on Arithmetic and Normal Probability Co-ordinates Using Word Probability as the Basic Variable

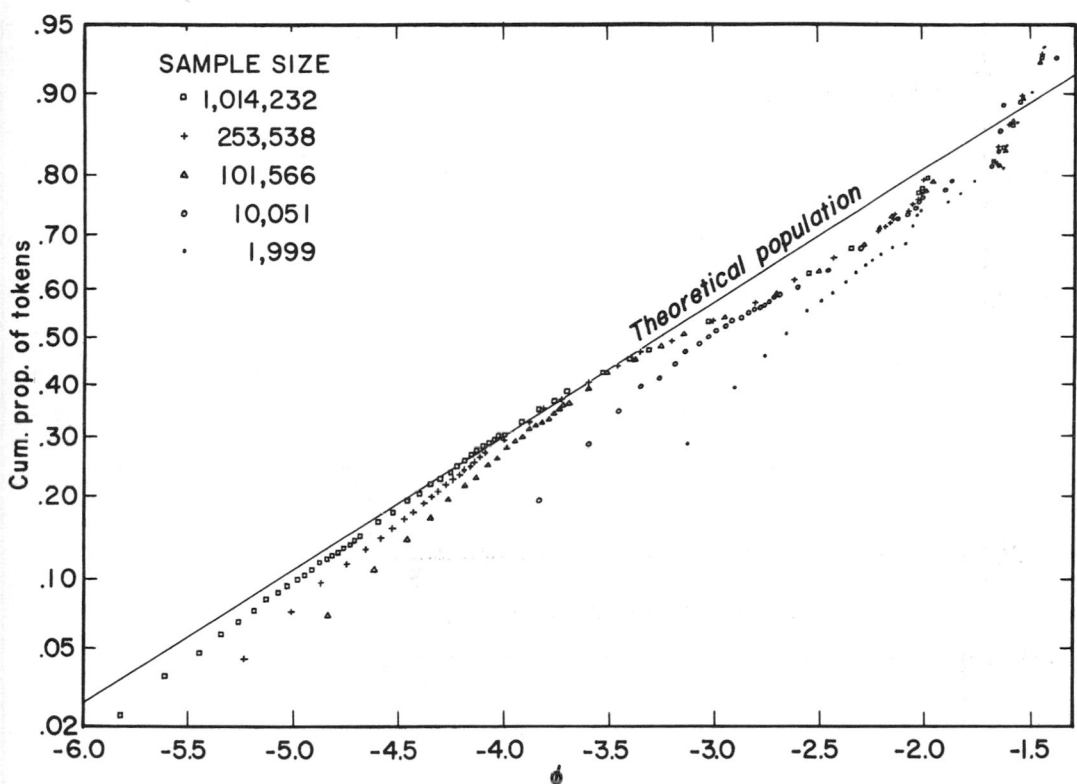

In the case of the larger samples only selected points are plotted. The theoretical population line is for the parameters $\mu = -3.2370$ and $\sigma = -1.4116$, as estimated from the data of the Corpus as a whole ($N = 1,014,232$).

Graph EIII   Cumulative Absolute Number of Types as a Function of Word Probability (ϕ) for Four Sample Sizes and as Predicted for the Theoretical Population

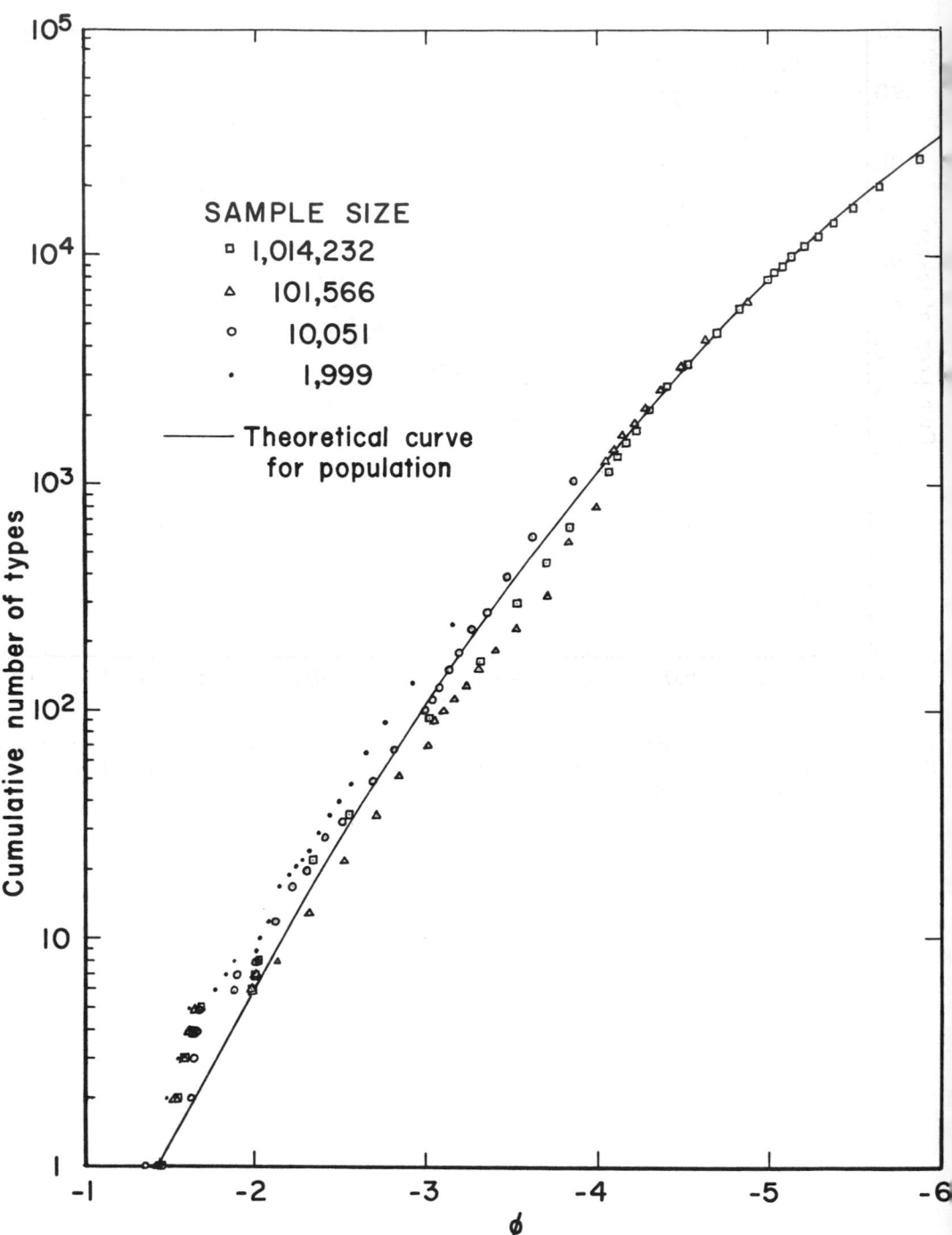

In the case of the larger samples only selected points are plotted.

Graph Eıv   Lognormal Plots of Observed Data for the Corpus as a Whole as Compared with the Plot Predicted for a Sample of This Size from the Theoretical Population with $\mu = -3.2370$ and $\sigma = 1.4116$

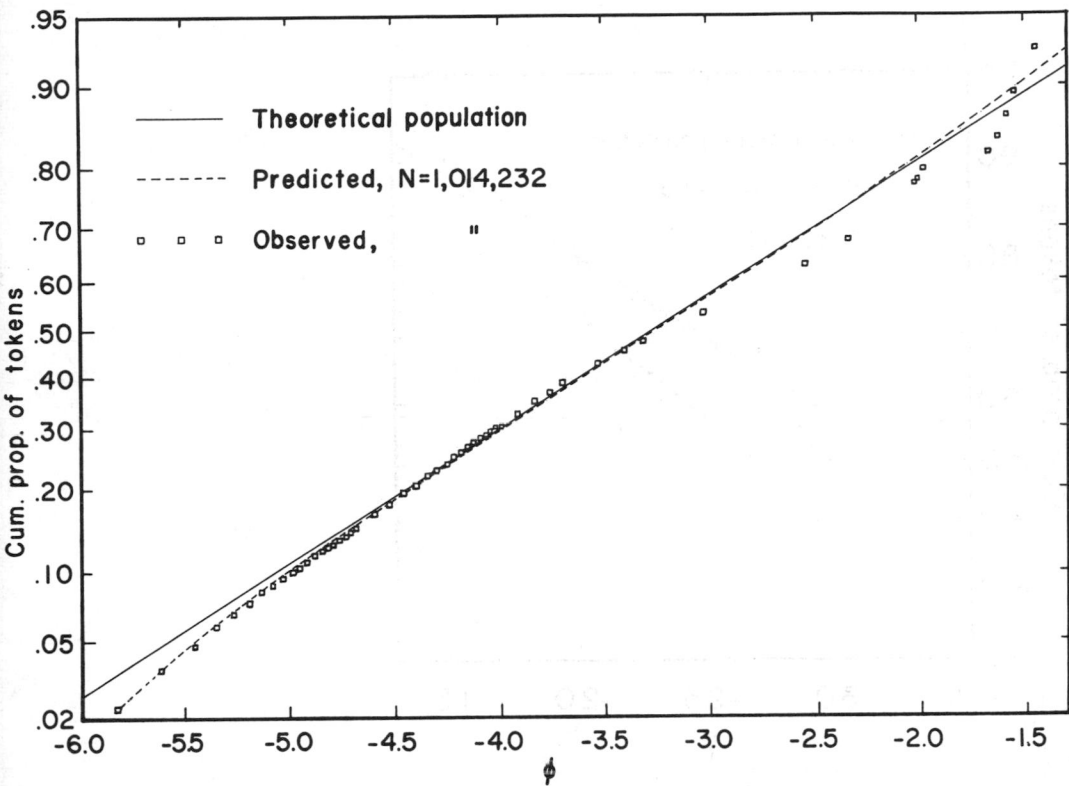

Only selected points from the total of 545 available are plotted for the observed data.

Graph Ev   Lognormal Plots of Observed
Data for Sample E06 as Compared with the
Plot Predicted for a Sample of This Size
from the Theoretical Population with $\mu = -3.2370$ and $\sigma = 1.4116$

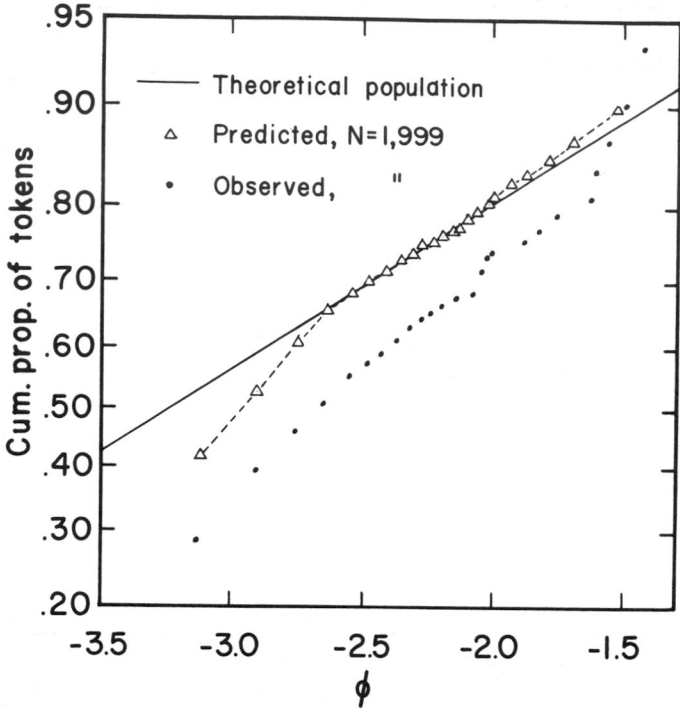

All available points are plotted both for the observed (25
points) and the predicted (23 points) data, except, of course,
for the point at which the cumulative proportion becomes
1.000.

Graph Evı   Number of Types as a Function of the Number of Tokens for Five Samples and as Predicted from a Theoretical Word-Frequency Distribution with $\mu = -3.2370$ and $\sigma = 1.4116$

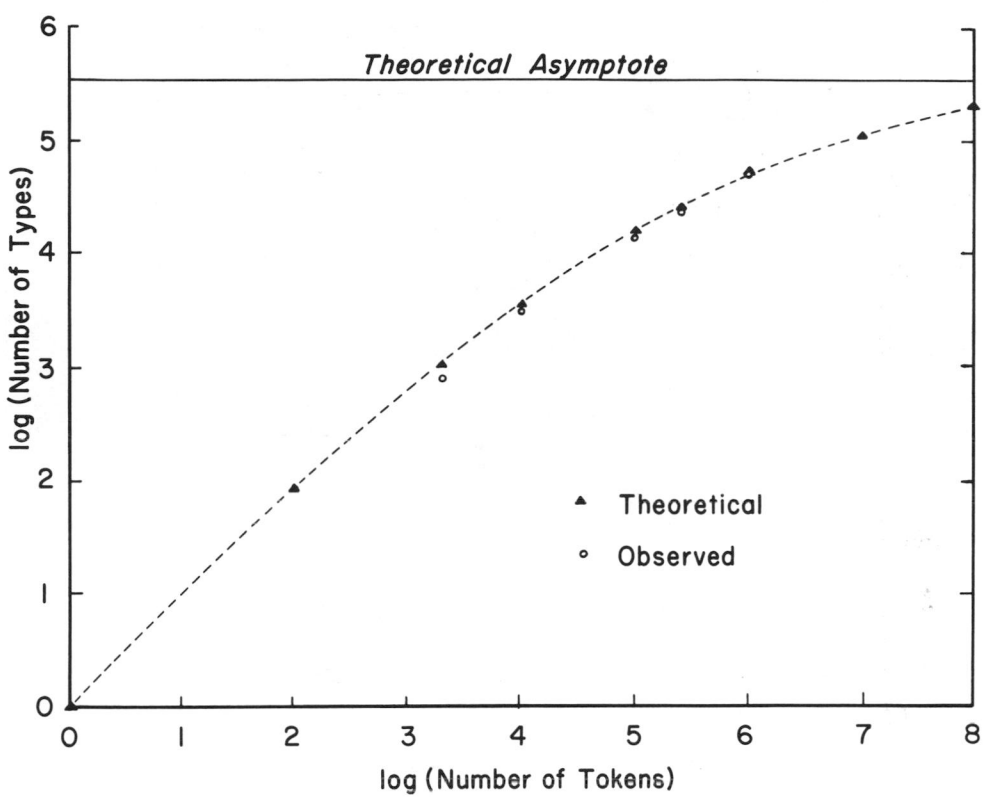

Graph EVII   Lognormal Plots for the Distribution of Word-Types in
Four Samples and as Predicted for a Theoretical Population of Word
Probabilities with $\mu = -3.2370$ and $\sigma = 1.4116$

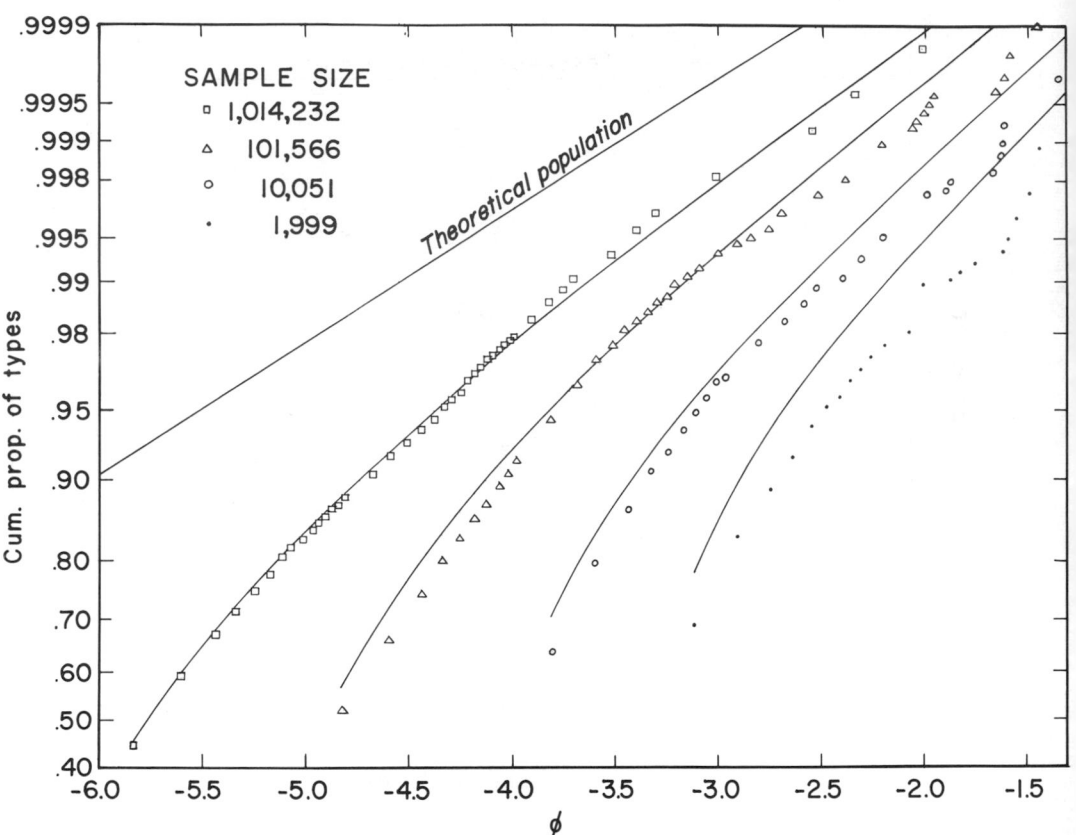

The parameters for the word-type distribution are $\mu_t = -7.8252$ and $\sigma = 1.4116$. For each sample size the distribution of word-types expected for a sample of this size from the theoretical population is depicted by a solid line.